HISTORICAL STATISTICS
OF THE
UNITED STATES

HISTORICAL STATISTICS OF THE UNITED STATES

Earliest Times to the Present

MILLENNIAL EDITION

VOLUME THREE

PART C
ECONOMIC STRUCTURE AND PERFORMANCE

Editors in Chief

Susan B. Carter

Scott Sigmund Gartner

Michael R. Haines

Alan L. Olmstead

Richard Sutch

Gavin Wright

CAMBRIDGE
UNIVERSITY PRESS

CAMBRIDGE UNIVERSITY PRESS
Cambridge, New York, Melbourne, Madrid, Cape Town, Singapore, São Paulo

Cambridge University Press
40 West 20th Street, New York, NY 10011-4211, USA

http://www.cambridge.org
Information on this title: www.cambridge.org/9780521817912

First published 2006

Printed in the United States of America

A catalog record for this publication is available from the British Library.

Library of Congress Cataloging in Publication Data

Historical statistics of the United States : earliest times to the present / Susan B. Carter ... [et al.]. – Millennial ed.
    p. cm.
  Rev. update of: Historical statistics of the United States, colonial times to 1970. Bicentennial ed. Washington : U.S. Dept. of Commerce, Bureau of the Census, 1975.
  Includes bibliographical references and index.
  ISBN 0-521-81791-9 (set)
  1. United States – Statistics.   I. Carter, Susan B.   II. Historical statistics of the United States, colonial times to 1970.   III. Title.

HA202.H57 2006
317.3 – dc22
                                                2005027089

ISBN-13 978-0-521-81791-2 (set of five volumes hardback)
ISBN-10 0-521-81791-9 (set of five volumes hardback)

ISBN-13 978-0-521-58496-8 (volume 1 hardback)
ISBN-10 0-521-58496-5 (volume 1 hardback)

ISBN-13 978-0-521-58540-8 (volume 2 hardback)
ISBN-10 0-521-58540-6 (volume 2 hardback)

ISBN-13 978-0-521-81790-5 (volume 3 hardback)
ISBN-10 0-521-81790-0 (volume 3 hardback)

ISBN-13 978-0-521-85389-7 (volume 4 hardback)
ISBN-10 0-521-85389-3 (volume 4 hardback)

ISBN-13 978-0-521-85390-3 (volume 5 hardback)
ISBN-10 0-521-85390-7 (volume 5 hardback)

ISBN-13 978-0-511-13297-1 (on-line edition)
ISBN-10 0-511-13297-2 (on-line edition)

SUMMARY CONTENTS

DETAILED CONTENTS OF VOLUME THREE

GUIDE TO THE MILLENNIAL EDITION

Monty Hindman and Richard Sutch

Editions and Copyright

Previous editions. This is the fourth edition of *Historical Statistics of the United States*. The U.S. Bureau of the Census published the prior editions in 1949, 1960, and 1975, the last known as the Bicentennial Edition. Cambridge University Press publishes this, the Millennial Edition, with the permission of the Census Bureau. Some of the data and table documentation presented here are used without explicit quotation, but with permission, from the earlier editions. The Census Bureau takes no responsibility for the design of this edition or the accuracy of its content, which rests solely with the contributors, the editors, and Cambridge University Press.

Electronic edition. This edition of *Historical Statistics of the United States* is available in electronic form from Cambridge University Press. A compact disk containing the Bicentennial Edition of *Historical Statistics of the United States* is also available from the Press.

Copyright. Permission to quote or reprint copyright material should be obtained directly from the copyright owner. Much of the data reproduced in this work were originally published by agencies of the U.S. government and are in the public domain. Generally speaking, original data that have been published elsewhere under copyright protection may be freely used for educational, scholarly, or journalistic purposes (but not commercial purposes) with proper citation to the original source under the fair use provision of U.S. copyright law. Cambridge University Press has made every effort to secure, where necessary, permission to reproduce protected material. In almost every case the permission requested was freely granted. In a few instances, however, the copyright owner requested a specific citation. These citations may be found in the listing of Copyright Citations at the end of Volume 5.

Data Revisions and Updates

Reproduction and revision of data from prior editions. Although this volume provides many data series from prior editions of *Historical Statistics of the United States*, users should be aware that some data from these editions have subsequently been revised. Our contributors sought to present the most recently available data, and thus users probably will wish to use the data presented here rather than that in previous editions. In some cases, data from the earlier editions were judged to be unreliable or obsolete and were not reproduced.

Data updates. The data series in *Historical Statistics of the United States* do not have a uniform end date; instead, each table reports the data available at the time the contributor compiled the data. Many series in these volumes are continued on a regular basis with periodic updates and revisions by the agency, group, or individual responsible for the original data. Figures for many of the current series are presented in the *Statistical Abstract of the United States*, published annually by the U.S. Bureau of the Census. The updating of industrial statistics will be complicated by the switch in 1997 from the Standard Industrial Classification (SIC) system to the North American Industrial Classification System (NAICS); see the Introduction to Part D.

Additional data. In many cases, additional data can be found in the source documents, in references mentioned in the table documentation or chapter essays, and through the Internet sites of the groups or agencies noted in the sources for the data presented here.

Errors. In a work as large as this, errors of both commission and omission are likely to have occurred. Users who discover errors are urged to communicate them to Cambridge University Press, 40 West 20th Street, New York, New York 10011-4211, USA.

Data Selection

General principles. The criteria for the selection of data to be included in this edition varied broadly, depending on the particular subject matter. Generally, summary measures or aggregates at gross levels and immediately below were given highest priority for inclusion. Below such levels, selection was governed by the interplay of the following: the amount of space already devoted to a particular subject; the attempt to achieve a relatively balanced presentation among subject fields; whether other data already covered a particular topic; the quantity and quality of the data available; and the extent to which the data might enhance the value of other material in the book. During the early phases of the project these selection criteria were conveyed to our contributors, upon whose judgment we ultimately relied.

Data reliability. Our contributors have attempted to select data that they consider to be generally reliable and to reproduce faithfully the data reported in their sources. They have also provided citations and technical descriptions to assist users in making independent assessments of both the data's reliability and their suitability for a project at hand.

Original versus derived data. Primary emphasis was placed on the presentation of original, unmodified figures rather than derived data because they offer greater flexibility to users. Derived data – for example, averages, percentages, ratios, and index numbers – were provided if they were the accepted standard for presentation (for example, unemployment rates), if the table contributor judged that the derived data would be particularly helpful, or if the use of derived data saved a significant amount of space.

Topical coverage. Because the last thirty years have witnessed the expansion of data collection into areas that were only inadequately covered, if at all, in the 1970s, this edition has a broader topical scope than its predecessors. A tentative list of topics emerged after extensive discussions between the project's editors in chief and Cambridge University Press. The outline was widely circulated to scholars, reference librarians, and government statistical bureaus. After a revision of that outline, the project recruited contributors, who offered additional suggestions. What emerged from this process was an outline for the project that was both designed by the profession and feasible to accomplish.

Temporal coverage. Contributors were asked to take the data series under their charge as far backward and forward in time as possible. They were also encouraged to include important lapsed series – those that begin and terminate in the past – because such series are sometimes available only in out-of-print documents. Most data series in *Historical Statistics of the United States* provide annual or decennial data spanning at least twenty years, with the main exceptions being for special topics (the colonial period and the Confederate States of America), for newly developed series providing the only data available to represent an important subject field, and for short series that served as important extensions of longer series.

Data frequency. Annual data were given preference for inclusion, but certain series are presented only for years in which a national census was conducted and, in some instances, only for scattered dates, as dictated by data availability. When both annual figures and benchmark data exist, both series are sometimes shown. A major exception was made for Chapter Cb, which presents many of its series on a monthly or quarterly basis. Although this volume mainly provides annual data, underlying data are sometimes available more frequently from the original sources.

Geographical coverage. The data in *Historical Statistics of the United States* generally cover the nation as a whole, defined by the recognized borders of the country for the year in question. As new states were admitted to the Union, the coverage of the typical statistical series in this volume expands to include the new additions, without any special notation in the table documentation. The documentation should be consulted to determine if such changes in the boundaries of the United States are likely to have affected the series. When the year of a state's inclusion in a series differs significantly from its year of statehood, this fact was noted in the documentation whenever possible. Refer to Appendix 2 for the dates of statehood.

Subnational data. Because of limitations of space, data are generally not shown for regions, states, or localities. The underlying sources sometimes provide data in finer geographical detail than shown here. Some tables provide data for U.S. census regions or divisions; see Appendix 2 for more information on such regional classifications.

Outlying areas. In almost all cases, outlying areas are not included in the national totals reported here. Refer to Chapter Ef for additional information on such areas.

Organization of the Volume

Arrangement of the data. In this edition of *Historical Statistics of the United States,* data are arranged by broad subjects in five parts, each published in a separate volume and each volume containing several chapters. The tables in most chapters are further organized into various subsections (see the Detailed Table of Contents in each volume).

Essays. Each chapter is introduced by one or more essays that provide a general guide to the data, the sources, and the historical trends that have been emphasized in the scholarly literature. They contain a list of references that may be consulted by those interested in more detail.

Series identifiers. Each data series is assigned a unique alphanumeric identifier. The two letters in the identifier indicate the chapter in which the series resides. Within a chapter, series are numbered sequentially. Sets of contiguous series are identified by means of a series range (for example, series Da42–47). Source citations and table documentation are linked to the data series by means of such identifiers, which may be preferred over page numbers for use in reference citations.

Table identifiers. An entire table is identified by the range of series that it contains. For example, the first two tables in the chapter on vital statistics contain ten and twenty series, respectively; thus, they are identified as Table Ab1–10 and Table Ab11–30. Similarly, a group of contiguous tables is identified by a series range. Using the same example, these two tables could be referred to jointly as Tables Ab1–30.

Table Documentation

Table contributors. Each table provides the names of the contributors who selected, collected, and described the data. The editorial staff also reviewed the data and table documentation for accuracy, completeness, and clarity of presentation.

Sources. In most cases, full citations are given for data sources; however, when numerous issues of a publication were used, the source citations are usually limited to "annual issues" or similar notations. When data are reproduced from the Bicentennial Edition, the source citation lists the original source rather than the Bicentennial Edition, except under special circumstances.

Unpublished data. Nearly all the data reported here have been previously published or accepted for publication. Rare exceptions for previously unpublished data were allowed if a contributor felt that the data were particularly important and if peer review accepted the data for inclusion.

Integrated Public Use Microdata Series. A number of series reported in this edition are extracted from the Integrated Public Use Microdata Series (IPUMS). The IPUMS is composed of representative samples drawn from the returns of the decennial censuses of the population. All censuses from 1850 to 1990 are included, with the exception of 1930, which is under development, and 1890, the manuscripts for which were destroyed by fire. The IPUMS data and documentation are available over the Internet.*

Internet sources. Some data series in *Historical Statistics of the United States* are based on electronic sources; however, owing to the fleeting nature of specific Internet addresses or Web-based

---

* Steven Ruggles, Matthew Sobek, et al., *Integrated Public Use Microdata Series: Version 2.0* (Historical Census Projects, University of Minnesota, 1997).

file names, we do not use them when identifying sources. Instead, we use more general phrasing to direct users to the Internet source.

Table documentation. Most tables are accompanied by documentation defining relevant terms and concepts, providing methodological and historical background, noting unusual values or comparability issues, explaining methods used to calculate derived data, and providing references to sources containing more detailed data or more extensive discussion. Unlike prior editions, which consolidated table documentation at the beginning of chapters, this edition locates the documentation with the tables, the intent being to increase its visibility, convenience, and thus use. Many tables are fully self-documenting, without cross references to other parts of this work; however, when cross references to other tables or essays are provided, the user is encouraged to follow those references.

Footnotes. There is no sharp demarcation between the type of information conveyed in the ordinary table documentation and that conveyed in the footnotes. Roughly speaking, footnotes are used for two purposes: to draw attention to issues of particular importance (footnotes as warnings) or to comment on matters related to specific columns, rows, or cells in a table.

Footnote order. Within a table, footnotes are numbered sequentially as follows: first the general footnotes that apply to the entire table; then left-to-right across the table header (the footnotes governing specific series); and finally footnotes attached to the table stub and the data area, proceeding in top-to-bottom, then left-to-right fashion (as used here, the directional terms apply to tables with standard page orientation). A footnote's first appearance within a table determines its position within the sequential numbering.

Total and subtotals. In most cases, a table's header structure will clearly indicate the total–subtotal relationships among the series. The typical practice in this volume is to provide the total series first, followed by its components. Often the sum of the components will equal the total, perhaps with small deviations attributable to rounding or other causes; however, sometimes the breakdowns provided in a table are not exhaustive, and the components will add to an amount less than the total. Users should consult the table documentation and exercise caution in this regard.

Race and ethnicity. Many tables provide disaggregations by race or ethnicity. This volume typically uses the terms "white," "black," "Asian" (or "Asian American"), "Indian" (or "Amerindian" or "Native American"), and "Hispanic." Note that a person identified as Hispanic may be of any race. See the essay on definitions and measurement of race and ethnicity in the Introduction to Part A for a discussion of racial classification and identification as it applies to the collection of historical statistics in the United States.

Dates

Date ranges. Throughout the table documentation and the chapter essays, date ranges are inclusive: for example, 1964–1987 includes both 1964 and 1987.

Year of record. The identification of the year of record – in other words, the precise meaning of the years shown in a table stub – was complicated by the failure of some sources to state whether the data were prepared on a calendar year, fiscal year, or some other basis; by changes in the year of record over time; and, in some instances, by imprecision or silence in the source concerning the beginning or ending date for the year of record. Table contributors

attempted to clarify such matters, but ambiguity remains in some tables.

Transition quarters. Sometimes the year of record changes in the middle of a table, and values are provided for the "transition quarter" – the gap between the end of the old year of record and beginning of the new. In such cases, users will see a (TQ) designation in the table stub. Nearly all transition quarters in this volume are associated with the year 1976, when the federal government changed the end of its fiscal year from June 30 to September 30. In rare cases, the (TQ) designation will be for a transition period that is not actually a quarter, but some other fraction of a year.

Units, Measures, and Monetary Values

Units of measure. Series are usually expressed in the units reported in the original source. In some cases, however, units were converted to make two or more data series comparable, or to create a single series when splicing data from multiple sources. The approach taken in these volumes was to restrict the units information to true *measures* and to rely on the table title and layered headers to convey other details about the things being counted or measured. Sometimes series are expressed in units too complex for pithy statement; in these rare cases, a generic unit of measure is given, with further elaboration left to the table documentation.

Billion and trillion. The American and Canadian definitions of billion (10^9) and trillion (10^{12}) are used throughout, not the definitions used in England, Germany, and many other countries.

Index numbers. Some series are expressed in terms of index numbers. In such cases, the base period of the index is provided where the unit of measure would normally be found. For a discussion of index numbers, see the essay on prices and price indexes in Chapter Cc and the essay on national income and product in Chapter Ca.

Weights and measures. Most data series are expressed in American units (the U.S. Customary System) rather than metric units (the International System). For a discussion of these two systems and for conversion information, see Appendix 1.

Monetary values. Unless otherwise noted, monetary values are expressed in current or nominal terms – in other words, the actual historical values (usually U.S. dollars), not adjusted for previous or subsequent changes in prices. This standard was adopted to avoid attaching the word "current" or "nominal" to every reference to a monetary unit. When monetary values have been adjusted in some fashion, this is stated explicitly and the relevant base period is given. For a discussion of monetary values, see Appendix 1 and the essay on prices and price indexes in Chapter Cc.

Data Values

Data precision and significant digits. In making decisions regarding the precision with which data values should be presented, fidelity to sources was our primary consideration. Thus, the underlying data files for *Historical Statistics of the United States* – available in the electronic edition – retain the full precision provided by table contributors, even though this level of detail might be deemed excessive by scientific standards for the reporting of significant digits. In most cases, the detail comes straight from the sources themselves; therefore, exact reproduction provides a valuable check for researchers wanting to trace the provenance of a number or hunt down an anomaly. In other cases, excessive precision comes from spreadsheet calculations made by table contributors (for example, in the computation of derived data). Here, too, we did not impose our judgments concerning the appropriate precision and instead retained the full detail provided by contributors. Users should note that historical sources sometimes change the precision with which they report data over time. Also, some tables contain series reported in the sources at different levels of detail but that, for ease of comparison, are provided here in consistent units. The usual indication of varying precision – whether in a single series or across multiple series within a table – is a run of data values with trailing zeros, either before or after the decimal point. In such cases, users will need to exercise judgment concerning the precision of the data.

Decimal precision for display purposes. While the underlying data files retain all of the detail provided by table contributors, the data displayed in the print edition of *Historical Statistics of the United States* are shown in rounded fashion, typically with no more than three digits following the decimal point. Similarly, tables generated for display purposes by the electronic edition are formatted using the same rounding conventions; however, the underlying files available for downloading provide the values at full precision.

Zero values and (Z). A zero in a data series means exactly that: a reported value of zero. In some cases, an underlying data value may be so small that it rounds to zero when displayed at the level of decimal precision chosen for the series. In such cases, a (Z) marker is used rather than a zero value. Stated more precisely, the (Z) notation indicates a *nonzero value that is not shown or possibly not known*. In the former case – a nonzero value not shown – (Z) means that the value falls below the threshold of our rounding convention: the number rounds to zero, as displayed in this volume (full precision for such values is available through the electronic edition). In the latter case – a nonzero value not known – (Z) means that the original source did not provide a specific value. Owing to these complexities, the meaning of the (Z) marker is specifically documented in every table that uses the device.

Dash as a data value. The "—" marker means that a value is not being reported. There are several possible reasons: the data are not available anywhere; the data were not provided in the source but conceivably could be found with sufficient research; the data were available in the source but the table contributor decided that they should not be reported (for example, unreliable data); or the data might conceivably be reported as a zero, but the table contributor decided for conceptual reasons to represent it as "no value reported" (for example, if a category or program covered by the series did not yet exist). Some sources do not carefully distinguish between zero values and missing data. Table contributors attempted to eliminate such confusion, but in some cases the "—" marker could mean that the value, if shown, would be zero.

Historical Statistics of the United States

Millennial Edition

Volume 3

Part C
Economic Structure and Performance

CHAPTER Ca
National Income and Product

Editor: Richard Sutch

NATIONAL INCOME AND PRODUCT

Richard Sutch

The Purposes of National Income Accounting

National product is a comprehensive measure of a nation's total annual production of commodities and services. Gross domestic product (GDP), the standard measure of national product for the United States, is defined as the market value of the goods and services produced in the United States. National income is the counterpart of national product. It represents the sum of all the incomes earned in producing national output. The two concepts – national income and national product – are equivalent, because the creation of output generates a valuable good or service that did not previously exist and the individuals whose labor or capital participated in the act of production count as their income their share of the value newly produced.

Estimates of the total output of the national economy are put to three main uses. First, when divided by estimates of the population they can be used as a rough index of the average standard of living. Calculated in this way, they can be used to compare the material standard of living in one country with that in another or the standard in one year with that in another. To make such comparisons meaningful, care must be taken to ensure that the evaluation of the myriad of goods and services that constitute national output is consistent across countries or across time. Second, time series of national output are used to study the progress of economic growth as the economy evolves and expands (or contracts) over time. Estimates of national output divided by the labor force provide estimates of labor productivity and its growth over time. Third, fluctuations in the total output are taken as indicators of booms and recessions, as the economy experiences what are often referred to as business cycles.

Economic Welfare

For the United States, GDP per capita has grown twenty-eight-fold since 1790 (series Ca13). This is the great success story of American history. J. Bradford DeLong (1998) has estimated that worldwide, GDP per capita per day in 1750 was between 50 cents and $1.80. For the world as a whole, in 2001 the average value of output per person per day was about $21. For the United States, among the countries with the highest GDP per capita, the figure was more than $90. For the poorest countries, in sub-Saharan Africa, the average was less than $2 (United Nations 2003). In 1790 the United States had a national output per capita per day of approximately $3.20 (series Ca13).

Although per capita national product is widely used as an index of the average standard of living or well-being, it is often criticized by economic historians and development economists as a poor indicator of changes, or differences between countries, in the material level of living provided by economic activity. The aggregate figures do not reflect changes in the distribution of income between the rich and the poor, in consumption needs arising from changes in the age composition of the population, or in worker-hours spent in economic activity. A significant problem in making comparisons of living standards in far distant times is that our high standard of living today derives not only from our highly productive manufacturing technology but also from our ability to manufacture whole new types of commodities. Some of the new goods do a better job of meeting our needs than the goods they replaced. It is in this sense that electric lighting is superior to whale-oil lamps. Other new goods meet wants today that no one even imagined in the distant past (e.g., personal computers, Botox injections, and air transportation). William Nordhaus (1997) has argued that the expansion in choice presented by the appearance of new goods adds enormously to our welfare. National output measures of the standard of living do not take into account this component of well-being.

There are other elements that influence our well-being that are perhaps as important as national output per capita. Frequently mentioned in this regard are reductions in infant mortality, rise in life expectancy, expanded opportunities for leisure time, reduced economic and social discrimination, and improvements in hygiene, health, education, and working conditions. These topics are dealt with in other chapters of *Historical Statistics*, so they need not delay us here. However, it is worth noting that the United Nations (2003) has produced estimates of life expectancy, school enrollment, and other indicators of welfare for many countries. All of these are highly correlated with national output per capita.

Acknowledgments

Richard Sutch acknowledges advice and assistance from Susan Carter, Robert J. Gordon, Paul Rhode, and Gavin Wright. Paul Rhode and Richard Sutch acknowledge advice and assistance from Susan Carter, Peter Coclanis, Paul David, Joseph Davis, Lance Davis, Michael Edelstein, Stanley Engerman, Nancy Folbre, Louis Johnston, Matthew Gallman, Robert Gallman, Claudia Goldin, Tom Mroz, Thomas Weiss, and Samuel Williamson. Financial support was provided by the Center for Social and Economic Policy, University of California, Riverside.

Economic Growth

Economic growth is a sustained process that expands national output over a significant period of time. When real output grows faster than the population, per capita output expands, reflecting the productive achievements of the economy. Because of the interest in long-term economic growth, considerable effort has gone into making estimates of national output for the United States extending back to 1790. Table Ca9–19 summarizes the work of many researchers by presenting estimates of national output for 1789–2002 (both in current and constant dollars, as well as in per capita terms). Figure Ca-A graphs the trend in real GDP over more than two centuries. The exponential expansion of per capita output is evident. However, it is more useful to plot these data on a logarithmic scale, which is displayed in Figure Ca-B. On such a graph a constant rate of economic growth will appear as a straight line. The steeper the slope is, the faster the rate of growth. The second graph also makes the annual fluctuations in output in the earlier

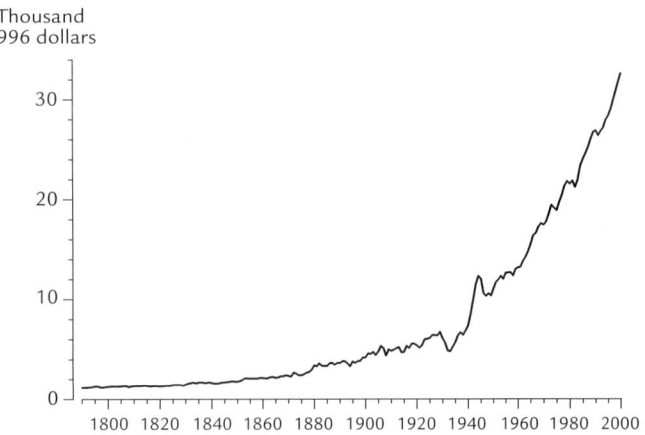

FIGURE Ca-A   Real gross domestic product per capita: 1790–2000

Source
Series Ca13.

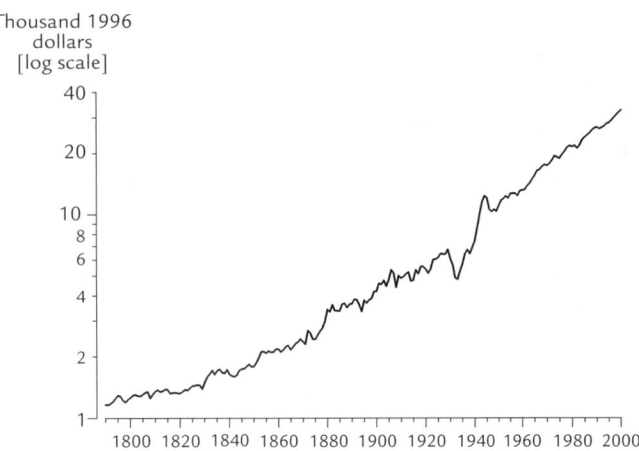

FIGURE Ca-B   Real gross domestic product per capita – log scale: 1790–2000

Source
Series Ca13.

years more apparent, but the predominant feature is still the strong and continuous expansion of the economy.

As may be evident from an inspection of Figure Ca-B, the rate of growth was substantially lower before 1820 than after. Table Ca-C enables us to specify the change more precisely. This type of table is called a growth triangle. In the table one can find the annual rate of growth between any two census benchmark dates. For example, the number 1.6 in the lower left corner of the triangle tells us that the rate of growth over the entire period 1790–2000 has been 1.6 percent.

The only negative number in the table is for the decade 1810–1820 (–0.2 percent), and it is followed by a substantial rebound in the 1830s (1.3 percent). If we believe the annual numbers in series Ca13, a sharp change in the rate of growth occurred in the mid-1820s. As an illustration, the rate of growth before 1828 was only 0.6 percent whereas the rate between 1828 and 1860 was more than twice this value. Following the Civil War, the decadal rates of growth have averaged 2.0 percent (between 1870 and 2000), and only infrequently have they fallen below 1.3 percent. This remarkable record of sustained economic growth has been an object of intense interest to both economic theorists (for an introduction see Solow 2000) and quantitative economic historians (Gallman 2000; Abramovitz and David 2000). However, many objections raised to using real GDP per capita as a measure of welfare carry over as objections to using the growth of real GDP per capita as a measure of economic progress. It measures only marketed output, leaving out household work, the increased enjoyment of leisure time activity, improvements in health and longevity, and many intangible elements of economic progress (Fogel 1999).

Economic Fluctuations

The long-term trends displayed in the figures are punctuated by recurrent fluctuations in output per capita. There are several bursts of very rapid growth and a number of setbacks, most of them brief. However, the Great Depression of the 1930s followed by the wartime boom of the 1940s stand out as a particularly sharp roller-coaster movement. These recurrent, but not periodic, fluctuations are often called business cycles. They have long been a major preoccupation of macroeconomists, and those investigating the cause and consequences of these fluctuations closely scrutinize data on national output. Yet the annual time series presented in this chapter (particularly those that apply to the period before 1929) are not well suited for this purpose. Chapter Cb, on business fluctuations and cycles, presents national output data (and many other series) on a quarterly and monthly basis. This higher frequency of reporting is important for studying economic fluctuations.

For GDP to serve all three purposes passably well means that it serves none of them perfectly. Yet despite misgivings about this measure of national output, it has become the standard index of the size of the economic system. Although rival estimates have been proposed for addressing various difficulties associated with GDP, none have succeeded in replacing aggregate national output as the universally understood and universally cited measure of economic activity. There are several explanations for the wide acceptance of these figures. First, the U.S. government has designated measures of national output as the "official" measure of economic activity, and the United Nations extended this official approval to all other

TABLE Ca-C Real gross domestic product per capita – average annual growth rates: 1790–2000

Terminal year	Initial year																				
	1790	1800	1810	1820	1830	1840	1850	1860	1870	1880	1890	1900	1910	1920	1930	1940	1950	1960	1970	1980	1990
1800	0.8	—	—	—	—	—	—	—	—	—	—	—	—	—	—	—	—	—	—	—	—
1810	0.7	0.7	—	—	—	—	—	—	—	—	—	—	—	—	—	—	—	—	—	—	—
1820	0.4	0.2	−0.2	—	—	—	—	—	—	—	—	—	—	—	—	—	—	—	—	—	—
1830	0.6	0.6	0.5	1.3	—	—	—	—	—	—	—	—	—	—	—	—	—	—	—	—	—
1840	0.7	0.7	0.7	1.1	0.9	—	—	—	—	—	—	—	—	—	—	—	—	—	—	—	—
1850	0.7	0.7	0.7	1.0	0.9	0.9	—	—	—	—	—	—	—	—	—	—	—	—	—	—	—
1860	0.9	0.9	1.0	1.3	1.2	1.4	1.9	—	—	—	—	—	—	—	—	—	—	—	—	—	—
1870	0.9	0.9	0.9	1.2	1.2	1.2	1.4	0.9	—	—	—	—	—	—	—	—	—	—	—	—	—
1880	1.2	1.3	1.3	1.6	1.7	1.9	2.2	2.3	3.8	—	—	—	—	—	—	—	—	—	—	—	—
1890	1.2	1.2	1.3	1.5	1.5	1.6	1.8	1.7	2.2	0.6	—	—	—	—	—	—	—	—	—	—	—
1900	1.2	1.2	1.3	1.5	1.5	1.6	1.7	1.7	1.9	1.0	1.4	—	—	—	—	—	—	—	—	—	—
1910	1.2	1.2	1.3	1.5	1.5	1.6	1.7	1.6	1.8	1.2	1.5	1.5	—	—	—	—	—	—	—	—	—
1920	1.2	1.2	1.3	1.4	1.4	1.5	1.6	1.5	1.7	1.1	1.3	1.3	1.0	—	—	—	—	—	—	—	—
1930	1.2	1.2	1.3	1.4	1.4	1.5	1.5	1.5	1.6	1.2	1.3	1.3	1.1	1.2	—	—	—	—	—	—	—
1940	1.2	1.3	1.3	1.4	1.5	1.5	1.6	1.5	1.6	1.3	1.4	1.4	1.4	1.6	1.9	—	—	—	—	—	—
1950	1.4	1.5	1.5	1.6	1.7	1.8	1.8	1.8	1.9	1.7	1.9	2.0	2.1	2.4	3.0	4.1	—	—	—	—	—
1960	1.4	1.5	1.5	1.7	1.7	1.7	1.8	1.8	1.9	1.7	1.8	1.9	2.0	2.3	2.6	2.9	1.7	—	—	—	—
1970	1.5	1.6	1.6	1.7	1.8	1.8	1.9	1.9	2.0	1.8	2.0	2.1	2.1	2.4	2.7	2.9	2.3	2.9	—	—	—
1980	1.5	1.6	1.6	1.8	1.8	1.9	1.9	1.9	2.0	1.9	2.0	2.1	2.1	2.3	2.6	2.7	2.2	2.5	2.1	—	—
1990	1.6	1.6	1.7	1.8	1.8	1.9	2.0	2.0	2.0	1.9	2.0	2.1	2.2	2.3	2.5	2.6	2.2	2.4	2.2	2.2	—
2000	1.6	1.6	1.7	1.8	1.8	1.9	2.0	2.0	2.0	1.9	2.0	2.1	2.1	2.3	2.4	2.5	2.2	2.3	2.1	2.1	1.9

Source

Computed from series Ca13.

Documentation

To find the growth rate (in percentage points) between any two years shown, select the initial year at the top of the table and the terminal year at the left. The growth rate is found at the intersection of the column and the row selected.

member nations. Second, there is wide agreement on the proper means of defining, constructing, and interpreting GDP. Moreover, once GDP had been defined, collecting the required information to measure aggregate output became, if not easy, at least a transparent accounting task. Devising a superior measure for any of the three purposes mentioned earlier typically would require incorporating aspects of human welfare, economic progress, or economic dynamics that are not so precisely defined or readily measured. Third, despite the inadequacies of the existing measures, economists generally believe that the official estimates are close to conceptually superior indexes and, even if one wished to depart from the official estimates, they would typically be the starting place for any more sophisticated analysis.

The detailed series that record the components of national output are as important as the bottom-line measurement of the level of the total. The definition of the various components is partly the result of the bureaucratic origins of much of the underlying data, but, more significantly, these components are deemed to be significant by the prevailing theories of macroeconomic dynamics. John Maynard Keynes, in *The General Theory of Employment, Interest and Money* (1936), used the components of national product and expenditure organized by economic sector and controlled by distinct classes of economic agents as the basis for his theory of the determination of income, output, and employment. Thus, national income and product accounts are the core of our macroeconomic information. They are critical in the formulation of the federal budget, they provide Congress and the White House with the vital signs of the economy's health, they guide business decisions, and they are the evidence evoked in most empirical analyses in macroeconomics since the mid-twentieth century.

The History of National Income Accounting

The conceptualization and implementation of a consistent scheme of national income and product accounts for producing a reliable, impartial, and accurate series of statistics has been called "one of the major achievements of economics in the twentieth century" (Ruggles 1983, p. 15; Daley 2000). In recognition of this achievement, Simon Kuznets, the economist most responsible for developing the concepts underlying the system of national income accounting used in the United States, received the Nobel Prize in Economic Science in 1971 in part for his contribution to their invention and implementation (Langley 1999, p. 58). The economics prize awarded to Richard Stone in 1984 for "fundamental contributions to the development of systems of national accounts" (which he made in England under Keynes's guidance) simply reemphasized the importance of national accounting systems for the systematic study of the social sciences.

The conceptualization and estimation of national output was initiated during the early 1930s when lack of comprehensive data hindered the government's efforts to combat the Great Depression. In response to the need for better data (and at the request of the Senate in 1932), the Department of Commerce commissioned Kuznets, of the National Bureau of Economic Research, to develop a system of accounts and to make estimates of national output. Kuznets presented the national income and product accounts system in a report to the Senate in 1934 with annual estimates for 1929–1932 (Kuznets 1934). He later extended his estimates back to 1919 and forward to 1938 (Kuznets 1941). The entry of the United States into World War II accelerated efforts to collect and summarize national economic data (Kuznets 1945). After the war,

Kuznets (1946) pushed his estimates back to 1869 and forward to 1943. At that point, the task of maintaining and continuing the national accounts was assigned to the Department of Commerce's Office of Business Economics (OBE, later to become the U.S. Bureau of Economic Analysis, BEA). The first report published by the OBE appeared in 1947 with annual estimates going back to 1929. Ever since, the OBE and its successor, the BEA, have been the keepers of the national accounts (Carson 1975). The BEA periodically revises and updates the entire historical record of accounts. The figures reported here reflect the 1996 comprehensive revision (U.S. Bureau of Economic Analysis 1998a, 1998b).

References

See the references at the conclusion of the essay on estimates of national product before 1929, in this chapter.

NATIONAL INCOME AND PRODUCT ACCOUNTS: OFFICIAL ESTIMATES

Richard Sutch

The NIPA Accounts

The national income and product accounts (NIPA) of the United States measure the total value of output produced by the American economy (gross domestic product, or GDP; see Table Ca1–8). Behind this statistical report is a precise double-entry accounting system that is used to keep track of the entire economy and that yields the GDP, a broad measure of the health of the economy, as its bottom line. Even more important, the accounts provide a wealth of underlying detail on the components of GDP so that systematic interrelationships may be investigated and structural features of the economy may be discerned.

The components of GDP are summarized in five basic accounts:

Account 1: National income and product

Account 2: Personal income and outlay

Account 3: Government receipts and expenditures

Account 4: Foreign transactions

Account 5: Gross saving and investment

Each account in the system is presented in Table Ca-D as a traditional T account with sources of funds (credits) recorded on the right-hand side and uses of funds (debits) recorded on the left-hand side. Of course, whether a particular item is a "source" or a "use" of funds is a matter of perspective. For this reason, each of the five accounts takes a different perspective. Each item that appears on the right of one account as a source will appear on the left of another account as a use. The two sides of each account sum to precisely the same total. Table Ca-D presents a simplified view of these five accounts with data for 1996, which is the base year for reporting GDP in constant prices (series Ca6).

Account 1 in Table Ca-D takes the "income approach" to calculating the national product on the left and the "expenditure approach" on the right. The right-hand side of account 1 defines GDP from the perspective of output (also see Tables Ca1–8, Ca20–63, and Ca74–148) and calculates it by assembling data on expenditures. All of the goods and services purchased are allocated into one of the following four broad categories: consumption (line 33), investment (line 37), government purchases (line 47), and net exports to the rest of the world (ROW) (line 44). The production of the goods enumerated on the right-hand side is the source of the incomes distributed on the left-hand side of account 1.

The left-hand side of account 1 totals the incomes earned by the producers of output (also see Tables Ca20–34). These income flows are categorized as labor income (line 1), owners' profits (line 6), rents received (line 7), corporate profits (line 8), and net interest received (line 17). These total to national income (line 18), which does not include depreciation (line 22), indirect taxes (such as sales taxes, line 20), and several other items (lines 19 and 21). To move from the national income concept to the domestic income concept, the net income paid to the ROW must be added (lines 28 and 29). In principle, gross domestic income (GDI) should exactly equal gross domestic product (GDP). However, in practice the match is not exact. The U.S. Bureau of Economic Analysis (BEA) believes that the product side of the account is more accurately measured, so GDP is defined by the expenditure approach. To close the gap between GDI and GDP, a statistical discrepancy, calculated as the difference between GDP and GDI, is added to the left-hand side to balance the account. In recent years the discrepancy has generally been less than 1 percent of GDP.

The double-entry accounting system used in national income accounting recognizes the two-sided nature of every transaction. For each purchase, there is a sale; for each payment, there is a receipt. Unlike business accounting, which takes the perspective of an individual firm, the NIPA are examples of social accounting that assume the perspective of the entire society. Each entry in the accounts has an equal counterentry. Again, take the right-hand side of account 1 as an example. Personal consumption expenditures (line 33) are also entered on the left-hand side of account 2 (line 3), where consumption appears as one of the uses to which personal income is put. In Table Ca-D the counterentries are given in parentheses following the designation of the entry; thus, in account 1 "33 personal consumption expenditures (2-3)" indicates that line 33 of account 1 records personal consumption and that the counterentry can be found in account 2 on line 3.

Account 2 presents the sources of personal income (on the right side) and the uses (or outlays) of that income (on the left). Note that personal saving (line 6) is calculated as a residual by subtracting taxes and personal outlays from personal income. Thus, the two sides of account 2 are in balance by construction.

Account 3 presents the sources of government revenue (on the right side) and government expenditures (on the left). All governments (federal, state, and local) are aggregated together in this simplified version; however, separate accountings at each level of government are available in the original source. In this account the balancing item, which is calculated as a residual, is the "current surplus or deficit" and is entered on the left-hand side. Note that the government surplus here is somewhat different in concept than that presented in government budgets and is distinguished from the latter by the notation "NIPA" in line 10.

Account 4 balances the country's receipts of money from the ROW with payments to the ROW. Thus, U.S. exports (line 1) generate receipts. Payments are made to the ROW in exchange for imports (line 4). In this account net foreign investment (line 10)

TABLE Ca-D   Summary of the national income and product accounts: 1996

ACCOUNT 1 – NATIONAL INCOME AND PRODUCT

	National income	
1	Compensation of employees	4,395.6
2	Wage and salary accruals (2-8, 3-8, and 5-6)	3,630.1
3	Supplements to wages and salaries	765.4
4	Employer contributions for social insurance (3-15)	275.4
5	Other labor income (2-9)	490.0
6	Proprietors' income with inventory valuation and capital consumption adjustments (2-10)	544.7
7	Rental income of persons with capital consumption adjustment (2-11)	129.7
8	Corporate profits with inventory valuation and capital consumption adjustments	754.0
9	Corporate profits with inventory valuation adjustment	729.4
10	Profits before tax	726.3
11	Profits tax liability (3-13)	223.6
12	Profits after tax	502.7
13	Dividends (2-12 and 3-6)	297.7
14	Undistributed profits (5-7)	205.0
15	Inventory valuation adjustment (5-7)	3.1
16	Capital consumption adjustment (5-7)	24.6
17	Net interest (2-4, 2-13, and 3-5)	386.3
18	**National Income**	**6,210.4**
19	Business transfer payments (2-14 and 4-9)	34.4
20	Indirect business tax and nontax liability (3-14)	620.0
21	Less: subsidies less current surplus of government enterprises (3-7)	22.6
22	Consumption of fixed capital	956.2
23	Private (5-8)	781.9
24	Government (5-12)	174.3
25	General government	149.2
26	Government enterprises	25.0
27	**Gross National Income**	**7,798.4**
28	Less: income receipts from the rest of the world (4-2)	245.6
29	Plus: income payments to the rest of the world (4-5)	227.5
30	**Gross Domestic Income**	**7,780.3**
31	*Statistical discrepancy (5-19)*	*32.8*
32	**Gross Domestic Product**	**7,813.2**

	National product	
33	Personal consumption expenditures (2-3)	5,237.5
34	Durable goods	616.5
35	Nondurable goods	1,574.1
36	Services	3,047.0
37	Gross private domestic investment (5-1)	1,242.7
38	Fixed investment	1,212.7
39	Nonresidential	899.4
40	Structures	225.0
41	Equipment and software	674.4
42	Residential	313.3
43	Change in private inventories	30.0
44	Net exports of goods and services	−89.0
45	Exports (4-1)	874.2
46	Less: imports (4-4)	963.1
47	Government consumption expenditures and gross investment (3-1 and 5-2)	1,421.9
48	Federal	531.6
49	National defense	357.0
50	Nondefense	174.6
51	State and local	890.4
52	**Gross Domestic Product**	**7,813.2**

ACCOUNT 2 – PERSONAL INCOME AND OUTLAY

	Personal outlays	
1	Personal tax and nontax payments (3-12)	869.7
2	Personal outlays	5,405.6
3	Personal consumption expenditures (1-33)	5,237.5
4	Interest paid by persons (1-17)	149.9
5	Personal transfer payments to the rest of the world (4-7)	18.2
6	*Personal saving (5-5)*	*272.1*
7	**Personal Taxes, Outlays, and Saving**	**6,547.4**

	Personal income	
8	Wage and salary disbursements (1-2)	3,626.5
9	Other labor income (1-5)	490.0
10	Proprietors' income with inventory valuation and capital consumption adjustments (1-6)	544.7
11	Rental income of persons with capital consumption adjustments (1-7)	129.7
12	Personal dividend income (1-13)	297.4
13	Personal interest income (1-17)	810.6
14	Transfer payments to persons (1-19 and 3-3)	928.8
15	Less: personal contributions for social insurance (3-15)	280.4
16	**Personal Income**	**6,547.4**

(continued)

TABLE Ca-D   Summary of the national income and product accounts: 1996   *Continued*

ACCOUNT 3 – GOVERNMENT RECEIPTS AND EXPENDITURES

	Government expenditures				Government receipts	
1	Consumption expenditures (1-47)	1,171.8		12	Personal tax and nontax payments (2-1)	869.7
2	Transfer payments	916.0		13	Corporate profits tax liability (1-11)	223.6
3	To persons (2-14)	902.4				
4	To the rest of the world (net) (4-8)	13.6		14	Indirect business tax and nontax liability (1-20)	620.0
5	Net interest paid (1-17)	274.4		15	Contributions for social insurance (1-4 and 2-15)	555.8
6	Less: Dividends received by government (1-13)	0.3				
7	Subsidies less current surplus of government enterprises (1-21)	22.6				
8	Less: Wage accruals less disbursements (1-2)	0.0				
9	**CURRENT EXPENDITURES**	**2,384.5**				
10	*Current surplus or deficit (–), NIPA (5-15)*	*–115.4*				
11	**Government Current Expenditures and Surplus**	**2,269.1**		**16**	**Government Current Receipts**	**2,269.1**

ACCOUNT 4 – FOREIGN TRANSACTIONS

	Receipts from rest of world (ROW)				Payments to rest of world (ROW)	
1	Exports of goods and services (1-45)	874.2		4	Imports of goods and services (1-46)	963.1
2	Income receipts from ROW (1-28)	245.6		5	Income payments to ROW (1-29)	227.5
				6	Transfer payments to ROW (net)	39.8
				7	From persons (net) (2-5)	18.2
				8	From government (net) (3-4)	13.6
				9	From business (1-19)	8.0
				10	*Net foreign investment (5-3)*	*–110.7*
3	**Receipts from Row**	**1,119.7**		**11**	**Payments to Row**	**1,119.7**

ACCOUNT 5 – GROSS SAVING AND INVESTMENT

	Investment				Saving	
1	Gross private domestic investment (1-37)	1,242.7		5	Personal saving (2-6)	272.1
2	Gross government investment (1-47)	250.1		6	Wage accruals less disbursements (private) (1-2)	3.6
3	Net foreign investment (4-10)	–110.7		7	Undistributed corporate profits with inventory and capital consumption adjustments (1-14, 1-15, and 1-16)	232.7
				8	Private consumption of fixed capital (1-23)	782.0
				9	Corporate consumption of fixed capital	543.5
				10	Noncorporate consumption of fixed capital	238.5
				11	**GROSS PRIVATE SAVING**	**1,290.4**
				12	Government consumption of fixed capital (1-24)	174.2
				13	Federal	85.3
				14	State and local	88.9
				15	Government current surplus and deficit (–), NIPA (3-10)	–115.4
				16	Federal	–136.8
				17	State and local	21.4
				18	**GROSS GOVERNMENT SAVING**	**58.9**
				19	Statistical discrepancy (1-31)	32.8
4	**Gross Investment**	**1,382.1**		**20**	**Gross Saving and Statistical Discrepancy**	**1,382.1**

Source

For the table layout: U.S. Bureau of Economic Analysis (BEA), "A Guide to the NIPAs," in *National Income and Product Accounts, 1929–97* (1998), Table A. For the 1996 data values: BEA Internet site, downloaded August 12, 2003; published August 1, 2003.

Documentation

Items in bold are totals or subtotals. Items in italics in accounts 1 through 4 are calculated as a residual. The line numbers are for cross reference; they are not assigned by the BEA. The numbers in parentheses after some item descriptions indicate the account and line number of the counterentry. For example, "Personal consumption expenditures (2-3)" in account 1, line 33, has its counterentry in account 2, line 3.

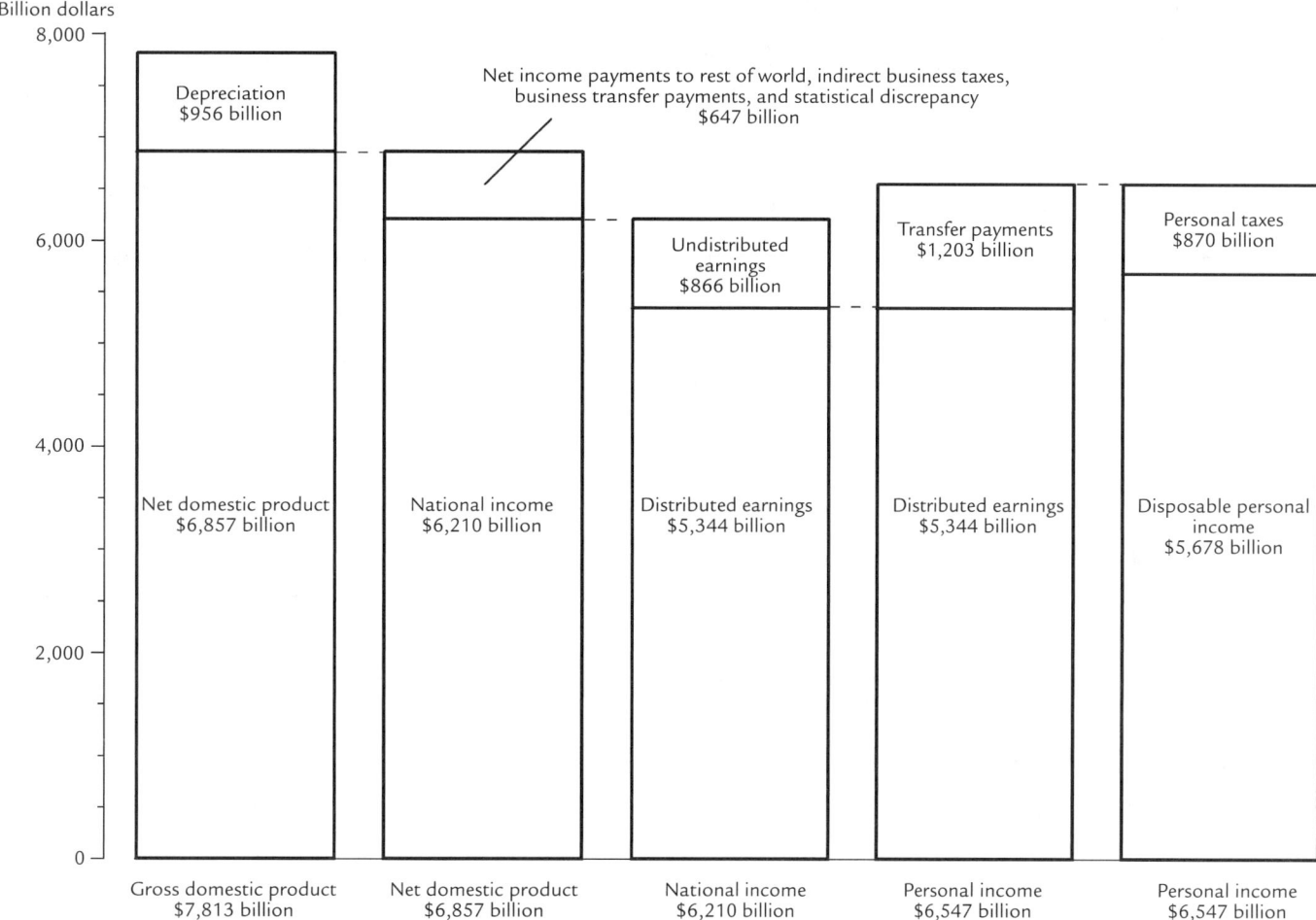

FIGURE Ca-E Relationships among the major NIPA aggregates: 1996

Source
Table Ca-D.

is calculated as a residual. When net foreign investment is positive, it means that Americans, on balance, have invested funds in foreign countries. When it is negative, as was the case in 1996, it means that, on balance, the ROW has invested in the U.S. economy.

Account 5 closes the system by organizing the remaining counterentries as a balance between saving (on the right) and investment (on the left). Note that the investment side records gross investment. Net investment is gross investment (line 4) less the consumption of fixed capital (the sum of lines 8 and 12).

Although the basic structure is summarized in the five accounts, there are other ways of disaggregating GDP. For example, Table Ca135–148 presents GDP based on sector of origin. A full set of the NIPA currently consists of 148 tables. The extent of detail presented in *Historical Statistics* is limited by space requirements; the full set of accounts is available on the BEA's Internet site, where the underlying data are constantly updated and frequently revised. The tables provided here for the period beginning in 1929 present only a hint of the rich detail available in the full accounts.

Greater detail on the account structure can be found in a publication of the BEA, *A Guide to the NIPAs*, which is also available on the BEA Internet site (Seskin and Parker 1998). The basic reference sources for concepts and methodology are "An Introduction

to National Income Accounting," "GNP: An Overview of Source Data and Estimating Methods," and "Updated Summary of NIPA Methodologies" (Young and Tice 1985; Carson 1987; U.S. Bureau of Economic Analysis 1998b).

Table Ca1–8 presents several major aggregates, including GDP, national income, and personal income. The relationship among these aggregates is depicted in Figure Ca-E. The difference between GDP and net domestic product is called capital consumption allowances, which is an estimate of the depreciation of the capital stock. The difference between net domestic product and national income is composed of (1) net income payments to the ROW, (2) indirect business tax and nontax liabilities that are chargeable as business expenses (primarily taxes on sales, property, and production, as well as excise taxes, but neither employer contributions to social insurance nor corporate income taxes), (3) business transfer payments to persons and the ROW (less subsidies to business), and (4) the statistical discrepancy discussed earlier. Indirect business taxes are the most significant of these four deductions. National income can be divided into undistributed earnings (consisting of corporate retained earnings, corporate profits tax, employer and employee contributions to social insurance, dividends paid to government, and any excess of wage accruals over disbursements) and distributed earnings. Distributed earnings plus transfer payments (which include net interest paid by the government and both business and government transfers to persons) constitute personal income. Personal income can be divided into personal taxes and disposable personal income (see Table Ca64–73).

Sources of Data

Most statistical data are collected for purposes other than for use in compiling the national accounts. There is no overarching database from which the NIPA tables are derived. Instead, the BEA relies on a large number of independently designed surveys and data collection protocols. However, it is true that many of these data sources have been shaped in part keeping in mind specific NIPA requirements. Many of the sources are agencies of the government, but private data sources are also used. Even when the source is a government agency, it is often the case that the government must rely on the cooperation of private firms and individuals to supply data and respond to surveys.

This state of affairs means that it is impossible to calculate formal measures of statistical reliability (Fixler and Grimm 2002). The sources used are generally reliable, but many are based on samples rather than a complete census of the economic activity. Users of the national accounts concerned about the accuracies of the measurements of a particular component will need to review the sources of data and the methodologies used by the BEA. Joseph Ritter provides an overview, which would serve as a good starting place (Ritter 2000).

Real versus Nominal National Product

Nominal GDP, calculated using the expenditure approach (the right-hand side of account 1 in Table Ca-D), is valued in terms of current transaction prices. When GDP measured in this way increases from one year to the next, it can be because the country produced more goods and services or because higher prices were paid. Often, the explanation involves a combination of both. If the chief cause of an increase in GDP is an increase in output, it means that the material standard of living has improved. If the primary reason for the change is a general increase in prices, then the cost of living has increased, with a very different implication for the average well-being of residents. It is important to decompose the change in nominal GDP into two components, the portion attributable to changing prices and the portion attributable to a change in production. The change in production is measured by a statistic called real GDP.

The proper accounting methods for calculating real GDP are the subject of a long-sustained dispute, which really has no unique solution. The accepted textbook definition of real GDP is the value of the final goods and services produced during the year when valued at "constant" prices. Typically, a "base year" is chosen to establish these prices, which are then used to evaluate GDP in all other years of interest. The BEA now uses the year 1996 as its base year and presents real GDP estimates (and its components) back to 1929 and forward beyond 1996 in terms of the 1996 prices (series Ca6–8). However, as a practical matter, each item in the GDP is not evaluated at 1996 prices. Given the countless transactions that make up the GDP, this ideal would be impossible to achieve. Furthermore, for some items produced in the years following 1996,

there was no "1996 price" for the simple reason that those products were first introduced in a subsequent year. In practice, the BEA uses the "deflation method" for the majority of the components of real GDP. In 1997, 83.6 percent of real GDP was estimated by deflation (Eldridge 1999).

The deflation approach calculates a quantity index by dividing the current dollar estimate by an appropriate price index. In its simplest form, the formula can be written as

$$\text{Real quantity} = \text{Nominal quantity}/\text{Price index}$$

The price index is constructed so that it equals 1 in the base year. This formula is not applied for each and every product but is instead applied to commodity groupings and thus sidesteps the problems of new goods. When used by the BEA, the deflation method is applied separately to detailed components of GDP using component estimates of the consumer price index (CPI), the producer price index (PPI), and several other indexes. For an extended discussion of price indexes, see Chapter Cc, on prices. For a discussion of the BEA's use of the deflation method, see the review by Lucy Eldridge (1999).

The traditional way in which the BEA defined real GDP was to total the real expenditures in each of the categories. The result is termed fixed-weight real GDP because the weights are the fixed prices of the base year. With both the fixed-weight real GDP and the nominal current-dollar GDP time series, the BEA then calculated an "implicit price deflator" (IPD) as the ratio of nominal GDP to real GDP.

Although this traditional method is intuitive and makes real GDP easy to interpret as *the value of output had all prices remained at the level of the base year*, it has several weaknesses. The first problem with this approach is that the choice of the base year is to some extent arbitrary, and yet the resulting rates of change of real GDP will depend on the particular base year chosen. If a commodity or service has an unusually low relative price in the base year, that component will receive a lower weight in the calculation of real GDP for all years than in a calculation in which a base year had been chosen in which that component had a relatively high price. The choice of a base year can have a profound effect on calculated growth rates. Take the change in GDP from 1997 to 1998 as an example. When 1995 is chosen as the base year, the growth rate would be calculated as 4.5 percent; using 1990 prices, it would be 6.5 percent (Whalen 2000).

The further back in time the base year is established, the higher will be the rate of growth for real GDP when adjusted by a fixed-weight index. Termed a substitution bias, this phenomenon is a consequence of consumers' tendency to substitute one category of goods for another as relative prices change. As an historical regularity, the economic sectors that had the most rapidly declining relative prices grew the most rapidly in terms of output. A base year further in the past, when prices in the rapidly growing sectors were relatively high, gives those sectors a large fixed weight and thus contributes to an exaggerated measured growth rate for real GDP in years when those sectors are expanding rapidly. Take the computer sector as an example. In 1970, the computer industry was still in its infancy; the sector was small, and prices were quite high. Over the next quarter century, computer prices tumbled, and the output of computers boomed. Using 1970 prices to evaluate the real growth of the sector produces enormous numbers for recent years that swamp the more modest growth rates of many of the other sectors. Thus, the growth rate of fixed-weight real GDP in 1998 – if measured using 1970 prices, when computers were very expensive – would be an astonishing 37.4 percent (Whalen 2000).

To minimize the effect of substitution bias on recent growth rates, BEA's practice was to move the base year forward periodically. Although this had the desired effect of making the growth estimates more reliable for the recent years, it made them worse for the distant past. Moreover, every time the base year was moved forward, the historical growth rates would change. Although this is awkward for those conducting historical research, the best advice for those using fixed-weight indexes is to choose a base year close to the historical period under study.

In 1996, BEA abandoned its traditional method and adopted the chain-linked method to calculate real GDP (Landefeld and Parker 1995, 1997). To address the problem that the choice of a base year is arbitrary, the new method calculates two price indexes, each with a base in a different but adjacent year, and then averages them. The price change between 1996 and 1997, for example, is calculated using 1996 prices in a fixed-weight index and then is reestimated using 1997 prices. The two estimates are then geometrically averaged (a geometric average is obtained by taking the square root of the product of the two numbers). This average, called a Fisher index, is a rough compromise between the upward substitution bias inherent in the 1996 base-year index and the downward bias that would be present in the index based on 1997 prices (Fisher 1922). The Fisher estimate of the 1996–1997 real change in GDP alleviates much of the problem associated with substitution bias. Annual real changes are calculated in this way for each adjacent pair of years and these are then "chained" together to form a continuous series that passes through the nominal GDP in the year chosen as the base.

Real GDP measured in "chained 1996 dollars" has several desirable properties. The ratio of nominal to real GDP is itself a Fisher index, thus allowing the continued use of this ratio as an implicit deflator for GDP (Table Ca149–158). As each year's output is evaluated at prices appropriate to that year, the chained-price real GDP avoids the need to update the base year routinely and the consequent "rewriting of economic history" whenever the base is changed (Landefeld and Parker 1997, p. 60). The new procedure has also eliminated distortions attributed to using price structures from a recent base year to examine events in the past when relative prices were quite different. The BEA provides a striking example:

> As measured by the old 1987 fixed-weighted index, real GDP dropped 25 percent from 1944 to 1947, reflecting the post–World War II demobilization and the associated sharp cutbacks in defense spending. However, much of this drop reflects the use of 1987 prices for defense equipment. As measured by the more appropriate price weights of BEA's new chain-type indexes, the postwar drop in real GDP is 13 percent. (Landefeld and Parker 1997, p. 60)

There is, however, a major drawback to the use of the new definition for real GDP. The components of real GDP will not sum to the total value. This is because the quantity indexes are forced to pass through the nominal estimates of GDP and its components in the base year (currently 1996). Thus, apart from that year, the 1996-dollar levels are based inconsistently on the annual weights

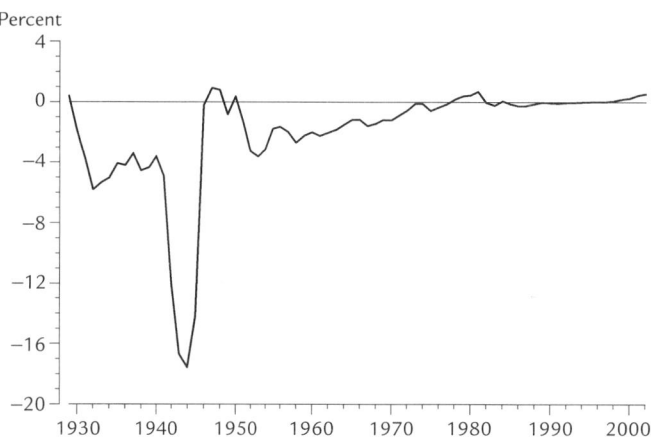

FIGURE Ca-F   The residual as a percentage of chain-weighted real GDP: 1929–2002

Source
Series Ca90 as a percentage of series Ca84.

involved in the chained growth rates *and* the quantity weights from the arbitrarily chosen base year. If one adds up the major components of chain-weighted real GDP (consumption, investment, government purchases, and exports minus imports; series Ca85–89) and then subtracts the result from chain-weighted real GDP (series Ca84), a "residual" is obtained (series Ca90). Figure Ca-F graphs this residual as a percent of real GDP.

As can be seen, the residual is generally larger the further back in time one looks. Very large residuals are shown for World War II and its immediate aftermath as the component weights from 1996 are strikingly different from those of the wartime economy.

The lack of additivity complicates the use of the chain-weighted components. Specifically, one cannot calculate the "share" of real GDP contributed by a component by using the data on the real components. Shares should be calculated using the nominal estimates of GDP and its components. In general, any calculations that involve ratios, sums, or differences between chain-weighted real series should be avoided. The BEA and Karl Whelan provide useful suggestions for users of the chain-weighted components (Landefeld and Parker 1997; Whalen 2000).

Because of the changing structure of the economy, it is best to use a base year for chained-dollar GDP that is close to the period of interest and to avoid using chained real GDP for studies of long-run trends. The interested user can "rebase" chained real GDP and its major components to an alternative base year by using BEA's "chain-type quantity indexes" (Howell 1997). These are presented in Table Ca159–168. For example, to create real GDP estimates in chained 1952 dollars, we take the current-dollar values of GDP (or one of its major components) from Table Ca74–90. The chain-type quantity indexes for a span of years preceding and following 1952 are then taken from Table Ca159–168. These are used to extrapolate the 1952 current-dollar figures forward and backward. The calculations are illustrated in Table Ca-G. This methodology produces a usable approximation for calculating the shares of each component of real GDP for years close to the new base year, as indicated by the small residuals. BEA publishes a small set of chained real GDP estimates with alternative base years (U.S. Bureau of Economic Analysis 1998a, 1998b). The one for

TABLE Ca-G   An illustration of rebasing estimates of real gross domestic product and its components

	Year	Gross domestic product	Personal consumption expenditures	Gross private domestic investment	Exports of goods and services	Imports of goods and services	Government consumption expenditures and gross investment	Residual
Chain-type quantity indexes (1996 = 100)	1948	19.97	19.06	17.33	6.84	5.65	23.13	—
	1949	19.85	19.58	13.22	6.78	5.45	25.83	—
	1950	21.59	20.83	18.71	5.93	6.44	25.84	—
	1951	23.23	21.14	18.77	7.27	6.69	35.16	—
	1952	24.16	21.81	16.99	6.93	7.28	42.56	—
	1953	25.26	22.86	17.78	6.47	7.97	45.54	—
	1954	25.09	23.33	16.96	6.78	7.57	42.40	—
	1955	26.87	25.02	21.09	7.50	8.49	40.82	—
	1956	27.40	25.75	20.81	8.75	9.17	40.85	—
GDP in chained 1952 dollars	1948	296.4	192.0	55.1	16.1	11.9	45.6	−0.5
	1949	294.6	197.2	42.0	15.9	11.5	50.9	0.0
	1950	320.5	209.8	59.5	13.9	13.5	50.9	−0.2
	1951	344.8	213.0	59.7	17.1	14.1	69.3	−0.2
	1952	358.6	219.7	54.0	16.3	15.3	83.9	0.0
	1953	374.9	230.3	56.5	15.2	16.8	89.8	−0.1
	1954	372.4	235.0	53.9	15.9	15.9	83.6	−0.1
	1955	398.8	252.0	67.0	17.6	17.8	80.5	−0.5
	1956	406.7	259.4	66.1	20.6	19.3	80.5	−0.7

Sources

Chain-type quantity indexes: Table Ca159–168. Gross domestic product (GDP) and its major components for 1952: Table Ca74–90.

Documentation

The chain-type quantity indexes in the top panel are used to extrapolate the 1952 data forward and backward. For example, GDP in chained 1952 dollars can be computed as follows:

For years before the base year: $GDP_t = GDP_{t+1} * (I_t/I_{t+1})$

$$GDP_{1951} = GDP_{1952} * (I_{1951}/I_{1952})$$

$$344.8 = 358.6 * (23.23/24.16)$$

For years after the base year: $GDP_t = GDP_{t-1} * (I_t/I_{t-1})$

$$GDP_{1953} = GDP_{1952} * (I_{1953}/I_{1952})$$

$$374.9 = 358.6 * (25.26/24.16)$$

1929–1947 uses 1937 dollars; for 1942–1962 the base is 1952 dollars, and so on.

References

See the references at the conclusion of the essay on estimates of national product before 1929, in this chapter.

ESTIMATES OF NATIONAL PRODUCT BEFORE 1929

Paul W. Rhode and Richard Sutch

The official estimates of national income and product provided by the Bureau of Economic Analysis (BEA) begin in 1929. The broad interest in long-term trends has generated a number of attempts to estimate national product for the earlier period. We briefly summarize this work, concentrating on annual estimates of real national output suitable for estimating economic and productivity growth. One product of this effort is a new annual series on real per capita gross product for 1790–2000 (Table Ca9–19).

Although estimates of aggregate output for the nineteenth and early twentieth centuries are undoubtedly valuable for the study of economic growth, the increase in the average standard of living, and other long-run trends, a concern arises because aggregate measures of output presented as annual time series are also used to study fluctuations in economic activity. However, the standards of precision in the estimates of national output required for examination of short-run changes, study of business cycles, or analysis of macroeconomic dynamics are much higher than those required to assess the pace and pattern of long-term economic growth. In Chapter Cb, data on economic fluctuations are described in detail. This chapter deals with estimates of national product that are intended primarily to focus on trends rather than fluctuations.

It is important to note that all pre-1929 estimates are based on fragmentary data that were not originally collected for the purpose of making national product estimates. This means that the series are less precise than the official estimates. Moreover, the further back in time these estimating methods are pushed, the more degraded the quality of existing data and the more scarce reliable detailed series become. These problems force the investigator to fill the gaps with interpolated data, rough estimates, and conjectural relationships between available and missing data. Finally, most experts in the field regard all of the available annual estimates of gross product before 1909 as unfinished "work in progress." Simon Kuznets, John Kendrick, and Robert Gallman, whose work on pre-1929 gross national product (GNP) is the foundation for all existing estimates, did not publish their annual series for the early period (Kuznets 1946, 1961; Kendrick 1961; Gallman 1966). They were interested in long-run trends and the factors underlying economic growth, not in annual economic fluctuations. Their annual estimates were not intended to accurately measure the timing and magnitude of recessions and depressions. At the time of his death in 1998, Gallman still regarded his annual series as subject to revision (Rhode 2002).

Attempts to estimate aggregate national output actually predate the work of Kuznets initiated in the 1930s by the Department of Commerce. Writing in 1806, Samuel Blodget was the pioneer of this field. He produced an estimate of national income in 1805 by classifying all employed persons into seven different categories, ranging from slaves to professionals. He then estimated the number of workers and dependents in each class and the average income for members of the seven classes. Totaling the products for each class, Blodget produced the aggregate for the country (Blodget 1806, p. 89). In 1843, George Tucker, a former member of Congress, based an estimate of the national product on the returns of the Census of 1840, and in 1855 he produced a second edition of his book with estimates of both national income and national product for 1850 (Tucker 1843–1855). Ezra Seaman also produced estimates of national product based on the 1840 and 1850 Censuses (Seaman 1846, 1852). In the 1890s, Charles Spahr produced estimates of national income for 1880 and 1890 based on the censuses of those years (Spahr 1896). Willford I. King extended this work to 1910 and back to 1850 (King 1915).

Kuznets–Kendrick Series

Modern estimates of long-term change in national product are based on the pioneering work of Simon Kuznets. In 1941, Kuznets extended his annual estimates of GNP, which originally spanned 1929–1932, back to 1919 (Kuznets 1941). He later published estimates for overlapping decades for 1869–1878 through 1914–1923 (Kuznets 1946). In 1961, he revised and finalized his annual estimates for 1869–1918. However, he published the annual estimates only for 1889–1918. He presented the earlier data only as overlapping decadal averages for 1869–1878 to 1884–1893, explaining that they "did not seem sufficiently reliable as *annual* measures to warrant presentation" (Kuznets 1961, p. 534). The underlying annual data, however, were widely circulated in mimeographed form by the National Bureau of Economic Research and have been widely used by subsequent researchers (Kuznets circa 1961).

Kuznets produced four variants of his estimates for GNP. These he labeled "Component Series, Variants I and III" and "Regression Series, Variants I and III." Variants I and III differ in the way that services were estimated. Variant I estimates services as a residual by subtracting all of the other components of GNP from an independently measured estimate of national income. Variant III estimates services directly (Kuznets 1961, p. 472). Variant II was not estimated as an annual series for the years before 1919.

The Component Series estimated each of ten components of GNP separately and then summed the components to arrive at the comprehensive total. Kuznets expressed the view that these estimates were excessively volatile and would exaggerate the amplitude of the business cycle (Kuznets 1961, p. 546). He made and published alternative estimates of GNP, which he labeled the Regression Series. This series extrapolates real GNP for the period 1889–1908 on an index of finished commodity output, derived from the work of William Shaw, using a nonlinear regression of GNP on commodity output estimated with data from the period spanning 1909–1938 (Shaw 1947; Kuznets 1961, pp. 536–8, series R-21(6)). Shaw's aggregates are reproduced in Table Ca169–183. Shaw's finished commodity output, which was adjusted and used

by Kuznets, is series Ca183. As intended, the effect of Kuznets's regression method was to damp the fluctuations in estimated GNP below those of commodity output.

The long-run trend of all of the Kuznets variants relies on a single set of benchmarks calculated largely with data drawn from the federal Censuses of Agriculture and Manufacturing. From 1840 through 1930 these censuses were conducted at the same time as the population census (in years ending in zero), but the outputs that were collected from each farm and firm were those of the previous calendar year (years ending in nine). Because the Censuses of Agriculture and Manufacturing were quite comprehensive, they provide strong statistical bases for estimating national product for 1839, 1849, 1859, 1869, 1879, 1889, 1899, 1909, and 1919. In addition, supplementary manufacturing censuses allowed for the creation of benchmarks for 1904, 1914, and 1924.

The Component Series bridged the gap between benchmarks by interpolating with available annual series for each of the ten components. Generally speaking, there exist fewer – and less reliable – data for the intercensal years, so a variety of interpolation techniques were used. For physical goods Kuznets relied heavily on the commodity flow statistics compiled by Shaw. Kuznets's Regression Series interpolated between the benchmarks for aggregate GNP and is thus available only for the aggregate and not for its component parts. Both Variants I and III of Kuznets's component GNP estimates are presented in Table Ca184–191. Despite Kuznets's preference for the less volatile regression estimates, most subsequent work has employed his directly estimated Component Series because only they provide component detail.

The definition that Kuznets adopted for GNP differed from the concept of gross domestic product (GDP) used by the Department of Commerce today. At the time he was writing, the Department of Commerce also preferred the GNP concept. It was not until 1991 that the official series was shifted from GNP to GDP. The difference between GDP and GNP is net receipts of income from the rest of the world (U.S. Bureau of Economic Analysis 1991, p. 8). For the years before 1929, the distinction between GNP and GDP is small.

Kuznets's definition of GNP also differed in concept from the Department of Commerce's definition of GNP. Kuznets treated government purchases quite differently and excluded the unpaid services of financial intermediaries. He regarded much of government output as an intermediate rather than a final product, basing his argument on the idea that GNP should be a measure of the satisfaction of final wants. Many government services, such as those that contribute to business productivity or maintain social stability (including nondurable national security outlays), he argued, were a means to better satisfy end wants rather than services directly desired for their own utility.

Shortly after the appearance of Kuznets's estimates, his former student John Kendrick undertook adjustments to Kuznets's Component Series, Variant III, to bring Kuznets's series into conceptual and statistical alignment with the official estimates of GNP published by the U.S. Department of Commerce (Kendrick 1961). These involved adopting the official treatment of government expenditure and adding an imputed series on the unpaid services provided by financial intermediaries (Kendrick 1961, pp. 238–46, and Table A-IIb, pp. 296–7). The resulting adjustment raised Kuznets's estimates by a fairly stable, slightly contracyclical, 3 to 4 percent throughout the entire period 1869–1908. Kendrick's estimates of GNP are presented as series Ca188–189. Series Ca191 gives Kendrick's estimates of GDP. Kendrick's series has an advantage over Kuznets's insofar as consistency with the official estimates after 1929 is desirable. However, Kendrick's estimates of government purchases of goods and services are somewhat rough, and users who do not care about this consistency or who are persuaded by Kuznets's argument for his treatment of government may prefer the original.

Gallman Series

Robert Gallman, another of Kuznets's students, undertook the task of revising Kuznets's GNP series and extending it back to 1839. The Gallman estimates were originally published in 1966 as overlapping decade averages. Gallman never published the annual data, in part because he worried that they would be used to analyze business cycle movements, a purpose for which they were not designed. In the best scholarly tradition, he did make his numbers available through the avenue of personal correspondence, with the appropriate caveats, to other economists and economic historians "for testing purposes." They are published here for the first time, with the warning that they are not appropriate for studies of economic fluctuations or dynamics.

Gallman produced estimates for the periods 1834–1859 and 1869–1909, using the same basic methodological framework, but those for the earlier period required substantially more original work (Tables Ca192–207 and Ca219–232). Construction of the series generally involved establishing solid benchmarks every five or ten years and then using a less comprehensive set of annual time series to interpolate values for the intervening years. Gallman did not make annual estimates for 1861–1869 because he did not believe he had reliable interpolating series for the decade that witnessed the American Civil War. Gallman's pre–Civil War estimates will be discussed after the description of the post–Civil War period.

For the post–Civil War period, Gallman largely adjusted estimates made by Kuznets, working with Kuznets's Variant I Component Series. Gallman made a number of adjustments to Kuznets's series that increased his benchmark estimates for the early years and reduced the trend rate of growth before 1889 but left the year-to-year movements proportionally unaffected. Gallman's principal adjustments to the Kuznets series are (1) substitution of new estimates for firewood, animal products, and federal excise taxes for the Shaw series used by Kuznets; (2) incorporation of new estimates of distribution costs, based on Harold Barger's work (Barger 1955); (3) separation of railroad construction from other building activity, based on series taken from Melville Ulmer (Ulmer 1960); and (4) deflation of the current-value GNP series by Dorothy Brady's detailed final price indexes, using an 1860 base (Brady 1966). By construction, the large upward revisions for the early years gradually taper to a "smooth link at 1909 with the Kuznets series" (Gallman 1966, p. 31).

Two points deserve attention. The first is that the Gallman estimates incorporated the most up-to-date data available in the early 1960s. To the extent that researchers over the past four decades have generated new statistics on the production or prices of individual goods and services, it should be possible for today's scholars to produce improved national product figures. Second, the annual national product series between the benchmark years is interpolated or extrapolated using a less comprehensive set of products than is used in the benchmark years. The main issue is how representa-

tive the movements in this data series are. For the post–Civil War period, many scholars believe that the Gallman–Kuznets series is reasonably reliable for studying long-run trends (see our comments on the excess volatility debate and the Balke–Gordon series in the following sections).

As we have emphasized, the interpolation and extrapolation procedures were designed to determine long-run trends, but as Gallman noted, they are problematic for analyzing business cycle fluctuations. This is especially true for investigations of the changing volatility of the macroeconomy or for comparison of one specific cycle with another. This message carries double weight for analyses contrasting the behavior of the antebellum and postbellum series, which are constructed in significantly different ways.

At the time of his death in 1998, Gallman had made several revisions to his post–Civil War series. Two seem particularly important to the overall research agenda designed to produce meaningful estimates of both long-term growth and cyclical changes. Gallman had prepared a revised version of railroad construction, based on data from Albert Fishlow, that corrected serious deficiencies in his earlier railroad construction estimates, and he had calculated estimates of the change in business inventories that, when added to his original GNP estimates, would bring his aggregate closer to the conventional definition of GNP, which includes this form of investment (and which is of importance to any study of business fluctuations). The series we present in Table Ca192–207 include these revisions. While preparing the Gallman series for publication, Paul Rhode also corrected several errors and made other minor revisions to the original Gallman numbers. See the documentation for Table Ca192–207 and Rhode (2002) for details. For this reason, the totals for GNP (series Ca192) and for GNP excluding inventory change differ from those that underlay the overlapping decade averages published by Gallman.

Standard Series

With two different revisions proposed to the Kuznets series for 1869–1909 – one by Kendrick to bring it into conceptual alignment with the Department of Commerce estimates and another set of improvements by Gallman – economists have tended to accept both revisions. This has produced a series known as the "Standard Series" (Balke and Gordon 1989, p. 49). Table Ca208–212 presents this series and documents the methods used in its computation. Because the version of Gallman's series that is reported here differs somewhat from the original Gallman data, this version of the Standard Series also incorporates the improvements introduced by Rhode.

Although there is room for dispute and much scope for improvement, most experts are now inclined to accept the Standard Series estimates for the period 1869–1909 as the best currently available. They especially depend on the Gallman series, and, as Rhode has concluded, Gallman's estimates "remain among the best numbers we have for this period." Gallman's data set also provides details on the components of GNP that no subsequent research has replaced.

Excess Volatility Debate

Neither Kuznets nor Gallman approved of the use of their annual series for the study of short-term economic fluctuations. Yet the temptation for others to use them for this purpose was strong. Economists have used annual data for 1869–1908 as evidence about the degree of price, output, and employment flexibility in the American economy (Gordon 1981, 1982; Friedman and Schwartz 1982; DeLong and Summers 1986; Allen 1992). In particular, comparison of the volatility of the Standard Series with the fluctuation of the official post–World War II data has led many to the conclusion that economic fluctuations have moderated since World War II (Bailey 1978; Gordon 1986; Zarnowitz 1992). In 1999, the Secretary of Commerce, when naming national income accounting as the department's "achievement of the century," attributed the reduced harshness of the business cycle to the development of reliable national accounts data, which led to better macroeconomic policy. To bolster this claim, he presented a chart that joined data from Kendrick with the official series beginning in 1929 (Daley 2000).

Yet in an influential series of articles, Christina Romer has argued forcefully that this conclusion is inappropriate (Romer 1986a, 1986b, 1988, 1989; Miron and Romer 1990). In particular, she claims that the Standard Series on GNP exaggerates the fluctuations in economic activity in the period before World War I (Romer 1989). She explains that Kuznets's component estimates implicitly assume that output valued in market prices moves proportionately with commodity output measured in producer prices. She claims that this "might not be true." Moreover, she suggests that both "economic theory and modern experience suggest that GNP actually moves much less over the cycle than commodity output" because the service components are less affected by "aggregate shocks" (Romer 1989, p. 2). Because she believed that the Standard Series exhibited excess volatility, Romer undertook to revise that series by adopting Kuznets's regression method to damp the fluctuations in GNP. By design, Romer's regression estimates are less volatile than the Standard Series. They are reproduced in Table Ca213–218.

Critics of Romer's work have joined, but not resolved, the ensuing debate (Lebergott 1986; Balke and Gordon 1989; Zarnowitz 1992, pp. 77–9; Weir 1992). There are three basic issues.

(1) Although it is granted that much of the direct evidence used by Kuznets and Gallman consisted of cyclically volatile series, this was well known to them, and they took care to avoid introducing spurious volatility in the broad aggregates. Moreover, excess volatility in some components was offset, at least partially, by inadequately measured volatility in other components. A number of the series were converted from fiscal year observations to calendar years by averaging, thus reducing the volatility of the series. When there was inadequate interpolating data, smooth interpolations were used for some of the components. Ultimately, the volatility displayed by the annual series is the product of explicit, conscious data collection and assembly choices. The possibility of a bias, as Zarnowitz notes, results "from the lack of data and so has no real solution short of introducing new pertinent historical information" (Zarnowitz 1992, p. 78).

(2) Kuznets's and Romer's regression procedures are intended to reduce the volatility of the component estimates, and, by design, they do. However, we have no direct way of determining whether a reduction in volatility is in fact warranted and, if so, whether either of these damping procedures gets it right. Romer makes six changes to Kuznets's procedures, yet there are neither theoretical nor historical reasons to prefer her choices to those of Kuznets.

(3) The regression procedures impose recent relationships between commodity output and GNP on the more distant past. In Romer's case, data as recent as 1985 are employed to estimate those relationships, which are then applied to years as far back as 1869. This ignores the structural changes that have occurred in the economy during this period of more than a century. These structural changes include the growth of government, with its stable spending patterns; the secular decline in agriculture, which was a majority activity in 1869; the growth of services; and the revolutions in manufacturing technology, business organization, and distribution. More fundamentally, the presumed stability in the structure of the economy precludes any possibility that macroeconomic policy guided by national income statistics *could have* moderated the business cycle. The method rules out the possibility that the application of Keynesian stabilization policy and the establishment of the independent Federal Reserve System to manage credit and monetary policy worked to prevent financial crises.

Balke–Gordon Series

Alone among Romer's critics, Nathan S. Balke and Robert J. Gordon not only rejected Romer's procedures but also undertook the estimation of a new annual series for real GNP for 1869–1908 (Balke and Gordon 1989). Their innovation was to introduce a multivariate regression procedure to estimate GNP. The three independent variables were Kuznets's estimates of real commodity output (based on Shaw) and two indexes, one that directly measured real output in trade and transportation and one that directly measured the real value of nonfarm buildings. Romer's method used only the commodity output series. All variables were measured as a percentage deviation from trend. The sample period was 1909–1938. The estimated regression parameters were then used to backcast GNP to 1869, using the data on all three independent variables.

The Balke–Gordon estimates "are as volatile on average over the business cycle as the . . . [Standard S]eries" and are more volatile than Romer's series (Balke and Gordon 1989, p. 38). Although they "judge the components method [used to calculate the Standard Series] to be superior in theory, in practice the two methods yield almost identical conclusions regarding prewar GNP volatility" (Balke and Gordon 1989, p. 85). Balke and Gordon also constructed new annual deflators based primarily on the consumer price indexes prepared by Ethel Hoover and Albert Rees (Hoover 1960; Rees 1961), in contrast to Kuznets's deflator, which was based on wholesale price indexes (Balke and Gordon 1989, pp. 71–5). These estimates are distinctly less volatile than the traditional series. Their new deflator allowed them to calculate a current-dollar series (see Table Ca213–218). Because the new deflator is probably superior to the deflators implicit in the Standard Series, one might use the Balke–Gordon deflator to convert the real Standard Series in Table Ca208–212 into a current-dollar series (note that the base of the Balke–Gordon deflator would have to be shifted to 1929 dollars).

Pre–Civil War Estimates

Gallman constructed his pre–Civil War national product series by (1) taking his benchmark figures for commodity production (agriculture, mining, and manufacturing) for the years 1834, 1836,

1839, 1844, 1849, 1854, and 1859 (Gallman 1960); (2) adding estimates for the value of services based largely on capital stock series; and (3) interpolating the series in the intervening years using scattered annual data on numerous economic activities. The "major" benchmarks (1839, 1849, and 1859) were primarily based on materials from the U.S. Census, whereas the "minor" benchmarks (1834, 1836, 1844, and 1854) used several state censuses. Gallman believed that the use of more frequent benchmarks for the pre–Civil War series reduced some of the problems of interpolation that plagued the post–Civil War estimates. Gallman's estimates are presented in Table Ca219–232.

There remains the question of how reliable the interbenchmark estimates for the pre–Civil War period are. This comes down to a question of the adequacy of the series used to interpolate between the benchmarks. Gallman noted that the statistics on net imports "receive relatively too much weight," industrial equipment is "inadequately represented," many of the major groups rely on one or a few underlying series, and the flow of materials into production (such as wheat, corn, raw cotton and wool, and lumber) tended to dominate the series. He adds, lest these warnings "raise too many doubts, bear in mind that the interpolations and extrapolations generally carry over only four years, and frequently fewer years than this" (Gallman 1966, pp. 64–71).

As with the post–Civil War series, Gallman did not publish his annual numbers, and he was generally opposed to work using his annual national product series to compare the volatility of pre- and postwar business cycles. However, he also took strong issue with claims that his procedures to estimate noncommodity production over the 1839–1859 period generated excessively volatile series. In his view, any bias in volatility due to his construction procedure was likely to be weak or to work in the opposite direction from what is usually suggested. The pre–Civil War series was not constructed using Kuznets's ratio method to estimate service flows, but rather using the growth of housing stocks, which was far smoother. Services, which accounted for about 24 percent of Gallman's real value estimate of national product over the 1834–1859 period, were estimated as a smooth series between the benchmarks. In addition, the estimates for firewood production, which accounted for about 6 percent of national product, relied on straight-line interpolation. One offsetting force was the interpolation using net imports, which tended to "oscillate fairly widely" over the 1834–1842 period, but Gallman "attempted to dilute the effect of these oscillations by bringing the leather series into the interpolator" (Gallman 1966, pp. 64 and 71).

Gallman's definition of GDP for the pre–Civil War era was the same as that used by Kuznets (1961) for the years following the Civil War; thus, it is not consistent with the Standard Series, which has been adjusted to the Department of Commerce definitions. However, because the government was relatively small before the Civil War, Kendrick-like adjustments would increase Gallman's figures by only a small and stable percentage.

Slave Economy Concept of GDP

A more fundamental, perhaps even philosophical, issue arises concerning the proper definition of GNP for a slave economy. Simon Kuznets hinted that the consumption of slaves should not be viewed as final goods, because slaves were like "tools" and hence their consumption would be intermediate inputs into production (Kuznets 1961, p. 466). This approach would treat slaves as work animals or

machines rather than as human beings. At first blush, such a view will undoubtedly offend modern sensibilities, but from a strictly economic point of view, slaves were assets rather than citizens. They were not free agents allowed to earn a living and make consumption choices as they pleased. It comes down to what purpose the aggregate statistics will be used for. For those interested in GNP as an index of the well-being of all residents of the country, slaves included, the Gallman definition is appropriate. However, if one is interested in capital formation, saving, and the mechanisms of economic growth, then a modified definition of GNP might be seen as more appropriate (Ransom and Sutch 1988).

To adjust the Gallman estimates in Table Ca219–232 to a slave economy definition of GNP, we must subtract the value of slave consumption and add the value of the increase in the slave stock. The latter can be thought of as a form of capital formation. Table Ca233–240 makes a rough adjustment along these lines. The net effects are to lower GNP and raise the rate of capital formation. To calculate real GNP *per capita* using the Gallman concept, one simply divides his estimates by the total population. However, when using the slave economy concept, only the *free* population is included in the denominator (series Ca238). The slave economy estimate of material well-being is larger than the Gallman estimate because only the welfare of the free population is measured. The standard of living was higher for the free population (an average of $146 in 1859, when measured in 1860 prices) than for the slave population (only $29.45).

Statistical Dark Age: 1790–1840

The long-run trends in real national product are defined by the decennial benchmarks based on the U.S. Censuses of Population, Agriculture, and Manufacturing. Because the first census that comprehensively surveyed manufacturing and agriculture was the Census of 1840 (with economic data for 1839), direct estimates of gross product are not possible before that date. This led Paul David to label the pre-1839 period the "statistical dark age" (David 1967b). The absence of direct data, however, has not prevented scholars from making conjectures about the likely trend of output per capita going back to the beginning of the nineteenth century. Several estimates are presented in Table Ca9–19. Users must be cautioned about the fragility of these estimates. The paragraphs that follow describe the procedures used to make output estimates for the period 1790–1840.

Dividing the standard Kuznets–Gallman series for real GNP (series Ca212) by the population (series Aa9) allows us to estimate the rate of economic growth for the period 1869–1929. This statistic is remarkably stable at about 1.7 percent per annum. Interestingly, the annual estimates of the rate of growth of per capita GNP based on the work of Robert Gallman also grow at approximately 1.7 percent, whether one uses Gallman's GNP concept or the slave economy concept (series Ca239–240). Raymond Goldsmith first called attention to this remarkable stability in the rate of growth over the century from 1840 to 1940 (Goldsmith 1959). Given that stability, we may be tempted to extrapolate these growth rates backward into the statistical dark age. However, if we succumb to that temptation, we soon observe improbably low figures (North 1966, p. 16). Thus, Goldsmith postulated that there must have been an acceleration in growth sometime "not very long before 1839" (Goldsmith 1959, pp. 277–8). W. W. Rostow argued (on the basis of little evidence) that the acceleration or "take-off," as he called it, was an abrupt shift from little or no growth to sustained economic growth. He placed the break around the 1840s and argued that the development of the railroad network in the 1838–1845 period was the proximate cause of the change (Rostow 1960).

It had seemed impossible to Goldsmith, Rostow, and North to get solid numbers on which to estimate national output for the period before 1839. The underlying data on production, particularly on the crucial manufacturing sector, simply did not exist. Yet this did not quell a lively debate about Rostow's take-off hypothesis, his dating of the take-off, and its connection to railroad construction (Fogel 1964; Fishlow 1965; North 1966).

Paul David introduced an ingenious method for extending the numbers back before 1840 (David 1967a). GNP per capita can be decomposed into the product of worker productivity (i.e., average output per worker) and the rate of labor force participation (workers per capita). Stanley Lebergott made a major contribution by estimating the size of the labor force at each census date from the first Census in 1790 (Lebergott 1964). He also estimated the proportion of the total labor force that worked in agriculture (Table Ba814–830). Average productivity for the economy could be calculated, David observed, as a weighted average of agricultural productivity and nonagricultural productivity, with the weights determined by the relative proportion of the labor force in the two sectors. A fundamental ingredient for the application of David's methodology was a decennial series on crop output estimated by Marvin Towne and Wayne Rasmussen (Table Da1277–1287) (Towne and Rasmussen 1960). By deflating the Towne–Rasmussen output series by Lebergott's series on agricultural labor force, David was able to compute an index of agricultural labor productivity for 1800–1840. This series showed little (or no) growth between 1800 and 1820 and then rose rapidly between 1820 and 1840, spurred on by the opening of the highly fertile new lands in the Ohio valley and the Alabama–Mississippi cotton belt.

Next turning to Gallman's estimates of GDP for 1839–1840, David was able to obtain an estimate of agricultural productivity based on Gallman's agricultural output and Lebergott's agricultural labor force in that year. This established a point on which he could peg the Towne–Rasmussen index (see point A in Figure Ca-H). At the time David was writing, virtually nothing was known about the level of nonagricultural productivity in the antebellum period. However, David could calculate the level of nonagricultural productivity in 1840 implied by Gallman's work. Lebergott's estimates gave him the respective proportions of the total labor force in agriculture and nonagriculture; he had calculated the level of agricultural productivity from the Towne and Rasmussen data (point A); and Gallman's work, of course, gave him the level of output per capita (point B). Thus, David could establish that nonagricultural productivity was at the (relative) level of point C.

If we take time to think about it, this is an astonishing result. Because agricultural productivity was so far below overall productivity, a worker off the farm produced twice as much output as a farmer, and this in a country that had a level of agricultural productivity higher than had been seen in world history. Indeed, if such an enormous gap in productivity were a feature of the half-century between 1790 and 1840, it would have been an enormous engine of growth. Workers willing to take the risk and leave the security and independence of agriculture for a job in manufacturing could double their incomes. No wonder the proportion of the labor force in agriculture fell dramatically over the fifty-year period. As more

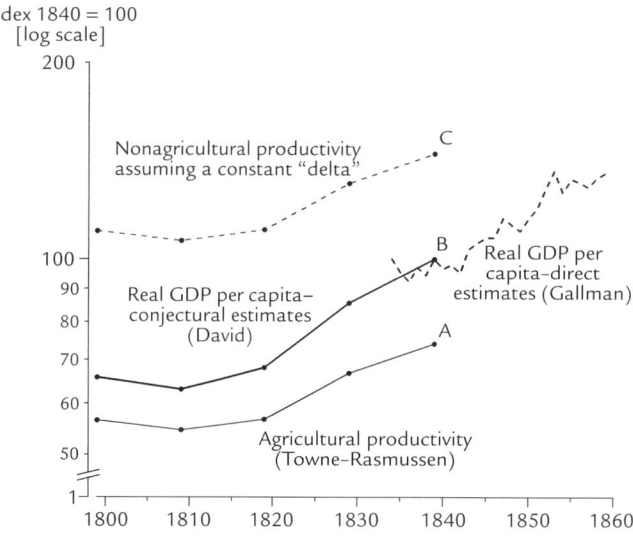

Index 1840 = 100 [log scale]

FIGURE Ca-H   Paul David's method of extrapolating real GDP per capita back to 1799

Source

See discussion in the text.

and more workers poured into nonagricultural jobs, the overall productivity of the economy rose.

Having no information on the trend of nonagricultural productivity between 1800 and 1840, David adopted the expedient of assuming that the ratio of nonagricultural productivity to agricultural productivity remained a constant over the forty-year period. This constant he called "delta." Although obviously arbitrary, the assumption of a constant productivity advantage was not entirely indefensible. There would have been two offsetting forces operating on this productivity gap. Working to close the gap would be the rising fraction of the labor force working in the nonagricultural sector. The higher wages possible in the manufacturing sector would attract some workers away from agriculture. The flood of workers into manufacturing and other nonagricultural pursuits should have slowed the productivity advance of that sector, whereas the slower growth of the agricultural labor force would (other things being equal) encourage productivity growth in that sector. On the other hand, the appearance and rapid expansion of manufacturing could be supposed to be accompanied by very rapid productivity gains as new methods of production were devised, learning by doing took place, and technological obstacles were overcome. David's assumption of a constant delta amounts to assuming that the classical equilibrating mechanism just offset the forces that might have otherwise exaggerated the gap between nonagricultural and agricultural productivity. The projection of nonagricultural productivity back to 1799–1800 from point C in the diagram reflects this guess.

Average economy-wide productivity is a weighted average of the productivities in the two sectors. The weights are the proportions of the labor force in agriculture and elsewhere. In 1800 and 1810, most Americans worked in agriculture, so David's conjectural estimates of GDP per capita are close to the level established by agricultural productivity. After 1810, the changing weights pull the average up and closer to the productivity line reflecting off-farm productivity. By 1840, economy-wide productivity is at point B.

David's conjectural estimates were a blow to Rostow's take-off thesis. They show no sharp acceleration in the rate of growth before 1820. The impact of the railroad age initiated in the late 1830s is not evident in the aggregate figures (although the railroads were undoubtedly part of the process that kept the rate of growth sustained at 1.7 percent for the next seven decades). David's work has stood as a foundation for the picture of American economic growth in the period before 1840. However, work by Thomas Weiss, Nancy Folbre, and Barnet Wagman suggests that revisions in David's estimates are warranted. These scholars accept the basic methodology but challenge the underlying data.

Weiss proposed three refinements to David's data inputs. First, and central to Weiss's research agenda, he proposed revisions in Lebergott's labor force data (Table Ba814–830) (Weiss 1992). The revisions change both the overall labor force participation rate of the population and its division into farm and nonfarm occupations. Second, Weiss revised the Towne–Rasmussen agricultural output series by expanding the definition of agricultural productivity to include the rental value of farm structures and the production of firewood for home use and sale, and he revised the Towne–Rasmussen estimates of home manufactures and the value created by land clearing and other farm "improvement" activities (Weiss 1993). Third, Weiss used estimates made by Kenneth Sokoloff of manufacturing productivity growth between 1820 and 1840 to challenge David's assumption of a constant productivity gap (delta) (Sokoloff 1986). However, Weiss adopted – consistent with David – a constant delta gap for the period 1800–1820.

The effect of the agricultural productivity revisions is to slow the rate of growth in that sector, because Weiss's estimates of imputed rents, firewood, and land improvements all grow more slowly than crop output. Weiss also reduces the rate at which the labor force moves from agricultural to nonagricultural pursuits, further slowing the rate of overall growth. Working against these revisions, which slowed the conjectural rate of growth over the 1820–1840 period, was Weiss's relaxation of David's constant advantage of nonagriculture over the farm sector. Making use of Kenneth Sokoloff's analysis of the McLane report on manufacturing (McLane 1833), Weiss argued that manufacturing productivity grew much faster than agricultural productivity between 1820 and 1840. Of course, not all nonagriculture is manufacturing. So Weiss assumed that manufacturing grew at Sokoloff's 2.3 percent per annum between 1820 and 1840, but that nonmanufacturing, nonagricultural productivity grew at the same rate as agricultural productivity. He assumed that nonagricultural production grew at the same rate as agricultural output before 1820. Because Weiss's revised estimates of agricultural productivity do not show growth prior to 1820, the end result he proposes is a flattening of the growth rate before 1820 compared to David's original estimate.

Nancy Folbre and Barnet Wagman were unhappy with the treatment of women in the David–Weiss framework (Folbre and Wagman 1993). They made three points: (1) Kuznets-defined GNP excludes housework, child care, and all other contributions to output made by women outside of the system of production for the market; (2) Weiss's labor force estimates – and Lebergott's as well – undercount females' contribution to market production; and (3) the true labor force participation of women and children differed markedly depending on which sector the husband/father labored in; however, Weiss's numbers (by assumption) do not allow for those differences.

The most vexing of the Folbre–Wagman objections is the second one, because Folbre and Wagman had no solid data source on which to make a better estimate of adult female labor force participation. However, expanding the standard definition of economic activity to explicitly include the production of services and goods produced by women for their families and outside of the market sector – thus addressing the first of Folbre and Wagman's complaints – obviated the need to estimate accurately the fraction of women's labor time devoted to the two activities. Folbre and Wagman increased female labor force participation rates to equal those of males and also imputed a value to the housework, child care, and other nonmarketed production of women. They did not, however, attempt to adjust for the third problem.

For the purposes of Table Ca9–19, we take a different approach to these problems. To retain comparability with the estimates of national output prepared by Gallman, Kuznets, and the BEA, we accept Kuznets's approach to housework and other nonmarketed production of women; we do not count it. Comparability, of course, would be of no value if the results were grossly misleading. In this case, they are not. In fact, the Folbre–Wagman approach does not have a noticeable impact on the *trends* in per capita income growth. The reason for this is that the Folbre–Wagman method imputes productivity in the nonmarket sector that increases at the same rate as productivity in the market sector.

In Table Ca9–19 we finesse the need to improve the estimate of the labor force participation of women and children by a different trick. We calculate productivity on a per-adult-male basis. Because we are interested only in the growth rate of a productivity index, the distortion of the level of productivity does not matter. The underlying assumption is that the man's wife and unmarried children live and work in the same sector he does. This is reasonably plausible. The major departure would be the practice of some young New England farm women of leaving home before marriage to work in the textile mills. This they did in sizable numbers beginning in the 1820s. However, if roughly the same number of young single men also left farming for urban pursuits, the assumption underlying the method adopted here would remain intact.

This approach will also automatically measure the output changes that were caused by evolving changes in the labor force participation rate of women and children in market activity. As men moved from agricultural work to nonagricultural work, some of the change in (per-male) productivity came directly from the elevated productivity in the nonagricultural sector, and some of it came from the different rates of labor force participation by his family. We do not have to measure that second component directly, nor even know the direction of the change, to incorporate it into the productivity index. The figures given for the benchmark years 1800, 1810, 1820, 1830, and 1840 for series Ca9 represent the conjectural estimates of GDP per capita estimated in this way. These estimates adopt Weiss's estimates of the adult male labor force participation and his division between the agricultural and nonagricultural sectors. They accept Weiss's revision of the Towne–Rasmussen index of agricultural output. They also accept Sokoloff's estimate of the rate of growth of manufacturing between 1820 and 1840. The result of these revisions is to flatten growth from 1800 to 1820 to a virtual standstill. A sharp take-off is located sometime between 1810 and 1830.

Just how reliable are these conjectural estimates? The answer is that they are quite fragile. Zero growth from 1800 to 1820 and the appearance of sustained growth after 1820 is the consequence of three pieces of evidence, each of which is open to criticism:

1. The adult male labor force estimates suggest that labor does not begin to shift out of agricultural occupations before 1820. However, after 1820 the proportional rise in the nonagricultural sector is rapid.
2. Agricultural output is estimated to have grown only slightly faster than the adult male labor force engaged in agriculture between 1800 and 1820. Indeed, agricultural productivity (per adult male) does not grow much even after 1820.
3. Nonagricultural productivity is assumed to grow at the same rate as agricultural productivity (that is, not at all) before 1820, but rises rapidly after 1820, on the authority of Sokoloff's study.

Although this may leave us quite uncertain about the validity of the conjectural estimates, one should not conclude that nothing has been gained by the extensive examination of David's methodology and the available evidence. We can be quite confident that the changes inspired by the work of Weiss, Sokoloff, and Folbre and Wagman are all in the right direction and all of those changes work to flatten the growth rate between 1800 and 1820 relative to that between 1820 and 1840. Even David now agrees. In a still unpublished paper, Paul David revised his earlier estimates, replacing the assumption of a constant delta with a model in which the gap between manufacturing productivity and agricultural productivity widened particularly rapidly after 1820 (David 1996). David's revised estimates are much closer to our own than to his original estimates. However, we hope that it is clear that our knowledge about the rate of economic growth (however measured) before 1840 remains uncertain. This remains a subject of active research, and refinements and revisions of the estimates are a likely future result.

References

Abramovitz, Moses, and Paul A. David. 2000. "Growth in the Era of Knowledge-Based Progress: The Long Run Perspective." In Stanley L. Engerman and Robert E. Gallman, editors. *The Cambridge Economic History of the United States,* volume 3, *The Twentieth Century.* Cambridge University Press.

Allen, Steven G. 1992. "Changes in the Cyclical Sensitivity of Wages in the United States, 1891–1987." *American Economic Review* 82 (March): 122–40.

Bailey, Martin Neil. 1978. "Stabilization Policy and Private Economic Behavior." *Brookings Papers on Economic Activity* 1: 11–50.

Balke, Nathan S., and Robert J. Gordon. 1989. "The Estimation of Prewar Gross National Product: Methodology and New Evidence." *Journal of Political Economy* 97 (February): 38–92.

Barger, Harold. 1955. *Distribution's Place in the American Economy since 1869.* Princeton University Press.

Blodget, Samuel. 1806. *Economica: A Statistical Manual for the United States of America.* Privately printed; reprinted Augustus M. Kelley, 1964.

Brady, Dorothy. 1966. "Price Deflators for Final Product Estimates." In *Output, Employment, and Productivity in the United States after 1800.* Columbia University Press.

Carson, Carol S. 1975. "The History of the United States National Income and Product Accounts: The Development of an Analytical Tool." *Review of Income and Wealth* series 21 (June): 153–82.

Carson, Carol S. 1987. "GNP: An Overview of Source Data and Estimating Methods." NIPA Methodology Paper number 4.

Daley, William M. 2000. "GDP: One of the Great Inventions of the 20th Century." *Survey of Current Business* 80 (January): 6–14.

David, Paul. 1967a. "The Growth of Real Product in the United States before 1840: New Evidence, Controlled Conjectures." *Journal of Economic History* 27 (June): 151–95.

David, Paul. 1967b. "New Light on a Statistical Dark Age: U.S. Real Product Growth before 1840." *American Economic Review* 57 (May): 294–306.

David, Paul. 1996. "Real Income and Economic Welfare Growth in the Early Republic, or Another Try at Getting the American Story Straight." University of Oxford Discussion Papers in Economic and Social History Number 5 (March).

DeLong, J. Bradford. 1998. "Estimating World GDP, One Million B.C.–Present." DeLong Web site (May).

DeLong, J. Bradford, and Lawrence H. Summers. 1986. "The Changing Cyclical Variability of Economic Activity in the United States." In Robert J. Gordon, editor. *The American Business Cycle: Continuity and Change.* University of Chicago Press.

Eldridge, Lucy P. 1999. "How Price Indexes Affect BLS Productivity Measures." *Monthly Labor Review* 122 (February): 35–46.

Fisher, Irving. 1922. *The Making of Index Numbers.* Houghton Mifflin.

Fishlow, Albert. 1965. *American Railroads and the Transformation of the Ante-Bellum Economy.* Harvard University Press.

Fixler, Dennis J., and Bruce T. Grimm. 2002. "Reliability of GDP and Related NIPA Estimates." *Survey of Current Business* 82 (January): 9–27.

Fogel, Robert W. 1964. *Railroads and American Economic Growth: Essays in Econometric History.* Johns Hopkins University Press.

Fogel, Robert W. 1999. "Catching Up with the Economy." *American Economic Review* 89 (March): 1–21.

Folbre, Nancy, and Barnet Wagman. 1993. "Counting Housework: New Estimates of Real Product in the United States, 1800–1860." *Journal of Economic History* 53 (June): 275–88.

Friedman, Milton, and Anna J. Schwartz. 1982. *Monetary Trends in the United States and the United Kingdom: Their Relation to Income, Prices, and Interest Rates, 1867–1975.* University of Chicago Press.

Gallman, Robert E. 1960. "Commodity Output, 1839–1899." In William N. Parker, editor. *Trends in the American Economy in the Nineteenth Century.* Princeton University Press.

Gallman, Robert E. 1966. "Gross National Product in the United States, 1834–1909." In *Conference on Research in Income and Wealth, Output, Employment, and Productivity in the United States after 1800.* Columbia University Press.

Gallman, Robert E. 2000. "Economic Growth and Structural Change in the Long Nineteenth Century." In Stanley L. Engerman and Robert E. Gallman, editors. *The Cambridge Economic History of the United States.* Cambridge University Press.

Goldsmith, Raymond W. 1959. In U.S. Congress, *Hearings before the Joint Economic Committee,* part 2, *Historical and Comparative Rates of Production, Productivity and Prices.* 86th Congress, 1st session (April 7).

Gordon, Robert J. 1981. "Output Fluctuations and Gradual Price Adjustment." *Journal of Economic Literature* 19 (June): 493–530.

Gordon, Robert J. 1982. "Price Inertia and Policy Ineffectiveness in the United States, 1890–1980." *Journal of Political Economy* 90 (December): 1087–1117.

Gordon, Robert J. 1986. "Introduction." In Robert J. Gordon, editor. *The American Business Cycle: Continuity and Change.* University of Chicago Press.

Hoover, Ethel D. 1960. "Retail Prices after 1850." In William N. Parker, editor. *Trends in the American Economy in the Nineteenth Century.* Princeton University Press.

Howell, Stephanie L. 1997. "Note on Computing Alternative Chained Dollar Indexes and Contributions to Growth." *Survey of Current Business* 77 (May): 63.

Kendrick, John W., assisted by Maude R. Pech. 1961. *Productivity Trends in the United States.* Princeton University Press.

Keynes, John Maynard. 1936. *The General Theory of Employment, Interest and Money.* Macmillan.

King, Willford Isbell. 1915. *Wealth and Income of the People of the United States.* Macmillan.

Kuznets, Simon. 1934. "National Income, 1929–32." Report prepared for U.S. Senate. 73rd Congress, 2nd session. Document 124, serial set 9788 (January).

Kuznets, Simon, assisted by Lillian Epstein and Elizabeth Jenks. 1941. *National Income and Its Composition, 1919–1938*. 2 volumes. National Bureau of Economic Research.

Kuznets, Simon. 1945. *National Product in Wartime*. National Bureau of Economic Research.

Kuznets, Simon, assisted by Lillian Epstein and Elizabeth Jenks. 1946. *National Product since 1869*. National Bureau of Economic Research.

Kuznets, Simon, assisted by Elizabeth Jenks. 1961. *Capital in the American Economy: Its Formation and Financing*. Princeton University Press.

Kuznets, Simon. Circa 1961. "Annual Estimates, 1869–1953, T-Tables 1–15 (Technical Tables Underlying Series in *Supplement to Summary Volume on Capital Formation and Financing*)." Mimeograph, National Bureau of Economic Research.

Landefeld, J. Steven, and Robert P. Parker. 1995. "Preview of the Comprehensive Revision of the National Income and Product Accounts: BEA's New Featured Measures of Output and Prices." *Survey of Current Business* 75 (July): 31–9.

Landefeld, J. Steven, and Robert P. Parker. 1997. "BEA's Chain Indexes, Time Series, and Measures of Long Term Growth." *Survey of Current Business* 77 (May): 58–68.

Langley, Veronica B. 1999. *The Nobel Prize: The Winners and Their Achievements*. Barnes and Noble.

Lebergott, Stanley. 1964. *Manpower in Economic Growth: The American Record since 1800*. McGraw-Hill.

Lebergott, Stanley. 1986. "Discussion [of Romer (1986a)]." *Journal of Economic History* 46 (June): 367–71.

McLane, Louis. 1833. *Documents Relative to the Manufactures in the United States*. 2 volumes. Duff Green; reprinted Augustus M. Kelley, 1969.

Miron, Jeffrey A., and Christina D. Romer. 1990. "A New Monthly Index of Industrial Production, 1884–1940." *Journal of Economic History* 50 (June): 321–37.

Nordhaus, William. 1997. "Do Real Wage and Output Series Capture Reality? The History of Lighting Suggests Not." In Timothy Bresnahan and Robert Gordon, editors. *The Economics of New Goods*. University of Chicago Press.

North, Douglass C. 1966. *Growth and Welfare in the American Past: A New Economic History*. Prentice Hall.

Ransom, Roger L., and Richard Sutch. 1988. "Capitalists without Capital: The Burden of Slavery and the Impact of Emancipation." *Agricultural History* 62 (Summer); reprinted in Morton Rothstein and Daniel Field, editors. 1993. *Quantitative Studies in Agrarian History*. Iowa State University Press.

Rees, Albert. 1961. *Real Wages in Manufacturing, 1890–1914*. Princeton University Press.

Rhode, Paul W. 2002. "Gallman's Annual Output Series for the United States, 1834–1909." National Bureau of Economic Research Working Paper 8860 (April).

Ritter, Joseph A. 2000. "Feeding the National Accounts." *Review of the Federal Reserve Bank of St. Louis* 82 (March/April): 11–20.

Romer, Christina D. 1986a. "New Estimates of Prewar Gross National Product and Unemployment." *Journal of Economic History* 46 (June): 341–52.

Romer, Christina D. 1986b. "Spurious Volatility in Historical Unemployment Data." *Journal of Political Economy* 94 (February): 1–37.

Romer, Christina D. 1988. "World War I and the Postwar Depression: A Reinterpretation Based on Alternative Estimates of GNP." *Journal of Monetary Economics* 22 (July): 91–115.

Romer, Christina D. 1989. "The Prewar Business Cycle Reconsidered: New Estimates of Gross National Product, 1869–1908." *Journal of Political Economy* 97 (February): 1–37.

Rostow, W. W. 1960. *The Stages of Economic Growth: A Non-Communist Manifesto*. Cambridge University Press.

Ruggles, Richard. 1983. "The United States National Income Accounts, 1947–1977: Their Conceptual Basis and Evolution." In Murray F. Foss, editor. *The U.S. National Income and Product Accounts: Selected Topics*. University of Chicago Press.

Seaman, Ezra C. 1846. *Essay on the Progress of Nations*. 1st edition. Baker and Scribner.

Seaman, Ezra C. 1852. *Essay on the Progress of Nations*. 2nd edition. Scribner.

Seskin, Eugene P., and Robert P. Parker. 1998. "A Guide to the NIPAs." *Survey of Current Business* 78 (March): 26–48.

Shaw, William Howard. 1947. *Value of Commodity Output since 1869*. National Bureau of Economic Research.

Sokoloff, Kenneth L. 1986. "Productivity Growth in Manufacturing during Early Industrialization: Evidence from the American Northeast, 1820–1860." In Stanley L. Engerman and Robert E. Gallman, editors. *Long-Term Factors in American Economic Growth*. University of Chicago Press.

Solow, Robert M. 2000. *Growth Theory: An Exposition*. 2nd edition. Oxford University Press.

Spahr, Charles. 1896. *An Essay on the Present Distribution of Wealth in the United States*. Crowell.

Towne, Marvin W., and Wayne D. Rasmussen. 1960. "Farm Gross Product and Gross Investment in the Nineteenth Century." In William N. Parker, editor. *Trends in the American Economy in the Nineteenth Century*. Princeton University Press.

Tucker, George. 1843–1855. *Progress of the United States in Population and Wealth in Fifty Years as Exhibited by the Decennial Census from 1790 to 1840, with an Appendix Containing an Abstract of the Census of 1850*. Press of Hunt's Merchant's Magazine; reprinted Augustus M. Kelley, 1964.

Ulmer, Melville J. 1960. *Capital in Transportation, Communications, and Public Utilities: Its Formation and Financing*. Princeton University Press.

United Nations. 2003. *Human Development Report*. Web site.

U.S. Bureau of Economic Analysis. 1991. "Gross Domestic Product as a Measure of U.S. Production." *Survey of Current Business* 71 (August): 8.

U.S. Bureau of Economic Analysis. 1998a. *National Income and Product Accounts of the United States, 1929–94*. U.S. Government Printing Office.

U.S. Bureau of Economic Analysis. 1998b. "Updated Summary of NIPA Methodologies." *Survey of Current Business* 78 (September): 14–35.

U.S. Bureau of Economic Analysis. Various years. *National Account Data*. Bureau of Economic Analysis Web site, updated regularly.

Weir, David R. 1992. "A Century of U.S. Unemployment, 1890–1990: Revised Estimates and Evidence for Stabilization." *Research in Economic History* 14: 301–46.

Weiss, Thomas. 1992. "U.S. Labor Force Estimates and Economic Growth, 1800–1860." In Robert E. Gallman and John Joseph Wallis, editors. *The Standard of Living in the United States before 1860*. University of Chicago Press.

Weiss, Thomas. 1993. "Estimates of Gross Domestic Product for the United States, 1800 to 1860." Unpublished paper, University of Kansas (July).

Whalen, Karl. 2000. "A Guide to the Use of Chain Aggregated NIPA Data." Federal Reserve Board of Governors Web site (June).

Young, Allan H., and Helen Stone Tice. 1985. "An Introduction to National Income Accounting." *Survey of Current Business* 65 (March): 59–76.

Zarnowitz, Victor. 1992. *Business Cycles: Theory, History, Indicators, and Forecasting*. University of Chicago Press.

AGGREGATE MEASURES AND LONG-TERM GROSS DOMESTIC PRODUCT SERIES

Richard Sutch

TABLE Ca1–8   Aggregate measures of economic activity: 1929–2002

Contributed by Richard Sutch

	Nominal dollars					Real (chained 1996) dollars		
	Gross domestic product	Gross national product	Final sales to domestic purchasers	National income	Aggregate personal income	Gross domestic product	Gross national product	Final sales to domestic purchasers
	Ca1	Ca2	Ca3	Ca4	Ca5	Ca6	Ca7	Ca8
Year	Billion dollars	Billion dollars	Billion dollars	Billion dollars	Billion dollars	Billion chained 1996 dollars	Billion chained 1996 dollars	Billion chained 1996 dollars
1929	103.7	104.5	101.8	86.8	85.3	822.2	828.9	847.4
1930	91.3	92.0	91.2	75.6	76.5	751.5	757.9	792.0
1931	76.6	77.1	77.7	60.4	65.5	703.6	708.8	747.9
1932	58.8	59.2	61.1	43.9	50.0	611.8	616.1	664.3
1933	56.4	56.7	57.8	41.4	46.9	603.3	606.8	644.0
1934	66.0	66.3	66.3	50.2	53.8	668.3	671.4	702.7
1935	73.3	73.7	72.4	57.9	60.5	728.3	731.9	753.0
1936	83.7	84.0	82.7	65.8	68.8	822.5	825.5	849.5
1937	91.9	92.3	89.2	74.0	74.3	865.8	869.9	882.2
1938	86.1	86.5	85.7	67.4	68.6	835.6	840.0	861.1
1939	92.0	92.5	91.0	72.9	73.1	903.5	908.0	925.2
1940	101.3	101.7	97.5	81.1	78.6	980.7	984.5	981.7
1941	126.7	127.2	121.4	104.3	96.3	1,148.8	1,153.8	1,148.9
1942	161.8	162.2	160.2	137.6	123.8	1,360.0	1,364.8	1,404.2
1943	198.4	198.8	201.5	171.4	152.4	1,583.7	1,588.2	1,674.0
1944	219.7	220.1	222.7	184.3	166.3	1,714.1	1,718.8	1,810.6
1945	223.0	223.4	225.4	183.3	171.9	1,693.3	1,697.1	1,782.0
1946	222.3	223.0	209.2	182.3	179.5	1,505.5	1,511.0	1,469.8
1947	244.4	245.6	234.2	198.6	192.1	1,495.1	1,502.7	1,487.4
1948	269.6	271.1	258.5	223.3	211.1	1,560.0	1,569.0	1,549.5
1949	267.7	269.0	265.2	216.7	208.2	1,550.9	1,559.1	1,584.8
1950	294.3	295.8	287.9	241.0	229.9	1,686.6	1,695.6	1,699.4
1951	339.5	341.5	327.2	278.7	258.7	1,815.1	1,826.3	1,804.2
1952	358.6	360.7	354.1	293.3	276.1	1,887.3	1,899.2	1,914.9
1953	379.9	381.9	378.8	308.2	292.6	1,973.9	1,985.1	2,022.7
1954	381.1	383.3	382.7	308.4	295.2	1,960.5	1,972.5	2,019.3
1955	415.2	417.8	409.8	338.5	316.8	2,099.5	2,113.0	2,131.8
1956	438.0	440.8	431.7	358.7	340.0	2,141.1	2,156.0	2,172.7
1957	461.5	464.7	456.8	375.0	359.3	2,183.9	2,199.6	2,223.2
1958	467.9	470.7	467.9	377.3	370.0	2,162.8	2,176.3	2,225.7
1959	507.4	510.3	505.2	411.5	394.0	2,319.0	2,332.8	2,376.0
1960	527.4	530.6	521.7	427.5	412.7	2,376.7	2,391.9	2,419.7
1961	545.7	549.3	539.3	442.5	430.3	2,432.0	2,448.8	2,475.2
1962	586.5	590.7	578.0	477.1	457.9	2,578.9	2,598.0	2,617.6
1963	618.7	623.2	609.8	504.4	481.0	2,690.4	2,710.8	2,728.1
1964	664.4	669.0	654.1	542.1	515.8	2,846.5	2,868.5	2,880.8
1965	720.1	725.5	707.0	589.6	557.4	3,028.5	3,051.7	3,059.0
1966	789.3	794.5	773.8	646.7	606.4	3,227.5	3,248.9	3,255.6
1967	834.1	839.5	822.8	681.7	650.4	3,308.3	3,330.4	3,362.5
1968	911.5	917.6	903.7	743.6	714.5	3,466.1	3,489.8	3,540.2
1969	985.3	991.5	977.4	802.7	780.8	3,571.4	3,594.1	3,649.3
1970	1,039.7	1,046.1	1,036.5	837.5	841.1	3,578.0	3,600.6	3,671.1
1971	1,128.6	1,136.2	1,123.3	903.9	905.1	3,697.7	3,722.9	3,782.0
1972	1,240.4	1,249.1	1,239.3	1,000.4	994.3	3,898.4	3,925.7	3,993.5
1973	1,385.5	1,398.2	1,369.0	1,127.4	1,113.4	4,123.4	4,161.0	4,167.4
1974	1,501.0	1,516.7	1,490.2	1,211.9	1,225.6	4,099.0	4,142.3	4,118.2
1975	1,635.2	1,648.4	1,627.9	1,302.2	1,331.7	4,084.4	4,117.7	4,119.6
1976	1,823.9	1,841.0	1,809.1	1,456.4	1,475.4	4,311.7	4,351.4	4,331.1
1977	2,031.4	2,052.1	2,032.7	1,635.8	1,637.1	4,511.8	4,556.6	4,553.3
1978	2,295.9	2,318.0	2,296.2	1,860.2	1,848.3	4,760.6	4,805.3	4,797.0
1979	2,566.4	2,599.3	2,572.4	2,075.6	2,081.5	4,912.1	4,973.9	4,938.4

(continued)

TABLE Ca1–8   Aggregate measures of economic activity: 1929–2002   *Continued*

	Nominal dollars					Real (chained 1996) dollars		
	Gross domestic product	Gross national product	Final sales to domestic purchasers	National income	Aggregate personal income	Gross domestic product	Gross national product	Final sales to domestic purchasers
	Ca1	Ca2	Ca3	Ca4	Ca5	Ca6	Ca7	Ca8
Year	Billion dollars	Billion dollars	Billion dollars	Billion dollars	Billion dollars	Billion chained 1996 dollars	Billion chained 1996 dollars	Billion chained 1996 dollars
1980	2,795.6	2,830.8	2,816.8	2,243.0	2,323.9	4,900.9	4,962.3	4,890.3
1981	3,131.3	3,166.1	3,116.5	2,497.1	2,599.4	5,021.0	5,075.4	4,958.6
1982	3,259.2	3,295.7	3,294.7	2,603.0	2,768.4	4,919.3	4,973.6	4,951.7
1983	3,534.9	3,571.8	3,592.3	2,796.5	2,946.9	5,132.3	5,184.9	5,215.9
1984	3,932.7	3,968.1	3,969.3	3,162.3	3,274.8	5,505.2	5,553.8	5,569.5
1985	4,213.0	4,238.4	4,305.4	3,380.4	3,515.0	5,717.1	5,750.9	5,865.0
1986	4,452.9	4,468.3	4,578.2	3,525.8	3,712.4	5,912.4	5,932.5	6,096.6
1987	4,742.5	4,756.2	4,857.6	3,803.4	3,962.5	6,113.3	6,130.8	6,261.9
1988	5,108.3	5,126.8	5,196.1	4,151.1	4,272.1	6,368.4	6,391.1	6,474.0
1989	5,489.1	5,509.4	5,542.1	4,392.1	4,599.8	6,591.8	6,615.5	6,648.3
1990	5,803.2	5,832.2	5,860.1	4,642.1	4,903.2	6,707.9	6,740.0	6,752.6
1991	5,986.2	6,010.9	6,007.1	4,756.6	5,085.4	6,676.4	6,703.4	6,693.5
1992	6,318.9	6,342.3	6,331.7	4,994.9	5,390.4	6,880.0	6,905.8	6,884.1
1993	6,642.3	6,666.7	6,681.7	5,251.9	5,610.0	7,062.6	7,087.8	7,101.8
1994	7,054.3	7,071.1	7,078.9	5,556.8	5,888.0	7,347.7	7,364.3	7,372.2
1995	7,400.5	7,420.9	7,451.7	5,876.7	6,200.9	7,543.8	7,564.0	7,590.3
1996	7,813.2	7,831.2	7,872.1	6,210.4	6,547.4	7,813.2	7,831.2	7,872.1
1997	8,318.4	8,325.4	8,344.8	6,618.4	6,937.0	8,159.5	8,168.1	8,207.3
1998	8,781.5	8,778.1	8,860.1	7,041.4	7,426.0	8,508.9	8,508.4	8,644.0
1999	9,274.3	9,297.1	9,464.7	7,468.7	7,786.5	8,859.0	8,883.7	9,095.1
2000	9,824.6	9,848.0	10,126.6	7,984.4	8,406.6	9,191.4	9,216.2	9,490.7
2001	10,082.2	10,104.1	10,491.4	8,122.0	8,685.3	9,214.5	9,237.3	9,644.9
2002	10,446.2	10,436.7	10,866.0	8,340.1	8,922.2	9,439.9	9,433.5	9,874.1

Source

U.S. Bureau of Economic Analysis Internet site, Tables 1.1, 1.2, 1.5, 1.6, 1.9, and 1.10; downloaded August 18, 2003.

Documentation

The data reported in this table reflect the 1996 comprehensive revision of the national income and product accounts (NIPA). This is the tenth revision since the Commerce Department began publishing national income statistics in 1942. For a discussion of the tenth revision and the definitional changes from earlier NIPA data, see Robert P. Parker and Eugene P. Seskin, "Preview of the Comprehensive Revision of the National Income and Product Accounts: New and Redesigned Tables," *Survey of Current Business* 75 (October 1995): 30–9, and "Improved Estimates of the National Income and Product Accounts: Results of the Comprehensive Revision," *Survey of Current Business* 76 (January/February 1996): 1–31.

Nominal dollar measures are calculated using the prices at which goods and services were sold; these are sometimes called current-dollar measures. Real-dollar measures are an effort to remove the effect of inflation and are calculated using prices that reflect values in a convenient base year. In the base year, nominal and real values are the same.

Series Ca1. Gross domestic product (GDP) is the official and standard measure of aggregate economic activity in the market economy. It is defined as the market value of all goods and services produced by labor and property located in the United States during the year. The workers and suppliers of property may be either U.S. residents or residents of the rest of the world. GDP does not include goods and services unless they are produced for and sold in the marketplace. It excludes, for example, the value of housework and child care (unless these are paid for) and the value of the services provided by consumer durables owned by individuals. Thus, for example, the transportation services of an automobile or the services of household appliances and furniture are excluded. GDP also excludes the value of illegal products and services (e.g., illegal drugs). The measure is "gross" because it does not deduct for depreciation of capital goods used up in production. For the components of GDP, see Table Ca74–90; for sectoral detail, see Table Ca135–148.

Series Ca2. Gross national product (GNP) was the standard measure of aggregate economic performance preferred by the Bureau of Economic Analysis before 1991 and is still frequently cited or used as an alternative to GDP. GNP is defined as the market value of all goods and services produced by labor and property owned by individuals *residing* in the United States regardless of the location of the property. To move from GNP to GDP, one must add payments of income to both labor and capital in the rest of the world and subtract receipts of income from the rest of the world. Until recently, GNP exceeded GDP, indicating that U.S. residents earned more abroad than foreign residents earned by producing within the United States. For the United States, the difference between GDP and GNP is small. For most of the period since 1929, it has been less than 1 percent of GDP. Furthermore, since the early 1980s, the gap between the two measures has been shrinking, and in the last few years GDP has actually exceeded GNP.

Series Ca3. Final sales of domestic product represent that proportion of GDP that is actually purchased by final consumers residing in the United States. To move from final sales to GDP, one must add any change in inventories and net exports.

Series Ca4. National income is the sum of all incomes earned by residents of the United States in return for producing the GNP. It differs from GNP in that the latter includes an allowance for the consumption of fixed capital (depreciation), indirect business taxes, and business gifts to American residents or the rest of the world. In practice there is also a "statistical discrepancy," which may be positive or negative, that arises as a result of inaccuracies in data collecting and estimating procedures. For the components of national income, see Table Ca20–27; for national income by legal form of organization, see Table Ca28–34.

Series Ca5. Aggregate personal income is the income received by persons from all sources – that is, from participation in production and from both government and business transfer payments (including interest paid by the government). In this measure, "persons" include nonprofit institutions (churches, private schools, or private trust funds) that primarily serve individuals. The retained earnings of businesses are not included. Employer and employee contributions for social insurance are not included. For personal income by source, see Table Ca54–63.

Series Ca6–8. "Real" values are alternative representations of the aggregates designed to remove the impact of a change in prices on the value of output.

TABLE Ca1–8   Aggregate measures of economic activity: 1929–2002   *Continued*

Changes in the real aggregates thus measure the changes in the quantities of goods and services produced, not both the changes in quantity and the changes in price. These real series are sometimes called inflation-adjusted data. The real values presented here are measured in terms of chained dollars with the value of the dollar in 1996 taken as the standard of comparison. Chained-dollar measures of real output were introduced with the 1996 revisions of the national accounts and replaced the fixed-weighted, or Laspeyres, measures of real output used previously. The chain-type annual-weighted indexes are also known as Fisher indexes; see Irving Fisher, *The Making of Index Numbers* (Houghton Mifflin, 1922). For a detailed discussion of the use of chained dollars in national income and product accounting, see J. Steven Landefeld and Robert P. Parker, "BEA's Chain Indexes, Time Series, and Measures of Long-Term Economic Growth," *Survey of Current Business* 77 (May 1997): 58–68. Because the chain-type index can be applied only to the aggregates of goods and services, only the product side of the national income and product accounts (GDP, GNP, and final sales) has chained-dollar variants. Aggregates of income (national income, personal income), however, are frequently deflated by a price index or a price deflator so that they may represent the real purchasing power of the income. Implicit price deflators for GDP and its components are given in Table Ca159–168.

TABLE Ca9–19   Gross domestic product: 1790–2002   [Continuous annual series]

Contributed by Richard Sutch

	GDP – Millennial Edition series						Real GDP per capita – alternative estimates				
	Real	Nominal	Per capita Real	Per capita Nominal	Price deflator	Resident population	Slave-economy concept	Johnston and Williamson (EH.net)	Berry	Real net income from abroad	Index of industrial production (Davis)
	Ca9	Ca10	Ca11	Ca12	Ca13	Ca14	Ca15	Ca16	Ca17	Ca18	Ca19
Year	Million 1996 dollars	Million dollars	1996 dollars	Dollars	Index 1996 = 100	Thousand	1996 dollars	1996 dollars	1929 dollars	Million 1996 dollars	Index 1849–1850 = 100
1790	4,571	—	1,163	—	—	3,929	—	1,158	93	—	4.291
1791	4,734	—	1,169	—	—	4,048	—	1,146	92	—	4.490
1792	4,975	—	1,192	—	—	4,172	—	1,184	96	—	4.881
1793	5,281	—	1,228	—	—	4,299	—	1,200	97	—	5.441
1794	5,591	—	1,262	—	—	4,429	—	1,226	99	—	6.014
1795	5,895	—	1,292	—	—	4,563	—	1,300	105	—	6.578
1796	6,035	—	1,284	—	—	4,701	—	1,357	109	—	6.699
1797	6,016	—	1,242	—	—	4,844	—	1,288	104	—	6.374
1798	6,066	—	1,216	—	—	4,990	—	1,297	105	—	6.213
1799	6,323	—	1,230	—	—	5,141	—	1,360	110	—	6.615
1800	6,671	519	1,259	98	7.78	5,297	—	1,357	110	—	7.273
1801	7,003	—	1,282	—	—	5,461	—	1,500	122	—	7.745
1802	7,341	—	1,303	—	—	5,632	—	1,341	110	—	8.210
1803	7,442	—	1,281	—	—	5,809	—	1,379	114	—	7.977
1804	7,666	—	1,280	—	—	5,991	—	1,405	118	—	8.077
1805	8,080	—	1,307	—	—	6,180	1,549	1,469	125	—	8.699
1806	8,489	—	1,331	—	—	6,379	1,576	1,397	121	—	9.283
1807	8,855	—	1,344	—	—	6,588	1,591	1,424	123	—	9.718
1808	8,492	—	1,249	—	—	6,797	1,477	1,301	115	—	8.063
1809	9,189	—	1,311	—	—	7,009	1,550	1,407	126	—	9.389
1810	9,735	827	1,348	114	8.49	7,224	1,590	1,426	129	—	10.258
1811	10,225	—	1,375	—	—	7,436	1,618	1,399	127	—	11.299
1812	10,338	—	1,351	—	—	7,651	1,588	1,320	121	—	11.253
1813	10,746	—	1,366	—	—	7,867	1,605	1,411	129	—	12.063
1814	11,251	—	1,392	—	—	8,085	1,635	1,472	135	—	13.172
1815	11,518	—	1,386	—	—	8,308	1,629	1,468	135	—	13.564
1816	11,359	—	1,330	—	—	8,540	1,561	1,475	136	—	12.595
1817	11,684	—	1,329	—	—	8,790	1,559	1,490	138	—	13.119
1818	12,071	—	1,333	—	—	9,057	1,562	1,579	146	—	13.838
1819	12,416	—	1,330	—	—	9,335	1,558	1,500	141	—	14.412
1820	12,720	832	1,322	86	6.54	9,618	1,549	1,466	137	−73	14.834
1821	13,295	—	1,343	—	6.35	9,899	1,574	1,445	136	−73	15.792
1822	14,063	—	1,380	—	6.61	10,189	1,618	1,590	150	−71	17.291
1823	14,317	—	1,365	—	6.13	10,488	1,599	1,506	143	−80	17.081
1824	15,129	—	1,402	—	5.81	10,795	1,642	1,482	143	−83	18.559
1825	15,927	—	1,433	—	6.08	11,115	1,678	1,637	160	−76	19.886
1826	16,522	—	1,443	—	6.07	11,449	1,690	1,537	151	−74	20.535
1827	17,099	—	1,449	—	6.08	11,797	1,696	1,560	154	−71	21.073
1828	17,615	—	1,449	—	5.92	12,158	1,694	1,587	158	−73	21.391
1829	17,547	—	1,401	—	5.86	12,525	1,637	1,589	161	−78	20.117

(continued)

TABLE Ca9–19   Gross domestic product: 1790–2002   [Continuous annual series]   *Continued*

	GDP – Millennial Edition series						Real GDP per capita – alternative estimates				
			Per capita		Price deflator	Resident population	Slave-economy concept	Johnston and Williamson (EH.net)	Berry	Real net income from abroad	Index of industrial production (Davis)
	Real	Nominal	Real	Nominal							
	Ca9	Ca10	Ca11	Ca12	Ca13	Ca14	Ca15	Ca16	Ca17	Ca18	Ca19
Year	Million 1996 dollars	Million dollars	1996 dollars	Dollars	Index 1996 = 100	Thousand	1996 dollars	1996 dollars	1929 dollars	Million 1996 dollars	Index 1849–1850 = 100
1830	19,387	1,113	1,503	86	5.74	12,901	1,751	1,574	160	−76	23.801
1831	21,172	—	1,595	—	5.71	13,277	1,851	1,597	163	−79	28.085
1832	22,612	—	1,653	—	5.78	13,676	1,918	1,653	167	−88	31.533
1833	24,098	—	1,711	—	5.74	14,086	1,983	1,725	176	−98	35.148
1834	23,623	—	1,629	—	5.77	14,504	1,884	1,793	167	−113	33.579
1835	25,229	—	1,691	—	6.07	14,917	1,956	1,716	182	−130	37.573
1836	26,329	—	1,716	—	6.52	15,340	1,983	1,662	194	−134	40.249
1837	26,236	—	1,662	—	6.59	15,790	1,916	1,754	185	−141	39.679
1838	26,726	—	1,647	—	6.44	16,224	1,898	1,720	185	−181	40.697
1839	28,768	—	1,727	—	6.63	16,656	1,990	1,825	201	−193	46.056
1840	28,113	1,730	1,642	101	6.15	17,120	1,893	1,764	183	−162	43.881
1841	28,314	1,744	1,608	99	6.16	17,612	1,856	1,772	200	−129	46.349
1842	28,893	1,670	1,594	92	5.78	18,124	1,839	1,710	192	−131	47.656
1843	30,189	1,636	1,619	88	5.42	18,641	1,868	1,668	193	−129	53.103
1844	32,705	1,814	1,707	95	5.55	19,157	1,970	1,864	201	−138	59.452
1845	34,172	1,956	1,734	99	5.73	19,708	2,000	1,882	209	−150	65.358
1846	35,435	2,062	1,744	102	5.82	20,313	2,011	1,866	207	−173	75.927
1847	37,562	2,335	1,790	111	6.22	20,987	2,061	1,982	230	−188	87.366
1848	39,849	2,373	1,836	109	5.95	21,706	2,112	1,921	205	−196	94.887
1849	40,191	2,344	1,789	104	5.83	22,464	2,055	1,861	214	−214	98.330
1850	41,781	2,537	1,796	109	6.07	23,261	2,056	1,930	224	−233	102.385
1851	45,045	2,710	1,869	112	6.02	24,095	2,133	2,009	224	−287	107.339
1852	49,099	2,969	1,964	119	6.05	24,999	2,237	2,164	217	−343	125.865
1853	54,360	3,431	2,098	132	6.31	25,911	2,387	2,107	222	−353	145.319
1854	56,499	3,881	2,104	145	6.87	26,856	2,388	2,156	223	−328	150.604
1855	57,065	4,046	2,058	146	7.09	27,727	2,332	2,272	227	−321	151.226
1856	59,859	4,196	2,101	147	7.01	28,497	2,379	2,242	222	−270	160.181
1857	60,211	4,316	2,055	147	7.17	29,298	2,325	2,202	242	−209	157.835
1858	62,087	4,068	2,065	135	6.55	30,068	2,335	2,301	215	−296	149.332
1859	65,276	4,287	2,121	139	6.57	30,780	2,398	2,320	247	−370	170.928
1860	68,594	4,485	2,177	142	6.54	31,513	2,461	2,342	229	−372	173.907
1861	68,671	4,671	2,132	145	6.80	32,215	—	2,257	226	−388	173.544
1862	72,308	5,510	2,199	168	7.62	32,889	—	2,226	226	−395	186.954
1863	78,660	7,341	2,341	218	9.33	33,607	—	2,190	227	−345	211.392
1864	83,109	9,528	2,418	277	11.46	34,376	—	2,606	276	−342	228.704
1865	80,667	9,412	2,293	268	11.67	35,182	—	2,336	253	−409	218.129
1866	82,026	9,153	2,275	254	11.16	36,052	—	2,319	255	−486	222.829
1867	86,869	8,865	2,350	240	10.21	36,970	—	2,286	257	−608	242.163
1868	90,212	8,680	2,381	229	9.62	37,885	—	2,323	264	−706	255.436
1869	94,998	8,591	2,444	221	9.04	38,870	—	2,372	276	−690	275.144
1870	94,758	8,153	2,375	204	8.60	39,905	—	2,486	270	−799	282.175
1871	94,450	8,025	2,303	196	8.50	41,010	—	2,512	270	−843	297.448
1872	113,082	9,358	2,688	222	8.28	42,066	—	2,544	296	−942	322.480
1873	113,376	9,300	2,623	215	8.20	43,225	—	2,614	295	−1,027	354.713
1874	108,530	8,645	2,443	195	7.97	44,429	—	2,521	296	−1,053	354.586
1875	110,962	8,467	2,439	186	7.63	45,492	—	2,594	298	−1,068	335.949
1876	118,329	8,682	2,547	187	7.34	46,459	—	2,561	300	−1,037	348.518
1877	127,195	9,186	2,683	194	7.22	47,400	—	2,595	320	−938	354.127
1878	133,680	9,067	2,767	188	6.78	48,319	—	2,649	303	−950	374.333
1879	147,057	9,683	2,985	197	6.58	49,264	—	2,923	312	−1,018	424.919
1880	172,474	11,942	3,431	238	6.92	50,262	—	3,203	345	−1,031	477.951
1881	171,935	11,838	3,341	230	6.89	51,466	—	3,245	341	−1,072	570.084
1882	191,309	13,446	3,617	254	7.03	52,893	—	3,365	361	−1,052	607.448
1883	184,207	12,506	3,384	230	6.79	54,435	—	3,343	351	−1,122	624.552
1884	188,250	12,226	3,372	219	6.49	55,826	—	3,314	356	−1,157	602.431
1885	192,454	12,186	3,369	213	6.33	57,128	—	3,273	350	−1,209	585.107
1886	212,015	13,422	3,639	230	6.33	58,258	—	3,296	362	−1,290	656.359
1887	218,490	13,838	3,681	233	6.33	59,357	—	3,386	379	−1,383	720.971
1888	212,295	13,659	3,502	225	6.43	60,614	—	3,300	393	−1,495	783.040
1889	225,659	14,549	3,646	235	6.45	61,893	—	3,441	394	−1,572	805.302

TABLE Ca9–19   Gross domestic product: 1790–2002   [Continuous annual series]   *Continued*

	GDP – Millennial Edition series						Real GDP per capita – alternative estimates				
	Real	Nominal	Per capita		Price deflator	Resident population	Slave-economy concept	Johnston and Williamson (EH.net)	Berry	Real net income from abroad	Index of industrial production (Davis)
			Real	Nominal							
	Ca9	Ca10	Ca11	Ca12	Ca13	Ca14	Ca15	Ca16	Ca17	Ca18	Ca19
Year	Million 1996 dollars	Million dollars	1996 dollars	Dollars	Index 1996 = 100	Thousand	1996 dollars	1996 dollars	1929 dollars	Million 1996 dollars	Index 1849–1850 = 100
1890	230,545	14,513	3,656	230	6.30	63,056	—	3,426	415	−1,679	931.165
1891	247,493	15,560	3,841	241	6.29	64,432	—	3,461	425	−1,638	945.586
1892	252,421	15,673	3,829	238	6.21	65,920	—	3,535	455	−1,638	1,015.912
1893	244,052	15,203	3,617	225	6.23	67,470	—	3,453	423	−1,563	927.836
1894	230,942	13,623	3,351	198	5.90	68,910	—	3,280	403	−1,596	860.857
1895	266,467	15,476	3,803	221	5.81	70,076	—	3,610	444	−1,638	1,009.668
1896	262,393	15,294	3,686	215	5.83	71,188	—	3,470	428	−1,762	978.804
1897	277,417	15,924	3,830	220	5.74	72,441	—	3,700	460	−2,084	1,042.738
1898	285,172	16,580	3,875	225	5.81	73,600	—	3,723	463	−1,952	1,228.429
1899	313,405	18,513	4,190	248	5.91	74,793	—	4,078	497	−1,795	1,347.034
1900	319,874	19,290	4,204	253	6.03	76,094	—	4,087	502	−1,654	1,409.530
1901	356,749	21,632	4,598	279	6.06	77,584	—	4,498	549	−1,481	1,522.690
1902	360,636	22,196	4,556	280	6.15	79,163	—	4,484	543	−1,299	1,632.723
1903	384,225	24,262	4,765	301	6.31	80,632	—	4,527	560	−1,166	1,693.529
1904	364,978	23,256	4,442	283	6.37	82,166	—	4,600	542	−1,133	1,613.424
1905	402,148	25,618	4,798	306	6.37	83,822	—	4,927	571	−1,075	1,866.779
1906	457,753	30,133	5,357	353	6.58	85,450	—	5,032	625	−943	1,961.295
1907	449,193	30,869	5,163	355	6.87	87,008	—	4,862	624	−960	2,042.788
1908	390,035	26,234	4,397	296	6.73	88,710	—	4,509	561	−1,042	1,724.670
1909	454,861	30,640	5,027	339	6.74	90,490	—	4,940	618	−910	2,033.567
1910	450,817	31,609	4,879	342	7.01	92,407	—	4,859	611	−885	2,127.062
1911	465,967	32,597	4,964	347	7.00	93,863	—	4,933	621	−1,059	2,048.329
1912	488,273	34,991	5,122	367	7.17	95,335	—	5,140	640	−993	2,264.356
1913	507,625	36,716	5,221	378	7.23	97,225	—	5,235	653	−976	2,354.875
1914	467,488	34,275	4,717	346	7.33	99,111	—	4,742	592	−728	2,115.357
1915	479,930	36,021	4,773	358	7.51	100,546	—	4,834	601	819	2,330.073
1916	546,817	44,694	5,363	438	8.17	101,961	—	5,532	675	1,489	—
1917	531,780	52,051	5,142	503	9.79	103,414	—	5,454	650	2,258	—
1918	581,178	66,820	5,559	639	11.50	104,550	—	5,806	702	2,713	—
1919	583,754	76,571	5,556	729	13.12	105,063	—	5,587	706	4,458	—
1920	574,987	87,062	5,401	818	15.14	106,461	—	5,410	689	3,160	—
1921	560,932	73,940	5,168	681	13.18	108,538	—	5,123	660	2,680	—
1922	594,388	72,819	5,401	662	12.25	110,049	—	5,398	689	4,731	—
1923	673,487	84,908	6,016	758	12.61	111,947	—	6,048	767	5,782	—
1924	690,094	87,023	6,048	763	12.61	114,109	—	6,099	774	5,128	—
1925	711,823	91,349	6,145	789	12.83	115,829	—	6,138	782	6,013	—
1926	755,262	97,456	6,433	830	12.90	117,397	—	6,423	821	6,080	—
1927	763,581	96,802	6,415	813	12.68	119,035	—	6,368	818	6,146	—
1928	769,888	96,805	6,389	803	12.57	120,509	—	6,406	817	6,634	—
1929	822,200	103,700	6,752	852	12.61	121,767	—	6,751	847	6,700	—
1930	751,500	91,300	6,106	742	12.15	123,077	—	6,102	754	6,400	—
1931	703,600	76,600	5,672	618	10.88	124,040	—	5,668	690	5,200	—
1932	611,800	58,800	4,901	471	9.61	124,840	—	4,894	585	4,300	—
1933	603,300	56,400	4,804	449	9.36	125,579	—	4,802	570	3,500	—
1934	668,300	66,000	5,288	522	9.88	126,374	—	5,286	617	3,100	—
1935	728,300	73,300	5,723	576	10.07	127,250	—	5,721	674	3,600	—
1936	822,500	83,700	6,423	654	10.18	128,053	—	6,419	763	3,000	—
1937	865,800	91,900	6,721	713	10.61	128,825	—	6,715	798	4,100	—
1938	835,600	86,100	6,436	663	10.30	129,825	—	6,432	752	4,400	—
1939	903,500	92,000	6,903	703	10.19	130,880	—	6,899	810	4,500	—
1940	980,700	101,300	7,396	764	10.33	132,594	—	7,391	866	3,800	—
1941	1,148,800	126,700	8,580	946	11.03	133,894	—	8,514	997	5,000	—
1942	1,360,000	161,800	10,047	1,195	11.89	135,361	—	10,047	1,114	4,800	—
1943	1,583,700	198,400	11,539	1,446	12.53	137,250	—	11,512	1,244	4,500	—
1944	1,714,100	219,700	12,339	1,582	12.81	138,916	—	12,310	1,315	4,700	—
1945	1,693,300	223,000	12,055	1,588	13.17	140,468	—	12,031	1,279	3,800	—
1946	1,505,500	222,300	10,607	1,566	14.77	141,936	—	10,568	1,114	5,500	—
1947	1,495,100	244,400	10,333	1,689	16.35	144,698	—	10,297	1,084	7,600	—
1948	1,560,000	269,600	10,597	1,831	17.28	147,208	—	10,597	—	9,000	—
1949	1,550,900	267,700	10,355	1,787	17.26	149,767	—	10,349	—	8,200	—

(continued)

TABLE Ca9–19   Gross domestic product: 1790–2002   [Continuous annual series]   *Continued*

	GDP – Millennial Edition series						Real GDP per capita – alternative estimates				
	Real	Nominal	Per capita		Price deflator	Resident population	Slave-economy concept	Johnston and Williamson (EH.net)	Berry	Real net income from abroad	Index of industrial production (Davis)
			Real	Nominal							
	Ca9	Ca10	Ca11	Ca12	Ca13	Ca14	Ca15	Ca16	Ca17	Ca18	Ca19
Year	Million 1996 dollars	Million dollars	1996 dollars	Dollars	Index 1996 = 100	Thousand	1996 dollars	1996 dollars	1929 dollars	Million 1996 dollars	Index 1849–1850 = 100
1950	1,686,600	294,300	11,076	1,933	17.45	152,271	—	11,033	—	9,000	—
1951	1,815,100	339,500	11,720	2,192	18.71	154,878	—	11,687	—	11,200	—
1952	1,887,300	358,600	11,979	2,276	19.00	157,553	—	11,932	—	11,900	—
1953	1,973,900	379,900	12,323	2,372	19.25	160,184	—	12,298	—	11,200	—
1954	1,960,500	381,100	12,026	2,338	19.44	163,026	—	12,023	—	12,000	—
1955	2,099,500	415,200	12,653	2,502	19.78	165,931	—	12,596	—	13,500	—
1956	2,141,100	438,000	12,677	2,593	20.45	168,903	—	12,670	—	14,900	—
1957	2,183,900	461,500	12,698	2,683	21.13	171,984	—	12,676	—	15,700	—
1958	2,162,800	467,900	12,367	2,676	21.64	174,882	—	12,351	—	13,500	—
1959	2,319,000	507,400	13,041	2,853	21.88	177,830	—	12,990	—	13,800	—
1960	2,376,700	527,400	13,155	2,919	22.19	180,671	—	13,118	—	15,200	—
1961	2,432,000	545,700	13,240	2,971	22.44	183,691	—	13,229	—	16,800	—
1962	2,578,900	586,500	13,825	3,144	22.74	186,538	—	13,777	—	19,100	—
1963	2,690,400	618,700	14,217	3,269	23.00	189,242	—	14,215	—	20,400	—
1964	2,846,500	664,400	14,834	3,462	23.34	191,889	—	14,800	—	22,000	—
1965	3,028,500	720,100	15,586	3,706	23.78	194,303	—	15,543	—	23,200	—
1966	3,227,500	789,300	16,420	4,016	24.46	196,560	—	16,382	—	21,400	—
1967	3,308,300	834,100	16,649	4,198	25.21	198,712	—	16,607	—	22,100	—
1968	3,466,100	911,500	17,270	4,541	26.30	200,706	—	17,239	—	23,700	—
1969	3,571,400	985,300	17,621	4,861	27.59	202,677	—	17,614	—	22,700	—
1970	3,578,000	1,039,700	17,449	5,070	29.06	205,052	—	17,410	—	22,600	—
1971	3,697,700	1,128,600	17,806	5,435	30.52	207,661	—	17,769	—	25,200	—
1972	3,898,400	1,240,400	18,573	5,910	31.82	209,896	—	18,533	—	27,300	—
1973	4,123,400	1,385,500	19,458	6,538	33.60	211,909	—	19,442	—	37,600	—
1974	4,099,000	1,501,000	19,167	7,019	36.62	213,854	—	19,125	—	43,300	—
1975	4,084,400	1,635,200	18,912	7,571	40.03	215,973	—	18,891	—	33,300	—
1976	4,311,700	1,823,900	19,775	8,365	42.30	218,035	—	19,767	—	39,700	—
1977	4,511,800	2,031,400	20,486	9,224	45.02	220,239	—	20,478	—	44,800	—
1978	4,760,600	2,295,900	21,388	10,315	48.23	222,585	—	21,385	—	44,700	—
1979	4,912,100	2,566,400	21,826	11,403	52.25	225,055	—	21,817	—	61,800	—
1980	4,900,900	2,795,600	21,568	12,303	57.04	227,225	—	21,565	—	61,400	—
1981	5,021,000	3,131,300	21,881	13,646	62.37	229,466	—	21,877	—	54,400	—
1982	4,919,300	3,259,200	21,235	14,069	66.25	231,664	—	21,194	—	54,300	—
1983	5,132,300	3,534,900	21,952	15,120	68.88	233,792	—	21,943	—	52,600	—
1984	5,505,200	3,932,700	23,344	16,676	71.44	235,825	—	23,322	—	48,600	—
1985	5,717,100	4,213,000	24,029	17,707	73.69	237,924	—	23,999	—	33,800	—
1986	5,912,400	4,452,900	24,621	18,543	75.31	240,133	—	24,611	—	20,100	—
1987	6,113,300	4,742,500	25,231	19,574	77.58	242,289	—	25,218	—	17,500	—
1988	6,368,400	5,108,300	26,047	20,893	80.21	244,499	—	26,012	—	22,700	—
1989	6,591,800	5,489,100	26,707	22,239	83.27	246,819	—	26,700	—	23,700	—
1990	6,707,900	5,803,200	26,872	23,248	86.51	249,623	—	26,840	—	32,100	—
1991	6,676,400	5,986,200	26,391	23,663	89.66	252,981	—	26,366	—	27,000	—
1992	6,880,000	6,318,900	26,821	24,634	91.84	256,514	—	26,821	—	25,800	—
1993	7,062,600	6,642,300	27,172	25,555	94.05	259,919	—	27,162	—	25,200	—
1994	7,347,700	7,054,300	27,925	26,810	96.01	263,126	—	27,895	—	16,600	—
1995	7,543,800	7,400,500	28,331	27,792	98.10	266,278	—	28,316	—	20,200	—
1996	7,813,200	7,813,200	29,000	29,003	100.00	269,394	—	28,991	—	18,000	—
1997	8,159,500	8,318,400	29,927	30,510	101.95	272,647	—	29,892	—	8,600	—
1998	8,508,900	8,781,500	30,846	31,834	103.20	275,854	—	30,813	—	−500	—
1999	8,858,963	9,274,319	31,748	33,237	104.69	279,040	—	31,716	—	24,737	—
2000	9,191,413	9,824,639	32,579	34,824	106.89	282,125	—	32,574	—	24,787	—
2001	9,214,540	10,082,151	—	—	109.42	—	—	—	—	22,760	—
2002	9,439,900	10,446,200	—	—	110.66	—	—	—	—	−6,400	—

Sources

Thomas Senior Berry, *Revised Annual Gross National Product: Preliminary Annual Estimates of Four Major Components of Demand, 1789–1889*, Bostwick Paper number 3 (Bostwick Press, 1978), Table 1B, p. 38.

Thomas Senior Berry, *Production and Population since 1789: Revised GNP Series in Constant Dollars*, Bostwick Paper number 6 (Bostwick Press, 1988), Tables 7 and 9:1, pp. 23–9.

Joseph H. Davis, "An Annual Index of U.S. Industrial Production, 1790–1915," personal communication (October 2003).

Louis D. Johnston and Samuel H. Williamson, "Source Note for US GDP, 1789–Present," EH.net Internet site, Economic History Services (March 2003), downloaded September 6, 2003.

John W. Kendrick assisted by Maude R. Pech, *Productivity Trends in the United States* (Princeton University Press, 1961), Table A-III, column 4.

TABLE Ca9-19   Gross domestic product: 1790-2002   [Continuous annual series]   *Continued*

Douglass C. North, "The United States Balance of Payments, 1790–1860," in William N. Parker, editor, *Trends in the American Economy in the Nineteenth Century* (Princeton University Press, 1960), pp. 573–628.

Matthew Simon, "The United States Balance of Payments, 1861–1900," in William N. Parker, editor, *Trends in the American Economy in the Nineteenth Century* (Princeton University Press, 1960), pp. 629–716.

Thomas Weiss, "Estimates of Gross Domestic Product for the United States, 1800 to 1860," unpublished paper (July 1993).

Documentation
GDP – Millennial Edition Series
The real gross domestic product (GDP) series reported as the "Millennial Edition series" are actually a pastiche reflecting the work of many contributors. For a full discussion, see the following detailed notes and the essay on national income and product in this chapter.

Two warnings are in order. First, the further one goes back in time, the less reliable are the numbers. In particular, the data before 1840 are based on conjectural estimates. There is a discussion in the essay on national income and product in this chapter concerning the underlying assumptions on which they rest. Second, before 1929 the intercensal data are generally less reliable than the figures for the census benchmark years (those ending in nine for 1869–1929 and ending in zero for 1790–1860). These continuous series are of value primarily for indicating long-run trends. They should not be used to study economic fluctuations or the interrelationship between price change and output movements.

For the data before 1929, the figures are based on the constant-dollar series provided by our sources. The constant-price estimates are regarded as substantially more reliable than the nominal-dollar series. Many components of the real series are based on interpolations and extrapolations from base-year values using real output values, or series on employment and estimates of real productivity. The current-dollar estimates of GDP reported here for the years before 1929 are calculated from the real GDP estimates using the price deflator shown. The several price deflators chosen and linked together are believed to reflect adequately the long-run changes in the prices of goods and services entering GDP for 1840–1929; however, strictly speaking these are not implicit deflators obtained by dividing an estimate of nominal GDP by real GDP. We report deflators for the census years spanning 1800–1840; however, we have no reliable method for interpolating those deflators for the intercensal years.

The official data, beginning in 1929, rest on a much firmer foundation. The Bureau of Economic Analysis (BEA) calculates real and current GDP separately, and the implicit deflator is calculated by division. However, the user should consult the discussion of "chain indexes," which the BEA uses to calculate GDP, in the section "Real versus Nominal National Product" of the essay on national income and product accounts in this chapter.

The per capita estimates are calculated by dividing the gross dollar figures by the resident population (series Ca14). (See the discussion of series Aa9 for the method of calculation of the intercensal estimates before 1900.)

Series Ca9. Beginning with the most recent data, several different series are linked together to create a continuous series going back to 1790.

1929–2002. BEA estimates, identical to series Ca6.

1869–1929. The standard estimates of real gross *national* product (GNP) (series Ca211) were converted to 1996 prices. These figures were then converted to gross *domestic* product by subtracting net income earned abroad (series Ca18). The resulting time series was then shifted to make a smooth link at 1929. The standard series was chosen because it is the only one based directly on data and, according to Nathan S. Balke and Robert J. Gordon ("The Estimation of Prewar Gross National Product: Methodology and New Evidence," *Journal of Political Economy* 97 (1989): 38–92), it is no more volatile on average than the regression-filtered series they proposed in response to the challenge by Christina D. Romer ("The Prewar Business Cycle Reconsidered: New Estimates of Gross National Product, 1869–1908," *Journal of Political*

Economy 97 (1989): 1–37). The Balke-Gordon and Romer alternatives are presented in Table Ca213–218.

1860–1869. There are no direct annual estimates of national output for the years 1861–1868. The figure for 1869 was estimated as described previously. The figure for 1860 is taken from Weiss as described later. These estimates for the endpoints were divided into farm output and nonfarm output, as indicated by the original sources. Farm output was interpolated on an exponential trend between 1860 and 1869. Nonfarm output was interpolated using the Davis index of industrial production (series Ca19). The estimates for the intervening years were obtained by summing these interpolated estimates for farm output and nonfarm output. Because of the wartime disruptions in record keeping, the data for the Civil War decade is less reliable than the estimates for the 1850s or the 1870s.

1840–1860. Weiss's estimates of GDP in 1840 prices for 1840, 1850, and 1860 established three benchmarks. Weiss's estimates differ from Gallman's both conceptually and by construction. Weiss includes the imputed value of home manufactures and farm improvements. The intercensal years were estimated by an interpolation based on Gallman's annual estimates of GNP (series Ca219). First, Gallman's estimates were converted to GDP by subtracting net income from abroad. Net income from abroad for calendar years were estimated from North's fiscal-year estimates and converted to 1860 prices (see the discussion of series Ca18). The census-interval GDP series was then converted to a calendar-year basis by taking a weighted average of sequential years with the weights of 7 and 5.

1800–1840. Benchmark estimates for 1800, 1810, 1820, and 1830 were established by the conjectural method (pioneered by Paul David, "The Growth of Real Product in the United States before 1840: New Evidence, Controlled Conjectures," *Journal of Economic History* 27 (1967): 151–95) described in the essay on national income and product in this chapter. These estimates are the sum of farm output and nonfarm output. In 1840, the division between farm output and nonfarm output is that indicated by Weiss. Farm output per adult male agricultural worker was extrapolated back to 1800 using the trends described by Marvin W. Towne and Wayne D. Rasmussen ("Farm Gross Product and Gross Investment in the Nineteenth Century," in William N. Parker, editor, *Trends in the American Economy in the Nineteenth Century* (Princeton University Press, 1960)), as adjusted by Weiss. Nonfarm output per adult male nonfarm worker was extrapolated back to 1820 using the trend for manufacturing suggested by Kenneth L. Sokoloff ("Productivity Growth in Manufacturing during Early Industrialization: Evidence from the American Northeast, 1820–1860," in Stanley L. Engerman and Robert E. Gallman, editors, *Long-Term Factors in American Economic Growth* (University of Chicago Press, 1986)). The trend for nonfarm, nonmanufacturing output per adult male in that sector was assumed to be the same as the trend in the agricultural sector. For 1800 and 1810, the gap between farm and nonfarm outputs per adult male worker was assumed to be the same as that in 1820. The intercensal estimates were made by exponential interpolation of the farm output and by using the Davis index of industrial production (series Ca19) to interpolate the nonfarm output.

1790–1800. Based on the sum of farm output and nonfarm output. Farm output was extrapolated backward from 1800 on the exponential trend observed for 1800–1810. Nonfarm output was extrapolated backward using the Davis index of industrial production (series Ca19) and the exponential trend observed for 1800–1810.

Series Ca10. 1790–1929: Equals series Ca9 multiplied by series Ca13 and divided by 100. 1929–2002: Equals series Ca1.

Series Ca11–12. Series Ca9-10 were converted to per capita terms by dividing by series Ca14.

(continued)

TABLE Ca9–19   Gross domestic product: 1790–2002   [Continuous annual series]   *Continued*

Series Ca13. The price deflator for GPD is based on the following:

1929–2002. Equals series Ca149.

1869–1929. Balke-Gordon implicit deflator of GNP (series Ca215) and converted to 1996 base by linking at 1929. Strictly speaking, we should have a deflator for GDP, but no such estimates exist. In practice, it may make little difference because net income from abroad is a small percentage of GNP and was itself deflated by an index of U.S. output prices (Kendrick 1961, p. 248).

1860–1869. Interpolated between the values for 1860 and 1869 using the David-Solar consumer price index, series Cc2.

1840–1860. Interpolated between Weiss's estimates for 1840, 1850, and 1860 using a simple average of the David-Solar consumer price index, series Cc2, and the Bezanson Philadelphia wholesale price index for all commodities, series Cc155, converted to a 1996 base by linking at 1860.

1800–1840. Weiss's estimates for 1800, 1810, 1820, 1830, and 1840, converted to a 1996 base by linking at 1860.

Series Ca14. Identical to series Aa9.

Real GDP Per Capita – Alternative Estimates

Series Ca15. See the discussion of Table Ca233–240 as well as the essay on national income and product in this chapter for extended discussions of the slave-economy concept. The series here is defined as series Ca9 minus the value of slave consumption (converting from 1860 prices to 1996 prices and from census-interval years to calendar years), plus the increase in the value of the stock of slaves evaluated at 1860 prices converted to 1996 prices and divided by the number in the nonslave population and expressed in calendar years. The slave population given in series Bb214 is used as the basis for these estimates; see the discussion of series Ca233–234 for details.

Series Ca16. Equals the real GDP series from Louis D. Johnston and Samuel H. Williamson (2003) converted to per capita terms using series Ca14. The Johnston-Williamson series is another pastiche constructed along lines similar to those described for series Ca9. Their data beginning in 1929 are identical to series Ca9. Those for 1869–1929 are based on Balke and Gordon's indirect estimates, series Ca213, rather than the standard series used for series Ca9. Johnston and Williamson use Weiss's benchmarks for all the census years between 1800 and 1860. They interpolate across the Civil War decade using the GNP estimates made by Berry (series Ca17). They extrapolate back to 1834 and interpolate between 1840 and 1850 and between 1850 and 1860 using Gallman's annual estimates of GNP (series Ca219), but they make no adjustments to convert Gallman's estimates to a calendar-year basis or to GDP. They interpolate between Weiss's estimates for 1800, 1810, 1820, and 1830 and their own estimate for 1834 and extrapolate back to 1789 from 1800 using Berry.

Series Ca17. Equals the real GNP series of Thomas Berry converted to per capita terms using series Ca14. Thomas Berry employed a variation of the regression approach to backcast GNP to 1789. He used an ad hoc collection of series to establish a fixed relationship to GNP during the period 1876–1926 and then imposed that relationship to estimate GNP for 1789–1875, despite the considerable differences in the structure of the economy during the two periods. Berry's estimates are not recommended for use; see the appraisal by Stanley E. Engerman and Robert E. Gallman ("U.S. Economic Growth, 1783–1860," *Research in Economic History* 8 (1983): 1–46). We present them

here because others, including Johnston and Williamson, have used them (see the discussion of series Ca16). Before the annual data that we present for 1790–1834, Berry's were the only annual estimates available.

Net Income from Abroad

Series Ca18. Net income from abroad is the difference between GNP and GDP. For the years before 1929, the standard estimates of national product were made for GNP. However, for the purposes of constructing a long-run view of American economic progress, GDP is the preferred concept. To convert the source data from GNP to GDP, we have subtracted the numbers in series Ca18 to series Ca9 to obtain a series on real GNP. For the purposes of constructing a welfare measure, GNP is the preferred concept. The series was constructed by linking data from various sources as follows:

1929–2002. BEA estimates, equal to series Ca7 minus series Ca6.

1889–1929. Estimates made by Kendrick, Table A-III, converted to 1996 prices and linked at 1929 to the BEA estimate.

1869–1889. Kendrick did not present annual estimates for 1869–1888. Instead, he provided decadal averages for 1869–1878 and 1879–1888. The series presented here interpolates those averages using data from Matthew Simon (1960, Table 27, row 25) converted from a fiscal-year to a calendar-year basis and converted to constant dollars using the Balke-Gordon GNP deflator (series Ca13).

1860–1869. Matthew Simon's estimates of the current value of the net balance of interest and dividends (1960, Table 27, row 25) converted from fiscal year to calendar year and converted to constant dollars using the David-Solar consumer price index (series Cc2).

1820–1860. Douglass North's estimates of the current value of the net balance of interest and dividends (1960, Table B-4, column 2, with the signs reversed; see Table B-5, column 7), converted from fiscal year to calendar year, and converted to constant dollars using the interpolated Weiss deflator (series Ca13).

1790–1820. No estimates available, which may not matter much because the difference between GNP and GDP was small, and the errors in the estimates of GDP are very likely to swamp the value of net income from abroad.

Index of Industrial Production

Series Ca19. The index of industrial production from Joseph H. Davis incorporates forty-three quantity-based annual series in the manufacturing and mining industries that are consistently defined over time. The index is consistent with the infrequent broad benchmarks for the pre–Civil War period and is markedly less volatile than annual indexes previously constructed for the post–Civil War era. The index weighs the relative importance of each of the forty-three components using the value added of the industrial sector that each series represents. The index rests on the value-added weights derived in two different base census years: 1849/50 and 1879/80. Index observations beginning in 1879 and thereafter reflect the 1879/80 census-year weights; observations for 1850 and before reflect the 1849/50 census-year weights. For the intervening observations from 1851–1878, the index is "chain-linked" by taking a time-weighted average of the two fixed-based annual indexes. The inadequacy of annual price data and more detailed census manufacturing data on many final goods in the Davis index prohibits a more sophisticated chain-linking procedure.

NATIONAL INCOME

Richard Sutch

TABLE Ca20-27   National income, by type of income: 1929-2002

Contributed by Richard Sutch

	National income	Compensation of employees	Proprietors' income			Rental income of persons	Corporate profits	Net interest
			Total	Nonfarm	Farm			
	Ca20	Ca21	Ca22	Ca23	Ca24	Ca25	Ca26	Ca27
Year	Billion dollars	Billion dollars	Billion dollars	Billion dollars	Billion dollars	Billion dollars	Billion dollars	Billion dollars
1929	86.8	51.1	14.9	8.7	6.2	5.6	10.6	4.6
1930	75.6	46.9	11.7	7.3	4.4	4.9	7.3	4.8
1931	60.4	39.8	9.1	5.6	3.5	4.0	2.8	4.8
1932	43.9	31.1	5.6	3.5	2.1	3.2	−0.4	4.4
1933	41.4	29.6	5.8	3.2	2.6	2.5	−0.3	3.9
1934	50.2	34.3	7.6	4.6	2.9	2.1	2.3	3.9
1935	57.9	37.4	10.7	5.4	5.3	2.2	3.8	3.9
1936	65.8	42.9	11.0	6.6	4.3	2.3	5.9	3.7
1937	74.0	48.0	13.1	7.1	6.0	2.6	6.7	3.6
1938	67.4	45.0	11.2	6.8	4.4	3.1	4.6	3.5
1939	72.9	48.1	11.7	7.3	4.4	3.3	6.2	3.5
1940	81.1	52.2	12.9	8.4	4.5	3.4	9.5	3.2
1941	104.3	64.8	17.3	10.9	6.4	4.0	15.0	3.2
1942	137.6	85.3	24.1	14.0	10.1	5.0	20.0	3.1
1943	171.4	109.6	29.1	17.0	12.0	5.6	24.5	2.7
1944	184.3	121.3	30.3	18.3	12.0	5.9	24.6	2.3
1945	183.3	123.3	31.7	19.3	12.4	6.1	20.1	2.1
1946	182.3	119.6	36.5	21.7	14.8	7.0	17.4	1.8
1947	198.6	130.1	35.6	20.5	15.1	7.0	23.5	2.4
1948	223.3	142.0	40.4	22.9	17.5	7.6	30.8	2.4
1949	216.7	142.0	35.7	23.1	12.7	7.8	28.6	2.6
1950	241.0	155.4	38.6	25.1	13.5	8.7	35.4	3.0
1951	278.7	181.5	43.8	27.8	16.0	9.5	40.4	3.5
1952	293.3	196.3	44.3	29.2	15.1	10.5	38.4	3.8
1953	308.2	210.3	43.3	30.3	13.0	11.5	38.7	4.4
1954	308.4	209.3	43.5	31.0	12.5	12.5	37.9	5.3
1955	338.5	225.8	45.5	34.0	11.5	12.8	48.5	6.0
1956	358.7	244.6	47.0	35.7	11.3	13.1	47.4	6.6
1957	375.0	257.6	49.0	37.7	11.3	13.8	47.0	7.7
1958	377.3	259.6	51.4	38.3	13.1	14.5	42.4	9.4
1959	411.5	281.0	51.8	40.9	10.9	15.2	53.7	9.7
1960	427.5	296.4	51.9	40.4	11.4	16.2	52.3	10.7
1961	442.5	305.3	54.4	42.3	12.1	16.9	53.5	12.4
1962	477.1	327.2	56.5	44.4	12.1	17.8	61.6	14.1
1963	504.4	345.3	57.8	45.8	11.9	18.5	67.6	15.2
1964	542.1	370.7	60.6	49.9	10.8	18.6	74.8	17.3
1965	589.6	399.5	65.2	52.2	13.1	19.2	86.0	19.7
1966	646.7	442.6	69.6	55.5	14.1	19.9	92.0	22.6
1967	681.7	475.2	71.1	58.4	12.8	20.4	89.6	25.4
1968	743.6	524.3	75.4	62.6	12.8	20.2	96.5	27.2
1969	802.7	577.6	78.9	64.7	14.2	20.3	93.7	32.2
1970	837.5	617.2	79.8	65.5	14.3	20.3	81.6	38.4
1971	903.9	658.8	86.1	71.2	14.9	21.2	95.1	42.6
1972	1,000.4	725.1	97.7	78.9	18.8	21.6	109.8	46.2
1973	1,127.4	811.2	115.2	84.5	30.7	23.1	123.9	53.9
1974	1,211.9	890.2	115.5	90.3	25.2	23.0	114.5	68.8
1975	1,302.2	949.0	121.6	98.1	23.5	22.0	133.0	76.6
1976	1,456.4	1,059.3	134.3	115.6	18.7	21.5	160.6	80.8
1977	1,635.8	1,180.4	148.3	130.8	17.5	20.4	190.9	95.7
1978	1,860.2	1,336.0	170.1	148.5	21.5	22.4	217.2	114.5
1979	2,075.6	1,500.8	183.7	160.0	23.7	24.5	222.5	144.2

(continued)

TABLE Ca20-27   National income, by type of income: 1929-2002 *Continued*

		Compensation	Proprietors' income			Rental income		
	National income	of employees	Total	Nonfarm	Farm	of persons	Corporate profits	Net interest
	Ca20	Ca21	Ca22	Ca23	Ca24	Ca25	Ca26	Ca27
Year	Billion dollars	Billion dollars	Billion dollars	Billion dollars	Billion dollars	Billion dollars	Billion dollars	Billion dollars
1980	2,243.0	1,651.7	177.6	164.5	13.1	31.3	198.5	183.9
1981	2,497.1	1,825.7	186.2	165.9	20.3	39.6	219.0	226.5
1982	2,603.0	1,926.0	179.9	165.4	14.4	39.6	201.2	256.3
1983	2,796.5	2,042.7	195.5	188.3	7.2	36.9	254.1	267.2
1984	3,162.3	2,255.9	247.5	225.9	21.6	39.5	309.8	309.6
1985	3,380.4	2,425.2	267.0	245.5	21.5	39.1	322.4	326.7
1986	3,525.8	2,570.7	278.6	255.6	23.0	32.2	300.7	343.6
1987	3,803.4	2,755.6	303.9	274.8	29.0	35.8	346.6	361.5
1988	4,151.1	2,973.8	338.8	312.7	26.0	44.1	405.0	389.4
1989	4,392.1	3,151.0	361.8	329.6	32.2	40.5	395.7	443.1
1990	4,642.1	3,351.0	381.0	349.9	31.1	49.1	408.6	452.4
1991	4,756.6	3,454.9	384.2	357.8	26.4	56.4	431.2	429.8
1992	4,994.9	3,644.8	434.3	401.7	32.7	63.3	453.1	399.5
1993	5,251.9	3,814.4	461.8	431.7	30.1	90.9	510.5	374.3
1994	5,556.8	4,016.2	476.6	444.6	31.9	110.3	573.2	380.5
1995	5,876.7	4,202.5	497.7	475.5	22.2	117.9	668.8	389.8
1996	6,210.4	4,395.6	544.7	510.5	34.3	129.7	754.0	386.3
1997	6,618.4	4,651.3	581.2	551.5	29.7	128.3	833.8	423.9
1998	7,041.4	4,989.6	623.8	598.2	25.6	138.6	777.4	511.9
1999	7,468.7	5,308.8	678.4	650.7	27.7	149.1	805.8	526.6
2000	7,984.4	5,723.4	714.8	692.2	22.6	146.6	788.1	611.5
2001	8,122.0	5,874.9	727.9	708.8	19.0	137.9	731.6	649.8
2002	8,340.1	5,969.5	756.5	743.7	12.9	142.4	787.4	684.2

Source

U.S. Bureau of Economic Analysis Internet site, Table 1.14, downloaded August 18, 2003.

Documentation

The figures are official Department of Commerce estimates. The relative accuracy of the various series as evaluated by the department is, in terms of decreasing reliability: employee compensation, corporate profits, net interest, proprietors' income, and rental income. In particular, the entrepreneurial income estimates (including rental income) are subject to significant shortcomings compared to the other income shares.

Series Ca20. The definition of national income is given in Table Ca1-8.

Series Ca21. Compensation of employees is the income accruing to persons in an employee status as remuneration for their work. It is the sum of wages and salaries and supplements to wages and salaries. Wages and salaries consist of the monetary remuneration of employees, inclusive of executives' compensation, commissions, tips, and bonuses, and of payments in kind that represent income to the recipients. Supplements to wages and salaries consist of employer contributions for social insurance and of "other labor income." Employer contributions for social insurance comprise employer payments under social security, federal and state unemployment insurance, railroad retirement and unemployment insurance, government retirement, and a few other minor social insurance programs. "Other labor income" is presented as series Ca57. It comprises employer contributions to private pension, health, unemployment, and welfare funds; compensation for injuries; directors' fees; pay of the military reserve; and a few other minor items.

Series Ca22-24. Proprietors' income measures the monetary earnings and income in kind of sole proprietorships, partnerships, and producers' cooperatives from their current business operations – other than the supplementary income of individuals derived from renting property. These series include the

inventory valuation adjustment, which is the difference between the book cost of inventories used in production and their replacement cost, and capital consumption adjustments, which are the other adjustments to taxable income described under corporate profits (series Ca26).

Series Ca25. Rental income of persons consists of the monetary earnings of persons from the rental of real property, except the earnings of persons primarily engaged in the real estate business; the imputed net rental returns to owner-occupants of nonfarm dwellings; and the royalties received by persons from patents, copyrights, and rights to natural resources. This series includes the capital consumption adjustments, which are the other adjustments to taxable income described under corporate profits (series Ca26).

Series Ca26. Corporate profits (before tax) are the earnings of corporations organized for profit that accrue to residents of the nation, measured before federal and state profits taxes, without deduction of depletion charges, exclusive of capital gains and losses and intercorporate dividends, and including inventory valuation adjustment. This series includes the profits of stock life insurance companies and of mutual financial institutions. Bad debt expenses are measured by actual losses, not additions to reserves, and the profit or loss of bankrupt firms includes the gain from unsatisfied debt. Corporate profits include net receipts of dividends and branch profits from abroad, as reflected in the balance of payments statistics, in addition to profits earned in domestic operations. In other major respects, the definition of profits is in accordance with federal income tax regulations.

Series Ca27. Net interest measures the excess of interest payments of the domestic business system over its interest receipts, plus net interest received from abroad. In addition to monetary interest flows, net interest includes imputed interest arising in connection with the operations of financial intermediaries.

TABLE Ca28–34   National income, by legal form of organization: 1929–2001

Contributed by Richard Sutch

	Private business enterprises			Government activities		Households and institutions	Rest of the world
	Corporate business	Sole proprietorships and partnerships	Other private business	Government enterprises	General government	Households and institutions	Rest of the world
	Ca28	Ca29	Ca30	Ca31	Ca32	Ca33	Ca34
Year	Billion dollars	Billion dollars	Billion dollars	Billion dollars	Billion dollars	Billion dollars	Billion dollars
1929	45.9	24.2	8.0	0.8	4.4	2.9	0.8
1930	39.4	20.3	7.2	0.8	4.6	2.7	0.7
1931	29.6	16.3	6.3	0.8	4.7	2.3	0.5
1932	19.9	11.2	5.4	0.7	4.5	1.9	0.4
1933	18.7	10.8	4.5	0.6	4.7	1.7	0.3
1934	24.5	13.1	4.2	0.7	5.6	1.8	0.3
1935	28.0	16.7	4.3	0.8	6.0	1.9	0.3
1936	33.3	17.7	4.4	0.8	7.3	2.0	0.3
1937	38.1	20.7	4.7	0.9	6.9	2.3	0.4
1938	32.6	18.5	5.2	0.9	7.7	2.2	0.4
1939	36.7	19.4	5.4	0.9	7.6	2.3	0.4
1940	42.8	21.1	5.5	1.0	7.8	2.4	0.4
1941	56.9	27.6	6.2	1.1	9.5	2.5	0.5
1942	73.2	37.3	7.3	1.2	15.2	2.9	0.5
1943	88.8	44.1	7.8	1.5	25.6	3.2	0.4
1944	91.6	46.8	8.0	1.5	32.3	3.7	0.5
1945	84.1	49.6	8.2	1.6	35.3	4.1	0.4
1946	86.3	57.2	9.3	1.9	22.4	4.5	0.7
1947	104.7	58.4	9.5	2.0	17.6	5.1	1.2
1948	120.4	64.9	10.5	2.3	18.1	5.6	1.5
1949	115.9	59.9	11.0	2.6	20.1	5.9	1.3
1950	132.4	64.4	12.3	2.7	21.2	6.5	1.5
1951	152.7	72.7	13.6	3.0	27.7	6.9	2.0
1952	158.9	74.9	15.0	3.5	31.5	7.2	2.1
1953	170.5	75.5	16.6	3.5	32.4	7.8	2.0
1954	167.9	75.5	18.1	3.6	33.0	8.1	2.2
1955	190.5	78.6	19.2	3.8	34.8	9.1	2.5
1956	202.4	82.0	20.3	4.0	37.2	9.9	2.9
1957	210.1	85.3	21.9	4.2	39.8	10.6	3.2
1958	204.0	87.4	23.9	4.7	42.9	11.5	2.7
1959	230.8	89.7	25.9	5.0	44.9	12.4	2.9
1960	239.4	89.7	27.8	5.5	48.1	13.9	3.2
1961	245.6	91.8	29.7	5.7	51.6	14.5	3.6
1962	268.9	94.9	31.9	6.1	55.5	15.6	4.2
1963	286.1	97.3	33.8	6.6	59.3	16.7	4.6
1964	309.7	102.7	35.4	7.1	64.4	17.9	5.0
1965	341.6	108.8	37.5	7.7	69.3	19.3	5.4
1966	377.6	116.2	39.8	8.3	78.4	21.3	5.2
1967	396.2	118.8	41.5	8.9	87.4	23.4	5.5
1968	435.0	125.4	43.3	9.9	97.8	26.1	6.2
1969	471.7	131.3	45.6	11.0	107.5	29.5	6.2
1970	484.0	134.5	47.9	12.8	119.4	32.4	6.4
1971	521.3	142.5	51.9	14.0	130.9	35.6	7.7
1972	581.0	157.2	56.3	15.2	143.1	38.9	8.7
1973	653.0	183.8	62.7	16.8	155.4	43.0	12.7
1974	700.6	191.1	68.4	19.3	169.8	47.1	15.7
1975	750.2	202.5	72.5	22.2	189.6	52.0	13.2
1976	850.6	223.0	78.1	24.0	206.4	57.1	17.1
1977	971.0	244.7	86.1	25.9	225.1	62.4	20.7
1978	1,116.9	277.9	100.4	28.4	244.8	69.7	22.1
1979	1,243.1	307.4	117.3	31.4	266.3	77.3	32.9
1980	1,334.1	314.8	140.2	35.8	295.7	87.1	35.3
1981	1,494.8	338.8	165.0	40.6	325.5	97.6	34.7
1982	1,537.3	343.4	181.8	42.8	353.1	108.2	36.4
1983	1,658.4	367.8	192.5	46.0	375.8	119.2	36.9
1984	1,876.3	444.7	214.5	49.3	411.0	131.2	35.3
1985	2,002.2	479.5	234.6	53.6	444.3	141.0	25.4
1986	2,079.3	503.5	247.1	55.6	471.1	153.7	15.5
1987	2,264.5	526.5	266.6	58.9	499.9	173.3	13.7
1988	2,456.3	593.5	291.3	64.0	532.6	195.1	18.4
1989	2,570.2	644.1	308.3	67.2	567.3	214.6	20.4

(continued)

TABLE Ca28–34   National income, by legal form of organization: 1929–2001   *Continued*

	Private business enterprises			Government activities			
	Corporate business	Sole proprietorships and partnerships	Other private business	Government enterprises	General government	Households and institutions	Rest of the world
	Ca28	Ca29	Ca30	Ca31	Ca32	Ca33	Ca34
Year	Billion dollars	Billion dollars	Billion dollars	Billion dollars	Billion dollars	Billion dollars	Billion dollars
1990	2,687.7	671.4	333.5	73.2	609.4	237.9	29.0
1991	2,731.4	671.8	349.5	76.7	645.1	257.5	24.7
1992	2,860.0	722.8	356.2	81.2	671.8	279.5	23.4
1993	3,018.6	758.3	376.1	81.7	695.8	297.0	24.4
1994	3,234.9	793.1	395.7	86.0	717.0	313.3	16.8
1995	3,445.6	832.5	423.8	88.4	735.8	330.3	20.3
1996	3,658.2	890.9	445.0	90.2	759.4	348.6	18.1
1997	3,952.1	953.2	460.2	92.6	790.0	363.2	7.1
1998	4,215.1	1,044.3	486.5	95.4	819.7	383.8	−3.4
1999	4,454.3	1,116.4	518.9	98.4	854.8	403.1	22.7
2000	4,778.4	1,191.7	552.6	104.6	902.6	431.1	23.4
2001	4,762.7	1,248.3	567.4	110.0	952.1	459.6	21.9

Source

U.S. Bureau of Economic Analysis Internet site, Table 1.15, downloaded August 18, 2003.

Documentation

These series present an allocation of national income (series Ca4) among seven legal forms of organization. Certain types of income, by definition, fall into one of the seven legal forms of organization distinguished in these series, such as corporate profits, proprietors' income, and rental income of persons. Net interest is estimated separately for each of the relevant legal forms, and a breakdown of compensation of employees among the three forms

of private business enterprises is derived for benchmark years by applying distributions for each industry developed largely from economic censuses. A description of the various types of income may be found in the text for Table Ca20–27.

Series Ca31. Covers the essentially commercial enterprises of the government, such as the U.S. Postal Service.

Series Ca34. Provides a measure of the net income originating in the rest of the world that accrues to U.S. residents.

TABLE Ca35–53   National income, by industry group: 1929–2002

Contributed by Susan B. Carter

		Domestic industries							
			Private sector						
							Manufacturing		
	Total	Total	Total	Agriculture, forestry, and fisheries	Mining	Contract construction	Total	Durable goods	Nondurable goods
	Ca35	Ca36	Ca37	Ca38	Ca39	Ca40	Ca41	Ca42	Ca43
Year	Billion dollars	Billion dollars	Billion dollars	Billion dollars	Billion dollars	Billion dollars	Billion dollars	Billion dollars	Billion dollars
1929	88.2	87.4	82.3	8.7	2.1	3.8	22.0	11.3	10.7
1930	76.7	76.0	70.7	6.6	1.7	3.2	18.3	8.5	9.8
1931	61.0	60.5	55.1	5.3	1.0	2.2	12.5	4.9	7.6
1932	44.2	43.8	38.6	3.6	0.7	1.1	7.3	2.0	5.3
1933	41.6	41.3	36.0	3.9	0.6	0.8	7.7	2.6	5.0
1934	50.8	50.6	44.3	4.3	1.2	1.1	11.0	4.5	6.5
1935	58.5	58.2	51.4	6.7	1.2	1.3	13.3	6.0	7.4
1936	66.4	66.1	58.0	5.9	1.6	2.0	16.3	8.0	8.3
1937	75.2	74.8	67.0	7.7	2.0	2.1	19.5	9.8	9.6
1938	68.8	68.4	59.8	6.1	1.6	2.0	15.1	6.7	8.4
1939	74.1	73.7	65.1	6.1	1.6	2.3	18.1	8.9	9.1
1940	82.5	82.2	73.4	6.2	1.9	2.6	22.5	12.1	10.3
1941	105.9	105.4	94.9	8.5	2.4	4.2	33.2	20.3	12.9
1942	139.2	138.7	122.4	12.7	2.6	6.5	45.5	28.8	16.6
1943	172.5	172.1	145.0	15.0	2.8	5.5	58.3	38.6	19.7
1944	184.8	184.4	150.6	15.2	3.0	4.1	60.3	39.3	21.0
1945	183.7	183.4	146.4	15.7	2.8	4.3	52.2	31.0	21.2
1946	185.9	185.2	160.9	18.5	3.0	6.5	49.2	24.3	24.9
1947	202.9	201.7	182.1	19.3	4.3	8.5	59.6	31.5	28.1
1948	228.3	226.8	206.4	22.2	5.4	11.0	68.8	35.9	32.9
1949	221.5	220.1	197.5	17.3	4.5	10.9	64.9	34.3	30.6

TABLE Ca35–53   National income, by industry group: 1929–2002   *Continued*

		Domestic industries							
			Private sector						
							Manufacturing		
	Total	Total	Total	Agriculture, forestry, and fisheries	Mining	Contract construction	Total	Durable goods	Nondurable goods
	Ca35	Ca36	Ca37	Ca38	Ca39	Ca40	Ca41	Ca42	Ca43
Year	Billion dollars	Billion dollars	Billion dollars	Billion dollars	Billion dollars	Billion dollars	Billion dollars	Billion dollars	Billion dollars
1950	245.8	244.2	220.3	18.3	5.3	12.4	76.4	43.0	33.4
1951	284.3	282.3	251.5	21.2	5.8	14.7	90.5	52.0	38.5
1952	298.5	296.3	261.3	20.3	5.5	15.9	92.7	54.4	38.3
1953	312.5	310.5	274.6	18.1	5.5	16.4	100.6	60.3	40.3
1954	311.6	309.4	272.8	17.5	5.3	16.5	94.9	55.1	39.8
1955	340.4	337.9	299.3	16.5	5.9	17.6	108.2	64.0	44.2
1956	361.4	358.5	317.3	16.5	6.6	19.6	113.4	67.1	46.4
1957	378.0	374.8	330.8	16.7	6.6	20.5	116.6	70.1	46.5
1958	380.1	377.4	329.8	18.9	5.7	20.0	108.2	62.2	46.0
1959	413.6	410.8	360.9	16.9	5.5	21.8	124.6	73.2	51.5
1960	429.2	425.9	372.4	17.7	5.6	22.3	125.5	73.4	52.1
1961	443.5	439.8	382.5	18.6	5.6	23.3	125.3	72.3	52.9
1962	475.1	470.9	409.3	19.0	5.5	25.0	136.5	81.1	55.4
1963	501.1	496.6	430.6	19.0	5.8	26.7	144.4	86.6	57.7
1964	538.1	533.1	461.5	18.4	6.0	29.3	154.9	93.5	61.4
1965	585.2	579.8	502.9	21.2	6.1	32.1	172.0	105.8	66.2
1966	642.5	637.3	550.6	22.7	6.3	35.1	190.7	117.9	72.7
1967	677.7	672.2	575.9	21.7	6.4	36.7	194.7	119.5	75.2
1968	740.4	734.2	626.5	22.5	7.1	40.1	211.9	129.9	82.0
1969	799.7	793.5	675.1	24.8	7.3	44.9	222.7	136.6	86.1
1970	836.1	829.7	697.5	25.6	8.3	47.2	215.9	127.8	88.2
1971	904.0	896.3	751.4	27.0	8.4	51.8	227.4	134.8	92.5
1972	999.4	990.7	832.5	32.2	9.3	57.3	253.2	154.2	99.0
1973	1,127.2	1,114.5	942.3	46.6	11.2	65.1	286.1	176.9	109.3
1974	1,217.6	1,201.9	1,012.9	43.4	16.7	69.5	302.3	181.6	120.8
1975	1,317.9	1,304.7	1,092.9	44.4	20.9	69.7	318.0	185.2	132.8
1976	1,476.2	1,459.0	1,228.6	42.7	21.5	79.8	366.6	215.9	150.7
1977	1,656.0	1,635.4	1,384.4	42.9	25.2	88.4	416.7	249.5	167.2
1978	1,885.0	1,862.9	1,589.7	51.1	27.5	104.6	471.7	286.7	185.0
1979	2,107.5	2,074.6	1,776.9	58.6	33.1	117.9	518.4	310.3	208.1
1980	2,282.9	2,247.6	1,916.0	52.2	45.7	120.9	536.6	311.8	224.7
1981	2,523.4	2,488.7	2,122.6	63.5	51.7	121.3	594.1	341.4	252.7
1982	2,620.2	2,583.7	2,187.9	61.2	50.2	119.2	576.7	322.3	254.4
1983	2,788.1	2,751.2	2,329.4	54.7	40.3	128.2	598.0	340.0	257.9
1984	3,126.5	3,091.1	2,630.8	70.2	43.8	153.0	672.5	400.6	271.9
1985	3,318.1	3,292.8	2,795.0	69.0	40.1	171.8	691.3	408.1	283.2
1986	3,475.8	3,460.3	2,933.6	70.7	28.4	191.8	686.8	412.3	274.5
1987 [1]	3,760.3	3,746.6	3,187.9	78.9	28.6	202.9	739.8	441.3	298.5
1987 [1]	3,760.3	3,746.6	3,187.9	78.9	28.6	202.9	739.8	440.5	299.3
1988	4,112.1	4,093.6	3,497.1	78.2	35.9	218.9	822.2	481.2	341.0
1989	4,366.9	4,346.5	3,712.1	85.5	36.2	227.1	853.4	497.3	356.1
1990	4,640.5	4,611.6	3,929.0	89.0	40.8	230.5	879.0	498.1	380.9
1991	4,769.1	4,744.4	4,022.6	83.6	40.2	214.6	863.9	484.6	379.3
1992	5,018.2	4,994.8	4,241.8	90.7	39.7	215.6	886.0	499.7	386.3
1993	5,267.9	5,243.5	4,466.0	91.9	40.5	228.3	929.1	533.2	395.9
1994	5,576.4	5,559.6	4,756.6	93.7	43.9	252.8	1,006.0	582.3	423.7
1995	5,884.4	5,864.0	5,039.9	86.9	45.7	266.7	1,058.5	606.8	451.6
1996	6,206.4	6,188.3	5,338.7	101.9	50.7	290.3	1,073.9	614.0	459.9
1997	6,599.6	6,592.6	5,709.9	101.6	58.2	309.3	1,119.3	643.8	475.5
1998	7,013.2	7,016.6	6,101.6	102.4	54.2	349.6	1,145.4	671.0	474.4
1999	7,424.5	7,401.8	6,448.5	111.3	48.6	389.4	1,180.5	688.0	492.6
2000	7,958.7	7,935.3	6,928.0	109.7	62.9	422.9	1,250.7	729.2	521.4
2001	8,053.5	8,031.5	6,969.4	111.1	69.5	438.9	1,132.2	640.5	491.8
2002	8,174.8	8,184.4	7,068.4	109.5	59.1	442.0	1,122.2	628.4	493.8

Note appears at end of table

(continued)

TABLE Ca35-53   National income, by industry group: 1929-2002   *Continued*

					Domestic industries					
					Private sector					
	Transportation and public utilities									Rest of the world
	Total	Transportation	Communications	Electric, gas, and sanitary services	Wholesale trade	Retail trade and automobile services	Finance, insurance, and real estate	Services	Government	
	Ca44	Ca45	Ca46	Ca47	Ca48	Ca49	Ca50	Ca51	Ca52	Ca53
Year	Billion dollars	Billion dollars	Billion dollars	Billion dollars	Billion dollars	Billion dollars	Billion dollars	Billion dollars	Billion dollars	Billion dollars
1929	9.4	6.6	1.1	1.7	4.4	9.5	13.7	8.8	5.1	0.8
1930	8.4	5.6	1.1	1.7	4.2	8.5	11.6	8.3	5.3	0.7
1931	7.0	4.4	1.0	1.6	3.3	6.9	9.7	7.2	5.5	0.5
1932	5.5	3.2	0.8	1.5	2.3	4.6	8.0	5.6	5.2	0.4
1933	5.1	3.1	0.7	1.3	1.9	4.0	6.9	5.1	5.4	0.3
1934	5.6	3.4	0.8	1.4	2.6	5.9	6.7	5.7	6.3	0.3
1935	6.0	3.7	0.8	1.5	3.0	6.6	7.1	6.1	6.8	0.3
1936	6.7	4.3	0.9	1.6	3.4	7.6	7.7	6.8	8.2	0.3
1937	7.4	4.6	1.0	1.7	4.0	8.5	8.3	7.5	7.8	0.4
1938	6.8	4.1	1.0	1.7	3.9	8.4	8.9	7.2	8.6	0.4
1939	7.5	4.6	1.1	1.8	3.9	8.8	9.2	7.5	8.6	0.4
1940	8.1	5.0	1.1	1.9	4.6	10.1	9.5	8.0	8.8	0.4
1941	9.6	6.3	1.2	2.1	5.3	12.2	10.6	8.8	10.6	0.5
1942	12.3	8.6	1.5	2.2	6.3	14.3	12.0	10.2	16.4	0.5
1943	14.8	10.8	1.7	2.3	6.9	17.1	13.0	11.8	27.1	0.4
1944	15.3	11.2	1.8	2.2	7.7	18.2	13.7	13.1	33.8	0.5
1945	14.8	10.5	1.9	2.3	8.3	19.8	14.5	14.1	36.9	0.4
1946	15.2	10.4	2.2	2.6	10.5	24.2	17.1	16.6	24.3	0.7
1947	16.8	11.6	2.3	2.8	11.7	26.0	18.0	18.1	19.6	1.2
1948	18.8	12.8	2.8	3.2	13.8	26.3	20.1	20.0	20.4	1.5
1949	18.8	12.1	3.0	3.7	13.1	26.1	21.4	20.4	22.7	1.3
1950	20.7	13.4	3.4	3.9	14.3	27.1	23.8	22.0	23.9	1.5
1951	23.5	15.1	3.9	4.6	16.5	29.3	26.1	24.0	30.7	2.0
1952	25.0	15.6	4.3	5.1	16.8	30.7	28.8	25.7	35.0	2.1
1953	26.3	16.0	4.8	5.5	17.0	31.3	31.7	27.7	35.9	2.0
1954	25.9	14.8	5.1	6.0	17.1	32.3	34.5	28.8	36.6	2.2
1955	28.2	16.2	5.7	6.3	19.2	34.3	37.1	32.3	38.6	2.5
1956	30.2	17.3	6.2	6.7	20.8	35.5	39.3	35.3	41.2	2.9
1957	31.6	17.8	6.7	7.1	21.9	37.1	41.9	38.1	44.0	3.2
1958	31.5	16.9	7.1	7.6	22.4	37.7	45.1	40.2	47.6	2.7
1959	34.3	18.2	7.8	8.2	24.2	41.2	48.3	44.1	49.9	2.9
1960	35.9	18.5	8.3	9.1	24.9	41.8	51.6	47.0	53.5	3.2
1961	36.9	18.7	8.7	9.5	25.7	42.6	54.4	50.2	57.3	3.6
1962	38.9	19.6	9.4	9.9	27.2	45.5	57.6	54.0	61.6	4.2
1963	41.2	20.6	10.0	10.5	28.4	47.4	60.0	57.6	66.0	4.6
1964	43.9	21.8	10.8	11.2	30.5	52.0	63.7	62.9	71.5	5.0
1965	47.0	23.7	11.6	11.7	32.5	55.7	68.2	68.0	76.9	5.4
1966	50.9	25.5	12.9	12.5	35.6	59.6	74.1	75.7	86.7	5.2
1967	52.6	26.0	13.5	13.1	37.7	64.1	78.7	83.3	96.3	5.5
1968	56.8	28.0	14.7	14.1	41.2	70.5	85.2	91.2	107.7	6.2
1969	61.1	29.9	16.3	14.9	45.0	76.2	91.8	101.3	118.4	6.2
1970	64.3	31.2	17.8	15.3	47.7	80.6	97.8	110.1	132.2	6.4
1971	70.2	34.4	18.7	17.0	51.3	87.6	108.6	119.1	144.9	7.7
1972	77.3	38.2	20.7	18.4	58.0	94.5	118.4	132.2	158.3	8.7
1973	85.3	42.8	22.9	19.5	65.7	104.0	129.9	148.5	172.2	12.7
1974	92.8	47.6	25.1	20.1	77.0	107.7	140.2	163.3	189.0	15.7
1975	101.4	48.0	27.1	26.4	83.4	121.6	152.0	181.5	211.8	13.2
1976	116.8	56.1	30.8	29.9	90.3	137.6	168.7	204.6	230.4	17.1
1977	130.7	62.9	34.3	33.4	100.2	151.8	194.7	233.8	251.0	20.7
1978	148.5	71.3	39.9	37.2	114.3	170.7	232.2	269.1	273.2	22.1
1979	160.5	78.7	43.6	38.1	132.6	184.5	266.3	304.9	297.7	32.9
1980	178.3	83.5	48.9	45.8	143.3	193.1	300.9	345.1	331.6	35.3
1981	198.7	88.4	55.9	54.4	159.6	212.2	334.1	387.5	366.1	34.7
1982	212.4	86.5	61.5	64.5	162.3	224.5	355.2	426.2	395.8	36.4
1983	223.8	93.3	63.2	67.3	166.5	249.6	397.6	470.6	421.8	36.9
1984	250.0	106.6	67.0	76.4	192.3	278.4	439.6	531.1	460.3	35.3

TABLE Ca35–53   National income, by industry group: 1929–2002   *Continued*

	Domestic industries									Rest of the world
	Private sector									
	Transportation and public utilities									
Year	Total	Transportation	Communications	Electric, gas, and sanitary services	Wholesale trade	Retail trade and automobile services	Finance, insurance, and real estate	Services	Government	Rest of the world
	Ca44	Ca45	Ca46	Ca47	Ca48	Ca49	Ca50	Ca51	Ca52	Ca53
	Billion dollars	Billion dollars	Billion dollars	Billion dollars	Billion dollars	Billion dollars	Billion dollars	Billion dollars	Billion dollars	Billion dollars
1985	255.3	107.3	70.7	77.3	198.4	301.1	484.9	583.0	497.8	25.4
1986	267.9	115.5	75.6	76.8	206.8	315.6	528.8	636.8	526.7	15.5
1987 [1]	286.2	123.4	80.5	82.3	215.3	330.7	599.6	706.0	558.8	13.7
1987 [1]	286.2	123.4	80.5	82.3	215.9	330.1	599.7	705.9	558.8	13.7
1988	303.6	132.7	84.9	86.0	239.7	351.7	651.5	795.3	596.5	18.4
1989	313.7	133.7	86.4	93.6	256.7	373.9	691.6	873.8	634.5	20.4
1990	330.5	138.7	94.2	97.6	266.0	385.3	738.5	969.5	682.6	29.0
1991	351.1	146.1	100.1	104.9	271.5	395.8	786.4	1,015.6	721.8	24.7
1992	366.1	152.9	105.2	108.0	284.9	413.8	841.5	1,103.6	753.0	23.4
1993	392.2	163.2	115.7	113.4	290.5	431.0	897.1	1,165.4	777.5	24.4
1994	423.2	176.6	126.2	120.4	314.0	460.7	932.7	1,229.5	803.0	16.8
1995	440.7	183.9	129.4	127.3	328.2	481.8	1,013.5	1,318.1	824.2	20.3
1996	461.6	194.7	136.1	130.8	354.7	509.8	1,088.0	1,407.8	849.6	18.1
1997	473.7	207.2	135.5	131.0	381.8	551.8	1,197.1	1,517.2	882.6	7.1
1998	495.9	224.6	142.8	128.5	420.5	585.6	1,309.5	1,638.6	915.1	−3.4
1999	511.4	234.0	144.1	133.2	444.4	619.3	1,379.3	1,764.2	953.3	22.7
2000	530.5	243.7	149.4	137.4	481.1	659.1	1,521.5	1,889.8	1,007.3	23.4
2001	529.9	236.6	148.4	144.9	458.4	686.1	1,571.1	1,972.0	1,062.1	21.9
2002	514.3	236.2	136.8	141.3	465.8	702.8	1,635.8	2,016.8	1,116.0	−9.6

[1] Two sets of values are presented for 1987, one based on the 1972 Standard Industrial Classification (SIC) and the other based on the 1987 SIC (see text).

Source
U.S. Bureau of Economic Analysis Internet site, Tables 6.1a, 6.1b, and 6.1c; downloaded August 27, 2003.

Documentation
National income is the total of factor incomes earned in the production of the gross national product (GNP). Factor incomes include the compensation of employees, proprietors' income, rental income of persons, corporate profits, and net interest. The figures presented here are without capital consumption adjustment, that is, excluding the value of fixed capital "used up" in the production process during the accounting period.

The industrial groupings in this table are based on the Standard Industrial Classification (SIC) system: The data for 1929–1948 are based on the 1942 SIC; those for 1948–1987 are based on the 1972 SIC; and those for 1987 and later are based on the 1987 SIC. See the Introduction to Part D for a discussion of industrial classification. Estimates for the overlap years, 1948 and 1987, were calculated twice, once using the SIC for the earlier period and a second time using the SIC for the later period. The 1948 estimates using the two different schemes are identical; however, for 1987 the two classification schemes produced slightly different estimates. Both sets of values are presented here for 1987.

Industrial distributions for private activities are based on data collected from establishments or from companies (also called enterprises or firms).

Establishments, as defined in the SIC, are economic units, generally at a single physical location where business is conducted or where services or industrial operations are performed. Companies consist of one or more establishments owned by the same legal entities or group of affiliated entities. Establishments are classified into an SIC industry on the basis of their principal product or service, and companies are classified into an SIC industry on the basis of the principal SIC industry of all of their establishments. Because large multiestablishment companies typically own establishments classified in different SIC industries, the industrial distribution of the same economic activity on an establishment basis can differ significantly from that on a company basis. Industrial distributions on a consistent establishment or company basis are not available for all national income components. As a result, the industrial distribution of national income reflects a mix of establishment and company data.

Individual industry series are not fully comparable over time. First, the composition of industries may change because of changes in the SIC basis that is used for the estimates. This factor affects estimates based on establishment data and on company data. Second, historical comparability is affected because the industrial classification of the same establishment or company may change over time.

Industrial distributions of government activities are not provided; instead, they are combined into a single category.

TABLE Ca54–63   Personal income, by source: 1929–2002

Contributed by Richard Sutch

	Wage and salary disbursements			Other labor income	Proprietors' income	Rental income of persons	Personal dividend income	Personal interest income	Transfer payments to persons	Less: personal contributions for social insurance
	Total	Private-sector employees	Government employees							
	Ca54	Ca55	Ca56	Ca57	Ca58	Ca59	Ca60	Ca61	Ca62	Ca63
	Billion dollars	Billion dollars	Billion dollars	Billion dollars	Billion dollars	Billion dollars	Billion dollars	Billion dollars	Billion dollars	Billion dollars
Year										
1929	50.5	45.5	5.0	0.7	14.9	5.6	5.8	6.8	1.2	0.1
1930	46.2	41.0	5.2	0.6	11.7	4.9	5.5	6.3	1.2	0.1
1931	39.2	33.9	5.3	0.6	9.1	4.0	4.1	6.3	2.3	0.1
1932	30.5	25.5	5.0	0.6	5.6	3.2	2.5	5.9	1.7	0.1
1933	29.0	23.9	5.2	0.5	5.8	2.5	2.0	5.4	1.7	0.1
1934	33.7	27.6	6.1	0.6	7.6	2.1	2.6	5.5	1.8	0.1
1935	36.7	30.2	6.5	0.6	10.7	2.2	2.8	5.5	2.0	0.1
1936	42.0	34.1	7.9	0.8	11.0	2.3	4.5	5.3	3.1	0.1
1937	46.1	38.6	7.5	0.8	13.1	2.6	4.7	5.4	2.0	0.4
1938	43.0	34.8	8.3	0.8	11.2	3.1	3.2	5.3	2.4	0.4
1939	46.0	37.7	8.2	0.9	11.7	3.3	3.8	5.3	2.5	0.4
1940	49.9	41.4	8.5	0.9	12.9	3.4	4.0	5.3	2.7	0.5
1941	62.1	51.9	10.2	1.0	17.3	4.0	4.4	5.4	2.7	0.6
1942	82.1	66.1	16.0	1.2	24.1	5.0	4.3	5.3	2.7	0.9
1943	105.6	79.0	26.6	1.5	29.1	5.6	4.4	5.2	2.5	1.5
1944	116.9	84.0	33.0	2.0	30.3	5.9	4.6	5.3	3.1	1.8
1945	117.5	82.6	34.9	2.3	31.7	6.1	4.6	6.0	5.6	1.9
1946	112.0	91.3	20.7	2.5	36.5	7.0	5.6	6.8	10.5	1.6
1947	123.1	105.6	17.5	3.0	35.6	7.0	6.3	7.8	10.8	1.6
1948	135.5	116.5	19.0	3.5	40.4	7.6	7.0	8.3	10.3	1.6
1949	134.8	114.0	20.8	3.9	35.7	7.8	7.2	9.0	11.3	1.5
1950	147.2	124.6	22.6	4.8	38.6	8.7	8.8	10.0	13.9	2.1
1951	171.5	142.3	29.2	5.9	43.8	9.5	8.6	10.8	11.2	2.5
1952	185.6	152.3	33.3	6.5	44.3	10.5	8.6	11.5	11.8	2.8
1953	199.0	164.7	34.4	7.2	43.3	11.5	8.9	13.0	12.6	2.9
1954	197.2	162.4	34.9	7.4	43.5	12.5	9.3	14.3	14.5	3.5
1955	212.1	175.6	36.6	8.5	45.5	12.8	10.5	15.6	15.7	3.9
1956	229.0	190.2	38.8	10.0	47.0	13.1	11.3	17.4	16.6	4.3
1957	239.9	198.9	41.0	11.3	49.0	13.8	11.7	19.4	19.2	5.0
1958	241.3	197.2	44.1	12.0	51.4	14.5	11.6	21.0	23.3	5.0
1959	259.8	213.8	46.0	13.4	51.8	15.2	12.6	23.0	24.2	6.0
1960	272.8	223.7	49.2	14.4	51.9	16.2	13.4	25.6	25.7	7.2
1961	280.5	228.0	52.4	15.2	54.4	16.9	13.9	27.3	29.5	7.4
1962	299.3	243.0	56.3	16.7	56.5	17.8	15.0	30.2	30.3	7.9
1963	314.8	254.8	60.0	18.0	57.8	18.5	16.2	33.0	32.0	9.3
1964	337.7	272.9	64.9	20.3	60.6	18.6	18.2	36.9	33.2	9.8
1965	363.7	293.8	69.9	22.7	65.2	19.2	20.2	40.8	35.9	10.3
1966	400.3	321.9	78.3	25.5	69.6	19.9	20.7	45.3	39.6	14.5
1967	428.9	342.5	86.4	28.2	71.1	20.4	21.5	49.4	47.6	16.8
1968	471.9	375.3	96.6	32.5	75.4	20.2	23.5	54.1	55.6	18.7
1969	518.3	412.7	105.5	36.6	78.9	20.3	24.2	62.3	61.6	21.4
1970	551.5	434.3	117.1	41.9	79.8	20.3	24.3	71.5	74.3	22.5
1971	583.9	457.4	126.5	48.0	86.1	21.2	25.0	77.5	88.2	24.7
1972	638.7	501.2	137.4	55.3	97.7	21.6	26.8	84.2	98.0	28.0
1973	708.7	560.0	148.7	62.8	115.2	23.1	29.9	97.6	111.9	35.7
1974	772.6	611.8	160.9	73.3	115.5	23.0	33.2	116.1	132.3	40.5
1975	814.6	638.6	176.0	87.6	121.6	22.0	32.9	128.0	167.5	42.6
1976	899.5	710.8	188.6	105.3	134.3	21.5	39.0	140.5	182.3	46.9
1977	993.9	791.6	202.3	125.3	148.3	20.4	44.7	161.9	194.6	52.0
1978	1,120.7	901.2	219.6	143.4	170.1	22.4	50.7	191.3	209.3	59.7
1979	1,255.8	1,018.7	237.1	162.6	183.7	24.5	57.4	233.5	234.2	70.2
1980	1,377.5	1,116.2	261.3	185.4	177.6	31.3	64.0	286.4	279.0	77.2
1981	1,517.2	1,231.7	285.6	204.8	186.2	39.6	73.6	352.7	317.2	92.1
1982	1,593.4	1,286.1	307.3	222.8	179.9	39.6	76.1	401.6	354.2	99.1
1983	1,684.7	1,359.8	325.0	238.6	195.5	36.9	83.5	431.6	382.2	106.1
1984	1,854.6	1,507.0	347.6	262.1	247.5	39.5	90.8	505.3	393.4	118.4

TABLE Ca54–63 Personal income, by source: 1929–2002 *Continued*

Year	Wage and salary disbursements			Other labor income	Proprietors' income	Rental income of persons	Personal dividend income	Personal interest income	Transfer payments to persons	Less: personal contributions for social insurance
	Total	Private-sector employees	Government employees							
	Ca54	Ca55	Ca56	Ca57	Ca58	Ca59	Ca60	Ca61	Ca62	Ca63
	Billion dollars	Billion dollars	Billion dollars	Billion dollars	Billion dollars	Billion dollars	Billion dollars	Billion dollars	Billion dollars	Billion dollars
1985	1,995.4	1,621.7	373.8	282.3	267.0	39.1	97.5	546.4	420.9	133.6
1986	2,114.4	1,717.8	396.6	298.4	278.6	32.2	106.1	579.2	449.0	145.6
1987	2,270.2	1,848.0	422.2	319.1	303.9	35.8	112.1	609.7	468.6	156.8
1988	2,452.7	2,001.8	450.9	336.5	338.8	44.1	129.4	650.5	496.9	176.8
1989	2,596.8	2,117.1	479.7	360.5	361.8	40.5	154.8	736.5	540.4	191.6
1990	2,754.6	2,237.9	516.7	390.0	381.0	49.1	165.4	772.4	594.4	203.7
1991	2,824.2	2,278.6	545.6	415.6	384.2	56.4	178.3	771.8	669.9	215.1
1992	2,982.6	2,414.9	567.7	449.5	434.3	63.3	185.3	750.1	751.7	226.6
1993	3,085.2	2,500.3	584.9	482.8	461.8	90.9	203.0	725.5	798.6	237.8
1994	3,236.7	2,632.8	603.9	507.5	476.6	110.3	234.7	742.4	833.9	254.1
1995	3,424.7	2,802.0	622.7	497.0	497.7	117.9	254.0	792.5	885.9	268.8
1996	3,626.5	2,985.5	641.0	490.0	544.7	129.7	297.4	810.6	928.8	280.4
1997	3,888.9	3,224.7	664.3	475.4	581.2	128.3	334.9	864.0	962.2	297.9
1998	4,192.8	3,500.1	692.7	490.6	623.8	138.6	348.3	964.4	983.7	316.3
1999	4,470.4	3,746.3	724.2	510.2	678.4	149.1	328.0	969.2	1,018.5	337.4
2000	4,836.3	4,067.4	768.9	544.2	714.8	146.6	375.7	1,077.0	1,070.3	358.4
2001	4,950.6	4,139.8	810.8	570.4	727.9	137.9	409.2	1,091.3	1,170.4	372.3
2002	4,996.4	4,143.6	852.8	610.6	756.5	142.4	433.8	1,078.5	1,288.0	384.0

Source

U.S. Bureau of Economic Analysis Internet site, Table 2.1, downloaded August 18, 2003.

Documentation

This table distributes aggregate personal income net of personal contributions for social insurance (series Ca5) by source. In this measure, "persons" includes nonprofit institutions that primarily serve individuals (churches, private schools, private trust funds). Series Ca5 is the sum of series Ca55–62, less series Ca63. For a definition of personal income, see Table Ca1–8.

Series Ca54–56. Wage and salary disbursements consist of the monetary remuneration of employees, inclusive of executives' compensation, commissions, tips, and bonuses, and of payments in kind that represent income to the recipients.

Series Ca57. Other labor income comprises employer contributions to private pension, health, unemployment, and welfare funds; compensation for injuries; directors' fees; pay of the military reserve; and a few other minor items.

Series Ca58–59. Equal series Ca22 and Ca25, respectively.

Series Ca60. Personal dividend income is from all sources. It equals dividends paid by corporations less dividends received by governments, primarily for state and local retirement systems.

Series Ca61. Personal interest income includes imputed interest as well as monetary interest received by persons. It equals net interest (series Ca27) plus interest paid by government and interest paid by individuals (except mortgage interest, which is reflected in net rental income of persons).

Series Ca62. Transfer payments to persons consist of income received by persons, generally in monetary form, for which no services are rendered currently. They include transfers both from business and government. The latter include benefits from Social Security, unemployment benefits, veterans' benefits, disability insurance, food stamps, public assistance (including medical care and family assistance), educational assistance, and other programs. Government payments to nonprofit institutions (except payment for work under research and development contracts) are also included.

Series Ca63. Personal contributions for social insurance are subtracted. This includes payments by employees, the self-employed, and others who participate in the following government programs: Old-Age, Survivors, and Disability Insurance (Social Security); hospital insurance; supplementary medical insurance; unemployment insurance; government employee retirement; railroad retirement; veterans' life insurance; and temporary disability insurance.

TABLE Ca64–73   Personal income and its disposition: 1929–2002
Contributed by Richard Sutch

Year	Total personal income	Less: payments to general government			Equals: disposable income	Less: outlays				Equals: personal saving
		Total	Contributions for social insurance	Tax and nontax payments		Total	Consumption expenditures	Interest paid by persons	Transfers to the rest of the world (net)	
	Ca64	Ca65	Ca66	Ca67	Ca68	Ca69	Ca70	Ca71	Ca72	Ca73
	Billion dollars	Billion dollars	Billion dollars	Billion dollars	Billion dollars	Billion dollars	Billion dollars	Billion dollars	Billion dollars	Billion dollars
1929	85.4	2.2	0.1	2.1	83.2	79.3	77.5	1.5	0.3	3.9
1930	76.6	2.0	0.1	1.9	74.6	71.3	70.2	0.9	0.3	3.2
1931	65.6	1.4	0.1	1.3	64.2	61.6	60.7	0.7	0.3	2.6
1932	50.1	1.1	0.1	1.0	49.1	49.5	48.7	0.5	0.2	−0.4
1933	47.0	1.1	0.1	1.0	45.9	46.6	45.9	0.5	0.2	−0.7
1934	53.9	1.2	0.1	1.1	52.7	52.1	51.5	0.5	0.2	0.6
1935	60.6	1.4	0.1	1.3	59.2	56.6	55.9	0.5	0.2	2.6
1936	68.9	1.6	0.1	1.5	67.3	63.0	62.2	0.6	0.2	4.3
1937	74.7	2.5	0.4	2.1	72.2	67.7	66.8	0.7	0.2	4.5
1938	69.0	2.5	0.4	2.1	66.5	65.1	64.2	0.7	0.2	1.5
1939	73.5	2.1	0.4	1.7	71.4	68.0	67.2	0.7	0.2	3.4
1940	79.1	2.4	0.5	1.9	76.7	72.2	71.2	0.8	0.2	4.5
1941	96.9	3.1	0.6	2.5	93.8	82.1	81.0	0.9	0.2	11.7
1942	124.7	6.0	0.9	5.1	118.7	89.7	88.9	0.7	0.1	29.0
1943	153.9	18.5	1.5	17.0	135.4	100.4	99.7	0.5	0.2	34.9
1944	168.1	19.8	1.8	18.0	148.3	109.3	108.5	0.5	0.4	39.0
1945	173.8	21.7	1.9	19.8	152.1	120.8	119.8	0.5	0.5	31.4
1946	181.1	19.1	1.6	17.5	162.0	145.6	144.2	0.7	0.7	16.3
1947	193.7	21.7	1.6	20.1	172.1	164.0	162.3	1.1	0.7	8.1
1948	212.7	21.2	1.6	19.6	191.6	177.5	175.4	1.4	0.7	14.1
1949	209.7	18.6	1.5	17.1	191.1	181.1	178.8	1.8	0.5	10.0
1950	232.0	21.4	2.1	19.3	210.6	195.4	192.7	2.3	0.4	15.2
1951	261.2	30.0	2.5	27.5	231.2	211.5	208.6	2.5	0.4	19.7
1952	278.9	35.3	2.8	32.5	243.6	223.0	219.7	2.9	0.4	20.6
1953	295.5	36.7	2.9	33.8	258.8	237.5	233.4	3.6	0.5	21.3
1954	298.7	34.2	3.5	30.7	264.5	244.8	240.5	3.8	0.5	19.8
1955	320.7	37.3	3.9	33.4	283.4	263.8	259.0	4.4	0.4	19.5
1956	344.3	41.5	4.3	37.2	302.8	277.4	271.9	5.1	0.5	25.4
1957	364.3	44.6	5.0	39.6	319.7	292.9	287.0	5.5	0.5	26.8
1958	375.0	44.2	5.0	39.2	330.8	302.6	296.6	5.6	0.4	28.2
1959	400.0	48.8	6.0	42.8	351.2	324.7	318.1	6.1	0.5	26.5
1960	419.9	53.8	7.2	46.6	366.2	339.8	332.3	7.0	0.5	26.4
1961	437.7	55.3	7.4	47.9	382.4	350.5	342.7	7.3	0.5	31.9
1962	465.8	60.2	7.9	52.3	405.6	372.2	363.8	7.8	0.5	33.5
1963	490.3	64.6	9.3	55.3	425.8	392.7	383.1	8.9	0.7	33.1
1964	525.6	62.6	9.8	52.8	463.0	422.4	411.7	10.0	0.7	40.5
1965	567.7	68.7	10.3	58.4	498.9	456.2	444.3	11.1	0.8	42.7
1966	620.9	81.8	14.5	67.3	539.1	494.6	481.8	12.0	0.8	44.5
1967	667.2	91.0	16.8	74.2	576.2	522.3	508.7	12.5	1.0	54.0
1968	733.2	107.0	18.7	88.3	626.2	573.6	558.7	13.8	1.0	52.7
1969	802.2	127.3	21.4	105.9	675.0	622.3	605.5	15.7	1.1	52.6
1970	863.6	127.1	22.5	104.6	736.5	667.0	648.9	16.8	1.3	69.5
1971	929.8	128.1	24.7	103.4	801.7	721.6	702.4	17.8	1.3	80.1
1972	1,022.3	153.6	28.0	125.6	868.6	791.7	770.7	19.6	1.4	76.9
1973	1,149.1	170.2	35.7	134.5	979.0	876.5	852.5	22.4	1.5	102.5
1974	1,266.1	193.8	40.5	153.3	1,072.3	957.9	932.4	24.2	1.3	114.3
1975	1,374.3	192.9	42.6	150.3	1,181.4	1,056.2	1,030.3	24.5	1.3	125.2
1976	1,522.3	222.4	46.9	175.5	1,299.9	1,177.8	1,149.8	26.6	1.3	122.1
1977	1,689.1	253.2	52.0	201.2	1,436.0	1,310.4	1,278.4	30.7	1.3	125.6
1978	1,908.0	293.2	59.7	233.5	1,614.8	1,469.4	1,430.4	37.5	1.5	145.4
1979	2,151.7	343.5	70.2	273.3	1,808.2	1,642.4	1,596.3	44.5	1.6	165.8
1980	2,401.1	381.4	77.2	304.2	2,019.8	1,814.1	1,762.9	49.4	1.8	205.6
1981	2,691.5	443.6	92.1	351.5	2,247.9	2,004.2	1,944.2	54.6	5.5	243.7
1982	2,867.5	460.7	99.1	361.6	2,406.8	2,144.6	2,079.3	58.8	6.5	262.2
1983	3,053.0	467.0	106.1	360.9	2,586.0	2,358.2	2,286.4	65.0	6.8	227.8
1984	3,393.2	505.6	118.4	387.2	2,887.6	2,581.1	2,498.4	75.0	7.7	306.5

TABLE Ca64–73   Personal income and its disposition: 1929–2002   *Continued*

	Total personal income	Less: payments to general government			Equals: disposable income	Less: outlays			Transfers to the rest of the world (net)	Equals: personal saving
		Total	Contributions for social insurance	Tax and nontax payments		Total	Consumption expenditures	Interest paid by persons		
	Ca64	Ca65	Ca66	Ca67	Ca68	Ca69	Ca70	Ca71	Ca72	Ca73
Year	Billion dollars	Billion dollars	Billion dollars	Billion dollars	Billion dollars	Billion dollars	Billion dollars	Billion dollars	Billion dollars	Billion dollars
1985	3,648.6	562.1	133.6	428.5	3,086.5	2,803.9	2,712.6	83.2	8.1	282.6
1986	3,858.0	595.5	145.6	449.9	3,262.5	2,994.7	2,895.2	90.6	9.0	267.8
1987	4,119.3	659.8	156.8	503.0	3,459.5	3,206.7	3,105.3	91.5	9.9	252.8
1988	4,448.9	696.5	176.8	519.7	3,752.4	3,460.1	3,356.6	92.9	10.6	292.3
1989	4,791.4	775.1	191.6	583.5	4,016.3	3,714.4	3,596.7	106.4	11.4	301.8
1990	5,106.9	813.3	203.7	609.6	4,293.6	3,959.3	3,831.5	115.8	12.0	334.3
1991	5,300.5	825.6	215.1	610.5	4,474.8	4,103.2	3,971.2	118.9	13.0	371.7
1992	5,617.0	862.4	226.6	635.8	4,754.6	4,340.9	4,209.7	118.7	12.5	413.7
1993	5,847.8	912.4	237.8	674.6	4,935.3	4,584.5	4,454.7	115.4	14.4	350.8
1994	6,142.1	976.7	254.1	722.6	5,165.4	4,849.9	4,716.4	117.9	15.6	315.5
1995	6,469.7	1,047.1	268.8	778.3	5,422.6	5,120.2	4,969.0	134.7	16.5	302.4
1996	6,827.8	1,150.1	280.4	869.7	5,677.7	5,405.6	5,237.5	149.9	18.2	272.1
1997	7,234.9	1,266.7	297.9	968.8	5,968.2	5,715.3	5,529.3	164.8	21.2	252.9
1998	7,742.3	1,386.7	316.3	1,070.4	6,355.6	6,054.1	5,856.0	173.7	24.3	301.5
1999	8,123.9	1,496.5	337.4	1,159.1	6,627.4	6,453.3	6,246.5	179.5	27.3	174.0
2000	8,765.0	1,644.8	358.4	1,286.4	7,120.2	6,918.6	6,683.7	205.4	29.5	201.5
2001	9,057.6	1,664.4	372.3	1,292.1	7,393.2	7,223.5	6,987.0	205.4	31.1	169.7
2002	9,306.2	1,495.9	384.0	1,111.9	7,810.3	7,524.5	7,303.7	188.4	32.3	285.8

Source

U.S. Bureau of Economic Analysis Internet site, Table 2.1, downloaded August 18, 2003.

Documentation

Disposable personal income is the income remaining to persons after the deduction of personal payments to general government (series Ca65). Individuals spend this income in various outlays (series Ca69), and the residual (which may be positive or negative) is personal saving (series Ca73).

Series Ca64. Equals aggregate personal income shown in series Ca5 plus personal contributions for social insurance (series Ca66).

Series Ca66. Equals series Ca63.

Series Ca67. Personal tax and nontax payments refer to tax payments (net of refunds) by U.S. residents that are not chargeable to business expense and certain other personal payments to government agencies (except government enterprises) that are treated like taxes. Personal taxes include taxes on income, including realized net capital gains, and on personal property. Nontaxes include donations and fees, fines, and forfeitures. Personal contributions for social insurance are not included. Taxes paid by U.S. residents to foreign governments and taxes paid by foreigners to the U.S. government are both included in transfer payments to the rest of the world (net) and are not part of personal tax and nontax payments.

Series Ca70. Personal consumption expenditures refer to goods and services purchased by U.S. residents. It consists mainly of purchases of new goods and of services by individuals from private business. In addition, it includes purchases of new goods and of services by nonprofit institutions (including compensation of employees), net purchases of used goods by individuals and nonprofit institutions, and purchases abroad of goods and services by U.S. residents. It also includes purchases of certain goods and services provided by general government and government enterprises, such as tuition payments for higher education, charges for medical care, and charges for water and other sanitary services. Finally, it includes imputed purchases that keep it invariant to changes in the way that certain activities are carried out – for example, whether housing is rented or owned, whether financial services are explicitly charged, or whether employees are paid in cash or in kind.

Series Ca71. Interest paid by persons consists of all interest paid by individuals except mortgage interest, which is reflected in rental income of persons.

Series Ca72. Personal transfer payments to the rest of the world (net) consist of personal remittances in kind and in cash to abroad, net of such remittances from abroad.

Series Ca73. Personal saving is personal income less the sum of personal outlays and personal tax and nontax payments. It is the current saving of individuals (including proprietors and partnerships), nonprofit institutions that primarily serve individuals, life insurance carriers, private noninsured welfare funds, private noninsured pension plans, publicly administered government employee retirement plans, and private trust funds. Personal saving may also be viewed as the net acquisition of financial assets (such as cash and deposits, securities, and the change in life insurance and pension fund reserves), plus the net investment in produced assets (such as residential housing, less depreciation), less the net increase in financial liabilities (such as mortgage debt, consumer credit, and security credit), less net capital transfers received.

NATIONAL PRODUCT

Richard Sutch

TABLE Ca74–90 Gross domestic product, by major component: 1929–2002

Contributed by Richard Sutch

						Government consumption expenditures and gross investment						Real (chained 1996) dollars						
	Gross domestic product	Personal consumption expenditure	Gross private domestic investment	Exports of goods and services	Imports of goods and services			Federal			State and local	Gross domestic product	Personal consumption expenditure	Gross private domestic investment	Exports of goods and services	Imports of goods and services	Government consumption expenditures and gross investment	Residual
						Total	Total	Defense	Nondefense									
	Ca74	Ca75	Ca76	Ca77	Ca78	Ca79	Ca80	Ca81	Ca82	Ca83	Ca84	Ca85	Ca86	Ca87	Ca88	Ca89	Ca90
Year	Billion dollars	Billion dollars	Billion dollars	Billion dollars	Billion dollars	Billion dollars	Billion dollars	Billion dollars	Billion dollars	Billion dollars	Billion chained 1996 dollars	Billion chained 1996 dollars	Billion chained 1996 dollars	Billion chained 1996 dollars	Billion chained 1996 dollars	Billion chained 1996 dollars	Billion chained 1996 dollars
1929	103.7	77.5	16.5	5.9	5.6	9.4	1.7	0.9	0.8	7.7	822.2	625.7	93.6	35.8	46.3	110.1	3.3
1930	91.3	70.2	10.8	4.4	4.1	10.0	1.8	0.9	0.8	8.2	751.5	592.3	62.5	29.6	40.3	121.3	−13.9
1931	76.6	60.7	5.9	2.9	2.9	9.9	1.8	0.9	0.9	8.1	703.6	574.3	39.2	24.6	35.1	126.6	−26.0
1932	58.8	48.7	1.3	2.0	1.9	8.8	1.8	0.9	0.9	7.0	611.8	523.0	11.8	19.3	29.2	122.4	−35.5
1933	56.4	45.9	1.7	2.0	1.9	8.7	2.3	0.9	1.4	6.5	603.3	511.0	17.5	19.4	30.4	118.0	−32.2
1934	66.0	51.5	3.7	2.6	2.2	10.6	3.2	0.8	2.4	7.3	668.3	546.9	31.6	21.5	31.0	133.0	−33.7
1935	73.3	55.9	6.7	2.8	3.0	10.9	3.3	1.0	2.3	7.6	728.3	580.6	58.4	22.7	40.7	137.0	−29.7
1936	83.7	62.2	8.6	3.0	3.2	13.1	5.5	1.2	4.2	7.6	822.5	639.6	74.9	23.9	40.2	158.9	−34.6
1937	91.9	66.8	12.2	4.0	4.0	12.8	5.0	1.3	3.7	7.8	865.8	663.5	93.6	30.1	45.2	153.2	−29.4
1938	86.1	64.2	7.1	3.8	2.8	13.8	5.6	1.4	4.2	8.2	835.6	652.6	61.9	29.8	35.2	164.6	−38.1
1939	92.0	67.2	9.3	3.9	3.1	14.7	5.9	1.5	4.4	8.9	903.5	689.0	79.6	31.4	36.9	179.7	−39.3
1940	101.3	71.2	13.6	4.8	3.4	15.1	6.4	2.5	3.9	8.7	980.7	724.9	110.9	35.7	37.8	182.4	−35.4
1941	126.7	81.0	18.1	5.4	4.4	26.6	17.9	14.3	3.6	8.7	1,148.8	776.7	135.4	36.7	46.5	303.0	−56.5
1942	161.8	88.9	10.4	4.3	4.6	62.8	54.1	51.2	2.9	8.7	1,360.0	758.3	71.6	24.1	42.2	711.1	−162.9
1943	198.4	99.7	6.1	3.9	6.3	94.9	86.5	84.2	2.2	8.5	1,583.7	779.1	42.3	20.1	53.2	1,059.9	−264.5
1944	219.7	108.5	7.8	4.8	6.9	105.5	97.0	94.6	2.4	8.5	1,714.1	801.7	52.2	21.6	55.7	1,195.6	−301.3
1945	223.0	119.8	10.8	6.7	7.5	93.2	84.2	82.1	2.1	9.0	1,693.3	851.8	69.0	30.5	59.2	1,041.0	−239.8
1946	222.3	144.2	31.1	14.1	7.0	39.8	29.0	25.3	3.6	10.8	1,505.5	956.9	175.0	66.5	49.1	359.7	−3.5
1947	244.4	162.3	35.0	18.7	7.9	36.4	22.6	18.2	4.3	13.9	1,495.1	976.4	168.6	75.9	46.6	307.1	13.7
1948	269.6	175.4	48.1	15.5	10.1	40.6	24.2	18.4	5.8	16.5	1,560.0	998.1	215.3	59.8	54.4	328.9	12.3
1949	267.7	178.8	36.9	14.4	9.2	46.8	27.6	19.9	7.8	19.2	1,550.9	1,025.3	164.3	59.2	52.5	367.3	−12.7
1950	294.3	192.7	54.1	12.3	11.6	46.9	26.0	19.6	6.4	20.9	1,686.6	1,090.9	232.5	51.8	62.0	367.4	6.0
1951	339.5	208.6	60.2	17.0	14.6	68.3	45.0	39.3	5.8	23.3	1,815.1	1,107.1	233.2	63.5	64.5	500.0	−24.2
1952	358.6	219.7	54.0	16.3	15.3	83.9	59.2	52.4	6.8	24.7	1,887.3	1,142.4	211.1	60.6	70.1	605.1	−61.8
1953	379.9	233.4	56.4	15.2	16.0	90.8	64.4	56.0	8.4	26.4	1,973.9	1,197.2	221.0	56.5	76.7	647.5	−71.6
1954	381.1	240.5	53.8	15.7	15.4	86.5	57.3	49.3	8.0	29.2	1,960.5	1,221.9	210.8	59.3	72.9	602.9	−61.5
1955	415.2	259.0	69.0	17.6	17.2	86.8	54.9	47.0	7.9	31.9	2,099.5	1,310.4	262.1	65.6	81.7	580.4	−37.3
1956	438.0	271.9	72.0	21.2	18.9	91.8	56.7	49.3	7.4	35.1	2,141.1	1,348.8	258.6	76.5	88.4	580.8	−35.2
1957	461.5	287.0	70.5	23.9	19.9	100.1	61.3	53.7	7.6	38.8	2,183.9	1,381.8	247.4	83.1	92.1	606.7	−43.0
1958	467.9	296.6	64.5	20.4	20.0	106.5	63.9	55.5	8.4	42.6	2,162.8	1,393.0	226.5	71.8	96.4	626.2	−58.3
1959	507.4	318.1	78.5	20.6	22.3	112.5	67.4	56.0	11.4	45.1	2,319.0	1,470.7	272.9	72.4	106.6	661.4	−51.8

	Nominal dollars					Government consumption expenditures and gross investment		Federal				Real (chained 1996) dollars						
	Gross domestic product	Personal consumption expenditure	Gross private domestic investment	Exports of goods and services	Imports of goods and services	Total	Total	Defense	Nondefense	State and local	Gross domestic product	Personal consumption expenditure	Gross private domestic investment	Exports of goods and services	Imports of goods and services	Government consumption expenditures and gross investment	Residual
	Ca74	Ca75	Ca76	Ca77	Ca78	Ca79	Ca80	Ca81	Ca82	Ca83	Ca84	Ca85	Ca86	Ca87	Ca88	Ca89	Ca90
Year	Billion dollars	Billion dollars	Billion dollars	Billion dollars	Billion dollars	Billion dollars	Billion dollars	Billion dollars	Billion dollars	Billion dollars	Billion chained 1996 dollars	Billion chained 1996 dollars	Billion chained 1996 dollars	Billion chained 1996 dollars	Billion chained 1996 dollars	Billion chained 1996 dollars	Billion chained 1996 dollars
1960	527.4	332.3	78.9	25.3	22.8	113.8	65.9	55.2	10.7	47.9	2,376.7	1,510.8	272.8	87.5	108.0	661.3	−47.7
1961	545.7	342.7	78.2	26.0	22.7	121.5	69.5	58.1	11.3	52.0	2,432.0	1,541.2	271.0	88.9	107.3	693.2	−55.0
1962	586.5	363.8	88.1	27.4	25.0	132.2	76.9	62.8	14.1	55.3	2,578.9	1,617.3	305.3	93.7	119.5	735.0	−52.9
1963	618.7	383.1	93.8	29.4	26.1	138.5	78.5	62.7	15.8	59.9	2,690.4	1,684.0	325.7	100.7	122.7	752.4	−49.7
1964	664.4	411.7	102.1	33.6	28.1	145.1	79.8	61.8	18.0	65.3	2,846.5	1,784.8	352.6	114.2	129.2	767.1	−43.0
1965	720.1	444.3	118.2	35.4	31.5	153.7	82.1	62.4	19.7	71.6	3,028.5	1,897.6	402.0	116.5	142.9	791.1	−35.8
1966	789.3	481.8	131.3	38.9	37.1	174.3	94.4	73.8	20.7	79.9	3,227.5	2,006.1	437.3	124.3	164.2	862.1	−38.1
1967	834.1	508.7	128.6	41.4	39.9	195.3	106.8	85.8	21.0	88.6	3,308.3	2,066.2	417.2	127.0	176.2	927.1	−53.0
1968	911.5	558.7	141.2	45.3	46.6	212.8	114.0	92.2	21.8	98.8	3,466.1	2,184.2	441.3	136.3	202.4	956.6	−49.9
1969	985.3	605.5	156.4	49.3	50.5	224.6	116.1	92.6	23.5	108.5	3,571.4	2,264.8	466.9	143.7	213.9	952.5	−42.6
1970	1,039.7	648.9	152.4	57.0	55.8	237.1	116.4	90.9	25.5	120.7	3,578.0	2,317.5	436.2	159.3	223.1	931.1	−43.0
1971	1,128.6	702.4	178.2	59.3	62.3	251.0	117.6	89.0	28.6	133.5	3,697.7	2,405.2	485.8	160.4	235.0	913.8	−32.5
1972	1,240.4	770.7	207.6	66.2	74.2	270.1	125.6	93.5	32.2	144.4	3,898.4	2,550.5	543.0	173.5	261.3	914.9	−22.2
1973	1,385.5	852.5	244.5	91.8	91.2	287.9	127.8	93.9	33.9	160.1	4,123.4	2,675.9	606.5	211.4	273.4	908.3	−5.3
1974	1,501.0	932.4	249.4	124.3	127.5	322.4	138.2	99.7	38.5	184.2	4,099.0	2,653.7	561.7	231.6	267.2	924.8	−5.6
1975	1,635.2	1,030.3	230.2	136.3	122.7	361.1	152.1	107.9	44.2	209.0	4,084.4	2,710.9	462.2	230.0	237.5	942.5	−23.7
1976	1,823.9	1,149.8	292.0	148.9	151.1	384.5	160.6	113.2	47.4	223.9	4,311.7	2,868.9	555.5	243.6	284.0	943.3	−15.6
1977	2,031.4	1,278.4	361.3	158.8	182.4	415.3	176.0	122.6	53.5	239.3	4,511.8	2,992.1	639.4	249.7	315.0	952.7	−7.1
1978	2,295.9	1,430.4	436.0	186.1	212.3	455.6	191.9	132.0	59.8	263.8	4,760.6	3,124.7	713.0	275.9	342.3	982.2	7.1
1979	2,566.4	1,596.3	490.6	228.7	252.7	503.5	211.6	146.7	65.0	291.8	4,912.1	3,203.2	735.4	302.4	347.9	1,001.1	17.9
1980	2,795.6	1,762.9	477.9	278.9	293.8	569.7	245.3	169.6	75.6	324.4	4,900.9	3,193.0	655.3	334.8	324.8	1,020.9	21.7
1981	3,131.3	1,944.2	570.8	302.8	317.8	631.4	281.8	197.8	84.0	349.6	5,021.0	3,236.0	715.6	338.6	333.4	1,030.0	34.2
1982	3,259.2	2,079.3	516.1	282.6	303.2	684.4	312.8	228.3	84.5	371.6	4,919.3	3,275.5	615.2	314.6	329.2	1,046.0	−2.8
1983	3,534.9	2,286.4	564.2	277.0	328.6	735.9	344.4	252.5	92.0	391.5	5,132.3	3,454.3	673.7	306.9	370.7	1,081.0	−12.9
1984	3,932.7	2,498.4	735.5	303.1	405.1	800.8	376.4	283.5	92.8	424.4	5,505.2	3,640.6	871.5	332.6	461.0	1,118.4	3.1
1985	4,213.0	2,712.6	736.3	303.0	417.2	878.3	413.4	312.4	101.0	464.9	5,717.1	3,820.9	863.4	341.6	490.7	1,190.5	−8.6
1986	4,452.9	2,895.2	747.2	320.3	452.2	942.3	438.7	332.2	106.5	503.6	5,912.4	3,981.2	857.7	366.8	531.9	1,255.2	−16.6
1987	4,742.5	3,105.3	781.5	365.6	507.9	997.9	460.4	351.2	109.3	537.5	6,113.3	4,113.4	879.3	408.0	564.2	1,292.5	−15.7
1988	5,108.3	3,356.6	821.1	446.9	553.2	1,036.9	462.6	355.9	106.8	574.3	6,368.4	4,279.5	902.8	473.5	585.6	1,307.5	−9.3
1989	5,489.1	3,596.7	872.9	509.0	589.7	1,100.2	482.6	363.2	119.3	617.7	6,591.8	4,393.7	936.5	529.4	608.8	1,343.5	−2.5
1990	5,803.2	3,831.5	861.7	557.2	628.6	1,181.4	508.4	374.9	133.6	673.0	6,707.9	4,474.5	907.3	575.7	632.2	1,387.3	−4.7
1991	5,986.2	3,971.2	800.2	601.6	622.3	1,235.5	527.4	384.5	142.9	708.1	6,676.4	4,466.6	829.5	613.2	629.0	1,403.4	−7.3
1992	6,318.9	4,209.7	866.6	636.8	664.6	1,270.5	534.5	378.5	156.0	736.0	6,880.0	4,594.5	899.8	651.0	670.8	1,410.0	−4.5
1993	6,642.3	4,454.7	955.1	658.0	718.5	1,293.0	527.3	364.9	162.4	765.7	7,062.6	4,748.9	977.9	672.7	731.8	1,398.8	−3.9
1994	7,054.3	4,716.4	1,097.1	725.1	812.1	1,327.9	521.1	355.1	165.9	806.8	7,347.7	4,928.1	1,107.0	732.8	819.4	1,400.1	−0.9
1995	7,400.5	4,969.0	1,143.8	818.6	902.8	1,372.0	521.5	350.6	170.9	850.5	7,543.8	5,075.6	1,140.6	808.2	886.6	1,406.4	−0.4
1996	7,813.2	5,237.5	1,242.7	874.2	963.1	1,421.9	531.6	357.0	174.6	890.4	7,813.2	5,237.5	1,242.7	874.2	963.1	1,421.9	0.0
1997	8,318.4	5,529.3	1,390.5	966.4	1,055.8	1,487.9	538.2	352.6	185.6	949.7	8,159.5	5,423.9	1,393.3	981.5	1,094.8	1,455.4	0.2
1998	8,781.5	5,856.0	1,538.7	964.9	1,116.7	1,538.5	539.2	349.1	190.1	999.3	8,508.9	5,683.7	1,558.0	1,002.4	1,223.5	1,483.3	5.0
1999	9,274.3	6,246.5	1,636.7	989.3	1,239.2	1,641.0	565.0	364.3	200.7	1,076.0	8,859.0	5,964.5	1,660.5	1,036.3	1,356.8	1,540.6	13.9
2000	9,824.6	6,683.7	1,755.4	1,101.1	1,466.6	1,751.0	589.2	374.9	214.3	1,161.8	9,191.4	6,223.9	1,762.9	1,137.2	1,536.0	1,582.5	20.9
2001	10,082.2	6,987.0	1,586.0	1,034.1	1,383.0	1,858.0	628.1	399.9	228.2	1,229.9	9,214.5	6,377.2	1,574.6	1,076.1	1,492.0	1,640.4	38.2
2002	10,446.2	7,303.7	1,593.2	1,014.9	1,438.5	1,972.9	693.7	447.4	246.3	1,279.2	9,439.9	6,576.0	1,589.6	1,058.8	1,547.4	1,712.8	50.1

(continued)

TABLE Ca74–90   Gross domestic product, by major component: 1929–2002   *Continued*

Source
U.S. Bureau of Economic Analysis Internet site, Tables 1.1 and 1.2, downloaded August 15, 2003.

Documentation
Gross domestic product (GDP) is the official measure of aggregate economic activity in the market economy. It is defined as the market value of all goods and services produced by labor and property located in the United States during the year. GDP is estimated from the expenditures side of the national income and product accounts (NIPA). See the text for Table Ca1–8.

Series Ca74. Equals the sum of series Ca75–77, plus series Ca79, minus series Ca78.

Series Ca75. Personal consumption expenditure (PCE) represents the market value of purchases of goods and services by individuals and nonprofit institutions and the value of food, clothing, housing, and financial services received by them as income in kind. It includes the rental value of owner-occupied houses but does not include purchases of dwellings, which are classified under gross private domestic investment. For the components of PCE, see Table Ca91–97. Also see the extended definition for the identical series Ca70.

Series Ca76. Gross private domestic investment (GPDI) consists of net acquisitions of fixed capital goods by private domestic business and domestic nonprofit institutions including commissions arising in sale and purchase of new and existing fixed assets, principally real estate, and of the value of the change in the volume of inventories held by business. It covers all private new dwellings, including those acquired by owner-occupants. Investment can be thought of as any transaction that will aid in the economy's ability to produce future output. For the components of GPDI, see Table Ca98–108.

Series Ca77. Exports of goods and services to the rest of the world, excluding transfers under military grants. For the components of exports, see Table Ca109–119.

Series Ca78. Imports of goods and services from the rest of the world. For the components of imports, see Table Ca109–119.

Series Ca79–83. Government consumption expenditures and gross investment are made up of the net expenditures on goods and services by the three levels of government and the gross investment of government enterprises.

Among the items included in government expenditures of goods and services are compensation of government employees; construction expenditures on highways, bridges, and schools; and net purchases of equipment and supplies from business and abroad. Excluded from this category are purchases or the acquisition of land, current outlays of government enterprises, transfer payments, government interest, subsidies, and transactions in financial claims. The recent NIPA revision modified the definition of government expenditures to include the consumption of fixed capital and the government's contribution to civilian and military retirement programs. For further discussion, see Robert P. Parker and Eugene P. Seskin, "Improved Estimates of the National Income and Product Accounts: Results of the Comprehensive Revision," *Survey of Current Business* 76 (January/February 1996): 1–31. For the components of government consumption expenditures and gross investment, see Table Ca120–134.

Series Ca84. Gross domestic product in chained (1996) dollars is an estimate of real GDP obtained by first calculating a quantity index for each component of nominal GDP by deflating using an appropriate Fisher index. These indexes are then weighted by the nominal dollar values of the corresponding component in the base year 1996. Because of this procedure, the components of GDP will not sum to the total, thus producing a residual (series Ca90). See the essay on national income and product in this chapter for a discussion (and a warning) about the use of these real GDP numbers.

Series Ca85–89. The components of GDP expressed in chained (1996) dollars.

Series Ca87–88. The table presents chain-weighted estimates of real exports and real imports. It is not possible to use the chain index deflation procedure on net exports (exports minus imports) because that series can become negative and the Fisher price indexes involve taking a square root, which is not defined for a negative number. Because of the nonadditive properties of the chain-weighted index, users should be cautious in calculating an estimate of real net exports by subtracting series Ca88 from series Ca87. See the essay on national income and product in this chapter for a discussion.

Series Ca90. Equals series Ca84, minus series Ca85–87, minus series Ca89, plus series Ca88. See the essay on national income and product in this chapter for a discussion.

TABLE Ca91–97   Personal consumption expenditures, by major component: 1929–2002

Contributed by Richard Sutch

Year	Nominal dollars			Real (chained 1996) dollars			
	Durable goods	Nondurable goods	Services	Durable goods	Nondurable goods	Services	Residual
	Ca91	Ca92	Ca93	Ca94	Ca95	Ca96	Ca97
	Billion dollars	Billion dollars	Billion dollars	Billion chained 1996 dollars	Billion chained 1996 dollars	Billion chained 1996 dollars	Billion chained 1996 dollars
1929	9.2	37.7	30.5	—	—	—	—
1930	7.2	34.0	29.0	—	—	—	—
1931	5.5	29.0	26.3	—	—	—	—
1932	3.6	22.7	22.4	—	—	—	—
1933	3.5	22.3	20.2	—	—	—	—
1934	4.2	26.7	20.5	—	—	—	—
1935	5.1	29.3	21.5	—	—	—	—
1936	6.3	32.9	23.0	—	—	—	—
1937	6.9	35.2	24.7	—	—	—	—
1938	5.7	34.0	24.6	—	—	—	—
1939	6.7	35.1	25.4	—	—	—	—
1940	7.8	37.0	26.4	—	—	—	—
1941	9.7	42.9	28.5	—	—	—	—
1942	6.9	50.8	31.3	—	—	—	—
1943	6.5	58.6	34.6	—	—	—	—
1944	6.7	64.3	37.4	—	—	—	—

TABLE Ca91–97   Personal consumption expenditures, by major component: 1929–2002   *Continued*

	Nominal dollars			Real (chained 1996) dollars			
	Durable goods	Nondurable goods	Services	Durable goods	Nondurable goods	Services	Residual
	Ca91	Ca92	Ca93	Ca94	Ca95	Ca96	Ca97
Year	Billion dollars	Billion dollars	Billion dollars	Billion chained 1996 dollars	Billion chained 1996 dollars	Billion chained 1996 dollars	Billion chained 1996 dollars
1945	8.0	71.9	40.0	—	—	—	—
1946	15.8	82.7	45.8	—	—	—	—
1947	20.4	90.9	51.0	—	—	—	—
1948	22.9	96.6	55.9	—	—	—	—
1949	25.1	94.9	58.9	—	—	—	—
1950	30.7	98.2	63.7	—	—	—	—
1951	29.9	109.2	69.6	—	—	—	—
1952	29.3	114.7	75.6	—	—	—	—
1953	32.7	117.8	82.9	—	—	—	—
1954	31.9	119.7	88.9	—	—	—	—
1955	38.8	124.7	95.4	—	—	—	—
1956	38.1	130.8	102.9	—	—	—	—
1957	40.0	137.1	109.9	—	—	—	—
1958	37.4	141.7	117.4	—	—	—	—
1959	42.7	148.5	127.0	—	—	—	—
1960	43.3	152.9	136.1	—	—	—	—
1961	41.8	156.6	144.3	—	—	—	—
1962	46.9	162.8	154.1	—	—	—	—
1963	51.6	168.2	163.4	—	—	—	—
1964	56.7	178.7	176.4	—	—	—	—
1965	63.3	191.6	189.5	—	—	—	—
1966	68.3	208.8	204.7	—	—	—	—
1967	70.4	217.1	221.2	—	—	—	—
1968	80.8	235.7	242.3	—	—	—	—
1969	85.9	253.2	266.4	—	—	—	—
1970	85.0	272.0	292.0	—	—	—	—
1971	96.9	285.5	320.0	—	—	—	—
1972	110.4	308.0	352.3	—	—	—	—
1973	123.5	343.1	385.9	—	—	—	—
1974	122.3	384.5	425.5	—	—	—	—
1975	133.5	420.7	476.1	—	—	—	—
1976	158.9	458.3	532.6	—	—	—	—
1977	181.2	497.2	600.0	—	—	—	—
1978	201.7	550.2	678.4	—	—	—	—
1979	214.4	624.4	757.4	—	—	—	—
1980	214.2	696.1	852.7	—	—	—	—
1981	231.3	758.9	954.0	—	—	—	—
1982	240.2	787.6	1,051.5	—	—	—	—
1983	281.2	831.2	1,174.0	—	—	—	—
1984	326.9	884.7	1,286.9	—	—	—	—
1985	363.3	928.8	1,420.6	—	—	—	—
1986	401.3	958.5	1,535.4	—	—	—	—
1987	419.7	1,015.3	1,670.3	455.2	1,274.5	2,379.3	4.4
1988	450.2	1,082.9	1,823.5	481.5	1,315.1	2,477.2	5.7
1989	467.8	1,165.4	1,963.5	491.7	1,351.0	2,546.0	5.0
1990	467.6	1,246.1	2,117.8	487.1	1,369.6	2,616.2	1.6
1991	443.0	1,278.8	2,249.4	454.9	1,364.0	2,651.8	−4.1
1992	470.8	1,322.9	2,415.9	479.0	1,389.7	2,729.7	−3.9
1993	513.4	1,375.2	2,566.1	518.3	1,430.3	2,802.5	−2.2
1994	560.8	1,438.0	2,717.6	557.7	1,485.1	2,886.2	−0.9
1995	589.7	1,497.3	2,882.0	583.5	1,529.0	2,963.4	−0.3
1996	616.5	1,574.1	3,047.0	616.5	1,574.1	3,047.0	−0.1
1997	642.5	1,641.6	3,245.2	657.3	1,619.9	3,147.0	−0.3
1998	693.2	1,708.5	3,454.3	726.7	1,686.4	3,273.4	−2.8
1999	755.9	1,830.1	3,660.5	812.5	1,765.1	3,395.4	−8.5
2000	803.9	1,972.9	3,906.9	878.9	1,833.8	3,524.5	−13.3
2001	835.9	2,041.3	4,109.9	931.9	1,869.8	3,594.9	−19.4
2002	871.9	2,115.0	4,316.8	999.9	1,929.5	3,675.6	−29.0

Source

U.S. Bureau of Economic Analysis (BEA) Internet site, Tables 1.1 and 1.2, downloaded August 15, 2003.

Documentation

See the text for Table Ca1–8.

This table disaggregates personal consumption expenditure, series Ca75, into three components: series Ca91–93. The BEA does not publish estimates of the consumption subaggregates in chained 1996 dollars for the years before 1987. Because of the procedures used to calculate chained real data,

(continued)

TABLE Ca91–97   Personal consumption expenditures, by major component: 1929–2002   *Continued*

the sum of series Ca94–96 will not equal series Ca85, hence the residual presented here as series Ca97. See the essay on national income and product in this chapter for a discussion (and a warning) about the use of these real gross domestic product numbers.

Series Ca91 and Ca94. Personal consumption expenditure on durable goods represents the portion of personal consumption expenditure that individuals and nonprofit institutions spend on the purchase of goods and the value of clothing and housing received by them as income in kind. These goods are generally defined as having an average life of three years or longer.

Series Ca92 and Ca95. Personal consumption expenditure on nondurable goods is the portion of personal consumption expenditure that individuals

and nonprofit institutions spend on the purchase of goods and the value of food received by them as income in kind. These goods are generally defined as having an average life of less than three years.

Series Ca93 and Ca96. Personal consumption expenditure on services is the remaining portion of personal consumption expenditure that individuals and nonprofit institutions spend on services and the value of financial services received by them as income in kind. It includes the rental values of owner- and tenant-occupied houses as well as dental visits and educational and recreational expenses.

Series Ca97. Calculated as series Ca85 less series Ca94–96. See the essay on national income and product in this chapter for a discussion.

TABLE Ca98–108   Gross private domestic investment, by major component: 1929–2002

Contributed by Richard Sutch

	Nominal dollars						Real (chained 1996) dollars				
	Gross private domestic fixed investment						Gross private domestic fixed investment				
				Nonresidential					Nonresidential		
					Equipment and software	Change in private inventories			Equipment and software	Change in private inventories	
	Total	Residential	Total	Structures			Residential	Structures			Residual
	Ca98	Ca99	Ca100	Ca101	Ca102	Ca103	Ca104	Ca105	Ca106	Ca107	Ca108
Year	Billion dollars	Billion dollars	Billion dollars	Billion dollars	Billion dollars	Billion dollars	Billion chained 1996 dollars	Billion chained 1996 dollars	Billion chained 1996 dollars	Billion chained 1996 dollars	Billion chained 1996 dollars
1929	14.9	4.0	11.0	5.5	5.5	1.5	—	—	—	—	—
1930	11.0	2.4	8.6	4.4	4.2	−0.2	—	—	—	—	—
1931	7.0	1.8	5.3	2.6	2.6	−1.1	—	—	—	—	—
1932	3.6	0.8	2.9	1.4	1.5	−2.4	—	—	—	—	—
1933	3.1	0.6	2.5	1.1	1.4	−1.4	—	—	—	—	—
1934	4.3	0.9	3.3	1.2	2.1	−0.6	—	—	—	—	—
1935	5.6	1.3	4.3	1.4	2.8	1.1	—	—	—	—	—
1936	7.5	1.7	5.8	1.9	3.9	1.2	—	—	—	—	—
1937	9.5	2.1	7.5	2.7	4.8	2.6	—	—	—	—	—
1938	7.7	2.1	5.5	2.1	3.4	−0.6	—	—	—	—	—
1939	9.1	3.0	6.1	2.2	3.9	0.2	—	—	—	—	—
1940	11.2	3.5	7.7	2.6	5.2	2.4	—	—	—	—	—
1941	13.8	4.1	9.7	3.3	6.4	4.3	—	—	—	—	—
1942	8.5	2.2	6.3	2.2	4.1	1.9	—	—	—	—	—
1943	6.9	1.4	5.4	1.8	3.7	−0.7	—	—	—	—	—
1944	8.7	1.4	7.4	2.4	5.0	−0.9	—	—	—	—	—
1945	12.3	1.7	10.6	3.3	7.3	−1.5	—	—	—	—	—
1946	25.1	7.8	17.3	7.4	9.9	6.0	—	—	—	—	—
1947	35.5	12.1	23.5	8.1	15.3	−0.6	—	—	—	—	—
1948	42.4	15.6	26.8	9.5	17.3	5.7	—	—	—	—	—
1949	39.6	14.6	24.9	9.2	15.7	−2.7	—	—	—	—	—
1950	48.3	20.5	27.8	10.0	17.8	5.8	—	—	—	—	—
1951	50.3	18.4	31.8	12.0	19.9	9.9	—	—	—	—	—
1952	50.5	18.6	31.9	12.2	19.7	3.5	—	—	—	—	—
1953	54.5	19.4	35.1	13.6	21.5	1.9	—	—	—	—	—
1954	55.8	21.1	34.7	13.9	20.8	−1.9	—	—	—	—	—
1955	64.0	25.0	39.0	15.2	23.9	5.0	—	—	—	—	—
1956	68.1	23.6	44.5	18.2	26.3	3.9	—	—	—	—	—
1957	69.7	22.2	47.5	19.0	28.6	0.8	—	—	—	—	—
1958	64.9	22.3	42.5	17.6	24.9	−0.4	—	—	—	—	—
1959	74.6	28.1	46.5	18.1	28.4	3.9	—	—	—	—	—
1960	75.7	26.3	49.4	19.6	29.8	3.2	—	—	—	—	—
1961	75.2	26.4	48.8	19.7	29.1	3.0	—	—	—	—	—
1962	82.0	29.0	53.1	20.8	32.3	6.1	—	—	—	—	—
1963	88.1	32.1	56.0	21.2	34.8	5.6	—	—	—	—	—
1964	97.2	34.3	63.0	23.7	39.2	4.8	—	—	—	—	—

TABLE Ca98–108   Gross private domestic investment, by major component: 1929–2002   *Continued*

	Nominal dollars						Real (chained 1996) dollars				
	Gross private domestic fixed investment						Gross private domestic fixed investment				
			Nonresidential					Nonresidential			
Year	Total	Residential	Total	Structures	Equipment and software	Change in private inventories	Residential	Structures	Equipment and software	Change in private inventories	Residual
	Ca98	Ca99	Ca100	Ca101	Ca102	Ca103	Ca104	Ca105	Ca106	Ca107	Ca108
	Billion dollars	Billion dollars	Billion dollars	Billion dollars	Billion dollars	Billion dollars	Billion chained 1996 dollars	Billion chained 1996 dollars	Billion chained 1996 dollars	Billion chained 1996 dollars	Billion chained 1996 dollars
1965	109.0	34.2	74.8	28.3	46.5	9.2	—	—	—	—	—
1966	117.7	32.3	85.4	31.3	54.0	13.6	—	—	—	—	—
1967	118.7	32.4	86.4	31.5	54.9	9.9	—	—	—	—	—
1968	132.1	38.7	93.4	33.6	59.9	9.1	—	—	—	—	—
1969	147.3	42.6	104.7	37.7	67.0	9.2	—	—	—	—	—
1970	150.4	41.4	109.0	40.3	68.7	2.0	—	—	—	—	—
1971	169.9	55.8	114.1	42.7	71.5	8.3	—	—	—	—	—
1972	198.5	69.7	128.8	47.2	81.7	9.1	—	—	—	—	—
1973	228.6	75.3	153.3	55.0	98.3	15.9	—	—	—	—	—
1974	235.4	66.0	169.5	61.2	108.2	14.0	—	—	—	—	—
1975	236.5	62.7	173.7	61.4	112.4	−6.3	—	—	—	—	—
1976	274.8	82.5	192.4	65.9	126.4	17.1	—	—	—	—	—
1977	339.0	110.3	228.7	74.6	154.1	22.3	—	—	—	—	—
1978	410.2	131.6	278.6	91.4	187.2	25.8	—	—	—	—	—
1979	472.7	141.0	331.6	114.9	216.7	18.0	—	—	—	—	—
1980	484.2	123.2	360.9	133.9	227.0	−6.3	—	—	—	—	—
1981	541.0	122.6	418.4	164.6	253.8	29.8	—	—	—	—	—
1982	531.0	105.7	425.3	175.0	250.3	−14.9	—	—	—	—	—
1983	570.0	152.5	417.4	152.7	264.7	−5.8	—	—	—	—	—
1984	670.1	179.8	490.3	176.0	314.3	65.4	—	—	—	—	—
1985	714.5	186.9	527.6	193.3	334.3	21.8	—	—	—	—	—
1986	740.7	218.1	522.5	175.8	346.8	6.6	—	—	—	—	—
1987	754.3	227.6	526.7	172.1	354.7	27.1	290.7	224.3	360.0	29.6	−25.3
1988	802.7	234.2	568.4	181.6	386.8	18.5	289.2	227.1	386.9	18.4	−18.8
1989	845.2	231.8	613.4	193.4	420.0	27.7	277.3	232.7	414.0	29.6	−17.1
1990	847.2	216.8	630.3	202.5	427.8	14.5	253.5	236.1	415.7	16.5	−14.5
1991	800.4	191.5	608.9	183.4	425.4	−0.2	221.1	210.1	407.2	−1.0	−7.9
1992	851.6	225.5	626.1	172.2	453.9	15.0	257.2	197.3	437.5	17.1	−9.3
1993	934.0	251.8	682.2	179.4	502.8	21.1	276.0	198.9	487.1	20.0	−4.1
1994	1,034.6	286.0	748.6	187.5	561.1	62.6	302.7	200.5	544.9	66.8	−7.9
1995	1,110.7	285.6	825.1	204.6	620.5	33.0	291.7	210.1	607.6	30.4	0.8
1996	1,212.7	313.3	899.4	225.0	674.4	30.0	313.3	225.0	674.4	30.0	0.0
1997	1,327.7	328.2	999.4	255.8	743.6	62.9	319.7	245.4	764.2	63.8	0.2
1998	1,465.6	364.4	1,101.2	282.4	818.9	73.1	345.1	262.2	875.4	76.7	−1.4
1999	1,577.2	403.7	1,173.5	283.7	889.8	59.5	368.3	258.6	975.9	62.8	−5.1
2000	1,691.8	426.0	1,265.8	314.2	951.6	63.6	372.4	275.5	1,056.0	65.0	−6.0
2001	1,646.3	444.8	1,201.6	324.5	877.1	−60.3	373.5	270.9	988.2	−61.4	3.4
2002	1,589.3	471.9	1,117.4	269.3	848.1	3.9	388.2	226.4	971.1	5.2	−1.3

Source

U.S. Bureau of Economic Analysis (BEA) Internet site, Tables 1.1 and 1.2; downloaded August 15, 2003.

Documentation

This table disaggregates gross private domestic investment, series Ca76, into two components: series Ca98 and Ca103. The BEA does not publish estimates of the investment subaggregates in chained 1996 dollars for the years before 1987. Because of the procedures used to calculate chained real data, the sum of series Ca104–107 will not equal series Ca86, hence the residual presented here as series Ca108. See the essay on national income and product in this chapter for a discussion (and a warning) about the use of these real gross domestic product numbers.

Series Ca99 and Ca104. Gross residential investment is the market (or real) value of purchases of new and existing fixed capital goods, such as housing, by households and landlords and includes commissions arising in the sale and purchase of new and existing fixed assets.

Series Ca100. Gross nonresidential investment represents the purchase of plant and equipment by firms.

Series Ca101 and Ca105. Gross nonresidential structure investment encompasses the purchase of items such as buildings for industrial and farm use.

Series Ca102 and Ca106. Gross nonresidential equipment and software expenditures are defined in terms of items having an average life of one or more years. This measure includes the purchase of equipment such as new and used vehicles for use by businesses.

Series Ca103. Change in business inventories is defined as the difference in inventories at the end of one period and inventories at the end of the preceding period. Prior to 1959, construction is included in nondurable goods, but it is reallocated to durable goods after 1959.

Series Ca107. The nominal change in business inventories, series Ca103, can be either positive or negative. Because of the negative values, chain-type indexes cannot be calculated for it. The real change in business inventories is calculated from inventory stock series that have been derived using the chain-type formula used to calculate the other series.

Series Ca108. The residual is equal to series Ca86 minus the sum of series Ca104–107. See the essay on national income and product in this chapter for a discussion.

TABLE Ca109–119   Exports and imports of goods and services: 1929–2002

Contributed by Richard Sutch

		Nominal dollars						Real (chained 1996) dollars			
		Exports			Imports			Exports		Imports	
	Net exports	Total	Goods	Services	Total	Goods	Services	Goods	Services	Goods	Services
	Ca109	Ca110	Ca111	Ca112	Ca113	Ca114	Ca115	Ca116	Ca117	Ca118	Ca119
Year	Billion dollars	Billion dollars	Billion dollars	Billion dollars	Billion dollars	Billion dollars	Billion dollars	Billion chained 1996 dollars	Billion chained 1996 dollars	Billion chained 1996 dollars	Billion chained 1996 dollars
1929	0.3	5.9	5.3	0.6	5.6	4.5	1.1	—	—	—	—
1930	0.3	4.4	3.9	0.5	4.1	3.1	1.0	—	—	—	—
1931	0.0	2.9	2.5	0.4	2.9	2.1	0.8	—	—	—	—
1932	0.1	2.0	1.7	0.3	1.9	1.3	0.6	—	—	—	—
1933	0.1	2.0	1.7	0.3	1.9	1.5	0.4	—	—	—	—
1934	0.4	2.6	2.2	0.3	2.2	1.8	0.5	—	—	—	—
1935	−0.2	2.8	2.4	0.4	3.0	2.5	0.5	—	—	—	—
1936	−0.2	3.0	2.6	0.4	3.2	2.5	0.6	—	—	—	—
1937	0.0	4.0	3.5	0.6	4.0	3.2	0.8	—	—	—	—
1938	1.0	3.8	3.2	0.5	2.8	2.2	0.7	—	—	—	—
1939	0.8	3.9	3.3	0.6	3.1	2.4	0.7	—	—	—	—
1940	1.4	4.8	4.1	0.7	3.4	2.7	0.7	—	—	—	—
1941	1.0	5.4	4.5	0.9	4.4	3.4	1.0	—	—	—	—
1942	−0.3	4.3	3.4	0.9	4.6	2.7	1.9	—	—	—	—
1943	−2.4	3.9	2.9	1.0	6.3	3.4	2.8	—	—	—	—
1944	−2.1	4.8	3.6	1.2	6.9	3.8	3.1	—	—	—	—
1945	−0.8	6.7	5.4	1.3	7.5	3.9	3.7	—	—	—	—
1946	7.1	14.1	11.8	2.3	7.0	5.1	1.9	—	—	—	—
1947	10.8	18.7	16.1	2.6	7.9	6.0	2.0	—	—	—	—
1948	5.4	15.5	13.3	2.2	10.1	7.6	2.5	—	—	—	—
1949	5.2	14.4	12.2	2.2	9.2	6.9	2.4	—	—	—	—
1950	0.7	12.3	10.2	2.1	11.6	9.1	2.5	—	—	—	—
1951	2.4	17.0	14.2	2.8	14.6	11.2	3.4	—	—	—	—
1952	1.0	16.3	13.4	2.9	15.3	10.8	4.5	—	—	—	—
1953	−0.8	15.2	12.4	2.8	16.0	11.0	5.0	—	—	—	—
1954	0.3	15.7	12.9	2.8	15.4	10.4	5.1	—	—	—	—
1955	0.4	17.6	14.4	3.2	17.2	11.5	5.7	—	—	—	—
1956	2.3	21.2	17.6	3.6	18.9	12.8	6.1	—	—	—	—
1957	4.0	23.9	19.6	4.3	19.9	13.3	6.7	—	—	—	—
1958	0.4	20.4	16.4	4.0	20.0	13.0	7.1	—	—	—	—
1959	−1.7	20.6	16.5	4.2	22.3	15.3	7.0	—	—	—	—
1960	2.5	25.3	20.5	4.8	22.8	15.2	7.6	—	—	—	—
1961	3.3	26.0	20.9	5.1	22.7	15.1	7.6	—	—	—	—
1962	2.4	27.4	21.7	5.7	25.0	16.9	8.1	—	—	—	—
1963	3.3	29.4	23.3	6.1	26.1	17.7	8.4	—	—	—	—
1964	5.5	33.6	26.7	6.9	28.1	19.4	8.7	—	—	—	—
1965	3.9	35.4	27.8	7.6	31.5	22.2	9.3	—	—	—	—
1966	1.8	38.9	30.7	8.2	37.1	26.3	10.7	—	—	—	—
1967	1.5	41.4	32.2	9.2	39.9	27.8	12.2	—	—	—	—
1968	−1.3	45.3	35.3	10.0	46.6	33.9	12.6	—	—	—	—
1969	−1.2	49.3	38.3	11.0	50.5	36.8	13.7	—	—	—	—
1970	1.2	57.0	44.5	12.4	55.8	40.9	14.9	—	—	—	—
1971	−3.0	59.3	45.6	13.8	62.3	46.6	15.8	—	—	—	—
1972	−8.0	66.2	51.8	14.4	74.2	56.9	17.3	—	—	—	—
1973	0.6	91.8	73.9	17.8	91.2	71.8	19.3	—	—	—	—
1974	−3.2	124.3	101.0	23.3	127.5	104.5	22.9	—	—	—	—
1975	13.6	136.3	109.6	26.7	122.7	99.0	23.7	—	—	—	—
1976	−2.2	148.9	117.8	31.1	151.1	124.6	26.5	—	—	—	—
1977	−23.6	158.8	123.7	35.1	182.4	152.6	29.8	—	—	—	—
1978	−26.2	186.1	145.4	40.7	212.3	177.4	34.8	—	—	—	—
1979	−24.0	228.7	184.0	44.7	252.7	212.8	39.9	—	—	—	—
1980	−14.9	278.9	225.8	53.2	293.8	248.6	45.3	—	—	—	—
1981	−15.0	302.8	239.1	63.7	317.8	267.8	49.9	—	—	—	—
1982	−20.6	282.6	215.0	67.6	303.2	250.5	52.6	—	—	—	—
1983	−51.6	277.0	207.3	69.7	328.6	272.7	56.0	—	—	—	—
1984	−102.0	303.1	225.6	77.5	405.1	336.3	68.8	—	—	—	—

TABLE Ca109-119   Exports and imports of goods and services: 1929-2002   *Continued*

		Nominal dollars						Real (chained 1996) dollars			
		Exports			Imports			Exports		Imports	
	Net exports	Total	Goods	Services	Total	Goods	Services	Goods	Services	Goods	Services
	Ca109	Ca110	Ca111	Ca112	Ca113	Ca114	Ca115	Ca116	Ca117	Ca118	Ca119
Year	Billion dollars	Billion dollars	Billion dollars	Billion dollars	Billion dollars	Billion dollars	Billion dollars	Billion chained 1996 dollars	Billion chained 1996 dollars	Billion chained 1996 dollars	Billion chained 1996 dollars
1985	−114.2	303.0	222.2	80.8	417.2	343.3	73.9	—	—	—	—
1986	−131.9	320.3	226.0	94.3	452.2	370.0	82.2	—	—	—	—
1987	−142.3	365.6	257.5	108.1	507.9	414.8	93.1	271.4	139.1	445.8	120.2
1988	−106.3	446.9	325.8	121.1	553.2	452.1	101.1	322.6	152.0	463.9	123.4
1989	−80.7	509.0	371.7	137.3	589.7	484.5	105.2	363.2	166.7	483.4	126.9
1990	−71.4	557.2	398.5	158.6	628.6	508.0	120.6	393.2	183.5	497.9	136.6
1991	−20.7	601.6	426.4	175.2	622.3	500.7	121.6	421.1	192.9	497.6	133.4
1992	−27.8	636.8	448.7	188.1	664.6	544.9	119.8	449.8	201.7	543.7	128.0
1993	−60.5	658.0	459.7	198.3	718.5	592.8	125.7	463.4	209.9	598.4	134.0
1994	−87.0	725.1	509.6	215.5	812.1	676.7	135.4	508.2	225.1	677.9	141.9
1995	−84.2	818.6	583.8	234.7	902.8	757.6	145.2	568.8	239.5	739.1	147.7
1996	−89.0	874.2	618.4	255.8	963.1	808.3	154.8	618.4	255.8	808.3	154.8
1997	−89.3	966.4	688.9	277.5	1,055.8	885.1	170.7	708.1	273.6	923.1	171.7
1998	−151.7	964.9	681.3	283.6	1,116.7	930.0	186.7	722.9	279.8	1,031.4	192.2
1999	−249.9	989.3	697.3	292.0	1,239.2	1,045.3	193.9	750.0	286.8	1,157.5	200.3
2000	−365.5	1,101.1	785.0	316.1	1,466.6	1,243.1	223.5	834.7	304.1	1,313.7	223.6
2001	−348.9	1,034.1	733.5	300.6	1,383.0	1,167.2	215.8	785.2	292.0	1,270.5	222.4
2002	−423.6	1,014.9	703.6	311.3	1,438.5	1,192.1	246.4	756.9	301.5	1,320.1	227.2

Source

U.S. Bureau of Economic Analysis (BEA) Internet site, Tables 1.1 and 1.2, downloaded August 18, 2003.

Documentation

Gross domestic product (GDP) is the sum of consumption expenditures, gross private domestic investment, government purchases of goods and services, and net exports. Net exports are exports to the rest of the world, less imports of goods and services from the rest of the world. Imports must be subtracted because imported items are included in the aggregates for consumption, investment, and government purchases; however, these imported goods and services are not part of U.S. GDP; they are part of the GDP of other countries. Because chained real components of GDP are not additive, users should be cautioned against calculating a real net export series by subtracting real imports from real exports. The BEA does not publish estimates of the components of exports and imports in chained dollars for the years before 1987.

Series Ca109. Equals series Ca110 minus series Ca113. Receipts and payments of factor income and transfer payments to the rest of the world (net) are excluded.

Series Ca110 and Ca113. Equals series Ca77-78, respectively.

Series Ca112, Ca115, Ca117, and Ca119. Exports and imports of certain goods, primarily military equipment purchased and sold by the federal government, are included in services. Beginning in 1986, repairs and alterations of equipment are reclassified from goods to services.

TABLE Ca120–134   Government consumption expenditures and gross investment, by level of government: 1929–2002

Contributed by Richard Sutch

	Nominal dollars									Real (chained 1996) dollars					
	Federal						State and local			Federal				State and local	
		National defense			Nondefense					National defense		Nondefense			
	Total	Consumption expenditures	Gross investment	Total	Consumption expenditures	Gross investment	Total	Consumption expenditures	Gross investment	Consumption expenditures	Gross investment	Consumption expenditures	Gross investment	Consumption expenditures	Gross investment
Year	Ca120	Ca121	Ca122	Ca123	Ca124	Ca125	Ca126	Ca127	Ca128	Ca129	Ca130	Ca131	Ca132	Ca133	Ca134
	Billion dollars	Billion dollars	Billion dollars	Billion dollars	Billion dollars	Billion dollars	Billion dollars	Billion dollars	Billion dollars	Billion chained 1996 dollars	Billion chained 1996 dollars	Billion chained 1996 dollars	Billion chained 1996 dollars	Billion chained 1996 dollars	Billion chained 1996 dollars
1929	0.9	0.9	0.0	0.8	0.6	0.2	7.7	5.1	2.6	—	—	—	—	—	—
1930	0.9	0.9	0.1	0.8	0.6	0.2	8.2	5.3	2.9	—	—	—	—	—	—
1931	0.9	0.9	0.1	0.9	0.7	0.3	8.1	5.4	2.6	—	—	—	—	—	—
1932	0.9	0.9	0.1	0.9	0.6	0.3	7.0	5.2	1.8	—	—	—	—	—	—
1933	0.9	0.8	0.1	1.4	0.9	0.5	6.5	5.1	1.3	—	—	—	—	—	—
1934	0.8	0.7	0.1	2.4	1.6	0.8	7.3	5.5	1.8	—	—	—	—	—	—
1935	1.0	0.9	0.1	2.3	1.2	1.1	7.6	6.0	1.6	—	—	—	—	—	—
1936	1.2	1.0	0.3	4.2	3.3	1.0	7.6	4.7	2.9	—	—	—	—	—	—
1937	1.3	1.0	0.3	3.7	2.8	0.9	7.8	5.2	2.6	—	—	—	—	—	—
1938	1.4	1.0	0.3	4.2	3.3	0.9	8.2	5.2	3.0	—	—	—	—	—	—
1939	1.5	1.2	0.3	4.4	3.6	0.8	8.9	5.5	3.4	—	—	—	—	—	—
1940	2.5	1.7	0.8	3.9	3.1	0.8	8.7	5.9	2.8	—	—	—	—	—	—
1941	14.3	7.1	7.2	3.6	2.2	1.4	8.7	6.4	2.2	—	—	—	—	—	—
1942	51.2	25.2	26.0	2.9	1.9	1.0	8.7	7.2	1.5	—	—	—	—	—	—
1943	84.2	46.8	37.4	2.2	1.4	0.8	8.5	7.6	0.9	—	—	—	—	—	—
1944	94.6	59.2	35.4	2.4	1.9	0.5	8.5	7.8	0.7	—	—	—	—	—	—
1945	82.1	59.4	22.7	2.1	1.4	0.6	9.0	8.2	0.8	—	—	—	—	—	—
1946	25.3	23.8	1.5	3.6	3.2	0.4	10.8	9.3	1.6	—	—	—	—	—	—
1947	18.2	17.3	0.9	4.3	3.5	0.8	13.9	11.0	2.8	—	—	—	—	—	—
1948	18.4	16.4	2.0	5.8	4.8	1.0	16.5	12.5	4.0	—	—	—	—	—	—
1949	19.9	16.9	2.9	7.8	6.3	1.4	19.2	13.8	5.3	—	—	—	—	—	—
1950	19.6	17.2	2.4	6.4	4.8	1.6	20.9	15.1	5.9	—	—	—	—	—	—
1951	39.3	30.1	9.1	5.8	4.2	1.5	23.3	16.3	7.0	—	—	—	—	—	—
1952	52.4	38.9	13.4	6.8	5.2	1.6	24.7	17.4	7.3	—	—	—	—	—	—
1953	56.0	41.3	14.7	8.4	7.1	1.4	26.4	18.5	7.9	—	—	—	—	—	—
1954	49.3	37.1	12.1	8.0	6.8	1.2	29.2	20.0	9.2	—	—	—	—	—	—
1955	47.0	36.9	10.1	7.9	7.0	0.9	31.9	21.9	10.0	—	—	—	—	—	—
1956	49.3	38.8	10.5	7.4	6.2	1.2	35.1	23.8	11.3	—	—	—	—	—	—
1957	53.7	43.2	10.5	7.6	6.2	1.4	38.8	26.2	12.5	—	—	—	—	—	—
1958	55.5	44.2	11.3	8.4	6.8	1.6	42.6	29.0	13.5	—	—	—	—	—	—
1959	56.0	42.2	13.7	11.4	9.8	1.7	45.1	31.1	13.9	—	—	—	—	—	—
1960	55.2	42.8	12.3	10.7	8.7	2.0	47.9	34.0	13.9	—	—	—	—	—	—
1961	58.1	44.3	13.9	11.3	8.9	2.4	52.0	37.0	15.0	—	—	—	—	—	—
1962	62.8	48.3	14.5	14.1	11.2	2.9	55.3	39.4	15.9	—	—	—	—	—	—
1963	62.7	50.1	12.6	15.8	12.3	3.5	59.9	42.4	17.5	—	—	—	—	—	—
1964	61.8	50.3	11.5	18.0	13.9	4.2	65.3	46.3	19.0	—	—	—	—	—	—

	Nominal dollars									Real (chained 1996) dollars					
	Federal						State and local			Federal				State and local	
	National defense			Nondefense						National defense		Nondefense			
	Total	Consumption expenditures	Gross investment	Total	Consumption expenditures	Gross investment	Total	Consumption expenditures	Gross investment	Consumption expenditures	Gross investment	Consumption expenditures	Gross investment	Consumption expenditures	Gross investment
Year	Ca120	Ca121	Ca122	Ca123	Ca124	Ca125	Ca126	Ca127	Ca128	Ca129	Ca130	Ca131	Ca132	Ca133	Ca134
	Billion dollars	Billion dollars	Billion dollars	Billion dollars	Billion dollars	Billion dollars	Billion dollars	Billion dollars	Billion dollars	Billion chained 1996 dollars	Billion chained 1996 dollars	Billion chained 1996 dollars	Billion chained 1996 dollars	Billion chained 1996 dollars	Billion chained 1996 dollars
1965	62.4	52.4	10.1	19.7	15.0	4.7	71.6	50.8	20.8	—	—	—	—	—	—
1966	73.8	61.4	12.3	20.7	15.8	4.9	79.9	56.8	23.1	—	—	—	—	—	—
1967	85.8	71.5	14.3	21.0	16.9	4.2	88.6	63.2	25.3	—	—	—	—	—	—
1968	92.2	79.0	13.2	21.8	18.0	3.8	98.8	71.1	27.7	—	—	—	—	—	—
1969	92.6	80.1	12.5	23.5	19.9	3.6	108.5	80.2	28.3	—	—	—	—	—	—
1970	90.9	78.7	12.3	25.5	21.7	3.8	120.7	92.0	28.7	—	—	—	—	—	—
1971	89.0	79.3	9.7	28.6	24.4	4.2	133.5	103.4	30.1	—	—	—	—	—	—
1972	93.5	82.3	11.2	32.2	27.6	4.5	144.4	113.8	30.6	—	—	—	—	—	—
1973	93.9	82.6	11.3	33.9	29.0	4.9	160.1	126.9	33.2	—	—	—	—	—	—
1974	99.7	87.5	12.3	38.5	32.9	5.6	184.2	144.5	39.6	—	—	—	—	—	—
1975	107.9	93.4	14.5	44.2	37.7	6.5	209.0	165.4	43.6	—	—	—	—	—	—
1976	113.2	97.9	15.3	47.4	40.1	7.3	223.9	180.1	43.8	—	—	—	—	—	—
1977	122.6	105.8	16.7	53.5	45.5	8.0	239.3	196.5	42.8	—	—	—	—	—	—
1978	132.0	114.2	17.8	59.8	50.1	9.8	263.8	214.3	49.5	—	—	—	—	—	—
1979	146.7	125.3	21.4	65.0	54.7	10.2	291.8	235.0	56.8	—	—	—	—	—	—
1980	169.6	145.3	24.3	75.6	63.6	12.0	324.4	260.5	64.0	—	—	—	—	—	—
1981	197.8	168.9	28.9	84.0	71.0	13.0	349.6	284.6	65.0	—	—	—	—	—	—
1982	228.3	193.6	34.7	84.5	71.7	12.7	371.6	306.8	64.8	—	—	—	—	—	—
1983	252.5	210.6	41.9	92.0	77.4	14.5	391.5	325.1	66.4	—	—	—	—	—	—
1984	283.5	234.9	48.7	92.8	77.1	15.7	424.4	349.5	75.0	—	—	—	—	—	—
1985	312.4	254.9	57.5	101.0	84.1	16.9	464.9	380.5	84.4	—	—	—	—	—	—
1986	332.2	269.3	62.9	106.5	89.0	17.5	503.6	410.8	92.8	—	—	—	—	—	—
1987	351.2	284.8	66.4	109.3	89.9	19.4	537.5	439.0	98.4	373.2	76.3	125.4	21.5	577.3	118.8
1988	355.9	294.6	61.3	106.8	88.2	18.6	574.3	467.9	106.3	376.1	70.6	119.2	20.1	596.8	125.0
1989	363.2	300.5	62.7	119.3	99.1	20.3	617.7	503.0	114.7	372.4	70.8	129.6	21.5	617.9	131.8
1990	374.9	308.9	65.9	133.6	111.0	22.6	673.0	545.8	127.2	369.7	73.2	140.1	23.5	638.9	142.2
1991	384.5	321.1	63.4	142.9	118.1	24.8	708.1	576.1	132.1	369.5	68.9	140.9	25.4	653.4	145.5
1992	378.5	316.9	61.6	156.0	128.8	27.2	736.0	601.6	134.3	350.6	66.4	150.0	28.0	667.8	147.4
1993	364.9	309.2	55.7	162.4	133.4	28.9	765.7	629.5	136.2	336.1	58.6	147.8	29.5	680.4	146.6
1994	355.1	301.1	54.0	165.9	138.6	27.3	806.8	662.6	144.2	320.5	55.4	148.0	27.6	697.5	151.4
1995	350.6	297.5	53.1	170.9	141.8	29.2	850.5	694.7	155.8	308.7	53.2	145.7	29.0	711.3	158.6
1996	357.0	302.4	54.6	174.6	142.9	31.7	890.4	726.5	163.8	302.4	54.6	142.9	31.7	726.5	163.8
1997	352.6	304.2	48.4	185.6	152.7	32.9	949.7	766.4	183.3	298.5	49.1	148.6	33.3	745.7	180.2
1998	349.1	299.7	49.4	190.1	153.4	36.7	999.3	808.3	191.0	290.6	51.0	146.5	37.5	771.9	185.8
1999	364.3	312.0	52.3	200.7	159.6	41.1	1,076.0	864.7	211.3	295.3	53.7	147.6	41.6	801.2	201.4
2000	374.9	321.4	53.5	214.3	171.9	42.4	1,161.8	937.9	223.9	294.1	54.8	153.7	42.3	831.1	206.5
2001	399.9	344.5	55.5	228.2	184.0	44.2	1,229.9	993.7	236.2	308.9	57.3	161.1	43.6	856.8	212.8
2002	447.4	386.6	60.8	246.3	199.9	46.4	1,279.2	1,034.5	244.7	337.0	63.3	167.8	45.9	881.1	218.6

(continued)

TABLE Ca120–134   Government consumption expenditures and gross investment, by level of government: 1929–2002   *Continued*

Source

U.S. Bureau of Economic Analysis (BEA) Internet site, Tables 3.7 and 3.8, downloaded August 15, 2003.

Documentation

Government consumption expenditures and gross investment are the measure of government-sector final demand. As defined by the BEA, it consists of two major components: current consumption expenditures by general government and gross investment by both general government and government enterprises.

Consumption expenditures consist of compensation of general government employees (except those engaged in producing investment goods or software that will be used by the government agency), consumption of fixed capital owned by the general government, and net current purchases from business and net purchases of used goods. Consumption expenditures also include changes in inventories and from the rest of the world. Current receipts for certain goods and services provided by general government agencies – primarily tuition payments for higher education and charges for medical care – are defined as government sales, which are treated as deductions from government consumption expenditures.

Gross investment consists of purchases of new structures and of equipment and software by both general government and government enterprises, net purchases of used structures and equipment, and own-account production of structures and of software. Government consumption expenditures and gross investment do not include current transactions of government enterprises, transfer payments, interest paid or received by government, subsidies, or transactions in financial assets and nonproduced assets such as land.

The BEA does not publish estimates of the government purchases subaggregates in chained 1996 dollars for the years before 1987. Because of the procedures used to calculate chained real data, the sum of the components shown here will not equal series Ca89. See the essay on national income and product in this chapter for a discussion (and a warning) about the use of these real gross domestic product numbers.

Series Ca121 and Ca129. Includes Department of Defense military functions, military assistance to other nations, development and control of atomic energy, and stockpiling of strategic materials.

TABLE Ca135–148   Gross domestic product, by sector of origin: 1929–2002

Contributed by Richard Sutch

	Nominal dollars							Real (chained 1996) dollars						
					General government								General government		
	Nonfarm business	Farm business	Private households	Nonprofit institutions	Total	Federal	State and local	Nonfarm business	Farm business	Private households	Nonprofit institutions	Federal	State and local	Residual
	Ca135	Ca136	Ca137	Ca138	Ca139	Ca140	Ca141	Ca142	Ca143	Ca144	Ca145	Ca146	Ca147	Ca148
Year	Billion dollars	Billion dollars	Billion dollars	Billion dollars	Billion dollars	Billion dollars	Billion dollars	Billion chained 1996 dollars	Billion chained 1996 dollars	Billion chained 1996 dollars	Billion chained 1996 dollars	Billion chained 1996 dollars	Billion chained 1996 dollars	Billion chained 1996 dollars
1929	86.0	9.7	1.7	1.1	5.2	1.1	4.1	560.2	29.3	30.4	27.1	26.6	91.5	56.6
1930	75.6	7.6	1.5	1.2	5.4	1.1	4.2	504.8	27.7	28.4	27.6	28.5	95.2	39.7
1931	62.6	6.3	1.1	1.1	5.5	1.1	4.3	458.5	32.7	25.2	27.2	27.3	98.4	35.4
1932	47.3	4.5	0.8	1.0	5.2	1.1	4.1	388.9	31.8	21.6	26.3	26.1	98.0	21.8
1933	44.7	4.6	0.7	0.9	5.5	1.4	4.1	381.7	30.6	20.6	25.8	32.2	98.7	16.2
1934	53.0	4.7	0.9	1.0	6.5	2.0	4.6	435.9	24.6	23.3	26.1	42.9	104.7	13.5
1935	57.5	7.0	0.9	1.0	6.9	2.1	4.8	471.5	30.2	24.4	26.6	47.5	109.7	21.4
1936	67.0	6.4	1.0	1.0	8.3	3.9	4.4	546.6	26.2	25.9	27.4	78.4	103.9	17.7
1937	73.3	8.2	1.2	1.1	8.0	3.4	4.6	574.2	31.6	27.4	28.0	67.9	107.0	33.4
1938	68.5	6.5	1.0	1.1	8.8	3.9	4.9	546.4	30.7	25.0	28.4	76.7	111.4	20.6
1939	74.6	6.3	1.1	1.1	8.8	3.9	5.0	594.6	34.0	26.8	28.7	78.2	113.5	31.5
1940	83.3	6.4	1.2	1.2	9.1	4.0	5.1	659.4	30.2	28.1	31.5	85.5	114.9	35.2
1941	104.0	8.9	1.2	1.3	11.2	5.9	5.3	774.9	33.6	26.6	33.4	130.7	115.8	38.5
1942	127.4	13.0	1.5	1.4	18.4	12.8	5.6	898.9	36.3	27.1	34.7	264.2	114.3	−10.1
1943	148.3	15.3	1.6	1.6	31.6	25.7	5.9	1,008.5	35.4	22.4	35.7	513.2	111.4	−136.5
1944	159.7	15.3	1.9	1.8	40.9	34.9	6.1	1,074.4	35.0	21.4	36.8	650.7	108.9	−206.1

	Nominal dollars				General government			Real (chained 1996) dollars				General government		
	Nonfarm business	Farm business	Private households	Nonprofit institutions	Total	Federal	State and local	Nonfarm business	Farm business	Private households	Nonprofit institutions	Federal	State and local	Residual
Year	Ca135	Ca136	Ca137	Ca138	Ca139	Ca140	Ca141	Ca142	Ca143	Ca144	Ca145	Ca146	Ca147	Ca148
	Billion dollars	Billion dollars	Billion dollars	Billion dollars	Billion dollars	Billion dollars	Billion dollars	Billion chained 1996 dollars	Billion chained 1996 dollars	Billion chained 1996 dollars	Billion chained 1996 dollars	Billion chained 1996 dollars	Billion chained 1996 dollars	Billion chained 1996 dollars
1945	157.7	16.0	2.1	2.0	45.3	38.8	6.5	1,055.7	34.8	21.2	37.3	651.5	111.1	−211.8
1946	166.0	18.8	2.1	2.4	33.0	25.6	7.4	1,044.2	35.1	19.5	40.9	306.0	116.9	−51.0
1947	191.2	20.2	2.4	2.8	27.9	19.1	8.8	1,087.6	31.8	20.9	43.6	215.7	124.5	−22.9
1948	213.4	23.3	2.4	3.2	27.3	17.2	10.2	1,136.2	36.4	20.5	50.3	198.5	127.8	−3.4
1949	214.6	18.7	2.4	3.6	28.4	17.3	11.1	1,132.3	35.1	20.4	52.7	188.9	136.2	−9.6
1950	239.3	19.9	2.6	3.9	28.7	16.9	11.8	1,246.9	36.9	22.3	55.0	188.4	140.9	2.2
1951	273.8	22.9	2.7	4.3	35.8	22.7	13.2	1,340.3	35.0	21.9	57.3	247.2	144.6	−24.9
1952	288.8	22.1	2.6	4.6	40.5	26.1	14.4	1,386.2	36.8	20.1	59.7	275.4	149.4	−34.6
1953	309.8	20.1	2.7	5.1	42.2	26.7	15.5	1,455.7	38.6	19.8	62.8	276.7	156.0	−29.8
1954	309.9	19.5	2.6	5.5	43.5	26.6	16.9	1,439.9	39.9	18.6	65.5	269.8	162.9	−31.4
1955	341.6	18.6	3.1	6.1	45.9	27.6	18.2	1,558.9	40.8	22.1	69.8	263.4	170.5	−20.5
1956	360.4	18.4	3.3	6.6	49.2	28.8	20.4	1,590.3	40.8	23.1	73.8	260.6	181.1	−23.5
1957	380.0	18.3	3.3	7.3	52.6	30.0	22.6	1,626.3	39.3	22.6	77.3	259.7	191.0	−28.0
1958	380.0	20.5	3.5	8.0	55.9	31.2	24.7	1,600.4	40.5	23.2	81.8	252.4	202.7	−35.3
1959	417.7	18.9	3.6	8.9	58.4	32.0	26.5	1,738.5	40.2	22.6	86.1	250.4	211.1	−26.5
1960	431.5	19.8	3.8	10.1	62.1	33.2	28.9	1,775.1	42.2	22.8	94.1	255.3	222.3	−32.6
1961	445.0	20.1	3.7	10.7	66.1	34.5	31.6	1,815.5	42.5	22.1	96.1	260.8	233.7	−37.0
1962	479.8	20.2	3.8	11.8	70.9	36.7	34.2	1,938.9	41.7	21.9	101.0	271.7	242.3	−36.7
1963	506.0	20.4	3.8	12.8	75.7	38.6	37.1	2,029.0	42.9	21.6	104.7	274.1	254.9	−34.9
1964	546.0	19.3	3.9	14.0	81.3	40.9	40.4	2,163.6	41.5	21.4	108.9	276.6	270.2	−33.2
1965	592.1	21.9	4.0	15.3	86.8	42.6	44.2	2,314.5	43.8	20.7	115.0	278.4	286.6	−27.5
1966	648.2	22.9	4.0	17.2	97.0	47.4	49.6	2,478.3	42.4	19.9	121.5	296.8	303.7	−31.2
1967	681.1	22.2	4.2	19.2	107.3	51.8	55.5	2,525.7	45.2	20.0	126.3	316.4	316.4	−38.8
1968	743.4	22.7	4.4	21.7	119.3	56.7	62.5	2,657.6	43.7	19.0	132.2	322.1	335.4	−40.4
1969	800.2	25.2	4.4	25.0	130.5	60.5	70.0	2,740.2	44.9	18.0	138.7	323.5	350.7	−41.7
1970	836.9	26.2	4.5	27.9	144.2	64.7	79.5	2,743.0	46.3	16.9	138.7	310.0	366.2	−41.3
1971	907.6	28.1	4.6	31.0	157.3	68.6	88.7	2,850.0	48.4	16.1	143.3	296.4	381.2	−36.1
1972	997.3	32.6	4.6	34.3	171.5	73.6	97.9	3,040.7	48.3	15.6	148.6	282.9	394.5	−29.6
1973	1,107.1	49.8	4.8	38.2	185.7	76.4	109.3	3,256.4	48.1	15.2	153.2	272.7	408.1	−26.3
1974	1,203.1	47.4	4.6	42.6	203.4	81.6	121.8	3,223.9	47.0	13.1	157.1	271.4	422.9	−36.2
1975	1,308.1	48.8	4.6	47.3	226.4	89.1	137.2	3,177.1	55.5	12.3	163.8	269.5	435.8	−31.4
1976	1,475.1	46.4	5.4	51.6	245.3	95.6	149.7	3,397.0	53.3	12.7	165.4	269.4	441.5	−26.0
1977	1,655.6	47.2	5.9	56.4	266.2	103.6	162.7	3,577.7	56.0	12.9	170.4	269.2	448.3	−19.2
1978	1,882.5	54.7	6.5	63.2	288.9	111.0	177.9	3,810.5	54.1	13.3	173.3	272.3	458.7	−17.0
1979	2,110.5	64.5	6.4	70.9	314.2	118.7	195.5	3,940.8	58.3	11.8	179.5	271.7	466.9	−13.7
1980	2,302.7	56.1	6.1	81.0	349.7	132.1	217.5	3,921.0	56.5	10.4	187.0	275.7	473.2	−26.4
1981	2,577.4	69.9	6.2	91.4	386.5	148.3	238.2	4,005.4	72.6	9.7	192.6	279.8	473.0	−17.6
1982	2,664.6	65.1	6.3	102.0	421.2	163.1	258.1	3,892.4	75.7	9.3	199.0	283.9	476.0	−26.4
1983	2,918.9	49.2	6.3	112.9	447.7	173.0	274.7	4,125.4	50.5	9.2	203.8	290.2	474.1	−26.0
1984	3,245.3	68.5	7.3	123.9	487.7	194.0	293.7	4,454.1	67.4	10.4	207.6	296.5	476.9	−10.0

(continued)

TABLE Ca135–148 Gross domestic product, by sector of origin: 1929–2002 *Continued*

	Nominal dollars							Real (chained 1996) dollars						
	Nonfarm business	Farm business	Private households	Nonprofit institutions	General government			Nonfarm business	Farm business	Private households	Nonprofit institutions	General government		Residual
					Total	Federal	State and local					Federal	State and local	
Year	Ca135	Ca136	Ca137	Ca138	Ca139	Ca140	Ca141	Ca142	Ca143	Ca144	Ca145	Ca146	Ca147	Ca148
	Billion dollars	Billion dollars	Billion dollars	Billion dollars	Billion dollars	Billion dollars	Billion dollars	Billion chained 1996 dollars	Billion chained 1996 dollars	Billion chained 1996 dollars	Billion chained 1996 dollars	Billion chained 1996 dollars	Billion chained 1996 dollars	Billion chained 1996 dollars
1985	3,479.7	67.1	7.3	133.6	525.3	206.3	319.1	4,620.5	80.7	10.1	214.7	304.7	490.6	−6.2
1986	3,678.0	63.0	7.7	146.0	558.2	213.9	344.3	4,788.7	77.5	10.4	225.5	309.9	504.8	−5.5
1987	3,910.9	65.1	7.7	165.6	593.1	224.5	368.7	4,958.5	78.8	10.2	237.6	318.0	514.5	−5.1
1988	4,217.4	63.8	8.3	186.8	632.0	235.9	396.2	5,183.8	70.2	10.6	254.8	321.8	532.1	−5.3
1989	4,524.7	76.2	8.9	205.7	673.6	247.6	426.0	5,362.5	79.5	11.1	268.6	325.6	548.5	−4.4
1990	4,762.4	79.6	9.4	228.6	723.3	259.7	463.6	5,440.8	84.2	11.4	280.1	331.4	564.7	−5.2
1991	4,889.2	73.2	9.1	248.4	766.3	275.8	490.4	5,391.6	85.6	10.5	290.4	333.3	571.2	−7.6
1992	5,161.6	80.5	10.1	269.4	797.3	282.8	514.5	5,575.3	95.7	11.3	297.3	326.2	579.4	−6.3
1993	5,444.4	73.6	10.7	286.3	827.3	287.0	540.3	5,753.4	85.8	11.7	308.0	319.7	587.1	−3.5
1994	5,803.0	83.6	11.1	302.2	854.5	287.4	567.0	6,013.7	100.3	11.8	319.1	309.9	596.1	−3.5
1995	6,116.9	73.2	11.9	318.4	880.1	286.8	593.3	6,210.3	85.5	12.2	329.3	299.1	607.7	−0.4
1996	6,463.8	92.2	12.0	336.5	908.7	292.0	616.7	6,463.8	92.2	12.0	336.5	292.0	616.7	0.1
1997	6,922.2	88.3	12.0	351.2	944.6	295.4	649.2	6,778.9	103.6	11.7	348.8	287.9	629.3	−0.8
1998	7,337.4	80.6	14.0	369.8	979.8	298.6	681.2	7,107.7	100.3	13.3	358.6	286.2	642.5	0.0
1999	7,772.5	75.2	12.7	390.4	1,023.5	307.6	715.9	7,434.4	108.1	11.7	367.5	285.2	653.7	−2.1
2000	8,233.6	77.8	13.6	417.5	1,082.1	323.4	758.7	7,729.2	120.5	12.0	376.9	289.4	669.0	−6.5
2001	8,402.1	80.6	11.9	447.7	1,139.8	332.8	807.0	7,724.7	114.3	10.1	388.7	291.3	687.0	−2.4
2002	8,680.2	78.9	10.8	475.3	1,201.1	355.6	845.5	7,917.7	114.7	8.8	398.9	297.5	703.1	−3.7

Source

U.S. Bureau of Economic Analysis (BEA) Internet site, Tables 1.7 and 1.8, downloaded August 18, 2003.

Documentation

The classification by sector of origin shows the same total of gross domestic product as series Ca74. These series are estimates of the gross product originating in the particular sectors of the nation's economy: farm and nonfarm business and three nonbusiness groups (households, nonprofit institutions, and government). The output of the three nonbusiness sectors is measured by the incomes originating in them.

To estimate real product series, the nominal series are deflated using chained price indexes and then calibrated to 1996 nominal levels. Because of the procedures used to calculate chained real data, the sum of the components shown here will not equal series Ca84, hence the residual displayed as series Ca148. See the essay on national income and product in this chapter for a discussion (and a warning) about the use of these real gross domestic product numbers.

Series Ca135 and Ca142. Gross domestic product originating in nonfarm business in current dollars is calculated as a residual. Series Ca135 is equal to series Ca74 less series Ca136–139. The business sector consists of all entities that produce goods and services for sale at a price intended at least to approximate the costs of production; corporate and noncorporate private entities organized for profit; and certain other entities that are treated as business by the BEA. These "other entities" include mutual financial institutions, private noninsured pension funds, cooperatives, nonprofit organizations that primarily serve business, Federal Reserve banks, federally sponsored credit agencies, and government enterprises. Business production also includes the services of owner-occupied housing and of

buildings and equipment and software owned and used by nonprofit institutions that primarily serve individuals.

Series Ca136 and Ca143. The contribution of the farm business sector is estimated as the total value of output is, in principle, equal to the sum of purchases from nonfarm business. The resulting measure of output is, in principle, equal to the sum of income derived from farm production plus certain other charges, mainly indirect business taxes and depreciation.

Series Ca137 and Ca144. Private households may consist of families, individuals living alone, or groups of unrelated individuals. Gross product of households is measured by the compensation paid to domestic workers.

Series Ca138 and Ca145. Nonprofit institutions include those nonprofit institutions (designated by the Internal Revenue Service) that primarily serve individuals. Nonprofit institutions that primarily serve business are included in the business sector. Gross domestic product originating in this sector consists of compensation paid to the employees of these nonprofit institutions.

Series Ca139. The output of general government is defined as the production of all federal, state, and local government agencies except government enterprises. Government enterprises are government agencies that cover a substantial portion of their operating costs by selling goods and services to the public and that maintain their own separate accounts. Gross product of general government is measured as the sum of the compensation of the employees of these agencies plus general government consumption of fixed capital.

Series Ca148. Calculated by subtracting the real series at the finest level of detail (as shown in the source) from series Ca84.

TABLE Ca149–158   Implicit price deflators for gross domestic product and major components: 1929–2002
Contributed by Richard Sutch

					Government consumption expenditures and gross investment				
							Federal		
Year	Gross domestic product	Personal consumption expenditure	Gross private domestic investment	Exports of goods and services	Imports of goods and services	Total	Total	National defense	Nondefense	State and local
	Ca149	Ca150	Ca151	Ca152	Ca153	Ca154	Ca155	Ca156	Ca157	Ca158
	Index 1996 = 100	Index 1996 = 100	Index 1996 = 100	Index 1996 = 100	Index 1996 = 100	Index 1996 = 100	Index 1996 = 100	Index 1996 = 100	Index 1996 = 100	Index 1996 = 100
1929	12.62	12.38	17.60	16.60	12.00	8.54	8.97	9.20	8.92	6.57
1930	12.15	11.85	17.23	15.02	10.23	8.27	8.55	8.90	8.36	6.39
1931	10.88	10.57	15.12	11.82	8.27	7.85	8.50	8.76	8.39	6.00
1932	9.61	9.32	10.71	10.25	6.63	7.15	8.13	8.60	7.82	5.40
1933	9.36	8.99	9.97	10.26	6.35	7.38	8.29	8.39	8.26	5.59
1934	9.88	9.41	11.70	11.89	7.22	7.93	8.83	8.78	8.88	6.03
1935	10.07	9.63	11.47	12.17	7.33	7.96	8.83	9.10	8.75	6.07
1936	10.18	9.72	11.54	12.55	7.85	8.24	9.60	9.30	9.72	6.10
1937	10.61	10.07	12.99	13.30	8.76	8.38	9.71	9.60	9.78	6.24
1938	10.30	9.84	11.44	12.68	8.09	8.39	9.82	9.67	9.90	6.20
1939	10.19	9.75	11.74	12.45	8.49	8.20	9.53	9.66	9.52	6.09
1940	10.33	9.83	12.31	13.49	9.06	8.26	9.63	9.30	9.77	6.13
1941	11.03	10.43	13.38	14.75	9.57	8.78	10.15	9.93	10.04	6.53
1942	11.89	11.72	14.58	17.86	10.96	8.83	9.97	9.73	10.42	7.19
1943	12.53	12.80	14.50	19.56	11.80	8.96	10.05	9.80	10.48	7.69
1944	12.81	13.53	14.93	22.02	12.39	8.83	9.86	9.62	10.06	7.98
1945	13.17	14.07	15.72	21.88	12.74	8.95	9.98	9.71	11.02	8.24
1946	14.77	15.07	17.80	21.17	14.21	11.07	12.71	12.44	13.23	9.01
1947	16.35	16.62	20.73	24.61	17.02	11.87	13.33	13.30	12.78	10.10
1948	17.28	17.57	22.34	25.91	18.50	12.36	13.25	13.31	12.41	11.30
1949	17.26	17.44	22.44	24.34	17.63	12.74	13.86	13.80	13.32	11.39
1950	17.45	17.66	23.25	23.70	18.72	12.77	13.83	13.83	13.11	11.49
1951	18.71	18.85	25.80	26.78	22.63	13.66	14.50	14.47	13.87	12.68
1952	19.00	19.23	25.59	26.98	21.81	13.86	14.52	14.38	14.61	13.24
1953	19.25	19.50	25.54	26.90	20.88	14.03	14.65	14.48	14.98	13.51
1954	19.44	19.68	25.54	26.56	21.16	14.34	15.01	14.90	14.98	13.74
1955	19.78	19.76	26.34	26.81	21.05	14.96	15.86	15.77	15.62	14.00
1956	20.45	20.16	27.85	27.71	21.42	15.81	16.68	16.66	15.92	14.91
1957	21.13	20.77	28.48	28.76	21.66	16.50	17.41	17.41	16.53	15.56
1958	21.64	21.29	28.47	28.50	20.76	17.00	18.15	18.08	17.68	15.76
1959	21.88	21.63	28.78	28.53	20.95	17.00	17.88	17.77	17.71	16.11
1960	22.19	22.00	28.92	28.88	21.15	17.21	18.01	17.87	17.97	16.41
1961	22.44	22.23	28.84	29.29	21.15	17.53	18.28	18.09	18.55	16.79
1962	22.74	22.49	28.87	29.27	20.90	17.98	18.69	18.46	19.12	17.32
1963	23.00	22.75	28.79	29.22	21.30	18.41	19.15	18.91	19.59	17.70
1964	23.34	23.07	28.95	29.42	21.75	18.92	19.79	19.47	20.54	18.06
1965	23.78	23.41	29.41	30.38	22.06	19.43	20.32	20.03	20.93	18.56
1966	24.46	24.01	30.03	31.32	22.57	20.22	21.00	20.68	21.71	19.48
1967	25.21	24.62	30.83	32.56	22.66	21.07	21.64	21.33	22.30	20.56
1968	26.30	25.58	31.99	33.23	23.00	22.25	22.89	22.53	23.77	21.66
1969	27.59	26.74	33.50	34.29	23.60	23.58	24.12	23.74	24.98	23.11
1970	29.06	28.00	34.93	35.77	25.00	25.47	26.00	25.47	27.46	25.01
1971	30.52	29.20	36.68	36.98	26.53	27.47	28.27	27.73	29.68	26.79
1972	31.82	30.22	38.23	38.18	28.40	29.52	30.88	30.66	31.29	28.37
1973	33.60	31.86	40.31	43.40	33.34	31.70	33.04	32.95	33.08	30.56
1974	36.62	35.13	44.40	53.68	47.70	34.86	35.87	35.85	35.67	33.93
1975	40.03	38.01	49.81	59.24	51.67	38.31	39.48	39.27	39.73	37.26
1976	42.30	40.08	52.56	61.11	53.22	40.76	42.17	42.08	42.09	39.53
1977	45.02	42.73	56.51	63.58	57.92	43.59	45.43	45.23	45.61	42.05
1978	48.23	45.78	61.15	67.48	62.01	46.39	48.24	48.33	47.72	44.83
1979	52.25	49.83	66.72	75.63	72.62	50.29	51.95	52.20	51.06	48.84
1980	57.04	55.21	72.92	83.32	90.45	55.80	57.45	57.95	55.99	54.32
1981	62.37	60.08	79.77	89.41	95.32	61.30	63.05	63.70	61.21	59.71
1982	66.25	63.48	83.88	89.83	92.10	65.43	67.53	68.44	65.07	63.57
1983	68.88	66.19	83.74	90.24	88.65	68.08	69.96	70.87	67.50	66.39
1984	71.44	68.63	84.40	91.13	87.88	71.60	74.13	75.95	69.22	69.36

(continued)

TABLE Ca149–158   Implicit price deflators for gross domestic product and major components: 1929–2002
Continued

						Government consumption expenditures and gross investment				
							Federal			
Year	Gross domestic product	Personal consumption expenditure	Gross private domestic investment	Exports of goods and services	Imports of goods and services	Total	Total	National defense	Nondefense	State and local
	Ca149	Ca150	Ca151	Ca152	Ca153	Ca154	Ca155	Ca156	Ca157	Ca158
	Index 1996 = 100	Index 1996 = 100	Index 1996 = 100	Index 1996 = 100	Index 1996 = 100	Index 1996 = 100	Index 1996 = 100	Index 1996 = 100	Index 1996 = 100	Index 1996 = 100
1985	73.69	70.99	85.29	88.70	85.02	73.77	75.66	77.23	71.44	72.07
1986	75.31	72.72	87.12	87.33	85.01	75.07	76.10	77.27	73.06	74.10
1987	77.58	75.49	88.88	89.62	90.02	77.21	77.03	78.00	74.58	77.26
1988	80.21	78.43	90.95	94.39	94.46	79.31	78.83	79.65	76.85	79.60
1989	83.27	81.86	93.21	96.15	96.87	81.89	81.14	81.93	79.27	82.41
1990	86.51	85.63	94.98	96.79	99.43	85.16	83.79	84.57	81.95	86.16
1991	89.66	88.91	96.47	98.10	98.93	88.04	87.18	87.70	86.07	88.64
1992	91.84	91.62	96.31	97.82	99.09	90.11	89.82	90.75	87.71	90.28
1993	94.05	93.81	97.67	97.82	98.18	92.44	92.18	92.45	91.58	92.59
1994	96.01	95.70	99.11	98.94	99.12	94.84	94.51	94.49	94.55	95.04
1995	98.10	97.90	100.28	101.28	101.83	97.56	97.21	96.88	97.90	97.77
1996	100.00	100.00	100.00	100.00	100.00	100.00	100.00	100.00	100.00	100.00
1997	101.95	101.94	99.80	98.47	96.44	102.23	101.63	101.41	102.06	102.58
1998	103.20	103.03	98.77	96.26	91.27	103.72	102.63	102.22	103.41	104.34
1999	104.69	104.73	98.57	95.47	91.33	106.52	105.08	104.44	106.29	107.33
2000	106.89	107.39	99.58	96.83	95.49	110.64	108.23	107.53	109.55	111.98
2001	109.42	109.56	100.73	96.10	92.70	113.27	110.09	109.27	111.63	115.01
2002	110.66	111.07	100.23	95.85	92.97	115.19	113.12	111.86	115.45	116.33

Source

U.S. Bureau of Economic Analysis Internet site, Table 7.1, downloaded August 17, 2003.

Documentation

Implicit price deflators shown here are index numbers with 1996 = 100. They are calculated as the ratio of current to chained-dollar output multiplied by 100. Definitions of gross domestic product and its components are given in Table Ca74–90. See the essay on national income and product in this chapter for a discussion of price indexes.

TABLE Ca159–168   Chain-type quantity indexes for gross domestic product and major components: 1929–2002
Continued

	Gross domestic product	Personal consumption expenditure	Gross private domestic investment	Exports of goods and services	Imports of goods and services	Government consumption expenditures and gross investment				
						Total	Federal			State and local
							Total	Defense	Nondefense	
	Ca159	Ca160	Ca161	Ca162	Ca163	Ca164	Ca165	Ca166	Ca167	Ca168
Year	Index 1996 = 100	Index 1996 = 100	Index 1996 = 100	Index 1996 = 100	Index 1996 = 100	Index 1996 = 100	Index 1996 = 100	Index 1996 = 100	Index 1996 = 100	Index 1996 = 100
1929	10.52	11.95	7.54	4.10	4.81	7.75	3.55	2.78	4.99	13.18
1930	9.62	11.31	5.03	3.39	4.18	8.53	3.94	2.98	5.78	14.50
1931	9.01	10.97	3.16	2.82	3.65	8.90	4.08	3.00	6.18	15.15
1932	7.83	9.99	0.95	2.21	3.03	8.61	4.16	3.01	6.40	14.46
1933	7.72	9.76	1.41	2.22	3.15	8.30	5.11	2.91	9.55	12.96
1934	8.55	10.44	2.54	2.46	3.22	9.35	6.88	2.59	15.61	13.62
1935	9.32	11.09	4.70	2.60	4.22	9.63	7.03	3.15	14.90	14.08
1936	10.53	12.21	6.03	2.73	4.17	11.18	10.72	3.75	24.90	14.02
1937	11.08	12.67	7.53	3.44	4.70	10.77	9.74	3.77	21.88	14.07
1938	10.70	12.46	4.98	3.41	3.65	11.58	10.74	3.93	24.59	14.87
1939	11.56	13.16	6.40	3.60	3.83	12.64	11.57	4.30	26.35	16.37
1940	12.55	13.84	8.92	4.08	3.93	12.83	12.51	7.44	23.08	15.88
1941	14.70	14.83	10.90	4.19	4.83	21.31	33.22	40.37	20.58	14.91
1942	17.41	14.48	5.76	2.75	4.38	50.01	102.01	147.30	16.09	13.59
1943	20.27	14.88	3.40	2.30	5.53	74.54	161.79	240.74	12.27	12.40
1944	21.94	15.31	4.20	2.47	5.78	84.08	185.15	275.58	13.86	11.97
1945	21.67	16.26	5.55	3.49	6.15	73.21	158.67	236.74	10.83	12.29
1946	19.27	18.27	14.08	7.61	5.10	25.29	42.88	57.01	15.78	13.52
1947	19.14	18.64	13.57	8.69	4.84	21.60	31.88	38.40	19.47	15.41
1948	19.97	19.06	17.33	6.84	5.65	23.13	34.30	38.60	26.82	16.39
1949	19.85	19.58	13.22	6.78	5.45	25.83	37.49	40.33	33.34	18.88
1950	21.59	20.83	18.71	5.93	6.44	25.84	35.34	39.65	28.00	20.45
1951	23.23	21.14	18.77	7.27	6.69	35.16	58.41	76.03	23.80	20.61
1952	24.16	21.81	16.99	6.93	7.28	42.56	76.67	102.00	26.68	20.94
1953	25.26	22.86	17.78	6.47	7.97	45.54	82.70	108.29	32.24	21.97
1954	25.09	23.33	16.96	6.78	7.57	42.40	71.75	92.61	30.67	23.88
1955	26.87	25.02	21.09	7.50	8.49	40.82	65.10	83.51	28.88	25.63
1956	27.40	25.75	20.81	8.75	9.17	40.85	63.99	82.92	26.63	26.43
1957	27.95	26.38	19.91	9.51	9.56	42.67	66.27	86.44	26.38	27.98
1958	27.68	26.60	18.23	8.21	10.01	44.04	66.23	86.00	27.19	30.34
1959	29.68	28.08	21.96	8.28	11.07	46.52	70.91	88.19	37.04	31.42
1960	30.42	28.85	21.95	10.00	11.21	46.51	68.81	86.49	34.05	32.79
1961	31.13	29.43	21.81	10.17	11.14	48.75	71.46	90.02	34.98	34.81
1962	33.01	30.88	24.57	10.72	12.40	51.69	77.38	95.29	42.21	35.87
1963	34.43	32.15	26.21	11.52	12.74	52.91	77.16	92.88	46.30	38.04
1964	36.43	34.08	28.37	13.06	13.41	53.95	75.85	88.86	50.33	40.61
1965	38.76	36.23	32.35	13.33	14.84	55.64	76.00	87.28	53.82	43.34
1966	41.31	38.30	35.19	14.22	17.05	60.63	84.59	99.90	54.54	46.08
1967	42.34	39.45	33.57	14.53	18.29	65.20	92.84	112.64	53.98	48.37
1968	44.36	41.70	35.51	15.59	21.02	67.27	93.69	114.65	52.60	51.22
1969	45.71	43.24	37.58	16.44	22.21	66.99	90.57	109.24	53.92	52.71
1970	45.80	44.25	35.10	18.22	23.16	65.48	84.21	100.03	53.09	54.21
1971	47.33	45.92	39.09	18.35	24.40	64.26	78.24	89.85	55.19	55.96
1972	49.90	48.70	43.70	19.84	27.13	64.34	76.53	85.39	58.89	57.18
1973	52.78	51.09	48.81	24.19	28.39	63.87	72.77	79.86	58.70	58.84
1974	52.46	50.67	45.20	26.49	27.75	65.04	72.47	77.91	61.78	60.96
1975	52.28	51.76	37.20	26.32	24.66	66.28	72.47	76.96	63.71	62.99
1976	55.19	54.78	44.70	27.87	29.49	66.34	71.63	75.35	64.45	63.62
1977	57.75	57.13	51.45	28.57	32.70	67.00	72.89	75.92	67.14	63.90
1978	60.93	59.66	57.38	31.56	35.54	69.07	74.82	76.51	71.83	66.08
1979	62.87	61.16	59.18	34.59	36.13	70.40	76.63	78.69	72.89	67.12
1980	62.73	60.96	52.73	38.30	33.73	71.80	80.31	81.99	77.39	67.08
1981	64.26	61.79	57.59	38.74	34.61	72.44	84.08	86.98	78.60	65.75
1982	62.96	62.54	49.51	35.99	34.18	73.56	87.13	93.46	74.35	65.66
1983	65.69	65.95	54.22	35.11	38.49	76.02	92.61	99.79	78.03	66.24
1984	70.46	69.51	70.13	38.05	47.86	78.65	95.50	104.57	76.81	68.73

(continued)

TABLE Ca159–168   Chain-type quantity indexes for gross domestic product and major components: 1929–2002 *Continued*

Year	Gross domestic product Ca159 Index 1996 = 100	Personal consumption expenditure Ca160 Index 1996 = 100	Gross private domestic investment Ca161 Index 1996 = 100	Exports of goods and services Ca162 Index 1996 = 100	Imports of goods and services Ca163 Index 1996 = 100	Government consumption expenditures and gross investment Total Ca164 Index 1996 = 100	Federal Total Ca165 Index 1996 = 100	Federal Defense Ca166 Index 1996 = 100	Federal Nondefense Ca167 Index 1996 = 100	State and local Ca168 Index 1996 = 100
1985	73.17	72.95	69.48	39.08	50.95	83.72	102.79	113.32	80.97	72.44
1986	75.67	76.01	69.02	41.96	55.23	88.28	108.45	120.44	83.47	76.34
1987	78.24	78.54	70.76	46.67	58.58	90.89	112.45	126.10	83.93	78.13
1988	81.51	81.71	72.65	54.17	60.81	91.95	110.41	125.15	79.57	81.02
1989	84.37	83.89	75.36	60.56	63.21	94.48	111.88	124.18	86.22	84.18
1990	85.85	85.43	73.01	65.85	65.64	97.56	114.16	124.15	93.38	87.73
1991	85.45	85.28	66.75	70.15	65.31	98.69	113.80	122.80	95.10	89.73
1992	88.06	87.72	72.41	74.47	69.64	99.16	111.95	116.83	101.89	91.56
1993	90.39	90.67	78.69	76.95	75.98	98.37	107.60	110.57	101.55	92.88
1994	94.04	94.09	89.08	83.83	85.08	98.46	103.71	105.28	100.52	95.34
1995	96.55	96.91	91.79	92.45	92.05	98.91	100.92	101.37	100.02	97.71
1996	100.00	100.00	100.00	100.00	100.00	100.00	100.00	100.00	100.00	100.00
1997	104.43	103.56	112.12	112.27	113.67	102.35	99.62	97.40	104.15	103.98
1998	108.91	108.52	125.37	114.67	127.03	104.32	98.84	95.67	105.29	107.56
1999	113.39	113.88	133.62	118.55	140.88	108.34	101.16	97.71	108.15	112.59
2000	117.64	118.83	141.86	130.09	159.48	111.29	102.42	97.66	112.06	116.52
2001	117.94	121.76	126.71	123.10	154.91	115.36	107.33	102.51	117.10	120.11
2002	120.82	125.56	127.92	121.13	160.66	120.46	115.37	112.04	122.18	123.51

Source

U.S. Bureau of Economic Analysis Internet site, Table 7.1, downloaded August 17, 2003.

Documentation

Chain-type quantity indexes are calculated from weighted averages of the detailed output series used to prepare gross domestic product (GDP) and its components. Definitions of GDP and its components are given in Table Ca74–90. See the essay on national income and product in this chapter for a discussion and a description of how to use these indexes to calculate real estimates with a base of any chosen year.

NATIONAL PRODUCT BEFORE 1929

Paul W. Rhode and Richard Sutch

TABLE Ca169–183　Value of finished commodity output: 1869–1919

Contributed by Richard Sutch

	Total		Shaw: value of finished commodities destined for domestic use										Kuznets: value of finished commodities		
			Consumer goods								Producer durables				
			Current prices				1913 prices								
	Current prices	1913 prices	Total	Perishable	Semidurable	Durable	Total	Perishable	Semidurable	Durable	Current prices	1913 prices	Destined for domestic use	Balance of exports over imports	Domestic production
	Ca169	Ca170	Ca171	Ca172	Ca173	Ca174	Ca175	Ca176	Ca177	Ca178	Ca179	Ca180	Ca181	Ca182	Ca183
Year	Million dollars	Million 1913 dollars	Million dollars	Million dollars	Million dollars	Million dollars	Million 1913 dollars	Million 1913 dollars	Million 1913 dollars	Million 1913 dollars	Million dollars	Million 1913 dollars	Billion 1929 dollars	Billion 1929 dollars	Billion 1929 dollars
1869	2,813	1,947	2,522	1,594	665	263	1,769	1,129	420	220	291	178	3.77	−0.10	3.67
1870	—	—	—	—	—	—	—	—	—	—	—	—	3.76	−0.06	3.69
1871	—	—	—	—	—	—	—	—	—	—	—	—	3.81	−0.13	3.68
1872	—	—	—	—	—	—	—	—	—	—	—	—	4.87	−0.21	4.66
1873	—	—	—	—	—	—	—	—	—	—	—	—	5.08	−0.03	5.05
1874	—	—	—	—	—	—	—	—	—	—	—	—	5.09	0.01	5.10
1875	—	—	—	—	—	—	—	—	—	—	—	—	5.15	0.01	5.16
1876	—	—	—	—	—	—	—	—	—	—	—	—	5.49	0.22	5.70
1877	—	—	—	—	—	—	—	—	—	—	—	—	5.99	0.20	6.18
1878	—	—	—	—	—	—	—	—	—	—	—	—	6.38	0.47	6.85
1879	3,442	3,807	3,129	1,996	828	304	3,479	2,304	810	366	313	328	7.19	0.41	7.60
1880	—	—	—	—	—	—	—	—	—	—	—	—	8.45	0.28	8.73
1881	—	—	—	—	—	—	—	—	—	—	—	—	8.74	0.24	8.98
1882	—	—	—	—	—	—	—	—	—	—	—	—	9.43	0.02	9.45
1883	—	—	—	—	—	—	—	—	—	—	—	—	9.45	0.16	9.61
1884	—	—	—	—	—	—	—	—	—	—	—	—	9.66	0.19	9.85
1885	—	—	—	—	—	—	—	—	—	—	—	—	9.77	0.17	9.94
1886	—	—	—	—	—	—	—	—	—	—	—	—	10.40	0.08	10.50
1887	—	—	—	—	—	—	—	—	—	—	—	—	10.90	0.01	10.90
1888	—	—	—	—	—	—	—	—	—	—	—	—	10.70	−0.06	10.70
1889	5,080	5,700	4,538	2,906	1,133	499	5,084	3,291	1,185	609	543	615	11.10	0.09	11.20
1890	5,002	5,698	4,440	2,705	1,196	539	5,057	3,143	1,260	654	562	641	11.80	0.06	11.90
1891	5,284	6,164	4,719	2,965	1,197	557	5,466	3,497	1,292	678	566	697	12.40	0.24	12.70
1892	5,331	6,466	4,744	2,909	1,256	579	5,732	3,646	1,356	731	587	734	13.70	0.18	13.80
1893	5,500	6,539	4,935	3,314	1,124	496	5,818	3,912	1,243	663	565	721	13.20	0.18	13.30
1894	4,752	6,178	4,317	2,916	971	429	5,622	3,822	1,207	593	436	557	12.50	0.30	12.80
1895	5,227	7,028	4,731	3,119	1,115	498	6,341	4,158	1,446	737	496	687	14.00	0.05	14.10
1896	5,003	7,092	4,484	2,944	1,065	475	6,305	4,151	1,410	744	520	787	13.70	0.66	14.40
1897	5,376	7,456	4,883	3,223	1,154	507	6,807	4,476	1,528	803	493	649	14.60	0.73	15.40
1898	5,708	7,578	5,136	3,432	1,176	529	6,885	4,581	1,521	782	572	693	14.60	1.22	15.90
1899	6,586	8,530	5,830	3,821	1,374	634	7,672	5,069	1,698	905	757	859	16.10	0.87	17.00

(continued)

TABLE Ca169–183   Value of finished commodity output: 1869–1919   Continued

	Shaw: value of finished commodities destined for domestic use												Kuznets: value of finished commodities		
	Total		Consumer goods								Producer durables				
			Current prices				1913 prices								
	Current prices	1913 prices	Total	Perishable	Semidurable	Durable	Total	Perishable	Semidurable	Durable	Current prices	1913 prices	Destined for domestic use	Balance of exports over imports	Domestic production
	Ca169	Ca170	Ca171	Ca172	Ca173	Ca174	Ca175	Ca176	Ca177	Ca178	Ca179	Ca180	Ca181	Ca182	Ca183
Year	Million dollars	Million 1913 dollars	Million dollars	Million dollars	Million dollars	Million dollars	Million 1913 dollars	Million 1913 dollars	Million 1913 dollars	Million 1913 dollars	Million dollars	Million 1913 dollars	Billion 1929 dollars	Billion 1929 dollars	Billion 1929 dollars
1900	7,121	8,653	6,225	4,101	1,466	659	7,659	5,114	1,690	854	896	995	16.60	1.10	17.70
1901	7,782	9,622	6,868	4,621	1,528	719	8,594	5,802	1,865	926	914	1,028	18.50	1.01	19.50
1902	8,228	9,769	7,165	4,765	1,614	786	8,584	5,668	1,933	983	1,063	1,185	19.10	0.63	19.70
1903	8,702	10,345	7,573	5,013	1,735	826	9,035	6,021	2,016	998	1,129	1,310	20.00	0.78	20.80
1904	8,734	10,180	7,741	5,168	1,746	827	9,062	6,042	2,031	989	993	1,118	19.60	0.66	20.30
1905	9,451	10,763	8,284	5,404	1,925	955	9,462	6,216	2,128	1,118	1,167	1,301	20.80	0.71	21.50
1906	10,752	12,138	9,286	5,913	2,244	1,130	10,520	6,968	2,286	1,266	1,466	1,618	23.30	0.74	24.00
1907	11,524	12,339	9,941	6,453	2,310	1,178	10,647	7,190	2,251	1,206	1,583	1,691	23.90	0.73	24.60
1908	10,191	10,942	9,155	5,988	2,155	1,011	9,781	6,488	2,246	1,046	1,037	1,161	21.30	0.96	22.20
1909	11,825	12,265	10,582	6,922	2,447	1,213	10,947	7,141	2,465	1,341	1,243	1,318	23.60	0.36	24.00
1910	12,659	12,808	11,135	7,386	2,417	1,332	11,209	7,389	2,396	1,424	1,524	1,600	24.50	0.41	24.90
1911	12,749	13,181	11,402	7,491	2,571	1,339	11,822	7,785	2,639	1,398	1,348	1,359	24.80	0.82	25.60
1912	14,028	13,946	12,394	8,101	2,754	1,538	12,272	7,879	2,794	1,599	1,634	1,674	26.20	0.80	27.00
1913	14,633	14,633	12,805	8,230	2,900	1,675	12,805	8,230	2,900	1,675	1,827	1,827	27.50	0.94	28.50
1914	14,054	14,128	12,576	8,296	2,710	1,570	12,655	8,184	2,807	1,664	1,478	1,474	26.10	0.45	26.60
1915	13,986	13,883	12,416	8,080	2,636	1,700	12,408	7,793	2,732	1,883	1,570	1,475	25.30	2.44	27.70
1916	18,389	15,991	15,863	9,893	3,574	2,396	13,894	8,204	3,040	2,651	2,526	2,096	28.30	3.45	31.70
1917	24,546	16,531	20,764	13,174	4,791	2,799	13,932	8,179	2,976	2,777	3,782	2,600	28.20	2.66	30.90
1918	29,980	16,870	24,530	15,807	6,076	2,647	13,768	8,649	2,947	2,171	5,450	3,102	28.30	2.26	30.60
1919	33,265	17,571	27,907	17,215	6,770	3,921	14,674	8,612	3,188	2,875	5,358	2,896	29.30	2.76	32.00

Sources

William H. Shaw, *Value of Commodity Output since 1869* (National Bureau of Economic Research, 1947), Tables I.1 (4) and I.3 (7, 13, 24, and 38), pp. 34–5, 39–40, 51–2, 61–3, and 70–7.

Simon Kuznets assisted by Elizabeth Jenks, *Capital in the American Economy: Its Formation and Financing* (Princeton University Press, 1961), Table R-21 (1, 5, and 6), pp. 553–4.

Simon Kuznets, *Commodity Flow and Capital Formation*, volume 1 (National Bureau of Economic Research, 1938).

Simon Kuznets assisted by Lillian Epstein and Elizabeth Jenks, *National Product since 1869* (National Bureau of Economic Research, 1946).

Documentation

Final output consists of "finished" commodities that have reached the form in which ultimate recipients will purchase them – chiefly households in the case of consumers' goods, and business and public enterprises in the case of producers' goods. Thus, intermediate goods are not included (for example, flour purchased by a manufacturer of macaroni or bread). The amount "destined for domestic use" is derived as the sum of domestic production, minus exports, plus imports. The estimates presented here exclude transportation and distribution costs incurred after the production stage, and hence are not in terms of prices to final users; rather, the output is valued at producers' prices. Nor do the estimates precisely measure domestic consumption, for they make no allowance for inventory changes.

Shaw's estimates are derived from Census of Manufactures data, taken decennially 1869–1899 and quinquennially 1899–1919, supplemented by less complete data for nonmanufactured finished commodities and bridged for the intercensal years by (often rough) interpolations. The annual interpolations for the period 1889–1899 are judged by Shaw to be less reliable than those for 1899–1919, which are described as "fairly reliable." Data in this table may be joined with the data in the source to extend the series to 1939. The estimates for 1920–1939 were based on the work of Simon Kuznets (1938, pp. 136–8 and 348). They were revised by Shaw to make them more compatible with his data for 1869–1919 and to correct certain errors or difficulties with Kuznets's data. They are not reproduced here, however, because they have been supplanted by the more recent estimates of Lebergott (Tables Cd1–152), the Bureau of Economic Analysis (Table Cd153–263), and Olney (Table Cd411–423).

The data for series Ca170 and Ca175–178 are expressed in the prices of 1913. Owing to a lack of specific price indexes, not all commodity series were separately deflated in all years. Those that could not be independently deflated were adjusted by the average price index for the other commodities in the same commodity group. The deficiencies in some of the price indexes probably make the estimates in 1913 prices less accurate than the basic ones in current prices; however, Shaw believes the constant-price series prices are reliable enough to approximate changes in physical output. As the quality of most commodities improved during the period and at least some of their improvement is reflected in higher prices, it is likely that the rising trend in real domestic use is slightly understated.

TABLE Ca169–183   Value of finished commodity output: 1869–1919   *Continued*

Series Ca169. Equals the sum of series Ca171 and Ca179.

Series Ca170. Equals the sum of series Ca175 and Ca180.

Series Ca171. Equals the sum of series Ca172–174.

Series Ca172–174 and Ca176–178. Perishable commodities include those usually lasting less than six months; semidurable includes those usually lasting between six months and three years; and durable includes those usually lasting more than three years. For a detailed discussion of underlying sources and procedures, see the sources.

Series Ca172 and Ca176. Derived by summing separate series on food and kindred products; tobacco products, drugs, and toilet and household preparations; magazines, newspapers, stationery, and miscellaneous paper products; and fuel and lighting products.

Series Ca173 and Ca177. Derived by summing separate series on dry goods and notions; clothing and personal furnishings; shoes and other footwear; semidurable house furnishings; toys, games, and sporting goods; and tires and tubes.

Series Ca174 and Ca178. Derived by summing separate series on household furniture and durable house furnishings; heating, cooking, and household appliances; floor coverings; china and household utensils; musical instruments; jewelry, silverware, clocks, and watches; books; luggage; automobiles; motor vehicle accessories (other than tires and tubes); horse-drawn vehicles and accessories; motorcycles and bicycles; pleasure craft; ophthalmic products and artificial limbs; and monuments and tombstones.

Series Ca175. Equals the sum of series Ca176–178.

Series Ca179–180. Derived by summing separate series on industrial machinery and equipment; tractors; farm equipment; industrial and commercial electrical equipment; office and store machinery and equipment; office and store furniture and fixtures; locomotives and railroad cars; ships and boats; business motor vehicles; business horse-drawn vehicles; aircraft; professional and scientific equipment; carpenters' and mechanics' tools; and miscellaneous producer durable equipment.

Series Ca181–183. Kuznets began with Shaw's final output destined for domestic use in 1913 prices (series Ca170). He converted the series to 1929 prices, interpolated between 1869 and 1889 using a variety of indicators (Kuznets 1946). Rather than undoing Shaw's adjustments for net exports, Kuznets added his own estimates of the balance of exports over imports (series Ca182) to obtain his series on finished commodity output (series Ca183). In other words, series Ca183 equals the sum of series Ca181–182.

Series Ca182. Figures are calendar-year totals of monthly figures reported in various issues of U.S. Department of Commerce, *Monthly Survey of Foreign Commerce.*

TABLE Ca184–191   Gross national product and gross domestic product: 1869–1929   [Kuznets and Kendrick]
Contributed by Richard Sutch

	Kuznets: gross national product				Kendrick			
	Component Series, Variant I		Component Series, Variant III		Gross national product		Net factor income from abroad	Gross domestic product
	Current dollars	1929 dollars	Current dollars	1929 dollars	Current dollars	1929 dollars		
	Ca184	Ca185	Ca186	Ca187	Ca188	Ca189	Ca190	Ca191
Year	Million dollars	Million 1929 dollars	Million dollars	Million 1929 dollars	Million dollars	Million 1929 dollars	Million 1929 dollars	Million 1929 dollars
1869	6,206	7,855	6,282	8,053	—	—	—	—
1870	5,875	7,838	5,937	8,022	—	—	—	—
1871	6,158	7,935	6,220	8,108	—	—	—	—
1872	7,423	10,218	7,493	10,457	—	—	—	—
1873	7,553	10,635	7,639	10,903	—	—	—	—
1874	7,407	10,723	7,503	10,997	—	—	—	—
1875	7,310	10,977	7,404	11,252	—	—	—	—
1876	7,507	11,918	7,622	12,208	—	—	—	—
1877	7,865	12,974	7,989	13,290	—	—	—	—
1878	7,836	13,920	7,981	14,255	—	—	—	—
1879	8,375	15,573	8,532	15,937	—	—	—	—
1880	10,619	17,939	10,757	18,336	—	—	—	—
1881	10,495	18,155	10,649	18,573	—	—	—	—
1882	11,543	19,401	11,701	19,851	—	—	—	—
1883	11,353	19,469	11,519	19,925	—	—	—	—
1884	11,132	20,167	11,328	20,647	—	—	—	—
1885	10,544	20,393	10,745	20,886	—	—	—	—
1886	11,022	21,602	11,227	22,113	—	—	—	—
1887	11,470	22,282	11,682	22,812	—	—	—	—
1888	11,415	21,875	11,622	22,411	—	—	—	—
1889	11,944	22,750	12,150	23,284	12,485	24,391	−190	24,581
1890	12,560	24,514	12,759	25,042	13,129	26,196	−203	26,399
1891	12,918	25,632	13,134	26,200	13,530	27,365	−198	27,563
1892	13,649	28,194	13,871	28,783	14,273	30,010	−198	30,208
1893	13,172	26,701	13,402	27,306	13,849	28,569	−189	28,758
1894	11,904	25,758	12,154	26,351	12,619	27,756	−193	27,949
1895	13,202	29,091	13,480	29,744	13,928	31,082	−198	31,280
1896	12,519	28,416	12,814	29,104	13,295	30,444	−213	30,657
1897	13,804	31,124	14,119	31,855	14,617	33,327	−252	33,579
1898	14,418	31,488	14,740	32,255	15,388	34,068	−236	34,304
1899	16,381	34,578	16,738	35,443	17,356	37,172	−217	37,389

(continued)

TABLE Ca184–191   Gross national product and gross domestic product: 1869–1929   [Kuznets and Kendrick]
Continued

	Kuznets: gross national product				Kendrick			
	Component Series, Variant I		Component Series, Variant III		Gross national product		Net factor income from abroad	Gross domestic product
	Current dollars	1929 dollars	Current dollars	1929 dollars	Current dollars	1929 dollars		
	Ca184	Ca185	Ca186	Ca187	Ca188	Ca189	Ca190	Ca191
Year	Million dollars	Million 1929 dollars	Million dollars	Million 1929 dollars	Million dollars	Million 1929 dollars	Million 1929 dollars	Million 1929 dollars
1900	17,705	35,678	18,075	36,574	18,684	38,197	−200	38,397
1901	19,638	39,931	20,088	40,931	20,668	42,587	−179	42,766
1902	20,450	40,293	20,924	41,337	21,554	43,004	−157	43,161
1903	21,615	42,280	22,136	43,391	22,864	45,123	−141	45,264
1904	21,618	41,668	22,179	42,836	22,850	44,559	−137	44,696
1905	23,739	44,659	24,350	45,947	25,116	47,870	−130	48,000
1906	27,252	50,080	27,929	51,544	28,720	53,420	−114	53,534
1907	28,726	50,688	29,445	52,201	30,404	54,277	−116	54,393
1908	25,734	45,744	26,466	47,203	27,699	49,790	−126	49,916
1909	30,361	52,002	31,165	53,615	32,166	55,893	−110	56,003
1910	31,453	52,580	32,320	54,263	33,360	56,499	−107	56,606
1911	31,891	53,669	32,810	55,341	34,268	58,312	−128	58,440
1912	34,883	56,479	35,836	58,171	37,311	61,058	−120	61,178
1913	36,713	59,079	37,722	60,828	39,067	63,475	−118	63,593
1914	33,864	53,986	34,966	55,755	36,424	58,636	−88	58,724
1915	36,031	55,588	37,269	57,434	38,738	60,424	99	60,325
1916	47,250	64,298	48,576	66,356	49,768	68,870	180	68,690
1917	57,191	62,505	58,402	64,692	59,945	67,264	273	66,991
1918	65,580	61,432	66,660	63,640	76,176	73,361	328	73,033
1919	74,013	67,800	75,027	70,271	78,907	74,158	539	73,619
1920	85,340	68,525	86,815	71,383	88,856	73,313	382	72,931
1921	68,700	65,454	71,081	68,355	73,938	71,583	324	71,259
1922	69,536	70,379	71,825	73,150	73,990	75,788	572	75,216
1923	81,242	79,962	83,711	82,994	86,115	85,819	699	85,120
1924	81,814	81,589	84,954	85,222	87,561	88,361	620	87,741
1925	85,975	84,317	88,530	87,359	91,308	90,529	727	89,802
1926	92,006	89,821	95,021	93,438	97,694	96,405	735	95,670
1927	90,356	90,634	93,409	94,161	96,279	97,337	743	96,594
1928	92,235	91,852	95,537	95,715	98,164	98,503	802	97,701
1929	98,379	98,030	101,465	101,444	104,436	104,436	810	103,626

Sources

Simon Kuznets, "Annual Estimates, 1869–1953, T-Tables 1–15 (Technical tables underlying series in *Supplement to Summary Volume on Capital Formation and Financing*)" (National Bureau of Economic Research, circa 1961), Tables T-4 (3 and 6) and T-5 (3 and 6). For notes and less precise estimates, see Simon Kuznets assisted by Elizabeth Jenks, *Capital in the American Economy: Its Formation and Financing* (Princeton University Press, 1961), Tables R-25, R-26, R-1, and R-2.

John W. Kendrick assisted by Maude R. Pech, *Productivity Trends in the United States* (Princeton University Press, 1961), Table A-IIb (11), Table A-IIa (11), and pp. 291–5; Table A-III (4) and p. 248; and Table A-IIIb (5).

Documentation

Kuznets produced two variants of his Component Series for gross national product (GNP). These he labeled "Component Series, Variants I and III." Variants I and III differ in the way that services were estimated. Variant I estimates services as a residual by subtracting all of the other components of GNP from an independently measured estimate of national income. Variant III estimates services directly (Kuznets 1961, p. 472). Variant II was not estimated as an annual series for the years before 1919. The component series estimated each of ten components of GNP separately and then summed the components to arrive at the comprehensive total. Generally speaking, there exist fewer – and less reliable – data for the intercensal years, so a variety of interpolation techniques were used. For physical goods, Kuznets relied heavily on the commodity flow statistics compiled by Shaw (see the text for Table Ca169–183).

John Kendrick undertook adjustments to Kuznets's Variant III to bring Kuznets's series into conceptual and statistical alignment with the official estimates of GNP published by the U.S. Department of Commerce. These involved adopting the official treatment of government expenditure and adding an imputed series on the unpaid services provided by financial intermediaries (Kendrick 1961, pp. 238–46 and Table A-IIb, pp. 296–7). For a detailed discussion of how Kendrick made these adjustments, see Kendrick 1961, pp. 234–46 and Table A-II.

At the time Kuznets was writing, the Department of Commerce used the GNP concept. It was not until 1991 that the official series was shifted from GNP to gross domestic product (GDP). GDP is the market value of all final goods and services produced by labor and property *located in the United States*. GNP is the value of the goods and services produced with labor and property *supplied by U.S. residents*. The difference between GDP and GNP is net receipts of income from the rest of the world (U.S. Bureau of Economic Analysis, "Gross Domestic Product as a Measure of U.S. Production," *Survey of Current Business* 71 (August 1991): 8). Kendrick estimated net factor income from abroad and then derived a series for GDP: series Ca191 equals series Ca189 minus series Ca190.

TABLE Ca192–207 Gross national product: 1869–1909 [Gallman]

Contributed by Paul W. Rhode and Richard Sutch

Year	Total, including or excluding inventory changes		Gross national product (GNP)													Price deflator for GNP (excluding inventory change)
			Consumption							Capital formation						
				Consumer goods							Gross new construction					
	Including	Excluding	Total	Total	Perishable	Semidurable	Durable	Services	Total	Producers' durables	Total	Railroad	Other	Inventory changes	Changes in claims against foreigners	Index
	Ca192	Ca193	Ca194	Ca195	Ca196	Ca197	Ca198	Ca199	Ca200	Ca201	Ca202	Ca203	Ca204	Ca205	Ca206	Ca207
	Million 1860 dollars	Million 1860 dollars	Million 1860 dollars	Million 1860 dollars	Million 1860 dollars	Million 1860 dollars	Million 1860 dollars	Million 1860 dollars	Million 1860 dollars	Million 1860 dollars	Million 1860 dollars	Million 1860 dollars	Million 1860 dollars	Million 1860 dollars	Million 1860 dollars	1860 = 100
1869	—	5,347	4,193	3,184	2,166	669	349	1,009	1,154	360	930	158	772	—	−136	138.3
1870	—	5,324	4,125	3,167	2,103	734	330	958	1,199	375	936	202	734	—	−112	133.4
1871	5,465	5,353	4,226	3,251	2,095	831	325	975	1,239	375	895	232	663	112	−143	134.2
1872	6,709	6,317	4,809	3,750	2,449	876	425	1,059	1,900	537	1,165	208	957	392	−194	129.6
1873	6,632	6,464	4,941	3,829	2,577	810	442	1,112	1,691	564	1,043	128	915	168	−84	129.0
1874	6,322	6,341	5,087	3,892	2,697	806	389	1,195	1,235	431	907	69	838	−19	−84	127.8
1875	6,484	6,413	5,193	3,939	2,595	894	450	1,254	1,291	384	924	69	855	71	−88	120.2
1876	6,979	6,846	5,513	4,140	2,772	921	447	1,373	1,466	427	889	80	809	133	17	114.3
1877	7,555	7,250	5,946	4,497	2,991	1,020	486	1,449	1,609	441	860	77	783	305	3	110.2
1878	7,941	7,692	6,165	4,684	3,187	1,023	474	1,481	1,776	517	887	122	765	249	123	107.8
1879	8,813	8,464	6,814	5,176	3,456	1,170	550	1,638	1,999	583	982	197	785	349	85	104.4
1880	10,391	9,760	7,729	5,938	3,958	1,385	595	1,791	2,662	869	1,123	315	808	631	39	114.3
1881	10,181	10,144	7,609	5,868	3,891	1,304	673	1,741	2,572	1,052	1,462	407	1,055	37	21	112.5
1882	11,388	10,735	8,216	6,370	4,204	1,429	737	1,846	3,172	1,166	1,435	384	1,051	653	−82	114.4
1883	10,831	10,660	8,244	6,412	4,240	1,420	752	1,832	2,587	1,108	1,333	203	1,130	171	−25	112.4
1884	11,073	10,764	8,474	6,623	4,497	1,368	758	1,851	2,599	889	1,420	131	1,289	309	−19	107.6
1885	11,278	10,989	8,727	6,861	4,470	1,524	867	1,866	2,551	845	1,460	209	1,251	289	−43	100.3
1886	12,491	11,907	8,851	6,994	4,421	1,575	998	1,857	3,640	1,254	1,892	397	1,495	584	−90	97.0
1887	12,819	12,410	9,003	7,149	4,505	1,567	1,077	1,854	3,816	1,555	1,979	376	1,603	409	−127	96.6
1888	12,335	12,101	9,019	7,183	4,494	1,597	1,092	1,836	3,316	1,448	1,789	229	1,560	234	−155	98.0
1889	13,162	12,531	9,276	7,439	4,686	1,665	1,088	1,837	3,886	1,571	1,774	201	1,573	631	−90	97.9
1890	13,475	13,240	9,237	7,417	4,492	1,763	1,162	1,820	4,238	1,643	2,476	197	2,279	235	−116	97.2
1891	14,474	13,862	9,822	7,904	4,921	1,800	1,183	1,918	4,652	1,813	2,254	168	2,086	612	−27	95.3
1892	14,804	14,753	10,022	8,043	4,904	1,886	1,253	1,979	4,782	1,928	2,859	159	2,700	51	−56	92.4
1893	14,105	14,343	10,196	8,218	5,381	1,723	1,114	1,978	3,909	1,895	2,294	119	2,175	−238	−42	95.0
1894	13,231	13,528	9,832	7,907	5,248	1,671	988	1,925	3,399	1,474	2,220	79	2,141	−297	2	90.8
1895	15,707	14,971	10,950	8,805	5,626	1,973	1,206	2,145	4,757	1,844	2,319	77	2,242	736	−142	87.6
1896	15,237	15,101	10,862	8,708	5,608	1,913	1,187	2,154	4,375	2,162	1,977	94	1,883	136	100	84.3
1897	16,279	15,841	11,632	9,326	5,998	2,058	1,270	2,306	4,647	1,758	2,295	133	2,162	438	156	87.2
1898	16,467	16,225	11,759	9,411	6,137	2,044	1,230	2,348	4,708	1,832	2,191	194	1,997	242	443	90.6
1899	18,499	17,721	13,022	10,420	6,727	2,290	1,403	2,602	5,477	2,297	2,122	235	1,887	778	280	93.2
1900	18,756	18,592	13,080	10,398	6,762	2,301	1,335	2,682	5,676	2,696	2,404	268	2,136	164	412	97.7
1901	21,180	20,373	14,572	11,564	7,586	2,549	1,429	3,008	6,608	2,793	2,671	298	2,373	807	337	97.2
1902	21,171	20,856	14,590	11,503	7,337	2,643	1,523	3,087	6,581	3,190	2,926	305	2,621	315	150	99.9
1903	22,599	21,965	15,399	12,103	7,783	2,774	1,546	3,296	7,200	3,626	2,719	248	2,471	634	221	99.6
1904	21,260	21,396	15,507	12,113	7,791	2,801	1,521	3,394	5,753	3,083	2,658	215	2,443	−136	148	102.9

(continued)

TABLE Ca192–207   Gross national product: 1869–1909   [Gallman]   Continued

	Gross national product (GNP)															
Year	Total, including or excluding inventory changes		Consumption						Capital formation							Price deflator for GNP (excluding inventory change)
	Including	Excluding	Total	Consumer goods				Services	Total	Producers' durables	Gross new construction			Inventory changes	Changes in claims against foreigners	
				Total	Perishable	Semidurable	Durable				Total	Railroad	Other			
	Ca192	Ca193	Ca194	Ca195	Ca196	Ca197	Ca198	Ca199	Ca200	Ca201	Ca202	Ca203	Ca204	Ca205	Ca206	Ca207
	Million 1860 dollars	Million 1860 dollars	Million 1860 dollars	Million 1860 dollars	Million 1860 dollars	Million 1860 dollars	Million 1860 dollars	Million 1860 dollars	Million 1860 dollars	Million 1860 dollars	Million 1860 dollars	Million 1860 dollars	Million 1860 dollars	Million 1860 dollars	Million 1860 dollars	Index 1860 = 100
1905	23,655	22,908	16,313	12,688	8,013	2,941	1,734	3,625	7,342	3,637	2,805	262	2,543	747	153	104.5
1906	27,274	25,796	18,066	14,050	8,910	3,172	1,968	4,016	9,208	4,559	3,034	283	2,751	1,478	137	105.7
1907	26,350	26,345	18,334	14,169	9,155	3,128	1,886	4,165	8,016	4,810	3,097	220	2,877	5	104	110.4
1908	21,995	23,454	17,092	13,035	8,265	3,137	1,633	4,057	4,903	3,328	2,833	182	2,651	-1,459	201	114.0
1909	26,957	25,758	18,945	14,516	9,046	3,427	2,043	4,429	8,012	3,778	3,169	206	2,963	1,199	-134	114.2

Source

Paul W. Rhode, "Gallman's Annual Output Series for the United States, 1834–1909," National Bureau of Economic Research Working Paper 8860, April 2002: Tables 2 and 3.

Documentation

The data refer to calendar years and were constructed for determining long-term trends. These data are not constructed for analysis as annual series (see the essay on national income and product in this chapter). For data in current prices, see the source, Table 3. The totals reported here use Gallman's revised data on railroad construction made in 1996–1997 and Rhode's revised data on inventory change made in 2001 and thus do not duplicate the data published by Gallman before 1997.

For the most part, Gallman adjusted estimates made by Kuznets, working with Component Series, Variant I (see Table Ca184–191). Gallman made the following adjustments to the Kuznets series: (1) he substituted new estimates for firewood, animal products, and federal excise taxes for Shaw's series, thereby substantially raising estimated national product in 1869 and lowering growth rates over the 1870s and 1880s relative to the Kuznets series; (2) he incorporated new estimates of distribution costs based on Harold Barger, *Distribution's Place in the American Economy since 1869* (Princeton University Press, 1955); (3) he separated railroad construction from other building activity; and (4) he deflated the current-value gross national product (GNP) series by Dorothy Brady's detailed final price indexes, using an 1860 base. See Dorothy Brady, "Price Deflators for Final Product Estimates," in Dorothy S. Brady, editor, *Output, Employment, and Productivity in the United States after 1800*, Studies in Income and Wealth, volume 30 (Columbia University Press, 1966).

In addition to the source, the user interested in the details of the estimation procedure and the sources of the underlying data should consult Robert E. Gallman, "Gross National Product in the United States, 1834–1909," in Dorothy S. Brady, editor, *Output, Employment, and Productivity in the United States after 1800*, Studies in Income and Wealth, volume 30 (Columbia University Press, 1966).

Series Ca192. Equals the sum of series Ca193 and Ca205.

Series Ca193. Equals the sum of consumption and gross capital formation (except for inventory changes) – series Ca194, Ca201–202, and Ca206.

Series Ca194. Consumption is the sum of goods flowing to consumers and services, series Ca195 and Ca199.

Series Ca195. Equals the sum of series Ca196–198.

Series Ca196–198. Perishable goods are those usually lasting six months or less. Semidurable goods are those that usually last between six months and three years. Durable goods are those that usually last three or more years.

Series Ca199. Personal services include domestic servants, professional and educational services, and the like. A major component of services is rent, measuring the flow of services from dwellings (including imputed rents from owner-occupied housing).

Series Ca200. Capital formation, also known as gross domestic investment, is the sum of purchases of producer durables, gross new construction, inventory change, and changes in claims against foreigners – series Ca201–202 and Ca205–206.

Series Ca201. Producer durables include tools, machines, power machinery, and the like.

Series Ca203. The railroad construction figures presented here were revised for 1870–1909 by Gallman in 1996–1997 at the suggestion of Richard Sutch and using data supplied by Albert Fishlow. See the source for details. The figure for 1869 may not be consistent with those that follow.

Series Ca204. Other construction includes housing construction, farm building (including land clearing), construction of structures for manufacturing, capital used in navigation (including canals), transportation (vessels and rolling stock), fisheries, and public property (other than railroad mileage) such as roads, bridges, forts, harbors, public buildings, and churches.

Series Ca205. The figures for inventory change were constructed using Gallman's methods, as revised by Rhode.

Series Ca206. The changes in claims against foreigners represent net foreign investment by Americans. A negative number indicates an inflow of capital from abroad, which must be deducted to obtain the U.S. GNP.

Series Ca207. Gallman's implicit deflator for GNP is 100 multiplied by the ratio of GNP (excluding inventory change) in current prices (from Rhode 2002, Table 3) to GNP (excluding inventory change) in 1860 prices (from Rhode 2002, Table 2). The data for GNP included in this table as series Ca193 are different from the series taken from Rhode's Table 2, because the figures reported here use Gallman's revised railroad data rather than his original data. Neither Gallman nor Rhode have presented a corrected railroad series in current dollars.

TABLE Ca208–212   Gross national product: 1869–1929   [Standard series]

Contributed by Richard Sutch

Year	GNP Gallman-Kuznets	Kendrick adjustments	Adjustments for change in business inventories	GNP standard series	
				Standard series	Linked to BEA estimates
	Ca208	Ca209	Ca210	Ca211	Ca212
	Million 1929 dollars	Million 1929 dollars	Million 1929 dollars	Million 1929 dollars	Million 1929 dollars
1869	10,795	693	—	11,488	11,881
1870	10,748	696	—	11,445	11,837
1871	10,807	700	−106	11,402	11,792
1872	12,753	704	202	13,659	14,127
1873	13,050	707	−73	13,684	14,153
1874	12,802	711	−422	13,090	13,539
1875	12,947	714	−277	13,385	13,844
1876	13,821	718	−252	14,286	14,776
1877	14,637	722	21	15,379	15,906
1878	15,529	725	−86	16,168	16,722
1879	17,088	729	−27	17,789	18,399
1880	19,704	767	414	20,884	21,600
1881	20,478	804	−469	20,813	21,527
1882	21,672	842	662	23,176	23,971
1883	21,521	880	−99	22,302	23,067
1884	21,731	918	142	22,790	23,572
1885	22,184	956	156	23,296	24,095
1886	24,038	994	638	25,669	26,549
1887	25,053	1,031	362	26,446	27,353
1888	24,429	1,069	179	25,678	26,557
1889	25,298	1,107	891	27,296	28,232
1890	26,728	1,154	−5	27,878	28,833
1891	27,986	1,165	798	29,948	30,974
1892	29,785	1,227	−463	30,548	31,595
1893	28,957	1,263	−681	29,538	30,550
1894	27,311	1,405	−780	27,937	28,894
1895	30,224	1,338	698	32,260	33,365
1896	30,487	1,340	−79	31,748	32,836
1897	31,980	1,472	85	33,538	34,687
1898	32,756	1,813	−69	34,499	35,681
1899	35,776	1,729	454	37,959	39,260
1900	37,534	1,623	−392	38,765	40,093
1901	41,129	1,656	494	43,280	44,763
1902	42,105	1,667	4	43,776	45,276
1903	44,344	1,732	591	46,667	48,266
1904	43,196	1,723	−593	44,326	45,845
1905	46,248	1,923	691	48,862	50,537
1906	52,077	1,876	1,701	55,654	57,561
1907	53,186	2,076	−653	54,609	56,480
1908	47,349	2,587	−2,545	47,391	49,015
1909	52,002	2,278	1,026	55,306	57,201
1910	52,580	2,236	—	54,816	56,695
1911	53,669	2,971	—	56,640	58,581
1912	56,479	2,887	—	59,366	61,400
1913	59,079	2,647	—	61,726	63,841
1914	53,986	2,881	—	56,867	58,816
1915	55,588	2,990	—	58,578	60,585
1916	64,298	2,514	—	66,812	69,102
1917	62,505	2,572	—	65,077	67,307
1918	61,432	9,721	—	71,153	73,591
1919	67,800	3,887	—	71,687	74,144
1920	68,525	1,930	—	70,455	72,869
1921	65,454	3,228	—	68,682	71,036
1922	70,379	2,638	—	73,017	75,519
1923	79,962	2,825	—	82,787	85,624
1924	81,589	3,139	—	84,728	87,632
1925	84,317	3,170	—	87,487	90,485
1926	89,821	2,967	—	92,788	95,968
1927	90,634	3,176	—	93,810	97,025
1928	91,852	2,788	—	94,640	97,883
1929	98,030	2,992	—	101,022	104,484

(continued)

TABLE Ca208–212 Gross national product: 1869–1929 [Standard series] *Continued*

Sources

John W. Kendrick assisted by Maude R. Pech, *Productivity Trends in the United States* (Princeton University Press, 1961).

Simon Kuznets, "Annual Estimates, 1869–1953, T-Tables 1–15 (Technical tables underlying series in *Supplement to Summary Volume on Capital Formation and Financing*)" (National Bureau of Economic Research, circa 1961).

Paul W. Rhode, "Gallman's Annual Output Series for the United States, 1834–1909," National Bureau of Economic Research Working Paper 8860, April 2002.

Documentation

The "standard" series for real gross national product (GNP) was first formally defined by both Balke and Gordon (pp. 87–8) and Romer (pp. 17–18). See Nathan S. Balke and Robert J. Gordon, "The Estimation of Prewar Gross National Product: Methodology and New Evidence," *Journal of Political Economy* 97 (1989): 38–92; and Christina D. Romer, "The Prewar Business Cycle Reconsidered: New Estimates of Gross National Product, 1869–1908," *Journal of Political Economy* 97 (1989): 1–37.

Balke and Gordon named it the standard series because it, or a very close variant, had been widely accepted and used for about a quarter century following the work of Kuznets (Simon Kuznets assisted by Elizabeth Jenks, *Capital in the American Economy: Its Formation and Financing* (Princeton University Press, 1961)) and Kendrick (1961). Both Balke and Gordon and Romer use the standard series as a starting point for their own work. See the essay on national income and product in this chapter and the text for Table Ca213–218. Balke and Gordon and Romer, when defining the standard series, accept the modifications to Kuznets's Component Series, Variant I, proposed by Gallman (Robert E. Gallman, "Gross National Product in the United States, 1834–1909," in Dorothy S. Brady, editor, *Output, Employment, and Productivity in the United States after 1800*, Studies in Income and Wealth, volume 30 (Columbia University Press, 1966)) and make the adjustments proposed by Kendrick to bring the Gallman-Kuznets series into conceptual and statistical conformity with the official estimates of the Department of Commerce. The series is then adjusted to make a smooth link to the official series in 1929.

The standard series is real GNP expressed in constant dollars, presented here as 1929 dollars. There is no agreed-upon current-dollar version. The user may wish to convert the constant-dollar figures given here into current-dollar figures using one of the GNP deflator series given in Table Ca213–218. To do so, however, would depart from the tradition that has labeled the GNP given here as a "standard." Furthermore, such an ad hoc conversion, although perhaps a suitable approximation for some purposes, would not be strictly appropriate because the deflators given in Table Ca213–218 are intended to apply to alternative real GNP series.

Both Balke and Gordon and Romer report a complicated procedure to extract Gallman's annual estimates. The details differ but the results are similar. They apparently calculated Gallman's annual estimates for 1869–1909 by taking the data on net national product in 1929 dollars from Friedman and Schwartz (Milton Friedman and Anna J. Schwartz, *Monetary Trends in the United States and the United Kingdom: Their Relation to Income, Prices, and*

Interest Rates, 1867–1975 (University of Chicago Press, 1982), pp. 122–9) and adding in Kuznets's estimates of real capital consumption. Balke and Gordon obtained the capital consumption figures by unraveling Kuznets's five-year moving average of these numbers (Kuznets 1961, series R-8(6) and R-29(5)). Romer reports using the unpublished annual series from Kuznets's worksheets (Table T-8). For 1909–1928, Balke and Gordon substitute the Department of Commerce estimates published in 1986 for the Gallman estimates. These estimates were originally made by John Kendrick but they have been superceded by Kendrick (1961). However, Kendrick's estimates are based on Kuznets's Variant III, whereas Gallman's are based on Variant I.

Both Balke and Gordon and Romer then add the "Kendrick adjustments" to the Gallman estimates. The adjustments were obtained by subtracting the Kuznets Variant III estimates from the Kendrick estimates. For the period 1869–1888, both Balke and Gordon and Romer use a "linear interpolation" of the difference between the Kendrick and Kuznets decadal averages.

Because of the inconsistencies in the two procedures used to compute the standard series and the availability of the Rhode corrections and the Gallman revisions reported by Rhode, the annual Gallman series as revised by Rhode is reported here.

Series Ca208. For 1910–1929, equals series Ca185, which is Kuznets's Component Series, Variant I (includes inventory change). For 1869–1909, equals series Ca193 converted from 1860 prices to 1929 prices by linking with series Ca185 in 1909 (does not include inventory change).

Series Ca209. For 1889–1929, the Kendrick adjustments were derived by subtracting the Kuznets Variant III estimates from the Kendrick estimates – in other words, series Ca189 minus series Ca187. For 1869–1888, the difference is available only as decadal averages. We followed the interpolation procedure described by Romer (1989, footnote 11) and Balke and Gordon (1989, p. 88). As Romer notes, this "procedure is valid because Kendrick calculates the correction factors incorporated in the decadal averages largely by similar interpolation." The unusually high figure for 1918 is the result of the difference between Kuznets's treatment of government spending for the military during World War I and the Department of Commerce's treatment of military spending.

Series Ca210. For 1869–1909, series Ca208 excludes inventory change; however, Kendrick's series Ca189 includes Kuznets's series on net changes in inventories. Gallman has proposed a revised series for 1871–1909, which we deem superior. Thus, the inventory adjustment in series Ca210 is calculated as the revised Gallman series (see series Ca205) minus the Kuznets series (Kuznets circa 1961, Table T-13(2)).

Series Ca211. Equals the sum of series Ca208–210.

Series Ca212. Series Ca211 has the value of $101.022 billion in 1929, whereas the revised official estimate from the U.S. Bureau of Economic Analysis is now $104.484 billion, as reported in series Ca2 (both values in 1929 dollars). Series Ca212 inflates series Ca211 by the constant ratio of 104.484 divided by 101.022 to make a smooth join at 1929.

TABLE Ca213-218   Gross national product: 1869-1929   [Alternative estimates – Balke–Gordon and Romer]
Contributed by Richard Sutch

	Balke–Gordon			Romer		
	Gross national product			Gross national product		
	Constant dollars	Current dollars	Implicit GNP deflator	Constant dollars	Current dollars	Implicit GNP deflator
	Ca213	Ca214	Ca215	Ca216	Ca217	Ca218
Year	Billion 1982 dollars	Billion dollars	Index 1982 = 100	Billion 1982 dollars	Billion dollars	Index 1982 = 100
1869	78.2	8.21	10.49	75.609	7.745	10.244
1870	84.2	8.41	9.98	76.464	7.387	9.661
1871	88.1	8.69	9.86	76.952	7.517	9.769
1872	91.7	8.81	9.60	89.605	8.444	9.423
1873	96.3	9.17	9.51	94.863	8.849	9.329
1874	95.7	8.85	9.25	96.205	8.821	9.169
1875	100.7	8.92	8.85	97.684	8.738	8.945
1876	101.9	8.68	8.51	104.628	8.934	8.539
1877	105.2	8.82	8.38	110.797	9.093	8.207
1878	109.6	8.63	7.87	118.906	9.069	7.627
1879	123.1	9.41	7.64	127.675	9.420	7.378
1880	137.6	11.06	8.03	139.990	11.431	8.166
1881	142.5	11.39	7.99	143.580	11.483	7.998
1882	151.6	12.37	8.16	149.307	12.343	8.267
1883	155.3	12.24	7.88	152.097	12.382	8.141
1884	158.1	11.92	7.53	155.684	12.035	7.730
1885	159.3	11.71	7.35	157.789	11.455	7.260
1886	164.1	12.06	7.35	164.375	11.791	7.173
1887	171.5	12.61	7.35	169.453	12.269	7.240
1888	170.7	12.75	7.47	168.940	12.420	7.352
1889	181.3	13.57	7.48	175.030	12.955	7.402
1890	183.9	13.44	7.30	182.964	13.276	7.256
1891	189.9	13.86	7.30	191.757	13.742	7.166
1892	198.8	14.33	7.21	204.279	14.081	6.893
1893	198.7	14.37	7.23	202.616	14.257	7.036
1894	192.9	13.21	6.85	200.819	13.260	6.603
1895	215.5	14.53	6.74	215.668	14.046	6.513
1896	210.6	14.25	6.76	221.438	14.044	6.342
1897	227.8	15.18	6.66	233.655	14.914	6.383
1898	233.2	15.74	6.75	241.459	15.869	6.572
1899	260.3	17.85	6.86	254.728	17.319	6.799
1900	265.4	18.58	7.00	264.540	18.879	7.136
1901	297.9	20.97	7.04	284.908	20.187	7.086
1902	303.0	21.65	7.14	291.572	21.386	7.335
1903	311.7	22.85	7.33	306.239	22.724	7.420
1904	323.5	23.93	7.39	307.127	23.041	7.502
1905	353.2	26.12	7.40	323.162	24.807	7.676
1906	367.7	28.10	7.64	351.499	27.674	7.873
1907	362.0	28.88	7.98	361.920	29.701	8.206
1908	342.2	26.72	7.81	346.800	28.247	8.145
1909	382.1	29.88	7.82	368.872	31.066	8.422
1910	383.8	31.24	8.14	383.888	33.187	8.645
1911	396.0	32.16	8.12	391.858	33.712	8.603
1912	418.9	34.85	8.32	407.112	36.412	8.944
1913	435.4	36.56	8.40	424.492	38.242	9.009
1914	402.4	34.25	8.51	414.599	37.741	9.103
1915	417.3	36.36	8.71	443.048	41.655	9.402
1916	485.0	46.02	9.49	476.498	50.442	10.586
1917	484.9	55.10	11.36	473.896	61.896	13.061
1918	522.2	69.70	13.35	498.458	75.786	15.204
1919	507.1	77.22	15.23	503.873	78.503	15.580
1920	496.3	87.24	17.58	498.132	88.399	17.746
1921	478.8	73.27	15.30	486.377	73.560	15.124
1922	513.2	72.99	14.22	514.949	73.612	14.295
1923	585.0	85.62	14.63	583.105	85.676	14.693
1924	600.5	87.91	14.64	600.377	87.115	14.510
1925	614.1	91.49	14.90	615.108	90.839	14.768
1926	651.0	97.52	14.98	655.033	97.194	14.838
1927	654.6	96.34	14.72	661.365	95.785	14.483
1928	666.7	97.32	14.60	669.288	97.663	14.592
1929	709.6	103.90	14.64	709.600	103.900	14.640

(continued)

TABLE Ca213–218 Gross national product: 1869–1929 [Alternative estimates – Balke–Gordon and Romer]
Continued

Sources

Nathan S. Balke and Robert J. Gordon, "The Estimation of Prewar Gross National Product: Methodology and New Evidence," *Journal of Political Economy* 97 (1989): 38–92; data are from Table 10.

Christina D. Romer, "The Prewar Business Cycle Reconsidered: New Estimates of Gross National Product, 1869–1908," *Journal of Political Economy* 97 (1989): 1–37; data are from Table 2.

Documentation

Both Balke and Gordon and Romer begin with a standard series of gross national product (GNP) estimates based on the estimates of Kuznets, Kendrick, and Gallman (Simon Kuznets assisted by Elizabeth Jenks, *Capital in the American Economy: Its Formation and Financing* (Princeton University Press, 1961); John W. Kendrick assisted by Maude R. Pech, *Productivity Trends in the United States* (Princeton University Press, 1961); Robert E. Gallman, "Gross National Product in the United States, 1834–1909," in Dorothy S. Brady, editor, *Output, Employment, and Productivity in the United States after 1800*, Studies in Income and Wealth, volume 30 (Columbia University Press, 1966)). However, they describe slightly different procedures for deriving the standard series, both of which differ from those reported as series Ca212, although the differences are minor. See Table Ca208–212 for a description of the standard series. Both Balke and Gordon and Romer replace the annual estimates for 1869–1909 with regression estimates interpolated between several standard series benchmarks. They use the same benchmarks: 1873, 1884, 1891, 1900, and 1910 (see Balke and Gordon 1989, p. 56).

Regression techniques to smooth and backcast annual numbers were first used by Kuznets (Kuznets 1961, pp. 536–8). Romer made six changes to Kuznets's regression methodology. (1) She used linear regression where Kuznets used a nonlinear version. (2) In both cases, the regression was estimated on post-1908 data with the deviations of GNP from its trend as the dependent variable and deviations of commodity output from its trend as an independent variable. Romer differs from Kuznets by fitting her trends through "normal" years rather than "average" years. (3) Romer estimated her regression for the period 1909–1985, omitting 1929–1946. Kuznets fit his regression for the unbroken period 1909–1938. (4) Romer allowed the coefficient to trend downward over time. Kuznets's nonlinear relationship was estimated to be stable in time. (5) Romer used log differences from trend rather than ratio differences. (6) Romer explicitly estimated the parameter for first-order serial correlation simultaneously with the elasticity estimate. Romer's modifications produced a substantially greater damping effect than Kuznets's procedure did. This difference is produced primarily by her modifications 1, 3, and 6 (Balke and Gordon 1989, pp. 68–71).

Balke and Gordon's innovation was to introduce a multivariate regression procedure to estimate GNP. As in Romer's procedure, the dependent variable of the regression was the log differences of the standard series of real gross domestic product (GDP) from trend, and the estimates were linear in the log differences from trend. The three independent variables were Kuznets's estimates of real commodity output (like Romer, Balke and Gordon based this on Shaw) and two indexes, one that directly measured real output in trade and transportation and one that directly measured the real value of nonfarm buildings (William Howard Shaw, *Value of Commodity Output since 1869* (National Bureau of Economic Research, 1947)). Romer's method used only the commodity output series. All variables were measured as a percentage deviation from trend. The estimated regression parameters were then used to backcast GNP to 1869 using the data on all three independent variables. Balke and Gordon's indicator of output in the transportation and communications sector was an index developed by Edwin Frickey linked to indexes developed by Kendrick (Balke and Gordon 1989, p. 53; Edwin Frickey, *Production in the United States, 1860–1914* (Harvard University Press, 1947), p. 117; Kendrick 1961, pp. 541–2, 583–7). Balke and Gordon used Manuel Gottlieb's direct estimates of the value of nonfarm buildings as an indicator for construction (Balke and Gordon 1989, pp. 53–4; Manuel Gottlieb, "New Measures of Value of Nonfarm Building for the United States, Annually 1850–1939," *Review of Economics and Statistics* 47 (November 1965): 417).

Like Kuznets, but unlike Romer, the sample period for Balke and Gordon was 1909–1938. Unlike Romer, Balke and Gordon have constant coefficients, and they exclude a serial correlation coefficient. The Balke and Gordon estimates "are as volatile on average over the business cycle as the traditional . . . [standard] series" (Balke and Gordon 1989, p. 38).

Balke and Gordon also constructed new annual deflators based primarily on the consumer price indexes prepared by Ethel Hoover and Albert Rees, in contrast to Kuznets's deflator, which was based on wholesale price indexes (Balke and Gordon 1989, pp. 71–5; Ethel D. Hoover, "Retail Prices after 1850," in William N. Parker, editor, *Trends in the American Economy in the Nineteenth Century*, Studies in Income and Wealth, volume 24 (Princeton University Press, 1960); Albert Rees, *Real Wages in Manufacturing, 1890–1914* (Princeton University Press, 1961)). These estimates are distinctly less volatile than the traditional series.

Series Ca218. A typographical error in the source for 1929 has been corrected.

TABLE Ca219–232   Gross national product: 1834–1859   [Gallman]
Contributed by Paul W. Rhode

		Consumption						Capital formation (excluding inventory changes)						
			Consumer goods							Gross new construction				Changes in claims against foreigners
	Total	Total	Total	Perishable	Semidurable	Durable	Services	Total	Producer durables	Total	Railroad	Canal	Other	
	Ca219	Ca220	Ca221	Ca222	Ca223	Ca224	Ca225	Ca226	Ca227	Ca228	Ca229	Ca230	Ca231	Ca232
Census year	Million 1860 dollars	Million 1860 dollars	Million 1860 dollars	Million 1860 dollars	Million 1860 dollars	Million 1860 dollars	Million 1860 dollars	Million 1860 dollars	Million 1860 dollars	Million 1860 dollars	Million 1860 dollars	Million 1860 dollars	Million 1860 dollars	Million 1860 dollars
1834	1,402.9	1,322.9	903.9	753.6	124.8	25.5	419	80.0	32.0	81.5	9.3	5.5	66.7	−33.5
1835	1,377.7	1,308.5	882.5	703.3	148.5	30.7	426	69.2	33.7	97.2	11.2	5.1	80.9	−61.7
1836	1,370.7	1,263.4	831.4	688.7	113.9	28.8	432	107.3	31.7	96.5	13.9	7.5	75.1	−20.9
1837	1,487.0	1,328.9	888.9	754.6	99.9	34.4	440	158.1	33.3	129.8	16.1	12.3	101.4	−5.0
1838	1,492.8	1,355.1	906.1	718.5	150.9	36.7	449	137.7	33.9	150.7	16.9	15.6	118.2	−46.9
1839	1,622.6	1,422.2	965.2	826.3	107.8	31.1	457	200.4	27.1	140.1	15.1	16.9	108.1	33.2
1840	1,609.1	1,452.0	987.0	832.7	125.3	29.0	465	157.1	25.5	139.9	12.6	16.3	111.0	−8.3
1841	1,679.0	1,510.3	1,036.3	859.5	140.6	36.2	474	168.7	31.2	130.5	10.0	9.5	111.0	7.0
1842	1,679.8	1,507.1	1,023.1	894.1	89.0	40.0	484	172.7	32.4	113.5	6.5	2.7	104.3	26.8
1843	1,880.2	1,726.1	1,233.1	1,044.6	146.7	41.8	493	154.1	34.2	114.2	5.8	1.3	107.1	5.7
1844	1,974.1	1,780.0	1,278.0	1,008.7	217.4	51.9	502	194.1	44.4	145.5	7.2	1.9	136.4	4.2
1845	2,069.7	1,841.3	1,327.3	1,057.7	209.4	60.2	514	228.4	51.0	176.5	10.1	2.4	164.0	0.9
1846	2,135.7	1,840.3	1,309.3	1,022.1	218.8	68.4	531	295.4	59.9	208.5	16.9	4.2	187.4	27.0
1847	2,367.5	2,068.7	1,518.7	1,133.2	302.6	82.9	550	298.8	75.5	217.5	27.2	5.8	184.5	5.8
1848	2,395.9	2,103.2	1,533.2	1,144.7	298.2	90.3	570	292.7	68.6	215.3	33.4	4.8	177.1	8.8
1849	2,429.1	2,170.9	1,576.9	1,145.4	334.9	96.6	594	258.2	66.5	217.4	35.1	5.0	177.3	−25.7
1850	2,635.2	2,304.6	1,688.6	1,178.0	402.1	108.5	616	330.6	75.7	259.3	41.9	5.7	211.7	−4.4
1851	2,831.5	2,446.7	1,799.7	1,270.5	401.4	127.8	647	384.8	86.9	312.0	55.3	4.7	252.0	−14.1
1852	3,159.2	2,745.9	2,063.9	1,409.2	498.1	156.6	682	413.3	102.6	368.6	72.3	4.1	292.2	−57.9
1853	3,490.7	2,994.7	2,273.7	1,513.1	598.6	162.0	721	496.0	112.3	417.9	86.8	4.7	326.4	−34.2
1854	3,365.6	2,823.2	2,065.2	1,457.0	445.9	162.3	758	542.4	124.1	430.5	78.1	5.5	346.9	−12.2
1855	3,648.9	3,073.9	2,283.9	1,551.7	555.2	177.0	790	575.0	143.1	441.9	61.4	5.1	375.4	−10.0
1856	3,696.6	3,076.6	2,248.6	1,496.1	565.5	187.0	828	620.3	154.7	480.4	62.3	4.1	414.0	−14.8
1857	3,718.0	3,097.6	2,234.6	1,617.1	433.3	184.2	863	620.4	138.3	460.6	62.7	3.4	394.5	21.5
1858	3,982.8	3,481.4	2,589.4	1,824.5	567.4	197.5	892	501.4	124.1	403.0	54.4	2.5	346.1	−25.7
1859	4,099.9	3,567.8	2,648.8	1,825.9	622.5	200.4	919	532.1	133.1	391.8	44.3	1.6	345.9	7.2

Source

Paul W. Rhode, "Gallman's Annual Output Series for the United States, 1834–1909," National Bureau of Economic Research Working Paper 8860, April 2002, Table 1.

Documentation

The data refer to census years (that is, the census year 1839 refers to June 1, 1839, to May 31, 1840). They were originally constructed for determining long-term trends. These data are not constructed for analysis as annual series (see the essay on national income and product in this chapter). Gallman did not make annual estimates of gross national product (GNP) in current prices for the years 1839–1860 because the relevant price deflators were available only intermittently.

Gallman constructed his antebellum national product series by (1) taking his benchmark figures for commodity production (agriculture, mining, and manufacturing) for the years 1834, 1836, 1839, 1844, 1849, 1854, and 1859 (Robert Gallman, "Commodity Output, 1839–1899," in William N.

Parker, editor, *Trends in the American Economy in the Nineteenth Century*, Studies in Income and Wealth, volume 24 (Princeton University Press, 1960)); (2) adding estimates for the value of services based largely on capital stock series; and (3) interpolating the series in the intervening years using scattered annual data on numerous economic activities. The "major" benchmarks (1839, 1849, and 1859) were primarily based on materials from the U.S. census, whereas the "minor" benchmarks (1834, 1836, 1844, and 1854) used several state censuses. The benchmarks for commodity production relied primarily on the sectoral value-added data described in Gallman (1960). There were only small adjustments and shifts of commodity production between categories.

In addition to the source, the user interested in the details of the estimation procedure and the sources of the underlying data should consult Robert E. Gallman, "Gross National Product in the United States, 1834–1909," in Dorothy S. Brady, editor, *Output, Employment, and Productivity in the United States after 1800*, Studies in Income and Wealth, volume 30 (Columbia University Press, 1966).

(continued)

TABLE Ca219–232   Gross national product: 1834–1859   [Gallman]   *Continued*

Series Ca219. Equals the sum of series Ca220 and Ca226.

Series Ca220. Equals the sum of series Ca221 and Ca225.

Series Ca221–224. Perishable goods are those usually lasting six months or less. Semidurable goods are those that usually last between six months and three years. Durable goods are those that usually last three or more years. Series Ca221 equals the sum of series Ca222–224.

Series Ca225. Personal services include domestic servants, professional and educational services, and the like. A major component of services is rent, measuring the flow of services from dwellings (including imputed rents from owner-occupied housing).

Series Ca226. Capital formation, also known as gross domestic investment, is the sum of series Ca227–228 and Ca232.

Series Ca227. Producer durables include tools, machines, power machinery, and the like.

Series Ca228. Equals the sum of series Ca229–231.

Series Ca231. Other construction includes housing construction; farm building (including land clearing); construction of structures for manufacturing; capital used in navigation, transportation (vessels and rolling stock), and fisheries; and public property (other than railroad or canal property) such as roads, bridges, forts, harbors, public buildings, and churches.

Series Ca232. The changes in claims against foreigners represent net foreign investment by Americans. A negative number indicates an inflow of capital from abroad, which must be deducted to obtain the U.S. GNP.

TABLE Ca233–240   Gross national product: 1834–1859   [Slave-economy concept]

Contributed by Richard Sutch

Year	Slave consumption Ca233 Million 1860 dollars	Increase in the stock of slaves Ca234 Million 1860 dollars	Gross national product, slave-economy concept			Free population Ca238 Thousand	Per capita gross national product	
			Total Ca235 Million 1860 dollars	Consumption, excluding the consumption of slaves Ca236 Million 1860 dollars	Gross capital formation, including slaves Ca237 Million 1860 dollars		Gallman Ca239 1860 dollars	Slave-economy concept Ca240 1860 dollars
1834	64.4	36.7	1,375.2	1,258.5	116.7	12,316	96.73	111.66
1835	65.8	37.5	1,349.4	1,242.7	106.7	12,682	92.36	106.41
1836	67.3	38.4	1,341.8	1,196.1	145.7	13,056	89.35	102.77
1837	68.7	39.2	1,457.5	1,260.2	197.3	13,457	94.17	108.31
1838	70.2	40.0	1,462.6	1,284.9	177.7	13,841	92.01	105.68
1839	71.7	40.9	1,591.8	1,350.5	241.3	14,221	97.42	111.93
1840	73.3	49.6	1,585.5	1,378.7	206.7	14,633	93.99	108.35
1841	75.1	50.9	1,654.8	1,435.2	219.6	15,061	95.33	109.87
1842	77.1	52.2	1,655.0	1,430.0	224.9	15,507	92.68	106.72
1843	79.0	53.6	1,854.7	1,647.1	207.7	15,957	100.86	116.23
1844	81.1	54.9	1,948.0	1,698.9	249.0	16,404	103.05	118.75
1845	83.1	56.3	2,042.9	1,758.2	284.7	16,885	105.02	120.99
1846	85.3	57.8	2,108.2	1,755.0	353.2	17,417	105.14	121.04
1847	87.5	59.3	2,339.3	1,981.2	358.1	18,017	112.81	129.84
1848	89.7	60.8	2,367.0	2,013.5	353.5	18,660	110.38	126.85
1849	92.0	62.3	2,399.4	2,078.9	320.5	19,340	108.13	124.07
1850	94.4	52.9	2,593.8	2,210.2	383.5	20,057	113.29	129.32
1851	96.4	54.1	2,789.2	2,350.3	438.9	20,823	117.51	133.95
1852	98.4	55.2	3,116.0	2,647.5	468.5	21,657	126.37	143.88
1853	100.5	56.4	3,446.6	2,894.2	552.4	22,498	134.72	153.19
1854	102.6	57.6	3,320.5	2,720.6	600.0	23,371	125.32	142.08
1855	104.8	58.8	3,602.9	2,969.1	633.8	24,168	131.60	149.08
1856	107.0	60.1	3,649.9	2,969.6	680.4	24,862	129.73	146.81
1857	109.3	61.3	3,670.0	2,988.3	681.7	25,586	126.90	143.44
1858	111.6	62.6	3,933.8	3,369.8	564.0	26,277	132.46	149.71
1859	114.0	64.0	4,049.9	3,453.8	596.1	26,908	133.20	150.50

Sources

Roger Ransom and Richard Sutch, "Capitalists without Capital: The Burden of Slavery and the Impact of Emancipation," *Agricultural History* 62 (Summer 1988): 133–60.

Roger Ransom and Richard Sutch, "Who Pays for Slavery?" in Richard F. America, editor, *The Wealth of Races: The Present Value of Benefits from Past Injustices* (Greenwood, 1990), Appendix Tables A.1 and A.2, pp. 47–50.

Documentation

Gross national product (GNP) for a slave economy treats slaves as capital assets and consumption by slaves as an intermediate input into production. Gallman's definition of GNP for the period 1834–1859 treats slaves as final consumers and their consumption as final product. To adjust the Gallman estimates in Table Ca219–232, we subtract an estimate of slave consumption and add an estimate of the value of the increase in the stock of slaves. See Ransom and Sutch (1988, 1990). To calculate per capita GNP using the Gallman approach, his reported GNP is divided by the entire population including slaves. Under the slave-economy definition of GNP, the base population is the free population because under this concept slaves are inputs rather than final consumers.

Series Ca233. Slave consumption is calculated as the number of slaves (series Bb214) multiplied by $29.45, the value of the average consumption of slaves in 1860 prices (Ransom and Sutch 1990, Table A.1, pp. 47–8). This estimate of slave consumption is based on Ransom and Sutch's estimate of $28.95 in 1859 in current prices (Roger L. Ransom and Richard Sutch, *One Kind of Freedom: The Economic Consequences of Emancipation*, 1st edition (Cambridge University Press, 1977), 2nd edition (Cambridge University Press, 2001), Table A.5,

p. 211). This was converted to 1860 prices using prices of corn, salt pork, cloth and clothing, medical care, boots and shoes, and other commodities included in the slave consumption estimates.

Series Ca234. Increase in the value of the stock of slaves is the numerical increase in the slave population (series Bb214) multiplied by $778, the average price of a slave in 1860 (series Bb212). The price of slaves in 1860 was relatively high, and this may distort the data somewhat. Also note that this measure does not include capital gains on slaves. On the importance of capital gains on slaves and the need to distinguish these from other economic returns to slave ownership, see Richard Sutch, "The Profitability of Ante Bellum Slavery – Revisited," *Southern Economic Journal* 31 (April 1965): 365–77.

Series Ca235. GNP under the slave-economy concept is Gallman's estimate of GNP (series Ca219) minus slave consumption (series Ca233), plus the increase in the stock of slaves (series Ca234). It is also equal to the sum of series Ca236–237.

Series Ca236. Equals Gallman's estimate of consumption (series Ca220) minus the consumption of slaves (series Ca233).

Series Ca237. Equals Gallman's estimate of gross capital formation (series Ca226) plus the increase in the value of slave assets (series Ca234).

Series Ca238. The free population is the total population (series Aa9) minus the slave population (series Bb214).

Series Ca239. Equals series Ca219 divided by series Aa9.

Series Ca240. Equals series Ca235 divided by series Ca238.

CHAPTER Cb

Business Fluctuations and Cycles

Editor: Richard Sutch

ECONOMIC FLUCTUATIONS, RECESSIONS, AND DEPRESSIONS

Richard Sutch

If one takes the long view, the story of the American economy has been one of steady growth. The output of the economy has grown more rapidly than the population, thus raising the standard of living over time. The per capita output of the economy has grown at a rate of about 2 percent per year from at least the 1850s to the present day (Table Ca9–19). However, if one takes the short view – which is, after all, the view of most contemporaries – then the performance of the economy is decidedly mixed. The growth path of the American economy has been punctuated by recurrent episodes of absolute decline. Short periods when the economy is in decline are called recessions; if the decline is particularly severe and sustained, the term "depression" is used. Short periods during which an economy recovers from an episode of interrupted growth are called expansions. When used technically, the terms "recession" and "depression" refer only to the contraction phase of a downturn. However, it is also common to refer to the entire period during which the economy operates below its potential as a recession or a depression (see Figure Cb-A). For example, the "Great Depression of the 1930s" is a term historians apply to the entire period of decline, 1929–1933, and then the slow recovery lasting until 1940.

These fluctuations are a simultaneous movement of output and employment in many industries across nearly all sectors of the economy. In other words, they are a "macroeconomic" phenomenon.[1] A recession is more than an isolated setback in one or two industries or within a localized region. Simultaneous declines and expansions in many industries and regions can occur because the economy is a complex, highly interconnected network of businesses, consumers, and income earners. The misfortunes of one sector or group are quickly transmitted to other industries through these connections. When other industries respond in parallel, the downturn widens as it deepens in a self-reinforcing downward spiral. For example, if consumers as a group become cautious or feel nervous about their future economic situation, they may decide to cut back purchases of new automobiles. In the face of uncertainty, they decide that they can get along with the old car for another year. The resulting decline in new car sales leads to cutbacks in automobile production, which in turn means fewer orders by auto manufacturers for new tires and automobile radios. With the fall in new auto sales, there is a diminished need for truck drivers to transport new cars to dealers. When autoworkers and truck drivers are put out of work because of the decline in sales, they cut back on their consumption of many goods, thus transmitting the decline in demand even more broadly.

Precisely what forces precipitate the change from boom to bust or from bust to boom in American history is still a subject of unsettled debate. The issue has led to the creation of a vast literature. Historians have typically examined each episode as an isolated event and have placed the blame on a diverse set of disturbances, such as shocks to key industries, political upheavals, bad weather, financial panics, and, in the twentieth century, on mistakes or even deliberate mismanagement of the economy by political leaders. Economists, by contrast, have focused on the periodic recurrence of economic fluctuations and the broadly similar patterns of downturn and recovery, and typically have chosen to study the business cycle as a single analytic entity. It was once thought that the business cycle had a mathematical regularity and predictability that could be uncovered by systematic study. This view is no longer held widely. Instead, most economists view economic fluctuations as complex, varied, and unpredictable, with multiple causes and uncertain dynamics. Some economists view them as inherent in market-oriented economies and others consider them accidental departures from a position of "economic equilibrium." An excellent introduction to the topic with a good review of the history of thought on the subject is Zarnowitz (1992). David Glasner (1997) has edited a valuable general reference.

A classic study of the business cycle was undertaken by Arthur F. Burns and Wesley C. Mitchell (1946). They defined a cycle as beginning at a peak in business activity and consisting of a contraction to a trough followed by an expansion composed of a recovery to the previous peak and then a continued expansion toward the next peak. Table Cb1–4 reproduces the chronology of the Burns–Mitchell business cycles beginning with 1790 and running to 1855. The table dates the peaks and troughs by year and gives the length of each contraction and expansion. Table Cb5–8, using dating by

---

[1] The study of economic fluctuations, together with the study of economic growth, constitutes one of the two main branches of economics. Called "macroeconomics," this subdiscipline takes a systemic approach that looks at the economic system as a whole. Two standard introductions to macroeconomics are J. Bradford DeLong (2002) and Robert J. Gordon (2000).

Acknowledgments

Richard Sutch acknowledges the advice of Susan Carter, Robert J. Gordon, and Gavin Wright. Jeffrey A. Miron and Christina D. Romer made their data on industrial production available, and Daniel Feenberg provided advice and assistance in accessing the National Bureau of Economic Research Macro-history Database. Financial support was provided by the Center for Social and Economic Policy, University of California, Riverside.

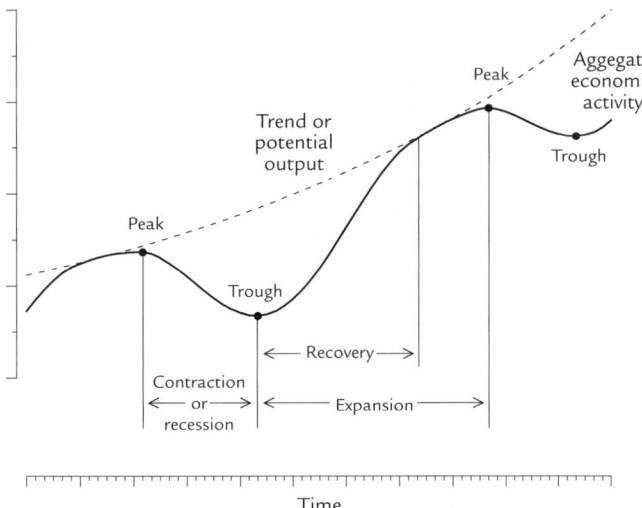

FIGURE Cb-A   Nomenclature of the business cycle

Documentation

This stylized picture of a business cycle graphs a measure of aggregate economic activity, such as real per capita gross domestic product or an index of industrial production, as a solid line. The level of potential output is assumed to grow exponentially along the dashed trend line. An exponential trend has the property that the annual percentage change in the series is a constant. The constant is the rate of growth. A peak in economic activity occurs when the measured series reaches a local maximum. Two such peaks are shown in the figure. A trough is reached when the series is at a local minimum. A contraction in economic activity, commonly called a recession, occurs as output or production falls from the peak to a trough. A recovery lasts from a trough until the economy returns to its long-run growth path. In general usage, an expansion is measured from trough to peak.

month rather than calendar year, extends the chronology up through March 2001.

Burns and Mitchell established the dates up through World War II using a rather complex procedure that required the contraction phase to be substantial in magnitude (depth), sufficiently sustained (duration), and broadly felt (diffusion). Since World War II, the National Bureau of Economic Research (NBER), a private not-for-profit research organization in Cambridge, Massachusetts, has maintained the generally accepted business cycle chronology. The NBER's Business Cycle Dating Committee does not use a mechanical empirical formula for dating the start or end of a recession. Instead, the committee members are asked to use their educated judgment in making these determinations (Hall 2002). Although the NBER is in the Burns and Mitchell tradition, the modern procedures are different and somewhat inconsistent with the procedures used to date the pre–World War II recessions. For a discussion and an alternative set of dates for the period 1887–1940, see Romer (1994). Defined by the Burns-Mitchell-NBER methodology, business cycles last more than one year.

This chapter differs from other chapters in *Historical Statistics of the United States* in two ways. Other chapters focus on presenting long time series of annual data to document trends and slowly evolving developments in American history (see, for example, Chapter Ca, on national income accounting). With few exceptions, the time series reported in the other chapters are not presented more frequently than with annual observations, although in many cases monthly or even daily data are available in the original source or in historical archives. Economic fluctuations that are

the subject of this chapter, however, are best studied using data that are recorded monthly or quarterly. Second, the other chapters of *Historical Statistics of the United States* set out to survey the entire quantitative historical record of the subject matter under review. This chapter cannot provide a comprehensive and exhaustive review and at the same time present time series on a monthly basis. This task would fill many volumes, not a single chapter. Here, our objective is different. This chapter is meant to help the user of *Historical Statistics of the United States* analyze the trends and long-term movements documented in the other chapters with a greater sensitivity to the disruptions in those trends caused by economic fluctuations.

Although the presentation of data here is sparse, there are several machine-readable data bases that provide access to a large volume of historical time-series data on economic fluctuations. A standard source, available on the Internet, is the NBER business cycle archive, which has good coverage of the period between World War I and World War II (and thus the Great Depression) (Feenberg, Miron, et al. 1967). A proprietary source for the period from 1947 to date is Standard and Poor's DRI BASIC Economics Database. There are only a few monthly time series with extensive track records for the period before World War I. One compilation of such data for the period 1860–1880 is Mitchell (1908). For the period 1879–1911, see Mitchell (1913). A review of available monthly time series for the period before World War II with a bibliography of sources can be found in Burns and Mitchell (1946).

Trend-Cycle Decomposition

In a stagnant economy with no population growth, it would be easy to observe fluctuations in aggregate economic activity as time series such as real gross domestic product (GDP) or total employment moved up and down. However, because the American economy has grown throughout its history, its economic fluctuations cycle about a rising trend. When the growth is strong and the fluctuations are weak, the trend may mask or distort the fluctuations. Thus, the study of fluctuations is intrinsically bound to the study of growth.

An illustration may help. Figure Cb-B presents a time plot of real GDP per capita using quarterly data for the period 1947–2003. GDP is a measure of the total annual economic output of the country. "Real" GDP is the national GDP adjusted to eliminate the impact of inflation on the figures. Real GDP is divided by the population to obtain real per capita GDP (series Cb11). This series is often taken as a measure of aggregate economic activity. As is clear from the graph (which uses a logarithmic scale), the series exhibits a long-term upward trend that is perturbed by periodic, but irregular, fluctuations. We wish to decompose the series into two components, its trend and the departures from the trend. Neither component is observed, so we must have additional information or impose restrictive assumptions before we can separate the two components. For example, if by a priori assumption or theorizing we can characterize the trend component sufficiently, we can extract the fluctuation component from the series by subtraction. Alternatively, if theory or assumption allows us to characterize the properties of economic fluctuations, then the trend component can be extracted by subtraction.

Burns and Mitchell (1946) conceived of the business cycle as a continuous sequence – a contraction followed by revival, which

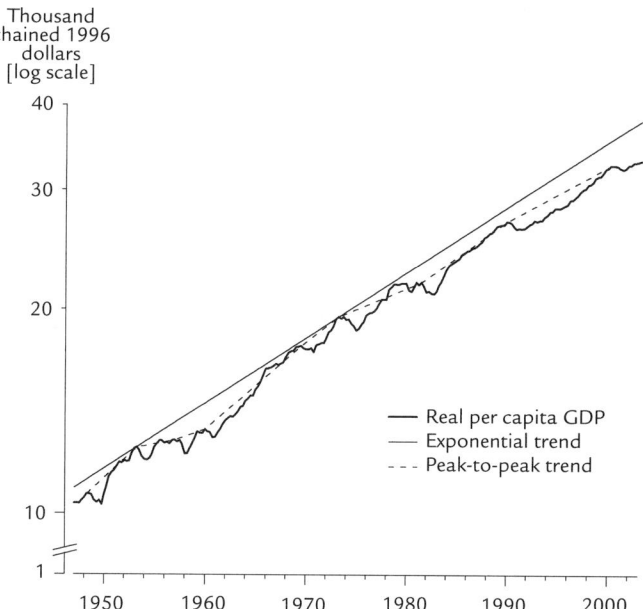

FIGURE Cb-B   Real per capita gross domestic product with trends: 1947–2003

Sources
Series Cb11–12 and Cb14.

would be followed by a resumed expansion, which would terminate with a new contraction. This conception defines the trend as a line of constant growth rate that moves from peak to peak of the series. Such a trend for real per capita GDP is provided in series Cb14 and is displayed in Figure Cb-B. Although the Burns–Mitchell approach to trend-cycle decomposition has an intuitive appeal, it is subject to two objections. First, the method proposed for dating the peaks of the series is both arbitrary and vague: the peaks had to be more than a year apart, and the resulting cycle could not be divisible into "shorter cycles of similar character" (Burns and Mitchell 1946, pp. 5–8). Second, in principle there is no reason why a cyclical peak in a given series should represent a point on the long-run trend. Indeed, several recessions, including the Great Depression of the 1930s, exhibit a W-shape. In such recessions, economic activity fell, began to revive, but then fell again before a full recovery was reached.

To avoid these difficulties, macroeconomists in the 1950s and 1960s adopted the simplifying assumption that aggregate economic activity would grow at a constant exponential rate for long periods spanning multiple business cycles. To implement this assumption, one needs to choose only two points through which the trend passes and calculate the rate of growth between them. Series Cb12, also graphed in Figure Cb-B, is a simple exponential trend for real per capita GDP calculated in this manner for the period 1947:1 to 2003:2. The line passes through the observations of real per capita GDP for 1953:1 and 1973:2. The two dates were chosen so that all of the actual data lie below the trend line. All departures from the trend (series Cb13) could be said to measure how far actual economic performance is below a ceiling defined by the trend. Throughout the entire time span shown, the trend grows at a constant rate of 2.24 percent per year.

As an alternative to selecting two points, the rate of exponential growth may be calculated as one element in an econometric time-series analysis of the macroeconomy. With this approach, output would be modeled as a function of several economic variables and a time trend or, equivalently, the change in output would be modeled as a function of economic variables and a constant. Typically, such models are estimated by linear or logarithmic regression, and the trend is thus estimated in such a way as to minimize the sum of the squared deviations from the trend. With this methodology, deviations are balanced between positive and negative departures from the trend. A pioneering study in this tradition is by Lawrence R. Klein (1950, Chapter 3, model III).

The exponential approach implemented either by the point-to-point method or by regression analysis was soon found to be unsatisfactory. The deviations from the trend did not correspond well with other measures of poor economic performance, such as the unemployment rate. For example, series Cb13 implies that the entire period from 1953 through 1969 was of suboptimal performance, but many macroeconomists would argue that 1957, late 1959 to early 1960, and the period 1965–1969 represented reasonably satisfactory, if not optimal, aggregate economic activity. Extrapolating the trend beyond 1973 produces a widening divergence, suggesting that the trend rate of growth may have been lower in the 1980s and 1990s than during the twenty years prior to 1973.

In principle there is no reason why a trend could not change its rate of growth. Economists' notions of the causes of economic growth make reference to the stock of productive capital relative to the labor force, the training and education of the labor force, and the progress of science and technology. These underlying determinants of growth may change at different speeds or even move in different directions at various times in the economy's history, causing potential output or trend output to grow more or less rapidly as a consequence. For example, in Figure Cb-B it would appear that the rate of growth of real per capita GDP in the 1960s was substantially higher than the rate of growth in either the 1950s or the 1970s.

Unfortunately, the sources of economic growth are difficult if not impossible to measure accurately. Technological progress in particular has never been adequately quantified (Gordon 1999, Abramovitz and David 2000; see also Denison 1962 and 1969, Jorgenson and Griliches 1967). Thus, some researchers specified a variable trend and sought to estimate it by statistical inspection of data on aggregate economic activity (for a review, see Stock and Watson 1988).

This approach soon uncovered a major problem. There was no way to know in advance – or to estimate statistically – how variable the trend may be. One economist's "trend" could be another's "cycle." The smoother the trend component is assumed to be, the larger will be the estimated fluctuations. The more irregularity in the trend, the smaller will be the amplitude of fluctuations. In the extreme case, one can imagine that *all* movements in economic time series represent variations in the trend rate of growth and that there is no business cycle at all. Such a view, however, would be contradicted by economic history. We have ample evidence that recessions in economic activity are coincident with human suffering in the face of unutilized or underutilized resources. They are associated with widespread unemployment, excess productive capacity, high rates of business and bank failures, and falling real income to a degree that seems unrelated to probable changes in capital, education, or technology. As the study of business cycles is motivated in no small part by the desire to mitigate these economic failures, assuming a highly variable growth trend that defines away the cycle has little appeal. The problem is further exacerbated if we imagine, as seems innocent enough, that our observations of economic data contain a random element, either because of measurement error or simply because human behavior has a random component. Beveridge and Nelson (1981) and Nelson and Plosser (1982) argue that many macroeconomic variables have time series properties that make them appear indistinguishable from a randomly variable trend (described in the literature as a "random walk with drift" or a "stochastic trend"). If this is true, a mechanical econometric solution to separating a variable trend from the cycle that relies on no data other than the series under study is not possible. Thus, new evidence needs to be brought to the problem (see Craine 1997).

On the other hand, moving in the opposite direction, assuming very little variability in the rate of growth would make all of the series' idiosyncrasies (and measurement errors) part of the deviations, thus confounding the study of the business cycle. This view, too, has little appeal. Moreover, detrending a series in this fashion can create spurious cycles. A famous study by Simon Kuznets (1958) postulated a cycle of approximately twenty years. To reveal the twenty-year cycle, Kuznets first used a five-year moving average to remove the business cycle and then an eleven-year differing operation to remove the trend. G. S. Fishman (1969) demonstrated that this technique was capable of creating a cycle of 20.3 years.

One alternative approach to the problem of separating trend from cycle is to make assumptions not about the trend but about the nature of the transitory component of a series. For example, if we believe that movements in the unemployment rate, business failure rate, level of consumer confidence, or other macroeconomic variables trace out (or define) the business cycle, we can then use data on these movements to estimate the cyclical component of aggregate economic activity. The best-known advocate of this approach was Arthur M. Okun (1962). Okun pointed out the close negative correlation between the rate of growth of real gross national product $(100\,(\Delta Y/Y_{t-1}))$ and the change in the rate of unemployment (U):

$$100\,(\Delta Y/Y_{t-1}) = a - b\,(U_t - U_{t-1})$$

Although the exact quantitative form of this relationship has changed somewhat over the last forty years, it has remained remarkably stable.

In his original research, Okun found that a one-percentage-point decline in the unemployment rate was associated with an increase of three percentage points in the rate of growth. Subsequent research has recalibrated the estimates of the parameters a and b, using GDP (rather than gross national product) and a much longer period of observation, to state that a one-point change in the unemployment rate is associated with an additional output growth of 2 percent ($b = 2.0$) (Altig, Fitzgerald, and Rupert 1997, Gordon 2000, pp. 55–6). Although only a handy rule of thumb, this two-for-one relationship between output growth and the unemployment rate has come to be known as Okun's law.

The parameter a in the equation can be interpreted as the rate of growth when unemployment remains stable. Okun called this the "potential rate of growth," which in his original research was a constant. Using annual data for 1960–2002 (series Ba485 and Ca84 updated to 2002), the potential rate of growth is estimated as 3.32. However, few economists would accept the notion that the potential rate of growth has been a constant over many decades. The 1970s are generally conceded to have witnessed a productivity slowdown. Moreover, the relationship between growth and unemployment is

thought to have shifted over time as demographic shifts and other developments have changed labor market dynamics. The primary demographic shift affecting this relationship was the move of the baby boom generation, born in the late 1940s and early 1950s, into the labor force. This caused the rate of unemployment at "full employment" to rise in the 1970s and then fall in the 1990s (Perry 1970; Easterlin 1987, pp. 114–27; Katz and Krueger 1999).

For these reasons, a modification of the Okun approach has gained favor. This brings another observed statistical relationship, the Phillips curve, to the problem of separating trend from fluctuations. The Phillips relationship is between the rate of inflation and unemployment. Named after A. W. H. Phillips, who first pointed out the statistical correlation (Phillips 1958), the relationship was made a central element of the analysis of economic fluctuations by Paul Samuelson and Robert Solow (1960), who explained that when unemployment was low and labor markets were tight, there would be upward pressure on inflation as bottlenecks appeared for goods in short supply relative to their brisk demand and as workers successfully competed for higher wages. This idea led to the concept of the nonaccelerating inflation rate of unemployment (NAIRU), which is the rate of unemployment at which there is neither an upward nor a downward pressure on the rate of inflation. Because this rate is unlikely to be a constant, most models postulate a time-varying NAIRU that is consistent with maintaining a stable rate of inflation, called the time-varying, nonaccelerating inflation rate of unemployment or TV-NAIRU (Gordon 1997, 1998). With this modification of Okun's method, the potential rate of output growth is defined as the rate of growth that holds the rate of unemployment equal to NAIRU.

Laurence Ball and N. Gregory Mankiw (2002) use the Phillips relationship to generate a time series that gives an estimate of NAIRU for each period. When the current rate of unemployment is more than this value of NAIRU, there is a downward pressure on inflation because the economy is operating below its full potential. When the actual rate is less than NAIRU, the tight labor market signals an imminent rise in the rate of inflation. Only when the rate is close to NAIRU is the economy close to operating at its noninflationary potential. Following this logic, whenever the value of the unemployment rate minus NAIRU (a measure of economic slack) changes from positive to negative or from negative to positive, we know that real GDP must be equal to its trend value. Once we have established the trend, the deviations from trend can be estimated by subtraction. Table Cb18–22 presents a decomposition of real per capita GDP using a simplified variation of the Okun–Phillips methodology.

It should be emphasized that the statistical relationships between output growth, unemployment, and inflation presumed in such calculations, although persistent and strong, are neither mechanical nor precisely measured. All kinds of other phenomena are capable of perturbing the interrelationships. In addition to the changes in the demographic features of the labor force, changes in labor productivity and in hours per worker and developments such as the rise of the temporary help industry, the greater emphasis on general skills rather than firm-specific skills (accelerated by the spread of computers), and the changing sectoral mix of output can have important consequences for both the trend in potential output and the fluctuations of actual output about this trend. Many investigators have sought to incorporate such secondary influences into the analysis to improve the estimates of NAIRU and Okun's law (see, for example, Weiner 1993; Staiger, Stock, and Watson

1997; Ball and Mankiw 2002). Although these investigators' estimates differ in detail, the broad picture obtained remains similar. One estimate of potential output that has special interest is the one prepared by the Congressional Budget Office (Arnold 2001). This series is reported in Table Cb23.

This discussion about trends and cycles may sound like a technical issue best left to experts, yet it is very important. The decomposition of an economic time series into trend and cycle can have important and far-reaching policy implications. The Employment Act of 1946 established the primary objective of macroeconomic policy to be the mitigation of the fluctuating component in aggregate economic output. Thus, the President and his Council of Economic Advisors must begin with some notion of which movements in economic variables constitute unhealthy fluctuations that would call forth compensatory policies and which movements are natural and unavoidable changes in the trend of potential output.

Selected Cyclical Indicators

The data on GDP are available on a quarterly basis, but not on a monthly basis. For this reason, several series of data that are available monthly are often used as "cyclical indicators" to track the performance of the economy on a month-to-month basis. The most natural cyclical indicator and the one most frequently used to measure the timing and depth of a recession is the unemployment rate. This measure is based on a survey of households conducted each month since the 1940s by the Bureau of the Census and analyzed by the Bureau of Labor Statistics. The unemployment rate measures the percentage of the civilian labor force that is not employed and is actively seeking work. The civilian labor force includes all individuals 16 years of age and older who are not institutionalized (in a prison, hospital, or a similar institution) or in military service, and who are either employed for pay or profit or unemployed. This concept excludes people without jobs who do not wish to work or who are not actively looking for work (see Chapter Ba, on labor, for further details). Table Cb24–27 presents the official unemployment rate on a monthly basis in both its original form and on a "seasonally adjusted" basis (series Cb25–26). The Bureau of Labor Statistics carries out the seasonal adjustment to remove the predictable seasonal fluctuations from the original data to help distinguish the movements in labor force utilization more clearly. The seasonally adjusted series is the "official" unemployment rate routinely cited in news accounts and political debate.

Table Cb24–27 also includes a measure of the unemployment rate for married men living with their wives. Unemployment among this group is consistently lower than the overall level of unemployment, and the series shows less erratic behavior. This is because single men, especially teenagers, and women experience higher rates of unemployment that seem to be more sensitive to economic fluctuations than the rate for married men is (see Chapter Ba, on labor, for further discussion). Because of its less volatile nature and the fact that it is less subject to shifts caused by demographic fluctuations, this series is sometimes preferred as a cyclical indicator.

Another widely cited cyclical indicator is the index of industrial production. The Federal Reserve System's Board of Governors has continuously calculated this series on a monthly basis since 1919. For this reason it is often called the FRB index. The index is a comprehensive indicator of industrial activity that measures the changes in the physical volume of manufacturing, mining, and

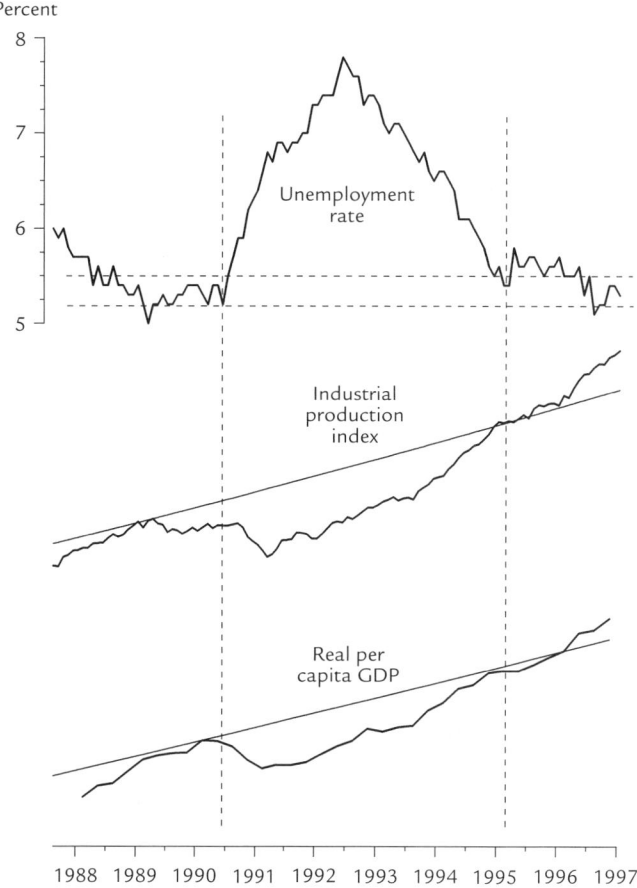

FIGURE Cb-C   The recession of 1990–1991

Sources

Series Cb11, Cb26, and Cb31.

Documentation

The graph shows the unemployment rate, the Federal Reserve Board's index of industrial production, and the level of real per capita gross domestic product (GDP) for the period July 1987 through December 1997. The unemployment rate is expressed as a percentage of the labor force (with a scale to the left). Both the index of industrial production and real per capita GDP are displayed as logarithms so that constant growth rates appear as a straight line. The annual rate of growth of the trend shown for industrial production is 2.09 percent. The annual rate of growth of the trend for real per capita GDP is 1.22 percent. It would appear that the rise in unemployment began sometime in 1990, although 1989 saw no growth in industrial production. The National Bureau of Economic Research dated the peak in July 1990. Recovery, judged by the return of the unemployment rate to the range of 5.2 to 5.5 percent, was in early 1995. It would appear that during the recession and recovery the trend rate of growth of real per capita GDP was only half that of the post–World War II long-term rate of growth of 2.24 percent, as measured by series Cb12.

electric and gas utilities. Output at all stages of production (including intermediate as well as final products) is included. It does not cover production on farms or in the construction industry, transportation, retail or wholesale trade, government, or other services. Since its introduction in the 1920s, it has been revised from time to time to take account of the growing complexity of the economy and to make use of an increasingly rich set of statistical indicators. Table Cb28–31 presents the FRB index on a monthly basis in both seasonally adjusted and unadjusted formats.

Figure Cb-C displays the seasonally adjusted unemployment rate and FRB index along with the real per capita GDP for the recession of 1990–1991. All three indicators trace out a roughly similar pattern.

A broad comprehensive index of monthly industrial activity, comparable in quality to the FRB index, is not available for the period before 1919. Jeffrey A. Miron and Christina D. Romer (1990) have calculated an index of industrial production based on thirteen component series for the period 1884–1940 (series Cb28). The Miron–Romer index is not consistent with the FRB index because it is based on a very limited number of series. It is based heavily on inputs to the production process (for example, pig iron, coal, crude petroleum, cattle, and hog receipts at Chicago) and the output of very simple manufacturing processes (flour, coke) rather than on the output of highly fabricated products. The FRB index is preferred to the Miron–Romer index for the period 1919–1940; however, the data for this period are presented for both series so that a comparison of the two can be made and for the use of those who wish to have a consistent series that spans both the pre–World War I era and the period between World War I and World War II.

Students of business cycles have discovered a number of individual series that seem to move roughly in coincidence with fluctuations in the overall economy, among which are the unemployment rate and the index of industrial production. Others that can be mentioned in this regard include real personal income (less transfer payments), real manufacturing and trade sales, and total employee hours in nonagricultural establishments. In Table Cb32–34 a composite index of coincident indicators is presented, along with a composite index of leading indicators and an estimate of the probability that the economy will be in a recession within six months from the date of the index. For example, the recession index for May gives the estimated probability in May that the economy will be in a recession in November. These indexes were derived at the NBER by James H. Stock and Mark W. Watson (1989a, 1989b) and are described as "experimental." The search for coincident and leading indicators has a long tradition dating back to at least 1938 (Mitchell and Burns 1938).

Seasonal Adjustments

Some of the series in Tables Cb24–31 are presented in both their original form and after a seasonal adjustment has been made. Seasonal adjustments are designed to remove any predictable seasonal variations from the data so that the underlying change in the intensity of economic activity can be seen more clearly. In the cases of unemployment rates and the FRB index of industrial production, the seasonal adjustments are performed by the governmental statistical agency that published the numbers. The procedures used are often complex, but they all rely on a statistical analysis of the historical experience of the seasonal movements in the data. As an illustration, Figure Cb-D displays the difference between the unadjusted unemployment rate and the seasonally adjusted rate (series Cb25–26) for the twenty-four months between the beginning of 1998 and the end of 1999. Unemployment is typically higher than "normal" in June and July as students join the labor force and look for work. It is typically lower in the fall, and particularly in December, as employees are hired in the period of high activity associated with Christmas and holiday sales. Unemployment usually rises in the new year as holiday workers are laid off and inclement weather reduces the level of outdoor construction activity. This pattern is repeated year after year. Experts at the Bureau of Labor

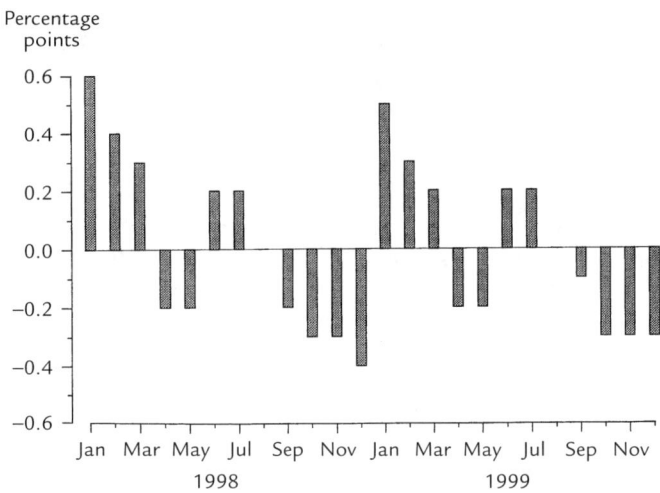

FIGURE Cb-D   Seasonal adjustments for the unemployment rate: 1998–1999

Sources
Series Cb25 (unadjusted) minus series Cb26 (adjusted).

Statistics estimate these regular fluctuations and then adjust the unemployment rate to remove them. That is, the seasonally adjusted unemployment rate for December is adjusted to be higher than the actual unemployment rate to remove the purely seasonal drop associated with the holiday season.

Many economic time series exhibit some seasonal fluctuations, and in some cases the seasonal component dominates the other fluctuations in magnitude. The major difference between seasonal fluctuations and business cycles is that the former are predictable and anticipated, whereas the economic fluctuations of the business cycle are not. It is tempting, then, to employ seasonally adjusted data, which bring the business cycle fluctuations into view without the distraction of the seasonal fluctuations. However, seasonal adjustment, like the techniques used for detrending data, can introduce spurious elements into a data series or confound the search for statistical relationships between multiple time series. Thus, many statisticians prefer to work with unadjusted data and to include explicit seasonal elements (or seasonal dummy variables) directly into their statistical analysis (Barsky and Miron 1989).

The Great Depression of the 1930s

By all accounts, the most disastrous recession in U.S. history was the Great Depression of the 1930s. The only other episode that rivals the Great Depression in both severity and length was the depression of the 1890s, which began with a collapse in late 1893. The economy persisted in a depressed state until after the turn of the century (Carter and Sutch 1992). The Depression of the 1930s is dated from a peak in mid-1929 and persisted for more than twelve years. The economy did not return to full-capacity production until 1942, after receiving the stimulus of wartime spending. According to the chronology of business cycles presented in Table Cb1–4, the Great Depression was actually two back-to-back recessions, one that lasted forty-three months, from August 1929 to March 1933, and a second that lasted thirteen months, from May 1937 to June 1938. However, the recovery from March 1933 to May 1937 was incomplete. The unemployment rate in 1937 was 9.2 percent, much higher than the rates of 2.9 percent in 1929 and 3.1 percent in 1942 (series Ba475). Thus, the Great Depression is a classic case of a W-shaped recession.

A number of long-lasting changes in the economy, the culture, and society seem to originate in or derive from the crisis years, though perhaps not as many as some would claim (Bordo, Goldin, and White 1998). The impact of the Depression on individual sectors of the economy both during the decade of the 1930s and in the decades to follow may be judged by surveying the numerous annual time series provided in the other chapters of *Historical Statistics of the United States*. Yet, the importance of the Great Depression and the interest in its evolution over the decade of the 1930s suggest that it is appropriate to provide a number of monthly data series to more closely track the events of that fateful decade (see Tables Cb35–76). An additional purpose is served by presenting this sampling of data. It will alert readers to the vast amount of detailed high-frequency data that exists for the period between World Wars I and II.

References

Abramovitz, Moses, and Paul A. David. 2000. "Growth in the Era of Knowledge-Based Progress: The Long Run Perspective." In Stanley L. Engerman and Robert E. Gallman, editors, *The Cambridge Economic History of the United States*, volume 3, *The Twentieth Century*. Cambridge University Press.

Altig, David, Terry Fitzgerald, and Peter Rupert. 1997. "Okun's Law Revisited: Should We Worry about Low Unemployment?" Federal Reserve Bank of Cleveland, *Economic Commentary* (May).

Arnold, Robert. 2001. "CBO's Method for Estimating Potential Output: An Update." Congressional Budget Office, Macroeconomic Analysis Division, August.

Ball, Laurence, and N. Gregory Mankiw. 2002. "The NAIRU in Theory and Practice." *NBER Working Paper* number 8940, May.

Barsky, Robert B., and Jeffrey A. Miron. 1989. "The Seasonal Cycle and the Business Cycle." *Journal of Political Economy* 97 (June): 503–34.

Beveridge, Stephen, and Charles R. Nelson. 1981. "A New Approach to Decomposition of Economic Time Series into Permanent and Transitory Components with Particular Attention to Measurement of the 'Business Cycle.'" *Journal of Monetary Economics* 7 (March): 151–74.

Bordo, Michael D., Claudia Goldin, and Eugene N. White, editors. 1998. *The Defining Moment: The Great Depression and the American Economy in the Twentieth Century*. University of Chicago Press.

Burns, Arthur F., and Wesley C. Mitchell. 1946. *Measuring Business Cycles*. National Bureau of Economic Research.

Carter, Susan B., and Richard Sutch. 1992. "The Great Depression of the 1890s: New Suggestive Estimates of the Unemployment Rate, 1890–1905." *Research in Economic History* 14: 347–76.

Craine, Roger. 1997. "Trends and Random Walks." In David Glasner, editor, *Business Cycles and Depressions: An Encyclopedia*. Garland.

DeLong, J. Bradford. 2002. *Macroeconomics*. McGraw-Hill.

Denison, Edward F. 1962. *The Sources of Economic Growth in the United States and the Alternatives before Us*. Committee for Economic Development.

Denison, Edward F. 1969. "Some Major Issues in Productivity Analysis: An Examination of Estimates by Jorgenson and Griliches." *Survey of Current Business* 49 (May 1969): part 2. Reprinted with additional rejoinders and corrections in *The Measurement of Productivity*, Brookings Reprint 244. Brookings Institution Press, 1972.

Easterlin, Richard A. 1987. *Birth and Fortune: The Impact of Numbers on Personal Welfare*. 2nd edition. University of Chicago Press.

Feenberg, Daniel, Jeffrey Miron, Esther D. Reichner, and Hanna Stern. 1967. *Catalog of Business Cycle Series*. NBER Macrohistory Database.

Fishman, G. S. 1969. *Spectral Methods in Economics*. Harvard University Press.

Glasner, David, editor. 1997. *Business Cycles and Depressions: An Encyclopedia*. Garland.

Gordon, Robert J. 1997. "Time-Varying NAIRU and Its Implications for Economic Growth." *Journal of Economic Perspectives* 11 (Winter): 11–32.

Gordon, Robert J. 1998. "Foundations of the Goldilocks Economy: Supply Shocks and the Time-Varying NAIRU." In *Brookings Papers on Economic Activity*. Brookings Institution.

Gordon, Robert J. 1999. "U.S. Economic Growth since 1870: One Big Wave?" *American Economic Review* 89 (May): 123–8.

Gordon, Robert J. 2000. *Macroeconomics*. 8th edition. Addison-Wesley.

Hall, Robert (Chair, Business Cycle Dating Committee, National Bureau of Economic Research). 2002. "The NBER's Recession Dating Procedure." NBER Internet site, June.

Jorgenson, Dale W., and Zvi Griliches. 1967. "The Explanation of Productivity Change." *Review of Economic Studies* 99 (July). Reprinted in the *Survey of Current Business* 49 (May 1969): part 2, and reprinted with additional rejoinders and corrections in *The Measurement of Productivity*, Brookings Reprint 244. Brookings Institution Press, 1972.

Katz, Lawrence F., and Alan B. Krueger. 1999. "The High-Pressure U.S. Labor Market of the 1990s." In *Brookings Papers on Economic Activity*. Brookings Institution.

Klein, Lawrence R. 1950. *Economic Fluctuations in the United States, 1921–1941*. Wiley.

Kuznets, Simon. 1958. "Long Swings in Population Growth and Related Economic Variables." *Proceedings of the American Philosophical Society* 102: 25–52.

Miron, Jeffrey A., and Christina D. Romer. 1990. "A New Monthly Index of Industrial Production, 1884–1940." *Journal of Economic History* 50 (June): 321–37.

Mitchell, Wesley C. 1908. *Gold, Prices, and Wages under the Greenback Standard*. University of California Publications in Economics, volume 1. University of California Press.

Mitchell, Wesley Clair. 1913. *Business Cycles*. University of California Press.

Mitchell, Wesley C., and Arthur F. Burns. 1938. "Statistical Indicators of Cyclical Revivals." *National Bureau of Economic Research Bulletin* 69 (May 28): 4–8.

Nelson, Charles R., and Charles I. Plosser. 1982. "Trends and Random Walks in Macroeconomic Time Series: Some Evidence and Implications." *Journal of Monetary Economics* 10 (September): 139–62.

Okun, Arthur M. 1962. "Potential GNP: Its Measurement and Significance." In *Proceedings of the Business and Economics Section*. American Statistical Association.

Perry, George. 1970. "Changing Labor Markets and Inflation." In *Brookings Papers on Economic Activity*. Brookings Institution.

Phillips, A. W. H. 1958. "The Relation between Unemployment and the Rate of Change of Money Wage Rates in the United Kingdom, 1861–1957." *Economica* ns 25 (November): 283–99.

Romer, Christina D. 1994. "Remeasuring Business Cycles." *Journal of Economic History* 54 (September): 573–690.

Samuelson, Paul A., and Robert M. Solow. 1960. "Analytical Aspects of Anti-Inflation Policy." *American Economic Review* 50 (May): 177–94.

Staiger, Douglas, James H. Stock, and Mark W. Watson. 1997. "The NAIRU, Unemployment, and Monetary Policy." *Journal of Economic Perspectives* 11 (Winter): 33–49.

Stock, James H., and Mark W. Watson. 1988. "Variable Trends in Economic Time Series." *Journal of Economic Perspectives* 2 (Summer): 147–74.

Stock, James H., and Mark W. Watson. 1989a. "Indexes of Coincident and Leading Economic Indicators." *NBER Reporter* (Spring): 3–5.

Stock, James H., and Mark W. Watson. 1989b. "New Indexes of Coincident and Leading Economic Indicators." In *NBER Macroeconomics Annual 1989*. National Bureau of Economic Research.

Weiner, Stuart. 1993. "New Estimates of the Natural Rate of Unemployment." Federal Reserve Bank of Kansas City, *Economic Review* (fourth quarter): 53–69.

Zarnowitz, Victor. 1992. *Business Cycles: Theory, History, Indicators, and Forecasting*. University of Chicago Press.

BUSINESS CYCLE CHRONOLOGY

Richard Sutch

TABLE Cb1–4   Business cycle turning dates and duration – annual: 1790–1855

Contributed by Richard Sutch

		Contraction (peak to trough)	Expansion (trough to peak)	Full cycle	
				Trough to trough	Peak to peak
		Cb1	Cb2	Cb3	Cb4
Trough	Peak	Years	Years	Years	Years
1790	1796	—	6.0	—	—
1799	1802	3.0	3.0	9	6.0
1804	1807	2.0	3.0	5	5.0
1810	1812	3.0	1.5	6	4.5
1812	1815	0.5	3.0	2	3.5
1821	1822	6.0	1.0	9	7.0
1823	1825	1.0	2.0	2	3.0
1826	1828	1.0	2.0	3	3.0
1829	1833	1.0	4.0	3	5.0
1834	1836	1.0	2.0	5	3.0
1838	1839	2.0	1.0	4	3.0
1843	1845	4.0	2.0	5	6.0
1846	1847	1.0	1.0	3	2.0
1848	1853	1.0	5.0	2	6.0
1855	—	2.0	—	7	—

Sources

Geoffrey H. Moore and Victor Zarnowitz "The NBER's Business Cycle Chronologies," in Robert Gordon, editor, *The American Business Cycle: Continuity and Change* (University of Chicago Press, 1986), Table A.2, p. 746. Moore and Zarnowitz cite the following sources: for 1790–1833, Willard L. Thorp, *Business Annals* (National Bureau of Economic Research, 1926) pp. 113–26; and for 1834–1855, Arthur F. Burns and Wesley C. Mitchell, *Measuring Business Cycles* (National Bureau of Economic Research, 1946), Table 16, p. 78.

Documentation

The era covered by this table comprises the rise of market-oriented capitalism and the rise of manufacturing. The business cycles in this period averaged about four and a half years, whether measured from trough to trough or peak to peak. However, five of the identified cycles fall in the early turbulent period of almost continuous wars that ended in 1815.

Given the absence of annual aggregate data on economic performance during this period and the limitations of the available business cycle indicators, identifying and dating the historical business cycles relies on the researcher's judgment after reviewing the voluminous business annals compiled during the period and numerous time series covering diverse economic activities. It is likely that measurement errors in such series are large. The Burns and Mitchell (1946) definition of a business cycle implies that the cyclical turns of a broad array of economic time series will bunch together at about the same time. In practice, it was found that the clusters of peaks and troughs typically extended over many months, but also showed rather definite points of concentration, allowing the researcher to identify the year of peak or trough in the otherwise unobservable level of "aggregate economic activity" (Moore and Zarnowitz 1986, pp. 745–7).

In 1812 there was a "brief recession" followed by a revival. The corresponding duration measures in these series are based on the assumption that the recession occurred in the first half of the year before the outbreak of the war with England.

TABLE Cb5–8   Business cycle turning dates and duration – monthly: 1854–2001

Contributed by Richard Sutch

Trough	Peak	Contraction (peak to trough)	Expansion (trough to peak)	Full cycle	
				Trough to trough	Peak to peak
		Cb5	Cb6	Cb7	Cb8
		Months	Months	Months	Months
Dec 1854	Jun 1857	—	30	—	—
Dec 1858	Oct 1860	18	22	48	40
Jun 1861	Apr 1865	8	46	30	54
Dec 1867	Jun 1869	32	18	78	50
Dec 1870	Oct 1873	18	34	36	52
Mar 1879	Mar 1882	65	36	99	101
May 1885	Mar 1887	38	22	74	60
Apr 1888	Jul 1890	13	27	35	40
May 1891	Jan 1893	10	20	37	30
Jun 1894	Dec 1895	17	18	37	35
Jun 1897	Jun 1899	18	24	36	42
Dec 1900	Sep 1902	18	21	42	39
Oct 1904	May 1907	23	33	44	56
Jun 1908	Jan 1910	13	19	46	32
Jan 1912	Jan 1913	24	12	43	36
Dec 1914	Aug 1918	23	44	35	67
Mar 1919	Jan 1920	7	10	51	17
Jul 1921	May 1923	18	22	28	40
Jul 1924	Oct 1926	14	27	36	41
Nov 1927	Aug 1929	13	21	40	34
Mar 1933	May 1937	43	50	64	93
Jun 1938	Feb 1945	13	80	63	93
Oct 1945	Nov 1948	8	37	88	45
Oct 1949	Jul 1953	11	45	48	56
May 1954	Aug 1957	10	39	55	49
Apr 1958	Apr 1960	8	24	47	32
Feb 1961	Dec 1969	10	106	34	116
Nov 1970	Nov 1973	11	36	117	47
Mar 1975	Jan 1980	16	58	52	74
Jul 1980	Jul 1981	6	12	64	18
Nov 1982	Jul 1990	16	92	28	108
Mar 1991	Mar 2001	8	120	100	128

Sources

U.S. Department of Commerce, *Survey of Current Business* 74 (October 1994), Table C-51; National Bureau of Economic Research, Business Cycle Dating Committee, *Report*, June 7, 2002.

Documentation

The first version of this chronology was published in Arthur F. Burns and Wesley C. Mitchell, *Measuring Business Cycles* (National Bureau of Economic Research, 1946), and later revised by Geoffrey H. Moore, *Business Cycle Indicators*, volume 1 (Princeton University Press, 1961), Appendix A, pp. 669–71.

The Business Cycle Dating Committee of the National Bureau of Economic Research (NBER) determines the "official" dates for recessions and expansions. The NBER defines a recession as "a recurring period of decline in total output, income, employment, and trade, usually lasting from six months to a year, and marked by widespread contractions in many sectors of the economy." At the time of writing this documentation (July 2002), the last expansion ended in March 2001. Further discussion of the NBER concepts can be found in NBER, *Business Cycles, Inflation and Forecasting*, 2nd edition (Ballinger, 1983).

A depression is a recession that is major in both scale and duration. There is, however, no official definition of a depression. Economic historians have generally described the period from October 1873 to March 1879 as the "Depression of 1873–1878," the period from March 1882 to May of 1885 as the "Depression of 1882–1885," the period from January 1893 to June 1897 as the "Depression of the 1890s," and the period from August 1929 to June 1938 as the "Great Depression." All other contractions are generally characterized as recessions, business crises, or business panics. For a general reference, see David Glasner, editor, *Business Cycles and Depressions: An Encyclopedia* (Garland, 1997).

BUSINESS CYCLE INDICATORS

Richard Sutch

TABLE Cb9–17   Gross domestic product – trends and fluctuations: 1946–2003

Contributed by Richard Sutch

	Gross domestic product			Trend in real per capita gross domestic product					
	Nominal	Real	Real per capita	Exponential trend	Deviations from exponential trend	Peak-to-peak trend	Deviations from peak-to-peak trend	Population	Implicit deflator
	Cb9	Cb10	Cb11	Cb12	Cb13	Cb14	Cb15	Cb16	Cb17
Year: Quarter	Billion dollars	Billion chained 1996 dollars	Chained 1996 dollars	Chained 1996 dollars	Chained 1996 dollars	Chained 1996 dollars	Chained 1996 dollars	Million	Index 1996 = 100
1946: 1	210.6	—	—	—	—	—	—	140.9	—
1946: 2	218.4	—	—	—	—	—	—	141.2	—
1946: 3	228.2	—	—	—	—	—	—	141.8	—
1946: 4	232.0	—	—	—	—	—	—	142.7	—
1947: 1	237.5	1,481.7	10,347	10,906	559	—	—	143.2	16.03
1947: 2	240.7	1,489.4	10,357	10,967	610	—	—	143.8	16.16
1947: 3	244.9	1,493.1	10,333	11,028	695	—	—	144.5	16.40
1947: 4	254.7	1,516.4	10,451	11,089	639	—	—	145.1	16.80
1948: 1	260.8	1,537.9	10,548	11,151	603	—	—	145.8	16.95
1948: 2	267.7	1,562.0	10,677 [1]	11,213	536	10,677	0	146.3	17.14
1948: 3	274.3	1,568.4	10,669	11,275	606	10,762	92	147.0	17.49
1948: 4	275.6	1,571.4	10,639	11,338	699	10,848	208	147.7	17.54
1949: 1	270.4	1,549.4	10,448	11,401	953	10,934	486	148.3	17.45
1949: 2	266.6	1,545.1	10,377	11,465	1,088	11,021	644	148.9	17.25
1949: 3	268.0	1,562.6	10,452	11,528	1,076	11,109	657	149.5	17.15
1949: 4	265.6	1,546.5	10,296	11,592	1,296	11,198	901	150.2	17.17
1950: 1	275.7	1,610.5	10,673	11,657	984	11,287	614	150.9	17.12
1950: 2	285.1	1,658.8	10,956	11,722	765	11,377	420	151.4	17.19
1950: 3	302.5	1,723.0	11,336	11,787	451	11,467	132	152.0	17.56
1950: 4	313.9	1,753.9	11,486	11,852	366	11,559	73	152.7	17.89
1951: 1	329.3	1,773.5	11,569	11,918	350	11,651	82	153.3	18.57
1951: 2	336.9	1,803.7	11,720	11,985	265	11,744	24	153.9	18.68
1951: 3	343.7	1,839.8	11,893	12,051	159	11,837	−55	154.7	18.68
1951: 4	348.1	1,843.3	11,862	12,118	257	11,932	70	155.4	18.89
1952: 1	351.5	1,864.7	11,953	12,186	232	12,027	74	156.0	18.85
1952: 2	352.4	1,866.2	11,917	12,253	336	12,123	206	156.6	18.88
1952: 3	358.8	1,878.0	11,939	12,322	383	12,219	280	157.3	19.11
1952: 4	371.8	1,940.2	12,280	12,390	110	12,317	37	158.0	19.16
1953: 1	378.9	1,976.0	12,459	12,459	0	12,415	−44	158.6	19.17
1953: 2	382.5	1,992.2	12,514 [1]	12,528	14	12,514	0	159.2	19.20
1953: 3	381.7	1,979.5	12,372	12,598	226	12,534	162	160.0	19.28
1953: 4	376.6	1,947.8	12,121	12,668	547	12,555	434	160.7	19.33
1954: 1	376.0	1,938.1	12,008	12,738	730	12,575	567	161.4	19.40
1954: 2	376.7	1,941.0	11,981	12,809	828	12,596	614	162.0	19.41
1954: 3	381.5	1,962.0	12,052	12,881	829	12,616	565	162.8	19.45
1954: 4	390.1	2,000.9	12,230	12,952	722	12,637	407	163.6	19.50
1955: 1	403.1	2,058.1	12,526	13,024	498	12,658	131	164.3	19.59
1955: 2	411.4	2,091.0	12,680	13,097	416	12,678	−2	164.9	19.67
1955: 3	419.9	2,118.9	12,788	13,169	382	12,699	−88	165.7	19.82
1955: 4	426.4	2,130.1	12,793	13,243	449	12,720	−73	166.5	20.02
1956: 1	428.8	2,121.0	12,685	13,316	631	12,741	55	167.2	20.22
1956: 2	434.7	2,137.7	12,732	13,390	658	12,762	30	167.9	20.33
1956: 3	439.7	2,135.3	12,657	13,465	808	12,782	125	168.7	20.59
1956: 4	448.6	2,170.4	12,805	13,540	735	12,803	−1	169.5	20.67
1957: 1	457.6	2,182.7	12,824 [1]	13,615	791	12,824	0	170.2	20.96
1957: 2	459.6	2,177.7	12,743	13,691	948	12,864	121	170.9	21.10
1957: 3	466.8	2,198.9	12,807	13,767	960	12,903	97	171.7	21.23
1957: 4	462.0	2,176.0	12,614	13,844	1,229	12,943	328	172.5	21.23
1958: 1	454.6	2,117.4	12,232	13,920	1,688	12,983	751	173.1	21.47
1958: 2	458.9	2,129.7	12,254	13,998	1,744	13,023	769	173.8	21.55
1958: 3	472.4	2,177.5	12,479	14,076	1,597	13,063	584	174.5	21.70
1958: 4	485.8	2,226.5	12,701	14,154	1,453	13,103	402	175.3	21.82

Notes appear at end of table

TABLE Cb9–17 Gross domestic product – trends and fluctuations: 1946–2003 *Continued*

	Gross domestic product			Trend in real per capita gross domestic product					
	Nominal	Real	Real per capita	Exponential trend	Deviations from exponential trend	Peak-to-peak trend	Deviations from peak-to-peak trend	Population	Implicit deflator
	Cb9	Cb10	Cb11	Cb12	Cb13	Cb14	Cb15	Cb16	Cb17
Year: Quarter	Billion dollars	Billion chained 1996 dollars	Chained 1996 dollars	Chained 1996 dollars	Chained 1996 dollars	Chained 1996 dollars	Chained 1996 dollars	Million	Index 1996 = 100
1959: 1	496.1	2,273.0	12,915	14,233	1,318	13,143	228	176.0	21.83
1959: 2	509.2	2,332.4	13,200	14,312	1,112	13,184	−16	176.7	21.83
1959: 3	510.2	2,331.4	13,135	14,391	1,257	13,224	89	177.5	21.88
1959: 4	514.2	2,339.1	13,119	14,472	1,353	13,265	146	178.3	21.98
1960: 1	527.9	2,391.0	13,306 [1]	14,552	1,247	13,306	0	179.7	22.08
1960: 2	527.1	2,379.2	13,196	14,633	1,437	13,405	210	180.3	22.15
1960: 3	529.9	2,383.6	13,162	14,714	1,553	13,506	344	181.1	22.23
1960: 4	524.6	2,352.9	12,935	14,796	1,861	13,607	672	181.9	22.30
1961: 1	528.9	2,366.5	12,960	14,878	1,918	13,709	749	182.6	22.35
1961: 2	539.9	2,410.8	13,152	14,961	1,809	13,812	660	183.3	22.40
1961: 3	550.3	2,450.4	13,310	15,044	1,734	13,916	606	184.1	22.46
1961: 4	563.4	2,500.4	13,523	15,128	1,605	14,020	497	184.9	22.53
1962: 1	576.8	2,544.0	13,707	15,212	1,505	14,125	419	185.6	22.67
1962: 2	583.9	2,571.5	13,810	15,297	1,486	14,231	421	186.2	22.71
1962: 3	591.0	2,596.8	13,894	15,382	1,488	14,338	444	186.9	22.76
1962: 4	594.4	2,603.3	13,869	15,467	1,598	14,446	576	187.7	22.83
1963: 1	603.4	2,634.1	13,989	15,553	1,565	14,554	565	188.3	22.91
1963: 2	612.1	2,668.4	14,126	15,640	1,514	14,663	537	188.9	22.94
1963: 3	624.9	2,719.6	14,344	15,727	1,383	14,773	430	189.6	22.98
1963: 4	634.3	2,739.4	14,388	15,814	1,427	14,884	497	190.4	23.16
1964: 1	650.4	2,800.5	14,662	15,902	1,240	14,996	334	191.0	23.22
1964: 2	659.6	2,833.8	14,790	15,991	1,201	15,108	318	191.6	23.28
1964: 3	671.2	2,872.0	14,935	16,080	1,145	15,222	287	192.3	23.37
1964: 4	676.3	2,879.5	14,927	16,169	1,242	15,336	409	192.9	23.49
1965: 1	696.5	2,950.1	15,246	16,259	1,013	15,451	205	193.5	23.61
1965: 2	709.0	2,989.9	15,412	16,349	938	15,567	155	194.0	23.71
1965: 3	726.2	3,050.7	15,677	16,440	764	15,684	7	194.6	23.81
1965: 4	748.7	3,123.6	15,994	16,532	538	15,801	−192	195.3	23.97
1966: 1	772.3	3,201.1	16,349	16,624	275	15,920	−429	195.8	24.13
1966: 2	781.5	3,213.2	16,369	16,716	347	16,039	−329	196.3	24.32
1966: 3	794.8	3,233.6	16,423	16,809	387	16,160	−263	196.9	24.58
1966: 4	808.6	3,261.8	16,515	16,903	387	16,281	−234	197.5	24.79
1967: 1	819.3	3,291.8	16,625	16,997	371	16,403	−222	198.0	24.89
1967: 2	823.9	3,289.7	16,573	17,091	518	16,526	−46	198.5	25.05
1967: 3	838.7	3,313.5	16,651	17,186	535	16,650	(Z)	199.0	25.31
1967: 4	854.4	3,338.3	16,725	17,282	557	16,775	50	199.6	25.59
1968: 1	881.4	3,406.2	17,031	17,378	347	16,901	−130	200.0	25.88
1968: 2	905.7	3,464.8	17,281	17,475	194	17,028	−253	200.5	26.14
1968: 3	920.9	3,489.2	17,359	17,572	212	17,156	−204	201.0	26.39
1968: 4	937.8	3,504.1	17,390	17,669	279	17,284	−106	201.5	26.76
1969: 1	961.9	3,558.3	17,615	17,768	152	17,414	−201	202.0	27.03
1969: 2	977.0	3,567.6	17,626	17,866	240	17,545	−82	202.4	27.39
1969: 3	997.2	3,588.3	17,676 [1]	17,966	289	17,676	0	203.0	27.79
1969: 4	1,005.3	3,571.4	17,541	18,066	525	17,794	253	203.6	28.15
1970: 1	1,018.2	3,566.5	17,474	18,166	692	17,912	438	204.1	28.55
1970: 2	1,034.4	3,573.9	17,459	18,267	808	18,031	572	204.7	28.94
1970: 3	1,051.9	3,605.2	17,552	18,369	817	18,151	599	205.4	29.18
1970: 4	1,054.2	3,566.5	17,305	18,471	1,166	18,272	967	206.1	29.56
1971: 1	1,099.9	3,666.1	17,728	18,574	846	18,394	666	206.8	30.00
1971: 2	1,120.6	3,686.2	17,773	18,677	904	18,516	743	207.4	30.40
1971: 3	1,140.8	3,714.5	17,858	18,781	923	18,639	781	208.0	30.71
1971: 4	1,153.1	3,723.8	17,851	18,885	1,034	18,763	912	208.6	30.96
1972: 1	1,192.5	3,796.9	18,158	18,990	832	18,888	730	209.1	31.41
1972: 2	1,227.5	3,883.8	18,530	19,096	566	19,013	484	209.6	31.61
1972: 3	1,252.0	3,922.3	18,660	19,202	542	19,140	480	210.2	31.92
1972: 4	1,289.7	3,990.5	18,939	19,309	370	19,267	328	210.7	32.32
1973: 1	1,338.4	4,092.3	19,376	19,416	40	19,395	19	211.2	32.71
1973: 2	1,374.4	4,133.3	19,524 [1]	19,524	0	19,524	0	211.7	33.25
1973: 3	1,394.1	4,117.0	19,402	19,633	231	19,594	192	212.2	33.86
1973: 4	1,435.3	4,151.1	19,516	19,742	226	19,664	148	212.7	34.58

Notes appear at end of table

(continued)

TABLE Cb9–17 Gross domestic product – trends and fluctuations: 1946–2003 *Continued*

	Gross domestic product			Trend in real per capita gross domestic product					
	Nominal	Real	Real per capita	Exponential trend	Deviations from exponential trend	Peak-to-peak trend	Deviations from peak-to-peak trend	Population	Implicit deflator
	Cb9	Cb10	Cb11	Cb12	Cb13	Cb14	Cb15	Cb16	Cb17
Year: Quarter	Billion dollars	Billion chained 1996 dollars	Chained 1996 dollars	Chained 1996 dollars	Chained 1996 dollars	Chained 1996 dollars	Chained 1996 dollars	Million	Index 1996 = 100
1974: 1	1,450.0	4,119.3	19,330	19,852	522	19,734	404	213.1	35.20
1974: 2	1,487.6	4,130.4	19,337	19,962	625	19,804	467	213.6	36.02
1974: 3	1,514.8	4,084.5	19,078	20,073	996	19,875	797	214.1	37.09
1974: 4	1,551.6	4,062.0	18,919	20,185	1,266	19,946	1,026	214.7	38.20
1975: 1	1,567.2	4,010.0	18,642	20,297	1,655	20,017	1,374	215.1	39.08
1975: 2	1,603.1	4,045.2	18,754	20,410	1,656	20,088	1,334	215.7	39.63
1975: 3	1,659.9	4,115.4	19,026	20,524	1,497	20,160	1,133	216.3	40.33
1975: 4	1,710.5	4,167.2	19,221	20,638	1,416	20,232	1,010	216.8	41.05
1976: 1	1,770.3	4,266.1	19,632	20,752	1,120	20,304	672	217.3	41.50
1976: 2	1,803.1	4,301.5	19,750	20,868	1,118	20,376	626	217.8	41.92
1976: 3	1,837.0	4,321.9	19,798	20,984	1,186	20,449	651	218.3	42.50
1976: 4	1,885.3	4,357.4	19,906	21,101	1,195	20,522	616	218.9	43.27
1977: 1	1,939.1	4,410.5	20,103	21,218	1,115	20,595	492	219.4	43.97
1977: 2	2,006.6	4,489.8	20,408	21,336	928	20,668	260	220.0	44.69
1977: 3	2,067.5	4,570.6	20,719	21,455	736	20,742	23	220.6	45.23
1977: 4	2,112.4	4,576.1	20,688	21,574	886	20,816	128	221.2	46.16
1978: 1	2,150.4	4,588.9	20,699	21,694	995	20,890	192	221.7	46.86
1978: 2	2,276.6	4,765.7	21,438	21,815	376	20,965	−473	222.3	47.77
1978: 3	2,338.5	4,811.7	21,587	21,936	349	21,039	−547	222.9	48.60
1978: 4	2,418.0	4,876.0	21,807	22,058	251	21,114	−692	223.6	49.59
1979: 1	2,470.9	4,888.3	21,803	22,181	377	21,190	−614	224.2	50.55
1979: 2	2,529.3	4,891.4	21,769	22,304	535	21,265	−503	224.7	51.71
1979: 3	2,601.3	4,926.2	21,855	22,428	573	21,341	−514	225.4	52.81
1979: 4	2,663.8	4,942.6	21,860	22,553	692	21,417	−443	226.1	53.90
1980: 1	2,732.9	4,958.9	21,865	22,678	813	21,494	−371	226.8	55.11
1980: 2	2,736.9	4,857.8	21,362	22,804	1,442	21,570	208	227.4	56.34
1980: 3	2,793.6	4,850.3	21,264	22,931	1,667	21,647	383	228.1	57.60
1980: 4	2,918.8	4,936.6	21,585	23,059	1,473	21,724	139	228.7	59.13
1981: 1	3,052.6	5,032.5	21,957	23,187	1,230	21,802	−155	229.2	60.66
1981: 2	3,086.2	4,997.3	21,756	23,316	1,560	21,879	124	229.7	61.76
1981: 3	3,183.5	5,056.8	21,957 [1]	23,445	1,488	21,957	0	230.3	62.95
1981: 4	3,203.1	4,997.1	21,642	23,576	1,934	22,091	449	230.9	64.10
1982: 1	3,193.8	4,914.3	21,237	23,707	2,470	22,225	988	231.4	64.99
1982: 2	3,248.9	4,935.5	21,283	23,839	2,556	22,360	1,078	231.9	65.83
1982: 3	3,278.6	4,912.1	21,127	23,971	2,844	22,496	1,369	232.5	66.75
1982: 4	3,315.6	4,915.6	21,088	24,105	3,017	22,633	1,545	233.1	67.45
1983: 1	3,378.5	4,972.4	21,295	24,239	2,944	22,771	1,476	233.5	67.95
1983: 2	3,489.6	5,089.8	21,751	24,374	2,622	22,909	1,158	234.0	68.56
1983: 3	3,582.9	5,180.4	22,082	24,509	2,427	23,049	967	234.6	69.16
1983: 4	3,688.8	5,286.8	22,478	24,645	2,167	23,189	711	235.2	69.77
1984: 1	3,813.4	5,402.3	22,930	24,782	1,852	23,330	400	235.6	70.59
1984: 2	3,909.4	5,493.8	23,269	24,920	1,651	23,472	203	236.1	71.16
1984: 3	3,974.7	5,541.3	23,411	25,059	1,648	23,614	204	236.7	71.73
1984: 4	4,033.5	5,583.1	23,538	25,198	1,661	23,758	221	237.2	72.24
1985: 1	4,109.7	5,629.7	23,684	25,338	1,654	23,903	219	237.7	73.00
1985: 2	4,170.1	5,673.8	23,819	25,479	1,660	24,048	228	238.2	73.50
1985: 3	4,252.9	5,758.6	24,115	25,621	1,506	24,194	79	238.8	73.85
1985: 4	4,319.3	5,806.0	24,252	25,763	1,511	24,341	89	239.4	74.39
1986: 1	4,375.3	5,858.9	24,422	25,907	1,484	24,489	67	239.9	74.68
1986: 2	4,415.2	5,883.3	24,473	26,051	1,578	24,638	165	240.4	75.05
1986: 3	4,483.4	5,937.9	24,639	26,196	1,557	24,788	149	241.0	75.51
1986: 4	4,537.5	5,969.5	24,718	26,341	1,623	24,939	220	241.5	76.01
1987: 1	4,612.3	6,013.3	24,848	26,488	1,639	25,090	242	242.0	76.70
1987: 2	4,695.8	6,077.2	25,061	26,635	1,575	25,243	182	242.5	77.27
1987: 3	4,770.2	6,128.1	25,208	26,783	1,575	25,397	188	243.1	77.84
1987: 4	4,891.6	6,234.4	25,582	26,932	1,350	25,551	−31	243.7	78.46
1988: 1	4,957.0	6,275.9	25,700	27,082	1,382	25,706	7	244.2	78.98
1988: 2	5,066.5	6,349.8	25,949	27,233	1,283	25,863	−87	244.7	79.79
1988: 3	5,151.5	6,382.3	26,008	27,384	1,376	26,020	12	245.4	80.71
1988: 4	5,258.3	6,465.2	26,281	27,536	1,255	26,178	−103	246.0	81.33

Notes appear at end of table

TABLE Cb9–17   Gross domestic product – trends and fluctuations: 1946–2003   *Continued*

	Gross domestic product			Trend in real per capita gross domestic product						
	Nominal	Real	Real per capita	Exponential trend	Deviations from exponential trend	Peak-to-peak trend	Deviations from peak-to-peak trend	Population	Implicit deflator
	Cb9	Cb10	Cb11	Cb12	Cb13	Cb14	Cb15	Cb16	Cb17
Year: Quarter	Billion dollars	Billion chained 1996 dollars	Chained 1996 dollars	Chained 1996 dollars	Chained 1996 dollars	Chained 1996 dollars	Chained 1996 dollars	Million	Index 1996 = 100
1989: 1	5,379.0	6,543.8	26,547	27,689	1,143	26,337	−209	246.5	82.20
1989: 2	5,461.7	6,579.4	26,637	27,843	1,206	26,498	−140	247.0	83.01
1989: 3	5,527.5	6,610.6	26,688	27,998	1,310	26,659	−29	247.7	83.62
1989: 4	5,588.0	6,633.5	26,705	28,154	1,449	26,821	116	248.4	84.24
1990: 1	5,720.8	6,716.3	26,984 [1]	28,311	1,327	26,984	0	248.9	85.18
1990: 2	5,800.0	6,731.7	26,981	28,468	1,487	27,110	129	249.5	86.16
1990: 3	5,844.9	6,719.4	26,845	28,626	1,781	27,237	391	250.3	86.99
1990: 4	5,847.3	6,664.2	26,529	28,786	2,256	27,364	835	251.2	87.74
1991: 1	5,886.3	6,631.4	26,315	28,946	2,631	27,492	1,177	252.0	88.76
1991: 2	5,962.0	6,668.5	26,379	29,107	2,728	27,620	1,242	252.8	89.40
1991: 3	6,015.9	6,684.9	26,350	29,268	2,919	27,749	1,400	253.7	89.99
1991: 4	6,080.7	6,720.9	26,398	29,431	3,033	27,879	1,481	254.6	90.47
1992: 1	6,183.6	6,783.3	26,570	29,595	3,025	28,009	1,439	255.3	91.16
1992: 2	6,276.6	6,846.8	26,735	29,760	3,025	28,140	1,405	256.1	91.67
1992: 3	6,345.8	6,899.7	26,837	29,925	3,088	28,272	1,435	257.1	91.97
1992: 4	6,469.8	6,990.6	27,095	30,091	2,996	28,404	1,308	258.0	92.55
1993: 1	6,521.6	6,988.7	27,004	30,259	3,255	28,537	1,532	258.8	93.32
1993: 2	6,596.7	7,031.2	27,085	30,427	3,342	28,670	1,585	259.6	93.82
1993: 3	6,655.5	7,062.0	27,120	30,596	3,476	28,804	1,684	260.4	94.24
1993: 4	6,795.5	7,168.7	27,435	30,766	3,332	28,938	1,504	261.3	94.79
1994: 1	6,887.8	7,229.4	27,593	30,938	3,344	29,074	1,481	262.0	95.28
1994: 2	7,015.7	7,330.2	27,893	31,110	3,217	29,210	1,317	262.8	95.71
1994: 3	7,096.0	7,370.2	27,960	31,283	3,323	29,346	1,386	263.6	96.28
1994: 4	7,217.7	7,461.1	28,219	31,457	3,238	29,483	1,264	264.4	96.74
1995: 1	7,297.5	7,488.7	28,238	31,631	3,394	29,621	1,383	265.2	97.45
1995: 2	7,342.6	7,503.3	28,219	31,807	3,589	29,759	1,541	265.9	97.86
1995: 3	7,432.8	7,561.4	28,352	31,984	3,633	29,898	1,547	266.7	98.30
1995: 4	7,529.3	7,621.9	28,482	32,162	3,680	30,038	1,556	267.6	98.78
1996: 1	7,629.6	7,676.4	28,611	32,341	3,730	30,178	1,567	268.3	99.39
1996: 2	7,782.7	7,802.9	29,007	32,521	3,514	30,319	1,312	269.0	99.74
1996: 3	7,859.0	7,841.9	29,066	32,702	3,636	30,461	1,396	269.8	100.22
1996: 4	7,981.4	7,931.3	29,299	32,884	3,584	30,603	1,304	270.7	100.63
1997: 1	8,124.2	8,016.4	29,526	33,066	3,540	30,746	1,220	271.5	101.34
1997: 2	8,279.8	8,131.9	29,875	33,250	3,376	30,890	1,015	272.2	101.82
1997: 3	8,390.9	8,216.6	30,086	33,435	3,349	31,034	948	273.1	102.12
1997: 4	8,478.6	8,272.9	30,193	33,621	3,428	31,180	986	274.0	102.49
1998: 1	8,627.8	8,396.3	30,565	33,808	3,243	31,325	760	274.7	102.76
1998: 2	8,697.3	8,442.9	30,657	33,996	3,339	31,472	815	275.4	103.01
1998: 3	8,816.5	8,528.5	30,867	34,185	3,318	31,619	752	276.3	103.38
1998: 4	8,984.5	8,667.9	31,281	34,375	3,095	31,766	486	277.1	103.65
1999: 1	9,092.7	8,733.2	31,426	34,567	3,141	31,915	489	277.9	104.12
1999: 2	9,171.7	8,775.5	31,499	34,759	3,260	32,064	565	278.6	104.51
1999: 3	9,316.5	8,886.9	31,807	34,952	3,145	32,214	407	279.4	104.83
1999: 4	9,516.4	9,040.1	32,252	35,146	2,895	32,364	113	280.3	105.27
2000: 1	9,649.5	9,097.4	32,364	35,342	2,978	32,516	152	281.1	106.07
2000: 2	9,820.7	9,205.7	32,667 [1]	35,539	2,871	32,667	0	281.8	106.68
2000: 3	9,874.8	9,218.7	32,633	35,736	3,104	—	—	282.5	107.12
2000: 4	9,953.6	9,243.8	32,641	35,935	3,294	—	—	283.2	107.68
2001: 1	10,028.1	9,229.9	32,523	36,135	3,612	—	—	283.8	108.65
2001: 2	10,049.9	9,193.1	32,325	36,336	4,011	—	—	284.4	109.32
2001: 3	10,097.7	9,186.4	32,210	36,538	4,327	—	—	285.2	109.92
2001: 4	10,152.9	9,248.8	32,350	36,741	4,391	—	—	285.9	109.78
2002: 1	10,313.1	9,363.2	32,681	36,945	4,264	—	—	286.5	110.14
2002: 2	10,376.9	9,392.4	32,715	37,151	4,436	—	—	287.1	110.48
2002: 3	10,506.2	9,485.6	32,959	37,357	4,398	—	—	287.8	110.76
2002: 4	10,588.8	9,518.2	32,992	37,565	4,573	—	—	288.5	111.25
2003: 1	10,688.4	9,552.0	33,040	37,774	4,734	—	—	289.1	111.90
2003: 2	10,777.3	9,608.1	33,154	37,984	4,830	—	—	289.8	112.17

Notes appear on next page

(continued)

TABLE Cb9–17   Gross domestic product – trends and fluctuations: 1946–2003   *Continued*

(Z) Less than 0.5 chained 1996 dollars (in absolute value).

[1] Denotes a peak year used for calculating series Cb14.

Source

U.S. Bureau of Economic Analysis Internet site, Tables 1.1, 1.2, 2.1, and 7.1; downloaded August 18, 2003.

Documentation

The U.S. Bureau of Economic Analysis (BEA) calculates gross domestic product (GDP). See Chapter Ca, on national income and product, for details.

Cb9–10. These series are seasonally adjusted, and the data are presented at annual rates. The series for real GDP is derived by dividing series Cb9 by series Cb17.

Series Cb11. Equals series Cb10 divided by series Cb16.

Series Cb12. Figures represent a 2.2431 percent rate of exponential growth of real per capita GDP passing through the observations of series Cb11 for 1953:1 and 1973:2. Those two quarters were chosen so that the exponential trend would lie everywhere above the data in series Cb11.

Series Cb13. Equals series Cb12 minus series Cb11.

Series Cb14. Figures are an exponential trend growing at a constant rate between each pair of business cycle peaks indicated with a footnote. Two tests established the dates of the cyclical peaks used in this table. First, the level of real per capita GDP at the date had to exceed both the levels of one and two quarters earlier and the levels of one and two quarters later. Second, any peak that was dominated by a higher peak within the next five quarters was eliminated. These rules were designed to be consistent

with those advocated by Burns and Mitchell, who defined business cycles to be "more than one year" and "not divisible into shorter cycles of similar character" (Arthur F. Burns and Wesley C. Mitchell, *Measuring Business Cycles* (National Bureau of Economic Research, 1947), pp. 7–8). They add this "rule is necessary as a 'brake' on the investigator's pattern sense which, while the source of all true knowledge, may lead to mischievous fictions" (p. 8). The peaks and the rate of growth between them are as presented here.

Initial peak	Concluding peak	Rate of growth between peaks
1948:2	1953:2	3.2264
1953:2	1957:1	0.6557
1957:1	1960:1	1.2354
1960:1	1969:3	3.0351
1969:3	1973:2	2.6870
1973:2	1981:3	1.4336
1981:3	1990:1	2.4548
1990:1	2002:2	1.8823

Series Cb15. Equals series Cb14 minus series Cb11.

Series Cb16. Values are estimates of the population at midperiod.

Series Cb17. The implicit deflator for gross domestic product. The BEA uses a chain price index. For details, see the essay on national income and product in Chapter Ca, and J. Steven Landerfeld and Robert P. Parker, "BEA's Chain Indexes, Time Series, and Measures of Long-Term Economic Growth," *Survey of Current Business* 77 (May 1997): 58–68.

TABLE Cb18–22   Real gross domestic product – trends and fluctuations: 1952–2001 [Okun–Phillips decomposition]

Contributed by Richard Sutch

			Okun–Phillips decomposition of real GDP		
Year: Quarter	Unemployment rate	Rate of inflation	Nonaccelerating inflation rate of unemployment (NAIRU)	Noninflationary potential real GDP	Deviation from potential real GDP
	Cb18	Cb19	Cb20	Cb21	Cb22
	Percent	Percent	Percent	Billion chained 1996 dollars	Billion chained 1996 dollars
1952:2	3.0	1.07	4.55	1,742.6	123.6
1952:3	3.2	2.30	4.61	1,769.3	108.7
1952:4	2.8	1.43	4.56	1,796.4	143.8
1953:1	2.7	1.70	4.41	1,823.9	152.1
1953:2	2.6	1.69	4.20	1,851.8	140.4
1953:3	2.7	0.89	3.97	1,880.1	99.4
1953:4	3.7	0.89	3.76	1,908.9	38.9
1954:1	5.2	1.20	3.67 [1]	1,938.1	0.0
1954:2	5.8	1.09	3.63	1,967.8	−26.8
1954:3	6.0	0.88	3.78	1,997.9	−35.9
1954:4	5.4	0.88	4.00	2,028.4	−27.5
1955:1	4.7	0.98	4.20	2,059.5	−1.4
1955:2	4.4	1.34	4.38 [2]	2,091.0	0.0
1955:3	4.1	1.90	4.47	2,093.4	25.5
1955:4	4.2	2.67	4.56	2,095.8	34.3
1956:1	4.0	3.22	4.65	2,098.2	22.8
1956:2	4.2	3.36	4.76	2,100.6	37.1
1956:3	4.1	3.88	4.89	2,103.0	32.3
1956:4	4.1	3.25	4.99	2,105.4	65.0
1957:1	4.0	3.66	5.08	2,107.8	74.9
1957:2	4.1	3.79	5.14	2,110.2	67.5
1957:3	4.2	3.11	5.18	2,112.6	86.3
1957:4	4.9	2.71	5.22	2,115.0	61.0

Notes appear at end of table

TABLE Cb18–22 Real gross domestic product – trends and fluctuations: 1952–2001 [Okun–Phillips decomposition] *Continued*

Year: Quarter	Unemployment rate	Rate of inflation	Nonaccelerating inflation rate of unemployment (NAIRU)	Noninflationary potential real GDP	Deviation from potential real GDP
	Cb18	Cb19	Cb20	Cb21	Cb22
	Percent	Percent	Percent	Billion chained 1996 dollars	Billion chained 1996 dollars
1958:1	6.3	2.43	5.25 [1]	2,117.4	0.0
1958:2	7.4	2.13	5.28	2,155.3	−25.6
1958:3	7.3	2.21	5.30	2,193.8	−16.3
1958:4	6.4	2.78	5.32	2,233.1	−6.6
1959:1	5.8	1.68	5.33 [2]	2,273.0	0.0
1959:2	5.1	1.30	5.37	2,294.8	37.6
1959:3	5.3	0.83	5.42	2,316.9	14.5
1959:4	5.6	0.73	5.48 [1,2]	2,339.1	0.0
1960:1	5.2	1.15	5.56	2,342.5	48.5
1960:2	5.2	1.47	5.63	2,346.0	33.2
1960:3	5.6	1.60	5.70	2,349.4	34.2
1960:4	6.3	1.46	5.78 [1]	2,352.9	0.0
1961:1	6.8	1.22	5.84	2,388.9	−22.4
1961:2	7.0	1.13	5.84	2,425.5	−14.7
1961:3	6.8	1.03	5.81	2,462.7	−12.3
1961:4	6.2	1.03	5.74 [2]	2,500.4	0.0
1962:1	5.6	1.43	5.67	2,526.6	17.4
1962:2	5.5	1.38	5.65	2,553.0	18.5
1962:3	5.6	1.34	5.61	2,579.8	17.0
1962:4	5.5	1.33	5.58	2,606.8	−3.5
1963:1	5.8	1.06	5.52 [1]	2,634.1	0.0
1963:2	5.7	1.01	5.44	2,674.7	−6.3
1963:3	5.5	0.97	5.38	2,716.0	3.6
1963:4	5.6	1.45	5.34	2,757.9	−18.5
1964:1	5.5	1.35	5.30 [2]	2,800.5	0.0
1964:2	5.2	1.48	5.23	2,827.8	6.0
1964:3	5.0	1.70	5.14	2,855.4	16.6
1964:4	5.0	1.42	5.02	2,883.3	−3.8
1965:1	4.9	1.68	4.90	2,911.5	38.6
1965:2	4.7	1.85	4.81	2,939.9	50.0
1965:3	4.4	1.88	4.74	2,968.6	82.1
1965:4	4.1	2.04	4.69	2,997.6	126.0
1966:1	3.9	2.20	4.62	3,026.8	174.3
1966:2	3.8	2.57	4.55	3,056.4	156.8
1966:3	3.8	3.23	4.46	3,086.2	147.4
1966:4	3.7	3.42	4.39	3,116.3	145.5
1967:1	3.8	3.15	4.35	3,146.8	145.0
1967:2	3.8	3.00	4.33	3,177.5	112.2
1967:3	3.8	2.97	4.34	3,208.5	105.0
1967:4	3.9	3.23	4.35	3,239.8	98.5
1968:1	3.7	3.98	4.37	3,271.4	134.8
1968:2	3.5	4.35	4.38	3,303.4	161.4
1968:3	3.5	4.27	4.41	3,335.6	153.6
1968:4	3.4	4.57	4.43	3,368.2	135.9
1969:1	3.4	4.44	4.48	3,401.1	157.2
1969:2	3.4	4.78	4.54	3,434.3	133.3
1969:3	3.6	5.31	4.62	3,467.8	120.5
1969:4	3.6	5.19	4.70	3,501.6	69.8
1970:1	4.2	5.62	4.79	3,535.8	30.7
1970:2	4.8	5.66	4.88	3,570.3	3.6
1970:3	5.2	5.00	4.96 [1]	3,605.2	0.0
1970:4	5.8	5.01	5.04	3,643.7	−77.2
1971:1	5.9	5.08	5.09	3,682.7	−16.6
1971:2	5.9	5.04	5.13	3,722.1	−35.9
1971:3	6.0	5.24	5.19	3,761.9	−47.4
1971:4	6.0	4.74	5.29	3,802.1	−78.3

Notes appear at end of table   (continued)

TABLE Cb18–22   Real gross domestic product – trends and fluctuations: 1952–2001 [Okun–Phillips decomposition] *Continued*

			Okun–Phillips decomposition of real GDP		
	Unemployment rate	Rate of inflation	Nonaccelerating inflation rate of unemployment (NAIRU)	Noninflationary potential real GDP	Deviation from potential real GDP
	Cb18	Cb19	Cb20	Cb21	Cb22
Year: Quarter	Percent	Percent	Percent	Billion chained 1996 dollars	Billion chained 1996 dollars
1972: 1	5.8	4.70	5.41	3,842.7	−45.8
1972: 2	5.7	3.98	5.55 [2]	3,883.8	(Z)
1972: 3	5.6	3.94	5.68	3,895.1	27.2
1972: 4	5.3	4.39	5.83	3,906.4	84.1
1973: 1	5.0	4.14	5.99	3,917.8	174.5
1973: 2	4.9	5.19	6.16	3,929.2	204.1
1973: 3	4.8	6.08	6.32	3,940.7	176.3
1973: 4	4.8	6.99	6.43	3,952.1	199.0
1974: 1	5.1	7.61	6.51	3,963.6	155.7
1974: 2	5.2	8.33	6.56	3,975.2	155.2
1974: 3	5.6	9.54	6.61	3,986.8	97.7
1974: 4	6.6	10.47	6.65	3,998.4	63.6
1975: 1	8.2	11.02	6.69 [1]	4,010.0	(Z)
1975: 2	8.9	10.02	6.71	4,062.8	−17.6
1975: 3	8.5	8.74	6.74	4,116.3	−0.9
1975: 4	8.3	7.46	6.75	4,170.5	−3.3
1976: 1	7.7	6.19	6.73	4,225.5	40.6
1976: 2	7.6	5.78	6.72	4,281.1	20.4
1976: 3	7.7	5.38	6.72	4,337.5	−15.6
1976: 4	7.8	5.41	6.74	4,394.7	−37.3
1977: 1	7.5	5.95	6.80	4,452.5	−42.0
1977: 2	7.1	6.61	6.86	4,511.2	−21.4
1977: 3	6.9	6.42	6.88 [2]	4,570.6	(Z)
1977: 4	6.6	6.68	6.90	4,593.3	−17.2
1978: 1	6.3	6.57	6.93	4,616.1	−27.2
1978: 2	6.0	6.89	6.96	4,639.0	126.7
1978: 3	6.0	7.45	6.98	4,662.0	149.7
1978: 4	5.9	7.43	7.00	4,685.1	190.9
1979: 1	5.9	7.87	7.05	4,708.4	179.9
1979: 2	5.7	8.25	7.10	4,731.7	159.7
1979: 3	5.9	8.66	7.19	4,755.2	171.0
1979: 4	5.9	8.69	7.27	4,778.8	163.8
1980: 1	6.3	9.02	7.34	4,802.5	156.4
1980: 2	7.3	8.95	7.39	4,826.4	31.4
1980: 3	7.7	9.07	7.42 [1,2]	4,850.3	0.0
1980: 4	7.4	9.70	7.43	4,879.3	57.3
1981: 1	7.4	10.07	7.44	4,908.5	124.0
1981: 2	7.4	9.62	7.44	4,937.9	59.4
1981: 3	7.4	9.29	7.45	4,967.4	89.4
1981: 4	8.2	8.41	7.47 [1]	4,997.1	0.0
1982: 1	8.8	7.14	7.48	5,040.6	−126.3
1982: 2	9.4	6.59	7.50	5,084.4	−148.9
1982: 3	9.9	6.04	7.52	5,128.7	−216.6
1982: 4	10.7	5.23	7.56	5,173.3	−257.7
1983: 1	10.4	4.55	7.62	5,218.3	−245.9
1983: 2	10.1	4.15	7.65	5,263.7	−173.9
1983: 3	9.4	3.61	7.67	5,309.5	−129.1
1983: 4	8.5	3.44	7.64	5,355.7	−68.9
1984: 1	7.9	3.89	7.59 [2]	5,402.3	(Z)
1984: 2	7.5	3.79	7.57	5,453.7	40.1
1984: 3	7.4	3.72	7.56	5,505.7	35.6
1984: 4	7.3	3.54	7.55	5,558.1	25.0
1985: 1	7.3	3.41	7.54	5,611.0	18.7
1985: 2	7.3	3.29	7.48	5,664.5	9.3
1985: 3	7.2	2.96	7.39	5,718.4	40.2
1985: 4	7.0	2.98	7.26	5,772.8	33.2

Notes appear at end of table

TABLE Cb18–22   Real gross domestic product – trends and fluctuations: 1952–2001 [Okun–Phillips decomposition]   *Continued*

			Okun–Phillips decomposition of real GDP		
	Unemployment rate	Rate of inflation	Nonaccelerating inflation rate of unemployment (NAIRU)	Noninflationary potential real GDP	Deviation from potential real GDP
	Cb18	Cb19	Cb20	Cb21	Cb22
Year: Quarter	Percent	Percent	Percent	Billion chained 1996 dollars	Billion chained 1996 dollars
1986: 1	7.0	2.30	7.11	5,827.8	31.1
1986: 2	7.2	2.11	6.95 [1]	5,883.3	(Z)
1986: 3	7.0	2.25	6.78	5,926.3	11.6
1986: 4	6.8	2.18	6.61	5,969.7	−0.2
1987: 1	6.6	2.70	6.46 [2]	6,013.3	(Z)
1987: 2	6.3	2.96	6.35	6,050.2	27.0
1987: 3	6.0	3.09	6.27	6,087.3	40.8
1987: 4	5.9	3.22	6.22	6,124.6	109.8
1988: 1	5.7	2.97	6.20	6,162.2	113.7
1988: 2	5.5	3.26	6.17	6,200.0	149.8
1988: 3	5.5	3.69	6.17	6,238.0	144.3
1988: 4	5.3	3.66	6.18	6,276.3	188.9
1989: 1	5.2	4.08	6.21	6,314.8	229.0
1989: 2	5.2	4.04	6.24	6,353.5	225.9
1989: 3	5.3	3.61	6.25	6,392.5	218.1
1989: 4	5.4	3.58	6.24	6,431.7	201.8
1990: 1	5.3	3.63	6.22	6,471.2	245.1
1990: 2	5.3	3.79	6.21	6,510.9	220.8
1990: 3	5.7	4.03	6.20	6,550.8	168.6
1990: 4	6.1	4.15	6.21	6,591.0	73.2
1991: 1	6.6	4.20	6.21 [1]	6,631.4	(Z)
1991: 2	6.8	3.76	6.21	6,682.7	−14.2
1991: 3	6.9	3.45	6.19	6,734.4	−49.5
1991: 4	7.1	3.11	6.17	6,786.5	−65.6
1992: 1	7.4	2.70	6.18	6,839.0	−55.7
1992: 2	7.6	2.54	6.19	6,891.9	−45.1
1992: 3	7.6	2.20	6.21	6,945.2	−45.5
1992: 4	7.4	2.30	6.22	6,999.0	−8.4
1993: 1	7.2	2.37	6.23	7,053.1	−64.4
1993: 2	7.1	2.35	6.21	7,107.7	−76.5
1993: 3	6.8	2.47	6.20	7,162.7	−100.7
1993: 4	6.6	2.42	6.19	7,218.1	−49.4
1994: 1	6.6	2.10	6.16	7,273.9	−44.5
1994: 2	6.2	2.01	6.12 [2]	7,330.2	(Z)
1994: 3	6.0	2.16	6.06	7,387.7	−17.5
1994: 4	5.6	2.06	6.00	7,445.6	15.5
1995: 1	5.5	2.28	5.93	7,504.0	−15.3
1995: 2	5.7	2.25	5.85	7,562.9	−59.6
1995: 3	5.7	2.10	5.75	7,622.2	−60.8
1995: 4	5.6	2.11	5.63	7,681.9	−60.0
1996: 1	5.5	1.99	5.52	7,742.2	−65.8
1996: 2	5.5	1.92	5.41 [1,2]	7,802.9	(Z)
1996: 3	5.3	1.95	5.31	7,866.8	−24.9
1996: 4	5.3	1.87	5.21 [1]	7,931.3	(Z)
1997: 1	5.2	1.96	5.11 [2]	8,016.4	0.0
1997: 2	5.0	2.09	5.03	8,077.3	54.6
1997: 3	4.9	1.90	4.92	8,138.7	77.9
1997: 4	4.7	1.85	4.83	8,200.5	72.4
1998: 1	4.6	1.40	4.75	8,262.8	133.5
1998: 2	4.4	1.17	4.69	8,325.6	117.3
1998: 3	4.5	1.23	4.69	8,388.8	139.7
1998: 4	4.4	1.13	4.70	8,452.6	215.3
1999: 1	4.3	1.32	4.71	8,516.8	216.4
1999: 2	4.3	1.46	4.71	8,581.5	194.0
1999: 3	4.3	1.40	4.71	8,646.7	240.2
1999: 4	4.1	1.56	4.70	8,712.4	327.7

Notes appear at end of table   (continued)

**TABLE Cb18–22   Real gross domestic product – trends and fluctuations: 1952–2001
[Okun–Phillips decomposition]   *Continued***

			Okun–Phillips decomposition of real GDP		
	Unemployment rate	Rate of inflation	Nonaccelerating inflation rate of unemployment (NAIRU)	Noninflationary potential real GDP	Deviation from potential real GDP
	Cb18	Cb19	Cb20	Cb21	Cb22
				Billion chained 1996 dollars	Billion chained 1996 dollars
Year: Quarter	Percent	Percent	Percent		
2000: 1	4.0	1.87	4.71	8,778.6	318.8
2000: 2	4.0	2.08	4.69	8,845.3	360.4
2000: 3	4.0	2.18	4.67	8,912.5	306.2
2000: 4	3.9	2.29	4.68	8,980.2	263.6
2001: 1	4.2	2.43	4.68	9,048.4	181.5
2001: 2	4.4	2.47	4.69	9,117.1	76.0
2001: 3	4.8	2.61	4.69 [1]	9,186.4	0.0

(Z) Less than 0.05 billion chained 1996 dollars (in absolute value).

[1] The first quarter that the unemployment rate rises above nonaccelerating inflation rate of unemployment (NAIRU), denoting a quarter when real gross domestic product (GDP) is assumed to be equal to "potential" real GDP. These dates are used for calculating series Cb21.

[2] The last quarter that the unemployment rate is above NAIRU before it falls below it, denoting a quarter when real GDP is assumed to be equal to "potential" real GDP. These dates are used for calculating series Cb21.

Sources

Series Cb18. U.S. Bureau of Labor Statistics Internet site; downloaded August 20, 2003.

Series Cb19–22. Calculated based on data from the U.S. Bureau of Economic Analysis Internet site, Tables 1.2 and 7.1; downloaded August 18, 2003.

Documentation

The Okun–Phillips decomposition and the role played by the NAIRU are discussed in the essay in this chapter. The NAIRU is estimated by a procedure proposed by J. Bradford DeLong, "The NAIRU: Non-Accelerating Inflation Rate of Unemployment," *Semi-Daily Journal: Brad DeLong's Thoughts of the Moment on Economics, and on Other Topics as Well*, DeLong's Internet site, July 2002. The change in the rate of inflation ($\Delta\pi$) is estimated as a linear function of the unemployment rate (U_t), using ordinary least-squares regression:

$\Delta\pi$ = change in the rate of inflation (that is, the difference between the rate of inflation four quarters ahead and the current rate of inflation)

$$\Delta\pi = a - bU_t$$

The parameter *b* is called the Phillips curve slope. When estimated with annual data for 1960 through 2002, *b* is equal to 0.37723. The level of unemployment that would keep inflation stable (U^*) is then calculated using quarterly data as

$$U^* = U_t + b\Delta\pi$$

Following DeLong, NAIRU is estimated as a twenty-seven-quarter centered moving average. The purpose of the moving average is to smooth out the "noise" in the estimate of NAIRU, because in theory NAIRU should change only slowly over time as the economy and labor markets evolve.

The "noninflationary" potential real GDP is defined to be equal to actual real GDP when the unemployment rate is equal to NAIRU. Exponential interpolation between the benchmarks defines the time series of noninflationary potential real GDP.

Series Cb18. The values refer to the noninstitutionalized civilian labor force, aged 16 years and older.

Series Cb19. The rate of inflation of the implicit deflator for GDP, series Cb17.

Series Cb20. The NAIRU is a centered twenty-seven-quarter moving average of U^*, as defined earlier. Data from the sources that lie outside of the date range of this table were required for some of the calculations shown here.

Series Cb21. For quarters marked with a footnote on the values for series Cb20, the value of noninflationary potential real GDP is the value of real GDP given in series Cb10. All other values are exponentially interpolated between these values.

Series Cb22. Deviation from natural real GDP is the value of real GDP (series Cb10) minus the value of series Cb21.

TABLE Cb23 Potential real gross domestic product: 1950–1997 [Congressional Budget Office estimates]

Contributed by Richard Sutch

Year	Potential real gross domestic product Cb23 Billion chained 1996 dollars	Year	Potential real gross domestic product Cb23 Billion chained 1996 dollars	Year	Potential real gross domestic product Cb23 Billion chained 1996 dollars	Year	Potential real gross domestic product Cb23 Billion chained 1996 dollars	Year	Potential real gross domestic product Cb23 Billion chained 1996 dollars
1950	1,665	1960	2,402	1970	3,596	1980	5,009	1990	6,714
1951	1,743	1961	2,497	1971	3,719	1981	5,137	1991	6,895
1952	1,825	1962	2,597	1972	3,845	1982	5,266	1992	7,068
1953	1,900	1963	2,702	1973	3,980	1983	5,413	1993	7,247
1954	1,965	1964	2,813	1974	4,124	1984	5,575	1994	7,439
1955	2,026	1965	2,931	1975	4,268	1985	5,752	1995	7,647
1956	2,091	1966	3,060	1976	4,411	1986	5,944	1996	7,882
1957	2,162	1967	3,196	1977	4,559	1987	6,137	1997	8,145
1958	2,236	1968	3,335	1978	4,719	1988	6,331		
1959	2,316	1969	3,469	1979	4,873	1989	6,525		

Source

Robert Arnold, "CBO's Method for Estimating Potential Output: An Update," Congressional Budget Office, Macroeconomic Analysis Division, August 2001.

Documentation

The essay in this chapter discusses the concept of potential product and the role of the nonaccelerating inflation rate of unemployment (NAIRU). Also see the text for Table Cb18–22. The Congressional Budget Office (CBO) uses a somewhat more complex method to estimate potential output. Each of several components of potential GDP is estimated separately. The CBO method uses its variant of Okun's law and its own annual estimates of NAIRU. The source also provides estimates for 1998 through 2000, but these are inconsistent with the latest revision of real gross domestic product released by the U.S. Bureau of Economic Analysis, and projections to 2011, neither of which is shown here.

TABLE Cb24–27 Unemployment rates: 1940–2003

Contributed by Richard Sutch

Year: Month	14 and older, seasonally adjusted Cb24 Percent	16 and older Not seasonally adjusted Cb25 Percent	16 and older Seasonally adjusted Overall Cb26 Percent	16 and older Seasonally adjusted Married men (spouse present) Cb27 Percent	Year: Month	14 and older, seasonally adjusted Cb24 Percent	16 and older Not seasonally adjusted Cb25 Percent	16 and older Seasonally adjusted Overall Cb26 Percent	16 and older Seasonally adjusted Married men (spouse present) Cb27 Percent
1940: 3	15.4	—	—	—	1942: 5	4.9	—	—	—
1940: 4	16.0	—	—	—	1942: 6	4.4	—	—	—
1940: 5	15.5	—	—	—	1942: 7	4.2	—	—	—
1940: 6	12.9	—	—	—	1942: 8	3.6	—	—	—
1940: 7	13.6	—	—	—	1942: 9	3.2	—	—	—
1940: 8	14.6	—	—	—	1942: 10	3.2	—	—	—
1940: 9	13.2	—	—	—	1942: 11	3.2	—	—	—
1940: 10	14.7	—	—	—	1942: 12	2.9	—	—	—
1940: 11	14.4	—	—	—	1943: 1	2.5	—	—	—
1940: 12	13.6	—	—	—	1943: 2	2.4	—	—	—
1941: 1	12.5	—	—	—	1943: 3	2.1	—	—	—
1941: 2	12.0	—	—	—	1943: 4	2.0	—	—	—
1941: 3	12.1	—	—	—	1943: 5	1.8	—	—	—
1941: 4	12.4	—	—	—	1943: 6	2.0	—	—	—
1941: 5	10.9	—	—	—	1943: 7	2.1	—	—	—
1941: 6	9.5	—	—	—	1943: 8	1.8	—	—	—
1941: 7	8.9	—	—	—	1943: 9	1.7	—	—	—
1941: 8	9.3	—	—	—	1943: 10	1.6	—	—	—
1941: 9	8.9	—	—	—	1943: 11	1.4	—	—	—
1941: 10	7.8	—	—	—	1943: 12	1.4	—	—	—
1941: 11	7.4	—	—	—	1944: 1	1.4	—	—	—
1941: 12	7.0	—	—	—	1944: 2	1.2	—	—	—
1942: 1	7.2	—	—	—	1944: 3	1.3	—	—	—
1942: 2	6.9	—	—	—	1944: 4	1.2	—	—	—
1942: 3	6.5	—	—	—					
1942: 4	5.8	—	—	—					

(continued)

TABLE Cb24–27 Unemployment rates: 1940–2003 *Continued*

Year: Month	14 and older, seasonally adjusted	16 and older			Year: Month	14 and older, seasonally adjusted	16 and older		
		Not seasonally adjusted	Seasonally adjusted				Not seasonally adjusted	Seasonally adjusted	
			Overall	Married men (spouse present)				Overall	Married men (spouse present)
	Cb24	Cb25	Cb26	Cb27		Cb24	Cb25	Cb26	Cb27
	Percent	Percent	Percent	Percent		Percent	Percent	Percent	Percent
1944: 5	1.4	—	—	—	1949: 1	—	5.0	4.3	—
1944: 6	1.4	—	—	—	1949: 2	—	5.8	4.7	—
1944: 7	1.4	—	—	—	1949: 3	—	5.6	5.0	—
1944: 8	1.2	—	—	—	1949: 4	—	5.4	5.3	—
1944: 9	1.2	—	—	—	1949: 5	—	5.7	6.1	—
1944: 10	0.9	—	—	—	1949: 6	—	6.4	6.2	—
1944: 11	1.0	—	—	—	1949: 7	—	7.0	6.7	—
1944: 12	1.0	—	—	—	1949: 8	—	6.3	6.8	—
1945: 1	1.1	—	—	—	1949: 9	—	5.9	6.6	—
1945: 2	1.1	—	—	—	1949: 10	—	6.1	7.9	—
1945: 3	1.1	—	—	—	1949: 11	—	5.7	6.4	—
1945: 4	1.0	—	—	—	1949: 12	—	6.0	6.6	—
1945: 5	1.1	—	—	—	1950: 1	—	7.6	6.5	—
1945: 6	1.4	—	—	—	1950: 2	—	7.9	6.4	—
1945: 7	1.5	—	—	—	1950: 3	—	7.1	6.3	—
1945: 8	1.5	—	—	—	1950: 4	—	6.0	5.8	—
1945: 9	3.4	—	—	—	1950: 5	—	5.3	5.5	—
1945: 10	3.3	—	—	—	1950: 6	—	5.6	5.4	—
1945: 11	3.6	—	—	—	1950: 7	—	5.3	5.0	—
1945: 12	4.0	—	—	—	1950: 8	—	4.1	4.5	—
1946: 1	4.1	—	—	—	1950: 9	—	4.0	4.4	—
1946: 2	4.1	—	—	—	1950: 10	—	3.3	4.2	—
1946: 3	4.3	—	—	—	1950: 11	—	3.8	4.2	—
1946: 4	3.9	—	—	—	1950: 12	—	3.9	4.3	—
1946: 5	4.3	—	—	—	1951: 1	—	4.4	3.7	—
1946: 6	3.9	—	—	—	1951: 2	—	4.2	3.4	—
1946: 7	3.4	—	—	—	1951: 3	—	3.8	3.4	—
1946: 8	3.6	—	—	—	1951: 4	—	3.2	3.1	—
1946: 9	3.9	—	—	—	1951: 5	—	2.9	3.0	—
1946: 10	4.0	—	—	—	1951: 6	—	3.4	3.2	—
1946: 11	4.0	—	—	—	1951: 7	—	3.3	3.1	—
1946: 12	4.2	—	—	—	1951: 8	—	2.9	3.1	—
1947: 1	3.9	—	—	—	1951: 9	—	3.0	3.3	—
1947: 2	3.6	—	—	—	1951: 10	—	2.8	3.5	—
1947: 3	3.5	—	—	—	1951: 11	—	3.2	3.5	—
1947: 4	3.9	—	—	—	1951: 12	—	2.9	3.1	—
1947: 5	3.4	—	—	—	1952: 1	—	3.7	3.2	—
1947: 6	3.6	—	—	—	1952: 2	—	3.8	3.1	—
1947: 7	3.7	—	—	—	1952: 3	—	3.3	2.9	—
1947: 8	3.6	—	—	—	1952: 4	—	3.0	2.9	—
1947: 9	3.5	—	—	—	1952: 5	—	2.9	3.0	—
1947: 10	3.3	—	—	—	1952: 6	—	3.2	3.0	—
1947: 11	3.3	—	—	—	1952: 7	—	3.3	3.2	—
1947: 12	3.2	—	—	—	1952: 8	—	3.1	3.4	—
1948: 1	3.3	4.0	3.4	—	1952: 9	—	2.7	3.1	—
1948: 2	3.7	4.7	3.8	—	1952: 10	—	2.4	3.0	—
1948: 3	3.6	4.5	4.0	—	1952: 11	—	2.5	2.8	—
1948: 4	3.5	4.0	3.9	—	1952: 12	—	2.5	2.7	—
1948: 5	3.1	3.4	3.5	—	1953: 1	—	3.4	2.9	—
1948: 6	3.1	3.9	3.6	—	1953: 2	—	3.2	2.6	—
1948: 7	3.1	3.9	3.6	—	1953: 3	—	2.9	2.6	—
1948: 8	3.2	3.6	3.9	—	1953: 4	—	2.8	2.7	—
1948: 9	3.4	3.4	3.8	—	1953: 5	—	2.5	2.5	—
1948: 10	3.2	2.9	3.7	—	1953: 6	—	2.7	2.5	—
1948: 11	3.6	3.3	3.8	—	1953: 7	—	2.7	2.6	—
1948: 12	3.7	3.6	4.0	—	1953: 8	—	2.4	2.7	—

TABLE Cb24–27   Unemployment rates: 1940–2003   *Continued*

Year: Month	14 and older, seasonally adjusted	16 and older Not seasonally adjusted	16 and older Seasonally adjusted Overall	16 and older Seasonally adjusted Married men (spouse present)	Year: Month	14 and older, seasonally adjusted	16 and older Not seasonally adjusted	16 and older Seasonally adjusted Overall	16 and older Seasonally adjusted Married men (spouse present)
	Cb24	Cb25	Cb26	Cb27		Cb24	Cb25	Cb26	Cb27
	Percent	Percent	Percent	Percent		Percent	Percent	Percent	Percent
1953: 9	—	2.6	2.9	—	1958: 5	—	7.1	7.4	5.6
1953: 10	—	2.5	3.1	—	1958: 6	—	7.6	7.3	5.8
1953: 11	—	3.2	3.5	—	1958: 7	—	7.4	7.5	5.7
1953: 12	—	4.2	4.5	—	1958: 8	—	6.7	7.4	5.6
1954: 1	—	5.7	4.9	—	1958: 9	—	6.0	7.1	5.1
1954: 2	—	6.3	5.2	—	1958: 10	—	5.5	6.7	4.9
1954: 3	—	6.4	5.7	—	1958: 11	—	5.6	6.2	4.5
1954: 4	—	6.1	5.9	—	1958: 12	—	6.0	6.2	4.5
1954: 5	—	5.7	5.9	—	1959: 1	—	7.0	6.0	4.1
1954: 6	—	5.7	5.6	—	1959: 2	—	7.0	5.9	4.0
1954: 7	—	5.7	5.8	—	1959: 3	—	6.4	5.6	3.7
1954: 8	—	5.4	6.0	—	1959: 4	—	5.2	5.2	3.2
1954: 9	—	5.3	6.1	—	1959: 5	—	4.9	5.1	3.2
1954: 10	—	4.6	5.7	—	1959: 6	—	5.4	5.0	3.1
1954: 11	—	4.9	5.3	—	1959: 7	—	5.2	5.1	3.3
1954: 12	—	4.8	5.0	—	1959: 8	—	4.8	5.2	3.4
1955: 1	—	5.8	4.9	3.3	1959: 9	—	4.7	5.5	3.7
1955: 2	—	5.7	4.7	3.2	1959: 10	—	4.7	5.7	3.9
1955: 3	—	5.2	4.6	3.2	1959: 11	—	5.3	5.8	4.2
1955: 4	—	4.9	4.7	3.3	1959: 12	—	5.1	5.3	3.3
1955: 5	—	4.2	4.3	2.7	1960: 1	—	6.1	5.2	3.3
1955: 6	—	4.4	4.2	2.6	1960: 2	—	5.7	4.8	2.9
1955: 7	—	4.0	4.0	2.4	1960: 3	—	6.1	5.4	3.6
1955: 8	—	3.8	4.2	2.5	1960: 4	—	5.2	5.2	3.4
1955: 9	—	3.5	4.1	2.5	1960: 5	—	4.8	5.1	3.4
1955: 10	—	3.4	4.3	2.6	1960: 6	—	5.8	5.4	3.6
1955: 11	—	3.8	4.2	2.4	1960: 7	—	5.5	5.5	3.7
1955: 12	—	3.9	4.2	2.3	1960: 8	—	5.2	5.6	3.9
1956: 1	—	4.7	4.0	2.5	1960: 9	—	4.7	5.5	3.9
1956: 2	—	4.8	3.9	2.5	1960: 10	—	5.0	6.1	4.4
1956: 3	—	4.7	4.2	2.5	1960: 11	—	5.6	6.1	4.4
1956: 4	—	4.1	4.0	2.5	1960: 12	—	6.4	6.6	4.7
1956: 5	—	4.2	4.3	2.6	1961: 1	—	7.7	6.6	4.7
1956: 6	—	4.7	4.3	2.6	1961: 2	—	8.1	6.9	4.8
1956: 7	—	4.4	4.4	2.8	1961: 3	—	7.7	6.9	4.8
1956: 8	—	3.7	4.1	2.4	1961: 4	—	7.0	7.0	4.9
1956: 9	—	3.4	3.9	2.7	1961: 5	—	6.6	7.1	5.1
1956: 10	—	3.1	3.9	2.5	1961: 6	—	7.3	6.9	4.8
1956: 11	—	3.9	4.3	2.8	1961: 7	—	6.9	7.0	4.8
1956: 12	—	4.0	4.2	2.8	1961: 8	—	6.2	6.6	4.7
1957: 1	—	4.9	4.2	2.6	1961: 9	—	5.8	6.7	4.6
1957: 2	—	4.7	3.9	2.4	1961: 10	—	5.5	6.5	4.2
1957: 3	—	4.3	3.7	2.3	1961: 11	—	5.6	6.1	4.1
1957: 4	—	4.0	3.9	2.6	1961: 12	—	5.8	6.0	3.9
1957: 5	—	3.9	4.1	2.6	1962: 1	—	6.7	5.8	3.7
1957: 6	—	4.6	4.3	2.6	1962: 2	—	6.5	5.5	3.3
1957: 7	—	4.1	4.2	2.6	1962: 3	—	6.2	5.6	3.6
1957: 8	—	3.7	4.1	2.7	1962: 4	—	5.5	5.6	3.7
1957: 9	—	3.7	4.4	3.0	1962: 5	—	5.1	5.5	3.5
1957: 10	—	3.6	4.5	3.1	1962: 6	—	5.9	5.5	3.7
1957: 11	—	4.6	5.1	3.5	1962: 7	—	5.3	5.4	3.6
1957: 12	—	5.0	5.2	3.7	1962: 8	—	5.3	5.7	3.6
1958: 1	—	6.8	5.8	4.0	1962: 9	—	4.9	5.6	3.4
1958: 2	—	7.7	6.4	4.7	1962: 10	—	4.5	5.4	3.5
1958: 3	—	7.7	6.7	5.2	1962: 11	—	5.3	5.7	3.5
1958: 4	—	7.5	7.4	5.5	1962: 12	—	5.3	5.5	3.6

(continued)

TABLE Cb24–27 Unemployment rates: 1940–2003 *Continued*

Year: Month	14 and older, seasonally adjusted	16 and older			Year: Month	14 and older, seasonally adjusted	16 and older		
		Not seasonally adjusted	Seasonally adjusted				Not seasonally adjusted	Seasonally adjusted	
			Overall	Married men (spouse present)				Overall	Married men (spouse present)
	Cb24	Cb25	Cb26	Cb27		Cb24	Cb25	Cb26	Cb27
	Percent	Percent	Percent	Percent		Percent	Percent	Percent	Percent
1963: 1	—	6.6	5.7	3.7	1967: 9	—	3.7	3.8	1.8
1963: 2	—	6.9	5.9	3.7	1967: 10	—	3.8	4.0	1.8
1963: 3	—	6.3	5.7	3.6	1967: 11	—	3.7	3.9	1.7
1963: 4	—	5.6	5.7	3.4	1967: 12	—	3.5	3.8	1.8
1963: 5	—	5.5	5.9	3.4	1968: 1	—	4.0	3.7	1.8
1963: 6	—	6.2	5.6	3.2	1968: 2	—	4.2	3.8	1.8
1963: 7	—	5.6	5.6	3.2	1968: 3	—	3.8	3.7	1.7
1963: 8	—	5.2	5.4	3.0	1968: 4	—	3.2	3.5	1.5
1963: 9	—	4.8	5.5	3.0	1968: 5	—	2.9	3.5	1.5
1963: 10	—	4.7	5.5	3.0	1968: 6	—	4.5	3.7	1.7
1963: 11	—	5.3	5.7	3.3	1968: 7	—	4.0	3.7	1.6
1963: 12	—	5.3	5.5	3.4	1968: 8	—	3.5	3.5	1.6
1964: 1	—	6.4	5.6	3.1	1968: 9	—	3.3	3.4	1.6
1964: 2	—	6.2	5.4	3.0	1968: 10	—	3.2	3.4	1.6
1964: 3	—	5.9	5.4	3.0	1968: 11	—	3.3	3.4	1.6
1964: 4	—	5.3	5.3	2.9	1968: 12	—	3.1	3.4	1.4
1964: 5	—	4.8	5.1	2.6	1969: 1	—	3.7	3.4	1.4
1964: 6	—	5.9	5.2	2.8	1969: 2	—	3.7	3.4	1.4
1964: 7	—	4.9	4.9	2.7	1969: 3	—	3.5	3.4	1.4
1964: 8	—	4.8	5.0	2.5	1969: 4	—	3.2	3.4	1.4
1964: 9	—	4.5	5.1	2.8	1969: 5	—	2.9	3.4	1.5
1964: 10	—	4.4	5.1	2.9	1969: 6	—	4.1	3.5	1.5
1964: 11	—	4.5	4.8	2.4	1969: 7	—	3.8	3.5	1.6
1964: 12	—	4.7	5.0	2.7	1969: 8	—	3.5	3.5	1.5
1965: 1	—	5.5	4.9	2.7	1969: 9	—	3.7	3.7	1.7
1965: 2	—	5.7	5.1	2.6	1969: 10	—	3.5	3.7	1.6
1965: 3	—	5.1	4.7	2.5	1969: 11	—	3.3	3.5	1.5
1965: 4	—	4.7	4.8	2.5	1969: 12	—	3.2	3.5	1.7
1965: 5	—	4.3	4.6	2.5	1970: 1	—	4.2	3.9	1.9
1965: 6	—	5.3	4.6	2.3	1970: 2	—	4.7	4.2	2.0
1965: 7	—	4.5	4.4	2.3	1970: 3	—	4.6	4.4	2.2
1965: 8	—	4.2	4.4	2.4	1970: 4	—	4.3	4.6	2.3
1965: 9	—	3.8	4.3	2.2	1970: 5	—	4.1	4.8	2.5
1965: 10	—	3.6	4.2	2.0	1970: 6	—	5.6	4.9	2.5
1965: 11	—	3.9	4.1	2.0	1970: 7	—	5.3	5.0	2.7
1965: 12	—	3.7	4.0	1.9	1970: 8	—	5.0	5.1	2.8
1966: 1	—	4.4	4.0	2.0	1970: 9	—	5.2	5.4	2.9
1966: 2	—	4.2	3.8	1.9	1970: 10	—	5.1	5.5	3.0
1966: 3	—	4.0	3.8	2.0	1970: 11	—	5.5	5.9	3.2
1966: 4	—	3.6	3.8	1.8	1970: 12	—	5.6	6.1	3.4
1966: 5	—	3.7	3.9	1.7	1971: 1	—	6.6	5.9	3.3
1966: 6	—	4.6	3.8	1.9	1971: 2	—	6.6	5.9	3.2
1966: 7	—	3.9	3.8	2.0	1971: 3	—	6.3	6.0	3.2
1966: 8	—	3.6	3.8	1.9	1971: 4	—	5.7	5.9	3.1
1966: 9	—	3.3	3.7	1.8	1971: 5	—	5.3	5.9	3.2
1966: 10	—	3.2	3.7	1.8	1971: 6	—	6.5	5.9	3.1
1966: 11	—	3.4	3.6	1.8	1971: 7	—	6.2	6.0	3.1
1966: 12	—	3.5	3.8	1.8	1971: 8	—	5.9	6.1	3.2
1967: 1	—	4.2	3.9	1.9	1971: 9	—	5.8	6.0	3.3
1967: 2	—	4.2	3.8	1.7	1971: 10	—	5.4	5.8	3.0
1967: 3	—	3.9	3.8	1.8	1971: 11	—	5.7	6.0	3.4
1967: 4	—	3.5	3.8	1.9	1971: 12	—	5.5	6.0	3.2
1967: 5	—	3.2	3.8	1.8	1972: 1	—	6.5	5.8	3.0
1967: 6	—	4.6	3.9	1.9	1972: 2	—	6.4	5.7	2.9
1967: 7	—	4.1	3.8	1.8	1972: 3	—	6.1	5.8	2.8
1967: 8	—	3.7	3.8	1.8	1972: 4	—	5.5	5.7	2.8

TABLE Cb24–27   Unemployment rates: 1940–2003   *Continued*

Year: Month	14 and older, seasonally adjusted	16 and older			Year: Month	14 and older, seasonally adjusted	16 and older		
		Not seasonally adjusted	Seasonally adjusted				Not seasonally adjusted	Seasonally adjusted	
			Overall	Married men (spouse present)				Overall	Married men (spouse present)
	Cb24	Cb25	Cb26	Cb27		Cb24	Cb25	Cb26	Cb27
	Percent	Percent	Percent	Percent		Percent	Percent	Percent	Percent
1972: 5	—	5.1	5.7	2.8	1977: 1	—	8.3	7.5	4.1
1972: 6	—	6.2	5.7	2.8	1977: 2	—	8.5	7.6	4.1
1972: 7	—	5.9	5.6	2.8	1977: 3	—	7.9	7.4	3.8
1972: 8	—	5.5	5.6	2.7	1977: 4	—	6.9	7.2	3.7
1972: 9	—	5.4	5.5	2.8	1977: 5	—	6.4	7.0	3.6
1972: 10	—	5.1	5.6	2.8	1977: 6	—	7.5	7.2	3.5
1972: 11	—	4.9	5.3	2.5	1977: 7	—	7.0	6.9	3.4
1972: 12	—	4.8	5.2	2.4	1977: 8	—	6.8	7.0	3.4
1973: 1	—	5.5	4.9	2.4	1977: 9	—	6.6	6.8	3.3
1973: 2	—	5.6	5.0	2.4	1977: 10	—	6.4	6.8	3.6
1973: 3	—	5.2	4.9	2.4	1977: 11	—	6.5	6.8	3.3
1973: 4	—	4.8	5.0	2.4	1977: 12	—	6.0	6.4	3.2
1973: 5	—	4.4	4.9	2.3	1978: 1	—	7.1	6.4	3.1
1973: 6	—	5.4	4.9	2.2	1978: 2	—	6.9	6.3	3.0
1973: 7	—	5.0	4.8	2.1	1978: 3	—	6.6	6.3	3.1
1973: 8	—	4.7	4.8	2.2	1978: 4	—	5.8	6.1	2.8
1973: 9	—	4.7	4.8	2.1	1978: 5	—	5.5	6.0	2.8
1973: 10	—	4.2	4.6	2.2	1978: 6	—	6.2	5.9	2.8
1973: 11	—	4.6	4.8	2.2	1978: 7	—	6.3	6.2	2.6
1973: 12	—	4.6	4.9	2.3	1978: 8	—	5.9	5.9	2.7
1974: 1	—	5.7	5.1	2.4	1978: 9	—	5.8	6.0	2.7
1974: 2	—	5.8	5.2	2.4	1978: 10	—	5.4	5.8	2.6
1974: 3	—	5.3	5.1	2.3	1978: 11	—	5.6	5.9	2.5
1974: 4	—	4.8	5.1	2.4	1978: 12	—	5.7	6.0	2.7
1974: 5	—	4.6	5.1	2.2	1979: 1	—	6.4	5.9	2.7
1974: 6	—	5.8	5.4	2.5	1979: 2	—	6.4	5.9	2.8
1974: 7	—	5.7	5.5	2.7	1979: 3	—	6.1	5.8	2.7
1974: 8	—	5.3	5.5	2.8	1979: 4	—	5.5	5.8	2.7
1974: 9	—	5.7	5.9	2.8	1979: 5	—	5.2	5.6	2.4
1974: 10	—	5.5	6.0	3.0	1979: 6	—	6.0	5.7	2.6
1974: 11	—	6.2	6.6	3.4	1979: 7	—	5.9	5.7	2.8
1974: 12	—	6.7	7.2	3.8	1979: 8	—	5.9	6.0	2.9
1975: 1	—	9.0	8.1	4.6	1979: 9	—	5.7	5.9	2.8
1975: 2	—	9.1	8.1	4.7	1979: 10	—	5.6	6.0	2.9
1975: 3	—	9.1	8.6	5.1	1979: 11	—	5.6	5.9	3.0
1975: 4	—	8.6	8.8	5.5	1979: 12	—	5.7	6.0	2.9
1975: 5	—	8.3	9.0	5.7	1980: 1	—	6.9	6.3	3.5
1975: 6	—	9.1	8.8	5.5	1980: 2	—	6.8	6.3	3.3
1975: 7	—	8.7	8.6	5.4	1980: 3	—	6.6	6.3	3.5
1975: 8	—	8.2	8.4	5.2	1980: 4	—	6.7	6.9	4.1
1975: 9	—	8.1	8.4	5.3	1980: 5	—	7.1	7.5	4.5
1975: 10	—	7.8	8.4	5.2	1980: 6	—	7.8	7.6	4.7
1975: 11	—	7.8	8.3	4.9	1980: 7	—	7.9	7.8	4.9
1975: 12	—	7.8	8.2	4.7	1980: 8	—	7.6	7.7	4.9
1976: 1	—	8.8	7.9	4.4	1980: 9	—	7.2	7.5	4.7
1976: 2	—	8.7	7.7	4.2	1980: 10	—	7.1	7.5	4.5
1976: 3	—	8.1	7.6	4.2	1980: 11	—	7.1	7.5	4.3
1976: 4	—	7.4	7.7	4.1	1980: 12	—	6.9	7.2	4.1
1976: 5	—	6.8	7.4	4.1	1981: 1	—	8.2	7.5	4.2
1976: 6	—	8.0	7.6	4.4	1981: 2	—	8.0	7.4	4.2
1976: 7	—	7.8	7.8	4.4	1981: 3	—	7.7	7.4	4.2
1976: 8	—	7.6	7.8	4.1	1981: 4	—	7.0	7.2	3.8
1976: 9	—	7.4	7.6	4.4	1981: 5	—	7.1	7.5	4.0
1976: 10	—	7.2	7.7	4.2	1981: 6	—	7.7	7.5	4.3
1976: 11	—	7.4	7.8	4.3	1981: 7	—	7.3	7.2	4.0
1976: 12	—	7.4	7.8	4.2	1981: 8	—	7.2	7.4	4.1

(continued)

TABLE Cb24–27   Unemployment rates: 1940–2003   *Continued*

Year: Month	14 and older, seasonally adjusted Cb24 Percent	16 and older Not seasonally adjusted Cb25 Percent	Seasonally adjusted Overall Cb26 Percent	Married men (spouse present) Cb27 Percent	Year: Month	14 and older, seasonally adjusted Cb24 Percent	16 and older Not seasonally adjusted Cb25 Percent	Seasonally adjusted Overall Cb26 Percent	Married men (spouse present) Cb27 Percent
1981: 9	—	7.3	7.6	4.3	1986: 5	—	7.0	7.2	4.5
1981: 10	—	7.5	7.9	4.6	1986: 6	—	7.3	7.2	4.5
1981: 11	—	7.9	8.3	4.9	1986: 7	—	7.0	7.0	4.5
1981: 12	—	8.3	8.5	5.4	1986: 8	—	6.7	6.9	4.3
1982: 1	—	9.4	8.6	5.4	1986: 9	—	6.8	7.0	4.3
1982: 2	—	9.6	8.9	5.4	1986: 10	—	6.6	7.0	4.5
1982: 3	—	9.5	9.0	5.7	1986: 11	—	6.6	6.9	4.4
1982: 4	—	9.2	9.3	6.0	1986: 12	—	6.3	6.6	4.3
1982: 5	—	9.1	9.4	6.1	1987: 1	—	7.3	6.6	4.2
1982: 6	—	9.8	9.6	6.5	1987: 2	—	7.2	6.6	4.1
1982: 7	—	9.8	9.8	6.7	1987: 3	—	6.9	6.6	4.1
1982: 8	—	9.6	9.8	6.8	1987: 4	—	6.2	6.3	4.0
1982: 9	—	9.7	10.1	7.1	1987: 5	—	6.1	6.3	4.0
1982: 10	—	9.9	10.4	7.4	1987: 6	—	6.3	6.2	4.1
1982: 11	—	10.4	10.8	7.5	1987: 7	—	6.1	6.1	3.9
1982: 12	—	10.5	10.8	7.5	1987: 8	—	5.8	6.0	3.7
1983: 1	—	11.4	10.4	7.2	1987: 9	—	5.7	5.9	3.7
1983: 2	—	11.3	10.4	7.2	1987: 10	—	5.7	6.0	3.7
1983: 3	—	10.8	10.3	7.2	1987: 11	—	5.6	5.8	3.5
1983: 4	—	10.0	10.2	7.1	1987: 12	—	5.4	5.7	3.4
1983: 5	—	9.8	10.1	7.0	1988: 1	—	6.3	5.7	3.5
1983: 6	—	10.2	10.1	6.6	1988: 2	—	6.2	5.7	3.4
1983: 7	—	9.4	9.4	6.1	1988: 3	—	5.9	5.7	3.4
1983: 8	—	9.2	9.5	6.4	1988: 4	—	5.3	5.4	3.0
1983: 9	—	8.8	9.2	6.0	1988: 5	—	5.4	5.6	3.3
1983: 10	—	8.4	8.8	5.7	1988: 6	—	5.5	5.4	3.2
1983: 11	—	8.1	8.5	5.5	1988: 7	—	5.5	5.4	3.1
1983: 12	—	8.0	8.3	5.2	1988: 8	—	5.4	5.6	3.4
1984: 1	—	8.8	8.0	5.0	1988: 9	—	5.2	5.4	3.1
1984: 2	—	8.4	7.8	4.8	1988: 10	—	5.0	5.4	3.1
1984: 3	—	8.1	7.8	4.7	1988: 11	—	5.2	5.3	3.3
1984: 4	—	7.6	7.7	4.7	1988: 12	—	5.0	5.3	3.1
1984: 5	—	7.2	7.4	4.6	1989: 1	—	6.0	5.4	3.1
1984: 6	—	7.4	7.2	4.5	1989: 2	—	5.6	5.2	3.1
1984: 7	—	7.5	7.5	4.5	1989: 3	—	5.2	5.0	2.9
1984: 8	—	7.3	7.5	4.6	1989: 4	—	5.1	5.2	3.1
1984: 9	—	7.1	7.3	4.6	1989: 5	—	5.0	5.2	2.9
1984: 10	—	7.0	7.4	4.5	1989: 6	—	5.5	5.3	2.8
1984: 11	—	6.9	7.2	4.4	1989: 7	—	5.3	5.2	3.0
1984: 12	—	7.0	7.3	4.5	1989: 8	—	5.1	5.2	3.1
1985: 1	—	8.0	7.3	4.5	1989: 9	—	5.1	5.3	3.3
1985: 2	—	7.8	7.2	4.4	1989: 10	—	5.0	5.3	3.1
1985: 3	—	7.5	7.2	4.2	1989: 11	—	5.2	5.4	3.1
1985: 4	—	7.1	7.3	4.3	1989: 12	—	5.1	5.4	3.1
1985: 5	—	7.0	7.2	4.0	1990: 1	—	6.0	5.4	3.4
1985: 6	—	7.5	7.4	4.6	1990: 2	—	5.9	5.3	3.1
1985: 7	—	7.4	7.4	4.4	1990: 3	—	5.5	5.2	3.1
1985: 8	—	6.9	7.1	4.3	1990: 4	—	5.3	5.4	3.3
1985: 9	—	6.9	7.1	4.4	1990: 5	—	5.2	5.4	3.2
1985: 10	—	6.8	7.1	4.1	1990: 6	—	5.4	5.2	3.1
1985: 11	—	6.7	7.0	4.2	1990: 7	—	5.6	5.5	3.4
1985: 12	—	6.7	7.0	4.3	1990: 8	—	5.5	5.7	3.5
1986: 1	—	7.3	6.7	4.3	1990: 9	—	5.6	5.9	3.5
1986: 2	—	7.8	7.2	4.4	1990: 10	—	5.5	5.9	3.7
1986: 3	—	7.5	7.2	4.5	1990: 11	—	5.9	6.2	3.9
1986: 4	—	7.0	7.1	4.2	1990: 12	—	6.0	6.3	3.9

TABLE Cb24–27   Unemployment rates: 1940–2003   *Continued*

	14 and older, seasonally adjusted	16 and older				14 and older, seasonally adjusted	16 and older		
		Not seasonally adjusted	Seasonally adjusted				Not seasonally adjusted	Seasonally adjusted	
			Overall	Married men (spouse present)				Overall	Married men (spouse present)
	Cb24	Cb25	Cb26	Cb27		Cb24	Cb25	Cb26	Cb27
Year: Month	Percent	Percent	Percent	Percent	Year: Month	Percent	Percent	Percent	Percent
1991: 1	—	7.1	6.4	4.1	1995: 9	—	5.4	5.6	3.4
1991: 2	—	7.3	6.6	4.3	1995: 10	—	5.2	5.5	3.1
1991: 3	—	7.2	6.8	4.4	1995: 11	—	5.3	5.6	3.3
1991: 4	—	6.5	6.7	4.5	1995: 12	—	5.2	5.6	3.1
1991: 5	—	6.7	6.9	4.4	1996: 1	—	6.3	5.6	3.2
1991: 6	—	7.0	6.9	4.5	1996: 2	—	6.0	5.5	3.0
1991: 7	—	6.8	6.8	4.3	1996: 3	—	5.8	5.5	3.1
1991: 8	—	6.6	6.9	4.4	1996: 4	—	5.4	5.6	3.0
1991: 9	—	6.5	6.9	4.5	1996: 5	—	5.4	5.6	3.0
1991: 10	—	6.5	7.0	4.3	1996: 6	—	5.5	5.3	3.0
1991: 11	—	6.7	7.0	4.7	1996: 7	—	5.6	5.5	3.0
1991: 12	—	6.9	7.3	4.9	1996: 8	—	5.1	5.1	2.9
1992: 1	—	8.1	7.3	4.9	1996: 9	—	5.0	5.2	3.0
1992: 2	—	8.2	7.4	5.1	1996: 10	—	4.9	5.2	3.0
1992: 3	—	7.8	7.4	4.8	1996: 11	—	5.0	5.4	3.1
1992: 4	—	7.2	7.4	4.9	1996: 12	—	5.0	5.4	2.9
1992: 5	—	7.3	7.6	5.1	1997: 1	—	5.9	5.3	2.8
1992: 6	—	8.0	7.8	5.2	1997: 2	—	5.7	5.2	2.8
1992: 7	—	7.7	7.7	5.2	1997: 3	—	5.5	5.2	2.8
1992: 8	—	7.4	7.6	5.3	1997: 4	—	4.8	5.1	2.7
1992: 9	—	7.3	7.6	5.3	1997: 5	—	4.7	4.9	2.7
1992: 10	—	6.9	7.3	5.2	1997: 6	—	5.2	5.0	2.7
1992: 11	—	7.1	7.4	5.0	1997: 7	—	5.0	4.9	2.7
1992: 12	—	7.1	7.4	4.9	1997: 8	—	4.8	4.8	2.6
1993: 1	—	8.0	7.3	4.6	1997: 9	—	4.7	4.9	2.6
1993: 2	—	7.8	7.1	4.6	1997: 10	—	4.4	4.7	2.6
1993: 3	—	7.4	7.0	4.6	1997: 11	—	4.3	4.6	2.4
1993: 4	—	6.9	7.1	4.6	1997: 12	—	4.4	4.7	2.5
1993: 5	—	6.8	7.1	4.6	1998: 1	—	5.2	4.6	2.5
1993: 6	—	7.2	7.0	4.5	1998: 2	—	5.0	4.6	2.4
1993: 7	—	7.0	6.9	4.5	1998: 3	—	5.0	4.7	2.5
1993: 8	—	6.6	6.8	4.4	1998: 4	—	4.1	4.3	2.3
1993: 9	—	6.4	6.7	4.3	1998: 5	—	4.2	4.4	2.4
1993: 10	—	6.4	6.8	4.4	1998: 6	—	4.7	4.5	2.3
1993: 11	—	6.2	6.6	4.1	1998: 7	—	4.7	4.5	2.3
1993: 12	—	6.1	6.5	4.0	1998: 8	—	4.5	4.5	2.3
1994: 1	—	7.3	6.6	4.1	1998: 9	—	4.4	4.6	2.3
1994: 2	—	7.1	6.6	4.4	1998: 10	—	4.2	4.5	2.3
1994: 3	—	6.8	6.5	4.1	1998: 11	—	4.1	4.4	2.2
1994: 4	—	6.2	6.4	3.9	1998: 12	—	4.0	4.4	2.3
1994: 5	—	5.9	6.1	3.7	1999: 1	—	4.8	4.3	2.3
1994: 6	—	6.2	6.1	3.6	1999: 2	—	4.7	4.4	2.3
1994: 7	—	6.2	6.1	3.6	1999: 3	—	4.4	4.2	2.1
1994: 8	—	5.9	6.0	3.5	1999: 4	—	4.1	4.3	2.3
1994: 9	—	5.6	5.9	3.3	1999: 5	—	4.0	4.2	2.3
1994: 10	—	5.4	5.8	3.3	1999: 6	—	4.5	4.3	2.3
1994: 11	—	5.3	5.6	3.3	1999: 7	—	4.5	4.3	2.3
1994: 12	—	5.1	5.5	3.2	1999: 8	—	4.2	4.2	2.3
1995: 1	—	6.2	5.6	3.3	1999: 9	—	4.1	4.2	2.2
1995: 2	—	5.9	5.4	3.2	1999: 10	—	3.8	4.1	2.2
1995: 3	—	5.7	5.4	3.2	1999: 11	—	3.8	4.1	2.0
1995: 4	—	5.6	5.8	3.4	1999: 12	—	3.7	4.0	2.2
1995: 5	—	5.5	5.6	3.4	2000: 1	—	4.5	4.0	2.0
1995: 6	—	5.8	5.6	3.4	2000: 2	—	4.4	4.1	2.1
1995: 7	—	5.9	5.7	3.4	2000: 3	—	4.3	4.0	1.9
1995: 8	—	5.6	5.7	3.3	2000: 4	—	3.7	3.8	1.8

(continued)

TABLE Cb24–27   Unemployment rates: 1940–2003   *Continued*

Year: Month	14 and older, seasonally adjusted	16 and older			Year: Month	14 and older, seasonally adjusted	16 and older		
		Not seasonally adjusted	Seasonally adjusted				Not seasonally adjusted	Seasonally adjusted	
			Overall	Married men (spouse present)				Overall	Married men (spouse present)
	Cb24	Cb25	Cb26	Cb27		Cb24	Cb25	Cb26	Cb27
	Percent	Percent	Percent	Percent		Percent	Percent	Percent	Percent
2000: 5	—	3.8	4.1	1.9	2002: 1	—	6.3	5.6	3.5
2000: 6	—	4.1	4.0	1.9	2002: 2	—	6.1	5.6	3.4
2000: 7	—	4.2	4.1	2.0	2002: 3	—	6.1	5.7	3.5
2000: 8	—	4.1	4.1	2.1	2002: 4	—	5.7	5.9	3.9
2000: 9	—	3.8	4.0	2.1	2002: 5	—	5.5	5.8	3.6
2000: 10	—	3.6	3.9	2.1	2002: 6	—	6.0	5.8	4.0
2000: 11	—	3.7	4.0	2.2	2002: 7	—	5.9	5.8	3.5
2000: 12	—	3.7	3.9	2.2	2002: 8	—	5.7	5.8	3.5
2001: 1	—	4.7	4.1	2.3	2002: 9	—	5.4	5.7	3.6
2001: 2	—	4.6	4.2	2.3	2002: 10	—	5.3	5.8	3.6
2001: 3	—	4.5	4.2	2.4	2002: 11	—	5.6	5.9	3.6
2001: 4	—	4.2	4.4	2.4	2002: 12	—	5.7	6.0	3.7
2001: 5	—	4.1	4.4	2.6	2003: 1	—	6.5	5.7	3.5
2001: 6	—	4.7	4.6	2.6	2003: 2	—	6.4	5.8	3.6
2001: 7	—	4.7	4.6	2.7	2003: 3	—	6.2	5.8	3.8
2001: 8	—	4.9	4.9	2.9	2003: 4	—	5.8	6.0	3.7
2001: 9	—	4.7	5.0	2.8	2003: 5	—	5.8	6.1	3.9
2001: 10	—	5.0	5.4	3.2	2003: 6	—	6.5	6.4	4.4
2001: 11	—	5.3	5.6	3.3	2003: 7	—	6.3	6.2	3.9
2001: 12	—	5.4	5.8	3.4					

Sources

Series Cb24. Geoffrey H. Moore, *Business Cycle Indicators*, volume 2, *Basic Data on Cyclical Indicators* (Princeton University Press, 1961), Series 14.0. Moore cites the original source as U.S. Bureau of the Census, *Current Population Reports*, series P-50, numbers 2, 13, and following.

Series Cb25–27. U.S. Bureau of Labor Statistics, Internet site. Also see the Bureau's *Monthly Labor Review*.

Documentation

These unemployment rates refer to the non-institutionalized civilian labor force, 14 years old and older (series Cb24) or 16 years old and older (series Cb25–27). Data refer to the calendar week that contains the eighth of the month before July 1955 and the twelfth of the month thereafter.

Series Cb24. Persons on temporary layoff or waiting to start new jobs within thirty days were classified as employed. For the period 1940:3 to 1943:6, persons employed on federal emergency and work projects are classified as unemployed.

Series Cb25–26. Persons on temporary layoff or waiting to start new jobs within thirty days were classified as unemployed, unlike the classification used for series Cb24. These monthly data correspond to the annual series presented in series Ba485; see that text for a full description of the methodology used by the U.S. Bureau of Labor Statistics (BLS) to define and measure the unemployment rate. The seasonal adjustment performed by the BLS is intended to remove the regular seasonal fluctuation from the original data to give a better indication of the trends in labor force utilization.

TABLE Cb28–31   Indexes of industrial production: 1884–2003
Contributed by Richard Sutch

	Miron–Romer, not seasonally adjusted		Federal Reserve Board			Miron–Romer, not seasonally adjusted		Federal Reserve Board	
	13-component index	Alternative index (less wool receipts)	Not seasonally adjusted	Seasonally adjusted		13-component index	Alternative index (less wool receipts)	Not seasonally adjusted	Seasonally adjusted
	Cb28	Cb29	Cb30	Cb31		Cb28	Cb29	Cb30	Cb31
Year: Month	Index 1909 = 100	Index 1909 = 100	Index 1997 = 100	Index 1997 = 100	Year: Month	Index 1909 = 100	Index 1909 = 100	Index 1997 = 100	Index 1997 = 100
1884: 1	32.663	—	—	—	1888: 9	45.294	—	—	—
1884: 2	29.431	—	—	—	1888: 10	48.058	—	—	—
1884: 3	27.334	—	—	—	1888: 11	48.079	—	—	—
1884: 4	32.417	—	—	—	1888: 12	47.629	—	—	—
1884: 5	33.379	—	—	—	1889: 1	42.128	—	—	—
1884: 6	32.529	—	—	—	1889: 2	44.540	—	—	—
1884: 7	30.341	—	—	—	1889: 3	41.061	—	—	—
1884: 8	33.642	—	—	—	1889: 4	41.480	—	—	—
1884: 9	31.086	—	—	—	1889: 5	44.462	—	—	—
1884: 10	39.220	—	—	—	1889: 6	46.024	—	—	—
1884: 11	41.070	—	—	—	1889: 7	51.524	—	—	—
1884: 12	42.527	—	—	—	1889: 8	44.493	—	—	—
1885: 1	35.326	—	—	—	1889: 9	45.283	—	—	—
1885: 2	31.070	—	—	—	1889: 10	53.171	—	—	—
1885: 3	31.372	—	—	—	1889: 11	53.015	—	—	—
1885: 4	33.941	—	—	—	1889: 12	50.542	—	—	—
1885: 5	34.757	—	—	—	1890: 1	49.559	—	—	—
1885: 6	34.386	—	—	—	1890: 2	46.276	—	—	—
1885: 7	30.918	—	—	—	1890: 3	47.928	—	—	—
1885: 8	31.329	—	—	—	1890: 4	48.316	—	—	—
1885: 9	33.523	—	—	—	1890: 5	50.961	—	—	—
1885: 10	43.127	—	—	—	1890: 6	53.711	—	—	—
1885: 11	47.974	—	—	—	1890: 7	56.701	—	—	—
1885: 12	42.973	—	—	—	1890: 8	55.166	—	—	—
1886: 1	39.204	—	—	—	1890: 9	54.878	—	—	—
1886: 2	37.032	—	—	—	1890: 10	58.035	—	—	—
1886: 3	36.119	—	—	—	1890: 11	61.391	—	—	—
1886: 4	37.557	—	—	—	1890: 12	51.690	—	—	—
1886: 5	39.065	—	—	—	1891: 1	55.409	—	—	—
1886: 6	42.485	—	—	—	1891: 2	54.288	—	—	—
1886: 7	38.719	—	—	—	1891: 3	56.316	—	—	—
1886: 8	38.624	—	—	—	1891: 4	48.469	—	—	—
1886: 9	41.653	—	—	—	1891: 5	47.600	—	—	—
1886: 10	43.643	—	—	—	1891: 6	51.910	—	—	—
1886: 11	47.502	—	—	—	1891: 7	57.242	—	—	—
1886: 12	45.893	—	—	—	1891: 8	55.833	—	—	—
1887: 1	39.015	—	—	—	1891: 9	56.872	—	—	—
1887: 2	39.705	—	—	—	1891: 10	64.819	—	—	—
1887: 3	39.667	—	—	—	1891: 11	69.095	—	—	—
1887: 4	38.546	—	—	—	1891: 12	64.993	—	—	—
1887: 5	38.505	—	—	—	1892: 1	60.392	—	—	—
1887: 6	37.058	—	—	—	1892: 2	59.742	—	—	—
1887: 7	36.082	—	—	—	1892: 3	59.295	—	—	—
1887: 8	39.074	—	—	—	1892: 4	56.494	—	—	—
1887: 9	41.553	—	—	—	1892: 5	58.457	—	—	—
1887: 10	47.254	—	—	—	1892: 6	62.885	—	—	—
1887: 11	48.023	—	—	—	1892: 7	61.492	—	—	—
1887: 12	43.236	—	—	—	1892: 8	60.001	—	—	—
1888: 1	39.480	—	—	—	1892: 9	58.238	—	—	—
1888: 2	38.688	—	—	—	1892: 10	60.800	—	—	—
1888: 3	40.647	—	—	—	1892: 11	61.882	—	—	—
1888: 4	39.423	—	—	—	1892: 12	57.369	—	—	—
1888: 5	39.557	—	—	—	1893: 1	55.857	—	—	—
1888: 6	40.647	—	—	—	1893: 2	56.202	—	—	—
1888: 7	43.737	—	—	—	1893: 3	55.670	—	—	—
1888: 8	42.953	—	—	—	1893: 4	58.165	—	—	—

(continued)

TABLE Cb28–31 Indexes of industrial production: 1884–2003 *Continued*

	Miron–Romer, not seasonally adjusted		Federal Reserve Board			Miron–Romer, not seasonally adjusted		Federal Reserve Board	
	13-component index	Alternative index (less wool receipts)	Not seasonally adjusted	Seasonally adjusted		13-component index	Alternative index (less wool receipts)	Not seasonally adjusted	Seasonally adjusted
	Cb28	Cb29	Cb30	Cb31		Cb28	Cb29	Cb30	Cb31
Year: Month	Index 1909 = 100	Index 1909 = 100	Index 1997 = 100	Index 1997 = 100	Year: Month	Index 1909 = 100	Index 1909 = 100	Index 1997 = 100	Index 1997 = 100
1893: 5	55.306	—	—	—	1898: 1	63.100	—	—	—
1893: 6	53.950	—	—	—	1898: 2	68.674	—	—	—
1893: 7	51.272	—	—	—	1898: 3	62.222	—	—	—
1893: 8	44.536	—	—	—	1898: 4	59.078	—	—	—
1893: 9	42.720	—	—	—	1898: 5	63.879	—	—	—
1893: 10	48.753	—	—	—	1898: 6	58.679	—	—	—
1893: 11	47.575	—	—	—	1898: 7	59.430	—	—	—
1893: 12	48.109	—	—	—	1898: 8	60.896	—	—	—
1894: 1	46.837	—	—	—	1898: 9	63.750	—	—	—
1894: 2	44.769	—	—	—	1898: 10	66.165	—	—	—
1894: 3	46.241	—	—	—	1898: 11	70.770	—	—	—
1894: 4	50.988	—	—	—	1898: 12	70.569	—	—	—
1894: 5	48.067	—	—	—	1899: 1	68.140	—	—	—
1894: 6	54.994	—	—	—	1899: 2	66.931	—	—	—
1894: 7	46.403	—	—	—	1899: 3	68.664	—	—	—
1894: 8	59.508	—	—	—	1899: 4	63.411	—	—	—
1894: 9	57.723	—	—	—	1899: 5	67.595	—	—	—
1894: 10	61.238	—	—	—	1899: 6	73.302	—	—	—
1894: 11	63.783	—	—	—	1899: 7	74.476	—	—	—
1894: 12	54.676	—	—	—	1899: 8	74.717	—	—	—
1895: 1	54.305	—	—	—	1899: 9	74.161	—	—	—
1895: 2	59.056	—	—	—	1899: 10	75.746	—	—	—
1895: 3	56.091	—	—	—	1899: 11	77.117	—	—	—
1895: 4	56.810	—	—	—	1899: 12	74.992	—	—	—
1895: 5	58.480	—	—	—	1900: 1	73.861	—	—	—
1895: 6	61.422	—	—	—	1900: 2	75.214	—	—	—
1895: 7	65.404	—	—	—	1900: 3	74.329	—	—	—
1895: 8	68.532	—	—	—	1900: 4	75.783	—	—	—
1895: 9	62.433	—	—	—	1900: 5	69.295	—	—	—
1895: 10	71.535	—	—	—	1900: 6	68.664	—	—	—
1895: 11	71.750	—	—	—	1900: 7	64.911	—	—	—
1895: 12	66.012	—	—	—	1900: 8	68.232	—	—	—
1896: 1	63.328	—	—	—	1900: 9	65.118	—	—	—
1896: 2	57.547	—	—	—	1900: 10	61.941	—	—	—
1896: 3	58.877	—	—	—	1900: 11	67.613	—	—	—
1896: 4	55.293	—	—	—	1900: 12	68.823	—	—	—
1896: 5	57.166	—	—	—	1901: 1	69.643	—	—	—
1896: 6	57.992	—	—	—	1901: 2	71.739	—	—	—
1896: 7	54.103	—	—	—	1901: 3	78.872	—	—	—
1896: 8	52.800	—	—	—	1901: 4	75.537	—	—	—
1896: 9	52.593	—	—	—	1901: 5	80.885	—	—	—
1896: 10	60.533	—	—	—	1901: 6	80.181	—	—	—
1896: 11	61.256	—	—	—	1901: 7	80.838	—	—	—
1896: 12	66.485	—	—	—	1901: 8	86.653	—	—	—
1897: 1	55.224	—	—	—	1901: 9	81.543	—	—	—
1897: 2	65.597	60.798	—	—	1901: 10	79.826	—	—	—
1897: 3	66.613	57.812	—	—	1901: 11	85.057	—	—	—
1897: 4	84.313	59.811	—	—	1901: 12	81.344	—	—	—
1897: 5	70.553	63.079	—	—	1902: 1	81.893	—	—	—
1897: 6	69.415	63.925	—	—	1902: 2	78.801	—	—	—
1897: 7	68.310	60.042	—	—	1902: 4	81.721	—	—	—
1897: 8	64.985	—	—	—	1902: 5	73.539	—	—	—
1897: 9	66.984	—	—	—	1902: 6	74.498	—	—	—
1897: 10	69.954	—	—	—	1902: 7	73.900	—	—	—
1897: 11	71.567	—	—	—	1902: 8	83.154	—	—	—
1897: 12	67.950	—	—	—					

TABLE Cb28–31   Indexes of industrial production: 1884–2003   *Continued*

Year: Month	Miron–Romer, not seasonally adjusted		Federal Reserve Board		Year: Month	Miron–Romer, not seasonally adjusted		Federal Reserve Board	
	13-component index	Alternative index (less wool receipts)	Not seasonally adjusted	Seasonally adjusted		13-component index	Alternative index (less wool receipts)	Not seasonally adjusted	Seasonally adjusted
	Cb28	Cb29	Cb30	Cb31		Cb28	Cb29	Cb30	Cb31
	Index 1909 = 100	Index 1909 = 100	Index 1997 = 100	Index 1997 = 100		Index 1909 = 100	Index 1909 = 100	Index 1997 = 100	Index 1997 = 100
1902: 9	76.571	—	—	—	1907: 5	95.414	—	—	—
1902: 10	76.403	—	—	—	1907: 6	97.813	—	—	—
1902: 11	86.707	—	—	—	1907: 7	99.264	—	—	—
1902: 12	84.516	—	—	—	1907: 8	105.710	—	—	—
1903: 1	83.149	—	—	—	1907: 9	97.179	—	—	—
1903: 2	84.555	—	—	—	1907: 10	93.398	—	—	—
1903: 3	85.724	—	—	—	1907: 11	81.228	—	—	—
1903: 4	84.833	—	—	—	1907: 12	71.268	—	—	—
1903: 5	83.485	—	—	—	1908: 1	73.117	—	—	—
1903: 6	89.291	—	—	—	1908: 2	75.614	—	—	—
1903: 7	87.148	—	—	—	1908: 3	74.413	—	—	—
1903: 8	93.639	—	—	—	1908: 4	70.207	—	—	—
1903: 9	87.414	—	—	—	1908: 5	75.243	—	—	—
1903: 10	73.288	—	—	—	1908: 6	79.211	—	—	—
1903: 11	75.042	—	—	—	1908: 7	80.613	—	—	—
1903: 12	72.568	—	—	—	1908: 8	85.906	—	—	—
1904: 1	74.276	—	—	—	1908: 9	80.305	—	—	—
1904: 2	86.334	—	—	—	1908: 10	86.419	—	—	—
1904: 3	81.760	—	—	—	1908: 11	96.892	—	—	—
1904: 4	77.899	—	—	—	1908: 12	94.622	—	—	—
1904: 5	81.020	—	—	—	1909: 1	91.660	—	—	—
1904: 6	87.263	—	—	—	1909: 2	99.782	—	—	—
1904: 7	78.118	—	—	—	1909: 3	97.895	—	—	—
1904: 8	85.829	—	—	—	1909: 4	90.816	—	—	—
1904: 9	72.676	—	—	—	1909: 5	94.327	—	—	—
1904: 10	84.970	—	—	—	1909: 6	99.274	—	—	—
1904: 11	89.464	—	—	—	1909: 7	99.357	—	—	—
1904: 12	86.404	—	—	—	1909: 8	99.562	—	—	—
1905: 1	93.714	—	—	—	1909: 9	101.209	—	—	—
1905: 2	96.550	—	—	—	1909: 10	108.008	—	—	—
1905: 3	92.465	—	—	—	1909: 11	111.270	—	—	—
1905: 4	93.843	—	—	—	1909: 12	106.841	—	—	—
1905: 5	89.031	—	—	—	1910: 1	109.875	—	—	—
1905: 6	97.103	—	—	—	1910: 2	111.897	—	—	—
1905: 7	86.292	—	—	—	1910: 3	105.637	—	—	—
1905: 8	93.886	—	—	—	1910: 4	92.770	—	—	—
1905: 9	89.297	—	—	—	1910: 5	90.781	—	—	—
1905: 10	95.278	—	—	—	1910: 6	93.088	—	—	—
1905: 11	93.436	—	—	—	1910: 7	93.689	—	—	—
1905: 12	93.880	—	—	—	1910: 8	104.906	—	—	—
1906: 1	93.360	—	—	—	1910: 9	93.698	—	—	—
1906: 2	99.239	—	—	—	1910: 10	98.192	—	—	—
1906: 3	91.993	—	—	—	1910: 11	96.383	—	—	—
1906: 4	83.824	—	—	—	1910: 12	91.205	—	—	—
1906: 5	84.996	—	—	—	1911: 1	92.979	—	—	—
1906: 6	88.810	—	—	—	1911: 2	96.479	—	—	—
1906: 7	91.710	—	—	—	1911: 3	95.179	—	—	—
1906: 8	96.470	—	—	—	1911: 4	95.804	—	—	—
1906: 9	96.620	—	—	—	1911: 5	91.739	—	—	—
1906: 10	95.191	—	—	—	1911: 6	94.220	—	—	—
1906: 11	96.123	—	—	—	1911: 7	100.463	—	—	—
1906: 12	97.484	—	—	—	1911: 8	100.931	—	—	—
1907: 1	95.781	—	—	—	1911: 9	96.579	—	—	—
1907: 2	97.889	—	—	—	1911: 10	102.223	—	—	—
1907: 3	96.950	—	—	—	1911: 11	100.462	—	—	—
1907: 4	97.378	—	—	—	1911: 12	99.965	—	—	—

(continued)

TABLE Cb28–31 Indexes of industrial production: 1884–2003 *Continued*

Year: Month	Miron–Romer, not seasonally adjusted		Federal Reserve Board		Year: Month	Miron–Romer, not seasonally adjusted		Federal Reserve Board	
	13-component index	Alternative index (less wool receipts)	Not seasonally adjusted	Seasonally adjusted		13-component index	Alternative index (less wool receipts)	Not seasonally adjusted	Seasonally adjusted
	Cb28	Cb29	Cb30	Cb31		Cb28	Cb29	Cb30	Cb31
	Index 1909 = 100	Index 1909 = 100	Index 1997 = 100	Index 1997 = 100		Index 1909 = 100	Index 1909 = 100	Index 1997 = 100	Index 1997 = 100
1912: 1	102.967	—	—	—	1916: 9	129.589	—	—	—
1912: 2	111.696	—	—	—	1916: 10	141.590	—	—	—
1912: 3	112.279	—	—	—	1916: 11	143.638	—	—	—
1912: 4	101.905	—	—	—	1916: 12	151.944	—	—	—
1912: 5	100.992	—	—	—	1917: 1	167.560	—	—	—
1912: 6	107.427	—	—	—	1917: 2	138.983	—	—	—
1912: 7	115.469	—	—	—	1917: 3	159.420	—	—	—
1912: 8	121.329	—	—	—	1917: 4	167.068	—	—	—
1912: 9	113.269	—	—	—	1917: 5	169.931	—	—	—
1912: 10	114.721	—	—	—	1917: 6	180.591	—	—	—
1912: 11	114.222	—	—	—	1917: 7	150.507	—	—	—
1912: 12	114.916	—	—	—	1917: 8	168.540	—	—	—
1913: 1	118.687	—	—	—	1917: 9	159.861	—	—	—
1913: 2	117.834	—	—	—	1917: 10	157.079	—	—	—
1913: 3	112.744	—	—	—	1917: 11	158.831	—	—	—
1913: 4	108.121	—	—	—	1917: 12	151.446	—	—	—
1913: 5	106.299	—	—	—	1918: 1	138.945	—	—	—
1913: 6	111.631	—	—	—	1918: 2	148.571	—	—	—
1913: 7	109.059	—	—	—	1918: 3	151.569	—	—	—
1913: 8	115.755	—	—	—	1918: 4	159.383	—	—	—
1913: 9	116.286	—	—	—	1918: 5	181.297	—	—	—
1913: 10	108.856	—	—	—	1918: 6	165.793	—	—	—
1913: 11	107.716	—	—	—	1918: 7	177.825	—	—	—
1913: 12	107.199	—	—	—	1918: 8	152.389	—	—	—
1914: 1	98.734	—	—	—	1918: 9	161.296	—	—	—
1914: 2	108.798	—	—	—	1918: 10	151.073	—	—	—
1914: 3	115.228	—	—	—	1918: 11	152.910	—	—	—
1914: 4	117.876	—	—	—	1918: 12	146.861	—	—	—
1914: 5	112.619	—	—	—	1919: 1	142.696	—	6.095	6.198
1914: 6	107.625	—	—	—	1919: 2	149.133	—	5.855	5.924
1914: 7	109.263	—	—	—	1919: 3	175.749	—	5.718	5.753
1914: 8	98.375	—	—	—	1919: 4	174.088	—	5.821	5.856
1914: 9	103.849	—	—	—	1919: 5	165.780	—	5.992	5.890
1914: 10	95.612	—	—	—	1919: 6	151.116	—	6.368	6.267
1914: 11	90.894	—	—	—	1919: 7	183.409	—	6.574	6.643
1914: 12	92.329	—	—	—	1919: 8	147.749	—	6.711	6.746
1915: 1	95.962	—	—	—	1919: 9	158.924	—	6.745	6.609
1915: 2	112.322	—	—	—	1919: 10	151.000	—	6.711	6.541
1915: 3	122.909	—	—	—	1919: 11	184.366	—	6.574	6.438
1915: 4	123.367	—	—	—	1919: 12	183.408	—	6.129	6.541
1915: 5	126.742	—	—	—	1920: 1	188.548	—	6.985	7.157
1915: 6	119.807	—	—	—	1920: 2	200.361	—	7.019	7.157
1915: 7	122.857	—	—	—	1920: 3	205.850	—	7.019	7.020
1915: 8	124.795	—	—	—	1920: 4	184.287	—	6.574	6.643
1915: 9	129.052	—	—	—	1920: 5	155.123	—	6.985	6.815
1915: 10	134.790	—	—	—	1920: 6	165.860	—	6.985	6.883
1915: 11	145.126	—	—	—	1920: 7	160.519	—	6.608	6.712
1915: 12	156.137	—	—	—	1920: 8	163.336	—	6.745	6.746
1916: 1	158.881	—	—	—	1920: 9	134.146	—	6.608	6.506
1916: 2	161.200	—	—	—	1920: 10	124.872	—	6.437	6.232
1916: 3	154.670	—	—	—	1920: 11	142.416	—	5.821	5.719
1916: 4	148.696	—	—	—	1920: 12	121.442	—	5.102	5.376
1916: 5	152.434	—	—	—	1921: 1	123.392	—	4.999	5.068
1916: 6	153.823	—	—	—	1921: 2	131.139	—	4.930	4.965
1916: 7	131.197	—	—	—	1921: 3	130.893	—	4.793	4.828
1916: 8	140.186	—	—	—	1921: 4	123.679	—	4.828	4.828

TABLE Cb28-31   Indexes of industrial production: 1884–2003   *Continued*

	Miron–Romer, not seasonally adjusted		Federal Reserve Board			Miron–Romer, not seasonally adjusted		Federal Reserve Board	
	13-component index	Alternative index (less wool receipts)	Not seasonally adjusted	Seasonally adjusted		13-component index	Alternative index (less wool receipts)	Not seasonally adjusted	Seasonally adjusted
	Cb28	Cb29	Cb30	Cb31		Cb28	Cb29	Cb30	Cb31
Year: Month	Index 1909 = 100	Index 1909 = 100	Index 1997 = 100	Index 1997 = 100	Year: Month	Index 1909 = 100	Index 1909 = 100	Index 1997 = 100	Index 1997 = 100
1921: 5	106.174	—	5.067	4.965	1926: 1	231.678	—	7.909	8.184
1921: 6	114.304	—	4.999	4.931	1926: 2	215.503	—	8.183	8.184
1921: 7	108.381	—	4.828	4.897	1926: 3	226.918	—	8.354	8.287
1921: 8	119.869	—	5.067	5.068	1926: 4	211.027	—	8.320	8.287
1921: 9	117.457	—	5.204	5.102	1926: 5	192.517	—	8.320	8.219
1921: 10	133.106	—	5.547	5.411	1926: 6	178.711	—	8.320	8.321
1921: 11	143.169	—	5.410	5.342	1926: 7	210.252	—	8.183	8.356
1921: 12	151.867	—	4.965	5.308	1926: 8	184.094	—	8.594	8.458
1922: 1	152.772	—	5.410	5.513	1926: 9	208.725	—	8.902	8.595
1922: 2	176.200	—	5.786	5.753	1926: 10	195.042	—	8.902	8.595
1922: 3	169.564	—	6.129	6.061	1926: 11	219.704	—	8.594	8.561
1922: 4	137.692	—	5.855	5.856	1926: 12	207.721	—	8.046	8.527
1922: 5	134.225	—	6.231	6.164	1927: 1	223.671	—	8.183	8.493
1922: 6	157.703	—	6.540	6.472	1927: 2	190.618	—	8.594	8.561
1922: 7	171.185	—	6.368	6.472	1927: 3	202.582	—	8.765	8.664
1922: 8	150.457	—	6.266	6.335	1927: 4	232.712	—	8.594	8.458
1922: 9	141.971	—	6.745	6.678	1927: 5	212.356	—	8.628	8.527
1922: 10	202.040	—	7.259	7.054	1927: 6	209.936	—	8.560	8.493
1922: 11	185.052	—	7.464	7.362	1927: 7	213.196	—	8.183	8.390
1922: 12	211.121	—	7.190	7.568	1927: 8	201.001	—	8.457	8.390
1923: 1	213.366	—	7.190	7.397	1927: 9	189.340	—	8.560	8.253
1923: 2	207.595	—	7.430	7.499	1927: 10	187.029	—	8.423	8.082
1923: 3	219.442	—	7.772	7.739	1927: 11	200.560	—	8.046	8.082
1923: 4	218.093	—	7.909	7.910	1927: 12	177.709	—	7.635	8.116
1923: 5	220.596	—	8.115	8.013	1928: 1	210.119	—	7.978	8.287
1923: 6	218.777	—	8.012	7.945	1928: 2	203.581	—	8.354	8.356
1923: 7	183.047	—	7.738	7.876	1928: 3	213.080	—	8.560	8.424
1923: 8	164.666	—	7.772	7.739	1928: 4	214.013	—	8.560	8.390
1923: 9	136.006	—	7.772	7.568	1928: 5	197.230	—	8.628	8.493
1923: 10	159.379	—	7.772	7.534	1928: 6	190.558	—	8.628	8.561
1923: 11	156.197	—	7.567	7.534	1928: 7	193.207	—	8.491	8.664
1923: 12	189.616	—	6.985	7.362	1928: 8	190.626	—	8.936	8.835
1924: 1	174.347	—	7.293	7.534	1928: 9	211.114	—	9.279	8.903
1924: 2	203.993	—	7.601	7.671	1928: 10	223.226	—	9.450	9.075
1924: 3	171.978	—	7.601	7.534	1928: 11	206.807	—	9.142	9.246
1924: 4	207.044	—	7.327	7.294	1928: 12	224.832	—	8.628	9.417
1924: 5	166.825	—	7.053	6.986	1929: 1	263.791	—	9.142	9.554
1924: 6	155.102	—	6.711	6.678	1929: 2	294.849	—	9.518	9.520
1924: 7	141.532	—	6.437	6.575	1929: 3	241.635	—	9.655	9.554
1924: 8	146.605	—	6.848	6.815	1929: 4	255.798	—	9.929	9.725
1924: 9	161.537	—	7.293	7.054	1929: 5	246.418	—	10.169	9.897
1924: 10	192.922	—	7.464	7.225	1929: 6	240.253	—	10.066	9.965
1924: 11	201.284	—	7.396	7.362	1929: 7	237.105	—	9.861	10.102
1924: 12	186.075	—	7.190	7.568	1929: 8	221.448	—	10.032	9.999
1925: 1	211.625	—	7.601	7.808	1929: 9	217.829	—	10.237	9.931
1925: 2	191.158	—	7.772	7.808	1929: 10	215.283	—	10.066	9.760
1925: 3	207.232	—	7.875	7.808	1929: 11	222.017	—	9.142	9.280
1925: 4	189.900	—	7.909	7.876	1929: 12	221.397	—	8.217	8.869
1925: 5	194.892	—	7.909	7.842	1930: 1	223.833	—	8.457	8.869
1925: 6	185.285	—	7.772	7.773	1930: 2	226.560	—	8.765	8.835
1925: 7	189.792	—	7.772	7.979	1930: 3	218.751	—	8.697	8.698
1925: 8	192.751	—	7.909	7.842	1930: 4	219.995	—	8.799	8.629
1925: 9	179.293	—	8.012	7.739	1930: 5	209.518	—	8.765	8.493
1925: 10	198.567	—	8.286	8.047	1930: 6	223.314	—	8.423	8.253
1925: 11	215.119	—	8.217	8.219	1930: 7	201.930	—	7.772	7.876
1925: 12	220.923	—	7.875	8.321	1930: 8	202.824	—	7.738	7.705

(continued)

TABLE Cb28–31   Indexes of industrial production: 1884–2003 *Continued*

Year: Month	Miron–Romer, not seasonally adjusted		Federal Reserve Board		Year: Month	Miron–Romer, not seasonally adjusted		Federal Reserve Board	
	13-component index	Alternative index (less wool receipts)	Not seasonally adjusted	Seasonally adjusted		13-component index	Alternative index (less wool receipts)	Not seasonally adjusted	Seasonally adjusted
	Cb28	Cb29	Cb30	Cb31		Cb28	Cb29	Cb30	Cb31
	Index 1909 = 100	Index 1909 = 100	Index 1997 = 100	Index 1997 = 100		Index 1909 = 100	Index 1909 = 100	Index 1997 = 100	Index 1997 = 100
1930: 9	184.965	—	7.875	7.568	1935: 5	146.230	—	7.430	7.362
1930: 10	210.960	—	7.601	7.362	1935: 6	170.133	—	7.430	7.465
1930: 11	167.043	—	7.053	7.191	1935: 7	198.033	—	7.327	7.465
1930: 12	182.274	—	6.574	7.020	1935: 8	172.670	—	7.738	7.739
1931: 1	176.986	—	6.608	6.986	1935: 9	173.749	—	8.046	7.945
1931: 2	185.612	—	6.985	7.020	1935: 10	171.206	—	8.423	8.184
1931: 3	192.290	—	7.156	7.157	1935: 11	145.481	—	8.423	8.356
1931: 4	197.385	—	7.327	7.191	1935: 12	180.875	—	8.217	8.458
1931: 5	179.835	—	7.259	7.089	1936: 1	164.985	—	8.046	8.321
1931: 6	210.721	—	6.985	6.917	1936: 2	173.532	—	8.046	8.116
1931: 7	202.097	—	6.711	6.815	1936: 3	162.884	—	8.183	8.219
1931: 8	179.401	—	6.574	6.575	1936: 4	197.327	—	8.765	8.732
1931: 9	172.174	—	6.540	6.267	1936: 5	178.358	—	9.039	8.903
1931: 10	180.480	—	6.231	6.027	1936: 6	194.893	—	9.073	9.075
1931: 11	198.151	—	5.923	5.958	1936: 7	198.554	—	9.073	9.246
1931: 12	201.333	—	5.581	5.924	1936: 8	194.232	—	9.381	9.383
1932: 1	152.278	—	5.547	5.753	1936: 9	213.904	—	9.758	9.554
1932: 2	140.377	—	5.649	5.616	1936: 10	193.485	—	10.032	9.691
1932: 3	167.411	—	5.512	5.548	1936: 11	202.694	—	10.066	9.965
1932: 4	153.193	—	5.273	5.171	1936: 12	227.087	—	10.066	10.273
1932: 5	141.321	—	5.102	5.000	1937: 1	215.962	—	9.792	10.239
1932: 6	159.795	—	4.930	4.828	1937: 2	232.051	—	10.203	10.376
1932: 7	145.559	—	4.622	4.691	1937: 3	207.278	—	10.614	10.616
1932: 8	147.121	—	4.793	4.828	1937: 4	216.205	—	10.683	10.616
1932: 9	141.451	—	5.376	5.137	1937: 5	223.829	—	10.820	10.650
1932: 10	153.656	—	5.512	5.308	1937: 6	232.285	—	10.511	10.513
1932: 11	135.835	—	5.273	5.308	1937: 7	200.692	—	10.340	10.581
1932: 12	136.726	—	4.965	5.205	1937: 8	220.668	—	10.511	10.513
1933: 1	129.017	—	4.965	5.102	1937: 9	234.997	—	10.443	10.170
1933: 2	113.479	—	5.136	5.137	1937: 10	221.343	—	9.792	9.417
1933: 3	115.877	—	4.793	4.828	1937: 11	215.345	—	8.594	8.493
1933: 4	109.910	—	5.239	5.171	1937: 12	231.944	—	7.601	7.739
1933: 5	128.269	—	6.129	6.027	1938: 1	177.320	—	7.259	7.568
1933: 6	151.576	—	7.019	6.952	1938: 2	171.663	—	7.327	7.499
1933: 7	221.452	—	7.464	7.602	1938: 3	161.271	—	7.430	7.499
1933: 8	210.920	—	7.259	7.294	1938: 4	140.976	—	7.259	7.362
1933: 9	207.182	—	7.122	6.883	1938: 5	138.488	—	7.190	7.191
1933: 10	190.378	—	6.608	6.541	1938: 6	139.900	—	7.190	7.260
1933: 11	170.434	—	6.095	6.164	1938: 7	130.150	—	7.567	7.671
1933: 12	162.880	—	5.923	6.198	1938: 8	149.443	—	8.149	8.082
1934: 1	184.349	—	6.129	6.404	1938: 9	157.510	—	8.628	8.321
1934: 2	164.288	—	6.711	6.712	1938: 10	164.739	—	8.868	8.527
1934: 3	170.521	—	7.053	7.020	1938: 11	167.273	—	9.039	8.869
1934: 4	187.549	—	7.190	7.020	1938: 12	167.767	—	8.799	8.972
1934: 5	197.562	—	7.293	7.157	1939: 1	172.516	—	9.039	8.972
1934: 6	202.631	—	7.156	7.020	1939: 2	156.213	—	9.039	9.040
1934: 7	187.067	—	6.505	6.541	1939: 3	182.798	—	9.039	9.075
1934: 8	140.726	—	6.540	6.472	1939: 4	158.482	—	8.868	9.040
1934: 9	150.742	—	6.403	6.095	1939: 5	184.297	—	8.902	9.006
1934: 10	134.765	—	6.505	6.369	1939: 6	172.813	—	9.210	9.212
1934: 11	159.877	—	6.300	6.438	1939: 7	179.191	—	9.381	9.486
1934: 12	100.768	—	6.540	6.849	1939: 8	179.728	—	9.518	9.623
1935: 1	164.291	—	7.156	7.397	1939: 9	192.803	—	10.237	10.225
1935: 2	201.865	—	7.567	7.534	1939: 10	215.692	—	10.888	10.718
1935: 3	184.372	—	7.533	7.499	1939: 11	207.562	—	11.196	10.992
1935: 4	171.052	—	7.430	7.362	1939: 12	281.021	—	11.128	10.992

TABLE Cb28-31   Indexes of industrial production: 1884-2003   *Continued*

	Miron–Romer, not seasonally adjusted		Federal Reserve Board			Miron–Romer, not seasonally adjusted		Federal Reserve Board	
	13-component index	Alternative index (less wool receipts)	Not seasonally adjusted	Seasonally adjusted		13-component index	Alternative index (less wool receipts)	Not seasonally adjusted	Seasonally adjusted
	Cb28	Cb29	Cb30	Cb31		Cb28	Cb29	Cb30	Cb31
Year: Month	Index 1909 = 100	Index 1909 = 100	Index 1997 = 100	Index 1997 = 100	Year: Month	Index 1909 = 100	Index 1909 = 100	Index 1997 = 100	Index 1997 = 100
1940: 1	275.583	—	10.956	10.855	1944: 9	—	—	21.023	21.197
1940: 2	200.597	—	10.511	10.513	1944: 10	—	—	21.023	21.266
1940: 3	232.237	—	10.237	10.273	1944: 11	—	—	20.852	21.094
1940: 4	262.499	—	10.306	10.479	1944: 12	—	—	20.715	21.026
1940: 5	221.192	—	10.648	10.787	1945: 1	—	—	20.749	20.820
1940: 6	252.392	—	11.093	11.129	1945: 2	—	—	20.817	20.752
1940: 7	282.412	—	11.128	11.266	1945: 3	—	—	20.749	20.615
1940: 8	285.488	—	11.265	11.335	1945: 4	—	—	20.406	20.238
1940: 9	320.230	—	11.641	11.574	1945: 5	—	—	19.961	19.690
1940: 10	304.910	—	11.915	11.746	1945: 6	—	—	19.585	19.245
1940: 11	309.145	—	12.223	12.020	1945: 7	—	—	18.900	18.800
1940: 12	372.697	—	12.566	12.431	1945: 8	—	—	16.880	16.848
1941: 1	—	—	12.840	12.739	1945: 9	—	—	15.305	15.341
1941: 2	—	—	13.114	13.115	1945: 10	—	—	14.620	14.725
1941: 3	—	—	13.456	13.526	1945: 11	—	—	15.168	15.273
1941: 4	—	—	13.387	13.561	1945: 12	—	—	15.134	15.341
1941: 5	—	—	14.038	14.177	1946: 1	—	—	14.483	14.485
1941: 6	—	—	14.278	14.280	1946: 2	—	—	13.833	13.766
1941: 7	—	—	14.312	14.451	1946: 3	—	—	15.305	15.204
1941: 8	—	—	14.552	14.622	1946: 4	—	—	14.997	14.930
1941: 9	—	—	14.689	14.622	1946: 5	—	—	14.449	14.382
1941: 10	—	—	14.894	14.759	1946: 6	—	—	15.442	15.273
1941: 11	—	—	14.997	14.828	1946: 7	—	—	15.784	15.786
1941: 12	—	—	15.168	15.067	1946: 8	—	—	16.366	16.369
1942: 1	—	—	15.442	15.376	1946: 9	—	—	16.674	16.677
1942: 2	—	—	15.647	15.649	1946: 10	—	—	16.880	16.985
1942: 3	—	—	15.784	15.821	1946: 11	—	—	16.948	17.088
1942: 4	—	—	15.271	15.376	1946: 12	—	—	16.914	17.190
1942: 5	—	—	15.339	15.410	1947: 1	—	—	17.256	17.396
1942: 6	—	—	15.476	15.444	1947: 2	—	—	17.599	17.499
1942: 7	—	—	15.750	15.821	1947: 3	—	—	17.667	17.601
1942: 8	—	—	16.298	16.300	1947: 4	—	—	17.325	17.464
1942: 9	—	—	16.674	16.677	1947: 5	—	—	17.222	17.533
1942: 10	—	—	17.256	17.225	1947: 6	—	—	17.359	17.533
1942: 11	—	—	17.667	17.636	1947: 7	—	—	16.366	17.430
1942: 12	—	—	18.044	18.047	1947: 8	—	—	17.599	17.533
1943: 1	—	—	18.249	18.218	1947: 9	—	—	18.044	17.670
1943: 2	—	—	18.694	18.697	1947: 10	—	—	18.558	17.841
1943: 3	—	—	18.900	18.834	1947: 11	—	—	18.421	18.081
1943: 4	—	—	19.105	19.074	1947: 12	—	—	18.078	18.149
1943: 5	—	—	19.277	19.211	1948: 1	—	—	18.181	18.252
1943: 6	—	—	19.277	19.108	1948: 2	—	—	18.386	18.286
1943: 7	—	—	19.653	19.690	1948: 3	—	—	18.112	18.081
1943: 8	—	—	20.098	20.101	1948: 4	—	—	17.941	18.115
1943: 9	—	—	20.509	20.615	1948: 5	—	—	18.078	18.423
1943: 10	—	—	20.817	20.923	1948: 6	—	—	18.421	18.663
1943: 11	—	—	21.023	21.197	1948: 7	—	—	17.599	18.663
1943: 12	—	—	20.715	20.923	1948: 8	—	—	18.626	18.594
1944: 1	—	—	21.125	21.163	1948: 9	—	—	18.934	18.457
1944: 2	—	—	21.399	21.334	1948: 10	—	—	19.345	18.594
1944: 3	—	—	21.434	21.300	1948: 11	—	—	18.694	18.355
1944: 4	—	—	21.434	21.300	1948: 12	—	—	18.112	18.184
1944: 5	—	—	21.399	21.163	1949: 1	—	—	17.907	18.012
1944: 6	—	—	21.434	21.094	1949: 2	—	—	17.941	17.841
1944: 7	—	—	21.125	21.060	1949: 3	—	—	17.599	17.499
1944: 8	—	—	21.331	21.334	1949: 4	—	—	17.222	17.396

(continued)

TABLE Cb28–31   Indexes of industrial production: 1884–2003   *Continued*

	Miron–Romer, not seasonally adjusted		Federal Reserve Board			Miron–Romer, not seasonally adjusted		Federal Reserve Board	
	13-component index	Alternative index (less wool receipts)	Not seasonally adjusted	Seasonally adjusted		13-component index	Alternative index (less wool receipts)	Not seasonally adjusted	Seasonally adjusted
	Cb28	Cb29	Cb30	Cb31		Cb28	Cb29	Cb30	Cb31
Year: Month	Index 1909 = 100	Index 1909 = 100	Index 1997 = 100	Index 1997 = 100	Year: Month	Index 1909 = 100	Index 1909 = 100	Index 1997 = 100	Index 1997 = 100
1949: 5	—	—	16.880	17.156	1954: 1	—	—	22.940	23.012
1949: 6	—	—	16.948	17.122	1954: 2	—	—	23.283	23.080
1949: 7	—	—	16.092	17.088	1954: 3	—	—	23.180	22.943
1949: 8	—	—	17.462	17.259	1954: 4	—	—	22.906	22.806
1949: 9	—	—	17.907	17.430	1954: 5	—	—	22.940	22.943
1949: 10	—	—	17.530	16.780	1954: 6	—	—	23.214	23.012
1949: 11	—	—	17.462	17.225	1954: 7	—	—	21.844	23.046
1949: 12	—	—	17.359	17.533	1954: 8	—	—	22.940	23.012
1950: 1	—	—	17.804	17.841	1954: 9	—	—	23.419	23.046
1950: 2	—	—	18.044	17.910	1954: 10	—	—	23.933	23.320
1950: 3	—	—	18.626	18.492	1954: 11	—	—	24.002	23.697
1950: 4	—	—	19.071	19.108	1954: 12	—	—	23.899	24.005
1950: 5	—	—	19.242	19.553	1955: 1	—	—	24.481	24.553
1950: 6	—	—	19.996	20.135	1955: 2	—	—	25.131	24.861
1950: 7	—	—	19.414	20.786	1955: 3	—	—	25.713	25.443
1950: 8	—	—	21.605	21.437	1955: 4	—	—	25.919	25.751
1950: 9	—	—	21.776	21.300	1955: 5	—	—	26.124	26.162
1950: 10	—	—	22.358	21.437	1955: 6	—	—	26.433	26.197
1950: 11	—	—	21.605	21.402	1955: 7	—	—	24.960	26.402
1950: 12	—	—	21.571	21.779	1955: 8	—	—	26.227	26.368
1951: 1	—	—	21.708	21.848	1955: 9	—	—	26.878	26.539
1951: 2	—	—	22.187	21.985	1955: 10	—	—	27.699	26.984
1951: 3	—	—	22.358	22.087	1955: 11	—	—	27.425	27.053
1951: 4	—	—	22.118	22.122	1955: 12	—	—	27.015	27.155
1951: 5	—	—	21.742	22.053	1956: 1	—	—	27.083	27.327
1951: 6	—	—	21.981	21.950	1956: 2	—	—	27.357	27.087
1951: 7	—	—	20.372	21.608	1956: 3	—	—	27.391	27.087
1951: 8	—	—	21.468	21.402	1956: 4	—	—	27.562	27.292
1951: 9	—	—	21.981	21.539	1956: 5	—	—	27.152	27.053
1951: 10	—	—	22.153	21.505	1956: 6	—	—	27.288	26.813
1951: 11	—	—	21.879	21.676	1956: 7	—	—	24.686	25.991
1951: 12	—	—	21.571	21.813	1956: 8	—	—	27.015	27.053
1952: 1	—	—	21.913	22.053	1956: 9	—	—	28.007	27.669
1952: 2	—	—	22.427	22.190	1956: 10	—	—	28.555	27.909
1952: 3	—	—	22.563	22.259	1956: 11	—	—	28.007	27.669
1952: 4	—	—	21.981	22.053	1956: 12	—	—	27.734	28.080
1952: 5	—	—	21.605	21.848	1957: 1	—	—	27.734	27.977
1952: 6	—	—	21.673	21.642	1957: 2	—	—	28.418	28.251
1952: 7	—	—	20.098	21.300	1957: 3	—	—	28.453	28.217
1952: 8	—	—	22.632	22.670	1957: 4	—	—	27.871	27.840
1952: 9	—	—	23.899	23.491	1957: 5	—	—	27.665	27.738
1952: 10	—	—	24.378	23.731	1957: 6	—	—	28.247	27.806
1952: 11	—	—	24.378	24.210	1957: 7	—	—	26.569	27.977
1952: 12	—	—	24.002	24.347	1957: 8	—	—	28.110	27.977
1953: 1	—	—	24.241	24.416	1957: 9	—	—	28.179	27.738
1953: 2	—	—	24.892	24.553	1957: 10	—	—	28.007	27.327
1953: 3	—	—	25.200	24.758	1957: 11	—	—	27.015	26.676
1953: 4	—	—	24.960	24.861	1957: 12	—	—	25.850	26.162
1953: 5	—	—	24.960	24.998	1958: 1	—	—	25.508	25.683
1953: 6	—	—	25.029	24.895	1958: 2	—	—	25.234	25.135
1953: 7	—	—	23.796	25.204	1958: 3	—	—	24.960	24.827
1953: 8	—	—	24.960	25.067	1958: 4	—	—	24.481	24.416
1953: 9	—	—	24.823	24.553	1958: 5	—	—	24.618	24.656
1953: 10	—	—	24.960	24.347	1958: 6	—	—	25.782	25.306
1953: 11	—	—	23.796	23.765	1958: 7	—	—	24.549	25.683
1953: 12	—	—	22.837	23.183	1958: 8	—	—	26.261	26.197

TABLE Cb28–31   Indexes of industrial production: 1884–2003   *Continued*

Year: Month	Miron–Romer, not seasonally adjusted 13-component index Cb28 Index 1909 = 100	Miron–Romer, not seasonally adjusted Alternative index (less wool receipts) Cb29 Index 1909 = 100	Federal Reserve Board Not seasonally adjusted Cb30 Index 1997 = 100	Federal Reserve Board Seasonally adjusted Cb31 Index 1997 = 100	Year: Month	Miron–Romer, not seasonally adjusted 13-component index Cb28 Index 1909 = 100	Miron–Romer, not seasonally adjusted Alternative index (less wool receipts) Cb29 Index 1909 = 100	Federal Reserve Board Not seasonally adjusted Cb30 Index 1997 = 100	Federal Reserve Board Seasonally adjusted Cb31 Index 1997 = 100
1958: 9	—	—	27.152	26.436	1963: 5	—	—	34.513	34.312
1958: 10	—	—	27.425	26.745	1963: 6	—	—	35.163	34.415
1958: 11	—	—	27.802	27.532	1963: 7	—	—	32.835	34.278
1958: 12	—	—	27.220	27.566	1963: 8	—	—	33.794	34.347
1959: 1	—	—	27.699	27.977	1963: 9	—	—	35.300	34.689
1959: 2	—	—	28.555	28.525	1963: 10	—	—	35.882	34.929
1959: 3	—	—	29.172	28.936	1963: 11	—	—	35.232	35.100
1959: 4	—	—	29.719	29.553	1963: 12	—	—	34.239	35.032
1959: 5	—	—	30.062	29.998	1964: 1	—	—	34.684	35.340
1959: 6	—	—	30.644	30.032	1964: 2	—	—	35.711	35.580
1959: 7	—	—	28.144	29.313	1964: 3	—	—	35.882	35.580
1959: 8	—	—	28.316	28.320	1964: 4	—	—	36.465	36.162
1959: 9	—	—	28.863	28.286	1964: 5	—	—	36.636	36.367
1959: 10	—	—	28.898	28.080	1964: 6	—	—	37.218	36.470
1959: 11	—	—	28.453	28.251	1964: 7	—	—	35.027	36.710
1959: 12	—	—	29.480	29.998	1964: 8	—	—	36.396	36.949
1960: 1	—	—	30.336	30.785	1964: 9	—	—	37.868	37.086
1960: 2	—	—	30.507	30.511	1964: 10	—	—	37.560	36.573
1960: 3	—	—	30.438	30.237	1964: 11	—	—	37.800	37.703
1960: 4	—	—	30.199	29.998	1964: 12	—	—	37.321	38.148
1960: 5	—	—	30.130	29.964	1965: 1	—	—	37.937	38.559
1960: 6	—	—	30.199	29.587	1965: 2	—	—	38.930	38.798
1960: 7	—	—	28.384	29.484	1965: 3	—	—	39.751	39.312
1960: 8	—	—	29.343	29.450	1965: 4	—	—	39.751	39.483
1960: 9	—	—	29.788	29.142	1965: 5	—	—	40.060	39.792
1960: 10	—	—	29.925	29.107	1965: 6	—	—	41.018	40.100
1960: 11	—	—	28.863	28.696	1965: 7	—	—	38.793	40.476
1960: 12	—	—	27.597	28.149	1965: 8	—	—	39.991	40.648
1961: 1	—	—	27.734	28.183	1965: 9	—	—	41.326	40.750
1961: 2	—	—	28.042	28.149	1965: 10	—	—	42.285	41.161
1961: 3	—	—	28.418	28.320	1965: 11	—	—	41.600	41.333
1961: 4	—	—	29.137	28.902	1965: 12	—	—	40.916	41.846
1961: 5	—	—	29.582	29.347	1966: 1	—	—	41.498	42.257
1961: 6	—	—	30.438	29.758	1966: 2	—	—	42.662	42.531
1961: 7	—	—	28.898	30.100	1966: 3	—	—	43.518	43.113
1961: 8	—	—	30.370	30.374	1966: 4	—	—	43.449	43.182
1961: 9	—	—	31.089	30.340	1966: 5	—	—	43.757	43.593
1961: 10	—	—	31.808	30.922	1966: 6	—	—	44.750	43.798
1961: 11	—	—	31.534	31.402	1966: 7	—	—	41.977	44.038
1961: 12	—	—	31.055	31.676	1966: 8	—	—	43.484	44.072
1962: 1	—	—	30.815	31.402	1966: 9	—	—	45.504	44.483
1962: 2	—	—	31.774	31.915	1966: 10	—	—	45.983	44.791
1962: 3	—	—	32.253	32.087	1966: 11	—	—	44.750	44.483
1962: 4	—	—	32.390	32.155	1966: 12	—	—	43.620	44.586
1962: 5	—	—	32.390	32.121	1967: 1	—	—	43.894	44.796
1962: 6	—	—	32.835	32.052	1967: 2	—	—	44.347	44.288
1962: 7	—	—	31.192	32.361	1967: 3	—	—	44.279	44.038
1962: 8	—	—	32.185	32.395	1967: 4	—	—	44.530	44.454
1962: 9	—	—	33.417	32.600	1967: 5	—	—	44.168	44.066
1962: 10	—	—	33.554	32.635	1967: 6	—	—	45.178	44.060
1962: 11	—	—	32.938	32.771	1967: 7	—	—	42.207	43.960
1962: 12	—	—	32.116	32.771	1967: 8	—	—	44.520	44.802
1963: 1	—	—	32.390	33.011	1967: 9	—	—	45.822	44.729
1963: 2	—	—	33.452	33.388	1967: 10	—	—	46.110	45.094
1963: 3	—	—	33.897	33.593	1967: 11	—	—	45.938	45.739
1963: 4	—	—	34.171	33.902	1967: 12	—	—	45.147	46.231

(continued)

TABLE Cb28-31   Indexes of industrial production: 1884–2003 *Continued*

	Miron–Romer, not seasonally adjusted		Federal Reserve Board			Miron–Romer, not seasonally adjusted		Federal Reserve Board	
	13-component index	Alternative index (less wool receipts)	Not seasonally adjusted	Seasonally adjusted		13-component index	Alternative index (less wool receipts)	Not seasonally adjusted	Seasonally adjusted
	Cb28	Cb29	Cb30	Cb31		Cb28	Cb29	Cb30	Cb31
Year: Month	Index 1909 = 100	Index 1909 = 100	Index 1997 = 100	Index 1997 = 100	Year: Month	Index 1909 = 100	Index 1909 = 100	Index 1997 = 100	Index 1997 = 100
1968: 1	—	—	45.238	46.181	1972: 9	—	—	54.799	53.625
1968: 2	—	—	46.418	46.347	1972: 10	—	—	55.729	54.288
1968: 3	—	—	46.833	46.492	1972: 11	—	—	55.586	54.912
1968: 4	—	—	46.590	46.559	1972: 12	—	—	54.757	55.655
1968: 5	—	—	47.251	47.081	1973: 1	—	—	55.146	56.088
1968: 6	—	—	48.484	47.254	1973: 2	—	—	57.041	56.847
1968: 7	—	—	45.388	47.182	1973: 3	—	—	57.194	56.904
1968: 8	—	—	46.746	47.313	1973: 4	—	—	56.803	56.725
1968: 9	—	—	48.607	47.493	1973: 5	—	—	57.202	57.121
1968: 10	—	—	48.780	47.587	1973: 6	—	—	58.423	57.172
1968: 11	—	—	48.551	48.202	1973: 7	—	—	55.580	57.411
1968: 12	—	—	47.162	48.355	1973: 8	—	—	56.578	57.220
1969: 1	—	—	47.619	48.647	1973: 9	—	—	58.587	57.678
1969: 2	—	—	49.051	48.958	1973: 10	—	—	59.334	58.047
1969: 3	—	—	49.679	49.342	1973: 11	—	—	58.804	58.249
1969: 4	—	—	49.232	49.161	1973: 12	—	—	56.899	58.129
1969: 5	—	—	49.124	48.975	1974: 1	—	—	56.686	57.817
1969: 6	—	—	50.710	49.453	1974: 2	—	—	57.522	57.575
1969: 7	—	—	47.684	49.715	1974: 3	—	—	57.766	57.642
1969: 8	—	—	49.560	49.829	1974: 4	—	—	57.174	57.627
1969: 9	—	—	51.103	49.818	1974: 5	—	—	58.030	57.932
1969: 10	—	—	51.050	49.832	1974: 6	—	—	59.071	57.861
1969: 11	—	—	49.579	49.362	1974: 7	—	—	56.124	57.835
1969: 12	—	—	47.917	49.230	1974: 8	—	—	56.858	57.197
1970: 1	—	—	47.174	48.318	1974: 9	—	—	58.277	57.238
1970: 2	—	—	48.352	48.286	1974: 10	—	—	58.277	56.977
1970: 3	—	—	48.482	48.224	1974: 11	—	—	55.647	55.124
1970: 4	—	—	48.141	48.100	1974: 12	—	—	52.539	53.145
1970: 5	—	—	48.164	48.044	1975: 1	—	—	51.704	52.547
1970: 6	—	—	49.143	47.888	1975: 2	—	—	51.477	51.386
1970: 7	—	—	46.277	48.006	1975: 3	—	—	50.868	50.836
1970: 8	—	—	47.806	47.920	1975: 4	—	—	50.919	50.783
1970: 9	—	—	48.867	47.590	1975: 5	—	—	50.558	50.638
1970: 10	—	—	47.739	46.638	1975: 6	—	—	51.963	51.006
1970: 11	—	—	46.452	46.356	1975: 7	—	—	49.736	51.354
1970: 12	—	—	46.018	47.420	1975: 8	—	—	51.797	51.939
1971: 1	—	—	46.607	47.785	1975: 9	—	—	53.460	52.574
1971: 2	—	—	47.821	47.694	1975: 10	—	—	53.690	52.682
1971: 3	—	—	47.898	47.642	1975: 11	—	—	53.134	52.805
1971: 4	—	—	47.981	47.910	1975: 12	—	—	52.732	53.492
1971: 5	—	—	48.320	48.153	1976: 1	—	—	53.471	54.257
1971: 6	—	—	49.600	48.355	1976: 2	—	—	55.115	54.883
1971: 7	—	—	46.376	48.214	1976: 3	—	—	55.292	54.896
1971: 8	—	—	47.953	47.935	1976: 4	—	—	54.878	55.296
1971: 9	—	—	50.143	48.714	1976: 5	—	—	55.633	55.483
1971: 10	—	—	50.395	49.078	1976: 6	—	—	56.747	55.461
1971: 11	—	—	49.443	49.287	1976: 7	—	—	54.025	55.767
1971: 12	—	—	48.106	49.856	1976: 8	—	—	55.716	56.168
1972: 1	—	—	49.799	51.053	1976: 9	—	—	56.979	56.225
1972: 2	—	—	51.383	51.550	1976: 10	—	—	57.347	56.295
1972: 3	—	—	51.939	51.955	1976: 11	—	—	57.425	57.117
1972: 4	—	—	52.630	52.446	1976: 12	—	—	56.981	57.759
1972: 5	—	—	52.650	52.482	1977: 1	—	—	56.676	57.499
1972: 6	—	—	53.807	52.609	1977: 2	—	—	58.522	58.214
1972: 7	—	—	50.500	52.634	1977: 3	—	—	59.528	58.996
1972: 8	—	—	52.880	53.250	1977: 4	—	—	59.474	59.526

TABLE Cb28–31   Indexes of industrial production: 1884–2003   *Continued*

Year: Month	Miron–Romer, not seasonally adjusted		Federal Reserve Board		Year: Month	Miron–Romer, not seasonally adjusted		Federal Reserve Board	
	13-component index	Alternative index (less wool receipts)	Not seasonally adjusted	Seasonally adjusted		13-component index	Alternative index (less wool receipts)	Not seasonally adjusted	Seasonally adjusted
	Cb28	Cb29	Cb30	Cb31		Cb28	Cb29	Cb30	Cb31
	Index 1909 = 100	Index 1909 = 100	Index 1997 = 100	Index 1997 = 100		Index 1909 = 100	Index 1909 = 100	Index 1997 = 100	Index 1997 = 100
1977: 5	—	—	60.027	59.923	1982: 1	—	—	61.413	61.524
1977: 6	—	—	61.669	60.295	1982: 2	—	—	63.302	62.702
1977: 7	—	—	58.831	60.539	1982: 3	—	—	62.831	62.236
1977: 8	—	—	59.892	60.578	1982: 4	—	—	61.283	61.709
1977: 9	—	—	61.586	60.850	1982: 5	—	—	60.639	61.235
1977: 10	—	—	61.972	60.995	1982: 6	—	—	61.647	60.997
1977: 11	—	—	61.175	61.055	1982: 7	—	—	59.463	60.825
1977: 12	—	—	60.275	61.156	1982: 8	—	—	60.388	60.310
1978: 1	—	—	59.616	60.483	1982: 9	—	—	60.689	60.081
1978: 2	—	—	61.081	60.613	1982: 10	—	—	60.028	59.480
1978: 3	—	—	62.163	61.748	1982: 11	—	—	59.172	59.288
1978: 4	—	—	63.422	62.954	1982: 12	—	—	58.299	58.767
1978: 5	—	—	63.188	63.214	1983: 1	—	—	59.761	59.886
1978: 6	—	—	64.833	63.621	1983: 2	—	—	60.195	59.585
1978: 7	—	—	61.598	63.648	1983: 3	—	—	60.612	60.026
1978: 8	—	—	63.126	63.855	1983: 4	—	—	60.624	60.836
1978: 9	—	—	64.844	63.994	1983: 5	—	—	60.700	61.265
1978: 10	—	—	65.494	64.463	1983: 6	—	—	62.360	61.627
1978: 11	—	—	65.037	64.930	1983: 7	—	—	61.168	62.578
1978: 12	—	—	64.443	65.319	1983: 8	—	—	63.278	63.263
1979: 1	—	—	63.973	65.000	1983: 9	—	—	64.999	64.191
1979: 2	—	—	65.758	65.293	1983: 10	—	—	65.230	64.663
1979: 3	—	—	66.323	65.482	1983: 11	—	—	64.607	64.899
1979: 4	—	—	64.420	64.902	1983: 12	—	—	64.501	65.217
1979: 5	—	—	65.359	65.378	1984: 1	—	—	66.635	66.617
1979: 6	—	—	66.552	65.330	1984: 2	—	—	67.482	66.770
1979: 7	—	—	63.288	65.137	1984: 3	—	—	67.955	67.256
1979: 8	—	—	64.239	64.651	1984: 4	—	—	67.439	67.652
1979: 9	—	—	65.604	64.720	1984: 5	—	—	67.361	67.999
1979: 10	—	—	65.951	65.032	1984: 6	—	—	69.007	68.234
1979: 11	—	—	65.112	65.000	1984: 7	—	—	66.812	68.452
1979: 12	—	—	64.398	65.050	1984: 8	—	—	68.571	68.491
1980: 1	—	—	64.563	65.449	1984: 9	—	—	69.206	68.298
1980: 2	—	—	65.841	65.438	1984: 10	—	—	68.747	68.255
1980: 3	—	—	65.948	65.235	1984: 11	—	—	68.136	68.475
1980: 4	—	—	63.673	63.915	1984: 12	—	—	67.638	68.489
1980: 5	—	—	61.957	62.352	1985: 1	—	—	68.304	68.306
1980: 6	—	—	62.267	61.512	1985: 2	—	—	69.439	68.648
1980: 7	—	—	59.416	60.906	1985: 3	—	—	69.190	68.649
1980: 8	—	—	61.256	61.236	1985: 4	—	—	68.111	68.626
1980: 9	—	—	63.118	62.257	1985: 5	—	—	68.030	68.662
1980: 10	—	—	63.675	62.940	1985: 6	—	—	69.500	68.624
1980: 11	—	—	64.095	64.073	1985: 7	—	—	66.721	68.237
1980: 12	—	—	63.931	64.427	1985: 8	—	—	68.718	68.500
1981: 1	—	—	63.568	64.048	1985: 9	—	—	69.734	68.794
1981: 2	—	—	64.310	63.786	1985: 10	—	—	68.962	68.528
1981: 3	—	—	64.826	64.114	1985: 11	—	—	68.352	68.745
1981: 4	—	—	63.489	63.783	1985: 12	—	—	68.660	69.403
1981: 5	—	—	63.832	64.259	1986: 1	—	—	69.875	69.755
1981: 6	—	—	65.337	64.559	1986: 2	—	—	70.073	69.335
1981: 7	—	—	63.504	65.036	1986: 3	—	—	68.994	68.932
1981: 8	—	—	64.907	64.960	1986: 4	—	—	68.811	68.906
1981: 9	—	—	65.027	64.532	1986: 5	—	—	68.228	68.970
1981: 10	—	—	64.665	64.053	1986: 6	—	—	69.708	68.782
1981: 11	—	—	63.306	63.329	1986: 7	—	—	67.494	68.960
1981: 12	—	—	62.286	62.598	1986: 8	—	—	69.389	69.005

(continued)

TABLE Cb28–31   Indexes of industrial production: 1884–2003   *Continued*

	Miron–Romer, not seasonally adjusted		Federal Reserve Board			Miron–Romer, not seasonally adjusted		Federal Reserve Board	
	13-component index	Alternative index (less wool receipts)	Not seasonally adjusted	Seasonally adjusted		13-component index	Alternative index (less wool receipts)	Not seasonally adjusted	Seasonally adjusted
	Cb28	Cb29	Cb30	Cb31		Cb28	Cb29	Cb30	Cb31
Year: Month	Index 1909 = 100	Index 1909 = 100	Index 1997 = 100	Index 1997 = 100	Year: Month	Index 1909 = 100	Index 1909 = 100	Index 1997 = 100	Index 1997 = 100
1986: 9	—	—	70.174	69.165	1991: 5	—	—	75.033	75.768
1986: 10	—	—	69.897	69.469	1991: 6	—	—	77.674	76.433
1986: 11	—	—	69.307	69.782	1991: 7	—	—	74.884	76.518
1986: 12	—	—	69.474	70.362	1991: 8	—	—	77.587	76.470
1987: 1	—	—	69.978	69.973	1991: 9	—	—	78.390	77.152
1987: 2	—	—	71.704	70.903	1991: 10	—	—	77.850	77.026
1987: 3	—	—	71.638	71.050	1991: 11	—	—	76.476	76.865
1987: 4	—	—	70.718	71.454	1991: 12	—	—	75.445	76.607
1987: 5	—	—	71.231	71.862	1992: 1	—	—	75.828	76.135
1987: 6	—	—	73.392	72.264	1992: 2	—	—	76.977	76.745
1987: 7	—	—	71.098	72.779	1992: 3	—	—	77.695	77.364
1987: 8	—	—	73.782	73.290	1992: 4	—	—	76.800	77.844
1987: 9	—	—	74.267	73.469	1992: 5	—	—	77.358	78.156
1987: 10	—	—	75.056	74.448	1992: 6	—	—	79.248	78.093
1987: 11	—	—	74.358	74.735	1992: 7	—	—	76.846	78.749
1987: 12	—	—	74.049	75.045	1992: 8	—	—	79.567	78.473
1988: 1	—	—	75.062	75.106	1992: 9	—	—	79.762	78.619
1988: 2	—	—	76.009	75.421	1992: 10	—	—	80.088	79.135
1988: 3	—	—	75.925	75.563	1992: 11	—	—	79.383	79.538
1988: 4	—	—	75.206	75.864	1992: 12	—	—	78.887	79.587
1988: 5	—	—	75.130	75.815	1993: 1	—	—	79.542	79.900
1988: 6	—	—	77.105	75.907	1993: 2	—	—	80.413	80.152
1988: 7	—	—	74.444	76.108	1993: 3	—	—	80.673	80.283
1988: 8	—	—	77.054	76.543	1993: 4	—	—	79.396	80.483
1988: 9	—	—	77.403	76.297	1993: 5	—	—	79.321	80.176
1988: 10	—	—	77.360	76.651	1993: 6	—	—	81.501	80.311
1988: 11	—	—	76.464	76.851	1993: 7	—	—	78.889	80.623
1988: 12	—	—	76.097	77.133	1993: 8	—	—	81.742	80.525
1989: 1	—	—	77.037	77.376	1993: 9	—	—	82.309	81.072
1989: 2	—	—	77.458	77.002	1993: 10	—	—	82.359	81.508
1989: 3	—	—	77.019	77.288	1993: 11	—	—	81.672	81.878
1989: 4	—	—	77.192	77.280	1993: 12	—	—	81.457	82.364
1989: 5	—	—	76.018	76.774	1994: 1	—	—	82.446	82.778
1989: 6	—	—	77.922	76.737	1994: 2	—	—	83.104	82.841
1989: 7	—	—	74.148	75.970	1994: 3	—	—	83.943	83.573
1989: 8	—	—	77.342	76.638	1994: 4	—	—	83.050	84.054
1989: 9	—	—	77.561	76.430	1994: 5	—	—	83.514	84.526
1989: 10	—	—	77.102	76.329	1994: 6	—	—	86.377	85.098
1989: 11	—	—	76.211	76.466	1994: 7	—	—	82.957	85.246
1989: 12	—	—	76.271	76.993	1994: 8	—	—	86.901	85.711
1990: 1	—	—	76.324	76.543	1994: 9	—	—	87.523	85.816
1990: 2	—	—	77.524	77.257	1994: 10	—	—	87.409	86.497
1990: 3	—	—	77.891	77.650	1994: 11	—	—	86.808	87.030
1990: 4	—	—	76.304	77.640	1994: 12	—	—	87.119	87.983
1990: 5	—	—	76.950	77.675	1995: 1	—	—	87.663	88.392
1990: 6	—	—	79.227	77.965	1995: 2	—	—	88.689	88.484
1990: 7	—	—	76.290	77.814	1995: 3	—	—	89.145	88.491
1990: 8	—	—	78.813	77.916	1995: 4	—	—	86.692	88.370
1990: 9	—	—	79.397	78.023	1995: 5	—	—	87.408	88.600
1990: 10	—	—	78.394	77.547	1995: 6	—	—	90.416	88.932
1990: 11	—	—	76.337	76.564	1995: 7	—	—	86.478	88.595
1990: 12	—	—	75.228	76.081	1995: 8	—	—	91.104	89.796
1991: 1	—	—	75.708	75.803	1995: 9	—	—	92.112	90.173
1991: 2	—	—	75.452	75.240	1995: 10	—	—	90.890	89.957
1991: 3	—	—	74.558	74.834	1995: 11	—	—	90.225	90.345
1991: 4	—	—	74.673	75.015	1995: 12	—	—	90.043	90.731

TABLE Cb28–31   Indexes of industrial production: 1884–2003   *Continued*

	Miron–Romer, not seasonally adjusted		Federal Reserve Board			Miron–Romer, not seasonally adjusted		Federal Reserve Board	
	13-component index	Alternative index (less wool receipts)	Not seasonally adjusted	Seasonally adjusted		13-component index	Alternative index (less wool receipts)	Not seasonally adjusted	Seasonally adjusted
	Cb28	Cb29	Cb30	Cb31		Cb28	Cb29	Cb30	Cb31
Year: Month	Index 1909 = 100	Index 1909 = 100	Index 1997 = 100	Index 1997 = 100	Year: Month	Index 1909 = 100	Index 1909 = 100	Index 1997 = 100	Index 1997 = 100
1996: 1	—	—	89.460	90.048	2000: 1	—	—	111.939	113.200
1996: 2	—	—	91.412	91.275	2000: 2	—	—	113.177	113.947
1996: 3	—	—	91.686	91.056	2000: 3	—	—	115.084	114.446
1996: 4	—	—	90.543	91.881	2000: 4	—	—	113.641	115.299
1996: 5	—	—	91.246	92.487	2000: 5	—	—	114.430	115.982
1996: 6	—	—	94.932	93.319	2000: 6	—	—	118.535	116.202
1996: 7	—	—	90.815	93.295	2000: 7	—	—	113.238	115.926
1996: 8	—	—	95.261	93.881	2000: 8	—	—	117.860	115.667
1996: 9	—	—	96.656	94.436	2000: 9	—	—	118.691	116.071
1996: 10	—	—	95.566	94.560	2000: 10	—	—	117.065	115.631
1996: 11	—	—	95.273	95.456	2000: 11	—	—	114.884	115.506
1996: 12	—	—	94.899	96.057	2000: 12	—	—	114.478	115.144
1997: 1	—	—	95.483	96.340	2001: 1	—	—	113.483	114.196
1997: 2	—	—	97.570	97.687	2001: 2	—	—	113.094	113.622
1997: 3	—	—	98.058	98.071	2001: 3	—	—	113.909	113.075
1997: 4	—	—	97.869	98.516	2001: 4	—	—	110.130	112.550
1997: 5	—	—	97.631	98.883	2001: 5	—	—	110.761	111.847
1997: 6	—	—	100.843	99.352	2001: 6	—	—	113.375	111.145
1997: 7	—	—	97.449	99.761	2001: 7	—	—	108.469	110.996
1997: 8	—	—	102.198	100.780	2001: 8	—	—	113.260	110.696
1997: 9	—	—	103.988	101.667	2001: 9	—	—	112.456	109.933
1997: 10	—	—	103.740	102.485	2001: 10	—	—	110.793	109.512
1997: 11	—	—	102.831	103.094	2001: 11	—	—	108.109	108.845
1997: 12	—	—	102.342	103.365	2001: 12	—	—	106.905	108.327
1998: 1	—	—	102.461	103.830	2002: 1	—	—	108.028	108.967
1998: 2	—	—	103.777	104.098	2002: 2	—	—	108.696	109.197
1998: 3	—	—	105.032	104.416	2002: 3	—	—	109.704	109.641
1998: 4	—	—	103.164	105.032	2002: 4	—	—	109.341	110.113
1998: 5	—	—	104.418	105.536	2002: 5	—	—	109.644	110.447
1998: 6	—	—	106.613	105.029	2002: 6	—	—	113.190	110.818
1998: 7	—	—	103.275	104.903	2002: 7	—	—	109.235	111.577
1998: 8	—	—	108.682	106.748	2002: 8	—	—	114.017	111.305
1998: 9	—	—	108.839	106.555	2002: 9	—	—	113.877	111.242
1998: 10	—	—	108.925	107.278	2002: 10	—	—	112.089	110.580
1998: 11	—	—	106.456	106.977	2002: 11	—	—	109.663	110.797
1998: 12	—	—	105.825	107.064	2002: 12	—	—	108.093	109.889
1999: 1	—	—	106.654	107.811	2003: 1	—	—	110.004	110.670
1999: 2	—	—	107.659	108.181	2003: 2	—	—	110.338	110.735
1999: 3	—	—	109.333	108.648	2003: 3	—	—	110.489	110.082
1999: 4	—	—	107.460	108.876	2003: 4	—	—	108.348	109.479
1999: 5	—	—	108.299	109.447	2003: 5	—	—	108.792	109.538
1999: 6	—	—	111.782	109.578	2003: 6	—	—	111.532	109.523
1999: 7	—	—	107.676	110.316	2003: 7	—	—	107.686	110.037
1999: 8	—	—	113.043	110.817					
1999: 9	—	—	113.078	110.737					
1999: 10	—	—	113.238	111.688					
1999: 11	—	—	111.577	112.343					
1999: 12	—	—	111.768	113.125					

Sources

Series Cb28–29. Jeffrey A. Miron and Christina D. Romer, "A New Monthly Index of Industrial Production, 1884–1940," *Journal of Economic History* 50 (June 1990): 321–35, with corrections to the original supplied by the authors.

Series Cb30–31. U.S. Board of Governors of the Federal Reserve System, Internet site, Tables 1 and 2; downloaded August 26, 2003.

Documentation

The production index measures real output and is expressed as a percentage of real output in a base year. The Miron–Romer indexes use 1909 as the base year. The Federal Reserve indexes currently use 1997 as the base year and are computed as Fisher indexes since 1972; the weights are based on annual estimates of value added.

Series Cb28–29. The Miron–Romer index is a weighted average of thirteen component indexes all measured in physical quantities. See the source for details. The alternative series for mid-1897 excludes wool receipts at Boston because a change in the tariff on wool imports distorted wool receipts so dramatically that it introduced a spike in the production index. The authors

(continued)

TABLE Cb28–31   Indexes of industrial production: 1884–2003   *Continued*

recommend that the alternative index should be used for most purposes. See Christina D. Romer, "Remeasuring Business Cycles," *Journal of Economic History* 54 (September 1994): 573–690.

Series Cb30–31. The Federal Reserve Board's index of industrial production measures output in manufacturing, mining, and electric and gas utility industries. It does not include farming, transportation, trade, service, or construction. Based on about fifty series in 1919–1922, the number of component series was increased substantially in 1923 and again in 1939. Since then, coverage has been expanded several times to add new industries. For the period since 1992, the total index has been constructed from 267 individual series that measure either output in physical units (for example, tons of steel or barrels of oil) or data on inputs to the production process (for example, electric power use or production-worker hours) from which output is inferred. For details see U.S. Federal Reserve System Board of Governors,

Industrial Production: 1986 Edition; *Industrial Production: 1976 Edition*; *Industrial Production: 1959 Revision* (all Federal Reserve System); and *Federal Reserve Bulletin* (particularly December 1953, April 1990, June 1990, June 1993, March 1994, January 1995, January 1996, February 1997, February 1998, January 1999, and March 2000). For details on the construction of the index during the period between World War I and World War II, see *Federal Reserve Bulletin* (August 1940).

Series Cb29–30. The data for 1919–1922 are not strictly compatible with the data beginning in 1923; the index for these years was calculated by averaging two indexes, one with 1919 weights and one with 1922 weights.

Series Cb31. The seasonally adjusted series is calculated by the Federal Reserve. For the period 1919–1976, the seasonal-adjustment procedure is applied to the unadjusted series. Beginning in 1977, the adjusted series is obtained by aggregating seasonally adjusted versions of the component series.

TABLE Cb32–34   NBER composite cyclical indicators: 1959–2003

Contributed by Richard Sutch

Year: Month	Composite coincident index Cb32 Index July 1967 = 100	Composite leading index Cb33 Percent	Recession index Cb34 Percent	Year: Month	Composite coincident index Cb32 Index July 1967 = 100	Composite leading index Cb33 Percent	Recession index Cb34 Percent
1959: 2	71.5	2.9	—	1962: 5	78.3	3.0	5
1959: 3	71.6	2.9	—	1962: 6	78.3	3.0	6
1959: 4	73.1	2.9	—	1962: 7	78.5	2.9	6
1959: 5	73.9	2.9	—	1962: 8	78.7	2.5	6
1959: 6	74.2	2.9	—	1962: 9	79.0	3.7	3
1959: 7	73.4	2.9	—	1962: 10	79.1	4.1	2
1959: 8	72.0	2.9	—	1962: 11	79.5	3.9	3
1959: 9	71.6	2.9	—	1962: 12	79.3	4.5	2
1959: 10	71.3	2.9	—	1963: 1	79.5	5.2	1
1959: 11	71.7	2.9	—	1963: 2	80.0	5.8	1
1959: 12	74.2	2.9	—	1963: 3	80.4	6.4	1
1960: 1	75.2	2.9	—	1963: 4	81.0	6.6	1
1960: 2	75.1	4.8	—	1963: 5	81.5	7.8	1
1960: 3	74.6	2.2	—	1963: 6	81.8	6.4	1
1960: 4	74.5	0.3	—	1963: 7	81.9	4.7	4
1960: 5	74.2	−2.0	—	1963: 8	81.9	3.4	7
1960: 6	73.7	−2.9	—	1963: 9	82.4	4.0	6
1960: 7	73.5	−2.6	—	1963: 10	82.9	4.4	5
1960: 8	73.5	−0.5	—	1963: 11	83.0	3.6	5
1960: 9	73.2	−0.7	—	1963: 12	83.2	4.5	3
1960: 10	73.1	−0.8	—	1964: 1	83.3	5.0	2
1960: 11	72.6	−1.5	—	1964: 2	84.0	6.1	2
1960: 12	71.5	−0.5	—	1964: 3	84.1	5.0	3
1961: 1	71.3	1.2	21	1964: 4	85.0	3.5	5
1961: 2	71.3	−0.2	29	1964: 5	85.5	3.4	5
1961: 3	71.7	1.3	13	1964: 6	85.8	3.8	4
1961: 4	72.3	3.0	4	1964: 7	86.2	5.4	2
1961: 5	72.9	4.5	2	1964: 8	86.5	6.5	1
1961: 6	73.8	6.2	1	1964: 9	86.9	6.0	1
1961: 7	74.2	6.0	1	1964: 10	86.3	4.9	3
1961: 8	74.8	6.8	1	1964: 11	87.7	5.8	3
1961: 9	74.8	5.6	1	1964: 12	88.8	4.5	3
1961: 10	75.7	6.0	1	1965: 1	89.5	4.9	2
1961: 11	76.6	6.1	1	1965: 2	89.9	4.8	2
1961: 12	77.0	5.8	1	1965: 3	90.7	5.0	2
1962: 1	76.5	6.1	1	1965: 4	91.1	5.3	2
1962: 2	77.2	7.2	1				
1962: 3	77.7	5.6	1				
1962: 4	78.2	4.9	2				

TABLE Cb32–34   NBER composite cyclical indicators: 1959–2003   *Continued*

Year: Month	Composite coincident index Cb32 Index July 1967 = 100	Composite leading index Cb33 Percent	Recession index Cb34 Percent	Year: Month	Composite coincident index Cb32 Index July 1967 = 100	Composite leading index Cb33 Percent	Recession index Cb34 Percent
1965: 5	91.5	4.6	2	1970: 5	108.3	−1.9	67
1965: 6	91.7	5.3	2	1970: 6	108.1	−3.0	79
1965: 7	92.3	5.2	2	1970: 7	108.4	−2.4	57
1965: 8	92.7	5.1	2	1970: 8	108.3	−0.2	21
1965: 9	92.9	5.7	2	1970: 9	107.5	1.6	9
1965: 10	93.8	6.9	1	1970: 10	106.3	2.4	9
1965: 11	94.5	7.5	1	1970: 11	105.7	2.3	11
1965: 12	95.5	7.8	1	1970: 12	107.1	4.0	2
1966: 1	96.2	8.1	1	1971: 1	107.9	3.4	1
1966: 2	96.7	6.6	1	1971: 2	108.1	3.2	1
1966: 3	97.7	6.8	1	1971: 3	108.2	4.6	1
1966: 4	97.8	5.7	2	1971: 4	108.6	5.3	1
1966: 5	98.0	3.7	5	1971: 5	109.0	7.0	1
1966: 6	98.5	0.8	18	1971: 6	109.4	7.2	1
1966: 7	98.8	0.0	28	1971: 7	109.1	6.2	2
1966: 8	99.0	1.5	12	1971: 8	109.1	5.0	5
1966: 9	99.4	2.4	7	1971: 9	109.9	4.5	3
1966: 10	99.9	2.3	5	1971: 10	110.1	4.6	2
1966: 11	99.8	1.9	12	1971: 11	111.0	5.4	1
1966: 12	100.0	0.5	24	1971: 12	112.1	6.3	1
1967: 1	100.4	1.8	16	1972: 1	113.6	8.1	1
1967: 2	99.8	−1.3	54	1972: 2	114.1	8.1	1
1967: 3	99.7	−1.5	50	1972: 3	114.8	5.9	1
1967: 4	99.9	0.2	20	1972: 4	115.7	5.8	1
1967: 5	99.6	1.9	8	1972: 5	116.0	5.6	1
1967: 6	100.0	5.6	1	1972: 6	116.2	5.6	1
1967: 7	100.0	5.7	2	1972: 7	116.3	7.0	1
1967: 8	101.0	6.3	2	1972: 8	117.5	8.1	1
1967: 9	101.1	5.5	3	1972: 9	118.4	8.8	1
1967: 10	101.4	6.3	2	1972: 10	119.8	9.6	1
1967: 11	102.5	5.8	2	1972: 11	121.0	9.0	1
1967: 12	103.5	6.1	1	1972: 12	122.2	10.8	1
1968: 1	103.3	6.1	1	1973: 1	122.8	8.9	1
1968: 2	103.7	7.2	1	1973: 2	123.9	6.7	3
1968: 3	104.0	7.5	1	1973: 3	124.2	4.6	8
1968: 4	104.1	4.8	5	1973: 4	124.1	3.1	11
1968: 5	104.8	3.9	7	1973: 5	124.5	3.7	8
1968: 6	105.3	2.5	9	1973: 6	124.6	2.7	25
1968: 7	105.8	1.9	10	1973: 7	125.2	−0.9	69
1968: 8	105.9	3.0	8	1973: 8	124.7	−2.1	85
1968: 9	106.3	5.0	3	1973: 9	125.2	−1.7	65
1968: 10	106.7	5.1	3	1973: 10	126.0	−1.8	40
1968: 11	107.5	5.3	2	1973: 11	127.1	−2.5	32
1968: 12	107.6	4.3	4	1973: 12	127.0	−1.6	20
1969: 1	108.0	5.1	3	1974: 1	126.4	0.2	11
1969: 2	108.3	5.6	3	1974: 2	125.9	1.5	16
1969: 3	108.9	3.5	8	1974: 3	125.8	1.7	44
1969: 4	109.0	1.8	19	1974: 4	125.0	−1.2	88
1969: 5	109.1	−0.9	53	1974: 5	125.7	−3.4	96
1969: 6	109.6	−1.8	62	1974: 6	125.8	−8.1	100
1969: 7	110.0	−1.9	57	1974: 7	125.9	−8.6	99
1969: 8	110.5	−1.8	52	1974: 8	125.0	−11.0	99
1969: 9	110.7	−2.1	62	1974: 9	124.7	−10.5	96
1969: 10	111.0	−1.5	47	1974: 10	124.3	−8.8	90
1969: 11	110.3	−1.5	49	1974: 11	121.9	−10.5	97
1969: 12	110.2	−0.2	38	1974: 12	119.1	−6.3	84
1970: 1	109.0	−2.8	76	1975: 1	117.9	−5.7	82
1970: 2	108.9	−3.0	75	1975: 2	116.3	−5.4	80
1970: 3	108.7	−1.8	59	1975: 3	115.1	−3.2	71
1970: 4	108.5	−1.7	61	1975: 4	115.0	−0.3	28

(continued)

TABLE Cb32–34   NBER composite cyclical indicators: 1959–2003   *Continued*

Year: Month	Composite coincident index Cb32 Index July 1967 = 100	Composite leading index Cb33 Percent	Recession index Cb34 Percent	Year: Month	Composite coincident index Cb32 Index July 1967 = 100	Composite leading index Cb33 Percent	Recession index Cb34 Percent
1975: 5	115.1	2.8	4	1980: 5	138.6	−4.3	56
1975: 6	115.7	3.8	2	1980: 6	137.5	−0.9	34
1975: 7	116.1	5.5	1	1980: 7	136.8	2.1	32
1975: 8	117.3	5.3	1	1980: 8	137.7	2.2	32
1975: 9	118.3	5.0	1	1980: 9	139.3	3.0	28
1975: 10	118.7	5.5	1	1980: 10	141.1	0.7	56
1975: 11	118.9	5.6	1	1980: 11	142.6	−2.1	90
1975: 12	119.8	6.0	1	1980: 12	143.2	−2.3	75
1976: 1	121.4	6.3	1	1981: 1	143.2	−0.8	48
1976: 2	122.4	6.2	1	1981: 2	142.7	−0.2	32
1976: 3	122.7	6.1	1	1981: 3	142.7	0.6	32
1976: 4	123.2	6.5	1	1981: 4	141.7	−1.3	74
1976: 5	123.5	5.4	1	1981: 5	142.1	−2.4	71
1976: 6	123.7	4.8	1	1981: 6	142.5	−3.8	86
1976: 7	124.2	6.6	1	1981: 7	143.2	−5.1	89
1976: 8	124.4	7.0	1	1981: 8	143.1	−5.8	91
1976: 9	124.7	8.0	1	1981: 9	141.6	−4.5	84
1976: 10	124.8	6.9	1	1981: 10	141.1	−3.6	64
1976: 11	126.1	7.3	1	1981: 11	140.4	−2.5	53
1976: 12	127.2	7.6	1	1981: 12	139.4	−2.1	56
1977: 1	126.7	6.3	1	1982: 1	137.3	−2.2	72
1977: 2	128.1	7.7	1	1982: 2	139.0	−1.0	43
1977: 3	129.3	8.4	1	1982: 3	138.8	−2.0	44
1977: 4	130.1	8.4	1	1982: 4	138.4	−2.5	48
1977: 5	130.8	7.6	1	1982: 5	138.0	−2.0	64
1977: 6	131.3	7.7	1	1982: 6	137.4	−2.3	66
1977: 7	131.9	6.4	1	1982: 7	136.7	−0.3	29
1977: 8	132.2	6.1	1	1982: 8	135.7	−2.4	56
1977: 9	132.9	6.0	2	1982: 9	135.3	−1.8	28
1977: 10	133.6	6.0	2	1982: 10	134.3	1.2	9
1977: 11	134.2	6.7	2	1982: 11	134.1	1.8	7
1977: 12	134.5	6.9	2	1982: 12	133.8	4.7	1
1978: 1	133.1	5.2	5	1983: 1	135.5	6.7	1
1978: 2	133.8	5.1	5	1983: 2	134.9	6.8	1
1978: 3	135.7	5.5	4	1983: 3	135.9	7.1	1
1978: 4	138.7	6.7	2	1983: 4	137.2	7.7	1
1978: 5	139.3	4.8	5	1983: 5	138.1	8.6	1
1978: 6	140.0	5.3	4	1983: 6	138.9	8.7	1
1978: 7	139.9	3.5	12	1983: 7	140.5	8.3	1
1978: 8	140.3	2.8	16	1983: 8	140.9	6.0	1
1978: 9	140.6	2.8	20	1983: 9	142.6	5.1	1
1978: 10	141.4	3.1	27	1983: 10	143.9	6.8	1
1978: 11	142.4	3.2	20	1983: 11	144.6	6.9	1
1978: 12	143.2	3.8	12	1983: 12	145.9	6.9	1
1979: 1	142.7	0.4	31	1984: 1	147.8	8.4	1
1979: 2	142.8	0.5	26	1984: 2	148.6	9.3	1
1979: 3	143.8	4.5	5	1984: 3	149.1	7.5	1
1979: 4	142.0	4.0	6	1984: 4	150.3	6.1	1
1979: 5	143.3	4.4	7	1984: 5	150.8	4.8	3
1979: 6	143.5	3.7	10	1984: 6	151.4	4.3	2
1979: 7	143.8	1.8	27	1984: 7	151.8	3.1	3
1979: 8	143.5	0.1	61	1984: 8	152.3	2.0	2
1979: 9	143.3	−0.8	82	1984: 9	152.4	2.4	2
1979: 10	143.5	−3.6	94	1984: 10	152.2	2.5	2
1979: 11	143.6	−5.2	95	1984: 11	152.9	5.4	1
1979: 12	143.8	−5.0	91	1984: 12	153.3	6.2	1
1980: 1	144.2	−3.6	88	1985: 1	153.3	6.6	1
1980: 2	144.0	−4.4	99	1985: 2	153.5	6.8	1
1980: 3	143.0	−8.3	99	1985: 3	154.0	5.6	1
1980: 4	140.8	−5.9	66	1985: 4	154.0	5.4	1

TABLE Cb32–34   NBER composite cyclical indicators: 1959–2003   *Continued*

Year: Month	Composite coincident index	Composite leading index	Recession index	Year: Month	Composite coincident index	Composite leading index	Recession index
	Cb32	Cb33	Cb34		Cb32	Cb33	Cb34
	Index July 1967 = 100	Percent	Percent		Index July 1967 = 100	Percent	Percent
1985: 5	154.6	5.1	1	1990: 5	176.0	−0.2	21
1985: 6	154.5	5.9	1	1990: 6	176.7	1.1	12
1985: 7	154.1	5.5	1	1990: 7	176.6	2.0	11
1985: 8	155.0	5.3	1	1990: 8	176.7	2.0	17
1985: 9	155.5	6.2	1	1990: 9	176.0	0.4	39
1985: 10	155.7	4.8	3	1990: 10	174.7	−0.3	47
1985: 11	156.0	3.5	5	1990: 11	173.3	−0.7	52
1985: 12	156.6	4.5	3	1990: 12	172.7	−0.9	44
1986: 1	157.2	4.7	4	1991: 1	171.5	−1.1	40
1986: 2	156.7	3.1	9	1991: 2	170.8	−0.6	32
1986: 3	156.7	4.0	5	1991: 3	170.5	0.4	20
1986: 4	157.5	4.3	4	1991: 4	170.9	0.2	14
1986: 5	157.4	2.3	16	1991: 5	171.8	1.2	7
1986: 6	157.2	1.3	28	1991: 6	172.5	1.6	6
1986: 7	157.3	2.5	13	1991: 7	172.7	2.3	3
1986: 8	157.7	3.6	5	1991: 8	172.8	2.6	4
1986: 9	158.7	3.0	6	1991: 9	173.4	2.4	4
1986: 10	158.8	2.4	8	1991: 10	173.2	2.1	5
1986: 11	159.2	1.6	11	1991: 11	173.0	2.1	8
1986: 12	160.2	4.3	3	1991: 12	172.4	4.0	3
1987: 1	159.5	3.2	9	1992: 1	172.4	4.7	1
1987: 2	161.4	2.9	12	1992: 2	173.3	4.8	1
1987: 3	161.7	2.4	15	1992: 3	173.9	3.1	1
1987: 4	161.6	0.7	37	1992: 4	174.7	2.8	1
1987: 5	162.4	0.0	40	1992: 5	175.0	2.4	2
1987: 6	163.2	1.0	15	1992: 6	175.2	2.6	2
1987: 7	164.1	1.8	6	1992: 7	175.9	3.5	2
1987: 8	164.8	0.8	13	1992: 8	175.2	3.3	3
1987: 9	164.6	−0.8	45	1992: 9	175.8	4.3	1
1987: 10	166.1	−0.2	33	1992: 10	176.5	3.9	1
1987: 11	166.7	−0.7	40	1992: 11	177.2	2.8	1
1987: 12	167.7	0.4	17	1992: 12	179.1	3.3	1
1988: 1	167.7	0.3	13	1993: 1	178.2	3.4	1
1988: 2	168.7	2.2	3	1993: 2	178.5	3.8	1
1988: 3	169.5	3.1	2	1993: 3	178.2	2.2	4
1988: 4	170.3	2.6	5	1993: 4	179.3	2.5	4
1988: 5	170.3	2.7	7	1993: 5	179.6	2.9	4
1988: 6	170.6	2.9	4	1993: 6	180.2	3.2	3
1988: 7	171.0	1.3	9	1993: 7	180.3	3.7	2
1988: 8	171.4	1.1	8	1993: 8	180.3	3.8	2
1988: 9	171.5	1.4	9	1993: 9	181.2	4.1	2
1988: 10	172.5	2.7	7	1993: 10	182.0	4.3	1
1988: 11	172.8	3.0	12	1993: 11	182.8	4.5	1
1988: 12	173.8	2.6	13	1993: 12	184.6	5.4	1
1989: 1	174.3	2.4	13	1994: 1	183.7	4.7	1
1989: 2	173.9	0.7	19	1994: 2	183.9	4.9	1
1989: 3	174.0	−0.1	23	1994: 3	185.8	5.2	2
1989: 4	174.5	1.4	10	1994: 4	187.0	4.4	4
1989: 5	173.8	2.1	8	1994: 5	188.0	3.2	8
1989: 6	173.4	1.9	9	1994: 6	188.6	2.9	8
1989: 7	172.5	1.3	19	1994: 7	188.8	2.5	8
1989: 8	173.7	1.1	19	1994: 8	189.9	3.1	5
1989: 9	173.6	0.7	24	1994: 9	190.4	3.6	5
1989: 10	173.6	2.0	14	1994: 10	191.7	3.3	6
1989: 11	174.5	2.5	11	1994: 11	192.3	1.8	17
1989: 12	174.9	4.0	5	1994: 12	193.8	2.3	9
1990: 1	174.5	6.4	3	1995: 1	194.5	2.0	7
1990: 2	175.6	3.8	10	1995: 2	194.5	1.8	8
1990: 3	176.3	0.9	15	1995: 3	194.3	2.1	11
1990: 4	175.6	−0.3	23	1995: 4	193.9	3.0	10

(continued)

TABLE Cb32-34   NBER composite cyclical indicators: 1959-2003   *Continued*

Year: Month	Composite coincident index Cb32 Index July 1967 = 100	Composite leading index Cb33 Percent	Recession index Cb34 Percent	Year: Month	Composite coincident index Cb32 Index July 1967 = 100	Composite leading index Cb33 Percent	Recession index Cb34 Percent
1995: 5	194.0	3.3	9	1999: 9	230.0	1.6	19
1995: 6	194.8	3.7	5	1999: 10	231.5	3.3	9
1995: 7	194.8	3.6	5	1999: 11	232.8	3.4	7
1995: 8	196.3	3.2	5	1999: 12	234.3	3.7	5
1995: 9	196.8	2.3	7	2000: 1	235.6	4.2	4
1995: 10	196.8	1.9	8	2000: 2	236.1	3.6	4
1995: 11	197.5	2.7	6	2000: 3	236.8	3.4	4
1995: 12	198.0	3.5	4	2000: 4	237.8	2.7	5
1996: 1	196.0	4.4	3	2000: 5	238.2	1.6	13
1996: 2	198.3	5.2	2	2000: 6	238.3	3.1	6
1996: 3	198.7	3.6	5	2000: 7	238.2	3.8	5
1996: 4	200.0	3.3	7	2000: 8	237.9	3.4	5
1996: 5	201.1	4.0	5	2000: 9	238.5	3.5	5
1996: 6	202.3	4.6	3	2000: 10	238.2	3.6	7
1996: 7	202.5	3.4	4	2000: 11	238.0	3.6	9
1996: 8	203.6	3.2	5	2000: 12	237.5	3.2	7
1996: 9	204.4	2.8	5	2001: 1	236.8	4.6	4
1996: 10	205.0	3.9	3	2001: 2	236.3	4.1	6
1996: 11	206.2	4.8	2	2001: 3	235.8	3.9	5
1996: 12	206.6	4.7	2	2001: 4	234.8	3.0	6
1997: 1	205.5	3.8	3	2001: 5	234.2	2.7	7
1997: 2	207.0	3.5	4	2001: 6	233.2	0.7	22
1997: 3	207.7	2.7	6	2001: 7	233.5	1.2	18
1997: 4	208.8	1.9	10	2001: 8	233.7	2.4	8
1997: 5	209.1	1.7	13	2001: 9	232.0	0.9	18
1997: 6	209.9	3.2	6	2001: 10	231.5	0.3	27
1997: 7	210.9	4.5	2	2001: 11	230.8	0.6	23
1997: 8	212.2	4.4	3	2001: 12	231.0	2.2	7
1997: 9	213.5	3.5	3	2002: 1	231.7	3.4	2
1997: 10	214.4	3.4	5	2002: 2	231.4	3.8	2
1997: 11	215.4	3.5	5	2002: 3	231.8	3.5	3
1997: 12	216.2	3.4	4	2002: 4	232.1	2.3	7
1998: 1	217.4	4.1	2	2002: 5	232.6	3.0	6
1998: 2	218.2	4.8	3	2002: 6	233.4	3.8	4
1998: 3	218.9	4.4	4	2002: 7	233.7	3.9	4
1998: 4	219.4	3.8	6	2002: 8	233.8	3.0	5
1998: 5	220.2	3.0	7	2002: 9	233.5	3.4	3
1998: 6	220.0	2.2	9	2002: 10	233.0	3.1	4
1998: 7	220.1	2.1	10	2002: 11	233.2	2.3	8
1998: 8	222.0	3.1	8	2002: 12	232.4	3.2	8
1998: 9	222.1	2.4	12	2003: 1	233.3	2.9	9
1998: 10	223.3	4.7	6	2003: 2	232.3	1.9	12
1998: 11	223.7	4.2	9	2003: 3	231.8	1.2	15
1998: 12	224.7	3.8	8	2003: 4	231.3	1.1	17
1999: 1	225.3	3.8	7	2003: 5	231.5	2.4	10
1999: 2	226.3	2.8	7	2003: 6	231.5	3.4	6
1999: 3	226.9	1.9	9				
1999: 4	227.2	2.1	6				
1999: 5	228.0	2.9	4				
1999: 6	228.7	3.3	5				
1999: 7	229.5	3.3	7				
1999: 8	230.3	3.1	8				

Source

James H. Stock and Mark W. Watson, "New Indexes of Coincident and Leading Economic Indicators," in *NBER Macroeconomic Annual 1989* (National Bureau of Economic Research, 1989), with revisions and updating from the National Bureau of Economic Research (NBER) Internet site, downloaded August 25, 2003.

Documentation

Series Cb32. This series is a weighted average of the current and recent values of the growth rates of four coincident series of economic activity.

The four series are industrial production, real personal income less transfer payments, total real manufacturing and trade sales, and total employee-hours in nonagricultural establishments. Stock and Watson name this series XCI.

Series Cb33. This series is a forecast of the growth of the coincident index in series Cb32 for the six months subsequent to date of the index. It is stated in percentage terms on an annual basis and is identified by Stock and Watson as series XLI. The index is a weighted average of seven leading indica-tors: (1) housing authorizations (building permits) for new private dwellings;

TABLE Cb32–34   NBER composite cyclical indicators: 1959–2003   *Continued*

(2) real manufacturers' unfilled orders, durable goods industries; (3) trade-weighted index of nominal exchange rates between the United States and the United Kingdom, Germany, France, Italy, and Japan; (4) the number of people working part-time in nonagricultural industries because of slack work; (5) the yield on a constant-maturity portfolio of ten-year U.S. Treasury bonds; (6) the difference between the interest rate on three-month commercial paper and the interest rate on three-month U.S. Treasury bills; and (7) the difference between the yield on a constant-maturity portfolio of ten-year U.S. Treasury bonds and one-year U.S. Treasury bonds. The series reporting leading indicators (2) through (5) have been smoothed.

Series Cb34. This series is an estimate of the probability that the economy would be in an NBER recession (see the text for Table Cb5–8) six months from the date of the index. Computation of the index uses all four of the components of the coincident index and all seven components of the leading index. The probability is expressed as a percentage. Thus, if the recession index is 25 in February, the model underlying the index predicts that the economy would be in recession in August with a probability of 25 percent. Stock and Watson call this index XRI.

THE GREAT DEPRESSION

Richard Sutch

TABLE Cb35–44   Production of consumer and producer goods – indexes and selected commodities: 1919–1939

Contributed by Richard Sutch

	Indexes of production									
Year: Month	Producer goods	Consumer goods	Consumer goods, excluding automobiles	Passenger cars	Pig iron	Bituminous coal	Polished plate glass	Hogs slaughtered	Cigarettes	Women's shoes
	Cb35	Cb36	Cb37	Cb38	Cb39	Cb40	Cb41	Cb42	Cb43	Cb44
	Index 1923–1925 = 100	Index 1923–1925 = 100	Index 1923–1925 = 100	Thousand	Thousand gross tons	Million short tons	Million square feet	Thousand	Billion	Million pairs
1919: 1	97.2	74.4	85.5	—	106.5	42.2	7.08	5,846	3.08	—
1919: 2	91.2	69.1	77.8	—	105.0	32.1	6.28	4,266	3.13	—
1919: 3	82.7	66.1	74.1	—	99.7	34.3	7.72	3,443	3.84	—
1919: 4	80.9	68.3	76.7	—	82.6	32.7	7.19	3,208	2.65	—
1919: 5	76.1	72.1	81.0	—	68.0	38.2	8.07	3,743	2.77	—
1919: 6	88.1	72.9	81.6	—	70.5	37.7	7.63	3,728	3.14	—
1919: 7	95.5	74.0	82.3	—	78.3	43.4	7.02	2,884	3.58	—
1919: 8	103.0	74.9	82.4	—	88.5	43.6	7.91	1,949	3.92	—
1919: 9	92.0	77.1	83.9	—	82.9	48.2	7.31	1,997	4.28	—
1919: 10	85.1	80.8	86.6	—	60.1	57.2	7.80	2,686	5.03	—
1919: 11	93.6	87.5	92.2	—	79.8	19.0	7.72	3,270	4.77	—
1919: 12	95.8	87.3	93.8	—	84.9	37.2	7.36	4,790	4.58	—
1920: 1	97.0	88.7	94.0	—	97.3	49.7	7.60	5,079	4.53	—
1920: 2	98.0	81.2	86.0	—	102.7	41.1	7.42	3,104	3.54	—
1920: 3	96.2	80.7	86.1	—	108.9	47.9	8.28	3,482	4.37	—
1920: 4	90.1	74.4	82.9	—	91.3	38.8	8.36	2,590	3.77	—
1920: 5	91.7	78.5	85.6	—	96.3	39.8	8.20	3,585	3.95	—
1920: 6	96.8	81.2	87.6	—	101.5	46.1	7.31	3,566	4.09	—
1920: 7	94.2	81.7	87.5	—	98.9	46.0	6.92	2,644	3.05	—
1920: 8	98.2	79.8	84.4	—	101.5	50.0	6.65	2,191	3.57	—
1920: 9	94.7	77.2	82.1	—	104.3	50.2	6.95	1,979	3.56	—
1920: 10	89.1	74.3	80.1	—	106.2	53.3	8.15	2,487	3.84	—
1920: 11	81.1	75.8	80.9	—	97.8	52.6	7.82	3,329	3.53	—
1920: 12	78.5	71.0	76.4	—	87.2	53.3	7.88	3,985	2.82	—
1921: 1	71.3	61.8	69.7	—	78.0	41.1	8.77	4,347	3.90	—
1921: 2	65.8	61.9	69.7	—	69.2	31.5	8.66	3,799	4.12	—
1921: 3	62.1	64.2	71.9	—	51.5	31.1	9.88	3,047	4.47	—
1921: 4	58.8	64.1	70.5	—	39.8	28.2	9.96	3,003	3.80	—
1921: 5	61.9	68.9	75.7	—	39.4	34.1	9.92	3,274	4.14	—
1921: 6	60.9	71.1	75.7	—	35.5	34.6	10.00	3,618	4.22	—
1921: 7	58.6	74.3	78.7	—	27.9	31.0	10.04	2,821	4.16	—
1921: 8	62.0	76.6	81.2	—	30.8	35.3	10.44	2,530	5.14	—
1921: 9	63.9	73.9	78.9	—	32.9	35.9	10.41	2,422	4.80	—
1921: 10	66.6	77.0	82.8	—	40.2	44.7	10.84	2,866	4.88	—
1921: 11	69.9	76.1	81.6	—	47.2	36.8	10.00	3,447	4.24	7.03
1921: 12	70.7	73.4	80.4	—	53.2	31.6	9.61	3,808	3.00	8.06
1922: 1	71.2	75.3	82.5	78	53.1	38.9	11.18	3,985	3.71	8.45
1922: 2	73.3	79.5	87.0	103	58.2	42.4	10.98	3,480	3.13	9.10
1922: 3	75.6	79.3	86.7	149	65.7	51.9	12.10	3,350	3.64	11.09
1922: 4	80.2	82.1	88.0	194	69.1	16.3	11.17	2,946	3.45	9.91
1922: 5	84.4	84.1	89.0	229	74.4	21.0	11.49	3,716	4.60	9.49
1922: 6	88.5	88.2	91.8	250	78.7	23.1	13.05	4,046	5.30	8.76
1922: 7	90.6	88.7	91.9	221	77.6	17.6	11.20	3,104	5.25	7.92
1922: 8	86.0	91.2	93.2	244	58.6	26.8	11.75	2,888	6.37	9.36
1922: 9	88.7	87.5	91.9	185	67.8	42.5	11.91	2,747	5.55	9.14
1922: 10	96.7	92.0	95.3	209	85.1	46.7	11.65	3,332	4.50	10.16
1922: 11	101.0	98.8	100.3	207	95.0	46.9	10.11	4,318	4.52	9.68
1922: 12	108.7	100.7	101.3	203	99.6	48.1	7.65	5,201	3.54	9.03
1923: 1	103.0	97.5	98.4	223	104.2	51.9	9.02	5,134	5.35	10.44
1923: 2	101.3	99.7	99.9	253	106.9	43.6	10.41	4,231	4.62	10.46
1923: 3	104.2	102.6	103.7	321	113.7	48.4	12.38	4,838	5.04	12.80
1923: 4	107.3	101.4	102.6	337	118.3	44.1	10.96	4,179	4.71	11.03

TABLE Cb35–44   Production of consumer and producer goods – indexes and selected commodities: 1919–1939
Continued

	Indexes of production									
	Producer goods	Consumer goods	Consumer goods, excluding automobiles	Passenger cars	Pig iron	Bituminous coal	Polished plate glass	Hogs slaughtered	Cigarettes	Women's shoes
	Cb35	Cb36	Cb37	Cb38	Cb39	Cb40	Cb41	Cb42	Cb43	Cb44
Year: Month	Index 1923–1925 = 100	Index 1923–1925 = 100	Index 1923–1925 = 100	Thousand	Thousand gross tons	Million short tons	Million square feet	Thousand	Billion	Million pairs
1923: 5	107.8	99.4	100.6	347	124.8	47.7	10.22	4,325	5.55	10.58
1923: 6	105.7	95.1	95.2	335	122.6	47.1	8.50	4,303	5.84	9.61
1923: 7	105.7	94.9	94.4	299	118.7	46.7	9.43	3,983	5.84	8.35
1923: 8	103.6	94.0	92.3	313	111.3	50.6	11.29	3,556	5.86	9.69
1923: 9	102.3	96.6	94.6	299	104.2	47.8	9.95	3,212	5.57	9.30
1923: 10	97.4	99.4	97.0	335	101.6	50.9	9.25	4,328	6.28	10.15
1923: 11	96.7	100.8	97.4	285	96.5	44.4	9.12	5,341	5.36	8.29
1923: 12	98.5	103.4	99.1	277	94.2	41.2	7.92	5,904	4.43	7.31
1924: 1	99.6	100.2	97.7	286	97.4	52.5	8.82	5,911	6.26	8.68
1924: 2	101.0	103.2	99.5	335	106.0	47.3	10.69	5,006	4.85	9.23
1924: 3	99.5	101.0	100.0	345	111.8	41.3	11.95	4,536	5.27	10.63
1924: 4	94.0	96.9	97.7	335	107.8	30.4	10.56	4,073	5.32	10.18
1924: 5	83.0	91.3	94.9	275	84.4	32.3	10.88	4,278	6.39	8.96
1924: 6	77.2	91.5	96.8	220	67.5	31.5	11.35	4,288	6.46	7.64
1924: 7	76.5	93.2	96.5	239	57.6	33.3	9.97	4,114	6.58	7.26
1924: 8	85.9	96.4	98.2	252	60.9	35.9	12.16	3,070	6.32	9.17
1924: 9	91.5	98.0	99.2	261	68.4	42.4	10.90	2,857	6.27	10.46
1924: 10	93.7	98.4	99.8	258	79.9	48.4	11.14	3,498	6.49	11.53
1924: 11	97.5	103.5	104.8	202	83.7	42.1	11.65	4,641	5.36	8.79
1924: 12	106.8	103.6	106.2	177	95.5	46.3	10.58	6,600	5.44	7.85
1925: 1	109.0	101.5	103.7	210	108.7	51.6	11.43	5,979	6.65	8.40
1925: 2	105.4	101.2	102.3	247	114.8	38.8	11.29	4,447	5.68	9.03
1925: 3	107.6	101.2	101.4	326	115.0	37.4	13.14	3,299	6.27	10.65
1925: 4	103.0	102.0	101.3	381	108.6	33.5	12.55	3,037	6.05	10.37
1925: 5	100.4	101.3	100.9	371	94.5	35.3	12.78	3,186	6.47	8.86
1925: 6	97.7	100.1	100.0	357	89.1	37.0	12.28	3,732	7.43	8.12
1925: 7	100.6	103.9	102.5	354	85.9	39.4	13.06	2,819	7.61	8.67
1925: 8	103.6	99.9	104.0	222	87.2	44.6	14.72	2,453	6.98	10.66
1925: 9	104.4	102.7	104.4	266	90.8	46.6	14.01	2,598	7.12	11.39
1925: 10	105.1	108.2	104.0	392	97.5	52.9	14.62	3,314	6.93	11.50
1925: 11	110.4	110.3	104.8	329	100.8	50.5	12.13	3,646	6.52	8.01
1925: 12	116.4	110.7	107.8	281	104.9	52.5	8.48	4,533	6.25	7.70
1926: 1	110.6	107.8	106.3	276	107.0	53.2	10.02	4,501	6.94	8.34
1926: 2	109.1	107.2	104.3	323	104.4	46.2	9.80	3,351	6.24	9.25
1926: 3	107.9	105.9	104.5	385	111.0	45.7	10.42	3,562	7.63	11.00
1926: 4	108.3	104.4	103.9	385	115.0	39.7	11.43	3,105	6.97	9.50
1926: 5	104.0	102.0	101.8	375	112.3	38.7	12.57	3,131	7.26	8.64
1926: 6	106.1	102.3	103.5	341	107.8	41.6	9.13	3,430	8.49	8.88
1926: 7	107.3	104.6	105.4	317	104.0	43.1	8.33	3,127	7.96	9.10
1926: 8	112.9	112.1	109.0	381	103.2	46.0	5.52	2,834	8.07	11.22
1926: 9	112.5	112.1	110.4	352	104.5	48.6	7.98	2,616	8.09	11.62
1926: 10	112.2	109.4	110.4	290	107.6	54.1	8.58	2,976	8.06	11.48
1926: 11	108.7	105.5	106.3	220	107.9	59.2	7.10	3,610	7.35	8.52
1926: 12	110.7	103.1	107.8	138	99.7	57.2	4.94	4,394	6.39	7.67
1927: 1	108.0	104.3	106.9	198	100.1	56.7	7.32	4,514	7.27	7.96
1927: 2	109.3	105.6	106.1	263	105.0	52.7	8.88	3,395	6.61	9.15
1927: 3	110.8	107.3	108.3	344	112.4	59.9	10.59	3,837	8.03	10.78
1927: 4	108.8	107.9	109.8	357	114.1	34.5	10.17	3,330	7.88	10.02
1927: 5	111.1	107.8	109.4	357	109.4	35.3	9.47	3,766	8.54	8.92
1927: 6	107.0	105.0	110.1	280	103.0	36.5	7.55	4,253	8.74	9.38
1927: 7	107.2	105.8	110.8	238	95.2	33.5	7.22	3,431	8.28	9.60
1927: 8	108.9	105.6	108.1	276	95.1	41.5	6.31	3,050	9.33	13.32
1927: 9	107.7	105.2	109.4	226	92.5	41.8	4.80	2,534	8.99	13.01
1927: 10	103.4	102.7	108.4	183	89.8	43.8	4.81	2,969	8.55	12.08
1927: 11	101.7	103.2	105.4	110	88.3	40.5	3.69	3,688	8.09	8.24
1927: 12	104.4	99.7	105.9	106	87.0	41.1	6.15	4,869	6.87	7.14
1928: 1	108.2	107.4	110.0	206	92.6	44.9	5.25	5,479	8.37	9.21
1928: 2	108.8	112.4	113.0	291	100.0	42.0	6.23	5,780	7.53	10.98
1928: 3	106.9	113.0	113.5	371	103.2	44.7	4.62	5,140	8.47	12.86
1928: 4	111.0	110.2	111.4	364	106.2	32.7	5.26	3,446	7.51	10.23

(continued)

TABLE Cb35–44　Production of consumer and producer goods – indexes and selected commodities: 1919–1939
Continued

	Indexes of production									
	Producer goods	Consumer goods	Consumer goods, excluding automobiles	Passenger cars	Pig iron	Bituminous coal	Polished plate glass	Hogs slaughtered	Cigarettes	Women's shoes
	Cb35	Cb36	Cb37	Cb38	Cb39	Cb40	Cb41	Cb42	Cb43	Cb44
Year: Month	Index 1923–1925 = 100	Index 1923–1925 = 100	Index 1923–1925 = 100	Thousand	Thousand gross tons	Million short tons	Million square feet	Thousand	Billion	Million pairs
1928: 5	108.5	106.9	108.2	375	105.9	37.2	3.15	3,884	8.89	9.64
1928: 6	106.3	107.2	108.8	356	102.7	36.5	5.14	4,078	9.69	9.34
1928: 7	110.3	111.2	111.3	338	99.1	36.9	2.85	2,984	9.72	10.35
1928: 8	113.9	114.7	111.8	399	101.2	41.8	1.84	2,545	10.63	13.58
1928: 9	116.1	116.5	114.3	358	102.1	42.0	3.57	2,508	9.13	12.73
1928: 10	115.8	113.3	112.7	339	108.8	51.2	4.12	3,713	9.92	13.22
1928: 11	116.0	111.7	113.7	216	110.1	46.8	4.72	4,455	8.54	8.36
1928: 12	120.8	114.7	116.3	204	108.7	44.1	4.48	5,782	7.52	7.02
1929: 1	118.5	118.4	115.0	348	111.0	52.4	6.19	5,738	10.16	10.09
1929: 2	115.9	122.3	116.6	406	114.5	48.1	4.96	4,478	8.06	10.85
1929: 3	121.4	125.7	119.1	514	119.8	40.1	4.88	3,645	8.69	12.72
1929: 4	121.4	120.6	115.4	538	122.1	37.6	4.68	3,761	9.61	11.03
1929: 5	128.0	119.6	115.8	516	125.7	40.9	7.92	3,798	11.17	10.34
1929: 6	127.8	121.6	119.5	453	123.9	38.8	9.50	3,756	10.84	9.63
1929: 7	127.6	119.8	117.1	426	122.1	41.4	11.35	3,597	10.72	11.38
1929: 8	127.2	122.1	118.2	442	121.2	44.7	11.33	3,130	10.93	14.49
1929: 9	125.9	120.9	119.1	364	116.6	45.3	8.92	3,104	10.35	14.06
1929: 10	119.1	114.1	114.8	319	115.7	52.2	5.79	3,857	11.20	14.07
1929: 11	106.2	108.1	112.3	170	106.0	46.5	4.17	4,499	9.04	8.43
1929: 12	101.5	104.5	111.8	92	91.5	47.0	6.35	5,083	8.26	7.32
1930: 1	102.8	107.0	108.6	234	91.2	50.4	7.61	5,001	10.21	9.99
1930: 2	107.3	110.3	110.6	280	101.4	40.1	7.44	4,034	8.47	10.32
1930: 3	104.2	108.4	109.7	331	104.7	36.2	10.12	3,392	9.17	11.87
1930: 4	104.8	111.1	112.8	373	106.1	36.3	8.87	3,480	9.54	11.47
1930: 5	99.5	108.6	110.9	361	104.3	36.4	8.05	3,823	10.30	8.98
1930: 6	94.7	105.0	109.2	286	97.8	34.1	6.81	3,689	11.75	8.30
1930: 7	88.9	100.4	105.8	222	85.1	35.2	7.54	3,187	11.86	9.12
1930: 8	88.9	99.6	105.5	184	81.4	36.1	7.74	2,724	10.58	11.80
1930: 9	87.6	98.8	105.0	176	75.9	39.1	6.98	2,773	10.19	12.08
1930: 10	83.1	93.2	101.6	114	69.8	44.7	7.82	3,492	10.95	10.59
1930: 11	77.9	94.2	100.3	101	62.2	38.6	6.87	4,024	7.95	5.18
1930: 12	75.6	92.9	97.4	122	53.7	40.2	8.70	4,647	8.67	5.53
1931: 1	74.9	94.6	99.6	138	55.3	38.9	13.36	5,362	9.37	7.87
1931: 2	78.1	94.8	98.9	180	61.0	31.7	13.72	4,142	8.84	10.15
1931: 3	82.3	97.1	101.9	231	65.6	34.2	16.53	3,523	9.80	12.86
1931: 4	81.8	100.7	105.3	287	67.3	28.8	17.00	3,488	9.47	12.28
1931: 5	80.5	101.5	106.8	271	64.3	28.6	14.58	3,408	10.45	11.42
1931: 6	74.5	94.2	101.0	210	54.6	29.5	13.16	3,251	11.51	10.42
1931: 7	75.6	95.7	102.5	184	47.2	30.1	13.91	2,767	10.70	10.88
1931: 8	71.7	94.0	100.7	155	41.3	30.9	14.53	2,500	9.52	13.57
1931: 9	69.2	89.7	98.2	109	39.0	32.3	14.40	2,955	9.70	12.43
1931: 10	63.6	86.5	96.8	58	37.8	36.1	16.59	3,772	8.96	8.58
1931: 11	63.3	89.3	98.0	49	36.8	30.4	15.91	4,218	7.85	4.11
1931: 12	60.7	91.6	97.4	98	31.6	30.6	16.11	5,387	7.30	5.73
1932: 1	60.3	91.3	98.3	99	31.4	28.3	17.47	5,027	8.96	8.67
1932: 2	57.5	88.7	97.6	94	33.3	28.4	14.01	4,590	7.68	11.22
1932: 3	55.3	85.1	95.6	99	31.2	32.7	16.24	3,664	8.45	13.20
1932: 4	48.1	82.2	92.6	121	28.4	20.6	19.67	3,714	7.56	10.83
1932: 5	46.0	85.9	94.5	158	25.3	18.6	19.41	3,940	8.69	8.81
1932: 6	44.5	84.2	91.9	160	20.9	18.0	16.42	3,320	10.56	9.17
1932: 7	45.2	81.3	90.5	95	18.5	18.1	16.61	2,802	9.53	8.18
1932: 8	51.0	77.0	86.1	76	17.1	22.8	18.92	2,970	9.56	14.28
1932: 9	57.4	84.1	94.4	65	19.8	26.7	19.77	3,252	9.31	14.08
1932: 10	56.4	82.1	93.2	35	20.8	33.1	21.07	3,605	8.35	11.60
1932: 11	53.9	81.0	89.0	48	21.0	31.0	13.23	3,778	7.61	5.70
1932: 12	51.9	83.1	88.6	86	17.6	31.5	7.45	4,584	7.32	6.19
1933: 1	52.1	81.2	86.1	110	18.3	27.9	7.06	4,700	8.62	9.64
1933: 2	50.3	81.2	88.9	90	19.8	27.9	20.68	3,647	7.85	11.76
1933: 3	45.5	75.6	84.7	97	17.5	24.4	22.97	3,602	7.97	12.08
1933: 4	55.3	86.6	96.2	150	20.8	19.8	24.31	3,847	7.97	11.44

TABLE Cb35–44   Production of consumer and producer goods – indexes and selected commodities: 1919–1939
Continued

	Indexes of production									
Year: Month	Producer goods	Consumer goods	Consumer goods, excluding automobiles	Passenger cars	Pig iron	Bituminous coal	Polished plate glass	Hogs slaughtered	Cigarettes	Women's shoes
	Cb35	Cb36	Cb37	Cb38	Cb39	Cb40	Cb41	Cb42	Cb43	Cb44
	Index 1923–1925 = 100	Index 1923–1925 = 100	Index 1923–1925 = 100	Thousand	Thousand gross tons	Million short tons	Million square feet	Thousand	Billion	Million pairs
1933: 5	67.6	92.4	101.8	181	28.6	22.5	21.52	4,286	12.82	12.96
1933: 6	86.5	99.3	107.6	208	42.2	25.5	21.48	4,626	12.46	12.99
1933: 7	97.8	103.2	110.8	191	57.8	29.7	16.99	3,914	9.53	12.97
1933: 8	88.4	97.5	103.7	191	59.1	34.4	19.82	3,477	11.19	14.98
1933: 9	74.0	92.3	98.7	157	50.7	29.7	18.25	9,449	9.53	12.61
1933: 10	67.9	87.0	95.0	105	43.8	30.3	16.45	3,058	9.18	11.45
1933: 11	60.1	86.1	95.4	42	36.2	31.2	13.86	4,501	6.84	7.04
1933: 12	63.4	88.1	96.6	51	38.1	30.3	9.88	4,530	7.80	6.94
1934: 1	65.4	90.1	96.5	113	39.2	33.5	5.57	5,391	11.48	10.99
1934: 2	69.9	96.7	100.7	187	45.1	32.7	2.90	3,433	9.17	12.89
1934: 3	72.8	93.8	96.0	279	52.2	38.5	4.14	3,039	9.33	14.76
1934: 4	78.2	99.0	102.3	288	57.6	24.7	4.16	3,411	9.29	14.03
1934: 5	78.6	97.2	102.1	274	65.9	27.4	4.21	4,218	11.17	13.78
1934: 6	72.1	97.0	101.5	261	64.3	25.9	6.48	3,763	12.05	10.14
1934: 7	57.6	101.8	107.6	223	39.5	24.9	5.99	3,324	11.36	12.10
1934: 8	58.7	98.4	104.9	184	34.0	27.5	8.35	2,641	11.81	15.43
1934: 9	54.3	100.6	110.0	125	29.9	27.9	9.66	2,601	10.29	10.83
1934: 10	61.4	107.8	101.4	84	30.7	33.0	14.00	3,545	10.72	9.05
1934: 11	63.1	91.0	100.5	49	31.9	31.0	14.02	4,312	9.73	6.37
1934: 12	73.7	101.5	106.6	111	33.1	32.5	13.81	4,197	9.21	7.94
1935: 1	82.2	94.5	94.6	228	47.7	37.1	13.40	3,048	11.34	12.74
1935: 2	83.1	101.0	99.9	274	57.4	35.1	11.16	2,409	9.31	13.86
1935: 3	81.1	100.0	97.9	359	57.1	39.0	12.94	2,158	10.20	15.42
1935: 4	80.3	100.8	98.5	387	55.4	22.1	7.98	2,178	10.70	14.98
1935: 5	78.8	96.5	99.3	306	55.7	27.0	8.82	2,172	11.71	11.99
1935: 6	80.0	95.9	97.7	294	51.6	30.3	10.20	1,828	12.12	9.58
1935: 7	81.1	96.8	98.6	274	49.0	22.5	6.82	1,712	13.14	13.63
1935: 8	86.8	92.5	98.2	181	56.8	26.3	11.47	1,668	11.97	16.28
1935: 9	93.5	91.2	103.1	56	59.2	25.3	15.00	1,453	10.77	13.63
1935: 10	92.4	97.0	100.7	213	63.8	38.1	20.16	2,135	12.71	12.17
1935: 11	92.5	105.7	99.8	337	68.9	33.7	17.36	2,422	10.80	7.34
1935: 12	102.5	112.6	105.2	343	68.0	35.8	20.28	2,875	9.84	10.15
1936: 1	93.2	113.5	111.5	298	65.4	40.2	—	3,428	12.72	14.56
1936: 2	89.5	107.5	110.8	224	62.9	41.5	—	2,319	10.77	15.02
1936: 3	86.0	105.8	106.2	343	65.8	31.8	—	2,617	11.19	15.54
1936: 4	99.1	111.4	111.0	416	80.1	30.8	—	2,559	11.87	14.14
1936: 5	99.2	112.6	114.1	385	85.4	28.8	—	2,579	12.02	12.84
1936: 6	102.7	109.8	110.5	375	86.2	29.6	—	2,739	14.01	11.14
1936: 7	111.4	119.0	119.2	372	83.7	32.3	—	2,692	14.80	14.98
1936: 8	112.9	113.5	120.7	209	87.5	33.5	—	2,254	13.43	18.18
1936: 9	112.6	106.9	119.6	90	91.0	37.7	—	2,403	14.34	17.24
1936: 10	117.3	115.7	123.3	190	96.5	43.9	—	3,492	13.20	14.41
1936: 11	110.9	122.6	118.9	341	98.2	42.5	—	4,292	11.56	8.47
1936: 12	125.9	135.6	127.0	425	100.5	46.4	—	4,681	13.25	11.80
1937: 1	119.6	119.7	117.8	309	103.6	41.4	—	3,519	13.44	16.75
1937: 2	117.5	123.3	124.7	297	107.1	42.7	—	2,842	12.33	17.74
1937: 3	122.3	123.1	123.4	404	111.6	51.9	—	3,033	12.79	20.50
1937: 4	123.0	121.2	121.4	440	113.1	26.2	—	2,810	12.21	16.82
1937: 5	121.5	120.2	121.0	425	114.1	30.3	—	2,099	13.07	14.25
1937: 6	114.5	115.5	115.4	411	103.6	32.0	—	2,110	14.26	12.88
1937: 7	117.3	115.4	115.6	360	112.9	32.2	—	1,643	15.29	15.47
1937: 8	122.1	116.9	118.6	311	116.3	34.2	—	1,590	15.10	17.76
1937: 9	112.5	102.9	113.3	119	113.7	39.4	—	2,033	14.85	14.44
1937: 10	94.0	109.6	110.1	299	93.3	41.1	—	2,711	13.89	10.95
1937: 11	74.4	107.4	104.2	295	66.9	36.7	—	3,295	12.79	6.19
1937: 12	66.7	110.2	109.4	244	48.1	37.4	—	3,958	12.61	8.16

(continued)

TABLE Cb35–44   Production of consumer and producer goods – indexes and selected commodities: 1919–1939
Continued

	Indexes of production									
	Producer goods	Consumer goods	Consumer goods, excluding automobiles	Passenger cars	Pig iron	Bituminous coal	Polished plate glass	Hogs slaughtered	Cigarettes	Women's shoes
	Cb35	Cb36	Cb37	Cb38	Cb39	Cb40	Cb41	Cb42	Cb43	Cb44
Year: Month	Index 1923–1925 = 100	Index 1923–1925 = 100	Index 1923–1925 = 100	Thousand	Thousand gross tons	Million short tons	Million square feet	Thousand	Billion	Million pairs
1938: 1	63.7	104.4	109.8	156	46.1	31.5	—	4,201	13.06	12.61
1938: 2	62.6	97.4	104.6	139	46.4	27.9	—	2,833	11.49	15.39
1938: 3	64.5	96.3	104.6	174	46.9	27.3	—	2,610	13.73	18.76
1938: 4	61.7	94.0	103.7	176	45.9	22.0	—	2,462	12.53	15.90
1938: 5	61.4	93.3	102.7	155	40.5	21.7	—	2,585	14.42	13.43
1938: 6	64.1	91.0	101.4	137	35.4	22.9	—	2,533	14.72	9.78
1938: 7	73.6	92.4	103.3	107	38.8	23.8	—	2,254	13.78	13.72
1938: 8	87.2	100.2	114.1	59	48.2	29.0	—	2,467	15.89	18.99
1938: 9	84.6	102.3	115.8	65	56.0	32.8	—	2,671	14.71	15.59
1938: 10	90.1	109.4	116.2	187	66.2	35.7	—	3,311	13.26	12.07
1938: 11	99.9	118.2	115.0	320	75.7	36.6	—	3,913	13.51	7.95
1938: 12	102.1	124.3	120.4	326	71.3	37.2	—	4,346	12.66	10.19
1939: 1	96.5	116.4	116.1	281	70.2	36.3	—	4,043	13.86	15.60
1939: 2	91.4	111.5	114.6	243	73.6	34.6	—	2,890	11.78	17.35
1939: 3	92.0	—	—	300	77.2	36.0	—	3,229	14.24	20.78
1939: 4	—	—	—	273	68.5	9.9	—	2,931	12.27	15.26
1939: 5	—	—	—	238	55.4	18.2	—	3,416	15.45	13.90
1939: 6	—	—	—	247	70.6	28.3	—	3,185	16.59	12.56
1939: 7	—	—	—	151	76.0	29.5	—	2,778	14.26	15.54
1939: 8	—	—	—	61	85.8	35.2	—	2,792	16.57	19.60
1939: 9	—	—	—	162	96.0	38.6	—	2,885	14.79	15.04
1939: 10	—	—	—	252	117.0	46.6	—	3,545	15.38	13.26
1939: 11	—	—	—	285	124.0	43.5	—	4,437	14.46	10.15
1939: 12	—	—	—	374	121.5	38.2	—	5,236	12.80	10.81

Sources

Daniel Feenberg, Jeffrey Miron, Hanna Stern, and Esther D. Reichner, Macrohistory Database (National Bureau of Economic Research), machine-readable data file. The original sources according to National Bureau of Economic Research (NBER) records are as follows:

Series Cb35–37. The data for 1919–1933 were originally compiled by Y. S. Leong for the National Recovery Agency and were continued to 1939:9 by George Hervey of the Agricultural Adjustment Administration.

Series Cb38. U.S. Bureau of the Census, *Survey of Current Business* 7 (June 1927), and subsequent issues.

Series Cb39. 1919–1921: Frederick R. Macauley, *The Movements of Interest Rates, Bond Yields, and Stock Prices in the U.S. since 1856* (National Bureau of Economic Research, 1938), Table 27. 1922–1939: Successive issues of *Iron Age*, the main trade journal of the iron and steel industry.

Series Cb40. 1919–1922: U.S. Geological Survey, *Mineral Resources of the U.S.* (1922), part 2, pp. 464–5. 1923–1931: U.S. Bureau of Mines, *Mineral Resources of the U.S.*, successive annual issues. 1932–1939: U.S. Bureau of Mines, *Mineral Yearbook*, successive annual issues.

Series Cb41. U.S. Bureau of the Census, *Survey of Current Business, 1932 Annual Supplement,* and following annual issues. Plate Glass Manufacturers of America, a trade association, provided revised figures for 1925–1927 to the NBER. The original data were adjusted by NBER to account for nonreporting firms.

Series Cb42. U.S. Bureau of Agricultural Economics, *Livestock, Meats, and Wool, Market Statistics and Related Data* (1940), p. 34.

Series Cb43. 1919: Standard Statistics Company, *Standard Statistics Bulletin* (January 1932). The data were adjusted by NBER to remove imports from Puerto Rico and the Philippines. 1920–1939: *Survey of Current Business* 2–4 (May 1922–August 1924) and *Supplements* for 1932, 1936, 1938, and 1940.

Series Cb44. Computed by NBER by summing women's shoe production, production of all fabric shoes (satin, canvas, and so on), and production of part-fabric and part-leather shoes as reported in *Survey of Current Business*, various issues and *Supplements*.

Documentation

Series Cb35–37. These are seasonally adjusted; the other series are not. Figures are on a daily average output basis (in physical units) and were seasonally adjusted by Feenberg, Miron, et al.

Series Cb38. Figures represent factory production, and they exclude foreign assemblies of parts manufactured in the United States.

Series Cb39. Figures are on a daily average output basis.

Series Cb40. There was a significant decline in bituminous coal production in April and May 1939, when close to 500,000 miners were kept out of work by the failure of the United Mine Workers and the coal operators to agree on the provisions of a new labor contract.

Series Cb42. Data are presented for federally inspected hogs. During the weeks ending August 25 through October 6, 1933, 6,411,000 pigs and sows were purchased and destroyed under the authority of the Emergency Hog Production Control Act. These hogs are included in the data for 1933:9. Because of the slaughter of so many sows and young pigs, hog production was sharply reduced in subsequent months.

Series Cb43. Cigarettes are defined as those tobacco items weighing not more than three pounds per 1,000. The figures represent tax-paid withdrawals from factories and bonded customs warehouses, computed on the basis of sales of revenue stamps.

TABLE Cb45–51   Employment and average weekly hours in manufacturing, by sex: 1919–1939
Contributed by Richard Sutch

	Manufacturing production workers				Manufacturing wage earners – average weekly hours		
	Number employed		Average weekly hours				
	Not seasonally adjusted	Seasonally adjusted	Not seasonally adjusted	Seasonally adjusted	Both sexes	Male	Female
	Cb45	Cb46	Cb47	Cb48	Cb49	Cb50	Cb51
Year: Month	Thousand	Thousand	Hours	Hours	Hours	Hours	Hours
1919: 1	8,440	8,577	—	—	—	—	—
1919: 2	8,178	8,303	—	—	—	—	—
1919: 3	8,216	8,175	—	—	—	—	—
1919: 4	8,234	8,226	—	—	—	—	—
1919: 5	8,290	8,298	—	—	—	—	—
1919: 6	8,393	8,410	—	—	—	—	—
1919: 7	8,613	8,674	—	—	—	—	—
1919: 8	8,832	8,762	—	—	—	—	—
1919: 9	8,995	8,819	—	—	—	—	—
1919: 10	8,958	8,843	—	—	—	—	—
1919: 11	9,053	9,026	—	—	—	—	—
1919: 12	9,202	9,323	—	—	—	—	—
1920: 1	9,237	9,387	—	—	—	—	—
1920: 2	9,157	9,296	—	—	—	—	—
1920: 3	9,338	9,292	—	—	—	—	—
1920: 4	9,211	9,202	—	—	—	—	—
1920: 5	8,976	8,985	—	—	—	—	—
1920: 6	8,891	8,909	—	—	49.4	50.2	44.9
1920: 7	8,681	8,733	—	—	49.5	50.5	44.5
1920: 8	8,680	8,611	—	—	49.3	50.4	43.7
1920: 9	8,570	8,410	—	—	48.7	49.6	43.9
1920: 10	8,246	8,132	—	—	48.3	49.4	42.8
1920: 11	7,726	7,695	—	—	46.4	47.5	41.0
1920: 12	7,111	7,190	—	—	45.8	47.0	39.9
1921: 1	6,423	6,521	—	—	44.2	45.0	40.1
1921: 2	6,604	6,691	—	—	44.2	44.7	41.8
1921: 3	6,698	6,658	—	—	45.0	45.6	42.1
1921: 4	6,650	6,637	—	—	44.7	45.2	42.5
1921: 5	6,628	6,621	—	—	44.5	44.7	43.6
1921: 6	6,557	6,557	—	—	44.6	44.9	43.4
1921: 7	6,438	6,483	—	—	45.2	45.6	43.0
1921: 8	6,552	6,513	—	—	45.8	46.3	43.7
1921: 9	6,706	6,594	—	—	46.0	46.4	44.1
1921: 10	6,759	6,679	—	—	47.7	48.3	44.7
1921: 11	6,761	6,734	—	—	47.1	47.6	44.3
1921: 12	6,684	6,752	—	—	47.6	48.0	45.1
1922: 1	6,658	6,759	—	—	—	—	—
1922: 2	6,831	6,893	—	—	—	—	—
1922: 3	6,930	6,875	—	—	—	—	—
1922: 4	6,921	6,893	—	—	—	—	—
1922: 5	7,104	7,097	—	—	—	—	—
1922: 6	7,236	7,251	—	—	—	—	—
1922: 7	7,315	7,419	—	—	48.0	48.7	43.9
1922: 8	7,518	7,510	—	—	48.7	49.7	44.0
1922: 9	7,686	7,565	—	—	49.0	49.8	44.6
1922: 10	7,802	7,694	—	—	49.6	50.4	45.5
1922: 11	7,915	7,883	—	—	49.7	50.4	45.9
1922: 12	8,007	8,080	—	—	49.9	50.7	45.9
1923: 1	8,095	8,210	—	—	50.0	50.8	45.7
1923: 2	8,276	8,301	—	—	49.7	50.5	45.4
1923: 3	8,453	8,369	—	—	50.1	50.9	45.8
1923: 4	8,490	8,448	—	—	50.2	51.0	46.0
1923: 5	8,504	8,487	—	—	49.9	50.7	45.7
1923: 6	8,543	8,569	—	—	49.5	50.3	45.3
1923: 7	8,451	8,580	—	—	49.2	50.1	44.4
1923: 8	8,468	8,493	—	—	48.8	49.5	44.9

(continued)

TABLE Cb45–51   **Employment and average weekly hours in manufacturing, by sex: 1919–1939**   *Continued*

	Manufacturing production workers				Manufacturing wage earners – average weekly hours		
	Number employed		Average weekly hours				
	Not seasonally adjusted	Seasonally adjusted	Not seasonally adjusted	Seasonally adjusted	Both sexes	Male	Female
	Cb45	Cb46	Cb47	Cb48	Cb49	Cb50	Cb51
Year: Month	Thousand	Thousand	Hours	Hours	Hours	Hours	Hours
1923: 9	8,505	8,404	—	—	48.0	48.6	44.7
1923: 10	8,401	8,310	—	—	48.5	49.2	44.4
1923: 11	8,302	8,285	—	—	48.2	48.9	44.4
1923: 12	8,170	8,203	—	—	48.2	49.0	43.7
1924: 1	8,086	8,176	—	—	48.2	49.2	43.6
1924: 2	8,218	8,193	—	—	48.2	49.2	43.6
1924: 3	8,237	8,147	—	—	47.6	48.7	43.8
1924: 4	8,092	8,052	—	—	47.7	48.6	42.8
1924: 5	7,824	7,840	—	—	46.6	47.5	42.3
1924: 6	7,576	7,622	—	—	45.7	46.6	40.9
1924: 7	7,324	7,451	—	—	45.0	45.8	40.4
1924: 8	7,430	7,452	—	—	45.5	46.3	41.1
1924: 9	7,613	7,523	—	—	46.4	47.1	43.0
1924: 10	7,674	7,591	—	—	47.5	48.3	43.4
1924: 11	7,633	7,625	—	—	46.9	47.7	43.1
1924: 12	7,760	7,791	—	—	48.0	48.8	43.7
1925: 1	7,803	7,890	—	—	48.5	49.2	44.9
1925: 2	7,945	7,921	—	—	48.5	49.2	45.0
1925: 3	8,019	7,932	—	—	48.6	49.4	44.6
1925: 4	8,010	7,962	—	—	48.1	49.0	43.7
1925: 5	7,967	7,991	—	—	48.0	48.8	44.0
1925: 6	7,953	8,009	—	—	47.4	48.3	43.1
1925: 7	7,944	8,090	—	—	47.4	48.3	43.2
1925: 8	8,082	8,106	—	—	47.6	48.3	43.9
1925: 9	8,236	8,122	—	—	48.4	49.3	43.8
1925: 10	8,293	8,187	—	—	48.4	49.3	44.0
1925: 11	8,261	8,253	—	—	48.6	49.4	44.4
1925: 12	8,225	8,266	—	—	49.0	49.9	45.0
1926: 1	8,159	8,275	—	—	48.4	49.4	43.2
1926: 2	8,242	8,226	—	—	49.0	50.0	44.1
1926: 3	8,287	8,205	—	—	48.8	49.9	43.7
1926: 4	8,226	8,185	—	—	48.1	49.0	43.5
1926: 5	8,142	8,175	—	—	47.9	49.0	43.1
1926: 6	8,145	8,202	—	—	47.9	49.0	43.0
1926: 7	8,057	8,205	—	—	47.5	48.5	43.2
1926: 8	8,228	8,228	—	—	47.5	48.5	42.4
1926: 9	8,400	8,251	—	—	48.5	49.5	43.4
1926: 10	8,370	8,238	—	—	48.7	49.6	44.2
1926: 11	8,213	8,205	—	—	47.6	48.4	44.0
1926: 12	8,103	8,160	—	—	47.7	48.5	43.7
1927: 1	7,965	8,103	—	—	48.1	49.1	43.4
1927: 2	8,092	8,108	—	—	48.4	49.4	43.8
1927: 3	8,153	8,112	—	—	48.3	49.1	44.1
1927: 4	8,101	8,085	—	—	47.9	48.7	43.9
1927: 5	8,049	8,089	—	—	48.2	49.0	43.7
1927: 6	8,055	8,104	—	—	47.7	48.5	43.5
1927: 7	7,966	8,063	—	—	47.0	47.8	43.0
1927: 8	8,077	8,037	—	—	47.6	48.5	43.5
1927: 9	8,175	8,007	—	—	47.7	48.5	43.8
1927: 10	8,094	7,943	—	—	47.4	48.1	44.0
1927: 11	7,914	7,906	—	—	47.1	47.8	43.8
1927: 12	7,800	7,887	—	—	47.3	48.0	43.8
1928: 1	7,702	7,875	—	—	48.0	48.8	43.5
1928: 2	7,849	7,888	—	—	48.4	49.3	44.0
1928: 3	7,931	7,907	—	—	48.2	49.1	43.7
1928: 4	7,899	7,883	—	—	47.4	48.4	41.8
1928: 5	7,906	7,938	—	—	47.7	48.6	42.7
1928: 6	7,958	7,990	—	—	48.0	48.8	43.1
1928: 7	7,952	8,049	—	—	47.6	48.4	43.0
1928: 8	8,170	8,121	—	—	47.9	48.8	43.4

TABLE Cb45–51   Employment and average weekly hours in manufacturing, by sex: 1919–1939   *Continued*

	Manufacturing production workers				Manufacturing wage earners – average weekly hours		
	Number employed		Average weekly hours				
	Not seasonally adjusted	Seasonally adjusted	Not seasonally adjusted	Seasonally adjusted	Both sexes	Male	Female
	Cb45	Cb46	Cb47	Cb48	Cb49	Cb50	Cb51
Year: Month	Thousand	Thousand	Hours	Hours	Hours	Hours	Hours
1928: 9	8,341	8,138	—	—	48.3	49.2	43.7
1928: 10	8,365	8,185	—	—	47.9	48.7	44.2
1928: 11	8,288	8,271	—	—	47.7	48.6	44.0
1928: 12	8,248	8,348	—	—	48.0	48.9	43.9
1929: 1	8,216	8,435	—	—	48.6	49.5	44.0
1929: 2	8,411	8,487	—	—	49.1	49.9	44.5
1929: 3	8,517	8,526	—	—	49.0	49.9	44.2
1929: 4	8,619	8,610	—	—	48.8	49.7	44.3
1929: 5	8,609	8,635	—	—	48.6	49.3	44.6
1929: 6	8,630	8,673	—	—	48.4	49.1	44.3
1929: 7	8,674	8,753	—	—	48.4	49.3	44.0
1929: 8	8,826	8,747	—	—	48.3	49.0	44.4
1929: 9	8,912	8,652	—	—	48.8	49.5	44.8
1929: 10	8,805	8,607	—	—	49.3	50.0	45.2
1929: 11	8,447	8,447	—	—	46.2	46.8	43.1
1929: 12	8,133	8,240	—	—	46.6	47.2	43.5
1930: 1	7,930	8,158	—	—	46.2	46.9	42.1
1930: 2	7,944	8,016	—	—	46.7	47.4	42.6
1930: 3	7,909	7,917	—	—	45.9	46.6	41.7
1930: 4	7,865	7,857	—	—	45.8	46.7	41.0
1930: 5	7,727	7,742	—	—	44.9	45.8	40.1
1930: 6	7,566	7,612	—	—	44.5	45.3	40.1
1930: 7	7,304	7,400	—	—	42.9	43.4	39.6
1930: 8	7,243	7,193	—	—	42.4	43.0	38.7
1930: 9	7,323	7,089	—	—	42.4	43.1	38.5
1930: 10	7,169	6,981	—	—	42.6	43.0	40.5
1930: 11	6,894	6,873	—	—	41.0	41.2	39.7
1930: 12	6,698	6,772	—	—	41.4	41.5	40.9
1931: 1	6,467	6,653	—	—	40.2	40.3	39.0
1931: 2	6,522	6,568	—	—	42.3	42.4	41.0
1931: 3	6,559	6,612	—	—	42.3	42.3	41.5
1931: 4	6,557	6,583	—	—	41.9	42.1	40.2
1931: 5	6,507	6,546	—	—	42.8	42.9	41.3
1931: 6	6,362	6,400	—	—	41.3	41.3	40.7
1931: 7	6,271	6,334	—	—	40.1	40.1	39.8
1931: 8	6,290	6,222	—	—	39.7	39.7	39.8
1931: 9	6,318	6,087	—	—	39.4	39.4	39.8
1931: 10	6,091	5,908	—	—	38.1	38.3	38.3
1931: 11	5,869	5,857	—	—	37.8	37.8	37.3
1931: 12	5,806	5,888	—	—	38.4	38.2	38.7
1932: 1	5,648	5,841	38.6	39.5	35.9	35.6	36.6
1932: 2	5,743	5,778	39.7	39.4	37.7	37.4	38.8
1932: 3	5,657	5,691	39.1	38.5	36.1	35.7	37.6
1932: 4	5,470	5,486	37.8	37.1	34.2	34.1	34.8
1932: 5	5,259	5,285	37.7	37.1	33.7	33.9	33.0
1932: 6	5,097	5,133	36.8	36.6	32.8	32.8	32.7
1932: 7	4,923	4,983	36.0	36.7	31.9	31.5	33.7
1932: 8	5,059	4,999	36.7	37.0	32.1	31.9	33.5
1932: 9	5,333	5,138	39.0	39.2	35.2	34.4	37.9
1932: 10	5,423	5,270	40.2	39.7	36.5	35.6	39.7
1932: 11	5,350	5,350	39.0	39.5	36.5	35.9	38.9
1932: 12	5,252	5,316	38.6	38.8	35.1	34.3	37.8
1933: 1	5,110	5,273	37.7	38.6	35.1	34.6	36.3
1933: 2	5,227	5,253	38.4	38.1	35.6	35.1	37.2
1933: 3	5,029	5,059	36.7	36.2	32.1	31.7	34.3
1933: 4	5,160	5,181	38.2	37.5	34.0	33.7	34.1

(continued)

TABLE Cb45–51   Employment and average weekly hours in manufacturing, by sex: 1919–1939   *Continued*

	Manufacturing production workers				Manufacturing wage earners – average weekly hours		
	Number employed		Average weekly hours				
	Not seasonally adjusted	Seasonally adjusted	Not seasonally adjusted	Seasonally adjusted	Both sexes	Male	Female
	Cb45	Cb46	Cb47	Cb48	Cb49	Cb50	Cb51
Year: Month	Thousand	Thousand	Hours	Hours	Hours	Hours	Hours
1933: 5	5,399	5,437	40.9	40.3	37.6	37.2	37.5
1933: 6	5,781	5,839	42.9	42.6	41.5	41.5	41.2
1933: 7	6,155	6,223	42.8	43.6	42.9	42.9	42.9
1933: 8	6,570	6,467	38.5	38.8	38.2	38.4	38.0
1933: 9	6,860	6,609	36.3	36.4	36.3	36.2	35.6
1933: 10	6,827	6,635	35.8	35.4	36.1	36.4	35.4
1933: 11	6,555	6,555	34.3	34.8	33.8	33.9	34.0
1933: 12	6,413	6,491	34.1	34.3	33.8	34.1	33.2
1934: 1	6,354	6,551	33.7	34.5	34.0	34.2	32.9
1934: 2	6,747	6,788	35.7	35.6	35.6	35.8	34.7
1934: 3	7,026	7,068	36.1	35.6	36.4	36.6	35.1
1934: 4	7,156	7,178	36.0	35.4	35.8	36.0	34.6
1934: 5	7,176	7,227	35.5	35.0	35.4	35.6	34.1
1934: 6	7,077	7,148	34.8	34.6	35.5	35.8	34.0
1934: 7	6,954	7,038	33.2	33.8	34.1	34.2	33.3
1934: 8	7,046	6,949	33.9	34.0	33.5	33.5	33.4
1934: 9	6,735	6,514	33.3	33.5	33.4	33.5	33.1
1934: 10	6,928	6,733	34.2	33.9	33.9	33.9	33.8
1934: 11	6,800	6,780	33.9	34.2	33.7	33.6	33.6
1934: 12	6,910	6,966	35.1	35.1	35.1	35.0	35.3
1935: 1	7,002	7,204	35.2	36.0	36.3	36.4	35.4
1935: 2	7,232	7,298	36.4	36.3	37.2	37.5	35.9
1935: 3	7,349	7,408	36.5	36.0	36.8	37.0	35.7
1935: 4	7,366	7,403	36.3	35.8	36.8	37.1	35.0
1935: 5	7,260	7,319	35.6	35.2	36.0	36.4	33.7
1935: 6	7,130	7,231	35.3	35.2	36.1	36.5	33.7
1935: 7	7,171	7,236	35.3	35.9	36.3	36.7	33.7
1935: 8	7,412	7,288	36.7	36.6	37.0	37.4	35.1
1935: 9	7,591	7,356	37.5	37.6	37.9	38.3	35.7
1935: 10	7,701	7,477	38.2	37.9	38.6	39.1	35.9
1935: 11	7,654	7,616	37.7	38.1	38.5	39.0	35.9
1935: 12	7,618	7,679	38.6	38.6	38.4	38.8	36.1
1936: 1	7,469	7,716	37.4	38.3	38.1	38.6	34.9
1936: 2	7,507	7,598	37.5	37.4	37.8	38.2	35.7
1936: 3	7,605	7,613	38.6	38.0	38.3	38.9	35.7
1936: 4	7,731	7,731	38.7	38.4	39.1	39.7	35.2
1936: 5	7,806	7,861	39.2	39.0	39.0	39.8	34.6
1936: 6	7,856	8,008	39.2	39.4	39.0	39.8	34.9
1936: 7	7,969	8,090	38.6	39.4	38.8	39.3	35.5
1936: 8	8,203	8,098	39.6	39.4	39.8	40.3	37.1
1936: 9	8,407	8,162	38.9	39.0	40.3	41.0	37.0
1936: 10	8,499	8,268	40.6	40.0	40.8	41.5	37.3
1936: 11	8,500	8,408	40.6	40.9	41.1	41.7	38.1
1936: 12	8,619	8,610	41.2	41.0	41.4	42.0	38.7
1937: 1	8,473	8,699	39.7	40.5	40.3	40.8	38.0
1937: 2	8,698	8,813	40.6	40.6	41.3	42.0	38.6
1937: 3	8,894	8,921	41.1	40.7	41.4	42.0	38.9
1937: 4	8,988	9,015	40.4	40.4	40.6	41.2	37.5
1937: 5	9,004	9,113	39.9	39.9	40.2	40.8	37.2
1937: 6	8,910	9,101	39.3	39.6	39.8	40.4	37.1
1937: 7	8,956	9,120	38.1	38.8	38.7	39.2	36.6
1937: 8	9,079	8,989	38.8	38.5	38.5	39.1	36.1
1937: 9	9,091	8,826	37.6	37.5	37.9	38.5	34.9
1937: 10	8,952	8,658	37.7	36.9	37.4	38.0	34.2
1937: 11	8,474	8,316	35.6	35.6	35.2	35.8	32.0
1937: 12	7,965	7,917	34.6	34.4	33.6	33.9	32.3
1938: 1	7,434	7,632	33.5	34.2	32.2	32.5	30.3
1938: 2	7,494	7,593	34.5	34.7	33.1	33.3	31.6
1938: 3	7,473	7,503	34.8	34.5	33.0	33.3	31.1
1938: 4	7,328	7,372	34.4	34.5	32.7	33.1	30.2

TABLE Cb45–51 Employment and average weekly hours in manufacturing, by sex: 1919–1939 *Continued*

	Manufacturing production workers				Manufacturing wage earners – average weekly hours		
	Number employed		Average weekly hours				
	Not seasonally adjusted	Seasonally adjusted	Not seasonally adjusted	Seasonally adjusted	Both sexes	Male	Female
	Cb45	Cb46	Cb47	Cb48	Cb49	Cb50	Cb51
Year: Month	Thousand	Thousand	Hours	Hours	Hours	Hours	Hours
1938: 5	7,148	7,249	34.6	34.6	32.5	32.9	30.3
1938: 6	7,026	7,177	34.6	34.8	32.9	33.3	30.8
1938: 7	7,073	7,217	35.1	35.8	33.7	33.9	32.1
1938: 8	7,434	7,375	36.6	36.3	35.5	35.7	34.1
1938: 9	7,723	7,498	37.2	37.1	36.0	36.3	34.4
1938: 10	7,778	7,522	37.7	36.8	36.8	37.1	35.1
1938: 11	7,876	7,714	36.7	36.7	36.7	37.0	34.9
1938: 12	7,955	7,884	37.5	37.2	36.6	36.8	36.1
1939: 1	7,795	7,917	36.7	37.4	36.7	36.9	35.4
1939: 2	7,926	8,001	37.2	37.3	36.9	36.9	36.4
1939: 3	8,037	8,107	37.5	37.2	37.1	37.2	36.5
1939: 4	8,037	8,125	36.7	37.0	36.7	37.1	35.4
1939: 5	7,992	8,100	36.9	37.0	36.5	37.0	34.0
1939: 6	8,038	8,123	37.4	37.6	37.2	37.7	35.1
1939: 7	8,081	8,145	36.7	37.4	37.1	37.5	35.6
1939: 8	8,375	8,272	38.2	37.8	37.9	38.2	36.3
1939: 9	8,722	8,540	38.0	37.7	38.2	38.7	35.8
1939: 10	8,987	8,789	39.2	38.3	39.0	39.5	36.4
1939: 11	8,947	8,820	38.7	38.9	39.1	39.7	36.3
1939: 12	8,882	8,833	38.7	38.5	39.1	39.5	36.6

Sources

Series Cb46–48. U.S. Bureau of Labor Statistics, "Employment, Hours, and Earnings, United States, 1909–94," *BLS Bulletin* 2445, two volumes (September 1994): 68–9, 1167–8, and 1183. The original seasonally unadjusted data for 1919–1938 were distributed in "Production-Worker Employment, Payroll, Hours and Earnings in Manufacturing Industries, 1909, 1914–1938," *BLS Release* LS 53-0902 (September 1952). The data for 1939 were originally published in *Release* LS 53-2884 (February 1953).

Series Cb49–51. For 1920–1933: National Industrial Conference Board, *Wages, Hours, and Employment in the U.S., 1914–1936*, (National Industrial Conference Board, 1939), pp. 44–7. For 1934–1939: *The Conference Board Economic Record* (March 28, 1940): 115–16.

Documentation

Series Cb45–48. The U.S. Bureau of Labor Statistics (BLS) collects employment data in a wide variety of industries in a monthly survey of establishments through a project known as the Current Employment Statistics. See the text for Table Ba840–848 for more detail. The origins of this effort date back to the early years of the twentieth century; however, monthly data earlier than 1939 are available from this survey only for the manufacturing sector. The data were compiled from a large-scale survey of cooperating private manufacturing establishments. Workers at government manufacturing operations (such as shipyards and arsenals) are excluded. Firms reported the number of full-time and part-time production workers and related employees who were paid for any part of the pay period ending the nearest to the fifteenth of the month. This definition considers workers to be employed even if they did not work because they were on paid vacation or paid sick leave.

Series Cb45–46. Production workers and related employees include working foremen and all nonsupervisory workers (including trainees) engaged in "fabricating, processing, assembling, inspecting, receiving, storing, handling, packing, warehousing, shipping, trucking, hauling, maintenance, repair, janitorial, guard services, product development, auxiliary production for the plant's own use (e.g., power plant), recordkeeping, and other services closely associated with the above production operations." Persons with two or more jobs would be counted for each job they held. The survey results are benchmarked to the Census of Occupations for 1920 and 1930; for 1939, they are benchmarked to tabulations prepared under the state unemployment insurance programs, the U.S. Bureau of Old Age and Survivors Insurance (Social Security) plan, and special establishment censuses. The series are calculated

to move between benchmarks by using a procedure called chain indexing. This procedure takes the last monthly employment estimate and applies to it the change for identical establishments reporting in that and the following month. Moving this way from month to month, the series ultimately closes the gap between two adjacent benchmarks. Then, when the next benchmark is reached, any error in matching it is spread back across the gap between benchmarks in what is called a linear wedge back procedure. The use of changes in employment at firms reporting in two consecutive months to interpolate the series means that employment fluctuations resulting from the entry and exit of plants are not included in the employment counts. For a more complete account of the BLS procedure, see U.S. Bureau of Labor Statistics, "Techniques of Preparing Major BLS Statistical Series," *BLS Bulletin* number 1168 (December 1954). For a description of the seasonal adjustment procedure used, see the source, pp. 1229–30. For evidence that the employment series calculated by the chain index and wedge back procedures is excessively stable, see Susan B. Carter and Richard Sutch, "The Great Depression of the 1890s: New Suggestive Estimates of the Unemployment Rate, 1890–1905," *Research in Economic History* 14 (1992): 347–76.

Series Cb47–48. Beginning in 1932, the BLS began collecting and publishing statistics on the length of the average workweek. These were also collected from a (smaller) group of cooperating establishments. Dividing the total production worker hours paid per week in manufacturing by the corresponding number of workers gives the average workweek in hours. Only hours actually paid for are counted. This is not the same as the nominal workweek, which is the number of hours of plant operating time. The number of hours reported include hours paid for holidays, vacations, and sick leave. For an extended discussion of weekly hours, see Gerhard Bry, "The Average Workweek as an Economic Indicator," National Bureau of Economic Research Occasional Paper 69 (1959).

Series Cb49–50. The National Industrial Conference Board (NICB) collected data on the average workweek for wage earners in twenty-five manufacturing industries for the period from 1920 to 1948. The definition of the workweek was the same as the one the BLS later adopted. The term "wage earner" referred to workers paid on an hourly or piece-rate basis. Because of its narrower coverage and smaller sample, the NICB data are usually viewed as inferior to the BLS data on the length of the workweek. They are included here because they allow the workweek data to be extended back to the beginning of the 1920s and provide separate series for men and women.

TABLE Cb52–54   Stock market indicators: 1919–1939

Contributed by Richard Sutch

Year: Month	Shares sold on the New York Stock Exchange	Stock price indexes	
		Dow-Jones	Standard and Poor's
	Cb52	Cb53	Cb54
	Million	Dollars per share	Index 1935–1939 = 100
1919: 1	11.86	81.65	66.7
1919: 2	12.26	82.45	67.0
1919: 3	21.34	86.55	69.0
1919: 4	28.76	91.15	71.3
1919: 5	34.73	99.40	76.2
1919: 6	33.54	103.60	78.3
1919: 7	34.69	109.70	80.8
1919: 8	24.37	103.25	75.4
1919: 9	24.06	108.20	76.6
1919: 10	37.37	113.90	80.5
1919: 11	30.27	111.60	78.1
1919: 12	25.02	105.80	75.8
1920: 1	20.02	105.90	75.0
1920: 2	22.11	96.50	68.8
1920: 3	29.00	97.95	73.7
1920: 4	28.43	99.45	73.1
1920: 5	16.63	91.10	68.5
1920: 6	9.33	91.70	67.3
1920: 7	12.58	90.70	67.2
1920: 8	13.81	85.25	64.6
1920: 9	15.43	86.50	66.9
1920: 10	13.66	84.85	67.0
1920: 11	22.29	79.30	63.6
1920: 12	24.35	72.20	57.9
1921: 1	16.13	74.75	60.4
1921: 2	10.27	75.70	60.0
1921: 3	15.96	75.05	58.5
1921: 4	15.74	77.00	58.7
1921: 5	17.12	76.70	60.5
1921: 6	18.41	69.20	55.7
1921: 7	9.25	68.60	55.5
1921: 8	11.05	66.95	54.8
1921: 9	12.76	69.35	56.2
1921: 10	13.13	71.70	56.9
1921: 11	15.32	75.70	60.0
1921: 12	17.64	79.80	62.1
1922: 1	15.49	80.60	62.0
1922: 2	16.16	83.75	63.4
1922: 3	22.62	87.20	65.8
1922: 4	30.67	91.30	69.8
1922: 5	29.64	93.95	72.5
1922: 6	24.51	93.55	71.8
1922: 7	15.42	95.00	72.3
1922: 8	17.90	98.50	75.0
1922: 9	21.90	99.20	72.0
1922: 10	25.75	99.75	78.7
1922: 11	21.06	95.75	74.8
1922: 12	19.77	97.00	74.6
1923: 1	20.47	98.20	75.6
1923: 2	22.83	100.80	78.9
1923: 3	25.94	103.90	80.1
1923: 4	20.20	100.55	77.3
1923: 5	23.27	95.50	73.7
1923: 6	19.93	92.55	70.9
1923: 7	12.64	89.30	68.5
1923: 8	13.45	90.45	68.8
1923: 9	14.69	90.75	69.3
1923: 10	15.89	88.15	68.2
1923: 11	22.59	90.65	70.3
1923: 12	24.59	94.10	72.7
1924: 1	27.07	97.80	75.0
1924: 2	20.63	98.80	75.4
1924: 3	18.39	95.60	73.9
1924: 4	17.83	91.95	72.2
1924: 5	13.59	90.40	72.0
1924: 6	16.98	93.30	73.3
1924: 7	24.33	99.25	76.7
1924: 8	22.84	103.55	79.4
1924: 9	18.47	102.90	78.6
1924: 10	17.91	101.65	77.6
1924: 11	42.13	107.65	81.9
1924: 12	43.88	115.45	86.3
1925: 1	42.17	121.55	89.9
1925: 2	33.38	120.45	90.7
1925: 3	39.17	120.35	88.3
1925: 4	25.34	119.70	87.4
1925: 5	36.97	125.55	90.2
1925: 6	31.22	128.90	91.8
1925: 7	33.05	133.90	94.3
1925: 8	33.08	138.85	95.6
1925: 9	37.45	142.45	97.8
1925: 10	54.69	150.65	101.0
1925: 11	49.72	153.80	104.2
1925: 12	43.49	154.55	105.9
1926: 1	39.25	156.10	107.5
1926: 2	35.73	158.40	107.5
1926: 3	52.32	144.25	101.2
1926: 4	30.53	140.55	98.1
1926: 5	23.45	140.30	98.4
1926: 6	38.03	148.15	102.6
1926: 7	37.06	156.80	105.6
1926: 8	44.83	163.50	108.7
1926: 9	37.39	161.20	110.1
1926: 10	40.10	152.70	107.3
1926: 11	31.33	153.95	108.9
1926: 12	41.85	159.30	111.3
1927: 1	34.60	154.65	111.5
1927: 2	44.56	158.15	113.9
1927: 3	49.69	160.10	115.2
1927: 4	49.89	164.05	117.3
1927: 5	46.82	168.80	120.6
1927: 6	48.28	168.85	121.9
1927: 7	39.06	175.35	123.8
1927: 8	51.27	183.85	128.8
1927: 9	52.07	195.30	134.8
1927: 10	50.87	189.80	133.8
1927: 11	51.80	189.95	136.9
1927: 12	62.80	198.00	140.5
1928: 1	57.68	198.95	141.9
1928: 2	47.09	195.35	139.7
1928: 3	86.01	204.50	145.6
1928: 4	81.63	212.45	154.1
1928: 5	84.80	216.30	160.6
1928: 6	65.34	211.50	153.4
1928: 7	38.83	210.85	152.3
1928: 8	68.81	227.25	156.6
1928: 9	92.33	239.30	165.4
1928: 10	99.63	247.45	168.0
1928: 11	116.05	274.90	180.7
1928: 12	92.69	278.65	181.0

TABLE Cb52–54   Stock market indicators: 1919–1939   *Continued*

Year: Month	Shares sold on the New York Stock Exchange Cb52 Million	Stock price indexes Dow-Jones Cb53 Dollars per share	Stock price indexes Standard and Poor's Cb54 Index 1935–1939 = 100	Year: Month	Shares sold on the New York Stock Exchange Cb52 Million	Stock price indexes Dow-Jones Cb53 Dollars per share	Stock price indexes Standard and Poor's Cb54 Index 1935–1939 = 100
1929: 1	110.80	307.25	195.6	1934: 1	54.57	102.85	79.9
1929: 2	77.97	309.00	196.9	1934: 2	56.83	106.90	85.0
1929: 3	105.63	308.85	199.7	1934: 3	29.90	102.30	81.3
1929: 4	82.59	309.20	197.0	1934: 4	29.85	103.55	84.1
1929: 5	91.31	310.25	198.3	1934: 5	25.34	96.20	75.8
1929: 6	69.55	316.45	201.4	1934: 6	16.80	95.90	77.6
1929: 7	93.38	341.45	218.9	1934: 7	21.11	92.25	75.4
1929: 8	95.60	359.15	230.3	1934: 8	16.69	91.60	71.6
1929: 9	100.06	362.35	237.8	1934: 9	12.64	90.20	70.7
1929: 10	141.67	291.50	213.0	1934: 10	15.66	93.00	71.1
1929: 11	72.46	228.20	159.6	1934: 11	20.87	98.30	73.3
1929: 12	83.58	247.20	162.4	1934: 12	23.59	101.80	73.1
1930: 1	62.31	255.65	165.0	1935: 1	19.41	103.20	73.6
1930: 2	68.72	267.40	174.8	1935: 2	14.40	103.70	71.5
1930: 3	96.56	278.25	182.0	1935: 3	15.85	100.00	68.0
1930: 4	111.04	285.50	191.1	1935: 4	22.41	105.45	71.3
1930: 5	78.04	266.70	180.0	1935: 5	30.44	112.75	77.2
1930: 6	76.59	243.15	161.4	1935: 6	22.34	115.25	80.3
1930: 7	47.75	229.80	157.7	1935: 7	29.43	122.65	83.8
1930: 8	39.87	228.80	155.9	1935: 8	42.93	126.95	88.0
1930: 9	53.55	225.00	157.1	1935: 9	34.73	130.70	89.8
1930: 10	65.50	198.75	134.7	1935: 10	46.66	134.80	90.9
1930: 11	51.95	180.95	123.2	1935: 11	57.46	144.75	99.5
1930: 12	58.76	172.15	115.5	1935: 12	45.59	141.70	101.1
1931: 1	42.50	167.25	118.5	1936: 1	67.20	146.30	107.3
1931: 2	64.18	181.55	126.5	1936: 2	60.88	152.00	112.6
1931: 3	65.66	180.05	128.4	1936: 3	51.02	154.60	114.8
1931: 4	54.35	158.00	115.3	1936: 4	39.61	152.85	112.6
1931: 5	46.66	141.45	103.5	1936: 5	20.61	149.50	107.6
1931: 6	58.64	139.30	100.4	1936: 6	21.43	155.00	111.5
1931: 7	33.55	145.35	103.7	1936: 7	34.79	162.25	116.2
1931: 8	24.83	139.80	100.8	1936: 8	26.56	164.95	119.2
1931: 9	51.04	118.35	86.3	1936: 9	30.87	167.40	120.5
1931: 10	47.90	98.10	73.7	1936: 10	44.00	172.95	126.6
1931: 11	37.36	103.40	75.7	1936: 11	50.47	180.80	131.1
1931: 12	50.11	82.80	61.0	1936: 12	48.60	179.05	130.0
1932: 1	34.36	78.55	61.3	1937: 1	58.67	182.30	133.5
1932: 2	31.72	78.90	59.6	1937: 2	50.25	188.40	136.7
1932: 3	33.03	81.05	60.0	1937: 3	50.35	187.10	136.6
1932: 4	31.47	64.05	46.3	1937: 4	34.61	177.65	128.1
1932: 5	23.14	51.85	42.0	1937: 5	18.55	171.90	123.3
1932: 6	23.00	46.85	35.9	1937: 6	16.45	170.30	119.6
1932: 7	23.06	47.75	37.9	1937: 7	20.72	177.85	126.0
1932: 8	82.63	64.40	56.3	1937: 8	17.21	182.95	127.3
1932: 9	67.38	71.00	61.5	1937: 9	33.85	160.25	111.0
1932: 10	29.20	65.30	52.7	1937: 10	51.13	139.90	94.3
1932: 11	23.05	62.20	50.2	1937: 11	29.25	124.75	87.6
1932: 12	23.20	58.85	50.1	1937: 12	28.42	124.35	85.7
1933: 1	18.72	61.85	51.8	1938: 1	24.15	127.25	87.4
1933: 2	19.31	55.15	47.5	1938: 2	14.53	125.45	85.2
1933: 3	20.10	57.75	45.6	1938: 3	23.00	114.75	79.2
1933: 4	52.90	66.70	50.2	1938: 4	17.12	111.00	76.5
1933: 5	104.21	83.30	66.4	1938: 5	14.00	113.55	78.0
1933: 6	125.62	93.80	79.1	1938: 6	24.37	122.80	79.7
1933: 7	120.27	98.55	85.0	1938: 7	38.77	139.75	93.6
1933: 8	42.46	98.85	79.3	1938: 8	20.73	140.95	94.0
1933: 9	43.33	99.45	79.0				
1933: 10	39.37	91.65	73.3				
1933: 11	33.65	95.45	73.0				
1933: 12	34.88	99.05	74.3				

(continued)

TABLE Cb52–54   Stock market indicators: 1919–1939   *Continued*

Year: Month	Shares sold on the New York Stock Exchange	Stock price indexes		Year: Month	Shares sold on the New York Stock Exchange	Stock price indexes	
		Dow-Jones	Standard and Poor's			Dow-Jones	Standard and Poor's
	Cb52	Cb53	Cb54		Cb52	Cb53	Cb54
	Million	Dollars per share	Index 1935–1939 = 100		Million	Dollars per share	Index 1935–1939 = 100
1938: 9	23.83	136.50	89.6	1939: 5	12.94	133.00	88.4
1938: 10	41.56	148.65	98.5	1939: 6	11.96	135.10	89.9
1938: 11	27.92	152.25	99.4	1939: 7	18.07	138.20	91.8
1938: 12	27.49	151.10	97.1	1939: 8	17.37	137.80	90.7
1939: 1	25.18	145.65	97.0	1939: 9	57.09	144.40	99.7
1939: 2	13.88	144.85	95.1	1939: 10	23.73	152.55	100.7
1939: 3	24.56	142.05	96.0	1939: 11	19.23	149.15	98.9
1939: 4	20.25	127.10	85.0	1939: 12	17.77	148.35	97.0

Sources

Daniel Feenberg, Jeffrey Miron, Hanna Stern, and Esther D. Reichner, Macrohistory Database (National Bureau of Economic Research), machine-readable computer file. The original sources according to National Bureau of Economic Research (NBER) records are as follows:

Series Cb52. *Commercial and Financial Chronicle*, various issues.

Series Cb53. Data computed by Dow Jones and Company from quotations in the *Wall Street Journal*. Data were taken from *The Dow Jones Averages,* 13th edition (Dow Jones, 1948). Also see Phyllis S. Pierce, editor, *The Dow Jones Averages, 1885–1985: Centennial Edition* (Dow Jones, 1986).

Series Cb54. Standard and Poor's Corporation, *Security Price Index Record* (Standard and Poor's, 1955).

Documentation

The New York Stock Exchange emerged in the early twentieth century as the premier market for the open trading of the securities (common stocks) of American corporations. See Robert Sobel, *The Big Board: A History of the New York Stock Market* (Free Press, 1965). About the middle of the 1920s, the volume of transactions on the exchange began to rise from a level of around 20 million shares exchanged monthly to a peak of more than 140 million shares in late 1929. This rise in transactions accompanied the "Giant Bull Market" of 1924–1929, which saw a general rise in the price of stocks, reaching new heights month after month. The two best-known indexes of the general movement of stock prices in the 1920s and 1930s are the Dow Jones Index of industrial stock prices and Standard and Poor's (S&P) index of common stock prices. These were the indexes that were widely followed by contemporaries.

Series Cb53. The Dow Jones index is an average of the daily closing prices on a changing list of industrial common stocks as sold on the New York exchange. The monthly series reproduced here is an average of the highest and lowest index numbers recorded for the month. From 1919 through October 1, 1928, twenty stocks were included in the index. After this date, the number was increased to thirty stocks. The stocks included are changed from time to time to reflect the "current representativeness" of the list. To maintain statistical continuity, adjustment has been made for stock splits and stock dividends.

Series Cb54. The monthly S&P index is an average of S&P's weekly composite index numbers with 1935–1939 set equal to 100. The weekly index is based on Wednesday's closing prices or the last preceding sales price. This series is the predecessor to today's S&P 500, which was introduced in 1957. For the period shown here, the number of stocks covered increased from 198 in 1918 to 480 in 1957. The index formula is adjusted to offset arbitrary price changes caused by mergers, splits, stock dividends, and the issue of rights.

TABLE Cb55   Percentage of corporations with profits: 1920–1963

Contributed by Richard Sutch

Year: quarter	Percentage of corporations with profits — Cb55 Percent	Year: quarter	Percentage of corporations with profits — Cb55 Percent	Year: quarter	Percentage of corporations with profits — Cb55 Percent	Year: quarter	Percentage of corporations with profits — Cb55 Percent
1920: 1	96.0	1929: 1	92.1	1938: 1	61.5	1954: 1	92.8
1920: 2	96.2	1929: 2	94.1	1938: 2	56.0	1954: 2	95.6
1920: 3	91.3	1929: 3	94.3	1938: 3	68.1	1954: 3	93.8
1920: 4	69.6	1929: 4	89.8	1938: 4	77.8	1954: 4	93.0
1921: 1	70.7	1930: 1	84.1	1946: 1	82.3	1955: 1	95.1
1921: 2	58.5	1930: 2	83.0	1946: 2	93.6	1955: 2	95.7
1921: 3	63.4	1930: 3	71.6	1946: 3	95.5	1955: 3	95.6
1921: 4	65.9	1930: 4	65.2	1946: 4	95.6	1955: 4	95.2
1922: 1	74.6	1931: 1	67.2	1947: 1	95.9	1956: 1	96.5
1922: 2	81.5	1931: 2	63.1	1947: 2	96.0	1956: 2	96.1
1922: 3	90.8	1931: 3	59.3	1947: 3	96.3	1956: 3	97.2
1922: 4	93.9	1931: 4	50.9	1947: 4	97.4	1956: 4	96.9
1923: 1	95.7	1932: 1	45.7	1948: 1	97.4	1957: 1	97.7
1923: 2	96.9	1932: 2	40.2	1948: 2	97.8	1957: 2	97.4
1923: 3	87.2	1932: 3	39.5	1948: 3	97.8	1957: 3	95.9
1923: 4	86.2	1932: 4	41.8	1948: 4	94.2	1957: 4	91.9
1924: 1	90.4	1933: 1	38.6	1949: 1	92.2	1958: 1	92.1
1924: 2	84.3	1933: 2	52.3	1949: 2	89.3	1958: 2	91.6
1924: 3	85.3	1933: 3	70.0	1949: 3	89.6	1958: 3	93.9
1924: 4	87.9	1933: 4	64.6	1949: 4	92.6	1958: 4	94.6
1925: 1	95.3	1934: 1	69.7	1950: 1	94.9	1959: 1	96.8
1925: 2	93.4	1934: 2	72.2	1950: 2	96.4	1959: 2	98.0
1925: 3	94.1	1934: 3	64.4	1950: 3	98.2	1959: 3	94.2
1925: 4	92.8	1934: 4	65.6	1950: 4	98.2	1959: 4	95.8
1926: 1	93.6	1935: 1	74.7	1951: 1	97.3	1960: 1	96.2
1926: 2	93.7	1935: 2	76.2	1951: 2	97.1	1960: 2	95.9
1926: 3	94.4	1935: 3	78.9	1951: 3	96.7	1960: 3	93.2
1926: 4	92.8	1935: 4	87.9	1951: 4	95.9	1960: 4	91.9
1927: 1	92.1	1936: 1	84.8	1952: 1	96.1	1961: 1	89.8
1927: 2	86.9	1936: 2	88.3	1952: 2	95.2	1961: 2	97.3
1927: 3	90.1	1936: 3	89.4	1952: 3	96.4	1961: 3	95.0
1927: 4	84.8	1936: 4	89.0	1952: 4	97.2	1961: 4	95.4
1928: 1	88.3	1937: 1	90.3	1953: 1	96.2	1962: 1	95.0
1928: 2	91.1	1937: 2	89.5	1953: 2	97.1	1962: 2	96.8
1928: 3	90.6	1937: 3	85.7	1953: 3	96.1	1962: 3	95.1
1928: 4	93.4	1937: 4	75.1	1953: 4	95.3	1962: 4	95.2
						1963: 1	92.9
						1963: 2	97.3

Sources

1920–1958: Geoffrey H. Moore, editor, *Business Cycle Indicators,* volume 2, *Basic Data on Cyclical Indicators* (Princeton University Press, 1961), pp. 22, 106.
1959–1963: Daniel Feenberg, Jeffrey Miron, Hanna Stern, and Esther D. Reichner, Macrohistory Database (National Bureau of Economic Research), machine-readable data file.

Documentation

Data were collected by the First National City Bank and compiled by the National Bureau of Economic Research. In the interwar period, the data are based on a sample of corporations in manufacturing and mining that expanded in number from 25 in 1920, to 224 in 1930, and to 260 in 1938. Beginning in 1946, the sample was expanded to cover all industrial sectors except utilities. For 1954–1963, utilities have been included. Financial corporations are excluded throughout. The sample is biased toward including large manufacturing firms.

TABLE Cb56–63   Selected interest rates – bond and security yields, bank loans, and the Federal Reserve discount rate: 1919–1941

Contributed by Richard Sutch

	Yields on securities and bonds						Loan rates	
			Corporate bonds		Government securities, adjusted yields			
Year: Month	Short-term U.S. securities	Long-term U.S. government bonds	Aaa-rated	Baa-rated	3 months	20 years	Customer loans by banks in principal cities	Discount rate, Federal Reserve Bank of New York
	Cb56	Cb57	Cb58	Cb59	Cb60	Cb61	Cb62	Cb63
	Percent per annum	Percent per annum	Percent per annum	Percent per annum	Percent per annum	Percent per annum	Percent per annum	Percent per annum
1919: 1	—	4.63	5.35	7.12	—	—	5.80	4.56
1919: 2	—	4.70	5.35	7.20	—	—	5.67	4.56
1919: 3	—	4.73	5.39	7.15	—	—	5.70	4.56
1919: 4	—	4.72	5.44	7.23	—	—	5.75	4.56
1919: 5	—	4.67	5.39	7.09	—	—	5.65	4.56
1919: 6	—	4.69	5.40	7.04	—	—	5.67	4.56
1919: 7	—	4.72	5.44	7.06	—	—	5.73	4.56
1919: 8	—	4.78	5.56	7.13	—	—	5.72	4.56
1919: 9	—	4.73	5.60	7.27	—	—	5.72	4.56
1919: 10	—	4.71	5.54	7.34	—	—	5.77	4.56
1919: 11	—	4.81	5.66	7.54	—	—	5.75	4.74
1919: 12	—	4.90	5.73	7.77	—	—	5.84	4.75
1920: 1	4.50	4.93	5.75	7.78	—	—	6.02	5.11
1920: 2	4.50	5.05	5.86	7.94	—	—	6.13	6.00
1920: 3	4.75	5.09	5.92	7.97	—	—	6.24	6.00
1920: 4	5.25	5.28	6.04	8.17	—	—	6.43	6.00
1920: 5	5.50	5.58	6.25	8.39	—	—	6.47	6.00
1920: 6	5.75	5.54	6.38	8.39	—	—	6.63	7.00
1920: 7	5.81	5.57	6.34	8.52	—	—	6.81	7.00
1920: 8	5.83	5.67	6.30	8.39	—	—	6.79	7.00
1920: 9	5.81	5.43	6.22	8.14	—	—	6.87	7.00
1920: 10	5.75	5.08	6.05	7.99	—	—	6.87	7.00
1920: 11	5.75	5.21	6.08	8.21	—	—	6.93	7.00
1920: 12	5.88	5.40	6.26	8.56	—	—	6.79	7.00
1921: 1	5.67	5.23	6.14	8.50	—	—	6.93	7.00
1921: 2	5.30	5.28	6.08	8.42	—	—	6.94	7.00
1921: 3	5.38	5.27	6.08	8.55	—	—	6.91	7.00
1921: 4	5.20	5.24	6.06	8.53	—	—	6.90	7.00
1921: 5	5.16	5.25	6.11	8.52	—	—	6.89	6.56
1921: 6	4.99	5.27	6.18	8.56	—	—	6.81	6.25
1921: 7	4.60	5.26	6.12	8.48	—	—	6.72	5.82
1921: 8	4.75	5.22	5.99	8.51	—	—	6.60	5.50
1921: 9	4.75	5.12	5.93	8.34	—	—	6.55	5.35
1921: 10	4.21	4.83	5.84	8.34	—	—	6.47	5.00
1921: 11	4.03	4.64	5.60	7.88	—	—	6.32	4.53
1921: 12	3.90	4.47	5.50	7.61	—	—	6.16	4.50
1922: 1	3.90	4.45	5.34	7.70	—	—	6.02	4.50
1922: 2	3.81	4.50	5.29	7.55	—	—	5.91	4.50
1922: 3	3.55	4.41	5.23	7.45	—	—	5.82	4.50
1922: 4	3.21	4.28	5.15	7.14	—	—	5.67	4.50
1922: 5	3.25	4.26	5.13	6.89	—	—	5.53	4.50
1922: 6	3.25	4.24	5.08	6.97	—	—	5.46	4.35
1922: 7	3.20	4.14	5.00	6.89	—	—	5.46	4.00
1922: 8	3.13	4.12	4.96	6.85	—	—	5.27	4.00
1922: 9	3.34	4.19	4.93	6.75	—	—	5.21	4.00
1922: 10	3.71	4.30	4.97	6.78	—	—	5.24	4.00
1922: 11	3.66	4.33	5.09	6.98	—	—	5.35	4.00
1922: 12	3.65	4.32	5.08	7.02	—	—	5.38	4.00
1923: 1	3.66	4.32	5.04	6.98	—	—	5.32	4.00
1923: 2	3.65	4.33	5.07	6.97	—	—	5.37	4.11
1923: 3	4.12	4.38	5.18	7.09	—	—	5.43	4.50
1923: 4	4.13	4.39	5.22	7.17	—	—	5.56	4.50
1923: 5	3.95	4.37	5.16	7.17	—	—	5.56	4.50
1923: 6	3.84	4.34	5.15	7.21	—	—	5.50	4.50
1923: 7	3.91	4.34	5.14	7.34	—	—	5.55	4.50
1923: 8	3.86	4.35	5.08	7.38	—	—	5.58	4.50

TABLE Cb56–63   Selected interest rates – bond and security yields, bank loans, and the Federal Reserve discount rate: 1919–1941 *Continued*

	Yields on securities and bonds						Loan rates	
	Short-term U.S. securities	Long-term U.S. government bonds	Corporate bonds		Government securities, adjusted yields		Customer loans by banks in principal cities	Discount rate, Federal Reserve Bank of New York
			Aaa-rated	Baa-rated	3 months	20 years		
	Cb56	Cb57	Cb58	Cb59	Cb60	Cb61	Cb62	Cb63
Year: Month	Percent per annum	Percent per annum	Percent per annum	Percent per annum	Percent per annum	Percent per annum	Percent per annum	Percent per annum
1923: 9	4.01	4.36	5.12	7.38	—	—	5.61	4.50
1923: 10	4.22	4.40	5.11	7.46	—	—	5.61	4.50
1923: 11	3.94	4.37	5.09	7.40	—	—	5.60	4.50
1923: 12	3.88	4.35	5.09	7.38	—	—	5.53	4.50
1924: 1	3.76	4.30	5.09	7.24	—	—	5.56	4.50
1924: 2	3.54	4.28	5.09	7.14	—	—	5.42	4.50
1924: 3	3.57	4.28	5.10	7.08	—	—	5.41	4.50
1924: 4	3.38	4.23	5.08	7.03	—	—	5.36	4.50
1924: 5	2.29	4.15	5.04	6.97	—	—	5.29	4.00
1924: 6	2.44	3.98	4.99	6.82	—	—	5.12	3.68
1924: 7	1.92	3.94	4.95	6.67	—	—	4.95	3.50
1924: 8	1.90	3.91	4.95	6.69	—	—	4.78	3.11
1924: 9	2.14	3.92	4.95	6.73	—	—	4.84	3.00
1924: 10	2.41	3.87	4.92	6.62	—	—	4.88	3.00
1924: 11	2.58	3.90	4.94	6.54	—	—	4.78	3.00
1924: 12	2.57	3.96	4.95	6.46	—	—	4.86	3.00
1925: 1	2.61	3.96	4.95	6.44	—	—	4.80	3.00
1925: 2	2.62	3.95	4.95	6.36	—	—	4.88	3.04
1925: 3	2.78	3.96	4.91	6.36	—	—	4.97	3.50
1925: 4	2.78	3.93	4.87	6.41	—	—	4.97	3.50
1925: 5	2.73	3.87	4.83	6.30	—	—	4.93	3.50
1925: 6	2.86	3.79	4.83	6.18	—	—	4.93	3.50
1925: 7	3.06	3.79	4.87	6.20	—	—	4.95	3.50
1925: 8	3.01	3.85	4.90	6.24	—	—	4.95	3.50
1925: 9	3.17	3.85	4.87	6.20	—	—	5.03	3.50
1925: 10	3.53	3.82	4.85	6.17	—	—	5.08	3.50
1925: 11	3.65	3.79	4.84	6.17	—	—	5.10	3.50
1925: 12	3.51	3.80	4.85	6.15	—	—	5.13	3.50
1926: 1	3.49	3.77	4.82	6.09	—	—	5.09	3.89
1926: 2	3.18	3.71	4.77	6.02	—	—	5.12	4.00
1926: 3	3.14	3.71	4.79	6.05	—	—	5.10	4.00
1926: 4	3.08	3.70	4.74	5.98	—	—	5.12	3.87
1926: 5	3.17	3.67	4.71	5.86	—	—	5.08	3.50
1926: 6	2.93	3.67	4.72	5.80	—	—	4.96	3.50
1926: 7	3.11	3.68	4.71	5.79	—	—	4.91	3.50
1926: 8	3.27	3.70	4.72	5.81	—	—	4.99	3.81
1926: 9	3.42	3.70	4.72	5.79	—	—	5.13	4.00
1926: 10	3.58	3.68	4.71	5.81	—	—	5.19	4.00
1926: 11	3.35	3.62	4.68	5.77	—	—	5.14	4.00
1926: 12	3.07	3.56	4.68	5.68	—	—	5.16	4.00
1927: 1	3.23	3.51	4.66	5.61	—	—	5.08	4.00
1927: 2	3.29	3.48	4.67	5.59	—	—	5.04	4.00
1927: 3	3.20	3.37	4.62	5.54	—	—	4.99	4.00
1927: 4	3.39	3.35	4.58	5.48	—	—	5.00	4.00
1927: 5	3.33	3.31	4.57	5.50	—	—	5.02	4.00
1927: 6	3.07	3.34	4.58	5.55	—	—	4.99	4.00
1927: 7	2.96	3.36	4.60	5.55	—	—	4.96	4.00
1927: 8	2.70	3.32	4.56	5.48	—	—	4.90	3.56
1927: 9	2.68	3.30	4.54	5.42	—	—	4.89	3.50
1927: 10	3.08	3.29	4.51	5.38	—	—	4.90	3.50
1927: 11	3.04	3.23	4.49	5.35	—	—	4.87	3.50
1927: 12	3.17	3.17	4.46	5.32	—	—	4.91	3.50
1928: 1	3.31	3.18	4.46	5.35	—	—	4.89	3.50
1928: 2	3.33	3.19	4.46	5.33	—	—	4.87	3.97
1928: 3	3.27	3.17	4.46	5.32	—	—	4.94	4.00
1928: 4	3.62	3.20	4.46	5.33	—	—	5.02	4.00

(continued)

TABLE Cb56–63   Selected interest rates – bond and security yields, bank loans, and the Federal Reserve discount rate: 1919–1941   *Continued*

	Yields on securities and bonds						Loan rates	
	Short-term U.S. securities	Long-term U.S. government bonds	Corporate bonds		Government securities, adjusted yields		Customer loans by banks in principal cities	Discount rate, Federal Reserve Bank of New York
			Aaa-rated	Baa-rated	3 months	20 years		
	Cb56	Cb57	Cb58	Cb59	Cb60	Cb61	Cb62	Cb63
Year: Month	Percent per annum	Percent per annum	Percent per annum	Percent per annum	Percent per annum	Percent per annum	Percent per annum	Percent per annum
1928: 5	3.90	3.24	4.49	5.42	—	—	5.16	4.23
1928: 6	3.92	3.29	4.57	5.55	—	—	5.35	4.50
1928: 7	4.12	3.42	4.61	5.58	—	—	5.56	4.81
1928: 8	4.36	3.48	4.64	5.61	—	—	5.64	5.00
1928: 9	4.57	3.46	4.61	5.59	—	—	5.75	5.00
1928: 10	4.70	3.47	4.61	5.58	—	—	5.76	5.00
1928: 11	4.26	3.38	4.58	5.55	—	—	5.75	5.00
1928: 12	4.26	3.45	4.61	5.60	—	—	5.82	5.00
1929: 1	4.66	3.52	4.62	5.63	4.72	3.51	5.84	5.00
1929: 2	4.39	3.62	4.66	5.66	4.75	3.70	5.84	5.00
1929: 3	4.60	3.74	4.70	5.79	5.03	3.79	5.91	5.00
1929: 4	4.80	3.64	4.69	5.80	5.09	3.58	5.97	5.00
1929: 5	5.09	3.64	4.70	5.80	5.19	3.71	6.02	5.00
1929: 6	4.80	3.69	4.77	5.94	4.86	3.54	6.03	5.00
1929: 7	4.55	3.64	4.77	5.95	4.94	3.35	6.04	5.00
1929: 8	4.70	3.71	4.79	6.04	4.69	3.60	6.12	5.74
1929: 9	4.58	3.70	4.80	6.12	4.89	3.50	6.19	6.00
1929: 10	4.37	3.61	4.77	6.11	4.00	2.96	6.21	6.00
1929: 11	3.47	3.35	4.76	6.03	3.01	3.10	6.08	4.73
1929: 12	3.03	3.36	4.67	5.95	2.82	3.26	5.94	4.50
1930: 1	3.39	3.43	4.66	5.92	3.84	3.31	5.87	4.50
1930: 2	3.36	3.41	4.69	5.89	3.04	3.23	5.66	4.11
1930: 3	2.95	3.29	4.62	5.73	2.71	3.24	5.53	3.71
1930: 4	3.00	3.37	4.60	5.70	2.96	3.31	5.30	3.50
1930: 5	2.41	3.31	4.60	5.72	2.07	3.17	5.17	3.02
1930: 6	1.89	3.25	4.57	5.78	1.78	3.11	5.08	2.82
1930: 7	1.83	3.25	4.52	5.77	1.54	3.26	4.93	2.50
1930: 8	1.53	3.26	4.47	5.73	2.09	3.12	4.88	2.50
1930: 9	1.77	3.24	4.42	5.65	1.42	3.28	4.81	2.50
1930: 10	1.74	3.21	4.42	5.94	1.76	3.19	4.81	2.50
1930: 11	1.40	3.19	4.47	6.25	1.53	3.30	4.73	2.50
1930: 12	1.48	3.22	4.52	6.71	1.25	3.28	4.72	2.37
1931: 1	1.24	3.20	4.42	6.41	1.10	3.50	4.73	2.00
1931: 2	1.06	3.30	4.43	6.38	1.50	3.19	4.74	2.00
1931: 3	1.38	3.27	4.39	6.44	1.33	3.31	4.70	2.00
1931: 4	1.49	3.26	4.40	6.72	1.20	3.30	4.66	2.00
1931: 5	0.88	3.16	4.37	7.15	0.65	3.17	4.60	1.61
1931: 6	0.55	3.13	4.36	7.36	0.60	3.06	4.61	1.50
1931: 7	0.41	3.15	4.36	7.08	0.35	2.98	4.56	1.50
1931: 8	0.42	3.18	4.40	7.47	0.40	3.29	4.53	1.50
1931: 9	0.45	3.25	4.55	8.07	1.37	3.16	4.53	1.50
1931: 10	1.70	3.63	4.99	9.04	2.50	3.56	4.72	2.76
1931: 11	1.77	3.63	4.94	8.93	2.40	3.57	4.99	3.50
1931: 12	2.41	3.93	5.32	10.42	2.75	4.01	5.00	3.50
1932: 1	2.48	4.26	5.20	9.13	2.30	4.14	5.10	3.50
1932: 2	2.42	4.11	5.23	8.87	2.37	3.73	5.13	3.43
1932: 3	2.25	3.92	4.98	8.83	1.75	3.77	5.14	3.00
1932: 4	1.11	3.68	5.17	10.46	0.55	3.46	5.11	3.00
1932: 5	0.31	3.76	5.36	11.63	0.25	3.78	5.08	3.00
1932: 6	0.34	3.76	5.41	11.52	0.25	3.49	5.09	2.88
1932: 7	0.22	3.58	5.26	10.79	0.25	3.46	5.00	2.50
1932: 8	0.14	3.45	4.91	8.22	0.20	3.42	5.05	2.50
1932: 9	0.03	3.42	4.70	7.61	0.10	3.28	4.95	2.50
1932: 10	—[1]	3.43	4.64	7.87	0.10	3.29	4.92	2.50
1932: 11	—[1]	3.45	4.63	8.24	0.05	3.22	4.81	2.50
1932: 12	0.04	3.35	4.59	8.42	0.05	3.15	4.86	2.50

Notes appear at end of table

TABLE Cb56–63   Selected interest rates – bond and security yields, bank loans, and the Federal Reserve discount rate: 1919–1941   *Continued*

	Yields on securities and bonds						Loan rates	
	Short-term U.S. securities	Long-term U.S. government bonds	Corporate bonds		Government securities, adjusted yields		Customer loans by banks in principal cities	Discount rate, Federal Reserve Bank of New York
			Aaa-rated	Baa-rated	3 months	20 years		
	Cb56	Cb57	Cb58	Cb59	Cb60	Cb61	Cb62	Cb63
Year: Month	Percent per annum	Percent per annum	Percent per annum	Percent per annum	Percent per annum	Percent per annum	Percent per annum	Percent per annum
1933: 1	0.07	3.22	4.44	8.01	0.05	2.96	4.83	2.50
1933: 2	0.01	3.31	4.48	8.37	0.63	3.42	4.80	2.50
1933: 3	1.34	3.42	4.68	8.91	1.00	3.34	5.30	3.44
1933: 4	0.45	3.42	4.78	9.12	0.35	3.22	5.00	3.10
1933: 5	0.29	3.30	4.63	7.74	0.20	3.17	4.92	2.90
1933: 6	0.07	3.21	4.46	7.07	0.15	2.95	4.86	2.50
1933: 7	0.19	3.20	4.36	6.62	0.25	3.14	4.72	2.50
1933: 8	0.01	3.21	4.30	6.77	0.12	3.01	4.68	2.50
1933: 9	0.04	3.19	4.36	7.27	0.05	3.01	4.61	2.50
1933: 10	0.09	3.22	4.34	7.49	0.15	3.13	4.54	2.31
1933: 11	0.22	3.46	4.54	7.98	0.35	3.29	4.45	2.00
1933: 12	0.29	3.53	4.50	7.75	0.50	3.58	4.45	2.00
1934: 1	0.25	3.50	4.35	7.01	0.60	3.53	4.50	2.00
1934: 2	0.08	3.32	4.20	6.27	0.15	3.24	4.39	1.52
1934: 3	0.01	3.20	4.13	6.26	0.15	2.91	4.36	1.50
1934: 4	0.18	3.11	4.07	6.01	0.15	3.07	4.37	1.50
1934: 5	0.14	3.02	4.01	6.05	0.15	2.72	4.31	1.50
1934: 6	0.07	2.98	3.93	6.06	0.15	2.67	4.22	1.50
1934: 7	0.07	2.92	3.89	6.13	0.15	2.58	4.12	1.50
1934: 8	0.20	3.03	3.93	6.49	0.20	2.78	4.11	1.50
1934: 9	0.27	3.20	3.96	6.57	0.25	3.16	4.09	1.50
1934: 10	0.21	3.10	3.90	6.40	0.25	2.95	4.10	1.50
1934: 11	0.22	3.07	3.86	6.37	0.25	2.92	4.03	1.50
1934: 12	0.14	3.01	3.81	6.23	0.20	2.68	3.98	1.50
1935: 1	0.14	2.88	3.77	5.98	0.20	2.48	3.90	1.50
1935: 2	0.11	2.79	3.69	5.95	0.15	2.24	3.87	1.50
1935: 3	0.15	2.77	3.67	6.20	0.15	2.67	3.80	1.50
1935: 4	0.17	2.74	3.66	6.13	0.15	2.66	3.75	1.50
1935: 5	0.15	2.72	3.65	5.94	0.15	2.59	3.74	1.50
1935: 6	0.13	2.72	3.61	5.77	0.15	2.62	3.68	1.50
1935: 7	0.07	2.69	3.56	5.67	0.15	2.69	3.65	1.50
1935: 8	0.10	2.76	3.60	5.58	0.20	2.48	3.65	1.50
1935: 9	0.21	2.85	3.59	5.53	0.20	2.81	3.62	1.50
1935: 10	0.19	2.85	3.52	5.54	0.20	2.77	3.63	1.50
1935: 11	0.14	2.83	3.47	5.43	0.15	2.79	3.59	1.50
1935: 12	0.09	2.83	3.44	5.30	0.15	2.74	3.56	1.50
1936: 1	0.10	2.80	3.37	5.00	0.20	2.72	3.53	1.50
1936: 2	0.08	2.77	3.32	4.80	0.20	2.71	3.52	1.50
1936: 3	0.11	2.71	3.29	4.86	0.20	2.65	3.50	1.50
1936: 4	0.10	2.68	3.29	4.91	0.20	2.62	3.42	1.50
1936: 5	0.18	2.66	3.27	4.94	0.20	2.63	3.41	1.50
1936: 6	0.23	2.66	3.24	4.90	0.15	2.73	3.39	1.50
1936: 7	0.14	2.65	3.23	4.84	0.15	2.73	3.43	1.50
1936: 8	0.18	2.61	3.21	4.74	0.20	2.66	3.34	1.50
1936: 9	0.16	2.60	3.18	4.62	0.18	2.71	3.33	1.50
1936: 10	0.13	2.62	3.18	4.54	0.10	2.76	3.36	1.50
1936: 11	0.10	2.53	3.15	4.52	0.11	2.69	3.34	1.50
1936: 12	0.21	2.51	3.10	4.53	0.20	2.74	3.31	1.50
1937: 1	0.36	2.47	3.10	4.49	0.22	2.72	3.30	1.50
1937: 2	0.38	2.46	3.22	4.53	0.25	2.67	3.29	1.50
1937: 3	0.58	2.60	3.32	4.68	0.60	3.03	3.28	1.50
1937: 4	0.70	2.80	3.42	4.84	0.60	2.96	3.32	1.50
1937: 5	0.65	2.76	3.33	4.84	0.45	3.15	3.32	1.50
1937: 6	0.56	2.76	3.28	4.93	0.39	3.14	3.23	1.50
1937: 7	0.49	2.72	3.25	4.91	0.32	3.05	3.24	1.50
1937: 8	0.52	2.72	3.24	4.92	0.42	3.08	3.25	1.42

(continued)

TABLE Cb56–63 Selected interest rates – bond and security yields, bank loans, and the Federal Reserve discount rate: 1919–1941 *Continued*

	Yields on securities and bonds						Loan rates	
	Short-term U.S. securities	Long-term U.S. government bonds	Corporate bonds		Government securities, adjusted yields		Customer loans by banks in principal cities	Discount rate, Federal Reserve Bank of New York
			Aaa-rated	Baa-rated	3 months	20 years		
	Cb56	Cb57	Cb58	Cb59	Cb60	Cb61	Cb62	Cb63
Year: Month	Percent per annum	Percent per annum	Percent per annum	Percent per annum	Percent per annum	Percent per annum	Percent per annum	Percent per annum
1937: 9	0.53	2.77	3.28	5.16	0.25	3.17	3.25	1.00
1937: 10	0.34	2.76	3.27	5.52	0.23	3.19	3.26	1.00
1937: 11	0.15	2.71	3.24	5.82	0.12	3.12	3.31	1.00
1937: 12	0.10	2.67	3.21	5.73	0.12	3.17	3.26	1.00
1938: 1	0.10	2.65	3.17	5.89	0.14	3.12	3.25	1.00
1938: 2	0.08	2.64	3.20	5.97	0.12	3.16	3.20	1.00
1938: 3	0.07	2.64	3.22	6.30	0.12	3.24	3.22	1.00
1938: 4	0.08	2.62	3.30	6.47	0.08	3.14	3.20	1.00
1938: 5	0.03	2.51	3.22	6.06	0.08	2.75	3.22	1.00
1938: 6	0.02	2.52	3.26	6.25	0.08	2.63	3.25	1.00
1938: 7	0.05	2.52	3.22	5.63	0.08	2.68	3.18	1.00
1938: 8	0.05	2.51	3.18	5.49	0.08	3.03	3.13	1.00
1938: 9	0.10	2.58	3.21	5.65	0.12	2.71	3.17	1.00
1938: 10	0.02	2.48	3.15	5.36	0.05	2.64	3.20	1.00
1938: 11	0.02	2.50	3.10	5.23	0.05	2.68	3.18	1.00
1938: 12	0.01	2.49	3.08	5.27	0.05	2.59	3.25	1.00
1939: 1	(Z)	2.47	3.01	5.12	0.01	2.56	3.23	1.00
1939: 2	(Z)	2.44	3.00	5.05	0.05	2.55	3.18	1.00
1939: 3	0.01	2.34	2.99	4.89	0.05	2.50	—	1.00
1939: 4	0.02	2.30	3.02	5.15	0.05	2.44	—	1.00
1939: 5	0.01	2.17	2.97	5.07	0.05	2.32	—	1.00
1939: 6	0.01	2.13	2.92	4.91	0.05	2.54	—	1.00
1939: 7	0.02	2.16	2.89	4.84	0.05	2.44	—	1.00
1939: 8	0.06	2.21	2.93	4.85	0.10	2.55	—	1.00
1939: 9	0.10	2.65	3.25	5.00	0.10	2.81	—	1.00
1939: 10	0.03	2.60	3.15	4.88	0.05	2.56	—	1.00
1939: 11	0.02	2.46	3.00	4.85	0.05	2.45	—	1.00
1939: 12	0.01	2.35	2.94	4.92	0.05	2.49	—	1.00
1940: 1	—[1]	2.30	2.88	4.86	0.05	2.51	—	1.00
1940: 2	(Z)	2.32	2.86	4.83	0.05	2.54	—	1.00
1940: 3	—[1]	2.25	2.84	4.80	0.05	2.43	—	1.00
1940: 4	(Z)	2.25	2.82	4.74	0.05	2.45	—	1.00
1940: 5	0.04	2.38	2.93	4.94	0.08	2.82	—	1.00
1940: 6	0.07	2.39	2.96	5.11	0.08	2.68	—	1.00
1940: 7	0.01	2.28	2.88	4.80	0.06	2.65	—	1.00
1940: 8	0.02	2.25	2.85	4.76	0.06	2.49	—	1.00
1940: 9	0.02	2.18	2.82	4.66	0.06	2.46	—	1.00
1940: 10	—[1]	2.10	2.79	4.56	0.06	2.49	—	1.00
1940: 11	(Z)	1.97	2.75	4.48	0.06	2.46	—	1.00
1940: 12	—[1]	1.89	2.71	4.45	0.06	2.39	—	1.00
1941: 1	—	1.99	2.75	4.38	—	—	—	1.00
1941: 2	—	2.10	2.78	4.42	—	—	—	1.00
1941: 3	—	2.01	2.80	4.38	—	—	—	1.00
1941: 4	—	1.96	2.82	4.33	—	—	—	1.00
1941: 5	—	1.92	2.81	4.32	—	—	—	1.00
1941: 6	—	1.91	2.77	4.31	—	—	—	1.00
1941: 7	—	1.90	2.74	4.28	—	—	—	1.00
1941: 8	—	1.94	2.74	4.27	—	—	—	1.00
1941: 9	—	1.94	2.75	4.30	—	—	—	1.00
1941: 10	—	1.88	2.73	4.28	—	—	—	1.00
1941: 11	—	1.85	2.72	4.28	—	—	—	1.00
1941: 12	—	1.96	2.80	4.38	—	—	—	1.00

TABLE Cb56–63   Selected interest rates – bond and security yields, bank loans, and the Federal Reserve discount rate: 1919–1941   *Continued*

(Z) Less than 0.005 percent per annum.

[1] Negative.

Sources

Series Cb56–59. U.S. Federal Reserve System, Board of Governors, *Banking and Monetary Statistics: 1914–1941* (September 1943), Table 122 (series Cb56), and Table 128 (series Cb57–59), except series Cb56, 1934:1 to 1934:3, which were provided by the Federal Reserve Board to the National Bureau of Economic Research (NBER); Daniel Feenberg, Jeffrey Miron, Hanna Stern, and Esther D. Reichner, Macrohistory Database (National Bureau of Economic Research), machine-readable data file.

Series Cb60–61. Stephen G. Cecchetti, "The Case of the Negative Nominal Interest Rates: New Estimates of the Term Structure of Interest Rates during the Great Depression," *Journal of Political Economy* 96 (December 1988), Table A1.

Series Cb62. 1919–1929: *Banking and Monetary Statistics: 1914–1941* (September 1943), Table 124; 1930–1939: provided by the Federal Reserve Board to the NBER in Feenberg, Miron, et al., Macrohistory Database.

Series Cb63. Feenberg, Miron, et al., Macrohistory Database. According to the NBER the original sources were the Federal Reserve Board, *Discount Rates of Federal Reserve Banks, 1914–1921* (Federal Reserve, 1922) and *Annual Reports* for 1931–1942.

Documentation

Series Cb56. During the Great Depression, the business environment became increasingly pessimistic. The demand for loans fell, and banks were often unwilling to take risks by lending to customers with uncertain prospects. As a consequence, the supply of short-term open-market paper (commercial notes, bankers' acceptances, and brokers' call loans) declined sharply, and banks increasingly invested in securities issued by the U.S. government. For the period 1920:1 to 1934:3, series Cb56 represents the average daily yields per annum on three- to six-month Treasury notes and certificates, except that for 1920:1 to 1921:12, the figures represent daily yield for the week nearest the fifteenth of each month. The series was discontinued in 1934 because the yields were continuously negative. Yields were also negative for October and November 1932. The negative observations were reported in the original source merely as "negative." Beginning with 1934:4, the series is continued with the new issue rate on U.S. Treasury bills. Bills are sold on a discount basis rather than with a fixed coupon. They were first introduced in 1929, but initially offerings of bills were irregular. A continuous series is available in the source beginning in 1931. Interest on Treasury bills was tax-exempt before 1941. Because of the change in tax status, the series here is carried only to the end of 1940. For discussion of the negative interest rates, see Cecchetti (1988).

Series Cb57. The U.S. bond yield represents, for the period from January 1919 to mid-October 1925, an unweighted average of daily figures for bonds exceeding eight years in maturity. After October 14, 1925, only bonds of twelve years or more to maturity were included. Before July 1928, the two series were identical. If a callable issue sells above par, the maturity of the bond is taken to be the call date. For further detail, see the *Federal Reserve Bulletin* for December 1938.

Series Cb58–59. Two series are provided for the yields on corporate bonds. Series Cb58 is for high-grade bonds, rated Aaa by Moody's Investor Service. Series Cb59 is for higher-risk bonds, rated Baa by Moody's. Because of the risk of default, purchasers of corporate bonds were promised a substantially higher yield than purchasers of U.S. bonds. The gap between the corporate bond yields and those of U.S. bonds is a measure of the implied risk of default.

Series Cb60–61. Cecchetti points out that the yields on government securities presented in series Cb56–57 are distorted, particularly at short maturities, because holders had the right to purchase newly issued securities at par at a future date. During most of the 1920s, new issues were given coupon rates that caused them to sell above par. Thus, the prices of existing issues were higher than they would have otherwise been, thus depressing the calculated yields. Cecchetti makes an adjustment for the "exchange privilege premium" and then uses a curve fitting technique to estimate the adjusted term structure of interest rates. These series present Cecchetti's estimates of the yield at three months to maturity (bond yield equivalent) and at twenty years to maturity.

Series Cb62. The interest rates charged by banks on loans made to their customers are based on quotations from twenty-two cities through 1924, for thirty-four cities for 1925–1928, and for thirty-six cities thereafter. The series was discontinued in 1939. The rates charged in these large cities are thought to be considerably lower than the average charged in smaller cities or by rural banks.

Series Cb63. A major innovation of the Federal Reserve Act was to provide a mechanism by which member banks could borrow reserves from the System by using short-term commercial and agricultural paper as collateral. The Federal Reserve discount rate is the rate charged member banks by the Federal Reserve for loans backed by discountable paper. The figures presented were calculated by the National Bureau of Economic Research by taking a simple average of the discount rates for commercial, agricultural, and livestock paper and weighting them by the number of days in each month that each rate was in force. See *Banking and Monetary Statistics: 1914–1941*, pp. 422–4, for more detail.

TABLE Cb64–70   Money and banking – money supply, monetary base, and banks suspended: 1919–1939

Contributed by Richard Sutch

	Money supply			Monetary base – high-powered money		Deposits in U.S. postal savings system	Banks suspended
	Total	Currency held by public	Adjusted demand deposits at commercial banks	Total	Bank reserves		
	Cb64	Cb65	Cb66	Cb67	Cb68	Cb69	Cb70
Year: Month	Million dollars	Million dollars	Million dollars	Million dollars	Million dollars	Million dollars	Number
1919: 1	20,352	3,962	16,390	6,461	2,499	170	—
1919: 2	20,085	3,954	16,131	6,427	2,473	173	—
1919: 3	20,787	3,944	16,843	6,462	2,518	174	—
1919: 4	21,051	3,962	17,089	6,569	2,607	175	—
1919: 5	21,035	3,936	17,099	6,563	2,627	171	—
1919: 6	21,390	3,888	17,502	6,517	2,629	170	—
1919: 7	21,748	3,958	17,790	6,593	2,635	169	—
1919: 8	22,034	3,963	18,071	6,635	2,672	165	—
1919: 9	22,363	4,002	18,361	6,671	2,669	162	—
1919: 10	22,772	4,053	18,719	6,793	2,740	159	—
1919: 11	23,038	4,121	18,917	6,874	2,753	159	—
1919: 12	23,465	4,213	19,252	6,874	2,661	159	—
1920: 1	23,256	4,179	19,077	6,909	2,730	159	—
1920: 2	23,626	4,309	19,317	7,059	2,750	158	—
1920: 3	23,906	4,372	19,534	7,134	2,762	157	—
1920: 4	23,783	4,418	19,365	7,202	2,784	158	—
1920: 5	23,745	4,414	19,331	7,195	2,781	159	—
1920: 6	23,592	4,463	19,129	7,214	2,751	159	—
1920: 7	23,593	4,500	19,093	7,253	2,753	161	—
1920: 8	23,545	4,574	18,971	7,304	2,730	160	—
1920: 9	23,508	4,624	18,884	7,295	2,671	160	—
1920: 10	23,342	4,657	18,685	7,330	2,673	160	—
1920: 11	22,914	4,534	18,380	7,181	2,647	160	—
1920: 12	23,148	4,487	18,661	7,173	2,686	161	—
1921: 1	22,474	4,317	18,157	6,955	2,638	163	63
1921: 2	22,268	4,278	17,990	6,888	2,610	161	29
1921: 3	21,752	4,220	17,532	6,753	2,533	159	45
1921: 4	21,430	4,160	17,270	6,725	2,565	157	42
1921: 5	21,379	4,129	17,250	6,638	2,509	155	40
1921: 6	20,955	4,047	16,908	6,549	2,502	153	21
1921: 7	20,729	3,987	16,742	6,470	2,483	152	30
1921: 8	20,786	3,938	16,848	6,376	2,438	151	36
1921: 9	20,550	3,905	16,645	6,386	2,481	150	29
1921: 10	20,657	3,805	16,852	6,262	2,457	148	57
1921: 11	20,705	3,744	16,961	6,215	2,471	146	63
1921: 12	20,645	3,735	16,910	6,246	2,511	145	50
1922: 1	20,451	3,614	16,837	6,085	2,471	144	57
1922: 2	20,648	3,614	17,034	6,142	2,528	143	42
1922: 3	20,684	3,632	17,052	6,226	2,594	142	30
1922: 4	21,219	3,626	17,593	6,221	2,595	141	32
1922: 5	21,400	3,606	17,794	6,262	2,656	139	29
1922: 6	21,618	3,625	17,993	6,321	2,696	138	19
1922: 7	21,723	3,608	18,115	6,253	2,645	136	12
1922: 8	21,731	3,657	18,074	6,295	2,638	135	24
1922: 9	22,038	3,717	18,321	6,358	2,641	134	19
1922: 10	22,126	3,725	18,401	6,339	2,614	132	26
1922: 11	22,084	3,742	18,342	6,423	2,681	132	34
1922: 12	22,838	3,778	19,060	6,476	2,698	131	42
1923: 1	22,698	3,730	18,968	6,532	2,802	130	35
1923: 2	22,788	3,793	18,995	6,545	2,752	130	36
1923: 3	22,398	3,854	18,544	6,624	2,770	130	46
1923: 4	22,688	3,894	18,794	6,607	2,713	131	31
1923: 5	22,821	3,956	18,865	6,680	2,724	131	29
1923: 6	22,653	3,988	18,665	6,682	2,694	132	30
1923: 7	22,634	3,982	18,652	6,670	2,688	132	48
1923: 8	22,588	3,999	18,589	6,734	2,735	132	52

TABLE Cb64–70   Money and banking – money supply, monetary base, and banks suspended: 1919–1939   *Continued*

	Money supply			Monetary base – high-powered money		Deposits in U.S. postal savings system	Banks suspended
	Total	Currency held by public	Adjusted demand deposits at commercial banks	Total	Bank reserves		
	Cb64	Cb65	Cb66	Cb67	Cb68	Cb69	Cb70
Year: Month	Million dollars	Million dollars	Million dollars	Million dollars	Million dollars	Million dollars	Number
1923: 9	22,714	3,999	18,715	6,747	2,748	133	53
1923: 10	22,818	3,966	18,852	6,740	2,774	132	71
1923: 11	22,849	4,018	18,831	6,802	2,784	132	102
1923: 12	22,937	3,978	18,959	6,748	2,770	131	113
1924: 1	22,761	3,897	18,864	6,714	2,817	129	152
1924: 2	22,690	3,955	18,735	6,773	2,818	130	90
1924: 3	22,733	3,978	18,755	6,787	2,809	131	69
1924: 4	22,831	3,969	18,862	6,802	2,833	132	72
1924: 5	22,997	3,991	19,006	6,827	2,836	133	80
1924: 6	23,226	3,944	19,282	6,851	2,907	133	52
1924: 7	23,525	3,911	19,614	6,913	3,002	133	45
1924: 8	23,847	3,904	19,943	6,920	3,016	133	35
1924: 9	24,111	3,854	20,257	6,886	3,032	133	34
1924: 10	24,217	3,905	20,312	6,990	3,085	134	40
1924: 11	24,607	3,927	20,680	7,008	3,081	133	48
1924: 12	24,402	3,915	20,487	7,019	3,104	133	58
1925: 1	24,724	3,930	20,794	7,007	3,077	133	100
1925: 2	24,914	3,936	20,978	7,077	3,141	132	62
1925: 3	24,800	3,943	20,857	6,974	3,031	132	42
1925: 4	24,937	3,926	21,011	6,980	3,054	132	45
1925: 5	25,125	3,931	21,194	6,988	3,057	132	55
1925: 6	25,362	3,926	21,436	6,951	3,025	132	37
1925: 7	25,468	3,943	21,525	7,017	3,074	131	27
1925: 8	25,941	3,917	22,024	7,018	3,101	131	19
1925: 9	26,241	3,908	22,333	7,036	3,128	132	28
1925: 10	26,230	3,938	22,292	7,054	3,116	132	53
1925: 11	26,143	3,921	22,222	7,054	3,133	132	77
1925: 12	26,087	3,964	22,123	7,161	3,197	133	73
1926: 1	26,096	3,960	22,136	7,107	3,147	133	71
1926: 2	26,201	3,980	22,221	7,131	3,151	134	51
1926: 3	26,104	3,954	22,150	7,124	3,170	134	53
1926: 4	25,879	4,014	21,865	7,166	3,152	134	57
1926: 5	26,128	3,972	22,156	7,126	3,154	134	66
1926: 6	26,082	3,978	22,104	7,130	3,152	134	81
1926: 7	25,857	4,024	21,833	7,173	3,149	135	142
1926: 8	25,968	3,987	21,981	7,130	3,143	135	49
1926: 9	25,892	3,974	21,918	7,148	3,174	135	42
1926: 10	25,687	3,976	21,711	7,093	3,117	136	87
1926: 11	25,728	3,955	21,773	7,056	3,101	137	154
1926: 12	25,439	3,983	21,456	7,093	3,110	139	123
1927: 1	25,526	3,991	21,535	7,092	3,101	140	135
1927: 2	25,663	3,996	21,667	7,084	3,088	142	80
1927: 3	25,831	4,008	21,823	7,210	3,202	144	75
1927: 4	25,724	4,015	21,709	7,211	3,196	146	48
1927: 5	26,164	3,980	22,184	7,196	3,216	147	46
1927: 6	25,796	3,951	21,845	7,238	3,287	147	40
1927: 7	25,830	3,964	21,866	7,198	3,234	147	35
1927: 8	25,977	3,906	22,071	7,161	3,255	147	26
1927: 9	25,822	3,942	21,880	7,200	3,258	148	36
1927: 10	25,930	3,905	22,025	7,146	3,241	148	51
1927: 11	26,488	3,950	22,538	7,246	3,296	148	42
1927: 12	25,741	3,859	21,882	7,183	3,324	148	55
1928: 1	26,137	3,825	22,312	7,109	3,284	148	56
1928: 2	26,211	3,802	22,409	7,114	3,312	149	48
1928: 3	26,223	3,871	22,352	7,164	3,293	150	64
1928: 4	26,579	3,878	22,701	7,211	3,333	151	47

(continued)

TABLE Cb64–70   Money and banking – money supply, monetary base, and banks suspended: 1919–1939   *Continued*

	Money supply			Monetary base – high-powered money		Deposits in U.S. postal savings system	Banks suspended
	Total	Currency held by public	Adjusted demand deposits at commercial banks	Total	Bank reserves		
	Cb64	Cb65	Cb66	Cb67	Cb68	Cb69	Cb70
Year: Month	Million dollars	Million dollars	Million dollars	Million dollars	Million dollars	Million dollars	Number
1928: 5	26,383	3,875	22,508	7,159	3,284	151	30
1928: 6	25,761	3,925	21,836	7,150	3,225	152	29
1928: 7	25,975	3,881	22,094	7,071	3,190	152	24
1928: 8	25,809	3,903	21,906	7,091	3,188	151	20
1928: 9	26,041	3,870	22,171	7,066	3,196	152	20
1928: 10	26,209	3,819	22,390	7,042	3,223	152	41
1928: 11	26,402	3,913	22,489	7,185	3,272	153	77
1928: 12	26,436	3,834	22,602	7,118	3,284	153	42
1929: 1	26,109	3,828	22,281	7,155	3,327	152	58
1929: 2	26,258	3,849	22,409	7,139	3,290	153	70
1929: 3	26,286	3,902	22,384	7,152	3,250	153	52
1929: 4	26,346	3,866	22,480	7,019	3,153	153	40
1929: 5	26,066	3,883	22,183	7,048	3,165	153	66
1929: 6	26,189	3,911	22,278	7,102	3,191	154	79
1929: 7	26,683	3,887	22,796	7,123	3,236	158	67
1929: 8	26,471	3,919	22,552	7,155	3,236	158	18
1929: 9	26,415	3,822	22,593	7,075	3,253	160	37
1929: 10	28,264	3,832	24,432	7,345	3,513	161	41
1929: 11	25,503	3,852	21,651	7,152	3,300	163	70
1929: 12	26,434	3,800	22,634	6,978	3,178	163	61
1930: 1	25,677	3,752	21,925	6,980	3,228	164	90
1930: 2	25,938	3,748	22,190	6,999	3,251	166	87
1930: 3	26,336	3,717	22,619	6,963	3,246	167	80
1930: 4	25,935	3,670	22,265	6,908	3,238	169	90
1930: 5	25,325	3,694	21,631	6,905	3,211	171	59
1930: 6	25,293	3,681	21,612	6,908	3,227	176	67
1930: 7	25,400	3,669	21,731	6,925	3,256	181	64
1930: 8	25,061	3,704	21,357	6,953	3,249	186	67
1930: 9	25,042	3,634	21,408	6,829	3,195	189	67
1930: 10	24,986	3,594	21,392	6,817	3,223	192	71
1930: 11	25,027	3,674	21,353	6,935	3,261	200	256
1930: 12	24,922	3,809	21,113	7,125	3,316	244	352
1931: 1	24,561	3,818	20,743	7,152	3,334	277	198
1931: 2	24,713	3,823	20,890	7,076	3,253	291	76
1931: 3	24,758	3,861	20,897	7,090	3,229	302	86
1931: 4	24,250	3,897	20,353	7,119	3,222	313	64
1931: 5	23,890	3,897	19,993	7,130	3,233	324	91
1931: 6	23,883	3,995	19,888	7,302	3,307	346	167
1931: 7	23,802	4,058	19,744	7,321	3,263	371	93
1931: 8	23,429	4,177	19,252	7,375	3,198	422	158
1931: 9	23,369	4,289	19,080	7,498	3,209	469	305
1931: 10	22,710	4,537	18,173	7,570	3,033	537	522
1931: 11	22,355	4,503	17,852	7,458	2,955	564	175
1931: 12	21,894	4,604	17,290	7,735	3,131	604	358
1932: 1	21,507	4,896	16,611	7,704	2,808	665	342
1932: 2	21,310	4,824	16,486	7,537	2,713	691	119
1932: 3	21,110	4,743	16,367	7,539	2,796	705	45
1932: 4	20,882	4,751	16,131	7,644	2,893	721	74
1932: 5	20,531	4,746	15,785	7,710	2,964	741	82
1932: 6	20,449	4,959	15,490	7,788	2,829	783	151
1932: 7	20,152	5,048	15,104	7,858	2,810	828	132
1932: 8	20,189	4,988	15,201	7,850	2,862	847	85
1932: 9	20,211	4,941	15,270	7,897	2,956	857	67
1932: 10	20,256	4,863	15,393	7,896	3,033	870	102
1932: 11	20,555	4,842	15,713	7,978	3,136	883	93
1932: 12	20,341	4,830	15,511	8,028	3,198	900	161

TABLE Cb64–70   Money and banking – money supply, monetary base, and banks suspended: 1919–1939 *Continued*

Year: Month	Money supply			Monetary base – high-powered money		Deposits in U.S. postal savings system	Banks suspended
	Total	Currency held by public	Adjusted demand deposits at commercial banks	Total	Bank reserves		
	Cb64	Cb65	Cb66	Cb67	Cb68	Cb69	Cb70
	Million dollars	Million dollars	Million dollars	Million dollars	Million dollars	Million dollars	Number
1933: 1	20,627	4,979	15,648	8,272	3,293	941	236
1933: 2	19,982	5,588	14,394	8,807	3,219	1,005	150
1933: 3	19,052	5,509	13,543	8,414	2,905	1,112	3,460
1933: 4	19,039	5,202	13,837	8,074	2,872	1,158	30
1933: 5	19,449	5,019	14,430	7,915	2,896	1,178	12
1933: 6	19,232	4,949	14,283	7,944	2,995	1,185	11
1933: 7	19,087	4,886	14,201	7,891	3,005	1,176	12
1933: 8	19,115	4,850	14,265	7,961	3,111	1,177	22
1933: 9	19,171	4,830	14,341	8,089	3,259	1,179	13
1933: 10	19,313	4,803	14,510	8,116	3,313	1,187	17
1933: 11	19,558	4,844	14,714	8,165	3,321	1,196	8
1933: 12	19,759	4,839	14,920	8,302	3,463	1,206	29
1934: 1	19,720	4,491	15,229	7,947	3,456	1,198	23
1934: 2	20,298	4,513	15,785	8,411	3,898	1,198	6
1934: 3	20,748	4,550	16,198	8,998	4,448	1,197	4
1934: 4	20,880	4,556	16,324	9,094	4,538	1,195	5
1934: 5	20,997	4,566	16,431	9,158	4,592	1,194	1
1934: 6	21,068	4,584	16,484	9,260	4,676	1,195	5
1934: 7	21,539	4,609	16,930	9,422	4,813	1,188	3
1934: 8	22,127	4,628	17,499	9,491	4,863	1,190	2
1934: 9	22,024	4,627	17,397	9,402	4,775	1,190	1
1934: 10	22,557	4,590	17,967	9,330	4,740	1,196	3
1934: 11	23,017	4,631	18,386	9,570	4,939	1,201	2
1934: 12	22,774	4,559	18,215	9,505	4,946	1,205	2
1935: 1	23,648	4,621	19,027	9,998	5,377	1,198	3
1935: 2	24,353	4,700	19,653	10,159	5,459	1,203	0
1935: 3	24,259	4,714	19,545	10,163	5,449	1,200	3
1935: 4	24,586	4,708	19,878	10,337	5,629	1,198	4
1935: 5	24,773	4,715	20,058	10,468	5,753	1,203	2
1935: 6	25,199	4,708	20,491	10,693	5,985	1,202	4
1935: 7	25,434	4,687	20,747	10,707	6,020	1,187	5
1935: 8	26,804	4,752	22,052	10,936	6,184	1,189	1
1935: 9	26,381	4,805	21,576	10,968	6,163	1,189	3
1935: 10	26,714	4,838	21,876	11,288	6,450	1,194	1
1935: 11	27,268	4,875	22,393	11,524	6,649	1,196	3
1935: 12	27,032	4,879	22,153	11,578	6,699	1,198	5
1936: 1	27,062	4,924	22,138	11,672	6,748	1,205	1
1936: 2	27,539	4,982	22,557	11,778	6,796	1,211	5
1936: 3	27,581	5,016	22,565	11,372	6,356	1,213	9
1936: 4	28,137	5,005	23,132	11,593	6,588	1,212	5
1936: 5	28,945	5,030	23,915	11,825	6,795	1,211	5
1936: 6	29,630	5,250	24,380	11,698	6,448	1,229	2
1936: 7	29,789	5,222	24,567	12,322	7,100	1,241	4
1936: 8	29,691	5,225	24,466	12,564	7,339	1,246	2
1936: 9	30,196	5,278	24,918	12,729	7,451	1,248	3
1936: 10	30,158	5,316	24,842	12,994	7,678	1,252	2
1936: 11	30,418	5,378	25,040	13,128	7,750	1,253	1
1936: 12	30,852	5,466	25,386	13,257	7,791	1,257	5
1937: 1	30,602	5,469	25,133	13,197	7,728	1,263	—
1937: 2	30,877	5,490	25,387	13,302	7,812	1,266	—
1937: 3	31,071	5,480	25,591	13,511	8,031	1,268	—
1937: 4	30,977	5,521	25,456	13,537	8,016	1,267	—
1937: 5	30,601	5,501	25,100	13,496	7,995	1,264	—
1937: 6	30,587	5,512	25,075	13,485	7,973	1,264	—
1937: 7	30,519	5,547	24,972	13,385	7,838	1,268	—
1937: 8	30,311	5,616	24,695	13,344	7,728	1,269	—

(continued)

TABLE Cb64–70   Money and banking – money supply, monetary base, and banks suspended: 1919–1939   *Continued*

	Money supply			Monetary base – high-powered money		Deposits in U.S. postal savings system	Banks suspended
	Total	Currency held by public	Adjusted demand deposits at commercial banks	Total	Bank reserves		
	Cb64	Cb65	Cb66	Cb67	Cb68	Cb69	Cb70
Year: Month	Million dollars	Million dollars	Million dollars	Million dollars	Million dollars	Million dollars	Number
1937: 9	30,153	5,608	24,545	13,628	8,020	1,266	—
1937: 10	29,563	5,589	23,974	13,376	7,787	1,266	—
1937: 11	29,339	5,573	23,766	13,407	7,834	1,266	—
1937: 12	29,089	5,524	23,565	13,652	8,128	1,266	—
1938: 1	29,310	5,485	23,825	13,680	8,195	1,269	—
1938: 2	29,513	5,451	24,062	13,818	8,367	1,268	—
1938: 3	29,603	5,460	24,143	14,111	8,651	1,265	—
1938: 4	29,421	5,433	23,988	14,177	8,744	1,258	—
1938: 5	29,057	5,451	23,606	14,284	8,833	1,252	—
1938: 6	29,173	5,428	23,745	14,609	9,181	1,248	—
1938: 7	29,479	5,453	24,026	14,778	9,325	1,248	—
1938: 8	30,225	5,455	24,770	14,794	9,339	1,249	—
1938: 9	30,570	5,531	25,039	14,832	9,301	1,245	—
1938: 10	30,944	5,553	25,391	15,224	9,671	1,247	—
1938: 11	31,542	5,582	25,960	15,540	9,958	1,247	—
1938: 12	31,729	5,598	26,131	15,568	9,970	1,249	—
1939: 1	31,668	5,682	25,986	15,903	10,221	1,255	—
1939: 2	31,553	5,749	25,804	15,901	10,152	1,260	—
1939: 3	32,016	5,807	26,209	16,393	10,586	1,263	—
1939: 4	32,301	5,900	26,401	16,926	11,026	1,261	—
1939: 5	32,485	5,904	26,581	17,103	11,199	1,258	—
1939: 6	32,586	5,946	26,640	17,298	11,352	1,259	—
1939: 7	33,455	5,980	27,475	17,674	11,694	1,265	—
1939: 8	34,341	6,073	28,268	18,326	12,253	1,267	—
1939: 9	35,084	6,136	28,948	18,857	12,721	1,263	—
1939: 10	35,467	6,169	29,298	19,083	12,914	1,267	—
1939: 11	36,394	6,201	30,193	18,996	12,795	1,271	—
1939: 12	36,011	6,214	29,797	19,293	13,079	1,275	—

Sources

Series Cb64–69. Milton Friedman and Anna Jacobson Schwartz, *A Monetary History of the United States* (Princeton University Press, 1963): series Cb64, sum of series Cb65–66; series Cb65, Table A-1, column 1; series Cb66, Table A-1, column 2; series Cb67, sum of series Cb65–68; series Cb68, Table A-2, sum of columns 1 and 2; and series Cb69, Table A-1, column 6.

Series Cb70. U.S. Federal Reserve System, Board of Governors, "Bank Suspensions, 1921–1936," *Federal Reserve Bulletin* 23 (September 1937): 907.

Documentation
Series Cb64–69

Figures are seasonally adjusted.

Friedman and Schwartz undertook an exhaustive effort to estimate the money supply of the United States. These estimates are generally regarded as the standard. Also see the same authors' *Monetary Statistics of the United States: Estimates, Sources, Methods* (Columbia University Press, 1970), Table 1, in which slightly different definitions are used. For the most part, however, the underlying data of the two sources are the same and the differences between the series are small. The major difference is that in *Monetary Statistics* the deposits in postal savings banks (series Cb69) and in mutual savings banks are included as part of currency held by the public. Because the definitions in *Monetary History* are considered orthodox but those in *Monetary Statistics* are yet to be widely accepted, we present the former here. As a practical matter, the differences are small.

As traditionally defined, the money supply consists of currency in the hands of the public (excluding the monetary authorities and all banks) (series Cb65) plus the sum on deposit at commercial banks (series Cb66). Because of the fractional reserve system of banking in the United States, the monetary authority of the government cannot perfectly control the money supply. When a member of the public deposits currency in a commercial bank, the money is a loan of funds to the bank, which retains only a fraction as bank reserves and loans the balance to others. Series Cb68 gives the level of bank reserves, which is easily seen to be considerably less than the volume of deposits. In this sense, then, the banking system can "create" money by creating loans backed only by fractional reserves. Bank reserves are the sum of currency in bank vaults plus reserves on deposit in Federal Reserve Banks. Because the partitioning of a customer's deposit between reserves and loans is at the discretion of the bank (after it has met its minimum required reserves), the monetary authorities do not have control over the total money supply. Instead, they control the monetary base, also called "high-powered money" (series Cb67). This is the sum of currency in the hands of the public (series Cb65) plus bank reserves (series Cb68).

Series Cb70

The number of bank suspensions is the number of banks closed to the public, either temporarily or permanently, either by supervisory authorities or voluntarily, on account of financial difficulties. Banks that closed under a special "banking holiday" declared by civil authorities but reopened after the holidays are not considered in suspension. Banks that have merged with other banks without actually closing are not counted as suspended. However, banks that closed but were later reopened or taken over by other institutions are included in the number of suspensions. Banks that reached agreements with their depositors to defer withdrawal or to forfeit a portion of deposits are not considered to be in suspension. The figures for 1933 include banks suspended before the banking holiday declared on March 9, banks suspended or placed on a restricted basis following the holiday, and all banks not granted a license to reopen by June 30, 1933. See the discussion in the *Federal Reserve Bulletin* (December 1937).

With the advent of Federal Deposit Insurance in January 1934, bank suspensions became very infrequent and remained so until banking deregulation in the 1980s led to another wave of bank failures.

TABLE Cb71–76   Prices and wages – producer and consumer price indexes, and weekly manufacturing earnings: 1919–1939

Contributed by Richard Sutch

	Price indexes				Average weekly earnings of manufacturing production workers	
	Producer prices					
Year: Month	All commodities	Industrial commodities	Prices received by farmers	Consumer prices	Nominal	Real
	Cb71	Cb72	Cb73	Cb74	Cb75	Cb76
	Index 1929 = 100	Index 1929 = 100	Index 1929 = 100	Index 1929 = 100	Dollars	1929 dollars
1919: 1	141.2	135.4	141.7	96.4	21.36	22.17
1919: 2	136.4	132.2	135.6	94.2	20.97	22.26
1919: 3	137.6	129.0	137.6	95.4	21.04	22.06
1919: 4	139.4	128.3	144.4	97.1	20.80	21.41
1919: 5	141.9	129.6	149.2	98.5	20.89	21.21
1919: 6	142.5	135.4	149.2	98.7	21.23	21.51
1919: 7	147.9	141.8	153.9	101.4	21.33	21.03
1919: 8	151.6	148.2	153.9	103.2	22.12	21.44
1919: 9	147.9	148.9	147.1	103.8	22.69	21.87
1919: 10	148.6	150.8	148.5	105.5	22.22	21.06
1919: 11	151.6	152.7	153.9	108.0	22.87	21.17
1919: 12	158.3	158.5	153.9	110.4	24.09	21.82
1920: 1	165.6	167.5	155.3	112.5	24.76	22.00
1920: 2	165.0	173.9	155.3	113.9	24.64	21.64
1920: 3	166.2	177.8	155.3	115.1	25.81	22.43
1920: 4	173.5	184.2	159.3	118.4	25.51	21.55
1920: 5	175.3	186.1	160.0	120.3	26.32	21.88
1920: 6	174.7	186.1	158.0	122.1	26.89	22.03
1920: 7	174.1	189.3	153.9	121.3	26.55	21.89
1920: 8	169.3	190.6	143.1	118.2	26.69	22.59
1920: 9	163.2	182.9	136.3	116.8	26.66	22.82
1920: 10	151.6	172.6	126.8	116.2	26.65	22.93
1920: 11	140.0	157.2	113.9	115.4	26.12	22.63
1920: 12	126.6	145.7	100.3	112.9	25.80	22.85
1921: 1	119.3	135.4	95.6	111.0	24.12	21.74
1921: 2	110.2	124.5	87.5	107.5	23.30	21.68
1921: 3	107.8	120.0	86.1	106.7	23.24	21.78
1921: 4	103.5	118.1	80.0	105.3	22.78	21.63
1921: 5	101.1	114.9	77.3	103.4	22.44	21.71
1921: 6	98.0	111.7	75.9	102.8	22.14	21.54
1921: 7	98.0	108.4	78.6	103.0	21.38	20.76
1921: 8	98.0	105.9	82.0	103.4	21.59	20.89
1921: 9	98.0	105.9	84.7	102.2	20.99	20.54
1921: 10	98.6	109.1	88.8	102.0	20.45	20.05
1921: 11	98.6	111.0	87.5	101.4	20.16	19.88
1921: 12	97.4	109.1	85.4	100.8	20.88	20.71
1922: 1	95.6	107.2	80.7	98.7	20.08	20.34
1922: 2	97.4	106.5	86.1	98.5	20.41	20.72
1922: 3	97.4	105.9	87.5	97.3	20.62	21.18
1922: 4	98.0	106.5	86.8	97.3	20.43	20.99
1922: 5	101.1	111.7	90.2	97.3	20.81	21.38
1922: 6	101.1	111.7	90.8	97.5	21.24	21.78
1922: 7	104.1	116.1	89.5	97.7	21.07	21.56
1922: 8	103.5	116.8	86.1	96.8	21.49	22.21
1922: 9	104.1	116.8	86.1	97.0	21.75	22.43
1922: 10	104.7	114.9	90.2	97.5	21.85	22.40
1922: 11	105.3	113.6	94.2	97.9	22.39	22.86
1922: 12	105.3	113.6	96.9	98.3	22.67	23.06
1923: 1	107.2	116.8	96.9	97.9	22.28	22.75
1923: 2	108.4	119.4	96.9	97.7	22.71	23.24
1923: 3	109.6	120.6	96.9	98.1	23.32	23.77
1923: 4	109.0	120.0	97.6	98.5	23.49	23.85

(continued)

TABLE Cb71–76   Prices and wages – producer and consumer price indexes, and weekly manufacturing earnings: 1919–1939   Continued

	Price indexes				Average weekly earnings of manufacturing production workers	
	Producer prices					
Year: Month	All commodities	Industrial commodities	Prices received by farmers	Consumer prices	Nominal	Real
	Cb71	Cb72	Cb73	Cb74	Cb75	Cb76
	Index 1929 = 100	Index 1929 = 100	Index 1929 = 100	Index 1929 = 100	Dollars	1929 dollars
1923: 5	106.5	117.4	95.6	98.7	24.25	24.57
1923: 6	105.3	114.9	94.2	99.3	24.10	24.27
1923: 7	103.5	112.9	92.2	100.3	23.38	23.32
1923: 8	102.9	111.7	90.8	99.9	23.39	23.42
1923: 9	104.7	111.0	95.6	100.5	23.44	23.33
1923: 10	104.1	109.7	97.6	100.6	24.22	24.06
1923: 11	103.5	108.4	99.7	100.8	24.04	23.84
1923: 12	102.9	108.4	99.7	100.8	24.15	23.95
1924: 1	104.7	111.7	99.7	100.6	23.50	23.35
1924: 2	104.7	112.9	98.3	100.3	24.43	24.37
1924: 3	103.5	112.3	93.6	99.7	24.37	24.45
1924: 4	101.7	111.0	94.9	99.3	24.23	24.40
1924: 5	100.5	109.1	93.6	99.3	23.97	24.14
1924: 6	99.8	107.2	92.2	99.3	23.32	23.49
1924: 7	100.5	106.5	93.6	99.5	22.39	22.51
1924: 8	101.7	106.5	99.0	99.3	23.04	23.21
1924: 9	101.7	106.5	94.9	99.7	23.32	23.40
1924: 10	102.9	106.5	99.7	100.1	23.67	23.65
1924: 11	104.1	107.8	99.7	100.5	23.42	23.31
1924: 12	106.5	109.7	102.4	100.6	24.17	24.01
1925: 1	107.8	111.0	106.4	100.8	23.64	23.44
1925: 2	109.0	113.6	105.1	100.5	24.41	24.30
1925: 3	109.0	112.3	107.8	100.6	24.62	24.46
1925: 4	106.5	110.4	105.1	100.5	24.10	23.99
1925: 5	106.5	111.0	104.4	100.8	24.46	24.26
1925: 6	107.8	112.3	106.4	102.0	23.97	23.50
1925: 7	109.6	112.9	107.8	103.4	23.57	22.80
1925: 8	109.0	111.7	107.8	103.4	23.80	23.02
1925: 9	108.4	111.7	103.7	103.0	23.20	22.53
1925: 10	108.4	112.3	105.8	103.4	24.40	23.60
1925: 11	109.6	112.9	105.8	105.1	24.43	23.24
1925: 12	108.4	112.9	105.1	104.5	24.65	23.58
1926: 1	108.4	112.3	104.4	104.5	23.93	22.89
1926: 2	107.2	111.0	104.4	104.2	24.65	23.67
1926: 3	105.3	109.7	101.0	103.6	24.86	24.00
1926: 4	105.3	109.1	102.4	104.5	24.50	23.44
1926: 5	105.3	109.1	101.0	104.0	24.43	23.50
1926: 6	105.3	109.1	99.0	103.2	24.47	23.72
1926: 7	104.1	108.4	95.6	102.2	23.71	23.20
1926: 8	104.1	108.4	94.9	101.6	24.24	23.85
1926: 9	104.7	108.4	96.9	102.2	24.03	23.51
1926: 10	104.1	108.4	94.2	102.6	24.80	24.17
1926: 11	103.5	108.4	94.9	103.0	24.41	23.70
1926: 12	102.9	107.2	93.6	103.0	24.55	23.84
1927: 1	99.8	105.2	92.9	102.2	23.79	23.28
1927: 2	101.1	104.6	92.9	101.4	24.89	24.54
1927: 3	100.5	103.3	90.8	100.8	25.11	24.90
1927: 4	99.2	102.0	90.8	100.8	24.91	24.70
1927: 5	98.6	102.0	92.2	101.6	25.02	24.62
1927: 6	98.6	102.0	92.9	102.6	24.61	23.99
1927: 7	98.6	102.0	92.2	100.6	23.90	23.75
1927: 8	99.8	102.0	94.9	100.1	24.38	24.36
1927: 9	101.1	102.7	100.3	100.6	23.99	23.84
1927: 10	101.7	102.0	101.0	101.2	24.37	24.07
1927: 11	101.1	101.4	101.0	101.0	24.01	23.76
1927: 12	101.1	102.0	101.0	100.8	24.64	24.43

TABLE Cb71–76   Prices and wages – producer and consumer price indexes, and weekly manufacturing earnings: 1919–1939 *Continued*

	Price indexes				Average weekly earnings of manufacturing production workers	
	Producer prices					
Year: Month	All commodities	Industrial commodities	Prices received by farmers	Consumer prices	Nominal	Real
	Cb71	Cb72	Cb73	Cb74	Cb75	Cb76
	Index 1929 = 100	Index 1929 = 100	Index 1929 = 100	Index 1929 = 100	Dollars	1929 dollars
1928: 1	101.1	101.4	100.3	100.6	24.09	23.93
1928: 2	100.5	101.4	98.3	99.7	24.96	25.04
1928: 3	100.5	101.4	99.7	99.7	25.08	25.16
1928: 4	101.7	101.4	101.7	99.9	24.64	24.67
1928: 5	102.3	101.4	105.1	100.5	24.87	24.76
1928: 6	101.7	101.4	101.7	99.7	24.79	24.87
1928: 7	102.3	101.4	102.4	99.7	24.22	24.30
1928: 8	102.3	101.4	98.3	99.9	24.61	24.64
1928: 9	103.5	101.4	101.0	100.6	24.45	24.29
1928: 10	101.7	101.4	100.3	100.5	25.16	25.05
1928: 11	100.5	101.4	99.0	100.3	24.61	24.55
1928: 12	100.5	101.4	100.3	99.9	24.91	24.94
1929: 1	100.5	100.7	98.3	99.7	24.27	24.35
1929: 2	99.8	100.1	100.3	99.5	25.30	25.43
1929: 3	101.1	100.7	100.3	99.1	25.49	25.72
1929: 4	100.5	100.1	99.7	98.7	25.43	25.76
1929: 5	99.2	100.1	97.6	99.3	25.51	25.69
1929: 6	99.8	100.1	98.3	99.7	25.09	25.17
1929: 7	101.1	100.1	101.7	100.6	24.05	23.89
1929: 8	101.1	99.5	102.4	101.0	24.70	24.45
1929: 9	101.1	100.1	101.0	100.8	24.67	24.46
1929: 10	99.8	100.1	101.0	100.8	24.81	24.60
1929: 11	98.0	99.5	99.7	100.6	23.85	23.70
1929: 12	98.0	98.8	99.7	100.1	23.90	23.88
1930: 1	96.8	97.5	98.3	99.7	23.37	23.45
1930: 2	95.6	96.9	95.6	99.3	24.09	24.26
1930: 3	94.4	96.3	92.2	98.7	24.23	24.55
1930: 4	94.4	96.3	92.9	99.3	24.08	24.25
1930: 5	93.2	95.6	90.2	98.7	23.91	24.22
1930: 6	91.3	93.7	86.8	98.1	23.58	24.03
1930: 7	88.3	92.4	79.3	96.8	22.37	23.12
1930: 8	88.3	91.1	78.0	96.2	22.23	23.12
1930: 9	88.3	91.1	80.7	96.8	22.24	22.99
1930: 10	87.1	89.8	77.3	96.2	22.23	23.12
1930: 11	85.2	88.6	74.6	95.4	21.52	22.56
1930: 12	83.4	87.3	70.5	94.0	21.61	22.98
1931: 1	82.2	86.0	67.8	92.7	20.86	22.51
1931: 2	80.4	85.3	64.4	91.3	21.91	24.00
1931: 3	79.8	84.1	65.8	90.7	22.23	24.50
1931: 4	78.5	82.8	65.8	90.1	21.86	24.25
1931: 5	76.7	82.1	61.0	89.2	21.72	24.36
1931: 6	75.5	80.9	57.6	88.2	21.08	23.90
1931: 7	75.5	80.9	56.9	88.0	20.37	23.15
1931: 8	75.5	80.9	55.6	87.8	20.25	23.06
1931: 9	74.9	80.9	54.2	87.4	19.39	22.18
1931: 10	73.7	79.6	51.5	86.8	19.48	22.44
1931: 11	73.7	80.2	54.2	85.9	19.07	22.21
1931: 12	71.8	78.9	51.5	85.1	19.10	22.45
1932: 1	70.6	78.3	48.1	83.3	18.37	22.05
1932: 2	69.4	77.6	46.1	82.2	18.62	22.66
1932: 3	69.4	77.0	47.5	81.8	18.06	22.09
1932: 4	68.8	77.0	46.1	81.2	17.35	21.37
1932: 5	67.6	76.4	42.7	80.0	17.15	21.43
1932: 6	67.0	76.4	40.0	79.4	16.41	20.66
1932: 7	67.6	75.7	42.7	79.4	15.95	20.08
1932: 8	68.2	76.4	44.1	78.5	15.78	20.11

(continued)

TABLE Cb71-76   Prices and wages – producer and consumer price indexes, and weekly manufacturing earnings: 1919–1939 *Continued*

	Price indexes				Average weekly earnings of manufacturing production workers	
	Producer prices					
	All commodities	Industrial commodities	Prices received by farmers	Consumer prices	Nominal	Real
	Cb71	Cb72	Cb73	Cb74	Cb75	Cb76
Year: Month	Index 1929 = 100	Index 1929 = 100	Index 1929 = 100	Index 1929 = 100	Dollars	1929 dollars
1932: 9	68.8	76.4	44.7	78.1	16.15	20.69
1932: 10	67.6	76.4	42.7	77.5	16.52	21.32
1932: 11	67.0	76.4	42.7	77.1	16.03	20.79
1932: 12	65.8	75.1	42.0	76.3	15.86	20.78
1933: 1	63.9	73.2	40.0	75.1	15.31	20.37
1933: 2	62.7	71.9	36.6	74.0	15.51	20.97
1933: 3	63.3	71.9	38.0	73.4	14.86	20.25
1933: 4	63.3	71.2	40.7	73.2	15.32	20.93
1933: 5	65.8	72.5	47.5	73.4	16.28	22.18
1933: 6	68.2	75.1	48.1	74.2	16.90	22.78
1933: 7	72.5	78.9	56.3	76.3	17.08	22.38
1933: 8	73.1	80.9	52.9	77.1	17.67	22.92
1933: 9	74.3	83.4	52.9	77.1	17.71	22.97
1933: 10	74.9	84.1	52.9	77.1	17.65	22.89
1933: 11	74.9	84.1	54.2	77.1	17.01	22.06
1933: 12	74.3	84.7	52.2	76.7	17.15	22.36
1934: 1	75.5	85.3	51.5	77.1	17.22	22.34
1934: 2	77.3	86.0	56.3	77.7	18.21	23.44
1934: 3	77.3	86.0	56.9	77.7	18.45	23.75
1934: 4	77.3	86.0	55.6	77.5	18.76	24.21
1934: 5	77.3	86.0	55.6	77.7	18.71	24.09
1934: 6	78.5	85.3	56.9	77.9	18.41	23.64
1934: 7	78.5	85.3	58.3	77.9	17.70	22.73
1934: 8	80.4	85.3	64.4	78.1	18.00	23.06
1934: 9	81.6	85.3	68.5	79.2	17.78	22.44
1934: 10	80.4	85.3	67.8	78.7	18.16	23.09
1934: 11	80.4	85.3	68.5	78.5	18.03	22.98
1934: 12	81.0	85.3	68.5	78.3	18.88	24.12
1935: 1	82.8	84.7	73.2	79.4	19.04	23.97
1935: 2	83.4	84.7	75.9	80.0	19.77	24.71
1935: 3	83.4	84.7	75.9	79.8	19.93	24.97
1935: 4	84.0	84.1	77.3	80.6	19.86	24.64
1935: 5	84.0	84.7	75.3	80.2	19.47	24.27
1935: 6	84.0	85.3	71.9	80.0	19.38	24.22
1935: 7	83.4	85.3	70.5	79.6	19.17	24.08
1935: 8	84.6	85.3	71.2	79.6	19.93	25.03
1935: 9	84.6	84.7	71.9	80.0	20.18	25.22
1935: 10	84.6	85.3	73.2	80.0	20.63	25.78
1935: 11	84.6	86.0	73.2	80.4	20.47	25.46
1935: 12	85.2	86.0	76.6	80.6	21.11	26.19
1936: 1	84.6	86.0	73.9	80.6	20.46	25.39
1936: 2	84.6	86.0	75.3	80.2	20.48	25.53
1936: 3	83.4	86.0	72.5	79.8	21.11	26.45
1936: 4	83.4	86.0	73.2	79.8	21.25	26.62
1936: 5	82.2	86.0	72.5	79.8	21.56	27.01
1936: 6	83.4	86.0	73.9	80.6	21.56	26.75
1936: 7	84.6	86.6	78.0	81.0	21.15	26.12
1936: 8	85.2	86.6	82.0	81.6	21.62	26.50
1936: 9	85.2	86.6	82.0	81.8	21.12	25.83
1936: 10	85.2	87.3	80.7	81.6	22.29	27.33
1936: 11	86.5	88.6	80.7	81.6	22.49	27.57
1936: 12	88.3	89.8	83.4	81.6	23.40	28.69
1937: 1	90.1	91.1	86.1	82.2	22.67	27.59
1937: 2	90.7	91.8	86.8	82.3	23.39	28.40
1937: 3	91.9	93.0	89.5	82.9	24.17	29.14
1937: 4	92.5	94.3	89.5	83.3	24.72	29.67

TABLE Cb71-76   Prices and wages – producer and consumer price indexes, and weekly manufacturing earnings: 1919-1939   *Continued*

	Price indexes				Average weekly earnings of manufacturing production workers	
	Producer prices					
	All commodities	Industrial commodities	Prices received by farmers	Consumer prices	Nominal	Real
	Cb71	Cb72	Cb73	Cb74	Cb75	Cb76
Year: Month	Index 1929 = 100	Index 1929 = 100	Index 1929 = 100	Index 1929 = 100	Dollars	1929 dollars
1937: 5	91.9	94.3	88.1	83.7	24.90	29.74
1937: 6	91.3	93.7	84.7	83.9	24.64	29.37
1937: 7	92.5	94.3	85.4	84.3	24.04	28.52
1937: 8	91.9	93.7	82.7	84.5	24.48	28.97
1937: 9	91.9	93.7	80.7	85.3	23.69	27.78
1937: 10	89.5	93.0	76.6	84.9	24.05	28.33
1937: 11	87.7	91.8	73.9	84.3	22.71	26.94
1937: 12	85.8	91.1	72.5	84.1	22.01	26.17
1938: 1	85.2	91.1	70.5	82.9	21.17	25.53
1938: 2	84.0	90.5	67.1	82.2	21.60	26.29
1938: 3	83.4	90.5	67.1	82.2	21.78	26.51
1938: 4	82.2	89.8	65.8	82.5	21.43	25.96
1938: 5	82.2	89.2	64.4	82.2	21.49	26.16
1938: 6	82.2	88.6	64.4	82.2	21.42	26.07
1938: 7	82.8	89.2	65.8	82.3	21.45	26.05
1938: 8	81.6	89.2	63.1	82.2	22.22	27.05
1938: 9	82.2	89.2	64.4	82.2	22.62	27.53
1938: 10	81.6	88.6	63.7	81.8	23.22	28.40
1938: 11	81.6	87.9	65.1	81.6	22.79	27.94
1938: 12	81.0	87.3	67.1	81.8	23.40	28.62
1939: 1	81.0	87.3	65.1	81.4	22.94	28.19
1939: 2	81.0	87.3	64.4	81.0	23.21	28.66
1939: 3	80.4	87.9	64.4	80.8	23.44	29.01
1939: 4	79.8	87.9	63.7	80.6	22.94	28.46
1939: 5	79.8	87.9	63.1	80.6	23.10	28.66
1939: 6	79.1	87.3	61.7	80.6	23.41	29.05
1939: 7	79.1	87.3	61.7	80.6	22.75	28.23
1939: 8	78.5	87.3	61.0	80.6	23.61	29.29
1939: 9	82.8	89.8	67.1	82.2	23.64	28.78
1939: 10	83.4	91.1	67.1	81.8	24.70	30.21
1939: 11	82.8	91.8	67.8	81.8	24.61	30.10
1939: 12	83.4	91.8	67.1	81.4	25.00	30.72

Sources

Series Cb71–72 and Cb74. U.S. Bureau of Labor Statistics (BLS) Internet site, series WPU00000000, WPU03THRU15, and MWUR0000AA0, downloaded July 16, 2000, and adjusted to a 1929 base.

Series Cb73. Daniel Feenberg, Jeffrey Miron, Hanna Stern, and Esther D. Reichner, Macrohistory Database (National Bureau of Economic Research), machine-readable data file. The original source, according to National Bureau of Economic Research (NBER) records, is U.S. Department of Agriculture, *Agricultural Prices*, Supplement Number 1 (May 15, 1955).

Series Cb75. U.S. Bureau of Labor Statistics, "Employment, Hours, and Earnings, United States, 1909–94": *BLS Bulletin* 2445, two volumes (September 1994): 71, series EEU30000004.

Series Cb76. Based on series Cb74–75.

Documentation

Series Cb71–73. Not seasonally adjusted. The producer price index (PPI, previously called the wholesale price index or WPI) measures the prices received by domestic producers of commodities at all stages of processing. The two producer indexes given here are based on selling prices voluntarily reported by establishments. See Chapter 16 in *BLS Handbook of Methods*, Bulletin 2285 (April 1988).

Series Cb73. Not seasonally adjusted. The index of prices received by farmers is not the same as the producer price index for farm products (available from BLS), which tracks prices for farm products at all stages of processing. Instead, this index is calculated by the U.S. Department of Agriculture and is based on farm gate prices for output received by farmers.

Series Cb74. The consumer price index (CPI) follows the prices of goods and services purchased by consumers for day-to-day living. The weights used in calculating the index were established in a survey of consumption patterns of urban workers taken in 1917–1919. The weights were revised in 1935 on the basis of a second survey of consumers taken in that year. See *The Consumer Price Index: History and Techniques*, BLS Bulletin 1517 (1966) and Chapter 19 in the *BLS Handbook of Methods* for further information.

Series Cb75. Corresponds to the series on the number of manufacturing production workers reported in series Cb45. The BLS calculates weekly earnings by multiplying average weekly hours by average hourly earnings.

Series Cb76. Calculated by dividing series Cb75 by series Cb74.

CHAPTER Cc
Prices

Editor: Christopher Hanes

Associate Editors: Peter H. Lindert and Robert A. Margo

PRICES AND PRICE INDEXES

Christopher Hanes

This chapter presents series that measure changes over time in prices, excluding the price series closely associated with the national income and product accounts. Some of the series included in this chapter represent prices of specific things, such as nails or turpentine, but most are constructed from prices of many different goods and services in a general class, combined or "aggregated" to produce a series with one number for each point in time. Movements in series that aggregate relatively wide classes of things are often taken to indicate "changes in the price level." This phrase usually refers to changes in prices that are in some sense universal, common to all or nearly all goods and services in an economy. A general increase in prices – an increase in the price level – is called price inflation, or simply inflation. A general decrease in prices – a decrease in the price level – is deflation. The price level is stable when there are no general changes in prices.

The Basics: How Price Indexes Are Constructed and Used

Table Cc-A shows some examples of price series for individual goods taken from Table Cc205–266. Column 1 of the table lists prices for cotton sheeting in each year for the period 1820–1830 (series Cc231). Column 2 shows an "index number" constructed from the prices in column 1 by dividing the price of cotton cloth in each year by the price in one particular year, the base year. The year chosen to be the base year was 1820, though any other year would have done as well. The resulting index number equals 1 in 1820. The proportional or percent change in the index number between any two years is the same as the corresponding change in the price found in column 1. In any year, the index number equals that year's cotton cloth price as a proportion or multiple of the price in 1820. Thus, the value of the cotton cloth price index in 1830, which is 0.64, indicates that the 1830 price was 64 percent of the 1820 price.

Column 3 of the table lists prices for cut nails sold in Philadelphia from 1820 through 1828 (series Cc248). This series

is unavailable for years after 1828. Column 4 is an index number constructed from the Philadelphia nails prices, with 1820 as the base year. Column 5 lists prices for cut nails sold in New York City from 1828 through 1830 (series Cc249). This series is unavailable for years before 1828. Column 6 is an index number constructed from the New York nails prices, with 1828 chosen to be the base year as there is no 1820 value for the New York price. Because the Philadelphia and New York price series overlap in 1828 – in that year values are available for *both* series – the price index for Philadelphia nails can be "linked" to the price index for New York nails, to give the series shown in column 7. For years from 1820 through 1828, column 7 is the same as column 4. For years after that, column 7 increases or decreases in proportion to the change between the same years in column 6 (or column 5). Thus, between years from 1820 through 1828, the percent change in column 7 is the same as the percent change in column 4 (or column 3); between years from 1828 through 1830, the percent change in the index in column 7 is the same as the percent change in column 6 (or column 5). If one could assume that percent changes in nail prices from year to year were the same in Philadelphia and New York – which may or may not have been the case – one could take the value of the index number in 1830, which is 0.53, to indicate that in either city the price of nails in 1830 was 53 percent of the 1820 price.

Columns 8–11 show examples of *aggregate* price indexes constructed from price indexes for cotton cloth and nails seen in columns 2 and 7. Column 8 is an arithmetic average, with the cotton cloth price index weighted 30 percent and the nails price index weighted 70 percent. Column 9 is an arithmetic average with the reverse set of weights: 70 percent cotton, 30 percent nails. Columns 10 and 11 are *geometric* rather than arithmetic averages (see the formulas shown with Table Cc-A). Although many people are unfamiliar with geometric averages, many price indexes incorporate them in one way or another. Note that the choice of weights makes a difference for either the arithmetic or geometric average: column 9 can be different from column 8; column 11 can be different from column 10. The use of geometric rather than arithmetic averages also matters, although in this particular case it matters less than the choice of weights: column 10 can be a bit different from 8; column 11 can be different from 9. For the year 1830, the values of the aggregate price indexes range from 0.561 to 0.607 – that is, from 56.1 to 60.7 percent of their values for 1820. One might take these numbers to indicate the general level of prices in 1830 for the class "cotton cloth and nails" relative to the 1820 price level. But one would have to decide which was the appropriate set of weights and averaging method.

Acknowledgments
Christopher Hanes thanks Michael Haines, John James, Peter Lindert, and Robert Margo for comments that improved the essay.

TABLE Cc-A Examples of price index construction

	Cotton cloth		Nails						Aggregate price indexes – cotton and nails			
			Philadelphia		New York				Arithmetic		Geometric	
	Price	Price index	Price	Price index	Price	Price index	Linked price index					
	Dollars per piece	1820 = 1	Dollars per 100 pounds	1820 = 1	Dollars per 100 pounds	1828 = 1	1820 = 1	30% cotton 70% nails	70% cotton 30% nails	30% cotton 70% nails	70% cotton 30% nails
Year	Column 1	Column 2	Column 3	Column 4	Column 5	Column 6	Column 7	Column 8	Column 9	Column 10	Column 11
1820	16.00	1.000	9.80	1.000	—	—	1.000	1.000	1.000	1.000	1.000
1821	16.00	1.000	9.80	1.000	—	—	1.000	1.000	1.000	1.000	1.000
1822	15.00	0.938	9.80	1.000	—	—	1.000	0.981	0.957	0.981	0.956
1823	14.50	0.906	9.80	1.000	—	—	1.000	0.972	0.934	0.971	0.933
1824	9.80	0.613	8.87	0.905	—	—	0.905	0.817	0.701	0.805	0.689
1825	10.52	0.658	7.33	0.748	—	—	0.748	0.721	0.685	0.720	0.684
1826	9.94	0.621	7.21	0.736	—	—	0.736	0.702	0.656	0.699	0.653
1827	9.17	0.573	6.76	0.690	—	—	0.690	0.655	0.608	0.653	0.606
1828	8.99	0.562	7.08	0.722	7.50	1.000	0.722	0.674	0.610	0.670	0.606
1829	9.44	0.590	—	—	7.10	0.947	0.684	0.656	0.618	0.654	0.617
1830	10.24	0.640	—	—	5.50	0.733	0.530	0.563	0.607	0.561	0.605

Documentation

The mathematical formulas for the price indexes shown in this table are as follows:

(Column 2) = (Column 1)/16.0

(Column 4) = (Column 3)/9.8

(Column 6) = (Column 5)/7.5

(Column 7) = (Column 4) for 1820−1828.

Thereafter, values are computed so that year-to-year percent changes match those in column 6. For example, the 1829 value for column 7 equals $0.722 * (0.947/1.000)$.

(Column 8) = $0.30 * $(Column 2) $+ 0.70 * $(Column 7)

(Column 9) = $0.70 * $(Column 2) $+ 0.30 * $(Column 7)

(Column 10) = (Column 2)$^{0.30} * $(Column 7)$^{0.70}$

(Column 11) = (Column 2)$^{0.70} * $(Column 7)$^{0.30}$

Most of the aggregate price indexes presented in this chapter were constructed like the examples in Table Cc-A, although they incorporate prices of many more goods (or services) and are meant to represent classes that are more meaningful than cotton cloth and nails.

Cost-of-living or consumer price indexes (CPIs) aggregate *prices paid by consumers* for the class of goods and services typically purchased by households – that is, families or individuals living alone – for their own use. CPIs are often used as measures of the "price level." They are also used to "deflate" measures of wages or family incomes at different points in time, converting them to "real" values. That is, values for wages or incomes originally expressed in dollars are divided by the values of the CPI for the corresponding points in time. The resulting ratio, sometimes referred to as the real wage or income, remains the same from one period to the next if the percent change in the wage or income measure between the periods is exactly the same as the percent change in the CPI. The ratio increases – real income rises – if the percent change in the wage or income measure is bigger than the percent change in the CPI. The ratio decreases – real income falls – if the percent change in wages or incomes is less than the percent change in the CPI.

Producer price indexes (PPIs) aggregate prices *received by producers* – firms, farms, or other institutions that produce goods and services for sale. Wholesale price indexes (WPIs) are constructed from prices in "wholesale markets," that is, prices paid or received in transactions somewhere preceding sale to the final consumer. In the United States, WPIs have been superseded by PPIs, but for historical periods in which PPIs are unavailable, WPIs are often used as a substitute. Like CPIs, WPIs and PPIs are often used to indicate movements in the price level. They are also used along with measures of production costs and other data relating to the situation of producers.

Changes in the Price Level, 1800–1997

The lower panel of Figure Cc-B plots one of the CPIs presented in this chapter along with a series of linked WPIs and PPIs. Both the CPI and the WPI-PPI were "rebased" to equal 1 in the year 1800 (original series values for each year were divided by values for 1800), so that values for each year are expressed as proportions or multiples of 1800 values. The upper panel of Figure Cc-B presents the same data as the lower panel, except it excludes the years after 1950 and expands the vertical scale to focus on the fluctuations in the price level during the late eighteenth, nineteenth, and early twentieth centuries. Figure Cc-C plots annual inflation rates, that is, the percentage change in the indexes from the previous year. The CPI and the WPI-PPI follow broadly similar paths over time. If the common movements in the two series are taken to indicate changes in the U.S. price level, how would one describe the evolution of the price level over the nineteenth and twentieth centuries?

From 1800 through the early 1890s, the long-run trend in the price level was flat or falling. In the mid-1890s, the price level was not much more than half of what it had been at the beginning of the nineteenth century. During two periods in the nineteenth century, the price level rose sharply above its long-run trend and remained relatively high for years while gradually falling back to the trend. The first of these periods coincided with the War of 1812. The second began with the Civil War: from 1861 through 1864, inflation rates were very high, whereas there was deflation in most years from 1866 through the 1870s.

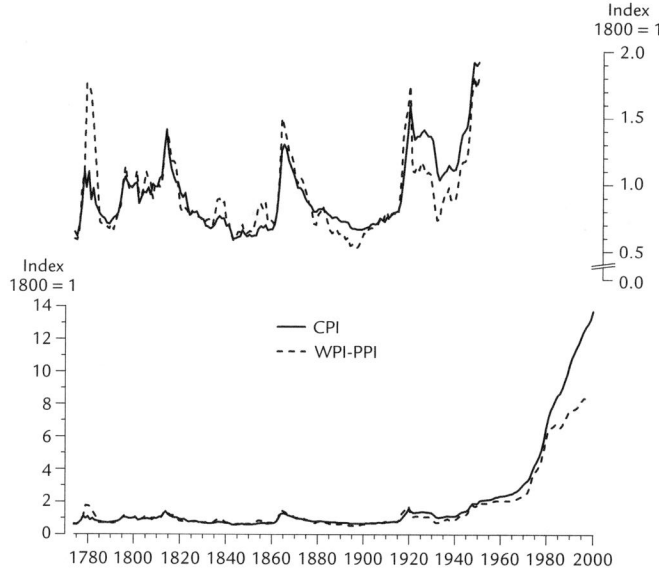

FIGURE Cc-B   Consumer and wholesale-producer price indexes: 1774–2000

Sources

Consumer price index (CPI): series Cc1, rebased to the year 1800. Wholesale-producer price index (WPI-PPI): series Cc113 linked to series Cc66, rebased to the year 1800.

Documentation

By excluding the modern period, the top half of this figure is able to illustrate the fluctuations in the price level during the late eighteenth, nineteenth, and early twentieth centuries.

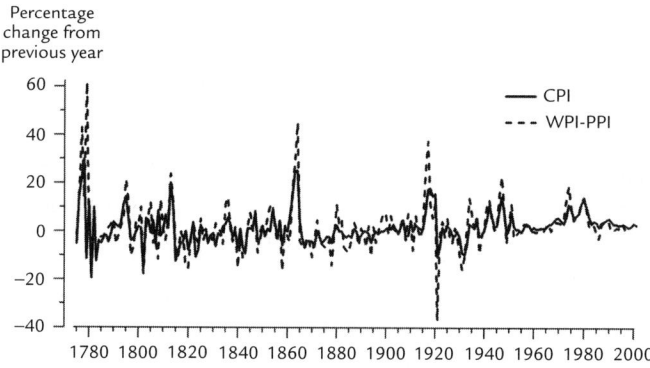

FIGURE Cc-C   Annual rate of inflation in the consumer and wholesale-producer price indexes: 1774–2000

Sources

See the source for Figure Cc-B.

Documentation

This figure plots the annual percentage change in the indexes shown in Figure Cc-B.

Around the turn of the twentieth century, the long-run trend in the price level turned up. There were several years of inflation from the late 1890s through 1914. The First World War, like the earlier wars, was marked by sharp inflation. The price level fell after the war but remained above its prewar trend until the early 1930s, when another spell of deflation left the price level close to its 1800 value. Thus, there had been very little net movement in the price level over 130 years.

After the 1930s, the behavior of the price level diverged from its earlier patterns. The price level did not rise much during the Second World War; instead it popped up *after* the war and never returned to its prewar trend. The price level rose at an accelerating rate over the 1960s and 1970s. Similar rates of inflation had occurred in the past, but not so persistently, year after year. Inflation slowed in the 1980s and remained low in the 1990s, but the price level continued to rise. By 1997, prices were far above the levels of the 1930s and the 1800s.

What accounts for the behavior of the price level from 1800 through 2000, especially the shift from long-run price stability before the 1930s to persistent inflation from the 1940s on?

For much of the earlier period, a dollar was effectively defined to be a certain amount and fineness of gold, in the sense that anyone owed a certain number of "dollars" by a private debtor or a government agency (such as the U.S. Treasury or a Federal Reserve bank) could demand to be paid the corresponding quantity and quality of gold. Money units of some other nations, most importantly Great Britain, were similarly defined to be quantities of gold. Governments did not attempt to control shipments of gold between countries or exchanges of one country's money for another's. This state of affairs is referred to as the international gold standard. Under the international gold standard, rates of exchange between the dollar and other gold-defined monies were fixed within narrow limits: the points at which it became worthwhile to convert dollars to gold, ship the gold to the foreign country, and convert the gold to the foreign money unit, or vice versa. The U.S. price level could not persistently rise or fall faster than price levels in other countries with gold money; otherwise, all transportable goods would be shipped to the country where they fetched the highest gold price (where the price level was highest relative to the fixed exchange rate). The international gold standard ceased to operate in periods when important countries redefined their monies to be something other than gold, or blocked international exchanges. Countries often went "off gold" during major wars, in order to allow the government to pay war expenses with issues of paper currency and other forms of "fiat" money. Britain was off gold during and after the Napoleonic Wars (1797–1819). Most countries other than the United States were off gold for periods during and after the First World War. The United States was off gold from 1862 through 1878. During that period, most dollar debts could be settled with paper "greenbacks" printed by the U.S. Treasury Department, and the Treasury refused to exchange gold for greenbacks at any fixed rate.

When the international gold standard was in operation, the trend price level in all gold-standard countries was determined by the balance between the world's gold supply and the demand for gold by households, businesses, and institutions, such as banks that held stocks of gold to settle current payments or as a reserve against debts that might come due at unpredictable times. Growth in the volume of payments and debt in gold-standard countries tended to increase the demand for gold relative to the supply and raise the price of gold relative to other goods and services, which is to say, *decrease* the price level. Production of new gold, and financial innovations that allowed greater volumes of debt to perch on a given base of gold, tended to increase the supply of gold relative to the demand and, hence, *increase* the price level. In principle, the balance of these forces could tip toward deflation or inflation, or happen to poise precisely at price stability. In fact, the balance tipped to deflation through most of the nineteenth century. The balance reversed in the later 1890s, when gold supply was boosted by the opening of rich new mines in Alaska and South Africa and by the discovery of the cyanide process for extracting gold from ore. In the 1920s, the concentration of gold in central banks and the practice by some central banks of holding short-term foreign assets rather than gold (the "gold exchange standard") tended to reduce gold demand and support a higher price level. As a matter of happy accident, however – or perhaps because a low price level (high gold price) tended to draw forth greater monetary gold supply – the balance of world gold supply and demand never tipped in one direction very much for very long. Thus, the trend of the U.S. price level was fairly stable outside of the Napoleonic Wars, the Civil War, and the First World War. At the same time, the operation of the international gold standard did not ensure a stable price level from year to year. Figure Cc-C shows many years of sharp inflation or deflation even when the United States and other major countries were on gold.

In the 1930s, the international gold standard broke down once and for all. During the Great Depression and the Second World War, nearly all countries other than the United States imposed controls on international exchanges and ceased to define their monies in terms of gold. The U.S. Treasury continued to exchange gold for dollars at a fixed rate, but only for payments to foreigners: U.S. residents were forced to accept payments in paper currency or in "reserve balances" at Federal Reserve banks. In the early 1970s, the Treasury ceased to give *anyone* gold in exchange for dollars at any fixed rate. Thus, since the 1930s, the U.S. price level has been determined mainly by the policies followed by the Federal Reserve (often under pressure from Congress or the President) with respect to the supply of currency and reserve balances. In the late 1960s and 1970s, Federal Reserve policies allowed the supply of this money to grow rapidly relative to demand, resulting in a great inflation. Since then, the Federal Reserve has managed to hold inflation to a lower rate, but it does not attempt to fix the price *level*. Apart from the effects of Federal Reserve policy, U.S. government agencies have occasionally attempted to control inflation directly by laying out guidelines for businesses, setting prices, and punishing those who violate the guidelines. In 1933 and 1934, the National Recovery Administration tried to force prices *up*. During the Second World War, controls were applied to hold prices *down*. At the end of the war, controls were released and prices popped up to the level determined by Federal Reserve policies. Controls meant to reduce inflation were also applied during the Korean War (from 1951 through early 1953) and the early 1970s (1971–1974).

In addition to the movements common to the CPI and the WPI-PPI, Figures Cc-B and Cc-C show some obvious differences in the behavior of the two series. Short-term ups and downs are bigger in the WPI-PPI than in the CPI. Beginning in the 1950s, the CPI tends to rise faster than the WPI-PPI. The 1997 CPI is more than twelve times its average value for the nineteenth century, while the WPI-PPI is only about nine times its nineteenth-century average value. To some degree, these differences reflect changes in markups of retail prices over wholesale or producer prices, and differences in the methods by which individual price series were averaged to create the two sets of aggregate series. More important, however, are differences in the classes of things covered by CPIs and WPIs or PPIs, especially the particular WPI-PPI series plotted here. Prices of housing and services such as medical care are important components of the CPI, but not the WPI-PPI, which is dominated by prices of goods produced by farms, mines, and factories. Since the 1950s, prices of housing and services as measured for the CPI have risen faster than measured prices of commodities and manufactures.

Using a Price Index to Deflate Another Series: An Example

Table Cc-D shows an example of using a price index to deflate a number originally expressed in terms of dollars. Column 1 of the table gives estimates of average salaries of assistant professors in public universities in three years: 1929, 1936, and 1997. Column 2 shows the percentage changes in the average salary from 1929 to 1936 and from 1936 to 1997. Column 3 shows an index for the price of nails constructed like column 7 in Table Cc-A, but with a 1929 base year. Column 5 shows the average assistant professor's salary deflated by the nails price index. That is to say, column 5 is the salaries as originally expressed in dollars (column 1) *divided by* the price index (column 3). The change in the deflated salary between two years is equivalent to the change in the quantity of nails that could be bought with an assistant professor's salary, if a professor bought nothing but nails. Thus, from 1929 to 1936, assistant professors' dollar salaries fell by 7.6 percent, but nail prices fell more, and so the deflated salary rose 10.5 percent: that is to say, the average assistant professor's salary bought 10.5 percent more nails in 1936 than it bought in 1929. From 1936 to 1997, assistant professors' dollar salaries rose by 1,561 percent (about 16 times the amount of the 1936 salary), but the price of nails rose almost as much, and so the deflated salary rose by only about 5.6 percent, which is to say that one could buy 5.6 percent more nails with an assistant professor's salary in 1997 than one could buy with an assistant professor's salary in 1936. Of course, professors do not actually buy a lot of nails, and so it is hard to imagine why anyone might care about these numbers.

Columns 9 and 10 show results of deflating the average assistant professor's salary by a CPI. Column 7 shows the level of the CPI, here rebased so that the 1929 value is equal to 1. Column 9 shows the salary deflated by the CPI (column 1 divided by column 7). At first glance, this exercise appears no more complicated than deflation by the nails price index, and it may be much more interesting. One may take the CPI to measure changes in the general level of prices for the class "things people consume." Under that interpretation, column 9 would indicate the change in the quantity of consumer goods and services that could be bought with an assistant professor's salary. Thus, from 1929 to 1936, while dollar salaries fell by 7.6 percent, consumer prices fell by 19.0 percent, and so the real consumption value of the average assistant professor's salary actually increased by 14.1 percent. From 1936 to 1997, while dollar salaries rose by about 1,561 percent, consumer prices rose by 1,055 percent, leaving a 43.8 percent increase in the quantity of real consumer goods and services that could be bought with the average assistant professor's salary.

The meaning of Table Cc-D cannot be quite as simple as that, however. Some things a professor could buy in 1936 were unavailable to most people in 1997 – for example, public transportation and groceries delivered to one's home. Other things professors routinely bought in 1936 had become prohibitively expensive in 1997, as their prices rose much more than the CPI or professors' salaries. For example, in 1936, many families with incomes equal

TABLE Cc-D Example: average assistant professor's salary deflated by two price indexes

	Average assistant professor's salary		Price index for nails		Salary deflated by price index for nails		Consumer price index		Salary deflated by consumer price index	
	Dollars	Percentage change	1929 = 1	Percentage change	Index	Percentage change	1929 = 1	Percentage change	Index	Percentage change
Year	Column 1	Column 2	Column 3	Column 4	Column 5	Column 6	Column 7	Column 8	Column 9	Column 10
1929	2,691	—	1	—	2691	—	1.000	—	2691	—
1936	2,486	−7.6	0.836	−16.4	2975	10.5	0.810	−19.0	3070	14.1
1997	41,300	1561.3	13.151	1473.6	3140	5.6	9.356	1055.4	4414	43.8

Sources

Average salary of assistant professors in state universities: 1929 and 1936, from George J. Stigler, Employment and Compensation in Education, National Bureau of Economic Research Occasional Paper number 33 (1950), Table 28, p. 42; 1997, from U.S. Bureau of the Census, *Statistical Abstract of the United States, 1998*, Table 314, p. 195.

Price index for nails: constructed from series Cc250–252, in the same manner described for Table Cc-A. These series lack a value for the year 1961. For the purpose of this example, the price of nails was assumed to remain constant from 1960 to 1962.

Consumer price index: series Cc2, rebased to 1929.

to the average assistant professor's salary employed full-time domestic servants.[1] That would hardly have been possible in 1997 on the average assistant professor's salary. Likewise, many goods and services a professor could buy in 1997 could not be bought by anyone in 1936 – for example, televisions and antibiotics. Thus, the numbers in columns 9 and 10 cannot mean that in 1997, the average assistant professor's salary would buy 43.8 percent more of the real goods and services that assistant professors could buy in 1936 with a 1936 salary. Nor can they mean that, compared to 1936, the 1997 salary bought 43.8 percent more of the goods and services that assistant professors bought in 1997.

Undoubtedly, the salary deflated by the CPI is a better measure of an assistant professor's consumption opportunities than is the undeflated dollar salary or the salary deflated by nails' prices. At the same time, it is not clear *exactly* what the CPI-deflated salary means.

The Construction of Aggregate Price Indexes, and Cautions for the User

Anyone using aggregate price indexes should be aware of some problems that complicate the interpretation of any aggregate price index. There are also some problems that apply specifically to historical price series – that is, series that cover periods relatively far in the past.

Price Indexes Depend on the Items Covered and the Aggregation Formula

Some events affect almost all prices in an economy, more or less proportionately. The results of these events are what most people mean by "changes in the price level." Other events affect just a few prices, or the relation between one price and another price. These are often described as changes in "relative prices" as distinct from

the price level. It would be easy to construct aggregate price indexes if most movements in prices reflected the events that affect all prices proportionately; then just about any sample of prices, averaged together in just about any way, would give a price index suitable for most purposes. In American data, however, the opposite is usually the case. Over most periods, factors that affect different types of prices in different ways seem to be much more important. Movements in retail prices are different from movements in prices for the same items at wholesale; prices in one place move differently from prices in another place; prices of goods purchased by rich people move differently from prices of things purchased by poor people; and so on. Thus, the behavior of an aggregate price index constructed from American data depends on the types of prices included in the class the index is meant to cover.

Within any class, prices of individual items can evolve in quite different ways, and so the behavior of an aggregate price index also depends on the exact formula that is applied to combine individual prices into one series. Economic theory can guide the selection of an appropriate formula, but the formula that is ideal from a theoretical point of view usually depends on the purpose to which the price index is to be applied and relies on a set of debatable assumptions about human behavior. Almost always, the ideal formula requires more information than the statistician can get, and so the formula applied in practice is a compromise between theory and the data, and the resulting index is less than ideal from any point of view.

Goods Change over Time

Some goods have remained essentially unchanged over many years. A steel nail, a bottle of bourbon whiskey, or a man's haircut produced in 1999 is not very different from the 1899 version. But other goods, as conventionally defined, have changed very much, for example, "an automobile" or "surgery." Any general class of goods is subject to the occasional introduction of goods that are so novel they seem to be entirely new goods, rather than new versions of old goods, while goods that had once been important practically disappear. In essence, all these developments are changes in the *set* of goods making up the class that an aggregate price index is meant to represent. Is there a sensible way to define a change from one period to the next in prices per se when the set of goods is changing, too?

Consider how a statistician constructing a PPI ought to deal with a change in the set of goods produced. From a producer's point of

[1] A survey of consumer expenditures in 1935–1936 asked families whether they employed domestic servants, and if so, the number of days servants were employed (U.S. Bureau of Labor Statistics 1941b, Table 8). One type of family surveyed was made up of a husband, a wife, and two young children, with annual income between $2,250 and $2,499, a range that includes the average assistant professor's salary in 1936. In the northeastern United States, 37 percent of such families employed servants; in the Southeast, 78 percent did. The average number of employment days implies that most families employing servants had them at least forty hours per week.

view, what matters is the way the change affects cost and profit: Does the new set of goods cost more or less to make than the old one? Thus, economic theory prescribes that a PPI should account for a change in goods by linking the price of the old good(s) to the price of the new *minus* any associated increase in production cost (or *plus* the cost savings, if the new is cheaper to produce). Unfortunately, it can be quite hard for a statistician to come up with a solid number for a production cost differential. (Indeed, any accountant will tell you that it is often hard for a firm's managers to come up with a cost differential between two goods, even if the firm is producing both goods at the same time.) Worse, the cost differential can vary across producers. It might be relatively small, for example, for the firm that was the first to produce a new good. (Why else would that particular firm have been first?) Also, cost differentials can vary over time: a good may be especially costly to make when it is first introduced, but less so later on. Whose cost differential, at what point in time, should be used to adjust a producer price index?

A CPI is subject to similar problems when there is a change in the set of goods purchased, although here what matters is whether the consumer prefers the new good(s) to the old one(s), that is, whether the consumer would choose the new (an improvement in quality) or the old (a deterioration in quality) *absent* any difference in price. In principle, a consumer can place a money value on any change in goods; it is the price differential that would make the consumer just indifferent between buying the new good(s) and the old. Intuitively, it seems sensible to link the price of the old good or set of goods to the price of the new *minus* this price premium (for an improvement in quality) or *plus* the discount (for a deterioration). That is indeed the technique prescribed by economic theory. But how is the statistician to come up with this value? One method is to use the difference in price between the new good(s) and the old that was observed to hold at a time and place when both goods or sets of goods were being purchased in meaningful quantities, under the same conditions. This differential was obviously enough to persuade *someone* to buy the new item(s) rather than the old, and vice versa. Unfortunately, it is often impossible to observe prices in the right circumstances.

Worse, just as production costs vary across producers, different consumers place different values on the special qualities of a novel good. Consider, for example, the introduction of central air-conditioning systems for houses in the 1950s. Then as now, some people would have been willing to pay a great deal for central air-conditioning, perhaps because they were rich and could pay a lot for anything, or because they lived in especially hot places or were gluttons for comfort. Other people would have been willing to pay almost nothing for the same good because they were poor, or lived in cool climates, or were ascetics. Most people would have been somewhere between the extremes. At any point in time, the prevailing price for a central air-conditioning system (or the price premium for an air-conditioned house) must have been *less* than some people were willing to pay and *more* than others were willing to pay. Otherwise, everyone would have had a centrally air-conditioned house, which is not the case even today. Whose valuation should be used in the construction of a CPI?

In general, it can be hard to defend any particular number for the change in consumption value or production cost associated with a change in goods. But there is no way to sidestep the issue. Suppose a statistician simply ignores a change in goods and calculates the price change from one period to the next to be equal to the difference

between the price of the old good(s) in the earlier period and the new good(s) in the later period. That is equivalent to choosing a value of *zero* for the difference in production cost or consumption quality. Alternatively, suppose a slightly more careful statistician finds a point in time at which there are prices for both the new and old good(s) and the statistician "links" the price series at that point, so that changes in the series up to that point from earlier points reflect the evolution of the price of the old good(s), while changes after the point of the link reflect changes in the price of the new good(s). In the case of a PPI, that would be equivalent to an assumption that all producers faced a production cost differential exactly as big as the differential in price prevailing at the point in time that the price series are linked. (Then why is any producer bothering to produce the new good?) In a CPI, it would mean that the statistician effectively assumes that all consumers are willing to pay that price differential to gain the novelty – nothing more, nothing less.

Cautions for the User of Any Aggregate Price Index

In reality, there is probably no such thing as the price level. There is certainly no such thing as a universal aggregate price index suitable for all purposes. The user of these volumes will find a variety of price indexes for any given historical period. Each series can be thought of as an approximation to a particular theoretical definition of a price level. Take care to choose the price series that is most appropriate for your purpose: for example, a CPI *versus* a PPI. Think about the aggregation formula and the way the index deals with changes in goods. Inevitably, the best available series will fall short of the ideal. Consider how its shortcomings could affect your results. Is it possible that some changes in the actual price level, however defined for your purpose, do not show up in the index – that is, could the index give *incomplete* measures of price changes? Could some movements in the index reflect the error in the price index rather than changes in the "true" price level – that is, could the index give *noisy* measures of changes in the price level? Could the error have a trend over time? Could it be systematically related to economic variables?

Special Cautions for Users of Historical Price Series

Most price indexes covering periods relatively far in the past are worse than their counterparts covering recent years. Some historical series were created long ago, when statisticians were less able (and, in some cases, less willing) than they are nowadays to define meaningful classes of prices, collect representative price samples, and follow economic theory in creating aggregation formulas and techniques for dealing with changes in goods. Other series were constructed retrospectively by researchers who had to use whatever scanty data history had left behind. Either way, historical series are on shaky ground. Gaps in time series are bridged by questionable interpolations. Information is absent for whole categories of prices within the class the index is meant to represent; other types of prices serve as proxies. Little is known about characteristics of priced goods, and so there may be unaccounted-for changes in quality. The aggregation formula may be hard to defend from any theoretical point of view.

Thus, the user of a historical series should keep in mind that it is probably subject to bigger errors than its modern counterpart. It may be a *noisier* and *less complete* measure of the price level, however defined. Its errors may be differently related to economic variables and have a different trend. This complicates interpretation of the behavior of price series and variables deflated by price series over long spans of time, or comparisons across historical periods. What appear to be changes over time in the behavior of prices or deflated variables may actually reflect differences in the behavior of the price index error.

After all these warnings, the user may agree with an economist of the 1890s who wrote that "the only possible conclusion seems to be that all attempts to calculate and represent average movements of prices, either by index-numbers or otherwise, ought to be abandoned" (Pierson 1896). A hundred years later, an economist known for his work on price indexes expressed particular doubt about comparisons using historical series:

> As far as long-run comparisons are concerned, I do not think that they are really possible.... We have now, approximately, three times the [real] per capita income of what our grandparents had, perhaps even more. Are we three times as happy as they were? Are we that much wealthier? I do not think that is a question that can really be answered. One can easily think of things that go in the other direction that have been lost. (Griliches 1993, p. 358)

On the other hand, John Maynard Keynes observed that there was an "unavoidable element of vagueness which admittedly attends the concept of the general price-level," but he argued that this

> need not, of course, prevent us from making approximate statistical comparisons, depending on some broad element of judgement rather than of strict calculation, which may possess significance and validity within certain limits. But the proper place for such things as net real output and the general level of prices lies within the field of historical and statistical description, and their purpose should be to satisfy historical or social curiosity, a purpose for which perfect precision... is neither usual nor necessary. (Keynes 1936, pp. 39, 40)

The essential thing is to keep the limits in mind and not pretend to more precision than the data allow.

A Brief History of U.S. Wholesale and Producer Price Series

Early Work

In 1806, Samuel Blodgett Jr. published a collection of prices for sixteen commodities over the period 1785–1805 in *Economica: A Statistical Manual for the United States of America*. In 1881, Horatio C. Burchard, the Director of the U.S. Mint, presented a report to the Secretary of the Treasury that contained time series of wholesale prices and an index number. In 1891, data on wholesale prices over the period 1840–1891 were collected for a Senate committee. They were published in 1893 as part of the "Aldrich Reports" (U.S. Senate Committee on Finance 1893). The report included a wholesale price index constructed by Roland Falkner that was inaccurately described as an index of wage earners' cost of living.

Interest in price statistics heightened in the late 1890s, stimulated by a turnaround in the secular trend of prices from deflation to inflation. In 1900, Falkner extended his indexes to 1899 with data collected by the U.S. Department of Labor (a function now performed by the U.S. Bureau of Labor Statistics), and John R. Commons published a wholesale price index covering the period 1878–

1900 (U.S. Department of Labor 1900, pp. 237–313; Commons 1900). Bradstreet's indexes of wholesale prices were established in 1897 and carried back to 1890. Dun's index numbers were published in *Dun's Review* beginning in 1901 and extended back to 1860.

Series by the U.S. Bureau of Labor Statistics

In 1902, the agency that became the U.S. Bureau of Labor Statistics (BLS) began regular publication of wholesale price indexes, with monthly series carried back to 1890. This program has been maintained continuously ever since, evolving into today's BLS *Producer Price Index*.

In the beginning, the class of prices covered by the program was vaguely defined to be "prices at which commodities could be purchased in the wholesale market" (U.S. Department of Labor 1902, p. 214). The prices actually collected were chiefly those that were easy to get, for goods that were easy to define. This included prices of some imports (for example, raw rubber) but excluded most finished goods, and so coverage was largely limited to raw materials and goods in the early stages of processing. Most prices in the sample were taken from trade journals. Index numbers were constructed as unweighted arithmetic averages of "price relatives." A price relative was the price for an individual good expressed as a ratio to its price in a base year. A comprehensive "all commodities" index was meant to indicate changes in the overall wholesale price level. Indexes were also constructed for various "commodity groups." Ten "major" groups were defined haphazardly by end-use or material composition. For example, the major group "building materials" included goods such as lumber, bricks, and ingredients for paint, while the goods in the "metals and metal products" ranged from pig iron to farm machinery. In addition to the commodity group series, series were constructed on other classification schemes that were thought to be useful for one reason or another. For example, starting in 1913, the BLS constructed special indexes for goods classified as "raw," "semimanufactured," or "manufactured."

In 1914, the BLS recalculated its indexes back to 1890 as *weighted* arithmetic averages of price relatives. Weights corresponded to estimated total U.S. sales or "shipments" of the good represented by a price series. Changes in commodities or sets of commodities in a group were dealt with by linking the old series to the new one, so that changes in the series from that point to earlier periods reflected the evolution of the price of the old set of goods, while changes from that point forward reflected the prices of the new set. Over the 1920s, 1930s, and 1940s, the BLS gradually expanded the geographic areas and number of goods covered by its price samples, and occasionally revised weights in response to new information on shipments. Lower-level commodity groupings were reorganized from time to time, but the set of major groups remained the same.

In 1952, the BLS introduced a new set of major commodity groups and roughly doubled the number of goods covered by its price samples. It also began regular publication of series organized on an alternative scheme, by "economic sectors," under which prices were categorized by type of buyer and degree of processing. Both of the new sets of series were carried back to 1947. The aggregation formula for indexes was still arithmetic averaging of price relatives weighted by estimates of shipment values, but otherwise, techniques were somewhat different from the early days. The weight for a good was now the value of shipments for a good *and* other goods whose price movements were assumed to behave similarly. Most prices were now collected by mail from the manufacturer or other producer. Sellers were clearly and specifically requested to report prices not including excise taxes, f.o.b. the production or central marketing point (that is, excluding shipping charges), *less* any discounts received by most buyers. Prices for imported commodities were those received by the first seller of the good in the United States. Price samples represented finished goods as well as less-finished commodities. New items were added to the sample when "they have become established in the market." For some changes in goods, "an attempt is made to obtain data from the reporters on the value of the additional (or deleted) features and to adjust the price index accordingly" (U.S. Bureau of Labor Statistics 1966b, pp. 96 and 93).

In 1978, the BLS changed the name of the program to "Producer Price Index" and shifted its focus to the series categorized by type of buyer and degree of processing, which were now referred to as "stage-of-processing" series. The series for "finished goods, total" replaced the "all commodities" series as the standard measure of overall changes in the price level. These rather abrupt innovations reflected changes in BLS thinking that had actually developed quite gradually during previous years. The BLS had come to understand that the old commodity group scheme was subject to an indefensible form of double-counting: goods that passed through many stages of sale received more weight than goods that moved directly from primary processors to final user. The BLS had also come to define the class of prices covered by the program as producer prices, that is, prices received by producers of goods, specifically revenue received by *domestic* producers in the first commercial transaction for a good. Under this definition, prices of imports were excluded from the aggregates, and weights reflected shipments by domestic producers alone. When possible, adjustments for changes in goods' quality were based on estimates of differentials in production cost – "the usual method for quality adjustment involves the collection of data from reporting companies on the costs they have incurred in connection with a quality change" (U.S. Bureau of Labor Statistics 1997, p. 132).

Retrospective Historical Series

In 1929, the International Scientific Committee on Price History was formed. In the United States, the committee supported a project by George F. Warren and Frank A. Pearson (1933) to create wholesale price indexes for the entire nineteenth century that would "correspond with" the BLS wholesale price indexes, which began with 1890. Most of the price data used by Warren and Pearson came from newspapers and government reports, and they referred specifically to prices at New York City. Like the BLS data for the 1890s, they covered few finished goods, and so movements in the indexes largely reflected movements in prices of raw materials and goods in the early stages of processing. Working in association with Warren and Pearson, Herman M. Stoker extended the series back into the eighteenth century. The Warren and Pearson and Stoker series are presented here in Table Cc113–124.

The committee also sponsored research to create wholesale price indexes for cities other than New York, focusing on periods before the Civil War. The resulting series for Charleston, South Carolina; Philadelphia; Cincinnati; and New Orleans are presented here as Tables Cc138–187. (Series were also constructed for Boston, but they are especially unreliable and are not presented here.) The data underlying these series were taken from newspapers, merchants' price lists, and account books and are generally scantier than the New York data used by Warren and Pearson. The committee planned to construct series for San Francisco but "with considerable regret, this area was stricken from the original list" because of "lack of funds" (Cole 1938, p. xxiii). Years later, Thomas Senior Berry, who had constructed the committee-sponsored series for Cincinnati, fulfilled the original plan by constructing the series for San Francisco given here as Table Cc188–204 (Berry 1943).

A Brief History of U.S. Consumer Price Series

Early Work

Although nineteenth-century discussions of economic matters often turned on questions about consumer prices, early statisticians collected less information about retail prices than wholesale prices. A special report for the 1880 census, overseen by Joseph D. Weeks and usually referred to as the Weeks Report, included data on retail prices and house rents from 1851 through 1880 (U.S. Bureau of the Census 1886). In 1891, retail prices for more than 200 commodities over twenty-eight months ending September 1891 were collected for a Senate committee and published in the Aldrich Report (U.S. Senate Committee on Finance 1892). In 1904, the agency that became the BLS began to publish indexes of retail food prices, beginning with data for 1890 (U.S. Department of Labor 1904).

The BLS Consumer Price Index

Today's BLS CPI originated in disputes among labor unions, employers, and government arbitrators during the First World War. To provide information for wage negotiations in the shipbuilding industry, the BLS collected data on blue-collar workers' household budgets in 1918 and 1919, as well as rents and retail prices in a set of industrial cities in December of each year from 1914 through 1917 (U.S. Bureau of Labor Statistics 1924). Following up on this study, the BLS collected retail prices and rents in December 1918 and June 1919. In the *Monthly Labor Review* for October 1919, the BLS published a time-series index of retail prices and rents, weighted by average budget shares in the 1918–1919 expenditure surveys, beginning with December 1914. Later BLS publications began consumer price series with a number for 1913, but that is merely an extrapolation based on data for retail food prices and *wholesale* prices of some consumer commodities (U.S. Bureau of Labor Statistics 1920, p. 97). In 1921, the BLS began to collect retail prices and rents on a regular basis in two months of each year and to publish indexes constructed from them. In 1935, the BLS began to collect data one month in each quarter, and in late 1940, for every month in the year. Monthly BLS CPI series for periods before 1940 are interpolations based mainly on food prices (U.S. Bureau of Labor Statistics 1966a, p. 10). Genuine monthly data on consumer prices during the 1920s and 1930s were collected by the National Industrial Conference Board (Sayre 1948).

In the beginning, the BLS program focused specifically on goods and services purchased by families of urban, male, employed "wage-earners and lower-salaried clerical workers," each having a wife and at least one child (U.S. Bureau of Labor Statistics 1924). In 1953, the target population was expanded to include families of all urban wage and clerical workers; in 1964, workers without families were added. In 1978, the population was expanded to include all urban residents, of any social status (except members of the armed forces and inmates of prisons, hospitals, and insane asylums). The current CPI-U series is based on consumption patterns of all urban consumers, while the CPI-W continues the older approach, with weights based on consumption of employed urban wage earners and clerical workers.

The theoretical concepts underlying the series were at first quite vague. From its inception through the early 1940s, its official name was the "Cost of Living" index. In practice, it was an arithmetically weighted index of rents and retail prices of goods and a few services, for the same list of items of the same qualities and bought from the same stores from one period to the next. During the Second World War, this method became controversial. Union leaders claimed that the index failed to account for increases in the "true cost of living" caused by schemes to evade rent and price controls, such as quality downgrades on "standard" grades of products. In response, the BLS changed the name of the index, in September 1945, to "Consumers' Price Index" and began to state clearly and often that the index was *not* meant to measure the cost of maintaining a certain standard of living or welfare, but rather the cost of purchasing an unchanging "basket" of goods and services (U.S. Bureau of Labor Statistics 1966a, p. 6).

Indeed, as a proxy for a true cost-of-living (or "constant-utility") price index, the CPI of the period from the 1920s through the 1950s has some obvious flaws. New goods were introduced only at the time of a major survey of household spending patterns, which was performed rarely. The survey following the original 1918–1919 survey was performed in 1934–1936. Important new goods of the 1920s, such as automobiles, radios, and electric refrigerators, did not enter the index until 1935, even though they had been important to working-class families long before that and had already affected consumption patterns in a variety of ways.[2] New goods of the late 1940s, such as television sets and frozen foods, entered the index in 1950 (U.S. Bureau of Labor Statistics 1966a, p. 12). Changes in goods were dealt with mainly by attempting to specify as precisely as possible the characteristics of goods included in the CPI basket, so that the priced goods did not change at all from one period to the next (Weiss 1955). When an old good disappeared from stores, it was usually replaced by a new good with the price series linked at the point of changeover, so that none of the price differential between the two goods was treated as a price change. As late as the 1940s, however, for some important goods such as automobiles, radios, and large appliances, a change in price from one period to the next was taken to be equal to the raw difference in price between an old model and a newer model, even if the newer model had significantly different characteristics.[3] In 1959, the BLS began

to adjust changes in new automobile prices by estimates of the *cost* of model changes obtained from manufacturers (Stotz 1966).

In 1960, a federally sponsored commission on price indexation headed by George Stigler recommended that "the CPI should be moved toward becoming an index of welfare or constant utility." The BLS rejected this recommendation but accepted in principle the importance of making explicit adjustments for quality changes and more timely introduction of new goods (U.S. Bureau of Labor Statistics 1966a, p. 8). In practice, little was done to improve the CPI along these lines until 1978, when procedures were adopted that allowed for more frequent introduction of new items and points of purchase; similar steps were taken in 1987 (Shishkin 1974; U.S. Bureau of Labor Statistics 1978; Cage 1996). In 1991, the BLS began to adjust clothing prices for changes in quality using statistical estimates of price differentials associated with clothing characteristics (Liegey 1994). In 1996, a federally sponsored commission chaired by Michael Boskin echoed the advice of the 1960 commission and recommended that the BLS "adopt production of a cost-of-living [constant-utility] index as its objective." This time the BLS replied that they had already done just that (Greenleas and Mason 1996, p. 2).

The late 1990s saw many important innovations to CPI procedures, including the adjustment of personal computer and television prices for changes in quality using methods similar to those already applied to clothing. The most radical innovation was the application of a method long recommended by economists but previously scorned by the BLS: geometric rather than arithmetic averaging of individual goods' prices to construct an index number (Fisher 1922). In January 1999, the BLS began to use geometric averaging within groups of very closely related goods, for example, to combine prices of different types of apples for an "apple" group index. Arithmetic averaging was still applied to combine component indexes for larger groups and aggregate series (Dalton, Greenlees, and Stewart 1998). The total effect of these and other technical changes of the late 1990s was to reduce the rate of growth of the CPI-U by about one-half percent per year, relative to the rate of growth the CPI would have shown had the BLS stuck with the methods of the early 1990s (U.S. Council of Economic Advisers 1999, p. 93; Stewart and Reed 1999).

Other than issues associated with new goods and quality changes, the most vexing problem faced by the BLS in CPI construction has been the treatment of housing costs. Housing costs are especially tricky even in theory because many people own their own homes.[4] At first, housing costs were represented by rents for apartments and houses. In 1956, house purchase prices, mortgage rates, and property taxes were incorporated into the index to account for housing costs for families that owned their homes. In the 1980s (1983 for the CPI-U, 1985 for the CPI-W), the 1956 move was reversed, so that the housing cost component was once again based on rents alone (including a calculation of "rental equivalence" cost of homeowning) (U.S. Bureau of Labor Statistics 1985, p. 346). BLS research indicates that such changes in the treatment of housing costs may have had a bigger effect on CPI growth rates than the innovations of the late 1990s (Stewart and Reed 1999).

---

[2] In 1940, it was observed that "in recent years, baby carriages have become increasingly difficult to price in stores patronized by wage-earners and lower-salaried workers. Demand for new baby carriages has fallen off among families in this group. Those with automobiles are apt to take the baby to ride in a basket in the car" (U.S. Bureau of Labor Statistics 1940, p. 377).

[3] "When new models of automobiles, radios, refrigerators, vacuum cleaners, and washing machines are introduced, the practice is to use the price of the largest selling lines of the current model . . . and allow the full effect of price changes of the most popular model to enter into the index. Thus, when refrigerator prices went down more than 10 percent in the spring of 1940 this decline was reflected in the cost-of-living index without adjustment, even though quality had improved so that price, without regard to quality, might have shown a greater decline" (U.S. Bureau of Labor Statistics 1941a, p. 8).

---

[4] For example, for a homeowner, an increase in house prices or rents relative to money income, as usually defined, need not reduce real consumption. That is because the increase in the implicit cost of "housing services" is offset by an increase in wealth – the value of the house – or income more broadly defined.

Retrospective Historical Series

Because historical data on retail prices and rents are so scarce, CPIs covering years before the beginning of the BLS series in 1914 may be less reliable than wholesale price series for the same periods. Many historical CPI series use wholesale prices as stand-ins for retail prices. Some contain component indexes of "rents" that are really indexes of construction costs or straight-line interpolations benchmarked to actual housing costs in just a few widely spaced years. In most cases, the underlying data are from the Northeast and Midwest, rather than the country as a whole. Like the BLS CPI for years before the 1970s, the series are designed to indicate changes in the cost of goods and services purchased by lower-class households.

Series covering years from the 1850s through 1880 are arguably the best of a bad lot because they can draw on the data originally collected for the Weeks Report. In 1908, Wesley C. Mitchell published an index of retail prices and rents spanning 1860–1880 constructed from a selection of Weeks Report data (Mitchell 1908, p. 91). In 1960, Ethel Hoover published a CPI for 1851–1880, given here as Table Cc49–57 and the 1851–1860 portion of Table Cc1–2, based mainly on the Weeks Report (Hoover 1960). Stanley Lebergott constructed a CPI for 1860–1880, given here as the 1860–1880 portion of Table Cc1–2, using Mitchell's food price indexes, Hoover's indexes for clothing and fuel, and, as a proxy for house rents, an index of construction costs benchmarked to data on rents in 1860 and 1868 (Lebergott 1964).

Series for 1890 through 1914 can rely on BLS retail price series for food and, starting in 1907, fuel. In 1926, Paul H. Douglas published an index of the "Cost of Living for Workingmen's Families" spanning 1890 to 1914, constructed from the BLS series supplemented by wholesale price data. Douglas did not attempt to construct measures of rents.[5] In 1958, Albert Rees published an index for 1890–1914, given here as the 1890–1914 portion of Table Cc1–2, based on Douglas's series for food, tobacco, and alcohol, combined with mail-order catalog prices for clothing, house furnishings, and house rents collected from newspaper advertisements.[6]

Series for periods before 1851 and between 1880 and 1890 are the product of heroic research and equally heroic assumptions. They must be used with special care. In the 1940s, T. M. Adams published series on retail prices paid by Vermont farmers over the period 1790–1940, based on figures spotted in farmers' journals and general store daybooks (Adams 1944). Clarence Long constructed a consumer price index for 1880–1890, given here as the 1880–1890 portion of Table Cc1–2, from scanty retail price data and a series for rent that is nothing more than a straight-line interpolation between observations for 1880 and 1890 (Long 1960). A series for years before 1851, given here as the early portion of Table Cc1–2, was constructed by Paul David and Peter Solar (David and Solar 1977, p. 2). For 1800–1851, the retail price component of this series is from Adams's Vermont farmers' prices, benchmarked on more comprehensive retail price data from Massachusetts and Pennsylvania in 1809, 1834, 1836, 1839, 1844, and 1849, while the rent component is actually an index of construction costs benchmarked on house prices in 1839, 1849, and 1859. For years before

1800, the series is a transformation of the Philadelphia wholesale price series given here as Table Cc155–169.

References

Adams, Thurston Madison. 1944. "Prices Paid by Farmers for Goods and Services and Received by Them for Farm Products, 1790–1940: Wages of Vermont Farm Labor, 1780–1940." Vermont Agricultural Experiment Station, Bulletin number 507, February.

Berry, Thomas. 1943. *Western Prices before 1861*. Harvard University Press.

Cage, Robert. 1996. "New Methodology for Selecting CPI Outlet Samples." *Monthly Labor Review* 119 (December): 49–56.

Cole, Arthur Harrison. 1938. *Wholesale Commodity Prices in the United States 1700–1861*. Harvard University Press.

Commons, John R. 1900. *Quarterly Bulletin of the Bureau of Economic Research* 1 (1 and 2) (July and October).

Dalton, Kenneth V., John S. Greenlees, and Kenneth J. Stewart. 1998. "Incorporating a Geometric Mean Formula into the CPI." *Monthly Labor Review* 121 (October): 3–7.

David, Paul A., and Peter Solar. 1977. "A Bicentenary Contribution to the History of the Cost of Living in America." *Research in Economic History* 2: 1–80.

Douglas, Paul H. 1926. "The Movement of Real Wages and Its Economic Significance." *American Economic Review* 16 (1) supplement: 17–53.

Douglas, Paul H. 1930. *Real Wages in the United States, 1890–1926*. Houghton Mifflin.

Fisher, Irving. 1922. *The Making of Index Numbers*. Houghton Mifflin.

Greenleas, John S., and Charles C. Mason. 1996. "Overview of the 1998 Revision of the Consumer Price Index." *Monthly Labor Review* 119 (12): 3–9.

Griliches, Zvi. 1993. "Panel Discussion: Implications of BEA's Treatment of Computer Prices and Productivity Measurement." In Murray F. Foss, Marilyn E. Manser, and Allan H. Young, editors. *Price Measurements and Their Uses*. University of Chicago Press.

Hoover, Ethel D. 1960. "Prices in the 19th Century." In *Trends in the American Economy in the Nineteenth Century*. Studies in Income and Wealth, volume 24. Princeton University Press.

Keynes, John Maynard. 1936. *The General Theory of Employment, Interest and Money*. Harcourt, Brace.

Lebergott, Stanley. 1964. *Manpower in Economic Growth*. McGraw-Hill.

Liegey, Paul R., Jr. 1994. "Apparel Price Indexes: Effects of Hedonic Adjustment." *Monthly Labor Review* 117 (May): 38–45.

Long, Clarence. 1960. *Wages and Earnings in the United States 1860–1890*. Princeton University Press.

Mitchell, Wesley C. 1908. *Gold, Prices, and Wages under the Greenback Standard*. University of California Publications in Economics, volume 1, March.

National Bureau of Economic Research. 1958. *Thirty-eighth Annual Report*. National Bureau of Economic Research, May.

Pierson, N. G. 1896. "Further Considerations on Index-Numbers." *Economic Journal* 6 (21): 127–31.

Rees, Albert. 1961. *Real Wages in Manufacturing, 1890–1914*. General Series number 70. Princeton University Press for the National Bureau of Economic Research.

Sayre, Robert A. 1948. *Consumers' Prices, 1914–1948*. National Industrial Conference Board.

Shishkin, Julius. 1974. "Updating the Consumer Price Index: An Overview." *Monthly Labor Review* 97 (July): 3–20.

Stewart, Kenneth J., and Stephen B. Reed. 1999. "Consumer Price Index Research Series Using Current Methods, 1978–98." *Monthly Labor Review* 122 (June): 29–38.

Stotz, Margaret S. 1966. "Introductory Prices of 1966 Automobile Models." *Monthly Labor Review* 89 (February): 178–81.

U.S. Bureau of Labor Statistics. 1920. "Changes in Cost of Living in the United States, 1913 to October 1919." *Monthly Labor Review* 10 (January): 97.

U.S. Bureau of Labor Statistics. 1924. *Cost of Living in the United States*. Bulletin number 357, May.

U.S. Bureau of Labor Statistics. 1940. "The Bureau of Labor Statistics' New Index of Cost of Living." *Monthly Labor Review* 51 (August): 367–404.

---

[5] Douglas 1926; series also given in Douglas 1930, p. 60.

[6] National Bureau of Economic Research 1958, pp. 59–60; series also given in Rees 1961.

U.S. Bureau of Labor Statistics. 1941a. *Changes in Costs of Living in Large Cities in the United States, 1913–41*. Bulletin number 699.

U.S. Bureau of Labor Statistics. 1941b. *Family Expenditures in Selected Cities*, volume 1, *Housing*. Bulletin number 648.

U.S. Bureau of Labor Statistics. 1966a. *The Consumer Price Index: History and Techniques*. Bulletin number 1,517.

U.S. Bureau of Labor Statistics. 1966b. *Handbook of Methods for Surveys and Studies*. Bulletin number 1,458.

U.S. Bureau of Labor Statistics. 1978. *The Consumer Price Index: Concepts and Contents over the Years*. Report number 517, May.

U.S. Bureau of Labor Statistics. 1985. *Handbook of Labor Statistics*. Bulletin number 2,217, June.

U.S. Bureau of Labor Statistics. 1997. *BLS Handbook of Methods*. Bulletin number 2,490, April.

U.S. Bureau of the Census. 1886. *Tenth Census of the United States*, volume 20, *Report on the Statistics of Wages in Manufacturing Industries*. U.S. Government Printing Office.

U.S. Council of Economic Advisers. 1999. "Economic Report of the President." February.

U.S. Department of Labor. 1900. "Wholesale Prices: 1890 to 1899." Bulletin number 27.

U.S. Department of Labor. 1902. *Course of Wholesale Prices, 1890–1901*. Bulletin number 39, March.

U.S. Department of Labor. 1904. *Eighteenth Annual Report of the Commissioner of Labor, 1903: Cost of Living and Retail Prices of Food*. U.S. Government Printing Office.

U.S. Senate Committee on Finance. 1892. *Retail Prices and Wages* (3 parts). Senate Report number 986. U.S. Government Printing Office.

U.S. Senate Committee on Finance. 1893. *Wholesale Prices, Wages, and Transportation* (4 parts). Senate Report number 1,394. U.S. Government Printing Office.

Warren, George F., and Frank A. Pearson. 1933. *Prices*. Wiley.

Weiss, Samuel. 1955. "The Development of Index Numbers in the BLS." *Monthly Labor Review* 78 (January): 20–5.

CONSUMER PRICE INDEXES

Peter H. Lindert and Robert A. Margo

TABLE Cc1–2   Consumer price indexes, for all items: 1774–2003

Contributed by Peter H. Lindert and Richard Sutch

	BLS-based	David–Solar-based		BLS-based	David–Solar-based		BLS-based	David–Solar-based
	Cc1	Cc2		Cc1	Cc2		Cc1	Cc2
Year	Index 1982–1984 = 100	Index 1860 = 100	Year	Index 1982–1984 = 100	Index 1860 = 100	Year	Index 1982–1984 = 100	Index 1860 = 100
1774	8.070	97	1830	9.235	111	1885	9.651	116
1775	7.654	92	1831	8.652	104	1886	9.401	113
1776	8.735	105	1832	8.569	103	1887	9.484	114
1777	10.649	128	1833	8.403	101	1888	9.484	114
1778	13.810	166	1834	8.569	103	1889	9.235	111
1779	12.230	147	1835	8.819	106	1890	9.068	109
1780	13.727	165	1836	9.318	112	1891	9.068	109
1781	11.065	133	1837	9.567	115	1892	9.068	109
1782	12.146	146	1838	9.318	112	1893	8.985	108
1783	10.649	128	1839	9.318	112	1894	8.569	103
1784	10.233	123	1840	8.652	104	1895	8.403	101
1785	9.734	117	1841	8.735	105	1896	8.403	101
1786	9.484	114	1842	8.153	98	1897	8.319	100
1787	9.318	112	1843	7.404	89	1898	8.319	100
1788	8.902	107	1844	7.488	90	1899	8.319	100
1789	8.819	106	1845	7.571	91	1900	8.403	101
1790	9.151	110	1846	7.654	92	1901	8.486	102
1791	9.401	113	1847	8.236	99	1902	8.569	103
1792	9.567	115	1848	7.903	95	1903	8.819	106
1793	9.900	119	1849	7.654	92	1904	8.902	107
1794	10.982	132	1850	7.820	94	1905	8.819	106
1795	12.562	151	1851	7.654	92	1906	8.985	108
1796	13.228	159	1852	7.737	93	1907	9.401	113
1797	12.729	153	1853	7.737	93	1908	9.235	111
1798	12.313	148	1854	8.403	101	1909	9.068	109
1799	12.313	148	1855	8.652	104	1910	9.484	114
1800	12.562	151	1856	8.486	102	1911	9.484	114
1801	12.729	153	1857	8.735	105	1912	9.734	117
1802	10.732	129	1858	8.236	99	1913	9.900	119
1803	11.314	136	1859	8.319	100	1914	10.000	120
1804	11.814	142	1860	8.319	100	1915	10.100	121
1805	11.730	141	1861	8.819	106	1916	10.900	130
1806	12.230	147	1862	10.067	121	1917	12.800	153
1807	11.564	139	1863	12.562	151	1918	15.100	180
1808	12.562	151	1864	15.724	189	1919	17.300	207
1809	12.313	148	1865	16.306	196	1920	20.000	240
1810	12.313	148	1866	15.890	191	1921	17.900	214
1811	13.145	158	1867	14.809	178	1922	16.800	200
1812	13.311	160	1868	14.226	171	1923	17.100	204
1813	15.973	192	1869	13.644	164	1924	17.100	204
1814	17.554	211	1870	13.062	157	1925	17.500	210
1815	15.391	185	1871	12.230	147	1926	17.700	211
1816	14.060	169	1872	12.230	147	1927	17.400	208
1817	13.311	160	1873	11.980	144	1928	17.100	205
1818	12.729	153	1874	11.398	137	1929	17.100	205
1819	12.729	153	1875	10.982	132	1930	16.700	200
1820	11.730	141	1876	10.732	129	1931	15.200	182
1821	11.314	136	1877	10.483	126	1932	13.700	163
1822	11.730	141	1878	9.983	120	1933	13.000	155
1823	10.483	126	1879	9.983	120	1934	13.400	160
1824	9.651	116	1880	10.233	123	1935	13.700	164
1825	9.900	119	1881	10.233	123	1936	13.900	166
1826	9.900	119	1882	10.233	123	1937	14.400	172
1827	9.983	120	1883	10.067	121	1938	14.100	169
1828	9.484	114	1884	9.817	118	1939	13.900	166
1829	9.318	112						

TABLE Cc1–2   Consumer price indexes, for all items: 1774–2003 *Continued*

	BLS-based	David–Solar-based		BLS-based	David–Solar-based		BLS-based	David–Solar-based
	Cc1	Cc2		Cc1	Cc2		Cc1	Cc2
Year	Index 1982–1984 = 100	Index 1860 = 100	Year	Index 1982–1984 = 100	Index 1860 = 100	Year	Index 1982–1984 = 100	Index 1860 = 100
1940	14.000	168	1965	31.500	377	1990	130.700	1,562
1941	14.700	176	1966	32.400	388	1991	136.200	1,627
1942	16.300	195	1967	33.400	399	1992	140.300	1,676
1943	17.300	207	1968	34.800	416	1993	144.500	1,726
1944	17.600	210	1969	36.700	438	1994	148.200	1,771
1945	18.000	215	1970	38.800	464	1995	152.400	1,821
1946	19.500	233	1971	40.500	484	1996	156.900	1,875
1947	22.300	267	1972	41.800	500	1997	160.500	1,918
1948	24.100	288	1973	44.400	531	1998	163.000	1,947
1949	23.800	285	1974	49.300	589	1999	166.600	1,990
1950	24.100	288	1975	53.800	643	2000	172.200	2,057
1951	26.000	310	1976	56.900	680	2001	177.100	2,116
1952	26.500	317	1977	60.600	724	2002	179.900	2,149
1953	26.700	320	1978	65.200	779	2003	184.000	2,198
1954	26.900	321	1979	72.600	867			
1955	26.800	320	1980	82.400	984			
1956	27.200	325	1981	90.900	1,086			
1957	28.100	336	1982	96.500	1,153			
1958	28.900	346	1983	99.600	1,190			
1959	29.100	348	1984	103.900	1,241			
1960	29.600	354	1985	107.600	1,286			
1961	29.900	358	1986	109.600	1,309			
1962	30.200	362	1987	113.600	1,357			
1963	30.600	366	1988	118.300	1,413			
1964	31.000	371	1989	124.000	1,481			

Sources

1774–1974, Paul A. David and Peter Solar, "A Bicentenary Contribution to the History of the Cost of Living in America," *Research in Economic History* 2 (1977): 1–80 (Table 1, pp. 16–17). 1913–2003, U.S. Bureau of Labor Statistics (BLS) consumer price index for all urban consumers (also called CPI-U, Series CUUR0000SA0). The BLS data are available from the BLS's Internet site.

Documentation

The user should refer to series Cc2 (base year 1860) to reduce rounding error for the pre-1913 era, when the absolute numbers were small. For more recent comparisons, refer to series Cc1 (base year 1982–1984).

David and Solar's consumer price index is calculated from multiple underlying price series using the following expenditure weights:

For 1774–1851: David and Solar modified the farm and urban expenditure weights for the 1830s from Dorothy Brady, with cross reference to those for working-class families in the early 1830s from Matthew Carey (their Appendix A, pp. 40–3).

For 1851–1880: David and Solar drew weights from Ethel Hoover, "Retail Prices after 1850," in *Trends in the American Economy in the Nineteenth Century: A Report of the National Bureau of Economic Research,* Studies in Income and Wealth, volume 24 (Princeton University Press, 1960), Table 4, p. 150.

For 1880–1890: David and Solar used weights from Clarence Long, *Wages and Earnings in the United States, 1860–1890* (Princeton University Press, 1960), Table B-3, column 2, pp. 158–60.

For 1890–1914: The weights are from Albert Rees, *Real Wages in Manufacturing, 1890–1914* (Princeton University Press, 1961), Table 42, row 4, p. 114.

For 1914–1924: The David–Solar weights are from U.S. Department of Labor, *The Cost of Living in the United States,* BLS Bulletin number 357 (1924), Table 2, row 16, p. 5.

For 1924–1930: A simple average of the weights in U.S. Department of Labor (1924) and U.S. Department of Labor, *Handbook of Labor Statistics,* BLS Bulletin number 1,790 (1973).

For 1930–1974: David and Solar used the weights from U.S. Department of Labor (1973), Table 125, p. 290. The weights came from its columns 1–4 for the following year ranges, respectively: 1930–1949, 1949–1953, 1953–1963, and 1963–1974.

The BLS calculates the CPI-U using expenditures of urban wage earners and clerical workers, professional, managerial, and technical workers, the self-employed, short-term workers, and the unemployed, retirees, and others not in the labor force. User fees (such as water and sewer service) and sales and excise taxes paid by the consumer are also included. Income taxes and investment items (such as stocks, bonds, and life insurance) are not included. Prices for the goods and services used to calculate the CPI-U are collected in eighty-seven urban areas throughout the country and from about 23,000 retail and service establishments. Data on rents are collected from about 50,000 landlords or tenants. The weight for an item is derived from reported expenditures on that item as estimated by the BLS Consumer Expenditure Survey.

Series Cc1. For 1774–1912, this series is the David–Solar series (series Cc2) divided by 12.02, to splice at the year 1913 to a base of 1982–1984 = 100. For 1913–2003, it is the BLS consumer price index for all urban consumers.

Series Cc2. For 1774–1974, this series is the David–Solar index from their Table 1. For 1975–2003, this series is the BLS consumer price index for all urban consumers (series Cc1) multiplied by the ratio 589/49.3 to create a splice at 1974.

David and Solar's primary sources for consumer price series are as follows: 1774–1851: David and Solar (1977), Appendix A, pp. 40–3; 1851–1860: David and Solar use Hoover (1960), Table 1, column 1, p. 142; 1860–1880: Stanley Lebergott, *Manpower in Economic Growth* (McGraw-Hill, 1964), Table A-33, column 1, p. 549; 1880–1890, Long (1960), Table B-2, column 1, p. 157; 1890–1914, Rees (1961), Table 22, column 1, p. 74; 1914–1972, U.S. Department of Labor (1973), Table 121, p. 287; 1972–1974, U.S. Department of Labor (1973), Table 22, column 1, p. 95.

TABLE Cc3–5   Consumer price indexes, for three broad groups: 1913–1996

Contributed by Peter H. Lindert

Year	All food Cc3 Index 1982–1984 = 100	Residential rent Cc4 Index 1982–1984 = 100	Apparel commodities Cc5 Index 1982–1984 = 100	Year	All food Cc3 Index 1982–1984 = 100	Residential rent Cc4 Index 1982–1984 = 100	Apparel commodities Cc5 Index 1982–1984 = 100
1913	10.0	21.0	16.1	1960	30.0	38.7	49.0
1914	10.2	21.0	16.2	1961	30.4	39.2	49.3
1915	10.0	21.1	16.6	1962	30.6	39.7	49.5
1916	11.3	21.3	18.2	1963	31.1	40.1	50.0
1917	14.5	21.2	21.8	1964	31.5	40.5	50.4
1918	16.7	21.5	29.5	1965	32.2	40.9	50.8
1919	18.6	23.3	39.2	1966	33.8	41.5	52.1
1920	21.0	27.4	46.6	1967	34.1	42.2	54.3
1921	15.9	31.5	35.9	1968	35.3	43.3	57.3
1922	14.9	32.4	29.2	1969	37.1	44.7	60.8
1923	15.4	33.2	29.3	1970	39.2	46.5	63.3
1924	15.2	34.4	29.0	1971	40.4	48.7	65.2
1925	16.5	34.6	28.4	1972	42.1	50.4	66.6
1926	17.0	34.2	28.0	1973	48.2	52.5	69.0
1927	16.4	33.7	27.4	1974	55.1	55.2	73.9
1928	16.3	32.9	27.0	1975	59.8	58.0	76.7
1929	16.5	32.1	26.7	1976	61.6	61.1	79.2
1930	15.6	31.2	26.2	1977	65.5	64.8	82.3
1931	12.9	29.6	23.8	1978	72.0	69.3	84.5
1932	10.7	26.5	21.1	1979	79.9	74.3	87.5
1933	10.4	22.9	20.3	1980	86.8	80.9	92.9
1934	11.6	21.4	22.3	1981	93.6	87.9	96.5
1935	12.4	21.4	22.4	1982	97.4	94.6	98.3
1936	12.6	21.9	22.7	1983	99.4	100.1	100.2
1937	13.1	22.9	23.9	1984	103.2	105.3	101.5
1938	12.1	23.7	23.7	1985	105.6	111.8	104.0
1939	11.8	23.7	23.3	1986	109.0	118.3	104.2
1940	12.0	23.7	23.6	1987	113.5	123.1	108.9
1941	13.1	24.2	24.9	1988	118.2	127.8	113.7
1942	15.4	24.7	29.0	1989	125.1	132.8	116.7
1943	17.1	24.7	30.4	1990	132.4	138.4	122.0
1944	16.9	24.8	32.5	1991	136.3	143.3	126.4
1945	17.3	24.8	34.2	1992	137.9	146.9	129.4
1946	19.8	25.0	37.7	1993	140.9	150.3	131.0
1947	24.1	25.8	43.7	1994	144.3	154.0	130.4
1948	26.1	27.5	46.4	1995	148.4	157.8	128.7
1949	25.0	28.7	44.5	1996	153.3	162.0	128.2
1950	25.4	29.7	44.0				
1951	28.2	30.9	48.2				
1952	28.7	32.2	47.6				
1953	28.3	33.9	47.1				
1954	28.2	35.1	46.9				
1955	27.8	35.6	46.6				
1956	28.0	36.3	47.4				
1957	28.9	37.0	47.9				
1958	30.2	37.6	47.9				
1959	29.7	38.2	48.3				

Sources

U.S. Census Bureau series on consumer price indexes, by major groups. 1913–1970: *Historical Statistics of the United States* (1975), based on U.S. Bureau of Labor Statistics, *Consumer Price Indexes for Urban Wage Earners and Clerical Workers; U.S. City Averages.* 1971–1996: *Statistical Abstract of the United States*, based on U.S. Bureau of Labor Statistics, *Monthly Labor Review* and *Handbook of Labor Statistics*, published periodically.

Documentation

The 1913–1992 figures represent annual averages of monthly figures and reflect buying patterns of all urban consumers.

TABLE Cc6–48 Consumer price indexes for all urban consumers, for selected items and groups: 1935–1997
Contributed by Peter H. Lindert

		All food and beverages													
				Food and beverages											
					Food at home										
							Meats, poultry, fish, seafood, and eggs								
Year	All items	All food and beverages	All food	All alcoholic beverages	All food at home	Cereal and bakery products	All meats, poultry, fish, seafood, and eggs	Meats	Poultry	Fish and seafood	Eggs	Dairy products	Nonalcoholic beverages	Processed fruits and vegetables	Food away from home
	Cc6	Cc7	Cc8	Cc9	Cc10	Cc11	Cc12	Cc13	Cc14	Cc15	Cc16	Cc17	Cc18	Cc19	Cc20
	Index 1982–1984 = 100	Index 1982–1984 = 100	Index 1982–1984 = 100	Index 1982–1984 = 100	Index 1982–1984 = 100	Index 1982–1984 = 100	Index 1982–1984 = 100	Index 1982–1984 = 100	Index 1982–1984 = 100	Index 1982–1984 = 100	Index 1982–1984 = 100	Index 1982–1984 = 100	Index 1982–1984 = 100	Index 1982–1984 = 100	Index 1982–1984 = 100
1935	13.7	—	12.4	—	—	13.3	—	12.4	36.3	5.1	37.1	15.5	—	16.5	—
1936	13.9	—	12.6	—	—	13.2	—	12.2	38.4	6.2	36.7	16.0	—	15.7	—
1937	14.4	—	13.1	—	—	13.5	—	13.1	39.9	6.3	36.0	16.6	—	16.6	—
1938	14.1	—	12.1	—	—	13.1	—	12.1	39.7	6.4	35.7	15.7	—	15.1	—
1939	13.9	—	11.8	—	—	12.4	—	12.0	35.6	6.3	32.4	15.1	—	14.5	—
1940	14.0	—	12.0	—	—	12.7	—	11.7	36.0	6.9	33.4	15.9	—	14.7	—
1941	14.7	—	13.1	—	—	12.8	—	13.1	38.8	7.8	39.9	17.6	—	15.6	—
1942	16.3	—	15.4	—	—	13.8	—	15.2	46.6	10.2	48.5	19.7	—	19.5	—
1943	17.3	—	17.1	—	—	14.1	—	15.4	55.5	13.0	57.6	21.2	—	21.2	—
1944	17.6	—	16.9	—	—	14.2	—	14.6	57.3	13.0	54.8	21.0	—	21.3	—
1945	18.0	—	17.3	—	—	14.3	—	14.6	58.7	13.6	58.5	21.0	—	21.5	—
1946	19.5	—	19.8	—	—	16.4	—	18.7	66.0	14.8	60.0	26.0	—	23.4	—
1947	22.3	—	24.1	—	25.8	20.4	—	26.6	69.6	17.0	71.5	29.3	12.0	29.0	—
1948	24.1	—	26.1	—	28.0	22.4	—	30.2	77.1	19.6	74.3	32.2	13.1	27.6	—
1949	23.8	—	25.0	—	26.9	22.3	—	28.4	72.7	19.7	71.6	29.4	14.2	26.3	—
1950	24.1	—	25.4	—	27.3	22.6	—	29.9	69.6	19.4	61.8	29.0	20.0	25.5	—
1951	26.0	—	28.2	—	30.3	24.7	—	33.9	73.0	22.1	75.2	32.4	22.1	28.8	—
1952	26.5	—	28.7	—	30.8	25.3	—	33.6	73.2	21.5	68.7	33.8	22.2	28.4	—
1953	26.7	—	28.3	39.6	30.3	25.8	—	31.4	71.4	20.7	72.8	33.2	22.8	29.1	21.5
1954	26.9	—	28.2	40.6	30.1	26.4	—	31.2	64.5	20.9	60.9	32.1	27.1	28.9	21.9
1955	26.8	—	27.8	40.5	29.5	26.8	—	28.7	67.1	20.4	62.9	32.1	24.3	29.1	22.1
1956	27.2	—	28.0	41.0	29.6	27.2	—	27.7	58.8	20.4	62.5	32.9	25.4	30.0	22.6
1957	28.1	—	28.9	42.1	30.6	28.3	—	30.8	57.3	20.7	59.6	33.9	25.2	29.4	23.4
1958	28.9	—	30.2	42.0	32.0	28.8	—	34.3	56.7	22.1	62.6	34.4	23.4	31.4	24.1
1959	29.1	—	29.7	42.4	31.2	29.1	—	33.1	51.6	22.5	54.9	34.6	21.3	32.8	24.8
1960	29.6	—	30.0	43.1	31.5	29.7	—	32.5	52.5	22.5	59.1	35.4	21.1	31.6	25.4
1961	29.9	—	30.4	43.3	31.8	30.3	—	32.9	47.4	23.0	59.1	35.9	21.1	32.9	26.0
1962	30.2	—	30.6	43.4	32.0	30.9	—	33.6	50.1	24.0	55.8	35.7	20.8	32.0	26.7
1963	30.6	—	31.1	43.8	32.4	31.4	—	33.0	49.3	23.9	56.7	35.6	21.1	33.8	27.3
1964	31.0	—	31.5	44.2	32.7	31.5	—	32.5	48.2	23.4	56.1	35.9	23.6	34.6	27.8
1965	31.5	—	32.2	44.6	33.5	31.9	—	35.0	49.7	24.1	54.8	36.0	23.4	33.5	28.4
1966	32.4	—	33.8	45.4	35.2	33.3	—	38.2	52.4	25.6	62.4	38.3	23.3	34.3	29.7
1967	33.4	35.0	34.1	46.4	35.1	34.0	—	37.2	49.1	26.5	52.2	40.0	23.1	34.1	31.3
1968	34.8	36.2	35.3	48.0	36.3	34.2	—	38.1	50.6	26.9	56.3	41.3	23.5	36.0	32.9
1969	36.7	38.1	37.1	49.7	38.0	35.2	—	41.5	53.5	28.4	66.2	42.7	24.2	36.3	34.9

(continued)

TABLE Cc6–48   Consumer price indexes for all urban consumers, for selected items and groups: 1935–1997   Continued

	All items	All food and beverages	All food	All alcoholic beverages	Food and beverages — Food at home		Meats, poultry, fish, seafood, and eggs								Food away from home
					All food at home	Cereal and bakery products	All meats, poultry, fish, seafood, and eggs	Meats	Poultry	Fish and seafood	Eggs	Dairy products	Nonalcoholic beverages	Processed fruits and vegetables	
	Cc6	Cc7	Cc8	Cc9	Cc10	Cc11	Cc12	Cc13	Cc14	Cc15	Cc16	Cc17	Cc18	Cc19	Cc20
Year	Index 1982–1984 = 100	Index 1982–1984 = 100	Index 1982–1984 = 100	Index 1982–1984 = 100	Index 1982–1984 = 100	Index 1982–1984 = 100	Index 1982–1984 = 100	Index 1982–1984 = 100	Index 1982–1984 = 100	Index 1982–1984 = 100	Index 1982–1984 = 100	Index 1982–1984 = 100	Index 1982–1984 = 100	Index 1982–1984 = 100	Index 1982–1984 = 100
1970	38.8	40.1	39.2	52.1	39.9	37.1	44.6	43.8	53.2	31.3	65.6	44.7	27.1	37.2	37.5
1971	40.5	41.4	40.4	54.2	40.9	38.8	—	43.5	53.5	34.5	56.6	46.1	28.1	39.6	39.4
1972	41.8	43.1	42.1	55.4	42.7	39.0	—	48.1	54.2	37.6	56.2	46.8	28.0	41.0	41.0
1973	44.4	48.8	48.2	56.8	49.7	43.5	—	60.0	76.0	43.1	83.6	51.2	30.1	44.3	44.2
1974	49.3	55.5	55.1	61.1	57.1	56.5	—	61.1	72.1	49.7	83.9	60.7	35.9	58.1	49.8
1975	53.8	60.2	59.8	65.9	61.8	62.9	67.0	66.3	79.7	53.9	82.4	62.6	41.3	60.7	54.5
1976	56.9	62.1	61.6	68.1	63.1	61.5	—	66.4	76.4	60.2	90.0	67.7	49.4	62.3	58.2
1977	60.6	65.8	65.5	70.0	66.8	62.5	—	64.9	76.9	66.7	87.1	69.5	74.4	64.3	62.6
1978	65.2	72.2	72.0	74.1	73.8	68.1	—	77.0	84.9	73.0	82.4	74.2	78.7	71.1	68.3
1979	72.6	79.9	79.9	79.9	81.8	74.9	89.0	90.1	89.1	80.1	90.2	82.8	82.6	77.2	75.9
1980	82.4	86.7	86.8	86.4	88.4	83.9	92.0	92.7	93.7	87.5	88.6	90.9	91.4	82.6	83.4
1981	90.9	93.5	93.6	92.5	94.8	92.3	96.0	96.0	97.5	94.8	95.9	97.4	95.3	92.5	90.9
1982	96.5	97.3	97.4	96.7	98.1	96.5	99.6	100.7	95.8	98.2	93.3	98.8	97.9	97.4	95.8
1983	99.6	99.5	99.4	100.4	99.1	99.6	99.2	99.5	97.0	99.3	97.7	100.0	99.8	98.4	100.0
1984	103.9	103.2	103.2	103.0	102.8	103.9	101.3	99.8	107.3	102.5	109.1	101.3	102.3	104.3	104.2
1985	107.6	105.6	105.6	106.4	104.3	107.9	100.1	98.9	106.2	107.5	91.0	103.2	104.3	107.0	108.3
1986	109.6	109.1	109.0	111.1	107.3	110.9	104.5	102.0	114.2	117.4	97.2	103.3	110.4	105.3	112.5
1987	113.6	113.5	113.5	114.1	111.9	114.8	110.5	109.6	112.6	129.9	91.5	105.9	107.5	109.0	117.0
1988	118.3	118.2	118.2	118.6	116.6	122.1	114.3	112.2	120.7	137.4	93.6	108.4	107.5	117.6	121.8
1989	124.0	124.9	125.1	123.5	124.2	132.4	121.3	116.7	132.7	143.6	118.5	115.6	111.3	125.0	127.4
1990	130.7	132.1	132.4	129.3	132.3	140.0	130.0	128.5	132.5	146.7	124.1	126.5	113.5	132.7	133.4
1991	136.2	136.8	136.3	142.8	135.8	145.8	132.6	132.5	131.5	148.3	121.2	125.1	114.1	130.2	137.9
1992	140.3	138.7	137.9	147.3	136.8	151.5	130.9	130.7	131.4	151.7	108.3	128.5	114.3	133.7	140.7
1993	144.5	141.6	140.9	149.6	140.1	156.6	135.5	134.6	136.9	156.6	117.1	129.4	—	—	—
1994	148.2	144.9	144.3	151.5	144.1	163.0	137.2	135.4	141.5	163.7	114.3	131.7	—	134.5	145.7
1995	152.4	148.9	148.4	153.9	148.8	167.5	138.8	135.5	143.5	171.6	120.5	132.8	—	137.5	149.0
1996	156.9	153.7	153.3	158.5	154.3	174.0	144.8	140.2	152.4	173.1	142.1	142.1	—	144.4	152.7
1997	160.5	157.7	—	—	—	—	—	—	—	—	—	—	—	—	—

		Housing									Apparel and upkeep				
	All housing	Shelter		Fuel and other utilities							All apparel and upkeep	Apparel commodities			
		Overall	Rent, residential	All fuel and other utilities	Fuel oil	Fuel oil and other	Utility gas (piped)	Gas (piped) and electricity	Electricity	Telephone services		All apparel	Men and boys	Women and girls	Footwear
	Cc21	Cc22	Cc23	Cc24	Cc25	Cc26	Cc27	Cc28	Cc29	Cc30	Cc31	Cc32	Cc33	Cc34	Cc35
Year	Index 1982–1984 = 100	Index 1982–1984 = 100	Index 1982–1984 = 100	Index 1982–1984 = 100	Index 1982–1984 = 100	Index 1982–1984 = 100	Index 1982–1984 = 100	Index 1982–1984 = 100	Index 1982–1984 = 100	Index 1982–1984 = 100	Index 1982–1984 = 100	Index 1982–1984 = 100	Index 1982–1984 = 100	Index 1982–1984 = 100	Index 1982–1984 = 100
1935	—	—	21.4	—	5.6	5.7	12.8	20.4	31.5	36.8	20.8	22.4	20.8	29.8	14.0
1936	—	—	21.9	—	5.8	5.8	12.7	20.0	30.5	36.6	21.0	22.7	21.1	30.1	14.2
1937	—	—	22.9	—	6.7	5.9	12.6	19.6	29.9	36.1	22.0	23.9	22.2	31.6	15.0
1938	—	—	23.7	—	6.4	5.9	12.7	19.6	29.4	36.1	21.9	23.7	22.1	31.4	15.0
1939	—	—	23.7	—	5.8	5.7	12.9	19.6	28.9	36.1	21.6	23.3	21.7	31.0	14.8
1940	—	—	23.7	—	6.1	5.9	12.8	19.4	28.6	36.1	21.8	23.6	22.1	31.2	15.0
1941	—	—	24.2	—	6.3	6.3	12.7	19.3	28.4	36.3	22.8	24.9	23.2	32.6	15.6
1942	—	—	24.7	—	7.2	6.7	12.6	19.2	28.3	38.3	26.7	29.0	27.0	37.7	17.6
1943	—	—	24.7	—	7.8	7.0	12.5	19.1	28.2	39.5	27.8	30.4	28.3	39.4	18.5
1944	—	—	24.8	—	7.9	7.3	12.4	19.0	28.2	40.7	29.8	32.5	29.7	42.4	19.3
1945	—	—	24.8	—	7.5	7.4	12.3	18.8	28.0	41.3	31.4	34.2	30.9	44.7	19.8
1946	—	—	25.0	—	7.6	7.9	12.1	18.3	26.9	41.3	34.4	37.7	35.1	48.0	22.2
1947	—	—	25.8	—	9.0	9.0	12.2	18.2	26.6	42.0	39.9	43.7	41.6	55.6	27.7
1948	—	—	27.5	—	11.5	10.6	12.6	18.7	26.8	44.1	42.5	46.4	43.9	58.9	30.3
1949	—	—	28.7	—	10.9	10.9	13.1	19.2	27.1	46.0	40.8	44.5	42.7	55.7	30.1
1950	—	—	29.7	—	11.0	11.3	13.2	19.2	27.2	49.5	40.3	44.0	42.5	53.8	30.5
1951	—	—	30.9	—	11.6	11.8	13.1	19.3	27.4	50.6	43.9	48.2	46.0	57.9	34.5
1952	—	—	32.2	—	11.9	12.1	13.4	19.5	27.6	52.5	43.5	47.6	46.2	57.2	33.8
1953	—	22.0	33.9	22.5	12.5	12.6	13.8	19.9	28.0	54.3	43.1	47.1	45.9	56.6	33.8
1954	—	22.5	35.1	22.6	12.6	12.6	14.1	20.2	28.1	53.4	43.1	46.9	45.6	56.1	34.2
1955	—	22.7	35.6	23.0	13.0	12.7	14.6	20.7	28.5	52.9	42.9	46.6	45.1	55.6	34.5
1956	—	23.1	36.3	23.6	13.6	13.3	14.9	20.9	28.6	53.5	43.7	47.4	45.9	56.0	36.4
1957	—	24.0	37.0	24.3	14.3	14.0	15.1	21.1	28.7	54.5	44.5	47.9	46.6	56.3	37.5
1958	—	24.5	37.6	24.8	13.5	13.7	16.0	21.9	29.1	56.1	44.6	47.9	46.4	56.2	38.1
1959	—	24.7	38.2	25.4	13.7	13.9	16.5	22.4	29.5	57.4	45.0	48.3	46.3	56.5	39.7
1960	—	25.2	38.7	26.0	13.5	13.8	17.6	23.3	29.9	58.3	45.7	49.0	47.2	56.7	41.1
1961	—	25.4	39.2	26.3	14.0	14.1	17.9	23.5	29.9	58.5	46.1	49.3	47.7	56.9	41.4
1962	—	25.8	39.7	26.3	14.0	14.2	17.9	23.5	29.9	58.5	46.3	49.5	48.0	56.8	42.0
1963	—	26.1	40.1	26.6	14.3	14.4	17.9	23.5	29.9	58.6	46.9	50.0	48.6	57.3	42.5
1964	—	26.5	40.5	26.6	14.0	14.4	17.9	23.5	29.8	58.6	47.3	50.4	49.3	57.6	42.6
1965	—	27.0	40.9	26.6	14.3	14.6	18.0	23.5	29.7	57.7	47.8	50.8	49.9	58.1	43.4
1966	—	27.8	41.5	26.7	14.7	15.0	18.1	23.6	29.7	56.5	49.0	52.1	51.2	59.2	46.0
1967	30.8	28.8	42.2	27.1	15.1	15.5	18.1	23.7	29.9	57.3	51.0	54.3	53.1	61.9	48.2
1968	32.0	30.1	43.3	27.4	15.6	16.0	18.2	23.9	30.2	57.3	53.7	57.3	56.1	65.6	50.8
1969	34.0	32.6	44.7	28.0	15.9	16.3	18.6	24.3	30.8	58.0	56.8	60.8	59.7	69.2	53.9
1970	36.4	35.5	46.5	29.1	16.5	17.0	19.6	25.4	31.8	58.7	59.2	63.3	62.2	71.8	56.8
1971	38.0	37.0	48.7	31.1	17.6	18.2	21.0	27.1	33.9	61.6	61.1	65.2	63.9	74.4	58.6
1972	39.4	38.7	50.4	32.5	17.6	18.3	22.1	28.5	35.6	65.0	62.3	66.6	64.7	76.2	60.3
1973	41.2	40.5	52.5	34.3	20.4	21.1	23.1	29.9	37.4	66.7	64.6	69.0	67.1	78.8	62.8
1974	45.8	44.4	55.2	40.7	32.2	33.2	26.0	34.5	44.1	69.5	69.4	73.9	72.4	83.5	66.6

(continued)

TABLE Cc6–48   Consumer price indexes for all urban consumers, for selected items and groups: 1935–1997   Continued

	Housing										Apparel and upkeep				
	All housing	Shelter		Fuel and other utilities							All apparel and upkeep	Apparel commodities			
		Overall	Rent, residential	All fuel and other utilities	Fuel oil	Fuel oil and other	Utility gas (piped)	Gas (piped) and electricity	Electricity	Telephone services		All apparel	Men and boys	Women and girls	Footwear
Year	Cc21 Index 1982–1984 = 100	Cc22 Index 1982–1984 = 100	Cc23 Index 1982–1984 = 100	Cc24 Index 1982–1984 = 100	Cc25 Index 1982–1984 = 100	Cc26 Index 1982–1984 = 100	Cc27 Index 1982–1984 = 100	Cc28 Index 1982–1984 = 100	Cc29 Index 1982–1984 = 100	Cc30 Index 1982–1984 = 100	Cc31 Index 1982–1984 = 100	Cc32 Index 1982–1984 = 100	Cc33 Index 1982–1984 = 100	Cc34 Index 1982–1984 = 100	Cc35 Index 1982–1984 = 100
1975	50.7	48.8	58.0	45.4	34.9	36.4	31.1	40.1	50.0	71.7	72.5	76.7	75.5	85.5	69.6
1976	53.8	51.5	61.1	49.4	37.4	38.8	36.3	44.7	53.1	74.3	75.2	79.2	78.1	87.9	72.3
1977	57.4	54.9	64.8	54.7	42.4	43.9	43.2	50.5	56.6	75.2	78.6	82.3	81.7	90.6	75.7
1978	62.4	60.5	69.3	58.5	44.9	46.2	47.5	55.0	60.9	76.0	81.4	84.5	83.5	92.4	79.0
1979	70.1	68.9	74.3	64.8	63.1	62.4	55.1	61.0	65.6	75.8	84.9	87.5	85.4	94.0	85.3
1980	81.1	81.0	80.9	75.4	87.7	86.1	65.7	71.4	75.8	77.7	90.9	92.9	89.4	96.0	91.8
1981	90.4	90.5	87.9	86.4	107.3	104.6	74.9	81.9	87.2	84.6	95.3	96.5	94.2	97.5	96.7
1982	96.9	96.9	94.6	94.9	105.0	103.4	89.8	93.2	95.8	93.2	97.8	98.3	97.6	98.5	99.1
1983	99.5	99.1	100.1	100.2	96.5	97.2	104.7	101.5	98.9	99.2	100.2	100.2	100.3	100.2	99.8
1984	103.6	104.0	105.3	104.8	98.5	99.4	105.5	105.4	105.3	107.5	102.1	101.5	102.1	101.3	101.1
1985	107.7	109.8	111.8	106.5	94.6	95.9	104.8	107.1	108.9	111.7	105.0	104.0	105.0	104.9	102.3
1986	110.9	115.8	118.3	104.1	74.1	77.6	99.7	105.7	110.4	117.2	105.9	104.2	106.2	104.0	101.9
1987	114.2	121.3	123.1	103.0	75.8	77.9	95.1	103.8	110.0	116.5	110.6	108.9	109.1	110.4	105.1
1988	118.5	127.1	127.8	104.4	75.8	78.1	94.5	104.6	111.5	116.0	115.4	113.7	113.4	114.9	109.9
1989	123.0	132.8	132.8	107.8	80.3	81.7	97.1	107.5	114.7	117.2	118.6	116.7	117.0	116.4	114.4
1990	128.5	140.0	138.4	111.6	98.6	99.3	97.3	109.3	117.4	117.7	124.1	122.0	120.4	122.6	117.4
1991	133.6	146.3	143.3	115.3	92.4	94.6	98.5	112.6	121.8	119.7	128.7	126.4	124.2	127.6	120.9
1992	137.5	151.2	146.9	117.8	88.0	90.7	100.3	114.8	124.2	120.4	131.9	129.4	126.5	130.4	125.0
1993	141.2	155.7	150.3	121.3	87.2	90.3	106.5	118.5	126.7	121.2	133.7	131.0	127.5	132.6	125.9
1994	144.8	160.5	154.0	122.8	85.6	88.8	108.5	119.2	126.7	123.1	133.4	130.4	126.4	130.9	126.0
1995	148.5	165.7	157.8	123.7	84.8	88.1	102.9	119.2	129.6	124.0	132.0	128.7	126.2	126.9	125.4
1996	152.8	171.0	162.0	127.5	97.0	99.2	107.2	122.1	131.8	125.9	131.7	128.2	127.7	124.7	126.6
1997	156.8	—	—	—	—	—	—	—	—	—	132.9	—	—	—	—

		Transportation				Medical care							
		Private transportation											
	All transportation	All private transportation	New vehicles	Motor fuel	Public transportation	All medical care	Physicians	Dental	Hospital room	Prescription drugs	Personal care	Entertainment	Energy
	Cc36	Cc37 [1]	Cc38	Cc39 [2]	Cc40	Cc41	Cc42	Cc43	Cc44	Cc45	Cc46	Cc47	Cc48
Year	Index 1982–1984 = 100	Index 1982–1984 = 100	Index 1982–1984 = 100	Index 1982–1984 = 100	Index 1982–1984 = 100	Index 1982–1984 = 100	Index 1982–1984 = 100	Index 1982–1984 = 100	Index 1982–1984 = 100	Index 1982–1984 = 100	Index 1982–1984 = 100	Index 1982–1984 = 100	Index 1982–1984 = 100
1935	14.2	14.5	20.3	13.1	9.1	10.2	11.1	13.4	2.1	30.6	14.2	—	—
1936	14.3	14.9	20.4	13.6	9.0	10.2	11.2	13.4	2.1	30.6	14.4	—	—
1937	14.5	15.4	20.8	14.2	8.9	10.3	11.2	13.7	2.1	30.8	15.2	—	—
1938	14.6	15.5	21.8	13.8	9.0	10.3	11.2	13.8	2.2	31.0	15.5	—	—
1939	14.3	14.9	21.3	12.9	9.1	10.3	11.2	13.8	2.2	31.0	15.5	—	—
1940	14.2	14.7	21.4	12.7	9.1	10.4	11.2	13.8	2.2	31.0	15.4	—	—
1941	14.7	15.5	23.0	13.3	9.1	10.4	11.3	13.8	2.3	31.4	15.8	—	—
1942	16.0	17.7	0.0	14.1	9.1	10.7	11.5	14.2	2.5	32.2	17.4	—	—
1943	15.9	17.4	0.0	14.3	9.2	11.2	12.3	14.8	2.6	32.5	19.2	—	—
1944	15.9	17.4	0.0	14.3	9.2	11.6	12.8	15.6	2.7	33.1	20.5	—	—
1945	15.9	17.3	0.0	14.2	9.2	11.9	13.1	16.3	2.9	33.5	21.2	—	—
1946	16.7	18.3	0.0	14.5	9.4	12.5	13.7	17.2	3.2	34.6	22.7	—	—
1947	18.5	20.8	34.1	16.4	9.9	13.5	14.6	18.7	3.8	38.1	25.4	—	—
1948	20.6	23.0	37.3	18.6	11.2	14.4	15.2	19.7	4.4	41.2	26.3	—	—
1949	22.1	24.4	40.9	19.1	12.4	14.8	15.5	20.5	4.8	42.2	26.2	—	—
1950	22.7	24.5	41.2	19.0	13.4	15.1	15.7	21.0	4.9	43.4	26.2	—	—
1951	24.1	25.6	43.1	19.5	14.8	15.9	16.3	21.8	5.4	45.5	28.7	—	—
1952	25.7	27.3	46.8	20.0	15.8	16.7	17.0	22.3	5.9	46.0	29.0	—	—
1953	26.5	27.8	47.3	21.2	16.8	17.3	17.4	23.0	6.3	46.0	29.3	—	—
1954	26.1	27.1	46.5	21.8	18.0	17.8	18.0	23.7	6.6	46.9	29.4	—	—
1955	25.8	26.7	44.9	22.1	18.5	18.2	18.6	24.0	6.9	47.6	29.9	—	—
1956	26.2	27.1	46.1	22.8	19.2	18.9	19.1	24.4	7.3	49.0	31.2	—	—
1957	27.7	28.6	48.6	23.8	19.9	19.7	20.0	25.0	7.9	50.7	32.3	—	—
1958	28.6	29.5	50.1	23.4	20.9	20.6	20.6	25.8	8.3	53.0	33.4	—	—
1959	29.8	30.8	52.3	23.7	21.5	21.5	21.3	26.4	8.7	54.2	34.1	—	—
1960	29.8	30.6	51.6	24.4	22.2	22.3	21.9	27.0	9.3	54.0	34.6	—	22.4
1961	30.1	30.8	51.6	24.1	23.2	22.9	22.4	27.1	9.9	52.2	34.8	—	22.5
1962	30.8	31.4	51.4	24.3	24.0	23.5	23.1	27.8	10.6	50.1	35.4	—	22.6
1963	30.9	31.6	51.1	24.2	24.3	24.1	23.6	28.6	11.1	48.9	35.9	—	22.6
1964	31.4	32.0	50.9	24.1	24.7	24.6	24.2	29.4	11.7	48.3	36.3	—	22.5
1965	31.9	32.5	49.8	25.1	25.2	25.2	25.1	30.3	12.3	47.8	36.6	—	22.9
1966	32.3	32.9	48.9	25.6	26.1	26.3	26.5	31.3	13.6	47.7	37.3	—	23.3
1967	33.3	33.8	49.3	26.4	27.4	28.2	28.4	32.8	16.2	46.8	38.4	40.7	23.8
1968	34.3	34.8	50.7	26.8	28.7	29.9	30.0	34.6	18.4	46.0	40.0	43.0	24.2
1969	35.7	36.0	51.5	27.6	30.9	31.9	32.1	37.1	20.9	46.6	42.0	45.2	24.8
1970	37.5	37.5	53.1	27.9	35.2	34.0	34.5	39.2	23.6	47.4	43.5	47.5	25.5
1971	39.5	39.4	55.3	28.1	37.8	36.1	36.9	41.7	26.5	47.4	44.9	50.0	26.5
1972	39.9	39.7	54.8	28.4	39.3	37.3	38.0	43.4	28.2	47.2	46.0	51.5	27.2
1973	41.2	41.0	54.8	31.2	39.7	38.8	39.3	44.8	29.6	47.1	48.1	52.9	29.4
1974	45.8	46.2	58.0	42.2	40.6	42.4	42.9	48.2	32.7	48.2	52.8	56.9	38.1

Notes appear at end of table

(continued)

TABLE Cc6–48   Consumer price indexes for all urban consumers, for selected items and groups: 1935–1997   Continued

| | Transportation | | | | | Medical care | | | | | | | |
| | All transportation | All private transportation [1] | New vehicles | Motor fuel [2] | Public transportation | All medical care | Physicians | Dental | Hospital room | Prescription drugs | Personal care | Entertainment | Energy |
Year	Cc36 Index 1982–1984 = 100	Cc37 Index 1982–1984 = 100	Cc38 Index 1982–1984 = 100	Cc39 Index 1982–1984 = 100	Cc40 Index 1982–1984 = 100	Cc41 Index 1982–1984 = 100	Cc42 Index 1982–1984 = 100	Cc43 Index 1982–1984 = 100	Cc44 Index 1982–1984 = 100	Cc45 Index 1982–1984 = 100	Cc46 Index 1982–1984 = 100	Cc47 Index 1982–1984 = 100	Cc48 Index 1982–1984 = 100
1975	50.1	50.6	63.0	45.1	43.5	47.5	48.1	53.2	38.3	51.2	57.9	62.0	42.1
1976	55.1	55.6	67.0	47.0	47.8	52.0	53.5	56.5	43.6	53.9	61.7	65.1	45.1
1977	59.0	59.7	70.5	49.7	50.0	57.0	58.5	60.8	48.6	57.2	65.7	68.3	49.4
1978	61.7	62.5	75.9	51.8	51.5	61.8	63.4	65.1	54.0	61.6	69.9	71.9	52.5
1979	70.5	71.7	81.9	70.1	54.9	67.5	69.2	70.5	60.1	66.4	75.2	76.7	65.7
1980	83.1	84.2	88.5	97.4	69.0	74.9	76.5	78.9	68.0	72.5	81.9	83.6	86.0
1981	93.2	93.8	93.9	108.5	85.6	82.9	84.9	86.5	78.1	80.8	89.1	90.1	97.7
1982	97.0	97.1	97.5	102.8	94.9	92.5	92.9	93.1	90.4	90.2	95.4	96.0	99.2
1983	99.3	99.3	99.9	99.4	99.5	100.6	100.1	99.4	100.6	100.1	100.3	100.1	99.9
1984	103.7	103.6	102.6	97.9	105.7	106.8	107.0	107.5	109.0	109.7	104.3	103.8	100.9
1985	106.4	106.2	106.1	98.7	110.5	113.5	113.3	114.2	115.4	120.1	108.3	107.9	101.6
1986	102.3	101.2	110.6	77.1	117.0	122.0	121.5	120.6	122.3	130.4	111.9	111.6	88.2
1987	105.4	104.2	114.4	80.2	121.1	130.1	130.4	128.8	131.1	140.8	115.1	115.3	88.6
1988	108.7	107.6	116.5	80.9	123.3	138.6	139.8	137.5	143.9	152.0	119.4	120.3	89.3
1989	114.1	112.9	119.2	88.5	129.5	149.3	150.1	146.1	160.5	165.2	125.0	126.5	94.3
1990	120.5	118.8	121.4	101.2	142.6	162.8	160.8	155.8	178.0	181.7	130.4	132.4	102.1
1991	123.8	121.9	126.0	99.4	148.9	177.0	170.5	167.4	191.9	199.7	134.9	138.4	102.5
1992	126.5	124.6	129.2	99.0	151.4	190.1	181.2	178.7	208.7	214.7	138.3	142.3	103.0
1993	130.4	127.5	132.7	98.0	167.0	201.4	191.3	188.1	226.4	223.0	141.5	145.8	104.2
1994	134.3	131.4	137.6	98.5	172.0	211.0	199.8	197.1	239.2	230.6	144.6	150.1	104.6
1995	139.1	136.3	141.0	100.0	175.9	220.5	208.8	206.8	251.2	235.0	147.1	153.9	—
1996	143.0	140.0	143.7	106.3	181.9	228.2	216.4	216.5	261.0	242.9	150.1	159.1	—
1997	144.3	—	—	—	—	234.6	—	—	—	—	—	—	—

[1] Includes direct pricing of new trucks and motorcycles beginning September 1982.

[2] Includes direct pricing of diesel fuel and gasohol beginning September 1981.

Sources

1935–1992: U.S Bureau of Labor Statistics (BLS), *Monthly Labor Review and CPI Detailed Report* (January issues), 1992–1996: *Statistical Abstract of the United States, 1997.* 1996–1997: Series CUUR0000SAO and so on from the BLS's Internet site.

Documentation

Represents annual averages of monthly figures, with 1982–1984 = 100.

Since 1978, the data reflect buying patterns of all urban consumers; earlier data are for urban wage earners and clerical workers.

TABLE Cc49-57   Consumer price indexes, for selected groups: 1851–1880   [Hoover]

Contributed by Peter H. Lindert

Year	Overall	All items except food	All items except rent	All items except food and rent	Food	Clothing	Rent	Fuel and light	Other
	Cc49	Cc50	Cc51	Cc52	Cc53	Cc54	Cc55	Cc56	Cc57
	Index 1860 = 100	Index 1860 = 100	Index 1860 = 100	Index 1860 = 100	Index 1860 = 100	Index 1860 = 100	Index 1860 = 100	Index 1860 = 100	Index 1860 = 100
1851	92	99	90	99	86	100	100	99	95
1852	93	100	91	100	87	101	100	99	95
1853	93	100	92	100	88	100	100	102	95
1854	101	103	101	103	100	100	102	113	96
1855	104	102	104	102	105	99	103	109	97
1856	102	102	102	101	102	100	103	106	96
1857	105	102	106	102	108	100	100	109	98
1858	99	100	99	100	99	99	100	103	98
1859	100	99	101	98	102	98	100	98	99
1860	100	100	100	100	100	100	100	100	100
1861	101	103	102	107	99	110	95	103	102
1862	113	120	115	131	107	143	101	112	105
1863	139	151	144	173	129	197	113	136	115
1864	176	187	185	222	167	261	130	155	141
1865	175	181	183	209	170	238	134	159	147
1866	167	163	172	178	169	194	138	152	146
1867	157	149	161	157	163	166	135	140	144
1868	154	141	157	143	164	148	138	133	144
1869	147	141	148	141	151	148	141	132	145
1870	141	137	141	135	143	141	142	126	143
1871	135	133	134	127	137	128	144	125	142
1872	135	132	133	125	136	126	144	122	141
1873	133	128	131	122	136	122	139	120	142
1874	129	122	128	116	134	115	133	114	141
1875	123	116	122	108	129	105	129	110	140
1876	119	118	118	106	124	104	123	106	138
1877	118	109	117	101	125	99	123	98	138
1878	111	107	108	96	113	95	124	93	135
1879	108	105	105	95	110	94	122	92	134
1880	110	108	106	96	111	94	127	95	133

Source

Ethel D. Hoover, "Prices in the 19th Century," in *Trends in the American Economy in the Nineteenth Century: A Report of the National Bureau of Economic Re-* *search,* Studies in Income and Wealth, volume 24 (Princeton University Press, 1960).

TABLE Cc58–59   Price indexes for rental housing in the New York metropolitan area: 1831–1860

Contributed by Robert A. Margo

Year	New York City Cc58 Index 1860 = 100	Outside New York City Cc59 Index 1860 = 100	Year	New York City Cc58 Index 1860 = 100	Outside New York City Cc59 Index 1860 = 100
1831	73.9	—	1850	84.9	84.9
1832	76.1	—	1851	92.6	88.6
1833	78.3	—	1852	93.4	87.6
1834	83.1	—	1853	94.1	80.1
1835	87.8	—	1854	94.7	95.0
1836	87.9	—	1855	97.8	83.6
1837	83.2	—	1856	90.1	77.0
1838	78.5	—	1857	97.2	79.0
1839	82.3	75.8	1858	108.0	87.1
1840	86.0	69.0	1859	112.3	82.5
1841	80.7	62.3	1860	100.0	100.0
1842	66.3	62.1			
1843	63.9	68.2			
1844	73.3	74.2			
1845	78.6	75.5			
1846	80.0	72.0			
1847	76.0	82.8			
1848	94.6	84.3			
1849	78.9	76.8			

Source

Robert A. Margo, "The Rental Price of Housing in New York City, 1830–1860," *Journal of Economic History* 56 (September 1996): 623.

Documentation

Data were collected from microfilm copies of advertisements for rental housing appearing in the *New York Daily Advertiser*, *New York Tribune*, and *New York Times*. The sampling procedure excluded advertisements that did not list a price or size of unit. Rents were generally stated by the week, month, or year. All information on the characteristics of the unit, including the street address, was recorded. From 1852 to 1860, the advertisements were selected from those appearing in the month of April, when the frequency of advertisements was greatest. Before 1852, advertisements were recorded throughout the year.

Approximately 1,000 housing units were included in the sample, 72 percent of which pertain to New York City proper, with the remainder (referred to as "outside New York City proper") located in Harlem, Brooklyn, or nearby locations in New York or New Jersey.

Price indexes were derived from hedonic regressions. The dependent variable was the logarithm of rental price, expressed on a per diem basis. Independent variables were the location of the unit, as indicated by neighborhood (for example, the Lower East Side) or distance in meters to New York City Hall (located in Lower Manhattan); characteristics of the unit (for example, the number of rooms, presence of bath facilities); and the time period (year, or group of years) in which the advertisement appeared. The coefficients of the time period variables were used to produce the price index, with 1860 set equal to 100. In the original article, the 1860 index value for housing units outside New York City was scaled so as to reflect the difference in rent for an unfurnished three-room apartment located in the Manhattan Central Business District compared with a Brooklyn location. For the purposes of this volume, this index value has been reset at 100. To convert the "outside New York City proper" index back to its original scale, multiply the index values for each year by 0.604.

TABLE Cc60   Rent indexes for dwelling units in five large cities: 1860–1880

Contributed by Robert A. Margo

| | Rent indexes for dwelling units | | | Rent indexes for dwelling units |
| | Cc60 | | | Cc60 |
Year	Index 1860 = 100	Year	Index 1860 = 100
1860	100	1875	162
1861	101	1876	147
1862	101	1877	148
1863	123	1878	152
1864	168	1879	148
1865	175	1880	151
1866	187		
1867	167		
1868	179		
1869	187		
1870	180		
1871	173		
1872	173		
1873	173		
1874	166		

Source

George F. Warren and Frank A. Pearson, *Prices* (Wiley, 1933), p. 267.

Documentation

The five cities are Boston, Philadelphia, Cincinnati, Louisville, and St. Louis.

The rental data were obtained from the special report by J. D. Weeks, "Report on the Average Retail Prices of Necessaries of Life in the United States," volume 20, *Tenth Census of the United States*, pp. 104–7. No information on the method of calculating the index was given in the source.

TABLE Cc61–62   Price of light, current and real: 1800–1992

Contributed by Robert A. Margo

| | Current price of light | Index of real price of light | | Current price of light | Index of real price of light |
| | Cc61 | Cc62 | | Cc61 | Cc62 |
Year	Dollars per 10,000 lumen-hours	Index 1800 = 100	Year	Dollars per 10,000 lumen-hours	Index 1800 = 100
1800	4.029	100.000	1916	0.035	0.997
1818	4.087	100.114	1920	0.063	0.984
1827	1.863	58.186	1930	0.051	0.954
1830	1.832	61.835	1940	0.032	0.720
1835	4.039	138.745	1950	0.024	0.314
1840	3.694	145.888	1960	0.021	0.219
1850	2.320	92.940	1970	0.018	0.142
1855	2.978	107.298	1980	0.045	0.170
1860	1.096	41.083	1990	0.060	0.144
1870	0.404	9.634	1992	0.012	0.029
1880	0.504	15.340			
1883	0.923	28.581			
1890	0.157	5.410			
1900	0.269	9.987			
1910	0.138	4.550			

Source

William D. Nordhaus, "Do Real-Output and Real-Wage Measures Capture Reality? The History of Lighting Suggests Not," in Timothy F. Bresnahan and Robert J. Gordon, editors, *The Economics of New Goods* (University of Chicago Press, 1997), pp. 46–7.

Documentation

The author used a variety of historical and contemporary sources to compute the current dollar cost of producing 1,000 lumen-hours of illumination from best-practice technology of the period (for example, candles in the early nineteenth century or light bulbs since their invention by Thomas Edison). These estimates have been converted into 10,000-lumen-hour units for ease of interpretation. To compute the "real price," the author converted the current price series into index number form (1800 = 100) and then deflated by the consumer price index (CPI). For further details on the methods of construction, consult the original article.

TABLE Cc63–65   Quality-adjusted price indexes for new and used automobiles: 1906–1983

Contributed by Robert A. Margo

Year	New automobiles Cc63 Index 1906 = 100	New automobiles Cc64 Index 1967 = 100	Late-model used automobiles Cc65 Index 1967 = 100	Year	New automobiles Cc63 Index 1906 = 100	New automobiles Cc64 Index 1967 = 100	Late-model used automobiles Cc65 Index 1967 = 100
1906	100.0	—	—	1960	—	98.0	98.0
1908	70.0	—	—	1961	—	99.0	97.0
1910	54.0	—	—	1962	—	103.0	98.0
1912	49.3	—	—	1963	—	101.0	106.2
1914	43.3	—	—	1964	—	100.0	106.2
1916	33.1	—	—	1965	—	98.0	104.1
1918	38.4	—	—	1966	—	99.0	94.2
1920	53.4	—	—	1967	—	100.0	100.0
1922	47.9	—	—	1968	—	104.1	107.3
1924	41.2	—	—	1969	—	102.0	104.1
1926	37.3	—	—	1970	—	105.1	103.0
1928	34.8	—	—	1971	—	112.7	120.9
1930	33.4	—	—	1972	—	108.3	128.4
1932	27.4	—	—	1973	—	106.2	127.1
1934	25.3	—	—	1974	—	113.9	131.0
1936	25.5	—	—	1975	—	133.6	160.0
1938	30.2	—	—	1976	—	140.5	178.6
1940	28.8	—	—	1977	—	144.8	176.8
1947	—	67.7	124.6	1978	—	166.5	205.3
1948	—	77.9	147.7	1979	—	173.3	201.4
1949	—	91.4	112.7	1980	—	193.5	224.8
1950	—	87.8	112.7	1981	—	243.5	274.6
1951	—	95.1	122.1	1982	—	263.8	300.4
1952	—	97.0	132.3	1983	—	274.6	335.4
1953	—	97.0	124.6				
1954	—	94.2	112.7				
1955	—	99.0	108.3				
1956	—	97.0	106.2				
1957	—	98.0	110.5				
1958	—	97.0	103.0				
1959	—	99.0	104.1				

Sources

Series Cc63. Daniel M. G. Raff and Manuel Trajtenberg, "Quality-Adjusted Prices for the American Automobile Industry: 1906-1940," in Timothy F. Bresnahan and Robert J. Gordon, editors, *The Economics of New Goods* (University of Chicago Press, 1997), p. 90.

Series Cc64–65. Robert J. Gordon, *The Measurement of Durable Goods Prices* (University of Chicago Press, 1990), p. 345.

Documentation

Series Cc63. The primary data source consists of tables specifying the characteristics of particular automobile models and the manufacturer's list price, as taken from trade publications printed contemporaneously with the New York Auto Show. Approximately 11,000 observations are contained in the data set. Owing to constraints on the scale of the project, the authors were able to collect data only for alternate pairs of years, starting in 1906. The authors estimate hedonic regressions for pairs of years (for example, 1910 and 1912), in which the dependent variable is the logarithm of the list price, and the independent variables are vehicle size, engine power, various technological indicators of the principal engineering systems (such as the rear axle, clutch, and so forth), and a dummy variable for the second year (in the preceding example, 1912). The coefficients of the year dummy variables are used to construct the price index, setting the value of the index for 1906 equal to 100. The price index is "quality-adjusted" because it controls (via the hedonic regression) for changes over time in the characteristics of automobiles (such as engine power), presumed by the authors to be related to the quality of the product. For further details, consult the series source, pp. 81-6.

Series Cc63–64. Data come from two sources. For 1947-1969, the source is the July 1 edition of National Market Reports, *Red Book: National Used Car Market Report,* yearly. For 1969-1983, the source is the National Automobile Dealers's Association, *Official Used Car Guide,* yearly. Both sources list new car prices, physical characteristics of cars, and estimated average retail prices for U.S. domestically produced automobiles (and, for some years, imports). Prices of new cars are manufacturer's list prices, which include cost of standard equipment, exclusive of state and local taxes, shipping, and dealer preparation costs. Used car prices are derived from information on retail and wholesale transactions by automobile dealers, and from wholesale auctions. The sample includes new car price information on all four-door sedans made by Chrysler, Ford, General Motors, and – beginning in 1977 – American Motors. "Luxury" makes (for example, Cadillac) are excluded. Prices pertain to so-called stripped models: all accessories are excluded except for a radio and heater. Sufficient information was available in the data sources to deduct the cost of other equipment (such as air-conditioning) that was standard on some models. The used-car sample consists of one- and two-year-old versions of the same makes and models in the new-car sample. The author estimates hedonic regressions for adjacent years (for example, 1970 and 1971), in which the dependent variable is the logarithm of the price of car, and the independent variables are physical characteristics (such as weight, length, "trim" line, engine power) and a dummy variable for the second year (in the preceding example, 1971). The coefficients of the year dummies are used to construct the price indexes. For further details, consult the series source, pp. 335-50.

Series Cc63–64. A single price index combining the new-car series for 1906-1940 with the new-car series for 1947-1983 can be constructed by multiplying each of the 1947-1983 index numbers by 0.513. For details on the splicing procedure, see Raff and Trajtenberg (1997), p. 90.

WHOLESALE AND PRODUCER PRICE INDEXES

Christopher Hanes

TABLE Cc66–83   Wholesale and producer price indexes, by commodity group: 1890–1997
[Bureau of Labor Statistics]

Contributed by Christopher Hanes

Year	All commodities	Industrial commodities	Farm products	Processed foods and feeds	Textile products and apparel	Hides, skins, leather, and related products	Fuels and related products and power	Chemicals and allied products	Rubber and plastic products
	Cc66	Cc67	Cc68	Cc69	Cc70	Cc71	Cc72	Cc73	Cc74
	Index 1982 = 100	Index 1982 = 100	Index 1982 = 100	Index 1982 = 100	Index 1982 = 100	Index 1982 = 100	Index 1982 = 100	Index 1982 = 100	Index 1982 = 100
1890	9.7	—	—	—	—	—	—	—	—
1891	9.6	—	—	—	—	—	—	—	—
1892	9.0	—	—	—	—	—	—	—	—
1893	9.2	—	—	—	—	—	—	—	—
1894	8.3	—	—	—	—	—	—	—	—
1895	8.4	—	—	—	—	—	—	—	—
1896	8.0	—	—	—	—	—	—	—	—
1897	8.0	—	—	—	—	—	—	—	—
1898	8.4	—	—	—	—	—	—	—	—
1899	9.0	—	—	—	—	—	—	—	—
1900	9.7	—	—	—	—	—	—	—	—
1901	9.5	—	—	—	—	—	—	—	—
1902	10.2	—	—	—	—	—	—	—	—
1903	10.3	—	—	—	—	—	—	—	—
1904	10.3	—	—	—	—	—	—	—	—
1905	10.4	—	—	—	—	—	—	—	—
1906	10.7	—	—	—	—	—	—	—	—
1907	11.2	—	—	—	—	—	—	—	—
1908	10.9	—	—	—	—	—	—	—	—
1909	11.7	—	—	—	—	—	—	—	—
1910	12.1	—	—	—	—	—	—	—	—
1911	11.2	—	—	—	—	—	—	—	—
1912	11.9	—	—	—	—	—	—	—	—
1913	12.0	11.9	18.0	—	—	—	—	—	—
1914	11.7	11.3	18.0	—	—	—	—	—	—
1915	12.0	11.6	18.0	—	—	—	—	—	—
1916	14.7	15.0	21.3	—	—	—	—	—	—
1917	20.3	19.5	32.6	—	—	—	—	—	—
1918	22.6	21.1	37.4	—	—	—	—	—	—
1919	23.9	22.0	39.8	—	—	—	—	—	—
1920	26.6	27.4	38.1	—	—	—	—	—	—
1921	16.8	17.8	22.3	—	—	—	—	—	—
1922	16.7	17.4	23.7	—	—	—	—	—	—
1923	17.4	17.8	24.9	—	—	—	—	—	—
1924	16.9	17.0	25.2	—	—	—	—	—	—
1925	17.9	17.5	27.7	—	—	—	—	—	—
1926	17.3	17.0	25.3	—	—	17.1	10.3	—	47.1
1927	16.4	16.0	25.1	—	—	18.4	9.1	—	35.7
1928	16.7	15.8	26.7	—	—	20.7	8.7	—	28.3
1929	16.4	15.6	26.4	—	—	18.6	8.6	—	24.6
1930	14.9	14.5	22.3	—	—	17.1	8.1	—	21.5
1931	12.5	12.8	16.4	—	—	14.7	7.0	—	18.3
1932	11.2	11.9	12.2	—	—	12.5	7.3	—	15.9
1933	11.4	12.1	13.0	—	—	13.8	6.9	16.2	16.7
1934	12.9	13.3	16.5	—	—	14.8	7.6	17.0	19.5
1935	13.8	13.3	19.9	—	—	15.3	7.6	17.7	19.6
1936	13.9	13.5	20.4	—	—	16.3	7.9	17.8	21.1
1937	14.9	14.5	21.9	—	—	17.9	8.0	18.6	24.9
1938	13.6	13.9	17.3	—	—	15.8	7.9	17.7	24.4
1939	13.3	13.8	16.5	—	—	16.3	7.5	17.6	25.4

(continued)

TABLE Cc66–83   Wholesale and producer price indexes, by commodity group: 1890–1997
[Bureau of Labor Statistics]   *Continued*

Year	All commodities	Industrial commodities	Farm products	Processed foods and feeds	Textile products and apparel	Hides, skins, leather, and related products	Fuels and related products and power	Chemicals and allied products	Rubber and plastic products
	Cc66	Cc67	Cc68	Cc69	Cc70	Cc71	Cc72	Cc73	Cc74
	Index 1982 = 100	Index 1982 = 100	Index 1982 = 100	Index 1982 = 100	Index 1982 = 100	Index 1982 = 100	Index 1982 = 100	Index 1982 = 100	Index 1982 = 100
1940	13.5	14.1	17.1	—	—	17.2	7.4	17.9	23.7
1941	15.0	15.1	20.8	—	—	18.4	7.9	19.5	25.5
1942	17.0	16.2	26.7	—	—	20.1	8.1	21.6	29.7
1943	17.8	16.5	30.9	—	—	20.1	8.3	21.9	30.5
1944	17.9	16.7	31.2	—	—	19.9	8.6	22.2	30.1
1945	18.2	17.0	32.4	—	—	20.1	8.7	22.3	29.2
1946	20.8	18.6	37.5	—	—	23.3	9.3	24.1	29.3
1947	25.6	22.7	45.2	33.0	50.7	31.7	11.1	32.0	29.2
1948	27.7	24.6	48.5	35.3	52.9	32.1	13.1	32.8	30.1
1949	26.3	24.1	41.9	32.0	48.4	30.4	12.4	30.0	29.2
1950	27.3	25.0	44.1	33.2	50.2	32.8	12.6	30.4	35.5
1951	30.4	27.6	51.2	36.9	56.0	37.7	13.0	34.8	43.7
1952	29.6	26.9	48.4	36.4	50.6	30.5	13.0	33.0	39.6
1953	29.2	27.1	43.8	34.8	49.3	30.9	13.3	33.4	36.9
1954	29.3	27.2	43.2	35.4	48.2	29.6	13.2	33.9	37.4
1955	29.4	27.8	40.5	33.8	48.2	29.4	13.2	33.7	42.4
1956	30.3	29.1	40.0	33.7	48.2	31.2	13.6	33.9	43.0
1957	31.2	29.9	41.1	34.8	48.3	31.2	14.3	34.6	42.8
1958	31.6	30.0	42.8	36.5	47.4	31.6	13.7	34.9	42.8
1959	31.7	30.5	40.2	35.6	48.1	35.9	13.7	34.8	42.6
1960	31.7	30.5	40.1	35.6	48.6	34.6	13.9	34.8	42.7
1961	31.6	30.4	39.8	36.2	47.8	34.9	14.0	34.5	41.1
1962	31.7	30.4	40.4	36.5	48.2	35.3	14.0	33.9	39.9
1963	31.6	30.3	39.6	36.8	48.2	34.3	13.9	33.5	40.1
1964	31.6	30.5	39.0	36.7	48.5	34.4	13.5	33.6	39.6
1965	32.3	30.9	40.7	38.0	48.8	35.9	13.8	33.9	39.7
1966	33.3	31.6	43.7	40.2	49.0	39.4	14.1	34.0	40.5
1967	33.4	32.0	41.3	39.8	48.9	38.1	14.4	34.2	41.5
1968	34.2	32.9	42.3	40.7	50.7	39.3	14.3	34.1	42.8
1969	35.6	33.9	45.0	42.7	51.8	41.5	14.6	34.2	43.6
1970	36.9	35.2	45.8	44.6	52.3	42.0	15.3	35.0	44.9
1971	38.1	36.5	46.6	45.5	53.3	43.4	16.6	35.6	45.2
1972	39.8	37.7	51.6	48.0	55.5	50.0	17.1	35.6	45.3
1973	45.0	40.3	72.8	58.9	60.5	54.5	19.4	37.6	46.6
1974	53.5	49.2	77.5	67.9	68.0	55.2	30.1	50.2	56.4
1975	58.4	54.9	77.0	72.6	67.4	56.6	35.4	62.0	62.2
1976	61.1	58.4	78.8	70.8	72.4	63.9	38.3	64.0	66.0
1977	64.9	62.5	79.4	74.0	75.3	68.3	43.6	66.0	69.4
1978	69.9	67.1	87.7	80.6	78.1	76.1	46.5	68.0	72.4
1979	78.7	75.7	99.6	88.5	82.5	96.1	58.9	76.0	80.5
1980	89.8	88.0	102.9	95.9	89.7	94.7	82.8	89.1	90.1
1981	98.0	97.4	105.2	98.9	97.6	99.3	100.2	98.4	96.4
1982	100.0	100.0	100.0	100.0	100.0	100.0	100.0	100.0	100.0
1983	101.3	101.1	102.4	101.8	100.3	103.2	95.9	100.3	100.8
1984	103.7	103.3	105.5	105.4	102.7	109.0	94.7	102.9	102.3
1985	103.2	103.7	95.1	103.5	102.9	108.9	91.4	103.7	101.9
1986	100.2	100.0	92.9	105.4	103.2	113.0	69.8	102.6	101.9
1987	102.8	102.6	95.5	107.9	105.1	120.4	70.2	106.4	103.0
1988	106.9	106.3	104.9	112.7	109.2	131.4	66.7	116.3	109.3
1989	112.2	111.6	110.9	117.8	112.3	136.3	72.9	123.0	112.6
1990	116.3	115.8	112.2	121.9	115.0	141.7	82.3	123.6	113.6
1991	116.5	116.5	105.7	121.9	116.3	138.8	81.2	125.6	115.1
1992	117.2	117.4	103.6	122.1	117.8	140.4	80.4	125.9	115.1
1993	118.9	119.0	107.1	124.0	118.0	143.7	80.0	128.2	116.0
1994	120.5	120.7	106.3	125.5	118.3	148.5	77.8	132.1	117.7
1995	124.8	125.5	107.4	127.0	120.8	153.7	78.0	142.5	124.3
1996	127.7	127.3	122.4	133.3	122.4	150.5	85.8	142.1	123.8
1997	127.6	127.7	112.9	134.0	122.7	154.2	86.1	143.6	123.2

TABLE Cc66–83   Wholesale and producer price indexes, by commodity group: 1890–1997
    [Bureau of Labor Statistics]   *Continued*

Year	Lumber and wood products Cc75 Index 1982 = 100	Pulp, paper, and allied products Cc76 Index 1982 = 100	Metals and metal products Cc77 Index 1982 = 100	Machinery and equipment Cc78 Index 1982 = 100	Furniture and household durables Cc79 Index 1982 = 100	Nonmetallic mineral products Cc80 Index 1982 = 100	Transportation equipment Cc81 Index 1982 = 100	Motor vehicles and equipment Cc82 Index 1982 = 100	Miscellaneous products Cc83 Index 1982 = 100
1926	9.3	—	13.7	—	28.5	16.4	—	16.7	—
1927	8.8	—	12.9	—	27.9	15.7	—	16.0	—
1928	8.5	—	12.9	—	27.2	16.2	—	16.2	—
1929	8.8	—	13.3	—	26.9	16.0	—	16.7	—
1930	8.0	—	12.0	—	26.5	15.9	—	15.7	—
1931	6.5	—	10.8	—	24.4	14.9	—	14.9	—
1932	5.6	—	9.9	—	21.5	13.9	—	14.5	—
1933	6.7	—	10.2	—	21.5	14.7	—	13.9	—
1934	7.8	—	11.2	—	23.4	15.7	—	14.6	—
1935	7.5	—	11.2	—	23.2	15.7	—	14.0	—
1936	7.9	—	11.4	—	23.6	15.7	—	13.9	—
1937	9.3	—	13.1	—	26.1	16.1	—	14.9	—
1938	8.5	—	12.6	—	25.5	15.6	—	15.9	—
1939	8.7	—	12.5	14.8	25.4	15.3	—	15.6	—
1940	9.6	—	12.5	14.8	26.0	15.3	—	16.1	—
1941	11.5	—	12.8	15.1	27.6	15.7	—	17.2	—
1942	12.5	—	13.0	15.3	29.8	16.3	—	18.8	—
1943	13.2	—	12.9	15.2	29.6	16.3	—	18.8	—
1944	14.3	—	12.9	15.1	30.5	16.7	—	18.9	—
1945	14.5	—	13.1	15.1	30.5	17.4	—	19.2	—
1946	16.6	—	14.7	16.6	32.4	18.5	—	22.3	—
1947	25.8	25.1	18.2	19.3	37.2	20.7	—	25.5	26.6
1948	29.5	26.2	20.7	20.9	39.4	22.4	—	28.2	27.7
1949	27.3	25.1	20.9	21.9	40.1	23.0	—	30.1	28.2
1950	31.4	25.7	22.0	22.6	41.0	23.5	—	30.0	28.7
1951	34.1	30.5	24.5	25.3	44.4	25.0	—	31.6	30.4
1952	33.2	29.7	24.5	25.3	43.5	25.0	—	33.4	30.2
1953	33.1	29.6	25.3	25.9	44.4	26.0	—	33.3	30.9
1954	32.5	29.6	25.5	26.3	44.8	26.6	—	33.3	31.2
1955	34.1	30.4	27.2	27.2	45.1	27.3	—	34.4	31.3
1956	34.6	32.4	29.6	29.4	46.3	28.5	—	36.3	31.7
1957	32.8	33.0	30.1	31.4	47.5	29.6	—	37.9	32.6
1958	32.4	33.4	30.0	32.1	47.9	29.9	—	39.1	33.3
1959	34.7	33.7	30.6	32.8	48.0	30.3	—	39.9	33.4
1960	33.5	33.9	30.7	33.0	47.8	30.4	—	39.4	33.6
1961	32.0	33.0	30.5	33.0	47.5	30.5	—	39.2	33.8
1962	32.1	33.4	30.2	33.0	47.2	30.5	—	39.2	33.9
1963	32.9	33.1	30.3	33.1	46.9	30.3	—	38.9	34.2
1964	33.5	33.0	31.1	33.3	47.1	30.4	—	39.1	34.4
1965	33.7	33.3	32.0	33.7	46.8	30.4	—	39.2	34.7
1966	35.2	34.2	32.8	34.7	47.4	30.7	—	39.2	35.3
1967	35.1	34.6	33.2	35.9	48.3	31.2	—	39.8	36.2
1968	39.8	35.0	34.0	37.0	49.7	32.4	—	40.9	37.0
1969	44.0	36.1	36.0	38.2	50.7	33.6	40.4	41.7	38.0
1970	39.9	37.5	38.7	40.0	51.9	35.3	41.9	43.2	39.8
1971	44.7	38.1	39.4	41.4	53.1	38.2	44.2	45.7	40.9
1972	50.7	39.3	40.9	42.3	53.8	39.4	45.6	47.0	41.4
1973	62.2	42.3	44.0	43.7	55.6	40.7	46.1	47.4	43.3
1974	64.5	52.6	57.0	50.0	61.8	47.8	50.3	51.4	48.1
1975	62.1	59.0	61.6	57.9	67.5	54.4	56.7	57.6	53.4
1976	72.2	62.2	65.0	61.4	70.3	58.2	60.6	61.2	55.6
1977	83.0	64.6	69.3	65.2	73.2	62.6	64.6	65.2	59.4
1978	96.9	67.7	75.3	70.3	77.5	69.6	69.5	70.1	66.7
1979	105.5	75.9	86.0	76.7	82.8	77.6	75.3	75.8	75.5
1980	101.5	86.3	95.0	86.0	90.7	88.4	82.9	83.1	93.6
1981	102.8	94.9	99.6	94.5	95.9	96.7	94.3	94.6	96.1
1982	100.0	100.0	100.0	100.0	100.0	100.0	100.0	100.0	100.0
1983	107.9	103.3	101.9	102.8	103.4	101.6	102.8	102.2	104.8
1984	108.0	110.3	104.8	105.1	105.7	105.3	105.2	104.1	107.0

(continued)

TABLE Cc66–83   Wholesale and producer price indexes, by commodity group: 1890–1997
[Bureau of Labor Statistics]   *Continued*

Year	Lumber and wood products	Pulp, paper, and allied products	Metals and metal products	Machinery and equipment	Furniture and household durables	Nonmetallic mineral products	Transportation equipment	Motor vehicles and equipment	Miscellaneous products
	Cc75	Cc76	Cc77	Cc78	Cc79	Cc80	Cc81	Cc82	Cc83
	Index 1982 = 100	Index 1982 = 100	Index 1982 = 100	Index 1982 = 100	Index 1982 = 100	Index 1982 = 100	Index 1982 = 100	Index 1982 = 100	Index 1982 = 100
1985	106.6	113.3	104.4	107.2	107.1	108.6	107.9	106.4	109.4
1986	107.3	116.2	103.2	108.8	108.2	110.0	110.5	109.1	111.6
1987	112.8	121.8	107.1	110.4	109.9	110.0	112.5	111.7	114.9
1988	118.9	130.4	118.7	113.2	113.1	111.2	114.3	113.1	120.2
1989	126.7	137.8	124.1	117.4	116.9	112.6	117.7	116.2	126.5
1990	129.7	141.2	122.9	120.7	119.2	114.7	121.5	118.2	134.2
1991	132.1	142.9	120.2	123.0	121.2	117.2	126.4	122.1	140.8
1992	146.6	145.2	119.2	123.3	122.2	117.3	130.4	124.9	145.3
1993	174.0	147.4	119.2	124.0	123.7	120.0	133.7	128.0	145.4
1994	180.0	152.5	124.8	125.1	126.1	124.2	137.2	131.4	141.9
1995	178.1	172.2	134.5	126.6	128.2	129.0	139.6	133.0	145.4
1996	176.1	168.7	131.0	126.5	130.4	131.0	141.8	134.1	147.7
1997	183.8	167.9	131.8	125.9	130.8	133.2	141.6	132.7	150.9

Source

For 1890–1926: U.S. Bureau of Labor Statistics (BLS), *Handbook of Labor Statistics,* Bulletin number 1,016 (1950), p. 118. For 1926–1977: U.S. Bureau of Labor Statistics, *Handbook of Labor Statistics,* Bulletin number 2,000 (1978), p. 437. For 1977–1997: BLS Internet site. For updates, see the BLS's Internet site.

Documentation

The index numbers are annual averages of monthly figures, with 1982 = 100.

The current BLS producer price indexes by commodity group were begun in 1952 but calculated back to 1947. A series was spliced to an old wholesale price index series (in Table Cc84–95) by linking as of January 1947, if the value aggregate of commodities in the old series represented 50 percent or more of the value of shipments in 1947 for all commodities (priced and unpriced) in the new series. The new series Cc67 for industrial commodities was spliced to the old series for all commodities other than farm products and foods, included in this volume as series Cc85.

For a more complete description of techniques used in compiling the index, see BLS Bulletin number 1,458, *Handbook of Methods for Surveys and Studies* (1966), Chapter 11, and BLS Bulletin number 2,414, *BLS Handbook of Methods* (1992), Chapter 16.

TABLE Cc84-95　Wholesale price indexes, by commodity group: 1890-1951　[Bureau of Labor Statistics]

Contributed by Christopher Hanes

Year	All commodities Cc84 Index 1926 = 100	All commodities other than farm products and foods Cc85 Index 1926 = 100	Farm products Cc86 Index 1926 = 100	Foods Cc87 Index 1926 = 100	Hides and leather products Cc88 Index 1926 = 100	Textile products Cc89 Index 1926 = 100	Fuel and lighting Cc90 Index 1926 = 100	Metals and metal products Cc91 Index 1926 = 100	Building materials Cc92 Index 1926 = 100	Chemicals and allied products Cc93 Index 1926 = 100	House furnishing goods Cc94 Index 1926 = 100	Miscellaneous goods Cc95 Index 1926 = 100
1890	56.2	—	50.4	55.5	47.5	57.8	38.1	105.3	46.5	73.2	49.9	97.9
1891	55.8	—	54.2	54.8	47.9	54.6	37.0	92.2	44.2	74.0	50.4	94.3
1892	52.2	—	49.5	51.0	47.2	55.2	34.8	84.0	41.7	74.6	48.1	86.6
1893	53.4	—	51.3	54.7	45.1	54.1	35.3	76.8	41.6	72.7	48.1	89.0
1894	47.9	—	44.6	48.2	43.0	46.1	34.3	65.7	39.8	65.5	45.3	86.4
1895	48.8	—	43.9	47.3	49.4	44.3	40.3	70.4	38.8	64.7	43.5	88.9
1896	46.5	—	39.6	44.1	45.2	43.1	39.5	71.2	38.9	65.0	43.4	90.2
1897	46.6	—	42.5	45.5	45.9	42.9	33.9	65.0	37.4	70.9	42.5	92.5
1898	48.5	—	44.9	47.8	48.3	44.9	34.5	65.3	39.6	77.4	44.0	93.4
1899	52.2	—	45.8	47.7	49.4	47.7	41.2	100.0	43.6	81.1	45.0	97.4
1900	56.1	—	50.5	50.8	49.4	53.3	46.3	98.0	46.2	82.1	48.9	102.0
1901	55.3	—	52.8	50.5	48.9	48.1	44.6	93.1	44.3	84.2	48.9	93.4
1902	58.9	—	58.4	53.3	50.8	49.4	51.8	91.0	45.3	86.5	49.2	88.1
1903	59.6	—	55.6	52.0	49.9	52.8	60.3	90.2	46.7	84.1	50.9	98.9
1904	59.7	—	58.5	54.0	49.7	52.9	53.3	79.9	45.0	84.1	50.3	109.5
1905	60.1	—	56.4	55.1	53.9	54.1	49.6	89.1	48.1	82.3	49.7	117.4
1906	61.8	—	57.3	53.4	57.7	58.7	52.0	102.4	54.0	76.8	51.3	115.3
1907	65.2	—	62.2	57.0	58.0	65.5	54.4	109.8	56.8	78.5	55.0	108.2
1908	62.9	—	62.2	58.7	55.6	54.8	53.7	86.3	52.0	79.6	51.6	97.8
1909	67.6	—	69.6	62.6	61.5	56.5	51.6	84.5	53.7	79.9	51.7	129.6
1910	70.4	—	74.3	64.9	60.2	58.4	47.6	85.2	55.3	82.0	54.0	152.7
1911	64.9	—	66.8	62.0	58.8	55.5	46.7	80.8	55.3	81.6	52.7	108.6
1912	69.1	—	72.6	66.8	64.5	55.7	51.4	89.5	55.9	80.7	53.0	106.4
1913	69.8	70.0	71.5	64.2	68.1	57.3	61.3	90.8	56.7	80.2	56.1	93.1
1914	68.1	66.4	71.2	64.7	70.9	54.6	56.6	80.2	52.7	81.4	56.5	89.9
1915	69.5	68.0	71.5	65.4	75.5	54.1	51.8	86.3	53.5	112.0	56.0	86.9
1916	85.5	88.3	84.4	75.7	93.4	70.4	74.3	116.5	67.6	160.7	61.4	100.6
1917	117.5	114.2	129.0	104.5	123.8	98.7	105.4	150.6	88.2	165.0	74.2	122.1
1918	131.3	124.6	148.0	119.1	125.7	137.2	109.2	136.5	98.6	182.3	93.3	134.4
1919	138.6	128.8	157.6	129.5	174.1	135.3	104.3	130.9	115.6	157.0	105.9	139.1
1920	154.4	161.3	150.7	137.4	171.3	164.8	163.7	149.4	150.1	164.7	141.8	167.5
1921	97.6	104.9	88.4	90.6	109.2	94.5	96.8	117.5	97.4	115.0	113.0	109.2
1922	96.7	102.4	93.8	87.6	104.6	100.2	107.3	102.9	97.3	100.3	103.5	92.8
1923	100.6	104.3	98.6	92.7	104.2	111.3	97.3	109.3	108.7	101.1	108.9	99.7
1924	98.1	99.7	100.0	91.0	101.5	106.7	92.0	106.3	102.3	98.9	104.9	93.6
1925	103.5	102.6	109.8	100.2	105.3	108.3	96.5	103.2	101.7	101.8	103.1	109.0
1926	100.0	100.0	100.0	100.0	100.0	100.0	100.0	100.0	100.0	100.0	100.0	100.0
1927	95.4	94.0	99.4	96.7	107.7	95.6	88.3	96.3	94.7	96.1	97.5	91.0
1928	96.7	92.9	105.9	101.0	121.4	95.5	84.3	97.0	94.1	95.0	95.1	85.4
1929	95.3	91.6	104.9	99.9	109.1	90.4	83.0	100.5	95.4	94.0	94.3	82.6

(continued)

TABLE Cc84–95 Wholesale price indexes, by commodity group: 1890–1951 [Bureau of Labor Statistics] Continued

Year	All commodities Cc84 Index 1926 = 100	All commodities other than farm products and foods Cc85 Index 1926 = 100	Farm products Cc86 Index 1926 = 100	Foods Cc87 Index 1926 = 100	Hides and leather products Cc88 Index 1926 = 100	Textile products Cc89 Index 1926 = 100	Fuel and lighting Cc90 Index 1926 = 100	Metals and metal products Cc91 Index 1926 = 100	Building materials Cc92 Index 1926 = 100	Chemicals and allied products Cc93 Index 1926 = 100	House furnishing goods Cc94 Index 1926 = 100	Miscellaneous goods Cc95 Index 1926 = 100
1930	86.4	85.2	88.3	90.5	100.0	80.3	78.5	92.1	89.9	88.7	92.7	77.7
1931	73.0	75.0	64.8	74.6	86.1	66.3	67.5	84.5	79.2	79.3	84.9	69.8
1932	64.8	70.2	48.2	61.0	72.9	54.9	70.3	80.2	71.4	73.9	75.1	64.4
1933	65.9	71.2	51.4	60.5	80.9	64.8	66.3	79.8	77.0	72.1	75.8	62.5
1934	74.9	78.4	65.3	70.5	86.6	72.9	73.3	86.4	86.2	75.3	81.5	69.7
1935	80.0	77.9	78.8	83.7	89.6	70.9	73.5	86.4	85.3	79.0	80.6	68.3
1936	80.8	79.6	80.9	82.1	95.4	71.5	76.2	87.0	86.7	78.7	81.7	70.5
1937	86.3	85.3	86.4	85.5	104.6	76.3	77.6	95.7	95.2	82.6	89.7	77.8
1938	78.6	81.7	68.5	73.6	92.8	66.7	76.5	95.7	90.3	77.0	86.8	73.3
1939	77.1	81.3	65.3	70.4	95.6	69.7	73.1	94.4	90.5	76.0	86.3	74.8
1940	78.6	83.0	67.7	71.3	100.8	73.8	71.7	95.8	94.8	77.0	88.5	77.3
1941	87.3	89.0	82.4	82.7	108.3	84.8	76.2	99.4	103.2	84.4	94.3	82.0
1942	98.8	95.5	105.9	99.6	117.7	96.9	78.5	103.8	110.2	95.5	102.4	89.7
1943	103.1	96.9	122.6	106.6	117.5	97.4	80.8	103.8	111.4	94.9	102.7	92.2
1944	104.0	98.5	123.3	104.9	116.7	98.4	83.0	103.8	115.5	95.2	104.3	93.6
1945	105.8	99.7	128.2	106.2	118.1	100.1	84.0	104.7	117.8	95.2	104.5	94.7
1946	121.1	109.5	148.9	130.7	137.2	116.3	90.1	115.5	132.6	101.4	111.6	100.3
1947	152.1	135.2	181.2	168.7	182.4	141.7	108.7	145.0	179.7	127.3	131.1	115.5
1948	165.1	151.0	188.3	179.1	188.8	149.8	134.2	163.6	199.1	135.7	144.5	120.5
1949	155.0	147.3	165.5	161.4	180.4	140.4	131.7	170.2	193.4	118.6	145.3	112.3
1950	161.5	153.2	170.4	166.2	191.9	148.0	133.2	173.6	206.0	122.7	153.2	120.9
1951	180.4	169.4	196.1	186.9	221.4	172.2	138.2	189.2	225.5	143.3	176.0	141.0

Sources

For 1890–1950: U.S. Bureau of Labor Statistics (BLS), *Handbook of Labor Statistics* (1950), p. 118. For 1951: U.S. Bureau of Labor Statistics, *Handbook of Labor Statistics* (1951), supplement, p. 42.

Documentation

The index numbers are annual averages of monthly figures, with 1926 = 100.

These series were the standard BLS wholesale price indexes (WPIs) prior to the major revision of the WPI program in 1952. Even before 1952, there were important changes from time to time in lists of items, weighting factors, base periods, and methods of computing the indexes.

The BLS began regular publication of wholesale price indexes in 1902. The first published indexes were unweighted averages of price relatives on a base 1890–1899 (U.S. Bureau of Labor, Bulletin number 39, March 1902). In 1914, the BLS recalculated its WPI series back to 1890 using weights that reflected the quantity of each priced item marketed in 1909. The system of classification for group indexes was generally according to origin, rather than end use, and each commodity was included in only one group index. From 1914 until 1921, the index series were continued with little change except for occasional rebasing and additions to the list of priced items.

In 1921, a revision of the indexes extended the commodity coverage to include about 400 items, as compared with 250 to 325 in previous years. The weighting factors were changed to represent quantities marketed in 1919. An important change was made in the method of grouping commodities. Articles properly classified in more than one major group were included in the appropriate groups with their total weights, but in the all-commodities index, the weights for such articles were counted only once.

In 1927, a 1926 base period was adopted and the indexes were recalculated back to 1913 with new sets of weights (see U.S. Bureau of Labor Statistics, Bulletin number 473, *Wholesale Prices, 1913 to 1927*, pp. 2–5). The figures for 1890–1912 were converted, not recalculated in detail.

In subsequent years, weights were occasionally revised. Major additions to the lists of priced items in 1931 and again in 1940 provided better coverage of manufactured articles.

Because of changes in the list of commodities and in the weighting factors, the indexes were calculated by the chain relative method. In this way, comparisons between any two periods were based on the same commodities, with the same weights.

The following table contains a summary of the number of commodities and the weights used for the indexes from 1890 through 1951.

Price quotations were obtained by mail from leading manufacturers or selling agents, or from sources such as trade publications, reports of boards of trade, and produce exchanges. Prices were usually net cash prices, f.o.b. (free on board, that is, exclusive of freight, insurance, and any taxes), unless it was customary for an industry to quote on the delivered basis. For articles subject to frequent fluctuations in price, monthly averages were made up of daily quotations or quotations for one day in each week. For other articles, monthly, quarterly, or semiannual quotations were secured. Before 1913, most prices were from the New York market, but after 1913, quotations were obtained in several major markets for a number of important commodities.

The BLS generally attempted to specify the quality of a priced item as precisely as possible, including the principal price-determining characteristics, terms of sale, and other details. By 1931, the BLS had developed a formal specification for each commodity in the index. Over subsequent years, specifications were refined and improved.

Number of price series and weighting factors used in BLS wholesale price index [All commodities: 1890 to 1951]

Year	Number of series	Weights used
1890–1912	251–261	Quantities marketed 1909
1913	252	Quantities marketed 1909 and 1914
1914–1919	296–371	Quantities marketed 1914 and 1919
1920–1921	390–450	Quantities marketed 1919 and 1921
1922–1923	450–478	Quantities marketed 1921 and 1923
1924–1925	526–528	Quantities marketed 1921 and 1923
1926–1929	404–550	Quantities marketed 1923 and 1925
1930	550	Quantities marketed 1923 and 1925
1931	784	Quantities marketed 1925 and 1927
1932–1933	784	Quantities marketed 1927 and 1929
1934–1937	784	Quantities marketed 1927 and 1929
1938–1939	813	Quantities marketed 1927 and 1929
1940–1948	881–890	Quantities marketed 1927 and 1929
1949–1951	900–947	Quantities marketed 1929 and 1931

TABLE Cc96–108   Producer price indexes, by stage of processing and commodity group: 1947–1998   [Bureau of Labor Statistics]

Contributed by Christopher Hanes

	Finished goods			Intermediate goods								Crude materials				
				All intermediate goods	Materials and components											
	All finished goods	Consumer goods	Capital equipment		For construction	For manufacturing	Processed fuels and lubricants	Containers	Supplies		All crude materials	Foodstuffs and feedstuffs	Nonfood materials, except fuel	Fuel
	Cc96	Cc97	Cc98	Cc99	Cc100	Cc101	Cc102	Cc103	Cc104		Cc105	Cc106	Cc107	Cc108
Year	Index 1982 = 100	Index 1982 = 100	Index 1982 = 100	Index 1982 = 100	Index 1982 = 100	Index 1982 = 100	Index 1982 = 100	Index 1982 = 100	Index 1982 = 100		Index 1982 = 100	Index 1982 = 100	Index 1982 = 100	Index 1982 = 100
1947	26.4	28.6	19.8	23.3	22.5	24.9	14.4	23.4	28.5		31.7	45.1	24.0	7.5
1948	28.5	30.8	21.6	25.2	24.9	26.8	16.4	24.4	29.8		34.7	48.8	26.7	8.9
1949	27.7	29.4	22.7	24.2	24.9	25.7	14.9	24.5	28.0		30.1	40.5	24.3	8.8
1950	28.2	29.9	23.2	25.3	26.2	26.9	15.2	25.2	29.0		32.7	43.4	27.8	8.8
1951	30.8	32.7	25.5	28.4	28.7	30.5	15.9	29.6	32.6		37.6	50.2	32.0	9.0
1952	30.6	32.3	25.9	27.5	28.5	29.3	15.7	28.0	32.6		34.5	47.3	27.8	9.0
1953	30.3	31.7	26.3	27.7	29.0	29.7	15.8	28.0	31.0		31.9	42.3	26.6	9.3
1954	30.4	31.7	26.7	27.9	29.1	29.8	15.8	28.5	31.7		31.6	42.3	26.1	8.9
1955	30.5	31.5	27.4	28.4	30.3	30.5	15.8	28.9	31.2		30.4	38.4	27.5	8.9
1956	31.3	32.0	29.5	29.6	31.8	32.0	16.3	31.0	32.0		30.6	37.6	28.6	9.5
1957	32.5	32.9	31.3	30.3	32.0	32.7	17.2	32.4	32.3		31.2	39.2	28.2	10.1
1958	33.2	33.6	32.1	30.4	32.0	32.8	16.2	33.2	33.1		31.9	41.6	27.1	10.2
1959	33.1	33.3	32.7	30.8	32.9	33.3	16.2	33.0	33.5		31.1	38.8	28.1	10.4
1960	33.4	33.6	32.8	30.8	32.7	33.3	16.6	33.4	33.3		30.4	38.4	26.9	10.5
1961	33.4	33.6	32.9	30.6	32.2	32.9	16.8	33.2	33.7		30.2	37.9	27.2	10.5
1962	33.5	33.7	33.0	30.6	32.1	32.7	16.7	33.6	34.5		30.5	38.6	27.1	10.4
1963	33.4	33.5	33.1	30.7	32.2	32.7	16.6	33.2	35.0		29.9	37.5	26.7	10.5
1964	33.5	33.6	33.4	30.8	32.5	33.1	16.2	32.9	34.7		29.6	36.6	27.2	10.5

(continued)

TABLE Cc96–108 Producer price indexes, by stage of processing and commodity group: 1947–1998 [Bureau of Labor Statistics] *Continued*

	Finished goods			Intermediate goods						Crude materials			
	All finished goods	Consumer goods	Capital equipment	All intermediate goods	Materials and components								
					For construction	For manufacturing	Processed fuels and lubricants	Containers	Supplies	All crude materials	Foodstuffs and feedstuffs	Nonfood materials, except fuel	Fuel
	Cc96	Cc97	Cc98	Cc99	Cc100	Cc101	Cc102	Cc103	Cc104	Cc105	Cc106	Cc107	Cc108
Year	Index 1982 = 100	Index 1982 = 100	Index 1982 = 100	Index 1982 = 100	Index 1982 = 100	Index 1982 = 100	Index 1982 = 100	Index 1982 = 100	Index 1982 = 100	Index 1982 = 100	Index 1982 = 100	Index 1982 = 100	Index 1982 = 100
1965	34.1	34.2	33.8	31.2	32.8	33.6	16.5	33.5	35.0	31.1	39.2	27.7	10.6
1966	35.2	35.4	34.6	32.0	33.6	34.3	16.8	34.5	36.5	33.1	42.7	28.3	10.9
1967	35.6	35.6	35.8	32.2	34.0	34.5	16.9	35.0	36.8	31.3	40.3	26.5	11.3
1968	36.6	36.5	37.0	33.0	35.7	35.3	16.5	35.9	37.1	31.8	40.9	27.1	11.5
1969	38.0	37.9	38.3	34.1	37.7	36.5	16.6	37.2	37.8	33.9	44.1	28.4	12.0
1970	39.3	39.1	40.1	35.4	38.3	38.0	17.7	39.0	39.7	35.2	45.2	29.1	13.8
1971	40.5	40.2	41.7	36.8	40.8	38.9	19.5	40.8	40.8	36.0	46.1	29.4	15.7
1972	41.8	41.5	42.8	38.2	43.0	40.4	20.1	42.7	42.5	39.9	51.5	32.3	16.8
1973	45.6	46.0	44.2	42.4	46.5	44.1	22.2	45.2	51.7	54.5	72.6	42.9	18.6
1974	52.6	53.1	50.5	52.5	55.0	56.0	33.6	53.3	56.8	61.4	76.4	54.5	24.8
1975	58.2	58.2	58.2	58.0	60.1	61.7	39.4	60.0	61.8	61.6	77.4	50.0	30.6
1976	60.8	60.4	62.1	60.9	64.1	64.0	42.3	63.1	65.8	63.4	76.8	54.9	34.5
1977	64.7	64.3	66.1	64.9	69.3	67.4	47.7	65.9	69.3	65.5	77.5	56.3	42.0
1978	69.8	69.4	71.3	69.5	76.5	72.0	49.9	71.0	72.9	73.4	87.3	61.9	48.2
1979	77.6	77.5	77.5	78.4	84.2	80.9	61.6	79.4	80.2	85.9	100.0	75.5	57.3
1980	88.0	88.6	85.8	90.3	91.3	91.7	85.0	89.1	89.9	95.3	104.6	91.8	69.4
1981	96.1	96.6	94.6	98.6	97.9	98.7	100.6	96.7	96.9	103.0	103.9	109.8	84.8
1982	100.0	100.0	100.0	100.0	100.0	100.0	100.0	100.0	100.0	100.0	100.0	100.0	100.0
1983	101.6	101.3	102.8	100.6	102.8	101.2	95.4	100.4	101.8	101.3	101.8	98.8	105.1
1984	103.7	103.3	105.2	103.1	105.6	104.1	95.7	105.9	104.1	103.5	104.7	101.0	105.1
1985	104.7	103.8	107.5	102.7	107.3	103.3	92.8	109.0	104.4	95.8	94.8	94.3	102.7
1986	103.2	101.4	109.7	99.1	108.1	102.2	72.7	110.3	105.6	87.7	93.2	76.0	92.2
1987	105.4	103.6	111.7	101.5	109.8	105.3	73.3	114.5	107.7	93.7	96.2	88.5	84.1
1988	108.0	106.2	114.3	107.1	116.1	113.2	71.2	120.1	113.7	96.0	106.1	85.9	82.1
1989	113.6	112.1	118.8	112.0	121.3	118.1	76.4	125.4	118.1	103.1	111.2	95.8	85.3
1990	119.2	118.2	122.9	114.5	122.9	118.7	85.9	127.7	119.4	108.9	113.1	107.3	84.8
1991	121.7	120.5	126.7	114.4	124.5	118.1	85.3	128.1	121.4	101.2	105.5	97.5	82.9
1992	123.2	121.7	129.1	114.7	126.5	117.9	84.5	127.7	122.7	100.4	105.1	94.2	84.0
1993	124.7	123.0	131.4	116.2	132.0	118.9	84.7	126.4	125.0	102.4	108.4	94.1	87.1
1994	125.5	123.3	134.1	118.5	136.6	122.1	83.1	129.7	127.0	101.8	106.5	97.0	82.4
1995	127.9	125.6	136.7	124.9	142.1	130.4	84.2	148.8	132.1	102.7	105.8	105.8	72.1
1996	131.3	129.5	138.3	125.7	143.6	128.6	90.0	141.1	135.9	113.8	121.5	105.7	92.6
1997	131.8	130.2	138.2	125.6	146.5	128.3	89.3	136.0	135.9	111.1	112.2	103.5	101.3
1998	130.6	128.9	137.5	123.0	146.8	126.1	81.1	140.9	134.8	96.7	103.8	84.5	86.4

TABLE Cc96–108   Producer price indexes, by stage of processing and commodity group: 1947–1998   [Bureau of Labor Statistics]   *Continued*

Sources

1947–1953: Eva E. Jacobs, editor, *Handbook of U.S. Labor Statistics: Employment, Earnings, Prices, Productivity, and other Labor Data* (Bernan Press, 1998). 1954–1998: U.S. Council of Economic Advisers, "Economic Report of the President" (February 1999). For updates, see the U.S. Bureau of Labor Statistics (BLS) Internet site.

Documentation

The index numbers are annual averages of monthly figures, with 1982 = 100.

Producer price indexes (PPIs) by stage of processing were the focus of the BLS producer price index program as of the end of the twentieth century, with the PPI for finished goods, series Cc96, serving as the "headline" number in releases of PPI data. These series originated in the 1952 overhaul of the wholesale price index program and were carried back to 1947.

For more information see U.S. Bureau of Labor Statistics, *BLS Handbook of Methods*, Bulletin number 2,490 (April 1997), Chapter 14.

Series Cc96–98. Finished goods are commodities ready for sale to the final-demand user. Consumer goods are goods for which private households are generally the final-demand users. Examples include processed goods, such as automobiles, household furniture, apparel, and home fuels, and unprocessed goods, such as eggs and fresh vegetables. Capital equipment includes durable investment goods, such as heavy motor trucks, tractors, and machine tools.

Series Cc99–104. Intermediate materials, supplies, and components are commodities that have undergone some processing but will undergo further processing before sale to the final user (for example, flour, cotton yarn, steel mill products, and lumber) and nondurable, physically complete goods purchased by business enterprises for their operations (such as diesel fuel, belts and belting, paper boxes, and fertilizers).

Series Cc105–108. Crude materials for further processing are unprocessed commodities not sold directly to final consumers. Foodstuffs and feedstuffs include items such as grain and livestock. Fuel includes crude petroleum, natural gas to pipelines, and coal. Nonfood materials include such items as raw cotton, gravel, and iron and steel scrap.

TABLE Cc109–112   Wholesale price indexes, by stage of processing: 1913–1951   [Bureau of Labor Statistics]

Contributed by Christopher Hanes

Year	All commodities Cc109 Index 1926 = 100	Raw materials Cc110 Index 1926 = 100	Semimanufactured articles Cc111 Index 1926 = 100	Manufactured articles Cc112 Index 1926 = 100	Year	All commodities Cc109 Index 1926 = 100	Raw materials Cc110 Index 1926 = 100	Semimanufactured articles Cc111 Index 1926 = 100	Manufactured articles Cc112 Index 1926 = 100
1913	69.8	68.8	74.9	69.4	1935	80.0	77.1	73.6	82.2
1914	68.1	67.6	70.0	67.8	1936	80.8	79.9	75.9	82.0
1915	69.5	67.2	81.2	68.9	1937	86.3	84.8	85.3	87.2
1916	85.5	82.6	118.3	82.3	1938	78.6	72.0	75.4	82.2
1917	117.5	122.6	150.4	109.2	1939	77.1	70.2	77.0	80.4
1918	131.3	135.8	153.8	124.7	1940	78.6	71.9	79.1	81.6
1919	138.6	145.9	157.9	130.6	1941	87.3	83.5	86.9	89.1
1920	154.4	151.8	198.2	149.8	1942	98.8	100.6	92.6	98.6
1921	97.6	88.3	96.1	103.3	1943	103.1	112.1	92.9	100.1
1922	96.7	96.0	98.9	96.5	1944	104.0	113.2	94.1	100.8
1923	100.6	98.5	118.6	99.2	1945	105.8	116.8	95.9	101.8
1924	98.1	97.6	108.7	96.3	1946	121.1	134.7	110.8	116.1
1925	103.5	106.7	105.3	100.6	1947	152.1	165.6	148.5	146.0
1926	100.0	100.0	100.0	100.0	1948	165.1	178.4	158.0	159.4
1927	95.4	96.5	94.3	95.0	1949	155.0	163.9	150.2	151.2
1928	96.7	99.1	94.5	95.9	1950	161.5	172.4	156.0	156.8
1929	95.3	97.5	93.9	94.5	1951	180.4	192.4	177.6	174.0
1930	86.4	84.3	81.8	88.0					
1931	73.0	65.6	69.0	77.0					
1932	64.8	55.1	59.3	70.3					
1933	65.9	56.5	65.4	70.5					
1934	74.9	68.6	72.8	78.2					

Source

U.S. Bureau of Labor Statistics, *Wholesale Prices and Price Indexes,* Bulletin number 1,235 (1957), p. 34.

Documentation

The index numbers are annual averages of monthly figures, with 1926 = 100.

These series were based on the data collected for the Wholesale Price Index (WPI) program prior to the major revision of 1952. Each commodity was classed in one of three groups: raw, semimanufactured, or manufactured. The list of commodities included in each class is shown in U.S. Bureau of Labor Statistics, *Wholesale Prices, 1913 to 1927,* Bulletin number 473 (1929), p. 62. Prices were weighted using quantities as specified for the series presented in Table Cc84–95.

These indexes differ significantly in structure, classification, and measurement from those in Table Cc96–108, which are based on the scheme adopted in the 1952 revision. The series most nearly comparable with series Cc110–112 are as follows, respectively: series Cc105, all crude materials; series Cc101, intermediate materials and components for manufacturing; and series Cc96, all finished goods.

TABLE Cc113–124   Wholesale price indexes, by commodity group: 1749–1890   [Warren and Pearson]
Contributed by Christopher Hanes

Year	All commodities Cc113 Index 1910–1914 = 100	Farm products Cc114 Index 1910–1914 = 100	Foods Cc115 Index 1910–1914 = 100	Hides and leather products Cc116 Index 1910–1914 = 100	Textile products Cc117 Index 1910–1914 = 100	Fuel and lighting Cc118 Index 1910–1914 = 100	Metals and metal products Cc119 Index 1910–1914 = 100	Building materials Cc120 Index 1910–1914 = 100	Chemicals and drugs Cc121 Index 1910–1914 = 100	House furnishing goods Cc122 Index 1910–1914 = 100	Spirits Cc123 Index 1910–1914 = 100	Miscellaneous Cc124 Index 1910–1914 = 100
1749	68	—	—	—	—	—	—	—	—	—	—	—
1750	60	—	—	—	—	—	—	—	—	—	—	—
1751	65	—	—	—	—	—	—	—	—	—	—	—
1752	66	—	—	—	—	—	—	—	—	—	—	—
1753	65	—	—	—	—	—	—	—	—	—	—	—
1754	65	—	—	—	—	—	—	—	—	—	—	—
1755	66	—	—	—	—	—	—	—	—	—	—	—
1756	66	—	—	—	—	—	—	—	—	—	—	—
1757	65	—	—	—	—	—	—	—	—	—	—	—
1758	70	—	—	—	—	—	—	—	—	—	—	—
1759	79	—	—	—	—	—	—	—	—	—	—	—
1760	79	—	—	—	—	—	—	—	—	—	—	—
1761	77	—	—	—	—	—	—	—	—	—	—	—
1762	87	—	—	—	—	—	—	—	—	—	—	—
1763	79	—	—	—	—	—	—	—	—	—	—	—
1764	74	—	—	—	—	—	—	—	—	—	—	—
1765	72	—	—	—	—	—	—	—	—	—	—	—
1766	73	—	—	—	—	—	—	—	—	—	—	—
1767	77	—	—	—	—	—	—	—	—	—	—	—
1768	74	—	—	—	—	—	—	—	—	—	—	—
1769	77	—	—	—	—	—	—	—	—	—	—	—
1770	77	—	—	—	—	—	—	—	—	—	—	—
1771	79	—	—	—	—	—	—	—	—	—	—	—
1772	89	—	—	—	—	—	—	—	—	—	—	—
1773	84	—	—	—	—	—	—	—	—	—	—	—
1774	76	—	—	—	—	—	—	—	—	—	—	—
1775	75	—	—	—	—	—	—	—	—	—	—	—
1776	86	—	—	—	—	—	—	—	—	—	—	—
1777	123	—	—	—	—	—	—	—	—	—	—	—
1778	140	—	—	—	—	—	—	—	—	—	—	—
1779	226	—	—	—	—	—	—	—	—	—	—	—
1780	225	—	—	—	—	—	—	—	—	—	—	—
1781	216	—	—	—	—	—	—	—	—	—	—	—
1785	92	—	—	—	—	—	—	—	—	—	—	—
1786	90	75	—	—	—	—	—	—	—	—	—	—
1787	90	78	103	—	—	127	236	36	—	—	15	148
1789	86	68	94	—	—	99	250	35	—	—	16	152
1790	90	68	104	—	—	95	247	35	—	—	17	141
1791	85	57	99	—	—	100	240	34	—	—	19	148
1793	102	75	125	—	—	122	240	39	—	—	22	163
1794	108	76	135	—	—	125	258	40	—	—	23	158

Year	All commodities Cc113 Index 1910–1914 = 100	Farm products Cc114 Index 1910–1914 = 100	Foods Cc115 Index 1910–1914 = 100	Hides and leather products Cc116 Index 1910–1914 = 100	Textile products Cc117 Index 1910–1914 = 100	Fuel and lighting Cc118 Index 1910–1914 = 100	Metals and metal products Cc119 Index 1910–1914 = 100	Building materials Cc120 Index 1910–1914 = 100	Chemicals and drugs Cc121 Index 1910–1914 = 100	House furnishing goods Cc122 Index 1910–1914 = 100	Spirits Cc123 Index 1910–1914 = 100	Miscellaneous Cc124 Index 1910–1914 = 100
1795	131	102	163	—	—	155	259	56	—	—	25	220
1796	146	116	186	—	—	150	284	58	—	—	31	204
1797	131	98	163	—	—	144	299	54	—	—	26	177
1798	122	93	145	65	226	131	304	51	442	—	26	177
1799	126	98	147	62	227	150	310	51	523	—	24	206
1800	129	99	157	62	225	159	322	51	427	—	25	194
1801	142	113	177	71	236	167	348	55	445	—	27	173
1802	117	84	132	80	230	153	301	55	377	—	24	145
1803	118	83	135	83	232	152	290	53	431	—	25	138
1804	126	89	142	84	252	182	300	56	493	—	23	149
1805	141	106	162	85	270	196	309	58	511	—	24	165
1806	134	95	150	85	280	153	328	58	519	—	23	179
1807	130	92	142	82	274	161	327	59	440	—	22	173
1808	115	71	113	79	279	148	336	57	455	—	23	164
1809	130	83	129	73	323	147	350	60	538	—	27	197
1810	131	90	139	75	278	167	332	59	483	—	29	208
1811	126	82	140	73	243	166	325	57	570	—	31	204
1812	131	81	141	72	257	185	356	58	735	—	34	234
1813	162	104	172	77	291	334	419	63	848	—	37	251
1814	182	112	181	96	300	525	464	69	814	—	48	246
1815	170	117	187	85	300	318	399	76	538	—	41	202
1816	151	119	172	86	274	190	310	68	376	—	34	177
1817	151	126	184	95	268	141	277	60	327	—	31	156
1818	147	117	172	113	275	149	279	56	318	—	29	149
1819	125	87	140	101	233	162	285	55	306	—	24	144
1820	106	68	109	83	211	157	270	53	300	—	22	124
1821	102	64	102	89	215	142	261	50	306	—	21	129
1822	106	70	109	93	218	138	257	50	342	—	21	118
1823	103	64	108	97	209	131	247	49	320	—	20	119
1824	98	61	99	97	191	133	242	48	304	—	19	119
1825	103	67	100	99	198	131	279	50	313	—	22	114
1826	99	62	98	91	188	138	269	52	298	—	21	110
1827	98	59	100	87	186	137	243	51	287	—	21	112
1828	97	58	99	90	190	138	234	51	251	—	19	113
1829	96	59	100	85	182	133	227	49	222	—	19	117
1830	91	58	94	85	181	116	209	47	207	—	19	111
1831	94	61	98	91	179	112	209	49	211	—	23	111
1832	95	63	99	85	161	137	212	49	226	—	22	110
1833	95	69	100	76	162	111	205	51	220	—	22	105
1834	90	64	93	70	161	101	201	52	212	—	19	109
1835	100	75	107	74	170	111	206	52	225	—	23	126
1836	114	89	128	78	177	130	241	53	251	—	25	130
1837	115	84	132	80	167	130	243	70	264	—	25	119
1838	110	82	128	80	157	121	219	70	257	—	25	120
1839	112	86	126	90	159	122	220	70	250	—	25	122

(continued)

TABLE Cc113–124   Wholesale price indexes, by commodity group: 1749–1890   [Warren and Pearson]   Continued

Year	All commodities Cc113 Index 1910–1914 = 100	Farm products Cc114 Index 1910–1914 = 100	Foods Cc115 Index 1910–1914 = 100	Hides and leather products Cc116 Index 1910–1914 = 100	Textile products Cc117 Index 1910–1914 = 100	Fuel and lighting Cc118 Index 1910–1914 = 100	Metals and metal products Cc119 Index 1910–1914 = 100	Building materials Cc120 Index 1910–1914 = 100	Chemicals and drugs Cc121 Index 1910–1914 = 100	House furnishing goods Cc122 Index 1910–1914 = 100	Spirits Cc123 Index 1910–1914 = 100	Miscellaneous Cc124 Index 1910–1914 = 100
1840	95	65	102	80	146	105	204	65	238	128	21	108
1841	92	64	90	86	140	111	204	67	220	121	19	113
1842	82	53	80	72	132	94	183	62	203	113	17	111
1843	75	48	77	69	114	87	172	58	188	99	19	109
1844	77	52	72	66	125	90	179	59	187	108	20	96
1845	83	58	84	63	125	96	189	64	178	107	21	85
1846	83	58	84	57	122	88	191	64	164	110	20	86
1847	90	72	96	66	117	90	186	61	156	117	24	99
1848	82	59	87	56	113	93	170	61	153	111	22	99
1849	82	62	88	64	111	93	155	58	152	110	21	92
1850	84	71	84	67	116	95	147	61	154	114	21	88
1851	83	71	84	65	115	87	141	61	153	117	20	86
1852	88	77	95	70	113	93	144	64	156	118	19	89
1853	97	83	98	84	119	102	186	67	169	128	22	96
1854	108	93	117	100	124	121	191	70	174	129	27	103
1855	110	98	126	104	125	102	176	71	178	129	31	103
1856	105	84	116	121	129	97	174	73	176	128	30	114
1857	111	95	123	139	138	97	173	73	171	130	27	107
1858	93	76	97	110	123	90	154	67	168	121	23	102
1859	95	82	99	115	120	93	150	64	168	118	24	98
1860	93	77	96	102	119	98	149	65	175	117	23	98
1861	89	75	89	90	120	80	152	63	174	110	21	98
1862	104	86	107	108	147	87	180	69	206	124	28	122
1863	133	113	123	133	206	125	236	88	234	165	45	146
1864	193	162	189	164	264	197	354	114	297	222	106	189
1865	185	148	180	152	266	214	306	118	300	214	150	175
1866	174	140	173	146	245	160	278	128	283	220	154	170
1867	162	133	167	132	220	144	248	120	229	196	146	162
1868	158	138	171	126	197	149	225	116	204	178	117	153
1869	151	128	154	134	194	166	227	110	227	178	86	136
1870	135	112	139	128	179	134	200	101	199	164	78	128
1871	130	102	130	126	170	152	203	102	177	154	74	120
1872	136	108	121	130	177	153	257	107	175	159	73	125
1873	133	103	122	132	175	148	243	106	181	160	75	115
1874	126	102	126	128	151	135	194	101	176	149	78	111
1875	118	99	120	123	141	128	175	90	149	134	88	98
1876	110	89	113	104	138	127	157	84	140	123	86	98
1877	106	89	115	109	125	108	141	80	136	118	86	95
1878	91	72	93	95	115	93	126	72	127	109	82	88
1879	90	72	90	100	114	80	134	74	120	105	82	90
1880	100	80	96	113	128	92	166	81	120	117	83	91
1881	103	89	106	109	119	91	150	83	120	109	81	90
1882	108	99	114	108	119	92	157	88	114	109	80	93
1883	101	87	103	107	116	89	144	85	110	110	83	93
1884	93	82	93	111	109	77	124	84	105	105	81	78

Year	All commodities Cc113 Index 1910–1914 = 100	Farm products Cc114 Index 1910–1914 = 100	Foods Cc115 Index 1910–1914 = 100	Hides and leather products Cc116 Index 1910–1914 = 100	Textile products Cc117 Index 1910–1914 = 100	Fuel and lighting Cc118 Index 1910–1914 = 100	Metals and metal products Cc119 Index 1910–1914 = 100	Building materials Cc120 Index 1910–1914 = 100	Chemicals and drugs Cc121 Index 1910–1914 = 100	House furnishing goods Cc122 Index 1910–1914 = 100	Spirits Cc123 Index 1910–1914 = 100	Miscellaneous Cc124 Index 1910–1914 = 100
1885	85	72	84	105	105	72	109	81	100	99	79	78
1886	82	68	78	101	100	70	110	82	99	94	79	74
1887	85	71	86	92	98	70	119	81	97	92	77	75
1888	86	75	86	86	98	72	121	80	103	94	80	73
1889	81	67	79	80	99	71	116	81	101	94	74	80
1890	82	71	86	74	103	72	123	84	90	91	—	89

Source

George F. Warren and Frank A. Pearson, "Wholesale Prices for 213 Years, 1720 to 1932," Cornell University Agricultural Experiment Station Memoir number 142 (November 1932), pp. 7–10 and 84–111. The indexes are also presented in George F. Warren and Frank A. Pearson, *Prices* (Wiley, 1933).

Documentation

The index numbers are annual averages of monthly figures, with the average value over 1910–1914 = 100.

Warren and Pearson constructed indexes for the period 1797–1890. Series for years before 1797 were created by Herman M. Stoker.

Commodity groups correspond to those used by the U.S. Bureau of Labor Statistics (BLS) before the 1952 overhaul of the wholesale price index program – that is, the groups for the indexes presented in Table Cc84–95. Warren and Pearson also constructed a price index for spirits. The bulk of the prices comprised by the indexes relate to New York City and were obtained from newspapers, supplemented with prices published in the *Report of the Secretary of the Treasury on the State of the Finances* (usually referred to as the U.S. Finance Report) for 1863.

The index numbers for 1797–1890 are weighted arithmetic averages of relatives, computed first on an 1876–1891 base and then linked to the BLS index numbers for corresponding commodity groups (Table Cc84–95) and converted to a base where the average value of the linked series is 100 over the period 1910–1914. The number of commodities included in the all-commodities index varies from a low of 113 in 1830 to 146 in 1880. When one commodity was substituted for another, a linking procedure was employed. Two all-commodity indexes were prepared from the commodity group indexes: one with fixed group weights and one with group weights that vary over time. The latter is presented here. Within each group, weights change over time and were meant to reflect the relative importance of commodities in the trade of the United States, as indicated by censuses, imports, exports, and similar official figures. Such information was meager for early years, and so some arbitrary weight assignments were necessary. Specific mention should be made of the reduction in the importance of cotton during the years of the Civil War. In this period, cotton was scarce and prices very high, and so weights were based on the amount available for consumption for 1861–1866 and on production for 1867–1871.

In attempting to extend the series to years before 1797, Stoker encountered serious gaps in source materials. Over 1783–1796, prices for seventy-one commodities were available for most years, and Stoker could use the same commodity group classifications and methods of calculation as those employed by Warren and Pearson. For 1749–1781, Stoker found continuous series for only eleven to nineteen items, nearly all farm products and foods. The all-commodities index for 1749–1781 is based on that small set of prices. Series covering scattered months over 1720–1748 are given in the source.

TABLE Cc125–137   Wholesale price indexes for historical comparisons, by commodity group: 1860–1990[1]   [Hanes]

Contributed by Christopher Hanes

Year	All commodities Cc125 Index	All commodities other than farm products Cc126 Index	Farm products Cc127 Index	Foods Cc128 Index	Hides and leather products Cc129 Index	Textile products Cc130 Index	Fuel and lighting Cc131 Index	Metals and metal products Cc132 Index	Building materials Cc133 Index	Chemicals and drugs Cc134 Index	House furnishing goods Cc135 Index	Spirits Cc136 Index	Miscellaneous products Cc137 Index
INDEX 1890–1914 = 100													
1860	105.4	108.1	97.5	110.4	116.7	122.3	119.9	138.1	68.6	177.7	130.3	29.5	100.1
1861	100.0	101.6	95.0	102.4	103.0	123.4	97.9	140.9	66.5	176.6	122.5	26.9	100.1
1862	116.9	119.5	108.9	123.1	123.6	151.1	106.5	166.9	72.9	209.1	138.1	35.9	124.6
1863	150.2	152.6	143.1	141.5	152.2	211.8	153.0	218.8	92.9	237.6	183.7	57.6	149.1
1864	217.6	221.7	205.2	217.4	187.7	271.4	241.1	328.2	120.4	301.5	247.2	135.8	193.1
1865	210.4	218.4	187.4	207.1	174.0	273.5	261.9	283.7	124.6	304.6	238.3	192.1	178.8
1866	195.9	202.3	177.3	199.0	167.1	251.9	195.8	257.7	135.2	287.3	245.0	197.2	173.7
1867	182.4	187.1	168.4	192.1	151.1	226.2	176.2	229.9	126.7	232.5	218.2	187.0	165.5
1868	179.4	180.8	174.8	196.7	144.2	202.5	182.3	208.6	122.5	207.1	198.2	149.9	156.3
1869	171.6	174.8	162.1	177.2	153.4	199.4	203.1	210.5	116.2	230.5	198.2	110.1	138.9

Note appears at end of table

(continued)

TABLE Cc125–137 Wholesale price indexes for historical comparisons, by commodity group: 1860–1990 [Hanes] Continued

Year	All commodities Cc125 Index	All commodities other than farm products Cc126 Index	Farm products Cc127 Index	Foods Cc128 Index	Hides and leather products Cc129 Index	Textile products Cc130 Index	Fuel and lighting Cc131 Index	Metals and metal products Cc132 Index	Building materials Cc133 Index	Chemicals and drugs Cc134 Index	House furnishing goods Cc135 Index	Spirits Cc136 Index	Miscellaneous products Cc137 Index
1870	152.3	155.8	141.8	159.9	146.5	184.0	164.0	185.4	106.7	202.0	182.6	99.9	130.8
1871	147.6	153.9	129.2	149.5	144.2	174.8	186.0	188.2	107.7	179.7	171.5	94.8	122.6
1872	153.0	158.6	136.8	139.2	148.8	182.0	187.2	238.3	113.0	177.7	177.0	93.5	127.7
1873	149.7	156.3	130.4	140.3	151.1	179.9	181.1	225.3	111.9	183.8	178.2	96.1	117.5
1874	141.8	146.1	129.2	144.9	146.5	155.2	165.2	179.9	106.7	178.7	165.9	99.9	113.4
1875	134.0	136.9	125.4	138.0	140.8	145.0	156.6	162.2	95.0	151.3	149.2	112.7	100.1
1876	125.0	129.2	112.7	130.0	119.0	141.9	155.4	145.6	88.7	142.1	137.0	110.1	100.1
1877	120.3	122.8	112.7	132.3	124.8	128.5	132.2	130.7	84.5	138.1	131.4	110.1	97.0
1878	102.4	106.3	91.2	107.0	108.7	118.2	113.8	116.8	76.0	128.9	121.4	105.0	89.9
1879	100.9	104.2	91.2	103.5	114.5	117.2	97.9	124.2	78.1	121.8	116.9	105.0	91.9
1880	112.2	115.9	101.3	110.4	129.3	131.6	112.6	153.9	85.5	121.8	130.3	106.3	93.0
1881	115.7	116.6	112.7	121.9	124.8	122.3	111.4	139.1	87.7	121.8	121.4	103.7	91.9
1882	122.5	121.3	125.4	131.1	123.6	122.3	112.6	145.6	92.9	115.7	121.4	102.5	95.0
1883	113.4	114.3	110.2	118.5	122.5	119.3	108.9	133.5	89.8	111.7	122.5	106.3	95.0
1884	104.9	105.1	103.9	107.0	127.0	112.1	94.2	115.0	88.7	106.6	116.9	103.7	79.7
1885	96.0	97.6	91.2	96.6	120.2	107.9	88.1	101.1	85.5	101.5	110.2	101.2	79.7
1886	92.2	94.2	86.1	89.7	115.6	102.8	85.7	102.0	86.6	100.5	104.7	101.2	75.6
1887	95.3	97.1	89.9	98.9	105.3	100.8	85.7	110.3	85.5	98.5	102.4	98.6	76.6
1888	96.9	97.4	95.0	98.9	98.4	100.8	88.1	112.2	84.5	104.6	104.7	102.5	74.6
1889	91.5	93.8	84.9	90.9	91.6	101.8	86.9	107.5	85.5	102.5	104.7	94.8	81.7
1890	95.6	97.6	89.9	98.9	84.7	105.9	88.1	114.0	88.7	91.4	101.3	84.5	90.9
1891	97.0	97.3	96.3	102.2	85.3	101.4	96.3	102.4	85.4	82.8	99.3	88.6	95.3
1892	90.6	91.6	87.4	90.7	81.0	99.9	95.1	95.3	84.0	93.8	94.7	86.2	90.4
1893	92.9	93.5	91.2	98.5	78.0	101.3	95.4	89.9	84.2	88.0	94.0	85.9	90.0
1894	82.8	83.9	79.8	87.6	72.1	87.7	82.9	78.2	79.7	79.7	88.6	90.8	86.7
1895	81.9	83.0	78.5	83.5	91.6	85.6	79.2	80.8	78.6	75.7	83.8	97.1	80.7
1896	77.9	80.2	70.9	74.8	78.5	84.6	82.2	86.1	77.4	74.4	83.9	96.4	78.6
1897	78.6	79.4	76.0	78.3	83.4	82.8	81.7	73.9	74.1	91.9	82.3	94.9	81.6
1898	82.0	82.7	79.8	85.1	92.3	82.4	79.9	74.7	76.9	102.6	84.6	98.0	85.0
1899	87.5	89.6	81.1	84.3	97.3	89.9	77.9	111.7	84.7	107.3	89.7	99.6	87.2
1900	94.8	96.5	89.9	88.5	98.8	97.0	97.6	116.4	91.5	108.6	100.9	99.9	93.9
1901	94.8	95.2	93.7	90.7	98.3	90.8	100.0	103.1	91.9	114.2	100.1	103.1	96.2
1902	101.4	100.6	103.9	99.8	101.9	93.7	104.0	106.3	96.8	120.6	101.0	105.4	99.3
1903	100.4	101.0	98.8	92.3	97.4	99.6	119.4	105.9	99.8	117.1	103.1	102.7	101.3
1904	101.4	100.6	103.9	97.5	95.2	100.9	114.2	93.1	101.6	118.1	103.5	101.8	100.8
1905	101.6	102.1	100.1	96.9	103.7	100.7	109.4	103.5	105.9	116.5	101.1	101.1	102.1
1906	105.5	106.9	101.3	96.8	111.5	108.1	109.0	117.5	118.3	102.1	104.1	103.3	103.6
1907	112.5	113.3	110.2	101.3	111.7	121.3	111.6	130.2	125.4	102.1	112.1	105.3	104.3
1908	108.4	107.9	110.2	107.3	105.9	103.9	113.5	100.5	116.2	102.7	111.0	108.8	104.5
1909	115.2	112.2	124.1	115.4	117.9	107.2	109.3	101.1	119.9	101.8	108.3	108.9	147.7
1910	118.8	114.5	131.7	118.3	114.5	113.1	107.6	104.8	124.2	100.8	109.4	106.2	148.5
1911	113.1	111.1	119.1	113.6	110.2	109.9	108.0	98.6	123.8	100.8	108.2	107.2	116.8
1912	120.0	116.9	129.2	124.8	122.2	108.5	110.1	108.3	124.5	100.8	108.9	109.1	109.5
1913	119.6	117.2	126.7	121.3	130.1	113.6	113.9	107.7	125.2	100.8	112.9	105.6	104.0
1914	119.0	116.4	126.7	125.2	136.5	109.9	113.6	95.8	121.3	105.2	113.4	109.6	101.3

Year	All commodities Cc125 Index	All commodities other than farm products Cc126 Index	Farm products Cc127 Index	Foods Cc128 Index	Hides and leather products Cc129 Index	Textile products Cc130 Index	Fuel and lighting Cc131 Index	Metals and metal products Cc132 Index	Building materials Cc133 Index	Chemicals and drugs Cc134 Index	House furnishing goods Cc135 Index	Spirits Cc136 Index	Miscellaneous products Cc137 Index
1915	120.2	117.9	127.2	126.7	149.4	105.4	110.5	94.7	119.9	146.4	119.8	110.0	145.1
1916	143.1	140.8	150.1	148.9	182.5	138.7	132.4	105.6	133.8	259.2	143.3	114.4	208.7
1917	200.6	191.1	229.5	214.7	236.8	202.7	178.5	135.6	171.7	230.3	196.1	162.1	217.4
1918	227.4	215.5	263.3	224.9	219.5	282.3	187.3	161.5	204.1	253.8	270.2	212.8	222.6
1919	250.1	240.1	280.3	258.9	291.1	292.5	187.8	193.4	244.5	176.2	270.4	208.4	192.7
1920	276.5	279.3	268.1	258.9	263.2	352.5	265.3	262.6	332.0	210.1	352.2	227.0	202.7
1921	184.4	193.3	157.2	169.5	145.3	199.7	224.4	192.4	243.3	146.7	260.9	204.9	130.5
1922	183.8	189.3	166.9	161.9	148.5	207.4	236.5	182.8	231.2	135.5	224.5	202.0	102.2
1923	192.2	197.7	175.4	169.4	145.3	238.2	225.4	195.0	246.6	117.4	246.8	203.6	106.6
1924	188.0	191.2	177.9	174.4	134.4	223.9	213.7	181.3	229.2	108.2	241.8	206.1	106.8
1925	197.0	197.5	195.3	196.8	145.6	221.7	212.3	176.4	223.1	95.7	229.6	208.6	122.2
1926	188.4	191.8	177.9	192.9	134.8	199.7	218.9	170.3	215.3	97.7	223.7	208.4	115.3
1927	181.9	183.5	176.8	182.8	160.3	193.5	212.2	161.9	204.7	99.9	219.4	160.7	110.6
1928	182.4	180.4	188.4	188.4	192.7	197.6	178.5	158.8	200.8	101.7	211.2	115.9	108.3
1929	178.9	176.2	186.6	181.4	156.9	193.1	174.7	167.1	205.4	104.8	206.1	117.8	108.3
1930	157.0	157.2	157.1	158.2	131.9	168.2	169.1	143.3	191.9	97.6	198.2	113.6	101.0
1931	126.5	130.8	115.3	120.5	102.3	134.0	159.9	125.4	171.6	90.1	180.3	107.3	88.8
1932	106.1	113.8	85.7	98.6	79.3	108.2	157.2	114.8	151.1	86.7	165.0	107.1	81.4
1933	113.5	121.8	91.4	106.1	94.4	128.2	154.9	122.6	160.6	90.4	167.1	107.1	76.0
1934	133.3	139.8	116.2	126.5	93.0	148.7	169.2	135.6	176.8	93.3	181.7	184.0	78.3
1935	146.7	149.3	140.2	150.1	105.9	147.4	171.8	135.8	174.5	93.4	176.5	193.4	80.5
1936	148.3	150.1	143.9	148.1	113.3	144.0	173.9	138.4	179.2	94.0	194.5	193.8	87.1
1937	160.3	162.9	153.7	155.7	134.7	157.0	175.0	169.1	200.5	99.4	199.0	195.9	94.0
1938	139.4	146.0	121.8	133.1	105.4	131.3	174.7	154.6	189.3	96.3	187.1	200.5	80.2
1939	136.3	143.9	116.2	123.9	111.6	138.5	171.0	155.1	188.5	97.5	187.6	205.5	81.4
1940	139.8	147.1	120.4	124.5	115.7	148.4	172.5	156.5	188.7	98.1	192.2	229.9	84.5
1941	163.1	169.4	146.6	148.2	130.0	180.7	187.6	172.7	211.9	99.2	218.2	283.7	88.8
INDEX 1947–1990 = 100													
1947	56.6	52.0	70.3	63.5	57.6	68.2	29.9	30.9	41.1	35.5	44.9	81.6	53.3
1948	59.5	54.2	75.5	66.2	54.5	66.3	35.1	36.2	45.3	37.5	47.5	73.9	54.4
1949	52.5	48.3	65.3	58.6	49.4	59.8	33.6	36.3	42.2	39.6	47.2	33.2	50.1
1950	55.8	51.6	68.5	59.6	56.9	66.9	34.3	38.2	46.8	41.0	50.4	46.7	57.6
1951	64.2	59.1	79.8	66.9	66.0	77.2	36.5	44.1	51.0	45.0	56.8	79.0	67.3
1952	60.3	55.2	75.3	66.3	42.9	68.5	35.7	44.0	49.5	45.0	53.4	60.2	58.8
1953	57.3	53.7	68.2	62.7	45.2	66.8	37.6	43.8	49.2	47.4	53.9	49.1	55.1
1954	56.6	53.0	67.2	63.9	39.9	63.5	35.8	44.1	48.7	49.3	54.0	45.7	57.1
1955	55.3	52.7	63.1	60.2	39.9	64.5	35.2	47.8	51.1	49.8	54.6	45.4	61.9
1956	56.2	54.2	62.2	60.1	42.7	65.4	37.4	51.4	52.7	51.0	57.0	51.0	60.7
1957	56.9	54.6	63.9	61.1	41.6	64.5	40.7	50.9	50.6	51.7	58.2	53.7	60.3
1958	57.8	54.8	66.7	62.9	42.8	61.9	40.3	50.4	50.2	52.3	58.2	54.7	59.6
1959	57.1	55.3	62.6	59.3	56.0	64.0	40.1	52.2	53.1	52.6	59.0	57.8	63.2
1960	57.3	55.6	62.4	60.9	47.9	66.3	39.7	53.1	51.4	53.0	60.2	57.8	64.1
1961	56.4	54.6	61.8	60.0	49.9	64.4	38.9	52.1	49.4	53.2	60.1	57.8	62.8
1962	57.2	55.3	62.9	61.3	50.4	65.7	38.1	52.2	50.0	53.2	60.8	57.8	63.2
1963	56.7	55.1	61.7	60.8	45.3	66.5	38.6	52.3	50.8	53.1	60.9	57.8	62.8
1964	57.3	56.2	60.8	62.1	46.1	66.7	39.4	55.1	51.7	53.5	61.7	56.9	62.9

(continued)

TABLE Cc125–137   Wholesale price indexes for historical comparisons, by commodity group: 1860–1990   [Hanes]   Continued

Year	All commodities Cc125 Index	All commodities other than farm products Cc126 Index	Farm products Cc127 Index	Foods Cc128 Index	Hides and leather products Cc129 Index	Textile products Cc130 Index	Fuel and lighting Cc131 Index	Metals and metal products Cc132 Index	Building materials Cc133 Index	Chemicals and drugs Cc134 Index	House furnishing goods Cc135 Index	Spirits Cc136 Index	Miscellaneous products Cc137 Index
1965	59.3	58.0	63.4	65.5	51.0	66.0	38.9	58.2	52.2	54.7	61.9	57.1	64.5
1966	61.8	59.7	68.0	68.4	59.4	65.9	39.3	57.7	54.7	56.0	63.8	57.2	64.0
1967	59.9	58.4	64.2	65.7	49.4	64.9	40.1	58.4	55.0	58.9	65.5	57.4	62.2
1968	61.7	60.4	65.8	66.4	51.0	66.0	41.3	60.3	62.4	62.4	67.8	57.2	61.7
1969	65.5	64.0	69.9	70.9	55.7	66.9	44.7	64.2	68.6	63.3	70.1	55.6	61.0
1970	67.4	66.0	71.3	73.7	52.8	67.4	55.2	68.8	61.7	63.1	72.2	56.3	64.4
1971	70.1	69.2	72.5	73.8	56.0	68.7	64.7	69.9	71.5	64.0	76.0	56.4	66.0
1972	76.4	75.0	80.3	78.4	78.7	74.9	67.7	73.7	81.4	64.4	80.4	54.8	66.7
1973	95.4	89.5	113.2	99.4	91.1	90.5	76.1	79.5	101.2	66.8	85.1	55.0	74.2
1974	113.8	111.6	120.5	124.0	81.6	105.3	116.7	110.8	108.4	82.8	94.9	86.5	90.6
1975	119.6	119.5	119.9	127.8	77.8	102.1	144.5	123.8	105.4	116.1	104.8	123.8	107.0
1976	122.8	122.9	122.7	116.9	101.9	122.3	141.4	127.5	122.4	125.0	111.1	133.2	113.2
1977	127.3	128.5	123.6	118.4	110.3	120.0	147.4	137.1	142.2	129.0	116.3	136.8	115.4
1978	140.4	141.7	136.5	132.8	133.4	131.1	158.6	146.7	163.0	133.4	125.7	131.6	123.6
1979	157.4	158.2	155.0	145.7	199.1	139.7	168.4	167.7	180.1	140.6	134.9	150.0	139.7
1980	167.1	169.4	160.2	163.0	161.2	155.1	186.1	175.6	172.3	163.9	156.5	203.8	160.6
1981	174.7	178.3	163.8	165.5	164.4	162.6	218.1	182.8	175.0	196.6	166.8	218.3	175.8
1982	171.8	177.2	155.7	163.7	160.1	159.1	229.8	180.8	170.0	211.2	173.3	198.8	179.8
1983	175.2	180.5	159.4	163.5	170.0	163.2	225.6	185.1	188.3	200.8	183.5	193.6	179.1
1984	180.7	186.2	164.2	170.8	191.4	169.3	227.3	190.7	188.7	199.1	192.2	196.7	186.8
1985	172.4	180.6	148.0	162.0	181.5	165.2	224.9	186.1	185.7	204.2	193.1	188.7	186.4
1986	169.9	178.4	144.6	160.9	196.7	163.8	214.4	181.2	186.2	201.2	193.8	178.9	182.1
1987	176.1	185.3	148.7	165.1	225.5	171.7	213.0	193.2	196.4	199.5	198.3	179.7	183.7
1988	187.0	194.8	163.3	169.9	268.1	180.4	210.3	220.3	203.3	213.1	207.8	177.1	197.7
1989	196.3	204.2	172.6	183.1	272.8	183.0	215.4	233.8	209.8	229.9	218.2	190.2	207.4
1990	199.5	207.8	174.6	188.4	284.1	187.4	223.3	231.0	209.4	235.9	227.4	184.8	211.0

¹ The basis of the indexes changes over time. See the following documentation.

Source

Christopher Hanes, "Consistent Wholesale Price Series for the United States, 1860–1990," in Trevor J. O. Dick, editor, *Business Cycles since 1820: New International Perspectives from Historical Evidence* (Edward Elgar, 1998), p. 205.

Documentation

The basis of the indexes changes over time: for 1860–1941, index 1890–1914 = 100; for 1947–1990, index 1947–1990 = 100.

These series present Warren and Pearson indexes for 1860–1890 alongside series for 1890–1941 and 1947–1990 that were constructed so as to resemble the Warren and Pearson indexes in aggregation methods and the set of products comprised in the indexes. They may be suitable for comparisons of price behavior between different historical periods, especially between periods before the First World War and later periods, and comparisons of movements at relatively high frequencies (for example, year-to-year movements during business cycles). Standard U.S. Bureau of Labor Statistics (BLS) wholesale and producer price indexes like those presented in Table Cc66–83 may be less suitable for such comparisons because of differences between periods in aggregation methods and the types of goods comprised in the series.

To construct the series for 1890–1941 and 1947–1990, Hanes matched each good in the Warren and Pearson series as of 1890 to a BLS price index for the same good, a similar good, or a similar class of goods over years from 1890 through 1941, and from 1947 through 1990. The train of BLS

price indexes corresponding to a Warren and Pearson good was linked, converted to price relatives on successive bases – 1890–1914, 1914–1928, 1928–1941, and 1947–1990 – and arithmetically averaged into commodity group indexes using Warren and Pearson's weights for the year 1889 (George F. Warren and Frank A. Pearson, "Wholesale Prices for 213 Years, 1720 to 1932," Cornell University Agricultural Experiment Station Memoir number 142, November 1932, p. 121, presented in Warren and Pearson, *Prices* (Wiley, 1933)). (Within each base period, some of Warren and Pearson's component goods could not be matched. The weight for those goods was allocated to the other goods in the group.) An exception to this process was the "farm products" group index, for which Hanes used the standard BLS commodity group series (series Cc68) because the nature of this particular BLS group remained fairly stable across historical periods.

Group indexes were aggregated into two comprehensive indexes: one for all commodities and one for all commodities other than farm products, using Warren and Pearson's group weights for 1889. Finally, commodity group and comprehensive indexes on the succession of bases from 1890 through 1941 were spliced to each other and to the corresponding Warren and Pearson indexes (series Cc114–124). The 1890–1941 "all commodities" series was linked to Warren and Pearson's "all commodities" index with constant group weights" (Warren and Pearson, p. 69). The 1890–1941 "all commodities other than farm products" was linked to an index constructed from Warren and Pearson's commodity group indexes, excluding the farm products group. The resulting series for 1860–1941 and 1947–1990 were rebased to the average value over 1890–1914. The indexes for 1947–1990 were left on the average 1947–1990 base.

TABLE Cc138–154   Wholesale price indexes for Charleston – export staples, other domestic products, and foreign imports: 1732–1861

Contributed by Christopher Hanes

		Taylor indexes: 1843–1861				Taylor indexes: 1818–1842			
	All commodities	All commodities	South Carolina export staples	U.S. products other than South Carolina export staples	Foreign imports	All commodities	South Carolina export staples	U.S. products other than South Carolina export staples	Foreign imports
	Cc138	Cc139	Cc140	Cc141	Cc142	Cc143	Cc144	Cc145	Cc146
Year	Index 1818–1842 = 100	Index 1843–1861 = 100	Index 1843–1861 = 100	Index 1843–1861 = 100	Index 1843–1861 = 100	Index 1818–1842 = 100	Index 1818–1842 = 100	Index 1818–1842 = 100	Index 1818–1842 = 100
1732	62	—	—	—	—	—	—	—	—
1733	62	—	—	—	—	—	—	—	—
1734	84	—	—	—	—	—	—	—	—
1735	82	—	—	—	—	—	—	—	—
1736	75	—	—	—	—	—	—	—	—
1737	92	—	—	—	—	—	—	—	—
1738	98	—	—	—	—	—	—	—	—
1739	65	—	—	—	—	—	—	—	—
1740	60	—	—	—	—	—	—	—	—
1741	76	—	—	—	—	—	—	—	—
1742	66	—	—	—	—	—	—	—	—
1743	54	—	—	—	—	—	—	—	—
1744	50	—	—	—	—	—	—	—	—
1745	36	—	—	—	—	—	—	—	—
1746	35	—	—	—	—	—	—	—	—
1747	54	—	—	—	—	—	—	—	—
1748	68	—	—	—	—	—	—	—	—
1749	75	—	—	—	—	—	—	—	—
1750	78	—	—	—	—	—	—	—	—
1751	65	—	—	—	—	—	—	—	—
1752	76	—	—	—	—	—	—	—	—
1753	88	—	—	—	—	—	—	—	—
1754	67	—	—	—	—	—	—	—	—
1755	67	—	—	—	—	—	—	—	—
1756	60	—	—	—	—	—	—	—	—
1757	61	—	—	—	—	—	—	—	—
1758	67	—	—	—	—	—	—	—	—
1759	87	—	—	—	—	—	—	—	—
1760	72	—	—	—	—	—	—	—	—
1761	62	—	—	—	—	—	—	—	—
1762	60	—	—	—	—	—	—	—	—
1763	72	—	—	—	—	—	—	—	—
1764	67	—	—	—	—	—	—	—	—
1765	68	—	—	—	—	—	—	—	—
1766	78	—	—	—	—	—	—	—	—
1767	74	—	—	—	—	—	—	—	—
1768	80	—	—	—	—	—	—	—	—
1769	81	—	—	—	—	—	—	—	—
1770	72	—	—	—	—	—	—	—	—
1771	84	—	—	—	—	—	—	—	—
1772	107	—	—	—	—	—	—	—	—
1773	91	—	—	—	—	—	—	—	—
1774	81	—	—	—	—	—	—	—	—
1775	80	—	—	—	—	—	—	—	—
1780	118	—	—	—	—	—	—	—	—
1781	138	—	—	—	—	—	—	—	—
1782	192	—	—	—	—	—	—	—	—
1784	110	—	—	—	—	—	—	—	—
1785	100	—	—	—	—	—	—	—	—
1786	108	—	—	—	—	—	—	—	—
1787	108	—	—	—	—	—	—	—	—
1788	97	—	—	—	—	—	—	—	—
1789	88	—	—	—	—	—	—	—	—

(continued)

TABLE Cc138–154 Wholesale price indexes for Charleston – export staples, other domestic products, and foreign imports: 1732–1861 *Continued*

		Taylor indexes: 1843–1861				Taylor indexes: 1818–1842			
	All commodities	All commodities	South Carolina export staples	U.S. products other than South Carolina export staples	Foreign imports	All commodities	South Carolina export staples	U.S. products other than South Carolina export staples	Foreign imports
	Cc138	Cc139	Cc140	Cc141	Cc142	Cc143	Cc144	Cc145	Cc146
Year	Index 1818–1842 = 100	Index 1843–1861 = 100	Index 1843–1861 = 100	Index 1843–1861 = 100	Index 1843–1861 = 100	Index 1818–1842 = 100	Index 1818–1842 = 100	Index 1818–1842 = 100	Index 1818–1842 = 100
1790	97	—	—	—	—	—	—	—	—
1791	92	—	—	—	—	—	—	—	—
1796	145	—	—	—	—	—	—	—	—
1797	122	—	—	—	—	—	—	—	—
1798	129	—	—	—	—	—	—	—	—
1799	133	—	—	—	—	—	—	—	—
1800	123	—	—	—	—	—	—	—	—
1801	136	—	—	—	—	—	—	—	—
1802	106	—	—	—	—	—	—	—	—
1803	112	—	—	—	—	—	—	—	—
1804	114	—	—	—	—	—	—	—	—
1805	126	—	—	—	—	—	—	—	—
1806	109	—	—	—	—	—	—	—	—
1807	107	—	—	—	—	—	—	—	—
1808	87	—	—	—	—	—	—	—	—
1809	90	—	—	—	—	—	—	—	—
1810	96	—	—	—	—	—	—	—	—
1811	96	—	—	—	—	—	—	—	—
1812	95	—	—	—	—	—	—	—	—
1813	109	—	—	—	—	—	—	—	—
1814	123	—	—	—	—	—	—	—	—
1815	149	—	—	—	—	—	—	—	—
1816	172	—	—	—	—	—	—	—	—
1817	189	—	—	—	—	—	—	—	—
1818	179	—	—	—	—	179	220	160	135
1819	133	—	—	—	—	133	131	138	128
1820	110	—	—	—	—	110	121	97	114
1821	101	—	—	—	—	101	103	92	113
1822	108	—	—	—	—	108	100	108	122
1823	98	—	—	—	—	98	94	94	111
1824	93	—	—	—	—	93	99	82	102
1825	109	—	—	—	—	109	133	84	110
1826	92	—	—	—	—	92	83	96	104
1827	87	—	—	—	—	87	77	87	104
1828	85	—	—	—	—	85	80	81	103
1829	82	—	—	—	—	82	72	85	97
1830	82	—	—	—	—	82	78	80	93
1831	81	—	—	—	—	81	70	88	86
1832	86	—	—	—	—	86	78	91	89
1833	93	—	—	—	—	93	94	93	89
1834	93	—	—	—	—	93	97	91	91
1835	108	—	—	—	—	108	123	100	91
1836	121	—	—	—	—	121	129	124	100
1837	108	—	—	—	—	108	92	133	90
1838	103	—	—	—	—	103	88	123	92
1839	107	—	—	—	—	107	108	114	90
1840	83	—	—	—	—	83	75	90	83
1841	85	—	—	—	—	85	81	88	86
1842	74	—	—	—	—	74	67	80	75
1843	66	77	66	74	106	—	—	—	—
1844	68	80	73	74	106	—	—	—	—
1845	70	82	72	82	102	—	—	—	—
1846	75	88	83	85	105	—	—	—	—
1847	90	105	110	100	107	—	—	—	—
1848	67	79	66	86	92	—	—	—	—
1849	73	86	85	85	90	—	—	—	—

TABLE Cc138–154   Wholesale price indexes for Charleston – export staples, other domestic products, and foreign imports: 1732–1861 *Continued*

		Taylor indexes: 1843–1861				Taylor indexes: 1818–1842			
	All commodities	All commodities	South Carolina export staples	U.S. products other than South Carolina export staples	Foreign imports	All commodities	South Carolina export staples	U.S. products other than South Carolina export staples	Foreign imports
	Cc138	Cc139	Cc140	Cc141	Cc142	Cc143	Cc144	Cc145	Cc146
Year	Index 1818–1842 = 100	Index 1843–1861 = 100	Index 1843–1861 = 100	Index 1843–1861 = 100	Index 1843–1861 = 100	Index 1818–1842 = 100	Index 1818–1842 = 100	Index 1818–1842 = 100	Index 1818–1842 = 100
1850	87	102	123	88	91	—	—	—	—
1851	78	92	97	90	84	—	—	—	—
1852	77	91	96	91	79	—	—	—	—
1853	84	99	108	96	89	—	—	—	—
1854	88	103	100	111	93	—	—	—	—
1855	98	115	108	132	95	—	—	—	—
1856	97	114	116	116	109	—	—	—	—
1857	106	125	135	123	109	—	—	—	—
1858	90	106	120	99	94	—	—	—	—
1859	94	111	120	112	92	—	—	—	—
1860	94	111	116	113	96	—	—	—	—
1861	113	133	105	144	166	—	—	—	—

		Taylor Indexes: 1813–1822			Taylor Indexes: 1796–1812			Taylor Indexes: 1732–1791	
	All commodities	South Carolina export staples	Other than South Carolina export staples	All commodities	South Carolina export staples	Other than South Carolina export staples	South Carolina products	Other than South Carolina products
	Cc147 [1]	Cc148 [1]	Cc149 [1]	Cc150 [1]	Cc151 [1]	Cc152 [1]	Cc153 [1]	Cc154 [1]
Year	Index 1813–1822 = 100	Index 1813–1822 = 100	Index 1813–1822 = 100	Index 1796–1812 = 100	Index 1796–1812 = 100	Index 1796–1812 = 100	Index 1762–1774 = 100	Index 1781, 1784–1791 = 100
1732	—	—	—	—	—	—	79	—
1733	—	—	—	—	—	—	80	—
1734	—	—	—	—	—	—	108	—
1735	—	—	—	—	—	—	105	—
1736	—	—	—	—	—	—	96	—
1737	—	—	—	—	—	—	117	—
1738	—	—	—	—	—	—	125	—
1739	—	—	—	—	—	—	84	—
1740	—	—	—	—	—	—	77	—
1741	—	—	—	—	—	—	97	—
1742	—	—	—	—	—	—	85	—
1743	—	—	—	—	—	—	70	—
1744	—	—	—	—	—	—	64	—
1745	—	—	—	—	—	—	46	—
1746	—	—	—	—	—	—	45	—
1747	—	—	—	—	—	—	69	—
1748	—	—	—	—	—	—	88	—
1749	—	—	—	—	—	—	96	—
1750	—	—	—	—	—	—	100	—
1751	—	—	—	—	—	—	83	—
1752	—	—	—	—	—	—	97	—
1753	—	—	—	—	—	—	112	—
1754	—	—	—	—	—	—	86	—
1755	—	—	—	—	—	—	86	—
1756	—	—	—	—	—	—	77	—
1757	—	—	—	—	—	—	78	—
1758	—	—	—	—	—	—	86	—
1759	—	—	—	—	—	—	112	—

(continued)

TABLE Cc138–154   Wholesale price indexes for Charleston – export staples, other domestic products, and foreign imports: 1732–1861   *Continued*

	Taylor Indexes: 1813–1822			Taylor Indexes: 1796–1812			Taylor Indexes: 1732–1791	
	All commodities	South Carolina export staples	Other than South Carolina export staples	All commodities	South Carolina export staples	Other than South Carolina export staples	South Carolina products	Other than South Carolina products
	Cc147 [1]	Cc148 [1]	Cc149 [1]	Cc150 [1]	Cc151 [1]	Cc152 [1]	Cc153 [1]	Cc154 [1]
Year	Index 1813–1822 = 100	Index 1813–1822 = 100	Index 1813–1822 = 100	Index 1796–1812 = 100	Index 1796–1812 = 100	Index 1796–1812 = 100	Index 1762–1774 = 100	Index 1781, 1784–1791 = 100
1760	—	—	—	—	—	—	92	—
1761	—	—	—	—	—	—	80	—
1762	—	—	—	—	—	—	77	—
1763	—	—	—	—	—	—	92	—
1764	—	—	—	—	—	—	86	—
1765	—	—	—	—	—	—	87	—
1766	—	—	—	—	—	—	100	—
1767	—	—	—	—	—	—	94	—
1768	—	—	—	—	—	—	102	—
1769	—	—	—	—	—	—	104	—
1770	—	—	—	—	—	—	93	—
1771	—	—	—	—	—	—	108	—
1772	—	—	—	—	—	—	137	—
1773	—	—	—	—	—	—	116	—
1774	—	—	—	—	—	—	104	—
1775	—	—	—	—	—	—	102	—
1780	—	—	—	—	—	—	137	146
1781	—	—	—	—	—	—	170	150
1782	—	—	—	—	—	—	250	178
1784	—	—	—	—	—	—	150	86
1785	—	—	—	—	—	—	135	84
1786	—	—	—	—	—	—	142	98
1787	—	—	—	—	—	—	142	97
1788	—	—	—	—	—	—	128	87
1789	—	—	—	—	—	—	113	86
1790	—	—	—	—	—	—	119	106
1791	—	—	—	—	—	—	110	106
1796	—	—	—	128	134	122	—	—
1797	—	—	—	108	108	108	—	—
1798	—	—	—	114	123	106	—	—
1799	—	—	—	117	125	110	—	—
1800	—	—	—	108	114	103	—	—
1801	—	—	—	120	122	118	—	—
1802	—	—	—	93	96	91	—	—
1803	—	—	—	98	106	90	—	—
1804	—	—	—	101	100	102	—	—
1805	—	—	—	111	116	105	—	—
1806	—	—	—	97	101	92	—	—
1807	—	—	—	94	100	88	—	—
1808	—	—	—	76	70	83	—	—
1809	—	—	—	79	74	85	—	—
1810	—	—	—	85	80	91	—	—
1811	—	—	—	85	70	100	—	—
1812	—	—	—	84	63	106	—	—
1813	79	57	101	—	—	—	—	—
1814	90	70	110	—	—	—	—	—
1815	109	102	115	—	—	—	—	—
1816	125	134	116	—	—	—	—	—
1817	138	145	131	—	—	—	—	—
1818	135	160	110	—	—	—	—	—
1819	98	96	99	—	—	—	—	—
1820	78	86	71	—	—	—	—	—
1821	71	74	67	—	—	—	—	—
1822	77	75	79	—	—	—	—	—

TABLE Cc138–154   Wholesale price indexes for Charleston – export staples, other domestic products, and foreign imports: 1732–1861   *Continued*

[1] Series has no data after 1822.

Source

Arthur H. Cole, *Wholesale Commodity Prices in the United States, 1700–1861* (Harvard University Press, 1938), pp. 153, 155–7, and 159–67. See also articles by George Rogers Taylor, "Wholesale Commodity Prices at Charleston, S.C., 1732–1791," *Journal of Economic and Business History* 4 (February 1932): 356–77, and "Wholesale Commodity Prices at Charleston, S.C., 1796–1861," *Journal of Economic and Business History* 4 (August 1932) supplement: 848–68.

Documentation

These series were constructed by George Rogers Taylor as part of the project directed by the International Scientific Committee on Price History (see the essay in this chapter).

Taylor's research in commodity prices at Charleston, South Carolina, was presented in separate sets of index numbers for eight different periods, summarized here in five sets. The choice of time periods was made partly to reflect business conditions in Charleston and partly to take account of availability of data. Newspapers and original manuscript materials produced price series for a maximum of thirty-two items for 1818–1842 and a minimum of six for 1732–1747. Gaps were frequent, and no quotations at all appeared for 1792–1795. Quotations for 1738, 1775, 1780, and 1782 cover only part of the year. Series Cc138 splices the all-commodities indexes for the separate periods. The all-commodities index for 1732–1791 is the same as series Cc138.

Indexes for each period are weighted arithmetic averages of price relatives. Weights approximately represent the importance of each commodity in South Carolina commerce. Weights are the same for all years within a given time period but change from period to period. The all-commodities series comprises prices of six articles over 1732–1747, ten articles over 1748–1761, and sixteen articles over 1762–1775. In each of these three early periods, rice represents 50–64 percent of the total weight. For the five later periods, the number of commodities comprised in the all-commodities series were as follows: 1780–1791, 20; 1796–1812, 18; 1813–1822, 13; 1818–1842, 32; 1843–1861, 20. Across these periods the importance of rice declines from about 37 percent of the total weight to 5–7 percent. The importance of cotton increases from zero in 1791 to almost 35 percent in 1843–1861.

TABLE Cc155–169   Wholesale price indexes for Philadelphia, by commodity group: 1720–1861

Contributed by Christopher Hanes

Year	All commodities Cc155 Index 1821–1825 = 100	Domestically produced commodities Cc156 Index 1821–1825 = 100	Imported commodities Cc157 Index 1821–1825 = 100	Agricultural commodities Cc158 Index 1821–1825 = 100	Industrial commodities Cc159 Index 1821–1825 = 100	Farm products, crops Cc160 Index 1821–1825 = 100	Farm products, derivatives Cc161 Index 1821–1825 = 100	Imported foods Cc162 Index 1821–1825 = 100	Lumber products and naval stores Cc163 Index 1821–1825 = 100	Industrial commodities, raw Cc164 Index 1821–1825 = 100	Industrial commodities, consumption Cc165 Index 1821–1825 = 100	Fish Cc166 Index 1821–1825 = 100	Furs Cc167 Index 1821–1825 = 100	Wine Cc168 Index 1821–1825 = 100	Twelve commodities Cc169 Index 1741–1745 = 100
1720	—	—	—	—	—	—	—	—	—	—	—	—	—	—	86.2
1721	—	—	—	—	—	—	—	—	—	—	—	—	—	—	78.6
1722	—	—	—	—	—	—	—	—	—	—	—	—	—	—	81.6
1723	—	—	—	—	—	—	—	—	—	—	—	—	—	—	84.3
1724	—	—	—	—	—	—	—	—	—	—	—	—	—	—	88.9
1725	—	—	—	—	—	—	—	—	—	—	—	—	—	—	96.6
1726	—	—	—	—	—	—	—	—	—	—	—	—	—	—	101.0
1727	—	—	—	—	—	—	—	—	—	—	—	—	—	—	97.6
1728	—	—	—	—	—	—	—	—	—	—	—	—	—	—	92.8
1729	—	—	—	—	—	—	—	—	—	—	—	—	—	—	92.5
1730	—	—	—	—	—	—	—	—	—	—	—	—	—	—	98.0
1731	—	—	—	—	—	—	—	—	—	—	—	—	—	—	87.1
1732	—	—	—	—	—	—	—	—	—	—	—	—	—	—	83.6
1733	—	—	—	—	—	—	—	—	—	—	—	—	—	—	90.0
1734	—	—	—	—	—	—	—	—	—	—	—	—	—	—	87.2
1735	—	—	—	—	—	—	—	—	—	—	—	—	—	—	87.8
1736	—	—	—	—	—	—	—	—	—	—	—	—	—	—	83.6
1737	—	—	—	—	—	—	—	—	—	—	—	—	—	—	91.1
1738	—	—	—	—	—	—	—	—	—	—	—	—	—	—	91.1
1739	—	—	—	—	—	—	—	—	—	—	—	—	—	—	82.2
1740	—	—	—	—	—	—	—	—	—	—	—	—	—	—	87.3
1741	—	—	—	—	—	—	—	—	—	—	—	—	—	—	112.6
1742	—	—	—	—	—	—	—	—	—	—	—	—	—	—	108.3
1743	—	—	—	—	—	—	—	—	—	—	—	—	—	—	95.6
1744	—	—	—	—	—	—	—	—	—	—	—	—	—	—	90.9
1745	—	—	—	—	—	—	—	—	—	—	—	—	—	—	92.7
1746	—	—	—	—	—	—	—	—	—	—	—	—	—	—	99.7
1747	—	—	—	—	—	—	—	—	—	—	—	—	—	—	110.6
1748	—	—	—	—	—	—	—	—	—	—	—	—	—	—	124.7
1749	—	—	—	—	—	—	—	—	—	—	—	—	—	—	121.5
1750	—	—	—	—	—	—	—	—	—	—	—	—	—	—	113.0
1751	—	—	—	—	—	—	—	—	—	—	—	—	—	—	112.8
1752	—	—	—	—	—	—	—	—	—	—	—	—	—	—	111.9
1753	—	—	—	—	—	—	—	—	—	—	—	—	—	—	109.9
1754	—	—	—	—	—	—	—	—	—	—	—	—	—	—	109.1
1755	—	—	—	—	—	—	—	—	—	—	—	—	—	—	107.3
1756	—	—	—	—	—	—	—	—	—	—	—	—	—	—	109.6
1757	—	—	—	—	—	—	—	—	—	—	—	—	—	—	107.1
1758	—	—	—	—	—	—	—	—	—	—	—	—	—	—	109.6
1759	—	—	—	—	—	—	—	—	—	—	—	—	—	—	125.0
1760	—	—	—	—	—	—	—	—	—	—	—	—	—	—	125.7
1761	—	—	—	—	—	—	—	—	—	—	—	—	—	—	121.2
1762	—	—	—	—	—	—	—	—	—	—	—	—	—	—	133.4
1763	—	—	—	—	—	—	—	—	—	—	—	—	—	—	136.4
1764	—	—	—	—	—	—	—	—	—	—	—	—	—	—	119.4

Year	All commodities Cc155 (Index 1821–1825 = 100)	Domestically produced commodities Cc156 (Index 1821–1825 = 100)	Imported commodities Cc157 (Index 1821–1825 = 100)	Agricultural commodities Cc158 (Index 1821–1825 = 100)	Industrial commodities Cc159 (Index 1821–1825 = 100)	Farm products, crops Cc160 (Index 1821–1825 = 100)	Farm products, derivatives Cc161 (Index 1821–1825 = 100)	Imported foods Cc162 (Index 1821–1825 = 100)	Lumber products and naval stores Cc163 (Index 1821–1825 = 100)	Industrial commodities, raw Cc164 (Index 1821–1825 = 100)	Industrial commodities, consumption Cc165 (Index 1821–1825 = 100)	Fish Cc166 (Index 1821–1825 = 100)	Furs Cc167 (Index 1821–1825 = 100)	Wine Cc168 (Index 1821–1825 = 100)	Twelve commodities Cc169 (Index 1741–1745 = 100)
1765	—	—	—	—	—	—	—	—	—	—	—	—	—	—	118.4
1766	—	—	—	—	—	—	—	—	—	—	—	—	—	—	124.7
1767	—	—	—	—	—	—	—	—	—	—	—	—	—	—	123.7
1768	—	—	—	—	—	—	—	—	—	—	—	—	—	—	119.7
1769	—	—	—	—	—	—	—	—	—	—	—	—	—	—	115.9
1770	—	—	—	—	—	—	—	—	—	—	—	—	—	—	121.6
1771	—	—	—	—	—	—	—	—	—	—	—	—	—	—	126.7
1772	—	—	—	—	—	—	—	—	—	—	—	—	—	—	141.0
1773	—	—	—	—	—	—	—	—	—	—	—	—	—	—	133.7
1774	—	—	—	—	—	—	—	—	—	—	—	—	—	—	127.5
1784	100.1	104.8	97.7	107.0	96.9	101.7	111.8	122.0	104.3	103.9	87.4	127.9	76.9	59.1	172.6
1785	94.1	97.0	93.5	101.8	90.9	105.9	98.4	110.7	92.4	100.6	78.3	121.9	72.4	66.0	158.0
1786	91.0	90.0	93.8	101.6	88.6	106.1	97.9	113.0	69.6	95.9	78.7	117.8	65.4	69.1	145.0
1787	88.4	85.4	92.7	97.5	88.3	104.2	92.1	110.9	59.9	93.7	80.8	116.2	55.3	69.1	135.8
1788	83.3	78.1	89.7	84.5	85.4	89.3	80.6	107.5	56.5	91.7	76.8	103.5	52.8	65.2	120.5
1789	82.4	76.5	88.8	80.7	85.2	84.6	77.4	102.7	60.5	91.1	77.1	103.5	55.8	62.7	128.6
1790	86.5	83.4	89.9	93.5	85.4	96.6	90.8	109.3	67.0	89.9	79.2	105.5	58.9	64.0	160.3
1791	89.7	84.7	96.5	88.4	87.0	88.3	88.4	128.7	74.2	87.3	86.5	117.1	57.7	67.1	149.2
1792	91.5	85.5	99.3	88.0	89.4	88.4	87.7	132.5	72.4	88.7	90.6	116.5	62.2	71.3	156.5
1793	96.3	91.2	103.0	97.8	92.8	98.8	96.9	133.3	79.1	91.7	94.4	113.8	61.9	78.6	174.9
1794	109.6	101.6	120.7	108.7	110.7	104.6	112.3	143.7	86.6	104.2	121.0	141.9	59.3	83.3	—
1795	130.7	125.3	141.3	129.6	130.4	124.1	134.6	173.3	114.2	124.9	138.9	200.3	70.1	86.5	257.8
1796	139.1	140.7	142.6	144.6	136.0	147.8	141.8	178.3	130.7	126.1	152.0	211.0	85.7	87.1	295.8
1797	133.5	134.4	135.8	135.9	130.0	142.8	130.2	169.3	133.9	125.4	137.1	226.3	75.1	85.7	266.7
1798	127.1	123.4	131.9	128.8	129.0	136.6	122.4	152.3	122.7	125.4	134.6	189.5	58.1	81.5	—
1799	127.3	115.6	142.2	123.3	133.4	127.4	120.0	158.7	104.8	132.9	134.2	146.2	60.5	89.9	—
1800	128.3	121.1	138.0	129.6	130.5	129.0	130.1	155.3	116.2	131.5	129.1	124.6	74.4	93.9	274.4
1801	131.9	129.5	137.4	140.8	131.6	142.7	144.8	144.2	120.5	132.1	130.9	169.4	77.6	101.7	211.2
1802	122.5	118.1	129.5	120.5	124.0	121.7	119.4	137.3	115.2	125.7	121.4	167.1	72.4	103.6	212.1
1803	120.2	115.9	124.9	114.7	123.1	120.6	109.9	130.8	125.0	126.1	118.9	138.2	72.9	98.7	241.0
1804	128.1	123.9	132.6	126.9	129.5	130.9	123.4	142.2	126.6	131.6	126.5	147.9	85.3	103.5	262.9
1805	131.5	131.6	130.8	142.0	131.9	145.5	139.0	142.8	124.7	130.9	133.3	163.0	81.7	96.7	233.1
1806	128.1	125.8	128.8	135.5	131.7	132.3	138.2	138.3	114.8	135.3	126.4	171.7	75.0	89.4	217.9
1807	123.7	121.9	123.7	126.0	128.4	125.9	126.0	128.8	114.3	133.9	120.7	167.6	82.7	89.1	192.6
1808	123.1	112.4	133.6	109.4	132.6	108.7	110.0	135.7	113.9	136.3	127.4	128.1	78.5	97.7	224.0
1809	135.6	121.9	151.1	119.3	145.9	115.7	122.5	146.8	131.3	148.1	142.6	136.9	83.8	113.0	249.6
1810	138.7	131.6	147.3	133.4	146.2	130.3	136.1	134.2	138.6	151.3	138.9	140.2	90.7	128.9	260.2
1811	135.3	134.2	139.4	129.4	141.8	122.2	135.9	127.0	132.5	146.1	135.7	157.7	97.6	137.0	257.3
1812	142.3	125.6	158.6	126.3	153.7	120.5	131.6	143.8	120.7	158.3	147.0	165.0	93.5	151.9	286.3
1813	161.0	135.5	187.8	133.4	175.9	133.2	133.7	182.4	132.9	177.0	174.2	174.7	90.7	164.5	371.3
1814	189.7	159.0	223.4	151.5	205.6	147.5	154.9	217.7	176.6	209.5	199.9	227.8	89.6	192.0	337.1
1815	173.1	160.8	186.4	161.1	175.1	154.1	167.3	194.8	165.8	175.1	175.0	220.5	111.5	167.1	298.3
1816	151.9	159.5	146.6	177.8	143.2	185.0	171.8	157.8	146.3	141.8	145.1	196.8	107.0	147.9	307.6
1817	132.6	145.1	122.9	178.0	121.8	183.5	173.5	133.0	123.4	117.2	128.8	155.1	93.7	122.7	276.2
1818	130.6	138.8	125.0	160.3	121.8	162.5	158.4	136.6	126.9	118.3	127.0	164.4	80.3	123.0	223.2
1819	119.4	123.8	116.4	132.9	113.5	136.7	129.6	126.1	121.5	109.6	119.4	137.9	75.0	122.8	—

(continued)

TABLE Cc155–169   Wholesale price indexes for Philadelphia, by commodity group: 1720–1861   *Continued*

Year	All commodities Cc155 Index 1821–1825 = 100	Domestically produced commodities Cc156 Index 1821–1825 = 100	Imported commodities Cc157 Index 1821–1825 = 100	Agricultural commodities Cc158 Index 1821–1825 = 100	Industrial commodities Cc159 Index 1821–1825 = 100	Farm products, crops Cc160 Index 1821–1825 = 100	Farm products, derivatives Cc161 Index 1821–1825 = 100	Imported foods Cc162 Index 1821–1825 = 100	Lumber products and naval stores Cc163 Index 1821–1825 = 100	Industrial commodities, raw Cc164 Index 1821–1825 = 100	Industrial commodities, consumption Cc165 Index 1821–1825 = 100	Fish Cc166 Index 1821–1825 = 100	Furs Cc167 Index 1821–1825 = 100	Wine Cc168 Index 1821–1825 = 100	Twelve commodities Cc169 Index 1741–1745 = 100
1820	106.6	108.6	104.7	109.2	105.7	112.9	106.2	107.7	109.1	101.8	111.8	108.5	73.4	114.0	180.7
1821	102.0	100.5	103.8	97.5	104.7	95.3	99.4	103.5	95.6	101.8	109.3	99.2	82.6	109.3	160.2
1822	104.2	105.4	102.9	107.9	103.3	107.7	108.1	103.6	102.5	102.2	104.9	106.8	103.8	103.4	183.4
1823	98.6	99.7	97.3	101.5	98.2	101.8	101.3	95.3	100.1	97.6	99.1	105.0	101.0	95.4	179.3
1824	94.3	94.4	93.8	92.6	94.9	91.4	93.7	92.3	97.8	95.5	93.9	99.4	99.0	92.1	163.0
1825	98.5	97.4	99.9	97.0	97.0	100.5	94.1	102.4	102.8	101.0	91.4	89.3	111.8	99.1	163.6
1826	95.9	96.3	94.7	100.3	94.0	106.7	95.1	96.1	98.0	97.2	89.4	84.1	101.0	96.4	160.4
1827	93.0	93.2	92.3	95.0	92.2	96.8	93.4	91.9	95.5	94.4	89.0	95.4	93.1	92.2	161.5
1828	91.0	90.7	91.6	89.5	90.2	86.5	92.2	90.1	96.2	91.8	87.9	96.4	101.4	90.9	165.4
1829	88.8	90.2	88.6	90.9	88.7	91.1	90.7	84.9	89.8	89.9	87.0	91.4	97.6	87.6	172.4
1830	84.0	84.7	85.4	87.3	84.2	84.3	89.9	80.7	80.9	85.3	82.7	88.0	85.2	82.5	150.2
1831	87.7	89.7	87.1	97.0	87.1	94.3	99.4	81.2	84.7	88.6	84.9	97.1	86.8	83.3	165.2
1832	89.3	91.8	86.6	99.7	88.2	99.6	99.8	84.4	87.4	88.7	87.5	86.3	84.9	84.8	166.7
1833	88.1	93.8	81.6	101.9	88.3	102.2	101.7	71.7	91.6	90.1	85.7	92.8	85.4	85.9	171.2
1834	85.8	91.6	79.1	97.6	86.4	101.3	94.6	68.0	94.1	90.1	81.3	91.8	88.4	81.6	163.0
1835	90.7	99.9	81.4	115.4	87.3	126.6	106.5	74.8	99.0	89.9	83.6	111.5	83.2	80.2	181.9
1836	97.6	113.0	82.4	135.7	93.8	142.8	129.8	75.0	105.2	97.4	88.6	124.9	92.2	77.3	217.7
1837	95.3	109.7	80.5	131.0	95.3	132.0	130.3	68.6	97.6	97.2	92.6	120.3	88.8	72.4	233.8
1838	91.9	103.2	80.2	123.3	92.6	123.9	122.9	67.4	94.0	94.7	89.6	130.7	66.1	71.2	211.4
1839	95.9	110.8	82.0	136.6	95.6	146.7	128.5	67.2	95.0	99.3	90.5	177.5	72.0	70.6	203.8
1840	87.4	96.8	78.2	107.6	89.8	109.5	106.0	63.7	90.1	93.1	85.2	139.7	74.3	68.7	165.4
1841	85.2	93.6	77.5	102.2	87.1	111.8	94.6	65.0	88.6	90.9	81.8	131.8	70.2	68.0	152.3
1842	79.1	85.1	74.1	89.0	83.2	97.1	82.6	60.8	83.0	87.2	77.5	109.3	61.1	64.7	135.7
1843	75.4	77.2	74.6	81.1	78.7	88.0	75.5	64.3	75.7	81.7	74.3	107.7	45.4	66.5	131.4
1844	76.9	77.4	77.3	81.1	79.0	87.7	75.9	68.6	70.2	82.4	74.2	126.5	56.6	73.6	129.3
1845	79.7	82.3	78.4	90.1	78.6	94.2	86.6	73.1	75.5	81.4	74.7	128.3	65.5	73.4	142.5
1846	80.1	83.4	78.3	93.2	78.9	101.7	86.4	71.7	75.4	80.9	76.1	119.6	64.5	71.1	144.1
1847	83.5	90.7	78.4	112.8	80.6	123.1	104.6	72.2	75.3	82.6	77.7	123.1	57.3	71.9	177.5
1848	78.5	84.2	74.9	97.4	78.7	103.7	92.4	54.8	72.6	80.6	75.9	118.4	56.0	69.9	149.3
1849	76.5	81.6	72.9	94.0	76.1	100.1	89.1	54.3	73.2	78.1	73.1	104.0	56.0	68.7	146.8
1850	79.9	85.2	76.7	98.6	77.1	109.2	90.3	71.5	79.1	80.1	72.8	126.1	56.0	70.6	147.3
1851	80.3	86.4	76.7	102.2	75.9	110.0	95.9	71.3	87.9	78.9	71.6	118.7	56.0	70.3	144.8
1852	80.4	89.5	74.8	107.7	75.1	107.6	107.7	65.4	92.9	78.2	70.7	135.7	57.1	70.3	152.8
1853	87.7	96.8	82.3	117.4	82.8	116.4	118.3	71.8	101.2	86.8	77.2	146.5	54.5	74.2	171.9
1854	95.8	105.6	91.5	131.8	90.7	135.5	128.7	75.1	111.0	92.1	88.8	156.7	45.4	90.4	211.6
1855	99.3	107.6	96.5	142.5	93.1	147.7	138.2	75.1	100.2	92.7	93.6	153.4	44.4	125.6	234.9
1856	99.1	103.7	99.2	128.8	93.9	129.9	127.9	83.0	92.5	94.3	93.4	156.8	51.4	126.4	194.6
1857	100.9	106.1	99.9	134.8	92.5	136.8	133.1	86.5	99.9	93.8	90.5	161.9	54.3	130.8	198.4
1858	89.7	94.8	88.0	115.4	85.3	115.6	115.2	66.0	97.2	86.9	82.9	136.5	49.4	127.2	165.3
1859	89.4	98.7	83.0	123.3	84.0	124.3	122.4	63.1	103.3	87.1	79.6	152.4	49.9	108.5	176.5
1860	88.8	95.7	84.9	118.0	83.2	113.8	121.7	64.7	100.0	87.0	77.8	150.8	47.6	122.2	164.3
1861	88.2	94.7	85.3	111.6	79.9	117.9	106.4	67.3	125.0	82.5	76.2	118.5	50.6	125.0	167.5

TABLE Cc155–169   Wholesale price indexes for Philadelphia, by commodity group: 1720–1861   *Continued*

Source

Anne Bezanson, Robert D. Gray, and Miriam Hussey, *Wholesale Prices in Philadelphia, 1784–1861,* part 1, Industrial Research Study number 29 (Industrial Research Department, Wharton School of Finance and Commerce, University of Pennsylvania, 1936), p. 392.

Documentation

The index numbers are annual averages of monthly figures.

These series were constructed under the direction of Anne Bezanson as part of the International Scientific Committee on Price History project (see the essay in this chapter). Bezanson and her associates found continuous price reports for 140 commodities over the period 1784–1861 and 157 commodities over 1819–1861.

For the period 1784–1861, they computed a comprehensive all-commodities index (series Cc155) comprising prices of 140 commodities

and indexes for a variety of commodity groups (series Cc156–168), as unweighted *geometric* averages of price relatives.

Price reports covering the colonial period were much scarcer, with many gaps in the data. For the period 1720–1861, Bezanson and her associates calculated an index (series Cc169) that is an unweighted *arithmetic* average of price relatives for twelve commodities (beef, bread, corn, flour, molasses, pitch, pork, rum, salt, sugar, tar, and wheat). Monthly relative prices for the individual commodities and descriptions of the commodities included in the indexes are given in Bezanson, Gray, and Hussey (1936). In addition to the indexes presented here, Bezanson and her associates constructed corresponding indexes for 1852–1896. See Bezanson, *Wholesale Prices in Philadelphia, 1852–1896* (University of Pennsylvania Press, 1954).

TABLE Cc170–175   Wholesale price indexes for Cincinnati and for the Ohio River valley: 1788–1861

Contributed by Christopher Hanes

	Cincinnati			Ohio River valley		
	All commodities	Commodities identified with Northern agriculture	Commodities not identified with Northern agriculture	All commodities	Commodities identified with Northern agriculture	Commodities not identified with Northern agriculture
	Cc170	Cc171	Cc172	Cc173	Cc174	Cc175
Year	Index 1824–1846 = 100	Index 1824–1846 = 100	Index 1824–1846 = 100	Index 1788–1817 = 100	Index 1788–1817 = 100	Index 1788–1817 = 100
1788	—	—	—	104	93	130
1789	—	—	—	102	87	139
1790	—	—	—	98	90	118
1791	—	—	—	92	88	104
1792	—	—	—	98	101	92
1793	—	—	—	106	110	96
1794	—	—	—	96	95	100
1795	—	—	—	111	110	114
1796	—	—	—	127	125	132
1797	—	—	—	133	134	129
1798	—	—	—	109	108	113
1799	—	—	—	97	89	117
1800	—	—	—	93	88	106
1801	—	—	—	90	89	94
1802	—	—	—	88	84	99
1803	—	—	—	84	82	88
1804	—	—	—	87	85	90
1805	—	—	—	86	86	89
1806	—	—	—	95	95	96
1807	—	—	—	95	92	104
1808	—	—	—	95	89	110
1809	—	—	—	90	87	97
1810	—	—	—	87	88	85
1811	—	—	—	79	78	82
1812	—	—	—	77	84	60
1813	—	—	—	106	114	86
1814	—	—	—	122	134	90
1815	—	—	—	108	117	86
1816	196	164	289	116	131	75
1817	205	175	272	125	145	75
1818	190	160	264	—	—	—
1819	193	164	265	—	—	—
1820	140	112	237	—	—	—
1821	86	68	160	—	—	—
1822	98	78	166	—	—	—
1823	101	87	129	—	—	—
1824	98	85	122	—	—	—

(continued)

TABLE Cc170–175   Wholesale price indexes for Cincinnati and for the Ohio River valley: 1788–1861   *Continued*

	Cincinnati			Ohio River valley		
	All commodities	Commodities identified with Northern agriculture	Commodities not identified with Northern agriculture	All commodities	Commodities identified with Northern agriculture	Commodities not identified with Northern agriculture
	Cc170	Cc171	Cc172	Cc173	Cc174	Cc175
Year	Index 1824–1846 = 100	Index 1824–1846 = 100	Index 1824–1846 = 100	Index 1788–1817 = 100	Index 1788–1817 = 100	Index 1788–1817 = 100
1825	100	85	127	—	—	—
1826	93	81	115	—	—	—
1827	91	79	114	—	—	—
1828	92	81	113	—	—	—
1829	98	91	112	—	—	—
1830	93	86	106	—	—	—
1831	99	100	98	—	—	—
1832	101	103	98	—	—	—
1833	102	101	102	—	—	—
1834	95	93	97	—	—	—
1835	117	125	102	—	—	—
1836	145	159	121	—	—	—
1837	131	142	112	—	—	—
1838	129	137	115	—	—	—
1839	138	150	116	—	—	—
1840	104	111	91	—	—	—
1841	89	91	87	—	—	—
1842	72	70	76	—	—	—
1843	72	73	70	—	—	—
1844	77	81	71	—	—	—
1845	87	97	68	—	—	—
1846	76	81	69	—	—	—
1847	90	102	76	—	—	—
1848	75	83	65	—	—	—
1849	77	87	65	—	—	—
1850	86	98	72	—	—	—
1851	90	107	68	—	—	—
1852	93	112	68	—	—	—
1853	104	118	84	—	—	—
1854	110	128	85	—	—	—
1855	123	153	81	—	—	—
1856	121	141	93	—	—	—
1857	128	154	94	—	—	—
1858	102	120	77	—	—	—
1859	114	140	79	—	—	—
1860	110	133	80	—	—	—
1861	103	123	76	—	—	—

Sources

Series Cc170. For 1816–1860: annual averages of monthly data from Arthur H. Cole, *Wholesale Commodity Prices in the United States, 1700–1861* (Harvard University Press, 1938), p. 185. For 1861: estimated by Ethel Hoover from series Cc171–172 using weights given in Cole (1938), p. 81.

Series Cc171–175. Thomas S. Berry, *Western Prices before 1861* (Harvard University Press, 1943), pp. 563–4.

Documentation

These series were constructed by Thomas S. Berry, originally as part of the International Scientific Committee on Price History project (see the essay in this chapter).

From Cincinnati in the period 1816–1825, Berry found continuous records of prices for 21 commodities. Thirteen were "identified with northern agriculture," that is, agricultural commodities and close derivatives produced in the Ohio valley region, such as flour, pork, and whiskey. Eight were not identified with northern agriculture, principally manufactured goods and foods and raw materials brought in from outside the region. For 1824–1846, the

number of commodities increased to a total of 37, 20 of which were identified with northern agriculture. For 1846–1861, the number of commodities increased further to a total of 50, 29 identified with northern agriculture. To construct indexes, Berry calculated weighted arithmetic averages of price relatives for each period separately and then linked the resulting series. Weights for 1816–1825 reflect New Orleans receipts in 1825. Weights for the two later periods reflect Cincinnati receipts in 1845–1848 and 1852–1856. Prices for individual goods are given in Berry, *Western Prices before 1861*.

For years before 1816, there were not enough price records from Cincinnati alone to construct series, and so Berry expanded his geographical coverage to include three other Ohio River valley cities in addition to Cincinnati: Pittsburgh, Lexington, and Louisville. Berry found prices for 14 commodities in "account books of backwoods merchants" and local journals. Indexes were computed as *unweighted* averages of price relatives. The price used to calculate the price relative for a commodity in a given year was the *median* value of all available price quotations for the good in that year, across all four of the cities.

TABLE Cc176–187 Wholesale price indexes for New Orleans – Louisiana and other domestic products, and foreign imports: 1800–1861

Contributed by Christopher Hanes

Year	Taylor indexes: 1840–1861					Taylor indexes: 1815–1842			Taylor indexes: 1804–1811			Taylor index: 1800–1811
	All commodities	All commodities	Louisiana products	U.S. products, other than Louisiana	Foreign imports	Louisiana products	U.S. products, other than Louisiana	Foreign imports	All commodities	Domestic products, U.S. and Louisiana	Foreign imports	Louisiana products
	Cc176	Cc177	Cc178	Cc179	Cc180	Cc181	Cc182	Cc183	Cc184	Cc185	Cc186	Cc187
	Index 1824–1842 = 100	Index 1843–1861 = 100	Index 1843–1861 = 100	Index 1843–1861 = 100	Index 1843–1861 = 100	Index 1824–1842 = 100	Index 1824–1842 = 100	Index 1824–1842 = 100	Index 1805–1811 = 100	Index 1805–1811 = 100	Index 1805–1811 = 100	Index 1805–1811 = 100
1800	138	—	—	—	—	—	—	—	—	—	—	114
1801	146	—	—	—	—	—	—	—	—	—	—	120
1802	130	—	—	—	—	—	—	—	—	—	—	106
1803	115	—	—	—	—	—	—	—	—	—	—	95
1804	126	—	—	—	—	—	—	—	100	100	101	99
1805	147	—	—	—	—	—	—	—	117	118	111	124
1806	142	—	—	—	—	—	—	—	113	114	106	118
1807	133	—	—	—	—	—	—	—	106	109	92	112
1808	112	—	—	—	—	—	—	—	89	90	83	89
1809	120	—	—	—	—	—	—	—	95	91	112	88
1810	119	—	—	—	—	—	—	—	95	91	108	87
1811	110	—	—	—	—	—	—	—	87	87	89	83
1815	170	—	—	—	—	178	142	—	—	—	—	—
1816	214	—	—	—	—	227	184	182	—	—	—	—
1817	197	—	—	—	—	218	150	151	—	—	—	—
1818	200	—	—	—	—	224	146	220	—	—	—	—
1819	151	—	—	—	—	160	127	200	—	—	—	—
1820	119	—	—	—	—	126	98	190	—	—	—	—
1821	115	—	—	—	—	130	83	160	—	—	—	—
1822	124	—	—	—	—	140	94	152	—	—	—	—
1823	105	—	—	—	—	112	90	132	—	—	—	—
1824	110	—	—	—	—	122	90	123	—	—	—	—
1825	130	—	—	—	—	155	96	123	—	—	—	—
1826	95	—	—	—	—	97	88	116	—	—	—	—
1827	90	—	—	—	—	88	87	112	—	—	—	—
1828	91	—	—	—	—	92	86	110	—	—	—	—
1829	90	—	—	—	—	84	94	108	—	—	—	—
1830	86	—	—	—	—	85	82	103	—	—	—	—
1831	80	—	—	—	—	74	86	97	—	—	—	—
1832	88	—	—	—	—	84	92	102	—	—	—	—
1833	99	—	—	—	—	103	95	95	—	—	—	—
1834	96	—	—	—	—	99	95	87	—	—	—	—
1835	123	—	—	—	—	133	114	95	—	—	—	—
1836	132	—	—	—	—	140	129	103	—	—	—	—
1837	108	—	—	—	—	103	118	98	—	—	—	—
1838	107	—	—	—	—	98	123	96	—	—	—	—
1839	116	—	—	—	—	105	136	93	—	—	—	—

(continued)

TABLE Cc176–187   Wholesale price indexes for New Orleans – Louisiana and other domestic products, and foreign imports: 1800–1861   *Continued*

	Taylor indexes: 1840–1861				Taylor indexes: 1815–1842			Taylor indexes: 1804–1811			Taylor index: 1800–1811
	All commodities	All commodities	Louisiana products	U.S. products, other than Louisiana	Foreign imports	Louisiana products	U.S. products, other than Louisiana	Foreign imports	All commodities	Domestic products, U.S. and Louisiana	Foreign imports	Louisiana products
	Cc176	Cc177	Cc178	Cc179	Cc180	Cc181	Cc182	Cc183	Cc184	Cc185	Cc186	Cc187
Year	Index 1824–1842 = 100	Index 1843–1861 = 100	Index 1843–1861 = 100	Index 1843–1861 = 100	Index 1843–1861 = 100	Index 1824–1842 = 100	Index 1824–1842 = 100	Index 1824–1842 = 100	Index 1805–1811 = 100	Index 1805–1811 = 100	Index 1805–1811 = 100	Index 1805–1811 = 100
1840	91	97	88	106	105	78	110	82	—	—	—	—
1841	93	100	102	97	104	89	100	85	—	—	—	—
1842	75	78	76	79	93	73	78	75	—	—	—	—
1843	70	74	75	70	89	—	—	—	—	—	—	—
1844	75	80	84	74	84	—	—	—	—	—	—	—
1845	74	79	77	80	85	—	—	—	—	—	—	—
1846	78	83	88	77	83	—	—	—	—	—	—	—
1847	93	99	108	90	82	—	—	—	—	—	—	—
1848	68	73	66	81	80	—	—	—	—	—	—	—
1849	80	85	85	85	81	—	—	—	—	—	—	—
1850	103	110	123	95	95	—	—	—	—	—	—	—
1851	89	95	98	93	86	—	—	—	—	—	—	—
1852	85	90	91	91	84	—	—	—	—	—	—	—
1853	91	97	94	101	96	—	—	—	—	—	—	—
1854	90	96	82	114	101	—	—	—	—	—	—	—
1855	103	110	96	129	107	—	—	—	—	—	—	—
1856	114	121	121	124	107	—	—	—	—	—	—	—
1857	136	144	156	136	115	—	—	—	—	—	—	—
1858	104	111	118	104	106	—	—	—	—	—	—	—
1859	107	114	118	110	106	—	—	—	—	—	—	—
1860	105	112	113	110	110	—	—	—	—	—	—	—
1861	117	125	102	138	206	—	—	—	—	—	—	—

Source

Arthur H. Cole, *Wholesale Commodity Prices in the United States, 1700–1861* (Harvard University Press, 1938), pp. 170–9.

Documentation

These series were constructed by George Rogers Taylor as part of the International Scientific Committee on Price History project (see the essay in this chapter).

All of the index numbers were calculated as weighted arithmetic averages of price relatives. Weights represent the importance of the commodities in New Orleans trade. Series Cc176 splices the all-commodities indexes for the separate periods. The all-commodities index for 1815–1842 is the same as series Cc176.

New Orleans price indexes were prepared for four separate periods because the volume of price information varied so much over time. The index for the period 1800–1811, covering Louisiana products only, comprises prices of 8 commodities, mostly agricultural products, from the month of July. The indexes for 1804–1811 comprise prices of 29 commodities in the domestic products index and 15 commodities in the imported products index, mostly from the month of April. The indexes for 1815–1842 comprise prices of 5 Louisiana products, 34 U.S. products other than Louisiana products, and 11 foreign imports. The indexes for 1840–1861 comprise 4 Louisiana products, 37 U.S. products other than Louisiana products, and 8 foreign products.

TABLE Cc188–204   Wholesale price indexes and gold-dollar exchange rates for San Francisco, by commodity group: 1847–1900

Contributed by Christopher Hanes

	Wholesale price index, in gold dollars									
	Farm products and foods				Industrial materials and products					
	All commodities	All farm products and foods	Farm products	Foods	All industrial materials and products	Textiles and clothing	Fuel and lighting materials	Metals and metal products	Building materials and naval stores	Chemicals and drugs
	Cc188	Cc189	Cc190	Cc191	Cc192	Cc193	Cc194	Cc195	Cc196	Cc197
Year	Index 1881–1885 = 100	Index 1881–1885 = 100	Index 1881–1885 = 100	Index 1881–1885 = 100	Index 1881–1885 = 100	Index 1881–1885 = 100	Index 1881–1885 = 100	Index 1881–1885 = 100	Index 1881–1885 = 100	Index 1881–1885 = 100
1847	254	265	151	292	367	185	364	409	141	—
1848	226	210	136	228	341	162	351	326	186	3,526
1849	319	348	372	342	427	137	467	408	928	1,174
1850	236	285	352	269	257	158	359	287	248	538
1851	162	205	249	195	152	106	169	171	180	324
1852	211	282	271	286	201	106	323	194	229	233
1853	168	207	183	214	178	94	302	143	203	181
1854	147	158	125	168	173	87	327	136	143	188
1855	141	172	143	179	142	95	227	128	108	162
1856	142	176	162	179	137	91	211	129	120	148
1857	143	176	146	185	133	97	181	129	115	170
1858	148	184	134	200	133	102	193	125	105	152
1859	127	142	115	151	128	92	181	134	100	155
1860	113	118	98	125	127	89	188	124	101	150
1861	114	116	98	123	135	98	206	121	106	158
1862	129	136	123	143	144	142	179	119	102	166
1863	131	126	107	136	160	182	184	129	105	154
1864	148	160	159	161	162	205	158	130	110	153
1865	162	179	170	183	177	224	192	125	108	163
1866	138	133	111	143	165	191	176	133	118	163
1867	129	127	119	131	144	149	160	130	114	152
1868	126	132	128	135	136	131	161	121	116	141
1869	121	122	104	138	135	131	155	127	116	142
1870	118	122	111	131	126	130	130	130	94	142
1871	130	139	152	127	135	127	167	138	101	135
1872	127	124	130	119	147	133	184	157	111	145
1873	122	123	125	120	137	129	149	159	116	135
1874	118	119	118	120	131	119	145	164	104	131
1875	114	116	117	116	119	110	131	133	106	122
1876	108	110	104	115	112	104	127	112	103	117
1877	113	122	129	116	109	100	121	105	103	126
1878	105	110	111	109	102	101	98	98	100	125
1879	100	101	103	99	100	100	95	97	97	123
1880	103	102	105	100	106	108	100	112	95	123
1881	103	103	100	105	106	108	104	104	100	112
1882	107	110	111	110	104	107	97	107	104	109
1883	105	109	112	107	102	101	104	101	106	101
1884	97	95	91	97	97	95	101	95	102	95
1885	89	84	87	81	90	90	95	94	88	83
1886	87	83	88	79	89	91	87	96	87	81
1887	93	92	96	89	93	92	89	106	99	81
1888	95	91	87	94	103	94	129	107	96	78
1889	91	88	85	92	95	97	100	105	85	77
1890	92	88	89	88	96	95	104	112	83	77
1891	94	95	100	90	94	98	98	105	77	78
1892	89	87	89	86	88	94	91	97	71	79
1893	86	83	76	89	86	90	87	95	71	77
1894	78	73	63	81	81	88	83	81	70	71
1895	74	68	59	76	74	71	83	76	69	67
1896	74	71	66	76	72	65	80	81	67	66
1897	79	78	80	76	73	71	80	79	66	66
1898	81	80	84	78	75	71	85	81	72	65
1899	81	76	72	79	81	79	84	97	74	64
1900	85	76	68	82	88	84	95	106	87	66

(continued)

TABLE Cc188–204   Wholesale price indexes and gold-dollar exchange rates for San Francisco, by commodity group: 1847–1900   *Continued*

	Wholesale price index, in gold dollars				Value of gold dollar, in U.S. currency cents		
	Miscellaneous products						
	All miscellaneous products	Hides and leather	Alcoholic beverages	Miscellaneous items	At San Francisco	At New York City	At San Francisco in U.S. currency exchange in East Coast cities
	Cc198	Cc199	Cc200	Cc201	Cc202	Cc203	Cc204
Year	Index 1881–1885 = 100	Index 1881–1885 = 100	Index 1881–1885 = 100	Index 1881–1885 = 100	Cents	Cents	Cents
1847	54	—	56	40	—	—	—
1848	78	93	47	95	—	—	—
1849	84	—	69	70	—	—	—
1850	96	152	73	85	—	—	—
1851	84	107	63	81	—	—	—
1852	71	83	57	73	—	—	—
1853	65	80	52	60	—	—	—
1854	83	115	66	66	—	—	—
1855	76	98	68	61	—	—	—
1856	78	110	58	65	—	—	—
1857	88	140	54	69	—	—	—
1858	95	162	52	68	—	—	—
1859	94	163	52	65	—	—	—
1860	82	133	49	61	—	—	—
1861	75	114	49	60	—	—	—
1862	89	121	52	95	112.1	121.0	114.9
1863	96	118	55	114	142.5	145.2	136.0
1864	101	121	72	111	187.3	203.3	185.4
1865	105	115	90	110	149.9	157.3	148.4
1866	110	107	102	111	136.6	140.9	135.6
1867	110	102	104	123	137.2	138.2	132.8
1868	100	94	94	111	139.5	139.7	137.5
1869	95	92	91	101	131.8	133.0	130.1
1870	99	97	89	110	113.5	114.9	112.7
1871	100	104	88	109	111.0	111.7	110.3
1872	100	105	90	104	111.6	112.4	110.8
1873	97	100	92	99	113.0	113.8	112.5
1874	98	104	93	98	110.7	111.2	110.4
1875	101	102	96	104	114.3	114.9	113.7
1876	98	94	97	104	110.9	111.5	110.7
1877	101	102	96	104	104.1	104.8	104.0
1878	100	102	95	103	100.5	100.8	100.2
1879	100	103	96	100	—	—	—
1880	100	100	98	101	—	—	—
1881	100	99	101	100	—	—	—
1882	101	101	101	101	—	—	—
1883	101	102	97	104	—	—	—
1884	100	103	97	100	—	—	—
1885	98	95	104	95	—	—	—
1886	94	91	106	88	—	—	—
1887	91	89	106	84	—	—	—
1888	91	87	108	81	—	—	—
1889	92	81	109	89	—	—	—
1890	93	82	109	90	—	—	—
1891	92	84	108	85	—	—	—
1892	93	83	109	89	—	—	—
1893	92	85	106	87	—	—	—
1894	86	79	100	83	—	—	—
1895	91	97	99	78	—	—	—
1896	87	86	99	78	—	—	—
1897	91	99	100	75	—	—	—
1898	91	97	101	77	—	—	—
1899	97	104	101	86	—	—	—
1900	104	114	101	98	—	—	—

TABLE Cc188–204   Wholesale price indexes and gold-dollar exchange rates for San Francisco, by commodity group: 1847–1900   *Continued*

Source

Thomas Senior Berry, *Early California: Gold, Prices, Trade* (Bostwick Press, 1984). Series Cc188–201: pp. 235–6. Series Cc202: calculated from series given in column A, p. 155. Series Cc203: column D, p. 155. Series Cc204: column E, p. 155.

Documentation

From 1862 through 1878, the U.S. government had suspended convertibility of U.S. currency into gold, and prices in most of the United States were quoted in terms of fiat currency ("greenbacks"). In California, however, prices were generally quoted in terms of gold dollars – that is, dollars corresponding to the quantity of gold coin or bullion prescribed by the prewar dollar–gold exchange rate. The index numbers presented here for 1862–1878 represent prices in gold dollars, following the California practice. In order to convert them to index numbers of prices in terms of U.S. fiat currency, they can be multiplied by series representing the exchange value of gold dollars in U.S. fiat currency. Three gold-dollar exchange rates are given here. Series Cc202 is the reciprocal of the price at San Francisco of a U.S. currency dollar in gold dollars. Series Cc203 is the price at New York of a gold dollar in U.S. currency dollars. Series Cc204 is the reciprocal of the price at San Francisco, in gold dollars, of a claim to a U.S. currency dollar in East Coast cities.

Berry constructed two sets of series, one for the period 1847–1888 and one for the period 1881–1900, corresponding to two different sets of price information. The two sets of series were linked at 1881. For some commodity groups, the number of commodities covered was greater in the earlier period; for other groups, the number of commodities was greater in the later period. The number of commodities covered in the comprehensive "all commodities" index was 176 for most of the earlier period and 186 for most of the later period. Indexes are weighted arithmetic averages of price relatives, with weights corresponding to estimates of total receipts in that commodity at San Francisco over 1881–1885, except for the relative weights for flour and wheat.

The original source gives monthly values for the price indexes. The price series presented here are averages of monthly values, except for 1847, for which prices were available from the month of March only. For 1848, prices were available for months from March through June. For 1849, prices were available for July through December. Thereafter, prices were available for all twelve months of each year. In the exchange-rate series (series Cc202–204), values for 1862 are averages over months from June through December; values for other years are averages over twelve months.

COMMODITY PRICES

Michael R. Haines

TABLE Cc205–266 Wholesale prices of selected commodities: 1784–1998

Contributed by Michael R. Haines

Year	Wheat Philadelphia Cc205 Dollars per bushel	Wheat Northern Cc206 Dollars per bushel	Wheat Chicago Cc207 Dollars per bushel	Wheat Spring and winter Cc208 Dollars per bushel	Wheat BLS index Cc209 Dollars per bushel	Wheat flour Philadelphia Cc210 Dollars per 196-pound barrel	Wheat flour New York Cc211 Dollars per 196-pound barrel	Wheat flour Aldrich Cc212 Dollars per 196-pound barrel	Wheat flour Winter straights Cc213 Dollars per 196-pound barrel	Wheat flour Kansas City Cc214 Dollars per 196-pound barrel	Wheat flour Carlots Cc215 Dollars per hundredweight	Wheat flour Enriched Cc216 Dollars per hundredweight	Wheat flour BLS index Cc217 Dollars per hundredweight	Sugar Philadelphia Cc218 Dollars per pound	Sugar New York "Cuba" Cc219 Dollars per pound
1784	1.02	—	—	—	—	6.47	—	—	—	—	—	—	—	0.08	—
1785	1.06	—	—	—	—	5.87	—	—	—	—	—	—	—	0.07	—
1786	0.99	—	—	—	—	5.58	—	—	—	—	—	—	—	0.07	—
1787	0.89	—	—	—	—	5.00	—	—	—	—	—	—	—	0.07	—
1788	0.79	—	—	—	—	4.61	—	—	—	—	—	—	—	0.07	—
1789	0.92	—	—	—	—	5.21	—	—	—	—	—	—	—	0.08	—
1790	1.34	—	—	—	—	6.86	—	—	—	—	—	—	—	0.09	—
1791	0.99	—	—	—	—	5.22	—	—	—	—	—	—	—	0.11	—
1792	0.96	—	—	—	—	5.05	—	—	—	—	—	—	—	0.14	—
1793	1.12	—	—	—	—	6.17	—	—	—	—	—	—	—	0.13	—
1794	1.19	—	—	—	—	7.00	—	—	—	—	—	—	—	0.12	—
1795	1.83	—	—	—	—	11.23	—	—	—	—	—	—	—	0.12	—
1796	1.95	—	—	—	—	12.54	—	—	—	—	—	—	—	0.13	—
1797	1.40	—	—	—	—	8.91	—	—	—	—	—	—	—	0.16	—
1798	1.30	—	—	—	—	8.17	—	—	—	—	—	—	—	0.14	—
1799	1.59	—	—	—	—	9.65	—	—	—	—	—	—	—	0.14	—
1800	1.78	—	—	—	—	10.03	—	—	—	—	—	—	—	0.13	—
1801	1.84	—	—	—	—	10.40	—	—	—	—	—	—	—	0.12	—
1802	1.19	—	—	—	—	6.90	—	—	—	—	—	—	—	0.11	—
1803	1.13	—	—	—	—	6.85	—	—	—	—	—	—	—	0.12	—
1804	1.36	—	—	—	—	8.21	—	—	—	—	—	—	—	0.14	—
1805	1.95	—	—	—	—	10.07	—	—	—	—	—	—	—	0.14	—
1806	1.38	—	—	—	—	7.27	—	—	—	—	—	—	—	0.13	—
1807	1.31	—	—	—	—	7.12	—	—	—	—	—	—	—	0.12	—
1808	1.00	—	—	—	—	5.53	—	—	—	—	—	—	—	0.12	—
1809	1.25	—	—	—	—	6.86	—	—	—	—	—	—	—	0.13	—
1810	1.80	—	—	—	—	9.65	—	—	—	—	—	—	—	0.13	—
1811	1.85	—	—	—	—	10.06	—	—	—	—	—	—	—	0.13	—
1812	1.77	—	—	—	—	9.34	—	—	—	—	—	—	—	0.14	—
1813	1.62	—	—	—	—	8.94	—	—	—	—	—	—	—	0.21	—
1814	1.48	—	—	—	—	8.11	—	—	—	—	—	—	—	0.22	—
1815	1.57	—	—	—	—	8.57	—	—	—	—	—	—	—	0.22	—
1816	1.94	—	—	—	—	9.80	—	—	—	—	—	—	—	0.18	—
1817	2.41	—	—	—	—	11.72	—	—	—	—	—	—	—	0.16	—
1818	1.98	—	—	—	—	9.97	—	—	—	—	—	—	—	0.15	—
1819	1.34	—	—	—	—	6.89	—	—	—	—	—	—	—	0.15	—

	Wheat					Wheat flour								Sugar	
	Philadelphia	Northern	Chicago	Spring and winter	BLS index	Philadelphia	New York	Aldrich	Winter straights	Kansas City	Carlots	Enriched	BLS index	Philadelphia	New York "Cuba"
	Cc205	Cc206	Cc207	Cc208	Cc209	Cc210	Cc211	Cc212	Cc213	Cc214	Cc215	Cc216	Cc217	Cc218	Cc219
Year	Dollars per bushel	Dollars per bushel	Dollars per bushel	Dollars per bushel	Dollars per bushel	Dollars per 196-pound barrel	Dollars per 196-pound barrel	Dollars per 196-pound barrel	Dollars per 196-pound barrel	Dollars per 196-pound barrel	Dollars per hundredweight	Dollars per hundredweight	Dollars per hundredweight	Dollars per pound	Dollars per pound
1820	0.93	—	—	—	—	4.71	—	—	—	—	—	—	—	0.12	—
1821	0.88	—	—	—	—	4.78	—	—	—	—	—	—	—	0.11	—
1822	1.25	—	—	—	—	6.58	—	—	—	—	—	—	—	0.12	—
1823	1.35	—	—	—	—	6.84	—	—	—	—	—	—	—	0.12	—
1824	1.10	—	—	—	—	5.61	—	—	—	—	—	—	—	0.12	—
1825	0.92	1.00	—	—	—	5.11	5.13	—	—	—	—	—	—	0.12	0.09
1826	—	0.94	—	—	—	—	4.81	—	—	—	—	—	—	—	0.08
1827	—	0.99	—	—	—	—	5.14	—	—	—	—	—	—	—	0.09
1828	—	1.22	—	—	—	—	5.58	—	—	—	—	—	—	—	0.09
1829	—	1.25	—	—	—	—	6.45	—	—	—	—	—	—	—	0.08
1830	—	1.07	—	—	—	—	4.99	—	—	—	—	—	—	—	0.07
1831	—	1.19	—	—	—	—	5.71	—	—	—	—	—	—	—	0.06
1832	—	1.26	—	—	—	—	5.77	—	—	—	—	—	—	—	0.07
1833	—	1.19	—	—	—	—	5.57	—	—	—	—	—	—	—	0.07
1834	—	1.06	—	—	—	—	4.98	—	—	—	—	—	—	—	0.07
1835	—	1.22	—	—	—	—	5.86	—	—	—	—	—	—	—	0.08
1836	—	1.78	—	—	—	—	7.50	—	—	—	—	—	—	—	0.09
1837	—	1.78	—	—	—	—	9.14	—	—	—	—	—	—	—	0.07
1838	—	1.92	—	—	—	—	7.96	—	—	—	—	—	—	—	0.07
1839	—	1.25	—	—	—	—	7.30	—	—	—	—	—	—	—	0.07
1840	—	1.06	—	—	—	—	5.30	—	—	—	—	—	—	—	0.06
1841	—	1.19	—	—	—	—	5.59	—	—	—	—	—	—	—	0.06
1842	—	1.14	—	—	—	—	5.57	—	—	—	—	—	—	—	0.05
1843	—	0.98	—	—	—	—	4.86	—	—	—	—	—	—	—	0.06
1844	—	0.98	—	—	—	—	4.67	—	—	—	—	—	—	—	0.06
1845	—	1.04	—	—	—	—	4.94	—	—	—	—	—	—	—	0.06
1846	—	1.09	—	—	—	—	5.06	—	—	—	—	—	—	—	0.09
1847	—	1.37	—	—	—	—	6.69	—	—	—	—	—	—	—	0.08
1848	—	1.18	—	—	—	—	5.96	—	—	—	—	—	—	—	0.07
1849	—	1.24	—	—	—	—	4.51	—	—	—	—	—	—	—	0.07
1850	—	1.28	—	—	—	—	5.55	—	—	—	—	—	—	—	0.07
1851	—	1.08	—	—	—	—	4.52	—	—	—	—	—	—	—	0.08
1852	—	1.11	—	—	—	—	5.01	—	—	—	—	—	—	—	0.07
1853	—	1.39	—	—	—	—	5.78	—	—	—	—	—	—	—	0.07
1854	—	2.21	—	—	—	—	8.95	—	—	—	—	—	—	—	0.07
1855	—	2.44	—	—	—	—	8.76	—	—	—	—	—	—	—	0.07
1856	—	1.76	—	—	—	—	6.42	—	—	—	—	—	—	—	0.10
1857	—	1.68	—	—	—	—	5.79	—	—	—	—	—	—	—	0.12
1858	—	1.33	—	—	—	—	4.30	—	—	—	—	—	—	—	0.09
1859	—	1.44	—	—	—	—	5.11	—	—	—	—	—	—	—	0.09
1860	—	1.50	—	—	—	—	5.19	—	—	—	—	—	—	—	0.09
1861	—	1.43	—	—	—	—	4.97	—	—	—	—	—	—	—	—
1862	—	1.39	—	—	—	—	5.17	—	—	—	—	—	—	—	—
1863	—	1.64	—	—	—	—	5.69	—	—	—	—	—	—	—	—
1864	—	1.94	—	—	—	—	8.06	—	—	—	—	—	—	—	—

(continued)

TABLE Cc205–266 Wholesale prices of selected commodities: 1784–1998 *Continued*

	Wheat					Wheat flour								Sugar	
	Philadelphia	Northern	Chicago	Spring and winter	BLS index	Philadelphia	New York	Aldrich	Winter straights	Kansas City	Carlots	Enriched	BLS index	Philadelphia	New York "Cuba"
Year	Cc205	Cc206	Cc207	Cc208	Cc209	Cc210	Cc211	Cc212	Cc213	Cc214	Cc215	Cc216	Cc217	Cc218	Cc219
	Dollars per bushel	Dollars per bushel	Dollars per bushel	Dollars per bushel	Dollars per bushel	Dollars per 196-pound barrel	Dollars per 196-pound barrel	Dollars per 196-pound barrel	Dollars per 196-pound barrel	Dollars per 196-pound barrel	Dollars per hundredweight	Dollars per hundredweight	Dollars per hundredweight	Dollars per pound	Dollars per pound
1865	—	2.16	—	—	—	—	7.71	—	—	—	—	—	—	—	—
1866	—	2.95	—	—	—	—	7.92	—	—	—	—	—	—	—	—
1867	—	2.84	—	—	—	—	9.16	—	—	—	—	—	—	—	—
1868	—	2.54	—	—	—	—	7.91	—	—	—	—	—	—	—	—
1869	—	1.65	—	—	—	—	5.73	—	—	—	—	—	—	—	—
1870	—	1.37	—	—	—	—	5.03	9.28	—	—	—	—	—	—	—
1871	—	1.58	—	—	—	—	—	10.25	—	—	—	—	—	—	—
1872	—	1.78	—	—	—	—	—	12.14	—	—	—	—	—	—	—
1873	—	1.79	—	—	—	—	—	11.50	—	—	—	—	—	—	—
1874	—	1.52	—	—	—	—	—	10.73	—	—	—	—	—	—	—
1875	—	1.40	—	—	—	—	—	10.22	—	—	—	—	—	—	—
1876	—	1.32	—	—	—	—	—	9.90	—	—	—	—	—	—	—
1877	—	1.69	—	—	—	—	—	10.81	—	—	—	—	—	—	—
1878	—	1.25	—	—	—	—	—	9.10	—	—	—	—	—	—	—
1879	—	1.22	—	—	—	—	—	8.63	—	—	—	—	—	—	—
1880	—	1.25	—	—	—	—	—	8.90	—	—	—	—	—	—	—
1881	—	—	1.15	—	—	—	—	8.90	—	—	—	—	—	—	—
1882	—	—	1.20	—	—	—	—	9.02	—	—	—	—	—	—	—
1883	—	—	1.04	—	—	—	—	7.74	—	—	—	—	—	—	—
1884	—	—	0.91	—	—	—	—	7.04	—	—	—	—	—	—	—
1885	—	—	0.86	—	—	—	—	6.28	—	—	—	—	—	—	—
1886	—	—	0.80	—	—	—	—	6.12	—	—	—	—	—	—	—
1887	—	—	0.77	—	—	—	—	5.82	—	—	—	—	—	—	—
1888	—	—	0.89	—	—	—	—	6.12	—	—	—	—	—	—	—
1889	—	—	0.90	—	—	—	—	6.54	—	—	—	—	—	—	—
1890	—	—	0.87	0.89	—	—	—	6.04	4.65	—	—	—	—	—	—
1891	—	—	—	0.96	—	—	—	—	4.91	—	—	—	—	—	—
1892	—	—	—	0.79	—	—	—	—	4.12	—	—	—	—	—	—
1893	—	—	—	0.68	—	—	—	—	3.28	—	—	—	—	—	—
1894	—	—	—	0.56	—	—	—	—	2.75	—	—	—	—	—	—
1895	—	—	—	0.60	—	—	—	—	3.23	—	—	—	—	—	—
1896	—	—	—	0.64	—	—	—	—	3.62	—	—	—	—	—	—
1897	—	—	—	0.80	—	—	—	—	4.36	—	—	—	—	—	—
1898	—	—	—	0.89	—	—	—	—	4.15	—	—	—	—	—	—
1899	—	—	—	0.71	—	—	—	—	3.38	—	—	—	—	—	—
1900	—	—	—	0.70	—	—	—	—	3.35	—	—	—	—	—	—
1901	—	—	—	0.72	—	—	—	—	3.31	—	—	—	—	—	—
1902	—	—	—	0.74	—	—	—	—	3.49	—	—	—	—	—	—
1903	—	—	—	0.79	—	—	—	—	3.59	—	—	—	—	—	—
1904	—	—	—	1.04	—	—	—	—	4.83	—	—	—	—	—	—
1905	—	—	—	1.01	—	—	—	—	4.54	—	—	—	—	—	—
1906	—	—	—	0.79	—	—	—	—	3.62	—	—	—	—	—	—
1907	—	—	—	0.91	—	—	—	—	3.99	—	—	—	—	—	—
1908	—	—	—	0.99	—	—	—	—	4.29	—	—	—	—	—	—
1909	—	—	—	1.20	—	—	—	—	5.45	—	—	—	—	—	—

	Wheat					Wheat flour								Sugar	
	Philadelphia	Northern	Chicago	Spring and winter	BLS index	Philadelphia	New York	Aldrich	Winter straights	Kansas City	Carlots	Enriched	BLS index	Philadelphia	New York "Cuba"
	Cc205	Cc206	Cc207	Cc208	Cc209	Cc210	Cc211	Cc212	Cc213	Cc214	Cc215	Cc216	Cc217	Cc218	Cc219
Year	Dollars per bushel	Dollars per bushel	Dollars per bushel	Dollars per bushel	Dollars per bushel	Dollars per 196-pound barrel	Dollars per 196-pound barrel	Dollars per 196-pound barrel	Dollars per 196-pound barrel	Dollars per 196-pound barrel	Dollars per hundredweight	Dollars per hundredweight	Dollars per hundredweight	Dollars per pound	Dollars per pound
1910	—	—	—	1.10	—	—	—	—	4.69	—	—	—	—	—	—
1911	—	—	—	0.98	—	—	—	—	3.98	—	—	—	—	—	—
1912	—	—	—	1.05	—	—	—	—	4.69	—	—	—	—	—	—
1913	—	—	—	0.95	0.88	—	—	—	4.31	3.85	—	—	—	—	—
1914	—	—	—	—	0.94	—	—	—	—	4.13	—	—	—	—	—
1915	—	—	—	—	1.29	—	—	—	—	5.61	—	—	—	—	—
1916	—	—	—	—	1.33	—	—	—	—	6.09	—	—	—	—	—
1917	—	—	—	—	2.30	—	—	—	—	10.55	—	—	—	—	—
1918	—	—	—	—	2.16	—	—	—	—	10.30	—	—	—	—	—
1919	—	—	—	—	2.42	—	—	—	—	10.70	—	—	—	—	—
1920	—	—	—	—	2.46	—	—	—	—	—	—	—	—	—	—
1921	—	—	—	—	1.33	—	—	—	—	—	—	—	—	—	—
1922	—	—	—	—	1.21	—	—	—	—	—	—	—	—	—	—
1923	—	—	—	—	1.11	—	—	—	—	—	—	—	—	—	—
1924	—	—	—	—	1.23	—	—	—	—	—	—	—	—	—	—
1925	—	—	—	—	1.67	—	—	—	—	—	—	—	—	—	—
1926	—	—	—	—	1.50	—	—	—	—	—	—	—	—	—	—
1927	—	—	—	—	1.37	—	—	—	—	—	—	—	—	—	—
1928	—	—	—	—	1.32	—	—	—	—	—	—	—	—	—	—
1929	—	—	—	—	1.18	—	—	—	—	—	—	—	—	—	—
1930	—	—	—	—	0.90	—	—	—	—	—	—	—	—	—	—
1931	—	—	—	—	0.61	—	—	—	—	—	—	—	—	—	—
1932	—	—	—	—	0.49	—	—	—	—	—	—	—	—	—	—
1933	—	—	—	—	0.72	—	—	—	—	—	—	—	—	—	—
1934	—	—	—	—	0.93	—	—	—	—	—	—	—	—	—	—
1935	—	—	—	—	1.04	—	—	—	—	—	—	—	—	—	—
1936	—	—	—	—	1.12	—	—	—	—	—	—	—	—	—	—
1937	—	—	—	—	1.20	—	—	—	—	—	—	—	—	—	—
1938	—	—	—	—	0.78	—	—	—	—	—	—	—	—	—	—
1939	—	—	—	—	0.76	—	—	—	—	—	—	—	—	—	—
1940	—	—	—	—	0.87	—	—	—	—	—	—	—	—	—	—
1941	—	—	—	—	0.99	—	—	—	—	—	—	—	—	—	—
1942	—	—	—	—	1.19	—	—	—	—	—	3.17	—	—	—	—
1943	—	—	—	—	1.44	—	—	—	—	—	3.18	—	—	—	—
1944	—	—	—	—	1.60	—	—	—	—	—	—	—	—	—	—
1945	—	—	—	—	1.66	—	—	—	—	—	3.18	—	—	—	—
1946	—	—	—	—	1.90	—	—	—	—	—	4.49	—	—	—	—
1947	—	—	—	—	2.60	—	—	—	—	—	6.20	—	—	—	—
1948	—	—	—	—	2.41	—	—	—	—	—	5.45	—	—	—	—
1949	—	—	—	—	2.15	—	—	—	—	—	5.04	—	—	—	—
1950	—	—	—	—	2.23	—	—	—	—	—	5.22	5.43	—	—	—
1951	—	—	—	—	2.40	—	—	—	—	—	—	5.75	—	—	—
1952	—	—	—	—	2.39	—	—	—	—	—	—	5.48	—	—	—
1953	—	—	—	—	2.24	—	—	—	—	—	—	5.65	—	—	—
1954	—	—	—	—	2.31	—	—	—	—	—	—	6.13	—	—	—

(continued)

TABLE Cc205–266 Wholesale prices of selected commodities: 1784–1998 *Continued*

	Wheat					Wheat flour								Sugar	
	Philadelphia	Northern	Chicago	Spring and winter	BLS index	Philadelphia	New York	Aldrich	Winter straights	Kansas City	Carlots	Enriched	BLS index	Philadelphia	New York "Cuba"
	Cc205	Cc206	Cc207	Cc208	Cc209	Cc210	Cc211	Cc212	Cc213	Cc214	Cc215	Cc216	Cc217	Cc218	Cc219
Year	Dollars per bushel	Dollars per bushel	Dollars per bushel	Dollars per bushel	Dollars per bushel	Dollars per 196-pound barrel	Dollars per 196-pound barrel	Dollars per 196-pound barrel	Dollars per 196-pound barrel	Dollars per 196-pound barrel	Dollars per hundredweight	Dollars per hundredweight	Dollars per hundredweight	Dollars per pound	Dollars per pound
1955	—	—	—	—	2.26	—	—	—	—	—	—	5.94	—	—	—
1956	—	—	—	—	2.22	—	—	—	—	—	—	5.68	—	—	—
1957	—	—	—	—	2.20	—	—	—	—	—	—	5.68	—	—	—
1958	—	—	—	—	2.03	—	—	—	—	—	—	5.42	—	—	—
1959	—	—	—	—	1.98	—	—	—	—	—	—	5.08	—	—	—
1960	—	—	—	—	1.99	—	—	—	—	—	—	4.99	—	—	—
1961	—	—	—	—	2.01	—	—	—	—	—	—	5.17	—	—	—
1962	—	—	—	—	—	—	—	—	—	—	—	5.62	—	—	—
1963	—	—	—	—	2.18	—	—	—	—	—	—	5.37	—	—	—
1964	—	—	—	—	1.88	—	—	—	—	—	—	5.39	—	—	—
1965	—	—	—	—	1.56	—	—	—	—	—	—	5.47	—	—	—
1966	—	—	—	—	1.79	—	—	—	—	—	—	5.99	—	—	—
1967	—	—	—	—	1.67	—	—	—	—	—	—	5.62	—	—	—
1968	—	—	—	—	1.47	—	—	—	—	—	—	—	—	—	—
1969	—	—	—	—	1.39	—	—	—	—	—	—	5.44	—	—	—
1970	—	—	—	—	1.48	—	—	—	—	—	—	5.57	—	—	—
1971	—	—	—	—	1.58	—	—	—	—	—	—	5.45	—	—	—
1972	—	—	—	—	1.84	—	—	—	—	—	—	5.87	—	—	—
1973	—	—	—	—	3.58	—	—	—	—	—	—	8.52	—	—	—
1974	—	—	—	—	4.68	—	—	—	—	—	—	11.06	—	—	—
1975	—	—	—	—	3.81	—	—	—	—	—	—	9.37	—	—	—
1976	—	—	—	—	3.34	—	—	—	—	—	—	8.31	—	—	—
1977	—	—	—	—	2.53	—	—	—	—	—	—	6.23	—	—	—
1978	—	—	—	—	3.17	—	—	—	—	—	—	7.48	—	—	—
1979	—	—	—	—	3.98	—	—	—	—	—	—	9.27	—	—	—
1980	—	—	—	—	4.30	—	—	—	—	—	—	10.08	—	—	—
1981	—	—	—	—	4.33	—	—	—	—	—	—	10.34	—	—	—
1982	—	—	—	—	4.02	—	—	—	—	—	—	—	9.12	—	—
1983	—	—	—	—	3.96	—	—	—	—	—	—	—	9.47	—	—
1984	—	—	—	—	3.81	—	—	—	—	—	—	—	9.35	—	—
1985	—	—	—	—	3.41	—	—	—	—	—	—	—	9.23	—	—
1986	—	—	—	—	2.95	—	—	—	—	—	—	—	8.73	—	—
1987	—	—	—	—	2.84	—	—	—	—	—	—	—	8.57	—	—
1988	—	—	—	—	3.65	—	—	—	—	—	—	—	9.75	—	—
1989	—	—	—	—	4.39	—	—	—	—	—	—	—	10.56	—	—
1990	—	—	—	—	3.47	—	—	—	—	—	—	—	9.58	—	—
1991	—	—	—	—	3.14	—	—	—	—	—	—	—	9.03	—	—
1992	—	—	—	—	3.91	—	—	—	—	—	—	—	10.26	—	—
1993	—	—	—	—	3.70	—	—	—	—	—	—	—	10.22	—	—
1994	—	—	—	—	3.93	—	—	—	—	—	—	—	10.36	—	—
1995	—	—	—	—	4.58	—	—	—	—	—	—	—	11.55	—	—
1996	—	—	—	—	5.43	—	—	—	—	—	—	—	12.78	—	—
1997	—	—	—	—	4.25	—	—	—	—	—	—	—	11.08	—	—
1998	—	—	—	—	3.38	—	—	—	—	—	—	—	10.20	—	—

	Sugar		Cotton, raw					Wool					Cotton sheeting		
Year	Refined	BLS	Cole and Hammond	New York	Ten markets	BLS index	Philadelphia	New York	Boston	Ohio	BLS	Philadelphia	Aldrich	BLS reports	BLS index
	Cc220	Cc221	Cc222	Cc223	Cc224	Cc225	Cc226	Cc227	Cc228	Cc229	Cc230	Cc231	Cc232	Cc233	Cc234
	Dollars per pound	Dollars per pound	Dollars per pound	Dollars per pound	Dollars per pound	Dollars per pound	Dollars per pound	Dollars per pound	Dollars per pound	Dollars per pound	Dollars per pound	Dollars per piece	Dollars per yard	Dollars per yard	Dollars per yard
1784	—	—	0.29	—	—	—	—	—	—	—	—	13.02	—	—	—
1785	—	—	0.32	—	—	—	—	—	—	—	—	13.74	—	—	—
1786	—	—	0.40	—	—	—	—	—	—	—	—	13.93	—	—	—
1787	—	—	0.40	—	—	—	—	—	—	—	—	14.03	—	—	—
1788	—	—	0.36	—	—	—	—	—	—	—	—	12.00	—	—	—
1789	—	—	0.28	—	—	—	—	—	—	—	—	12.00	—	—	—
1790	—	—	0.15	—	—	—	—	—	—	—	—	12.00	—	—	—
1791	—	—	0.26	—	—	—	—	—	—	—	—	12.00	—	—	—
1792	—	—	0.29	—	—	—	—	—	—	—	—	12.25	—	—	—
1793	—	—	0.32	—	—	—	—	—	—	—	—	15.28	—	—	—
1794	—	—	0.33	—	—	—	—	—	—	—	—	17.33	—	—	—
1795	—	—	0.36	—	—	—	—	—	—	—	—	15.78	—	—	—
1796	—	—	0.37	—	—	—	—	—	—	—	—	16.28	—	—	—
1797	—	—	0.35	—	—	—	—	—	—	—	—	16.83	—	—	—
1798	—	—	0.39	—	—	—	—	—	—	—	—	17.97	—	—	—
1799	—	—	0.44	—	—	—	—	—	—	—	—	17.65	—	—	—
1800	—	—	0.24	—	—	—	—	—	—	—	—	17.38	—	—	—
1801	—	—	0.44	—	—	—	—	—	—	—	—	17.35	—	—	—
1802	—	—	0.19	—	—	—	—	—	—	—	—	16.00	—	—	—
1803	—	—	0.19	—	—	—	—	—	—	—	—	16.00	—	—	—
1804	—	—	0.20	—	—	—	—	—	—	—	—	19.21	—	—	—
1805	—	—	0.23	—	—	—	—	—	—	—	—	21.27	—	—	—
1806	—	—	0.22	—	—	—	—	—	—	—	—	21.83	—	—	—
1807	—	—	0.22	—	—	—	—	—	—	—	—	20.69	—	—	—
1808	—	—	0.19	—	—	—	—	—	—	—	—	22.50	—	—	—
1809	—	—	0.16	—	—	—	—	—	—	—	—	25.17	—	—	—
1810	—	—	0.16	—	—	—	—	—	—	—	—	21.58	—	—	—
1811	—	—	0.16	—	—	—	—	—	—	—	—	19.04	—	—	—
1812	—	—	0.11	—	—	—	—	—	—	—	—	19.04	—	—	—
1813	—	—	0.13	—	—	—	2.75 [3]	—	—	—	—	21.60	—	—	—
1814	—	—	0.15	—	—	—	3.31	—	—	—	—	22.68	—	—	—
1815	—	—	0.21	—	—	—	1.33	—	—	—	—	20.00	—	—	—
1816	—	—	0.30	—	—	—	0.98	—	—	—	—	19.47	—	—	—
1817	—	—	0.27	—	—	—	0.75	—	—	—	—	17.96	—	—	—
1818	—	—	0.24	—	—	—	0.89	—	—	—	—	16.99	—	—	—
1819	—	—	0.24	—	—	—	0.83	—	—	—	—	16.50	—	—	—
1820	—	—	0.17	—	—	—	0.75	—	—	—	—	16.00	—	—	—
1821	—	—	0.14	—	—	—	0.75	—	—	—	—	16.00	—	—	—
1822	—	—	0.14	—	—	—	0.75	—	—	—	—	15.00	—	—	—
1823	—	—	0.11	—	—	—	0.72	—	—	—	—	14.50	—	—	—
1824	—	—	0.15	—	—	—	0.55	—	—	—	—	9.80	—	—	—

Notes appear at end of table

(continued)

TABLE Cc205–266   Wholesale prices of selected commodities: 1784–1998   Continued

	Sugar		Cotton, raw						Wool				Cotton sheeting		
	Refined	BLS	Cole and Hammond	New York	Ten markets	BLS index	Philadelphia	New York	Boston	Ohio	BLS	Philadelphia	Aldrich	BLS reports	BLS index
Year	Cc220	Cc221	Cc222	Cc223	Cc224	Cc225	Cc226	Cc227	Cc228	Cc229	Cc230	Cc231	Cc232	Cc233	Cc234
	Dollars per pound	Dollars per pound	Dollars per pound	Dollars per pound	Dollars per pound	Dollars per pound	Dollars per pound	Dollars per pound	Dollars per pound	Dollars per pound	Dollars per pound	Dollars per piece	Dollars per yard	Dollars per yard	Dollars per yard
1825	—	—	0.19	—	—	—	0.53	0.59	—	—	—	10.52	—	—	—
1826	—	—	0.12	—	—	—	—	0.50	—	—	—	9.94	—	—	—
1827	—	—	0.09	—	—	—	—	0.39	—	—	—	9.17	—	—	—
1828	—	—	0.10	—	—	—	—	0.37	—	—	—	8.99	—	—	—
1829	—	—	0.10	—	—	—	—	0.35	—	—	—	9.44	—	—	—
1830	—	—	0.10	—	—	—	—	0.39	—	—	—	10.24	—	—	—
1831	—	—	0.10	—	—	—	—	0.54	—	—	—	10.00	—	—	—
1832	—	—	0.09	—	—	—	—	0.48	—	—	—	9.28	—	—	—
1833	—	—	0.12	—	—	—	—	0.49	—	—	—	8.74	—	—	—
1834	—	—	0.13	—	—	—	—	0.49	—	—	—	8.53	—	—	—
1835	—	—	0.18	—	—	—	—	0.54	—	—	—	8.62	—	—	—
1836	—	—	0.17	—	—	—	—	0.59	—	—	—	10.50	—	—	—
1837	—	—	0.13	—	—	—	—	0.42	—	—	—	10.56	—	—	—
1838	—	—	0.10	—	—	—	—	0.38	—	—	—	9.60	—	—	—
1839	—	—	0.13	—	—	—	—	0.51	—	—	—	9.22	—	—	—
1840	—	—	0.09	—	—	—	—	0.39	—	—	—	9.26	—	—	—
1841	—	—	0.10	—	—	—	—	0.44	—	—	—	8.92	—	—	—
1842	—	—	0.08	—	—	—	—	0.32	—	—	—	8.57	—	—	—
1843	—	—	0.07	—	—	—	—	0.31	—	—	—	7.92	—	—	—
1844	—	—	0.08	—	—	—	—	0.40	—	—	—	7.67	—	—	—
1845	—	—	0.06	—	—	—	—	0.35	—	—	—	8.10	—	—	—
1846	—	—	0.08	—	—	—	—	0.32	—	—	—	8.45	—	—	—
1847	—	—	0.11	—	—	—	—	0.35	—	—	—	8.50	0.08	—	—
1848	—	—	0.08	—	—	—	—	0.34	—	—	—	—	0.07	—	—
1849	—	—	0.08	—	—	—	—	0.36	—	—	—	—	0.06	—	—
1850	—	—	0.12	—	—	—	—	0.40	0.83	—	—	—	0.07	—	—
1851	—	—	0.12	—	—	—	—	—	0.86	—	—	—	0.07	—	—
1852	—	—	0.10	—	—	—	—	—	0.82	—	—	—	0.07	—	—
1853	—	—	0.11	—	—	—	—	—	1.07	—	—	—	0.07	—	—
1854	—	—	0.11	—	—	—	—	—	0.91	—	—	—	0.08	—	—
1855	—	—	0.10	—	—	—	—	—	0.86	—	—	—	0.07	—	—
1856	—	—	0.10	—	—	—	—	—	1.05	—	—	—	0.07	—	—
1857	—	—	0.14	—	—	—	—	—	1.02	—	—	—	0.09	—	—
1858	—	—	0.12	—	—	—	—	—	0.83	—	—	—	0.08	—	—
1859	—	—	0.12	—	—	—	—	—	1.09	—	—	—	0.08	—	—
1860	0.10	—	0.11	—	—	—	—	—	1.03	—	—	—	0.08	—	—
1861	0.09	—	0.13	—	—	—	—	—	0.83	—	—	—	0.09	—	—
1862	0.11	—	0.31	—	—	—	—	—	0.94	—	—	—	0.18	—	—
1863	0.15	—	0.67	—	—	—	—	—	1.52	—	—	—	0.34	—	—
1864	0.24	—	1.02	—	—	—	—	—	1.77	—	—	—	0.51	—	—
1865	0.21	—	0.83	—	—	—	—	—	1.66	—	—	—	0.37	—	—
1866	0.17	—	0.43	—	—	—	—	—	1.31	—	—	—	0.24	—	—
1867	0.16	—	0.32	—	—	—	—	—	1.13	—	—	—	0.17	—	—
1868	0.16	—	0.25	—	—	—	—	—	0.89	—	—	—	0.16	—	—
1869	0.16	—	0.29	—	—	—	—	—	0.91	—	—	—	0.15	—	—

Year	Sugar		Cotton, raw				Wool					Cotton sheeting			
	Refined	BLS	Cole and Hammond	New York	Ten markets	BLS index	Philadelphia	New York	Boston	Ohio	BLS	Philadelphia	Aldrich	BLS reports	BLS index
	Cc220	Cc221	Cc222	Cc223	Cc224	Cc225	Cc226	Cc227	Cc228	Cc229	Cc230	Cc231	Cc232	Cc233	Cc234
	Dollars per pound	Dollars per pound	Dollars per pound	Dollars per pound	Dollars per pound	Dollars per pound	Dollars per pound	Dollars per pound	Dollars per pound	Dollars per pound	Dollars per pound	Dollars per piece	Dollars per yard	Dollars per yard	Dollars per yard
1870	0.14	—	0.24	—	—	—	—	—	0.90	—	—	—	0.14	—	—
1871	0.13	—	0.17	—	—	—	—	—	1.07	—	—	—	0.13	—	—
1872	0.12	—	0.21	—	—	—	—	—	1.57	—	—	—	0.14	—	—
1873	0.11	—	0.18	—	—	—	—	—	1.20	—	—	—	0.13	—	—
1874	0.11	—	0.17	—	—	—	—	—	1.15	—	—	—	0.11	—	—
1875	0.11	—	0.15	—	—	—	—	—	1.05	—	—	—	0.10	—	—
1876	0.11	—	0.13	—	—	—	—	—	0.87	—	—	—	0.08	—	—
1877	0.11	—	0.12	—	—	—	—	—	0.91	—	—	—	0.08	—	—
1878	0.09	—	0.11	—	—	—	—	—	0.75	—	—	—	0.07	—	—
1879	0.09	—	0.10	—	—	—	—	—	0.72	—	—	—	0.08	—	—
1880	0.10	—	0.12	—	—	—	—	—	1.03	—	—	—	0.08	—	—
1881	0.10	—	0.11	—	—	—	—	—	0.96	—	—	—	0.08	—	—
1882	0.10	—	0.12	—	—	—	—	—	0.91	—	—	—	0.08	—	—
1883	0.09	—	0.11	—	—	—	—	—	0.86	—	—	—	0.08	—	—
1884	0.07	—	0.11	—	—	—	—	—	0.81	—	—	—	0.07	—	—
1885	0.06	—	0.11	—	—	—	—	—	0.71	—	—	—	0.07	—	—
1886	0.06	—	0.09	—	—	—	—	—	0.74	—	—	—	0.06	—	—
1887	0.06	—	0.10	—	—	—	—	—	0.73	—	—	—	0.07	—	—
1888	0.07	—	0.10	—	—	—	—	—	0.68	—	—	—	0.07	—	—
1889	0.08	—	0.11	—	—	—	—	—	0.74	—	—	—	0.07	—	—
1890	0.06	0.06	0.12	0.11	—	—	—	—	0.73	0.72	—	—	0.07	0.07	—
1891	—	0.05	—	0.09	—	—	—	—	—	0.69	—	—	0.13	0.07	—
1892	—	0.04	—	0.08	—	—	—	—	—	0.61	—	—	0.14	0.07	—
1893	—	0.05	—	0.08	—	—	—	—	—	0.56	—	—	0.13	0.07	—
1894	—	0.04	—	0.07	—	—	—	—	—	0.45	—	—	0.11	0.06	—
1895	—	0.04	—	0.07	—	—	—	—	—	0.38	—	—	0.10	0.06	—
1896	—	0.05	—	0.08	—	—	—	—	—	0.39	—	—	0.08	0.06	—
1897	—	0.05	—	0.07	—	—	—	—	—	0.50	—	—	0.08	0.06	—
1898	—	0.05	—	0.06	—	—	—	—	—	0.62	—	—	0.07	0.05	—
1899	—	0.05	—	0.07	—	—	—	—	—	0.62	—	—	0.08	0.05	—
1900	—	0.05	—	0.10	—	—	—	—	—	0.66	—	—	0.08	0.06	—
1901	—	0.05	—	0.09	—	—	—	—	—	0.55	—	—	0.08	0.06	—
1902	—	0.05	—	0.09	—	—	—	—	—	0.58	—	—	0.08	0.06	—
1903	—	0.05	—	0.11	—	—	—	—	—	0.66	—	—	0.08	0.07	—
1904	—	0.05	—	0.12	—	—	—	—	—	0.69	—	—	0.07	0.08	—
1905	—	0.05	—	0.10	—	—	—	—	—	0.76	—	—	0.07	0.08	—
1906	—	0.05	—	0.11	—	—	—	—	—	0.72	—	—	0.06	0.08	—
1907	—	0.05	—	0.12	—	—	—	—	—	0.72	—	—	0.07	0.08	—
1908	—	0.05	—	0.11	—	—	—	—	—	0.72	—	—	0.07	0.08	—
1909	—	0.05	—	0.12	—	—	—	—	—	0.74	—	—	0.07	0.08	—
1910	—	0.05	—	0.15	—	—	—	—	—	0.69	—	—	0.07	0.08	—
1911	—	0.05	—	0.13	—	—	—	—	—	0.65	—	—	—	0.09	—
1912	—	0.05	—	0.12	—	—	—	—	—	0.65	—	—	—	0.08	—
1913	—	0.04	—	0.13	—	—	—	—	—	0.59	0.56	—	—	0.08	—
1914	—	0.05	—	0.12	—	—	—	—	—	—	0.59	—	—	0.08	—

(continued)

TABLE Cc205–266   Wholesale prices of selected commodities: 1784–1998   Continued

Year	Sugar		Cotton, raw						Wool			Cotton sheeting			
	Refined	BLS	Cole and Hammond	New York	Ten markets	BLS index	Philadelphia	New York	Boston	Ohio	BLS	Philadelphia	Aldrich	BLS reports	BLS index
	Cc220	Cc221	Cc222	Cc223	Cc224	Cc225	Cc226	Cc227	Cc228	Cc229	Cc230	Cc231	Cc232	Cc233	Cc234
	Dollars per pound	Dollars per pound	Dollars per pound	Dollars per pound	Dollars per pound	Dollars per pound	Dollars per pound	Dollars per pound	Dollars per pound	Dollars per pound	Dollars per pound	Dollars per piece	Dollars per yard	Dollars per yard	Dollars per yard
1915	—	0.06	—	0.10	—	—	—	—	—	—	0.71	—	—	0.07	—
1916	—	0.07	—	0.15	—	—	—	—	—	—	0.85	—	—	0.09	—
1917	—	0.08	—	0.24	—	—	—	—	—	—	1.57	—	—	0.15	—
1918	—	0.08	—	0.32	—	—	—	—	—	—	1.82	—	—	0.24	—
1919	—	0.09	—	0.33	—	—	—	—	—	—	1.78	—	—	0.23	—
1920	—	0.13	—	0.34	—	—	—	—	—	—	1.60	—	—	0.29	—
1921	—	0.06	—	0.15	—	—	—	—	—	—	0.83	—	—	0.13	—
1922	—	0.06	—	0.21	—	—	—	—	—	—	1.24	—	—	0.13	—
1923	—	0.08	—	0.29	—	—	—	—	—	—	1.38	—	—	0.16	—
1924	—	0.07	—	0.29	—	—	—	—	—	—	1.41	—	—	0.16	—
1925	—	0.06	—	0.24	—	—	—	—	—	—	1.39	—	—	0.15	—
1926	—	0.06	—	0.18	—	—	—	—	—	—	1.15	—	—	0.12	—
1927	—	0.06	—	0.18	—	—	—	—	—	—	1.11	—	—	0.12	—
1928	—	0.06	—	0.20	—	—	—	—	—	—	1.16	—	—	0.14	—
1929	—	0.05	—	0.19	—	—	—	—	—	—	0.99	—	—	0.13	—
1930	—	0.05	—	0.14	—	—	—	—	—	—	0.76	—	—	0.11	—
1931	—	0.04	—	0.09	—	—	—	—	—	—	0.62	—	—	0.07	—
1932	—	0.04	—	0.06	—	—	—	—	—	—	0.46	—	—	0.06	—
1933	—	0.04	—	0.09	—	—	—	—	—	—	0.66	—	—	0.09	—
1934	—	0.04	—	0.12	—	—	—	—	—	—	0.82	—	—	0.11	—
1935	—	0.05	—	0.12	—	—	—	—	—	—	0.72	—	—	0.11	—
1936	—	0.05	—	0.12	—	—	—	—	—	—	0.88	—	—	0.10	—
1937	—	0.05	—	0.11	—	—	—	—	—	—	0.97	—	—	0.11	—
1938	—	0.05	—	0.09	—	—	—	—	—	—	0.69	—	—	0.08	—
1939	—	0.05	—	0.10	—	—	—	—	—	—	0.82	—	—	0.08	—
1940	—	0.04	—	0.10	0.14	—	—	—	—	—	0.97	—	—	0.09	0.12
1941	—	0.05	—	0.15	0.19	—	—	—	—	—	1.09	—	—	0.12	0.14
1942	—	0.06	—	—	0.21	—	—	—	—	—	1.20	—	—	—	0.14
1943	—	0.06	—	—	0.21	—	—	—	—	—	1.18	—	—	—	0.15
1944	—	0.06	—	—	—	—	—	—	—	—	1.19	—	—	—	—
1945	—	0.05	—	—	0.23	—	—	—	—	—	1.19	—	—	—	0.15
1946	—	0.06	—	—	0.31	—	—	—	—	—	1.03	—	—	—	0.20
1947	—	0.08	—	—	0.35	—	—	—	—	—	1.24	—	—	—	0.26
1948	—	0.08	—	—	0.34	—	—	—	—	—	1.65	—	—	—	0.24
1949	—	0.08	—	—	0.32	—	—	—	—	—	1.66	—	—	—	0.21
1950	—	0.08	—	—	0.36	—	—	—	—	—	1.98	—	—	—	0.26
1951	—	0.08	—	—	0.42	—	—	—	—	—	2.70	—	—	—	0.28
1952	—	0.08	—	—	0.39	—	—	—	—	—	1.67	—	—	—	0.23
1953	—	0.09	—	—	0.33	—	—	—	—	—	1.73	—	—	—	0.22
1954	—	0.09	—	—	0.34	—	—	—	—	—	1.71	—	—	—	0.21

	Sugar		Cotton, raw				Wool					Cotton sheeting			
	Refined	BLS	Cole and Hammond	New York	Ten markets	BLS index	Philadelphia	New York	Boston	Ohio	BLS	Philadelphia	Aldrich	BLS reports	BLS index
	Cc220	Cc221	Cc222	Cc223	Cc224	Cc225	Cc226	Cc227	Cc228	Cc229	Cc230	Cc231	Cc232	Cc233	Cc234
Year	Dollars per pound	Dollars per pound	Dollars per pound	Dollars per pound	Dollars per pound	Dollars per pound	Dollars per pound	Dollars per pound	Dollars per pound	Dollars per pound	Dollars per pound	Dollars per piece	Dollars per yard	Dollars per yard	Dollars per yard
1955	—	0.08	—	—	0.34	—	—	—	—	—	1.42	—	—	—	0.21
1956	—	0.09	—	—	0.35 [1]	0.34 [2]	—	—	—	—	1.37	—	—	—	0.23
1957	—	0.09	—	—	—	0.34	—	—	—	—	1.61	—	—	—	0.21
1958	—	0.09	—	—	—	0.35	—	—	—	—	1.19	—	—	—	0.20
1959	—	0.09	—	—	—	0.33	—	—	—	—	1.22	—	—	—	0.21
1960	—	0.09	—	—	—	0.31	—	—	—	—	1.16	—	—	—	0.22
1961	—	0.09	—	—	—	0.32	—	—	—	—	1.18	—	—	—	0.22
1962	—	0.09	—	—	—	—	—	—	—	—	1.25	—	—	—	0.23
1963	—	0.11	—	—	—	0.34	—	—	—	—	1.32	—	—	—	0.22
1964	—	0.10	—	—	—	0.32	—	—	—	—	1.39	—	—	—	0.23
1965	—	0.10	—	—	—	0.30	—	—	—	—	1.25	—	—	—	0.23
1966	—	0.10	—	—	—	0.26	—	—	—	—	1.35	—	—	—	0.25
1967	—	0.10	—	—	—	0.23	—	—	—	—	1.22	—	—	—	0.26
1968	—	0.10	—	—	—	—	—	—	—	—	1.21	—	—	—	0.24
1969	—	0.11	—	—	—	0.26	—	—	—	—	1.22	—	—	—	0.24
1970	—	0.11	—	—	—	0.25	—	—	—	—	1.03	—	—	—	0.25
1971	—	0.12	—	—	—	—	—	—	—	—	0.67	—	—	—	0.26
1972	—	0.12	—	—	—	0.34	—	—	—	—	1.15	—	—	—	0.31
1973	—	0.13	—	—	—	0.56	—	—	—	—	2.50	—	—	—	0.32
1974	—	0.32	—	—	—	0.58	—	—	—	—	1.78	—	—	—	0.41
1975	—	0.31	—	—	—	0.45	—	—	—	—	1.49	—	—	—	—
1976	—	0.21	—	—	—	0.68	—	—	—	—	1.82	—	—	—	—
1977	—	0.18	—	—	—	0.61	—	—	—	—	1.83	—	—	—	—
1978	—	0.22	—	—	—	0.58	—	—	—	—	1.90	—	—	—	—
1979	—	0.23	—	—	—	0.63	—	—	—	—	2.16	—	—	—	—
1980	—	0.43	—	—	—	0.82	—	—	—	—	2.37	—	—	—	—
1981	—	0.33	—	—	—	0.72	—	—	—	—	2.53	—	—	—	—
1982	—	0.31	—	—	—	0.60	—	—	—	—	2.19	—	—	—	—
1983	—	0.33	—	—	—	0.68	—	—	—	—	1.89	—	—	—	—
1984	—	0.33	—	—	—	0.68	—	—	—	—	2.16	—	—	—	—
1985	—	0.32	—	—	—	0.59	—	—	—	—	1.76	—	—	—	—
1986	—	0.32	—	—	—	0.53	—	—	—	—	1.77	—	—	—	—
1987	—	0.33	—	—	—	0.63	—	—	—	—	2.23	—	—	—	—
1988	—	0.34	—	—	—	0.57	—	—	—	—	3.22	—	—	—	—
1989	—	0.37	—	—	—	0.63	—	—	—	—	3.01	—	—	—	—
1990	—	0.38	—	—	—	0.71	—	—	—	—	1.96	—	—	—	—
1991	—	0.38	—	—	—	0.70	—	—	—	—	1.52	—	—	—	—
1992	—	0.37	—	—	—	0.54	—	—	—	—	1.78	—	—	—	—
1993	—	0.37	—	—	—	0.55	—	—	—	—	1.24	—	—	—	—
1994	—	0.37	—	—	—	0.73	—	—	—	—	1.76	—	—	—	—
1995	—	0.37	—	—	—	0.94	—	—	—	—	2.18	—	—	—	—
1996	—	0.38	—	—	—	0.78	—	—	—	—	1.71	—	—	—	—
1997	—	0.38	—	—	—	0.70	—	—	—	—	2.01	—	—	—	—
1998	—	0.37	—	—	—	0.67	—	—	—	—	1.43	—	—	—	—

Notes appear at end of table

(continued)

TABLE Cc205–266   Wholesale prices of selected commodities: 1784–1998   *Continued*

	Coal, anthracite								Steel rails					Nails		
	Philadelphia	New York	White ash lump	Chestnut	Railroad, gross	Railroad, net	F.O.B.	BLS index	Iron rails	Bessemer	Open hearth	Standard	Carbon steel	Philadelphia	Cut nails	Fence and common
	Cc235	Cc236	Cc237	Cc238	Cc239	Cc240	Cc241	Cc242	Cc243	Cc244	Cc245	Cc246	Cc247	Cc248	Cc249	Cc250
Year	Dollars per 80-pound bushel	Dollars per ton	Dollars per gross ton	Dollars per gross ton	Dollars per gross ton	Dollars per net ton	Dollars per net ton	Dollars per ton	Dollars gross ton	Dollars per gross ton	Dollars per gross ton	Dollars per hundredweight	Dollars per hundredweight	Dollars per hundredweight	Dollars per hundredweight	Dollars per hundredweight
1784	—	—	—	—	—	—	—	—	—	—	—	—	—	10.53	—	—
1785	0.20 [4]	—	—	—	—	—	—	—	—	—	—	—	—	10.48	—	—
1786	0.20	—	—	—	—	—	—	—	—	—	—	—	—	10.38	—	—
1787	0.20	—	—	—	—	—	—	—	—	—	—	—	—	10.45	—	—
1788	0.17	—	—	—	—	—	—	—	—	—	—	—	—	9.99	—	—
1789	0.18	—	—	—	—	—	—	—	—	—	—	—	—	10.06	—	—
1790	0.19	—	—	—	—	—	—	—	—	—	—	—	—	9.67	—	—
1791	0.21	—	—	—	—	—	—	—	—	—	—	—	—	10.28	—	—
1792	0.21	—	—	—	—	—	—	—	—	—	—	—	—	10.00	—	—
1793	0.22	—	—	—	—	—	—	—	—	—	—	—	—	10.00	—	—
1794	0.29	—	—	—	—	—	—	—	—	—	—	—	—	10.00 [6]	—	—
1795	0.32	—	—	—	—	—	—	—	—	—	—	—	—	12.25	—	—
1796	0.39	—	—	—	—	—	—	—	—	—	—	—	—	12.00	—	—
1797	0.32	—	—	—	—	—	—	—	—	—	—	—	—	12.00	—	—
1798	0.33	—	—	—	—	—	—	—	—	—	—	—	—	12.00	—	—
1799	0.31	—	—	—	—	—	—	—	—	—	—	—	—	11.78	—	—
1800	0.31	—	—	—	—	—	—	—	—	—	—	—	—	10.67	—	—
1801	0.30	—	—	—	—	—	—	—	—	—	—	—	—	10.67	—	—
1802	0.29	—	—	—	—	—	—	—	—	—	—	—	—	11.65	—	—
1803	0.29	—	—	—	—	—	—	—	—	—	—	—	—	10.52	—	—
1804	0.29	—	—	—	—	—	—	—	—	—	—	—	—	10.50	—	—
1805	0.40	—	—	—	—	—	—	—	—	—	—	—	—	10.50	—	—
1806	0.32	—	—	—	—	—	—	—	—	—	—	—	—	9.50	—	—
1807	0.30	—	—	—	—	—	—	—	—	—	—	—	—	9.50	—	—
1808	0.28	—	—	—	—	—	—	—	—	—	—	—	—	9.50	—	—
1809	0.30	—	—	—	—	—	—	—	—	—	—	—	—	9.50	—	—
1810	0.37	—	—	—	—	—	—	—	—	—	—	—	—	9.50	—	—
1811	0.37	—	—	—	—	—	—	—	—	—	—	—	—	9.33	—	—
1812	0.41	—	—	—	—	—	—	—	—	—	—	—	—	8.50	—	—
1813	0.92	—	—	—	—	—	—	—	—	—	—	—	—	8.50	—	—
1814	1.13	—	—	—	—	—	—	—	—	—	—	—	—	11.25	—	—
1815	0.60	—	—	—	—	—	—	—	—	—	—	—	—	12.50	—	—
1816	0.36	—	—	—	—	—	—	—	—	—	—	—	—	12.83	—	—
1817	0.32	—	—	—	—	—	—	—	—	—	—	—	—	10.90	—	—
1818	0.33	—	—	—	—	—	—	—	—	—	—	—	—	9.60	—	—
1819	0.34	—	—	—	—	—	—	—	—	—	—	—	—	9.67	—	—
1820	0.32	—	—	—	—	—	—	—	—	—	—	—	—	9.80	—	—
1821	0.33	—	—	—	—	—	—	—	—	—	—	—	—	9.80	—	—
1822	0.33	—	—	—	—	—	—	—	—	—	—	—	—	9.80	—	—
1823	0.33	—	—	—	—	—	—	—	—	—	—	—	—	9.80	—	—
1824	0.30	—	—	—	—	—	—	—	—	—	—	—	—	8.87	—	—

	Coal, anthracite								Steel rails					Nails		
	Philadelphia	New York	White ash lump	Chestnut	Railroad, gross	Railroad, net	F.O.B.	BLS index	Iron rails	Bessemer	Open hearth	Standard	Carbon steel	Philadelphia	Cut nails	Fence and common
	Cc235	Cc236	Cc237	Cc238	Cc239	Cc240	Cc241	Cc242	Cc243	Cc244	Cc245	Cc246	Cc247	Cc248	Cc249	Cc250
Year	Dollars per 80-pound bushel	Dollars per ton	Dollars per gross ton	Dollars per gross ton	Dollars per gross ton	Dollars per net ton	Dollars per net ton	Dollars per ton	Dollars per gross ton	Dollars per gross ton	Dollars per gross ton	Dollars per hundredweight	Dollars per hundredweight	Dollars per hundredweight	Dollars per hundredweight	Dollars per hundredweight
1825	0.25	9.16	—	—	—	—	—	—	—	—	—	—	—	7.33	—	—
1826	—	10.92	—	—	—	—	—	—	—	—	—	—	—	7.21	—	—
1827	—	11.34	—	—	—	—	—	—	—	—	—	—	—	6.76	7.50	—
1828	—	10.92	—	—	—	—	—	—	—	—	—	—	—	7.08	7.10	—
1829	—	10.72	—	—	—	—	—	—	—	—	—	—	—	—	—	—
1830	—	9.05	—	—	—	—	—	—	—	—	—	—	—	—	5.50	—
1831	—	7.08	—	—	—	—	—	—	—	—	—	—	—	—	5.60	—
1832	—	10.21	—	—	—	—	—	—	—	—	—	—	—	—	5.80	—
1833	—	6.82	5.23	—	—	—	—	—	—	—	—	—	—	—	5.00	—
1834	—	—	4.84	—	—	—	—	—	—	—	—	—	—	—	5.50	—
1835	—	—	4.84	—	—	—	—	—	—	—	—	—	—	—	6.00	—
1836	—	—	6.64	—	—	—	—	—	—	—	—	—	—	—	6.00	—
1837	—	—	6.72	—	—	—	—	—	—	—	—	—	—	—	6.00	—
1838	—	—	5.27	—	—	—	—	—	—	—	—	—	—	—	6.00	—
1839	—	—	5.00	—	—	—	—	—	—	—	—	—	—	—	6.12	—
1840	—	—	4.91	—	—	—	—	—	—	—	—	—	—	—	5.50	—
1841	—	—	5.79	—	—	—	—	—	—	—	—	—	—	—	5.25	—
1842	—	—	4.18	—	—	—	—	—	—	—	—	—	—	—	4.75	—
1843	—	—	3.27	—	—	—	—	—	—	—	—	—	—	—	4.25	—
1844	—	—	3.20	—	—	—	—	—	—	—	—	—	—	—	4.50	—
1845	—	—	3.46	—	—	—	—	—	—	—	—	—	—	—	4.75	—
1846	—	—	3.90	—	—	—	—	—	—	—	—	—	—	—	4.50	—
1847	—	—	3.80	—	—	—	—	—	69.34	—	—	—	—	—	4.50	—
1848	—	—	3.50	—	—	—	—	—	62.25	—	—	—	—	—	4.25	—
1849	—	—	3.62	—	—	—	—	—	53.87	—	—	—	—	—	4.00	—
1850	—	—	3.64	—	—	—	—	—	47.87	—	—	—	—	—	3.71	—
1851	—	—	3.34	—	—	—	—	—	45.62	—	—	—	—	—	3.28	—
1852	—	—	3.46	—	—	—	—	—	48.37	—	—	—	—	—	3.13	—
1853	—	—	3.70	—	—	—	—	—	77.25	—	—	—	—	—	4.85	—
1854	—	—	5.19	—	—	—	—	—	80.12	—	—	—	—	—	4.76	—
1855	—	—	4.49	—	—	—	—	—	62.87	—	—	—	—	—	4.10	—
1856	—	—	4.11	—	—	—	—	—	64.37	—	—	—	—	—	3.92	—
1857	—	—	3.87	—	—	—	—	—	64.25	—	—	—	—	—	3.72	—
1858	—	—	3.43	—	—	—	—	—	50.00	—	—	—	—	—	3.53	—
1859	—	—	3.25	—	—	—	—	—	49.37	—	—	—	—	—	3.86	—
1860	—	—	3.40	—	—	—	—	—	48.00	—	—	—	—	—	3.13	—
1861	—	—	3.39	—	—	—	—	—	42.37	—	—	—	—	—	2.75	—
1862	—	—	4.14	—	—	—	—	—	41.75	—	—	—	—	—	3.47	—
1863	—	—	6.06	—	—	—	—	—	76.87	—	—	—	—	—	5.13	—
1864	—	—	8.39	—	—	—	—	—	126.00	—	—	—	—	—	7.85	—
1865	—	—	7.86	—	—	—	—	—	98.62	—	—	—	—	—	7.08	—
1866	—	—	5.80	—	—	—	—	—	86.75	—	—	—	—	—	6.97	—
1867	—	—	4.37	—	—	—	—	—	83.12	166.00	—	—	—	—	5.92	—
1868	—	—	3.86	—	—	—	—	—	—	158.50	—	—	—	—	5.17	—
1869	—	—	5.31	—	—	—	—	—	—	132.25	—	—	—	—	4.87	—

Notes appear at end of table

(continued)

TABLE Cc205–266   Wholesale prices of selected commodities: 1784–1998   *Continued*

Year	Coal, anthracite Philadelphia Cc235 Dollars per 80-pound bushel	Coal, anthracite New York Cc236 Dollars per ton	Coal, anthracite White ash lump Cc237 Dollars per gross ton	Coal, anthracite Chestnut Cc238 Dollars per gross ton	Coal, anthracite Railroad, gross Cc239 Dollars per gross ton	Coal, anthracite Railroad, net Cc240 Dollars per net ton	Coal, anthracite F.O.B. Cc241 Dollars per net ton	Coal, anthracite BLS index Cc242 Dollars per ton	Iron rails Cc243 Dollars gross ton	Bessemer Cc244 Dollars per gross ton	Steel rails Open hearth Cc245 Dollars per gross ton	Steel rails Standard Cc246 Dollars per hundredweight	Steel rails Carbon steel Cc247 Dollars per hundredweight	Nails Philadelphia Cc248 Dollars per hundredweight	Nails Cut nails Cc249 Dollars per hundredweight	Nails Fence and common Cc250 Dollars per hundredweight
1870	—	—	4.39	—	—	—	—	—	—	106.79	—	—	—	—	—	—
1871	—	—	4.46	—	—	—	—	—	—	102.52	—	—	—	—	4.40	—
1872	—	—	3.74	—	—	—	—	—	—	111.94	—	—	—	—	4.52	—
1873	—	—	4.27	—	—	—	—	—	—	120.58	—	—	—	—	5.46	—
1874	—	—	4.55	—	—	—	—	—	—	94.28	—	—	—	—	4.90	—
1875	—	—	4.39	—	—	—	—	—	—	68.75	—	—	—	—	3.99	—
1876	—	—	3.87	—	—	—	—	—	—	59.25	—	—	—	—	3.42	—
1877	—	—	2.59	—	—	—	—	—	—	45.58	—	—	—	—	2.98	—
1878	—	—	3.22	—	—	—	—	—	—	42.21	—	—	—	—	2.57	—
1879	—	—	2.70	—	—	—	—	—	—	48.21	—	—	—	—	2.31	—
1880	—	—	4.53	—	—	—	—	—	—	67.52	—	—	—	—	2.69	—
1881	—	—	4.53	—	—	—	—	—	—	61.08	—	—	—	—	3.68	—
1882	—	—	4.61	—	—	—	—	—	—	48.50	—	—	—	—	3.09	—
1883	—	—	4.54	—	—	—	—	—	—	37.75	—	—	—	—	3.47	—
1884	—	—	4.42	—	—	—	—	—	—	30.75	—	—	—	—	3.06	—
1885	—	—	4.10	—	—	—	—	—	—	28.52	—	—	—	—	2.39	—
1886	—	—	4.00	—	—	—	—	—	—	34.52	—	—	—	—	2.33	—
1887	—	—	4.05	—	—	—	—	—	—	37.08	—	—	—	—	2.27	—
1888	—	—	4.21	—	—	—	—	—	—	29.83	—	—	—	—	2.30	—
1889	—	—	4.04	—	—	—	—	—	—	29.25	—	—	—	—	2.03	—
1890	—	—	3.92	3.35	—	—	—	—	—	31.78	—	—	—	—	2.00	2.97
1891	—	—	—	3.46	—	—	—	—	—	29.92	—	—	—	—	2.00	2.47
1892	—	—	—	3.94	—	—	—	—	—	30.00	—	—	—	—	—	2.19
1893	—	—	—	4.17	—	—	—	—	—	28.13	—	—	—	—	—	1.99
1894	—	—	—	3.54	—	—	—	—	—	24.00	—	—	—	—	—	1.65
1895	—	—	—	2.98	—	—	—	—	—	24.33	—	—	—	—	—	2.12
1896	—	—	—	3.56	—	—	—	—	—	28.00	—	—	—	—	—	2.93
1897	—	—	—	3.74	—	—	—	—	—	18.75	—	—	—	—	—	1.49
1898	—	—	—	3.55	—	—	—	—	—	17.63	—	—	—	—	—	1.44
1899	—	—	—	3.65	—	—	—	—	—	28.13	—	—	—	—	—	2.39
1900	—	—	—	3.92	—	—	—	—	—	32.29	—	—	—	—	—	2.63
1901	—	—	—	4.33	—	—	—	—	—	27.33	—	—	—	—	—	2.37
1902	—	—	—	4.46	—	—	—	—	—	28.00	—	—	—	—	—	2.10
1903	—	—	—	4.83	—	—	—	—	—	28.00	—	—	—	—	—	2.08
1904	—	—	—	4.83	—	—	—	—	—	28.00	—	—	—	—	—	1.91
1905	—	—	—	4.82	—	—	—	—	—	28.00	—	—	—	—	—	1.90
1906	—	—	—	4.86	—	—	—	—	—	28.00	—	—	—	—	—	1.96
1907	—	—	—	4.82	—	—	—	—	—	28.00	—	—	—	—	—	2.12
1908	—	—	—	4.82	—	—	—	—	—	28.00	—	—	—	—	—	2.10
1909	—	—	—	4.82	—	—	—	—	—	28.00	—	—	—	—	—	1.92

	Coal, anthracite								Steel rails					Nails		
	Philadelphia	New York	White ash lump	Chestnut	Railroad, gross	Railroad, net	F.O.B.	BLS index	Iron rails	Bessemer	Open hearth	Standard	Carbon steel	Philadelphia	Cut nails	Fence and common
Year	Cc235	Cc236	Cc237	Cc238	Cc239	Cc240	Cc241	Cc242	Cc243	Cc244	Cc245	Cc246	Cc247	Cc248	Cc249	Cc250
	Dollars per 80-pound bushel	Dollars per ton	Dollars per gross ton	Dollars per gross ton	Dollars per gross ton	Dollars per net ton	Dollars per net ton	Dollars per ton	Dollars gross ton	Dollars per gross ton	Dollars per gross ton	Dollars per hundredweight	Dollars per hundredweight	Dollars per hundredweight	Dollars per hundredweight	Dollars per hundredweight
1910	—	—	—	4.81	—	—	—	—	—	28.00	—	—	—	—	—	1.89
1911	—	—	—	5.00	—	—	—	—	—	28.00	—	—	—	—	—	1.80
1912	—	—	—	5.28	—	—	—	—	—	28.00	30.00	—	—	—	—	1.74
1913	—	—	—	5.31	—	—	—	—	—	28.00	30.00	—	—	—	—	1.82
1914	—	—	—	5.32	—	—	—	—	—	—	30.00	—	—	—	—	1.68
1915	—	—	—	5.33	—	—	—	—	—	—	30.00	—	—	—	—	1.75
1916	—	—	—	5.57	—	—	—	—	—	—	33.33	—	—	—	—	2.60
1917	—	—	—	5.94	—	—	—	—	—	—	40.00	—	—	—	—	3.63
1918	—	—	—	6.86	—	—	—	—	—	—	56.00	—	—	—	—	3.60
1919	—	—	—	8.27	—	—	—	—	—	—	49.26	—	—	—	—	3.52
1920	—	—	—	9.50	—	—	—	—	—	—	58.83	—	—	—	—	4.19
1921	—	—	—	10.53	—	—	—	—	—	—	45.65	—	—	—	—	3.06
1922	—	—	—	10.60	—	—	—	—	—	—	40.69	—	—	—	—	2.61
1923	—	—	—	10.88	—	—	—	—	—	—	43.00	—	—	—	—	3.04
1924	—	—	—	11.37	—	—	—	—	—	—	43.00	—	—	—	—	2.99
1925	—	—	—	11.19	—	—	—	—	—	—	43.00	—	—	—	—	2.82
1926	—	—	—	11.48	—	—	—	—	—	—	43.00	—	—	—	—	2.75
1927	—	—	—	10.95	—	—	—	—	—	—	43.00	—	—	—	—	2.64
1928	—	—	—	10.93	13.00	—	—	—	—	—	43.00	—	—	—	—	2.68
1929	—	—	—	—	12.89	—	—	—	—	—	43.00	—	—	—	—	2.67
1930	—	—	—	—	12.72	—	—	—	—	—	43.00	—	—	—	—	2.19
1931	—	—	—	—	12.77	11.40	—	—	—	—	43.00	—	—	—	—	1.98
1932	—	—	—	—	—	10.88	—	—	—	—	42.38	—	—	—	—	2.05
1933	—	—	—	—	—	10.06	—	—	—	—	39.33	—	—	—	—	2.09
1934	—	—	—	—	—	9.64	—	—	—	—	36.38	—	—	—	—	2.62
1935	—	—	—	—	—	9.59	—	—	—	—	36.38	—	—	—	—	2.63
1936	—	—	—	—	—	9.74	—	—	—	—	36.63	—	—	—	—	2.23
1937	—	—	—	—	—	9.37	—	—	—	—	41.89	—	—	—	—	2.77
1938	—	—	—	—	—	9.44	—	—	—	—	41.79	—	—	—	—	2.58
1939	—	—	—	—	—	9.14	—	—	—	—	40.00	—	—	—	—	2.46
1940	—	—	—	—	—	9.55	—	—	—	—	40.00	—	—	—	—	2.55
1941	—	—	—	—	—	10.01	—	—	—	—	40.00	—	—	—	—	2.55
1942	—	—	—	—	—	10.31	—	—	—	—	40.00	—	—	—	—	2.55
1943	—	—	—	—	—	10.89	—	—	—	—	40.00	—	—	—	—	2.55
1944	—	—	—	—	—	11.47	—	—	—	—	40.00	—	—	—	—	2.55
1945	—	—	—	—	—	11.89	—	—	—	—	42.94	—	—	—	—	2.85
1946	—	—	—	—	—	13.06	—	—	—	—	47.90	—	—	—	—	3.48
1947	—	—	—	—	—	14.11	10.33	—	—	—	—	2.61	—	—	—	3.97
1948	—	—	—	—	—	—	11.57	—	—	—	—	2.94	—	—	—	—
1949	—	—	—	—	—	—	12.04	—	—	—	—	3.21	—	—	—	—
1950	—	—	—	—	—	—	12.58	—	—	—	—	3.42	—	—	—	—
1951	—	—	—	—	—	—	14.19	—	—	—	—	3.60	—	—	—	—
1952	—	—	—	—	—	—	14.30	—	—	—	—	3.67	—	—	—	—
1953	—	—	—	—	—	—	15.45	—	—	—	—	3.78 [6]	4.09 [7]	—	—	—
1954	—	—	—	—	—	—	14.01	—	—	—	—	—	4.46	—	—	—

Notes appear at end of table

(continued)

TABLE Cc205–266   Wholesale prices of selected commodities: 1784–1998   Continued

	Coal, anthracite							Iron rails	Steel rails				Nails		
	Philadelphia	New York	White ash lump	Chestnut	Railroad, gross	Railroad, net	F.O.B.	BLS index		Bessemer	Open hearth	Standard	Carbon steel	Philadelphia	Cut nails	Fence and common
Year	Cc235	Cc236	Cc237	Cc238	Cc239	Cc240	Cc241	Cc242	Cc243	Cc244	Cc245	Cc246	Cc247	Cc248	Cc249	Cc250
	Dollars per 80-pound bushel	Dollars per ton	Dollars per gross ton	Dollars per gross ton	Dollars per gross ton	Dollars per net ton	Dollars per net ton	Dollars per ton	Dollars gross ton	Dollars per gross ton	Dollars per gross ton	Dollars per hundredweight	Dollars per hundredweight	Dollars per hundredweight	Dollars per hundredweight	Dollars per hundredweight
1955	—	—	—	—	—	—	12.93	—	—	—	—	—	4.66	—	—	—
1956	—	—	—	—	—	—	13.53	—	—	—	—	—	4.95	—	—	—
1957	—	—	—	—	—	—	14.67	—	—	—	—	—	5.44	—	—	—
1958	—	—	—	—	—	—	14.24	—	—	—	—	—	5.68	—	—	—
1959	—	—	—	—	—	—	14.18	—	—	—	—	—	5.83	—	—	—
1960	—	—	—	—	—	—	13.95	—	—	—	—	—	5.83	—	—	—
1961	—	—	—	—	—	—	13.35	—	—	—	—	—	5.83	—	—	—
1962	—	—	—	—	—	—	13.05	—	—	—	—	—	5.83	—	—	—
1963	—	—	—	—	—	—	13.36	—	—	—	—	—	5.83	—	—	—
1964	—	—	—	—	—	—	13.90	—	—	—	—	—	5.83	—	—	—
1965	—	—	—	—	—	—	12.98	—	—	—	—	—	5.83	—	—	—
1966	—	—	—	—	—	—	—	—	—	—	—	—	5.89	—	—	—
1967	—	—	—	—	—	—	12.89 [5]	—	—	—	—	—	6.08	—	—	—
1968	—	—	—	—	—	—	13.71 [5]	—	—	—	—	—	6.33	—	—	—
1969	—	—	—	—	—	—	15.02	—	—	—	—	—	6.58	—	—	—
1970	—	—	—	—	—	—	16.57	—	—	—	—	—	6.80	—	—	—
1971	—	—	—	—	—	—	17.67	—	—	—	—	—	7.59	—	—	—
1972	—	—	—	—	—	—	18.23	—	—	—	—	—	8.00	—	—	—
1973	—	—	—	—	—	—	20.04	—	—	—	—	—	8.35	—	—	—
1974	—	—	—	—	—	—	29.97	—	—	—	—	—	10.53	—	—	—
1975	—	—	—	—	—	—	44.86	—	—	—	—	—	12.72	—	—	—
1976	—	—	—	—	—	—	—	46.34	—	—	—	—	14.17	—	—	—
1977	—	—	—	—	—	—	—	47.20	—	—	—	—	15.17	—	—	—
1978	—	—	—	—	—	—	—	48.52	—	—	—	—	16.90	—	—	—
1979	—	—	—	—	—	—	—	49.46	—	—	—	—	18.80	—	—	—
1980	—	—	—	—	—	—	—	55.69	—	—	—	—	21.35	—	—	—
1981	—	—	—	—	—	—	—	68.93	—	—	—	—	23.70	—	—	—
1982	—	—	—	—	—	—	—	77.88	—	—	—	—	24.23 [8]	—	—	—
1983	—	—	—	—	—	—	—	75.31	—	—	—	—	—	—	—	—
1984	—	—	—	—	—	—	—	74.53	—	—	—	—	—	—	—	—
1985	—	—	—	—	—	—	—	75.47	—	—	—	—	—	—	—	—
1986	—	—	—	—	—	—	—	75.43	—	—	—	—	—	—	—	—
1987	—	—	—	—	—	—	—	75.78	—	—	—	—	—	—	—	—
1988	—	—	—	—	—	—	—	76.79	—	—	—	—	—	—	—	—
1989	—	—	—	—	—	—	—	78.82	—	—	—	—	—	—	—	—
1990	—	—	—	—	—	—	—	80.37	—	—	—	—	—	—	—	—
1991	—	—	—	—	—	—	—	80.92	—	—	—	—	—	—	—	—
1992	—	—	—	—	—	—	—	81.08	—	—	—	—	—	—	—	—
1993	—	—	—	—	—	—	—	81.15	—	—	—	—	—	—	—	—
1994	—	—	—	—	—	—	—	81.70	—	—	—	—	—	—	—	—
1995	—	—	—	—	—	—	—	80.45	—	—	—	—	—	—	—	—
1996	—	—	—	—	—	—	—	80.45	—	—	—	—	—	—	—	—
1997	—	—	—	—	—	—	—	80.61	—	—	—	—	—	—	—	—
1998	—	—	—	—	—	—	—	81.08	—	—	—	—	—	—	—	—

TABLE Cc205–266 Wholesale prices of selected commodities: 1784–1998 *Continued*

	Nails		Copper						Turpentine					Brick		
	Common	BLS index	Philadelphia	Sheathing	Lake copper	New York	Connecticut	BLS index	Philadelphia	New York	Spirits	New York	BLS index	New York	Common	Building
	Cc251	Cc252	Cc253	Cc254	Cc255	Cc256	Cc257	Cc258	Cc259	Cc260	Cc261	Cc262	Cc263	Cc264	Cc265	Cc266
Year	Dollars per hundredweight	Dollars per 50 pounds	Dollars per pound	Dollars per pound	Dollars per pound	Dollars per pound	Dollars per pound	Dollars per pound	Dollars per 31.5-gallon barrel	Dollars per gallon	Dollars per gallon	Dollars per gallon	Dollars per gallon	Dollars per thousand	Dollars per thousand	Dollars per thousand
1784	—	—	0.24	—	—	—	—	—	3.99	—	—	—	—	—	—	—
1785	—	—	0.25	—	—	—	—	—	2.87	—	—	—	—	—	—	—
1786	—	—	0.25	—	—	—	—	—	1.84	—	—	—	—	—	—	—
1787	—	—	0.26	—	—	—	—	—	1.47	—	—	—	—	—	—	—
1788	—	—	0.25	—	—	—	—	—	1.63	—	—	—	—	—	—	—
1789	—	—	0.25	—	—	—	—	—	1.77	—	—	—	—	—	—	—
1790	—	—	0.25	—	—	—	—	—	2.39	—	—	—	—	—	—	—
1791	—	—	0.25	—	—	—	—	—	2.11	—	—	—	—	—	—	—
1792	—	—	—	—	—	—	—	—	1.84	—	—	—	—	—	—	—
1793	—	—	—	—	—	—	—	—	2.17	—	—	—	—	—	—	—
1794	—	—	—	—	—	—	—	—	2.29	—	—	—	—	—	—	—
1795	—	—	0.37 [3]	—	—	—	—	—	3.04	—	—	—	—	—	—	—
1796	—	—	0.36	—	—	—	—	—	3.49	—	—	—	—	—	—	—
1797	—	—	0.38	—	—	—	—	—	3.54	—	—	—	—	—	—	—
1798	—	—	0.43	—	—	—	—	—	3.50 [9]	—	—	—	—	—	—	—
1799	—	—	0.51	—	—	—	—	—	2.60 [10]	—	—	—	—	—	—	—
1800	—	—	0.53	—	—	—	—	—	2.50 [11]	—	—	—	—	—	—	—
1801	—	—	0.50	—	—	—	—	—	2.67	—	—	—	—	—	—	—
1802	—	—	0.41	—	—	—	—	—	2.98	—	—	—	—	—	—	—
1803	—	—	0.43	—	—	—	—	—	3.63	—	—	—	—	—	—	—
1804	—	—	0.48	—	—	—	—	—	3.50	—	—	—	—	—	—	—
1805	—	—	0.51	—	—	—	—	—	3.61	—	—	—	—	—	—	—
1806	—	—	0.52	—	—	—	—	—	2.98	—	—	—	—	—	—	—
1807	—	—	0.51	—	—	—	—	—	2.55	—	—	—	—	—	—	—
1808	—	—	0.46	—	—	—	—	—	3.05	—	—	—	—	—	—	—
1809	—	—	0.45	—	—	—	—	—	3.84	—	—	—	—	—	—	—
1810	—	—	0.43	—	—	—	—	—	3.94	—	—	—	—	—	—	—
1811	—	—	0.36	—	—	—	—	—	3.23	—	—	—	—	—	—	—
1812	—	—	0.46	—	—	—	—	—	2.43	—	—	—	—	—	—	—
1813	—	—	0.50	—	—	—	—	—	3.08	—	—	—	—	—	—	—
1814	—	—	0.60	—	—	—	—	—	6.67	—	—	—	—	—	—	—
1815	—	—	0.45	—	—	—	—	—	4.48	—	—	—	—	—	—	—
1816	—	—	0.36	—	—	—	—	—	3.69	—	—	—	—	—	—	—
1817	—	—	0.27	—	—	—	—	—	2.90	—	—	—	—	—	—	—
1818	—	—	0.29	—	—	—	—	—	3.54	—	—	—	—	—	—	—
1819	—	—	0.30	—	—	—	—	—	2.88	—	—	—	—	—	—	—
1820	—	—	0.29	—	—	—	—	—	2.37	—	—	—	—	—	—	—
1821	—	—	0.30	—	—	—	—	—	2.22	—	—	—	—	—	—	—
1822	—	—	0.28	—	—	—	—	—	2.54	—	—	—	—	—	—	—
1823	—	—	0.26	—	—	—	—	—	2.69	—	—	—	—	—	—	—
1824	—	—	0.25	—	—	—	—	—	2.56	—	—	—	—	—	—	—

Notes appear at end of table

(continued)

TABLE Cc205–266   Wholesale prices of selected commodities: 1784–1998   *Continued*

	Nails		Copper						Turpentine					Brick		
	Common	BLS index	Philadelphia	Sheathing	Lake copper	New York	Connecticut	BLS index	Philadelphia	New York	Spirits	New York	BLS index	New York	Common	Building
	Cc251	Cc252	Cc253	Cc254	Cc255	Cc256	Cc257	Cc258	Cc259	Cc260	Cc261	Cc262	Cc263	Cc264	Cc265	Cc266
Year	Dollars per hundredweight	Dollars per 50 pounds	Dollars per pound	Dollars per pound	Dollars per pound	Dollars per pound	Dollars per pound	Dollars per pound	Dollars per 31.5-gallon barrel	Dollars per gallon	Dollars per gallon	Dollars per gallon	Dollars per gallon	Dollars per thousand	Dollars per thousand	Dollars per thousand
1825	—	—	0.30	0.30	—	—	—	—	2.62 [12]	0.41	—	—	—	—	—	—
1826	—	—	—	0.30	—	—	—	—	—	0.30	—	—	—	—	—	—
1827	—	—	—	0.26	—	—	—	—	—	0.37	—	—	—	—	—	—
1828	—	—	—	0.25	—	—	—	—	—	0.38	—	—	—	—	—	—
1829	—	—	—	0.24	—	—	—	—	—	0.36	—	—	—	—	—	—
1830	—	—	—	0.22	—	—	—	—	—	0.29	—	—	—	—	—	—
1831	—	—	—	0.22	—	—	—	—	—	0.29	—	—	—	—	—	—
1832	—	—	—	0.23	—	—	—	—	—	0.37	—	—	—	—	—	—
1833	—	—	—	0.23	—	—	—	—	—	0.42	—	—	—	—	—	—
1834	—	—	—	0.24	—	—	—	—	—	0.47	—	—	—	—	—	—
1835	—	—	—	0.24	—	—	—	—	—	0.55	—	—	—	—	—	—
1836	—	—	—	0.27	—	—	—	—	—	0.55	—	—	—	—	—	—
1837	—	—	—	0.27	—	—	—	—	—	0.39	—	—	—	—	—	—
1838	—	—	—	0.26	—	—	—	—	—	0.32	—	—	—	—	—	—
1839	—	—	—	0.25	—	—	—	—	—	0.34	—	—	—	—	—	—
1840	—	—	—	0.25	—	—	—	—	—	0.28	0.27	—	—	—	—	—
1841	—	—	—	0.25	—	—	—	—	—	—	0.32	—	—	—	—	—
1842	—	—	—	0.23	—	—	—	—	—	—	0.34	—	—	—	—	—
1843	—	—	—	0.21	—	—	—	—	—	—	0.34	—	—	—	—	—
1844	—	—	—	0.22	—	—	—	—	—	—	0.34	—	—	—	—	—
1845	—	—	—	0.23	—	—	—	—	—	—	0.41	—	—	—	—	—
1846	—	—	—	0.24	—	—	—	—	—	—	0.45	—	—	—	—	—
1847	—	—	—	0.23	—	—	—	—	—	—	0.40	—	—	—	—	—
1848	—	—	—	0.22	—	—	—	—	—	—	0.37	—	—	—	—	—
1849	—	—	—	0.22	—	—	—	—	—	—	0.33	—	—	3.85	—	—
1850	—	—	—	0.22	—	—	—	—	—	—	0.33	—	—	4.85	—	—
1851	—	—	—	0.21	—	—	—	—	—	—	0.35	—	—	4.69	—	—
1852	—	—	—	0.24	—	—	—	—	—	—	0.45	—	—	4.63	—	—
1853	—	—	—	0.29	—	—	—	—	—	—	0.59	—	—	5.42	—	—
1854	—	—	—	0.30	—	—	—	—	—	—	0.56	—	—	4.89	—	—
1855	—	—	—	0.30	—	—	—	—	—	—	0.43	—	—	4.31	—	—
1856	—	—	—	0.31	—	—	—	—	—	—	0.40	—	—	4.29	—	—
1857	—	—	—	0.30	—	—	—	—	—	—	0.45	—	—	4.21	—	—
1858	—	—	—	0.26	—	—	—	—	—	—	0.46	—	—	3.96	—	—
1859	—	—	—	0.26	—	—	—	—	—	—	0.48	—	—	5.00	—	—
1860	—	—	—	0.26	0.23	—	—	—	—	—	0.42	—	—	4.49	—	—
1861	—	—	—	—	0.22	—	—	—	—	—	0.83	—	—	3.88	—	—
1862	—	—	—	—	0.22	—	—	—	—	—	1.57	—	—	4.16	—	—
1863	—	—	—	—	0.34	—	—	—	—	—	2.92	—	—	6.41	—	—
1864	—	—	—	—	0.47	—	—	—	—	—	2.98	—	—	8.27	—	—
1865	—	—	—	—	0.39	—	—	—	—	—	1.53	—	—	9.67	—	—
1866	—	—	—	—	0.34	—	—	—	—	—	0.81	—	—	11.44	—	—
1867	—	—	—	—	0.25	—	—	—	—	—	0.64	—	—	10.85	—	—
1868	—	—	—	—	0.23	—	—	—	—	—	0.51	—	—	12.08	—	—
1869	—	—	—	—	0.24	—	—	—	—	—	0.46	—	—	11.33	—	—

	Nails		Copper						Turpentine					Brick		
	Common	BLS index	Philadelphia	Sheathing	Lake copper	New York	Connecticut	BLS index	Philadelphia	New York	Spirits	New York	BLS index	New York	Common	Building
Year	Cc251	Cc252	Cc253	Cc254	Cc255	Cc256	Cc257	Cc258	Cc259	Cc260	Cc261	Cc262	Cc263	Cc264	Cc265	Cc266
	Dollars per hundredweight	Dollars per 50 pounds	Dollars per pound	Dollars per pound	Dollars per pound	Dollars per pound	Dollars per pound	Dollars per pound	Dollars per 31.5-gallon barrel	Dollars per gallon	Dollars per gallon	Dollars per gallon	Dollars per gallon	Dollars per thousand	Dollars per thousand	Dollars per thousand
1870	—	—	—	—	0.21	—	—	—	—	—	0.43	—	—	8.40	—	—
1871	—	—	—	—	0.24	—	—	—	—	—	0.55	—	—	9.31	—	—
1872	—	—	—	—	0.36	—	—	—	—	—	0.62	—	—	9.96	—	—
1873	—	—	—	—	0.28	—	—	—	—	—	0.50	—	—	8.02	—	—
1874	—	—	—	—	0.22	—	—	—	—	—	0.40	—	—	7.44	—	—
1875	—	—	—	—	0.23	—	—	—	—	—	0.35	—	—	7.00	—	—
1876	—	—	—	—	0.21	—	—	—	—	—	0.37	—	—	5.71	—	—
1877	—	—	—	—	0.19	—	—	—	—	—	0.36	—	—	4.94	—	—
1878	—	—	—	—	0.17	—	—	—	—	—	0.30	—	—	4.89	—	—
1879	—	—	—	—	0.19	—	—	—	—	—	0.32	—	—	5.26	—	—
1880	—	—	—	—	0.22	—	—	—	—	—	0.38	—	—	6.94	—	—
1881	—	—	—	—	0.18	—	—	—	—	—	0.48	—	—	7.50 [12]	—	—
1882	—	—	—	—	0.19	—	—	—	—	—	0.52	—	—	7.58 [13]	—	—
1883	—	—	—	—	0.16	—	—	—	—	—	0.43	—	—	8.14	—	—
1884	—	—	—	—	0.14	—	—	—	—	—	0.33	—	—	6.52	—	—
1885	—	—	—	—	0.11	—	—	—	—	—	0.35	—	—	6.36	—	—
1886	—	—	—	—	0.11	—	—	—	—	—	0.40	—	—	7.58	—	—
1887	—	—	—	—	0.11	—	—	—	—	—	0.36	—	—	7.40	—	—
1888	—	—	—	—	0.17	—	—	—	—	—	0.40	—	—	6.52	—	—
1889	—	—	—	—	0.14	—	—	—	—	—	0.46	—	—	7.00	—	—
1890	—	—	—	—	0.16	—	—	—	—	—	0.41	0.41	—	6.56	—	—
1891	—	—	—	—	0.13	—	—	—	—	—	—	0.38	—	5.71	—	—
1892	—	—	—	—	0.12	—	—	—	—	—	—	0.32	—	5.77	—	—
1893	—	—	—	—	0.11	—	—	—	—	—	—	0.30	—	5.83	—	—
1894	—	—	—	—	0.10	—	—	—	—	—	—	0.29	—	5.00	—	—
1895	—	—	—	—	0.11	—	—	—	—	—	—	0.29	—	5.31	—	—
1896	—	—	—	—	0.11	—	—	—	—	—	—	0.27	—	5.06	—	—
1897	—	—	—	—	0.11	—	—	—	—	—	—	0.29	—	4.94	—	—
1898	—	—	—	—	0.12	—	—	—	—	—	—	0.32	—	5.75	—	—
1899	—	—	—	—	0.18	—	—	—	—	—	—	0.46	—	5.69	—	—
1900	—	—	—	—	0.17	—	—	—	—	—	—	0.48	—	5.25	—	—
1901	—	—	—	—	0.17	—	—	—	—	—	—	0.37	—	5.77	—	—
1902	—	—	—	—	0.12	—	—	—	—	—	—	0.47	—	5.39	—	—
1903	—	—	—	—	0.14	—	—	—	—	—	—	0.57	—	5.91	—	—
1904	—	—	—	—	0.13	—	—	—	—	—	—	0.58	—	7.49	—	—
1905	—	—	—	—	0.16	—	—	—	—	—	—	0.63	—	8.10	—	—
1906	—	—	—	—	0.20	0.21	—	—	—	—	—	0.67	—	8.55	—	—
1907	—	—	—	—	0.21	0.13	—	—	—	—	—	0.63	—	6.16	—	—
1908	—	—	—	—	—	0.13	—	—	—	—	—	0.45	—	5.10	—	—
1909	—	—	—	—	—	—	—	—	—	—	—	0.49	—	6.39	—	—
1910	—	—	—	—	—	0.13	—	—	—	—	—	0.68	—	5.72	—	—
1911	—	—	—	—	—	0.13	—	—	—	—	—	0.68	—	5.89	—	—
1912	—	—	—	—	—	0.16	—	—	—	—	—	0.47	—	6.76	—	—
1913	—	—	—	—	—	0.16	—	—	—	—	—	0.43	—	6.56	—	—
1914	—	—	—	—	—	0.13	—	—	—	—	—	0.47	—	5.53	—	—

Notes appear at end of table

(continued)

TABLE Cc205–266   Wholesale prices of selected commodities: 1784–1998   *Continued*

	Nails		Copper						Turpentine					Brick		
	Common	BLS index	Philadelphia	Sheathing	Lake copper	New York	Connecticut	BLS index	Philadelphia	New York	Spirits	New York	BLS index	New York	Common	Building
	Cc251	Cc252	Cc253	Cc254	Cc255	Cc256	Cc257	Cc258	Cc259	Cc260	Cc261	Cc262	Cc263	Cc264	Cc265	Cc266
Year	Dollars per hundredweight	Dollars per 50 pounds	Dollars per pound	Dollars per pound	Dollars per pound	Dollars per pound	Dollars per pound	Dollars per pound	Dollars per 31.5-gallon barrel	Dollars per gallon	Dollars per gallon	Dollars per gallon	Dollars per gallon	Dollars per thousand	Dollars per thousand	Dollars per thousand
1915	—	—	—	—	—	0.17	—	—	—	—	—	0.46	—	6.05	—	—
1916	—	—	—	—	—	0.28	—	—	—	—	—	0.49	—	8.04	—	—
1917	—	—	—	—	—	0.29	—	—	—	—	—	0.49	—	8.89	—	—
1918	—	—	—	—	—	0.25	—	—	—	—	—	0.59	—	11.93	—	—
1919	—	—	—	—	—	0.19	—	—	—	—	—	1.21	—	15.96	—	—
1920	—	—	—	—	—	0.18	—	—	—	—	—	1.73	—	21.85	—	—
1921	—	—	—	—	—	0.13	—	—	—	—	—	0.68	—	15.21	—	—
1922	—	—	—	—	—	0.13	—	—	—	—	—	1.15	—	17.34	—	—
1923	—	—	—	—	—	0.15	—	—	—	—	—	1.17	—	19.81	—	—
1924	—	—	—	—	—	0.13	—	—	—	—	—	0.91	—	17.04	—	—
1925	—	—	—	—	—	0.14	—	—	—	—	—	1.01	—	14.70	—	—
1926	—	—	—	—	—	0.14	—	—	—	—	—	0.93	—	16.46	—	—
1927	—	—	—	—	—	0.13	0.13	—	—	—	—	0.62	—	13.88	—	—
1928	—	—	—	—	—	—	0.15	—	—	—	—	0.57	—	13.00	—	—
1929	—	—	—	—	—	—	0.18	—	—	—	—	0.55	—	10.73	—	—
1930	—	—	—	—	—	—	0.13	—	—	—	—	0.47	—	10.10	—	—
1931	—	—	—	—	—	—	0.08	—	—	—	—	0.45	—	10.02	—	—
1932	—	—	—	—	—	—	0.06	—	—	—	—	0.43	—	9.54	—	—
1933	—	—	—	—	—	—	0.07	—	—	—	—	0.46	—	9.19	10.53	—
1934	—	—	—	—	—	—	0.09	—	—	—	—	0.53	—	—	12.00	—
1935	—	—	—	—	—	—	0.09	—	—	—	—	0.50	—	—	11.77	—
1936	—	—	—	—	—	—	0.10	—	—	—	—	0.44	—	—	11.74	—
1937	—	—	—	—	—	—	0.13	—	—	—	—	0.39	—	—	12.05	—
1938	—	—	—	—	—	—	0.10	—	—	—	—	0.29	—	—	12.00	—
1939	—	—	—	—	—	—	0.11	—	—	—	—	0.31	—	—	12.05	—
1940	—	—	—	—	—	—	0.12	—	—	—	—	0.37	—	—	12.13	—
1941	—	—	—	—	—	—	0.12	—	—	—	—	0.62	—	—	12.59	—
1942	—	—	—	—	—	—	0.12	—	—	—	—	0.71	0.62	—	13.21	—
1943	—	—	—	—	—	—	0.12	—	—	—	—	—	0.67	—	13.43	—
1944	—	—	—	—	—	—	0.12	—	—	—	—	—	0.78	—	14.29	—
1945	—	—	—	—	—	—	0.12	—	—	—	—	—	0.79	—	15.89	—
1946	—	—	—	—	—	—	0.14	—	—	—	—	—	0.95	—	18.13	—
1947	4.47	—	—	—	—	—	0.21	—	—	—	—	—	0.75	—	20.50	20.98
1948	5.82	—	—	—	—	—	0.22	—	—	—	—	—	0.48	—	—	23.65
1949	6.14	—	—	—	—	—	0.20	—	—	—	—	—	0.39	—	—	24.73
1950	6.34	—	—	—	—	—	0.22	—	—	—	—	—	0.53	—	—	25.67
1951	6.93	—	—	—	—	—	0.25	—	—	—	—	—	0.81	—	—	27.33
1952	7.12	—	—	—	—	—	0.25	—	—	—	—	—	0.63	—	—	27.35
1953	7.44	—	—	—	—	—	0.29	—	—	—	—	—	0.59	—	—	27.85
1954	7.65	—	—	—	—	—	0.30	—	—	—	—	—	0.65	—	—	28.22
1955	8.18	—	—	—	—	—	0.37	—	—	—	—	—	0.64	—	—	29.15
1956	8.92	—	—	—	—	—	0.42	—	—	—	—	—	0.65	—	—	30.61
1957	9.60	—	—	—	—	—	0.30	—	—	—	—	—	0.66	—	—	30.86
1958	9.83	—	—	—	—	—	0.26	—	—	—	—	—	0.63	—	—	34.07
1959	9.83	—	—	—	—	—	0.31	—	—	—	—	—	0.54	—	—	31.67

Year	Nails Common Cc251 (Dollars per hundredweight)	Nails BLS index Cc252 (Dollars per 50 pounds)	Copper Philadelphia Cc253 (Dollars per pound)	Copper Sheathing Cc254 (Dollars per pound)	Copper Lake copper Cc255 (Dollars per pound)	Copper New York Cc256 (Dollars per pound)	Copper Connecticut Cc257 (Dollars per pound)	Copper BLS index Cc258 (Dollars per pound)	Turpentine Philadelphia Cc259 (Dollars per 31.5-gallon barrel)	Turpentine New York Cc260 (Dollars per gallon)	Turpentine Spirits Cc261 (Dollars per gallon)	Turpentine New York Cc262 (Dollars per gallon)	Turpentine BLS index Cc263 (Dollars per gallon)	Brick New York Cc264 (Dollars per thousand)	Brick Common Cc265 (Dollars per thousand)	Brick Building Cc266 (Dollars per thousand)
1960	9.60	—	—	—	—	—	0.33	—	—	—	—	—	0.49	—	—	35.40
1961	—	4.72	—	—	—	—	0.30	—	—	—	—	—	0.33	—	—	35.53
1962	—	4.62	—	—	—	—	0.31	—	—	—	—	—	0.20	—	—	35.89
1963	—	4.65	—	—	—	—	0.31	—	—	—	—	—	0.31	—	—	36.37
1964	—	4.65	—	—	—	—	0.32	—	—	—	—	—	0.43	—	—	36.62
1965	—	4.35	—	—	—	—	0.35	—	—	—	—	—	0.55	—	—	30.46
1966	—	4.34	—	—	—	—	0.36	—	—	—	—	—	0.56	—	—	31.32
1967	—	4.34	—	—	—	—	0.38	—	—	—	—	—	0.57	—	—	33.68
1968	—	4.67	—	—	—	—	—	—	—	—	—	—	0.72	—	—	40.13
1969	—	—	—	—	—	—	0.48	—	—	—	—	—	1.09	—	—	36.17
1970	—	—	—	—	—	—	—	—	—	—	—	—	—	—	—	43.53
1971	—	5.51	—	—	—	—	0.53	—	—	—	—	—	1.20	—	—	45.35
1972	—	5.90	—	—	—	—	0.59	—	—	—	—	—	1.16	—	—	42.17
1973	—	6.21	—	—	—	—	0.69	—	—	—	—	—	0.83	—	—	45.57
1974	—	9.15	—	—	—	—	0.77	—	—	—	—	—	—	—	—	49.94
1975	—	10.67	—	—	—	—	0.64	—	—	—	—	—	—	—	—	56.09
1976	—	10.74	—	—	—	—	0.69	—	—	—	—	—	—	—	—	62.76
1977	—	11.52	—	—	—	—	0.66	—	—	—	—	—	—	—	—	72.32
1978	—	12.06	—	—	—	—	—	0.65	—	—	—	—	—	—	—	82.68
1979	—	13.16	—	—	—	—	0.91	0.91	—	—	—	—	—	—	—	92.80
1980	—	14.63	—	—	—	—	—	0.97	—	—	—	—	—	—	—	99.04
1981	—	15.85	—	—	—	—	—	0.82	—	—	—	—	—	—	—	116.52
1982	—	16.22	—	—	—	—	—	0.72	—	—	—	—	—	—	—	121.25
1983	—	15.90	—	—	—	—	—	0.76	—	—	—	—	—	—	—	131.07
1984	—	16.13	—	—	—	—	—	0.66	—	—	—	—	—	—	—	135.92
1985	—	16.26	—	—	—	—	—	0.66	—	—	—	—	—	—	—	139.44
1986	—	16.19	—	—	—	—	—	0.66	—	—	—	—	—	—	—	144.52
1987	—	16.42	—	—	—	—	—	0.81	—	—	—	—	—	—	—	148.78
1988	—	16.99	—	—	—	—	—	1.20	—	—	—	—	—	—	—	152.35
1989	—	17.91	—	—	—	—	—	1.35	—	—	—	—	—	—	—	154.13
1990	—	18.56 [1]	—	—	—	—	—	1.26	—	—	—	—	—	—	—	158.12
1991	—	18.67	—	—	—	—	—	1.12	—	—	—	—	—	—	—	159.49
1992	—	18.80	—	—	—	—	—	1.09	—	—	—	—	—	—	—	161.96
1993	—	19.14	—	—	—	—	—	0.92	—	—	—	—	—	—	—	167.60
1994	—	19.44	—	—	—	—	—	1.13	—	—	—	—	—	—	—	172.68
1995	—	19.37	—	—	—	—	—	1.44	—	—	—	—	—	—	—	177.35
1996	—	19.39	—	—	—	—	—	1.13	—	—	—	—	—	—	—	179.27
1997	—	—	—	—	—	—	—	1.09	—	—	—	—	—	—	—	181.47
1998	—	—	—	—	—	—	—	0.79	—	—	—	—	—	—	—	186.83

1 July through December.
2 January through July.
3 December.
4 June through December.
5 Eleven-month average.
6 January through April.
7 May through December.
8 January through June.
9 January through November.
10 Five-month average.
11 June through December.
12 July.
13 January.

(continued)

TABLE Cc205–266   Wholesale prices of selected commodities: 1784–1998 *Continued*

Sources

Arthur H. Cole, *Wholesale Commodity Prices in the United States, 1700–1861*, Statistical Supplement (Harvard University Press, 1938); *Annual Report of the Director of the Mint to the Secretary of the Treasury for the Fiscal Year Ended June 30, 1881* (U.S. Government Printing Office, 1881); *Wholesale Prices, Wages, and Transportation*, Senate Report number 1,394, 52d Congress, 2d Session, part 2, 1893 (one of the reports usually referred to as the *Aldrich Reports* and referred to here as "*Aldrich Report*"); data compiled from U.S. Bureau of Labor Statistics (BLS) reports and records (referred to here as "BLS reports"); BLS annual producer price indexes for individual commodities seasonally unadjusted, found at the bureau's Internet site (referred to here as "BLS producer price indexes"); American Metal Market and Daily Iron and Steel Report, *Metal Statistics* (1921), p. 91; Matthew B. Hammond, *The Cotton Industry, an Essay in American Economic History*, American Economic Association, New Series number 1 (Macmillan 1897); American Iron and Steel Association, *Statistics of the American and Foreign Iron Trades for 1896* (Philadelphia, 1897).

For the BLS reports, in general, annual average prices, when available, were taken from annual reports, *Wholesale Prices and Price Indexes*, through the year 1963. Thereafter, annual average prices were computed from monthly prices as published in monthly reports, *Wholesale Prices and Price Indexes*, and from annual issues of *Statistical Abstract of the United States*.

Documentation

All data are in current dollars.

The wholesale prices for selected commodities from 1784 through 1998 provide an indication of price levels (in current dollars) for selected basic commodities at a particular point in time. These series provide only a general indication of price trends, owing to the changes in descriptions (specifications) for the commodities, in markets from which prices were obtained, in quality of the product that takes place over time, and other factors that affect prices.

From among the several hundred commodities for which wholesale prices have been published in various reports, twelve were selected for publication in the form of actual prices. Generally, consideration was given to representation of commodities in different product groups, importance in U.S. trade, and the length of the series available.

The descriptions for each commodity, insofar as they could be determined, and the sources from which the prices were compiled are shown here in the detailed notes for each series. When annual averages were not available in the original source, they were computed for this publication. If twelve monthly figures were presented, a simple average was calculated, but if only quarterly figures were given, straight-line interpolation was used to estimate missing months.

It was not possible to obtain one continuously comparable series for the full period. The data were assembled from several sources for each commodity, and there were, frequently, changes in the basis of quotation even in the same source. Two prices are shown for years in which a change in the series occurred, if it was possible to obtain the information. In some series, mostly prior to 1890, changes in the basis of quotation occurred and no overlapping prices were available. Such changes are noted here in the text for each series.

Prices for earlier years for some commodities are available in the same sources as those indicated for 1784 and in other publications. Figures prior to 1784 were not included in this chapter. For example, prices of wheat back to 1700 may be found in the publication by Cole (1938), cited as the source for wheat prices for 1784–1825. Wheat prices in the New England colonies at ten-year intervals for 1630–1750 are included with prices for several other commodities in U.S. Bureau of Labor Statistics, Bulletin number 604, *History of Wages in the United States from Colonial Times to 1928* (1934), p. 19.

The *Annual Report of the Director of the Mint*, cited as the source for practically all series for some part of the period 1825–1880, was used despite the lack of commodity descriptions. The prices included in this report were summaries of the New York prices included in the *U.S. Finance Reports* of 1868, 1873, and 1874, which had been compiled from the newspaper *The New York Shipping and Commercial List*. Prices for 1875–1880 were also compiled from this source. Such descriptions as appear in the notes for each series of prices taken from *U.S. Finance Reports* were obtained from the report for 1863.

An alternate source for many of the price series included in the *Aldrich Reports* (cited for data prior to 1890) is *Monthly Summary of Commerce and Finance*

in the United States, 57th Congress, 2d Session, House Document number 15, part 1, 1902, pp. 59–100. The *Summary* not only covers the years included in the *Aldrich Report* but also extends the data through July 1902.

Some of the earlier prices were quoted in the British units of account (that is, pounds, shillings, pence). Those prices were converted to dollars at a rate of $1 = 7.5 shillings. This conversion is from John J. McCusker, *How Much Is That in Real Money? A Historical Price Index for Use as a Deflator of Money Values in the Economy of the United States* (American Antiquarian Society, 1992), Table A-3, exchange rate for Pennsylvania for 1782–1796.

Discussions and source details relevant to specific series follow:

Series Cc205–209, Wheat

Data sources: 1784–1825, Cole (1938); 1825–1880, *1881 Report of the Director of the Mint*, p. 50; 1880–1890, *Aldrich Report*, p. 61; 1890–1981, BLS reports; 1982–1998, BLS producer price indexes.

For 1784–1825, prices are for Philadelphia (commodity description not available). For 1825–1880, prices are for New York, "Northern" wheat; the *1863 U.S. Finance Report* (from which these prices were partially compiled) shows prices for "genesee" for most years, 1825–1863, but for a few years prices refer to "North River," "prime white," "western," "western red," or "mixed and red." For 1880–1890, prices are for "wheat No. 2, Winter, Chicago." For 1890–1913, prices are for Chicago "Range No. 1 Northern Spring and No. 2 Red Winter" in carlots. For 1913–1948, prices are for Kansas City, "No. 2, hard (ordinary)" in carlots. For 1949–1961, prices are for Kansas City, "No. 2, hard winter, closing spot market price, carlots, f.o.b. track." The term "f.o.b." means free on board, that is, not including freight, insurance, and any taxes. From 1962 to 1981, prices are for Kansas City, "No. 1, hard winter." For 1982 to 1998, nominal prices were calculated from the BLS price index retrieved from its Internet site using the series WPU01210101 "Hard red winter wheat." The index was converted to nominal prices using the actual price for 1981.

Series Cc210–217, Wheat Flour

Data sources: 1784–1825, Cole (1938), 1825–1870, *1881 Report of the Director of the Mint*, p. 50; 1870–1890, *Aldrich Report*, p. 79; 1890–1981, BLS reports; 1982–1998, BLS producer price indexes.

For 1784–1825, prices are for Philadelphia, "Superfine" flour, per barrel of 196 pounds. For 1825–1870, prices are for New York, "Superfine" flour, per barrel. For 1870–1890, prices were provided by a New York firm (commodity description not available). For 1890–1913, prices are for "winter straights, f.o.b., New York," per barrel. For 1913–1943, prices are for "Straights, hard winter, white, in carlots, f.o.b., Kansas City," per barrel. During 1943, the basis of quotation was changed from per barrel to flour in sacks, per 100 pounds. For 1950–1981, prices are for "hard winter, bakery, short patents, plain or enriched, in 100-pound sacks, carlots, f.o.b. mill, Kansas City," per 100 pounds. During 1918 and a part of 1946, prices were quoted on the standard provided under government regulation. For 1982 to June 1983, nominal prices were calculated from the BLS price index retrieved from its Internet site using the series WPU02120109 "Soft red winter wheat flour 100 lbs." For July 1983 to 1998 nominal prices were calculated from the BLS price index retrieved from its Internet site using the series WPU02120201 "Wheat flour 100 lbs." The index was converted to nominal prices using the actual price for 1981.

Series Cc218–221, Sugar

Data sources: 1784–1825, Cole (1938); 1825–1860, *1881 Report of the Director of the Mint*, p. 50; 1860–1890, *Aldrich Report*, p. 114; 1890–1981, BLS reports; 1982–1998, BLS producer price indexes.

For 1784–1825, prices are for the Philadelphia market. Prices for 1784–1796 (January) refer to "Muscovado." Prices for 1796 (February)–1800 refer to "Muscovado, brown"; 1801–1802 (October), "Muscovado"; 1802 (November)–1813 (October), "Muscovado, first quality"; 1813 (November)–1815 (April), "Muscovado, unspecified"; 1815 (May)–1825, "Muscovado, prime." For 1825–1860, prices are for New York, "Cuba" sugar; the *1863 U.S. Finance Report* (from which the data were compiled) quoted "Muscovado" for 1825–1829 and 1845–1860, "Cuba Muscovado" for 1830–1836, and "Cuba" for 1837–1844. For 1860–1890, prices are for "Refined, granulated" sugar (no market specified). For 1890–1946, prices are for New York, "Granulated" sugar. Prices were quoted for sugar in barrels

TABLE Cc205-266   Wholesale prices of selected commodities: 1784-1998 *Continued*

until 1955 when the basis of quotation was changed to 100-pound paper bags. For 1947-1970, the description was amplified to "granulated, domestic, cane, refined, New York," per pound. Prices for 1934-1970 include the excise tax of $53\frac{1}{2}$ cents per 100 pounds, effective in May 1934. Prices after 1970 exclude the excise tax. Prices 1975-1981 are for "Sugar, granulated (5 lb.)." For 1982 to 1998, nominal prices were calculated from the BLS price index retrieved from its Internet site using the series WPU0253 "Refined sugar." The index was converted to nominal prices using the actual price for 1981.

Series Cc222-225, Cotton, Raw
Data sources: 1784-1789, Cole (1938); 1790-1890, Hammond (1897), p. 358; 1890-1981, BLS reports; 1982-1998, BLS producer price indexes.

For 1784-1789, prices refer to "Unspecified grade" for the Philadelphia market. For 1790-1890, prices refer to "Middling uplands" cotton for the New York market. For 1790-1820, prices are estimates made by merchants or government officials. For 1821-1890, prices were taken from James L. Watkin, *Production and Price of Cotton for One Hundred Years,* published by the U.S. Department of Agriculture,1895. For 1890-1941, prices are for New York, "Upland, Middling" cotton, spot. In 1936, "$\frac{7}{8}$ inch" was added to the description. For 1941-1954 (July), prices are for "Middling, $\frac{15}{16}$ inch," ten spot-market average. For 1954 (July)-1956 (August), the number of markets included in the average was increased from ten to fourteen. The July 1954 average for ten markets was $0.342 per pound and for fourteen markets, $0.341 per pound. For 1956 (August)-1957, prices are for "Middling, 1-inch," fourteen spot-market average. In August 1956, the average for $\frac{15}{16}$ inch staple was $0.348 per pound and for 1-inch staple, $0.357 per pound. Beginning September 1962, prices are for one-market average. Beginning July 1968, prices are for "$1\frac{1}{16}$ middling," twelve spot-market average. For 1970 to 1981, prices are for "Cotton, raw." For 1982 to 1998, nominal prices were calculated from the BLS price index retrieved from its Internet site using the series WPU01510101 "Raw Cotton." The index was converted to nominal prices using the actual price for 1981.

Series Cc226-230, Wool
Data sources: 1813-1825, Cole (1938); 1825-1850, *1881 Report of the Director of the Mint,* p. 60; 1850-1890, *Aldrich Report,* p. 387; 1890-1981, BLS reports; 1982-1998, BLS producer price indexes.

For 1813-1825, prices are for Philadelphia, "Merino clean" wool, except for 1819 and 1820 when description was "Merino" wool. For 1825-1850, prices are for New York, "Merino" wool. For 1850-1890, prices are for Boston, "Ohio, fine fleece, scoured." For 1890-1913, prices are for "Domestic, Ohio, fine fleece (x and xx grades), scoured"; for 1913-1945, for Boston, "Domestic, Territory, staple, fine and fine medium, scoured"; for 1946-1949, for Boston, "Domestic, Territory, staple, fine combing, graded, scoured." For 1950-1981, the description was changed with no difference in price level to "Domestic, fine, good French combing and staple, clean basis." For 1982 to 1998, nominal prices were calculated from the BLS price index retrieved from its Internet site using the series WPU0152 "Wool." The index was converted to nominal prices using the actual price for 1981.

Series Cc231-234, Cotton Sheeting
Data sources: 1784-1847, Cole (1938); 1847-1890, *Aldrich Report,* p. 155; 1890-1969, BLS reports; 1970-1974, BLS producer price indexes.

Prices are for Philadelphia, "Russian, Brown" for 1784-1787 (May), "Russian, unspecified" for 1787 (June)-1804, "Russian, brown" for 1805-1814 and 1824-1847, and "Russian, half bleached" for 1815-1823. Prices were shown "per piece" (approximately 100 yards). For 1847-1890, prices are for "sheeting, brown, 4-4, Atlantic A," per yard (no market specified). For 1890-1912, prices are for "brown, Indian head, 4-4, 2.85 yards to pound, factory." For 1913-1941, the description is the same except that the width designation was changed in 1913 to "36-inch" instead of "4-4," and "48 × 48, carded yarn" was added in 1923. For 1941-1943 (May), prices are for "Unbleached, 36-inch, 48 × 48, 2.85 yards per pound, Class A, non-feeler, f.o.b. mill." For 1943 (May)-1947, the description changed from "48 × 48" to "48 × 44." The other elements remained the same. For 1948-1969, the description changed again, replacing "36 = inch, 48 × 44" with "40 = inch, 48 × 48." As an indication of the significance of this last change, we note that the January 1948 price for 36 = inch, 48 × 44 was $0.279 and that in the same month the price for 40 = inch, 48 ×48 was $0.289. The

1970-1974 nominal prices were calculated from the BLS price index retrieved from its Internet site using the series WPU03120221 "Sheeting, class A, 2.85 yd./lb. yd." The index was converted to nominal prices using the actual price for 1967.

Series Cc235-242, Coal, Anthracite
Data sources: 1784-1825, Cole (1938); 1825-1833, *1881 Report of the Director of the Mint*; 1833-1890, *Statistics of the American and Foreign Iron Trades for 1896,* p. 91; 1890-1981, BLS reports; 1982-1998, BLS producer price indexes.

Prices are for Philadelphia, "Unspecified" for 1785-1795 and 1798-1799; "Virginia" coal for 1796-1797, 1800-1811, and 1814-1825; and "Domestic" for 1812 and 1813. There was no description for 1826-1833. For 1825-1833, prices are for New York, "anthracite coal (Schuylkill)." For 1833-1890, prices are for "Schuylkill white ash lump" coal, by the cargo, at Philadelphia, per gross ton. For 1890-1975, prices are for "Pennsylvania anthracite, chestnut," but the basis of quotation was changed several times. For 1890-1928, the basis was "New York Tidewater," per gross ton; for 1928-1931, "destination on tracks," per gross ton; for 1931-1947, per net ton (2,000 pounds); and for 1947-1975, "f.o.b. cars" per net ton. For 1976, prices are for "Prepared anthracite shipped." For 1976-1998, nominal prices were calculated from the BLS price index retrieved from its Internet site using the series WPU051101 "Prepared anthracite shipped." The index was converted to nominal prices using the actual price for 1975.

Series Cc243-247, Iron and Steel Rails
Data sources: 1847-1890, *Metal Statistics,* p. 91; 1891-1981, BLS reports; 1982, BLS producer price indexes.

For 1847-1867, prices are for "Iron rails, Eastern Pennsylvania mill" (production of steel rails did not exceed production of iron rails until 1877). The source also shows prices of iron rails of this description for 1868-1882. For 1867-1870, prices are for New York, "Steel rails, Bessemer," per gross ton. For 1871-1890, prices are for "Steel rails, Pennsylvania mill." For 1891-1913, prices are for "Bessemer, Standard, f.o.b. mill, Pittsburgh," per long ton; for 1913-1946, for "Open hearth, standard, f.o.b. mill"; for 1947-1953 (April), for "Standard, heavier than 60 pounds, No. 1 open hearth, f.o.b. mill" (refinement of previous specification and quoted per 100 pounds – no break in series); thereafter, for "Standard, carbon steel, No. 1 open hearth, 115 pounds per linear yard, control cooled, base quantity, f.o.b. mill." Nominal price for 1982 (January through June) calculated from the BLS price index retrieved from its Internet site using the series WPU10130241 "Rails, standard, carbon 100 lb." The index was converted to nominal prices using the actual price for 1967.

Series Cc248-252, Nails
Data sources: 1784-1828, Cole (1938); 1828-1834, *1881 Report of the Director of the Mint,* p. 54; 1835-1890, *Metal Statistics,* p. 87; 1890-1981, BLS reports; 1982-1998, BLS producer price indexes.

For 1835-1849, prices were compiled from the *Report of the Secretary of the Treasury,* 1849; for 1850-1859, by the American Iron and Steel Association from the books of the Duncannon Iron Company; and for 1860-1890, by an official of the Duncannon Iron Company.

For 1784-1828, prices are for the Philadelphia market. For 1814-1827, prices are for "Cut nails, all sizes"; for other years, "assorted sizes." For 1828-1834, prices are for New York, "Nails, cut." For 1835-1890, prices are for "Cut nails." For 1890-1953, prices refer to "wire, 8 penny, fence and common, 10-pound keg, f.o.b. Pittsburgh." "Base price" was added to the description in 1926, and fence nails were not included after 1947. For 1953-1959, prices refer to "wire, carbon steel 8d, common, carload lots, f.o.b. mill." The April 1953 price for the former specification was $7.41, and for the new specification, $7.33 per 100 pounds. "Packed in fiberboard boxes" was added to the description for 1955. "Carload lots" was changed to "in lots of 30,000 lb. or over" in October 1960. The change was not considered to affect comparability of prices before or after. For 1975-1981, the description is "Nails, wire, 8d, common" with the price for units of 50 pounds. For 1982-1998, the description is "Bright nails." For 1982-1998, nominal prices were calculated from the BLS price index retrieved from its Internet site using the series WPU10880211 "Bright nails." The index was converted to nominal prices using the actual price for 1981.

(continued)

TABLE Cc205–266   Wholesale prices of selected commodities: 1784–1998   *Continued*

Series Cc253–258, Copper
Data sources: 1784–1825, Cole (1938); 1825–1860, *1881 Report of the Director of the Mint*, p. 52; 1860–1889, *Metal Statistics*, p. 299; 1890–1981, BLS reports; 1982–1998, BLS producer price indexes.

For 1784–1825, prices are for the Philadelphia market. Prices are for "Copper in sheets," 1784–1789, 1795 (December)–1801 (April), and 1805 (June)–1809 (June); "Copper bottoms," 1790–1791; "Sheathing unspecified," 1801 (May)–1802 (December), 1809 (July)–1818 (April), and 1824 (September)–1825; "Sheathing, cold rolled," 1803–1805 (May); and "Sheathing unspecified," 1818 (May)–1824 (August). For 1825–1860, prices are for New York, "Sheathing." For 1860–1889, prices are for New York, "Lake Copper." The price shown for 1890 is the same as that in *Metal Statistics, 1921*. For 1890–1907, prices are for New York, "Lake Copper"; for 1907–1927, for "Copper ingot, electrolytic, early delivery, refinery in New York"; for 1927–1953, for "Copper, electrolytic, delivered, Connecticut Valley"; for 1954–1969, for "Copper ingot, electrolytic"; for 1970–1979, "Copper wirebar, domestic origin"; for 1980–1996, "Domestic copper cathode"; and for 1997–1998, "Copper cathode and refined copper." For 1979–1996, nominal prices were calculated from the BLS price index retrieved from its Internet site using the series WPU10220123 "Domestic copper cathode" and for 1997–1998 using the series WPU10220131 "Copper cathode and refined copper." The index was converted to nominal prices using the actual price for 1977.

Series Cc259–263, Turpentine
Data sources: 1784–1825, Cole (1938); 1825–1840, *1881 Report of the Director of the Mint*, p. 56; 1840–1890, *Aldrich Report*, p. 240; 1890–1969, BLS reports.

For 1784–1825, prices are for the Philadelphia market, per barrel (31½ gallons per barrel). No description was available, but a comparison of prices indicates that they may be for "soft" turpentine. For 1825–1840, prices are for the New York market (no description is available). For 1840–1890, prices are for New York, "Spirits of turpentine." For 1890–1942, prices are for "Southern, barrels, at New York." The description was amplified in 1936 by the addition of "carlots, ex dock, gum spirits." For 1942–1951, prices refer to "Gum spirits, bulk, f.o.b. Savannah, Ga." For 1952–1956 (October), quotations are for "Spirits of turpentine, tank cars, at New York." The January 1952 price for the former specification (Savannah) was $0.80 per gallon and for the new (New York), $0.76 per gallon. For 1956 (November)–1958 (January), prices are for "gum, tank cars" at New York. For 1959 (March)–1969, prices are for carlots or truckload quantities f.o.b. in cars or trucks at processing plants in Georgia and Florida. "Midpoint of range for week" was added in 1961.

Series Cc264–266, Brick
Data sources: 1849–1890, *Aldrich Report*, p. 222; 1890–1981, BLS reports; 1982–1998, BLS producer price indexes.

For 1849–1890, prices are for "common domestic building" (market not indicated). For 1890–1933, prices are for "Common, Red, Domestic, at New York"; 1933–1947, for "Common building, f.o.b. plant" (composite of approximately fifty firms); for 1947–1961, for "Building brick, f.o.b. plant or New York dock" (composite of approximately twenty-five firms); and for 1962–1981, for "Building brick, f.o.b. plant." Changes in list of firms from time to time did not result in any significant differences in the annual average prices. For 1982–1984, nominal prices were calculated from the BLS price index retrieved from its Internet site using the series WPU13410101 "Building brick per thousand" and for 1985–1998 using the series WPU134201 "Brick, except ceramic, glazed and refractory." The index was converted to nominal prices using the actual price for 1981.

CHAPTER Cd

Consumer Expenditures

Editor: Lee A. Craig

CONSUMER EXPENDITURES

Lee A. Craig

"Consumer expenditures" refer to purchases of goods and services by families and households. They include items destined for immediate consumption – food, haircuts, and entertainment – and items that will yield a flow of services over several years – automobiles, refrigerators, and pianos. By convention, consumer expenditures do not include purchases of new or used homes.[1] Also by convention, consumer expenditures do not include consumption goods purchased either by businesses or by other private enterprises. Major components of such business or governmentally purchased consumption goods are life, health, and retirement insurance.

Since the time of Adam Smith, economists have recognized that consumption is a primary, if not the ultimate, objective of economic activity. According to Smith, "Consumption is the sole end and purpose of all production" (Smith 1976 [1776], volume 2, p. 179). Following Smith's admonition, today consumer expenditure data are used as an indicator of the standard of living and quality of life. Because they measure consumption directly, they are better standard-of-living indicators than output and income. This is partly because many households save rather than spend a portion of their income. For these households, income is greater than consumption. Other households draw down their earlier savings or borrow money and go into debt in order to finance consumption. For these households, income is less than consumption. Moreover, the propensities to save, dissave, and borrow change over time, and at any point in time they differ among the different segments of the population. For example, during World War II, gross domestic product (GDP) and personal income rose faster than consumer expenditures. The difference between income and consumption – savings – was lent by households, through their purchases of war bonds, to the government, which used the resources to finance the war. After the war, consumption grew faster than income as consumers redeemed their government bonds, moved back to peacetime spending patterns, and purchased automobiles and refrigerators. Furthermore,

at any point in time there are differences among segments of the population in the relationship between income and consumption. Young people tend to borrow and accumulate debt; people in their middle years tend to save; and retirees eventually tend to draw down assets such as pension accumulations and savings accounts.

At the same time, it is important to note that even though consumer expenditures are a better measure of consumption than output or income, they may be misleading as well, because they omit the value of household production and governmentally provided services. For example, a home-baked loaf of bread will be recorded as the value of the purchased inputs of flour and liquids. The labor services of the home-baker will be absent, whereas store-bought bread will reflect the market value of those services, thus indicating larger consumption expenditures – though a loaf of bread was consumed in each case. Therefore, on the one hand, because home production has fallen over time, expenditure data tend to overstate the long-term rise in consumption.[2] On the other hand, exclusion of the consumption of publicly provided goods and services – such as roads, schools, water and sanitation services, and libraries – biases the measure in the other direction (Galbraith 1958). The absence of these publicly provided goods and services from consumer expenditures will understate the true level of the standard of living at any one point in time, though it is difficult to determine the net trend over time in this missing component.

Consumer expenditure data are also useful in comprehending, in human terms, the implications for standard-of-living and quality-of-life changes over long periods of time. It might be difficult to imagine how anyone could have survived on the low incomes typical of, say, the early nineteenth century. Consumer expenditure data on what people bought with that income – what and how much they ate, what household implements and clothing they purchased, and what they wasted – are helpful in evaluating the human dimensions of economic growth (Martin 1942; Brady 1972; Easterlin 2000). In the same way, consumer expenditure data may be more helpful than income data in assessing the social meaning of poverty, income inequality, and the social "distance" between classes. Poverty in a society in which the poorest members consume above a bare subsistence level of food, shelter, and clothing would be judged less onerous than in societies where the poorest suffer malnutrition, exposure, and starvation (Sen 1986). Still, the position equating greater levels of consumption with greater well-being has not gone unchallenged (Veblen 1934; Easterlin 1974; Scitovsky 1976).

Acknowledgments

Lee A. Craig thanks Jeannette Espinoza, Raymond Mikus, and Laura Phillips for their assistance in preparing the tables in this chapter. Alastair Hall provided valuable comments on the essay. This work was made possible in part by funding from the College of Management and the College of Agriculture and Life Sciences at North Carolina State University; Dean John Bartley, former Dean Richard Lewis, and Director of Graduate Programs Wally Thurman were particularly supportive. In addition, Susan Carter offered considerable editorial guidance with the chapter in general and the essay in particular.

[1] Such expenditures are treated separately in Chapter Dc, on construction, housing, and mortgages.

[2] See the essay and tables dealing with household production in Chapter Ba, on labor.

Consumer expenditure data can also indicate important social, political, economic, and cultural changes that are difficult to observe directly. For example, changes over time in women's economic roles and options can be glimpsed in statistics on the relative importance of domestic service expenditures in family budgets, of restaurant meals as a share of all food expenditures, and of relative spending on women's and men's clothing. In addition, scholars use consumer expenditures as indexes of social trends. Corsets, processed flour, and tail fins on 1958 Chevrolets are but a few of the individual items that have been viewed as emblematic of complex social patterns (Cummings 1940; Reid 1968; Horowitz 1985; Levenstein 1988; Lebergott 1993, 1996). Highlighting the role of mass consumption as an "Americanizer," Daniel Boorstin writes: "Men who never saw or knew one another were held together by their common use of objects so similar that they could not be distinguished even by their owners. These consumption communities were quick; they were nonideological; they were democratic; they were public, and vague, and rapidly shifting" (Boorstin 1973, p. 90). One could say the same about mass consumption in the global economy today. At the same time, consumer behavior can be used to maintain group identity and check assimilation. Ethnic foods and traditional clothing can serve this function.

Finally, consumer expenditure patterns are thought to be responsible for certain features of American economic development. For example, the "American system" of manufacturing, which relied on the mass production of identical products using highly specialized machinery and interchangeable parts, is believed to have depended, in large part, on the development of a vast domestic market for inexpensive, standardized products (Rosenberg 1972; David 1975; Hounshell 1984). Another example is the "consumer durables revolution" of the 1920s – that is, the rapid growth of new goods such as automobiles, furniture, and appliances – which is thought to have made the economy more unstable and thus to have contributed to the economic disaster of the Great Depression of the 1930s (Olney 1991).

Sources of Consumer Expenditure Data

The earliest systematic evidence on consumer expenditures for the United States was collected in a series of surveys of households in the late nineteenth century. Prompted by the social unrest generated in the wake of industrialization, unemployment, immigration, urbanization, unionization, and the factory employment of women and children, Carroll D. Wright (1840–1909), Commissioner of the Massachusetts Bureau of Labor Statistics, initiated the systematic collection of a set of objective and comparative survey questions. Wright believed that the first step to developing intelligent public policy was to gain a better understanding of underlying conditions. Wright said he wanted to "show the actual condition of the workingman . . . and his comparative situation as regards his fellow laborers in other states and foreign countries" (Commonwealth of Massachusetts 1875, p. 192). To this end, Wright first organized and administered a survey of the earnings and expenditures of 397 families of skilled and unskilled workers in Massachusetts in 1875 (for a summary of key findings, see Table Cd456–464). What gave Wright's data credibility at the time, and what makes this evidence valuable today, is the care and thought that Wright and his colleagues put into the selection of their samples, the design of a survey instrument that was relatively objective and unambiguous, and the scrupulous tabulation and publication of the findings.

Wright eventually became Commissioner of the U.S. Bureau of Labor, and there he supervised similar large-scale studies in 1888–1891 and 1901 (see Tables Cd465–482). Wright's leadership and example inspired labor commissioners in other states and in foreign nations, scholars, and other investigators to conduct literally hundreds of similar studies in the half-century that followed his pioneering effort. Williams and Zimmerman (1935) and U.S. Bureau of Labor Statistics (1959) are valuable, annotated guides to the evidence collected from these studies.

During the First World War, the U.S. Bureau of Labor Statistics (BLS) began to conduct national cross-section studies of consumer expenditure patterns at irregular intervals. Data from some of the larger and better-known surveys are presented in Tables Cd483–502, Cd521–539, and Cd597–616. The BLS's *How American Buying Habits Change* (1959) offers a useful guide to comparability across many of these surveys.

In 1980, the BLS initiated its Consumer Expenditure Survey program, and in 1984 it began its publication of annual, representative, and comparable data on the buying patterns of the American people. Data from these surveys, including the major components of consumer expenditures, are shown in Table Cd424–455. Among their many important uses, these data are inputs into periodic revisions of the Consumer Price Index (CPI). Williamson (1967), Horowitz (1985), Carter, Ransom, and Sutch (1991), and Brown (1994) provide recent appraisals of these data collection efforts and the implications of their findings. Micro-level data from some of these surveys are available in electronic form at the Interuniversity Consortium for Political and Social Research (ICPSR) at the University of Michigan.

Beginning in 1929, a conceptually distinct source of data on consumer expenditures was collected by the Bureau of Economic Analysis (BEA) in the U.S. Department of Commerce and published as part of the *National Income and Product Accounts of the United States*. Data from this source, including the major components of consumer expenditures, are displayed in Tables Cd153–377. Stanley Lebergott (1996) used the BEA framework to develop conceptually similar estimates of consumer expenditures for the period 1900 through 1929. These are displayed in Tables Cd1–152. Lebergott's estimates are directly comparable with the 1993 revision of the BEA series.

Consumer Expenditures at a Point in Time

Consumer expenditure data were originally collected in order to understand the behavior of families in different economic and social circumstances. Perhaps the most important regularity such studies reveal is known as "Engel's Law" – the proposition that, as expenditures or income rise, the proportion devoted to food falls. This "law" is named in honor of the German statistician Ernst Engel (1821–1896), who first observed the relationship in 1857 in cross-sectional data. The intuition behind the principal is that people prioritize their expenditures, putting food purchases before all others. At very low levels of income, households spend most or all of their income on food. As their incomes rise, they purchase other necessities such as housing and clothing. As their incomes rise further still, and after their basic needs are met, they expand their expenditures to include luxuries. Engel's Law holds even though households with higher incomes purchase more and better-quality food. Tables Cd483–502, Cd521–539, Cd558–577, Cd597–616, and Cd636–655 contain family or household expenditures on sixteen categories for the years 1917–1919, 1935–1936, 1950, 1972–1973, and 1988. The patterns of food expenditures in these tables are all consistent with Engel's Law, although the precise character of the relationship varies over time. Engel's Law has also been used to describe the pattern of saving at different levels of income – namely, as income rises, savings grow.

Consumer expenditure patterns depend upon households' needs and preferences and the relative cost of different goods, in addition to resources available. For these reasons, scholars have uncovered systematic relations between the occupation, education, location, and class of the household head and the household's buying patterns. A particularly detailed description of expenditure differences across socioeconomic classes, and their change over time, was developed by Clair Brown (Brown 1994). Her estimates are displayed in Tables Cd503–520, Cd540–557, Cd578–596, Cd617–635, and Cd656–673.

Trends in Consumer Expenditures over Time

Historical trend data can reveal important society-wide changes in consumer expenditures. For instance, the rise in food expenditures per capita over the twentieth century is displayed in Figure Cd-A. Over this hundred-year period when real per capita income rose more than five-fold, real per capita food expenditures rose almost three times. The three episodes when real food expenditures per capita fell are exceptions that prove the rule. The declines in the

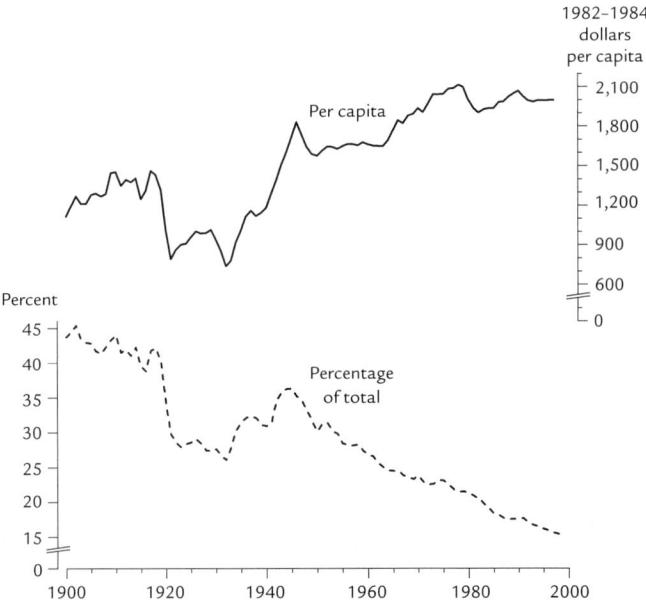

FIGURE Cd-A   Consumption expenditures on food, alcohol, and tobacco – per capita and as a percentage of total expenditures: 1900–1999

Sources

Consumption expenditures: series Cd1–2 and Cd153–154. Population: series Aa110. Consumer price index: series Cc1.

Documentation

To create a continuous series for display purposes, series from Tables Cd1–77 and Cd153–263 were joined at the year 1929. Also, in computing constant-dollar per capita expenditures, the values were deflated using the consumer price index from series Cc1. These constant-dollar figures differ, therefore, from the constant-dollar values found in Tables Cd78–152 and Cd264–377.

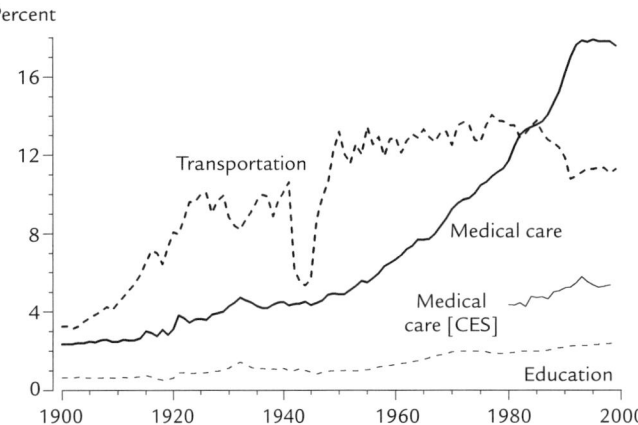

FIGURE Cd-B   Consumption expenditures on medical care, transportation, and education as a percentage of total expenditures: 1900–1999

Sources

Aggregate consumption expenditures: for 1900–1928, series Cd39, Cd52, and Cd68 expressed as a percentage of series Cd1; and for 1929–1999, series Cd194, Cd218, and Cd254 expressed as a percentage of series Cd153.

Health care expenditures of consumer units, based on the Consumer Expenditure Survey (CES): series Cd445 expressed as a percentage of series Cd428.

1920s and again in the 1930s are, in part, the result of substantial declines in the relative price of food (see Table Cc3–5), while the decline during the early 1940s resulted from wartime rationing.

One can also observe a version of Engel's Law in Figure Cd-A, which displays fluctuations in the ratio of food expenditures to total expenditures over the twentieth century. With the exception of the three periods mentioned earlier, this ratio falls from a level of more than 40 percent in 1900 to less than 15 percent a hundred years later. Because real expenditures on food rose over the same period, the substantial fall in food's share of expenditures suggests that the standard of living must have risen, and risen rather dramatically. To understand this conclusion, consider that by the end of the century, food needs could be satisfied with a much smaller share of total income, despite the fact that more and better food was being consumed. This meant that more income was available to meet other basic needs and to purchase luxuries.

Figure Cd-B shows the long-term change for certain goods and services that claimed an increasing share of income over the twentieth century. They include medical care, transportation, and education. The statistics may overstate this growth to the extent that during earlier periods such goods were relatively more likely than the basics to be provided in the home rather than the market. We know, for example, that this may be a problem with the statistics on medical care because in 1900 a large share of nursing services was provided by relatives in the home. Still, properly interpreted, these statistics highlight profound changes in the pattern of peoples' lives over the past hundred years.

Engel's Law suggests that these long-term changes are evidence of improvements in the standard of living and quality of life. Lebergott, for example, offers the following vivid suggestion of the consequences of the increase over the century in expenditures for transportation services.

In 1900 the United States led most nations in wealth. With so much open land, it fed horses at low cost. Yet only one urban family in five had its own horse and could therefore travel at need, or whim. Fewer still had carriages, enabling several family members to travel together. Most Americans still walked to work, living within a mile of their workplaces. . . .

When the twentieth century opened, the automobile appeared to be only a plaything for the rich and reckless. In the 1920s it became the center of a new society. Its promise of instant mobility made it "essential" for millions. Between 1900 and 1980, the number of cars increased from 8,000 to 100,000,000. . . .

At the beginning of the twentieth century, Americans made few contacts outside their family. If youngsters left home to live in another state, they rarely saw their parents again. But by 1990, contact with other families, other modes of belief and behavior, was almost incessant. Cheap transport, more than almost any other force, made "the melting pot" a reality. (Lebergott 1993, pp. 128, 130, 135)

Other observers have drawn more pessimistic conclusions (Scitovsky 1976; Easterlin 1974; Galbraith 1958).

A second clear pattern is that over time, consumers have purchased more ready-to-use goods and have reduced their time spent in household production. For example, instead of buying flour and baking bread at home, more households buy bakery bread, purchase ready-made sandwiches, and eat out at restaurants.[3]

The third regularity is the expansion in variety and the appearance of new goods. Clair Brown documents the increase in the variety of goods consumed by households at every socioeconomic rung. By the end of the century the variety of goods consumed by the lowest classes rivaled that of the upper classes a century earlier (Brown 1994, pp. 466–7). New Goods are also important. For example, Lebergott calculates that in 1900, 88 percent of American homes were lighted by coal, oil, or kerosene, but that by 1990 all but a relative handful relied on electricity (Lebergott 1993, p. 40).

Aggregate Consumer Expenditures

The rapid growth of the U.S. economy during the 1920s and its subsequent dramatic decline during the Great Depression of the 1930s prompted economists' systematic investigation of the behavior of aggregate consumer expenditures. A number of scholars, including Joseph Schumpeter and Peter Temin, attributed the Great Depression to this decline, though this position is not without controversy.[4]

Regardless of its causes, as a response to the crisis, an intensive effort focused on the development of estimates of aggregate consumer expenditures (Lough 1935; Kuznets 1938; Landefeld 2000). These efforts initiated an ongoing data collection and publication effort that continues to this day. These data are collected by the BEA in the Department of Commerce and published as part of the *National Income and Product Accounts of the United States*. Data from this source, including the major components of consumer expenditures, are displayed in Tables Cd153–377. They have been a durable element of ongoing economic analysis ever since. They underlie the early pathbreaking studies of aggregate saving and consumption (Brady and Friedman 1947; Duesenberry 1949; Modigliani 1949; Houthakker and Taylor 1966).

The value of these consumer expenditure estimates prompted William Shaw to compile estimates for the nineteenth and early twentieth centuries (Shaw 1947). These are shown in Table Cd378–410. More recently, Stanley Lebergott constructed improved estimates of real and nominal personal consumption expenditures by twelve major and sixty-four minor categories from 1900 through 1929 (Lebergott 1996). These are reported in Tables Cd1–152. Although Lebergott placed considerable weight on Shaw's figures, Lebergott's estimates have the advantage of being annual, of including a substantially larger number of categories, and of being based on a larger, more diverse set of sources. Furthermore, Lebergott's figures are directly comparable to the 1993 revision of the consumption figures in the national income and product accounts.

Because we now have one hundred years worth of high-quality annual estimates of detailed expenditures, these data can be used to indicate long-term changes in the distribution of consumers' expenditures across various categories. Indeed, Figures Cd-A and Cd-B make use of them in just this way. These figures should not be used uncritically, however. Unlike the household expenditure data discussed earlier, aggregate consumer expenditure data include the expenditures of businesses and governments. For goods such as food and clothing – that is, goods for which consumption decisions are made by households – the difference is not very important. But for a category such as medical expenditures, the difference is enormous, as Figure Cd-B illustrates in the comparison between the two series for medical expenditures. The difference is caused by the fact that consumers themselves pay only a small and falling share of these expenses, with the remainder being paid by businesses and governments.

References

Atack, Jeremy, and Peter Passell. 1994. *A New Economic View of American History*, 2nd edition. Norton.

Boorstin, Daniel J. 1973. *Americans: The Democratic Experience*. Random House.

Brady, Dorothy S. 1972. "Consumption and the Style of Life." In Lance E. Davis, Richard A. Easterlin, et al. *American Economic Growth: An Economist's History of the United States*. Harper & Row.

Brady, Dorothy S., and Rose D. Friedman. 1947. "Savings and the Income Distribution." In Conference on Research in Income and Wealth, *Studies in Income and Wealth*, volume 10. National Bureau of Economic Research.

Brown, Clair. 1994. *American Standards of Living*. Blackwell.

Carter, Susan B., Roger L. Ransom, and Richard Sutch. 1991. "The Historical Labor Statistics Project at the University of California." *Historical Methods* 24 (2): 52–65.

Commonwealth of Massachusetts. 1875. *Sixth Annual Report on the Statistics of Labor*, Part 4, *Conditions of Workingmen's Families*. Wright & Potter.

Cummings, Richard Osborn. 1940. *The American and His Food: A History of Food Habits in the United States*. University of Chicago Press.

David, Paul A. 1975. *Technical Choice, Innovation and Economic Growth: Essays on American and British Experience in the Nineteenth Century*. Cambridge University Press.

Duesenberry, James S. 1949. *Income, Saving and the Theory of Consumer Behavior*. Harvard Economic Studies, volume 87. Harvard University Press.

Easterlin, Richard A. 1974. "Does Economic Growth Improve the Human Lot?" In Paul A. David and Melvin W. Reder, editors. *Nations and Households in Economic Growth: Essays in Honor of Moses Abramovitz*. Academic Press.

Easterlin, Richard A. 2000. "The Worldwide Standard of Living since 1800." *Journal of Economic Perspectives* 14 (1): 7–26.

Gabaccia, Donna R. 1998. *We Are What We Eat: Ethnic Food and the Making of Americans*. Harvard University Press.

Galbraith, John Kenneth. 1958. *The Affluent Society*. Houghton Mifflin.

---

[3] See the essay and tables on household production in Chapter Ba, on labor.
[4] Schumpeter (1939) and Temin (1976). On the controversy, see the summary in Atack and Passell (1994), Chapter 21.

Giedion, Sigfried. 1948. *Mechanization Takes Command*. Oxford University Press.

Horowitz, Daniel. 1985. *The Morality of Spending: Attitudes toward the Consumer Society in America, 1875–1940*. Johns Hopkins University Press.

Hounshell, David A. 1984. *From the American System to Mass Production, 1800–1932*. Johns Hopkins University Press.

Houthakker, H. S., and Lester D. Taylor. 1966. *Consumer Demand in the United States, 1929–1970: Analyses and Projections*. Harvard University Press.

Kuznets, Simon. 1938. *Commodity Flow and Capital Formation*. National Bureau of Economic Research.

Landefeld, J. Steven. 2000. "GDP: One of the Great Inventions of the 20th Century." *Survey of Current Business* (January): 6–8.

Lebergott, Stanley. 1993. *Pursuing Happiness: American Consumers in the Twentieth Century*. Princeton University Press.

Lebergott, Stanley. 1996. *Consumer Expenditures: New Measures and Old Motives*. Princeton University Press.

Leiby, James. 1960. *Carroll Wright and Labor Reform: The Origins of Labor Statistics*. Harvard University Press.

Levenstein, Harvey A. 1988. *Revolution at the Table: The Transformation of the American Diet*. Oxford University Press.

Lough, William H. 1935. *High-Level Consumption*. McGraw-Hill.

Martin, Edgar S. 1942. *The Standard of Living in 1860: American Consumption Levels on the Eve of the Civil War*. University of Chicago Press.

Modigliani, Franco. 1949. "Fluctuations in the Saving–Income Ratio: A Problem in Economic Forecasting." In Conference on Research in Income and Wealth, *Studies in Income and Wealth*, volume 11. National Bureau of Economic Research.

Olney, Martha L. 1991. *Buy Now, Pay Later: Advertising, Credit, and Consumer Durables*. University of North Carolina Press.

Pillsbury, Richard. 1998. *No Foreign Food: The American Diet in Time and Place*. Westview Press.

Putnam, Robert D. 2000. *Bowling Alone: The Collapse and Revival of American Community*. Simon & Schuster.

Reid, Margaret G. 1968. "Consumers: Consumption Levels and Standards." In David L. Sills, editor. *International Encyclopedia of the Social Sciences*. Macmillan and Free Press.

Rosenberg, Nathan. 1972. *Technology and American Economic Growth*. Harper & Row.

Schumpeter, Joseph. 1939. *Business Cycles*. McGraw-Hill.

Scitovsky, Tibor. 1976. *The Joyless Economy*. Oxford University Press.

Sen, Amartya. 1986. *The Standard of Living*. Cambridge University Press.

Shaw, William. 1947. *Value of Commodity Output since 1869*. National Bureau of Economic Research.

Smith, Adam. 1976 [1776]. *An Inquiry into the Nature and Causes of the Wealth of Nations*. General editors, R. H. Campbell and A. S. Skinner; textual editor, W. B. Todd. Liberty Classics.

Temin, Peter. 1976. *Did Monetary Forces Cause the Great Depression?* Norton.

U.S. Bureau of Labor Statistics. 1959. *How American Buying Habits Change*. U.S. Government Printing Office.

Veblen, Thorstein. 1934. *Essays in Our Changing Order*. Viking.

Williams, Faith M., and Carle C. Zimmerman. 1935. "Studies of Family Living in the United States and Other Countries: An Analysis of Material and Method." U.S. Department of Agriculture, Miscellaneous Publication number 223. U.S. Government Printing Office.

Williamson, Jeffrey G. 1967. "Consumer Behavior in the Nineteenth Century: Carroll D. Wright's Massachusetts Workers in 1875." *Explorations in Entrepreneurial History*, Second Series, 4 (2): 98–135.

CLASSIFIED BY TYPE

Lee A. Craig

TABLE Cd1–77 Consumption expenditures, by type: 1900–1929

Contributed by Lee A. Craig

Year	Total	Food, alcohol, and tobacco						Clothing							
		Total	Purchased food and meals (excluding alcohol)	Food furnished to employees	Food consumed on farms	Alcohol [1]	Tobacco	Total	Shoes	Civilian clothing			Military clothing	Jewelry	Clothing services
										Total	Women's	Men's			
	Cd1	Cd2	Cd3	Cd4	Cd5	Cd6	Cd7	Cd8	Cd9	Cd10	Cd11	Cd12	Cd13	Cd14	Cd15
	Million dollars	Million dollars	Million dollars	Million dollars	Million dollars	Million dollars	Million dollars	Million dollars	Million dollars	Million dollars	Million dollars	Million dollars	Million dollars	Million dollars	Million dollars
1900	16,393	7,164	4,892	97	822	955	398	2,127	428	1,262	500	762	3	147	287
1901	17,785	7,902	5,444	89	917	1,022	430	2,254	485	1,297	530	767	3	153	316
1902	19,079	8,653	6,069	99	956	1,101	428	2,381	484	1,385	583	802	3	173	336
1903	19,904	8,650	6,059	78	911	1,145	457	2,596	525	1,526	661	865	3	178	364
1904	20,768	8,913	6,286	81	928	1,169	449	2,689	551	1,577	689	888	3	179	381
1905	22,208	9,499	6,741	86	967	1,230	475	2,895	593	1,670	754	916	3	214	415
1906	23,897	9,958	7,012	89	984	1,342	531	3,450	674	2,059	942	1,117	3	260	454
1907	25,222	10,425	7,326	94	1,085	1,378	542	3,536	684	2,095	971	1,124	4	270	483
1908	25,026	10,607	7,563	98	1,107	1,303	536	3,386	683	2,025	951	1,074	4	193	481
1909	27,499	11,921	8,710	114	1,196	1,322	579	3,820	708	2,302	1,095	1,207	4	264	542
1910	29,059	12,786	9,375	123	1,269	1,393	626	3,828	739	2,229	1,077	1,152	4	276	580
1911	29,109	12,079	8,786	113	1,129	1,429	622	4,142	764	2,479	1,216	1,263	4	273	622
1912	31,042	13,001	9,558	124	1,224	1,460	635	4,368	814	2,643	1,316	1,327	4	278	629
1913	32,410	13,309	9,759	127	1,247	1,488	688	4,597	897	2,757	1,393	1,364	5	281	657
1914	33,140	14,001	10,456	137	1,258	1,468	682	4,277	808	2,570	1,317	1,253	5	219	675
1915	32,234	12,745	9,286	122	1,275	1,409	653	4,173	806	2,476	1,272	1,204	5	202	684
1916	37,811	14,672	10,835	143	1,448	1,531	715	5,457	1,096	3,283	1,690	1,593	7	308	763
1917	46,448	19,410	14,386	225	2,124	1,812	863	6,737	1,346	4,267	2,200	2,067	33	300	791
1918	53,209	22,421	15,693	950	2,376	2,215	1,187	8,433	1,632	5,490	2,837	2,653	207	263	841
1919	59,353	23,923	17,509	321	2,476	2,240	1,377	9,701	1,864	6,260	3,242	3,018	83	548	946
1920	62,949	21,621	17,317	263	2,409	—	1,632	10,854	2,042	7,213	3,804	3,409	30	495	1,074
1921	51,942	15,445	12,315	184	1,509	—	1,437	8,379	1,429	5,525	2,966	2,559	19	343	1,063
1922	55,947	16,015	12,961	193	1,493	—	1,368	9,404	1,494	6,408	3,490	2,918	14	430	1,058
1923	61,890	17,280	14,218	208	1,426	—	1,433	10,518	1,705	7,223	3,994	3,229	14	514	1,062
1924	62,716	17,784	14,669	214	1,437	—	1,464	9,453	1,611	6,252	3,470	2,782	15	486	1,089
1925	68,234	19,505	16,087	237	1,688	—	1,493	10,198	1,592	6,954	3,880	3,074	14	518	1,120
1926	71,847	20,885	17,367	254	1,727	—	1,537	10,395	1,643	7,042	3,992	3,050	13	542	1,155
1927	71,997	20,485	17,067	248	1,582	—	1,588	10,756	1,655	7,361	4,238	3,123	12	531	1,197
1928	74,603	20,464	17,002	248	1,621	—	1,593	10,910	1,657	7,431	4,395	3,036	13	547	1,262
1929	77,457	21,239	17,688	257	1,599	—	1,695	11,193	1,675	7,682	4,662	3,020	12	560	1,264

	Personal care			Housing					Household operation							
										Furnishings						
										Durable						
	Total	Toilet articles	Barber and beauty	Total	Owner-occupied	Tenant-occupied	Rent of farmhouse	Other	Total	Furniture and mattresses	Kitchen appliances	China	Other	Semidurable	Cleaners and polishes	Stationery
Year	Cd16	Cd17	Cd18	Cd19	Cd20	Cd21	Cd22	Cd23	Cd24	Cd25	Cd26	Cd27	Cd28	Cd29	Cd30	Cd31
	Million dollars	Million dollars	Million dollars	Million dollars	Million dollars	Million dollars	Million dollars	Million dollars	Million dollars	Million dollars	Million dollars	Million dollars	Million dollars	Million dollars	Million dollars	Million dollars
1900	119	64	55	2,426	1,266	804	307	49	1,810	172	103	147	203	80	64	17
1901	134	74	60	2,570	1,331	868	319	52	1,891	191	118	155	207	80	73	17
1902	147	84	63	2,617	1,316	905	340	56	2,073	207	132	166	236	86	82	18
1903	157	89	68	2,831	1,422	1,003	345	61	2,254	223	132	191	246	87	87	21
1904	160	89	71	3,141	1,560	1,112	405	64	2,275	229	124	193	236	86	87	21
1905	187	109	78	3,280	1,634	1,207	370	69	2,395	258	144	229	253	90	107	22
1906	201	117	84	3,514	1,724	1,303	413	74	2,533	306	174	258	186	113	115	23
1907	222	133	89	3,793	1,861	1,432	421	79	2,788	298	171	253	297	111	132	28
1908	218	129	89	3,784	1,878	1,459	427	80	2,634	246	142	196	239	98	128	31
1909	241	141	100	3,942	1,897	1,520	435	90	2,891	316	157	216	300	122	141	32
1910	256	151	105	4,146	1,992	1,613	445	96	3,037	336	163	239	323	140	151	37
1911	271	158	113	4,220	2,002	1,652	464	102	3,116	350	174	244	314	139	157	37
1912	278	164	114	4,361	2,060	1,699	498	104	3,350	391	219	255	337	153	163	36
1913	286	167	119	4,561	2,108	1,827	518	108	3,566	432	207	271	361	176	165	40
1914	286	164	122	4,727	2,183	1,903	529	112	3,486	418	181	262	334	170	163	41
1915	313	190	123	4,870	2,231	1,959	563	117	3,430	410	196	262	322	162	185	39
1916	381	244	137	5,179	2,373	2,062	614	130	4,089	539	232	334	422	224	234	58
1917	452	300	152	5,344	2,486	2,043	671	144	4,945	612	315	460	526	322	282	75
1918	551	377	174	5,650	2,652	2,092	739	167	5,528	688	351	409	591	421	350	76
1919	604	396	208	6,325	3,030	2,274	824	197	6,591	1,060	424	476	702	458	361	95
1920	712	460	252	7,498	3,680	2,745	835	238	8,252	1,152	589	625	946	564	421	114
1921	615	346	269	8,066	3,884	3,180	769	233	6,758	872	342	391	623	410	315	85
1922	675	386	289	8,553	4,114	3,445	767	227	7,400	945	407	392	788	462	342	87
1923	743	432	311	9,267	4,496	3,686	850	235	8,460	1,100	542	557	1,016	580	372	118
1924	784	445	339	9,944	4,848	4,006	854	236	8,456	1,175	550	422	934	562	373	114
1925	848	477	371	10,487	5,132	4,236	868	251	9,221	1,201	612	557	1,041	659	386	121
1926	895	487	408	11,050	5,423	4,479	869	279	9,849	1,240	676	628	1,028	714	390	121
1927	969	523	446	11,303	5,563	4,561	878	301	9,695	1,224	653	529	1,025	659	420	124
1928	1,069	573	496	11,637	5,734	4,687	883	333	10,253	1,241	625	634	1,110	679	459	137
1929	1,116	591	525	11,672	5,868	4,542	913	349	10,664	1,192	699	628	1,148	717	485	143

Note appears at end of table

(continued)

TABLE Cd1-77 Consumption expenditures, by type: 1900–1929 Continued

	Household operation							Medical care						Personal business		
	Electricity	Gas	Water	Wood, gas, and coal	Telephone and telegraph	Domestic services	Other household operations	Total	Drugs	Ophthalmology	Medical, dental, and other professional services	Hospitals	Health insurance	Total	Brokerage	Banking and financial services
	Cd32	Cd33	Cd34	Cd35	Cd36	Cd37	Cd38	Cd39	Cd40	Cd41	Cd42	Cd43	Cd44	Cd45	Cd46	Cd47
Year	Million dollars	Million dollars	Million dollars	Million dollars	Million dollars	Million dollars	Million dollars	Million dollars	Million dollars	Million dollars	Million dollars	Million dollars	Million dollars	Million dollars	Million dollars	Million dollars
1900	15	72	50	399	13	419	56	384	103	11	253	15	2	754	103	249
1901	17	86	52	387	17	430	61	417	118	12	269	16	2	866	149	287
1902	20	97	54	420	22	476	57	451	132	14	286	17	2	916	135	316
1903	22	109	59	489	26	493	69	481	139	14	307	18	3	983	130	329
1904	24	120	60	472	30	514	68	498	139	14	323	19	3	1,027	135	321
1905	26	127	65	446	34	523	71	552	162	17	344	25	4	1,154	181	406
1906	29	134	68	466	38	546	77	581	167	19	361	30	4	1,209	199	436
1907	34	139	72	510	51	613	79	643	181	23	394	42	3	1,158	169	396
1908	39	146	76	509	57	645	82	644	168	23	414	35	4	1,109	155	350
1909	45	155	80	513	62	661	91	679	177	26	431	41	4	1,156	170	363
1910	56	164	89	506	69	682	82	715	189	26	435	60	5	1,213	161	388
1911	66	174	93	497	77	695	99	752	198	27	460	61	6	1,253	143	410
1912	79	185	96	546	84	709	97	787	207	26	485	61	8	1,318	144	454
1913	89	195	99	611	94	723	103	828	212	31	506	69	10	1,377	125	506
1914	102	208	103	579	100	719	106	877	208	39	543	75	12	1,419	106	543
1915	110	222	107	544	104	657	110	965	237	50	576	87	15	1,586	140	633
1916	118	241	110	694	116	648	119	1,102	300	60	609	116	17	1,912	173	868
1917	129	264	117	919	133	667	124	1,278	364	92	655	147	20	2,114	169	995
1918	157	290	128	1,083	154	695	135	1,643	450	179	742	248	24	2,471	163	1,147
1919	197	341	137	1,138	187	865	150	1,675	465	147	833	196	34	2,814	302	1,361
1920	248	389	150	1,589	220	1,070	175	1,961	499	171	995	254	42	2,938	349	1,169
1921	268	433	168	1,330	243	1,092	186	1,983	347	118	1,256	234	28	2,809	319	1,134
1922	288	446	190	1,450	269	1,140	194	2,053	386	123	1,239	252	53	2,905	396	1,114
1923	332	463	208	1,368	292	1,301	211	2,129	432	117	1,239	280	61	3,090	459	1,088
1924	362	471	222	1,330	323	1,393	225	2,258	447	122	1,314	310	65	3,184	472	1,150
1925	420	478	237	1,426	371	1,466	246	2,482	480	117	1,455	360	70	3,488	576	1,196
1926	465	521	258	1,588	418	1,535	267	2,574	486	117	1,480	409	82	3,397	558	1,066
1927	522	543	268	1,371	459	1,607	291	2,775	516	125	1,579	449	106	3,654	591	1,201
1928	561	539	274	1,578	509	1,595	312	2,923	567	122	1,621	500	113	3,686	712	1,013
1929	616	542	285	1,608	569	1,716	316	3,104	604	131	1,692	569	108	3,886	784	1,048

Year	Personal business				Transportation								Recreation		
	Life insurance	Legal services	Funeral	Other	Total	Motor vehicles and wagons	Tires and accessories	Automobile repair	Gasoline and oil	Auto insurance and tolls	Purchased transportation Local	Purchased transportation Intercity	Total	Books and maps	Magazines and newspapers
	Cd48	Cd49	Cd50	Cd51	Cd52	Cd53	Cd54	Cd55	Cd56	Cd57	Cd58	Cd59	Cd60	Cd61	Cd62
	Million dollars	Million dollars	Million dollars	Million dollars	Million dollars	Million dollars	Million dollars	Million dollars	Million dollars	Million dollars	Million dollars	Million dollars	Million dollars	Million dollars	Million dollars
1900	100	81	185	36	533	57	6	—	—	2	247	220	498	64	88
1901	110	81	191	48	581	74	5	1	1	2	259	239	561	69	97
1902	121	85	198	61	601	70	4	1	1	2	255	268	631	72	109
1903	135	90	216	83	649	70	3	1	2	2	284	287	666	75	111
1904	144	90	243	94	727	81	6	2	2	2	331	303	685	78	116
1905	147	94	239	87	818	100	10	3	3	3	377	322	755	83	126
1906	140	96	252	86	919	129	15	5	5	4	414	347	803	82	134
1907	130	100	268	95	1,013	158	20	7	9	5	430	384	860	83	144
1908	133	102	274	95	1,062	188	26	11	10	6	435	386	770	79	115
1909	146	106	282	89	1,121	212	33	19	14	7	452	384	889	93	154
1910	154	111	303	96	1,291	267	47	26	28	9	486	428	915	89	153
1911	167	116	311	106	1,383	264	54	32	42	11	533	447	963	88	153
1912	179	116	315	110	1,581	365	75	41	54	12	584	450	1,039	99	169
1913	190	119	323	114	1,756	426	103	46	73	14	620	474	1,133	116	175
1914	193	122	334	121	1,953	449	112	54	187	16	656	479	1,119	102	182
1915	221	127	348	117	2,098	586	132	77	182	18	663	440	1,158	111	182
1916	223	137	387	124	2,696	932	209	111	248	23	703	470	1,438	116	250
1917	250	152	412	136	3,258	1,065	366	161	360	29	730	547	1,829	137	288
1918	281	175	552	153	3,414	820	476	189	429	35	785	680	1,836	152	314
1919	355	206	406	184	4,321	1,347	570	225	471	40	892	776	2,281	196	322
1920	439	255	497	229	5,073	1,700	689	211	556	41	1,028	848	2,534	215	353
1921	434	302	405	215	4,144	1,165	346	173	630	37	1,035	758	2,225	188	370
1922	471	329	415	180	4,889	1,616	412	278	779	52	1,045	707	2,377	194	390
1923	568	314	496	165	5,937	2,290	506	441	793	73	1,077	757	2,709	204	431
1924	576	323	502	161	6,028	2,012	523	540	1,084	86	1,081	702	2,914	227	440
1925	664	360	530	162	6,824	2,451	734	649	1,108	102	1,097	683	3,152	236	482
1926	720	346	543	164	7,231	2,625	784	694	1,224	108	1,125	671	3,441	246	496
1927	762	385	551	164	6,510	2,064	747	706	1,141	114	1,120	618	3,597	274	509
1928	813	394	592	162	7,211	2,396	730	748	1,482	125	1,104	562	4,072	287	520
1929	880	402	607	165	7,721	2,697	648	776	1,814	134	1,117	535	4,356	309	538

(continued)

TABLE Cd1-77   Consumption expenditures, by type: 1900–1929   *Continued*

	Recreation					Education				Religion and welfare			Net foreign travel		
	Nondurable toys	Durable toys and wheel goods	Music, radio, and television	Flowers and plants	Recreational services	Total	Higher education	Elementary education	Other education and research	Total	Religion	Welfare	Net total	Foreign travel by U.S. residents	Travel in the United States by aliens
	Cd63	Cd64	Cd65	Cd66	Cd67	Cd68	Cd69	Cd70	Cd71	Cd72	Cd73	Cd74	Cd75	Cd76	Cd77
Year	Million dollars	Million dollars	Million dollars	Million dollars	Million dollars	Million dollars	Million dollars	Million dollars	Million dollars	Million dollars	Million dollars	Million dollars	Million dollars	Million dollars	Million dollars
1900	37	45	80	47	137	105	14	42	51	326	226	100	149	157	8
1901	48	50	92	57	153	115	15	42	60	325	225	100	162	170	8
1902	50	49	108	65	178	121	16	41	66	327	227	100	153	162	9
1903	52	45	123	66	194	135	18	48	71	337	237	100	157	166	9
1904	55	49	109	68	210	135	19	48	70	337	237	100	170	183	13
1905	61	55	134	70	226	141	20	48	75	338	238	100	191	209	18
1906	68	58	154	69	238	147	21	50	78	345	245	100	222	250	28
1907	63	72	167	79	252	159	26	50	85	362	262	100	244	280	36
1908	61	49	120	83	263	166	30	52	86	366	266	100	264	304	40
1909	74	60	146	90	272	171	31	54	88	365	265	100	286	328	42
1910	79	63	149	93	289	181	34	63	91	357	257	100	308	347	39
1911	85	70	158	87	322	193	37	65	96	377	277	100	336	378	42
1912	89	73	188	91	330	199	39	74	97	387	287	100	350	400	50
1913	98	91	208	91	354	218	42	82	105	397	297	100	356	407	51
1914	105	85	185	84	376	234	45	82	110	422	314	108	316	356	40
1915	113	87	184	85	396	243	49	85	112	446	332	114	184	209	25
1916	175	126	239	98	434	254	52	84	122	461	346	115	139	161	22
1917	305	201	281	129	488	266	53	86	130	683	366	317	96	131	35
1918	194	140	304	152	580	277	54	89	137	867	411	456	64	109	45
1919	225	161	528	153	696	329	74	96	162	647	442	205	104	161	57
1920	216	163	581	141	865	398	93	110	199	835	523	312	181	249	68
1921	190	119	370	103	885	459	116	128	220	840	574	266	185	262	77
1922	199	123	446	110	915	504	139	137	233	884	618	266	256	318	62
1923	253	166	553	131	971	531	160	146	234	929	664	265	267	340	73
1924	238	153	664	150	1,042	552	179	146	232	1,014	729	285	317	396	79
1925	257	161	716	172	1,128	594	201	155	243	1,038	790	248	369	454	85
1926	277	179	832	176	1,235	644	221	166	263	1,088	832	256	375	487	112
1927	286	179	754	190	1,405	682	249	173	267	1,147	867	280	407	523	116
1928	314	199	945	226	1,581	727	278	184	271	1,180	905	275	462	586	124
1929	336	219	1,012	221	1,721	769	298	188	283	1,247	949	298	490	632	142

[1] Sales of alcoholic beverages were illegal, 1920–1932.

Source

Stanley Lebergott, *Consumer Expenditures: New Measures and Old Motives* (Princeton University Press, 1996), Table A1.

Documentation

The first detailed estimates of aggregate consumer expenditures for goods and services in the United States before the construction of unified national income and product accounts appeared in William H. Lough (with the assistance of Martin Gainsbrugh), *High-Level Consumption* (McGraw-Hill, 1935). These pioneer estimates covered the years 1909, 1914, 1919, 1921, 1923, 1925, 1927, 1929, and 1931. The data for the later years were revised and extended by Harold Barger and are reported in his *Outlay and Income in the United States, 1921–1938* (National Bureau of Economic Research, 1942).

Those estimates were revised in J. Frederic Dewhurst, *America's Needs and Resources* (Twentieth Century Fund, 1947). In particular, the recreational expenditures were expanded to take account of estimates reported in Julius Weinberger, "The Economic Aspects of Recreation," *Harvard Business Review* (Summer 1937). Those figures served as the base for those reported for 1909–1929 by J. Frederic Dewhurst in *America's Needs and Resources* (Twentieth Century Fund, 1955), pp. 965–80; and in U.S. Bureau of the Census, *Historical Statistics of the United States, Bicentennial Edition* (1975), part 1, p. 320.

The estimates for 1900–1929 reported in Tables Cd1–152 were constructed by Stanley Lebergott and are reported in his *Consumer Expenditures* (1996). Lebergott created his series to be consistent with, and benchmarked to, the Bureau of Economic Analysis (BEA) data for the United States (1993 revision). The details of Lebergott's procedures and sources for estimating expenditures on goods can be found in *Consumer Expenditures*, chapter 9, part 1. Those for most service expenditures were reported separately in Stanley Lebergott, *The American Economy: Income, Wealth and Want* (Princeton University Press, 1976), pp. 326–76, with a few additions explained in *Consumer Expenditures*, chapter 9, part 2.

Although Lebergott benchmarked his series to the BEA's, the expenditure categories that the BEA currently reports differ slightly from those reported by Lebergott. In particular, the BEA has divided expenditures into durable and nondurable goods and services, and this division means that some expenditures in Lebergott's tables are spread over more than one category in the BEA data (Tables Cd153–377).

Series Cd2–7. The value of food at the farm level was derived from gross income to farmers from the production of food as calculated by Frederick Strauss and Louis Bean and reported in *Gross Income and Indices of Farm Production in the United States*, U.S. Department of Agriculture, Technical Bulletin number 703 (1940). Exports of "crude" and "manufactured" food were deducted from the total value of food after adjusting them for the port-to-farm difference and after excluding the value added by manufacturing. For the details of these adjustments, see Lebergott (1996), pp. 73–4, 260.

Series Cd3. Data on purchased food and meals (excluding alcohol) are derived by subtracting the value of food furnished to employees, series Cd4, and food consumed on the farm, series Cd5, from the adjusted total value of food.

Series Cd4. Data on food furnished to employees were estimated by first calculating the ratio of persons in the armed forces and domestic service to the U.S. population. That ratio was then multiplied by the estimates of the value of food (see earlier discussion) for the entire United States. The resulting series was adjusted for the fact that wartime expenditures per soldier were higher than those for civilians. See Lebergott (1996), p. 75.

Series Cd5. In order to estimate the value of food consumed on the farm, Lebergott first estimated a volume index based on figures in U.S. Department of Agriculture, *Agricultural Economics Report*, number 138 (1968), p. 163. He then multiplied it by a price index derived from the prices used in the calculation of the value of food at the farm level (see earlier discussion).

Series Cd6. Lebergott calculated the alcohol series by computing a benchmark for 1899 from the production series reported in the 1900 Census. He then extrapolated between 1900 and 1919 using the annual product of gallons of distilled spirits and malt liquor consumed, as reported in the *Statistical Abstract of the United States*, 1922, p. 697. He used prices from Clark Warburton, *The Economic Results of Prohibition* (Columbia University Press, 1932), p. 112.

Series Cd7–14 and Cd24–67. Except as noted for particular series, expenditures on goods were derived from output series calculated by William H. Shaw and reported in his *Value of Commodity Output since 1869* (National Bureau of Economic Research, 1947), Tables I-1 and I-2. Those figures were adjusted to obtain retail purchases by using margin data by Harold Barger reported in his *Distribution's Place in the American Economy since 1869* (National Bureau of Economic Research, 1955).

Series Cd15. Derived from Lebergott (1976), pp. 326–76.

Series Cd16–18. Shaw (1947), Tables I-1 and II-2, included expenditures on toilet articles and preparations with his series for cleaning and polishing, and drug preparations and sundries. Lebergott separated the expenditures on these items based on their relative shares of benchmark output figures from Shaw (1947), Tables I-1 and II-2. The series, such as those for expenditures on toilet articles, were then constructed by interpolating the shares between the benchmark figures and multiplying the resulting series by Shaw's group figures. Those series were then adjusted to obtain retail purchases by using margin data from Barger (1955). Expenditures on services were derived from Lebergott (1976), pp. 326–76.

Series Cd19–23. In constructing his housing series, Lebergott rejected all earlier estimates of housing services. Instead he employed "present-day BEA procedures" to construct a rent index for both owner-occupied and rental housing. The original housing stock estimates seem to be derived from Leo Grebler, David M. Blank, and Louis Winnick, *Capital Formation in Residential Real Estate* (Princeton University Press, 1956). The discussion of the construction of the housing series is rather subtle, and for more detail, interested readers should consult Lebergott (1996), pp. 81–2, 263.

Series Cd30 and Cd39–44. Shaw included expenditures on cleaning and polishing with his series for toilet articles and preparations, and drug preparations and sundries. Lebergott separated the expenditures on these items based on benchmark output figures. For more information on that procedure, see the preceding text for series Cd16–18 and Lebergott (1996), p. 76.

Series Cd31. Shaw included expenditures on stationery with those on magazines and newspapers. Lebergott separated the expenditures on these items based on benchmark output figures. He then interpolated using the product of the quantity of postage stamps sold and Shaw's price index for the combined group reported in Shaw (1947), Table IV-1.

Series Cd35. The expenditures on fuel and ice were derived from various original series reported by Shaw, though these had to be recombined into their current form. Shaw omitted expenditures on wood for fuel; these are calculated in Lebergott (1996), pp. 77–8.

Series Cd63–64. Expenditures on nondurable toys and wheel goods are based on comparable figures reported in Shaw (1947), with minor adjustments discussed in Lebergott (1996), p. 79.

Series Cd66. Personal consumption expenditures on flowers and seeds, which is a component of this series, are based on figures from a number of sources. See Lebergott (1996), pp. 79, 263.

Series Cd68–77. With one exception, the underlying data used to generate these series are based on the corresponding series in Lebergott (1976). The exception is "expenditures abroad by U.S. government personnel," which is a component of foreign travel by U.S. residents, series Cd76. The adjustments to this component are based primarily on the size of the American Expeditionary Force. See Lebergott (1996), p. 79.

TABLE Cd78–152 Consumption expenditures, by type: 1900–1929 [1987 dollars]
Contributed by Lee A. Craig

		Food, alcohol, and tobacco						Clothing						Personal care		
	Total	Total	Purchased food and meals (excluding alcohol)	Food furnished to employees	Food consumed on farms	Alcohol	Tobacco	Total	Shoes	Civilian clothing	Military clothing	Jewelry	Clothing services	Total	Toilet articles	Barber and beauty
	Cd78	Cd79	Cd80	Cd81	Cd82	Cd83 [1]	Cd84	Cd85	Cd86	Cd87	Cd88	Cd89	Cd90	Cd91	Cd92	Cd93
Year	Million 1987 dollars	Million 1987 dollars	Million 1987 dollars	Million 1987 dollars	Million 1987 dollars	Million 1987 dollars	Million 1987 dollars	Million 1987 dollars	Million 1987 dollars	Million 1987 dollars	Million 1987 dollars	Million 1987 dollars	Million 1987 dollars	Million 1987 dollars	Million 1987 dollars	Million 1987 dollars
1900	248,699	107,793	79,821	1,820	7,975	12,871	5,307	20,738	6,037	8,845	18	999	4,838	2,139	454	1,686
1901	268,622	115,838	86,246	1,616	8,637	13,681	5,658	22,781	6,898	9,437	19	945	5,482	2,363	524	1,838
1902	274,973	119,084	88,869	1,674	8,323	14,660	5,558	23,191	6,874	10,324	19	1,069	4,905	2,421	533	1,888
1903	282,827	120,655	90,154	1,335	8,061	15,246	5,859	25,152	7,344	11,375	19	1,100	5,313	2,567	569	1,997
1904	291,955	123,948	93,069	1,379	8,167	15,649	5,684	26,285	7,614	11,865	19	1,086	5,700	2,649	587	2,062
1905	313,193	132,889	100,302	1,477	8,557	16,689	5,864	27,560	7,764	12,565	19	1,299	5,913	2,914	692	2,222
1906	326,145	135,090	100,469	1,471	8,384	18,209	6,556	31,290	8,088	15,197	19	1,667	6,319	3,118	725	2,393
1907	328,213	136,756	100,756	1,614	8,870	18,825	6,691	31,363	8,122	14,963	24	1,684	6,570	3,278	818	2,460
1908	326,164	138,444	102,952	1,537	8,959	18,378	6,617	30,868	8,313	15,165	25	1,366	5,997	3,168	735	2,433
1909	348,920	149,439	112,926	1,694	9,216	18,541	7,061	33,495	8,161	16,913	26	1,972	6,423	3,422	767	2,655
1910	358,726	154,279	115,909	1,757	9,332	19,647	7,634	33,871	8,556	16,616	25	2,061	6,612	3,493	782	2,711
1911	357,208	146,679	109,190	1,612	8,341	20,042	7,494	36,520	8,886	18,479	25	2,039	7,090	3,662	822	2,840
1912	370,431	150,976	112,600	1,678	8,571	20,477	7,651	37,614	8,967	19,231	25	2,010	7,381	3,761	873	2,888
1913	383,911	156,941	116,921	1,757	8,886	20,987	8,390	38,656	9,160	19,691	30	1,910	7,864	3,918	904	3,014
1914	386,609	161,676	122,577	1,853	8,771	20,055	8,420	36,437	8,251	18,520	31	1,474	8,161	3,910	871	3,040
1915	379,164	147,973	110,372	1,671	9,006	18,862	8,062	35,229	8,038	17,518	30	1,373	8,270	3,945	960	2,985
1916	410,715	154,119	115,094	1,974	9,145	19,185	8,720	41,862	10,002	21,094	38	1,774	8,954	4,180	1,050	3,131
1917	421,914	157,919	118,412	2,134	10,397	17,695	9,280	40,278	9,073	22,908	151	1,236	6,911	4,112	949	3,164
1918	415,593	148,488	108,161	7,543	9,737	12,354	10,694	39,450	9,690	22,356	717	903	5,785	4,369	1,198	3,171
1919	402,384	130,522	104,416	2,205	8,919	5,862	9,119	35,310	8,045	19,613	221	1,741	5,690	4,512	1,238	3,274
1920	388,848	119,317	98,941	1,729	8,185	—	10,462	34,409	7,860	19,062	67	1,385	6,035	4,680	1,352	3,327
1921	371,030	110,329	92,654	1,593	6,751	—	9,331	34,593	7,452	18,362	54	1,014	7,711	4,898	1,295	3,603
1922	407,375	123,085	104,180	1,784	7,135	—	9,985	44,932	8,856	25,096	47	1,484	9,450	5,552	1,642	3,910
1923	445,713	130,119	110,938	1,869	6,619	—	10,694	48,865	10,007	27,928	46	1,468	9,416	6,014	1,807	4,207
1924	455,703	135,884	115,510	1,935	6,727	—	11,712	45,091	9,518	24,425	50	1,371	9,727	6,351	1,874	4,476
1925	483,135	138,001	116,784	1,985	7,289	—	11,944	48,226	9,212	27,589	47	1,593	9,785	6,756	1,966	4,790
1926	503,494	143,738	122,157	2,060	7,225	—	12,296	49,409	9,553	28,227	44	1,780	9,805	7,053	1,954	5,099
1927	511,908	146,229	124,577	2,080	6,868	—	12,704	51,607	9,388	29,899	41	1,744	10,535	7,582	2,202	5,379
1928	531,579	148,085	125,478	2,107	7,114	—	13,387	51,810	8,765	30,336	45	1,796	10,867	8,222	2,555	5,667
1929	554,055	151,818	128,733	2,154	6,922	—	14,008	53,169	9,165	31,613	42	1,839	10,510	8,657	2,663	5,993

	Housing					Household operation									
							Furnishings								
							Durable								
Year	Total	Owner-occupied	Tenant-occupied	Rent of farmhouse	Other	Total	Furniture and mattresses	Kitchen appliances	China	Other	Semidurable	Cleaners and polishes	Stationery	Electricity	Gas
	Cd94	Cd95	Cd96	Cd97	Cd98	Cd99	Cd100	Cd101	Cd102	Cd103	Cd104	Cd105	Cd106	Cd107	Cd108
	Million 1987 dollars	Million 1987 dollars	Million 1987 dollars	Million 1987 dollars	Million 1987 dollars	Million 1987 dollars	Million 1987 dollars	Million 1987 dollars	Million 1987 dollars	Million 1987 dollars	Million 1987 dollars	Million 1987 dollars	Million 1987 dollars	Million 1987 dollars	Million 1987 dollars
1900	19,503	9,395	6,066	3,410	632	35,439	2,787	343	2,316	1,854	728	753	237	13	523
1901	20,251	9,628	6,384	3,583	656	36,778	3,149	389	2,612	1,934	797	887	241	15	635
1902	20,983	9,683	6,770	3,817	714	37,626	3,273	435	2,771	2,260	822	837	263	23	717
1903	21,471	9,871	7,080	3,784	735	38,949	3,393	431	3,022	2,299	796	888	318	26	805
1904	22,856	10,251	7,430	4,444	731	39,566	3,484	417	2,968	2,281	792	911	314	31	894
1905	23,415	10,657	8,003	3,975	780	41,560	3,894	479	3,761	2,533	793	1,067	329	37	946
1906	24,646	11,075	8,510	4,233	828	42,533	4,382	568	3,892	1,815	919	1,120	340	46	1,033
1907	25,536	11,525	9,018	4,153	841	43,589	3,802	542	3,410	2,686	815	1,253	390	60	1,102
1908	26,568	11,975	9,459	4,275	860	42,449	3,201	459	3,064	2,213	834	1,115	418	70	1,168
1909	27,769	12,371	10,079	4,302	1,017	45,203	4,194	483	3,273	2,740	1,006	1,169	416	83	1,252
1910	28,617	12,703	10,458	4,393	1,063	46,042	4,100	506	3,264	2,950	1,128	1,205	485	107	1,349
1911	29,762	13,056	10,954	4,600	1,153	46,674	3,760	563	3,564	2,840	1,179	1,253	488	130	1,464
1912	30,845	13,434	11,266	4,970	1,175	48,236	3,807	708	3,892	3,021	1,278	1,337	486	156	1,571
1913	31,425	13,343	11,758	5,140	1,184	50,425	4,682	676	3,822	3,208	1,471	1,379	543	186	1,672
1914	32,480	13,777	12,211	5,263	1,228	48,652	3,608	591	3,568	2,902	1,499	1,379	563	224	1,820
1915	33,323	14,018	12,516	5,519	1,270	48,254	3,524	641	3,999	2,670	1,427	1,565	536	253	1,961
1916	34,822	14,696	12,985	5,744	1,398	50,916	4,516	734	3,895	3,132	1,447	1,919	532	277	2,153
1917	35,608	15,508	12,958	5,579	1,564	52,082	4,637	887	3,409	3,340	1,455	1,724	546	314	2,382
1918	36,604	16,307	13,078	5,441	1,778	49,797	4,505	810	2,116	2,919	1,342	1,683	536	390	2,512
1919	37,569	17,160	13,094	5,368	1,947	50,116	5,415	894	2,554	2,754	1,504	1,518	589	479	2,677
1920	37,603	17,698	13,423	4,491	1,992	51,807	3,925	1,040	2,882	3,022	1,461	1,653	526	610	2,922
1921	37,148	16,389	13,643	5,412	1,703	49,880	3,838	627	2,914	2,369	1,943	1,598	564	667	2,729
1922	35,576	14,136	14,291	5,543	1,605	56,046	4,693	754	2,917	3,532	2,082	2,134	666	684	2,873
1923	40,385	17,918	14,937	5,900	1,631	59,165	5,303	888	3,578	4,237	2,314	2,308	850	846	3,051
1924	41,949	18,632	15,653	6,087	1,578	59,883	6,128	924	2,584	3,963	2,282	2,328	776	923	3,159
1925	44,093	19,635	16,479	6,311	1,668	64,896	6,506	1,081	3,663	4,512	2,692	2,359	775	1,110	3,200
1926	46,888	21,028	17,659	6,324	1,876	69,241	6,945	1,176	4,603	4,566	3,230	2,317	727	1,230	3,541
1927	48,576	21,867	18,228	6,430	2,050	68,579	7,033	1,146	4,132	4,658	3,053	2,582	737	1,417	3,722
1928	51,106	23,066	19,169	6,545	2,325	73,468	7,171	1,146	4,923	5,173	3,061	2,765	815	1,564	3,636
1929	52,406	24,169	19,021	6,713	2,502	76,199	6,969	1,268	4,914	5,400	3,418	2,818	844	1,813	3,685

Note appears at end of table

(continued)

TABLE Cd78–152　Consumption expenditures, by type: 1900–1929　[1987 dollars]　*Continued*

		Household operation				Medical care						Personal business			
	Water	Wood, gas, and coal	Telephone and telegraph	Domestic services	Other household operations	Total	Drugs	Ophthalmology	Medical, dental, and other professional services	Hospitals	Health insurance	Total	Brokerage	Banking and financial services	Life insurance
Year	Cd109	Cd110	Cd111	Cd112	Cd113	Cd114	Cd115	Cd116	Cd117	Cd118	Cd119	Cd120	Cd121	Cd122	Cd123
	Million 1987 dollars	Million 1987 dollars	Million 1987 dollars	Million 1987 dollars	Million 1987 dollars	Million 1987 dollars	Million 1987 dollars	Million 1987 dollars	Million 1987 dollars	Million 1987 dollars	Million 1987 dollars	Million 1987 dollars	Million 1987 dollars	Million 1987 dollars	Million 1987 dollars
1900	1,486	7,279	46	16,178	897	12,607	579	74	10,902	1,004	47	19,055	8,898	4,882	1,111
1901	1,510	7,027	60	16,538	984	13,391	695	85	11,502	1,063	46	24,378	12,263	6,097	1,325
1902	1,548	7,002	80	16,702	895	13,700	663	84	11,817	1,091	45	24,084	11,739	6,330	1,360
1903	1,666	7,260	93	16,884	1,066	14,291	704	85	12,315	1,122	65	24,675	11,429	6,573	1,517
1904	1,644	7,497	111	17,191	1,033	14,618	725	88	12,591	1,151	63	25,026	11,663	6,286	1,600
1905	1,766	7,340	126	17,433	1,056	15,462	815	102	12,996	1,467	82	30,454	15,146	8,125	1,652
1906	1,795	7,669	140	17,670	1,142	16,203	820	112	13,454	1,737	80	32,998	16,345	9,088	1,628
1907	1,820	8,393	194	17,977	1,145	17,631	881	135	14,204	2,353	58	29,547	14,113	7,923	1,461
1908	1,917	8,377	216	18,220	1,175	17,465	757	124	14,591	1,917	76	26,506	12,917	6,491	1,385
1909	2,014	8,552	242	18,515	1,265	17,716	768	135	14,585	2,156	73	28,852	14,316	6,973	1,570
1910	2,250	8,527	270	18,788	1,112	18,233	776	129	14,198	3,043	88	28,686	13,790	7,191	1,588
1911	2,328	8,717	301	18,784	1,302	18,438	816	134	14,416	2,970	102	28,052	12,599	7,454	1,687
1912	2,395	9,201	338	18,757	1,288	19,310	872	132	15,200	2,970	135	29,225	12,414	8,401	1,865
1913	2,318	9,992	379	18,731	1,365	20,184	908	160	15,636	3,313	167	29,992	11,312	9,727	2,043
1914	2,290	9,652	403	18,773	1,381	21,147	875	197	16,367	3,512	195	27,843	9,860	9,521	1,911
1915	2,368	9,351	431	18,135	1,393	22,015	948	240	16,678	3,914	234	32,009	11,618	11,295	2,210
1916	2,414	11,207	481	16,788	1,422	22,909	1,023	246	16,507	4,885	249	39,478	13,542	15,490	2,398
1917	2,540	13,067	552	15,881	1,351	23,183	1,005	306	16,022	5,587	264	40,218	12,269	17,463	2,475
1918	2,688	13,468	659	14,882	1,288	25,863	1,131	541	15,741	8,174	275	46,338	10,449	22,050	3,022
1919	2,313	12,539	753	14,888	1,239	22,631	1,152	438	15,164	5,544	334	55,575	16,825	25,210	3,660
1920	2,352	14,443	859	14,903	1,209	22,360	1,158	483	14,596	5,789	333	51,617	17,450	19,156	4,065
1921	2,422	12,425	897	15,578	1,309	22,368	1,028	420	16,074	4,653	193	48,686	14,566	18,893	4,056
1922	2,557	14,547	966	16,262	1,377	21,868	1,301	498	14,987	4,736	346	50,779	18,000	17,683	4,168
1923	2,740	13,565	1,048	16,940	1,498	24,182	1,431	466	16,175	5,679	430	56,295	19,935	18,759	5,462
1924	2,732	13,753	1,160	17,611	1,561	25,879	1,490	488	17,155	6,288	458	58,653	20,171	20,182	5,703
1925	2,898	14,845	1,265	18,325	1,665	26,741	1,567	459	17,523	6,736	455	64,966	24,589	20,627	6,385
1926	3,057	15,748	1,356	18,998	1,748	29,792	1,544	447	19,051	8,180	570	62,280	23,495	18,381	6,990
1927	3,034	14,064	1,465	19,694	1,841	29,869	1,717	498	18,710	8,266	678	67,432	24,447	21,076	7,545
1928	3,075	16,427	1,624	20,215	1,871	31,686	2,002	517	19,228	9,215	724	69,534	29,331	17,462	7,893
1929	3,098	16,612	1,775	21,500	1,892	34,124	2,146	560	20,179	10,543	695	74,423	31,360	18,714	8,800

	Personal business			Transportation								Recreation			
	Legal services	Funeral	Other	Total	Motor vehicles and wagons	Tires and accessories	Automobile repair	Gasoline and oil	Auto insurance and tolls	Purchased transportation		Total	Books and maps	Magazines and newspapers	Nondurable toys
										Local	Intercity				
	Cd124	Cd125	Cd126	Cd127	Cd128	Cd129	Cd130	Cd131	Cd132	Cd133	Cd134	Cd135	Cd136	Cd137	Cd138
Year	Million 1987 dollars	Million 1987 dollars	Million 1987 dollars	Million 1987 dollars	Million 1987 dollars	Million 1987 dollars	Million 1987 dollars	Million 1987 dollars	Million 1987 dollars	Million 1987 dollars	Million 1987 dollars	Million 1987 dollars	Million 1987 dollars	Million 1987 dollars	Million 1987 dollars
1900	1,929	1,927	308	10,763	265	3	3	—	19	7,577	2,896	6,334	1,072	1,047	207
1901	2,077	2,170	444	11,607	343	3	6	6	19	8,045	3,185	7,054	1,155	1,154	286
1902	2,024	2,106	526	12,030	327	2	9	6	19	8,041	3,626	7,845	1,206	1,297	290
1903	2,143	2,298	716	12,904	327	2	9	10	19	8,746	3,792	8,295	1,256	1,321	295
1904	2,143	2,531	803	14,437	417	3	19	10	19	10,029	3,939	8,803	1,306	1,380	312
1905	2,238	2,543	750	15,980	340	4	23	17	23	11,397	4,177	9,397	1,390	1,499	327
1906	2,400	2,769	768	17,218	378	5	34	26	27	12,317	4,430	9,754	1,373	1,595	338
1907	2,381	2,851	819	17,594	402	6	44	44	31	12,339	4,728	9,979	1,390	1,714	298
1908	2,267	2,686	760	18,062	477	7	69	48	38	12,619	4,805	9,717	1,323	1,369	310
1909	2,409	2,848	736	19,414	888	21	160	72	59	13,348	4,866	10,744	1,557	1,833	365
1910	2,413	2,942	762	20,997	1,213	24	227	167	80	13,996	5,289	11,204	1,490	1,821	382
1911	2,522	2,962	828	22,484	1,264	29	281	268	98	15,108	5,437	11,768	1,474	1,821	427
1912	2,578	3,088	880	25,019	2,099	49	395	291	112	16,589	5,485	12,248	1,658	2,011	439
1913	2,705	3,263	942	26,042	2,545	68	446	313	139	16,966	5,565	13,122	1,942	2,083	478
1914	2,542	3,093	917	27,611	3,167	87	554	889	158	17,327	5,429	13,227	1,708	2,166	528
1915	2,702	3,283	900	28,774	4,467	117	813	941	189	17,315	4,931	13,573	1,859	2,166	568
1916	3,114	3,909	1,025	32,561	7,632	179	1,172	936	242	17,406	4,993	15,389	1,942	2,975	723
1917	3,167	3,815	1,030	33,362	8,503	254	1,604	1,211	287	16,271	5,231	17,240	2,294	3,427	924
1918	3,977	5,576	1,264	27,134	5,973	286	1,684	1,249	313	12,853	4,777	17,737	2,545	3,737	459
1919	4,478	3,942	1,460	30,150	8,330	375	1,756	1,435	308	13,068	4,878	19,568	3,282	3,832	518
1920	5,000	4,322	1,624	29,880	9,399	408	1,420	1,570	277	12,412	4,393	19,593	3,010	3,803	408
1921	6,040	3,584	1,547	28,405	7,158	266	1,220	2,266	261	13,113	4,121	17,777	1,958	3,986	548
1922	6,208	3,487	1,233	35,706	12,219	491	2,104	2,643	400	13,833	4,016	17,911	2,020	4,150	614
1923	6,408	4,509	1,222	44,838	18,553	636	3,396	3,091	562	14,290	4,310	19,501	1,894	4,586	718
1924	6,729	4,648	1,220	44,780	16,485	777	4,105	4,534	662	14,248	3,970	20,537	2,107	4,682	726
1925	7,347	4,818	1,200	49,656	20,501	1,024	4,871	4,352	750	14,330	3,828	21,352	2,191	5,129	809
1926	7,208	4,982	1,224	53,124	23,123	1,078	5,143	4,627	794	14,618	3,741	22,945	2,101	5,278	925
1927	8,021	5,102	1,242	48,481	17,739	1,374	5,062	5,534	803	14,529	3,440	24,410	2,340	5,416	1,049
1928	8,208	5,431	1,209	51,704	19,737	1,584	5,094	7,063	845	14,266	3,116	26,522	2,451	5,533	1,197
1929	8,553	5,726	1,269	55,428	21,418	1,636	5,224	9,064	905	14,252	2,929	28,077	2,639	5,628	1,291

(continued)

TABLE Cd78–152   Consumption expenditures, by type: 1900–1929   [1987 dollars]   Continued

Year	Recreation				Education				Religion and welfare			Net foreign travel		
	Durable toys and wheel goods	Music, radio, and television	Flowers and plants	Recreational services	Total	Higher education	Elementary education	Other education and research	Total	Religion	Welfare	Net total	Foreign travel by U.S. residents	Travel in the United States by aliens
	Cd139	Cd140	Cd141	Cd142	Cd143	Cd144	Cd145	Cd146	Cd147	Cd148	Cd149	Cd150	Cd151	Cd152
	Million 1987 dollars	Million 1987 dollars	Million 1987 dollars	Million 1987 dollars	Million 1987 dollars	Million 1987 dollars	Million 1987 dollars	Million 1987 dollars	Million 1987 dollars	Million 1987 dollars	Million 1987 dollars	Million 1987 dollars	Million 1987 dollars	Million 1987 dollars
1900	227	69	526	3,185	2,999	380	1,506	1,113	9,975	7,279	2,695	1,355	1,307	147
1901	249	78	571	3,583	3,130	396	1,462	1,272	9,681	7,064	2,617	1,373	1,325	144
1902	222	83	609	4,137	3,209	417	1,410	1,382	9,433	6,890	2,543	1,366	1,333	154
1903	202	94	661	4,466	3,315	431	1,517	1,366	9,164	6,779	2,385	1,389	1,352	154
1904	225	85	681	4,813	3,469	475	1,586	1,408	8,970	6,626	2,344	1,328	1,363	221
1905	236	98	681	5,167	3,581	499	1,580	1,502	8,741	6,476	2,265	1,240	1,370	305
1906	249	112	671	5,415	3,611	507	1,593	1,512	8,607	6,415	2,191	1,078	1,389	461
1907	289	114	706	5,469	3,754	609	1,546	1,599	8,213	6,231	1,982	972	1,407	569
1908	205	85	705	5,721	3,921	701	1,605	1,615	8,105	6,166	1,939	892	1,396	628
1909	253	105	701	5,930	4,036	723	1,663	1,650	7,928	6,030	1,898	902	1,415	637
1910	268	108	696	6,440	4,416	789	1,930	1,697	7,851	5,925	1,925	1,037	1,452	567
1911	291	112	724	6,919	4,549	842	1,952	1,755	7,638	5,865	1,773	985	1,456	608
1912	328	144	693	6,975	4,814	875	2,191	1,748	7,472	5,787	1,685	911	1,482	697
1913	400	155	673	7,391	4,957	887	2,287	1,782	7,350	5,736	1,614	901	1,489	714
1914	397	147	615	7,667	5,046	940	2,261	1,846	7,439	5,696	1,743	1,141	1,527	546
1915	382	137	629	7,832	5,137	1,002	2,295	1,840	7,485	5,645	1,840	1,449	1,597	343
1916	578	186	625	8,359	5,268	1,050	2,239	1,979	7,428	5,572	1,856	1,782	1,795	274
1917	908	216	565	8,906	5,084	994	2,130	1,960	10,644	5,589	5,056	2,182	2,234	352
1918	525	194	595	9,681	4,975	954	2,076	1,945	12,170	5,632	6,538	2,667	2,636	371
1919	501	280	566	10,590	5,377	1,202	2,059	2,115	8,317	5,783	2,535	2,737	2,792	409
1920	429	260	532	11,150	5,673	1,325	2,069	2,279	9,326	5,850	3,475	2,586	2,696	448
1921	334	177	600	10,175	5,756	1,446	2,106	2,204	8,690	5,911	2,779	2,500	2,759	618
1922	383	236	663	9,844	5,825	1,596	2,078	2,151	7,344	6,103	1,240	2,753	2,893	525
1923	463	263	794	10,784	6,096	1,803	2,173	2,120	7,709	6,495	1,215	2,543	2,796	606
1924	412	304	904	11,402	6,194	1,986	2,139	2,069	8,137	6,852	1,285	2,366	2,688	655
1925	465	352	861	11,546	6,526	2,183	2,222	2,121	9,287	7,066	2,221	2,636	2,934	665
1926	505	400	881	12,855	6,836	2,319	2,300	2,218	9,769	7,469	2,300	2,419	2,941	853
1927	494	354	1,012	13,745	7,040	2,533	2,324	2,183	9,763	7,375	2,388	2,339	2,915	899
1928	546	441	1,162	15,192	7,328	2,758	2,410	2,160	9,838	7,543	2,295	2,276	2,919	959
1929	604	475	1,128	16,314	7,511	2,893	2,410	2,208	10,140	7,713	2,427	2,103	2,893	1,084

1 Sales of alcoholic beverages were illegal, 1920–1932.

Source

Stanley Lebergott, *Consumer Expenditures: New Measures and Old Motives* (Princeton University Press, 1996), Table A2.

Documentation

These series are deflated versions of those in Table Cd1–77.

To deflate the nominal expenditures reported in Table Cd1–77, Lebergott employed the fixed-weight price deflators formerly used by the Bureau of Economic Analysis (BEA). These deflators have the advantage of computational ease, and the resulting series are additive. Subsequently, BEA converted to a chained annual-weight index, the so-called Fisher index, which is essentially a geometric mean of the conventional fixed-weight Laspeyres and Paasche indexes. The chained series, which are used to generate real consumption expenditures (Table Cd264–377), are neither additive nor strictly comparable to those generated by Lebergott. For a summary of these issues, see the text for Table Cd264–377. For a detailed discussion of the methodology, see J. Steven Landefeld and Robert P. Parker, "BEA's Chain Indexes, Time Series, and Measures of Long-Term Economic Growth," *Survey of Current Business* (May 1997): 58–68.

The details of the construction of the individual series can be found in Lebergott (1996) and Lebergott, *The American Economy: Income, Wealth and Want* (Princeton University Press, 1976).

Series Cd80–82. The nominal expenditures on food were deflated for 1900–1913 by creating a price index from the original retail price indexes for individual food items reported in U.S. Bureau of Labor,

Retail Prices of Food, 1890–1902, Bulletin number 77 (1908), pp. 181–332; and U.S. Bureau of Labor, *Retail Prices of Food, 1907 to June 1915,* Bulletin number 184 (1916), pp. 14–15. For 1913–1929, Lebergott used the retail food price index calculated by the U.S. Bureau of Labor Statistics (BLS) and reported in U.S. Bureau of the Census, *Historical Statistics of the United States* (1975), p. 211.

Series Cd83. To deflate the nominal expenditures on alcohol, Lebergott first constructed a benchmark for 1900 based on the retail prices of whiskey, beer, and wine reported in U.S. Department of the Treasury, *Imports, Exports, Immigration, and Navigation of the United States, 1886,* Quarterly Report, Chief, Bureau of Statistics (1887), pp. 393–5. That benchmark was extrapolated using wholesale price data from the Cincinnati area. See Lebergott (1996), pp. 83–4, 264.

Series Cd84. Nominal expenditures on tobacco for 1912–1929 were deflated by the average retail price of Camel and Chesterfield brand cigarettes reported in William Nicholls, *Price Policies in the Cigarette Industry* (Vanderbilt University Press, 1951), pp. 46, 80. This index was extrapolated to 1900 by the wholesale price index for tobacco products in William H. Shaw, *Value of Commodity Output since 1869* (National Bureau of Economic Research, 1947), Table IV-1.

Series Cd86–88. Nominal expenditures on shoes and clothing were deflated for 1914–1929 using the apparel series from U.S. Bureau of the Census, *Historical Statistics of the United States* (1975), p. 211. For earlier years, apparel figures were taken from Albert Rees, *Real Wages in Manufacturing, 1890–1914* (Princeton University Press, 1961), p. 74.

Series Cd89. Nominal expenditures on jewelry were deflated using the jewelry index in Shaw (1947), Table IV-1.

Series Cd90. Nominal expenditures on clothing services were deflated by the wage earnings index from Lebergott, *Manpower and Economic Growth* (McGraw-Hill, 1964), p. 526. That index was adjusted for productivity changes reported in John Kendrick, *Productivity Trends in the United States* (Princeton University Press, 1961).

Series Cd92. Expenditures on toilet articles were deflated using the deflator for the series entitled "drug, toilet, and household preparations" in Shaw (1947), Table IV-1, with minor adjustments explained in Lebergott (1996), p. 84.

Series Cd93. Barber and beauty expenditures were deflated by the wage earnings index for personal service from Lebergott (1964), p. 526. That index was adjusted for productivity changes reported in Kendrick (1961).

Series Cd94–98. Expenditures on housing were deflated for 1913–1929 using the rental housing series from U.S. Bureau of the Census, *Historical Statistics of the United States* (1975), p. 211. For earlier years the series was deflated using the rent index in Rees (1961), p. 74.

Series Cd100–104. Expenditures on furniture, furnishings, and appliances for 1913–1929 were deflated using the housefurnishings series from U.S. Bureau of the Census, *Historical Statistics of the United States* (1975), p. 211. For earlier years, housefurnishings figures were taken from Rees (1961), p. 74.

Series Cd105. Expenditures on cleaning materials before 1914 were deflated by first deriving benchmark estimates for census years and then interpolating using the price index for drugs, toilet, and household preparations from Shaw (1947), Table IV-1. After 1914, Lebergott used the price index for soap from U.S. Bureau of Labor Statistics, *Wholesale Prices 1913 to 1928,* Bulletin number 493 (1929), p. 212.

Series Cd106. Expenditures on stationery were deflated using benchmark prices on "fine writing paper" from U.S. Census, *Manufactures* (various years), which were then interpolated based on the price index for newspapers and magazines from Shaw (1947), Table IV-1.

Series Cd107. The deflators used on nominal expenditures on electricity were derived from the sources used to construct the usage figures reported in U.S. Bureau of the Census, *Historical Statistics of the United States* (1975), pp. 814, 827, with some additional interpolation. For the details, see Lebergott (1996), pp. 85, 265.

Series Cd108. Expenditures on gas were deflated for 1900–1914 using estimates from Rees (1961), p. 107. After 1914, the series was extrapolated by manufactured gas prices from U.S. Bureau of Labor Statistics, *Retail Prices, 1890 to 1929,* Bulletin number 495 (1929), p. 208.

Series Cd109. Expenditures on water (and refuse collection) were deflated using estimates of the annual pay of municipal employees in 1909–1925 from Willford I. King, *The National Income and Its Purchasing Power* (National Bureau of Economic Research, 1930), p. 365. This series was extrapolated to 1900–1908 and 1925–1929 by the average annual earnings of all state and local employees reported in Lebergott (1964), p. 526.

Series Cd110. Expenditures on fuel and ice were deflated using a series for fuel prices in 1900–1914 from Rees (1961), p. 110. That series was extrapolated to 1929 by a weighted average of prices for bituminous coal, anthracite coal, kerosene, and gas from various sources cited in Lebergott (1996), p. 265.

Series Cd111. Expenditures on telephone and telegraph service were deflated using an index of phone rates calculated from average operating revenue of phone companies from local calls per telephone in service in 1900 and 1920–1929 from U.S. Bureau of the Census, *Historical Statistics of the United States* (1975), pp. 783, 785–6. Figures for 1901–1919 were interpolated linearly.

Series Cd112. Expenditures on domestic service were deflated using the annual earnings of full-time employees in domestic service from Lebergott (1964), Table A-18.

Series Cd113. Expenditures on other household operation were deflated using the annual earnings of employees in personal service from Lebergott (1964), p. 526, adjusted for productivity changes derived from Kendrick (1961).

Series Cd115–116. Expenditures on drugs and ophthalmic appliances were deflated using the price index for drugs, toilet, and household preparations from Shaw (1947), Table IV-1.

Series Cd117. Expenditures on medical, dental, and other professional services were deflated using an index of average annual earning of all workers in those fields and derived from data in Lebergott (1964), Table A-18.

Series Cd118. With respect to expenditures for hospital care, Lebergott reports that "the percentage change in the average daily patient cost in hospitals for 1900 to 1923 is virtually identical with the change shown in the medical price index," though it is not clear to which medical price index this statement refers (1996), pp. 86–7.

Series Cd121. Expenditures on brokerage services were deflated using a weighted average of two indexes: "the average commission rate for brokers and dealers, and an index of real estate prices" (Lebergott 1996), p. 87. The source of the original data is Raymond Goldsmith, *A Study of Savings in the United States* (Princeton University Press, 1955), volume 1, pp. 527, 529, 625.

Series Cd125. Expenditures on funeral costs were deflated using a series derived from expenditure data and discussed in Lebergott (1976), pp. 362–3.

Series Cd122–123 and Cd126. Lebergott notes that expenditures on "other personal business" were deflated using "annual earnings of full-time equivalent employees in finance, insurance, and real estate, adjusted for the trend in their productivity" (1996), p. 87. This methodology seems to have been employed to deflate banking and financial services and life insurance as well.

Series Cd128–129. Expenditures on motor vehicles and wagons, and on auto tires, tubes, and accessories, were deflated using the corresponding series in Shaw (1947), Table IV-1.

(continued)

TABLE Cd78–152   Consumption expenditures, by type: 1900–1929   [1987 dollars]   Continued

Series Cd130. Expenditures on automobile repairs were deflated using a weighted average of indexes for materials and labor. The materials series is from Shaw (1947), Table IV-1. The labor series is from Lebergott (1964), p. 526.

Series Cd131. Expenditures on gasoline and oil for 1918–1929 were deflated using the retail prices of gasoline in fifty cities and reported in American Petroleum Institute, *Petroleum Facts and Figures*, Centennial Edition (Petroleum Institute, 1959).

Series Cd132. Expenditures on auto insurance and tolls were deflated using average annual earnings in finance, real estate, and insurance from Lebergott (1964), p. 527.

Series Cd133–134. Expenditures on public transportation were deflated using average annual earnings in local and intercity rail transport from Lebergott (1964), p. 525, with adjustments discussed in Lebergott (1996), p. 266.

Series Cd136–137. Lebergott constructed price indexes to deflate expenditures on books, maps, magazines, and newspapers from sets of specific publications reported in Lebergott (1996), p. 88.

Series Cd138–139. Expenditures on toys and wheel goods were deflated using a price series for semidurable consumption goods reported in Shaw (1947), Table IV-1.

Series Cd140. Music and radio expenditures for 1900–1923 were deflated using the price index for musical instruments from Shaw (1947), Table IV-1. Because of changes in the radio market after 1923, Lebergott (1996, pp. 88–9) adjusted Shaw's series using price data from the Census of Manufactures.

Series Cd141. Lebergott reports that the deflator for expenditures on flowers and plants from "the index for prices received by farmers for food grains was used to extrapolate the unpublished BEA index" (1996, p. 267).

Series Cd142. Expenditures on recreational services were deflated using the average annual earnings of workers in personal services, from Lebergott (1964), p. 526, adjusted for productivity changes calculated from Kendrick (1961).

Series Cd143–146. Expenditures on education were deflated using the average annual earnings in private education in Lebergott (1964), p. 527.

Series Cd148. Expenditures on religion were deflated using an index of ministerial salaries based on benchmarks for 1906 and 1916 from the *Census of Religious Bodies: 1916* (U.S. Government Printing Office, 1919), p. 94. These were then extrapolated by the average salary of ministers as estimated by Paul Douglas, *Real Wages in the United States, 1890–1926* (Houghton Mifflin, 1930), p. 386, and by Simon Kuznets, *National Income and Its Composition, 1919–1938* (National Bureau of Economic Research, 1941), pp. 762, 765.

Series Cd149. Expenditures on welfare were deflated using an index of earnings of social workers for 1913–1925 calculated from data reported in Ralph Hurlin, *Social Work Salaries* (Russell Sage Foundation, 1926), p. 6. That series was extrapolated back to 1900 using the index of ministerial salaries employed in the construction of series Cd148.

Series Cd150. Net foreign travel before 1915 was deflated using data from Paul Dickens, *The Transition Period in American International Financing: 1897–1914* (unpublished manuscript, June 1933). From 1915 through 1929, the data are from August Maffry, U.S. Bureau of Foreign and Domestic Commerce, *Economic Series Number 4, Overseas Travel and Travel Expenditures in the Balance of International Payments of the United States, 1919–1938* (1939).

Series Cd151–152. The component series were deflated, respectively, by UK prices reported in Charles H. Feinstein, *National Income, Expenditure and Outlay of the United Kingdom, 1855–1965* (Cambridge University Press, 1972), Table 62, and the series for food, housing, and transportation reported in Table Cd1–77.

TABLE Cd153–263　Consumption expenditures, by type: 1929–1999
Contributed by Lee A. Craig

Year	Total	Food and tobacco									Clothing, accessories, and jewelry						
		Total	Food purchased for off-premises consumption	Purchased meals and beverages	Food furnished to employees	Food produced and consumed on farms	Tobacco products	Food, excluding alcoholic beverages	Total	Shoes	Clothing, and accessories, except shoes				Cleaning storage, and repair of clothing and shoes	Jewelry and watches	Other
											Total	Women's and children's	Men's and boys'	Standard clothing issued to military personnel			
	Cd153	Cd154	Cd155	Cd156	Cd157	Cd158	Cd159	Cd160	Cd161	Cd162	Cd163	Cd164	Cd165	Cd166	Cd167	Cd168	Cd169
	Billion dollars	Billion dollars	Billion dollars	Billion dollars	Billion dollars	Billion dollars	Billion dollars	Billion dollars	Billion dollars	Billion dollars	Billion dollars	Billion dollars	Billion dollars	Billion dollars	Billion dollars	Billion dollars	Billion dollars
1929	77.5	21.2	14.8	2.9	0.3	1.6	1.7	19.5	11.2	1.7	7.7	4.7	3.0	0.0	1.1	0.6	0.2
1930	70.2	19.4	13.5	2.8	0.2	1.4	1.5	18.0	9.7	1.4	6.7	4.1	2.6	0.0	1.0	0.5	0.1
1931	60.7	16.2	10.8	2.5	0.2	1.2	1.5	14.7	8.2	1.2	5.7	3.5	2.2	0.0	0.9	0.3	0.1
1932	48.7	12.7	8.2	2.1	0.2	0.9	1.3	11.4	6.0	1.0	4.0	2.4	1.6	0.0	0.7	0.3	0.1
1933	45.9	12.8	8.6	1.8	0.2	0.9	1.2	10.9	5.4	0.9	3.7	2.3	1.5	0.0	0.6	0.2	0.1
1934	51.5	15.6	10.8	2.2	0.2	1.0	1.4	12.2	6.6	1.1	4.6	2.8	1.8	0.0	0.6	0.2	0.1
1935	55.9	17.6	12.2	2.6	0.2	1.2	1.4	13.6	7.0	1.0	5.0	3.1	1.9	0.0	0.7	0.2	0.1
1936	62.2	20.0	13.9	3.0	0.2	1.3	1.5	15.3	7.7	1.1	5.4	3.2	2.2	0.0	0.8	0.3	0.1
1937	66.8	21.6	14.8	3.5	0.3	1.3	1.7	16.5	8.1	1.3	5.5	3.3	2.3	0.0	0.8	0.3	0.1
1938	64.2	20.6	14.1	3.4	0.2	1.1	1.7	15.6	8.0	1.3	5.5	3.3	2.2	0.0	0.8	0.3	0.1
1939	67.2	20.9	14.2	3.6	0.3	1.1	1.8	15.7	8.4	1.2	5.9	3.6	2.3	0.0	0.8	0.4	0.1
1940	71.2	22.0	14.9	3.9	0.3	1.1	1.9	16.6	8.9	1.3	6.2	3.8	2.4	0.0	0.9	0.4	0.1
1941	81.0	25.4	17.0	4.6	0.5	1.3	2.1	19.2	10.5	1.4	7.1	4.3	2.8	0.2	1.0	0.6	0.1
1942	88.9	30.7	20.1	5.7	0.9	1.6	2.3	23.3	13.1	1.8	8.5	5.3	3.2	0.7	1.2	0.7	0.2
1943	99.7	35.8	22.3	7.1	1.7	2.1	2.6	27.4	16.0	1.9	10.5	6.9	3.5	1.0	1.5	0.9	0.2
1944	108.5	39.3	24.1	8.1	2.4	2.1	2.6	29.9	17.5	2.0	11.6	7.8	3.8	1.0	1.6	1.0	0.2
1945	119.8	43.5	26.2	9.5	2.8	2.2	2.9	33.2	19.6	2.3	13.1	8.8	4.3	1.1	1.7	1.2	0.3
1946	144.2	50.7	32.7	10.9	1.3	2.5	3.4	39.0	22.0	2.8	15.1	9.7	5.4	0.4	2.2	1.4	0.2
1947	162.3	56.1	37.9	10.9	1.0	2.6	3.7	43.7	22.8	3.0	15.6	9.9	5.6	0.2	2.4	1.4	0.2
1948	175.4	58.2	39.6	11.0	1.0	2.5	4.0	46.3	24.2	3.1	16.8	10.9	5.9	0.2	2.5	1.4	0.2
1949	178.8	56.6	38.6	10.8	1.0	2.1	4.1	44.8	23.3	3.1	16.0	10.2	5.8	0.2	2.5	1.3	0.2
1950	192.7	58.1	39.8	11.1	1.1	1.9	4.3	46.0	23.7	3.3	16.0	10.0	6.0	0.3	2.5	1.3	0.2
1951	208.6	65.2	44.2	12.7	1.6	2.2	4.5	52.4	25.6	3.3	17.5	10.9	6.6	0.4	2.7	1.4	0.2
1952	219.7	69.0	46.7	13.6	1.8	2.1	4.9	55.3	26.6	3.3	18.5	11.6	6.8	0.3	2.8	1.5	0.3
1953	233.4	70.5	47.8	14.1	1.7	1.9	5.1	56.3	27.0	3.3	18.7	12.0	6.8	0.2	2.9	1.6	0.3
1954	240.5	71.7	49.3	14.4	1.5	1.7	4.9	57.7	27.2	3.3	18.9	12.0	6.8	0.1	2.9	1.7	0.3
1955	259.0	73.6	50.9	14.9	1.3	1.6	5.1	59.3	28.4	3.6	19.6	12.5	7.1	0.1	3.0	1.8	0.3
1956	271.9	76.7	53.1	15.6	1.2	1.5	5.3	61.7	29.7	3.8	20.5	13.1	7.4	0.1	3.1	1.8	0.4
1957	287.0	80.7	56.2	16.3	1.2	1.4	5.7	65.2	30.0	3.8	20.6	13.3	7.4	0.1	3.2	1.8	0.4
1958	296.6	83.9	58.8	16.4	1.2	1.4	6.0	67.9	30.3	4.1	20.7	13.5	7.2	0.1	3.1	1.9	0.4
1959	318.1	87.2	60.8	17.5	1.2	1.2	6.6	70.1	32.0	4.4	22.0	14.3	7.7	0.1	3.2	2.0	0.5
1960	332.3	89.2	62.0	18.1	1.2	1.1	6.9	71.6	32.7	4.5	22.4	14.6	7.8	0.0	3.3	1.9	0.5
1961	342.7	91.1	63.2	18.5	1.3	1.0	7.1	73.2	33.5	4.6	23.0	15.0	8.0	0.1	3.3	1.9	0.6
1962	363.8	93.3	64.2	19.6	1.3	0.9	7.2	74.6	35.0	4.8	24.2	15.8	8.3	0.1	3.4	2.0	0.6
1963	383.1	95.8	65.6	20.5	1.4	0.9	7.5	76.4	36.0	4.8	24.9	16.4	8.5	0.1	3.5	2.2	0.6
1964	411.7	101.1	69.5	21.9	1.4	0.8	7.6	81.2	39.1	5.2	27.1	17.8	9.3	0.1	3.6	2.4	0.7

(continued)

TABLE Cd153–263 Consumption expenditures, by type: 1929–1999 Continued

		Food and tobacco							Clothing, accessories, and jewelry								
	Total	Total	Food purchased for off-premises consumption	Purchased meals and beverages	Food furnished to employees	Food produced and consumed on farms	Tobacco products	Food, excluding alcoholic beverages	Clothing, and accessories, except shoes		Total	Women's and children's	Men's and boys'	Standard clothing issued to military personnel	Cleaning storage, and repair of clothing and shoes	Jewelry and watches	Other
									Total	Shoes							
Year	Cd153	Cd154	Cd155	Cd156	Cd157	Cd158	Cd159	Cd160	Cd161	Cd162	Cd163	Cd164	Cd165	Cd166	Cd167	Cd168	Cd169
	Billion dollars	Billion dollars	Billion dollars	Billion dollars	Billion dollars	Billion dollars	Billion dollars	Billion dollars	Billion dollars	Billion dollars	Billion dollars	Billion dollars	Billion dollars	Billion dollars	Billion dollars	Billion dollars	Billion dollars
1965	444.3	108.8	74.5	23.9	1.5	0.8	8.1	87.8	41.4	5.4	28.6	18.6	9.9	0.1	3.8	2.7	0.8
1966	481.8	117.9	80.8	25.9	1.8	0.8	8.5	95.5	45.5	6.0	31.2	20.2	11.0	0.2	4.0	3.2	0.9
1967	508.7	121.4	83.0	26.8	1.9	0.7	8.9	98.4	47.8	6.4	32.6	20.9	11.8	0.2	4.1	3.5	1.0
1968	558.7	131.7	89.4	30.2	2.0	0.7	9.4	106.9	52.5	7.1	35.9	23.0	12.9	0.2	4.3	3.8	1.2
1969	605.5	141.3	96.0	32.7	2.1	0.7	9.8	114.8	56.2	7.8	38.5	24.6	13.9	0.2	4.5	4.0	1.2
1970	648.9	154.6	104.4	36.5	2.1	0.8	10.8	125.1	57.6	7.8	39.8	25.6	14.3	0.2	4.5	4.1	1.3
1971	702.4	161.0	108.2	38.8	2.0	0.7	11.3	129.3	61.8	8.1	43.4	28.1	15.3	0.1	4.3	4.4	1.3
1972	770.7	173.6	115.5	43.0	2.0	0.9	12.2	139.3	67.1	8.9	47.4	30.4	17.0	0.1	4.5	4.8	1.5
1973	852.5	192.9	128.0	48.4	2.2	1.1	13.2	155.6	74.7	9.8	52.6	33.7	18.9	0.1	4.4	6.0	1.8
1974	932.4	215.9	144.8	53.2	2.7	1.1	14.1	175.6	79.3	9.9	56.0	36.0	20.0	0.1	4.4	7.0	1.9
1975	1,030.3	238.3	158.6	60.4	3.2	1.1	15.1	194.6	85.6	10.3	60.4	38.8	21.6	0.1	4.5	8.1	2.2
1976	1,149.8	259.3	169.8	68.0	3.6	1.1	16.8	211.9	93.7	11.1	65.5	42.1	23.3	0.1	4.7	9.8	2.5
1977	1,278.4	279.6	182.8	75.0	3.7	1.1	17.0	229.5	102.8	12.2	71.8	45.9	25.8	0.1	4.9	11.0	2.7
1978	1,430.4	307.8	199.2	85.0	4.3	1.1	18.3	253.4	115.1	14.1	80.1	51.7	28.4	0.1	5.3	12.3	3.2
1979	1,596.3	343.8	221.7	96.7	4.9	1.3	19.2	283.8	123.4	16.0	85.0	55.0	30.1	0.1	5.5	13.0	3.7
1980	1,762.9	376.8	243.4	105.9	5.5	1.2	20.9	310.6	132.3	17.4	89.8	58.0	31.8	0.2	5.7	15.0	4.2
1981	1,944.2	406.3	260.4	115.8	6.2	1.1	22.8	334.4	143.8	19.3	97.7	63.2	34.5	0.1	5.9	16.0	4.8
1982	2,079.3	427.7	272.5	123.3	6.5	1.0	24.3	351.7	147.0	19.2	101.1	65.7	35.5	0.2	5.8	15.6	5.1
1983	2,286.4	451.3	283.1	133.3	6.4	1.0	27.5	369.3	161.1	20.4	110.3	72.1	38.2	0.2	6.3	17.4	6.5
1984	2,498.4	476.7	297.7	142.4	6.4	0.9	29.2	391.5	175.8	21.6	120.8	79.4	41.4	0.2	6.9	19.8	6.7
1985	2,712.6	498.5	310.5	150.0	6.2	0.9	30.8	408.7	188.3	22.9	129.1	85.3	43.8	0.1	7.3	21.1	7.8
1986	2,895.2	524.2	323.7	161.5	6.0	0.9	32.2	429.9	204.1	24.5	138.5	92.1	46.4	0.2	7.7	24.3	9.0
1987	3,105.3	549.8	332.1	176.7	5.7	0.7	34.5	452.2	218.9	26.0	148.2	98.4	49.8	0.2	8.4	26.2	9.9
1988	3,356.6	588.3	351.3	195.4	6.1	0.7	34.7	486.8	235.7	27.6	157.7	104.2	53.5	0.2	9.6	28.3	12.3
1989	3,596.7	630.5	374.7	210.1	6.5	0.6	38.6	521.1	252.6	30.4	168.4	110.7	57.6	0.2	10.7	29.2	13.8
1990	3,831.5	677.9	401.6	227.8	6.8	0.7	41.0	558.7	261.7	31.5	172.4	113.0	59.4	0.2	11.5	30.3	15.8
1991	3,971.2	700.0	413.5	236.5	6.9	0.6	42.4	575.7	263.7	31.3	177.2	115.6	61.5	0.2	11.2	30.2	13.7
1992	4,209.7	717.3	415.7	246.0	7.1	0.6	48.0	586.8	280.9	32.9	188.7	123.4	65.3	0.3	11.4	31.6	16.0
1993	4,454.7	742.8	428.3	261.7	7.4	0.6	44.9	612.6	294.0	34.0	196.8	128.4	68.3	0.3	11.4	34.1	17.4
1994	4,716.4	773.6	445.5	274.5	7.6	0.5	45.4	639.4	307.2	35.8	204.6	132.3	72.3	0.3	11.6	36.2	18.6
1995	4,969.0	802.5	459.8	287.5	8.0	0.5	46.7	663.2	317.3	37.1	210.4	135.5	74.9	0.3	12.2	38.1	19.2
1996	5,237.5	834.1	476.7	300.5	8.2	0.5	48.2	689.1	333.3	38.8	219.5	140.8	78.6	0.3	12.7	40.3	21.7
1997	5,529.3	862.0	486.5	316.6	8.5	0.5	49.8	710.9	348.0	40.1	231.3	148.0	83.3	0.3	13.2	41.2	22.0
1998	5,850.9	900.2	504.2	332.2	8.9	0.5	54.4	737.8	368.3	41.7	244.4	156.2	88.2	0.3	13.5	44.2	24.2
1999	6,268.7	963.8	531.8	356.3	9.1	0.5	66.0	782.3	397.2	43.3	263.4	168.7	94.7	0.3	14.2	48.8	27.3

Year	Personal care			Housing					Household operation						
	Total	Toilet articles and preparations	Barbershops, beauty parlors, and health clubs	Total	Owner-occupied nonfarm dwellings – space rent	Tenant-occupied nonfarm dwellings – rent	Rental value of farm dwellings	Other	Total	Furniture	Kitchen and other household appliances	China, glassware, tableware, and utensils	Other durable housefurnishings	Semidurable housefurnishings	Cleaning and polishing preparations, and miscellaneous household supplies and paper products
	Cd170	Cd171	Cd172	Cd173	Cd174	Cd175	Cd176	Cd177	Cd178	Cd179	Cd180	Cd181	Cd182	Cd183	Cd184
	Billion dollars	Billion dollars	Billion dollars	Billion dollars	Billion dollars	Billion dollars	Billion dollars	Billion dollars	Billion dollars	Billion dollars	Billion dollars	Billion dollars	Billion dollars	Billion dollars	Billion dollars
1929	1.1	0.6	0.5	11.7	5.9	4.5	0.9	0.3	10.7	1.2	0.7	0.6	1.1	0.7	0.5
1930	1.0	0.5	0.5	11.2	5.6	4.5	0.9	0.3	9.5	0.9	0.6	0.4	0.9	0.6	0.5
1931	1.0	0.5	0.5	10.5	5.1	4.3	0.8	0.3	8.4	0.8	0.5	0.4	0.8	0.5	0.4
1932	0.8	0.4	0.4	9.2	4.4	3.9	0.7	0.2	6.8	0.5	0.3	0.4	0.6	0.4	0.3
1933	0.7	0.3	0.3	8.1	3.8	3.4	0.6	0.2	6.4	0.5	0.4	0.4	0.5	0.4	0.3
1934	0.8	0.4	0.4	7.8	3.6	3.3	0.6	0.2	7.2	0.5	0.5	0.4	0.6	0.4	0.4
1935	0.8	0.4	0.4	7.9	3.6	3.3	0.7	0.3	7.7	0.7	0.6	0.4	0.6	0.5	0.4
1936	0.9	0.4	0.5	8.2	3.8	3.5	0.7	0.3	8.8	0.8	0.7	0.5	0.8	0.6	0.4
1937	1.0	0.4	0.5	8.8	4.0	3.8	0.7	0.3	9.4	0.9	0.8	0.5	0.9	0.6	0.5
1938	1.0	0.4	0.5	9.2	4.1	4.0	0.7	0.3	8.8	0.8	0.6	0.5	0.8	0.6	0.5
1939	1.0	0.5	0.5	9.4	4.2	4.1	0.7	0.3	9.6	0.9	0.7	0.5	0.9	0.7	0.5
1940	1.0	0.5	0.5	9.7	4.3	4.3	0.7	0.3	10.4	1.1	0.8	0.5	1.0	0.7	0.5
1941	1.2	0.6	0.6	10.4	4.7	4.6	0.8	0.4	11.8	1.3	1.1	0.6	1.2	0.9	0.6
1942	1.4	0.7	0.6	11.2	5.2	4.8	0.8	0.4	12.7	1.3	0.7	0.7	1.3	1.1	0.7
1943	1.6	0.9	0.7	11.8	5.6	4.8	0.9	0.5	13.1	1.2	0.3	0.6	1.4	1.3	0.8
1944	1.8	1.0	0.8	12.3	6.1	4.8	1.0	0.5	14.0	1.3	0.2	0.6	1.4	1.5	0.8
1945	2.0	1.1	0.9	12.8	6.5	4.7	1.1	0.6	15.5	1.5	0.3	0.8	1.5	1.5	0.7
1946	2.1	1.1	1.0	14.2	7.4	4.9	1.3	0.6	19.9	2.2	1.6	1.3	2.2	2.0	0.9
1947	2.2	1.2	1.0	16.0	8.5	5.3	1.4	0.8	23.7	2.5	2.9	1.3	2.4	2.1	1.5
1948	2.3	1.3	1.0	17.9	9.7	5.9	1.5	0.8	26.1	2.8	3.1	1.4	2.7	2.4	1.6
1949	2.3	1.3	1.0	19.6	11.0	6.5	1.4	0.8	25.6	2.7	2.8	1.4	2.7	2.3	1.6
1950	2.4	1.4	1.1	21.7	12.4	7.1	1.5	0.8	29.1	3.1	3.6	1.5	3.1	2.6	1.8
1951	2.7	1.5	1.2	24.3	14.1	7.7	1.6	0.9	31.1	3.2	3.5	1.6	3.5	2.8	2.0
1952	2.9	1.6	1.3	27.0	15.9	8.4	1.7	0.9	31.5	3.5	3.5	1.6	3.2	2.6	1.9
1953	3.1	1.7	1.4	29.9	17.9	9.2	1.8	1.0	33.0	3.7	3.6	1.6	3.1	2.6	2.1
1954	3.4	1.8	1.6	32.3	19.7	9.8	1.7	1.1	33.7	3.8	3.7	1.6	2.9	2.4	2.3
1955	3.7	1.9	1.7	34.4	21.4	10.1	1.7	1.1	37.3	4.4	4.1	1.7	3.3	2.6	2.5
1956	4.6	2.4	2.2	39.3	25.0	10.5	1.7	1.2	39.8	4.6	4.3	1.8	3.6	2.7	2.7
1957	4.1	2.2	2.0	36.7	23.2	11.2	1.8	1.4	41.2	4.5	4.3	1.7	3.8	2.7	2.9
1958	4.9	2.6	2.3	42.0	27.0	11.8	1.9	1.4	42.3	4.5	4.1	1.7	3.8	2.6	3.1
1959	5.2	2.7	2.5	45.0	29.0	12.5	2.0	1.4	45.0	4.8	4.4	1.7	4.1	2.7	3.5
1960	5.6	3.0	2.6	48.2	31.3	13.3	2.1	1.5	46.7	4.7	4.3	1.7	4.2	2.8	3.7
1961	6.1	3.3	2.8	51.2	33.3	14.2	2.2	1.5	48.2	4.8	4.3	1.8	4.3	2.9	4.2
1962	6.7	3.6	3.1	54.7	35.7	15.1	2.3	1.6	51.0	5.1	4.3	1.9	4.6	3.2	4.6
1963	7.0	3.9	3.2	58.0	37.8	16.0	2.4	1.8	54.0	5.5	4.5	1.9	5.1	3.3	4.9
1964	7.5	4.2	3.4	61.4	40.0	17.0	2.4	1.9	58.4	6.1	4.9	2.1	5.8	3.7	5.3

(continued)

TABLE Cd153–263   Consumption expenditures, by type: 1929–1999   Continued

	Personal care			Housing					Household operation						
	Total	Toilet articles and preparations	Barbershops, beauty parlors, and health clubs	Total	Owner-occupied nonfarm dwellings – space rent	Tenant-occupied nonfarm dwellings – rent	Rental value of farm dwellings	Other	Total	Furniture	Kitchen and other household appliances	China, glassware, tableware, and utensils	Other durable housefurnishings	Semidurable housefurnishings	Cleaning and polishing preparations, and miscellaneous household supplies and paper products
	Cd170	Cd171	Cd172	Cd173	Cd174	Cd175	Cd176	Cd177	Cd178	Cd179	Cd180	Cd181	Cd182	Cd183	Cd184
Year	Billion dollars	Billion dollars	Billion dollars	Billion dollars	Billion dollars	Billion dollars	Billion dollars	Billion dollars	Billion dollars	Billion dollars	Billion dollars	Billion dollars	Billion dollars	Billion dollars	Billion dollars
1965	8.1	4.5	3.6	65.4	42.7	18.2	2.5	2.1	62.1	6.5	4.9	2.4	6.3	3.9	5.7
1966	9.0	5.0	4.0	69.5	45.3	19.2	2.6	2.3	67.3	7.0	5.3	2.7	6.9	4.3	6.3
1967	9.8	5.4	4.4	74.1	48.3	20.4	2.7	2.6	71.0	7.3	5.5	2.9	7.2	4.6	6.7
1968	10.5	5.9	4.6	79.7	51.9	22.2	2.8	2.8	76.4	7.9	6.2	3.3	7.9	4.9	7.1
1969	10.9	6.2	4.6	86.8	56.6	24.0	3.0	3.1	81.3	8.4	6.8	3.4	8.0	4.9	7.6
1970	11.5	6.6	4.9	94.0	61.3	26.0	3.3	3.4	85.0	8.6	7.3	3.5	7.9	4.9	8.2
1971	11.7	6.9	4.8	102.7	67.3	28.4	3.5	3.5	90.3	9.2	7.9	3.6	8.1	5.0	8.4
1972	12.3	7.4	4.9	112.1	73.7	30.8	3.7	3.9	99.7	10.4	9.0	4.0	9.0	5.3	8.9
1973	13.6	8.3	5.2	122.7	81.0	33.7	3.8	4.3	111.7	11.8	9.9	4.6	10.3	5.9	10.0
1974	14.8	9.3	5.5	134.1	89.7	35.8	3.9	4.7	123.8	12.5	10.3	5.1	11.5	6.3	11.4
1975	16.1	10.3	5.8	147.0	98.8	39.0	4.0	5.3	136.0	12.8	10.6	5.6	12.0	6.6	12.5
1976	17.5	11.3	6.2	161.5	108.7	42.6	4.1	6.2	152.6	14.1	11.5	6.3	13.5	7.2	13.5
1977	19.9	12.6	7.3	179.5	121.3	47.0	4.3	6.8	171.4	16.3	12.7	7.1	15.2	7.9	14.6
1978	21.9	14.0	8.0	201.7	138.1	51.1	4.6	7.8	190.5	18.0	13.6	8.3	17.0	8.7	16.8
1979	23.8	15.5	8.3	226.5	156.9	55.7	4.9	9.1	212.7	20.3	14.8	9.3	18.9	9.7	19.4
1980	25.5	16.9	8.6	255.1	178.4	61.8	5.1	9.8	233.8	20.7	15.1	10.3	20.0	10.6	21.9
1981	27.1	18.4	8.7	287.7	200.9	71.0	5.2	10.6	255.0	21.7	15.5	11.5	21.2	11.8	24.0
1982	28.0	19.3	8.7	313.0	217.9	78.6	5.0	11.4	272.4	21.0	15.2	12.5	21.7	12.4	25.7
1983	31.8	21.4	10.5	338.7	235.6	85.5	5.1	12.5	297.3	23.8	16.8	13.0	24.5	13.7	27.1
1984	34.7	23.7	11.0	370.3	257.2	94.4	5.1	13.6	323.2	27.2	18.4	13.7	27.7	15.4	29.2
1985	37.6	25.7	11.9	406.8	279.3	107.8	5.0	14.6	344.0	29.3	19.8	14.0	29.4	16.4	30.6
1986	40.7	27.7	12.9	442.0	303.1	118.9	4.9	15.2	360.8	32.5	21.2	14.8	32.7	18.3	32.0
1987	44.5	30.0	14.5	476.4	328.2	126.5	4.9	16.8	377.8	34.5	21.8	14.7	36.3	19.3	33.1
1988	47.7	31.8	15.9	511.9	356.1	132.4	4.8	18.5	399.8	35.9	22.7	15.9	38.3	20.8	35.1
1989	51.0	33.9	17.1	546.4	383.1	138.5	5.0	19.8	423.4	39.5	23.9	17.1	38.6	21.7	37.1
1990	53.7	36.0	17.7	585.6	410.7	148.7	5.1	21.0	433.6	38.4	23.7	17.9	38.6	22.5	38.9
1991	54.9	36.9	18.0	616.0	434.1	154.5	5.2	22.1	444.3	37.7	23.3	18.1	37.3	23.3	39.7
1992	58.0	37.9	20.1	641.3	452.3	159.3	5.3	24.3	463.6	39.0	24.3	19.6	38.8	25.6	41.1
1993	60.1	40.0	20.1	666.5	475.2	160.3	5.6	25.5	497.2	41.8	25.9	20.8	41.3	26.8	43.1
1994	63.3	42.5	20.8	704.7	502.6	169.3	5.9	27.0	528.2	45.1	27.5	22.5	45.1	28.5	45.4
1995	67.4	45.0	22.4	740.8	529.3	177.0	6.0	28.5	555.0	47.5	29.1	23.8	47.7	29.7	47.3
1996	71.6	48.0	23.5	772.5	555.4	180.6	6.2	30.2	589.2	50.9	30.0	25.4	50.5	31.0	49.8
1997	76.1	50.6	25.5	810.5	585.5	186.1	6.4	32.5	617.8	53.8	30.8	27.2	53.5	33.1	51.4
1998	80.5	53.4	27.1	858.2	622.7	193.8	6.7	35.0	643.8	56.4	32.2	29.2	57.4	35.2	53.5
1999	86.0	57.5	28.5	906.2	661.1	200.6	7.0	37.5	682.5	60.3	34.5	31.8	62.8	38.3	57.1

Year	Stationery and writing supplies Cd185	Household operation — Total Cd186	Electricity Cd187	Gas Cd188	Water and other sanitary services Cd189	Fuel oil and coal Cd190	Telephone and telegraph Cd191	Domestic service Cd192	Other Cd193	Medical care — Total Cd194	Drug preparations and sundries Cd195	Ophthalmic products and orthopedic appliances Cd196	Physicians Cd197	Dentists Cd198	Other professional services Cd199
	Billion dollars	Billion dollars	Billion dollars	Billion dollars	Billion dollars	Billion dollars	Billion dollars	Billion dollars	Billion dollars	Billion dollars	Billion dollars	Billion dollars	Billion dollars	Billion dollars	Billion dollars
1929	0.1	3.1	0.6	0.5	0.3	1.6	0.6	1.7	0.3	3.1	0.6	0.1	1.0	0.5	0.3
1930	0.1	3.1	0.7	0.6	0.3	1.5	0.6	1.5	0.3	3.0	0.6	0.1	0.9	0.5	0.2
1931	0.1	2.9	0.7	0.6	0.3	1.3	0.6	1.1	0.3	2.7	0.5	0.1	0.8	0.4	0.2
1932	0.1	2.6	0.7	0.5	0.3	1.1	0.5	0.8	0.3	2.3	0.4	0.1	0.7	0.3	0.2
1933	0.1	2.6	0.6	0.5	0.3	1.2	0.4	0.7	0.2	2.1	0.4	0.1	0.6	0.3	0.1
1934	0.1	2.7	0.7	0.5	0.3	1.3	0.4	0.9	0.3	2.3	0.5	0.1	0.7	0.3	0.1
1935	0.1	2.8	0.7	0.5	0.3	1.3	0.5	0.9	0.3	2.4	0.5	0.1	0.7	0.3	0.2
1936	0.1	3.0	0.7	0.5	0.3	1.4	0.5	1.0	0.3	2.6	0.5	0.1	0.8	0.3	0.2
1937	0.1	3.0	0.8	0.5	0.3	1.4	0.5	1.2	0.3	2.8	0.6	0.2	0.9	0.4	0.2
1938	0.1	3.0	0.8	0.5	0.3	1.3	0.5	1.0	0.3	2.8	0.6	0.2	0.8	0.4	0.2
1939	0.1	3.1	0.8	0.5	0.3	1.4	0.6	1.1	0.3	3.0	0.6	0.2	0.9	0.4	0.2
1940	0.2	3.4	0.9	0.6	0.4	1.5	0.6	1.2	0.4	3.2	0.6	0.2	0.9	0.4	0.2
1941	0.2	3.6	1.0	0.6	0.4	1.7	0.7	1.2	0.4	3.5	0.7	0.2	1.0	0.5	0.2
1942	0.2	3.9	1.0	0.6	0.4	1.9	0.8	1.5	0.5	3.9	0.8	0.3	1.0	0.5	0.2
1943	0.3	4.1	1.0	0.6	0.4	2.0	1.0	1.6	0.6	4.4	1.0	0.3	1.1	0.5	0.2
1944	0.4	4.2	1.1	0.7	0.4	2.0	1.1	1.9	0.7	4.9	1.1	0.3	1.3	0.6	0.2
1945	0.4	4.5	1.2	0.7	0.4	2.2	1.2	2.1	0.8	5.2	1.1	0.3	1.4	0.6	0.3
1946	0.4	5.0	1.3	0.8	0.5	2.5	1.3	2.1	0.8	6.4	1.3	0.4	1.8	0.8	0.3
1947	0.4	5.8	1.5	0.9	0.5	3.0	1.4	2.3	0.9	7.4	1.3	0.4	2.1	0.8	0.4
1948	0.5	6.6	1.7	1.0	0.5	3.4	1.6	2.4	1.0	8.5	1.5	0.4	2.4	0.9	0.5
1949	0.5	6.5	1.9	1.0	0.6	3.1	1.7	2.4	1.0	8.8	1.6	0.5	2.5	0.9	0.5
1950	0.5	7.3	2.1	1.2	0.6	3.4	1.9	2.6	1.1	9.4	1.7	0.5	2.6	1.0	0.5
1951	0.6	2.7	1.0	0.5	7.9	2.4	1.3	0.7	3.5	2.2	2.7	1.2	10.2	2.0	0.5
1952	0.6	8.3	2.7	1.5	0.7	3.5	2.4	2.6	1.3	11.2	2.1	0.6	3.0	1.1	0.5
1953	0.7	8.7	2.9	1.6	0.8	3.4	2.7	2.7	1.4	12.4	2.2	0.6	3.3	1.2	0.6
1954	0.7	9.4	3.2	1.8	0.8	3.5	2.8	2.6	1.5	13.4	2.2	0.6	3.7	1.4	0.6
1955	0.8	10.2	3.5	2.0	0.9	3.8	3.1	3.1	1.6	14.2	2.4	0.6	3.8	1.5	0.7
1956	0.8	11.0	3.8	2.3	1.0	3.9	3.3	3.3	1.7	15.5	2.7	0.7	4.2	1.7	0.7
1957	0.9	11.6	4.1	2.4	1.1	4.1	3.6	3.3	1.8	17.1	3.0	0.7	4.6	1.8	0.8
1958	0.9	12.3	4.4	2.7	1.1	4.2	3.9	3.5	1.9	18.7	3.2	0.7	5.1	1.9	0.9
1959	1.1	12.9	4.7	2.9	1.2	4.0	4.2	3.6	2.1	20.6	3.5	0.6	5.5	2.0	1.3
1960	1.1	13.5	5.1	3.3	1.4	3.8	4.5	3.8	2.3	22.1	3.9	0.6	5.8	2.0	1.5
1961	1.1	14.1	5.3	3.5	1.5	3.8	4.8	3.7	2.3	23.6	4.3	0.6	5.9	2.1	1.7
1962	1.2	14.8	5.7	3.8	1.6	3.8	5.1	3.8	2.4	26.2	4.6	0.8	6.5	2.3	2.1
1963	1.3	15.7	6.0	3.9	1.8	4.0	5.5	3.8	2.6	28.2	4.8	0.8	6.9	2.3	2.4
1964	1.4	16.5	6.3	4.1	1.9	4.1	5.9	3.9	2.8	31.7	5.0	0.9	8.2	2.7	2.9

(continued)

TABLE Cd153–263   Consumption expenditures, by type: 1929–1999   Continued

		Household operation								Medical care					
	Stationery and writing supplies	Household utilities					Telephone and telegraph	Domestic service	Other	Total	Drug preparations and sundries	Ophthalmic products and orthopedic appliances	Physicians	Dentists	Other professional services
		Total	Electricity	Gas	Water and other sanitary services	Fuel oil and coal									
Year	Cd185	Cd186	Cd187	Cd188	Cd189	Cd190	Cd191	Cd192	Cd193	Cd194	Cd195	Cd196	Cd197	Cd198	Cd199
	Billion dollars	Billion dollars	Billion dollars	Billion dollars	Billion dollars	Billion dollars	Billion dollars	Billion dollars	Billion dollars	Billion dollars	Billion dollars	Billion dollars	Billion dollars	Billion dollars	Billion dollars
1965	1.5	17.4	6.6	4.3	2.1	4.4	6.5	4.0	3.1	34.1	5.2	1.0	8.5	2.8	3.3
1966	1.7	18.3	7.0	4.5	2.2	4.7	7.0	4.0	3.5	37.2	5.4	1.1	9.1	3.0	3.6
1967	1.8	19.3	7.5	4.7	2.2	4.8	7.7	4.2	3.9	40.6	5.8	1.0	10.0	3.4	3.1
1968	2.0	20.1	8.1	4.9	2.4	4.7	8.3	4.4	4.2	46.8	6.4	1.2	10.9	3.7	3.4
1969	2.3	21.4	8.9	5.2	2.8	4.6	9.3	4.4	4.6	53.1	7.0	1.3	12.4	4.3	3.4
1970	2.3	22.9	9.8	5.6	3.2	4.4	10.1	4.5	4.8	60.0	8.1	1.5	14.0	4.9	3.7
1971	2.2	25.0	10.9	6.0	3.6	4.6	11.0	4.6	5.2	67.0	8.6	1.6	15.3	5.1	3.9
1972	2.4	27.8	12.2	6.6	4.0	5.1	12.4	4.6	5.8	75.0	9.3	1.8	16.6	5.6	4.3
1973	2.7	31.1	13.7	6.7	4.4	6.3	14.1	4.8	6.4	83.5	10.1	2.0	18.4	6.6	5.2
1974	2.9	36.8	16.6	7.4	4.9	7.8	15.5	4.6	7.0	93.6	11.0	2.1	20.3	7.3	5.9
1975	3.1	43.1	20.0	9.1	5.5	8.4	17.7	4.7	7.3	107.7	12.0	2.4	23.5	8.2	7.2
1976	3.3	49.3	22.4	10.8	6.0	10.1	19.8	5.5	8.7	122.1	13.1	2.5	25.8	9.3	8.9
1977	3.7	56.2	26.0	12.4	6.7	11.1	21.5	6.1	10.0	139.5	14.2	2.7	29.6	10.3	10.3
1978	4.5	62.1	29.0	14.0	7.5	11.5	23.9	6.6	11.1	159.2	16.3	2.9	32.5	11.3	11.5
1979	5.0	70.5	31.8	16.0	8.4	14.4	25.7	6.4	12.7	180.4	19.1	3.2	36.8	12.3	13.0
1980	5.5	82.4	38.4	19.1	9.4	15.4	27.6	6.1	13.6	206.5	21.8	3.4	42.8	13.7	14.7
1981	6.2	91.1	43.9	20.9	10.5	15.8	30.9	6.2	15.0	241.5	24.9	3.6	50.4	16.1	17.8
1982	6.6	100.3	48.6	25.6	11.7	14.5	35.1	6.5	15.5	270.8	27.6	3.9	55.2	17.4	18.7
1983	7.1	109.1	53.3	29.1	13.1	13.6	38.6	6.6	16.8	303.7	31.4	4.4	62.5	18.9	23.0
1984	8.0	115.3	57.2	29.3	14.9	13.9	41.8	7.7	18.9	335.1	35.2	5.3	69.9	20.6	26.9
1985	8.5	121.3	61.2	29.5	17.0	13.6	46.0	7.7	20.8	367.4	38.7	6.2	78.0	22.6	31.2
1986	9.0	119.6	62.6	26.6	19.1	11.3	49.3	8.2	23.1	396.7	42.7	7.2	86.4	24.2	35.8
1987	10.0	123.2	65.4	25.5	21.1	11.2	51.9	8.2	24.8	437.1	47.0	8.4	100.8	26.8	40.4
1988	11.1	130.8	69.1	27.2	22.9	11.7	54.4	9.0	25.9	492.1	51.8	10.3	115.0	28.4	46.9
1989	12.4	138.2	72.0	29.0	25.3	11.9	58.0	9.8	27.1	548.6	58.0	11.4	125.7	30.3	53.3
1990	13.2	141.1	74.2	26.8	27.1	12.9	60.5	10.4	28.4	619.7	65.4	13.7	140.4	32.4	65.0
1991	13.9	148.6	79.2	28.2	28.8	12.4	63.7	10.2	28.4	675.0	71.4	12.5	152.0	34.1	74.3
1992	14.9	151.4	79.3	29.5	30.3	12.2	70.7	11.4	27.1	741.5	75.9	13.0	167.3	37.6	85.2
1993	15.7	164.7	85.9	32.7	33.3	12.9	74.6	11.9	30.5	794.6	80.5	13.5	173.0	39.9	95.1
1994	16.7	169.5	87.2	32.6	36.2	13.5	82.7	12.4	32.9	838.1	85.8	15.0	181.0	42.9	103.6
1995	17.7	175.0	91.0	31.5	38.4	14.1	87.8	13.3	36.1	888.6	92.1	15.8	192.4	46.5	112.9
1996	18.8	185.0	93.3	35.5	40.7	15.6	97.1	13.6	37.1	932.3	100.3	17.6	199.1	48.4	119.7
1997	20.0	188.1	93.8	36.6	42.6	15.1	105.0	13.9	41.2	984.4	110.6	19.1	208.8	51.9	125.9
1998	21.4	185.8	96.1	32.4	44.5	12.8	113.0	16.0	43.6	1,040.9	121.8	20.6	221.2	55.0	132.3
1999	23.1	189.8	96.2	32.7	46.5	14.4	121.7	17.4	45.7	1,102.6	136.8	22.1	232.3	57.8	137.2

	Medical care										Personal business			
	Hospitals and nursing homes					Health insurance								
		Hospitals												
Year	Total	Total	Nonprofit	Proprietary	Government	Nursing homes	Total	Medical care and hospitalization	Income loss	Workers' compensation	Total	Brokerage charges and investment counseling	Bank service charges, trust services, and safe-deposit box rental	Services furnished without payment by financial intermediaries
	Cd200	Cd201	Cd202	Cd203	Cd204	Cd205	Cd206	Cd207	Cd208	Cd209	Cd210	Cd211	Cd212	Cd213
	Billion dollars	Billion dollars	Billion dollars	Billion dollars	Billion dollars	Billion dollars	Billion dollars	Billion dollars	Billion dollars	Billion dollars	Billion dollars	Billion dollars	Billion dollars	Billion dollars
1929	0.6	—	—	—	—	—	0.1	—	—	—	3.9	0.8	0.1	1.0
1930	0.6	—	—	—	—	—	0.1	—	—	—	3.5	0.5	0.1	0.9
1931	0.6	—	—	—	—	—	0.1	—	—	—	3.0	0.3	0.1	0.7
1932	0.5	—	—	—	—	—	0.1	—	—	—	2.6	0.2	0.1	0.5
1933	0.5	—	—	—	—	—	0.1	—	—	—	2.5	0.4	0.1	0.4
1934	0.5	—	—	—	—	—	0.1	—	—	—	2.5	0.2	0.1	0.4
1935	0.5	—	—	—	—	—	0.1	—	—	—	2.8	0.2	0.1	0.5
1936	0.6	—	—	—	—	—	0.1	—	—	—	3.0	0.3	0.1	0.6
1937	0.6	—	—	—	—	—	0.1	—	—	—	3.2	0.3	0.1	0.6
1938	0.6	—	—	—	—	—	0.1	—	—	—	3.1	0.2	0.1	0.6
1939	0.6	—	—	—	—	—	0.2	—	—	—	3.1	0.2	0.1	0.6
1940	0.7	—	—	—	—	—	0.2	—	—	—	3.2	0.1	0.1	0.6
1941	0.7	—	—	—	—	—	0.2	—	—	—	3.3	0.1	0.2	0.7
1942	0.8	—	—	—	—	—	0.2	—	—	—	3.4	0.1	0.2	0.7
1943	0.9	—	—	—	—	—	0.3	—	—	—	3.7	0.2	0.2	0.7
1944	1.0	—	—	—	—	—	0.3	—	—	—	3.9	0.2	0.2	0.7
1945	1.1	—	—	—	—	—	0.4	—	—	—	4.2	0.3	0.2	0.8
1946	1.4	—	—	—	—	—	0.4	—	—	—	4.8	0.3	0.2	1.2
1947	1.7	—	—	—	—	—	0.8	—	—	—	5.3	0.3	0.3	1.3
1948	1.9	—	—	—	—	—	0.8	0.3	0.3	0.3	5.8	0.3	0.3	1.4
1949	2.1	—	—	—	—	—	0.8	0.2	0.3	0.3	6.0	0.3	0.3	1.5
1950	2.3	—	—	—	—	—	0.9	0.3	0.3	0.3	6.6	0.5	0.4	1.7
1951	2.6	—	—	—	—	—	0.9	0.3	0.3	0.3	7.2	0.5	0.4	1.8
1952	2.9	—	—	—	—	—	1.1	0.4	0.3	0.3	7.5	0.4	0.4	1.9
1953	3.2	—	—	—	—	—	1.3	0.5	0.4	0.4	8.4	0.4	0.5	2.5
1954	3.5	—	—	—	—	—	1.4	0.6	0.4	0.4	9.1	0.6	0.5	2.7
1955	3.8	—	—	—	—	—	1.4	0.6	0.4	0.4	10.1	0.7	0.6	3.1
1956	4.2	—	—	—	—	—	1.4	0.6	0.4	0.4	11.0	0.7	0.7	3.4
1957	4.7	—	—	—	—	—	1.6	0.7	0.5	0.4	11.8	0.7	0.7	3.5
1958	5.4	—	—	—	—	—	1.5	1.1	0.0	0.4	12.7	0.9	0.8	3.7
1959	6.0	5.7	4.2	0.5	0.9	0.3	1.7	0.7	0.5	0.4	13.6	1.2	0.9	4.0
1960	6.5	6.1	4.5	0.5	1.0	0.5	1.8	0.8	0.5	0.5	14.6	1.2	0.9	4.4
1961	7.0	6.5	4.9	0.6	1.0	0.5	2.0	0.9	0.6	0.5	15.8	1.6	1.0	4.5
1962	7.8	7.3	5.4	0.7	1.2	0.5	2.2	1.0	0.6	0.5	16.4	1.5	1.0	4.7
1963	8.7	8.1	6.0	0.7	1.3	0.6	2.2	1.1	0.6	0.6	17.2	1.7	1.1	4.8
1964	9.7	8.8	6.5	0.8	1.5	0.9	2.4	1.2	0.6	0.6	19.0	1.9	1.2	5.4

(continued)

TABLE Cd153–263 Consumption expenditures, by type: 1929–1999 *Continued*

Year	Total	Hospitals and nursing homes					Medical care — Health insurance				Personal business			
		Hospitals				Nursing homes	Total	Medical care and hospitalization	Income loss	Workers' compensation	Total	Brokerage charges and investment counseling	Bank service charges, trust services, and safe-deposit box rental	Services furnished without payment by financial intermediaries
		Total	Nonprofit	Proprietary	Government									
	Cd200	Cd201	Cd202	Cd203	Cd204	Cd205	Cd206	Cd207	Cd208	Cd209	Cd210	Cd211	Cd212	Cd213
	Billion dollars	Billion dollars	Billion dollars	Billion dollars	Billion dollars	Billion dollars	Billion dollars	Billion dollars	Billion dollars	Billion dollars	Billion dollars	Billion dollars	Billion dollars	Billion dollars
1965	10.6	9.7	7.1	0.9	1.7	0.9	2.7	1.3	0.7	0.7	20.7	2.2	1.3	5.8
1966	12.1	11.0	8.0	1.0	2.0	1.2	3.0	1.4	0.8	0.8	22.8	2.6	1.4	6.5
1967	14.3	12.8	9.3	1.1	2.4	1.5	3.1	1.3	0.9	1.0	24.4	3.0	1.6	7.1
1968	17.2	15.2	10.9	1.3	3.0	1.9	4.0	2.0	1.0	1.1	26.9	3.5	1.7	7.8
1969	20.4	17.7	12.8	1.5	3.4	2.7	4.2	1.9	1.2	1.1	29.7	3.0	1.9	9.7
1970	23.5	20.2	14.7	1.8	3.7	3.2	4.4	2.1	1.1	1.1	32.6	2.3	2.0	11.4
1971	27.7	23.5	17.0	2.0	4.5	4.2	4.9	2.6	1.3	0.9	34.8	3.0	2.2	11.9
1972	31.3	26.7	19.0	2.3	5.4	4.6	6.0	3.5	1.6	0.9	38.2	3.4	2.3	13.1
1973	34.9	29.7	21.0	2.5	6.1	5.3	6.4	3.6	1.7	1.1	42.3	2.5	2.6	15.4
1974	40.5	34.1	24.3	2.9	6.9	6.3	6.4	3.6	1.7	1.1	47.2	2.1	2.8	18.0
1975	47.8	40.4	29.0	3.5	7.8	7.5	6.6	3.2	2.2	1.2	54.0	2.9	3.1	21.5
1976	55.6	47.1	33.8	4.1	9.2	8.5	7.0	3.6	2.2	1.2	60.6	3.6	3.4	22.7
1977	63.1	53.3	38.6	4.7	10.1	9.8	9.4	5.4	2.4	1.5	67.4	3.6	3.9	25.3
1978	72.8	61.5	44.5	5.4	11.6	11.2	11.9	6.4	3.4	2.1	81.7	4.4	4.4	33.1
1979	83.6	70.7	50.5	6.4	13.8	12.9	12.4	7.2	2.3	2.9	92.1	4.9	5.1	38.5
1980	97.2	82.2	58.8	7.5	15.8	15.0	12.8	7.6	1.9	3.4	103.6	6.9	6.5	41.0
1981	114.1	96.9	69.0	9.0	19.0	17.1	14.6	9.1	1.9	3.6	110.7	6.9	8.3	40.7
1982	130.2	111.5	78.7	10.7	22.1	18.7	17.9	11.8	2.5	3.6	123.8	8.8	10.4	43.9
1983	144.3	123.3	86.3	12.1	24.9	21.0	19.2	14.5	2.1	2.6	147.7	12.7	11.5	58.7
1984	154.7	131.6	91.8	13.6	26.2	23.1	22.4	18.9	2.1	1.4	160.9	12.3	13.4	63.7
1985	166.5	141.1	97.5	15.4	28.3	25.3	24.3	20.6	2.1	1.6	188.1	15.2	15.6	75.5
1986	180.0	152.4	104.5	17.3	30.6	27.6	20.3	16.5	2.4	1.4	212.9	20.3	18.2	86.8
1987	194.9	165.6	113.7	19.2	32.7	29.3	18.9	14.1	2.2	2.6	238.1	23.4	19.9	102.9
1988	215.7	183.0	126.0	21.5	35.6	32.7	23.9	18.7	2.5	2.6	254.4	19.6	21.4	107.9
1989	238.5	201.6	138.7	23.8	39.2	36.9	31.4	26.0	2.4	3.0	268.2	22.3	23.6	108.2
1990	265.0	222.2	153.0	26.1	43.1	42.9	37.7	31.7	2.6	3.4	284.7	22.1	25.5	115.0
1991	292.9	245.9	168.5	28.5	48.9	46.9	37.8	33.6	1.8	2.4	316.7	24.7	28.2	129.0
1992	319.2	269.0	183.5	30.3	55.2	50.2	43.3	37.6	2.1	3.6	342.6	28.8	30.9	141.5
1993	339.2	286.8	194.5	30.9	61.4	52.4	53.5	44.7	1.3	7.4	365.9	33.6	34.0	145.5
1994	353.9	299.9	200.8	32.4	66.6	54.1	55.8	44.4	1.6	9.8	381.6	33.4	35.5	156.3
1995	370.9	312.3	206.0	35.2	71.1	58.6	58.0	46.4	1.2	10.4	406.8	36.5	38.3	166.1
1996	390.8	327.6	213.5	38.7	75.4	63.2	56.6	45.3	1.0	10.3	435.1	43.2	42.9	177.0
1997	408.9	339.6	221.7	41.5	76.3	69.3	59.3	48.5	1.2	9.6	489.0	50.9	47.9	204.2
1998	428.7	355.1	233.1	42.6	79.3	73.6	61.3	51.7	1.4	8.3	533.7	59.1	55.8	222.6
1999	451.8	375.0	245.5	46.0	83.5	76.8	64.6	55.2	1.5	7.8	586.2	70.6	63.5	243.8

	Personal business				Transportation									
						User-operated transportation								
Year	Expenses of handling life insurance and pension plans	Legal services	Funeral and burial expenses	Other	Total	Total	New autos	Net purchases of used autos	Other motor vehicles	Tires, tubes, accessories, and other parts	Repair, greasing, washing, parking, storage, rental, and leasing	Gasoline and oil	Bridge, tunnel, ferry, and road tolls	Insurance
	Cd214	Cd215	Cd216	Cd217	Cd218	Cd219	Cd220	Cd221	Cd222	Cd223	Cd224	Cd225	Cd226	Cd227
	Billion dollars	Billion dollars	Billion dollars	Billion dollars	Billion dollars	Billion dollars	Billion dollars	Billion dollars	Billion dollars	Billion dollars	Billion dollars	Billion dollars	Billion dollars	Billion dollars
1929	0.9	0.4	0.6	0.2	7.7	6.1	2.6	0.0	0.1	0.6	0.8	1.8	0.0	0.1
1930	0.9	0.4	0.5	0.1	6.2	4.7	1.6	0.0	0.1	0.5	0.6	1.7	0.0	0.1
1931	0.9	0.4	0.5	0.1	5.1	3.8	1.1	0.0	0.1	0.4	0.5	1.5	0.0	0.1
1932	0.9	0.3	0.4	0.1	4.0	3.0	0.6	0.0	0.0	0.3	0.4	1.5	0.0	0.1
1933	0.9	0.3	0.4	0.1	4.0	3.1	0.8	0.0	0.0	0.3	0.4	1.5	0.0	0.1
1934	0.9	0.4	0.4	0.1	4.7	3.6	1.0	0.0	0.1	0.3	0.4	1.6	0.0	0.1
1935	1.0	0.4	0.4	0.1	5.4	4.3	1.5	0.0	0.1	0.4	0.5	1.7	0.0	0.1
1936	1.0	0.4	0.5	0.2	6.2	5.0	1.9	0.0	0.1	0.4	0.5	1.9	0.0	0.1
1937	1.0	0.4	0.5	0.3	6.6	5.4	2.0	0.0	0.1	0.4	0.5	2.1	0.0	0.1
1938	1.0	0.4	0.5	0.3	5.7	4.5	1.2	0.0	0.1	0.4	0.5	2.1	0.0	0.1
1939	1.0	0.4	0.5	0.3	6.5	5.2	1.6	0.0	0.1	0.5	0.6	2.2	0.0	0.1
1940	1.0	0.4	0.5	0.3	7.2	6.0	2.1	0.1	0.1	0.5	0.6	2.3	0.1	0.2
1941	1.0	0.5	0.6	0.3	8.6	7.2	2.6	0.2	0.1	0.7	0.8	2.6	0.1	0.2
1942	1.0	0.5	0.6	0.4	5.5	3.6	0.1	0.3	0.0	0.3	0.6	2.1	0.0	0.1
1943	1.1	0.5	0.6	0.4	5.5	2.9	0.1	0.3	0.0	0.4	0.6	1.3	0.0	0.2
1944	1.1	0.5	0.7	0.5	5.8	3.0	0.1	0.3	0.0	0.4	0.7	1.4	0.0	0.2
1945	1.1	0.6	0.7	0.4	6.8	4.0	0.0	0.3	0.0	0.7	1.0	1.8	0.0	0.2
1946	1.2	0.6	0.7	0.5	12.5	9.5	2.0	0.4	0.3	1.4	1.7	3.4	0.1	0.3
1947	1.4	0.7	0.8	0.6	15.9	13.0	4.0	0.8	0.4	1.4	2.0	4.0	0.1	0.4
1948	1.6	0.8	0.8	0.6	18.5	15.6	5.0	1.2	0.5	1.3	2.2	4.8	0.1	0.5
1949	1.6	0.8	0.9	0.6	21.8	18.9	7.7	1.3	0.4	1.2	2.4	5.3	0.1	0.6
1950	1.8	0.9	0.9	0.6	25.4	22.6	10.3	1.4	0.5	1.5	2.5	5.5	0.1	0.8
1951	1.9	1.0	1.0	0.7	25.1	22.1	8.6	1.5	0.5	1.5	2.9	6.1	0.1	0.9
1952	2.0	1.0	1.0	0.7	25.4	22.4	8.0	1.4	0.4	1.6	3.1	6.8	0.1	1.0
1953	2.1	1.1	1.1	0.7	29.3	26.3	11.1	0.9	0.4	1.5	3.5	7.4	0.2	1.3
1954	2.2	1.3	1.1	0.7	28.9	25.9	10.8	0.2	0.4	1.3	3.6	7.8	0.2	1.5
1955	2.5	1.4	1.1	0.8	34.8	31.8	13.8	1.8	0.5	1.6	3.9	8.6	0.2	1.4
1956	2.8	1.4	1.2	0.8	34.1	31.1	11.6	1.9	0.6	1.7	4.3	9.4	0.2	1.4
1957	3.1	1.6	1.3	0.9	37.1	34.0	12.6	2.4	0.6	2.0	4.6	10.2	0.2	1.4
1958	3.3	1.8	1.4	0.9	35.4	32.3	9.7	2.8	0.5	2.1	4.8	10.6	0.3	1.6
1959	3.2	2.0	1.4	1.0	40.7	37.5	13.2	2.7	0.6	2.4	5.2	11.3	0.3	1.9
1960	3.6	2.0	1.5	1.1	42.9	39.5	14.0	2.6	0.6	2.5	5.5	12.0	0.3	2.0
1961	3.8	2.3	1.5	1.1	41.5	38.1	12.1	2.6	0.5	2.6	5.8	12.0	0.3	2.1
1962	3.9	2.4	1.6	1.2	46.3	42.8	15.0	2.9	0.7	2.8	6.2	12.6	0.4	2.1
1963	4.2	2.6	1.7	1.2	50.0	46.5	17.2	3.2	0.9	3.0	6.6	13.0	0.4	2.1
1964	4.7	2.8	1.7	1.3	53.0	49.2	18.3	3.4	1.0	3.2	7.1	13.6	0.4	2.1

(continued)

TABLE Cd153–263 Consumption expenditures, by type: 1929–1999 Continued

	Personal business				Transportation									
	Expenses of handling life insurance and pension plans	Legal services	Funeral and burial expenses	Other	Total	User-operated transportation								
						Total	New autos	Net purchases of used autos	Other motor vehicles	Tires, tubes, accessories, and other parts	Repair, greasing, washing, parking, storage, rental, and leasing	Gasoline and oil	Bridge, tunnel, ferry, and road tolls	Insurance
Year	Cd214	Cd215	Cd216	Cd217	Cd218	Cd219	Cd220	Cd221	Cd222	Cd223	Cd224	Cd225	Cd226	Cd227
	Billion dollars	Billion dollars	Billion dollars	Billion dollars	Billion dollars	Billion dollars	Billion dollars	Billion dollars	Billion dollars	Billion dollars	Billion dollars	Billion dollars	Billion dollars	Billion dollars
1965	5.2	3.0	1.8	1.4	59.1	55.1	21.4	3.8	1.3	3.5	7.6	14.8	0.5	2.4
1966	5.4	3.4	1.9	1.6	62.2	57.8	21.0	3.9	1.5	3.8	8.1	16.0	0.5	2.8
1967	5.4	3.6	2.0	1.7	64.4	59.5	20.0	4.3	1.6	4.0	8.8	17.1	0.5	3.0
1968	6.0	3.8	2.1	1.9	73.5	68.0	24.5	4.6	2.3	4.6	9.7	18.6	0.6	3.0
1969	6.5	4.2	2.2	2.2	79.8	73.3	25.1	5.0	2.8	5.4	10.9	20.5	0.6	3.0
1970	7.2	4.9	2.3	2.4	81.1	74.2	21.9	4.8	2.7	6.1	12.3	21.9	0.7	3.8
1971	7.4	5.4	2.5	2.5	94.8	87.1	28.2	5.3	3.9	7.1	13.9	23.2	0.7	4.9
1972	8.0	6.0	2.6	2.8	105.3	96.7	31.6	5.9	5.6	8.0	15.1	24.4	0.8	5.4
1973	9.1	6.9	2.7	3.1	115.4	106.1	33.9	6.4	6.9	8.9	15.8	28.1	0.8	5.2
1974	10.2	7.6	2.8	3.5	119.0	108.4	27.0	6.6	6.4	9.5	17.0	36.1	0.8	5.0
1975	11.7	7.9	2.9	4.0	130.2	118.9	29.3	7.4	7.7	10.3	19.8	39.7	0.8	3.8
1976	14.3	8.7	3.3	4.5	155.7	142.6	38.2	9.7	12.1	11.4	22.1	43.0	0.9	5.3
1977	16.4	9.6	3.5	5.1	179.6	164.9	44.4	10.4	15.9	12.9	25.7	46.9	0.9	7.8
1978	19.1	11.0	3.8	5.8	196.7	181.1	48.5	11.1	19.1	14.4	28.5	50.1	1.0	8.4
1979	21.5	11.7	4.0	6.3	218.8	201.4	49.3	11.3	16.6	16.3	32.2	66.2	1.0	8.5
1980	24.7	13.1	4.5	7.0	238.4	218.3	46.4	10.8	11.8	17.9	34.0	86.7	1.1	9.4
1981	26.9	15.5	4.8	7.6	262.4	241.1	50.7	12.8	12.8	19.6	37.2	97.9	1.2	8.9
1982	30.3	17.2	5.1	8.2	268.0	246.0	53.3	13.6	15.6	20.4	38.5	94.1	1.3	9.2
1983	31.7	18.9	5.4	8.8	299.4	275.4	66.0	15.6	23.0	22.3	43.7	93.1	1.3	10.4
1984	34.6	21.4	6.0	9.5	337.0	310.1	77.1	21.4	30.7	23.2	51.6	94.6	1.4	10.1
1985	40.2	24.5	6.8	10.3	372.8	344.9	86.3	24.4	40.8	24.3	60.5	97.2	1.5	10.0
1986	42.0	27.2	7.1	11.2	379.7	350.9	99.0	23.8	45.0	24.6	64.0	80.1	1.8	12.7
1987	41.8	30.8	7.5	11.8	396.7	365.8	91.3	28.4	48.2	25.2	69.8	85.4	2.0	15.5
1988	49.1	34.6	8.3	13.5	423.6	390.1	96.7	28.9	52.7	27.8	77.7	87.7	1.9	16.8
1989	52.7	37.6	8.8	15.0	445.0	410.0	92.9	31.0	59.0	28.5	82.5	97.0	2.3	16.8
1990	55.0	40.9	9.5	16.6	455.4	419.0	89.7	29.3	57.5	29.9	84.9	107.3	2.3	18.1
1991	65.3	41.7	10.1	17.6	428.1	392.5	72.3	28.9	52.2	29.5	81.9	102.5	2.5	22.8
1992	66.9	44.9	11.0	18.6	460.1	424.0	78.0	31.2	60.5	30.5	90.3	104.9	2.8	25.7
1993	74.8	46.4	11.7	19.9	494.9	456.4	82.1	38.8	68.9	32.4	97.6	106.6	3.1	27.0
1994	75.3	47.4	12.1	21.6	532.1	492.3	86.5	43.0	77.7	35.2	110.0	109.0	3.3	27.8
1995	81.8	48.0	13.3	22.7	560.3	517.8	82.2	50.0	80.2	36.9	122.2	113.3	3.4	29.7
1996	81.3	51.5	14.5	24.8	594.6	550.2	81.9	51.4	84.3	38.7	134.2	124.2	3.7	31.8
1997	89.3	55.0	15.2	26.6	626.7	578.9	82.5	53.1	89.0	39.6	146.3	128.1	4.0	36.3
1998	92.2	58.7	16.3	29.1	648.6	599.4	87.8	55.3	104.0	41.7	153.1	115.2	4.2	38.0
1999	98.0	62.3	16.2	31.9	705.5	654.6	97.3	58.7	119.9	44.8	162.1	128.3	4.4	39.1

	Transportation								Recreation			
	Purchased local transportation			Purchased intercity transportation								Nondurable toys and sport supplies
	Total	Mass transit systems	Taxicab	Total	Railway	Bus	Airline	Other	Total	Books and maps	Magazines, newspapers, and sheet music	
	Cd228	Cd229	Cd230	Cd231	Cd232	Cd233	Cd234	Cd235	Cd236	Cd237	Cd238	Cd239
Year	Billion dollars	Billion dollars	Billion dollars	Billion dollars	Billion dollars	Billion dollars	Billion dollars	Billion dollars	Billion dollars	Billion dollars	Billion dollars	Billion dollars
1929	1.1	0.9	0.2	0.5	0.4	0.1	0.0	0.1	4.4	0.3	0.5	0.3
1930	1.1	0.8	0.2	0.4	0.3	0.1	0.0	0.0	4.0	0.3	0.5	0.3
1931	0.9	0.8	0.2	0.3	0.2	0.1	0.0	0.0	3.3	0.3	0.5	0.3
1932	0.8	0.7	0.1	0.3	0.2	0.0	0.0	0.0	2.5	0.2	0.4	0.2
1933	0.7	0.6	0.1	0.2	0.2	0.0	0.0	0.0	2.2	0.2	0.4	0.2
1934	0.8	0.7	0.1	0.3	0.2	0.0	0.0	0.0	2.5	0.2	0.4	0.2
1935	0.8	0.7	0.1	0.3	0.2	0.1	0.0	0.0	2.6	0.2	0.5	0.2
1936	0.8	0.7	0.1	0.3	0.2	0.1	0.0	0.0	3.0	0.2	0.5	0.2
1937	0.9	0.7	0.1	0.4	0.2	0.1	0.0	0.0	3.4	0.2	0.5	0.3
1938	0.8	0.7	0.1	0.3	0.2	0.1	0.0	0.0	3.3	0.2	0.5	0.3
1939	0.9	0.7	0.2	0.4	0.2	0.1	0.0	0.0	3.5	0.2	0.6	0.3
1940	0.9	0.8	0.2	0.4	0.2	0.1	0.0	0.0	3.8	0.2	0.6	0.3
1941	1.0	0.8	0.2	0.4	0.2	0.1	0.0	0.0	4.3	0.3	0.6	0.4
1942	1.3	1.0	0.3	0.7	0.4	0.2	0.0	0.0	4.7	0.3	0.7	0.4
1943	1.6	1.3	0.4	1.0	0.7	0.3	0.0	0.0	5.0	0.4	0.8	0.4
1944	1.7	1.4	0.4	1.1	0.7	0.3	0.0	0.0	5.4	0.5	0.9	0.5
1945	1.7	1.4	0.4	1.1	0.7	0.3	0.1	0.0	6.2	0.5	1.0	0.6
1946	1.9	1.4	0.5	1.0	0.6	0.3	0.1	0.0	8.6	0.6	1.1	0.8
1947	1.9	1.4	0.5	1.0	0.5	0.3	0.1	0.0	9.3	0.5	1.2	0.9
1948	2.0	1.5	0.5	1.0	0.5	0.3	0.1	0.0	9.7	0.6	1.4	1.1
1949	2.0	1.5	0.5	0.9	0.5	0.3	0.1	0.0	10.0	0.6	1.5	1.2
1950	1.9	1.4	0.5	0.9	0.4	0.3	0.1	0.0	11.2	0.7	1.5	1.4
1951	2.0	1.5	0.5	1.0	0.4	0.3	0.2	0.0	11.7	0.8	1.6	1.7
1952	2.0	1.5	0.5	1.1	0.5	0.4	0.2	0.0	12.3	0.8	1.7	1.7
1953	2.0	1.5	0.5	1.1	0.4	0.3	0.3	0.0	13.1	0.8	1.8	1.7
1954	1.9	1.4	0.5	1.0	0.4	0.3	0.3	0.0	13.6	0.8	1.8	1.6
1955	1.9	1.4	0.5	1.1	0.4	0.3	0.3	0.0	14.6	0.9	1.9	1.8
1956	2.0	1.4	0.6	1.1	0.4	0.3	0.4	0.0	15.5	1.0	1.9	2.0
1957	2.0	1.4	0.6	1.2	0.4	0.3	0.4	0.0	15.9	1.0	2.0	2.0
1958	1.9	1.3	0.6	1.1	0.3	0.3	0.5	0.0	16.3	1.0	2.1	2.1
1959	2.0	1.4	0.6	1.2	0.3	0.3	0.6	0.0	17.7	1.1	2.1	2.4
1960	2.0	1.4	0.6	1.3	0.3	0.3	0.7	0.0	18.5	1.1	2.2	2.5
1961	2.0	1.4	0.6	1.4	0.3	0.3	0.8	0.0	19.3	1.2	2.0	2.7
1962	2.0	1.4	0.6	1.5	0.3	0.3	0.9	0.0	20.8	1.3	2.3	2.9
1963	2.0	1.4	0.6	1.5	0.3	0.3	0.9	0.0	22.5	1.4	2.5	3.1
1964	2.0	1.4	0.6	1.7	0.3	0.3	1.1	0.0	24.6	1.6	2.5	3.4

(continued)

TABLE Cd153–263   Consumption expenditures, by type: 1929–1999   *Continued*

	Transportation								Recreation			
	Purchased local transportation			Purchased intercity transportation								
	Total	Mass transit systems	Taxicab	Total	Railway	Bus	Airline	Other	Total	Books and maps	Magazines, newspapers, and sheet music	Nondurable toys and sport supplies
	Cd228	Cd229	Cd230	Cd231	Cd232	Cd233	Cd234	Cd235	Cd236	Cd237	Cd238	Cd239
Year	Billion dollars	Billion dollars	Billion dollars	Billion dollars	Billion dollars	Billion dollars	Billion dollars	Billion dollars	Billion dollars	Billion dollars	Billion dollars	Billion dollars
1965	2.1	1.4	0.6	2.0	0.3	0.4	1.3	0.1	26.9	1.7	2.7	3.6
1966	2.1	1.5	0.6	2.3	0.3	0.4	1.5	0.1	30.9	1.8	3.2	4.0
1967	2.2	1.5	0.7	2.7	0.3	0.5	1.8	0.1	33.1	1.9	3.3	4.3
1968	2.4	1.6	0.9	3.1	0.2	0.5	2.2	0.1	36.7	2.0	3.4	4.8
1969	2.7	1.7	1.0	3.7	0.2	0.5	2.8	0.2	40.0	2.3	3.7	5.2
1970	3.0	1.8	1.2	4.0	0.2	0.5	3.1	0.2	43.1	2.9	4.1	5.5
1971	3.3	1.9	1.4	4.4	0.2	0.6	3.5	0.2	46.0	3.0	4.4	5.8
1972	3.4	1.9	1.6	5.2	0.2	0.6	4.1	0.2	51.5	2.9	4.8	6.6
1973	3.5	1.9	1.6	5.9	0.2	0.6	4.7	0.3	57.6	3.1	5.3	7.4
1974	3.7	2.0	1.7	6.9	0.3	0.7	5.5	0.4	63.4	3.2	5.9	8.2
1975	4.0	2.1	2.0	7.3	0.3	0.7	5.9	0.4	70.5	3.6	6.4	9.0
1976	4.4	2.2	2.2	8.6	0.3	0.8	7.1	0.5	78.2	3.6	7.0	10.0
1977	4.8	2.4	2.4	9.9	0.3	0.8	8.3	0.6	85.5	4.1	7.7	10.8
1978	4.8	2.5	2.2	10.9	0.2	0.9	9.1	0.6	95.9	5.0	9.1	12.3
1979	4.8	2.8	2.0	12.6	0.3	1.1	10.4	0.8	108.4	5.7	10.9	13.6
1980	4.8	2.9	1.9	15.4	0.3	1.4	12.8	0.9	116.7	6.5	12.0	14.6
1981	5.0	3.3	1.7	16.3	0.3	1.6	13.4	1.0	129.5	7.3	13.0	16.0
1982	5.4	3.8	1.5	16.6	0.3	1.7	13.5	1.2	138.9	8.0	13.8	17.1
1983	5.8	4.0	1.9	18.1	0.4	1.5	14.9	1.3	155.0	9.0	14.6	18.4
1984	6.4	4.1	2.3	20.5	0.4	1.5	17.2	1.4	172.9	10.0	15.7	20.5
1985	6.8	4.2	2.6	21.1	0.5	1.3	17.6	1.7	187.6	10.6	15.9	21.4
1986	7.1	4.5	2.5	21.8	0.5	1.1	18.3	1.8	204.7	11.4	16.5	22.9
1987	6.9	4.6	2.4	23.9	0.6	1.4	19.9	2.1	224.5	13.0	17.6	25.3
1988	7.3	5.0	2.3	26.2	0.6	1.7	21.3	2.6	248.4	14.2	19.2	27.7
1989	7.5	5.2	2.3	27.5	0.7	1.5	22.4	2.9	268.2	15.0	20.1	30.7
1990	8.4	5.8	2.6	28.1	0.7	1.3	22.7	3.3	284.9	16.2	21.6	32.8
1991	8.8	6.1	2.6	26.9	0.7	1.6	21.4	3.3	295.3	16.4	22.1	34.6
1992	9.0	6.5	2.6	27.1	0.6	1.6	21.3	3.6	313.8	17.1	22.0	36.5
1993	9.5	6.7	2.8	29.1	0.6	1.6	23.3	3.6	340.1	18.8	23.1	39.5
1994	10.0	7.1	3.0	29.8	0.6	1.5	23.7	4.0	368.7	20.8	24.9	43.4
1995	10.4	7.1	3.2	32.1	0.6	1.6	25.5	4.3	401.6	23.1	26.2	47.2
1996	11.2	7.7	3.5	33.3	0.6	1.8	26.2	4.7	429.6	24.9	27.6	50.6
1997	11.6	7.8	3.7	36.2	0.7	1.8	29.0	4.7	456.6	26.3	29.1	53.2
1998	12.1	8.0	4.1	37.2	0.7	2.1	29.5	4.9	489.8	27.8	32.5	57.3
1999	12.3	8.2	4.0	38.7	0.7	2.2	30.7	5.1	534.9	29.8	37.0	63.1

Year	Wheel goods, sports and photographic equipment, boats, and pleasure aircraft	Video and audio goods, musical instruments, and computer goods			Radio and television repair	Flowers, seeds, and potted plants	Recreation — Admissions to specified spectator amusements				Clubs and fraternal organizations	Commercial participant amusements	Pari-mutuel net receipts	Other
		Total	Video and audio goods, and musical instruments	Computers, peripherals, and software			Total	Motion picture theaters	Legitimate theaters and opera, and entertainments of nonprofit institutions	Spectator sports				
	Cd240	Cd241	Cd242	Cd243	Cd244	Cd245	Cd246	Cd247	Cd248	Cd249	Cd250	Cd251	Cd252	Cd253
	Billion dollars	Billion dollars	Billion dollars	Billion dollars	Billion dollars	Billion dollars	Billion dollars	Billion dollars	Billion dollars	Billion dollars	Billion dollars	Billion dollars	Billion dollars	Billion dollars
1929	0.2	1.0	1.0	—	0.0	0.2	0.9	0.7	0.1	0.1	0.3	0.2	0.0	0.3
1930	0.2	0.9	0.9	—	0.0	0.2	0.9	0.7	0.1	0.1	0.3	0.2	0.0	0.3
1931	0.2	0.5	0.5	—	0.0	0.1	0.9	0.7	0.1	0.1	0.3	0.1	0.0	0.2
1932	0.1	0.3	0.3	—	0.0	0.1	0.6	0.5	0.1	0.0	0.3	0.1	0.0	0.2
1933	0.1	0.2	0.2	—	0.0	0.1	0.6	0.5	0.0	0.1	0.2	0.1	0.0	0.2
1934	0.1	0.2	0.2	—	0.0	0.1	0.6	0.5	0.0	0.1	0.2	0.1	0.0	0.2
1935	0.1	0.2	0.2	—	0.0	0.1	0.7	0.6	0.0	0.1	0.2	0.1	0.0	0.2
1936	0.2	0.3	0.3	—	0.0	0.2	0.8	0.6	0.1	0.1	0.2	0.1	0.0	0.3
1937	0.2	0.4	0.4	—	0.0	0.2	0.8	0.7	0.1	0.1	0.2	0.2	0.0	0.3
1938	0.2	0.3	0.3	—	0.0	0.2	0.8	0.7	0.1	0.1	0.2	0.1	0.0	0.3
1939	0.2	0.4	0.4	—	0.0	0.2	0.8	0.7	0.1	0.1	0.2	0.2	0.0	0.3
1940	0.3	0.5	0.5	—	0.0	0.2	0.9	0.7	0.1	0.1	0.2	0.2	0.1	0.3
1941	0.3	0.6	0.6	—	0.0	0.2	1.0	0.8	0.1	0.1	0.2	0.2	0.1	0.3
1942	0.3	0.6	0.6	—	0.0	0.2	1.2	1.0	0.1	0.1	0.2	0.2	0.1	0.4
1943	0.3	0.4	0.4	—	0.1	0.3	1.5	1.3	0.1	0.1	0.3	0.2	0.1	0.4
1944	0.3	0.3	0.3	—	0.1	0.3	1.6	1.3	0.1	0.1	0.3	0.2	0.1	0.4
1945	0.4	0.3	0.3	—	0.1	0.4	1.7	1.5	0.1	0.1	0.3	0.2	0.2	0.5
1946	0.8	1.1	1.1	—	0.1	0.4	2.1	1.7	0.2	0.2	0.4	0.3	0.2	0.5
1947	1.0	1.4	1.4	—	0.1	0.4	2.0	1.6	0.2	0.2	0.5	0.3	0.3	0.6
1948	1.0	1.5	1.5	—	0.2	0.4	1.9	1.5	0.2	0.2	0.5	0.3	0.3	0.6
1949	0.8	1.7	1.7	—	0.2	0.5	1.9	1.5	0.2	0.2	0.5	0.4	0.2	0.6
1950	0.9	2.4	2.4	—	0.3	0.5	1.8	1.4	0.2	0.2	0.5	0.4	0.2	0.7
1951	0.9	2.2	2.2	—	0.4	0.5	1.8	1.3	0.2	0.2	0.6	0.4	0.3	0.7
1952	1.0	2.4	2.4	—	0.4	0.5	1.7	1.3	0.2	0.2	0.6	0.4	0.3	0.8
1953	1.1	2.6	2.6	—	0.5	0.6	1.7	1.3	0.2	0.2	0.6	0.4	0.4	0.9
1954	1.2	2.8	2.8	—	0.5	0.6	1.8	1.4	0.2	0.2	0.6	0.5	0.4	1.0
1955	1.4	2.9	2.9	—	0.6	0.6	2.0	1.5	0.2	0.2	0.7	0.5	0.4	1.1
1956	1.6	3.0	3.0	—	0.6	0.6	2.1	1.5	0.3	0.2	0.7	0.6	0.4	1.2
1957	1.7	2.9	2.9	—	0.7	0.6	1.8	1.2	0.3	0.3	0.8	0.6	0.4	1.3
1958	1.9	2.8	2.8	—	0.8	0.6	1.7	1.1	0.3	0.3	0.8	0.7	0.5	1.4
1959	2.0	3.1	3.1	—	0.8	0.6	1.7	1.0	0.3	0.3	0.9	0.9	0.5	1.6
1960	2.0	3.0	3.0	—	0.9	0.7	1.8	1.0	0.3	0.4	0.9	1.1	0.5	1.8
1961	2.0	3.2	3.2	—	0.9	0.7	1.8	1.0	0.3	0.4	1.0	1.2	0.6	1.9
1962	2.0	3.4	3.4	—	1.0	0.9	1.9	1.0	0.4	0.5	1.0	1.4	0.7	2.1
1963	2.2	3.7	3.7	—	1.0	1.0	1.9	1.0	0.4	0.5	1.1	1.5	0.7	2.4
1964	2.5	4.3	4.3	—	1.0	1.1	2.0	1.0	0.4	0.6	1.1	1.6	0.8	2.6

(continued)

TABLE Cd153–263   Consumption expenditures, by type: 1929–1999   Continued

	Wheel goods, sports and photographic equipment, boats, and pleasure aircraft	Video and audio goods, musical instruments, and computer goods			Radio and television repair	Flowers, seeds, and potted plants	Recreation		Admissions to specified spectator amusements			Clubs and fraternal organizations	Commercial participant amusements	Pari-mutuel net receipts	Other
		Total	Video and audio goods, and musical instruments	Computers, peripherals, and software			Total	Motion picture theaters	Legitimate theaters and opera, and entertainments of nonprofit institutions	Spectator sports				
Year	Cd240	Cd241	Cd242	Cd243	Cd244	Cd245	Cd246	Cd247	Cd248	Cd249	Cd250	Cd251	Cd252	Cd253
	Billion dollars	Billion dollars	Billion dollars	Billion dollars	Billion dollars	Billion dollars	Billion dollars	Billion dollars	Billion dollars	Billion dollars	Billion dollars	Billion dollars	Billion dollars	Billion dollars
1965	2.9	5.1	5.1	—	1.0	1.3	2.2	1.2	0.4	0.7	1.2	1.6	0.8	2.8
1966	3.6	6.3	6.3	—	1.0	1.4	2.4	1.2	0.4	0.7	1.3	1.7	0.8	3.2
1967	4.1	7.0	7.0	—	1.1	1.5	2.5	1.2	0.5	0.8	1.3	1.8	0.9	3.5
1968	4.8	7.6	7.6	—	1.2	1.7	2.9	1.4	0.5	1.0	1.4	1.9	0.9	4.1
1969	5.2	8.0	8.0	—	1.3	1.7	3.1	1.5	0.5	1.1	1.5	2.1	1.0	4.8
1970	5.2	8.5	8.5	—	1.4	1.8	3.3	1.6	0.5	1.1	1.5	2.4	1.1	5.4
1971	5.6	8.9	8.9	—	1.5	1.9	3.5	1.7	0.5	1.2	1.5	2.6	1.2	6.0
1972	7.4	10.1	10.1	—	1.7	2.2	3.5	1.7	0.6	1.2	1.5	3.0	1.3	6.6
1973	8.5	11.3	11.3	—	1.9	2.3	3.5	1.6	0.6	1.2	1.6	3.5	1.4	7.8
1974	9.0	12.1	12.1	—	2.0	2.6	4.0	2.0	0.7	1.2	1.8	4.2	1.6	9.1
1975	10.1	13.5	13.5	—	2.2	2.7	4.3	2.2	0.8	1.3	2.0	4.9	1.7	10.4
1976	11.4	14.8	14.8	—	2.3	2.9	4.4	2.1	0.9	1.4	2.1	5.6	1.8	12.1
1977	12.8	15.8	15.8	0.0	2.5	2.9	5.0	2.4	1.1	1.6	2.2	6.4	1.9	13.4
1978	14.1	17.3	17.3	0.1	2.4	3.6	5.9	2.8	1.3	1.8	2.1	7.2	2.0	14.9
1979	16.2	19.4	19.3	0.1	2.4	4.2	6.4	2.8	1.5	2.1	2.5	8.0	2.1	16.8
1980	15.6	20.6	20.4	0.2	2.5	4.7	6.6	2.6	1.8	2.3	2.9	9.1	2.3	19.4
1981	16.4	22.2	21.8	0.4	2.5	5.3	7.1	2.7	2.0	2.4	3.4	10.8	2.5	23.0
1982	16.3	23.0	21.7	1.4	2.6	5.7	8.0	3.1	2.1	2.7	4.1	11.6	2.6	26.0
1983	16.9	28.5	25.6	2.9	2.8	6.0	8.7	3.2	2.4	3.1	4.4	12.9	2.6	30.4
1984	20.4	32.0	29.0	3.0	2.8	6.5	9.7	3.4	2.8	3.5	4.7	13.8	2.8	34.1
1985	21.2	35.9	33.0	2.9	3.2	6.9	9.7	3.2	3.2	3.3	5.5	15.1	2.8	39.2
1986	23.0	41.8	36.6	5.2	3.2	7.7	10.5	3.3	3.9	3.3	6.1	16.0	2.9	42.7
1987	25.6	46.2	40.0	6.2	3.5	9.2	10.8	3.4	4.0	3.4	6.7	17.3	3.0	46.3
1988	27.7	50.8	42.6	8.2	3.8	9.7	11.9	3.9	4.4	3.6	7.1	19.8	3.4	53.0
1989	29.3	52.4	44.0	8.3	3.7	10.5	13.3	4.6	4.4	4.3	8.0	21.8	3.3	59.9
1990	29.7	52.9	43.9	8.9	3.7	10.9	14.8	5.1	5.2	4.5	8.7	24.6	3.5	65.4
1991	29.5	55.1	43.2	11.9	3.4	11.0	15.6	5.2	5.4	4.9	9.5	25.7	3.4	68.8
1992	30.1	57.0	45.0	12.1	3.4	12.0	16.1	4.9	6.0	5.1	10.2	29.9	3.4	76.1
1993	32.5	62.6	48.1	14.5	3.3	12.5	17.5	5.0	6.8	5.7	11.1	34.0	3.3	81.9
1994	35.2	71.0	53.0	18.0	3.3	13.2	18.2	5.2	7.2	5.8	11.8	38.6	3.4	84.7
1995	38.5	77.0	55.9	21.0	3.6	13.8	19.2	5.5	7.6	6.1	12.7	43.9	3.5	93.1
1996	40.5	80.0	56.4	23.6	3.7	14.9	20.7	5.8	8.0	6.9	14.0	48.3	3.5	100.8
1997	42.8	83.7	57.9	25.9	4.0	15.3	22.1	6.3	8.6	7.1	14.6	52.8	3.6	109.1
1998	46.4	90.7	62.1	28.6	4.0	16.3	23.6	6.9	9.1	7.6	15.0	56.4	3.7	116.0
1999	51.3	99.1	67.3	31.9	3.9	17.5	25.8	7.4	10.2	8.2	15.8	63.1	3.8	124.6

	Education and research				Religious and welfare activities	Foreign travel and other				
	Total	Higher education	Nursery, elementary, and secondary schools	Other		Foreign travel and other, net	Foreign travel by U.S. residents	Expenditures abroad by U.S. residents	Less: expenditures in the United States by nonresidents	Less: personal remittances in kind to nonresidents
Year	Cd254	Cd255	Cd256	Cd257	Cd258	Cd259	Cd260	Cd261	Cd262	Cd263
	Billion dollars	Billion dollars	Billion dollars	Billion dollars	Billion dollars	Billion dollars	Billion dollars	Billion dollars	Billion dollars	Billion dollars
1929	0.8	0.3	0.2	0.3	1.2	0.5	0.6	0.0	0.1	0.0
1930	0.8	0.4	0.2	0.3	1.2	0.5	0.6	0.0	0.1	0.0
1931	0.8	0.4	0.2	0.2	1.1	0.4	0.4	0.0	0.1	0.0
1932	0.7	0.3	0.2	0.2	1.0	0.3	0.3	0.0	0.1	0.0
1933	0.6	0.3	0.1	0.2	0.9	0.2	0.3	0.0	0.1	0.0
1934	0.6	0.3	0.1	0.1	0.9	0.2	0.3	0.0	0.1	0.0
1935	0.6	0.3	0.1	0.2	0.9	0.2	0.3	0.0	0.1	0.0
1936	0.7	0.3	0.1	0.2	0.9	0.3	0.4	0.0	0.1	0.0
1937	0.7	0.4	0.2	0.2	0.9	0.3	0.4	0.0	0.1	0.0
1938	0.7	0.4	0.2	0.2	0.9	0.3	0.4	0.0	0.1	0.0
1939	0.7	0.4	0.2	0.2	1.0	0.2	0.3	0.0	0.1	0.0
1940	0.8	0.4	0.2	0.2	1.0	0.1	0.2	0.0	0.1	0.0
1941	0.8	0.4	0.2	0.2	1.1	0.1	0.2	0.0	0.1	0.0
1942	0.9	0.4	0.2	0.3	1.2	0.2	0.1	0.2	0.1	0.0
1943	1.1	0.5	0.2	0.4	1.5	0.3	0.1	0.3	0.1	0.0
1944	1.1	0.5	0.3	0.3	1.7	0.6	0.2	0.6	0.2	0.0
1945	1.1	0.5	0.3	0.3	1.8	1.2	0.3	1.2	0.2	0.1
1946	1.2	0.6	0.3	0.3	2.0	-0.1	0.5	0.1	0.4	0.3
1947	1.5	0.8	0.3	0.5	2.1	0.0	0.6	0.2	0.4	0.3
1948	1.7	0.9	0.4	0.4	2.3	0.3	0.7	0.3	0.4	0.3
1949	1.8	0.9	0.4	0.4	2.3	0.6	0.9	0.4	0.5	0.2
1950	1.9	1.0	0.5	0.5	2.4	0.7	0.9	0.3	0.5	0.1
1951	2.1	1.0	0.5	0.5	2.6	0.9	0.9	0.6	0.6	0.1
1952	2.2	1.1	0.6	0.5	3.0	1.1	1.0	0.8	0.6	0.1
1953	2.3	1.1	0.6	0.6	3.1	1.5	1.2	1.1	0.7	0.1
1954	2.5	1.2	0.7	0.6	3.3	1.5	1.3	1.1	0.7	0.1
1955	2.7	1.3	0.7	0.7	3.5	1.6	1.5	1.1	0.8	0.1
1956	3.0	1.5	0.8	0.7	3.9	1.7	1.6	1.1	0.9	0.1
1957	3.4	1.7	0.9	0.8	4.1	1.7	1.7	1.1	1.0	0.1
1958	3.7	1.8	1.0	0.9	4.4	1.9	1.9	1.1	1.0	0.1
1959	4.0	2.0	1.1	0.9	5.0	2.0	2.1	1.1	1.1	0.1
1960	4.4	2.2	1.3	1.0	5.3	2.1	2.3	1.1	1.1	0.1
1961	4.7	2.4	1.4	0.9	5.6	2.0	2.3	1.0	1.1	0.1
1962	5.1	2.6	1.6	0.9	5.8	2.3	2.6	1.0	1.1	0.1
1963	5.6	2.8	1.7	1.0	6.2	2.5	2.8	1.0	1.2	0.1
1964	6.2	3.2	1.9	1.1	7.2	2.6	3.0	1.1	1.4	0.1
1965	7.0	3.8	2.0	1.2	7.8	2.9	3.3	1.2	1.6	0.2
1966	8.0	4.3	2.2	1.4	8.5	3.1	3.6	1.5	1.8	0.2
1967	8.9	4.8	2.4	1.8	9.5	3.8	4.2	1.6	1.8	0.2
1968	10.1	5.4	2.6	2.1	10.4	3.7	4.2	1.7	2.0	0.2
1969	11.3	6.1	2.8	2.4	11.1	4.0	4.7	1.9	2.3	0.2

(continued)

TABLE Cd153–263 Consumption expenditures, by type: 1929–1999 *Continued*

	Education and research					Foreign travel and other				
	Total	Higher education	Nursery, elementary, and secondary schools	Other	Religious and welfare activities	Foreign travel and other, net	Foreign travel by U.S. residents	Expenditures abroad by U.S. residents	Less: expenditures in the United States by nonresidents	Less: personal remittances in kind to nonresidents
	Cd254	Cd255	Cd256	Cd257	Cd258	Cd259	Cd260	Cd261	Cd262	Cd263
Year	Billion dollars	Billion dollars	Billion dollars	Billion dollars	Billion dollars	Billion dollars	Billion dollars	Billion dollars	Billion dollars	Billion dollars
1970	12.7	7.0	3.2	2.6	12.2	4.5	5.4	2.0	2.7	0.3
1971	13.9	7.8	3.5	2.7	13.7	4.8	5.9	2.1	2.9	0.2
1972	15.3	8.6	3.8	2.9	15.4	5.2	6.8	1.9	3.3	0.2
1973	16.9	9.3	4.3	3.2	16.5	4.7	7.3	1.6	4.0	0.3
1974	18.5	10.0	5.0	3.4	18.1	4.7	8.1	1.5	4.6	0.3
1975	20.6	10.7	5.7	4.2	19.8	4.4	8.8	1.3	5.4	0.3
1976	22.5	11.6	6.1	4.9	22.4	3.8	9.4	1.2	6.5	0.3
1977	24.2	12.6	6.3	5.3	24.7	4.3	10.3	1.2	7.0	0.2
1978	26.8	13.3	7.5	6.1	28.7	4.3	11.1	1.5	8.1	0.2
1979	29.8	14.8	8.3	6.7	32.5	4.1	12.1	1.7	9.4	0.3
1980	33.5	16.6	9.5	7.4	37.2	3.5	13.3	2.2	11.6	0.4
1981	37.6	19.1	10.4	8.1	41.9	0.4	15.0	2.5	16.6	0.4
1982	41.3	22.0	10.9	8.4	45.9	2.5	16.5	3.1	16.7	0.4
1983	45.3	24.2	12.0	9.1	50.0	5.2	18.4	3.2	15.9	0.5
1984	49.4	26.5	13.2	9.7	56.1	6.4	26.1	3.3	22.5	0.5
1985	53.8	28.7	14.3	10.9	60.4	7.5	27.9	3.9	23.5	0.7
1986	58.1	31.1	15.1	11.9	67.1	4.1	27.8	3.7	26.6	0.7
1987	63.2	33.6	16.5	13.0	71.7	6.7	33.9	3.9	30.3	0.8
1988	70.2	36.4	17.7	16.1	81.2	3.2	37.3	3.5	36.6	1.0
1989	77.6	40.0	19.8	17.9	88.1	−2.9	38.4	3.6	44.0	0.9
1990	83.7	43.8	21.2	18.7	97.1	−6.3	42.7	3.6	51.6	1.0
1991	89.2	47.9	21.9	19.5	101.8	−13.7	41.7	3.5	57.7	1.1
1992	96.0	52.2	23.1	20.7	112.4	−18.0	45.9	2.6	64.9	1.6
1993	101.2	55.7	23.8	21.8	116.6	−19.3	48.7	2.5	68.7	1.7
1994	107.2	59.2	25.0	23.0	127.9	−16.2	53.0	2.4	69.9	1.6
1995	114.5	62.9	26.4	25.2	134.9	−20.7	54.1	2.3	75.4	1.6
1996	122.3	66.1	27.4	28.8	146.8	−24.1	57.6	2.2	82.4	1.5
1997	130.5	69.4	29.0	32.1	149.5	−21.8	63.6	2.9	86.7	1.6
1998	139.4	73.2	29.9	36.3	162.6	−15.2	68.9	3.2	85.6	1.6
1999	148.9	76.7	30.8	41.3	170.2	−15.4	72.9	3.5	89.9	1.9

Source

U.S. Bureau of Economic Analysis, *National Income and Product Accounts of the United States, 1929–94* (1998), volume 1, Table 2.4, with revisions and updates from the bureau's Internet site, downloaded June 22, 2001. Regular updates and revisions of the components of the national income and product accounts are reported in *Survey of Current Business*.

Documentation

As defined by the Department of Commerce, personal consumption expenditures represent the market value of purchases of goods and services by individuals resident in the United States and by nonprofit institutions and the value of food, clothing, housing, and financial services received by them as income in kind. Personal consumption expenditures consist primarily of new goods and services purchased from domestic businesses or from abroad. Only the *net* purchases of used goods are included.

Personal consumption expenditures also include certain goods and services provided by government agencies, such as tuition for education provided by public institutions of higher education, charges for medical care at public hospitals, and charges for water and sanitary services.

Some items included are imputed purchases that keep expenditures invariant to changes in the way certain activities are carried out – for example, whether housing is rented or owner-occupied, whether financial services are explicitly charged, or whether employees are paid in kind or in cash. Rental value of owner-occupied houses is included; purchases of dwellings, which are classified as capital goods, are excluded.

Unless noted otherwise, for most goods the U.S. Bureau of Economic Analysis (BEA) uses the commodity-flow method, starting with manufacturers' shipments from the Census Bureau's quinquennial census and including an adjustment for exports and imports from the Census Bureau's foreign trade data. The commodity flow approach was developed by Simon Kuznets and explained in his *Commodity Flow and Capital Formation* (National Bureau of Economic Research, 1938). Estimates of personal consumption expenditures for services are based on a variety of source materials, which cannot be summarized briefly. For most services, figures for benchmark years are derived from data on receipts and expenses from the Census Bureau's quinquennial census.

For a detailed explanation of the estimation of personal consumption expenditures, see U.S. Bureau of Economic Analysis, *Personal Consumption Expenditures*, Methodology Paper Series, MP-6 (1990). For other series and figures and details concerning methodologies and sources, see U.S. Bureau of Economic Analysis (1990) and BEA, "Updated Summary NIPA Methodologies," *Survey of Current Business* (September 1997): 12–17.

For a discussion of the estimates of consumption expenditures before 1929, see Table Cd1–77.

Series Cd156. Consists of purchases (including tips) of meals and beverages from retail, service, and amusement establishments, hotels, dining and buffet cars, schools, school fraternities, institutions, clubs, and industrial lunchrooms. Includes meals and beverages consumed both on- and off-premises.

Series Cd157. Includes military. Food furnished to employees for benchmark years is derived for nonmilitary personnel by multiplying the number of employees of appropriate industries from Bureau of Labor Statistics tabulations times BEA estimates of per capita expenditures for food; for military personnel, estimates are based on outlays reported in the *Budget of the United States* prepared by the Office of Management and Budget. For nonbenchmark years, see U.S. Bureau of Economic Analysis (1997).

Series Cd163. Includes luggage.

Series Cd169. Consists of watch, clock, and jewelry repairs, costume and dress suit rental, and miscellaneous personal services.

Series Cd174. Consists of rent for space and for heating and plumbing facilities, water heaters, lighting fixtures, kitchen cabinets, linoleum, storm windows and doors, window screens, and screen doors, but excludes rent for appliances and furniture and purchases of fuel and electricity.

Series Cd175. Consists of space rent (see the text for series Cd174) and rent for appliances, furnishings, and furniture.

Series Cd176. The rental value of farm dwellings for benchmark years is based on data on the housing stock and average annual rent from the Census Bureau's decennial census of housing and survey of residential finance. For other years, see U.S. Bureau of Economic Analysis (1997).

Series Cd177. Consists of transient hotels, motels, clubs, schools, and other group housing.

Series Cd179. Includes mattresses and bedsprings.

Series Cd180. Consists of refrigerators and freezers, cooking ranges, dishwashers, laundry equipment, stoves, room air conditioners, sewing machines, vacuum cleaners, and other appliances.

Series Cd182. Includes housefurnishings such as floor coverings, comforters, quilts, blankets, pillows, picture frames, mirrors, art products, portable lamps, and clocks. Also includes writing equipment and hand, power, and garden tools.

Series Cd183. Consists largely of textile housefurnishings, including piece goods allocated to housefurnishing use. Also includes lamp shades, brooms, and brushes.

Series Cd192. Expenditures for domestic services for benchmark years are derived for cleaning services from receipts recorded in the Census Bureau's quinquennial census. For other domestic services the number of workers is multiplied by weekly hours, which is in turn multiplied by earnings (all from the Bureau of Labor Statistics). For other years, see U.S. Bureau of Economic Analysis (1997).

Series Cd193. Consists of maintenance services for appliances and housefurnishings, moving and warehouse expenses, postage and express charges, premiums for fire and theft insurance on personal property less benefits and dividends, and miscellaneous household operation services.

Series Cd195. Excludes drug preparations and related products dispensed by physicians, hospitals, and other medical services.

Series Cd199. Consists of osteopathic physicians, chiropractors, private-duty nurses, chiropodists, podiatrists, and others providing health and allied services, not elsewhere classified.

Series Cd200–205. Consists of (1) current expenditures (including consumption of fixed capital) of nonprofit hospitals and nursing homes; and (2) payments by patients to proprietary and government hospitals and nursing homes.

Series Cd207. Consists of (1) premiums, less benefits and dividends, for health, hospitalization, and accidental death and dismemberment insurance provided by commercial insurance carriers; and (2) administrative expenses (including consumption of fixed capital) of nonprofit and self-insured health plans.

Series Cd208. Consists of premiums, less benefits and dividends, for income loss insurance.

Series Cd209. Consists of premiums, less benefits and dividends, for privately administered workers' compensation.

Series Cd213. Excludes life insurance carriers.

Series Cd214. Consists of (1) operating expenses of commercial life insurance carriers; (2) administrative expenses of private noninsured pension plans and publicly administered government employee retirement plans; and (3) premiums, less benefits and dividends, of fraternal benefit societies. For commercial life insurance carriers, excludes expenses for accident and health insurance and includes profits of stock companies and services furnished without payment by banks, credit agencies, and investment companies. For pension and retirement plans, excludes services furnished without payment by banks, credit agencies, and investment companies.

Series Cd217. Consists of current expenditures (including consumption of fixed capital) of trade unions and professional associations, employment agency fees, money order fees, spending for classified advertisements, tax return preparation services, and other personal business services.

Series Cd220. The value of expenditures on new autos is estimated by multiplying the physical quantity purchased times average retail price. Unit sales, information to allocate sales among consumers and other purchasers, and average list price with options, adjusted for transportation charges, sales tax, dealer discounts, and rebates, are all collected from trade sources.

Series Cd221. For benchmark years, net purchases of used autos are derived from change in the consumer stock of autos from trade sources. For dealers' margin, retail sales are from the Census Bureau's quinquennial census and the margin rate is from the Census Bureau's annual survey of retail trade. For other years, see U.S. Bureau of Economic Analysis (1997).

Series Cd222. For benchmark years, expenditures on new trucks, a component of this series, are estimated using the BEA's commodity-flow method, starting with manufacturers' shipments from the Census Bureau's quinquennial census and including an adjustment for exports and imports from the Census Bureau's foreign trade data. For an explanation of the commodity-flow method, see U.S. Bureau of Economic Analysis (1990). For other years, see U.S. Bureau of Economic Analysis (1997).

(continued)

TABLE Cd153–263   Consumption expenditures, by type: 1929–1999   *Continued*

Series Cd225. Expenditures on gasoline and oil are estimated for benchmark years by multiplying the physical quantity purchased times average retail price. The gallons consumed are from U.S. Department of Transportation data, and the allocation of that total among consumers and other purchasers is derived from various federal agencies and trade sources. Average retail price is from the Census Bureau's quinquennial census. For other years, see U.S. Bureau of Economic Analysis (1997).

Series Cd227. Consists of premiums, less benefits and dividends, for motor vehicle insurance.

Series Cd235. Consists of baggage charges, coastal and inland waterway fares, travel agents' fees, and airport bus fares.

Series Cd248. Excludes athletics.

Series Cd249. Consists of admissions to professional and amateur athletic events and to racetracks.

Series Cd250. Consists of dues and fees, excluding insurance premiums.

Series Cd251. Consists of billiard parlors; bowling alleys; dancing, riding, shooting, skating, and swimming places; amusement devices and parks; golf courses; sightseeing buses and guides; private flying operations; casino gambling; and other commercial participant amusements.

Series Cd253. Consists of net receipts of lotteries and expenditures for purchases of pets and pet care services, cable TV, film processing, photographic studios, sporting and recreation camps, videocassette rentals, and recreational services not elsewhere classified.

Series Cd255. For private institutions, equals current expenditures (including consumption of fixed capital) less receipts – such as those from meals, rooms, and entertainments – accounted for separately

in consumer expenditures, and less expenditures for research and development financed under contracts or grants. For government institutions, equals student payments of tuition.

Series Cd256. For private institutions, equals current expenditures (including consumption of fixed capital) less receipts – such as those from meals, rooms, and entertainments – accounted for separately in consumer expenditures. For government institutions, equals student payments of tuition. Excludes child day care services, which are included in religious and welfare activities.

Series Cd257. Consists of (1) fees paid to commercial, business, trade, and correspondence schools and for educational services not elsewhere classified; and (2) current expenditures (including consumption of fixed capital) by research organizations and foundations for education and research.

Series Cd258. For nonprofit institutions, equals current expenditures (including consumption of fixed capital) of religious, social welfare, foreign relief, and political organizations, museums, libraries, and foundations. The expenditures are net of receipts – such as those from meals, rooms, and entertainments – accounted for separately in consumer expenditures, and exclude relief payments within the United States and expenditures by foundations for education and research. For proprietary and government institutions, equals receipts from users.

Series Cd260. Beginning with 1981, includes U.S. students' expenditures abroad; these expenditures were $0.3 billion in 1981.

Series Cd262. Beginning with 1981, includes nonresidents' student and medical care expenditures in the United States; student expenditures were $2.2 billion and medical expenditures were $0.4 billion in 1981.

TABLE Cd264–377 Consumption expenditures, by type: 1987–1999 [Chained 1996 dollars]
Contributed by Lee A. Craig

		Food and tobacco									Clothing, accessories, and jewelry	
	Total	Total	Food purchased for off-premises consumption	Purchased meals and beverages	Food furnished to employees	Food produced and consumed on farms	Tobacco products	Food, excluding alcoholic beverages	Alcoholic beverages purchased for off-premises consumption	Other alcoholic beverages	Total	Shoes
	Cd264	Cd265	Cd266	Cd267	Cd268	Cd269	Cd270	Cd271	Cd272	Cd273	Cd274	Cd275
Year	Billion chained 1996 dollars	Billion chained 1996 dollars	Billion chained 1996 dollars	Billion chained 1996 dollars	Billion chained 1996 dollars	Billion chained 1996 dollars	Billion chained 1996 dollars	Billion chained 1996 dollars	Billion chained 1996 dollars	Billion chained 1996 dollars	Billion chained 1996 dollars	Billion chained 1996 dollars
1987	4,113.4	721.7	425.3	231.0	7.4	0.7	59.2	579.2	53.6	31.4	236.9	29.1
1988	4,279.5	744.7	436.9	245.5	7.5	0.7	54.7	603.2	54.0	33.1	246.2	29.7
1989	4,393.7	757.1	442.7	252.5	7.7	0.6	54.0	614.2	55.1	34.0	258.5	31.5
1990	4,474.5	774.4	452.4	261.8	7.7	0.6	52.0	628.2	57.6	36.5	258.2	32.0
1991	4,466.6	769.9	451.7	261.6	7.6	0.6	48.3	631.8	53.2	36.2	254.5	31.2
1992	4,594.5	776.2	450.8	266.6	7.6	0.6	50.4	637.9	50.2	37.6	268.5	32.0
1993	4,748.9	790.6	458.3	278.5	7.8	0.5	45.5	655.7	51.4	38.1	281.6	33.0
1994	4,928.1	812.9	468.8	287.5	8.0	0.5	48.0	672.5	53.8	38.6	297.2	35.1
1995	5,075.6	825.1	473.7	294.6	8.2	0.5	48.1	681.9	55.4	39.6	312.9	36.8
1996	5,237.5	834.5	476.7	300.5	8.2	0.5	48.2	689.1	56.1	40.7	333.3	38.8
1997	5,423.9	842.1	477.6	308.0	8.3	0.5	47.6	695.5	57.2	41.8	348.8	40.1
1998	5,678.7	858.8	488.6	315.3	8.5	0.5	46.2	708.9	61.8	42.1	376.3	42.2
1999	5,978.8	887.8	506.9	329.9	8.5	0.5	43.4	737.3	66.4	42.2	411.5	45.0

	Clothing, accessories, and jewelry							Personal care			Housing	
	Total	Women's and children's	Men's and boys'	Standard clothing issued to military personnel	Cleaning, storage, and repair of clothing and shoes	Jewelry and watches	Other	Total	Toilet articles and preparations	Barbershops, beauty parlors, and health clubs	Total	Owner-occupied nonfarm dwellings – space rent
	Cd276	Cd277	Cd278	Cd279	Cd280	Cd281	Cd282	Cd283	Cd284	Cd285	Cd286	Cd287
Year	Billion chained 1996 dollars	Billion chained 1996 dollars	Billion chained 1996 dollars	Billion chained 1996 dollars	Billion chained 1996 dollars	Billion chained 1996 dollars	Billion chained 1996 dollars	Billion chained 1996 dollars	Billion chained 1996 dollars	Billion chained 1996 dollars	Billion chained 1996 dollars	Billion chained 1996 dollars
1987	153.2	98.8	54.3	0.2	11.1	30.2	13.1	55.6	36.5	19.1	644.8	445.5
1988	158.0	101.5	56.5	0.2	12.3	30.9	15.6	57.7	37.5	20.3	663.4	462.3
1989	166.9	107.5	59.3	0.2	12.9	30.7	16.7	59.2	38.5	20.7	679.9	477.4
1990	165.1	105.4	59.7	0.2	13.3	30.1	18.3	60.1	39.5	20.6	696.2	488.3
1991	166.5	106.3	60.2	0.2	12.4	29.1	15.2	59.5	39.2	20.3	709.8	501.6
1992	176.6	113.1	63.5	0.3	12.3	30.1	17.4	61.5	39.4	22.2	719.3	509.0
1993	185.3	118.6	66.7	0.3	12.1	32.7	18.4	62.6	40.9	21.7	728.1	520.8
1994	196.2	124.7	71.5	0.3	12.0	34.5	19.2	64.8	42.9	21.9	749.1	535.7
1995	207.2	132.3	74.9	0.3	12.4	36.7	19.5	68.3	45.2	23.1	763.7	546.1
1996	219.5	140.8	78.6	0.3	12.7	40.3	21.7	71.6	48.0	23.5	772.6	555.4
1997	231.2	148.4	82.8	0.3	12.8	42.9	21.4	75.2	50.5	24.7	787.2	569.0
1998	249.8	161.2	88.5	0.3	13.0	47.8	23.4	78.2	52.5	25.7	807.7	586.7
1999	273.3	177.6	95.7	0.3	13.5	54.0	25.8	81.9	55.7	26.2	828.3	605.7

(continued)

TABLE Cd264–377 Consumption expenditures, by type: 1987–1999 [Chained 1996 dollars] *Continued*

	Housing			Household operation							
	Tenant-occupied nonfarm dwellings—rent	Rental value of farm dwellings	Other	Total	Furniture	Kitchen and other household appliances	China, glassware, tableware, and utensils	Other durable housefurnishings	Semidurable housefurnishings	Cleaning and polishing preparations, and miscellaneous household supplies and paper products	Stationery and writing supplies
	Cd288	Cd289	Cd290	Cd291	Cd292	Cd293	Cd294	Cd295	Cd296	Cd297	Cd298
Year	Billion chained 1996 dollars	Billion chained 1996 dollars	Billion chained 1996 dollars	Billion chained 1996 dollars	Billion chained 1996 dollars	Billion chained 1996 dollars	Billion chained 1996 dollars	Billion chained 1996 dollars	Billion chained 1996 dollars	Billion chained 1996 dollars	Billion chained 1996 dollars
1987	167.7	7.2	24.3	440.7	38.8	21.4	15.7	39.9	19.5	39.9	13.6
1988	168.6	7.2	25.3	458.9	39.6	22.3	16.7	41.3	20.4	41.4	14.8
1989	169.6	7.0	25.8	476.0	43.7	23.4	17.7	41.1	21.2	41.6	15.9
1990	174.6	6.9	26.2	476.8	42.2	23.4	18.2	40.1	21.8	42.4	16.4
1991	174.9	7.0	26.2	477.3	41.4	23.2	18.0	38.1	22.6	42.1	16.7
1992	175.6	6.8	27.9	490.0	41.7	24.4	19.1	39.2	24.6	43.4	17.0
1993	172.4	6.6	28.3	517.2	44.0	26.0	20.4	41.7	25.8	45.6	17.6
1994	177.8	6.4	29.2	541.9	46.3	27.2	21.8	45.3	27.4	48.0	18.3
1995	181.6	6.3	29.7	564.2	48.1	29.1	23.5	47.8	29.0	48.5	18.4
1996	180.6	6.2	30.2	589.2	50.9	30.0	25.4	50.5	31.0	49.8	18.8
1997	181.0	6.0	31.1	611.6	53.8	30.9	27.3	53.3	33.8	50.9	19.2
1998	182.9	5.9	32.2	641.1	56.6	32.8	28.9	57.0	36.8	52.1	19.9
1999	183.7	5.7	33.4	681.9	60.6	36.0	32.2	63.1	40.5	54.6	21.7

	Household operation								Medical care		
	Household utilities										
	Total	Electricity	Gas	Water and other sanitary services	Fuel oil and coal	Telephone and telegraph	Domestic services	Other	Total	Drug preparations and sundries	Ophthalmic products and orthopedic appliances
	Cd299	Cd300	Cd301	Cd302	Cd303	Cd304	Cd305	Cd306	Cd307	Cd308	Cd309
Year	Billion chained 1996 dollars	Billion chained 1996 dollars	Billion chained 1996 dollars	Billion chained 1996 dollars	Billion chained 1996 dollars	Billion chained 1996 dollars	Billion chained 1996 dollars	Billion chained 1996 dollars	Billion chained 1996 dollars	Billion chained 1996 dollars	Billion chained 1996 dollars
1987	155.8	78.1	28.7	34.8	14.2	52.8	10.9	34.8	711.3	69.5	11.2
1988	162.8	81.5	30.8	35.6	14.7	56.0	11.5	34.5	745.6	72.6	13.1
1989	166.1	82.6	32.0	37.0	14.4	59.8	12.2	35.1	768.9	76.3	14.0
1990	162.8	83.2	29.5	37.1	13.1	62.6	12.6	36.1	807.6	80.3	16.1
1991	165.8	85.6	30.7	36.6	12.9	65.4	11.7	33.6	830.3	81.7	14.3
1992	164.9	84.1	31.5	35.9	13.2	72.5	12.6	31.0	861.6	82.2	14.2
1993	173.7	89.3	32.8	37.4	14.0	76.2	12.9	33.8	874.3	84.7	14.4
1994	176.5	90.6	32.2	38.7	15.0	82.6	13.2	35.7	887.2	88.4	15.7
1995	180.8	92.5	32.8	39.8	15.7	88.1	13.7	37.2	907.8	94.1	16.0
1996	185.0	93.3	35.5	40.7	15.6	97.1	13.6	37.1	932.3	100.3	17.6
1997	184.1	93.5	34.1	41.6	15.0	104.7	13.5	40.1	963.2	109.0	18.9
1998	186.1	99.6	30.8	42.1	14.0	114.4	15.1	41.5	997.0	117.4	19.9
1999	189.4	100.3	30.9	43.0	15.5	126.3	16.0	42.0	1,030.0	127.2	21.2

Medical care

Year	Physicians Cd310 Billion chained 1996 dollars	Dentists Cd311 Billion chained 1996 dollars	Other professional services Cd312 Billion chained 1996 dollars	Total Cd313 Billion chained 1996 dollars	Hospitals and nursing homes Total Cd314 Billion chained 1996 dollars	Hospitals Nonprofit Cd315 Billion chained 1996 dollars	Hospitals Proprietary Cd316 Billion chained 1996 dollars	Hospitals Government Cd317 Billion chained 1996 dollars	Nursing homes Cd318 Billion chained 1996 dollars	Health insurance Total Cd319 Billion chained 1996 dollars	Health insurance Medical care and hospitalization Cd320 Billion chained 1996 dollars
1987	162.2	44.6	57.3	309.4	264.8	168.3	36.4	61.8	44.7	62.4	45.3
1988	172.8	44.4	63.0	319.6	272.4	174.9	37.1	61.6	47.3	64.6	46.8
1989	175.9	44.6	68.0	328.3	277.9	180.9	36.9	60.9	50.4	65.5	47.5
1990	183.3	44.8	78.8	340.5	285.7	189.1	36.6	60.3	54.9	66.0	47.9
1991	187.4	43.9	85.8	352.5	295.5	197.2	36.2	62.1	57.1	66.7	48.6
1992	194.1	45.4	94.6	364.4	305.5	205.9	35.4	64.2	58.8	68.3	50.1
1993	190.1	45.8	102.4	371.4	312.1	210.6	34.0	67.4	59.3	66.3	49.7
1994	189.4	47.1	107.5	375.6	316.4	211.4	34.3	70.7	59.2	63.8	49.7
1995	193.8	48.7	114.9	381.5	320.0	211.1	36.1	72.8	61.6	58.9	47.1
1996	199.1	48.4	119.7	390.8	327.6	213.5	38.7	75.4	63.2	56.6	45.3
1997	206.0	49.6	121.1	401.1	334.2	217.3	41.2	75.7	66.8	57.8	46.7
1998	213.7	50.5	124.3	410.4	342.0	222.0	41.9	78.1	68.3	61.0	48.2
1999	219.5	50.6	126.8	422.3	353.4	228.2	44.5	80.8	68.9	62.7	50.2

Medical care — Health insurance

Year	Income loss Cd321 Billion chained 1996 dollars	Workers' compensation Cd322 Billion chained 1996 dollars
1987	0.8	21.0
1988	0.8	22.6
1989	0.8	23.0
1990	0.8	23.5
1991	0.7	24.2
1992	0.9	21.3
1993	0.9	17.2
1994	0.9	13.5
1995	0.9	10.9
1996	1.0	10.3
1997	0.9	10.2
1998	0.9	12.3
1999	0.9	11.4

Personal business

Year	Total Cd323 Billion chained 1996 dollars	Brokerage charges and investment counseling Cd324 Billion chained 1996 dollars	Bank service charges, trust services, and safe-deposit box rental Cd325 Billion chained 1996 dollars	Services furnished without payment by financial intermediaries Cd326 Billion chained 1996 dollars	Expense of handling life insurance and pension plans Cd327 Billion chained 1996 dollars	Legal services Cd328 Billion chained 1996 dollars	Funeral and burial expenses Cd329 Billion chained 1996 dollars	Other Cd330 Billion chained 1996 dollars
1987	336.1	20.7	33.8	144.3	63.3	46.0	11.7	17.3
1988	345.6	17.4	34.4	146.4	70.1	49.8	12.5	18.7
1989	355.3	19.2	36.0	147.5	72.2	51.1	12.6	19.9
1990	363.2	19.1	36.5	154.2	71.2	51.9	12.9	20.9
1991	378.7	21.5	37.3	157.2	81.3	50.1	12.9	21.2
1992	383.8	24.9	38.8	156.8	78.8	51.3	13.4	21.6
1993	404.9	30.2	40.4	163.2	84.9	51.0	13.7	22.4
1994	414.6	32.6	39.7	172.3	83.0	50.6	13.5	23.3
1995	424.4	36.1	40.5	173.9	87.0	49.7	14.0	23.6
1996	435.1	43.2	42.9	177.0	81.3	51.5	14.5	24.8
1997	462.1	50.5	45.6	188.4	84.6	52.8	14.4	25.7
1998	485.9	60.3	51.7	195.8	82.9	53.9	14.9	27.2
1999	520.4	74.6	57.1	209.5	83.7	54.7	14.4	28.8

Transportation — User-operated transportation

Year	Total Cd331 Billion chained 1996 dollars	Total Cd332 Billion chained 1996 dollars	New autos Cd333 Billion chained 1996 dollars
1987	519.6	481.4	111.3
1988	542.4	503.4	115.8
1989	544.5	505.9	109.2
1990	532.2	493.5	104.0
1991	486.0	448.0	81.0
1992	509.3	471.7	85.5
1993	534.1	496.1	87.8
1994	561.5	521.2	89.7
1995	574.7	532.3	83.5
1996	594.6	550.2	81.9
1997	619.3	573.5	82.4
1998	656.0	608.5	88.4
1999	698.3	649.1	98.8

(continued)

TABLE Cd264–377   Consumption expenditures, by type: 1987–1999   [Chained 1996 dollars]   *Continued*

Transportation

	User-operated transportation							Purchased local transportation			Purchased intercity transportation	
	Net purchases of used autos	Other motor vehicles	Tires, tubes, accessories, and other parts	Repair, greasing, washing, parking, storage, rental, and leasing	Gasoline and oil	Bridge, tunnel, ferry, and road tolls	Insurance	Total	Mass transit systems	Taxicab	Total	Railway
	Cd334	Cd335	Cd336	Cd337	Cd338	Cd339	Cd340	Cd341	Cd342	Cd343	Cd344	Cd345
Year	Billion chained 1996 dollars	Billion chained 1996 dollars	Billion chained 1996 dollars	Billion chained 1996 dollars	Billion chained 1996 dollars	Billion chained 1996 dollars	Billion chained 1996 dollars	Billion chained 1996 dollars	Billion chained 1996 dollars	Billion chained 1996 dollars	Billion chained 1996 dollars	Billion chained 1996 dollars
1987	41.1	63.2	26.1	92.9	112.8	2.8	31.0	10.0	6.5	3.5	28.1	0.8
1988	41.6	68.2	28.3	99.6	114.9	2.5	31.9	10.1	7.0	3.2	28.8	0.9
1989	41.5	74.2	28.5	101.7	116.4	2.9	31.2	10.2	7.0	3.1	28.5	0.9
1990	42.0	69.7	29.7	100.8	113.1	2.8	31.0	10.8	7.4	3.4	28.1	0.9
1991	40.8	60.7	29.1	93.7	109.4	2.9	30.3	10.7	7.5	3.2	27.2	0.8
1992	41.7	68.4	29.9	100.2	112.5	3.3	30.1	10.6	7.5	3.0	27.1	0.7
1993	46.9	75.3	32.2	105.1	115.4	3.3	30.1	10.8	7.6	3.2	27.5	0.7
1994	48.5	81.7	35.2	115.0	117.4	3.4	30.2	11.3	8.0	3.3	29.2	0.7
1995	51.2	81.9	36.8	124.5	120.2	3.5	30.6	11.4	7.8	3.6	31.0	0.7
1996	51.4	84.3	38.7	134.2	124.2	3.7	31.8	11.2	7.7	3.5	33.3	0.6
1997	54.4	88.1	39.9	144.2	128.1	3.9	32.5	11.3	7.7	3.6	34.5	0.7
1998	57.7	103.2	42.3	148.3	131.2	3.8	33.6	12.0	8.0	4.0	35.6	0.7
1999	60.3	117.9	45.7	153.9	134.2	3.8	34.2	12.3	8.3	4.0	37.0	0.7

Transportation / Recreation

	Purchased intercity transportation			Recreation					Video and audio goods, musical instruments, and computer goods		
	Bus	Airline	Other	Total	Books and maps	Magazines, newspapers, and sheet music	Nondurable toys and sport supplies	Wheel goods, sports and photographic equipment, boats, and pleasure aircraft	Total	Video and audio goods, and musical instruments	Computers, peripherals, and software
	Cd346	Cd347	Cd348	Cd349	Cd350	Cd351	Cd352	Cd353	Cd354	Cd355	Cd356
Year	Billion chained 1996 dollars	Billion chained 1996 dollars	Billion chained 1996 dollars	Billion chained 1996 dollars	Billion chained 1996 dollars	Billion chained 1996 dollars	Billion chained 1996 dollars	Billion chained 1996 dollars	Billion chained 1996 dollars	Billion chained 1996 dollars	Billion chained 1996 dollars
1987	1.5	22.8	2.8	247.6	17.1	24.9	28.5	30.0	25.7	31.6	1.0
1988	1.9	22.6	3.4	268.3	18.2	26.3	29.9	31.4	29.4	34.7	1.5
1989	1.6	22.4	3.7	282.7	18.5	26.4	32.1	32.4	31.2	36.6	1.7
1990	1.3	22.0	3.9	292.6	18.9	27.2	33.7	31.8	33.0	37.3	2.1
1991	1.5	21.2	3.8	296.4	18.6	26.2	35.2	30.7	36.2	37.5	3.4
1992	1.5	20.8	4.1	313.0	18.9	25.2	36.7	30.9	40.3	39.8	4.5
1993	1.6	21.4	3.8	338.3	20.3	25.7	39.5	33.4	47.7	43.4	7.0
1994	1.5	22.9	4.2	365.2	22.0	26.8	43.1	35.5	57.1	49.2	10.0
1995	1.6	24.3	4.4	398.7	23.9	27.2	47.4	38.5	67.3	53.6	14.6
1996	1.8	26.2	4.7	429.6	24.9	27.6	50.6	40.5	80.0	56.4	23.6
1997	1.8	27.3	4.6	463.7	26.0	28.8	53.7	43.1	97.0	60.4	38.1
1998	2.0	28.2	4.7	507.3	26.8	31.5	60.7	47.2	122.1	68.1	60.8
1999	2.0	29.5	4.7	567.5	29.2	35.0	71.1	53.3	154.3	79.0	92.3

Recreation

Year	Radio and television repair Cd357 Billion chained 1996 dollars	Flowers, seeds, and potted plants Cd358 Billion chained 1996 dollars	Admissions to specified spectator amusements Total Cd359 Billion chained 1996 dollars	Motion picture theaters Cd360 Billion chained 1996 dollars	Legitimate theaters and opera, and entertainments of nonprofit institutions Cd361 Billion chained 1996 dollars	Spectator sports Cd362 Billion chained 1996 dollars	Clubs and fraternal organizations Cd363 Billion chained 1996 dollars	Commercial participant amusements Cd364 Billion chained 1996 dollars	Pari-mutuel net receipts Cd365 Billion chained 1996 dollars	Other Cd366 Billion chained 1996 dollars
1987	4.7	10.5	15.6	4.9	5.8	4.8	8.8	23.1	4.4	63.7
1988	4.9	10.9	16.4	5.3	6.0	5.0	9.0	25.6	4.4	70.5
1989	4.8	11.5	17.1	5.9	5.7	5.5	9.7	27.1	4.3	76.3
1990	4.6	11.5	18.0	6.2	6.3	5.5	10.3	29.2	4.2	78.7
1991	4.1	11.1	17.9	6.0	6.2	5.6	10.9	29.3	4.0	78.5
1992	3.9	11.7	18.3	5.6	6.9	5.8	11.4	33.1	3.7	84.1
1993	3.6	12.5	19.7	5.6	7.7	6.3	12.1	36.7	3.5	87.5
1994	3.5	13.2	19.8	5.7	7.8	6.3	12.5	40.6	3.5	89.3
1995	3.7	13.4	20.2	5.8	8.0	6.4	13.1	45.1	3.6	96.2
1996	3.7	14.9	20.7	5.8	8.0	6.9	14.0	48.3	3.5	100.8
1997	3.9	15.8	21.5	6.1	8.4	6.9	14.3	51.5	3.5	105.3
1998	3.9	16.6	22.5	6.6	8.7	7.2	14.2	54.1	3.5	108.6
1999	3.8	18.3	23.4	6.7	9.2	7.4	14.6	58.8	3.6	113.7

Education and research　　　　　**Foreign travel and other**

Year	Total Cd367 Billion chained 1996 dollars	Higher education Cd368 Billion chained 1996 dollars	Nursery, elementary, and secondary schools Cd369 Billion chained 1996 dollars	Other Cd370 Billion chained 1996 dollars	Religious and welfare activities Cd371 Billion chained 1996 dollars	Foreign travel and other, net Cd372 Billion chained 1996 dollars	Foreign travel by U.S. residents Cd373 Billion chained 1996 dollars	Expenditures abroad by U.S. residents Cd374 Billion chained 1996 dollars	Less: expenditures in the United States by nonresidents Cd375 Billion chained 1996 dollars	Less: personal remittances in kind to nonresidents Cd376 Billion chained 1996 dollars	Residual Cd377 Billion chained 1996 dollars
1987	95.2	55.6	22.4	17.6	96.8	10.9	46.4	5.5	40.1	1.0	−36.7
1988	100.0	56.7	22.8	20.6	104.1	5.2	48.2	4.7	46.6	1.2	−35.8
1989	104.9	58.6	24.2	22.1	108.0	−0.8	49.4	4.9	54.1	1.0	−31.9
1990	107.6	60.1	25.0	22.4	115.3	−5.3	51.7	4.3	60.1	1.1	−34.0
1991	108.9	61.4	25.1	22.5	116.6	−13.1	47.3	4.0	63.2	1.2	−32.0
1992	111.8	62.8	25.6	23.3	125.1	−18.5	49.7	2.8	69.2	1.7	−23.8
1993	113.5	63.5	25.9	24.1	126.8	−18.6	52.7	2.8	72.3	1.8	−14.9
1994	115.8	64.3	26.7	24.8	136.5	−16.1	55.8	2.6	72.9	1.7	−7.8
1995	119.2	65.6	27.4	26.2	138.7	−21.4	55.3	2.3	77.4	1.7	−2.9
1996	122.3	66.1	27.4	28.8	146.8	−24.1	57.6	2.2	82.4	1.5	0.1
1997	126.0	66.9	28.1	31.0	145.5	−20.6	62.4	3.3	84.7	1.6	−2.1
1998	130.0	67.9	28.1	34.0	154.0	−11.2	69.3	3.6	82.4	1.6	−16.0
1999	133.9	69.1	28.1	36.6	156.1	−10.8	71.5	3.8	84.2	1.9	−41.5

(continued)

TABLE Cd264–377   Consumption expenditures, by type: 1987–1999   [Chained 1996 dollars]   *Continued*

Source

U.S. Bureau of Economic Analysis, *National Income and Product Accounts of the United States, 1929–94* (1998), volume 1, Table 2.5, with revisions and updates from the bureau's Internet site, downloaded June 22, 2001. Regular updates and revisions of the components of the national income and product accounts are reported in *Survey of Current Business*.

Documentation

See the text for the corresponding series in Table Cd153–263.

The series in Table Cd153–263 were deflated to generate the corresponding real series in this table. Prior to 1996, the U.S. Bureau of Economic Analysis (BEA) typically deflated consumption expenditures with a fixed-weight Laspeyres index. In 1996, however, as part of a comprehensive revision of the national income and product accounts, BEA began using a chained annual-weight index, the so-called Fisher index, which is a geometric mean of the conventional Laspeyres index (in which the weights were from the first or base period) and a Paasche index (in which the weights are from the second period). For the theoretical discussion of these indexes, see Irving Fisher, *The Making of Index Numbers* (Houghton Mifflin, 1922). For the details of the BEA's use of those indexes, see J. Steven Landefeld and Robert P. Parker, "BEA's Chain Indexes, Time Series, and Measures of Long-Term Economic Growth," *Survey of Current Business* (May 1997): 58–68.

In general, the chained indexes are more accurate than the fixed-weight indexes, particularly as the series moves farther away from the base year. In addition, the chained series avoid the so-called substitution bias, which reflects the fact that goods and services for which consumption grows rapidly are often those for which prices, that is, the weights in the Laspeyres quantity index, are often falling or at least increasing less than prices on average.

The chained Fisher index is more difficult to calculate than the fixed-weight estimates. Furthermore, and particularly troubling to some, is the fact that the chained series are not additive. This observation explains the presence of the residual, series Cd377, which represents the difference between the total and the sum of the component series. Of additional concern is the fact that the residual tends to expand as one moves away from the base period. Using the same base period for the old Laspeyres index yielded series with components that added up precisely to the totals. Landefeld and Parker note that the BEA employed such measures at least partly because users considered this property to be useful. In particular, the Laspeyres indexes for particular series could be grouped into various aggregates while maintaining additivity.

TABLE Cd378–410 Value of commodities destined for domestic consumption, by type: 1869–1919

Contributed by Lee A. Craig

		Perishable							Semidurable		
		Food and kindred products				Magazines, newspapers, stationery and supplies, and miscellaneous	Fuel and lighting products				
	Total	Manufactured	Nonmanufactured	Cigars, cigarettes, and tobacco	Drugs, toilet and household preparations	paper products	Manufactured	Nonmanufactured	Total	Dry goods and notions	Clothing and personal furnishings
	Cd378	Cd379	Cd380	Cd381	Cd382	Cd383	Cd384	Cd385	Cd386	Cd387	Cd388
Year	Thousand dollars	Thousand dollars	Thousand dollars	Thousand dollars	Thousand dollars	Thousand dollars	Thousand dollars	Thousand dollars	Thousand dollars	Thousand dollars	Thousand dollars
1869	1,594,193	673,101	699,082	74,685	37,677	30,551	29,361	49,736	665,400	224,478	229,802
1879	1,996,100	962,935	716,507	119,676	40,381	61,461	39,678	55,462	828,229	263,131	358,234
1889	2,905,690	1,434,264	956,639	202,528	81,629	93,863	59,524	77,243	1,132,923	281,673	560,813
1890	2,705,314	1,155,484	991,441	215,375	90,070	97,334	75,432	80,178	1,195,977	299,556	588,836
1891	2,964,881	1,308,518	1,079,222	226,550	97,901	101,170	62,670	88,850	1,196,860	289,254	603,250
1892	2,908,827	1,251,447	1,062,266	230,487	104,730	109,273	52,137	98,487	1,255,775	297,164	632,831
1893	3,314,358	1,555,299	1,182,710	218,492	104,872	98,327	54,006	100,652	1,124,216	259,363	566,942
1894	2,916,319	1,337,867	1,012,266	218,118	102,895	92,925	61,902	90,346	970,869	209,854	478,129
1895	3,119,121	1,443,718	1,079,016	202,379	111,298	94,076	95,753	92,881	1,114,670	265,749	542,192
1896	2,944,027	1,436,187	927,538	193,016	112,689	89,957	92,770	91,870	1,064,607	215,548	549,474
1897	3,222,644	1,633,679	1,032,104	197,321	115,551	92,569	62,381	89,039	1,153,957	232,276	596,824
1898	3,431,733	1,707,906	1,121,390	226,864	122,411	103,191	63,941	86,030	1,175,751	227,358	608,187
1899	3,820,907	1,955,505	1,160,890	267,371	134,559	113,030	87,729	101,823	1,374,420	255,779	743,651
1900	4,100,837	2,083,885	1,249,132	303,976	136,197	122,290	100,332	105,025	1,465,700	271,943	817,364
1901	4,620,511	2,364,955	1,420,870	327,931	155,189	134,899	84,707	131,960	1,528,490	271,081	837,949
1902	4,764,692	2,403,132	1,519,311	325,098	174,015	151,263	89,704	102,169	1,613,823	298,710	892,775
1903	5,012,723	2,516,662	1,518,942	346,009	183,112	154,180	111,522	182,296	1,734,666	302,082	981,795
1904	5,167,699	2,601,491	1,614,914	339,232	182,257	159,729	109,242	160,834	1,746,493	285,066	992,585
1905	5,403,555	2,856,673	1,540,049	357,192	215,752	172,477	94,420	166,992	1,925,320	318,314	1,099,733
1906	5,912,688	3,121,037	1,719,638	398,130	225,360	184,314	102,875	161,334	2,244,158	348,180	1,314,701
1907	6,452,678	3,389,702	1,886,923	405,162	249,297	196,653	128,457	196,484	2,310,071	375,512	1,335,411
1908	5,988,070	2,974,683	1,915,699	399,755	234,127	156,762	125,789	181,255	2,155,465	295,451	1,286,987
1909	6,922,092	3,617,655	2,112,522	430,506	250,290	210,551	124,746	175,822	2,447,035	368,034	1,459,721
1910	7,386,035	3,823,456	2,306,102	463,966	266,834	209,866	120,973	194,838	2,417,299	349,526	1,408,347
1911	7,491,275	3,980,074	2,235,742	460,372	278,791	211,325	119,064	205,907	2,571,369	326,339	1,560,044
1912	8,100,756	4,342,294	2,410,531	468,913	289,430	233,604	142,004	213,980	2,754,388	363,153	1,656,668
1913	8,230,180	4,441,948	2,315,912	506,812	294,939	243,945	191,304	235,320	2,900,185	348,647	1,721,595
1914	8,296,467	4,484,813	2,380,096	500,889	288,983	254,407	160,355	226,924	2,709,518	337,785	1,598,100
1915	8,079,807	4,342,078	2,310,325	478,613	330,970	255,583	141,697	220,541	2,635,735	317,012	1,533,914
1916	9,893,244	5,380,148	2,693,620	522,394	420,685	352,219	262,503	261,675	3,573,718	461,560	2,025,344
1917	13,174,069	6,925,675	3,907,237	629,498	511,523	407,531	425,717	366,888	4,790,623	620,291	2,622,704
1918	15,807,190	8,583,600	4,280,803	863,979	636,099	445,493	580,684	416,532	6,076,066	854,779	3,361,106
1919	17,215,450	9,312,376	4,709,015	1,000,045	660,130	458,683	630,668	444,533	6,770,232	890,859	3,817,927

(continued)

TABLE Cd378–410   Value of commodities destined for domestic consumption, by type: 1869–1919   Continued

	Semidurable				Durable						
	Shoes and other footwear	Housefurnishings	Toys, games, and sporting goods	Tires and tubes	Total	Household furniture	Heating and cooking apparatus and household appliances, except electrical	Electrical household appliances and supplies	Floor coverings	Miscellaneous housefurnishings	China and household utensils
	Cd389	Cd390	Cd391	Cd392	Cd393	Cd394	Cd395	Cd396	Cd397	Cd398	Cd399
Year	Thousand dollars	Thousand dollars	Thousand dollars	Thousand dollars	Thousand dollars	Thousand dollars	Thousand dollars	Thousand dollars	Thousand dollars	Thousand dollars	Thousand dollars
1869	185,268	12,843	13,009	—	262,657	58,457	26,407	—	25,749	14,356	26,017
1879	173,685	16,219	16,960	—	304,293	65,199	22,992	—	31,276	25,425	31,239
1889	236,057	32,114	22,266	—	499,203	93,396	38,937	—	46,340	51,249	46,360
1890	249,816	34,482	23,287	—	538,703	95,276	37,924	—	50,054	53,832	49,326
1891	244,161	35,349	24,846	—	556,837	100,473	39,122	—	60,418	54,457	51,745
1892	263,807	36,954	25,019	—	579,295	114,992	38,886	—	56,168	56,437	52,855
1893	233,550	35,918	28,443	—	496,302	100,204	35,296	—	46,623	53,510	43,460
1894	228,042	32,416	22,428	—	429,337	82,431	30,970	—	40,602	48,311	39,306
1895	235,967	36,427	26,429	7,906	497,667	93,965	35,483	—	49,695	52,947	45,923
1896	228,871	35,499	25,414	9,801	475,184	90,208	45,611	—	39,524	51,109	51,004
1897	246,300	35,655	24,799	18,103	506,534	88,420	50,733	—	44,084	51,923	50,980
1898	261,925	35,863	23,407	19,011	528,943	89,399	46,341	—	43,622	51,819	51,974
1899	292,860	42,462	26,952	12,716	634,259	104,084	59,233	1,858	54,499	61,053	60,885
1900	289,810	49,809	28,980	7,794	658,679	106,942	61,914	2,384	56,051	70,733	69,503
1901	327,386	49,392	36,483	6,199	718,903	118,721	70,677	2,550	59,367	69,384	73,492
1902	325,854	53,238	37,784	5,462	786,325	129,380	78,550	3,236	71,441	75,359	78,523
1903	352,508	53,871	40,142	4,268	825,680	139,249	78,828	3,753	76,536	75,999	90,829
1904	368,937	52,869	41,299	5,737	826,912	142,404	73,552	3,298	70,773	75,465	91,681
1905	395,933	55,741	46,268	9,331	954,843	160,818	85,770	4,737	78,327	78,377	108,734
1906	448,926	69,510	50,377	12,464	1,129,501	190,303	103,387	8,021	91,793	93,981	122,601
1907	454,372	68,241	60,899	15,636	1,178,064	185,079	101,247	10,181	93,116	89,702	120,668
1908	452,149	60,122	43,255	17,501	1,011,019	152,564	84,174	7,722	71,288	75,793	93,556
1909	467,901	75,043	52,928	23,408	1,212,801	192,007	93,795	11,816	93,044	91,146	102,873
1910	486,032	82,995	54,403	35,996	1,331,623	202,368	97,318	16,312	97,597	98,055	114,140
1911	500,830	79,983	58,722	45,451	1,339,236	204,061	104,138	15,734	93,152	94,388	116,733
1912	531,389	85,532	59,317	58,329	1,538,377	220,539	131,461	19,657	101,171	97,961	122,374
1913	583,800	95,519	63,989	86,635	1,675,078	236,725	124,900	22,229	102,214	107,134	130,242
1914	523,801	89,990	67,094	92,748	1,570,382	222,514	110,470	18,772	91,861	98,846	125,889
1915	520,639	85,836	73,483	104,851	1,700,183	212,317	119,408	23,742	85,152	96,263	160,144
1916	705,530	112,166	113,046	156,072	2,396,129	271,683	142,462	41,235	110,784	124,075	160,878
1917	863,354	156,681	198,471	329,122	2,799,029	300,573	194,207	58,793	121,757	166,813	221,718
1918	1,043,187	199,889	125,817	491,288	2,646,898	328,980	216,790	67,537	120,094	199,987	197,585
1919	1,187,561	212,029	146,446	515,410	3,921,240	494,718	263,452	84,524	158,503	216,652	230,140

Durable

Year	Musical instruments Cd400	Jewelry, silverware, clocks, and watches Cd401	Printing and publishing, books Cd402	Luggage Cd403	Motorized passenger vehicles Cd404	Motor vehicle accessories Cd405	Horse-drawn passenger vehicles and accessories Cd406	Motorcycles and bicycles Cd407	Pleasure craft Cd408	Ophthalmic products and artificial limbs Cd409	Monuments and tombstones Cd410
	Thousand dollars	Thousand dollars	Thousand dollars	Thousand dollars	Thousand dollars	Thousand dollars	Thousand dollars	Thousand dollars	Thousand dollars	Thousand dollars	Thousand dollars
1869	10,797	41,577	8,440	7,674	—	—	35,666	—	550	386	6,581
1879	14,330	43,306	19,122	7,115	—	—	35,074	—	920	752	7,543
1889	28,191	74,456	34,656	10,669	—	—	54,039	1,907	1,460	2,296	15,247
1890	32,948	90,232	33,883	13,436	—	—	60,448	—	1,454	2,625	17,265
1891	32,966	86,688	33,419	13,938	—	—	62,364	—	1,589	2,936	16,722
1892	34,569	90,333	34,898	15,604	—	—	63,298	—	1,462	3,225	16,568
1893	23,165	71,650	34,288	12,931	—	—	58,539	—	1,395	3,303	11,938
1894	19,861	58,301	28,361	11,081	—	—	50,907	—	1,036	3,302	14,868
1895	27,935	69,217	35,586	8,917	—	—	45,154	14,067	1,315	3,674	13,789
1896	22,842	58,496	34,640	9,211	—	—	39,317	14,861	1,201	3,806	13,354
1897	24,529	63,608	33,730	8,837	—	—	40,890	27,025	1,195	3,951	16,629
1898	27,795	74,011	40,762	8,798	—	—	43,514	27,765	1,399	4,285	17,459
1899	34,235	97,086	45,016	12,592	4,172	—	53,482	18,870	2,065	4,806	20,323
1900	42,359	99,974	44,348	12,028	5,976	—	50,090	10,524	2,698	4,729	18,426
1901	48,846	103,634	47,403	13,131	7,789	—	64,092	7,693	3,742	5,218	23,164
1902	57,222	116,961	49,150	14,863	9,291	—	58,835	6,409	3,539	5,698	27,868
1903	65,101	120,524	51,504	15,845	11,314	—	56,704	4,208	3,584	5,814	25,888
1904	57,732	120,883	53,607	18,900	21,381	2,451	57,825	2,478	3,149	5,644	25,689
1905	71,062	144,060	56,719	20,146	35,626	4,280	61,245	5,402	3,783	7,099	28,658
1906	81,150	173,984	55,947	23,880	62,719	7,828	62,351	4,894	4,320	7,874	34,468
1907	87,802	180,936	56,763	27,681	89,586	11,261	63,767	6,545	6,055	9,360	38,315
1908	63,014	128,617	53,837	23,646	132,169	17,295	48,845	4,904	3,351	9,307	40,937
1909	76,812	175,868	62,927	28,455	154,308	21,141	49,827	5,599	4,301	10,477	38,405
1910	77,583	186,149	60,332	32,786	203,781	26,919	53,330	7,295	4,437	10,653	42,568
1911	81,321	186,092	59,114	36,061	209,182	26,323	45,936	9,405	4,283	10,928	42,385
1912	95,182	190,851	66,348	33,938	311,333	39,330	41,557	11,997	3,871	10,557	40,250
1913	104,361	196,019	77,789	34,023	372,803	46,112	40,137	21,850	4,090	12,304	42,146
1914	91,581	154,634	68,087	26,451	399,584	49,878	35,569	16,177	3,616	15,476	40,977
1915	90,172	144,051	73,311	25,894	537,823	60,999	30,547	13,312	3,363	20,172	37,513
1916	116,249	221,663	76,702	39,641	873,667	103,971	31,045	16,289	3,986	23,904	37,895
1917	134,716	219,183	89,776	36,698	996,717	120,477	38,792	16,690	3,321	36,514	42,284
1918	144,231	194,944	99,214	52,172	762,697	85,817	35,275	18,919	1,501	71,119	50,036
1919	248,262	409,740	127,357	64,159	1,286,866	167,960	26,387	18,981	5,137	45,041	73,361

Source

William Howard Shaw, *Value of Commodity Output since 1869* (National Bureau of Economic Research, 1947), pp. 30–52.

Documentation

Perishable commodities are those usually lasting six months or less. Semidurable commodities are those usually lasting from six months to three years. Consumer durables are commodities manufactured for sale to final consumers that have an estimated life of three years or more.

Shaw's figures refer to output of firms that is destined for domestic consumption. His calculations begin with the total output of firms. He then deducts the value of output that was exported and adds

the value of imported items to arrive at his estimate of domestic consumption. This measure of "consumption" differs from that presented in Table Cd424–455 in two ways. First, it is based on the output of firms rather than on the purchases of households. Second, it includes not only output destined for final consumption but also output purchased by other firms and used as an input into their own production processes. For example, perishable commodity output, series Cd378, includes the output of both flour and bread. Some of the flour was purchased by bakeries that then used it as an input in their production of bread. This means that Shaw's totals double-count some items. In the preceding example, some flour is counted twice – first as the output of flour producers and second as a portion of the value created by bread producers. Because of this double-counting, Shaw's aggregated series

(continued)

TABLE Cd378–410 Value of commodities destined for domestic consumption, by type: 1869–1919 *Continued*

are a poor measure of the overall output of the economy in any year, and they are a poor measure of change in output over time because the share of double-counted items has grown. Shaw's figures are useful as indicators of the relative importance of individual sectors of the economy at different points in time.

For census years, Shaw took the value of the component series from the *Census of Manufactures*. Shaw used related or complementary series, often from a limited number of states rather than the nation as a whole, to interpolate values between census benchmarks. The availability of such related and complementary series varied from year to year and across commodities. For example, intercensal estimates of the output of musical instruments are interpolated on the output of only two piano producers. In some cases, complementary series existed for only a subset of the component series.

Series Cd379–380. The series on food and kindred products were interpolated for 1889–1899 using mineral waters, rice, peanuts, butter, cheese, condensed and evaporated milk, coffee imports, slaughtering; and sugar meltings for 1899–1919. Shaw added flour to these and related products, and for 1909–1919 he added the production of canned tomatoes, peas, and corn, "multiplied by the appropriate prices" (1947, p. 213).

Series Cd381. The value of cigars, cigarettes, and tobacco was interpolated using annual production figures, again multiplied by the appropriate price.

Series Cd384–385. The value of fuel and lighting products was interpolated using series on coke sold for domestic consumption, and the production of crude petroleum, lubricating oil, kerosene, and gasoline.

Series Cd390. Shaw interpolated the benchmark data using tonnage from the Interstate Commerce Commission for household goods and furniture.

Series Cd391. After 1914, Shaw used exports of firearms.

Series Cd392. For 1889–1904, the figures were interpolated using a "combined automobile & bicycle series" (Shaw 1947, p. 214), by which Shaw apparently means his durable series (series Cd404 and Cd407). State series were used between 1904 and 1914, and after 1914 Shaw used state figures on the number of casings renewed annually and prices from the Bureau of Labor Statistics.

Series Cd394 and Cd398. Shaw interpolated the benchmark data using state-level data and tonnage from the Interstate Commerce Commission for household goods and furniture.

Series Cd395–397, Cd401–403, Cd406, and Cd408. Shaw used the state-level data exclusively to interpolate the benchmark figures.

Series Cd399. Interpolated using a small number of specific items, for example, "red earthenware; . . . delft and belleek ware" (p. 214) and so forth.

Series Cd400. Interpolated using state-level data and "sales of two piano companies" (p. 214).

Series Cd404–405. Interpolated using the series for factory sales of passenger cars.

Series Cd407. Interpolated using some state-level data in addition to exports of bicycles and motorcycles as well as production figures from the Indian Motorcycle Company.

Series Cd409. For data prior to 1909, Shaw interpolated using the series he created for drugs and toilet and household preparations, series Cd382; beginning 1909, he used state-level data.

Series Cd410. Shaw used "granite monumental stone" (p. 215), which appears to be from Massachusetts state data.

TABLE Cd411–423 Consumption expenditures on consumer durables, by major commodity group: 1869–1986

Contributed by Lee A. Craig

Year	Total	Automobiles and parts	Horse-drawn vehicles	Other motor vehicles	Furniture	Household appliances	China and tableware	Housefurnishings	Radios and musical instruments	Jewelry and watches	Orthopedic and ophthalmic products	Books and maps	Other
	Cd411	Cd412	Cd413	Cd414	Cd415	Cd416	Cd417	Cd418	Cd419	Cd420	Cd421	Cd422	Cd423
	Million dollars	Million dollars	Million dollars	Million dollars	Million dollars	Million dollars	Million dollars	Million dollars	Million dollars	Million dollars	Million dollars	Million dollars	Million dollars
1869	403	0	36	0	107	30	56	65	20	57	1	12	19
1870	400	0	35	0	106	29	56	66	20	56	1	13	19
1871	424	0	37	0	112	30	59	71	21	59	2	14	20
1872	562	0	48	0	147	38	78	96	28	77	2	21	27
1873	528	0	44	0	137	35	74	92	27	71	2	21	25
1874	473	0	39	0	122	30	66	84	24	63	2	20	23
1875	487	0	39	0	125	30	68	88	25	64	2	22	23
1876	452	0	36	0	115	27	63	83	24	59	2	21	22
1877	457	0	35	0	116	27	64	85	24	58	2	23	22
1878	427	0	32	0	108	24	60	81	23	54	2	22	21
1879	478	0	35	0	120	26	67	92	26	59	2	26	23
1880	618	0	46	0	153	34	86	120	34	77	3	34	30
1881	622	0	46	0	152	34	86	122	35	78	4	35	29
1882	669	0	49	0	162	37	92	132	39	85	4	38	31
1883	665	0	48	0	159	37	91	132	39	85	5	38	31
1884	649	0	47	0	153	36	88	129	39	83	5	38	29
1885	668	0	48	0	156	38	90	134	41	86	5	40	30
1886	732	0	53	0	169	41	97	148	46	95	6	44	32
1887	750	0	54	0	171	43	99	153	48	98	7	46	32
1888	752	0	54	0	170	43	98	154	49	99	7	46	32
1889	770	0	55	0	172	44	100	159	51	102	8	48	32

TABLE Cd411–423   Consumption expenditures on consumer durables, by major commodity group: 1869–1986
Continued

Year	Total	Automobiles and parts	Horse-drawn vehicles	Other motor vehicles	Furniture	Household appliances	China and tableware	Housefurnishings	Radios and musical instruments	Jewelry and watches	Orthopedic and ophthalmic products	Books and maps	Other
	Cd411	Cd412	Cd413	Cd414	Cd415	Cd416	Cd417	Cd418	Cd419	Cd420	Cd421	Cd422	Cd423
	Million dollars	Million dollars	Million dollars	Million dollars	Million dollars	Million dollars	Million dollars	Million dollars	Million dollars	Million dollars	Million dollars	Million dollars	Million dollars
1890	829	0	61	0	175	43	106	169	60	124	9	47	35
1891	866	0	63	0	185	44	112	187	60	119	10	46	41
1892	905	0	64	0	211	44	114	183	63	124	11	48	43
1893	790	0	59	0	184	40	94	163	42	98	11	47	52
1894	678	0	51	0	151	35	85	145	36	80	11	39	44
1895	796	6	46	0	172	40	99	167	51	95	12	49	59
1896	762	8	40	0	165	52	110	147	42	80	13	48	59
1897	815	15	41	0	162	58	110	156	45	87	13	46	82
1898	848	15	44	0	164	53	112	155	51	102	14	56	83
1899	992	14	54	0	191	69	131	188	62	133	16	62	71
1900	1,042	11	51	0	196	73	150	206	77	142	16	61	59
1901	1,160	12	65	0	228	87	158	219	95	147	17	67	65
1902	1,266	12	59	0	249	97	169	250	112	167	19	69	62
1903	1,344	13	57	0	269	98	196	260	127	171	19	73	60
1904	1,329	24	58	0	275	91	198	249	113	171	19	76	56
1905	1,535	39	62	1	310	108	234	267	138	204	23	80	68
1906	1,792	66	63	1	367	132	264	316	158	246	26	79	73
1907	1,851	93	64	2	356	132	260	311	171	257	31	80	93
1908	1,515	133	49	3	294	109	202	250	123	183	31	76	63
1909	1,839	157	50	3	370	125	222	313	149	249	34	89	77
1910	1,989	211	54	4	390	135	246	333	151	264	35	85	81
1911	2,072	225	46	4	410	151	253	333	170	264	36	92	87
1912	2,324	325	42	6	444	190	262	356	199	272	35	103	90
1913	2,538	401	41	7	477	184	280	375	219	279	41	120	114
1914	2,371	434	36	8	448	162	271	342	192	219	51	106	102
1915	2,488	565	31	10	427	179	271	332	189	204	66	114	100
1916	3,409	898	31	16	547	230	348	443	244	315	78	119	140
1917	4,216	1,152	39	19	605	316	477	551	282	311	120	140	204
1918	3,928	676	36	9	663	357	426	650	302	278	234	154	143
1919	5,548	1,422	25	22	936	410	466	719	490	570	139	186	163
1920	6,645	1,436	14	22	1,227	617	595	1,014	587	527	166	220	220
1921	6,049	1,984	11	33	1,062	414	431	748	429	417	132	221	166
1922	5,590	1,583	6	28	991	429	375	820	448	450	120	198	141
1923	7,152	2,300	11	39	1,113	558	521	1,018	539	519	140	201	192
1924	7,295	2,259	9	39	1,248	601	417	983	682	513	123	236	185
1925	7,938	2,495	10	47	1,264	669	552	1,080	731	542	117	243	188
1926	8,459	2,774	9	45	1,277	732	616	1,044	837	554	116	249	206
1927	8,222	2,525	7	36	1,313	742	542	1,079	793	561	130	289	205
1928	8,533	2,733	6	38	1,252	677	621	1,108	940	548	120	285	205
1929	9,299	3,240	6	125	1,204	702	628	1,148	1,020	565	131	310	220
1930	7,470	2,425	5	91	939	614	442	937	928	518	133	265	173
1931	5,740	1,803	2	65	798	516	429	783	482	331	117	254	160
1932	4,140	1,427	1	38	510	314	406	562	270	254	93	154	111
1933	4,084	1,660	2	42	463	373	364	472	196	174	92	153	93
1934	4,388	1,518	0	65	515	473	404	573	231	200	124	166	119
1935	5,011	1,741	0	80	667	562	407	617	250	235	131	184	137
1936	5,951	1,922	0	103	850	670	456	827	335	267	140	209	172
1937	6,610	2,062	0	106	925	773	515	885	388	336	165	244	211
1938	5,465	1,379	0	77	829	650	472	800	342	326	157	222	211
1939	6,597	2,044	0	103	951	707	475	908	423	358	172	227	229
1940	7,760	2,696	0	108	1,062	806	510	991	498	413	186	235	255
1941	9,550	3,214	0	151	1,324	1,059	623	1,214	612	555	227	256	315
1942	6,328	145	0	7	1,288	739	658	1,266	639	729	258	292	307
1943	5,962	164	0	9	1,245	266	612	1,369	406	944	307	368	272
1944	6,074	112	0	11	1,318	157	643	1,398	313	1,013	333	452	324
1945	7,189	147	0	16	1,563	331	800	1,519	347	1,193	349	522	402
1946	14,267	2,197	0	387	2,254	1,640	1,256	2,185	1,124	1,440	396	591	797
1947	19,239	4,867	0	440	2,559	2,880	1,341	2,444	1,408	1,408	400	533	959
1948	21,705	6,227	0	518	2,793	3,149	1,442	2,742	1,461	1,387	431	586	969
1949	24,701	9,698	0	456	2,709	2,846	1,391	2,679	1,688	1,310	454	630	840

(continued)

TABLE Cd411–423   Consumption expenditures on consumer durables, by major commodity group: 1869–1986
Continued

Year	Total	Automobiles and parts	Horse-drawn vehicles	Other motor vehicles	Furniture	Household appliances	China and tableware	Housefurnishings	Radios and musical instruments	Jewelry and watches	Orthopedic and ophthalmic products	Books and maps	Other
	Cd411	Cd412	Cd413	Cd414	Cd415	Cd416	Cd417	Cd418	Cd419	Cd420	Cd421	Cd422	Cd423
	Million dollars	Million dollars	Million dollars	Million dollars	Million dollars	Million dollars	Million dollars	Million dollars	Million dollars	Million dollars	Million dollars	Million dollars	Million dollars
1950	29,600	11,891	0	589	3,100	3,596	1,498	3,121	2,439	1,330	486	677	873
1951	29,182	10,757	0	644	3,259	3,543	1,593	3,468	2,258	1,431	546	779	904
1952	29,275	10,601	0	642	3,521	3,498	1,557	3,156	2,378	1,551	580	791	1,000
1953	32,694	13,123	0	662	3,761	3,662	1,614	3,109	2,626	1,595	604	833	1,105
1954	33,787	14,043	0	573	3,877	3,715	1,628	2,905	2,773	1,676	595	809	1,193
1955	38,342	16,395	0	768	4,437	4,103	1,732	3,326	2,920	1,790	592	871	1,408
1956	38,597	15,256	0	873	4,663	4,356	1,790	3,600	2,991	1,861	655	955	1,597
1957	39,421	16,115	0	785	4,537	4,340	1,726	3,770	2,877	1,865	674	987	1,745
1958	37,289	14,121	0	695	4,518	4,169	1,697	3,766	2,865	1,898	663	1,026	1,871
1959	41,575	16,745	0	786	4,824	4,441	1,741	4,088	3,079	1,969	778	1,092	2,032
1960	42,474	17,727	0	840	4,792	4,311	1,739	4,150	3,061	1,951	758	1,144	2,001
1961	41,417	16,425	0	779	4,798	4,304	1,756	4,262	3,221	1,920	767	1,217	1,968
1962	46,253	19,585	0	993	5,135	4,343	1,859	4,596	3,413	2,063	935	1,292	2,039
1963	51,478	22,809	0	1,129	5,529	4,532	1,900	5,058	3,733	2,179	986	1,419	2,204
1964	55,029	22,725	0	1,295	6,183	4,896	2,125	5,783	4,341	2,446	1,064	1,621	2,550
1965	62,288	27,034	0	1,553	6,556	4,923	2,371	6,252	5,138	2,724	1,157	1,659	2,921
1966	64,939	24,685	0	1,828	7,086	5,369	2,738	6,865	6,326	3,229	1,296	1,854	3,663
1967	69,555	26,682	0	2,012	7,323	5,563	2,947	7,239	7,086	3,495	1,211	1,863	4,134
1968	79,195	31,346	0	2,704	7,977	6,254	3,254	7,912	7,665	3,862	1,408	2,024	4,789
1969	82,984	31,638	0	3,230	8,531	6,840	3,418	8,044	8,052	4,053	1,628	2,318	5,232
1970	83,072	29,853	0	3,155	8,654	7,291	3,471	7,901	8,604	4,133	1,861	2,934	5,215
1971	93,985	36,569	0	4,442	9,284	7,981	3,640	8,114	8,980	4,452	1,884	2,988	5,651
1972	104,033	37,965	0	6,109	10,529	9,039	3,978	8,952	10,126	4,828	2,151	2,956	7,400
1973	119,307	43,384	0	7,623	11,908	9,942	4,594	10,330	11,360	6,067	2,375	3,066	8,658
1974	118,124	37,118	0	7,170	12,638	10,383	5,079	11,477	12,186	7,060	2,568	3,205	9,240
1975	129,120	40,466	0	8,694	12,945	10,631	5,586	12,027	13,590	8,172	2,862	3,585	10,562
1976	152,543	50,157	0	13,161	14,195	11,560	6,345	13,467	14,958	9,934	3,042	3,591	12,133
1977	174,073	57,506	0	16,932	16,464	12,785	7,134	15,213	15,855	11,085	3,231	4,091	13,777
1978	195,626	64,137	0	20,413	18,325	14,054	7,882	16,938	17,079	12,521	3,727	4,774	15,776
1979	209,594	68,038	0	18,864	20,516	15,623	8,626	18,756	18,967	13,401	4,272	5,174	17,357
1980	209,044	65,796	0	13,576	21,087	16,450	9,262	19,765	20,037	15,520	4,669	5,618	17,264
1981	224,993	70,317	0	14,618	22,288	17,567	10,037	21,075	22,185	16,896	4,998	6,199	18,813
1982	238,936	76,662	0	17,731	21,780	17,802	10,394	21,517	24,700	16,806	5,541	6,578	19,425
1983	273,363	90,331	0	23,528	23,998	19,713	11,183	24,372	28,430	18,114	5,948	7,214	20,532
1984	317,070	107,953	0	30,006	26,721	21,724	12,237	27,142	31,757	20,026	6,743	7,800	24,961
1985	348,146 [1]	120,551	0	35,576	28,334	23,635	12,755	28,300	36,395	20,932	7,400	8,200	26,068
1986	379,677	131,997	0	39,326	30,855	24,842	13,400	30,300	41,133	23,649	8,300	8,700	27,175

[1] Correction of error in the original.

Source

Martha L. Olney, *Buy Now, Pay Later: Advertising, Credit, and Consumer Durables* (University of North Carolina Press, 1991), Table A6.

Documentation

Consumer durables are goods with an estimated life of three years or more that are sold to final customers. Olney's estimates of expenditures on consumer durables before 1929 are based on those of Raymond Goldsmith, *A Study of Savings in the United States*, 3 volumes (Princeton University Press, 1955). Goldsmith, in turn, derived his figures by adjusting those of William H. Shaw, *Value of Commodity Output since 1869* (National Bureau of Economic Research, 1947), Tables I-1 and I-2. Shaw's figures are summarized in Table Cd378–410. Olney splices these to figures collected and published by the Bureau of Economic Analysis beginning in the year when these become available.

TABLE Cd424–455 Average expenditures of consumer units, by type of expenditure: 1980–1998
Contributed by Lee A. Craig

					Average annual expenditures											
	Consumer units in the sample	Persons per consumer unit	Earners per consumer unit	Average income before taxes	Total	Food			Alcoholic beverages	Housing						Apparel and services
						Total	Food at home	Food away from home		Total	Shelter	Utilities, fuels, and public services	Household operations	Housekeeping supplies	Housefurnishings and equipment	
Year	Cd424	Cd425	Cd426	Cd427	Cd428	Cd429	Cd430	Cd431	Cd432	Cd433	Cd434	Cd435	Cd436	Cd437	Cd438	Cd439
	Number	Number	Number	Dollars	Dollars	Dollars	Dollars	Dollars	Dollars	Dollars	Dollars	Dollars	Dollars	Dollars	Dollars	Dollars
1980	67,610	2.7	1.4	19,127	16,723	3,185	2,398	787	278	4,899	2,726	1,184	274	—	715	895
1981	68,980	2.6	1.4	20,842	17,588	3,263	2,424	839	282	5,199	2,904	1,340	248	—	707	974
1982	70,610	2.6	1.4	22,256	18,071	3,075	2,184	891	283	5,582	3,174	1,436	257	—	715	975
1983	72,531	2.6	1.3	23,126	19,692	3,198	2,224	974	286	5,980	3,349	1,540	284	—	808	1,084
1984	90,223	2.6	1.4	23,464	21,975	3,290	1,970	1,320	275	6,674	3,489	1,638	315	307	926	1,319
1985	91,564	2.6	1.4	25,127	23,490	3,477	2,037	1,441	306	7,087	3,833	1,648	346	325	936	1,420
1986	94,044	2.6	1.4	25,460	23,866	3,448	1,993	1,455	271	7,292	3,979	1,645	354	316	998	1,346
1987	94,150	2.6	1.4	27,326	24,414	3,664	2,099	1,565	289	7,569	4,154	1,671	371	341	1,032	1,446
1988	94,862	2.6	1.4	28,540	25,892	3,748	2,136	1,612	269	8,079	4,493	1,747	394	361	1,083	1,489
1989	95,818	2.6	1.4	31,308	27,810	4,152	2,390	1,762	284	8,609	4,835	1,835	460	394	1,086	1,582
1990	96,968	2.6	1.4	31,889	28,381	4,296	2,485	1,811	293	8,703	4,836	1,890	446	406	1,125	1,618
1991	97,918	2.6	1.4	33,901	29,614	4,271	2,651	1,620	297	9,252	5,191	1,990	448	424	1,200	1,735
1992	100,019	2.5	1.3	33,854	29,846	4,273	2,643	1,631	301	9,477	5,411	1,984	487	433	1,162	1,710
1993	100,049	2.5	1.3	34,868	30,692	4,399	2,735	1,664	268	9,636	5,415	2,112	469	410	1,230	1,676
1994	102,210	2.5	1.3	36,181	31,731	4,411	2,712	1,698	278	10,106	5,686	2,189	490	393	1,348	1,644
1995	103,123	2.5	1.3	36,918	32,264	4,505	2,803	1,702	277	10,458	5,928	2,191	509	430	1,401	1,704
1996	104,212	2.5	1.3	38,014	33,797	4,698	2,876	1,823	309	10,747	6,064	2,347	522	464	1,350	1,752
1997	105,576	2.5	1.3	39,926	34,819	4,801	2,880	1,921	309	11,272	6,344	2,412	548	455	1,512	1,729
1998	107,182	2.5	1.3	41,622	35,535	4,810	2,780	2,030	309	11,713	6,680	2,405	546	482	1,601	1,674

Note appears at end of table

(continued)

TABLE Cd424–455   Average expenditures of consumer units, by type of expenditure: 1980–1998   Continued

Average annual expenditures

Year	Transportation					Health care	Entertainment	Personal care products and services	Reading	Education	Tobacco products and supplies	Miscellaneous	Cash contributions	Personal insurance and pensions		
	Total	Vehicle purchases (net outlay)	Gasoline and motor oil	Other vehicle expenses	Public transportation									Total	Life and other personal insurance	Pensions and social security
	Cd440	Cd441	Cd442	Cd443	Cd444	Cd445	Cd446	Cd447	Cd448	Cd449	Cd450	Cd451	Cd452	Cd453	Cd454	Cd455
	Dollars	Dollars	Dollars	Dollars	Dollars	Dollars	Dollars	Dollars	Dollars	Dollars	Dollars	Dollars	Dollars	Dollars	Dollars	Dollars
1980 [1]	3,416	1,169	1,184	852	210	730	724	153	114	209	175	259	481	1,204	255	949
1981 [1]	3,490	1,179	1,167	907	239	762	799	162	120	228	176	260	520	1,323	274	1,049
1982 [1]	3,504	1,236	1,060	991	218	804	820	168	122	255	194	256	563	1,469	251	1,218
1983 [1]	3,914	1,565	1,064	1,047	239	839	919	184	131	293	215	283	588	1,777	265	1,513
1984	4,304	1,813	1,058	1,178	255	1,049	1,055	289	132	303	228	451	706	1,897	300	1,598
1985	4,587	2,043	1,035	1,241	268	1,108	1,170	303	141	321	219	529	805	2,016	278	1,738
1986	4,842	2,338	915	1,342	248	1,135	1,149	303	140	314	230	522	746	2,127	292	1,834
1987	4,600	2,022	888	1,417	273	1,135	1,193	330	142	337	232	562	741	2,175	294	1,881
1988	5,093	2,361	932	1,521	279	1,298	1,329	334	150	342	242	578	693	2,249	314	1,935
1989	5,187	2,291	985	1,627	284	1,407	1,424	366	157	367	261	643	900	2,472	346	2,125
1990	5,120	2,129	1,047	1,642	302	1,480	1,422	364	153	406	274	842	816	2,592	345	2,248
1991	5,151	2,111	995	1,741	304	1,554	1,472	399	163	447	276	860	950	2,787	356	2,431
1992	5,228	2,189	973	1,776	290	1,634	1,500	387	162	426	275	765	958	2,750	353	2,397
1993	5,453	2,319	977	1,843	314	1,776	1,626	385	166	455	268	715	961	2,908	399	2,509
1994	6,044	2,725	986	1,953	381	1,755	1,567	397	165	460	259	749	960	2,938	398	2,540
1995	6,014	2,638	1,006	2,015	355	1,732	1,612	403	162	471	269	766	925	2,964	373	2,591
1996	6,382	2,815	1,082	2,058	427	1,770	1,834	513	159	524	255	855	940	3,060	353	2,707
1997	6,457	2,736	1,098	2,230	393	1,841	1,813	528	164	571	264	847	1,001	3,223	379	2,844
1998	6,616	2,964	1,017	2,206	429	1,903	1,746	401	161	580	273	860	1,109	3,381	398	2,982

[1] Urban households only. Complete data available only for diary surveys. See text.

Sources

U.S. Department of Labor, *Survey of Consumer Expenditures, 1960–61,* "Consumer Expenditures and Income: Detail of Expenditures and Income, Total United States, Urban and Rural, 1960–61," Supplement 3, Part A, to U.S. Bureau of Labor Statistics *Report* number 237-93 (May 1966), pp. 2–15.

U.S. Department of Labor, *Consumer Expenditure Survey: Integrated Diary and Interview Survey Data, 1972–73,* Bulletin number 1992 (1978), pp. 24–35.

U.S. Department of Labor, *Consumer Expenditure Survey: Interview Survey, 1982–83,* Bulletin number 2246 (1986), p. 3.

U.S. Department of Labor, *Consumer Expenditure Survey: Interview Survey, 1984–86,* Bulletin number 2333 (August 1989), p. 2.

U.S. Department of Labor, *Consumer Expenditure Survey: Integrated Survey Data, 1987,* Bulletin number 2354 (June 1990), p. 2.

U.S. Department of Labor, *Consumer Expenditure Survey, 1988–89,* Bulletin number 2383 (August 1991), p. 2.

U.S. Department of Labor, *Consumer Expenditure Survey, 1990–91,* Bulletin number 2425 (September 1993), p. 2.

U.S. Department of Labor, *Consumer Expenditure Survey, 1992–93,* Bulletin number 2462 (September 1995), p. 2.

U.S. Department of Labor, "Consumer Expenditures in 1994," *Report* number 902 (February 1996), p. 3.

Data are also available at the U.S. Bureau of Labor Statistics (BLS) Internet site, Consumer Expenditures Survey.

Documentation

For historical background and general information, see the text for Tables Cd456–464 and Cd483–502.

These series display the results of the BLS's Consumer Expenditure Survey program, begun in 1980. The Consumer Expenditure Survey, which is conducted by the U.S. Bureau of the Census for the BLS, consists of two components: a diary or recordkeeping survey completed by participating consumer units for two consecutive one-week periods and an interview survey in which expenditures of consumer units are obtained in five interviews conducted every three months. Survey participants record dollar amounts for goods and services purchased during the reporting period and whether or not payment is made at the time of purchase. Expenditure amounts include all sales and excise taxes for all items purchased by the consumer unit for itself or for others. Excluded from both surveys are all business-related expenditures and expenditures for which the consumer unit is reimbursed.

The surveys from 1980 through 1983 included only urban units; furthermore, the complete data for those years are reported for the diary surveys only. The data reported for 1984 and thereafter are from both rural and urban units and from "integrating" the diary and interview surveys. The methodology for sampling the consumer units and integrating the surveys is described in Appendix B of each *Consumer Expenditure Survey* cited earlier. With only a few minor changes noted later, the series are comparable across years.

Series Cd424. Comprises either (1) all members of a particular household who are related by blood, marriage, adoption, or other legal arrangements; (2) a person living alone or sharing a household with others or living as a boarder in a private home or lodging house or in permanent living quarters in a hotel or motel, but who is financially independent; or (3) two or more persons living together who pool their income to make joint expenditure decisions. Financial independence is determined by the

TABLE Cd424–455   Average expenditures of consumer units, by type of expenditure: 1980–1998 *Continued*

three major expense categories: housing, food, and other living expenses. To be considered financially independent, at least two of the three major expense categories have to be provided by the respondent.

Series Cd425. The ratio of the number of persons whose usual place of residence at the time of the interview was in a sample unit, divided by the number of units.

Series Cd426. Consumer unit members, 14 years of age or older, who reported having worked at least one week during the twelve months prior to the interview date.

Series Cd427. Total money earnings and selected money receipts during the twelve months prior to the interview date. See the individual surveys cited as sources for specific details.

Series Cd428. The dollar value of transactions, including excise and sales taxes, involving goods and services. This includes gifts but excludes purchases assignable to business purposes. Periodic or installment credit payments are excluded as well.

Series Cd430. Includes total expenditures for food purchased at grocery or other food stores and food prepared by the consumer unit on trips. Excludes the purchase of nonfood items.

Series Cd431. Includes all meals at restaurants, carryouts, and vending machines, including tips, plus meals as pay, special catered affairs such as weddings, bar mitzvahs, and confirmations, and meals away from home on trips.

Series Cd432. Includes beer and ale, wine, whiskey, gin, vodka, rum, and other alcoholic beverages.

Series Cd435. Includes natural gas, electricity, fuel oil, wood, kerosene, coal, bottled gas, water, garbage and trash collection, sewerage maintenance, septic tank cleaning, telephone charges, and other public services.

Series Cd436. Represents the sum of expenditures for domestic or personal services, such as babysitters, and other household expenses, such as gardening and lawn care services.

Series Cd437. Includes laundry and cleaning supplies, cleaning and toilet tissues, stationery supplies, postage, miscellaneous household products, and lawn and garden supplies.

Series Cd438. Represents the sum of expenditures on household textiles, furniture, floor coverings, major appliances, small appliances and miscellaneous housewares, and miscellaneous household equipment.

Series Cd439. Represents the sum of expenditures on men's and boys' apparel; women's and girls' apparel; apparel for children younger than age 2; footwear; and other apparel products and services, such as repair and dry cleaning.

Series Cd441. Includes the net outlay (purchase price minus trade-in value) on new and used domestic and imported cars and trucks; other vehicles include attachable campers, trailers, motorcycles, and private planes.

Series Cd442. Includes gasoline, diesel fuel, and motor oil.

Series Cd443. Represents the sum of expenditures on finance charges; maintenance and repairs; insurance; and rental, license, and other charges.

Series Cd444. Includes fares for mass transit, buses, trains, airlines, taxis, private school buses, and boats.

Series Cd445. Represents the sum of expenditures on health insurance, medical services, drugs, and medical supplies.

Series Cd446. Represents the sum of expenditures on fees and admission; television, radios, and sound equipment; pets, toys, and playground equipment; other entertainment supplies, equipment, and services.

Series Cd447. Includes products for the hair, oral hygiene products, shaving needs, cosmetics and bath products, electric personal care appliances, other personal care products, and personal care services for males and females.

Series Cd448. Includes expenditures on subscriptions for newspapers, magazines, and books through book clubs, as well as the purchase of single copy newspapers and magazines, newsletters, books, and encyclopedias and other reference books.

Series Cd449. Includes tuition, fees, textbooks, supplies, and equipment for public and private nursery schools, elementary and high schools, colleges and universities, and other schools.

Series Cd450. Includes cigarettes, cigars, snuff, loose smoking tobacco, chewing tobacco, and smoking accessories such as cigarette or cigar holders, pipes, flints, lighters, pipe cleaners, and other smoking products and accessories.

Series Cd451. Includes expenditures on safe-deposit box rental; checking account fees and other bank services; legal fees; accounting fees; funerals; cemetery lots; union dues; occupational expenses; and finance charges other than for mortgage and vehicles.

Series Cd452. Includes cash contributed to persons or organizations outside the consumer unit including alimony and child support payments; care of students away from home; and contributions to religious, educational, charitable, or political organizations.

Series Cd454. Includes expenditures on premiums for whole life and term insurance; endowments; income and other life insurance; premiums for personal liability, accident and disability, and other nonhealth insurance, other than that for homes and vehicles.

Series Cd455. Includes all Social Security contributions paid by employees; employee's contributions to railroad retirement, government retirement, and private pension programs; and contributions to retirement programs for self-employed workers.

CLASSIFIED BY FAMILY CHARACTERISTICS

Lee A. Craig

TABLE Cd456–464   Consumption expenditures of families, by income class: 1874–1875 [Massachusetts wage earners]

Contributed by Lee A. Craig

Income class	Families in the sample	Average family size	Average income before taxes	Average consumption expenditures					
				Total	Food	Clothing	Rent	Fuel	Sundry expenses
	Cd456	Cd457	Cd458	Cd459	Cd460 [1]	Cd461	Cd462	Cd463	Cd464
	Number	Number	Dollars	Dollars	Dollars	Dollars	Dollars	Dollars	Dollars
All	397	5.1	763	738	427	106	117	44	44
$300–$450	6	5.0	395	410	262	29	82	25	12
$450–$600	52	5.2	549	555	350	58	86	33	28
$600–$750	143	4.8	679	668	401	94	94	40	40
$750–$1,200	188	5.3	871	832	466	125	141	50	50
$1,200 or more	8	6.9	1,383	1,212	618	230	182	60	121

[1] Includes kerosene, which was primarily used for lighting.

Source

Massachusetts Bureau of Statistics of Labor, *Sixth Annual Report*, March 1875, Public Document number 31 (Wright and Potter, 1875), pp. 221–354, 372, 373, 441.

Documentation

General Note for Tables Cd424–673

Collection of data on consumer expenditures, and especially wage earners' expenditures, began in the United States in the 1870s. Initially the data collection was undertaken on a small scale by state agencies using a variety of methods. The most important of these studies was the one made for Massachusetts by Carroll D. Wright, Bureau of Statistics of Labor, Massachusetts. He undertook a carefully planned survey of the earnings and expenditures of families of skilled and unskilled workers in 1874–1875.

The data for 1874–1875 were collected from families of wage earners in fifteen cities and twenty-one towns by trained agents of the Massachusetts Bureau of Statistics of Labor. Agents approached 1,000 families, of which 397 were willing and able to have "their private life inquired into" (p. 202) and thus to provide enough information about their affairs to answer the questions put to them. The families included about equal numbers of skilled and unskilled workers, and were those which, with few exceptions, had dependent children in the household.

The general categories reported in Tables Cd456–482 were calculated from expenditure items in the original report, which include groceries, meat, fish, milk, boots and shoes, dry goods, books and papers, societies, and religion. Expenditures not specifically for food, clothing, rent, and fuel and light were listed as sundries. The report states that sundry items of expense are those which "although . . . not absolutely necessary for the life of the body, are, in their way, imperative necessity in a man's social life" (p. 433). Some specified sundries include furniture, carpets, books and papers, societies, religion, charity, sickness, care of parents, care of house, recreation, house girl, travel to work, and life insurance. In addition, the report contains a brief description of the living conditions of each household, for example, family number 142, "House is well furnished, and the parlor carpeted. Own a sewing-machine. Family dresses well and attends church" (p. 268). The data are reported by income class in Table Cd456–464. The income categories were created to promote comparability across Tables Cd456–482.

The usefulness of the Massachusetts data led Congress to request further studies of this type on a broader base by the newly formed U.S. Bureau of Labor, of which Wright had become Commissioner. The Bureau of Labor undertook large-scale studies for 1888–1991 and 1901. The data on food expenditures obtained in the 1901 survey were used to provide the design for

an index of prices of food purchased by workingmen. This index was used generally as a deflator for workers' incomes and expenditures for all kinds of goods until World War I.

The data for 1888–1891 were only from 2,562 so-called normal families. "Normal" families had both a husband and wife; had no more than five children, none of them over 14 years of age; had no dependents or boarders; did not own their own dwelling place; and had expenditures for rent, fuel, lighting, clothing, and food. The study covered workers in the following industries: pig iron, bar iron, steel, bituminous coal, coke, iron ore, cotton, wool, and glass. The data are reported by income class in Table Cd465–473.

The data for 1901 were for families with wage and salary incomes not exceeding $1,200 a year, and they were collected through personal interviews by experienced special agents of the U.S. Bureau of Labor. About 15 percent of these families had incomes from boarders and lodgers and other sources. The latter raised total income above $1,200 for a few families. Therefore, their expenditures could be, and were, above $1,200. Altogether, data were collected from 25,440 families of all types, but only those from the 11,156 families defined as "normal" were summarized by income levels. These "normal" families had a husband at work, a wife, and not more than five children (with none over 14 years of age); had no dependents, boarders, lodgers, or servants; and provided data on expenditures for rent, fuel, lighting, food, clothing, and sundries. The study had a wide city and industry coverage in thirty-two states and the District of Columbia, and it appears to have provided a good picture of "normal" families with a wage earner or salaried worker. The selection of the number of persons interviewed in each geographical area was roughly apportioned in accordance with the number of persons employed in the manufacturing industries of the states. The data are reported by income class in Table Cd474–482.

Table Cd456–464

The figures in the table were calculated from data in the Massachusetts report that show, by income class, the number of families from whom figures were received, their aggregate earnings and expenses in each class, and percentages of expenditure as regards income, by income class, for five major categories of expense. The resulting weighted averages for all families' earnings and expenses were found to correspond with all family averages shown elsewhere in the report. Average figures on money earnings, expenses for all goods and services, and expenses for fuel also corresponded with such averages in the report. The figures on expenses for food, rent, and sundries corresponded within a few dollars. The differences were small enough that they may have resulted from rounding, though errors in reporting or arithmetic in the original document cannot be ruled out.

TABLE Cd465–473 Consumption expenditures of families, by income class: 1888–1891 [Workers in nine basic industries]

Contributed by Lee A. Craig

	Families in the sample	Average family size	Average income before taxes	Average consumption expenditures					
				Total	Food	Clothing	Housing	Fuel and light	Sundry expenses
	Cd465	Cd466	Cd467	Cd468	Cd469	Cd470	Cd471	Cd472	Cd473
Income class	Number	Number	Dollars	Dollars	Dollars	Dollars	Dollars	Dollars	Dollars
All	2,562	3.9	573	534	219	82	80	32	121
Under $400	524	3.7	327	357	163	50	53	26	65
$400–$600	1,168	3.9	486	476	212	70	73	31	90
$600–$800	492	3.9	674	608	245	97	95	34	137
$800–$1,200	292	4.1	936	785	278	128	119	37	222
$1,200 or more	86	4.3	1,450	1,128	323	177	142	34	452

Sources

U.S. Bureau of Labor, Sixth Annual Report of the Commissioner of Labor, 1890, *Cost of Production*, part 3 (1891), pp. 790–801, 914–25, 984–9, 1076–85, 1128–31, 1160–2.

U.S. Bureau of Labor, Seventh Annual Report of the Commissioner of Labor, 1891, *Cost of Production*, volume 2, part 2 (1892), pp. 1170–1206, 1374–90, 1552–69, 1826–39, 1887–98, 2012, 2013.

Documentation

For general information, see the text for Table Cd456–464.

Family size, income, and expenditures were tabulated from the Sixth Annual Report and the Seventh Annual Report. Those data provided the basis for calculation of average family size, income, and total expenditures for all "normal" families by income class. The percentage distributions of total expenditures for "normal" families in the Seventh Annual Report were applied to the appropriate averages to estimate the dollar expenditure by income class.

TABLE Cd474–482 Consumption expenditures of families, by income class: 1901

Contributed by Lee A. Craig

	Families in the sample	Average family size	Average income before taxes	Average consumption expenditures					
				Total	Food	Clothing	Rent	Fuel and light	Sundry expenses
	Cd474	Cd475	Cd476	Cd477	Cd478	Cd479	Cd480	Cd481	Cd482
Income class	Number	Number	Dollars	Dollars	Dollars	Dollars	Dollars	Dollars	Dollars
All	11,156	4.0	651	618	266	80	112	35	124
Under $400	692	3.7	—	367	176	36	68	26	61
$400–$600	3,940	3.9	—	509	236	60	94	32	86
$600–$800	4,430	3.9	—	650	276	86	119	36	134
$800–$1,200	1,926	4.2	—	820	329	117	142	40	191
$1,200 or more	168	3.8	—	1,052	384	165	183	53	267

Source

U.S. Bureau of Labor, Eighteenth Annual Report of the Commissioner of Labor, Document number 23, 1903, *Cost of Living and Retail Prices of Food,* pp. 581, 592, 593.

Documentation

For general information, see the text for Table Cd456–464.

The figures in the table were calculated from data in the Eighteenth Annual Report that show, by income class, the number of families for whom data were reported; the nativity of the head of the family; the families' average income and expenditures in each class; and expenditures, by income class, for the six major categories of expense. Fuel and lighting expenditures have been combined for comparability with Tables Cd456–473.

TABLE Cd483–502 Consumption expenditures of urban families, by income class: 1917–1919

Contributed by Lee A. Craig

				Average consumption expenditures						
	Families in the sample	Average family size	Average income after taxes	Total	Food	Alcoholic beverages	Tobacco	Housing	Fuel, light, and refrigeration	Household operation
	Cd483	Cd484	Cd485	Cd486	Cd487	Cd488	Cd489	Cd490 [1]	Cd491	Cd492
Income class	Number	Number	Dollars	Dollars	Dollars	Dollars	Dollars	Dollars	Dollars	Dollars
All	12,096	4.9	1,505	1,352	549	7	17	187	74	37
Under $900	332	4.3	810	804	372	4	12	122	57	18
$900–$1,200	2,423	4.5	1,070	1,016	456	7	14	150	64	14
$1,200–$1,500	3,959	4.7	1,336	1,234	516	7	15	180	73	32
$1,500–$1,800	2,730	5.0	1,622	1,452	572	7	17	207	79	41
$1,800–$2,100	1,594	5.1	1,914	1,656	627	7	20	232	87	51
$2,100–$2,500	705	5.7	2,261	1,937	712	9	21	248	93	61
$2,500 or more	353	6.4	2,777	2,331	860	16	28	260	102	63

			Average consumption expenditures								
	Furnishings and equipment	Clothing	Transportation		Medical care	Personal care	Recreation	Reading	Education	Miscellaneous
			Automobile	Other						
	Cd493	Cd494	Cd495	Cd496	Cd497	Cd498	Cd499	Cd500	Cd501	Cd502
Income class	Dollars	Dollars	Dollars	Dollars	Dollars	Dollars	Dollars	Dollars	Dollars	Dollars
All	62	238	16	26	64	14	33	11	7	10
Under $900	28	112	1	11	36	9	8	6	4	4
$900–$1,200	43	156	4	18	46	11	15	8	3	7
$1,200–$1,500	54	206	9	23	58	13	25	10	5	8
$1,500–$1,800	71	257	18	29	71	15	38	11	8	11
$1,800–$2,100	79	307	31	32	78	17	52	13	11	12
$2,100–$2,500	93	384	50	43	87	19	69	15	16	17
$2,500 or more	105	503	58	54	102	24	97	16	22	21

[1] Excludes 301 families whose rent included the cost of heat or light, or both.

Source

U.S. Bureau of Labor Statistics (BLS), *Cost of Living in the United States, 1917–19*, Bulletin number 357 (May 1924).

Documentation

For historical background, see the text for Table Cd456–464. For a general definition of the expenditure categories, see the text for Table Cd424–455.

General Note for Tables Cd483–673

The data on food expenditures obtained in the 1901 survey (Table Cd474–482) were used to design an index of prices of food purchased by "workingmen." This index was used generally as a deflator for workers' incomes and expenditures for all kinds of goods until World War I. During that period, the need for a more inclusive index of retail prices became clearer because food prices rose much faster than those of many other commodities or housing. A nationwide study of the expenditures of wage earners and clerical workers was undertaken in 1918 to provide a list of items to be priced for such an index and also to provide data on the relative importance of each item. Because of the number of wage disputes in the shipbuilding centers, the survey was first undertaken in seacoast cities. It was later expanded into what was regarded as a representative sample of industrial centers in the United States (Table Cd483–502).

Subsequently, data on the consumption expenditures of city wage- and clerical-worker families of two or more persons were collected at irregular intervals and for a variety of purposes. With the 1950 BLS *Study of Consumer Expenditures*, the samples began representing families of all types in these occupational groups in cities of all sizes throughout the country. Insofar as the original publications make it possible, the figures from the earlier studies have been adjusted as to definition and classification of consumer expenditures in order to conform to those used in 1950.

The years and surveys from which the data in Tables Cd483–673 come were chosen so that expenditures by both income and occupation class could be presented.

Several other studies conducted before 1960–1961 were summarized in *Historical Statistics of the United States* (1975). For example, in 1934 the Brookings Institution published estimates of expenditure patterns at different income levels of farm and nonfarm families and single individuals in 1929 (see M. Leven, H. G. Moulton, and C. Warburton, *America's Capacity to Consume* (Brookings Institution, 1934)). The figures were prepared by Clark Warburton on the basis of scattered sample studies made during the 1920s and early 1930s and correlated with national income estimates made by Maurice Leven. In 1935, estimates of aggregate consumer expenditures in detail for 1909 and 1929 and selected years between were prepared by Martin Gainsbrugh and published in William H. Lough, *High-Level Consumption* (McGraw-Hill, 1935). This book included a comparison with the Brookings Institution's aggregates for 1929 showing that the two estimates were very close for expense and reasonably close for attire and home maintenance, but the estimates by Lough and Gainsbrugh of expenditures for all other items were much higher than the Brookings Institution's figures.

Dramatic increases in productivity in industry and agriculture during the 1920s and the subsequent economic collapse led a number of economists to study the factors affecting consumer expenditures and to estimate changes in consumption patterns over time. The pioneer investigation in this field was made by Simon Kuznets, *Commodity Flow and Capital Formation* (National Bureau of Economic Research, 1938), which shows national aggregates for four types of consumer goods and services.

In the mid-1930s, two national cross-sectional studies of consumer expenditure patterns were undertaken. The first, conducted by the BLS, covered employed city wage and clerical workers and was initiated to provide a new list of items and weights for the Consumer Price Index (CPI) of the BLS (Table Cd483–502). The second, the Study of Consumer Purchases,

TABLE Cd483–502 Consumption expenditures of urban families, by income class: 1917–1919 *Continued*

conducted jointly by the BLS and the Bureau of Home Economics in the Department of Agriculture, related to families (with native-born heads) who were not on public relief rolls during the survey year. It was initiated to provide data relating the effect on expenditure patterns of income, occupation of the head, race, family composition, and type of community. The results of the second study were used by the National Resources Planning Board as the basis for a national estimate of consumer expenditures. The data from this study were supplemented by information from the Bureau of Internal Revenue (now the Internal Revenue Service) on income distribution and receipts from excise taxes, and from a few studies of the expenditures of families on public relief rolls and of those with foreign-born heads. A small nationwide survey conducted in 1941 by the BLS and the Bureau of Home Economics provides detailed data on the expenditure patterns of rural and urban families in the same year. The BLS also conducted a sample national study of urban family expenditures in 1944. Another BLS urban study covering 1950, intended primarily to serve as a basis for revision of the CPI, subsequently provided detailed tabulations of consumer expenditures, income, and savings (Table Cd558–577).

Data from the following studies were reported in *Historical Statistics of the United States* (1975) but are not included here: U.S. National Resources Planning Board, *Family Expenditures in the United States, Statistical Tables and Appendixes* (1941), pp. 61, 120, 157; U.S. Bureau of Labor Statistics, *Family Spending and Saving in Wartime*, Bulletin number 822 (1942), pp. 68, 70, 71, 76, 102, 109; U.S. Bureau of Labor Statistics, *Monthly Labor Review* (January 1946), p. 4; U.S. Bureau of Labor Statistics, *Wartime Food Purchases*, Bulletin number 838 (1945), pp. 1–4 and appendix; U.S. Bureau of Labor Statistics, *Study of Consumer Expenditures, Incomes and Savings; Statistical Tables: Urban U.S. 1950* (University of Pennsylvania, 1956); and U.S. Bureau of Labor Statistics, *Survey of Consumer Expenditures, 1960–61*.

For a discussion of the BLS surveys after 1960–1961, see the text for Table Cd424–455. In addition to the sources cited there, there have been a number of nationwide surveys of consumer expenditures by income level for specified types of goods. See, for example, individual reports in the series published by the Department of Agriculture, *Household Food Consumption Survey*, 1965–1966. The reports of this survey provide detailed data for farm and nonfarm households on quantities and values of food consumed and on dietary levels by money income after taxes in the United States as a whole and in four major regions. The "Surveys of Consumer Finances," conducted annually for 1946–1995 for the Board of Governors of the Federal Reserve System by the Survey Research Center of the University of Michigan, yield data on consumer purchases of selected durable goods by income level of all "spending units" in the United States. Reports of these surveys appear annually in the *Federal Reserve Bulletin*.

The lack of continuity in the income categories in Tables Cd483–502, Cd521–539, Cd558–577, Cd597–616, and Cd636–655 is, at least in part, owing to the fact that the coverage and definitions used in obtaining the data differ from study to study. Also, because of inflation, the categories have tended to "broaden" over time: were one to use the same expenditure categories in, say, 1988, as were used in 1917–1919, all of the 1988 households would be in the highest income category ($2,500 and over).

Population coverage is discussed in the notes to each of the subsequent tables. The classification and definition of goods and services purchased primarily affect the figures on income and expenditures for housing and for "sundries" or "miscellaneous goods and services." The figures on income represent annual income after the deduction of direct personal taxes, that is, income, poll, and personal property taxes. In the case of the 1935–1936 sample, the (reported) income before taxes was adjusted. Direct personal taxes, as well as indirect taxes, were generally tabulated as an item of current expenditure in the consumer expenditure surveys made before the 1930s. Since the Consumer Purchases Study of 1935–1936, such taxes have been presented separately and have not been included in consumer expenditures. For the series presented here, direct personal taxes were deducted from expenditure figures in the earlier surveys, wherever possible, to ensure greater comparability with the most recent surveys.

The treatment of imputed income resulting from expenditures for owned homes varies considerably from one series to another. In the early

studies of wage earners' expenditures, the statistical difficulties of handling homeowners' housing expenditures were avoided by excluding homeowners from the "normal" family group and including only renters. In studies done since the mid-1930s, emphasis has been placed on homeowners' current-year expenditures for housing and for investments in their homes, but in some surveys, data on rental value are also available in the original sources.

Conceptually, premiums paid on life insurance policies may be classified wholly as current expenditures or partly as savings and partly as current expenditures, depending on the type of policy; but in sample surveys it was difficult to obtain from respondents information on the type of policies on which premiums are paid. In sample surveys of consumer expenditures made before the 1930s, the difficulty of obtaining information on the types of insurance policies held resulted in classifying payments on such premiums in the sundries or miscellaneous group as current expenditures. In expenditure surveys made since 1930, it has been the practice to exclude insurance premiums from current expenditure data, handling them either as savings or as a separate class of disbursements.

The early studies on consumer expenditures focused on urban families, but beginning with a study made in Livingston County, N.Y., in 1909, consumer expenditures of farm families were also reviewed. In the early 1920s, the U.S. Department of Agriculture initiated a cooperative project on the subject with the State Agricultural Experiment Stations under the direction of E. L. Kirkpatrick. In 1925, it was decided, for lack of any other data on farm family expenditures extending across state lines, to average the data that had been collected in eleven states covering one year in the period 1923–1925. The Department of Agriculture, in cooperation with the Bureau of the Census, conducted a survey of farm family expenditures in 1955 to obtain data to revise the Parity Index and improve the basis for estimating farm operators' production expenses, which provides detailed data on farm family expenditures. In the early studies of wage earners' incomes and expenditures, no attempt was made to evaluate the products received by a family from its garden, poultry, hogs, or cows; however, most studies of the incomes and expenditures of farm-operator families include data on the value of food and fuel produced by the family for its own use, sometimes valued at prices that would have been paid for them had they been purchased through nearby trade channels, and sometimes at prices that would have been received if the products had been sold. Although space prohibits the inclusion of the data from those and later studies on the expenditure of farm families, *Historical Statistics of the United States* (1975) contained similar data from the following sources: E. L. Kirkpatrick, *The Farmer's Standard of Living: A Socio-Economic Study of 2,886 White Farm Families of Selected Localities in 11 States,* U.S. Department of Agriculture, Bulletin number 1466 (1924), pp. 29, 34; M. Leven, H. G. Moulton, and C. Warburton, *America's Capacity to Consume* (Brookings Institution, 1934), p. 260; U.S. National Resources Planning Board, *Family Expenditures in the United States, Statistical Tables and Appendixes* (June 1941), pp. 51, 120, 157; U.S. Department of Agriculture, *Rural Family Spending and Saving in Wartime*, Miscellaneous Bulletin number 520 (June 1943), pp. 156, 159; U.S. Department of Agriculture, *Farmers' Expenditures in 1955 by Regions*, Statistical Bulletin number 224 (1958); and U.S. Agricultural Research Service, *Consumer Expenditures and Income, Rural Farm Population* (1961), p. 6.

Until the 1960–1961 survey, farm studies included operator families only, in some cases defined to cover nonresident operators and resident operators of urban farms as well as those living on rural farms. In the 1960–1961 survey, the three population groups were defined by place of residence. Farm families in that survey are limited to those living on rural farms and include families other than operator families.

Table Cd483–502

The data in this table have been chosen to correspond with those organized by occupation and presented in Table Cd503–520.

These data were collected from white urban families consisting of at least one worker, a husband and wife, and at least one child who was not a boarder or lodger. The families could have no boarders and not more than three lodgers; at least 75 percent of family income had to come from the principal breadwinner or others who contributed all earnings to the family fund; slum or charity families and non-English-speaking families who had been in the United States fewer than five years were excluded.

TABLE Cd483–502 Consumption expenditures of urban families, by income class: 1917–1919 *Continued*

This survey was first undertaken in shipbuilding centers for the purpose of providing market baskets that could be used in computing consumer price indexes for those cities most affected by the inflation associated with World War I. It was later broadened to cover ninety-two cities and localities throughout the country.

The income and expenditure figures presented in BLS Bulletin number 357 (1924) were adjusted for comparability with definitions and classifications used in the 1950 *Study of Consumer Expenditures* (Table Cd558–577). Thus, average money income after taxes was derived by deducting dues to labor organizations, personal property and poll taxes, and expenditures for

tools (BLS Bulletin number 357 (1924), pp. 448 and 454) from total average income per family (BLS Bulletin number 357 (1924), p. 4). Average expenditures for current consumption, series Cd486, were derived by deducting from total average yearly expenses per family (BLS Bulletin number 357 (1924), p. 5) the same items deducted from income and, in addition, life insurance premiums; contributions to church, charity, and patriotic purposes; and gifts (BLS Bulletin number 357 (1924), pp. 447 and 448). Each consumption group was adjusted for maximum comparability with the corresponding groups as classified in the 1950 study (when they differed from the original published table).

TABLE Cd503–520 Consumption expenditures of urban families, by race and occupation class: 1918

Contributed by Lee A. Craig

| | | | | Average consumption expenditures | | | | |
Race or occupation class	Percentage of families in each race or occupation class	Average family size	Average earners per family	Average income	Total	Food and alcoholic beverages	Clothing	Rent	Fuel, light, and refrigeration
	Cd503	Cd504	Cd505	Cd506	Cd507	Cd508	Cd509	Cd510	Cd511
	Percent	Number	Number	Dollars	Dollars	Dollars	Dollars	Dollars	Dollars
Black	7	4.2	—	—	791	376	105	100	47
Laborer	18	4.5	1.2	1,037	1,075	462	156	149	64
Wage earner	40	4.7	1.2	1,344	1,298	521	207	180	74
Salaried	12	5.7	1.6	2,272	2,053	721	384	248	92

| | Average consumption expenditures | | | | | | | | |
Race or occupation class	Furniture and furnishings	Transportation	Recreation and education	Household operation	Medical care	Personal care	Gifts and contributions	Personal insurance	Other
	Cd512	Cd513	Cd514	Cd515	Cd516	Cd517	Cd518	Cd519	Cd520
	Dollars	Dollars	Dollars	Dollars	Dollars	Dollars	Dollars	Dollars	Dollars
Black	28	—	—	—	—	—	—	—	—
Laborer	40	22	41	26	46	11	20	30	6
Wage earner	50	32	59	35	59	13	25	37	8
Salaried	86	92	125	66	88	18	60	57	16

Source

Clair Brown, *American Standards of Living* (Blackwell, 1994), pp. 10–11, 42–3.

Documentation

See the text for Table Cd483–502.

"Laborers" include service workers. "Wage earners" include clerical, sales, and craft and operative workers. "Salaried" workers include professional and managerial workers. Population percentages represent urban population in race or occupation class.

Brown organized these data by race and occupation in order to analyze changes in the standard of living and what she refers to as "economic distance" between socioeconomic classes over time (see the essay in Chapter Df, on transportation). The original data for white families are from U.S. Bureau of Labor Statistics (BLS), *Cost of Living in the United States, 1917–19,* Bulletin number 357 (May 1924), and for blacks, *Monthly Labor Review* 6 (2) (1927). For details concerning BLS Bulletin number 357 (1924), see the text for Table Cd483–502. The categories reported by Brown are similar, though not identical, to those reported in that table.

TABLE Cd521–539   Consumption expenditures of urban families, by income class: 1935–1936

Contributed by Lee A. Craig

	Families in the sample	Average family size	Average income after taxes	Average consumption expenditures						
				Total	Food and alcoholic beverages	Tobacco	Housing	Fuel, light, and refrigeration	Household operation	Furnishings and equipment
	Cd521	Cd522	Cd523	Cd524	Cd525	Cd526	Cd527	Cd528	Cd529	Cd530
Income class	Number	Number	Dollars	Dollars	Dollars	Dollars	Dollars	Dollars	Dollars	Dollars
All Classes	14,469	3.6	1,518	1,463	508	29	259	108	58	60
$500–$600	116	3.1	550	637	250	11	132	64	20	13
$600–$900	1,215	3.2	775	832	315	15	169	76	30	28
$900–$1,200	2,952	3.4	1,062	1,081	398	20	215	94	38	39
$1,200–$1,500	3,444	3.5	1,348	1,332	472	26	246	106	49	55
$1,500–$1,800	2,937	3.6	1,634	1,576	540	31	281	114	63	70
$1,800–$2,100	2,185	3.8	1,928	1,804	597	36	300	123	77	77
$2,100–$2,400	810	4.0	2,241	2,075	683	44	324	136	92	90
$2,400–$2,700	391	4.3	2,507	2,305	756	51	346	131	102	96
$2,700–$3,000	188	4.4	2,867	2,590	837	58	370	131	119	83
$3,000 or more	231	4.8	3,450	3,093	1,021	75	411	148	142	112

		Average consumption expenditures								
	Clothing	Transportation		Medical care	Personal care	Recreation	Reading	Education	Miscellaneous
		Automobile	Other						
	Cd531	Cd532	Cd533	Cd534	Cd535	Cd536	Cd537	Cd538	Cd539
Income class	Dollars	Dollars	Dollars	Dollars	Dollars	Dollars	Dollars	Dollars	Dollars
All Classes	160	87	38	59	30	38	15	7	7
$500–$600	49	9	17	22	13	11	6	2	18
$600–$900	74	20	25	33	17	15	8	2	5
$900–$1,200	102	40	29	42	22	23	11	4	4
$1,200–$1,500	136	73	33	53	27	32	14	5	5
$1,500–$1,800	173	99	40	64	32	40	16	7	6
$1,800–$2,100	211	137	43	78	37	49	19	11	9
$2,100–$2,400	258	162	52	81	43	62	23	14	11
$2,400–$2,700	309	161	65	97	51	73	28	19	20
$2,700–$3,000	388	197	78	109	59	88	31	17	25
$3,000 or more	471	212	115	115	71	116	41	22	21

Source
U.S. Bureau of Labor Statistics, unpublished data.

Documentation
For historical background and general information, see the text for Tables Cd456–464 and Cd483–502. For a general definition of the expenditure categories, see the text for Table Cd424–455.

The data in this table have been chosen to correspond with those organized by occupation and presented in Table Cd540–557.

These series were derived from data in Faith M. Williams and Alice C. Hanson, *Money Disbursements of Wage Earners and Clerical Workers*, Bureau of Labor Statistics, Bulletin number 638, summary volume (1941), and were adjusted by Faith M. Williams to be comparable with definitions and classifications in the 1950 *Study of Consumer Expenditures* (Table Cd558–577). For details of the adjustments, see U.S. Bureau of the Census, *Historical Statistics of the United States* (1975), discussion of series G515–533, Part 1, p. 308.

The data in this 1934–1936 study were gathered to provide the basis for revising the Bureau of Labor Statistics Consumer Price Index (CPI). The survey was restricted to families of two or more in large cities that had incomes of at least $500 and whose members had not been on public relief rolls during the survey year; thus, the spending habits of workers on "relief" and those employed so irregularly that their purchases could not have been typical of long-range consumption patterns were excluded from the weights calculated to construct the CPI. The survey covered 12,903 white families and 1,566 "Negro" families in forty-two cities with populations of 50,000 or more.

TABLE Cd540–557   Consumption expenditures of urban families, by race and occupation class: 1935

Contributed by Lee A. Craig

	Percentage of families in each race or occupation class	Average family size	Average number of gainful workers per family	Average income	Average consumption expenditures				
					Total	Food and alcoholic beverages	Clothing	Rent	Fuel, light, and refrigeration
	Cd540	Cd541	Cd542	Cd543	Cd544	Cd545	Cd546	Cd547	Cd548
Race or occupation class	Percent	Number	Number	Dollars	Dollars	Dollars	Dollars	Dollars	Dollars
Black	8	3.4	1.41	758	697	256	63	124	68
Laborer	10	3.4	1.23	1,071	1,165	402	102	217	99
Wage earner	44	3.5	1.29	1,355	1,439	472	136	246	111
Salaried	9	3.3	1.35	2,260	2,285	603	231	340	137

	Average consumption expenditures								
	Furniture and furnishings	Transportation	Recreation and education	Household operation	Medical care	Personal care	Gifts and contributions	Personal insurance	Other
	Cd549	Cd550	Cd551	Cd552	Cd553	Cd554	Cd555	Cd556	Cd557
Race or occupation class	Dollars	Dollars	Dollars	Dollars	Dollars	Dollars	Dollars	Dollars	Dollars
Black	22	28	34	16	27	15	16	25	3
Laborer	38	68	60	33	42	22	28	50	3
Wage earner	55	105	80	45	53	27	37	68	4
Salaried	73	242	185	107	103	48	78	126	9

Source

Clair Brown, *American Standards of Living* (Blackwell, 1994), pp. 10–11, 106–7.

Documentation

See the text for Tables Cd503–539.

The original data are from Faith M. Williams and Alice C. Hanson, *Money Disbursements of Wage Earners and Clerical Workers*, Bureau of Labor Statistics,

Bulletin number 638, summary volume (1941); and U.S. Bureau of Labor Statistics, *Study of Consumer Purchases, Urban Series, 1935–36*, Bulletin number 648. For a discussion of BLS Bulletin number 357 (1924), see the text for Table Cd483–502. The categories reported by Brown are similar, though not identical, to those reported in Table Cd521–539.

TABLE Cd558–577   Consumption expenditures of urban families, by income class: 1950

Contributed by Lee A. Craig

	Families in the sample	Average family size	Average income after taxes	Average consumption expenditures						
				Total	Food	Alcoholic beverages	Tobacco	Housing	Fuel, light, and refrigeration	Household operation
	Cd558	Cd559	Cd560	Cd561	Cd562	Cd563	Cd564	Cd565	Cd566	Cd567
Income class	Number	Number	Dollars	Dollars	Dollars	Dollars	Dollars	Dollars	Dollars	Dollars
All	7,007	3.4	3,923	3,925	1,205	70	79	415	163	155
Under $1,000	64	2.3	651	1,683	540	8	29	283	122	77
$1,000–$2,000	498	2.9	1,629	1,924	690	25	50	249	111	71
$2,000–$3,000	1,423	3.1	2,564	2,795	946	41	66	336	140	108
$3,000–$4,000	2,180	3.4	3,487	3,573	1,139	58	73	390	158	135
$4,000–$5,000	1,453	3.5	4,454	4,408	1,324	82	88	454	174	169
$5,000–$6,000	749	3.7	5,434	5,262	1,514	102	96	511	194	213
$6,000–$7,500	427	3.9	6,606	6,187	1,691	134	107	590	208	245
$7,500–$10,000	164	4.2	8,394	7,161	1,992	158	130	606	228	304
$10,000 or more	49	4.5	13,292	10,342	2,656	289	126	976	287	814

TABLE Cd558–577   Consumption expenditures of urban families, by income class: 1950   _Continued_

	Average consumption expenditures									
	Furnishings and equipment	Clothing	Transportation		Medical care	Personal care	Recreation	Reading	Education	Miscellaneous
			Automobile	Other						
	Cd568	Cd569	Cd570	Cd571	Cd572	Cd573	Cd574	Cd575	Cd576	Cd577
Income class	Dollars	Dollars	Dollars	Dollars	Dollars	Dollars	Dollars	Dollars	Dollars	Dollars
All	278	453	472	69	200	91	177	34	17	47
Under $1,000	86	131	107	25	112	35	33	14	1	81
$1,000–$2,000	117	197	131	37	102	51	46	17	6	25
$2,000–$3,000	193	286	248	53	150	69	93	26	7	34
$3,000–$4,000	242	385	421	56	194	84	155	33	14	37
$4,000–$5,000	331	508	561	73	221	99	219	38	20	49
$5,000–$6,000	388	648	737	98	246	118	256	44	29	70
$6,000–$7,500	462	822	887	113	294	132	324	50	39	89
$7,500–$10,000	435	1,026	1,052	158	333	161	397	55	43	84
$10,000 or more	805	1,588	1,002	202	411	212	605	80	84	206

Source

U.S. Department of Labor, _How American Buying Habits Change_ (1959).

Documentation

For historical background and general information, see the text for Tables Cd456–464 and Cd483–502. For a general definition of the expenditure categories, see the text for Table Cd424–455.

The data in this table have been chosen to correspond with those organized by occupation and presented in Table Cd578–596.

The survey of consumer expenditures in 1950 was conducted by the U.S. Bureau of Labor Statistics (BLS) to provide the basis for revising its Consumer Price Index (CPI). The survey was undertaken during the first half of 1951 in ninety-one urban areas throughout the United States ranging in size from places of 2,500 inhabitants to the greater New York area with a population of 9 million. Complete and usable reports were obtained from 12,489 consumer units. Since the study was directed toward the determination of expenditure weights for the revised CPI, the data for family expenditures for individual consumption goods and services purchased by the 7,007 wage-earner and clerical-worker families of two or more persons were tabulated and averaged for each of the ninety-one cities surveyed.

Subsequently, the same data were tabulated in considerable detail and published as part of the study of consumer expenditures, income, and savings that was made by the Wharton School of Finance and Commerce in cooperation with the BLS under a grant from the Ford Foundation.

Although the original source of the data is _How American Buying Habits Change_, the data are reported in _Study of Consumer Expenditures, Incomes and Savings; Statistical Tables: Urban U.S. 1950_, a joint study by the BLS and the Wharton School of Finance and Commerce (University of Pennsylvania, 1956, 18 volumes). See in particular volumes 1, 2, 3, 9, and 10.

To obtain data for wage-earner and clerical-worker families of two or more, the following groups were excluded: single consumers; self-employed; salaried professionals; officials and the like; and persons not gainfully employed. Within the nine classes of cities averaged for the Wharton School publications (large cities, suburbs, and small cities in the North, South, and West), averages were based on the sample families as weights; in combining the resulting averages, universe weights were used (total consumer units, that is, families and single consumers).

TABLE Cd578–596   Consumption expenditures of urban families, by race and occupation class: 1950

Contributed by Lee A. Craig

	Percentage of families in each race or occupation class	Average family size	Average earners per family	Average income after taxes	Average consumption expenditures					
					Total	Food	Alcoholic beverages	Clothing	Rent	Fuel, light, and refrigeration
	Cd578	Cd579	Cd580	Cd581	Cd582	Cd583	Cd584	Cd585	Cd586	Cd587
Race or occupation class	Percent	Number	Number	Dollars	Dollars	Dollars	Dollars	Dollars	Dollars	Dollars
Black	7	3.3	—	2,320	2,543	879	55	303	270	132
Laborer	18	2.6	1.31	2,538	2,947	943	39	272	353	130
Wage earner	40	3.2	1.39	3,489	3,874	1,174	56	377	404	156
Salaried	12	3.4	1.40	4,467	4,835	1,385	74	504	474	176

	Average consumption expenditures								
	Furniture and furnishings	Transportation	Recreation and education	Household operation	Medical care	Personal care	Gifts and contributions	Personal insurance	Other
	Cd588	Cd589	Cd590 [1]	Cd591	Cd592	Cd593	Cd594	Cd595 [2]	Cd596
Race or occupation class	Dollars	Dollars	Dollars	Dollars	Dollars	Dollars	Dollars	Dollars	Dollars
Black	174	192	149	94	90	76	57	97	30
Laborer	172	309	194	115	152	63	96	108	41
Wage earner	236	487	283	145	203	82	121	165	40
Salaried	331	647	383	186	230	97	163	206	52

Notes appear at end of table   (continued)

TABLE Cd578–596   Consumption expenditures of urban families, by race and occupation class: 1950   *Continued*

[1] Includes tobacco.

[2] Includes employee withholding for the Social Security program Old Age Security and Disability Insurance (OASDI).

Source

Clair Brown, *American Standards of Living* (Blackwell, 1994), pp. 10–11, 188.

Documentation

See the text for Tables Cd503–520 and Cd558–577.

The original source for these data is U.S. Department of Labor, *How American Buying Habits Change* (1959). However, the data were compiled as *Study of Consumer Expenditures, Incomes and Savings; Statistical Tables: Urban U.S. 1950*, a joint study by the U.S. Bureau of Labor Statistics and the Wharton School of Finance and Commerce (University of Pennsylvania, 1956, 18 volumes). See in particular volumes 1, 2, 3, 9, and 10. The categories reported by Brown are similar, though not identical, to those reported in Table Cd558–577.

TABLE Cd597–616   Consumption expenditures of families, by income class: 1972–1973

Contributed by Lee A. Craig

	Families in the sample	Average family size	Average income after taxes	Average consumption expenditures						
				Total	Food	Alcoholic beverages	Tobacco products and smoking supplies	Shelter	Fuel and utilities	Household operation
	Cd597	Cd598	Cd599	Cd600	Cd601	Cd602	Cd603	Cd604	Cd605	Cd606
Income class	Number	Number	Dollars	Dollars	Dollars	Dollars	Dollars	Dollars	Dollars	Dollars
All classes	71,220	2.9	9,731	8,270	1,596	110	130	1,311	409	443
Under $3,000	9,065	1.4	1,636	3,211	722	36	67	735	218	206
$3,000–$3,999	3,991	1.9	3,347	4,173	958	47	79	853	260	265
$4,000–$4,999	3,624	2.1	4,252	4,774	1,096	60	88	893	284	292
$5,000–$5,999	3,282	2.4	5,084	5,400	1,220	74	100	967	315	316
$6,000–$6,999	3,401	2.5	5,928	6,023	1,259	81	110	1,052	329	342
$7,000–$7,999	3,251	2.7	6,715	6,501	1,392	87	120	1,073	343	371
$8,000–$9,999	6,594	2.8	7,911	7,332	1,516	105	132	1,215	357	387
$10,000–$11,999	6,278	3.2	9,491	8,284	1,656	124	144	1,266	413	415
$12,000–$14,999	8,375	3.4	11,485	9,388	1,903	127	154	1,382	458	490
$15,000–$19,999	9,996	3.6	14,541	11,065	2,108	154	174	1,592	521	558
$20,000–$24,999	5,028	3.8	18,370	13,073	2,405	188	169	1,778	568	638
$25,000 or more	4,560	3.8	30,461	17,290	2,845	265	161	2,603	685	954
Incomplete	3,773	3.0	1,645	9,084	1,375	75	142	1,479	491	531

			Average consumption expenditures							
	Furnishings and equipment	Clothing	Transportation		Health care	Personal care	Recreation	Reading	Education	Miscellaneous
			Automobile	Other						
	Cd607	Cd608	Cd609	Cd610	Cd611	Cd612	Cd613	Cd614	Cd615	Cd616
Income class	Dollars	Dollars	Dollars	Dollars	Dollars	Dollars	Dollars	Dollars	Dollars	Dollars
All classes	387	565	1,534	63	528	165	708	48	106	85
Under $3,000	99	141	399	38	234	63	155	16	11	26
$3,000–$3,999	148	218	539	43	307	82	243	22	17	33
$4,000–$4,999	161	249	729	45	371	93	271	24	20	40
$5,000–$5,999	214	302	816	49	403	111	352	30	19	44
$6,000–$6,999	237	336	1,073	73	457	125	364	30	24	50
$7,000–$7,999	281	395	1,169	49	446	131	436	37	29	68
$8,000–$9,999	309	452	1,368	51	510	141	532	41	41	92
$10,000–$11,999	373	539	1,678	55	536	169	638	45	62	92
$12,000–$14,999	439	612	1,902	50	592	186	784	54	78	99
$15,000–$19,999	572	794	2,222	61	662	227	1,006	65	143	114
$20,000–$24,999	682	993	2,595	90	765	263	1,371	81	250	138
$25,000 or more	915	1,427	2,999	157	966	341	2,000	112	500	210
Incomplete	455	761	1,676	96	542	184	849	50	201	67

Source

U.S. Department of Labor, *Consumer Expenditure Survey: Integrated Diary and Interview Survey Data, 1972–73*, Bulletin number 1992 (1978), pp. 24–35.

Documentation

For historical background and general information, see the text for Tables Cd456–464 and Cd483–502. For a general definition of the expenditure categories, see the text for Table Cd424–455.

The data in this table have been chosen to correspond with those organized by occupation and presented in Table Cd617–635.

The expenditure surveys dating from the late nineteenth century were largely limited to specific racial or income groups in particular cities or regions. Beginning in 1960–1961, the Bureau of Labor Statistics became more ambitious in its consumer expenditure surveys and more consistent in the definition of the series on which it collected information. The data reported in this table include urban and rural families as well as single consumers, and they represent the "integrated" summary from the diary and interview surveys. The methodology for sampling the consumer units and integrating the surveys is described in U.S. Department of Labor (1978), pp. 2–20.

TABLE Cd617-635   Consumption expenditures of families, by occupation class: 1973

Contributed by Lee A. Craig

	Percent of families in each occupation class	Average family size	Average earners per family	Average income after taxes	Average consumption expenditures					
					Total	Food	Alcoholic beverages	Clothing	Housing	Fuel and utilities
	Cd617	Cd618	Cd619	Cd620	Cd621	Cd622	Cd623	Cd624	Cd625	Cd626
Occupation class	Percent	Number	Number	Dollars	Dollars	Dollars	Dollars	Dollars	Dollars	Dollars
Low Income	—	2.76	—	3,669	4,853	1,190	22	277	1,006	290
Laborer	14	2.90	1.51	9,025	9,039	1,704	78	489	1,406	395
Wage earner	53	3.17	1.76	11,094	10,517	1,885	88	566	1,544	440
Salaried	25	3.47	2.06	15,716	13,813	2,394	127	826	1,873	547
Seniors	—	1.62	—	4,536	5,041	1,143	28	213	841	319

	Average consumption expenditures								
	Furnishings	Transportation	Recreation and education	Household operation	Medical care	Personal care	Gifts and contributions	Personal insurance	Other
	Cd627	Cd628	Cd629	Cd630	Cd631	Cd632	Cd633	Cd634	Cd635
Occupation class	Dollars	Dollars	Dollars	Dollars	Dollars	Dollars	Dollars	Dollars	Dollars
Low Income	173	557	317	323	274	77	148	172	28
Laborer	326	1,615	742	480	477	149	359	725	93
Wage earner	422	1,836	906	595	525	186	417	974	132
Salaried	606	2,351	1,322	697	576	224	619	1,479	171
Seniors	158	513	321	398	547	106	297	90	67

Source

Clair Brown, *American Standards of Living* (Blackwell, 1994), pp. 10–11, 270.

Documentation

See the text for Tables Cd503–520 and Cd597–616.

The original data are from U.S. Department of Labor, *Consumer Expenditure Survey Series: Interview Survey, 1972–73*, Bulletin number 1985 (August 1978). For a discussion of the 1972–1973 surveys, see the text for Table Cd597–616. The categories reported by Brown are similar, though not identical, to those reported in Table Cd597–616.

TABLE Cd636-655   Consumption expenditures of consumer units, by income class: 1988

Contributed by Lee A. Craig

	Consumer units in the sample	Average number of persons in consumer unit	Average income after taxes	Average consumption expenditures						
				Total	Food	Alcoholic beverages	Tobacco	Shelter	Utilities, fuel, and public services	Household operation
	Cd636	Cd637	Cd638	Cd639	Cd640	Cd641	Cd642	Cd643	Cd644	Cd645
Income class	Number	Number	Dollars	Dollars	Dollars	Dollars	Dollars	Dollars	Dollars	Dollars
All classes	81,354	2.6	26,149	26,389	3,804	282	242	4,470	1,726	387
Under $5,000	6,893	1.7	2,373	10,793	1,911	125	158	2,354	1,048	111
$5,000–$9,999	11,916	1.9	7,196	11,545	2,082	150	198	2,222	1,223	179
$10,000–$14,999	9,433	2.2	11,892	16,789	2,777	183	221	3,043	1,413	201
$15,000–$19,999	8,219	2.5	16,345	19,558	3,195	235	250	3,139	1,543	223
$20,000–$29,999	14,586	2.7	22,963	24,896	3,765	291	263	4,125	1,711	310
$30,000–$39,999	10,901	2.9	31,660	31,660	4,587	344	293	5,050	1,925	449
$40,000–$49,999	7,198	3.2	40,100	37,562	5,282	353	249	5,901	2,089	531
$50,000 or more	12,209	3.1	66,345	52,320	6,296	506	270	8,909	2,593	955

(continued)

TABLE Cd636-655   Consumption expenditures of consumer units, by income class: 1988   *Continued*

				Average consumption expenditures					
Income class	Furnishings and equipment	Clothing	Private transportation	Public transportation	Health care	Personal care products and services	Entertainment	Reading	Education	Miscellaneous
	Cd646	Cd647	Cd648	Cd649	Cd650	Cd651	Cd652	Cd653	Cd654	Cd655
	Dollars	Dollars	Dollars	Dollars	Dollars	Dollars	Dollars	Dollars	Dollars	Dollars
All classes	1,485	1,537	5,140	266	1,282	346	1,349	152	324	598
Under $5,000	488	532	1,676	125	683	148	428	59	385	321
$5,000–$9,999	547	664	1,728	107	959	152	469	77	167	214
$10,000–$14,999	838	886	3,127	152	1,385	249	802	93	187	346
$15,000–$19,999	1,042	1,086	3,841	156	1,300	282	856	114	119	475
$20,000–$29,999	1,365	1,406	5,303	239	1,328	325	1,191	142	190	553
$30,000–$39,999	1,837	1,847	6,704	294	1,367	420	1,510	185	323	770
$40,000–$49,999	2,087	2,396	7,779	321	1,532	479	1,995	230	349	811
$50,000 or more	3,261	3,154	9,715	635	1,568	651	3,148	287	836	1,182

Source

U.S. Department of Labor, *Consumer Expenditure Survey, 1988–89*, Bulletin number 2383 (August 1991), pp. 51–4.

Documentation

For historical background and general information, see the text for Tables Cd456–464 and Cd483–502. For a general definition of the expenditure categories, see the text for Table Cd424–455.

The data in this table have been chosen to correspond with those organized by occupation and presented in Table Cd656–673.

The data reported in these series include both urban and rural consumer units, as did the data for 1972–1973 in Table Cd597–616. The surveys from 1980 through 1983, however, included only urban units; furthermore, the complete data for those years are reported for the diary surveys only. The data reported for 1984 and thereafter are from both rural and urban units and from "integrating" the diary and interview surveys. The methodology for sampling the consumer units and integrating the surveys is described in Appendix B of U.S. Department of Labor (1991).

TABLE Cd656-673   Consumption expenditures of families, by occupation class: 1988

Contributed by Lee A. Craig

	Percentage of families in each occupation class	Average family size	Average earners per family	Average income after taxes	Average consumption expenditures				
					Total	Food and alcoholic beverages	Clothing	Housing	Fuel and utilities
	Cd656	Cd657	Cd658	Cd659	Cd660	Cd661	Cd662	Cd663	Cd664
Occupation class	Percent	Number	Number	Dollars	Dollars	Dollars	Dollars	Dollars	Dollars
Poor	—	3.04	—	6,115	14,363	3,070	610	2,682	947
Laborer	14	2.63	1.33	22,484	25,508	3,925	1,172	4,496	1,110
Wage earner	52	2.91	1.65	30,903	32,781	4,609	1,526	5,071	1,318
Salaried	30	3.11	2.20	47,613	44,624	5,541	2,121	6,918	1,586
Seniors	—	1.83	—	15,926	18,091	3,081	600	2,512	1,209

				Average consumption expenditures					
	Furnishings	Transportation	Recreation and education	Household operation	Medical care	Personal care	Gifts and contributions	Personal insurance	Other
	Cd665	Cd666	Cd667	Cd668	Cd669	Cd670	Cd671	Cd672	Cd673
Occupation class	Dollars	Dollars	Dollars	Dollars	Dollars	Dollars	Dollars	Dollars	Dollars
Poor	334	2,108	1,377	1,039	775	205	505	373	339
Laborer	680	4,486	2,352	1,470	1,002	373	1,683	2,204	555
Wage earner	972	6,496	3,058	1,801	1,177	437	2,223	3,395	697
Salaried	1,639	7,576	5,155	2,139	1,389	604	3,316	5,414	1,227
Seniors	528	2,637	1,396	1,197	2,268	306	1,383	433	540

Source

Clair Brown, *American Standards of Living* (Blackwell, 1994), pp. 10–11, 367.

Documentation

See the text for Tables Cd503–520 and Cd636–655.

The original data were reported in U.S. Department of Labor, *Consumer Expenditure Survey, 1988–89*, Bulletin number 2383 (August 1991). The categories reported by Brown are similar, though not identical, to those reported in Table Cd636–655.

CHAPTER Ce
Saving, Capital, and Wealth

Editor: Richard Sutch

SAVING, CAPITAL, AND WEALTH

Richard Sutch

Definitions and Distinctions

There are two, somewhat opposing, reasons to be interested in how and why society saves. First, saving is one of two primary influences on the rate of long-term growth in per capita output, technological innovation being the other determinant of growth. The creation of capital is closely related to technological change because most technological innovations are achieved through investment and are thus "embodied" in capital. Second, saving may not be an unmixed blessing. In the short run, saving too much while investing too little (underconsumption) could mean that private demand falls short of the economy's capacity to produce, leading either to unemployment and recession or to the need for compensatory government spending to fill the gap. The opposite problem of too little saving could induce the unhappy consequence of inflation as aggregate demand exceeds capacity.

Saving and Savings

In economics, "saving" is defined and measured as a *flow*, the portion of the flow of personal (or national) income that is accumulated rather than spent or transferred. "Savings" (a singular noun ending in *s*) refers to an accumulated *stock* of saving, as in the term "savings account." In common use, saving refers to *net* saving, the difference between income and outlays. However, some of those outlays are for the repair or replacement of the existing capital stock; so gross saving is defined to include allowances for the "consumption of fixed capital." Refer to Table Ce-A for the variant definitions of saving. Account 5 in Table Ca-D and the discussion in the essay on national income and product in Chapter Ca provide additional details on how saving is defined in the national accounts.

National saving consists of personal saving (by households and nonprofit entities), corporate saving, and government saving. Corporate saving is often called retained earnings. Government saving is also called the government budget surplus (when positive) or the government deficit (when negative). Gross national saving includes the allowances for the consumption of fixed capital. By definition,

gross national saving, which is based on the income side of the national accounts, should equal gross investment, which is calculated from the product side. In practice they do not, so gross investment actually equals gross saving plus the statistical discrepancy (see Chapter Ca on national income and product).

Saving is equal to current income less current consumption. To be more precise, then, we must turn to the definitions of the components. In most treatments, current income is thought of as earned income after taxes, or disposable income. Disposable income excludes capital gains, whether realized or not. The preferred definition of current consumption for the purpose of defining saving is the total current outlays on *nondurable* goods and services. This definition of saving, which we label the "standard concept" (it was so named by Raymond Goldsmith), includes the outlays for consumer durables as part of saving (Goldsmith 1955, volume 1, p. 30). When individuals purchase a consumer durable (say an automobile or refrigerator), the outlay represents an investment in an asset that will yield a flow of services (transportation services or refrigeration services) over the life of the durable. The household is saving when it purchases a consumer durable because it is forgoing current consumption in exchange for a flow of services in the future.

For this treatment of consumer durables to be consistent with the standard concept of saving, the definition of income and consumption would need to be expanded beyond the concept used by the Bureau of Economic Analysis (BEA) when it calculates the national income and product accounts (NIPA). See the bottom row of Table Ce-A. Both income and consumption should include the flow of consumption services produced by the stock of consumer durables. However, if we constrain our attention to saving, that flow would cancel out because it would be part of both current income and current consumption.

Saving may be defined on either a gross or a net basis. The difference is an accounting allowance for capital consumption (depreciation). Business accounting practice typically makes a charge against income for the estimated cost of depreciation. Often, however, only the original cost of the capital (book value) is depreciated and then often on an ad hoc basis. The BEA replaces this business estimate of depreciation with its own estimates of the "consumption of fixed capital," defined as the decline in the value of the stock of assets "due to wear and tear, obsolescence, accidental damage, and aging." Because a key reason for the interest in saving is its role in expanding the productive capital stock, saving is usually expressed in net terms.

Acknowledgments

Richard Sutch acknowledges the helpful comments and advice received from Susan Carter, Paul David, Monty Hindman, Franco Modigliani, Alan Olmstead, Roger Ransom, and Gavin Wright. Financial support was provided by the John Simon Guggenheim Memorial Foundation, the National Science Foundation, the Institute of Business and Economic Research at the University of California, Berkeley, the Division of Humanities and Social Sciences of the California Institute of Technology, and the Center for Social and Economic Policy at the University of California, Riverside.

TABLE Ce-A Relation among various definitions of saving

Components of national saving			Various saving concepts						
			Net saving; change in earned net worth				**Gross saving; net saving PLUS consumption of fixed capital**		**Change in total net worth**
			Narrow	Standard	Broad	Expanded	Narrow	Standard	Standard [6]
	Private saving	Personal saving [1]	Personal disposable income; LESS personal outlays [2]	PLUS expenditures for consumer durables	PLUS net agricultural capital improvements. PLUS increase in the value of the slave population	PLUS net increase in human capital [5]	PLUS wage accruals less disbursements	PLUS capital consumption allowances for consumer durables	PLUS realized and unrealized capital gains; LESS change in net liabilities
		Corporate saving	Undistributed corporate profits [3]			PLUS corporate research and development expenditures	PLUS capital consumption allowances for corporate fixed capital		
	Government saving		Government surplus [4]			PLUS government research and development expenditures	PLUS capital consumption allowances for government fixed capital		

Corresponding definition of personal income							
Narrow	Standard	Broad	Expanded	Narrow	Standard	Standard [6]	
Bureau of Economic Analysis (BEA) definition	PLUS flow of services from consumer durables	PLUS increase in the value of the slave population; LESS consumption by slaves	PLUS income forgone while in school; PLUS corporate and government expenditure on training and education	Bureau of Economic Analysis (BEA) definition	PLUS flow of services from consumer durables	PLUS realized and unrealized capital gains; LESS change in net liabilities	

[1] Includes nonprofit organizations and unincorporated businesses.

[2] Personal disposable income is personal income less personal tax and nontax payments. Personal outlays include personal consumption expenditures, interest paid by persons, and personal transfers to the rest of the world.

[3] Includes inventory valuation and capital consumption adjustments.

[4] Government surplus or deficit (−) on national income accounts basis.

[5] Includes increases in human capital financed by government and corporations.

[6] Net or gross as desired.

The standard concept of net saving is distinguished from the official BEA definition because the latter excludes consumer durables. For this reason, the official definition is sometimes called the "narrow concept." In addition, we also wish to propose a "broad concept" of saving that would expand the standard concept by including (1) the capital value created by members of farm families when they engage in land clearing, soil improvement, and farm building and (2) the value of the increase in the stock of slaves. Although the broad concept has little relevance in today's economy, it is significant in historical studies of saving and capital formation in the early nineteenth century.

Other variations on the concept of net saving are, of course, possible. For example, some would expand the concept to include activities that increase human capital, such as formal education and skill acquisition (Schultz 1960; Schultz, 1962; Becker 1964/1993). To do that, not only the current outlay for education (tuition, cost of books, etc.) but also the income lost while the individual was attending classes would have to be included as a form of saving (and investment). As another example, some have suggested that business expenditures on research and development be classified as investment (rather than as an intermediary product) because they are intended to increase the future productivity of the economy. The result would be to increase corporate and government saving and thus national saving (Kendrick 1961, p. 25).

There is an alternative to the definition of saving as a flow. For any unit, saving may also be defined as the *change* in earned net worth during the year. This difference is not estimated from the income account but rather from the balance sheet. The balance sheet records the net worth of the economic unit by including all assets and liabilities. If consistent methods of accounting are observed, the two measures of saving are identical. Every dollar of income that is not spent on services and nondurable commodities must be used either to increase the holdings of financial assets and the ownership of tangible capital (consumer durables), or to reduce financial liabilities (consumer debt). Thus, saving is equal to the change in assets minus the change in liabilities. To exclude capital gains and losses, only the change in *earned* net worth is considered.

Saving and Wealth

Broadly speaking, the purpose of saving is to increase wealth. At the individual level, this is often accomplished by depositing the excess income into a cash account or by purchasing one or more of a wide variety of financial assets, such as bonds, stocks, or shares in a mutual fund. The terms "financial capital" and "financial wealth" refer to the value of these resources. Purchasing real estate or durable goods will also increase personal wealth, though these physical assets are most often acquired for the flow of services they provide. Command over financial assets gives individuals and households a buffer that allows them to stabilize consumption in the face of fluctuating income. These stocks can also provide protection in the event of an unexpected diminution of income caused by ill health, unemployment, or other catastrophe. Saving can also be motivated by a desire to accumulate sufficient money to meet a large expenditure planned for the future, as when we save for a vacation or for a child's college education.

A major motivation for saving is to build a stock of assets that can be used to finance retirement. In the United States today, most individuals save to supplement the benefits they are due under the Social Security system. They save heavily during their peak earning years by contributing to their employer-established pension fund, by accumulating equity in their homes, and by acquiring financial assets such as equities and government and corporate bonds. At a later point in life, they plan to draw upon these assets to finance a flow of consumption that exceeds their income. Thus, at any one point in time, some individuals will be saving and others will be "dissaving."

Generally speaking, the saving of savers will exceed the dissaving of those who are drawing down their stock of assets. This phenomenon occurs for several reasons. Population is growing, so the young and middle-aged savers outnumber the older dissavers in the population. Throughout most periods of U.S. history, the productivity of labor has grown, so the young and middle-aged savers will be saving to finance a retirement standard of living that they anticipate will be higher than the standard of living enjoyed by those currently in retirement (Modigliani 1966). Immigrants to the country also tend to help ensure that the overall level of saving is high. Most immigrants come as young adults in their peak earning years, swelling the ranks of savers relative to the older dissavers. Moreover, immigrants may be heavy savers compared to their native-born counterparts because they will have expended some of the wealth they accumulated before immigration in the costs of migration, including financing their consumption during the period they were in transit and establishing themselves before they secured their first U.S. employment. Restoring this wealth to the level commensurate with their new income will require, at least temporarily, a high saving rate (Carter and Sutch 1999, pp. 327–30).

Accumulating financial wealth is a way for an individual to move resources earned in the present into the future. However, society as a whole cannot do this. In the future, what society will consume, for the most part, will be goods and services produced in the future. We do not literally stockpile food and other nondurable commodities produced today for consumption decades later. Even if that were practical, services produced today have no physical manifestation and so cannot be saved for future consumption. Rather than stockpiling commodities, individuals stockpile purchasing power. The individual converts savings into money (or some other financial asset). For this strategy to be attractive, one needs to have the confidence that the value of money and the enforceability of contracts will hold up reasonably well and the expectation that one will be able to buy what is needed and desired some years far in the future. Thus, stable financial and political institutions will promote saving, while uncertainty and instability will reduce it.

Saving and Investment

Output that is not purchased for consumption in the year that it is produced is, by definition, invested. Much of this would be intended investment, though some of it may be manifest in an unintended increase in the inventory of goods, goods that went unsold because demand from consumers was not what was anticipated.

"Investment" refers to both the act of investing and the amount invested. "Investing" is the commitment of money (or other resources) in the hope of future gain. Business enterprises invest in tangible capital (machines, tools, vehicles, buildings) with the expectation that the production made possible with the help of capital will lead to an overall profit. Individuals acquire (and thus invest in) human capital through education and skill acquisition with the expectation that their future incomes, enhanced by the productivity attributable to additional knowledge, will increase enough to generate a positive rate of return. Much of the commitment made by those investing in human capital takes the form of forgone income during the period of schooling or training. Thus, it is convenient to think of that forgone income as income saved to finance the human capital (Becker 1964/1993).

The act of investment will be based on the investor's expectations about the returns that will be earned from the expanded capacity to produce. A general optimism about such matters will raise the level of investment; a general pessimism will decrease it. The cost of devoting the resources to a potential investment should also influence the willingness to undertake the investment. Those costs can be direct, as when the money must be borrowed and interest paid for the privilege of using someone else's money, or indirect, as when the money is diverted from another investment, thus sacrificing a rate of return elsewhere. Generally speaking, the higher the rate of interest is, the lower the volume of investment spending becomes. A fall in the rate of interest should stimulate investment.

Interestingly, saving is much less likely to be sensitive to the interest rate than investment because, in most cases, the motivation for saving is to achieve some target for accumulated assets. On the one hand, a high rate of interest represents a higher reward to saving and can be expected to increase the size of the desired target and thus the required rate of saving. However, with a high rate of return on financial assets, one can achieve any given target with less saving, as the interest payments received will be larger. The empirical studies that have been done suggest that the two effects approximately offset each other, leaving saving largely unaffected by changes in interest rates, at least within the range of variation of interest rates experienced in the last century (Modigliani 1975; Modigliani 1989, p. 44).

As with saving, a distinction is made between net investment and gross investment. Gross investment includes an allowance for the consumption of fixed capital. Thus, net investment must be positive for the capital stock to grow. Moreover, the capital stock must grow faster than the labor force, if the capital–labor ratio is to rise. When this happens, the process is called capital deepening.

National Saving and Private Saving

For the economy as a whole, national saving is the sum of private saving and government saving, while private saving is the sum of personal saving (generated by households and nonprofit institutions) and corporate saving (see Table Ce-A) The national saving rate is national saving expressed as a percentage of gross *national* product (GNP) because gross *domestic* product (GDP) excludes income earned abroad. Figure Ce-B plots the rate of gross national saving (as defined by the NIPA without consumer durables). A substantial proportion of gross saving is used to replace fixed capital lost through depreciation, obsolescence, or destruction (see Table Ce69–90). Net saving, plotted on the same figure, excludes the allowances for capital consumption.

Because government's contribution to net national saving is the government budget surplus, government deficits reduce national saving and reduce net investment in fixed capital. When the government runs a budget deficit, it borrows from the public by selling government bonds. From the point of view of a saver, government bonds are one of many assets that can be acquired to augment personal wealth. So government debt displaces tangible capital from the national portfolio (Modigliani 1961).

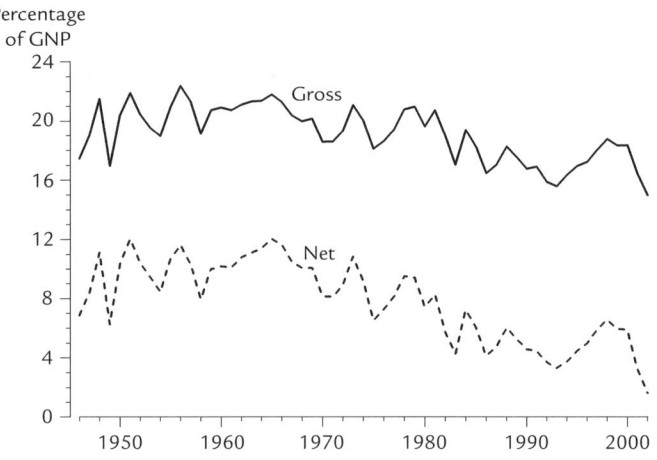

FIGURE Ce-B National savings rates, without consumer durables: 1946–2002

Sources
Series Ce125–126.

Estimating Personal Saving

There are two widely cited data series on personal saving. The BEA calculates one as a residual component of the NIPA. The Board of Governors of the Federal Reserve System (FRB or the Fed) calculates the alternative measure as part of its Flow of Funds Accounts. Conceptually, the two measures should be identical, but they differ because of both practical measurement problems and different treatments of several components.

The BEA measure is calculated as the difference between income and outlays (including outlays for consumer durables) and thus represents a narrow definition of saving (series Ce71). However, the standard definition of saving can be computed from the BEA data on purchases of consumer durables (series Ca91) and the stocks of these assets that are included in the BEA's estimates of tangible wealth (series Ce295). The BEA treats government-employee insurance and pensions as a component of government saving (series Ce79) rather than personal saving (for more detail, see Larkins 1999).

The FRB measures personal saving as the change in the net worth of households and nonprofit organizations (Table Ce91–121). Net worth includes both financial and tangible assets offset by household liabilities. The FRB treats both consumer durables and residential structures as tangible assets and includes the insurance and pension funds of government employees and thus represents the standard definition of saving.

The personal saving *rate* is defined as personal saving expressed as a percentage of disposable personal income, that is, income after tax (series Ca68). Figure Ce-C plots the BEA measure of the personal saving rate from the NIPA and the FRB flow of funds measure, which was adjusted to be comparable by excluding consumer durables. One notable feature, which has been widely remarked upon, is that both measures document a steady decline in the personal saving rate during the last twenty years of the twentieth century. One common explanation for this decline is the impact of stock market capital gains (Peach and Steindel 2000; Poterba 2000). When the value of stock market holdings increases, some may feel more prepared for retirement and thus free to consume more and save less.

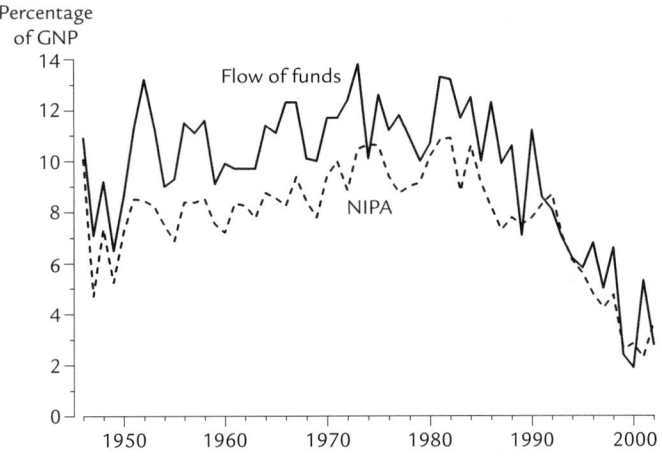

FIGURE Ce-C   Personal saving rate, without consumer durables: 1946–2002

Sources

Series Ce122 and Ce124.

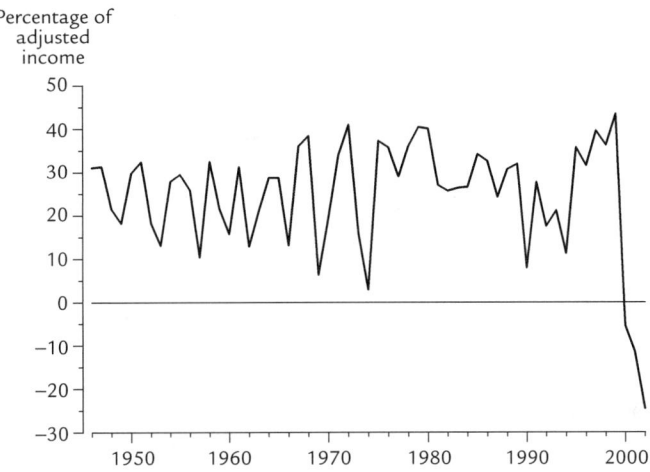

FIGURE Ce-D   Personal saving rate, including capital gains: 1946–2002

Sources

Series Ca68, Ce71, and Ce127.

Documentation

The personal saving rate shown here includes both realized and unrealized capital gains. The series plotted is the annual change in the net worth of households and nonprofit organizations (computed from series Ce127), as a percentage of adjusted income. Adjusted income is equal to disposable income (series Ca68) less the Bureau of Economic Analysis concept of personal saving (series Ce71) plus the change in net worth (computed from series Ce127).

By definition, changes in net worth are produced either by saving or by capital gains. If we take a very broad definition of income to include all capital gains, whether realized or not, then saving would be redefined as the change in household net worth, that is, the change in series Ce127 (Peach and Steindel 2000). This broadened view of the saving rate is plotted in Figure Ce-D. The change in net worth is divided by adjusted income, which is defined as disposable income minus personal saving plus the change in net worth. This view puts personal saving at a much higher rate, with a decline in the 1980s and a recovery in the 1990s. The rapid fall to

negative rates after 2000 is caused by a dramatic decline in stock market values.

The official figures on personal saving based on the flow of funds accounts begin with 1946. These can be extended back to 1897 using the estimates of personal saving made by Raymond Goldsmith (Tables Ce1–68). Goldsmith also presents estimates for net national saving, business saving, and government saving (Table Ce1–12). Except for corporate saving, Goldsmith estimates saving as the change in earned net worth. In this respect, his method resembles that used by the FRB when calculating saving.

Goldsmith is candid about the fact that his estimates are imprecise. He describes the reliability of the estimates in the following terms:

> Evaluation of the possible errors in the individual series from which the estimates of group and national saving have been constructed indicates that the margin of error is hardly under 10 percent for any given year or for the average annual figure in any series, that it is probably in the order of magnitude of 20 to 30 percent in many of them, that it may run even higher in not a few cases, but that the relative margin of error in most cases is reduced for sequences of several years and generally the smaller the longer the period.
>
> The quality of most of the individual series used in the measurement of saving has undoubtedly improved. It would seem to be substantially poorer for the period before the thirties than for the last two decades, and within the earlier period, in turn, to be particularly poor for the years before approximately 1905. . . . There is, however, evidence . . . that the error is . . . in the direction of an overstatement of saving in the first three decades and an understatement during the thirties. (Goldsmith 1955, volume 1, pp. 40–1)

Nineteenth-Century Transformation of Saving Behavior

Robert Gallman (1966) discovered that the American economy experienced a dramatic rise in the rate of gross capital formation during the nineteenth century. Because of the accounting relationship between gross investment and gross saving, the rise in gross capital formation implies a rise in the saving rate. Figure Ce-E plots Gallman's estimates of gross private saving (GPS), including consumer durables as a percentage of GNP. GPS as a percentage of GNP averaged 15.5 percent for the period 1839–1859. It then jumped to 28.3 percent for the decade 1869–1879. For the 1880s, the average rate was double what Gallman reported for the pre–Civil War period. By the end of the nineteenth century, GPS rates were near one third of GNP.

Particularly puzzling is the substantial jump in the saving rate that occurred during the decade of the Civil War (1860–1868). Ransom and Sutch explain part of the jump by the emancipation of the slaves. Slaves were a component of the wealth of slave owners. Thus, from the point of view of the free population, the growth of the slave population represented a change in net worth and thus a form of saving (Moes 1961; Sutch 1967; Ransom and Sutch 1986b). Using the slave-economy concept of GNP (described in Chapter Ca on national income and product), we can calculate GPS including slave capital. This is also plotted in Figure Ce-E. The emancipation of the slaves without compensation to their owners destroyed this form of wealth. The resulting "asset shortage" generated a temporary increase in the aggregate saving rate until asset stocks were restored to their desired level (Ransom and Sutch

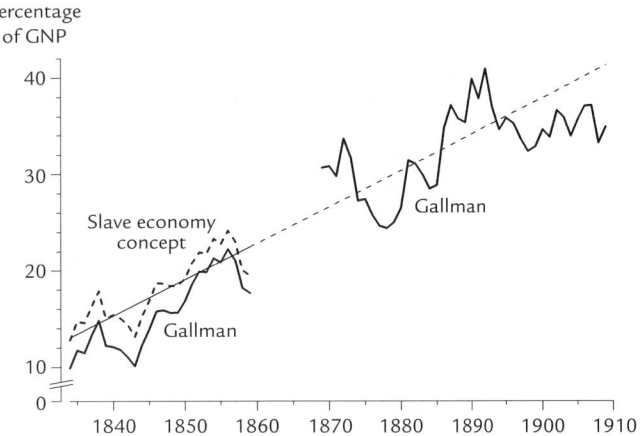

FIGURE Ce-E   Gross private saving rate, including consumer durables: 1834–1909

Sources

Gallman, 1834–1859: computed as capital formation excluding inventory changes (series Ca226) minus changes in claims against foreigners (series Ca232) plus durable consumer goods (series Ca224), and then expressed as a percentage of gross national product (GNP) (series Ca219).

Slave economy concept, 1834–1859: computed as capital formation excluding inventory changes (series Ca226) minus changes in claims against foreigners (series Ca232) plus durable consumer goods (series Ca224) plus increase in the stock of slaves (series Ca234), and then expressed as a percentage of GNP under the slave-economy concept (series Ca235).

Gallman, 1869–1909: computed as capital formation (series Ca200) plus durable consumer goods (series Ca198) minus inventory changes (series Ca205) minus changes in claims against foreigners (series Ca206), and then expressed as a percentage of GNP (series Ca193).

1988, pp. 143–9). Figure Ce-E extrapolates (with a straight line) the pre–Civil War trend of GPS augmented by the inclusion of slave capital in the postwar period. This exercise suggests that the unusually high saving rates of the early 1870s may be attributed to the temporarily high saving required to replace the wealth previously represented by the ownership of the slave population.

There is broad agreement that by the end of the nineteenth century the primary reasons for personal saving were a mix of the life-cycle motive to save for retirement and a bequest motive to provide for heirs; however, there is some debate on which motive was stronger (Kotlikoff and Summers 1981; Modigliani 1988; Dynan, Skinner, and Zeldes 2002). What we know is that retirement rates were relatively high for men older than 60 years of age (Ransom and Sutch 1986a; Carter and Sutch 1996), that self-financed and company-sponsored pension plans were widespread (Ransom and Sutch 1987; Ransom, Sutch, and Williamson 1993a, 1993b), and that the dynamic behavior of saving in the early twentieth century was consistent with the life-cycle model of saving (Modigliani 1966; David and Scadding 1974). Franco Modigliani estimates that if one considers the stock of wealth at any point in time, less than one fourth of it was acquired as a result of intergenerational transfer. Thus, more than three fourths was acquired through saving and capital gains (Modigliani 1988, p. 81).

We have no reliable data on capital formation or saving for the period before 1834. There is, however, a presumption that the rate was low before 1815, if for no other reason than that life-cycle saving was likely to be rare at that early date (Ransom and Sutch 2001, pp. 260–4). Saving for future consumption requires the existence of reliable markets. Markets are required for consumption

items as well as for assets because the household's savings must be held in the form of marketable assets that will be sold later to finance the purchase of consumption items. It is doubtful that either asset or consumption markets were sufficiently developed in the eighteenth century to warrant reliance on the life-cycle strategy, especially outside of cities such as Boston, New York, and Philadelphia (Schumacher 1949; Rothenberg 1992). The major asset of the time – land, with its improvements – was encumbered with the restrictions of common law upon sale, partition, or alienation (Bidwell and Falconer 1925; Hughes 1976).

Financial assets did not appear with any great regularity in probate records from 1774 (Jones 1980, pp. 127–34). A longitudinal study of the probate records of Middlesex County, Massachusetts, undertaken by Winifred Rothenberg, revealed that financial assets were only a small fraction of the decedent's wealth in the eighteenth century, but the proportion rose dramatically in the nineteenth century (Rothenberg 1985).

It would appear, then, that there was a sustained rise in saving rates beginning perhaps as early as 1815, and almost certainly before 1834, and that this rise continued throughout the nineteenth century. There is no shortage of competing explanations designed to account for the increase in saving. Paul David has suggested that a rise in the cost of capital was triggered by an increase in the demand for capital produced by the rapid pace of technological change (David 1977). In response, he suggests, the interest rate and the volume of saving rose. Lance Davis, Robert Gallman, and Robert Cull consider that the growth of financial intermediation motivated more people to save and to save more (Davis and Gallman 1973; Davis and Cull 2000). Jeffrey Williamson (1974) has suggested that post–Civil War debt repayment by the government "crowded in" physical investment – just the opposite of the crowding-out effect of government budget deficits. In another place, Williamson (1979) suggested that rising wealth inequality might have increased saving. If the wealthy saved more than the poor, a redistribution from poor to rich would increase saving. Williamson's calculations on the magnitude of this effect, however, indicated that it was likely to be small. John James and Jonathan Skinner proposed a variant of the redistribution argument with a potentially larger impact (James and Skinner 1987). James and Skinner suggest that workers in the trades, manufacturing, and personal and professional services had a much higher propensity to save than did farmers. The relative growth of those high-saving sectors at the expense of the agricultural sector produced the aggregate increase in saving. Frank Lewis (1983) attributes the rise in saving to a fall in the dependency ratio. For a review of this extensive literature, see Davis and Gallman (1994).

What is clear is that, over the course of the nineteenth century, there was a rise in life-cycle-motivated saving. This transition has been called the life-cycle revolution (Sutch 1991) and seems to have been associated with significant and wide-ranging changes in the attitudes and in the economic, demographic, and social behavior of rural Americans (Rothenberg 1992, pp. 119–20; Parkerson 1995; Carter, Ransom, and Sutch 2003, pp. 298–9). Young adults freed themselves from patriarchal control and began to choose their own marriage partners and to time their marriages to suit themselves (Smith 1973; Folbre 1985). Children were sent to school, and less work was expected of them on the farm (Fishlow 1966a, 1966b; Kaestle and Vinovskis 1980). Inheritance patterns changed toward more equality and less sexism (Newell 1986). Fertility fell from the biological maximum of about eight children per woman to fewer than four children in about two generations (Carter, Ransom, and Sutch 2003). Savings banks arose to collect the assets of savers (Payne and Davis 1956; Olmstead 1976; Steckel 1992).

The shift was toward self-reliance in providing for old age and away from reliance on one's grown children for support in old age. In the eighteenth century, this support was ensured by high fertility, thus producing many children to share the burden, and the threat of disinheritance to compel agreement (Carter, Ransom, and Sutch 2003). A prerequisite for such a change was the development of consumer and financial markets, secure property rights, enforceable contracts, and confidence that the real value of assets (both tangible and financial) would remain secure over a lifetime. The life-cycle strategy also requires a compatible philosophy – a set of values that places the individual over the family line, abhors dependency, and views children with empathy. Adoption of life-cycle strategies of saving and the abandonment of the bequest mechanism would permit parents to give their children much greater freedom – freedom to marry whom and when they choose, and freedom to leave home to take up superior opportunities in other agricultural communities or in the expanding urban sector. The parents would also stand to gain a measure of individual freedom. They no longer would have to look forward to a period of dependency in old age, and their decisions about the disposition of the family farm and other assets would not have to take the wishes of the children into account.

It should not be inferred from the foregoing discussion that the values of individualism and modernization were simply lying dormant in the colonial population waiting to be unleashed by the rise of markets and the removal of restrictions on the sale of land. It is much more likely that the change in values, the rise of asset markets, the restructuring of family responsibilities, the appearance of manufacturing development, and the adoption of life-cycle behavior were phenomena that evolved together. A proximate cause of all of these changes, if indeed a cause should be sought, was the opening of new lands west of the Appalachian Mountains and the resulting flow of population westward.

Although migration into the lands of western New York, western Pennsylvania, and the Ohio River valley was halted temporarily by the 1812–1815 conflict with England, it resumed soon after the war and was greatly stimulated by the fact that many who fought had been paid in part with land script redeemable for western land. This bounty script was transferable, so those who did not wish to move could sell their rights to others. Malcolm Rohrbough offers a useful account of the migration west during this period that is complemented by Hal Barron's study of those who did not migrate (Rohrbough 1978; Barron 1984).

One effect of Jeffersonian land policy was to reduce the value of land everywhere and thus weaken the hold parents could exercise over their children by offering a guaranteed legacy (Barron 1984, pp. 94–7). The terms of the bargain had shifted in favor of children and against their parents. Indeed, the opportunities in the West attracted the young, and many left. Estimates of interregional migration based on calculations by Peter McClelland and Richard Zeckhauser suggest that most young migrants left their parents behind (McClelland and Zeckhauser 1982; Carter, Ransom, and Sutch 2003, p. 298). After the migration had begun, no couple could depend with confidence on their children's continued presence in the community.

One response to this threat was for the parents to view the family farm not as a legacy for the next generation but as ultimate insurance for their old age. Under the circumstances, parents without grown children living nearby felt free to sell the farm or to lease the land to support themselves. It was even common for the parents to sell the family farm to one of their own children (Barron 1984, pp. 99–100). The bequest motive gave way to the greater exigencies of circumstance. Members of the younger generation, observing and perhaps even precipitating this stress in their parents' generation, were likely to adopt a life-cycle outlook from the outset.

Assets that could be bought and sold became the parents' substitute for a large and captive family. And if the assets accumulated during a lifetime of hard work were needed for the support of the parents when they grew older, there might not remain much of a bequest to pass on to their children. So wealth was transferred between generations when the children were young and their parents alive. Sometimes these gifts took the form of land or other assets, but more often the gift was education. Children were sent to school rather than put to work on farm; the loss in family income was probably significant (Craig 1993). Education may have well increased the desire for independence and heightened awareness of the opportunities that lay elsewhere. Parents permitted grown children to leave the family farm at an early age. In doing this, parents were giving up a great deal because those departing would no longer contribute labor to the parental farm.

There is direct evidence of a change in attitudes motivating saving, wealth holding, and bequests recorded in letters, diaries, and legal documents. For example, the personal recollections of John H. Latrobe regarding the quick sale of Baltimore and Ohio Railroad stock in 1827 contain the following account:

> Then came a scene which almost beggars description. By this time public excitement had gone far beyond fever heat and reached the boiling point. Everybody wanted stock. . . . Before a survey had been made – before common sense had been consulted, even, the possession of stock in any quantity was regarded as a provision for old age and great was the scramble to obtain it.

Latrobe's account was set down in 1868. We have taken the quote from Julius Rubin (1960, p. 75). This vignette is typical in that it describes the old-age security motivation for saving as both new and passionate. In this context, it is particularly apt because it links life-cycle behavior directly to the creation of tangible physical capital.

Denison's Law and Twentieth-Century Trends in Private Saving

Private saving, as indicated in Table Ce-A, is the sum of personal saving and saving by corporate businesses. Private saving rates for the twentieth century are known to exhibit no strong trend. Edward Denison (1958) called attention to the remarkable long-term stability of the ratio of GPS to GNP after an examination of data for the years 1948–1956. This phenomenon, known to economists as Denison's law, has been verified with data for a longer period extending back to 1900, first by Franco Modigliani (1966) and later by Paul David and John Scadding (1974). Figure Ce-F displays a three-year moving average of the GPS rate (including consumer durables) for the twentieth century. The rate plotted here is the percentage of GNP that is represented by GPS. Strictly speaking, GNP should be augmented by the flow of services produced by the stock of consumer durables; however, lack of reliable data led us to omit this adjustment.

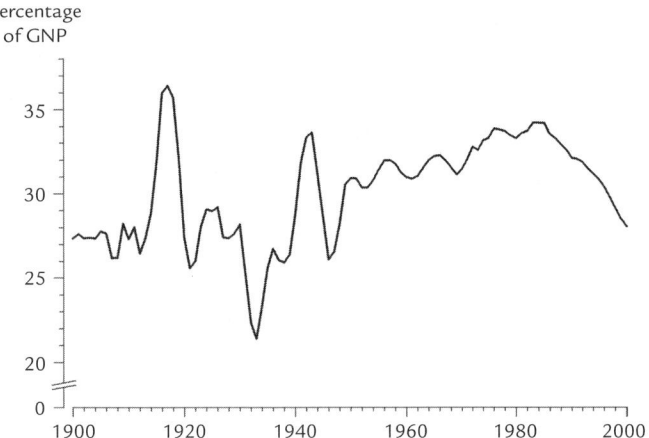

Percentage of GNP

FIGURE Ce-F   Gross private saving rate, including consumer durables: 1900–2000

Sources

The gross private saving (GPS) rate plotted is a three-year moving average of GPS (including consumed durables), expressed as a percentage of gross national product (series Ca211). GPS has three components: net private saving (Goldsmith 1955), an estimate of the consumption of capital (except consumer durables) (Kendrick 1961), and an estimate of the consumption of consumer durable capital (Olney 1991). Net private saving is the sum of series Ce3–4 and Ce10, converted to 1929 dollars using Goldsmith's GNP deflator, series T-16(1) (Goldsmith 1955, volume 1, p. 377). Allowances for capital consumption (Bureau of Economic Analysis concept) are from Kendrick, series A-III(2) (Kendrick 1961, pp. 298–9). Allowances for the depreciation of consumer durables are from Olney, series A-12(TOT) (Olney 1991, pp. 266–7).

Private saving rose during the two world wars when consumption was restrained; however, a significant reduction in saving was evident during the Great Depression of the 1930s. Following the postwar recovery, the saving rate seems to trend slowly upward for more than three decades between the late 1940s and the early 1980s. Robert Mundell (1963) suggested that this trend may, in part, be the result of inflation because the price increases would reduce the real value of financial wealth and induce individuals to restore their lost wealth with a boost in their saving. It may also reflect efforts by households to expand their stock of consumer durables as they increasingly planned to own more than one automobile. Had the denominator of the saving rate displayed here been augmented by the flow of services from consumer durables, the rise in the 1950s would not be so evident. The ratio of the stock of consumer durables to GNP reaches a peak in 1958 (series Ce295 and series Ca2). Since the mid-1980s, the GPS rate has slowly declined. As already suggested, this may, in part, be the result of capital gains in the stock market, which would increase wealth and reduce saving.

Franco Modigliani argued that both the short-term fluctuations and the long-term stability of the saving–income ratio could be explained by the simple version of the life-cycle hypothesis of saving originally proposed by Modigliani and Richard Brumburg (1954, 1980). Paul David and John Scadding noted that the stability of the GPS ratio implies, first, that saving is interest inelastic and, second, that individuals exhibit an ultrarationality that allows them to treat corporate saving as equivalent to personal saving (David and Scadding 1974, pp. 239–40, 243). Both of these observations are consistent with the life-cycle saving hypothesis. This model includes corporate saving in the definition of saving (Modigliani

1966, pp. 184–5, 216; also see Miller and Modigliani 1961) and (in most versions) assumes that the income effect of interest rate changes cancels the substitution effect, leaving GPS insensitive to interest rate movements (Modigliani 1966, 1975).

Estimating National Wealth

In principle, a national balance sheet could be derived by summing similar balance sheets for all sectors in the economy: nonfarm households, agriculture, unincorporated business, corporations, and so forth. The balance sheet of each group in turn would be derived by summing the balance sheets of the constituent units, based as far as possible on a comparable valuation of assets and liabilities. In deriving the national balance sheet, no creditor–debtor or owner–issuer relationships among units are eliminated; for example, the debts of households to corporations appear on one side as assets of corporations and on the other as liabilities of households.

The Federal Reserve calculates balance sheets for three sectors: (1) households and nonprofit institutions, (2) nonfarm/nonfinancial corporate businesses, and (3) nonfarm/noncorporate business. They also prepare (4) a consolidated statement of financial asset holdings by federal, state, and local governments. The asset sides of these statements are reproduced here as Tables Ce127–208.[1] The BEA calculates government ownership of tangible capital (series Ce293–294). The Department of Agriculture publishes the *Balance Sheet of the Farming Sector*, formerly called *The Balance Sheet of Agriculture* (Table Da1312–1322). Missing from this list is a consolidated balance sheet for financial corporations. However, see the balance sheets for banks and other financial institutions provided in Chapter Cj on financial markets and institutions. These estimates fall somewhat short of the goal of a comprehensive summary of the assets, liabilities, and net worth of all transactors in the economy because, for lack of data, obligations among households are not included, and, in the case of corporations with subsidiaries, the balance sheet of the parent company is used, thus eliminating relationships among the subsidiary units. In addition, intangibles such as goodwill and patent rights are excluded from the balance sheet.

Table Ce127–146 presents the asset side of the balance sheet for households. Figure Ce-G plots the trends in net worth, tangible assets, and financial assets since 1945 (evaluated in the prices of 2002). Particularly striking is the rapid growth of stock market equities owned (directly or indirectly) by households. Especially in the 1950s and 1990s, the rapid growth of stock prices generated considerable capital gains. The decline in net worth in 2001 and 2002 was produced by the decline in stock prices in those years.

The expansion of wealth has implications for consumption. When an individual's wealth expands, the individual must either spend that increase while living or pass it on to beneficiaries at death. Even if the original owner refrained from spending the wealth, the individuals who inherit that wealth will spend it. The question of timing is the central issue regarding the impact of an increase in wealth on consumption. Estimates of the wealth effect have ranged widely, partly because of the difficulty in pinning down the timing, which might be thought to vary with the distribution

---

[1] See Board of Governors of the Federal Reserve System, *Guide to the Flow of Funds Accounts*, 1993, for a full description.

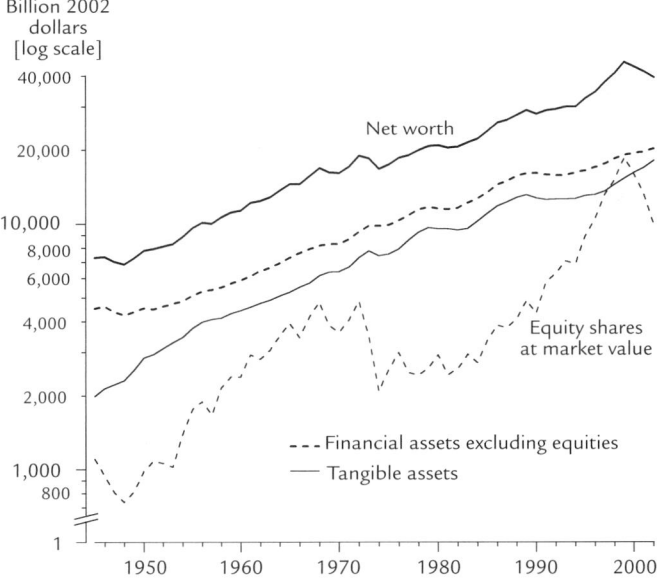

FIGURE Ce-G Net worth and asset holdings of households and nonprofit organizations: 1945–2002

Sources

Net worth: series Ce127. Tangible assets: series Ce129. Equity shares at market value: series Ce133. Financial assets excluding equities: series Ce130 minus series Ce133. Values were converted to 2002 dollars using the consumer price index for urban workers (series Cc1 extended to 2002 using data from the Internet site of the Bureau of Labor Statistics).

of asset ownership, consumer confidence, the demographic composition of wealth owners, and other factors, and partly because wealth is so unequally distributed that the behavior of the extremely wealthy is likely to dominate the results. See James Poterba (2000) for a review of these issues. Information on the distribution of wealth can be found in Chapter Be on economic inequality and poverty.

When all creditor–debtor relationships are canceled, the national balance sheet reduces to a national wealth statement. National wealth consists of reproducible tangible assets, land and natural resources, and net foreign assets. From a strict accounting standpoint, the value of slaves would also be a component of national wealth for the period before 1863 when slavery was legal. The category of reproducible tangible assets consists of physical capital including structures, equipment, and livestock; inventories of durable goods; and monetary stocks of gold and silver. In principle, inventories of perishable goods should also be included; however, reliable data on these holdings by households are not available.

Total national wealth will be less than the total of all assets in the national balance sheet. For example, in the balance sheet the net worth for a corporation is added to the net worth of the stockholders. In the national wealth statement, however, they are consolidated. That is, the outstanding stock of the corporation is canceled against the holdings of the owners, leaving only the net worth of the stockholders and the undistributed earnings of the corporations.

Raymond Goldsmith has estimated national wealth for selected years, using the "perpetual inventory method." The stocks of tangible assets in existence at a given point in time is estimated from annual output totals extending back over a period equal to the average life of the asset, the output total for every year being depreciated

to the end of the period, and the results summed. Military assets are excluded from Goldsmith's estimates (see Tables Ce209–280).

The BEA has made annual estimates of fixed, reproducible tangible wealth beginning in 1925 with details provided for (1) residential capital, (2) fixed nonresidential business capital, (3) consumer durable goods, and (4) stocks of business inventories (see Tables Ce281–310). As with Goldsmith, the BEA estimates for structures, equipment, and consumer durables are computed by the perpetual inventory method, which derives capital stock estimates for a given year by cumulating past investment and deducting the cumulated value of the investment that is used up. The data used to implement this method are taken from the NIPA from 1929 onward and from various private studies prior to that time. The series published here represent just one of a number of variants of capital stock estimates made by BEA reflecting different valuations, service lives, and depreciation techniques (see source for additional estimates). Martha Olney has published alternative estimates for consumer durables that extend back in some cases to 1869 (see Table Cd411–423).

The stocks of business inventories estimated by the BEA were calculated by cumulating the annual inventory changes, in book values and in constant prices, respectively, that are estimated in the NIPA. An estimate of the level of each book value and constant price series was made for some single benchmark point in time for which appropriate data were available; that stock was then moved forward through time by adding the estimated annual changes and backward through time by subtracting annual changes.

Estimates of the national stock of land (in acres) are available in Tables Cf101–144.

References

Barron, Hal S. 1984. *Those Who Stayed Behind: Rural Society in Nineteenth-Century New England.* Cambridge University Press.

Becker, Gary S. 1964. *Human Capital: A Theoretical and Empirical Analysis, with Special Reference to Education,* 3rd edition. University of Chicago Press, 1993.

Bidwell, Percy Wells, and John I. Falconer. 1925. *History of Agriculture in the Northern United States, 1620–1860.* Carnegie Institution of Washington; reprinted, Peter Smith, 1941.

Board of Governors of the Federal Reserve System. 1993. *Guide to the Flow of Funds Accounts.* Internet site.

Carter, Susan B., Roger L. Ransom, and Richard Sutch. 2003. "Family Matters: The Life-Cycle Transition and the Antebellum American Fertility Decline." In Timothy W. Guinnane, William A. Sundstrom, and Warren Whatley, editors. *History Matters: Essays on Economic Growth, Technology, and Demographic Change.* Stanford University Press.

Carter, Susan B., and Richard Sutch. 1996. "Myth of the Industrial Scrap Heap: A Revisionist View of Turn-of-the-Century American Retirement." *Journal of Economic History* 56 (1): 5–38.

Carter, Susan B., and Richard Sutch. 1999. "Historical Perspectives on the Economic Consequences of Immigration into the United States." In Charles Hirschman, Philip Kasinitz, and Joshua DeWind, editors. *The Handbook of International Migration: The American Experience.* Russell Sage Foundation.

Craig, Lee A. 1993. *To Sow One Acre More: Childbearing and Farm Productivity in the Antebellum North.* Johns Hopkins University Press.

David, Paul A. 1977. "Invention and Accumulation in America's Economic Growth: A Nineteenth Century Parable." *Carnegie-Rochester Conference Series on Public Policy* 6: 179–240.

David, Paul A., and John L. Scadding. 1974. "Private Savings: Ultrarationality, Aggregation, and 'Denison's Law.'" *Journal of Political Economy* 82 (2, part 1): 225–49.

Davis, Lance E., and Robert J. Cull. 2000. "International Capital Movements, Domestic Capital Markets, and American Economic Growth, 1820–1914." In Stanley L. Engerman and Robert E. Gallman, editors. *Cambridge Economic History of the United States*, volume 2. Cambridge University Press.

Davis, Lance E., and Robert E. Gallman. 1973. "The Share of Savings and Investment in Gross National Product during the 19th Century in the U.S.A." In F.C. Lane, editor. *Fourth International Conference of Economic History, Bloomington, 1968*. Mouton La Hage.

Davis, Lance E., and Robert E. Gallman. 1994. "Savings, Investment, and Economic Growth: The United States in the Nineteenth Century." In John A. James and Mark Thomas, editors. *Capitalism in Context: Essays on Economic Development and Cultural Change in Honor of R. M. Hartwell*. University of Chicago Press.

Denison, Edward F. 1958. "A Note on Private Savings." *Review of Economics and Statistics* 40 (August): 261–7.

Dynan, Karen E., Jonathan Skinner, and Stephen P. Zeldes. 2002. "The Importance of Bequests and Life-Cycle Saving in Capital Accumulation: A New Answer." *American Economic Review* 92 (2): 274–8.

Fishlow, Albert. 1966a. "The American Common School Revival: Fact or Fancy?" In Henry Rosovsky, editor. *Industrialization in Two Systems: Essays in Honor of Alexander Gerschenkron*. Wiley.

Fishlow, Albert. 1966b. "Levels of Nineteenth-Century American Investment in Education." *Journal of Economic History* 26 (4): 418–36.

Folbre, Nancy R. 1985. "The Wealth of Patriarchs: Deerfield, Massachusetts, 1760–1840." *Journal of Interdisciplinary History* 16 (2): 199–220.

Gallman, Robert E. 1966. "Gross National Product in the United States, 1834–1909." Conference on Research in Income and Wealth. *Output, Employment, and Productivity in the United States after 1800*. Columbia University Press.

Goldsmith, Raymond W. 1955. *A Study of Saving in the United States*. 3 volumes. Princeton University Press.

Hughes, Jonathan R. T. 1976. *Social Control in the Colonial Economy*. University Press of Virginia.

James, John A., and Jonathan S. Skinner. 1987. "Sources of Savings in the Nineteenth Century United States." In Peter Kilby, editor. *Quantity and Quiddity: Essays in U.S. Economic History*. Wesleyan University Press.

Jones, Alice Hanson. 1980. *Wealth of a Nation to Be: The American Colonies on the Eve of the Revolution*. Columbia University Press.

Kaestle, Carl F., and Maris A. Vinovskis. 1980. *Education and Social Change in Nineteenth-Century Massachusetts*. Cambridge University Press.

Kendrick, John W., assisted by Maude R. Pech. 1961. *Productivity Trends in the United States*. Princeton University Press.

Kotlikoff, Laurence J., and Lawrence H. Summers. 1981. "The Role of Intergenerational Transfers in Aggregate Capital Formation." *Journal of Political Economy* 89 (4): 706–32.

Larkins, Daniel. 1999. "Note on the Personal Saving Rate." *Survey of Current Business* (February): 8–9.

Lewis, Frank D. 1983. "Fertility and Savings in the United States: 1830–1900." *Journal of Political Economy* 91 (5): 825–40.

McClelland, Peter D., and Richard J. Zeckhauser. 1982. *Demographic Dimensions of the New Republic: American Interregional Migration, Vital Statistics, and Manumissions, 1800–1860*. Cambridge University Press.

Miller, Merton H., and Franco Modigliani. 1961. "Dividend Policy, Growth, and the Valuation of Shares." *Journal of Business* 34 (4): 411–33.

Modigliani, Franco. 1961. "Long-Run Implications of Alternative Fiscal Policies and the Burden of the National Debt." *Economic Journal* 71 (284): 730–56.

Modigliani, Franco. 1966. "The Life Cycle Hypothesis of Saving, the Demand for Wealth and the Supply of Capital." *Social Research* 33 (2): 160–217.

Modigliani, Franco. 1975. "The Life Cycle Hypothesis of Saving Twenty Years Later." In M. Parkin, editor. *Contemporary Issues in Economics*. Manchester University Press.

Modigliani, Franco. 1988. "The Role of Intergenerational Transfers and Life Cycle Saving in the Accumulation of Wealth." *Journal of Economic Perspectives* 2 (2): 15–40.

Modigliani, Franco. 1989. "Life Cycle, Individual Thrift and the Wealth of Nations." Nobel Prize Lecture. In Simon Johnson, editor. *The Collected Papers of Franco Modigliani*, volume 5. MIT Press.

Modigliani, Franco, and Richard Brumberg. 1954. "Utility Analysis and the Consumption Function: An Interpretation of Cross-Section Data." In

Kenneth K. Kurihara, editor. *Post Keynesian Economics*. Rutgers University Press.

Modigliani, Franco, and Richard Brumberg. 1980. "Utility Analysis and Aggregate Consumption Functions: An Attempt at Integration." In Andrew Abel, editor. *The Collected Papers of Franco Modigliani*, volume 2. MIT Press.

Moes, John E. 1961. "The Absorption of Capital in Slave Labor in the Ante-Bellum South and Economic Growth." *American Journal of Economics and Sociology* 21 (October): 535–41.

Mundell, Robert, 1963. "Inflation and Real Interest." *Journal of Political Economy* 71 (June): 280–3.

Newell, William H. 1986. "Inheritance on the Maturing Frontier: Butler County, Ohio, 1803–65." In Stanley Engerman and Robert Gallman, editors. *Long-Term Factors in American Economic Growth*. University of Chicago Press.

Olmstead, Alan L. 1976. *New York City Mutual Savings Banks. 1819–1861*. University of North Carolina Press.

Olney, Martha L. 1991. *Buy Now, Pay Later: Advertising, Credit, and Consumer Durables in the 1920s*. University of North Carolina Press.

Parkerson, Donald H. 1995. *The Agricultural Transition in New York State: Markets and Migration in Mid-Nineteenth-Century America*. Iowa State University Press.

Payne, Peter Lester, and Lance Edwin Davis. 1956. *The Savings Bank of Baltimore, 1818–1866: A Historical and Analytical Study*. Johns Hopkins University Press.

Peach, Richard, and Charles Steindel. 2000. "A Nation of Spendthrifts? An Analysis of Trends in Personal and Gross Saving." Federal Reserve of New York, *Current Issues in Economics and Finance* 6 (September): 1–6.

Poterba, James. 2000. "Stock Market Wealth and Consumption." *Journal of Economic Perspectives* 14: 99–118.

Ransom, Roger L., and Richard Sutch. 1986a. "The Labor of Older Americans: Retirement of Men On and Off the Job, 1870–1937." *Journal of Economic History* 46 (March): 1–30.

Ransom, Roger L., and Richard Sutch. 1986b. "The Life-Cycle Transition: A Preliminary Report on Wealth-Holding in America." *Income and Wealth Distribution in Historical Perspective*, volume 1. University of Utrecht.

Ransom, Roger L., and Richard Sutch. 1987. "Tontine Insurance and the Armstrong Investigation: A Case of Stifled Innovation, 1868–1905." *Journal of Economic History* 47 (June): 379–90.

Ransom, Roger L., and Richard Sutch. 1988. "Capitalists Without Capital: The Burden of Slavery and the Impact of Emancipation." *Agricultural History* 62 (Summer): 133–60.

Ransom, Roger L., and Richard Sutch. 2001. "Conflicting Visions: The American Civil War as a Revolutionary Event." *Research in Economic History*, volume 20. Elsevier.

Ransom, Roger L., Richard Sutch, and Samuel H. Williamson. 1993a. "Counting Pensions: A Statistical Appendix to 'The Origins of the Company-Provided Pension in the United States, 1900–1940.' " Working Papers on the History of Retirement 2. Institute of Business and Economic Research, University of California.

Ransom, Roger L., Richard Sutch, and Samuel H. Williamson. 1993b. "Inventing Pensions: The Origins of the Company-Provided Pension in the United States, 1900–1940." In K. Warner Schaie and W. Andrew Achenbaum, editors. *Societal Impact on Aging: Historical Perspectives*. Springer.

Rohrbough, Malcolm J. 1978. *The Trans-Appalachian Frontier: People, Societies, and Institutions, 1775–1850*. Oxford University Press.

Rothenberg, Winifred Barr 1985. "The Emergence of Capital Markets in Rural Massachusetts, 1730–1838." *Journal of Economic History* 45 (December): 781–808.

Rothenberg, Winifred Barr. 1992. *From Market-Places to a Market Economy: The Transformation of Rural Massachusetts, 1750–1850*. University of Chicago Press.

Rubin, Julius. 1960. "Canal or Railroad?" *Transactions of the American Philosophical Society* New Series 50 (July).

Schultz, Theodore W. 1960. "Capital Formation by Education." *Journal of Political Economy* 68 (6) (December): 571–83.

Schultz, Theodore W., editor. 1962. "Symposium: Investment in Human Beings." *Journal of Political Economy* 70 (5, part 2): 1–157.

Schumacher, Max George. 1949. *The Northern Farmer and His Markets during the Late Colonial Period*. Ph.D. dissertation, University of California, Berkeley; reprinted Arno Press, 1975.

Smith, Daniel Scott. 1973. "Parental Power and Marriage Patterns: An Analysis of Historical Trends in Hingham, Massachusetts." *Journal of Marriage and the Family* 35 (3): 419–28.

Steckel, Richard H. 1992. "The Fertility Transition in the United States: Test of Alternative Hypotheses." In Claudia Goldin and Hugh Rockoff, editors. *Strategic Factors in Nineteenth Century American Economic History: A Volume to Honor Robert W. Fogel*. University of Chicago Press.

Sutch, Richard. 1967. "Slavery as an Obstacle to Economic Growth in the United States: A Panel Discussion," with Alfred H. Conrad and others. *Journal of Economic History* 27: 518–60.

Sutch, Richard. 1991. "All Things Reconsidered: The Life-Cycle Perspective and the Third Task of Economic History." *Journal of Economic History* 51 (June): 1–18.

Williamson, Jeffrey G. 1974. "Watersheds and Turning Points: Conjectures on the Long-Term Impact of Civil War Financing." *Journal of Economic History* 34 (September): 636–61.

Williamson, Jeffrey G. 1979. "Inequality, Accumulation, and Technological Imbalance: A Growth-Equity Conflict in American History?" *Economic Development and Cultural Change* 28 (January 1979): 231–53.

SAVING

John A. James, Richard Sutch, and Richard Sylla

TABLE Ce1–12   Net national saving – personal, corporate, and government: 1897–1949   [Goldsmith]

Contributed by Susan B. Carter, John A. James, and Richard Sutch

	Net national saving		Personal saving							Corporate saving	Government saving	
	Including consumer durables	Excluding consumer durables	Excluding consumer durables				Consumer durables				State and local	Federal
			Total	Nonagricultural households	Agricultural households	Unincorporated business	Total	Nonagricultural households	Agricultural households			
Year	Ce1	Ce2	Ce3	Ce4	Ce5	Ce6	Ce7	Ce8	Ce9	Ce10	Ce11	Ce12
	Million dollars	Million dollars	Million dollars	Million dollars	Million dollars	Million dollars	Million dollars	Million dollars	Million dollars	Million dollars	Million dollars	Million dollars
1897	934	787	400	537	17	−154	147	122	25	294	69	24
1898	1,620	1,496	1,164	721	211	232	124	102	22	370	68	−106
1899	2,820	2,583	1,953	1,518	76	359	237	206	31	546	71	13
1900	2,102	1,920	1,092	911	−54	235	182	157	25	672	124	32
1901	2,220	2,000	1,143	1,582	−374	−65	220	196	24	648	118	91
1902	3,946	3,673	2,669	1,968	451	250	273	246	27	724	216	64
1903	2,766	2,483	1,218	1,349	−163	32	283	259	24	1,067	143	55
1904	2,043	1,805	1,186	1,355	54	−223	238	209	29	396	226	−3
1905	4,313	3,939	3,084	2,533	61	490	374	337	37	678	139	38
1906	4,206	3,690	2,724	2,442	35	247	516	455	61	730	115	121
1907	3,128	2,698	1,668	1,866	−319	121	430	383	47	773	158	99
1908	2,451	2,350	1,895	2,239	−10	−334	101	64	37	413	81	−39
1909	3,687	3,234	2,547	2,720	0	−173	453	358	95	418	224	45
1910	4,597	4,112	2,759	2,406	−107	460	485	387	98	1,104	161	88
1911	2,934	2,582	1,742	2,495	−718	−35	352	287	65	577	199	64
1912	5,230	4,754	3,763	3,482	188	93	476	396	80	565	296	130
1913	4,137	3,695	2,225	2,441	−698	482	442	405	37	916	451	103
1914	3,511	3,346	2,380	1,948	358	74	165	122	43	741	199	26
1915	6,272	6,061	4,473	4,339	123	11	211	127	84	1,246	197	145
1916	9,579	8,740	4,724	5,137	−1,225	812	839	716	123	3,192	215	609
1917	9,926	9,253	9,399	8,300	898	201	673	352	321	2,525	160	−2,831
1918	1,607	1,908	12,987	11,292	1,426	269	−301	−376	75	422	61	−11,562
1919	6,566	6,105	9,303	10,079	−1,967	1,191	461	252	209	2,484	132	−5,814
1920	9,969	9,455	6,054	5,769	−1,420	1,705	514	728	−214	3,437	−187	151
1921	2,261	2,562	1,587	2,762	−1,293	118	−301	248	−549	1,338	88	−451
1922	7,949	7,053	5,404	4,889	−27	542	896	1,067	−171	948	500	201
1923	13,607	11,423	7,696	7,666	289	−259	2,184	2,142	42	2,354	412	961
1924	12,134	10,293	6,775	5,884	594	297	1,841	1,854	−13	1,455	1,267	796
1925	15,453	12,819	8,110	8,091	−136	155	2,634	2,432	202	2,369	1,321	1,019
1926	15,891	13,194	7,406	6,692	−136	850	2,697	2,603	94	3,394	1,222	1,172
1927	13,692	12,012	8,394	8,435	−56	15	1,680	1,738	−58	1,368	1,108	1,142
1928	10,907	9,246	4,353	4,718	14	−379	1,661	1,566	95	2,105	1,753	1,035
1929	15,968	14,017	9,534	9,163	−8	379	1,951	1,816	135	2,136	1,248	1,099

	Net national saving		Personal saving								Government saving	
	Including consumer durables	Excluding consumer durables	Excluding consumer durables				Consumer durables			Corporate saving	State and local	Federal
			Total	Nonagricultural households	Agricultural households	Unincorporated business	Total	Nonagricultural households	Agricultural households			
	Ce1	Ce2	Ce3	Ce4	Ce5	Ce6	Ce7	Ce8	Ce9	Ce10	Ce11	Ce12
Year	Million dollars	Million dollars	Million dollars	Million dollars	Million dollars	Million dollars	Million dollars	Million dollars	Million dollars	Million dollars	Million dollars	Million dollars
1930	5,820	5,886	5,683	7,923	-45	-2,195	-66	66	-132	-514	903	-186
1931	-3,305	-2,209	3,562	6,853	257	-3,548	-1,096	-848	-248	-3,360	-478	-1,933
1932	-10,491	-8,392	-1,174	1,077	495	-2,746	-2,099	-1,796	-303	-5,032	-953	-1,233
1933	-8,851	-7,351	-2,305	-2,063	196	-438	-1,500	-1,320	-180	-4,687	765	-1,124
1934	-4,417	-3,755	-292	-798	-1,120	1,626	-662	-653	-9	-2,718	1,411	-2,156
1935	237	-323	1,789	184	1,127	478	560	439	121	-1,287	750	-1,575
1936	1,560	-208	3,507	2,674	-203	1,036	1,768	1,587	181	-1,405	1,227	-3,537
1937	7,286	5,322	5,358	4,503	1,143	-288	1,964	1,816	148	-553	1,309	-792
1938	2,002	1,863	3,576	3,777	431	-632	139	177	-38	-574	1,501	-2,640
1939	4,842	3,489	5,499	4,863	693	-57	1,353	1,219	134	-89	804	-2,725
1940	10,983	8,749	6,309	4,386	862	1,061	2,234	2,149	85	1,618	1,845	-1,023
1941	14,309	11,228	10,890	7,709	2,491	690	3,081	2,835	246	1,697	1,724	-3,083
1942	4,500	5,814	34,551	25,152	5,007	4,392	-1,314	-1,351	37	2,863	1,816	-33,416
1943	-3,642	-2,137	37,672	29,371	4,379	3,922	-1,505	-1,525	20	4,234	2,720	-46,763
1944	-7,280	-5,620	40,959	32,213	4,441	4,305	-1,660	-1,435	-225	4,787	3,166	-54,532
1945	-7,311	-6,563	37,157	29,920	3,754	3,483	-748	-606	-142	2,507	2,587	-48,814
1946	25,035	18,634	16,126	12,886	2,560	680	6,401	5,634	767	2,103	2,145	-1,740
1947	32,358	23,279	11,107	11,208	416	-517	9,079	8,076	1,003	4,254	1,603	6,315
1948	42,165	33,636	18,194	15,015	3,084	95	8,529	7,644	885	8,974	1,095	5,373
1949	31,164	22,378	13,671	11,607	995	1,069	8,786	7,982	804	9,473	1,271	-2,037

Source

Raymond W. Goldsmith, *A Study of Saving in the United States*, volume 1 (Princeton University Press, 1955), Table T-1, pp. 344–5; Table T-8(5), p. 359; and Table A-3(5), p. 756.

Documentation

These series were developed by Raymond W. Goldsmith to provide a comprehensive quantitative description of the saving process in the United States in the first half of the twentieth century that could serve as a basis for understanding "the process of financing the country's economic growth" (1955, volume 1, p. ix). Because of his focus on growth, rather than on cyclical change of the economy, Goldsmith defined saving differently from the Bureau of Economic Analysis (BEA) savings estimates presented in Table Ce69–90. The Goldsmith estimates in this table include all forms of net saving covered by the BEA figures and, in addition, cover saving in the form of consumer durables and of brokers' and dealers' commissions and profits made when existing assets change hands. Another difference between the Goldsmith and BEA estimates is that Goldsmith's estimates of net saving and capital consumption allowances have been valued at replacement cost, whereas the BEA estimates are valued in terms of current outlays. Neither set of figures includes saving in the form of soil improvement or additions to military assets.

Goldsmith estimates the components of net saving (with the exception of corporate saving) as the change in earned net worth. All valuation changes are omitted, allowances are made for accruals,

and capital consumption allowances are based on replacement cost and straight-line depreciation. In this respect, they are similar to the Federal Reserve's flow of funds approach. By contrast, the BEA estimates were derived by measuring the flows of expenditures and income. Goldsmith's figures, with the exception of series Ce10 for corporate saving, were obtained by the balance sheet method.

Goldsmith's estimates are imprecise. See the discussion in the essay in this chapter.

Goldsmith also calculates national saving by two other more inclusive concepts not reported here: the business accounting concept, which followed the prevailing business practices of not eliminating realized capital gains and losses, calculating depreciation on the basis of original cost, and accepting all depletion allowances made by owners, and the cash flow, or gross, concept of saving, which ignores capital consumption allowances and other accruals (volume 1, pp. 25–35; volume 2, pp. 3–34).

Series Ce1. Equals the sum of series Ce3, Ce7, and Ce10-12.

Series Ce2. Equals series Ce1 minus series Ce7.

Series Ce3. Equals the sum of series Ce4-6.

Series Ce4. Equals the sum of series Ce8-9.

TABLE Ce13–41 Personal saving, by major components of assets and liabilities: 1897–1949 [Goldsmith]

Contributed by John A. James and Richard Sylla

		Change in tangible assets					
		Structures			Durables		
		Nonfarm					
	Total	Residential	Nonresidential	Farm	Consumer	Producer	Inventories
	Ce13	Ce14	Ce15	Ce16	Ce17	Ce18	Ce19
Year	Million dollars	Million dollars	Million dollars	Million dollars	Million dollars	Million dollars	Million dollars
1897	547	70	152	74	147	−43	−105
1898	1,288	41	125	86	124	−9	271
1899	2,190	71	118	82	237	24	207
1900	1,274	3	198	95	182	34	193
1901	1,363	138	188	108	220	58	−569
1902	2,942	270	227	121	273	136	543
1903	1,501	402	149	116	283	94	−38
1904	1,424	358	106	116	238	65	−133
1905	3,458	546	126	116	374	95	270
1906	3,240	611	181	122	516	165	247
1907	2,098	680	242	119	430	177	−238
1908	1,996	548	137	128	101	49	−30
1909	3,000	729	140	159	453	101	−63
1910	3,244	731	134	179	485	110	472
1911	2,094	651	98	155	352	74	−446
1912	4,239	721	150	181	476	153	511
1913	2,667	733	204	171	442	158	−207
1914	2,545	597	93	165	165	57	499
1915	4,684	607	60	171	211	−2	409
1916	5,563	688	169	287	839	131	−817
1917	10,072	376	133	435	673	277	1,185
1918	12,686	−58	−8	413	−301	246	−168
1919	9,764	752	67	635	461	233	556
1920	6,568	540	240	385	514	359	1,970
1921	1,286	904	272	−37	−301	−370	−796
1922	6,300	2,186	400	44	896	−116	107
1923	9,880	3,158	471	93	2,184	183	471
1924	8,616	3,748	509	63	1,841	71	−915
1925	10,744	4,000	720	82	2,634	234	104
1926	10,103	3,788	848	59	2,697	314	30
1927	10,074	3,166	806	148	1,680	202	−227
1928	6,014	2,725	691	98	1,661	182	−263
1929	11,485	1,454	645	50	1,951	357	196
1930	5,617	−74	451	−127	−66	25	−729
1931	2,466	−512	40	−230	−1,096	−438	−228
1932	−3,273	−1,447	−243	−291	−2,099	−704	−539
1933	−3,805	−1,604	−406	−255	−1,500	−589	−819
1934	−954	−1,499	−435	−256	−662	−345	−1,311
1935	2,349	−992	−435	−141	560	1	800
1936	5,275	−311	−247	−99	1,768	329	−671
1937	7,322	−61	−165	−42	1,964	518	900
1938	3,715	143	−214	−90	139	86	−24
1939	6,852	952	−188	−24	1,353	201	134
1940	8,543	1,285	−158	16	2,234	489	555
1941	13,971	1,776	−97	93	3,081	833	789
1942	33,237	−262	−386	−39	−1,314	150	1,643
1943	36,167	−1,193	−495	−50	−1,505	−184	−170
1944	39,299	−1,442	−440	−108	−1,660	464	354
1945	36,409	−1,327	−303	−167	−748	672	50
1946	22,527	1,764	269	713	6,401	1,536	120
1947	20,186	3,294	90	1,135	9,079	2,514	−2,191
1948	26,723	4,880	448	1,234	8,529	3,023	2,850
1949	22,457	4,341	530	1,076	8,786	2,665	−1,374

TABLE Ce13-41   Personal saving, by major components of assets and liabilities: 1897-1949   [Goldsmith]   *Continued*

		Net acquisition of financial assets					
		Deposits					
Year	Currency	Commercial bank	Savings bank	Credit unions and cooperatives	Savings and loan associations	Mortgage holdings	Life insurance reserves
	Ce20	Ce21	Ce22	Ce23	Ce24	Ce25	Ce26
	Million dollars	Million dollars	Million dollars	Million dollars	Million dollars	Million dollars	Million dollars
1897	27	184	91	5	−20	62	83
1898	40	325	118	5	1	57	96
1899	116	588	119	5	−20	61	103
1900	63	292	193	5	−5	49	113
1901	43	625	131	7	−5	53	140
1902	60	453	145	6	6	55	151
1903	56	223	121	7	14	71	148
1904	−72	136	130	7	17	65	170
1905	219	1,123	183	6	16	68	191
1906	63	474	168	7	31	42	208
1907	116	−279	71	7	43	69	170
1908	−280	−101	55	6	43	78	178
1909	64	674	174	7	55	58	213
1910	42	464	148	7	60	216	205
1911	−71	785	163	6	75	253	245
1912	88	764	201	7	89	259	233
1913	51	502	186	20	82	621	234
1914	−136	212	132	20	81	472	200
1915	299	1,726	168	20	102	267	272
1916	326	2,923	352	21	90	548	354
1917	605	2,853	152	26	131	1,111	394
1918	962	1,462	176	26	105	506	367
1919	−21	4,061	441	31	172	1,144	529
1920	365	−1,017	506	32	280	2,236	520
1921	−914	−1,364	283	32	283	276	526
1922	129	2,471	403	33	348	−180	664
1923	85	1,254	435	34	450	180	791
1924	−31	2,075	508	33	602	−463	821
1925	−104	1,581	465	33	599	426	1,021
1926	−38	−355	538	29	630	684	1,136
1927	−53	2,642	664	31	741	1,318	1,249
1928	−55	−1,745	586	33	685	1,650	1,290
1929	0	−795	158	27	526	1,891	1,115
1930	−2	−899	761	−4	198	781	1,006
1931	752	−3,663	1,028	−1	−229	−183	766
1932	312	−1,979	313	−2	−421	−232	268
1933	191	−1,833	−19	1	−358	−899	535
1934	−12	2,139	337	47	−242	−533	1,127
1935	178	2,483	211	55	−300	133	1,510
1936	528	2,767	350	63	−175	100	1,693
1937	200	349	232	67	−90	92 [1]	1,624
1938	−9	339	189	66	−3	−202	1,606
1939	448	2,440	364	81	170	−292	1,722
1940	894	2,004	248	106	287	−280	1,842
1941	2,129	2,537	26	149	401	80	2,197
1942	4,214	6,256	284	109	297	−232	2,496
1943	4,665	9,979	1,566	111	612	−238	2,871
1944	4,578	10,588	2,322	165	833	18	3,188
1945	2,867	13,258	2,747	207	1,107	646	3,381
1946	77	8,677	1,986	248	1,267	1,582	3,382
1947	−323	1,477	1,209	348	1,304	1,680	3,568
1948	−435	−2,131	703	271	1,327	1,203	3,632
1949	−723	−634	888	288	1,629	615	3,790

Note appears at end of table   (continued)

TABLE Ce13–41   Personal saving, by major components of assets and liabilities:
1897–1949   [Goldsmith]   *Continued*

	Net acquisition of financial assets							Share in saving of foreign corporations
	Pension and retirement funds			Securities				
	U.S. government	State and local	Private	U.S. government	State and local	Corporate and foreign bonds	Stocks	
	Ce27	Ce28	Ce29	Ce30	Ce31	Ce32	Ce33	Ce34
Year	Million dollars	Million dollars	Million dollars	Million dollars	Million dollars	Million dollars	Million dollars	Million dollars
1897	—	0	—	−24	31	58	105	1
1898	—	1	—	92	26	121	99	1
1899	—	1	—	129	56	287	543	1
1900	—	1	—	−45	18	235	259	1
1901	—	1	—	−33	31	393	561	1
1902	—	1	—	−16	2	465	715	1
1903	—	1	—	−24	15	82	475	2
1904	—	1	—	−24	20	302	356	2
1905	—	1	—	−7	45	664	353	2
1906	—	1	—	7	67	417	805	2
1907	—	1	—	−75	122	81	692	2
1908	—	2	—	3	212	610	656	3
1909	—	1	—	−32	10	529	745	3
1910	—	1	—	8	138	−26	804	4
1911	—	0	—	19	109	407	250	4
1912	—	1	—	4	143	667	929	4
1913	—	3	—	−1	8	198	536	4
1914	—	0	—	−2	226	471	456	4
1915	—	5	—	−3	299	1,459	688	5
1916	—	7	—	−123	218	1,089	1,380	7
1917	—	8	—	3,401	213	692	956	9
1918	6	14	—	8,670	497	1,005	956	10
1919	9	14	—	3,148	28	524	1,999	10
1920	21	22	—	−668	682	1,668	1,818	11
1921	34	27	10	−611	696	1,400	956	12
1922	35	29	30	−2,686	745	1,262	1,347	14
1923	35	39	10	−277	624	1,567	1,228	18
1924	90	43	20	−1,516	195	1,436	1,254	22
1925	160	41	30	−295	225	1,937	2,093	26
1926	161	46	40	−639	149	1,895	1,761	30
1927	130	60	70	−2,260	446	2,019	2,075	34
1928	127	66	80	−975	379	1,628	3,406	39
1929	157	70	160	−473	508	660	4,789	44
1930	125	71	50	−227	585	666	1,278	30
1931	−401	72	50	720	1,781	556	599	30
1932	−38	73	50	689	128	−398	227	30
1933	29	87	50	1,108	−912	−100	437	30
1934	53	106	50	−233	−857	39	420	30
1935	137	120	50	−898	−8	−938	−67	30
1936	452	130	80	978	−360	−915	185	30
1937	1,245	157	60	1,026	97	−1,059	831	30
1938	961	159	60	4	−45	−45	228	32
1939	1,108	178	50	−80	−118	−674	568	34
1940	1,138	189	50	289	−129	−416	491	36
1941	1,684	204	75	3,401	−151	−963	627	38
1942	2,424	223	125	10,574	−183	61	189	40
1943	3,710	240	200	14,666	−150	−653	470	42
1944	4,413	259	600	17,797	−76	−1,141	519	44
1945	4,801	253	800	11,843	−306	−1,580	1,246	47
1946	3,354	335	800	−2,273	−218	−1,226	1,818	50
1947	3,494	392	1,050	1,259	411	−694	2,074	55
1948	2,935	528	1,050	1,171	1,184	574	1,441	60
1949	1,929	578	1,050	1,089	906	94	1,620	60

TABLE Ce13–41   Personal saving, by major components of assets and liabilities: 1897–1949 [Goldsmith] *Continued*

	Net increase in liabilities						
	Nonfarm mortgage debt			Debt to banks			
	Residential corporations	Nonresidential structures	Farm mortgage debt	and other institutions	Borrowing on securities	Consumer and other debt	Tax liabilities
	Ce35	Ce36	Ce37	Ce38	Ce39	Ce40	Ce41
Year	Million dollars	Million dollars	Million dollars	Million dollars	Million dollars	Million dollars	Million dollars
1897	−1	22	74	135	71	32	18
1898	19	28	77	68	71	50	19
1899	26	30	80	219	109	55	19
1900	64	40	83	233	111	60	19
1901	63	40	85	301	149	72	18
1902	97	49	89	266	76	79	16
1903	110	53	92	281	71	74	15
1904	132	59	96	40	30	62	17
1905	169	66	99	332	143	109	15
1906	187	73	103	343	42	130	16
1907	135	58	107	−29	−49	93	17
1908	134	60	110	34	36	13	15
1909	228	84	115	299	105	173	16
1910	236	85	314	157	8	122	16
1911	204	78	408	142	52	135	16
1912	217	79	418	317	104	163	44
1913	411	137	359	111	−15	137	138
1914	356	125	284	14	108	99	181
1915	249	99	265	644	397	190	235
1916	328	117	570	628	284	323	676
1917	617	186	711	1,038	137	264	605
1918	271	103	600	408	367	152	299
1919	362	150	1,312	1,776	792	652	−15
1920	1,166	349	1,772	916	−669	574	−192
1921	811	196	486	−1,477	−84	−145	245
1922	996	297	89	−210	655	129	−95
1923	1,700	546	−111	644	−104	301	177
1924	1,737	553	−742	−828	842	147	81
1925	2,179	804	−190	209	1,478	643	145
1926	2,603	544	−45	−40	−2	453	187
1927	2,393	540	109	−231	1,327	353	376
1928	2,500	554	10	189	1,645	981	395
1929	1,949	389	−116	46	−1,329	1,091	−25
1930	566	212	−223	−990	−2,051	1,281	−513
1931	−563	71	−284	−1,223	−2,010	1,144	−188
1932	−1,147	−144	−598	−879	−1,026	435	329
1933	−1,260	−80	−706	−953	−45	−455	478
1934	14	−90	−26	−231	−284	−851	385
1935	−225	−100	−86	171	−114	230	264
1936	−203	23	−194	146	−27	1,102	553
1937	106	−59	−149	281	−520	1,216	−222
1938	196	−58	−156	−102	−97	419	−537
1939	566	−108	−183	276	−153	1,100	77
1940	781	−75	−85	490	−277	1,303	490
1941	955	−55	−109	815	−90	978	2,444
1942	−231	−144	−421	−545	64	−4,199	−1,092
1943	−545	−186	−562	−41	563	−1,509	607
1944	−108	−90	−456	54	1,567	307	702
1945	394	35	−251	475	1,384	1,459	−411
1946	4,241	445	95	1,690	−2,662	3,115	1,211
1947	4,940	548	105	1,654	−477	3,703	566
1948	4,901	518	226	971	−116	2,550	−1,296
1949	3,914	498	305	−156	197	1,642	346

[1] Error in source corrected; see Goldsmith (1955), Tables M-1(1) and A-53(7).

Source

Raymond W. Goldsmith, *A Study of Saving in the United States*, volume 1 (Princeton University Press, 1955), Table T-6, pp. 352–5.

Documentation

For a description of Goldsmith's methodology, see the text for Table Ce1–12.

Total personal saving, series Ce13, is defined as the sum of series Ce14–34 less series Ce35–41.

Series Ce34. Excludes U.S. subsidiaries.

TABLE Ce42–68   Personal saving, by major components of assets and liabilities – nonagricultural individuals and nonprofit institutions: 1897–1949   [Goldsmith]

Contributed by John A. James and Richard Sylla

						Nonagricultural individuals								
	Change in tangible assets					Net acquisition of financial assets								
		Real estate							Mortgage holdings			Pension and retirement funds		
		1- to 4-family homes	Multifamily homes	Farm land and subdivisions	Consumer durables	Currency and commercial bank deposits	Savings bank and other deposits	Savings and loan associations	Farm	Nonfarm	Life insurance reserves	U.S. government	State and local	Private
	Total	Ce43	Ce44	Ce45	Ce46	Ce47	Ce48	Ce49	Ce50	Ce51	Ce52	Ce53	Ce54	Ce55
	Ce42													
Year	Million dollars	Million dollars	Million dollars	Million dollars	Million dollars	Million dollars	Million dollars	Million dollars	Million dollars	Million dollars	Million dollars	Million dollars	Million dollars	Million dollars
1897	659	63	7	57	122	137	91	−20	54	3	74	—	0	—
1898	823	35	6	57	102	173	118	1	53	0	85	—	1	—
1899	1,724	66	5	58	206	317	119	−20	48	8	91	—	1	—
1900	1,068	−1	4	63	157	232	193	−5	39	7	101	—	1	—
1901	1,778	120	18	69	196	361	131	−5	39	11	125	—	1	—
1902	2,214	248	22	74	246	306	145	6	42	10	136	—	1	—
1903	1,608	365	37	79	259	205	121	14	46	21	134	—	1	—
1904	1,564	322	36	84	209	101	130	17	45	16	152	—	1	—
1905	2,870	499	47	89	337	793	183	16	37	28	172	—	1	—
1906	2,897	568	43	94	455	307	168	31	17	23	188	—	1	—
1907	2,249	633	47	100	383	36	71	43	45	21	154	—	1	—
1908	2,303	509	39	105	64	−116	55	43	56	17	159	—	2	—
1909	3,078	669	60	110	358	600	174	55	20	36	188	—	1	—
1910	2,793	664	67	113	387	360	148	60	172	30	182	—	1	—
1911	2,782	592	59	115	287	620	163	75	205	30	218	—	0	—
1912	3,878	657	64	117	396	582	201	89	211	30	207	—	1	—
1913	2,846	671	62	119	405	321	186	82	218	385	208	—	3	—
1914	2,070	528	69	118	122	−49	132	81	157	302	177	—	0	—
1915	4,466	531	76	125	127	1,392	168	102	115	142	243	—	5	—
1916	5,853	614	74	132	716	1,991	353	90	204	258	319	—	7	—
1917	8,652	331	45	142	352	3,018	153	131	341	654	355	—	8	—
1918	10,916	−54	−4	153	−376	1,577	177	105	128	261	330	6	14	—
1919	10,331	683	69	181	252	3,231	442	172	793	141	477	9	14	—
1920	6,497	485	55	−201	728	−1,048	508	280	834	1,126	469	18	22	—
1921	3,010	835	69	−166	248	−1,271	285	283	50	218	477	30	27	10
1922	5,956	1,999	187	−154	1,067	2,060	406	348	−164	147	604	31	29	30
1923	9,808	2,851	307	−135	2,142	1,286	439	450	−345	704	721	32	39	10
1924	7,738	3,402	346	−114	1,854	1,958	511	602	−611	339	751	79	43	20
1925	10,523	3,551	449	345	2,432	1,271	468	599	−263	812	935	142	41	30
1926	9,295	3,265	523	326	2,603	−653	542	630	−135	916	1,043	143	46	40
1927	10,173	2,624	542	314	1,738	2,710	670	741	−6	1,326	1,149	115	60	70
1928	6,284	2,286	439	297	1,566	−1,897	594	685	74	1,572	1,184	124	66	80
1929	10,979	1,199	255	288	1,816	−783	160	526	−24	1,919	1,027	146	70	160
1930	7,989	−81	7	17	66	−279	757	198	−74	864	926	117	71	50
1931	6,005	−478	−34	16	−848	−1,495	1,027	−229	−123	−46	706	−344	72	50
1932	−719	−1,329	−118	4	−1,796	−1,307	311	−421	−207	−3	248	−28	73	50
1933	−3,383	−1,481	−123	5	−1,320	−1,308	−18	−358	−358	−505	494	28	87	50
1934	−1,451	−1,353	−146	5	−653	1,131	344	−242	−274	−208	1,041	48	106	50
1935	623	−857	−135	−5	439	2,291	226	−300	−2	148	1,398	125	120	50
1936	4,261	−253	−58	−6	1,587	2,433	373	−175	−103	215	1,569	413	130	80
1937	6,319	−45	−16	−6	1,816	627	264	−90	−56	155	1,507	1,243	157	60
1938	3,954	188	−45	−5	177	158	220	−3	−44	−153	1,491	958	159	60
1939	6,082	947	5	−5	1,219	2,506	409	170	−34	−254	1,601	1,108	178	50
1940	6,535	1,292	−7	−92	2,149	1,790	305	287	−37	−239	1,713	1,138	189	50
1941	10,544	1,776	0	−93	2,835	3,102	97	401	−36	120	2,050	1,682	204	75
1942	23,801	−199	−63	−103	−1,351	6,772	302	297	−71	−155	2,347	2,398	223	125
1943	27,846	−1,144	−49	−121	−1,525	9,903	1,581	612	−56	−177	2,710	3,651	240	200
1944	30,778	−1,386	−56	−136	−1,435	11,181	2,363	833	−67	91	3,006	4,298	259	600
1945	29,314	−1,244	−83	86	−606	10,879	2,781	1,107	7	639	3,179	4,589	253	800
1946	18,520	1,807	−43	101	5,634	6,780	2,046	1,267	95	1,479	3,179	3,164	335	800
1947	19,284	3,311	−17	108	8,076	618	1,302	1,304	59	1,617	3,358	3,397	392	1,050
1948	22,659	4,816	64	116	7,644	−1,264	813	1,327	102	1,092	3,420	2,897	528	1,050
1949	19,589	4,199	142	113	7,982	−458	1,012	1,629	93	514	3,569	1,862	578	1,050

TABLE Ce42–68   Personal saving, by major components of assets and liabilities – nonagricultural individuals and nonprofit institutions: 1897–1949   [Goldsmith]   *Continued*

	Nonagricultural individuals										Nonprofit institutions		
	Net acquisition of financial assets					Net increase in liabilities					Change in tangible assets		
	Securities				Share in saving of foreign corporations	Mortgage debt							Net increase in mortgage debt
	U.S. government	State and local	Corporate and foreign bonds	Stocks		1- to 4-family homes	Multifamily homes	Borrowing on securities	Consumer debt	Net tax liabilities	Real estate	Equipment	
	Ce56	Ce57	Ce58	Ce59	Ce60	Ce61	Ce62	Ce63	Ce64	Ce65	Ce66	Ce67	Ce68
Year	Million dollars	Million dollars	Million dollars	Million dollars	Million dollars	Million dollars	Million dollars	Million dollars	Million dollars	Million dollars	Million dollars	Million dollars	Million dollars
1897	−24	31	58	105	1	−6	5	71	45	17	50	2	20
1898	92	26	121	99	1	12	7	71	61	19	42	1	20
1899	129	56	287	543	1	19	7	109	57	18	39	0	20
1900	−45	18	235	259	1	54	10	111	49	19	67	5	20
1901	−33	31	393	561	1	45	18	149	61	17	65	4	20
1902	−16	2	465	715	1	74	23	76	74	7	78	7	20
1903	−24	15	82	475	2	86	24	71	72	6	52	3	20
1904	−24	20	302	356	2	105	27	30	44	17	38	0	20
1905	−7	45	664	353	2	137	32	143	91	14	47	1	20
1906	7	67	417	805	2	151	36	42	104	15	65	7	20
1907	−75	122	81	692	2	104	31	−49	90	8	88	9	20
1908	3	212	610	656	3	102	32	36	−24	6	58	1	21
1909	−32	10	529	745	3	183	45	105	150	0	55	1	21
1910	8	138	−26	804	4	186	50	8	95	14	55	0	21
1911	19	109	407	250	4	155	49	52	134	−1	42	−3	21
1912	4	143	667	929	4	164	53	104	113	36	66	0	20
1913	−1	8	198	536	4	330	81	−15	106	111	81	4	31
1914	−2	226	471	456	4	280	76	108	87	177	41	−4	31
1915	−3	299	1,459	688	5	186	63	397	131	214	24	−10	31
1916	−123	218	1,089	1,380	7	252	76	284	219	659	52	−7	31
1917	2,601	213	692	956	9	496	121	137	24	573	43	−10	31
1918	7,120	497	1,005	956	10	198	73	367	30	280	11	−21	31
1919	2,698	28	524	1,999	10	253	109	792	310	−97	25	−15	35
1920	−218	682	1,668	1,818	11	930	236	−669	409	−282	−58	−22	36
1921	−111	696	1,400	956	12	603	208	−84	52	218	10	−8	43
1922	−2,336	745	1,262	1,347	14	700	296	655	163	−105	85	12	54
1923	−27	624	1,567	1,228	18	1,241	459	−104	351	162	109	18	121
1924	−1,466	195	1,436	1,254	22	1,236	501	842	271	76	145	23	125
1925	−195	225	1,937	2,093	26	1,507	672	1,478	655	135	194	35	157
1926	−589	149	1,895	1,761	30	1,811	792	−2	557	172	204	36	150
1927	−2,360	446	2,019	2,075	34	1,644	749	1,327	192	351	223	38	92
1928	−1,075	379	1,628	3,406	39	1,673	827	1,645	775	375	199	31	98
1929	−373	508	660	4,789	44	1,275	674	−1,329	976	−45	184	25	66
1930	−77	585	666	1,278	30	137	429	−2,051	−699	−543	171	22	52
1931	770	1,781	556	599	30	−537	−26	−2,010	−1,195	−188	78	1	40
1932	689	128	−398	227	30	−1,029	−118	−1,026	−1,349	349	−24	−23	−2
1933	1,108	−912	−100	437	30	−1,023	−237	−45	−203	498	−112	−39	−2
1934	−183	−857	39	420	30	254	−240	−284	463	385	−131	−42	−2
1935	−864	−8	−938	−67	30	−61	−164	−114	933	284	−116	−36	−2
1936	841	−360	−915	185	30	−108	−95	−27	1,284	573	−73	−27	−2
1937	870	97	−1,059	831	30	155	−49	−520	622	−212	−81	−23	−34
1938	−50	−45	−45	228	32	254	−58	−97	−323	−512	−80	−18	−35
1939	−166	−118	−674	568	34	518	48	−153	877	92	−92	−13	−25
1940	186	−129	−416	491	36	762	19	−277	1,099	515	−71	−7	−25
1941	2,742	−151	−963	627	38	950	5	−90	612	2,464	−57	1	−35
1942	8,924	−183	61	189	40	−172	−59	64	−3,144	−1,062	−149	−13	−37
1943	11,992	−150	−653	470	42	−416	−129	563	−1,161	627	−216	−20	−40
1944	14,618	−76	−1,141	519	44	−3	−105	1,567	399	702	−206	−11	−40
1945	9,759	−306	−1,580	1,246	47	408	−14	1,384	778	−451	−173	−1	−40
1946	−2,579	−218	−1,226	1,818	50	4,143	98	−2,662	3,259	1,161	−9	32	−7
1947	982	411	−694	2,074	55	4,751	189	−477	3,230	491	62	48	45
1948	2,528	1,184	574	1,441	60	4,637	264	−116	2,519	−1,347	237	82	95
1949	1,063	906	94	1,620	60	3,610	304	197	2,425	298	427	113	145

(continued)

TABLE Ce42–68   Personal saving, by major components of assets and liabilities – nonagricultural individuals and nonprofit institutions: 1897–1949   [Goldsmith]   *Continued*

Source

Raymond W. Goldsmith, *A Study of Saving in the United States*, volume 1 (Princeton University Press, 1955), Table T-8, pp. 358–61.

Documentation

For a description of Goldsmith's methodology, see the text for Table Ce1–12. The difference between personal saving presented in Table Ce13–41 and that

presented in this table is the savings of farm households and unincorporated businesses.

Series Ce42. Defined as the sum of series Ce43–60, less series Ce61–65, plus series Ce66–67, less series Ce68.

Series Ce60. Excludes U.S. subsidiaries.

TABLE Ce69–90   Gross saving and investment, by sector and type: 1929–2002   [BEA concept]

Contributed by Richard Sutch

	Gross saving									
		Private								
				Undistributed corporate profits, with adjustments				Consumption of fixed capital		
	Total	Total	Personal saving	Total	Undistributed profits	Inventory valuation adjustment	Capital consumption adjustment	Corporate	Noncorporate	Wage accruals, less disbursements
	Ce69	Ce70	Ce71	Ce72	Ce73	Ce74	Ce75	Ce76	Ce77	Ce78
Year	Billion dollars	Billion dollars	Billion dollars	Billion dollars	Billion dollars	Billion dollars	Billion dollars	Billion dollars	Billion dollars	Billion dollars
1929	19.2	15.7	3.9	3.4	3.4	0.5	−0.5	5.0	3.4	0.0
1930	14.9	12.4	3.2	1.0	−2.0	3.3	−0.3	4.9	3.4	0.0
1931	8.2	8.5	2.6	−1.8	−4.2	2.4	0.0	4.6	3.1	0.0
1932	3.1	3.0	−0.4	−3.3	−4.4	1.0	0.0	4.1	2.6	0.0
1933	3.1	2.8	−0.7	−2.9	−0.8	−2.1	0.1	3.8	2.5	0.0
1934	6.2	6.2	0.6	−1.0	−0.2	−0.6	−0.2	4.0	2.6	0.0
1935	9.5	9.2	2.6	0.0	0.4	−0.2	−0.2	4.0	2.6	0.0
1936	11.3	11.1	4.3	0.0	1.0	−0.7	−0.3	4.1	2.7	0.0
1937	16.1	12.5	4.5	0.6	1.3	0.0	−0.7	4.5	3.0	0.0
1938	11.6	9.7	1.5	0.4	0.2	1.0	−0.8	4.7	3.1	0.0
1939	13.5	12.1	3.4	1.0	2.4	−0.7	−0.7	4.6	3.1	0.0
1940	18.3	15.2	4.5	2.6	3.6	−0.2	−0.8	4.8	3.2	0.0
1941	29.7	23.6	11.7	2.9	6.3	−2.5	−0.9	5.4	3.6	0.0
1942	39.8	43.5	29.0	4.4	6.4	−1.2	−0.8	6.2	4.0	0.0
1943	44.8	51.3	34.9	6.0	7.0	−0.8	−0.3	6.1	4.1	0.2
1944	39.8	56.3	39.0	7.0	6.9	−0.3	0.4	6.1	4.3	−0.2
1945	29.6	46.9	31.4	4.8	4.7	−0.6	0.7	6.2	4.5	0.0
1946	38.9	31.6	16.3	2.7	10.3	−5.3	−2.3	7.5	5.2	0.0
1947	46.8	29.5	8.1	5.9	14.4	−5.9	−2.5	8.9	6.7	0.0
1948	58.3	43.8	14.1	11.4	16.4	−2.2	−2.9	10.4	7.9	0.0
1949	45.6	41.1	10.0	11.1	12.2	1.9	−2.9	11.4	8.7	0.0
1950	60.3	45.6	15.2	8.6	16.5	−5.0	−2.9	12.2	9.5	0.0
1951	74.8	54.0	19.7	9.3	13.7	−1.2	−3.2	14.0	10.9	0.0
1952	73.8	57.6	20.6	10.4	12.3	1.0	−2.8	14.9	11.7	−0.1
1953	74.6	58.9	21.3	9.5	12.5	−1.0	−2.0	15.8	12.2	0.0
1954	72.7	60.0	19.8	11.0	12.4	−0.3	−1.1	16.6	12.7	0.0
1955	87.4	66.5	19.5	16.0	17.4	−1.7	0.3	17.6	13.4	0.0
1956	98.6	73.9	25.4	14.1	17.2	−2.7	−0.4	19.8	14.6	0.0
1957	99.0	78.0	26.8	13.8	15.9	−1.5	−0.5	21.9	15.4	0.0
1958	90.1	78.8	28.2	11.9	12.4	−0.3	−0.3	22.8	16.0	0.0
1959	105.8	84.2	26.5	17.5	17.5	−0.3	0.3	23.7	16.5	0.0
1960	110.9	84.4	26.4	16.3	15.5	−0.2	1.0	24.7	17.1	0.0
1961	113.9	91.5	31.9	16.8	14.8	0.3	1.7	25.2	17.6	0.0
1962	124.6	100.4	33.5	22.6	17.9	0.0	4.6	26.2	18.1	0.0
1963	132.8	104.3	33.1	25.2	19.5	0.1	5.6	27.2	18.7	0.0
1964	143.0	117.6	40.5	28.6	22.7	−0.5	6.4	28.7	19.7	0.0
1965	158.1	129.4	42.7	34.9	28.9	−1.2	7.2	30.8	21.0	0.0
1966	169.1	138.5	44.5	37.6	32.1	−2.1	7.6	33.7	22.6	0.0
1967	171.1	150.8	54.0	35.4	29.1	−1.6	7.9	37.1	24.3	0.0
1968	183.3	153.7	52.7	33.6	29.3	−3.7	8.0	41.1	26.4	0.0
1969	199.8	157.0	52.6	29.8	27.2	−5.9	8.5	45.6	29.0	0.0

TABLE Ce69–90 Gross saving and investment, by sector and type: 1929–2002 [BEA concept] *Continued*

Gross saving

Private

				Undistributed corporate profits, with adjustments				Consumption of fixed capital		
	Total	Total	Personal saving	Total	Undistributed profits	Inventory valuation adjustment	Capital consumption adjustment	Corporate	Noncorporate	Wage accruals, less disbursements
	Ce69	Ce70	Ce71	Ce72	Ce73	Ce74	Ce75	Ce76	Ce77	Ce78
Year	Billion dollars	Billion dollars	Billion dollars	Billion dollars	Billion dollars	Billion dollars	Billion dollars	Billion dollars	Billion dollars	Billion dollars
1970	194.3	174.3	69.5	23.0	21.9	−6.6	7.6	50.5	31.4	0.0
1971	211.4	202.6	80.1	32.4	29.7	−4.6	7.3	55.4	34.4	0.4
1972	241.6	217.0	76.9	41.1	38.6	−6.6	9.0	60.9	38.5	−0.3
1973	294.6	256.4	102.5	44.8	55.0	−19.6	9.4	66.8	42.3	0.0
1974	304.0	270.7	114.3	29.5	61.8	−38.2	5.9	78.5	48.4	0.0
1975	298.4	323.5	125.2	49.1	60.9	−10.5	−1.2	94.0	55.2	0.0
1976	342.7	344.0	122.1	57.3	75.4	−14.1	−4.0	104.5	60.0	0.0
1977	398.2	383.1	125.6	73.1	91.2	−15.7	−2.4	117.5	66.9	0.0
1978	481.6	439.1	145.4	82.9	110.6	−23.7	−4.0	134.5	76.2	0.0
1979	544.9	487.8	165.8	77.0	124.6	−40.1	−7.4	156.4	88.5	0.0
1980	555.5	537.8	205.6	49.6	102.6	−42.1	−10.8	181.1	101.5	0.0
1981	656.5	631.7	243.7	64.1	86.0	−24.6	2.7	210.1	113.7	0.0
1982	625.7	681.6	262.2	61.9	56.2	−7.5	13.3	233.4	124.0	0.0
1983	608.0	693.8	227.8	93.2	70.5	−7.4	30.2	244.4	128.3	0.0
1984	769.4	824.8	306.5	124.7	81.0	−4.0	47.7	260.2	133.4	0.0
1985	772.5	833.4	282.6	128.3	61.0	0.0	67.2	280.9	141.7	0.0
1986	735.9	806.5	267.8	88.0	30.6	7.1	50.3	302.1	148.7	0.0
1987	810.4	838.3	252.8	107.3	75.3	−16.2	48.2	320.8	157.4	0.0
1988	936.2	943.0	292.3	138.3	115.2	−22.2	45.3	344.3	168.1	0.0
1989	967.6	955.1	301.8	99.2	80.2	−16.3	35.3	370.6	183.4	0.0
1990	977.7	1,016.2	334.3	102.4	95.3	−12.9	19.9	391.1	188.4	0.0
1991	1,015.8	1,098.9	371.7	119.2	104.1	4.9	10.2	411.2	196.8	0.0
1992	1,007.4	1,164.6	413.7	124.4	122.9	−2.8	4.3	427.9	214.3	−15.8
1993	1,039.4	1,159.4	350.8	142.0	141.9	−4.0	4.1	448.5	211.6	6.4
1994	1,155.9	1,199.3	315.5	151.6	151.8	−12.4	12.2	482.7	231.9	17.6
1995	1,257.5	1,266.0	302.4	203.6	203.3	−18.3	18.6	512.1	231.5	16.4
1996	1,349.3	1,290.4	272.1	232.7	205.0	3.1	24.6	543.5	238.5	3.6
1997	1,502.3	1,343.7	252.9	261.3	220.0	8.4	32.9	581.5	250.9	−2.9
1998	1,647.2	1,375.0	301.5	189.9	133.6	18.3	38.0	620.2	264.2	−0.7
1999	1,704.1	1,356.1	174.0	229.6	185.9	−4.2	47.9	665.5	281.8	5.2
2000	1,807.9	1,372.1	201.5	152.6	146.8	−15.0	20.8	721.1	296.8	0.0
2001	1,662.4	1,399.3	169.7	122.7	61.2	5.0	56.5	789.1	317.7	0.0
2002	1,565.1	1,589.6	285.8	139.9	17.6	−6.9	129.1	827.5	336.4	0.0

	Gross saving							Gross investment				
	Government											
		Federal			State and local							
	Total	Total	Consumption of fixed capital	Surplus or deficit	Total	Consumption of fixed capital	Surplus or deficit	Total	Private domestic	Government	Net foreign	Statistical discrepancy
	Ce79	Ce80	Ce81	Ce82	Ce83	Ce84	Ce85	Ce86	Ce87	Ce88	Ce89	Ce90
Year	Billion dollars	Billion dollars	Billion dollars	Billion dollars	Billion dollars	Billion dollars	Billion dollars	Billion dollars	Billion dollars	Billion dollars	Billion dollars	Billion dollars
1929	3.5	1.3	0.2	1.1	2.2	0.7	1.5	20.1	16.5	2.8	0.8	0.9
1930	2.5	0.4	0.2	0.2	2.1	0.7	1.3	14.6	10.8	3.2	0.7	−0.3
1931	−0.2	−1.9	0.2	−2.1	1.7	0.7	0.9	9.1	5.9	3.0	0.2	0.9
1932	0.1	−1.2	0.2	−1.3	1.3	0.6	0.6	3.6	1.3	2.1	0.2	0.5
1933	0.4	−0.7	0.2	−0.9	1.1	0.7	0.3	3.8	1.7	1.9	0.2	0.7
1934	0.1	−1.9	0.2	−2.2	2.0	0.8	1.2	6.8	3.7	2.7	0.4	0.5
1935	0.3	−1.6	0.3	−1.9	1.9	0.8	1.1	9.4	6.7	2.8	−0.1	−0.1
1936	0.3	−2.9	0.3	−3.2	3.2	0.9	2.3	12.7	8.6	4.1	−0.1	1.3
1937	3.5	0.6	0.3	0.2	3.0	1.0	2.0	16.2	12.2	3.8	0.2	0.1
1938	2.0	−0.9	0.4	−1.3	2.9	1.0	1.9	12.4	7.1	4.2	1.2	0.8
1939	1.3	−1.7	0.4	−2.1	3.0	1.0	2.0	14.9	9.3	4.5	1.0	1.4

(continued)

TABLE Ce69–90   Gross saving and investment, by sector and type: 1929–2002   [BEA concept]   *Continued*

	Gross saving							Gross investment				
		Government										
		Federal			State and local							
	Total	Total	Consumption of fixed capital	Surplus or deficit	Total	Consumption of fixed capital	Surplus or deficit	Total	Private domestic	Government	Net foreign	Statistical discrepancy
	Ce79	Ce80	Ce81	Ce82	Ce83	Ce84	Ce85	Ce86	Ce87	Ce88	Ce89	Ce90
Year	Billion dollars	Billion dollars	Billion dollars	Billion dollars	Billion dollars	Billion dollars	Billion dollars	Billion dollars	Billion dollars	Billion dollars	Billion dollars	Billion dollars
1940	3.1	0.1	0.4	−0.3	3.0	1.1	1.9	19.6	13.6	4.4	1.5	1.2
1941	6.1	3.0	0.8	2.2	3.1	1.2	1.9	30.2	18.1	10.8	1.3	0.5
1942	−3.7	−6.6	2.1	−8.7	2.9	1.4	1.5	38.9	10.4	28.5	−0.1	−0.9
1943	−6.4	−9.3	4.8	−14.1	2.9	1.5	1.4	43.1	6.1	39.1	−2.1	−1.7
1944	−16.4	−19.4	7.6	−27.0	3.0	1.4	1.5	42.5	7.8	36.6	−2.0	2.6
1945	−17.3	−20.2	8.8	−29.1	2.9	1.4	1.6	33.6	10.8	24.1	−1.3	4.0
1946	7.3	4.3	9.4	−5.1	3.0	1.5	1.4	39.6	31.1	3.5	4.9	0.7
1947	17.3	14.1	8.8	5.2	3.2	1.8	1.4	48.8	35.0	4.6	9.3	2.1
1948	14.4	11.2	7.6	3.5	3.3	2.1	1.2	57.5	48.1	7.0	2.4	−0.7
1949	4.5	1.0	6.6	−5.7	3.5	2.1	1.4	47.4	36.9	9.7	0.9	1.8
1950	14.7	11.4	5.9	5.5	3.4	2.1	1.3	62.0	54.1	9.8	−1.8	1.7
1951	20.8	15.8	6.1	9.6	5.1	2.6	2.5	78.7	60.2	17.6	0.9	3.9
1952	16.2	10.6	6.9	3.7	5.7	2.7	2.9	77.0	54.0	22.3	0.6	3.1
1953	15.7	9.5	7.7	1.8	6.3	2.8	3.4	79.2	56.4	24.0	−1.3	4.6
1954	12.7	6.6	8.3	−1.7	6.1	2.9	3.2	76.6	53.8	22.5	0.2	3.9
1955	20.9	14.4	8.7	5.7	6.5	3.1	3.4	90.5	69.0	21.0	0.4	3.1
1956	24.7	16.8	9.3	7.5	7.9	3.5	4.3	97.7	72.0	22.9	2.8	−0.9
1957	21.1	13.1	9.9	3.2	8.0	3.9	4.1	99.6	70.5	24.4	4.8	0.6
1958	11.3	4.5	10.0	−5.5	6.8	4.0	2.8	91.9	64.5	26.5	0.9	1.7
1959	21.6	13.6	10.4	3.2	8.0	4.2	3.8	106.7	78.5	29.3	−1.2	0.8
1960	26.5	17.8	10.7	7.1	8.7	4.4	4.3	110.4	78.9	28.3	3.2	−0.6
1961	22.5	13.5	11.0	2.5	9.0	4.7	4.3	113.8	78.2	31.3	4.3	−0.2
1962	24.2	14.0	11.6	2.4	10.2	5.0	5.2	125.3	88.1	33.3	3.9	0.7
1963	28.5	17.5	12.3	5.2	11.0	5.4	5.7	132.4	93.8	33.6	5.0	−0.4
1964	25.5	13.4	12.5	0.8	12.1	5.7	6.4	144.2	102.1	34.6	7.5	1.2
1965	28.8	16.0	12.8	3.2	12.7	6.2	6.5	160.0	118.2	35.6	6.2	1.9
1966	30.7	16.1	13.3	2.7	14.6	6.9	7.7	175.6	131.3	40.4	3.9	6.4
1967	20.3	5.8	14.2	−8.3	14.5	7.5	7.0	175.9	128.6	43.8	3.5	4.8
1968	29.6	13.8	15.1	−1.3	15.8	8.3	7.5	187.6	141.2	44.7	1.7	4.3
1969	42.8	25.5	15.9	9.6	17.3	9.3	8.0	202.7	156.4	44.4	1.8	2.9
1970	20.0	2.3	16.7	−14.4	17.6	10.6	7.1	201.2	152.4	44.8	4.0	6.9
1971	8.8	−9.5	17.4	−26.8	18.2	11.8	6.4	222.7	178.2	44.0	0.6	11.3
1972	24.6	−3.8	18.7	−22.5	28.4	12.9	15.6	250.3	207.6	46.3	−3.6	8.7
1973	38.2	8.3	19.5	−11.2	30.0	14.3	15.7	302.6	244.5	49.4	8.7	8.0
1974	33.3	6.4	20.2	−13.9	27.0	17.7	9.3	314.0	249.4	57.4	7.1	10.0
1975	−25.1	−47.7	21.6	−69.3	22.7	20.2	2.4	316.1	230.2	64.5	21.4	17.7
1976	−1.3	−29.9	23.2	−53.0	28.6	21.3	7.3	367.2	292.0	66.4	8.9	24.5
1977	15.1	−20.6	24.6	−45.2	35.7	22.6	13.1	419.8	361.3	67.5	−9.0	21.6
1978	42.5	−0.6	26.3	−26.9	43.1	24.4	18.7	502.6	436.0	77.1	−10.4	21.0
1979	57.1	16.6	28.0	−11.4	40.5	27.4	13.0	580.6	490.6	88.5	1.4	35.7
1980	17.7	−22.8	30.9	−53.8	40.6	31.7	8.8	589.5	477.9	100.3	11.4	33.9
1981	24.8	−18.9	34.7	−53.7	43.8	36.3	7.5	684.0	570.8	106.9	6.3	27.5
1982	−55.9	−93.1	39.5	−132.6	37.2	39.5	−2.3	628.2	516.1	112.3	−0.2	2.5
1983	−85.7	−131.5	42.4	−173.9	45.7	40.9	4.8	655.0	564.2	122.8	−32.0	47.0
1984	−55.4	−121.6	46.4	−168.1	66.2	42.4	23.8	787.9	735.5	139.4	−87.0	18.6
1985	−60.9	−127.9	49.3	−177.1	67.0	44.7	22.3	784.2	736.3	158.8	−110.9	11.7
1986	−70.5	−139.2	52.9	−192.1	68.7	47.9	20.8	779.8	747.2	173.2	−140.6	43.9
1987	−27.9	−91.6	56.3	−147.9	63.7	51.5	12.2	813.8	781.5	184.3	−152.0	3.3
1988	−6.7	−77.2	60.2	−137.4	70.5	54.9	15.6	894.0	821.1	186.2	−113.2	−42.2
1989	12.5	−65.6	64.4	−130.0	78.1	58.8	19.3	983.9	872.9	197.7	−86.7	16.3
1990	−38.6	−104.3	68.7	−173.0	65.7	63.1	2.6	1,008.2	861.7	215.8	−69.2	30.6
1991	−83.2	−142.3	73.0	−215.3	59.1	66.9	−7.8	1,035.4	800.2	220.3	14.9	19.6
1992	−157.2	−222.2	75.4	−297.5	65.0	69.9	−4.9	1,051.1	866.6	223.1	−38.7	43.7
1993	−120.0	−195.4	78.7	−274.1	75.4	73.9	1.5	1,103.2	955.1	220.9	−72.9	63.8
1994	−43.4	−130.9	81.4	−212.3	87.5	78.9	8.6	1,214.4	1,097.1	225.6	−108.3	58.5

TABLE Ce69–90 Gross saving and investment, by sector and type: 1929–2002 [BEA concept] *Continued*

	Gross saving							Gross investment				
	Government											
		Federal			State and local							
Year	Total	Total	Consumption of fixed capital	Surplus or deficit	Total	Consumption of fixed capital	Surplus or deficit	Total	Private domestic	Government	Net foreign	Statistical discrepancy
	Ce79	Ce80	Ce81	Ce82	Ce83	Ce84	Ce85	Ce86	Ce87	Ce88	Ce89	Ce90
	Billion dollars	Billion dollars	Billion dollars	Billion dollars	Billion dollars	Billion dollars	Billion dollars	Billion dollars	Billion dollars	Billion dollars	Billion dollars	Billion dollars
1995	−8.5	−108.0	84.0	−192.0	99.4	84.1	15.3	1,284.0	1,143.8	238.2	−98.0	26.5
1996	58.9	−51.5	85.3	−136.8	110.4	88.9	21.4	1,382.1	1,242.7	250.1	−110.7	32.8
1997	158.6	33.4	86.8	−53.3	125.1	94.2	31.0	1,532.1	1,390.5	264.6	−123.1	29.7
1998	272.2	132.0	88.2	43.8	140.2	99.5	40.7	1,616.2	1,538.7	277.1	−199.7	−31.0
1999	348.1	203.4	91.5	111.9	144.7	106.4	38.3	1,665.4	1,636.7	304.7	−276.0	−38.8
2000	435.8	302.8	95.9	206.9	133.0	115.0	18.0	1,679.4	1,755.4	319.8	−395.8	−128.5
2001	263.1	170.7	98.7	72.0	92.4	123.7	−31.3	1,545.1	1,586.0	335.8	−376.7	−117.3
2002	−24.5	−100.2	101.9	−202.1	75.7	127.7	−52.0	1,456.2	1,593.2	351.9	−488.9	−108.8

Source

Bureau of Economic Analysis, Internet site, Table 5.1, downloaded September 23, 2003.

Documentation

The national income and product accounts (NIPA) are a consistent set of double-entry accounts in which gross saving plus the statistical discrepancy is equal to gross investment at the aggregate level each year (see the essay on national income and product in Chapter Ca).

Series Ce71. Personal saving is personal income less the sum of personal outlays and personal tax and nontax payments. It is the current saving of individuals (including proprietors and partnerships), nonprofit institutions that primarily serve individuals, life insurance carriers, private noninsured welfare funds, and private trust funds. For more information on the calculation of personal saving in the NIPA, see U.S. Bureau of Economic Analysis, *A Guide to the NIPA's Methodology, National Income and Product Accounts, 1929–1997* (June 2001). Also see the text for Table Ca64–73.

Series Ce73. Undistributed profits are corporate profits after taxes and after the payment of dividends. Dividends are payments in cash or other assets, excluding the corporations' own stock, that are made by corporations located in the United States and abroad to stockholders who are U.S. residents. The payments are measured net of dividends received by U.S. corporations. Dividends paid to state and local governments' social insurance funds and general government are included.

Series Ce74. Inventory valuation adjustment (IVA) for corporations is the difference between the cost of inventory withdrawals as valued in the source data used to determine profits before tax and the cost of withdrawals valued at replacement cost. It is needed because inventories, as reported in the source data, are often charged to cost of sales (that is, withdrawn) at their acquisition (historical) cost rather than at their replacement cost (the concept underlying the NIPA). As prices change, companies that value inventory withdrawals at acquisition cost may realize profits or losses. Inventory profits, a capital-gains-like element in profits, result from a decrease in inventory prices. In the NIPA, inventory profits or losses are shown as adjustments to business income (corporate profits and nonfarm proprietors' income); they are shown as the IVA with the sign reversed. In other words, if inventory prices fall and firms find that inventory replacements are less expensive than the originals, the IVA would be positive, but inventory profits would be negative. No adjustment is needed to farm proprietors' income because farm inventories are measured on a current-market-cost basis.

Series Ce75. Capital consumption adjustment is the difference between the value of corporate-owned capital used up in the production process and the tax-return corporate charges for depreciation.

Series Ce76–77, Ce81, and Ce84. Consumption of fixed capital is a charge for the using up of fixed capital such as equipment and structures located in the United States. It is based on studies of prices of used equipment and structures in resale markets.

Series Ce80–85. Government saving totals are the sum of the consumption of fixed capital and the current surplus or deficit. The current surplus or deficit is the sum government receipts less expenditures. Includes net capital grants received by the United States, not shown separately.

Series Ce87–88. Gross private domestic investment and gross government investment represent the sum of fixed investment and change in business inventories. Fixed investment consists of both nonresidential fixed investment and residential fixed investments. It consists of purchases of fixed assets, which are commodities that will be used in a production process for more than one year, including replacements and additions to the capital stock, and it is measured before a deduction for consumption of fixed capital. Gross private domestic investment covers all investment by private businesses and by nonprofit institutions in the United States, regardless of whether the investment is owned by U.S. residents. It excludes investment by U.S. residents in other countries. Gross government investment covers all such investment by government.

Series Ce89. Net foreign investment is U.S. exports of goods and services, receipts of factor income, and capital grants received by the United States (net) less imports of goods and services by the United States, payments of factor income, and transfer payments to the rest of the world (net). It may also be viewed as the acquisition of U.S. assets by foreign residents. It includes the statistical discrepancy in the balance of payments accounts.

Series Ce90. The statistical discrepancy is gross domestic product (GDP) less gross domestic income (GDI) or gross national product (GNP) less gross national income (GNI). It is recorded in the NIPA as an "income" component that reconciles the income and product sides of the accounts. It arises because the two sides are estimated using independent and imperfect data. For additional details, see "The Statistical Discrepancy" in Robert P. Parker and Eugene P. Seskin, "Annual Revision of the National Income and Product Accounts," *Survey of Current Business* (August 1997): 19.

TABLE Ce91–121 Derivation of personal saving: 1946–2002 [Flow of funds]

Contributed by Richard Sutch

	Personal saving		Net acquisition of financial assets					Securities								
	With consumer durables	Without consumer durables	Total	Foreign deposits	Checkable deposits and currency	Time and savings deposits	Money market fund shares	Total	Open market paper	U.S. government securities	Municipal securities	Corporate and foreign bonds	Corporate equities	Mutual fund shares	Life insurance reserves	Pension fund reserves
	Ce91	Ce92	Ce93	Ce94	Ce95	Ce96	Ce97	Ce98	Ce99	Ce100	Ce101	Ce102	Ce103	Ce104	Ce105	Ce106
Year	Billion dollars	Billion dollars	Billion dollars	Billion dollars	Billion dollars	Billion dollars	Billion dollars	Billion dollars	Billion dollars	Billion dollars	Billion dollars	Billion dollars	Billion dollars	Billion dollars	Billion dollars	Billion dollars
1946	22.7	17.6	19.4	0.0	5.6	6.3	0.0	−1.2	0.1	−1.5	−0.1	−0.9	0.9	0.2	3.8	1.3
1947	19.9	12.2	12.4	0.0	0.0	3.5	0.0	1.0	0.0	0.0	0.6	−0.8	1.0	0.2	3.2	2.3
1948	25.7	17.7	8.9	0.0	−3.0	2.3	0.0	2.3	0.1	0.9	0.2	0.0	0.9	0.1	2.8	2.5
1949	21.1	12.5	8.5	0.0	−2.0	2.6	0.0	0.9	0.1	1.4	−0.9	−0.4	0.4	0.3	2.8	2.8
1950	28.9	18.1	14.9	0.0	2.7	2.4	0.0	0.9	0.1	−0.8	1.7	−1.0	0.5	0.3	2.9	3.2
1951	34.7	26.2	19.4	0.0	4.6	4.8	0.0	2.0	0.3	−0.9	0.3	0.3	1.6	0.4	2.7	3.6
1952	39.5	32.1	29.6	0.0	1.6	7.4	0.0	8.3	0.2	1.6	5.2	−0.3	1.0	0.5	2.9	5.6
1953	37.3	29.1	24.6	0.0	1.0	8.2	0.0	5.0	0.3	0.8	2.9	0.0	0.7	0.4	3.0	5.0
1954	30.6	23.9	20.7	0.0	2.2	9.1	0.0	−0.6	−0.2	−2.0	2.1	−1.1	0.3	0.4	2.7	5.3
1955	36.2	26.3	28.0	0.0	1.2	8.5	0.0	7.8	0.3	3.2	3.2	0.1	0.4	0.6	2.9	5.8
1956	42.2	34.7	31.8	0.0	2.0	9.3	0.0	7.5	0.1	1.7	2.7	1.1	1.0	0.8	3.5	6.3
1957	43.4	35.4	29.6	0.0	−0.3	11.8	0.0	6.4	0.3	1.8	2.0	1.1	0.5	0.8	2.7	7.0
1958	44.4	38.4	32.5	0.0	3.9	13.8	0.0	−0.2	0.1	−3.5	0.8	0.7	0.3	1.4	3.1	7.6
1959	39.4	31.8	34.5	0.0	1.1	10.5	0.0	8.8	−0.2	4.4	3.7	0.3	−1.0	1.4	3.4	8.8
1960	43.2	36.2	33.9	0.0	1.0	12.0	0.0	5.2	0.9	−0.6	2.6	2.4	−1.2	1.0	3.2	8.7
1961	42.0	37.1	35.6	0.0	−0.7	18.1	0.0	1.3	−0.4	−0.7	1.5	0.2	−1.1	1.7	3.4	9.1
1962	48.9	39.3	40.2	0.0	−1.1	25.8	0.0	−0.7	0.8	1.4	−0.4	−0.6	−2.7	0.9	3.8	9.8
1963	53.0	41.4	45.6	0.0	4.5	25.9	0.0	−1.5	1.2	−1.1	0.0	−0.1	−2.6	1.0	4.2	10.2
1964	65.6	53.0	56.4	0.0	6.3	25.9	0.0	3.9	1.0	0.9	2.8	0.1	−1.9	0.9	4.4	12.7
1965	72.5	55.2	56.2	0.0	6.7	27.5	0.0	0.8	0.9	2.1	1.7	−1.1	−4.8	2.1	4.8	13.0
1966	83.6	66.4	62.7	0.0	2.4	18.8	0.0	17.3	2.3	9.0	4.6	2.7	−3.5	2.2	4.7	15.5
1967	88.4	70.8	71.1	0.0	10.5	34.9	0.0	−0.9	1.8	0.4	−3.0	4.4	−5.5	0.9	5.2	14.5
1968	87.2	63.1	66.5	0.0	9.5	30.3	0.0	−0.2	2.0	2.8	−1.6	5.1	−10.6	2.2	4.8	16.3
1969	87.1	67.2	69.2	0.0	−1.8	9.7	0.0	26.2	6.3	15.5	13.3	4.5	−15.7	2.2	5.0	18.3
1970	103.2	86.5	79.8	0.0	7.3	42.5	0.0	−4.8	−2.3	−6.2	−1.0	8.1	−4.4	1.0	5.3	20.5
1971	115.9	93.7	110.2	0.0	13.5	65.5	0.0	−21.1	−3.9	−9.0	−3.5	7.1	−11.7	0.0	6.4	24.0
1972	135.0	107.6	136.7	0.0	13.0	72.6	0.0	−20.7	−5.2	−2.5	0.5	1.9	−13.8	−1.7	6.9	43.6
1973	168.6	135.4	149.4	0.0	12.5	63.0	0.0	8.3	4.1	8.6	5.8	2.9	−10.5	−2.6	7.3	34.5
1974	134.3	108.2	153.3	0.0	5.1	55.3	2.4	30.8	5.6	10.4	8.2	11.6	−3.5	−1.5	7.1	37.5
1975	173.2	149.2	178.5	0.0	1.3	78.2	1.3	14.5	−15.4	11.2	4.0	10.0	5.0	−0.2	10.2	63.6
1976	178.2	145.5	197.8	0.0	12.2	101.6	−0.3	−0.1	−3.9	−7.6	2.5	8.2	3.6	−2.9	9.2	51.7
1977	209.6	169.1	241.2	0.0	16.8	105.4	−0.4	9.4	14.4	−4.3	3.9	2.5	−7.0	−0.1	10.0	71.0
1978	222.8	175.5	283.7	0.0	16.7	104.2	5.4	20.8	13.8	3.7	25.3	−9.6	−12.1	−0.3	11.6	83.4
1979	225.0	181.1	311.0	0.0	20.5	76.9	29.8	39.8	7.1	42.0	16.0	−6.0	−17.3	−1.9	10.9	93.2
1980	241.2	216.9	319.4	0.0	12.1	121.3	23.9	0.5	−5.0	17.0	8.3	−14.4	−5.2	−0.2	10.3	118.5
1981	327.2	298.3	360.1	0.0	44.4	69.7	85.9	−38.1	−11.7	−12.2	26.2	1.3	−46.1	4.3	9.6	119.4
1982	342.4	316.5	414.9	0.0	18.6	116.5	32.2	61.3	3.6	28.9	39.1	12.3	−25.1	2.5	7.8	144.0
1983	353.7	302.8	478.5	0.3	15.9	203.0	−31.2	68.0	−5.3	38.0	41.2	−4.1	−23.4	21.6	8.8	175.6
1984	440.6	361.6	551.6	0.0	16.5	229.6	41.8	67.1	17.0	68.1	39.1	−5.2	−67.8	16.0	6.1	151.8
1985	409.0	310.1	590.8	0.8	29.7	130.4	2.3	53.0	−7.0	6.9	95.5	2.7	−118.4	73.3	11.5	282.3
1986	518.3	402.7	564.6	0.8	115.7	94.0	38.8	55.2	−4.4	0.5	6.7	31.0	−91.6	112.9	18.3	175.8
1987	455.9	341.1	460.5	−0.1	3.2	124.3	21.1	86.4	2.3	30.4	99.6	33.0	−140.2	61.3	26.9	158.9
1988	505.6	397.4	590.8	0.9	3.1	167.3	17.5	74.1	34.4	95.8	58.0	−4.4	−118.2	8.6	26.1	235.9
1989	402.0	285.7	474.4	0.8	0.6	80.9	76.9	1.5	−10.4	58.9	24.1	7.6	−105.1	26.3	29.6	218.7
1990	570.0	481.9	538.8	1.4	−9.8	33.6	27.8	190.6	6.2	125.8	27.6	57.1	−48.6	22.5	26.5	207.7
1991	436.3	386.5	444.9	1.0	51.6	−68.6	9.9	129.0	−29.9	15.6	40.0	57.2	−52.2	98.3	26.8	228.8
1992	469.3	384.3	441.9	1.2	114.9	−92.3	−38.6	195.8	−3.3	88.7	−34.2	−2.4	18.1	128.9	29.1	223.2
1993	464.9	347.1	430.3	−1.1	49.6	−105.2	0.8	134.4	15.6	−8.0	−40.5	23.3	−56.1	200.1	37.1	260.2
1994	441.0	320.4	483.9	3.1	−18.2	−26.0	14.9	162.0	1.2	282.0	−50.2	37.5	−172.1	63.6	35.5	256.0
1995	451.6	314.6	534.3	4.6	−27.1	131.4	99.6	21.1	1.3	5.6	−51.0	96.1	−96.9	66.0	45.8	158.8
1996	513.0	384.7	647.4	12.4	−53.9	156.9	52.7	169.6	6.7	81.1	−31.1	87.4	−185.3	210.8	44.5	148.3
1997	462.3	297.8	633.6	6.5	−11.3	142.6	83.5	36.4	1.5	−112.4	38.5	102.1	−273.8	280.6	59.3	201.4
1998	626.7	420.1	915.8	0.1	18.7	175.6	139.4	124.6	7.5	−7.7	5.3	118.6	−280.0	281.0	48.0	217.4
1999	381.7	160.5	712.1	5.2	−35.8	101.3	118.3	108.2	4.1	164.5	24.1	53.6	−304.8	166.7	50.8	181.8
2000	379.6	137.2	687.9	15.0	−59.6	308.7	154.2	−331.8	10.9	−129.5	11.1	74.8	−465.5	166.3	50.2	209.0
2001	658.7	388.6	831.8	−5.0	55.0	256.9	158.2	−34.1	−36.9	−142.1	48.3	127.8	−219.9	188.8	77.2	210.8
2002	467.8	219.6	799.9	10.7	58.8	279.2	−39.2	119.0	5.8	−228.0	108.8	180.4	−76.2	128.2	60.1	215.1

TABLE Ce91–121   Derivation of personal saving: 1946–2002   [Flow of funds]   *Continued*

	Net acquisition of financial assets		Net investment in tangible assets					Net increase in liabilities							Net capital transfers
	Investment in bank personal trusts	Miscellaneous and other assets	Total	Residential fixed investment	Other fixed assets	Consumer durables	Inventories	Total	Mortgage debt on nonfarm homes	Other mortgage debt	Consumer credit	Policy loans	Security credit	Other liabilities	
	Ce107	Ce108	Ce109	Ce110	Ce111	Ce112	Ce113	Ce114	Ce115	Ce116	Ce117	Ce118	Ce119	Ce120	Ce121
Year	Billion dollars	Billion dollars	Billion dollars	Billion dollars	Billion dollars	Billion dollars	Billion dollars	Billion dollars	Billion dollars	Billion dollars	Billion dollars	Billion dollars	Billion dollars	Billion dollars	Billion dollars
1946	0.0	3.6	12.6	3.9	3.5	5.0	0.1	10.2	4.4	1.0	2.9	−0.1	−0.7	2.6	−0.9
1947	0.0	2.5	18.3	8.7	3.7	7.6	−1.7	11.8	5.1	0.8	3.5	0.0	0.0	2.2	−1.0
1948	0.0	2.0	26.8	11.8	4.1	8.1	2.8	11.0	5.1	1.2	3.1	0.1	0.0	1.6	−1.1
1949	0.0	1.4	21.6	10.6	3.1	8.6	−0.7	9.9	4.3	1.5	3.1	0.2	0.4	0.5	−0.9
1950	0.0	2.7	31.0	16.1	3.9	10.8	0.2	17.8	7.5	2.1	4.6	0.2	0.5	2.8	−0.8
1951	0.0	1.6	26.8	13.5	3.4	8.5	1.4	12.4	6.5	2.3	1.4	0.2	−0.1	2.0	−0.9
1952	0.0	3.8	24.5	13.3	2.2	7.4	1.5	15.5	6.7	2.1	5.2	0.1	0.1	1.3	−1.0
1953	0.0	2.4	25.7	13.9	2.9	8.1	0.8	14.1	7.5	1.6	4.1	0.2	0.4	0.2	−1.1
1954	0.0	2.0	25.2	15.3	3.2	6.6	0.1	16.6	9.3	2.3	1.3	0.2	0.8	2.6	−1.2
1955	0.0	1.7	33.4	18.8	5.0	9.9	−0.3	26.5	12.5	1.9	7.0	0.2	0.4	4.5	−1.3
1956	0.0	3.4	28.1	16.9	4.4	7.4	−0.7	19.4	10.8	3.0	3.6	0.3	0.0	1.6	−1.6
1957	0.0	1.9	27.3	15.3	3.8	8.0	0.2	15.2	8.7	2.1	2.6	0.4	−0.3	1.8	−1.8
1958	0.0	4.3	27.3	15.1	4.4	6.0	1.8	17.0	9.8	3.6	0.3	0.4	0.9	2.1	−1.7
1959	0.0	1.9	31.3	20.3	4.9	7.5	−1.3	28.3	13.0	5.0	7.7	0.5	0.0	2.1	−1.8
1960	0.0	3.7	30.2	18.1	4.4	7.0	0.7	23.1	11.2	4.7	4.0	0.7	−0.1	2.6	−2.2
1961	0.0	4.4	28.1	17.8	4.4	5.0	1.0	24.2	12.5	6.2	2.2	0.6	1.0	1.8	−2.5
1962	0.0	2.6	35.7	19.9	5.5	9.6	0.9	29.7	14.2	6.6	5.9	0.5	−0.1	2.6	−2.6
1963	0.0	2.2	40.7	22.5	5.7	11.7	0.8	36.1	16.6	7.3	8.5	0.5	1.5	1.7	−2.9
1964	0.0	3.2	43.1	24.1	7.3	12.6	−0.9	37.2	17.3	7.2	9.5	0.5	−0.5	3.2	−3.3
1965	0.0	3.3	51.5	23.5	9.5	17.3	1.2	38.7	17.2	7.9	10.1	0.6	0.3	2.6	−3.6
1966	0.0	4.1	48.7	20.9	10.4	17.3	0.2	31.6	13.0	7.2	5.9	1.5	0.0	4.1	−3.9
1967	0.0	6.9	48.2	20.3	9.0	17.6	1.3	34.8	13.4	6.1	5.1	1.0	3.0	6.2	−4.0
1968	0.0	5.7	60.5	25.9	8.7	24.2	1.8	43.9	17.2	11.8	10.8	1.3	2.6	0.2	−4.1
1969	8.0	3.8	59.2	28.3	10.4	19.9	0.5	45.9	18.2	11.9	9.9	2.6	−3.3	6.6	−4.6
1970	4.9	3.9	52.4	26.1	10.4	16.7	−0.7	33.8	13.3	4.4	4.4	2.3	−1.3	10.7	−4.8
1971	13.5	8.4	73.9	38.7	10.9	22.3	2.0	73.9	26.6	18.9	15.6	1.0	2.5	9.3	−5.8
1972	9.5	11.9	90.4	49.8	12.5	27.4	0.7	98.9	38.2	25.2	19.5	1.0	3.6	11.4	−6.8
1973	13.6	10.2	105.9	53.6	16.9	33.2	2.3	93.3	42.9	4.6	22.5	2.2	−4.2	25.3	−6.6
1974	6.4	8.7	78.9	41.4	13.4	26.1	−1.9	104.3	36.2	26.5	8.9	2.7	−1.5	31.5	−6.3
1975	−4.8	14.1	72.9	35.6	10.4	24.0	2.9	84.7	38.6	12.9	7.8	1.6	0.9	22.9	−6.4
1976	8.6	15.1	96.8	52.9	11.2	32.7	0.1	123.7	60.1	17.4	22.0	1.4	3.9	19.0	−7.2
1977	8.4	20.5	138.9	76.6	16.3	40.5	5.4	179.7	91.4	23.8	35.5	1.7	2.0	25.3	−9.3
1978	9.8	31.9	164.9	92.6	22.5	47.3	2.6	233.0	109.9	29.9	46.4	2.6	2.6	41.5	−7.2
1979	7.7	32.1	172.9	95.5	29.2	43.9	4.3	266.5	116.2	47.8	43.3	4.7	0.3	54.1	−7.5
1980	4.1	28.8	113.2	71.7	23.3	24.3	−6.1	200.1	93.3	49.9	3.4	6.7	7.3	39.5	−8.8
1981	19.0	50.1	136.9	65.8	32.4	29.0	9.8	179.0	68.1	42.7	19.8	7.4	−1.7	42.8	−9.3
1982	−1.0	35.5	101.2	44.7	25.9	25.9	4.7	183.7	54.4	56.2	18.8	4.2	2.8	47.3	−10.1
1983	3.8	34.4	145.4	88.7	20.7	50.8	−14.9	278.5	115.4	65.2	48.2	1.1	8.4	40.4	−8.3
1984	15.1	23.6	233.3	112.8	32.9	78.9	8.7	352.7	133.8	89.7	81.7	0.4	−2.3	49.4	−8.4
1985	11.2	69.7	259.4	114.5	39.3	98.9	6.6	450.1	173.6	84.4	84.0	−0.1	18.9	89.4	−8.9
1986	16.9	49.3	291.7	142.0	35.1	115.6	−1.1	347.9	202.7	65.9	55.8	−0.1	6.7	16.9	−9.9
1987	16.3	23.4	294.8	146.3	38.3	114.9	−4.7	309.7	238.5	35.8	32.3	0.0	−16.3	19.5	−10.4
1988	0.9	65.0	288.4	147.4	43.1	108.2	−10.4	384.6	221.6	73.7	46.6	0.0	1.7	41.0	−11.0
1989	19.3	46.3	295.1	135.7	41.7	116.3	1.4	379.9	227.1	43.1	47.0	3.2	−1.0	60.5	−12.4
1990	32.9	28.1	250.3	120.0	39.2	88.1	3.0	234.5	207.1	−0.3	15.1	4.1	−3.7	12.2	−15.5
1991	17.5	48.8	161.3	89.8	22.8	49.8	−1.1	185.1	167.8	−5.4	−8.8	4.8	16.3	10.5	−15.2
1992	−7.1	15.6	208.2	106.5	11.3	85.0	5.5	196.5	170.1	−20.2	9.2	5.7	−1.6	33.3	−15.8
1993	0.9	53.6	271.1	135.0	22.9	117.8	−4.6	254.2	160.0	−16.2	61.0	5.6	22.6	21.1	−17.7
1994	17.8	38.8	304.5	147.9	22.5	120.6	13.4	367.3	180.8	−20.3	134.8	7.8	−1.1	65.3	−20.0
1995	6.4	93.7	318.9	154.7	34.4	136.9	−7.1	421.6	176.9	5.7	147.2	10.5	3.5	77.7	−19.9
1996	−5.1	122.1	351.5	174.4	39.9	128.3	9.0	508.9	240.8	29.1	103.6	4.5	15.8	115.0	−23.0
1997	−53.0	168.1	376.2	174.1	31.6	164.5	5.9	573.9	258.1	31.8	72.0	3.2	36.8	172.0	−26.4
1998	−46.1	238.0	450.3	203.3	35.9	206.6	4.5	771.1	383.2	85.7	86.7	0.1	21.6	193.8	−31.7
1999	−8.1	190.5	533.4	239.5	71.3	221.1	1.6	899.7	422.2	108.5	120.2	−5.1	75.2	178.6	−35.7
2000	56.6	285.6	590.9	255.6	91.8	242.4	1.1	934.2	416.2	111.4	166.2	2.8	7.2	230.4	−35.1
2001	−59.9	172.6	601.0	259.6	72.7	270.1	−1.5	808.7	530.6	117.7	126.0	2.2	−38.8	70.9	−34.6
2002	−2.4	98.6	555.8	275.9	31.1	248.2	0.6	920.1	720.5	112.6	79.2	1.1	−48.2	54.8	−32.1

(continued)

TABLE Ce91–121 Derivation of personal saving: 1946–2002 [Flow of funds] *Continued*

Source
Board of Governors of the Federal Reserve System, Internet site, *Flow of Funds Accounts*, Table F.10, downloaded September 24, 2003.

Documentation
Personal saving may be viewed as the net acquisition of financial assets (such as cash and deposits, securities, and the change in life insurance and pension fund reserves) plus the net investment in produced assets (such as residential housing, less depreciation) less the net increase in financial liabilities (such as mortgage debt, consumer credit, and security credit) less net capital transfers. This account consolidates the household sector with nonfarm, noncorporate business and farm business.

Series Ce91. Equals series Ce93 plus series Ce109 minus series Ce114 and Ce121.

Series Ce92. Equals series Ce91 minus series Ce112.

Series Ce93. Equals the sum of series Ce94–98 and Ce105–108.

Series Ce98. Equals the sum of series Ce99–104.

Series Ce103. Corporate equities includes only securities directly held or held in closed-end and exchange-traded funds. Other corporate equities are included in mutual funds, life insurance and pension funds, and personal bank trusts (series Ce104–107).

Series Ce109. Equals the sum of series Ce110–113. Net investment is gross investment less consumption of fixed capital.

Series Ce111. Other fixed assets includes corporate farms.

Series Ce114. Equals the sum of series Ce115–120.

Series Ce121. Net capital transfers consist of net immigrants' transfers received by persons less estate and gift taxes paid by persons.

TABLE Ce122–126 Personal and national savings rates: 1929–2002

Contributed by Richard Sutch

	Personal saving rate			National saving rate (NIPA)	
	NIPA concept without consumer durables	Flow of funds concept		Gross	Net
		With consumer durables	Without consumer durables		
	Ce122	Ce123	Ce124	Ce125	Ce126
Year	Percent	Percent	Percent	Percent	Percent
1929	4.7	—	—	18.4	9.5
1930	4.3	—	—	16.2	6.2
1931	4.0	—	—	10.6	−0.5
1932	−0.8	—	—	5.2	−7.4
1933	−1.5	—	—	5.5	−7.4
1934	1.1	—	—	9.4	−2.1
1935	4.4	—	—	12.9	2.4
1936	6.4	—	—	13.5	4.0
1937	6.2	—	—	17.4	7.9
1938	2.3	—	—	13.4	2.9
1939	4.8	—	—	14.6	4.6
1940	5.9	—	—	18.0	8.6
1941	12.5	—	—	23.3	14.7
1942	24.4	—	—	24.5	16.2
1943	25.8	—	—	22.5	14.2
1944	26.3	—	—	18.1	9.3
1945	20.6	—	—	13.2	3.9
1946	10.1	14.0	10.9	17.4	6.9
1947	4.7	11.5	7.1	19.1	8.4
1948	7.4	13.4	9.2	21.5	11.1
1949	5.2	11.0	6.5	17.0	6.2
1950	7.2	13.7	8.6	20.4	10.3
1951	8.5	15.0	11.3	21.9	12.0
1952	8.5	16.2	13.2	20.5	10.4
1953	8.2	14.4	11.3	19.5	9.4
1954	7.5	11.6	9.0	19.0	8.4
1955	6.9	12.8	9.3	20.9	10.7
1956	8.4	13.9	11.5	22.4	11.6
1957	8.4	13.6	11.1	21.3	10.3
1958	8.5	13.4	11.6	19.1	7.9
1959	7.5	11.2	9.1	20.7	10.0
1960	7.2	11.8	9.9	20.9	10.2
1961	8.3	11.0	9.7	20.7	10.1
1962	8.3	12.0	9.7	21.1	10.8
1963	7.8	12.5	9.7	21.3	11.1
1964	8.7	14.2	11.4	21.4	11.4

TABLE Ce122–126   Personal and national savings rates: 1929–2002   *Continued*

Year	Personal saving rate			National saving rate (NIPA)	
	NIPA concept without consumer durables	Flow of funds concept		Gross	Net
		With consumer durables	Without consumer durables		
	Ce122	Ce123	Ce124	Ce125	Ce126
	Percent	Percent	Percent	Percent	Percent
1965	8.6	14.5	11.1	21.8	12.0
1966	8.3	15.5	12.3	21.3	11.6
1967	9.4	15.3	12.3	20.4	10.5
1968	8.4	13.9	10.1	20.0	10.1
1969	7.8	12.9	10.0	20.2	10.1
1970	9.4	14.0	11.7	18.6	8.1
1971	10.0	14.5	11.7	18.6	8.1
1972	8.9	15.5	12.4	19.3	8.9
1973	10.5	17.2	13.8	21.1	10.9
1974	10.7	12.5	10.1	20.0	9.2
1975	10.6	14.7	12.6	18.1	6.5
1976	9.4	13.7	11.2	18.6	7.3
1977	8.7	14.6	11.8	19.4	8.1
1978	9.0	13.8	10.9	20.8	9.5
1979	9.2	12.4	10.0	21.0	9.4
1980	10.2	11.9	10.7	19.6	7.4
1981	10.8	14.6	13.3	20.7	8.3
1982	10.9	14.2	13.2	19.0	5.7
1983	8.8	13.7	11.7	17.0	4.3
1984	10.6	15.3	12.5	19.4	7.2
1985	9.2	13.3	10.0	18.2	6.0
1986	8.2	15.9	12.3	16.5	4.1
1987	7.3	13.2	9.9	17.0	4.7
1988	7.8	13.5	10.6	18.3	6.0
1989	7.5	10.0	7.1	17.6	5.3
1990	7.8	13.3	11.2	16.8	4.6
1991	8.3	9.8	8.6	16.9	4.5
1992	8.7	9.9	8.1	15.9	3.7
1993	7.1	9.4	7.0	15.6	3.3
1994	6.1	8.5	6.2	16.3	3.7
1995	5.6	8.3	5.8	16.9	4.4
1996	4.8	9.0	6.8	17.2	5.0
1997	4.2	7.7	5.0	18.0	5.9
1998	4.7	9.9	6.6	18.8	6.6
1999	2.6	5.8	2.4	18.3	6.0
2000	2.8	5.3	1.9	18.4	5.9
2001	2.3	8.9	5.3	16.5	3.3
2002	3.7	6.0	2.8	15.0	1.6

Sources

Bureau of Economic Analysis, Internet site, Tables 2.1 and 5.1, downloaded September 23, 2003. Board of Governors of the Federal Reserve System, Internet site, *Flow of Funds Accounts*, Table F.10, downloaded September 24, 2003.

Documentation

Series Ce122. Equals personal savings as defined by the U.S. Bureau of Economic Analysis (BEA) divided by disposable personal income – in other words, series Ce71 expressed as a percentage of series Ca68.

Series Ce123. Equals personal savings as defined by the Federal Reserve Board (FRB) *Flow of Funds Accounts* divided by disposable personal income – in other words, series Ce91 expressed as a percentage of series Ca68.

Series Ce124. Equals personal savings without consumer durables as defined by the FRB *Flow of Funds Accounts* divided by disposable personal income – in other words, series Ce92 expressed as a percentage of series Ca68.

Series Ce125. Equals gross savings as defined by the BEA divided by gross national product (GNP) – in other words, series Ce69 expressed as a percentage of series Ca2.

Series Ce126. Equals gross saving (series Ce69) less consumption of fixed capital (the sum of series Ce76-77, Ce81, and Ce84), expressed as a percentage of GNP (series Ca2).

NATIONAL BALANCE SHEETS

Richard Sutch

TABLE Ce127–146   Net worth of households and nonprofit organizations: 1945–2002

Contributed by Richard Sutch

							Assets				
								Financial			
									Equity shares at market value		
								Total		Indirectly held	
	Net worth	Total	Tangible	Total	Deposits	Credit market instruments	Total	Excluding defined benefit plans	Directly held	Total	Bank personal trusts and estates
	Ce127	Ce128	Ce129	Ce130	Ce131	Ce132	Ce133	Ce134	Ce135	Ce136	Ce137
Year	Billion dollars	Billion dollars	Billion dollars	Billion dollars	Billion dollars	Billion dollars	Billion dollars	Billion dollars	Billion dollars	Billion dollars	Billion dollars
1945	731.4	761.7	198.9	562.8	104.2	91.0	110.5	110.5	109.5	1.0	0.0
1946	797.0	834.1	231.4	602.7	115.5	90.3	102.3	102.3	101.3	1.1	0.0
1947	871.9	917.9	275.1	642.8	118.8	91.5	100.0	100.0	98.8	1.2	0.0
1948	920.6	975.3	308.7	666.6	118.6	93.7	98.7	98.7	97.5	1.2	0.0
1949	961.0	1,024.0	336.0	688.0	119.4	94.6	107.7	107.7	105.0	2.7	0.0
1950	1,044.2	1,120.5	381.7	738.8	124.3	96.2	131.6	131.6	128.7	2.9	0.0
1951	1,145.7	1,230.7	425.2	805.4	133.3	96.9	156.3	156.2	151.1	5.2	0.0
1952	1,195.6	1,293.0	458.3	834.7	142.7	104.6	156.2	154.7	151.0	5.2	0.0
1953	1,231.4	1,341.5	488.2	853.3	152.0	109.6	151.7	149.8	145.8	6.0	0.0
1954	1,326.0	1,448.4	515.9	932.5	162.9	109.5	207.5	204.8	198.8	8.6	0.0
1955	1,436.5	1,580.0	559.8	1,020.2	172.4	117.6	261.5	256.4	248.2	13.2	0.0
1956	1,533.2	1,692.0	602.7	1,089.3	183.4	124.9	286.1	280.3	271.0	15.2	0.0
1957	1,567.2	1,738.5	637.9	1,100.6	194.3	131.9	259.7	253.4	244.5	15.2	0.0
1958	1,712.8	1,896.1	664.4	1,231.7	210.4	132.7	345.9	336.3	322.3	23.6	0.0
1959	1,802.5	2,008.3	698.0	1,310.2	223.9	142.8	386.2	374.1	357.3	28.9	0.0
1960	1,866.1	2,089.5	729.6	1,359.9	237.6	150.9	391.7	377.9	359.8	32.0	0.0
1961	2,025.4	2,266.6	761.7	1,504.9	254.5	154.9	487.2	468.0	443.2	44.0	0.0
1962	2,080.5	2,343.8	795.4	1,548.3	279.9	158.2	472.1	453.6	431.2	40.9	0.0
1963	2,185.3	2,477.3	831.0	1,646.3	310.6	159.8	520.8	497.2	469.9	50.9	0.0
1964	2,355.2	2,676.4	875.7	1,800.7	339.2	166.2	605.0	576.0	544.1	60.8	0.0
1965	2,539.2	2,889.9	921.5	1,968.4	373.3	170.2	689.7	654.6	616.1	73.6	0.0
1966	2,614.1	2,988.0	995.2	1,992.9	394.4	190.8	619.2	584.8	548.3	70.9	0.0
1967	2,908.8	3,306.9	1,063.2	2,243.7	439.7	196.3	776.2	731.4	682.1	94.1	0.0
1968	3,265.8	3,699.0	1,188.4	2,510.6	479.4	206.7	929.1	874.1	815.3	113.8	0.0
1969	3,308.3	3,771.6	1,294.7	2,476.9	483.6	217.0	787.3	730.8	587.4	199.9	92.8
1970	3,468.8	3,947.5	1,375.2	2,572.3	531.9	216.3	779.3	718.9	572.5	206.8	91.4
1971	3,840.5	4,365.7	1,500.2	2,865.5	609.1	204.0	913.4	831.5	650.9	262.5	109.8
1972	4,389.7	4,976.8	1,694.9	3,281.9	691.3	199.5	1,125.9	1,022.8	813.7	312.2	129.1
1973	4,556.4	5,211.1	1,920.4	3,290.7	760.6	220.6	861.9	771.5	597.5	264.4	110.9
1974	4,586.1	5,296.7	2,034.6	3,262.1	822.2	262.3	570.5	498.0	373.4	197.1	78.6
1975	5,212.4	5,978.2	2,253.5	3,724.8	902.1	278.0	762.8	660.8	499.0	263.8	95.3
1976	5,867.4	6,722.6	2,503.9	4,218.8	1,012.2	280.2	947.8	827.4	637.4	310.4	113.6
1977	6,403.7	7,390.0	2,902.9	4,487.0	1,128.0	290.2	835.2	716.2	542.5	292.7	103.2
1978	7,233.6	8,383.5	3,357.2	5,026.3	1,247.6	330.1	877.1	735.6	550.3	326.8	106.9
1979	8,347.8	9,670.1	3,900.6	5,769.5	1,364.8	400.6	1,044.0	884.1	674.9	369.0	116.7
1980	9,558.2	11,011.2	4,378.0	6,633.3	1,520.7	425.4	1,340.1	1,133.3	875.4	464.7	139.4
1981	10,300.4	11,865.6	4,837.9	7,027.7	1,717.0	443.7	1,230.1	1,023.1	780.1	450.0	128.8
1982	11,039.6	12,678.6	5,063.0	7,615.6	1,873.3	506.7	1,383.1	1,116.8	832.5	550.6	138.9
1983	11,881.1	13,688.3	5,307.0	8,381.3	2,053.9	589.7	1,632.8	1,287.8	936.2	696.6	159.2
1984	12,816.3	14,834.0	5,933.9	8,900.1	2,333.4	694.5	1,573.5	1,229.7	863.1	710.3	153.2
1985	14,274.8	16,642.6	6,609.5	10,033.1	2,484.2	849.5	2,005.8	1,547.0	1,058.1	947.6	181.8
1986	15,725.3	18,358.8	7,205.1	11,153.7	2,721.2	866.2	2,355.9	1,855.6	1,330.3	1,025.6	183.1
1987	16,753.7	19,594.1	7,762.1	11,831.9	2,864.8	1,027.6	2,380.9	1,885.5	1,306.2	1,074.7	176.1
1988	18,287.0	21,426.9	8,414.2	13,012.7	3,055.3	1,228.5	2,707.2	2,191.4	1,585.7	1,121.4	189.1
1989	20,030.0	23,480.1	9,064.0	14,416.1	3,211.9	1,316.1	3,361.7	2,722.1	1,946.5	1,415.2	231.9

TABLE Ce127–146   Net worth of households and nonprofit organizations: 1945–2002   *Continued*

							Assets				
							Financial				
									Equity shares at market value		
							Total			Indirectly held	
Year	Net worth	Total	Tangible	Total	Deposits	Credit market instruments	Total	Excluding defined benefit plans	Directly held	Total	Bank personal trusts and estates
	Ce127	Ce128	Ce129	Ce130	Ce131	Ce132	Ce133	Ce134	Ce135	Ce136	Ce137
	Billion dollars	Billion dollars	Billion dollars	Billion dollars	Billion dollars	Billion dollars	Billion dollars	Billion dollars	Billion dollars	Billion dollars	Billion dollars
1990	20,374.2	24,094.3	9,255.3	14,839.1	3,259.3	1,556.1	3,135.6	2,507.0	1,781.4	1,354.2	214.1
1991	21,944.1	25,879.5	9,505.8	16,373.7	3,253.3	1,634.9	4,363.2	3,521.0	2,548.6	1,814.6	271.7
1992	22,868.4	27,009.8	9,830.5	17,179.4	3,219.7	1,676.5	4,896.2	3,976.8	2,869.2	2,027.0	268.7
1993	24,098.8	28,508.3	10,138.0	18,370.3	3,156.1	1,647.9	5,686.4	4,623.6	3,237.0	2,449.4	262.0
1994	24,712.6	29,451.5	10,446.2	19,005.3	3,109.6	1,935.4	5,673.2	4,587.0	3,081.6	2,591.6	263.6
1995	27,558.8	32,640.5	11,044.3	21,596.1	3,298.0	1,944.1	7,598.8	6,190.0	4,137.1	3,461.6	365.2
1996	30,049.1	35,501.1	11,490.8	24,010.3	3,440.8	2,142.6	9,165.9	7,511.6	4,856.1	4,309.8	439.3
1997	33,791.9	39,620.9	12,140.5	27,480.5	3,622.3	2,145.2	11,792.4	9,776.6	6,219.9	5,572.5	555.1
1998	37,234.6	43,543.4	13,107.9	30,435.5	3,904.6	2,256.3	13,718.0	11,427.4	7,020.0	6,698.0	599.2
1999	42,183.7	49,072.9	14,167.9	34,905.0	4,022.8	2,564.4	17,235.5	14,639.2	8,992.1	8,243.4	698.6
2000	41,825.2	49,293.3	15,456.2	33,837.1	4,355.6	2,490.1	15,312.6	12,841.5	7,421.4	7,891.2	645.5
2001	41,080.0	49,129.6	16,663.9	32,465.7	4,774.7	2,475.8	13,100.8	10,916.1	6,151.8	6,949.0	527.0
2002	39,600.2	48,381.3	18,081.5	30,299.8	5,068.1	2,497.6	10,035.2	8,291.0	4,570.1	5,465.1	385.0

					Assets				
					Financial				
					Equity shares at market value				
					Indirectly held				
		Private pension funds							
Year	Life insurance companies	Total	Defined benefit plans	Defined contribution plans	State and local government retirement funds	Federal government retirement funds	Mutual funds	Other	Liabilities
	Ce138	Ce139	Ce140	Ce141	Ce142	Ce143	Ce144	Ce145	Ce146
	Billion dollars	Billion dollars	Billion dollars	Billion dollars	Billion dollars	Billion dollars	Billion dollars	Billion dollars	Billion dollars
1945	0.0	0.0	0.0	0.0	0.0	0.0	1.0	257.0	30.3
1946	0.0	0.0	0.0	0.0	0.0	0.0	1.0	294.6	37.1
1947	0.0	0.0	0.0	0.0	0.0	0.0	1.2	332.6	46.1
1948	0.0	0.0	0.0	0.0	0.0	0.0	1.2	355.6	54.7
1949	0.0	0.0	0.0	0.0	0.0	0.0	2.7	366.3	63.0
1950	0.0	0.0	0.0	0.0	0.0	0.0	2.9	386.7	76.3
1951	1.9	0.3	0.0	0.3	0.0	0.0	2.9	419.0	85.0
1952	0.0	1.8	1.5	0.4	0.1	0.0	3.3	431.1	97.4
1953	0.0	2.4	1.9	0.5	0.1	0.0	3.5	439.9	110.1
1954	0.0	3.2	2.5	0.6	0.1	0.0	5.4	452.7	122.4
1955	0.0	6.1	4.9	1.2	0.2	0.0	6.9	468.7	143.5
1956	0.0	7.1	5.7	1.4	0.2	0.0	7.9	494.8	158.8
1957	0.0	7.5	6.0	1.5	0.3	0.0	7.4	514.6	171.2
1958	0.0	11.6	9.2	2.3	0.4	0.0	11.7	542.7	183.3
1959	0.0	14.5	11.6	2.9	0.5	0.0	13.9	557.4	205.7
1960	0.0	16.5	13.2	3.3	0.6	0.0	14.8	579.7	223.4
1961	0.0	22.9	18.3	4.6	0.9	0.0	20.3	608.3	241.2
1962	0.0	21.9	17.5	4.4	1.0	0.0	18.0	638.0	263.3
1963	0.0	27.7	22.1	5.5	1.5	0.0	21.7	655.1	292.0
1964	0.1	33.7	27.0	6.7	2.0	0.0	25.0	690.4	321.2
1965	0.2	40.8	32.6	8.2	2.5	0.0	30.2	735.1	350.7
1966	0.5	39.5	31.6	7.9	2.8	0.0	28.1	788.5	373.9
1967	1.1	51.1	40.9	10.2	3.9	0.0	38.0	831.4	398.1
1968	1.9	61.5	49.2	12.3	5.8	0.0	44.6	895.3	433.2
1969	2.8	61.4	49.1	12.3	7.3	0.0	35.6	989.0	463.3

(continued)

TABLE Ce127–146 Net worth of households and nonprofit organizations: 1945–2002 *Continued*

	Assets								
	Financial								
	Equity shares at market value								
	Indirectly held								
		Private pension funds			State and local government retirement funds	Federal government retirement funds			
	Life insurance companies	Total	Defined benefit plans	Defined contribution plans			Mutual funds	Other	Liabilities
	Ce138	Ce139	Ce140	Ce141	Ce142	Ce143	Ce144	Ce145	Ce146
Year	Billion dollars	Billion dollars	Billion dollars	Billion dollars	Billion dollars	Billion dollars	Billion dollars	Billion dollars	Billion dollars
1970	4.0	67.1	50.3	16.8	10.1	0.0	34.3	1,044.7	478.7
1971	6.5	88.7	66.5	22.2	15.4	0.0	42.2	1,139.0	525.2
1972	8.7	107.8	80.9	27.0	22.2	0.0	44.4	1,265.2	587.2
1973	7.9	93.6	70.2	23.4	20.2	0.0	31.8	1,447.6	654.8
1974	6.1	74.8	56.1	18.7	16.4	0.0	21.2	1,607.1	710.6
1975	9.3	108.0	77.8	30.2	24.3	0.0	26.9	1,781.8	765.8
1976	12.2	125.5	90.4	35.1	30.1	0.0	29.0	1,978.6	855.2
1977	10.9	123.6	89.0	34.6	30.0	0.0	24.9	2,233.6	986.3
1978	11.5	150.3	108.2	42.1	33.3	0.0	24.9	2,571.5	1,149.9
1979	12.8	175.4	122.8	52.6	37.1	0.0	27.0	2,960.2	1,322.3
1980	17.6	232.0	162.4	69.6	44.3	0.0	31.3	3,347.1	1,453.0
1981	16.8	227.5	159.2	68.2	47.8	0.0	29.1	3,636.9	1,565.2
1982	20.3	294.4	206.1	88.3	60.2	0.0	36.8	3,852.6	1,639.0
1983	24.8	364.8	255.4	109.5	89.6	0.0	58.1	4,104.8	1,807.2
1984	23.8	374.6	247.2	127.4	96.5	0.0	62.2	4,298.7	2,017.7
1985	33.3	520.9	338.6	182.2	120.1	0.0	91.5	4,693.6	2,367.7
1986	38.3	528.1	350.1	178.0	150.2	0.0	125.9	5,210.4	2,633.5
1987	44.0	540.2	325.3	214.9	170.1	0.0	144.4	5,558.7	2,840.4
1988	45.7	524.0	303.1	220.9	212.6	0.0	150.0	6,021.7	3,139.9
1989	59.3	649.5	361.8	287.7	277.8	0.1	196.7	6,526.3	3,450.1
1990	57.8	622.3	344.0	278.3	284.6	0.3	175.1	6,888.0	3,720.1
1991	93.8	839.9	463.2	376.8	379.1	1.0	229.0	7,122.3	3,935.5
1992	113.3	928.4	490.8	437.5	428.5	2.4	285.7	7,386.9	4,141.4
1993	163.5	1,096.1	565.5	530.6	497.3	4.4	426.0	7,879.9	4,409.5
1994	199.6	1,135.9	578.6	557.3	507.6	6.2	478.7	8,287.0	4,738.9
1995	274.7	1,490.4	729.9	760.5	678.9	11.5	641.1	8,755.3	5,081.7
1996	373.3	1,701.3	825.9	875.5	828.5	18.8	948.6	9,261.0	5,452.0
1997	510.5	2,053.5	931.0	1,122.5	1,084.8	29.9	1,338.7	9,920.7	5,829.0
1998	665.4	2,457.0	1,056.7	1,400.3	1,233.9	44.9	1,697.6	10,556.6	6,308.8
1999	904.4	2,875.3	1,253.2	1,622.1	1,343.2	59.1	2,362.8	11,082.3	6,889.2
2000	882.8	2,720.3	1,136.0	1,584.3	1,335.1	59.1	2,248.2	11,678.8	7,468.1
2001	806.5	2,348.2	962.8	1,385.4	1,221.9	51.4	1,994.1	12,114.3	8,049.6
2002	692.5	1,783.4	733.0	1,050.4	1,004.3	48.5	1,551.4	12,699.0	8,781.0

Source

Board of Governors of the Federal Reserve System, Internet site, *Flow of Funds Accounts*, Table B.100e, downloaded on September 25, 2003.

Documentation

The data in Tables Ce127–208 are part of the U.S. *Flow of Funds Accounts* produced at the Federal Reserve Board. The *Flow of Funds Accounts* measures financial flows across sectors of the economy, tracking funds as they move from those sectors that serve as sources of capital through intermediaries (such as banks, mutual funds, and pension funds) to sectors that use the capital to acquire physical and financial assets. With data extending back more than half a century, the accounts provide a broadly consistent set of time-series data for measuring financial flows in the economy. For a description see Albert M. Teplin, "The U.S. Flow of Funds Accounts and Their Uses," *Federal Reserve Bulletin* (July 2001).431–41.

Tables Ce127–208 display the balance sheets of various sectors of the economy: Table Ce127–146, the balance sheet of the household and nonprofit sector; Table Ce147–168, the balance sheet of the nonfarm, nonfinancial corporate business sector; Table Ce169–189, the balance sheet of the nonfarm, noncorporate business sector; and Table Ce190–208, the financial assets and liabilities of government.

Figures in this table are amounts outstanding at the end of the year and are not seasonally adjusted. Additional details on liabilities and assets at historical cost are provided in the source.

Series Ce127. Net worth is the difference between assets and liabilities, series Ce128 and Ce146.

Series Ce128. Assets are disaggregated according to tangible assets (such as automobiles and refrigerators) and financial assets (such as bank deposits, money market accounts, stocks and bonds, life insurance and retirement accounts).

Series Ce130. Financial assets is the sum of deposits in commercial banks, credit market instruments, equity shares at market value, and other financial assets (series Ce131–133 and Ce145).

Series Ce133. Equity shares at market value is the sum of those held directly by the household and nonprofit sector, series Ce135, and those held indirectly by mutual funds, pension plans, insurance companies, and other agents of households and the nonprofit sector, series Ce136.

Series Ce134. Equals series Ce133 minus series Ce140 and Ce142, and minus part of series Ce143. Prior to 1985, all pension assets are assumed to have been in defined benefit plans.

TABLE Ce147–168   Net worth of nonfarm, nonfinancial corporate businesses: 1945–2002

Contributed by Richard Sutch

			Assets								
			Tangible assets				Financial assets				
Year	Net worth	Total	Total	Real estate	Equipment and software	Inventories	Total	Foreign deposits	Checkable deposits and currency	Time and savings deposits	Money market fund shares
	Ce147	Ce148	Ce149	Ce150	Ce151	Ce152	Ce153	Ce154	Ce155	Ce156	Ce157
	Billion dollars	Billion dollars	Billion dollars	Billion dollars	Billion dollars	Billion dollars	Billion dollars	Billion dollars	Billion dollars	Billion dollars	Billion dollars
1945	194.6	264.8	196.0	130.6	32.0	33.4	68.8	0.0	19.0	0.9	0.0
1946	220.8	301.0	233.8	158.2	39.2	36.5	67.2	0.1	19.5	0.9	0.0
1947	259.7	352.7	276.8	186.3	48.0	42.5	75.9	0.1	21.4	0.9	0.0
1948	280.9	382.7	301.3	197.9	55.9	47.5	81.4	0.0	21.9	0.9	0.0
1949	291.0	392.1	306.9	202.4	61.1	43.4	85.3	0.0	22.9	0.9	0.0
1950	319.4	443.1	341.0	219.2	68.8	53.1	102.1	0.1	24.2	0.9	0.0
1951	350.2	486.6	376.5	238.9	76.6	61.0	110.1	0.1	25.9	0.9	0.0
1952	367.7	509.0	393.5	249.6	82.2	61.7	115.5	0.1	26.6	0.9	0.0
1953	381.5	527.6	409.0	257.2	88.4	63.4	118.5	0.1	26.6	0.9	0.0
1954	393.0	542.3	418.3	262.9	93.4	61.9	124.0	0.2	28.3	1.1	0.0
1955	424.5	595.8	454.4	282.9	102.9	68.6	141.4	0.1	29.3	1.0	0.0
1956	466.3	649.8	503.3	310.9	116.6	75.8	146.4	0.1	29.0	1.0	0.0
1957	491.1	684.0	533.0	327.1	128.4	77.5	151.0	0.1	29.0	1.0	0.0
1958	502.1	704.5	541.9	334.5	133.6	73.9	162.5	0.1	30.1	1.9	0.0
1959	520.1	739.2	561.6	344.3	140.5	76.8	177.6	0.1	29.2	1.5	0.0
1960	524.9	754.5	574.0	348.5	145.8	79.7	180.5	0.1	28.2	3.0	0.0
1961	540.7	782.8	589.6	357.9	149.6	82.1	193.1	0.2	31.7	4.1	0.0
1962	557.7	815.0	609.9	366.9	155.9	87.1	205.1	0.8	34.6	5.0	0.0
1963	574.3	852.2	631.7	375.6	163.5	92.6	220.5	0.7	33.4	5.7	0.0
1964	601.1	901.1	666.1	393.2	173.7	99.3	235.0	1.1	32.7	6.7	0.0
1965	640.2	975.4	713.0	417.1	187.5	108.5	262.4	0.8	33.1	9.0	0.0
1966	687.8	1,057.0	780.2	446.4	209.8	124.0	276.8	0.9	32.4	8.6	0.0
1967	738.2	1,135.3	840.7	474.9	231.7	134.1	294.6	1.1	34.8	9.7	0.0
1968	798.7	1,244.7	917.1	515.8	257.3	143.9	327.6	1.6	37.5	9.1	0.0
1969	876.6	1,377.0	1,015.1	570.8	285.7	158.6	361.9	1.2	43.1	3.7	0.0
1970	952.3	1,491.9	1,108.7	627.8	314.4	166.5	383.2	0.8	44.1	5.3	0.0
1971	1,048.2	1,633.5	1,208.9	695.9	337.6	175.5	424.7	1.2	42.6	9.5	0.0
1972	1,159.2	1,808.8	1,315.9	762.9	363.9	189.0	492.9	2.2	44.9	11.9	0.0
1973	1,309.1	2,069.9	1,499.1	867.2	406.2	225.7	570.8	3.3	46.3	16.6	0.0
1974	1,687.2	2,451.8	1,836.6	1,043.8	500.8	292.0	615.2	4.9	47.8	20.5	0.0
1975	1,701.8	2,788.8	2,015.7	1,147.8	572.8	295.1	773.0	2.6	58.3	24.1	0.0
1976	1,897.7	3,087.0	2,224.4	1,263.2	631.5	329.7	862.6	3.4	63.0	28.8	0.0
1977	2,102.2	3,437.6	2,474.2	1,397.4	711.1	365.6	963.4	5.7	66.7	35.5	0.2
1978	2,377.6	3,909.9	2,812.0	1,580.3	808.7	423.0	1,097.9	8.3	73.0	38.2	0.6
1979	2,736.3	4,525.7	3,249.3	1,811.2	936.8	501.3	1,276.4	10.1	79.1	40.4	3.0
1980	3,148.7	5,159.9	3,716.8	2,057.0	1,092.2	567.6	1,443.0	9.7	78.7	45.0	7.0
1981	3,511.6	5,805.1	4,168.8	2,340.0	1,208.0	620.8	1,636.3	12.4	57.7	55.0	18.4
1982	3,671.5	6,125.2	4,379.3	2,491.2	1,276.3	611.9	1,746.0	10.1	68.0	63.6	19.0
1983	3,827.9	6,437.5	4,515.2	2,561.3	1,320.4	633.5	1,922.3	14.4	89.6	70.0	11.2
1984	4,064.2	6,992.7	4,797.2	2,706.6	1,387.5	703.1	2,195.5	13.3	102.7	69.1	16.1
1985	4,167.4	7,475.6	5,011.0	2,829.4	1,468.3	713.4	2,464.6	16.0	125.7	69.3	14.5
1986	4,308.3	7,806.5	5,173.9	2,916.3	1,548.4	709.2	2,632.6	19.2	127.2	85.5	14.9
1987	4,517.2	8,291.2	5,428.3	3,053.2	1,609.9	765.1	2,862.9	16.3	136.8	85.9	15.8
1988	4,826.2	9,017.8	5,777.0	3,252.5	1,697.8	826.7	3,240.8	21.6	150.7	82.3	10.3
1989	5,031.8	9,564.5	6,097.2	3,438.8	1,789.4	869.0	3,467.4	14.7	159.8	80.6	10.4
1990	5,025.1	9,754.5	6,179.1	3,385.4	1,892.2	901.5	3,575.5	14.7	165.8	74.6	19.7
1991	4,775.8	9,605.6	5,907.5	3,066.1	1,954.2	887.3	3,698.1	16.4	172.7	77.6	24.1
1992	4,634.9	9,744.6	5,885.4	2,958.8	2,024.7	902.0	3,859.2	15.8	168.4	76.0	37.6
1993	4,899.6	10,288.2	6,081.0	3,028.9	2,117.6	934.5	4,207.2	14.5	188.9	92.0	33.9
1994	5,255.1	10,882.5	6,405.1	3,157.9	2,240.3	1,007.0	4,477.3	15.7	200.6	96.4	37.1
1995	5,726.0	11,735.6	6,777.1	3,317.7	2,389.6	1,069.8	4,958.5	17.4	205.1	99.7	60.0
1996	6,346.0	12,724.6	7,266.8	3,660.9	2,515.2	1,090.7	5,457.7	28.2	244.3	99.7	67.6
1997	7,051.9	13,680.6	7,871.9	4,100.9	2,641.4	1,129.6	5,808.7	23.1	251.9	119.4	87.8
1998	7,509.5	14,967.1	8,151.0	4,209.2	2,770.7	1,171.0	6,816.1	30.5	275.0	112.6	126.4
1999	8,268.8	16,676.1	8,582.3	4,400.2	2,923.7	1,258.4	8,093.8	31.5	331.0	136.9	154.9
2000	9,441.2	19,052.5	9,280.1	4,804.4	3,124.5	1,351.2	9,772.5	24.0	381.4	137.3	191.4
2001	9,186.0	19,086.0	9,174.9	4,697.7	3,214.3	1,262.9	9,911.1	15.6	371.3	132.9	301.9
2002	9,261.4	19,397.9	9,393.9	4,891.5	3,213.8	1,288.6	10,004.0	20.7	317.7	141.5	329.3

(continued)

TABLE Ce147-168   Net worth of nonfarm, nonfinancial corporate businesses: 1945-2002 *Continued*

	Assets										
	Financial assets										
Year	Security repurchase agreements	Commercial paper	U.S. government securities	Municipal securities	Mortgages	Consumer credit	Trade receivables	Mutual fund shares	Miscellaneous assets	Liabilities	Net worth (historical cost)
	Ce158	Ce159	Ce160	Ce161	Ce162	Ce163	Ce164	Ce165	Ce166	Ce167	Ce168
	Billion dollars	Billion dollars	Billion dollars	Billion dollars	Billion dollars	Billion dollars	Billion dollars	Billion dollars	Billion dollars	Billion dollars	Billion dollars
1945	0.0	0.0	18.5	0.3	0.0	2.8	19.8	0.0	7.5	70.2	119.2
1946	0.0	0.0	12.8	0.3	0.0	3.3	22.6	0.0	7.7	80.2	126.3
1947	0.0	0.1	12.3	0.4	0.0	4.1	27.6	0.0	9.0	93.0	139.3
1948	0.0	0.2	12.9	0.5	0.0	4.9	29.6	0.0	10.6	101.8	151.1
1949	0.0	0.3	14.7	0.5	0.0	5.5	28.6	0.0	11.9	101.1	160.7
1950	0.0	0.1	17.9	0.7	0.0	6.6	38.6	0.0	13.0	123.6	174.2
1951	0.0	0.1	18.7	0.8	0.0	7.2	42.0	0.0	14.4	136.4	191.6
1952	0.0	0.2	17.6	0.8	0.0	7.1	45.9	0.0	16.3	141.2	205.3
1953	0.0	0.2	19.2	1.0	0.0	7.3	45.0	0.0	18.2	146.1	218.6
1954	0.0	0.3	17.5	1.0	0.0	7.7	48.4	0.0	19.6	149.3	230.7
1955	0.0	0.2	21.6	1.2	0.0	8.3	58.0	0.0	21.6	171.3	247.4
1956	0.0	0.3	17.1	1.3	0.1	8.6	63.8	0.0	25.0	183.5	266.2
1957	0.0	0.4	16.4	1.5	0.1	8.7	65.4	0.0	28.4	192.9	282.3
1958	0.0	0.2	16.7	2.0	0.1	8.8	71.8	0.0	30.8	202.4	297.5
1959	0.0	0.7	22.8	1.8	0.0	10.1	77.4	0.0	33.9	219.2	317.7
1960	0.0	0.8	16.9	2.4	0.0	9.6	82.3	0.0	37.1	229.6	330.9
1961	0.0	1.1	15.3	2.4	0.0	9.6	88.3	0.0	40.4	242.1	351.0
1962	0.0	1.3	13.6	2.7	0.1	10.4	92.8	0.2	43.8	257.4	370.9
1963	0.0	1.0	16.7	3.8	0.1	11.3	99.1	0.2	48.4	277.9	390.8
1964	0.3	1.7	15.5	3.7	0.1	12.3	107.6	0.3	53.1	300.0	411.1
1965	0.6	1.4	13.8	4.6	0.1	13.2	120.9	0.3	64.7	335.2	445.9
1966	0.9	2.9	12.1	3.6	0.1	13.4	133.3	0.4	68.3	369.2	477.2
1967	0.7	4.0	9.6	3.3	0.1	13.7	141.6	0.6	75.5	397.0	510.5
1968	1.1	5.1	10.4	3.8	0.1	13.8	160.1	0.8	84.2	446.0	543.4
1969	3.3	7.6	7.3	2.8	0.2	13.9	183.0	0.7	94.9	500.4	586.7
1970	0.2	9.4	7.5	2.2	0.2	14.7	191.4	0.6	106.8	539.6	615.6
1971	1.1	11.3	10.0	3.2	0.2	17.3	203.8	0.7	123.8	585.3	657.6
1972	2.7	14.2	7.9	4.2	0.2	18.0	230.2	0.7	155.7	649.5	735.5
1973	11.3	14.9	4.5	4.0	0.3	19.2	269.3	0.8	180.3	760.8	802.8
1974	5.5	16.5	5.6	4.7	0.7	20.3	245.5	0.8	242.4	764.6	968.9
1975	1.2	8.4	17.5	4.8	9.7	21.2	271.4	0.9	352.8	1,086.9	865.6
1976	1.5	10.5	24.4	4.2	10.4	23.5	302.4	1.0	389.5	1,189.3	956.5
1977	2.1	9.4	19.2	4.4	13.6	24.4	346.4	0.8	435.1	1,335.3	1,043.4
1978	2.5	9.5	17.8	4.6	15.5	26.5	407.3	0.6	493.4	1,532.3	1,153.7
1979	3.1	9.6	15.3	4.5	18.8	28.3	479.7	1.1	583.6	1,789.3	1,279.7
1980	3.9	9.1	15.9	9.4	27.4	29.4	529.4	1.5	676.7	2,011.2	1,412.2
1981	1.8	8.2	24.4	10.6	35.9	30.3	574.1	1.6	805.8	2,293.5	1,563.6
1982	2.4	7.9	24.3	12.2	38.2	30.8	569.1	3.1	897.2	2,453.7	1,664.1
1983	3.2	12.2	34.3	18.3	40.0	35.4	626.5	4.5	962.7	2,609.6	1,848.9
1984	3.9	9.7	41.8	22.5	51.4	38.4	694.1	7.2	1,125.2	2,928.5	2,046.3
1985	3.4	10.5	45.1	25.6	57.0	42.5	739.3	10.8	1,304.8	3,308.2	2,165.0
1986	5.1	10.2	42.7	25.1	50.2	47.0	741.5	15.7	1,448.4	3,498.2	2,288.3
1987	3.4	15.0	34.4	19.4	51.5	54.0	805.3	12.8	1,612.2	3,774.0	2,436.9
1988	5.0	13.6	34.0	16.8	68.1	60.8	895.9	10.6	1,871.1	4,191.7	2,601.9
1989	2.8	14.3	60.6	32.4	54.4	63.8	938.0	11.7	2,024.0	4,532.7	2,678.0
1990	2.1	13.8	40.9	24.7	52.8	67.1	967.2	9.7	2,122.3	4,729.4	2,773.3
1991	1.6	14.7	48.5	44.8	59.0	63.0	961.4	14.8	2,199.4	4,829.8	2,934.2
1992	5.1	17.0	69.2	45.8	60.0	65.7	988.9	21.1	2,288.4	5,109.7	3,000.1
1993	2.5	19.4	67.9	54.7	52.3	76.9	1,035.4	29.8	2,539.0	5,388.6	3,282.2
1994	2.2	18.8	70.7	56.7	56.4	86.6	1,107.0	31.1	2,698.2	5,627.4	3,563.5
1995	2.4	20.1	80.5	36.8	57.9	85.1	1,184.9	45.7	3,062.9	6,009.5	3,928.6
1996	3.9	31.5	75.6	31.0	54.4	77.7	1,273.1	59.9	3,410.8	6,378.6	4,354.2
1997	4.6	36.1	34.8	27.4	80.2	78.9	1,366.6	69.1	3,628.7	6,628.8	4,768.6
1998	4.2	39.4	34.2	25.7	67.3	74.9	1,452.9	95.5	4,477.5	7,457.6	5,289.1
1999	5.8	47.6	31.8	25.0	41.2	80.3	1,653.4	133.7	5,420.8	8,407.3	5,993.1
2000	4.2	57.8	33.5	31.9	43.5	82.7	1,938.1	122.8	6,723.8	9,611.4	6,893.5
2001	3.9	59.5	34.2	29.4	46.1	68.0	1,820.7	105.9	6,921.9	9,900.0	6,963.4
2002	6.1	65.7	49.6	29.0	48.1	56.9	1,914.6	90.5	6,934.4	10,136.5	6,993.6

TABLE Ce147–168 Net worth of nonfarm, nonfinancial corporate businesses: 1945–2002 *Continued*

Source

Board of Governors of the Federal Reserve System, Internet site, *Flow of Funds Accounts*, Table B.102, downloaded on September 25, 2003.

Documentation

See the text for Table Ce127–146. Figures in this table are amounts outstanding at the end of the year and are not seasonally adjusted. Additional details on liabilities and assets at historical cost are provided in the source.

Series Ce147. Equals series Ce148 minus series Ce167.

Series Ce148. Equals the sum of series Ce149 and Ce153.

Series Ce149-152. Series Ce149 equals the sum of series Ce150-152. Tangible assets are stated at either market value (for real estate) or replacement value (for equipment and software and for inventories).

Series Ce153. Equals the sum of series Ce154–166.

Series Ce158. A security repurchase agreement (also called a repo) is a secured loan. The lender, in this case a corporation, holds securities provided by the borrower as collateral. The seller of securities commits to repurchase the same securities at a specified time and price.

Series Ce165. Mutual fund shares at market value.

Series Ce168. Evaluates tangible assets at historical cost rather than current value.

TABLE Ce169–189 Net worth of nonfarm, noncorporate businesses: 1945–2002

Contributed by Richard Sutch

					Assets					
					Tangible assets					
					Real estate			Equipment and software		
	Net worth	Total	Total	Total	Residential	Nonresidential	Total	Durable goods in rental properties	Nonresidential	Inventories
	Ce169	Ce170	Ce171	Ce172	Ce173	Ce174	Ce175	Ce176	Ce177	Ce178
Year	Billion dollars	Billion dollars	Billion dollars	Billion dollars	Billion dollars	Billion dollars	Billion dollars	Billion dollars	Billion dollars	Billion dollars
1945	117.9	125.4	109.8	98.5	82.2	16.3	7.0	1.3	5.8	4.3
1946	133.9	144.9	128.0	114.6	93.8	20.8	8.8	1.6	7.3	4.6
1947	154.9	167.9	150.1	133.1	107.5	25.5	11.8	2.0	9.8	5.2
1948	165.8	180.2	162.2	142.1	114.7	27.5	14.2	2.3	11.9	5.9
1949	170.2	185.8	167.2	146.3	118.8	27.5	15.4	2.4	12.9	5.5
1950	183.0	201.6	181.5	156.9	126.9	30.0	17.8	2.8	15.0	6.7
1951	195.8	216.3	195.7	168.2	134.6	33.5	19.9	3.2	16.7	7.6
1952	202.7	225.4	202.7	174.2	139.5	34.8	20.8	3.4	17.4	7.7
1953	207.0	231.4	208.1	178.0	142.8	35.2	22.0	3.6	18.4	8.1
1954	209.2	237.1	213.1	182.2	146.3	35.9	22.8	3.8	19.0	8.1
1955	217.3	248.9	224.6	191.1	151.8	39.3	25.1	3.9	21.2	8.5
1956	227.1	262.0	235.9	200.0	156.3	43.7	27.4	4.1	23.2	8.6
1957	231.1	267.4	240.9	203.2	157.3	45.9	28.9	4.3	24.5	8.9
1958	237.1	276.5	247.7	207.0	160.2	46.7	29.8	4.6	25.2	11.0
1959	240.9	283.8	256.5	212.7	164.2	48.5	29.9	3.6	26.3	14.0
1960	251.1	298.2	271.0	226.8	177.0	49.8	30.4	3.8	26.6	13.8
1961	263.0	314.8	287.0	243.4	191.1	52.3	30.5	3.9	26.6	13.1
1962	276.2	332.8	305.2	260.8	205.4	55.3	31.1	4.0	27.1	13.4
1963	278.0	339.0	311.4	266.6	208.0	58.5	32.0	4.2	27.7	12.9
1964	292.6	358.7	330.5	284.1	220.9	63.2	33.6	4.5	29.1	12.9
1965	307.6	379.1	350.6	301.5	232.5	69.0	35.3	4.7	30.6	13.7
1966	334.3	411.0	381.6	328.8	253.0	75.7	38.5	4.9	33.6	14.3
1967	351.6	435.7	405.3	349.1	267.2	81.9	41.2	5.3	35.9	15.0
1968	385.6	477.1	447.5	387.4	297.0	90.4	44.7	5.6	39.0	15.4
1969	412.7	517.8	486.6	421.6	320.8	100.8	49.1	6.2	42.9	16.0
1970	438.8	556.1	523.6	453.3	340.8	112.5	53.6	6.8	46.8	16.8
1971	488.6	628.4	586.8	510.4	382.6	127.8	57.4	7.4	50.0	18.9
1972	541.2	712.2	661.6	579.6	436.9	142.7	61.1	8.2	52.9	20.9
1973	614.3	822.3	759.3	668.1	503.6	164.5	67.5	9.4	58.0	23.7
1974	698.2	945.9	878.6	772.6	577.4	195.1	79.9	11.7	68.2	26.1
1975	750.2	1,014.7	945.6	834.5	624.1	210.4	87.2	13.3	74.0	23.9
1976	819.3	1,108.5	1,030.5	912.2	684.0	228.3	93.7	14.7	79.0	24.5
1977	939.4	1,261.2	1,167.6	1,038.6	782.4	256.3	103.2	16.4	86.8	25.8
1978	1,074.1	1,445.7	1,332.2	1,185.4	890.2	295.2	118.1	18.8	99.3	28.7
1979	1,241.8	1,682.6	1,549.8	1,381.3	1,033.6	347.8	137.2	21.4	115.9	31.3

(continued)

TABLE Ce169–189   Net worth of nonfarm, noncorporate businesses: 1945–2002   *Continued*

		Assets								
			Tangible assets							
				Real estate			Equipment and software			
	Net worth	Total	Total	Total	Residential	Nonresidential	Total	Durable goods in rental properties	Nonresidential	Inventories
	Ce169	Ce170	Ce171	Ce172	Ce173	Ce174	Ce175	Ce176	Ce177	Ce178
Year	Billion dollars	Billion dollars	Billion dollars	Billion dollars	Billion dollars	Billion dollars	Billion dollars	Billion dollars	Billion dollars	Billion dollars
1980	1,422.7	1,928.8	1,784.1	1,595.2	1,186.1	409.2	157.8	24.7	133.1	31.1
1981	1,593.8	2,153.8	1,978.0	1,769.8	1,291.8	478.0	177.4	28.0	149.4	30.9
1982	1,669.3	2,316.5	2,130.7	1,912.3	1,386.6	525.7	187.7	30.5	157.1	30.7
1983	1,737.9	2,471.6	2,258.2	2,028.9	1,470.9	558.0	197.8	32.7	165.1	31.6
1984	1,821.1	2,690.3	2,450.7	2,202.0	1,589.1	612.9	214.2	34.8	179.4	34.6
1985	1,934.4	2,941.7	2,671.4	2,400.9	1,723.5	677.4	233.7	36.7	197.0	36.8
1986	2,091.0	3,185.3	2,880.9	2,590.4	1,863.2	727.3	254.6	39.7	214.9	35.9
1987	2,183.4	3,342.4	3,044.0	2,729.2	1,952.1	777.1	275.6	42.4	233.1	39.3
1988	2,305.4	3,588.3	3,239.7	2,897.4	2,052.5	845.0	299.9	45.6	254.3	42.4
1989	2,411.7	3,774.2	3,418.3	3,053.0	2,140.4	912.6	319.6	48.4	271.2	45.7
1990	2,469.9	3,818.9	3,462.7	3,080.7	2,172.5	908.3	334.5	50.5	284.0	47.4
1991	2,450.8	3,768.9	3,406.6	3,022.3	2,162.7	859.7	337.5	51.5	286.1	46.7
1992	2,398.3	3,708.1	3,321.4	2,935.9	2,137.6	798.4	338.0	53.0	285.0	47.5
1993	2,464.1	3,759.8	3,348.4	2,946.0	2,185.2	760.8	353.3	55.7	297.6	49.2
1994	2,623.8	3,951.5	3,478.6	3,051.6	2,258.3	793.3	373.9	58.7	315.3	53.0
1995	2,801.2	4,201.9	3,653.8	3,203.4	2,383.2	820.2	394.1	61.0	333.1	56.3
1996	2,957.8	4,491.9	3,848.7	3,370.4	2,534.8	835.6	421.0	64.1	356.9	57.4
1997	3,177.5	4,900.5	4,126.6	3,626.4	2,727.1	899.3	440.8	65.5	375.3	59.5
1998	3,394.5	5,399.4	4,410.3	3,872.3	2,903.3	969.0	476.3	67.6	408.7	61.6
1999	3,592.4	5,910.8	4,732.9	4,132.5	3,143.7	988.8	534.2	69.3	464.9	66.2
2000	3,814.3	6,487.4	5,063.8	4,501.4	3,423.5	1,077.9	491.3	72.9	418.5	71.1
2001	3,878.7	6,771.5	5,204.9	4,598.5	3,551.8	1,046.7	539.9	75.9	464.1	66.5
2002	4,076.2	7,150.3	5,456.8	4,795.4	3,725.6	1,069.8	593.6	76.5	517.0	67.8

		Assets									
		Financial assets									
	Total	Checkable deposits and currency	Time and savings deposits	Money market fund shares	Treasury securities	Municipal securities	Mortgages	Consumer credit	Trade receivables	Miscellaneous assets	Liabilities
	Ce179	Ce180	Ce181	Ce182	Ce183	Ce184	Ce185	Ce186	Ce187	Ce188	Ce189
Year	Billion dollars	Billion dollars	Billion dollars	Billion dollars	Billion dollars	Billion dollars	Billion dollars	Billion dollars	Billion dollars	Billion dollars	Billion dollars
1945	15.6	9.7	0.0	0.0	0.0	0.0	0.0	0.6	4.5	0.8	7.4
1946	16.9	9.7	0.0	0.0	0.0	0.0	0.0	0.7	5.6	0.9	11.0
1947	17.8	10.1	0.0	0.0	0.0	0.0	0.0	0.8	5.9	1.1	13.0
1948	18.0	9.9	0.0	0.0	0.0	0.0	0.0	0.9	5.9	1.2	14.4
1949	18.6	10.3	0.0	0.0	0.0	0.0	0.0	1.0	6.0	1.3	15.5
1950	20.2	10.5	0.0	0.0	0.0	0.0	0.0	1.1	7.1	1.4	18.6
1951	20.6	10.8	0.0	0.0	0.0	0.0	0.0	1.3	7.0	1.5	20.5
1952	22.7	10.4	0.0	0.0	0.0	0.0	0.0	2.7	7.8	1.7	22.7
1953	23.3	10.4	0.0	0.0	0.0	0.0	0.0	2.8	8.2	1.9	24.5
1954	24.0	10.9	0.0	0.0	0.0	0.0	0.0	2.8	8.2	2.1	27.9
1955	24.3	11.2	0.0	0.0	0.0	0.0	0.0	2.9	7.9	2.3	31.6
1956	26.1	11.5	0.0	0.0	0.0	0.0	0.0	3.1	9.1	2.4	34.8
1957	26.4	12.4	0.0	0.0	0.0	0.0	0.0	3.1	8.4	2.6	36.3
1958	28.8	13.6	0.0	0.0	0.0	0.0	0.0	3.1	9.4	2.7	39.4
1959	27.3	12.7	0.0	0.0	0.0	0.0	0.0	3.4	8.2	2.9	42.8
1960	27.2	12.4	0.0	0.0	0.0	0.0	0.0	3.2	8.6	3.0	47.1
1961	27.8	12.5	0.0	0.0	0.0	0.0	0.0	3.1	8.9	3.2	51.7
1962	27.6	12.5	0.0	0.0	0.0	0.0	0.0	3.3	8.5	3.3	56.6
1963	27.6	12.5	0.0	0.0	0.0	0.0	0.0	3.6	8.0	3.5	61.0
1964	28.2	12.5	0.0	0.0	0.0	0.0	0.0	3.8	8.1	3.8	66.2

TABLE Ce169–189   Net worth of nonfarm, noncorporate businesses: 1945–2002   *Continued*

					Assets							
					Financial assets							
	Total	Checkable deposits and currency	Time and savings deposits	Money market fund shares	Treasury securities	Municipal securities	Mortgages	Consumer credit	Trade receivables	Miscellaneous assets		Liabilities
	Ce179	Ce180	Ce181	Ce182	Ce183	Ce184	Ce185	Ce186	Ce187	Ce188		Ce189
Year	Billion dollars	Billion dollars	Billion dollars	Billion dollars	Billion dollars	Billion dollars	Billion dollars	Billion dollars	Billion dollars	Billion dollars		Billion dollars
1965	28.6	12.5	0.0	0.0	0.0	0.0	0.0	4.0	7.9	4.1		71.5
1966	29.4	12.5	0.0	0.0	0.0	0.0	0.0	4.0	8.5	4.4		76.7
1967	30.4	12.5	0.0	0.0	0.1	0.0	0.0	3.9	9.0	4.8		84.1
1968	29.6	12.5	0.0	0.0	0.3	0.0	0.0	3.9	7.7	5.3		91.5
1969	31.1	12.5	0.0	0.0	0.5	0.0	0.3	3.7	8.1	6.0		105.1
1970	32.4	12.5	1.4	0.0	0.7	0.0	0.7	3.8	6.6	6.7		117.3
1971	41.6	12.5	3.0	0.0	0.9	0.0	1.9	3.7	8.1	11.5		139.8
1972	50.7	12.5	4.6	0.0	1.1	0.0	3.0	3.6	8.8	17.1		171.1
1973	63.0	16.9	6.2	0.0	1.2	0.0	3.3	3.4	11.1	20.9		208.0
1974	67.3	17.3	7.8	0.0	1.2	0.0	3.4	3.1	13.3	21.3		247.7
1975	69.1	17.8	8.1	0.0	1.3	0.0	3.3	2.7	14.6	21.5		264.5
1976	78.0	19.8	9.5	0.0	1.5	0.0	4.2	2.5	15.8	24.8		289.2
1977	93.6	22.4	12.1	0.0	2.4	0.0	5.5	2.0	20.0	29.2		321.9
1978	113.5	25.6	15.5	0.0	3.2	0.0	8.1	1.5	26.0	33.6		371.7
1979	132.8	28.3	21.3	0.0	2.8	0.0	11.0	0.9	30.2	38.4		440.8
1980	144.7	31.1	24.2	0.0	2.6	0.0	12.2	0.2	32.5	41.9		506.1
1981	175.8	33.3	25.7	0.0	3.3	0.0	20.3	0.0	37.0	56.1		560.0
1982	185.8	36.8	28.1	0.0	3.2	0.0	25.0	0.0	45.0	47.7		647.2
1983	213.4	45.0	31.7	0.0	6.0	0.0	29.3	0.0	52.4	48.9		733.7
1984	239.6	49.8	35.1	0.0	5.5	0.0	39.3	0.0	59.3	50.6		869.2
1985	270.3	61.3	40.6	0.0	5.8	0.0	44.0	0.0	63.8	54.8		1,007.3
1986	304.4	63.5	42.3	3.2	10.8	0.0	44.7	0.0	74.8	65.1		1,094.2
1987	298.4	64.2	40.4	3.1	9.8	0.0	37.9	0.0	76.3	66.7		1,159.0
1988	348.6	68.5	47.0	5.3	10.3	0.0	47.8	0.0	88.3	81.4		1,283.0
1989	355.9	69.4	48.4	5.8	11.9	0.0	35.1	0.0	95.1	90.2		1,362.5
1990	356.2	71.2	51.0	6.7	12.5	0.0	31.1	0.0	97.8	85.9		1,349.0
1991	362.3	72.7	53.2	7.4	12.2	0.0	26.0	0.0	96.7	94.0		1,318.1
1992	386.7	77.3	60.2	9.7	13.0	0.0	25.2	0.0	103.8	97.5		1,309.8
1993	411.4	79.5	63.6	10.9	13.6	1.5	21.9	0.0	108.7	111.7		1,295.8
1994	472.9	91.5	67.2	15.1	18.3	1.6	23.8	0.0	125.0	130.3		1,327.6
1995	548.1	104.7	71.5	17.0	23.6	2.2	21.7	0.0	140.3	167.0		1,400.7
1996	643.2	124.0	75.0	19.2	28.6	2.6	20.4	0.0	169.8	203.5		1,534.1
1997	773.8	146.2	85.7	22.9	32.2	3.2	18.7	0.0	204.9	259.9		1,722.9
1998	989.1	178.3	94.8	32.6	38.0	2.8	26.7	0.0	233.8	382.1		2,004.9
1999	1,177.9	217.6	117.5	40.7	37.2	2.7	24.7	0.0	272.5	465.0		2,318.4
2000	1,423.7	274.1	137.6	49.4	40.2	2.4	23.3	0.0	342.1	554.6		2,673.1
2001	1,566.7	289.7	157.8	59.0	38.6	2.6	26.6	0.0	357.0	635.2		2,892.9
2002	1,693.5	302.3	159.4	61.3	40.7	2.8	27.8	0.0	384.6	714.6		3,074.1

Source

Board of Governors of the Federal Reserve System, Internet site, *Flow of Funds Accounts*, Table B.103, downloaded on September 25, 2003.

Documentation

See the text for Table Ce127–146. Figures in this table are amounts outstanding at the end of the year and are not seasonally adjusted. Additional details on liabilities are provided in the source.

Series Ce169. Equals series Ce170 minus Ce189.

Series Ce170. Equals the sum of series Ce171 and Ce179.

Series Ce171. Equals the sum of series Ce172, Ce175, and Ce178.

Series Ce172. Evaluated at market prices.

Series Ce175 and Ce178. Evaluated at current replacement cost.

Series Ce179. Equals the sum of series Ce180–188.

TABLE Ce190–208   Financial assets and liabilities of federal, state, and local governments: 1945–2002

Contributed by Richard Sutch

					Financial assets				
		Gold, SDRs, and official foreign exchange	Checkable deposits and currency	Time and savings deposits	Security repurchase agreements	Credit market instruments			
	Total					Total	Open market paper	Agency securities	Municipal securities	Corporate and foreign bonds
	Ce190	Ce191	Ce192	Ce193	Ce194	Ce195	Ce196	Ce197	Ce198	Ce199
Year	Billion dollars	Billion dollars	Billion dollars	Billion dollars	Billion dollars	Billion dollars	Billion dollars	Billion dollars	Billion dollars	Billion dollars
1945	50.7	0.0	30.7	0.6	0.0	6.7	0.0	0.2	1.8	0.0
1946	29.3	−0.1	8.8	0.8	0.0	9.4	0.0	0.1	1.5	0.0
1947	37.9	1.3	9.0	1.0	0.0	13.7	0.0	0.1	1.4	0.0
1948	42.5	1.7	10.7	1.3	0.0	15.2	0.0	0.3	1.4	0.0
1949	42.9	1.9	11.2	1.5	0.0	17.0	0.0	0.3	1.7	0.0
1950	52.0	1.6	11.4	1.6	0.0	17.9	0.0	0.2	2.0	0.0
1951	59.9	1.6	12.0	1.8	0.0	19.2	0.0	0.4	2.1	0.0
1952	52.9	1.6	14.6	2.0	0.2	20.8	0.0	0.6	2.1	0.0
1953	52.3	1.5	13.5	2.3	0.2	23.3	0.0	0.5	2.3	0.0
1954	50.6	1.3	13.5	2.8	0.2	23.8	0.0	0.7	2.5	0.0
1955	53.2	1.2	13.3	2.7	0.7	24.5	0.0	0.7	2.5	0.0
1956	54.5	1.8	12.4	2.7	1.3	25.2	0.0	0.8	2.5	0.0
1957	55.8	2.1	11.9	3.1	1.8	26.0	0.0	0.8	2.6	0.0
1958	56.3	2.0	12.0	3.9	1.4	27.5	0.0	0.6	2.7	0.0
1959	61.7	2.1	14.4	3.5	0.6	29.3	0.0	0.5	2.7	0.0
1960	64.6	1.7	15.4	4.8	−0.2	30.9	0.0	1.1	2.7	0.0
1961	68.4	1.9	15.2	5.7	−0.1	33.1	0.0	1.6	2.8	0.0
1962	73.2	1.2	16.3	6.7	0.5	34.9	0.0	1.9	2.6	0.0
1963	78.2	1.2	16.8	8.4	−0.7	36.7	0.0	2.4	2.3	0.0
1964	84.0	1.0	18.6	10.1	−1.8	40.0	0.0	2.9	2.2	0.0
1965	89.0	1.4	16.6	12.4	−0.7	42.8	0.0	3.1	2.2	0.0
1966	94.7	0.9	16.7	13.7	0.8	46.7	0.0	3.7	2.1	0.0
1967	105.6	1.3	18.6	16.0	0.3	51.6	0.0	4.0	2.1	0.0
1968	115.7	3.3	15.5	19.2	−1.3	59.8	0.0	7.6	2.2	0.0
1969	121.4	4.7	19.3	13.3	2.6	64.1	0.0	7.6	2.2	0.0
1970	127.0	3.6	21.1	23.5	−1.4	65.5	0.0	5.2	2.4	0.0
1971	141.0	2.2	25.3	30.8	−0.9	65.9	0.0	3.0	2.1	0.0
1972	156.2	2.6	26.0	37.6	−1.0	71.8	0.0	6.3	1.8	0.0
1973	179.5	2.9	25.3	44.0	0.5	83.7	0.0	13.0	2.1	0.0
1974	196.4	4.3	21.2	49.0	−1.3	96.4	0.0	16.0	2.6	0.0
1975	217.3	4.6	24.5	47.5	−2.1	116.0	0.0	18.2	5.0	0.0
1976	243.4	7.0	27.4	49.8	−1.9	127.6	0.0	20.4	7.3	0.0
1977	269.4	7.6	28.1	56.6	−2.0	144.8	0.0	26.7	7.9	0.0
1978	324.4	5.4	32.1	63.9	2.2	178.0	0.0	39.5	7.2	0.0
1979	385.5	5.3	32.2	61.8	11.8	223.0	0.0	59.4	6.8	0.0
1980	429.1	10.6	28.6	59.6	17.0	256.3	0.0	59.7	7.0	0.0
1981	461.7	13.8	28.3	61.7	13.7	296.2	0.0	69.1	7.1	0.0
1982	507.1	17.1	33.9	66.0	16.1	319.9	0.0	70.2	7.4	0.0
1983	537.1	19.0	25.2	59.3	32.7	337.5	0.0	70.1	8.0	1.0
1984	614.2	20.3	35.6	60.1	53.1	367.0	0.0	74.6	9.0	5.0
1985	733.1	25.1	48.8	67.1	74.1	421.3	0.0	105.1	9.6	8.0
1986	774.1	28.0	50.1	69.7	79.0	440.8	0.0	103.7	10.4	10.0
1987	800.2	29.1	38.0	77.0	90.9	444.0	0.2	108.9	10.2	12.0
1988	838.7	27.7	51.6	74.8	89.9	462.7	0.7	131.7	10.3	13.0
1989	908.3	31.7	46.0	71.8	106.0	495.6	1.6	162.6	10.8	15.0
1990	985.1	39.7	44.0	68.9	111.8	526.2	4.0	151.0	11.6	16.0
1991	1,075.7	39.1	76.0	58.0	118.4	556.0	9.0	162.7	11.6	18.0
1992	1,082.3	38.8	58.0	51.2	123.1	563.3	14.1	174.9	10.5	20.9
1993	1,112.2	40.2	80.4	49.6	133.7	557.5	17.9	175.0	9.5	26.5
1994	1,092.8	41.4	57.8	56.0	118.6	564.8	22.3	186.6	8.6	31.9
1995	1,136.3	53.8	55.5	62.9	115.7	546.6	39.4	151.5	5.1	39.0
1996	1,187.7	44.9	66.1	74.9	147.8	544.0	59.7	116.2	4.6	49.7
1997	1,227.3	42.0	73.8	81.8	151.4	566.4	74.0	115.4	3.9	51.0
1998	1,346.2	51.0	51.5	95.8	158.5	681.5	102.0	179.0	2.5	61.2
1999	1,541.8	44.4	120.1	107.5	163.5	752.3	108.9	190.0	1.0	71.3
2000	1,553.5	41.0	57.4	117.8	173.3	783.4	116.5	192.0	1.6	75.0
2001	1,660.5	43.1	105.1	129.7	154.9	779.5	90.0	194.4	1.9	84.4
2002	1,712.4	51.1	94.3	163.9	147.7	790.1	86.2	194.0	0.5	86.2

TABLE Ce190–208   Financial assets and liabilities of federal, state, and local governments: 1945–2002   *Continued*

	Financial assets								Liabilities
	Credit market instruments								
	Mortgages	Consumer credit	Other loans and advances	Corporate equities	Mutual fund shares	Trade receivables	Taxes receivable	Miscellaneous assets	Liabilities
	Ce200	Ce201	Ce202	Ce203	Ce204	Ce205	Ce206	Ce207	Ce208
Year	Billion dollars	Billion dollars	Billion dollars	Billion dollars	Billion dollars	Billion dollars	Billion dollars	Billion dollars	Billion dollars
1945	1.4	0.0	3.3	0.0	0.0	0.9	10.1	1.7	274.8
1946	1.1	0.0	6.8	0.0	0.0	0.1	8.7	1.5	251.5
1947	1.0	0.0	11.1	0.0	0.0	0.0	11.2	1.7	245.6
1948	1.1	0.0	12.4	0.0	0.0	0.0	12.1	1.5	241.7
1949	1.6	0.0	13.3	0.0	0.0	0.0	9.8	1.5	246.0
1950	2.0	0.0	13.6	0.0	0.0	0.4	17.3	1.7	250.9
1951	2.6	0.0	14.1	0.0	0.0	1.3	22.5	1.5	254.6
1952	3.3	0.0	14.7	0.0	0.0	2.3	10.2	1.2	266.4
1953	3.8	0.0	16.7	0.0	0.0	2.2	8.2	1.2	278.3
1954	4.0	0.0	16.6	0.0	0.0	2.4	5.3	1.4	285.8
1955	4.3	0.0	17.0	0.0	0.0	2.3	6.9	1.7	289.2
1956	4.4	0.0	17.6	0.0	0.0	2.4	6.5	2.2	287.8
1957	4.8	0.0	17.8	0.0	0.0	2.3	5.7	2.9	291.0
1958	5.5	0.0	18.7	0.0	0.0	1.7	4.5	3.2	306.8
1959	7.0	0.0	19.1	0.0	0.0	1.7	6.7	3.4	322.1
1960	7.4	0.0	19.7	0.0	0.0	1.8	6.1	4.1	328.5
1961	8.1	0.0	20.7	0.0	0.0	1.8	6.2	4.5	345.0
1962	8.4	0.0	22.1	0.0	0.0	2.0	6.7	4.9	360.7
1963	8.2	0.0	23.8	0.0	0.0	2.5	7.9	5.3	374.1
1964	8.4	0.0	26.4	0.0	0.0	2.7	8.0	5.3	390.8
1965	8.6	0.0	28.9	0.0	0.0	3.1	7.9	5.4	404.2
1966	9.8	0.0	31.1	0.0	0.0	4.4	5.8	5.8	421.3
1967	10.8	0.0	34.7	0.0	0.0	5.8	6.3	5.6	449.8
1968	12.5	0.0	37.6	0.0	0.0	6.4	7.3	5.4	477.9
1969	13.9	0.0	40.3	0.0	0.0	7.3	4.7	5.5	490.3
1970	15.1	0.0	42.8	0.0	0.0	6.6	2.4	5.7	521.8
1971	15.8	0.0	45.0	0.0	0.0	4.9	6.9	5.8	571.6
1972	16.5	0.0	47.2	0.0	0.0	4.0	9.2	5.9	608.0
1973	17.6	0.0	51.1	0.0	0.0	4.3	11.9	6.9	639.4
1974	23.8	0.0	53.9	0.0	0.0	5.3	14.5	7.0	678.9
1975	32.0	0.0	60.9	0.0	0.0	6.5	14.2	6.1	797.6
1976	33.6	0.0	66.3	0.0	0.0	6.9	20.4	6.1	892.2
1977	38.4	0.0	71.8	0.0	0.0	6.2	21.3	6.8	967.5
1978	45.1	0.0	86.2	0.0	0.0	8.9	26.5	7.5	1,065.5
1979	58.1	0.0	98.7	0.0	0.0	11.3	31.6	8.5	1,154.7
1980	75.4	0.0	114.1	0.0	0.0	15.1	31.8	10.1	1,275.2
1981	88.1	0.0	131.9	0.0	0.0	17.6	19.5	10.9	1,400.2
1982	95.7	0.0	146.7	0.0	0.0	22.4	19.3	12.4	1,619.1
1983	104.8	0.0	153.8	0.0	0.0	26.2	24.1	13.1	1,865.0
1984	115.9	0.0	162.5	0.0	0.0	31.3	31.0	15.9	2,137.6
1985	127.5	0.0	171.1	0.0	0.0	35.0	38.4	23.3	2,500.1
1986	140.4	0.0	176.4	0.2	0.0	32.6	48.1	25.4	2,799.5
1987	143.8	0.0	168.9	0.7	0.0	40.6	49.5	30.5	3,054.0
1988	146.7	0.0	160.3	1.7	0.1	40.7	58.4	31.1	3,340.4
1989	152.2	0.0	153.3	3.3	1.5	43.9	61.2	47.3	3,604.6
1990	193.1	0.0	150.6	4.8	4.8	42.1	59.6	83.2	3,910.9
1991	212.0	0.0	142.7	6.3	9.4	37.5	53.4	121.6	4,304.7
1992	200.0	0.0	142.8	7.8	14.9	30.8	54.4	140.1	4,702.6
1993	193.3	0.4	135.0	9.3	21.3	28.4	58.0	133.7	5,054.8
1994	181.5	6.3	127.6	10.6	29.1	24.7	52.6	137.2	5,309.0
1995	171.3	9.7	130.7	26.2	35.0	23.1	45.2	172.3	5,521.4
1996	167.9	17.4	128.6	46.8	41.0	24.0	46.8	151.2	5,770.8
1997	167.0	28.2	126.8	79.0	33.6	20.8	46.9	131.8	5,918.3
1998	170.3	37.2	129.2	102.0	21.3	22.3	49.5	112.7	5,967.8
1999	207.5	50.9	122.7	115.0	25.6	22.9	72.0	118.5	6,007.0
2000	211.2	67.0	120.1	115.1	26.4	28.1	87.9	123.0	5,799.1
2001	214.8	80.1	113.9	126.3	31.5	35.5	129.9	125.0	5,943.1
2002	220.2	92.8	110.2	112.9	26.0	33.1	123.9	169.5	6,377.1

(continued)

TABLE Ce190–208   Financial assets and liabilities of federal, state, and local governments: 1945–2002   *Continued*

Source

Board of Governors of the Federal Reserve System, Internet site, *Flow of Funds Accounts*, Table L.106c, downloaded on September 25, 2003.

Documentation

See the text for Table Ce127–146. Figures in this table are amounts outstanding at the end of the year and are not seasonally adjusted. Additional details on liabilities are provided in the source.

Series Ce190. Equals the sum of series Ce191–195 and Ce203–207.

Series Ce191. An SDR is a "special drawing right."

Series Ce194. A security repurchase agreement (also called a repo) is a secured loan. The lender, in this case the government, holds securities provided by the borrower as collateral. The seller of securities commits to repurchase the same securities at a specified time and price.

Series Ce197. Agency securities holdings by state and local governments may include small amounts of agency securities issued by the federal government.

Series Ce202. Other loans and advances excludes loans to state and local governments.

NATIONAL WEALTH

Susan B. Carter and Richard Sutch

TABLE Ce209–232   National wealth, by type of asset: 1850–1958[1]   [Goldsmith]

Contributed by Susan B. Carter and Richard Sutch

Year	Total	Reproducible tangible assets Total	Structures Total	Nonfarm Residential	Nonfarm Nonresidential	Farm	Institutional	Government	Equipment Total	Producer durables	Consumer durables
	Ce209	Ce210	Ce211	Ce212	Ce213	Ce214	Ce215 [2]	Ce216 [2]	Ce217	Ce218	Ce219
	Billion dollars	Billion dollars	Billion dollars	Billion dollars	Billion dollars	Billion dollars	Billion dollars	Billion dollars	Billion dollars	Billion dollars	Billion dollars
1850	—	4.5	—	0.8	1.1 [3]	0.7	0.1	—	—	0.2 [3]	0.3
1880	—	25.8	13.3	4.9	5.8	2.0	0.6	—	5.4	3.0	2.4
1890	—	46.1	25.0	10.8	10.3	2.7	1.2	—	10.3	5.8	4.5
1900 [1]	—	63.8	35.0	15.0	14.3	3.6	2.1	—	15.3	9.3	6.0
1900 [1]	87.9	59.3	35.0	15.8	12.9	3.3	1.1	2.0	12.6	6.5	6.1
1912	165.4	109.3	62.5	25.4	23.5	5.6	2.0	5.9	27.3	13.8	13.6
1922	334.5	233.4	134.5	56.6	45.9	12.4	4.1	15.5	61.8	30.8	31.0
1929	439.4	313.5	189.8	89.5	59.1	12.2	5.6	23.4	80.6	38.4	42.2
1933	330.5	241.3	159.4	69.6	50.1	8.7	4.8	26.2	54.9	29.2	25.7
1939	396.8	307.4	188.5	86.3	54.1	9.0	5.4	33.8	66.8	34.2	32.5
1945 [1]	571.4	442.3	265.1	124.6	67.6	15.7	6.4	50.7	101.3	50.3	51.0
1945 [1]	576.2	457.0	285.6	141.1	63.8	16.3	7.0	57.4	94.9	48.6	46.2
1946	700.9	556.2	345.4	165.0	81.4	19.3	9.3	70.4	118.2	58.5	59.6
1947	843.5	668.4	414.7	200.8	95.4	22.9	11.5	83.9	147.1	73.7	73.4
1948	928.4	736.5	449.5	217.9	104.9	24.2	12.5	90.1	172.8	87.5	85.3
1949	932.0	742.2	446.1	215.0	105.2	24.6	12.4	88.9	188.1	96.9	91.2
1950	1,067.1	851.8	507.3	249.3	118.5	26.8	13.9	98.6	221.3	110.0	111.3
1951	1,164.6	928.6	545.4	266.2	127.9	29.3	15.2	106.9	246.1	123.6	122.5
1952	1,214.1	972.9	578.7	280.7	135.4	30.3	16.5	115.8	259.6	132.0	127.6
1953	1,259.3	1,015.3	605.7	291.9	144.4	31.0	17.6	121.0	275.5	140.8	134.8
1954	1,306.3	1,052.6	631.3	302.5	150.8	31.7	18.8	127.5	288.2	149.5	138.7
1955	1,401.9	1,130.4	683.6	328.2	163.7	33.0	20.4	138.4	307.4	156.6	150.8
1956	1,518.1	1,226.2	736.6	351.4	177.2	34.4	22.3	151.3	340.8	177.4	163.4
1957	1,629.8	1,311.3	790.2	367.2	200.6	35.2	24.3	163.0	366.8	193.1	173.6
1958	1,702.8	1,367.6	833.7	385.0	211.2	36.0	26.3	175.2	378.6	199.8	178.8

Year	Reproducible tangible assets Inventories Total	Private Livestock	Private Crops	Private Nonfarm	Public	Monetary gold and silver	Land Total	Private Agricultural	Private Nonfarm Residential	Private Nonfarm Nonresidential	Forests	Public	Net foreign assets
	Ce220	Ce221	Ce222	Ce223	Ce224	Ce225	Ce226	Ce227	Ce228	Ce229	Ce230	Ce231	Ce232
	Billion dollars	Billion dollars	Billion dollars	Billion dollars	Billion dollars	Billion dollars	Billion dollars	Billion dollars	Billion dollars	Billion dollars	Billion dollars	Billion dollars	Billion dollars
1850	1.1	0.5	0.2	0.5	—	0.2	—	—	—	—	—	—	−0.2
1880	6.6	2.0	—	4.6	—	0.6	—	—	—	—	—	—	−0.5
1890	9.6	2.6	—	7.0	—	1.2	—	—	—	—	—	—	−1.6
1900 [1]	11.8	3.3	—	8.5	—	1.7	—	—	—	—	—	—	−1.1
1900 [1]	10.0	3.1	1.4	5.4	(Z)	1.6	31.0	14.6	4.4	6.5	1.5	4.0	−2.3
1912	16.7	5.7	2.6	8.4	(Z)	2.5	58.3	31.6	7.0	10.2	2.0	7.5	−2.1
1922	32.6	5.4	3.1	24.0	0.1	4.4	92.8	41.5	15.4	19.8	3.5	12.6	8.2
1929	38.0	6.5	3.0	28.4	0.1	4.8	113.5	34.9	24.1	36.1	3.1	15.3	12.4
1933	21.9	3.2	1.8	16.9	0.1	4.7	81.2	22.8	18.7	22.1	2.2	15.4	8.1
1939	30.5	5.1	2.2	22.2	1.0	19.6	88.6	23.2	22.9	22.2	2.9	17.4	1.7
1945 [1]	52.3	9.7	5.6	34.2	2.7	22.9	128.1	44.5	31.1	24.9	3.6	24.0	1.7
1945 [1]	52.6	9.7	6.0	34.3	2.7	23.9	121.6	43.5	22.6	31.9	3.1	20.5	−2.3
1946	68.2	11.9	7.2	47.6	1.5	24.4	141.9	46.5	26.3	39.4	3.8	25.9	2.8
1947	80.0	13.3	9.2	56.3	1.2	26.7	164.2	49.8	31.9	46.7	6.1	29.7	10.9
1948	86.0	14.4	7.8	61.8	2.0	28.2	178.9	51.9	34.6	54.4	7.6	30.4	12.9
1949	79.6	12.9	6.0	57.3	3.4	28.5	176.0	50.9	34.2	53.0	8.3	29.6	13.8

Notes appear at end of table

(continued)

TABLE Ce209-232   National wealth, by type of asset: 1850-1958   [Goldsmith] *Continued*

	Reproducible tangible assets						Land						Net foreign assets
	Inventories					Monetary gold and silver	Private						
		Private							Nonfarm				
Year	Total	Livestock	Crops	Nonfarm	Public		Total	Agricultural	Residential	Nonresidential	Forests	Public	
	Ce220	Ce221	Ce222	Ce223	Ce224	Ce225	Ce226	Ce227	Ce228	Ce229	Ce230	Ce231	Ce232
	Billion dollars	Billion dollars	Billion dollars	Billion dollars	Billion dollars	Billion dollars	Billion dollars	Billion dollars	Billion dollars	Billion dollars	Billion dollars	Billion dollars	Billion dollars
1950	96.5	17.1	7.3	69.3	2.8	26.8	201.8	58.4	39.6	56.4	11.9	35.5	13.4
1951	110.4	19.5	8.6	79.9	2.4	26.8	221.6	66.3	42.2	61.2	14.3	37.6	14.4
1952	106.9	14.8	8.4	80.9	2.8	27.4	226.7	66.9	44.4	65.5	13.3	36.6	14.7
1953	107.8	11.8	7.2	83.1	5.7	26.3	228.1	64.2	46.2	69.7	12.0	36.0	15.9
1954	107.1	11.2	7.5	81.4	7.0	26.0	238.3	66.4	47.8	75.0	12.6	36.5	15.4
1955	113.3	10.7	6.7	88.8	7.1	26.1	256.2	68.9	51.8	82.0	15.0	38.4	15.4
1956	122.3	11.1	7.1	97.1	7.1	26.5	274.1	74.0	55.4	90.3	14.7	39.7	17.9
1957	126.8	14.1	6.5	100.1	6.1	27.5	295.7	79.9	57.9	101.8	15.0	41.0	22.8
1958	129.9	18.1	8.0	95.7	8.1	25.4	310.8	87.6	60.7	108.0	13.7	40.8	24.3

(Z) Less than $50 million.

[1] Two sets of values are shown for the years 1900 and 1945. In each case, the first set is comparable with data from earlier years; the second with that from later years. See text.

[2] Through the first set of values for 1900, government and institutional are combined under institutional.

[3] Producer durables in the hands of nonagricultural business included with nonfarm, nonresident construction.

Sources

1850-1900: Raymond W. Goldsmith, "The Growth of Reproducible Wealth of the United States of America from 1805 to 1950," in International Association for Research in Income and Wealth, *Income and Wealth of the United States: Trends and Structure*, Income and Wealth Series II (Bowes and Bowes, 1952), p. 306.

1900-1958: Raymond W. Goldsmith, *The National Wealth of the United States in the Postwar Period* (Princeton University Press, 1962), Appendixes A and B.

Goldsmith summarized his calculations of long-term change in national wealth in U.S. Bureau of the Census, *Historical Statistics of the United States* (1975). This table is adapted from series F 422–445 in that publication.

Documentation

The departure point for Goldsmith's estimates for 1850 appear in the Census Office, *Preliminary Report of the Eighth Census* (1862), p. 195. The benchmarks for Goldsmith's estimates for 1880, 1890, and 1900 are in Simon Kuznets's, *National Product since 1869* (National Bureau of Economic Research, 1946), pp. 202-15. The basic sources for these earlier estimates were returns on stocks of various assets in the Industrial Censuses and Censuses of Wealth. Hence, there is a sharp break in the method of derivation between the earlier and later estimates. However, the figures for the overlap year, 1900, agree reasonably well. The figures for 1850 exclude the value of slaves. In every case, the departure-point figures were adjusted by Goldsmith (for 1880 substantially) to improve their comparability with his estimates for 1900-1958.

For the estimates for 1850-1900, which are primarily from the federal censuses, the basis of valuation is not always certain and is not uniform among types of assets and among industries. It is possible that the figures may approximate either current market values or original cost, depreciated or undepreciated, or some combination of the two. Some assurance as to the comparability of the earlier and later sets of figures on this score is provided, however, by the overlapping values for 1900, though this comparison applies only to a single year.

As to the reliability of the estimates for 1850-1900, the source (*Income and Wealth of the United States: Trends and Structure*) states (1) the margin of error amounts to hardly less than 10-20 percent at any date, (2) this rel-

ative margin increases going back in time, and (3) comparability may not be impaired by as much as the size of the margin would imply because the error probably tends in the same direction for most if not all benchmarks, although the understatement is probably more pronounced in the early part of the period than in the latter.

Concerning the estimates for 1900-1958, derived by the perpetual inventory method, the most important source of error is considered to reside in the estimates of construction expenditures. For some of the components of total wealth, reliability is strengthened because of the availability of checks against alternative estimates, as is the case for residential real estate, farm structures, inventories, and international assets. Checks are less satisfactory for nonfarm business structures and equipment; however, the information in corporate balance sheets submitted to the Internal Revenue Service gives assurance that the perpetual inventory estimates are not too far off for the years after 1929. The only sectors of reproducible tangible wealth in which the perpetual inventory estimates are not subject to checks, or only to very unsatisfactory checks, are consumers' durables and government fixed assets.

The estimates for 1900-1958 were constructed by Goldsmith by means of the perpetual inventory method. In this method, the stock of an asset in existence at a given point in time is estimated from annual output totals extending back over a period equal to the average life of the asset, the output total for every year being depreciated to the end of the period, and the results summed. Goldsmith excluded military assets.

The estimates for 1900-1958 are in "current prices" – that is, each asset is valued at its replacement cost in the given year. This is preferable to valuation at original cost, whether depreciated or undepreciated. Assets appearing in the wealth statement for any given date were produced in different years, and since prices change from year to year, summation of original cost values would often result in an arithmetic aggregate without economic meaning.

The relatively small differences between the two sets of data given for 1945 are the result of the use of more recent data for the series comparable with later years and to different methods of estimation; there are no conceptual differences.

Goldsmith (1952) also produced estimates for 1805; however, he chose not to present them in U.S. Bureau of the Census (1975) "because of questionable reliability" (Goldsmith 1975, p. 247).

The source also presents considerably greater detail than given here (for example, annual estimates for 1896-1949). Estimates of national wealth by contemporaries are also available for various dates during the nineteenth century. See, for example, Samuel Blodget Jr., *Economica: A Statistical Manual for the United States* (printed for the author, 1806), and U.S. Bureau of the Mint, *Annual Report of the Director of the Mint* (1881).

Data are as of end of year, except for the figures for 1850 through the first set of values for 1900, which are as of June 1.

TABLE Ce209–232   National wealth, by type of asset: 1850–1958   [Goldsmith]   *Continued*

Goldsmith derived the estimates in Tables Ce233–280 by adjusting the current dollar figures for a given class of assets shown in Table Ce209–232 for the change in price or cost of construction of that type of asset between each year and the base year. Thus, conceptually, changes over time in the constant price value of a category of assets reflect changes in the physical stock of that asset and not in its value. For 1945–1958, a different base year was necessary because estimates in 1929 prices for the most recent years were not available. This shift in base years introduces some element of incomparability because the relative weights of individual assets in the price index differ between the two years.

For the years 1900–1958, Goldsmith made an attempt to adjust for price changes by fairly narrow classes of assets, using construction cost or price indexes referring specifically to the assets in each class. For 1880, 1890, and 1900, a more summary adjustment was used. Only three separate deflators were employed for construction (residential, other private, and farm), and a single deflator was used for all types of equipment. For 1850, the same price index (Snyder's index of the general price level) was applied to all types of structures and equipment, although for the adjustment of inventories the wholesale price index was used.

Goldsmith states that the conceptual significance of a constant price estimate for land is open to question. If land is carried for all dates at its absolute value in the base year, the relation to the constant price value of re-producible assets tends to become unrealistic, particularly at dates fairly far removed from the base year. In the present estimate, an alternative procedure is followed, a constant price value of land being derived, generally speaking, as a fixed proportion of the constant price value of structures. This permits derivation of a constant price series for aggregate national wealth, but it should be recognized that the deflated estimates of land values included in the totals cannot be conceived as reflecting changes in physical units alone.

The adjustment for price changes introduces errors in the estimates in addition to those discussed in connection with the series shown in Table Ce209–232. On balance, any error is likely to lead toward an overstatement of the price rise over the period and hence an understatement of growth rates because the techniques used in adjusting for price change fail to make adequate allowance for improvement in the quality of the assets; there is no evidence that the error is larger for one part of the period than for another, although the possibilities of error are certainly greater in the nineteenth century than in the twentieth. In addition, it is likely that the failure to allow for quality improvement has a differential effect on the different components of wealth. In particular, it leads to a more serious understatement in the growth of components such as producer and consumer than for structures and inventories.

Series Ce226–231. Changes over time in the estimates of the value of land reflect improvements as well as acreage growth.

TABLE Ce233–256   National wealth, by type of asset: 1850–1945[1]   [Goldsmith, 1929 prices]

Contributed by Susan B. Carter and Richard Sutch

		Reproducible tangible assets									
		Structures							Equipment		
				Nonfarm							
	Total	Total	Total	Residential	Nonresidential	Farm	Institutional	Government	Total	Producer durables	Consumer durables
	Ce233	Ce234	Ce235	Ce236	Ce237	Ce238	Ce239 [2]	Ce240 [2]	Ce241	Ce242	Ce243
Year	Billion dollars	Billion dollars	Billion dollars	Billion dollars	Billion dollars	Billion dollars	Billion dollars	Billion dollars	Billion dollars	Billion dollars	Billion dollars
1850	—	10.8	—	2.1	3.0 [3]	1.7	0.3	—	—	0.4 [3]	0.8
1880	—	53.7	31.1	11.6	13.2	4.9	1.4	—	11.2	4.7	6.5
1890	—	99.7	58.4	26.0	23.2	6.5	2.7	—	24.3	11.7	12.6
1900 [1]	—	139.0	81.5	35.4	32.9	8.5	4.7	—	36.5	19.9	16.6
1900 [1]	179.5	122.6	73.0	33.1	25.7	6.8	2.3	5.1	30.0	13.5	16.6
1912	265.3	186.3	113.2	48.2	40.7	9.4	3.8	11.2	49.6	24.6	25.0
1922	336.6	238.0	140.4	60.8	48.1	12.0	4.3	15.1	60.7	31.8	28.9
1929	445.8	318.7	193.5	90.6	61.0	12.5	5.6	23.8	83.0	39.1	43.8
1933	421.5	301.5	194.1	87.4	59.6	11.3	5.7	30.1	72.0	33.9	38.1
1939	424.8	317.8	191.7	86.3	54.3	10.4	5.1	35.5	78.8	34.7	44.1
1945 [1]	435.6	331.5	185.3	84.0	49.7	10.1	4.4	37.2	89.4	42.6	46.9

	Reproducible tangible assets							Land							
	Inventories							Private							
		Private								Nonfarm					
	Total	Livestock	Crops	Nonfarm	Public	Monetary gold and silver		Total	Agricultural	Residential	Nonresidential	Forests	Public	Net foreign assets
	Ce244	Ce245	Ce246	Ce247	Ce248	Ce249		Ce250	Ce251	Ce252	Ce253	Ce254	Ce255	Ce256
Year	Billion dollars	Billion dollars	Billion dollars	Billion dollars	Billion dollars	Billion dollars		Billion dollars	Billion dollars	Billion dollars	Billion dollars	Billion dollars	Billion dollars	Billion dollars
1850	2.2	1.1	0.3	0.8	—	0.3		—	—	—	—	—	—	−0.3
1880	10.8	4.5	2.0	4.3	—	0.6		—	—	—	—	—	—	−1.0
1890	15.6	6.2	2.3	7.1	—	1.2		—	—	—	—	—	—	−3.6
1900 [1]	19.3	6.4	2.6	10.3	—	1.7		—	—	—	—	—	—	−3.1
1900 [1]	18.2	6.4	2.6	9.2	—	1.3		61.6	28.0	9.2	15.2	2.5	6.7	−4.7
1912	21.3	6.5	3.6	11.2	—	2.1		82.2	36.3	13.3	20.2	2.6	9.9	−3.2
1922	32.9	7.2	3.2	22.4	0.1	4.0		90.4	35.5	16.6	22.7	3.2	12.4	8.2
1929	38.0	6.5	3.0	28.4	0.1	4.3		114.7	34.9	24.4	37.0	3.1	15.3	12.4
1933	31.2	7.1	3.0	21.1	0.1	4.2		109.2	34.5	23.4	28.5	2.9	20.0	10.8
1939	36.4	6.6	3.2	24.9	1.6	10.9		105.0	31.8	22.9	26.4	3.4	20.4	2.1
1945 [1]	44.0	7.2	3.9	30.8	2.1	12.7		103.3	35.9	20.9	22.5	3.1	20.8	0.8

[1] Two sets of values are shown for 1900. The first set is comparable with data from earlier years; the second, with that from later years. This table is based on the first set of 1945 values from Table Ce209–232. See text.

[2] Through the first set of values for 1900, government and institutional are combined under institutional.

[3] Producer durables in the hands of nonagricultural business are included with nonfarm, nonresidential construction.

Source

See the source for Table Ce209–232.

Documentation

See the text for Table Ce209–232.

TABLE Ce257–280 National wealth, by type of asset: 1900–1958[1]   [Goldsmith, 1947–1949 prices]

Contributed by Susan B. Carter and Richard Sutch

		Reproducible tangible assets									
		Structures							Equipment		
			Nonfarm								
	Total	Total	Total	Residential	Nonresidential	Farm	Institutional	Government	Total	Producer durables	Consumer durables
	Ce257	Ce258	Ce259	Ce260	Ce261	Ce262	Ce263	Ce264	Ce265	Ce266	Ce267
Year	Billion dollars	Billion dollars	Billion dollars	Billion dollars	Billion dollars	Billion dollars	Billion dollars	Billion dollars	Billion dollars	Billion dollars	Billion dollars
1900	314.6	221.9	144.7	68.1	48.9	13.6	4.7	9.5	42.1	20.5	21.7
1912	464.7	335.6	223.6	99.0	77.3	18.8	7.5	21.0	70.3	17.6	32.7
1922	588.2	428.5	277.3	125.0	91.6	23.9	8.6	28.2	87.8	50.1	37.8
1929	778.0	572.3	382.7	186.2	116.0	24.7	11.2	44.5	118.4	61.1	57.3
1933	742.2	546.5	382.9	179.4	113.4	22.5	11.4	56.3	102.6	52.8	49.8
1939	748.4	572.0	378.0	177.3	103.3	20.7	10.2	66.5	112.4	54.8	57.6
1945 [1]	763.7	591.1	365.6	172.6	94.5	20.1	8.8	69.6	128.6	67.3	61.3
1945 [1]	788.1	622.3	407.9	195.6	92.8	22.2	11.6	85.6	118.9	61.3	57.5
1946	812.7	644.1	411.1	197.4	95.1	22.5	11.6	84.6	131.4	66.7	64.7
1947	845.9	669.2	416.7	200.9	97.0	23.0	11.5	84.4	149.4	75.6	73.8
1948	882.6	702.3	426.5	206.8	99.4	23.6	11.7	85.0	167.0	84.8	82.2
1949	910.4	726.4	437.0	211.9	101.4	24.2	12.1	87.5	181.0	90.6	90.4
1950	949.2	761.9	451.4	219.8	103.7	24.8	12.6	90.6	199.7	96.8	102.9
1951	990.8	798.2	465.6	226.6	106.8	25.5	13.2	93.6	213.5	103.4	110.2
1952	1,022.5	828.0	479.9	233.2	109.9	26.2	13.6	97.0	225.2	109.4	115.8
1953	1,055.3	858.9	495.5	240.5	113.7	26.7	14.1	100.5	239.0	115.7	123.3
1954	1,086.3	887.0	512.3	248.2	117.5	27.1	14.8	104.7	249.6	119.8	129.8
1955	1,131.6	928.2	553.4	258.7	122.5	27.4	15.5	109.4	265.1	123.8	141.3
1956	1,174.6	965.2	533.4	268.0	127.3	27.7	16.1	114.0	279.4	129.9	149.5
1957	1,216.3	998.9	572.9	275.9	132.4	27.9	17.0	119.7	292.0	135.7	156.3
1958	1,244.4	1,022.3	592.8	283.6	136.4	28.2	17.8	126.8	297.0	137.4	159.7

	Reproducible tangible assets						Land						
	Inventories						Private						
		Private				Monetary gold and silver			Nonfarm				Net foreign assets
	Total	Livestock	Crops	Nonfarm	Public		Total	Agricultural	Residential	Nonresidential	Forests	Public	
	Ce268	Ce269	Ce270	Ce271	Ce272	Ce273	Ce274	Ce275	Ce276	Ce277	Ce278	Ce279	Ce280
Year	Billion dollars	Billion dollars	Billion dollars	Billion dollars	Billion dollars	Billion dollars	Billion dollars	Billion dollars	Billion dollars	Billion dollars	Billion dollars	Billion dollars	Billion dollars
1900	32.6	13.6	4.8	14.2	(Z)	2.3	98.8	41.7	19.0	22.4	4.2	11.5	−6.9
1912	37.8	13.7	6.6	17.4	0.1	3.7	132.5	54.1	27.2	29.8	4.5	16.9	−4.8
1922	56.0	15.2	6.0	34.6	0.1	7.1	146.9	52.9	34.0	33.6	5.3	21.1	12.0
1929	63.3	13.7	5.5	44.0	0.1	7.5	188.1	52.1	49.9	54.7	5.1	26.2	18.2
1933	53.2	15.0	5.5	32.6	0.1	7.3	180.5	51.5	48.0	42.0	4.8	34.1	15.8
1939	61.4	14.0	6.0	38.6	3.0	19.0	174.2	47.4	47.0	39.0	5.7	35.0	3.1
1945 [1]	73.8	15.1	7.3	47.7	3.7	22.3	170.0	53.5	43.0	33.3	4.6	35.5	1.2
1945 [1]	74.2	14.9	7.9	47.8	3.6	21.7	168.7	53.8	31.3	47.7	6.4	29.5	−2.7
1946	79.4	14.3	8.3	55.3	1.6	22.2	165.7	50.9	31.5	48.6	6.4	28.2	3.0
1947	78.6	13.6	7.1	56.8	1.1	24.5	166.1	50.3	32.0	48.6	6.5	28.7	10.6
1948	83.0	13.4	8.9	58.7	2.1	26.0	168.1	49.3	32.8	50.1	6.5	29.4	12.2
1949	82.1	13.6	7.5	57.2	3.8	26.2	171.2	49.6	33.6	51.2	6.6	30.3	12.9
1950	86.4	14.0	7.9	62.0	2.5	24.5	175.3	50.9	34.8	51.7	6.6	31.3	12.0
1951	94.5	14.6	8.0	69.7	2.2	24.5	180.5	51.3	35.9	53.5	6.6	33.2	12.3
1952	97.5	14.8	8.3	71.7	2.8	25.0	182.1	50.7	36.9	54.5	6.7	33.3	12.5
1953	100.9	14.6	7.8	72.5	6.0	23.9	183.1	50.2	38.0	55.6	6.7	32.6	13.4
1954	101.6	14.8	8.2	70.9	7.6	23.6	186.5	50.2	39.1	57.1	6.8	33.2	12.8
1955	106.2	15.0	8.4	74.4	8.5	23.6	190.9	50.1	40.7	58.9	6.8	34.4	12.5
1956	108.9	14.7	8.3	78.1	7.9	23.9	194.8	50.9	42.2	61.0	6.8	34.0	14.5
1957	109.2	14.3	9.0	79.5	6.5	24.8	199.3	51.6	43.4	63.0	6.9	34.5	18.0
1958	110.0	14.9	10.7	75.4	8.9	22.7	203.2	52.9	44.6	64.6	6.9	34.2	18.9

(Z) Less than $50 million.

[1] Two sets of values are shown for 1945. The first set is comparable with data from earlier years; the second, with that from later years. This table is based on the second set of 1900 values from Table Ce209–232. See text.

Source
See the source for Table Ce209–232.

Documentation
See the text for Table Ce209–232.

TABLE Ce281–295 Fixed reproducible tangible wealth, by type of asset: 1925–2000 [BEA, current dollars]

Contributed by Susan B. Carter and Richard Sutch

		Fixed assets													Consumer durable goods
			Private					Government							
				Nonresidential					Nonresidential				By government level		
					By type of asset					By type of asset					
	Total	Total	Total	Total	Equipment and software	Structures	Residential	Total	Total	Equipment and software	Structures	Residential	Federal	State and local	Total
	Ce281	Ce282	Ce283	Ce284	Ce285	Ce286	Ce287	Ce288	Ce289	Ce290	Ce291	Ce292	Ce293	Ce294	Ce295
Year	Million dollars	Million dollars	Million dollars	Million dollars	Million dollars	Million dollars	Million dollars	Million dollars	Million dollars	Million dollars	Million dollars	Million dollars	Million dollars	Million dollars	Million dollars
1925	297,047	265,014	226,984	126,506	28,346	98,161	100,477	38,030	38,030	2,860	35,170	0	9,168	28,862	32,033
1926	307,205	273,754	234,870	130,015	29,876	100,139	104,855	38,884	38,884	2,806	36,078	0	8,992	29,892	33,451
1927	315,788	281,148	241,418	133,073	30,899	102,174	108,345	39,731	39,731	2,779	36,951	0	8,702	31,028	34,640
1928	326,032	290,323	249,786	135,245	31,403	103,842	114,541	40,537	40,537	2,769	37,768	0	8,482	32,055	35,709
1929	331,060	294,555	253,987	135,530	31,941	103,589	118,457	40,568	40,563	2,444	38,119	6	7,893	32,675	36,504
1930	315,787	281,424	241,958	129,183	30,690	98,493	112,775	39,466	39,456	2,382	37,075	10	7,451	32,015	34,363
1931	280,309	250,163	214,277	116,838	28,292	88,546	97,439	35,887	35,874	2,323	33,551	12	6,832	29,055	30,145
1932	255,843	229,331	193,841	107,550	25,634	81,916	86,291	35,490	35,476	2,304	33,172	14	6,676	28,814	26,512
1933	265,173	239,421	197,850	107,729	24,570	83,160	90,120	41,572	41,553	2,313	39,240	18	7,562	34,009	25,752
1934	275,749	250,036	204,437	110,392	24,752	85,640	94,045	45,599	45,576	2,540	43,036	23	8,591	37,008	25,713
1935	282,198	256,520	208,000	112,284	24,784	87,500	95,717	48,520	48,485	2,817	45,667	35	9,884	38,636	25,678
1936	303,945	276,835	222,883	119,255	26,300	92,956	103,627	53,952	53,845	2,936	50,908	107	11,380	42,572	27,111
1937	323,191	294,533	237,555	126,267	28,846	97,422	111,287	56,979	56,763	3,116	53,647	216	12,578	44,400	28,657
1938	327,246	298,719	239,647	125,461	28,939	96,522	114,186	59,071	58,811	3,342	55,469	261	13,351	45,720	28,528
1939	335,976	306,511	245,070	126,566	29,378	97,188	118,504	61,441	61,108	3,604	57,504	332	14,000	47,441	29,465
1940	361,859	329,583	262,190	133,868	31,680	102,188	128,322	67,393	66,833	3,956	62,877	560	15,711	51,682	32,276
1941	411,086	373,875	289,487	148,486	35,779	112,707	141,000	84,388	83,327	7,810	75,517	1,061	24,429	59,959	37,212
1942	469,986	428,404	310,373	158,416	36,662	121,753	151,957	118,031	116,328	22,251	94,078	1,703	50,901	67,130	41,582
1943	522,428	477,265	326,320	162,088	36,298	125,790	164,232	150,946	148,328	47,331	100,997	2,618	82,708	68,238	45,162
1944	564,778	517,562	344,078	167,335	37,404	129,931	176,743	173,484	170,480	69,204	101,276	3,003	106,827	66,657	47,216
1945	609,410	561,472	374,808	184,508	42,575	141,933	190,300	186,664	183,353	74,074	109,280	3,311	117,424	69,240	47,938
1946	695,461	639,902	445,719	221,061	52,098	168,963	224,658	194,183	189,956	64,588	125,368	4,227	116,596	77,586	55,559
1947	811,034	744,146	529,479	263,664	65,198	198,466	265,815	214,667	208,194	61,795	146,399	6,473	121,705	92,962	66,887
1948	872,984	796,477	582,248	291,475	77,239	214,236	290,773	214,229	209,222	52,139	157,083	5,007	113,025	101,204	76,507
1949	896,557	811,057	611,476	304,077	85,263	218,814	307,399	199,581	194,228	44,183	150,045	5,353	106,959	96,622	85,500
1950	984,154	883,167	671,502	332,013	96,927	235,085	339,489	211,665	204,990	40,509	164,481	6,675	102,693	108,973	100,987
1951	1,085,902	972,819	735,896	365,893	108,275	257,617	370,003	236,923	228,601	44,192	184,409	8,322	114,318	122,606	113,082
1952	1,150,482	1,030,434	776,339	386,386	115,469	270,917	389,953	254,095	246,502	50,686	195,817	7,592	124,199	129,895	120,049
1953	1,195,898	1,067,621	807,950	401,721	123,500	278,221	406,229	259,670	251,192	57,456	193,736	8,478	131,110	128,560	128,277
1954	1,249,704	1,117,646	842,207	415,045	129,587	285,458	427,162	275,439	264,404	63,975	200,429	11,035	141,159	134,280	132,058
1955	1,343,778	1,202,140	905,673	448,424	142,179	306,245	457,249	296,467	288,908	69,432	219,476	7,559	147,393	149,074	141,638
1956	1,457,577	1,304,981	976,125	494,558	158,824	335,733	481,567	328,857	319,774	73,966	245,807	9,083	159,798	169,059	152,596
1957	1,527,693	1,365,654	1,022,657	526,384	172,831	353,553	496,273	342,997	333,471	76,195	257,276	9,526	165,855	177,142	162,039
1958	1,582,347	1,416,796	1,055,203	543,182	179,710	363,472	512,021	361,593	351,187	77,866	273,321	10,406	172,287	189,306	165,551
1959	1,643,059	1,471,551	1,099,393	564,929	188,662	376,266	534,465	372,158	360,856	82,336	278,520	11,302	176,502	195,657	171,507

		Fixed assets													
		Private						Government							
				Nonresidential						Nonresidential			By government level		
Year	Total	Total	Total	Total	Equipment and software	Structures	Residential	Total	Total	Equipment and software	Structures	Residential	Federal	State and local	Consumer durable goods
	Ce281	Ce282	Ce283	Ce284	Ce285	Ce286	Ce287	Ce288	Ce289	Ce290	Ce291	Ce292	Ce293	Ce294	Ce295
	Million dollars	Million dollars	Million dollars	Million dollars	Million dollars	Million dollars	Million dollars	Million dollars	Million dollars	Million dollars	Million dollars	Million dollars	Million dollars	Million dollars	Million dollars
1960	1,693,739	1,516,923	1,131,424	575,856	194,834	381,022	555,568	385,499	373,548	85,162	288,386	11,951	180,468	205,031	176,815
1961	1,752,246	1,572,306	1,167,363	591,394	198,985	392,410	575,968	404,943	392,195	89,106	303,089	12,749	187,611	217,332	179,940
1962	1,826,504	1,640,285	1,208,983	611,521	206,456	405,065	597,462	431,302	417,679	96,443	321,235	13,624	198,674	232,629	186,219
1963	1,894,840	1,698,322	1,245,483	632,828	215,723	417,106	612,654	452,839	438,956	99,104	339,852	13,883	204,694	248,145	196,518
1964	2,011,944	1,804,942	1,330,288	668,428	228,521	439,907	661,859	474,654	459,905	101,969	357,936	14,750	209,997	264,677	207,002
1965	2,141,750	1,923,155	1,418,149	714,546	246,023	468,523	703,603	505,006	489,546	104,606	384,940	15,460	216,927	288,079	218,595
1966	2,323,991	2,084,984	1,538,680	777,984	273,822	504,163	760,696	546,304	529,786	110,009	419,777	16,519	228,058	318,246	239,007
1967	2,501,833	2,240,446	1,649,165	838,074	300,832	537,242	811,091	591,282	573,889	117,416	456,472	17,393	243,545	347,737	261,387
1968	2,748,401	2,457,962	1,815,703	918,567	332,515	586,052	897,136	642,258	622,702	122,940	499,763	19,556	256,205	386,053	290,439
1969	2,998,609	2,681,555	1,973,745	1,013,214	368,233	644,981	960,531	707,810	686,073	128,131	557,941	21,737	271,694	436,116	317,054
1970	3,258,789	2,918,141	2,129,580	1,113,896	404,558	709,338	1,015,684	788,562	765,350	135,103	630,247	23,212	290,932	497,630	340,647
1971	3,586,824	3,224,422	2,366,389	1,225,585	434,473	791,112	1,140,804	858,033	831,995	140,299	691,696	26,038	308,631	549,403	362,401
1972	3,946,367	3,553,867	2,613,524	1,334,583	468,376	866,207	1,278,941	940,343	911,182	150,671	760,512	29,161	338,234	602,109	392,500
1973	4,456,376	4,022,217	2,968,194	1,500,373	525,240	975,133	1,467,821	1,054,024	1,021,083	152,204	868,879	32,941	363,859	690,164	434,159
1974	5,275,954	4,775,962	3,489,429	1,821,697	648,759	1,172,938	1,667,733	1,286,533	1,249,721	160,670	1,089,050	36,812	411,377	875,155	499,992
1975	5,717,471	5,167,344	3,815,176	2,010,064	740,502	1,269,562	1,805,112	1,352,168	1,311,877	176,590	1,135,287	40,291	436,502	915,666	550,127
1976	6,235,791	5,633,492	4,207,473	2,204,037	818,891	1,385,146	2,003,436	1,426,019	1,381,064	189,802	1,191,262	44,955	470,390	955,629	602,299
1977	6,969,040	6,301,198	4,787,426	2,448,959	920,301	1,528,658	2,338,466	1,513,772	1,462,013	204,722	1,257,291	51,759	493,187	1,020,585	667,842
1978	7,876,129	7,123,339	5,472,965	2,772,742	1,047,984	1,724,758	2,700,223	1,650,373	1,590,642	215,210	1,375,432	59,732	528,408	1,121,965	752,790
1979	9,061,725	8,216,890	6,339,915	3,202,606	1,220,885	1,981,721	3,137,309	1,876,975	1,805,875	230,370	1,575,505	71,100	586,729	1,290,246	844,835
1980	10,293,977	9,363,352	7,212,686	3,675,903	1,420,129	2,255,773	3,536,783	2,150,666	2,072,703	256,475	1,816,228	77,963	652,727	1,497,939	930,625
1981	11,318,715	10,321,068	7,949,746	4,145,785	1,575,632	2,570,153	3,803,961	2,371,322	2,285,843	294,735	1,991,108	85,478	709,137	1,662,185	997,647
1982	11,918,727	10,884,618	8,376,086	4,402,703	1,665,730	2,736,973	3,973,382	2,508,532	2,417,865	324,457	2,093,408	90,667	752,531	1,756,001	1,034,109
1983	12,327,687	11,234,765	8,667,556	4,532,780	1,724,231	2,808,549	4,134,776	2,567,209	2,466,696	356,688	2,110,008	100,513	791,342	1,775,867	1,092,922
1984	13,005,009	11,832,037	9,163,472	4,794,620	1,814,414	2,980,206	4,368,853	2,668,565	2,563,482	376,470	2,187,013	105,082	826,493	1,842,072	1,172,972
1985	13,705,300	12,439,828	9,657,761	5,056,417	1,920,649	3,135,768	4,601,344	2,782,067	2,675,868	397,113	2,278,754	106,199	855,560	1,926,506	1,265,472
1986	14,604,994	13,215,197	10,266,626	5,298,800	2,035,134	3,263,666	4,967,826	2,948,571	2,838,519	422,053	2,416,467	110,052	895,487	2,053,084	1,389,797
1987	15,458,322	13,959,905	10,857,300	5,573,999	2,130,594	3,443,405	5,283,301	3,102,605	2,982,632	445,114	2,537,518	119,973	929,450	2,173,155	1,498,416
1988	16,423,101	14,803,138	11,540,896	5,934,825	2,264,893	3,669,932	5,606,071	3,262,242	3,126,528	479,335	2,647,193	135,714	985,920	2,276,323	1,619,963
1989	17,363,919	15,635,976	12,197,239	6,285,064	2,400,238	3,884,827	5,912,174	3,438,738	3,293,807	515,831	2,777,976	144,930	1,039,464	2,399,274	1,727,942
1990	18,186,533	16,371,917	12,760,342	6,622,673	2,541,947	4,080,726	6,137,669	3,611,576	3,461,866	558,776	2,903,090	149,710	1,087,074	2,524,502	1,814,615
1991	18,614,536	16,753,894	13,021,507	6,760,468	2,622,815	4,137,653	6,261,038	3,732,387	3,581,629	590,390	2,991,239	150,759	1,129,791	2,602,596	1,860,642
1992	19,384,774	17,477,280	13,582,631	6,986,782	2,708,167	4,278,615	6,595,849	3,894,649	3,735,047	619,073	3,115,975	159,602	1,176,047	2,718,602	1,907,494
1993	20,396,609	18,403,646	14,318,030	7,327,079	2,828,576	4,498,504	6,990,951	4,085,616	3,914,692	644,787	3,269,905	170,924	1,228,962	2,856,654	1,992,963
1994	21,617,704	19,526,130	15,203,720	7,731,509	2,992,448	4,739,061	7,472,211	4,322,411	4,140,114	671,952	3,468,162	182,297	1,279,232	3,043,179	2,091,574
1995	22,617,033	20,441,473	15,908,450	8,124,204	3,182,826	4,941,378	7,784,245	4,533,024	4,344,180	685,578	3,658,602	188,844	1,314,386	3,218,638	2,175,559
1996	23,700,986	21,447,285	16,722,529	8,527,229	3,352,197	5,175,032	8,195,300	4,724,756	4,528,590	691,903	3,836,687	196,166	1,343,208	3,381,548	2,253,701
1997	24,924,786	22,596,001	17,653,109	9,006,806	3,519,778	5,487,028	8,646,303	4,942,891	4,739,083	693,530	4,045,553	203,808	1,366,952	3,575,939	2,328,785
1998	26,218,656	23,791,268	18,649,609	9,457,771	3,711,580	5,746,191	9,191,838	5,141,659	4,928,396	697,664	4,230,731	213,263	1,381,353	3,760,306	2,427,388
1999	27,757,073	25,197,122	19,767,331	9,986,814	3,959,184	6,027,631	9,780,516	5,429,791	5,203,724	720,262	4,483,461	226,068	1,423,500	4,006,292	2,559,951
2000	29,639,626	26,907,415	21,164,786	10,693,610	4,245,428	6,448,182	10,471,177	5,742,629	5,505,679	740,634	4,765,045	236,950	1,463,280	4,279,349	2,732,211

(continued)

TABLE Ce281–295   Fixed reproducible tangible wealth, by type of asset: 1925–2000   [BEA, current dollars]   Continued

Source

U.S. Bureau of Economic Analysis, Internet site, *Fixed Asset Tables*, downloaded on October 28, 2001; last revised October 1, 2001.

Documentation

These series display the total wealth stock and its components as defined by the Bureau of Economic Analysis (BEA). These figures are current cost estimates so assets are valued in the prices of the given period. They are end-of-year prices for net stocks and annual averages for depreciation.

For a description of concepts and methods see, U.S. Bureau of Economic Analysis, "Fixed Assets and Consumer Durables: Introductory and Definitional Information," September 2001.

Series Ce281. The wealth stock consists of total fixed assets plus durable goods owned by consumers, series Ce282 and Ce295.

Series Ce282. Total fixed assets are the sum of private and government fixed assets, series Ce283 and Ce288.

Series Ce283. Fixed private assets consists of equipment and structures that are owned by private business or nonprofit institutions, including owner-occupied housing, located in the United States.

Series Ce285 and Ce290. Covers equipment and software with a life expectancy of at least one year.

Series Ce288. Fixed government assets consist of equipment and structures owned by the federal government and state and local government entities, including government enterprises, located in the United States, except in the case of national defense equipment and U.S. embassies abroad, for which coverage is worldwide. This series equals the sum of government nonresidential and residential fixed assets, series Ce289 and Ce292. Fixed government assets are also disaggregated according to government level, series Ce293–294.

Series Ce295. Durable goods are goods purchased by households for their nonbusiness use with a life expectancy of at least three years.

TABLE Ce296–310   Fixed reproducible tangible wealth, by type of asset: 1987–2000   [BEA, chained 1996 dollars]

Contributed by Susan B. Carter and Richard Sutch

All values in Million chained 1996 dollars.

Year	Total (Ce296)	Fixed assets — Total (Ce297)	Private — Total (Ce298)	Private Nonresidential — Total (Ce299)	Private Nonresidential — Equipment and software (Ce300)	Private Nonresidential — Structures (Ce301)	Private — Residential (Ce302)	Government — Total (Ce303)	Government Nonresidential — Total (Ce304)	Government Nonresidential — Equipment and software (Ce305)	Government Nonresidential — Structures (Ce306)	Government — Residential (Ce307)	Government By level — Federal (Ce308)	Government By level — State and local (Ce309)	Consumer durable goods (Ce310)
1987	19,087,645	17,291,505	13,537,248	6,899,094	2,505,777	4,401,985	6,637,789	3,918,378	3,754,781	542,526	3,214,100	163,563	1,220,845	2,697,957	1,647,551
1988	19,636,149	17,731,572	13,893,278	7,071,255	2,578,593	4,500,647	6,821,947	4,006,084	3,838,497	569,357	3,270,420	167,598	1,245,416	2,761,000	1,745,857
1989	20,167,768	18,165,969	14,242,865	7,248,991	2,657,781	4,598,341	6,993,753	4,094,491	3,923,332	598,633	3,325,454	171,138	1,267,825	2,826,809	1,834,937
1990	20,650,376	18,578,742	14,561,558	7,418,871	2,722,479	4,703,522	7,142,388	4,192,374	4,017,294	628,839	3,388,653	175,082	1,291,169	2,901,153	1,899,027
1991	20,984,075	18,894,724	14,790,210	7,538,234	2,769,804	4,775,443	7,251,382	4,283,528	4,105,172	650,690	3,454,346	178,462	1,307,856	2,975,464	1,914,744
1992	21,348,962	19,220,995	15,033,071	7,648,812	2,826,252	4,828,212	7,384,193	4,370,535	4,188,485	668,804	3,519,284	182,170	1,321,662	3,048,575	1,949,684
1993	21,795,926	19,603,534	15,344,825	7,798,334	2,914,899	4,886,940	7,546,472	4,444,518	4,259,270	678,187	3,580,781	185,329	1,326,864	3,117,418	2,009,477
1994	22,291,432	20,017,146	15,693,586	7,973,451	3,035,710	4,938,996	7,720,216	4,511,547	4,323,746	683,417	3,640,200	187,912	1,326,117	3,185,395	2,087,340
1995	22,829,383	20,468,760	16,074,893	8,190,637	3,183,018	5,007,606	7,884,271	4,584,930	4,393,860	687,432	3,706,461	191,038	1,325,890	3,259,039	2,169,567
1996	23,450,348	20,995,538	16,521,129	8,447,526	3,354,005	5,093,534	8,073,597	4,667,736	4,474,399	694,558	3,779,827	193,337	1,333,907	3,333,816	2,261,473
1997	24,126,422	21,760,395	17,009,824	8,749,103	3,554,608	5,197,595	8,261,147	4,749,421	4,553,730	699,302	3,854,138	195,671	1,328,945	3,420,128	2,368,712
1998	24,908,022	22,407,119	17,571,377	9,099,675	3,796,465	5,314,135	8,473,967	4,834,508	4,636,999	709,026	3,927,429	197,616	1,327,037	3,506,641	2,508,109
1999	25,769,587	23,093,469	18,160,190	9,462,412	4,065,725	5,420,946	8,703,095	4,932,210	4,732,706	724,223	4,008,015	199,568	1,328,851	3,601,588	2,694,613
2000	26,679,930	23,806,306	18,779,567	9,857,840	4,359,636	5,541,205	8,931,982	5,026,638	4,825,460	737,885	4,086,976	201,339	1,328,198	3,695,535	2,910,584

Source

U.S. Bureau of Economic Analysis, Internet site, *Fixed Asset Tables*, downloaded on October 28, 2001; last revised October 1, 2001.

Documentation

See the text for Table Ce281–295. The figures here are expressed in real (chained 1996) dollars, rather than current dollars.

CHAPTER Cf

Geography and the Environment

Editor: Gavin Wright

Associate Editors: Scott Farrow and Myron P. Gutmann

NATURAL RESOURCES AND THE ENVIRONMENT

Gavin Wright

The United States has long been rich in natural resources, an abundance that has had a profound influence on the country's prosperity and economic preeminence in the world. What is perhaps less well appreciated is that natural resources have a history. Territorial expansion as a feature of nineteenth-century American history is well known; but even within U.S. political jurisdiction, the economic meaning and significance of a given land area depended on settlement, ownership, transportation, the application of technologies, and the state of knowledge, to offer only a partial list of contributing factors. Although the temperate-zone regions of the country were blessed with naturally fertile soils, expansion of cropland throughout the nineteenth century required an arduous struggle to clear these lands of their original forest. Further extensions of agriculture during the twentieth century have been possible only with the aid of artificial irrigation and other forms of human intervention.

In this chapter, the term "natural resources" encompasses land, water, the environment, and climate. Information on resource-based economic activity in mining, energy, forestry, and fisheries may be found in Chapter Db, on natural resource industries. The attention given to these subjects by observers and reformers has varied widely through American history, as national priorities have evolved from resource development in the nineteenth century to conservation in the twentieth, and increasingly to the quality of life in the twenty-first. Partly as a consequence of these changing foci, the availability of data on particular topics varies considerably. Because competing resources have interacted historically, and interpretive themes often overlap, readers are encouraged to consult more than one of the essays and their associated groups of tables.

Land Area and the Public Domain

The United States is by no means a "natural" geographic unit; instead, the country's size and boundaries have been shaped by historical events and forces dating back to the eighteenth century, continuing even into the mid-twentieth century when Alaska and Hawai'i became states in 1959. These noncontiguous states are the most obvious deviations from purely geographic logic, but regional divisions dictated by waterways, mountain ranges, or differences in soil and climate could readily have formed the basis for smaller national units. For that matter, an even larger American national entity is not difficult to imagine, but for limits set by military or diplomatic exigencies at particular historical junctures.

Each one of the events that led to an expansion of the American domain may appear to have been inevitable in retrospect, and indeed it would be hard to claim that any of them were mere "historical accidents." But to say that territorial expansion reflected powerful historical forces is not the same as saying that the breadth of the country as we know it was geographically inevitable. The original thirteen colonies were only a subset of British North America, a potentially larger national unit that until that time had functioned in many respects as an integrated economy. After independence, the country's western boundary was commonly shown as a line marking the area closed to settlement and reserved by treaty for Indians. The westward movement of this boundary was ultimately driven by military pressures. Perhaps the clearest example of historical contingency is provided by the Civil War, in which one major section of the country – distinguished by geographic as well as institutional features – attempted to secede and form a new national entity. Thus, when we review the quantitative record of America's land and resources, we are viewing the outcomes of a rich and complex set of historical events and developments, not a simple count of the bounties of nature.

Territorial Expansion: The Continental United States

Table Cf1 lists the major additions to U.S. land area after 1790, and Map Cf-A depicts the territorial expansion of the United States

Acknowledgments

The preparation of data for the tables on land and water was partly supported by a grant from the National Institute of Child Health and Human Development.

Gavin Wright and Scott Farrow would like to thank Carroll Curtis for her substantial assistance on numerous environmental tables. Her work was made possible by funding from the Office of Environmental Information, U.S. Environmental Protection Agency, and from the Council on Environmental Quality.

The preparation of data for the tables on weather was partly supported by a grant from the National Institute of Child Health and Human Development. Myron P. Gutmann, Christie S. Wilson, and Timothy G. F. Kittel are grateful to J. Andrew Royle and Nan A. Rosenbloom for the work done to prepare these data. The data described as drawn from the VEMAP2 source are from the Vegetation/Ecosystem Modeling and Analysis Project, with support from the National Aeronautics and Space Administration, the Electric Power Research Institute, and the U.S. Department of Agriculture Forest Service.

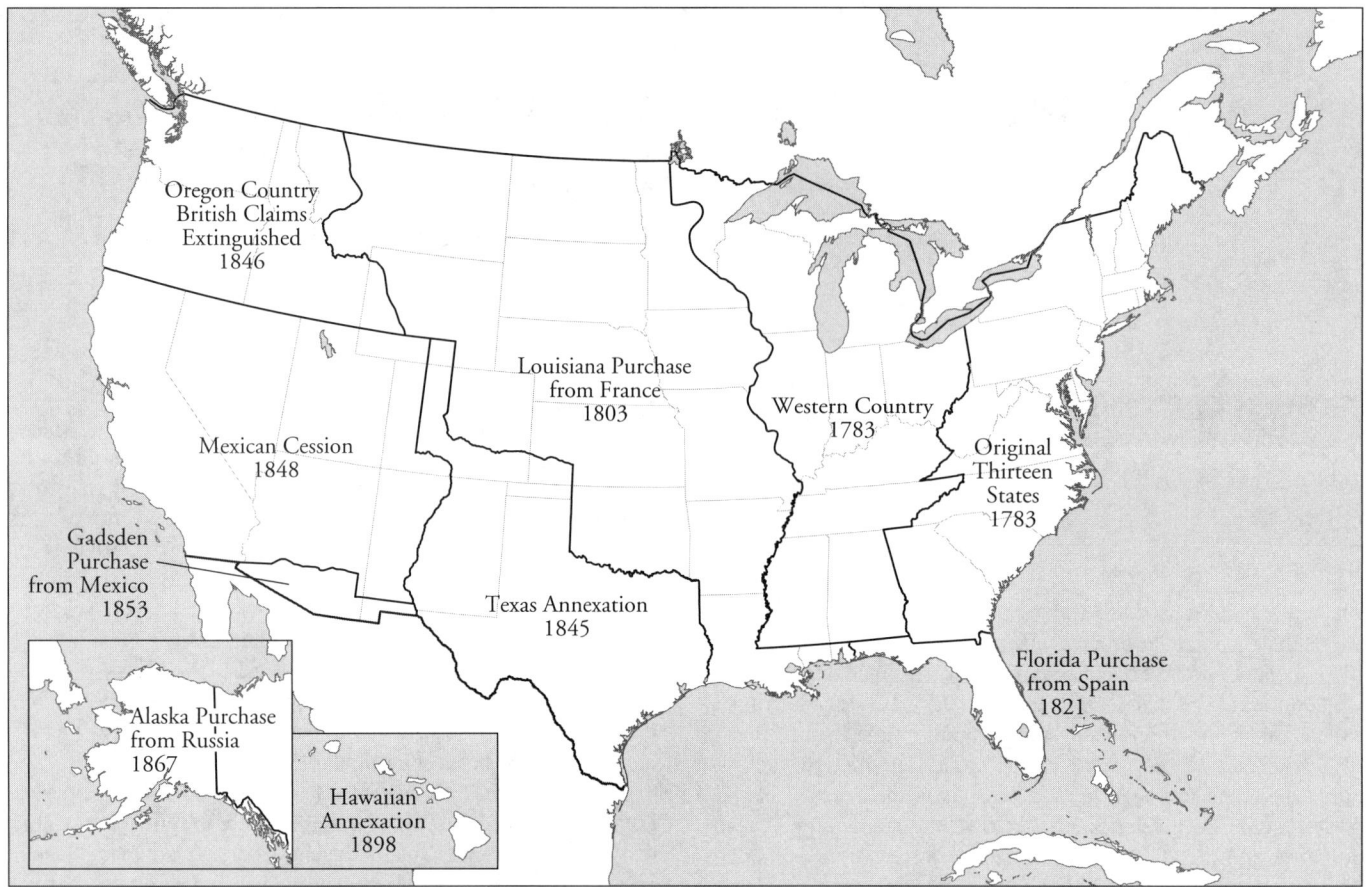

MAP Cf-A   Territorial expansion of the United States: 1783–1898

Source

Charles O. Paullin, *Atlas of the Historical Geography of the United States* (Carnegie Institution of Washington, 1932), plate 46C; see also plates 46B and 89–101.

Documentation

The area shown for the original thirteen states depicts their western boundaries as established by the Ordinance of 1784. Note that this region also includes the area that would become the state of Vermont (1791). The northern and eastern boundaries of what would become Maine (which was part of Massachusetts at the time) and the northern boundary of New Hampshire were not finalized with Great Britain until 1842. The modern boundaries are shown here.

The Western Country was recognized as the territory of the United States by the Treaty of Paris (1783). The western boundary between the Lake of the Woods and the headwaters of the Mississippi River is ambiguous because of misconceptions about the locations of the lake and the course of the river

with respect to the 49th parallel. Ongoing boundary negotiations with Great Britain became moot with the Louisiana Purchase.

The northern boundary of the Louisiana Purchase, originally defined by the drainage of the Mississippi and Missouri Rivers, was formally established with Great Britain as the 49th Parallel running westward from the Lake of the Woods in 1818. The western boundary north of the 42nd Parallel was the continental divide. The United States claimed all of the land westward to the Rio Grande. Spain, however, disputed both the legitimacy of the purchase and the western boundary. As part of the larger settlement with Spain in 1819 (ratified in 1821), which ceded East and West Florida to the United States, the western boundary was established as shown.

The Texas–Mexico boundary was agreed upon in 1848, following the Mexican-American War. The United States acquired the Mexican Cession at the same time.

from 1783 to 1898. The vehicles of expansion ranged from outright purchase to military conquest.

In 1803 President Thomas Jefferson secured the new country's status as a continental power by purchasing from the French Republic the Louisiana Territory comprising the entire river basin west of the Mississippi River. The price was 60 million francs, about $15 million; $11,250,000 was paid directly. The U.S. assumption of the French debts to American citizens covered the balance. Napoleon Bonaparte had acquired the territory from Spain only in 1800. But after the French loss of Hispaniola, when Haitian slaves led by Toussaint L'Ouverture seized power in 1801, Napoleon abandoned his vision of a vast French empire in the New World. Facing a war with Great Britain, he could not spare the troops to defend the territory and he needed funds to support his European

campaigns. Accordingly, in April 1803 he offered to sell Louisiana to the United States.

The purchase set the precedent for territorial expansion even though the Constitution did not specifically grant this power to the federal government. The newly acquired land became part of the general territory mentioned in the Constitution and might be admitted as one or more states at the discretion of Congress. The principle was established that Congress has powers in the territories that it may not exercise in the states, and that the constitutional limitations of power are applicable only to the area within the states.[1]

---

[1] See Ogg (1904) for a history of the Louisiana Purchase and the early political history of the territory.

Spain had never recognized the validity of the French sale of Louisiana, which they deemed to have been prohibited by the treaty wherein Spain had transferred the territory to France. Spain, however, was soon distracted by the South American wars of liberation led by Simón Bolívar in the North and José de San Martín in the South. In 1818 Andrew Jackson, then the American military commander in the South, invaded East Florida under the pretext that Florida had become a haven for escaped American slaves. The next year Spain agreed to cede both Floridas to the United States and to relinquish any claim it may have had on the Oregon Territory in exchange for establishing the western boundary of the Louisiana Purchase (delineating it from Texas). The so-called "Transcontinental Treaty" was ratified in 1821.

In 1836 Anglo-Texans, unhappy with the Mexican government's attempt to discourage further immigration of Americans and to prohibit the importation of slaves, proclaimed the independence of Texas from Mexico. In 1844 the further westward expansion of the country became a political issue when Democrats linked the southern interest in the annexation of Texas – as a slave state – with the assertion of U.S. claims to the Oregon Territory, including the area north of the Columbia River as far north as the Russian boundary of Alaska, which had been ruled for decades by the British Hudson's Bay Company. The claim to "all of Oregon" – presumably as territory free of slaves – had political appeal in the North. In 1845, Texas, bypassing territorial status, was admitted to the Union. The boundary between Texas and Mexico was, however, still very much in dispute.

The next year, using the boundary issue as a pretext, the United States declared war on Mexico. Military victories on Mexican soil, the collapse of the Mexican government in California, and the capture of Mexico City by General Winfield Scott led Mexico to agree to the Treaty of Guadalupe Hidalgo, which offered Mexico essentially the same terms the United States was prepared to offer before the war. For $15 million and the assumption of Mexican debts to American citizens, Mexico gave up California and New Mexico, and it agreed to the Rio Grande as the Texas–Mexican boundary. The treaty was ratified in 1848.

Meanwhile, another treaty ratified in the same year settled the dispute with Great Britain over the Oregon Territory by establishing the 49th parallel as the boundary between the two countries (rather than the line of 54° 40′) and by giving British Canada all of Vancouver Island.

Gold was discovered in California in 1848 simultaneously with the Mexican cession of that territory. The discovery spurred the great Gold Rush of 1849 and hastened the admission of California as a state in 1850 as part of the famous Compromise of 1850. In 1853, to secure a favorable railroad right-of-way for a southern route for a transcontinental railroad, the government purchased a strip of land from Mexico along the border between New Mexico Territory and Mexico for $10 million. The land was named for the American railroad entrepreneur and diplomat James Gadsden. The purchase also clarified a misunderstanding arising from the Treaty of Guadalupe Hidalgo, which defined the border between Mexico and the United States on the basis of an inaccurate map. The Southern Pacific Railroad was eventually built through the region.

Territorial Expansion: Outlying Areas

With the Gadsden Purchase, the territorial boundaries of the 48 contiguous states were essentially complete. Subsequently, a series of acquisitions added a diverse set of possessions in outlying areas.

In 1856 Congress passed the Guano Act, which authorized the President to claim any uninhabited and unclaimed island valuable for its deposits of guano, which was highly prized as a natural fertilizer in the era before chemical fertilizers were developed. More than 100 islands, reefs, banks, and cays were claimed in the Pacific and the Caribbean during the next three years. Midway Island in the Pacific was occupied in 1867 under the provisions of the Guano Act.

That same year, 1867, the United States purchased Alaska from the Russian czar for $7.2 million despite the lack of public enthusiasm.

In 1893, American business interests engineered a coup in the Hawaiian Islands against the native queen. The reluctance of President Cleveland to act thwarted the attempts to annex the Islands immediately.

In 1895, the Cuban Revolution against Spain broke out. With the issue of slavery removed from both the American and Cuban agendas, there was strong national support for the revolutionary side and even calls for America to intervene against Spain. The issue did not come to a head, however, until the Spanish instituted a brutal program of repression against the revolutionaries. When the U.S. battleship Maine exploded in Havana Harbor in Cuba many Americans assumed the Spanish were responsible. Congress declared war against Spain in 1898. The American Pacific fleet demolished the Spanish in the Battle of Manila Bay, Philippines, and the Atlantic squadron systematically destroyed the Spanish ships in Santiago Harbor, Cuba. The Spanish possessions of Puerto Rico and Guam fell to the Americans without any real resistance. Within months, Spain conceded and signed a treaty of peace. Spain relinquished Cuba, Puerto Rico, the Philippines, and Guam. The United States annexed the last three named territories and incorporated Hawai'i, Wake Island, and Palmyra Atoll into the list of territories at the same time. Cuba was occupied and became a U.S. protectorate in 1903, a state of affairs that lasted until 1934. An insurrection arose against U.S. rule in the Philippines that dragged on until 1901.

In the 1890s, the British, German, and American governments all vied for political domination of the Samoan Islands. After an American attempt to take the Islands by a show of force was thwarted by a typhoon, an 1899 treaty in which Germany and the United States divided the Samoan archipelago settled the international rivalries. The United States formally occupied its portion – a smaller group of eastern islands – the following year.

The Virgin Islands were purchased in 1917 from Denmark for $25 million.

Following the defeat of Japan in World War II, the United Nations established the Trust Territory of the Pacific Islands under U.S. stewardship. It was composed of the former Japanese mandates of the Marshall Islands, the Northern Mariana Islands, Palau, and the four islands of Kosrae, Ponape (now Pohnpei), Truk (now Chuuk), and Yap. In 1986 the Northern Mariana Islands became a commonwealth in political union with the United States. The Marshall Islands, Palau, and the Federated States of Micronesia (Kosrae, Pohnpei, Chuuk, and Yap) became independent in free association with the United States.

The Philippines were granted their independence in 1946. The Corn Islands were ceded to Nicaragua in 1971 and the U.S. lease on the Swan Islands from Honduras was terminated that same year.

Guano banks were ceded to Colombia in 1972. The Phoenix and Line Islands and a number of atolls in the Ellice Islands (also claimed under the Guano Act) were transferred to Kiribati and Tuvalu in 1979. In 1980 guano atolls were transferred to Tokelau, New Zealand, and the Cook Islands. Pursuant to an agreement reached in 1977 the Panama Canal Zone was transferred to Panama in 1999.

This sequence of events left the United States with five major possessions (Puerto Rico, Guam, American Samoa, the U.S. Virgin Islands, and the Northern Mariana Islands), an entity known as the United States Minor Outlying Islands (none of which have indigenous inhabitants), and three states in free association (Marshall Islands, Palau, and the Federated States of Micronesia). In almost all cases the outlying areas are not included in the national totals reported here. As always, users are cautioned to examine the documentation for the series of interest to determine whether and in which time periods various outlying areas are included in the national aggregates.[2]

The Public Domain

The fact that the United States acquired sovereignty over an area does not mean that the federal government thereby gained title to that land. Only land that was not retained by individual states and their political subdivisions, or by private owners, is included under the heading "public domain." Comparison of series Cf65 with series Cf8 shows that the share of the public domain in total national land area peaked at more than 40 percent in 1850, declining to less than 15 percent a century later. During this period the federal government relinquished title to approximately 800 million acres, primarily through a series of active "privatization" measures that permeated national politics in the nineteenth century. Today the unclaimed or "vacant" public domain is still very substantial (242 million acres as shown in series Cf71), but most of this is remote and of low market value.

The first phase of liberalized land policy is depicted in Table Cf79–82, which records annual data on public land sales between 1800 and 1860. These numbers may be compared to those in Table Cf83–87, which represent the more active uses of federal land to promote westward settlement and economic development, through support for what were known as "internal improvements": wagon roads, canals, river improvements, and railroads. The tables show that prior to the Civil War, the largest shares of lands were released through sales to private buyers. After survey, these lands were offered at auction, with a minimum price ($2.00 per acre from 1796 to 1820, $1.25 per acre thereafter) and a minimum required acreage (which declined from 640 acres in 1796 to 40 acres after 1832). Schoene (1981) shows that the great majority of sales were "private" or post-auction sales, generally at the minimum price. Land was often occupied prior to purchase, a practice known as "squatting" that was legitimated by a series of special "preemption" acts between 1801 and 1841, at which point preemption became standard.[3]

Legal changes notwithstanding, the marked cyclical fluctuation in the volume of land sales has been used to argue that the pace of westward settlement was driven by economic forces, because the major surges (of 1815–1818, 1833–1836, and 1853–1855) were associated with peaks in commodity prices (North 1961). During these periods, competitive bidding sometimes drove average land prices well above the minimum. Prior to the Civil War, revenues from these sales represented a substantial share of federal revenues, peaking at nearly 50 percent of the total in 1836 (see series Cf82 and Table Ea588–593). But the political pressures toward more generous land distribution policies were inexorable, culminating in the Homestead Act of 1862, and effectively reducing land sales to a minor revenue role. The Homestead Act did not abolish earlier measures, however, and throughout the nineteenth century land was released to private hands under any number of prior or subsequent laws.

Table Cf83–87 does confirm, however, that the Civil War era marked a major watershed in policies regarding the public domain and economic development. The Republican Party was formed in the 1850s in opposition to the extension of slavery into the territories, but also in favor of homestead legislation and activist policies to promote railroad construction in the West. When southern representatives walked out at the time of the secession crisis, the Republican Congress was free to pursue this agenda, through the Homestead Act and the Pacific Railway Act of 1862, in addition to tariff legislation and other measures. Series Cf84 shows the surge in acreage granted to aid in construction of railroads, more than 100 million acres in total, between 1863 and 1871. Whereas the railroad land grants were concentrated in that one decade, acreage released under the Homestead Act continued to rise throughout the nineteenth century, beginning its historical descent only after World War I. This pattern may be seen in series Cf76–78.

Neither of these sets of acreage figures should be taken as straightforward measures of the federal contribution. Grants of public land to railroads were only a part of a much broader program, which included bond subsidies, construction financing, and other forms of assistance. The measure of the *value* of the land grant subsidy is itself subject to ambiguity and debate, because rising land values were one of the anticipated consequences of railroad building. Support in the form of land grants could be viewed therefore as an incentive scheme, whereby railroads internalized much of the return to the enterprise as appreciated land value. In response, transcontinental railroads engaged in extensive efforts to recruit settlers and facilitate migration, sometimes even engaging in research on farming techniques and livestock varieties. Also, the typical pattern was for the federal government to provide alternate sections along the right-of-way, doubling the minimum price on the remainder in hopes that the government would also share in these gains. Although the land-grant program may be rationalized in these ways, it is also clear that vast individual fortunes were made in the course of federally supported railroad construction, and that corruption was not infrequent. The economic effects of the program, and the returns to society and to private entrepreneurs, have been extensively debated by economic historians (see Gates 1954; Fleisig 1975; and Mercer 1982).

The Homestead Act is also subject to interpretation and debate. Although the Act was clearly a response to the long-standing demand for free farmland in family-size units, by the 1860s the frontier of settlement had passed the point where the size specified (160 acres) was commercially viable. Even by the 1850s, the

---

[2] Chapter Ef, on outlying areas, treats the statistical history of the remaining five insular possessions, the three states in free association, as well as Alaska, Hawai'i, the Canal Zone, and the Philippines during the period these last four were territories.

[3] These legal changes are conveniently summarized in Davis, Easterlin, et al. (1972), pp. 104–5.

cost of acquiring the land itself was only a small part of the total costs of setting up a working commercial farm. Thus large numbers of "original" Homestead entries were recorded, but less than half of these ultimately resulted in a transfer of title under the terms of the Act. Nonetheless, vast acreages did pass into private hands by means of the Homestead Act, one way or another. A key provision of the Act allowed a homestead to be "commuted" (i.e., converted into clear title through payment of the statutory minimum price) after only six months of residence. Very often the purpose of commutation was to sell to a cattle rancher, lumber company, or mining firm.[4]

The total acreage disposed, as recorded in series Cf73, includes not just Homestead land but also land claimed under several other statutes. The major acts were: the Timber Culture Act (1873), which offered 160 acres free to settlers who cultivated trees on one quarter of the plot (reduced to one sixteenth in 1878); the Desert Land Act (1877), which offered 640 acres at $1.25 per acre, on condition that the land be irrigated within three years; and the Enlarged Homestead Act (1909) and the Stock-Raising Homestead Act (1916), both of which offered land in larger sizes in semiarid areas suitable only for grazing. These incentives were often ineffective, or observed only with the aid of fraud. But on the whole, the system was not ineffective in encouraging rapid settlement.

Land Utilization

Around the turn of the twentieth century, attention turned from territorial expansion to the balance in allocations of land among alternative uses. Tracking land utilization historically is hazardous, however, because the country has not maintained a national land inventory on a consistent basis over any extended stretch of history. The Census of 1850 may be considered the first attempt, when land on farms was divided into "improved" and "unimproved" acreage. The Census of Agriculture continued to be responsible for land utilization figures, but the farm-based series reported in Table Cf101–118 became less and less informative over time; hence the thoroughly revised set of categories found in Table Cf119–134, which have been extended back to 1945 by the U.S. Department of Agriculture's (USDA's) Economic Research Service. Yet another categorization appears in Table Cf135–144, in which major uses are listed separately, according to whether the land is owned by private parties or by public agencies (federal, state, and local). Any comprehensive account of the history of land utilization will have to make use of each one of these frameworks, which themselves reflect changes in public attention and concerns.

Despite problems of comparability, the broad impression that these tables convey is that patterns of American land utilization have been surprisingly stable across the twentieth century. The "big three" land uses in terms of area have continued to be cropland, grazing land, and forest. Total cropland acreage has declined only modestly from its peak in 1930 (series Cf103 and Cf120). The area actually "used for crops" (series Cf121) has fallen by perhaps ten percent, but this largely reflects a decline in intensity of use, as acreage has been shifted into cover crops (series Cf122). Contrary to popular impression, the amounts of both public and private

forest acreage have actually been rising since World War II (series Cf138 and Cf143), as land that had been cut over and abandoned has regenerated its forests. The only change that stands out as discontinuous is the addition of Alaska in 1959; this is perhaps more an accounting measure than a new development in land utilization, but that one state is large enough to have a notable impact on total area (series Cf101 and Cf119), "other land uses" (series Cf134), and total public land (series Cf140).

Perhaps the surprise is that urban land still looms so small as a share of the total (series Cf130). Although the acreage classified as "urban" quadrupled between 1945 and 1992, this still only came to 2.6 percent of the nation's land area in that year. One can justifiably conclude that the country is still land-rich by world standards. But it would be unjustified to argue as a result that urban land-use issues are of minor importance. The *value* of urban land clearly exceeds the value of most rural American land, an indication that well-located property does indeed have scarcity value. As a result, conversion of farmland to urban uses is a lively issue in many localities, but not one to be evaluated with national aggregate data.

The aggregate data do, however, allow us to dismiss the fear that agricultural production has been or will be severely constrained by a shortage of cropland. As noted, acreage harvested is well below its historic peak. The U.S. Conservation Service estimates that for every hundred acres presently in cropland, there are thirty-six acres of potential cropland of roughly comparable quality. Earlier analyses of the dangers of soil erosion are now known to have exaggerated the magnitude of the losses, while underestimating the recuperative powers of the soil. As yields per acre have risen steadily since the 1930s – through greater attention to soils, improved hybrid strains, and increased use of fertilizer – production has been limited much more by export demand than by land availability.[5]

Despite these successes, fears about the sustainability of the country's agricultural path deserve to be taken seriously. A particular concern is the supply of water, a scarce resource that in many parts of the country has long been priced below its true social cost. Enthusiasm for public water projects was high after World War II, expanding the area of irrigated farmland by more than 25 million acres in the western states (series Cf153). But such projects largely ceased after 1980, as the reality of limits has become more fully appreciated. Series Cf158 shows that consumption of groundwater in irrigation grew rapidly until that year, but has since declined. In California and elsewhere, rising salinity levels and land subsidence threaten not only agriculture, but also supplies of water for urban uses.[6]

The impact of public opinion is discernible elsewhere in the tables. The Department of the Interior has long been criticized for allowing private grazing on the public domain. Lacking incentives to conserve, grazers have often been accused of exploitative practices on public range land. Tables Cf95–100 and Cf135–144 show that grazing on the public domain, particularly by sheep and goats, has greatly declined since the 1970s. Against this, the area allocated to rural parks and wildlife area has expanded (series Cf129), and recreational use of these areas continues to climb (see series Db402 for data on visitor-days to national forests). A major challenge

---

[4] The social and economic consequences of the Homestead Act are discussed in Shannon (1945).

[5] For a more thorough discussion of these issues, see Crosson (1991).

[6] Annual updates on California water quality may be found at the U.S. Geological Survey Internet site, "Water Resources of California," part of the National Water Data System.

facing the Forest Service is balancing these recreational demands against the environmentalist pressure to conserve and preserve ecological relationships in wooded and wilderness areas.

Environmental Indicators

Information on the "environment," broadly defined, is scattered throughout these volumes. Examples include land utilization, forests, fisheries, crop yields, nutrition and public health, and many others. Missing from coverage under other headings tend to be data on the unwanted byproducts of human activity, such as pollution of air, land, and water, as well as the effects of such byproducts on wildlife habitats and the preservation of the nation's natural heritage – in short, the state of the "environment" as it has come to be defined as a policy objective in recent decades. Tables Cf168–285 address these topics.

Unfortunately, there are few long national series on measures of environmental quality. Most of the systematic evidence dates only from the rise of the modern environmental movement in the 1960s, much of it collected by the Council on Environmental Quality, the Environmental Protection Agency, the National Oceanic and Atmospheric Agency (all created in 1970), and other relatively recent federal monitoring agencies. To be sure, many of the issues – water pollution, air quality, wildlife preservation – have a much longer history. But until recent times, pollution policies were considered to be primarily a local responsibility. Some local series extending over longer periods have been assembled.[7] At the national level, however, most data on environmental indicators is available only for the period since World War II, sometimes only for the years since the 1960s or even later.

Even within this constricted historical range of observation, the evidence shows the remarkable expansion in the scope of federal involvement in environmental policy since 1970 and, broadly speaking, the effectiveness of these policies in arresting previous trends toward environmental deterioration. Table Cf177–182 shows the expansion of expenditures for the implementation of environmental regulations, the largest percentage increase being federal spending, of which the Environmental Protection Agency accounts for only about half (series Cf178–179). The table also shows that the majority of environmental expenditures are private rather than public, but these too represent the effects of federally mandated standards (series Cf182). Table Cf168–176 demonstrates that this intensified compliance has not been concentrated on any one form of pollution or environmental medium. Chemicals, water, land, air, and radiation all received substantial increases in compliance expenditures between 1972 and 1999.

Trends in Air and Water Quality

Have these expenditures been effective in improving the environment? The most readily observable trend reversal is in emissions of air pollutants, for which annual data go back to 1940, and estimates have been extended back to 1900 by the Environmental Protection

Agency (EPA).[8] Almost all of the major criteria pollutants – sulfur dioxide, nitrogen oxides, volatile organic compounds, carbon monoxide, and lead – show a rising trend until 1970, after which they have declined, or (in the case of nitrogen oxides) at least stopped rising (see Table Cf203–210 and Figure Cf-B).[9] The timing suggests that the decisive steps were taken in 1970, when a series of amendments to the Clean Air Act of 1963 created the EPA and charged it with developing three sets of standards: National Ambient Air Quality Standards (NAAQS); motor vehicle emission standards; and new source performance standards (NSPS). Because on-road vehicles have been significant contributors to rising levels of nearly all of these pollutants (with the exception of sulfur dioxide), it is notable that these improvements have occurred despite substantial increases in vehicle miles traveled, along with population and national per-person income. The most dramatic change has been in emissions of lead, which steadily declined after 1972 as the result of EPA mandates progressively reducing the lead content of gasoline, culminating in a complete ban as of 1996 (series Cf204). In 1998, on-road vehicles accounted for less than 1 percent of national lead emissions, down from 82 percent in 1980.

Monitoring of air concentrations of these pollutants by the Office of Air Quality and Standards dates only from 1977 (Table Cf197–202). Even across this relatively brief span, the data show striking reductions in air pollutant levels for sulfur dioxide, carbon monoxide, ozone, nitrogen dioxide, PM-10 particulates, and lead, averaged over hundreds of monitoring sites.

Another side effect of fossil fuel consumption is the acidification of rain, as sulfur dioxide and nitrous oxide emissions are transformed into sulfuric and nitric acid, which inflict damage on trees, lakes, rivers, fish, crops, soils, and buildings. Although these effects have been observed since the nineteenth century, both monitoring and regulations targeted at acid rain were long delayed by a combination of skepticism among scientists and political conflicts arising from the interstate and international (U.S.–Canadian) character of the problem. A major breakthrough occurred with the 1990 amendments to the Clean Air Act, which mandated specific reductions in sulfur dioxide and nitrous oxide emissions. A noteworthy policy initiative was the introduction of a system of "tradable pollution permits," allowing power companies to buy and sell sulfur dioxide emission allowances each year. Observations on these programs are still relatively early, but suggest some success in acid rain reduction, at least in the eastern region of the country (Table Cf183–196).[10]

A partial exception to this generally optimistic picture is the long-term trend in emissions of carbon dioxide, the byproduct of the consumption of fossil fuels. Series Cf209 shows that aggregate national emissions of carbon dioxide grew steadily from 1940 through the 1970s (extending a much longer trend); after a brief hiatus in the 1980s, expansion resumed in the 1990s, setting new all-time records every year. The United States is easily the world's largest source of fossil fuel–related carbon dioxide emissions, more than 50 percent larger than the People's Republic of China, which is in second place. Per capita emissions are also highest in the United

---

[7] See, for example, the water quality data in the Storage and Retrieval System for Water and Biological Monitoring Data (STORET); air quality data in the Aerometric Information Retrieval System (AIRS); the data of the Ohio River Valley Water Sanitation Commission (ORSANCO); and individual studies such as Davidson (1979).

[8] See *National Air Pollutant Emission Trends, 1900–1998.*

[9] The much earlier peak for particulate (PM-10) emissions is attributable to state air pollution statutes enacted in the 1950s, aimed at controlling smoke and particulates from both residential and industrial sources.

[10] For evidence of the effectiveness of the program in reducing regulated emissions, see Schmalensee, Joskow, et al. (1998) and Stavins (1998).

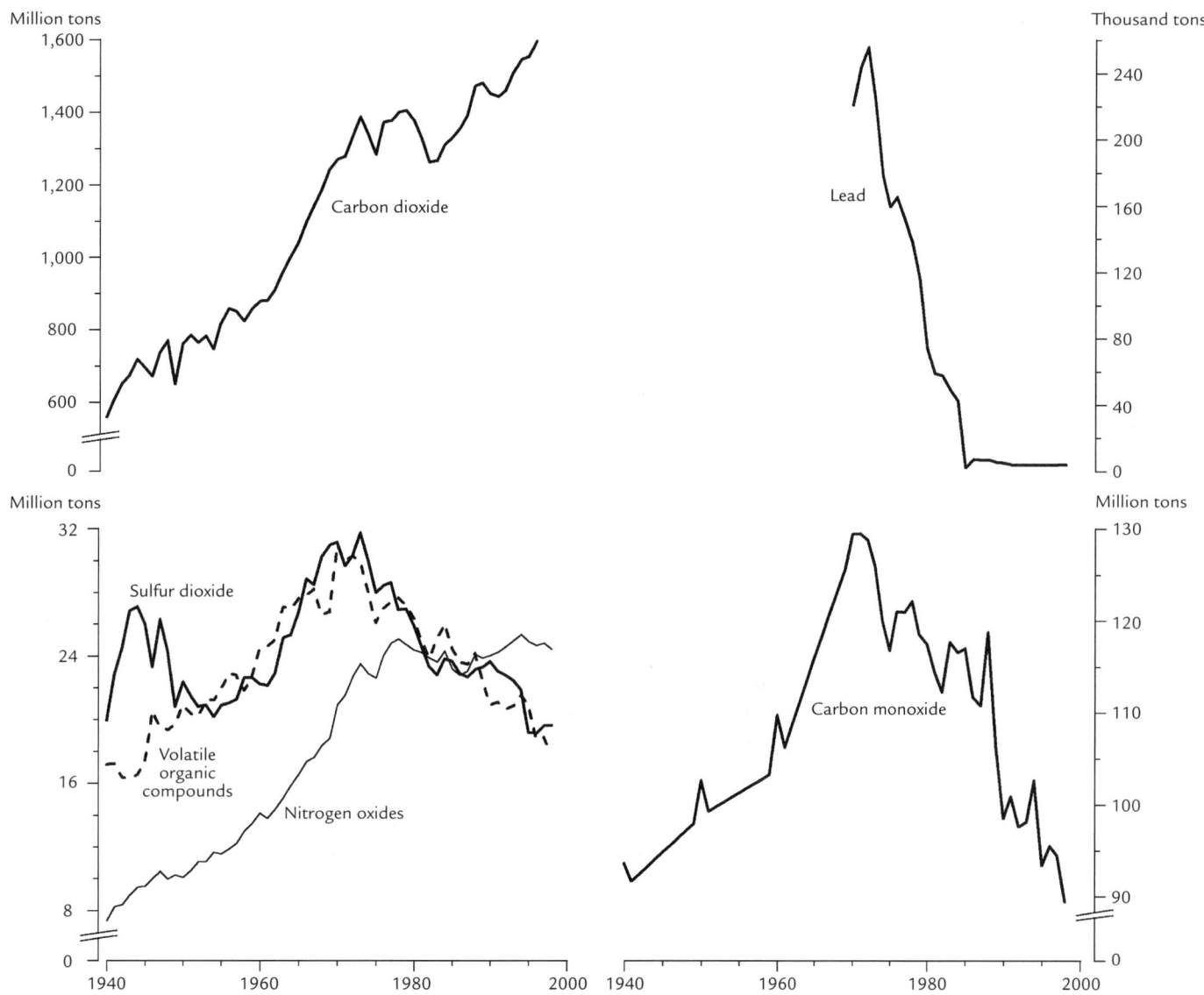

FIGURE Cf-B   Emissions of air pollutants – sulfur dioxide, volatile organic compounds, and nitrogen oxides: 1940–1998

Sources
Series Cf205–206 and Cf208.

States, but in the 1990s were still somewhat below the peaks of the 1970s (see Marland, Boden, et al. 2002). The proximate reason for the absence of further progress on this front was apparently the decline in the relative prices of petroleum and coal between the 1970s and the 1990s.

National data on water quality are much more limited, even though the techniques and sophistication of water quality indicators have a much longer history. Municipalities began to employ scientists and engineers to analyze sewage-polluted waters in the mid-nineteenth century. In 1912, Congress assigned the Public Health Service (PHS) the task of investigating "the diseases of man and conditions influencing the propagation and spread thereof, including sanitation and sewage and the pollution, either directly or indirectly, of the navigable streams and lakes of the United States." The PHS investigations were especially important in improving understanding of the comparative effects of both sewage and organic wastes on stream quality, the natural assimilative characteristics of

streams, and the measurement of stream pollution. In conjunction with various editions of the Standard Methods of Water Analysis formulated by the American Public Health Association, the PHS standards came to define basic measures of water quality throughout the nation. In the 1960s, partially stimulated by the publication of Rachel Carson's *Silent Spring* (1962), concern over the environmental effects of insecticides and pesticides accelerated, leading to monitoring for various trace elements and toxics that could not be identified in the past. The data presented in Table Cf223–227 suggest that violation rates for such pollutants as dissolved oxygen, phosphorus, cadmium, and lead had fallen to insignificance by the 1990s.

Municipal Solid Waste Disposal

Along with sewage, the growth of economic activity and population generates unwanted byproducts in the form of solid waste.

Although solid waste disposal is an inherently local issue, the emergence of the EPA has made it possible to monitor national trends in municipal solid waste (MSW) generation and disposal. The EPA also plays an active role in shaping waste disposal policies. Local choices are of course constrained by federal and state environmental regulations, and the volume of waste generation is influenced by efforts at "source reduction" strategies that are often implemented at higher governmental levels – package designs, recyclability of products or packaging, product durability, and so forth. The evidence presented in Table Cf211–216 suggests that heightened environmental concerns have had a major impact on the nation's way of handling its garbage.

The table distinguishes "gross discards" from "net discards," the former being the volume of waste generated by business and residential activity, the latter being the portion of that waste remaining after recycling and compost recovery. This net figure is then further divided into a portion that is burned and a remainder discarded in landfills. Gross discards nearly tripled between 1960 and 1990, but show only slow growth during the 1990s, as per capita MSW generation has largely stabilized at around 4.5 pounds per person day (series Cf211). Series Cf212–213 show the remarkable expansion of recycling and composting, from less than 10 percent of MSW in 1980 to nearly 30 percent in 1998. Because the combustion levels have been relatively stable, the result has been an absolute decline in the tonnage of MSW discarded to landfills (series Cf216). The number of landfills in the country declined from 8,000 in 1988 to 2,314 in 1998, although their average size has increased. In 1998, there were more than 9,300 curbside recycling programs, and approximately 3,800 yard trimmings composting programs in the United States. These trends are now closely monitored by the Municipal and Industrial Solid Waste Division of the EPA, whose annual reports may be found at the EPA Internet site.

Wildlife Preservation

Hunting enthusiasts, concerned about the decline in wildlife populations, were one of the organized forces behind the creation of national forests and national parks in the late nineteenth and early twentieth centuries. Early legislative achievements of this campaign include the Lacey Act (1900), regulating imports of, and interstate commerce in, birds and mammals; the Norbeck–Andresen Migratory-Bird Conservation Act (1929), which provided for a system of national refuges; and legislation of 1934 and 1937 taxing hunters of migratory fowl, the funds to be used for wildlife preservation programs. The U.S. Wildlife Refuge System was established in 1940 and is administered by the Fish and Wildlife Service of the Department of the Interior. By far the most numerous are the waterfowl refuges, which supply breeding areas, wintering areas, and rest and feeding areas along major flyways during migration. Refuges have also been established by private individuals and societies, such as the Nature Conservancy and the Audubon Society.

As part of the trend toward environmental consciousness in recent decades, the hunters were joined by an increasing sentiment in favor of the appreciative or "nongame" protection of wildlife in the 1960s and 1970s, confirmed by public opinion polls. Their impact was reflected in the passage of the Endangered Species

Acts of 1966, 1969, 1973, 1978, 1982, and 1988, constructing an elaborate set of restrictions and procedures to be followed when proposed projects may have an impact on wildlife habitat. Wildlife preservation has thus made its way onto the agenda of any number of federal agencies, and monitoring responsibilities are widely dispersed. The tables presented here are only a small sampling of recent trends, and they are not necessarily representative. The number of threatened and endangered species has increased steadily since 1980.[11] On the other hand, populations of ospreys, bald eagles, and peregrine falcons have recovered robustly since the ban on dichlorodiphenyltrichloroethane (DDT) in 1972.

Table Cf263–268 presents evidence of major gains in North American goose and swan populations between 1970 and the 1990s. Estimates of North American duck populations show a more mixed trend (Table Cf269–280). The number of pintails declined from more than 10 million in 1956 to fewer than 2 million in 1991, with some recovery in the 1990s. The numbers of scaups and widgeons drifted downward in the 1990s, while the number of black ducks has steadily declined on both the Atlantic and Mississippi flyways. Populations of all other major duck varieties are either stable or substantially increased since the 1950s.

Not all wildlife preservation policies take the direct form of refuge maintenance. Of equal importance is the preservation of natural habitats threatened by the encroachment of human settlements or by air and water pollution. One measure of progress in this area is the number of closures of shellfish beds, recorded by the Strategic Environmental Assessments Division of the National Oceanic and Atmospheric Administration (Table Cf228–235). The table shows that between 1966 and 1990, the number and rate of bed closures significantly increased in both the North Atlantic and Gulf of Mexico regions, followed by improvements in the 1990s. In the South Atlantic and Pacific Coast regions, the number of closures steadily declined after 1971. One should note, however, that water contamination is only one of several possible reasons for prohibiting shellfish harvests in a locality.

Another index of habitat conditions is the contamination of herring gull eggs in the Great Lakes, monitored by the Canadian Wildlife Service. Table Cf238–262 records remarkable improvements between 1974 and 1999, for all contaminants on every one of the Great Lakes.

Possibly the most infamous human assaults on wildlife have been the major spills of oil in environmentally sensitive areas; the largest was the Exxon Valdez, which spilled 11 million gallons in Prince William Sound, Alaska, in 1989. In fact, hundreds of such spills occur every year, from pipelines and storage tanks as well as from oil-carrying vessels. Since the 1970s, oil polluting incidents have been monitored by the U.S. Coast Guard. The evidence in Table Cf236–237 shows that although the average annual number of such incidents has not declined, the volume of oil spillage has fallen to a tiny fraction of what was common in the 1970s. The decline in the early 1990s is attributable to increased attention to the issue on the part of companies, in the wake of the Exxon Valdez incident, as well as increased audit and inspection activity. Another response to the same incident was the Oil Pollution Act of 1990,

---

[11] Fish and Wildlife Service, *Endangered Species Bulletin*, bimonthly.

which mandated a phase-in of double hulls on oil-carrying vessels, beginning in 1995.[12]

References

Carson, Rachel. 1962. *Silent Spring*. Riverside.

Commission on Engineering and Technical Systems of the National Academy of Sciences. 1998. *Double-Hull Tanker Legislation: Assessment of the Oil Pollution Act of 1990*. Available at the National Academy Press Internet site.

Crosson, Pierre. 1991. "Cropland and Soils." In Kenneth D. Frederick and Rodger A. Sedjo, editors. *America's Renewable Resources*. Resources for the Future.

Davidson, Cliff. 1979. "Air Pollution in Pittsburgh: A Historical Perspective." *Air Pollution Control Association Journal* 29: 1035–41.

Davis, Lance, Richard Easterlin, et al. 1972. *American Economic History*. Harper and Row.

Fleisig, Heywood. 1975. "The Central Pacific and the Railroad Land Grant Controversy." *Journal of Economic History* 35: 552–66.

Gates, Paul. 1954. "The Railroad Land Grant Legend." *Journal of Economic History* 19 (Spring): 143–6.

Marland, G., T. A. Boden, et al. 2002. "Global, Regional and National CO_2 Emissions." In *Trends: A Compendium of Data on Global Change*. Carbon Dioxide Information Analysis Center, Oak Ridge National Laboratory.

Mercer, Lloyd. 1982. *Railroads and Land Grant Policy*. Academic Press.

North, Douglass C. 1961. *The Economic Growth of the United States, 1790–1860*. Prentice-Hall.

Ogg, Frederick Austin. 1904. *The Opening of the Mississippi: A Struggle for Supremacy in the American Interior*. Cooper Square.

Schmalensee, Richard, Paul L. Joskow, et al. 1998. "An Interim Evaluation of Sulfur Dioxide Emissions Trading." *Journal of Economic Perspectives* 12 (Summer): 53–68.

Schoene, Steven W. 1981. "The Economics of U.S. Public Land Policy Prior to 1860." Ph.D. dissertation, University of North Carolina at Chapel Hill.

Shannon, Fred. 1966. *The Farmer's Last Frontier*. Holt, Rinehart and Winston (first published 1945).

Stavins, Robert N. 1998. "What Have We Learned from the Grand Policy Experiment? Lessons from SO_2 Allowance Trading." *Journal of Economic Perspectives* 12 (Summer): 69–88.

U.S. Environmental Protection Agency, Office of Air Quality, Planning and Standards. 2000. *National Air Pollutant Emission Trends, 1900–1998*. U.S. Environmental Protection Agency, Office of Air Quality, Planning and Standards.

---

[12] For a full review, see Commission on Engineering and Technical Systems of the National Academy of Sciences (1998).

WEATHER

Myron P. Gutmann and Ben Tausig

Weather Research and Climatological Data

The data in Tables Cf286–569 represent a microscopic portion of the vast amount of data collected and preserved in the service of understanding and predicting the weather of the United States. The quantity and quality of the data have grown and improved over the past two centuries, thereby advancing knowledge of weather processes achieved by American and other scientists. The double goal of meteorologists and climatologists has been to understand current weather and climate, and to predict future weather and climate, for general scientific purposes and to contribute to the overall social, economic, and political good of the United States. The mass of data that have accumulated are the consequence in large part of an institutional commitment by the U.S. government to support weather forecasting and science to ensure the quality of life of many Americans, including parents planning school day clothing for their children; farmers planning planting, irrigation, and harvest; and NASA planning its operations in space.[1]

The early history of climatological recording in the United States was marked largely by guesswork and nonstandardized analytical techniques, although several trends in the nineteenth century helped to transform observation from casual study into the highly useful and practical science of meteorology. During those years, American settlers moving west in search of fertile farming territory relied increasingly on information about the weather in making decisions about where to settle. Although such information remained hit-or-miss for many decades, this process established a link between accurate weather data and successful farms.

In the United States, 1814 was the first watershed year in weather observation, as the U.S. Army Medical Department, in coordination with a small group of academics, began recording data at military posts. Previously such activity had been restricted to hobbyists and expeditioners such as Lewis and Clark. Thanks to increased interest from scientific communities and the government, by the middle of the century every state in the Great Plains and Western United States had at least one weather observation site.

In 1847, the Smithsonian Institution began a meteorological project that extended a network of observation across North America. This project, whose existence was catalyzed by leading meteorologists such as Elias Loomis and James Pollard Espy as well as Smithsonian director Joseph Henry, had long been a dream of scientists who surmised that weather observation could move drastically forward only through the work of a geographically broad and well-organized association of data recorders. With hundreds of observers, the Smithsonian network represented just such an organization, and indeed dominated weather data collection for nearly twenty years. Unfortunately, the Civil War and a building fire eventually ravaged the network irreparably. To the dismay of many scientists, in 1873 the U.S. Army Signal Office assumed control of the work the Smithsonian had previously done.

Despite increased scholarly and governmental attention to monitoring weather and understanding climatological issues, farmers and settlers remained generally uninformed. Folklore persistently acted as a crucial means of predicting and reacting to weather. The climatic volatility of the central and western United States further complicated this problem. Storms, floods, and freezing temperatures alternated with extended periods of drought and heat. Some scholars have even asserted that the mid-nineteenth century was a "little ice age," during which typically dry regions experienced increased precipitation and cooler temperatures. While more rain aided travelers along the Oregon Trail, it also contributed to widespread confusion about the nature of climate in the Western states. The inadequate work of the Signal Office led to misinformation and inaccurate forecasts. The scientific community criticized

---

[1] This review of the early history of American meteorology draws upon Whitnah (1961), Hughes (1970), and Fleming (1990).

the office for their poor research methods, and farmers had little reason to trust a poorly run government agency as opposed to a localized volunteer network.

Consequently, the government and meteorologists shifted to a state-level, farm-oriented approach to observing weather. The growth of western settlement and the need for farms gave meteorology a new importance. Which regions could be settled, and with what crops? How large and diverse should farms be? These questions hinged on accurate, regionally specific weather data and thus necessitated increasingly scientific methods.

Two major events of the 1890s altered the course of weather research in the United States. The first was the transfer of responsibility for government weather monitoring from the Signal Corps (formerly Signal Office) to the U.S. Department of Agriculture. This move signaled a strengthening of the ties between farming and meteorology. The second was the extended period of drought in the Great Plains, which forced a revision of certain inaccurate folk theories, such as the idea that cultivation and precipitation enjoyed a causal relationship.

In this period and immediately after, not only were measurements further standardized and instrumentation greatly advanced, but the functioning of the entire network of weather observation was also encouraged by the needs of industry. In the early twentieth century, commercial interests and local government worked together to avoid disasters such as crop failure or fire resulting from the lack of warning regarding weather phenomena. For example, the Weather Bureau aided farmers in the 1910s when it created reports on water availability and gave advance forecasts of fire hazards. Later, the growth of aviation provided a strong stimulus to the active development of meteorological reporting and forecasting, spurred by economic needs and by the opportunities for observation made possible by increased access to higher altitudes with balloons and aircraft.

At the turn of the twentieth century weather data were still backward by later standards, despite new levels of government intervention and the abandonment of archaic theories. The Progressive-era notion of dry farming, for instance, thought to be a means of combating drought, was ineffective despite its pretension toward a scientific basis. Such theories relied on pseudoscientific conclusions, suggesting that meteorology at the beginning of the century still retained many of its old problems. As the first half of the twentieth century progressed, however, scientific advances in meteorological science and in weather mapping and forecasting gradually brought improvements in the quality of forecasts and the strength of the underlying science.

Meteorology truly became an effective and practical tool after the Dust Bowl of the 1930s, when effective forecasting began and people began to realize the potential for human environmental impact. One of the weaknesses of the period between the two World Wars was the growing difficulty in dealing with the very large quantity of data that had begun to accumulate from regular daily (and sometimes hourly) observations at hundreds of weather stations throughout the United States. Only when data processing methods (initially punched cards) began to be widely used were scientists able to make use of more of the data that had been collected for so long. At first, these methods were extensions of earlier analog traditions of mapping weather and its progress across space and through time, but eventually digital processes were invented. (See Nebeker 1995, 1996; Cressman 1996; Kutzbach 1996; and Monmonier 1999.)

Numerical methods for studying weather phenomena had begun to be explored in the first decades of the twentieth century, but despite successes in identifying the role of mathematics in the study of weather processes, only slow progress was made until the advent of electronic computers in the 1940s. Then, led by innovators who saw the possibility of using computers to understand weather, and the possibility of using weather data and forecasting to advance the development of computers, matters changed rapidly in the late 1940s and early 1950s. Nearly all meteorology has become computational in the five decades since.

High-speed computing has given value to the large volume of numerical weather data that have been collected for the United States since the 1890s. Not only are they used to understand the past and to predict the near future, but they are also increasingly important in the effort to understand the risk of climatic change that most scientists believe exists today. In response to the need for continuous series of historical climatological data, the National Climatic Data Center has created the U.S. Historical Climatalogical Network as a digital record of the best and most representative data for the United States in the past century. Most of the climate data in this chapter are drawn from the USHCN publications. The products of USHCN and others have made possible the creation of data sets – such as VEMAP (Vegetation/Ecosystem Modeling and Analysis Project) – that allow the testing of competing models of climate change in the past and future. (See Karl, Williams, et al. 1990; Kittel, Rosenbloom, et al. 1995; and Kittel, Royle, et al. 1997.)

The temperature and precipitation measures that are included here represent a small portion of the information that is available and useful for the analysis and prediction of weather and climate. They are important because they allow those who study historical events, patterns, and trends to see local phenomena across the United States in great detail in the twenty-first century; in earlier times this was also possible but with lower resolution.

History of American Weather

A comprehensive history of American weather has not yet been written. One reason for this omission may be that the weather is not intrinsically a "national" phenomenon. The famous "year without a summer" in 1816 was attributable to the eruption of Mount Tambora in eastern Java, half a world away. The effect was felt in Western Europe and China as well as in the eastern United States, and is now thought to have interacted with a cooling cycle already underway for several years (Harington 1992). In our tables, the effect is observable only in the temperature and rainfall series for New Haven, Connecticut (series Cf556–557). Much more recently, the stormy seasons associated with the term "El Niño" are traceable to a warming of ocean waters off the coast of Chile (Changnon 2000). These effects are readily observable in the more abundant data available for modern times. See, for example, the extraordinary precipitation recorded for San Francisco in 1998 (series Cf563).

Furthermore, weather conditions and fluctuations within the United States are by no means uniform. On the basis of weather proxies such as tree rings, types of vegetation, amounts of snowfall as recorded in ice cores, and so forth, researchers have documented significant regional climate fluctuations over the centuries. The western part of the country went through a long hot spell known as the Altithermal from about 7,000 years ago to about 4,500 years ago, after which temperature and rainfall settled into patterns similar to what they are today (Laskin 1996, p. 26). In recent times, the experience of global warming has been highly uneven. The Southeast is one of the handful of places in the world that have actually experienced cooling across the twentieth century, perhaps because of the increased presence of sulfate aerosols, changes in atmospheric circulation regimens, or changes in cloud cover (National Assessment Synthesis Team 2001, p. 29). In light of these divergences, any aggregation of rainfall and temperature figures into national averages is distinctly artificial.

But weather fluctuations in particular times and places have certainly played an important role in American history. The first general migration from New England to the Middle West occurred in 1817, immediately following the year without a summer. Evidently, this pattern persisted throughout the nineteenth century. Historians have documented an association between out-migration from Maine and unusually cold, wet summers (Smith, Born, et al. 1981, pp. 451–56).

Perhaps the most famous weather-based episode in American history is the migration of farmers onto the western Great Plains during the 1880s, on the basis of several years of unusually high rainfall. Developers promoted the theory that rainfall patterns could be favorably influenced by human settlement, summarized in the slogan "Rain follows the plow." Although much of this was mere unscrupulous propaganda, Libecap and Hansen (2002) show that farmers at that time lacked reliable data on which to base their decisions. Instead, they learned the hard way from experience that western Kansas is normally too dry to support agriculture on a nonirrigated basis.

Some historians maintain, however, that the impacts of the weather on American life and activities have been greatly exaggerated. William B. Meyer argues that "The opposite is closer to the truth." Meyer's (2000, p. vii) complaint is that changes in the weather (the "less visible and less important sources of change") have received far more attention than the social changes (changes "in plain sight") transforming relationships between weather and society. For example, the shift from canals and rivers to railroads reduced the vulnerability of the country's transportation to frost and snow. Improvements in transportation and distribution facilities have greatly diminished the impact of weather fluctuations on food and fuel supplies. Technological improvements, most notably air conditioning but also long-distance trade in water, have encouraged migration and development in areas previously considered inhospitable for human settlement. When the full history of American weather is written, in other words, it will have to acknowledge that interactions between activity and the weather have historically operated in both directions.

Nonetheless, the temptation is irresistible to use these abundant data to ask whether there have been long-term changes in American weather, most notably whether the country has in fact shared in the worldwide experience of global warming. Because systematically recorded temperature data are available only for modern times, however, students of long-term temperature trends are forced to compare proxy records with instrumental evidence. Such comparisons do show rising temperatures beginning in the late nineteenth century, roughly coincident with the rising volume of fossil fuel emissions. The same methods show that the pattern has been essentially similar for the United States, albeit with regional variations and even one regional exception in the Southeast (National

Assessment Synthesis Team 2001, pp. 21–31). Over most areas of the country, warming of more than 1 degree Fahrenheit has occurred, consistent with global averages. Warming has been greatest in the Northeast, the Southwest, and the upper Midwest, reaching as much as 3 degrees Fahrenheit in the northern Great Plains. Correspondingly, the number of days on which the temperature falls below freezing has dropped by about two days per year. Over the same period, precipitation in the coterminous United States has increased by 5 to 10 percent, which is broadly consistent with global changes in the midlatitudes.

Because these conclusions are derived from sophisticated statistical procedures, often requiring supplemental data to adjust for subtle geographic and climatological effects, no attempt is made to replicate them here. The scientific community has not yet reached full consensus on the causes of these warming trends; other possibilities include changes in solar radiation, a decline in the impact of volcanic eruptions, or a change in the linkage between the atmosphere and oceans. The most recent comprehensive assessment rejects these alternative possibilities and supports the conclusion that the primary causal factor has been the increasing concentrations of greenhouse gases and aerosols (National Assessment Synthesis Team 2001, p. 24). The weather information presented in the tables here will be useful for historians, but specialized scientific researchers will undoubtedly want to utilize more detailed sources of technical data.

References

Changnon, Stanley A., editor. 2000. *El Niño 1997–1998: The Climate Event of the Century*. Oxford University Press.

Cressman, George P. 1996. "The Origin and Rise of Numerical Weather Prediction." In James Rodger Fleming, editor. *Historical Essays on Meteorology, 1919–1995: The Diamond Anniversary History Volume of the American Meteorological Society*. American Meteorological Society.

Fleming, James Rodger. 1990. *Meteorology in America, 1800–1870*. Johns Hopkins University Press.

Harington, C. R., editor. 1992. *The Year without a Summer? World Climate in 1816*. Canadian Museum of Nature.

Hughes, Patrick. 1970. *A Century of Weather Service: A History of the Birth and Growth of the National Weather Service, 1870–1970*. Gordon and Breach.

Karl, T. R., C. N. Williams Jr., et al. 1990. *United States Historical Climatology Network (HCN) Serial Temperature and Precipitation Data*. Environmental Science Division, Publication number 3404, Carbon Dioxide Information and Analysis Center, Oak Ridge National Laboratory. See also the U.S. Historical Climatology Network, available at the Internet site of the National Climatic Data Center.

Kittel, T. G. F., N. A. Rosenbloom, et al., and VEMAP Modeling Participants. 1995. "The VEMAP Integrated Database for Modeling United States Ecosystem/Vegetation Sensitivity to Climate Change." *Journal of Biogeography* 22 (4–5): 857–62.

Kittel, T. G. F., J. A. Royle, et al., and VEMAP2 Participants. 1997. "A Gridded Historical (1895–1993) Bioclimate Dataset for the Conterminous United States." In *Proceedings of the 10th Conference on Applied Climatology, 20–24 October 1997, Reno, Nevada*. American Meteorological Society.

Kutzbach, John E. 1996. "Steps in the Evolution of Climatology: From Descriptive to Analytic." In James Rodger Fleming, editor. *Historical Essays on Meteorology, 1919–1995: The Diamond Anniversary History Volume of the American Meteorological Society*. American Meteorological Society.

Laskin, David 1996. *Braving the Elements: The Stormy History of American Weather*. Doubleday.

Libecap, Gary D., and Zeynep Kocabiyik Hansen. 2002. "'Rain Follows the Plow' and Dryfarming Doctrine: The Climate Information Problem and Homestead Failure in the Upper Great Plains, 1890–1925." *Journal of Economic History* 62: 86–120.

Meyer, William B. 2000. *Americans and Their Weather.* Oxford University Press.

Monmonier, Mark. 1999. *Air Apparent: How Meteorologists Learned to Map, Predict, and Dramatize Weather.* University of Chicago Press.

National Assessment Synthesis Team. 2001. *Climate Change Impacts on the United States: The Potential Consequences of Climate Variability and Change.* Report for the U.S. Global Change Research Program. Cambridge University Press.

Nebeker, Frederik. 1995. *Calculating the Weather: Meteorology in the 20th Century.* Academic Press.

Nebeker, Frederik. 1996. "A History of Calculating Aids in Meteorology." In James Rodger Fleming, editor. *Historical Essays on Meteorology, 1919–1995: The Diamond Anniversary History Volume of the American Meteorological Society.* American Meteorological Society.

Smith, David C., Harold W. Borns, et al. 1981. "Climatic Stress and Maine Agriculture, 1785–1885." In T. M. L. Wigley, M. J. Ingram, and G. Farmer, editors. *Climate and History.* Cambridge University Press.

Whitnah, Donald Robert. 1961. *A History of the United States Weather Bureau.* University of Illinois Press.

LAND AND WATER

Myron P. Gutmann

TABLE Cf1   Territorial expansion of the United States – land area, by accession: 1790–2000

Contributed by Richard Sutch

Accession	Year(s)	Land area Cf1 Square miles
United States in 2000	—	3,536,278
Territory in 1790	—	895,415
Louisiana Purchase	1803	909,380
By treaty with Spain:	—	—
Florida	1819	53,937
West Florida	1819	4,729
Definition of Louisiana–Texas boundary:	—	—
Gain	1819	22,834
Loss	1819	−97,150
Texas annexation:	—	—
Texas	1845	261,914
Other	1845	126,773
Oregon Territory	1846	286,541
Mexican cession	1848	529,189
Gadsden Purchase	1853	29,670
Alaska Purchase	1867	570,374
Hawaiian annexation	1898	6,423
Insular areas in 2000:	—	—
Puerto Rico	1898	3,427
Guam	1898	210
American Samoa	1900	77
Virgin Islands of the United States	1917	134
Northern Mariana Islands	1947	179
Minor outlying areas:	—	—
Navassa Island	1857	2
Baker Island	1857	1
Howland Island	1857	1
Jarvis Island	1857	2
Kingman Reef	1858	(Z)
Johnston Atoll	1858	1
Midway Islands	1867	2
Wake Island	1898	3
Palmyra Atoll	1898	5

Accession	Year(s)	Land area Cf1 Square miles
Freely Associated States:	—	—
Marshall Islands	1947–1986	70
Micronesia	1947–1986	271
Palau	1947–1994	177
Former possessions:	—	—
The Philippines	1898–1946	115,124 [1]
Canal Zone (Panama)	1904–1999	553 [1]
Corn Islands (Nicaragua)	1914–1971	4
Phoenix Islands (Kiribati)	1856–1979	—
Line Islands (Kiribati)	1856–1979	—
Atolls of the Union Islands (Tokelau)	1856–1980	4
Atolls in the Ellice Islands (Tuvalu)	1856–1979	—
Swan Islands (Honduras)	1863–1971	1
Atolls of the Northern Cook Islands (Cook Islands)	1856–1980	—
Colombian Banks (Colombia)	1856–1972	—
Disputed possessions:	—	—
Serranilla Bank (Colombia)	1856	—
Bajo Nuevo Bank (Jamaica)	1856	—

(Z) Less than 0.5 square miles.

[1] Gross area (land plus water) as of 1976.

Sources

U.S. Department of Commerce, *Statistical Abstract of the United States, 1994,* Table 352, p. 226; *Statistical Abstract of the United States, 2000,* Table 380, p. 227; *Statistical Abstract of the United States, 1976,* Table 301, p. 179; U.S. Central Intelligence Agency, *The World Factbook, 2000;* The U.S. Department of the Interior, Office of Insular Affairs, *Fact Sheet,* August 2000; Frederick Austin Ogg, *The Opening of the Mississippi: A Struggle for Supremacy in the American Interior* (Cooper Square, 1904); Charles O. Paullin, *Atlas of the Historical Geography of the United States* (Carnegie Institution of Washington, 1932).

Documentation

Boundaries of territories listed under the United States were indefinite, at least in part, at the time of acquisition. Area figures shown here represent precise determinations of specific territories that have been marked on maps, based on interpretations of the several treaties of cession, which are necessarily debatable. A committee consisting of representatives of various governmental agencies made these determinations in 1912. Subsequently these figures were adjusted to bring them into agreement with remeasurements made in 1990. The data in this table reflect those remeasurements.

The sum of the land area of 1790 plus all of the accessions listed exceeds the area of the United States in 2000 because those portions of the Louisiana Purchase north of the 49th parallel were later granted to Great Britain. There were also other adjustments to the boundaries between Canada and the United States and Mexico and the United States. For an extensive discussion of the boundary changes see Paullin (1932).

Territory in 1790 includes part of the drainage basin of the Red River of the North south of the 49th parallel that was sometimes considered part of the Louisiana Purchase.

The Louisiana Purchase has been generally understood to include New Orleans, the island on which the city stands, and the entire Mississippi Valley west of the River, together with the north shore of the Gulf of Mexico westward to the Sabine River. However, the eastern boundary that separated the territory acquired from France from West Florida, which was retained by Spain, was far from clear (Ogg 1904, pp. 533–36).

The Treaty with Spain in 1819 gave the United States both East Florida (the present state of Florida) and West Florida (a strip of land south of the 31st parallel along the gulf coast). At the same time the western boundary between the purchase and Texas was redefined. The United States ceded 97,150 square miles and gained 22,834.

The Compact of Free Association with Palau was approved in 1986 and ratified by the United States in 1993. Palau gained independence in 1994.

The agreement for the complete transfer of the Panama Canal to Panama was signed in 1977. Control of certain portions of the Canal Zone and increasing responsibility over the Canal transferred to Panama beginning in 1977. The entire Panama Canal, area supporting the Canal, and remaining U.S. military bases were turned over to Panama on December 31, 1999.

For a brief history of the acquisition of insular areas and other territories, see the essays on natural resources and the environment in this chapter, and on outlying areas in Chapter Ef.

TABLE Cf2-7   Land and water area: 1790–1990

Contributed by Michelle L. Butler and Myron P. Gutmann

	Conterminous U.S.			United States		
	Total	Land	Water	Total	Land	Water
	Cf2 [1]	Cf3 [1]	Cf4 [1]	Cf5	Cf6	Cf7
Year	Square miles	Square miles	Square miles	Square miles	Square miles	Square miles
1790	888,811	864,746	24,065	—	—	—
1800	888,811	864,746	24,065	—	—	—
1810	1,716,003	1,681,828	34,175	—	—	—
1820	1,788,006	1,749,462	38,544	—	—	—
1830	1,788,006	1,749,462	38,544	—	—	—
1840	1,788,006	1,749,462	38,544	—	—	—
1850	2,992,747	2,940,042	52,705	—	—	—
1860	3,022,387	2,969,640	52,747	—	—	—
1870	3,022,387	2,969,640	52,747	—	—	—
1880	3,022,387	2,969,640	52,747	—	—	—
1890	3,022,387	2,969,640	52,747	—	—	—
1900	3,002,387	2,969,834	52,553	—	—	—
1910	3,022,387	2,969,565	52,822	—	—	—
1920	3,022,387	2,969,451	52,936	—	—	—
1930	3,022,387	2,977,128	45,259	—	—	—
1940	3,022,387	2,977,128	45,259	—	—	—
1950	3,022,387	2,974,726	47,661	3,615,211	3,552,206	63,005
1960	3,002,261	2,968,054	54,207	3,615,123	3,540,911	74,212
1970	—	—	—	3,615,122	3,536,855	78,267
1980	—	—	—	3,618,770	3,539,289	79,481
1990	—	—	—	3,717,796	3,536,278	78,937

[1] Excludes Alaska and Hawai'i.

Sources

U.S. Bureau of the Census, Reports of Fourteenth, Fifteenth, Sixteenth, Seventeenth, Eighteenth, and Nineteenth Censuses, *Population*, volume 1, and unpublished data; 1980, *1980 Census of Population*, volume 1, Chapter A, part 1, Table 11, pp. 1–47; 1990, *Statistical Abstract of the United States, 1996*, number 362, p. 227.

Documentation

Area measurements within the United States began with the country as a whole and developed, as mapping progressed, to measurements for the states. The annual report of the U.S. General Land Office for 1850 contained the first reference to the areas of the states and territories, although there was no indication of the method used in obtaining the measurements.

In 1881, as part of the 1880 Census of Population, the Bureau of the Census laid the foundation for accurate and detailed area measurement in the United States. For the first time an account was given of the method and maps employed, the water bodies included, and the outer limits of the United States used as a basis for measurement. As part of the 1940 Census, the Bureau published "Areas of the United States: 1940," presenting data on the total land and water areas of the states, counties, cities, and minor civil divisions. For reports of the 1950 and 1960 Censuses, adjustments in selected area figures were made for reasons of changes in boundaries, development of water reservoirs, or improvement in maps from which measurements are made.

Figures are as of the following dates: 1790 (August 2); 1800 (August 4); 1810 (August 6); 1820 (August 7); 1830–1900 (June 1); 1910 (April 15); 1920 (January 1), and 1930–1990 (April 1).

TABLE Cf8-64   Land area, by state and territory: 1790–1990

Contributed by Michelle L. Butler, Myron P. Gutmann, and Michael R. Haines

	United States	States													
		Alabama	Alaska	Arizona	Arkansas	California	Colorado	Connecticut	Delaware	District of Columbia	Florida	Georgia	Hawai'i	Idaho	Illinois
	Cf8	Cf9	Cf10	Cf11	Cf12	Cf13	Cf14	Cf15	Cf16	Cf17	Cf18	Cf19	Cf20	Cf21	Cf22
Year	Square miles	Square miles	Square miles	Square miles	Square miles	Square miles	Square miles	Square miles	Square miles	Square miles	Square miles	Square miles	Square miles	Square miles	Square miles
1790	867,980	—	—	—	—	—	—	4,820	1,965	—	—	145,196	—	—	—
1800	867,980	—	—	—	—	—	—	4,820	1,965	90	—	111,877	—	—	—
1810	1,685,865	—	—	—	—	—	—	4,820	1,965	90	—	58,725	—	—	192,381
1820	1,753,588	51,279	—	—	105,275	—	—	4,820	1,965	90	54,861	58,725	—	—	56,002
1830	1,753,588	51,279	—	—	52,525	—	—	4,820	1,965	90	54,861	58,725	—	—	56,002
1840	1,753,588	51,279	—	—	52,525	—	—	4,820	1,965	90	54,861	58,725	—	—	56,002
1850	2,944,337	51,279	—	—	52,525	155,900	—	4,820	1,965	58	54,861	58,725	—	—	56,002
1860	2,973,965	51,279	—	—	52,525	155,900	103,658	4,820	1,965	58	54,861	58,725	—	—	56,002
1870	2,973,965	51,279	—	113,840	52,525	155,900	103,658	4,820	1,965	58	54,861	58,725	—	83,360	56,002
1880	2,973,965	51,279	—	113,840	52,525	155,900	103,658	4,820	1,965	58	54,861	58,725	—	83,354	56,002

TABLE Cf8–64 Land area, by state and territory: 1790–1990 *Continued*

Year	United States	Alabama	Alaska	Arizona	Arkansas	California	Colorado	Connecticut	Delaware	District of Columbia	Florida	Georgia	Hawai'i	Idaho	Illinois
	Cf8	Cf9	Cf10	Cf11	Cf12	Cf13	Cf14	Cf15	Cf16	Cf17	Cf18	Cf19	Cf20	Cf21	Cf22
	Square miles	Square miles	Square miles	Square miles	Square miles	Square miles	Square miles	Square miles	Square miles	Square miles	Square miles	Square miles	Square miles	Square miles	Square miles
1890	2,973,965	51,279	—	113,840	52,525	155,900	103,658	4,820	1,965	58	54,861	58,725	—	83,354	56,002
1900	2,974,159	51,279	—	113,840	52,525	156,092	103,658	4,820	1,965	60	54,861	58,725	—	83,354	56,002
1910	2,973,890	51,279	—	113,810	52,525	155,652	103,658	4,820	1,965	60	54,861	58,725	—	83,354	56,043
1920	2,973,774	51,279	—	113,810	52,525	155,652	103,658	4,820	1,965	60	54,861	58,725	—	83,354	56,043
1930	2,973,776	51,279	—	113,810	52,525	155,652	103,658	4,820	1,965	62	54,861	58,725	—	83,354	56,043
1940	2,977,128	51,078	—	113,580	52,725	156,803	103,967	4,899	1,978	61	54,262	58,518	—	82,808	55,947
1950	2,974,726	51,078	—	113,575	52,675	156,740	103,922	4,899	1,978	61	54,262	58,483	—	82,769	55,935
1960	3,540,911	50,851	566,432	113,563	52,175	156,537	103,794	4,870	1,982	61	54,136	58,197	6,425	82,677	55,875
1970	3,536,855	50,708	566,432	113,417	51,945	156,361	103,766	4,862	1,982	61	54,090	58,073	6,425	82,677	55,748
1980	3,539,289	50,767	570,833	113,508	52,078	156,299	103,595	4,872	1,932	63	54,153	58,056	6,425	82,412	55,645
1990	3,536,338	50,750	570,374	113,642	52,075	155,973	103,729	4,845	1,955	61	53,997	57,919	6,423	82,751	55,593

Year	Indiana	Iowa	Kansas	Kentucky	Louisiana	Maine	Maryland	Massachusetts	Michigan	Minnesota	Mississippi	Missouri	Montana	Nebraska
	Cf23	Cf24	Cf25	Cf26	Cf27	Cf28	Cf29	Cf30	Cf31	Cf32	Cf33	Cf34	Cf35	Cf36
	Square miles	Square miles	Square miles	Square miles	Square miles	Square miles	Square miles	Square miles	Square miles	Square miles	Square miles	Square miles	Square miles	Square miles
1790	—	—	—	40,181	—	29,895	9,999	8,041	—	—	—	—	—	—
1800	252,084	—	—	40,181	—	29,895	9,941	8,041	—	—	33,319	—	—	—
1810	42,933	—	—	40,181	34,065	29,895	9,941	8,041	42,625	—	97,641	—	—	—
1820	35,885	—	—	40,181	45,409	29,895	9,941	8,041	186,052	—	46,362	65,618	—	—
1830	35,885	—	—	40,181	45,409	29,895	9,941	8,041	186,052	—	46,362	65,618	—	—
1840	35,885	191,656	—	40,181	45,409	29,895	9,941	8,041	57,480	—	46,362	68,727	—	—
1850	35,885	55,586	—	40,181	45,409	29,895	9,941	8,041	57,480	163,457	46,362	68,727	—	—
1860	35,885	55,586	81,774	40,181	45,409	29,895	9,941	8,039	57,480	80,858	46,362	68,727	—	118,915
1870	35,885	55,586	81,774	40,181	45,409	29,895	9,941	8,039	57,480	80,858	46,362	68,727	146,195	76,172
1880	35,885	55,586	81,774	40,181	45,409	29,895	9,941	8,039	57,480	80,858	46,362	68,727	146,201	76,172
1890	35,885	55,586	81,774	40,181	45,409	29,895	9,941	8,039	57,480	80,858	46,362	68,727	146,201	76,808
1900	35,885	55,586	81,774	40,181	45,409	29,895	9,941	8,039	57,480	80,858	46,362	68,727	146,201	76,808
1910	36,045	55,586	81,774	40,181	45,409	29,895	9,941	8,039	57,480	80,858	46,362	68,727	146,201	76,808
1920	36,045	55,586	81,774	40,181	45,409	29,895	9,941	8,039	57,480	80,858	46,362	68,727	146,131	76,808
1930	36,045	55,586	81,774	40,181	45,409	29,895	9,941	8,039	57,480	80,858	46,362	68,727	146,131	76,808
1940	36,205	55,986	82,113	40,109	45,177	31,040	9,887	7,907	57,022	80,009	47,420	69,270	146,316	76,653
1950	36,205	56,045	82,108	39,864	45,162	31,040	9,881	7,867	57,022	80,009	47,248	69,226	145,878	76,663
1960	36,189	56,043	82,056	39,851	45,131	30,933	9,891	7,833	56,817	79,289	47,358	69,046	145,603	76,522
1970	36,097	55,941	81,787	39,650	44,930	30,920	9,891	7,826	56,817	79,289	47,296	68,995	145,587	76,483
1980	35,932	55,965	81,778	39,669	44,521	30,995	9,837	7,824	56,954	79,548	47,233	68,945	145,388	76,644
1990	35,870	55,875	81,823	39,732	43,566	30,865	9,775	7,838	56,809	79,617	46,914	68,898	145,556	76,878

Year	Nevada	New Hampshire	New Jersey	New Mexico	New York	North Carolina	North Dakota	Ohio	Oklahoma	Oregon	Pennsylvania	Rhode Island	South Carolina	South Dakota
	Cf37	Cf38	Cf39	Cf40	Cf41	Cf42	Cf43	Cf44	Cf45	Cf46	Cf47	Cf48	Cf49	Cf50
	Square miles	Square miles	Square miles	Square miles	Square miles	Square miles	Square miles	Square miles	Square miles	Square miles	Square miles	Square miles	Square miles	Square miles
1790	—	9,031	7,514	—	47,652	48,740	—	—	—	—	44,832	1,067	30,495	—
1800	—	9,031	7,514	—	47,652	48,740	—	40,228	—	—	44,832	1,067	30,495	—
1810	—	9,031	7,514	—	47,652	48,740	—	40,228	—	—	44,832	1,067	30,495	—
1820	—	9,031	7,514	—	47,652	48,740	—	40,228	—	—	44,832	1,067	30,495	—
1830	—	9,031	7,514	—	47,652	48,740	—	40,228	—	—	44,832	1,067	30,495	—
1840	—	9,031	7,514	—	47,652	48,740	—	40,740	—	—	44,832	1,067	30,495	—
1850	—	9,031	7,514	236,548	47,652	48,740	—	40,740	—	282,257	44,832	1,067	30,495	—
1860	61,260	9,031	7,514	247,782	47,654	48,740	—	40,740	—	95,607	44,832	1,067	30,495	—
1870	109,821	9,031	7,514	122,503	47,654	48,740	—	40,740	—	95,607	44,832	1,067	30,495	—
1880	109,821	9,031	7,514	122,503	47,654	48,740	—	40,740	—	95,607	44,832	1,067	30,495	—

(continued)

TABLE Cf8–64   Land area, by state and territory: 1790–1990   *Continued*

Year	Nevada	New Hampshire	New Jersey	New Mexico	New York	North Carolina	North Dakota	Ohio	Oklahoma	Oregon	Pennsylvania	Rhode Island	South Carolina	South Dakota
	Cf37	Cf38	Cf39	Cf40	Cf41	Cf42	Cf43	Cf44	Cf45	Cf46	Cf47	Cf48	Cf49	Cf50
	Square miles	Square miles	Square miles	Square miles	Square miles	Square miles	Square miles	Square miles	Square miles	Square miles	Square miles	Square miles	Square miles	Square miles
1890	109,821	9,031	7,514	122,503	47,654	48,740	70,183	40,740	38,624	95,607	44,832	1,067	30,495	76,868
1900	109,821	9,031	7,514	122,503	47,654	48,740	70,183	40,740	38,624	95,607	44,832	1,067	30,495	76,868
1910	109,821	9,031	7,514	122,503	47,654	48,740	70,183	40,740	69,414	95,607	44,832	1,067	30,495	76,868
1920	109,821	9,031	7,514	122,503	47,654	48,740	70,183	40,740	69,414	95,607	44,832	1,067	30,495	76,868
1930	109,821	9,031	7,514	122,503	47,654	48,740	70,183	40,740	69,414	95,607	44,832	1,067	30,495	76,868
1940	109,802	9,024	7,522	121,511	47,929	49,142	70,054	41,122	69,283	96,350	45,045	1,058	30,594	76,536
1950	109,789	9,017	7,522	121,511	47,944	49,097	70,057	41,000	69,031	96,315	45,045	1,058	30,305	76,536
1960	109,889	9,033	7,532	121,445	47,869	48,880	69,280	41,018	68,983	96,209	45,025	1,049	30,280	75,956
1970	109,889	9,027	7,521	121,412	47,831	48,798	69,273	40,975	68,782	96,184	44,966	1,049	30,225	75,955
1980	109,894	8,993	7,468	121,335	47,377	48,843	69,300	41,004	68,655	96,184	44,888	1,055	30,203	75,952
1990	109,806	8,969	7,419	121,365	47,224	48,718	68,994	40,953	68,679	96,003	44,820	1,045	30,111	75,896

Year	Tennessee	Texas	Utah	Vermont	Virginia	Washington	West Virginia	Wisconsin	Wyoming	Indian and unorganized	Territory northwest of Ohio River	Territory south of Tennessee	Missouri	Dakota
													(Territories)	
	Cf51	Cf52	Cf53	Cf54	Cf55	Cf56	Cf57	Cf58	Cf59	Cf60	Cf61	Cf62	Cf63	Cf64
	Square miles	Square miles	Square miles	Square miles	Square miles	Square miles	Square miles	Square miles	Square miles	Square miles	Square miles	Square miles	Square miles	Square miles
1790	46,977	—	—	9,124	64,284	—	—	—	—	—	318,167	—	—	—
1800	41,687	—	—	9,124	64,252	—	—	—	—	—	25,855	5,290	—	—
1810	41,687	—	—	9,124	64,252	—	—	—	—	—	—	—	777,940	—
1820	41,687	—	—	9,124	64,252	—	—	—	—	—	—	—	608,565	—
1830	41,687	—	—	9,124	64,252	—	—	—	—	52,750	—	—	608,565	—
1840	41,687	—	—	9,124	64,252	—	—	82,643	—	511,967	—	—	—	—
1850	41,687	262,398	230,610	9,124	64,284	—	—	55,256	—	535,003	—	—	—	—
1860	41,687	262,398	122,887	9,124	64,284	183,254	—	55,256	—	69,414	—	—	—	312,094
1870	41,687	262,398	82,184	9,124	40,262	66,836	24,022	55,256	97,594	69,414	—	—	—	147,687
1880	41,687	262,398	82,184	9,124	40,262	66,836	24,022	55,256	97,594	69,414	—	—	—	147,687
1890	41,687	262,398	82,184	9,124	40,262	66,836	24,022	55,256	97,594	30,790	—	—	—	—
1900	41,687	262,398	82,184	9,124	40,262	66,836	24,022	55,256	97,594	30,790	—	—	—	—
1910	41,687	262,398	82,184	9,124	40,262	66,836	24,022	55,256	97,594	—	—	—	—	—
1920	41,687	262,398	82,184	9,124	40,262	66,836	24,022	55,256	97,548	—	—	—	—	—
1930	41,687	262,398	82,184	9,124	40,262	66,836	24,022	55,256	97,548	—	—	—	—	—
1940	41,961	263,644	82,346	9,278	39,899	66,977	24,090	54,715	97,506	—	—	—	—	—
1950	41,797	263,513	82,346	9,278	39,893	66,786	24,080	54,705	97,506	—	—	—	—	—
1960	41,366	262,970	82,381	9,274	39,841	66,663	24,084	54,466	97,281	—	—	—	—	—
1970	41,328	262,134	82,096	9,267	39,780	66,570	24,070	54,464	97,203	—	—	—	—	—
1980	41,155	262,017	82,073	9,273	39,704	66,511	24,119	54,426	96,989	—	—	—	—	—
1990	41,220	261,914	82,168	9,249	39,598	66,581	24,087	54,314	97,105	—	—	—	—	—

Sources

U.S. Bureau of the Census. 1790–1920, *Fourteenth Census of the United States: 1920*, vol. I, *Population*, Table 14; 1930, *Fifteenth Census of the United States, 1930*, volume I, *Population*, Table 7; 1940, *Sixteenth Census of the United States: 1940, Areas of the United States, 1940*, Table 1; 1950, *Census of Population: 1950*, volume II, *Characteristics of the Population*, part 1, U.S. Summary, Table 9; 1960, *Area Measurement Reports*, 1960, series GE-20; 1970, *U.S. Census of Population: 1970*, volume I, part 1, section 1, Table 11; 1980, *1980 Census of Population*, volume 1, *Characteristics of the Population*, Chapter A, part 1, Table 11, p. 1-47; 1990, *1990 Census of Population and Housing, Summary Population and Housing Characteristics, United States*, Table 8, p. 360.

Documentation

Area measurements were first conducted for the United States as a whole and gradually were extended to the individual states. The annual report of the U.S. General Land Office for 1850 contained the first reference to measurements of areas of states and territories. In 1881, as part of the 1880 Census of Population, the Bureau of the Census laid the foundation for accurate and detailed area measurement in the United States. For the first time, an account was given of the methods and maps employed, the bodies of water included, and the outer limits of the United States used as a basis for measurement.

Area measurements of the states and former territories rest on several periods of measurement. The first period is for the 1880 Census of Population when, under Henry Gannett, Census Geographer, "the foundation for accurate and detailed area measurement in the United States" was laid (Proudfoot, *Measurement of Geographic Area*, 1946, p. 27). The second period is for the 1940 Census when, under Batschelet and Proudfoot, a basic remeasurement of all the areas was accomplished, which still remains the basis for subsequent remeasurements. According to the 1940 definitions of land and water areas (used also in the 1960s), ponds, lakes, or similar areas were counted as inland water if their areas measured 40 acres or more; streams and canals had to be $\frac{1}{8}$ mile or more in width to be counted. All other areas were tabulated as land with the exception of "water other than inland water" such as the Great Lakes, coastal waters, bays, and so forth. The definitions

TABLE Cf8–64   Land area, by state and territory: 1790–1990   *Continued*

were based on maps, not on inspection of the surface of the earth. Accordingly, features such as new reservoirs that were not shown in the maps used in the measurement work were reported as land rather than water.

The third period was during the 1960s. In 1964 the Census Bureau undertook new area measurement of the areas of places with at least 1,000 inhabitants, minor civil division, and census county divisions of the 1960 Census. The results are published in *Area Measurement Reports*, series GE-20, a series of state reports, and a U.S. summary. The fourth period was in connection with the 1980 Census. For 1980, the areas of all states and counties were completely remeasured, using newer large-scale maps and more modern equipment. The land area results for these areas are published in *U.S. Census of Population: 1980*, volume 1, Chapter A Reports (Series PC80-1-A). Data for areas and selected minor civil divisions with a population of 2,500 and over, metropolitan areas, and urbanized areas, as well as for states and counties, are contained in a U.S. summary report.

Finally, for the 1990 Census, area measurements were calculated by computer based on the information contained in a single, consistent geographic database, the TIGER file (Topologically Integrated Geographic Encoding and Referencing System), rather than relying on historical, local, and manually calculated information. This especially affects water area figures reported in 1990; these had included only those bodies of water of at least 40 acres and those streams with a width of at least one-eighth of a statute mile from 1940 to 1980. Water area figures for 1990 increased because the data reflected all water recorded in the Census Bureau's geographic database, including coastal, Great Lakes, and territorial waters. The TIGER System is a joint project of the U.S. Census Bureau and the U.S. Geological Survey.

Remeasurements of land and water areas between and since those three periods occurred but they were largely in terms of adjusting the earlier figures because of relatively minor boundary changes or because of land and water changes resulting mainly from the construction of known dams and reservoirs.

The land areas shown for the United States, which are consistent with data available for states and territories, differ slightly from the figures shown in Table Aa1–5. The latter figures reflect adjustments made only at the national level.

TABLE Cf65–69   Acquisition of the public domain – land and water area and cost, by accession: 1781–1867

Contributed by Michelle L. Butler and Myron P. Gutmann

	Acquisition	Area			Cost
		Total	Land	Inland water	
	Cf65	Cf66	Cf67	Cf68	Cf69
Year(s)	—	Thousand acres	Thousand acres	Thousand acres	dollars
Total	—	1,837,763	1,807,682	30,081	85,079
1781–1802	State Cessions	236,826	233,416	3,410	6,200 [4]
1803 [1]	Louisiana Purchase	529,912	523,446	6,465	23,214
1819	Cession from Spain	46,145	43,343	2,802 [3]	6,674
1819	Red River Basin [2]	29,602	29,067	535	—
1846	Oregon Compromise	183,386	180,644	2,742	—
1848 [1]	Mexican Cession	338,681	334,479	4,202	16,295
1850	Purchase from Texas	78,927	78,843	84	15,496
1853	Gadsden Purchase	18,989	18,962	27	10,000
1867	Alaska Purchase	375,296	365,482	9,814	7,200

[1] The data for the Louisiana Purchase exclude areas eliminated by the Treaty of 1819 with Spain. Such areas are included in the figures for the Mexican Cession.

[2] Represents drainage basin of the Red River of the North, south of the 49th parallel. Authorities differ as to the method and exact date of its acquisition. Some hold it as part of the Louisiana Purchase; others maintain it was acquired from Great Britain.

[3] Includes 33,920 acres subsequently recognized as part of the State of Texas, which is not a public-domain state.

[4] Figure is only for the purchase of the Georgia cession in 1802 (59,689,920 acres); see Donaldson (1884).

Sources
U.S. Bureau of Land Management, Public Land Statistics, 1970, p. 4.

Series Cf69. 1781–1802: Thomas Donaldson, *The Public Domain, Its History, with Statistics*, 1884. Other years: U.S. Geological Survey, *Boundaries, Areas, Geographic Centers*, 1939.

Documentation
The U.S. government acquired sovereignty over its present area through a series of international agreements and treaties. However, the federal government did not gain title to all of the lands covered by such agreements; title to much of the land was retained by individual states and their political subdivisions or by private owners.

"Original public-domain land" embraces all of the area that title was vested in the U.S. government by virtue of its sovereignty. Any of the lands that the government has not disposed of under public-land laws are generally referred to as "public-domain lands."

In addition to public-domain lands, the federal government has acquired – by purchase, condemnation, and gift – tracts of land needed for various public purposes, such as sites for public buildings, defense installations, and natural resources conservation activities. Such lands are referred to as "acquired lands."

Series Cf66. Presents the original public-domain lands acquired from 1781 through 1867. During the period from 1781 through 1802, seven of the original thirteen states relinquished to the federal government, by acts of cession, their claims to what was then described as "western lands." Roughly, the western lands covered the area north of the Ohio River and east of the Mississippi River and the area embraced by the present states of Alabama and Mississippi. The State of Maryland ceded the present area of the District of Columbia in 1788. In 1850, the State of Texas sold its land outside its present boundaries to the United States. During the period from 1803 through 1867, title to the remaining area west of the Mississippi River (except the State of Texas) and to Florida passed to the federal government. With the exception of land in the District of Columbia, the total of 1,808 million acres of land is vested in the United States government as original public-domain land.

Series Cf67. Presents the areas of inland waters that were acquired with the original public-domain lands.

TABLE Cf70   Area of the public domain: 1802–2000

Contributed by Michelle L. Butler and Myron P. Gutmann

| | Public domain | | Public domain | | Public domain | | Public domain | | Public domain |
| | Cf70 | | Cf70 | | Cf70 | | Cf70 | | Cf70 |
Year	Thousand acres	Year	Thousand acres	Year	Thousand acres	Year	Thousand acres	Year	Thousand acres
1802	200,000 [1]	1961	767,766	1971	760,204	1981	730,816	1993	650,322
1850	1,200,000 [1]	1962	770,797	1972	760,676	1982	729,821	1994	676,615
1880	900,000 [1]	1963	769,903	1973	760,999	1983	732,042	1995	549,474
1912	600,000 [1]	1964	770,514	1974	760,532	1986	727,113	1996	563,129
1946	413,000 [1]	1965	765,797	1975	760,415	1987	724,066	1997	563,081
1950	412,000 [1]	1966	764,762	1976	762,192	1988	688,253	1998	654,885
1955	407,896	1967	760,364	1977	741,509	1989	662,158	1999	630,266
1958	408,553	1968	755,345	1978	775,249	1990	649,802	2000	635,355
1959	768,640	1969	762,514	1979	744,146	1991	649,346		
1960	771,512	1970	761,301	1980	719,522	1992	651,094		

[1] Estimated from limited data available.

Source

1802–1950, U.S. Bureau of Land Management; 1955–2000, *U.S. General Services Administration, Inventory Report on Real Property Owned by the United States throughout the World*, annual.

Documentation

This table presents the total of the public domain and acquired lands owned by the United States. It excludes any federally owned land outside the United States.

TABLE Cf71–78   Vacant lands and disposal of public lands: 1802–2001

Contributed by Michelle L. Butler and Myron P. Gutmann

	Vacant public lands	Land granted to states	All entries, selections, patents, certifications			Homestead entries		
			Original entries and selections	Final entries	Patents and certifications	Original entries		Final entries
						Number	Acreage	
	Cf71	Cf72	Cf73 [1]	Cf74	Cf75	Cf76	Cf77	Cf78
Fiscal year	Million acres	Thousand acres	Thousand acres	Thousand acres	Thousand acres	Number	Thousand acres	Thousand acres
1802	—	24	—	—	—	—	—	—
1803	—	793	—	—	—	—	—	—
1812	—	807	—	—	—	—	—	—
1816	—	740	—	—	—	—	—	—
1818	—	1,186	—	—	—	—	—	—
1819	—	986	—	—	—	—	—	—
1820	—	1,317	—	—	—	—	—	—
1823	—	92	—	—	—	—	—	—
1826	—	25	—	—	—	—	—	—
1827	—	46	—	—	—	—	—	—
1831	—	6	—	—	—	—	—	—
1832	—	24	—	—	—	—	—	—
1836	—	2,146	—	—	—	—	—	—
1841	—	7,807	—	—	—	—	—	—
1845	—	2,076	—	—	—	—	—	—
1846	—	1,081	—	—	—	—	—	—
1849	—	9,491	—	—	—	—	—	—
1850	—	55,401	—	—	—	—	—	—
1853	—	5,587	—	—	—	—	—	—
1855	—	46	—	—	—	—	—	—

Notes appear at end of table

TABLE Cf71-78   Vacant lands and disposal of public lands: 1802-2001   *Continued*

			All entries, selections, patents, certifications			Homestead entries		
	Vacant public lands	Land granted to states	Original entries and selections	Final entries	Patents and certifications	Original entries		Final entries
						Number	Acreage	
	Cf71	Cf72	Cf73 [1]	Cf74	Cf75	Cf76	Cf77	Cf78
Fiscal year	Million acres	Thousand acres	Thousand acres	Thousand acres	Thousand acres	Number	Thousand acres	Thousand acres
1857	—	2,974	—	—	—	—	—	—
1859	—	3,498	—	—	—	—	—	—
1861	—	3,052	—	—	—	—	—	—
1862	—	9,420	—	—	—	—	—	—
1863	—	—	—	—	—	8,223	—	—
1864	—	4,955	—	—	—	9,405	—	—
1865	—	—	—	—	—	8,924	—	—
1866	—	226	—	—	—	15,355	—	—
1867	—	4	—	—	—	16,957	—	—
1868	—	—	—	—	—	23,746	—	355
1869	—	—	6,678	—	—	25,628	—	504
1870	—	—	6,663	—	—	33,972	—	520
1871	—	—	7,119	—	—	39,768	—	629
1872	—	—	7,248	—	—	38,742	—	707
1873	—	—	6,386	—	—	31,561	—	1,225
1874	—	—	4,784	—	—	29,126	—	1,586
1875	—	3,842	3,792	—	—	20,668	—	2,069
1876	—	—	4,292	—	—	25,104	—	2,591
1877	—	—	3,495	—	—	18,675	—	2,408
1878	—	—	7,210	—	—	35,630	—	2,663
1879	—	—	8,724	—	—	41,005	—	2,071
1880	—	(Z)	9,152	—	—	47,293	—	1,938
1881	—	276	10,763	—	—	36,999	5,028	1,928
1882	—	—	13,999	—	—	45,331	6,348	2,219
1883	—	—	19,031	—	—	56,565	8,172	2,504
1884	—	46	26,834	—	—	54,982	7,832	2,946
1885	—	—	20,114	—	—	60,877	7,416	3,033
1886	—	—	20,992	—	—	61,688	9,145	2,664
1887	—	—	25,111	—	—	52,028	7,594	2,749
1888	—	(Z)	24,161	—	—	46,236	6,677	3,175
1889	—	15,367	17,026	—	—	42,183	6,029	3,682
1890	—	7,678	12,666	—	—	40,244	5,532	4,061
1891	—	(Z)	10,357	—	—	37,602	5,040	3,955
1892	—	8	13,567	—	—	55,113	7,716	3,260
1893	—	—	11,802	—	—	48,436	6,809	3,477
1894	—	8,470	10,377	—	—	56,632	8,047	2,930
1895	—	69	8,364	—	—	37,336	5,009	2,981
1896	—	—	13,174	—	—	36,548	4,831	2,790
1897	—	(Z)	7,754	—	—	33,250	4,452	2,778
1898	—	5,600	8,422	—	—	44,980	6,207	3,095
1899	—	50	9,091	—	—	45,776	6,178	3,134
1900	—	8	13,391	—	—	61,270	8,478	8,478
1901	—	—	15,453	—	—	68,648	9,497	5,241
1902	—	(Z)	19,372	—	—	98,829	14,033	4,343
1903	—	—	22,824	—	—	80,188	11,193	3,577
1904	474	20	16,332	—	—	69,175	10,171	3,233
1905	449	(Z)	17,057	—	—	70,844	12,896	3,419
1906	424	3,114	19,431	—	—	89,600	13,975	3,527
1907	406	(Z)	20,998	—	—	93,957	14,755	3,741
1908	387	16	19,090	—	—	87,057	13,586	4,243
1909	363	(Z)	19,893	—	—	75,445	12,302	3,699
1910	344	17,150	26,391	—	—	98,598	18,329	3,796
1911	327	—	19,211	—	—	70,720	17,639	4,620
1912	315	— [3]	14,575	—	—	52,991	13,624	4,306
1913	298	—	15,867	—	—	57,800	11,222	10,009
1914	291	—	16,523	—	—	62,229	12,117	9,291
1915	280	2	16,861	—	—	62,360	12,440	7,181
1916	255	4	18,708	—	—	65,282	13,628	7,278
1917	231	(Z)	16,202	—	—	58,896	12,021	8,497
1918	222	—	10,147	—	—	35,875	7,420	8,236
1919	213	—	11,871	—	—	39,341	10,204	6,525

Notes appear at end of table

(continued)

TABLE Cf 71–78   Vacant lands and disposal of public lands: 1802–2001   *Continued*

			All entries, selections, patents, certifications			Homestead entries		
	Vacant public lands	Land granted to states	Original entries and selections	Final entries	Patents and certifications	Original entries		Final entries
						Number	Acreage	
	Cf 71	Cf 72	Cf 73 [1]	Cf 74	Cf 75	Cf 76	Cf 77	Cf 78
Fiscal year	Million acres	Thousand acres	Thousand acres	Thousand acres	Thousand acres	Number	Thousand acres	Thousand acres
1920	200	—	16,437	9,778	13,327	48,532	13,511	8,373
1921	190	(Z)	15,632	8,772	10,930	43,813	13,662	7,727
1922	183	—	10,367	8,074	13,761	29,263	8,980	7,307
1923	186	—	6,415	6,201	10,352	18,942	5,524	5,594
1924	187	(Z)	4,564	5,229	9,082	13,886	3,873	4,791
1925	185	1	3,641	4,489	5,627	11,010	3,041	4,049
1926	196 [2]	—	3,243	3,962	4,600	10,354	2,875	3,451
1927	194	55	3,595	3,011	4,586	10,500	3,237	2,584
1928	194	252	3,726	2,168	2,519	10,429	3,367	1,816
1929	190	100	4,613	2,030	2,648	11,598	4,178	1,701
1930	179	1	5,435	1,577	2,253	12,708	4,723	1,371
1931	177	2	5,219	1,537	2,126	12,640	4,757	1,353
1932	173	77	4,552	1,333	2,013	10,639	3,914	1,210
1933	172	193	3,118	980	1,866	7,527	2,642	907
1934	166	3	3,585	1,225	1,362	7,507	2,787	1,124
1935	—	(Z)	1,759	1,772	1,610	3,297	1,166	1,640
1936	—	200	426	1,938	1,359	1,209	357	1,765
1937	—	1	125	2,026	2,184	561	111	1,915
1938	—	2	131	1,478	1,944	447	78	1,362
1939	—	—	302	1,198	1,982	378	66	1,089
1940	—	—	54	756	1,904	349	46	652
1941	172	—	76	491	1,039	400	51	390
1942	174	—	135	252	1,055	283	37	188
1943	169	—	63	168	637	211	29	102
1944	168	—	91	85	402	157	20	51
1945	170	—	40	61	217	182	22	35
1946	170	—	27	61	154	143	18	29
1947	170	—	76	53	403	474	55	26
1948	171	—	117	56	287	635	73	18
1949	170	—	134	116	390	681	82	40
1950	170	—	142	150	492	523	78	46
1951	174	—	121	198	388	363	49	63
1952	172	—	113	165	374	458	59	38
1953	171	—	310	177	364	482	61	39
1954	171	—	306	289	416	474	60	43
1955	170	—	251	250	539	482	60	37
1956	170	—	151	267	629	455	57	42
1957	169	—	180	279	561	662	79	66
1958	168	—	146	257	915	524	70	43
1959	438	104,569	303	280	850	1,181	147	42
1960	438	—	1,295	270	512	1,077	148	45
1961	441	—	2,211	451	482	615	77	57
1962	439	—	2,453	622	756	674	83	51
1963	437	—	880	254	835	383	46	57
1964	434	—	5,696	507	1,224	291	31	63
1965	428	—	2,403	220	768	182	22	30
1966	427	—	1,787	214	3,407	115	16	33
1967	426	—	474	942	1,622	51	7	23
1968	425	—	1,171	405	906	33	4	10
1969	417	—	319	264	821	26	4	8
1970	159	—	124	298	582	13	2	6
1971	159	—	48	104	334	7	1	5
1972	174	—	45	155	293	67	8	22
1973	173	—	132	430	566	32	3	6
1974	159	—	1,092	3,287	3,584	92	10	5
1975	159	—	11,762	728	807	13	2	4
1976	158	—	102,810	8,206	8,302	6	(Z)	4
1977	159	—	10,518	1,163	1,161	13	2	5
1978	159	—	860	1,365	108	0	0	1
1979	159	—	18,649	277	616	1	(Z)	1

Notes appear at end of table

TABLE Cf71–78   Vacant lands and disposal of public lands: 1802–2001   *Continued*

	Vacant public lands	Land granted to states	All entries, selections, patents, certifications			Homestead entries		
			Original entries and selections	Final entries	Patents and certifications	Original entries		Final entries
						Number	Acreage	
	Cf71	Cf72	Cf73 [1]	Cf74	Cf75	Cf76	Cf77	Cf78
Fiscal year	Million acres	Thousand acres	Thousand acres	Thousand acres	Thousand acres	Number	Thousand acres	Thousand acres
1980	158	—	1,167	175	2,495	1	(Z)	1
1981	159	—	1,311	340	1,258	12	1	2
1982	161	—	10,390	18,121	411	3	(Z)	1
1983	161	—	5,350	16,907	723	1	(Z)	1
1984	161	—	1,835	4,837	1,449	20	2	3
1985	161	—	1,404	6,491	4,217	4	1	2
1986	318	—	4	683	3,704	0	0	0
1987	317	—	1	1,812	3,000	0	0	0
1988	255	—	1	1,387	5,419	0	0	0
1989	254	—	1	579	780	0	0	0
1990	254	—	7	238	1,052	0	0	0
1991	251	—	1	436	476	0	0	0
1992	251	—	1	1,219	1,585	0	0	0
1993	250	—	0	819	1,460	0	0	0
1996	243	—	0	58	818	0	0	0
1997	242	—	0	36	537	5	(Z)	0
1998	242	—	0	13	547	0	0	0
1999	242	—	0	0	448	0	0	0
2000	242	—	0	0	285	0	0	0
2001	238	—	—	—	473	—	—	—

(Z) Series Cf77, through 1983: less than 500 acres. All other series and years: less than 1,000 acres.

[1] Figures for years before 1911 include some classes of final entries and patents.

[2] The increase in area over 1925 was reported as the result of a "special check" of field office records that was "used as a basis for a complete revision of the vacant land statistics."

[3] In 1912, there were grants of unsurveyed lands to Wisconsin for forestry purposes; area not determined.

Sources

Series Cf71. U.S. Bureau of Land Management, *Public Land Statistics* (*Annual Report of the Director* prior to 1962), annual issues, and unpublished data.

Series Cf72. U.S. Bureau of Land Management, *Annual Report of the Commissioner of the General Land Office, 1946, Statistical Appendix*, pp. 108–119, and *Public Land Statistics*, 1970, p. 7. See also *General Land Office Information Bulletin No. 1, 1939 series*.

Series Cf73–75. 1869–1919, U.S. Department of Commerce, Statistical Abstract of the United States, various issues, 1879–1919; 1920–2001, U.S. Bureau of Land Management, Public Land Statistics (*Annual Report of the Director* prior to 1962), annual issues.

Series Cf76. 1863–1883, Thomas Donaldson, *The Public Domain, Its History, with Statistics*, 1884, pp. 351–355 (reprinted 1970, Johnson Reprint Corporation); 1884–2000, U.S. Bureau of Land Management, *Public Land Statistics* (*Annual Report of the Director* prior to 1962), annual issues.

Series Cf77. 1881–1945, U.S. Department of Commerce, *Statistical Abstract of the United States*, various issues; 1946–2000, U.S. Bureau of Land Management, *Public Land Statistics* (*Annual Report of the Director* prior to 1962), annual issues.

Series Cf78. U.S. Department of the Interior, 1868–1940, *Annual Report of the Commissioner of the General Land Office, 1946*; 1941–1960, *Annual report of the Director, 1961 Statistical Appendix*; 1961–2000, *Public Land Statistics*, annual issues.

Documentation

Series Cf71. The vacant public lands of the United States are public-domain lands that are not reserved for any purpose other than for reclassification and are not covered by any non-Federal right or claim other than permits, leases, rights-of-way, or unreported mining claims. They are subject to acquisition by applicants under appropriate laws, such as the laws governing homesteads or grants to States. For the most part, entries and selections are made based on these laws. The Bureau of Land Management administers the public-land laws relating to such entries and elections, a function transferred to it from the General Land Office as a part of Reorganization Plan No. 3 of 1946 (U.S. Congress). Data prior to 1959 exclude Alaska.

Series Cf72. Includes grants for such public purposes as the following: educational, penal, and other public institutions and buildings; bridges, reservoirs, and other internal improvements; reclamation of swamp and arid lands; experiment stations; recreational areas; wildlife and forestry areas; military camps; and payment of bonds issued by local governments. It excludes 46,600,000 acres granted to states for aid in construction of railroads, wagon roads, canals, and so forth (see Table Cf83–87). It does not include acreage of swamplands lost to the states, for which the states received indemnity in cash.

Series Cf72. The data on land grants to the states for various public purposes are presented according to the calendar year in which Congress passed the granting legislation. Some variation in the series is possible because the language of some of the statutes, including that of amendatory legislation, offers alternatives in the selection of the year to which individual grants could be assigned. As with the land grants for the construction of canals and other transportation improvements (Table Cf83–87), many of these grants were satisfied through delivery of evidence of legal title throughout the years.

Series Cf73–74 and Cf76–78. These series were no longer reported separately in *Public Land Statistics* after 2000.

Series Cf73–75. The data on entries, selections, patents, and certifications refer to transactions that involve the disposal, under the public-land laws, including the homestead laws, of federal public-domain lands to non-federal owners. In general terms, original entries and selections are applications to secure title to public-domain lands that have been accepted as properly filed. Some types of applications are not reported until the final certificate is issued, and they are not included in series Cf73.

Series Cf73–75. Applications become final entries on issuance of a final certificate that is given to the applicant after he or she has complied fully with the requirements of the laws relating to his application. These requirements may include, in particular cases, settlement on and improvement of the lands entered, or payment of statutory fees or purchase money. A final

(continued)

TABLE Cf71–78   Vacant lands and disposal of public lands: 1802–2001 *Continued*

certificate passes equitable title to the land to the applicant. With respect to certain state selections, no final certificate is issued. Such cases are not included in series Cf74. Patents are instruments that pass legal title to the lands to the applicant. Certifications are issued in lieu of patents in connection with certain state selections.

Series Cf73–75. Data include disposals of lands in Alaska. The data do not include the area of certain lands that were granted to the states to aid in the support of common schools. Title to such lands usually passes to the states on survey of the lands by the federal government. Owing to legal complexities, detailed statistical records were not kept of these lands. Figures for 1970 and earlier published here have been subjected to minor adjustments to improve comparability. They have not been checked, however, for internal accuracy or for strict comparability that would require analysis of supporting records.

Series Cf76–77. Figures for original homestead entries exclude applications that were accepted for lands ceded by the Indians to the United States with the provision that proceeds from their disposal would be covered into the Treasury to the credit of the Indians. Detailed statistics on such homestead entries were not published in the reports of the Commissioner of the General Land Office prior to 1924. Such reports contain general information as to the disposal of ceded Indian lands. The records upon which the reports were based are for the most part on file in the National Archives.

Series Cf78. Acreage figures of final entries do not include commuted homesteads. A commuted homestead entry is a homestead entry not exceeding 160 acres in connection with which the entryman pays the minimum statutory price for the land in consideration for reduction in residence and other requirements. Only certain classes of homestead entries can be commuted.

TABLE Cf79–82   Public land sales – area and receipts: 1800–1860

Contributed by Gavin Wright

Year	Sales Cf79 Acres	Sold at auction Cf80 Acres	Mexican War military bounty land Cf81 Acres	Receipts from sales Cf82 Dollars	Year	Sales Cf79 Acres	Sold at auction Cf80 Acres	Mexican War military bounty land Cf81 Acres	Receipts from sales Cf82 Dollars
1800	640	—	—	—	1835	12,504,143	962,339	—	16,165,420
1801	676,979	—	—	—	1836	21,196,957	1,255,464	—	24,933,766
1803	167,552	—	—	—	1837	5,713,401	59,194	—	6,940,918
1804	479,816	—	—	—	1838	1,426,879	762,894	—	4,010,964
1805	434,112	—	—	—	1839	5,712,874	1,471,699	—	6,487,782
1806	269,742	—	—	427,281	1840	2,627,071	755,078	—	2,746,988
1807	100,062	—	—	215,788	1841	1,513,085	35,564	—	1,511,610
1808	184,630	—	—	2,071,469	1842	1,222,156	133,374	—	1,452,778
1809	247,507	—	—	534,855	1843	1,675,081	272,592	—	2,050,114
1810	249,216	—	—	394,251	1844	1,914,935	131,918	—	2,240,905
1811	515,644	—	—	464,741	1845	2,112,668	64,564	—	2,461,777
1812	318,339	—	—	739,013	1846	2,465,121	92,350	—	2,870,768
1813	483,257	—	—	2,357,107	1847	2,728,902	204,690	239,980	3,275,117
1814	1,079,515	—	—	2,541,829	1848	2,090,163	40,781	2,288,960	2,533,424
1815	1,447,352	—	—	2,171,893	1849	1,434,157	2,755	3,405,520	1,392,860
1816	1,372,563	—	—	3,639,804	1850	1,466,760	3,872	2,167,680	1,814,113
1817	1,158,199	—	—	5,082,980	1851	2,071,137	26,913	2,829,147	2,520,940
1818	1,505,612	—	—	13,608,901	1852	1,060,118	62,767	4,671,837	1,392,306
1819	991,297	—	—	8,980,456	1853	4,038,490	48,376	4,772,490	4,838,969
1820	503,881	—	—	1,736,216	1854	11,642,880	85,349	2,374,100	11,502,141
1821	985,601	252,732	—	1,279,022	1855	11,437,968	122,145	4,864,030	11,287,880
1822	803,470	95,364	—	1,017,353	1856	4,078,978	7,249	7,333,200	4,756,402
1823	621,570	125,249	—	807,360	1857	5,861,095	302,256	6,043,035	3,066,044
1824	1,185,068	181,568	—	1,589,283	1858	3,987,506	28,018	4,358,425	1,793,081
1825	1,009,607	102,568	—	1,292,332	1859	4,030,530	29,774	2,848,741	1,868,812
1826	900,928	98,475	—	1,129,798	1860	2,580,441	43,859	2,400,111	1,506,916
1827	1,106,481	144,279	—	1,404,985					
1828	973,947	98,445	—	1,219,263					
1829	1,725,359	133,453	—	2,162,844					
1830	1,912,979	139,841	—	2,408,756					
1831	2,672,162	274,368	—	3,365,744					
1832	2,246,942	44,067	—	2,802,822					
1833	3,254,313	376,500	—	4,173,071					
1834	4,623,970	625,097	—	6,063,575					

Sources

Series Cf79–81. Stephen Walter Schoene, "The Economics of U.S. Public Land Policy Prior to 1860" (Ph.D. dissertation, University of North Carolina, 1981).

Series Cf82. Arthur H. Cole, "Cyclical and Sectional Variations in the Sale of Public Lands," *Review of Economics and Statistics* 9 (January 1926): 41–53.

TABLE Cf79–82   Public land sales – area and receipts: 1800–1860   *Continued*

Documentation

Series Cf79–81. Drawing upon General Land Office documents in the National Archives, Schoene corrects earlier series published by Gates and Hibbard, putting them on a standard calendar-year basis. Hibbard reports a total of 1,281,860 acres sold prior to 1800: Benjamin Hibbard, *A History of the Public Land Policies* (University of Wisconsin Press, 1965; first published 1924), p. 100. See also Paul W. Gates, *A History of Public Land Law Development* (Public Land Law Review Commission, 1968).

Series Cf79–80. Public lands were offered at auction periodically, but the great majority of sales were "private" or post-auction sales, generally at the minimum price.

Series Cf81. "Mexican War Military Bounty Land" refers to warrants used to recruit troops for the Mexican War.

Series Cf82. Data prior to 1816 are incomplete, but derive from Cole's research in the General Land Office records. The superiority of Cole's series is emphasized by Schoene, on the grounds that alternatives rely on published Land Office figures, which are unreliable.

TABLE Cf83–87   Public land grants to aid the construction of railroads, wagon roads, canals, and river improvements: 1823–1871

Contributed by Michelle L. Butler and Myron P. Gutmann

Year	Total	Railroads	Wagon roads	Canals	River improvements
	Cf83	Cf84	Cf85	Cf86	Cf87
	Thousand acres	Thousand acres	Thousand acres	Thousand acres	Thousand acres
1823	49	—	49	—	—
1827	2,273	—	202	2,071	—
1828	1,338	—	—	938	400
1838	139	—	—	139	—
1847	1,845	840	—	—	1,005
1851	3,752	3,752	—	—	—
1852	1,773	1,773	—	—	—
1853	3,379	2,629	—	750	—
1856	14,085	14,085	—	—	—
1857	6,689	6,689	—	—	—
1863	31,401	30,877	524	—	—
1864	2,349	2,349	—	—	—
1865	42,794	41,452	941	401	—
1866	200	—	—	200	—
1867	25,173	23,535	1,538	100	—
1869	105	—	105	—	—
1870	129	129	—	—	—
1871	3,253	3,253	—	—	—

Source

U.S. Bureau of Land Management, *Annual Report of the Commissioner of the General Land Office, 1946, Statistical Appendix*, pp. 100–7.

Documentation

Figures include only the area of lands for which title passed to the grantee states and corporations. The exact extent of practically all of these grants was, owing to their terms, indeterminate at the time the Congress passed the granting acts. The procedures for the satisfaction of the grants generally required the grantees to submit lists of lands to which they requested evidence of legal title on the basis of the provisions of the authorizing legislation.

In this table, the areas shown in the instruments of title that were issued for each grant over the years were totaled and shown as of the fiscal year in which the grant was originally enacted, even though in certain instances grants were revived at a later date after the expiration of statutory time limits, while others were enlarged by subsequent legislation. Because the tabulation is based on instruments of title, the data do not reflect the area of those portions of grants that could not be satisfied under the law for various reasons or of those grants or portions of grants that were forfeited.

TABLE Cf88–94   Revenue from public-domain, revested, and acquired land: 1881–2001

Contributed by Michelle L. Butler and Myron P. Gutmann

Fiscal year	Total	Sales of public domain	Fees and commissions	Timber sales from O & C land and public domain	Mineral leases	Outer continental shelf leases	Miscellaneous
	Cf88	Cf89	Cf90	Cf91	Cf92	Cf93	Cf94
	Million dollars	Million dollars	Million dollars	Million dollars	Million dollars	Million dollars	Million dollars
1881	5.4	3.5	0.9	—	—	—	1.0
1882	8.4	6.6	1.1	—	—	—	0.6
1883	11.7	9.7	1.4	—	—	—	0.6
1884	12.8	10.3	1.5	—	—	—	0.9
1885	8.6	6.2	1.5	—	—	—	0.9
1886	9.0	5.8	1.7	—	—	—	1.6
1887	12.3	9.2	1.5	—	—	—	1.5
1888	13.5	11.2	1.5	—	—	—	0.8
1889	9.7	8.0	1.3	—	—	—	0.4
1890	7.8	6.3	1.1	—	—	—	0.3
1891	5.4	4.2	0.9	—	—	—	0.3
1892	4.9	3.3	1.1	—	—	—	0.5
1893	4.5	3.2	1.0	—	—	—	0.3
1894	2.8	1.7	1.0	—	—	—	0.1
1895	2.0	1.1	0.8	—	—	—	0.2
1896	2.1	1.1	0.8	—	—	—	0.3
1897	2.1	0.9	0.7	—	—	—	0.5
1898	2.3	1.3	0.9	—	—	—	0.1
1899	3.1	1.7	0.9	—	—	—	0.5
1900	4.4	2.9	1.2	—	—	—	0.3
1901	5.0	3.0	1.3	—	—	—	0.7
1902	6.3	4.1	1.7	—	—	—	0.4
1903	11.0	9.0	1.6	—	—	—	0.5
1904	9.3	7.4	1.3	—	—	—	0.5
1905	7.0	4.8	1.3	—	—	—	0.9
1906	7.6	4.9	1.6	—	—	—	1.1
1907	11.6	7.7	1.8	—	—	—	2.0
1908	12.7	9.8	1.7	—	—	—	1.2
1909	12.2	7.7	1.5	—	—	—	3.0
1910	11.5	6.3	2.0	—	—	—	3.1
1911	11.1	5.8	1.5	—	—	—	3.8
1912	10.0	5.4	1.2	—	—	—	3.3
1913	7.0	2.7	1.5	—	—	—	2.7
1914	6.1	2.6	1.7	—	—	—	1.9
1915	5.4	2.2	1.6	—	—	—	1.6
1916	5.4	1.8	1.7	—	—	—	2.0
1917	6.1	1.9	1.6	—	—	—	2.6
1918	5.4	2.1	1.2	—	—	—	2.2
1919	4.3	1.5	1.2	—	—	—	1.6
1920	6.1	2.0	1.6	—	—	—	2.6
1921	14.5	2.0	1.7	—	9.7	—	1.5
1922	11.8	0.9	1.1	—	8.8	—	1.0
1923	10.7	0.6	0.8	—	7.6	—	1.6
1924	16.4	0.6	0.7	—	13.6	—	1.5
1925	10.8	0.6	0.6	—	8.3	—	1.3
1926	11.4	0.7	0.4	—	8.4	—	1.9
1927	9.2	0.6	0.5	—	6.7	—	1.4
1928	6.7	0.4	0.4	—	4.7	—	1.2
1929	6.2	0.3	0.5	—	3.9	—	1.5
1930	6.8	0.4	0.4	—	4.7	—	1.2
1931	4.8	0.3	0.4	—	3.5	—	0.6
1932	4.1	0.2	0.3	—	3.2	—	0.4
1933	3.9	0.1	0.3	—	3.3	—	0.2
1934	4.0	0.1	0.3	—	3.2	—	0.5
1935	4.8	0.1	0.2	—	3.9	—	0.6
1936	5.2	0.1	0.1	—	4.4	—	0.6
1937	7.4	0.1	0.1	—	5.6	—	1.6
1938	8.4	0.1	0.1	—	6.5	—	1.7
1939	7.8	0.2	0.1	—	5.7	—	1.7

TABLE Cf88–94   Revenue from public-domain, revested, and acquired land: 1881–2001   *Continued*

Fiscal year	Total	Sales of public domain	Fees and commissions	Timber sales from O & C land and public domain	Mineral leases	Outer continental shelf leases	Miscellaneous
	Cf88	Cf89	Cf90	Cf91	Cf92	Cf93	Cf94
	Million dollars	Million dollars	Million dollars	Million dollars	Million dollars	Million dollars	Million dollars
1940	7.5	0.1	0.1	—	5.2	—	2.2
1941	8.7	0.2	0.1	—	5.7	—	2.8
1942	9.9	0.1	(Z)	—	6.9	—	2.8
1943	10.5	0.1	(Z)	—	7.2	—	3.2
1944	15.2	0.1	0.1	—	10.9	—	4.2
1945	14.1	0.2	0.1	—	10.1	—	3.9
1946	13.8	0.1	0.1	—	10.0	—	3.6
1947	21.0	0.1	0.1	3.0	15.1	—	2.6
1948	33.3	0.3	0.2	4.7	24.4	—	3.9
1949	37.1	0.5	0.3	3.9	29.0	—	3.5
1950	36.2	0.5	0.4	4.3	27.0	—	4.1
1951	49.1	0.5	0.4	7.8	35.0	—	5.5
1952	64.5	0.7	0.8	9.6	41.9	—	11.6
1953	66.8	1.0	0.4	13.8	43.5	—	8.0
1954	77.5	1.2	0.6	13.4	52.5	—	9.8
1955	239.5	1.9	0.7	25.0	60.0	142.4	9.6
1956	154.8	2.3	0.8	24.9	61.6	53.8	11.4
1957	112.1	3.4	1.0	21.4	72.3	2.2	11.7
1958	127.4	3.0	1.2	24.6	81.4	3.5	13.7
1959	136.7	4.2	1.3	31.8	83.5	3.4	12.5
1960	371.1	5.1	1.8	36.4	84.1	229.5	14.3
1961	159.2	4.3	2.5	32.1	89.2	7.3	23.9
1962	173.5	3.6	2.8	34.7	105.2	11.6	15.6
1963	530.7	3.4	3.0	33.6	102.6	366.8	21.3
1964	199.1	3.2	3.7	47.2	107.1	16.5	21.4
1965	234.4	3.1	3.8	44.9	107.3	53.5	21.9
1966	433.7	2.3	3.9	47.6	108.0	248.3	23.6
1967	821.5	2.6	3.3	47.1	110.2	637.3	21.1
1968	1,158.9	2.5	3.9	56.2	113.8	961.3	21.3
1969	651.1	1.8	4.9	69.7	123.3	428.3	23.1
1970	407.4	2.1	4.5	65.4	127.1	186.9	21.4
1971	1,287.9	2.0	4.1	70.7	135.2	1,050.5	25.3
1972	525.1	1.9	5.4	83.5	129.8	279.4	25.1
1973	4,230.1	1.8	6.8	104.6	133.4	3,955.6	27.9
1974	7,177.7	2.1	12.5	127.8	252.8	6,748.4	34.2
1975	2,919.6	20.3	18.3	108.2	302.6	2,428.0	42.3
1976	3,191.9	5.8	19.4	130.8	320.8	2,662.4	52.7
(TQ)	1,460.2	1.5	6.2	67.0	63.1	1,311.1	11.3
1977	3,008.1	2.8	26.8	235.3	315.1	2,373.0	55.0
1978	2,923.9	1.6	31.8	195.4	369.8	2,259.3	66.0
1979	4,052.0	9.2	39.7	218.2	446.0	3,276.4	62.4
1980	5,079.3	7.8	28.6	216.1	618.1	4,100.9	107.8
1981	11,279.4	4.8	43.8	215.7	738.8	10,138.0	138.2
1982	7,879.9	3.6	4.4	87.4	1,169.3	6,249.6	365.6
1983	1,188.2	11.5	2.3	106.9	886.2	—	181.3
1984	215.0	13.5	2.4	153.2	1.8	—	44.0
1985	227.2	12.4	2.0	137.6	1.6	—	73.5
1986	244.1	13.9	1.5	162.2	1.2	—	65.3
1987	219.6	8.3	1.7	152.7	1.2	—	55.7
1988	297.0	7.3	2.6	240.9	0.4	—	45.8
1989	312.8	15.2	2.6	253.3	3.0	—	38.8
1990	298.9	21.6	2.0	234.4	2.6	—	38.2
1991	236.0	18.5	1.8	168.0	7.6 [1]	—	40.1
1992	261.8	9.7	1.3	204.7	6.7	—	39.4
1993	265.6	11.5	1.3	150.7	61.9	—	40.1
1994	157.6	8.7	1.3	70.7	34.6	—	42.4
1995	125.9	14.2	1.2	45.5	25.8	—	39.2
1996	181.1	12.6	0.9	92.9	36.4	—	38.2
1997	179.3	19.4	1.0	82.6	37.2	—	39.1
1998	140.2	9.0	1.1	53.6	31.4	—	45.1
1999	170.6	22.0	0.9	65.5	49.9	—	32.3
2000	214.7	25.0	0.8	39.9	110.2	—	38.8
2001	185.9	78.1	0.8	16.8	55.3	—	34.9

Notes appear at end of table   (continued)

TABLE Cf88–94 Revenue from public-domain, revested, and acquired land: 1881–2001 *Continued*

(TQ) Transition quarter.

(Z) Less than $50,000.

[1] Includes mining claim and holding fees beginning 1991.

Sources

U.S. General Land Office, 1785–1939, *Annual Report of the Commissioner, 1946, Statistical Appendix*, Table 90; U.S. Bureau of Land Management, 1940–1946, *Annual Report of the Director, 1958, Statistical Appendix*, Table 116; 1947–1960, *Public Land Statistics, 1962*, Table 111; 1961–1970, *Public Land Statistics, 1970*, Table 112; 1971–1980, *Public Land Statistics, 1980*, Table 105, p. 163; 1981–1990, *Public Land Statistics, 1990*, Table 62, p. 112; 1991–2001, *Public Land Statistics*, annual. Total revenues for 1785–1880 are reported as $208.1 million by J. R. Mahoney, *Natural Resources Activity of the Federal Government*, Public Affairs Bulletin No. 76, Library of Congress, 1950.

Documentation

Figures are for fiscal years and represent the total receipts of the General Land Office and Bureau of Land Management (BLM) transferred to the Treasury. They include the relatively small receipts from land and resources in Alaska. They do not include the receipts that other government agencies realized from their operations on federal lands, although they do include some receipts from lands under the administration of such agencies. For example, mineral leases for public-domain lands within areas administered by the National Forest Service were issued by the General Land Office, which also collected the mineral rentals, royalties, and bonuses from such lands. Also, for 1935 through part of 1940, the General Land Office collected grazing fees for lands within grazing districts; and, for 1908 through the first half of 1913, it collected water-right charges in connection with the Bureau of Reclamation irrigation projects. Other examples of multiple jurisdiction exist.

Series Cf91. Excludes revenues from years prior to 1947, totaling $21.4 million, which are included in series Cf94. Annual data for years prior to 1947 are not available separately; cumulative totals are as follows (in million dollars): 1911–1920, 0.8; 1921–1930, 7.5; 1931–1940, 4.3; and 1941–1946, 8.8. O & C lands are those areas granted to the Oregon and California Railroad Company in 1866. Later the federal government repossessed this land because the terms of the grant were not carried out.

Series Cf92. From Act of February 25, 1920 (41Stat. 437; 20 U.S.C. 181 seq.). The collection and distribution responsibilities for receipts under this act were transferred to the Minerals Management Service (MMS) as of October 1, 1983. BLM has continued to collect oil and gas pipeline rights-of-way rents; rents, bonuses, and royalties from Bankhead-Jones lands and National Petroleum Reserve lands; and royalties due Oklahoma for the South Half of the Red River. The Mineral Leases column amounts have been changed for 1991 and subsequent years to include oil and gas receipts collected by BLM, some of which were previously reported under series Cf94. All other mineral and oil and gas receipts are collected and reported by MMS.

Series Cf94. Includes the sales of Indian lands, revenues from grazing, rental of land, and revenues from other miscellaneous sources.

TABLE Cf95–100 Grazing on public-domain land – receipts and usage: 1935–2002

Contributed by Michelle L. Butler and Myron P. Gutmann

	Receipts			Usage		
	Total	In grazing districts	Outside grazing districts	Total	Cattle and horses	Sheep and goats
	Cf95 [1]	Cf96	Cf97	Cf98 [2]	Cf99 [2,3]	Cf100 [2]
Fiscal year	Thousand dollars	Thousand dollars	Thousand dollars	Thousand animal-unit months	Thousand animal-unit months	Thousand animal-unit months
1935	1	1	—	6,507	—	—
1936	48	48	—	11,106	—	—
1937	488	415	73	14,383	—	—
1938	850	800	49	13,376	—	—
1939	1,038	886	152	13,789	—	—
1940	747	595	152	13,832	—	—
1941	1,113	922	191	15,369	—	—
1942	1,095	900	195	15,271	—	—
1943	979	785	194	15,061	—	—
1944	1,015	813	202	15,745	—	—
1945	996	765	231	15,572	—	—
1946	964	736	228	15,254	—	—
1947	1,046	819	221	14,993	9,195	5,798
1948	1,415	1,165	244	14,726	9,078	5,648
1949	1,239	1,060	173	14,522	9,117	5,405
1950	1,534	1,146	383	14,461	9,205	5,256
1951	1,694	1,382	306	14,331	9,211	5,120
1952	1,985	1,658	322	15,403	10,157	5,246
1953	2,095	1,764	328	15,780	10,483	5,297
1954	2,039	1,678	359	15,686	10,371	5,315
1955	2,219	1,879	339	15,367	10,186	5,181
1956	2,386	2,050	355	15,301	10,223	5,078
1957	2,286	1,902	384	14,661	9,725	4,936
1958	2,763	2,388	376	14,797	9,919	4,878
1959	3,228	2,713	515	14,750	9,898	4,852

Notes appear at end of table

TABLE Cf95–100   Grazing on public-domain land – receipts and usage: 1935–2002
Continued

	Receipts			Usage		
	Total	In grazing districts	Outside grazing districts	Total	Cattle and horses	Sheep and goats
	Cf95 [1]	Cf96	Cf97	Cf98 [2]	Cf99 [2, 3]	Cf100 [2]
Fiscal year	Thousand dollars	Thousand dollars	Thousand dollars	Thousand animal-unit months	Thousand animal-unit months	Thousand animal-unit months
1960	3,488	2,729	759	12,454	8,738	3,716
1961	2,982	2,311	671	12,097	8,478	3,619
1962	2,780	2,190	590	12,000	8,557	3,443
1963	3,772	3,355	418	12,051	8,710	3,341
1964	4,142	3,611	531	11,861	8,713	3,148
1965	3,990	3,467	523	11,773	8,830	2,943
1966	4,371	3,817	554	11,801	9,064	2,738
1967	4,287	3,718	569	11,635	8,948	2,686
1968	4,326	3,788	538	11,665	9,060	2,605
1969	5,257	4,663	594	11,238	8,821	2,416
1970	5,380	4,647	733	10,981	8,626	2,354
1971	7,151	6,223	928	10,287	8,235	2,052
1972	7,611	6,576	1,035	10,410	8,441	1,968
1973	8,831	7,680	1,151	10,383	8,598	1,785
1974	11,134	9,671	1,463	10,393	8,708	1,685
1975	11,134	9,585	1,549	10,239	8,686	1,553
1976	15,549	13,511	2,038	10,228	8,797	1,431
1977	16,800	14,300	2,500	9,094	7,855	1,239
1978	15,590	13,246	2,344	9,385	8,162	1,224
1979	18,976	16,190	2,786	9,173	8,024	1,149
1980	23,514	20,035	3,479	8,875	7,754	1,121
1981	24,009	20,599	3,410	10,483	9,045	1,438
1982	20,032	17,319	2,713	10,657	9,237	1,420
1983	16,067	13,901	2,166	10,336	8,938	1,398
1984	15,015	12,967 [4]	2,049	11,067	9,564	1,503
1985	14,190	12,189	2,001	11,218	9,805	1,413
1986	14,077	12,100	1,977	10,447	9,118	1,329
1987	13,803	11,892	1,911	11,178	9,659	1,518
1988	14,456	12,417	2,039	10,099	8,720	1,380
1989	17,183	14,720	2,463	11,043	9,654	1,389
1990	17,345	14,878	2,468	10,844	9,399	1,445
1991	18,122	15,571	2,550	9,602	8,409	1,193
1992	17,745	15,186	2,559	10,088	8,801	1,287
1993	16,693	14,165	2,527	9,758	8,547	1,211
1996	13,896	11,959	1,937	9,739	8,752	986
1997	14,103	11,704	1,826	9,445	8,460	985
1998	14,350	11,886	1,886	10,352	9,341	1,011
1999	14,023	11,581	1,864	10,088	9,122	964
2000	13,936	11,488	1,866	9,838	8,945	892
2001	13,156	10,766	1,848	9,436	8,600	836
2002	12,788	10,482	1,793	8,871	8,136	734

[1] Includes minor receipts from grazing on privately owned lands within grazing districts (Pierce Act) that were administered by the Bureau of Land Management.

[2] Beginning in 1960, data are for calendar years. From 1978, data are for grazing fee years, March 1 through the last day of February.

[3] Beginning in 1974, burros and mules are included in the figures for horses.

[4] Includes the data for Land Utilization Project (LUP) lands purchased by the federal government under Title III of the Bankhead-Jones Farm Tenant Act and subsequently transferred to the Department of the Interior.

Source
U.S. Bureau of Land Management, *Public Land Statistics* (*Annual Report of the Director*, prior to 1962), annual issues.

Documentation
Data on grazing exclude grazing on reclamation land, land utilization projects that are not part of a grazing district, O & C lands (see documentation for series Cf91), and Alaskan grazing. They include lands rented and sublet under the Pierce Act (43 U.S.C. 315M).

Grazing receipts are credited to the year received even though part of the period covered extends into the following year.

Series Cf98–100. The amount of grazing in districts includes free-use, crossing, and trailing permits in addition to regular paid use. Beginning in 1964, it does not include non-use permits or exchange-of-use permits for grazing district lands. Beginning in 1978, it does not include trailing permits. An animal-unit month represents the forage required to maintain five sheep, five goats, one horse, one cow, or four reindeer, all over six months of age, for a month.

TABLE Cf101–118   Land area, by use: 1850–1969   [Pre-1974 land use categories]

Contributed by Michelle L. Butler and Myron P. Gutmann

		Land in farms										Land not in farms					
			Cropland				Woodland										
Year	Total land area	Total	Total	Used for crops	Idle or in cover crops	Grassland pasture	Total	Pastured	Not pastured	Special uses and other uses	Special uses	Other uses	Total	Grazing	Forest land not used for grazing	Special uses and other uses	Special uses	Other uses
	Cf101	Cf102	Cf103	Cf104	Cf105	Cf106	Cf107	Cf108	Cf109	Cf110	Cf111	Cf112	Cf113	Cf114	Cf115	Cf116	Cf117	Cf118
	Million acres	Million acres	Million acres	Million acres	Million acres	Million acres	Million acres	Million acres	Million acres	Million acres	Million acres	Million acres	Million acres	Million acres	Million acres	Million acres	Million acres	Million acres
1850	1,884	294	113	—	—	—	181	—	—	—	—	—	1,590	—	—	—	—	—
1860	1,903	407	163	—	—	—	244	—	—	—	—	—	1,496	—	—	—	—	—
1870	1,903	408	189	—	—	—	219	—	—	—	—	—	1,495	—	—	—	—	—
1880	1,903	536	188	—	—	122	190	—	—	36	—	—	1,367	883	368	116	—	—
1890	1,903	623	248	—	—	144	190	—	—	41	—	—	1,280	818	344	118	—	—
1900	1,903	839	319	—	—	276	191	87	103	54	—	—	1,064	768	175	121	—	—
1910	1,903	879	347	324	23	284	191	98	93	57	—	—	1,024	739	162	123	—	—
1920	1,903	956	402	374	28	328	168	77	91	58	—	—	947	661	160	126	—	—
1925	1,903	924	391	365	26	331	144	77	67	58	—	—	979	646	203	130	—	—
1930	1,903	987	413	379	34	379	150	85	65	—	21	24	916	578	208	—	53	77
1935	1,903	1,055	416	375	41	410	185	108	77	44	—	—	848	533	184	131	—	—
1940	1,905	1,061	399	363	36	461	157	100	57	44	—	—	844	504	203	137	—	—
1945	1,905	1,142	403	379	24	529	166	95	71	—	20	24	763	428	186	—	76	73
1950	1,904	1,159	409	387	22	485	220	135	85	—	21	24	745	400	201	—	81	63
1954	1,904	1,158	399	380	19	526	197	121	76	—	13	23	746	353	238	—	87	68
1959	2,271	1,124	392	359	33	532	163	93	70	—	10	27	1,147	319	438	—	141	249
1964	2,266	1,110	387	335	52	547	146	82	64	—	9	21	1,156	293	443	—	158	262
1969	2,264	1,064	384	333	51	540	112	62	50	—	9	19	1,200	288	475	—	169	268

Sources

U.S. Department of Agriculture, 1850–1900, *Major Uses of the Land in the United States: Summary for 1954*, Agriculture Information Bulletin No. 168, 1957, pp. 36 and 37; 1910–1968, *Agricultural Statistics, 1972*, p. 506; 1969, *Major Uses of the Land in the United States, Summary for 1969*, Agricultural Economics Report No. 247.

These data are based on estimates from Department of Agriculture publications as follows: *Major Uses of Land and Water in the United States, Summary for 1954*, Agricultural Economics Report 149, 1968; *Major Uses of Land and Water in the United States: Summary for 1959*, Agricultural Economics Report No. 13, 1962; *Major Uses of Land in the United States*, Technical Bulletin No. 1082, and Supplement, *Basic Land Use Statistics, 1950*; *Inventory of Major Land Uses, United States, 1945*, Miscellaneous publication 663, 1948; *Pasture Land on Farms in the United States*, Bulletin No. 626, 1918; *Agricultural Yearbook, 1923, 1924*; and Natural Resources Board, *A Report on National Planning and Public Works*, 1934.

Documentation

The source separates "land in farms" from "land not in farms," a distinction no longer maintained in the source after 1969. The modern categories are presented in Table Cf119–134 for 1945–1997.

Total land area, as defined by the Census Bureau in 1940 and subsequent years, includes "dry land and land temporarily or partially covered by water, such as marshland, swamps and river flood plains . . . (except tidal flats) . . . streams, sloughs, estuaries, and canals less than 1/8 of a statute mile in width; and lakes, reservoirs, and ponds having less than 40 acres of area."

See also U.S. Bureau of the Census reports, *U.S. Census of Population*, volume 1, for 1920, 1930, 1940, 1950, and 1960; *Areas of the United States, 1940*; and *Area Measurement Reports* (for individual States, 1960 area), series GE-20, 1964–1967.

Series Cf102–112. Cropland used for crops includes cropland harvested, crop failure, and cultivated summer fallow. Cropland idle or in cover crops includes temporarily idle land as well as some poorer cropland abandoned for crop purposes and soil-improvement crops not harvested and not pastured. Grassland pasture includes cropland used only for pasture in the year indicated and all other non-forested pasture in farms. Farm woodland includes grazed or ungrazed farm wood lots or timber tracts, natural or planted, and cutover land with young growth, which has or will have value as wood or timber. Chaparral and woody shrubs are omitted. Special uses in farms include farmsteads, farm roads, and farm lanes. Other land in farms includes miscellaneous unclassified uses and wasteland.

Series Cf113–118. Nonfarm grazing land comprises the open grassland and shrub grazing lands and the woodland and forest area grazed. Nonfarm forest land not used for grazing excludes forested areas in parks, wildlife refuges, military areas, recreation sites, and arid woodland, brushland, and forest land used for grazing. Special uses not in farms includes urban areas, highways and roads, railroads, airports, parks and related recreational areas, wildlife refuges, and military reservations. Other nonfarm land includes various unclassified uses and unused areas such as desert, rock, swamp, and tundra.

TABLE Cf119–134 Land area, by use: 1945–1997 [1992 land use categories]

Contributed by Michelle L. Butler and Myron P. Gutmann

Year	Total U.S. land area Cf119	Cropland				Grassland pasture and range Cf124	Forest-use land			Special uses						Other land uses Cf134
		Total Cf120	Used for crops Cf121	Idle or in cover crops Cf122	Used for pasture Cf123		Total Cf125	Grazed Cf126	Not grazed Cf127	Total Cf128	Rural parks and wildlife areas Cf129	Urban areas Cf130	Defense and industrial areas Cf131	Rural transportation Cf132	Miscellaneous farmland Cf133	
	Thousand acres	Thousand acres	Thousand acres	Thousand acres	Thousand acres	Thousand acres	Thousand acres	Thousand acres	Thousand acres	Thousand acres	Thousand acres	Thousand acres	Thousand acres	Thousand acres	Thousand acres	Thousand acres
1945	1,905,362	450,693	363,163	40,081	47,448	659,498	601,717	345,000	256,717	100,031	22,580	15,012	24,762	22,607	15,071	93,423
1949	1,903,825	477,838	382,892	25,614	69,332	631,078	605,570	319,450	286,120	105,333	27,641	18,283	21,458	22,880	15,071	84,006
1954	1,903,825	465,327	380,542	18,715	66,070	632,417	615,384	301,253	314,131	110,198	27,504	18,561	27,395	24,494	12,244	80,499
1959	2,271,343	458,007	358,785	33,603	65,612	633,127	745,177	244,635	500,542	141,869	46,939	27,217	31,122	25,219	11,372	293,163
1964	2,266,273	444,196	335,145	51,632	57,419	640,439	731,775	224,520	507,255	173,157	75,510	29,268	31,880	25,987	10,512	276,706
1969	2,263,587	472,097	332,968	50,909	88,220	603,615	722,670	198,043	524,627	174,228	81,337	31,013	25,587	25,953	10,338	290,977
1974	2,263,587	465,084	361,340	21,008	82,736	597,833	718,177	179,419	538,758	181,709	87,466	34,851	25,041	26,318	8,067	300,784
1978	2,263,587	470,842	368,574	26,109	76,159	586,721	702,627	171,771	530,856	202,545	97,951	44,646	24,901	26,632	8,415	300,852
1982	2,265,147	469,286	382,755	21,498	65,033	596,664	655,280	158,000	497,280	319,921	211,020	50,182	23,951	26,733	8,035	223,996
1987	2,265,147	464,001	330,877	68,143	64,981	591,083	648,164	155,023	493,141	335,241	224,858	56,642	20,917	25,696	7,128	226,658
1992	2,263,254	460,044	337,553	55,684	66,807	591,176	648,046	145,494	502,552	339,549	228,849	58,910	20,478	25,235	6,206	224,439
1997	2,263,254	455,052	348,701	38,839	67,512	580,165	641,536	140,777	500,759	351,081	237,119	65,537	16,443	25,420	6,560	235,420

Source

U.S. Department of Agriculture (USDA), Economic Research Service, *Major Uses of Land in the United States*, issues for 1945–1997. Figures in the originally published data have been updated with corrections, to form a coherent, consistent set of series, using the 1992 categories. Data are available on the USDA Internet site.

Documentation

Some of the major categories in which these estimates differ from those published in previous Major Land Use (MLU) series reports include:

1. Published urban land use estimates for 1969 were based on U.S. Census of Population data for areas with at least 1,000 inhabitants. However, estimates for both previous years and subsequent years were based on a 2,500 population standard. Here, unpublished Economic Research Service (ERS) estimates have been substituted for those published in the 1969 MLU report.

2. The 1978 and 1982 MLU reports contained no urban land use data. Urban land was part of the other land uses category. Estimates for urban land use have been developed for those years, to fill the data gaps and enhance the value of the time series. Previously published data on other land uses have been adjusted to reflect the subtraction of urban land from this category.

3. In the forestland category for 1959, a 27 million acre overlap between forest cover and other land uses was counted entirely as forest land. To improve comparability, much of the 27 million acres of land in question has been subtracted from forestland and reallocated to other land uses.

Series Cf120. Includes five components: cropland harvested, crop failure, cultivated summer fallow, cropland used only for pasture, and idle cropland. Three of these components – cropland harvested, crop failure, and cultivated summer fallow – are collectively termed cropland used for crops, series Cf121.

Series Cf124. Consists of all open land used primarily for pasture and grazing. It includes shrub and brushland types of pasture and grazing land such as sagebrush and scattered mesquite, all tame and native grasses, legumes, and other forage. Grassland pasture and range are not always clearly distinguishable from other types of pasture and range.

Series Cf128. Includes areas in highway, road, and railroad rights-of-way and airports; federal and state parks, wilderness areas, and wildlife refuges; national defense and industrial uses; and urban areas. The 1992 value fails to equal the sum of series Cf129–133. This discrepancy exists in the source and can be traced to deviations for the states of Massachusetts, Connecticut, and New Jersey.

Series Cf129. Includes federal and state parks, wilderness areas, and wildlife refuges.

Series Cf130. Incorporated and unincorporated places of 2,500 population or more.

Series Cf132. Highways, roads, and railroad rights-of-way plus airport facilities.

Series Cf134. Includes miscellaneous special uses such as industrial and commercial sites in rural areas, cemeteries, golf courses, mining areas, quarry sites, marshes, swamps, sand dunes, bare rocks, deserts, tundra, and other unclassified land.

TABLE Cf135-144   Private and public land area, by use: 1920-1997

Contributed by Michelle L. Butler and Myron P. Gutmann

	Private land					Public land				
	Total	Cropland	Pasture and grazing land	Forest and woodland not grazed	Other land	Total	Cropland	Pasture and grazing land	Forest and woodland not grazed	Other land
	Cf135	Cf136	Cf137	Cf138	Cf139	Cf140	Cf141	Cf142	Cf143	Cf144
Year	Million acres	Million acres	Million acres	Million acres	Million acres	Million acres	Million acres	Million acres	Million acres	Million acres
1920	1,404	401	766	145	92	499	1	300	106	92
1930	1,409	411	745	168	85	494	2	297	105	90
1940	1,404	398	766	150	90	501	1	299	110	91
1945	1,396	401	748	156	91	509	2	304	109	94
1950	1,399	405	724	184	86	505	4	296	102	103
1954	1,399	396	704	211	88	505	3	296	103	103
1959	1,385	389	659	255	82	886	3	285	246	352
1964	1,378	384	660	253	81	888	3	262	254	369
1969	1,367	381	621	271	94	897	3	269	254	371
1974	1,367	462	400	433	72	897	3	198	315	381
1978	1,367	468	396	413	90	897	3	191	324	379
1982	1,380	466	406	406	102	885	3	191	315	376
1987	1,379	462	404	393	120	517	2	185	208	122
1992	1,417	457	405	410	142	846	3	186	327	333
1997	1,366	450	352	420	145	842	3	192	317	331

Sources

U.S. Department of Agriculture, Economic Research Service, 1920, unpublished data; 1930-1954, *Major Uses of Land in the United States: Summary for 1954*, Agricultural Information Bulletin 168, 1957; 1959, *Major Uses of Land and Water in the United States: Summary for 1959*, Agricultural Economics Report 13, 1962; 1964, *Major Uses of Land and Water in the United States: Summary for 1964*, Agricultural Economics Report 149, 1968; 1969, U.S. Department of Agriculture, Economic Research Service, *Major Uses of Land in the United States, 1969* issue; 1974, *Major Uses of Land in the United States: 1974*, Table 12, p. 21; 1978, *Major Uses of Land in the United States: 1978*, Table 12, p. 14; 1982, *Major Uses of Land in the United States: 1982*, Table 14, p. 14; 1987, *Major Uses of Land in the United States: 1987*, Table 14, p. 14; 1992, *Major Uses of Land in the United States, 1992*, Table 15, p. 19; 1997, *Major Uses of Land in the United States*, 1997, Table 17, p. 23.

Documentation

Private land is land held or owned by private individuals, groups, and corporations, and is generally used for private purposes. Indian lands held in trust and administered by the federal government for the benefit and use of groups or tribes of the Indian people are included in private land, as more than three fourths of this land is used directly for farming and grazing by Indian farmers and stockmen. Much of the rest is leased for farming and grazing to other farmers and ranchers and the proceeds go to the Indian owners.

Public land as used here is land owned or administered by federal, state, county, municipal, or other governments for common or public purposes such as highways, airports, national defense, flood control, water supply, forests, and parks. Public land frequently is used for farming and grazing by private parties under a system of permits or leases. However, most of it is dry, rough, rocky, swampy, or otherwise unsuited for farming. When used by individuals, public land is sometimes included in reporting statistics about acreages in farms. More often, when public land is used in common by several persons, it is not reported as in farms.

TABLE Cf145-155   Agricultural land drainage and irrigation – acreage, farms, and drainage projects: 1890-1992

Contributed by Michelle L. Butler and Myron P. Gutmann

	Drainage				Irrigation						
	Drainage on farms		Drainage projects		Total		Seventeen western states			All other states	
	Farms with artificial drainage	Acreage drained	Number	Acreage in drainage projects	Farms with irrigated land	Acreage irrigated	Farms with irrigated land	Land in irrigated farms	Acreage irrigated	Farms with irrigated land	Acreage irrigated
	Cf145	Cf146	Cf147	Cf148	Cf149	Cf150	Cf151	Cf152	Cf153	Cf154	Cf155
Year	Number	Thousand acres	Number	Thousand acres	Number	Thousand acres	Number	Thousand acres	Thousand acres	Number	Thousand acres
1890	—	—	—	—	—	3,717	54,136	—	3,632	—	85
1900	—	—	—	—	—	7,789	109,298	—	7,543	—	246
1910	—	—	—	—	—	11,667	159,801	—	11,259 [3]	—	408
1920	924,810	53,025	56,949	65,495	—	14,482	215,152	—	13,883 [3]	—	599
1930	651,172	44,524	67,927	84,408	—	14,689	258,463	77,083	14,086	—	603
1940	—	—	39,597	86,967	299,604	17,983	283,089	110,942	17,243	16,515	740
1945	—	—	—	—	288,195	20,539	270,629	—	19,431	17,566	1,108
1950	—	—	14,533	102,688 [2]	305,061	25,787	281,476	166,074	24,271	23,585	1,516
1954	—	—	—	—	320,236	29,552	279,896	188,898	26,971	40,340	2,581
1959	—	—	8,461 [1]	101,870 [1]	307,783	33,163	262,614	211,564	30,738	45,169	2,425

Notes appear at end of table

TABLE Cf145-155 Agricultural land drainage and irrigation – acreage, farms, and drainage projects: 1890-1992
Continued

	Drainage				Irrigation						
	Drainage on farms		Drainage projects		Total		Seventeen western states			All other states	
	Farms with artificial drainage	Acreage drained	Number	Acreage in drainage projects	Farms with irrigated land	Acreage irrigated	Farms with irrigated land	Land in irrigated farms	Acreage irrigated	Farms with irrigated land	Acreage irrigated
	Cf145	Cf146	Cf147	Cf148	Cf149	Cf150	Cf151	Cf152	Cf153	Cf154	Cf155
Year	Number	Thousand acres	Number	Thousand acres	Number	Thousand acres	Number	Thousand acres	Thousand acres	Number	Thousand acres
1964	—	—	—	—	297,387	37,056	23,304	226,334	33,208	64,347	3,848
1969	338,696	59,551	—	—	257,147	39,122	205,848	216,189	34,786	51,299	4,336
1974	225,818	42,784	—	—	236,733	41,243	192,846	208,792	36,648	43,877	4,595
1978	—	105,278	—	—	302,674	50,838	235,116	225,771	43,629	67,558	7,209
1982	—	—	—	—	278,277	49,002	216,623	153,210	41,284	61,654	7,718
1987	—	—	—	—	291,628	46,386	215,078	159,681	37,507	76,550	8,879
1992	—	—	—	—	279,357	49,404	149,351	143,289	32,053	130,006	17,351

[1] The census date for the Census of Drainage Projects is January 1, 1960.

[2] Data include 4,110,000 acres reported drained by irrigation organizations.

[3] Data were interpolated from the special censuses of irrigation organizations for 1910 and 1920.

Sources

U.S. Bureau of the Census. Series Cf145-148, 1920-1969, *1969 Census of Agriculture*, volume 6, *Drainage of Agricultural Lands*, 1969, p. x; series Cf145-146, 1974, *1974 Census of Agriculture*, volume 2, part 9, *Irrigation and Drainage on Farms*, p. II-4; 1978, *1978 Census of Agriculture*, volume 5, part 5, *Drainage of Agricultural Lands*, p. 4.

U.S. Bureau of the Census. Series Cf149-155. 1890-1954: *Irrigation of Agricultural Lands*, 1950, and 1959. 1959-1969: 1969 *Census of Agriculture*, volume 4, *Irrigation*, p. 2. 1974: *1974 Census of Agriculture*, volume 2, part 9, *Irrigation and Drainage on Farms*, p. I-12. 1978: 1978 *Census of Agriculture*, volume 4, *Irrigation*, pp. 14-16. 1982-1987: *1987 Census of Agriculture*, volume 3, part ,1 *Farm and Ranch Irrigation Survey (1988)*, pp. 1-2; 1992: *1992 Census of Agriculture*, volume 3, part 1, *Farm and Ranch Irrigation Survey (1994)*, pp. vii, 1-2.

Documentation

Drainage and irrigation are the two major reclamation means by which additional land can be brought under cultivation. Land that is drained greatly exceeds land that is irrigated in terms of acreage already developed. Drainage activities are concentrated in the North Central States and lower Mississippi Valley. Other highly drained areas are the Gulf Coast area of Texas, Southern Florida, and the Sacramento and San Joaquin River areas of California. Irrigation is practiced predominantly in the arid and semiarid areas of the West. In irrigated areas, particularly areas where water is applied by flooding or by furrows and ditches, drainage is necessary to carry away excess water.

The Bureau of the Census has collected drainage and irrigation statistics by means of three censuses: (1) The censuses of agriculture, which represent a direct enumeration of farms; (2) the special censuses of drainage projects; and (3) the special censuses of irrigation organizations. The censuses of agriculture have collected statistics on drainage on farms for 1920, 1930, and 1969, and statistics on irrigation on farms since 1890. The special censuses of drainage projects were taken decennially from 1920 to 1960 and collected information in only those states where projects existed. Changes in census procedures for collecting drainage project statistics have shifted the census year from 1969 to 1971 and limited the projects enumerated to publicly organized projects. The special censuses of irrigation organizations have been taken decennially since 1910 and collect information from irrigation organizations in those states where organizations exist. In addition, a special census of irrigation was taken in 1902; the statistics were published in 1904 in Bulletin 16 of the Census Bureau.

Series Cf145-146. Statistics were collected from all farms in the forty-eight states and the District of Columbia in the censuses of agriculture for 1920 and 1930. For 1969 and 1974, statistics were collected from all fifty states for farms with sales of $2,500 and more. In 1978, statistics were collected for all farms. Comparable data could not be found for series Cf145 after 1974 or for series Cf146 after 1978.

Series Cf147-148. The date of each special census of drainage projects was January 1 of the census year. The number of states covered in the five censuses of drainage projects taken between 1920 and 1960 has varied from census to census. The New England States, Pennsylvania, and West Virginia have never been included. The number of states included in each census is as follows: 1920, 34; 1930, 35; 1940, 38; 1950, 40; and 1960, 39. The special census of drainage projects has always been primarily a census of community or public drainage undertakings and of the larger private drainage undertakings. Variation in the methods employed and the scope of the census have had the most effect on the number of projects covered but have not greatly affected the comparability of other items. The major changes have been, beginning with 1950: (1) exclusion of projects of less than 500 acres, (2) elimination in the enumeration of numerous projects that had been taken over by a later project, and (3) the consolidation into a single report of undertakings under common management; and in 1960 the elimination of drainage undertakings required solely because of the irrigation of the land.

Series Cf149-155. For reasons of comparability, the irrigation data presented here are from the censuses of agriculture. In 1982 and 1987 the irrigation data are from the *1987 Census of Agriculture*, volume 3, part 1, *Farm and Ranch Irrigation Survey (1988)*. The data listed in 1987 were collected in 1988, and the data for 1982 were from 1984. In 1992 the irrigation data were collected in 1994 and published in the *1992 Census of Agriculture*, volume 3, part 1, *Farm and Ranch Irrigation Survey (1994)*.

Series Cf151-153. The seventeen Western states are Arizona, California, Colorado, Idaho, Kansas, Montana, Nebraska, Nevada, New Mexico, North Dakota, Oklahoma, Oregon, South Dakota, Texas, Utah, Washington, and Wyoming.

Series Cf154-155. For 1910-1930, data referred only to Louisiana and Arkansas. For 1940, 1945, and 1950, they referred to thirty-one states and the District of Columbia. The thirty-one states are Alabama, Arkansas, Connecticut, Delaware, Florida, Georgia, Illinois, Indiana, Iowa, Kentucky, Louisiana, Maine, Maryland, Massachusetts, Michigan, Minnesota, Mississippi, Missouri, New Hampshire, New Jersey, New York, North Carolina, Ohio, Pennsylvania, Rhode Island, South Carolina, Tennessee, Vermont, Virginia, West Virginia, and Wisconsin. In 1954, they referred to only the thirty-one states. In 1959, Hawai'i was included, and the series referred to thirty-two states. Alaska was included in 1964, and for 1964-1992, the series referred to all thirty-three other states.

TABLE Cf156–167   Estimated daily water use – irrigation, public utility, and self-supplied water: 1900–1990[1]

Contributed by Michelle L. Butler and Myron P. Gutmann

	Total water use		Irrigation		Public water utilities		Self-supplied					
							Rural domestic		Industrial and miscellaneous		Steam electric utilities	
	Total	Groundwater	Total	Groundwater	Total	Groundwater	Total	Groundwater	Total	Groundwater	Total	Groundwater
	Cf156	Cf157	Cf158	Cf159	Cf160	Cf161	Cf162	Cf163	Cf164	Cf165	Cf166	Cf167
Year	Billion gallons	Billion gallons	Billion gallons	Billion gallons	Billion gallons	Billion gallons	Billion gallons	Billion gallons	Billion gallons	Billion gallons	Billion gallons	Billion gallons
1900	40.19	7.28	20.19	2.22	3.00	1.05	2.00	1.60	10.00	2.40	5.00	0.01
1910	66.44	11.68	39.04	5.27	4.70	1.49	2.20	1.76	14.00	3.15	6.50	0.01
1920	91.54	15.78	55.94	8.17	6.00	1.79	2.40	1.94	18.00	3.87	9.20	0.01
1930	110.50	18.18	60.20	9.09	8.00	2.30	2.90	2.40	21.00	4.37	18.40	0.02
1940	136.43	22.56	71.03	11.22	10.10	2.82	3.10	2.64	29.00	5.86	23.20	0.02
1944	178.43	29.19	80.65	13.55	12.00	3.30	3.18	2.76	48.00	9.55	34.60	0.03
1945	170.46	28.33	83.06	14.12	12.00	3.28	3.20	2.78	41.00	8.12	31.20	0.03
1946	165.74	27.88	86.44	15.04	12.00	3.25	3.50	3.06	33.00	6.50	30.80	0.03
1950	202.70	35.19	100.00	19.80	14.10	3.78	4.60	4.09	38.10	7.47	45.90	0.05
1955	263.80	47.79	116.30	29.08	16.30	4.27	5.40	4.91	49.20	9.45	76.60	0.08
1958	299.26	54.02	127.52	32.78	19.72	5.12	5.76	5.31	56.40	10.72	89.86	0.09
1960	322.90	58.17	135.00	35.24	22.00	5.68	6.00	5.58	61.20	11.57	98.70	0.10
1961	334.72	60.46	138.54	36.60	22.71	5.88	6.12	5.70	64.22	12.14	103.13	0.14
1962	344.48	62.09	141.16	37.58	23.31	6.00	6.22	5.81	66.62	12.55	107.17	0.15
1963	352.18	63.04	142.86	38.18	23.80	6.04	6.30	5.91	68.40	12.80	110.82	0.11
1964	361.94	64.67	145.48	39.16	24.40	6.16	6.40	6.03	70.80	13.21	114.86	0.11
1965	269.62	48.57	110.85	30.04	23.74	5.96	4.08	3.86	46.41	8.63	84.54	0.08
1966	379.60	67.68	150.28	40.95	25.40	6.35	6.58	6.22	75.76	14.04	121.58	0.12
1967	387.50	69.08	152.46	41.76	25.80	6.42	6.66	6.31	78.32	14.47	124.26	0.12
1968	395.40	70.48	154.64	42.57	26.20	6.49	6.74	6.39	80.88	14.90	126.94	0.13
1969	403.30	71.87	156.82	43.39	26.60	6.56	6.82	6.47	83.44	15.32	129.62	0.13
1970	327.30	54.27	119.18	33.13	27.03	6.65	4.34	4.13	55.95	10.24	120.80	0.12
1975	420.00	83.00	140.00	57.00	29.00	11.00	4.90	3.90	44.40	10.58	130.00	1.40
1980	450.00	89.00	150.00	60.00	34.00	12.00	5.60	4.40	45.30	10.93	150.00	1.60
1985	399.00	74.00	137.00	45.70	36.50	14.60	7.79	6.27	30.47	6.73	186.61	0.61
1990	408.40	80.62	137.00	51.00	38.50	15.10	7.89	5.95	29.95	8.11	194.00	0.53

[1] Figures include Puerto Rico and the U.S. Virgin Islands beginning in 1975.

Sources

1900–1970, all series. U. S. Department of Commerce, Business and Defense Services Administration, *Water Use in the United States, 1900–1980*, March 1960, and Bureau of Domestic Commerce, Table 1, p. 2, unpublished data; 1975–1990, U.S. Department of the Interior, Geological Survey, *Estimated Use of Water, 1975, 1980, 1985*, and *1990*.

Series Cf156–157. 1975–1990, *Estimated Use of Water, 1975*, Table 10, p. 31. 1980, *Estimated Use of Water, 1980*, Table 15, p. 37. 1985, *Estimated Use of Water, 1985*, Table 23, p. 57. 1990, *Estimated Use of Water, 1990*, series Cf156, combined totals from Table 1, p. 9 and Table 4, p. 13; series Cf157, combined totals from Table 1, p. 9 and Table 8, p. 17.

Series Cf158–159. 1975–1990, *Estimated Use of Water, 1975*, Table 7, p. 25; 1980, *Estimated Use of Water, 1980*, Table 6, p. 19; 1985, *Estimated Use of Water, 1985*, Table 7, p. 23; 1990, *Estimated Use of Water, 1990*, Table 15, p. 35.

Series Cf160–161. 1975–1990, *Estimated Use of Water, 1975*, Table 5, p. 21; 1980, *Estimated Use of Water, 1980*, Table 2, p. 2; 1985, *Estimated Use of Water, 1985*, Table 1, p. 11; 1990, *Estimated Use of Water, 1990*, Table 9, p. 23.

Series Cf162–163. 1975–1990, *Estimated Use of Water, 1975*, Table 6, p. 23; 1980, *Estimated Use of Water, 1980*, Table 4, p. 15; 1985, *Estimated Use of Water, 1985*, combined totals from Table 3, p. 15 and Table 10, p. 29; 1990, *Estimated Use of Water, 1990*, combined totals from Table 11, p. 27 and Table 17, p. 39.

Series Cf164–167. 1975–1990, *Estimated Use of Water, 1975*, Table 8, p. 27; 1980, *Estimated Use of Water, 1980*, Table 7, p. 23; 1985: *Estimated Use of Water, 1985*; series Cf164–165, combined totals from Table 5, p. 19, Table 11, p. 31, and Table 13, p. 35; series Cf166–167, Table 15, p. 39; 1990, *Estimated Use of Water, 1990*; series Cf164–165, combined totals from Table 13, p. 31, Table 19, p. 43, and Table 21, p. 47; series Cf166–167, Table 23, p. 51.

Documentation

The estimates of water use from 1900 to 1970 are based on estimates developed initially in 1948 but revised on the basis of information available from federal surveys and censuses in 1954 and later years.

The year 1954 was used as a benchmark because of the availability of detailed data on water use during that year, such as the 1954 censuses of manufactures and mineral industries; Inventory of Major Public Water Utilities; Survey of Water Use in Steam Generation of Electric Power by Public Electric Utilities; and Survey of Water Use by the Department of Defense. Adjustments were also made after comparison with surveys of water use by the U.S. Geological Survey in 1950 and 1955, and studies of projections of water requirements by several river basin committees and state water survey commissions.

Series Cf158–159. For 1900–1970, figures equal the total take, including delivery losses but not including reservoir evaporation.

Series Cf162–163. For 1900–1970, includes rural farm and nonfarm household and garden use, and water for farm stock and dairies. For 1975–1990, includes domestic and livestock use of water.

Series Cf164–165. For 1900–1960, figures include manufacturing industries, mineral industries, rural commercial industries, air conditioning, resorts, hotels, motels, military and other state and federal agencies, and other miscellaneous uses. In 1970, they include manufacturing, mining and mineral processing, ordnance, and construction. In 1975, the figures include water use for fish farming, fish hatcheries, and log ponds. In 1980, they include, but are not limited to, steel, chemical and allied products, paper and allied products, mining, and petroleum refining. For 1975 and 1980, these figures came from the "other industrial" uses of water and did not include water used for thermoelectric utilities. The U.S. Geological Survey's *Estimated Use of Water* stopped using the "other industrial" category in 1985. For 1985 and 1990, the figures include commercial, industrial, and mining uses of water. The commercial category consists of water used in motels, hotels, restaurants, office buildings, other commercial facilities, and civilian and military institutions. Industrial includes water used in steel, chemical and allied products, paper and allied products, petroleum refining, and other industries.

THE ENVIRONMENT

Scott Farrow

TABLE Cf168–176   Government expenditures on natural resources and the environment: 1962–1999

Contributed by Scott Farrow

	Federal					State and local			
	Total	Water resources	Conservation and land management	Recreational resources	Pollution control and abatement	Natural resources	Parks and recreation	Sewerage	Solid waste management
	Cf168	Cf169	Cf170	Cf171	Cf172	Cf173	Cf174	Cf175	Cf176
Year	Million 1996 dollars	Million 1996 dollars	Million 1996 dollars	Million 1996 dollars	Million 1996 dollars	Million 1996 dollars	Million 1996 dollars	Million 1996 dollars	Million 1996 dollars
1962	8,989	5,673	1,530	668	308	—	—	—	—
1963	9,787	6,296	1,404	787	378	—	—	—	—
1964	10,129	6,260	1,401	874	501	—	—	—	—
1965	10,643	6,501	1,434	917	563	7,820	4,630	6,600	3,320
1966	11,116	6,966	1,247	861	646	8,340	4,870	6,990	3,520
1967	11,380	6,684	1,464	1,071	754	9,280	5,120	6,510	3,530
1968	11,361	6,251	1,529	1,228	947	9,390	5,360	6,580	3,730
1969	7,715	4,233	713	984	806	6,780	4,390	5,050	2,850
1970	10,547	5,210	1,294	1,249	1,321	9,390	6,500	7,470	4,300
1971	12,828	5,793	1,599	1,514	2,300	10,090	6,910	8,680	4,720
1972	13,328	6,122	1,398	1,622	2,401	9,810	7,290	10,250	5,000
1973	14,211	6,610	952	1,628	3,339	9,760	7,620	10,710	5,120
1974	15,557	6,008	404	1,761	5,557	9,990	8,060	11,140	5,240
1975	18,351	6,515	1,636	2,006	6,303	10,540	8,640	13,140	5,450
1976	19,348	6,482	1,454	2,052	7,251	11,020	9,130	14,040	5,440
1977	22,283	7,137	1,308	2,188	9,505	9,000	10,930	15,660	5,260
1978	22,772	7,114	2,134	2,919	8,221	8,770	10,930	14,800	5,660
1979	23,225	7,374	1,571	2,846	9,009	9,010	11,290	16,840	5,720
1980	24,295	7,404	1,829	2,940	9,660	9,660	11,430	17,340	5,820
1981	21,754	6,625	1,910	2,561	8,289	9,910	11,320	17,830	6,060
1982	19,620	5,959	1,636	2,166	7,565	9,920	11,320	16,320	6,230
1983	18,397	5,668	2,182	2,111	6,189	10,280	11,690	16,320	6,330
1984	17,627	5,697	1,823	2,213	5,661	10,390	11,670	16,130	6,590
1985	18,126	5,594	2,010	2,200	6,059	11,340	12,430	16,540	7,070
1986	18,110	5,366	1,843	2,009	6,415	12,040	13,490	17,670	7,750
1987	17,225	4,876	1,899	2,016	6,276	12,810	14,200	19,530	8,380
1988	18,210	5,029	2,729	2,086	6,024	12,770	15,050	20,360	9,160
1989	19,433	5,129	3,992	2,182	5,858	13,320	15,530	20,460	10,480
1990	19,743	5,087	4,107	2,169	5,976	14,250	16,560	21,170	11,720
1991	20,699	4,870	4,514	2,383	6,538	14,030	17,770	21,950	12,650
1992	21,804	4,964	4,988	2,589	6,628	14,210	17,130	22,150	13,120
1993	21,519	4,527	5,079	2,786	6,456	14,000	17,000	24,130	13,520
1994	21,900	4,678	5,375	2,728	6,307	14,570	17,370	22,520	14,620
1995	22,339	4,718	5,421	2,855	6,639	15,550	18,240	24,040	15,280
1996	21,524	4,539	5,396	2,673	6,182	15,820	19,140	24,670	14,700
1997	20,829	4,331	4,972	2,733	6,174	16,290	20,350	25,180	15,590
1998	21,627	4,510	5,310	2,894	6,228	16,960	21,690	24,870	15,630
1999	22,912	4,520	5,429	3,344	6,594	17,430	22,380	25,790	15,360

Source

The Council on Environmental Quality, "Environmental Quality Statistics," online update of *Environmental Quality*, annual: Tables 2.2 and 2.3.

Documentation

The federal data are tabulations of outlays that comprise the U.S. budget subfunction "300 Natural Resources and Environment," from the Budget of the United States Government, Office of Management and Budget, using implicit gross domestic product price deflators from the Bureau of Economic Analysis (April 2000). These price deflators are available in the source, and were also used to deflate the series on state and local expenditures. State and local data were updated from U.S. Bureau of the Census, "United States State and Local Government Finances." Additional precision is available in original source. Data for the transition quarter in 1976 are not included.

Series Cf168. The totals include other expenditures not listed separately.

TABLE Cf177–182 Environmental expenditures – governmental and private: 1972–1999

Contributed by Scott Farrow

	Total	Federal		State	Local	Private
		EPA	Non-EPA			
	Cf177	Cf178	Cf179	Cf180	Cf181	Cf182
Year	Million 1986 dollars	Million 1986 dollars	Million 1986 dollars	Million 1986 dollars	Million 1986 dollars	Million 1986 dollars
1972	26,481	978	87	1,542	7,673	16,201
1973	30,261	1,174	98	1,548	8,250	19,191
1974	33,614	1,636	1,129	1,612	8,996	20,241
1975	36,842	1,738	1,352	1,698	9,801	22,254
1976	41,572	2,348	1,507	1,769	10,376	25,572
1977	46,509	3,046	1,624	1,842	10,937	29,060
1978	50,482	3,423	1,713	1,916	11,542	31,887
1979	54,824	3,960	1,832	2,051	12,135	34,846
1980	57,969	4,574	1,932	2,230	12,857	36,376
1981	60,539	4,981	1,678	2,320	13,758	37,802
1982	61,237	5,155	1,712	2,343	14,624	37,403
1983	65,477	5,342	1,819	2,394	15,371	40,550
1984	69,925	5,591	1,861	2,546	16,155	43,772
1985	74,021	5,890	2,184	2,731	17,091	46,125
1986	80,046	6,240	2,605	2,967	18,301	49,933
1987	85,290	6,758	2,649	3,025	19,162	53,696
1988	88,490	7,118	2,863	3,061	19,733	55,715
1989	94,280	7,509	3,412	3,193	20,770	59,396
1990	99,850	7,865	3,865	3,313	21,779	63,027
1991	107,221	8,291	4,427	3,444	23,333	67,726
1992	113,123	8,432	5,591	3,558	24,678	70,864
1993	117,811	8,703	6,427	3,678	25,867	73,137
1994	120,510	8,944	7,256	3,788	26,868	73,654
1995	125,056	9,161	7,970	3,911	27,913	76,101
1996	129,368	9,386	8,648	4,030	28,909	78,395
1997	133,948	9,628	9,392	4,147	29,850	80,932
1998	139,507	9,879	10,146	4,269	30,879	84,333
1999	143,396	10,139	10,902	4,375	31,778	86,203

Source

U.S. Environmental Protection Agency, *Environmental Investments: The Cost of a Clean Environment*, Tables 8-12 and 8-12A (November 1990).

Documentation

These data represent estimates of direct regulatory implementation and compliance costs for the present level of implementation of environmental regulations. They are the out-of-pocket costs to those entities that implement control measures and undertake compliance activities. Capital costs are annualized at 7 percent. All governmental costs for program implementation and administration are listed as operating costs. For industry and some state and local expenditure information, the cost data are based on the survey of Pollution Abatement and Control Costs by the U.S. Department of Commerce, Bureau of Economic Analysis, as published in the *Survey of Current Business* and in annual Current Industrial Reports of the Bureau of the Census which also contain a breakdown of costs by major industry. The survey was discontinued in 1994, but an updated survey was carried out in 1999. Other data on state and local governments are based on U.S. Bureau of the Census reports, *Government Finances*; federal government budget documents; and special studies. Cost forecasts are based on the implementation of environmental laws up to and including the 1990 Clean Air Act Amendments.

TABLE Cf183–196 Precipitation chemistry, by region: 1985–1998

Contributed by Scott Farrow

	Eastern region							Western region						
	Levels in precipitation							Levels in precipitation						
	Acidity	Hydrogen ion	Sulfate ion	Nitrate ion	Ammonium ion	Calcium ion	Precipitation	Acidity	Hydrogen ion	Sulfate ion	Nitrate ion	Ammonium ion	Calcium ion	Precipitation
	Cf183	Cf184	Cf185	Cf186	Cf187	Cf188	Cf189	Cf190	Cf191	Cf192	Cf193	Cf194	Cf195	Cf196
Year	pH units	Micrograms per liter	Milligrams per liter	Milligrams per liter	Milligrams per liter	Milligrams per liter	Centimeters	pH Units	Micrograms per liter	Milligrams per liter	Milligrams per liter	Milligrams per liter	Milligrams per liter	Centimeters
1985	4.43	37.57	2.02	1.25	0.23	0.15	106.7	5.13	7.40	0.82	0.71	0.18	0.23	62.0
1986	4.42	38.16	2.14	1.30	0.24	0.13	102.2	5.18	6.57	0.78	0.68	0.17	0.19	72.4
1987	4.42	38.06	2.09	1.33	0.26	0.14	100.7	5.11	7.82	0.83	0.83	0.24	0.19	62.2
1988	4.43	37.05	2.14	1.33	0.21	0.17	95.9	5.10	7.93	0.93	0.83	0.16	0.27	56.6
1989	4.47	34.25	2.01	1.35	0.31	0.15	110.8	5.23	5.84	0.87	0.91	0.29	0.25	56.7
1990	4.49	32.71	1.80	1.18	0.27	0.12	122.6	5.21	6.22	0.80	0.87	0.29	0.22	66.2
1991	4.47	34.00	1.87	1.27	0.26	0.14	111.0	5.20	6.31	0.77	0.80	0.24	0.21	68.4
1992	4.49	32.04	1.77	1.22	0.25	0.12	108.4	5.23	5.86	0.77	0.83	0.28	0.18	65.1
1993	4.47	33.64	1.78	1.28	0.26	0.11	113.7	5.27	5.41	0.71	0.76	0.23	0.18	74.4
1994	4.48	33.07	1.71	1.24	0.28	0.13	111.9	5.07	8.53	0.76	0.92	0.28	0.20	62.0
1995	4.55	28.17	1.47	1.23	0.28	0.13	109.3	5.11	7.73	0.70	0.79	0.27	0.19	77.7
1996	4.55	28.01	1.49	1.22	0.28	0.14	123.0	5.15	6.99	0.70	0.86	0.29	0.21	74.5
1997	4.52	30.44	1.55	1.28	0.26	0.18	105.8	5.07	8.48	0.67	0.83	0.24	0.18	74.9
1998	4.54	28.80	1.60	1.26	0.30	0.13	110.2	5.10	7.92	0.68	0.82	0.26	0.18	75.6

Source

National Trends Network of the National Atmospheric Deposition Program (NADP), unpublished, as prepared for the Council on Environmental Quality, *Environmental Quality*, annual report.

Documentation

Data are from seventy-three sites in the eastern United States and thirty-nine sites in the western United States. Sites included are those where precipitation amounts are available for at least 90 percent of the summary period and at least 60 percent of the precipitation during the summary period is represented by valid samples. Data are available for individual sites starting in 1978 and can be found at the NADP Internet site.

TABLE Cf197–202 Concentrations of air pollutants: 1977–1999

Contributed by Scott Farrow

Year	Sulfur dioxide Cf197 Parts per million	Carbon monoxide Cf198 Parts per million	Ozone Cf199 Parts per million	Nitrogen dioxide Cf200 Parts per million	PM-10 particulates Cf201 Micrograms per cubic meter	Lead Cf202 Micrograms per cubic meter
1977	0.0133	10.9	0.152	0.026	—	1.35
1978	0.0128	10.5	0.156	0.027	—	1.26
1979	0.0125	10.1	0.141	0.026	—	1.06
1980	0.0112	9.3	0.143	0.024	—	0.73
1981	0.0108	8.9	0.131	0.023	—	0.59
1982	0.0100	8.2	0.127	0.022	—	0.50
1983	0.0098	8.2	0.144	0.022	—	0.40
1984	0.0099	8.1	0.128	0.023	—	0.36
1985	0.0092	7.3	0.127	0.023	—	0.25
1986	0.0091	7.3	0.122	0.022	—	0.16
1987	0.0089	6.7	0.124	0.021	—	0.16
1988	0.0089	6.4	0.133	0.022	32.2	0.12
1989	0.0087	6.4	0.116	0.021	31.7	0.09
1990	0.0081	5.9	0.113	0.020	29.4	0.09
1991	0.0078	5.6	0.114	0.020	29.1	0.07
1992	0.0073	5.2	0.106	0.019	26.8	0.06
1993	0.0071	4.9	0.108	0.019	26.0	0.05
1994	0.0068	5.1	0.108	0.020	26.0	0.05
1995	0.0056	4.5	0.113	0.019	24.9	0.04
1996	0.0056	4.2	0.106	0.019	23.9	0.04
1997	0.0054	3.9	0.105	0.018	23.8	0.04
1998	0.0053	3.8	0.110	0.018	23.7	0.04
1999	0.0052	3.7	0.107	0.018	23.9	0.04

Source

U.S. Environmental Protection Agency, Office of Air Quality Planning and Standards, *National Air Quality and Emissions Trends Report*, annual. Recent data may be found on the Environmental Protection Agency's Internet site.

Documentation

Data are national composite mean concentrations of the specified criteria air pollutant. Under 1970 amendments to the Clean Air Act of 1963, National Ambient Air Quality Standards (NAAQS) set maximum allowable concentrations for each pollutant. The six series here are for common air pollutants designated as "criteria" pollutants. The standards are as follows: sulfur dioxide, 0.03 parts per million (ppm); carbon monoxide, 9 ppm; ozone,

0.12 ppm; nitrogen dioxide, 0.053 ppm; PM-10, 50 micrograms per cubic meter ($\mu g/m^3$); and lead, 1.5 $\mu g/m^3$.

Data are composite averages from all sites. The number of sites varies by report year. The number of sites for 1977–1986 and 1987–1996 are listed respectively below, along with data computation details. Sulfur dioxide: 178 and 479 sites; annual arithmetic means. Nitrogen dioxide: 65 and 214 sites; annual arithmetic means. Carbon monoxide: 168 and 345 sites; arithmetic means of second maximum nonoverlapping 8-hour concentrations. Ozone: 238 and 600 sites; arithmetic means of second daily maximum 1-hour concentrations. Lead: 122 and 208 sites; arithmetic means of maximum quarterly measurements. PM-10 (particulate matter less than 10 μm in diameter): 0 and 900 sites; weighted annual arithmetic means.

TABLE Cf203–210 Emissions of air pollutants and carbon dioxide: 1940–2000

Contributed by Scott Farrow

Year	PM-10 particulate Cf203 Thousand tons	Lead Cf204 Tons	Sulfur dioxide Cf205 Thousand tons	Volatile organic compound Cf206 Thousand tons	Carbon monoxide Cf207 Thousand tons	Nitrogen oxides Cf208 Thousand tons	Carbon dioxide Cf209 Thousand metric tons	Carbon dioxide concentration Cf210 Parts per million
1940	15,957	—	19,952	17,161	93,616	7,374	506,732	—
1941	16,074	—	22,857	17,235	91,657	8,262	553,466	—
1942	16,192	—	24,541	16,358	92,449	8,389	592,489	—
1943	16,309	—	26,846	16,323	93,241	8,972	612,491	—
1944	16,427	—	27,092	16,539	94,033	9,455	652,733	—
1945	16,545	—	26,007	17,308	94,825	9,548	631,014	—
1946	16,663	—	23,297	20,549	95,617	9,993	608,629	—
1947	16,780	—	26,298	19,507	96,409	10,470	671,101	—
1948	16,898	—	24,284	19,349	97,202	9,985	699,510	—
1949	17,016	—	20,801	19,720	97,993	10,247	589,091	—

TABLE Cf203–210   Emissions of air pollutants and carbon dioxide: 1940–2000   *Continued*

	Emissions							Carbon dioxide concentration
	PM-10 particulate	Lead	Sulfur dioxide	Volatile organic compound	Carbon monoxide	Nitrogen oxides	Carbon dioxide	
	Cf203	Cf204	Cf205	Cf206	Cf207	Cf208	Cf209	Cf210
Year	Thousand tons	Tons	Thousand tons	Thousand tons	Thousand tons	Thousand tons	Thousand metric tons	Parts per million
1950	17,133	—	22,357	20,936	102,609	10,093	692,091	—
1951	16,976	—	21,477	20,398	99,285	10,535	712,885	—
1952	16,818	—	20,826	20,208	99,784	11,056	694,524	—
1953	16,661	—	20,920	21,258	100,283	11,104	711,090	—
1954	16,503	—	20,181	21,232	100,782	11,663	677,606	—
1955	16,345	—	20,883	21,973	101,281	11,563	742,731	—
1956	16,188	—	21,039	22,902	101,780	11,867	778,532	—
1957	16,031	—	21,272	22,784	102,279	12,248	771,873	—
1958	15,873	—	22,634	21,846	102,778	13,012	747,956	—
1959	15,715	—	22,654	22,703	103,278	13,486	778,480	316
1960	15,558	—	22,227	24,459	109,745	14,140	796,643	317
1961	15,286	—	22,142	24,584	106,207	13,809	799,075	317
1962	15,014	—	22,955	25,036	108,637	14,408	828,582	318
1963	14,742	—	25,133	27,062	111,067	15,100	872,512	319
1964	14,470	—	25,301	26,948	113,498	15,871	909,595	—
1965	14,198	—	26,750	27,630	115,928	16,579	944,815	320
1966	13,926	—	28,849	27,827	118,358	17,390	996,098	321
1967	13,654	—	28,493	28,209	120,788	17,635	1,035,509	322
1968	13,382	—	30,263	26,568	123,219	18,372	1,077,381	323
1969	13,110	—	30,961	26,764	125,649	18,847	1,128,385	324
1970	13,042	220,869	31,161	30,982	129,444	20,928	1,152,145	326
1971	11,335	243,415	29,686	30,039	129,491	21,559	1,159,217	326
1972	10,734	255,555	30,390	30,297	128,779	22,740	1,211,838	327
1973	10,237	223,686	31,754	29,873	125,935	23,529	1,259,274	330
1974	9,636	178,693	30,032	28,042	119,978	22,915	1,214,830	330
1975	7,671	159,659	28,011	26,079	116,757	22,632	1,164,477	331
1976	7,906	165,349	28,435	26,991	120,963	24,051	1,244,362	332
1977	7,739	152,467	28,623	27,426	120,868	24,808	1,248,602	334
1978	7,865	137,964	26,877	27,655	122,150	25,070	1,270,297	335
1979	7,571	116,786	26,941	27,161	118,475	24,716	1,274,776	337
1980	7,119	74,153	25,905	26,336	117,434	24,384	1,248,748	339
1981	6,605	58,884	24,612	24,956	114,396	24,211	1,204,805	340
1982	5,274	57,666	23,319	23,866	112,260	23,875	1,145,066	341
1983	6,021	49,232	22,807	25,078	117,675	23,639	1,149,186	343
1984	6,281	42,217	23,816	26,015	116,533	24,322	1,188,813	344
1985	3,662	22,890	23,658	24,428	117,013	23,198	1,208,060	346
1986	3,500	7,296	22,892	23,617	111,688	22,808	1,231,104	347
1987	3,504	6,840	22,675	23,470	110,798	23,068	1,263,787	349
1988	3,721	7,053	23,135	24,167	118,729	24,124	1,328,802	351
1989	3,502	5,468	23,293	22,513	106,439	23,893	1,337,681	353
1990	3,340	4,975	23,679	21,053	99,119	24,170	1,314,813	354
1991	3,253	4,169	23,044	21,249	101,797	24,338	1,313,745	356
1992	3,292	3,810	22,813	20,862	99,007	24,732	1,315,580	356
1993	3,174	3,916	22,474	21,099	99,791	25,116	1,392,124	357
1994	3,136	4,047	21,875	21,683	103,713	25,474	1,417,184	359
1995	3,165	3,929	19,189	20,918	94,058	25,051	1,417,701	361
1996	2,967	4,077	19,447	19,885	104,600	26,065	1,440,154	363
1997	2,974	4,137	19,939	20,285	105,466	26,357	1,491,763	364
1998	2,888	4,057	20,059	19,238	101,246	26,011	1,497,410	367
1999	2,900	4,199	19,349	19,399	102,356	24,971	1,499,846	368
2000	2,947	4,228	18,202	20,345	109,300	24,443	—	369

Sources

Series Cf203–208. U.S. Environmental Protection Agency, Office of Air Quality Planning and Standards, *National Air Quality and Emissions Trends Report, 2000*, Tables A-2 to A8; and *National Air Pollutant Emission Trends, 1990–1998*, Table 3-13.

Series Cf209. G. Marland, T. Boden, and R. J. Andres, "Global, Regional, and National CO₂ Emissions," in *Trends: A Compendium of Data on Global Change* (Carbon Dioxide Information Analysis Center, Oak Ridge National Laboratory, U.S. Department of Energy, 2002).

Series Cf210. C. D. Keeling, and T. P. Whorf, "Atmospheric CO₂ Records from Sites in the SIO Air Sampling Network," in *Trends: A Compendium of Data on Global Change* (Carbon Dioxide Information Analysis Center, Oak Ridge National Laboratory, U.S. Department of Energy, 2002).

Recent data for series Cf203–208 may be found at the U.S. Environmental Protection Agency's Internet site, and for series Cf209–210 at the Carbon Dioxide Information Analysis Center's Internet site.

(continued)

TABLE Cf203–210   Emissions of air pollutants and carbon dioxide: 1940–2000 *Continued*

Documentation

Series Cf203–208. These series cover criteria air pollutants (see the text for Table Cf197–202). Emission trend reports are made annually with a ten-year rolling average for estimated emissions. In 1985 the method for estimating particulate matter (PM-10) was changed, and the reported series now includes PM-10 from "fugitive dust" and other miscellaneous sources. Series

Cf203 maintains the narrower definition to preserve continuity. Sources of emissions for all pollutants are available in the data source.

Series Cf209. Values expressed as thousand metric tons of carbon. Estimates extend back to 1800 in the electronic source.

Series Cf210. Measurements from Mauna Loa, Hawai'i.

TABLE Cf211–216   Disposition of municipal solid waste: 1960–2000

Contributed by Scott Farrow

Year	Gross discards	Recovery for recycling	Recovery for composting	Net discards	Combustion	Discards to landfills
	Cf211	Cf212	Cf213	Cf214	Cf215	Cf216
	Million tons	Million tons	Million tons	Million tons	Million tons	Million tons
1960	88.1	5.6	(Z)	82.5	27.0	55.5
1970	121.1	8.0	(Z)	113.0	25.1	87.9
1980	151.6	14.5	(Z)	137.1	13.7	123.4
1990	205.2	29.0	4.2	172.0	31.9	140.1
1994	214.2	42.2	8.5	163.6	32.5	131.1
1995	211.4	45.3	9.6	156.5	35.5	120.9
1996	209.2	46.4	10.9	151.9	36.1	115.8
1997	216.4	47.3	12.1	156.3	36.7	119.6
1998	220.2	49.0	13.1	158.1	—	—
1999	231.0	50.1	14.7	166.2	—	132.1
2000	231.9	53.4	16.5	162.0	—	128.3

(Z) Less than 50,000 tons.

Source

U.S. Environmental Protection Agency, Office of Solid Waste and Emergency Response. *Characterization of Municipal Solid Waste in the United States*, annual.

Documentation

Discards include paper, glass, aluminum, nonaluminum metals, rubber, leather, textiles, wood, food, plastics, and yard waste as major categories.

Breakdowns for these categories for generation and recovery are available in the source. Selected individual years are available in revised annual updates.

Net discards equal gross discards less those recovered for recycling and composting. Net discards are disposed of in landfills or through combustion. Total combustion tonnage is no longer available as of the end of 1997, but combustion for energy recovery is now monitored.

TABLE Cf217–222   Inventory of nuclear waste and spent nuclear fuel: 1962–1997

Contributed by Scott Farrow

	Nuclear waste				Spent nuclear fuel	
	Low-level		High-level		Boiling-water reactors	Pressurized-water reactors
	Volume	Radioactivity	Volume	Radioactivity		
	Cf217	Cf218	Cf219	Cf220	Cf221	Cf222
Year	Thousand cubic meters	Million curies	Thousand cubic meters	Million curies	Metric tons	Metric tons
1962	2	—	—	—	—	—
1963	8	0.042	—	—	—	—
1964	20	0.204	—	—	—	—
1965	34	0.273	—	—	—	—
1966	49	0.355	—	—	—	—
1967	71	0.428	—	—	—	—
1968	91	0.529	—	—	—	—
1969	112	0.687	—	—	—	—
1970	138	0.855	—	—	—	—
1971	169	2.000	—	—	81	83
1972	208	2.287	—	—	226	183
1973	255	2.732	—	—	320	250
1974	309	2.754	—	—	562	458

TABLE Cf217–222   Inventory of nuclear waste and spent nuclear fuel: 1962–1997   *Continued*

	Nuclear waste				Spent nuclear fuel	
	Low-level		High-level		Boiling-water reactors	Pressurized-water reactors
	Volume	Radioactivity	Volume	Radioactivity		
	Cf217	Cf218	Cf219	Cf220	Cf221	Cf222
Year	Thousand cubic meters	Million curies	Thousand cubic meters	Million curies	Metric tons	Metric tons
1975	367	3.040	—	—	787	780
1976	442	3.268	—	—	1,085	1,181
1977	514	3.765	—	—	1,469	1,648
1978	593	4.383	—	—	1,852	2,346
1979	676	4.539	—	—	2,252	3,068
1980	768	4.547	329.7	1,362.6	2,872	3,686
1981	852	4.483	339.3	1,628.5	3,331	4,362
1982	929	4.568	342.0	1,369.4	3,688	5,002
1983	1,007	4.732	352.7	1,299.7	4,179	5,773
1984	1,083	4.954	363.5	1,355.2	4,677	6,614
1985	1,160	5.282	357.1	1,459.5	5,209	7,475
1986	1,213	5.059	365.9	1,419.0	5,667	8,472
1987	1,265	4.924	381.4	1,303.1	6,264	9,581
1988	1,306	4.793	384.9	1,206.7	6,799	10,697
1989	1,352	5.284	381.1	1,113.9	7,497	11,913
1990	1,387	4.979	372.3	1,050.8	8,130	13,417
1991	1,426	5.272	370.7	1,007.4	8,718	14,688
1992	1,476	5.708	370.7	1,081.2	9,413	16,284
1993	1,499	5.709	375.4	1,045.3	10,113	17,816
1994	1,524	5.841	354.8	958.8	10,788	19,024
1995	1,544	5.376	349.5	915.4	11,415	20,538
1996	1,551	5.020	347.3	894.8	12,105	22,148
1997	1,560	5.030	341.7	847.8	—	—

Source

U.S. Department of Energy, Office of Environmental Management, *Integrated Data Base Report: U.S. Spent Fuel and Radioactive Waste Inventories, Projections, and Characteristics*, annual.

Documentation

Volumes, radioactivity, and spent fuel are all expressed as cumulative inventories. Radioactivity data are calculated decayed values. For details, see the source.

High-level waste includes highly radioactive residue created by spent fuel reprocessing, mostly for defense purposes. Low-level waste (along with mill tailings and transuranic waste) represents a large share of the volume, but less than 1 percent of the U.S. total of radioactivity. Spent nuclear fuel refers to fuel rods that have been permanently withdrawn from a nuclear reactor because they can no longer efficiently sustain a nuclear chain reaction.

Series Cf217–220. Covers Department of Energy, Department of Defense, and commercial sites.

Series Cf221–222. Values expressed in terms of metric tons of initial heavy metal.

TABLE Cf223–227   Ambient water quality – percent of rivers and streams in violation of environmental standards: 1975–1997

Contributed by Scott Farrow

Year	Fecal coliform bacteria	Dissolved oxygen	Phosphorus	Dissolved cadmium	Dissolved lead
	Cf223	Cf224	Cf225	Cf226	Cf227
	Percent	Percent	Percent	Percent	Percent
1975	36	5	5	—	—
1976	32	6	5	—	—
1977	34	11	5	—	—
1978	35	5	5	—	—
1979	34	4	3	4	13
1980	31	5	4	1	5
1981	30	4	4	1	3
1982	33	5	3	1	2
1983	34	4	3	1	5
1984	30	3	4	(Z)	(Z)

Note appears at end of table   (continued)

TABLE Cf223–227   Ambient water quality – percent of rivers and streams in violation of environmental standards: 1975–1997   *Continued*

Year	Fecal coliform bacteria Cf223 Percent	Dissolved oxygen Cf224 Percent	Phosphorus Cf225 Percent	Dissolved cadmium Cf226 Percent	Dissolved lead Cf227 Percent
1985	28	3	3	(Z)	(Z)
1986	24	3	3	(Z)	(Z)
1987	23	2	3	(Z)	(Z)
1988	22	2	4	(Z)	(Z)
1989	30	3	2	(Z)	(Z)
1990	26	2	3	(Z)	(Z)
1991	15	2	2	(Z)	(Z)
1992	28	2	2	(Z)	(Z)
1993	31	(Z)	2	—	—
1994	28	2	2	—	—
1995	35	1	4	—	—
1996	—	1	1	(Z)	(Z)
1997	—	1	2	(Z)	(Z)

(Z) Less than 0.5 percent.

Source

Council on Environmental Quality, *President's Annual Report on Environmental Quality*, annual, as derived from U.S. Geological Survey national-level data.

Documentation

Violation levels are based on the following U.S. Environmental Protection Agency (EPA) water quality criteria: fecal coliform bacteria, above 200 cells per 100 milliliters; dissolved oxygen, below 5 milligrams (mg) per liter; phosphorus, above 1.0 mg per liter; dissolved cadmium, above 10 micrograms (µg) per liter; and dissolved lead, above 50 µg per liter.

Large amounts of site-specific water quality information are available in Storage and Retrieval System for Water and Biological Monitoring Data (STORET) at the EPA's Internet site.

TABLE Cf228–235   Shellfish bed closures, by region: 1966–1995

Contributed by Scott Farrow

Year	North Atlantic Number Cf228 Thousand acres	North Atlantic Percent Cf229 Percent	South Atlantic Number Cf230 Thousand acres	South Atlantic Percent Cf231 Percent	Gulf of Mexico Number Cf232 Thousand acres	Gulf of Mexico Percent Cf233 Percent	Pacific coast Number Cf234 Thousand acres	Pacific coast Percent Cf235 Percent
1966	443	9	790	29	524	21	3	—
1971	710	10	1,702	35	592	10	317	—
1974	711	10	1,897	39	829	14	317	—
1980	782	11	878	18	889	15	318	—
1985	709	11	613	22	1,649	24	313	57
1990	1,125	14	631	21	2,406	34	202	31
1995	1,067	11	590	15	1,015	13	129	31

Source

U.S. National Oceanic and Atmospheric Administration, National Ocean Survey, Office of Ocean Resources Conservation and Assessment, Strategic Environmental Assessments Division, *The 1995 National Shellfish Register of Classified Growing Waters* (1997), and earlier reports in this series.

Documentation

Data refer to classified shellfish beds. The total acreage of classified shellfish-growing waters varies with each report. Percentages refer to the percent of classified shellfish-growing water closed in each region. There may be several reasons why shellfish harvest is prohibited, including water quality problems, lack of funding for complete surveying and monitoring, conservation measures, and other management or administrative actions.

Regions are organized by bay or estuary as follows.

The North Atlantic region consists of Passamaquoddy Bay, Englishman Bay, Narraguagus Bay, Blue Hill Bay, Penobscot Bay, Muscongus Bay, Sheepscot Bay, Casco Bay, Saco Bay, Merrimack River, Massachusetts Bay, and Cape Cod Bay.

The Middle Atlantic region consists of Buzzards Bay, Narragansett Bay, Gardiners Bay, Long Island Sound, Great South Bay, Hudson River/Raritan Bay, Barnegat Bay, New Jersey Inland Bays, Delaware Bay, Delaware Inland Bays, Chincoteague Bay, and Chesapeake Bay.

The South Atlantic region consists of Albemarle/Pamlico Sounds, Bogue Sound, New River, Cape Fear River, Winyeh Bay, North Santee/South Santee Rivers, Charleston Harbor, St. Helena Sound, Broad River, Savannah River, Ossabaw Sound, St. Catherines/Sapelo Sounds, Altamaha River, St. Andrews/St. Simons Sounds, St. Marys River/Cumberland Sound, St. Johns River, Indian River, and Biscayne Bay.

The Gulf of Mexico Region includes Florida Bay, South Ten Thousand Islands, North Ten Thousand Islands, Rookery Bay, Charlotte Harbor, Sarasota Bay, Tampa Bay, Suwannee River, Apalachee Bay, Apalachicola Bay, St. Andrews Bay, Choctawahatchee Bay, Pensacola Bay, Perdido Bay, Mobile Bay, Mississippi Sound, Breton/Chandeleur Sounds, Mississippi River, Barataria Bay, Terrebonne/Timbalier Bays, Atchafalaya/Vermilion Bays, Calcasieu Lake, Sabine Lake, Galveston Bay, Brazos River, Matagorda Bay, San Antonio Bay, Aransas Bay, Corpus Christi Bay, Upper Laguna Madre, Lower Laguna Madre, and the Rio Grande River.

The Pacific Coast Region includes the Tijuana Estuary, San Diego Bay, Mission Bay, Newport Bay, San Pedro Bay, Santa Monica Bay, Morro Bay, Monterey Bay, San Francisco Bay, Drake's Estero, Tomales Bay, Eel River, Humboldt Bay, Klamath River, Rogue River, Coos Bay, Umpqua River, Siuslaw River, Alsea River, Yaquina Bay, Siletz Bay, Netarts Bay, Tillamook Bay, Nehalem River, Columbia River, Willapa Bay, Grays Harbor, and Puget Sound.

TABLE Cf236–237   Oil spills in and around U.S. waters: 1970–2000

Contributed by Scott Farrow

	Incidents	Volume of oil		Incidents	Volume of oil
	Cf236	Cf237		Cf236	Cf237
Year	Number	Thousand gallons	Year	Number	Thousand gallons
1970	3,711	15,253	1990	8,177	7,915
1971	8,736	8,840	1991	8,569	1,876
1972	9,931	18,806	1992	9,491	1,876
1973	9,014	15,254	1993	8,972	2,067
1974	9,999	15,699	1994	8,960	2,489
1975	9,292	21,520	1995	9,038	2,638
1976	9,422	18,518	1996	9,335	3,118
1977	9,459	8,189	1997	8,624	943
1978	10,644	10,864	1998	8,315	885
1979	9,834	20,894	1999	8,539	1,172
1980	8,383	12,597	2000	8,354	1,431
1981	7,811	8,921			
1982	7,484	10,345			
1983	7,916	8,380			
1984	8,258	18,006			
1985	6,169	8,436			
1986	4,993	4,282			
1987	4,841	3,609			
1988	4,998	6,586			
1989	6,613	13,479			

Source

U.S. Coast Guard, *Pollution Incidents in and around U.S. Waters: A Spill/Release Compendium*, updated annually.

Documentation

Includes oil spills in and around U.S. waters for vessels and nonvessel facilities such as pipelines and other, sometimes unknown, sources.

TABLE Cf238–262   Contaminants in herring gull eggs in the Great Lakes: 1974–1999

Contributed by Scott Farrow

	Lake Superior					Lake Michigan					Lake Huron		
	DDE	Dieldrin	Mirex	HCB	PCB	DDE	Dieldrin	Mirex	HCB	PCB	DDE	Dieldrin	Mirex
	Cf238	Cf239	Cf240	Cf241	Cf242	Cf243	Cf244	Cf245	Cf246	Cf247	Cf248	Cf249	Cf250
Year	Parts per million	Parts per million	Parts per million	Parts per million	Parts per million	Parts per million	Parts per million	Parts per million	Parts per million	Parts per million	Parts per million	Parts per million	Parts per million
1974	16.59	0.51	1.04	0.26	62.08	—	—	—	—	—	17.40	0.50	1.34
1975	23.10	0.38	0.96	0.18	76.24	—	—	—	—	—	14.03	0.36	0.51
1976	—	—	—	—	—	33.40	0.82	0.36	0.14	118.42	—	—	—
1977	11.92	0.38	0.33	0.24	55.22	29.25	0.68	0.14	0.24	107.80	16.17	0.54	0.44
1978	9.64	0.39	0.28	0.12	41.57	22.36	0.87	0.21	0.12	90.74	6.53	0.22	0.21
1979	6.83	0.60	0.26	0.14	58.74	—	—	—	—	—	2.30	0.30	0.19
1980	3.67	0.34	0.13	0.08	25.58	12.17	0.70	0.10	0.09	57.83	2.71	0.24	0.11
1981	5.74	0.44	0.14	0.12	33.84	—	—	—	—	—	3.82	0.24	0.26
1982	6.29	0.39	0.37	0.08	34.74	15.86	0.81	0.09	0.09	65.41	4.43	0.28	0.48
1983	3.17	0.33	0.15	0.05	21.42	6.46	0.61	0.05	0.05	30.27	2.74	0.22	0.15
1984	2.94	0.36	0.12	0.05	16.91	7.85	0.53	0.09	0.06	31.47	2.56	0.22	0.34
1985	3.13	0.32	0.11	0.05	15.89	6.98	0.47	0.12	0.05	31.94	2.77	0.30	0.22
1986	3.22	0.34	0.11	0.05	14.10	7.48	0.38	0.07	0.07	27.25	2.05	0.21	0.12
1987	2.52	0.20	0.10	0.04	12.35	3.95	0.33	0.06	0.04	16.58	1.32	0.22	0.08
1988	2.94	0.34	0.06	0.05	13.43	5.04	0.55	0.03	0.04	19.14	1.40	0.22	0.07
1989	2.50	0.34	0.07	0.05	15.09	4.74	0.54	0.04	0.04	21.00	1.57	0.20	0.09

(continued)

TABLE Cf238–262   Contaminants in herring gull eggs in the Great Lakes: 1974–1999   *Continued*

	Lake Superior					Lake Michigan					Lake Huron		
	DDE	Dieldrin	Mirex	HCB	PCB	DDE	Dieldrin	Mirex	HCB	PCB	DDE	Dieldrin	Mirex
	Cf238	Cf239	Cf240	Cf241	Cf242	Cf243	Cf244	Cf245	Cf246	Cf247	Cf248	Cf249	Cf250
Year	Parts per million	Parts per million	Parts per million	Parts per million	Parts per million	Parts per million	Parts per million	Parts per million	Parts per million	Parts per million	Parts per million	Parts per million	Parts per million
1990	2.64	0.30	0.06	0.03	11.62	8.12	0.54	0.06	0.05	32.19	1.86	0.14	0.11
1991	3.60	0.27	0.07	0.04	14.09	10.52	0.34	0.12	0.05	31.27	1.97	0.16	0.11
1992	3.69	0.40	0.07	0.05	13.96	6.70	0.41	0.05	0.04	20.25	2.36	0.16	0.05
1993	4.09	0.19	0.08	0.03	15.68	9.56	0.32	0.09	0.06	33.75	3.18	0.19	0.06
1994	2.39	0.15	0.10	0.03	12.31	9.29	0.37	0.09	0.05	30.81	2.19	0.13	0.10
1995	2.48	0.11	0.08	0.02	11.17	6.38	0.19	0.05	0.03	23.28	1.60	0.10	0.06
1996	2.79	0.13	0.06	0.03	11.02	5.02	0.18	0.06	0.04	19.78	2.00	0.13	0.14
1997	1.83	0.07	0.02	0.01	8.30	7.40	0.18	0.03	0.02	33.32	1.26	0.06	0.03
1998	2.66	0.07	0.04	0.01	12.96	5.15	0.09	0.03	0.01	24.61	0.98	0.02	0.02
1999	2.06	0.10	0.03	0.02	9.66	5.04	0.14	0.02	0.02	23.42	1.30	0.07	0.05

	Lake Huron		Lake Erie					Lake Ontario				
	HCB	PCB	DDE	Dieldrin	Mirex	HCB	PCB	DDE	Dieldrin	Mirex	HCB	PCB
	Cf251	Cf252	Cf253	Cf254	Cf255	Cf256	Cf257	Cf258	Cf259	Cf260	Cf261	Cf262
Year	Parts per million	Parts per million	Parts per million	Parts per million	Parts per million	Parts per million	Parts per million	Parts per million	Parts per million	Parts per million	Parts per million	Parts per million
1974	0.38	71.01	7.13	0.35	0.64	0.29	72.46	22.30	0.47	6.99	0.58	152.37
1975	0.21	42.67	7.41	0.33	0.32	0.19	62.30	22.80	0.29	4.70	0.33	143.11
1976	—	—	—	—	—	—	—	—	—	—	—	—
1977	0.36	70.28	7.49	0.40	0.45	0.37	68.70	14.88	0.39	2.48	0.80	102.50
1978	0.11	32.38	4.29	0.24	0.20	0.09	44.43	10.65	0.26	1.59	0.32	72.43
1979	0.10	28.66	3.10	0.25	0.17	0.11	48.44	8.94	0.21	1.89	0.21	69.60
1980	0.07	20.41	2.98	0.21	0.18	0.09	46.38	7.62	0.19	1.65	0.17	56.43
1981	0.07	25.39	3.90	0.22	0.25	0.09	56.49	11.00	0.28	2.67	0.24	78.90
1982	0.08	34.29	3.07	0.25	0.13	0.08	58.89	10.04	0.28	3.05	0.16	62.90
1983	0.05	18.28	2.39	0.20	0.17	0.05	37.31	4.78	0.18	1.43	0.08	42.59
1984	0.07	19.95	3.23	0.33	0.22	0.06	46.20	6.26	0.21	1.87	0.12	51.11
1985	0.06	16.90	2.83	0.19	0.14	0.06	38.41	6.02	0.15	1.47	0.07	35.58
1986	0.05	12.00	2.77	0.23	0.14	0.06	33.35	4.41	0.16	1.10	0.07	27.86
1987	0.02	8.33	1.77	0.14	0.12	0.03	23.16	2.60	0.13	0.68	0.04	16.48
1988	0.04	8.83	2.07	0.17	0.10	0.05	27.50	4.25	0.15	0.82	0.07	23.53
1989	0.03	10.19	2.69	0.17	0.18	0.05	39.21	5.28	0.22	1.15	0.07	32.45
1990	0.03	11.34	2.01	0.10	0.11	0.03	30.09	3.36	0.10	0.64	0.03	18.44
1991	0.03	10.00	2.12	0.08	0.07	0.02	26.55	3.53	0.14	0.58	0.03	17.06
1992	0.05	10.20	1.68	0.13	0.05	0.04	24.44	5.01	0.13	0.77	0.05	21.18
1993	0.03	10.95	1.49	0.10	0.07	0.02	21.69	5.27	0.13	0.82	0.04	21.06
1994	0.03	11.25	1.55	0.08	0.08	0.03	22.89	3.83	0.13	0.80	0.04	19.73
1995	0.03	8.95	1.21	0.08	0.07	0.03	23.57	2.22	0.05	0.57	0.02	13.56
1996	0.08	10.05	1.25	0.06	0.09	0.03	15.51	3.03	0.10	0.68	0.04	16.12
1997	0.02	5.53	0.74	0.05	0.02	0.01	13.58	2.39	0.05	0.46	0.02	12.83
1998	0.01	4.58	0.83	0.03	0.03	0.01	15.59	2.01	0.03	0.39	0.01	13.29
1999	0.02	5.84	0.76	0.05	0.02	0.01	12.81	2.20	0.05	0.45	0.02	11.91

Source

Environment Canada, Canadian Wildlife Service, Canada Centre for Inland Waters, Organochlorine Contaminant Concentrations in Herring Gull Eggs from Great Lakes Colonies, unpublished, as reported in annual reports of the Council on Environmental Quality.

Documentation

Data are measured in whole egg samples, wet weight. DDE is a derivative of dichlorodiphenyltrichloroethane (DDT); HCB is hexachlorobenzene; PCBs are polychlorinated biphenyls. Details on these organochlorine contaminants are described by the National Toxicology Program at the National Institute for Environmental Sciences Internet site.

TABLE Cf263–268   North American goose and swan population estimates: 1970–2002

Contributed by Scott Farrow

	Goose				Tundra swan	
	Canada	Snow	Greater white-fronted	Brant	Eastern	Western
	Cf263	Cf264	Cf265	Cf266	Cf267	Cf268
Nesting year	Thousand	Thousand	Thousand	Thousand	Thousand	Thousand
1970	244	908	51	142	55	31
1971	367	1,191	39	300	58	99
1972	550	1,467	46	198	63	83
1973	648	1,180	43	166	57	34
1974	536	1,371	43	219	64	70
1975	535	1,277	40	211	67	54
1976	810	1,751	53	249	79	51
1977	727	1,344	50	221	76	47
1978	724	2,191	53	209	70	46
1979	604	1,485	49	173	79	54
1980	610	2,126	132	215	64	65
1981	923	1,819	161	291	93	84
1982	1,027	2,767	182	227	73	91
1983	1,024	2,328	154	233	87	67
1984	859	2,310	183	260	81	62
1985	1,012	2,741	182	291	94	49
1986	925	2,358	172	246	91	66
1987	1,148	2,754	179	220	95	53
1988	1,307	2,322	207	278	77	59
1989	2,482	2,828	278	273	91	79
1990	2,615	2,595	322	287	90	40
1991	2,238	3,298	377	279	97	48
1992	3,280	3,240	409	303	110	64
1993	2,885	2,927	330	225	77	63
1994	3,314	3,446	1,126	287	85	79
1995	3,829	3,966	1,187	282	81	53 [1]
1996	3,721	3,662	1,552	233	79	98
1997	4,577	4,002	1,087	279	86	123
1998	4,682	4,193	941	276	97	71
1999	5,706	3,967	1,471	301	109	120
2000	5,584	3,928	1,317	292	90	103
2001	4,885	3,941	1,499	270	87	98
2002	5,379	3,883	1,070	318	59	104

[1] Survey incomplete.

Source

U.S. Department of the Interior, Fish and Wildlife Service, Office of Migratory Bird Management in Conjunction with the Canadian Wildlife Service, *Waterfowl Population Status*, and earlier annual reports.

Documentation

Data for Canada goose are aggregate population totals for thirteen separate populations that nest in North America. The year listed is the latter part of an estimating period that crosses calendar years (that is, 1995 means 1994–1995). Additional bird population information can be found through the U.S. Fish and Wildlife Service's Internet site.

TABLE Cf269-280 North American duck population estimates: 1955-2002

Contributed by Scott Farrow

	Northern pintail	Mallard	Canvasback	Redhead	Gadwall	Green wing teal	Blue wing teal	Scaup	American widgeon	Northern shoveler	Black duck Atlantic flyway	Black duck Mississippi River flyway
	Cf269	Cf270	Cf271	Cf272	Cf273	Cf274	Cf275	Cf276	Cf277	Cf278	Cf279	Cf280
Year	Million	Million	Million	Million	Million	Million	Million	Million	Million	Million	Million	Million
1955	9.78	8.78	0.59	0.54	0.65	1.81	5.31	5.62	3.32	1.64	0.58	0.18
1956	10.37	10.45	0.70	0.76	0.77	1.53	5.00	5.99	3.15	1.78	0.42	0.21
1957	6.61	9.30	0.63	0.51	0.67	1.10	4.30	5.77	2.92	1.48	0.42	0.23
1958	6.04	11.23	0.75	0.46	0.50	1.35	5.46	5.35	2.56	1.38	0.28	0.26
1959	5.87	9.02	0.49	0.50	0.59	2.65	5.10	7.04	3.79	1.58	0.31	0.18
1960	5.72	7.37	0.61	0.50	0.78	1.43	4.29	4.87	2.99	1.82	0.34	0.17
1961	4.22	7.33	0.44	0.32	0.65	1.73	3.66	5.38	3.05	1.38	0.32	0.16
1962	3.62	5.54	0.36	0.51	0.91	0.72	3.01	5.29	1.96	1.27	0.34	0.11
1963	3.85	6.75	0.51	0.41	1.06	1.24	3.72	5.44	1.82	1.40	0.33	0.14
1964	3.29	6.06	0.64	0.53	0.87	1.56	4.02	5.13	2.59	1.72	0.37	0.22
1965	3.59	5.13	0.52	0.60	1.26	1.28	3.60	4.64	2.30	1.42	0.33	0.16
1966	4.81	6.73	0.66	0.71	1.68	1.62	3.73	4.44	2.32	2.15	0.30	0.15
1967	5.28	7.51	0.50	0.74	1.38	1.59	4.49	4.93	2.33	2.32	0.29	0.21
1968	3.49	7.09	0.56	0.50	1.95	1.43	3.46	4.41	2.30	1.69	0.34	0.14
1969	5.90	7.53	0.50	0.63	1.57	1.49	4.14	5.14	2.94	2.16	0.33	0.15
1970	6.39	9.99	0.58	0.62	1.61	2.18	4.86	5.66	3.47	2.23	0.28	0.14
1971	5.85	9.42	0.45	0.53	1.61	1.89	4.61	5.14	3.27	2.01	0.26	0.13
1972	7.00	9.27	0.43	0.55	1.62	1.95	4.28	8.00	3.20	2.47	0.27	0.14
1973	4.36	8.08	0.62	0.50	1.25	1.95	3.33	6.26	2.88	1.62	0.27	0.15
1974	6.60	6.88	0.51	0.63	1.59	1.87	4.98	5.78	2.67	2.01	0.25	0.08
1975	5.90	7.73	0.60	0.83	1.64	1.67	5.89	6.46	2.78	1.98	0.24	0.12
1976	5.48	7.93	0.61	0.67	1.25	1.55	4.75	5.82	2.51	1.75	0.28	0.15
1977	3.93	7.40	0.66	0.63	1.30	1.29	4.46	6.26	2.58	1.45	0.26	0.10
1978	5.11	7.43	0.37	0.73	1.56	2.17	4.50	5.98	3.28	1.98	0.27	0.09
1979	5.38	7.88	0.58	0.70	1.76	2.07	4.88	7.66	3.11	2.41	0.24	0.08
1980	4.51	7.71	0.74	0.73	1.39	2.05	4.90	6.38	3.60	1.91	0.20	0.08
1981	3.48	6.41	0.62	0.60	1.40	1.91	3.72	5.99	2.95	2.33	0.24	0.08
1982	3.71	6.41	0.51	0.62	1.63	1.54	3.66	5.53	2.46	2.15	0.24	0.07
1983	3.51	6.46	0.53	0.72	1.52	1.88	3.37	7.17	2.64	1.88	0.20	0.09
1984	2.97	5.42	0.53	0.67	1.52	1.41	4.00	6.02	3.02	1.62	0.23	0.06
1985	2.52	4.96	0.38	0.58	1.30	1.48	3.50	5.10	2.05	1.70	0.22	0.06
1986	2.74	6.12	0.44	0.56	1.55	1.68	4.48	5.24	1.74	2.13	0.23	0.10
1987	2.63	5.79	0.45	0.50	1.31	2.01	3.53	4.86	2.01	1.95	0.20	0.07
1988	2.01	6.37	0.44	0.44	1.35	2.06	4.01	4.67	2.21	1.68	0.23	0.11
1989	2.11	5.65	0.48	0.51	1.42	1.84	3.13	4.34	1.97	1.54	0.24	0.07
1990	2.26	5.45	0.54	0.48	1.67	1.80	2.78	4.29	1.86	1.76	0.23	0.01
1991	1.80	5.45	0.49	0.45	1.58	1.56	3.77	5.26	2.25	1.72	0.23	0.05
1992	2.10	5.98	0.48	0.60	2.03	1.77	4.33	4.64	2.21	1.95	0.20	0.08
1993	2.05	5.71	0.47	0.49	1.76	1.69	3.19	4.08	2.05	2.05	0.21	0.08
1994	2.97	6.98	0.53	0.65	2.32	2.11	4.62	4.53	2.38	2.91	0.22	0.08
1995	2.76	8.27	0.77	0.89	2.84	2.30	5.14	4.45	2.62	2.86	0.21	0.09
1996	2.74	7.94	0.85	0.83	2.98	2.50	6.41	4.22	2.27	3.45	0.20	0.04
1997	3.56	9.94	0.69	0.92	3.90	2.51	6.12	4.11	3.12	4.12	0.20	0.04
1998	2.52	9.64	0.69	1.01	3.74	2.09	6.40	3.47	2.86	3.18	0.20	0.04
1999	3.06	10.81	0.72	0.97	3.24	2.63	7.15	4.41	2.92	3.89	0.27	0.05
2000	2.91	9.47	0.71	0.93	3.16	3.19	7.43	4.03	2.73	3.52	—	—
2001	3.30	7.90	0.58	0.71	2.68	2.51	5.76	3.69	2.49	3.31	—	—
2002	1.79	7.50	0.49	0.56	2.24	2.33	4.21	3.52	2.33	2.14	—	—

Source

U.S. Department of the Interior, Fish and Wildlife Service, Office of Migratory Bird Management in Conjunction with the Canadian Wildlife Service, Status of Waterfowl and Fall Flight Forecast, annual, as reported in Council on Environmental Quality, *Environmental Quality*.

Documentation

Additional bird population information can be found at the U.S. Fish and Wildlife Service's Internet site.

TABLE Cf281–285   Forestland damaged by insects: 1968–2000

Contributed by Scott Farrow

Year	Spruce budworm Cf281 Million acres	Western spruce budworm Cf282 Million acres	Gypsy moth Cf283 Million acres	Mountain pine beetle Cf284 Million acres	Southern pine beetle Cf285 Million acres
1968	1.3	5.3	0.1	—	—
1969	1.2	4.6	0.3	—	—
1970	2.0	4.0	1.0	—	—
1971	1.6	4.8	1.9	—	—
1972	2.8	5.5	1.4	—	—
1973	4.2	4.4	1.8	—	—
1974	10.8	5.5	0.8	—	—
1975	9.2	5.3	0.5	—	—
1976	9.1	5.8	0.9	—	—
1977	10.3	6.5	1.6	—	—
1978	7.7	5.2	1.3	4.0	—
1979	6.6	5.0	0.6	4.4	15.0
1980	6.6	4.0	5.0	4.7	12.1
1981	4.5	5.5	12.9	4.7	0.9
1982	4.2	8.7	8.2	4.2	7.3
1983	6.5	11.0	2.4	3.6	11.4
1984	6.1	10.6	1.0	3.3	—
1985	5.2	12.8	1.7	3.3	15.5
1986	1.0	13.2	2.4	3.5	26.4
1987	0.8	8.0	1.3	2.4	13.8
1988	0.3	6.1	0.7	2.2	7.9
1989	0.2	3.1	3.0	1.6	5.3
1990	0.2	4.6	7.3	0.9	4.2
1991	0.1	7.2	4.2	0.6	10.7
1992	0.1	4.6	3.1	15.8 [1]	14.3
1993	0.1	0.5	1.8	0.8	10.4
1994	1.0	0.5	0.9	0.4	5.3
1995	0.8	0.5	1.4	0.6	21.7
1996	0.5	0.3	0.2	0.3	7.3
1997	0.4	0.4	(Z)	0.3	8.5
1998	0.4	0.8	0.4	0.3	6.8
1999	0.1	0.5	0.5	0.4	6.2
2000	(Z)	0.6	1.6	0.5	12.1

(Z) Less than 50,000 acres.

[1] Includes 15.2 million acres in California not previously reported.

Sources

Forest Insect and Disease Conditions in the United States, 1979–1983 (U.S. Forest Service, 1985) and *Forest Insect and Disease Conditions in the United States* (U.S. Forest Service, annual from 1986). Related data can be found at the U.S. Forest Service's Internet site.

Documentation

Series Cf281. Includes damage by the spruce budworm in Alaska as it is the same species as in the eastern United States (it is not the western spruce budworm).

WEATHER

Myron P. Gutmann and Timothy G. F. Kittel

TABLE Cf286–351   Normal temperatures – thirty-year annual and monthly averages: 1961–1990   [Reference climatological stations]

Contributed by Myron P. Gutmann, Timothy G. F. Kittel, and Christie S. Wilson

Month	Muscle Shoals, Alabama	Selma, Alabama	Grand Canyon National Park, Arizona [1,2]	Fayetteville Experiment Station, Arkansas	Davis Experiment Farm, California	Death Valley, California	Indio Fire Station, California	Boulder, Colorado	Montrose #2, Colorado	Groton, Connecticut	Saint Leo, Florida	Savannah WSO AP, Georgia	Grace, Idaho	Porthill, Idaho	Urbana, Illinois	Marion 2N, Indiana
	Cf286	Cf287	Cf288	Cf289	Cf290	Cf291	Cf292	Cf293	Cf294	Cf295	Cf296	Cf297	Cf298	Cf299	Cf300	Cf301
	Degrees F	Degrees F	Degrees F	Degrees F	Degrees F	Degrees F	Degrees F	Degrees F	Degrees F	Degrees F	Degrees F	Degrees F	Degrees F	Degrees F	Degrees F	Degrees F
Annual	60.6	65.0	47.6	57.4	59.8	75.9	74.0	51.5	49.0	49.9	72.2	66.3	42.9	45.0	51.5	49.8
Jan	38.7	45.6	30.3	34.0	44.5	51.7	55.9	32.6	24.8	27.7	59.9	48.9	20.3	24.1	23.8	23.1
Feb	43.2	49.4	33.2	38.4	49.7	59.2	60.8	35.9	31.6	29.4	61.7	51.8	24.5	29.5	28.3	26.0
Mar	52.2	57.7	37.2	47.9	53.0	66.6	65.6	41.0	39.5	37.6	67.1	59.2	31.8	36.5	40.0	37.6
Apr	61.0	65.3	44.1	58.0	57.8	74.9	72.0	49.2	48.0	46.7	71.7	66.0	42.0	45.6	51.9	49.1
May	68.7	72.7	52.7	65.6	64.6	84.8	79.3	58.0	57.2	56.4	77.0	73.5	50.9	53.9	62.7	59.9
June	76.3	79.2	62.0	73.5	71.1	94.6	87.3	67.1	66.6	65.4	80.7	79.1	58.8	60.9	71.8	69.5
July	79.7	81.6	67.9	78.7	74.1	100.8	92.6	73.0	72.5	71.4	81.9	81.8	65.9	65.9	75.0	73.3
Aug	78.6	81.2	65.7	77.2	73.1	98.8	91.5	71.0	70.0	70.7	82.0	81.0	64.3	64.9	72.7	71.0
Sept	72.7	76.3	59.3	70.0	69.9	90.0	86.1	62.4	61.5	63.3	80.4	76.6	55.6	55.4	66.5	64.8
Oct	61.2	65.7	49.1	59.3	62.9	76.7	76.4	52.9	50.4	53.0	74.5	67.3	45.4	43.9	54.5	52.7
Nov	51.5	56.4	38.3	48.0	52.3	61.9	63.9	40.8	37.7	43.9	67.7	59.1	32.6	33.5	42.1	41.6
Dec	42.8	48.9	31.2	38.0	44.9	50.8	56.0	33.6	27.6	33.0	62.1	51.7	22.2	26.2	29.2	29.0

Month	Belle Plain, Iowa	Lawrence, Kansas	Hopkinsville, Kentucky	Calhoun Research Station, Louisiana	New Orleans Audubon, Louisiana	Presque Isle, Maine	Baltimore WSO City, Maryland	Blue Hill, Massachusetts	Ann Arbor, University of Michigan, Michigan	Chatham Experimental Farm #2, Michigan [1,3]	Itasca, University of Minnesota, Minnesota	Greenville, Mississippi	Sweet Springs, Missouri	Bozeman, Montana State University, Montana	Glasgow WSO AP, Montana	Crete, Nebraska
	Cf302	Cf303	Cf304	Cf305	Cf306	Cf307	Cf308	Cf309	Cf310	Cf311	Cf312	Cf313	Cf314	Cf315	Cf316	Cf317
	Degrees F	Degrees F	Degrees F	Degrees F	Degrees F	Degrees F	Degrees F	Degrees F	Degrees F	Degrees F	Degrees F	Degrees F	Degrees F	Degrees F	Degrees F	Degrees F
Annual	48.2	56.2	56.5	63.8	69.5	40.1	58.2	48.6	49.4	41.6	37.8	63.2	54.9	44.2	42.4	52.1
Jan	18.2	29.2	32.0	43.3	52.7	11.5	34.9	25.3	23.2	15.9	2.4	41.2	27.9	22.9	10.6	23.8
Feb	23.3	34.3	36.1	47.6	55.8	14.5	37.3	27.3	25.7	17.5	9.5	46.1	33.1	28.1	17.5	29.2
Mar	35.9	45.5	46.6	55.8	63.0	25.6	46.6	35.8	36.3	26.8	23.1	54.6	44.8	33.4	29.4	40.5
Apr	49.3	57.3	57.0	64.4	69.8	38.2	56.6	45.9	48.3	39.7	39.0	64.1	56.1	42.6	44.3	53.1
May	60.6	66.4	65.6	71.6	76.0	51.6	66.8	56.6	59.8	51.6	52.5	72.2	65.2	51.5	55.0	63.4
June	69.7	74.9	74.0	78.5	81.2	61.7	76.0	65.3	68.9	59.9	62.4	79.4	73.8	60.0	64.4	73.0
July	74.0	80.3	77.7	81.8	82.9	66.3	80.4	71.2	73.0	65.9	67.5	81.9	78.7	67.3	70.8	77.7
Aug	71.4	78.1	76.3	81.2	82.7	63.9	78.7	69.6	70.9	64.4	65.1	80.7	76.4	65.8	69.4	75.2
Sept	63.2	70.1	69.9	75.5	79.4	55.1	71.6	61.9	64.2	56.7	54.4	74.8	68.7	55.7	57.3	66.4
Oct	51.8	59.4	58.1	64.5	70.9	44.4	60.0	51.9	52.5	46.6	42.9	64.1	57.4	46.2	46.1	55.4
Nov	37.7	45.6	47.5	55.3	62.8	31.7	49.6	41.7	40.9	33.6	26.3	54.0	44.6	32.8	29.2	40.5
Dec	23.4	33.2	36.9	46.6	56.2	17.0	39.3	30.1	28.5	21.2	9.0	45.3	32.2	24.3	15.2	27.5

Month	Reno WSFO AP, Nevada Cf318 Degrees F	Searchlight, Nevada Cf319 Degrees F	Hanover, New Hampshire Cf320 Degrees F	Carlsbad, New Mexico Cf321 Degrees F	Chama, New Mexico Cf322 Degrees F	Albany, WSFOAP New York Cf323 Degrees F	Geneva Resr Farm, New York Cf324 Degrees F	New York Central Park, New York Cf325 Degrees F	Cape Hatteras WSO, North Carolina Cf326 Degrees F	Dickinson Experiment Station, North Dakota Cf327 Degrees F	Wooster Experiment Station, Ohio Cf328 Degrees F	Goodwell Research Station, Oklahoma Cf329 Degrees F	Muskogee, Oklahoma Cf330 Degrees F	Newport, Oregon Cf331 Degrees F	Union Experiment Station, Oregon Cf332 Degrees F	Harrisburg Capital City, Pennsylvania Cf333 Degrees F	Charleston City, South Carolina Cf334 Degrees F
Annual	50.8	63.3	45.1	62.2	41.8	47.4	47.0	54.7	62.0	40.8	48.8	55.0	60.9	50.5	47.7	52.9	66.1
Jan	32.9	44.5	17.8	41.7	20.9	20.6	22.3	31.5	44.6	11.0	24.3	31.9	37.3	43.9	30.0	28.6	48.4
Feb	38.0	48.7	21.2	47.0	24.9	23.5	23.3	33.6	45.5	14.8	26.9	36.1	42.1	45.7	35.2	31.3	51.0
Mar	42.8	52.7	32.0	54.2	31.1	34.3	33.2	42.4	51.6	27.0	37.7	43.9	52.0	46.2	40.2	41.2	57.9
Apr	48.6	60.2	43.9	63.1	39.7	46.4	44.9	52.5	58.9	40.8	47.8	54.5	62.0	47.5	45.9	51.6	65.4
May	56.5	69.1	56.1	71.1	48.4	57.6	56.1	62.7	67.0	52.1	58.1	63.2	69.1	51.0	52.5	61.8	72.8
June	65.1	79.0	65.1	78.8	57.2	66.9	65.2	71.6	74.2	62.3	66.8	73.1	77.0	54.8	60.0	70.9	78.8
July	71.6	84.5	70.0	81.0	63.3	71.8	70.4	76.8	78.3	68.6	70.7	78.5	82.2	57.1	66.5	75.7	81.8
Aug	69.6	82.5	68.0	79.3	61.2	69.6	68.6	75.5	78.4	67.6	69.0	76.4	81.1	57.6	66.2	74.1	81.0
Sept	60.4	75.4	59.7	72.6	54.3	61.3	61.3	68.2	74.2	55.0	62.4	68.1	73.5	56.8	57.5	66.4	76.8
Oct	50.8	65.3	47.9	62.5	44.7	50.2	50.2	57.5	65.4	43.9	51.3	56.8	62.6	52.9	48.2	54.7	67.9
Nov	40.3	52.6	36.7	51.7	32.4	39.7	40.0	47.6	57.0	29.2	41.1	43.8	50.9	48.2	39.0	44.4	59.7
Dec	32.7	44.8	23.2	43.7	23.5	26.5	28.0	36.6	49.0	16.1	29.7	33.9	40.6	44.2	31.5	33.6	52.2

Month	Winthrop College, South Carolina Cf335 Degrees F	Cottonwood 2E, South Dakota Cf336 Degrees F	Lewisburg Experiment Station, Tennessee Cf337 Degrees F	Rogersville 1NE, Tennessee Cf338 Degrees F	Beeville 5NE, Texas Cf339 Degrees F	El Paso WSO AP, Texas Cf340 Degrees F	Marshall, Texas Cf341 Degrees F	Temple, Texas Cf342 Degrees F	Logan, Utah State University, Utah Cf343 Degrees F	Charlottesville 2W, Virginia Cf344 Degrees F	Hot Springs, Virginia Cf345 Degrees F	Seattle Urban Site, Washington Cf346 Degrees F	Spokane WSO AP, Washington Cf347 Degrees F	Martinsburg FAA Airport, West Virginia Cf348 Degrees F	Oshkosh, Wisconsin Cf349 Degrees F	Cheyenne WSFO, Wyoming Cf350 Degrees F	Sheridan Field Station, Wyoming Cf351 Degrees F
Annual	61.0	45.8	57.1	55.7	69.5	63.2	63.6	66.2	47.8	56.5	50.9	52.8	47.3	53.2	44.8	45.6	43.9
Jan	40.9	18.0	34.8	34.3	51.7	42.8	43.3	45.4	23.6	34.5	29.1	41.3	27.1	29.6	14.8	26.5	18.6
Feb	44.3	22.8	38.5	38.1	55.2	48.1	47.6	49.7	28.5	37.1	31.7	44.3	33.3	32.6	18.6	29.3	24.2
Mar	52.8	32.0	47.7	47.8	63.0	55.1	55.8	58.1	37.0	46.6	41.0	46.6	38.7	42.6	30.3	33.6	32.7
Apr	61.1	45.3	57.1	56.2	70.7	63.4	64.2	66.7	46.3	56.4	50.3	50.4	45.9	52.4	44.3	42.5	43.5
May	68.9	56.5	65.3	64.0	76.2	71.8	70.9	73.4	55.5	64.9	59.5	56.1	53.9	62.2	57.1	52.0	52.9
June	75.7	66.7	73.3	70.9	81.0	80.4	77.8	80.2	64.4	72.6	67.0	61.4	62.0	70.9	66.7	61.3	62.4
July	79.1	74.4	76.9	74.3	83.4	82.3	81.6	84.0	73.0	76.4	70.7	65.3	68.8	75.2	71.8	68.4	69.9
Aug	78.1	72.0	76.0	73.6	83.4	80.1	81.3	84.1	71.4	75.0	69.8	65.7	68.4	73.6	68.9	66.4	68.1
Sept	72.3	60.5	69.7	67.7	79.6	74.4	75.1	78.0	61.3	68.9	63.2	60.8	58.9	66.3	60.2	57.4	56.7
Oct	61.7	47.8	58.0	56.3	71.5	64.0	64.5	68.4	50.1	58.1	52.5	53.5	47.3	54.4	49.1	47.0	45.6
Nov	52.9	32.6	48.4	47.0	63.1	52.0	55.1	57.6	36.9	49.0	42.8	46.3	35.1	44.6	34.9	35.2	31.6
Dec	44.3	20.6	39.1	38.2	55.0	44.1	46.5	48.8	25.7	38.3	33.3	41.6	27.8	34.5	20.6	20.8	20.8

1 Different source; see text.

2 U.S. Historical Climatology Network data incomplete for the months of January, February, October, and November.

3 USHCN data incomplete for the months of March, April, May, and October.

Sources

Except as noted, data are published in the state publications in this series: *Climatography of the United States, Monthly Station Normals of Temperature, Precipitation, and Heating and Cooling Degree Days, 1961–90* (U.S. National Climatic Data Center, 1992). T. R. Karl, C. N. Williams Jr, et al., "United States Historical Climatology Network (USHCN) Serial Temperature and Precipitation Data," Environmental Science Division, Publication number 3404 (Carbon Dioxide Information and Analysis Center, Oak Ridge National Laboratory, 1990); T. G. F. Kittel, J. A. Royle, et al., "A Gridded Historical (1895–1993) Bioclimate Dataset for the Conterminous United States," in *Proceedings of the 10th Conference on Applied Climatology*, 20–24 October 1997 (American Meteorological Society, 1997), pp. 219–22; T. G. F. Kittel, N. A. Rosenbloom, et al., "VEMAP Phase 2 Historical and Future Scenario Climate Database for the Conterminous US" (2000, revised 2002), available online from the ORNL Distributed Active

(continued)

TABLE Cf286–351   Normal temperatures – thirty-year annual and monthly averages: 1961–1990   [Reference climatological stations]   *Continued*

Archive Center, Oak Ridge National Laboratory, Oak Ridge, Tennessee; T. G. F. Kittel, N. A. Rosenbloom, et al., "The VEMAP Phase 2 Bioclimatic Database. I: A Gridded Historical (20th Century) Climate Dataset for Modeling Ecosystem Dynamics Across the Conterminous United States," *Climate Research* (2004). Data are also from the Internet site of the National Climatic Data Center.

Documentation

National weather data collection for selected locations in the United States extends as far back as the 1780s. Data from a large number of weather stations began in the 1890s. The Weather Bureau, Air Force, and Navy Tabulation Units in New Orleans, LA, were combined and formed into the National Weather Records Center in Asheville, NC, in November 1951. The Center was eventually renamed the National Climatic Data Center (NCDC). NCDC archives weather data obtained by the National Weather Service, Military Services, Federal Aviation Administration, and Coast Guard, as well as data from voluntary cooperative observers.

From these national data the U.S. Historical Climatology Network (USHCN) compiled digital and nondigital data sets archived at NCDC (including data from climatological publications, universities, federal agencies, individuals, and data archives) to maintain a monthly database of weather data from more than 1,200 stations nationwide. The stations included in the USHCN are those considered to be consistent and reliable over a long period of time. The USHCN (Karl, Williams, et al. 1990) is a high-quality moderate-sized data set of monthly averaged maximum, minimum, and mean temperatures and total monthly precipitation developed to assist in the detection of regional climate change. The USHCN comprises 1,221 high-quality stations from the U.S. Cooperative Observing Network within the 48 contiguous United States.

The raw data from each station may have incomplete data or data that have significant biases owing to inconsistency in recording, instrument moves, station relocation, or the effects of urbanization. In some instances, the USHCN includes adjusted data to compensate for inadequacies in the raw data file. When necessary, the creators of USHCN computed a series of data they call "filnet" values, which are time-of-observation data adjusted for Maximum/Minimum Temperature System (MMTS) bias, station moves and changes, and estimated values for missing and outlier data. When these data are used they are referred to as filnet data.

Another source of data comes from the historical climate data set developed by the Vegetation/Ecosystem Modeling and Analysis Project (VEMAP), an ongoing multi-institutional, international effort addressing the response of biogeography and biogeochemistry to environmental variability in climate and other drivers in both space and time. Other data are drawn from adjusted and estimated station data prepared by the VEMAP2 research group as a step in the preparation of their gridded data set. These data are statistically in-filled using a local kriging (spatial autocorrelation) model. For more details about the VEMAP2 process, see Kittel, Royle, et al. (1997); Kittel, Royle, et al. (in preparation); and the VEMAP Internet site. These data are used selectively in the *Historical Statistics* weather data.

In Tables Cf286–549, sixty-six stations were chosen to represent geographical and climatic diversity. For these sixty-six stations temperature and precipitation data are reported. The tables report normal mean temperature and normal precipitation on a monthly and annual basis, where available, for the sixty-six stations. The normal temperatures are based on monthly mean maximum and minimum temperature records for each year in the thirty-year period 1961–1990. The normal precipitation data are based on monthly total precipitation records for each year in the thirty-year period 1961–1990. Except for Grand Canyon National Park and Chatham Experimental Farm number 2, the NCDC has published monthly and annual station normals for all the stations. In those publications, adjustments are made in the data to estimate missing data, adjust for time-of-observation bias, and adjust for exposure changes. For further details in the methodology for computing normals, see the source publication.

For Grand Canyon National Park and Chatham Experimental Farm, normals are arithmetic means of available monthly data. The monthly mean temperatures and monthly normal precipitation are based on raw data, meaning that they have not made use of any of the corrected series mentioned earlier. These data come from the USHCN files. If the raw data were not available for each month for a given station, the reliable readings were averaged, with the number of years reduced accordingly. For example, if monthly data for a given station existed for only twenty-seven Januarys during the 1961–1990 time period, the averages reported would be based on only those twenty-seven years. For the annual figures, VEMAP2 estimated values were used for those with missing or unreliable raw data values, so that the annual averages are all based on the entire thirty-year period.

TABLE Cf352–417 Normal precipitation – thirty-year annual and monthly averages: 1961–1990 [Reference climatological stations]

Contributed by Myron P. Gutmann, Timothy G. F. Kittel, and Christie S. Wilson

Month	Muscle Shoals, Alabama Cf352	Selma, Alabama Cf353	Grand Canyon National Park, Arizona Cf354 [1,2]	Fayetteville Experiment Station, Arkansas Cf355	Davis Experiment Farm, California Cf356	Death Valley, California Cf357	Indio Fire Station, California Cf358	Boulder, Colorado Cf359	Montrose #2, Colorado Cf360	Groton, Connecticut Cf361	Saint Leo, Florida Cf362	Savannah WSO AP, Georgia Cf363	Grace, Idaho Cf364	Porthill, Idaho Cf365	Urbana, Illinois Cf366	Marion 2N, Indiana Cf367
	Inches	Inches	Inches	Inches	Inches	Inches	Inches	Inches	Inches	Inches	Inches	Inches	Inches	Inches	Inches	Inches
Annual	53.85	53.74	15.69	44.04	18.13	2.28	3.81	18.58	9.68	48.16	54.09	49.22	15.74	20.63	39.71	37.56
Jan	4.48	5.22	1.45	1.84	3.94	0.24	0.58	0.59	0.47	4.15	3.14	3.59	1.24	2.23	1.83	2.01
Feb	4.45	5.31	1.38	2.49	2.86	0.41	0.53	0.72	0.42	3.83	3.80	3.22	1.17	1.58	1.97	2.09
Mar	5.90	6.75	1.80	3.88	2.65	0.31	0.42	1.63	0.66	4.33	4.03	3.78	1.29	1.49	3.30	3.20
Apr	4.41	4.58	1.10	4.29	1.10	0.15	0.07	2.16	0.76	4.28	1.82	3.03	1.40	1.38	3.94	3.61
May	5.10	3.69	0.62	5.02	0.28	0.08	0.07	3.00	0.85	4.05	4.71	4.09	1.65	1.72	3.97	3.84
June	4.07	3.96	0.56	4.97	0.15	0.04	0.01	2.22	0.61	3.47	7.19	5.66	1.73	1.81	4.07	3.66
July	4.58	4.44	1.72	2.88	0.03	0.15	0.22	1.97	1.01	3.25	7.79	6.38	1.02	1.07	4.46	4.29
Aug	3.29	3.90	2.11	3.57	0.06	0.18	0.51	1.31	1.11	3.71	8.04	7.46	1.16	1.27	4.03	3.35
Sept	4.08	3.73	1.13	4.49	0.29	0.17	0.42	1.86	1.17	3.61	6.22	4.47	1.39	1.41	3.36	2.85
Oct	3.20	2.86	1.14	3.77	1.08	0.11	0.19	1.27	1.14	3.89	2.22	2.39	1.16	1.38	2.66	2.50
Nov	4.52	3.77	1.38	3.73	2.83	0.23	0.38	1.07	0.83	4.94	2.48	2.19	1.28	2.77	3.10	3.13
Dec	5.77	5.53	1.42	3.11	2.86	0.21	0.41	0.78	0.65	4.65	2.65	2.96	1.25	2.52	3.02	3.03

Month	Belle Plain, Iowa Cf368	Lawrence, Kansas Cf369	Hopkinsville, Kentucky Cf370	Calhoun Research Station, Louisiana Cf371	New Orleans Audubon, Louisiana Cf372	Presque Isle, Maine Cf373	Baltimore WSO City, Maryland Cf374	Blue Hill, Massachusetts Cf375	Ann Arbor, University of Michigan, Michigan Cf376	Chatham Experimental Farm #2, Michigan Cf377 [1]	Itasca, University of Minnesota, Minnesota Cf378	Greenville, Mississippi Cf379	Sweet Springs, Missouri Cf380	Bozeman, Montana State University, Montana Cf381	Glasgow WSO AP, Montana Cf382	Crete, Nebraska Cf383
	Inches	Inches	Inches	Inches	Inches	Inches	Inches	Inches	Inches	Inches	Inches	Inches	Inches	Inches	Inches	Inches
Annual	35.66	39.28	50.79	53.34	61.33	35.25	42.38	48.95	32.81	34.10	26.68	53.38	39.76	19.20	10.96	29.47
Jan	0.99	1.24	3.81	4.80	4.85	2.16	3.14	4.15	1.71	2.12	0.92	4.56	1.34	0.87	0.37	0.56
Feb	1.12	1.12	4.25	4.85	5.25	1.61	3.18	4.31	1.73	1.56	0.60	4.87	1.50	0.67	0.27	0.79
Mar	2.56	2.80	5.25	5.46	4.75	2.03	3.63	4.41	2.55	1.91	1.44	5.63	3.15	1.42	0.41	2.27
Apr	3.54	3.46	4.69	4.21	4.72	2.14	3.24	4.05	3.21	2.14	2.25	5.01	4.02	1.87	0.69	2.68
May	3.87	4.96	4.81	5.39	4.49	3.36	4.05	3.80	2.88	2.82	2.81	5.05	4.87	3.18	1.77	4.19
June	4.65	5.82	3.53	4.06	5.75	3.15	3.31	3.43	3.47	3.42	4.31	4.00	4.35	2.86	2.11	4.26
July	4.41	3.97	4.35	4.02	6.72	4.12	3.72	3.49	3.02	3.27	3.39	3.95	3.76	1.35	1.72	3.20
Aug	4.63	4.06	3.43	3.22	6.64	4.01	4.28	3.92	3.37	3.78	3.51	2.41	3.68	1.50	1.35	3.29
Sept	3.86	4.52	3.45	3.46	5.70	3.61	3.50	3.82	3.11	4.04	2.96	2.97	4.65	1.95	1.00	3.84
Oct	2.61	3.35	3.19	3.79	2.97	3.17	2.98	3.94	2.15	3.36	2.34	3.25	3.54	1.60	0.61	2.21
Nov	1.95	2.24	4.90	4.52	4.29	3.33	3.60	4.92	2.83	3.10	1.15	5.85	2.76	1.19	0.28	1.25
Dec	1.47	1.74	5.13	5.56	5.20	2.56	3.75	4.71	2.78	2.56	1.00	5.83	2.14	0.74	0.38	0.93

Notes appear at end of table   (continued)

TABLE Cf352–417 Normal precipitation – thirty-year annual and monthly averages: 1961–1990 [Reference climatological stations] Continued

Month	Reno WSFO AP, Nevada Cf384	Searchlight, Nevada Cf385	Hanover, New Hampshire Cf386	Carlsbad, New Mexico Cf387	Chama, New Mexico Cf388	Albany, WSFOAP, New York Cf389	Geneva Resr Farm, New York Cf390	New York Central Park, New York Cf391	Cape Hatteras WSO, North Carolina Cf392	Dickinson Experiment Station, North Dakota Cf393	Wooster Experiment Station, Ohio Cf394	Goodwell Research Station, Oklahoma Cf395	Muskogee, Oklahoma Cf396	Newport, Oregon Cf397	Union Experiment Station, Oregon Cf398	Harrisburg Capital City, Pennsylvania Cf399	Charleston City, South Carolina Cf400
	Inches	Inches	Inches	Inches	Inches	Inches	Inches	Inches	Inches	Inches	Inches	Inches	Inches	Inches	Inches	Inches	Inches
Annual	7.53	7.42	37.40	13.32	21.61	36.17	32.92	47.25	56.09	16.67	36.19	16.91	41.74	71.93	13.78	40.50	48.52
Jan	1.07	0.73	2.54	0.37	1.77	2.36	1.76	3.42	5.30	0.34	1.95	0.27	1.80	11.11	1.16	2.84	3.36
Feb	0.99	0.72	2.35	0.46	1.58	2.27	1.78	3.27	4.12	0.30	1.97	0.42	2.31	8.13	0.90	2.93	3.06
Mar	0.71	0.77	2.65	0.34	1.99	2.93	2.06	4.08	4.29	0.66	2.92	0.87	3.55	8.24	1.18	3.28	4.30
Apr	0.38	0.41	2.88	0.62	1.27	2.99	2.91	4.20	3.53	1.84	3.06	1.23	4.08	4.84	1.24	3.24	2.44
May	0.69	0.23	3.56	1.16	1.11	3.41	3.00	4.42	4.00	2.62	4.01	3.11	5.12	3.50	1.64	4.26	3.53
June	0.46	0.12	3.25	1.59	1.12	3.62	3.67	3.67	4.11	3.63	3.47	2.68	4.29	2.69	1.56	3.85	5.83
July	0.28	0.89	3.28	1.76	2.24	3.18	2.95	4.35	4.98	2.11	4.05	2.52	2.64	1.04	0.61	3.59	6.05
Aug	0.32	1.21	3.62	2.08	2.82	3.47	3.14	4.01	6.00	1.68	3.72	2.16	2.84	1.26	0.94	3.31	7.31
Sept	0.39	0.60	3.30	2.67	2.23	2.95	3.22	3.89	5.27	1.63	3.24	1.68	4.51	2.63	1.04	3.51	4.67
Oct	0.38	0.47	3.32	1.17	1.96	2.83	2.90	3.56	4.98	1.00	2.25	0.96	4.15	5.36	1.00	2.93	2.78
Nov	0.87	0.55	3.54	0.64	1.72	3.23	3.06	4.47	4.97	0.45	2.93	0.73	3.55	10.87	1.32	3.52	2.29
Dec	0.99	0.72	3.11	0.46	1.80	2.93	2.47	3.91	4.54	0.41	2.62	0.28	2.90	12.26	1.19	3.24	2.90

Month	Winthrop College, South Carolina Cf401	Cottonwood 2E, South Dakota Cf402	Lewisburg Experiment Station, Tennessee Cf403	Rogersville 1NE, Tennessee Cf404	Beeville 5NE, Texas Cf405	El Paso WSO AP, Texas Cf406	Marshall, Texas Cf407	Temple, Texas Cf408	Logan, Utah State University, Utah Cf409	Charlottesville 2W, Virginia Cf410	Hot Springs, Virginia Cf411	Seattle Urban Site, Washington Cf412	Spokane WSO AP, Washington Cf413	Martinsburg FAA Airport, West Virginia Cf414	Oshkosh, Wisconsin Cf415	Cheyenne WSFO, Wyoming Cf416	Sheridan Field Station, Wyoming Cf417
	Inches	Inches	Inches	Inches	Inches	Inches	Inches	Inches	Inches	Inches	Inches	Inches	Inches	Inches	Inches	Inches	Inches
Annual	48.65	16.46	54.70	45.23	32.05	8.81	47.65	34.87	19.52	47.29	42.14	38.00	16.49	37.45	31.15	14.40	14.81
Jan	4.36	0.29	4.49	3.81	1.98	0.40	3.82	1.89	1.40	3.15	2.93	5.35	1.98	2.35	1.23	0.40	0.55
Feb	4.26	0.40	4.12	3.72	1.90	0.41	4.00	2.74	1.65	3.32	2.92	4.03	1.49	2.50	1.08	0.39	0.46
Mar	5.08	1.06	5.97	4.18	1.21	0.29	4.00	2.51	2.02	3.75	3.69	3.77	1.49	3.14	2.25	1.03	0.81
Apr	2.99	1.82	4.67	3.88	2.29	0.20	4.44	2.90	2.15	3.34	3.43	2.51	1.18	3.17	2.85	1.37	1.66
May	3.76	2.97	5.66	4.33	3.62	0.25	4.91	4.63	2.04	4.88	4.15	1.84	1.41	4.06	3.15	2.39	2.64
June	4.28	3.11	3.85	3.38	3.80	0.67	4.44	3.64	1.57	3.74	3.36	1.59	1.26	3.42	3.29	2.08	2.77
July	4.30	2.16	5.19	4.33	2.78	1.54	3.01	1.95	0.78	4.75	4.49	0.85	0.67	3.53	3.28	2.09	0.99
Aug	4.30	1.47	3.25	3.67	2.94	1.58	2.51	2.26	0.97	4.71	3.70	1.22	0.72	3.30	3.88	1.69	0.95
Sept	4.31	1.15	3.79	3.36	4.81	1.70	3.78	3.82	1.62	4.10	3.39	1.94	0.73	2.81	3.82	1.27	1.50
Oct	3.66	1.13	3.81	2.86	3.10	0.76	3.91	3.33	1.87	4.57	3.77	3.25	0.99	3.42	2.37	0.74	1.17
Nov	3.48	0.51	4.85	3.52	2.01	0.44	4.32	2.88	1.73	3.66	3.47	5.65	2.15	3.08	2.30	0.53	0.73
Dec	3.87	0.39	5.05	4.19	1.61	0.57	4.51	2.32	1.72	3.32	2.84	6.00	2.42	2.67	1.65	0.42	0.58

1 Different source; see text.

2 U.S. Historical Climatology Network data incomplete for the months of February, April, October, and November.

Source
See the text for Table Cf286–351.

Documentation
For a description of the data, see the text for Table Cf286–351.

TABLE Cf418–483 Annual mean temperature: 1895–1998 [Reference climatological stations]

Contributed by Myron P. Gutmann, Timothy G. F. Kittel, and Christie S. Wilson

Year	Muscle Shoals, Alabama	Selma, Alabama	Grand Canyon National Park, Arizona	Fayetteville Experiment Station, Arkansas	Davis Experiment Farm, California	Death Valley, California	Indio Fire Station, California	Boulder, Colorado	Montrose #2, Colorado	Groton, Connecticut	Saint Leo, Florida	Savannah WSO AP, Georgia
	Cf418	Cf419	Cf420	Cf421	Cf422	Cf423	Cf424	Cf425	Cf426	Cf427	Cf428	Cf429
	Degrees F	Degrees F	Degrees F	Degrees F	Degrees F	Degrees F	Degrees F	Degrees F	Degrees F	Degrees F	Degrees F	Degrees F
1895	59.9 [1]	64.5 [1]	46.8 [1]	57.2	59.7 [1]	75.2 [1]	75.5	48.5 [1]	48.4 [1]	48.8	70.7 [2]	65.4
1896	61.9 [1]	66.4 [1]	48.4 [1]	60.6	60.2 [1]	76.5 [1]	72.1	51.6 [1]	50.7 [1]	48.9	72.0	67.4
1897	61.7 [1]	65.7	47.1 [1]	59.5	61.2	75.3 [1]	71.4	50.4 [1]	47.5 [1]	48.6	72.6	67.5
1898	61.2 [1]	65.2	46.9 [1]	58.3	60.7	75.9 [1]	71.9	49.6	47.5 [1]	48.4	72.4	67.2
1899	60.6 [1]	65.3	47.7 [1]	57.8 [2]	61.3	76.1 [1]	73.7	49.6	48.6 [1]	49.0	72.3	67.0
1900	61.1 [1]	65.0 [1]	48.1 [1]	59.0 [2]	60.7	76.1 [1]	72.0	52.7	49.5 [1]	51.8	72.3	67.2
1901	59.4 [1]	62.9 [1]	47.9 [1]	58.4 [2]	61.4	76.5 [1]	73.9	51.9	49.8 [1]	49.4	70.1 [2]	65.0
1902	60.8 [1]	65.1	47.4 [1]	58.1 [2]	59.0 [1]	75.7 [1]	73.1	51.7	49.0 [1]	49.2	72.0	67.0
1903	59.9 [1]	63.5	49.0 [1]	55.7 [1]	61.0	76.1 [1]	74.5 [2]	50.0	47.8 [1]	49.6	70.3	65.9
1904	60.2 [1]	66.2 [1]	49.4 [1]	56.4 [2]	61.9	76.9 [1]	75.5 [2]	52.2	47.0 [2]	47.6	70.6	65.7
1905	59.9 [1]	65.1	47.0 [2]	56.2 [2]	64.1	76.0 [1]	72.7	50.1	45.4 [2]	49.3	71.3	66.3
1906	60.8 [1]	65.6	48.0	57.9 [2]	64.8	76.0 [1]	73.1	50.6	46.5 [2]	50.8	71.2 [2]	66.5
1907	61.1 [1]	65.8	48.9	60.2	65.1	75.2 [1]	73.2 [2]	52.0 [2]	48.3 [2]	49.0	72.3 [2]	67.3
1908	61.7 [1]	65.0	45.1	59.8	61.4 [2]	75.0 [1]	72.6 [2]	51.6	46.0	51.5	71.9	67.3
1909	61.2 [1]	64.5	45.2	60.9 [2]	58.4	74.6 [1]	72.3 [2]	49.3	45.3	50.4	71.5	66.7
1910	60.4 [1]	63.8 [1]	48.7	59.3	58.0 [2]	76.8 [1]	74.9 [2]	53.2 [1]	46.8 [2]	51.0	69.5	65.6
1911	62.7 [1]	67.1	45.0	61.1	57.0 [2]	74.3 [1]	72.3	50.6 [1]	49.2 [2]	51.7	72.9	67.7
1912	59.8 [1]	64.1	43.2 [2]	57.4	58.3	73.1	71.9	48.2 [1]	47.5	51.1	71.6	66.3
1913	61.7 [1]	65.5 [2]	46.6	59.2	59.4 [2]	77.4	71.9	48.7	47.4	53.6	71.8	67.2
1914	60.7 [1]	64.1	48.3 [2]	59.7	59.2	81.0	73.9	51.6	48.9	51.2	70.9	66.0
1915	61.0 [1]	64.8	46.0 [2]	58.7	60.6	79.8 [1]	72.4	49.7 [2]	48.1	52.4	70.5	66.9
1916	60.9 [1]	63.9 [2]	46.5 [2]	60.2 [2]	59.5	75.0 [1]	72.5 [2]	51.2	48.8	51.1	71.1	67.3
1917	59.1 [1]	63.0 [1]	47.1 [2]	57.1 [2]	60.8	75.1	72.9	51.0	47.4	49.3	70.2	65.9
1918	61.7 [1]	65.9 [1]	47.5 [2]	59.5	60.1 [2]	72.3 [2]	73.3	52.1	47.7	50.7	71.0	66.9
1919	61.6 [1]	66.5 [1]	47.8 [2]	59.1 [2]	59.4	71.8	72.9	52.5	47.8	51.9	70.8	67.6
1920	60.4 [1]	64.8 [2]	46.8 [1]	58.3 [2]	60.0	71.0	71.7	49.1	47.7	49.8	69.4	65.7
1921	63.3 [1]	69.3 [1]	48.1	62.3 [2]	60.2 [2]	72.5 [1]	73.6	52.5 [2]	51.5	52.4	71.4	68.6
1922	62.8 [1]	69.7	47.9	60.1 [2]	59.5	76.2 [1]	73.0	50.7 [2]	49.2	51.3	71.1	68.0
1923	61.3 [1]	67.5 [2]	47.5 [1]	59.8 [2]	59.7 [2]	74.4	73.0	48.5 [2]	48.4	50.4	70.9	67.3
1924	59.9 [1]	66.5 [2]	49.0	57.0	58.9	75.2	73.9	49.6	46.6	49.7	71.9	66.0
1925	62.5 [1]	68.4	48.6	60.0 [2]	59.5	75.6	73.0	50.9	48.7	51.1	72.9	68.0
1926	61.0 [1]	66.4	50.0 [2]	58.3	61.1	77.6	73.9	50.8	49.4	48.9	70.9	66.7
1927	62.7 [1]	69.3	49.6	59.7	59.3	75.7	72.5	50.5 [2]	49.3	51.2	71.3	68.6
1928	60.8 [1]	66.6	50.3	58.7 [2]	59.6	72.7 [1]	73.3	49.6	48.8	51.1 [1]	70.0	66.5
1929	61.1 [1]	67.1	49.3	57.9	59.1	76.0 [1]	73.4	49.0	46.4	50.9	71.9	67.2
1930	61.5 [1]	66.3	48.4	58.9	58.8	76.4 [1]	73.1	50.5	47.4	51.9	69.3	66.6
1931	62.5 [1]	67.3 [1]	49.9	60.3	61.2 [2]	76.3 [1]	73.2	52.1	49.4	52.9	69.9	68.2
1932	61.6 [1]	67.8	49.8	59.6	59.7	75.7 [1]	72.0	50.0	48.4	52.1	72.9	68.7
1933	62.9 [1]	68.6 [2]	50.7	61.0	59.6	75.7 [2]	72.7	53.4	49.0	51.0	72.2	69.0
1934	61.7 [1]	66.4	51.9	60.8	62.2	79.1 [2]	76.5	54.7	53.2	49.1	70.8	67.7
1935	61.5 [1]	66.6 [2]	49.0	59.0	59.0	76.6 [2]	72.8	50.8	50.4	50.3	70.5	68.1
1936	61.8 [1]	67.2	49.7	60.2	61.1	77.2 [1]	73.8	51.4	49.9	50.9	71.9	67.9
1937	61.3 [1]	66.3	49.4 [2]	58.2	59.7	76.2	73.8	49.7	47.4	52.1	72.0	67.8
1938	62.6 [1]	67.1 [2]	49.2 [2]	61.4	59.3	76.0 [2]	72.7 [2]	50.7	48.0	52.3 [1]	72.2	68.8
1939	61.8 [1]	66.6 [2]	49.8	61.1	60.4	76.2 [2]	73.4	51.2	49.5	51.4	72.9	69.2
1940	59.8 [1]	63.8 [2]	50.6	57.0	61.6	77.2	74.3	49.4	50.1	49.0 [1]	70.3	66.4
1941	62.1	66.3 [2]	47.9	60.0	61.3	74.5 [2]	71.8	48.4 [2]	49.2	50.8 [1]	72.1	68.3
1942	60.9	65.1	50.0	58.7	60.3 [2]	76.2 [2]	73.2 [2]	48.9	49.6	51.6	71.7	67.7
1943	61.4	65.9 [1]	50.7	59.3	60.7 [2]	77.3 [2]	73.3	51.5	51.3	50.8	71.5	67.6
1944	61.7	66.0	48.2	58.7	59.7	74.3	71.0	49.0	49.5	51.4 [1]	72.4	67.9
1945	61.3	66.7	49.1	57.9	60.1	73.0	71.7 [2]	49.5	49.2	51.9	72.5	68.2
1946	62.3	66.6	49.1	59.8	58.7	76.5 [1]	72.5 [2]	51.3	49.8	52.6	73.6	68.2
1947	60.6	65.1	49.2 [2]	57.9	60.3	77.7 [2]	73.5	51.0 [1]	49.5	51.6	72.3	66.4
1948	61.4	65.8 [1]	48.6	58.0	58.6	74.3 [1]	71.5	52.3	48.5	51.4 [2]	74.4	67.5
1949	62.2 [2]	66.9 [2]	46.9	57.7	59.3	75.3 [2]	71.6	53.0 [2]	48.7	54.1 [2]	73.8 [2]	68.4
1950	61.1	67.2	50.5 [2]	56.9	60.8 [2]	76.5	73.5	53.4	50.2	51.0 [1]	72.5	66.7
1951	61.5	67.8 [2]	48.8	57.4	60.4	76.9	72.1	50.8	48.9	52.7 [1]	72.4	66.6
1952	61.8	67.0 [2]	48.1	59.1	60.5	75.8	73.0 [2]	53.6	49.1	52.1 [1]	72.1	66.7
1953	62.5	67.2	49.9 [2]	59.7	60.8	76.9	73.1	54.8	49.6	52.3 [2]	72.9	66.7
1954	63.1	67.8	51.0 [2]	60.3	60.1	77.4	73.9	56.1	51.7	50.9	72.0	66.4

Notes appear at end of table

(continued)

TABLE Cf418–483   Annual mean temperature: 1895–1998   [Reference climatological stations]   *Continued*

Year	Muscle Shoals, Alabama Cf418 Degrees F	Selma, Alabama Cf419 Degrees F	Grand Canyon National Park, Arizona Cf420 Degrees F	Fayetteville Experiment Station, Arkansas Cf421 Degrees F	Davis Experiment Farm, California Cf422 Degrees F	Death Valley, California Cf423 Degrees F	Indio Fire Station, California Cf424 Degrees F	Boulder, Colorado Cf425 Degrees F	Montrose #2, Colorado Cf426 Degrees F	Groton, Connecticut Cf427 Degrees F	Saint Leo, Florida Cf428 Degrees F	Savannah WSO AP, Georgia Cf429 Degrees F
1955	61.7	66.5 [2]	48.7 [2]	58.6	60.1	75.5 [1]	71.7 [2]	52.4	49.0	51.0 [1]	72.1	65.8
1956	62.4	66.1	50.1	59.1	60.3	76.0 [1]	72.8	54.4	50.1 [2]	50.2 [1]	71.9	66.5
1957	62.0	66.8	48.4 [2]	57.3	60.7	76.6 [1]	73.7 [2]	52.3	49.6	50.2 [1]	73.0	66.3
1958	59.3	64.3	49.4 [2]	56.7	62.6	77.7 [1]	75.3 [2]	53.3	51.5	47.8	71.1 [2]	64.4
1959	61.4	66.1	49.2 [2]	57.4 [2]	62.7	78.7 [2]	74.9 [2]	51.2	49.8	50.0	72.6 [2]	66.3
1960	59.0	65.0	48.7	56.9	60.6	78.2 [1]	74.5 [2]	52.6	48.6	49.3	71.4	64.7
1961	59.2	65.2	48.3	57.4	59.4	77.1 [2]	73.8	51.3	48.3	49.4	72.5	65.8
1962	60.5	66.5	49.2	58.6 [2]	58.8	77.5	74.0	52.3	49.5	48.0	72.2 [2]	65.6
1963	60.3	65.1	49.5 [2]	59.5	58.1	76.7	73.0	53.6	49.5	48.7	71.7 [1]	64.8
1964	61.2	65.7	47.6	59.3	58.8	76.3	71.2 [2]	52.2	47.1	49.3	72.0	65.5
1965	61.1	66.3	47.1	59.8 [2]	59.0	75.2 [2]	71.8 [2]	51.7	48.4	49.1	72.3	65.7
1966	61.5	65.0 [2]	49.1 [2]	57.9	60.2	76.5 [2]	73.5 [2]	52.8	49.2	49.4	70.9	64.5 [2]
1967	60.5	66.1	48.8 [2]	58.9 [2]	59.8	76.5 [2]	72.8 [2]	51.9	48.0	48.5	72.2	65.8
1968	60.0	65.3	47.5	57.7 [2]	60.4	76.9	73.6	51.5	45.8	49.5	70.3	64.9
1969	59.9	65.2	47.4	58.8 [2]	60.5	76.9 [2]	74.3	51.7	47.5	49.9	70.6	64.3
1970	61.6	65.8 [2]	47.7	58.7 [2]	60.8	76.8	73.0 [2]	51.4	47.0	49.3	71.1	66.0
1971	60.7	66.6	47.5 [2]	59.3 [2]	59.0	76.5	72.3 [2]	50.6	47.9	50.1	72.3 [2]	67.0
1972	60.5	67.4	48.5 [2]	58.7 [2]	59.4	76.5	73.5 [2]	50.8	49.8	48.6	73.0 [2]	67.1
1973	61.0	66.8 [2]	47.8 [2]	59.0 [2]	60.4	76.7 [2]	73.2 [2]	50.1	47.8	50.9 [2]	71.7 [1]	66.9
1974	60.1	66.2 [2]	48.8 [1]	59.2	60.4	77.5	73.7 [2]	51.3	48.3	50.1	72.6 [1]	67.3
1975	60.0	66.2 [2]	47.5 [1]	58.8	58.7	76.2	72.1 [2]	50.5	47.5	50.9	73.5	67.5
1976	58.0	63.9 [2]	47.5 [1]	56.9 [2]	60.0	76.0	72.9	51.1	48.9	49.3	70.9	64.4
1977	61.3	66.0 [2]	48.0 [2]	58.2 [2]	59.6	77.0	73.6 [2]	52.4	50.8	49.8	71.0	66.1
1978	60.2	65.6 [2]	47.5 [2]	56.3 [2]	60.5	76.5 [2]	73.2 [2]	50.2 [2]	50.1	48.2	71.6	66.1
1979	58.8	64.7 [2]	46.5 [2]	55.0	60.1	76.0 [2]	73.1 [2]	50.8 [1]	48.2	50.5 [2]	72.0	66.0
1980	60.4	65.4 [1]	48.0 [2]	58.3 [2]	59.4	76.7 [2]	73.8 [2]	52.7	50.9	50.1	72.1	66.2
1981	60.2	65.2 [1]	48.9 [2]	57.7 [2]	61.1 [2]	78.5	75.2 [2]	53.3 [2]	51.7	50.0	71.9 [2]	65.7
1982	60.4	66.9 [1]	46.2	56.9	58.4	74.3 [2]	72.4 [1]	51.0 [1]	48.9	50.6	74.0	67.6
1983	60.0	63.7 [1]	47.2	56.2	60.2 [1]	75.0	73.0 [1]	49.9 [1]	49.6	51.9 [2]	72.0	65.6
1984	61.2	65.2	46.5 [1]	57.1	60.7	75.6 [2]	73.8 [1]	50.2 [2]	48.6	51.4	72.5	67.0
1985	60.3	65.6 [2]	45.9	55.9 [2]	59.0	75.3 [2]	74.0 [1]	49.7 [2]	49.5 [2]	51.0	73.6	67.6
1986	62.1	66.8 [2]	47.3	58.7	60.9	77.2 [2]	75.8	52.6 [2]	50.6	50.3 [2]	73.6	68.7
1987	62.1	66.3 [2]	45.6	58.3	60.5	76.7 [2]	74.0 [1]	51.6	49.5 [2]	50.4 [2]	71.8	66.6
1988	60.6	65.1 [2]	46.3	57.5	61.1	76.6 [2]	74.8	52.0	49.8 [2]	49.6	71.5	65.7
1989	60.0	64.4	47.6 [1]	56.4 [2]	59.2 [2]	76.9 [2]	74.6	51.0 [1]	49.8	49.6 [1]	73.4	67.0
1990	63.0	67.3	47.0	59.5	60.5	75.6	73.7 [1]	51.1 [1]	49.4	52.0	74.4	69.4
1991	62.9	65.8	47.1	59.3	61.1	75.6 [1]	73.8 [1]	51.0	46.9	52.6	72.9	68.5
1992	60.8	63.8 [1]	46.8 [2]	57.8	62.1	76.8	74.2 [1]	51.0	48.6	49.3 [2]	71.1	66.8
1993	61.2 [2]	64.0	46.1	56.3 [2]	60.6	75.6	74.1 [2]	49.0 [1]	48.3	50.1 [2]	72.2	67.2
1994	61.8 [2]	64.8	47.7 [2]	—	59.3	76.9	75.1	51.6 [2]	49.8	49.9 [2]	73.7	68.0
1995	—	65.6	48.0	57.6	61.4	76.7	76.2	50.9	49.8	50.5 [2]	72.9	67.5
1996	—	64.5	—	56.4	61.8	77.4	77.0	51.1	49.8	49.2	71.7	66.0
1997	—	64.5	—	56.6	62.3	76.2 [2]	—	50.4	48.7	49.9	73.2	65.6
1998	—	66.8	—	60.5	—	73.3 [2]	—	—	49.9 [2]	—	74.4	68.0

Notes appear at end of table

TABLE Cf418–483 Annual mean temperature: 1895–1998 [Reference climatological stations] *Continued*

Year	Grace, Idaho	Porthill, Idaho	Urbana, Illinois	Marion 2N, Indiana	Belle Plain, Iowa	Lawrence, Kansas	Hopkinsville, Kentucky	Calhoun Research Station, Louisiana	New Orleans Audubon, Louisiana	Presque Isle, Maine	Baltimore WSO City, Maryland	Blue Hill, Massachusetts
	Cf430	Cf431	Cf432	Cf433	Cf434	Cf435	Cf436	Cf437	Cf438	Cf439	Cf440	Cf441
	Degrees F	Degrees F	Degrees F	Degrees F	Degrees F	Degrees F	Degrees F	Degrees F	Degrees F	Degrees F	Degrees F	Degrees F
1895	41.6[1]	44.7	49.4	50.3	47.2	53.3[2]	56.1[1]	62.6	66.7	39.8[1]	54.2	47.3
1896	42.8[1]	44.8	51.8	52.2	47.5	55.3[2]	58.6[1]	65.7[2]	68.7[1]	39.1[1]	55.8	46.9
1897	41.9[1]	46.7	51.2[1]	51.4	46.0[1]	54.7	59.1	65.4[1]	69.1	39.4[1]	55.1	47.3
1898	41.5[1]	47.1[2]	51.2[1]	52.1	46.3[1]	54.3[2]	59.4	64.0[1]	67.3[1]	40.0[1]	56.4	48.3
1899	42.2[1]	42.2[2]	50.8[1]	51.5	47.6[1]	53.5	57.7	63.5[2]	67.7	39.6[1]	55.1[2]	47.7
1900	44.3[1]	44.2	52.2	52.8	49.0[1]	55.2	58.1	64.4[1]	68.4[2]	39.5[1]	57.1[2]	48.7
1901	43.8[1]	44.0[2]	50.5[1]	51.0	48.7[1]	55.6	57.3	62.6[1]	66.6	39.5[1]	54.4	46.8
1902	42.8[1]	44.0	50.4[1]	51.3	47.2[2]	53.6	58.1	63.2[1]	68.7	40.2[1]	55.2	47.6
1903	41.2[1]	43.5	49.9	50.6	46.3	53.2	56.9	62.9[1]	67.5[2]	40.7[1]	55.0	47.4
1904	43.4[1]	46.0	48.8	48.3	45.4	53.0	56.6	64.3[1]	68.8	37.8[1]	52.7	44.7
1905	42.4[1]	44.9	50.1	50.4	46.7	53.1	56.9	63.1[1]	68.7	38.8[1]	54.8	46.6
1906	42.9[1]	46.7	51.5	52.0	47.7[2]	54.3	57.9	64.6[1]	68.8	39.9[1]	56.0	47.7
1907	45.8[1]	44.5	50.2[2]	50.1	47.3[1]	54.2	57.3	66.3[1]	70.0	38.8[1]	53.7	45.6
1908	44.0[2]	45.3	52.1[2]	52.6	49.1	55.1	59.1	65.8[1]	69.7	40.2[1]	56.2	48.7
1909	44.5[2]	43.5	50.6	51.0	47.4	53.8[2]	59.3	65.9[2]	69.9[2]	40.1[1]	55.9	47.6
1910	46.7[2]	45.4	51.0	50.9	48.5	54.5	57.8	65.3[2]	69.4	40.5[2]	55.8	48.1
1911	43.2	42.9	52.6[2]	52.6	49.2	56.0	60.7	66.9	71.8	39.5[2]	56.6	48.1
1912	43.1[2]	44.4	49.5[2]	49.7	46.7	52.7	56.9	63.5	68.6	39.6[1]	55.1	47.4
1913	44.1	42.8	53.2	53.2	50.1	55.8[1]	59.8	64.3[1]	69.2	41.3[1]	57.9	49.4
1914	46.2[2]	44.7	51.8	52.0	49.6	55.7	57.9	64.6[2]	68.5	36.6	55.4	46.5
1915	45.3[2]	45.9	51.0	51.3	48.1	54.0	58.5	64.6[2]	68.7	40.6	55.9	48.0
1916	43.9[2]	41.1	51.2	51.9	47.6	54.6[1]	59.0	65.2[2]	68.8	39.5[1]	55.2	46.2
1917	43.7[1]	43.9	48.4	49.0	45.0	53.2[2]	56.1	62.8	68.0	36.4	53.4	45.0
1918	45.4[2]	45.7	51.1	51.4	49.0	56.1[1]	59.0	64.4[2]	69.2	37.4[1]	55.8	46.7
1919	46.4	44.0	52.4	51.9	48.8	55.3[2]	59.9	64.0[1]	68.8	39.0[1]	56.7	47.1
1920	42.3[2]	44.5	50.8	50.3	48.7	54.5[1]	58.1[2]	63.2[2]	67.2	38.8	55.3	45.8
1921	43.1	44.8	55.3[2]	56.2	52.8	58.0[2]	62.0[2]	66.0[2]	69.8	40.4	58.3	48.7
1922	40.4	43.2	53.2[2]	53.4	50.9	56.5[1]	59.7[2]	65.0[2]	70.0	38.8[2]	56.9	48.3
1923	40.4	44.3	51.7[2]	51.6	49.5	55.2	59.2	64.9[1]	69.2	37.2	56.6	46.9
1924	41.3	43.1	49.4	49.2	47.2	53.2	57.1	64.4[1]	68.9[2]	37.6	54.7	47.2
1925	44.1	45.6	52.0	51.1	49.2[2]	55.4[2]	59.8	66.6[1]	70.0[2]	37.6[2]	56.5	49.1
1926	44.1	47.2	50.5	49.9	48.5[2]	55.0[2]	58.6	64.9[2]	68.6[1]	36.9[2]	54.8	46.5
1927	41.9	44.3	52.3	51.5	49.6	54.9[2]	59.9	67.2[1]	71.1[1]	39.3	56.7	48.9
1928	41.7	44.7	51.4	50.2	49.7	55.8[2]	57.7	65.1[2]	68.5[1]	38.6[1]	56.6	48.2
1929	40.6	42.6	50.1	49.3	46.7	53.4[2]	57.7	64.8[1]	69.2[2]	39.1	56.8	48.4
1930	40.5	44.7	53.1[2]	51.3	50.1	56.2	59.8	65.5	68.7[2]	40.6[2]	58.1	49.1
1931	41.9	46.6	55.4	54.2	53.6	58.3	61.4	65.7[2]	69.0[2]	41.5	59.2	49.6
1932	40.3	44.7	52.6	51.6	49.1	55.1	59.7	66.0[2]	69.5[2]	40.4	57.9	48.9
1933	42.3	45.4	54.2	53.5	50.9	57.7	60.4	67.5[1]	71.4[2]	39.1	57.6	47.8
1934	46.6	47.8	53.4	52.9	51.4	59.0	58.7	66.8[2]	69.5[2]	37.9	56.3	46.7
1935	42.2	43.8	51.7	51.3	48.4	55.9	58.1	66.2	69.7	38.7	56.0	46.9
1936	42.6[2]	44.7	52.2	51.3	48.3	57.3	58.8	65.6[1]	69.0[2]	38.8	56.4	47.4
1937	41.8	43.6	51.0	50.2	47.3	55.1	57.9	65.3[2]	70.3[2]	41.2	57.0	48.9
1938	43.2	46.2	54.4	53.7	51.1	58.8	59.9	67.2[2]	70.8[1]	38.6[1]	58.0	49.2
1939	43.9	46.0	53.7	53.4	50.6	58.8[2]	59.2	67.0[1]	71.0	38.6[2]	58.3	47.9
1940	45.0	47.5	51.2	49.9	48.4	54.7	55.7	64.0[2]	68.8[1]	38.7	55.1	45.9
1941	42.2	47.2	53.7	52.5	51.7	57.2	58.7	65.9	71.3[2]	40.5	58.3	48.9
1942	40.8	45.7	52.3	51.3	49.3	56.0	58.0[2]	65.4	69.5[2]	41.5	57.5[2]	48.6
1943	42.8	43.9	51.8	50.5	47.7	55.3	58.0	66.0	69.4[1]	39.2	56.9	48.0
1944	39.8	46.6	52.9	52.3	49.5	56.1	59.1	65.5	70.2[1]	41.3	57.0	49.0
1945	40.5	46.7	51.3	50.9	47.8	55.2	57.4	65.9	70.3[1]	41.2	57.4	49.0
1946	42.4	44.9	54.4	53.6	50.7	58.5	58.7	67.1	70.0[2]	41.1	58.4[2]	49.7
1947	42.5	45.9	52.0	50.9	49.2	55.9	56.0	65.6[2]	68.5[1]	41.0[1]	56.6[2]	48.8
1948	41.2	44.3	52.6	51.8[2]	49.2	55.5	56.3	66.3[2]	69.6[1]	40.1	57.0	48.4
1949	41.3	43.8[2]	54.1	52.7	49.5	55.7	57.9[2]	67.4[2]	71.1[1]	41.5[2]	59.2	51.4
1950	41.7	43.8	50.7	49.1	46.6	54.1	56.6[2]	66.3[1]	70.3[1]	40.6	56.7	48.7
1951	40.7	44.1	50.7[2]	49.7	46.0	53.5	57.4[2]	66.9[2]	71.0[1]	40.7[2]	57.4	49.7
1952	40.9	45.9	53.6[2]	51.8	49.5	56.6	58.8[2]	66.3[2]	70.3[1]	41.3	58.2	50.2
1953	44.4	47.8[1]	54.8	52.0[1]	50.4	58.3	59.7[2]	66.9[2]	70.1[1]	42.5[2]	59.0[2]	51.2
1954	43.6	45.3	54.8	51.1[2]	50.7	58.8	58.6	67.5[2]	70.2[1]	40.0[2]	58.7	48.8

Notes appear at end of table

(continued)

TABLE Cf418–483   Annual mean temperature: 1895–1998   [Reference climatological stations]   *Continued*

Year	Grace, Idaho	Porthill, Idaho	Urbana, Illinois	Marion 2N, Indiana	Belle Plain, Iowa	Lawrence, Kansas	Hopkinsville, Kentucky	Calhoun Research Station, Louisiana	New Orleans Audubon, Louisiana	Presque Isle, Maine	Baltimore WSO City, Maryland	Blue Hill, Massachusetts
	Cf430	Cf431	Cf432	Cf433	Cf434	Cf435	Cf436	Cf437	Cf438	Cf439	Cf440	Cf441
	Degrees F	Degrees F	Degrees F	Degrees F	Degrees F	Degrees F	Degrees F	Degrees F	Degrees F	Degrees F	Degrees F	Degrees F
1955	39.9	43.2	53.3	50.3	49.6	56.4	57.6	65.5	70.6 [1]	39.8	57.4	48.6
1956	41.2	45.0	53.0	49.8 [2]	49.7	57.6	58.1	66.3 [2]	69.4	38.9	58.2	48.0
1957	41.9 [2]	44.3	52.3	49.5 [2]	49.0	55.9 [2]	57.6	65.6	70.0 [2]	40.4	59.0	50.0
1958	43.9 [2]	47.8 [2]	50.6	47.5 [2]	48.0	55.5	55.0	64.2 [2]	66.5 [2]	39.0	55.8	47.1
1959	43.6	44.4	52.7	50.0 [2]	48.1	56.0 [2]	57.5	65.7	68.9 [2]	40.0	59.3	48.8
1960	42.6	44.6	50.8 [2]	48.2	47.5	55.0	55.8	64.3	68.3 [2]	40.9	57.2	48.5
1961	43.8	46.1 [2]	51.8	49.8 [2]	48.2	54.7	56.2	63.0	68.2	40.0	57.5	48.6
1962	43.5	45.5	51.4	49.1 [2]	47.4	56.0	56.6	64.9	69.6	39.0	56.4	47.2
1963	44.4	45.3	51.0 [2]	48.1	48.4	57.4	56.4	64.1 [2]	69.4	39.5	56.6	48.1
1964	40.5	43.8	53.0	50.0 [2]	49.8	57.1	57.7	64.2 [2]	68.6	40.0	58.3	48.6
1965	42.7	45.5	52.5	50.1	48.1	57.4	58.0	65.1 [2]	69.1	39.0	58.0	48.0
1966	42.8	46.3	51.1	48.8 [2]	47.7	55.7 [1]	56.2	63.4	67.7	41.4	57.6	48.7
1967	42.8 [2]	47.2	50.7	48.6	47.8	55.6	55.9	63.6 [2]	68.2	39.1	57.1	47.5
1968	41.8	44.9 [2]	51.4	49.5	48.9	55.7	55.4	62.2	67.3 [2]	39.5	59.0	48.0
1969	43.1	45.2	51.4	49.0	47.5	55.0 [2]	56.3	63.6	68.6	40.7	58.4	48.6
1970	42.7	45.5 [2]	51.7	49.8	48.4	56.0	56.9	63.6	68.0	39.5	58.2	48.2
1971	41.6	45.2	53.0	50.2	48.9	56.1	57.7	64.4	70.0 [2]	39.8	57.9	48.7
1972	42.6	45.0	50.7	48.8	46.6	55.4	56.8	64.3	69.3 [2]	37.9	56.9	47.1
1973	42.2	46.5	53.9	51.9 [2]	50.1 [1]	56.9	58.7	64.5	69.1 [2]	41.7	59.4	50.4
1974	43.3 [2]	46.6	51.8	49.6	48.5	56.2	57.6	64.2	70.4 [2]	38.9	57.9	48.6
1975	41.2 [2]	43.6 [2]	52.4	50.9	49.0	54.9	56.9	64.1	70.1 [2]	40.2 [2]	58.8	49.7
1976	42.5 [2]	44.5 [2]	50.5	48.8	48.4	54.4	55.2 [2]	62.5	67.3	38.8	58.1	48.4
1977	44.1 [2]	45.0	51.7	49.9	49.8	55.5 [2]	57.1	63.9	70.6	40.3	58.8	48.9
1978	42.5 [1]	44.0 [2]	49.7	47.6 [2]	46.8	54.9	55.5 [2]	62.8	70.1	39.6	57.5	47.2
1979	42.0 [2]	45.6 [2]	49.5	48.1 [2]	46.6 [2]	54.3 [2]	54.9 [2]	62.2	69.1 [2]	42.2	58.0	49.2
1980	43.3 [2]	44.8	51.3	49.1	49.3	57.9	56.1	64.2 [2]	71.5	39.3 [2]	57.7	47.9
1981	45.2 [2]	45.5 [2]	51.3	49.2	50.4	57.9	55.4	64.2	71.3	41.8	57.8	48.6
1982	41.5 [2]	44.1 [2]	50.5	49.3	47.8	55.8 [2]	55.4	64.6	71.6	39.7 [1]	57.7	47.9
1983	43.5 [1]	46.3 [2]	52.0	51.0	49.7	55.8	55.6	62.3	68.6	42.0	58.3	49.6
1984	40.1 [2]	45.1 [2]	51.5	49.8	49.4	56.5	56.7	64.1	69.2	41.1	57.8	49.3
1985	40.3 [1]	43.4 [2]	50.7 [2]	50.0 [2]	47.7	54.4	56.0 [2]	64.0	69.1	39.8 [2]	59.3	48.5
1986	44.9 [1]	46.4 [2]	52.2 [2]	50.7	49.8	58.4	57.2 [2]	65.2	70.8	39.7	59.2	48.3
1987	44.9 [2]	47.3 [2]	53.3	51.7	52.3	58.7	58.1	64.2	69.8	41.1	59.3	48.7
1988	44.4 [2]	46.7 [2]	51.8	49.7	49.5	58.2	56.1	63.6	69.6	41.0	57.6	49.0
1989	43.7 [2]	45.5 [2]	50.2	48.6	47.1	55.8 [2]	55.0	63.0	69.8	39.4 [1]	58.0	48.1
1990	44.3	46.6 [1]	53.1 [1]	52.0	50.2	58.3 [1]	57.9 [1]	65.8	71.6	41.8	61.1	50.9
1991	43.1	45.8 [2]	53.9	52.4	49.6	58.6	58.2	64.9 [1]	70.7 [1]	40.9	61.2	50.8 [1]
1992	45.0	47.2 [2]	51.9	49.8	48.2 [2]	56.3	56.0 [1]	63.7	69.2 [1]	39.7	58.7	47.6
1993	40.5	44.1	50.4	49.4	46.3	54.3 [1]	55.5	63.2	69.4	39.4	57.7	48.6
1994	45.3	47.3 [2]	51.5	50.2	47.6	56.6	56.3	64.2	70.5	39.9	58.1	49.3
1995	46.1	46.5 [2]	51.4	50.7 [2]	47.5	55.5 [2]	—	64.7 [2]	70.5	—	—	49.1
1996	44.5	43.5 [2]	49.6	49.2	44.6	54.5	—	63.8	70.0 [2]	39.9	57.8 [2]	48.6
1997	43.2	—	50.5	49.6	46.3	—	—	63.4	69.8 [2]	39.1 [2]	—	48.9
1998	44.9	48.5 [2]	55.0	54.2	50.3	—	—	66.3	72.2	42.9	63.9 [2]	—

Notes appear at end of table

TABLE Cf418–483   Annual mean temperature: 1895–1998   [Reference climatological stations]   *Continued*

Year	Ann Arbor, University of Michigan Michigan	Chatham Experimental Farm #2, Michigan	Itasca, University of Minnesota, Minnesota	Greenville, Mississippi	Sweet Springs, Missouri	Bozeman, Montana State University, Montana	Glasgow WSO AP, Montana	Crete, Nebraska	Reno WSFO AP, Nevada	Searchlight, Nevada	Hanover, New Hampshire
	Cf442	Cf443	Cf444	Cf445	Cf446	Cf447	Cf448	Cf449	Cf450	Cf451	Cf452
	Degrees F	Degrees F	Degrees F	Degrees F	Degrees F	Degrees F	Degrees F	Degrees F	Degrees F	Degrees F	Degrees F
1895	46.4	39.5 [1]	36.8 [1]	62.1 [2]	54.2	41.1	39.3 [2]	50.7	48.3 [1]	62.4 [1]	43.6
1896	47.7	39.9 [1]	36.9 [1]	64.9	56.6 [1]	43.2 [2]	38.4	51.7	49.1	63.9 [1]	43.9
1897	47.6 [2]	39.5 [1]	37.0 [1]	64.6 [2]	57.5	42.9 [2]	38.7 [1]	51.2	47.5	62.8 [1]	43.7
1898	48.9	40.4 [1]	37.8 [1]	64.2	55.5 [1]	42.3 [1]	39.6 [1]	51.0	48.3 [2]	63.1 [1]	45.3
1899	48.3	39.5 [1]	36.8 [1]	63.8	54.3 [2]	41.1 [1]	36.8 [2]	50.2	49.1 [1]	63.4 [1]	43.9
1900	48.8 [2]	41.7 [1]	39.2 [1]	64.8	56.1 [1]	44.2	43.5 [2]	51.7 [1]	51.1 [2]	63.6 [1]	44.0 [2]
1901	47.3	40.6	38.1 [1]	63.5	56.2 [2]	42.9	43.2 [1]	52.3	49.2	63.6 [1]	44.0
1902	47.7 [2]	40.2	38.6 [1]	64.2	54.1 [2]	41.7	40.2 [1]	50.5 [1]	49.3 [1]	63.0 [1]	43.6
1903	46.9	39.9	36.3 [1]	62.6	54.2 [2]	40.8	40.8 [1]	50.3	48.3	63.3 [1]	44.2
1904	45.0 [2]	36.6	36.0 [1]	63.7	55.0 [1]	42.2	39.2 [2]	49.6	50.3	64.1 [1]	40.7
1905	47.3	38.5	37.4 [1]	63.2	55.0	40.8 [2]	39.6 [1]	50.5	49.6	62.8 [1]	42.6
1906	49.1 [2]	39.7	38.0 [1]	63.5	56.2	41.3 [2]	40.8 [2]	51.8	50.6	63.2 [1]	44.0 [2]
1907	45.3	37.0	36.3 [1]	64.7 [2]	56.0 [1]	40.9	37.6 [2]	51.1	49.9	63.4 [1]	42.3
1908	48.2	40.8	39.2 [1]	64.7	57.0	41.3	42.8 [1]	52.6 [2]	49.6	62.6 [1]	44.4
1909	47.3	39.1	37.4 [1]	64.7	56.2	40.2	40.0 [1]	50.6 [1]	50.0	62.6 [1]	43.6
1910	47.7	39.9	39.3 [1]	63.9	56.0	42.8	43.2 [1]	52.4 [2]	52.0	64.8 [1]	44.1 [2]
1911	49.0	39.9	39.8 [1]	66.0	57.9	39.6	38.3 [1]	53.1	48.6	62.2 [1]	44.1 [2]
1912	45.9	36.2	38.4 [1]	62.6	54.0 [1]	39.7	38.4 [2]	50.0 [2]	49.1	61.9 [1]	43.0
1913	49.1	39.4 [1]	38.7	64.6	57.6	40.1	40.6 [1]	52.6	49.9	62.4 [1]	46.2
1914	47.3	38.0	37.8	64.1	56.7	42.7	42.0 [1]	51.8	51.2	63.4	42.5
1915	46.9	39.9	38.4	64.0 [2]	55.5	41.8	42.3 [2]	50.0 [2]	51.4	61.8	45.5
1916	47.3	38.5 [1]	35.1 [2]	64.3	55.9	38.2	36.3 [2]	50.3	49.0	62.2	43.6
1917	44.2	34.3 [2]	34.8 [2]	61.9	53.7	41.2	38.6 [2]	49.1	50.2	63.4	41.4
1918	47.6	38.9 [2]	38.7	64.1	56.9	41.5	42.3	52.7 [2]	50.6	63.0	43.4
1919	48.9	39.7 [2]	38.3 [1]	65.0	56.2 [1]	41.5	41.2 [2]	50.9 [2]	50.1	62.7	44.6
1920	46.8	39.0 [1]	38.0 [1]	63.4 [1]	55.2 [1]	40.5	42.1 [2]	51.0	49.9	62.0	43.5
1921	50.7	42.8 [1]	40.6 [1]	67.7	58.6 [1]	42.5	44.1	54.8 [1]	51.9	63.8	46.3
1922	49.1	41.3 [1]	39.1 [2]	65.9	57.1 [1]	39.8	40.1 [2]	53.0 [2]	48.9	62.3	44.2
1923	47.5	40.1	38.1 [2]	64.6	56.2 [1]	42.4	42.6	52.2 [2]	49.2	62.3 [2]	42.8
1924	45.9	38.4 [1]	33.6 [1]	63.9	54.1 [1]	40.6	40.8 [2]	50.0 [2]	51.2	65.6 [2]	43.1
1925	47.8 [2]	40.3	36.1 [1]	66.4 [1]	56.6 [2]	43.6	42.8 [2]	52.6 [2]	51.4	63.6 [2]	44.0
1926	46.1	38.2	37.5 [2]	64.8	56.0 [1]	42.9	43.7	52.4	53.1	64.7	41.7
1927	48.9	40.2	36.2 [2]	66.0 [1]	55.0 [2]	40.7	39.4	51.6 [2]	50.9	65.7	45.0
1928	48.0 [2]	40.3	38.5 [1]	64.3	56.2 [1]	42.3	42.2	52.4 [2]	51.9	66.1 [2]	44.8
1929	47.3	38.6	35.5 [2]	64.9	53.8 [2]	40.6	40.4	49.9 [2]	51.3	65.0	44.2 [2]
1930	49.6	40.8 [1]	39.0 [2]	65.6	56.1 [2]	42.2	43.2	53.9 [2]	50.6	63.7	45.4
1931	51.9	45.0	42.6	65.9	58.6	43.8	45.9	55.3	52.6	62.6	46.2
1932	49.3	41.0	37.5 [2]	65.5	55.4 [2]	41.5	42.0 [2]	51.3	51.0	63.0 [1]	45.5
1933	50.1	40.3	38.4 [2]	67.1 [1]	57.6	44.0	43.1	54.9	51.7	62.6 [1]	45.0
1934	49.4	39.3 [1]	38.9 [2]	66.1	58.5	47.4	45.4	56.4	54.5	65.5	43.6
1935	48.0	40.0	37.6	65.3	55.6 [2]	42.0	40.9	53.1 [2]	50.8	61.8 [2]	43.5
1936	48.3	39.6	35.9	65.1	56.9	42.7	40.6	53.4 [2]	52.5	64.3	44.2
1937	48.5	40.9	36.5 [2]	64.6	54.9	41.2	41.7	51.1 [2]	49.5	63.6 [1]	45.5
1938	50.8	42.3	40.1 [1]	66.9	59.0	43.4	43.5	54.0 [2]	49.8	62.6 [1]	45.6
1939	50.3	41.0	39.6	66.1 [2]	58.5	44.5	43.9	54.5 [1]	52.4	63.0	43.8
1940	47.4	40.7	38.4	63.2 [2]	54.6	43.7	42.4	50.0 [1]	51.8	65.2 [1]	42.7
1941	50.6	44.0	41.3	65.6	57.7	43.3	44.3	52.4 [2]	50.1	62.1 [1]	44.8
1942	49.0	42.3	39.7	64.9	56.0	41.0	42.2 [2]	52.1 [2]	49.2	62.4 [1]	44.8
1943	47.8	40.1	38.2	65.4	56.0 [2]	42.1	42.4	52.0	50.1	63.5 [1]	42.4
1944	49.6	41.8	40.4	65.4	56.6 [2]	42.4	44.5	51.8 [2]	48.5	62.2 [1]	43.8
1945	48.4	40.0	37.4	65.0	55.7 [2]	42.3	41.9	51.0 [1]	49.5	62.9	44.5
1946	50.2	41.8	39.0	65.4	59.2 [2]	43.4	43.8 [2]	55.0 [2]	49.3	63.8	45.1
1947	47.6	40.7	38.2	63.5 [2]	56.4 [2]	43.6	43.3	52.6	50.0	64.5	44.3
1948	48.9 [2]	40.5	38.5 [1]	63.0	56.5 [2]	42.1	43.7	52.0 [2]	47.8	63.0	44.1
1949	50.9 [2]	42.9 [2]	38.7	64.4 [2]	56.9 [2]	42.6 [2]	42.4	51.4 [1]	47.7	63.0	47.2
1950	47.9 [1]	38.5 [2]	34.7 [2]	63.8 [2]	55.3 [1]	41.6 [1]	37.7	50.2	50.4	65.7	44.2
1951	48.1	40.3 [2]	35.7 [2]	63.6 [2]	54.6 [2]	40.0 [2]	37.9	49.2 [2]	49.3	62.6	45.2
1952	50.7	43.3 [2]	39.9 [2]	64.7 [2]	57.8 [2]	43.1	42.2	51.8 [1]	48.4	62.3	45.8
1953	51.4 [2]	43.9 [2]	40.7 [2]	65.2	59.5 [2]	46.0	45.5	54.1	49.2	63.5	47.6 [2]
1954	48.9 [1]	41.7 [2]	39.7 [2]	66.0	60.2 [2]	44.4	43.6	54.1 [2]	49.7	64.6	44.8

Notes appear at end of table   (continued)

TABLE Cf418–483   Annual mean temperature: 1895–1998   [Reference climatological stations]   *Continued*

Year	Ann Arbor, University of Michigan Michigan	Chatham Experimental Farm #2, Michigan	Itasca, University of Minnesota, Minnesota	Greenville, Mississippi	Sweet Springs, Missouri	Bozeman, Montana State University, Montana	Glasgow WSO AP, Montana	Crete, Nebraska	Reno WSFO AP, Nevada	Searchlight, Nevada	Hanover, New Hampshire
	Cf442	Cf443	Cf444	Cf445	Cf446	Cf447	Cf448	Cf449	Cf450	Cf451	Cf452
	Degrees F	Degrees F	Degrees F	Degrees F	Degrees F	Degrees F	Degrees F	Degrees F	Degrees F	Degrees F	Degrees F
1955	50.2 [1]	43.1 [2]	38.9	64.4 [2]	57.5 [2]	40.7	40.5	52.2	47.9	62.1	45.2
1956	49.5 [2]	41.2 [2]	38.8 [2]	64.8	58.3 [2]	43.5 [2]	41.5	52.8	48.0	63.8 [2]	44.0
1957	49.8 [2]	41.2	38.8 [2]	63.2	56.4 [2]	42.8	42.4	51.4	48.7	62.8 [1]	46.0
1958	48.7 [2]	41.3	39.6 [2]	60.4	55.3 [2]	45.0	43.4	50.8	50.7	64.1 [2]	43.6
1959	50.1 [2]	40.9	38.8 [2]	63.7	56.5 [2]	43.1	40.4	51.0	49.8	64.2 [1]	45.8
1960	48.4 [2]	41.1	39.0 [2]	62.0	55.6 [2]	43.2	41.9	49.7	49.3	63.9 [2]	45.1
1961	49.5 [1]	42.0	41.0	62.7	55.4 [2]	44.8	44.2	50.7	49.6	63.7 [2]	45.2
1962	49.5 [2]	40.7	39.1	64.0	56.4 [2]	43.4	42.8	51.9	48.2	63.9 [1]	43.7
1963	49.4 [2]	40.8	39.9	63.3	57.5 [2]	45.0	44.5	53.4	49.3	63.8 [2]	44.3
1964	51.0 [2]	42.6	38.1	63.1	57.6 [2]	43.1	42.8	53.2	49.0	62.1 [1]	44.8
1965	49.1	40.5 [2]	36.5	63.1	57.6	43.1	39.6	51.6	49.2	61.8 [2]	44.2
1966	49.9 [2]	42.0	36.3	62.7	56.3 [2]	44.7	40.2	51.5	50.2	63.3	44.6
1967	49.3 [2]	40.6	37.4 [2]	62.9	56.3 [2]	44.0	41.2	51.6	49.9	62.8	43.9 [2]
1968	50.4 [2]	42.1 [2]	39.5 [2]	61.8	55.4 [2]	42.6	41.9	51.9	49.7	63.2	43.9
1969	50.2	42.2 [2]	39.1 [2]	62.4	55.0	43.1	39.7	50.9	50.4	63.2	45.2
1970	50.5 [2]	41.6	38.1 [2]	64.4	56.2 [2]	43.8	41.1	52.6	51.0	63.1	44.7
1971	50.8 [2]	41.3	38.9 [2]	65.3	56.8	43.6	41.6	52.0	48.0	61.4	44.6 [2]
1972	48.7	38.4 [2]	36.6 [2]	64.9	55.6	43.5	40.1	51.2 [2]	49.0	63.2 [1]	43.6
1973	51.7	43.7 [2]	41.6	65.2 [1]	56.9 [2]	43.7 [2]	44.1	52.4	49.8	62.9 [2]	46.7
1974	49.4	41.0 [2]	39.4 [2]	65.0	54.2	45.2	44.2	53.0	49.2	63.8 [2]	44.4
1975	49.3	42.5 [2]	39.4	64.7 [2]	54.4	41.9	41.2	51.5 [2]	48.3	62.8 [2]	45.6
1976	47.8	40.8 [1]	39.8	63.4 [2]	53.4	45.4	44.1	52.9 [2]	48.8	63.1	44.1
1977	48.5	42.4 [2]	40.5 [2]	65.7	53.3	44.7	41.6	53.5	50.9	64.8	45.6
1978	47.1	40.4 [2]	38.7	64.0 [2]	51.1	43.2	38.2	49.5	49.3	63.4	43.5 [2]
1979	47.4	39.5 [2]	37.3	63.4	50.3	43.9	39.9	50.0	50.4	62.8 [2]	46.0 [1]
1980	47.7	41.3 [2]	39.8 [2]	65.1	53.4	44.9	44.0	53.3	51.0	64.1 [2]	44.8 [2]
1981	48.4	41.7	42.3 [2]	64.6	52.6	46.4	46.7	53.7 [2]	52.0	66.0 [2]	47.0 [2]
1982	48.4	40.3	37.6 [2]	64.0	51.3	42.4	39.1 [2]	50.4	48.5	61.3	45.3 [2]
1983	49.5	42.1	39.5 [2]	62.3 [1]	53.1	44.7	43.4	50.9	50.6	62.4	46.8 [2]
1984	49.3	41.8	39.2 [2]	63.8 [2]	53.5 [2]	44.1	44.4	52.2	50.3	63.4 [1]	45.9 [2]
1985	48.8	42.3	35.9 [2]	64.2 [2]	51.8	41.9	39.8	50.3	50.0	62.7 [1]	45.8 [2]
1986	49.5	43.2	39.5 [2]	65.6 [1]	56.9	45.7	44.2	53.8	52.7	64.1	45.6 [2]
1987	51.3	44.2	43.4	64.6 [2]	57.5	46.9	47.6	54.7	52.5	63.2	46.3
1988	49.4	42.4 [2]	38.0 [2]	63.2 [2]	55.9 [2]	47.0	45.6	54.2 [2]	53.0	64.2	45.7
1989	47.8	40.8	36.1	62.0 [2]	53.8	43.8	41.6	51.3	51.4	65.3 [2]	44.6 [1]
1990	50.8	43.8	39.6	64.9 [1]	57.3	45.7	44.9	53.8 [1]	51.6	63.7	47.7
1991	51.3	43.8	39.3	64.2	57.3	45.8	45.1	53.1 [1]	51.8	63.1	46.9
1992	48.3	41.6	38.0	62.5	55.6	46.4	45.3	52.3 [2]	53.7	63.4 [1]	44.2
1993	48.3	41.6 [2]	36.0	62.2	53.6	42.5	40.5	49.5	51.1	62.8	45.0
1994	49.2	41.8	38.3 [2]	63.2 [2]	55.5	46.5	42.7	52.0	53.8	64.4	45.3
1995	49.0	42.0	37.4	63.5	54.7	—	41.8	51.8 [2]	53.1	64.9	45.9 [2]
1996	47.7	39.8	34.5	62.8	53.8	43.7	38.2	50.1	51.6	66.3	45.6
1997	48.1	41.0	37.9	62.5 [2]	53.3	43.9	42.8	51.6	51.2	65.0	—
1998	53.2	45.1	42.1	65.8 [2]	56.4	44.8	45.7	54.0	51.4	62.0	—

Notes appear at end of table

TABLE Cf418–483   Annual mean temperature: 1895–1998   [Reference climatological stations]   *Continued*

Year	Carlsbad, New Mexico	Chama, New Mexico	Albany, WSFOAP, New York	Geneva Resr Farm, New York	New York Central Park, New York	Cape Hatteras WSO, North Carolina	Dickinson Experiment Station, North Dakota	Wooster Experiment Station, Ohio	Goodwell Research Station, Oklahoma	Muskogee, Oklahoma
	Cf453	Cf454	Cf455	Cf456	Cf457	Cf458	Cf459	Cf460	Cf461	Cf462
	Degrees F	Degrees F	Degrees F	Degrees F	Degrees F	Degrees F	Degrees F	Degrees F	Degrees F	Degrees F
1895	61.4 [2]	44.4 [1]	48.5	46.9	53.1	60.8	38.4 [1]	47.9	55.6 [1]	60.0 [1]
1896	64.0	47.2	48.5	48.0	53.6	62.1	37.8	49.6	58.7 [1]	62.9 [1]
1897	61.0	42.4 [1]	48.9	47.6	53.6	62.2	40.0	49.3	56.7 [1]	61.2 [1]
1898	59.8	41.1 [1]	50.3	49.3	55.1	62.3	40.6 [2]	50.5	55.9 [1]	60.7 [1]
1899	62.4 [2]	42.1 [1]	49.0	47.7	54.0	61.1	38.1	49.6	55.2 [1]	60.7 [1]
1900	60.6 [2]	42.9 [1]	50.1	48.4	54.1 [2]	62.8	45.3 [2]	50.7	57.0 [1]	61.0 [1]
1901	63.4 [1]	43.2 [1]	48.6	47.8	52.4 [2]	60.5	43.7	48.9	56.8 [1]	61.1
1902	65.0 [2]	42.6 [1]	48.0	48.0	53.0 [2]	61.6	39.1 [2]	49.5	56.8 [1]	59.8
1903	63.5 [2]	41.6 [1]	48.4	48.2	53.1	62.2	41.8 [2]	49.2	54.8 [1]	58.0
1904	65.0 [1]	42.7 [1]	45.4	45.9	50.9	60.9	40.4 [2]	47.1	56.4 [1]	59.2
1905	61.4 [2]	43.2 [2]	47.6	47.2	53.4	62.0	41.9	48.9	55.3 [1]	58.7
1906	62.0 [1]	44.3 [2]	48.7	48.8	54.9	62.9	41.3 [2]	50.7	56.0 [1]	59.2
1907	63.3	44.3	47.0	46.7	52.9	61.3	38.9 [2]	48.4	57.6 [1]	61.2
1908	62.3	42.6 [2]	49.1	48.8	55.0	63.1	42.1 [2]	51.1	57.0 [1]	61.3 [2]
1909	63.8	42.4	48.3	48.1	53.7	62.9	40.2 [2]	50.1	55.7 [1]	62.5 [2]
1910	65.2	44.4	48.5	47.9	53.5	62.4	42.5 [2]	49.1	58.4 [1]	61.7
1911	64.0	42.4	49.2	49.2	53.5	63.1	39.7 [2]	50.9	58.4 [1]	63.1 [2]
1912	61.0	40.7	47.6	47.8	52.7	62.6	39.1	47.9	53.7 [1]	60.0 [2]
1913	61.8	40.9	50.5	49.7	55.0 [2]	63.7	41.6	50.6	56.1 [1]	61.3 [1]
1914	63.3	42.4	47.2	47.5	52.0 [2]	62.0	41.5	49.3	57.6 [2]	61.2
1915	62.1	41.5	49.2	48.5	53.5	62.2	40.4	49.0	55.3 [1]	59.5
1916	64.0 [1]	43.0	47.8	47.9	52.2	62.5	37.9	49.0	57.8 [2]	60.2
1917	62.4 [1]	41.6	45.8	45.1	50.7	60.1	38.1	46.3	55.0 [1]	57.4 [1]
1918	60.5 [2]	42.0 [2]	48.2	48.0	53.2	61.5	41.2	50.5	56.2	60.3
1919	60.6	41.9 [1]	49.3	49.3	53.8	62.7	41.4 [2]	51.2	54.5 [1]	60.8
1920	61.7	41.7 [2]	47.7	48.3	52.3	61.0	40.8 [2]	49.2	56.3 [2]	60.2 [2]
1921	63.4 [2]	42.5 [2]	51.0	51.8	54.9	63.9	42.5	53.3	58.6 [1]	64.2
1922	61.7 [2]	40.5 [1]	49.3	49.1	53.5	63.1	39.4	51.4	57.4 [2]	62.6
1923	61.6 [2]	40.1 [1]	47.7	46.9	52.9	62.5	41.2	50.2	55.8 [1]	61.8
1924	61.3 [2]	39.3	47.4	46.2 [2]	51.9	61.0	38.4	48.1	54.7 [2]	59.7
1925	63.3 [2]	40.8	48.6	48.0	53.4	63.3	41.4	49.8	56.9	62.3
1926	62.2 [1]	40.9 [1]	46.5	45.7	51.2	61.9	41.4	48.5	56.0	60.7
1927	65.0	41.6	49.4	48.9	53.4	62.9	38.2	50.8	56.7 [2]	62.0
1928	63.2	40.8	49.8	49.1	53.6	62.9	41.0	50.1	54.9	61.3
1929	62.7 [1]	39.1	49.0	48.4	54.1	63.7	37.2	49.4	53.6 [1]	60.0 [2]
1930	63.7	39.9	50.3	49.6	54.5	63.2	40.7	51.3	55.9 [1]	61.6
1931	64.1	40.3	51.3	52.0	55.8	63.1	44.4	52.6	57.0 [2]	63.1
1932	61.8	39.6	50.1	50.1	55.1	64.6	39.7	51.2	55.3	61.9
1933	65.2	41.9	50.0	50.1	54.2	64.8	41.8	52.1	58.4	63.3
1934	66.3	47.0	48.0	48.3	53.0	62.7	43.8	50.5	59.5	63.3
1935	64.9	43.8 [2]	48.4	48.1	53.1	62.5	40.0	49.6	57.9	61.2
1936	63.8	43.9	49.3	49.0	53.4	62.8	39.5	49.9	57.4 [2]	63.2
1937	63.1	42.9	50.4	49.4	54.5	63.0	39.3	49.9	57.1 [2]	60.8
1938	65.3	42.7	49.5	50.4	55.2	63.8	41.6	51.2	58.6	64.0
1939	64.0	42.5	47.0	49.5	54.7	64.1	41.6	50.7	58.1	63.9
1940	62.4	43.2	45.0	46.8	51.9	60.6	41.1	47.4	56.5	59.9
1941	63.2	42.6	48.2	50.3	54.9	62.2	41.8	51.0	56.4	62.4
1942	63.5	42.4	47.8	49.6	54.1 [2]	63.3	40.3	49.1 [2]	57.0	61.3
1943	63.8	44.6	46.2	48.3	53.7	62.0	39.6	47.8	57.1 [1]	62.0
1944	62.5	42.7	47.6	49.6	54.6	62.6	39.6	49.2	55.6	61.9
1945	64.0	42.0	47.2	49.0	54.1	63.1	38.7	49.4	56.7	60.4
1946	64.1	43.0 [2]	48.4	50.3	55.3	63.6	42.3	51.1	58.3 [2]	63.5
1947	63.0 [2]	42.7 [2]	47.4	49.4	53.8	62.8	40.1	49.6	56.5 [1]	61.1
1948	64.1	42.7 [2]	46.8	48.5	54.0 [2]	63.8	40.5	49.4 [2]	56.0 [1]	59.4
1949	63.3 [2]	42.5 [1]	50.0	50.5 [2]	56.9 [2]	64.6	39.9 [2]	51.9 [2]	56.2 [1]	59.8 [2]
1950	64.1 [1]	42.6 [1]	46.8	47.4 [2]	53.6	63.6	36.3	48.5	57.2 [2]	60.5
1951	62.8 [2]	42.4	47.8	48.2	55.1	63.2	37.1 [2]	49.2	56.1 [1]	61.1
1952	61.8 [2]	42.2 [1]	48.7	49.2	55.8	63.8	41.6 [2]	50.5	57.8 [1]	62.3
1953	62.6 [1]	43.0 [1]	50.1	50.1	57.0	64.2	43.7 [2]	50.9	59.5 [1]	63.2
1954	64.3 [1]	45.5	48.0	48.4	54.9	63.7	42.5 [2]	50.0 [2]	60.0 [2]	65.1

Notes appear at end of table   (continued)

TABLE Cf418–483   Annual mean temperature: 1895–1998   [Reference climatological stations]   *Continued*

Year	Carlsbad, New Mexico	Chama, New Mexico	Albany, WSFOAP, New York	Geneva Resr Farm, New York	New York Central Park, New York	Cape Hatteras WSO, North Carolina	Dickinson Experiment Station, North Dakota	Wooster Experiment Station, Ohio	Goodwell Research Station, Oklahoma	Muskogee, Oklahoma
	Cf453	Cf454	Cf455	Cf456	Cf457	Cf458	Cf459	Cf460	Cf461	Cf462
	Degrees F	Degrees F	Degrees F	Degrees F	Degrees F	Degrees F	Degrees F	Degrees F	Degrees F	Degrees F
1955	62.5 [1]	40.9 [1]	48.1	49.1	54.7	62.5	40.3 [2]	49.7 [2]	57.1 [2]	62.4
1956	62.8 [1]	43.0 [1]	46.4	46.9	53.5	62.6	41.7 [2]	49.2 [2]	58.6 [2]	63.4
1957	62.3 [2]	42.9 [2]	48.6	48.5 [2]	55.4	64.3 [2]	41.4 [2]	49.5	56.4 [2]	61.3
1958	61.1 [2]	44.8	46.2	46.3	52.5	60.9	42.2 [2]	47.0	55.9 [2]	60.2
1959	61.3	43.9 [1]	48.6	48.7	55.4	63.9	40.2	50.1	56.3 [2]	61.0
1960	60.3	43.0	47.4	47.4	54.0	62.6	40.6 [2]	47.6 [2]	55.8 [1]	60.4 [2]
1961	61.1	43.0	47.6	47.7	55.1	62.6	42.6 [2]	48.4	55.5 [2]	60.2 [2]
1962	63.4 [2]	44.4	46.4	46.9	53.4	61.8	41.6	48.0	57.1 [2]	61.8
1963	62.9 [2]	44.1 [1]	46.2	46.2	53.6	60.9	43.1	46.4	58.6 [2]	62.4
1964	62.3	41.6 [2]	47.9	48.2	54.6	63.0 [1]	40.8	49.1 [2]	57.4 [2]	62.1 [2]
1965	62.7 [2]	42.8	46.8	46.5	54.2	62.4	38.8	49.2	57.2 [2]	61.9
1966	61.4 [2]	43.2 [1]	46.8	47.1	55.1	61.8	39.4	48.1	55.7 [2]	59.9
1967	62.6 [2]	42.7 [2]	46.2	46.9	53.0	61.8	40.3 [2]	48.5	57.7 [2]	60.2
1968	61.3 [1]	41.8	47.2	46.5	54.1	62.0 [2]	39.7	48.2	56.7	58.8
1969	63.0 [2]	42.4	46.6	46.5	54.8	62.0	40.0 [2]	48.0	56.5 [2]	60.4
1970	61.4 [1]	41.5 [2]	46.8	46.6	54.3	63.0 [2]	39.2 [2]	49.3	56.5 [2]	60.2
1971	62.2 [2]	40.7 [2]	46.3	46.7	55.2	63.8 [2]	39.5 [2]	49.3	56.5 [1]	60.4 [2]
1972	61.9 [1]	42.3 [2]	45.6	45.4	53.9	64.0	38.2	47.9	56.4	60.7
1973	61.8 [1]	40.6 [1]	49.1	48.5	56.1	65.0 [1]	42.2	51.3	53.1	60.7
1974	62.0 [1]	41.5 [2]	46.0	46.3	54.7	64.5 [1]	42.0	48.9	54.0	60.9
1975	60.7 [1]	39.5 [2]	48.0	48.0	54.9	64.2 [2]	40.1	50.0	55.5 [1]	60.4
1976	60.5 [1]	40.9 [2]	46.3	45.5 [2]	53.4	62.9 [2]	43.0	47.3	54.6 [1]	59.6 [2]
1977	63.7 [1]	41.9 [2]	47.6	47.1	54.3	63.3 [2]	41.5	48.7	56.1 [2]	62.2 [2]
1978	62.5 [1]	41.5 [2]	45.6	45.5	53.0	62.0 [2]	38.1	46.8	53.8	60.2 [1]
1979	61.1 [2]	40.3	47.9	46.9	55.7	63.0	38.6 [1]	47.8 [2]	53.9	58.9 [1]
1980	62.9 [2]	42.0	46.3	46.0	55.0	62.0 [2]	42.3 [2]	48.2 [2]	55.6	62.2 [1]
1981	63.0 [1]	43.1	46.7	47.3	55.2	61.1 [?]	44.1 [2]	48.3 [2]	57.3	61.8 [1]
1982	63.0 [1]	39.8	46.7	46.9	54.9	63.3	37.7	48.5 [2]	54.4	61.1 [1]
1983	62.6	41.1	47.9	47.9	56.0	63.3	41.3	49.7	53.5	60.1 [1]
1984	62.3 [2]	40.7	48.0	47.3	55.5	63.9 [2]	40.9 [1]	48.7	54.4	61.5 [1]
1985	62.8 [1]	41.0	47.8	46.8	55.5	65.3	38.1 [2]	48.2	54.6	60.8 [2]
1986	62.9 [1]	41.8 [2]	47.8	47.4	55.3	64.3 [2]	41.8	50.2 [2]	57.0 [2]	62.4
1987	61.3 [1]	40.5	48.2	48.0	55.1	63.2	44.5	50.9	54.9	62.1
1988	61.8 [1]	41.0 [2]	47.6	47.1	54.8	62.7	42.8 [2]	48.9 [2]	54.4 [1]	61.3
1989	63.2	41.9	47.2	45.8	54.0	63.4	40.5 [2]	48.6 [2]	54.5	59.8
1990	63.5	41.3	50.4	49.4 [1]	57.2	65.4	42.3	51.7	56.0	62.5
1991	62.5 [2]	40.4	49.9	49.4	57.1 [1]	65.4	42.9	52.3	56.0	62.1
1992	62.4	40.8	46.9	45.6	53.9	63.0	42.2	49.0	55.3	60.9
1993	62.8 [2]	41.1	47.5	46.0	55.5	63.4	38.7	49.5	53.8 [1]	60.2
1994	64.4	42.4	47.1	46.4	55.2	64.7	40.4 [2]	49.2	—	61.3 [2]
1995	64.0	42.5	48.2	47.1 [2]	55.3	63.6 [2]	41.6	48.9	56.5	61.3
1996	64.4	42.1	47.2	46.2	53.7	61.6 [2]	38.5	48.2 [2]	—	60.4
1997	62.1	42.0	47.1	46.5 [2]	54.3	61.7 [2]	41.9	48.4	55.7	60.5
1998	64.8	42.4	50.6	50.2	57.2	63.7	43.5 [2]	52.1 [2]	—	63.4 [2]

Notes appear at end of table

TABLE Cf418–483   Annual mean temperature: 1895–1998   [Reference climatological stations]   *Continued*

Year	Newport, Oregon	Union Experiment Station, Oregon	Harrisburg Capital City, Pennsylvania	Charleston City, South Carolina	Winthrop College, South Carolina	Cottonwood 2E, South Dakota	Lewisburg Experiment Station, Tennessee	Rogersville 1NE, Tennessee	Beeville 5NE, Texas	El Paso WSO AP, Texas	Marshall, Texas
	Cf463	Cf464	Cf465	Cf466	Cf467	Cf468	Cf469	Cf470	Cf471	Cf472	Cf473
	Degrees F	Degrees F	Degrees F	Degrees F	Degrees F	Degrees F	Degrees F	Degrees F	Degrees F	Degrees F	Degrees F
1895	50.2	47.2 [1]	51.3	64.7	60.2 [1]	45.2 [1]	57.2 [1]	55.6 [1]	68.9 [1]	62.3	63.8
1896	50.8 [1]	47.9 [1]	52.3	66.6	61.9 [1]	45.7 [1]	59.4 [1]	56.8	71.4	64.3	66.4 [1]
1897	50.9	47.5 [1]	52.4	67.1	61.3 [1]	45.5 [1]	59.2 [1]	56.7	71.2	63.2	67.5 [1]
1898	51.0	47.0 [1]	53.7	66.8	61.2 [1]	46.1 [1]	58.9 [1]	56.2	70.3	62.4	65.5 [1]
1899	49.9	46.7 [1]	52.3	66.6	61.1 [1]	44.0 [1]	59.4	56.0	69.0	63.4	65.0 [1]
1900	52.1	48.5 [1]	54.3	66.8	62.1 [2]	48.7 [1]	60.3 [2]	56.7	68.9	64.3	65.7 [1]
1901	50.9	47.9 [1]	51.9	64.3	59.0	47.6 [1]	57.7	53.9	69.1 [2]	64.2	64.5 [1]
1902	50.9	46.8 [1]	51.9	65.7	61.0 [2]	45.7 [1]	59.5	56.8 [2]	72.2 [1]	64.3	65.3 [1]
1903	51.1	46.5 [1]	51.8	65.1	60.8	45.2 [1]	58.6	56.7	68.5 [2]	62.7	63.9 [1]
1904	50.5	48.2 [1]	49.2	64.6	59.8 [2]	46.0 [1]	59.6	56.0	71.1 [2]	63.5	65.4 [1]
1905	51.7	47.2 [1]	51.5	65.5	60.6 [1]	45.1 [1]	59.5	56.8	69.4 [2]	62.6	64.3 [1]
1906	51.5 [1]	47.9 [1]	52.9	66.1	61.7	46.0 [1]	60.0	57.8	70.3 [2]	63.3	65.4 [1]
1907	53.3	47.6 [1]	50.4	66.4	61.1 [2]	45.3 [1]	59.6	57.2	72.0 [2]	64.5	66.6 [1]
1908	51.2 [2]	47.4 [1]	52.9	66.8	62.2 [2]	46.8 [1]	60.4	57.5	71.8 [2]	62.9	66.0 [1]
1909	50.2	47.0 [1]	52.5	66.1	62.1 [2]	45.8 [1]	59.7	57.1	72.0	63.3	66.8 [1]
1910	50.8	48.0 [1]	52.5	65.2	61.4 [2]	47.7 [1]	58.7	55.9 [2]	71.4	65.1	66.2 [2]
1911	50.3	46.1 [1]	53.4	67.3	63.2	48.8	61.8	58.9	72.6	63.4	67.8 [2]
1912	51.4	46.3	51.8	65.5	61.2	45.7 [2]	58.3	56.5	69.9	61.4	63.9 [2]
1913	49.3	45.7	54.7	66.4	61.9	47.7 [2]	60.5	58.6	69.4	61.4	65.2 [2]
1914	50.3	49.0	51.8	65.0	61.1 [2]	48.0 [2]	58.9	57.1	70.1 [2]	63.1	65.2 [2]
1915	51.3	48.5 [2]	52.7	66.0	61.6	44.0 [2]	58.8 [1]	57.4 [2]	71.6 [2]	62.2	65.3 [2]
1916	48.8 [2]	45.0 [2]	51.9	66.3	61.2 [2]	43.6 [2]	59.4	57.4	72.4	64.7	66.5 [2]
1917	49.4 [2]	46.4	50.1	64.6	58.2 [2]	43.8 [2]	57.0	55.1	70.5 [2]	63.6	64.6 [2]
1918	50.4 [2]	48.0	52.6	65.9	62.1	46.3	59.7	57.4 [2]	69.9	62.4	66.4 [2]
1919	49.1	46.4	53.3	67.3	62.9	45.1	60.1	58.5	69.1 [2]	62.8	65.0 [2]
1920	49.7 [2]	46.4	51.7	65.0	60.7 [2]	45.5 [2]	58.6 [2]	56.1 [2]	69.7 [2]	62.9	64.6 [2]
1921	50.7 [2]	47.9 [2]	55.1	67.9	63.2 [1]	49.0 [2]	62.1	59.3 [2]	72.2 [2]	64.8	69.7 [1]
1922	48.4	46.5	53.6	67.3	62.2 [1]	43.5	60.8	58.4	71.5	63.9	67.9
1923	49.1	47.5	53.0	66.3	61.8	45.6	58.7	57.2	70.7	63.1	67.1 [2]
1924	48.3 [2]	46.6 [1]	51.2	65.5	60.3	44.4	56.9 [1]	55.8 [2]	70.0	63.8	65.9
1925	49.5 [2]	49.4	52.8	67.0	63.3	47.3	60.7	59.0 [2]	70.2	64.2	68.1 [2]
1926	51.2	48.3 [1]	51.0	66.0	61.7	47.3 [2]	59.0	57.2	68.8	63.7	66.6
1927	48.3	46.4	52.8	67.5	62.9	44.4	61.4	58.7	73.3	65.7	69.7
1928	50.7	47.8	52.8	66.0	60.9	47.3 [1]	58.9	56.2 [2]	70.4	64.2	67.5
1929	50.4	46.4	52.9	66.4	61.1	44.0 [2]	59.5	57.1 [2]	69.8	63.3	65.6 [1]
1930	51.4	46.6	54.0	66.0	61.5 [2]	47.8	60.0	57.2 [2]	69.6	64.2	65.7
1931	52.6	47.7	55.5 [2]	67.0	62.7	50.0	60.7	58.6	70.1	64.6	66.4 [2]
1932	50.4 [1]	45.7	54.1	68.1	63.0	46.0	60.3	58.4	70.1	63.7	66.6 [2]
1933	49.4 [1]	46.4	53.6 [2]	68.0	63.2	48.7	61.4	58.4	72.4	65.0	68.2 [2]
1934	53.7	51.0	52.6	66.3	61.5	50.7	59.9	58.2 [1]	70.9 [2]	67.1	66.7
1935	50.1 [2]	46.9	52.4	66.4	61.4	48.0	59.0	58.8	70.0	64.8	65.8
1936	52.0	47.9	52.6	66.3	61.2	47.0	59.4	59.1	68.2	64.6	65.2
1937	51.1	47.0	53.0	66.2	61.8	46.3	58.8	57.9	71.0	65.1	65.2
1938	51.6	49.0	54.0	67.3	63.4	48.4	61.0 [2]	59.6	72.7	64.9	67.9
1939	51.9	49.1	54.0 [2]	67.5	63.4	49.6	59.4 [1]	59.7	72.8	64.9	68.0
1940	53.0	50.2	51.5	64.6	60.4	47.0	56.7 [2]	56.8	70.4	64.6	64.3
1941	53.4	49.6	55.5 [2]	66.3	62.2	48.9 [2]	60.1 [2]	59.4	70.5	64.0	65.7
1942	52.0	47.8 [2]	53.5	66.4	61.7	46.6 [2]	58.8 [2]	58.2	70.6	64.8	65.0
1943	51.6	47.4	53.0	65.6	62.4	46.5	59.0 [2]	58.2	70.7	64.0	66.0
1944	51.6	47.7 [2]	53.3	66.2	61.7	45.1 [1]	59.5	58.6 [1]	71.2	62.8	65.4
1945	50.7	47.9	53.0	67.2	62.7	46.9	58.8	59.6 [1]	72.5	64.1	65.2 [2]
1946	50.8	47.6	54.1	67.4	63.1	48.8 [2]	59.8	60.1	71.7	64.3	66.7 [2]
1947	52.5	48.5	52.9	65.8	61.4	47.4	57.9	57.6	70.2	63.3	65.6 [2]
1948	50.6	46.1	52.6	66.6	61.6	46.4 [2]	58.8 [2]	59.3 [2]	71.4 [2]	63.9	64.6 [1]
1949	50.4 [2]	47.2	54.8	67.9	62.0 [2]	46.1 [2]	59.8 [2]	60.5 [1]	71.8 [2]	62.9	65.9 [2]
1950	50.0 [1]	47.8	52.0	66.5	61.9 [2]	44.0 [2]	58.4 [2]	58.6	73.2	65.9	65.1 [2]
1951	50.3 [1]	47.5	52.9	66.3	61.8	43.4 [2]	59.0 [2]	58.5	72.9 [2]	64.4	65.9 [2]
1952	50.1	47.8	53.9	66.9	61.6	46.7 [2]	59.5	59.4 [1]	71.4	63.8	66.0 [2]
1953	51.7	49.3	55.0	67.3	61.2	48.9 [2]	60.0 [2]	59.1	72.0	64.5	66.4 [2]
1954	50.3 [2]	48.3	53.6	67.0	63.3	49.4 [2]	60.4	57.7	72.3	65.6	68.0 [2]

TABLE Cf418–483   Annual mean temperature: 1895–1998   [Reference climatological stations]   *Continued*

Year	Newport, Oregon	Union Experiment Station, Oregon	Harrisburg Capital City, Pennsylvania	Charleston City, South Carolina	Winthrop College, South Carolina	Cottonwood 2E, South Dakota	Lewisburg Experiment Station, Tennessee	Rogersville 1NE, Tennessee	Beeville 5NE, Texas	El Paso WSO AP, Texas	Marshall, Texas
	Cf463	Cf464	Cf465	Cf466	Cf467	Cf468	Cf469	Cf470	Cf471	Cf472	Cf473
	Degrees F	Degrees F	Degrees F	Degrees F	Degrees F	Degrees F	Degrees F	Degrees F	Degrees F	Degrees F	Degrees F
1955	48.1	45.8	53.6	66.4	62.7	47.2	58.9 [2]	57.3 [1]	71.5	63.9	66.4 [2]
1956	49.3 [2]	47.5	52.6	66.9	62.7	48.1 [2]	59.6	56.9 [2]	71.3	64.4	67.2 [2]
1957	50.8	46.9	53.8	66.4	62.7 [1]	46.6 [2]	59.7	58.6 [2]	69.8	64.5	66.1 [2]
1958	52.4 [2]	50.1 [2]	51.5	64.7	60.5	47.8 [2]	56.8	54.9 [2]	69.0 [2]	64.2	65.1 [2]
1959	50.2 [2]	47.3	54.4	66.5	62.3	47.4 [2]	58.5	57.0	68.1 [2]	64.8	65.3 [2]
1960	49.5 [2]	47.3	52.3	64.9	59.9	46.4 [1]	56.2	54.5	67.7 [2]	64.1	65.0 [2]
1961	50.2 [2]	48.9	52.7	65.9	60.3 [2]	47.9 [2]	57.8	55.8	68.7 [2]	63.3	64.7 [2]
1962	49.5 [2]	47.2	51.7	65.4	60.5	47.1 [1]	57.9	55.9 [1]	70.4	64.1	66.0 [2]
1963	51.3 [1]	48.4	51.7	64.9	60.1	48.9 [1]	56.5	54.3	70.5	64.4	64.0 [2]
1964	49.5 [1]	46.0	52.5	65.9	61.2	46.8 [2]	57.7	55.3	70.1	62.8	63.8
1965	50.6 [2]	48.0	53.0	66.3	61.9 [2]	46.6 [2]	57.8	55.9	70.5	63.9	64.2
1966	51.1 [1]	48.7	53.6	65.0	60.3	45.9	56.2 [2]	54.1	69.2	62.8	62.8
1967	50.7 [1]	49.0	51.7	65.8	60.7	47.1 [2]	56.6	55.6 [2]	70.6	63.1	63.6
1968	51.0	47.9	52.7	65.1	60.1	47.0 [2]	56.0 [2]	55.1 [2]	68.4	62.2	62.2
1969	50.5 [2]	47.9 [2]	52.8	64.7	59.8	46.7 [2]	55.9 [2]	55.6	69.8 [2]	65.2	63.7
1970	49.8	47.5	53.3	66.4	61.5 [2]	46.3 [2]	57.1	57.1	68.7 [2]	64.0	63.4
1971	49.0 [2]	46.9	53.6	66.6	60.9	46.0 [2]	57.6	57.1	71.1	63.3	64.4 [1]
1972	49.4	46.8	52.8	66.4	60.6	45.7 [2]	56.9	56.0 [1]	69.2	63.8	63.4 [1]
1973	50.1	48.6	54.4	66.6	61.9 [2]	48.0 [1]	58.2	56.5	68.9 [2]	61.9	63.2
1974	49.8	47.6 [2]	54.2	66.9	62.2 [2]	48.5 [1]	57.4	55.8	69.3 [2]	62.7	63.7 [2]
1975	49.3	45.7 [2]	53.6	67.5	62.1 [2]	46.1 [1]	57.6 [2]	56.8	70.0 [2]	62.5	63.3 [2]
1976	50.5	47.6 [2]	52.4	65.9 [2]	60.1 [2]	48.6 [2]	55.2 [2]	53.9 [2]	68.0 [2]	61.4	61.7 [2]
1977	50.7	48.3	52.7	66.7	61.5 [2]	47.6 [2]	57.3	56.2 [2]	69.2 [2]	63.8	63.8
1978	51.0	47.7 [2]	52.1	66.2	60.7 [2]	43.7 [1]	56.1	55.7	68.2 [2]	64.7	62.6 [2]
1979	51.4	47.8	52.2	65.1	60.0	44.3	55.9	55.0 [2]	67.7 [2]	62.4	61.5 [2]
1980	51.4 [1]	48.1	51.9	66.5	60.7	47.5 [2]	57.3	55.4 [2]	69.8 [2]	64.3	63.6 [2]
1981	52.2 [2]	49.0	52.0	65.4	60.0 [2]	48.7 [2]	56.5 [2]	54.9	70.0 [2]	65.0	63.0 [2]
1982	49.6	46.8 [2]	51.8	66.9 [2]	61.3	44.5	57.4	57.2	70.0	64.1	63.3 [1]
1983	51.5	48.5	52.4	64.7	59.8	46.3	56.2	55.9	68.2	63.2	62.0
1984	51.0	45.9	53.0	66.5	60.7	46.4	57.1	56.7	70.7 [2]	63.1	63.0
1985	49.0	44.5	54.5	67.6 [2]	60.8	44.1	56.9	56.2	69.6	62.2	62.2 [1]
1986	50.3	49.3	53.6	67.4	62.7	46.6 [2]	59.0 [2]	57.7 [2]	71.1 [2]	63.2	64.7 [2]
1987	51.4 [1]	49.6	53.5	65.6	61.5	47.6	58.5	57.1	69.4	61.4	64.3
1988	51.1 [2]	48.6	52.2	64.7	60.4	47.2	56.3 [2]	55.2 [2]	70.4	62.4	64.1 [2]
1989	51.2 [2]	46.9	51.8	66.2	61.3	45.9	55.6	55.3	69.9	64.1	64.2
1990	50.9	48.3	55.1	69.2	64.3	47.8	59.6	58.9	70.7	64.0	66.6 [1]
1991	51.4	48.2	55.5 [1]	68.1 [2]	63.6	47.3	59.1	59.4	69.5	63.0	64.3
1992	53.3	50.1	52.1 [1]	66.3	61.3	46.6	57.1	57.4	68.6	64.6	63.5
1993	51.9	46.0	52.5 [1]	66.5	62.1	43.0	57.0 [2]	57.3	69.1	65.7	63.0 [1]
1994	52.0	49.2	—	66.9 [2]	62.1 [2]	46.2	57.1	56.3	70.9	67.4	—
1995	53.4	48.9	—	66.5 [2]	61.0	45.9	57.1	57.2	71.0	65.9	64.7
1996	52.3 [2]	48.4	—	65.9 [2]	60.7	—	56.5	57.7	71.6	65.5 [2]	64.1
1997	53.7	48.8	—	66.9	62.0	46.0	56.5	58.5 [2]	69.8	63.9	63.2
1998	52.4	—	—	70.4	64.2	47.6	59.9 [2]	59.6 [2]	—	64.6	66.7

Notes appear at end of table

TABLE Cf418–483   Annual mean temperature: 1895–1998   [Reference climatological stations]   *Continued*

Year	Temple, Texas	Logan, Utah State University, Utah	Charlottesville 2W, Virginia	Hot Springs, Virginia	Seattle Urban Site, Washington	Spokane WSO AP, Washington	Martinsburg FAA Airport, West Virginia	Oshkosh, Wisconsin	Cheyenne WSFO, Wyoming	Sheridan Field Station, Wyoming
	Cf474	Cf475	Cf476	Cf477	Cf478	Cf479	Cf480	Cf481	Cf482	Cf483
	Degrees F	Degrees F	Degrees F	Degrees F	Degrees F	Degrees F	Degrees F	Degrees F	Degrees F	Degrees F
1895	64.2	45.4 [2]	55.4 [1]	50.8 [1]	52.1 [1]	48.1	51.3	46.1 [1]	43.7	41.0
1896	67.3 [1]	47.7 [2]	57.4 [1]	51.7 [1]	51.9 [1]	48.6	53.1	45.8 [1]	45.7	42.8
1897	66.1	46.6 [2]	57.2 [1]	53.3	52.0 [1]	48.2	53.1	45.0 [1]	44.5	42.2
1898	65.4	45.6 [2]	56.7 [1]	52.2 [1]	52.1 [1]	48.3	53.8	45.1 [1]	43.7	41.6 [2]
1899	65.7	47.1 [2]	56.4 [1]	50.3 [1]	52.1 [1]	47.3	52.4	45.5 [1]	43.3	41.0
1900	66.2	50.1 [2]	58.2 [1]	51.7 [1]	52.8 [1]	49.9 [2]	54.2	46.6 [1]	46.4	45.8 [1]
1901	67.0	49.5 [2]	55.5 [2]	48.6	51.8 [1]	49.0	51.2	46.1 [1]	45.6	45.7
1902	66.1	48.1 [2]	56.3 [2]	50.9 [1]	52.0 [1]	47.9	52.1	46.4 [2]	45.1	44.2 [1]
1903	62.4 [2]	46.0 [2]	56.1 [2]	49.7	51.7 [1]	47.5	51.3	44.9 [1]	43.7	43.7 [1]
1904	65.0	49.0 [2]	55.4	48.4	52.5 [1]	49.9	49.8	42.8 [1]	45.7	45.3 [1]
1905	63.5	48.7	56.0 [1]	49.5	52.3 [1]	48.3	52.0	44.4 [2]	43.5	44.0
1906	64.1	47.8 [2]	57.0 [2]	51.2	52.9 [1]	49.5	53.1	46.1 [2]	44.4	44.7 [2]
1907	66.2	48.1 [2]	55.6 [2]	49.6	51.9 [1]	47.7	50.4	43.8 [2]	45.5	43.4 [1]
1908	66.7 [2]	45.9 [2]	57.2 [2]	50.3	51.6 [1]	48.8	52.8	47.0 [2]	44.7	44.4 [1]
1909	67.4 [2]	47.6 [2]	57.3 [2]	50.3	49.1 [2]	47.4	52.8	44.5 [2]	44.2	42.4
1910	67.3 [2]	49.5	56.5	49.5	49.6 [2]	49.6	53.0 [2]	45.8 [2]	47.3	45.5 [2]
1911	68.2	46.1 [2]	58.2	51.2	49.3 [2]	47.8	54.7	46.3 [2]	45.2	43.0 [2]
1912	65.4 [2]	45.9	56.3	48.6 [1]	51.4 [2]	47.9	52.5	43.0 [2]	42.7	41.4
1913	65.5	47.4 [2]	58.5 [1]	53.0	50.6 [2]	46.9	55.1	45.5 [2]	43.4	43.6 [1]
1914	65.1	47.8	56.2 [1]	50.8	52.0 [2]	49.6	52.7	44.6 [2]	45.3	44.3
1915	66.7 [2]	49.7 [2]	56.9	50.8 [1]	52.6 [2]	49.9	53.7	45.1	43.6	43.0
1916	67.6	47.5 [2]	56.2	50.4	49.0	45.9	52.8	45.0 [2]	43.3	40.7
1917	66.7	46.5 [2]	54.2	48.8	50.5	48.7	50.9	42.2	42.9	43.1 [2]
1918	67.7	49.2	56.6	51.1	50.8 [2]	50.3	52.8	46.5	44.2 [2]	44.0 [2]
1919	65.9	48.6 [2]	57.3	52.4	50.7 [2]	47.8	53.7	47.0	45.2	44.6 [2]
1920	66.7	46.7 [2]	55.6	50.3	52.2 [2]	48.7	52.2	45.5	43.6	42.9
1921	70.5	48.7	59.1 [2]	53.8	51.4 [2]	48.9	56.0	49.9	46.5	46.2
1922	68.7	46.7 [2]	57.6	52.5	50.9	47.4 [2]	54.4 [1]	46.1 [1]	44.6	42.2
1923	68.5 [1]	46.5 [2]	57.1	51.8	52.4 [2]	49.0	53.2 [1]	46.6 [2]	43.7	44.4
1924	66.3	46.7 [2]	55.2	49.6	52.0	49.1	53.1 [1]	44.0 [2]	43.2	41.8
1925	69.0	49.8 [2]	57.7	51.9	53.0	51.1	54.7 [2]	45.3	45.7	45.7 [2]
1926	66.5	50.0 [2]	55.7	50.4	53.7	50.6	52.1	43.2	45.4	45.9
1927	69.1	48.7 [2]	57.3	51.7	51.2	48.1	53.0 [2]	45.1	44.4 [2]	41.8 [2]
1928	67.4	48.3 [2]	56.6	50.6	52.0	49.5	52.9 [2]	45.4	44.4	43.6 [2]
1929	67.3	47.6 [2]	57.0	51.0	50.6	47.2	53.3	43.0	43.0	41.3
1930	67.9	47.1 [2]	58.5	51.2	50.9	48.7	54.4 [2]	46.5	44.7 [2]	45.4
1931	67.4	48.2 [2]	59.4	52.8	53.2 [2]	50.1	56.4 [2]	49.9	46.6	47.2
1932	65.3 [2]	46.5 [2]	58.9	52.1	52.4	48.7	55.2 [2]	45.7	44.3	43.0
1933	70.2 [2]	48.9 [2]	58.4	51.9	51.4	49.0	55.2 [2]	46.7	47.1	45.3
1934	69.2	53.2 [2]	57.0	50.9	55.0	52.9	54.4 [2]	46.5	48.9 [2]	49.0
1935	65.2 [1]	48.9	56.1	51.2	52.2	48.5	54.2 [2]	44.7	45.5	44.5
1936	65.8	50.1 [2]	57.0	51.3	53.1	49.0	54.2 [2]	44.4	46.0	45.1
1937	66.5	48.4	56.2	50.2	52.5	48.1	54.4 [2]	45.0	44.5	43.0
1938	68.4	49.9 [2]	57.4	51.4	53.5	50.8	55.4	47.4 [2]	46.2	45.9
1939	68.1	49.8	58.0	51.0	53.4	50.7	55.4	47.2	46.7 [2]	46.3
1940	64.9	51.6	54.9	48.2	54.3	51.5	52.3	45.1	46.5	46.2
1941	66.9	48.5	58.2	50.4	54.6 [2]	50.5	55.1	48.2	45.9	46.0
1942	66.2	46.7	56.7	49.5	53.1 [2]	48.1	54.8	46.2	44.5	44.4
1943	66.7	49.5 [2]	56.6	49.0	52.3 [2]	47.4	54.8	44.6	46.3	44.8
1944	66.7	46.7 [2]	56.3	49.9	52.9 [2]	48.7	53.4	47.2	44.7	43.4
1945	66.9	47.2 [2]	57.2	50.7 [2]	52.2	48.5	52.8	44.8	44.5	43.2
1946	67.6	48.7 [2]	58.0	51.7	51.8 [2]	48.4	53.7	47.2	46.2	45.7
1947	66.4	48.2	56.2	49.9	53.1 [2]	48.7	52.6	45.8	44.7	44.0
1948	67.4	47.2 [2]	56.8 [2]	51.2 [2]	51.5	45.5	52.9	46.0	44.6	44.3
1949	68.0	47.2 [2]	58.6 [2]	52.3 [2]	51.9	46.3	54.7	47.3	44.8	43.0 [2]
1950	68.0 [1]	48.1	56.0 [2]	50.8 [1]	51.0	45.8	52.3	43.4	45.0	41.8
1951	67.9 [1]	47.0	57.1	51.1 [2]	52.4	46.7	53.2	43.3	42.8	42.3
1952	67.2 [2]	47.6	57.9	52.3 [2]	52.4 [2]	48.1	53.9	46.6	45.6	44.8 [2]
1953	67.5	50.1	59.8	52.7	53.6 [2]	49.4	55.0	47.5	46.7	47.2 [1]
1954	69.2	49.5 [2]	58.1	51.2	52.1 [2]	46.7	53.7	46.2	48.3	46.5 [1]

Notes appear at end of table

(continued)

TABLE Cf418–483   Annual mean temperature: 1895–1998   [Reference climatological stations]   *Continued*

Year	Temple, Texas Cf474 Degrees F	Logan, Utah State University, Utah Cf475 Degrees F	Charlottesville 2W, Virginia Cf476 Degrees F	Hot Springs, Virginia Cf477 Degrees F	Seattle Urban Site, Washington Cf478 Degrees F	Spokane WSO AP, Washington Cf479 Degrees F	Martinsburg FAA Airport, West Virginia Cf480 Degrees F	Oshkosh, Wisconsin Cf481 Degrees F	Cheyenne WSFO, Wyoming Cf482 Degrees F	Sheridan Field Station, Wyoming Cf483 Degrees F
1955	67.2 [1]	45.9 [2]	57.6	52.1	50.3 [2]	44.6	53.5	46.2	45.0	43.1 [2]
1956	68.1 [2]	48.0 [2]	57.5	52.3	52.5 [2]	47.0	53.0	44.7	46.2	44.5 [2]
1957	66.8 [2]	48.2 [2]	57.6	53.1	53.7 [2]	46.9	54.1	45.2 [2]	44.8	44.5 [2]
1958	65.7 [2]	49.9 [2]	55.0	50.1	55.8 [1]	50.6	51.4	44.7	46.3	45.6 [1]
1959	65.7 [2]	48.8 [2]	58.0	53.0 [2]	52.4 [2]	46.2	54.3	44.5 [2]	45.1	43.5 [2]
1960	66.2	48.3 [2]	56.1	50.9	52.2 [1]	46.6	51.8	45.0	46.5	45.5 [1]
1961	66.0	49.6 [2]	56.6	51.8	52.5 [1]	48.0	52.5	45.9	45.0	45.7 [2]
1962	67.4 [2]	48.8 [2]	55.5	51.5 [2]	52.6 [1]	47.0	51.5	44.4	45.8	44.8 [2]
1963	67.6	49.2 [2]	56.4	50.8 [2]	52.8 [2]	48.0	51.3	44.9	47.5	46.3 [2]
1964	66.9 [2]	46.1 [2]	57.2	52.3	51.1 [2]	45.2	52.8	46.8	44.8	43.8 [2]
1965	66.6	47.3	56.9	52.6	53.2	47.4	53.0	44.8	45.3	44.0 [2]
1966	65.4 [2]	47.8	56.2	50.4 [2]	53.2 [2]	48.4	52.1	44.9	47.1	44.8 [2]
1967	67.4 [2]	48.1	55.5	49.4	53.9	49.0	51.5	43.9	45.9	43.5 [2]
1968	65.3 [1]	46.5 [2]	56.6	49.8	52.8	47.1	52.3	46.3	46.0	41.7 [2]
1969	66.8 [1]	48.3	55.8 [2]	49.6	52.5	45.9	52.3	44.5	46.8	42.6 [1]
1970	66.1	48.2	57.0	51.9	52.5 [2]	47.3	52.8	45.4	45.5	43.7
1971	68.0	47.1	57.1	51.7 [2]	51.7	47.1	52.0	45.5	44.9	42.4
1972	66.9	48.4	55.8 [2]	51.1 [2]	52.1	46.8	52.1	43.2	44.7	41.7
1973	66.1	47.0	57.8	52.8	52.5	48.5	55.6	47.5	44.9	43.0 [2]
1974	66.5 [1]	48.7	57.3 [2]	52.0	52.9	47.7	55.8	45.5	46.4	43.2 [2]
1975	65.9 [1]	46.4	56.6 [2]	52.2	52.0	45.4	54.3	45.9	44.1	41.7
1976	65.0 [1]	47.0	55.6	50.0	52.8	47.1	53.5	44.4	45.3	45.8 [2]
1977	66.8 [1]	48.7	56.5 [2]	50.5 [2]	52.3	46.9	55.0	46.0	46.2	44.9 [2]
1978	65.7 [2]	48.2	55.2	49.8	52.7	45.7	53.2	44.2	44.5	41.3 [1]
1979	64.7 [1]	47.9	55.6 [2]	50.5	53.1	46.9	54.4	43.8	46.0	42.9 [2]
1980	66.6 [1]	48.4	56.8 [2]	50.9 [2]	53.0	47.3	55.0	45.2	47.0	45.5 [2]
1981	66.5	49.6	56.1 [2]	50.1 [2]	54.2	47.8	51.9	46.8 [2]	48.3	46.7 [2]
1982	66.5 [1]	45.7	55.9 [2]	51.9	52.4	47.1	53.0	45.0	44.8	41.9
1983	64.0	47.6	55.5 [2]	51.2	53.9	48.5	53.6	45.1	44.2	44.7
1984	66.9	44.2	56.7 [2]	52.0	52.9	46.3	53.3 [2]	45.5 [1]	43.7	43.6 [2]
1985	65.9	44.5	57.1 [2]	52.1 [1]	51.3	43.7	53.4	43.1	43.8	41.3
1986	67.1	49.1	57.3 [2]	52.7 [2]	54.2	47.7	53.8	45.7	47.2	45.2 [2]
1987	65.7	49.2	57.3 [1]	51.9	54.6	48.8	54.1	48.5	46.6	46.9 [2]
1988	66.2	49.2	56.0 [1]	49.7 [2]	53.1 [1]	48.1	53.4	46.2 [2]	46.5	46.4 [2]
1989	64.7	48.0	55.9 [2]	50.2	52.7	46.9	52.6	43.4 [2]	45.7	43.3
1990	67.5	49.5	58.7 [1]	53.4	53.2 [1]	48.1	55.6	46.8	45.7	44.8
1991	65.5 [1]	47.2	59.1	52.6 [1]	52.9	47.5	56.2	46.0	46.4	44.5
1992	66.4 [1]	49.7	55.1	50.1 [1]	54.1	49.5	52.3	45.0	47.0	45.7
1993	65.9	45.7	55.5 [2]	50.4 [1]	53.2	45.3	52.8 [2]	44.3	44.3	41.7 [2]
1994	—	50.8	56.3	—	54.0	49.0	53.5	45.4	48.0	45.7 [2]
1995	—	50.0	56.7	50.5	54.7 [2]	48.0	—	45.1	46.3	45.2
1996	66.4 [2]	49.9	55.8 [2]	49.7	52.8	45.4	53.1	43.0	45.4	—
1997	64.0 [2]	48.4	56.4	50.3 [2]	54.1	47.9	54.9	44.9	44.9	43.8
1998	—	—	59.6	53.5	—	50.3	58.4 [2]	49.6	46.7	45.9 [2]

[1] VEMAP2 estimated data.

[2] Incomplete data as reported in the original source, U.S. Historical Climatology Network data.

Source

See the text for Table Cf286–351.

Documentation

For a description of the data, see the text for Table Cf286–351.

Tables Cf418–549 report the mean annual temperature and total annual precipitation for each of the sixty-six stations beginning in 1895. Where possible, the reported figures are the raw data from the U.S. Historical Climatology Network. For those cases where the raw data were unavailable, the VEMAP2 estimated data were used. Where this was necessary, the mean minimum temperature and mean maximum temperature for each year were averaged in order to create the annual mean temperature.

TABLE Cf484–549   Annual precipitation: 1895–1998   [Reference climatological stations]

Contributed by Myron P. Gutmann, Timothy G. F. Kittel, and Christie S. Wilson

Year	Muscle Shoals, Alabama	Selma, Alabama	Grand Canyon National Park, Arizona	Fayetteville Experiment Station, Arkansas	Davis Experiment Farm, California	Death Valley, California	Indio Fire Station, California	Boulder, Colorado	Montrose #2, Colorado	Groton, Connecticut	Saint Leo, Florida
	Cf484	Cf485	Cf486	Cf487	Cf488	Cf489	Cf490	Cf491	Cf492	Cf493	Cf494
	Inches	Inches	Inches	Inches	Inches	Inches	Inches	Inches	Inches	Inches	Inches
1895	43.87 [1]	46.63	12.26 [1]	41.56	16.39	1.61 [1]	6.01	20.79 [1]	11.05 [2]	40.86	56.82 [2]
1896	42.15 [1]	38.61	12.09 [1]	38.52	26.31	1.24 [1]	0.92	15.86 [1]	6.47	30.05	58.82
1897	48.77 [1]	46.15	16.08 [1]	37.21	13.88	2.45 [1]	3.39	20.36 [1]	15.62 [2]	47.76	59.55
1898	43.74 [1]	40.24	11.51 [1]	66.06	8.20	0.39 [1]	1.70	16.03	5.71 [2]	59.31	55.88
1899	40.84 [1]	41.17	9.63 [1]	40.17	17.80	0.81 [1]	1.30	14.04	10.33 [2]	42.47	65.87 [2]
1900	57.80 [1]	56.14	8.38 [1]	37.69	11.49	1.31 [1]	2.74	16.89	5.88 [2]	37.01	82.82
1901	43.80 [1]	44.88	9.90 [1]	28.88	16.96	1.23 [1]	1.75	13.85	6.19	38.74	73.01 [2]
1902	48.05 [1]	45.46	11.65 [1]	48.16	17.18	1.18 [1]	2.00	18.44	6.52	34.85	45.52
1903	44.73 [1]	47.21	10.72 [1]	45.31	14.68	0.63 [1]	1.58	16.71	8.10 [2]	34.42	54.86 [2]
1904	37.66 [1]	36.85	17.62 [1]	43.51 [2]	22.47	0.90 [1]	2.43	17.78	7.53 [2]	38.93	50.69
1905	52.51 [1]	53.71	28.61 [2]	64.71	15.90	3.03 [1]	5.37	21.83	11.20 [2]	39.25	62.32
1906	49.25 [1]	45.22 [2]	22.27 [2]	51.56	31.74	3.66 [1]	7.10	26.20	13.39	51.19	60.03
1907	49.02 [1]	54.13	36.74	42.08 [2]	19.30	1.68 [1]	3.88	16.27	10.95 [2]	45.42	46.56
1908	49.57 [1]	40.76	22.53	50.46	11.96	1.81 [1]	3.64	17.88	9.87 [2]	43.92	41.69
1909	49.66 [1]	55.57	26.08 [2]	34.02	25.85	5.07 [1]	4.07	26.34	11.19	45.03	53.27
1910	41.37 [1]	49.46	15.66 [2]	33.42	6.98	0.50 [1]	1.05	12.02 [1]	6.63 [2]	37.36	53.78
1911	58.38 [1]	43.39	20.95 [2]	38.91	22.37	3.57 [1]	2.53	13.76 [1]	11.79	40.24	54.94
1912	56.87 [1]	68.42	11.50	40.41	11.04	1.40	4.50	21.00 [1]	10.91	38.86	64.10
1913	47.39 [1]	43.97	15.75	47.30	17.93	4.54	1.95	20.03	8.06	42.57	50.59
1914	40.00 [1]	44.75	13.01	38.82	22.25	1.65	2.74	18.33	13.23	35.77	51.92
1915	51.97 [1]	53.60	13.87	58.23	21.02	1.31	5.15	24.30	8.98	45.45	53.47
1916	45.13 [1]	49.23	14.47	42.97	20.10	2.23	5.12	19.65	13.13	41.59	50.55
1917	49.79 [1]	53.48	10.73	39.96	9.50	0.42	2.08	13.99	7.76	43.31	54.05
1918	45.18 [1]	57.29	19.86	39.51	16.69	1.12	1.99	18.84	11.00	44.79	54.37
1919	60.76 [1]	73.12	18.42 [2]	45.54	14.64	0.52	3.11	18.61	9.94	60.62	63.31
1920	56.99 [1]	56.18	12.04	44.23 [2]	15.41	2.90	6.80	18.70	10.08	48.42	50.31
1921	46.64 [1]	41.72	15.78	39.34	13.45	0.60	6.56	18.39	10.62	42.02	58.07
1922	53.78 [1]	54.36	16.45	35.75	22.63	1.76	1.67	13.80	7.64	44.01	61.83
1923	59.54 [1]	56.59	18.62	46.28	7.80	2.36	0.48	25.89	9.05	44.23	53.92
1924	43.93 [1]	47.85	15.60	38.75	13.85	0.44	0.70	13.08	9.13	37.77	62.23
1925	41.10 [1]	50.26	17.56	26.95	15.37	0.61	3.58	17.19	10.01	39.61	53.76
1926	51.66 [1]	61.23	17.43	42.51	22.99	0.83	6.19	17.90	10.83	40.89	55.40
1927	53.72 [1]	37.05	22.94	66.63	18.11	1.75	7.87	19.44	12.70	51.31	48.51
1928	47.06 [1]	47.17	13.06	52.90	13.88	0.87	0.74	20.51	11.28	43.36 [1]	64.81
1929	62.65 [1]	70.98	10.75	52.78	8.59	0.30	1.46	21.22	10.39	41.65	52.33
1930	39.68 [1]	35.00	14.70	40.15	12.08	1.45	3.28	15.98	9.08	32.56	51.86
1931	44.59 [1]	36.30	15.02	41.90	16.06	0.80	4.55	14.23	7.62	44.46	45.15
1932	69.18 [1]	54.13	12.74	45.12	8.40	0.15	3.49	11.85	8.88	57.11	40.49
1933	44.19 [1]	42.79	10.59	54.18	12.53	0.26	0.77	16.08	7.47	52.06	64.97
1934	43.91 [1]	56.08	10.53	39.97	11.24	1.53	0.53	14.02	7.93	55.92	69.85
1935	47.16 [1]	44.82	14.08	58.47	16.57	1.32	3.46	16.44	7.20	43.04	57.55
1936	50.56 [1]	55.86	15.83	29.28	18.16	3.08	6.76	20.25	7.57	55.73	55.85
1937	51.31 [1]	58.26	19.26	42.43	21.61	0.89	1.29	15.58	7.05	55.31	60.73
1938	48.31 [1]	47.20	17.18	48.32	20.64	3.86	4.09	29.09	13.29	60.61 [1]	49.16
1939	59.03 [1]	63.39	17.72	36.41	5.89	3.73	10.85	11.11	6.42	44.90	50.90
1940	43.47	53.22	22.69	40.48	29.42	2.17	4.90	20.29	10.14	50.22 [1]	43.87
1941	31.15	42.10	24.63	50.48	28.85	4.62	8.26	23.99	16.88	34.43 [1]	60.05
1942	38.58	51.43	9.68	56.88	18.35	0.75	1.20	26.23	7.76	45.47	60.09
1943	30.92	46.27	12.26	40.74	15.61	2.33	8.08	15.75	9.72	33.83	63.30
1944	53.91	62.20	10.91	47.97	19.51	2.49	2.95	18.65	10.44	43.64	54.30
1945	45.32	58.85	12.65	64.72	18.87	1.54	5.01	22.65	8.25	39.14	81.93
1946	58.96	63.81	18.70	52.62	10.84	3.50	1.82	18.64	9.07	35.46	51.79
1947	42.17	61.66	11.80	40.01	11.31	0.85	0.99	23.33 [1]	12.50	39.91	68.46
1948	61.05	58.41	13.51	48.28	16.01	0.21 [1]	1.97	17.11	10.82	41.75	51.33
1949	52.03	54.80	17.88	47.03	10.64	2.43	2.33	21.22	8.40	40.93	59.52 [2]
1950	63.37	48.31	10.27	50.72	19.95	1.22	0.74	14.16	6.82	39.98 [1]	57.35
1951	51.61	46.98	17.25	48.13	12.89	0.32	3.17	27.41	5.82	51.03 [1]	50.12
1952	41.18	46.50	17.82	34.83	21.53	3.37	6.46	17.15	9.66	41.58 [2]	42.62
1953	46.22	54.21	10.90	35.63	10.04	0.00 [3]	0.80	16.01	10.83	58.90 [2]	81.13
1954	40.74	30.00	12.51	35.33	18.26	2.92	2.68	10.91	8.61	52.11	45.02

Notes appear at end of table   (continued)

TABLE Cf484–549   Annual precipitation: 1895–1998   [Reference climatological stations]

Year	Muscle Shoals, Alabama	Selma, Alabama	Grand Canyon National Park, Arizona	Fayetteville Experiment Station, Arkansas	Davis Experiment Farm, California	Death Valley, California	Indio Fire Station, California	Boulder, Colorado	Montrose #2, Colorado	Groton, Connecticut	Saint Leo, Florida
	Cf484	Cf485	Cf486	Cf487	Cf488	Cf489	Cf490	Cf491	Cf492	Cf493	Cf494
	Inches	Inches	Inches	Inches	Inches	Inches	Inches	Inches	Inches	Inches	Inches
1955	48.58	47.30	11.87	37.75	21.52	0.47	1.79	15.25	7.66	44.54	41.37
1956	45.64	47.57 [2]	7.59	38.71	13.04	0.82	0.41	18.45	6.73	50.36	45.41
1957	52.14	54.18	20.58 [2]	62.51	15.31	2.15 [1]	3.03	27.43	15.40	44.79	58.83
1958	46.94	54.01	16.69	45.79	24.73	1.87 [2]	2.98	19.28	6.19	63.21	56.16
1959	44.97	59.44	13.79	38.90 [2]	12.93	1.86	2.66	18.85	8.74	50.97	70.41
1960	43.16	46.02	16.16	42.81	14.09	1.59 [2]	1.31	15.30	9.43	48.70	75.34
1961	53.72	70.90	14.38	56.79	13.06	1.41	1.35	22.39	11.29	55.20	36.61
1962	48.14	49.20	11.43 [2]	48.20	20.72	0.77	0.83	12.77	8.55	47.56	45.90
1963	40.10	47.90	13.87	21.56	21.77	2.42	4.74	16.95	8.60	38.76	61.00
1964	54.40	68.11	11.46 [2]	36.50	15.40	1.05	1.72	11.47	11.19	42.95	59.68
1965	42.80	48.46	20.70	39.78	15.59	3.32	5.86	19.47	13.97	31.33	57.82
1966	45.34	60.63	17.47 [2]	37.11	14.99	0.79	2.08	11.13	6.77	41.87	53.46
1967	52.32	48.95	12.55	38.41	19.65	1.39	3.34	24.89	10.89	52.19	43.47
1968	46.79	42.58	13.48 [2]	48.66	15.56	1.62	2.19	16.19	7.74	45.22	46.31
1969	62.88	49.15	16.81	44.35	25.10	3.42	2.63	27.52	11.16	49.69	65.75
1970	56.04	48.96	14.01	41.57	22.35	2.29	4.71	16.65	10.10	45.73	52.93
1971	55.06	65.94	10.37 [2]	35.17	8.86	0.96	0.40	18.69	8.22	41.90	52.27
1972	62.11	55.42	16.64	40.83 [2]	14.70	2.25	1.12	18.43	8.54	64.03	50.31
1973	64.20	64.27	14.46	66.05	28.09	2.31	1.11	20.21	8.85	50.47	58.38 [2]
1974	61.45	64.00	14.49 [2]	54.01 [2]	15.61	3.47	3.62	15.11	8.13 [2]	43.00 [2]	60.75 [2]
1975	78.78	70.74	13.85	47.75 [2]	13.97	1.51	0.93	18.24	7.36	50.14	49.87
1976	45.86	49.41	8.35 [2]	30.89 [2]	5.62	4.21	7.25	14.66	7.12	39.27	47.14
1977	54.46	49.76 [2]	10.25	40.93 [2]	12.85	2.80	5.85	13.49	7.43	53.09	49.66
1978	42.92	49.64	25.29	43.86 [2]	23.95	4.03	7.40	23.82	9.39	50.22	50.75
1979	67.41	60.82 [2]	16.12	36.74 [2]	21.83	1.87 [2]	5.31	24.20	8.53	53.69	66.95
1980	51.70	54.66 [2]	19.37	28.19	20.02	3.19	6.70	13.45	9.17	36.00	42.98
1981	43.47	49.91	20.17	44.83	19.09	1.74	4.31	16.91	9.05	39.80	52.87
1982	53.35	63.47 [1]	25.51	56.01	34.02	2.62	4.97 [1]	21.43 [1]	8.25	52.64 [2]	72.45
1983	65.85	71.55 [1]	22.02	34.44 [2]	38.15	4.15	11.17 [1]	24.51	13.42	64.50	75.89
1984	47.38	53.24	15.04 [1]	51.10	12.42	2.86 [1]	3.31 [1]	18.54	12.80	51.62	46.33
1985	42.75	34.17	15.96	51.72 [2]	14.89	0.89	2.17 [1]	17.44	12.00	48.90 [2]	54.22
1986	56.34	38.86	15.15	52.42	21.23	1.00	3.51	21.35	14.98	55.41 [2]	50.25
1987	39.18	35.63	18.52	53.41	15.99	3.74	3.94 [1]	25.82	9.81	38.43 [2]	64.81
1988	42.02	44.33	16.37	36.47	13.60	4.19	4.18 [1]	16.95	8.75	49.79	64.09
1989	70.59	52.19	9.06 [1]	36.41	11.82	0.00	1.42	17.36 [1]	5.58	61.62 [1]	47.80
1990	68.93	48.24	17.57	66.89	12.51	1.28	0.39 [1]	18.99 [1]	12.90	48.90	42.02 [2]
1991	77.17	60.39 [2]	14.38	44.74	15.22	1.31 [1]	4.75 [1]	21.17	7.56	49.40	51.91
1992	52.87	47.41 [1]	20.58 [2]	50.68	22.54	3.36	5.47 [1]	17.38	11.33	46.98 [2]	51.17
1993	46.43	46.66 [2]	20.11 [2]	54.34	25.79	2.58	6.41 [2]	21.48 [1]	9.97	42.81 [2]	47.56
1994	72.03	55.34	13.11	—	15.15	—	1.57	16.79	7.51	45.56	55.87
1995	—	52.80 [2]	21.26 [2]	44.84	30.41	3.27	4.38	29.43	12.62	42.85	50.40
1996	—	54.64 [2]	—	48.57 [2]	27.31	1.15	1.19	21.68	10.76	55.46 [2]	50.63
1997	—	54.21 [2]	—	43.87	17.86	2.81	—	28.49	12.31	37.14	68.51
1998	—	49.21	—	44.18	—	4.26	—	—	9.79 [2]	—	56.12

Notes appear at end of table

TABLE Cf484–549   Annual precipitation: 1895–1998   [Reference climatological stations]   *Continued*

Year	Savannah WSO AP, Georgia	Grace, Idaho	Porthill, Idaho	Urbana, Illinois	Marion 2N, Indiana	Belle Plain, Iowa	Lawrence, Kansas	Hopkinsville, Kentucky	Calhoun Research Station, Louisiana	New Orleans Audubon, Louisiansa	Presque Isle, Maine
	Cf495	Cf496	Cf497	Cf498	Cf499	Cf500	Cf501	Cf502	Cf503	Cf504	Cf505
	Inches	Inches	Inches	Inches	Inches	Inches	Inches	Inches	Inches	Inches	Inches
1895	54.84	10.49 [1]	16.81	29.12	22.63	25.96	47.15	42.44 [1]	48.35	69.87	30.48 [1]
1896	44.24	12.86 [1]	26.13 [2]	35.91	42.37	32.52	34.87	46.29 [1]	37.26 [2]	56.86	32.29 [1]
1897	54.08	13.97 [1]	31.84	33.92	37.35	32.83	23.79	42.29	45.54	54.29	35.82 [1]
1898	60.18	10.62 [1]	21.96 [2]	48.47	43.29	42.25	44.05	55.74	53.59	69.04	37.24 [1]
1899	42.17	12.50 [1]	24.29	29.56	35.63	37.29 [1]	30.96	49.72	30.72	43.60	30.47 [1]
1900	45.08	10.23 [1]	29.39	34.16	37.94	45.10 [2]	41.44	59.33	57.67	71.62	41.43 [1]
1901	36.84	11.67 [1]	24.23 [2]	28.64	32.35	26.53	29.11	37.11	36.69	54.43	36.83 [1]
1902	47.35	9.47 [1]	24.47	45.66	40.63	57.48 [2]	43.83	53.29	52.12	39.11	41.26 [1]
1903	53.67	13.42 [1]	20.01	32.48	40.27	34.43	41.29	45.43	50.26 [2]	47.79	28.91 [1]
1904	40.42	14.00 [1]	18.21	29.79	41.88	30.24	41.14	36.85	49.90 [2]	39.22	35.38 [1]
1905	45.49	10.87 [1]	18.16	29.60	39.64	41.35	43.52	49.89	65.34	71.97	23.90 [1]
1906	39.67	19.26 [1]	19.39	34.25	43.54	36.31	28.50	59.36	57.83 [2]	45.55	31.14 [1]
1907	42.45	19.73 [2]	24.87	40.20	43.73	43.52	36.17	52.56	47.51 [2]	69.36	33.35 [1]
1908	47.56	12.51	19.09	33.27	33.21	30.22	48.12	42.22	63.99 [2]	57.10	27.55 [1]
1909	38.30	21.47	19.64	47.05	48.60	37.63	48.15	53.80	44.74 [2]	68.65	39.94 [1]
1910	46.61	9.90	17.36	27.96	33.66	18.77	37.65	45.95	41.74	48.79	32.18
1911	36.17	15.36	15.32	32.31	40.82	38.43	29.54	42.52	54.41	60.73	26.28 [2]
1912	61.84	16.09	18.75	31.50	36.08	32.54	32.47	52.77	50.60	80.61	33.05 [2]
1913	40.00	10.81	17.14	38.20	44.46	31.15	38.66	45.62	62.73	65.86	31.88
1914	43.58	13.80	21.99	24.68	35.92	34.41	33.60	49.72	48.19	54.92	34.77
1915	52.15	10.77 [2]	19.78	34.23	41.34	46.46	51.61	48.71	48.75	73.63	35.52
1916	37.91	12.23	17.99	29.71	35.50	27.07	35.20	44.03	36.45	55.37	33.55
1917	42.15	13.36 [2]	16.09	32.23	33.30	30.91	24.72	46.22	39.02	33.07	41.34
1918	43.14	12.06 [2]	17.58	43.19	38.34	38.17	37.07	36.71	43.97	64.32	39.42 [2]
1919	48.23	9.01	16.44	35.25	42.83	41.88	30.42 [2]	66.42	59.63	74.14	31.57 [2]
1920	57.84	15.12	16.87	29.29	36.61	30.21	39.16	47.27	71.06	68.64	43.56
1921	42.01	16.98	16.40	41.66	35.23	43.83	43.60	54.30	49.50	46.97	31.11
1922	58.26	13.29	13.69	36.73	32.82	35.19	38.39	45.45	60.85	62.24	33.71
1923	32.62	16.96	18.63	40.38	42.84	29.87	38.00	74.18	72.76 [2]	63.69	30.23
1924	57.72	10.57	17.90	40.40	47.67	35.22	37.45	45.84	29.49 [2]	40.28	24.62
1925	41.69	16.56	15.46	29.38	36.95	25.88	27.58	48.55	54.61	48.56	33.37 [2]
1926	54.66	17.01	18.46	43.53	38.71	34.54	28.20	50.25	49.85	72.36	31.62 [2]
1927	35.18	16.10	24.57	55.64	48.70	33.78	43.13	62.94	49.83	70.12	35.59
1928	55.67	11.30	14.34	32.96	34.37	40.37	38.51	42.49	49.78	66.03	36.72
1929	53.90	12.87	12.49	44.13	42.77	31.62	32.35	51.25	43.10	90.78	29.69
1930	42.15	18.36	13.28	25.08	31.01	31.76	25.80	31.68	44.90	66.60	29.07 [2]
1931	22.00	11.29	15.66	36.46	40.18	35.36	38.23	41.65	58.58	56.94	37.11
1932	46.78	12.78	19.39	30.49	37.58	32.94	30.78	61.79	51.71	71.32	34.00
1933	48.63	12.69	21.19	34.47	43.10	26.97	30.05	57.06	62.81	51.33	32.50 [2]
1934	42.34	11.73	17.11	35.15	26.25	31.91	27.35	42.42	54.79	63.57	36.36
1935	43.89	8.65	12.65	37.21	31.29	37.88	42.93	50.91	48.42	54.79	28.39
1936	39.75	15.33	12.51	35.09	32.39	30.89	22.12	37.41	32.86	57.44	43.97
1937	51.47	14.34	19.34	37.65	41.02	34.65	21.59	58.01	62.14	73.45	31.81
1938	29.81	16.52	14.21	42.77	41.21	38.12	30.33	41.17	47.12	47.46	33.42
1939	35.96	9.80	14.68	38.05	32.46	28.04	31.11	50.31	44.98	52.13	36.62
1940	36.54	15.97	15.52	30.60	26.61	22.36	42.58	40.80	62.19	76.38	36.87
1941	45.30	20.12	20.07	42.87	29.43	38.18	46.88	34.64	54.56	56.36	32.95
1942	38.69	17.55	21.03	42.38	36.51	35.99	41.16	44.73	44.46	79.04	28.04
1943	40.83	12.13	17.40	35.54	40.15	40.23	34.47	36.27	32.22	56.42	33.76
1944	61.01	14.26	9.26	40.73	34.85	36.29	42.65	42.39	56.59	63.08 [1]	30.43
1945	55.91	20.99	20.47	48.01	40.44	34.90	43.58	47.01	61.92	63.48 [1]	37.11
1946	43.14	15.23	25.90	35.46	30.94	41.60	32.84	46.96	71.52	72.38	34.32
1947	67.25	14.87	21.92	36.90	37.23	40.96	42.70	39.89	57.11	74.70 [1]	34.11
1948	64.34	12.80	21.25	41.36	46.96	29.71	32.43	57.48	39.20	62.35 [1]	31.04
1949	41.16	18.62	19.03	45.53	41.02	30.26	41.52	56.18	52.96	68.71 [1]	33.49 [2]
1950	55.94	17.66	23.81	42.99	52.58	25.06	36.32	65.38 [2]	67.16	45.10 [1]	37.41
1951	48.66	15.27	24.71	38.39	38.15	42.06	50.68	57.57	48.44	47.86 [1]	40.21
1952	38.47	12.18	13.43	33.87	39.07	28.66	23.80	37.62	33.95 [2]	54.70 [2]	36.40
1953	55.25	12.03	20.96	26.09	30.85	25.11	20.99	42.16 [2]	54.64	72.23 [2]	35.39
1954	32.83	13.23	22.70	29.70	35.65	38.81	31.53	47.19	30.88	49.58 [2]	52.35

Notes appear at end of table

(continued)

TABLE Cf484–549 Annual precipitation: 1895–1998 [Reference climatological stations] *Continued*

Year	Savannah WSO AP, Georgia	Grace, Idaho	Porthill, Idaho	Urbana, Illinois	Marion 2N, Indiana	Belle Plain, Iowa	Lawrence, Kansas	Hopkinsville, Kentucky	Calhoun Research Station, Louisiana	New Orleans Audubon, Louisiansa	Presque Isle, Maine
	Cf495	Cf496	Cf497	Cf498	Cf499	Cf500	Cf501	Cf502	Cf503	Cf504	Cf505
	Inches	Inches	Inches	Inches	Inches	Inches	Inches	Inches	Inches	Inches	Inches
1955	38.52	17.48	25.93	37.17	40.16	21.08	25.78	47.47	51.14	70.40 [2]	30.51
1956	43.16	8.70	20.29	27.30	29.40	25.72	21.67	42.76	43.31	63.34	30.81
1957	63.96	15.20	19.84	41.64	47.48	31.65	37.48	71.17	69.11	60.70	31.34
1958	48.01	13.56	22.17 [2]	36.63	39.19	34.39	42.62	41.71	53.53	65.13 [2]	37.65
1959	68.00	12.05	24.87	36.60	48.37	44.62	38.75	47.06	45.53	78.48	35.52
1960	53.73	12.33	20.24	32.86	29.39	38.66	32.22	38.22	41.45	53.25	37.89
1961	49.00	13.00	25.75	42.10	36.73 [2]	38.55	55.03	55.80	72.42 [2]	83.88	44.43
1962	54.08	11.92 [2]	15.58	37.98	36.99	38.16	36.39	43.66	45.49	47.06	35.43
1963	50.83	20.11 [2]	19.98	26.89	27.98	30.70	22.60	28.47	36.93	54.72	40.02
1964	73.17	17.27 [2]	21.75	35.48	34.56	29.16	45.65	49.27	40.30 [2]	62.80	31.10
1965	45.81	16.97	19.48	44.44	36.83	45.87	44.89	49.49 [2]	41.37	56.48	28.53
1966	45.39	9.89	21.74	35.84	31.22	28.73	24.63	49.41	49.24	72.36	29.96
1967	41.27	16.87	18.38	34.80	38.43	33.01	51.87	48.55	37.11	62.42	37.74
1968	37.34	13.94	25.12	39.72	33.26	33.58	40.97	48.61	73.99	40.11	29.75
1969	60.84	12.51	21.56	37.05	35.47	40.72	44.06	54.25	39.15	54.67	42.36 [2]
1970	53.84	15.84	21.60	36.48	33.81	41.02	36.63	49.32	44.62	50.28	35.60
1971	61.34	21.18	22.18	37.15	34.53	32.06	37.31	42.64	49.31	59.80	31.69
1972	48.57	17.44	21.91	42.95	45.04	40.86	36.65	57.51	55.34	60.28	38.55
1973	45.40	16.76	19.27	49.20	43.11 [2]	38.23	59.25	52.18	61.82	81.58	44.50 [2]
1974	41.93	10.71 [2]	26.06 [2]	43.58	36.49	49.09	35.98	57.84	70.84	63.27	34.57 [2]
1975	51.18	11.74	20.86	45.89	37.65	32.28	29.91	54.99	75.97	68.58	27.71
1976	63.74	12.22 [2]	16.61	32.77	29.82	22.98	21.58 [2]	44.25	43.14	51.28	44.94
1977	41.84	15.07	16.58	42.90	41.18	40.26 [2]	54.55 [2]	47.11	43.69	71.41	40.33
1978	35.41	12.44 [2]	17.42	36.05	34.37	40.47	32.53 [2]	57.51	49.96	77.74	28.45 [2]
1979	61.92	9.30	16.60	37.76	39.01	38.77	34.61 [2]	71.97	64.55	61.82 [2]	37.15
1980	37.84	20.87	22.96 [2]	31.73	37.68	27.77	33.36 [2]	39.14	43.17 [2]	69.43	32.88
1981	40.06	20.03	24.74	45.87	38.25 [2]	34.13	45.07	46.54 [2]	31.35	62.87	41.81
1982	52.26	22.74 [2]	25.06 [2]	43.75	41.10 [2]	37.51	38.40	54.86 [2]	74.21	70.45	32.10 [1]
1983	54.51	26.60 [2]	24.13	50.28 [2]	36.61	42.65	35.67	59.81	60.02	86.09	41.88
1984	50.66	19.08	18.47	40.55	38.22	32.42	43.39 [2]	63.03	62.32	43.40	34.72 [2]
1985	38.64	15.55 [1]	14.49	45.64	49.42	29.96	53.25	48.98 [2]	55.39	69.22 [2]	30.45
1986	45.33	22.66 [1]	23.18 [2]	35.38	44.10	44.79	51.45 [2]	39.53	51.58	48.15 [2]	31.90
1987	56.70	15.38 [2]	15.32	41.39	37.64 [2]	34.96 [2]	40.86	37.01	48.28	51.04 [2]	27.90
1988	48.17	9.67	18.91	29.61	27.74 [2]	18.83 [2]	23.79	46.36 [2]	46.56	71.38	28.36 [2]
1989	46.87	11.29	17.37 [2]	34.84	39.46 [2]	28.23	29.14	62.78	67.54	50.26	29.13 [1]
1990	43.08	14.23	25.16 [1]	52.86 [1]	50.68	44.26	38.17 [1]	62.88	64.10	55.50 [2]	43.25 [2]
1991	68.42	16.11	18.59 [2]	34.87	35.34	39.21 [2]	33.00 [2]	48.03	72.29	113.74	33.68
1992	58.36	11.48	18.95	45.15	46.37	38.28 [2]	42.81	39.32 [1]	54.72	82.54	32.95 [2]
1993	48.05	17.84	19.88	58.54	45.18	55.79 [2]	62.37 [1]	43.41	44.03	52.06 [2]	38.90
1994	69.44	14.00 [2]	16.27 [2]	37.49	31.68	28.44 [2]	35.19 [2]	50.87	52.90	50.37 [2]	34.44 [2]
1995	51.11	15.83	25.74	36.49 [2]	30.73	33.01 [2]	40.19	—	45.83	66.58	—
1996	36.16	17.81	30.17	38.39	41.08 [2]	36.71 [2]	52.46	—	48.70	57.56	40.06 [2]
1997	—	17.91 [2]	—	36.90 [2]	34.24	32.02	32.88 [2]	—	65.98	51.54 [2]	33.89 [2]
1998	49.47	17.75	28.47 [2]	46.11	54.68	40.60	49.86	51.75 [2]	57.38	80.13	35.82

Notes appear at end of table

TABLE Cf484–549   Annual precipitation: 1895–1998   [Reference climatological stations]   *Continued*

Year	Baltimore WSO City, Maryland	Blue Hill, Massachusetts	Ann Arbor, University of Michigan, Michigan	Chatham Experimental Farm #2, Michigan	Itasca, University of Minnesota, Minnesota	Greenville, Mississippi	Sweet Springs, Missouri	Bozeman, Montana Station University, Montana	Glasgow WSO AP, Montana	Crete, Nebraska
	Cf506	Cf507	Cf508	Cf509	Cf510	Cf511	Cf512	Cf513	Cf514	Cf515
	Inches	Inches	Inches	Inches	Inches	Inches	Inches	Inches	Inches	Inches
1895	40.47 [2]	46.19	22.75	29.57 [1]	22.32 [1]	48.65 [2]	38.33 [1]	18.16	10.01	20.72
1896	38.59 [2]	47.44	30.05	36.04 [1]	30.17 [1]	31.57	27.74 [1]	19.06	14.07	40.99
1897	47.47 [2]	45.40	32.66	30.63 [1]	26.43 [1]	44.93	26.86	19.02 [1]	9.63 [2]	27.92
1898	36.46	58.69	32.90	29.77 [1]	24.18 [1]	50.70	54.83 [1]	17.21 [1]	16.15 [2]	22.78
1899	38.45 [2]	40.65	26.85	32.75 [1]	32.84 [1]	33.88	34.62	17.32 [1]	15.55	30.33
1900	31.57 [2]	48.14	28.55 [2]	37.80 [1]	27.32 [1]	54.92	37.56 [1]	15.48	9.41	34.01
1901	43.04	53.98	25.83	41.98	26.45 [1]	41.98	24.20	15.49	13.01 [2]	24.03
1902	50.13	42.72	39.97	34.78	26.06 [1]	44.14	43.80	16.89	11.98 [2]	42.88
1903	46.26	46.76	36.86	39.12	26.05 [1]	39.40	48.03	17.64	11.32 [2]	33.46
1904	36.09	46.19	27.52 [2]	32.47	22.82 [1]	39.82	39.41	16.19	11.79 [2]	30.24
1905	46.55	39.45	36.60	33.42	33.35 [1]	64.94	44.81	14.68	9.21 [2]	32.99
1906	46.82	45.53	31.58	30.68	33.16 [1]	54.65	32.03	16.88	20.02 [1]	29.73
1907	49.09	47.57	31.38	29.29	23.77 [1]	45.99	53.79 [1]	17.23	11.56 [1]	29.55
1908	35.41	37.74	31.05	27.64	23.96 [1]	59.44	53.09	25.27	9.86 [1]	38.10
1909	34.70	43.61	28.09	30.17	30.80 [1]	50.01	37.36	22.34	11.60 [1]	33.64
1910	34.97	34.27	25.89	27.91	14.47 [1]	47.50	34.38	18.74	7.99 [1]	25.28
1911	48.58	44.62	29.15	37.24	27.94 [1]	72.84	30.26 [1]	18.14	14.31 [2]	25.42
1912	45.13	40.40	29.10	27.02	17.82	52.48	34.89 [1]	21.65	17.90	23.79
1913	36.11	45.13	26.58	26.70	22.39	57.91	33.33	18.67	11.05 [2]	27.02
1914	36.40	40.30	32.86	33.01	28.01	47.97	37.83	16.46	17.14 [2]	29.63
1915	46.40	43.98	28.16	42.16	23.59 [2]	45.91	53.38	25.00	16.73	36.03
1916	36.04	45.50	36.52	41.88 [2]	26.46	41.05	43.33	21.19	20.47	23.87
1917	37.92	48.78	40.87	30.27 [2]	16.26	42.01	28.99	15.68	7.83	24.77
1918	37.54	44.86	35.20 [2]	36.41 [2]	18.91	35.87	34.97	18.89	11.65	26.24
1919	47.23	56.24	35.37	27.84 [2]	27.51 [2]	69.02	31.75 [1]	11.02	7.74	33.42
1920	48.43	63.81	34.27	30.38 [2]	23.61 [2]	67.91	39.89 [1]	19.25	10.10	27.44
1921	37.72	51.77	33.04	31.01 [2]	24.30 [2]	51.76	43.26 [1]	15.19	16.96	23.87
1922	42.51	54.00	26.14	34.70 [2]	24.86	66.19	38.22 [1]	17.74	15.18	23.04 [2]
1923	36.66	44.90	31.73 [2]	30.85	19.69	76.66	39.41 [1]	15.27	19.53	31.20 [2]
1924	49.04	42.80	26.53	35.55 [2]	22.15	40.16	37.92	20.94	18.28	22.48
1925	32.72	50.35	32.72	21.71	28.79	46.96	33.39	19.40	13.24	26.30
1926	45.18	48.89	33.64	37.80	21.01	51.21	42.08 [1]	19.82	11.74	26.36
1927	36.23	51.61	33.35	31.04	21.43	62.44	50.94	21.80	20.37	26.42
1928	43.40	46.84	27.02	36.11	26.97 [2]	45.83	42.93	16.18	9.79	28.19
1929	42.47	46.95	31.91	32.70	13.93	46.91	53.40	15.77	11.60	24.40
1930	21.55	41.27	21.98	26.93	21.45	46.86	23.71	14.17	8.28	22.50 [2]
1931	39.57	49.28	24.98	31.99	20.38	56.89	38.62	15.29	9.53	36.29
1932	49.58	48.88	37.23	40.92	20.83	61.70	36.54	17.34	15.08	27.33
1933	52.96	52.79	26.50	29.85	22.60	51.80	29.79	15.89	14.30	26.84
1934	50.88	41.17	18.95	32.62	18.63	60.37	33.89	10.54	6.83	17.22
1935	51.52	43.74	26.57	31.75	28.67	46.38	37.70	15.46	10.02	26.82
1936	44.60	59.14	24.55	25.53	17.60	35.02	24.55	12.78	7.93	12.38
1937	50.79	46.11	35.01	32.71	24.62	59.81	28.94	17.99	7.70	21.66
1938	34.79	58.51	28.55	34.09	25.39	46.20	41.71	20.35	20.85	28.30
1939	40.94	37.80	26.99	36.54	20.71	54.32	29.54	14.03	13.51	18.29
1940	44.33	45.00	32.94	38.45	21.93	60.70	32.51	18.63	14.40	21.16
1941	34.73	32.55	28.88	40.88	27.43	40.59	40.15	22.87	12.86	30.94
1942	46.68	46.32	37.03	32.84	29.52	41.49	46.35	17.24	13.39	29.50
1943	36.75	34.93	37.43	33.55	23.48	32.75	36.03	17.18	12.40	24.25
1944	45.45 [2]	45.61	27.28	33.09	32.60	62.27	49.81	20.93	14.15	38.47
1945	46.61	54.45	37.84	32.45	22.34	69.77	41.19	19.53	10.82	25.39
1946	37.65	41.96	24.67	28.96	27.70	61.80	38.36	18.58	13.76	27.82
1947	46.24 [2]	44.94	31.79	34.50	24.18	53.04	44.51	23.64	15.12	27.65
1948	54.71	47.80	29.30	27.32	23.47	52.20	38.08	19.50	14.24	28.62
1949	37.69	33.67	33.70	37.69 [2]	35.51	60.81	46.77	17.11	8.47	38.76
1950	43.96	42.02	37.00 [2]	33.33	29.88	57.21	31.56	18.19	19.02	30.71
1951	46.93	50.93	34.85	41.19 [2]	30.91	57.80	51.23	20.20	13.28	44.36
1952	55.89	39.76	27.89	31.72	21.77	31.35	31.09	19.57	12.79	35.08 [2]
1953	49.32	59.55	25.25	36.05	31.70	52.21	26.73 [2]	16.40	15.33	21.52
1954	30.46	57.38	34.63 [1]	32.23	25.39	42.99	32.98 [2]	12.68	16.24	33.67

Notes appear at end of table

(continued)

TABLE Cf484–549   Annual precipitation: 1895–1998   [Reference climatological stations]   *Continued*

Year	Baltimore WSO City, Maryland Cf506 Inches	Blue Hill, Massachusetts Cf507 Inches	Ann Arbor, University of Michigan, Michigan Cf508 Inches	Chatham Experimental Farm #2, Michigan Cf509 Inches	Itasca, University of Minnesota, Minnesota Cf510 Inches	Greenville, Mississippi Cf511 Inches	Sweet Springs, Missouri Cf512 Inches	Bozeman, Montana Station University, Montana Cf513 Inches	Glasgow WSO AP, Montana Cf514 Inches	Crete, Nebraska Cf515 Inches
1955	47.86	59.58	25.12 [1]	27.19	21.23	42.50	34.71	19.07	12.56	15.86
1956	41.26	59.24	28.08	25.17 [2]	20.66	42.92	21.13	11.30	9.19	24.42
1957	37.70	35.48	34.37	30.25	33.93	74.19	40.04	16.52 [2]	10.39	32.97
1958	50.44	59.89	22.47	27.48	20.34	71.82	35.79	18.11	7.07	30.93
1959	35.75	48.31	35.87 [2]	40.17	26.40	48.25	27.89 [1]	19.58	9.70	37.09
1960	43.91	46.69	28.30	44.42	27.28	47.60 [2]	45.28	14.61	7.30	33.31
1961	40.05	50.66	33.90 [2]	31.78	23.79	74.57	62.06	16.12	8.89	31.78
1962	38.06	51.58	25.53	27.43	31.32	37.52	27.29	19.97	17.77	29.86
1963	34.10	41.61	16.85	26.96	22.60	38.98 [2]	25.88 [2]	17.86	14.67	28.71
1964	37.19	40.22	24.35	40.27	31.26	43.51 [2]	36.42	19.85	10.53	21.14
1965	30.80	26.96	30.67	31.63	33.39	38.43	58.75	19.22	14.31	36.08
1966	39.79	41.14	26.78 [2]	35.51	29.69	42.02	31.54	14.63	12.58	20.44
1967	40.58	54.05	33.61	32.00 [2]	23.76	41.41	43.28	22.94	9.92	35.75
1968	40.06	49.89	40.33 [2]	42.89 [2]	32.63	68.64	37.88	23.56	7.65	36.44
1969	33.22	58.38	31.80 [2]	35.50 [2]	28.20	50.44	51.15	23.40	10.48	28.95
1970	36.04	48.30	30.92	36.51	22.74	53.81	39.27	19.64	10.25	28.72
1971	61.57	38.09	23.95	38.46	29.06	52.87	28.06	15.97	6.90	28.41
1972	56.72	65.51	28.88	34.90	26.72 [2]	53.81	32.03	17.82	15.22	30.41
1973	47.50	51.65	35.93	40.56 [2]	29.23	70.93 [2]	55.34	21.06	11.20	44.42
1974	41.46	48.11	27.82	34.66 [2]	24.10 [2]	73.42	47.03 [2]	16.27	13.12	17.72
1975	61.52	62.38	37.09	31.64	26.80	71.58	38.79 [2]	25.29	13.90	24.80 [2]
1976	44.11	44.71	27.38	28.01 [2]	12.24	50.37	27.51 [2]	19.36	13.53	18.30
1977	40.12	51.70	35.34	41.73 [2]	31.79	42.87	44.35	20.74	9.29	33.12
1978	45.29	43.49	30.03	42.37	24.84	54.21	35.62 [2]	20.33	15.86	33.81
1979	61.36	55.90	31.41	46.11 [2]	23.93	75.65	35.88 [2]	15.43	8.11	30.40
1980	32.41	32.99	37.70	28.64	18.90	50.30	34.50 [2]	21.23	8.95	24.03
1981	32.14 [2]	41.82	36.02	30.26	29.42	34.76	52.21 [2]	22.70 [2]	8.79	34.37
1982	34.38	52.24	36.66	42.93	22.99 [2]	68.99 [2]	53.38 [2]	22.42	12.21	33.37 [2]
1983	58.21	62.45	37.60	34.35	27.41	60.71 [1]	46.22 [2]	21.76	7.56	26.25
1984	37.78	54.91	30.50	32.34	30.59	59.80 [2]	45.26 [2]	20.60	6.74	41.76
1985	40.69	40.07	43.11	34.11	35.70	43.11 [2]	63.06 [2]	13.16	12.85	24.02
1986	37.83	49.95	35.74	25.01	30.65	45.64 [1]	46.32	18.39	13.40	39.51
1987	38.66	54.29	33.69	32.62	24.40	49.39 [2]	39.00	15.55	9.24	36.48 [2]
1988	35.62	47.29	37.89	33.21	29.65	36.56 [2]	29.47	15.61	7.48	19.25
1989	50.82	56.13	35.99	24.39	20.40	60.34 [1]	34.75	18.83	10.31	24.76
1990	43.22	52.12	47.19	26.31 [2]	22.66	57.03 [1]	47.12	16.14	6.84	22.10 [1]
1991	29.55	52.38 [1]	32.82	37.11	25.98	57.02 [2]	31.16	19.03	10.98	18.10 [1]
1992	38.94	48.77	39.04 [2]	27.25 [2]	23.08	44.67	43.49	22.07	9.24	32.43
1993	44.65	49.17	34.61	31.76 [2]	32.95	41.96 [2]	50.93	23.51	16.27	40.38 [2]
1994	41.42	52.66	34.31	22.45 [2]	30.53	53.89 [2]	42.82	17.77	10.02	27.55 [2]
1995	—	39.11	34.78	38.15	30.03	59.47	48.77	—	13.17	22.45 [2]
1996	—	69.35	34.03	39.74 [2]	24.42	51.40	42.89	18.15 [2]	10.40	32.43 [2]
1997	—	39.90	39.73	25.56	27.79	54.24	41.35 [2]	25.57	11.75	27.13 [2]
1998	—	—	39.15	26.90	29.14	52.37	53.33	17.51	14.82	35.15 [2]

Notes appear at end of table

TABLE Cf484–549 Annual precipitation: 1895–1998 [Reference climatological stations] *Continued*

Year	Reno WSFO AP, Nevada	Searchlight, Nevada	Hanover, New Hampshire	Carlsbad, New Mexico	Chama, New Mexico	Albany, WSFOAP, New York	Geneva Resr Farm, New York	New York Central Park, New York	Cape Hatteras WSO, North Carolina	Dickinson Experiment Station, North Dakota	Wooster Experiment Station, Ohio	Goodwell Research Station, Oklahoma
	Cf516	Cf517	Cf518	Cf519	Cf520	Cf521	Cf522	Cf523	Cf524	Cf525	Cf526	Cf527
	Inches	Inches	Inches	Inches	Inches	Inches	Inches	Inches	Inches	Inches	Inches	Inches
1895	5.53	3.90 [1]	31.75	12.92	28.53 [2]	29.80	22.04 [2]	35.37	67.28	11.76	30.91	16.63 [1]
1896	10.70	3.62 [1]	35.87	10.97	18.65	27.88	27.61	41.96	45.25	18.48	39.10	11.92 [1]
1897	8.00	6.01 [1]	43.38	9.85	28.16 [1]	40.79	23.78	44.55	58.82	13.52 [2]	36.76	18.68 [1]
1898	6.41	3.59 [1]	38.22	16.92	19.34 [1]	38.77	22.88	47.90	48.20	11.92	47.85	14.77 [1]
1899	8.21	3.59 [1]	31.31	9.40 [2]	17.73 [1]	28.92	19.35	38.57	61.88	17.27	32.93	17.08 [1]
1900	7.90 [2]	3.11 [1]	35.59	17.44 [2]	15.64 [1]	30.56	28.66	41.19 [2]	45.65	11.78	36.61	17.55 [1]
1901	11.36	3.22 [1]	34.88	12.24 [2]	16.15 [1]	40.53	33.16 [2]	48.69	50.11	12.92	35.89	11.93 [1]
1902	4.94	4.59 [1]	40.65	22.42	15.82 [1]	37.48	26.93	52.77	40.13	16.07 [2]	32.95	14.74 [1]
1903	6.55	4.01 [1]	34.73	8.05	16.97 [1]	34.09	38.71	58.32	48.87	16.90 [2]	40.44	14.69 [1]
1904	10.63	3.85 [1]	31.77	18.10	18.08 [1]	31.26	28.61	41.64	40.97	15.19	41.28	15.32 [1]
1905	5.69	12.69 [1]	36.54	21.87 [2]	15.67 [2]	26.98	32.38	37.44	41.77	16.55	42.93	22.72 [1]
1906	11.05	12.25 [1]	33.07	20.86	25.17	32.51	29.93	40.18	53.94	20.46	42.82	22.84 [1]
1907	11.27	5.77 [1]	36.32	15.82	25.30	33.63	23.73	45.48	44.56	13.67	40.00	17.44 [1]
1908	5.42	7.80 [1]	25.76	13.58	20.21	28.41	24.06	41.05	67.88	19.48	33.94	11.51 [1]
1909	11.16	13.24 [1]	31.21	8.08	21.31	27.96	20.87	41.67	34.43	21.26	44.22	17.80 [1]
1910	5.97	5.83 [1]	31.37	3.95	17.30	28.51	25.12	33.72	35.45	13.34	35.45	11.38 [2]
1911	10.57	5.39 [1]	36.34	16.82	30.49	32.10	26.25	48.82	29.64	15.62	47.15	15.53
1912	4.66	6.28 [1]	36.98	12.68	18.95	32.12	32.82	45.58	48.98	19.06	46.60	17.47
1913	11.57	5.12 [1]	34.06	15.33	23.02	26.39	31.59	58.00	43.40	11.93	51.18	18.99
1914	8.71	10.18	30.24	19.04	26.01	29.76	27.92	40.17	37.56	22.74	37.38	22.51
1915	5.62	8.67	36.75	18.57	26.50	37.62	28.43	45.73	37.99	19.98	42.06	26.75
1916	10.44	6.79	38.94	19.87	32.34	33.87	42.01	37.90	37.88	18.40	34.93	11.66
1917	5.43	6.32	30.79	5.73	15.93	28.66	35.45	41.04	44.92	9.25	31.86	16.56
1918	8.85	11.82	34.52	7.86	21.23	30.12	34.38	38.27	36.97	12.36	33.75	20.13
1919	9.64	9.49	36.22	19.10	26.75 [2]	35.52	35.40	53.29	33.16	8.37	43.08	19.15 [1]
1920	6.73	9.51	46.15	14.74	22.27 [2]	40.54	37.24	53.20	47.01	15.81	39.70	14.79
1921	7.27	15.22	31.65	9.71	23.80	29.71	29.41	37.76	47.55	15.76	41.90	16.91
1922	11.30	11.90	39.02	11.15	18.76	34.12	39.85	44.66	71.03	18.20	34.42	16.90
1923	7.22	8.83 [2]	37.38	14.87	23.76	34.89	31.25	40.57	51.68	19.67	36.30	24.12
1924	4.32	2.71	36.52	2.95	17.65	30.46	32.25	41.72	66.34	15.13	38.90	12.12
1925	7.87	4.84 [2]	39.02	9.69	21.91	31.37	36.84	41.43 [2]	37.09	12.19	30.40	15.93
1926	5.32	8.06	36.19	16.11	20.05	30.81	36.25	47.74 [2]	41.13	13.11	39.42	17.29
1927	8.13	8.35	36.82	3.85	29.49	39.90	42.76	56.06	48.23	19.59	43.28	16.34
1928	4.65	1.70	29.92	13.81	11.32	33.55	33.54	45.62	59.81	15.30	33.46	24.30
1929	6.41	3.50	32.49	12.32	25.25	31.69	35.48	40.38	70.41	17.21	44.35	18.37
1930	6.24	4.00	27.24	10.45	17.66	25.54	26.78	38.95	46.86	13.79	28.78	18.53
1931	8.09	13.23	39.43	13.88	27.24	33.22	31.72	36.07	41.55	16.17	35.66	16.24
1932	5.15	5.76 [2]	34.87	18.13	18.65	34.24	36.39	43.93	52.86	17.24	34.57	14.71
1933	8.28	5.29	39.63	9.61	17.22	38.18	26.87	53.53 [2]	61.75	11.50	33.53	12.62
1934	5.83	6.51	36.13	6.79	14.65	36.48	23.41	49.83 [2]	62.61	7.91	29.90	14.27
1935	6.42	9.22	35.68	14.01	22.37	33.74	35.52	33.84 [2]	50.02	15.00	46.32	11.69
1936	6.90	11.38	42.14	11.99	23.76	39.95	30.11	49.43	55.92	6.72	36.90	9.69
1937	7.02	5.05 [1]	42.09	11.91	20.49	38.50	38.16	52.97	61.60	16.28	42.25	11.26
1938	8.25	9.45 [2]	41.80	12.60	21.41	40.19	35.19	48.49	48.63	16.65	36.71	14.86
1939	5.73	17.44	31.16	7.89	14.46	31.17	28.86	38.55	54.96	15.75	30.68	13.64
1940	10.23	9.99 [2]	37.26	12.30	22.99	35.91	36.86	45.07 [2]	59.31	17.12	39.71	16.22
1941	7.64	18.34 [2]	31.30	33.94	30.95	24.58	30.19	39.04	44.50	31.16	29.88	26.25
1942	4.64	2.01 [2]	34.75	17.50	21.65	35.77	38.87	48.51	53.90	19.75	29.85	27.00
1943	9.01	12.95 [2]	39.93	10.84	20.25	32.62	37.12	36.74	43.63	15.06	30.22	14.95
1944	6.97	7.77 [2]	32.76	14.86	19.37	31.57	32.11	44.81	59.71	20.63	30.18	21.63
1945	8.84	9.79	45.49	12.73	13.45	41.18	40.41	44.85	54.57	12.22	39.11	15.46
1946	5.59	8.22	35.70	11.72	15.07	30.16	29.58	38.69	69.57	14.50	34.61	25.97
1947	1.55	4.52	33.30	5.96	19.29 [2]	32.20	35.73	40.79	61.20	17.17	45.40	23.30 [2]
1948	3.80	2.32	36.52	10.73	19.18	37.44	32.87	46.31	51.84	16.11	35.12	24.02
1949	6.53	7.72	32.11	18.48 [2]	16.70 [1]	25.73	22.81	36.80	67.18	10.77	32.78	22.25
1950	9.61	1.83	32.23	14.79 [2]	11.47 [1]	38.64	36.90	36.84	46.82	15.13	49.08	26.94
1951	8.12	9.61	43.53	6.43	17.74	45.21	31.30	44.38	48.05	16.70	41.02	16.17
1952	9.89	11.79	35.63	7.09 [2]	17.61	35.05	31.57	40.26	55.96	11.97	32.04	9.16
1953	4.57	3.09	35.62	5.97	14.29 [1]	42.08	26.34	45.20	74.65	19.39	25.88	12.19 [2]
1954	6.94	10.32	46.86	10.18	14.83	37.31	29.21	35.58	62.40	16.33	32.05	10.08

Notes appear at end of table

(continued)

TABLE Cf484–549   Annual precipitation: 1895–1998   [Reference climatological stations]   *Continued*

Year	Reno WSFO AP, Nevada	Searchlight, Nevada	Hanover, New Hampshire	Carlsbad, New Mexico	Chama, New Mexico	Albany, WSFOAP, New York	Geneva Resr Farm, New York	New York Central Park, New York	Cape Hatteras WSO, North Carolina	Dickinson Experiment Station, North Dakota	Wooster Experiment Station, Ohio	Goodwell Research Station, Oklahoma
	Cf516	Cf517	Cf518	Cf519	Cf520	Cf521	Cf522	Cf523	Cf524	Cf525	Cf526	Cf527
	Inches	Inches	Inches	Inches	Inches	Inches	Inches	Inches	Inches	Inches	Inches	Inches
1955	9.19	7.40	37.61	7.86	13.11	35.65	40.10 [2]	39.90	52.04	14.65	36.33	14.47
1956	7.09	1.64	37.37	4.40	8.72	35.18	34.18	36.25	51.18	12.70	43.42 [2]	10.29
1957	7.37	8.97	32.12	10.72	31.38	27.64	26.06	36.49	61.80	22.15	44.63	15.41
1958	8.87	9.78	36.08	20.96	18.65	32.39	37.74	40.94	62.70	12.18	36.44	20.98
1959	5.98	9.49	41.08	11.82 [2]	18.79 [2]	32.39	40.21	38.77	45.68	13.45 [2]	44.27 [2]	20.55
1960	5.78	6.74	38.53	16.56	15.25	38.35	27.12 [2]	46.39	56.82 [2]	10.23	27.38	21.65 [2]
1961	5.37	2.91	31.88	7.58	21.32	35.72	33.13	39.32	47.23	13.90	35.72	16.68
1962	9.05	3.21	37.87	13.06	14.82	29.30	29.77	37.15	71.98 [2]	18.34	27.89	21.52
1963	10.93	5.30	24.88 [2]	10.16	13.22 [2]	26.24	31.11 [2]	34.28	50.16	18.94	24.15	12.75
1964	7.73	1.95	31.48	4.47 [2]	18.88	21.55	26.65	32.99	58.36 [2]	18.74	38.96	11.54
1965	9.72	12.97	27.13	10.47	26.61	27.94	25.83	26.09	41.32	21.63	34.93	16.37 [2]
1966	3.27	5.49	30.94	13.83	19.90	33.37	28.66	39.90	52.49	16.69	30.15	13.97
1967	9.47	6.86	35.85	6.97	18.18	33.28	29.73	49.12	50.78	14.24	29.91	16.52
1968	5.45	3.48	39.18	15.30 [2]	20.22	32.28	37.93	43.57	49.02	15.73	36.30	17.58
1969	10.22	8.50	44.22	12.40	28.69	39.50	31.35	48.54	44.54	16.37	41.37	20.07
1970	6.95	5.03	31.09	8.09	19.14	30.52	34.62 [2]	35.29	62.75 [2]	20.16	38.42	12.94 [2]
1971	10.58	2.71	35.89	11.15	19.94	39.57	33.21	56.77	58.81	20.97	26.79	17.68 [2]
1972	5.52	5.38 [2]	43.00	18.74	20.09	47.18	44.91	67.03	59.15	20.76	41.69	17.99
1973	9.21	5.08 [2]	44.98 [2]	11.47 [2]	15.94	38.74	31.35	57.23	46.67	13.53	38.28 [2]	21.43
1974	5.38	7.26	36.44 [2]	23.11	15.09	38.47	35.95	47.69	56.58	14.17	35.77	13.15 [2]
1975	6.95	5.65	40.97	10.22 [2]	24.05 [2]	47.05	35.31	61.21	43.35	17.71	37.24	12.19 [2]
1976	5.06	12.30	44.59	11.26	15.24 [2]	42.54	40.52	41.28	54.81	12.68	30.05	14.72
1977	6.84	4.24	39.80 [2]	12.79 [2]	17.93	44.30	38.60	54.73	51.28 [2]	23.13	44.38	20.30
1978	7.93	18.65	33.88	23.50 [2]	24.61	33.46	27.61	49.81	46.60	17.63	34.80	14.68
1979	6.03	10.10	36.33 [1]	12.49	22.22	37.14	36.46	52.13	61.22	12.68 [2]	41.26	21.77
1980	9.20	12.34	24.89 [2]	19.42	25.34	32.59	30.35	44.55	55.18	12.59	39.93	14.77
1981	6.68	6.41	43.73 [2]	15.81 [2]	20.16	30.44	27.90	38.11	56.37	15.76	32.85	18.12
1982	11.10	14.48	31.04	12.85 [2]	28.32	32.07	25.51	41.40	56.93	26.58	34.55	16.08
1983	13.23	14.83	56.04	10.67	26.65	46.29	30.34	80.56	64.29	12.59	35.29	14.23 [2]
1984	4.28	11.83	43.97	24.23	23.49 [2]	37.13	35.41	57.03	38.99	15.38 [1]	36.69	14.79
1985	4.99	6.18 [2]	30.93 [2]	12.56	29.25	29.95	31.33	38.82	64.65	16.98	39.63 [2]	25.60
1986	8.94	7.16	42.78	18.12	31.04	43.96	38.29	42.95	50.85	21.68	37.30	15.78
1987	7.50	7.83	40.53	16.58 [2]	20.45	39.29	33.92 [2]	46.44	58.00	15.93	32.04	21.79
1988	5.30	5.65	31.51	14.94	22.67	29.55	23.14	44.67	46.78	9.20	35.34	17.85 [1]
1989	7.34	3.02	41.69 [1]	5.99 [2]	14.50	39.67	34.58	65.11	90.84	12.78	40.07	17.65
1990	5.26	5.99	44.12 [2]	11.44	30.58	46.01	43.16 [1]	60.92	47.69	12.37	53.29	14.15
1991	5.15	8.03	35.11	23.66	23.25	35.72	28.44 [2]	44.82 [1]	64.51	14.86	29.35	15.60 [2]
1992	5.36	14.45 [1]	33.87 [2]	15.76 [2]	24.11 [2]	31.38	38.88 [2]	43.35	62.08	14.21	42.71 [2]	17.21
1993	6.58	11.43	33.91 [2]	8.01	27.49	41.25	31.98	44.28	59.26	16.98 [2]	39.24 [2]	16.23 [2]
1994	5.20	6.59	38.91 [2]	7.20	29.50 [2]	34.72	31.11 [2]	47.39	63.37	17.61 [2]	37.25	—
1995	12.56	9.24	32.12 [2]	7.45	21.34 [2]	34.08	26.87 [2]	40.42	62.32 [2]	20.02 [2]	42.58	16.45
1996	12.21	4.37	49.11	13.98	20.08 [2]	45.89	41.78	56.19	55.15 [2]	17.07 [2]	52.30	—
1997	7.75	5.12	38.62	20.91 [2]	28.60	34.72	26.88	43.93	52.36 [2]	16.60 [2]	34.28	13.43
1998	12.03	12.21	34.17 [2]	7.84	23.79 [2]	38.94	33.46 [2]	48.69	61.81	24.04 [2]	40.60	19.21 [2]

Notes appear at end of table

TABLE Cf484–549   Annual precipitation: 1895–1998   [Reference climatological stations]   *Continued*

Year	Muskogee, Oklahoma	Newport, Oregon	Union Experiment Station, Oregon	Harrisburg Capital City, Pennsylvania	Charleston City, South Carolina	Winthrop College, South Carolina	Cottonwood 2E, South Dakota	Lewisburg Experiment Station, Tennessee	Rogersville 1NE, Tennessee	Beeville 5NE, Texas	El Paso WSO AP, Texas
	Cf528	Cf529	Cf530	Cf531	Cf532	Cf533	Cf534	Cf535	Cf536	Cf537	Cf538
	Inches	Inches	Inches	Inches	Inches	Inches	Inches	Inches	Inches	Inches	Inches
1895	39.62 [1]	74.59	10.24 [1]	26.02	55.18	43.08 [1]	12.90 [1]	46.90 [1]	36.44	28.88 [2]	10.20
1896	26.71 [1]	91.86 [2]	16.16 [1]	35.06	47.78	42.66 [1]	13.48 [1]	50.89 [1]	45.10	29.69	9.79
1897	36.19 [1]	69.28	16.73 [1]	33.66	50.65	43.12 [1]	13.10 [1]	52.97 [1]	48.28	20.21	12.41
1898	54.53 [1]	63.73	11.05 [1]	45.09	46.43	43.61 [1]	9.89 [1]	46.65 [1]	49.58	22.92	6.16
1899	35.62 [1]	90.19	18.74 [1]	33.98	44.33	45.15 [1]	11.59 [1]	47.45	44.44	28.86	7.30
1900	34.18 [1]	75.61	15.24 [1]	28.94	38.10	44.92	11.79 [1]	53.57	43.40	32.67	7.95
1901	26.32 [1]	70.00	12.93 [1]	29.81	32.70	64.14	16.97 [1]	44.97	53.84	22.08 [2]	8.68
1902	40.51	86.22	14.96 [1]	39.84	37.22	48.75	15.64 [1]	52.32	41.14	29.75	10.15
1903	36.92	60.09	13.49 [1]	35.90	42.86	43.56	15.95 [1]	51.07	42.15	49.13	11.63
1904	31.40	74.53	14.74 [1]	31.99	37.88	35.36	10.79 [1]	37.42	38.71	29.60 [2]	11.30
1905	48.25	52.16	13.32 [1]	36.02	34.85	45.47	20.99 [1]	62.81	42.34	39.65	17.80
1906	40.53	70.43	15.63 [1]	34.21	43.62	55.65	16.57 [1]	57.10	44.19	31.23	14.99
1907	31.69	63.82	14.00 [1]	36.25	31.71	49.30	13.11 [1]	51.52	50.00	19.10	8.41
1908	53.98	58.49	10.10 [1]	33.47	31.41	54.96	16.74 [1]	50.37	42.77	35.68	6.94
1909	28.58	74.47	13.72 [1]	28.16	38.68	40.89	15.64 [1]	50.54	49.68	30.81	4.33
1910	31.61	55.73	13.98 [1]	32.02	39.69	42.49	9.95	46.67	39.28	29.80	4.03
1911	37.18	43.83	12.58 [2]	37.90	31.68	40.05	12.31	60.32	44.85	23.46	10.88
1912	30.50	73.78	17.74	34.09	51.32	47.42	14.07	60.95	49.35	30.01	10.14
1913	35.31	73.31	17.29	38.42	41.49	52.43	10.48	53.08	45.04	32.77	7.09
1914	26.70	76.60	11.58	37.05	44.32	45.77	15.01	46.85	39.12	46.62	17.02
1915	55.20	69.80	16.91	44.78	46.55	48.04	27.62	57.36	44.46	13.14	10.26
1916	38.22	79.60	13.33	36.37	42.51	43.83	12.29	57.64	42.11	23.40	7.77
1917	30.30	72.38	15.02	39.21	33.57	40.61	13.16	52.83	50.86	12.09	6.49
1918	38.12	60.55	12.44	35.62	31.33	47.83	15.03	49.07	47.40	29.57	8.21
1919	35.21	77.67	9.52	40.82	36.68	54.18	15.99	55.10	43.03	47.44	9.87
1920	38.50	75.14	14.76	44.34	46.81	51.55	19.38	57.30	50.42	22.27	6.21
1921	35.38	85.02	14.79	30.08	45.62	40.07	10.90	50.07	42.17	27.54 [2]	6.92
1922	42.95	66.06	8.26	28.20	50.62	52.93	22.41	55.78	48.77	37.72	4.30
1923	60.86	60.75	17.46	30.01	46.58	47.99	22.30	59.15	44.96	46.45	8.13
1924	44.51	56.98	9.42	47.71	51.07	58.38	11.22	45.75	45.02	21.58	7.28
1925	37.22	57.43	11.56	42.37	33.42	32.56	10.45	42.45	32.98	31.18	6.51
1926	46.66	70.98	15.88	42.46	35.12	38.37	13.52	63.49	45.73	31.61	11.73
1927	51.17	69.09	16.48	38.99	29.86	43.77	21.02	54.53	46.10 [2]	20.59	6.25
1928	48.15	63.52	9.45	41.64	42.76	48.78	14.06	42.97	49.88	36.84	8.21
1929	41.48	38.45	10.99	47.39	44.96	60.81	18.15	58.05	49.82	38.38	9.29
1930	38.37	37.43	13.51	27.29	32.43	36.25	23.07	41.68 [2]	34.14	26.91	6.09
1931	39.31	73.27	9.88	31.00	28.80	49.97	9.58	41.32	34.35	37.75	10.79
1932	41.51	69.04 [1]	11.26	39.77	44.84	51.36	17.27	61.79	47.48	42.70	10.94
1933	43.32	78.65 [1]	12.69	47.24	52.85	32.59	14.53	49.60	42.07	29.66	5.93
1934	33.45	62.57 [1]	10.83	43.34	38.83	45.10	11.99	41.34	49.03	32.11	2.73
1935	67.70	43.46	8.04	31.44	54.06	39.29	15.68	46.82	45.53	33.20	5.65
1936	19.28	47.30	9.80	45.18	40.20	63.34	7.13	51.12	44.82	34.94	9.93
1937	36.01	83.30	12.85	49.73	48.76	55.33	14.65	64.40	41.91	23.30	6.23
1938	41.95	59.88	11.77	36.73	31.10	40.08	14.90	46.76	42.41	21.06	8.30
1939	32.80	53.99	6.11	34.42	49.04	46.91	8.35	59.38	33.75	16.73	5.91
1940	38.80	54.37	18.76	43.51	45.49	41.12	9.84	43.78	36.94	33.03	7.76
1941	53.47	57.60	21.27	27.43	62.63	45.24	18.62	38.57	29.28	47.53	15.65
1942	52.28	59.98	17.15	44.34	41.37	53.08	19.32	44.75	43.94	39.96	10.76
1943	40.75	53.37	12.35	34.46	36.17	39.93	10.98	42.10	36.15	33.57	6.55
1944	43.98	42.65	10.61	39.52	51.23	47.02	12.87	58.11	45.41	27.37	9.08
1945	58.77	64.95	14.36	49.23	74.87	45.15	11.39	62.52	49.73	25.74	6.74
1946	48.61	63.43	15.36	33.58	48.97	41.26	17.75	54.71	43.16	37.14	8.22
1947	41.95	61.44	14.64	36.05	67.41	51.14	12.97	41.43	45.74	22.37 [2]	7.12
1948	42.25	64.43	16.92	38.28	61.26	49.84	17.06	63.70	52.98	19.93	5.70
1949	45.78	55.84	10.04	32.96	46.05	55.24 [1]	14.77	49.81	49.22	35.51 [2]	8.76
1950	46.19	80.76 [1]	12.95	33.73	43.35	44.46	11.93	66.62	51.32	13.89	6.75
1951	48.43	71.44 [1]	13.89	33.55	38.23	37.17	20.92	52.92	48.59	25.47	6.47
1952	32.53	59.98	11.67	43.53	39.20	49.53 [2]	16.71 [2]	48.86	39.27	32.16	7.97
1953	34.14	94.14	18.33	39.80	44.03	42.08	18.58 [2]	48.14	36.87	19.27	4.42
1954	22.76	75.63	12.52	33.46	31.02	35.68	13.01	47.34	37.50	15.39	6.39

Notes appear at end of table

(continued)

TABLE Cf484–549   Annual precipitation: 1895–1998   [Reference climatological stations]   *Continued*

Year	Muskogee, Oklahoma	Newport, Oregon	Union Experiment Station, Oregon	Harrisburg Capital City, Pennsylvania	Charleston City, South Carolina	Winthrop College, South Carolina	Cottonwood 2E, South Dakota	Lewisburg Experiment Station, Tennessee	Rogersville 1NE, Tennessee	Beeville 5NE, Texas	El Paso WSO AP, Texas
	Cf528	Cf529	Cf530	Cf531	Cf532	Cf533	Cf534	Cf535	Cf536	Cf537	Cf538
	Inches	Inches	Inches	Inches	Inches	Inches	Inches	Inches	Inches	Inches	Inches
1955	29.23	79.21	13.72	34.45	40.48	40.51	13.95	55.81	45.47 [2]	19.52	6.70
1956	26.78	74.32	15.83	38.12	35.13	36.73	14.63	52.27	48.84	19.34	5.44
1957	56.26	66.34	15.60	28.98	51.79	50.04	22.51	65.27	51.53	40.07	11.20
1958	45.55	76.28	20.83	36.70	44.36	50.44	16.43	45.02	48.07	33.06	17.19
1959	50.95	70.93	14.15	35.62	58.64	69.49	15.53	54.82	51.48 [2]	30.86	4.99
1960	45.88	74.89	16.32	39.15	46.50	48.58	15.18 [2]	42.07	42.01	43.41	9.12
1961	49.51	82.73	11.66	40.47	48.91	53.21	14.08	56.42	49.91	23.75	7.69
1962	37.51	60.72	11.01	39.58	49.70	47.35	14.92	57.74 [2]	52.96 [2]	31.43	8.28
1963	23.75	67.53	13.06	30.09	48.32	41.00	17.37	45.26 [2]	44.09 [2]	17.84 [2]	4.92
1964	35.41	77.06 [2]	12.67	34.45	73.41	60.36	15.35	63.17 [2]	41.01	21.94	5.35
1965	37.50	66.35 [2]	13.40	31.19	52.23	40.18	17.35	51.62	40.76	32.84	5.41
1966	36.35	73.28 [2]	12.33	31.60	48.07	43.00	15.26 [2]	47.80	51.43	26.15	9.24
1967	40.18	75.61 [2]	11.18	41.09	42.55	50.81	20.18	57.09	50.92	42.07	5.72
1968	54.04	111.03	13.73	33.21	45.48	39.99	15.86	47.93	37.39 [2]	31.51	12.02
1969	37.63	73.05	13.43	36.68	54.51	41.90	20.05	54.62	44.70 [2]	29.48	4.34
1970	39.30	74.47	19.17	43.71	42.98	46.39	15.83 [2]	47.51	45.16 [2]	28.00	6.06
1971	47.35	90.47	15.91	41.42	63.77	58.82	26.36	53.38	46.62	44.22	7.24
1972	37.83	69.96	12.88	59.27	40.73	48.97	16.21	58.31	49.15 [2]	35.90	9.00
1973	70.18	82.49	11.75	43.81	60.76	50.98	15.60 [1]	70.82	52.62 [2]	46.29	7.53
1974	44.70	80.75	10.64	42.95	50.68 [2]	52.04	11.38 [1]	60.32	49.91	31.04	13.95
1975	40.10	86.67	14.77	54.22	40.20 [2]	64.29	15.77 [2]	65.57	52.54	29.42	6.21
1976	37.68	50.06	10.71	45.31	51.31	50.96	11.61 [2]	49.44	37.10 [2]	43.48	10.14
1977	35.71 [2]	67.15	14.12	39.70	42.12 [2]	46.19	20.28	58.36	57.10	30.37	5.50
1978	31.18	58.52	15.19	43.71	45.18	41.68 [2]	14.62	49.10	43.96 [2]	34.20	12.57
1979	38.7 [1]	72.71	12.83	46.60	49.16	67.69	17.03	71.26	57.31 [2]	37.74	5.84
1980	30.7 [1]	66.79 [2]	17.13	30.06	40.94	51.14	14.37	47.20	41.08 [2]	37.08	7.31
1981	45.02 [2]	72.57	16.98	34.78	40.37	44.23 [2]	17.12	43.90	42.55 [2]	46.67	12.63
1982	46.98 [1]	75.73	16.81	39.92	48.37 [1]	52.44	23.23	50.91	48.89 [2]	21.61	10.97
1983	33.34 [1]	90.88	18.06	48.57	48.38 [2]	46.81	15.01	68.02	41.11	35.86	7.99
1984	42.67	78.47	20.54	44.05	41.97	52.06	16.40	54.43	44.03	27.17	16.17
1985	49.79	50.23	12.21	33.81	42.28	48.70	13.48	42.92	40.03 [2]	31.34	8.16
1986	47.80	57.99 [2]	12.52	41.92	42.32	33.70	24.29	52.10	36.21 [2]	35.81	12.17
1987	49.01	58.15 [1]	9.98	39.52	52.33	45.49	13.67	37.61 [2]	35.14 [2]	35.82	10.94
1988	37.32 [2]	64.78 [2]	11.75	32.75	38.29	36.11	14.60	42.80	29.69 [2]	17.57	11.06
1989	35.36	54.21	14.06	46.51	56.45 [2]	54.67 [2]	12.73	76.12	55.18 [2]	18.47	7.26
1990	55.48 [2]	62.55	13.07	44.12	54.01	47.79	12.85	59.52	38.25 [2]	35.46	12.85
1991	46.30	53.79	15.60	30.15 [1]	45.60 [2]	49.91	21.32	68.13 [2]	48.60 [2]	35.39	12.38
1992	60.28 [2]	50.41	11.35	34.72 [1]	57.87	50.39	18.39	57.03	33.32 [2]	48.13	11.40
1993	49.97 [2]	46.25 [2]	15.39	45.66 [1]	36.63	41.80	20.67	51.55	43.92 [1]	37.48	9.63
1994	41.71	63.00	14.94	—	54.33 [2]	41.39	14.06	60.82 [2]	60.20	35.98	5.48
1995	40.99 [2]	78.83	19.65	—	42.13	50.18	17.49	61.12 [2]	43.15 [2]	—	8.06
1996	44.78 [2]	94.44	15.99 [2]	—	30.22	43.82	—	58.77 [2]	—	—	8.39 [2]
1997	48.83 [2]	80.57	15.73	—	51.92 [2]	46.79	26.14	60.52	45.17 [2]	40.53	9.63
1998	42.48 [2]	90.78	—	—	52.14	55.91	21.73	—	53.96	35.14	6.77

Notes appear at end of table

TABLE Cf484–549 Annual precipitation: 1895–1998 [Reference climatological stations] *Continued*

Year	Marshall, Texas	Temple, Texas	Logan, Utah State University, Utah	Charlottesville 2W, Virginia	Hot Springs, Virginia	Seattle Urban Site, Washington	Spokane WSO AP, Washington	Martinsburg FAA Airport, West Virginia	Oshkosh, Wisconsin	Cheyenne WSFO, Wyoming	Sheridan Field Station, Wyoming
	Cf539	Cf540	Cf541	Cf542	Cf543	Cf544	Cf545	Cf546	Cf547	Cf548	Cf549
	Inches	Inches	Inches	Inches	Inches	Inches	Inches	Inches	Inches	Inches	Inches
1895	62.65	36.98	13.51	36.98 [2]	29.51 [1]	30.57 [1]	13.46	28.98	19.14 [1]	14.76	16.13
1896	56.02 [1]	31.31 [2]	16.15	43.42 [2]	41.07 [1]	41.15 [1]	20.32	31.78	29.16 [1]	20.79	11.59
1897	45.48 [1]	37.05	17.45	39.90 [1]	35.54	36.95 [1]	23.80	35.34	25.80 [1]	17.25	10.68
1898	44.13 [1]	28.75	13.18	60.98 [2]	50.72 [2]	29.93 [1]	13.08	38.60	26.19 [1]	13.05	14.50
1899	33.04 [1]	33.46	12.57	44.65 [2]	41.99 [2]	46.43 [1]	20.08	33.76	24.47 [1]	14.18	18.79
1900	45.67 [1]	48.98	15.06	43.60 [2]	45.11 [2]	40.51 [1]	18.72	30.65	25.99 [1]	16.09	10.27
1901	33.77 [1]	20.92	14.47	65.29	55.47	33.58 [1]	15.99	50.36	30.56 [1]	14.99	15.00
1902	57.26 [1]	59.18	13.33	56.21 [2]	37.00 [2]	42.40 [1]	19.23	41.33	30.62	16.50	7.98 [2]
1903	39.75 [1]	31.99	13.97	49.35	47.66	40.50 [1]	16.55	40.15	28.50 [1]	12.25	12.20 [2]
1904	37.51 [1]	31.20 [1]	13.52 [2]	30.37	35.57	37.44 [1]	13.97	35.05	28.76 [1]	15.44 [1]	11.54 [2]
1905	66.43 [1]	49.82	12.51	46.90	44.08	33.19 [1]	16.68	39.60	37.20 [1]	22.68	16.75
1906	44.81 [1]	31.55	26.40	56.87 [2]	44.93	39.41 [1]	17.60	41.15	33.76	17.65	18.71
1907	43.44 [1]	36.11	21.96	46.08	46.31	31.47 [1]	17.69	46.18	31.63 [1]	12.34	15.32
1908	49.01 [1]	37.94	18.77	48.86	42.09	35.65 [1]	12.02	29.91	27.01 [2]	19.09	15.93
1909	34.19 [1]	30.45	22.31 [2]	30.11	38.05	35.40 [2]	16.21	33.29	27.59	17.62	16.62
1910	32.92	27.07	11.74	46.67	40.05	36.53	15.44	29.07	22.39	12.05	10.75
1911	40.75	27.22	19.07	39.41	45.64	22.83	11.86	41.61	33.67	10.85	9.91
1912	48.98	29.41	18.90	49.79	37.66	38.15	18.21	44.58	32.56	18.50	19.34
1913	53.52	43.29	17.82	49.39	47.13	24.47 [2]	16.74	39.59	28.04	15.84	15.61
1914	50.49	48.23	19.59	37.67 [2]	35.04 [1]	32.43	13.56	34.50	30.27 [1]	11.07	12.69
1915	50.49	33.44	15.17	43.78	38.27 [2]	37.22	16.35	43.53	31.20	19.00	22.51
1916	34.42	24.81	18.77	43.08	36.03 [1]	35.16 [2]	15.75	40.79	33.28	11.15	17.33
1917	35.51	17.04	18.14	42.97	34.38	28.14 [2]	11.88	38.71	32.05	14.06	11.32
1918	32.44 [1]	28.76	16.91	42.74	54.97	30.38 [2]	9.92	43.17	28.38	19.26	17.15
1919	53.42	44.44	15.70	47.41	44.59	32.60 [2]	13.85	39.92	28.23	13.85	8.53
1920	46.38	37.58	19.24	48.87	40.61	32.30 [2]	12.18	37.79	28.08	15.87	13.35
1921	48.70 [1]	45.40	18.33	33.66	37.92	40.90	12.57 [2]	43.56	26.68	13.25	10.06
1922	49.89	37.29	15.16	42.21	40.68	27.62 [2]	11.51	33.14 [1]	35.55 [2]	15.38	17.07
1923	46.49	42.35	16.91	38.84	42.26	27.16	16.02	35.21 [1]	22.65	21.74	25.09
1924	30.33	28.32	12.42	54.70	44.89	33.31	12.25	40.30	38.74 [2]	16.79	14.32
1925	42.83	20.86	16.32	29.55	34.25	29.15	12.35	32.39	27.30	17.14	17.89
1926	52.85	44.08	15.97	43.64	39.20	29.03	14.52	42.58	36.84	17.60	14.90
1927	52.32	40.71	18.38	41.87	47.04	33.51	23.28	39.32	28.76	20.06 [2]	22.03
1928	50.60	29.92	10.81 [2]	41.55	36.64	27.31 [2]	10.59	43.59	30.51	14.67	16.58
1929	39.22 [1]	39.92	15.97	49.39	42.01	23.18	7.54	40.99	30.94	18.42	16.98
1930	43.19	37.66	20.33	23.66	21.38	22.21 [2]	11.84	21.41 [2]	22.03	20.64	8.78
1931	49.63	24.19	12.32	44.97	39.55	36.88	13.61	34.75	28.14	12.79	14.73
1932	50.63	36.47	16.42	46.00	44.65	36.14	14.83	42.09	21.18	11.26	19.27
1933	58.64	23.68	11.93	46.58	36.57	44.33	14.37	42.65	24.95	16.88	15.84
1934	39.48	32.01	11.79	49.91	45.69	31.78	12.19 [2]	38.95	32.06	11.44	10.40
1935	47.88	46.91	13.47	49.17	50.46	28.81	8.74	33.11	26.30	17.69	13.00
1936	29.92	38.89	18.31	47.66	44.75	29.38	11.13	43.90	23.84	14.19	9.79
1937	45.10	31.40	20.41	72.07	44.89	42.29	16.40	47.08	27.96	14.48	16.97
1938	38.26	30.12	17.76	43.57	32.57	24.33	10.40	38.45	43.63	17.47	17.72
1939	41.33	26.39	12.42	37.54	36.74	32.85	11.13 [2]	38.33	25.67	9.84	17.43
1940	55.28	41.26	17.05	46.79	47.47	38.84	23.98	45.23	37.44	15.02	16.10
1941	58.62	46.22	19.62	29.11	25.36	36.41	17.74	30.67	31.19	18.96	17.25
1942	38.96	40.62	17.97	57.64	50.78	34.73	14.27	53.59	35.00	23.69	18.65
1943	29.58	25.23	18.12	32.51	36.97	26.24	13.66	30.74	26.53	13.95	16.78
1944	67.43	53.13	18.88	54.79	37.46	23.69	10.65	34.74	25.93	15.57	20.82
1945	59.22	41.37	24.57	42.91	39.32	42.24	17.36 [2]	45.22	31.08	16.51	17.02
1946	54.66	45.59	20.49	43.64	32.23	34.51	15.42	30.89	26.13	18.18	21.32
1947	43.57	29.00	18.77	42.26	40.57	35.82 [2]	18.56	28.43	30.37	16.97	18.18
1948	37.39 [1]	23.44	17.30	69.72	50.82 [1]	43.14	26.07	41.33	26.35	11.91	18.53
1949	55.14	31.58 [1]	19.77	44.01	51.07 [1]	31.18	13.91	37.58	22.39	20.50	16.83
1950	50.40	24.39 [1]	19.88	43.58	47.35	47.90	23.00	39.48	25.92	14.40	14.28
1951	41.54	26.90 [1]	18.92	43.49	43.72	34.85	19.30	34.81	29.89	17.16	15.18
1952	41.91	30.67	12.82	51.44	40.14 [2]	22.84 [2]	13.00	46.98	22.23	12.60	15.70
1953	49.32	35.46	14.00	38.19	32.12	39.77	17.23 [2]	32.68	25.10	15.24	15.60
1954	45.96	13.89	12.46 [2]	41.96	50.76 [2]	34.84 [2]	16.26	35.60	29.35	10.34	10.03

Notes appear at end of table   (continued)

TABLE Cf484–549   Annual precipitation: 1895–1998   [Reference climatological stations]   *Continued*

Year	Marshall, Texas	Temple, Texas	Logan, Utah State University, Utah	Charlottesville 2W, Virginia	Hot Springs, Virginia	Seattle Urban Site, Washington	Spokane WSO AP, Washington	Martinsburg FAA Airport, West Virginia	Oshkosh, Wisconsin	Cheyenne WSFO, Wyoming	Sheridan Field Station, Wyoming
	Cf539	Cf540	Cf541	Cf542	Cf543	Cf544	Cf545	Cf546	Cf547	Cf548	Cf549
	Inches	Inches	Inches	Inches	Inches	Inches	Inches	Inches	Inches	Inches	Inches
1955	44.30	36.95 [2]	20.17	42.75	33.34	36.12 [2]	19.78 [2]	34.39	24.31 [2]	15.46	17.18
1956	29.60	17.12	11.68	42.41	37.89	32.75	12.88	40.30	31.56	11.40	14.07
1957	64.45	46.74	17.80	42.65	43.85	30.26 [2]	18.09	28.57 [2]	25.37	19.84	16.90
1958	38.95	35.75	13.35	42.13	37.54 [2]	36.60 [2]	20.91	33.15	19.68	16.57	15.40
1959	47.79	45.48	16.38	47.40	45.90	43.06 [2]	19.57	33.19	35.73 [2]	13.07	10.57
1960	52.42	38.72	14.18	39.61	38.11 [2]	36.64 [2]	17.69 [2]	32.72	35.62 [2]	8.22	9.36
1961	53.26	32.76	14.75	55.55	51.38	37.93 [2]	19.30	38.77	34.32 [2]	16.99	14.07
1962	38.51	29.36	15.09	49.08	41.96 [2]	31.45 [2]	17.02	33.28	28.08 [2]	14.62	16.71
1963	33.17	21.18	19.72	30.39	32.12	37.74 [2]	15.26	31.35	23.77	14.89	17.75
1964	32.03	35.89	19.07	42.34	39.84	34.22 [2]	21.51	29.96	28.13	5.94	16.70
1965	38.06	43.71	19.79 [2]	35.61	39.48 [2]	31.16	14.46	29.82	33.63	14.02	13.34
1966	48.16	34.85	10.58	39.69	42.13	36.25	14.13	30.51	23.54	12.42	12.07 [2]
1967	35.02	32.31	21.12	44.63	41.39	34.29	13.89	37.70	29.87	15.39	16.00
1968	63.96	46.18	22.46	39.81	39.95	50.19	16.26	32.92	31.16	11.91	20.87
1969	45.18	29.10	16.85	55.97	40.05 [2]	36.05	13.70	27.75	29.11	10.93	11.46
1970	45.53	27.74	20.92	44.88	37.57	36.78	17.52	41.91	28.91 [2]	11.83	17.68
1971	35.93 [2]	33.99	22.37	56.22	42.34	39.38	18.48	40.49	28.98	13.90	15.34
1972	49.55 [2]	27.60	15.54	66.03	52.42	42.83	13.53	48.96	33.83 [2]	12.04	14.35
1973	62.92	46.05 [2]	21.47	49.16	44.33	35.01	17.11	43.27	36.11	17.58	17.97
1974	58.12	35.09 [2]	15.04	43.51	38.15	38.94	16.04	34.58	27.90	9.87	12.88
1975	53.24	37.68 [2]	19.89 [2]	59.81	44.54	45.00	21.27	51.50	31.09	10.71	16.78
1976	50.67	41.44 [2]	17.38	49.86	43.20	27.78	11.22	34.90	21.97	10.98	13.39
1977	42.04	25.07 [2]	20.20	31.86	36.11	38.33	15.57	34.66	36.81	13.65	16.73 [2]
1978	41.01 [2]	32.13	18.21	49.76	42.58	36.26	19.19	41.60	34.91	10.81	23.81 [2]
1979	70.17	45.68 [1]	12.84	61.29	56.40	34.87	14.35	45.41	32.94	17.19	12.09 [2]
1980	39.75	25.26 [2]	25.42	34.71	42.66 [2]	40.30	17.03	31.54	30.54	13.76	13.30
1981	51.03	46.14	22.37	36.39	33.70	39.77	14.91	35.11	29.96	16.71	14.66
1982	57.26 [1]	28.00 [1]	28.42 [2]	51.81	46.87	41.76	17.25	34.08	38.03	19.23	15.52
1983	45.93	34.06	35.85	57.56	46.30	46.11	22.64	44.93	32.44	20.69	11.12
1984	46.16	34.44	23.55	50.99	48.64 [2]	38.61	18.01	43.65	37.78	17.64	13.17
1985	38.78	50.75	19.79	47.54	46.76 [1]	28.54	11.21	37.58	35.85	19.94	11.92 [2]
1986	46.73	46.35	26.78	34.67	35.19	40.88	15.55	32.63	40.48	14.56	15.29
1987	51.29	34.54	17.23	56.30 [1]	40.00 [2]	31.59	17.68	38.31	28.45	15.29	13.34
1988	38.78 [2]	24.28	12.57	36.36 [1]	31.46 [2]	32.49 [1]	16.52	36.23	27.18	15.75	9.11
1989	60.32	28.76 [2]	14.50	55.05	49.06 [2]	32.70	14.71	38.60	22.29	12.73	13.68
1990	57.05	34.48	14.96	48.98 [1]	38.11 [2]	38.81 [1]	19.61	41.59	36.58 [2]	19.63	12.95
1991	74.88	48.44 [1]	20.33	44.04	36.05 [1]	34.31	14.45	26.32	28.78 [2]	18.65	12.69 [2]
1992	52.50	47.34 [2]	13.61	51.38	38.46 [1]	34.65	14.52	38.48	28.10 [2]	13.77	13.11 [2]
1993	53.46	38.29	20.59	47.93 [2]	40.63 [1]	29.54	13.63	46.82	37.28 [2]	18.91	14.90
1994	—	31.16	15.24 [2]	53.10	—	34.85	13.81	37.86	25.33 [2]	13.49	12.50 [2]
1995	43.02	20.30	19.78	47.12	38.29 [2]	42.91 [2]	21.67	—	34.41 [2]	20.09	16.60 [2]
1996	46.84	34.18 [2]	22.07 [2]	56.49 [2]	52.35 [2]	51.56	25.23	60.20	24.62 [2]	15.80	—
1997	64.27	47.06 [2]	22.32 [2]	45.31 [2]	37.49 [2]	45.37	17.45	30.69	29.43 [2]	19.84	16.94
1998	54.28	—	—	51.22	47.69 [2]	—	17.77	36.93	29.34 [2]	10.82	18.10

[1] VEMAP2 estimated data.

[2] Incomplete data as reported in the original source (U.S. Historical Climatology Network data).

[3] Trace of precipitation recorded.

Source
See the text for Table Cf286–351.

Documentation
See the text for Table Cf418–483.

TABLE Cf550-569   Annual mean temperature and total precipitation: 1780-1999   [Long-record city stations]

Contributed by Myron P. Gutmann, Timothy G. F. Kittel, and Christie S. Wilson

	Albany		Baltimore		Charleston		New Haven		New York	
	Mean temperature	Precipitation	Mean temperature	Precipitation	Mean temperature	Precipitation	Mean temperature	Precipitation	Mean temperature	Precipitation
	Cf550	Cf551	Cf552	Cf553	Cf554	Cf555	Cf556	Cf557	Cf558	Cf559
Year	Degrees F	Inches	Degrees F	Inches	Degrees F	Inches	Degrees F	Inches	Degrees F	Inches
1780	—	—	—	—	—	—	50	—	—	—
1781	—	—	—	—	—	—	50	—	—	—
1782	—	—	—	—	—	—	49	—	—	—
1783	—	—	—	—	—	—	48	—	—	—
1784	—	—	—	—	—	—	47	—	—	—
1785	—	—	—	—	—	—	48	—	—	—
1786	—	—	—	—	—	—	48	—	—	—
1787	—	—	—	—	—	—	48	—	—	—
1788	—	—	—	—	—	—	50	—	—	—
1789	—	—	—	—	—	—	50	—	—	—
1790	—	—	—	—	—	—	50	—	—	—
1791	—	—	—	—	—	—	50	—	—	—
1792	—	—	—	—	—	—	48	—	—	—
1793	—	—	—	—	—	—	50	—	—	—
1794	—	—	—	—	—	—	50	—	—	—
1795	50	—	—	—	—	—	—	—	—	—
1796	47	—	—	—	—	—	48	—	—	—
1797	—	—	—	—	—	—	48	—	—	—
1798	—	—	—	—	—	—	49	—	—	—
1799	—	—	—	—	—	—	48	—	—	—
1800	—	—	—	—	—	—	50	—	—	—
1801	—	—	—	—	—	—	51	—	—	—
1802	—	—	—	—	—	—	51	—	—	—
1803	—	—	—	—	—	—	51	—	—	—
1804	—	—	—	—	—	—	50	43.3	—	—
1805	—	—	—	—	—	—	52	40.8	—	—
1806	—	—	—	—	—	—	50	38.6	—	—
1807	—	—	—	—	—	42.2	49	45.3	—	—
1808	—	—	—	—	—	40.8	50	49.4	—	—
1809	—	—	—	—	—	66.0	49	44.6	—	—
1810	—	—	—	—	—	45.4	50	39.4	—	—
1811	—	—	—	—	—	49.3	50	47.7	—	—
1812	—	—	—	—	—	—	47	44.2	—	—
1813	48	—	—	—	—	—	49	53.4	—	—
1814	50	—	—	—	—	—	49	56.1	—	—
1815	—	—	—	—	—	—	47	50.6	—	—
1816	—	—	—	—	—	—	47	38.0	—	—
1817	—	—	55	49.0	—	—	46	43.4	—	—
1818	—	—	55	32.6	—	—	47	38.0	—	—
1819	—	—	57	28.8	—	—	49	33.9	—	—
1820	49	—	55	42.5	—	—	48	46.2	—	—
1821	48	—	56	50.2	—	—	48	44.6	—	—
1822	49	—	59	29.2	—	—	50	—	54	—
1823	47	—	56	44.6	65	—	48	—	51	—
1824	48	—	57	42.3	67	—	50	—	52	—
1825	50	—	58	26.2	67	—	51	—	54	—
1826	51	33.1	58	30.7	66	—	50	—	52	55.7
1827	49	49.8	58	32.7	67	—	49	51.4	52	51.1
1828	51	37.7	58	33.0	71	—	52	—	54	48.9
1829	48	38.1	55	52.3	66	—	49	—	52	45.8
1830	51	41.8	58	39.0	70	—	51	—	55	43.3
1831	49	39.5	55	37.4	66	—	49	—	52	38.8
1832	48	44.4	57	34.3	67	45.0	48	—	52	39.2
1833	48	41.8	57	41.3	66	48.4	48	—	52	37.7
1834	48	32.4	57	29.5	68	68.6	49	—	51	33.6
1835	46	40.5	54	34.1	67	49.0	47	—	50	28.8
1836	45	44.6	52	54.6	66	40.9	45	—	47	36.6
1837	46	41.2	54	45.0	67	56.4 [3]	46	—	49	32.1
1838	47	42.0	54	47.1	67	58.9	48	—	50	33.7
1839	48	38.1	56	51.7	67	53.0	49	—	51	33.4

Notes appear at end of table

(continued)

TABLE Cf550–569   Annual mean temperature and total precipitation: 1780–1999   [Long-record city stations]
Continued

	Albany		Baltimore		Charleston		New Haven		New York	
	Mean temperature	Precipitation	Mean temperature	Precipitation	Mean temperature	Precipitation	Mean temperature	Precipitation	Mean temperature	Precipitation
	Cf550	Cf551	Cf552	Cf553	Cf554	Cf555	Cf556	Cf557	Cf558	Cf559
Year	Degrees F	Inches	Degrees F	Inches	Degrees F	Inches	Degrees F	Inches	Degrees F	Inches
1840	49	44.4	54	37.5	67	46.1	49	—	51	35.5
1841	48	38.0	53	43.9	66	53.9	50	—	51	44.6
1842	48	46.0	55	35.1	66	42.1	50	—	53	41.6
1843	47	48.4	54	48.8	64	54.7	47	—	51	35.7
1844	48	35.0	54	32.5	66	36.4	50	—	52	39.8
1845	50	39.4	55	28.4	64	46.4	50	—	53	33.7
1846	50	39.8	55	40.7	65	44.3	50	—	52	35.9
1847	49	41.4	56	33.0	65	47.8	49	—	52	44.5
1848	50	48.2	57	34.4	65	43.4	49	—	52	32.8
1849	48	36.7	56	30.6	66	30.7	48	—	50	30.1
1850	48	51.8	58	44.8	66	23.7	49	—	51	44.6
1851	47	34.6	57	38.1	66	33.1	49	—	52	38.8
1852	48	32.0	55	51.5	66	49.7	49	—	51	35.3
1853	49	45.8	56	36.0	67	43.5	50	—	52	46.4
1854	49	34.1	57	59.2	66	37.6	49	—	51	43.5
1855	50	42.5	57	29.3	66	34.8	49	—	51	43.2
1856	47	39.1	54	22.9	64	49.1	47	—	50	35.0
1857	47	41.9	55	38.4	65	38.1	48	—	50	38.7
1858	—	34.0	57	46.1	66	48.1	48	—	51	36.7
1859	51	32.0	56	55.6	66	50.2	48	—	52	59.7
1860	48	32.2	54	37.5	68	44.4	49	—	52	31.1
1861	50	36.0	55	43.6	66	44.5	50	—	53	37.2
1862	46	37.8	54	35.5	67	52.3	50	—	52	46.8
1863	46	43.2	54	43.0	66	33.1	50	—	52	43.4
1864	48	27.9	57	23.0	67	57.2	50	—	53	39.5
1865	48	36.4	58	33.2	67	57.2	49	41.9	54	45.0
1866	47	34.3	56	27.5	67	36.3	48	47.0	52	38.3
1867	47	38.0	56	32.9	66	61.1	48	45.4	51	53.4
1868	46	41.9	55	32.6	66	61.1	47	—	50	57.4
1869	47	44.2	56	27.3	67	43.1	47	—	52	43.6
1870	50	55.8	58	22.4	66	48.3	49	—	53	37.8
1871	50	56.8	56	32.7	66	63.4 [3]	48	—	51	49.2
1872	50	39.1	56	34.8	64	57.1	48	—	51	40.3
1873	50	39.4	55	49.4	64	62.2	48	57.3	51	45.5
1874	47	37.9	55	33.6	65	62.5	49	55.8	51	44.2
1875	44	38.2	53	45.3	64	51.0	48	43.5	49	38.6
1876	47	38.2	54	46.7	65	78.4	51	54.1	52	40.6
1877	48	36.1	56	43.1	66	78.1	52	51.4	52	38.7
1878	49	49.4	57	50.1	66	77.4	53	58.1	53	46.0
1879	46	38.7	55	36.0	66	50.3	51	55.5	52	37.1
1880	49	32.5	56	41.9	67	46.7	52	46.5	53	34.7
1881	50	36.3	57	49.1	66	43.2 [3]	50	51.3	52	35.0
1882	50	33.8	56	42.1	67	57.0	49	47.9	52	43.0
1883	48	39.4	55	40.5	66	51.3 [3]	48	39.5	50	34.4
1884	48	38.9	56	45.9	66	60.2	49	49.3	52	49.7
1885	44	34.4	54	46.0	64	67.9 [3]	47	38.3	51	33.5
1886	46	34.0	54	52.1	64	35.9	48	42.3	51	38.3
1887	48	39.7	55	43.6	65	44.7	49	44.1	51	41.7
1888	46	44.7	54	43.5	65	49.5	47	60.3	49	51.0
1889	50	39.5	56	62.4	65	52.2	50	59.8	52	54.4
1890	48	44.9	57	47.0	67	47.8	49	49.0	52	43.7
1891	49	41.7	56	54.2	65	45.5	50	44.7	54	37.6
1892	48	34.8	54	45.0	64	53.3	49	37.8	52	34.1
1893	47	35.4	54	32.2	65	71.0	48	46.7	50	46.6
1894	49	35.1	56	38.3	66	56.8	50	37.7	52	39.3
1895	48	29.8	54	40.5	64	55.2	49	36.0	52	33.7
1896	48	27.9	56	38.6	66	47.8	49	38.4	53	40.1
1897	49	40.8	55	47.5	66	50.6	49	57.9	53	42.4
1898	50	38.8	56	36.5	66	46.4 [3]	50	53.7	54	46.2
1899	49	28.9	55	40.6	66	44.3	49	35.3	53	36.8

Notes appear at end of table

TABLE Cf550–569   Annual mean temperature and total precipitation: 1780–1999   [Long-record city stations]
Continued

	Albany		Baltimore		Charleston		New Haven		New York	
	Mean temperature	Precipitation	Mean temperature	Precipitation	Mean temperature	Precipitation	Mean temperature	Precipitation	Mean temperature	Precipitation
	Cf550	Cf551	Cf552	Cf553	Cf554	Cf555	Cf556	Cf557	Cf558	Cf559
Year	Degrees F	Inches	Degrees F	Inches	Degrees F	Inches	Degrees F	Inches	Degrees F	Inches
1900	50	30.6	57	31.6	66	38.1	51	34.8	54	39.4
1901	48	40.5	54	43.0	64	32.7	49	52.6	52	47.0
1902	48	37.5	55	50.1	65	37.2	49	44.3	53	50.3
1903	48	34.1	55	46.3	64	42.9	49	41.2	52	55.5
1904	45	31.3	53	36.1	64	37.9	47	41.7	50	39.5
1905	47	27.0	55	46.6	65	34.8	49	43.3	53	35.5
1906	48	32.5	56	46.8	65	43.6	50	51.3	54	39.4
1907	47	33.6	54	49.1	66	31.7	48	46.2	52	43.8
1908	49	28.4	56	35.4	66	31.4	51	43.3	55	39.4
1909	48	28.0	56	34.7	65	38.7	50	43.7	53	39.9
1910	48	28.5	56	35.0	64	39.7	50	39.8	53	32.7
1911	49	32.1	57	48.6	67	31.7	50	46.9	53	46.5
1912	47	32.1	55	45.1	65	51.3	50	44.8	52	44.2
1913	50	26.4	58	36.1	66	41.5	52	46.3	55	56.1
1914	47	29.8	55	36.4	64	44.3	49	43.8	52	38.5
1915	49	37.6	56	46.4	65	46.6	51	45.5	53	43.1
1916	47	33.9	55	36.0	66	42.5	49	40.1	52	36.7
1917	46	28.7	53	37.9	64	33.6	48	39.3	50	39.6
1918	48	30.1	56	37.5	65	31.3	50	44.9	53	36.9
1919	49	35.5	57	47.2	67	36.7	51	52.6	54	50.8
1920	47	40.5	55	48.4	64	46.8	49	53.2	52	53.2
1921	51	29.7	58	37.7	67	45.6	52	41.8	55	37.8
1922	49	34.1	57	42.5	67	50.6	51	43.3	54	44.7
1923	47	34.9	57	36.7	66	46.6	50	44.6	53	40.6
1924	47	30.5	55	49.0	65	51.1	49	38.3	52	41.7
1925	48	31.4	56	32.7	66	33.4	51	44.4	53	41.4
1926	46	30.8	55	45.2	65	35.1	48	43.8	51	47.8
1927	49	39.9	57	36.2	67	29.9	51	52.0	53	56.1
1928	49	33.6	56	43.4	65	42.8	51	45.0	54	45.6
1929	49	31.7	57	42.5	66	45.0	51	43.1	54	40.4
1930	50	25.5	58	21.6	65	32.4	52	34.7	54	39.0
1931	51	33.2	59	39.6	66	28.8	53	44.2	56	36.1
1932	50	34.2	58	49.6	67	44.8	52	45.6	55	43.9
1933	50	38.2	58	53.0	68	52.8	51	45.4	54	53.5
1934	48	36.5	56	50.9	66	38.8	50	49.0	53	49.8
1935	48	33.7	56	51.5	66	54.1	50	37.0	53	33.8
1936	49	40.0	56	44.6	66	40.2	50	59.6	53	49.8
1937	50	38.5	57	50.8	66	48.8	52	53.2	54	53.0
1938	49	40.2	58	34.8	67	31.1	52	57.8	55	48.5
1939	47	31.2	58	40.9	67	49.0	51	46.4	55	38.6
1940	45	35.9	55	44.3	64	45.5	49	48.7	52	45.1
1941	50	28.0	58	34.7	66	62.6	52	36.7	55	39.0
1942	50	44.2	58	46.0	66	41.4	51	57.7	54	43.5
1943	48	36.1	57	36.8	65	36.2	51	37.2	54	36.7
1944	49	39.6	57	45.5	66	51.2	52	49.1	55	45.0
1945	49	47.3	57	46.6	66	74.9	52	50.4	54	45.0
1946	50	33.0	58	37.6	67	49.0	52	40.6	55	38.4
1947	50	37.6	57	46.2	65	67.4	51	47.6	54	40.8
1948	49	39.9	57	54.7	66	61.3	51	50.7	54	46.9
1949	52	28.5	59	37.7	67	46.0	54	39.9	57	36.2
1950	49	37.8	57	44.0	66	43.4	51	42.5	54	36.9
1951	50	43.6	57	46.9	66	38.2	53	50.5	55	44.4
1952	51	39.2	58	55.9	66	39.2	53	49.7	55	41.5
1953	52	41.0	59	49.3	67	44.0	54	56.7	57	45.2
1954	50	41.0	59	30.5	66	31.0	52	48.5	55	35.6
1955	50	41.5	57	47.9	66	40.5	52	51.3	55	39.9
1956	49	32.6	58	37.8	66	35.1	51	48.4	54	36.2
1957	51	29.1	59	37.7	66	51.8	51	38.1	56	36.5
1958	48	38.0	56	50.4	65	44.4	49	51.9	52	40.9
1959	51	32.5	59	35.8	66	58.6	51	43.1	55	38.8

(continued)

TABLE Cf550–569   Annual mean temperature and total precipitation: 1780–1999   [Long-record city stations]
Continued

	Albany		Baltimore		Charleston		New Haven		New York	
	Mean temperature	Precipitation	Mean temperature	Precipitation	Mean temperature	Precipitation	Mean temperature	Precipitation	Mean temperature	Precipitation
	Cf550	Cf551	Cf552	Cf553	Cf554	Cf555	Cf556	Cf557	Cf558	Cf559
Year	Degrees F	Inches	Degrees F	Inches	Degrees F	Inches	Degrees F	Inches	Degrees F	Inches
1960	50	47.9	57	43.9	65	46.5	50	41.6	54	46.4
1961	50	34.0	58	40.0	66	48.9	51	41.3	55	39.3
1962	48	28.8	56	38.1	65	49.7	49	36.6	53	37.2
1963	48	25.0	57	34.1	65	48.3	50	38.2	54	34.3
1964	50	20.7	58	37.2	66	73.4	50	33.5	55	33.0
1965	48	26.7	58	30.8	66	52.2	50	27.7	54	26.1
1966	49	34.4	58	39.8	65	48.1	50	32.1	55	39.9
1967	49	35.6	57	40.6	66	42.6	50	40.6	53	49.1
1968	49	35.3	59	40.1	65	45.5	51	40.1	54	43.6
1969	49	39.9	58	33.2	65	54.5	51	41.3	55	48.5
1970	47	30.5	58	35.4	66	43.0	51	29.4	54	35.3
1971	46	39.6	58	61.6	67	63.8	—	—	55	56.8
1972	46	47.2	57	56.7	66	40.7	—	—	54	67.0
1973	49	38.7	59	47.5	67	60.8	—	—	56	57.2
1974	46	38.5	58	41.5	67	50.7 [2]	—	—	55	47.7
1975	48	47.1	59	61.5	68	40.2 [2]	—	—	55	61.2
1976	46	42.5	58	44.1	66 [2]	51.3	—	—	53	41.3
1977	48	44.3	59	40.1	67	42.1 [2]	—	—	54	54.7
1978	46	33.5	58	45.3	66	45.2	—	—	53	49.8
1979	48	37.1	58	61.4	65	49.2	—	—	56	52.1
1980	46	32.6	58	32.4	67	40.9	—	—	55	44.6
1981	47	30.4	58	32.1 [2]	65	40.4	—	—	55	38.1
1982	47	32.1	58	34.4	67 [2]	50.0 [1]	—	—	55	41.4
1983	48	46.3	58	58.2	65	48.4 [2]	—	—	56	80.6
1984	48	37.1	58	37.8	67	42.0	—	—	56	57.0
1985	48	30.0	59	40.7	68 [2]	42.3	—	—	56	38.8
1986	48	44.0	59	37.8	67	42.3	—	—	55	43.0
1987	48	39.3	59	38.7	66	52.3	—	—	55	46.4
1988	48	29.6	58	35.6	65	38.3	—	—	55	44.7
1989	47	39.7	58	50.8	66	56.5 [2]	—	—	54	65.1
1990	50	46.0	61	43.2	69	54.0	—	—	57	60.9
1991	50	35.7	61	29.6	68 [2]	45.6 [2]	—	—	57 [1]	44.8 [1]
1992	47	31.4	59	38.9	66	57.9	—	—	54	43.4
1993	48	41.3	58	44.7	67	36.6	—	—	56	44.3
1994	47	34.7	58	41.4	67 [2]	54.3 [2]	—	—	55	47.4
1995	48	34.1	59 [1]	33.6 [1]	67 [2]	42.1	—	—	55	40.4
1996	47	45.9	58 [2]	52.3 [1]	66 [2]	30.2	—	—	54	56.2
1997	47	34.7	60 [1]	35.2 [1]	67	51.9 [2]	—	—	54	43.9
1998	51	38.9	64 [2]	40.5 [1]	70	52.1	—	—	57	48.7
1999	—	—	—	—	—	—	—	—	—	—

	Philadelphia		San Francisco		Santa Fe		St. Louis		St. Paul	
	Mean temperature	Precipitation	Mean temperature	Precipitation	Mean temperature	Precipitation	Mean temperature	Precipitation	Mean temperature	Precipitation
	Cf560	Cf561	Cf562	Cf563	Cf564	Cf565	Cf566	Cf567	Cf568	Cf569
Year	Degrees F	Inches	Degrees F	Inches	Degrees F	Inches	Degrees F	Inches	Degrees F	Inches
1820	—	49.4	—	—	—	—	—	—	43	—
1821	—	36.2	—	—	—	—	—	—	43	—
1822	—	30.6	—	—	—	—	—	—	44	—
1823	—	44.5	—	—	—	—	—	—	44	—
1824	—	49.9	—	—	—	—	—	—	43	—
1825	54	29.7	—	—	—	—	—	—	48	—
1826	54	35.2	—	—	—	—	—	—	45	—
1827	52	38.5	—	—	—	—	—	—	46	—
1828	56	38.0	—	—	—	—	—	—	46	—
1829	53	41.9	—	—	—	—	—	—	46	—

Notes appear at end of table

TABLE Cf550-569   Annual mean temperature and total precipitation: 1780-1999   [Long-record city stations]
Continued

	Philadelphia		San Francisco		Santa Fe		St. Louis		St. Paul	
	Mean temperature	Precipitation	Mean temperature	Precipitation	Mean temperature	Precipitation	Mean temperature	Precipitation	Mean temperature	Precipitation
	Cf560	Cf561	Cf562	Cf563	Cf564	Cf565	Cf566	Cf567	Cf568	Cf569
Year	Degrees F	Inches	Degrees F	Inches	Degrees F	Inches	Degrees F	Inches	Degrees F	Inches
1830	55	45.1	—	—	—	—	—	—	48	—
1831	54	43.9	—	—	—	—	—	—	43	—
1832	54	39.5	—	—	—	—	—	—	46	—
1833	54	48.6	—	—	—	—	—	—	48	—
1834	55	34.2	—	—	—	—	—	—	47	—
1835	54	39.3	—	—	—	—	—	—	43	—
1836	50	42.7	—	—	—	—	53	—	43	—
1837	51	39.0	—	—	—	—	55	27.0	44	24.0
1838	51	45.3	—	—	—	—	53	31.5	42	27.7
1839	52	43.7	—	—	—	—	55	47.4	47	21.2
1840	53	47.4	—	—	—	—	56	41.6	45	23.2
1841	52	55.5	—	—	—	—	56	42.7	44	21.7
1842	53	48.5	—	—	—	—	56	32.3	43	25.2
1843	52	46.9	—	—	—	—	54	34.8	40	23.8
1844	53	40.2	—	—	—	—	57	45.8	43	30.2
1845	54	40.2	—	—	—	—	56	38.0	46	25.3
1846	54	44.4	—	—	—	—	57	45.4	48	26.1
1847	54	45.1	—	—	—	—	54	52.7	42	21.8
1848	55	35.0	—	—	—	—	54	65.4	42	23.2
1849	53	42.1	—	—	52	—	54	45.7	42	49.7
1850	54	54.6	—	17.4	—	9.1	55	50.5	44	25.5
1851	54	35.5	56	15.6	—	13.2	55	46.8	47	23.4
1852	53	45.8	—	27.3	—	21.7	55	47.0	44	15.1
1853	55	40.7	55	21.2	50	21.8	55	30.9	42	20.5
1854	55	40.2	56	22.4	50	24.8	57	40.6	45	26.6
1855	54	44.1	—	26.4	51	24.2	54	50.4	44	24.8
1856	52	34.0	—	22.3	50	23.1	52	42.6	43	22.6
1857	53	48.3	57	21.0	50	8.5	53	39.0	42	32.1
1858	54	39.8	56	23.5	49	11.4	56	68.8	44	27.6
1859	54	58.1	55	21.4	48	9.5	54	61.4	41	29.4
1860	54	44.2	—	21.2	51	8.8	56	29.8	43	29.3
1861	55	46.3	56	25.5	52	15.8	57	38.0	42	30.1
1862	54	45.0	55	38.5	—	11.3	56	44.0	41	28.2
1863	55	49.2	54	15.1	51	7.8	54	40.4	43	15.8
1864	55	46.0	56	21.6	50	21.8	55	37.6	43	15.5
1865	56	56.3	54	14.1	49	23.2	56	46.9	44	38.0
1866	54	45.3	54	36.3	—	11.5	55	43.2	40	27.5
1867	54	61.2	—	30.6 [3]	—	7.8	55	37.8	40	33.3
1868	53	51.4	54	30.2	49	8.9	54	45.6	42	31.0
1869	55	48.9	—	22.6	48	12.1	54	47.0	42	31.8
1870	57	44.1	—	16.2	53	13.9	56	27.1	46	30.5
1871	55	47.3	—	27.5	56	11.2 [3]	58	23.4	44	30.6
1872	52	48.4	56	22.4	48	9.9	54	30.5	42	29.8
1873	52	55.3	55	18.6	50	9.7	54	45.5	42	33.7
1874	53	46.2	55	22.5	49	19.9	57	37.9	44	35.5
1875	50	40.2	55	22.6	49	19.0	53	43.0	39	30.7
1876	53	47.4	56	23.5	48	15.1	56	48.5	42	23.7
1877	54	37.3	57	11.9	48	13.2	57	41.4	47	28.8
1878	55	34.5	56	33.3	48	19.6	58	40.8	48	22.8
1879	54	36.8	56	30.8	51	11.4	56	25.7	46	32.4
1880	55	33.6	54	30.1	46	9.9	55	34.7	44	29.8
1881	54	30.2	55	23.7	49	22.2	56	37.4	45	39.2
1882	55	45.6	54	18.7	49	11.4	56	43.2	46	23.1
1883	54	39.2	54	15.4	—	14.8	54	40.1	41	26.7
1884	54	39.3	55	38.8	—	19.7	56	40.6	44	26.1
1885	52	33.4	56	24.9	48	14.9	55	45.6	42	25.3
1886	54	37.2	56	20.0	48	15.9	53	44.3	43	22.9
1887	54	42.2	55	19.0	50	13.4	58	35.3	42	25.8
1888	53	44.1	56	23.0	50	12.0	54	41.2	41	25.9
1889	55	50.6	57	36.9	50	7.9	56	33.2	45	17.0

Notes appear at end of table

(continued)

TABLE Cf550–569   Annual mean temperature and total precipitation: 1780–1999   [Long-record city stations]
Continued

	Philadelphia		San Francisco		Santa Fe		St. Louis		St. Paul	
	Mean temperature	Precipitation	Mean temperature	Precipitation	Mean temperature	Precipitation	Mean temperature	Precipitation	Mean temperature	Precipitation
	Cf560	Cf561	Cf562	Cf563	Cf564	Cf565	Cf566	Cf567	Cf568	Cf569
Year	Degrees F	Inches	Degrees F	Inches	Degrees F	Inches	Degrees F	Inches	Degrees F	Inches
1890	55	34.0	55	25.4	50	12.9	56	37.7	44	23.4
1891	55	38.2	56	21.1	47	16.8	56	30.5	44	21.8
1892	54	34.8	55	22.1	49	11.6	55	41.6	43	32.6
1893	53	37.6	53	17.9	49	14.9	55	39.3	41	26.0
1894	55	40.3	54	24.3	49	13.3	57	27.4	46	25.8
1895	54	31.0	55	17.1	47	20.2	55	31.2	44	24.3
1896	54	32.2	55	28.2	50	14.3	58	37.6	44	34.7
1897	55	42.0	54	16.4	48	20.4	57	40.2	44	30.5
1898	56	49.2	54	9.3	48	13.0	57	49.2	45	25.3
1899	54	40.0	54	23.2	49	10.0	56	34.6	44	27.5
1900	56	40.9	55	15.3	50	15.9	58	29.5	46	34.2
1901	54	45.5	54	19.8	50	17.4	57	24.8	46	25.8
1902	54	49.8	54	19.2	50	13.4	56	38.4	45	31.8
1903	54	41.5	54	18.3	48	9.8	56	33.8	44	37.9
1904	52	39.8	55	24.7	49	14.2	54	33.7	43	34.1
1905	54	41.6	55	16.2	47	17.2	55	38.5	44	30.8
1906	55	51.9	55	26.3	48	16.6	55	35.5	45	33.2
1907	53	48.7	55	22.5	49	15.2	55	41.4	42	23.1
1908	56	38.1	54	16.4	48	12.8	57	34.2	46	31.6
1909	55	37.4	54	31.4	47	12.3	56	47.5	44	31.8
1910	55	39.6	54	12.4	50	8.6	55	37.3	46	10.2
1911	55	51.4	54	26.0	48	17.1	57	36.1	45	40.4
1912	54	47.0	56	15.6	47	10.3	54	44.6	43	21.2
1913	57	47.4	56	19.0	47	15.0	58	38.7	46	24.0
1914	54	39.1	56	24.0	49	17.3	57	35.6	45	24.6
1915	55	44.8	56	28.3	48	17.9	56	49.3	45	30.8
1916	54	32.3	55	28.1	49	16.4	56	41.8	43	24.5
1917	53	39.4	55	9.0	49	5.0	54	25.0	40	24.9
1918	55	37.7	56	20.8	48	15.2	57	35.9	45	30.2
1919	56	49.1	55	19.0	48	20.8	57	40.8	44	30.4
1920	54	46.2	55	18.3	48	13.2	56	31.5	45	24.7
1921	57	35.4	56	19.7	50	17.8	60	41.1	48	24.8
1922	56	29.3	55	25.7	49	10.3	58	32.3	46	25.0
1923	55	39.2	56	11.0	48	14.2	56	41.7	45	20.2
1924	54	43.1	56	20.2	49	8.9	54	36.5	42	30.6
1925	56	32.4	57	23.1	49	12.6	57	32.2	45	20.9
1926	54	44.9	58	26.7	49	13.0	56	33.4	44	27.3
1927	56	43.2	56	24.3	50	14.2	57	50.8	43	26.4
1928	55	39.4	56	19.0	49	13.1	56	38.6	45	24.8
1929	56	41.6	56	10.0	48	21.5	55	46.3	42	24.4
1930	57	34.0	57	16.7	48	13.2	58	23.2	46	20.0
1931	58	39.3	57	22.9	49	15.9	60	37.4	51	22.6
1932	57	44.5	56	12.0	48	15.4	57	38.0	45	23.6
1933	56	51.4	55	17.0	49	13.1	59	34.8	47	23.5
1934	55	38.4	58	15.9	52	13.3	58	29.2	47	22.7
1935	54	46.4	56	20.6	49	12.9	56	39.4	45	27.5
1936	55	38.7	57	22.4	50	14.4	57	26.1	44	18.5
1937	55	37.4	56	25.8	50	15.7	55	35.9	44	22.6
1938	56	46.9	56	22.2	50	15.6	59	41.2	47	29.8
1939	56	45.4	56	11.2	49	13.4	58	40.2	46	24.5
1940	53	44.8	57	34.8	50	16.4	56	25.0	44	28.5
1941	56	32.2	58	35.2	49	17.7	58	32.1	48	27.0
1942	56	41.2	56	24.9	49	13.0	57	45.1	46	30.6
1943	55	36.8	56	17.7	50	9.6	56	33.6	44	22.7
1944	56	39.5	55	25.6	48	14.6	57	33.5	47	29.1
1945	56	47.0	56	25.0	49	11.5	55	49.8	44	27.2
1946	57	40.9	55	12.3	50	13.5	59	57.1	46	29.0
1947	55	52.1	56	14.4	49	11.0	56	37.1	45	21.1
1948	55	49.5	55	16.5	49	16.9	57	34.5	46	17.0
1949	58	43.3	54	16.2	49	17.7	57	46.3	46	25.1

TABLE Cf550–569 Annual mean temperature and total precipitation: 1780–1999 [Long-record city stations]
Continued

Year	Philadelphia Mean temperature Cf560 Degrees F	Philadelphia Precipitation Cf561 Inches	San Francisco Mean temperature Cf562 Degrees F	San Francisco Precipitation Cf563 Inches	Santa Fe Mean temperature Cf564 Degrees F	Santa Fe Precipitation Cf565 Inches	St. Louis Mean temperature Cf566 Degrees F	St. Louis Precipitation Cf567 Inches	St. Paul Mean temperature Cf568 Degrees F	St. Paul Precipitation Cf569 Inches
1950	55	45.4	55	26.3	51	10.4	55	43.2	42	21.6
1951	56	42.0	54	22.9	50	9.3	55	38.6	42	34.6
1952	57	51.1	54	31.5	49	11.4	58	26.7	46	23.7
1953	58	50.5	56	12.6	50	12.8	60	23.0	47	27.9
1954	56	36.9	55	19.8	52	14.1	59	30.0	46	23.7
1955	56	33.7	54	21.0	49	10.8	58	33.0	46	21.1
1956	55	44.8	56	15.1	50	6.7	58	33.7	45	26.8
1957	56 [3]	35.0 [3]	56	22.8	49	17.6	57	52.7	46	27.8
1958	53	47.9	59	28.6	51	14.6	55	37.3	46	16.2
1959	56	38.4	59	12.5	50	12.9	57	30.8	46	26.9
1960	53	41.2	56	17.8	49	17.6	56	28.2	44	21.5
1961	53	41.1	57	14.6	48	14.8	56	44.7	44	25.7
1962	52	42.6	56	20.0	50	11.3	57	40.4	42	28.8
1963	52	35.0	57	18.8	50	14.2	57	28.2	44	19.6
1964	54	29.9	57	17.7	48	13.4	58	28.9	46	26.0
1965	53	29.3	57	19.9	49	20.7	58	33.0	43	39.9
1966	53	40.0	57	16.5	49	12.3	56	30.2	43	24.3
1967	53	44.8	57	24.3	49	15.1	56	38.7	43	25.4
1968	54	35.5	57	18.0	48	15.2	57 [4]	39.1 [4]	45	37.9
1969	54	43.4	57	27.0	50	19.6	57 [4]	39.2 [4]	45	19.4
1970	55	39.1	57	24.3	49	11.6	58 [4]	37.0 [4]	44	30.5
1971	56	47.8	56	12.3	48 [2]	12.4 [2]	56	33.7	44	29.4
1972	54	49.6	56	20.8	54 [2]	12.4 [2]	55	33.7	41	23.8
1973	56	46.1	56	31.8	49 [2]	12.9	56	39.8	47	21.1
1974	55	37.8	56	15.3	48 [2]	13.7	55	36.8	44	19.1
1975	56	52.1	56	16.0	49 [2]	12.6	55	40.2	45	35.2
1976	54	33.3	58	8.7	49	7.9	54	23.5	46	16.5
1977	54	49.4	57	11.5	51	13.2	55	43.4	45	34.9
1978	54	46.0	58	21.5	51	14.1	53	37.7	44	30.3
1979	55	52.8	58	22.1	49	16.2	54	29.5	43	31.1
1980	55	38.8	57	14.2	51 [2]	11.5	56	27.5	45	21.8
1981	54	37.8	57	19.6	52	13.5	56	45.5	46	28.0
1982	54	40.4	56	32.2	48	13.8 [2]	55	55.0	44	30.2
1983	55	54.4	59	43.8	51 [2]	11.6 [2]	56	44.8	46	39.1
1984	54	43.7	58	18.4	52 [2]	17.7 [2]	56	51.7	45	37.0
1985	55	35.2	59	15.7	52 [2]	18.0 [2]	55	50.7	43	31.7
1986	55	40.4	60	23.5	52	19.3	58	34.9	46	36.6
1987	56	33.4	59	19.8	51	11.2	58	38.4	50	32.2
1988	55	38.4	59	17.1	47 [2]	12.4 [2]	57	33.9	46	19.1
1989	55	48.7	58	12.4	52	10.3 [2]	56	28.6	44	23.3
1990	58	35.8	59	13.6	49 [2]	13.2 [2]	59	45.1	47	33.1
1991	58	36.2	59	16.9	49	19.5 [2]	59	33.5	46	36.7
1992	55	30.4	61	21.2	49	15.2 [2]	57	33.5	45	29.7
1993	57	42.2	60	23.8	49	13.3 [2]	56	54.8	44	32.2
1994	57	44.9	58	24.2	51	20.1 [2]	58	34.7	45	29.7
1995	57	31.5	60	28.6	51	10.4 [2]	57	41.7	46	25.7
1996	54	56.5	60 [2]	30.0	51 [2]	14.5 [2]	55	43.7	42	26.1
1997	55	32.5	60	20.8	49	17.8 [2]	55	31.2	44	34.4
1998	58	31.7	57	42.2	51 [2]	13.7 [2]	59	43.6	49	33.4
1999	57	48.5	56	21.4	53 [2]	12.6 [2]	58	34.1	48	30.5

[1] Raw value unavailable; corrected filnet value from U.S. Historical Climatology Network was used. See text for Table Cf286–351.

[2] Figure based on incomplete data.

[3] Value corrected for typographical errors in World Weather Record.

[4] St. Louis City closed June 1968; data are for Gateway Arch.

Sources
Through 1970
Except Baltimore and Philadelphia (precipitation). 1780–1940: H. H. Clayton, editor, *World Weather Records*, Smithsonian Miscellaneous Collections, volume 79 (1927), volume 90 (1934), volume 105 (1947). 1941–1960: U.S.

National Weather Service, *World Weather Records*, 1941 to 1950 (1959) and 1951 to 1960 (1965). 1961–1970: U.S. Environmental Data Service, *Local Climatological Data* (corrected to 24-hour means), annual editions.

Baltimore and Philadelphia (precipitation). *Local Climatological Data* and *Climatic Summary of the United States*, annual editions.

The data for Albany, Baltimore, Charleston, and New York are drawn from the raw data collected by the U.S. Historical Climatology Network (USHCN). When these data were unavailable, the figures reported come from the corrected filnet data reported in the same data source, as identified in the footnote in the table. See the text for Table Cf286–351.

(continued)

TABLE Cf550–569   Annual mean temperature and total precipitation: 1780–1999   [Long-record city stations]
Continued

Post-1970

Data for the following cities are available from USHCN through the National Climate Data Center's (NCDC) Internet site: Albany (NCDC station 300042; data through 1970 from station 300047); Baltimore (station 180470); Charleston (station 381549); New York (station 305801); St. Paul (monthly surface data from station 215435).

Data for other cities are from the following sources. Philadelphia (Pennsylvania State Climatologist Internet site); San Francisco (Western Regional Climate Center Internet site, NCDC station 047772); Santa Fe (Western Regional Climate Center Internet site, station 298072 until 1972, and station 298085 thereafter); and St. Louis (Midwestern Regional Climate Center, NCDC station 237455; data through 1970 from downtown St. Louis).

Documentation

The series for city stations selected for presentation here are among the longest-existing climatological series for the United States. They were selected with the realization that they are not homogeneous, but have comparative value in the earlier years and have been less frequently affected by changes of station location. The series, however, are not adjusted for known station changes, and coming as they do from growing cities, they contain climatic trends that in part are typical only of major metropolitan centers.

Records for five of the ten stations shown refer in recent years to airport locations; the observation program in New Haven city terminated in 1943, and that in St. Paul–Minneapolis terminated in 1937. In addition to these cities, complete data for Albany, Philadelphia, and St. Louis are only consistently available for recent years from the airport locations, which are reported here. The other records are continuously available from city locations, although the major part of National Weather Service activities has been transferred to airport stations.

CHAPTER Cg
Science, Technology, and Productivity

Editor: Gavin Wright

Associate Editor: Stanley L. Engerman

SCIENCE AND TECHNOLOGY

Stanley L. Engerman and Gavin Wright

The term "science" refers to a systematic body of knowledge about the physical world and its phenomena. In the modern world, scientific knowledge is pursued and codified through structured institutions such as universities, laboratories, and professional societies. By these criteria, the beginnings of American science might be traced to the founding of the American Philosophical Society by Benjamin Franklin in 1743. But it was not until well into the nineteenth century that American science began to assume anything resembling its modern shape, with the establishment of programs in mineralogy, chemistry, and geology at several universities (see Bruce 1987). "Technology," on the other hand, refers much more broadly to practical knowledge about techniques, methods, and procedures in productive activity, even when these practices are not well understood in a scientific sense. Thus, the history of American technology goes back to the earliest human settlements on these continents.

Nathan Rosenberg has written:

> One of the more misleading consequences of thinking about technology as the mere *application* of prior scientific knowledge is that this perspective obscures a very elemental point: Technology is itself a body of knowledge about certain classes of events and activities. It is not merely the application of knowledge brought from another sphere. It is a knowledge of techniques, methods and designs that work, and that work in certain ways and with certain consequences, even when we cannot explain exactly why .... Indeed, if the human race had been confined to technologies that were understood in a scientific sense, it would have passed from the scene long ago. (Rosenberg 1982, p. 143)

Acknowledgments

Stanley L. Engerman and Gavin Wright thank Nathan Rosenberg for helpful advice on the essay on science and technology in this chapter. They also extend thanks to Chris Meissner and Andrea Maestrejuan for research assistance for the tables on science and technology and to Sriniketh Nagavarapu for assistance with the productivity tables.

Daniel Johnson thanks Robert E. Evenson for the initial question that generated the impetus for the data in Tables Cg38–107. A preliminary version of the data benefited from comments made by Anne Knowles and other participants at the Social Sciences History Association meetings in Chicago, 1998. Kristine Ishii provided research help. Funding was provided by a Wellesley College Faculty Research Grant.

The relationship at any time between science and technology can be complex. New technologies have sometimes resulted from prior changes in science, but as Rosenberg points out, technological practice has historically preceded scientific understanding. Technologies became increasingly science-based in the twentieth century, so much so that the two modes of advance have often been mutually reinforcing. Even with a scientific base, it is important conceptually to distinguish between the introduction of new methods that increase society's technical potential and the benefits that flow from the diffusion, expanded use, and ongoing improvement in already existing technologies. Because of the complexity of these interactions, the capacity of statistical evidence to track historical changes in science and technology is inherently imperfect.

Measures of Technological Progress: Intellectual Property

Long before the United States became an important player in world science, the country's mechanics and inventors began to develop new and distinctive technologies in such fields as firearms, steamboats, farm machinery, sewing machines, and other machine tools.[1] The longest-running quantitative measure of this technological activity is the series on patents issued for inventions under the Patent Law of 1790, authorized under Article I, Section 8, of the Constitution of 1789 (series Cg30). The American patent system was far more accessible and inexpensive than its British counterpart, and perhaps as a result, the United States surpassed Great Britain in patents per capita as early as 1810 (Khan and Sokoloff 2001, p. 239).

In 1836 the Patent Office introduced the examination system, whereby applicants were required to demonstrate novelty and compliance with requirements of the statute. Hence, as of this date the data differentiate between patent applications (series Cg27) and patents issued (series Cg30). The initial effect of this tightening of standards was a sharp drop in patent applications. But the reform significantly increased potential returns to patenting, and patents per capita surged between the 1850s and the 1870s, reaching a peak shortly after the turn of the twentieth century, sometimes known as the "golden age of the individual inventor." The increase in numbers and potential value of patents led, in turn, to the rise of an elaborate set of institutions concerned with trade and litigation in patent rights (Lamoreaux and Sokoloff 1999).

---

[1] For accounts of these developments, see Habakkuk (1962), Rosenberg (1976, 1994), and Hounshell (1984).

Scholars such as Schmookler and Griliches have analyzed patent data as an indicator of the pace of innovative activity in the economy (Schmookler 1966; Griliches 1998). Such inferences must be drawn with caution, however, because patents constitute only one particular form of protection for technology, not equally appropriate for all sectors of the economy (Levin, Klevorik, et al. 1987). The decline in patents per capita in the twentieth century, for example, probably reflects the rise of corporate research labs and other patent substitutes rather than a decline in the pace of innovative activity (see Figure Cg-A). Another observable trend in the late twentieth century is the rise of patents issued to residents of foreign countries, reflecting the globalization of technology and markets for technology (series Cg37).

Copyrights are another form of intellectual property. The first U.S. copyright law also dates from 1790 – at which time it applied only to maps, charts, and books – but the statistical compilations begin only in 1870 (series Cg1). The definition of copyrighted material expanded over time to include prints (1802), musical compositions (1831), dramatic compositions (1856), photographs (1865), paintings and other works of fine art (1870), and motion pictures (1912). Meanwhile the period of copyright protection was extended from 14 to 28 years, which became renewable for another 28 years in 1909. Protected trademarks were introduced in 1870 and, with several changes in the law, were under the Act of 1946 for a time of 20 years, with renewal possible for successive 20-year terms.

Despite the ostensibly parallel histories of patents and copyrights, the issues involved and the trajectories of change have been very different for the two institutions. Although the United States was a center of innovation in technology, the country was a net importer of literary and artistic works throughout the nineteenth century. American copyright laws did not provide protection for foreign works, and, as a result, domestic producers freely pirated materials from overseas. Only in 1891 was copyright protection extended to citizens of countries with which the United States had reciprocal agreements. Copyright protection is significantly weaker than patent protection because of legal interpretations such as the right of "fair use" under specified circumstances. Attempts to deploy copyright law as an auxiliary form of protection for new

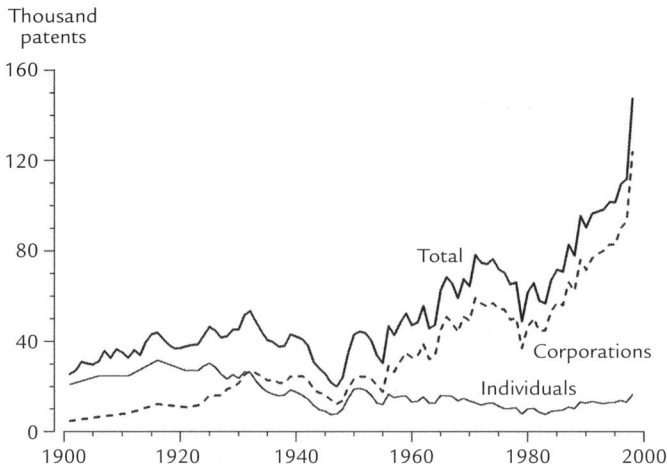

FIGURE Cg-B   Patents issued for inventions: 1901–1998

Sources
Series Cg30–33.

technologies have largely been turned back by American courts (Khan and Sokoloff 2001, p. 238).

The Rise of Organized Research

With the advent of industrial research laboratories around 1900, American technological innovation increasingly originated in structured institutional settings, which was the dominant trend in most of the twentieth century. The trend may be observed in the increased number of patents awarded to corporations, which surpassed the number awarded to individuals by the 1930s (series Cg32). See Figure Cg-B. The expansion of research laboratories was closely related to the increased employment of scientists and engineers by industrial firms, underscoring the synergies between organized innovation and the rise of the American research university.[2]

Although the trend toward organized and science-based research dates from the early twentieth century, the major stimulus for federal research support came with World War II and subsequently with the defense priorities of the Cold War. The dual justifications for federal research subsidies – to strengthen national defense but also to build the foundations for new technologies and economic growth – are popularly associated with the publication in 1945 of *Science, The Endless Frontier* by Vannevar Bush (1945), who as Director of the Office of Scientific Research and Development was responsible for 6,000 scientists involved in the war effort. The postwar structure of federal support, however, differed considerably from Bush's proposal for a single civilian agency overseeing all federal science policy and funding. By the 1950s, more than 85 percent of federal research and development (R&D) spending went to the Defense Department and the Atomic Energy Agency (Table Cg182–202).

Although federal support for R&D originated before World War II (the main prewar contributions being in agriculture and in aeronautics), national estimates by agency and by performing sector were compiled by the National Science Foundation only

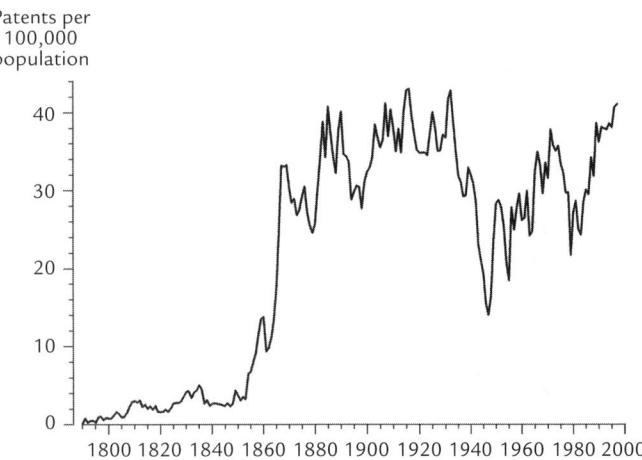

FIGURE Cg-A   Patents issued for inventions – per capita: 1790–1997

Sources
Series Aa7 and Cg30.

---

[2] For historical discussions, see Geiger (1986), Hounshell and Smith (1988), and Mowery and Rosenberg (1989, 1998).

beginning in 1953 (Tables Cg110–211). It seems safe to say that the figures represent a major increase in the level of national resources devoted to research, even though the concept of "R&D" as a distinct category of activity did not really exist before that time. The postwar volume of R&D activity was large not only relative to the nation's previous history but also relative to advances by other nations of the world. By the 1970s, however, the leading foreign industrial countries (West Germany, France, the United Kingdom, and Japan) had closed or greatly narrowed this gap in R&D spending as a share of GDP (Mowery and Rosenberg 1998, p. 30).

A number of broad trends may be seen in these tables. The growth of federal research funding reached a plateau in the 1990s with the end of the Cold War. Total national R&D expenditures continued to rise, however, as federal support was largely replaced by private expenditures, encouraged by the favorable tax treatment in expensing of such expenditures (series Cg110). The vast majority of expenditures by industry, however, have been for "applied" rather than "basic" research, much of it devoted to product development (Table Cg203–211).

Within federal R&D spending, the overwhelming dominance of the defense budget has receded, though it remains the single largest category. Since the 1980s, the most rapidly growing area of research has been health (series Cg193 and Cg195). Large infusions of federal funding have facilitated major advances in pharmaceuticals, medical devices, and biomedical science. Federal funds have been complementary to an even larger increase in research expenditures by private pharmaceutical firms.

An instructive if by no means comprehensive indicator of the rise of American science to world prominence is the international pattern of Nobel Prize awards (Table Cg212–235). Based upon a bequest of Alfred Nobel (1833–1896), the inventor of dynamite, the Nobel Prize has been awarded since 1901, in several different fields of science – physics, chemistry, physiology or medicine, literature, peace, and, starting in 1969, economic science. Seen as the outcome of worldwide competition, they are indicative of the caliber of individual research in different countries.

One clear pattern is the sharp increase in the proportion of scientific awards going to citizens of the United States after 1940, compared to the number in the first half-century of competition. The relative paucity of scientific awards before World War II, at a time where the United States had a higher productivity in the overall economy than did those countries whose scientists won a Nobel Prize, suggests that national scientific standing was not a necessary precondition for U.S. economic growth. The initial jump was associated with the out-migration of scientists from Europe that began in the 1930s. From 1943 to 1967, eleven of the twenty-two American winners of the Nobel Prize in Physics had been born in Europe (Table Ad938–949). Although many in this cohort were refugees, the educational and research opportunities provided by the expansion of American research universities after World War II have continued to attract foreigners, who are well-represented among American Nobel Prize winners. The dominance of the United States in the scientific awards is thus as much the result of economic growth as the cause.

Computer and Information Technology

Tables Cg241–264 deal with growth in the output of computers and their changing prices. They are meant to highlight the dramatic effects upon business and consumers of this most conspicuous and important technological change of recent years. The diffusion and improvement of computer technologies has been nothing short of spectacular, but the magnitude of the revolution was by no means obvious from the beginning. The first fully electronic digital computer is generally considered to be the ENIAC, developed at the University of Pennsylvania during World War II. The abstract analysis of John von Neumann formed the conceptual basis for the next machine (the EDVAC, the first stored-program computer) and for virtually all subsequent computers. These first-generation computers were gigantic, slow, and prone to breakdown, giving rise to the view before 1950 that total world demand could be satisfied by not much more than a handful of computers. Although computers quickly gained in speed and reliability, throughout the 1950s and 1960s the market was indeed dominated by large mainframe computers, of which the primary producer was IBM (Table Cg241–250). That company did not foresee the rapid spread of smaller and more portable machines, made possible by the commercialization of the integrated circuit microprocessor by the Intel Corporation in 1971. By 1995 the industry was selling more than two million personal computers per year, and the sale of mainframes had dwindled to a trickle (series Cg243).[3]

The rapid progress of the underlying technologies may be measured by any number of price indexes and performance indicators (Tables Cg251–264). The most famous of these is Moore's Law, which originated in 1965 with an observation by Intel founder Gordon E. Moore, who noted that the number of transistors per integrated circuit had doubled every eighteen months. Although Moore predicted that the trend would continue through 1975, the pace showed no signs of slackening through the end of the century (series Cg263). Many other measures of computer memory, speed, and capability have shown similarly persistent dynamic tendencies.

As costs have fallen and performance has improved, a major question has arisen regarding appropriate measures of the value of computer production and price deflators to use when measuring real output. The standard measure used to evaluate a machine is the cost of producing that machine, but where the machine has a specific use and the cost of its use falls sharply, economists often argue that a better measure of the value of the computer would be the cost per calculation or per task performed, the so-called hedonic measure of computer value. Such adjustments have a major impact on measured rates of productivity growth, as well as on comparisons of productivity growth between industries. As a result, these relatively technical issues have been central to the debate over the "productivity paradox," which refers to the observation that rapid technological progress and diffusion of computer technologies coincided with an apparent slowing of the rate of productivity growth in the U.S. economy between 1970 and 1995.[4]

References

Bruce, Robert V. 1987. *The Launching of Modern American Science, 1846–1876*. Knopf.

---

[3] These developments are described in Gordon (1990) and Mowery and Rosenberg (1998, Chapter 6).

[4] For alternative perspectives on this relationship, see David (1990), Griliches (1998), Brynjolfsson and Hitt (2000), Gordon (2000), and Oliner and Sichel (2000).

Brynjolfsson, Erik, and Lorin M. Hitt. 2000. "Beyond Computation: Information Technology, Organizational Transformation and Business Performance." *Journal of Economic Perspectives* 14 (Fall): 23–48.

Bush, Vannever. 1945. *Science, The Endless Frontier*. U.S. Government Printing Office.

David, Paul A. 1990. "The Computer and the Dynamo: A Historical Perspective on the Modern Productivity Paradox." *American Economic Review* 80: 355–61.

Geiger, Roger L. 1986. *To Advance Knowledge: The Growth of American Research Universities, 1900–1940*. Oxford University Press.

Gordon, Robert J. 1990. *The Measurement of Durable Goods Prices*. University of Chicago Press.

Gordon, Robert J. 2000. "Does the 'New Economy' Measure up to the Great Inventions of the Past?" *Journal of Economic Perspectives* 14 (Fall): 49–74.

Griliches, Zvi. 1998. *R&D and Productivity: The Econometric Evidence*. University of Chicago Press.

Habakkuk, H. J. 1962. *American and British Technology in the Nineteenth Century*. Cambridge University Press.

Hounshell, David A. 1984. *From the American System to Mass Production, 1800–1932*. Johns Hopkins University Press.

Hounshell, David, and John Kenly Smith Jr. 1988. *Science and Corporate Strategy: DuPont R&D, 1902–1980*. Cambridge University Press.

Khan, Zorina B., and Kenneth L. Sokoloff. 2001. "History Lessons: The Early Development of Intellectual Property Institutions in the United States." *Journal of Economic Perspectives* 15 (Summer): 233–46.

Lamoreaux, Naomi R., and Kenneth L. Sokoloff. 1999. "Investors, Firms, and the Market for Technology: United States Manufacturing in the Late Nineteenth and Early Twentieth Centuries." In Naomi Lamoreaux, Daniel M. G. Raff, and Peter Temin, editors. *Learning by Doing in Markets, Firms, and Countries*. University of Chicago Press.

Levin, Richard A., A. Klevorick, et al. 1987. "Appropriating the Returns from Industrial Research and Development," *Brookings Papers on Economic Activity* 3: 783–820.

Mowery, David, and Nathan Rosenberg. 1989. *Technology and the Pursuit of Economic Growth*. Cambridge University Press.

Mowery, David, and Nathan Rosenberg. 1998. *Paths of Innovation: Technological Change in Twentieth Century America*. Cambridge University Press. A version also appears in Stanley L. Engerman and Robert E. Gallman, editors. *The Cambridge Economic History of the United States*, Volume 3, *The Twentieth Century*. Cambridge University Press.

Oliner, Stephen D., and Daniel E. Sichel. 2000. "The Resurgence of Growth in the Late 1990s: Is Information Technology the Story?" *Journal of Economic Perspectives* 14 (Fall): 3–22.

Rosenberg, Nathan. 1976. *Perspectives on Technology*. Cambridge University Press.

Rosenberg, Nathan. 1982. *Inside the Black Box: Technology and Economics*. Cambridge University Press.

Rosenberg, Nathan. 1994. *Exploring the Black Box*. Cambridge University Press.

Schmookler, Jacob. 1966. *Invention and Economic Growth*. Harvard University Press.

PRODUCTIVITY

Gavin Wright

The term "productivity" may be defined as the ratio of an output measure to one or more of the inputs associated with that output. The most commonly used productivity index is output per unit of labor input, generally called labor productivity. The historical increase in labor productivity is important because it forms the primary component of the long-term increase in national product per person, which is to say the average income levels and standards of living for the population as a whole. To say that labor produc-

tivity is the "primary component" of long-term economic growth, however, is not to identify the causal mechanisms of the growth process in any simple way. Labor productivity reflects not just labor's effort but also other factors, including the state of technology, capital per worker, the efficiency of management, the pace of operations, and changes in the composition of the workforce. A variety of alternative input and output measures have been developed in productivity studies as part of the effort to understand the sources of historical productivity change.

Alternative Productivity Concepts and Measures

Productivity concepts have come in for considerable attention and debate in recent years as part of the national discussion about appropriate indicators of economic performance. Despite the apparent simplicity of the core concept, virtually every term in a productivity calculation requires some adjustment to make the resulting ratio meaningful in economic terms. Long-term productivity studies typically divide a measure of aggregate output (such as gross domestic product (GDP)) by an index of total worker-hours.[1] The computation of worker-hours entails defining which members of the population were in the labor force, and hence contributing to production, and estimating the average hours worked per year by each member of the labor force. The adjustment for labor-hours is appropriate, because U.S. economic growth has been characterized (as in other countries) by a long-term decline in the average work week, from more than sixty hours in the mid-nineteenth century to the forty hours that became standard in the 1930s. In the face of such large historical change, total hours worked seems a better measure of labor input than simply counting the number of workers.

Such adjustments can make a large difference during times of rapid change in the condition of labor. For example, between 1913 and 1950, real per capita GDP grew at 1.61 percent per year, according to Angus Maddison, but GDP per hour worked grew during the same period by 2.48 percent per year, more than 50 percent faster (Maddison 2001, pp. 186 and 352). The difference is explained by declines in the average workweek and in the share of the population in the labor force.

Tables Cg265–291 report such aggregate measures of labor productivity for extended overlapping historical periods. An aggregate output measure such as GDP is a value-added concept, which means that intermediate purchases of goods and services have been "netted out." Current-dollar GDP has the convenient property that it is equal to current-dollar value added summed across all industries. To convert current-dollar productivity into a "real" productivity measure, however, one must deflate them by an index of the general price level, thus introducing all of the "index number problems" that arise when relative prices change over the course of time. Thus, just as with price indexes, aggregate productivity indexes have a "base year," which must be changed from time to time in order to reflect changing relative prices and the changing composition of GDP. Because the choice of base year affects the trend, it is *not* advisable to join productivity series from Tables Cg265–291 by splicing them together using the overlap years. The three graphs in Figure Cg-C suggest that older series deviate increasingly from newer ones, the farther removed they are from the

---

[1] Standard references are Kendrick (1961, 1973) for U.S. historical data and Maddison (1991, 2001) for comparative international figures.

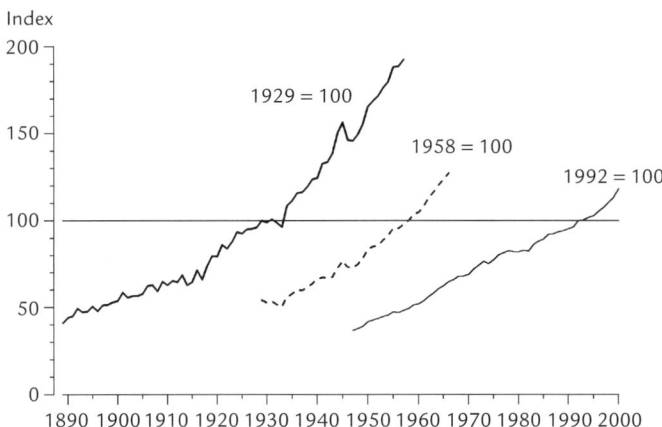

FIGURE Cg-C Nonfarm labor productivity: 1889–2000

Sources
Series Cg267, Cg275, and Cg285.

original base year.[2] For this reason, linking them at the endpoints is risky, but one may reasonably use different base-year series to compare rates of productivity growth between one historical period and another.

For various reasons, many analysts prefer to work with productivity aggregates that are not quite as broad as GDP. The measurement of labor inputs in the farm sector is particularly difficult because American farms have used part-time and unpaid family labor extensively. Hence, Tables Cg265–280 report productivity series separately for the farm and nonfarm sectors. Because measuring output accurately in government and nonprofit activities is generally difficult, the more recent data from the Bureau of Labor Statistics report separate series for the "business sector" and the "nonfarm business sector" (Table Cg281–291). Similarly, it is often argued that output is imperfectly measured in the financial sector, giving rise to a productivity series for "nonfinancial corporations" (series Cg286). Indeed, some argue that output measures are inaccurate in the service sectors generally, preferring to focus on manufacturing (series Cg281). Whether for measurement reasons or "real" reasons, one finds that observed productivity trends and fluctuations differ dramatically among these various indexes.[3]

Total Factor Productivity

Productivity may be calculated for other inputs besides labor, most often capital. "Capital" in such ratios refers to an aggregation of past investments in plant and equipment, adjusted for depreciation (that is, wear and tear, deterioration, and obsolescence). Although "capital productivity" is much less familiar than labor productivity, historical series of this index do show interesting trends and fluctuations, reflecting changes in the effective utilization of the capital stock. For example, series Cg269 shows that after a long period of relative stability, capital productivity jumped upward in the 1920s. After declines during the Great Depression of the 1930s,

the upward trend continued at least until the 1960s, reflecting an increase in the hours of operation in industrial plants, the result in turn of lower costs for electric lighting and power (Foss 1984).

The primary purpose for incorporating capital into the analysis, however, is to allow computation of total factor productivity (TFP), the ratio of output to a weighted index of capital and labor inputs.[4] In the modern literature on theories of economic growth, the seminal contribution was Solow (1957), who proposed that aggregate output could usefully be interpreted in terms of an aggregate "production function," as follows:

$$Q_t = A_t F(K_t, L_t)$$

where Q is output, K is capital, L is labor, and the subscripts refer to the time period of observation. If the production function F is characterized by constant returns to scale, and if shifts in this production function (represented by the parameter A) are "Hicksian neutral" (that is, the shifts do not affect the relative productivities of capital and labor), then the growth of output may be decomposed into separate contributions from capital, from labor, and from shifts of the aggregate production function, as follows:

$$\frac{\dot{A}}{A} = \frac{\dot{Q}}{Q} - s_K \frac{\dot{K}}{K} - s_L \frac{\dot{L}}{L}$$

where s_K and s_L are the elasticities of output with respect to capital and labor, respectively (typically approximated by the share of the factor in total product), and the symbol $\frac{\dot{X}}{X}$ refers to the percentage growth rate of the variable. In this formulation, the shift variable A is called total factor productivity, and $\frac{\dot{A}}{A}$ is the percentage growth rate of total factor productivity.[5]

TFP is commonly identified with "technological progress," but as Hulten makes clear, this usage is generally inappropriate (Hulten 2001). At best, TFP is measured only as a residual and, as such, includes conceptual or empirical errors throughout the analysis – a "measure of our ignorance," to quote Moses Abramovitz's famous phrase. But even if all of the inputs and outputs were accurately measured, conceptually TFP represents only costless improvements in the way inputs are transformed into real output. New technologies that result from investments in research and development (R&D) are appropriately viewed as forms of capital, as are improvements in the quality of labor that result from time devoted to education or training. Improvements in the organization of production or in the institutional arrangements of society would also be reflected in the residual.

Further, it is by no means clear that the assumption of neutrality between capital and labor is historically appropriate. Economic historians often portray technologies as progressing along "trajectories" of historical learning, which may have pronounced factor-saving biases (for examples, see David 1975; Rosenberg 1976). "Technological change" can take the form of augmenting the effective resource supplies available to the economy – land, minerals, or capital, as well as labor. In such cases, the pace of factor accumulation would itself be influenced by technology. Taking into account interactions between technological change and factor accumulation undermines the very distinction that this framework attempts to delineate.[6]

---

[2] Modern productivity data mitigate this transition problem by use of "superlative" index number formulas, of which the Tornqvist is one variant, that incorporate information from earlier and later periods in an even-handed way. The industry productivity indexes in Tables Cg292–345 are of this type.

[3] A useful review of alternative labor productivity concepts and their recent trends may be found in Steindel and Stiroh (2001).

---

[4] The Bureau of Labor Statistics refers to "multifactor productivity," but these terms are interchangeable.

[5] A useful analytical history of this concept is Hulten (2001).

[6] For elaboration on these points, see Nelson (1964) and Abramovitz (1993).

In response to these conceptual ambiguities, many researchers have set out to refine the measures of inputs into the aggregate production function, to reflect improvements in the quality of capital and labor, and changes in the utilization of the capital stock. Jorgenson and Griliches advanced the view that careful measurement of the relevant variables should cause the Solow residual to disappear entirely (Jorgenson and Griliches 1967). Reflecting the insights of the so-called New Growth Theory on the endogeneity of technological change (associated with Romer), subsequent studies have attempted to incorporate R&D spending directly into the growth accounting analysis, though with limited success owing to the absence of an observable knowledge "asset" and an associated income stream (Romer 1986; Griliches 1988). By elaborating and expanding the definitions of inputs into the production process, studies have indeed succeeded in reducing the size of the Solow residual as an explanatory factor in productivity growth accounting. In general, however, this research subjects the raw data in the national accounts to a substantial amount of refinement; hence, it does not lend itself to compilation of basic series in a reference work (for examples, see Jorgenson, Gollop, and Fraumeni 1987; Jorgenson and Stiroh 2000).

Trends and Fluctuations in Productivity

Since 1889, labor productivity in the United States has grown at an average annual rate in excess of 2 percent per year. The pace of this growth, however, has by no means been uniform over the entire period. Figure Cg-C displays the three major sets of productivity estimates for the nonfarm economy. The first of these shows distinct productivity acceleration after World War I. The third shows a marked deceleration in the early 1970s. Angus Maddison presents the following periodization (Maddison 2001, p. 352):

1870–1913	1.92 percent
1913–1950	2.48 percent
1950–1973	2.77 percent
1973–1998	1.74 percent

Such comparisons are extremely sensitive to the choice of end dates. Hansen conducts a systematic econometric test for the date at which a structural change occurred in productivity growth, concluding that such a break in the trend had almost certainly taken place by 1980; the verdict for 1973 is statistically less certain (Hansen 2001). For end dates such as 1978 to 1995, the productivity slowdown would be even more dramatic, falling to less than 1.50 percent per year over this period.

The labor productivity acceleration after World War I was also associated with an acceleration in total factor productivity growth (series Cg270 and Cg272), ushering in the era that Gordon refers to as the "One Big Wave" of American economic growth (Gordon 1999). Early growth-accounting studies (such as Abramovitz 1956; Solow 1957) found that most growth in labor productivity was not attributable to increases in capital per worker, giving rise to the stylized fact that the primary source of economic progress was not investment but technological change. Abramovitz and David emphasize, however, that this generalization fits the twentieth century much better than the nineteenth century (Abramovitz and David 2000). In their account of American economic history, changes in the proximate sources of growth were driven by a deep shift in the character of technological change from one century to the next,

from primary reliance on physical resources and tangible capital in the nineteenth century to a much greater use of human and intangible forms of capital (such as knowledge generated by R&D) in the twentieth century.[7]

This analysis makes the slowdown in productivity growth beginning in the 1970s all the more puzzling. The TFP residual virtually disappeared during this period, but the proposition that the pace of technological change came to a standstill at this historical point scarcely seems plausible (series Cg287–291). As Professor Solow put it in an oft-quoted comment: "We can see the computer age everywhere except in the productivity statistics." Understanding this "productivity paradox" has been one of the central preoccupations of economics in recent years.

Many proposed explanations deal with compositional issues and measurement biases. As one may confirm by inspection of Table Cg281–291, the productivity slowdown is less pronounced in manufacturing than in the business sector as a whole or in nonfinancial corporations. The detailed series in Tables Cg292–345 show a great range of productivity experience among specific industries. In general, however, the industry tables confirm that productivity growth in recent years has been substantially greater in most manufacturing industries than in service industries such as electric and gas utilities or the postal service (Tables Cg336–345). Some studies find zero or even negative productivity growth in large sectors such as construction, insurance, banking, and health. Because output is poorly measured in these sectors, it is sometimes suggested that the productivity slowdown is largely attributable to the growth of the relative size of that portion of the economy for which objective measures of productivity are inadequate.

But there are good reasons to believe that the productivity slowdown has been real, however uncertain its locus and magnitude may be. For one thing, many service industries have recorded large productivity gains in the past, and some, such as railroad transportation and telephone communications (series Cg341–342), have been well above the average even in recent decades. Measurement biases, including the failure of price indexes to account fully for quality change, improvements in speed and convenience, and so on, have always posed problems for productivity accounting, but it has not been shown that these problems became more severe during and after the 1970s than in earlier times. For another thing, the assignment of productivity change to sectors and industries is often arbitrary. As the measurement of productivity in computers and information technology has become more sophisticated – replacing mere machine counts with "hedonic" indicators reflecting improvements in speed, memory, and capability – the allocation of productivity between the computer-producing and the computer-consuming sectors may well be altered. Further, the rise of temporary employment services and other specialized service firms means that many tasks formerly carried out as part of "manufacturing" have now been shifted to other sectors, blurring comparisons of sector-specific productivity rates.

Another class of explanations attributes the slowdown to the completion of Gordon's "One Big Wave," a cluster of productivity-enhancing innovations and structural shifts that diffused through the economy between the 1920s and the 1970s. On this view, time lags between the invention of new technologies and their major

---

[7] For estimates of the stock of these unconventional forms of capital, see Kendrick (1976).

impact on productivity are only to be expected because both technology and its utilization often require organizational and institutional restructuring before its potential can be realized. Paul David has proposed an analogy between the computer and the electrification of manufacturing, for which the basic technological foundations had been in place for more than a generation prior to its dramatic impact on productivity in the 1920s (David 1990). Both of these would qualify as examples of general-purpose technologies, whose improvement and adoption typically require an extended period of learning and adaptation (Bresnahan and Trajtenberg 1995; Helpman 1998). According to this perspective, the rapid pace of change in computer and information technologies has, if anything, made it more difficult for business firms to adapt their organizations and personnel so as to take advantage of the potential of the new technologies to raise productivity. But a strong productivity effect should ultimately occur, and may have begun in the latter half of the 1990s (see series Cg281–286 and the industry data in Tables Cg292–345).

In the decade of the 1920s, technological transformations interacted with significant changes in the labor market – most notably, the sharp increase in the wages of unskilled labor associated with the end of mass European immigration – to accentuate both the diffusion of electric power and its deployment as a productivity-raising tool. A similar conjunction may have occurred in the late 1990s, when extremely tight labor market conditions prompted firms to speed up the process of adaptation to new computer and information technologies, restoring the growth of labor productivity after two decades of stagnation. Perhaps the best test among competing interpretations of the slowdown will be whether or not the increased rate of productivity change persists in the first decade of the new millennium.

References

Abramovitz, Moses. 1956. "Resource and Output Trends in the United States since 1870." *American Economic Review* 46 (May): 5–23.

Abramovitz, Moses. 1993. "The Search for the Sources of Growth: Areas of Ignorance, Old and New." *Journal of Economic History* 53 (June): 217–43.

Abramovitz, Moses, and Paul A. David. 2000. "Growth in the Era of Knowledge-Based Progress." In Stanley L. Engerman and Robert E. Gallman, editors. *The Cambridge Economic History of the United States.* Cambridge University Press.

Bresnahan, Timothy, and Manuel Trajtenberg. 1995. "General Purpose Technologies." *Journal of Econometrics* 65: 83–108.

David, Paul A. 1975. *Technical Choice, Innovation and Economic Growth.* Cambridge University Press.

David, Paul A. 1990. "The Computer and the Dynamo." *American Economic Review* 80 (May): 355–61.

Foss, Murray. 1984. *Changing Utilization of Fixed Capital: An Element in Long-Term Growth.* American Enterprise Institute for Public Policy Research.

Gordon, Robert J. 1999. "U.S. Economic Growth since 1870: One Big Wave?" *American Economic Review* 89 (May): 123–8.

Griliches, Zvi. 1988. "Research Expenditures and Growth Accounting." In Zvi Griliches, editor. *Technology, Education and Productivity.* Blackwell.

Hansen, Bruce E. "The New Econometrics of Structural Change: Dating Breaks in U.S. Labor Productivity." *Journal of Economic Perspectives* 15 (Fall): 117–28.

Helpman, Elhanan, editor. 1998. *General Purpose Technologies and Economic Growth.* MIT Press.

Hulten, Charles R. 2001. "Total Factor Productivity: A Short Biography." In Charles R. Hulten, Edwin R. Dean, and Michael J. Harper, editors. *New Developments in Productivity Analysis.* Studies in Income and Wealth, Volume 63. University of Chicago Press.

Jorgenson, Dale W., and Zvi Griliches. 1967. "The Explanation of Productivity Change." *Review of Economic Studies* 34 (July): 349–83.

Jorgenson, Dale W., Frank M. Gollop, and Barbara M. Fraumeni. 1987. *Productivity and U.S. Economic Growth.* Harvard University Press.

Jorgenson, Dale W., and Kevin J. Stiroh. 2000. "Raising the Speed Limit: U.S. Economic Growth in the Information Age." *Brookings Papers on Economic Activity*, issue 2: 125–211.

Kendrick, John W. 1961. *Productivity Trends in the United States.* Princeton University Press.

Kendrick, John W. 1973. *Postwar Productivity Trends in the United States, 1948–1969.* Columbia University Press.

Kendrick, John W. 1976. *The Formation and Stocks of Total Capital.* Columbia University Press.

Maddison, Angus. 1991. *Dynamic Forces in Capitalist Development.* Oxford University Press.

Maddison, Angus. 2001. *The World Economy: A Millennial Perspective.* Development Centre of the Organisation for Economic Co-Operation and Development.

Nelson, Richard R. 1964. "Aggregate Production Functions and Medium Range Growth Projections." *American Economic Review* 54 (September): 575–606.

Romer, Paul M. 1986. "Increasing Returns and Long-Run Growth." *Journal of Political Economy* 94: 1002–37.

Rosenberg, Nathan. 1976. *Perspectives on Technology.* Cambridge University Press.

Solow, Robert M. 1957. "Technical Change and the Aggregate Production Function." *Review of Economics and Statistics* 39 (August): 312–20.

Steindel, Charles, and Kevin J. Stiroh. 2001. "Productivity: What Is It, and Why Do We Care about It?" *Business Economics* (October): 13–31.

COPYRIGHTS, PATENTS, AND TRADEMARKS

Daniel K. N. Johnson and Gavin Wright

TABLE Cg1–15 Copyright registrations, by type: 1870–1977
Contributed by Gavin Wright

Year	Total Cg1 [1] Number	Books, including pamphlets, leaflets, etc. Total Cg2 [2] Number	Books and pamphlets printed abroad Cg3 Number	Periodicals Cg4 Number	Contributions to newspapers and periodicals Cg5 [2] Number	Dramatic or dramatico-musical compositions Cg6 Number	Musical compositions Cg7 Number	Maps Cg8 Number	Works of art, models, or designs Cg9 Number	Prints and pictorial illustrations Cg10 Number	Commercial prints and labels Cg11 Number	Motion pictures Cg12 Number	Sound recordings Cg13 Number	Miscellaneous Cg14 Number	Renewals Cg15 [3] Number
1870	5,600 [4]	—	—	—	—	—	—	—	—	—	—	—	—	—	—
1871	12,688	—	—	—	—	—	—	—	—	—	—	—	—	—	—
1872	14,164	—	—	—	—	—	—	—	—	—	—	—	—	—	—
1873	15,352	—	—	—	—	—	—	—	—	—	232	—	—	—	—
1874	16,283	—	—	—	—	—	—	—	—	—	—	—	—	—	—
1875	15,927	—	—	—	—	—	—	—	—	—	232	—	—	—	—
1876	14,882	—	—	—	—	—	—	—	—	—	472	—	—	—	—
1877	15,758	—	—	—	—	—	—	—	—	—	392	—	—	—	—
1878	15,798	—	—	3,424	—	372	3,772	—	—	—	492	—	—	—	—
1879	18,125	—	—	3,608	—	414	4,688	—	—	—	355	—	—	—	—
1880	20,686	—	—	4,369	—	496	5,628	—	—	—	203	—	—	—	—
1881	21,075	—	—	4,339	—	415	5,578	—	—	—	202	—	—	—	—
1882	22,918	—	—	4,612	—	458	6,143	—	—	—	304	—	—	—	—
1883	25,274	—	—	5,489	—	498	6,280	—	—	—	906	—	—	—	—
1884	26,893	—	—	5,570	—	587	6,241	—	—	—	513	—	—	—	—
1885	28,411	—	—	6,060	—	625	6,808	—	—	—	391	—	—	—	—
1886	31,241	—	—	6,089	—	672	7,514	—	—	—	378	—	—	—	—
1887	35,083	—	—	6,708	—	536	7,744	—	—	—	380	—	—	—	—
1888	38,225	—	—	7,086	—	589	8,066	—	—	—	327	—	—	—	—
1889	40,985	—	—	7,646	—	620	8,958	—	—	—	319	—	—	—	—
1890	42,794	—	—	8,164	—	715	9,132	—	—	—	304	—	—	—	—
1891	48,908	—	—	9,477	—	746	11,688	1,912	—	—	137	—	—	—	—
1892	54,735	—	—	10,327	—	813	14,649	—	—	—	6	—	—	—	—
1893	58,956	—	—	11,094	—	580	16,273	1,814	—	—	2	—	—	—	—
1894	62,762	—	—	12,149	—	465	18,460	1,922	—	—	4	—	—	—	—
1895	67,572	—	—	12,155	—	827	18,563	1,432	—	—	3	—	—	—	—
1896	72,470	—	—	12,892	—	907	20,951	1,198	—	—	33	—	—	—	—
1897	75,000	—	—	—	—	—	—	—	—	—	35	—	—	—	—
1898	75,545	—	—	—	—	—	—	—	—	—	89	—	—	—	—
1899	80,968	—	—	—	—	—	—	—	—	—	448	—	—	—	—
1900	94,798	—	—	—	—	—	—	—	—	—	775	—	—	—	—
1901	92,351	—	—	—	—	—	—	—	—	—	948	—	—	—	—
1902	92,978	24,272	—	21,071	—	1,448	19,706	—	—	—	913	—	—	—	—
1903	97,979	27,466	—	22,625	—	1,608	21,161	—	—	—	1,143	—	—	—	—
1904	103,130	27,824	—	21,496	—	1,571	23,110	—	—	—	1,301	—	—	—	—

Year	Total	Books, including pamphlets, leaflets, etc.		Periodicals	Contributions to newspapers and periodicals	Dramatic or dramatico-musical compositions	Musical compositions	Maps	Works of art, models, or designs	Prints and pictorial illustrations	Commercial prints and labels	Motion pictures	Sound recordings	Miscellaneous	Renewals
		Total	Books and pamphlets printed abroad												
	Cg1 [1]	Cg2 [2]	Cg3	Cg4	Cg5 [2]	Cg6	Cg7	Cg8	Cg9	Cg10	Cg11	Cg12	Cg13	Cg14	Cg15 [3]
	Number	Number	Number	Number	Number	Number	Number	Number	Number	Number	Number	Number	Number	Number	Number
1905	113,374	29,860	—	22,591	—	1,645	24,595	—	—	—	1,373	—	—	—	—
1906	117,704	29,261	—	23,163	—	1,879	26,435	—	—	—	1,095	—	—	—	—
1907	123,829	30,879	—	23,078	—	2,114	31,401	—	—	—	985	—	—	—	—
1908	119,742	30,191	—	22,409	—	2,382	28,427	—	—	—	915	—	—	—	—
1909	120,131	32,533	—	21,195	—	2,937	26,306	—	—	—	1,010	—	—	—	—
1910	109,074	24,740	1,351	21,608	—	3,911	24,345	2,622	4,383	11,925	235	—	—	14,533	1,007
1911	115,198	26,970	1,707	23,393	—	3,415	25,525	2,318	3,355	14,269	757	—	—	15,025	928
1912	120,931	29,286	2,294	23,580	—	3,767	26,777	2,158	3,224	17,639	893	—	—	14,151	1,349
1913	119,495	29,572	2,369	23,002	—	3,700	26,292	2,011	2,871	16,591	918	953	—	13,438	1,065
1914	123,154	31,891	2,860	24,134	—	3,957	28,493	1,950	3,021	15,438	1,059	2,148	—	10,891	1,231
1915	115,193	31,926	1,843	24,938	—	3,797	21,406	1,772	2,965	12,935	1,083	2,950	—	11,178	1,326
1916	115,967	32,897	1,276	26,553	—	3,223	20,644	1,612	2,220	12,722	1,235	3,240	—	11,228	1,628
1917	111,438	33,552	914	26,467	—	3,067	20,115	1,529	2,247	11,514	1,123	2,720	—	8,235	1,992
1918	106,728	33,617	636	25,822	—	2,711	21,849	1,269	1,858	9,161	708	1,838	—	6,746	1,857
1919	113,003	37,710	855	25,083	—	2,293	26,209	1,207	1,901	9,997	768	1,429	—	5,268	1,906
1920	126,562	39,090	939	28,935	—	2,906	29,151	1,498	2,115	10,945	780	1,714	—	8,096	2,112
1921	135,280	41,245	1,134	34,074	—	3,217	31,054	1,647	2,762	9,362	1,485	1,721	—	7,992	2,206
1922	138,633	46,307	1,309	35,471	—	3,418	27,381	1,930	2,954	9,139	2,101	1,487	—	7,820	2,726
1923	148,946	55,561	2,886	37,104	—	3,778	24,900	2,042	2,790	10,400	2,141	1,277	—	8,405	2,689
1924	162,694	61,982	2,306	39,806	—	3,409	26,734	2,265	2,873	11,170	2,016	1,473	—	9,549	3,433
1925	165,848	65,670	3,266	40,880	—	4,015	25,548	2,222	2,950	10,827	2,015	1,765	—	8,662	3,309
1926	177,635	73,455	3,430	41,169	—	4,130	25,484	2,647	3,173	13,382	2,544	1,623	—	8,543	4,029
1927	184,000	47,801	3,777	41,475	29,335	4,475	25,282	2,677	2,575	14,833	2,856	1,915	—	8,946	4,686
1928	193,914	50,095	4,405	47,364	26,986	4,473	26,897	2,862	3,152	14,272	2,801	2,304	—	10,062	5,447
1929	161,959	44,040	3,868	44,161	13,574	4,594	27,023	2,232	2,486	9,873	2,707	2,319	—	6,709	4,948
1930	172,792	47,248	4,664	43,939	14,587	5,734	32,129	2,554	2,734	9,170	2,333	2,195	—	6,565	5,937
1931	164,642	46,855	4,339	42,415	12,698	5,784	31,488	2,940	2,551	5,813	2,465	1,926	—	6,174	5,998
1932	151,735	46,576	4,784	39,177	10,489	6,296	29,264	1,774	2,590	3,354	1,975	1,539	—	4,788	5,888
1933	137,424	40,694	4,232	35,464	9,290	6,359	26,846	1,178	2,667	3,143	1,937	1,607	—	3,765	6,411
1934	139,047	40,658	3,593	35,819	7,740	5,945	27,001	1,250	5,447	2,834	2,170	1,513	—	3,851	6,989
1935	142,031	43,134	3,283	36,351	7,875	6,501	27,459	1,343	3,082	3,120	2,408	1,695	—	4,810	6,661
1936	156,962	47,667	3,853	38,418	7,082	6,569	33,250	1,444	2,977	4,117	2,306	1,708	—	5,550	8,180
1937	154,424	45,504	3,841	38,053	7,551	7,176	31,821	1,198	3,002	3,875	2,506	1,751	—	5,904	8,589
1938	166,248	49,156	3,646	39,249	8,195	7,369	35,334	1,200	3,330	3,010	2,415	1,889	—	7,576	9,940
1939	173,135	49,901	4,086	38,307	9,843	6,800	40,961	1,566	3,419	3,126	2,315	1,757	—	7,278	10,177
1940	176,997	50,125	2,504	40,173	13,926	6,450	37,975	1,622	3,081	4,699	2,470	1,611	—	7,128	10,207
1941	180,647	46,040	1,553	42,207	5,845	5,010	49,135	1,398	2,187	3,058	7,152	1,798	—	6,475	10,342
1942	182,232	45,157	651	45,145	5,119	4,803	50,023	1,217	2,110	2,917	7,162	2,219	—	4,872	11,488
1943	160,795	36,889	156	42,995	3,568	3,687	48,348	737	1,649	2,317	5,385	1,767	—	3,803	9,650
1944	169,269	35,952	82	44,364	4,730	4,875	52,087	494	1,743	2,426	5,953	1,872	—	4,526	10,247
1945	178,848	35,688	111	45,763	4,856	4,714	57,835	857	1,821	2,634	7,403	1,735	—	4,175	11,367
1946	202,144	42,356	3,513	48,289	5,504	5,356	63,367	1,304	3,094	5,384	7,975	2,024	—	4,975	12,516
1947	230,215	49,525	3,970	58,340	4,400	6,456	68,709	1,779	4,044	6,506	9,674	2,084	—	5,497	13,201
1948	238,121	48,811	2,545	59,699	5,963	6,128	72,339	1,456	3,938	6,686	10,619	1,631	—	5,035	15,816
1949	201,190	47,422	2,644	54,163	4,140	5,159	48,210	2,314	3,281	4,358	13,233	1,763	—	3,472	13,675

Notes appear at end of table

(continued)

TABLE Cg1-15   Copyright registrations, by type: 1870–1977   Continued

Year	Total	Books, including pamphlets, leaflets, etc. Total	Books and pamphlets printed abroad	Periodicals	Contributions to newspapers and periodicals	Dramatic or dramatico-musical compositions	Musical compositions	Maps	Works of art, models, or designs	Prints and pictorial illustrations	Commercial prints and labels	Motion pictures	Sound recordings	Miscellaneous	Renewals
	Cg1 [1]	Cg2 [2]	Cg3	Cg4	Cg5 [2]	Cg6	Cg7	Cg8	Cg9	Cg10	Cg11	Cg12	Cg13	Cg14	Cg15 [3]
	Number	Number	Number	Number	Number	Number	Number	Number	Number	Number	Number	Number	Number	Number	Number
1950	210,564	50,456	3,710	55,436	4,438	4,427	52,309	1,638	4,013	4,309	13,320	1,895	—	3,792	14,531
1951	200,354	47,125	3,536	55,129	3,408	3,992	48,319	1,992	3,428	3,590	11,981	2,149	—	2,869	16,372
1952	203,705	46,083	3,382	56,509	3,320	3,766	51,538	2,422	3,305	2,891	11,770	2,079	—	3,332	16,690
1953	218,506	49,059	3,875	59,371	3,288	3,884	59,302	2,541	3,029	3,126	12,025	2,175	—	3,605	17,101
1954	222,665	51,763	3,697	60,667	3,294	3,527	58,213	2,390	3,170	4,103	10,784	2,556	—	3,690	18,508
1955	224,732	54,414	3,694	59,448	3,746	3,493	57,527	2,013	3,456	3,793	10,505	2,650	—	4,168	19,519
1956	224,908	53,942	3,115	58,576	3,490	3,329	58,330	2,242	4,168	3,306	9,491	3,012	—	4,096	20,926
1957	225,807	53,503	2,915	59,724	3,214	2,764	59,614	2,084	4,557	3,409	8,687	3,198	—	3,580	21,473
1958	238,935	57,242	—	60,691	3,355	2,754	66,515	1,614	5,019	3,413	8,924	3,199	—	3,616	22,593
1959	241,735	55,967	—	62,246	3,042	2,669	70,707	1,865	4,593	3,186	8,786	3,724	—	3,417	21,533
1960	243,926	60,034	—	64,204	3,306	2,445	65,558	1,812	5,271	3,343	8,142	3,457	—	4,961	21,393
1961	247,014	62,415	—	66,251	3,398	2,762	65,500	2,010	5,557	2,955	7,564	4,654	—	5,754	18,194
1962	254,776	66,571	—	67,523	2,993	2,813	67,612	2,073	6,043	2,889	7,167	3,641	—	6,177	19,274
1963	264,845	68,445	—	69,682	2,535	2,730	72,583	2,002	6,262	2,594	7,318	4,216	—	6,314	20,164
1964	278,987	71,618	—	74,611	2,529	3,039	75,256	1,955	5,915	3,325	7,013	4,107	—	7,045	22,574
1965	293,617	76,098	—	78,307	2,095	3,343	80,881	3,262	5,735	2,927	7,509	3,752	—	6,188	23,520
1966	286,866	77,300	—	77,963	1,717	3,215	76,805	1,933	5,164	3,081	6,285	2,889	—	5,050	25,464
1967	294,406	80,910	—	81,647	1,696	3,371	79,291	2,840	4,855	2,740	5,862	2,696	—	4,999	23,499
1968	303,451	85,189	—	81,773	2,026	3,214	80,479	2,560	5,236	3,109	5,972	2,922	—	5,197	25,774
1969	301,258	83,603	—	80,706	1,676	3,213	83,608	2,024	5,630	2,837	4,798	2,364	—	5,132	25,667
1970	316,466	88,432	—	83,862	1,943	3,352	80,949	1,921	6,807	3,373	5,255	2,545	—	6,711	23,316
1971	329,696	96,124	—	84,491	1,884	3,553	95,202	1,677	7,916	4,209	4,424	2,395	—	6,986	20,835
1972	344,574	103,231	—	84,686	2,004	3,838	97,482	1,633	7,901	4,524	4,118	3,204	1,141	7,573	23,239
1973	353,648	104,523	—	88,553	2,074	3,980	95,296	1,914	8,621	4,441	4,216	2,869	6,718	7,372	23,071
1974	372,832	104,806	—	92,224	2,172	4,016	104,511	1,549	8,525	4,716	4,964	3,062	9,362	7,461	25,464
1975	401,274	111,887	—	95,062	2,554	4,914	114,790	1,847	11,010	5,042	4,663	3,038	8,938	9,287	28,202
1976	410,969	113,197	—	96,001	3,090	4,929	118,499	1,595	12,197	5,918	4,485	4,249	9,048	10,064	27,697
1977	452,702	122,080	—	106,474	3,371	5,462	131,236	1,845	13,749	6,689	5,039	5,141	10,628	10,035	30,953

1 Through 1940, commercial prints and labels not included in total; jurisdiction moved to copyright office in 1940.

2 Through 1928, contributions to periodicals included with books and pamphlets.

3 Through 1940, excludes renewals of commercial prints and labels.

4 July–December.

Sources

U.S. Library of Congress, *Annual Report of the Librarian of Congress and Annual Report of the Register of Copyrights*, various issues. Series Cg11 for 1874–1896 is from U.S. Patent Office, *Annual Report of the Commissioner of Patents*, various issues; and for 1897–1940, from unpublished data.

Documentation

Figures are on a calendar-year basis for 1870–1896, and on a fiscal-year basis thereafter. Prior to 1870, copyright claims were entered at federal district courts. For additional information on this period, see Martin A. Roberts, *Records in the Copyright Office Deposited by the United States Districts Courts Covering the Period 1790–1870* (1939).

The term "copyright" may be defined as the right to prevent copying. It has come to mean that body of exclusive rights granted by federal statute to authors for the protection of their writings. It includes the exclusive right to print, reprint, publish, copy, and vend the copyrighted work; to make other versions of the work; and, with certain limitations, to make recordings of the work and to perform the work in public.

The first law, 1790, applied only to maps, charts, and books. Subsequent amendments provided for prints (1802); musical compositions (1831); dramatic compositions with the right of public performance (1856); photographs (1865); paintings, drawings, sculpture, and models or designs for works of the fine arts (1870); performance rights in music (1897); motion pictures and photoplays (1912); and performance rights in nondramatic literary works (1952). The original term of copyright was fourteen years, with the privilege of renewal for fourteen years. In 1831, the first term was increased to twenty-eight years, and in 1909, the renewal term was also increased to twenty-eight years. Before 1891, only citizens of the United States could obtain copyrights. The act of 1891 extended the privilege to citizens of countries with which the United States had reciprocal copyright agreements.

Series Cg4. Periodicals are defined as serial publications issued at regular intervals less than one year; otherwise, they are considered books.

Series Cg6. Prior to 1909, pertains only to dramatic compositions.

Series Cg14. Miscellaneous copyrights include lectures, sermons, and addresses; reproductions of works of art; drawings or plastic works of a scientific or technical character; and photographs.

TABLE Cg16–26 Copyright registrations, by type: 1978–2001

Contributed by Gavin Wright

	Total	Monographs		Serials	Works in the performing arts		Works in the visual arts		Sound recordings		Renewals
		Published	Unpublished		Published	Unpublished	Published	Unpublished	Published	Unpublished	
	Cg16	Cg17	Cg18	Cg19	Cg20	Cg21	Cg22	Cg23	Cg24	Cg25	Cg26
Year	Number	Number	Number	Number	Number	Number	Number	Number	Number	Number	Number
1978	415,700	102,909	10,038	110,863	30,322	99,072	26,099	4,918	7,528	1,533	21,247
1979	429,004	103,938	18,878	109,648	29,900	91,204	26,893	8,365	7,873	2,800	27,001
1980	464,743	97,538	21,683	117,898	36,149	100,629	30,516	10,637	8,098	4,680	32,982
1981	471,178	94,390	24,708	118,523	34,207	107,575	30,601	9,193	7,957	5,541	34,243
1982	468,149	91,911	24,405	112,430	33,505	108,415	32,326	9,962	7,971	5,907	36,332
1983	488,256	100,922	28,338	106,135	36,102	110,452	24,383	13,028	9,284	12,465	39,092
1984	502,628	113,020	34,156	113,603	37,744	102,442	29,280	13,515	8,638	12,949	37,281
1985	540,081	115,466	39,114	120,000	37,400	110,536	33,491	16,552	8,422	14,321	43,863
1986	561,208	108,063	40,152	130,000	36,808	119,498	35,620	15,638	10,706	18,374	45,353
1987	582,239	125,237	40,029	119,643	38,223	123,389	38,727	18,466	12,060	19,919	45,583
1988	565,801	111,531	40,902	120,000	40,447	119,091	39,664	20,764	9,408	19,239	43,830
1989	619,543	110,338	43,468	133,932	47,427	149,860	43,911	22,374	12,880	15,498	38,626
1990	643,602	133,352	46,319	111,539	48,929	136,386	52,447	24,271	11,784	25,743	51,834
1991	663,684	139,127	54,680	109,222	51,014	140,185	53,215	26,010	11,227	25,541	52,255
1992	606,253	143,722	46,562	92,904	46,509	115,568	53,253	24,647	11,242	21,820	49,095
1993	604,894	150,073	49,164	87,777	47,708	115,430	55,564	23,164	11,867	22,839	40,340
1994	530,332	121,323	41,673	68,692	44,219	91,880	56,520	29,592	14,052	21,814	33,264
1995	609,195	141,107	54,892	80,988	50,329	113,293	64,937 [1]	30,613 [1]	13,602	20,406	30,606
1996	550,422	139,248	47,967	74,455	46,892	86,738	65,109	26,531	12,689	17,260	23,723
1997	569,226	131,762	44,626	74,156	46,259	108,153	59,022	30,613	14,610	21,132	28,649
1998	558,645	134,989	54,382	61,783	49,622	92,848	66,103	29,680	14,590	17,092	25,453
1999	594,501	151,830	55,716	64,289	51,134	104,091	62,779	30,838	14,994	23,082	23,896
2000	515,612	122,827	46,966	57,360	47,599	91,336	56,218	29,621	13,665	20,625	16,807
2001	601,659	157,160	55,014	49,993	55,296	101,054	64,289	35,617	20,027	30,505	19,752

[1] The source appears to have reversed the values for the number of published and unpublished works; this apparent error has been corrected here.

Source

U.S. Library of Congress, *Annual Report of the Librarian of Congress*, various issues.

Documentation

The categories presented in the *Annual Report* were completely reorganized beginning in 1978. Unlike earlier reports, published and unpublished works were differentiated. Total registrations should be reasonably comparable with the data in Table Cg1–15, but the detailed composition does change over time. Some reports provide more detailed breakdowns, but this practice has not been maintained.

Series Cg16. Includes categories not reported separately in this table, such as group daily newspapers, group serials, and mask work registrations.

Series Cg17–18. Includes computer software and machine-readable works after 1984.

Series Cg20–21. Total performing arts include musical works, dramatic works, choreography, pantomimes, motion pictures, and filmstrips.

Series Cg22–23. Works of the visual arts include two-dimensional works of fine and graphic art reproductions; sculptural works; technical drawings and models; photographs; commercial prints and labels; works of applied arts; cartographic works; and multimedia works.

TABLE Cg27–37 Patent applications filed and patents issued, by type of patent and patentee: 1790–2000

Contributed by Gavin Wright

	Patent applications filed			Patents issued							
						Inventions					To residents of foreign countries
							Corporations		U.S. government		
	Inventions	Designs	Botanical plants	Total	Individuals	U.S.	Foreign		Designs	Botanical plants	
	Cg27	Cg28	Cg29	Cg30	Cg31	Cg32	Cg33	Cg34	Cg35	Cg36	Cg37
Year	Number	Number	Number	Number	Number	Number	Number	Number	Number	Number	Number
1790	—	—	—	3	—	—	—	—	—	—	—
1791	—	—	—	33	—	—	—	—	—	—	—
1792	—	—	—	11	—	—	—	—	—	—	—
1793	—	—	—	20	—	—	—	—	—	—	—
1794	—	—	—	22	—	—	—	—	—	—	—
1795	—	—	—	12	—	—	—	—	—	—	—
1796	—	—	—	44	—	—	—	—	—	—	—
1797	—	—	—	51	—	—	—	—	—	—	—
1798	—	—	—	28	—	—	—	—	—	—	—
1799	—	—	—	44	—	—	—	—	—	—	—

(continued)

TABLE Cg27–37   Patent applications filed and patents issued, by type of patent and patentee: 1790–2000   *Continued*

	Patent applications filed			Patents issued								
						Inventions						To residents of foreign countries
							Corporations		U.S. government				
	Inventions	Designs	Botanical plants	Total	Individuals	U.S.	Foreign		Designs	Botanical plants	
	Cg27	Cg28	Cg29	Cg30	Cg31	Cg32	Cg33	Cg34	Cg35	Cg36	Cg37
Year	Number	Number	Number	Number	Number	Number	Number	Number	Number	Number	Number
1800	—	—	—	41	—	—	—	—	—	—	—
1801	—	—	—	44	—	—	—	—	—	—	—
1802	—	—	—	65	—	—	—	—	—	—	—
1803	—	—	—	97	—	—	—	—	—	—	—
1804	—	—	—	84	—	—	—	—	—	—	—
1805	—	—	—	57	—	—	—	—	—	—	—
1806	—	—	—	63	—	—	—	—	—	—	—
1807	—	—	—	99	—	—	—	—	—	—	—
1808	—	—	—	158	—	—	—	—	—	—	—
1809	—	—	—	203	—	—	—	—	—	—	—
1810	—	—	—	223	—	—	—	—	—	—	—
1811	—	—	—	215	—	—	—	—	—	—	—
1812	—	—	—	238	—	—	—	—	—	—	—
1813	—	—	—	181	—	—	—	—	—	—	—
1814	—	—	—	210	—	—	—	—	—	—	—
1815	—	—	—	173	—	—	—	—	—	—	—
1816	—	—	—	206	—	—	—	—	—	—	—
1817	—	—	—	174	—	—	—	—	—	—	—
1818	—	—	—	222	—	—	—	—	—	—	—
1819	—	—	—	156	—	—	—	—	—	—	—
1820	—	—	—	155	—	—	—	—	—	—	—
1821	—	—	—	168	—	—	—	—	—	—	—
1822	—	—	—	200	—	—	—	—	—	—	—
1823	—	—	—	173	—	—	—	—	—	—	—
1824	—	—	—	228	—	—	—	—	—	—	—
1825	—	—	—	304	—	—	—	—	—	—	—
1826	—	—	—	323	—	—	—	—	—	—	—
1827	—	—	—	331	—	—	—	—	—	—	—
1828	—	—	—	368	—	—	—	—	—	—	—
1829	—	—	—	447	—	—	—	—	—	—	—
1830	—	—	—	544	—	—	—	—	—	—	—
1831	—	—	—	573	—	—	—	—	—	—	—
1832	—	—	—	474	—	—	—	—	—	—	—
1833	—	—	—	586	—	—	—	—	—	—	—
1834	—	—	—	630	—	—	—	—	—	—	—
1835	—	—	—	752	—	—	—	—	—	—	—
1836	400 [1,2]	—	—	702	—	—	—	—	—	—	8
1837	650 [1]	—	—	426	—	—	—	—	—	—	7
1838	900 [1]	—	—	514	—	—	—	—	—	—	17
1839	800 [1]	—	—	404	—	—	—	—	—	—	10
1840	765	—	—	458	—	—	—	—	—	—	19
1841	847	—	—	490	—	—	—	—	—	—	21
1842	761	—	—	488	—	—	—	—	1	—	11
1843	819	—	—	493	—	—	—	—	14	—	8
1844	1,045	—	—	478	—	—	—	—	12	—	20
1845	1,246	—	—	473	—	—	—	—	17	—	12
1846	1,272	—	—	566	—	—	—	—	59	—	19
1847	1,531	—	—	495	—	—	—	—	60	—	21
1848	1,628	—	—	583	—	—	—	—	46	—	14
1849	1,955	—	—	984	—	—	—	—	49	—	17
1850	2,193	—	—	883	—	—	—	—	83	—	20
1851	2,258	—	—	752	—	—	—	—	90	—	17
1852	2,639	—	—	885	—	—	—	—	109	—	20
1853	2,673	—	—	844	—	—	—	—	86	—	26
1854	3,328	—	—	1,755	—	—	—	—	57	—	35
1855	4,435	—	—	1,881	—	—	—	—	70	—	41
1856	4,960	—	—	2,302	—	—	—	—	107	—	31
1857	4,771	—	—	2,674	—	—	—	—	113	—	45
1858	5,364	—	—	3,455	—	—	—	—	102	—	28
1859	6,225	—	—	4,160	—	—	—	—	107	—	47

Notes appear at end of table

TABLE Cg27–37   Patent applications filed and patents issued, by type of patent and patentee: 1790–2000   *Continued*

	Patent applications filed			Patents issued							
					Inventions						To residents of foreign countries
						Corporations					
Year	Inventions	Designs	Botanical plants	Total	Individuals	U.S.	Foreign	U.S. government	Designs	Botanical plants	
	Cg27	Cg28	Cg29	Cg30	Cg31	Cg32	Cg33	Cg34	Cg35	Cg36	Cg37
	Number	Number	Number	Number	Number	Number	Number	Number	Number	Number	Number
1860	7,653	—	—	4,357	—	—	—	—	183	—	49
1861	4,643	—	—	3,020	—	—	—	—	142	—	83
1862	5,038	—	—	3,214	—	—	—	—	195	—	80
1863	6,014	—	—	3,773	—	—	—	—	176	—	125
1864	6,932	—	—	4,630	—	—	—	—	139	—	181
1865	10,664	—	—	6,088	—	—	—	—	221	—	181
1866	15,269	—	—	8,863	—	—	—	—	294	—	244
1867	21,276	—	—	12,277	—	—	—	—	325	—	275
1868	20,420	—	—	12,526	—	—	—	—	445	—	337
1869	19,271	—	—	12,931	—	—	—	—	506	—	377
1870	19,171	—	—	12,137	—	—	—	—	737	—	644
1871	19,472	—	—	11,659	—	—	—	—	903	—	522
1872	18,246	—	—	12,180	—	—	—	—	884	—	581
1873	20,414	—	—	11,616	—	—	—	—	747	—	493
1874	21,602	—	—	12,230	—	—	—	—	886	—	547
1875	21,638	—	—	13,291	—	—	—	—	915	—	563
1876	21,425	—	—	14,169	—	—	—	—	802	—	787
1877	20,308	—	—	12,920	—	—	—	—	699	—	590
1878	20,260	—	—	12,345	—	—	—	—	590	—	581
1879	20,059	—	—	12,125	—	—	—	—	591	—	648
1880	21,761	634	—	12,903	—	—	—	—	514	—	786
1881	24,878	678	—	15,500	—	—	—	—	565	—	995
1882	30,270	948	—	18,091	—	—	—	—	858	—	1,135
1883	33,073	1,238	—	21,162	—	—	—	—	1,017	—	1,259
1884	34,192	1,230	—	19,118	—	—	—	—	1,150	—	1,284
1885	34,697	862	—	23,285	—	—	—	—	769	—	1,549
1886	35,161	645	—	21,767	—	—	—	—	594	—	1,489
1887	34,420	1,041	—	20,403	—	—	—	—	948	—	1,466
1888	34,713	971	—	19,551	—	—	—	—	832	—	1,536
1889	39,607	857	—	23,324	—	—	—	—	723	—	2,003
1890	39,884	1,046	—	25,313	—	—	—	—	886	—	2,105
1891	39,418	1,025	—	22,312	—	—	—	—	835	—	1,928
1892	29,514	1,130	—	22,647	—	—	—	—	816	—	2,051
1893	37,293	1,060	—	22,750	—	—	—	—	899	—	2,473
1894	36,987	1,357	—	19,855	—	—	—	—	927	—	2,166
1895	39,145	1,463	—	20,856	—	—	—	—	1,108	—	2,049
1896	42,077	1,828	—	21,822	—	—	—	—	1,441	—	2,027
1897	45,661	2,150	—	22,067	—	—	—	—	1,620	—	2,221
1898	33,915	1,843	—	20,377	—	—	—	—	1,799	—	2,752
1899	38,937	2,400	—	23,278	—	—	—	—	2,137	—	2,311
1900	39,673	2,225	—	24,644	—	—	—	—	1,754	—	3,483
1901	43,973	2,361	—	25,546	20,896	4,370	280	—	1,729	—	3,402
1902	48,320	1,170	—	27,119	—	—	—	—	639	—	3,499
1903	49,289	770	—	31,029	—	—	—	—	536	—	3,763
1904	51,168	818	—	30,258	—	—	—	—	553	—	3,285
1905	54,034	781	—	29,775	—	—	—	—	486	—	3,292
1906	55,471	806	—	31,170	24,750	6,040	380	—	620	—	3,471
1907	57,679	896	—	35,859	—	—	—	—	589	—	3,366
1908	60,142	1,131	—	32,735	—	—	—	—	755	—	3,338
1909	64,408	1,234	—	36,561	—	—	—	—	679	—	3,812
1910	63,293	1,155	—	35,141	—	—	—	—	636	—	3,719
1911	67,370	1,534	—	32,856	24,756	7,580	520	—	1,004	—	4,058
1912	63,968	1,850	—	36,198	—	—	—	—	1,341	—	4,489
1913	68,117	2,060	—	33,917	—	—	—	—	1,677	—	4,212
1914	67,774	2,454	—	39,892	—	—	—	—	1,711	—	4,595
1915	67,138	2,734	—	43,118	—	—	—	—	1,538	—	4,334
1916	68,075	2,684	—	43,892	31,742	11,540	610	—	1,745	—	3,767
1917	67,590	2,545	—	40,935	—	—	—	—	1,505	—	3,209
1918	57,347	2,234	—	38,452	—	—	—	—	1,206	—	2,883
1919	76,710	3,627	—	36,797	—	—	—	—	1,521	—	3,687

(continued)

TABLE Cg27–37   Patent applications filed and patents issued, by type of patent and patentee: 1790–2000   *Continued*

	Patent applications filed			Patents issued								
					Inventions							To residents of foreign countries
						Corporations		U.S. government		Botanical plants	
	Inventions	Designs	Botanical plants	Total	Individuals	U.S.	Foreign		Designs		
	Cg27	Cg28	Cg29	Cg30	Cg31	Cg32	Cg33	Cg34	Cg35	Cg36	Cg37
Year	Number	Number	Number	Number	Number	Number	Number	Number	Number	Number	Number
1920	81,915	4,660	—	37,060	—	—	—	—	2,481	—	3,762
1921	87,467	5,596	—	37,798	27,098	9,860	840	—	3,265	—	3,963
1922	83,962	4,763	—	38,369	27,369	10,300	700	—	1,609	—	4,455
1923	76,783	3,550	—	38,616	27,016	10,800	800	—	1,927	—	4,133
1924	87,987	3,635	—	42,574	29,174	12,400	1,000	—	2,670	—	4,723
1925	80,208	4,082	—	46,432	30,332	14,800	1,300	—	2,819	—	5,347
1926	81,365	4,343	—	44,733	28,633	15,200	900	—	2,597	—	5,103
1927	87,219	4,473	—	41,717	25,417	15,100	1,200	—	2,387	—	4,918
1928	87,603	4,761	—	42,357	23,357	17,800	1,200	—	3,182	—	5,218
1929	89,752	4,520	—	45,267	25,367	18,500	1,400	—	2,905	—	5,921
1930	89,554	4,182	16	45,226	23,726	19,700	1,800	—	2,710	—	6,085
1931	79,740	4,190	37	51,756	26,618	23,149	1,961	28	2,935	5	6,897
1932	67,006	4,345	46	53,458	26,274	24,822	2,325	37	2,942	46	7,376
1933	56,558	3,600	27	48,774	22,713	23,667	2,343	51	2,411	33	7,170
1934	56,643	4,399	28	44,420	19,731	22,529	2,131	29	2,919	32	6,489
1935	58,117	5,728	72	40,618	17,757	20,821	2,018	22	3,864	45	5,980
1936	62,599	6,478	66	39,782	16,639	21,207	1,903	33	4,556	49	5,734
1937	65,324	7,207	45	37,683	15,995	19,831	1,824	33	5,136	55	5,638
1938	66,874	8,084	48	38,061	16,304	19,635	2,063	59	5,026	41	5,776
1939	64,093	7,137	76	43,073	18,583	21,800	2,640	50	5,592	45	6,338
1940	60,863	8,530	91	42,238	17,627	22,165	2,406	40	6,145	85	6,148
1941	52,339	7,203	67	41,109	16,322	22,632	2,112	43	6,486	62	5,311
1942	45,549	4,218	60	38,449	14,534	22,019	1,286	62	3,728	65	3,943
1943	45,493	2,986	41	31,054	11,654	18,022	524	48	2,228	47	2,625
1944	54,190	5,063	42	28,053	9,636	16,769	645	106	2,914	38	2,564
1945	67,846	8,066	52	25,695	8,981	15,665	580	87	3,524	17	2,112
1946	81,056	10,698	72	21,803	7,444	13,486	585	147	2,778	56	1,656
1947	75,443	7,644	92	20,139	7,784	11,448	669	155	2,102	52	1,617
1948	68,740	7,048	59	23,963	9,812	13,124	628	352	3,968	44	1,984
1949	67,592	6,998	70	35,131	14,957	18,536	1,127	485	4,450	93	3,105
1950	67,264	6,739	105	43,040	18,960	21,782	1,660	622	4,718	89	4,408
1951	60,438	4,279	71	44,326	19,192	22,305	2,163	659	4,163	58	4,888
1952	64,554	4,993	84	43,616	18,538	22,340	2,035	695	2,959	101	5,635
1953	72,284	5,450	99	40,468	16,284	21,230	2,294	658	2,713	78	4,331
1954	77,185	5,465	95	33,809	12,531	18,319	2,301	658	2,536	101	4,433
1955	77,188	5,764	118	30,432	11,914	16,084	1,744	689	2,713	103	4,065
1956	74,906	4,824	104	46,817	16,643	25,502	3,690	982	2,977	101	6,646
1957	74,197	4,714	101	42,744	15,154	23,255	3,372	963	2,362	129	6,282
1958	77,495	4,923	134	48,330	15,706	27,116	4,230	1,278	2,374	120	7,395
1959	78,594	4,879	114	52,408	16,017	29,888	5,081	1,422	2,768	101	8,340
1960	79,590	4,525	131	47,170	13,069	28,187	4,670	1,244	2,543	116	7,850
1961	83,100	4,714	107	48,368	13,383	28,351	5,161	1,473	2,487	108	8,384
1962	85,029	4,897	151	55,691	15,470	32,560	6,380	1,281	2,300	91	10,255
1963	85,724	4,968	145	45,679	12,525	26,632	5,501	1,021	2,965	129	8,736
1964	87,597	5,259	120	47,376	12,504	27,836	5,854	1,182	2,686	128	9,168
1965	94,632	5,413	105	62,857	16,063	37,158	8,096	1,540	3,424	120	12,782
1966	88,293	4,853	104	68,406	16,018	41,634	9,222	1,532	3,188	114	14,008
1967	87,872	4,744	103	65,652	15,647	38,353	9,895	1,757	3,165	85	14,711
1968	93,136	5,171	95	59,102	13,555	34,886	9,172	1,489	3,352	72	13,722
1969	98,386	5,496	111	67,557	14,772	38,847	12,188	1,750	3,335	103	17,573
1970	102,868	5,996	188	64,427	13,511	36,896	12,294	1,726	3,214	52	17,872
1971	104,729	6,211	155	78,317	12,669	43,133	16,045	2,144	3,156	71	22,850
1972	99,298	5,867	135	74,810	11,652	39,927	16,980	1,771	2,901	199	23,810
1973	104,079	5,425	118	74,143	12,416	38,732	16,634	2,090	4,033	132	23,344
1974	102,538	5,318	155	76,278	12,678	38,186	18,715	1,727	4,304	261	26,514
1975	101,014	6,292	150	72,000	11,200	35,540	18,868	1,895	4,282	150	36,271
1976	102,344	7,061	175	70,226	10,097	34,390	19,770	1,823	4,564	176	27,134
1977	100,931	7,258	188	65,269	10,263	31,510	18,058	1,495	3,929	173	24,684
1978	100,916	7,538	194	66,102	10,418	31,355	19,070	1,241	3,862	186	25,711
1979	100,494	7,519	196	48,854	7,805	22,504	14,616	964	3,119	131	19,458

TABLE Cg27–37   Patent applications filed and patents issued, by type of patent and patentee: 1790–2000   *Continued*

	Patent applications filed			Patents issued								
						Inventions						To residents of foreign countries
							Corporations		U.S. government		Botanical plants	
	Inventions	Designs	Botanical plants	Total	Individuals	U.S.	Foreign		Designs		
	Cg27	Cg28	Cg29	Cg30	Cg31	Cg32	Cg33	Cg34	Cg35	Cg36	Cg37
Year	Number	Number	Number	Number	Number	Number	Number	Number	Number	Number	Number
1980	104,329	7,830	220	61,819	9,955	27,640	18,874	1,237	3,949	117	25,387
1981	106,413	7,375	178	65,771	10,264	29,433	20,788	1,121	4,745	183	27,752
1982	109,625	8,174	188	57,888	8,553	25,783	18,856	1,005	4,944	173	25,528
1983	103,703	8,082	255	56,860	7,574	25,677	19,246	1,048	4,563	197	25,331
1984	111,284	8,739	253	67,200	8,911	29,999	23,238	1,235	4,938	212	30,394
1985	117,006	9,551	231	71,661	9,265	31,181	25,957	1,139	5,066	242	33,795
1986	122,433	9,912	320	70,860	9,477	29,490	26,545	1,022	5,518	224	34,780
1987	127,917	11,153	385	82,952	10,887	33,726	32,371	981	5,959	229	41,587
1988	139,825	11,289	377	77,924	10,122	31,437	30,960	733	5,679	425	39,627
1989	152,750	12,615	383	95,537	13,028	38,664	37,506	880	6,092	587	47,802
1990	164,558	11,288	418	90,364	12,542	36,093	35,548	983	8,024	318	46,094
1991	164,306	13,061	463	96,513	13,207	39,133	37,594	1,183	9,569	353	48,944
1992	173,075	13,078	354	97,444	12,751	40,308	38,239	1,161	9,269	321	48,572
1993	174,743	13,635	361	98,343	12,281	41,826	38,401	1,166	10,630	442	48,531
1994	189,857	15,774	459	101,676	12,805	44,036	38,788	1,258	11,095	499	49,224
1995	212,377	15,409	452	101,419	12,885	44,035	38,688	1,028	11,712	387	49,327
1996	195,187	15,161	665	109,646	13,729	48,741	41,476	923	11,410	362	52,268
1997	215,257	16,546	621	111,984	12,914	50,220	42,907	944	11,414	394	54,108
1998	243,100	17,100	700	147,520	16,407	66,062	57,668	1,018	14,767	561	72,395
1999	270,200	17,800	900	153,500	22,800	69,400	60,300	1,000	14,700	400	75,100
2000	295,900	18,300	800	157,500	22,400	70,900	63,300	900	17,400	500	79,100

[1] Estimate.

[2] From July 4 to end of year.

Sources

1870–1970: U.S. Patent Office, *Annual Report of the Commissioner of Patents*, various issues, and unpublished data.

1971–2000: U.S. Department of Commerce, *Statistical Abstract of the United States*, various issues. Fiscal-year figures are published in the *Commissioner of Patents and Trademarks Annual Report*.

Documentation

A patent is a grant by the government to the inventor, or the inventor's heirs or assigns, of the right to exclude others from making, using, or selling the invention patented. Patents can be obtained for any new and useful machine, manufacture, composition of matter or process, or any new and useful improvement thereof, subject to the requirements and conditions of the law. An invention is "useful" if it has lawful purpose and is operative. The subject matter of a patent must be sufficiently new so as not to be obvious to one skilled in the art to which it relates.

Patents on inventions have been issued by the federal government since April 10, 1790. Both the fee charged and the term of patents have been changed occasionally by law. A total fee of $30 was charged on application in 1793. Whereas no fee was made prior to 1861 when a patent was granted, modern-day applicants pay an additional fee at that time. For 1790–1861, the term of a patent was fourteen years. From 1836 until the patents granted in 1861 expired, patents could be extended for an additional seven years upon application by the patentee and approval of a special board or the Commissioner. Since 1861, the term of patents on inventions has been fixed at seventeen years, with extensions possible only by special act of Congress.

From February 21, 1790, to July 4, 1836, patents were granted on demand of the applicant, upon compliance with the formal requirements, without examination as to novelty and other requirements. Consequently, statistics on patents issued during this period are more comparable to subsequent statistics on *applications* for patents for inventions than to subsequent statistics on patents issued. Since July 4, 1836, the U.S. Patent Office has examined applications for novelty and for compliance with the requirements of the statute. Patents for inventions are numbered serially, beginning with the first patent issued after the Patent Act of July 4, 1836.

Series Cg27–28. Applications for reissue are included with inventions, 1836–1876. Design applications are included with inventions, 1836–1879.

Series Cg30. Since 1942, this series includes patents issued to the Alien Property Custodian, not listed separately.

Series Cg34. The U.S. government series does not include patents issued to the Alien Property Custodian.

Series Cg35. Designs became patentable in 1842 and relate to the appearance, not to the structure or use, of articles of manufacture.

Series Cg36. Botanical plants became subject to patents for the first time in 1930. Patentable plants are those that are asexually reproduced – distinct and new varieties of plants other than tuber-propagated plants.

Series Cg37. Data are based on residence and not on citizenship. The volume of patents issued to citizens of foreign countries was influenced in the early years of the system by discriminatory legislation. For 1800–1836, only aliens who had resided in the United States for two years and who had declared their intention of becoming citizens could apply for U.S. patents. For 1836–1861, aliens paid higher fees than citizens on a theory of reciprocity. Discrimination based on nationality was eliminated in 1861. It includes patents on inventions, designs, and botanical plants.

TABLE Cg38–68   Patents granted, by industry of manufacture: 1840–1996

Contributed by Daniel K. N. Johnson

	Primary sectors (natural resources)				Secondary sectors (manufacturing)									Transport	
	Total	Agriculture	Forestry and fishing	Mining	Electrical appliances	Electrical lighting	Radio and television	Electrical industrial equipment	Other electrical equipment	Electronic equipment	Chemicals	Drugs	Petroleum	Aerospace	Motor vehicles
	Cg38	Cg39	Cg40	Cg41	Cg42	Cg43	Cg44	Cg45	Cg46	Cg47	Cg48	Cg49	Cg50	Cg51	Cg52
Year	Number	Number	Number	Number	Number	Number	Number	Number	Number	Number	Number	Number	Number	Number	Number
1840	459	1	(Z)	(Z)	8	(Z)	(Z)	8	1	10	14	1	(Z)	2	14
1841	491	1	(Z)	(Z)	8	1	(Z)	9	2	8	15	2	(Z)	3	17
1842	491	1	(Z)	(Z)	9	1	(Z)	9	3	9	18	3	1	2	15
1843	493	1	(Z)	(Z)	8	1	(Z)	10	2	9	16	2	(Z)	2	15
1844	482	1	(Z)	(Z)	10	1	(Z)	8	1	9	19	2	(Z)	3	13
1845	479	1	(Z)	(Z)	11	1	(Z)	9	2	10	15	3	(Z)	3	13
1846	569	2	(Z)	(Z)	11	1	(Z)	9	2	13	18	3	(Z)	3	22
1847	497	1	(Z)	(Z)	7	1	(Z)	9	2	10	20	2	(Z)	2	26
1848	589	2	(Z)	(Z)	10	3	1	12	3	13	19	1	1	1	20
1849	990	2	(Z)	(Z)	14	3	(Z)	18	5	26	25	2	1	4	41
1850	886	3	(Z)	(Z)	12	2	(Z)	16	4	22	32	2	1	4	39
1851	760	2	(Z)	(Z)	12	3	(Z)	15	4	22	27	3	(Z)	3	33
1852	890	3	(Z)	(Z)	11	3	(Z)	18	5	24	30	1	2	3	44
1853	846	1	(Z)	(Z)	11	3	(Z)	16	4	21	27	2	(Z)	4	27
1854	1,762	3	(Z)	(Z)	25	7	1	35	8	40	51	3	1	6	70
1855	1,895	3	(Z)	1	27	9	1	38	9	41	57	4	4	10	72
1856	2,325	4	(Z)	1	34	6	1	47	9	52	71	5	3	10	93
1857	2,689	5	(Z)	1	40	8	1	50	10	57	89	5	3	13	107
1858	3,465	6	(Z)	1	64	16	2	73	18	83	92	6	4	13	134
1859	4,183	8	(Z)	1	77	12	2	84	20	102	149	10	7	18	165
1860	4,378	11	(Z)	1	75	21	2	91	21	100	152	14	4	17	166
1861	3,033	5	(Z)	1	57	17	1	65	14	68	105	9	3	14	128
1862	3,223	5	(Z)	1	62	38	1	64	16	71	152	10	5	19	129
1863	3,791	8	(Z)	1	64	34	2	77	21	79	182	21	6	21	153
1864	4,654	10	(Z)	3	85	24	2	89	21	90	222	29	9	17	179
1865	6,110	13	(Z)	5	106	37	2	111	30	121	270	37	14	23	235
1866	8,896	20	(Z)	7	152	52	3	164	48	168	353	71	27	33	370
1867	12,310	37	(Z)	7	213	56	5	224	67	247	420	89	30	47	578
1868	12,594	46	(Z)	4	214	71	5	235	60	252	419	95	16	46	594
1869	12,980	38	(Z)	4	231	72	5	244	64	253	483	108	16	48	601
1870	12,192	35	(Z)	4	234	71	5	245	66	257	443	90	18	46	566
1871	11,717	26	(Z)	4	228	57	5	249	67	258	375	98	14	43	597
1872	12,269	31	(Z)	4	247	66	6	260	65	298	403	101	18	45	627
1873	11,747	26	(Z)	3	222	63	5	238	61	291	344	67	14	47	560
1874	12,331	31	(Z)	4	200	64	7	248	64	327	370	65	19	50	648
1875	13,375	33	(Z)	4	237	81	8	271	77	355	365	40	13	53	642
1876	14,259	39	(Z)	4	241	84	9	287	90	386	366	57	14	53	648
1877	12,991	39	(Z)	4	213	71	8	253	71	318	338	36	15	54	622
1878	12,413	40	(Z)	3	205	86	9	243	69	342	325	54	12	51	631
1879	12,215	43	(Z)	3	199	77	10	260	73	358	330	58	12	52	642
1880	12,985	38	(Z)	3	189	80	15	318	88	486	357	53	12	53	659
1881	15,602	50	(Z)	4	231	102	19	399	114	633	473	69	15	51	778
1882	18,182	51	(Z)	4	279	152	22	556	164	762	548	67	15	66	918
1883	21,225	66	(Z)	5	273	148	21	641	225	837	616	92	20	63	1,168
1884	19,230	65	(Z)	4	218	100	20	527	199	736	521	71	17	53	1,117
1885	23,401	71	1	5	299	134	24	650	213	926	622	93	18	73	1,250
1886	21,878	71	1	4	300	122	27	634	197	876	540	74	15	64	1,141
1887	20,536	69	(Z)	4	269	118	23	567	202	851	470	69	13	57	1,058
1888	19,710	56	(Z)	4	250	109	22	651	232	825	510	62	14	61	1,061
1889	23,443	51	(Z)	5	312	146	25	839	301	915	636	95	21	71	1,215
1890	25,434	77	1	5	337	153	30	968	342	1,111	635	93	20	70	1,345
1891	22,421	57	1	5	295	137	28	880	281	972	569	74	15	65	1,107
1892	22,744	64	1	5	293	149	30	812	274	1,035	528	61	16	61	1,152
1893	22,832	50	(Z)	4	296	148	28	894	270	1,064	612	59	13	72	1,252
1894	19,899	39	(Z)	5	246	125	24	836	245	981	541	54	16	58	1,070

Note appears at end of table

TABLE Cg38-68 Patents granted, by industry of manufacture: 1840–1996 *Continued*

	Primary sectors (natural resources)				Secondary sectors (manufacturing)										
														Transport	
		Forestry and fishing	Mining	Electrical appliances	Electrical lighting	Radio and television	Electrical industrial equipment	Other electrical equipment	Electronic equipment	Chemicals	Drugs	Petroleum	Aerospace	Motor vehicles
	Total	Agriculture													
	Cg38	Cg39	Cg40	Cg41	Cg42	Cg43	Cg44	Cg45	Cg46	Cg47	Cg48	Cg49	Cg50	Cg51	Cg52
Year	Number	Number	Number	Number	Number	Number	Number	Number	Number	Number	Number	Number	Number	Number	Number
1895	20,969	49	(Z)	5	262	124	23	771	230	994	538	47	16	63	1,258
1896	21,917	42	(Z)	4	291	148	27	788	244	1,055	564	50	14	59	1,307
1897	22,164	40	(Z)	4	283	171	27	753	260	1,066	543	61	14	68	1,315
1898	20,466	25	(Z)	4	263	128	21	657	206	789	620	57	13	67	1,240
1899	23,356	36	(Z)	6	272	136	31	746	246	948	775	74	30	72	1,303
1900	24,707	41	1	6	287	161	42	848	283	1,081	851	73	25	77	1,426
1901	25,613	34	(Z)	7	311	176	44	937	306	1,181	806	76	26	73	1,445
1902	27,143	33	1	9	332	158	38	985	331	1,237	881	79	33	90	1,510
1903	31,070	53	1	10	366	211	47	1,180	394	1,421	899	89	39	93	1,663
1904	30,350	43	1	10	342	194	56	1,161	369	1,607	830	79	40	86	1,641
1905	29,850	53	1	10	310	184	54	1,121	325	1,457	893	86	31	96	1,642
1906	31,260	56	1	8	339	197	53	1,083	330	1,551	866	79	30	102	1,725
1907	35,958	41	1	10	450	202	69	1,377	408	1,740	989	87	33	148	2,075
1908	32,815	54	1	9	397	204	76	1,227	400	1,663	978	98	27	157	1,845
1909	36,704	49	1	9	458	277	72	1,420	456	1,826	1,056	109	34	178	2,001
1910	35,255	44	1	9	447	281	68	1,343	428	1,603	1,038	102	34	180	1,921
1911	33,022	38	1	9	400	308	57	1,332	403	1,576	1,093	96	26	318	1,890
1912	36,444	30	1	8	431	351	74	1,356	441	1,680	1,181	121	26	335	2,138
1913	34,073	35	1	8	414	301	65	1,240	386	1,512	1,183	108	24	245	2,008
1914	40,154	44	1	10	485	373	83	1,560	466	2,022	1,343	111	37	242	2,569
1915	43,346	46	1	12	527	428	94	1,688	535	2,253	1,368	122	39	233	2,936
1916	44,091	34	1	11	537	485	107	1,694	582	2,303	1,332	129	41	237	3,086
1917	41,038	23	1	10	481	481	114	1,733	572	2,287	1,362	119	37	230	2,863
1918	38,544	19	1	10	432	433	100	1,597	530	2,037	1,263	119	41	246	2,706
1919	36,787	16	1	10	385	404	100	1,600	493	1,997	1,473	99	38	317	2,636
1920	37,088	14	1	10	445	391	105	1,596	522	1,892	1,242	90	38	311	2,610
1921	37,864	13	1	10	470	373	105	1,538	530	1,881	1,345	131	43	282	2,807
1922	38,478	12	1	11	463	428	114	1,503	492	1,853	1,474	120	54	261	2,851
1923	38,766	11	1	11	507	433	110	1,512	473	1,905	1,352	136	48	224	2,890
1924	42,703	17	1	14	530	521	108	1,821	687	2,293	1,471	157	65	263	2,940
1925	47,593	15	1	14	616	571	129	2,090	711	3,011	1,758	184	61	299	3,180
1926	43,816	11	1	15	536	562	123	1,820	651	2,630	1,676	193	85	221	2,950
1927	41,937	12	1	12	508	523	122	1,820	649	2,643	1,608	187	66	236	2,812
1928	42,556	9	(Z)	14	560	578	129	2,043	703	2,813	1,848	167	80	235	2,571
1929	45,515	12	1	12	585	562	138	2,157	701	2,910	2,005	173	68	322	2,712
1930	45,386	10	1	13	536	537	157	2,140	696	2,915	2,157	187	84	455	2,654
1931	51,886	9	1	16	629	577	191	2,339	741	3,402	2,713	194	91	509	3,062
1932	53,733	9	1	17	627	544	205	2,472	772	3,485	3,347	260	107	499	3,099
1933	49,007	8	1	18	609	555	182	2,457	756	3,386	3,291	310	136	330	2,818
1934	44,643	7	1	15	542	555	182	2,213	735	3,084	3,093	245	112	239	2,412
1935	40,868	7	1	15	535	476	170	1,778	596	2,890	3,052	268	106	240	2,220
1936	40,017	9	(Z)	15	517	427	171	1,702	574	2,986	3,143	267	114	203	2,251
1937	37,956	7	(Z)	13	464	429	171	1,693	556	2,881	3,056	281	96	207	2,117
1938	38,254	7	(Z)	14	432	458	158	1,672	570	2,857	3,183	274	97	242	2,093
1939	43,288	6	1	14	539	507	203	2,045	690	3,460	3,540	320	95	254	2,378
1940	42,502	7	1	15	509	506	210	1,973	657	3,535	3,631	293	101	238	2,308
1941	41,380	6	1	14	555	508	221	2,107	685	3,555	3,261	260	94	219	2,244
1942	38,666	5	(Z)	13	501	494	215	2,080	682	3,395	3,271	261	97	207	1,812
1943	31,214	4	(Z)	11	381	341	135	1,489	488	2,224	2,996	230	85	196	1,430
1944	28,136	4	(Z)	10	290	263	118	1,296	387	2,027	2,871	265	78	211	1,321
1945	25,790	2	(Z)	9	250	210	91	1,154	342	1,832	3,386	232	75	257	1,246
1946	21,822	2	(Z)	8	225	234	102	1,065	329	2,107	2,769	183	57	262	1,033
1947	20,207	4	(Z)	5	222	233	88	1,136	345	2,014	2,398	185	43	213	907
1948	24,087	4	(Z)	5	268	324	90	1,429	452	2,249	2,856	214	44	223	1,151
1949	35,287	8	1	9	396	414	156	2,047	577	3,369	4,032	296	61	320	1,669
1950	43,154	9	1	11	539	452	234	2,225	672	4,209	4,495	346	66	347	2,020
1951	44,402	6	1	12	506	438	228	2,034	630	4,082	4,632	382	77	318	2,161
1952	43,688	7	1	12	517	414	198	1,909	607	3,686	4,219	329	73	304	2,118
1953	40,582	7	1	12	493	375	185	1,820	611	3,297	3,883	289	71	294	1,974
1954	33,896	6	1	11	391	325	156	1,614	530	2,722	3,595	281	62	261	1,577

Note appears at end of table

(continued)

TABLE Cg38–68   Patents granted, by industry of manufacture: 1840–1996   *Continued*

	Primary sectors (natural resources)				Secondary sectors (manufacturing)									Transport	
	Total	Agriculture	Forestry and fishing	Mining	Electrical appliances	Electrical lighting	Radio and television	Electrical industrial equipment	Other electrical equipment	Electronic equipment	Chemicals	Drugs	Petroleum	Aerospace	Motor vehicles
	Cg38	Cg39	Cg40	Cg41	Cg42	Cg43	Cg44	Cg45	Cg46	Cg47	Cg48	Cg49	Cg50	Cg51	Cg52
Year	Number	Number	Number	Number	Number	Number	Number	Number	Number	Number	Number	Number	Number	Number	Number
1955	30,525	5	1	10	356	324	136	1,412	489	2,525	2,958	242	55	213	1,497
1956	46,910	8	1	16	512	509	209	2,329	727	4,108	5,217	418	98	315	2,244
1957	42,803	7	1	15	471	479	200	2,272	694	3,842	4,842	414	73	246	2,009
1958	48,419	8	1	19	468	521	272	2,457	787	4,720	6,029	507	120	298	2,376
1959	52,564	7	1	19	531	588	322	2,592	832	5,393	6,454	580	141	274	2,525
1960	47,218	6	1	17	443	508	298	2,257	761	5,085	5,588	536	122	519	2,256
1961	48,448	6	1	19	453	431	260	2,201	745	4,809	6,343	590	128	456	2,264
1962	55,785	7	1	22	527	484	291	2,531	848	5,364	7,418	756	140	470	2,374
1963	45,798	7	1	16	454	396	207	2,045	670	4,220	5,843	621	91	386	1,872
1964	47,485	9	1	16	403	425	204	2,251	733	4,521	6,231	618	84	411	1,952
1965	62,977	9	1	19	522	629	313	3,351	1,090	6,749	7,531	700	105	448	2,710
1966	68,631	12	1	22	557	675	341	3,619	1,204	7,292	9,832	906	144	448	2,733
1967	65,921	11	1	22	548	639	318	3,286	1,102	6,586	9,956	875	123	401	2,561
1968	59,262	8	1	21	514	571	300	2,871	968	5,997	8,518	666	119	356	2,435
1969	67,757	9	1	22	552	617	361	3,380	1,219	7,419	10,158	981	138	381	2,578
1970	64,588	9	1	18	491	618	407	3,227	1,192	7,746	9,393	919	119	327	2,423
1971	78,553	12	1	22	615	781	511	4,024	1,445	9,569	9,214	1,115	137	407	3,049
1972	75,070	10	1	24	546	669	476	3,342	1,256	8,188	13,164	1,376	166	349	2,774
1973	74,484	13	1	22	556	742	477	3,510	1,251	8,351	10,497	1,268	134	401	3,183
1974	78,075	14	1	24	553	727	474	3,375	1,305	7,996	11,455	1,501	146	355	3,383
1975	70,988	13	1	22	473	604	418	2,808	1,166	7,146	11,694	1,640	138	313	3,158
1976	70,726	12	1	21	451	588	442	2,825	1,178	7,312	12,350	1,870	140	337	2,864
1977	65,713	11	1	23	404	566	426	2,749	1,170	7,058	10,559	1,925	144	297	2,684
1978	66,664	10	1	23	446	572	417	2,777	1,183	6,816	10,843	1,899	157	271	2,901
1979	49,278	10	1	19	344	443	340	2,055	836	5,215	7,568	1,487	133	198	2,102
1980	62,246	12	1	22	431	553	442	2,481	1,070	6,553	9,210	1,973	147	261	2,613
1981	66,166	13	1	27	435	553	448	2,759	1,091	6,672	10,259	2,111	185	281	2,711
1982	58,224	11	1	21	417	545	480	2,753	997	6,622	8,451	1,936	142	202	2,430
1983	57,323	12	1	24	404	535	481	2,531	1,043	6,236	8,395	1,820	176	244	2,432
1984	67,792	12	1	26	501	604	517	3,087	1,176	7,395	9,285	2,177	172	298	3,081
1985	72,086	14	1	28	514	671	661	3,186	1,303	8,429	9,631	2,199	190	273	3,089
1986	71,061	15	1	24	489	676	698	3,037	1,211	8,783	8,625	2,249	152	282	2,998
1987	83,188	17	1	27	569	842	942	3,908	1,515	11,128	9,347	2,751	154	368	3,610
1988	78,146	18	1	25	511	847	806	3,338	1,445	10,185	9,222	2,740	148	356	3,370
1989	95,737	20	1	29	609	1,001	1,060	3,951	1,719	13,024	11,332	3,728	178	378	3,887
1990	90,671	20	1	24	593	978	915	3,590	1,621	12,061	11,181	3,502	146	339	3,710
1991	96,750	24	1	25	633	1,050	1,036	3,697	1,732	13,250	12,020	3,886	163	386	4,003
1992	97,728	28	1	25	573	1,028	1,075	3,701	1,766	13,462	12,490	4,096	152	437	3,810
1993	98,618	26	1	25	576	942	1,162	3,734	1,790	13,978	13,015	4,549	160	375	3,653
1994	101,796	35	1	28	628	974	1,264	3,753	1,836	16,138	12,099	4,271	174	368	3,556
1995	101,629	34	1	26	611	1,043	1,302	3,696	1,875	17,096	11,720	4,701	155	325	3,585
1996	109,949	56	1	26	633	1,105	1,441	4,095	2,074	19,319	12,054	5,634	159	326	3,997

TABLE Cg38–68 Patents granted, by industry of manufacture: 1840–1996 *Continued*

	Transport		Metals				Computers and peripherals	Other office machinery	Other machinery	Food and tobacco	Textiles	Rubber and plastic	Nonmetallic minerals	Paper	Wood	Other manufacturing
	Ships	Other	Ferrous metals	Nonferrous	Fabricated	Instruments										
	Cg53	Cg54	Cg55	Cg56	Cg57	Cg58	Cg59	Cg60	Cg61	Cg62	Cg63	Cg64	Cg65	Cg66	Cg67	Cg68
Year	Number	Number	Number	Number	Number	Number	Number	Number	Number	Number	Number	Number	Number	Number	Number	Number
1840	6	10	3	(Z)	78	22	4	2	209	1	13	12	4	3	8	25
1841	7	9	2	1	80	21	3	2	235	3	15	11	4	3	7	21
1842	5	5	2	(Z)	82	23	3	1	230	3	18	10	3	2	7	24
1843	5	6	2	(Z)	81	23	4	2	235	1	15	11	4	2	8	27
1844	4	5	2	1	75	22	3	2	233	2	15	12	5	3	5	24
1845	4	7	2	1	74	24	3	1	227	3	15	11	5	3	5	27
1846	3	10	2	1	95	32	4	2	259	3	20	13	5	2	8	26
1847	6	7	2	(Z)	72	24	3	1	230	2	14	12	5	3	9	25
1848	5	6	4	1	93	23	5	2	286	2	17	13	5	2	9	29
1849	8	17	5	2	150	43	10	4	463	5	32	25	6	6	20	53
1850	7	12	4	1	128	41	9	4	408	6	27	22	7	6	17	49
1851	4	16	4	1	110	35	9	3	342	2	25	18	7	4	15	42
1852	6	11	4	1	117	45	8	3	421	4	29	20	9	5	18	45
1853	9	7	5	1	108	37	10	4	422	3	26	22	7	7	19	42
1854	15	22	7	1	250	78	17	7	854	4	51	50	15	13	35	91
1855	20	19	9	4	272	78	18	8	933	6	57	49	15	13	30	88
1856	16	28	11	3	345	105	23	9	1,123	7	62	68	22	16	37	113
1857	25	26	14	4	366	124	24	10	1,331	7	64	76	23	20	45	140
1858	30	63	23	3	482	166	29	12	1,635	12	93	105	27	27	73	174
1859	32	82	28	4	568	190	36	17	1,943	15	110	129	35	33	89	218
1860	31	77	24	5	623	193	36	17	2,046	20	123	135	35	35	90	214
1861	19	44	18	3	429	135	22	11	1,378	19	92	97	21	25	56	177
1862	31	54	15	3	487	140	28	15	1,352	25	103	106	26	30	59	175
1863	38	58	19	6	594	168	25	12	1,582	21	123	126	32	42	68	209
1864	36	69	26	9	697	194	30	15	2,003	33	153	165	41	59	78	266
1865	40	108	36	10	896	272	45	22	2,623	44	188	220	52	72	114	362
1866	43	139	49	13	1,314	384	57	30	3,802	57	285	336	77	93	184	562
1867	73	250	74	17	1,895	548	82	38	5,009	65	380	495	120	137	304	803
1868	52	237	72	16	1,884	547	85	39	5,226	74	428	496	120	143	309	808
1869	70	285	83	23	2,004	527	79	38	5,325	88	380	484	132	143	336	816
1870	55	203	77	24	1,952	482	81	40	4,977	64	361	477	131	138	350	696
1871	49	228	64	17	1,834	476	84	36	4,743	61	346	455	111	131	355	705
1872	58	266	78	19	1,854	501	87	36	4,856	69	392	505	132	149	350	747
1873	55	311	79	19	1,787	469	89	36	4,688	66	370	478	124	142	343	748
1874	57	386	79	18	1,873	531	110	40	4,757	57	405	489	136	152	313	831
1875	53	322	82	18	2,140	634	119	47	5,081	65	421	580	126	182	404	923
1876	59	327	91	17	2,248	651	129	55	5,444	71	470	631	140	199	438	1,011
1877	56	261	76	15	2,101	594	113	54	4,942	85	431	601	122	207	352	942
1878	46	244	73	14	1,946	589	121	53	4,664	75	436	579	116	202	323	861
1879	42	257	76	17	1,793	565	108	52	4,631	66	468	561	112	195	293	862
1880	51	307	75	14	1,860	616	126	54	4,899	71	455	570	113	197	299	928
1881	60	399	86	16	2,190	712	148	61	5,786	96	596	651	134	201	394	1,132
1882	61	576	102	16	2,515	834	175	68	6,682	108	613	739	179	234	471	1,205
1883	90	631	129	25	3,033	975	213	88	7,792	84	704	874	207	273	518	1,412
1884	59	590	127	27	2,759	906	193	81	7,086	68	663	835	185	269	411	1,323
1885	77	664	166	28	3,428	1,151	243	103	8,618	103	780	943	212	294	637	1,571
1886	69	663	151	24	3,198	1,125	253	105	7,894	99	767	895	210	290	559	1,510
1887	66	660	152	21	3,005	1,066	270	107	7,213	75	773	835	184	274	547	1,518
1888	74	640	163	34	2,810	1,000	254	103	7,016	73	657	763	174	258	472	1,363
1889	66	777	186	31	3,379	1,163	340	148	8,417	87	674	923	225	336	542	1,516
1890	80	939	208	32	3,600	1,236	440	169	8,799	91	752	967	235	338	606	1,755
1891	69	829	164	26	3,098	1,147	395	155	7,847	87	630	860	218	304	535	1,573
1892	62	863	170	28	3,261	1,123	402	151	7,704	77	644	984	204	359	585	1,645
1893	60	900	171	25	3,160	1,108	364	137	7,870	95	609	949	212	315	545	1,549
1894	77	635	152	21	2,829	965	323	119	6,905	77	464	860	185	281	470	1,296
1895	75	692	149	21	3,013	1,015	324	128	7,233	78	569	903	183	292	499	1,414
1896	66	752	142	21	3,004	1,049	361	153	7,388	85	628	1,001	181	327	550	1,617
1897	70	684	157	31	3,112	1,071	363	161	7,395	96	588	1,114	194	364	558	1,598
1898	67	620	139	23	3,015	950	324	141	6,976	85	501	1,055	190	310	517	1,465
1899	90	616	148	25	3,302	1,148	384	157	8,216	95	617	1,073	220	363	568	1,660

Note appears at end of table

(continued)

TABLE Cg38–68   Patents granted, by industry of manufacture: 1840–1996 *Continued*

Secondary sectors (manufacturing)

	Transport		Metals				Computers and	Other office	Other	Food and		Rubber and	Nonmetallic			Other
	Ships	Other	Ferrous metals	Nonferrous	Fabricated	Instruments	peripherals	machinery	machinery	tobacco	Textiles	plastic	minerals	Paper	Wood	manufacturing
	Cg53	Cg54	Cg55	Cg56	Cg57	Cg58	Cg59	Cg60	Cg61	Cg62	Cg63	Cg64	Cg65	Cg66	Cg67	Cg68
Year	Number	Number	Number	Number	Number	Number	Number	Number	Number	Number	Number	Number	Number	Number	Number	Number
1900	96	630	170	35	3,375	1,215	380	154	8,642	119	625	1,156	221	390	580	1,719
1901	88	602	175	30	3,468	1,303	433	172	8,990	120	599	1,178	242	405	593	1,793
1902	95	740	212	36	3,675	1,384	463	171	9,275	132	673	1,253	270	429	607	2,013
1903	94	876	259	46	4,272	1,584	499	194	10,682	125	819	1,380	322	486	731	2,238
1904	75	886	272	34	4,126	1,561	545	219	10,359	122	741	1,385	307	495	697	2,065
1905	92	789	279	38	4,114	1,465	445	183	10,322	109	734	1,455	303	477	733	2,049
1906	101	909	292	44	4,266	1,548	496	207	10,802	121	757	1,493	333	471	796	2,203
1907	120	919	325	59	4,953	1,761	562	236	12,459	142	824	1,682	376	518	880	2,510
1908	95	823	305	50	4,335	1,628	564	222	11,055	127	887	1,588	323	537	800	2,339
1909	119	950	391	59	5,152	1,855	615	257	12,258	141	855	1,879	380	598	903	2,346
1910	107	819	322	58	4,904	1,752	576	249	12,270	140	800	1,698	375	517	874	2,294
1911	119	788	324	48	4,346	1,638	546	225	11,378	167	748	1,550	322	438	727	2,108
1912	122	861	349	65	4,714	1,844	570	235	12,583	167	844	1,858	361	525	811	2,364
1913	126	960	329	61	4,566	1,735	550	233	11,307	156	845	1,715	334	477	811	2,338
1914	172	1,003	352	70	5,135	2,068	648	267	13,430	154	1,044	1,985	395	587	850	2,648
1915	171	1,081	345	61	5,570	2,212	742	292	14,380	188	1,068	2,247	419	672	907	2,709
1916	178	982	339	62	5,629	2,291	765	292	14,371	199	1,034	2,290	427	674	957	3,022
1917	172	906	321	67	5,028	2,158	717	271	13,023	205	947	2,092	406	600	1,009	2,803
1918	205	835	273	64	4,553	2,102	682	244	12,428	180	939	1,927	366	538	935	2,741
1919	222	733	271	69	4,554	1,973	593	208	11,717	112	833	1,827	364	519	775	2,448
1920	159	690	303	93	4,688	1,894	561	206	12,046	125	834	1,841	379	538	855	2,610
1921	147	781	273	69	4,758	1,916	568	212	12,213	205	847	1,878	369	542	890	2,668
1922	125	801	261	65	4,890	1,896	583	230	12,567	164	821	1,973	398	582	856	2,625
1923	109	722	269	68	4,940	1,922	568	231	12,772	152	794	2,124	402	645	806	2,631
1924	119	770	302	82	5,276	2,241	642	260	13,984	202	988	2,094	408	647	820	2,982
1925	129	863	354	123	5,814	2,443	695	284	15,337	241	1,069	2,081	506	677	942	3,392
1926	104	810	319	93	5,401	2,327	631	272	14,051	194	985	2,036	488	658	900	3,075
1927	108	909	286	84	5,091	2,312	591	250	13,331	208	919	1,929	454	611	800	2,852
1928	112	760	312	105	5,105	2,224	583	250	13,574	179	924	1,942	457	639	873	2,765
1929	128	754	323	113	5,425	2,346	575	248	14,866	196	1,081	2,010	485	697	1,068	2,841
1930	153	724	329	104	5,381	2,266	597	250	15,142	197	1,012	1,889	487	616	968	2,731
1931	194	785	386	118	6,155	2,672	778	318	17,013	234	1,108	2,153	581	741	1,029	3,149
1932	150	819	386	138	6,119	2,833	787	323	17,599	280	1,086	2,229	632	751	1,086	3,069
1933	100	578	368	201	5,428	2,501	700	275	15,836	325	885	2,157	632	742	925	2,498
1934	70	534	308	143	4,815	2,579	643	264	14,336	287	887	1,983	579	692	814	2,271
1935	65	500	270	128	4,377	2,377	603	241	12,736	257	937	1,880	519	661	686	2,278
1936	74	543	295	174	4,197	2,349	625	230	12,366	224	912	1,750	490	583	648	2,176
1937	70	471	267	141	3,851	2,180	592	213	11,634	259	926	1,634	458	565	656	2,066
1938	75	450	269	163	3,897	2,170	559	208	11,621	283	967	1,648	465	593	698	2,129
1939	82	514	310	180	4,347	2,432	657	236	13,169	319	939	1,777	485	624	729	2,437
1940	78	507	298	183	4,242	2,454	664	243	13,015	303	849	1,612	502	549	686	2,334
1941	69	493	272	157	4,091	2,403	660	239	12,649	250	861	1,558	484	491	710	2,263
1942	80	356	269	152	3,805	2,321	621	219	11,671	269	793	1,563	464	495	644	1,911
1943	96	290	189	80	3,099	1,944	492	170	9,728	211	649	1,381	384	458	510	1,523
1944	96	252	164	64	2,780	1,780	465	160	9,004	191	582	1,142	325	366	404	1,219
1945	94	234	165	95	2,522	1,555	362	131	7,895	152	538	920	306	284	338	1,114
1946	81	209	125	60	1,987	1,342	336	98	6,186	107	471	738	260	208	253	987
1947	59	179	102	41	1,703	1,220	296	91	5,720	120	518	746	233	207	264	916
1948	52	180	144	52	2,102	1,510	328	102	6,628	149	581	883	269	227	347	1,222
1949	81	309	223	90	3,248	2,209	541	158	9,685	208	712	1,274	365	337	591	1,900
1950	104	376	230	93	4,007	2,747	727	214	12,010	263	867	1,647	408	477	805	2,556
1951	109	401	218	90	4,299	2,901	742	231	12,675	272	817	1,776	421	524	903	2,518
1952	85	368	191	78	4,331	2,950	690	243	13,240	277	805	1,725	417	514	850	2,530
1953	84	355	191	74	3,964	2,687	683	240	12,521	234	739	1,582	374	476	839	2,230
1954	76	248	180	79	3,155	2,288	541	178	10,481	198	626	1,320	328	383	601	1,685
1955	88	255	152	63	2,876	1,997	466	150	9,501	179	605	1,192	304	349	547	1,577
1956	98	373	257	125	4,239	2,938	709	242	14,278	273	790	1,843	471	551	719	2,293
1957	81	308	246	144	3,907	2,571	674	216	12,595	295	666	1,679	428	510	691	2,226
1958	99	370	284	154	4,294	3,019	792	249	13,712	293	684	1,791	473	525	770	2,325
1959	138	408	302	153	4,557	3,216	953	271	14,959	330	791	1,933	529	550	845	2,373

TABLE Cg38–68   Patents granted, by industry of manufacture: 1840–1996   *Continued*

							Secondary sectors (manufacturing)									
	Transport		Metals				Computers and peripherals	Other office machinery	Other machinery	Food and tobacco	Textiles	Rubber and plastic	Nonmetallic minerals	Paper	Wood	Other manufacturing
	Ships	Other	Ferrous metals	Nonferrous	Fabricated	Instruments										
	Cg53	Cg54	Cg55	Cg56	Cg57	Cg58	Cg59	Cg60	Cg61	Cg62	Cg63	Cg64	Cg65	Cg66	Cg67	Cg68
Year	Number	Number	Number	Number	Number	Number	Number	Number	Number	Number	Number	Number	Number	Number	Number	Number
1960	140	352	249	122	3,815	3,028	996	267	13,396	292	696	1,701	438	494	738	2,097
1961	180	354	254	137	4,005	3,097	1,004	258	13,739	291	740	1,818	471	526	720	2,148
1962	218	346	289	142	4,458	3,905	1,188	314	15,784	339	893	2,163	542	634	799	2,538
1963	209	294	252	120	3,753	3,019	973	279	13,354	266	729	1,809	477	539	670	2,227
1964	202	321	287	166	3,962	3,056	1,007	291	13,636	274	710	1,865	463	581	682	2,127
1965	203	435	378	183	5,347	4,210	1,381	379	17,779	305	810	2,389	604	723	893	2,780
1966	192	428	379	197	5,437	4,581	1,473	410	18,758	352	894	2,599	710	774	934	2,728
1967	201	374	392	213	5,281	4,265	1,300	372	18,193	353	914	2,630	695	789	924	2,594
1968	206	397	341	192	4,898	4,121	1,139	326	16,371	366	826	2,315	610	691	681	2,435
1969	201	397	387	182	5,178	5,076	1,430	367	17,872	393	963	2,488	725	699	736	2,848
1970	171	364	363	181	4,649	5,269	1,509	367	16,613	396	898	2,293	700	622	705	2,598
1971	250	492	456	238	5,865	6,403	2,004	505	21,045	477	1,082	2,833	853	808	915	3,424
1972	211	439	432	256	5,050	5,679	1,916	471	18,793	483	955	2,679	798	738	805	3,025
1973	240	493	425	259	5,410	5,941	1,822	458	19,481	422	1,001	2,593	774	747	840	3,174
1974	281	572	465	268	5,775	6,197	1,743	457	20,791	458	1,090	2,791	887	756	883	3,354
1975	230	473	400	206	5,008	5,611	1,495	414	18,094	499	928	2,630	795	736	751	3,125
1976	240	368	365	227	4,816	5,445	1,532	416	17,702	493	931	2,616	779	728	741	2,936
1977	191	342	352	211	4,631	5,098	1,532	402	16,613	409	871	2,259	749	622	690	2,725
1978	187	371	361	216	5,014	5,057	1,555	381	16,590	366	883	2,443	808	654	780	2,681
1979	109	249	268	164	3,561	4,044	1,191	290	12,237	308	618	1,773	550	507	483	2,177
1980	134	329	314	187	4,576	5,212	1,486	363	15,544	406	816	2,241	712	645	663	2,848
1981	173	340	331	174	4,917	5,569	1,534	387	16,520	433	886	2,424	749	674	627	2,883
1982	160	314	270	147	4,066	4,802	1,573	354	14,079	362	750	2,116	636	584	540	2,462
1983	131	262	303	202	4,040	4,770	1,487	373	14,080	351	781	2,104	650	595	534	2,326
1984	167	340	357	208	5,069	5,818	1,784	433	16,629	368	898	2,417	755	683	671	2,864
1985	192	335	350	201	5,131	6,224	2,000	481	17,650	442	987	2,554	790	759	695	3,108
1986	181	367	384	226	5,187	6,481	2,003	485	16,972	404	1,002	2,584	768	781	806	3,191
1987	257	420	409	223	5,916	7,909	2,432	550	18,946	432	1,185	2,927	894	859	944	3,708
1988	223	394	377	241	5,240	7,339	2,365	533	17,724	450	1,117	2,976	888	902	888	3,477
1989	260	445	457	310	6,386	9,307	3,099	666	20,600	621	1,351	3,573	1,078	1,121	1,078	4,466
1990	259	417	420	272	6,103	8,892	2,805	627	19,442	579	1,328	3,452	1,041	1,091	1,002	4,263
1991	259	443	435	283	6,230	9,434	3,050	657	20,461	572	1,449	3,593	1,186	1,121	1,047	4,623
1992	231	433	433	284	5,977	9,450	3,225	681	20,761	588	1,400	3,668	1,186	1,150	1,060	4,555
1993	229	441	404	261	5,803	9,671	3,533	671	20,324	533	1,315	3,683	1,174	1,169	981	4,439
1994	245	443	441	292	5,965	10,513	3,922	697	19,914	492	1,376	3,810	1,181	1,228	1,124	5,027
1995	239	448	411	269	5,637	10,581	4,240	697	19,043	517	1,406	3,765	1,066	1,226	1,085	4,830
1996	254	487	404	262	5,950	11,204	5,144	771	19,918	546	1,522	3,866	1,153	1,215	1,231	5,101

(Z) Less than 0.5.

Source

Data are based on the U.S. Historical Patent Set (USHiPS), downloaded from Daniel K. N. Johnson's Internet site.

Documentation

The data presented in Tables Cg38–107 are counts of U.S. patents. In this table, each series displays patents *created by* a particular economic sector ("industry of manufacture," or IOM), for use in a range of different applications. In Table Cg69–107, each series displays patents *used by* a particular economic sector ("sector of use," or SOU), as created by a range of different industries. The two tables combined show the supply of (IOM) and demand for (SOU) patented inventions. For example, a fertilizer to improve grain production would be listed here under the chemical series (because it is created by the chemical industry), while it would be listed under the agriculture series (because it is used by agriculture) in Table Cg69–107. A larger data set on the Internet site displays both aspects simultaneously.

The greatest benefit of using patent data to measure innovation or technological change is that each patent has achieved a degree of novelty and usefulness (as verified by the U.S. Patent Office). However, that benchmark level has varied over time and across industries, so these counts must be used with care. In addition, many innovations are never patented, and those that are patented vary widely in both private financial and social value.

To construct these series, two legal codes and two corresponding statistical tools were used. Recent data were prepared using only one statistical tool and U.S. Patent Office records. Since 1976, one or more International Patent Class (IPC) codes have been assigned to each patent, to document the type of technology protected. Because these legal codes did not correspond to economic definitions, the Yale Technology Concordance was developed as a statistical tool to count patents by industry. It uses the fact that the Canadian Patent Office assigned IPC, IOM, and SOU to more than 300,000 patent documents and calculates the probability that a given patent in an IPC will have a particular IOM or SOU. The original assignment of IOMs and SOUs by Canadian patent examiners assumed that service sectors could be users of patented technology, but not creators of it, so these tables remain consistent with that claim. See Robert E. Evenson, Samuel Kortum, et al., "Estimating Patent Counts by Industry Using the Yale-Canada Concordance," *Final Report to the National Science Foundation* (National Science Foundation, 1991), or for a more thorough discussion of tests and applications, see *Economic Systems Research* 9 (2) (1997): 161–192.

Prior to 1976, the United States had a separate legal code, a national patent classification system (U.S. Patent Classification (USPC)), which was

(continued)

TABLE Cg38–68   Patents granted, by industry of manufacture: 1840–1996   *Continued*

frequently updated and altered. The Wellesley Technology Concordance uses the overlap years of 1976–1996 to ascertain the probability that a given pre-1976 patent in a USPC would have a particular IPC. All pre-1976 U.S. patents were counted from U.S. Patent Office records and then assigned expected IPCs and processed through the Yale Technology Concordance to assign industries of manufacture and sectors of use. See Daniel K. N. Johnson, "150 Years of American Invention: Methodology and a First Geographical Application," Wellesley College Working Paper 99-01, January 1999.

The resulting data, then, as presented in these tables, are estimates of the number of patents granted in a given year that might be ascribed to each

IOM or SOU, if our current legal and economic classification system had been in place at the time of grant. The data are constructed to accord with the total patents recorded in a given year, so the only source of potential error is in the assignments to one sector or another. However, this does mean that inventions currently ascribed to one sector might be similarly interpreted in the historical series. For example, an adding device invented in 1995 might be listed as a "computer sector IOM"; in 1885, a similar device will be listed under the same IOM, although such a sector did not exist at the time. In defense of the data, very few such examples exist.

TABLE Cg69–107   Patents granted, by sector of use: 1840–1996

Contributed by Daniel K. N. Johnson

		Primary sectors (natural resources)			Secondary sectors (manufacturing)								
	Total	Agriculture	Forestry and fishing	Mining	Electrical appliances	Electrical lighting	Radio and television	Electrical industrial equipment	Other electrical equipment	Electronic equipment	Chemicals	Drugs	Petroleum
	Cg69	Cg70	Cg71	Cg72	Cg73	Cg74	Cg75	Cg76	Cg77	Cg78	Cg79	Cg80	Cg81
Year	Number	Number	Number	Number	Number	Number	Number	Number	Number	Number	Number	Number	Number
1840	459	27	7	13	6	(Z)	(Z)	2	1	5	13	1	1
1841	491	28	7	13	7	1	(Z)	2	2	4	10	1	1
1842	491	35	9	13	8	1	(Z)	2	2	4	13	1	2
1843	493	39	10	15	8	(Z)	(Z)	2	1	4	14	2	2
1844	482	37	7	11	10	1	(Z)	2	1	4	13	2	1
1845	479	27	8	12	9	(Z)	(Z)	2	1	6	12	3	2
1846	569	45	7	13	10	(Z)	(Z)	2	2	7	14	2	3
1847	497	35	7	11	7	1	(Z)	2	2	5	15	2	2
1848	589	49	9	13	9	1	1	3	3	8	16	2	3
1849	990	74	12	21	13	1	1	4	4	14	21	3	4
1850	886	75	13	22	11	1	1	5	3	13	24	3	4
1851	760	39	9	14	11	1	1	4	3	13	18	2	2
1852	890	69	11	20	10	1	1	5	4	13	22	2	7
1853	846	72	11	17	10	1	1	4	4	12	18	3	5
1854	1,762	115	27	41	25	3	1	8	6	22	38	4	10
1855	1,895	138	24	44	30	3	1	8	7	23	41	5	12
1856	2,325	210	36	42	34	3	2	11	7	27	46	6	16
1857	2,689	281	35	52	42	3	2	9	8	30	54	7	24
1858	3,465	349	49	69	68	6	4	16	13	45	70	8	32
1859	4,183	406	56	87	79	6	4	18	14	57	108	14	41
1860	4,378	478	60	100	77	7	4	20	14	52	111	14	28
1861	3,033	329	47	56	61	5	4	14	8	35	68	9	20
1862	3,223	260	35	65	63	10	3	11	9	36	87	11	27
1863	3,791	275	48	73	67	10	4	16	13	44	106	15	33
1864	4,654	358	64	102	86	8	4	18	15	49	136	22	31
1865	6,110	485	68	195	107	12	6	23	21	70	168	28	50
1866	8,896	735	122	235	153	17	8	37	32	96	250	36	80
1867	12,310	1,072	179	241	211	21	13	53	47	142	308	50	96
1868	12,594	1,206	201	235	206	24	12	53	42	139	290	52	70
1869	12,980	1,229	174	231	228	25	13	55	43	138	310	57	87
1870	12,192	1,002	155	216	231	25	12	59	46	143	282	52	84
1871	11,717	869	172	196	235	22	12	61	48	141	251	51	92
1872	12,269	795	154	214	259	24	13	63	47	166	266	57	90
1873	11,747	712	138	212	228	22	13	52	41	154	244	50	80
1874	12,331	787	150	212	200	23	16	60	43	177	253	48	89
1875	13,375	786	161	231	237	27	18	66	54	197	278	48	104
1876	14,259	999	179	267	239	30	20	74	59	208	271	58	90
1877	12,991	949	176	229	212	26	17	62	44	180	265	54	86
1878	12,413	898	153	232	202	29	19	63	45	193	250	57	73
1879	12,215	847	136	207	200	32	21	70	47	206	257	54	75

Note appears at end of table

TABLE Cg69–107   Patents granted, by sector of use: 1840–1996 *Continued*

	Total	Primary sectors (natural resources)			Secondary sectors (manufacturing)								
		Agriculture	Forestry and fishing	Mining	Electrical appliances	Electrical lighting	Radio and television	Electrical industrial equipment	Other electrical equipment	Electronic equipment	Chemicals	Drugs	Petroleum
	Cg69	Cg70	Cg71	Cg72	Cg73	Cg74	Cg75	Cg76	Cg77	Cg78	Cg79	Cg80	Cg81
Year	Number	Number	Number	Number	Number	Number	Number	Number	Number	Number	Number	Number	Number
1880	12,985	850	143	242	192	36	33	101	56	293	285	54	68
1881	15,602	983	177	290	238	50	43	135	68	394	356	74	96
1882	18,182	1,151	187	333	294	82	55	221	100	464	410	98	93
1883	21,225	1,307	212	360	287	76	53	264	139	515	439	102	142
1884	19,230	1,099	171	339	230	59	47	210	131	461	404	84	115
1885	23,401	1,474	232	377	319	70	55	246	140	558	465	97	134
1886	21,878	1,396	245	343	313	65	57	253	135	512	417	86	104
1887	20,536	1,267	212	282	273	56	50	216	138	486	350	76	86
1888	19,710	1,078	209	280	262	54	48	272	167	492	367	78	88
1889	23,443	1,181	222	348	328	79	56	354	217	525	479	109	154
1890	25,434	1,345	236	371	357	79	67	419	211	669	486	105	119
1891	22,421	1,139	222	331	314	70	60	381	155	579	419	95	96
1892	22,744	1,191	234	347	305	77	66	344	158	612	413	95	117
1893	22,832	1,112	212	311	311	81	67	389	154	635	474	104	125
1894	19,899	890	187	312	261	64	55	373	140	561	440	100	104
1895	20,969	934	185	328	269	67	52	314	130	578	425	106	116
1896	21,917	891	194	323	301	75	61	320	136	624	458	116	127
1897	22,164	904	211	321	293	86	60	298	150	662	466	120	157
1898	20,466	875	189	278	272	66	50	258	121	453	483	132	176
1899	23,356	978	210	341	283	75	66	290	155	561	585	163	288
1900	24,707	1,037	234	373	304	92	84	352	178	655	663	176	272
1901	25,613	1,023	231	392	330	101	90	389	185	722	637	165	231
1902	27,143	1,039	253	403	346	96	82	416	199	752	661	180	218
1903	31,070	1,291	291	480	384	114	103	513	234	862	745	172	247
1904	30,350	1,225	277	454	361	101	115	488	200	961	644	171	224
1905	29,850	1,268	297	475	329	92	106	482	172	854	694	190	232
1906	31,260	1,294	332	469	357	86	105	454	180	905	697	169	224
1907	35,958	1,389	371	562	465	102	129	616	209	1,042	791	188	230
1908	32,815	1,376	370	503	412	111	139	534	203	986	775	203	217
1909	36,704	1,393	332	526	475	136	141	632	238	1,093	843	211	229
1910	35,255	1,397	357	543	470	144	138	593	208	1,030	828	203	250
1911	33,022	1,272	349	532	430	145	120	596	188	969	824	202	219
1912	36,444	1,366	365	582	464	167	151	574	209	1,042	912	234	231
1913	34,073	1,271	348	541	443	152	127	520	193	899	891	238	219
1914	40,154	1,520	391	610	521	182	173	662	218	1,218	1,031	254	297
1915	43,346	1,500	396	666	572	199	192	732	268	1,405	1,080	263	273
1916	44,091	1,577	464	676	578	207	208	743	283	1,441	1,018	235	284
1917	41,038	1,402	417	603	529	208	216	802	263	1,464	986	220	228
1918	38,544	1,317	364	580	469	194	193	753	257	1,303	931	200	241
1919	36,787	1,087	333	611	420	190	195	744	250	1,274	986	204	211
1920	37,088	1,093	341	612	469	187	197	725	277	1,224	942	173	228
1921	37,864	1,039	337	634	495	178	195	696	296	1,210	968	194	259
1922	38,478	983	329	657	487	201	205	668	268	1,190	1,088	244	347
1923	38,766	1,051	424	647	520	199	197	657	242	1,276	1,019	255	290
1924	42,703	1,127	401	762	557	236	221	880	368	1,589	1,106	254	343
1925	47,593	1,250	429	806	660	286	285	974	361	2,087	1,227	282	340
1926	43,816	1,094	369	776	571	244	266	866	340	1,836	1,213	295	390
1927	41,937	1,060	333	767	536	252	272	883	313	1,876	1,142	283	324
1928	42,556	895	258	771	603	286	289	1,032	326	2,024	1,290	359	400
1929	45,515	1,056	323	806	627	277	303	1,061	311	2,117	1,426	381	448
1930	45,386	1,060	316	850	587	246	314	1,056	314	2,131	1,526	380	483
1931	51,886	1,219	393	1,034	677	290	381	1,130	338	2,435	1,859	476	608
1932	53,733	1,297	408	1,093	689	313	425	1,205	367	2,549	2,177	673	664
1933	49,007	1,134	330	942	687	323	410	1,258	364	2,542	2,168	472	706
1934	44,643	863	274	769	605	328	421	1,136	339	2,315	1,992	621	690
1935	40,868	774	265	766	575	311	387	850	301	2,094	1,911	654	552
1936	40,017	762	226	798	563	276	394	814	283	2,166	1,927	660	590
1937	37,956	708	216	734	500	264	399	829	268	2,093	1,835	658	549
1938	38,254	688	220	795	470	268	378	836	259	2,102	1,883	685	503
1939	43,288	860	294	918	588	325	473	1,020	326	2,563	2,081	783	523

(continued)

TABLE Cg69–107   Patents granted, by sector of use: 1840–1996   Continued

	Primary sectors (natural resources)				Secondary sectors (manufacturing)								
	Total	Agriculture	Forestry and fishing	Mining	Electrical appliances	Electrical lighting	Radio and television	Electrical industrial equipment	Other electrical equipment	Electronic equipment	Chemicals	Drugs	Petroleum
	Cg69	Cg70	Cg71	Cg72	Cg73	Cg74	Cg75	Cg76	Cg77	Cg78	Cg79	Cg80	Cg81
Year	Number	Number	Number	Number	Number	Number	Number	Number	Number	Number	Number	Number	Number
1940	42,502	882	295	950	567	309	477	989	306	2,602	2,122	762	524
1941	41,380	843	306	823	613	307	478	1,081	316	2,643	1,900	744	446
1942	38,666	706	224	765	562	298	452	1,097	312	2,559	1,917	678	526
1943	31,214	673	193	700	427	204	287	750	239	1,639	1,697	634	449
1944	28,136	559	164	617	327	170	247	639	190	1,477	1,621	644	444
1945	25,790	433	118	499	279	157	205	574	185	1,366	1,932	767	401
1946	21,822	312	105	399	248	181	248	549	162	1,554	1,545	666	298
1947	20,207	349	107	340	257	178	225	618	155	1,502	1,333	626	277
1948	24,087	403	154	376	308	240	261	803	199	1,706	1,603	720	275
1949	35,287	736	274	556	442	330	403	1,119	275	2,476	2,274	1,037	348
1950	43,154	1,132	413	685	583	330	516	1,155	313	3,098	2,522	1,224	370
1951	44,402	1,080	438	780	534	298	490	1,049	315	3,022	2,668	1,216	415
1952	43,688	1,141	471	869	544	297	445	931	330	2,672	2,493	1,022	431
1953	40,582	1,070	343	866	545	259	396	911	321	2,425	2,232	1,011	431
1954	33,896	885	269	755	441	225	333	835	281	2,017	2,028	994	383
1955	30,525	866	293	667	390	220	310	736	248	1,882	1,651	793	337
1956	46,910	1,219	435	1,032	575	348	491	1,225	341	3,127	2,916	1,473	640
1957	42,803	1,056	389	921	528	364	476	1,183	324	2,895	2,752	1,384	434
1958	48,419	1,094	345	999	534	402	612	1,274	399	3,567	3,337	1,636	541
1959	52,564	1,090	363	1,138	610	465	716	1,345	422	4,087	3,617	1,609	765
1960	47,218	971	296	959	524	396	646	1,159	386	3,817	3,090	1,393	603
1961	48,448	1,039	315	1,064	532	315	542	1,123	412	3,621	3,456	1,603	522
1962	55,785	1,185	389	1,255	608	359	589	1,298	465	4,050	4,000	1,913	500
1963	45,798	1,062	303	1,105	518	279	433	1,038	373	3,123	3,133	1,587	410
1964	47,485	1,062	307	1,077	481	295	455	1,192	374	3,408	3,242	1,857	429
1965	62,977	1,263	380	1,432	634	428	694	1,832	567	5,176	4,172	1,993	536
1966	68,631	1,245	353	1,434	677	479	760	1,953	668	5,631	5,236	2,638	654
1967	65,921	1,253	361	1,600	649	466	706	1,788	642	5,108	5,365	2,633	578
1968	59,262	1,068	298	1,484	600	446	670	1,518	570	4,615	4,768	2,074	559
1969	67,757	1,236	323	1,522	650	500	786	1,862	745	5,779	5,487	2,693	679
1970	64,588	1,237	310	1,338	588	478	840	1,812	718	6,078	4,957	2,519	624
1971	78,553	1,447	376	1,578	728	565	1,036	2,213	816	7,543	4,900	2,276	681
1972	75,070	1,343	364	1,453	642	484	920	1,815	736	6,420	6,831	3,541	755
1973	74,484	1,390	432	1,558	661	521	951	1,839	698	6,388	5,438	2,824	698
1974	78,075	1,448	449	1,611	650	506	944	1,782	748	6,167	5,967	3,241	769
1975	70,988	1,382	384	1,382	550	446	858	1,466	716	5,542	5,937	3,507	706
1976	70,726	1,405	401	1,356	525	424	868	1,480	729	5,705	6,320	3,583	753
1977	65,713	1,449	371	1,328	479	406	830	1,445	722	5,481	5,453	2,880	749
1978	66,664	1,370	329	1,396	523	406	798	1,445	740	5,280	5,650	2,747	789
1979	49,278	1,155	293	951	394	317	642	1,066	495	4,023	3,965	1,962	605
1980	62,246	1,458	370	1,253	495	379	812	1,283	660	5,078	4,824	2,444	720
1981	66,166	1,432	343	1,413	505	394	823	1,436	676	5,212	5,425	2,633	779
1982	58,224	1,257	287	1,105	487	407	864	1,454	597	5,089	4,470	2,194	695
1983	57,323	1,104	265	1,201	475	379	845	1,344	626	4,891	4,465	1,947	734
1984	67,792	1,355	359	1,536	583	440	930	1,634	688	5,759	4,870	2,233	781
1985	72,086	1,460	375	1,494	609	475	1,145	1,686	755	6,608	5,076	2,298	743
1986	71,061	1,404	387	1,461	564	466	1,206	1,629	684	6,928	4,480	2,174	628
1987	83,188	1,492	435	1,754	673	579	1,596	2,130	803	8,811	4,913	2,395	631
1988	78,146	1,516	435	1,473	604	544	1,394	1,812	779	8,183	4,827	2,357	597
1989	95,737	1,906	554	1,781	714	644	1,802	2,176	924	10,359	5,825	2,989	748
1990	90,671	1,875	491	1,590	675	629	1,587	1,972	871	9,632	5,726	2,974	685
1991	96,750	1,851	497	1,664	722	669	1,774	2,032	930	10,710	6,228	3,060	692
1992	97,728	1,842	511	1,649	675	638	1,817	2,030	968	10,916	6,602	3,253	656
1993	98,618	1,824	493	1,617	683	605	1,918	2,046	1,017	11,161	6,717	3,539	658
1994	101,796	1,847	531	1,718	727	620	2,068	2,094	1,051	12,823	6,209	3,190	675
1995	101,629	1,872	459	1,576	705	638	2,152	2,069	1,072	13,495	5,870	3,408	610
1996	109,949	2,103	520	1,607	750	653	2,381	2,317	1,205	15,104	5,902	3,751	556

TABLE Cg69–107   Patents granted, by sector of use: 1840–1996   *Continued*

							Secondary sectors (manufacturing)						
	Transport				Metals				Computers and peripherals	Other office machinery	Other machinery	Food and tobacco	Textiles
	Aerospace	Motor vehicles	Ships	Other	Ferrous metals	Nonferrous	Fabricated	Instruments					
	Cg82	Cg83	Cg84	Cg85	Cg86	Cg87	Cg88	Cg89	Cg90	Cg91	Cg92	Cg93	Cg94
Year	Number	Number	Number	Number	Number	Number	Number	TCHNumber	Number	Number	Number	Number	Number
1840	3	20	7	9	6	2	36	7	3	1	69	10	29
1841	3	24	10	9	6	3	39	7	2	1	91	14	34
1842	4	21	9	4	5	2	41	7	3	1	87	12	39
1843	3	22	6	6	8	4	45	7	3	1	80	9	34
1844	4	18	6	4	9	4	38	6	3	1	79	13	37
1845	3	18	6	6	5	3	38	8	2	1	72	12	43
1846	4	30	5	9	9	3	47	11	3	1	87	14	44
1847	3	34	8	6	7	4	31	7	3	1	83	9	33
1848	2	29	8	5	11	5	50	7	4	1	90	13	37
1849	6	55	9	18	14	6	78	15	9	2	161	24	81
1850	6	51	10	10	12	6	65	15	8	3	134	26	62
1851	4	45	8	17	15	6	63	14	9	2	118	15	61
1852	5	59	8	12	14	6	69	18	8	2	143	18	68
1853	6	38	12	7	12	5	65	14	9	3	145	18	65
1854	9	94	21	20	23	9	133	27	17	5	305	37	136
1855	13	98	25	17	23	10	138	28	15	5	336	37	150
1856	14	126	26	23	32	13	171	39	20	6	384	49	158
1857	18	147	31	24	46	16	196	47	21	7	453	52	174
1858	19	183	39	58	39	16	235	69	25	8	571	78	228
1859	25	219	43	75	47	20	269	69	29	10	677	103	250
1860	24	224	41	71	49	19	297	73	29	10	694	113	263
1861	18	168	25	40	38	14	195	48	19	7	476	79	211
1862	23	169	39	49	32	14	227	48	22	7	483	95	205
1863	26	204	48	55	44	20	293	57	21	7	568	98	247
1864	24	244	46	64	59	28	335	63	27	10	715	138	339
1865	34	326	57	99	85	39	432	94	39	13	945	169	394
1866	48	505	66	130	109	50	625	129	47	18	1,327	250	590
1867	68	780	96	222	154	65	847	191	70	23	1,755	325	718
1868	68	786	77	204	146	63	880	186	72	25	1,846	350	780
1869	69	793	93	254	170	75	885	181	69	25	1,898	361	733
1870	68	751	81	189	149	70	862	178	70	26	1,862	320	705
1871	63	777	82	214	149	61	808	167	74	24	1,809	307	720
1872	65	814	89	247	157	65	813	185	81	26	1,860	341	842
1873	67	739	85	298	145	57	794	169	79	26	1,769	319	859
1874	72	848	82	365	149	65	840	196	101	28	1,861	294	820
1875	79	850	81	300	151	60	940	232	107	34	1,957	362	842
1876	80	875	91	308	160	64	976	237	117	38	2,056	388	895
1877	78	830	88	233	145	60	882	210	96	36	1,884	390	802
1878	73	825	69	216	124	50	822	214	106	36	1,774	371	781
1879	74	832	64	234	124	53	753	208	91	34	1,791	354	831
1880	76	860	77	286	139	62	803	243	111	36	1,903	366	826
1881	79	1,020	87	382	161	66	975	276	134	40	2,198	450	1,095
1882	100	1,206	94	554	173	70	1,114	325	162	49	2,642	496	1,126
1883	104	1,521	129	611	252	97	1,331	381	196	61	3,114	498	1,247
1884	90	1,452	94	557	217	93	1,196	367	178	58	2,861	456	1,165
1885	120	1,652	123	645	288	106	1,546	446	225	74	3,416	547	1,411
1886	105	1,505	102	635	240	91	1,387	447	238	77	3,046	520	1,330
1887	98	1,401	100	614	235	87	1,324	414	256	77	2,796	441	1,310
1888	101	1,400	111	595	248	97	1,287	379	242	75	2,752	413	1,271
1889	115	1,614	102	754	298	121	1,573	431	323	110	3,343	510	1,331
1890	120	1,793	121	898	277	111	1,627	469	436	135	3,476	534	1,308
1891	111	1,495	107	805	235	95	1,381	450	384	122	3,162	486	1,228
1892	107	1,573	102	829	244	111	1,410	423	393	122	3,082	505	1,166
1893	118	1,696	102	880	243	108	1,431	421	361	111	3,179	518	1,207
1894	99	1,456	116	680	235	103	1,265	362	314	95	2,814	463	901
1895	106	1,677	116	724	200	95	1,313	375	311	101	2,959	486	1,128
1896	103	1,755	108	772	193	87	1,311	394	336	108	3,081	514	1,212
1897	116	1,800	113	703	212	101	1,344	401	339	114	3,117	568	1,127
1898	111	1,706	107	623	193	83	1,272	337	299	97	2,914	508	1,074
1899	120	1,780	134	607	219	97	1,451	408	370	121	3,355	557	1,280

(continued)

TABLE Cg69-107   Patents granted, by sector of use: 1840-1996   *Continued*

							Secondary sectors (manufacturing)						
	Transport				Metals				Computers				
	Aerospace	Motor vehicles	Ships	Other	Ferrous metals	Nonferrous	Fabricated	Instruments	and peripherals	Other office machinery	Other machinery	Food and tobacco	Textiles
	Cg82	Cg83	Cg84	Cg85	Cg86	Cg87	Cg88	Cg89	Cg90	Cg91	Cg92	Cg93	Cg94
Year	Number	Number	Number	Number	Number	Number	Number	Number	Number	Number	Number	Number	Number
1900	130	1,942	139	625	247	116	1,490	429	366	118	3,563	636	1,281
1901	129	1,966	132	607	275	123	1,577	465	423	133	3,810	663	1,279
1902	146	2,025	141	738	315	152	1,594	490	464	135	3,875	713	1,300
1903	158	2,228	146	880	358	189	1,863	557	485	148	4,492	756	1,514
1904	152	2,222	125	915	296	133	1,775	590	532	171	4,369	722	1,473
1905	162	2,254	134	831	334	164	1,780	528	425	138	4,267	708	1,316
1906	173	2,338	153	931	327	162	1,795	568	469	154	4,418	746	1,361
1907	234	2,807	180	939	381	193	2,069	646	540	187	5,235	847	1,623
1908	244	2,509	151	863	375	196	1,822	605	548	179	4,566	805	1,562
1909	274	2,803	178	964	436	208	2,209	693	601	203	5,059	923	1,645
1910	267	2,704	163	790	399	200	2,149	662	568	200	5,093	835	1,588
1911	411	2,673	178	769	357	175	1,922	635	534	176	4,787	823	1,531
1912	439	3,038	179	825	403	193	2,137	701	553	187	5,165	917	1,896
1913	336	2,858	172	924	363	186	1,967	656	537	186	4,749	827	1,671
1914	343	3,550	226	1,033	414	206	2,242	802	632	213	5,529	946	2,120
1915	341	4,021	234	1,122	409	198	2,420	864	739	233	6,107	1,087	2,255
1916	349	4,197	248	1,038	408	210	2,390	902	764	237	6,258	1,090	2,143
1917	334	3,945	230	953	372	187	2,169	840	716	217	5,694	1,009	1,967
1918	351	3,735	249	878	367	184	2,042	828	685	199	5,325	924	1,934
1919	416	3,614	264	805	410	209	2,120	780	597	171	5,117	787	1,619
1920	410	3,597	213	737	444	229	2,131	743	561	164	5,199	818	1,751
1921	380	3,839	205	835	399	196	2,204	757	575	174	5,258	943	1,841
1922	361	3,901	185	847	404	199	2,292	780	587	185	5,407	940	1,743
1923	320	3,974	177	775	447	214	2,295	764	576	186	5,528	1,009	1,746
1924	367	3,980	190	830	514	258	2,459	890	649	205	6,027	1,088	2,048
1925	406	4,225	211	944	624	332	2,663	974	694	221	6,489	1,171	2,198
1926	324	3,934	181	875	463	233	2,486	898	626	209	5,903	1,057	2,046
1927	335	3,769	177	963	410	202	2,289	919	584	193	5,769	1,078	1,864
1928	328	3,483	183	824	507	259	2,389	886	588	196	5,754	1,044	2,062
1929	427	3,632	207	835	558	289	2,566	922	584	198	6,176	1,135	2,374
1930	569	3,563	229	801	563	291	2,559	904	613	200	6,323	1,114	2,178
1931	641	4,099	280	902	628	332	2,905	1,100	799	254	7,159	1,234	2,292
1932	636	4,146	238	913	647	344	2,991	1,184	810	256	7,341	1,378	2,409
1933	456	3,784	181	672	649	370	2,802	1,123	743	229	6,619	1,422	2,047
1934	347	3,266	143	606	549	296	2,573	1,080	685	220	6,019	1,336	1,953
1935	340	2,992	126	575	473	256	2,190	979	620	191	5,330	1,240	2,108
1936	302	3,022	126	628	486	282	2,130	977	648	184	5,094	1,097	2,097
1937	296	2,835	127	562	431	247	1,938	901	616	177	4,808	1,129	2,027
1938	338	2,810	130	532	449	270	1,993	894	588	174	4,834	1,180	1,997
1939	363	3,206	147	601	515	291	2,233	1,011	702	200	5,561	1,314	2,108
1940	343	3,118	136	590	496	298	2,189	1,002	704	200	5,509	1,190	2,000
1941	322	3,038	134	570	484	278	2,142	981	705	204	5,482	1,097	1,922
1942	309	2,546	139	434	492	267	2,075	966	665	183	4,987	1,109	1,729
1943	280	2,017	142	345	325	164	1,698	805	511	138	4,015	943	1,411
1944	290	1,850	136	309	322	159	1,639	762	488	132	3,707	826	1,193
1945	334	1,721	129	280	309	178	1,517	656	378	108	3,344	650	1,069
1946	332	1,428	112	241	228	126	1,186	580	356	83	2,712	484	919
1947	272	1,268	87	205	195	103	1,009	506	322	80	2,447	503	949
1948	291	1,615	87	215	233	124	1,218	605	354	87	2,881	583	1,077
1949	421	2,311	141	356	361	198	1,823	912	577	134	4,230	868	1,394
1950	469	2,783	172	434	409	220	2,114	1,094	771	182	5,192	1,164	1,624
1951	441	2,956	171	460	378	211	2,198	1,149	796	199	5,452	1,242	1,573
1952	421	2,906	151	434	390	198	2,171	1,170	717	199	5,805	1,262	1,576
1953	403	2,696	149	417	353	187	1,982	1,069	707	199	5,511	1,140	1,486
1954	353	2,189	127	295	335	180	1,694	894	572	151	4,489	950	1,230
1955	292	2,042	130	299	289	158	1,506	794	500	127	3,986	835	1,169
1956	436	3,098	162	438	524	309	2,384	1,184	766	200	6,018	1,290	1,544
1957	353	2,770	131	370	542	325	2,163	1,049	733	182	5,335	1,268	1,296
1958	421	3,238	155	436	595	373	2,367	1,176	876	213	6,039	1,302	1,364
1959	404	3,477	206	480	563	349	2,494	1,276	1,079	234	6,495	1,376	1,656

TABLE Cg69-107   Patents granted, by sector of use: 1840-1996   *Continued*

	Secondary sectors (manufacturing)												
	Transport				Metals								
	Aerospace	Motor vehicles	Ships	Other	Ferrous metals	Nonferrous	Fabricated	Instruments	Computers and peripherals	Other office machinery	Other machinery	Food and tobacco	Textiles
	Cg82	Cg83	Cg84	Cg85	Cg86	Cg87	Cg88	Cg89	Cg90	Cg91	Cg92	Cg93	Cg94
Year	Number	Number	Number	Number	Number	Number	Number	Number	Number	Number	Number	Number	Number
1960	659	3,101	204	415	458	284	2,092	1,257	1,126	228	5,971	1,223	1,458
1961	597	3,114	251	419	484	293	2,203	1,297	1,139	231	6,017	1,260	1,522
1962	634	3,331	279	419	564	328	2,543	1,584	1,338	277	6,799	1,480	1,802
1963	518	2,643	253	344	481	279	2,105	1,204	1,070	229	5,604	1,252	1,565
1964	546	2,742	258	374	565	333	2,262	1,277	1,159	246	5,770	1,318	1,438
1965	629	3,786	282	517	797	423	3,014	1,771	1,596	322	7,622	1,599	1,626
1966	634	3,896	273	516	758	446	3,170	1,924	1,703	361	7,884	1,725	1,874
1967	573	3,615	267	447	807	474	2,996	1,734	1,506	324	7,329	1,730	1,947
1968	515	3,420	266	465	701	424	2,768	1,659	1,322	281	6,773	1,586	1,712
1969	561	3,690	268	470	811	471	3,112	2,074	1,721	318	7,308	1,679	1,981
1970	504	3,496	232	440	759	438	2,872	2,132	1,792	315	6,781	1,610	1,741
1971	618	4,402	333	584	1,028	567	3,639	2,567	2,342	440	8,606	1,978	2,046
1972	541	4,009	271	524	918	578	3,387	2,315	2,265	397	7,370	1,857	1,960
1973	596	4,468	306	579	949	571	3,395	2,330	2,115	393	7,907	1,797	1,905
1974	555	4,773	367	654	1,011	596	3,593	2,421	2,013	390	8,262	1,895	2,021
1975	486	4,405	309	547	837	498	3,066	2,146	1,719	347	7,194	1,886	1,787
1976	508	4,073	319	457	801	524	2,849	2,136	1,779	358	7,008	1,859	1,849
1977	453	3,792	259	419	830	512	2,792	1,978	1,777	338	6,418	1,543	1,605
1978	432	4,102	258	447	758	480	2,941	2,026	1,817	321	6,525	1,517	1,680
1979	319	2,995	154	302	580	364	2,139	1,574	1,389	246	4,792	1,198	1,114
1980	411	3,715	197	398	697	432	2,668	1,958	1,722	311	6,172	1,521	1,463
1981	435	3,886	238	412	726	441	2,838	2,063	1,777	322	6,492	1,614	1,581
1982	340	3,480	233	375	619	372	2,364	1,798	1,830	307	5,621	1,409	1,332
1983	385	3,505	205	327	671	415	2,526	1,807	1,743	318	5,505	1,343	1,428
1984	465	4,370	253	420	758	467	2,963	2,147	2,072	367	6,898	1,508	1,576
1985	449	4,418	291	418	773	478	3,075	2,294	2,312	411	7,431	1,739	1,708
1986	457	4,258	263	444	806	498	3,126	2,293	2,348	409	6,941	1,661	1,628
1987	576	5,106	361	519	815	492	3,377	2,798	2,871	476	7,912	1,823	1,829
1988	551	4,763	325	489	813	500	3,071	2,618	2,812	467	7,279	1,833	1,628
1989	615	5,533	369	555	871	555	3,636	3,269	3,689	581	8,452	2,274	1,972
1990	558	5,274	377	510	827	522	3,440	3,060	3,340	542	7,828	2,170	1,925
1991	617	5,654	374	547	855	541	3,572	3,236	3,639	590	8,349	2,226	2,028
1992	677	5,441	348	537	802	525	3,568	3,172	3,820	612	8,401	2,266	1,959
1993	612	5,262	346	547	815	529	3,495	3,222	4,236	621	8,255	2,212	1,881
1994	613	5,132	354	547	834	561	3,559	3,383	4,827	652	8,003	2,155	1,929
1995	565	5,165	340	551	756	508	3,364	3,409	5,195	669	7,602	2,211	1,937
1996	580	5,704	366	601	736	490	3,422	3,645	6,291	766	8,168	2,296	2,032

(continued)

TABLE Cg69–107 Patents granted, by sector of use: 1840–1996 *Continued*

	Secondary sectors (manufacturing)					Tertiary sectors (services)							
	Rubber and plastic	Nonmetallic minerals	Paper	Wood	Other manufacturing	Construction	Transportation and storage	Communication	Trade	Finance	Government and education	Health	Other services
	Cg95	Cg96	Cg97	Cg98	Cg99	Cg100	Cg101	Cg102	Cg103	Cg104	Cg105	Cg106	Cg107
Year	Number	Number	Number	Number	Number	Number	Number	Number	Number	Number	Number	Number	Number
1840	9	4	11	15	7	44	12	24	9	4	8	17	14
1841	10	6	10	13	8	42	10	24	11	3	6	14	14
1842	10	4	11	15	7	36	7	27	9	4	6	15	15
1843	9	6	12	12	9	37	7	24	11	4	5	18	14
1844	12	6	12	11	9	38	7	24	11	4	6	17	14
1845	9	7	14	12	10	42	8	22	10	3	5	18	17
1846	10	7	11	13	9	49	9	26	12	4	4	24	18
1847	10	7	16	15	9	42	9	18	9	3	7	20	15
1848	16	7	13	19	10	52	9	23	12	4	8	17	18
1849	17	7	19	35	20	78	20	36	21	7	20	33	28
1850	18	8	24	30	17	70	15	32	19	8	14	25	25
1851	19	9	22	26	17	58	12	23	17	7	11	21	24
1852	17	15	25	28	18	63	15	26	21	9	11	23	24
1853	17	9	25	31	17	57	16	31	20	6	13	25	27
1854	41	23	52	63	35	141	31	57	40	16	35	45	49
1855	38	22	47	61	36	159	35	63	44	14	47	46	51
1856	56	30	54	76	43	193	39	66	54	20	61	59	72
1857	57	24	74	79	52	216	53	71	64	24	55	65	78
1858	62	31	85	102	59	274	76	103	96	35	61	78	106
1859	93	43	87	111	75	327	101	134	116	34	84	120	137
1860	95	45	91	118	78	348	93	146	122	39	84	112	137
1861	53	22	60	68	60	237	63	87	88	27	94	81	100
1862	57	30	62	69	59	239	70	108	100	27	173	96	103
1863	82	36	97	88	67	282	77	127	106	32	163	132	111
1864	94	48	119	98	84	339	92	151	132	40	176	154	143
1865	129	61	152	138	120	447	124	198	180	53	156	202	192
1866	207	87	195	217	188	715	189	286	266	76	152	327	298
1867	281	127	248	342	265	1,094	298	363	385	120	161	441	446
1868	282	133	239	342	263	1,093	287	361	395	114	163	453	462
1869	256	134	251	362	302	1,177	296	380	391	120	210	442	469
1870	253	137	249	389	258	1,142	265	377	394	113	170	382	433
1871	228	114	246	369	247	1,020	247	373	365	105	186	399	418
1872	263	140	249	363	259	1,111	291	351	373	112	172	417	442
1873	235	125	238	355	272	1,091	296	334	369	110	169	374	431
1874	241	135	266	346	306	1,107	307	335	386	117	184	390	440
1875	277	134	294	417	323	1,231	323	392	455	142	219	461	510
1876	272	146	291	424	349	1,329	357	398	498	151	233	488	550
1877	260	125	280	358	321	1,200	311	371	447	147	211	428	506
1878	253	124	282	333	309	1,113	301	371	420	132	211	429	468
1879	258	125	291	301	316	1,053	301	364	406	125	212	424	454
1880	269	125	318	308	347	1,078	325	414	428	135	211	416	475
1881	311	148	331	399	439	1,268	374	483	518	150	237	522	563
1882	342	181	371	447	467	1,538	451	558	595	190	250	579	623
1883	417	210	441	528	534	1,881	566	609	678	230	331	674	701
1884	398	194	408	451	513	1,757	520	533	636	202	297	571	625
1885	437	207	495	625	592	2,131	629	662	744	248	347	769	763
1886	417	215	503	566	569	1,982	602	609	720	245	324	709	769
1887	361	177	463	533	581	1,890	592	567	694	240	334	707	752
1888	353	167	409	470	508	1,783	578	563	644	238	317	636	677
1889	441	237	603	538	569	2,070	684	716	759	281	309	768	790
1890	462	242	678	599	672	2,309	751	733	827	314	381	816	893
1891	418	211	613	512	612	2,003	641	654	737	282	306	730	793
1892	438	196	587	549	639	2,024	661	673	754	310	351	721	827
1893	416	215	548	517	605	2,022	673	686	739	285	281	709	796
1894	388	200	484	466	497	1,770	628	657	629	247	288	597	667
1895	407	188	522	477	549	1,841	638	691	650	256	295	651	719
1896	430	185	555	518	647	1,851	644	653	740	271	298	730	806
1897	448	206	554	503	651	1,897	639	652	776	282	278	721	786
1898	432	206	450	488	598	1,812	584	590	713	239	270	693	727
1899	486	261	668	520	639	1,955	624	706	774	303	349	798	794

TABLE Cg69–107   Patents granted, by sector of use: 1840–1996   *Continued*

	Secondary sectors (manufacturing)					Tertiary sectors (services)							
	Rubber and plastic	Nonmetallic minerals	Paper	Wood	Other manufacturing	Construction	Transportation and storage	Communication	Trade	Finance	Government and education	Health	Other services
	Cg95	Cg96	Cg97	Cg98	Cg99	Cg100	Cg101	Cg102	Cg103	Cg104	Cg105	Cg106	Cg107
Year	Number	Number	Number	Number	Number	Number	Number	Number	Number	Number	Number	Number	Number
1900	528	256	671	539	651	2,040	663	779	783	313	320	855	821
1901	530	274	689	558	665	2,094	700	790	813	322	362	896	859
1902	576	301	745	587	689	2,316	801	822	855	358	401	986	992
1903	643	348	813	647	799	2,758	935	971	994	397	406	1,117	1,050
1904	648	347	869	635	765	2,756	984	927	965	406	384	990	977
1905	725	373	775	641	749	2,731	972	908	952	381	455	1,014	942
1906	761	427	831	711	790	2,950	1,063	906	1,015	406	438	1,053	1,043
1907	814	434	938	779	944	3,431	1,137	1,042	1,180	457	478	1,134	1,216
1908	691	329	862	712	882	2,984	1,077	903	1,085	432	424	1,086	1,094
1909	827	404	976	814	876	3,535	1,220	1,013	1,198	485	516	1,192	1,223
1910	801	401	965	771	849	3,332	980	1,030	1,141	465	455	1,115	1,192
1911	693	329	852	657	783	3,035	972	976	1,020	434	469	993	1,011
1912	817	375	928	730	901	3,304	1,065	987	1,141	464	512	1,152	1,161
1913	712	307	878	715	857	3,150	1,020	929	1,097	455	484	1,127	1,071
1914	892	388	1,043	761	1,014	3,538	1,192	1,109	1,226	519	575	1,294	1,268
1915	1,060	475	1,157	826	1,048	3,657	1,218	1,221	1,316	564	587	1,329	1,334
1916	1,062	447	1,119	869	1,127	3,781	1,213	1,139	1,371	594	661	1,370	1,392
1917	958	419	1,002	847	1,027	3,488	1,108	1,110	1,321	570	623	1,334	1,259
1918	884	377	989	793	1,017	3,061	1,003	1,009	1,244	544	604	1,309	1,207
1919	906	406	858	700	914	2,901	965	972	1,117	490	887	1,179	1,079
1920	923	410	899	740	963	3,051	955	1,004	1,172	497	675	1,202	1,153
1921	976	393	934	765	976	3,001	976	970	1,235	540	580	1,245	1,167
1922	1,001	424	964	766	983	3,147	997	998	1,236	553	548	1,157	1,204
1923	1,026	435	986	703	925	3,204	963	1,028	1,247	554	525	1,148	1,235
1924	1,057	470	1,106	725	1,062	3,484	1,041	1,096	1,358	607	587	1,379	1,382
1925	1,180	617	1,277	859	1,213	3,905	1,133	1,324	1,482	661	636	1,499	1,694
1926	1,143	594	1,239	790	1,132	3,662	1,020	1,249	1,356	630	505	1,517	1,485
1927	1,060	528	1,110	710	1,021	3,468	990	1,212	1,269	601	485	1,456	1,433
1928	1,067	513	1,116	737	1,019	3,592	996	1,286	1,289	603	472	1,371	1,458
1929	1,070	520	1,241	850	1,068	3,767	1,070	1,391	1,433	655	505	1,470	1,437
1930	1,089	548	1,203	799	1,026	3,760	1,071	1,493	1,362	632	548	1,367	1,345
1931	1,194	683	1,502	866	1,162	4,212	1,218	1,608	1,553	771	657	1,484	1,511
1932	1,323	743	1,523	894	1,088	4,166	1,139	1,615	1,573	799	639	1,539	1,540
1933	1,361	712	1,335	791	952	3,705	940	1,555	1,402	713	513	1,190	1,404
1934	1,222	610	1,317	686	848	3,335	820	1,364	1,245	652	417	1,419	1,279
1935	1,129	548	1,189	579	832	2,951	796	1,199	1,145	599	434	1,397	1,212
1936	1,101	507	1,122	545	825	2,892	782	1,149	1,089	595	415	1,342	1,123
1937	999	453	1,062	535	757	2,725	736	1,078	1,040	559	464	1,307	1,093
1938	998	470	1,089	559	795	2,758	737	1,036	1,059	590	467	1,311	1,110
1939	1,105	498	1,180	592	890	3,074	808	1,182	1,161	659	451	1,385	1,297
1940	1,087	540	1,163	586	878	2,973	763	1,216	1,102	631	437	1,345	1,225
1941	1,075	542	1,051	607	849	2,906	712	1,175	1,082	591	408	1,350	1,173
1942	1,139	526	971	542	722	2,701	678	1,137	1,031	572	416	1,218	1,015
1943	1,013	418	842	454	571	2,208	590	864	826	479	431	1,022	813
1944	882	357	768	386	467	1,828	528	822	693	439	496	915	658
1945	801	339	657	330	429	1,584	453	735	583	365	481	864	578
1946	625	277	465	248	375	1,333	386	621	468	320	428	728	504
1947	559	247	447	247	362	1,183	362	565	474	293	360	722	486
1948	718	288	486	317	447	1,472	396	632	585	351	434	931	626
1949	1,012	422	665	512	703	2,157	597	972	890	534	594	1,244	988
1950	1,216	483	912	657	926	2,611	757	1,177	1,218	699	638	1,643	1,245
1951	1,327	483	1,034	795	897	2,854	794	1,199	1,215	717	550	1,785	1,220
1952	1,284	481	1,067	762	864	2,838	786	1,178	1,231	707	528	1,689	1,229
1953	1,104	425	1,018	743	787	2,636	738	1,087	1,145	644	480	1,554	1,114
1954	966	377	863	572	607	2,154	591	898	863	514	364	1,348	872
1955	855	342	782	527	564	1,992	556	782	794	454	373	1,168	813
1956	1,300	513	1,130	698	816	2,922	822	1,240	1,156	718	548	1,697	1,174
1957	1,195	461	953	665	802	2,666	735	1,156	1,067	640	593	1,532	1,118
1958	1,371	519	1,099	695	834	2,941	817	1,332	1,121	752	631	1,859	1,151
1959	1,565	584	1,228	736	881	3,177	857	1,440	1,237	832	629	1,879	1,204

(continued)

TABLE Cg69–107   Patents granted, by sector of use: 1840–1996   *Continued*

	Secondary sectors (manufacturing)					Tertiary sectors (services)							
	Rubber and plastic	Nonmetallic minerals	Paper	Wood	Other manufacturing	Construction	Transportation and storage	Communication	Trade	Finance	Government and education	Health	Other services
	Cg95	Cg96	Cg97	Cg98	Cg99	Cg100	Cg101	Cg102	Cg103	Cg104	Cg105	Cg106	Cg107
Year	Number	Number	Number	Number	Number	Number	Number	Number	Number	Number	Number	Number	Number
1960	1,420	512	1,100	643	806	2,620	810	1,269	1,125	786	712	1,600	1,102
1961	1,570	548	1,171	651	830	2,742	861	1,345	1,088	797	764	1,597	1,140
1962	1,892	592	1,451	731	948	3,160	1,027	1,499	1,241	938	766	2,232	1,354
1963	1,464	534	1,118	605	815	2,672	885	1,237	1,052	753	659	1,874	1,220
1964	1,487	560	1,228	614	811	2,667	879	1,350	1,101	782	701	1,682	1,158
1965	2,045	746	1,500	782	1,054	3,697	1,135	1,913	1,472	1,077	839	2,095	1,531
1966	2,490	881	1,771	834	1,083	3,906	1,145	2,141	1,483	1,222	875	2,369	1,535
1967	2,555	830	1,667	816	1,002	3,866	1,139	1,951	1,395	1,083	812	2,429	1,478
1968	2,214	684	1,496	632	946	3,443	1,001	1,790	1,201	1,023	762	2,132	1,374
1969	2,414	838	1,620	692	1,111	3,730	1,072	1,897	1,333	1,232	759	2,729	1,603
1970	2,356	819	1,565	660	1,025	3,336	939	1,888	1,278	1,249	700	2,727	1,430
1971	2,693	1,016	2,286	843	1,351	4,217	1,222	2,250	1,615	1,505	960	3,338	1,944
1972	2,960	915	2,079	759	1,217	3,679	1,073	2,039	1,412	1,371	856	3,280	1,732
1973	2,544	891	1,967	790	1,229	3,861	1,175	2,172	1,483	1,412	1,141	3,376	1,734
1974	2,863	1,006	2,064	847	1,294	4,218	1,230	2,276	1,543	1,411	898	3,820	1,818
1975	2,659	886	1,851	727	1,184	3,627	1,104	1,957	1,372	1,264	801	3,844	1,648
1976	2,747	875	1,795	700	1,129	3,500	1,007	2,057	1,309	1,285	843	3,879	1,573
1977	2,400	846	1,672	644	1,056	3,401	912	2,026	1,215	1,213	786	3,822	1,411
1978	2,685	868	1,623	752	1,091	3,675	935	2,012	1,253	1,208	690	3,639	1,456
1979	1,834	609	1,232	471	848	2,492	675	1,557	925	923	541	2,982	1,152
1980	2,229	784	1,596	640	1,103	3,193	822	1,964	1,185	1,136	644	4,113	1,399
1981	2,555	843	1,820	621	1,120	3,418	873	2,238	1,208	1,242	644	4,275	1,451
1982	2,136	746	1,457	540	978	2,905	786	1,925	1,035	1,078	610	3,767	1,307
1983	2,286	722	1,605	546	919	2,794	732	1,823	1,008	1,061	607	3,595	1,172
1984	2,469	777	1,760	659	1,089	3,467	856	2,139	1,229	1,298	727	4,442	1,446
1985	2,554	866	2,003	678	1,171	3,555	916	2,182	1,290	1,365	717	4,747	1,560
1986	2,373	795	1,931	753	1,184	3,680	925	2,157	1,305	1,417	728	5,111	1,599
1987	2,613	884	2,050	878	1,370	4,313	1,101	2,737	1,489	1,723	976	6,139	1,792
1988	2,716	895	2,065	801	1,277	3,802	1,036	2,486	1,447	1,607	822	5,833	1,735
1989	3,206	1,072	2,550	982	1,587	4,670	1,240	2,879	1,755	2,044	1,030	7,759	2,223
1990	3,119	1,004	2,532	901	1,548	4,414	1,167	2,640	1,680	1,911	1,006	7,453	2,211
1991	3,372	1,125	2,648	959	1,657	4,611	1,219	2,732	1,792	1,988	1,082	8,226	2,338
1992	3,569	1,161	2,720	966	1,631	4,436	1,194	2,905	1,752	1,983	1,015	8,459	2,252
1993	3,641	1,113	2,843	875	1,626	4,332	1,167	2,963	1,714	1,983	975	8,792	2,284
1994	3,518	1,109	2,863	955	1,776	4,415	1,215	3,009	1,800	2,107	996	9,384	2,547
1995	3,331	967	2,867	938	1,726	4,247	1,217	3,021	1,763	2,153	1,038	9,652	2,509
1996	3,389	1,030	3,000	1,056	1,801	4,683	1,274	3,354	1,870	2,313	1,034	10,624	2,577

(Z) Less than 0.5.

Source

Data are based on the U.S. Historical Patent Set (USHiPS), downloaded from Daniel K. N. Johnson's Internet site.

Documentation

See the text for Table Cg38–68.

TABLE Cg108–109   Trademarks registered and renewed: 1870–2002[1]

Contributed by Gavin Wright

| | Registered | Renewed | | Registered | Renewed | | Registered | Renewed | | Registered | Renewed |
| | Cg108 | Cg109 | | Cg108 | Cg109 | | Cg108 | Cg109 | | Cg108 | Cg109 |
Year	Number	Number	Year	Number	Number	Year	Number	Number	Year	Number	Number
1870	121	—	1905	4,490	—	1940	9,974	2,547	1975	30,931	6,132
1871	486	—	1906	10,568	—	1941	8,530	2,765	1976	26,326	6,754
1872	491	—	1907	7,878	—	1942	6,795	2,894	1977	25,858	6,060
1873	492	—	1908	5,191	—	1943	5,595	3,835	1978	29,630	5,454
1874	559	—	1909	4,184	—	1944	6,025	4,052	1979	20,485	5,407
1875	1,138	—	1910	4,239	—	1945	7,490	4,210	1980	14,614	5,862
1876	959	—	1911	4,205	—	1946	8,106	5,725	1981	31,306	5,884
1877	1,216	—	1912	5,020	—	1947	8,976	6,139	1982	39,025	6,070
1878	1,455	—	1913	5,065	—	1948	11,472	5,056	1983	41,179	5,695
1879	872	—	1914	6,817	48	1949	15,968	3,788	1984	45,475	5,678
1880	349	—	1915	6,262	57	1950	16,817	3,564	1985	63,122	5,177
1881	834	—	1916	6,791	55	1951	17,376	3,350	1986	48,971	5,550
1882	947	—	1917	5,339	52	1952	16,172	3,419	1987	47,522	4,415
1883	902	—	1918	4,061	38	1953	15,610	3,103	1988	46,704	5,884
1884	1,021	—	1919	4,208	64	1954	15,946	3,491	1989	51,802	9,209
1885	1,067	—	1920	10,268	73	1955	18,207	4,268	1990	56,515	7,122
1886	1,029	—	1921	11,636	117	1956	20,753	3,756	1991	43,152	6,416
1887	1,133	—	1922	12,793	254	1957	17,480	3,488	1992	62,067	5,733
1888	1,059	—	1923	14,834	251	1958	15,351	3,070	1993	74,349	6,182
1889	1,229	—	1924	15,727	227	1959	18,709	3,272	1994	59,797	6,136
1890	1,415	—	1925	13,815	2,278	1960	18,434	3,933	1995	65,662	6,785
1891	1,762	—	1926	14,955	4,273	1961	16,595	3,358	1996	78,674	7,346
1892	1,737	—	1927	14,579	3,063	1962	17,023	2,809	1997	97,294	7,389
1893	1,677	—	1928	14,133	2,049	1963	19,740	2,655	1998	89,634	6,504
1894	1,806	—	1929	14,514	1,750	1964	20,087	2,702	1999	87,774	6,280
1895	1,829	—	1930	13,246	1,661	1965	18,501	3,165	2000	106,383	8,821
1896	1,813	—	1931	11,400	1,643	1966	20,259	3,585	2001	102,314	31,477
1897	1,671	—	1932	9,603	1,587	1967	20,036	3,801	2002	133,225	29,957
1898	1,238	—	1933	9,130	1,671	1968	21,528	4,646			
1899	1,649	—	1934	11,362	2,445	1969	20,613	6,176			
1900	1,721	—	1935	10,886	1,874	1970	21,745	6,076			
1901	1,928	—	1936	10,722	1,888	1971	21,019	6,213			
1902	2,006	—	1937	11,242	1,524	1972	23,252	5,637			
1903	2,186	—	1938	10,204	1,051	1973	26,112	5,397			
1904	2,158	—	1939	10,521	1,398	1974	28,099	5,513			

[1] Beginning 1980, data are on a fiscal-year basis.

Sources

1870–1970, U.S. Patent Office, *Annual Report of the Commissioner of Patents*, various issues, and unpublished data.

1971–1979, U.S. Bureau of the Census, *Statistical Abstract of the United States*, various issues.

1980–2002, U.S. Patent Office, *Annual Report of the Commissioner*, various issues.

Documentation

A trademark is a symbol, picture, word, or phrase applied by a manufacturer or merchant to distinguish his or her goods from those of others. Trademark rights are acquired by adoption of a mark and use of it on the goods in trade. Federal law provides for the registration in the U.S. Patent Office of such marks that are used in interstate and foreign commerce. Applications for registration are examined and may be refused if the mark is of a characteristic-prohibited registration (national emblems, deceptive marks, purely descriptive marks, and so on), or if it conflicts with a prior registered mark. Federal registration does not create ownership but only gives additional advantages to the owner.

The first federal trademark law in 1870 was based on the patent and copyright clause of the Constitution instead of the interstate and foreign commerce clause and was held unconstitutional in 1879. The Trademark Act of 1881 was limited to marks used in foreign commerce. The Trademark Act of 1905 included marks used in interstate commerce as well. The Trademark Act of 1920 permitted registration of a secondary class of marks not previously registrable. The Trademark Act of 1946 provided for a Principal Register on which marks of the type registrable under the Acts of 1881 and 1905 could be registered, and a Supplemental Register on which marks of the type registrable under the Act of 1920 could be registered. Registrations under the Act of 1946 are for a term of twenty years, with renewal possible for successive twenty-year terms.

RESEARCH AND DEVELOPMENT

Gavin Wright

TABLE Cg110–181   Expenditures on research and development, by performing sector and source of funding: 1953–2000

Contributed by Gavin Wright

			Total research and development									
			Expenditures by industry				Expenditures by universities and colleges					
	Total U.S. expenditures	Expenditures by the federal government	Total	Federal government funds	Industry funds	Expenditures by industry FFRDCs	Total	Federal government funds	Nonfederal government funds	Industry funds	University and college funds	Nonprofit funds
	Cg110	Cg111	Cg112	Cg113	Cg114	Cg115	Cg116	Cg117	Cg118	Cg119	Cg120	Cg121
Year	Million dollars	Million dollars	Million dollars	Million dollars	Million dollars	Million dollars	Million dollars	Million dollars	Million dollars	Million dollars	Million dollars	Million dollars
1953 [1]	5,160	1,015	3,630	1,430	2,200	—	273	149	40	21	37	27
1954 [1]	5,621	963	4,070	1,750	2,320	—	301	165	45	24	40	29
1955	6,281	973	4,517	2,057	2,460	123	342	191	50	27	42	32
1956	8,500	1,130	6,272	2,995	3,277	333	391	221	57	32	46	36
1957	9,908	1,297	7,324	3,928	3,396	407	433	242	64	37	51	40
1958	10,915	1,507	8,066	4,436	3,630	323	491	280	72	39	56	45
1959	12,490	1,681	9,200	5,217	3,983	418	586	356	81	40	61	50
1960	13,711	1,801	10,032	5,604	4,428	477	705	453	90	40	67	55
1961	14,564	1,987	10,353	5,685	4,668	555	834	557	101	40	75	62
1962	15,636	2,188	11,037	6,008	5,029	426	993	687	112	41	84	70
1963	17,519	2,558	12,216	6,856	5,360	414	1,178	839	125	41	96	78
1964	19,103	2,965	13,049	7,257	5,792	463	1,375	995	138	41	114	88
1965	20,252	3,156	13,812	7,367	6,445	373	1,595	1,167	150	42	136	101
1966	22,072	3,308	15,193	7,977	7,216	355	1,818	1,335	160	45	165	114
1967	23,346	3,444	15,966	7,946	8,020	419	2,035	1,491	168	52	200	126
1968	24,666	3,497	17,014	8,145	8,869	415	2,187	1,586	185	58	221	139
1969	25,996	3,790	17,844	7,987	9,857	464	2,280	1,624	208	61	233	155
1970	26,271	4,154	17,594	7,306	10,288	473	2,418	1,686	237	66	259	171
1971	26,952	4,409	17,829	7,175	10,654	491	2,565	1,760	262	72	290	182
1972	28,740	4,676	19,004	7,469	11,535	548	2,757	1,890	282	79	312	195
1973	30,952	4,837	20,704	7,600	13,104	545	2,953	2,009	302	90	343	211
1974	33,359	5,132	22,239	7,572	14,667	648	3,216	2,160	320	104	393	239
1975	35,671	5,561	23,460	7,878	15,582	727	3,570	2,400	348	118	432	272
1976	39,435	5,890	26,107	8,671	17,436	890	3,899	2,619	369	131	480	300
1977	43,421	6,211	28,863	9,523	19,340	962	4,346	2,893	394	155	569	337
1978	48,774	6,962	32,222	10,107	22,115	1,082	4,996	3,329	443	182	679	364
1979	55,457	7,471	37,062	11,354	25,708	1,164	5,715	3,848	482	215	785	386
1980	63,273	7,831	43,228	12,752	30,476	1,277	6,455	4,335	519	264	920	419
1981	72,267	8,605	50,425	14,997	35,428	1,385	7,085	4,670	581	314	1,058	463
1982	80,848	9,501	57,166	17,061	40,105	1,484	7,603	4,879	621	363	1,207	534
1983	90,075	10,830	63,683	19,095	44,588	1,585	8,251	5,210	658	432	1,357	595
1984	102,344	11,916	73,061	21,657	51,404	1,739	9,154	5,748	721	518	1,514	654
1985	114,778	13,093	82,376	25,333	57,043	1,863	10,308	6,388	834	630	1,743	713
1986	120,337	13,504	85,932	26,000	59,932	1,891	11,540	7,028	969	745	2,019	780
1987	126,299	13,588	90,160	28,757	61,403	1,995	12,807	7,768	1,065	831	2,262	882
1988	133,930	14,342	94,893	28,221	66,672	2,122	14,220	8,592	1,165	933	2,527	1,003
1989	141,914	15,231	99,860	26,359	73,501	2,195	15,632	9,315	1,274	1,061	2,852	1,131
1990	152,051	15,671	107,404	25,802	81,602	2,323	16,936	9,936	1,399	1,166	3,187	1,249
1991	160,914	15,249	114,675	24,095	90,580	2,277	18,202	10,663	1,483	1,242	3,457	1,358
1992	165,358	15,853	116,757	22,369	94,388	2,353	19,384	11,524	1,525	1,320	3,568	1,448
1993	165,714	16,531	115,435	20,844	94,591	1,965	20,485	12,300	1,556	1,391	3,708	1,530
1994	169,214	16,355	117,392	20,261	97,131	2,202	21,591	12,985	1,621	1,455	3,936	1,594
1995	183,611	16,904	129,830	21,178	108,652	2,273	22,599	13,580	1,750	1,547	4,108	1,616
1996	197,330	16,585	142,371	21,356	121,015	2,297	23,686	14,067	1,858	1,667	4,430	1,665
1997	212,379	16,819	155,409	21,798	133,611	2,130	25,088	14,716	1,926	1,812	4,846	1,790
1998	226,872	17,362	167,102	22,086	145,016	2,078	26,664	15,589	1,987	1,971	5,183	1,934
1999	244,143	18,332	180,450	20,162	160,288	2,373	28,363	16,518	2,083	2,133	5,562	2,066
2000 [2]	264,622	19,143	197,280	19,635	177,645	2,575	30,154	17,475	2,197	2,310	5,969	2,203

Notes appear at end of table

TABLE Cg110–181   Expenditures on research and development, by performing sector and source of funding: 1953–2000 *Continued*

	Total research and development						Basic research					
		Expenditures by nonprofit institutions							Expenditures by industry			
	Expenditures by university and college FFRDCs	Total	Federal government funds	Industry funds	Nonprofit funds	Expenditures by nonprofit FFRDCs	Total U.S. expenditures	Expenditures by the federal government	Total	Federal government funds	Industry funds	Expenditures by industry FFRDCs
	Cg122	Cg123	Cg124	Cg125	Cg126	Cg127	Cg128	Cg129	Cg130	Cg131	Cg132	Cg133
Year	Million dollars	Million dollars	Million dollars	Million dollars	Million dollars	Million dollars	Million dollars	Million dollars	Million dollars	Million dollars	Million dollars	Million dollars
1953 [1]	131	112	58	26	28	—	460	102	151	19	132	—
1954 [1]	161	127	65	31	31	—	509	96	166	23	143	—
1955	187	131	64	35	32	9	579	98	189	27	162	—
1956	217	146	71	37	38	11	718	114	253	37	216	—
1957	267	167	79	37	51	14	814	124	271	41	230	—
1958	316	195	95	38	62	18	944	149	295	43	252	—
1959	349	234	125	42	67	22	1,087	165	320	72	248	—
1960	385	264	148	48	68	48	1,286	184	376	79	297	—
1961	440	304	169	49	86	92	1,512	230	395	81	314	—
1962	500	363	200	54	109	130	1,824	252	488	143	345	—
1963	580	408	234	55	119	165	2,115	285	522	147	375	—
1964	629	417	250	55	112	205	2,396	339	507	123	384	42
1965	630	472	286	62	124	215	2,664	375	563	157	406	29
1966	652	537	329	70	138	210	2,930	410	593	142	451	31
1967	696	561	342	74	145	225	3,168	434	595	168	427	34
1968	722	596	364	81	151	235	3,376	482	607	145	462	35
1969	731	642	388	93	161	245	3,491	545	581	123	458	37
1970	727	677	410	95	172	230	3,594	562	566	122	444	36
1971	735	709	427	98	184	215	3,720	581	557	101	456	33
1972	785	771	472	101	198	200	3,850	603	554	91	463	39
1973	841	882	566	105	211	190	4,099	652	595	96	499	36
1974	926	988	639	114	235	210	4,511	715	650	114	536	49
1975	1,067	1,062	675	124	262	225	4,875	760	677	104	573	53
1976	1,266	1,139	711	135	292	245	5,373	850	750	116	634	69
1977	1,551	1,213	740	147	326	275	6,075	943	836	135	701	75
1978	1,826	1,353	830	160	363	333	6,998	1,044	941	156	785	94
1979	2,091	1,564	985	174	405	390	7,864	1,112	1,054	161	893	104
1980	2,366	1,641	1,000	189	452	475	8,825	1,212	1,205	170	1,035	120
1981	2,483	1,747	1,038	206	504	538	9,844	1,343	1,477	164	1,313	137
1982	2,608	1,961	1,175	224	561	525	10,863	1,522	1,776	253	1,523	128
1983	2,944	2,182	1,313	244	626	600	12,110	1,733	2,106	346	1,760	117
1984	3,337	2,513	1,550	265	698	625	13,503	1,877	2,472	340	2,132	136
1985	3,709	2,767	1,700	289	778	663	14,885	1,947	2,731	358	2,373	131
1986	4,051	2,882	1,700	314	867	538	17,287	2,026	3,930	434	3,496	117
1987	4,369	2,878	1,569	342	967	501	18,551	2,047	4,181	598	3,583	142
1988	4,631	3,213	1,762	372	1,078	510	19,813	2,116	4,163	656	3,507	337
1989	4,781	3,669	2,062	405	1,202	547	21,908	2,309	4,818	986	3,832	398
1990	4,955	4,126	2,346	440	1,340	636	23,069	2,319	4,629	869	3,760	499
1991	5,163	4,652	2,679	479	1,494	696	27,201	2,378	7,376	1,251	6,125	461
1992	5,271	4,993	2,806	521	1,666	748	27,628	2,419	6,528	712	5,816	474
1993	5,283	5,267	2,843	567	1,857	749	28,754	2,621	6,427	466	5,961	492
1994	5,317	5,599	2,911	617	2,071	758	29,578	2,547	6,514	436	6,078	503
1995	5,372	5,827	2,847	671	2,308	808	29,560	2,689	5,569	190	5,379	530
1996	5,410	6,209	2,906	730	2,574	772	32,812	2,680	7,498	650	6,848	708
1997	5,486	6,626	3,014	809	2,804	821	36,270	2,746	9,795	1,029	8,766	625
1998	5,589	7,234	3,281	880	3,073	843	41,294	3,003	13,027	1,326	11,701	568
1999	5,698	8,017	3,718	976	3,323	909	44,625	3,312	14,024	1,211	12,813	649
2000 [2]	5,801	8,750	4,079	1,085	3,586	918	47,903	3,525	15,378	1,179	14,199	704

Notes appear at end of table

(continued)

TABLE Cg110–181   Expenditures on research and development, by performing sector and source of funding: 1953–2000   *Continued*

	Basic research											
	Expenditures by universities and colleges						Expenditures by university and college FFRDCs	Expenditures by nonprofit institutions				Expenditures by nonprofit FFRDCs
	Total	Federal government funds	Nonfederal government funds	Industry funds	University and college funds	Nonprofit funds		Total	Federal government funds	Industry funds	Nonprofit funds	
	Cg134	Cg135	Cg136	Cg137	Cg138	Cg139	Cg140	Cg141	Cg142	Cg143	Cg144	Cg145
Year	Million dollars	Million dollars	Million dollars	Million dollars	Million dollars	Million dollars	Million dollars	Million dollars	Million dollars	Million dollars	Million dollars	Million dollars
1953 [1]	123	82	7	13	6	16	36	48	27	9	12	—
1954 [1]	148	97	10	15	8	18	44	55	31	11	13	—
1955	180	117	14	17	12	21	50	63	36	13	14	—
1956	220	143	19	20	15	24	58	74	42	15	17	—
1957	261	167	25	23	20	27	72	87	49	15	23	—
1958	312	202	31	24	24	31	85	103	59	16	28	—
1959	388	263	38	24	28	36	95	120	72	18	30	—
1960	485	341	45	25	33	41	106	136	85	21	30	—
1961	598	432	54	25	40	48	126	164	105	22	37	—
1962	737	546	64	25	48	55	148	200	130	24	46	—
1963	909	689	75	25	58	63	175	225	150	25	50	—
1964	1,071	824	84	25	70	68	200	238	166	25	47	—
1965	1,221	944	94	27	86	70	218	260	179	29	52	—
1966	1,380	1,066	104	29	106	75	239	278	188	32	58	—
1967	1,554	1,188	114	34	136	83	263	289	194	34	61	—
1968	1,681	1,265	131	38	156	91	276	296	196	37	63	—
1969	1,754	1,288	153	40	171	103	272	302	192	43	67	—
1970	1,855	1,323	179	43	196	115	265	311	195	44	72	—
1971	1,968	1,385	194	50	214	127	252	329	207	45	77	—
1972	2,038	1,437	195	55	216	134	270	347	216	47	84	—
1973	2,103	1,489	196	59	223	137	343	371	232	49	90	—
1974	2,282	1,609	204	66	250	153	415	401	245	54	102	—
1975	2,480	1,768	212	72	264	164	476	430	255	59	116	—
1976	2,675	1,924	218	75	283	175	556	474	278	65	131	—
1977	2,967	2,114	232	89	334	198	734	521	301	72	148	—
1978	3,376	2,399	260	107	398	213	945	598	351	79	168	—
1979	3,828	2,719	286	128	466	229	1,077	689	413	87	190	—
1980	4,315	3,061	307	156	544	248	1,201	771	461	95	215	—
1981	4,737	3,331	338	183	615	269	1,299	853	505	105	243	—
1982	5,091	3,475	368	215	716	317	1,406	941	551	115	275	—
1983	5,518	3,689	396	260	816	358	1,587	1,050	613	127	311	—
1984	6,145	4,087	436	313	915	395	1,728	1,147	656	139	351	—
1985	7,025	4,606	515	389	1,076	440	1,821	1,231	681	153	397	—
1986	7,943	5,122	606	466	1,262	488	1,955	1,317	700	168	449	—
1987	8,644	5,527	659	514	1,399	545	2,139	1,399	707	185	507	—
1988	9,343	5,937	705	565	1,529	607	2,299	1,531	756	203	573	24
1989	10,218	6,422	766	637	1,714	680	2,390	1,730	860	223	647	46
1990	11,125	6,888	847	705	1,929	756	2,512	1,922	947	245	730	65
1991	12,061	7,423	912	764	2,127	836	2,719	2,129	1,036	269	825	77
1992	12,910	8,058	941	814	2,202	893	2,891	2,340	1,114	295	931	67
1993	13,642	8,636	952	851	2,268	936	2,968	2,532	1,157	324	1,051	72
1994	14,392	9,134	990	889	2,405	974	2,870	2,678	1,137	356	1,186	75
1995	15,137	9,628	1,069	945	2,509	987	2,661	2,899	1,170	390	1,338	75
1996	16,029	10,085	1,148	1,030	2,738	1,028	2,632	3,187	1,248	428	1,510	79
1997	17,015	10,608	1,190	1,119	2,993	1,105	2,660	3,322	1,317	449	1,557	108
1998	18,143	11,358	1,217	1,208	3,175	1,185	2,685	3,656	1,461	489	1,706	213
1999	19,439	12,154	1,281	1,312	3,421	1,271	2,759	4,092	1,705	542	1,845	351
2000 [2]	20,656	12,857	1,351	1,421	3,672	1,355	2,809	4,492	1,898	602	1,991	339

Notes appear at end of table

TABLE Cg110–181   Expenditures on research and development, by performing sector and source of funding: 1953–2000 *Continued*

			Applied research									
			Expenditures by industry				Expenditures by universities and colleges					
Year	Total U.S. expenditures	Expenditures by the federal government	Total	Federal government funds	Industry funds	Expenditures by industry FFRDCs	Total	Federal government funds	Nonfederal government funds	Industry funds	University and college funds	Nonprofit funds
	Cg146	Cg147	Cg148	Cg149	Cg150	Cg151	Cg152	Cg153	Cg154	Cg155	Cg156	Cg157
	Million dollars	Million dollars	Million dollars	Million dollars	Million dollars	Million dollars	Million dollars	Million dollars	Million dollars	Million dollars	Million dollars	Million dollars
1953 [1]	1,289	347	726	288	438	—	134	59	30	7	28	10
1954 [1]	1,378	330	814	322	492	—	137	60	32	8	28	10
1955	1,514	333	928	368	560	—	142	63	32	9	27	11
1956	1,928	387	1,268	474	794	—	146	65	33	10	27	11
1957	2,414	446	1,670	678	992	—	147	63	34	12	27	11
1958	2,758	516	1,911	774	1,137	—	152	66	35	12	27	12
1959	2,940	577	1,991	813	1,178	—	167	78	37	13	28	12
1960	3,065	615	2,029	833	1,196	—	186	93	39	13	29	12
1961	3,123	668	1,977	812	1,165	—	199	104	40	13	30	13
1962	3,698	709	2,449	1,011	1,438	—	216	119	41	14	30	13
1963	3,865	809	2,457	1,007	1,450	—	230	128	42	14	32	14
1964	4,201	947	2,538	978	1,560	62	256	142	45	14	37	18
1965	4,374	994	2,612	992	1,620	46	304	176	46	13	42	27
1966	4,653	1,012	2,790	986	1,804	53	351	208	47	14	48	34
1967	4,848	1,069	2,832	983	1,849	83	389	238	46	16	54	36
1968	5,137	1,112	3,037	956	2,081	87	405	250	46	16	55	39
1969	5,454	1,229	3,192	920	2,272	95	417	257	48	16	54	43
1970	5,752	1,334	3,330	952	2,378	97	451	280	51	18	56	47
1971	5,833	1,355	3,348	907	2,441	67	499	306	61	19	67	47
1972	6,147	1,434	3,407	845	2,562	107	619	391	74	21	82	52
1973	6,655	1,527	3,715	883	2,832	110	725	450	88	26	100	62
1974	7,344	1,652	4,168	905	3,263	120	794	477	96	32	118	72
1975	8,091	1,912	4,431	991	3,440	139	934	550	113	39	141	92
1976	8,976	2,068	4,945	1,033	3,912	167	1,042	596	127	45	166	109
1977	9,670	2,081	5,424	1,113	4,311	212	1,126	626	134	51	194	121
1978	10,710	2,242	6,065	1,195	4,870	235	1,247	676	151	61	232	128
1979	12,117	2,415	6,975	1,305	5,670	250	1,418	793	161	71	263	129
1980	13,745	2,546	8,175	1,625	6,550	275	1,622	912	174	88	308	140
1981	16,393	2,731	10,401	2,042	8,359	298	1,781	953	199	108	363	159
1982	18,286	2,802	11,956	2,593	9,363	367	1,915	1,007	207	121	402	178
1983	20,394	2,991	13,513	3,227	10,286	414	2,116	1,122	215	141	443	194
1984	22,517	2,961	15,218	3,677	11,541	547	2,332	1,226	234	168	491	212
1985	25,403	3,135	17,625	4,717	12,908	630	2,527	1,296	262	198	547	224
1986	27,251	3,204	19,131	4,049	15,082	629	2,779	1,393	298	229	620	240
1987	27,914	3,366	19,190	4,037	15,153	623	3,219	1,643	333	260	707	276
1988	29,545	3,362	20,377	3,846	16,531	371	3,779	1,957	377	302	818	325
1989	32,279	3,566	22,317	4,324	17,993	374	4,188	2,120	417	347	933	370
1990	34,974	3,652	24,399	5,967	18,432	386	4,405	2,139	453	377	1,031	404
1991	38,632	4,094	27,013	5,588	21,425	433	4,608	2,230	468	392	1,091	428
1992	37,938	4,337	25,660	4,476	21,184	507	4,879	2,412	479	414	1,120	454
1993	37,285	4,838	24,251	4,295	19,956	435	5,145	2,538	495	443	1,181	487
1994	36,613	4,985	22,988	3,616	19,372	503	5,385	2,640	517	464	1,256	508
1995	40,999	4,952	26,919	3,164	23,755	535	5,653	2,774	558	494	1,311	516
1996	43,169	4,872	29,010	3,640	25,370	231	5,870	2,856	582	522	1,388	522
1997	47,211	4,997	32,430	2,648	29,782	213	6,152	2,900	604	568	1,519	561
1998	45,702	5,146	30,341	2,533	27,808	230	6,475	2,957	631	626	1,646	614
1999	51,632	5,503	35,367	3,440	31,927	274	6,814	3,075	658	673	1,756	652
2000 [2]	55,041	5,826	37,648	2,252	35,396	285	7,260	3,259	693	729	1,884	695

Notes appear at end of table

(continued)

TABLE Cg110–181   Expenditures on research and development, by performing sector and source of funding: 1953–2000 *Continued*

	Applied research							Development					
	Expenditures by university and college FFRDCs	Expenditures by nonprofit institutions				Expenditures by nonprofit FFRDCs	Total U.S. expenditures	Expenditures by the federal government	Expenditures by industry				Expenditures by industry FFRDCs
		Total	Federal government funds	Industry funds	Nonprofit funds					Total	Federal government funds	Industry funds	
	Cg158	Cg159	Cg160	Cg161	Cg162	Cg163	Cg164	Cg165	Cg166	Cg167	Cg168	Cg169
Year	Million dollars	Million dollars	Million dollars	Million dollars	Million dollars	Million dollars	Million dollars	Million dollars	Million dollars	Million dollars	Million dollars	Million dollars
1953 [1]	48	35	14	11	10	—	3,412	567	2,753	1,123	1,630	—
1954 [1]	58	40	16	13	11	—	3,734	537	3,090	1,405	1,685	—
1955	68	43	18	14	11	—	4,189	543	3,523	1,785	1,738	—
1956	79	49	21	14	14	—	5,855	631	5,084	2,817	2,267	—
1957	94	58	24	14	20	—	6,681	728	5,790	3,616	2,174	—
1958	111	69	30	14	25	—	7,214	842	6,183	3,942	2,241	—
1959	121	85	43	15	27	—	8,463	940	7,307	4,750	2,557	—
1960	129	108	63	17	28	—	9,360	1,003	8,104	5,169	2,935	—
1961	145	135	83	17	35	—	9,930	1,090	8,536	5,347	3,189	—
1962	163	162	98	19	45	—	10,116	1,227	8,527	5,281	3,246	—
1963	186	183	115	19	49	—	11,540	1,465	9,651	6,116	3,535	—
1964	203	196	130	19	47	—	12,506	1,680	10,004	6,156	3,848	359
1965	206	213	140	21	52	—	13,215	1,789	10,637	6,218	4,419	298
1966	213	234	153	24	57	—	14,490	1,886	11,810	6,849	4,961	271
1967	225	251	166	25	60	—	15,332	1,943	12,539	6,795	5,744	302
1968	221	276	186	28	62	—	16,154	1,904	13,370	7,044	6,326	293
1969	213	308	210	32	66	—	17,051	2,016	14,071	6,944	7,127	332
1970	213	328	225	33	70	—	16,925	2,258	13,698	6,232	7,466	340
1971	216	349	241	34	74	—	17,399	2,473	13,924	6,167	7,757	391
1972	224	357	243	35	79	—	18,743	2,639	15,043	6,533	8,510	402
1973	203	376	257	36	83	—	20,197	2,657	16,394	6,621	9,773	399
1974	191	420	290	39	91	—	21,504	2,765	17,421	6,553	10,868	479
1975	219	456	315	42	100	—	22,706	2,890	18,352	6,783	11,569	535
1976	263	492	338	45	109	—	25,085	2,972	20,412	7,522	12,890	654
1977	305	523	355	48	120	—	27,677	3,188	22,603	8,275	14,328	675
1978	329	592	409	52	132	—	31,067	3,676	25,216	8,756	16,460	753
1979	380	680	480	55	144	—	35,475	3,944	29,033	9,888	19,145	810
1980	421	706	489	60	158	—	40,703	4,072	33,848	10,957	22,891	882
1981	423	758	521	64	173	—	46,030	4,530	38,547	12,791	25,756	950
1982	439	808	550	69	189	—	51,698	5,178	43,434	14,215	29,219	989
1983	494	866	585	74	207	—	57,571	6,106	48,064	15,522	32,542	1,054
1984	561	899	594	79	226	—	66,323	7,078	55,371	17,640	37,731	1,056
1985	573	913	581	85	247	—	74,489	8,011	62,020	20,258	41,762	1,102
1986	547	961	600	91	270	—	75,799	8,275	62,871	21,517	41,354	1,145
1987	531	986	593	98	295	—	79,833	8,176	66,789	24,122	42,667	1,230
1988	565	1,026	599	105	322	66	84,572	8,864	70,353	23,719	46,634	1,414
1989	605	1,159	695	112	352	70	87,727	9,355	72,725	21,049	51,676	1,423
1990	767	1,284	780	120	384	81	94,008	9,700	78,376	18,966	59,410	1,438
1991	929	1,468	921	129	419	86	95,081	8,778	80,286	17,256	63,030	1,383
1992	946	1,528	933	138	456	81	99,793	9,098	84,569	17,181	67,388	1,372
1993	969	1,544	900	148	497	103	99,676	9,071	84,757	16,083	68,674	1,038
1994	981	1,659	960	158	541	111	103,023	8,823	87,890	16,209	71,681	1,196
1995	1,119	1,692	934	170	589	129	113,053	9,262	97,342	17,824	79,518	1,208
1996	1,283	1,781	960	182	640	122	121,348	9,033	105,863	17,066	88,797	1,358
1997	1,364	1,926	1,011	205	711	128	128,898	9,077	113,184	18,121	95,063	1,292
1998	1,326	2,062	1,060	223	779	123	139,875	9,214	123,734	18,227	105,507	1,280
1999	1,276	2,284	1,194	247	842	114	147,886	9,517	131,060	15,512	115,548	1,450
2000 [2]	1,401	2,504	1,320	275	909	117	161,679	9,792	144,254	16,205	128,050	1,586

Notes appear at end of table

TABLE Cg110–181   Expenditures on research and development, by performing sector and source of funding: 1953–2000   *Continued*

	Development											
	Expenditures by universities and colleges						Expenditures by university and college FFRDCs	Expenditures by nonprofit institutions				Expenditures by nonprofit FFRDCs
	Total	Federal government funds	Nonfederal government funds	Industry funds	University and college funds	Nonprofit funds		Total	Federal government funds	Industry funds	Nonprofit funds	
	Cg170	Cg171	Cg172	Cg173	Cg174	Cg175	Cg176	Cg177	Cg178	Cg179	Cg180	Cg181
Year	Million dollars	Million dollars	Million dollars	Million dollars	Million dollars	Million dollars	Million dollars	Million dollars	Million dollars	Million dollars	Million dollars	Million dollars
1953 [1]	16	9	3	1	3	1	48	29	17	6	6	—
1954 [1]	17	9	3	1	3	1	59	32	18	7	7	—
1955	21	12	4	2	3	1	69	34	19	8	7	—
1956	25	14	4	2	4	2	81	35	20	8	7	—
1957	26	12	5	3	4	2	101	37	21	8	8	—
1958	28	13	6	3	4	2	120	42	25	8	9	—
1959	31	16	6	3	5	2	134	51	32	9	10	—
1960	35	19	6	3	5	2	151	69	49	10	10	—
1961	38	22	7	2	5	2	170	97	73	10	14	—
1962	40	23	8	2	6	2	190	132	103	11	18	—
1963	40	22	8	2	6	2	219	165	134	11	20	—
1964	49	30	8	2	7	3	227	188	159	11	18	—
1965	71	48	9	2	8	4	207	215	183	12	20	—
1966	87	61	9	2	10	5	200	236	199	14	23	—
1967	93	66	9	3	10	7	208	247	208	15	24	—
1968	102	72	8	4	9	9	226	259	217	16	26	—
1969	110	80	7	5	8	10	246	277	231	18	28	—
1970	112	84	6	5	7	10	249	268	220	18	30	—
1971	98	69	8	4	9	9	267	246	194	19	33	—
1972	101	63	12	4	14	9	291	267	213	19	35	—
1973	126	71	18	5	20	13	296	326	268	20	38	—
1974	141	75	20	7	25	15	321	377	314	22	42	—
1975	156	83	22	8	27	16	373	400	330	23	47	—
1976	182	100	24	12	31	16	447	418	341	25	52	—
1977	254	153	28	15	40	19	513	444	359	27	58	—
1978	373	254	32	15	49	24	552	496	403	30	64	—
1979	469	336	34	16	56	28	633	586	483	32	71	—
1980	518	362	38	19	68	31	744	639	525	35	79	—
1981	568	386	44	24	80	35	761	674	549	37	88	—
1982	597	397	46	27	88	39	763	737	599	40	98	—
1983	617	399	47	31	97	43	862	867	715	44	109	—
1984	677	435	51	37	108	47	1,048	1,093	925	47	120	—
1985	756	486	57	43	120	49	1,315	1,285	1,100	51	134	—
1986	818	513	65	50	136	53	1,549	1,141	938	55	149	—
1987	945	599	73	57	155	61	1,699	996	771	60	165	—
1988	1,098	698	83	66	180	71	1,767	655	407	65	183	420
1989	1,227	773	92	76	205	81	1,786	780	507	70	203	430
1990	1,407	909	99	83	226	89	1,676	920	619	75	226	490
1991	1,533	1,011	103	86	239	94	1,514	1,054	722	82	251	533
1992	1,595	1,054	105	91	246	100	1,435	1,125	758	88	279	599
1993	1,698	1,126	109	97	259	107	1,346	1,191	787	95	309	574
1994	1,814	1,211	114	102	276	112	1,466	1,261	815	103	343	573
1995	1,809	1,177	123	108	288	113	1,592	1,236	744	111	381	603
1996	1,787	1,125	128	115	305	115	1,495	1,241	698	120	423	571
1997	1,921	1,207	132	125	333	123	1,462	1,378	687	155	536	585
1998	2,046	1,274	139	137	361	135	1,577	1,516	760	168	588	507
1999	2,110	1,290	144	148	385	143	1,663	1,641	819	187	636	445
2000 [2]	2,238	1,360	152	160	413	153	1,592	1,754	860	208	686	463

[1] Expenditures of industry and nonprofit FFRDCs were not separated from total federal support; thus, the figures for federal support include support to FFRDCs.

[2] Preliminary.

Sources

Data were downloaded from the Internet site of the National Science Foundation, August 21, 2001. The data were derived from National Science Foundation/Division of Science Resource Studies (NSF/SRS), *Research and Development in Industry 1999*; NSF/SRS, *Academic Research and Development Expenditures: Fiscal Year 1999*; NSF/SRS, *Federal Funds for Research and Development: Fiscal Years*

1999, 2000, and 2001; and *NSF/SRS Survey of R&D Funding & Performance by Nonprofit Organizations*. Also see NSF/SRS, *National Patterns of R&D Resources*, published biennially.

Documentation

FFRDCs are Federally Funded Research and Development Centers.

National estimates of funds spent on the performance of research and development by the four major sectors of the economy have been made by the National Science Foundation since 1953. The data are derived basically from survey responses by performers of research and development (R&D) as

TABLE Cg110–181 Expenditures on research and development, by performing sector and source of funding: 1953–2000 _Continued_

to how much they spent on this activity and where their funds originated. Because of conceptual and practical limitations, the table should be considered as a general approximation rather than an exact statement.

R&D consists of basic and applied research in the sciences (including medical sciences) and in engineering and in activities in development, defined later. R&D excludes routine product testing, quality control, mapping surveys, collection of general-purpose statistics, experimental production, and activities concerned primarily with the dissemination of scientific information and the training of scientific manpower.

Basic research, for three of the sectors (federal government, universities and colleges, and other nonprofit institutions), is research directed toward increases of knowledge in science with "the primary aim of the investigator being a fuller knowledge or understanding of the subject under study, rather than a practical application thereof." To take account of an individual company's commercial goals, the definition for the industry sector is modified to indicate that basic research projects represent "original investigations for the advancement of scientific knowledge . . . which do not have specific commercial objectives, although they may be in fields of present or potential interest to the reporting company."

The NSF survey concept of development may be summarized as "the systematic use of scientific knowledge directed toward the production of useful materials, devices, systems or methods, including design and development of prototypes and processes."

The four-sector division followed by the NSF attempts to take into account both the legal nature and major functions of organizations active in financing and performing basic research, applied research, and development. However, grouping diverse types of organizations into discrete sectors requires certain arbitrary judgments because of the mixed nature of many organizations, particularly those in the university and other nonprofit sectors.

Expenditure levels for academic and federal government performers are in reference to calendar years. These levels are approximations based on fiscal-year data. For federal government expenditures starting in 1977, the calendar-year approximation is equal to 75 percent of the amount reported in the same fiscal year plus 25 percent of the amount reported in the subsequent fiscal year. For academic expenditures in all years and for federal government expenditures prior to 1977, the respective percentages are 50 and 50 because those fiscal years (for most academic institutions and the federal government before 1977) begin on July 1 instead of October 1.

Series Cg114, Cg132, Cg150, and Cg168. Industry sources of industry R&D expenditures include all nonfederal sources of industry R&D expenditures.

Series Cg118, Cg136, Cg154, and Cg172. Because of limitations in the survey information, data on nonfederal government funding to other performers are not available and are consequently included in other sectors' support for their own R&D performance. For example, nonfederal government support to nonprofits is included in nonprofits' support for their own R&D.

Series Cg122, Cg140, Cg158, and Cg176. Includes all R&D expenditures of FFRDCs administered by academic institutions.

TABLE Cg182-202   Federal obligations for research and development, by agency: 1947-2000

Contributed by Gavin Wright

	Total		Department							
					Defense					
	Excluding plant	Including plant	Agriculture	Commerce	Total	Army	Navy	Air Force	Other	Energy
	Cg182	Cg183	Cg184	Cg185	Cg186	Cg187 [1]	Cg188 [1]	Cg189 [1]	Cg190 [1]	Cg191
Fiscal year	Thousand dollars	Thousand dollars	Thousand dollars	Thousand dollars	Thousand dollars	Thousand dollars	Thousand dollars	Thousand dollars	Thousand dollars	Thousand dollars
1947	619,500	—	40,000	5,700	469,300	104,300	252,300	112,700	—	—
1948	776,500	—	45,700	8,900	485,800	97,700	247,300	140,800	—	—
1949	937,700	—	53,200	10,900	626,100	114,700	298,000	213,500	—	—
1950	972,600	—	56,900	22,400	599,700	119,000	257,600	223,100	—	—
1951	1,521,527	1,851,571	55,076	45,995	1,123,636	307,100	450,200	368,600	—	—
1952	1,909,665	2,216,848	55,291	27,684	1,506,540	458,800	551,100	498,600	—	—
1953	1,919,543	2,167,456	56,045	23,045	1,476,774	899,600	660,700	1,016,900	—	—
1954	1,761,840	1,918,046	59,459	16,920	1,282,936	763,300	615,300	941,400	—	—
1955	2,044,593	2,251,894	72,176	14,996	1,528,689	419,300	564,800	939,300	21,700	—
1956	2,988,203	3,266,903	83,038	18,210	2,268,547	408,000	673,300	1,142,800	44,500	—
1957	3,932,001	4,389,237	99,794	17,696	2,985,555	500,600	804,200	1,643,900	36,900	—
1958	4,569,722	4,906,015	110,242	18,254	3,403,278	603,300	867,900	1,858,600	73,500	—
1959	6,693,510	7,122,610	120,697	25,589	5,161,674	1,174,200	1,349,500	2,440,000	197,900	—
1960	7,551,746	8,080,015	125,759	31,396	5,711,532	1,117,000	1,535,500	2,815,500	243,600	—
1961	9,058,623	9,607,023	143,443	32,334	6,574,029	1,117,900	1,539,000	3,588,900	328,300	—
1962	10,289,947	11,069,059	157,167	40,101	6,722,867	1,203,500	1,539,100	3,569,800	410,600	—
1963	12,494,611	13,662,879	168,038	52,246	7,285,659	1,297,400	1,597,300	3,944,700	446,300	—
1964	14,225,354	15,323,870	189,034	53,828	7,261,867	1,376,900	1,621,200	3,784,000	479,700	—
1965	14,614,249	15,745,852	224,552	61,339	6,796,540	1,459,500	1,449,500	3,351,000	536,500	—
1966	15,320,334	16,178,640	234,896	55,186	7,023,647	1,585,400	1,601,700	3,342,300	494,200	—
1967	16,529,099	17,149,186	252,642	74,836	8,049,155	1,703,274	2,122,494	3,819,919	479,534	—
1968	15,921,208	16,525,038	253,540	83,900	7,709,319	1,593,903	2,078,402	3,724,498	503,544	—
1969	15,640,888	13,309,900	260,066	72,054	7,696,253	1,666,515	2,159,715	3,604,184	454,588	—
1970	15,338,937	15,863,385	281,157	121,571	7,360,368	1,687,021	2,276,120	3,049,117	484,600	—
1971	15,542,512	16,153,756	304,902	143,711	7,509,036	1,725,978	2,311,686	3,163,195	458,820	—
1972	16,495,895	17,097,951	349,573	187,259	8,318,145	2,103,651	2,559,735	3,325,086	500,433	—
1973	16,800,153	17,574,486	366,522	190,600	8,404,214	2,030,685	2,690,458	3,344,093	457,068	—
1974	17,410,128	18,176,457	378,706	180,585	8,420,386	2,041,974	2,772,553	3,283,941	464,140	1,488,903 [2]
1975	19,038,818	19,859,548	420,082	215,382	9,012,472	1,920,691	3,162,843	3,573,144	497,391	2,047,306 [2]
1976	20,779,658	21,616,382	462,449	228,853	9,654,722	2,025,976	3,373,805	3,799,627	573,947	2,463,809 [2]
1977	23,450,377	24,817,577	546,963	244,721	10,963,351	2,458,166	3,878,610	4,381,095	659,541	3,536,220
1978	25,845,137	27,140,849	621,282	283,665	11,553,638	2,556,527	4,046,716	4,422,449	724,486	4,244,827
1979	28,145,142	29,620,597	663,025	309,359	12,506,225	2,772,474	4,403,142	4,693,116	878,383	4,638,766
1980	29,830,432	31,386,095	687,586	342,549	13,981,012	2,993,787	4,789,332	5,319,029	1,049,184	4,753,688
1981	33,103,924	34,589,634	773,958	327,925	16,508,649	3,256,959	5,103,852	7,128,847	1,255,640	4,918,225
1982	36,432,589	37,822,363	797,274	336,278	20,622,574	3,785,189	6,000,956	9,442,558	1,643,334	4,708,158
1983	38,711,537	40,009,032	847,605	334,992	22,922,789	4,024,385	6,209,906	10,951,316	2,058,100	4,536,682
1984	42,224,865	44,012,149	866,171	358,226	25,372,870	4,281,732	7,779,022	12,377,040	1,405,728	4,673,578
1985	48,359,565	50,180,369	942,979	398,759	29,791,504	4,623,693	9,309,510	13,552,246	2,786,324	4,966,008
1986	51,412,364	52,951,181	928,528	399,166	32,937,939	4,863,270	9,747,910	13,723,864	4,771,925	4,688,304
1987	55,253,693	57,099,656	947,858	402,240	35,231,532	5,085,233	9,576,757	15,618,012	5,291,799	4,757,202
1988	56,769,425	58,826,512	1,016,627	388,949	35,248,856	4,898,837	9,588,941	15,011,031	5,957,328	5,036,400
1989	61,406,484	63,571,605	1,038,279	397,862	37,576,887	5,704,460	9,755,718	15,487,571	6,973,301	5,192,612
1990	63,559,471	65,831,189	1,108,380	438,168	37,268,148	5,737,212	9,646,613	15,153,595	6,996,807	5,630,554
1991	61,295,152	64,147,951	1,236,646	489,601	32,134,765	6,172,507	7,860,000	11,089,796	7,200,897	5,983,100
1992	65,592,590	68,577,184	1,327,112	651,165	36,129,467	6,876,232	8,126,830	13,606,830	7,670,465	6,172,230
1993	67,314,025	70,414,697	1,327,795	656,276	35,849,149	6,227,212	9,148,346	12,866,924	7,723,345	6,262,146
1994	67,235,390	69,450,776	1,399,883	826,081	34,553,204	5,576,196	9,005,096	12,626,759	7,367,814	6,047,985
1995	68,186,798	70,442,935	1,380,218	1,136,003	33,796,302	5,424,745	8,974,532	11,835,713	7,369,119	6,144,975
1996	67,653,047	69,399,164	1,300,326	1,067,520	34,535,389	4,879,718	8,614,428	13,066,490	7,742,017	5,344,937
1997	69,826,779	71,753,430	1,388,619	1,003,118	34,788,263	4,825,240	8,252,540	13,990,598	7,509,055	5,603,506
1998	71,903,293	73,743,457	1,441,046	948,578	35,286,223	5,041,671	8,190,828	13,865,245	7,981,858	5,873,804
1999	75,340,622	77,386,368	1,614,133	990,226	35,645,859	5,043,528	8,862,435	14,069,508	7,476,036	6,009,730
2000	79,470,264	81,772,642	1,752,045	1,041,435	36,875,907	5,444,698	9,398,833	14,268,277	7,555,653	6,305,572

Notes appear at end of table

(continued)

TABLE Cg182–202   Federal obligations for research and development, by agency: 1947–2000   *Continued*

	Department										
	Health, Education and Welfare								National Aeronautics		
	Total	National Institutes of Health	Education	Health and Human Services	Interior	Transportation	Veterans Affairs	Atomic Energy Commission	and Space Administration	National Science Foundation	Other
	Cg192	Cg193 [1]	Cg194 [1]	Cg195	Cg196	Cg197	Cg198	Cg199	Cg200	Cg201	Cg202
Fiscal year	Thousand dollars	Thousand dollars	Thousand dollars	Thousand dollars	Thousand dollars	Thousand dollars	Thousand dollars	Thousand dollars	Thousand dollars	Thousand dollars	Thousand dollars
1947	10,600	—	—	—	16,900	—	1,400	39,900	26,700	—	8,900
1948	24,300	—	—	—	20,300	—	3,100	145,400	33,000	—	10,000
1949	25,200	—	—	—	30,200	—	4,300	140,000	38,300	—	9,600
1950	34,200	—	—	—	28,700	—	3,800	172,200	42,800	—	11,800
1951	38,941	33,000	—	—	30,442	—	5,071	157,901	45,428	151	18,866
1952	44,607	38,000	—	—	30,709	—	3,872	168,844	50,536	1,244	20,338
1953	51,017	48,400	—	—	32,113	—	5,091	204,404	48,393	2,495	20,166
1954	59,745	—	—	—	38,832	—	5,343	229,552	47,358	4,552	17,143
1955	68,049	—	—	—	34,527	—	5,575	253,406	43,030	9,654	14,491
1956	85,976	124,700	—	—	36,110	—	6,471	410,727	49,524	15,989	13,611
1957	144,213	157,400	—	—	45,207	—	7,707	528,043	55,260	30,649	17,877
1958	184,870	211,700	—	—	51,119	16,312	9,976	644,003	77,058	33,584	21,026
1959	242,828	274,300	—	—	60,573	27,255	12,815	699,756	261,671	60,418	20,234
1960	319,778	375,400	—	—	63,991	47,902	15,087	761,657	369,278	74,720	30,646
1961	428,525	495,100	—	—	73,302	48,237	22,015	850,157	776,920	83,983	25,678
1962	576,936	566,000	—	—	85,645	66,228	27,456	1,029,195	1,439,208	113,943	31,201
1963	656,158	651,000	—	—	92,122	83,478	29,868	1,077,942	2,857,423	154,123	37,554
1964	776,947	715,100	—	—	106,437	62,786	33,742	1,235,979	4,286,550	170,229	47,955
1965	869,354	701,000	—	—	113,173	64,408	37,371	1,240,664	4,951,522	187,150	68,176
1966	1,014,389	802,800	—	—	143,203	171,746	40,057	1,212,377	5,050,006	243,669	131,148
1967	1,146,614	858,739	—	—	170,401	283,608	40,894	1,257,342	4,866,962	262,426	124,219
1968	1,251,816	909,318	—	—	190,597	171,671	44,658	1,368,999	4,429,407	283,457	133,844
1969	1,297,441	919,789	—	—	207,620	231,844	50,207	1,405,944	3,963,306	273,790	182,363
1970	1,220,975	893,192	—	—	156,806	327,808	58,612	1,345,989	3,799,946	288,978	376,727
1971	1,476,071	1,055,293	—	—	191,516	497,204	62,901	1,302,926	3,257,927	336,942	458,376
1972	1,751,112	1,321,104	—	—	218,722	310,505	69,087	1,297,668	3,157,237	454,840	381,747
1973	1,837,578	1,355,484	—	—	243,746	310,640	74,271	1,363,196	3,060,887	479,893	468,606
1974	2,290,114	1,777,273	—	—	192,427	369,789	84,805	—	3,002,172	556,413	445,828
1975	2,397,458	1,918,228	—	—	303,329	311,563	94,807	—	3,064,413	595,021	576,985
1976	2,583,563	2,092,472	—	—	333,198	294,500	97,679	—	3,446,830	609,256	604,799
1977	2,823,297	2,411,706	—	—	314,682	354,604	107,001	—	3,170,789	697,019	691,730
1978	3,207,254	2,654,220	—	—	358,974	408,250	113,991	—	3,333,260	748,775	971,221
1979	—	3,000,761	166,288	3,504,880	405,778	370,089	127,004	—	3,578,404	807,925	1,233,687
1980	—	3,211,203	139,372	3,780,221	411,258	361,230	133,400	—	3,234,088	881,792	1,263,608
1981	—	3,355,530	0	3,927,141	427,105	415,539	144,400	—	3,593,155	961,564	1,106,263
1982	—	3,452,572	127,981	3,940,745	381,074	310,083	137,300	—	3,077,859	975,327	1,145,917
1983	—	3,806,753	111,681	4,352,530	382,473	347,728	161,400	—	2,661,579	1,061,990	1,031,769
1984	—	4,285,228	115,702	4,830,693	410,877	448,335	190,300	—	2,821,900	1,202,820	1,049,095
1985	—	4,856,511	125,969	5,451,036	391,685	428,859	226,600	—	3,327,200	1,345,583	1,089,352
1986	—	5,034,472	127,907	5,657,604	385,219	385,474	186,200	—	3,419,800	1,353,335	1,070,795
1987	—	5,886,193	153,512	6,606,289	403,834	324,980	209,500	—	3,787,072	1,470,505	1,112,681
1988	—	6,309,927	145,853	7,158,041	416,768	304,590	215,300	—	4,330,358	1,532,773	1,120,763
1989	—	6,833,827	160,989	7,902,837	469,020	303,312	234,700	—	5,393,476	1,670,396	1,227,103
1990	—	7,221,300	178,846	8,405,641	508,509	366,554	237,700	—	6,533,246	1,689,535	1,373,036
1991	—	7,763,351	175,217	9,755,999	592,938	379,921	216,600	—	7,280,239	1,785,223	1,440,120
1992	—	8,491,354	170,893	8,987,823	609,178	445,012	223,900	—	7,657,606	1,868,397	1,520,700
1993	—	9,893,293	179,942	10,349,177	619,069	545,323	236,159	—	8,019,854	1,881,889	1,567,188
1994	—	10,439,854	178,422	11,021,519	694,095	620,747	247,979	—	8,296,247	2,040,358	1,487,292
1995	—	10,930,625	179,397	11,457,247	561,613	726,986	237,860	—	9,014,944	2,149,277	1,583,373
1996	—	11,377,862	173,690	11,951,108	567,535	552,457	256,075	—	8,570,100	2,188,313	1,319,287
1997	—	12,237,861	181,248	12,785,262	579,901	526,872	252,699	—	9,327,300	2,248,520	1,322,719
1998	—	13,137,530	204,455	13,704,232	531,969	566,117	277,094	—	9,568,029	2,289,337	1,416,864
1999	—	15,005,029	223,697	15,914,736	641,542	666,950	339,088	—	9,525,693	2,506,031	1,486,634
2000	—	17,228,564	246,804	18,140,350	565,974	700,138	366,706	—	9,568,073	2,655,593	1,498,471

TABLE Cg182–202   Federal obligations for research and development, by agency: 1947–2000   *Continued*

[1] Includes obligations for R&D plant.

[2] Figures are obligations for the U.S. Energy Research and Development Administration.

Sources

1947–1950: U.S. Bureau of the Budget (now U.S. Office of Management and Budget), unpublished data.

1951–2000: National Science Foundation (NSF), *Federal Funds for Research and Development Detailed Historical Tables: Fiscal Years 1951–2001*; Army, Navy, Air Force, Education, and National Institutes of Health figures: NSF, *Federal Funds for Research, Development and Other Activities*, available biennially from the NSF Internet site.

Documentation

Obligations represent orders placed, contracts awarded, services received, and similar transactions during a given period, regardless of when the funds were appropriated and when future payment of money is required. Because government accounting does not use research and development (R&D) as a uniform bookkeeping category for all agencies, the data represent estimates by informed persons. Figures for outlays (as opposed to obligations) are available from the source beginning with 1967. The trends in obligations and outlays are essentially similar, but in particular years the discrepancy may be substantial because of time lags.

R&D plant (or R&D facilities and fixed equipment, such as reactors, wind tunnel, and radio telescopes) includes acquisition of, major repairs to, or alterations in structures, works, equipment, facilities, or land, for use in R&D activities. Excluded from the R&D plant category are expendable equipment and office furniture and equipment.

Series Cg195. Federal Security Agency prior to 1952.

Series Cg198. The Veterans Administration became the Department of Veterans Affairs in 1989.

Series Cg200. National Advisory Committee for Aeronautics prior to 1958.

TABLE Cg203–211   Expenditures for industrial research and development: 1953–2000[1,2]

Contributed by Gavin Wright

		Federal				Company			
	Total	Total	Basic research	Applied research	Development	Total	Basic research	Applied research	Development
	Cg203	Cg204	Cg205	Cg206	Cg207	Cg208	Cg209	Cg210	Cg211
Year	Million dollars	Million dollars	Million dollars	Million dollars	Million dollars	Million dollars	Million dollars	Million dollars	Million dollars
1953	3,630	1,430	19	288	1,123	2,200	132	438	1,630
1954	4,070	1,750	23	322	1,405	2,320	143	492	1,685
1955	4,640	2,180	27	368	1,785	2,460	162	560	1,738
1956	6,605	3,328	37	474	2,817	3,277	216	794	2,267
1957	7,731	4,335	41	678	3,616	3,396	230	992	2,174
1958	8,389	4,759	43	774	3,942	3,630	252	1,137	2,241
1959	9,618	5,635	72	813	4,750	3,983	248	1,178	2,557
1960	10,509	6,081	79	833	5,169	4,428	297	1,196	2,935
1961	10,908	6,240	81	812	5,347	4,668	314	1,165	3,189
1962	11,464	6,434	143	1,011	5,281	5,029	345	1,438	3,246
1963	12,630	7,270	147	1,007	6,116	5,360	375	1,450	3,535
1964	13,512	7,720	165	1,040	6,515	5,792	384	1,560	3,848
1965	14,185	7,740	186	1,038	6,516	6,445	406	1,620	4,419
1966	15,548	8,332	173	1,039	7,120	7,216	451	1,804	4,961
1967	16,385	8,365	202	1,066	7,097	8,020	427	1,849	5,744
1968	17,429	8,560	180	1,043	7,337	8,869	462	2,081	6,326
1969	18,308	8,451	160	1,015	7,276	9,857	458	2,272	7,127
1970	18,067	7,779	158	1,049	6,572	10,288	444	2,378	7,466
1971	18,320	7,666	134	974	6,558	10,654	456	2,441	7,757
1972	19,552	8,017	130	952	6,935	11,535	463	2,562	8,510
1973	21,249	8,145	132	993	7,020	13,104	499	2,832	9,773
1974	22,887	8,220	163	1,025	7,032	14,667	536	3,263	10,868
1975	24,187	8,605	157	1,130	7,316	15,582	573	3,440	11,569
1976	26,997	9,561	185	1,200	8,176	17,436	634	3,912	12,890
1977	29,825	10,485	210	1,325	8,950	19,340	701	4,311	14,328
1978	33,304	11,189	250	1,430	9,509	22,115	785	4,670	16,460
1979	38,226	12,518	265	1,555	10,698	25,708	893	5,670	19,145
1980	44,505	14,029	290	1,900	11,639	30,476	1,035	6,550	22,891
1981	51,810	16,382	301	2,340	13,741	35,428	1,313	8,359	25,756
1982	58,650	18,545	381	2,960	15,204	40,105	1,523	9,363	29,219
1983	65,268	20,680	463	3,641	16,576	44,588	1,760	10,286	32,542
1984	74,800	23,396	476	4,224	18,696	51,404	2,132	11,541	37,731
1985	84,239	27,196	489	5,347	21,360	57,043	2,373	12,908	41,762
1986	87,823	27,891	551	4,678	22,662	59,932	3,496	15,082	41,354
1987	92,155	30,752	740	4,660	25,352	61,403	3,583	15,153	42,667
1988	97,015	30,343	993	4,217	25,133	66,672	3,507	16,531	46,634
1989	102,055	28,554	1,384	4,698	22,472	73,501	3,632	17,993	51,676

Notes appear at end of table   (continued)

TABLE Cg203–211   Expenditures for industrial research and development: 1953–2000   *Continued*

	Total	Federal				Company			
		Total	Basic research	Applied research	Development	Total	Basic research	Applied research	Development
	Cg203	Cg204	Cg205	Cg206	Cg207	Cg208	Cg209	Cg210	Cg211
Year	Million dollars	Million dollars	Million dollars	Million dollars	Million dollars	Million dollars	Million dollars	Million dollars	Million dollars
1990	109,727	28,125	1,368	6,353	20,404	81,602	3,760	18,432	59,410
1991	116,952	26,372	1,712	6,021	18,639	90,580	6,125	21,425	63,030
1992	119,110	24,722	1,186	4,983	18,555	94,388	5,816	21,184	67,385
1993	117,400	22,809	958	4,730	17,118	94,591	5,961	19,956	68,678
1994	119,595	22,463	939	4,119	17,405	97,131	6,078	19,372	71,683
1995	132,103	23,451	720	3,699	19,031	108,652	5,379	23,755	79,516
1996	144,667	23,653	1,358	3,871	18,423	121,015	6,848	25,370	88,798
1997	157,539	23,928	1,654	2,861	19,412	133,611	8,766	29,782	95,064
1998	169,180	24,164	1,894	2,763	19,507	145,016	11,701	27,808	105,506
1999	182,711	22,535	—	—	—	160,176	—	—	—
2000	199,539	19,118	—	—	—	180,421	—	—	—

[1] Data for 1953–1956 not directly comparable with data for later years; see text.

[2] As a result of new sample design, data beginning 1991 are not directly comparable with data for earlier years.

Source

National Science Foundation (NSF), *Research and Development in Industry*, annual reports, available on the NSF Internet site.

Documentation

This table reports data from the annual Survey of Industrial Research and Development conducted by the National Science Foundation. The NSF's Division of Science Resources Studies has sponsored and managed a survey of industrial research and development (R&D) since 1953. The 1953–1956 surveys were conducted by the U.S. Bureau of Labor Statistics using somewhat different methodology and, hence, are not directly comparable with later data collected by the U.S. Bureau of the Census.

The survey's primary focus is on U.S. industry as a performer of, rather than as a source of, funds for R&D. Thus, data on federal support of R&D activities performed by industry are collected, while statistics on industrial funding of R&D undertaken at universities and colleges and other nonprofit organizations are not collected or included. The result of collecting performer-reported statistics is that the totals differ from those reported by federal funding agencies, as reported in NSF/SRS, *National Patterns of R&D Resources* (see Table Cg110–181). One reason for the difference is that performers often expend federal funds in a year other than the one in which the federal government provides authorization, obligations, or outlays.

As used in the survey, R&D is the pursuit of a planned search for new knowledge or understanding of the subject under study. In industry, *basic research* is the pursuit of new scientific knowledge or understanding that does not have specific immediate commercial objectives, although it may be in fields of present or potential commercial interest; *applied research* is investigation that has specific commercial objectives with respect to products, processes, or services; *development* is the systematic use of knowledge toward the production of useful materials, devices, systems, or methods, including the design and development of prototypes and processes. Specifically excluded from the survey are quality control, routine product testing, market research, sales promotion, and sales service; routine technical services; and research in the social sciences or psychology.

Recent issues of the report contain the following note: "For accurate historical statistics for 1988–1997, use only the detailed statistical tables in the report and not those published earlier. As a result of a new sample design, statistics for 1988–1991 have been revised since their original publication.... Also, before the 1995 survey cycle, data for previous years were reviewed for consistency with current year responses and were revised systematically during processing. This practice of routinely revising already published statistics has been discontinued." (NSF, *Research and Development in Industry*, 1998, p. 2).

Series Cg208–211. "Company" expenditures include costs funded by the company itself or by any other nonfederal sources. A breakdown of expenditures by industry may be found in the source, but many of the figures have been withheld to avoid possible disclosure of information about individual companies.

TABLE Cg212–235   Nobel Prizes, by category and recipient's country of residence: 1901–1999

Contributed by Gavin Wright

	Chemistry						Economics					
	France	Germany	Russia	United Kingdom	United States	Other	France	Germany	Russia	United Kingdom	United States	Other
	Cg212	Cg213	Cg214	Cg215	Cg216	Cg217	Cg218	Cg219	Cg220	Cg221	Cg222	Cg223
Years	Number	Number	Number	Number	Number	Number	Number	Number	Number	Number	Number	Number
1901–1904	0.0	2.0	0.0	1.0	0.0	1.0	0	0.0	0.0	0.0	0.0	0.0
1905–1909	1.0	3.0	0.0	1.0	0.0	0.0	0	0.0	0.0	0.0	0.0	0.0
1910–1914	2.0	1.0	0.0	0.0	1.0	1.0	0	0.0	0.0	0.0	0.0	0.0
1915–1919	0.0	2.0	0.0	0.0	0.0	0.0	0	0.0	0.0	0.0	0.0	0.0
1920–1924	0.0	1.0	0.0	2.0	0.0	1.0	0	0.0	0.0	0.0	0.0	0.0
1925–1929	0.0	3.0	0.0	0.5	0.0	1.5	0	0.0	0.0	0.0	0.0	0.0
1930–1934	0.0	2.0	0.0	0.0	2.0	0.0	0	0.0	0.0	0.0	0.0	0.0
1935–1939	1.0	2.5	0.0	0.5	0.0	1.0	0	0.0	0.0	0.0	0.0	0.0
1940–1944	0.0	1.0	0.0	0.0	0.0	1.0	0	0.0	0.0	0.0	0.0	0.0
1945–1949	0.0	0.0	0.0	1.0	2.0	2.0	0	0.0	0.0	0.0	0.0	0.0
1950–1954	0.0	2.0	0.0	1.0	2.0	0.0	0	0.0	0.0	0.0	0.0	0.0
1955–1959	0.0	0.0	0.5	2.5	1.0	1.0	0	0.0	0.0	0.0	0.0	0.0
1960–1964	0.0	0.5	0.0	2.0	2.0	0.5	0	0.0	0.0	0.0	0.0	0.0
1965–1969	0.0	0.3	0.0	1.2	3.0	0.5	0	0.0	0.0	0.0	0.0	1.0
1970–1974	0.0	0.5	0.0	0.5	2.0	2.0	0	0.0	0.0	1.0	3.5	0.5
1975–1979	0.0	0.5	0.0	1.5	1.5	1.5	0	0.0	0.5	1.0	3.0	0.5
1980–1984	0.0	0.0	0.0	1.3	3.2	0.5	0	0.0	0.0	1.0	4.0	0.0
1985–1989	0.3	0.7	0.0	0.0	3.7	0.3	1	0.0	0.0	0.0	3.0	1.0
1990–1994	0.0	0.0	0.0	0.0	3.5	1.5	0	0.3	0.0	0.0	4.7	0.0
1995–1999	0.0	0.3	0.0	1.2	3.2	0.3	0	0.0	0.0	1.5	3.5	0.0

	Physics						Physiology or medicine					
	France	Germany	Russia	United Kingdom	United States	Other	France	Germany	Russia	United Kingdom	United States	Other
	Cg224	Cg225	Cg226	Cg227	Cg228	Cg229	Cg230	Cg231	Cg232	Cg233	Cg234	Cg235
Years	Number	Number	Number	Number	Number	Number	Number	Number	Number	Number	Number	Number
1901–1904	1.0	1.0	0.0	1.0	0.0	1.0	0.0	1.0	1	1.0	0.0	1.0
1905–1909	1.0	1.5	0.0	1.0	1.0	0.5	1.5	1.5	0	0.0	0.0	2.0
1910–1914	0.0	2.0	0.0	0.0	0.0	3.0	1.0	1.0	0	0.0	1.0	2.0
1915–1919	0.0	2.0	0.0	2.0	0.0	0.0	0.0	0.0	0	0.0	0.0	1.0
1920–1924	0.0	1.0	0.0	0.0	1.0	3.0	0.0	0.5	0	0.5	0.0	3.0
1925–1929	2.0	1.0	0.0	1.5	0.5	0.0	0.0	0.0	0	0.5	0.0	3.5
1930–1934	0.0	1.0	0.0	0.5	0.0	1.5	0.0	1.0	0	1.0	3.0	0.0
1935–1939	0.0	0.0	0.0	1.5	2.0	1.5	0.0	2.0	0	0.5	0.0	2.5
1940–1944	0.0	0.0	0.0	0.0	2.0	0.0	0.0	0.0	0	0.0	1.5	0.5
1945–1949	0.0	0.0	0.0	2.0	2.0	1.0	0.0	0.0	0	1.0	1.7	2.3
1950–1954	0.0	0.5	0.0	2.0	1.0	1.5	0.0	0.0	0	0.5	4.2	0.3
1955–1959	0.0	0.0	1.0	0.0	4.0	0.0	0.0	0.3	0	0.0	2.7	2.0
1960–1964	0.0	0.8	1.7	0.0	2.5	0.0	0.0	0.5	0	1.8	1.8	0.8
1965–1969	1.0	0.0	0.0	0.0	3.7	0.3	1.0	0.0	0	0.0	3.7	0.3
1970–1974	0.5	0.0	0.0	2.3	1.3	0.8	0.0	0.3	0	1.2	2.5	1.0
1975–1979	0.0	0.0	0.3	0.7	3.3	0.7	0.0	0.0	0	0.8	3.8	0.3
1980–1984	0.0	0.0	0.0	0.0	3.7	1.3	0.3	0.0	0	0.7	2.7	1.3
1985–1989	0.0	1.7	0.0	0.0	1.3	2.0	0.0	0.0	0	0.3	3.2	1.5
1990–1994	1.0	0.0	0.0	0.0	2.5	1.5	0.0	1.0	0	0.0	4.0	0.0
1995–1999	0.3	0.0	0.0	0.0	4.2	0.5	0.0	0.3	0	0.0	4.2	0.5

Source

Internet site of the Nobel Foundation.

Documentation

Country refers to the country of residence at the time the prize was awarded. This is often different from the country of birth.

Also see Table Ad938–949.

TABLE Cg236–240   Commercial space launches, by nation: 1982–1997

Contributed by Louis P. Cain

Year	Total Cg236 Number	United States Cg237 Number	Europe Cg238 Number	Russia Cg239 Number	China Cg240 Number	Year	Total Cg236 Number	United States Cg237 Number	Europe Cg238 Number	Russia Cg239 Number	China Cg240 Number
1982	3	2	1	0	0	1990	12	7	4	0	1
1983	8	6	2	0	0	1991	12	6	6	0	0
1984	6	2	4	0	0	1992	14	6	6	0	2
1985	6	3	3	0	0	1993	8	2	6	0	0
1986	2	0	2	0	0	1994	14	4	8	0	2
1987	3	1	2	0	0	1995	17	6	8	0	3
1988	7	0	7	0	0	1996	21	8	9	2	2
1989	7	1	6	0	0	1997	33	13	11	6	3

Source

U.S. Bureau of Transportation Statistics *National Transportation Statistics*, annual editions.

Documentation

The data in this table cover commercial satellite launches in the medium-to-large vehicle class.

COMPUTERS

Gavin Wright

TABLE Cg241–250   Purchases of computers, by type: 1955–1995
Contributed by Gavin Wright

	All computers		Mainframes		Minicomputers		Microcomputers		Workstations	
	Units	Value	Units	Value	Units	Value	Units	Value	Units	Value
	Cg241	Cg242	Cg243	Cg244	Cg245	Cg246	Cg247	Cg248	Cg249	Cg250
Year	Number	Million dollars	Number	Million dollars	Number	Million dollars	Number	Million dollars	Number	Million dollars
1955	150	63	150	63	—	—	—	—	—	—
1956	500	152	500	152	—	—	—	—	—	—
1957	660	235	660	235	—	—	—	—	—	—
1958	970	381	970	381	—	—	—	—	—	—
1959	1,150	475	1,150	475	—	—	—	—	—	—
1960	1,790	590	1,790	590	—	—	—	—	—	—
1961	2,700	880	2,700	880	—	—	—	—	—	—
1962	3,470	1,090	3,470	1,090	—	—	—	—	—	—
1963	4,200	1,300	4,200	1,300	—	—	—	—	—	—
1964	5,600	1,670	5,600	1,670	—	—	—	—	—	—
1965	5,610	1,799	5,350	1,770	260	29	—	—	—	—
1966	7,635	2,680	7,250	2,640	385	40	—	—	—	—
1967	11,920	3,968	11,200	3,900	720	69	—	—	—	—
1968	10,180	4,900	9,100	4,800	1,080	100	—	—	—	—
1969	7,770	4,302	6,000	4,150	1,770	152	—	—	—	—
1970	8,320	3,810	5,700	3,600	2,620	210	—	—	—	—
1971	10,400	4,118	7,600	3,900	2,800	218	—	—	—	—
1972	14,310	5,271	10,700	5,000	3,610	271	—	—	—	—
1973	19,270	5,769	14,000	5,400	5,270	369	—	—	—	—
1974	17,480	6,777	8,600	6,200	8,880	577	—	—	—	—
1975	23,470	6,128	6,700	5,410	11,670	642	5,100	77	—	—
1976	49,550	6,770	6,750	5,580	17,000	816	25,800	374	—	—
1977	91,950	8,563	8,900	6,600	24,550	1,203	58,500	761	—	—
1978	152,650	10,284	7,500	7,590	29,550	1,596	115,600	1,098	—	—
1979	202,330	10,856	7,200	7,330	35,130	2,038	160,000	1,488	—	—
1980	301,850	13,431	9,900	8,840	41,450	2,487	250,500	2,104	—	—
1981	1,164,800	15,382	10,700	9,540	44,100	2,699	1,110,000	3,143	—	—
1982	3,708,700	23,625	6,700	10,000	171,400	7,700	3,530,000	5,925	600	—
1983	7,132,900	30,979	7,600	11,300	222,000	9,800	6,900,000	9,779	3,300	100
1984	7,919,400	42,869	9,700	16,400	291,100	11,800	7,610,000	14,269	8,600	400
1985	7,103,000	45,877	10,700	15,900	321,800	12,200	6,750,000	17,077	20,500	700
1986	7,414,500	49,288	11,300	17,200	332,100	12,300	7,040,000	18,888	31,100	900
1987	8,804,100	52,984	6,500	14,648	396,400	13,485	8,340,000	23,458	61,200	1,391
1988	9,953,000	55,815	6,000	14,079	349,600	11,820	9,500,000	27,700	97,400	2,216
1989	6,591,400	47,386	4,200	13,023	304,700	10,705	6,147,000	20,773	135,500	2,885
1990	7,012,773	44,996	4,483	13,327	208,102	9,816	6,638,700	18,661	161,488	3,192
1991	7,418,500	46,603	3,785	10,589	151,574	7,967	7,052,600	24,589	210,541	3,458
1992	12,909,841	46,502	2,992	8,391	124,745	8,534	12,544,374	25,858	237,730	3,719
1993	15,147,237	46,119	2,334	5,344	107,034	6,705	14,775,000	29,695	262,869	4,375
1994	19,065,713	56,017	3,483	5,976	141,147	7,752	18,605,000	37,313	316,083	4,976
1995	23,149,503	66,430	2,830	4,384	206,008	8,623	22,582,900	47,708	357,765	5,715

Sources

Series Cg241–242. Based on sources described for the other series.

Series Cg243–246 and Cg249–250. 1955–1984: Robert J. Gordon, *The Measurement of Durable Goods Prices* (University of Chicago Press, 1990), Table 6.1, whose sources are Montgomery Phister, *Data Processing Technology and Economics*, second edition (DEC, 1979), and Marcus E. Einstein and James C. Franklin, "Computer Manufacturing Enters a New Era of Growth," *Monthly Labor Review* 109 (1986): 9–16. 1985–1995: *Statistical Abstract of the United States*, annual issues, whose source is Dataquest, Incorporated, *Consolidated Database* (Dataquest).

Series Cg247–248. 1955–1980: Gordon (1990) ["microcomputers"]. 1981–1995: *Statistical Abstract*, annual issues, whose sources are Future Computing/Datapro, Inc (Dallas, Texas) [1981–1988] and Dataquest, Incorporated [1989–1995].

Documentation

In principle, these series represent all domestic purchases of computers. Mainframes were the first commercial computers and are the largest, most powerful computers available. Minicomputers are smaller and are used for business, scientific, and engineering tasks. Personal computers are units for individual use. The lines between these categories were continually blurred

(continued)

TABLE Cg241–250   Purchases of computers, by type: 1955–1995   *Continued*

during the period covered by the table, and the sources ceased to report the data in this form after 1995. In practice, the distinctions represent price brackets: Mainframes are those valued at greater than $250,000; minis are multiuser units priced between $20,000 and $249,000; and personal computers are those priced below $10,000. Workstations were classified as "engineering and technical systems" until 1987.

Because of the source changes in the early 1980s, the series on personal computers (series Cg248–249) may exaggerate the discontinuity of the increase between 1980 and 1981. Einstein and Franklin (1986) report that units below $1,000 were excluded from their table, so the figures prior to 1980 are biased downward. Nonetheless, the table conveys an accurate picture of the rapid shift away from mainframes and minis to personal computers. *Statistical Abstract* identifies the figures as "shipments" rather than "purchases," but the two concepts track each other very closely during the years where they overlap (1981–1988). The series on personal computers probably reflects domestic production rather than purchases for the 1990s.

TABLE Cg251–257   Price indexes for computer processors and memory chips: 1951–1996

Contributed by Gavin Wright

	All models of computer processors	Metal oxide semiconductor memory chips					
		All	Dynamic random access memory (DRAM)	Read-only memory (ROM)	Static random access memory (SRAM)		Microprocessors
					Fast	Slow	
	Cg251	Cg252	Cg253	Cg254	Cg255	Cg256	Cg257
Year	Index 1984 = 100	Index 1992 = 100	Index 1992 = 100	Index 1992 = 100	Index 1992 = 100	Index 1992 = 100	Index 1992 = 100
1951	133,666	—	—	—	—	—	—
1954	33,293	—	—	—	—	—	—
1955	26,452	—	—	—	—	—	—
1956	25,373	—	—	—	—	—	—
1957	24,337	—	—	—	—	—	—
1958	23,344	—	—	—	—	—	—
1959	15,726	—	—	—	—	—	—
1960	13,948	—	—	—	—	—	—
1961	9,928	—	—	—	—	—	—
1962	9,349	—	—	—	—	—	—
1963	9,444	—	—	—	—	—	—
1964	5,992	—	—	—	—	—	—
1965	2,931	—	—	—	—	—	—
1966	1,583	—	—	—	—	—	—
1967	1,582	—	—	—	—	—	—
1968	1,296	—	—	—	—	—	—
1969	1,058	—	—	—	—	—	—
1970	1,065	—	—	—	—	—	—
1971	1,084	—	—	—	—	—	—
1972	1,099	—	—	—	—	—	—
1973	846	—	—	—	—	—	—
1974	831	177,837	471,340	—	—	—	—
1975	813	56,057	131,553	—	—	12,952	—
1976	606	34,362	80,519	—	—	8,131	—
1977	638	19,923	48,058	7,499	12,584	4,660	—
1978	554	11,668	26,755	4,562	9,569	3,691	—
1979	439	9,733	21,535	4,093	8,521	3,172	—
1980	307	6,897	17,599	3,113	4,129	2,349	—
1981	211	3,348	7,532	2,160	1,979	1,249	—
1982	138	2,073	3,825	1,582	1,138	751	—
1983	145	1,513	2,758	1,083	1,059	570	—
1984	—	1,186	2,157	882	1,085	479	—
1985	—	557	739	544	749	283	724
1986	—	361	434	398	500	197	489
1987	—	323	399	308	395	182	427
1988	—	387	508	200	392	262	377
1989	—	329	443	157	343	241	281
1990	—	183	214	129	219	138	187
1991	—	130	142	107	142	110	153
1992	—	100	100	100	100	100	100
1993	—	94	98	77	66	103	71
1994	—	94	101	84	62	101	44
1995	—	87	98	77	40	82	15
1996	—	47	40	71	35	69	6

TABLE Cg251–257   Price indexes for computer processors and memory chips: 1951–1996   *Continued*

Sources
Series Cg251. Robert J. Gordon, *The Measurement of Durable Goods Prices* (University of Chicago Press, 1990), Table 6.7.

Series Cg252–257. Bruce T. Grimm, "Price Indexes for Selected Semiconductors, 1974–1996," *Survey of Current Business* (February 1998), Tables 4, 5, 12.

Documentation
Series Cg251. Calculated by Robert J. Gordon using a method known as "hedonic regression." The method estimates the relationship between sales prices and various performance measures such as memory, memory cycle time, and millions of instructions per second (MIPS). Gordon included mainframes for the full period, 1955–1984; minicomputers for 1965–1984; and personal computers beginning 1982.

Series Cg252–256. Figures represent quality-adjusted price indexes for various types of metal oxide semiconductor (MOS) digital memory integrated circuits ("memory chips"), and an aggregate index for all memory chips. The aggregate index, series Cg252, reflects changes in the relative importance of the components, as well as the price indexes for individual chip types. In particular, the relative weight of DRAM increased from about one third of the total in the early 1980s to about two thirds in 1995–1996. The sharp declines in all of the series show the effects of continuing advances in chip-making technology. The temporary reversal in 1987–1988 reflects the impact of the U.S.-Japan Semiconductor Trade Agreement of late 1986.

Series Cg257. Figures are an aggregation of price indexes for two types of microprocessors, constructed using hedonic regression methods similar to those employed by Gordon. A full description of the methodology may be found in the source.

TABLE Cg258–264   Performance indicators of computers and transistors: 1946–2000
Contributed by Gavin Wright

Year	Model number	Memory	Memory cycle time	Knight commercial index	MIPS indicator	Transistors per chip	Clock speed of transistors
	Cg258	Cg259	Cg260	Cg261	Cg262	Cg263	Cg264
					Million instructions per second		
	—	Kilobytes	Milliseconds	Index		Thousand	Megahertz
1946	ENIAC	—	—	0.04	—	—	—
1951	UNIVAC I	8	220.00	0.29	—	—	—
1954	650	10	2,400.00	0.27	—	—	—
1955	704	108	12.00	3.79	—	—	—
1955	705	30	17.00	2.09	—	—	—
1958	709	108	12.00	10.23	—	—	—
1959	7090	197	2.20	45.47	—	—	—
1960	7070	37	6.00	5.14	—	—	—
1961	1410	45	4.50	4.70	—	—	—
1961	7074	88	4.00	31.70	—	—	—
1961	7080	100	2.20	30.90	—	—	—
1962	7094	197	2.00	95.90	—	—	—
1963	7010	70	2.40	11.50	—	—	—
1963	7044	122	2.00	23.40	—	⌐	—
1965	360-20	10	3.60	4.50	—	—	—
1965	360-30	36	1.50	17.10	—	—	—
1965	360-40	136	2.50	50.10	—	—	—
1965	360-50	288	2.00	149.00	—	—	—
1965	360-65	1,088	0.75	810.00	—	—	—
1966	360-44	144	1.00	858.00	—	—	—
1971	—	—	—	—	—	2.3	0.1
1972	370-135	304	0.94	172.00	0.16	2.5	0.2
1972	370-145	1,184	0.61	446.00	0.30	—	—
1972	370-155	1,152	0.12	1,203.00	0.55	—	—
1972	370-165	1,792	0.08	3,515.00	1.90	—	—
1973	370-125	176	0.48	70.00	0.08	—	—
1974	370-115	165	0.48	39.00	0.05	5.0	2.0
1975	370-158-3	3,328	0.12	2,423.00	0.83	—	—
1976	370-138	768	0.94	496.00	0.21	—	—
1977	370-148	1,000	0.23	1,014.00	0.42	—	—
1978	3031	2,000	0.12	2,317.00	1.05	—	—
1978	3032	2,000	0.08	6,921.00	2.50	29.0	10.0
1978	3033	2,000	0.06	19,019.00	5.90	—	—
1979	4341	2,000	0.12	1,863.00	0.72	—	—
1980	3081	16,000	0.03	—	10.40	—	—

(continued)

TABLE Cg258–264   Performance indicators of computers and transistors: 1946–2000
Continued

Year	Model number Cg258 –	Memory Cg259 Kilobytes	Memory cycle time Cg260 Milliseconds	Knight commercial index Cg261 Index	MIPS indicator Cg262 Number	Transistors per chip Cg263 Thousand	Clock speed of transistors Cg264 Megahertz
1981	8140	1,000	0.80	—	0.36	—	—
1981	3033-M	16,000	0.06	—	9.10	—	—
1982	4321	1,000	0.90	—	0.19	120.0	12.5
1984	4361-5	2,000	0.10	—	1.14	—	—
1984	4381-2	4,000	0.07	—	2.70	—	—
1985	—	—	—	—	—	275.0	16.0
1989	—	—	—	—	—	1,180.0	25.0
1993	—	—	—	—	—	3,100.0	60.0
1995	—	—	—	—	—	5,500.0	200.0
1997	—	—	—	—	—	7,500.0	300.0
1999	—	—	—	—	—	24,000.0	600.0
2000	—	—	—	—	—	42,000.0	—

Sources

Series Cg258–262. Robert J. Gordon, *The Measurement of Durable Goods Prices* (University of Chicago Press, 1990), Table 6.8, using data from Montgomery Phister, *Data Processing Technology and Economics*, second edition (DEC, 1979) and *Computerworld*.

Series Cg263. "Moore's Law," on the Intel Corporate Internet site.

Series Cg264. National Science Foundation, National Science Board, *Science and Engineering Indicators – 2000*, Appendix Table 9-1.

Documentation

Series Cg258–262. These IBM performance indicators were compiled by Gordon for use in his estimates of hedonic prices for computer attributes (see Table Cg251–257).

Series Cg261. The Knight index of computation power is a composite blend of memory and speed that uses a formula to weight together memory, processor time, and input–output factors.

Series Cg262. MIPS means millions of instructions per second.

Series Cg263. Moore's Law originated in an observation by Intel founder Gordon E. Moore in 1965. It states that the number of transistors per integrated circuit doubles every eighteen months. Moore predicted that the trend would continue through 1975, but in fact Moore's Law has been maintained ever since.

PRODUCTIVITY

Gavin Wright

TABLE Cg265–272   Indexes of national productivity, by sector and type of input: 1889–1957

Contributed by Gavin Wright

	Real gross private domestic product per labor hour			Real gross private domestic product per unit of input				
	Total economy	Farm sector	Nonfarm sector	Labor input	Capital input	Total factor input		
						Total economy	Farm sector	Nonfarm sector
	Cg265	Cg266	Cg267	Cg268	Cg269	Cg270	Cg271	Cg272
Year	Index 1929 = 100	Index 1929 = 100	Index 1929 = 100	Index 1929 = 100	Index 1929 = 100	Index 1929 = 100	Index 1929 = 100	Index 1929 = 100
1889	43.6	77.0	41.1	50.0	74.8	56.0	83.9	51.6
1890	45.7	74.7	44.1	52.4	77.8	58.6	81.3	55.2
1891	46.6	77.0	44.9	53.2	77.1	59.1	83.6	55.4
1892	49.4	72.5	49.4	56.0	79.6	61.8	78.3	60.4
1893	47.4	69.9	47.2	54.1	71.9	58.7	75.5	56.4
1894	47.7	71.7	47.7	55.3	67.6	58.5	77.3	55.6
1895	50.7	75.6	50.6	57.7	73.5	61.7	81.4	59.3
1896	49.5	80.3	47.9	56.3	69.2	59.5	86.3	55.2
1897	52.9	85.6	51.2	60.0	74.3	63.7	91.5	59.2
1898	53.7	88.6	51.6	60.9	73.3	64.1	94.2	59.0
1899	54.7	87.9	52.8	61.0	77.9	65.4	93.1	61.3
1900	55.6	87.9	53.6	61.7	77.0	65.7	92.3	61.5
1901	59.4	86.8	58.5	65.2	83.2	69.8	91.0	67.3
1902	57.2	85.6	55.7	61.9	80.7	66.7	90.6	64.1
1903	58.5	87.6	56.6	62.9	81.7	67.7	91.6	64.9
1904	58.4	89.4	56.5	63.5	78.0	67.2	93.8	63.8
1905	59.9	89.8	57.8	64.2	81.7	68.8	93.5	65.7
1906	64.4	94.0	62.3	68.5	88.1	73.5	97.5	70.6
1907	64.2	89.3	62.7	68.0	86.2	72.7	92.5	70.5
1908	61.1	90.5	59.3	65.6	76.2	68.2	93.7	64.9
1909	65.6	88.1	64.7	69.6	84.3	73.4	90.9	71.5
1910	64.4	90.0	62.7	67.7	82.4	71.6	92.5	68.9
1911	65.7	83.3	65.2	69.0	83.0	72.7	85.4	71.4
1912	66.9	97.2	64.4	69.7	85.1	73.7	99.8	70.2
1913	69.2	85.6	68.6	71.8	86.0	75.6	87.2	74.3
1914	64.7	92.7	62.7	67.9	76.6	70.3	95.3	66.9
1915	67.2	101.3	64.4	70.2	77.0	72.0	102.1	68.0
1916	72.3	89.6	71.3	73.7	87.5	77.4	89.9	76.1
1917	68.6	96.2	66.0	69.5	82.6	73.0	97.3	69.8
1918	74.1	86.2	74.1	75.0	86.1	78.0	87.3	77.1
1919	79.0	88.4	79.7	80.4	86.8	82.1	88.4	81.7
1920	78.3	85.8	79.4	79.6	85.4	81.2	86.5	80.9
1921	83.8	87.6	86.1	86.8	81.1	85.1	85.7	85.8
1922	83.0	90.4	84.0	84.9	85.7	85.1	90.2	84.9
1923	87.8	95.9	87.8	88.2	95.9	90.2	96.5	89.7
1924	91.7	90.0	93.4	92.9	95.3	93.6	91.2	94.2
1925	91.6	94.6	92.6	92.5	96.4	93.6	96.6	93.4
1926	94.1	93.4	95.0	94.4	99.2	95.7	95.3	95.9
1927	95.7	100.1	95.3	95.6	97.5	96.1	100.3	95.6
1928	95.7	96.1	96.1	95.9	96.1	96.0	96.7	96.0
1929	100.0	100.0	100.0	100.0	100.0	100.0	100.0	100.0
1930	97.5	94.0	98.9	98.8	89.0	96.3	93.9	96.5
1931	98.4	103.0	100.7	102.1	82.3	96.4	103.4	95.3
1932	95.0	102.2	98.7	100.8	71.9	91.9	100.9	90.5
1933	93.5	105.2	96.4	99.3	72.5	91.3	104.5	88.7
1934	104.5	101.0	108.5	108.6	82.0	100.8	97.2	101.2
1935	108.0	107.0	111.4	111.9	90.6	105.9	104.8	105.9
1936	113.3	102.9	115.6	114.4	102.2	111.2	99.9	112.6
1937	114.0	106.8	116.4	115.6	107.7	113.6	106.6	114.4
1938	117.8	119.8	119.4	120.3	100.8	115.2	116.8	115.0
1939	122.2	119.5	123.6	123.6	110.4	120.2	116.5	119.4

(continued)

TABLE Cg265-272 Indexes of national productivity, by sector and type of input: 1889–1957 *Continued*

Year	Real gross private domestic product per labor hour			Real gross private domestic product per unit of input				
	Total economy	Farm sector	Nonfarm sector	Labor input	Capital input	Total factor input		
						Total economy	Farm sector	Nonfarm sector
	Cg265	Cg266	Cg267	Cg268	Cg269	Cg270	Cg271	Cg272
	Index 1929 = 100	Index 1929 = 100	Index 1929 = 100	Index 1929 = 100	Index 1929 = 100	Index 1929 = 100	Index 1929 = 100	Index 1929 = 100
1940	124.0	119.9	124.4	124.4	114.9	122.0	115.7	122.4
1941	134.6	132.6	132.6	131.3	131.7	131.3	126.2	132.0
1942	136.6	136.7	133.6	131.3	140.2	133.1	130.4	132.5
1943	141.5	131.5	138.6	134.1	150.4	137.3	124.6	150.5
1944	152.6	134.0	150.3	144.5	161.3	147.9	126.6	148.7
1945	159.0	137.3	156.6	150.9	160.7	152.9	127.2	154.2
1946	150.9	145.4	146.2	143.1	150.3	144.5	133.0	144.3
1947	151.5	146.1	145.7	142.3	146.7	143.1	131.7	142.6
1948	156.7	161.3	149.5	146.4	144.6	145.9	142.8	144.5
1949	162.7	165.9	155.5	152.8	137.9	149.3	143.9	148.2
1950	175.4	182.5	165.6	162.8	145.5	158.7	153.0	157.3
1951	179.4	180.3	168.7	164.8	146.0	160.4	147.8	158.8
1952	183.5	189.7	171.7	167.7	145.6	162.5	152.8	161.0
1953	190.9	217.7	176.3	173.1	145.3	166.4	171.2	163.8
1954	195.4	232.7	179.9	178.4	138.9	168.4	181.1	165.1
1955	204.8	240.3	188.2	186.8	146.8	176.8	187.7	173.2
1956	206.5	252.5	188.7	188.0	145.1	177.1	194.1	173.0
1957	211.7	265.6	192.3	192.6	142.4	179.4	198.0	175.0

Sources

John W. Kendrick, *Productivity Trends in the United States* (Princeton University Press, 1961), and *Postwar Productivity Trends in the United States* (National Bureau of Economic Research, 1973).

Documentation

Productivity may be defined as the ratio relating output measures to one or more of the inputs associated with that output. Historically, the most commonly used measure of productivity has been output per unit of labor input, frequently called labor productivity. Such a measure reflects not just labor's effort but also other factors, including the state of technology, capital per worker, the efficiency of management, the pace of operations, and changes in the composition of the workforce. A variety of alternative input measures have been developed and used in productivity studies as part of the effort to understand the sources of historical productivity change. But labor productivity is perhaps the most basic concept because of its relatively close connection to changes in real income per person, the primary index of economic growth.

The output part of a productivity measure may also be defined in several ways. Industry productivity is typically derived from measures of physical output, where the components are physical units such as pounds, bushels, and tons. To arrive at total measures for an industry or an industry group, the units are weighted by man-hours or the closest equivalent. Estimates for broad aggregates, such as the total private economy or the farm sector, are constructed in terms of an output concept called value added or net output, where purchased "intermediate" products consumed in the production process are excluded. Changes in this type of measure reflect not only the average of individual industry productivity changes but also shifts in the relative importance of low- or high-productivity industries.

The specific year chosen for the weight base may affect the trend of the productivity series. In general, a current-year-weighted productivity index gives a lower trend than a base-year-weighted index because items that increase most in volume of output tend to be those with price declines or lower price increases. Because the base year affects the trend, it is *not* advisable simply to splice separate base-year series together to gain a longer series. One may reasonably compare rates of productivity growth across one base-year series and another. But compositional changes create an inherent ambiguity in comparing levels of productivity across long historical periods,

and this ambiguity is best acknowledged frankly as opposed to assuming it away.

The series in this table are measures of aggregate productivity for the total private economy, with a distinction between farm and nonfarm sectors in two cases. The numerator is derived from the U.S. Department of Commerce gross national product (GNP) series (with some adjustments), carried back from 1929 chiefly by the estimates of Simon Kuznets, supplemented by estimates of government purchases by John W. Kendrick. Although the numerator is adjusted GNP, the indexes are actually measures of the net productivity of the economy. This arises as a result of "netting" out all intermediate purchases of goods and services, thus eliminating duplication and measuring only the "end product" of the system. The indexes are "real" in that price fluctuations have been eliminated by use of average prices in the base period.

Series Cg265–267. Labor-hours is the physical unit of labor input. Estimates of labor-hours were obtained by multiplying employment of average hours worked per year in the various industrial groupings. These industry hours were combined without explicit weights, except for the farm sector, where the Agricultural Marketing Service estimates of farm labor requirements in terms of "average adult man-hour equivalents" were used.

Series Cg268. Labor-hours for industry groups were combined by average hourly earnings, using the same comparison period as for the output index. This adjustment provides one measure of the impact of labor force composition on productivity.

Series Cg269. Productivity is measured relative to real capital assets. The capital input was defined to include land and replaceable assets, such as residential and nonresidential structures, equipment, and inventories. The estimates are based primarily on those by Raymond Goldsmith, *A Study of Saving in the United States* (Princeton University Press, 1956). Index numbers for industry groups were combined using unit capital compensation as weights, parallel to the procedure in series Cg268.

Series Cg270–272. These series relate the quantity of output to the real quantity of total factor input, which is a weighted average of the index of labor input and the index of capital input. The weights are units of factor compensation.

TABLE Cg273–280   Indexes of national productivity, by sector and type of input: 1929–1970

Contributed by Gavin Wright

	Real gross private domestic product per labor hour			Real gross private domestic product per unit of input				
	Total economy	Farm sector	Nonfarm sector	Labor input	Capital input	Total factor input		
						Total economy	Farm sector	Nonfarm sector
	Cg273	Cg274	Cg275	Cg276	Cg277	Cg278	Cg279	Cg280
Year	Index 1958 = 100	Index 1958 = 100	Index 1958 = 100	Index 1958 = 100	Index 1958 = 100	Index 1958 = 100	Index 1958 = 100	Index 1958 = 100
1929	48.6	37.3	54.1	53.5	77.5	57.8	52.6	58.8
1930	46.8	35.6	52.5	52.3	68.1	55.1	50.1	55.6
1931	47.2	39.5	53.3	54.0	63.1	55.3	56.1	55.0
1932	45.4	39.8	51.6	53.2	56.2	53.0	55.8	51.9
1933	44.5	38.9	50.4	52.1	56.8	52.3	54.6	51.3
1934	49.0	36.2	55.9	56.2	62.1	56.7	48.7	57.6
1935	50.6	39.2	57.7	57.8	69.8	59.8	53.9	60.6
1936	53.2	37.0	60.2	59.2	78.6	62.7	50.1	64.7
1937	53.1	40.3	59.7	59.3	81.6	63.2	56.5	64.7
1938	54.7	43.3	61.4	61.5	76.4	64.1	59.1	65.0
1939	56.9	44.2	63.6	63.5	83.9	67.1	60.5	68.3
1940	58.5	42.7	66.1	64.9	89.3	69.3	58.3	71.5
1941	61.8	47.7	67.2	66.3	98.2	72.0	64.2	73.5
1942	62.0	49.9	66.7	65.7	102.9	72.3	67.9	73.2
1943	63.0	47.9	67.4	65.8	108.6	73.1	64.7	74.5
1944	67.2	47.6	72.7	70.1	115.7	77.8	64.3	80.3
1945	70.7	47.9	76.8	74.0	115.6	81.3	63.0	84.4
1946	68.7	51.4	73.3	71.7	109.4	78.4	66.7	80.5
1947	68.7	49.6	72.8	71.0	105.6	77.2	63.0	79.3
1948	71.4	56.2	74.8	73.5	106.7	79.5	70.0	81.0
1949	74.0	54.3	78.4	76.8	102.4	81.5	67.3	82.6
1950	80.1	61.9	83.8	82.3	109.1	87.1	74.1	88.3
1951	82.0	62.3	85.1	82.9	109.5	87.8	72.4	89.1
1952	83.5	68.0	85.6	83.8	106.7	87.9	77.1	88.7
1953	87.4	76.6	88.8	87.1	108.0	90.8	84.1	91.3
1954	89.9	80.1	91.2	90.3	103.2	92.8	86.7	93.2
1955	94.2	81.0	95.9	94.4	108.4	97.0	88.1	97.7
1956	94.6	84.6	95.6	94.4	105.6	96.6	90.4	96.9
1957	97.2	89.8	97.6	96.4	103.4	97.8	92.7	98.0
1958	100.0	100.0	100.0	100.0	100.0	100.0	100.0	100.0
1959	103.5	101.1	103.5	103.0	104.5	103.3	100.9	103.5
1960	104.9	106.5	104.7	104.5	104.1	104.4	105.4	104.6
1961	108.5	115.8	107.8	107.7	103.5	106.8	111.2	107.0
1962	113.5	118.2	113.0	112.4	108.0	111.4	112.1	111.8
1963	117.4	128.7	116.3	115.6	109.4	114.2	118.5	114.5
1964	121.6	131.7	120.3	119.4	111.9	117.7	118.9	118.3
1965	125.7	144.2	123.8	122.9	114.5	121.0	128.3	121.3
1966	129.5	149.4	127.1	125.4	115.3	123.2	126.6	123.7
1967	131.5	163.5	—	127.7	112.8	124.2	—	—
1968	135.2	164.6	—	131.0	113.5	126.8	—	—
1969	135.6	177.5	—	130.9	112.1	126.5	—	—
1970	137.2	—	—	132.6	107.5	126.4	—	—

Sources

John W. Kendrick, *Productivity Trends in the United States* (Princeton University Press, 1961), and *Postwar Productivity Trends in the United States* (National Bureau of Economic Research, 1973); 1967–1970 from unpublished data supplied by John W. Kendrick.

Documentation

See the text for Table Cg265–272.

TABLE Cg281–291   Indexes of national productivity, by sector and type of good: 1947–2000

Contributed by Gavin Wright

	Output per hour						Multifactor productivity				
	Manufacturing			Business sector	Nonfarm business sector	Nonfinancial corporations	Manufacturing			Business sector	Nonfarm business sector
	All	Durable goods	Nondurable goods				All	Durable goods	Nondurable goods		
	Cg281	Cg282	Cg283	Cg284	Cg285	Cg286	Cg287	Cg288	Cg289	Cg290	Cg291
Year	Index 1992 = 100	Index 1992 = 100	Index 1992 = 100	Index 1992 = 100	Index 1992 = 100	Index 1992 = 100	Index 1996 = 100	Index 1996 = 100	Index 1996 = 100	Index 1996 = 100	Index 1996 = 100
1947	—	—	—	31.8	36.7	—	—	—	—	—	—
1948	—	—	—	33.3	37.7	—	—	—	—	51.5	56.3
1949	33.5	31.5	35.0	34.0	39.0	—	59.7	53.3	72.1	52.1	57.4
1950	34.0	33.3	35.2	36.9	41.7	—	62.7	56.6	74.6	55.9	60.9
1951	33.8	32.1	36.2	38.0	42.7	—	62.9	56.2	75.4	57.2	62.5
1952	35.2	33.9	37.2	39.2	43.6	—	63.8	57.7	75.4	57.7	62.6
1953	36.4	35.8	37.8	40.7	44.6	—	65.0	58.6	76.7	59.0	63.3
1954	37.3	35.8	39.4	41.6	45.5	—	64.9	58.1	77.5	59.1	63.4
1955	38.8	37.4	41.0	43.3	47.4	—	66.9	60.4	78.6	61.9	66.3
1956	38.6	35.8	42.7	43.4	47.0	—	66.0	58.4	79.3	61.6	65.7
1957	39.4	36.3	43.8	44.7	48.2	—	66.4	58.5	80.1	62.5	66.4
1958	40.0	36.0	45.1	46.0	49.3	51.8	65.2	57.2	79.3	62.8	66.6
1959	40.9	37.3	46.2	47.9	51.3	54.4	68.1	59.8	82.3	64.9	68.9
1960	41.8	37.7	47.5	48.8	51.9	55.4	68.3	59.6	82.9	65.3	69.2
1961	42.8	38.3	48.8	50.6	53.7	57.3	68.9	60.2	83.5	66.7	70.3
1962	44.2	40.2	49.8	52.9	56.1	59.7	71.6	63.1	85.5	69.1	72.8
1963	45.7	41.9	51.5	55.0	58.1	61.7	73.6	65.2	87.1	71.2	74.8
1964	47.4	43.4	53.7	57.5	60.6	64.1	75.7	67.4	88.8	74.0	77.6
1965	48.5	45.6	53.7	59.6	62.4	65.8	77.7	69.7	89.8	76.4	79.8
1966	49.1	46.3	54.2	62.0	64.6	66.7	78.0	70.0	90.0	78.7	82.1
1967	50.9	47.2	57.1	63.4	65.8	67.7	77.5	69.2	90.2	78.8	82.0
1968	52.7	49.4	58.6	65.4	67.8	70.0	79.9	71.1	92.8	80.9	84.2
1969	53.5	50.1	60.0	65.7	67.9	70.0	80.5	71.2	93.9	80.4	83.4
1970	54.2	49.8	61.7	67.0	68.9	70.4	79.2	69.4	94.0	80.3	82.9
1971	57.8	54.0	64.6	69.9	71.8	73.3	81.4	71.5	96.0	82.8	85.4
1972	60.3	56.6	67.7	72.2	74.2	75.3	84.4	73.8	99.1	85.3	88.0
1973	61.4	58.9	67.9	74.5	76.6	76.1	85.9	76.0	99.1	87.6	90.4
1974	61.2	57.2	69.8	73.2	75.3	74.4	81.3	72.7	93.6	84.4	87.2
1975	64.3	59.1	72.4	75.8	77.4	77.2	78.9	70.5	91.6	85.2	87.4
1976	67.0	62.5	74.2	78.5	80.3	79.7	81.7	73.1	94.1	88.4	90.9
1977	69.7	65.7	76.9	79.8	81.5	81.6	82.9	74.5	94.8	89.8	92.2
1978	70.4	66.6	77.8	80.7	82.6	82.1	83.6	74.3	96.4	91.0	93.5
1979	69.8	66.7	76.7	80.7	82.2	81.5	82.7	73.4	95.9	90.6	92.9
1980	70.1	66.7	76.5	80.4	82.0	81.1	81.3	72.2	94.4	88.6	90.8
1981	70.7	67.5	76.9	82.0	83.0	82.6	81.9	73.5	94.0	88.8	90.3
1982	74.2	70.1	80.3	81.7	82.5	83.4	83.3	73.8	96.8	86.1	87.3
1983	76.7	74.0	81.4	84.6	86.3	85.9	85.2	76.1	97.9	88.5	90.5
1984	79.5	78.5	82.9	87.0	88.1	88.2	87.8	80.4	98.0	91.4	92.9
1985	82.3	80.5	86.5	88.7	89.3	89.9	89.2	82.2	98.5	92.4	93.3
1986	85.9	84.8	89.1	91.4	92.0	91.7	90.7	84.2	99.2	93.8	94.7
1987	88.3	87.8	90.8	91.9	92.3	94.7	93.5	87.7	100.8	94.1	94.8
1988	90.2	90.0	92.2	93.0	93.5	95.9	95.2	89.5	102.0	94.7	95.5
1989	90.3	90.1	91.8	93.9	94.2	94.7	93.4	88.5	99.7	95.3	95.8
1990	92.9	92.5	94.0	95.2	95.3	95.4	93.3	89.0	98.8	95.4	95.7
1991	95.0	93.9	96.0	96.3	96.4	97.7	92.4	88.2	98.1	94.5	94.8
1992	100.0	100.0	100.0	100.0	100.0	100.0	94.0	90.6	98.5	96.6	96.7
1993	101.9	103.4	100.6	100.5	100.5	100.7	94.9	92.2	98.6	97.1	97.2
1994	105.0	108.0	102.5	101.9	101.8	103.1	97.3	95.6	99.5	98.1	98.1
1995	109.0	113.1	105.6	102.6	102.8	104.2	99.2	98.1	100.6	98.4	98.6
1996	112.8	118.1	108.6	105.4	105.4	107.5	100.0	100.0	100.0	100.0	100.0
1997	117.6	124.2	113.1	107.8	107.5	108.4	103.5	104.6	101.9	101.2	101.0
1998	124.0	134.3	115.9	110.8	110.4	112.3	106.3	109.3	102.2	102.6	102.4
1999	129.6	143.6	117.7	113.8	113.2	116.2	109.4	114.6	102.5	103.5	103.0
2000	138.5	158.0	121.4	118.6	118.1	121.1	—	—	—	—	—

TABLE Cg281–291   Indexes of national productivity, by sector and type of good: 1947–2000   *Continued*

Source

U.S. Bureau of Labor Statistics (BLS), "Business and Manufacturing Productivity," from the BLS Internet site.

Documentation

Indexes of labor productivity, multifactor productivity, and related measures for broad economic sectors and manufacturing industries are maintained and published by the BLS. Aggregate sector measures such as these reflect not only the average of trends within industries but also shifts in the relative importance of low- or high-productivity industries. A detailed description of procedures, data sources, and their uses and limitations may be found in the BLS *Handbook of Methods*, Bulletin 2490 (April 1997), pp. 89–102.

Series Cg281–286. The traditional measure of labor productivity – output per hour – is available quarterly and updated and revised eight times a year. Output, measured net of price changes and interindustry transactions, is compared to labor input, measured as hours at work in the corresponding sector. The basis for the output components is real gross domestic product in the business and nonfarm business sectors; these output components are consistent with the National Income and Product Accounts prepared by the U.S. Bureau of Economic Analysis.

Series Cg284–285. The business sector excludes general government, non-profit institutions, paid employees of private households, and the rental value of owner-occupied dwellings (that is, many of the activities where it is difficult to draw inferences on productivity from conventional output measures).

The farm sector, which is subject to unique external forces, is also excluded to yield the nonfarm business sector, the principal focus of many productivity studies.

Series Cg286. Nonfinancial corporate output is similar to that of the business sector but also excludes unincorporated businesses and those corporations that are depository institutions, nondepository institutions, security and commodity brokers, insurance carriers, regulated investment offices, small business offices, and real estate investment trusts. The primary source of hours and employment data is the BLS Current Employment Statistics (CES) program, which provides monthly survey data on employment and average weekly hours of production and nonsupervisory workers in nonagricultural establishments. Jobs rather than persons are counted so that multiple jobholders are counted more than once. Because CES data include only nonfarm wage and salary workers, data from the Current Population Survey (CPS) are used for farm employment and for proprietors and unpaid family workers.

Series Cg287–289. Multifactor indexes for manufacturing provide measures of sector output per combined unit of capital, labor, energy, materials, and purchased services inputs – so-called KLEMS inputs.

Series Cg290–291. The multifactor productivity indexes for major sectors measure the value-added output per combined unit of labor and capital input in private business and private nonfarm business.

TABLE Cg292–296   Output per employee – mining and mineral industries: 1955–2000

Contributed by Gavin Wright

Year	Copper (recoverable metal) Cg292 Index 1987 = 100	Coal Cg293 Index 1987 = 100	Crude petroleum and natural gas Cg294 Index 1987 = 100	Nonmetallic minerals, except fuels Cg295 Index 1987 = 100	Crushed and broken stone Cg296 Index 1987 = 100
1955	31.5	36.0	—	—	—
1956	30.2	37.7	—	—	—
1957	30.5	36.6	—	—	—
1958	32.2	36.7	—	50.4	41.9
1959	32.2	39.8	90.6	52.9	44.5
1960	34.8	42.4	95.1	52.1	43.9
1961	36.6	47.3	101.3	54.6	45.6
1962	39.2	52.4	106.2	57.9	48.6
1963	39.9	58.0	112.7	60.9	51.1
1964	42.0	61.8	117.2	65.1	55.2
1965	41.2	66.9	123.3	67.8	59.4
1966	41.0	70.9	135.0	71.7	62.8
1967	34.5	72.6	145.7	70.6	62.2
1968	39.5	75.0	153.2	75.9	67.1
1969	42.5	75.1	160.3	79.0	69.4
1970	43.5	74.9	168.8	79.7	68.4
1971	41.3	68.4	167.6	79.2	67.1
1972	41.6	66.3	169.3	81.5	69.7
1973	40.3	65.5	171.5	87.8	79.0
1974	34.9	60.2	157.6	84.1	76.8
1975	35.0	54.4	138.8	79.4	72.8
1976	42.8	53.8	130.7	84.8	75.5
1977	44.2	54.7	125.3	89.2	81.0
1978	49.4	56.5	120.3	94.1	88.9
1979	47.3	53.2	110.5	92.8	88.9
1980	43.1	59.5	97.1	84.8	81.4
1981	46.8	64.7	83.4	82.2	75.9
1982	51.8	62.5	78.4	77.1	73.9
1983	59.8	71.2	78.4	85.8	82.7
1984	73.2	80.8	82.9	93.2	86.6

(continued)

TABLE Cg292–296   Output per employee – mining and mineral industries: 1955–2000
Continued

Year	Copper (recoverable metal)	Coal	Crude petroleum and natural gas	Nonmetallic minerals, except fuels	Crushed and broken stone
	Cg292	Cg293	Cg294	Cg295	Cg296
	Index 1987 = 100	Index 1987 = 100	Index 1987 = 100	Index 1987 = 100	Index 1987 = 100
1985	90.7	83.2	84.0	93.9	85.9
1986	105.5	89.2	92.2	93.9	86.3
1987	100.0	100.0	100.0	100.0	100.0
1988	110.7	111.0	101.2	101.5	101.1
1989	113.0	120.1	99.6	100.1	98.3
1990	108.2	123.6	99.0	101.0	100.3
1991	106.3	129.4	99.3	96.3	95.1
1992	118.8	138.5	102.8	101.3	101.1
1993	123.7	148.0	107.5	101.7	103.8
1994	132.1	158.3	114.1	106.4	109.7
1995	123.0	165.6	121.0	106.5	106.6
1996	122.8	182.0	125.0	107.6	109.8
1997	125.6	190.8	127.3	111.1	116.4
1998	127.7	199.3	128.8	110.4	112.6
1999	121.2	207.4	133.6	108.9	106.4
2000	141.2	219.0	140.8	104.5	104.8

Source

U.S. Bureau of Labor Statistics (BLS), "Industry Labor Productivity Tables," from the BLS Internet site.

Documentation

Studies of labor productivity in individual industries have been a part of the program of the Bureau of Labor Statistics since the nineteenth century. During the 1920s and 1930s, the BLS began the preparation and publication of industry indexes of output per employee and per hour, which were based on available production data from the periodic *Census of Manufactures* and employment statistics collected by the BLS. However, wartime disruptions and budget restrictions after 1952 prevented direct collection of data, with the result that the coverage of industries was very uneven until recent decades. The number of industries included continued to expand through 1998, at which point it had reached 100 percent of employment in manufacturing, 96 percent in mining, 90 percent in communications and utilities, 78 percent in trade, 57 percent in transportation, and 17 percent in finance and services. The series presented here represent a selection based on industry size

and on the length of continuously available data. They link the data reported as "1987 forward" with what the BLS calls "historical" data going back to various starting years.

The output measures are what is known as Tornqvist indexes, computed as a weighted average of the growth rates of the various industry products between two periods, with weights based on the products' shares in industry value of production. The weight for each product equals its average value share in the two periods. Therefore, the weights are allowed to change through time rather than being fixed. For a more complete discussion of the Tornqvist methodology, see Chapter 11 of the BLS *Handbook of Methods*, BLS Bulletin 2490 (April 1997), pp. 103–9.

Employment includes both production (nonsupervisory) and nonproduction (professional, technical, clerical, supervisory) workers. No distinction is made between different groups of employees.

Series Cg292. Links the series for "copper ores," 1955–1986, with "copper mining," beginning 1987.

TABLE Cg297–301   Output per hour – mining and mineral industries: 1955–2000

Contributed by Gavin Wright

Year	Copper (recoverable metal) Cg297 Index 1987 = 100	Coal Cg298 Index 1987 = 100	Crude petroleum and natural gas Cg299 Index 1987 = 100	Nonmetallic minerals, except fuels Cg300 Index 1987 = 100	Crushed and broken stone Cg301 Index 1987 = 100
1955	30.4	41.0	—	—	—
1956	29.7	42.7	—	—	—
1957	31.9	43.0	—	—	—
1958	35.3	46.4	—	52.2	43.7
1959	32.5	47.0	90.5	53.2	45.1
1960	33.7	50.0	95.7	53.5	45.7
1961	36.3	55.3	101.3	55.7	46.9
1962	39.6	59.4	106.2	58.6	49.6
1963	40.1	62.8	112.0	61.1	51.4
1964	42.4	66.4	116.9	64.5	55.6
1965	41.1	70.2	123.1	66.5	58.3
1966	41.0	73.4	134.8	70.3	61.8
1967	34.1	75.2	145.9	69.9	61.8
1968	36.2	78.6	153.4	75.9	67.0
1969	39.8	79.2	160.1	77.6	68.4
1970	42.3	77.3	169.1	80.1	69.2
1971	40.9	71.1	167.3	79.2	67.4
1972	43.5	68.1	168.4	82.1	71.2
1973	42.4	68.9	173.5	86.5	78.6
1974	37.1	67.2	161.5	83.4	76.8
1975	38.1	57.7	142.8	81.0	76.3
1976	46.8	56.5	131.9	86.1	78.2
1977	49.4	54.8	125.0	89.7	83.7
1978	53.2	58.4	119.7	94.3	90.6
1979	48.5	54.5	110.3	92.6	89.6
1980	45.3	61.7	97.2	86.9	84.7
1981	48.3	67.1	83.0	85.6	81.0
1982	57.4	65.6	78.1	80.8	78.8
1983	64.3	75.0	77.2	88.5	86.9
1984	75.9	83.4	81.9	94.0	88.4
1985	93.6	85.1	83.0	95.1	87.1
1986	109.7	92.4	90.3	95.1	87.4
1987	100.0	100.0	100.0	100.0	100.0
1988	109.2	110.5	101.0	101.0	101.3
1989	106.6	116.4	98.0	99.6	98.7
1990	102.7	118.3	97.0	101.4	102.2
1991	100.5	122.1	97.9	98.5	99.8
1992	115.2	132.7	102.1	103.0	105.0
1993	118.1	140.4	105.9	100.8	103.6
1994	126.0	147.3	112.4	104.4	108.7
1995	117.2	155.5	119.4	104.5	105.4
1996	116.5	167.2	123.9	104.3	107.2
1997	118.9	177.2	125.2	107.3	112.6
1998	118.3	187.8	127.4	108.6	110.2
1999	110.0	195.3	134.5	108.6	105.0
2000	122.6	206.9	206.9	103.3	101.9

Source

U.S. Bureau of Labor Statistics (BLS), "Industry Labor Productivity Tables," from the BLS Internet site.

Documentation

For background on BLS procedures and output measures, see the text for Table Cg292–296.

To compute hourly productivity, the output index is divided by an index of hours for each industry, computed by dividing an index of hours for each year by the hours for a base year. Prior to 1968, the estimates of average annual hours worked were calculated by multiplying the number of workweeks in the year times the scheduled weekly hours. Both employment and annual hour indexes are developed from basic data compiled by the BLS and the U.S. Bureau of the Census. The BLS and the Census differ in their definitions and in their sampling and reporting methods. In general, BLS data are preferred for these purposes. Census figures are averaged from four payroll periods

during the year, while BLS collects employment and hours monthly, and the employment levels are benchmarked each year to comprehensive data from the unemployment insurance programs. For more detailed discussion, see the BLS *Handbook of Methods*, BLS Bulletin 2490 (April 1997), Chapters 2 and 11.

Only employment data are available for nonproduction workers. From 1968 to 1977, the estimates of average annual hours for nonproduction workers were based on data collected in the BLS biennial surveys of employee compensation in the private nonfarm economy. Because these surveys are no longer being conducted, the 1977 levels of average annual hours per nonproduction worker are being carried forward until other data become available. For the mining industries, estimates for the hours of nonproduction workers are based on data collected by the U.S. Mine Safety and Health Administration.

Series Cg297. Links the series for "copper ores" (1955–1986) with "copper mining" (beginning 1987).

TABLE Cg302–307   Output per employee – food and beverage industries: 1947–2000

Contributed by Gavin Wright

Year	Dairy products Cg302 Index 1987 = 100	Preserved fruits and vegetables Cg303 Index 1987 = 100	Grain mill products Cg304 Index 1987 = 100	Bakery products Cg305 Index 1987 = 100	Malt beverages Cg306 Index 1987 = 100	Bottled and canned soft drinks Cg307 Index 1987 = 100
1947	—	40.0	—	53.5	12.4	—
1948	—	39.4	—	53.5	12.1	—
1949	—	40.1	—	52.2	12.9	—
1950	—	43.0	—	52.4	12.6	—
1951	—	46.4	—	51.6	12.9	—
1952	—	45.4	—	52.9	13.3	—
1953	—	48.8	—	55.3	13.1	—
1954	—	51.1	—	54.0	13.3	—
1955	—	51.0	—	54.4	13.7	—
1956	—	56.0	—	55.0	14.0	—
1957	—	53.3	—	56.6	14.3	—
1958	—	52.8	—	59.4	15.7	35.4
1959	—	53.0	—	59.2	16.5	37.6
1960	—	57.3	—	59.6	16.9	35.9
1961	—	59.1	—	60.2	17.7	36.9
1962	—	63.3	—	61.5	18.7	39.1
1963	—	63.0	44.1	65.5	20.6	40.7
1964	—	66.0	46.4	68.7	22.1	40.7
1965	—	67.4	47.3	69.6	23.3	40.9
1966	—	68.2	49.1	70.6	24.6	41.3
1967	42.1	68.1	51.0	73.0	25.9	40.0
1968	44.0	67.9	52.9	75.5	28.1	43.0
1969	46.1	68.0	53.7	74.9	30.3	41.8
1970	47.2	70.2	54.1	77.6	32.1	42.3
1971	51.7	72.6	56.1	80.0	33.8	45.2
1972	56.6	71.1	58.2	84.0	38.9	46.7
1973	58.4	76.9	55.7	83.8	43.4	49.0
1974	61.8	75.9	56.9	81.8	45.3	50.5
1975	65.3	77.3	57.5	82.0	50.0	55.2
1976	67.0	81.1	59.9	82.8	56.6	58.7
1977	69.1	82.4	65.6	87.9	58.0	61.7
1978	70.2	83.8	65.0	85.7	59.4	63.9
1979	71.3	81.2	67.2	84.4	63.6	64.0
1980	75.4	84.3	70.1	83.4	67.6	66.2
1981	81.2	82.7	75.2	85.8	68.0	68.5
1982	84.0	88.0	79.3	90.2	69.7	70.5
1983	88.8	92.2	81.5	93.0	73.8	75.1
1984	89.0	92.9	85.3	93.7	75.4	80.9
1985	92.6	92.7	90.1	96.3	72.8	84.8
1986	96.1	96.2	94.4	100.7	87.1	91.0
1987	100.0	100.0	100.0	100.0	100.0	100.0
1988	107.8	97.8	101.6	96.8	99.3	109.6
1989	107.3	100.3	107.7	96.0	106.4	119.5
1990	107.0	99.5	106.3	92.5	111.9	127.4
1991	108.1	102.9	106.4	89.8	110.1	136.0
1992	112.1	103.9	108.7	93.1	114.1	144.9
1993	110.7	109.9	110.5	94.3	111.9	146.0
1994	113.3	112.1	110.3	96.8	122.4	152.7
1995	118.6	112.5	117.4	97.6	123.1	161.6
1996	117.2	113.8	110.2	96.3	127.5	164.9
1997	121.4	116.4	121.2	100.2	136.8	167.5
1998	121.2	124.5	129.6	102.8	140.2	168.3
1999	116.4	127.1	130.7	107.6	130.8	167.8
2000	116.5	131.0	130.5	108.5	121.6	169.1

Source

U.S. Bureau of Labor Statistics (BLS), "Industry Labor Productivity Tables," from the BLS Internet site.

Documentation

See the text for Table Cg292–296.

TABLE Cg308–313   Output per hour – food and beverage industries: 1947–2000
Contributed by Gavin Wright

Year	Dairy products Cg308 Index 1987 = 100	Preserved fruits and vegetables Cg309 Index 1987 = 100	Grain mill products Cg310 Index 1987 = 100	Bakery products Cg311 Index 1987 = 100	Malt beverages Cg312 Index 1987 = 100	Bottled and canned soft drinks Cg313 Index 1987 = 100
1947	—	38.5	—	49.9	11.2	—
1948	—	38.0	—	49.9	10.9	—
1949	—	42.1	—	49.5	12.4	—
1950	—	44.2	—	49.9	12.3	—
1951	—	45.6	—	49.5	12.4	—
1952	—	45.5	—	51.0	12.9	—
1953	—	49.4	—	53.6	12.8	—
1954	—	50.6	—	53.1	13.2	—
1955	—	51.7	—	53.5	13.7	—
1956	—	55.7	—	54.6	14.0	—
1957	—	52.6	—	56.3	14.4	—
1958	—	52.1	—	58.4	15.9	35.9
1959	—	51.4	—	58.2	16.7	37.6
1960	—	55.2	—	58.3	17.4	36.3
1961	—	57.8	—	59.3	18.2	37.8
1962	—	61.1	—	60.5	19.1	40.5
1963	—	62.8	43.3	64.9	21.0	41.8
1964	—	65.0	45.2	66.7	22.6	42.0
1965	—	66.1	46.2	69.2	23.7	42.3
1966	—	67.2	48.0	69.9	24.9	42.4
1967	41.7	66.4	50.6	73.2	26.6	41.4
1968	45.4	68.2	53.2	74.7	29.1	44.9
1969	47.4	67.8	53.7	74.7	31.4	43.4
1970	48.3	70.2	54.6	77.1	32.7	43.6
1971	52.5	71.8	56.8	79.0	34.6	46.0
1972	56.7	70.3	57.4	82.6	38.9	47.0
1973	58.3	76.2	53.4	82.2	43.3	49.2
1974	61.6	75.0	56.9	81.8	44.8	50.8
1975	65.0	77.2	57.2	81.8	50.4	55.7
1976	66.8	82.3	59.7	82.2	55.7	59.2
1977	68.3	82.2	66.4	87.5	58.2	62.2
1978	70.3	84.2	65.9	85.7	59.0	64.2
1979	71.6	81.1	67.3	83.8	63.8	64.4
1980	75.2	82.9	70.8	82.4	67.1	66.5
1981	81.7	81.6	74.8	84.3	68.2	68.8
1982	84.7	88.5	81.4	90.3	70.4	71.1
1983	89.3	92.0	83.3	93.3	75.0	75.7
1984	89.5	92.7	87.6	93.7	77.7	81.6
1985	92.4	94.3	92.4	96.0	73.7	85.2
1986	96.3	98.9	95.5	100.2	85.0	91.4
1987	100.0	100.0	100.0	100.0	100.0	100.0
1988	108.4	97.0	101.3	96.8	99.1	109.8
1989	107.7	97.8	107.6	96.1	105.2	119.4
1990	107.3	95.6	105.4	92.7	110.6	126.7
1991	108.3	99.2	104.9	90.6	109.6	135.1
1992	111.4	100.5	107.8	93.8	113.4	144.2
1993	109.6	106.8	109.2	94.4	112.6	144.7
1994	111.8	107.6	108.4	96.4	117.5	150.4
1995	116.4	109.1	115.4	97.3	116.1	160.2
1996	116.0	109.2	108.0	95.6	119.0	163.2
1997	119.3	110.7	118.2	99.1	128.3	163.2
1998	119.3	117.8	126.2	100.8	130.4	162.5
1999	112.7	120.4	129.3	106.4	122.6	160.1
2000	113.5	123.5	127.5	107.6	113.2	161.9

Source
U.S. Bureau of Labor Statistics (BLS), "Industry Labor Productivity Tables," from the BLS Internet site.

Documentation
See the text for Table Cg297–301.

TABLE Cg314–324   Output per employee – manufacturing industries: 1947–2000

Contributed by Gavin Wright

Year	Petroleum refining Cg314 Index 1987 = 100	Tires and inner tubes Cg315 Index 1987 = 100	Footwear, except rubber Cg316 Index 1987 = 100	Glass containers Cg317 Index 1987 = 100	Hydraulic cement Cg318 Index 1987 = 100	Blast furnace and basic steel products Cg319 Index 1987 = 100	Primary aluminum Cg320 Index 1987 = 100	Metal cans Cg321 Index 1987 = 100	Motors and generators Cg322 Index 1987 = 100	Electric lamp bulbs and tubes Cg323 Index 1987 = 100	Motor vehicles and equipment Cg324 Index 1987 = 100
1947	19.5	22.1	63.7	54.5	22.6	32.9	30.6	31.7	—	—	—
1948	21.5	19.2	63.0	45.8	24.9	33.4	33.6	31.7	—	—	—
1949	21.1	22.9	61.6	48.8	25.3	32.7	32.5	33.9	—	—	—
1950	23.7	27.5	67.7	53.8	25.6	37.4	32.6	37.3	—	—	—
1951	24.7	26.7	68.3	51.5	26.5	38.3	33.5	36.2	—	—	—
1952	25.0	25.5	72.7	51.1	27.1	37.8	32.1	36.6	—	—	—
1953	25.2	26.5	72.7	53.1	30.1	39.0	31.4	36.7	—	—	—
1954	26.3	25.3	71.8	52.8	33.0	35.2	34.9	38.0	45.6	43.4	—
1955	28.9	29.7	77.8	55.5	35.0	42.4	38.4	40.3	45.9	47.3	—
1956	30.1	27.6	78.0	56.3	36.5	41.7	39.0	42.6	48.5	50.0	—
1957	30.2	29.3	78.7	55.5	34.0	39.5	39.3	41.3	47.1	47.0	—
1958	31.2	30.0	80.0	53.4	35.9	35.4	43.9	42.8	46.3	48.2	35.8
1959	35.3	33.9	86.0	55.4	39.1	41.4	52.9	45.8	53.7	53.2	40.4
1960	37.0	34.6	83.4	54.9	38.3	37.7	54.6	46.5	53.9	52.7	43.8
1961	39.8	36.0	83.6	55.2	41.9	39.8	56.6	49.3	57.4	52.6	43.4
1962	43.4	41.1	85.2	57.7	44.7	41.2	59.1	48.9	65.0	56.4	50.1
1963	46.3	43.4	88.7	59.6	47.6	44.4	61.0	48.0	67.0	57.7	52.5
1964	49.5	48.5	90.3	61.8	50.1	47.8	60.0	49.8	74.1	59.2	53.1
1965	53.3	49.8	89.3	65.0	50.8	49.5	63.7	52.4	79.0	63.9	58.1
1966	57.6	50.8	91.2	65.5	53.9	50.5	66.6	51.9	80.6	64.4	56.5
1967	59.5	47.5	88.9	67.6	53.3	48.2	65.1	55.3	79.4	61.4	54.5
1968	62.0	54.4	92.7	69.4	60.1	50.3	60.9	58.0	80.3	62.4	62.0
1969	66.6	53.1	84.7	72.0	61.5	51.7	67.5	58.1	78.8	63.0	59.2
1970	65.5	51.4	91.2	71.3	60.1	49.4	68.0	57.6	74.3	65.3	54.8
1971	68.4	55.3	93.1	72.2	66.5	51.2	73.1	56.1	78.9	63.7	64.8
1972	75.7	58.9	93.1	72.6	67.4	55.7	71.7	58.3	87.0	66.7	68.8
1973	82.1	55.7	89.5	74.6	70.6	61.3	73.0	59.6	90.3	62.2	70.9
1974	75.9	55.3	86.8	79.8	63.8	64.0	80.5	61.2	90.5	63.8	63.7
1975	78.0	52.8	90.1	77.3	58.0	54.1	70.5	62.7	82.6	63.5	67.4
1976	82.8	53.7	91.1	80.6	63.5	57.1	75.2	67.1	86.8	70.5	76.5
1977	87.7	60.0	90.8	80.2	69.2	57.5	74.5	71.5	91.2	72.0	83.2
1978	89.4	64.6	91.8	81.3	71.6	61.8	75.9	73.0	89.7	75.6	81.7
1979	82.6	62.3	89.8	82.9	67.9	62.2	74.9	74.8	90.4	76.8	76.6
1980	81.2	57.5	89.0	85.2	60.5	59.4	73.4	74.0	88.2	69.5	68.9
1981	72.8	67.9	87.2	88.2	62.5	64.3	76.7	77.2	91.3	72.6	71.8
1982	69.8	72.5	93.3	85.5	63.0	53.6	74.9	87.4	89.8	76.7	74.3
1983	71.3	81.6	92.7	85.1	74.3	67.7	86.6	93.0	88.5	88.5	88.5
1984	77.8	89.8	92.9	94.0	83.8	76.5	97.9	98.7	93.6	88.3	94.4
1985	83.2	86.1	95.8	94.8	89.5	81.3	93.7	98.5	94.3	94.3	98.4
1986	94.8	90.2	96.2	100.2	97.4	86.2	98.9	95.4	96.4	91.8	96.2
1987	100.0	100.0	100.0	100.0	100.0	100.0	100.0	100.0	100.0	100.0	100.0
1988	106.3	104.7	99.8	99.1	104.3	113.0	101.5	108.7	104.3	101.3	106.0
1989	110.3	103.5	100.0	103.0	109.9	107.4	102.9	108.8	105.2	92.9	106.1
1990	110.5	101.1	98.0	109.2	112.8	109.0	104.5	117.8	101.3	99.1	102.9
1991	107.2	99.1	90.8	110.7	108.2	105.6	109.0	123.3	105.6	104.4	96.5
1992	111.1	109.3	102.1	115.6	115.7	116.2	107.7	128.2	113.4	117.5	104.3
1993	121.0	116.0	106.0	110.6	121.4	134.4	101.8	133.6	129.9	108.6	110.2
1994	124.6	125.0	112.3	116.8	128.5	145.2	96.1	139.8	129.9	109.6	116.8
1995	131.9	131.9	115.4	116.9	129.0	144.8	98.7	142.8	146.0	100.3	112.5
1996	140.8	136.8	123.9	125.3	135.1	148.8	103.7	155.6	151.8	106.4	112.9
1997	147.5	148.5	120.2	133.5	140.8	158.7	106.8	162.5	158.4	119.3	122.7
1998	154.8	141.6	108.4	142.7	142.4	153.8	108.6	164.9	151.4	127.7	128.5
1999	164.0	141.7	129.9	150.6	145.8	160.1	113.5	165.9	147.3	115.9	143.9
2000	176.1	147.4	147.6	156.6	146.5	167.5	114.9	170.5	137.9	125.6	132.4

Source

U.S. Bureau of Labor Statistics (BLS), "Industry Labor Productivity Tables,"
from the BLS Internet site.

Documentation

See the text for Table Cg292–296.

TABLE Cg325–335   Output per hour – manufacturing industries: 1947–2000

Contributed by Gavin Wright

Year	Petroleum refining	Tires and inner tubes	Footwear, except rubber	Glass containers	Hydraulic cement	Blast furnace and basic steel products	Primary aluminum	Metal cans	Motors and generators	Electric lamp bulbs and tubes	Motor vehicles and equipment
	Cg325	Cg326	Cg327	Cg328	Cg329	Cg330	Cg331	Cg332	Cg333	Cg334	Cg335
	Index 1987 = 100	Index 1987 = 100	Index 1987 = 100	Index 1987 = 100	Index 1987 = 100	Index 1987 = 100	Index 1987 = 100	Index 1987 = 100	Index 1987 = 100	Index 1987 = 100	Index 1987 = 100
1947	19.0	22.0	62.9	51.6	21.5	36.6	28.4	32.0	—	—	—
1948	20.9	19.1	62.1	43.3	23.7	36.8	31.1	32.0	—	—	—
1949	21.1	24.2	66.2	47.1	24.7	37.1	29.0	33.6	—	—	—
1950	23.6	27.3	71.5	52.3	25.0	40.8	31.8	37.5	—	—	—
1951	24.7	26.3	73.2	50.4	26.1	41.0	31.1	37.0	—	—	—
1952	25.3	25.3	74.9	49.9	26.4	41.2	30.5	36.8	—	—	—
1953	25.8	26.6	74.9	52.7	29.2	42.1	30.7	38.2	—	—	—
1954	27.0	26.4	75.1	52.1	32.6	40.2	33.7	39.2	45.6	44.7	—
1955	29.6	28.1	78.5	54.4	34.5	45.7	37.3	41.5	45.3	47.8	—
1956	30.8	28.1	80.0	54.5	36.4	45.0	38.4	43.3	48.2	49.8	—
1957	30.9	29.6	81.5	54.4	35.5	43.9	38.5	42.5	47.3	47.9	—
1958	32.4	30.8	83.3	52.5	36.8	40.6	42.9	44.6	46.3	49.4	37.7
1959	36.4	34.2	87.6	55.3	39.5	45.1	51.0	46.2	53.0	52.8	41.2
1960	37.9	35.1	86.3	53.9	39.2	42.7	53.3	47.4	54.2	54.2	44.8
1961	40.9	36.4	86.9	54.8	43.4	44.5	55.5	50.0	57.6	53.4	45.3
1962	44.5	40.2	87.7	56.7	46.1	45.8	58.2	48.3	64.2	56.7	49.6
1963	47.9	43.3	90.9	58.6	48.8	48.3	60.2	48.0	65.4	57.9	51.7
1964	50.4	47.1	90.8	60.3	50.6	51.0	62.0	49.1	72.0	59.7	52.2
1965	54.7	48.1	90.3	64.4	52.2	52.7	63.5	50.4	76.6	63.6	55.7
1966	58.9	49.1	91.8	64.5	54.7	54.1	65.7	51.8	79.5	64.0	55.6
1967	60.5	49.0	89.9	66.4	54.9	52.4	65.2	54.2	77.9	62.7	55.8
1968	62.6	52.3	93.1	69.8	61.0	53.4	60.9	56.7	77.9	63.0	60.6
1969	65.3	50.6	86.8	72.0	61.6	54.6	66.8	58.1	76.2	64.3	59.4
1970	65.6	51.7	93.1	70.5	60.6	53.6	68.5	57.2	73.5	65.6	57.0
1971	69.1	55.6	95.0	71.9	66.7	56.0	74.5	57.1	77.3	64.6	66.2
1972	76.6	57.7	92.9	71.8	67.9	59.6	73.7	58.6	84.9	66.6	67.5
1973	84.0	56.0	90.7	75.2	71.3	64.2	73.6	59.2	89.0	62.1	68.7
1974	76.9	54.8	89.5	80.8	65.3	67.6	82.3	61.5	90.4	65.0	65.7
1975	80.0	54.1	93.6	80.3	60.6	59.3	71.7	63.1	82.7	64.4	70.2
1976	83.0	59.2	94.6	80.2	66.1	61.7	75.8	67.9	87.2	69.6	75.1
1977	88.7	59.5	94.8	81.9	71.5	61.8	75.0	71.7	90.9	71.5	79.8
1978	88.7	64.3	97.0	81.3	72.5	65.1	74.7	74.2	89.8	74.2	79.4
1979	82.6	63.9	94.5	83.8	68.7	65.9	74.7	75.2	89.7	76.1	77.7
1980	81.7	60.7	93.5	85.9	62.3	65.4	74.9	74.5	87.9	70.1	71.6
1981	72.7	70.0	90.3	89.7	65.3	69.3	77.8	78.4	91.6	72.4	73.4
1982	69.9	76.2	99.7	86.1	67.4	60.6	80.1	89.4	92.6	77.3	76.7
1983	71.5	81.4	97.2	85.4	77.5	73.8	91.6	95.9	90.5	85.4	86.8
1984	78.7	88.8	98.8	97.4	89.4	81.3	100.7	101.1	93.3	86.4	91.1
1985	84.7	89.3	100.3	93.4	91.8	85.8	97.6	99.2	94.9	94.2	95.3
1986	94.9	92.6	101.9	98.5	97.1	89.7	102.7	95.9	96.8	91.5	95.1
1987	100.0	100.0	100.0	100.0	100.0	100.0	100.0	100.0	100.0	100.0	100.0
1988	105.3	102.9	101.3	99.6	103.2	112.6	102.3	106.9	102.8	100.3	103.2
1989	109.6	103.8	101.1	101.6	110.2	108.1	104.8	108.1	103.6	92.7	103.3
1990	109.2	103.0	101.1	107.5	112.4	109.7	106.5	117.5	100.9	98.0	102.4
1991	106.6	102.4	94.4	108.1	108.3	107.8	110.6	123.8	104.4	101.8	96.6
1992	111.3	107.8	104.2	111.5	115.1	117.0	109.7	129.7	111.5	112.8	104.2
1993	120.1	116.5	105.2	106.0	119.9	133.6	105.7	134.6	127.1	100.9	106.2
1994	123.8	124.1	113.0	111.0	125.6	142.4	99.0	140.7	124.4	98.9	108.8
1995	132.3	131.1	117.1	110.2	124.3	142.6	101.7	147.2	143.8	92.8	106.7
1996	142.0	138.8	126.1	118.1	128.7	147.5	106.2	159.7	149.8	99.9	107.2
1997	149.2	149.1	121.4	125.4	133.1	155.0	107.1	164.6	156.0	113.2	116.3
1998	155.7	144.2	110.9	132.6	134.1	151.0	108.0	166.3	150.2	125.8	125.2
1999	170.2	142.1	132.6	141.5	138.6	155.6	112.3	160.1	143.6	111.5	136.7
2000	180.2	145.9	146.2	147.3	136.9	160.1	114.3	162.7	134.7	120.1	127.1

Source

U.S. Bureau of Labor Statistics (BLS), "Industry Labor Productivity Tables," from the BLS Internet site.

Documentation

See the text for Table Cg297–301.

For manufacturing industries, estimates of employee hours are derived by summing the aggregate hours for production workers and the estimated aggregate hours for nonproduction workers.

TABLE Cg336–340   Output per employee – services and utilities: 1947–2000
Contributed by Gavin Wright

Year	Railroad transportation	Telephone communications	Electric utilities	Gas utilities	Air transportation
	Cg336	Cg337	Cg338	Cg339	Cg340
	Index 1987 = 100	Index 1987 = 100	Index 1987 = 100	Index 1987 = 100	Index 1987 = 100
1947	19.7	—	—	—	7.6
1948	18.8	—	—	—	8.5
1949	17.5	—	—	—	9.6
1950	18.0	—	—	—	11.5
1951	18.6	11.3	—	—	13.2
1952	18.7	11.5	—	—	13.5
1953	18.6	11.8	—	—	14.6
1954	19.3	12.4	—	—	16.2
1955	20.8	13.7	—	—	18.1
1956	21.1	14.0	—	—	18.8
1957	20.9	15.1	—	—	19.6
1958	22.4	16.8	33.7	63.4	20.1
1959	24.0	19.2	37.6	67.1	21.6
1960	24.5	20.5	40.2	71.3	21.8
1961	26.4	22.1	42.7	74.0	23.1
1962	28.5	23.9	46.4	79.9	25.7
1963	30.1	25.8	49.8	83.7	28.3
1964	32.5	27.0	53.7	89.7	31.0
1965	35.7	28.3	57.3	92.4	34.6
1966	38.3	29.7	62.1	98.1	38.8
1967	38.5	30.9	64.7	102.6	41.4
1968	41.1	33.2	69.7	108.0	43.3
1969	42.5	34.4	74.3	114.7	44.4
1970	41.7	33.9	77.2	118.6	45.4
1971	41.8	35.3	81.5	123.4	48.4
1972	46.4	38.3	86.0	124.2	53.3
1973	50.3	41.0	89.7	122.8	54.3
1974	49.3	43.3	87.5	118.5	55.0
1975	46.3	46.5	91.6	114.7	55.6
1976	49.7	50.4	95.0	118.4	60.5
1977	52.1	55.2	99.5	113.9	63.3
1978	54.4	58.8	98.1	113.5	69.4
1979	55.3	61.6	96.5	115.6	75.5
1980	54.8	65.6	95.1	114.3	70.8
1981	56.4	69.0	93.0	108.3	70.4
1982	57.1	70.9	89.6	97.4	77.7
1983	70.7	81.6	90.6	92.6	85.5
1984	76.6	82.5	94.1	99.3	88.8
1985	78.5	88.2	93.9	97.7	92.0
1986	83.7	95.0	96.1	94.3	93.8
1987	100.0	100.0	100.0	100.0	100.0
1988	109.8	105.9	105.1	108.6	99.5
1989	113.1	110.3	109.0	113.4	95.8
1990	119.5	111.9	110.4	107.9	92.9
1991	124.7	117.5	113.4	112.3	92.5
1992	134.2	126.1	115.9	114.1	96.9
1993	142.0	134.5	122.5	125.6	100.2
1994	152.8	141.5	129.5	130.6	105.7
1995	161.8	148.1	137.9	141.4	108.6
1996	171.9	162.5	148.3	150.3	111.1
1997	176.9	162.5	152.2	163.7	111.6
1998	175.9	174.5	162.2	148.5	110.7
1999	182.4	187.2	164.1	151.1	109.1
2000	195.4	200.8	171.3	161.6	110.7

Source

U.S. Bureau of Labor Statistics (BLS), "Industry Labor Productivity Tables," from the BLS Internet site.

Documentation

See the text for Table Cg292–296.

TABLE Cg341–345   Output per hour – services and utilities: 1947–2000
Contributed by Gavin Wright

Year	Railroad transportation Cg341 Index 1987 = 100	Telephone communications Cg342 Index 1987 = 100	Electric utilities Cg343 Index 1987 = 100	Gas utilities Cg344 Index 1987 = 100	U.S. Postal Service Cg345 Index 1987 = 100
1947	14.5	—	—	—	—
1948	13.8	—	—	—	—
1949	13.7	—	—	—	—
1950	15.1	—	—	—	—
1951	15.8	12.0	—	—	—
1952	16.1	12.4	—	—	—
1953	16.2	12.6	—	—	—
1954	17.0	13.2	—	—	—
1955	18.1	14.3	—	—	—
1956	18.4	14.6	—	—	—
1957	18.4	16.1	—	—	—
1958	19.8	18.2	34.1	64.6	—
1959	21.3	20.3	38.1	67.7	—
1960	21.9	21.4	40.5	72.2	—
1961	23.6	23.3	43.3	74.8	—
1962	25.3	24.8	46.8	80.6	—
1963	26.7	26.6	50.2	84.0	—
1964	28.3	27.8	54.1	90.1	—
1965	31.5	28.9	57.3	92.3	—
1966	33.8	30.3	61.9	98.0	—
1967	34.8	32.6	64.6	102.7	81.5
1968	36.6	34.7	69.6	108.2	80.1
1969	37.9	35.3	73.7	115.2	80.6
1970	36.2	35.6	76.9	118.6	81.0
1971	38.6	38.3	81.4	124.4	82.8
1972	42.1	40.1	85.5	124.5	83.6
1973	46.5	42.7	88.4	123.2	88.6
1974	45.5	45.0	87.1	119.2	86.2
1975	43.3	49.3	92.5	115.6	86.1
1976	46.9	53.6	95.4	119.8	86.4
1977	49.1	57.3	99.7	114.9	90.2
1978	51.6	60.6	96.6	114.3	93.0
1979	54.3	63.5	95.2	116.6	91.9
1980	54.6	67.6	93.7	115.3	94.8
1981	55.1	71.1	92.8	109.0	96.0
1982	58.3	73.8	89.2	98.0	96.5
1983	72.0	84.6	90.4	93.1	96.9
1984	78.0	84.5	93.8	99.2	98.1
1985	81.5	88.9	93.0	98.0	98.4
1986	89.2	95.0	95.3	94.1	100.0
1987	100.0	100.0	100.0	100.0	100.0
1988	108.4	106.2	104.9	108.3	99.9
1989	114.6	111.6	107.7	111.2	99.7
1990	118.5	113.3	110.1	105.8	104.0
1991	127.8	119.8	113.4	109.6	103.7
1992	139.6	127.7	115.2	111.1	104.5
1993	145.4	135.5	120.6	121.8	107.1
1994	150.3	142.2	126.8	125.6	106.6
1995	156.2	148.1	135.0	137.1	106.5
1996	167.0	159.5	146.5	145.9	104.7
1997	169.8	160.9	150.5	158.6	108.3
1998	173.3	170.3	160.1	144.4	109.7
1999	182.5	186.3	162.0	147.2	110.9
2000	195.8	201.3	169.6	160.6	113.6

Source

U.S. Bureau of Labor Statistics (BLS), "Industry Labor Productivity Tables," from the BLS Internet site.

Documentation

See the text for Table Cg297–301.

For trade and services industries, all person-hour estimates are derived by summing the aggregate hours for paid employees and the estimated aggregate hours for partners, proprietors, and unpaid family workers. Output-per-hour indexes are not available for air transportation.

CHAPTER Ch

Business Organization

Editor: Naomi R. Lamoreaux

BUSINESS ORGANIZATION

Naomi R. Lamoreaux

Before one can count the number of elements in a set, one has to be able to specify clearly how the set is defined and how its elements can be distinguished from those of other related sets. In the case of business enterprises, these are not easy tasks. Even if one accepts the apparently simple and commonsense notion that businesses are undertakings that have as their purpose the generation of profits, there are all kinds of knotty theoretical issues to be confronted – most obviously the question of whether the set of business enterprises is identical to the set of "firms."

Theoretical Issues

When business history first emerged as a subdiscipline during the second quarter of the twentieth century, practitioners implicitly treated business enterprises and firms as if they were the same. Thus, N. S. B. Gras, the scholar generally regarded as the field's founding father, stated boldly in 1934 that business historians should devote themselves to writing "the collective biography of firms, large and small, past and present" (Gras 1934, p. 385).[1] What exactly he meant by the term "firm" was not clear, however, and scholars who worked in this tradition sometimes misclassified enterprises. For example, James B. Hedges wrote about some of the early Brown family trading ventures as if they were formal partnerships, whereas they now appear instead to have been informal long-term relationships (Hedges 1968a, 1968b).[2]

Gras's injunction that business historians should study the operation and organization of firms received explicit theoretical grounding with the publication in 1959 of Edith Penrose's *The Theory of the Growth of the Firm*. In this study, Penrose deliberately broke with the neoclassical view that essentially reduced firms to equation-solving entities that maximized profits by equating marginal revenue and marginal costs. As she pointed out, this conception of the firm "was constructed for the purpose of assisting in the theoretical investigation of . . . the way in which prices and the allocation of resources among different uses are determined" – that is, the way in which markets worked. Penrose postulated, by contrast, that firms were fundamentally different from markets and were, in fact, an alternative means of economic coordination. Whereas markets coordinated economic activity through the price mechanism, firms accomplished the same task administratively. The difference was an important one because administrative co-ordination was subject to improvement – firms could learn how to accomplish their tasks more efficiently. Moreover, as firms became better at coordinating economic activity, they could expand the scope of their responsibilities. The implication of Penrose's theory, therefore, was that, over time, as the coordination abilities of firms increased relative to the price mechanism, more and more economic activity would move within firms (Penrose 1959, especially pp. 9–30).

Two decades later Alfred D. Chandler Jr. took this basic idea and made it the core of his synthesis of American business history. Chandler argued that Penrosian-type administrative capabilities provided coordination mechanisms that were superior to the market in certain important types of industries. As he saw it, in the most capital- and energy-intensive sectors of the economy, firms that were able to maintain a large volume of throughput had a competitive advantage. They obtained this advantage in part by building plants large enough to capture economies of scale, but more importantly, they learned to substitute "the visible hand of management" for the invisible hand of the market. By integrating vertically – backward into raw materials to avoid supply bottlenecks and forward into marketing to assure themselves an outlet

---

[1] For a discussion of Gras's founding role, see Sass (1986), pp. 41–6.

[2] This approach to business history has recently been criticized by Angel Kwolek-Folland, who found it necessary to extend the term "business enterprise" beyond relationships conventionally thought of as firms in order to include the activities of women (Kwolek-Folland 1998, p. 5). Intriguingly, Hedges's focus on firms not only caused him to make classification errors but also, as the recent reprocessing of the Brown family's papers (led by Joyce Botelho at Brown University) has shown, to miss the important economic role played by Brown women. See the extended discussion on H-Business, an Internet forum devoted to topics in business history, about whether the firm

was a "fiction" that obscured as much as it revealed about business enterprises (begun on August 31, 1999, with the posting of Mary Yeager's review of Kwolek-Folland's book, archived on the EH-Net Internet site).

Acknowledgments

Naomi R. Lamoreaux thanks the many colleagues whose comments helped her conceptualize this essay. These include Ruth Bloch, Lance Davis, Stanley Engerman, Louis Galambos, Stephen Haber, David Lamoreaux, Kenneth Lipartito, John Majewski, Gregory Mark, Jean-Laurent Rosenthal, David Sicilia, Kenneth Sokoloff, John Wallis, and Mary Yeager. She is grateful for the research assistance of Juliette Levy, Victoria Nayak, and Andrea Maestrejuan; for the ongoing support and helpful comments of Susan Carter, Richard Sutch, Matt Sobek, and Monty Hindman; and for financial assistance from the All-UC Economic History Group. Fellowships from the National Endowment for the Humanities and the American Council of Learned Societies enabled her to take leave from teaching to pursue the research underlying this chapter.

for their product – and by investing in a managerial hierarchy that could coordinate the flow of product from raw material to final sale, they improved upon the workings of the market, captured the resulting efficiency gains, and reaped enormous competitive advantages. The only firms that could compete with them were ones that completely duplicated their vertically integrated structures and managerial hierarchies. Because of the enormous investment such duplication required, these kinds of industries came to be dominated by small numbers of very large firms (Chandler 1977, 1990).

Chandler's view of the dynamic of American business history obtained reinforcement from two new bodies of economic theory that emerged at approximately the same time. The one that was closest in spirit to what Chandler was trying to do was the evolutionary economics of Richard Nelson and Sidney Winter (Nelson and Winter 1982). Nelson and Winter took as their starting point the Penrosian notion that the essence of firms was the capabilities they built up over time. They argued that particular ways of coordinating economic activity – the term they used was "routines" – became embedded in the structure and culture of an enterprise. Routines became established in the first place because they worked. An enterprise innovated in a particular way, achieved good results, and then attempted to build on its success by expanding the same or similar practices to other areas. Firms that came to dominate their industries succeeded because their organization-specific capabilities had proved adaptive in an evolutionary sense. Moreover, because these capabilities typically depended on considerable firm-specific knowledge and attributes, competitors found them difficult to copy. Successful imitation involved replicating not only a product or production process but also the entire system in which it was embedded – something that it was extremely difficult for other firms even to learn about, let alone do. Thus, the learning – the routine building – that individual firms engaged in over time was an important source of sustained competitive advantage.

The second theoretical tradition that reinforced Chandler's synthesis was the so-called transaction-cost theory of the firm. This view harked back, not to Penrose, but to Ronald Coase's classic 1937 article, "The Nature of the Firm." Coase's starting point was the question why all economic activity did not occur through market exchange – why some of it was "managed" within firms. He reasoned that certain kinds of transactions were difficult to conduct in the market because they involved writing contracts that anticipated a myriad of possible contingencies. In such cases, economic actors could reduce their transaction costs by entering into more general, long-term contracts that gave one of the parties discretionary authority over the others. These contracts, Coase argued, were the essence of those entities that we call firms. During the 1970s, a number of scholars began to reinterpret and extend this view. They retained Coase's observation that firms existed to economize on transaction costs, but they tried to give this insight more explicit content by exploring the particular kinds of exchanges that were likely to be characterized by high transaction costs.[3] For example, Oliver Williamson analyzed exchanges where one party had to make investments that were highly specific to the transaction. Because the resulting assets could not readily be used for other

purposes, the party making the investment was susceptible to being held up – that is, to undue pressure to lower prices. Because it was extremely difficult to write contracts that would eliminate this risk, a straightforward way to elicit the desired investment was to integrate vertically – that is, to bring the asset within the bounds of the firm (see Williamson 1995, pp. 52–6). Williamson thought that this argument provided an effective theoretical underpinning for Chandler's view that, in capital- and energy-intensive industries, the visible hand of management provided a coordination mechanism that was superior to the invisible hand of the market, and in an article published in the *Journal of Economic Literature*, he undertook to translate Chandler's scholarship into the language of transaction costs (Williamson 1981).

None of these theories, however, offered a clear set of criteria for distinguishing firms from other kinds of business relationships. Any time economic actors are involved in a long-term relationship, whether it be organized formally or informally, they can engage in learning that makes them better able to coordinate their activities and expand the scope of their ventures. Should we include all such long-term relationships in the category of firms? Transaction-cost theorists like Steven Cheung have argued that logically there is no other choice. To illustrate the difficulty of the problem, Cheung posed the following question. Suppose an orchard owner contracted with a beekeeper to pollinate his plants. Did the contract create a new firm, or should the contract be conceptualized as binding two preexisting firms? Cheung argued that the question had no clear answer. Most economists, he suggested, would reply that there was one firm if the beekeeper agreed to work for wages but two if the contract took some other form – for example, an agreement whereby the orchard owner rented the hives. But he questioned whether this answer made sense – whether it was at all useful to make one's count of the number and size of firms dependent on the precise form of the contract between the parties involved. Furthermore, he pointed out, the count was likely to be different depending on whether the orchard owner rented the hives from the beekeeper or whether the beekeeper rented the orchard from the owner. Thus, Cheung concluded, "it is futile to press the issue of what is or is not a firm." The important question is "why contracts take the forms observed and what are the economic implications of different contractual and pricing arrangements" (Cheung 1983, pp. 16–18).

The question of what is and what is not a firm, however, is not a purely economic one. Even if one accepts Cheung's claim that it is impossible to draw up a set of economic criteria that distinguishes firms from other kinds of contracts, one nonetheless has to recognize that the distinction is a very real one from the standpoint of the legal system. As Peter Behrens has pointed out, the law differentiates between those parties to a contract that are risk bearers and those that are not, and effectively defines a firm in terms of the former group (Behrens 1985, p. 73). That is, the law delimits the set of contracts that will bear the designation "firm." More important, businesspeople do not in fact have complete freedom of contract when they organize their enterprises. The legal system effectively constrains the kinds of contracts that businesspeople can write by sorting them into categories – for example, ordinary contracts versus firms; and within the category of firms, partnerships, limited partnerships, corporations, and so on. Furthermore, the contracts that the legal system designates as firms have associated with them standard sets of terms, and these terms often dominate, even when they are contrary to the provisions that businesspeople actually

---

[3] For a survey of the literature that developed from Coase's initial insight, see Eggertsson (1990), especially Chapter 6.

write into their agreements. For example, the corporate form entailed a governance structure based on majority rule by stockholders, even though members of small corporations with closely held shares might prefer another type of voting system. At least until the post–World War II period, however, there was substantial risk that agreements based on alternative governance structures would not be enforced by the courts. (For examples, see Schwartz 1965, pp. 66–7. See also Weiner 1929, pp. 275–7.)

For the purpose of counting business enterprises, there are a couple of important implications to draw from the preceding discussion. First, such counts as we can make of the number and types of business enterprises must be based on legal rather than economic definitions of firms. There is not (and never has been) any general requirement in the United States that contracts be recorded and preserved. Hence, even if one accepts Cheung's argument that firms are indistinguishable from other types of long-term business relationships, it is not possible to get a count (or even any reasonable estimate) of the number of such contracts in effect at any given point in time. For the nineteenth century, the only business enterprises that it is possible to count are those for which legislatures required some kind of public registration or notice. During the early years of the century, the grant of a corporate charter required a special act of the legislature, and the result was a paper trail that is fairly easy to track (see Table Ch380–391). Similarly, the general incorporation laws that state legislatures subsequently passed in large number enabled any group that met specified statutory requirements to obtain a corporate charter but required that the corporation register (and pay fees) at the office of the Secretary of the State. Scholars have used these records to compile figures on the number of corporations chartered over time (see Table Ch293–318). Moreover, it should be possible, though it has not been done, to establish for at least some states the number of corporations that were active on a year-by-year basis. Limited partnerships also had to register in order to secure their limitation on liability. Unfortunately, because the requirement applied at the county level, and because these registrations typically were interspersed in local record books with other, more voluminous types of contracts (like deeds), the limited partnership form is very difficult to track and little effort has been made to establish its incidence (for one attempt, see Howard 1934). Ordinary partnerships are even harder to count because their contracts did not have to be registered. The law did, however, require partnerships to publish notices in local newspapers announcing their dissolution and any changes in the identity of their members. In theory, it should be possible to use a combination of newspapers and city directories to obtain estimates of the number of partnerships in operation in particular localities, but again this work has not yet been done.[4]

The ratification of the Sixteenth Amendment to the Constitution (income tax) in 1913 made more complete counts possible (see, for example, Table Ch1–18) because Congress used the standard legal forms of organization to sort businesses into different tax categories. Thus, the Internal Revenue Service (IRS) taxes corporations and individuals at different rates. Although partnership profits are taxed as income earned by individual partners, the IRS requires partners to submit information about the firm and its expenses and revenues along with their individual returns. The income tax system has also made it possible to obtain estimates of the number of single proprietorships because individuals who operate their own businesses can deduct costs from revenues if they file a separate business schedule along with their returns. Unfortunately, many individuals who are full-time employees also file these schedules (university professors, for example, often report income from their writing as a separate business), and so these numbers are inflated by the inclusion of many such part-time activities.

The second important point to make is that the proportion of enterprises taking one or another of these standard legal forms has been affected over the years by government actions that have altered the relative desirability of these different ways of organizing business activities. The most obvious example is tax policy. Since World War II, changes in the level of corporate tax rates relative to the top individual brackets have stimulated businesses first to shift toward the corporate form and then away from it (see, for example, Petska and Wilson 1994; Petska 1996). But changes in the terms associated with the standard legal forms of organization have also affected businesspeople's choices. For example, until the late twentieth century, a business enterprise had to organize as a corporation in order for all of its members to obtain the advantage of limited liability. But organizing as a corporation meant perforce adopting other provisions that could operate to the disadvantage of some of these members. Take, for example, the case of a small business. If it organized as a partnership, members who were dissatisfied with the actions of the other partners could move to dissolve the enterprise, even if they were in the minority. Because such an action raised the specter of liquidation, an outcome that could impose serious costs on all the members of the firm, this threat provided an incentive for the parties to resolve their differences in a mutually satisfactory way. This incentive did not exist, however, in the case of small corporations. Because the corporate form concentrated power in the hands of the majority, minority stockholders who were disadvantaged by the way the business was proceeding could do little to remedy the situation. Nor typically could they exit by selling their shares because small firms' securities were not normally sold on the market and thus lacked liquidity, and because investors would not be eager to buy a minority position in a company where there was already dissatisfaction about the policies of the majority. Hence, until their legal options changed during the late twentieth century, participants in small businesses who were considering adoption of the corporation form had to weigh the advantages of limited liability against the risks associated with becoming minority shareholders (Lamoreaux 2004).

The sections that follow trace over the course of U.S. history the ways in which governments have affected the menu (and relative attractiveness) of the main organizational forms available to businesspeople. As will be shown, although governments have sought to reduce uncertainty in the capital markets by maintaining clear legal definitions for the various forms, from time to time these definitions have themselves become a source of uncertainty and thus an impetus for change. At other times, governments have acted to revise the choices open to businesspeople in response to political pressures. Although in the early period these pressures were mainly associated with democratization, more recently they have been generated by the search for favorable tax treatment.

---

[4] For studies using city directories alone, see Lamoreaux (1997). The manuscript Census of Manufactures can provide counts of the number of enterprises on an industry-by-industry basis, but breakdowns by organizational form are problematic because classifications have to be made on the basis of the firm's name (Atack and Bateman 1995). A potential source is the records of firms compiled by R. G. Bun & Co. (see Table Ch408–413).

Proprietorships and Partnerships

The dominant form of enterprise during the early nineteenth century was the single proprietorship – that is, a business owned by just one person. This form of enterprise is still numerically preponderant. In 1997, for example, the Internal Revenue Service reported that there were more than 17 million nonfarm proprietors in the United States, as opposed to fewer than 2 million partnerships and fewer than 5 million corporations. Single-owner businesses, however, accounted for a smaller share of total economic activity than either of these other two forms. In 1997, their total receipts were about $870 billion as opposed to more than $1,500 billion for partnerships and more than $16,600 billion for corporations (see Table Ch1–18 as well as Figure Ch-A).

Proprietors enter into contractual relationships with other individuals or firms for a variety of purposes. For example, they often hire workers on wage contracts and borrow money from lenders on debt contracts. But proprietors are the sole residual claimants on the profits of their enterprise. Indeed, it is this characteristic that at law has distinguished proprietorships from partnerships, which have two or more residual claimants.

The partnership form of organization has a long history that can be traced back to Greco-Roman times (Lopez 1976, p. 74). Given all of these centuries of experience, one might think that the boundary between partnerships and proprietorships would have been well demarcated by the modern period, but in fact considerable confusion developed on precisely this frontier during the early nineteenth century. Partnerships, of course, were contracts by which two or more individuals entered into a business relationship with each other, but individuals could unite their interests through many different kinds of business contracts, only some of which were considered partnerships. Determining which contracts were partnerships and which were not was generally a matter of common, rather than statutory, law until states adopted the Uniform Partnership Act during the early twentieth century, and so it is to the common law that one must look for the source of the difficulty.

At the beginning of the nineteenth century, the courts based their definition of the partnership form on two long-standing principles of English common law, both of which aimed to safeguard the rights of creditors (Lamoreaux 1995, pp. 52–4). The first was the idea that a contract might be deemed a partnership even if the parties to the agreement did not so intend. If two or more businesspeople stood in relation to each other as partners, then according to this principle, they could not escape the resulting liability to creditors merely by claiming that they had not entered into a partnership agreement. The second was the idea that an agreement among two or more people to share the profits of a venture was by its very nature a partnership contract. As Justice Putnam of Massachusetts explained in 1821, "He who takes a moiety of all the profits indefinitely, shall by operation of law be made liable for losses, if losses arise; upon the principle that, by taking a part of the profits, he takes from the creditors a part of that fund, which is the proper security for the payment of their debts" (*John P. Rice v. Nathaniel Austin*, 17 Mass. 197 at 204).

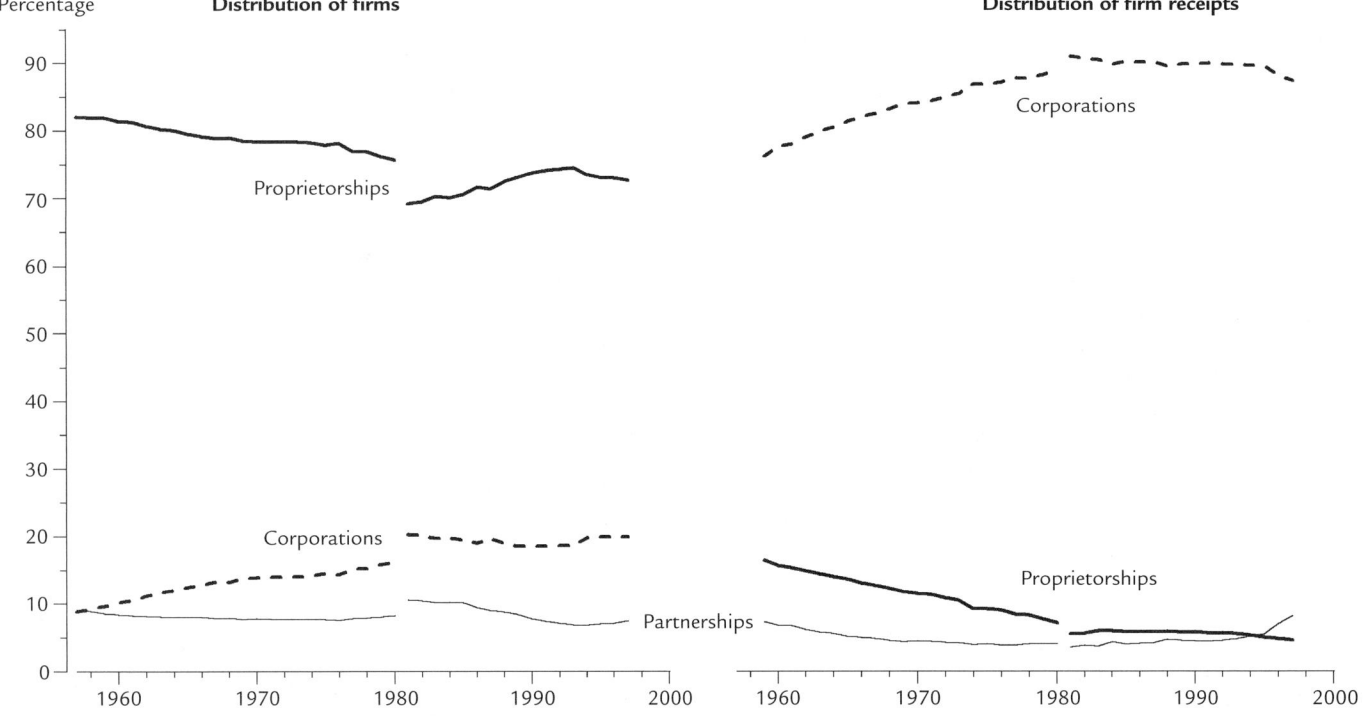

FIGURE Ch-A   Proprietorships, partnerships, and corporations – distribution of firms and firm receipts: 1959–1997

Sources

Proprietorships: through 1980, series Ch4; thereafter, series Ch7. Partnerships: series Ch10. Corporations: series Ch13. In each case, the values are expressed as a percentage of series Ch1.

Proprietorship receipts: through 1980, series Ch5; thereafter, series Ch8. Partnership receipts: series Ch11. Corporation receipts: series Ch14. In each case, the values are expressed as a percentage of series Ch2.

Documentation

Note that beginning in 1981 only nonfarm proprietorships are covered.

Although there were a few well-established exceptions to the rule that sharing in profits made an individual a partner in a firm (for example, seamen who contracted to work on whaling ships in exchange for a share of the catch were not considered partners), these two principles caused a great deal of difficulty during the early nineteenth century. As both the pace and uncertainty of economic life increased, a growing number of cases reached the courts in which creditors attempted to claim that parties who had entered into what were conventionally thought to be ordinary contracts had in fact formed partnerships and were thus liable for each other's debts. In Massachusetts, for example, ten cases of this type reached the appeals courts during the 1820s and fifteen during the years 1830 to 1845. The contracts asserted to be partnerships involved such widely varying matters as an individual's agreement to manage a foundry owned by others, a manufacturer's commitment to supply a mercantile firm with cloth to sell, and a loan to provide a dealer with working capital to fulfill a supply contract with the navy. All of these agreements involved the sharing of profits, sometimes in addition to a fixed form of compensation (Lamoreaux 1995, pp. 46, 50–2).

Although the appeals court justices knew that holding business-people liable for the debts of parties with whom they had entered into ordinary contracts would destabilize conventional business relationships, they had a great deal of difficulty avoiding this outcome, given the existing legal rules. Not surprisingly, the average length of the court's written opinions in these kinds of cases grew (from about five pages during the 1820s to over ten pages in the early 1840s), and the justices' reasoning became increasingly convoluted, as they tried to rationalize new distinctions between sharing in profits and sharing in profits *as profits* or tried to argue that partnerships differed from ordinary contracts in that they entailed sharing in losses as well as sharing in profits. None of these stratagems really worked, and the issue was not resolved until 1841, when U.S. Supreme Court Justice Joseph Story proposed (in a treatise on partnership law) the addition of a third legal principle that would enable the courts to recognize the existence of a category of ordinary contracts involving sharing in profits. In essence, Story argued that for an agreement to be considered a partnership, a claim on profits had to be accompanied by real power to direct the business of the enterprise. What mattered was whether the individual sharing in profits was acting in the capacity of a principal or agent: "If the participation in the profits can be clearly shown to be in the character of agent, then the presumption of partnership is repelled" (Story 1859, p. 59). Thus, the difference between a partnership contract specifying that one partner was to run a factory and the other to handle sales and an agency contract with the same division of labor was that in the former case each partner had full authority to dispose of any of the property involved in the transaction as if he were the sole owner, whereas in the latter case each party had ownership rights over only their own parts of the business (Lamoreaux 1995, pp. 46, 54–9).

Even as Story was clarifying the boundary between partnerships and proprietorships, however, the definition of what it meant to be a partnership was becoming more rigid. Indeed, the ownership rights that the partnership form conferred on all members of the firm had already become so critical an aspect of this organizational form that attempts to contract them away had lost legal standing. A good example was a Massachusetts dispute that ended up in the U.S. Supreme Court in 1831. In 1817, Amos and John Binney had formed a partnership with John Winship to manufacture soap and candles. Winship was responsible for the actual manufacturing enterprise. The Binneys provided capital for the business and tried to protect themselves by insisting that Winship sign an agreement not to endorse the notes of anyone outside the firm. Winship violated the agreement, but the Binneys were nonetheless held liable for the notes he endorsed on the grounds that creditors could not be expected to know of the provisions of the agreement. As John Marshall, Chief Justice of the U.S. Supreme Court, explained in *Winship v. The Bank of the United States*, specific clauses restricting the rights of any of the partners to act in the interest of the firm could not be employed to limit the firm's liabilities:

> The articles of copartnership are perhaps never published. They are rarely if ever seen, except by the partners themselves. The stipulations they may contain are to regulate the conduct and rights of the parties, as between themselves. The trading world, with whom the company is in perpetual intercourse, cannot individually examine these articles, but must trust to the general powers contained in all partnerships.[5]

Decisions such as Marshall's effectively prevented partners from negotiating binding governance structures for their firms that differed from the standard partnership template. Partners could, and did, continue to write copartnership agreements, but these arrangements were really only as good as the people making them and, indeed, depended for their enforcement on extralegal mechanisms, such as those provided by family and community. Although, in theory, an aggrieved partner might seek an injunction in equity against another member of the firm, such a remedy typically could do little more than force the dissolution of the partnership and a settlement of accounts. It was of no use whatsoever in a situation such as the Binneys found themselves, where their partner was essentially bankrupt. As Story reminded readers of his treatise, problems in a partnership were akin to those in marriage: "As in some relations in life, we enter into the connection for better or for worse" (Story 1859, p. 352).

Although there is no way to compare directly the use of the partnership device relative to ordinary contracts, scattered evidence suggests that partnerships were becoming an increasingly popular business form during the early to middle nineteenth century. Samples drawn from Boston city directories indicate that the number of partnerships relative to the city's total population nearly doubled between 1800 and 1860 (Lamoreaux 1997, p. 279). Moreover, Jeremy Atack and Fred Bateman have shown that, between 1850 and 1870, the number of partnerships increased relative to single proprietorships in the manufacturing sector (Atack and Bateman 1995).

It is somewhat surprising that increasing numbers of proprietors turned to the partnership form during this period to combine their skills and resources with those of other owners, especially after the courts made it possible to use profit-sharing arrangements to align the parties' incentives in ordinary contracts. One possible explanation is that, compared to ordinary contracts, partnership agreements offered superior protections against the various kinds of contracting problems that can occur whenever parties must make

---

[5] *John Winship and Others v. The Bank of the United States*, 5 Peter's Supreme Court Reports, 529 at 552–4, 561–2. See also Story (1859), pp. 163, 351–81.

investments, whether human capital or otherwise, that are specific to the enterprise. For example, as Harold Demsetz and Armen Alchian have pointed out, the kinds of ex ante compensation rules that must be written into ordinary contracts create an incentive for shirking whenever the parties' respective contributions to output cannot easily be distinguished. Members of partnerships have greater ability than parties to ordinary contracts to monitor each other's activities and thus reduce the possibility that shirking will undermine the profitability of the "team" enterprise (Alchian and Demsetz 1972). It is also possible that the threat of dissolution provides a mechanism not available in ordinary contracts that can effectively limit the extent of the rent-seeking behavior when the terms of the agreement are renegotiated. If a partner attempts to extract more than his or her fair share of income from the other partners, they (unlike parties to ordinary contracts) can respond by dissolving the firm, in which case all the parties will have to bear proportionately the cost of liquidating enterprise-specific investments unless they work out an amicable settlement. Finally, it is also possible that the mutual liabilities that the legal system imposes on partners, but not on parties to ordinary contracts, serve the useful purpose of enabling partners to bond themselves to the enterprise – to signal both to insiders and to outsiders their commitment to its ongoing vitality – by assuming responsibility for its debts. Hence, for certain kinds of ventures, particularly those that involved enterprise-specific investments, partnerships may have offered advantages over ordinary contracts that can explain their growing popularity during the early nineteenth century. As the century progressed, however, businesspeople could more easily exploit other organizational alternatives that enabled them to avoid some of the disadvantages of the partnership form. The first to become readily available was the limited partnership. Legislation permitting this type of organization was first passed by the New York and Connecticut legislatures in 1822 and then by most other states over the next couple of decades. Limited partnerships consisted of two types of partners: general partners, who ran the company and had unlimited liability for its debts, and special partners, who had no managerial authority but whose liabilities were limited to their investments. From the standpoint of a general partner, the limited partnership functioned much like an ordinary partnership but afforded greater possibilities for tapping external sources of capital. From the standpoint of a special partner, the form created the possibility of greater gains than could be obtained from a simple loan contract (especially given usury restrictions) without the risks that an ordinary partnership entailed.[6]

What is most interesting about the limited partnership form, however, is how rarely it was used, despite the advantages it would seem to offer over ordinary partnerships in raising capital. Stanley Howard searched the records of five New Jersey counties (representing about a third of the population of the state) over a period of nearly one hundred years and found that only 142 limited partnerships had been formed (Howard 1934, pp. 309–12). Because of the way the legislation in New Jersey and other states was written, special partners in limited partnerships were exposed to unlimited liability under certain circumstances beyond their control; nevertheless, these statutory deficiencies should have been easy to remedy. Except in a small number of Western states, however,

legislatures generally did not bother to do more than tinker in a minor way with the statutes until the movement to pass uniform laws that occurred during the second decade of the twentieth century. The most likely reason for the lack of interest was the growing availability of another organizational form, the corporation.[7]

Corporations

Like the partnership, the corporation has a long history that can be traced back to classical times. Unlike the partnership, however, the corporate form could not be freely used for private business purposes until the nineteenth century. In early modern England, the Tudor kings had used corporate charters as a device to help them consolidate their power. When these monarchs granted (or confirmed) charters to urban governments and other associations like churches and guilds, they offered these organizations privileges, mainly the right to create a set of rules that would be binding on their members – that is, the right to be a governing authority – in exchange for recognition that the ultimate source of this authority was the king. Over time, however, kings began to use their power to charter corporations for other purposes – for example, to promote trading companies. Although these ventures typically took the form of profit-oriented joint-stock enterprises whose shares were owned by private individuals, the crown justified the grants on the grounds that the charters furthered the geopolitical interests of the nation, and the companies generally received broad governmental powers as well as trading rights within their jurisdictions (Hurst 1970, pp. 2–4).

The corporate form retained its essentially public character in the United States after the American Revolution, though, in the absence of a king, the power to grant charters of incorporation became a legislative prerogative exercised primarily by individual state governments. The vast majority of charters issued during the late eighteenth and early nineteenth centuries were for towns and other governmental entities. Most of the rest went to churches and charitable associations of various kinds. A small number were granted to business associations, but these were restricted initially to projects deemed to be in the public interest (Maier 1993; Hurst 1970, pp. 15–18; Handlin and Handlin 1969, pp. 87–133). States chartered turnpike or bridge corporations as a way of encouraging badly needed transportation projects. Similarly, legislatures viewed banks as vehicles for providing vital community services, and merchants seeking to organize them had to couch their appeals for charters on public interest grounds. For example, petitioners for the Massachusetts Bank, incorporated in Boston in 1784, promised that their bank would make it possible for citizens of the Commonwealth to obtain credit at reasonable rates of interest, thus ensuring that "the enormous advantages made by the griping Usurer from the Necessities of those who want to borrow Money will be immediately checked & in great Measure Destroyed" (quoted in Gras 1937, pp. 212–14). Even charters for manufacturing ventures had to have a civic justification. Indeed, many were granted during the period of the Embargo and War of 1812, when manufacturing had come to be considered, as William Kessler has suggested,

---

[6] The 1822 statutes aimed to introduce to American practice the "commandite" form of enterprise that had been in use in Europe since the Middle Ages (Lopez 1976, pp. 76–7; Howard 1934, pp. 296–301; Lewis 1917, p. 716).

[7] Ironically, one of the original motivations for passing limited partnership statutes was fear of the economic dominance of corporations. On the lack of popularity and deficiencies of limited partnerships, see Howard (1934), Lewis (1917), pp. 718–21, and Warren (1929), pp. 306–10.

a "patriotic duty" (Kessler 1948, p. 51). When the Boston Associates sought a corporate charter for their first textile enterprise in Waltham in 1813, they believed that it was necessary to emphasize the social value of securing "the establishment of manufactures upon a more permanent foundation than has hitherto been found practicable in this commonwealth" (quoted in Dalzell 1987, p. 28).

The principle that charters should be restricted to public infrastructure projects was not incompatible with the expectation that these investments would earn profits for the corporations' shareholders. Quite the contrary, the idea was that the special privileges that went along with the grant of a corporate charter would make it possible for participants to earn a profitable rate of return and therefore encourage them to channel their savings into such socially useful investments. These privileges always included the right to hold property and sue or be sued as if the corporation were a natural person. Depending on the purpose of the corporation and the extent of the community's need, they might include other valuable boons – a grant of monopoly power or, in the case of banks, the right to issue currency in the form of banknotes. They also sometimes included a limitation on shareholders' liability for the corporation's debts.[8]

Although many early corporations were not profitable, the privileges that corporate charters conferred on those who were able to secure them became a source of heated political controversy.[9] Banks in particular were objects of criticism because they often lent substantial proportions of their funds to their own officers and directors, and because the currency that they alone were allowed to issue appeared to give them power over the community's money supply (see Lamoreaux 1994, especially pp. 31–51). At one extreme, critics proposed abolishing corporations entirely; at the other, they advocated the passage of general incorporation laws that would eliminate the element of privilege that inhered in corporate charters by enabling virtually any group that so desired to obtain a charter for their venture. Although both options were tried at different times and places and for different types of corporations, in the end the second group won out – in part because there was broad support for economic development and interest in participating in corporate ventures, and in part because incorporation fees were so lucrative that states that chartered large numbers of corporations could thereby reduce the property-tax burden on their citizens (Wallis, Sylla, and Legler 1994).

State legislatures generally responded to these pushes and pulls first by making it easier for petitioners to obtain special charters and then by passing general incorporation laws that enabled any group that paid a fee and met specified requirements (such as minimum capitalization) to take out a charter (Hurst 1970, pp. 13–57; Maier 1993).[10] As a result of this liberalization, the number

---

[8] Early charters were often silent on the issue of stockholders' liability, creating considerable uncertainty that, beginning in the second decade of the nineteenth century, was gradually resolved by the courts in favor of the presumption of limited liability. Where charters were not silent, they sometimes provided for limited liability but sometimes (especially in the case of manufacturing concerns) explicitly denied stockholders this privilege (Dodd 1954, pp. 365–437; Handlin and Handlin 1945, pp. 8–17; Perkins 1994, pp. 373–6).

[9] On the meager returns earned by many early transportation companies, see Majewski (2000). Paskoff (1983) has shown that corporations differed little in profitability or performance from other firms in the early-nineteenth-century iron industry.

[10] There are a number of studies of this process in different states; see especially Handlin and Handlin (1969), Cadman (1949), and Seavoy (1982).

FIGURE Ch-B   Business incorporations in New England, by type of incorporation law: 1700–1875

Source
Table Ch380-391.

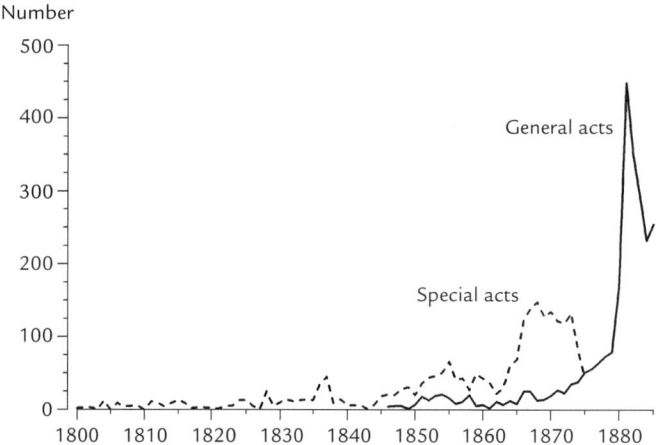

FIGURE Ch-C   Business incorporations in New Jersey, by type of incorporation law: 1800–1885

Sources
Series Ch306-308.

of corporations increased dramatically. Between 1800 and 1817, the New England states chartered about 850 corporations under special laws; between 1844 and 1862, they chartered more than 3,500, over 70 percent by means of special legislation (see Table Ch380–391 and Figure Ch-B). Similarly, between 1826 and 1835, New Jersey authorized on average 11 corporations per year using a special charter system; between 1846 and 1855, it granted on average 45 per year through a combination of special and general incorporation; between 1866 and 1875, 145 per year under a similar combination; and between 1876 and 1885, 202 per year using general incorporation alone (see Table Ch293–318 and Figure Ch-C).

As these numbers suggest, even after incorporation became routinely available, it was still possible for entrepreneurs who wished to secure more favorable provisions than those available under the general laws to petition their legislatures for special charters. Hence the controversy over corporations as vehicles of privilege continued, and the upshot, during the third quarter of the nineteenth century, was that many states added provisions to their constitutions forbidding the chartering of corporations by special legislative act.[11] Even before the passage of these amendments, it was increasingly common for legislatures to apply standard templates in writing charters for corporations in the various sectors of the economy. After the amendments, the extent of variation was dramatically reduced. Although some differences still existed among states and across sectors of the economy, certain features of the corporate form became standard – most typically, perpetual life, limited liability, and majority rule by stockholders entitled to one vote for each share they owned (Wallis 2003; Dunlavy 2004).

As their numbers increased, corporations inevitably lost much of their public character, and references to the larger civic good gradually disappeared from their petitions for charters. For example, although some applicants for bank charters in the 1820s and 1830s continued to invoke the public interest, many made more strictly personal appeals. Incorporators of the Smithfield (Rhode Island) Exchange Bank, for instance, declared that they desired an institution in which "they can become stockholders, and particularly if they can have one located and established in their own vicinity or neighborhood; in order to share or participate with their fellow Statesmen in equal privileges." As time went on, more and more petitioners made no attempt whatsoever to justify their requests. Their applications for charters consisted solely of a list of participants and a brief statement explaining that the undersigned wished to organize a bank.[12]

The growing use of the corporate device to organize ordinary private businesses also inevitably changed the way legal thinkers viewed the form. When incorporation required a special act of the legislature, the resulting charters defined both the powers of the company and the scope of its business. Corporations formed in this manner were thus clearly creations of the state – "artificial beings" to use Marshall's phrase in his famous *Dartmouth College* decision – and "being the mere creatures of law," it posed no problem to conceive of them as having in some respects the legal standing of natural persons (*Dartmouth College v. Woodward*, 17 U.S. 518 at 636). For example, according to the classic definition offered in Stewart Kyd's 1793 *Treatise on the Law of Corporations*, a corporation was a group of individuals united "in one body" that was "vested by the policy of the law, with a capacity of acting, in several respects, as an individual, particularly of taking and granting property, contracting obligations, and of suing and being sued." Kyd went on to state that corporations, like individuals, were similarly vested with the capacity "of enjoying privileges and immunities *in common*, and of exercising a variety of political rights, more or less extensive, according to the design of its institution" (quoted in Angell and Ames 1832, p. 1).

On the other hand, because corporations were creations of the state, it also posed no problem to conceive of them as having a legal status that was different from natural persons. For example, an individual was free to enter into any contract that was not contrary to law. A corporation, on the other hand, not only could "make no contracts forbidden by its charter, ... but in general [could] make no contracts which [were] not necessary either directly or

incidentally" to fulfill the purpose of its charter. Moreover, it was generally recognized that, unlike a natural person, a corporation could not "be deemed a moral agent, subject to moral obligation." Nor could it "be subject to personal suffering." Nor could it generally participate, like an ordinary citizen, "in the civil government of the country." Nor did it automatically receive the protections afforded natural citizens by the U.S. Constitution (Angell and Ames 1832, pp. 2–3).[13]

As more and more private businesses took out corporate charters, however, it became increasingly difficult for the individuals involved to accept the idea that they had lost some of their constitutional protections just because they used a particular organizational form. It also became increasingly difficult for the courts to maintain a clear distinction between the corporate and partnership forms, for as the number of ordinary private businesses using the corporate form increased, the number and kinds of disagreements involving these corporations inevitably increased as well, as did the number and kinds of lawsuits reaching the courts. Because widespread use of the corporate form was so new, in many cases judges did not have precedents in corporate law on which to base their decisions, so they turned for assistance to the one well-articulated body of business law they had available – cases involving partnerships.[14] In order to apply these precedents, however, they had to assert that corporations were, at least in certain respects, essentially similar to partnerships. For example, in his opinion finding that a stockholder in the Portland Bank was wrongly prevented by the directors from buying additional shares authorized by the bank's charter and voted to be issued by its stockholders, Justice Sedgwick of Massachusetts declared that "all the stockholders of the bank were *partners*." The decision followed from this premise, for "whenever a partnership adopts a project, within the principles of their agreement, for the purpose of profit, it must be for the benefit of all the partners, in proportion to their respective interests in the concern" (*Gray v. Portland Bank*, 3 Mass. 364, Tyng 364).[15]

As a result of these kinds of decisions, over the course of the nineteenth century corporate law grew more similar to partnership law, and the differences between the two forms of organization eroded. For example, although corporations made decisions by majority votes about important matters such as who was able to act on behalf of the firm, by the mid-nineteenth century the courts established the principle that any nontrivial change to a corporation's charter required stockholders' unanimous consent. The analogy to partnerships in these cases was explicit. As Chancellor Bennett of Vermont pointed out in *Stevens v. Rutland and Burlington Railroad Company*, partnerships and joint stock associations "cannot by a vote of the majority change or alter their fundamental articles of copartnership or association, against the will of the minority,

---

[11] For a summary of such constitutional provisions, see Evans (1948), p. 11. All the major industrial states outside New England passed such amendments during this period.

[12] See Rhode Island, General Assembly, "Charters," manuscript records, Rhode Island state archives. For the Smithfield application, see Volume 7 (1820–1823), p. 52.

---

[13] The last quotation is from Marshall, who qualified it with the phrase "unless that be the purpose for which it was created," again pointing to the importance of the specific provisions of the charter. For further discussion of the ascendancy of this "artificial person" theory of corporations during the first half of the nineteenth century, see Mark (1987), pp. 1447–55.

[14] It is important to realize that the use of the corporate form to organize ordinary businesses was not only new in the United States; it was new in the world. In Britain and on the continent of Europe, the corporate device was not as widely used until much later (Maier 1993).

[15] For similar comparisons of corporations to partnerships in very different kinds of cases, see *State of Connecticut, ex rel. Kilbourn v. Tudo*, 5 Day 329; *Slee v. Bloom*, 19 Johns. 456; and *Bissell v. Michigan Southern and Northern Indiana Railroad Companies*, 22 NY 258.

however small, unless there is an express or implied provision in the articles themselves that they may do it." The same principle must hold for corporations. To find otherwise would undermine the sanctity of contract because when an individual purchased a share in a corporation, he or she invested "for the purpose specified in the charter, . . . and there was at the same time a trust created, and an implied assumption on the part of the corporation, to apply it to that object, and none other." Altering the charter without the individual's consent violated his or her rights, for as Bennett put it, "no one can suppose, that upon the payment of his subscription, the personal identity of the plaintiff was merged in the corporation, or that he ceased to have distinct and independent rights."[16]

This growing similarity between corporate and partnership law provided the basis for the emergence during the late nineteenth century of the so-called aggregate theory of the corporation – that is, the idea that corporations were contracts into which business-people entered freely just as they did any other business form, and that, consequently, the legal status of corporations could not be distinguished from those of the natural persons of whom they were comprised. The most notable proponent of this view, Victor Morawetz, began his *Treatise on the Law of Private Corporations* with a critique of Marshall's definition of a corporation as an artificial being. "It is evident," he countered, that the corporation cannot be "in reality a person or a thing distinct from the corporators who compose it." As a result, "when it is said that a corporation is itself a person, or being, or creature, this must be understood in a figurative sense only."

> Although a corporation is frequently spoken of as a person or unit, it is essential to a clear understanding of many important branches of the law of corporations to bear in mind distinctly, that the existence of a corporation independently of its shareholders is a fiction; and that the rights and duties of an incorporated association are in reality the rights and duties of the persons who compose it, and not of an imaginary being. (Morawetz 1882, pp. 1–2)[17]

For Morawetz, "the ultimate object" of "every ordinary business corporation" was "the pecuniary profit of the individual members" (Morawetz 1882, p. 346). There is no talk in his treatise about corporations serving the public interest. Rather, they served the interests of their stockholders, who came together voluntarily to pursue some particular business purpose. From this basic assumption, Morawetz derived most of the important principles of corporate law. From his perspective, for example, corporations were forbidden to enter into contracts that were contrary to their charters (*ultra vires*), not because they were artificial creatures of the state, but because the charter delimited the boundaries of the business that the incorporators had themselves decided on when they formed the enterprise: "Those who become members of a corporation for purposes of pecuniary profit evidently intend that the object of their

company shall be to prosecute the enterprise expressly set forth in their charter or articles of association; and they evidently do not intend to join in any speculation which is not in pursuance of the purposes thus indicated" (Morawetz 1882, p. 148).

This view of the corporation was increasingly influential in the late nineteenth century and, as Gregory Mark and Morton Horwitz have convincingly argued, provided the logic that underpinned the Supreme Court's famous *Santa Clara* decision in 1886 – the first decision that extended Fourteenth Amendment protection against discriminatory legislation to corporations (Mark 1987, pp. 1460–4; Hovenkamp 1991, pp. 43–7; Horwitz 1992, pp. 66–70). The case originated in a suit brought by the Southern Pacific and other railroads to overturn property taxes based on a provision of the California constitution that the plaintiffs claimed discriminated against their businesses. Because the provision was written into the state constitution, the only way in which the railroads could obtain redress was to show that the tax violated the equal protection clause of the recently ratified Fourteenth Amendment to the federal Constitution. The issue of whether the amendment could be used to protect corporations in this way was settled even before lawyers for the two sides were able to make their oral arguments. Chief Justice Morrison R. Waite simply announced "the court does not wish to hear argument on the question whether the provision in the Fourteenth Amendment to the Constitution, which forbids a State to deny to any person within its jurisdiction the equal protection of the laws, applies to these corporations. We are all of opinion that it does" (*Santa Clara County v. Southern Pacific Railroad Company*, 118 U.S. 396). Waite provided no explanation for the Court's action, instead proceeding immediately to consideration of the technical aspects of the tax case, but as Mark and Horwitz have shown, the Court had accepted the logic, laid out by Justice Stephen Field in a series of lower-court decisions, that corporations were made up of people who did not lose the protections of the federal Constitution just because they had become members of firms that took a particular contractual form. As Field wrote in *County of San Mateo v. Southern Pacific Railroad Company*, "It would be a most singular result if a constitutional provision intended for the protection of every person against partial and discriminating legislation by the states, should cease to exert such protection the moment the person becomes a member of a corporation" (13 F. 744).

Although this effort to reinterpret corporate law in terms of the law of contract – to see corporations as essentially similar to partnerships – triumphed in the *Santa Clara* case, it was only partially successful elsewhere because many features of corporate law could not be reconciled with this view of the nature of the form. For example, shares in corporations could be held by women subject to coverture, by children, and by individuals who were mentally incompetent. That is, many members of corporations were people who could not legally enter into contracts on their own.[18] Similarly, the case law on investors who were induced to buy stock in corporations on the basis of fraudulent claims suggests that, in the eyes of the law, investors were viewed more like passive consumers than like parties who were actively contracting to participate in a business (Morawetz 1882, pp. 300–2).

There were many other significant differences as well. But the one that posed the most serious problems for Morawetz and other proponents of the aggregate theory was the fact that parties could

---

[16] 29 Vt. 545. For a summary of the case law, see Dodd (1954), pp. 134–48, and Morawetz (1882), pp. 47–9. Carney (1980) has shown that this unanimity rule was seriously weakened in the second half of the century as courts permitted firms effectively to liquidate and reorganize in order to bypass recalcitrant shareholders. But I would argue that this change too was consistent with partnership law. In a partnership, if one member disapproved of a new direction for the firm, the likely outcome was dissolution of the old firm and formation of a new one.

[17] On the rise of the aggregate theory of corporations, see Horwitz (1992), pp. 90–3, and Mark (1987), pp. 1455–64.

[18] Morawetz recognized this fact but ignored its implications (1882, p. 18).

not form corporations at will the way they could partnerships. Forming a corporation required permission from the state in the form of a corporate charter. Moreover, this permission was required because corporate charters were conceived of as conveying privileges that could not be acquired by means of ordinary contracts. Indeed, as late as the second decade of the twentieth century, many state laws defined corporations as associations "having any of the powers or privileges not possessed by individuals or partnerships" (Crane 1915, p. 778).[19]

The most important of these privileges was, of course, limited liability. Without a corporate charter from a state, parties who wrote contracts that imposed limits on their liabilities to creditors assumed significant risk that they might nonetheless find themselves judged fully liable for their enterprise's debts.[20] Morawetz argued that such contracts should be allowed – that individuals should be free to contract for corporate privileges such as limited liability. In his view "an assumption of the privilege of acting in a corporate capacity [did] not involve an infringement of the rights of other persons." Creditors could easily be protected, he argued, "by requiring due notice of the corporate organization to be given to the world." Indeed, he pointed out that states had already gone a long way in this direction by passing general incorporation laws that effectively "repeal the prohibition of the common law, and leave the right of forming a corporation and of acting in a corporate capacity free to all, subject merely to such limitations and safeguards as are required for the protection of the public" (Morawetz 1882, pp. 24–5).

This argument, however, did not carry the day, and though aggregate theory continued to be influential, it never vanquished other views of the corporation. In particular, the theory that corporations were artificial entities regained considerable power by the end of the nineteenth century. The reason was the sudden rise of large-scale business enterprises to positions of market dominance. In the context of a weak federal state, jurists latched onto the view that corporations were artificial creatures in order to provide a basis for greater government regulation. One ironic consequence was to increase the rigidity with which the courts imposed the standard corporate form on small businesses as well as on large.

The Rise of Big Business

Most corporations chartered during the nineteenth century were scarcely distinguishable in the scale and type of their operations from partnerships, but the form did permit some firms to expand beyond the size feasible for partnerships by selling equity. For most of the century, however, problems of asymmetric information on the securities markets made it difficult for corporations to exploit this possibility to its fullest potential. It was really not until the Great Merger Movement of the turn of the century (see Table Ch416–421) that industrials were able to tap the equity markets to any significant degree, but, even then, only the largest firms had access to this source of capital. The more general availability of equity finance awaited the passage during the 1930s of regulatory legislation to protect investors and provide them with better information, and the growth after World War II of retail brokerage houses aimed at middle-class savers. Even then, however, the

vast majority of corporations would continue to be private affairs whose stock was held by a relatively few individuals, generally either the firms' managers or their relatives and friends (Navin and Sears 1955; McCraw 1984, pp. 153–209; Baskin and Miranti 1997; Perkins 1999, pp. 145–236).

The first businesses that attempted to any significant degree to raise capital on broad, extralocal markets were the railroads. The earliest transportation ventures had been local enterprises whose investors had contributed capital, less for the return they thought they could earn on their shares (which was often meager) and more because they lived along the route and expected to benefit from cheaper freight rates. As longer railroads were constructed to link major cities, and as local roads expanded their routes or merged with others into systems of trunk and feeder lines, the profitability of railroad securities rose, and investors were increasingly attracted by the promise of high rates of return rather than indirect benefits (Taylor 1951, pp. 74–103; Majewski 1996; 2000, pp. 111–40). Although railroads were corporations and thus in theory could have raised capital by selling equity, investors' lack of information about the finances of individual roads (and the very real fear that insiders might deliberately manipulate the value of railroad equities to their own advantage) made bonds rather than stock the preferred instrument for attracting funds (Baskin and Miranti 1997, pp. 127–66; Chandler 1977, pp. 89–93). When railroads representing approximately a quarter of the nation's mileage went bankrupt during the depression of the nineties, however, J. P. Morgan and the other financiers who handled the reorganizations sought to reduce fixed charges by convincing bondholders to exchange debt for equity (in the form of some mixture of preferred and common stock). Morgan had painstakingly built a reputation for financial probity and fair dealing, and he exploited his stature in the eyes of investors to build a market for the railroads' stock. In the early stages of a reorganization, for example, he typically established a voting trust that would be under his control. The officers of the trust took responsibility for monitoring the corporation's business and, because they controlled a majority of the corporation's shares, had real power to shape its business practices. When these trusts expired at the end of some agreed-upon period, Morgan continued to protect investors' interests by putting one of his partners on the railroad's board and often on its finance committee as well (Carosso 1987, pp. 363–9; De Long 1991).

Banks and utilities did raise funds throughout the nineteenth century by selling shares of their stock, but trading in these securities was largely restricted to local markets where investors had reasonably good knowledge of the firms and their managers. It was much less common for industrials to raise capital by selling equity, even on local markets. For example, Joseph G. Martin, who published stock quotations for the Boston exchange, wrote as late as 1898 that "it was exceedingly difficult to obtain reliable quotations of" manufacturing stocks, even for the region's largest enterprises, because the securities rarely appeared on the market "except in stray shares or in the case of executors' sales." Virtually all the firms for which he provided quotations came from the top ranks of the region's textile enterprises. The securities of the vast majority of the manufacturing corporations in this heavily industrial region were never publicly traded (Martin 1898, p. 126).

Some manufacturing enterprises nonetheless were able to grow quite large by plowing back earnings and borrowing both short- and long-term to meet their needs for additional funds. Carnegie Steel, for example, never went to the equity markets for capital. Indeed,

---

[19] Crane listed eighteen states whose statutes defined corporations in this way.
[20] For a lengthy discussion (and defense) of the idea that corporate privileges could not be achieved by contract under common law but could only be granted by statute, see Warren (1929), especially pp. 327–404.

the firm was a limited partnership association until a lawsuit in 1900 by Henry Clay Frick forced the firm to revalue its assets and reorganize as a corporation – with a capitalization of $320 million (Bridge 1903, p. 301; Wall 1970, pp. 714–64). Other firms that grew large by drawing on traditional funding sources included Armour & Company, the Singer Sewing Machine Company, and the McCormick Harvesting Machinery Company (Doyle 1991; 2000, p. 213).[21]

In other cases, however, the lack of equity finance seems to have been more of a constraint. In many industries, firms initially drew on family resources and borrowed funds to build plants capable of exploiting new capital-intensive technologies. Often, however, a number of firms made similar investments at about the same time, and the result was severe competition, downward-spiraling prices, and poor (or even negative) earnings. Firms in this situation did not generate profits that they could plow back into growth. Nor, as price competition became more and more severe, were they good risks for lenders. The only possible way for a firm to escape this cycle of competition and decline was to raise enough capital to break away from the pack by investing in more efficient technology and/or vertically integrating to reduce costs and improve access to markets. With this option unavailable, firms concentrated instead on stopping the downward-spiraling price competition. After trying and failing repeatedly to achieve this result through collusive arrangements of escalating degrees of formality, firms in these industries ultimately turned to mergers for relief (Davis 1966; Lamoreaux 1985, pp. 46–86).

The first giant merger, Standard Oil, had been organized in 1882 to enable the leaders of the Standard Oil Alliance, a cartel of oil refiners, to make common managerial decisions. Members of the alliance had already taken the first step toward merger by exchanging stock in each other's concerns, but they lacked a governance structure that would enable them to shut down inefficient refineries and concentrate production in those with the lowest costs. With the help of a clever lawyer named S. C. T. Dodd, they devised an alternative form of organization – a trust company that would hold the stock of firms in the Alliance and whose officers would thereby have the managerial authority to reallocate production among the constituent firms (Chandler 1977, pp. 321–6).

In several other industries – most notably sugar, lead, whiskey, linseed oil, cottonseed oil, and cordage – firms joined together during the 1880s and adopted Standard Oil's trust form of organization. After the passage of the Sherman Antitrust Act in 1890, this type of organization became vulnerable to prosecution. But, eager for the revenues to be derived from chartering corporations operating primarily in other states, the New Jersey legislature had enacted a liberal general incorporation law for holding companies during its 1888–1889 session, making an alternative form of organization readily available. Most of the trusts subsequently reorganized as New Jersey corporations, and Morgan and other financiers of comparable stature showed that they could successfully market the equities of these giant consolidations on the exchanges.[22]

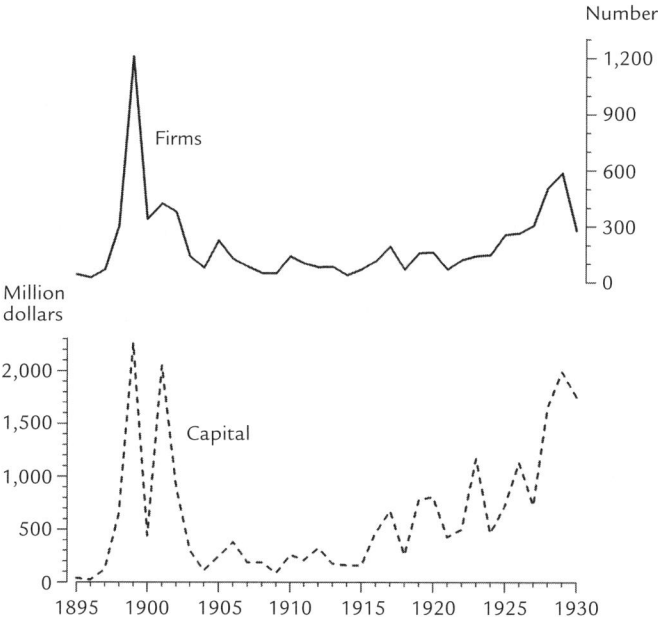

FIGURE Ch-D Mergers in manufacturing and mining – number and capitalization of firms that disappeared into consolidations or were acquired by larger firms: 1895–1930

Sources
Series Ch416–417.

A larger wave of mergers occurred during the period 1895–1904 and involved industries that had experienced unrelenting competition during the depression of the mid-1890s (see Figure Ch-D). In these industries prices did not rebound with the return of prosperity. The upturn did, however, stimulate a rise in activity on the securities markets. Morgan had demonstrated the usefulness of equities in the railroad reorganizations of the 1890s, and the trusts and mergers of the previous decade had shown that the stock of large industrial combinations could be sold on the exchanges. Now promoters began to apply these lessons on a larger scale by merging all the firms in industries experiencing severe competition into giant consolidations. The idea was to buy out existing owners by offering them the value of their firm in preferred stock with an equivalent amount of common stock as a sweetener. The expectation was that the preferred stock would find a ready market on the exchanges from investors eager to participate in the monopoly gains that consolidation would yield (under the oversight of well-known promoters). Then, when the firm did well, the desirability of the common stock would increase as well (Nelson 1959, pp. 89–100; Kolko 1963, pp. 17–25; De Long 1991).

The result was a flurry of consolidations. Only thirteen multi-firm consolidations were formed during the depression years 1895–1897, but in 1898 the number rose to sixteen and in 1899 suddenly to sixty-three. Thereafter the numbers began to trail off again – to twenty-one in 1900, nineteen in 1901, seventeen in 1902, five in 1903, and three in 1904. During the years 1895–1904, more than 1,800 manufacturing firms disappeared into consolidations, many of which acquired substantial shares (at least initially) of the markets in which they operated. Of the ninety-three consolidations whose market shares it is possible to estimate, around the time of their formation seventy-two controlled at least 40 percent of their industries, and forty-two controlled at least 70 percent. Even

---

[21] Doyle uses evidence from the sugar and meatpacking industries to argue that firms financed most capital investment in the traditional way and turned to the equity markets only to facilitate the reorganization of existing investment by means such as mergers.

[22] During the early twentieth century Delaware would surpass New Jersey in "charter mongering" (Grandy 1989; 1987; Roy 1997, pp. 221–58; Chandler 1977, pp. 326–31; Carosso 1987, pp. 390–4; Navin and Sears 1955).

assuming that none of the remaining mergers achieved significant market power, these figures meant that nearly half the consolidations absorbed more than 40 percent of their industries, and more than one quarter absorbed in excess of 70 percent (Lamoreaux 1985, pp. 1–5).[23]

Although many of these consolidations would subsequently lose market share and some would even fail, contemporaries reacted to the Great Merger Movement with alarm. The passage of liberal incorporation laws by states like New Jersey had enabled these mergers not only to occur but also to amass capital on a hitherto unheard of scale. At the same time, these laws seriously undermined the regulatory authority that other states could exercise. Although the power to charter corporations theoretically gave states the authority to determine the very conditions under which their "creations" could do business, giant consolidations could respond to efforts to regulate their behavior by obtaining a charter from a more friendly jurisdiction, or even by closing down their operations in a state (see Roy 1997, pp. 144–258).[24]

However weak the states' charter powers now were in practice, they nonetheless hamstrung the federal government (itself small and inexperienced in regulatory affairs) in its efforts to fill the power vacuum. The main legal tools that were available to national authorities to regulate giant corporations were the common-law prohibitions against restraint of trade and attempts to monopolize that had been embodied in the Sherman Antitrust Act of 1890. Although prosecutors found it relatively easy to wield these tools against pools and similar collusive devices that involved agreements between more than one firm, they had much greater difficulty using them against combinations that took the form of state-chartered corporations and whose existence therefore seemingly had received state sanction (McCurdy 1979; Freyer 1992, pp. 61–8, 90–102). Hence, the central questions in antitrust law during the first decade of the twentieth century became, first, how the federal government could assert regulatory authority over corporations operating in interstate commerce without undermining states' powers over corporations and, second, how the special status of corporations as creatures of the states could be used to bolster the federal government's otherwise weak position (Lamoreaux 1985, pp. 159–86).[25]

The ultimate solution to the first of these problems was the "rule of reason," articulated by the Supreme Court's Chief Justice Edward Douglass White in 1911 in the *Standard Oil* and *American Tobacco* decisions. White classified combinations into two distinct categories, for which two different tests of restraint of trade were required. First, there were those contracts or combinations whose "inherent nature or effect" was to restrain trade. This category included combinations involving more than one individual or corporation, such as gentlemen's agreements, pools, and other types of cartels. These combinations were illegal per se; that is, the Sherman Act applied literally to them. Combinations formed by merger, however, did not fall into the category of agreements

whose "inherent nature or effect" was to restrain trade. In order to find combinations in violation of the Sherman Act, the Court must have proof that the "evident purpose" of the combination was to restrain trade. If this proof was available, it did not matter that the combination took the form of a state-chartered corporation because states did not have the right to charter corporations whose purpose was to violate federal law (*Standard Oil Company v. United States*, 221 U.S. 1; *United States v. American Tobacco Company*, 221 U.S. 106; Lamoreaux 1985, pp. 159–86).

Demonstrating such purpose, however, was highly dependent on the continuing power of the artificial theory of the corporation, as an earlier Supreme Court decision involving one of the companies implicated in the *American Tobacco* case had demonstrated. The government had subpoenaed records of a number of firms for evidence of anticompetitive activity. The secretary-treasurer of one of these companies, MacAndrews & Forbes, had refused to produce the requested documents on a number of grounds, among them that by doing so he would violate the corporation's rights under the Fifth Amendment to the Constitution. In his opinion for the Court, Justice Henry B. Brown rejected the corporation's claim to Fifth Amendment protection, using the states' charter powers to bolster federal authority. The corporation, he pointed out, "is a creature of the State."

> It is presumed to be incorporated for the benefit of the public. It receives certain special privileges and franchises, and holds them subject to the laws of the State and the limitations of its charter.... Its rights to act as a corporation are only preserved to it so long as it obeys the laws of its creation. There is a reserved right in the legislature to investigate its contracts and find out whether it has exceeded its powers. (*Hale v. Henkel*, 210 U.S. 43 at 74–6)

Brown acknowledged that an individual "may lawfully refuse to answer incriminating questions unless protected by an immunity statute." But, he asserted, "it does not follow that a corporation, vested with special privileges and franchises, may refuse to show its hand when charged with an abuse of such privileges." Indeed, it would be "a strange anomaly" if a state could not, after chartering a corporation and granting it certain privileges, "demand the production of the corporate books and papers" to ensure that these privileges were legally employed. Because such privileges "must also be exercised in subordination to the power of Congress to regulate commerce," the federal government "may also assert a sovereign authority" over the corporation to make sure that its laws are being upheld. Thus, Brown put the state's charter powers in service of the federal government: "The powers of the General Government ... are the same as if the corporation had been created by an act of Congress."[26]

The heightened importance that the rise of big business gave to the states' charter powers also had broader implications, fueling among other things an increased tendency at the state level for

---

[23] For a more complete listing of mergers that includes smaller consolidations as well as acquisitions, see Table Ch416–421.

[24] An exception was Texas, which was able to use its petroleum resources to assert regulatory authority in that industry (Pratt 1980). For the contemporary reaction, see Galambos (1975).

[25] One manifestation of this concern was the attempt to secure a federal incorporation law during the first decade of the twentieth century (Sklar 1988, pp. 203–85).

[26] In a dissenting opinion, Justice David J. Brewer opposed this attempt to harness the states' powers in service of the federal governing, countering that such a supervisory power belonged only "to the creator of the corporation" – which in the case at hand was a state, not the federal, government (*Hale v. Henkel*, 210 U.S. 83-9). The corporation had also claimed Fourth Amendment protection against unreasonable searches and seizures, but Brown found this argument much more difficult to dismiss (mainly on aggregate-theory grounds) (Lamoreaux 2004).

judges to draw a rigid line between partnerships and corporations. A good example is the case of *Jackson v. Hooper*, decided by the New Jersey Appeals Court in 1910. Several years earlier, Walter M. Jackson and Horace E. Hooper had organized two corporations, one in Britain and one in the United States, to publish and distribute the *Encyclopaedia Britannica*. Jackson and Hooper divided the stock of the corporations equally between them and also contracted to run the two businesses as a partnership. They agreed that all decisions were to be made by mutual assent, and they bound the other directors, whose positions were merely nominal, to ratify whatever actions they took. By 1908, however, the two men had a falling out. Hooper, with the support of the dummy directors, effectively stripped Jackson of his power in the enterprise, and Jackson sued in equity to enforce the partnership agreement. Although Jackson initially secured an injunction to enforce his partnership rights, the order was reversed on appeal. The court adamantly declared that partnerships and corporations were different legal forms and that businesspeople could not "Proteus-like" become "at will a copartnership or a corporation, as the exigencies or purposes of their joint enterprise may from time to time require."

> If the parties have the rights of partners, they have the duties and liabilities imposed by law, and are responsible in solido to all their creditors. If they adopt the corporate form, with the corporate shield extended over them to protect them against personal liability, they cease to be partners, and have only the rights, duties, and obligations of stockholders. (*Jackson v. Hooper et al.*, 76 N.J. Eq. 592, 75 Atl. 568)

The subtext for this decision was the tremendous importance that the states' charter powers had acquired as a result of the rise of big business. To allow the partnership agreement between Jackson and Hooper to stand, the court declared, would render "nugatory and void the authority of the Legislature . . . in respect to the creation, supervision, and winding up of corporations." This result, the court underscored, could not "be tolerated" (75 Atl. 571).

A Dual Economy

The rigid distinction between partnerships and corporations that the New Jersey Appeals Court articulated in 1910 would persist until the middle of the century.[27] Throughout this period, however, there was ongoing debate about the nature of both partnerships and corporations. For example, a new breed of legal theorists emerged to challenge the resurgence of artificial entity theory by arguing that corporations should be regarded as "natural" entities that were comparable to human beings even to the extent of developing their own identities and personalities. According to Horwitz and Mark, this view of the corporation originated in Germany during the second half of the nineteenth century as part of a philosophical project stimulated by, and in reaction to, the growth of the modern nation-state. The writings of prominent German thinkers, the most influential of whom was Otto Gierke, were first introduced

to America at the turn of the century, where they immediately appealed to intellectuals seeking to legitimate the giant corporations that had emerged to dominate the American economy. Natural-entity theory, according to Horwitz and Mark, allowed these intellectuals to present corporations as existing in a Lockean sense prior to the state, as organisms which the law could "no more create . . . than it [could] a house out of a collection of loose bricks" (Arthur W. Machen, quoted in Horwitz 1992, p. 103).[28]

As Mark Hager has pointed out, however, natural-entity theory could serve very different political purposes as well. Some of the leading proponents were reformers searching for a more effective means of asserting the government's regulatory authority over large corporations. If corporations were equivalent to natural persons, then they could be subjected to the state's police powers just as ordinary citizens and not exempted from oversight on the grounds that they were creatures of state governments whose privileges were protected by their charters (Hager 1989). Moreover, it is clearly the case that some of the most vocal advocates of the natural-entity theory were not primarily concerned about corporations at all. Rather, they were intent on articulating a more general theory of the personality of groups that would apply to (and help to legitimate) other forms of organization – for example, labor unions – that were under attack as conspiracies or illegitimate restraints of trade. For example, when Harold Laski (the future head of the Labor Party in Britain) made the case in the *Harvard Law Review* that "less than the admission of a real personality [for corporations] results in illogic and injustice," this demonstration was only the first step in an argument that had as its ultimate purpose proving that the "unincorporate body was [not] any less the result of self-will than its corporate analogue" and that "the distinction between incorporate and voluntary association must be abolished" (Laski 1916, pp. 416–17, 424).

Theorists also applied this more general version of natural-entity theory to the case of partnerships. When the Conference on Uniform State Laws (a Progressive-era effort to standardize legal practice across states) in 1902 directed its Committee on Commercial Law to draft a new uniform law of partnerships, the committee initially delegated this task to James Barr Ames, dean of the Harvard Law School and a proponent of the new ideas about the personality of associations. Ames died before the bill could be completed, and the committee turned to William Draper Lewis of the University of Pennsylvania School of Law to complete the task. Apparently, some members of the committee were having doubts about Ames's approach, because Lewis was asked to prepare two drafts – one on the basis of real-entity theory, as Ames had done, and another on the standard (aggregate) theory of partnerships. After Lewis finished his work, the committee held a conference in 1911 attended by a number of experts in partnership law. Although, according to Lewis, virtually all the participants had originally supported the real-entity view, the consensus that emerged from the conference was that this draft should be abandoned. It seems that the changes that the revision entailed were now perceived to be too radical. Participants worried that the bill would effectively overturn much of the existing case law and that it might also have the undesirable consequence of weakening partners' sense of responsibility for their business dealings. In any event, the committee asked Lewis to write yet another draft based on the aggregate theory of

---

[27] For additional examples of cases where the courts overturned agreements that members of small businesses had used to circumvent some of the standard features of the corporate form, see Weiner (1929), pp. 275–7, and Schwartz (1965), pp. 66–7. Rutledge (1937) claimed that the more liberal incorporation laws that states like New Jersey and Delaware passed during the late nineteenth century had actually made the problem of small corporations worse by reducing the power of individual shareholders.

---

[28] Also see Horwitz (1992), pp. 71–4, 100–5; and Mark (1987), pp. 1464–78.

partnerships. This Lewis did, and after further discussion, the bill was accepted in 1914 and subsequently adopted by virtually all of the states (Lewis 1911, pp. 93–4; Williston 1915, pp. 206–12; Crane 1915, pp. 769–70; Lewis 1915, pp. 162–73; Warren 1929, pp. 293–301).

Hence, despite the growing strength of the view that all groups (including partnerships as well as corporations) were natural entities, the rigid legal differentiation between partnerships and corporations continued. Nor was there much innovation during this period in the sense of creating intermediate forms that would allow small businesses to obtain limited liability without having to accept all of the other aspects of the corporate form. After it completed its work on the partnership law, the Committee on Commercial Law did turn its attention to drafting a uniform limited partnership law. The act that emerged from the committee in 1916 remedied the defects of earlier laws under which ostensibly limited partners might find themselves through no fault of their own fully liable for their firms' debts. Nonetheless, the form continued to be little used. As late as 1980 there were only 170,336 limited partnerships in the entire United States, as opposed to 1,209,318 ordinary partnerships and 2,710,538 corporations (Lewis 1917; Howard 1934; see Table Ch157–168).[29]

It seems that members of small businesses preferred a form, like the corporation, that granted them all limited liability over a form, like the limited partnership, that afforded this privilege only to partners who did not participate in management.[30] As we have seen, however, this benefit of incorporation was potentially offset by costs associated with other aspects of the corporate form, most significantly the possibility that minority shareholders could be "held up" by those owning a majority of the stock. That growing numbers of businesspeople nonetheless chose the corporate form over the partnership during the early twentieth century (see Table Ch1–18) suggests that, in their minds, the advantages of limited liability more than offset the costs associated with the standard corporate governance structure. But it is also possible that members of firms, who typically were well acquainted with each other and likely to err on the side of trust, overly discounted the possibility

that something would go wrong with their relationship.[31] In any event, there were lots of problems with these kinds of firms and, as time went on, a growing volume of legal writings advocating remedial legislation on the grounds that the corporate form, with its one-size-fits-all character, was not well suited to the needs of small business.[32]

The first major statutory response occurred in North Carolina in 1955. That year several provisions were embedded in the state's new Business Corporation Act that aimed specifically at small businesses, including one declaring that agreements among all the shareholders of such corporations shall not, regardless of their form or purpose, "be invalidated on the ground that [their] effect is to make the parties partners among themselves."[33] A few other states passed similar statutes over the next decade or so, but the late 1960s and especially the 1970s brought forth a flood of new legislation that in most jurisdictions created a separate legal status for close corporations. In some cases, the new statutes not only gave members of small corporations flexibility to govern their enterprises like partnerships, but also provided greater ease of exit. For example, Delaware's law permitted close corporations to include in their charters provisions granting to one or more shareholders the right to "have the corporation dissolved at will or upon the occurrence of a specified event or contingency" (O'Neal 1958, pp. 876–8). Still other states followed South Carolina's lead and gave judges broad powers to intervene in the affairs of, and even dissolve, small corporations suffering from internal dissension. Protection of minority shareholders became a major legislative preoccupation, and during the 1970s and 1980s there was another wave of legislation that defined and established legal remedies for "corporate oppression" and other similar torts (O'Neal 1958, pp. 873–80; Mitchell 1990, pp. 1679–81).

Ironically, the rise of big business had facilitated the development of this separate legislative status for small corporations at the same time as it spurred the courts to enforce more rigidly the standard corporate template. The growth of a market for industrial securities that the Great Merger Movement had initially stimulated made it easier to distinguish public corporations (those whose equities were traded on the exchanges) from close corporations (those whose equities were not).[34] Moreover, there was growing

---

[29] In 1874, Pennsylvania passed a law providing for the creation of a new form of enterprise called the limited partnership association. Michigan followed suit in 1877, New Jersey in 1880, and Ohio in 1881, but the device did not spread beyond these four heavily industrial states. Moreover, even in these states the form was rarely adopted, most likely because the governance structure dictated by the legislation was highly restrictive. The statutes vested the power to incur debts in a board that had to consist of at least three managers elected by the members of the firm. Debts in excess of $500 required the signature of at least two managers, and there were situations in which the prior approval of a majority of the members was required before the managers could take action. Approval of a majority was also necessary for the transfer of shares to new members (even from decedents to heirs) and for the acquisition of additional shares by an existing member (Schwartz 1965).

[30] Even the corporate form, however, did not ensure that businesspeople would be able to limit their obligations to the amount they had invested in the firm. Indeed, stockholders of small firms often found that they had to assume personal liability for the enterprise's debts in order for it to secure loans at affordable rates (see Woodward 1985 and Forbes 1986). Limited liability did, however, resolve to an important degree the principal-agent problems that partners faced vis-à-vis each other because it eliminated the possibility that one member of a firm could unilaterally encumber the enterprise with debts that the others might have to repay out of their own assets. In a firm with limited liability, members were responsible personally only for obligations that they deliberately chose to assume.

[31] As Hetherington and Dooley have argued, small firms usually "are founded by individuals who have a virtually complete identity of interest and strong feelings of trust and confidence for one another." Even in such firms, however, "time and human nature may cause a divergence of interests and a breakdown in consensus," a situation that can be resolved relatively easily by dissolution in the case of partnerships but that poses more severe difficulties for corporations (1977, p. 3).

[32] F. Hodge O'Neal (1958) was a leader of this movement. For a survey of this literature, see O'Neal (1965), pp. 642–3.

[33] The North Carolina law also contained a provision that made it possible for any shareholder to precipitate a judicial dissolution if the corporation's charter or any other written agreement among all the shareholders entitled "the complaining shareholder to liquidation or dissolution of the corporation at will or upon the occurrence of some event which has subsequently occurred" (O'Neal 1965, pp. 646–8).

[34] This development did not completely solve the definitional problem, however. Indeed, as late as 1965, there was considerable confusion about how to draw the line between close and other corporations, and states adopted widely different strategies. Florida, for example, defined a close corporation as one whose securities were not generally traded on the markets, but Delaware placed limits on the number of shareholders a close corporation could have and insisted that its charter include restrictions on the transferability of its stock. Maryland

recognition that the economy had acquired a dual structure. The "center" portions of the economy were now dominated by a relatively small number of very large firms operating in oligopolistic markets – multiunit enterprises whose far-flung plants (often spanning a variety of different industries) and vertically integrated facilities were coordinated by managerial hierarchies (see Table Ch440–449). The economy's "periphery," on the other hand, consisted of small, mostly single-unit, owner-managed firms operating in competitive markets (Averitt 1968, pp. 1–21). It no longer seemed to make sense to force these small firms of the periphery to conform to the same organizational rules as center firms.

The increasingly burdensome character of the personal income tax may also have played a role in these changes by providing an incentive for firms that might not otherwise have chosen to do so to organize as corporations and thus confront the aspects of the form that were inappropriate for small businesses. Corporations paid a flat tax rate on their income that ranged from a post–World War II peak of 52 percent to a low of 46 percent on the eve of the Tax Reform Act of 1986. The top personal income tax rates were above this level (often substantially) during these years, increasing the attractiveness of the corporate form relative to partnerships. In addition, whereas the flat corporate tax rate was unaffected by inflation, the progressive personal income tax subjected individual taxpayers to bracket creep, forcing marginal rates relatively higher. In 1950, the amount of revenue raised by the corporate and personal income taxes had been about the same; by 1980, the personal income tax yielded four times the revenue of the corporate tax (Brownlee 1996, pp. 89–129).

Legislation during Ronald Reagan's presidency reversed this situation, first in 1981, by reducing the top personal tax rate to 50 percent, and then, with the Tax Reform Act of 1986, by reducing it to 28 percent (the 1986 Act also dropped the corporate rate from 46 to 34 percent). The impact of these changes on businesspeople's organizational choices was to a large extent counteracted, however, by legislation liberalizing the rules under which small corporations could claim Subchapter S status, which essentially allowed them to be taxed as partnerships. Especially after the 1986 Act, growing numbers of firms filed as S-corporations, but there was comparatively little shifting from the corporate to the partnership form (Petska and Wilson 1994; Petska 1996).

The 1986 law did, however, spur the American Bar Association to appoint a drafting committee to begin the process of revising the Uniform Partnership Act to make the form more attractive. The end result, the Revised Uniform Partnership Act (RUPA) of 1992, reversed the tack taken at the turn of the century and declared partnerships to be legal entities with the right to hold property and sue and be sued like an individual. Members of partnerships could still withdraw from their firms at will, but the Act also aimed to stabilize the form by reducing the number of circumstances under which partnerships would be dissolved. For example, the withdrawal of a member from a firm no longer automatically triggered dissolution but instead typically resulted in a buyout (Weidner 1991, pp. 427–8).

Tax incentives also fostered the growth of interest groups that pressured legislatures to expand the range of organizational choices

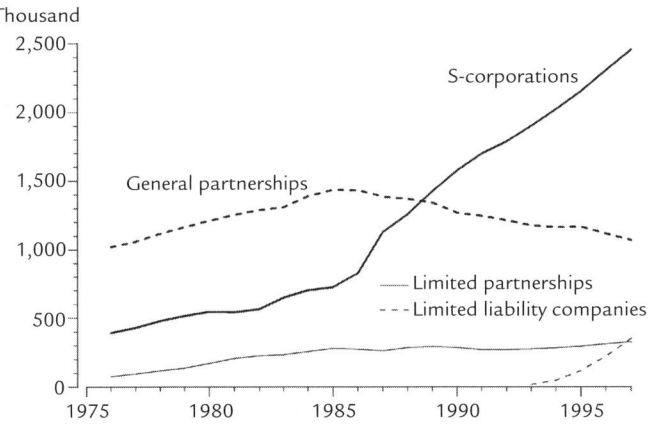

FIGURE Ch-E   General partnerships, limited partnerships, limited liability companies, and S-corporations: 1976–1997
Sources
Series Ch16, Ch160, Ch163, and Ch166.

available to small businesses. Wyoming, for example, passed enabling legislation for limited liability companies (LLCs) as early as 1977, consciously designing the form so as to allow firms to acquire the privilege of limited liability without losing the tax status of partnerships. Few states followed Wyoming's lead, however, until the IRS confirmed in 1988 the tax advantages of the new form (Gazur and Goff 1991, pp. 389–93). Then there was a wave of statutes establishing the LLC as a legal form of organization, followed by a second wave of enabling statutes for limited liability partnerships (LLPs). The latter laws permitted all members of an ordinary partnership to limit their liability for their firm's future debts simply by filing appropriate notice.[35]

The result of all this legislative action has been to create a dual economy organizationally as well as economically. (See Figure Ch-E for trends in corporate and partnership forms.) Businesspeople involved in small enterprises now have virtually complete freedom to organize their enterprises as best suits their needs and can contract on the extent of their liability, the governance rules to which they must adhere, and the ease with which they can exit from the firm. Large firms, on the other hand, still employ the traditional corporate form, though there is ongoing debate about the legal character of these entities. One of the two main conceptions of the corporation currently vying for dominance harks back to Morawetz's "aggregate theory" that the corporation is the private property of its owners, the stockholders. This view seeks implicitly to reverse the split that has arisen between small and large businesses by conceiving of all firms regardless of size or form as private contracts whose purpose is to advance the wealth of their owners. The opposing side conceives of the corporation as a social institution in which many groups besides stockholders (labor, for example) have a stake equivalent to ownership. According to this view, the directors of a corporation are not just representatives of shareholders but rather are officers vested with responsibility for mediating among the various stakeholders in the interests of the

---

required only that the charter include a statement saying that the firm was a close corporation (O'Neal 1958, pp. 875–7; 1965, p. 644).

[35] Although the initial Texas legislation creating the LLP form was apparently "a response to astronomical losses threatening lawyers and accountants as a result of their partners' involvement in the savings and loan crises of the late 1980s," the rapid spread of the form to other states owed more to tax considerations (Stover and Hamill 1999, pp. 815–16).

TABLE Ch-F Important events, legislation, and judicial decisions relating to business organization: 1811–1992

1811	New York passes legislation to encourage manufacturing by providing for the routine incorporation of businesses in certain specified industries.
1819	U.S. Supreme Court decision in *Dartmouth College v. Woodward* defines corporations as "artificial beings" having the legal standing of natural persons in some respects.
1822	New York and Connecticut pass legislation allowing limited partnerships.
1831	U.S. Supreme Court decision in *Winship v. Bank of the United States* rules that specific clauses restricting the rights of any of the partners to act in the interest of the firm could not be employed to limit the firm's liabilities.
1837	Connecticut passes a general incorporation act.
1845	Louisiana adopts a constitutional amendment prohibiting corporations from being chartered by special act of the legislature.
1882	Organization of the Standard Oil Trust.
1886	U.S. Supreme Court decision in *Santa Clara County v. Southern Pacific Railroad* extends the Fourteenth Amendment protection against discriminatory legislation to corporations.
1888	New Jersey passes a general incorporation law allowing the formation of holding companies.
1890	Congress passes the Sherman Antitrust Act authorizing the federal government to institute legal proceedings against trusts for the purpose of dissolving them.
1895–1904	The Great Merger Movement sees 157 consolidations and more than 1,800 firms disappearing into consolidations.
1906	U.S. Supreme Court decision in *Hale v. Henkel* defines the corporation as a "creature of the state ... presumed to be incorporated for the benefit of the public."
1911	U.S. Supreme Court decisions in *Standard Oil v. United States* and *United States v. American Tobacco* invoke the "rule of reason" to classify industrial combinations into two distinct categories, to which two different tests of restraint of trade applied.
1913	Ratification of the Sixteenth Amendment to the Constitution (income tax).
1914	Uniform Partnership Law standardizes criteria for determining which contracts are partnerships and which are not.
1916	Uniform Limited Partnership Law remedies defects of earlier laws under which ostensibly limited partners might find themselves, through no fault of their own, fully liable for their firms' debts.
1955	North Carolina passes a new Business Corporation Act with special provisions aimed at small businesses.
1977	Wyoming passes enabling legislation for limited liability companies (LLCs).
1986	Congress passes the Tax Reform Act reducing the top personal income tax rate below the corporate tax rate.
1991	Texas passes enabling legislation for limited liability partnerships (LLPs).
1992	Revised Uniform Partnership Act declares partnerships to be legal entities with the rights to hold property and sue and be sued like individuals.

enterprise as a whole. Both of these views have found support in the case law. As William T. Allen, Chancellor of the Delaware Court of Chancery (effectively the nation's primary court of corporate law) has argued, this "schizophrenic" state of the law is unlikely to end because at its root are ongoing, and largely unresolvable, political disagreements over the role of government in regulating large-scale capital. For a summary of the two positions, see Allen (1992), Blair (1995), and Blair and Stout (1999).

What We Are Missing

This narrative has, of necessity, focused on changes in the organizational forms that the legal system has designated as firms (see Table Ch-F for some of the key events). These are the forms whose numbers it is possible to count, and much can be learned by analyzing their relative incidence across industries and over time. Much can also be learned by analyzing the additional information that it is sometimes possible to collect for firms that took these standard forms. For example, using balance-sheet data of the sort reported in Table Ch510–524, we can track the effects of the development of a broad national securities market on corporations' sources of finance. Similarly, by comparing the data in this table with that provided for S-corporations in Table Ch645–658, we can get some sense of how the financial structures of small and large corporations differed. For example, we can compare their debt-to-equity

ratios or the ratio of their share capital to their accumulated surplus.[36]

It is important to bear in mind, however, that the figures in these tables represent only part of the economic activity that Cheung and other theorists think should be included in the study of business enterprises. It is impossible to estimate even roughly the relative magnitude of the missing portion, because many of the long-term contracts that structure these enterprises are private documents that are not recorded in any regular way. It is likely, however, that the relative size of this missing portion has changed dramatically over the course of U.S. history and that, as a result, we are severely handicapped in our efforts to understand both the magnitude and the determinants of organizational change. For example, as Chandler has argued, for approximately a century beginning during the 1870s, firms in a number of important industries grew and expanded their boundaries, first by integrating horizontally to acquire competitors, second by integrating vertically into supply and distribution functions, and third by diversifying into new product areas (Chandler 1990, pp. 47–233). During the last quarter of the twentieth century, however, this trend was significantly reversed. Large firms began actively selling off acquisitions and spinning off

---

[36] The IRS also published (although not in every year) aggregated balance-sheet data for partnerships. See its various *Statistics of Income* (SOI) volumes and the *SOI Bulletin*.

entire divisions into independent firms. They also began, in a process that Michael Dell has dubbed "virtual integration," to substitute long-term contracts for vertical integration. His Dell Computer Company is an excellent example (Lamoreaux, Raff, and Temin 2003).

These new virtually integrated networks of firms can be as much repositories of capabilities as the vertically integrated behemoths of Chandler's account. For example, Toyota, the model for many "new economy" firms such as Dell, involves its suppliers in its strategic planning and codevelops new technologies with them. Undoubtedly, these alternative organizational arrangements have both advantages and disadvantages over the type of vertical integration Chandler described, but unfortunately their relative invisibility in the quantitative record makes them difficult to study in any systematic way. As a result, we may never be able fully to answer the questions that Cheung argues are central to an understanding of business enterprises: "why contracts take the forms observed and what are the economic implications of different contractual and pricing arrangements" (Cheung 1983, p. 18).

References

Alchian, Armen A., and Harold Demsetz. 1972. "Production, Information Costs, and Economic Organization." *American Economic Review* 62 (5): 777–95.

Allen, William T. 1992. "Our Schizophrenic Conception of the Business Corporation." *Cardozo Law Review* 14 (2): 261–81.

Angell, Joseph K., and Samuel Ames. 1832. *A Treatise on the Law of Private Corporations Aggregate*. Hilliard, Gray, Little & Wilkins.

Atack, Jeremy, and Fred Bateman. 1995. "Preliminary Data on the Spread of Organizational Forms among American Manufacturing Firms in the Nineteenth Century." Unpublished paper.

Averitt, Robert T. 1968. *The Dual Economy: The Dynamics of American Industry Structure*. Norton.

Baskin, Jonathon Barron, and Paul J. Miranti Jr. 1997. *A History of Corporate Finance*. Cambridge University Press.

Behrens, Peter. 1985. "The Firm as a Complex Institution." *Journal of Institutional and Theoretical Economics* 141 (1): 62–75.

Blair, Margaret M. 1995. *Ownership and Control: Rethinking Corporate Governance for the Twenty-First Century*. Brookings Institution.

Blair, Margaret M., and Lynn A. Stout. 1999. "A Team Production Theory of Corporate Law." *Virginia Law Review* 85 (2): 247–328.

Bridge, James Howard. 1903. *The Inside History of the Carnegie Steel Company: A Romance of Millions*. Aldine.

Brownlee, W. Elliot. 1996. *Federal Taxation in America: A Short History*. Cambridge University Press.

Cadman, John W., Jr. 1949. *The Corporation in New Jersey: Business and Politics, 1791–1875*. Harvard University Press.

Carney, William J. 1980. "Fundamental Corporate Changes, Minority Shareholders, and Business Purposes." *American Bar Foundation Research Journal* 5 (1): 69–132.

Carosso, Vincent P. 1987. *The Morgans: Private International Bankers, 1854–1913*. Harvard University Press.

Chandler, Alfred D., Jr. 1977. *The Visible Hand: The Managerial Revolution in American Business*. Harvard University Press.

Chandler, Alfred D., Jr. 1990. *Scale and Scope: The Dynamics of Industrial Capitalism*. Harvard University Press.

Cheung, Steven N. S. 1983. "The Contractual Nature of the Firm." *Journal of Law and Economics* 26 (1): 1–21.

Coase, Ronald. 1937. "The Nature of the Firm." *Economica* 4 (16): 386–405.

Crane, Judson A. 1915. "The Uniform Partnership Act: A Criticism." *Harvard Law Review* 26 (8): 772–89.

Dalzell, Robert F., Jr. 1987. *Enterprising Elite: The Boston Associates and the World They Made*. Harvard University Press.

Davis, Lance E. 1966. "The Capital Markets and Industrial Concentration: The U.S. and U.K., a Comparative Study." *Economic History Review* 19 (3): 255–72.

De Long, J. Bradford. 1991. "Did J. P. Morgan's Men Add Value? An Economist's Perspective on Financial Capitalism." In Peter Temin, editor. *Inside the Business Enterprise: Historical Perspectives on the Use of Information*. University of Chicago Press.

Dodd, Edwin Merrick. 1954. *American Business Corporations until 1860: With Special Reference to Massachusetts*. Harvard University Press.

Doyle, William M. 1991. "The Evolution of Financial Practices and Financial Structures among American Manufacturers, 1875–1905: Case Studies of the Meat Packing and Sugar Refining Industries." Ph.D. dissertation, University of Tennessee.

Doyle, William M. 2000. "Capital Structure and the Financial Development of the U.S. Sugar-Refining Industry, 1875–1905." *Journal of Economic History* 60 (1): 190–215.

Dunlavy, Colleen A. 2004. "From Citizens to Plutocrats: 19th-Century Shareholder Voting Rights and Theories of the Corporation." In Kenneth Lipartito and David B. Sicilia, editors. *Constructing Corporate America: History, Politics, Culture*. Oxford University Press.

Eggertsson, Thrainn. 1990. *Economic Behavior and Institutions*. Cambridge University Press.

Evans, George Heberton, Jr. 1948. *Business Incorporation in the United States, 1800–1943*. National Bureau of Economic Research.

Forbes, Kevin F. 1986. "Limited Liability and the Development of the Business Corporation." *Journal of Law, Economics, and Organization* 2 (1): 163–77.

Freyer, Tony. 1992. *Regulating Big Business: Antitrust in Great Britain and America, 1880–1990*. Cambridge University Press.

Galambos, Louis. 1975. *The Public Image of Big Business in America, 1880–1940: A Quantitative Study in Social Change*. Johns Hopkins University Press.

Gazur, Wayne M., and Neil M. Goff. 1991. "Assessing the Limited Liability Company." *Case Western Reserve Law Review* 41 (2): 387–501.

Grandy, Christopher. 1987. "The Economics of Multiple Governments: New Jersey Corporate Chartermongering, 1875–1929." Unpublished Ph.D. dissertation, University of California, Berkeley.

Grandy, Christopher. 1989. "New Jersey Corporate Chartermongering, 1875–1929." *Journal of Economic History* 49 (3): 677–92.

Gras, N. S. B. 1934. "Business History." *Economic History Review* 4 (4): 385–98.

Gras, N. S. B. 1937. *The Massachusetts First National Bank of Boston, 1784–1934*. Harvard University Press.

Hager, Mark M. 1989. "Bodies Politic: The Progressive History of Organization 'Real Entity' Theory." *University of Pittsburgh Law Review* 50 (2): 575–654.

Handlin, Oscar, and Mary Flug Handlin. 1945. "Origins of the American Business Corporation." *Journal of Economic History* 5 (1): 1–23.

Handlin, Oscar, and Mary Flug Handlin. 1969. *Commonwealth: A Study of the Role of Government in the American Economy*. Revised edition. Harvard University Press.

Hartz, Louis. 1948. *Economic Policy and Democratic Thought: Pennsylvania, 1776–1860*. Quadrangle.

Hedges, James B. 1968a. *The Browns of Providence Plantations: Colonial Years*. Brown University Press.

Hedges, James B. 1968b. *The Browns of Providence Plantations: The Nineteenth Century*. Brown University Press.

Hetherington, J. A. C., and Michael P. Dooley. 1977. "Illiquidity and Exploitation: A Proposed Statutory Solution to the Remaining Close Corporation Problem." *Virginia Law Review* 63 (1): 1–62.

Horwitz, Morton J. 1992. *The Transformation of American Law, 1870–1960: The Crisis of Legal Orthodoxy*. Oxford University Press.

Hovenkamp, Herbert. 1991. *Enterprise and American Law, 1836–1937*. Harvard University Press.

Howard, Stanley E. 1934. "The Limited Partnership in New Jersey." *Journal of Business of the University of Chicago* 7 (3): 297–317.

Hurst, James Willard. 1970. *The Legitimacy of the Business Corporation in the Law of the United States, 1780–1970*. University Press of Virginia.

Kessler, William C. 1948. "Incorporation in New England: A Statistical Study, 1800–1875." *Journal of Economic History* 8 (1): 43–62.

Kolko, Gabriel. 1963. *The Triumph of Conservatism: A Reinterpretation of American History, 1900–1916*. Quadrangle.

Kwolek-Folland, Angel. 1998. *Incorporating Women: A History of Women and Business in the United States*. Twayne.

Lamoreaux, Naomi R. 1985. *The Great Merger Movement in American Business, 1895–1904*. Cambridge University Press.

Lamoreaux, Naomi R. 1994. *Insider Lending: Banks, Personal Connections, and Economic Development in Industrial New England*. Cambridge University Press.

Lamoreaux, Naomi R. 1995. "Constructing Firms: Partnerships and Alternative Contractual Arrangements in Early-Nineteenth-Century American Business." *Business and Economic History* 24 (2): 43–71.

Lamoreaux, Naomi R. 1997. "The Partnership Form of Organization: Its Popularity in Early-Nineteenth-Century Boston." In Conrad E. Wright and Katheryn P. Viens, editors. *Entrepreneurs: The Boston Business Community, 1750–1850*. Massachusetts Historical Society.

Lamoreaux, Naomi R. 2004. "Partnerships, Corporations, and the Limits on Contractual Freedom in U.S. History: An Essay in Economics, Law, and Culture." In Kenneth Lipartito and David B. Sicilia, editors. *Constructing Corporate America: History, Politics, Culture*. Oxford University Press.

Lamoreaux, Naomi R., Daniel M. G. Raff, and Peter Temin. 2003. "Beyond Markets and Hierarchies: A New Synthesis of American Business History." *American Historical Review* 108 (2): 404–33.

Laski, Harold J. 1916. "The Personality of Associations." *Harvard Law Review* 29 (4): 404–26.

Lewis, William Draper. 1911. "The Desirability of Expressing the Law of Partnership in Statutory Form." *University of Pennsylvania Law Review* 60 (2): 93–102.

Lewis, William Draper. 1915. "The Uniform Partnership Act – A Reply to Mr. Crane's Criticism." *Harvard Law Review* 29 (2): 158–92.

Lewis, William Draper. 1917. "The Uniform Limited Partnership Act." *University of Pennsylvania Law Review and American Law Register* 65 (8): 715–31.

Lopez, Robert S. 1976. *The Commercial Revolution of the Middle Ages, 950–1350*. Cambridge University Press.

Maier, Pauline. 1993. "The Revolutionary Origins of the American Corporation." *William and Mary Quarterly* 50 (1): 51–84.

Majewski, John. 1996. "Who Financed the Transportation Revolution? Regional Divergence and Internal Improvements in Virginia and Pennsylvania, 1790–1860." *Journal of Economic History* 56 (4): 763–88.

Majewski, John. 2000. *A House Dividing: Economic Development in Pennsylvania and Virginia before the Civil War*. Cambridge University Press.

Mark, Gregory A. 1987. "The Personification of the Business Corporation in American Law." *University of Chicago Law Review* 54 (4): 1441–83.

Martin, Joseph G. 1898. *A Century of Finance: Martin's History of the Boston Stock and Money Markets*. Privately printed.

McCraw, Thomas K. 1984. *Prophets of Regulation: Charles Francis Adams, Louis D. Brandeis, James M. Landis, Alfred E. Kahn*. Harvard University Press.

McCurdy, Charles W. 1979. "The *Knight* Sugar Decision of 1895 and the Modernization of American Corporate Law, 1869–1903." *Business History Review* 53 (3): 304–42.

Mitchell, Lawrence E. 1990. "The Death of Fiduciary Duty in Close Corporations." *University of Pennsylvania Law Review* 138 (6): 1675–1731.

Morawetz, Victor. 1882. *A Treatise on the Law of Private Corporations Other than Charitable*. Little, Brown.

Navin, Thomas R., and Marian V. Sears. 1955. "The Rise of a Market for Industrial Stocks, 1887–1902." *Business History Review* 29 (2): 105–38.

Nelson, Ralph L. 1959. *Merger Movements in American Industry, 1895–1956*. Princeton University Press.

Nelson, Richard R., and Sidney G. Winter. 1982. *An Evolutionary Theory of Economic Change*. Harvard University Press.

O'Neal, F. Hodge. 1958. *Close Corporations: Law and Practice*. 2 volumes. Callahan.

O'Neal, F. Hodge. 1965. "Developments in the Regulation of the Close Corporation." *Cornell Law Quarterly* 50 (4): 641–62.

O'Neal, F. Hodge. 1978. "Close Corporations: Existing Legislation and Recommended Reform." *Business Lawyer* 33 (2): 873–88.

Paskoff, Paul F. 1983. *Industrial Evolution: Organization, Structure, and Growth of the Pennsylvania Iron Industry, 1750–1860*. Johns Hopkins University Press.

Penrose, Edith Tilton. 1959. *The Theory of the Growth of the Firm*. Basil Blackwell.

Perkins, Edwin J. 1994. *American Public Finance and Financial Services, 1700–1815*. Ohio State University Press.

Perkins, Edwin J. 1999. *Wall Street to Main Street: Charles Merrill and Middle-Class Investors*. Cambridge University Press.

Petska, Thomas B. 1996. "Taxes and Organizational Choice: An Analysis of Trends, 1985–1992." *SOI Bulletin* 15 (4): 86–102.

Petska, Thomas B., and Robert A. Wilson. 1994. "Trends in Business Structure and Activity, 1980–1990." *SOI Bulletin* 13 (4): 27–72.

Pratt, Joseph A. 1980. "The Petroleum Industry in Transition: Antitrust and the Decline of Monopoly Control in Oil." *Journal of Economic History* 40 (4): 815–37.

Roy, William G. 1997. *Socializing Capital: The Rise of the Large Industrial Corporation in America*. Princeton University Press.

Rutledge, Wiley B., Jr. 1937. "Significant Trends in Modern Incorporation Statutes." *Washington University Law Quarterly* 22 (3): 305–43.

Sass, Steven A. 1986. *Entrepreneurial Historians and History: Leadership and Rationality in American Economic Historiography, 1940–1960*. Garland.

Schwartz, Edward R. 1965. "The Limited Partnership Association – An Alternative to the Corporation for the Small Business with 'Control' Problems?" *Rutgers Law Review* 20: 29–88.

Seavoy, Ronald E. 1982. *The Origins of the American Business Corporation, 1784–1855: Broadening the Concept of Public Service during Industrialization*. Greenwood Press.

Sklar, Martin J. 1988. *The Corporate Reconstruction of American Capitalism, 1890–1916: The Market, the Law, and Politics*. Cambridge University Press.

Story, Joseph. 1859. *Commentaries on the Law of Partnership, as a Branch of Commercial and Maritime Jurisprudence with Occasional Illustrations from the Civil and Foreign Law*. 5th edition. Little, Brown.

Stover, Fallany O., and Susan Pace Hamill. 1999. "The LLC Versus LLP Conundrum: Advice for Businesses Contemplating the Choice." *Alabama Law Review* 50 (3): 813–47.

Taylor, George Rogers. 1951. *The Transportation Revolution, 1815–1860*. Holt, Rinehart and Winston.

Wall, Joseph Frazier. 1970. *Andrew Carnegie*. Oxford University Press.

Wallis, John J. 2003. "Market Augmenting Government? The State and the Corporation in Nineteenth Century America." In Omar Azfar and Charles Cadwell, editors. *Market-Augmenting Government: The Institutional Foundations for Prosperity*. University of Michigan Press.

Wallis, John Joseph, Richard E. Sylla, and John B. Legler. 1994. "The Interaction of Taxation and Regulation in Nineteenth-Century U.S. Banking." In Claudia Goldin and Gary D. Libecap, editors. *The Regulated Economy: A Historical Approach to Political Economy*. University of Chicago Press.

Warren, Edward H. 1929. *Corporate Advantages without Incorporation*. Baker, Voorhis.

Weidner, Donald J. 1991. "Three Policy Decisions Animate Revision of Uniform Partnership Act." *The Business Lawyer* 46 (2): 427–70.

Weiner, Joseph L. 1929. "Legislative Recognition of the Close Corporation." *Michigan Law Review* 27 (3): 273–84.

Williamson, Oliver. 1981. "The Modern Corporation: Origins, Evolution, Attributes." *Journal of Economic Literature* 19 (4): 1537–68.

Williamson, Oliver. 1995. *The Economic Institutions of Capitalism*. Free Press–Macmillan.

Williston, Samuel. 1915. "The Uniform Partnership Act, with Some Remarks on Other Uniform Commercial Laws." *University of Pennsylvania Law Review* 63 (3): 206–13.

Woodward, Susan E. 1985. "Limited Liability in the Theory of the Firm." *Journal of Institutional and Theoretical Economics* 141 (4): 601–11.

BUSINESS POPULATION, BY LEGAL STATUS

Naomi R. Lamoreaux

TABLE Ch1–18   Active proprietorships, partnerships, and corporations – entities, receipts, and profit: 1916–1998 [All industries]

Contributed by Naomi R. Lamoreaux

	Total			Proprietorships					
				Total			Nonfarm		
	Entities	Receipts	Profit	Entities	Receipts	Profit	Entities	Receipts	Profit
	Ch1 [1,2]	Ch2 [1,2]	Ch3 [1,2]	Ch4	Ch5	Ch6	Ch7	Ch8	Ch9
Year	Number	Thousand dollars	Thousand dollars	Number	Thousand dollars	Thousand dollars	Number	Thousand dollars	Thousand dollars
1916	—	—	—	—	—	—	—	—	—
1917	—	—	—	—	—	—	—	—	—
1918	1,333,030	—	11,700,244	958,379 [4]	—	3,124,355 [4]	—	—	—
1919	1,592,107	—	—	1,124,385 [4]	—	3,877,550 [4]	—	—	—
1920	1,518,725	—	—	964,123 [4]	—	3,205,555 [4]	—	—	—
1921	1,395,350	—	—	807,374 [4]	—	2,366,319 [4]	—	—	—
1922	1,546,907	—	—	906,348 [4]	—	2,839,771 [4]	—	—	—
1923	2,423,823	—	—	1,746,144 [4]	—	4,733,033 [4]	—	—	—
1924	2,358,111	—	—	1,645,971 [4]	—	4,755,483 [4]	—	—	—
1925	1,704,734	—	—	978,792 [4]	—	3,688,804 [4]	—	—	—
1926	968,893	—	—	218,148 [5]	—	1,738,523 [5]	—	—	—
1927	921,435	—	—	212,919 [5]	—	1,704,175 [5]	—	—	—
1928	935,897	—	—	220,159 [5]	—	1,772,255 [5]	—	—	—
1929	948,015	—	—	228,475 [5]	—	1,836,329 [5]	—	—	—
1930	862,346	—	—	154,640 [5]	—	1,215,452 [5]	—	—	—
1931	787,890	—	—	97,779 [5]	—	766,730 [5]	—	—	—
1932	714,143	—	—	45,547 [5]	—	354,488 [5]	—	—	—
1933	719,433	—	—	57,710 [5]	2,525,814 [5]	367,024 [5]	—	—	—
1934	775,402	—	—	83,858 [5]	3,322,224 [5]	538,936 [5]	—	—	—
1935	800,443	—	—	101,037 [5]	3,909,495 [5]	653,754 [5]	—	—	—
1936	864,473	—	—	148,279 [5]	6,263,256 [5]	976,483 [5]	—	—	—
1937	893,636	—	—	154,328 [5]	6,636,725 [5]	1,008,194 [5]	—	—	—
1938	873,049	—	—	128,656 [5]	5,288,380 [5]	804,974 [5]	—	—	—
1939	1,792,637	171,146,381	10,776,918	1,052,002	23,505,169	2,477,956	912,242	22,289,239	23,398,715
1940	2,863,549	—	—	2,017,711	31,113,391	3,906,714	—	—	—
1941	4,091,667	—	—	3,168,850	37,547,755	6,225,508	2,007,505	32,561,575	36,736,151
1942	—	—	—	—	—	9,002,395	—	—	—
1943	6,032,750	—	—	5,120,685 [6]	57,951,447	10,668,237	2,560,695 [6]	46,447,442	7,173,121
1944	7,124,199	—	—	6,134,437 [6]	65,721,959	11,563,987	—	—	—
1945	6,737,647	381,776,816	39,976,167	5,689,473	79,027,600	12,069,496	3,030,109	64,800,391	8,728,666
1946	8,320,311	—	48,460,640	6,943,781 [6]	—	15,319,907	—	—	—
1947	8,064,969	529,509,827	54,205,915	6,624,300	101,124,485	15,104,686	3,720,389	82,743,483	9,936,278
1948	8,731,764	—	—	7,207,844 [6]	—	16,758,192	—	—	—
1949	8,445,583	—	—	6,901,253	110,027,888	14,459,012	3,913,831	91,034,401	10,187,394
1950	—	—	—	6,865,387 [6]	—	15,264,764	—	—	—
1951	—	—	—	7,339,811	131,864,551	16,551,545	4,201,200	109,771,250	—
1952	—	—	—	6,872,667 [6]	—	16,311,615	—	—	—
1953	9,371,078	782,019,314	64,886,166	7,714,512	143,791,575	17,007,213	4,589,001	122,474,831	13,633,710
1954	—	—	—	7,785,538	—	16,925,803	—	—	—
1955	—	—	—	8,239,328	138,840,548	17,588,176	4,822,747	118,061,053	14,945,977
1956	9,858,414	—	—	8,972,667	—	21,284,646	—	—	—
1957	10,648,439	—	72,793,991	8,737,665	162,686,506	20,220,171	5,394,441 [7]	140,270,068	16,987,528
1958	10,743,932	—	67,416,932	8,799,711	163,398,989	20,777,789	5,425,228 [7]	138,725,395	17,015,074
1959	11,165,875	1,071,410,666	77,158,851	9,142,359	176,204,711	21,516,876	5,775,479 [7]	149,925,350	18,869,924
1960	11,171,119	1,094,696,773	72,932,637	9,089,985	171,257,205	21,067,090	5,731,370 [7]	145,727,786	18,330,560
1961	11,371,007	1,118,865,884	77,279,512	9,241,755	170,981,413	22,696,990	5,879,704 [7]	144,690,795	19,345,798
1962	11,382,809	1,201,398,497	82,013,838	9,182,586	178,420,483	23,894,781	5,863,324 [7]	150,109,022	20,530,249
1963	11,383,417	1,263,568,460	86,723,434	9,135,954	181,551,305	23,770,528	5,927,865 [7]	153,266,343	21,021,494
1964	11,488,423	1,350,299,144	96,375,495	9,192,746	188,737,610	25,555,837	6,062,756 [7]	160,991,815	22,915,793

Notes appear at end of table

(continued)

TABLE Ch1–18   Active proprietorships, partnerships, and corporations – entities, receipts, and profit: 1916–1998
[All industries]   *Continued*

	Total			Proprietorships					
				Total			Nonfarm		
	Entities	Receipts	Profit	Entities	Receipts	Profit	Entities	Receipts	Profit
	Ch1 [1,2]	Ch2 [1,2]	Ch3 [1,2]	Ch4	Ch5	Ch6	Ch7	Ch8	Ch9
Year	Number	Thousand dollars	Thousand dollars	Number	Thousand dollars	Thousand dollars	Number	Thousand dollars	Thousand dollars
1965	11,416,661	1,469,243,895	111,146,383	9,078,466	199,384,594	27,557,417	6,014,914 [7]	169,476,149	24,501,455
1966	11,478,119	1,593,740,814	121,002,962	9,086,714	207,446,686	30,030,195	6,066,222 [7]	174,122,705	25,946,962
1967	11,566,624	1,666,108,563	119,455,254	9,126,082	211,372,116	30,407,572	6,096,017 [7]	178,236,353	27,049,863
1968	11,670,750	1,812,757,836	129,237,686	9,211,613	222,105,222	31,870,535	6,169,049 [7]	187,087,765	28,745,686
1969	12,009,398	2,002,022,084	124,572,675	9,429,822	234,334,588	33,867,537	6,340,336 [7]	196,721,521	30,310,830
1970	12,001,263	2,081,851,331	108,906,747	9,399,653	237,726,748	33,214,737	6,493,789 [7]	198,582,172	30,537,426
1971	12,436,884	2,261,052,672	123,296,471	9,744,640	255,242,662	34,450,038	6,803,193 [7]	214,329,874	32,032,324
1972	12,977,564	2,555,841,841	145,492,309	10,172,792	275,993,721	39,113,220	7,165,611 [7]	227,355,335	34,415,666
1973	13,591,964	2,993,065,472	176,335,995	10,648,202	311,374,523	46,673,063	7,445,136 [7]	248,785,404	38,058,018
1974	13,901,984	3,557,381,442	200,717,704	10,873,822	328,262,352	45,855,023	7,695,666 [7]	264,892,250	38,995,406
1975	13,978,710	3,686,266,787	194,985,646	10,881,969	339,221,398	44,611,250	7,759,576 [7]	273,954,741	39,636,453
1976	14,536,876	4,171,376,140	245,342,105	11,358,235	374,960,465	49,500,188	8,139,962 [7]	301,446,844	44,424,787
1977	14,740,901	4,703,025,361	283,896,182	11,345,616	393,871,922	51,388,971	8,413,806 [7]	324,492,975	49,436,518
1978	15,628,889	5,377,149,575	320,341,568	12,017,953	443,354,851	59,027,286	8,908,289 [7]	361,630,253	53,481,341
1979	16,186,369	6,344,694,449	360,580,068	12,329,982	487,807,384	60,758,789	9,343,603 [7]	395,669,594	56,528,403
1980	16,791,789	7,159,167,009	302,705,184	12,701,597	505,884,882	55,449,987	9,730,019 [7]	411,205,713	54,947,219
1981	13,857,712	7,725,544,701	263,985,693	—	—	—	9,584,790 [6]	427,063,055	53,071,628
1982	14,545,660	7,754,452,966	197,531,269	—	—	—	10,105,515 [6]	433,664,897	50,573,163
1983	15,244,531	7,891,981,399	246,063,040	—	—	—	10,703,921 [6]	465,168,637	60,359,153
1984	16,076,714	8,691,940,681	300,167,182	—	—	—	11,262,390 [6]	516,036,944	70,766,610
1985	16,919,395	9,305,441,172	310,007,924	—	—	—	11,928,573 [6]	540,045,430	78,772,578
1986	18,071,167	9,626,065,304	342,583,143	—	—	—	12,939,700 [6]	559,384,259	90,423,763
1987	18,351,297	10,634,345,667	452,987,687	—	—	—	13,091,132 [6]	610,822,732	105,460,627
1988	18,896,336	11,477,547,586	553,799,118	—	—	—	13,679,302 [6]	671,969,931	126,323,251
1989	19,560,585	12,178,632,771	535,847,630	—	—	—	14,297,558 [6]	692,810,938	132,737,680
1990	20,052,917	12,706,338,312	528,672,365	—	—	—	14,782,738 [6]	730,606,020	141,430,193
1991	20,498,855	12,711,822,184	507,782,184	—	—	—	15,180,722 [6]	712,567,989	141,515,783
1992	20,849,194	13,075,999,620	598,873,917	—	—	—	15,495,419 [6]	737,082,032	153,960,246
1993	21,280,315	13,683,048,601	721,270,265	—	—	—	15,848,119 [6]	757,215,452	156,458,803
1994	21,990,202	14,912,871,851	826,259,274	—	—	—	16,153,871 [6]	790,630,020	166,798,668
1995	22,478,939	16,236,845,715	990,285,230	—	—	—	16,423,872 [6]	807,363,638	169,262,663
1996	23,240,649	17,595,575,972	1,128,458,931	—	—	—	16,955,023 [6]	843,233,843	176,755,693
1997	23,645,197	19,019,497,493	1,270,281,273	—	—	—	17,176,487 [6]	870,392,286	186,643,910
1998	—	—	—	—	—	—	17,408,809 [6]	918,268,196	202,274,720

	Partnerships			Corporations					
				Total			S-corporations		
	Entities	Receipts	Profit	Entities	Receipts	Profit	Entities	Receipts	Profit
	Ch10	Ch11	Ch12	Ch13 [3]	Ch14 [3]	Ch15 [3]	Ch16	Ch17	Ch18
Year	Number	Thousand dollars	Thousand dollars	Number	Thousand dollars	Thousand dollars	Number	Thousand dollars	Thousand dollars
1916	—	—	—	341,253 [9,10]	35,327,631 [8]	8,109,005	—	—	—
1917	31,701 [7]	—	—	351,426 [9,10]	84,693,239 [8]	10,100,752	—	—	—
1918	100,728 [7]	8,337,349 [8]	901,375	273,923	86,461,918 [8]	7,674,514	—	—	—
1919	175,898 [7]	—	—	291,824	99,890,700 [8]	8,424,595	—	—	—
1920	240,767 [7]	—	—	313,835	117,904,166 [8]	5,936,882	—	—	—
1921	259,359 [7]	—	—	328,617	91,249,222 [8]	457,846	—	—	—
1922	287,959 [7]	—	—	352,600	101,314,557	4,770,035	—	—	—
1923	304,996 [7]	—	—	372,683	119,019,865	6,307,974	—	—	—
1924	321,158 [7]	—	—	390,982	119,746,703	5,362,726	—	—	—
1925	309,414 [7]	—	—	416,528	136,710,992	7,621,056	—	—	—
1926	295,425 [7]	—	—	455,320 [9]	142,629,445	7,504,693	—	—	—
1927	282,841 [7]	—	—	425,675	144,899,177	6,510,145	—	—	—
1928	272,127 [7]	—	—	443,611	157,848,366	8,226,617	—	—	—
1929	263,519 [7]	—	—	456,021	161,158,206	8,739,758	—	—	—

Notes appear at end of table

TABLE Ch1–18   Active proprietorships, partnerships, and corporations – entities, receipts, and profit: 1916–1998
[All industries]   *Continued*

	Partnerships			Corporations					
				Total			S-corporations		
	Entities	Receipts	Profit	Entities	Receipts	Profit	Entities	Receipts	Profit
	Ch10	Ch11	Ch12	Ch13 [3]	Ch14 [3]	Ch15 [3]	Ch16	Ch17	Ch18
Year	Number	Thousand dollars	Thousand dollars	Number	Thousand dollars	Thousand dollars	Number	Thousand dollars	Thousand dollars
1930	244,670 [7]	—	—	463,036	138,848,320	1,551,218	—	—	—
1931	230,407 [7]	—	—	459,704	108,056,952	−3,287,545	—	—	—
1932	216,712 [7]	—	—	451,884	81,637,988	−5,643,574	—	—	—
1933	214,881 [7]	—	—	446,842	84,234,006	−2,547,367	—	—	—
1934	221,740 [7]	—	—	469,804 [10]	101,494,854	94,170	—	—	—
1935	222,293 [7]	—	—	477,113 [10]	114,649,717	1,695,950	—	—	—
1936	237,367 [7]	—	—	478,827 [10]	132,722,602	7,326,218	—	—	—
1937	261,470 [7]	—	—	477,838 [10]	142,443,379	7,353,991	—	—	—
1938	273,361 [7]	—	—	471,032 [10]	120,453,946	3,672,882	—	—	—
1939	271,018	14,762,988	1,564,397	469,617 [10]	132,878,224	6,734,565	—	—	—
1940	372,796 [7]	—	—	473,042 [10]	148,236,788	8,919,429	—	—	—
1941	453,911 [7]	—	—	468,906 [10]	190,432,017	16,332,542	—	—	—
1942	490,320 [7]	—	—	442,665 [10]	217,680,512	23,051,612	—	—	—
1943	491,544 [7]	—	—	420,521	249,682,493	27,819,245	—	—	—
1944	577,295 [7]	—	—	412,467	262,200,531	26,304,481	—	—	—
1945	627,049	47,301,464	6,767,715	421,125	255,447,752	21,138,956	—	—	—
1946	885,378 [7]	—	7,947,847	491,152	288,954,237	25,192,886	—	—	—
1947	888,862	60,639,764	7,678,501	551,807	367,745,578	31,422,728	—	—	—
1948	929,677 [7]	—	—	594,243	410,965,648	34,425,024	—	—	—
1949	929,488 [7]	—	—	614,842	393,449,692	28,194,837	—	—	—
1950	—	—	—	629,314	458,130,069	42,613,304	—	—	—
1951	—	—	—	652,376	517,039,183	43,545,590	—	—	—
1952	—	—	—	672,071	531,307,298	38,456,179	—	—	—
1953	958,591	79,985,477	8,394,266	697,975	558,242,262	39,484,687	—	—	—
1954	—	—	—	722,805	554,822,450	36,328,435	—	—	—
1955	—	—	—	807,303	642,248,036	47,478,271	—	—	—
1956	—	—	—	885,747	679,868,168	46,884,912	—	—	—
1957	970,627	—	8,097,356	940,147	720,413,567	44,476,464	—	—	—
1958	953,840	—	8,116,274	990,381	735,338,092	38,522,869	43,945	11,579,638	88,890
1959	949,396	78,406,071	8,844,708	1,074,120	816,799,884	46,797,267	71,140	19,199,731	395,299
1960	940,560	74,307,629	8,360,373	1,140,574	849,131,939	43,505,174	90,221	23,417,799	382,479
1961	938,966	74,706,827	8,688,622	1,190,286	873,177,644	45,893,900	106,048	26,175,449	564,447
1962	932,181	73,672,672	8,513,019	1,268,042	949,305,342	49,606,038	123,666	29,808,701	707,097
1963	924,276	73,274,451	8,668,166	1,323,187	1,008,742,704	54,284,740	139,112	35,083,133	799,453
1964	922,160	74,822,051	9,244,464	1,373,517	1,086,739,483	61,575,194	157,855	40,112,212	1,040,197
1965	914,215	75,258,639	9,699,145	1,423,980	1,194,600,662	73,889,821	173,410	46,442,511	1,447,857
1966	922,680	79,776,231	10,445,061	1,468,725	1,306,517,897	80,527,706	181,851	50,909,933	1,655,084
1967	906,182	80,137,915	10,865,953	1,534,360	1,374,598,532	78,181,729	200,784	56,752,764	1,853,187
1968	917,500	82,866,910	11,405,163	1,541,637	1,507,785,704	85,961,988	217,134	61,765,015	1,947,535
1969	920,831	87,204,511	10,486,453	1,658,745	1,680,482,985	80,218,685	233,807	73,260,632	2,250,954
1970	936,133	93,348,080	9,790,396	1,665,477	1,750,776,503	65,901,614	257,475	77,631,396	1,851,508
1971	958,912	99,802,234	9,146,110	1,733,332	1,906,007,776	79,700,323	262,066	79,788,892	2,160,592
1972	992,012	108,638,271	9,618,447	1,812,760	2,171,209,849	96,760,642	287,906	90,999,639	2,875,101
1973	1,039,092	124,001,999	9,216,034	1,904,670	2,557,688,950	120,446,898	313,080	110,890,533	3,670,577
1974	1,062,268	139,417,727	8,864,873	1,965,894	3,089,701,363	145,997,808	333,099	123,143,669	3,549,831
1975	1,073,094	148,417,529	7,737,570	2,023,647	3,198,627,860	142,636,826	358,413	128,016,555	3,242,098
1976	1,096,441	160,943,693	10,422,811	2,082,200	3,635,471,982	185,419,106	391,685	148,438,448	3,671,196
1977	1,153,398	180,848,961	13,264,168	2,241,887	4,128,304,478	219,243,043	428,204	164,317,459	4,750,479
1978	1,234,157	219,192,109	14,446,809	2,376,779	4,714,602,615	246,867,473	478,679	194,224,117	5,348,741
1979	1,299,593	258,197,936	15,205,908	2,556,794	5,598,689,129	284,615,371	514,907	212,706,226	3,795,578
1980	1,379,654	291,998,115	8,248,655	2,710,538	6,361,284,012	239,006,542	545,389	210,322,424	2,518,912
1981	1,460,502	272,129,807	−2,734,897	2,812,420	7,026,351,839	213,648,962	541,489	212,514,030	1,870,746
1982	1,514,212	296,690,303	−7,314,587	2,925,933	7,024,097,766	154,272,693	564,219	243,056,569	3,047,943
1983	1,541,539	291,318,703	−2,610,041	2,999,071	7,135,494,059	188,313,928	648,267	300,248,422	5,075,351
1984	1,643,581	375,192,511	−3,500,024	3,170,743	7,800,711,226	232,900,596	701,339	385,026,843	6,906,667
1985	1,713,603	367,117,316	−8,883,674	3,277,219	8,398,278,426	240,119,020	724,749	430,641,781	7,602,450
1986	1,702,952	397,302,544	−17,370,860	3,428,515	8,669,378,501	269,530,240	826,214	483,986,301	82,933,241
1987	1,648,032	442,802,234	19,303,350	3,612,133	9,580,720,701	328,223,710	1,127,905 [11]	972,246,266	24,151,513
1988	1,654,245	540,710,194	14,493,114	3,562,789	10,264,867,461	412,982,753	1,257,191	1,263,988,377	33,403,456
1989	1,635,164	550,848,428	14,099,275	3,627,863	10,934,973,405	389,010,675	1,422,967	1,463,966,315	32,469,877

Notes appear at end of table

(continued)

TABLE Ch1–18 Active proprietorships, partnerships, and corporations – entities, receipts, and profit: 1916–1998 [All industries] *Continued*

	Partnerships			Corporations					
	Entities	Receipts	Profit	Total			S-corporations		
				Entities	Receipts	Profit	Entities	Receipts	Profit
	Ch10	Ch11	Ch12	Ch13 [3]	Ch14 [3]	Ch15 [3]	Ch16	Ch17	Ch18
Year	Number	Thousand dollars	Thousand dollars	Number	Thousand dollars	Thousand dollars	Number	Thousand dollars	Thousand dollars
1990	1,553,529	566,212,218	16,609,540	3,716,650	11,409,520,074	370,632,632	1,575,092	1,620,702,664	32,250,110
1991	1,515,345	562,779,428	21,406,607	3,802,788	11,436,474,767	344,859,794	1,698,271	1,682,984,576	29,074,913
1992	1,484,752	596,782,859	42,916,649	3,869,023	11,742,134,729	401,997,022	1,785,371	1,821,882,961	58,329,739
1993	1,467,567	656,111,439	66,652,288	3,964,629	12,269,721,710	498,159,174	1,901,505	1,997,596,803	66,233,497
1994	1,493,963	762,234,674	82,183,076	4,342,368	13,360,007,157	577,277,530	2,023,754	2,210,945,344	91,676,443
1995	1,580,900	890,431,963	106,829,196	4,474,167	14,539,050,114	714,193,371	2,153,119	2,405,073,461	99,128,672
1996	1,654,256	1,226,624,120	145,218,248	4,631,370	15,525,718,009	806,484,990	2,304,416	2,618,094,172	125,245,496
1997	1,758,627	1,539,397,905	168,240,726	4,710,083	16,609,707,302	915,396,637	2,452,254	2,895,237,519	153,063,011
1998	—	—	—	—	—	—	—	—	—

[1] Totals have not been generated independently, but are simply summations of the series for proprietorships, partnerships, and corporations.

[2] Beginning 1981, figures exclude farm proprietorships.

[3] Includes S-corporations.

[4] Includes only proprietorships with positive net income.

[5] Includes only proprietorships with net income greater than or equal to $5,000.

[6] Number of tax returns rather than the number of businesses.

[7] Includes all returns filed during the succeeding calendar year, including delinquent returns from prior years and those with a fiscal year ending after June 30.

[8] Gross income instead of total receipts.

[9] Includes inactive corporations.

[10] Affiliated corporations filed separate returns.

[11] Firms that shifted from fiscal to calendar years are counted twice.

Sources

U.S. Internal Revenue Service (and its predecessor, U.S. Bureau of Internal Revenue), *Statistics of Income (SOI)*, various issues; *SOI Bulletin*, various issues.

Documentation

When Congress passed the Revenue Act of 1916, the legislation that created the modern U.S. income tax system, it included a provision requiring that the Internal Revenue Service (IRS) compile an annual statistical report. The IRS issued the first report in 1918, and from the beginning the *Statistics of Income*, as the documents were titled, contained information on the number and earnings of corporations that filed tax returns. Over the years, the reports were expanded to include additional information on corporations, as well as data on single proprietorships and partnerships. Unfortunately, the amount of information contained in the reports has contracted as well as expanded from time to time, producing many breaks in the series. Yet other discontinuities resulted from the way the IRS handled the information. For example, the IRS shifted over time from the analysis of whole populations to sample data, with the dates of this transition varying by series, and with sampling and estimation methods changing over time. In addition, continuity has been affected by the many changes that have occurred in the tax law and in the incidence of the income tax since 1916. Only the most important breaks and discontinuities can be discussed in this note. For additional information, see Dan Rosa and Dorothy Collins, "Statistics of Income Studies of Business Income and Taxes," *SOI Bulletin* 8 (Fall 1988): 81–101; "A Chronological History of Statistics of Income," *SOI Bulletin* 13 (Summer 1993): 6–13; and Thomas B. Petska and Robert A. Wilson, "Trends in Business Structure and Activity," *SOI Bulletin* 13 (Spring 1994): 27–72. See also the individual *SOI* volumes and issues of the *SOI Bulletin*.

Within each organizational form, the number of entities, unless otherwise noted, is the (actual or estimated) number of tax or information returns filed by active enterprises. The numbers include part-year as well as full-year returns. Hence, if an enterprise changed ownership during a year, it was counted twice by the IRS. Unless otherwise noted, receipts consist of the *SOI* category "total receipts." They include business receipts (that is, gross operating revenues) plus income from investments. Also unless otherwise

indicated, net profits are the *SOI* category "net income less deficit." The series on receipts and net profits are not strictly comparable across organizational forms, mainly because of differences in reporting requirements for tax purposes. For example, in the case of sole proprietors, the IRS considers earnings from investments (including capital gains and losses) to be personal rather than business income, so they are not included in total receipts. Similarly, the IRS does not allow sole proprietorships to deduct salaries to owners in the calculation of net income.

Since 1938, the IRS has allocated firms to industries on the basis of the Standard Industrial Classification (SIC) system. Firms whose businesses involve multiple industries are assigned to the classification that accounts for the largest proportion of their total receipts. See the Introduction to Part D for a discussion of SIC codes.

The series on sole proprietorships cover unincorporated, single-owner businesses that were reported by their owners on individual tax returns (currently on Schedule C). The series does not include certain categories of persons who are defined as self-employed by the Internal Revenue Code. Examples include clergymen and public officials like sheriffs and notaries public. Before 1926, the IRS excluded from their counts businesses that generated losses and, from 1926 through 1938, businesses with net incomes of less than $5,000. After 1980, the *SOI* counted only one business per taxpayer so that the series effectively reports the number, receipts, and profits of proprietors rather than of individual proprietorships. It is claimed, however, that the discrepancy is not large – that the relationship between the number of businesses and the number of owners is about 1.1 to 1. For earlier years, the procedures that the IRS followed to generate its counts are not always clear. For most years, the IRS reported the total number of proprietorships, although sometimes it counted a maximum of three businesses per owner and sometimes it counted separately only those businesses that operated in different industries. Beginning in 1981, the IRS reported data only for non-farm proprietorships.

Although the IRS taxes partnership income as personal income earned by the individual partners, partnerships are required to submit tax forms for informational purposes. These forms are the basis for the series on partnerships. The partnership category includes all groups conducting business for profit unless classified as corporations for tax purposes. Thus, in addition to partnerships, the category includes a variety of unincorporated businesses such as syndicates, groups, pools, and joint ventures. Until 1939, virtually the only data that the *SOI* reported on partnerships were the numbers of returns filed. From 1939 until the late 1950s, when the annual series begins, the *SOI* sporadically published more complete reports that included information on receipts and profits. The series for 1939, 1945, 1947, 1953, and all subsequent years include returns for the calendar year and for fiscal years ending up to June 30 of the following year. For other years before 1953, the IRS simply counted all returns submitted during the succeeding calendar year, regardless of filing period. For 1939, this more casual method would have yielded a total of 290,876 partnerships, as opposed to the 271,018 reported in the table.

TABLE Ch1–18   Active proprietorships, partnerships, and corporations – number, receipts, and profit: 1916–1998 [All industries]   *Continued*

The series on corporations include data on all active corporations that filed income tax returns. The figures reported for any given year represent corporations whose fiscal years ended any time from July 1 of that year until June 30 of the next. The series provide reasonably comprehensive coverage of the corporate sector from the earliest years because all corporations were (and are) required to file tax returns regardless of size or amount of earnings. The tax definition of the term "corporation," however, is broader than the conventional legal meaning (it includes, for example, mutual insurance societies, savings and loan associations, publicly traded partnerships, and real estate investment trusts) and has changed somewhat over the years (for example, nonexempt corporate farmers' cooperatives were excluded after 1980). During the early years of the series there were a few important changes in the way the numbers were reported. First, the figures for 1916, 1917, and 1926 include inactive as well as active corporations. Judging by the numbers of inactive versus active corporations that are available for the next several years, the former could account for as much as 7 to 14 percent of the total. Second, between 1917 and 1918, there was a change in procedure (temporarily reversed again between 1934 and 1942) whereby corporations that were affiliated with each other were required to file consolidated rather than individual returns, causing a downward shift in the number of corporations counted. This filing change affected the relative distribution of

corporations across industries because firms operating in different industries were assigned to the industry that accounted for the major part of their output. It also meant that events such as merger waves or surges in the number of corporate spin-offs affected the year-to-year comparability of the data. Finally, for 1916 through 1922, the IRS reported gross income rather than total receipts.

Beginning in 1958, the tax law allowed certain kinds of closely held corporations (now called S-corporations) to be taxed like partnerships. The definition of an S-corporation has changed over time. For example, the maximum number of shareholders was raised from 15 to 25 in 1982 and again to 35 in 1983. Similarly, in 1982 the amount of revenues that could derive from passive investments was increased from 20 to 25 percent, and the limitation on receipts from foreign sources was abolished. The S-corporation became an especially appealing form as a result of the changes in marginal tax rates effected by the Tax Reform Act of 1986. Beginning in 1987, the IRS required S-corporations to use the same accounting periods as their owners, which were mostly calendar years. S-corporations that had been on other fiscal years had to file two part-year returns in 1987 and, as a result, were counted twice in the numbers for that year (though not in the data on receipts and profits). It has been estimated that this double counting added about 100,000 firms to the total for 1987.

TABLE Ch19–36   Active proprietorships, partnerships, and corporations – entities, receipts, and profit: 1918–1998 [Agriculture, forestry, and fishing]

Contributed by Naomi R. Lamoreaux

	Total			Proprietorships					
				Total			Nonfarm		
	Entities	Receipts	Profit	Entities	Receipts	Profit	Entities	Receipts	Profit
	Ch19 [1,2]	Ch20 [1,2]	Ch21 [1,2]	Ch22	Ch23	Ch24	Ch25	Ch26	Ch27
Year	Number	Thousand dollars	Thousand dollars	Number	Thousand dollars	Thousand dollars	Number	Thousand dollars	Thousand dollars
1918	—	—	—	372,336 [4]	—	1,222,532 [4]	—	—	—
1919	—	—	—	418,945 [4]	—	1,211,261 [4]	—	—	—
1920	—	—	—	271,805 [4]	—	637,425 [4]	—	—	—
1921	—	—	—	130,344 [4]	—	229,193 [4]	—	—	—
1922	—	—	—	104,834 [4]	—	231,290 [4]	—	—	—
1923	—	—	—	185,446 [4]	—	356,693 [4]	—	—	—
1924	—	—	—	164,669 [4]	—	371,706 [4]	—	—	—
1925	—	—	—	82,968 [4]	—	250,061 [4]	—	—	—
1926	—	—	—	14,767 [5]	—	84,435 [5]	—	—	—
1927	—	—	—	16,297 [5]	—	103,213 [5]	—	—	—
1928	—	—	—	18,861 [5]	—	121,723 [5]	—	—	—
1929	—	—	—	19,306 [5]	—	113,322 [5]	—	—	—
1930	—	—	—	9,708 [5]	—	51,379 [5]	—	—	—
1931	—	—	—	3,213 [5]	—	14,573 [5]	—	—	—
1932	—	—	—	1,415 [5]	—	6,185 [5]	—	—	—
1933	—	—	—	6,729 [5]	72,478 [5]	−114 [5]	—	—	—
1934	—	—	—	11,170 [5]	128,383 [5]	13,486 [5]	—	—	—
1935	—	—	—	13,703 [5]	161,052 [5]	24,924 [5]	—	—	—
1936	—	—	—	20,866 [5]	273,941 [5]	43,480 [5]	—	—	—
1937	—	—	—	23,152 [5]	286,630 [5]	38,630 [5]	—	—	—
1938	—	—	—	17,239 [5]	243,831 [5]	10,594 [5]	—	—	—
1939	172,565	2,270,510	185,411	143,521	1,290,873	114,476	3,761	74,943	8,022
1940	—	—	—	—	—	—	—	—	—
1941	—	—	—	1,177,237	5,135,144	1,672,921	15,892	148,964	28,017
1942	—	—	—	—	—	—	—	—	—
1943	—	—	—	2,588,435 [6]	11,762,480	3,538,530	28,445 [6]	258,475	43,415
1944	—	—	—	—	—	—	—	—	—

Notes appear at end of table

(continued)

TABLE Ch19–36   Active proprietorships, partnerships, and corporations – entities, receipts, and profit: 1918–1998
[Agriculture, forestry, and fishing]   *Continued*

	Total			Proprietorships					
				Total			Nonfarm		
	Entities	Receipts	Profit	Entities	Receipts	Profit	Entities	Receipts	Profit
	Ch19 [1,2]	Ch20 [1,2]	Ch21 [1,2]	Ch22	Ch23	Ch24	Ch25	Ch26	Ch27
Year	Number	Thousand dollars	Thousand dollars	Number	Thousand dollars	Thousand dollars	Number	Thousand dollars	Thousand dollars
1945	2,802,343	17,376,761	3,992,752	2,695,382	14,494,212	3,391,162	36,018	267,003	50,332
1946	—	—	—	—	—	—	—	—	—
1947	3,083,223	23,507,939	6,191,858	2,955,492	18,788,509	5,242,989	51,581	407,507	74,581
1948	—	—	—	—	—	—	—	—	—
1949		—	—	3,049,023	19,756,110	4,382,325	61,601	762,623	110,707
1950	—	—	—	—	—	—	—	—	—
1951	—	—	—	3,209,539	22,947,065	—	70,928	853,764	—
1952	—	—	—	—	—	—	—	—	—
1953	3,362,613	28,495,903	4,141,013	3,209,565	22,483,949	3,543,435	84,054	1,167,205	169,932
1954	—	—	—	—	—	—	—	—	—
1955	—	—	—	3,513,080	21,704,755	2,827,792	96,499	925,260	185,593
1956	—	—	—	—	—	—	—	—	—
1957	3,613,594		4,243,329	3,452,851	23,497,998	3,441,954	109,627 [7]	1,081,560	209,311
1958	3,648,024	—	4,811,778	3,489,164	25,913,881	4,016,594	114,681 [7]	1,240,287	253,879
1959	3,662,408	36,066,532	3,608,967	3,505,090	27,816,099	2,913,642	138,210 [7]	1,536,738	266,690
1960	3,633,640	36,226,392	3,589,513	3,480,195	27,369,780	2,997,639	121,580 [7]	1,840,361	261,109
1961	3,642,703	37,965,755	4,341,890	3,487,190	27,914,902	3,621,946	125,139 [7]	1,624,284	270,754
1962	3,599,893	41,565,744	4,512,105	3,444,116	30,200,142	3,695,945	124,854 [7]	1,888,681	331,413
1963	3,491,771	42,836,923	3,710,201	3,338,081	30,049,957	3,048,031	129,992 [7]	1,764,995	298,997
1964	3,445,165	40,889,406	3,748,919	3,288,873	29,532,128	2,998,897	158,883 [7]	1,786,333	358,853
1965	3,380,578	44,825,264	4,694,863	3,225,266	32,159,830	3,780,717	161,714 [7]	2,251,385	724,755
1966	3,325,785	49,503,415	5,537,941	3,172,739	35,485,823	4,498,417	152,247 [7]	2,161,842	415,184
1967	3,352,683	50,180,314	4,586,640	3,195,602	35,271,425	3,770,215	165,537 [7]	2,135,662	412,506
1968	3,357,686	52,337,847	4,467,353	3,205,683	37,361,795	3,545,128	163,119 [7]	2,344,338	420,279
1969	3,410,489	59,382,024	4,979,518	3,258,696	40,213,513	4,054,037	169,210 [7]	2,600,446	497,330
1970	3,239,658	64,015,771	3,887,069	3,078,255	41,819,207	3,168,068	172,391 [7]	2,674,631	490,757
1971	3,287,410	66,469,546	3,655,779	3,126,160	43,813,248	2,919,159	184,713 [7]	2,900,460	501,445
1972	3,363,781	78,349,340	6,487,021	3,206,381	51,596,105	5,228,996	199,200 [7]	2,957,719	531,442
1973	3,585,777	102,994,315	11,463,244	3,415,111	65,994,132	9,237,503	212,045 [7]	3,405,013	622,458
1974	3,561,171	105,517,749	9,074,113	3,385,088	66,866,949	7,468,758	206,932 [7]	3,496,847	609,141
1975	3,546,697	110,734,586	7,229,765	3,367,244	69,289,670	5,587,213	244,851 [7]	4,023,013	612,416
1976	3,652,064	123,947,548	7,393,255	3,470,438	77,709,573	5,738,144	252,165 [7]	4,195,952	662,743
1977	3,363,816	125,155,612	4,450,803	3,177,180	74,641,258	2,950,461	245,370 [7]	5,262,311	998,008
1978	3,583,874	148,292,307	9,178,545	3,386,965	87,514,766	6,646,711	277,301 [7]	5,790,168	1,100,766
1979	3,470,913	174,207,772	7,586,833	3,262,599	98,568,112	5,225,460	276,220 [7]	6,430,322	995,074
1980	3,486,413	176,533,489	2,424,012	3,279,306	101,112,780	1,279,306	307,728 [7]	6,433,611	776,538
1981	466,839	79,390,012	412,592	—	—	—	256,496 [6]	6,963,081	787,900
1982	518,200	81,755,777	−154,738	—	—	—	293,883 [6]	8,697,269	632,711
1983	532,231	77,811,052	713,966	—	—	—	303,503 [6]	9,975,351	1,055,340
1984	560,591	85,838,320	353,861	—	—	—	322,924 [6]	10,700,001	900,369
1985	558,064	91,864,712	−208,678	—	—	—	318,999 [6]	11,927,580	915,026
1986	578,424	98,007,599	1,381,277	—	—	—	324,258 [6]	11,618,715	1,170,993
1987	626,093	102,352,256	5,681,289	—	—	—	360,654 [6]	14,495,263	2,039,480
1988	593,194	—	4,791,519	—	—	—	351,244 [6]	15,357,049	2,096,952
1989	596,552	—	5,078,284	—	—	—	342,300 [6]	14,704,382	2,147,459
1990	614,192	—	5,206,433	—	—	—	362,740 [6]	17,231,926	2,383,217
1991	688,553	—	5,151,383	—	—	—	431,594 [6]	16,949,061	2,786,050
1992	673,577	—	6,964,837	—	—	—	411,180 [6]	18,413,532	3,130,501
1993	758,434	134,979,451	6,660,825	—	—	—	497,148 [6]	20,169,374	2,994,137
1994	785,479	137,748,098	6,270,686	—	—	—	515,336 [6]	19,437,487	3,348,127
1995	786,584	146,713,398	6,169,445	—	—	—	509,952 [6]	19,170,533	3,235,201
1996	841,915	161,734,234	7,194,875	—	—	—	552,107 [6]	20,279,907	3,223,406
1997	854,908	165,191,451	8,314,603	—	—	—	564,734 [6]	23,645,626	3,675,044
1998	—	—	—	—	—	—	549,684 [6]	27,992,915	3,823,486

Notes appear at end of table

TABLE Ch19–36   Active proprietorships, partnerships, and corporations – entities, receipts, and profit: 1918–1998 [Agriculture, forestry, and fishing]   Continued

	Partnerships			Corporations					
				Total			S-corporations		
	Entities	Receipts	Profit	Entities	Receipts	Profit	Entities	Receipts	Profit
	Ch28	Ch29	Ch30	Ch31 [3]	Ch32 [3]	Ch33 [3]	Ch34	Ch35	Ch36
Year	Number	Thousand dollars	Thousand dollars	Number	Thousand dollars	Thousand dollars	Number	Thousand dollars	Thousand dollars
1918	—	—	—	7,887	524,181 [10]	30,347	—	—	—
1919	—	—	—	8,298	791,458 [10]	64,172	—	—	—
1920	—	—	—	9,186	725,050 [10]	5,340	—	—	—
1921	—	—	—	8,724	675,598 [10]	−47,845	—	—	—
1922	—	—	—	9,092	706,394	6,809	—	—	—
1923	—	—	—	9,360	774,424	42,271	—	—	—
1924	—	—	—	9,758	810,958	1,732	—	—	—
1925	—	—	—	9,904	794,410	17,647	—	—	—
1926	—	—	—	10,688 [8]	865,406	15,147	—	—	—
1927	—	—	—	9,905	823,624	16,684	—	—	—
1928	—	—	—	9,183	826,443	30,384	—	—	—
1929	—	—	—	9,430	883,441	19,257	—	—	—
1930	—	—	—	9,906	671,901	−45,885	—	—	—
1931	—	—	—	9,900	492,724	−84,775	—	—	—
1932	—	—	—	9,768	368,966	−88,983	—	—	—
1933	—	—	—	9,261	396,091	−45,318	—	—	—
1934	—	—	—	9,326 [9]	539,474	−54,699	—	—	—
1935	—	—	—	9,055 [9]	591,110	3,648	—	—	—
1936	—	—	—	8,945 [9]	726,143	33,130	—	—	—
1937	—	—	—	8,703 [9]	783,452	23,736	—	—	—
1938	—	—	—	8,993 [9]	603,812	−3,162	—	—	—
1939	20,408	368,430	58,386	8,636 [9]	611,207	12,549	—	—	—
1940	—	—	—	8,400 [9]	643,420	16,963	—	—	—
1941	—	—	—	7,901 [9]	752,617	63,123	—	—	—
1942	—	—	—	7,318 [9]	804,639	80,485	—	—	—
1943	—	—	—	6,884	867,739	113,845	—	—	—
1944	—	—	—	6,417	929,627	119,922	—	—	—
1945	100,809	1,889,177	467,777	6,152	993,372	133,813	—	—	—
1946	—	—	—	6,663	1,274,595	183,575	—	—	—
1947	120,402	3,048,918	733,527	7,329	1,670,512	215,342	—	—	—
1948	—	—	—	7,694	1,861,942	219,546	—	—	—
1949	—	—	—	8,006	1,902,210	177,342	—	—	—
1950	—	—	—	8,300	2,130,965	294,497	—	—	—
1951	—	—	—	8,734	2,467,383	258,917	—	—	—
1952	—	—	—	8,869	2,560,447	138,962	—	—	—
1953	143,643	3,619,311	485,556	9,405	2,392,643	112,022	—	—	—
1954	—	—	—	8,779	2,272,577	122,283	—	—	—
1955	—	—	—	10,303	2,585,998	123,231	—	—	—
1956	—	—	—	10,973	2,759,462	128,947	—	—	—
1957	148,910	—	686,680	11,833	3,008,157	114,695	—	—	—
1958	144,915	—	651,623	13,945	3,613,666	143,561	542	90,939	4,821
1959	141,715	4,412,813	589,441	15,603	3,837,620	105,884	1,485	177,211	−4,868
1960	136,306	4,454,405	554,540	17,139	4,402,207	37,334	2,508	378,213	1,701
1961	136,532	4,711,307	609,793	18,981	5,339,546	110,151	3,367	546,707	11,692
1962	133,647	5,076,573	655,206	22,130	6,289,029	160,954	4,106	650,264	11,066
1963	130,420	4,800,591	566,518	23,270	7,986,375	95,652	4,988	918,384	16,892
1964	130,359	5,027,854	611,023	25,933	6,329,424	138,999	6,144	762,448	−797
1965	127,782	5,141,160	676,917	27,530	7,524,274	237,229	6,839	1,119,696	89
1966	125,101	5,412,976	750,310	27,945	8,604,616	289,214	7,427	1,237,971	28,141
1967	124,633	5,612,519	633,453	32,448	9,296,370	182,972	8,516	1,455,494	30,837
1968	120,759	5,525,537	654,300	31,244	9,450,515	267,925	8,579	1,265,102	18,607
1969	119,819	7,041,367	668,282	31,974	12,127,144	257,199	9,332	1,425,075	11,272
1970	124,165	7,918,857	653,706	37,238	14,277,707	65,295	11,634	1,915,731	−26,010
1971	121,318	8,258,526	528,570	39,932	14,397,772	208,050	12,040	2,332,672	21,161
1972	114,426	9,596,642	748,931	42,974	17,156,593	509,094	13,686	2,792,165	106,263
1973	123,541	13,390,801	1,289,605	47,125	23,609,382	936,136	14,465	3,735,387	170,928
1974	122,625	13,198,172	1,184,192	53,458	25,452,628	421,163	17,178	3,777,020	83,467

Notes appear at end of table

(continued)

TABLE Ch19–36   Active proprietorships, partnerships, and corporations – entities, receipts, and profit: 1918–1998
[Agriculture, forestry, and fishing]   *Continued*

Year	Partnerships			Corporations					
	Entities	Receipts	Profit	Total			S-corporations		
				Entities	Receipts	Profit	Entities	Receipts	Profit
	Ch28	Ch29	Ch30	Ch31 [3]	Ch32 [3]	Ch33 [3]	Ch34	Ch35	Ch36
	Number	Thousand dollars	Thousand dollars	Number	Thousand dollars	Thousand dollars	Number	Thousand dollars	Thousand dollars
1975	123,173	13,326,402	895,644	56,280	28,118,514	746,908	18,146	4,355,181	94,576
1976	121,337	13,804,826	1,014,820	60,289	32,433,149	640,291	18,825	4,891,679	73,545
1977	121,042	14,606,487	791,386	65,594	35,907,867	708,956	20,282	5,425,277	16,222
1978	126,938	19,359,983	1,234,872	69,971	41,417,558	1,296,962	26,214	6,732,204	245,500
1979	124,825	22,293,664	1,061,398	83,489	53,345,996	1,299,975	30,280	8,481,959	298,101
1980	126,224	23,330,794	471,548	80,883	52,089,915	673,158	31,732	8,393,556	−114,551
1981	124,973	7,364,972	−703,617	85,370	65,061,959	328,309	26,611	9,590,357	−120,254
1982	132,997	7,701,597	−701,031	91,320	65,356,911	−86,418	27,648	11,090,205	−212,614
1983	136,603	8,627,059	−144,846	92,125	59,208,642	−196,528	28,445	9,261,649	−531,020
1984	139,306	8,493,200	−749,030	98,361	66,645,119	202,522	32,995	11,946,454	−323,621
1985	135,909	9,445,646	−1,049,434	103,156	70,491,486	−74,270	32,258	13,209,197	−413,980
1986	147,532	8,886,669	−938,402	106,634	77,502,215	1,148,686	34,671	16,499,232	−211,872
1987	148,895	10,799,879	2,015,308	116,544	77,057,114	1,626,501	46,796 [11]	21,345,878	−16,575
1988	122,048	—	1,078,646	119,902	86,258,094	1,615,921	49,761	25,171,121	104,147
1989	131,057	—	1,380,245	123,195	86,627,044	1,550,580	52,349	26,650,251	57,837
1990	125,029	—	1,666,947	126,423	88,101,065	1,156,269	54,971	26,108,382	−138,250
1991	127,073	—	1,739,677	129,886	85,945,700	625,656	58,594	27,795,647	−272,493
1992	124,564	—	2,227,039	137,833	95,563,041	1,607,297	65,055	32,553,498	1,240,937
1993	119,960	16,509,001	2,018,963	141,326	98,301,076	1,647,725	64,764	35,129,407	479,617
1994	123,147	17,403,458	1,608,256	146,996	100,907,153	1,314,303	71,336	36,139,788	221,764
1995	129,105	19,960,892	1,329,763	147,527	107,581,973	1,604,481	72,085	40,130,194	17,984
1996	130,845	21,717,269	1,357,338	158,963	119,737,058	2,614,131	82,712	48,474,500	1,388,924
1997	127,060	24,158,270	1,925,633	163,114	117,387,555	2,713,926	88,270	51,202,714	2,450,167
1998	—	—	—	—	—	—	—	—	—

[1] Totals have not been generated independently, but are simply summations of the series for proprietorships, partnerships, and corporations.

[2] Beginning 1981, figures exclude farm proprietorships.

[3] Includes S-corporations.

[4] Includes only proprietorships with positive net income.

[5] Includes only proprietorships with net income greater than or equal to $5,000.

[6] Number of tax returns rather than the number of businesses.

[7] Computed by subtracting, from the total number of proprietorships in agriculture, forestry, and fishing, the difference between the total number of proprietorships in all industries and the number of nonfarm proprietorships in all industries.

[8] Includes inactive corporations.

[9] Affiliated corporations filed separate returns.

[10] Gross income instead of total receipts.

[11] Firms that shifted from fiscal to calendar years are counted twice.

Sources
U.S. Internal Revenue Service (and its predecessor, U.S. Bureau of Internal Revenue), *Statistics of Income* (*SOI*), various issues; *SOI Bulletin*, various issues.

Documentation
See the text for Table Ch1–18.

TABLE Ch37-51 Active proprietorships, partnerships, and corporations – entities, receipts, and profit: 1918–1998 [Mining]

Contributed by Naomi R. Lamoreaux

	Total			Proprietorships			Partnerships			Corporations — Total			Corporations — S-corporations		
	Entities	Receipts	Profit	Entities	Receipts	Profit	Entities	Receipts	Profit	Entities	Receipts	Profit	Entities	Receipts	Profit
	Ch37 [1]	Ch38 [1]	Ch39 [1]	Ch40	Ch41	Ch42	Ch43	Ch44	Ch45	Ch46 [2]	Ch47 [2]	Ch48 [2]	Ch49	Ch50	Ch51
Year	Number	Thousand dollars	Thousand dollars	Number	Thousand dollars	Thousand dollars	Number	Thousand dollars	Thousand dollars	Number	Thousand dollars	Thousand dollars	Number	Thousand dollars	Thousand dollars
1918	—	—	—	8,191 [3]	—	26,627 [3]	—	—	—	10,661	3,995,043 [8]	496,304	—	—	—
1919	—	—	—	7,321 [3]	—	26,624 [3]	—	—	—	18,469	4,677,648 [8]	251,670	—	—	—
1920	—	—	—	5,276 [3]	—	36,850 [3]	—	—	—	17,534	6,151,220 [8]	525,569	—	—	—
1921	—	—	—	3,871 [3]	—	11,168 [3]	—	—	—	17,660	3,888,876 [8]	-229,355	—	—	—
1922	—	—	—	3,006 [3]	—	15,932 [3]	—	—	—	17,093	3,706,636	5,981	—	—	—
1923	—	—	—	5,859 [3]	—	18,331 [3]	—	—	—	18,509	4,876,768	-50,688	—	—	—
1924	—	—	—	3,525 [3]	—	15,340 [3]	—	—	—	18,453	4,860,667	-66,949	—	—	—
1925	—	—	—	4,604 [3]	—	25,432 [3]	—	—	—	19,163	4,936,040	243,643	—	—	—
1926	—	—	—	1,546 [4]	—	25,785 [4]	—	—	—	19,252 [6]	4,561,462	15,146	—	—	—
1927	—	—	—	1,160 [4]	—	12,355 [4]	—	—	—	13,036	3,847,305	29,384	—	—	—
1928	—	—	—	1,112 [4]	—	10,716 [4]	—	—	—	12,933	3,599,883	125,263	—	—	—
1929	—	—	—	1,558 [4]	—	16,097 [4]	—	—	—	12,502	4,059,067	232,087	—	—	—
1930	—	—	—	915 [4]	—	9,623 [4]	—	—	—	12,233	3,009,567	-44,341	—	—	—
1931	—	—	—	550 [4]	—	5,340 [4]	—	—	—	12,123	2,237,212	-254,809	—	—	—
1932	—	—	—	517 [4]	—	5,188 [4]	—	—	—	12,046	1,672,288	-224,367	—	—	—
1933	—	—	—	721 [4]	13,875 [4]	4,502 [4]	—	—	—	11,848	1,966,418	-176,441	—	—	—
1934	—	—	—	1,125 [4]	27,641 [4]	7,804 [4]	—	—	—	13,543 [7]	2,546,100	-9,311	—	—	—
1935	—	—	—	1,255 [4]	22,412 [4]	8,844 [4]	—	—	—	13,715 [7]	2,633,330	-10,943	—	—	—
1936	—	—	—	1,623 [4]	42,655 [4]	12,118 [4]	—	—	—	13,788 [7]	3,070,588	175,902	—	—	—
1937	—	—	—	1,873 [4]	63,689 [4]	15,612 [4]	—	—	—	13,567 [7]	3,583,597	299,252	—	—	—
1938	—	—	—	1,451 [4]	61,721 [4]	12,295 [4]	—	—	—	10,942 [7]	2,741,386	47,181	—	—	—
1939	23,504	3,148,630	164,190	6,437	117,896	11,220	6,247	154,190	21,794	10,820 [7]	2,876,544	131,176	—	—	—
1940	—	—	—	10,701	195,302	23,740	—	—	—	10,383 [7]	3,264,372	205,507	—	—	—
1941	—	—	—	—	—	—	—	—	—	9,667 [7]	3,899,506	378,851	—	—	—
1942	—	—	—	16,167 [5]	348,245	35,802	—	—	—	8,915 [7]	4,002,786	389,707	—	—	—
1943	—	—	—	—	—	—	—	—	—	8,133	3,731,407	338,219	—	—	—
1944	—	—	—	—	—	—	—	—	—	7,620	4,027,595	317,374	—	—	—
1945	31,677	4,936,647	302,079	13,234	399,238	-5,802	11,147	583,727	65,493	7,296	3,953,682	242,388	—	—	—
1946	—	—	—	—	—	—	—	—	—	7,675	4,299,558	334,739	—	—	—
1947	40,639	7,407,867	942,693	18,766	531,398	33,144	13,579	839,866	123,498	8,294	6,036,603	786,051	—	—	—
1948	—	—	—	—	—	—	—	—	—	9,085	7,906,995	1,152,983	—	—	—
1949	—	—	—	19,657	685,620	15,644	—	—	—	9,151	6,825,473	1,692,777	—	—	—
1950	—	—	—	—	—	—	—	—	—	9,056	8,608,558	1,090,223	—	—	—
1951	—	—	—	21,000	813,839	—	—	—	—	9,036	9,690,851	1,120,071	—	—	—
1952	—	—	—	—	—	—	—	—	—	9,055	9,716,522	980,859	—	—	—
1953	51,959	11,490,377	877,859	21,169	781,033	-8,797	21,643	1,356,248	-58,477	9,147	9,353,096	945,133	—	—	—
1954	—	—	—	—	—	—	—	—	—	9,585	8,550,919	740,913	—	—	—
1955	—	—	—	29,981	934,705	-13,014	—	—	—	10,718	9,810,730	1,080,309	—	—	—
1956	—	—	—	—	—	—	—	—	—	11,743	10,872,050	1,165,232	—	—	—
1957	61,133	—	1,058,938	33,075	1,164,289	32,593	15,383	—	78,010	12,675	11,539,284	948,335	—	—	—
1958	65,605	—	790,160	35,413	1,286,608	4,358	18,075	—	-45,959	12,117	10,105,633	831,761	474	85,600	-2,012
1959	59,912	12,346,975	666,986	33,691	1,005,283	-4,607	13,301	986,837	25,719	12,920	10,354,855	645,874	832	130,206	261

Notes appear at end of table

(continued)

TABLE Ch37–51   Active proprietorships, partnerships, and corporations – entities, receipts, and profit: 1918–1998   [Mining]   Continued

Year	Total Entities Ch37 [1] Number	Total Receipts Ch38 [1] Thousand dollars	Total Profit Ch39 [1] Thousand dollars	Proprietorships Entities Ch40 Number	Proprietorships Receipts Ch41 Thousand dollars	Proprietorships Profit Ch42 Thousand dollars	Partnerships Entities Ch43 Number	Partnerships Receipts Ch44 Thousand dollars	Partnerships Profit Ch45 Thousand dollars	Corporations Total Entities Ch46 [2] Number	Corporations Total Receipts Ch47 [2] Thousand dollars	Corporations Total Profit Ch48 [2] Thousand dollars	S-corporations Entities Ch49 Number	S-corporations Receipts Ch50 Thousand dollars	S-corporations Profit Ch51 Thousand dollars
1960	61,750	13,475,537	593,004	33,036	1,501,474	-103,044	15,697	1,048,288	-42,816	13,017	10,925,775	738,864	1,009	225,075	4,174
1961	65,219	14,486,028	841,632	35,549	1,209,179	-12,580	15,939	1,018,877	-8,225	13,731	12,257,972	862,437	1,277	314,687	-3,618
1962	63,566	14,461,817	725,985	34,987	987,483	-63,855	15,040	944,894	-3,761	13,539	12,529,440	793,601	1,482	205,495	-3,500
1963	63,466	15,039,211	1,190,358	34,438	1,048,761	-9,875	14,150	935,143	-9,497	14,878	13,055,307	1,209,730	1,550	275,214	25,001
1964	61,066	15,327,100	1,297,633	32,147	985,308	47,105	14,432	1,027,521	22,953	14,487	13,314,271	1,227,575	1,606	302,685	6,791
1965	64,565	14,466,055	1,371,441	36,378	943,037	-7,430	14,902	920,931	-13,068	13,285	12,602,087	1,391,939	1,912	425,073	32,754
1966	70,765	16,666,316	1,652,919	42,696	1,117,131	-76,120	13,238	939,833	-10,534	14,831	14,609,352	1,739,573	2,227	771,034	20,769
1967	73,361	16,113,571	1,472,479	45,677	1,323,164	-56,996	13,243	1,110,685	65,000	14,441	13,679,722	1,464,256	1,896	409,590	22,021
1968	69,528	16,806,240	1,602,318	43,488	1,219,968	-73,873	13,227	1,035,817	72,806	12,813	14,550,455	1,603,385	2,075	388,149	21,447
1969	84,310	18,827,063	1,215,661	58,808	1,450,329	-96,630	11,475	1,143,406	-241,678	14,027	16,233,328	1,553,969	2,184	592,739	31,483
1970	79,514	20,472,358	1,578,408	50,666	1,446,607	-11,033	14,383	1,278,001	-244,874	14,465	17,747,750	1,834,315	1,857	593,637	26,055
1971	84,590	22,415,054	1,273,244	58,563	1,556,413	-17,795	13,414	1,378,948	-869,720	12,613	19,479,693	2,160,759	2,322	631,861	26,981
1972	79,184	25,794,279	2,800,431	51,411	1,651,406	-13,223	13,562	1,494,662	-385,716	14,211	22,648,211	3,199,370	2,875	616,107	2,517
1973	85,526	33,739,492	6,192,520	57,696	1,914,516	-37,036	15,019	1,746,392	-528,395	12,811	30,078,584	6,757,951	1,922	764,861	72,752
1974	86,818	71,561,602	26,226,040	57,033	2,991,449	364,630	14,053	3,765,311	-42,665	15,732	64,804,842	25,904,075	2,363	1,573,046	218,338
1975	85,413	73,682,422	23,357,930	55,600	3,530,555	283,053	15,571	4,241,873	-499,956	14,242	65,909,994	23,574,833	2,597	1,814,050	174,268
1976	93,150	93,648,369	30,148,175	59,732	3,588,318	170,395	17,812	5,731,042	-46,926	15,606	84,329,009	30,024,706	2,293	2,021,770	122,003
1977	112,333	104,615,473	30,881,446	71,151	1,586,603	77,700	21,966	6,364,117	-550,177	19,216	96,164,753	31,353,923	3,277	2,446,184	150,066
1978	125,113	106,504,921	24,662,423	82,360	4,744,164	-189,912	23,629	7,054,695	-2,857,247	19,124	94,706,062	27,709,582	3,033	1,958,497	10,883
1979	149,476	148,877,920	40,640,817	97,488	6,084,218	90,450	28,069	10,251,058	-2,508,231	23,919	132,542,644	43,058,598	6,212	4,221,304	298,101
1980	180,415	199,279,465	3,837,000	119,763	8,567,096	294,773	35,076	14,039,979	-4,208,334	25,576	176,672,390	7,750,561	5,198	5,150,691	80,681
1981	208,517	227,643,089	-4,666,449	123,786 [5]	10,444,566	-178,099	51,368	17,003,772	-10,109,096	33,363	200,194,751	5,620,746	6,870	5,318,366	-61,966
1982	230,701	234,690,225	-8,631,692	138,259 [5]	11,793,547	-345,446	55,766	19,798,121	-8,829,824	36,676	203,098,557	543,578	6,735	4,680,484	-149,693
1983	249,459	164,138,551	-5,445,037	152,797 [5]	12,242,108	250,819	59,596	19,476,693	-4,109,760	37,066	132,419,750	-1,586,096	8,404	3,741,208	-176,660
1984	250,557	158,741,208	80,772	153,445 [5]	13,190,105	364,844	56,548	22,054,470	69,112	40,564	123,496,633	-353,184	9,015	5,587,855	-105,845
1985	279,806	177,943,212	-528,809	176,017 [5]	12,502,896	532,977	62,363	23,401,721	1,481,701	41,426	142,038,595	-2,543,487	9,561	4,511,119	-10,702
1986	253,314	123,618,565	-7,269,183	159,818 [5]	7,210,024	-688,298	53,142	17,831,325	-3,458,320	40,354	98,577,216	-3,122,565	10,197	4,593,054	98,840
1987	260,839	120,712,354	-1,341,534	158,864 [5]	6,600,294	-256,665	59,925	17,306,189	-1,359,917	42,050	96,805,871	275,048	13,734 [9]	7,467,589	613,636
1988	229,242	—	5,006,895	140,028 [5]	7,041,752	-39,151	48,134	—	934,191	41,080	100,426,996	4,111,855	13,344	8,155,738	260,847
1989	242,068	—	5,640,647	154,900 [5]	6,525,670	530,756	45,537	—	1,965,205	41,631	102,378,796	3,144,686	15,323	10,425,281	384,752
1990	212,717	—	8,140,102	132,139 [5]	7,377,613	654,485	40,904	—	2,183,394	39,674	111,444,457	5,302,223	16,030	11,069,493	775,230
1991	227,769	—	4,990,802	149,548 [5]	6,861,582	209,959	39,022	—	779,487	39,199	103,286,287	4,001,356	16,126	10,743,329	403,049
1992	204,152	—	4,109,567	131,093 [5]	5,585,501	394,173	36,399	—	1,008,625	36,660	112,830,722	2,706,769	15,563	11,918,122	934,972
1993	191,375	140,454,290	4,870,403	124,138 [5]	6,334,808	93,626	31,892	21,998,332	2,148,057	35,345	112,121,150	2,628,720	16,645	12,545,527	1,374,190
1994	188,838	141,744,289	4,665,053	126,239 [5]	6,370,579	36,037	27,228	19,686,403	984,128	35,371	115,687,307	3,644,888	14,726	10,998,013	1,577,836
1995	180,552	152,958,127	6,548,072	119,322 [5]	4,623,965	-93,646	26,107	21,573,671	1,110,743	35,123	126,760,491	5,530,975	14,794	13,232,848	1,657,750
1996	168,642	176,250,255	13,298,991	107,516 [5]	5,951,643	290,019	25,327	29,020,520	4,856,365	35,799	141,278,092	8,152,607	15,950	14,563,056	2,290,463
1997	185,406	197,795,328	16,556,616	124,365 [5]	5,731,388	176,539	28,045	41,745,676	6,651,515	32,996	150,318,264	9,728,562	16,403	14,976,849	2,834,344
1998	—	—	—	119,376 [5]	5,060,080	-146,439	—	—	—	—	—	—	—	—	—

1 Totals have not been generated independently, but are simply summations of the series for proprietorships, partnerships, and corporations.

2 Includes S-corporations.

3 Includes only proprietorships with positive net income.

4 Includes only proprietorships with net income greater than or equal to $5,000.

5 Number of tax returns rather than the number of businesses.

6 Includes inactive corporations.

7 Affiliated corporations filed separate returns.

8 Gross income instead of total receipts.

9 Firms that shifted from fiscal to calendar years are counted twice.

Sources

U.S. Internal Revenue Service (and its predecessor, U.S. Bureau of Internal Revenue), *Statistics of Income* (SOI), various issues; *SOI Bulletin*, various issues.

Documentation

See the text for Table Ch1–18.

TABLE Ch52–66   Active proprietorships, partnerships, and corporations – entities, receipts, and profit: 1918–1998   [Construction]

Contributed by Naomi R. Lamoreaux

	Total			Proprietorships			Partnerships			Corporations Total			S-corporations		
	Entities	Receipts	Profit	Entities	Receipts	Profit	Entities	Receipts	Profit	Entities	Receipts	Profit	Entities	Receipts	Profit
	Ch52 [1]	Ch53 [1]	Ch54 [1]	Ch55	Ch56	Ch57	Ch58	Ch59	Ch60	Ch61 [2]	Ch62 [2]	Ch63 [2]	Ch64	Ch65	Ch66
Year	Number	Thousand dollars	Thousand dollars	Number	Thousand dollars	Thousand dollars	Number	Thousand dollars	Thousand dollars	Number	Thousand dollars	Thousand dollars	Number	Thousand dollars	Thousand dollars
1918	—	—	—	18,606 [3]	—	53,603 [3]	—	—	—	7,731	1,946,300 [8]	118,249	—	—	—
1919	—	—	—	27,310 [3]	—	82,924 [3]	—	—	—	8,242	2,010,074 [8]	140,602	—	—	—
1920	—	—	—	32,618 [3]	—	117,317 [3]	—	—	—	9,960	2,237,654 [8]	85,343	—	—	—
1921	—	—	—	33,045 [3]	—	110,027 [3]	—	—	—	10,361	1,773,308 [8]	15,858	—	—	—
1922	—	—	—	39,543 [3]	—	146,266 [3]	—	—	—	11,370	1,768,686	39,196	—	—	—
1923	—	—	—	90,677 [3]	—	267,050 [3]	—	—	—	12,551	2,226,569	69,195	—	—	—
1924	—	—	—	96,991 [3]	—	315,630 [3]	—	—	—	13,176	2,213,611	90,694	—	—	—
1925	—	—	—	60,436 [3]	—	246,794 [3]	—	—	—	15,338	2,308,715	113,145	—	—	—
1926	—	—	—	13,209 [4]	—	115,572 [4]	—	—	—	16,770 [6]	2,819,223	108,948	—	—	—
1927	—	—	—	12,304 [4]	—	111,392 [4]	—	—	—	16,352	3,059,013	111,743	—	—	—
1928	—	—	—	11,320 [4]	—	100,332 [4]	—	—	—	17,296	2,982,549	99,537	—	—	—
1929	—	—	—	11,551 [4]	—	102,023 [4]	—	—	—	18,358	3,085,752	108,310	—	—	—
1930	—	—	—	7,128 [4]	—	65,469 [4]	—	—	—	18,545	3,046,233	68,060	—	—	—
1931	—	—	—	3,504 [4]	—	34,138 [4]	—	—	—	18,132	2,239,573	−30,348	—	—	—
1932	—	—	—	937 [4]	—	8,928 [4]	—	—	—	17,319	1,442,802	−110,369	—	—	—
1933	—	—	—	840 [4]	53,475 [4]	6,211 [4]	—	—	—	16,252	1,083,031	−67,808	—	—	—
1934	—	—	—	1,502 [4]	100,140 [4]	11,973 [4]	—	—	—	15,941 [7]	1,260,502	−34,787	—	—	—
1935	—	—	—	2,041 [4]	117,880 [4]	15,136 [4]	—	—	—	16,050 [7]	1,495,907	−6,477	—	—	—
1936	—	—	—	4,294 [4]	295,293 [4]	35,862 [4]	—	—	—	16,645 [7]	2,013,692	36,831	—	—	—
1937	—	—	—	5,358 [4]	397,798 [4]	45,998 [4]	—	—	—	16,864 [7]	2,462,864	47,573	—	—	—
1938	—	—	—	4,060 [4]	308,029 [4]	32,384 [4]	—	—	—	16,341 [7]	1,964,134	25,148	—	—	—
1939	69,357	4,198,546	218,021	42,393	1,294,512	112,729	10,903	654,403	72,727	16,061 [7]	2,249,631	32,565	—	—	—
1940	—	—	—	130,264	388,488	308,835	—	—	—	15,749 [7]	2,527,985	67,841	—	—	—
1941	—	—	—	—	—	—	—	—	—	14,996 [7]	3,529,934	177,882	—	—	—
1942	—	—	—	—	—	—	—	—	—	13,697 [7]	4,786,663	339,602	—	—	—
1943	—	—	—	149,356 [5]	2,106,910	363,575	—	—	—	12,128	4,342,622	267,420	—	—	—
1944	—	—	—	—	—	—	—	—	—	11,514	3,181,965	139,133	—	—	—

Notes appear at end of table

(continued)

TABLE Ch52-66   Active proprietorships, partnerships, and corporations – entities, receipts, and profit: 1918–1998   [Construction]   Continued

Year	Total			Proprietorships			Partnerships			Corporations – Total			S-corporations		
	Entities	Receipts	Profit	Entities	Receipts	Profit	Entities	Receipts	Profit	Entities	Receipts	Profit	Entities	Receipts	Profit
	Ch52 [1]	Ch53 [1]	Ch54 [1]	Ch55	Ch56	Ch57	Ch58	Ch59	Ch60	Ch61 [2]	Ch62 [2]	Ch63 [2]	Ch64	Ch65	Ch66
	Number	Thousand dollars	Thousand dollars	Number	Thousand dollars	Thousand dollars	Number	Thousand dollars	Thousand dollars	Number	Thousand dollars	Thousand dollars	Number	Thousand dollars	Thousand dollars
1945	259,215	7,602,351	810,746	222,556	2,941,651	465,603	24,825	1,712,747	232,523	11,834	2,947,953	112,620	—	—	—
1946	—	—	—	—	—	—	—	—	—	15,849	4,320,561	232,078	—	—	—
1947	395,338	16,353,314	1,710,640	322,459	5,785,489	816,668	52,592	3,519,820	502,333	20,287	7,048,005	391,639	—	—	—
1948	—	—	—	—	—	—	—	—	—	23,480	9,389,035	577,020	—	—	—
1949	—	—	—	290,653	7,166,053	902,463	—	—	—	25,746	9,917,590	517,513	—	—	—
1950	—	—	—	—	—	—	—	—	—	27,694	11,561,779	562,017	—	—	—
1951	—	—	—	342,310	9,324,851	—	—	—	—	29,593	14,240,093	559,378	—	—	—
1952	—	—	—	—	—	—	—	—	—	31,817	15,297,052	598,758	—	—	—
1953	495,555	34,103,142	2,550,616	393,679	10,823,460	1,258,269	67,010	7,089,165	779,289	34,866	16,190,517	513,058	—	—	—
1954	—	—	—	—	—	—	—	—	—	36,130	17,490,821	487,594	—	—	—
1955	—	—	—	—	—	—	—	—	—	41,569	20,038,383	477,838	—	—	—
1956	—	—	—	524,944	12,428,301	1,508,842	—	—	—	48,292	23,508,854	676,797	—	—	—
1957	717,939	—	3,278,349	598,418	13,589,214	1,759,985	65,945	—	778,739	53,576	27,051,994	739,625	—	—	—
1958	725,702	—	3,065,933	604,910	13,561,916	1,691,236	60,945	—	715,803	59,847	28,561,305	658,894	3,765	985,095	9,991
1959	779,706	55,734,486	3,271,556	646,316	15,719,142	1,979,608	67,130	7,874,934	712,840	66,260	32,140,410	579,108	6,137	1,859,791	33,777
1960	789,938	54,498,683	2,915,452	655,155	14,941,971	1,898,455	62,451	6,663,365	637,785	72,332	32,893,347	379,212	8,290	2,185,466	27,352
1961	824,537	59,403,774	3,197,234	678,456	14,487,676	1,997,795	62,290	7,503,350	690,280	83,791	37,412,748	509,159	10,229	2,611,715	42,455
1962	835,955	63,482,702	3,319,500	687,187	15,539,360	2,108,195	58,164	6,877,933	594,149	90,604	41,065,409	617,156	12,289	3,117,909	83,182
1963	848,487	68,965,296	3,439,898	691,613	16,344,887	2,170,954	60,408	6,971,722	624,528	96,466	45,648,687	644,416	13,031	3,354,909	58,474
1964	856,765	73,527,488	3,959,471	695,333	17,100,609	2,334,785	57,298	6,685,456	681,596	104,134	49,741,423	943,090	14,901	4,110,290	111,054
1965	876,392	83,095,179	4,619,446	704,627	19,308,272	2,685,430	58,481	7,092,010	676,384	113,284	56,694,897	1,257,632	18,000	5,317,183	176,623
1966	858,330	90,058,786	4,895,673	689,842	19,163,506	2,733,249	56,115	7,865,406	763,489	112,373	63,029,874	1,398,935	17,603	5,299,487	160,119
1967	855,982	93,612,286	5,035,591	680,460	18,334,278	2,750,893	52,342	7,256,095	741,540	123,180	68,021,913	1,543,158	22,388	6,673,989	211,337
1968	838,988	99,072,137	5,400,734	663,301	19,333,780	2,886,567	49,688	7,475,564	800,748	125,999	72,262,793	1,713,419	20,882	6,728,252	239,786
1969	900,832	112,795,547	5,675,638	722,604	21,484,393	3,232,592	50,562	7,398,617	782,703	127,666	83,912,537	1,660,343	21,356	8,991,497	271,222
1970	874,549	118,110,804	5,363,881	684,643	20,099,158	3,075,841	51,001	7,701,002	749,622	138,905	90,310,644	1,538,418	26,066	9,661,472	251,421
1971	931,985	129,281,652	6,280,635	735,846	23,334,473	3,499,669	53,047	8,454,570	855,788	143,092	97,492,609	1,925,178	27,556	10,315,985	297,609
1972	1,019,891	145,417,527	6,862,054	804,528	27,108,554	4,073,412	60,945	9,571,398	907,826	154,418	108,737,575	1,880,816	30,308	12,124,532	358,559
1973	1,098,671	167,815,607	7,678,736	856,756	30,837,376	4,600,508	66,031	10,236,747	920,871	175,884	126,741,484	2,157,357	35,484	15,696,638	406,734
1974	1,145,090	181,403,305	7,265,577	896,431	32,743,263	4,561,215	63,096	11,635,703	856,145	185,563	137,024,339	1,848,217	37,770	15,353,158	358,491
1975	1,144,247	190,539,624	7,419,555	892,244	31,012,890	4,388,896	60,784	12,571,617	794,397	191,219	146,955,117	2,236,262	41,843	15,595,028	279,277
1976	1,219,036	205,387,280	9,585,320	962,713	37,953,980	5,620,085	60,390	13,336,424	1,139,001	195,933	154,096,876	2,826,234	43,476	16,045,513	291,817
1977	1,278,034	238,845,662	12,545,420	994,072	42,751,792	6,569,677	69,217	14,542,948	1,458,221	214,745	181,550,922	4,517,522	49,559	18,930,093	579,168
1978	1,375,249	284,325,230	15,750,859	1,068,560	51,272,856	8,104,290	78,032	16,342,214	1,770,242	228,657	216,710,160	5,876,327	52,916	22,431,178	564,927
1979	1,422,579	324,081,182	16,060,217	1,097,417	50,942,938	7,947,840	75,275	20,285,538	2,126,987	249,887	252,852,706	5,985,390	54,321	23,030,957	123,144
1980	1,412,323	333,802,077	14,292,178	1,073,301	47,834,507	7,460,876	66,590	18,762,214	1,560,093	272,432	267,205,356	5,271,209	57,533	23,468,220	364,761
1981	1,444,055	344,899,308	11,429,543	1,097,804 [5]	47,707,740	6,765,263	69,856	17,019,193	1,209,222	276,395	280,172,375	3,455,058	56,341	23,144,865	295,006
1982	1,550,979	349,473,380	10,348,877	1,202,872 [5]	49,124,529	6,605,428	65,762	18,600,983	1,419,497	282,345	281,747,868	2,323,952	57,289	24,625,841	480,269
1983	1,620,330	365,486,763	11,771,021	1,273,219 [5]	51,761,787	7,337,482	63,592	22,926,133	2,167,975	283,519	290,798,843	2,265,564	62,888	27,340,119	627,160
1984	1,757,612	428,734,726	15,226,557	1,386,099 [5]	66,311,253	10,126,530	64,607	23,847,838	2,193,322	306,906	338,575,635	2,906,705	70,787	35,692,736	887,097

	Total			Proprietorships			Partnerships			Corporations					
										Total			S-corporations		
	Entities	Receipts	Profit	Entities	Receipts	Profit	Entities	Receipts	Profit	Entities	Receipts	Profit	Entities	Receipts	Profit
	Ch52 [1]	Ch53 [1]	Ch54 [1]	Ch55	Ch56	Ch57	Ch58	Ch59	Ch60	Ch61 [2]	Ch62 [2]	Ch63 [2]	Ch64	Ch65	Ch66
Year	Number	Thousand dollars	Thousand dollars	Number	Thousand dollars	Thousand dollars	Number	Thousand dollars	Thousand dollars	Number	Thousand dollars	Thousand dollars	Number	Thousand dollars	Thousand dollars
1985	1,828,703	480,310,028	17,635,128	1,453,762 [5]	70,789,842	11,056,803	56,665	22,287,233	2,207,401	318,276	387,232,953	4,370,924	68,392	41,304,736	1,115,843
1986	1,979,918	527,637,307	21,094,544	1,576,677 [5]	87,539,701	12,815,063	61,425	27,620,392	2,497,759	341,816	412,477,214	5,781,722	79,452	47,887,133	1,432,793
1987	2,069,316	571,034,015	25,979,588	1,635,744 [5]	89,277,578	14,512,879	62,403	26,925,343	2,766,067	371,169	454,831,094	8,700,642	115,706 [9]	98,147,701	3,376,768
1988	2,151,923	—	31,090,391	1,695,865 [5]	96,781,683	16,462,790	74,559	—	3,283,681	381,499	499,690,338	11,343,920	122,551	130,182,358	4,874,614
1989	2,212,173	—	28,615,158	1,757,120 [5]	100,915,543	17,230,782	61,950	—	2,647,446	393,103	517,477,336	8,736,930	140,629	144,287,504	4,698,317
1990	2,248,468	—	25,099,507	1,782,125 [5]	99,235,747	16,366,981	59,469	—	1,907,918	406,874	534,654,044	6,824,608	158,045	166,931,987	4,669,354
1991	2,210,162	—	22,547,290	1,735,980 [5]	92,519,267	14,949,913	57,195	—	1,493,772	416,987	515,128,533	6,103,605	177,070	165,539,264	3,703,572
1992	2,375,804	—	24,267,370	1,908,511 [5]	96,631,722	16,856,521	59,412	—	1,905,787	407,881	499,405,033	5,505,062	178,761	167,362,892	4,932,620
1993	2,405,786	673,324,563	27,861,714	1,926,626 [5]	107,420,172	18,171,267	61,910	27,638,139	2,175,628	417,250	538,266,252	7,514,819	192,495	194,263,829	5,508,298
1994	2,484,171	740,382,792	34,670,765	1,985,561 [5]	115,853,044	20,443,346	65,645	31,769,358	2,653,523	432,965	592,760,390	11,573,896	201,354	217,455,805	7,706,863
1995	2,632,012	792,564,273	37,812,075	2,111,403 [5]	118,938,100	20,826,810	70,727	36,535,978	2,527,241	449,882	637,090,195	14,458,024	216,192	241,113,967	9,356,399
1996	2,642,161	884,161,624	42,698,988	2,096,767 [5]	127,357,252	21,706,292	74,164	46,337,149	3,114,236	471,230	710,467,223	17,878,460	234,047	276,283,862	11,441,644
1997	2,756,643	963,758,586	47,176,477	2,196,762 [5]	130,764,670	23,450,389	72,098	53,979,443	3,203,649	487,783	779,014,473	20,522,439	216,104	332,647,323	14,493,088
1998	—			2,228,593 [5]	142,416,515	25,808,901								—	

[1] Totals have not been generated independently, but are simply summations of the series for proprietorships, partnerships, and corporations.

[2] Includes S-corporations.

[3] Includes only proprietorships with positive net income.

[4] Includes only proprietorships with net income greater than or equal to $5,000.

[5] Number of tax returns rather than the number of businesses.

[6] Includes inactive corporations.

[7] Affiliated corporations filed separate returns.

[8] Gross income instead of total receipts.

[9] Firms that shifted from fiscal to calendar years are counted twice.

Sources

U.S. Internal Revenue Service (and its predecessor, U.S. Bureau of Internal Revenue), *Statistics of Income (SOI)*, various issues; *SOI Bulletin*, various issues.

Documentation

See the text for Table Ch1–18.

TABLE Ch67-81 Active proprietorships, partnerships, and corporations – entities, receipts, and profit: 1918–1998 [Manufacturing]

Contributed by Naomi R. Lamoreaux

	Total			Proprietorships			Partnerships			Corporations					
										Total			S-corporations		
	Entities	Receipts	Profit	Entities	Receipts	Profit	Entities	Receipts	Profit	Entities	Receipts	Profit	Entities	Receipts	Profit
	Ch67 [1]	Ch68 [1]	Ch69 [1]	Ch70	Ch71	Ch72	Ch73	Ch74	Ch75	Ch76 [2]	Ch77 [2]	Ch78 [2]	Ch79	Ch80	Ch81
Year	Number	Thousand dollars	Thousand dollars	Number	Thousand dollars	Thousand dollars	Number	Thousand dollars	Thousand dollars	Number	Thousand dollars	Thousand dollars	Number	Thousand dollars	Thousand dollars
1918	—	—	—	45,235 [3]	—	202,367 [3]	—	—	—	67,274	44,167,152 [8]	4,534,120	—	—	—
1919	—	—	—	55,542 [3]	—	307,181 [3]	—	—	—	67,852	52,289,577 [8]	4,852,599	—	—	—
1920	—	—	—	60,729 [3]	—	261,901 [3]	—	—	—	78,171	56,649,233 [8]	3,282,278	—	—	—
1921	—	—	—	55,919 [3]	—	186,335 [3]	—	—	—	79,748	38,441,924 [8]	−121,045	—	—	—
1922	—	—	—	59,513 [3]	—	220,385 [3]	—	—	—	82,485	44,762,655	2,641,007	—	—	—
1923	—	—	—	129,767 [3]	—	366,552 [3]	—	—	—	85,199	56,308,800	3,570,888	—	—	—
1924	—	—	—	125,559 [3]	—	380,098 [3]	—	—	—	86,803	53,994,723	2,763,472	—	—	—
1925	—	—	—	68,742 [3]	—	267,805 [3]	—	—	—	88,674	60,921,257	3,701,103	—	—	—
1926	—	—	—	14,036 [4]	—	128,306 [4]	—	—	—	93,244 [6]	62,583,773	3,007,644	—	—	—
1927	—	—	—	12,862 [4]	—	118,863 [4]	—	—	—	89,816	63,816,289	3,087,595	—	—	—
1928	—	—	—	12,681 [4]	—	118,846 [4]	—	—	—	91,573	67,368,001	3,910,526	—	—	—
1929	—	—	—	13,655 [4]	—	130,443 [4]	—	—	—	92,230	72,223,990	4,405,773	—	—	—
1930	—	—	—	8,653 [4]	—	75,398 [4]	—	—	—	91,504	60,976,432	1,117,664	—	—	—
1931	—	—	—	4,934 [4]	—	43,209 [4]	—	—	—	80,225	44,108,477	−822,970	—	—	—
1932	—	—	—	1,874 [4]	—	15,823 [4]	—	—	—	87,916	32,055,589	−1,806,354	—	—	—
1933	—	—	—	2,920 [4]	283,056 [4]	26,222 [4]	—	—	—	88,649	35,230,321	204,045	—	—	—
1934	—	—	—	4,375 [4]	388,984 [4]	38,477 [4]	—	—	—	91,292 [7]	41,156,801	979,915	—	—	—
1935	—	—	—	5,118 [4]	413,850 [4]	44,134 [4]	—	—	—	91,676 [7]	47,946,605	1,816,447	—	—	—
1936	—	—	—	8,077 [4]	677,027 [4]	72,503 [4]	—	—	—	92,030 [7]	56,977,336	3,701,539	—	—	—
1937	—	—	—	8,360 [4]	720,938 [4]	74,825 [4]	—	—	—	91,979 [7]	62,474,438	3,703,121	—	—	—
1938	—	—	—	5,896 [4]	548,587 [4]	51,730 [4]	—	—	—	88,067 [7]	51,143,458	1,589,515	—	—	—
1939	148,273	61,567,106	3,873,512	39,827	1,555,114	126,100	22,263	1,705,623	179,656	86,183 [7]	58,306,369	3,567,756	—	—	—
1940	—	—	—	80,299	2,479,726	290,641	—	—	—	85,588 [7]	66,690,782	5,306,540	—	—	—
1941	—	—	—	—	—	—	—	—	—	84,431 [7]	93,442,070	10,429,414	—	—	—
1942	—	—	—	—	—	—	—	—	—	82,174 [7]	119,440,882	13,650,102	—	—	—
1943	—	—	—	107,007 [5]	3,741,364	507,853	—	—	—	78,716	146,379,404	16,581,896	—	—	—
1944	—	—	—	—	—	—	—	—	—	76,619	154,215,393	14,850,939	—	—	—
1945	261,851	157,139,869	12,329,144	121,543	5,247,246	573,317	61,196	10,608,660	1,505,610	79,112	141,283,963	10,250,217	—	—	—
1946	—	—	—	—	—	—	—	—	—	98,131	139,421,332	11,693,964	—	—	—
1947	340,081	193,611,093	18,090,915	152,919	5,326,811	484,961	74,978	7,959,588	953,987	112,184	180,324,694	16,651,967	—	—	—
1948	—	—	—	164,687	4,841,844	411,260	—	—	—	116,746	200,011,406	18,113,988	—	—	—
1949	—	—	—	—	—	—	—	—	—	117,270	187,346,823	14,246,866	—	—	—
1950	—	—	—	157,278	6,263,630	—	—	—	—	115,872	220,302,937	23,721,535	—	—	—
1951	—	—	—	—	—	—	—	—	—	120,196	255,006,524	24,861,835	—	—	—
1952	—	—	—	—	—	—	—	—	—	119,399	261,095,156	20,318,120	—	—	—
1953	355,899	297,219,391	22,974,985	171,669	6,672,513	619,012	63,144	9,425,016	934,627	121,086	281,121,862	21,421,346	—	—	—
1954	—	—	—	—	—	—	—	—	—	120,896	268,327,923	18,289,865	—	—	—
1955	—	—	—	162,610	5,805,514	598,909	—	—	—	129,828	306,463,593	26,010,453	—	—	—
1956	—	—	—	—	—	—	—	—	—	132,835	319,313,746	24,628,749	—	—	—
1957	360,831	—	24,013,291	170,395	6,248,046	571,803	51,870	—	703,440	138,566	332,621,264	22,738,048	—	—	—
1958	381,408	—	19,775,226	179,967	6,323,870	608,824	50,745	—	665,908	150,696	329,432,571	18,500,494	8,019	2,445,281	68,547
1959	391,067	377,640,048	26,262,525	186,901	6,726,173	626,948	47,869	7,756,708	649,693	156,297	363,157,167	24,985,884	11,849	4,156,795	107,795

	Total			Proprietorships			Partnerships			Corporations					
										Total			S-corporations		
	Entities	Receipts	Profit	Entities	Receipts	Profit	Entities	Receipts	Profit	Entities	Receipts	Profit	Entities	Receipts	Profit
	Ch67 [1]	Ch68 [1]	Ch69 [1]	Ch70	Ch71	Ch72	Ch73	Ch74	Ch75	Ch76 [2]	Ch77 [2]	Ch78 [2]	Ch79	Ch80	Ch81
Year	Number	Thousand dollars	Thousand dollars	Number	Thousand dollars	Thousand dollars	Number	Thousand dollars	Thousand dollars	Number	Thousand dollars	Thousand dollars	Number	Thousand dollars	Thousand dollars
1960	405,679	385,452,601	23,392,559	192,634	6,935,367	645,495	47,183	7,424,192	602,274	165,862	371,093,042	22,144,790	14,240	4,549,450	102,931
1961	412,345	391,076,183	23,721,373	194,325	6,599,828	660,681	44,462	6,896,121	567,114	173,558	377,580,234	22,493,578	15,776	5,290,295	136,234
1962	407,045	421,277,926	26,599,894	180,805	6,710,267	654,001	43,091	6,702,990	594,927	183,149	407,864,669	25,350,966	18,152	5,664,272	162,346
1963	408,566	442,032,057	29,999,412	187,398	6,369,127	677,601	39,368	6,155,987	543,063	181,800	429,506,943	28,778,748	19,607	6,904,268	173,157
1964	410,683	478,125,899	33,870,556	185,311	6,708,523	706,345	40,411	6,597,833	608,277	184,961	464,819,543	32,555,934	21,659	7,576,416	285,471
1965	408,333	527,650,744	41,610,906	185,843	7,266,965	773,958	36,566	5,664,938	589,389	185,924	514,718,841	40,247,559	22,534	8,239,182	395,148
1966	403,835	584,298,898	45,892,986	179,649	7,145,493	872,148	36,544	6,144,233	617,142	187,642	571,009,172	44,403,696	21,737	9,421,868	476,177
1967	401,014	602,992,370	41,639,116	169,505	6,472,710	748,121	34,486	5,697,329	561,919	197,023	590,822,331	40,329,076	24,568	10,631,459	493,796
1968	396,908	661,219,611	45,713,246	172,333	6,672,726	757,474	32,665	5,582,083	544,305	191,910	648,964,802	44,411,467	25,951	10,808,629	464,186
1969	404,993	722,097,473	42,538,562	172,432	6,881,128	805,536	30,495	5,132,246	476,279	202,066	710,084,099	41,256,747	25,158	11,082,003	475,465
1970	409,768	734,877,174	32,991,370	183,466	6,701,707	734,199	28,495	5,264,148	411,093	197,807	722,911,319	31,846,078	29,980	12,140,257	371,743
1971	414,206	788,800,112	39,829,344	186,019	6,927,983	745,285	27,214	5,393,558	333,351	200,973	776,478,571	38,750,708	28,606	11,739,210	397,894
1972	463,190	884,146,585	49,582,505	202,776	7,916,205	948,859	30,176	5,766,973	400,443	230,238	870,463,407	48,233,203	30,761	12,357,672	510,218
1973	449,506	1,053,092,679	65,003,015	210,315	8,461,112	1,002,559	29,932	6,586,045	559,889	209,259	1,038,045,522	63,440,567	32,448	15,069,991	706,870
1974	455,047	1,314,076,275	74,245,980	212,864	9,117,843	1,138,147	30,620	7,692,639	574,347	211,563	1,297,265,793	72,533,486	33,909	16,794,060	680,400
1975	468,322	1,311,987,242	69,787,915	221,642	8,678,677	1,040,261	29,326	6,948,915	341,027	217,354	1,296,359,650	68,406,627	35,738	16,527,178	599,269
1976	466,248	1,480,294,170	90,771,918	223,148	9,449,795	1,029,507	30,767	8,191,523	470,054	212,333	1,462,652,852	89,272,357	34,027	19,773,097	803,655
1977	483,273	1,672,528,420	101,729,911	224,128	10,024,166	1,260,024	27,996	8,972,355	461,000	231,149	1,653,531,899	100,008,887	37,846	21,419,043	774,229
1978	492,265	1,859,127,301	115,668,653	240,863	11,836,156	1,489,852	27,931	10,738,885	660,015	223,471	1,836,552,260	113,518,786	37,467	22,439,698	1,100,000
1979	502,544	2,179,056,622	132,367,481	235,526	12,928,527	1,512,431	30,454	13,467,931	484,564	236,564	2,152,660,164	130,370,486	34,240	24,741,787	773,659
1980	568,852	2,434,839,890	126,869,525	296,216	14,846,538	1,673,759	30,086	15,669,508	−472,049	242,550	2,404,323,844	125,667,815	40,263	25,697,032	742,558
1981	539,090	2,641,745,571	117,691,168	257,490 [5]	13,647,822	1,356,424	30,306	14,585,168	−440,649	251,294	2,613,512,581	116,775,393	40,509	25,225,993	544,041
1982	531,638	2,513,509,459	75,867,506	249,342 [5]	10,033,072	891,880	23,190	15,144,472	−815,638	259,106	2,488,331,915	75,791,264	41,721	33,298,795	1,262,986
1983	618,903	2,582,822,835	95,726,224	330,525 [5]	15,445,367	1,139,323	26,451	14,546,750	−744,064	261,927	2,552,830,718	95,330,965	46,876	44,344,610	2,158,836
1984	621,759	2,805,368,836	121,550,227	320,103 [5]	18,176,274	1,435,916	29,606	18,944,907	−1,100,943	272,050	2,768,247,655	121,215,254	50,195	60,139,449	3,146,180
1985	632,972	2,871,139,816	113,947,877	326,447 [5]	16,937,385	1,274,419	29,980	23,139,935	−1,085,187	276,545	2,831,062,496	113,758,645	50,171	69,092,049	3,731,656
1986	641,864	2,853,081,271	102,826,132	329,238 [5]	19,638,481	1,456,702	27,507	22,729,009	−457,841	285,119	2,810,713,781	101,827,271	57,945	74,924,302	3,666,048
1987	689,092	3,193,565,726	148,376,656	360,210 [5]	18,934,642	2,076,303	34,671	33,224,640	806,462	294,211	3,141,406,444	145,493,891	83,980 [9]	178,761,781	8,405,308
1988	680,208	—	208,937,799	354,785 [5]	20,027,986	2,314,127	25,885	—	1,540,021	299,538	3,348,965,911	205,083,651	94,395	232,569,016	10,936,222
1989	758,739	—	185,103,226	431,130 [5]	25,400,029	3,228,762	26,263	—	1,398,440	301,346	3,531,219,028	180,476,024	105,874	273,493,232	11,403,618
1990	709,857	—	175,007,041	379,903 [5]	21,839,350	2,467,377	28,285	—	1,165,938	301,669	3,688,693,895	171,373,726	113,289	297,357,534	11,838,918
1991	750,793	—	135,769,002	426,697 [5]	23,354,542	2,595,448	23,974	—	904,329	300,122	3,658,501,307	132,269,225	115,417	300,579,225	10,719,612
1992	784,990	—	149,005,618	460,845 [5]	27,243,502	3,508,402	24,074	—	1,869,813	300,071	3,760,265,837	143,627,403	117,812	326,547,950	16,618,517
1993	804,818	4,011,775,742	180,376,048	472,334 [5]	27,157,994	3,216,585	25,065	93,869,477	3,939,506	307,419	3,890,747,271	173,219,957	127,046	352,827,742	17,854,158
1994	855,122	4,363,809,219	229,627,083	513,200 [5]	32,928,845	3,927,951	29,539	112,088,791	6,584,412	312,383	4,218,791,583	219,114,720	129,408	389,844,284	23,625,110
1995	847,634	4,749,802,973	274,274,893	497,780 [5]	32,101,683	4,143,519	30,155	132,151,529	9,221,427	319,699	4,585,549,761	260,909,947	138,856	431,543,312	24,934,073
1996	866,981	5,092,310,219	299,697,296	507,167 [5]	32,057,221	3,941,135	34,125	157,583,876	9,696,339	325,689	4,902,669,122	286,059,822	141,171	450,440,118	28,733,161
1997	845,432	5,403,787,960	321,401,050	480,365 [5]	33,254,751	4,377,188	40,022	192,869,439	11,065,708	325,045	5,177,663,770	305,958,154	153,249	488,763,265	27,970,457
1998	—	—	—	362,607 [5]	27,693,221	3,941,664	—	—	—	—	—	—	—	—	—

[1] Totals have not been generated independently, but are simply summations of the series for proprietorships, partnerships, and corporations.

[2] Includes S-corporations.

[3] Includes only proprietorships with positive net income.

[4] Includes only proprietorships with net income greater than or equal to $5,000.

[5] Number of tax returns rather than the number of businesses.

[6] Includes inactive corporations.

[7] Affiliated corporations filed separate returns.

[8] Gross income instead of total receipts.

[9] Firms that shifted from fiscal to calendar years are counted twice.

Sources

U.S. Internal Revenue Service (and its predecessor, U.S. Bureau of Internal Revenue), *Statistics of Income* (SOI), various issues; *SOI Bulletin*, various issues.

Documentation

See the text for Table Ch1–18.

TABLE Ch82–96 Active proprietorships, partnerships, and corporations – entities, receipts, and profit: 1918–1998
[Transportation, communications, and utilities]

Contributed by Naomi R. Lamoreaux

	Total			Proprietorships			Partnerships			Corporations			S-corporations		
	Entities	Receipts	Profit	Entities	Receipts	Profit	Entities	Receipts	Profit	Total			Entities	Receipts	Profit
	Ch82 [1]	Ch83 [1]	Ch84 [1]	Ch85	Ch86	Ch87	Ch88	Ch89	Ch90	Entities Ch91 [2]	Receipts Ch92 [2]	Profit Ch93 [2]	Ch94	Ch95	Ch96
Year	Number	Thousand dollars	Thousand dollars	Number	Thousand dollars	Thousand dollars	Number	Thousand dollars	Thousand dollars	Number	Thousand dollars	Thousand dollars	Number	Thousand dollars	Thousand dollars
1918	—	—	—	12,943 [3]	—	39,079 [3]	—	—	—	18,246	3,721,996 [8,9]	679,499	—	—	—
1919	—	—	—	19,563 [3]	—	63,780 [3]	—	—	—	20,547	5,153,415 [8,9]	878,950	—	—	—
1920	—	—	—	18,978 [3]	—	58,355 [3]	—	—	—	20,599	9,152,782 [8,9]	678,626	—	—	—
1921	—	—	—	23,886 [3]	—	51,143 [3]	—	—	—	19,105	9,000,756 [8,9]	498,502	—	—	—
1922	—	—	—	15,776 [3]	—	45,992 [3]	—	—	—	20,511	9,784,690	782,783	—	—	—
1923	—	—	—	35,150 [3]	—	81,868 [3]	—	—	—	21,113	10,560,623	1,131,760	—	—	—
1924	—	—	—	44,096 [3]	—	111,846 [3]	—	—	—	22,431	10,206,069	1,094,259	—	—	—
1925	—	—	—	26,531 [3]	—	84,080 [3]	—	—	—	23,613	11,911,494	1,333,948	—	—	—
1926	—	—	—	3,680 [4]	—	26,122 [4]	—	—	—	25,100 [6]	14,791,474	1,603,224	—	—	—
1927	—	—	—	3,116 [4]	—	22,594 [4]	—	—	—	20,837	15,165,612	1,391,237	—	—	—
1928	—	—	—	2,287 [4]	—	17,447 [4]	—	—	—	21,304	15,825,518	1,639,918	—	—	—
1929	—	—	—	2,567 [4]	—	19,694 [4]	—	—	—	21,608	17,113,511	1,901,962	—	—	—
1930	—	—	—	1,800 [4]	—	13,965 [4]	—	—	—	21,631	16,026,584	1,000,700	—	—	—
1931	—	—	—	1,258 [4]	—	9,804 [4]	—	—	—	21,555	13,418,874	297,386	—	—	—
1932	—	—	—	556 [4]	—	4,414 [4]	—	—	—	21,681	11,261,335	-130,884	—	—	—
1933	—	—	—	872 [4]	39,158 [4]	5,674 [4]	—	—	—	21,778	10,628,518	-85,844	—	—	—
1934	—	—	—	1,137 [4]	52,092 [4]	8,594 [4]	—	—	—	25,379 [7]	11,130,794	276,402	—	—	—
1935	—	—	—	1,311 [4]	58,847 [4]	9,819 [4]	—	—	—	25,433 [7]	11,604,014	355,097	—	—	—
1936	—	—	—	2,087 [4]	107,086 [4]	15,300 [4]	—	—	—	24,853 [7]	12,822,563	1,022,635	—	—	—
1937	—	—	—	2,098 [4]	96,564 [4]	14,289 [4]	—	—	—	24,672 [7]	13,457,869	1,093,017	—	—	—
1938	—	—	—	1,587 [4]	71,999 [4]	10,886 [4]	—	—	—	21,961 [7]	12,145,928	669,851	—	—	—
1939	44,183	13,564,470	1,240,412	18,012	336,504	46,691	4,107	134,355	25,194	22,064 [7]	13,093,611	1,168,527	—	—	—
1940	—	—	—	—	—	—	—	—	—	22,053 [7]	13,710,372	1,313,040	—	—	—
1941	—	—	—	69,379	641,954	132,774	—	—	—	21,921 [7]	15,948,578	1,927,205	—	—	—
1942	—	—	—	—	—	—	—	—	—	20,237 [7]	18,649,573	3,628,585	—	—	—
1943	—	—	—	127,490 [5]	1,151,154	244,847	—	—	—	19,279	21,337,650	4,494,517	—	—	—
1944	—	—	—	—	—	—	—	—	—	19,242	22,497,409	4,140,878	—	—	—
1945	197,709	24,728,116	3,296,070	165,673	1,457,452	257,022	12,300	607,313	101,972	19,736	22,663,351	2,937,076	—	—	—
1946	—	—	—	—	—	—	—	—	—	21,823	22,926,446	2,342,682	—	—	—
1947	311,406	29,500,465	3,178,512	266,901	1,929,306	337,236	20,776	774,605	125,169	23,729	26,796,554	2,716,107	—	—	—
1948	—	—	—	—	—	—	—	—	—	25,225	29,676,420	3,448,020	—	—	—
1949	—	—	—	238,152	2,281,279	365,753	—	—	—	25,908	28,723,748	2,873,761	—	—	—
1950	—	—	—	—	—	—	—	—	—	26,277	32,136,928	4,332,010	—	—	—
1951	—	—	—	262,582	2,795,939	—	—	—	—	26,828	36,221,314	4,685,941	—	—	—
1952	—	—	—	—	—	—	—	—	—	28,460	38,607,664	4,910,409	—	—	—
1953	319,961	44,661,945	5,699,542	269,675	2,870,366	495,836	20,349	981,449	166,590	29,937	40,810,130	5,037,116	—	—	—
1954	—	—	—	—	—	—	—	—	—	29,122	42,361,745	4,440,325	—	—	—
1955	—	—	—	253,209	2,973,700	512,160	—	—	—	33,017	48,219,480	5,775,740	—	—	—
1956	—	—	—	—	—	—	—	—	—	36,181	52,308,520	5,962,353	—	—	—
1957	350,197	—	6,425,521	295,561	3,682,743	528,251	16,873	—	139,948	37,763	56,075,459	5,757,322	—	—	—
1958	345,343	—	6,399,110	290,225	3,929,658	545,104	17,198	—	131,685	37,920	55,965,004	5,722,321	1,783	304,320	2,817
1959	344,671	67,472,877	7,475,961	283,553	4,044,718	553,519	17,623	1,119,613	131,646	43,495	62,308,546	6,790,796	2,510	416,805	16,538

	Total			Proprietorships			Partnerships			Corporations Total			Corporations S-corporations		
	Entities	Receipts	Profit	Entities	Receipts	Profit	Entities	Receipts	Profit	Entities	Receipts	Profit	Entities	Receipts	Profit
Year	Ch82[1] Number	Ch83[1] Thousand dollars	Ch84[1] Thousand dollars	Ch85 Number	Ch86 Thousand dollars	Ch87 Thousand dollars	Ch88 Number	Ch89 Thousand dollars	Ch90 Thousand dollars	Ch91[2] Number	Ch92[2] Thousand dollars	Ch93[2] Thousand dollars	Ch94 Number	Ch95 Thousand dollars	Ch96 Thousand dollars
1960	349,151	71,298,491	7,261,172	287,661	4,362,621	540,130	17,638	1,013,882	128,926	43,852	65,921,988	6,592,116	2,998	491,884	13,667
1961	353,820	73,434,685	8,202,953	286,672	4,100,142	570,078	18,100	1,180,641	146,189	49,048	68,153,902	7,486,686	4,109	674,614	50,981
1962	353,688	78,404,911	8,777,141	283,955	4,241,309	642,210	17,032	1,007,149	124,303	52,701	73,156,453	8,010,628	4,802	778,620	29,827
1963	380,034	83,976,623	9,762,829	307,103	4,969,278	694,347	16,640	1,137,189	143,171	56,291	77,870,156	8,925,311	5,734	906,563	29,173
1964	364,663	87,679,877	10,611,296	291,888	4,860,538	731,110	16,437	1,093,282	141,302	56,338	81,726,057	9,738,884	6,132	1,080,097	41,120
1965	374,076	95,821,630	11,672,496	296,621	5,526,927	826,392	17,779	1,338,184	146,795	59,676	88,956,519	10,699,309	7,090	1,170,673	56,678
1966	371,770	104,124,084	12,643,270	296,361	5,755,221	869,302	15,484	1,271,109	154,204	59,925	97,097,754	11,619,764	7,097	1,295,889	43,892
1967	359,088	109,274,125	11,557,280	277,807	5,538,856	812,199	15,236	1,336,826	142,173	66,045	102,398,443	10,602,908	8,598	1,363,641	78,192
1968	366,667	120,016,449	11,593,535	285,910	6,174,955	925,258	15,206	1,254,433	152,218	65,551	112,587,061	10,516,059	10,009	1,764,064	70,264
1969	366,212	132,714,897	11,079,479	284,708	6,174,338	921,872	14,560	1,278,744	103,776	66,944	125,261,815	10,053,831	9,160	1,819,101	67,251
1970	380,131	143,452,054	8,577,861	296,216	6,497,338	895,410	16,517	1,462,240	138,733	67,398	135,492,476	7,543,718	10,272	2,444,073	39,470
1971	386,116	158,238,167	9,033,074	300,158	7,124,099	995,258	14,854	1,391,875	138,549	71,104	149,722,193	7,899,267	11,673	2,221,588	72,625
1972	430,104	176,718,592	9,887,263	338,844	7,856,050	1,100,207	18,710	1,649,901	169,112	72,550	167,212,641	8,617,944	12,693	2,929,246	121,049
1973	434,172	198,407,961	10,333,152	341,396	9,417,737	1,244,138	15,824	1,995,096	158,869	76,952	186,995,128	8,930,145	14,757	3,624,653	94,224
1974	454,078	234,477,274	10,031,793	359,515	10,250,720	1,340,587	14,331	2,151,795	7,336	80,232	222,074,759	8,683,870	14,531	4,384,765	89,804
1975	453,113	255,992,452	11,335,210	355,255	10,008,997	1,260,800	17,157	2,502,818	−25,161	80,701	243,480,637	10,099,571	15,793	4,299,061	75,343
1976	443,912	296,603,107	15,767,426	345,679	11,233,209	1,365,707	16,860	2,611,564	−98,021	81,373	282,758,334	14,499,740	17,254	5,190,101	134,031
1977	487,374	347,886,196	20,411,093	385,322	13,879,398	1,815,203	16,837	3,894,449	202,488	85,215	330,112,349	18,393,402	19,113	6,166,054	145,740
1978	525,769	392,240,854	23,199,968	413,197	14,784,631	1,821,424	19,886	4,557,732	376,590	92,686	372,898,491	21,001,954	19,968	6,184,335	153,156
1979	539,020	469,540,277	20,680,334	415,472	18,069,893	1,956,999	19,778	5,492,363	367,734	103,770	445,978,021	18,355,601	24,195	7,742,175	43,812
1980	570,536	549,842,238	22,290,099	438,795	19,965,525	1,995,557	20,417	6,069,317	248,387	111,324	523,807,396	20,046,155	26,047	8,311,975	−88,152
1981	564,817	626,802,054	21,399,399	433,979[5]	21,868,362	2,053,514	21,711	6,425,698	−227,832	109,127	598,507,994	19,573,717	25,154	7,725,050	−276,151
1982	585,449	661,771,955	19,219,789	451,531[5]	22,661,685	1,644,591	18,448	6,815,828	−760,761	115,470	632,294,442	18,335,959	29,940	9,986,924	−260,571
1983	625,933	690,269,756	21,082,613	483,234[5]	25,357,957	2,293,767	20,132	7,490,312	−703,495	122,567	657,421,487	19,492,341	34,231	12,538,896	−176,381
1984	721,087	766,044,038	30,116,207	572,325[5]	29,087,904	3,271,595	20,578	11,324,902	−2,007,032	128,184	725,631,232	28,851,644	36,675	14,586,748	−88,742
1985	708,958	809,991,359	24,431,361	545,651[5]	25,885,652	2,410,045	24,970	11,747,519	−3,066,313	138,337	772,358,188	25,087,629	38,005	17,631,823	−133,560
1986	735,341	802,894,383	22,197,965	575,854[5]	27,416,165	3,423,725	21,059	13,247,016	−3,029,423	138,428	762,231,202	21,803,663	40,705	19,295,458	−211,837
1987	825,514	836,254,502	37,371,877	647,778[5]	29,733,523	3,686,399	29,843	20,341,513	−3,781,248	147,893	786,179,466	37,466,726	55,722[10]	36,193,733	323,197
1988	768,259	—	48,774,425	598,590[5]	30,260,148	4,122,939	20,421	—	−2,292,315	149,248	838,753,393	46,943,801	56,783	43,900,725	442,055
1989	801,543	—	41,716,968	623,046[5]	30,831,223	4,619,598	22,460	—	−1,976,583	156,037	906,501,335	39,073,953	62,230	53,188,436	−128,775
1990	800,172	—	39,401,318	614,639[5]	31,374,195	4,104,660	25,180	—	−116,938	160,353	936,277,062	35,413,596	63,957	60,312,629	−211,436
1991	851,514	—	40,963,113	660,427[5]	33,206,338	4,651,488	26,107	—	−1,441,340	164,980	954,944,592	37,742,965	70,009	63,753,848	34,906
1992	816,993	—	47,549,984	615,174[5]	33,306,527	4,706,577	23,535	—	1,053,599	178,284	997,640,581	41,789,809	74,886	70,076,118	1,771,652
1993	908,104	1,136,528,596	62,075,517	711,367[5]	35,886,552	5,071,564	20,757	63,485,606	4,118,603	175,980	1,037,156,438	52,885,350	76,855	78,223,735	1,984,944
1994	954,010	1,218,266,180	80,010,806	744,110[5]	40,406,804	6,118,329	23,426	74,647,122	5,627,377	186,474	1,103,212,254	68,265,100	82,080	86,185,775	4,474,160
1995	957,435	1,282,121,319	85,458,269	737,071[5]	39,811,359	5,797,110	25,908	85,599,981	6,749,983	194,456	1,156,709,979	72,911,176	91,822	94,665,458	3,175,980
1996	1,059,770	1,412,247,998	88,131,957	824,687[5]	42,124,760	5,680,369	29,806	113,112,599	7,051,416	205,277	1,257,010,639	75,400,172	98,311	109,038,953	5,214,707
1997	1,021,323	1,520,937,419	85,328,408	780,994[5]	45,690,042	6,941,712	30,917	144,520,946	−1,636,618	209,412	1,330,726,431	80,023,314	105,803	114,202,022	4,422,930
1998	—	—	—	890,856	48,978,573	7,264,484	—	—	—	—	—	—	—	—	—

1 Totals have not been generated independently, but are simply summations of the series for proprietorships, partnerships, and corporations.

2 Includes S-corporations.

3 Includes only proprietorships with positive net income.

4 Includes only proprietorships with net income greater than or equal to $5,000.

5 Number of tax returns rather than the number of businesses.

6 Includes inactive corporations.

7 Affiliated corporations filed separate returns.

8 Gross income instead of total receipts.

9 Values are understated because railroad and other utility corporations reported net rather than gross income.

10 Firms that shifted from fiscal to calendar years are counted twice.

Sources

U.S. Internal Revenue Service (and its predecessor, U.S. Bureau of Internal Revenue), *Statistics of Income* (SOI), various issues; *SOI Bulletin*, various issues.

Documentation

See the text for Table Ch1-18.

TABLE Ch97–111   Active proprietorships, partnerships, and corporations – entities, receipts, and profit: 1918–1998   [Wholesale and retail trade]
Contributed by Naomi R. Lamoreaux

Year	Total Entities Ch97 [1]	Total Receipts Ch98 [1]	Total Profit Ch99 [1]	Proprietorships Entities Ch100	Proprietorships Receipts Ch101	Proprietorships Profit Ch102	Partnerships Entities Ch103	Partnerships Receipts Ch104	Partnerships Profit Ch105	Corporations Total Entities Ch106 [2]	Corporations Total Receipts Ch107 [2]	Corporations Total Profit Ch108 [2]	S-corporations Entities Ch109	S-corporations Receipts Ch110	S-corporations Profit Ch111
	Number	Thousand dollars	Thousand dollars	Number	Thousand dollars	Thousand dollars	Number	Thousand dollars	Thousand dollars	Number	Thousand dollars	Thousand dollars	Number	Thousand dollars	Thousand dollars
1918	—	—	—	218,347 [3]	—	777,906 [3]	—	—	—	70,149	21,661,744 [8]	1,001,581	—	—	—
1919	—	—	—	254,645 [3]	—	1,006,377 [3]	—	—	—	70,159	25,438,135 [8]	1,379,344	—	—	—
1920	—	—	—	223,931 [3]	—	840,756 [3]	—	—	—	78,885	31,513,117 [8]	571,691	—	—	—
1921	—	—	—	240,486 [3]	—	712,884 [3]	—	—	—	88,179	27,344,350 [8]	-54,883	—	—	—
1922	—	—	—	297,133 [3]	—	891,372 [3]	—	—	—	95,683	28,697,453	695,319	—	—	—
1923	—	—	—	647,569 [3]	—	1,617,969 [3]	—	—	—	100,646	32,299,071	933,129	—	—	—
1924	—	—	—	614,459 [3]	—	1,603,555 [3]	—	—	—	105,323	35,129,501	802,069	—	—	—
1925	—	—	—	366,916 [3]	—	1,217,319 [3]	—	—	—	109,588	39,859,651	966,540	—	—	—
1926	—	—	—	56,316 [4]	—	415,492 [4]	—	—	—	112,705 [6]	40,950,472	834,560	—	—	—
1927	—	—	—	53,935 [4]	—	400,030 [4]	—	—	—	119,678	40,955,443	794,531	—	—	—
1928	—	—	—	58,248 [4]	—	424,815 [4]	—	—	—	126,347	43,286,710	891,348	—	—	—
1929	—	—	—	62,665 [4]	—	458,603 [4]	—	—	—	129,089	43,506,309	729,837	—	—	—
1930	—	—	—	36,863 [4]	—	253,524 [4]	—	—	—	131,487	37,227,078	-87,597	—	—	—
1931	—	—	—	20,625 [4]	—	136,337 [4]	—	—	—	132,848	30,605,553	-565,397	—	—	—
1932	—	—	—	6,534 [4]	—	43,185 [4]	—	—	—	132,214	23,145,961	-805,250	—	—	—
1933	—	—	—	12,068 [4]	1,175,136 [4]	79,011 [4]	—	—	—	132,896	24,213,588	-40,364	—	—	—
1934	—	—	—	18,927 [4]	1,725,886 [4]	125,666 [4]	—	—	—	140,876 [7]	33,027,953	321,174	—	—	—
1935	—	—	—	23,096 [4]	2,074,052 [4]	152,503 [4]	—	—	—	144,881 [7]	37,539,595	466,176	—	—	—
1936	—	—	—	36,536 [4]	3,295,549 [4]	251,383 [4]	—	—	—	145,520 [7]	43,277,581	923,370	—	—	—
1937	—	—	—	36,563 [4]	3,575,623 [4]	257,447 [4]	—	—	—	143,084 [7]	45,439,940	833,968	—	—	—
1938	—	—	—	27,751 [4]	2,663,372 [4]	184,676 [4]	—	—	—	139,192 [7]	39,048,466	415,663	—	—	—
1939	673,370	64,813,290	2,243,628	424,899	14,293,309	899,444	110,264	7,772,613	531,622	138,207 [7]	42,747,368	812,562	—	—	—
1940	—	—	—	—	—	—	—	—	—	139,849 [7]	47,216,043	1,082,223	—	—	—
1941	—	—	—	884,026	20,752,306	1,883,522	—	—	—	138,703 [7]	57,776,415	2,080,220	—	—	—
1942	—	—	—	—	—	—	—	—	—	128,969 [7]	55,992,116	2,569,016	—	—	—
1943	—	—	—	1,080,034 [5]	30,111,049	3,235,961	—	—	—	120,880	58,349,594	3,091,881	—	—	—
1944	—	—	—	—	—	—	—	—	—	117,363	61,723,762	3,253,262	—	—	—
1945	1,655,325	136,620,060	10,154,721	1,285,517	43,032,887	4,023,277	248,860	26,946,733	2,768,531	120,948	66,640,440	3,362,913	—	—	—
1946	—	—	—	—	—	—	—	—	—	151,511	96,733,544	5,582,036	—	—	—
1947	2,098,844	216,995,449	13,490,641	1,549,335	55,492,385	4,175,861	372,212	38,170,968	3,233,853	177,297	123,332,096	6,080,927	—	—	—
1948	—	—	—	—	—	—	—	—	—	196,748	137,505,300	5,758,361	—	—	—
1949	—	—	—	1,691,370	61,141,142	3,878,032	—	—	—	204,025	132,291,269	3,840,358	—	—	—
1950	—	—	—	—	—	—	—	—	—	209,339	155,102,744	6,314,708	—	—	—
1951	—	—	—	—	—	—	—	—	—	216,309	168,265,742	5,493,434	—	—	—
1952	—	—	—	1,723,534	72,612,998	—	—	—	—	221,314	168,657,120	4,418,821	—	—	—
1953	2,410,602	299,365,490	11,844,112	1,825,442	80,969,411	4,872,219	356,800	48,396,936	3,039,253	228,360	169,999,143	3,932,640	—	—	—
1954	—	—	—	—	—	—	—	—	—	238,523	173,303,172	3,647,762	—	—	—
1955	—	—	—	1,736,179	73,953,486	4,885,593	—	—	—	264,968	207,734,473	5,123,375	—	—	—
1956	—	—	—	—	—	—	—	—	—	286,252	218,166,977	5,242,583	—	—	—
1957	2,506,592	—	12,790,789	1,870,401	89,312,470	5,358,868	331,074	—	2,721,022	305,117	232,107,862	4,710,899	—	—	—
1958	2,509,264	—	12,241,900	1,880,131	85,157,755	5,281,021	317,656	—	2,535,901	311,477	228,759,100	4,424,978	20,167	7,055,596	30,455
1959	2,648,324	391,111,167	13,878,119	2,009,785	92,389,543	5,781,879	303,822	42,073,880	2,529,112	334,717	256,647,744	5,567,128	31,616	11,156,330	154,724

Year	Total			Proprietorships			Partnerships			Corporations — Total			Corporations — S-corporations		
	Entities Ch97[1]	Receipts Ch98[1]	Profit Ch99[1]	Entities Ch100	Receipts Ch101	Profit Ch102	Entities Ch103	Receipts Ch104	Profit Ch105	Entities Ch106[2]	Receipts Ch107[2]	Profit Ch108[2]	Entities Ch109	Receipts Ch110	Profit Ch111
	Number	Thousand dollars	Thousand dollars	Number	Thousand dollars	Thousand dollars	Number	Thousand dollars	Thousand dollars	Number	Thousand dollars	Thousand dollars	Number	Thousand dollars	Thousand dollars
1960	2,591,435	396,059,812	12,270,629	1,944,759	87,062,497	5,454,649	291,053	39,416,044	2,290,370	355,623	269,581,271	4,525,610	38,568	13,842,049	151,833
1961	2,585,318	394,231,990	12,367,600	1,942,804	85,639,324	5,579,784	277,567	37,745,960	2,224,007	364,947	270,846,706	4,563,809	43,822	14,456,503	211,661
1962	2,544,947	424,277,387	13,207,898	1,888,602	88,977,310	5,836,878	267,493	36,963,635	2,198,615	388,852	298,336,442	5,172,405	51,541	16,971,630	321,989
1963	2,496,782	435,239,470	13,321,124	1,836,746	89,775,198	5,807,485	256,601	35,874,352	2,157,013	403,435	309,589,920	5,356,626	57,585	19,433,793	329,061
1964	2,533,829	464,438,242	15,184,349	1,863,551	93,454,166	6,293,638	248,725	35,664,624	2,257,608	421,553	335,319,452	6,633,103	63,423	22,837,820	442,920
1965	2,529,539	497,115,227	16,460,750	1,853,913	97,190,462	6,623,844	235,322	34,758,290	2,216,142	440,304	365,166,475	7,620,764	68,219	25,904,288	540,257
1966	2,497,300	524,672,525	17,377,090	1,812,872	99,684,065	6,889,526	231,254	35,833,069	2,247,098	453,174	389,155,391	8,240,466	72,393	27,154,692	622,674
1967	2,527,162	547,867,093	18,259,353	1,840,621	102,629,235	7,061,582	220,700	34,867,091	2,265,989	465,841	410,369,867	8,931,782	76,929	30,303,021	710,559
1968	2,590,943	593,585,197	20,279,400	1,909,640	106,886,227	7,644,409	209,324	34,800,486	2,279,827	471,979	451,898,484	10,355,164	81,579	33,881,190	863,234
1969	2,689,379	652,963,725	20,705,567	1,958,469	110,286,226	7,694,711	206,343	34,412,586	2,244,585	524,567	508,264,913	10,766,271	92,537	41,196,613	917,668
1970	2,711,523	669,360,367	19,466,833	1,992,253	111,516,393	7,634,088	201,208	35,297,605	2,161,701	518,062	522,546,369	9,671,044	94,024	41,489,458	852,667
1971	2,849,114	731,626,447	21,509,929	2,115,092	120,143,547	7,957,817	195,358	35,753,390	2,189,261	538,664	575,729,510	11,362,851	96,659	43,070,043	956,667
1972	2,937,705	835,819,842	24,889,382	2,172,991	124,206,842	8,300,117	196,486	37,105,180	2,221,340	568,228	674,507,820	14,367,925	107,896	49,455,640	1,165,119
1973	2,944,491	964,724,820	31,804,936	2,163,860	134,061,517	9,575,275	198,764	40,770,862	2,555,478	581,867	789,892,441	19,674,183	112,179	58,494,882	1,608,138
1974	2,997,790	1,109,720,002	35,435,972	2,199,864	142,295,220	10,027,218	195,503	44,060,034	2,835,692	602,423	923,364,748	22,573,062	117,158	66,481,520	1,712,543
1975	3,001,316	1,163,907,209	35,007,537	2,193,218	148,327,660	9,859,533	193,466	45,640,677	2,658,574	614,632	969,938,872	22,489,430	123,493	69,830,765	1,633,085
1976	3,112,842	1,318,682,726	38,357,759	2,282,288	158,157,392	9,925,843	195,014	46,611,598	2,409,252	635,540	1,113,913,736	26,022,664	139,982	81,676,492	1,702,696
1977	3,130,553	1,449,575,565	42,568,486	2,264,847	160,494,441	9,761,395	193,312	49,198,951	2,626,944	672,394	1,239,882,173	30,180,147	147,140	85,989,328	1,869,618
1978	3,255,986	1,694,166,982	49,308,790	2,334,348	179,166,569	10,744,505	200,195	53,595,358	2,804,927	721,443	1,461,404,863	35,759,358	167,711	104,847,601	1,916,948
1979	3,432,234	2,007,288,044	54,213,575	2,454,720	195,654,840	11,173,789	204,916	58,924,271	2,858,401	772,598	1,752,708,933	40,181,385	180,298	113,721,649	1,565,889
1980	3,526,985	2,224,270,517	50,159,627	2,527,084	202,283,802	9,375,330	200,273	66,462,937	2,474,626	799,628	1,955,523,778	38,309,671	181,586	108,207,814	912,234
1981	3,487,539	2,309,078,970	43,030,569	2,453,895[5]	198,280,696	8,393,233	216,808	71,169,890	1,316,933	816,836	2,039,628,384	33,320,403	173,353	106,527,098	834,138
1982	3,531,282	2,284,705,938	36,679,995	2,486,593[5]	196,423,399	6,636,407	205,142	70,581,175	1,600,910	839,547	2,017,701,364	28,442,678	177,063	118,252,835	1,302,696
1983	3,460,777	2,375,496,362	44,915,122	2,414,632[5]	195,372,218	8,082,473	194,360	60,679,282	1,539,779	851,785	2,119,444,862	35,292,870	193,695	148,129,559	1,911,411
1984	3,462,203	2,576,946,850	51,415,530	2,380,838[5]	195,961,164	7,708,348	184,841	73,373,547	1,666,476	896,524	2,307,612,139	42,040,706	205,114	189,466,690	2,398,591
1985	3,407,029	2,749,374,048	43,437,107	2,289,196[5]	205,412,816	8,333,720	200,532	70,095,779	1,976,685	917,301	2,473,865,453	33,126,702	209,129	210,422,503	2,630,042
1986	3,381,949	2,809,420,167	47,210,968	2,268,672[5]	192,491,816	10,019,464	174,118	69,487,365	2,271,556	939,159	2,547,440,986	34,919,948	236,451	231,564,327	2,528,988
1987	3,525,035	3,054,588,105	51,944,537	2,368,480[5]	216,304,918	11,207,639	184,797	71,565,947	2,696,840	971,758	2,766,717,240	38,040,058	327,354[9]	477,666,231	7,173,128
1988	3,577,902	—	59,349,387	2,413,661[5]	230,010,195	13,153,248	179,688	—	3,351,256	984,553	2,977,982,750	42,844,883	355,292	623,745,693	10,299,835
1989	3,714,631	—	52,231,807	2,438,472[5]	234,071,082	13,547,817	173,179	—	2,528,553	1,102,980	3,184,946,370	36,155,437	383,772	721,195,005	9,153,524
1990	3,849,191	—	48,561,362	2,650,195[5]	249,734,337	15,857,424	175,939	—	2,609,860	1,023,057	3,308,988,336	30,094,078	419,833	777,891,193	9,015,665
1991	3,892,206	—	45,680,941	2,677,709[5]	245,891,502	13,101,670	170,963	—	2,628,050	1,043,534	3,380,598,972	29,951,221	444,791	821,865,946	8,480,458
1992	4,050,652	—	57,833,326	2,835,467[5]	247,260,829	13,936,753	162,472	—	2,552,791	1,052,713	3,503,944,396	41,343,782	467,234	889,290,904	15,354,623
1993	4,090,231	4,067,875,515	67,562,260	2,860,073[5]	244,689,874	14,771,612	157,178	113,690,896	3,075,840	1,072,980	3,709,494,745	49,714,808	497,321	969,967,843	17,019,396
1994	4,214,139	4,445,372,250	89,350,014	2,954,466[5]	247,975,952	16,575,923	153,310	145,170,482	4,301,147	1,106,363	4,052,225,816	68,472,944	517,812	1,075,844,032	23,887,745
1995	4,323,753	4,742,736,702	84,177,719	3,026,959[5]	257,278,099	16,615,003	164,385	175,111,656	3,996,004	1,132,409	4,310,346,947	63,566,712	537,539	1,137,934,320	24,075,672
1996	4,461,813	4,968,296,995	95,513,885	3,151,272[5]	261,111,146	16,696,463	168,050	217,112,241	5,464,154	1,142,491	4,490,073,608	73,353,268	556,908	1,225,474,736	29,972,943
1997	4,454,735	5,257,534,279	104,129,928	3,132,594[5]	254,642,287	17,215,295	173,009	299,075,139	5,329,996	1,149,132	4,703,816,853	81,584,637	583,006	1,337,278,598	38,345,586
1998				2,975,385[5]	249,758,597	17,811,549									

[1] Totals have not been generated independently, but are simply summations of the series for proprietorships, partnerships, and corporations.

[2] Includes S-corporations.

[3] Includes only proprietorships with positive net income.

[4] Includes only proprietorships with net income greater than or equal to $5,000.

[5] Number of tax returns rather than the number of businesses.

[6] Includes inactive corporations.

[7] Affiliated corporations filed separate returns.

[8] Gross income instead of total receipts.

[9] Firms that shifted from fiscal to calendar years are counted twice.

Sources

U.S. Internal Revenue Service (and its predecessor, U.S. Bureau of Internal Revenue), *Statistics of Income* (SOI), various issues; *SOI Bulletin*, various issues.

Documentation

See the text for Table Ch1–18.

TABLE Ch112–126   Active proprietorships, partnerships, and corporations – entities, receipts, and profit: 1918–1998   [Finance, insurance, and real estate]

Contributed by Naomi R. Lamoreaux

Year	Total			Proprietorships			Partnerships			Corporations – Total			Corporations – S-corporations		
	Entities	Receipts	Profit	Entities	Receipts	Profit	Entities	Receipts	Profit	Entities	Receipts	Profit	Entities	Receipts	Profit
	Ch112 [1]	Ch113 [1]	Ch114 [1]	Ch115	Ch116	Ch117	Ch118	Ch119	Ch120	Ch121 [2]	Ch122 [2]	Ch123 [2]	Ch124	Ch125	Ch126
	Number	Thousand dollars	Thousand dollars	Number	Thousand dollars	Thousand dollars	Number	Thousand dollars	Thousand dollars	Number	Thousand dollars	Thousand dollars	Number	Thousand dollars	Thousand dollars
1918	—	—	—	30,070 [3]	—	90,019 [3]	—	—	—	68,132	5,889,762 [8]	478,685	—	—	—
1919	—	—	—	45,882 [3]	—	184,105 [3]	—	—	—	72,813	6,459,366 [8]	703,135	—	—	—
1920	—	—	—	45,082 [3]	—	182,418 [3]	—	—	—	78,902	8,389,575 [8]	639,368	—	—	—
1921	—	—	—	26,688 [3]	—	96,591 [3]	—	—	—	82,858	7,551,096 [8]	376,131	—	—	—
1922	—	—	—	32,745 [3]	—	129,521 [3]	—	—	—	91,105	9,177,088	490,174	—	—	—
1923	—	—	—	54,771 [3]	—	196,828 [3]	—	—	—	96,772	8,758,175	457,270	—	—	—
1924	—	—	—	53,588 [3]	—	202,035 [3]	—	—	—	104,761	9,441,666	534,527	—	—	—
1925	—	—	—	37,784 [3]	—	221,567 [3]	—	—	—	115,947	12,814,966	1,067,604	—	—	—
1926	—	—	—	13,615 [4]	—	130,673 [3]	—	—	—	130,433 [6]	12,649,926	808,860	—	—	—
1927	—	—	—	12,866 [4]	—	126,967 [4]	—	—	—	122,682	13,556,930	956,657	—	—	—
1928	—	—	—	13,042 [4]	—	151,950 [4]	—	—	—	129,139	20,079,096	1,405,144	—	—	—
1929	—	—	—	12,695 [4]	—	140,645 [4]	—	—	—	133,937	16,045,037	1,188,712	—	—	—
1930	—	—	—	8,864 [4]	—	80,047 [4]	—	—	—	136,579	13,690,664	−501,862	—	—	—
1931	—	—	—	5,981 [4]	—	52,432 [4]	—	—	—	134,563	11,236,791	−1,686,341	—	—	—
1932	—	—	—	3,184 [4]	—	25,545 [4]	—	—	—	125,120	8,581,660	−2,047,508	—	—	—
1933	—	—	—	4,017 [4]	344,198 [4]	31,555 [4]	—	—	—	121,683	7,882,990	−2,013,237	—	—	—
1934	—	—	—	4,885 [4]	192,013 [4]	33,533 [4]	—	—	—	126,096 [7]	8,450,999	−1,204,775	—	—	—
1935	—	—	—	6,074 [4]	245,343 [4]	42,971 [4]	—	—	—	124,933 [7]	9,124,020	−778,319	—	—	—
1936	—	—	—	8,595 [4]	314,106 [4]	62,137 [4]	—	—	—	115,694 [7]	9,176,746	1,448,444	—	—	—
1937	—	—	—	8,763 [4]	268,461 [4]	55,944 [4]	—	—	—	117,079 [7]	9,393,578	1,341,153	—	—	—
1938	—	—	—	7,475 [4]	233,711 [4]	47,729 [4]	—	—	—	140,437 [7]	904,031	888,345	—	—	—
1939	212,222	11,708,798	1,196,118	38,319	582,649	112,688	31,571	1,911,440	147,332	142,332 [7]	9,214,709	936,098	—	—	—
1940	—	—	—	76,189	692,086	—	—	—	—	142,602 [7]	9,913,228	868,365	—	—	—
1941	—	—	—	—	868,506	185,444	—	—	—	143,494 [7]	10,705,913	1,112,684	—	—	—
1942	—	—	—	100,344 [5]	—	—	—	—	—	136,882 [7]	9,237,163	2,043,297	—	—	—
1943	—	—	—	—	—	259,951	—	—	—	133,655	9,199,597	2,377,353	—	—	—
1944	—	—	—	—	—	—	—	—	—	133,879	9,826,804	2,895,416	—	—	—
1945	320,770	13,247,545	4,342,076	120,719	1,207,651	373,818	64,478	1,213,119	474,357	135,573	10,826,775	3,493,901	—	—	—
1946	—	—	—	—	—	—	—	—	—	144,373	12,391,550	4,004,484	—	—	—
1947	388,003	16,917,270	4,856,852	149,313	1,552,775	458,444	87,647	1,529,546	556,886	151,043	13,834,949	3,841,522	—	—	—
1948	—	—	—	137,071	1,786,379	485,543	—	—	—	160,643	15,474,469	4,525,177	—	—	—
1949	—	—	—	—	—	—	—	—	—	166,277	17,048,059	5,283,987	—	—	—
1950	—	—	—	—	—	—	—	—	—	171,841	18,574,819	5,719,377	—	—	—
1951	—	—	—	205,077	2,880,825	—	—	—	—	177,832	20,356,610	5,932,944	—	—	—
1952	—	—	—	—	—	—	—	—	—	185,855	23,669,573	6,458,941	—	—	—
1953	586,243	29,832,325	8,827,553	259,665	3,386,166	955,732	131,371	271,245	950,510	195,207	26,174,914	6,921,311	—	—	—
1954	—	—	—	—	—	—	—	—	—	205,339	29,795,719	8,003,817	—	—	—
1955	—	—	—	397,571	4,250,655	1,327,231	—	—	—	234,019	32,806,720	8,190,386	—	—	—
1956	—	—	—	—	—	—	—	—	—	265,005	36,247,414	8,235,900	—	—	—
1957	875,271	—	11,115,305	425,156	5,056,909	1,372,545	170,180	—	1,065,671	279,935	39,571,953	8,677,089	—	—	—
1958	899,184	—	10,012,337	436,296	6,106,808	1,363,723	168,960	—	1,161,345	293,928	60,013,793	7,487,269	4,254	151,030	17,987
1959	950,760	75,063,577	9,858,511	446,995	4,406,676	1,504,794	185,173	4,745,143	1,201,105	318,592	65,911,758	7,152,612	7,480	325,581	58,675

	Total			Proprietorships			Partnerships			Corporations Total			S-corporations		
	Entities	Receipts	Profit	Entities	Receipts	Profit	Entities	Receipts	Profit	Entities	Receipts	Profit	Entities	Receipts	Profit
Year	Ch112 [1] Number	Ch113 [1] Thousand dollars	Ch114 [1] Thousand dollars	Ch115 Number	Ch116 Thousand dollars	Ch117 Thousand dollars	Ch118 Number	Ch119 Thousand dollars	Ch120 Thousand dollars	Ch121 [2] Number	Ch122 [2] Thousand dollars	Ch123 [2] Thousand dollars	Ch124 Number	Ch125 Thousand dollars	Ch126 Thousand dollars
1960	1,019,927	80,831,738	10,859,649	482,909	5,293,971	1,517,428	202,630	4,696,220	1,091,795	334,388	70,841,547	8,250,426	10,368	423,636	56,296
1961	1,009,537	86,302,133	11,647,840	461,649	5,275,142	1,548,197	207,678	5,442,938	1,117,534	340,210	75,584,053	8,982,109	12,135	513,138	81,545
1962	1,061,303	92,595,232	11,271,810	472,674	5,172,284	1,638,461	229,400	5,564,292	952,454	359,229	81,858,656	8,680,895	13,395	547,273	76,726
1963	1,115,002	104,932,153	11,095,468	506,111	5,467,484	1,781,505	233,516	6,121,802	931,617	375,375	93,342,867	8,382,346	15,948	886,222	119,360
1964	1,173,184	114,341,122	12,011,998	543,050	6,108,907	1,978,168	246,407	6,935,414	852,201	383,727	101,296,801	9,181,629	17,904	835,319	100,234
1965	1,176,858	125,069,819	13,978,140	539,443	7,022,354	2,150,652	248,987	7,581,963	983,111	388,428	110,465,502	10,844,377	19,336	1,036,488	160,361
1966	1,247,245	134,784,471	14,134,120	575,942	6,593,529	2,151,435	268,563	8,376,031	980,204	402,740	119,814,911	11,002,481	21,904	1,177,335	112,919
1967	1,222,496	147,852,090	16,511,123	548,651	6,738,222	2,242,242	274,730	9,130,915	1,121,657	399,115	131,982,953	13,147,224	20,340	1,030,872	123,900
1968	1,221,595	165,354,774	18,643,747	515,872	7,759,614	2,501,210	298,531	10,690,078	1,067,844	407,192	146,905,082	15,074,693	25,749	1,410,564	122,027
1969	1,254,325	185,055,463	15,990,852	515,688	7,986,239	2,570,646	309,668	12,778,287	405,753	428,969	164,290,937	13,014,453	28,610	2,231,634	225,624
1970	1,292,360	200,831,202	14,474,825	565,898	8,345,823	2,561,379	320,227	15,165,331	-300,633	406,235	177,320,048	12,214,079	29,317	1,725,317	144,215
1971	1,359,417	226,692,627	18,525,250	588,354	9,463,636	3,031,302	353,327	18,980,271	-463,456	417,736	198,468,720	15,957,404	30,011	1,938,809	230,743
1972	1,466,876	257,346,587	20,297,505	666,036	10,072,398	3,591,823	375,752	21,692,961	-949,200	425,088	225,581,228	17,654,882	35,764	2,640,156	315,068
1973	1,575,547	296,598,393	17,137,908	738,985	11,301,426	3,958,084	409,912	25,204,676	-2,679,739	426,650	260,092,291	15,859,563	37,615	2,727,294	248,819
1974	1,594,345	343,877,696	18,687,564	738,770	11,568,586	3,578,681	430,326	29,110,335	3,604,727	425,249	303,198,775	11,504,156	38,177	3,021,908	130,303
1975	1,590,109	360,339,798	11,773,381	743,906	12,137,847	3,761,853	434,357	32,405,970	-3,651,802	411,846	315,795,981	11,663,330	38,293	2,811,469	77,551
1976	1,685,831	406,678,372	22,803,773	826,859	15,271,974	5,277,016	446,988	37,632,363	-268,511	411,984	353,774,035	17,795,268	45,278	4,239,499	223,924
1977	1,804,250	468,346,614	33,058,843	894,941	19,320,207	6,361,253	476,390	43,894,814	-970,443	432,919	405,131,593	27,668,033	51,271	5,385,878	480,491
1978	1,954,069	558,074,173	40,642,319	983,633	20,561,255	6,655,179	516,135	62,822,429	113,206	454,301	474,690,489	33,873,934	55,830	6,561,924	731,326
1979	2,106,284	658,521,654	43,510,672	1,057,726	21,156,800	7,072,331	577,336	76,258,032	-520,929	471,222	561,106,822	36,959,270	61,735	6,027,879	497,228
1980	2,179,871	806,124,811	35,488,647	1,048,965	21,530,768	6,614,631	637,480	87,133,197	-4,248,776	493,426	697,460,846	33,122,792	66,652	6,375,372	251,252
1981	2,058,898	973,536,950	26,966,156	907,465 [5]	22,154,345	5,979,708	681,638	73,573,659	-5,360,047	469,795	877,808,946	26,346,495	57,686	6,176,245	238,224
1982	2,113,417	1,060,104,132	16,493,171	926,165 [5]	24,331,647	5,844,979	725,622	85,904,608	-11,155,896	461,630	949,867,877	21,804,088	59,346	7,096,159	31,281
1983	2,140,001	1,005,407,860	26,423,249	930,278 [5]	25,801,198	7,813,689	730,067	76,784,190	-13,105,211	479,656	902,822,472	31,714,771	74,695	11,257,848	440,993
1984	2,272,297	1,157,486,180	22,897,688	984,029 [5]	29,977,330	9,464,360	790,902	94,362,434	-19,243,718	497,366	1,033,146,416	32,677,046	90,968	14,488,752	310,360
1985	2,376,452	1,305,760,955	44,538,304	1,014,153 [5]	31,417,991	9,796,447	843,867	92,308,655	-25,928,669	518,432	1,182,034,309	60,670,526	101,930	17,440,244	61,124
1986	2,518,773	1,513,900,705	78,431,284	1,128,684 [5]	36,210,941	11,601,929	852,705	112,594,396	-32,979,553	537,384	1,365,095,368	99,808,908	121,857	21,764,366	135,119
1987	2,573,237	1,771,144,557	74,998,735	1,224,580 [5]	42,039,464	14,372,053	827,521	139,886,658	-26,776,536	521,136	1,589,218,435	87,403,218	135,672 [9]	42,117,731	1,612,181
1988	2,674,191	—	89,066,696	1,232,886 [5]	46,119,571	16,431,139	868,887	—	-19,257,397	572,418	1,714,352,381	91,892,954	185,688	56,382,432	2,247,876
1989	2,715,759	—	104,507,047	1,270,410 [5]	49,574,462	16,423,266	852,517	—	-20,823,570	592,832	1,868,003,359	108,907,351	220,191	57,214,013	1,673,348
1990	2,762,030	—	107,048,279	1,330,638 [5]	49,049,308	16,359,365	822,254	—	-19,212,967	609,138	1,954,709,651	109,901,881	241,530	60,388,316	-226,594
1991	2,711,998	—	127,199,343	1,290,603 [5]	43,632,470	15,440,236	803,838	—	-12,786,397	617,557	1,924,317,623	124,545,504	254,937	54,816,499	-803,199
1992	2,710,584	—	163,324,631	1,277,992 [5]	45,857,790	17,097,512	797,324	—	-751,856	635,268	1,900,428,224	146,978,975	273,415	61,223,859	4,580,011
1993	2,707,068	2,189,660,647	219,355,747	1,273,020 [5]	52,816,574	18,865,707	792,651	196,528,334	15,260,195	641,397	1,940,315,739	185,229,845	286,428	64,830,031	7,310,612
1994	2,835,880	2,258,956,361	213,399,382	1,344,676 [5]	54,130,754	19,971,684	809,533	228,334,259	24,124,681	681,671	1,976,491,348	169,303,017	314,490	71,621,176	8,576,635
1995	2,807,059	2,618,216,100	321,932,946	1,275,117 [5]	57,473,784	20,600,260	848,731	282,638,393	44,521,919	683,211	2,278,103,923	256,810,767	326,149	77,811,520	10,671,258
1996	2,886,725	2,836,488,668	391,224,108	1,271,394 [5]	64,606,561	22,351,241	891,577	365,026,857	69,723,674	723,754	2,406,855,250	299,149,193	356,778	87,396,401	15,088,860
1997	3,032,797	3,242,181,504	492,668,329	1,314,029 [5]	75,595,055	24,264,460	974,223	455,316,613	94,921,837	744,545	2,711,269,836	373,482,032	382,153	104,017,724	20,420,790
1998	—	—	—	1,409,882 [5]	100,957,574	30,333,369	—	—	—	—	—	—	—	—	—

1 Totals have not been generated independently, but are simply summations of the series for proprietorships, partnerships, and corporations.

2 Includes S-corporations.

3 Includes only proprietorships with positive net income.

4 Includes only proprietorships with net income greater than or equal to $5,000.

5 Number of tax returns rather than the number of businesses.

6 Includes inactive corporations.

7 Affiliated corporations filed separate returns.

8 Gross income instead of total receipts.

9 Firms that shifted from fiscal to calendar years are counted twice.

Sources

U.S. Internal Revenue Service (and its predecessor, U.S. Bureau of Internal Revenue), *Statistics of Income* (*SOI*), various issues; *SOI Bulletin*, various issues.

Documentation

See the text for Table Ch1–18.

TABLE Ch127–141   Active proprietorships, partnerships, and corporations – entities, receipts, and profit: 1918–1998   [Services]

Contributed by Naomi R. Lamoreaux

Year	Total Entities Ch127 [1] (Number)	Total Receipts Ch128 [1] (Thousand dollars)	Total Profit Ch129 [1] (Thousand dollars)	Proprietorships Entities Ch130 (Number)	Proprietorships Receipts Ch131 (Thousand dollars)	Proprietorships Profit Ch132 (Thousand dollars)	Partnerships Entities Ch133 (Number)	Partnerships Receipts Ch134 (Thousand dollars)	Partnerships Profit Ch135 (Thousand dollars)	Corporations Total Entities Ch136 [2] (Number)	Corporations Total Receipts Ch137 [2] (Thousand dollars)	Corporations Total Profit Ch138 [2] (Thousand dollars)	S-corporations Entities Ch139 (Number)	S-corporations Receipts Ch140 (Thousand dollars)	S-corporations Profit Ch141 (Thousand dollars)
1918	—	—	—	213,700 [3]	—	678,670 [3]	—	—	—	14,899	1,097,928 [8]	45,040	—	—	—
1919	—	—	—	257,554 [3]	—	852,040 [3]	—	—	—	15,723	1,471,143 [8]	102,841	—	—	—
1920	—	—	—	269,045 [3]	—	952,774 [3]	—	—	—	17,490	1,952,574 [8]	116,292	—	—	—
1921	—	—	—	231,395 [3]	—	795,403 [3]	—	—	—	19,103	1,755,088 [8]	58,934	—	—	—
1922	—	—	—	263,592 [3]	—	911,625 [3]	—	—	—	23,145	2,218,148	88,752	—	—	—
1923	—	—	—	481,779 [3]	—	1,530,652 [3]	—	—	—	25,114	2,420,815	129,227	—	—	—
1924	—	—	—	471,396 [3]	—	1,547,171 [3]	—	—	—	26,320	2,633,834	135,515	—	—	—
1925	—	—	—	287,553 [3]	—	1,223,867 [3]	—	—	—	28,981	2,841,191	174,200	—	—	—
1926	—	—	—	79,948 [4]	—	659,553 [4]	—	—	—	32,257 [6]	3,362,543	157,210	—	—	—
1927	—	—	—	83,471 [4]	—	688,882 [4]	—	—	—	31,146	3,588,636	127,399	—	—	—
1928	—	—	—	86,384 [4]	—	710,140 [4]	—	—	—	33,526	3,831,748	127,477	—	—	—
1929	—	—	—	91,587 [4]	—	762,533 [4]	—	—	—	35,967	4,193,380	160,212	—	—	—
1930	—	—	—	72,431 [4]	—	607,817 [4]	—	—	—	38,213	4,166,744	54,998	—	—	—
1931	—	—	—	52,900 [4]	—	440,497 [4]	—	—	—	38,225	3,680,803	-123,364	—	—	—
1932	—	—	—	27,551 [4]	—	227,197 [4]	—	—	—	43,282	3,094,202	-416,088	—	—	—
1933	—	—	—	25,809 [4]	405,629 [4]	195,017 [4]	—	—	—	42,985	2,823,456	-317,041	—	—	—
1934	—	—	—	36,304 [4]	553,605 [4]	275,617 [4]	—	—	—	45,912 [7]	3,376,582	-175,599	—	—	—
1935	—	—	—	42,918 [4]	638,932 [4]	325,051 [4]	—	—	—	49,647 [7]	3,709,617	-141,070	—	—	—
1936	—	—	—	58,798 [4]	942,304 [4]	438,778 [4]	—	—	—	59,703 [7]	4,650,087	-11,071	—	—	—
1937	—	—	—	61,369 [4]	1,088,192 [4]	470,814 [4]	—	—	—	60,208 [7]	4,838,473	15,661	—	—	—
1938	—	—	—	51,384 [4]	915,893 [4]	399,311 [4]	—	—	—	40,973 [7]	3,558,177	49,835	—	—	—
1939	373,328	7,715,758	1,461,150	288,894	2,862,581	958,815	43,404	1,184,797	422,235	41,030 [7]	3,668,380	80,100	—	—	—
1940	—	—	—	—	—	—	—	—	—	41,385 [7]	3,846,133	108,013	—	—	—
1941	—	—	—	673,330	4,547,599	1,616,888	—	—	—	40,494 [7]	4,183,574	183,130	—	—	—
1942	—	—	—	—	—	—	—	—	—	38,449 [7]	4,618,118	356,763	—	—	—
1943	—	—	—	804,192 [5]	6,059,091	2,208,872	—	—	—	35,594	5,157,580	546,447	—	—	—
1944	—	—	—	—	—	—	—	—	—	34,712	5,637,054	578,793	—	—	—
1945	1,067,835	17,006,588	4,356,351	942,262	7,826,810	2,707,677	90,466	3,207,785	1,046,979	35,107	5,971,993	601,695	—	—	—
1946	—	—	—	—	—	—	—	—	—	39,648	7,373,545	802,524	—	—	—
1947	1,309,681	22,713,200	5,413,071	1,132,752	9,876,255	3,342,704	130,954	4,340,642	1,346,793	45,975	8,496,303	723,574	—	—	—
1948	—	—	—	—	—	—	—	—	—	50,456	9,017,974	630,351	—	—	—
1949	—	—	—	1,251,207	11,677,036	3,895,397	—	—	—	53,978	9,285,575	557,399	—	—	—
1950	—	—	—	—	—	—	—	—	—	55,233	9,593,288	572,072	—	—	—
1951	—	—	—	1,355,389	13,367,054	—	—	—	—	58,268	10,671,994	632,657	—	—	—
1952	—	—	—	—	—	—	—	—	—	61,647	11,600,566	629,755	—	—	—
1953	1,694,774	33,715,943	7,864,649	1,484,804	15,337,857	5,195,298	146,453	6,277,536	2,061,000	63,517	12,100,550	608,351	—	—	—
1954	—	—	—	—	—	—	—	—	—	64,845	12,593,627	591,128	—	—	—
1955	—	—	—	1,578,709	16,246,282	5,875,383	—	—	—	72,892	14,477,311	704,098	—	—	—
1956	—	—	—	—	—	—	—	—	—	81,598	16,531,236	843,282	—	—	—
1957	2,071,426	—	10,317,899	1,825,599	19,533,328	7,026,428	155,230	—	2,502,416	90,597	18,230,523	789,055	—	—	—
1958	2,086,069	—	10,722,627	1,825,988	20,710,408	7,189,981	162,881	—	2,779,900	97,200	18,678,063	752,746	4,743	459,224	7,725
1959	2,250,198	54,874,928	12,016,264	1,979,695	23,480,681	8,084,421	160,498	9,166,991	2,963,591	110,005	22,227,256	968,252	8,652	962,596	28,430

Year	Total Entities Ch127 [1]	Total Receipts Ch128 [1]	Total Profit Ch129 [1]	Prop. Entities Ch130	Prop. Receipts Ch131	Prop. Profit Ch132	Part. Entities Ch133	Part. Receipts Ch134	Part. Profit Ch135	Corp. Total Entities Ch136 [2]	Corp. Total Receipts Ch137 [2]	Corp. Total Profit Ch138 [2]	S-corp Entities Ch139	S-corp Receipts Ch140	S-corp Profit Ch141
	Number	Thousand dollars	Thousand dollars	Number	Thousand dollars	Thousand dollars	Number	Thousand dollars	Thousand dollars	Number	Thousand dollars	Thousand dollars	Number	Thousand dollars	Thousand dollars
1960	2,246,452	56,048,302	11,964,571	1,966,068	23,256,055	8,059,667	159,360	9,445,464	3,055,552	121,024	23,346,783	849,352	11,760	1,316,266	24,163
1961	2,384,922	60,385,201	12,781,979	2,075,689	24,355,060	8,580,176	171,278	10,109,802	3,311,877	137,955	25,920,339	889,926	14,954	1,761,903	33,552
1962	2,449,570	64,691,434	13,516,128	2,132,751	26,079,027	9,289,343	166,737	10,517,086	3,393,644	150,082	28,095,321	833,141	17,537	1,868,164	25,046
1963	2,520,956	69,977,992	14,140,086	2,185,196	27,095,434	9,528,995	171,994	11,267,660	3,709,982	163,766	31,614,898	901,109	20,217	2,395,781	48,231
1964	2,583,901	75,158,905	15,688,550	2,240,321	29,290,178	10,465,517	166,678	11,767,574	4,064,028	176,902	34,101,153	1,159,005	25,610	2,600,552	54,219
1965	2,564,954	80,798,238	17,000,148	2,207,927	29,788,755	11,007,933	168,850	12,632,449	4,402,118	188,177	38,377,034	1,590,097	28,902	3,217,500	85,386
1966	2,645,188	88,916,830	18,751,223	2,270,739	31,990,956	11,999,126	172,384	13,842,881	4,924,450	202,065	43,082,993	1,827,647	30,918	4,532,303	177,976
1967	2,713,942	97,225,830	20,317,162	2,327,684	34,783,754	13,019,978	165,697	15,000,746	5,314,597	220,561	47,441,330	1,982,587	35,728	4,710,457	183,630
1968	2,795,421	104,059,918	21,490,524	2,390,247	36,547,905	13,645,498	176,276	16,465,740	5,823,150	228,898	51,046,273	2,021,876	42,150	5,472,363	146,711
1969	2,864,941	117,623,452	22,329,308	2,426,599	39,611,478	14,634,558	176,709	17,975,338	6,041,645	261,633	60,036,636	1,653,105	45,313	5,876,622	251,779
1970	2,964,013	129,501,440	22,450,844	2,506,995	40,869,473	15,063,044	175,800	19,060,539	6,189,097	281,218	69,571,428	1,198,703	53,491	7,622,199	194,610
1971	3,052,573	135,903,085	23,119,146	2,592,524	42,442,854	15,244,117	172,269	19,884,260	6,403,931	287,780	73,595,971	1,471,098	51,548	7,486,798	162,413
1972	3,180,785	150,299,909	24,554,653	2,693,126	44,863,778	15,787,423	172,864	21,448,386	6,462,732	314,795	83,987,745	2,304,498	51,498	7,988,358	300,458
1973	3,367,140	174,623,927	26,539,123	2,820,552	48,806,311	16,968,221	178,489	23,976,714	6,876,023	368,099	101,840,902	2,694,879	63,749	10,748,336	364,098
1974	3,523,574	194,700,260	26,721,456	2,943,592	51,340,474	17,170,867	191,150	27,770,644	7,050,409	388,832	115,589,142	2,500,180	71,381	11,623,934	266,542
1975	3,668,684	218,139,518	29,005,996	3,034,056	55,997,019	18,385,362	198,956	30,765,135	7,223,890	435,672	131,377,364	3,396,744	82,267	12,805,607	299,918
1976	3,826,680	244,370,135	32,389,111	3,153,115	61,201,598	20,266,088	207,248	33,010,892	7,802,578	466,317	150,157,645	4,320,445	90,364	14,490,497	314,820
1977	4,045,562	289,673,669	38,357,807	3,302,537	67,791,043	22,516,228	226,638	38,874,840	9,244,749	516,387	183,007,786	6,596,830	99,330	18,503,025	729,191
1978	4,246,837	327,890,377	41,608,292	3,472,508	72,563,683	23,597,886	214,313	44,720,621	10,344,281	560,016	210,606,073	7,666,125	113,759	22,447,968	608,814
1979	4,496,162	379,613,835	45,177,524	3,654,001	83,289,968	25,531,243	238,716	51,216,172	11,339,292	603,445	245,107,695	8,306,989	122,240	24,529,375	449,184
1980	4,777,528	428,378,091	47,051,405	3,842,790	87,964,739	26,433,341	263,400	60,530,165	12,424,161	671,338	279,883,187	8,193,903	135,473	24,282,133	373,422
1981	4,968,546	514,660,217	47,279,878	3,952,801 [5]	102,963,808	27,463,790	262,932	64,849,686	11,618,171	752,813	346,846,723	8,197,917	151,187	28,240,663	400,544
1982	5,374,254	560,550,808	47,301,236	4,275,377 [5]	108,254,050	28,199,813	279,171	71,529,364	11,902,165	819,706	380,767,394	7,199,258	160,865	33,557,573	607,356
1983	5,800,929	621,013,034	50,390,260	4,646,241 [5]	124,455,046	31,930,521	306,294	80,095,561	12,456,811	848,394	416,462,427	6,002,928	193,862	43,147,447	825,916
1984	6,220,472	735,593,642	57,872,624	4,989,999 [5]	147,438,458	36,825,238	331,103	97,822,373	15,583,256	899,370	490,332,811	5,464,130	195,015	51,204,331	719,114
1985	6,812,917	804,664,977	65,474,415	5,532,232 [5]	157,334,406	43,049,304	341,295	112,742,962	16,541,329	939,390	534,587,609	5,883,782	208,265	56,072,668	643,523
1986	7,155,810	881,747,839	74,850,200	5,758,498 [5]	168,972,768	48,838,556	325,134	120,925,356	18,563,621	1,072,178	591,849,715	7,448,023	238,837	66,719,390	927,458
1987	7,388,407	968,519,142	83,309,566	5,977,347 [5]	183,497,832	55,965,425	291,456	121,888,209	18,092,212	1,119,604	663,133,101	9,251,929	339,640 [9]	109,305,372	2,611,643
1988	7,748,704	—	103,188,252	6,456,871 [5]	211,968,486	68,273,074	296,408	—	25,638,547	995,425	695,265,170	9,276,631	373,950	143,512,717	4,258,628
1989	8,328,213	—	111,127,359	7,038,940 [5]	225,547,569	73,454,722	299,423	—	26,652,443	989,850	735,497,193	11,020,194	437,676	177,181,725	5,278,344
1990	8,631,779	—	121,231,906	7,334,996 [5]	252,307,538	84,162,121	267,336	—	26,452,993	1,029,447	779,329,609	10,616,792	501,733	219,873,675	6,531,943
1991	8,964,016	—	119,799,330	7,641,910 [5]	246,899,790	86,993,373	260,449	—	23,036,066	1,061,657	809,724,469	9,769,891	547,414	235,890,633	6,847,103
1992	8,975,877	—	144,673,922	7,622,911 [5]	259,526,265	93,144,225	252,517	—	33,004,354	1,100,449	869,533,422	18,525,343	587,071	261,504,463	12,824,428
1993	9,131,600	1,402,935,656	151,679,509	7,718,150 [5]	260,305,160	92,431,030	255,726	200,987,632	33,887,012	1,157,724	941,642,864	25,361,467	634,555	289,074,655	14,681,157
1994	9,488,944	1,684,943,109	167,602,639	7,803,277 [5]	271,707,333	95,716,323	261,273	215,205,825	36,317,808	1,424,394	1,198,029,951	35,568,508	687,981	322,211,588	21,567,432
1995	9,744,034	1,850,935,614	172,982,128	7,957,579 [5]	275,272,662	97,180,886	282,225	239,968,393	37,393,680	1,504,230	1,335,694,559	38,407,562	753,890	368,278,859	24,785,445
1996	10,088,149	2,060,137,501	189,819,320	8,233,940 [5]	287,494,755	101,984,543	296,808	276,427,194	43,882,573	1,557,401	1,496,215,552	43,952,204	815,494	406,198,180	31,113,590
1997	10,311,835	2,264,998,849	202,940,307	8,407,991 [5]	298,983,752	105,774,261	310,990	327,427,194	46,695,598	1,592,854	1,638,587,903	50,470,448	860,445	451,975,219	35,729,256
1998	—	—	—	8,524,300 [5]	309,352,287	111,356,622	—	—	—	—	—	—	—	—	—

[1] Totals have not been generated independently, but are simply summations of the series for proprietorships, partnerships, and corporations.

[2] Includes S-corporations.

[3] Includes only proprietorships with positive net income.

[4] Includes only proprietorships with net income greater than or equal to $5,000.

[5] Number of tax returns rather than the number of businesses.

[6] Includes inactive corporations.

[7] Affiliated corporations filed separate returns.

[8] Gross income instead of total receipts.

[9] Firms that shifted from fiscal to calendar years are counted twice.

Sources

U.S. Internal Revenue Service (and its predecessor, U.S. Bureau of Internal Revenue), *Statistics of Income (SOI)*, various issues; *SOI Bulletin*, various issues.

Documentation

See the text for Table Ch1–18.

TABLE Ch142–156   Active proprietorships, partnerships, and corporations – entities, receipts, and profit: 1918–1998   [All other industries]

Contributed by Naomi R. Lamoreaux

Year	Total			Proprietorships			Partnerships			Corporations — Total			Corporations — S-corporations		
	Entities	Receipts	Profit	Entities	Receipts	Profit	Entities	Receipts	Profit	Entities	Receipts	Profit	Entities	Receipts	Profit
	Ch142 [1]	Ch143 [1]	Ch144 [1]	Ch145	Ch146	Ch147	Ch148	Ch149	Ch150	Ch151 [2]	Ch152 [2]	Ch153 [2]	Ch154	Ch155	Ch156
	Number	Thousand dollars	Thousand dollars	Number	Thousand dollars	Thousand dollars	Number	Thousand dollars	Thousand dollars	Number	Thousand dollars	Thousand dollars	Number	Thousand dollars	Thousand dollars
1918	—	—	—	38,951 [3]	—	133,551 [3]	—	—	—	8,944	3,457,813 [8]	290,688	—	—	—
1919	—	—	—	37,677 [3]	—	143,256 [3]	—	—	—	9,721	1,599,884 [8]	51,281	—	—	—
1920	—	—	—	36,659 [3]	—	117,760 [3]	—	—	—	3,108	1,132,962 [8]	32,376	—	—	—
1921	—	—	—	61,740 [3]	—	173,573 [3]	—	—	—	2,879	818,225 [8]	-38,421	—	—	—
1922	—	—	—	90,206 [3]	—	247,388 [3]	—	—	—	2,116	492,458	20,284	—	—	—
1923	—	—	—	115,126 [3]	—	297,092 [3]	—	—	—	3,419	800,620	25,725	—	—	—
1924	—	—	—	71,688 [3]	—	208,102 [3]	—	—	—	3,957	455,376	7,481	—	—	—
1925	—	—	—	43,258 [3]	—	151,878 [3]	—	—	—	5,320	323,260	5,182	—	—	—
1926	—	—	—	21,031 [4]	—	152,584 [4]	—	—	—	14,871 [6]	45,166	3,683	—	—	—
1927	—	—	—	16,908 [4]	—	119,880 [4]	—	—	—	3,223	86,326	5,255	—	—	—
1928	—	—	—	16,224 [4]	—	116,316 [4]	—	—	—	2,310	48,417	2,980	—	—	—
1929	—	—	—	12,891 [4]	—	92,997 [4]	—	—	—	2,900	47,720	-6,392	—	—	—
1930	—	—	—	8,368 [4]	—	58,230 [4]	—	—	—	2,938	33,116	-10,518	—	—	—
1931	—	—	—	4,814 [4]	—	30,400 [4]	—	—	—	3,273	36,949	-16,928	—	—	—
1932	—	—	—	2,979 [4]	—	18,023 [4]	—	—	—	2,438	15,185	-13,771	—	—	—
1933	—	—	—	3,734 [4]	138,810 [4]	18,946 [4]	—	—	—	1,490	9,593	-5,359	—	—	—
1934	—	—	—	4,443 [4]	153,479 [4]	23,786 [4]	—	—	—	1,439 [7]	5,651	-4,150	—	—	—
1935	—	—	—	5,521 [4]	177,125 [4]	30,373 [4]	—	—	—	1,723 [7]	5,519	-8,608	—	—	—
1936	—	—	—	7,403 [4]	315,296 [4]	44,923 [4]	—	—	—	1,679 [7]	7,864	-4,561	—	—	—
1937	—	—	—	6,792 [4]	205,794 [4]	34,636 [4]	—	—	—	1,682 [7]	9,168	-3,490	—	—	—
1938	—	—	—	3,980 [4]	241,236 [4]	25,529 [4]	—	—	—	4,126 [7]	206,104	-9,494	—	—	—
1939	75,835	2,159,271	194,478	49,700	1,171,730	95,794	21,851	877,136	105,451	4,284 [7]	110,405	-6,767	—	—	—
1940	—	—	—	—	—	—	—	—	—	7,033 [7]	124,452	-49,063	—	—	—
1941	—	—	—	67,425	815,149	110,741	—	—	—	7,299 [7]	193,410	-199,968	—	—	—
1942	—	—	—	—	—	—	—	—	—	6,024 [7]	218,573	-5,945	—	—	—
1943	—	—	—	147,660 [5]	1,802,648	272,845	—	—	—	5,252	226,900	7,668	—	—	—
1944	—	—	—	—	—	—	—	—	—	5,101	160,922	8,763	—	—	—
1945	140,922	3,118,880	392,229	122,587	2,420,453	283,422	12,968	532,203	104,473	5,367	166,224	4,334	—	—	—
1946	—	—	—	—	—	—	—	—	—	5,479	212,880	16,804	—	—	—
1947	137,754	2,503,233	330,733	116,363	1,841,557	212,679	15,722	455,811	102,455	5,669	205,865	15,599	—	—	—
1948	—	—	—	—	—	—	—	—	—	4,166	122,107	-422	—	—	—
1949	—	—	—	59,433	692,425	122,595	—	—	—	4,481	108,945	1,834	—	—	—
1950	—	—	—	—	—	—	—	—	—	5,702	118,051	6,865	—	—	—
1951	—	—	—	63,102	558,350	—	—	—	—	5,580	118,672	413	—	—	—
1952	—	—	—	—	—	—	—	—	—	5,655	103,198	1,554	—	—	—
1953	93,472	693,298	105,837	78,844	466,820	76,209	8,178	127,071	35,918	6,450	99,407	-6,290	—	—	—
1954	—	—	—	43,045	273,150	65,280	—	—	—	9,586	125,947	4,748	—	—	—
1955	—	—	—	—	—	—	—	—	—	9,989	111,348	-7,159	—	—	—
1956	—	—	—	—	—	—	—	—	—	12,868	159,909	1,069	—	—	—
1957	94,456	—	211,702	66,209	601,509	127,744	15,162	—	82,562	13,085	207,071	1,396	—	—	—
1958	83,333	—	130,640	57,617	408,085	76,948	12,465	—	52,847	13,251	208,957	845	198	2,553	-423
1959	79,129	1,100,076	119,962	50,333	616,396	76,672	12,265	269,152	41,561	16,531	214,528	1,729	579	14,416	-63

	Total			Proprietorships			Partnerships			Corporations					
										Total			S-corporations		
	Entities	Receipts	Profit	Entities	Receipts	Profit	Entities	Receipts	Profit	Entities	Receipts	Profit	Entities	Receipts	Profit
	Ch142 [1]	Ch143 [1]	Ch144 [1]	Ch145	Ch146	Ch147	Ch148	Ch149	Ch150	Ch151 [2]	Ch152 [2]	Ch153 [2]	Ch154	Ch155	Ch156
Year	Number	Thousand dollars	Thousand dollars	Number	Thousand dollars	Thousand dollars	Number	Thousand dollars	Thousand dollars	Number	Thousand dollars	Thousand dollars	Number	Thousand dollars	Thousand dollars
1960	73,147	805,217	86,088	47,568	533,469	56,671	8,242	145,769	41,947	17,337	125,979	-12,530	480	5,760	56
1961	92,606	1,580,135	177,011	79,421	1,400,160	150,913	5,120	97,831	30,053	8,065	82,144	-3,955	379	5,887	-55
1962	66,842	641,344	83,377	57,509	513,301	93,603	1,577	18,120	3,482	7,756	109,923	-13,708	362	5,074	415
1963	58,353	568,735	64,058	49,268	431,179	71,485	1,179	10,005	1,771	7,906	127,551	-9,198	452	7,999	104
1964	59,167	817,105	96,933	52,272	697,253	94,482	1,413	28,493	5,476	5,482	91,359	-3,025	476	6,585	-815
1965	41,366	401,739	68,193	28,448	177,992	45,921	5,546	128,714	21,357	7,372	95,033	915	578	12,428	561
1966	57,902	715,489	117,740	45,874	510,962	93,112	3,998	90,693	18,698	8,030	113,834	5,930	545	19,354	12,417
1967	60,896	990,884	76,510	40,075	280,472	59,338	5,115	124,809	19,406	15,706	585,603	-2,234	1,821	174,251	-1,085
1968	33,014	305,663	46,829	25,139	148,252	38,864	1,824	37,172	9,965	6,051	120,239	-2,000	161	46,702	1,273
1969	33,916	562,440	58,090	31,818	246,944	50,215	1,200	43,920	5,108	898	271,576	2,767	157	45,348	-810
1970	49,747	881,918	115,656	41,261	431,042	93,741	4,337	200,357	31,951	4,149	250,519	-10,036	834	39,252	-2,663
1971	71,473	1,405,982	70,070	41,924	456,409	75,226	8,111	306,836	29,836	21,438	642,737	-34,992	1,649	31,926	-5,501
1972	63,048	1,948,595	131,495	36,699	722,383	95,606	9,091	311,583	42,979	17,258	914,629	-7,090	2,425	95,763	-1,450
1973	51,134	1,068,278	140,022	43,531	580,396	123,811	1,580	94,666	20,094	6,023	393,216	-3,883	—	—	—
1974	84,071	—	238,663	80,665	1,087,848	204,920	564	—	4,144	2,842	926,337	29,599	—	—	—
1975	20,809	943,936	68,367	18,804	238,083	44,289	304	14,122	957	1,701	691,731	23,121	—	—	—
1976	37,113	—	125,368	34,263	394,626	107,403	25	—	564	2,825	1,356,346	17,401	—	—	—
1977	—	—	—	31,438	383,014	77,030	—	—	—	4,268	3,015,136	-184,657	386	52,577	5,754
1978	42,627	—	321,719	35,519	910,772	157,351	98	—	-77	7,110	5,616,660	164,445	1,781	620,712	17,187
1979	67,157	—	352,976	55,033	1,112,087	248,246	224	—	-3,307	11,900	2,386,149	98,037	1,386	209,141	7,461
1980	88,867	—	292,692	75,376 [5]	1,779,126	322,414	107	—	-1,000	13,384	4,317,300	-28,722	906	435,632	-3,294
1981	119,412	—	442,840	101,074 [5]	3,032,635	449,895	911	—	-37,982	17,427	4,618,127	30,927	3,779	565,395	17,165
1982	109,742	—	282,883	81,493 [5]	2,345,699	462,801	8,115	—	25,969	20,134	4,931,458	-205,909	3,610	467,754	-13,768
1983	195,967	—	485,947	169,492 [5]	4,457,606	455,935	4,443	—	32,770	22,032	4,084,856	-2,858	5,171	487,087	-4,902
1984	210,134	37,186,883	683,718	152,625 [5]	5,194,456	669,410	26,091	24,968,840	88,533	31,418	7,023,587	-74,225	10,576	1,913,829	-36,467
1985	314,495	14,392,063	1,281,217	272,116 [5]	7,836,861	1,403,836	18,023	1,947,865	38,812	24,356	4,607,337	-161,431	7,037	957,441	-21,497
1986	339,773	15,757,465	1,859,957	272,001 [5]	8,285,646	1,785,629	40,329	3,981,016	159,743	27,443	3,490,803	-85,415	6,098	739,038	-68,298
1987	393,492	16,175,011	1,944,523	357,475 [5]	9,939,218	1,857,115	8,250	863,856	121,709	27,767	5,371,937	-34,301	9,303 [9]	1,240,251	52,225
1988	472,711	—	3,593,755	435,372 [5]	14,403,060	3,508,133	18,214	—	216,485	19,125	3,172,428	-130,863	5,426	368,578	-20,768
1989	280,906	—	1,827,134	241,240 [5]	5,240,978	1,554,517	22,777	—	327,096	16,889	2,322,943	-54,479	4,922	330,868	-51,088
1990	224,511	—	748,079	195,361 [5]	2,456,006	846,224	9,133	—	-47,605	20,017	7,321,955	-50,540	5,705	769,452	-4,720
1991	201,827	—	680,978	166,253 [5]	3,253,437	787,645	6,706	—	42,962	28,868	4,027,285	-149,629	13,913	2,000,186	-38,094
1992	256,565	—	1,144,659	232,247 [5]	6,256,366	1,185,580	4,454	—	46,498	19,864	2,523,472	-87,419	5,574	1,405,155	71,977
1993	282,898	—	828,241	265,262 [5]	2,434,914	843,274	2,428	269,739	28,483	15,208	1,676,176	-43,516	5,395	734,035	21,126
1994	183,619	3,842,398	662,843	167,005 [5]	1,819,222	660,948	861	121,821	-18,258	15,753	1,901,355	20,153	4,566	644,883	38,898
1995	199,876	—	—	188,689 [5]	2,693,452	957,193	3,556	—	—	7,631	1,212,287	-6,275	1,791	362,984	-11,519
1996	213,992	—	—	210,174 [5]	2,250,599	882,226	3,552	—	—	10,266	1,411,462	-74,867	3,046	224,366	1,204
1997	182,116	—	—	174,652 [5]	2,084,714	769,023	2,263	—	—	5,201	922,217	-8,240	1,821	173,806	21,991
1998	—	—	—	348,125 [5]	6,058,434	2,082,707	—	—	—	—	—	—	—	—	—

(continued)

[1] Totals have not been generated independently, but are simply summations of the series for proprietorships, partnerships, and corporations.

[2] Includes S-corporations.

[3] Includes only proprietorships with positive net income.

[4] Includes only proprietorships with net income greater than or equal to $5,000.

[5] Number of tax returns rather than the number of businesses.

[6] Includes inactive corporations.

[7] Affiliated corporations filed separate returns.

[8] Gross income instead of total receipts.

[9] Firms that shifted from fiscal to calendar years are counted twice.

TABLE Ch142–156   Active proprietorships, partnerships, and corporations – entities, receipts, and profit: 1918–1998   [All other industries]   *Continued*

Sources
U.S. Internal Revenue Service (and its predecessor, U.S. Bureau of Internal Revenue), *Statistics of Income (SOI)*, various issues; *SOI Bulletin*, various issues; *Statistics of Income Source Book: Partnership Returns*, 1957–1993.

Documentation
See the text for Table Ch1–18.
   "All other industries" is a residual category whose content has fluctuated considerably over time and is particularly liable to sampling error when numbers are small.

TABLE Ch157–168   General partnerships, limited partnerships, and limited liability companies – entities, partners, and profit: 1976–1997   [All industries]

Contributed by Naomi R. Lamoreaux

	All partnerships			General			Limited			Limited liability companies		
	Entities	Partners	Profit	Entities	Partners	Profit	Entities	Partners	Profit	Entities	Partners	Profit
	Ch157	Ch158	Ch159	Ch160	Ch161	Ch162	Ch163	Ch164	Ch165	Ch166	Ch167	Ch168
Year	Number	Number	Thousand dollars	Number	Number	Thousand dollars	Number	Number	Thousand dollars	Number	Number	Thousand dollars
1976	1,096,441	5,370,236	10,422,811	1,019,920 [1]	—	—	76,521	—	—	—	—	—
1977	1,153,398	6,079,860	13,264,168	1,058,220 [1]	4,773,824	—	95,178	1,306,036	—	—	—	—
1978	1,234,157	6,121,455	14,446,809	1,115,508 [1]	—	—	118,649	—	—	—	—	—
1979	1,299,593	6,954,767	15,205,908	1,163,481 [1]	4,602,389 [1]	20,925,444 [1]	136,112	2,352,378	−5,719,536	—	—	—
1980	1,379,654	8,419,899	8,248,655	1,209,318 [1]	4,799,863 [1]	17,641,454 [1]	170,336	3,620,036	−9,392,799	—	—	—
1981	1,460,502	9,095,165	−2,734,897	1,252,298 [1]	4,919,485 [1]	12,956,589 [1]	208,204	4,175,680	−15,691,486	—	—	—
1982	1,514,212	9,764,667	−7,314,587	1,288,326 [1]	5,054,587 [1]	10,173,441 [1]	225,886	4,710,080	−17,488,028	—	—	—
1983	1,541,539	10,589,338	−2,610,041	1,307,552 [1]	5,154,468	16,100,000 [2]	233,986	5,434,870	−18,700,000 [2]	—	—	—
1984	1,643,581	12,426,721	−3,500,024	1,386,417 [1]	5,742,000 [2]	19,133,300 [2]	257,164	6,685,000 [2]	−22,633,300 [2]	—	—	—
1985	1,713,603	13,244,824	−8,883,674	1,433,735 [1]	5,330,000 [2]	18,009,600 [2]	279,868	7,914,000 [2]	−26,893,300 [2]	—	—	—
1986	1,702,952	15,228,530	−17,370,860	1,429,876	5,487,000 [2]	18,146,200 [2]	273,076	9,814,000 [2]	−35,517,100 [2]	—	—	—
1987	1,648,032	16,963,258	19,303,350	1,385,824	5,440,000 [2]	22,750,000 [2]	262,210	11,523,000 [2]	−28,169,000 [2]	—	—	—
1988	1,654,245	17,291,178	14,493,114	1,369,093	5,618,000 [2]	38,503,534	285,152	11,673,000 [2]	−24,010,711	—	—	—
1989	1,635,164	18,431,918	14,099,275	1,341,527	5,208,241	35,660,018	293,637	13,223,676	−21,560,743	—	—	—
1990	1,553,529	17,094,966	16,609,540	1,267,760	5,108,423	37,770,771	285,769	11,986,542	−21,161,231	—	—	—
1991	1,515,345	15,801,047	21,406,607	1,244,665	4,535,511	38,108,885	270,681	11,265,537	−16,702,278	—	—	—
1992	1,484,752	15,734,691	42,916,649	1,214,004	4,421,208	46,194,340	270,748	11,313,483	−3,277,692	—	—	—
1993	1,467,567	15,626,848	66,652,288	1,175,179	4,345,028	55,983,743	275,042	11,197,286	10,405,272	17,335	84,534	263,273
1994	1,493,963	14,989,505	82,183,076	1,163,259	4,394,117	62,236,849	282,888	10,282,762	17,895,002	47,816	312,626	2,051,224
1995	1,580,900	15,605,686	106,829,196	1,167,036	4,669,004	69,402,490	295,304	10,223,901	32,542,951	118,559	712,781	4,883,755
1996	1,654,256	15,662,298	145,218,248	1,116,054	4,565,827	73,539,490	311,563	10,025,630	55,458,035	221,498	1,035,050	12,313,453
1997	1,758,627	16,183,715	168,240,726	1,069,250	4,414,901	79,795,969	328,210	10,167,018	62,946,099	349,054	1,524,256	17,059,601

[1] Calculated by subtracting the number for limited partnerships from the number for all partnerships.

[2] Rounded.

Sources
U.S. Internal Revenue Service, *Statistics of Income (SOI)*, various issues; *SOI Bulletin*, various issues.

Documentation
The IRS first began to collect data on limited partnerships in 1976, when it asked firms organized as such to check a box on the partnership income return. The IRS similarly began to collect information on limited liability companies (LLCs) in 1993. A limited partnership is a partnership consisting of two or more persons, including one or more general partners (that is, partners with unlimited liability and full managerial responsibility) and one or more limited partners (that is, partners with limited liability and no managerial authority). LLCs are entities that combine corporate and partnership attributes. All members of these firms have limited liability, whether they take an active role in management or not. For 1996 and 1997, the total number of partnerships is greater than the sum of general partnerships, limited partnerships, and LLCs because firms filing partnership returns had the option of checking an additional box labeled "other."

See also the text for Table Ch1–18.

TABLE Ch169–180   General partnerships, limited partnerships, and limited liability companies – entities, partners, and profit: 1976–1997   [Agriculture, forestry, and fishing]

Contributed by Naomi R. Lamoreaux

	All partnerships			General			Limited			Limited liability companies		
	Entities	Partners	Profit	Entities	Partners	Profit	Entities	Partners	Profit	Entities	Partners	Profit
	Ch169	Ch170	Ch171	Ch172	Ch173	Ch174	Ch175	Ch176	Ch177	Ch178	Ch179	Ch180
Year	Number	Number	Thousand dollars	Number	Number	Thousand dollars	Number	Number	Thousand dollars	Number	Number	Thousand dollars
1976	121,337	342,934	1,014,820	117,696 [1]	—	—	3,641	—	—	—	—	—
1977	121,042	353,897	791,386	116,546 [1]	306,196	—	4,496	47,701	—	—	—	—
1978	126,938	380,363	1,234,872	122,243 [1]	—	—	4,695	—	—	—	—	—
1979	124,825	375,386	1,061,398	120,344 [1]	322,847 [1]	1,222,620 [1]	4,481	52,539	−161,222	—	—	—
1980	126,224	380,982	471,548	121,079 [1]	325,689 [1]	729,525 [1]	5,145	55,293	−257,977	—	—	—
1981	124,973	405,594	−703,617	118,408 [1]	326,457 [1]	−355,727 [1]	6,565	79,137	−347,890	—	—	—
1982	132,997	449,872	−701,031	123,596 [1]	348,315 [1]	−235,664 [1]	9,401	101,557	−465,367	—	—	—
1983	136,603	466,132	−144,846	127,405 [1]	343,994 [2]	—	9,198	120,494 [2]	—	—	—	—
1984	139,306	494,392	−749,030	129,356 [1]	—	21,400 [3]	9,950	—	−770,400 [3]	—	—	—
1985	135,909	584,789	−1,049,434	126,853 [1]	—	−168,300 [3]	9,056	—	−881,200 [3]	—	—	—
1986	147,532	642,342	−938,402	138,450	—	−100,500 [3]	9,082	—	−837,900 [3]	—	—	—
1987	148,895	592,277	2,015,308	140,927	—	2,290,000 [3]	7,968	—	−275,000 [3]	—	—	—
1988	122,048	554,701	1,078,646	117,443	—	1,170,310	4,605	—	−91,664	—	—	—
1989	131,057	591,133	1,380,245	123,201	344,100	1,876,260	7,856	247,033	−496,016	—	—	—
1990	125,029	502,740	1,666,947	112,775	301,827	1,700,697	12,254	200,912	−33,750	—	—	—
1991	127,073	551,714	1,739,677	117,293	331,784	1,981,930	9,780	219,931	−242,252	—	—	—
1992	124,564	504,317	2,227,039	115,988	331,701	2,270,624	8,576	172,616	−43,585	—	—	—
1993	119,960	588,188	2,018,963	111,013	322,315	2,085,722	8,718	265,124	−29,803	—	—	—
1994	123,147	574,999	1,608,256	111,456	337,167	1,651,375	9,166	230,662	−7,076	2,526	7,169	−36,042
1995	129,105	602,779	1,329,763	114,478	340,934	1,806,269	9,406	247,699	−368,898	5,220	14,147	−107,608
1996	130,845	594,460	1,357,338	110,665	321,297	1,916,258	11,629	247,547	−262,246	8,487	25,103	−313,710
1997	127,060	576,382	1,925,633	102,506	304,389	2,160,390	11,504	227,509	45,452	12,179	42,338	−308,699

[1] Calculated by subtracting the number for limited partnerships from the number for all partnerships.

[2] Calculated by multiplying the number of partners by the reported average number of partners per partnership.

[3] Rounded.

Sources

U.S. Internal Revenue Service, *Statistics of Income* (*SOI*), various issues; *SOI Bulletin*, various issues.

Documentation

See the text for Table Ch157–168.

TABLE Ch181–192   General partnerships, limited partnerships, and limited liability companies – entities, partners, and profit: 1976–1997   [Mining]

Contributed by Naomi R. Lamoreaux

	All partnerships			General			Limited			Limited liability companies		
	Entities	Partners	Profit	Entities	Partners	Profit	Entities	Partners	Profit	Entities	Partners	Profit
	Ch181	Ch182	Ch183	Ch184	Ch185	Ch186	Ch187	Ch188	Ch189	Ch190	Ch191	Ch192
Year	Number	Number	Thousand dollars	Number	Number	Thousand dollars	Number	Number	Thousand dollars	Number	Number	Thousand dollars
1976	17,812	360,777	−46,926	14,039 [1]	—	—	3,773	—	—	—	—	—
1977	21,966	388,273	−550,177	16,952 [1]	143,616	—	5,014	244,657	—	—	—	—
1978	23,629	468,566	−2,857,247	20,363 [1]	—	—	8,266	—	—	—	—	—
1979	28,069	689,445	−2,508,231	18,426 [1]	162,474 [1]	−1,340,854 [1]	9,643	526,971	−1,167,377	—	—	—
1980	35,076	721,879	−4,208,334	21,877 [1]	191,932 [1]	−3,078,617 [1]	13,199	529,947	−1,129,717	—	—	—
1981	51,368	1,475,289	−10,109,096	30,890 [1]	316,599 [1]	−5,419,202 [1]	20,478	1,158,690	−4,689,894	—	—	—
1982	55,766	1,574,375	−8,829,824	35,131 [1]	361,056 [1]	−5,123,442 [1]	20,635	1,213,319	−3,706,382	—	—	—
1983	59,596	2,083,107	−4,109,760	36,117 [1]	949,877 [2]	—	23,418	1,580,715 [2]	—	—	—	—
1984	56,548	2,007,460	69,112	35,520 [1]	—	−662,000 [3]	21,028	—	731,100 [3]	—	—	—
1985	62,363	2,207,066	1,481,701	37,071 [1]	—	171,700 [3]	25,292	—	1,310,000 [3]	—	—	—
1986	53,142	2,350,587	−3,458,320	34,111	—	−2,965,900 [3]	19,031	—	−292,500 [3]	—	—	—
1987	59,925	2,742,346	−1,359,917	40,811	—	−3,633,000 [3]	19,114	—	2,273,000 [3]	—	—	—
1988	48,134	2,466,748	934,191	31,586	—	−1,529,681	16,548	—	2,463,872	—	—	—
1989	45,537	2,770,870	1,965,205	26,868	290,678	53,674	18,669	2,480,193	1,911,532	—	—	—
1990	40,904	2,148,754	2,183,394	21,752	196,390	−576,942	19,152	1,952,364	276,336	—	—	—
1991	39,022	1,414,487	779,487	22,728	216,247	−1,010,792	16,295	1,198,240	1,790,279	—	—	—
1992	36,399	1,388,608	1,008,625	21,254	191,629	−1,031,403	15,145	1,196,978	2,040,028	—	—	—
1993	31,892	1,431,073	2,148,057	18,875	235,156	−323,050	12,839	1,195,174	2,468,763	—	—	—
1994	27,228	1,009,805	984,128	16,526	228,592	−1,185,962	9,931	773,979	2,076,044	711	7,233	94,046
1995	26,107	827,935	1,110,743	14,380	202,987	−779,439	10,240	613,825	1,625,433	1,487	11,124	264,750
1996	25,327	746,362	4,856,365	11,929	140,605	525,249	10,186	592,771	3,665,411	3,192	12,909	674,049
1997	28,045	774,930	6,651,515	12,542	202,910	972,069	10,289	547,021	4,487,166	5,198	24,933	1,194,792

[1] Calculated by subtracting the number for limited partnerships from the number for all partnerships.

[2] Calculated by multiplying the number of partners by the reported average number of partners per partnership.

[3] Rounded.

Sources

U.S. Internal Revenue Service, *Statistics of Income* (SOI), various issues; *SOI Bulletin*, various issues.

Documentation

See the text for Table Ch157–168.

TABLE Ch193–204   General partnerships, limited partnerships, and limited liability companies – entities, partners, and profit: 1976–1997   [Construction]

Contributed by Naomi R. Lamoreaux

	All partnerships			General			Limited			Limited liability companies		
	Entities	Partners	Profit	Entities	Partners	Profit	Entities	Partners	Profit	Entities	Partners	Profit
	Ch193	Ch194	Ch195	Ch196	Ch197	Ch198	Ch199	Ch200	Ch201	Ch202	Ch203	Ch204
Year	Number	Number	Thousand dollars	Number	Number	Thousand dollars	Number	Number	Thousand dollars	Number	Number	Thousand dollars
1976	60,390	138,409	1,139,001	59,412 [1]	—	—	978	—	—	—	—	—
1977	69,217	156,429	1,458,221	67,180 [1]	150,837	—	2,037	5,592	—	—	—	—
1978	78,032	177,685	1,770,242	67,386 [1]	—	—	2,646	—	—	—	—	—
1979	75,275	168,549	2,126,987	73,452 [1]	160,328 [1]	1,979,613 [1]	1,823	8,221	147,374	—	—	—
1980	66,590	160,212	1,560,093	64,176 [1]	142,412 [1]	1,445,758 [1]	2,414	17,800	114,335	—	—	—
1981	69,856	165,054	1,209,222	67,643 [1]	155,132 [1]	165,054 [1]	2,213	9,922	78,302	—	—	—
1982	65,762	151,859	1,419,497	63,098 [1]	141,468 [1]	1,539,164 [1]	2,664	10,391	−119,667	—	—	—
1983	63,592	148,768	2,167,975	62,000 [1]	142,600 [2]	—	1,592	8,438 [2]	—	—	—	—
1984	64,607	173,273	2,193,322	61,583 [1]	—	2,271,100 [3]	3,024	—	−77,700 [3]	—	—	—
1985	56,665	134,034	2,207,401	55,394 [1]	—	2,175,700 [3]	1,271	—	31,700 [3]	—	—	—
1986	61,425	137,404	2,497,759	59,754	—	2,386,700 [3]	1,671	—	111,100 [3]	—	—	—
1987	62,403	153,150	2,766,067	59,066	—	2,587,000 [3]	3,337	—	184,000 [3]	—	—	—
1988	74,559	178,994	3,283,681	71,514	—	2,898,595	3,045	—	385,086	—	—	—
1989	61,950	164,869	2,647,446	60,024	128,479	2,373,229	1,926	36,390	274,217	—	—	—
1990	59,469	161,537	1,907,918	55,789	124,256	2,058,426	3,681	37,282	−150,509	—	—	—
1991	57,195	151,692	1,493,772	55,789	123,689	1,806,689	1,406	28,003	−312,608	—	—	—
1992	59,412	157,934	1,905,787	56,933	129,162	2,056,012	2,478	28,772	−150,226	—	—	—
1993	61,910	154,474	2,175,628	59,290	133,809	2,113,705	1,967	19,128	72,256	—	—	—
1994	65,645	159,367	2,653,523	61,648	137,106	2,384,823	1,802	16,189	176,285	2,195	6,072	92,415
1995	70,727	166,868	2,527,241	61,826	140,812	2,172,962	2,026	9,082	168,725	6,875	16,974	185,554
1996	74,164	178,782	3,114,236	60,043	134,727	2,564,070	2,525	12,122	168,020	11,416	31,538	375,167
1997	72,098	171,110	3,203,649	53,214	118,851	2,343,493	2,749	15,057	274,960	15,771	36,456	582,085

[1] Calculated by subtracting the number for limited partnerships from the number for all partnerships.

[2] Calculated by multiplying the number of partners by the reported average number of partners per partnership.

[3] Rounded.

Sources

U.S. Internal Revenue Service, *Statistics of Income* (*SOI*), various issues; *SOI Bulletin*, various issues.

Documentation

See the text for Table Ch157–168.

TABLE Ch205-216   General partnerships, limited partnerships, and limited liability companies – entities, partners, and profit: 1976-1997   [Manufacturing]

Contributed by Naomi R. Lamoreaux

	All partnerships			General			Limited			Limited liability companies		
	Entities	Partners	Profit	Entities	Partners	Profit	Entities	Partners	Profit	Entities	Partners	Profit
	Ch205	Ch206	Ch207	Ch208	Ch209	Ch210	Ch211	Ch212	Ch213	Ch214	Ch215	Ch216
Year	Number	Number	Thousand dollars	Number	Number	Thousand dollars	Number	Number	Thousand dollars	Number	Number	Thousand dollars
1976	30,767	82,891	470,054	29,922 [1]	—	—	845	—	—	—	—	—
1977	27,996	70,931	461,000	27,160 [1]	67,317	—	836	3,614	—	—	—	—
1978	27,931	75,100	660,015	26,511 [1]	—	—	1,420	—	—	—	—	—
1979	30,454	87,230	484,564	28,893 [1]	71,810 [1]	548,191 [1]	1,561	15,420	−63,627	—	—	—
1980	30,086	91,724	−472,049	28,005 [1]	76,573 [1]	−337,654 [1]	2,081	15,151	−134,395	—	—	—
1981	30,306	90,879	−440,649	28,284 [1]	66,998 [1]	−53,697 [1]	2,022	23,881	−386,952	—	—	—
1982	23,190	76,742	−815,638	21,773 [1]	54,113 [1]	−402,261 [1]	1,417	22,629	−413,377	—	—	—
1983	26,451	90,752	−744,064	25,665 [1]	61,596 [2]	—	786	27,903 [2]	—	—	—	—
1984	29,606	93,601	−1,100,943	28,490 [1]	—	−524,200 [3]	1,116	—	−576,800 [3]	—	—	—
1985	29,980	105,007	−1,085,187	28,419 [1]	—	−839,800 [3]	1,561	—	−245,400 [3]	—	—	—
1986	27,507	107,726	−457,841	25,905	—	−184,100 [3]	1,602	—	−273,700 [3]	—	—	—
1987	34,671	177,793	806,462	31,474	—	587,000 [3]	3,197	—	219,000 [3]	—	—	—
1988	25,885	173,443	1,540,021	24,341	—	1,221,652	1,544	—	318,369	—	—	—
1989	26,263	185,233	1,398,440	24,071	54,070	1,346,021	2,192	131,163	52,419	—	—	—
1990	28,285	246,210	1,165,938	26,695	57,962	873,733	1,590	188,248	292,205	—	—	—
1991	23,974	175,157	904,329	22,028	48,710	1,519,294	1,946	126,447	−614,965	—	—	—
1992	24,074	224,900	1,869,813	22,443	54,581	1,458,677	1,631	170,319	411,136	—	—	—
1993	25,065	231,080	3,939,506	21,829	51,119	2,437,965	2,586	177,677	1,431,982	—	—	—
1994	29,539	223,819	6,584,412	25,472	57,901	3,962,488	2,484	160,766	2,476,058	1,583	5,152	145,867
1995	30,155	223,381	9,221,427	23,716	55,767	5,035,493	2,364	150,352	3,974,454	4,075	17,272	211,480
1996	34,125	233,228	9,696,339	24,793	60,970	5,522,251	2,611	144,689	4,323,879	6,382	26,885	−146,632
1997	40,022	257,845	11,065,708	24,874	55,504	5,882,717	3,210	150,567	4,993,959	11,827	45,458	207,289

[1] Calculated by subtracting the number for limited partnerships from the number for all partnerships.

[2] Calculated by multiplying the number of partners by the reported average number of partners per partnership.

[3] Rounded.

Sources

U.S. Internal Revenue Service, *Statistics of Income* (*SOI*), various issues; *SOI Bulletin*, various issues.

Documentation

See the text for Table Ch157-168.

TABLE Ch217-228   General partnerships, limited partnerships, and limited liability companies – entities, partners, and profit: 1976-1997   [Transportation, communications, and utilities]

Contributed by Naomi R. Lamoreaux

	All partnerships			General			Limited			Limited liability companies		
	Entities	Partners	Profit	Entities	Partners	Profit	Entities	Partners	Profit	Entities	Partners	Profit
	Ch217	Ch218	Ch219	Ch220	Ch221	Ch222	Ch223	Ch224	Ch225	Ch226	Ch227	Ch228
Year	Number	Number	Thousand dollars	Number	Number	Thousand dollars	Number	Number	Thousand dollars	Number	Number	Thousand dollars
1976	16,860	49,079	−98,021	15,921 [1]	—	—	939	—	—	—	—	—
1977	16,837	45,022	202,488	15,908 [1]	39,118	—	929	5,904	—	—	—	—
1978	19,886	55,480	376,590	18,592 [1]	—	—	1,294	—	—	—	—	—
1979	19,778	61,036	367,734	18,374 [1]	46,979 [1]	482,081 [1]	1,404	14,057	−114,347	—	—	—
1980	20,417	73,192	248,387	19,100 [1]	52,599 [1]	356,229 [1]	1,317	20,593	−107,842	—	—	—
1981	21,711	73,005	−227,832	18,992 [1]	47,576 [1]	−548 [1]	2,719	25,429	−227,284	—	—	—
1982	18,448	93,329	−760,761	16,276 [1]	45,153 [1]	−328,408 [1]	2,172	48,176	−432,353	—	—	—
1983	20,132	103,035	−703,495	17,735 [1]	49,658 [2]	—	2,397	52,734 [2]	—	—	—	—
1984	20,578	142,091	−2,007,032	16,184 [1]	—	−1,032,000 [3]	4,394	—	−975,000 [3]	—	—	—
1985	24,970	186,326	−3,066,313	20,729 [1]	—	−1,931,500 [3]	4,241	—	−1,134,800 [3]	—	—	—
1986	21,059	223,272	−3,029,423	18,526	—	−1,614,100 [3]	2,533	—	−1,415,300 [3]	—	—	—
1987	29,843	428,859	−3,781,248	25,077	—	−2,241,000 [3]	4,766	—	−1,540,000 [3]	—	—	—
1988	20,421	433,357	−2,292,315	15,643	—	−755,086	4,778	—	−1,537,229	—	—	—
1989	22,460	434,573	−1,976,583	17,319	63,514	425,342	5,141	371,059	−2,401,925	—	—	—
1990	25,180	503,411	−116,938	21,068	76,828	1,717,524	4,113	426,583	−1,834,462	—	—	—
1991	26,107	519,142	−1,431,340	22,309	79,874	746,509	3,797	439,268	−2,177,849	—	—	—
1992	23,535	527,350	1,053,598	19,433	79,082	1,293,876	4,103	448,268	−240,277	—	—	—
1993	20,757	652,085	4,118,603	16,454	53,720	2,511,828	3,958	592,533	1,582,387	—	—	—
1994	23,426	634,782	5,627,377	18,045	76,149	3,034,160	4,425	520,323	2,355,315	956	38,310	237,903
1995	25,908	655,770	6,749,983	17,295	65,653	3,112,857	5,261	562,243	3,617,791	3,352	27,874	19,336
1996	29,806	646,709	7,051,416	20,050	86,983	4,609,034	4,842	536,737	3,043,358	4,789	22,337	−604,831
1997	30,917	620,597	−1,636,618	18,149	70,957	3,715,227	3,993	505,037	−2,622,505	8,746	44,528	−2,728,429

[1] Calculated by subtracting the number for limited partnerships from the number for all partnerships.

[2] Calculated by multiplying the number of partners by the reported average number of partners per partnership.

[3] Rounded.

Sources

U.S. Internal Revenue Service, *Statistics of Income* (*SOI*), various issues; *SOI Bulletin*, various issues.

Documentation

See the text for Table Ch157-168.

TABLE Ch229–240   General partnerships, limited partnerships, and limited liability companies – entities, partners, and profit: 1976–1997   [Wholesale and retail trade]

Contributed by Naomi R. Lamoreaux

	All partnerships			General			Limited			Limited liability companies		
	Entities	Partners	Profit	Entities	Partners	Profit	Entities	Partners	Profit	Entities	Partners	Profit
	Ch229	Ch230	Ch231	Ch232	Ch233	Ch234	Ch235	Ch236	Ch237	Ch238	Ch239	Ch240
Year	Number	Number	Thousand dollars	Number	Number	Thousand dollars	Number	Number	Thousand dollars	Number	Number	Thousand dollars
1976	195,014	468,773	2,409,252	190,770 [1]	—	—	4,244	—	—	—	—	—
1977	193,312	498,871	2,626,944	188,352 [1]	479,001	—	4,960	19,870	—	—	—	—
1978	200,195	478,481	2,804,927	194,304 [1]	—	—	5,881	—	—	—	—	—
1979	204,916	487,819	2,858,401	198,284 [1]	455,777 [1]	2,690,114 [1]	6,632	32,042	168,287	—	—	—
1980	200,273	487,362	2,474,626	193,213 [1]	455,506 [1]	2,350,563 [1]	7,060	31,856	124,063	—	—	—
1981	216,808	528,483	1,316,933	206,018 [1]	474,822 [1]	1,428,193 [1]	10,790	53,661	−111,260	—	—	—
1982	205,142	490,863	1,600,910	194,064 [1]	444,388 [1]	1,565,531 [1]	11,078	46,475	35,379	—	—	—
1983	194,360	478,893	1,539,779	184,774 [1]	427,259 [2]	—	7,494	50,256 [2]	—	—	—	—
1984	184,841	443,712	1,666,476	173,664 [1]	—	1,621,900 [3]	11,177	—	44,500 [3]	—	—	—
1985	200,532	492,511	1,976,685	190,305 [1]	—	1,798,800 [3]	10,227	—	177,900 [3]	—	—	—
1986	174,118	408,584	2,271,556	164,377	—	2,187,700 [3]	9,741	—	89,900 [3]	—	—	—
1987	184,797	475,961	2,696,840	175,088	—	2,483,000 [3]	9,709	—	214,000 [3]	—	—	—
1988	179,688	490,458	3,351,256	171,998	—	2,635,263	7,690	—	171,998	—	—	—
1989	173,179	495,773	2,528,553	158,024	356,174	2,083,329	15,155	139,599	445,224	—	—	—
1990	175,939	480,927	2,609,860	163,636	363,861	2,492,697	12,303	117,067	117,164	—	—	—
1991	170,963	447,833	2,628,050	157,342	351,055	2,249,053	13,640	96,779	378,997	—	—	—
1992	162,472	425,381	2,552,791	149,823	340,419	1,787,408	12,649	84,962	765,383	—	—	—
1993	157,178	471,412	3,075,840	145,985	337,160	2,314,368	8,744	127,704	898,864	—	—	—
1994	153,310	442,741	4,301,147	139,160	315,036	3,140,618	8,182	108,553	1,244,411	5,968	19,152	−83,882
1995	164,385	500,711	3,996,004	140,482	323,868	2,838,785	8,348	129,671	1,163,978	15,556	47,173	−6,758
1996	168,050	534,451	5,464,154	132,464	299,344	2,865,076	9,408	154,639	2,347,642	26,011	79,533	247,255
1997	173,009	584,212	5,329,996	124,315	285,605	3,586,302	8,317	180,983	2,033,370	40,139	116,942	−321,778

[1] Calculated by subtracting the number for limited partnerships from the number for all partnerships.

[2] Calculated by multiplying the number of partners by the reported average number of partners per partnership.

[3] Rounded.

Sources

U.S. Internal Revenue Service, *Statistics of Income* (*SOI*), various issues; *SOI Bulletin*, various issues.

Documentation

See the text for Table Ch157–168.

TABLE Ch241–252   General partnerships, limited partnerships, and limited liability companies – entities, partners, and profit: 1976–1997   [Finance, insurance, and real estate]

Contributed by Naomi R. Lamoreaux

	All partnerships			General			Limited			Limited liability companies		
	Entities	Partners	Profit	Entities	Partners	Profit	Entities	Partners	Profit	Entities	Partners	Profit
	Ch241	Ch242	Ch243	Ch244	Ch245	Ch246	Ch247	Ch248	Ch249	Ch250	Ch251	Ch252
Year	Number	Number	Thousand dollars	Number	Number	Thousand dollars	Number	Number	Thousand dollars	Number	Number	Thousand dollars
1976	446,988	3,250,369	−268,511	393,505 [1]	—	—	53,483	—	—	—	—	—
1977	476,390	3,814,396	−970,443	410,239 [1]	2,930,881	—	66,151	883,515	—	—	—	—
1978	516,135	3,702,421	113,206	433,314 [1]	—	—	82,821	—	—	—	—	—
1979	577,336	4,271,344	−520,929	479,877 [1]	2,727,185 [1]	3,866,073 [1]	97,459	1,544,159	−4,387,002	—	—	—
1980	637,480	5,566,294	−4,248,776	514,517 [1]	2,803,644 [1]	3,270,328 [1]	122,963	2,762,650	−7,519,104	—	—	—
1981	681,638	5,326,300	−5,360,047	538,029 [1]	2,793,135 [1]	3,496,417 [1]	143,609	2,533,165	−8,856,464	—	—	—
1982	725,622	5,756,896	−11,155,896	572,289 [1]	2,852,562 [1]	−704,594 [1]	153,333	2,904,334	−10,451,302	—	—	—
1983	730,067	5,926,901	−13,105,211	566,683 [1]	2,720,078 [2]	—	163,384	3,185,988 [2]	—	—	—	—
1984	790,902	7,408,313	−19,243,718	607,324 [1]	—	−960,100 [3]	183,578	—	−18,283,700 [3]	—	—	—
1985	843,867	7,754,557	−25,928,669	644,303 [1]	—	−2,967,700 [3]	199,564	—	−22,961,000 [3]	—	—	—
1986	852,705	9,459,473	−32,979,553	653,193	—	−3,505,000 [3]	199,512	—	−29,474,600 [3]	—	—	—
1987	827,521	10,327,352	−26,776,536	637,607	—	−863,000 [3]	189,914	—	−25,914,000 [3]	—	—	—
1988	868,887	10,879,684	−19,257,397	653,456	—	4,991,860	215,432	—	−24,249,548	—	—	—
1989	852,517	11,326,504	−20,823,570	639,507	3,089,859	−2,914,256	213,010	8,236,645	−17,909,314	—	—	—
1990	822,254	10,846,185	−19,212,967	616,875	3,118,136	−247,270	205,379	7,728,049	−18,965,697	—	—	—
1991	803,838	10,316,515	−12,786,397	602,335	2,642,348	982,822	201,502	7,674,167	−13,769,218	—	—	—
1992	797,324	10,328,122	−751,856	593,736	2,565,224	5,537,572	203,587	7,762,898	−6,289,429	—	—	—
1993	792,651	9,944,143	15,260,195	573,273	2,505,659	12,044,694	211,085	7,387,294	3,050,856	8,293	51,190	164,646
1994	809,533	9,880,982	24,124,681	564,455	2,512,433	15,529,196	222,674	7,200,233	7,864,877	22,404	168,317	730,608
1995	848,731	10,316,652	44,521,919	560,099	2,770,558	21,581,993	232,677	7,153,706	19,760,510	55,956	392,387	3,179,416
1996	891,577	10,262,431	69,723,674	536,635	2,810,446	24,511,605	245,358	6,838,804	36,875,024	107,702	600,122	8,232,434
1997	974,223	10,554,864	94,921,837	526,108	2,676,273	30,935,658	266,377	6,986,563	48,180,049	176,328	856,899	13,938,262

[1] Calculated by subtracting the number for limited partnerships from the number for all partnerships.

[2] Calculated by multiplying the number of partners by the reported average number of partners per partnership.

[3] Rounded.

Sources

U.S. Internal Revenue Service, *Statistics of Income (SOI)*, various issues; *SOI Bulletin*, various issues.

Documentation

See the text for Table Ch157–168.

TABLE Ch253–264   General partnerships, limited partnerships, and limited liability companies – entities, partners, and profit: 1976–1997   [Services]

Contributed by Naomi R. Lamoreaux

	All partnerships			General			Limited			Limited liability companies		
	Entities	Partners	Profit	Entities	Partners	Profit	Entities	Partners	Profit	Entities	Partners	Profit
	Ch253	Ch254	Ch255	Ch256	Ch257	Ch258	Ch259	Ch260	Ch261	Ch262	Ch263	Ch264
Year	Number	Number	Thousand dollars	Number	Number	Thousand dollars	Number	Number	Thousand dollars	Number	Number	Thousand dollars
1976	207,248	676,915	7,802,578	198,630 [1]	—	—	8,618	—	—	—	—	—
1977	226,638	752,041	9,244,749	215,883 [1]	656,858	—	10,755	95,183	—	—	—	—
1978	214,313	783,163	10,344,281	229,785 [1]	—	—	11,528	—	—	—	—	—
1979	238,716	813,459	11,339,292	225,621 [1]	654,554 [1]	11,478,555 [1]	13,095	158,905	−139,263	—	—	—
1980	263,400	938,027	12,424,161	247,242 [1]	751,280 [1]	12,906,325 [1]	16,158	186,747	−482,164	—	—	—
1981	262,932	1,024,751	11,618,171	243,238 [1]	733,253 [1]	12,734,351 [1]	19,694	291,498	−1,116,180	—	—	—
1982	279,171	1,146,522	11,902,165	254,478 [1]	787,734 [1]	13,749,299 [1]	24,693	358,788	−1,847,134	—	—	—
1983	306,294	1,274,934	12,456,811	280,756 [1]	870,344 [2]	—	25,538	398,393 [2]	—	—	—	—
1984	331,103	1,577,704	15,583,256	308,986 [1]	—	18,240,800 [3]	22,117	—	−2,657,600 [3]	—	—	—
1985	341,295	1,713,060	16,541,329	313,136 [1]	—	19,700,400 [3]	28,159	—	−3,159,100 [3]	—	—	—
1986	325,134	1,744,294	18,563,621	296,015	—	21,734,900 [3]	29,119	—	−3,171,300 [3]	—	—	—
1987	291,456	2,041,763	18,092,212	267,345	—	21,310,000 [3]	24,111	—	−3,218,000 [3]	—	—	—
1988	296,408	2,060,351	25,638,547	268,008	—	27,652,561	28,400	—	−2,014,014	—	—	—
1989	299,423	2,369,709	26,652,443	270,235	818,138	30,086,239	29,189	1,551,571	−3,433,796	—	—	—
1990	267,336	2,153,169	26,452,993	241,718	822,087	29,793,848	25,617	1,331,082	−3,340,855	—	—	—
1991	260,449	2,206,489	23,036,066	238,217	724,531	29,790,360	22,232	1,481,958	−1,754,293	—	—	—
1992	252,517	2,166,644	33,004,354	229,941	717,999	32,786,982	22,576	1,448,645	217,371	—	—	—
1993	255,726	2,146,425	33,887,012	226,283	698,662	32,774,831	24,906	1,432,113	925,163	4,537	15,650	187,018
1994	261,273	2,059,912	36,317,808	225,676	726,823	33,716,794	24,200	1,271,901	1,729,218	11,397	61,188	871,797
1995	282,225	2,296,467	37,393,680	231,519	754,129	33,648,797	24,857	1,356,976	2,600,928	25,849	185,362	1,143,955
1996	296,808	2,454,595	43,882,573	217,133	705,913	30,959,076	24,772	1,496,407	5,296,679	52,539	232,798	3,853,737
1997	310,990	2,642,024	46,695,598	206,186	695,193	30,165,157	21,348	1,552,713	5,545,489	78,384	355,738	4,455,787

[1] Calculated by subtracting the number for limited partnerships from the number for all partnerships.

[2] Calculated by multiplying the number of partners by the reported average number of partners per partnership.

[3] Rounded.

Sources

U.S. Internal Revenue Service, *Statistics of Income* (*SOI*), various issues; *SOI Bulletin*, various issues.

Documentation

See the text for Table Ch157–168.

TABLE Ch265–292 Firms in operation and new, discontinued, and transferred firms, by industry: 1929–1963[1]

Contributed by Naomi R. Lamoreaux

Year	Firms in operation							New firms						
	All industries	Contract construction	Manufacturing	Wholesale trade	Retail trade	Service	Not elsewhere classified	All industries	Contract construction	Manufacturing	Wholesale trade	Retail trade	Service	Not elsewhere classified
	Ch265	Ch266	Ch267	Ch268	Ch269	Ch270	Ch271	Ch272	Ch273	Ch274	Ch275	Ch276	Ch277	Ch278
	Thousand	Thousand	Thousand	Thousand	Thousand	Thousand	Thousand	Thousand	Thousand	Thousand	Thousand	Thousand	Thousand	Thousand
1929	3,029	234	257	148	1,327	591	472	—	—	—	—	—	—	—
1930	2,994	230	228	147	1,326	599	464	—	—	—	—	—	—	—
1931	2,916	219	195	144	1,317	592	449	—	—	—	—	—	—	—
1932	2,828	202	166	142	1,302	588	428	—	—	—	—	—	—	—
1933	2,782	185	167	142	1,291	575	422	—	—	—	—	—	—	—
1934	2,884	180	188	152	1,337	592	435	—	—	—	—	—	—	—
1935	2,992	180	205	157	1,387	616	447	—	—	—	—	—	—	—
1936	3,070	192	211	165	1,430	629	443	—	—	—	—	—	—	—
1937	3,136	199	214	171	1,469	631	452	—	—	—	—	—	—	—
1938	3,074	193	202	167	1,452	605	455	—	—	—	—	—	—	—
1939	3,222	199	221	176	1,535	615	476	—	—	—	—	—	—	—
1940	3,319	202	222	184	1,580	639	492	275	22	29	20	118	49	37
1941	3,276	194	230	190	1,561	615	486	290	20	31	23	117	62	38
1942	3,295	187	241	201	1,561	620	485	121	8	23	5	39	29	18
1943	3,030	164	243	182	1,401	579	461	146	9	25	8	50	28	26
1944	2,839	147	246	170	1,291	536	449	331	28	27	24	128	71	52
1945	2,995	160	253	186	1,356	567	472	423	56	37	30	161	84	54
1946	3,242	199	264	209	1,458	614	498	617	95	63	45	234	117	64
1947	3,651	268	302	243	1,627	686	523	461	74	40	30	180	90	48
1948	3,873	310	316	254	1,730	728	535	393	65	35	25	151	73	45
1949	3,984	339	322	260	1,783	739	541	331	54	26	21	136	58	37
1950	4,009	353	318	263	1,802	736	536	348	64	30	22	133	56	44
1951	4,067	377	323	269	1,821	733	545	327	54	28	21	123	53	48
1952	4,118	387	328	276	1,831	740	557	346	61	28	21	130	54	50
1953	4,188	405	331	283	1,846	750	573	352	60	28	21	140	56	47
1954	4,240	417	331	288	1,861	760	582	366	62	25	21	147	61	50
1955	4,287	430	326	292	1,874	773	592	408	69	29	22	161	67	59
1956	4,381	452	327	297	1,903	790	612	431	68	31	24	170	73	64
1957	4,471	465	332	304	1,926	810	634	398	57	25	23	166	71	56
1958	4,533	466	329	309	1,955	828	647	397	58	24	22	160	76	56
1959	4,583	464	323	312	1,977	848	658	422	67	27	23	161	82	62
1960	4,658	476	323	317	1,997	872	674	438	66	27	24	170	89	62
1961	4,713	477	322	322	2,011	895	686	431	62	25	25	170	89	61
1962	4,755	473	317	327	2,022	918	698	430	60	25	25	168	91	61
1963	4,797	470	313	332	2,032	942	708	—	—	—	—	—	—	—

Note appears at end of table

(continued)

TABLE Ch265–292 Firms in operation and new, discontinued, and transferred firms, by industry: 1929–1963 Continued

	Discontinued firms							Transferred firms						
	All industries	Contract construction	Manufacturing	Wholesale trade	Retail trade	Service	Not elsewhere classified	All industries	Contract construction	Manufacturing	Wholesale trade	Retail trade	Service	Not elsewhere classified
Year	Ch279	Ch280	Ch281	Ch282	Ch283	Ch284	Ch285	Ch286	Ch287	Ch288	Ch289	Ch290	Ch291	Ch292
	Thousand	Thousand	Thousand	Thousand	Thousand	Thousand	Thousand	Thousand	Thousand	Thousand	Thousand	Thousand	Thousand	Thousand
1929	—	—	—	—	—	—	—	—	—	—	—	—	—	—
1930	—	—	—	—	—	—	—	—	—	—	—	—	—	—
1931	—	—	—	—	—	—	—	—	—	—	—	—	—	—
1932	—	—	—	—	—	—	—	—	—	—	—	—	—	—
1933	—	—	—	—	—	—	—	—	—	—	—	—	—	—
1934	—	—	—	—	—	—	—	—	—	—	—	—	—	—
1935	—	—	—	—	—	—	—	—	—	—	—	—	—	—
1936	—	—	—	—	—	—	—	—	—	—	—	—	—	—
1937	—	—	—	—	—	—	—	—	—	—	—	—	—	—
1938	—	—	—	—	—	—	—	—	—	—	—	—	—	—
1939	—	—	—	—	—	—	—	—	—	—	—	—	—	—
1940	318	30	22	14	138	74	41	241	7	18	6	60	105	44
1941	271	27	21	12	117	56	38	320	10	23	9	74	158	48
1942	386	30	21	24	199	70	43	292	7	17	7	104	121	36
1943	337	26	22	20	160	71	38	250	4	17	7	122	60	39
1944	175	15	20	8	63	40	28	359	7	17	11	227	65	33
1945	176	17	26	7	59	38	28	473	10	21	16	308	83	36
1946	209	26	24	11	66	44	38	627	18	37	26	399	107	39
1947	239	32	27	18	76	49	38	572	18	31	20	375	94	34
1948	282	36	27	19	98	62	38	501	17	29	17	327	79	33
1949	306	41	31	18	116	61	41	435	16	22	16	286	66	29
1950	290	39	25	16	115	58	37	419	15	21	14	278	63	29
1951	276	44	23	13	113	47	37	358	11	16	11	241	53	25
1952	276	43	25	14	115	44	34	370	12	17	13	248	54	27
1953	299	48	28	16	124	46	37	378	14	17	13	253	55	26
1954	319	48	30	18	134	48	40	371	13	15	12	250	53	27
1955	314	47	28	17	133	50	38	384	13	17	13	259	55	28
1956	342	54	26	17	148	53	43	393	14	17	13	261	58	30
1957	335	57	29	17	137	53	43	376	13	15	12	252	56	28
1958	347	59	30	19	138	56	45	371	12	14	11	248	59	27
1959	346	56	27	18	140	59	46	—	—	—	—	—	—	—
1960	384	64	29	19	157	65	49	—	—	—	—	—	—	—
1961	389	65	30	21	159	65	50	—	—	—	—	—	—	—
1962	387	63	29	20	158	67	50	—	—	—	—	—	—	—
1963	—	—	—	—	—	—	—	—	—	—	—	—	—	—

[1] Figures are annual averages through 1939; thereafter, as of January 1.

Sources

1929–1939, U.S. Bureau of Economic Analysis (BEA, formerly Office of Business Economics), *Survey of Current Business* (January 1954): 12; 1940–1950, U.S. Bureau of the Census, *Historical Statistics of the United States* (1975), series V13–19, V31–37; 1951–1958, BEA, *Survey of Current Business* (May 1959): 18; 1959–1963, BEA, *Survey of Current Business* (June 1963): 2.

Documentation

The estimates are based on data from the Bureau of Old-Age and Survivors' Insurance and the Internal Revenue Service, and were revised from time to time by the Bureau of Economic Analysis. The BEA defined a firm as a business organization under one management. A self-employed person was considered a firm only if he or she had either at least one employee or an established place of business. Firms might have more than one plant or outlet, but the BEA made no effort to identify and combine firms owned or controlled by the same interests. The series covers all private nonfarm businesses except those operating in the professional service field. A firm conducting more than one kind of business was assigned to the industry that accounted for the major part of the firm's business.

New firms are businesses that were established during the preceding year. Discontinued firms include closures of all kinds regardless of the reason for going out of business. A firm that was maintained as a business entity but underwent a change of ownership counts as a transferred firm, not as a discontinuance. Partnerships in which a member was added or dropped, corporations that were reorganized or reincorporated, and firms that were sold or otherwise acquired by new owners or that changed their legal form of organization (for example, switched from partnership to corporation) count as transfers.

Series Ch271, Ch278, Ch285, and Ch292. Industries "not elsewhere classified" include the following: mining and quarrying; transportation, communications, and other public utilities; and finance, insurance, and real estate.

INCORPORATIONS, FAILURES, AND BANKRUPTCIES

Naomi R. Lamoreaux

TABLE Ch293–318   Business incorporations, by type of incorporation law: 1800–1943   [Sixteen states]
Contributed by Naomi R. Lamoreaux

Year	Arizona, general laws Ch293 Number	Colorado, general laws Ch294 Number	Connecticut, general laws Ch295 Number	Delaware, general laws Ch296 Number	Florida, general laws Ch297 Number	Illinois, general laws Ch298 Number	Louisiana, general laws Ch299 Number	Maine Total Ch300 Number	Maine Special acts Ch301 Number	Maine General laws Ch302 Number	Maryland Special acts Ch303 Number	Maryland General laws Ch304 Number	Massachusetts, general laws Ch305 Number
1800	—	—	—	—	—	—	—	—	—	—	0	—	—
1801	—	—	—	—	—	—	—	—	—	—	2	—	—
1802	—	—	—	—	—	—	—	—	—	—	0	—	—
1803	—	—	—	—	—	—	—	—	—	—	0	—	—
1804	—	—	—	—	—	—	—	—	—	—	1	—	—
1805	—	—	—	—	—	—	—	—	—	—	10	—	—
1806	—	—	—	—	—	—	—	—	—	—	2	—	—
1807	—	—	—	—	—	—	—	—	—	—	0	—	—
1808	—	—	—	—	—	—	—	—	—	—	5	—	—
1809	—	—	—	—	—	—	—	—	—	—	0	—	—
1810	—	—	—	—	—	—	—	—	—	—	11	—	—
1811	—	—	—	—	—	—	—	—	—	—	0	—	—
1812	—	—	—	—	—	—	—	—	—	—	9	—	—
1813	—	—	—	—	—	—	—	—	—	—	0	—	—
1814	—	—	—	—	—	—	—	—	—	—	11	—	—
1815	—	—	—	—	—	—	—	—	—	—	10	—	—
1816	—	—	—	—	—	—	—	—	—	—	23	—	—
1817	—	—	—	—	—	—	—	—	—	—	10	—	—
1818	—	—	—	—	—	—	—	—	—	—	12	—	—
1819	—	—	—	—	—	—	—	—	—	—	10	—	—
1820	—	—	—	—	—	—	—	3	3	—	2	—	—
1821	—	—	—	—	—	—	—	13	13	—	1	—	—
1822	—	—	—	—	—	—	—	10	10	—	3	—	—
1823	—	—	—	—	—	—	—	13	13	—	8	—	—
1824	—	—	—	—	—	—	—	10	10	—	4	—	—
1825	—	—	—	—	—	—	—	17	17	—	4	—	—
1826	—	—	—	—	—	—	—	18	18	—	7	—	—
1827	—	—	—	—	—	—	—	19	19	—	6	—	—
1828	—	—	—	—	—	—	—	12	12	—	16	—	—
1829	—	—	—	—	—	—	—	17	17	—	21	—	—
1830	—	—	—	—	—	—	—	13	13	—	6	—	—
1831	—	—	—	—	—	—	—	20	20	—	5	—	—
1832	—	—	—	—	—	—	—	21	21	—	22	—	—
1833	—	—	—	—	—	—	—	25	25	—	27	—	—
1834	—	—	—	—	—	—	—	47	47	—	13	—	—
1835	—	—	—	—	—	—	—	24	24	—	9	—	—
1836	—	—	—	—	—	—	—	131	131	—	36	—	—
1837	—	—	12 [1]	—	—	—	—	104	104	—	12	—	—
1838	—	—	23	—	—	—	—	34	34	—	13	—	—
1839	—	—	9	—	—	—	—	14	14	—	35	—	—
1840	—	—	4	—	—	—	—	3	3	—	10	—	—
1841	—	—	10	—	—	—	—	18	18	—	6	—	—
1842	—	—	4	—	—	—	—	11	11	—	4	—	—
1843	—	—	8	—	—	—	—	10	10	—	3	—	—
1844	—	—	9	—	—	—	—	17	17	—	8	—	—
1845	—	—	20	—	—	—	—	30	30	—	12	—	—
1846	—	—	18	—	—	—	—	44	44	—	22	—	—
1847	—	—	26	—	—	—	—	32	32	—	24	—	—
1848	—	—	14	—	—	—	—	27	27	—	34	—	—
1849	—	—	29	—	—	—	—	34	34	—	0	—	—
1850	—	—	38	—	—	—	—	27	27	—	71	—	—
1851	—	—	44	—	—	—	—	8	8	—	0	—	8 [1]
1852	—	—	85	—	—	—	—	52	52	—	18	—	20
1853	—	—	133	—	—	—	—	61	61	—	—	—	21
1854	—	—	106	—	—	—	—	63	63	—	—	—	13

Note appears at end of table

(continued)

TABLE Ch293–318   Business incorporations, by type of incorporation law: 1800–1943   [Sixteen states]   *Continued*

	Arizona, general laws	Colorado, general laws	Connecticut, general laws	Delaware, general laws	Florida, general laws	Illinois, general laws	Louisiana, general laws	Maine			Maryland		Massachusetts, general laws
								Total	Special acts	General laws	Special acts	General laws	
	Ch293	Ch294	Ch295	Ch296	Ch297	Ch298	Ch299	Ch300	Ch301	Ch302	Ch303	Ch304	Ch305
Year	Number	Number	Number	Number	Number	Number	Number	Number	Number	Number	Number	Number	Number
1855	—	—	48	—	—	—	—	33	33	—	—	—	31
1856	—	—	26	—	—	—	—	38	38	—	—	—	26
1857	—	—	28	—	—	—	—	39	39	—	—	—	26
1858	—	—	18	—	—	—	—	14	14	—	—	—	11
1859	—	—	22	—	—	—	—	29	29	—	—	—	20
1860	—	—	26	—	—	—	—	31	31	—	—	—	21
1861	—	—	14	—	—	—	—	16	16	—	—	—	16
1862	—	—	18	—	—	—	—	19	19	—	—	—	20
1863	—	—	27	—	—	—	—	16	16	—	—	—	56
1864	—	—	76	—	—	—	—	33	33	—	—	—	174
1865	—	—	93	—	—	—	—	38	38	—	—	—	136
1866	—	—	123	—	—	—	—	61	61	—	—	—	103
1867	—	—	66	—	—	—	—	55	55	—	—	—	87
1868	—	—	72	—	—	—	—	50	50	—	—	—	89
1869	—	—	68	—	—	—	—	65	65	—	—	—	56
1870	—	—	62	—	—	—	—	79	68	11	—	161	65
1871	—	—	—	—	—	—	—	73	54	19	—	172	84
1872	—	—	—	—	—	—	—	64	58	6	—	163	81
1873	—	—	—	—	—	—	—	91	68	23	—	109	88
1874	—	—	—	—	—	—	—	113	93	20	—	125	80
1875	—	—	—	—	—	—	—	78	66	12	—	80	86
1876	—	—	—	—	—	—	—	25	11	14	—	58	63
1877	—	—	—	—	—	—	—	45	4	41	—	64	80
1878	—	—	—	—	—	—	—	37	9	28	—	63	69
1879	—	—	—	—	—	—	—	66	11	55	—	32	77
1880	—	—	18 [1]	—	—	—	—	262	21	241	—	80	145
1881	—	—	85	—	—	—	—	265	34	231	—	78	149
1882	—	—	83	—	—	—	—	228	0	228	—	79	132
1883	—	—	98	—	—	—	—	258	36	222	—	99	132
1884	—	—	77	—	—	—	—	234	0	234	—	87	143
1885	—	—	90	—	—	—	—	240	32	208	—	92	111
1886	—	—	103	—	—	—	—	252	0	252	—	114	146
1887	—	—	128	—	—	—	—	373	81	292	—	147	153
1888	—	—	110	—	—	—	—	308	0	308	—	142	195
1889	—	—	110	—	—	—	—	466	96	370	—	144	233
1890	—	86 [1]	118	—	—	—	—	476	0	476	—	206	199
1891	—	738	163	—	—	—	—	534	98	436	—	216	203
1892	—	1,164	173	—	—	—	—	519	—	519	—	193	245
1893	—	822	137	—	—	—	—	456	—	456	—	172	227
1894	—	829	141	—	—	—	—	405	—	405	—	188	228
1895	—	1,164	139	—	—	—	—	457	—	457	—	208	251
1896	—	1,841	131	—	—	239 [1]	—	432	—	432	—	172	235
1897	—	990	137	—	—	1,165	—	490	—	490	—	205	259
1898	—	781	165	—	—	1,208	—	452	—	452	—	212	232
1899	—	912	179	421	—	1,319	—	697	—	697	—	252	256
1900	—	1,008	198	552	—	1,373	—	631	—	631	—	247	239
1901	—	983	236	734	132	1,567	—	862	—	862	—	333	254
1902	—	1,047	239	872	141	1,882	—	1,215	—	1,215	—	318	258
1903	—	1,007	276	746	167	2,127	—	1,178	—	1,178	—	301	535
1904	—	931	313	493	211	2,017	—	853	—	853	—	309	1,067
1905	—	990	322	550	305	2,127	—	993	—	993	—	407	1,272
1906	—	1,171	437	587	324	2,261	—	1,042	—	1,042	—	412	1,314
1907	—	1,193	343	671	350	2,189	—	1,027	—	1,027	—	354	1,213
1908	—	1,102 [1]	329	872	253	2,150	—	850	—	850	—	380	1,276
1909	—	—	390	1,318	324	2,331	—	920	—	920	—	539	1,343
1910	—	—	369	1,325	426	2,173	—	722	—	722	—	495	1,283
1911	—	—	421	1,342	470	2,209	—	710	—	710	—	531	1,383
1912	906 [1]	—	437	1,427	523	2,542	—	706	—	706	—	566	1,475
1913	668	—	499	1,613	578	2,587	—	572	—	572	—	541	1,501
1914	530	—	428	1,661	436	2,319	—	528	—	528	—	521	1,595

Note appears at end of table

TABLE Ch293–318   Business incorporations, by type of incorporation law: 1800–1943   [Sixteen states]   *Continued*

Year	Arizona, general laws	Colorado, general laws	Connecticut, general laws	Delaware, general laws	Florida, general laws	Illinois, general laws	Louisiana, general laws	Maine Total	Maine Special acts	Maine General laws	Maryland Special acts	Maryland General laws	Massachusetts, general laws
	Ch293	Ch294	Ch295	Ch296	Ch297	Ch298	Ch299	Ch300	Ch301	Ch302	Ch303	Ch304	Ch305
	Number	Number	Number	Number	Number	Number	Number	Number	Number	Number	Number	Number	Number
1915	656	—	473	1,916	439	2,667	—	485	—	485	—	562	1,719
1916	1,084	—	552	2,521	478	2,815	—	654	—	654	—	580	1,946
1917	1,029	—	527	3,314	488	2,686	—	548	—	548	—	563	1,965
1918	549	—	375	2,460	357	1,650 [1]	—	345	—	345	—	403	1,464
1919	717	—	697	4,731	568	—	—	485	—	485	—	864	2,678
1920	567	—	811	5,716	725	—	—	482	—	482	—	946	2,820
1921	359	—	623	4,527	701	—	—	391	—	391	—	852	2,152 [1]
1922	374	—	713	5,048	668 [1]	—	—	429	—	429	—	881	—
1923	338	—	743	5,030	—	—	—	427	—	427	—	903	—
1924	158 [1]	—	794	4,322	—	—	—	394	—	394	—	934	—
1925	—	—	848	4,997	—	5,591	—	386	—	386	—	1,032	—
1926	—	—	851	4,734	—	5,528	—	349	—	349	—	1,049	—
1927	—	—	933	5,367	—	5,615	—	390	—	390	—	1,045	—
1928	—	—	1,047	6,183	—	6,164	—	367	—	367	—	1,058	—
1929	—	—	1,182	7,474	—	6,410	—	389	—	389	—	1,141	—
1930	—	—	1,043	5,546	—	5,908	—	339	—	339	—	904	—
1931	—	—	1,006	4,166	—	6,262	—	307	—	307	—	870	—
1932	—	—	1,075	3,493	—	5,566	—	287	—	287	—	890	—
1933	—	—	—	2,972	—	5,796	—	352	—	352	—	1,012	—
1934	—	—	—	2,273	—	5,256	—	289	—	289	—	816	—
1935	—	—	—	2,274	—	5,524	—	328	—	328	—	771	—
1936	—	—	—	2,515	—	5,447	—	261	—	261	—	757	—
1937	—	—	—	2,134	—	5,394	745	220	—	220	—	748	—
1938	—	—	—	1,595	—	4,899	572	238	—	238	—	643	—
1939	—	—	—	1,387	—	4,736	491	183	—	183	—	667	—
1940	—	—	—	1,273	—	4,483	443	177	—	177	—	—	—
1941	—	—	—	1,210	—	3,749	395	193	—	193	—	—	—
1942	—	—	—	829	—	2,442	220	120	—	120	—	—	—
1943	—	—	—	832	—	2,339	217	120	—	120	—	—	—

Year	New Jersey Total	New Jersey Special acts	New Jersey General laws	New York Total	New York Special acts	New York General laws	Ohio Total	Ohio Special acts	Ohio General laws	Pennsylvania Special acts	Pennsylvania General laws	Texas, general laws	Virginia, general laws
	Ch306	Ch307	Ch308	Ch309	Ch310	Ch311	Ch312	Ch313	Ch314	Ch315	Ch316	Ch317	Ch318
	Number	Number	Number	Number	Number	Number	Number	Number	Number	Number	Number	Number	Number
1800	2	2	—	5	5	—	—	—	—	0	—	—	—
1801	3	3	—	13	13	—	—	—	—	2	—	—	—
1802	3	3	—	14	14	—	—	—	—	0	—	—	—
1803	0	0	—	9	9	—	2	2	—	6	—	—	—
1804	12	12	—	12	12	—	0	0	—	14	—	—	—
1805	0	0	—	28	28	—	0	0	—	4	—	—	—
1806	9	9	—	25	25	—	0	0	—	6	—	—	—
1807	4	4	—	12	12	—	0	0	—	9	—	—	—
1808	5	5	—	36	36	—	2	2	—	2	—	—	—
1809	5	5	—	25	25	—	3	3	—	13	—	—	—
1810	0	0	—	44	44	—	1	1	—	15	—	—	—
1811	11	11	—	55 [1]	43	12 [1]	1	1	—	17	—	—	—
1812	9	9	—	43	31	12	2	2	—	12	—	—	—
1813	4	4	—	54	25	29	1	1	—	11	—	—	—
1814	9	9	—	68	28	40	3	3	—	69	—	—	—
1815	13	13	—	38	19	19	1	1	—	15	—	—	—
1816	9	9	—	33	23	10	18	18	—	22	—	—	—
1817	2	2	—	32	27	5	18	18	—	23	—	—	—
1818	3	3	—	30	26	4	3	3	—	11	—	—	—
1819	3	3	—	29	28	1	2	2	—	24	—	—	—

Note appears at end of table   (continued)

TABLE Ch293–318   Business incorporations, by type of incorporation law: 1800–1943   [Sixteen states]   *Continued*

	New Jersey			New York			Ohio			Pennsylvania		Texas, general laws	Virginia, general laws
	Total	Special acts	General laws	Total	Special acts	General laws	Total	Special acts	General laws	Special acts	General laws		
	Ch306	Ch307	Ch308	Ch309	Ch310	Ch311	Ch312	Ch313	Ch314	Ch315	Ch316	Ch317	Ch318
Year	Number	Number	Number	Number	Number	Number	Number	Number	Number	Number	Number	Number	Number
1820	2	2	—	10	9	1	2	2	—	9	—	—	—
1821	1	1	—	10	7	3	0	0	—	4	—	—	—
1822	5	5	—	21	18	3	1	1	—	5	—	—	—
1823	5	5	—	38	32	6	0	0	—	11	—	—	—
1824	13	13	—	42	40	2	2	2	—	4	—	—	—
1825	13	13	—	66	56	10	3	3	—	12	—	—	—
1826	5	5	—	35	25	10	8	8	—	30	—	—	—
1827	0	0	—	32	24	8	7	7	—	16	—	—	—
1828	25	25	—	54	44	10	8	8	—	22	—	—	—
1829	5	5	—	46	37	9	12	12	—	18	—	—	—
1830	10	10	—	34	32	2	17	17	—	22	—	—	—
1831	14	14	—	48	40	8	8	8	—	37	—	—	—
1832	11	11	—	73	70	3	37	37	—	39	—	—	—
1833	13	13	—	54	48	6	14	14	—	38	—	—	—
1834	14	14	—	57	47	10	31	31	—	35	—	—	—
1835	13	13	—	38	26	12	38	38	—	30	—	—	—
1836	35	35	—	136	116	20	71	71	—	70	—	—	—
1837	45	45	—	61	44	17	92	92	—	31	—	—	—
1838	9	9	—	32	28	4	55	55	—	64	—	—	—
1839	14	14	—	40	36	4	67	67	—	43	—	—	—
1840	6	6	—	20	15	5	10	10	—	33	—	—	—
1841	6	6	—	29	17	12	9	9	—	31	—	—	—
1842	6	6	—	11	8	3	11	11	—	23	—	—	—
1843	1	1	—	6	6	0	10	10	—	31	—	—	—
1844	7	7	—	31	17	14	29	29	—	40	—	—	—
1845	18	18	—	30	17	13	53	53	—	25	—	—	—
1846	25	21	4 [1]	—	—	—	49	49	—	25	—	—	—
1847	25	20	5	—	—	—	22	22	—	17	—	—	—
1848	33	28	5	—	—	—	80	80	—	51	—	—	—
1849	32	31	1	—	—	—	103	103	—	90	—	—	—
1850	27	20	7	—	—	—	192	192	—	98	—	—	—
1851	54	36	18	—	—	—	170	170	—	131	—	—	—
1852	57	44	13	—	—	—	—	—	—	74	—	—	—
1853	65	46	19	—	—	—	—	—	—	147	—	—	—
1854	72	51	21	—	—	—	—	—	—	126	—	—	—
1855	82	66	16	—	—	—	7 [1]	—	7 [1]	90	—	—	—
1856	49	41	8	—	—	—	64	—	64	91	—	—	—
1857	54	43	11	—	—	—	47	—	47	117	—	—	—
1858	47	27	20	—	—	—	49	—	49	49	—	—	—
1859	54	49	5	—	—	—	97	—	97	122	—	—	—
1860	50	43	7	—	—	—	36	—	36	94	—	—	—
1861	39	37	2	—	—	—	25	—	25	—	—	—	—
1862	33	22	11	—	—	—	26	—	26	—	—	—	—
1863	37	30	7	—	—	—	51	—	51	—	—	—	—
1864	72	60	12	—	—	—	91	—	91	—	—	—	—
1865	77	69	8	—	—	—	358	—	358	—	—	—	—
1866	148	123	25	—	—	—	281	—	281	—	—	—	—
1867	165	140	25	—	—	—	266	—	266	—	—	—	—
1868	161	148	13	—	—	—	295	—	295	—	—	—	—
1869	142	128	14	—	—	—	333	—	333	—	—	—	—
1870	154	135	19	—	—	—	304	—	304	—	—	—	—
1871	149	122	27	—	—	—	336	—	336	—	—	—	—
1872	142	119	23	—	—	—	401	—	401	—	—	47	—
1873	168	133	35	—	—	—	360	—	360	—	—	78	—
1874	121	83	38	—	—	—	298	—	298	—	—	89	—
1875	95	44	51	—	—	—	333	—	333	—	188	199	—
1876	56	—	56	—	—	—	266	—	266	—	163	144	—
1877	64	—	64	—	—	—	237	—	237	—	135	69	—
1878	73	—	73	—	—	—	227	—	227	—	116	78	—
1879	79	—	79	—	—	—	286	—	286	—	155	77	—

Note appears at end of table

TABLE Ch293-318   Business incorporations, by type of incorporation law: 1800-1943   [Sixteen states]   *Continued*

	New Jersey			New York			Ohio			Pennsylvania		Texas, general laws	Virginia, general laws
	Total	Special acts	General laws	Total	Special acts	General laws	Total	Special acts	General laws	Special acts	General laws		
Year	Ch306	Ch307	Ch308	Ch309	Ch310	Ch311	Ch312	Ch313	Ch314	Ch315	Ch316	Ch317	Ch318
	Number	Number	Number	Number	Number	Number	Number	Number	Number	Number	Number	Number	Number
1880	168	—	168	—	—	—	391	—	391	—	215	85	—
1881	449	—	449	—	—	—	508	—	508	—	252	158	—
1882	351	—	351	—	—	—	598	—	598	—	288	187	—
1883	295	—	295	—	—	—	612	—	612	—	344	262	—
1884	232	—	232	—	—	—	477	—	477	—	399	253	—
1885	254	—	254	—	—	—	515	—	515	—	441	221	—
1886	386	—	386	—	—	—	626	—	626	—	482	157	—
1887	472	—	472	—	—	—	832	—	832	—	467	284	—
1888	567	—	567	—	—	—	661	—	661	—	477	264	—
1889	685	—	685	—	—	—	725	—	725	—	717	331	—
1890	897	—	897	—	—	—	768	—	768	—	667	416	—
1891	1,155	—	1,155	—	—	—	834	—	834	—	572	337	—
1892	1,212	—	1,212	—	—	—	854	—	854	—	760	304	—
1893	970	—	970	—	—	—	713	—	713	—	604	321	—
1894	890	—	890	—	—	—	835	—	835	—	578	263	—
1895	964	—	964	—	—	—	872	—	872	—	573	362	—
1896	859	—	859	—	—	—	763	—	763	—	530	325	—
1897	1,118	—	1,118	—	—	—	714	—	714	—	540	342	—
1898	1,104	—	1,104	—	—	—	701	—	701	—	484	315	—
1899	2,186	—	2,186	—	—	—	1,005	—	1,005	—	687	387	—
1900	1,995	—	1,995	—	—	—	1,102	—	1,102	—	854	494	—
1901	2,353	—	2,353	2,670	—	2,670	1,468	—	1,468	—	1,171	1,234	—
1902	2,255	—	2,255	3,577	—	3,577	1,459	—	1,459	—	1,530	873	—
1903	2,035	—	2,035	3,887	—	3,887	1,657	—	1,657	—	1,608	854	369 [1]
1904	1,635	—	1,635	4,420	—	4,420	2,086	—	2,086	—	1,345	852	496
1905	1,872	—	1,872	5,609	—	5,609	2,338	—	2,338	—	1,469	998	718
1906	2,086	—	2,086	6,347	—	6,347	2,397	—	2,397	—	1,528	1,455	967
1907	1,840	—	1,840	6,599	—	6,599	2,306	—	2,306	—	1,611	1,706	896
1908	1,643	—	1,643	7,185	—	7,185	2,146	—	2,146	—	1,114	845	687
1909	2,091	—	2,091	8,328	—	8,328	2,681	—	2,681	—	1,517	1,367	913
1910	1,909	—	1,909	7,998	—	7,998	2,275	—	2,275	—	1,523	1,232	839
1911	1,856	—	1,856	8,357	—	8,357	2,368	—	2,368	—	1,658	1,115	819
1912	1,900	—	1,900	8,668	—	8,668	2,328	—	2,328	—	1,659	1,275	841
1913	1,445	—	1,445	9,090	—	9,090	2,269	—	2,269	—	2,095	1,302	898
1914	1,280	—	1,280	9,327	—	9,327	2,374	—	2,374	—	1,322	991	813
1915	1,428	—	1,428	10,521	—	10,521	2,460	—	2,460	—	1,366	1,143	903
1916	1,622	—	1,622	11,830	—	11,830	3,098	—	3,098	—	1,694	1,174	1,013
1917	1,515	—	1,515	10,536	—	10,536	3,166	—	3,166	—	1,958	1,138	980
1918	1,272	—	1,272	8,504	—	8,504	2,151	—	2,151	—	1,277	765	660
1919	—	—	—	15,274	—	15,274	4,352	—	4,352	—	2,297	1,431	1,322
1920	—	—	—	15,103	—	15,103	4,643	—	4,643	—	2,918	1,097 [1]	1,379
1921	—	—	—	16,097	—	16,097	3,855	—	3,855	—	921 [1]	—	1,051
1922	—	—	—	18,160	—	18,160	4,233	—	4,233	—	—	—	1,103
1923	—	—	—	19,530	—	19,530	4,050	—	4,050	—	—	—	1,157
1924	—	—	—	19,549	—	19,549	3,640	—	3,640	—	—	—	1,051
1925	—	—	—	24,703	—	24,703	4,051	—	4,051	—	—	—	1,077
1926	—	—	—	25,388	—	25,388	3,893	—	3,893	—	—	—	1,023
1927	—	—	—	25,670	—	25,670	3,808	—	3,808	—	—	—	1,032
1928	—	—	—	26,817	—	26,817	4,151	—	4,151	—	—	—	1,154
1929	—	—	—	25,755	—	25,755	4,148	—	4,148	—	—	—	1,114
1930	—	—	—	23,867	—	23,867	3,872	—	3,872	—	—	—	1,028
1931	—	—	—	24,828	—	24,828	3,699	—	3,699	—	—	—	910
1932	—	—	—	24,901	—	24,901	3,463	—	3,463	—	—	—	901
1933	—	—	—	22,659	—	22,659	3,185	—	3,185	—	—	—	815
1934	—	—	—	18,537	—	18,537	2,743	—	2,743	—	—	—	696
1935	—	—	—	18,624	—	18,624	2,677	—	2,677	—	—	—	753
1936	—	—	—	18,805	—	18,805	2,858	—	2,858	—	—	—	698
1937	—	—	—	17,455	—	17,455	—	—	—	—	—	—	744
1938	—	—	—	15,649	—	15,649	—	—	—	—	—	—	626
1939	—	—	—	16,113	—	16,113	—	—	—	—	—	—	689

Note appears at end of table

(continued)

TABLE Ch293–318   Business incorporations, by type of incorporation law: 1800–1943   [Sixteen states]   *Continued*

	New Jersey			New York			Ohio			Pennsylvania		Texas, general laws	Virginia, general laws
	Total	Special acts	General laws	Total	Special acts	General laws	Total	Special acts	General laws	Special acts	General laws		
	Ch306	Ch307	Ch308	Ch309	Ch310	Ch311	Ch312	Ch313	Ch314	Ch315	Ch316	Ch317	Ch318
Year	Number	Number	Number	Number	Number	Number	Number	Number	Number	Number	Number	Number	Number
1940	—	—	—	16,040	—	16,040	—	—	—	—	—	—	741
1941	—	—	—	13,815	—	13,815	—	—	—	—	—	—	622
1942	—	—	—	8,696	—	8,696	—	—	—	—	—	—	—
1943	—	—	—	8,660	—	8,660	—	—	—	—	—	—	—

[1] Not a full year.

Source

George Heberton Evans Jr., *Business Incorporations in the United States, 1800–1943* (National Bureau of Economic Research, 1948), p. 12 and Appendix 3.

Documentation

Evans compiled his figures from published state documents and, in several instances, from lists of incorporations produced by other scholars. Unfortunately, these sources do not provide a comprehensive record of business incorporations in these sixteen states. Many years are missing, and the coverage is often incomplete. To give a few examples, there is no information at all on the large numbers of corporations chartered by special legislative acts in Connecticut and Massachusetts; the Illinois series does not include building and loan associations; and the Texas series misses on average approximately ten railroad corporations per year. Nonetheless, Evans worked hard to ensure comparability from year to year within each of his series. Evans defined business incorporations to be those with authorized capitalizations greater than zero, thereby excluding mutual insurance companies and other similar enterprises from his figures. Wherever the official documents classified corporations according to whether they were business enterprises or not, Evans accepted these designations (though, to be consistent, he excluded mutual insurance companies from the business category). In the event that neither authorized capital figures nor state classifications were available, he used the corporations' names to decide whether they were business enterprises. Evans's figures exclude recharters and renewals but include most reorganizations. Because some corporate charters were never actually taken up, the number of incorporations is not the same as the number of new corporate enterprises in existence.

At the beginning of the nineteenth century, the grant of a corporate charter required a special act of the legislature, but over time there was a shift toward general incorporation laws, and many states ultimately adopted constitutional provisions prohibiting incorporation by special act. Arizona adopted such a clause in 1911, Colorado in 1876, Delaware in 1897, Florida in 1900, Illinois in 1848, Louisiana in 1845, Maine in 1875 (though incorporation by special act nonetheless continued through 1891), Maryland in 1851, New Jersey in 1875, New York in 1846, Ohio in 1851, Pennsylvania in 1873, Texas in 1876, and Virginia in 1902. Connecticut and Massachusetts never adopted such provisions. See Evans's Table 5 for additional information.

TABLE Ch319–329   Authorized capital stock of business incorporations under general laws: 1846–1943
[Eleven states]

Contributed by Naomi R. Lamoreaux

Year	Colorado Ch319 Thousand dollars	Delaware Ch320 [1] Thousand dollars	Florida Ch321 Thousand dollars	Illinois Ch322 Thousand dollars	Maryland Ch323 Thousand dollars	Massachusetts Ch324 Thousand dollars	New Jersey Ch325 Thousand dollars	Ohio Ch326 Thousand dollars	Pennsylvania Ch327 Thousand dollars	Texas Ch328 Thousand dollars	Virginia Ch329 Thousand dollars
1846	—	—	—	—	—	—	275 [2]	—	—	—	—
1847	—	—	—	—	—	—	770	—	—	—	—
1848	—	—	—	—	—	—	700	—	—	—	—
1849	—	—	—	—	—	—	300	—	—	—	—
1850	—	—	—	—	—	—	680	—	—	—	—
1851	—	—	—	—	—	410 [2]	6,556	—	—	—	—
1852	—	—	—	—	—	986	2,665	—	—	—	—
1853	—	—	—	—	—	2,032	5,652	—	—	—	—
1854	—	—	—	—	—	783	4,469	—	—	—	—
1855	—	—	—	—	—	1,726	2,368	—	—	—	—
1856	—	—	—	—	—	1,812	1,815	—	—	—	—
1857	—	—	—	—	—	1,700	3,250	—	—	—	—
1858	—	—	—	—	—	564	5,670	—	—	—	—
1859	—	—	—	—	—	1,775	735	—	—	—	—
1860	—	—	—	—	—	3,525	916	—	—	—	—
1861	—	—	—	—	—	746	300	—	—	—	—
1862	—	—	—	—	—	1,211	3,258	—	—	—	—
1863	—	—	—	—	—	10,878	590	—	—	—	—
1864	—	—	—	—	—	43,878	2,891	—	—	—	—
1865	—	—	—	—	—	26,316	753	—	—	—	—
1866	—	—	—	—	—	14,451	4,776	—	—	—	—
1867	—	—	—	—	—	9,722	14,596	—	—	—	—
1868	—	—	—	—	—	10,870	1,660	—	—	—	—
1869	—	—	—	—	—	6,455	1,290	—	—	—	—
1870	—	—	—	—	30,765	6,085	3,605	—	—	—	—
1871	—	—	—	—	31,089	9,738	6,602	8,015 [2]	—	—	—
1872	—	—	—	—	36,838	10,588	7,095	135,665	—	19,976	—
1873	—	—	—	—	28,724	8,677	27,901	75,236	—	13,844	—
1874	—	—	—	—	31,656	6,310	16,954	68,574	—	13,028	—
1875	—	—	—	—	19,650	5,503	7,904	96,287	—	31,473	—
1876	—	—	—	—	10,838	4,101	10,022	48,068	—	22,779	—
1877	—	—	—	—	14,145	13,328	9,523	47,067	—	9,235	—
1878	—	—	—	—	17,414	6,091	37,299	54,471	—	4,918	—
1879	—	—	—	—	6,763	6,038	17,318	101,358	—	8,067	—
1880	—	—	—	—	20,014	19,733	146,124	104,007	—	27,290	—
1881	—	—	—	—	35,559	14,799	417,003	377,840	—	24,593	—
1882	—	—	—	—	23,827	9,351	433,781	247,145	—	34,378	—
1883	—	—	—	—	27,422	9,713	132,725	211,476	—	39,800	—
1884	—	—	—	—	26,753	9,676	56,613	143,732	—	29,451	—
1885	—	—	—	—	14,532	5,463	36,892	107,727	—	33,907	—
1886	—	—	—	—	25,951	5,513	84,704	157,333	—	8,163	—
1887	—	—	—	—	33,717	6,406	145,893	225,281	56,485 [2]	23,961	—
1888	—	—	—	—	49,171	10,594	170,460	114,433	95,641	41,568	—
1889	—	—	—	—	35,605	10,670	172,824	202,521	158,911	35,542	—
1890	23,929 [2]	—	—	—	40,407	7,935	400,625	214,017	123,059	44,391	—
1891	270,371	—	—	—	30,464	8,920	407,505	122,405	81,181	46,595	—
1892	560,778	—	—	—	15,607	13,702	390,086	109,492	130,773	26,719	—
1893	299,365	—	—	—	36,731	10,175	328,939	158,620	91,663	23,594	—
1894	256,538	—	—	—	37,873	9,038	179,259	59,973	141,011	14,145	—
1895	651,726	—	—	—	57,300	12,120	179,713	109,341	106,041	21,519	—
1896	1,417,374	—	—	8,563 [2]	50,912	8,624	194,999	87,120	65,462	15,204	—
1897	345,844	—	—	83,183	31,389	9,059	420,343	51,013	69,942	11,868	—
1898	199,883	—	—	99,201	36,609	8,057	810,089	52,812	46,973	12,097	—
1899	314,392	—	—	121,702	49,259	13,780	3,261,908	130,579	73,431	14,470	—
1900	328,330	—	—	127,937	35,645	9,675	1,329,803	79,633	96,514	22,991	—
1901	330,207	—	8,733	83,924	33,009	13,156	1,779,846	126,262	104,025	276,168	—
1902	360,592	—	12,635	82,016	24,142	10,906	1,517,655	106,328	138,691	86,932	—
1903	330,121	—	10,198	130,320	18,141	126,714	999,951	113,469	147,068	49,144	28,844 [2]
1904	256,240	—	12,998	63,216	15,935	67,429	641,559	129,807	108,529	44,772	64,917

Notes appear at end of table

(continued)

TABLE Ch319–329   Authorized capital stock of business incorporations under general laws: 1846–1943
[Eleven states]   *Continued*

Year	Colorado Ch319 Thousand dollars	Delaware Ch320 [1] Thousand dollars	Florida Ch321 Thousand dollars	Illinois Ch322 Thousand dollars	Maryland Ch323 Thousand dollars	Massachusetts Ch324 Thousand dollars	New Jersey Ch325 Thousand dollars	Ohio Ch326 Thousand dollars	Pennsylvania Ch327 Thousand dollars	Texas Ch328 Thousand dollars	Virginia Ch329 Thousand dollars
1905	229,640	—	23,719	72,869	31,061	64,902	769,070	189,335	109,661	44,416	49,186
1906	306,254	—	29,626	72,599	27,907	87,618	596,115	171,300	157,600	62,535	175,214
1907	270,375	—	24,792	60,114	25,958	61,214	304,371	130,920	161,263	67,025	114,990
1908	293,971 [2]	—	14,713	71,629	12,662	53,491	480,233	91,378	86,779	20,523	56,477
1909	—	—	17,758	163,789	21,541	71,098	644,583	111,225	134,519	44,843	97,488
1910	—	—	36,249	71,285	50,136	71,404	310,056	122,445	176,967	42,812	87,743
1911	—	—	41,163	57,373	29,256	114,857	364,372	119,979	174,763	48,758	140,740
1912	—	—	44,565	66,967	30,368	224,908	428,214	135,256	169,261	51,695	373,241
1913	—	—	44,196	110,012	28,800	161,408	228,754	88,073	203,060	41,384	212,385
1914	—	—	19,983	44,865	28,209	119,423	95,560	446,897	414,170	44,946	196,415
1915	—	—	23,412	53,536	65,451	119,506	105,178	97,368	169,085	28,479	275,931
1916	—	2,272,500	27,974	60,898	155,380	267,480	149,626	244,520	457,754	54,564	579,429
1917	—	3,764,200	33,786	73,400	138,636	176,656	170,683	212,696	414,337	62,410	446,474
1918	—	1,830,300	27,255	51,665 [2]	66,637	114,181	246,853	117,354	123,077	58,419	149,725
1919	—	11,077,900	47,920	—	266,929	305,632	—	138,618 [2]	609,451	163,669	—
1920	—	12,311,200	74,126	—	702,173	472,994	—	—	1,023,208	83,572 [2]	—
1921	—	6,591,900	69,911	—	246,560	241,202 [2]	—	—	273,294 [2]	—	—
1922	—	9,128,500	55,713 [2]	—	580,500	—	—	—	—	—	—
1923	—	8,124,600	—	—	711,095	—	—	—	—	—	—
1924	—	6,190,500	—	—	1,532,522	—	—	—	—	—	—
1925	—	10,793,500	—	—	3,544,195	—	—	—	—	—	—
1926	—	12,911,900	—	—	4,700,909	—	—	—	—	—	—
1927	—	14,222,200	—	—	1,070,086	—	—	—	—	—	—
1928	—	29,086,100	—	—	3,400,656	—	—	—	—	—	—
1929	—	85,723,400	—	—	7,670,131	—	—	—	—	—	—
1930	—	23,762,000	—	—	1,355,490	—	—	—	—	—	—
1931	—	9,790,400	—	—	408,078	—	—	—	—	—	—
1932	—	4,090,500	—	—	228,691	—	—	—	—	—	—
1933	—	3,224,400	—	—	259,542	—	—	—	—	—	—
1934	—	1,056,100	—	—	63,043	—	—	—	—	—	—
1935	—	1,276,400	—	—	65,992	—	—	—	—	—	—
1936	—	2,595,200	—	—	103,251	—	—	—	—	—	—
1937	—	1,379,600	—	—	291,558	—	—	—	—	—	—
1938	—	726,500	—	—	80,497	—	—	—	—	—	—
1939	—	585,800	—	—	59,710	—	—	—	—	—	—
1940	—	344,400	—	—	—	—	—	—	—	—	—
1941	—	275,300	—	—	—	—	—	—	—	—	—
1942	—	278,800	—	—	—	—	—	—	—	—	—
1943	—	367,400	—	—	—	—	—	—	—	—	—

[1] Rounded to nearest hundred thousand.

[2] Not a full year.

Source

George Heberton Evans Jr., *Business Incorporations in the United States, 1800–1943* (National Bureau of Economic Research, 1948), Appendix 3.

Documentation

See the text for Table Ch293–318.

Laws authorizing the use of nonpar shares were passed in Delaware in 1915, Maryland in 1916, Massachusetts around 1919, and Virginia in 1919. In calculating authorized capital for corporations with such issues, Evans treated the shares as if they had a par value of $100.

TABLE Ch330–379 Business incorporations, by industry: 1800–1930   [Five states]

Contributed by Naomi R. Lamoreaux

Year	Maryland										New Jersey					
	Total	Agriculture, forestry, and fishing	Mining	Construction	Manufacturing	Transportation, communications, and utilities	Wholesale and retail trade	Finance, insurance, and real estate	Services	Miscellaneous	Total	Agriculture, forestry, and fishing	Mining	Construction	Manufacturing	Transportation, communications, and utilities
	Ch330	Ch331	Ch332	Ch333	Ch334	Ch335	Ch336	Ch337	Ch338	Ch339	Ch340	Ch341	Ch342	Ch343	Ch344	Ch345
	Number	Number	Number	Number	Number	Number	Number	Number	Number	Number	Number	Number	Number	Number	Number	Number
1800	0	0	0	0	0	0	0	0	0	0	2	0	0	0	0	2
1801	2	0	0	0	0	2	0	0	0	0	3	0	0	0	1	2
1802	0	0	0	0	0	0	0	0	0	0	3	0	0	0	0	3
1803	0	0	0	0	0	0	0	0	0	0	0	0	0	0	0	0
1804	1	0	0	0	0	1	0	0	0	0	12	0	0	0	0	8
1805	10	0	0	0	0	5	0	5	0	0	0	0	0	0	0	0
1806	2	0	0	0	0	1	0	1	0	0	9	0	0	0	0	9
1807	0	0	0	0	0	0	0	0	0	0	4	0	0	0	0	3
1808	5	0	0	0	1	2	0	2	0	0	5	0	0	0	0	5
1809	0	0	0	0	0	0	0	0	0	0	5	0	0	0	1	4
1810	11	0	0	0	1	4	1	5	0	0	0	0	0	0	0	0
1811	0	0	0	0	0	0	0	0	0	0	11	0	1	0	1	9
1812	9	0	0	0	1	5	0	3	0	0	9	0	0	0	0	3
1813	0	0	0	0	0	0	0	0	0	0	4	0	0	0	1	3
1814	11	0	0	0	2	4	0	5	0	0	9	0	0	0	4	5
1815	10	0	0	0	5	4	0	1	0	0	13	0	0	0	4	7
1816	23	0	0	0	5	13	1	4	0	0	9	0	0	0	1	7
1817	10	0	1	0	1	8	0	1	0	0	2	0	0	0	0	2
1818	12	0	1	0	0	8	0	4	0	0	3	0	0	0	0	1
1819	10	0	4	0	1	7	0	2	0	0	3	0	0	0	0	3
1820	2	0	0	0	0	2	0	0	0	0	2	0	1	0	0	1
1821	1	0	0	0	0	1	0	0	0	0	1	0	0	0	1	0
1822	3	0	0	0	2	1	0	0	0	0	5	0	0	0	0	2
1823	8	0	0	0	4	4	0	0	0	0	5	0	0	0	1	2
1824	4	0	0	0	1	3	0	0	0	0	13	0	1	0	3	2
1825	4	0	0	0	1	3	0	0	0	0	13	1	1	0	3	6
1826	7	0	1	0	1	5	0	1	0	0	5	1	1	0	1	1
1827	6	0	0	0	2	2	0	1	0	0	0	0	0	0	0	0
1828	16	0	1	0	2	9	0	4	0	0	25	0	5	0	9	6
1829	21	1	4	0	4	9	0	3	0	0	5	0	0	0	4	1
1830	6	0	0	0	1	3	0	1	1	0	10	0	1	0	1	5
1831	5	0	1	0	1	2	0	1	0	0	14	0	1	0	2	9
1832	22	0	0	0	2	11	0	9	0	0	11	0	1	0	2	5
1833	27	0	0	0	1	8	0	18	0	0	13	0	1	0	8	4
1834	13	0	0	0	3	5	0	5	0	0	14	0	2	0	1	6
1835	9	0	0	0	6	2	0	1	0	0	13	0	1	0	5	4
1836	36	0	7	0	8	4	0	14	3	0	35	0	1	0	17	15
1837	12	0	1	0	2	6	0	2	1	0	45	0	1	0	21	13
1838	13	0	0	0	9	0	0	4	0	0	9	1	0	0	3	1
1839	35	0	4	0	25	3	0	2	1	0	14	1	1	0	5	6
1840	10	0	0	0	6	4	0	0	0	0	6	0	0	0	4	2
1841	6	0	2	0	0	2	0	1	1	0	6	1	1	0	2	3
1842	4	0	0	0	1	2	0	0	1	0	6	0	0	0	3	2
1843	3	0	0	0	0	3	0	0	0	0	1	0	0	0	1	0
1844	8	0	1	0	2	3	0	2	0	0	7	0	0	0	1	4

(continued)

TABLE Ch330–379   Business incorporations, by industry: 1800–1930   [Five states]   *Continued*

	Maryland										New Jersey					
	Total	Agriculture, forestry, and fishing	Mining	Construction	Manufacturing	Transportation, communications, and utilities	Wholesale and retail trade	Finance, insurance, and real estate	Services	Miscellaneous	Total	Agriculture, forestry, and fishing	Mining	Construction	Manufacturing	Transportation, communications, and utilities
	Ch330	Ch331	Ch332	Ch333	Ch334	Ch335	Ch336	Ch337	Ch338	Ch339	Ch340	Ch341	Ch342	Ch343	Ch344	Ch345
Year	Number	Number	Number	Number	Number	Number	Number	Number	Number	Number	Number	Number	Number	Number	Number	Number
1845	12	0	2	0	6	4	0	0	0	0	18	0	0	0	9	9
1846	22	0	5	0	8	7	0	2	0	0	25 [1]	0 [1]	1 [1]	0 [1]	18 [1]	5 [1]
1847	24	0	2	0	12	8	0	2	0	0	25	0	2	0	12	7
1848	34	1	9	0	3	16	0	5	0	0	33	0	9	0	6	14
1849	0	0	0	0	0	0	0	0	0	0	32	0	1	0	1	24
1850	71	0	11	0	11	25	0	23	1	0	27	0	0	0	7	17
1851	0	0	0	0	0	0	0	0	0	0	54	0	0	0	6	29
1852	18	0	2	0	0	12	0	3	1	0	57	0	0	0	12	35
1853	—	—	—	—	—	—	—	—	—	—	65	0	1	0	15	39
1854	—	—	—	—	—	—	—	—	—	—	72	0	3	0	20	37
1855	—	—	—	—	—	—	—	—	—	—	82	1	2	0	24	31
1856	—	—	—	—	—	—	—	—	—	—	49	0	1	0	15	25
1857	—	—	—	—	—	—	—	—	—	—	54	0	1	0	14	24
1858	—	—	—	—	—	—	—	—	—	—	47	0	0	0	15	18
1859	—	—	—	—	—	—	—	—	—	—	54	1	0	0	10	32
1860	—	—	—	—	—	—	—	—	—	—	50	0	3	0	15	24
1861	—	—	—	—	—	—	—	—	—	—	39	0	0	0	9	22
1862	—	—	—	—	—	—	—	—	—	—	33	0	0	0	6	16
1863	—	—	—	—	—	—	—	—	—	—	37	0	3	0	15	16
1864	—	—	—	—	—	—	—	—	—	—	72	0	1	1	27	32
1865	—	—	—	—	—	—	—	—	—	—	77	1	17	0	30	22
1866	—	—	—	—	—	—	—	—	—	—	148	3	12	1	44	55
1867	—	—	—	—	—	—	—	—	—	—	165	6	19	1	47	48
1868	—	—	—	—	—	—	—	—	—	—	161	7	6	1	52	48
1869	—	—	—	—	—	—	—	—	—	—	142	7	4	0	51	45
1870	—	—	—	—	—	—	—	—	—	—	154	6	4	1	47	47
1871	—	—	—	—	—	—	—	—	—	—	149	5	9	1	30	32
1872	—	—	—	—	—	—	—	—	—	—	142	8	4	2	40	32
1873	—	—	—	—	—	—	—	—	—	—	168	6	6	2	49	40
1874	—	—	—	—	—	—	—	—	—	—	121	1	4	2	37	28
1875	—	—	—	—	—	—	—	—	—	—	95	1	0	0	32	26
1876	—	—	—	—	—	—	—	—	—	—	56	2	4	0	23	20
1877	—	—	—	—	—	—	—	—	—	—	64	0	2	0	35	10
1878	—	—	—	—	—	—	—	—	—	—	73	1	4	1	30	19
1879	—	—	—	—	—	—	—	—	—	—	79	2	5	1	42	19
1880	—	—	—	—	—	—	—	—	—	—	168	0	26	10	69	45
1881	—	—	—	—	—	—	—	—	—	—	449	3	107	48	185	61
1882	—	—	—	—	—	—	—	—	—	—	351	3	55	27	182	43
1883	—	—	—	—	—	—	—	—	—	—	295	10	17	19	147	48
1884	—	—	—	—	—	—	—	—	—	—	232	6	9	5	128	49
1885	—	—	—	—	—	—	—	—	—	—	254	5	12	8	143	44
1886	—	—	—	—	—	—	—	—	—	—	386	7	13	25	200	74
1887	—	—	—	—	—	—	—	—	—	—	472	6	30	36	235	55
1888	—	—	—	—	—	—	—	—	—	—	567	4	23	22	322	72
1889	—	—	—	—	—	—	—	—	—	—	685	6	22	34	370	98

	Maryland										New Jersey					
	Total	Agriculture, forestry, and fishing	Mining	Construction	Manufacturing	Transportation, communications, and utilities	Wholesale and retail trade	Finance, insurance, and real estate	Services	Miscellaneous	Total	Agriculture, forestry, and fishing	Mining	Construction	Manufacturing	Transportation, communications, and utilities
	Ch330	Ch331	Ch332	Ch333	Ch334	Ch335	Ch336	Ch337	Ch338	Ch339	Ch340	Ch341	Ch342	Ch343	Ch344	Ch345
Year	Number	Number	Number	Number	Number	Number	Number	Number	Number	Number	Number	Number	Number	Number	Number	Number
1890	—	—	—	—	—	—	—	—	—	—	897	11	28	36	538	88
1891	—	—	—	—	—	—	—	—	—	—	1,155	7	44	47	658	91
1892	—	—	—	—	—	—	—	—	—	—	1,212	13	44	41	694	105
1893	—	—	—	—	—	—	—	—	—	—	970	11	36	40	525	93
1894	—	—	—	—	—	—	—	—	—	—	890	13	43	24	506	89
1895	—	—	—	—	—	—	—	—	—	—	964	5	31	40	517	103
1896	—	—	—	—	—	—	—	—	—	—	859	9	44	30	456	97
1897	—	—	—	—	—	—	—	—	—	—	1,118	10	92	59	552	108
1898	—	—	—	—	—	—	—	—	—	—	1,104	4	59	43	582	115
1899	—	—	—	—	—	—	—	—	—	—	2,186	25	176	76	1,100	224
1900	—	—	—	—	—	—	—	—	—	—	1,995	25	172	66	1,062	183
1901	—	—	—	—	—	—	—	—	—	—	2,353	23	200	105	1,236	221
1902	—	—	—	—	—	—	—	—	—	—	2,255	28	190	107	1,142	161
1903	—	—	—	—	—	—	—	—	—	—	2,035	30	129	92	1,021	135
1904	—	—	—	—	—	—	—	—	—	—	1,635	16	102	70	754	111
1905	—	—	—	—	—	—	—	—	—	—	1,872	26	87	124	751	136
1906	—	—	—	—	—	—	—	—	—	—	2,086	31	85	131	749	99
1907	—	—	—	—	—	—	—	—	—	—	1,840	16	71	140	659	82
1908	—	—	—	—	—	—	—	—	—	—	—	—	—	—	—	—
1909	—	—	—	—	—	—	—	—	—	—	—	—	—	—	—	—
1910	—	—	—	—	—	—	—	—	—	—	—	—	—	—	—	—
1911	—	—	—	—	—	—	—	—	—	—	—	—	—	—	—	—
1912	—	—	—	—	—	—	—	—	—	—	—	—	—	—	—	—
1913	—	—	—	—	—	—	—	—	—	—	—	—	—	—	—	—
1914	—	—	—	—	—	—	—	—	—	—	—	—	—	—	—	—
1915	—	—	—	—	—	—	—	—	—	—	—	—	—	—	—	—
1916	—	—	—	—	—	—	—	—	—	—	—	—	—	—	—	—
1917	—	—	—	—	—	—	—	—	—	—	—	—	—	—	—	—
1918	—	—	—	—	—	—	—	—	—	—	—	—	—	—	—	—
1919	—	—	—	—	—	—	—	—	—	—	—	—	—	—	—	—
1920	—	—	—	—	—	—	—	—	—	—	—	—	—	—	—	—
1921	—	—	—	—	—	—	—	—	—	—	—	—	—	—	—	—
1922	—	—	—	—	—	—	—	—	—	—	—	—	—	—	—	—
1923	—	—	—	—	—	—	—	—	—	—	—	—	—	—	—	—
1924	—	—	—	—	—	—	—	—	—	—	—	—	—	—	—	—
1925	—	—	—	—	—	—	—	—	—	—	—	—	—	—	—	—
1926	—	—	—	—	—	—	—	—	—	—	—	—	—	—	—	—
1927	—	—	—	—	—	—	—	—	—	—	—	—	—	—	—	—
1928	—	—	—	—	—	—	—	—	—	—	—	—	—	—	—	—
1929	—	—	—	—	—	—	—	—	—	—	—	—	—	—	—	—
1930	—	—	—	—	—	—	—	—	—	—	—	—	—	—	—	—

Note appears at end of table

(continued)

TABLE Ch330–379 Business incorporations, by industry: 1800–1930 [Five states] Continued

	New Jersey				New York										Ohio		
	Wholesale and retail trade	Finance, insurance, and real estate	Services	Miscellaneous	Total	Agriculture, forestry, and fishing	Mining	Construction	Manufacturing	Transportation, communications, and utilities	Wholesale and retail trade	Finance, insurance, and real estate	Services	Miscellaneous	Total	Agriculture, forestry, and fishing	Mining
Year	Ch346	Ch347	Ch348	Ch349	Ch350	Ch351	Ch352	Ch353	Ch354	Ch355	Ch356	Ch357	Ch358	Ch359	Ch360	Ch361	Ch362
	Number	Number	Number	Number	Number	Number	Number	Number	Number	Number	Number	Number	Number	Number	Number	Number	Number
1800	0	0	0	0	5	0	0	0	0	5	0	0	0	0	—	—	—
1801	0	0	0	0	13	0	0	0	0	11	0	2	0	0	—	—	—
1802	0	0	0	0	14	0	0	0	0	13	0	1	0	0	—	—	—
1803	0	0	0	0	9	0	0	0	0	8	0	1	0	0	2	0	0
1804	0	4	0	0	12	0	0	0	0	12	0	0	0	0	0	0	0
1805	0	0	0	0	28	0	0	0	0	26	0	2	0	0	0	0	0
1806	0	0	0	0	25	0	0	0	0	25	0	0	0	0	0	0	0
1807	0	1	0	0	12	0	0	0	0	10	1	2	0	0	0	0	0
1808	0	0	0	0	36	0	0	0	1	33	0	1	0	0	2	0	0
1809	0	0	0	0	25	0	0	0	8	16	0	1	0	0	3	0	0
1810	0	0	0	0	44	0	1	0	15	25	0	3	0	1	1	0	0
1811	0	0	0	0	55	0	1	0	24	22	1	7	1	1	1	0	0
1812	0	6	0	0	43	0	3	0	15	22	0	3	0	0	2	0	0
1813	0	0	0	0	54	0	2	0	33	14	1	4	0	0	1	0	0
1814	0	0	0	0	68	0	2	0	46	16	0	4	0	0	3	0	0
1815	0	2	0	0	38	0	0	0	20	16	0	2	0	0	1	0	0
1816	0	1	0	0	33	0	0	0	11	19	0	3	0	0	18	0	0
1817	0	0	0	0	32	0	0	0	5	21	0	6	0	0	18	0	0
1818	0	2	0	0	30	0	0	0	5	19	0	6	0	0	3	0	0
1819	0	0	0	0	29	0	0	0	1	23	0	5	0	0	2	0	0
1820	0	0	0	0	10	0	0	0	1	8	0	1	0	0	2	0	1
1821	0	0	0	0	10	0	0	0	3	3	0	4	0	0	0	0	0
1822	0	2	0	1	21	0	0	0	4	12	0	5	0	0	1	0	0
1823	0	1	0	1	38	0	2	0	7	23	2	4	0	0	0	0	0
1824	0	6	0	1	42	0	2	0	3	23	0	14	0	0	2	0	0
1825	0	2	0	0	66	0	0	0	18	24	0	24	0	0	3	0	0
1826	0	1	0	0	35	0	2	0	15	17	0	1	0	0	8	0	0
1827	0	0	0	2	32	0	0	0	12	20	0	0	0	0	7	0	0
1828	0	5	0	1	54	0	1	0	15	37	1	0	0	0	8	0	0
1829	0	0	0	1	46	0	0	0	10	23	0	13	0	0	12	0	0
1830	1	2	0	0	34	0	0	0	6	16	0	12	0	0	17	0	0
1831	0	2	0	0	48	1	2	0	11	21	0	15	0	0	8	0	0
1832	0	3	0	0	73	2	2	0	15	39	0	15	0	0	37	0	0
1833	0	0	0	0	54	3	0	0	12	20	0	19	0	0	14	0	0
1834	0	5	0	0	57	1	0	0	16	28	0	12	0	0	31	0	0
1835	1	1	0	1	38	0	0	0	19	18	0	1	0	0	38	0	0
1836	0	1	0	1	136	1	1	0	33	76	0	26	0	0	71	0	0
1837	0	8	0	2	61	0	2	0	20	36	1	2	0	0	92	0	1
1838	0	3	0	1	32	2	1	0	10	15	0	4	0	0	55	0	3
1839	0	2	0	0	40	2	2	0	12	17	0	9	0	0	67	0	0
1840	0	0	0	0	20	0	0	0	6	12	0	2	0	0	10	0	0
1841	0	0	0	0	29	0	1	0	16	10	0	2	0	0	9	0	0
1842	0	0	0	0	11	0	0	0	3	6	0	2	0	0	11	0	0
1843	0	0	0	0	6	0	0	0	—	6	0	0	0	0	10	0	0
1844	0	2	0	0	31	0	0	0	14	17	0	0	0	0	29	0	0

	New Jersey				New York										Ohio		
	Wholesale and retail trade	Finance, insurance, and real estate	Services	Miscellaneous	Total	Agriculture, forestry, and fishing	Mining	Construction	Manufacturing	Transportation, communications, and utilities	Wholesale and retail trade	Finance, insurance, and real estate	Services	Miscellaneous	Total	Agriculture, forestry, and fishing	Mining
Year	Ch346	Ch347	Ch348	Ch349	Ch350	Ch351	Ch352	Ch353	Ch354	Ch355	Ch356	Ch357	Ch358	Ch359	Ch360	Ch361	Ch362
	Number	Number	Number	Number	Number	Number	Number	Number	Number	Number	Number	Number	Number	Number	Number	Number	Number
1845	0	0	0	0¹	30	0	0	0	14	15	1	0	0	0	53	0	0
1846	0¹	1¹	0¹	0¹	—	—	—	—	—	—	—	—	—	—	49	0	1
1847	0	3	1	0	—	—	—	—	—	—	—	—	—	—	22	0	0
1848	0	4	0	0	—	—	—	—	—	—	—	—	—	—	80	0	0
1849	0	4	2	0	—	—	—	—	—	—	—	—	—	—	103	0	0
1850	0	1	2	0	—	—	—	—	—	—	—	—	—	—	192	0	1
1851	0	18	1	0	—	—	—	—	—	—	—	—	—	—	170	0	1
1852	0	8	2	1	—	—	—	—	—	—	—	—	—	—	—	—	—
1853	0	6	3	1	—	—	—	—	—	—	—	—	—	—	—	—	—
1854	0	9	3	0	—	—	—	—	—	—	—	—	—	—	—	—	—
1855	0	24	0	0	—	—	—	—	—	—	—	—	—	—	—	—	—
1856	0	6	2	0	—	—	—	—	—	—	—	—	—	—	64	0	6
1857	0	15	0	2	—	—	—	—	—	—	—	—	—	—	47	0	7
1858	0	10	3	1	—	—	—	—	—	—	—	—	—	—	49	0	3
1859	0	11	0	0	—	—	—	—	—	—	—	—	—	—	97	0	1
1860	0	7	1	0	—	—	—	—	—	—	—	—	—	—	36	0	5
1861	1	4	3	0	—	—	—	—	—	—	—	—	—	—	25	0	9
1862	0	11	0	0	—	—	—	—	—	—	—	—	—	—	26	0	2
1863	1	2	0	0	—	—	—	—	—	—	—	—	—	—	51	0	4
1864	0	3	8	0	—	—	—	—	—	—	—	—	—	—	91	0	36
1865	1	4	2	0	—	—	—	—	—	—	—	—	—	—	358	0	245
1866	1	23	9	0	—	—	—	—	—	—	—	—	—	—	281	0	106
1867	0	35	7	2	—	—	—	—	—	—	—	—	—	—	266	0	25
1868	2	37	8	0	—	—	—	—	—	—	—	—	—	—	295	1	28
1869	1	25	8	1	—	—	—	—	—	—	—	—	—	—	333	1	47
1870	2	40	5	2	—	—	—	—	—	—	—	—	—	—	304	0	32
1871	1	65	4	2	—	—	—	—	—	—	—	—	—	—	336	0	25
1872	0	43	8	5	—	—	—	—	—	—	—	—	—	—	401	2	56
1873	2	52	9	2	—	—	—	—	—	—	—	—	—	—	360	1	35
1874	3	30	13	3	—	—	—	—	—	—	—	—	—	—	298	2	35
1875	2	19	13	2	—	—	—	—	—	—	—	—	—	—	333	0	30
1876	1	2	4	2	—	—	—	—	—	—	—	—	—	—	266	1	17
1877	5	8	3	1	—	—	—	—	—	—	—	—	—	—	237	0	6
1878	0	9	8	1	—	—	—	—	—	—	—	—	—	—	227	8	13
1879	0	4	6	0	—	—	—	—	—	—	—	—	—	—	286	2	24
1880	2	8	8	0	—	—	—	—	—	—	—	—	—	—	391	1	34
1881	1	30	12	2	—	—	—	—	—	—	—	—	—	—	508	2	29
1882	7	17	14	3	—	—	—	—	—	—	—	—	—	—	598	10	42
1883	8	29	12	5	—	—	—	—	—	—	—	—	—	—	612	7	30
1884	4	18	11	2	—	—	—	—	—	—	—	—	—	—	477	9	29
1885	9	15	13	5	—	—	—	—	—	—	—	—	—	—	515	5	38
1886	17	23	23	4	—	—	—	—	—	—	—	—	—	—	626	7	72
1887	15	53	33	9	—	—	—	—	—	—	—	—	—	—	832	3	163
1888	25	62	28	9	—	—	—	—	—	—	—	—	—	—	661	2	49
1889	27	83	31	14	—	—	—	—	—	—	—	—	—	—	725	8	44

Note appears at end of table

(continued)

TABLE Ch330–379   Business incorporations, by industry: 1800–1930   [Five states]   *Continued*

	New Jersey				New York										Ohio		
	Wholesale and retail trade	Finance, insurance, and real estate	Services	Miscellaneous	Total	Agriculture, forestry, and fishing	Mining	Construction	Manufacturing	Transportation, communications, and utilities	Wholesale and retail trade	Finance, insurance, and real estate	Services	Miscellaneous	Total	Agriculture, forestry, and fishing	Mining
Year	Ch346	Ch347	Ch348	Ch349	Ch350	Ch351	Ch352	Ch353	Ch354	Ch355	Ch356	Ch357	Ch358	Ch359	Ch360	Ch361	Ch362
	Number	Number	Number	Number	Number	Number	Number	Number	Number	Number	Number	Number	Number	Number	Number	Number	Number
1890	52	83	47	14	—	—	—	—	—	—	—	—	—	—	768	11	51
1891	88	133	74	13	—	—	—	—	—	—	—	—	—	—	834	9	55
1892	102	122	73	18	—	—	—	—	—	—	—	—	—	—	854	4	51
1893	98	90	65	12	—	—	—	—	—	—	—	—	—	—	713	12	37
1894	72	61	66	16	—	—	—	—	—	—	—	—	—	—	835	6	62
1895	95	87	70	16	—	—	—	—	—	—	—	—	—	—	872	8	70
1896	69	76	62	16	—	—	—	—	—	—	—	—	—	—	763	5	94
1897	91	90	88	28	—	—	—	—	—	—	—	—	—	—	714	5	66
1898	92	112	76	21	—	—	—	—	—	—	—	—	—	—	701	3	37
1899	244	162	129	50	—	—	—	—	—	—	—	—	—	—	1,005	5	116
1900	175	160	116	36	—	—	—	—	—	—	—	—	—	—	1,102	1	118
1901	190	240	106	32	—	—	—	—	—	—	—	—	—	—	1,468	5	114
1902	195	257	138	37	—	—	—	—	—	—	—	—	—	—	1,459	11	149
1903	209	240	142	37	—	—	—	—	—	—	—	—	—	—	1,657	5	186
1904	194	221	108	59	—	—	—	—	—	—	—	—	—	—	2,086	22	209
1905	248	283	137	80	—	—	—	—	—	—	—	—	—	—	2,338	21	193
1906	358	345	176	112	—	—	—	—	—	—	—	—	—	—	2,397	15	145
1907	258	390	154	70	—	—	—	—	—	—	—	—	—	—	2,306	12	152
1908	—	—	—	—	—	—	—	—	—	—	—	—	—	—	2,146	18	241
1909	—	—	—	—	—	—	—	—	—	—	—	—	—	—	2,681	25	353
1910	—	—	—	—	—	—	—	—	—	—	—	—	—	—	2,275	29	168
1911	—	—	—	—	—	—	—	—	—	—	—	—	—	—	2,368	24	137
1912	—	—	—	—	—	—	—	—	—	—	—	—	—	—	2,328	15	117
1913	—	—	—	—	—	—	—	—	—	—	—	—	—	—	2,269	19	114
1914	—	—	—	—	—	—	—	—	—	—	—	—	—	—	2,374	16	265
1915	—	—	—	—	—	—	—	—	—	—	—	—	—	—	2,460	27	134
1916	—	—	—	—	—	—	—	—	—	—	—	—	—	—	3,098	19	175
1917	—	—	—	—	—	—	—	—	—	—	—	—	—	—	3,166	22	360
1918	—	—	—	—	—	—	—	—	—	—	—	—	—	—	2,151	16	229
1919	—	—	—	—	—	—	—	—	—	—	—	—	—	—	4,352	30	226
1920	—	—	—	—	—	—	—	—	—	—	—	—	—	—	4,643	51	374
1921	—	—	—	—	—	—	—	—	—	—	—	—	—	—	3,855	28	256
1922	—	—	—	—	—	—	—	—	—	—	—	—	—	—	4,233	19	197
1923	—	—	—	—	—	—	—	—	—	—	—	—	—	—	4,050	37	185
1924	—	—	—	—	—	—	—	—	—	—	—	—	—	—	3,640	36	136
1925	—	—	—	—	—	—	—	—	—	—	—	—	—	—	4,051	28	137
1926	—	—	—	—	—	—	—	—	—	—	—	—	—	—	3,893	34	96
1927	—	—	—	—	—	—	—	—	—	—	—	—	—	—	3,808	42	113
1928	—	—	—	—	—	—	—	—	—	—	—	—	—	—	4,151	54	119
1929	—	—	—	—	—	—	—	—	—	—	—	—	—	—	4,148	46	130
1930	—	—	—	—	—	—	—	—	—	—	—	—	—	—	3,872	50	94

Ohio

Pennsylvania

Year	Construction Ch363 Number	Manufacturing Ch364 Number	Transportation, communications, and utilities Ch365 Number	Wholesale, and retail trade Ch366 Number	Finance, insurance, and real estate Ch367 Number	Services Ch368 Number	Miscellaneous Ch369 Number	Total Ch370 Number	Agriculture, forestry, and fishing Ch371 Number	Mining Ch372 Number	Construction Ch373 Number	Manufacturing Ch374 Number	Transportation, communications, and utilities Ch375 Number	Wholesale, and retail trade Ch376 Number	Finance, insurance, and real estate Ch377 Number	Services Ch378 Number	Miscellaneous Ch379 Number
1800	—	—	—	—	—	—	—	—	—	—	—	—	—	—	—	—	—
1801	—	—	—	—	—	—	—	—	—	—	—	—	—	—	—	—	—
1802	—	—	—	—	—	—	—	—	—	—	—	—	—	—	—	—	—
1803	0	0	0	0	1	0	1	—	—	—	—	—	—	—	—	—	—
1804	0	0	0	0	0	0	0	—	—	—	—	—	—	—	—	—	—
1805	0	0	0	0	0	0	0	—	—	—	—	—	—	—	—	—	—
1806	0	0	0	0	0	0	0	—	—	—	—	—	—	—	—	—	—
1807	0	0	0	0	0	0	0	—	—	—	—	—	—	—	—	—	—
1808	0	0	0	0	2	0	0	—	—	—	—	—	—	—	—	—	—
1809	0	0	2	0	1	0	0	—	—	—	—	—	—	—	—	—	—
1810	0	0	1	0	0	0	0	—	—	—	—	—	—	—	—	—	—
1811	0	1	0	0	0	0	1	—	—	—	—	—	—	—	—	—	—
1812	0	0	0	0	2	0	1	—	—	—	—	—	—	—	—	—	—
1813	0	0	0	0	1	0	0	—	—	—	—	—	—	—	—	—	—
1814	0	1	2	0	0	0	0	—	—	—	—	—	—	—	—	—	—
1815	0	0	1	0	0	0	0	—	—	—	—	—	—	—	—	—	—
1816	0	0	5	0	12	0	1	—	—	—	—	—	—	—	—	—	—
1817	0	0	12	0	5	0	1	—	—	—	—	—	—	—	—	—	—
1818	0	1	1	0	1	0	0	—	—	—	—	—	—	—	—	—	—
1819	0	0	1	0	1	0	0	—	—	—	—	—	—	—	—	—	—
1820	0	0	1	0	0	0	0	—	—	—	—	—	—	—	—	—	—
1821	0	0	0	0	0	0	0	—	—	—	—	—	—	—	—	—	—
1822	0	0	1	0	0	0	0	—	—	—	—	—	—	—	—	—	—
1823	0	0	0	0	0	0	0	—	—	—	—	—	—	—	—	—	—
1824	0	2	2	0	3	1	0	—	—	—	—	—	—	—	—	—	—
1825	0	0	3	0	2	0	0	—	—	—	—	—	—	—	—	—	—
1826	0	1	5	0	2	0	0	—	—	—	—	—	—	—	—	—	—
1827	0	0	6	0	1	0	0	—	—	—	—	—	—	—	—	—	—
1828	0	0	8	0	0	0	0	—	—	—	—	—	—	—	—	—	—
1829	0	2	7	0	3	0	0	—	—	—	—	—	—	—	—	—	—
1830	0	6	9	0	2	0	0	—	—	—	—	—	—	—	—	—	—
1831	0	1	4	0	3	0	0	—	—	—	—	—	—	—	—	—	—
1832	0	5	29	0	3	0	1	—	—	—	—	—	—	—	—	—	—
1833	0	1	11	0	2	0	1	—	—	—	—	—	—	—	—	—	—
1834	0	3	13	0	14	1	0	—	—	—	—	—	—	—	—	—	—
1835	0	11	22	0	4	1	1	—	—	—	—	—	—	—	—	—	—
1836	0	9	55	0	5	1	1	—	—	—	—	—	—	—	—	—	—
1837	0	26	55	0	8	1	1	—	—	—	—	—	—	—	—	—	—
1838	0	11	38	0	2	0	1	—	—	—	—	—	—	—	—	—	—
1839	0	16	47	0	4	0	0	—	—	—	—	—	—	—	—	—	—
1840	0	2	8	0	0	0	0	—	—	—	—	—	—	—	—	—	—
1841	0	0	9	0	0	0	0	—	—	—	—	—	—	—	—	—	—
1842	0	2	8	0	1	0	0	—	—	—	—	—	—	—	—	—	—
1843	0	1	3	0	6	0	0	—	—	—	—	—	—	—	—	—	—
1844	0	2	22	0	5	0	0	—	—	—	—	—	—	—	—	—	—

(continued)

TABLE Ch330–379   Business incorporations, by industry: 1800–1930   [Five states]   *Continued*

	Ohio							Pennsylvania									
	Construction	Manufacturing	Transportation, communications and utilities	Wholesale and retail trade	Finance, insurance, and real estate	Services	Miscellaneous	Total	Agriculture, forestry, and fishing	Mining	Construction	Manufacturing	Transportation, communications, and utilities	Wholesale and retail trade	Finance, insurance, and real estate	Services	Miscellaneous
Year	Ch363	Ch364	Ch365	Ch366	Ch367	Ch368	Ch369	Ch370	Ch371	Ch372	Ch373	Ch374	Ch375	Ch376	Ch377	Ch378	Ch379
	Number	Number	Number	Number	Number	Number	Number	Number	Number	Number	Number	Number	Number	Number	Number	Number	Number
1845	0	4	42	0	7	0	0	—	—	—	—	—	—	—	—	—	—
1846	0	5	38	0	5	0	0	—	—	—	—	—	—	—	—	—	—
1847	0	1	19	0	2	0	0	—	—	—	—	—	—	—	—	—	—
1848	0	1	73	0	5	1	0	—	—	—	—	—	—	—	—	—	—
1849	0	1	94	0	8	0	0	—	—	—	—	—	—	—	—	—	—
1850	0	0	176	0	14	1	0	—	—	—	—	—	—	—	—	—	—
1851	0	7	137	0	17	8	0	—	—	—	—	—	—	—	—	—	—
1852	—	—	—	—	—	—	—	—	—	—	—	—	—	—	—	—	—
1853	—	—	—	—	—	—	—	—	—	—	—	—	—	—	—	—	—
1854	—	—	—	—	—	—	—	—	—	—	—	—	—	—	—	—	—
1855	—	—	—	—	—	—	—	—	—	—	—	—	—	—	—	—	—
1856	0	13	38	0	3	0	4	—	—	—	—	—	—	—	—	—	—
1857	0	17	17	0	2	0	4	—	—	—	—	—	—	—	—	—	—
1858	0	10	31	0	3	0	2	—	—	—	—	—	—	—	—	—	—
1859	0	15	72	0	8	0	1	—	—	—	—	—	—	—	—	—	—
1860	0	6	21	0	3	1	0	—	—	—	—	—	—	—	—	—	—
1861	0	2	14	0	0	0	0	—	—	—	—	—	—	—	—	—	—
1862	0	10	10	0	2	0	2	—	—	—	—	—	—	—	—	—	—
1863	0	12	26	0	6	0	3	—	—	—	—	—	—	—	—	—	—
1864	0	14	22	0	13	0	6	—	—	—	—	—	—	—	—	—	—
1865	0	29	42	0	28	4	10	—	—	—	—	—	—	—	—	—	—
1866	1	66	62	1	15	5	25	—	—	—	—	—	—	—	—	—	—
1867	6	71	74	5	53	6	26	—	—	—	—	—	—	—	—	—	—
1868	4	74	74	5	91	8	10	—	—	—	—	—	—	—	—	—	—
1869	1	88	76	5	85	10	20	—	—	—	—	—	—	—	—	—	—
1870	6	106	80	0	64	9	7	—	—	—	—	—	—	—	—	—	—
1871	0	128	85	2	89	6	1	—	—	—	—	—	—	—	—	—	—
1872	2	149	98	4	66	20	4	—	—	—	—	—	—	—	—	—	—
1873	1	160	60	3	90	10	0	—	—	—	—	—	—	—	—	—	—
1874	0	108	48	4	71	29	1	—	—	—	—	—	—	—	—	—	—
1875	4	92	62	12	95	32	6	—	—	—	—	—	—	—	—	—	—
1876	3	72	53	29	57	34	0	—	—	—	—	—	—	—	—	—	—
1877	1	80	61	12	41	36	0	—	—	—	—	—	—	—	—	—	—
1878	0	75	63	4	35	27	2	—	—	—	—	—	—	—	—	—	—
1879	1	119	64	4	47	24	1	—	—	—	—	—	—	—	—	—	—
1880	2	185	76	9	60	22	2	—	—	—	—	—	—	—	—	—	—
1881	10	207	154	14	63	24	5	—	—	—	—	—	—	—	—	—	—
1882	4	300	89	21	94	32	6	—	—	—	—	—	—	—	—	—	—
1883	4	302	89	17	115	43	5	—	—	—	—	—	—	—	—	—	—
1884	1	220	69	22	65	60	2	—	—	—	—	—	—	—	—	—	—
1885	4	238	80	19	65	44	22	—	—	—	—	—	—	—	—	—	—
1886	3	254	123	35	79	47	6	—	—	—	—	—	—	—	—	—	—
1887	4	296	164	54	102	40	6	—	—	—	—	—	—	—	—	—	—
1888	7	313	96	35	109	47	3	477	0	52	2	187	89	1	141	4	1
1889	6	337	123	46	111	46	4	717	1	74	1	243	167	1	221	6	3

Ohio

Year	Construction Ch363	Manufacturing Ch364	Transportation, communications, and utilities Ch365	Wholesale and retail trade Ch366	Finance, insurance, and real estate Ch367	Services Ch368	Miscellaneous Ch369
	Number	Number	Number	Number	Number	Number	Number
1890	6	387	106	46	115	38	8
1891	6	429	94	65	112	60	4
1892	8	451	89	77	89	78	7
1893	16	379	83	87	55	35	9
1894	16	418	104	86	75	59	9
1895	12	399	116	88	90	81	8
1896	12	353	69	87	69	69	5
1897	18	330	90	58	70	66	11
1898	24	335	106	79	59	50	8
1899	27	426	163	96	89	75	8
1900	21	501	178	82	125	75	1
1901	38	628	249	137	203	89	5
1902	34	657	197	119	179	88	25
1903	39	730	217	134	207	117	22
1904	62	1,023	180	208	176	174	32
1905	74	1,125	218	252	256	168	31
1906	91	1,108	215	307	298	204	14
1907	84	1,021	146	337	312	211	31
1908	71	938	116	310	249	186	17
1909	84	1,062	139	395	309	277	37
1910	84	936	116	372	337	201	32
1911	82	1,019	101	380	344	248	33
1912	78	918	106	423	375	257	39
1913	79	845	105	464	334	265	44
1914	100	811	94	439	339	265	45
1915	101	821	116	524	384	313	40
1916	126	1,023	131	665	590	336	33
1917	158	936	131	707	520	300	32
1918	67	729	92	526	285	183	24
1919	146	1,538	171	858	911	423	49
1920	156	1,542	159	955	932	408	66
1921	159	1,226	132	862	744	379	69
1922	164	1,389	145	883	987	409	40
1923	174	1,145	185	882	1,024	362	56
1924	176	948	152	809	940	393	50
1925	186	1,016	176	981	1,058	419	50
1926	238	950	192	1,035	888	437	23
1927	250	981	150	924	836	471	41
1928	251	1,044	217	1,051	909	463	43
1929	252	988	213	1,100	928	455	36
1930	176	816	178	1,169	844	506	39

Pennsylvania

Year	Total Ch370	Agriculture, forestry, and fishing Ch371	Mining Ch372	Construction Ch373	Manufacturing Ch374	Transportation, communications, and utilities Ch375	Wholesale and retail trade Ch376	Finance, insurance, and real estate Ch377	Services Ch378	Miscellaneous Ch379
	Number	Number	Number	Number	Number	Number	Number	Number	Number	Number
1890	667	3	76	5	255	150	0	169	9	0
1891	572	1	51	3	288	97	0	124	7	1
1892	760	1	69	1	324	173	0	178	9	5
1893	604	0	49	4	285	137	0	121	8	0
1894	578	0	50	1	261	123	0	127	11	5
1895	573	1	39	0	280	152	1	92	7	1
1896	530	0	41	3	268	121	15	76	6	0
1897	540	1	36	6	265	123	13	79	13	4
1898	484	1	23	6	253	118	15	60	6	2
1899	687	2	51	2	376	142	14	88	8	4
1900	854	0	104	5	399	198	23	108	13	4
1901	1,171	3	104	10	525	258	62	177	29	3
1902	1,530	7	135	41	637	265	136	248	55	6
1903	1,608	5	167	40	645	249	162	284	49	7
1904	1,345	9	117	45	559	201	162	188	53	11
1905	1,469	7	103	46	617	256	163	194	72	11
1906	1,528	13	115	61	610	184	192	249	85	19
1907	1,611	10	96	56	622	177	226	293	109	22
1908	1,114	8	68	39	440	134	183	156	70	16
1909	1,517	8	92	56	569	224	208	229	119	12
1910	1,523	7	85	42	496	303	200	268	111	11
1911	1,658	18	72	46	504	437	229	248	100	4
1912	1,659	17	104	61	508	444	229	212	78	6
1913	2,095	13	116	60	527	770	231	246	117	15
1914	1,322	18	97	46	477	95	229	239	106	15
1915	1,366	14	102	41	470	157	235	232	106	9
1916	1,694	12	124	59	533	215	290	333	101	27
1917	1,958	12	453	56	492	164	372	281	101	27
1918	1,277	9	237	34	415	70	246	159	78	29
1919	2,297	10	158	73	711	123	507	546	143	26
1920	2,918	15	310	77	778	151	641	747	168	31
1921	—	—	—	—	—	—	—	—	—	—
1922	—	—	—	—	—	—	—	—	—	—
1923	—	—	—	—	—	—	—	—	—	—
1924	—	—	—	—	—	—	—	—	—	—
1925	—	—	—	—	—	—	—	—	—	—
1926	—	—	—	—	—	—	—	—	—	—
1927	—	—	—	—	—	—	—	—	—	—
1928	—	—	—	—	—	—	—	—	—	—
1929	—	—	—	—	—	—	—	—	—	—
1930	—	—	—	—	—	—	—	—	—	—

[1] Not a full year.

Documentation

See the text for Table Ch293–318.

This table combines corporations chartered by special and general acts. For some states in some years, Evans created a separate category for corporations engaged in both mining and manufacturing. These corporations have been added here to the manufacturing category.

Source

George Heberton Evans Jr., *Business Incorporations in the United States, 1800–1943* (National Bureau of Economic Research, 1948), pp. 14, 17, 51–2, 154–68.

TABLE Ch380–391   Business incorporations in New England, by type of incorporation law: 1700–1875   [Six states]

Contributed by Naomi R. Lamoreaux

	Connecticut		Maine		Massachusetts		New Hampshire		Rhode Island		Vermont	
	Special acts	General laws	Special acts	General laws	Special acts	General laws	Special acts	General laws	Special acts	General laws	Special acts	General laws
	Ch380	Ch381	Ch382	Ch383	Ch384	Ch385	Ch386	Ch387	Ch388	Ch389	Ch390	Ch391
Period	Number	Number	Number	Number	Number	Number	Number	Number	Number	Number	Number	Number
1700–1780	2	0	0	0	1	0	0	0	3	0	0	0
1781–1799	35	0	22	0	53	0	29	0	11	0	15	0
1800–1817	103	0	86	0	318	0	174	0	57	0	111	0
1818–1830	131	0	148	0	328	0	130	0	70	0	66	0
1831–1843	91	71	473	0	523	0	149	0	83	0	137	0
1844–1862	177	726	691	0	893	249	346	0	163	0	281	7
1863–1875	250	783	624	91	398	1,246	223	39	403	0	492	46

Sources

Joseph S. Davis, *Essays in the Earlier History of American Corporations* (Russell & Russell, 1965), Volume 2, pp. 22–3; William C. Kessler, "Incorporation in New England: A Statistical Study, 1800–1875," *Journal of Economic History* 8 (May 1948): 46.

Documentation

Davis collected the data for the period before 1800 from the legislative records of each of the New England states. Because not all of these early records were extant, some corporations may be missing, though Davis considered "the list not far from complete." Kessler used similar legislative and incorporation records for the period 1800–1875. Because some corporate charters were never taken up, the number of incorporations is not the same as the number of new corporate enterprises created.

TABLE Ch392–401   Business incorporations in New England, by industry and type of incorporation law: 1700–1875

Contributed by Naomi R. Lamoreaux

	Total		Mining and manufacturing		Public utility and transportation		Finance and real estate		Other	
	Special acts	General laws	Special acts	General laws	Special acts	General laws	Special acts	General laws	Special acts	General laws
	Ch392	Ch393	Ch394	Ch395	Ch396	Ch397	Ch398	Ch399	Ch400	Ch401
Period	Number	Number	Number	Number	Number	Number	Number	Number	Number	Number
1700–1780	6	0	0	0	5	0	0	0	1	0
1781–1799	165	0	5	0	135	0	24	0	1	0
1800–1817	849	0	280	0	418	0	142	0	9	0
1818–1830	873	0	311	0	316	0	227	0	19	0
1831–1843	1,456	71	738	65	414	0	261	29	43	5
1844–1862	2,551	982	1,032	821	953	66	454	29	112	66
1863–1875	2,390	2,185	1,120	2,016	802	85	270	25	198	59

Sources

Joseph S. Davis, *Essays in the Earlier History of American Corporations* (Russell & Russell, 1965), Volume 2, pp. 22–3; William C. Kessler, "Incorporation in New England: A Statistical Study, 1800–1875," *Journal of Economic History* 8 (May 1948): 47.

Documentation

See the text for Table Ch380–391. Corporations chartered by special act were assigned to industry groups using the details of their charters. Corporations chartered by general law were categorized according to the terms of the legislation under which they were organized.

TABLE Ch402–407   Manufacturing companies chartered in New York, by industry and type of incorporation law: 1811–1848

Contributed by Naomi R. Lamoreaux

		General laws							General laws				
	Special act, total	Total	Textile	Metal	Glass	Mixed or miscellaneous		Special act, total	Total	Textile	Metal	Glass	Mixed or miscellaneous
	Ch402	Ch403	Ch404	Ch405	Ch406	Ch407		Ch402	Ch403	Ch404	Ch405	Ch406	Ch407
Year	Number	Number	Number	Number	Number	Number	Year	Number	Number	Number	Number	Number	Number
1811	13	11	6	2	1	2	1830	4	2	0	0	0	2
1812	5	12	10	1	0	1	1831	4	8	5	2	0	1
1813	4	29	25	3	1	0	1832	14	3	2	1	0	0
1814	4	39	33	3	1	2	1833	7	6	3	1	1	1
1815	1	10	17	2	0	0	1834	9	10	5	2	2	1
1816	1	8	6	2	0	0	1835	7	13	3	5	1	4
1817	0	5	2	1	0	2	1836	15	20	10	3	1	6
1818	1	4	4	0	0	0	1837	7	17	6	6	0	5
1819	0	1	1	0	0	0	1838	7	4	1	0	1	2
1820	0	1	1	0	0	0	1839	8	4	1	1	0	2
1821	0	3	1	0	0	2	1840	2	5	2	1	2	0
1822	1	3	2	0	0	1	1841	4	12	6	1	0	5
1823	1	6	4	2	0	0	1842	0	3	3	0	0	0
1824	1	2	1	0	0	1	1843	1	0	0	0	0	0
1825	9	10	2	2	0	6	1844	0	13	9	1	2	1
1826	7	10	2	5	0	3	1845	2	12	4	4	1	3
1827	0	9	5	3	0	1	1846	1	24	20	3	0	1
1828	9	9	3	3	1	2	1847	0	13	11	2	0	0
1829	1	9	8	0	0	1	1848	0	3	2	0	0	1

Source

W. C. Kessler, "A Statistical Study of the New York General Incorporation Act of 1811," *Journal of Political Economy* 48 (December 1948): 879.

Documentation

The New York "Act Relative to Incorporations for Manufacturing Purposes," passed in 1811 and renewed in 1821, was one of the earliest general incorporation laws in the United States. It permitted the incorporation of firms in the textile, glass, metal, and paint industries and, later, in clay, earthenware, and leather products (the latter only in a limited number of counties). Firms organized under the act were chartered for twenty years and had a maximum capitalization of $100,000. Kessler compiled his counts of corporations formed under this law and by special charter from the articles of incorporation filed with the office of the Secretary of State in Albany, New York.

TABLE Ch408–413   Business incorporations and failures – number and liabilities: 1857–1998

Contributed by Richard Sutch

Year	Active firms Ch408 Thousand	New business incorporations Ch409 Number	Index of net business formation Ch410 Index 1967 = 100	Business failures Number Ch411 Number	Business failures Per 10,000 Ch412 Per 10,000	Business failures Current liabilities Ch413 Million dollars	Year	Active firms Ch408 Thousand	New business incorporations Ch409 Number	Index of net business formation Ch410 Index 1967 = 100	Business failures Number Ch411 Number	Business failures Per 10,000 Ch412 Per 10,000	Business failures Current liabilities Ch413 Million dollars
1857	204	—	—	4,932	242	292	1915	1,675	—	—	22,156	132	302
1858	—	—	—	4,225	—	96	1916	1,708	—	—	16,993	99	196
1859	230	—	—	3,913	170	64	1917	1,733	—	—	13,855	80	182
1860	—	—	—	3,676	—	80	1918	1,708	—	—	9,982	58	163
1861	—	—	—	6,993	—	207	1919	1,711	—	—	6,451	38	113
1862	—	—	—	1,652	—	23	1920	1,821	—	—	8,881	49	295
1863	—	—	—	495	—	8	1921	1,927	—	—	19,652	102	627
1864	—	—	—	520	—	9	1922	1,983	—	—	23,676	119	624
1865	—	—	—	530	—	18	1923	1,996	—	—	18,718	94	539
1866	—	—	—	1,505	—	54	1924	2,047	—	—	20,615	101	543
1867	—	—	—	2,780	—	97	1925	2,113	—	—	21,214	100	444
1868	—	—	—	2,608	—	64	1926	2,158	—	—	21,773	101	409
1869	—	—	—	2,799	—	75	1927	2,184	—	—	23,146	106	520
1870	427	—	—	3,546	83	88	1928	2,187	—	—	23,842	109	490
1871	457	—	—	2,915	64	85	1929	2,203	—	—	22,909	104	483
1872	500	—	—	4,069	81	121	1930	2,160	—	—	26,355	122	668
1873	494	—	—	5,183	105	229	1931	2,127	—	—	28,285	133	736
1874	559	—	—	5,830	104	155	1932	2,066	—	—	31,822	154	928
1875	603	—	—	7,740	128	201	1933	1,986	—	—	19,859	100	458
1876	639	—	—	9,092	142	191	1934	1,982	—	—	12,091	61	334
1877	637	—	—	8,872	139	191	1935	1,975	—	—	12,244	62	311
1878	661	—	—	10,478	159	234	1936	2,001	—	—	9,607	48	203
1879	702	—	—	6,658	95	98	1937	2,063	—	—	9,490	46	183
1880	747	—	—	4,735	63	66	1938	2,104	—	—	12,836	61	247
1881	782	—	—	5,582	71	81	1939	2,344	—	—	14,768	63	183
1882	822	—	—	6,738	82	102	1940	2,162	—	—	13,619	63	167
1883	864	—	—	9,184	106	173	1941	2,154	—	—	11,848	55	136
1884	905	—	—	10,968	121	226	1942	2,090	—	—	9,405	45	101
1885	920	—	—	10,637	116	134	1943	2,013	—	—	3,221	16	45
1886	970	—	—	9,834	101	115	1944	1,746	—	—	1,222	7	32
1887	994	—	—	9,634	97	168	1945	2,023	—	—	809	4	30
1888	1,047	—	—	10,679	102	124	1946	2,258	132,916	—	1,129	5	67
1889	1,051	—	—	10,882	104	149	1947	2,481	112,897	—	3,474	14	205
1890	1,111	—	—	10,907	98	190	1948	2,625	96,346	112.5	5,250	20	235
1891	1,143	—	—	12,273	107	190	1949	2,719	85,640	87.9	9,246	34	308
1892	1,173	—	—	10,344	88	114	1950	2,695	93,092	93.1	9,162	34	248
1893	1,193	—	—	15,242	128	347	1951	2,599	83,778	98.2	8,058	31	260
1894	1,114	—	—	13,905	125	173	1952	2,624	92,946	98.1	7,611	29	283
1895	1,209	—	—	13,206	109	173	1953	2,685	102,706	94.4	8,862	33	394
1896	1,152	—	—	15,088	131	226	1954	2,640	117,411	91.3	11,086	42	463
1897	1,059	—	—	13,351	126	154	1955	2,612	139,915	98.9	10,969	42	449
1898	1,106	—	—	12,486	113	131	1956	2,643	141,163	95.0	12,686	48	563
1899	1,148	—	—	9,335	81	91	1957	2,642	137,112	90.3	13,739	52	615
1900	1,174	—	—	10,774	92	138	1958	2,672	150,781	89.4	14,964	56	728
1901	1,219	—	—	11,002	90	113	1959	2,703	193,067	96.7	14,053	52	693
1902	1,253	—	—	11,615	93	117	1960	2,710	182,713	92.4	15,445	57	939
1903	1,281	—	—	12,069	94	155	1961	2,668	181,535	88.4	17,075	64	1,090
1904	1,320	—	—	12,199	92	144	1962	2,587	182,057	90.7	15,782	61	1,214
1905	1,357	—	—	11,520	85	103	1963	2,567	186,404	93.3	14,374	56	1,353
1906	1,393	—	—	10,682	77	119	1964	2,547	197,724	97.2	13,501	53	1,329
1907	1,418	—	—	11,721	83	197	1965	2,550	203,897	98.5	13,514	53	1,322
1908	1,448	—	—	15,690	108	222	1966	2,512	200,010	98.2	13,061	52	1,386
1909	1,486	—	—	13,023	88	154	1967	2,523	206,569	100.1	12,364	49	1,265
1910	1,515	—	—	12,650	83	202	1968	2,471	233,635	109.8	9,636	39	941
1911	1,525	—	—	13,441	88	191	1969	2,474	274,267	116.2	9,154	37	1,142
1912	1,564	—	—	15,452	99	203							
1913	1,617	—	—	16,037	99	273							
1914	1,655	—	—	18,280	110	358							

(continued)

TABLE Ch408–413   Business incorporations and failures – number and liabilities: 1857–1998 *Continued*

Year	Active firms	New business incorporations	Index of net business formation	Business failures Number	Business failures Per 10,000	Current liabilities	Year	Active firms	New business incorporations	Index of net business formation	Business failures Number	Business failures Per 10,000	Current liabilities
	Ch408	Ch409	Ch410	Ch411	Ch412	Ch413		Ch408	Ch409	Ch410	Ch411	Ch412	Ch413
	Thousand	Number	Index 1967 = 100	Number	Per 10,000	Million dollars		Thousand	Number	Index 1967 = 100	Number	Per 10,000	Million dollars
1970	2,443	264,209	108.1	10,748	44	1,888	1985	4,979	664,235	121.2	57,253	115	36,937
1971	2,459	287,577	111.2	10,326	42	1,917	1986	5,135	702,738	120.4	61,616	120	44,724
1972	2,517	316,601	117.9	9,566	38	2,000	1987	5,991	685,572	121.2	61,111	102	34,724
1973	2,596	329,358	117.9	9,345	36	2,299	1988	5,826	685,095	124.1	57,097	98	39,573
1974	2,609	319,149	112.4	9,915	38	3,053	1989	7,748	676,565	—	50,361	65	42,329
1975	2,659	326,345	108.9	11,432	43	4,380	1990	8,209	647,366	—	60,747	74	56,130
1976	2,751	375,766	117.6	9,628	35	3,011	1991	8,237	628,604	—	88,140	107	96,825
1977	2,828	436,170	127.4	7,919	28	3,095	1992	8,824	666,800	—	97,069	110	94,318
1978	2,758	478,019	132.9	6,619	24	2,656	1993	7,902	706,537	—	86,133	109	47,756
1979	2,701	524,565	131.7	7,564	28	2,667	1994	8,321	741,778	—	71,558	86	28,978
1980	2,796	533,520	121.1	11,742	42	4,635	1995	8,674	766,988	—	71,128	82	37,284
1981	2,753	581,242	113.5	16,794	61	6,955	1996	8,991	786,482	—	71,931	80	29,569
1982	2,830	566,942	113.2	24,908	88	15,611	1997	9,475	798,779	—	83,384	88	37,437
1983	2,849	600,420	114.8	31,334	110	16,073	1998	—	765,868	—	—	—	—
1984	4,867	634,991	121.3	52,078	107	29,269							

Sources

Series Ch408. 1857–1919: "Dun & Bradstreet Reference Book and Failure Statistics" (an undated folder distributed by Dun & Bradstreet); 1920–1926: Dun & Bradstreet, Inc., *The Failure Record through 1971*, and unpublished data supplied by Dun & Bradstreet, Inc., and reproduced in *Historical Statistics of the United States* (1975), series V20; 1927–1997: calculated from series Ch411–412.

Series Ch409. Data provided by the Economic Analysis Department, Dun & Bradstreet Corporation.

Series Ch410. U.S. Bureau of Economic Analysis, *Business Conditions Digest*, June 1971 and subsequent issues, series B12.

Series Ch411 and Ch413. 1857–1919: "Dun & Bradstreet Reference Book and Failure Statistics"; 1920–1926: *The Failure Record through 1971*, and unpublished data supplied by Dun & Bradstreet and reproduced in *Historical Statistics of the United States* (1975), series V24; 1927–1997: Dun & Bradstreet Inc., *Business Failure Record* (1999). Several minor errors in series Ch411 were corrected by summing monthly data as reported in *Dun's Review,* January 5, 1895; January 1910; and January 1927.

Series Ch412. 1857–1926: calculated from series Ch408 and Ch411; 1927–1997: Dun & Bradstreet Inc., *Business Failure Record* (1999).

Documentation

In 1841, Lewis Tappan organized the Mercantile Agency to gather and disseminate impartial credit information regarding merchants seeking credit from suppliers. The name was changed to R. G. Dun & Co. in 1859. John Bradstreet founded a rival agency in 1849. In 1933, the R.G. Dun Corporation acquired the Bradstreet Company and renamed itself Dun & Bradstreet, Inc. For a history, see Roy A. Foulke, *The Sinews of American Commerce* (Dun & Bradstreet, 1941). Today the company's U.S. data base includes the detailed histories of over 11 million businesses.

Series Ch408. Represents the number of active firms each year in the company's data base. In the early years, this list of concerns was published in a periodic volume called the *Reference Book*. The *Reference Book* published nearest to July 1 of each year was used to make the count. Recent data for the total number of listed concerns is as of July 1. From 1857 through 1983 the listings included businesses, both incorporated and unincorporated, in man-

ufacturing; wholesale and retail trade; building contractors; and certain types of commercial service including public utilities, water carriers, motor carriers, and airlines. Specific businesses not covered are finance, insurance, and real estate companies; railroads; terminals; amusements; and many "one-man services." Neither professions nor farmers are included. Beginning in 1984, the series was revised to include agriculture; forestry and fishing; finance, insurance, and real estate; and the service sector in its entirety. According to Dun & Bradstreet (D&B), "all industries in the U.S. are now represented."

Series Ch409. Represents the total number of stock corporations issued charters under the general incorporation laws of the various states and (beginning with 1963) the District of Columbia. The statistics include completely new businesses that have incorporated, existing businesses changed from a noncorporate form to a corporation, existing corporations given certificates to operate in another state, and existing corporations transferred to another state. This series does not, therefore, represent net new business formation. That is the object of the D&B index of net business formation (series Ch410).

Series Ch410. Compiled from monthly national data on new business incorporations, number of business failures, and confidential data.

Series Ch411–413. Business failures do not represent total business closings, which consist of both failures and discontinuances. Business failures consist of businesses involved in court proceedings or in voluntary actions involving losses to creditors. Businesses that discontinue operations for reasons such as inadequate profits, ill health, and retirement are not recorded as failures if all creditors are paid in full. Since June 1934, with the enactment of the Bankruptcy Act, reorganization may or may not lead to discontinuance of operation. Since that date, however, bankruptcy under the act is included in the failure statistics.

Series Ch413. Liabilities of business failures refer to liabilities at the time of failure. They include all accounts and notes payable on secured or unsecured obligations held by banks, officers, affiliated companies, suppliers, or the government. Before 1933, the series includes liabilities arising from failures of real estate, insurance, holding, and financial companies; steamship lines; and travel agencies, even though these firms were not included in series Ch408 or series Ch412. Before 1939, the series does not include the losses from small concerns forced out of business with insufficient assets to cover all claims unless the closure was involuntary.

TABLE Ch414–415   Bankruptcy petitions filed by businesses and nonbusinesses: 1948–1998

Contributed by Naomi R. Lamoreaux

	Business	Nonbusiness		Business	Nonbusiness
	Ch414	Ch415		Ch414	Ch415
Year	Number	Number	Year	Number	Number
1948	4,973	13,537	1975	30,130	224,354
1949	6,877	19,144	1976	35,201	211,348
1950	8,352	25,040	1977	32,189	182,210
1951	7,387	27,806	1978	30,528	172,423
1952	6,542	28,331	1979	29,500	196,976
1953	6,772	33,315	1980 [1]	46,071	314,886
1954	8,888	44,248	1981	66,333	452,730
1955	9,185	50,219	1982	77,725	450,086
1956	9,478	52,608	1983	95,572	440,025
1957	10,144	63,617	1984	62,170	282,105
1958	11,404	80,264	1985	66,651	297,885
1959	11,729	88,943	1986	76,281	401,575
1960	12,284	97,750	1987	88,278	473,000
1961	15,241	131,402	1988	68,501	526,066
1962	15,655	132,125	1989	62,534	580,459
1963	16,302	139,191	1990	64,689	660,796
1964	16,510	155,209	1991	69,193	811,206
1965	16,910	163,413	1992	72,650	899,840
1966	16,430	175,924	1993	66,428	852,306
1967	16,600	191,729	1994	56,748	788,509
1968	16,545	181,266	1995	51,288	806,816
1969	15,430	169,500	1996	52,938	989,172
1970	16,197	178,202	1997	53,993	1,263,006
1971	19,103	182,249	1998	50,202	1,379,249
1972	18,132	164,737			
1973	17,490	155,707			
1974	20,746	168,767			

[1] Includes cases filed under both the Bankruptcy Act and the Bankruptcy Reform Act of 1978.

Sources

Administrative Office of the U.S. Courts, *Tables of Bankruptcy Statistics*, various issues; and U.S. Census Bureau, *Statistical Abstract of the United States*, various issues.

Documentation

Totals are for fiscal years ending June 30. The filing of a bankruptcy petition represents the commencement of a legal proceeding (by means of a petition to the court) through which an insolvent individual or company will either liquidate or restructure its obligations. Business bankruptcies include filings by merchants, manufacturers, farmers, professionals, and others in business. Nonbusiness bankruptcies include filings by employees and others not in business. After 1980, the series includes only cases filed under the Bankruptcy Reform Act of 1978, which took effect in that year.

Naomi R. Lamoreaux

TABLE Ch416–421   Mergers in manufacturing and mining – entities, capitalization, and type: 1895–1930

Contributed by Naomi R. Lamoreaux

	Firms that disappeared into consolidations or were acquired by larger firms		Percentage of mergers that were consolidations		Percentage of merger capital accounted for by consolidations	
	Entities	Capital	Including two-firm consolidations	Excluding two-firm consolidations	Including two-firm consolidations	Excluding two-firm consolidations
	Ch416	Ch417	Ch418	Ch419	Ch420	Ch421
Year	Number	Million dollars	Percent	Percent	Percent	Percent
1895	43	40.8	86.1	—	84.6	—
1896	26	24.7	84.6	—	89.1	—
1897	69	119.7	89.9	—	92.4	—
1898	303	650.6	93.1	—	94.6	—
1899	1,208	2,262.7	91.7	—	92.1	—
1900	340	442.4	89.9	—	88.1	—
1901	423	2,052.9	83.2	—	92.4	—
1902	379	910.8	70.7	—	76.2	—
1903	142	297.6	39.4	—	49.5	—
1904	79	110.5	45.6	—	28.1	—
1905	226	243.0	63.7	—	43.4	—
1906	128	377.8	35.9	—	57.1	—
1907	87	185.8	50.5	—	36.6	—
1908	50	187.6	72.0	—	89.8	—
1909	49	89.1	24.5	—	40.4	—
1910	142	257.0	52.8	—	44.8	—
1911	103	210.5	67.0	—	76.7	—
1912	82	322.4	45.1	—	58.5	—
1913	85	175.6	45.9	—	37.5	—
1914	39	159.6	48.7	—	38.2	—
1915	71	158.4	42.3	—	46.3	—
1916	117	470.0	38.5	—	44.9	—
1917	195	678.7	42.1	—	59.1	—
1918	71	254.2	9.9	—	21.3	—
1919	159	777.4	55.4	53.5	65.3	64.6
1920	163	809.4	36.9	35.1	63.5	63.3
1921	70	430.0	5.7	2.9	1.8	0.5
1922	122	501.8	31.7	27.6	16.7	15.3
1923	143	1,171.1	29.7	25.5	8.4	6.3
1924	149	466.0	40.3	35.6	45.4	36.5
1925	257	720.7	49.3	43.9	26.2	17.6
1926	265	1,135.0	50.0	47.7	25.6	23.8
1927	306	727.4	55.4	49.5	55.0	47.2
1928	507	1,653.2	49.7	46.0	32.1	28.6
1929	587	1,993.3	25.3	22.1	35.3	30.9
1930	281	1,756.8	14.2	10.6	27.8	26.1

Sources

1895–1918, Ralph L. Nelson, *Merger Movements in American Industry* (Princeton University Press, 1959), pp. 37, 60; 1919–1930, Carl Eis, *The 1919–1930 Merger Movement in American Industry* (Arno Press, 1978), pp. 40, 63–4.

Documentation

Nelson defined a merger as the combination into a single economic enterprise of two or more previously independent enterprises. He built up his series by recording all items on mergers reported in the investment news pages of the *Commercial and Financial Chronicle* from 1895 to 1920. For each item, he then verified that the merger had actually occurred by checking *Moody's Manual* and *Poor's Manual* for the year of the merger and for four subsequent years and by checking a variety of other sources. Nelson's measure of merger capitalization is essentially an estimate of the total size of the firms that disappeared into consolidations or were acquired by other firms. Where information on size was not available, Nelson imputed a value based on the average size of acquired firms in the relevant three-digit Standard Industrial Classification (SIC) industry group. See the Introduction to Part D for a discussion of SIC codes. Because of price changes, he computed separate averages for the 1895–1914 and 1915–1920 periods. The reported series exclude consolidations capitalized at less than $1,000,000 for the 1895–1914 period and $2,000,000 for the 1915–1920 period and acquisitions smaller than $35,000 for the former period and $65,000 for the later.

Eis's study was a doctoral dissertation written under Nelson's supervision, using Nelson's methods. The two studies report different numbers for 1919 and 1920, however, probably because Eis used a cut-off of $1,000,000 for consolidations and $100,000 for acquisitions. For 1919, Nelson reported 171 mergers (43.3 percent of which were disappearances into consolidations) and total merger capital of $981.7 million (61.9 percent accounted for by consolidations). For 1920, Nelson's figures were 206 (23.8 percent) and $1,088.6 million (51.1 percent), respectively.

Nelson classified mergers as consolidations if they involved the simultaneous combination of previously independent firms into a new entity. His list of consolidations included a number of combinations that involved only two firms. Eis defined two-firm consolidations as acquisitions, but, in order to maintain comparability with Nelson's work, also included tables that classified them as consolidations.

TABLE Ch422–429   Mergers, acquisitions, and joint ventures – number and assets: 1919–1979
Contributed by Naomi R. Lamoreaux

	Mergers and acquisitions						Large mergers and acquisitions– manufacturing and mining	
	Recorded							
	Manufacturing and mining	All industries	Completed	New joint ventures	American companies acquired by foreign companies	Foreign companies acquired by American companies	Number	Assets of acquired companies
	Ch422	Ch423	Ch424	Ch425 [1]	Ch426	Ch427	Ch428	Ch429
Year	Number	Number	Number	Number	Number	Number	Number	Million dollars
1919	438	—	—	—	—	—	—	—
1920	760	—	—	—	—	—	—	—
1921	487	—	—	—	—	—	—	—
1922	309	—	—	—	—	—	—	—
1923	311	—	—	—	—	—	—	—
1924	368	—	—	—	—	—	—	—
1925	554	—	—	—	—	—	—	—
1926	856	—	—	—	—	—	—	—
1927	870	—	—	—	—	—	—	—
1928	1,058	—	—	—	—	—	—	—
1929	1,245	—	—	—	—	—	—	—
1930	799	—	—	—	—	—	—	—
1931	464	—	—	—	—	—	—	—
1932	203	—	—	—	—	—	—	—
1933	120	—	—	—	—	—	—	—
1934	101	—	—	—	—	—	—	—
1935	130	—	—	—	—	—	—	—
1936	126	—	—	—	—	—	—	—
1937	124	—	—	—	—	—	—	—
1938	110	—	—	—	—	—	—	—
1939	87	—	—	—	—	—	—	—
1940	140	—	—	—	—	—	—	—
1941	111	—	—	—	—	—	—	—
1942	118	—	—	—	—	—	—	—
1943	213	—	—	—	—	—	—	—
1944	324	—	—	—	—	—	—	—
1945	333	—	—	—	—	—	—	—
1946	419	—	—	—	—	—	—	—
1947	404	—	—	—	—	—	—	—
1948	223	—	—	—	—	—	4	63.2
1949	126	—	—	—	—	—	6	89.0
1950	219	—	—	—	—	—	5	186.3
1951	235	—	—	—	—	—	9	201.5
1952	288	—	—	—	—	—	16	373.8
1953	295	—	—	—	—	—	23	779.1
1954	387	—	—	—	—	—	37	1,444.5
1955	683	—	—	—	—	—	67	2,165.7
1956	673	—	—	—	—	—	53	1,882.0
1957	585	—	—	—	—	—	17	1,202.3
1958	589	—	—	—	—	—	42	1,070.6
1959	835	—	—	—	—	—	49	1,431.1
1960	844	—	—	—	—	—	51	1,535.1
1961	954	1,724	—	—	—	—	46	2,003.3
1962	853	1,667	—	—	—	—	65	2,251.9
1963	861	1,479	—	—	—	—	54	2,535.8
1964	854	1,797	—	—	—	—	73	2,302.9
1965	1,008	1,893	—	—	—	—	64	3,253.7
1966	995	1,746	—	218	—	—	76	3,329.1
1967	1,496	2,384	—	171	—	—	138	8,258.5
1968	2,407	3,932	—	169	—	—	174	12,580.0
1969	2,307	4,542	—	204	—	—	138	11,043.2
1970	1,351	3,089	—	223	—	—	91	5,904.3
1971	1,011 [2]	2,633 [2]	—	244	—	—	59	2,459.9
1972	—	—	2,839	289	—	361	60	1,885.5
1973	—	—	2,359	247	76	332	64	3,148.8
1974	—	—	1,474	130	87	208	62	4,466.4

Notes appear at end of table

TABLE Ch422–429   Mergers, acquisitions, and joint ventures – number and assets: 1919–1979   *Continued*

	Mergers and acquisitions			New joint ventures	American companies acquired by foreign companies	Foreign companies acquired by American companies	Large mergers and acquisitions, manufacturing and mining	
	Recorded							
	Manufacturing and mining	All industries	Completed				Number	Assets of acquired companies
	Ch422	Ch423	Ch424	Ch425 [1]	Ch426	Ch427	Ch428	Ch429
Year	Number	Number	Number	Number	Number	Number	Number	Million dollars
1975	—	—	1,047	82	67	116	59	4,950.5
1976	—	—	1,164	106	55	84	82	6,301.8
1977	—	—	1,207	115	54	88	101	9,166.6
1978	—	—	1,279	114	105	123	111	10,724.6
1979	—	—	1,214	85	147	99	73	12,867.1

[1] Series changes in 1972; see text.

[2] Preliminary figures.

Sources

U.S. Federal Trade Commission, *Report on Corporate Mergers and Acquisitions, 1955*; *Current Trends in Merger Activity, 1971*; *Statistical Report on Mergers and Acquisitions, 1979*.

Documentation

The original Federal Trade Commission (FTC) series (1919–1971) was based on mergers in manufacturing and mining reported by Moody's Investors Service, Inc., and Standard and Poor's Corporation. The FTC discontinued this series in 1972. Beginning in 1961, however, the FTC also compiled a broader series that included mergers in trade, services, and other industries (mainly insurance, warehousing and storage, commercial farming, contract construction, and credit companies other than banks). The FTC collected this data from the same sources as the original series, but also from other publications such as the *Wall Street Journal*, the *Journal of Commerce*, and the *New York Times*. The FTC also discontinued this series in 1972 but replaced it with a similar one, based, however, on a broader range of commercial publications and including all industries under FTC jurisdiction (that is, all industries except commercial banking, transportation, and communications). This replacement series included only mergers that were actually completed, and was revised each year. The FTC stopped collecting data on mergers after 1979. To be included in these series, the acquired company must have been American

and must have been an independent company, a subsidiary of an independent company, or a division of such a subsidiary. The series included partial acquisitions of at least 10 percent of a company's or subsidiary's assets or stock. To be counted in the two series on large mergers and acquisitions, the acquired firm must have been primarily in manufacturing and mining and have had assets greater than $10 million. The FTC made only minor changes in the large merger series after 1971.

The 1972–1979 series on new joint ventures, acquisitions of American companies by foreign companies, and acquisitions of foreign companies by American companies are based on the same sources as the 1972–1979 series for completed mergers, except the last also draws on *Jane's Major Companies of Europe*, *Fortune's Directory of the 500 Largest Industrial Companies Outside the U.S.*, and *Dun and Bradstreet's International Directories*. New joint ventures were reported (not necessarily completed) formations of new companies jointly owned by two or more independent companies, at least one of which was American. Ventures that operated abroad as well as in the United States were included. The 1966–1971 series on joint ventures differed from the subsequent one in that it was compiled from a narrower range of sources (as for the 1961–1971 series on reported mergers) and included ventures that did not take the form of independent companies. All the mergers in the series on American companies acquired by foreign firms were included in the overall series as well. The mergers in the series on acquisitions of foreign companies by American firms were not included in the overall series. Moreover, this series included industries not under FTC jurisdiction in the United States.

TABLE Ch430–439   Mergers, acquisitions, divestitures, and leveraged buyouts – entities and value: 1984–1998

Contributed by Naomi R. Lamoreaux

	Mergers, acquisitions, divestitures, and leveraged buyouts		Divestitures		Leveraged buyouts		Foreign acquisitions of U.S. companies		U.S. acquisitions of foreign companies	
	Entities	Value	Entities	Value	Entities	Value	Entities	Value	Entities	Value
	Ch430	Ch431	Ch432	Ch433	Ch434	Ch435	Ch436	Ch437	Ch438	Ch439
Year	Number	Billion dollars	Number	Billion dollars	Number	Billion dollars	Number	Billion dollars	Number	Billion dollars
1984	2,243	153.2	801	44.8	106	15.3	—	—	—	—
1985	1,719	149.6	780	51.0	154	16.3	259	27.9	91	3.7
1986	2,497	223.1	1,090	84.7	233	46.5	345	31.4	111	3.4
1987	2,479	198.8	1,004	77.8	208	40.5	365	55.3	162	6.9
1988	2,970	281.8	1,274	115.8	291	55.2	536	66.0	223	11.1
1989	3,752	316.8	1,615	94.9	293	75.5	693	69.2	347	27.1
1990	4,239	205.6	1,907	90.8	177	17.6	773	56.4	392	20.5
1991	3,446	141.5	1,759	61.4	171	7.3	504	29.1	402	14.8
1992	3,502	125.3	1,598	57.2	199	7.2	361	17.6	455	13.7
1993	3,722	420.4	1,993	213.4	621	16.4	—	—	197	19.5
1994	4,383	524.9	2,005	236.9	173	10.6	—	—	207	21.1
1995	4,981	895.8	2,227	365.3	206	23.6	80	3.5	317	62.6
1996	5,639	1,059.3	2,423	319.0	169	17.4	73	2.9	364	59.3
1997	8,770	1,610.3	3,189	616.2	198	24.1	441	64.8	539	87.8
1998	9,634	2,480.2	3,304	554.8	238	27.2	483	232.5	746	127.8

Source

U.S. Census Bureau, *Statistical Abstract of the United States,* 1994–1999 (based on data collected for Securities Data Company for the Merger and Corporate Transactions Database).

Documentation

The series include only transactions valued at $5 million or more. The series on value include only those transactions for which price data were revealed.

Acquisitions include partial acquisitions that involve at least a 40 percent stake in the acquired company or an investment of $100 million. Divestitures are sales of a business, division, or subsidiary by a corporate owner to another party. Leveraged buyouts are acquisitions where the buyers use mostly borrowed money to finance the purchase.

ENTERPRISES

Sukkoo Kim

TABLE Ch440–449 Companies, establishments, and central administrative organizations – entities, employees, and payroll: 1954–1992

Contributed by Sukkoo Kim

	All companies								Single-unit companies	
				Establishments						
					Classified in the same industry as the parent company		Classified as central administrative organizations and auxiliaries			
	Entities	Employees	Payroll	Entities	Entities	Employees	Entities	Employees	Entities	Employees
	Ch440	Ch441	Ch442	Ch443	Ch444	Ch445	Ch446	Ch447	Ch448	Ch449
Year	Number	Number	Million dollars	Number	Number	Number	Number	Number	Number	Number
1954	2,783,977	29,496,604	106,900.1	3,074,427	2,966,195	24,992,877	33,469	1,316,946	2,715,844	14,149,026
1958	3,151,606	30,952,031	129,121.1	3,493,770	3,351,005	25,995,291	39,879	1,547,616	3,060,283	14,295,248
1963	3,293,313	33,270,321	167,798.5	3,687,556	3,517,542	26,678,750	46,617	1,795,456	3,198,384	14,694,761
1967	4,410,047	41,921,345	251,282.3	4,839,501	4,644,043	33,062,456	50,132	2,105,210	4,328,750	18,714,750
1972	5,026,743	45,810,804	358,762.2	5,605,383	5,340,577	35,312,820	73,190	2,536,191	4,908,459	19,457,016
1977	5,589,806	49,775,765	555,848.3	6,225,812	5,944,596	38,289,186	31,023	2,078,682	5,479,717	20,597,181
1982	4,256,243	61,660,233	913,861.7	5,014,025	4,690,141	49,175,227	76,815	3,464,848	4,125,614	29,954,356
1987	3,878,866	68,140,393	1,307,947.6	4,731,694	4,459,009	56,548,308	72,257	3,594,379	3,710,320	30,333,681
1992	4,610,829	86,856,851	2,124,984.5	5,829,983	—	—	—	—	—	—

Sources

U.S. Bureau of the Census, *Company Statistics: 1954 Censuses of Business, Manufactures, and Mineral Industries*, Census Bulletin CS-1 (1958); and *Enterprise Statistics*, 1958–1992.

Documentation

Enterprise Statistics reports data on companies as well as on establishments. The publication consists of two parts: a general report that provides information on the characteristics of American business firms, including data on single-establishment (single-unit) or multi-establishment (multiunit) companies and single-industry or multi-industry firms, and a specialized report that provides information on firms' central administrative offices and auxiliaries – that is, on the establishments that monitor, coordinate, or support the activities of multiunit enterprises. According to the Census's definitions, a company consists of all operating establishments (factories, mines, stores, sales offices, and so on) and administrative or auxiliary units (central offices, central warehouses, research and development laboratories, and other support services) reported as being under common ownership or control. An establishment is a business or industrial unit at a single physical location that produces goods or performs services. A central administrative office is an establishment primarily engaged in general administrative, supervisory, purchasing, accounting, and related management functions that are performed centrally for other establishments of the same company. An auxiliary unit is an establishment, such as a central warehouse, research laboratory, or repair shop that provides support services to the operating establishments of the company.

The series include data on companies that were in operation all or part of the year. Employment figures include both full- and part-time employees. Salaried officers and executives of corporations are counted but proprietors and partners of unincorporated businesses are not. The payroll total includes all forms of compensation (salaries, wages, commissions, bonuses, vacation and sick leave pay, and payments in kind) received by all employees before payroll deductions for such items as social security, group insurance, union dues, and so forth.

The industry categories used for *Enterprise Statistics* are based on the Standard Industrial Classification (SIC) system, and approximate, but differ somewhat from, the SIC's three-digit categories. The definitions of the categories also shifted over time because of revisions of the SIC codes. See the Introduction to Part D for an extended discussion of SIC codes. In series Ch440, companies are classified into approximately 180 "enterprise industry categories" according to their primary business activities. The data in series Ch441–443 are then allocated to the same industry categories as the companies to which they refer. The major industry groups for which *Enterprise Statistics* reported data varied from year to year. For example, data for the transportation sector were reported only for 1967, 1987, and 1992; data for public warehouses were reported only for 1954, 1958, and 1963; and data for finance, insurance, and real estate were reported only for 1992. Because so few years were reported, these data are not reproduced here.

TABLE Ch450–459   Mining companies, establishments, and central administrative organizations – entities, employees, and payroll: 1954–1992

Contributed by Sukkoo Kim

	All companies								Single-unit companies	
				Establishments						
					Classified in the same industry as the parent company		Classified as central administrative organizations and auxiliaries			
	Entities	Employees	Payroll	Entities	Entities	Employees	Entities	Employees	Entities	Employees
	Ch450	Ch451	Ch452	Ch453	Ch454	Ch455	Ch456	Ch457	Ch458	Ch459
Year	Number	Number	Million dollars	Number	Number	Number	Number	Number	Number	Number
1954	30,274	596,804	2,443.2	37,181	35,398	542,309	587	19,403	28,256	255,450
1958	30,133	574,759	2,765.7	36,613	33,490	490,541	744	23,095	28,267	248,938
1963	30,956	447,424	2,492.7	37,531	35,082	378,666	705	19,607	29,045	215,090
1967	20,035	379,537	2,583.3	26,179	23,328	315,063	630	18,689	18,751	159,031
1972	18,199	448,996	4,400.6	25,803	20,578	328,747	1,723	37,999	17,051	147,032
1977	22,358	645,975	10,005.9	30,613	24,800	475,793	753	40,523	21,275	229,003
1982	43,366	815,667	19,250.2	60,654	53,296	627,224	1,301	60,485	42,123	363,264
1987	25,145	473,296	12,822.5	32,074	28,229	378,273	968	34,924	23,922	202,038
1992	22,426	472,822	16,211.1	29,411	—	—	—	—	—	—

Sources

U.S. Bureau of the Census, *Company Statistics: 1954 Censuses of Business, Manufactures, and Mineral Industries*, Census Bulletin CS-1 (1958); and *Enterprise Statistics*, 1958–1992.

Documentation

See the text for Table Ch440–449.

TABLE Ch460–469   Construction companies, establishments, and central administrative organizations – entities, employees, and payroll: 1967–1992

Contributed by Sukkoo Kim

	All companies								Single-unit companies	
				Establishments						
					Classified in the same industry as the parent company		Classified as central administrative organizations and auxiliaries			
	Entities	Employees	Payroll	Entities	Entities	Employees	Entities	Employees	Entities	Employees
	Ch460	Ch461	Ch462	Ch463	Ch464	Ch465	Ch466	Ch467	Ch468	Ch469
Year	Number	Number	Million dollars	Number	Number	Number	Number	Number	Number	Number
1967	795,508	3,422,816	24,019.2	800,246	797,556	3,298,317	304	12,235	793,863	2,841,678
1972	893,933	4,167,772	39,718.6	905,012	897,972	3,954,305	846	24,574	889,156	3,269,712
1977	1,190,789	3,887,221	54,963.7	1,201,812	1,194,332	3,630,754	446	26,579	1,187,100	2,932,367
1982	449,388	4,321,677	80,065.5	461,704	452,902	4,017,161	780	34,366	445,968	3,297,236
1987	529,194	5,116,642	111,527.4	539,171	533,209	4,899,802	677	22,705	525,055	4,252,549
1992	566,144	4,671,756	116,976.5	575,163	—	—	—	—	—	—

Source

U.S. Bureau of the Census, *Enterprise Statistics*, 1967–1992.

Documentation

See the text for Table Ch440–449.

TABLE Ch470-479   Manufacturing companies, establishments, and central administrative organizations – entities, employees, and payroll: 1954-1992

Contributed by Sukkoo Kim

	All companies								Single-unit companies	
				Establishments						
					Classified in the same industry as the parent company		Classified as central administrative organizations and auxiliaries			
	Entities	Employees	Payroll	Entities	Entities	Employees	Entities	Employees	Entities	Employees
	Ch470	Ch471	Ch472	Ch473	Ch474	Ch475	Ch476	Ch477	Ch478	Ch479
Year	Number	Number	Million dollars	Number	Number	Number	Number	Number	Number	Number
1954	263,103	17,250,739	70,918.3	356,741	278,459	13,332,551	28,295	1,089,891	255,035	6,140,100
1958	269,834	17,272,957	85,314.0	379,896	286,385	13,087,806	32,545	1,286,859	258,210	5,624,596
1963	274,127	18,571,260	110,784.7	402,218	290,511	13,036,903	37,099	1,461,266	263,114	5,573,321
1967	266,985	21,376,976	148,159.8	420,607	284,453	13,988,369	40,328	1,689,956	256,061	5,459,158
1972	265,052	21,116,324	194,337.3	447,170	283,380	12,833,660	57,838	1,944,588	250,430	4,765,679
1977	296,146	21,952,260	298,042.8	485,439	320,006	13,220,552	14,297	1,289,444	280,273	4,853,534
1982	293,556	22,007,978	442,415.0	495,665	314,699	12,773,188	54,185	2,400,172	277,564	5,055,050
1987	307,120	21,447,990	543,922.7	473,353	335,197	13,691,888	46,791	2,256,927	287,962	5,111,330
1992	319,396	20,258,069	629,577.0	477,429	—	—	—	—	—	—

Sources

U.S. Bureau of the Census, *Company Statistics: 1954 Censuses of Business, Manufactures, and Mineral Industries*, Census Bulletin CS-1 (1958); and *Enterprise Statistics*, 1958–1992.

Documentation

See the text for Table Ch440-449.

TABLE Ch480-489   Wholesale companies, establishments, and central administrative organizations – entities, employees, and payroll: 1954-1992

Contributed by Sukkoo Kim

	All companies								Single-unit companies	
				Establishments						
					Classified in the same industry as the parent company		Classified as central administrative organizations and auxiliaries			
	Entities	Employees	Payroll	Entities	Entities	Employees	Entities	Employees	Entities	Employees
	Ch480	Ch481	Ch482	Ch483	Ch484	Ch485	Ch486	Ch487	Ch488	Ch489
Year	Number	Number	Million dollars	Number	Number	Number	Number	Number	Number	Number
1954	185,067	1,989,177	7,955.3	211,092	203,543	1,896,889	631	19,607	176,485	1,456,936
1958	213,054	2,100,808	9,230.2	246,175	234,210	2,028,741	864	16,531	198,711	1,474,421
1963	235,634	2,340,845	12,766.8	269,689	259,565	2,230,178	1,153	23,233	221,658	1,653,974
1967	232,786	2,644,103	16,894.0	269,236	258,142	2,479,095	1,212	27,482	219,764	1,786,914
1972	328,535	3,314,988	28,257.1	381,275	364,485	3,082,677	2,622	49,690	305,728	2,151,437
1977	293,522	3,571,992	44,144.8	358,039	335,339	3,248,955	2,409	54,312	269,807	2,148,783
1982	326,492	4,120,876	73,157.2	394,449	369,970	3,719,573	3,325	90,817	303,398	2,495,606
1987	354,676	4,756,294	105,976.9	431,869	408,145	4,282,036	3,407	123,080	326,011	2,708,514
1992	376,328	4,933,518	137,130.1	461,953	—	—	—	—	—	—

Sources

U.S. Bureau of the Census, *Company Statistics: 1954 Censuses of Business, Manufactures, and Mineral Industries*, Census Bulletin CS-1 (1958); and *Enterprise Statistics*, 1958–1992.

Documentation

See the text for Table Ch440-449.

TABLE Ch490-499   Retail companies, establishments, and central administrative organizations – entities, employees, and payroll: 1954–1992

Contributed by Sukkoo Kim

	All companies								Single-unit companies	
				Establishments						
					Classified in the same industry as the parent company		Classified as central administrative organizations and auxiliaries			
	Entities	Employees	Payroll	Entities	Entities	Employees	Entities	Employees	Entities	Employees
	Ch490	Ch491	Ch492	Ch493	Ch494	Ch495	Ch496	Ch497	Ch498	Ch499
Year	Number	Number	Million dollars	Number	Number	Number	Number	Number	Number	Number
1954	1,542,982	7,216,788	18,816.5	1,677,000	1,659,681	6,819,566	3,274	170,803	1,503,954	4,425,457
1958	1,688,322	8,034,128	22,524.5	1,839,234	1,811,937	7,500,478	3,854	199,204	1,641,091	4,801,922
1963	1,678,549	8,567,546	29,154.6	1,852,513	1,816,592	7,831,020	4,801	253,066	1,629,126	4,880,740
1967	1,683,420	9,710,319	38,531.1	1,862,673	1,827,570	8,761,335	5,546	319,471	1,645,268	5,396,777
1972	1,845,307	11,553,779	59,705.6	2,097,607	2,040,439	10,218,207	7,797	423,468	1,794,693	5,788,529
1977	1,776,253	13,560,387	94,782.1	2,064,427	2,000,545	11,946,459	10,451	601,115	1,730,754	6,562,903
1982	1,055,095	14,845,081	137,170.3	1,398,759	1,319,900	13,072,231	13,042	738,298	1,001,808	6,927,763
1987	1,069,713	18,622,014	203,977.8	1,484,922	1,415,822	16,654,828	14,532	859,710	1,005,849	7,675,108
1992	1,058,286	18,780,526	247,010.6	1,495,318	—	—	—	—	—	—

Sources

U.S. Bureau of the Census, *Company Statistics: 1954 Censuses of Business, Manufactures, and Mineral Industries*, Census Bulletin CS-1 (1958); and *Enterprise Statistics*, 1958–1992.

Documentation

See the text for Table Ch440-449.

TABLE Ch500-509   Selected service companies, establishments, and central administrative organizations – entities, employees, and payroll: 1954–1992

Contributed by Sukkoo Kim

	All companies								Single-unit companies	
				Establishments						
					Classified in the same industry as the parent company		Classified as central administrative organizations and auxiliaries			
	Entities	Employees	Payroll	Entities	Entities	Employees	Entities	Employees	Entities	Employees
	Ch500	Ch501	Ch502	Ch503	Ch504	Ch505	Ch506	Ch507	Ch508	Ch509
Year	Number	Number	Million dollars	Number	Number	Number	Number	Number	Number	Number
1954	755,859	2,352,499	6,474.3	784,972	781,816	2,312,520	650	16,803	745,668	1,802,897
1958	942,804	2,869,443	8,912.5	983,295	976,777	2,794,817	1,831	21,362	926,990	2,080,014
1963	1,066,282	3,244,647	12,153.1	1,116,664	1,107,120	3,106,997	2,793	37,705	1,048,111	2,302,606
1967	1,396,793	4,243,159	20,296.7	1,444,733	1,437,540	4,083,098	2,054	36,717	1,380,942	2,964,073
1972	1,675,717	5,208,945	32,343.0	1,748,516	1,733,723	4,895,224	2,364	55,872	1,651,401	3,334,627
1977	2,010,738	6,157,930	53,909.1	2,085,482	2,069,574	5,766,673	2,667	66,709	1,990,508	3,870,591
1982	1,220,631	10,792,294	153,621.6	1,333,812	1,311,123	10,222,214	4,115	139,403	1,187,660	7,149,948
1987	1,467,663	15,832,758	288,680.2	1,622,694	1,594,813	14,859,213	5,254	258,321	1,420,735	9,455,894
1992	1,698,254	25,686,028	597,843.3	1,954,948	—	—	—	—	—	—

Sources

U.S. Bureau of the Census, *Company Statistics: 1954 Censuses of Business, Manufactures, and Mineral Industries*, Census Bulletin CS-1 (1958); and *Enterprise Statistics*, 1958–1992.

Documentation

See the text for Table Ch440-449.

Selected services include businesses such as hotels and motels, laundries, cleaning and dyeing plants, beauty shops, barber shops, advertising and other business services, automobile repair shops, motion picture theaters, bowling alleys, billiard and pool halls, and other amusement and recreation services.

CORPORATE BALANCE SHEETS

Naomi R. Lamoreaux

TABLE Ch510–524 Corporate assets, liabilities, receipts, dividends, and income tax: 1926–1997 [All active corporations]

Contributed by Naomi R. Lamoreaux

	Corporate tax returns	Total assets or liabilities	Selected assets					Selected liabilities				Receipts		Income tax (not adjusted for credits)	Dividends paid other than own stock
			Cash	Notes and accounts receivable less allowance for bad debts	Inventories	Investments	Capital assets less reserves	Accounts payable and short-term debt	Long-term debt	Capital	Surplus and retained earnings	Total	Total less total deductions		
Year	Ch510 [1] Number	Ch511	Ch512	Ch513 [2]	Ch514	Ch515	Ch516 [3]	Ch517	Ch518	Ch519	Ch520	Ch521	Ch522	Ch523	Ch524
		Thousand dollars	Thousand dollars	Thousand dollars	Thousand dollars	Thousand dollars	Thousand dollars	Thousand dollars	Thousand dollars	Thousand dollars	Thousand dollars	Thousand dollars	Thousand dollars	Thousand dollars	Thousand dollars
1926	359,449 [4]	262,179,000	16,802,000	23,552,000	20,939,000	—	97,523,000	24,042,000	31,801,000	84,663,000	34,597,000	—	—	—	—
1927	379,156	287,542,000	16,851,000	50,959,000	21,005,000	—	104,945,000	24,126,000	37,740,000	91,881,000	40,522,000	—	—	—	—
1928	384,548	307,218,000	21,952,000	62,804,000	20,751,000	—	109,931,000	27,437,000	42,943,000	95,731,000	47,156,000	—	—	—	—
1929	398,815	335,778,000	22,371,000	66,810,000	21,911,000	66,182,000	116,446,000	29,453,000	46,643,000	105,258,000	55,111,000	—	—	—	—
1930	403,173	334,002,000	21,012,000	59,675,000	18,771,000	94,037,000	120,994,000	26,870,000	50,282,000	106,184,000	55,098,000	—	—	—	—
1931	381,088	296,497,000	15,880,000	48,667,000	15,140,000	85,972,000	114,303,000	23,251,000	48,101,000	99,011,000	44,352,000	105,238,000	487,000	393,000	6,092,000
1932	392,021	280,083,000	15,917,000	39,564,000	12,372,000	87,547,000	108,553,000	20,562,000	47,222,000	97,489,000	36,080,000	79,701,000	3,511,000	282,000	3,854,000
1933	388,564	268,206,000	15,236,000	35,835,000	13,597,000	84,045,000	104,958,000	19,362,000	45,883,000	92,482,000	35,096,000	82,148,000	639,000	417,000	3,091,000
1934	410,626	301,307,000	19,961,000	40,529,000	14,311,000	109,657,000	102,751,000	27,021,000	48,604,000	104,946,000	36,639,000	99,095,000	3,037,000	586,000	4,788,000
1935	415,205	303,150,000	23,664,000	38,690,000	14,788,000	112,026,000	100,480,000	25,332,000	49,822,000	102,266,000	36,665,000	112,098,000	5,500,000	722,000	5,896,000
1936	415,654	303,180,000	26,102,000	40,219,000	16,584,000	110,521,000	97,873,000	25,580,000	47,023,000	96,663,000	36,806,000	126,269,000	7,618,000	1,145,000	7,163,000
1937	416,902	303,357,000	24,346,000	40,329,000	18,515,000	109,053,000	100,320,000	25,121,000	49,326,000	95,703,000	45,930,000	138,907,000	7,777,000	1,246,000	7,281,000
1938	411,941	300,022,000	27,973,000	37,763,000	16,582,000	108,228,000	99,299,000	21,851,000	50,278,000	92,900,000	44,537,000	117,596,000	4,144,000	844,000	4,834,000
1939	412,759	306,801,000	34,054,000	39,451,000	17,718,000	108,508,000	100,226,000	22,533,000	49,388,000	90,695,000	46,169,000	130,365,000	7,236,000	1,217,000	5,639,000
1940	413,716	320,478,000	41,423,000	42,864,000	19,463,000	109,999,000	100,214,000	22,683,000	49,199,000	89,430,000	48,957,000	145,427,000	9,472,000	2,525,000	6,019,000
1941	407,053	340,452,000	41,629,000	49,255,000	25,058,000	116,902,000	100,698,000	25,592,000	49,542,000	87,791,000	54,800,000	186,137,000	16,592,000	7,064,000	6,556,000
1942	383,534	360,018,000	46,464,000	46,155,000	26,832,000	132,090,000	99,772,000	24,260,000	45,040,000	81,301,000	58,328,000	213,777,000	23,280,000	12,138,000	5,512,000
1943	366,870	389,524,000	50,271,000	45,728,000	27,187,000	158,719,000	97,728,000	24,265,000	43,735,000	79,548,000	66,116,000	245,796,000	27,933,000	15,752,000	5,628,000
1944	363,056	418,324,000	52,783,000	47,894,000	26,476,000	185,611,000	95,128,000	24,861,000	42,454,000	79,897,000	70,562,000	258,880,000	26,454,000	14,769,000	5,957,000
1945	374,950	441,461,000	57,717,000	51,630,000	26,067,000	203,961,000	92,057,000	24,663,000	40,987,000	79,511,000	75,014,000	252,636,000	21,220,000	10,702,000	6,009,000
1946	440,750	454,705,000	58,502,000	61,371,000	36,965,000	186,999,000	100,329,000	30,840,000	44,968,000	83,191,000	81,424,000	283,917,000	25,025,000	8,710,000	7,378,000
1947	496,821	494,615,000	64,369,000	75,959,000	44,009,000	187,137,000	112,194,000	36,826,000	50,108,000	87,470,000	93,097,000	361,521,000	31,207,000	10,787,000	8,285,000
1948	536,833	525,136,000	65,737,000	84,597,000	48,293,000	189,021,000	125,650,000	38,527,000	57,326,000	91,731,000	105,489,000	405,430,000	34,248,000	11,771,000	9,305,000
1949	554,573	543,562,000	63,864,000	85,526,000	44,726,000	202,121,000	135,617,000	36,697,000	61,851,000	94,309,000	113,987,000	387,636,000	28,130,000	9,688,000	9,464,000
1950	569,961	598,369,000	71,018,000	108,639,000	54,496,000	206,582,000	144,691,000	47,143,000	65,719,000	94,216,000	129,393,000	452,523,000	42,535,000	17,168,000	11,471,000
1951	596,385	647,524,000	76,853,000	119,314,000	63,776,000	213,822,000	159,325,000	52,592,000	72,835,000	98,399,000	140,638,000	511,849,000	43,495,000	21,902,000	11,219,000
1952	615,698	721,864,000	79,597,000	140,902,000	64,520,000	252,815,000	169,546,000	56,823,000	80,628,000	101,196,000	152,811,000	525,011,000	38,507,000	19,002,000	11,196,000
1953	640,073	761,877,000	80,171,000	148,282,000	65,519,000	270,787,000	180,612,000	56,948,000	86,607,000	103,936,000	168,900,000	551,984,000	39,582,000	19,693,000	11,533,000
1954	667,856	805,300,000	81,723,000	158,738,000	62,914,000	291,962,000	191,437,000	61,392,000	90,797,000	106,362,000	173,407,000	547,001,000	36,486,000	16,682,000	11,832,000
1955	746,962	888,621,000	87,375,000	191,779,000	70,920,000	311,456,000	206,388,000	76,048,000	98,399,000	112,628,000	192,820,000	634,508,000	47,601,000	21,536,000	13,468,000
1956	827,916	948,951,000	89,780,000	210,392,000	78,744,000	320,900,000	225,862,000	85,116,000	108,928,000	119,604,000	208,064,000	673,493,000	47,184,000	21,222,000	14,359,000
1957	940,147	996,400,000	89,222,000	198,226,000	80,560,000	357,977,000	244,463,000	90,735,000	122,515,000	124,360,000	219,990,000	720,414,000	45,073,000	20,582,000	14,914,000
1958	990,381	1,064,481,000	93,248,000	210,141,000	80,047,000	393,366,000	259,613,000	96,489,000	132,082,000	128,406,000	240,751,000	735,338,000	39,224,000	18,814,000	14,952,000
1959	1,074,120	1,136,668,000	91,856,000	227,994,000	88,304,000	418,733,000	275,772,000	105,926,000	142,913,000	135,095,000	253,909,000	816,800,000	47,655,000	22,525,000	16,242,000

Notes appear at end of table

(continued)

TABLE Ch510–524 Corporate assets, liabilities, receipts, dividends, and income tax: 1926–1997 [All active corporations] Continued

	Corporate tax returns	Total assets or liabilities	Selected assets					Selected liabilities				Receipts		Income tax (not adjusted for credits)	Dividends paid other than own stock
			Cash	Notes and accounts receivable less allowance for bad debts	Inventories	Investments	Capital assets less reserves	Accounts payable and short-term debt	Long-term debt	Capital	Surplus and retained earnings	Total	Total less total deductions		
Year	Ch510 ¹	Ch511	Ch512	Ch513 ²	Ch514	Ch515	Ch516 ³	Ch517	Ch518	Ch519	Ch520	Ch521	Ch522	Ch523	Ch524
	Number	Thousand dollars	Thousand dollars	Thousand dollars	Thousand dollars	Thousand dollars	Thousand dollars	Thousand dollars	Thousand dollars	Thousand dollars	Thousand dollars	Thousand dollars	Thousand dollars	Thousand dollars	Thousand dollars
1960	1,140,574	1,206,662,000	97,162,000	242,416,000	91,334,000	443,473,000	293,215,000	112,314,000	153,566,000	140,348,000	268,618,000	849,132,000	44,499,000	21,866,000	17,193,000
1961	1,190,286	1,289,516,000	101,965,000	259,541,000	94,818,000	477,642,000	310,266,000	121,056,000	165,521,000	146,371,000	287,822,000	873,178,000	47,034,000	22,188,000	18,038,000
1962	1,268,042	1,388,127,000	—	—	100,327,000	—	—	—	—	—	—	949,305,000	50,842,000	23,930,000	19,565,000
1963	1,323,187	1,481,236,000	108,775,000	330,953,000	106,340,000	533,567,000	342,026,000	164,078,000	180,952,000	154,602,000	321,953,000	1,008,743,000	55,737,000	26,298,000	21,105,000
1964	1,373,517	1,585,619,000	113,742,000	345,322,000	112,960,000	583,946,000	365,551,000	155,002,000	192,878,000	158,120,000	345,285,000	1,086,739,000	63,059,000	27,857,000	23,305,000
1965	1,423,980	1,723,524,000	117,060,000	392,252,000	126,341,000	620,294,000	395,297,000	174,279,000	210,274,000	161,357,000	374,641,000	1,194,601,000	74,742,000	31,662,000	25,997,000
1966	1,468,725	1,844,775,000	126,255,000	414,384,000	141,019,000	654,983,000	432,034,000	197,393,000	232,506,000	167,778,000	406,020,000	1,306,518,000	81,293,000	34,449,000	27,033,000
1967	1,534,360	2,010,443,000	139,984,000	449,222,000	151,581,000	712,083,000	467,446,000	215,344,000	252,423,000	176,709,000	444,171,000	1,374,599,000	79,250,000	33,301,000	28,239,000
1968	1,541,670	2,215,625,000	150,295,000	499,397,000	164,433,000	792,439,000	504,865,000	249,601,000	285,612,000	181,314,000	494,102,000	1,507,786,000	87,477,000	39,694,000	31,563,000
1969	1,658,820	2,445,628,000	162,615,000	562,102,000	184,583,000	848,793,000	561,306,000	301,526,000	326,039,000	195,548,000	542,319,000	1,680,482,000	82,135,000	39,374,000	32,951,000
1970	1,665,477	2,634,706,564	176,924,573	594,637,040	190,401,642	925,607,766	599,464,541	319,696,858	362,700,303	201,213,719	562,525,222	1,750,776,503	67,997,656	33,293,018	32,012,677
1971	1,733,332	2,889,221,468	196,335,069	649,708,586	199,091,682	1,103,825,728	633,695,428	333,739,186	402,715,090	210,224,732	611,885,003	1,906,007,776	81,944,686	37,510,264	32,592,946
1972	1,812,760	3,256,831,334	228,071,734	762,413,376	223,847,520	1,165,200,706	684,755,425	386,090,561	445,200,445	220,584,621	680,177,914	2,171,209,849	99,478,258	42,890,248	36,039,621
1973	1,904,670	3,648,919,824	258,711,569	890,742,489	262,566,242	1,261,546,875	750,492,153	460,814,405	493,152,166	228,377,837	747,939,416	2,557,688,950	122,645,162	52,438,603	41,829,368
1974	1,965,894	4,016,466,940	281,022,745	998,546,828	312,096,928	1,334,826,381	830,211,526	539,221,439	542,093,213	240,076,710	794,815,391	3,089,701,363	148,157,366	66,112,989	49,280,658
1975	2,023,647	4,286,556,273	290,426,439	1,019,509,808	317,718,545	1,490,452,256	891,926,208	535,541,135	586,703,526	251,715,862	866,121,556	3,198,627,860	145,953,263	66,144,308	45,224,392
1976	2,082,200	4,720,938,670	314,548,604	1,137,279,634	350,644,363	1,655,021,795	969,108,900	578,552,685	638,277,006	266,788,251	961,290,355	3,635,471,982	186,589,106	83,291,815	54,644,375
1977	2,241,887	5,326,389,281	361,549,924	1,303,557,066	396,032,639	1,862,518,544	1,075,809,074	666,326,899	694,119,251	286,775,916	1,090,818,299	4,128,304,478	219,522,757	96,340,453	61,536,761
1978	2,376,779	6,014,452,008	412,948,244	1,551,126,400	442,652,820	2,034,451,343	1,195,218,787	784,405,448	780,536,053	309,432,793	1,217,426,735	4,714,602,615	247,405,739	107,888,445	70,294,349
1979	2,556,794	6,835,056,963	461,750,680	1,656,996,419	503,033,064	2,289,742,102	1,348,011,782	933,315,209	884,636,968	352,811,534	1,406,863,760	5,598,689,129	282,964,117	120,047,034	86,613,794
1980	2,710,538	7,617,238,403	528,914,747	1,934,544,483	534,806,547	2,580,369,436	1,511,537,677	1,046,974,656	986,663,932	417,153,783	1,601,403,100	6,361,284,012	235,918,858	105,142,436	97,378,617
1981	2,812,420	8,547,161,872	533,472,168	2,195,352,166	588,219,956	2,836,755,133	1,693,789,884	1,205,916,970	1,058,070,877	532,560,826	1,840,571,302	7,026,351,839	212,510,484	102,257,851	120,295,338
1982	2,925,933	9,357,784,804	540,903,600	2,373,829,411	581,241,455	3,152,672,547	1,872,179,498	1,345,691,238	1,224,277,725	658,259,634	2,010,091,064	7,024,097,766	154,830,304	86,766,154	132,478,411
1983	2,999,071	10,201,084,144	590,386,817	2,626,205,349	599,445,162	3,465,856,597	1,963,031,852	1,431,031,514	1,323,209,421	787,278,549	2,147,952,124	7,135,494,059	190,036,702	92,218,567	128,298,545
1984	3,170,743	11,106,701,948	595,773,262	2,842,639,825	664,243,060	3,825,488,730	2,085,144,276	1,607,919,478	1,494,350,573	839,344,147	2,374,160,067	7,800,711,226	231,939,061	107,968,407	144,871,643
1985	3,277,219	12,773,093,888	683,204,264	3,256,054,856	714,722,928	4,588,774,149	2,261,490,330	1,892,909,238	1,699,272,481	920,182,882	2,786,583,758	8,398,278,426	240,134,300	111,340,839	—
1986	3,428,515	14,163,209,894	762,946,878	3,519,300,244	732,587,518	5,283,887,763	2,427,460,619	1,993,038,740	1,958,477,161	1,190,628,800	3,120,031,289	8,669,378,501	274,445,682	111,140,137	—
1987	3,612,133	15,310,615,602	754,042,297	3,668,026,414	829,272,682	5,774,830,776	2,558,653,257	2,245,219,754	2,141,169,042	1,291,674,344	3,404,850,757	9,580,720,701	336,816,848	118,484,975	—
1988	3,562,789	16,568,467,823	784,815,919	4,002,403,216	845,783,686	6,314,084,370	2,740,054,496	2,454,119,849	2,352,107,056	1,429,486,841	3,647,639,028	10,264,867,461	411,447,323	131,367,397	—
1989	3,627,863	17,647,120,286	823,705,622	4,091,972,823	879,318,508	6,509,095,140	2,976,436,801	2,691,962,510	2,490,067,919	1,477,273,520	4,117,668,479	10,934,973,405	390,267,875	127,754,021	—
1990	3,716,650	18,190,057,609	771,086,440	4,087,956,237	893,586,141	6,595,984,014	3,149,131,461	2,896,733,409	2,665,098,250	1,584,840,863	4,224,216,396	11,409,520,074	376,945,444	128,185,666	—
1991	3,802,788	19,029,508,839	786,735,219	4,076,755,770	883,913,179	7,347,861,870	3,225,042,316	3,180,760,294	2,697,909,300	1,740,894,708	4,698,011,114	11,436,474,767	349,355,256	121,121,231	—
1992	3,869,023	20,002,093,972	806,358,400	4,050,283,141	915,412,953	7,785,856,643	3,319,286,151	3,164,829,341	2,742,496,304	1,881,147,182	5,087,256,895	11,742,134,729	412,224,119	131,284,690	—
1993	3,964,629	21,815,869,373	812,077,106	4,415,256,282	947,287,758	8,617,604,887	3,427,503,819	3,034,725,447	2,871,045,770	2,042,497,435	5,884,920,539	12,269,721,710	504,977,653	154,447,416	—
1994	4,342,368	23,446,206,586	853,076,121	4,652,518,888	1,125,766,128	9,235,132,299	3,641,803,884	3,436,700,673	3,099,902,033	2,132,453,838	6,488,160,978	13,360,007,157	585,119,129	172,776,719	—
1995	4,474,167	26,013,689,001	962,083,261	5,185,230,671	1,045,010,082	10,506,136,494	3,879,666,215	3,783,175,628	3,335,426,303	2,194,368,322	7,637,393,681	14,539,050,114	717,772,533	198,786,648	—
1996	4,631,370	28,642,263,127	1,097,176,746	5,663,740,579	1,079,396,261	11,821,462,409	4,243,105,345	4,232,495,805	3,650,975,449	2,278,486,551	8,945,308,506	15,525,718,009	797,628,988	223,712,985	—
1997	4,710,083	33,029,652,126	1,299,322,671	6,509,122,299	1,114,311,184	14,128,157,659	4,575,360,269	4,692,796,151	4,072,058,514	2,950,770,321	10,365,912,855	16,609,707,302	905,465,066	239,394,206	—

[1] Through 1956, number of returns filing balance sheets.

[2] Through 1958, includes loans to stockholders.

[3] Through 1938, excludes intangible assets.

[4] Includes inactive corporations.

Sources

U.S. Internal Revenue Service (and its predecessor, U.S. Bureau of Internal Revenue), *Statistics of Income* and *Statistics of Income: Corporation Income Tax Returns*, various issues.

Documentation

See the text for Table Ch1–18.

The IRS has published aggregate balance-sheet data for U.S. corporations, broken down by major industry group, on an annual basis since 1926. The data derive from (end-of-fiscal-year) balance sheets submitted by corporations with their tax returns. The accounting methods that underpin these balance sheets have varied among firms, and, in addition, the popularity of different accounting practices has changed over time. For example, earlier in the century, firms typically used the FIFO (first in, first out) method of inventory valuation, but many switched by the late 1960s to LIFO (last in, first out).

For the years prior to 1950, the series are compilations of submitted balance sheets. Although a large number of small corporations did not include balance sheets with their returns, the IRS estimates that the missing amounts totaled only about 1 to 3 percent of the aggregate receipts of the corporate sector. Beginning during the 1950s (with the procedures evolving over the course of the decade), the IRS began to report estimates for the entire population of active corporations based on sample data.

The figures for 1926 through 1969 have been taken from the Bicentennial Edition of *Historical Statistics*. Some of the original series (V108–140) have been combined here so that the reported data are comparable to those broken down by major industry groups in series V167–181. The Bicentennial Edition rounded dollar values in these series to the nearest million. The series for "all active corporations" include data for corporations that the IRS was not able to allocate to a major industry group.

The asset category "Cash" includes bank deposits. "Investments" consists of investments in government obligations, mortgages and real estate loans, and other investments (for example, long-term nongovernment securities such as stocks and bonds). "Capital assets" consists of land, depreciable tangible assets such as buildings and equipment, depletable tangible assets such as natural resources, and intangible assets such as patents, trademarks, and goodwill. "Surplus and retained earnings" includes "Other retained earnings, 1120S" for years when this category was reported separately.

TABLE Ch525–539　Corporate assets, liabilities, receipts, dividends, and income tax: 1926–1997　[Agriculture, forestry, and fisheries]

Contributed by Naomi R. Lamoreaux

		Selected assets						Selected liabilities				Receipts			
	Corporate tax returns	Total assets or liabilities	Cash	Notes and accounts receivable less allowance for bad debts	Inventories	Investments	Capital assets less reserves	Accounts payable and short-term debt	Long-term debt	Capital	Surplus and retained earnings	Total	Total less total deductions	Income tax (not adjusted for credits)	Dividends paid other than own stock
	Ch525 [1]	Ch526	Ch527	Ch528 [2]	Ch529	Ch530	Ch531 [3]	Ch532	Ch533	Ch534	Ch535	Ch536	Ch537	Ch538	Ch539
Year	Number	Thousand dollars	Thousand dollars	Thousand dollars	Thousand dollars	Thousand dollars	Thousand dollars	Thousand dollars	Thousand dollars	Thousand dollars	Thousand dollars	Thousand dollars	Thousand dollars	Thousand dollars	Thousand dollars
1926	7,681 [4]	2,050,000	47,000	192,000	118,000	—	1,242,000	407,000	114,000	1,071,000	210,000	—	—	—	—
1927	7,195	2,177,000	57,000	197,000	217,000	—	1,230,000	387,000	178,000	1,082,000	202,000	—	—	—	—
1928	7,130	2,054,000	51,000	210,000	189,000	—	1,177,000	399,000	161,000	1,059,000	297,000	—	—	—	—
1929	7,443	2,140,000	60,000	218,000	198,000	230,000	1,231,000	376,000	222,000	1,051,000	341,000	—	—	—	—
1930	7,862	2,031,000	41,000	219,000	196,000	262,000	1,188,000	393,000	229,000	1,001,000	264,000	—	—	—	—
1931	7,567	2,136,000	57,000	203,000	155,000	246,000	1,334,000	362,000	240,000	975,000	373,000	467,000	−70,000	1,000	25,000
1932	7,716	2,143,000	51,000	168,000	150,000	307,000	1,340,000	370,000	234,000	1,152,000	187,000	354,000	−77,000	1,000	14,000
1933	7,295	1,913,000	58,000	144,000	147,000	211,000	1,217,000	311,000	231,000	1,047,000	159,000	380,000	−34,000	2,000	5,000
1934	7,445	2,243,000	68,000	169,000	187,000	409,000	1,303,000	447,000	219,000	1,227,000	175,000	513,000	−11,000	4,000	26,000
1935	7,143	2,107,000	76,000	151,000	187,000	340,000	1,229,000	392,000	217,000	1,135,000	186,000	566,000	18,000	6,000	35,000
1936	7,126	2,064,000	82,000	151,000	177,000	352,000	1,214,000	372,000	244,000	1,100,000	170,000	697,000	36,000	9,000	56,000
1937	7,046	1,987,000	77,000	141,000	179,000	346,000	1,174,000	362,000	254,000	1,055,000	214,000	746,000	26,000	8,000	48,000
1938	7,304	1,523,000	57,000	107,000	145,000	290,000	872,000	299,000	212,000	828,000	122,000	575,000	−1,000	4,000	19,000
1939	7,048	1,502,000	50,000	100,000	138,000	306,000	867,000	292,000	216,000	767,000	168,000	585,000	15,000	6,000	23,000
1940	6,816	1,516,000	62,000	107,000	141,000	259,000	900,000	233,000	224,000	762,000	216,000	617,000	19,000	9,000	25,000
1941	6,312	1,502,000	69,000	103,000	146,000	306,000	844,000	281,000	192,000	716,000	243,000	717,000	64,000	22,000	32,000
1942	5,893	1,409,000	85,000	109,000	152,000	232,000	793,000	195,000	159,000	675,000	284,000	771,000	81,000	39,000	25,000
1943	5,557	1,422,000	118,000	125,000	160,000	250,000	730,000	189,000	159,000	662,000	323,000	828,000	112,000	61,000	29,000
1944	5,224	1,436,000	117,000	174,000	160,000	262,000	684,000	215,000	141,000	631,000	357,000	896,000	119,000	62,000	31,000

Notes appear at end of table　　　(continued)

TABLE Ch525–539   Corporate assets, liabilities, receipts, dividends, and income tax: 1926–1997   [Agriculture, forestry, and fisheries]   Continued

	Corporate tax returns	Total assets or liabilities		Selected assets					Selected liabilities				Receipts			Dividends paid other than own stock
			Cash	Notes and accounts receivable less allowance for bad debts	Inventories	Investments	Capital assets less reserves	Accounts payable and short-term debt	Long-term debt	Capital	Surplus and retained earnings	Total	Total less total deductions	Income tax (not adjusted for credits)	
Year	Ch525 [1]	Ch526	Ch527	Ch528 [2]	Ch529	Ch530	Ch531 [3]	Ch532	Ch533	Ch534	Ch535	Ch536	Ch537	Ch538	Ch539
	Number	Thousand dollars	Thousand dollars	Thousand dollars	Thousand dollars	Thousand dollars	Thousand dollars	Thousand dollars	Thousand dollars	Thousand dollars	Thousand dollars	Thousand dollars	Thousand dollars	Thousand dollars	Thousand dollars
1945	5,114	1,477,000	120,000	183,000	168,000	305,000	662,000	242,000	135,000	615,000	397,000	965,000	133,000	63,000	26,000
1946	5,554	1,583,000	139,000	149,000	207,000	270,000	764,000	232,000	152,000	648,000	437,000	1,239,000	181,000	66,000	33,000
1947	6,153	1,757,000	145,000	172,000	250,000	264,000	873,000	273,000	173,000	665,000	535,000	1,599,000	206,000	74,000	58,000
1948	6,539	1,855,000	160,000	176,000	266,000	256,000	934,000	278,000	205,000	754,000	510,000	1,812,000	217,000	78,000	62,000
1949	6,820	1,934,000	164,000	183,000	254,000	295,000	990,000	286,000	232,000	762,000	554,000	1,833,000	172,000	64,000	59,000
1950	7,094	2,260,000	177,000	211,000	322,000	321,000	1,174,000	435,000	246,000	799,000	640,000	2,052,000	287,000	99,000	106,000
1951	7,618	2,462,000	186,000	369,000	360,000	349,000	1,138,000	499,000	323,000	827,000	671,000	2,404,000	254,000	105,000	99,000
1952	7,738	2,355,000	191,000	257,000	332,000	318,000	1,186,000	384,000	332,000	827,000	683,000	2,500,000	139,000	77,000	58,000
1953	8,259	2,392,000	190,000	256,000	299,000	304,000	1,264,000	354,000	356,000	855,000	689,000	2,333,000	119,000	72,000	49,000
1954	7,790	2,620,000	191,000	452,000	278,000	376,000	1,251,000	508,000	334,000	870,000	696,000	2,226,000	122,000	65,000	49,000
1955	9,023	2,600,000	207,000	269,000	284,000	338,000	1,380,000	499,000	379,000	881,000	697,000	2,508,000	122,000	67,000	46,000
1956	9,892	2,678,000	199,000	383,000	304,000	367,000	1,335,000	550,000	385,000	900,000	683,000	2,700,000	133,000	68,000	44,000
1957	10,676	2,885,000	190,000	355,000	318,000	382,000	1,529,000	588,000	524,000	953,000	651,000	2,953,000	114,000	62,000	48,000
1958	12,618	3,523,000	246,000	477,000	395,000	512,000	1,766,000	722,000	610,000	1,147,000	827,000	3,528,000	145,000	77,000	53,000
1959	15,603	3,587,000	214,000	429,000	434,000	494,000	1,837,000	703,000	676,000	1,168,000	792,000	3,838,000	106,000	62,000	32,000
1960	17,139	4,063,000	255,000	545,000	472,000	515,000	2,048,000	881,000	746,000	1,270,000	878,000	4,402,000	38,000	58,000	50,000
1961	18,981	4,691,000	272,000	599,000	568,000	534,000	2,432,000	1,026,000	899,000	1,406,000	968,000	5,340,000	111,000	71,000	52,000
1962	22,130	5,176,000	—	—	632,000	—	—	—	—	—	—	6,289,000	162,000	81,000	61,000
1963	23,270	5,946,000	358,000	741,000	711,000	736,000	3,074,000	1,348,000	1,280,000	1,618,000	1,065,000	7,986,000	99,000	90,000	147,000
1964	25,933	6,453,000	359,000	829,000	697,000	882,000	3,384,000	1,429,000	1,376,000	1,688,000	1,249,000	6,329,000	138,000	93,000	73,000
1965	27,530	6,845,000	411,000	811,000	794,000	861,000	3,619,000	1,560,000	1,527,000	1,855,000	1,186,000	7,524,000	238,000	111,000	97,000
1966	27,945	7,557,000	433,000	875,000	970,000	876,000	3,993,000	1,758,000	1,607,000	1,788,000	1,636,000	8,605,000	286,000	118,000	91,000
1967	32,448	8,411,000	491,000	967,000	878,000	836,000	4,651,000	2,108,000	1,797,000	1,980,000	1,805,000	9,296,000	184,000	99,000	86,000
1968	31,248	8,343,000	491,000	951,000	1,089,000	693,000	4,563,000	2,036,000	1,917,000	1,935,000	1,630,000	9,451,000	269,000	132,000	95,000
1969	31,979	10,407,000	480,000	982,000	1,232,000	1,066,000	5,474,000	2,453,000	2,730,000	2,035,000	2,028,000	12,127,000	258,000	138,000	92,000
1970	37,238	11,909,403	578,673	1,232,761	1,327,963	1,346,756	6,127,176	2,854,131	3,174,250	2,526,114	1,621,510	14,277,707	67,994	113,926	65,824
1971	39,932	11,800,386	686,751	1,227,807	1,529,256	1,149,054	6,339,882	3,237,189	3,116,340	2,512,916	1,649,986	14,397,772	208,229	138,244	92,926
1972	42,974	13,620,047	804,589	1,529,019	1,924,554	1,232,835	7,151,789	3,756,642	3,457,014	2,748,528	2,124,441	17,156,593	510,203	186,403	109,442
1973	47,125	16,820,935	1,084,659	1,814,150	2,265,106	1,746,623	7,679,383	4,479,376	4,237,875	2,918,478	2,996,554	23,609,382	939,424	322,497	138,617
1974	53,458	19,283,714	1,191,724	1,964,239	1,985,683	1,943,178	10,700,548	4,755,329	5,506,030	3,336,905	3,311,465	25,452,628	423,249	335,628	195,454
1975	56,280	21,177,941	1,309,844	2,056,740	2,350,028	2,186,397	11,466,985	5,306,079	6,220,321	3,601,550	3,567,650	28,118,514	749,228	354,747	244,524
1976	60,289	23,803,530	1,385,664	2,016,715	2,312,930	2,124,958	13,763,465	5,599,353	6,925,430	4,269,677	3,975,653	32,433,149	642,804	353,451	217,307
1977	65,594	28,902,259	1,665,861	2,548,012	2,838,025	2,759,502	16,409,165	6,778,389	9,175,057	4,742,216	4,732,169	35,907,867	708,690	401,946	387,651
1978	69,971	32,904,622	1,911,031	3,000,877	3,769,408	3,330,760	17,981,195	8,087,103	9,619,740	5,154,893	5,458,880	41,417,558	1,292,505	485,580	251,428
1979	83,489	37,976,331	2,254,593	3,180,499	4,309,825	3,756,813	21,155,364	8,856,222	11,632,659	6,148,452	6,234,001	53,345,996	1,295,272	530,849	349,294

		Total assets or liabilities		Selected assets					Selected liabilities				Receipts			
	Corporate tax returns		Cash	Notes and accounts receivable less allowance for bad debts	Inventories	Investments	Capital assets less reserves	Accounts payable and short-term debt	Long-term debt	Capital	Surplus and retained earnings	Total	Total less total deductions	Income tax (not adjusted for credits)	Dividends paid other than own stock
	Ch525 [1]	Ch526	Ch527	Ch528 [2]	Ch529	Ch530	Ch531 [3]	Ch532	Ch533	Ch534	Ch535	Ch536	Ch537	Ch538	Ch539
Year	Number	Thousand dollars	Thousand dollars	Thousand dollars	Thousand dollars	Thousand dollars	Thousand dollars	Thousand dollars	Thousand dollars	Thousand dollars	Thousand dollars	Thousand dollars	Thousand dollars	Thousand dollars	Thousand dollars
1980	80,883	40,738,977	2,371,775	3,256,431	4,243,601	4,285,290	22,536,043	9,696,906	13,363,285	6,020,729	5,828,578	52,089,915	671,635	544,487	304,733
1981	85,370	46,081,067	2,680,973	3,857,192	4,592,776	4,871,757	25,551,357	10,691,855	14,855,225	6,956,857	7,117,231	65,061,959	326,360	557,892	512,027
1982	91,320	50,409,537	2,849,448	4,247,151	4,971,985	5,400,967	27,838,905	11,848,982	16,640,904	7,774,465	6,925,729	65,356,911	−85,093	502,671	409,070
1983	92,125	50,292,891	3,082,182	4,390,569	4,760,167	5,080,498	27,476,812	12,151,235	16,424,895	7,755,901	6,467,906	59,208,642	−178,154	430,119	172,301
1984	98,361	50,699,926	3,251,201	4,354,622	4,648,552	4,556,651	28,183,321	11,849,235	15,879,263	8,030,388	7,013,718	66,645,119	208,830	509,081	417,177
1985	103,156	52,651,197	3,795,092	4,937,695	4,698,551	5,163,039	27,976,833	12,283,716	15,861,923	8,144,837	8,071,302	70,491,486	−67,992	540,671	—
1986	106,634	53,478,288	3,999,870	4,816,729	4,932,107	5,853,043	27,724,895	11,768,608	15,481,615	8,691,060	9,259,124	77,502,215	1,171,272	589,887	—
1987	116,544	55,374,698	4,020,884	4,950,539	6,255,324	5,591,984	28,393,857	12,115,845	15,107,663	8,285,087	10,893,147	77,057,114	1,634,401	508,012	—
1988	119,902	60,491,780	4,746,863	5,731,467	6,986,298	5,589,601	30,861,441	12,453,990	16,213,970	8,930,380	12,610,788	86,258,094	1,621,012	554,457	—
1989	123,195	63,413,253	4,779,025	6,215,720	7,188,371	6,341,838	32,014,980	13,218,769	16,694,788	8,296,573	14,207,062	86,627,044	1,561,956	605,850	—
1990	126,423	68,338,381	4,922,941	6,431,820	7,867,448	6,961,316	34,909,627	14,315,168	16,771,881	8,787,829	16,052,308	88,101,065	1,217,937	589,866	—
1991	129,886	67,756,553	4,957,939	5,789,779	7,284,831	6,294,356	35,969,885	13,568,341	16,988,309	8,723,249	15,659,626	85,945,700	614,130	520,185	—
1992	137,833	71,760,770	5,094,121	6,632,703	8,114,409	6,721,851	37,869,943	14,532,119	16,965,055	9,511,052	17,536,506	95,563,041	1,545,410	563,325	—
1993	141,326	74,646,834	5,578,602	6,994,786	8,405,157	6,954,778	39,401,556	14,769,564	17,460,756	9,345,689	20,181,076	98,301,076	1,644,447	613,080	—
1994	146,996	79,893,306	5,495,064	7,784,289	8,133,874	8,590,648	41,826,397	15,064,065	19,476,274	10,039,441	22,180,046	100,907,153	1,291,938	689,669	—
1995	147,527	86,298,574	6,294,322	7,904,282	8,389,466	9,941,172	44,619,253	15,752,168	21,396,689	9,835,656	22,974,308	107,581,973	1,614,613	661,579	—
1996	158,963	94,140,118	6,509,497	8,768,684	9,045,728	11,087,820	46,596,937	17,822,750	23,051,648	10,491,557	24,930,558	119,737,058	2,570,724	764,345	—
1997	163,114	91,984,030	6,306,978	8,420,170	8,564,678	12,085,093	46,772,805	17,456,886	22,526,161	10,211,809	25,439,190	117,387,555	2,713,926	659,642	—

[1] Through 1956, number of returns filing balance sheets.

[2] Through 1958, includes loans to stockholders.

[3] Through 1938, excludes intangible assets.

[4] Includes inactive corporations.

Sources

U.S. Internal Revenue Service (and its predecessor, U.S. Bureau of Internal Revenue), *Statistics of Income* and *Statistics of Income: Corporation Income Tax Returns*, various issues.

Documentation

See the text for Table Ch510–524.

TABLE Ch540–554   Corporate assets, liabilities, receipts, dividends, and income tax: 1926–1997   [Mining]

Contributed by Naomi R. Lamoreaux

	Corporate tax returns	Total assets or liabilities	Selected assets					Selected liabilities				Receipts			Dividends paid other than own stock
			Cash	Notes and accounts receivable less allowance for bad debts	Inventories	Investments	Capital assets less reserves	Accounts payable and short-term debt	Long-term debt	Capital	Surplus and retained earnings	Total	Total less total deductions	Income tax (not adjusted for credits)	
	Ch540 [1]	Ch541	Ch542	Ch543 [2]	Ch544	Ch545	Ch546 [3]	Ch547	Ch548	Ch549	Ch550	Ch551	Ch552	Ch553	Ch554
Year	Number	Thousand dollars	Thousand dollars	Thousand dollars	Thousand dollars	Thousand dollars	Thousand dollars	Thousand dollars	Thousand dollars	Thousand dollars	Thousand dollars	Thousand dollars	Thousand dollars	Thousand dollars	Thousand dollars
1926	11,641 [4]	12,172,000	409,000	763,000	636,000	—	7,967,000	902,000	1,008,000	671,400	1,638,000	—	—	—	—
1927	11,298	11,565,000	360,000	703,000	681,000	—	7,495,000	918,000	912,000	624,000	1,863,000	—	—	—	—
1928	10,366	10,799,000	413,000	745,000	516,000	—	6,647,000	354,000	976,000	579,300	2,004,000	—	—	—	—
1929	10,219	11,832,000	421,000	837,000	694,000	1,611,000	7,264,000	975,000	1,037,000	625,200	2,566,000	—	—	—	—
1930	10,025	11,395,000	331,000	730,000	444,000	1,734,000	7,259,000	1,028,000	941,000	578,500	2,166,000	2,191,000	-202,000	7,000	170,000
1931	9,576	10,050,000	242,000	603,000	474,000	1,455,000	6,633,000	849,000	996,000	556,400	1,776,000	1,653,000	-186,000	7,000	102,000
1932	10,020	9,485,000	236,000	515,000	392,000	1,366,000	6,415,000	768,000	957,000	546,000	1,528,000	1,936,000	-149,000	10,000	91,000
1933	9,950	9,007,000	255,000	504,000	411,000	1,213,000	6,053,000	730,000	928,000	504,600	1,460,000	2,361,000	67,000	22,000	265,000
1934	11,362	10,228,000	265,000	738,000	374,000	2,139,000	6,116,000	1,299,000	1,039,000	536,600	1,775,000	2,418,000	70,000	22,000	255,000
1935	11,491	9,519,000	295,000	597,000	317,000	1,840,000	5,914,000	1,172,000	1,047,000	480,700	1,750,000	2,756,000	168,000	36,000	274,000
1936	11,531	9,199,000	315,000	678,000	278,000	1,671,000	5,850,000	1,241,000	1,046,000	459,000	1,853,000	3,273,000	297,000	58,000	361,000
1937	11,467	9,146,000	333,000	677,000	340,000	1,737,000	5,748,000	1,004,000	1,125,000	445,800	2,165,000	2,489,000	52,000	28,000	200,000
1938	9,468	7,545,000	314,000	502,000	342,000	1,406,000	4,688,000	838,000	999,000	354,700	1,846,000	2,843,000	138,000	37,000	216,000
1939	9,287	7,331,000	408,000	550,000	321,000	1,372,000	4,450,000	804,000	1,000,000	337,400	1,858,000	3,219,000	212,000	67,000	280,000
1940	8,885	7,362,000	488,000	556,000	309,000	1,355,000	4,432,000	753,000	1,056,000	328,500	1,937,000	3,754,000	370,000	138,000	311,000
1941	8,227	7,065,000	482,000	568,000	339,000	1,354,000	4,128,000	712,000	941,000	300,900	2,014,000	3,945,000	192,000	195,000	264,000
1942	7,619	6,221,000	527,000	485,000	343,000	1,039,000	3,625,000	618,000	619,000	277,800	1,753,000	3,680,000	342,000	168,000	197,000
1943	7,036	5,434,000	516,000	476,000	281,000	1,013,000	2,980,000	547,000	578,000	227,700	1,614,000	3,969,000	118,000	156,000	187,000
1944	6,581	5,480,000	527,000	480,000	273,000	1,106,000	2,919,000	569,000	561,000	213,500	1,831,000	3,903,000	246,000	117,000	156,000
1945	6,394	5,563,000	556,000	492,000	306,000	1,140,000	2,906,000	602,000	550,000	209,300	1,987,000	4,240,000	332,000	131,000	207,000
1946	6,759	5,949,000	641,000	601,000	341,000	1,152,000	3,050,000	639,000	719,000	205,500	2,162,000	5,881,000	788,000	286,000	315,000
1947	7,280	7,186,000	785,000	789,000	410,000	1,506,000	3,516,000	825,000	830,000	226,600	2,755,000	7,782,000	1,143,000	408,000	468,000
1948	8,025	9,042,000	971,000	991,000	551,000	2,023,000	4,271,000	916,000	1,176,000	252,600	3,653,000	6,730,000	698,000	265,000	417,000
1949	8,094	9,261,000	871,000	889,000	569,000	2,000,000	4,636,000	933,000	1,278,000	249,300	3,901,000	8,493,000	1,086,000	443,000	549,000
1950	8,045	10,844,000	1,031,000	1,312,000	643,000	2,187,000	5,395,000	1,139,000	1,629,000	268,200	4,584,000	9,562,000	1,114,000	553,000	593,000
1951	8,136	11,659,000	1,032,000	1,415,000	755,000	2,273,000	5,878,000	1,258,000	1,610,000	275,500	5,030,000	9,475,000	973,000	504,000	613,000
1952	7,998	12,034,000	970,000	1,423,000	803,000	2,349,000	6,208,000	1,321,000	1,833,000	257,700	5,354,000	9,230,000	951,000	509,000	648,000
1953	8,164	11,967,000	917,000	1,426,000	761,000	2,721,000	5,866,000	1,277,000	1,677,000	251,500	5,545,000	8,181,000	736,000	425,000	736,000
1954	8,704	11,891,000	1,059,000	1,496,000	640,000	2,221,000	6,111,000	1,245,000	1,713,000	256,300	5,407,000	9,631,000	1,085,000	603,000	780,000
1955	9,683	13,265,000	1,119,000	1,706,000	631,000	2,483,000	6,959,000	1,580,000	2,067,000	266,700	5,819,000	10,732,000	1,157,000	640,000	837,000
1956	10,861	14,015,000	1,071,000	1,827,000	757,000	2,707,000	7,236,000	1,847,000	2,069,000	266,800	6,334,000	11,193,000	957,000	553,000	692,000
1957	11,532	14,572,000	1,041,000	1,811,000	923,000	2,763,000	7,643,000	1,876,000	2,122,000	294,100	6,595,000	9,992,000	855,000	483,000	758,000
1958	10,971	15,062,000	1,142,000	1,977,000	828,000	2,846,000	7,829,000	2,049,000	2,353,000	291,900	6,820,000	10,355,000	649,000	473,000	719,000
1959	12,920	16,039,000	1,034,000	1,991,000	883,000	2,979,000	8,618,000	1,877,000	3,009,000	295,400	7,114,000	10,926,000	741,000	505,000	814,000
1960	13,017	16,949,000	1,074,000	2,259,000	921,000	3,159,000	8,938,000	1,850,000	2,854,000	306,800	7,609,000	12,258,000	865,000	534,000	898,000
1961	13,731	17,944,000	1,217,000	2,409,000	1,000,000	3,229,000	9,437,000	2,061,000	2,977,000	315,000	8,035,000	12,529,000	797,000	534,000	946,000
1962	13,539	17,942,000	—	—	1,004,000	—	—	—	—	—	—	—	—	—	—
1963	14,878	17,341,000	1,150,000	2,602,000	948,000	2,922,000	8,676,000	2,124,000	2,752,000	286,700	7,936,000	13,055,000	1,213,000	660,000	1,067,000
1964	14,487	17,724,000	1,232,000	2,673,000	939,000	2,951,000	8,901,000	2,177,000	2,921,000	268,100	7,996,000	13,314,000	1,230,000	620,000	934,000

	Corporate tax returns	Total assets or liabilities	Selected assets					Selected liabilities				Receipts			Dividends paid other than own stock
			Cash	Notes and accounts receivable less allowance for bad debts	Inventories	Investments	Capital assets less reserves	Accounts payable and short-term debt	Long-term debt	Capital	Surplus and retained earnings	Total	Total less total deductions	Income tax (not adjusted for credits)	
Year	Ch540 [1] Number	Ch541 Thousand dollars	Ch542 Thousand dollars	Ch543 [2] Thousand dollars	Ch544 Thousand dollars	Ch545 Thousand dollars	Ch546 [3] Thousand dollars	Ch547 Thousand dollars	Ch548 Thousand dollars	Ch549 Thousand dollars	Ch550 Thousand dollars	Ch551 Thousand dollars	Ch552 Thousand dollars	Ch553 Thousand dollars	Ch554 Thousand dollars
1965	13,285	16,546,000	1,120,000	2,495,000	850,000	2,870,000	8,223,000	2,179,000	2,346,000	227,700	7,839,000	12,602,000	1,389,000	658,000	909,000
1966	14,831	17,605,000	1,182,000	2,683,000	890,000	3,000,000	8,879,000	2,498,000	2,666,000	260,400	7,910,000	14,609,000	1,725,000	832,000	1,088,000
1967	14,441	18,176,000	1,166,000	2,547,000	984,000	3,040,000	9,258,000	2,376,000	2,768,000	251,500	8,259,000	13,680,000	1,461,000	738,000	1,039,000
1968	12,813	19,813,000	1,318,000	2,725,000	1,064,000	3,423,000	9,956,000	2,630,000	3,214,000	231,600	9,066,000	14,550,000	1,602,000	898,000	1,181,000
1969	14,028	22,773,000	1,185,000	3,517,000	1,253,000	4,091,000	11,307,000	3,264,000	3,920,000	238,600	10,187,000	16,233,000	1,545,000	931,000	1,274,000
1970	14,465	23,972,812	1,251,647	3,347,947	1,289,480	4,519,159	11,744,421	3,321,811	4,157,797	2,685,704	11,013,188	17,747,750	1,820,402	1,051,738	1,177,550
1971	12,613	26,042,605	1,204,325	3,747,762	1,343,226	4,911,311	16,620,620	3,757,430	4,559,116	2,454,302	12,423,716	19,479,693	2,160,100	1,238,264	1,344,360
1972	14,211	30,461,410	1,479,920	4,538,341	1,494,154	5,751,708	14,430,999	4,512,517	5,582,397	2,615,073	13,914,653	22,648,211	3,182,297	1,740,471	1,986,779
1973	12,811	35,987,626	1,627,839	6,372,357	1,724,590	6,600,909	16,367,019	5,124,576	6,345,744	2,352,915	16,785,874	30,078,584	6,744,383	3,259,004	3,109,856
1974	15,732	47,039,718	2,381,681	11,060,077	3,014,709	7,840,914	18,984,822	5,689,983	7,538,624	2,970,961	18,788,429	64,804,842	25,878,148	12,257,873	7,729,679
1975	14,242	64,505,341	2,365,186	13,841,214	3,369,233	12,799,072	25,599,293	7,900,401	9,838,345	2,869,334	30,243,960	65,909,994	23,561,229	11,411,846	1,015,895
1976	15,606	76,701,653	3,037,747	16,130,428	3,864,203	16,093,243	31,617,172	9,949,259	12,299,490	3,460,629	34,873,266	84,329,009	29,987,384	14,549,609	4,088,323
1977	19,216	88,377,059	3,323,447	17,326,699	4,360,146	19,042,855	37,115,644	11,817,978	15,098,612	3,461,694	39,720,048	96,164,753	31,270,153	15,263,122	1,945,098
1978	19,124	97,670,205	3,068,877	19,873,644	4,739,477	19,474,857	41,195,422	12,134,637	20,039,817	3,597,033	42,067,744	94,706,062	27,547,910	13,837,808	2,194,973
1979	23,919	115,128,696	3,994,593	25,096,527	5,134,691	24,242,432	44,842,057	15,692,391	21,932,654	4,533,605	47,250,574	132,542,644	42,929,355	20,210,019	3,239,424
1980	25,576	126,947,880	4,895,248	25,045,558	5,543,183	31,524,506	48,799,111	24,453,656	26,898,761	5,488,751	49,351,133	176,672,390	7,620,766	4,083,078	4,757,780
1981	33,363	168,908,241	5,366,295	30,675,427	8,186,285	43,283,027	65,173,052	31,392,099	39,167,648	6,996,519	64,566,361	200,194,751	5,173,175	4,245,279	3,278,771
1982	36,676	192,380,473	5,811,313	28,814,200	8,852,449	55,264,818	76,422,262	33,983,125	48,020,816	8,953,599	72,218,905	203,098,557	52,822	3,330,610	3,926,230
1983	37,066	194,417,434	6,297,748	22,536,223	6,876,023	65,729,053	73,634,402	27,301,794	49,379,766	10,154,486	77,094,950	132,419,750	-1,885,989	2,100,692	2,710,318
1984	40,564	209,036,474	7,526,144	23,468,228	6,588,702	67,124,912	72,604,099	28,553,209	52,801,935	10,314,535	86,076,031	123,496,633	-1,131,332	2,381,154	3,057,411
1985	41,426	240,815,996	7,677,747	27,771,851	8,748,729	90,750,661	52,708,099	35,789,607	57,050,533	10,725,644	95,961,830	142,038,595	-3,350,920	1,810,559	—
1986	40,354	206,122,125	7,671,424	19,549,415	7,335,578	85,724,073	70,432,739	26,242,983	45,823,514	10,861,610	90,254,891	98,577,216	-3,516,755	1,453,090	—
1987	42,050	220,137,063	7,612,885	21,115,567	6,821,281	94,549,440	70,432,047	25,426,951	47,779,341	10,279,830	101,686,970	96,805,871	145,184	1,256,089	—
1988	41,080	225,639,336	7,168,561	21,604,025	7,213,538	90,213,701	76,551,331	25,634,632	48,719,957	9,794,318	100,426,816	100,426,996	3,661,583	1,815,670	—
1989	41,631	236,339,172	9,723,259	19,765,052	6,342,748	102,070,797	82,833,839	25,363,055	52,613,170	10,781,620	118,500,289	102,378,796	2,882,129	1,771,670	—
1990	39,674	219,197,640	8,574,514	22,897,736	6,199,727	85,207,014	79,822,443	25,789,061	49,466,030	10,232,669	104,394,105	111,444,457	4,977,949	2,223,977	—
1991	39,199	212,962,835	7,093,120	20,287,922	6,124,084	83,631,047	79,222,099	24,845,898	50,040,395	9,459,939	101,751,480	103,286,287	3,748,655	1,814,367	—
1992	36,660	218,211,769	8,239,232	19,097,388	6,454,160	81,286,200	66,468,753	24,656,450	49,702,581	10,998,006	99,795,120	112,830,722	2,529,200	1,657,953	—
1993	35,345	224,018,659	9,221,153	22,483,428	7,256,426	82,552,073	90,515,809	24,130,222	47,765,892	11,778,278	103,406,438	112,121,150	2,497,902	1,360,692	—
1994	35,371	239,893,306	8,511,987	26,920,888	6,958,895	82,768,666	94,971,294	25,244,714	50,745,967	13,371,145	108,976,648	115,687,307	3,420,748	1,605,727	—
1995	35,123	268,298,574	9,308,874	42,487,009	7,347,892	91,134,510	100,976,672	38,204,396	53,258,939	16,920,037	118,675,930	126,760,491	5,363,048	2,119,370	—
1996	35,799	299,106,231	11,343,335	42,685,822	7,674,818	104,742,658	108,707,763	32,843,362	56,629,422	19,056,325	136,467,375	141,278,092	7,892,269	2,525,467	—
1997	32,996	324,294,826	12,516,811	37,205,518	7,798,865	105,510,251	118,914,862	30,428,077	73,031,110	20,169,270	149,967,348	150,318,264	9,271,845	3,141,128	—

[1] Through 1956, number of returns filing balance sheets.
[2] Through 1958, includes loans to stockholders.
[3] Through 1938, excludes intangible assets.
[4] Includes inactive corporations.

Sources

U.S. Internal Revenue Service (and its predecessor, U.S. Bureau of Internal Revenue), *Statistics of Income* and *Statistics of Income: Corporation Income Tax Returns*, various issues.

Documentation

See the text for Table Ch510–524.

TABLE Ch555–569   Corporate assets, liabilities, receipts, dividends, and income tax: 1926–1997   [Construction]
Contributed by Naomi R. Lamoreaux

	Corporate tax returns	Total assets or liabilities	Selected assets					Selected liabilities				Receipts		Income tax (not adjusted for credits)	Dividends paid other than own stock
			Cash	Notes and accounts receivable less allowance for bad debts	Inventories	Investments	Capital assets less reserves	Accounts payable and short-term debt	Long-term debt	Capital	Surplus and retained earnings	Total	Total less total deductions		
Year	Ch555 [1] Number	Ch556 Thousand dollars	Ch557 Thousand dollars	Ch558 [2] Thousand dollars	Ch559 Thousand dollars	Ch560 Thousand dollars	Ch561 [3] Thousand dollars	Ch562 Thousand dollars	Ch563 Thousand dollars	Ch564 Thousand dollars	Ch565 Thousand dollars	Ch566 Thousand dollars	Ch567 Thousand dollars	Ch568 Thousand dollars	Ch569 Thousand dollars
1926	13,981 [4]	2,358,000	213,000	668,000	273,000	—	654,000	645,000	233,000	639,000	317,000	—	—	—	—
1927	14,955	2,739,000	191,000	743,000	306,000	—	743,000	691,000	237,000	738,000	426,000	—	—	—	—
1928	15,289	2,690,000	197,000	816,000	263,000	—	756,000	818,000	220,000	808,000	442,000	—	—	—	—
1929	16,355	3,095,000	208,000	876,000	305,000	476,000	857,000	846,000	350,000	881,000	510,000	—	—	—	—
1930	16,496	3,012,000	215,000	800,000	248,000	554,000	896,000	773,000	350,000	932,000	524,000	—	—	—	—
1931	15,350	2,475,000	155,000	643,000	180,000	545,000	704,000	580,000	297,000	809,000	450,000	2,131,000	-4,000	7,000	63,000
1932	15,382	2,141,000	132,000	479,000	138,000	517,000	674,000	448,000	274,000	791,000	332,000	1,384,000	-84,000	3,000	40,000
1933	14,398	1,833,000	100,000	390,000	125,000	479,000	555,000	376,000	235,000	734,000	263,000	1,035,000	-51,000	3,000	28,000
1934	14,082	1,700,000	110,000	418,000	125,000	325,000	546,000	392,000	131,000	707,000	198,000	1,220,000	-23,000	4,000	23,000
1935	14,117	1,613,000	123,000	426,000	125,000	288,000	485,000	372,000	140,000	668,000	158,000	1,425,000	5,000	7,000	29,000
1936	14,574	1,689,000	126,000	544,000	159,000	244,000	493,000	436,000	135,000	608,000	188,000	1,927,000	38,000	11,000	49,000
1937	14,807	1,702,000	140,000	543,000	170,000	240,000	494,000	415,000	152,000	604,000	287,000	2,355,000	47,000	14,000	49,000
1938	14,308	1,364,000	134,000	460,000	116,000	188,000	385,000	341,000	98,000	515,000	225,000	1,882,000	28,000	10,000	23,000
1939	14,162	1,370,000	146,000	529,000	121,000	159,000	326,000	395,000	95,000	482,000	213,000	2,159,000	35,000	11,000	28,000
1940	13,795	1,445,000	157,000	608,000	117,000	182,000	321,000	434,000	93,000	458,000	260,000	2,439,000	70,000	23,000	30,000
1941	12,894	1,714,000	195,000	768,000	140,000	205,000	325,000	532,000	107,000	444,000	358,000	3,406,000	178,000	81,000	32,000
1942	11,729	2,082,000	315,000	934,000	177,000	262,000	309,000	568,000	107,000	430,000	500,000	4,661,000	337,000	204,000	32,000
1943	10,707	1,826,000	315,000	678,000	147,000	291,000	308,000	410,000	115,000	415,000	506,000	4,177,000	255,000	165,000	30,000
1944	10,326	1,629,000	263,000	555,000	147,000	308,000	274,000	345,000	101,000	401,000	492,000	3,106,000	138,000	89,000	25,000
1945	10,726	1,619,000	257,000	559,000	159,000	275,000	291,000	364,000	102,000	405,000	482,000	2,903,000	113,000	62,000	29,000
1946	14,406	2,497,000	319,000	993,000	332,000	287,000	459,000	645,000	181,000	517,000	636,000	4,234,000	231,000	83,000	38,000
1947	18,398	3,419,000	409,000	1,457,000	460,000	328,000	651,000	897,000	252,000	633,000	866,000	6,899,000	386,000	137,000	42,000
1948	21,293	4,203,000	523,000	1,881,000	475,000	364,000	810,000	1,020,000	297,000	749,000	1,168,000	9,198,000	569,000	207,000	67,000
1949	23,402	4,637,000	693,000	2,052,000	428,000	429,000	889,000	1,043,000	291,000	832,000	1,388,000	9,691,000	511,000	196,000	71,000
1950	25,344	5,661,000	661,000	2,670,000	614,000	502,000	1,025,000	1,496,000	434,000	911,000	1,568,000	11,262,000	545,000	238,000	81,000
1951	27,315	6,698,000	788,000	3,149,000	773,000	596,000	1,199,000	1,859,000	629,000	972,000	1,783,000	13,946,000	554,000	287,000	72,000
1952	29,433	7,307,000	918,000	3,372,000	793,000	673,000	1,336,000	1,904,000	713,000	1,035,000	1,946,000	15,047,000	596,000	304,000	75,000
1953	32,158	7,414,000	974,000	3,474,000	664,000	680,000	1,346,000	1,976,000	628,000	1,115,000	1,959,000	15,914,000	512,000	271,000	74,000
1954	33,700	8,254,000	1,074,000	3,694,000	886,000	789,000	1,438,000	2,302,000	631,000	1,216,000	2,189,000	17,215,000	483,000	252,000	75,000
1955	38,653	9,319,000	1,052,000	4,530,000	693,000	1,042,000	1,664,000	2,864,000	784,000	1,347,000	2,354,000	19,722,000	479,000	251,000	85,000
1956	45,223	10,386,000	1,184,000	5,167,000	929,000	882,000	1,835,000	3,243,000	731,000	1,500,000	2,452,000	23,257,000	680,000	326,000	80,000
1957	50,425	11,935,000	1,401,000	5,894,000	1,040,000	1,057,000	2,117,000	3,520,000	1,034,000	1,692,000	2,838,000	26,744,000	745,000	383,000	95,000
1958	56,181	13,204,000	1,659,000	6,132,000	1,303,000	1,314,000	2,321,000	3,943,000	1,308,000	1,856,000	3,067,000	28,234,000	670,000	356,000	89,000
1959	66,260	14,222,000	1,559,000	5,589,000	1,562,000	1,424,000	2,639,000	5,096,000	1,344,000	1,971,000	3,068,000	32,140,000	581,000	332,000	91,000
1960	72,332	15,367,000	1,625,000	5,584,000	1,643,000	1,453,000	2,905,000	5,669,000	1,549,000	2,115,000	3,208,000	32,893,000	382,000	297,000	116,000
1961	83,791	17,745,000	1,781,000	6,130,000	2,535,000	1,753,000	3,279,000	6,438,000	1,962,000	2,383,000	3,575,000	37,413,000	512,000	329,000	140,000
1962	90,604	19,467,000	—	—	2,559,000	—	—	—	—	—	—	41,065,000	621,000	367,000	134,000
1963	96,466	21,395,000	2,153,000	7,295,000	2,635,000	2,089,000	4,234,000	7,741,000	2,637,000	2,674,000	3,928,000	45,649,000	650,000	369,000	143,000
1964	104,134	23,309,000	2,356,000	7,744,000	2,942,000	2,103,000	4,788,000	8,410,000	2,734,000	2,721,000	4,257,000	49,741,000	946,000	424,000	187,000

Year	Corporate tax returns Ch555 [1] Number	Total assets or liabilities Ch556 Thousand dollars	Cash Ch557 Thousand dollars	Notes and accounts receivable less allowance for bad debts Ch558 [2] Thousand dollars	Inventories Ch559 Thousand dollars	Investments Ch560 Thousand dollars	Capital assets less reserves Ch561 [3] Thousand dollars	Accounts payable and short-term debt Ch562 Thousand dollars	Long-term debt Ch563 Thousand dollars	Capital Ch564 Thousand dollars	Surplus and retained earnings Ch565 Thousand dollars	Total Ch566 Thousand dollars	Total less total deductions Ch567 Thousand dollars	Income tax (not adjusted for credits) Ch568 Thousand dollars	Dividends paid other than own stock Ch569 Thousand dollars
1965	113,284	26,725,000	2,673,000	9,098,000	3,532,000	2,223,000	5,525,000	10,126,000	3,051,000	2,939,000	4,917,000	56,695,000	1,258,000	519,000	240,000
1966	112,373	28,809,000	2,909,000	9,880,000	3,674,000	2,204,000	6,240,000	10,600,000	3,567,000	2,957,000	5,744,000	63,030,000	1,392,000	612,000	200,000
1967	123,180	32,538,000	3,210,000	10,793,000	4,434,000	2,411,000	7,139,000	11,145,000	4,026,000	3,141,000	6,622,000	68,022,000	1,549,000	699,000	282,000
1968	125,999	35,896,000	3,512,000	11,673,000	4,570,000	3,329,000	7,946,000	12,063,000	4,801,000	3,471,000	7,409,000	72,263,000	1,713,000	768,000	281,000
1969	127,670	39,643,000	3,616,000	13,505,000	5,059,000	3,065,000	8,704,000	13,866,000	4,815,000	3,367,000	7,964,000	83,913,000	1,660,000	814,000	398,000
1970	138,905	42,719,792	4,049,253	14,104,806	5,344,682	3,549,763	9,265,450	14,596,736	5,185,552	3,598,822	8,637,166	90,310,644	1,540,622	780,987	299,204
1971	143,092	48,242,866	4,777,308	15,187,255	6,263,716	4,098,932	10,331,310	16,184,566	6,460,969	3,741,114	9,865,788	97,492,609	1,924,652	908,429	329,253
1972	154,418	55,090,085	4,978,459	11,220,585	7,928,854	5,067,123	11,990,131	19,229,681	7,548,280	4,179,318	11,139,965	108,737,575	1,875,297	942,508	293,625
1973	175,884	66,417,838	5,633,851	19,944,918	10,347,870	6,409,781	14,312,847	24,205,663	9,562,054	4,311,750	12,974,006	126,741,484	2,167,618	1,088,356	400,447
1974	185,563	74,108,047	6,069,320	21,045,157	12,322,603	6,782,750	16,529,468	26,467,250	11,958,549	4,502,335	13,680,897	137,024,339	1,823,767	1,184,335	454,047
1975	191,219	76,691,947	7,328,173	20,796,335	12,554,152	6,972,063	18,389,244	25,747,455	12,637,295	4,855,437	15,242,444	146,955,117	2,237,808	1,332,299	464,553
1976	195,933	80,759,509	7,843,033	21,074,002	13,630,508	7,453,320	18,839,307	26,975,904	12,723,657	5,053,049	16,661,951	154,096,876	2,791,192	1,511,654	514,107
1977	214,745	91,222,022	8,712,907	24,734,482	15,693,140	7,038,091	21,280,902	31,373,515	14,103,707	5,903,557	18,442,600	181,550,922	4,457,556	1,919,876	556,171
1978	228,657	105,545,997	9,560,850	29,014,127	19,335,507	8,010,516	23,368,020	37,799,380	15,217,242	5,348,464	21,876,413	216,710,160	5,803,591	2,427,708	627,914
1979	249,887	123,261,127	11,275,366	34,243,201	21,078,815	10,059,615	27,264,424	43,406,398	19,032,360	5,674,266	25,449,996	252,852,706	5,862,029	2,545,393	681,853
1980	272,432	132,939,026	13,344,814	36,106,648	22,055,863	11,248,573	27,854,089	45,114,397	19,076,627	5,941,850	28,924,134	267,205,356	5,089,081	2,557,976	793,764
1981	276,395	150,764,144	14,236,832	37,977,456	23,059,162	14,554,793	32,256,598	45,625,560	21,596,688	6,607,863	32,661,190	280,172,375	3,427,774	2,360,800	889,557
1982	282,345	153,085,046	15,150,303	39,276,354	22,865,508	16,833,174	32,293,373	50,675,342	23,362,155	7,331,352	34,211,783	281,747,868	2,192,739	2,114,820	916,690
1983	283,519	161,365,795	15,251,451	39,950,909	24,107,031	19,539,454	32,809,157	49,303,765	30,985,665	7,390,565	36,948,119	290,798,843	2,224,266	1,859,927	846,579
1984	306,906	195,272,738	17,718,758	46,875,583	28,244,404	30,962,937	37,105,381	60,683,773	35,592,423	8,839,222	44,514,025	338,575,635	2,879,481	1,767,756	738,873
1985	318,276	215,297,771	18,258,973	53,048,415	30,964,501	34,909,649	39,084,185	70,420,213	35,987,365	9,173,765	48,971,215	387,232,953	4,409,840	2,312,846	—
1986	341,816	218,880,512	20,460,013	57,191,245	32,351,852	31,455,355	40,295,032	70,632,253	38,200,198	8,052,829	48,208,084	412,477,214	5,813,639	2,525,994	—
1987	371,169	222,064,937	22,947,739	57,244,779	33,352,955	29,573,027	41,275,855	70,140,245	41,641,804	7,757,070	49,943,339	454,831,094	8,734,446	2,459,657	—
1988	381,499	241,395,405	24,943,516	64,150,067	32,417,281	34,674,329	44,982,062	75,180,445	42,867,024	7,643,192	59,170,556	499,690,338	11,333,107	2,497,276	—
1989	393,103	249,711,210	25,378,919	67,193,557	34,156,301	35,582,057	46,679,466	76,786,152	45,173,077	8,108,527	62,620,759	517,477,336	8,688,605	2,327,882	—
1990	406,874	243,829,026	27,167,367	67,018,873	32,230,686	28,251,158	47,776,424	80,063,116	44,370,971	8,467,751	59,470,262	534,654,044	6,853,249	2,092,196	—
1991	416,987	243,035,939	27,267,065	64,880,524	29,616,722	35,519,764	48,442,055	74,775,526	42,923,484	9,260,422	65,309,162	515,128,533	5,880,805	2,008,680	—
1992	407,881	231,050,110	26,127,300	63,366,013	27,818,870	35,721,223	45,010,998	70,540,434	34,747,506	8,498,347	66,972,696	499,405,033	5,547,243	1,550,717	—
1993	417,250	240,435,575	26,855,813	67,042,954	30,296,203	33,576,210	46,421,393	75,064,109	34,237,422	8,883,697	70,773,937	538,266,252	7,568,835	1,654,270	—
1994	432,965	249,093,544	28,563,896	72,562,328	33,737,741	26,658,066	46,963,221	80,436,761	33,958,467	8,099,265	74,171,324	592,760,390	11,536,595	2,072,970	—
1995	449,882	265,812,616	31,508,759	79,176,244	34,006,965	29,125,549	50,953,386	84,570,076	35,146,050	8,441,826	82,406,676	637,090,195	14,468,211	2,462,222	—
1996	471,230	284,595,206	34,604,102	84,468,784	39,091,171	32,789,278	54,568,347	90,841,044	36,945,980	8,211,371	88,525,623	710,467,223	17,885,708	2,958,069	—
1997	487,783	314,551,349	39,548,824	94,190,275	39,991,175	35,439,694	59,140,937	102,764,537	42,048,183	8,804,901	94,747,262	779,014,473	20,585,350	2,953,440	—

[1] Through 1956, number of returns filing balance sheets.
[2] Through 1958, includes loans to stockholders.
[3] Through 1938, excludes intangible assets.
[4] Includes inactive corporations.

Sources

U.S. Internal Revenue Service (and its predecessor, U.S. Bureau of Internal Revenue), *Statistics of Income* and *Statistics of Income: Corporation Income Tax Returns*, various issues.

Documentation

See the text for Table Ch510–524.

TABLE Ch570–584 Corporate assets, liabilities, receipts, dividends, and income tax: 1926–1997 [Manufacturing]

Contributed by Naomi R. Lamoreaux

	Corporate tax returns	Total assets or liabilities	Selected assets					Selected liabilities				Receipts			
			Cash	Notes and accounts receivable less allowance for bad debts	Inventories	Investments	Capital assets less reserves	Accounts payable and short-term debt	Long-term debt	Capital	Surplus and retained earnings	Total	Total less total deductions	Income tax (not adjusted for credits)	Dividends paid other than own stock
	Number														
Year	Ch570 [1]	Ch571	Ch572	Ch573 [2]	Ch574	Ch575	Ch576 [3]	Ch577	Ch578	Ch579	Ch580	Ch581	Ch582	Ch583	Ch584
		Thousand dollars	Thousand dollars	Thousand dollars	Thousand dollars	Thousand dollars	Thousand dollars	Thousand dollars	Thousand dollars	Thousand dollars	Thousand dollars	Thousand dollars	Thousand dollars	Thousand dollars	Thousand dollars
1926	84,251 [4]	64,727,000	3,528,000	8,567,000	12,284,000	—	26,619,000	7,216,000	4,340,000	31,412,000	14,862,000	—	—	—	—
1927	84,776	65,582,000	3,525,000	8,946,000	11,884,000	—	26,007,000	7,349,000	4,806,000	31,553,000	16,496,000	—	—	—	—
1928	84,925	67,060,000	3,895,000	9,502,000	12,011,000	—	27,025,000	7,449,000	5,446,000	32,491,000	17,526,000	—	—	—	—
1929	86,112	70,282,000	3,847,000	9,572,000	12,614,000	9,154,000	28,235,000	7,418,000	5,450,000	33,228,000	19,466,000	—	—	—	—
1930	85,520	69,245,000	3,960,000	8,730,000	11,157,000	11,062,000	28,987,000	6,852,000	5,879,000	33,855,000	18,267,000	—	—	—	—
1931	80,106	63,801,000	3,458,000	7,819,000	9,003,000	10,120,000	27,286,000	6,017,000	5,581,000	32,329,000	15,310,000	43,534,000	-308,000	164,000	2,276,000
1932	82,083	59,023,000	3,343,000	6,541,000	7,310,000	11,651,000	25,622,000	5,507,000	5,226,000	31,186,000	12,790,000	31,850,000	-1,468,000	100,000	1,324,000
1933	82,836	57,753,000	3,084,000	6,765,000	8,084,000	11,481,000	24,384,000	5,722,000	5,021,000	30,398,000	12,943,000	34,943,000	502,000	206,000	1,159,000
1934	85,499	52,531,000	3,006,000	7,483,000	8,319,000	9,663,000	20,451,000	6,768,000	4,025,000	26,930,000	11,201,000	40,581,000	1,387,000	263,000	1,578,000
1935	85,817	52,682,000	3,389,000	7,376,000	8,735,000	9,688,000	20,231,000	6,745,000	4,387,000	25,882,000	11,729,000	47,473,000	2,494,000	355,000	2,184,000
1936	85,350	54,262,000	3,522,000	7,368,000	10,029,000	9,524,000	20,690,000	7,096,000	4,256,000	25,622,000	12,845,000	55,378,000	3,636,000	587,000	2,867,000
1937	85,474	55,723,000	3,283,000	7,004,000	11,454,000	9,525,000	21,537,000	7,271,000	4,904,000	25,951,000	15,288,000	61,560,000	3,686,000	641,000	2,899,000
1938	82,155	54,792,000	4,003,000	6,761,000	10,192,000	9,444,000	21,544,000	6,456,000	5,274,000	25,847,000	15,413,000	50,489,000	1,615,000	372,000	1,634,000
1939	80,860	56,739,000	4,570,000	7,427,000	10,993,000	9,507,000	23,060,000	6,996,000	5,255,000	25,640,000	16,756,000	57,603,000	3,571,000	629,000	2,170,000
1940	80,198	60,547,000	5,744,000	8,412,000	12,334,000	9,349,000	23,605,000	7,311,000	5,418,000	25,429,000	18,734,000	66,246,000	5,313,000	1,544,000	2,390,000
1941	78,645	70,071,000	6,149,000	10,858,000	16,178,000	10,781,000	24,727,000	9,151,000	5,702,000	25,476,000	22,922,000	91,606,000	10,310,000	4,881,000	2,800,000
1942	76,334	85,092,000	9,075,000	13,809,000	18,433,000	14,537,000	26,607,000	11,133,000	6,219,000	27,113,000	27,958,000	117,895,000	13,554,000	8,158,000	2,486,000
1943	73,149	94,768,000	11,752,000	15,010,000	19,155,000	18,501,000	27,037,000	12,540,000	6,573,000	27,378,000	33,310,000	144,560,000	16,428,000	10,430,000	2,596,000
1944	72,170	95,999,000	11,918,000	14,552,000	18,421,000	21,836,000	25,921,000	12,501,000	6,332,000	28,335,000	34,735,000	152,673,000	14,754,000	9,318,000	2,828,000
1945	75,215	91,030,000	11,270,000	13,569,000	17,256,000	21,076,000	25,145,000	11,056,000	6,385,000	28,445,000	35,705,000	140,155,000	10,179,000	6,064,000	2,801,000
1946	92,771	96,300,000	11,042,000	13,517,000	23,282,000	16,561,000	29,414,000	12,647,000	7,879,000	30,015,000	37,574,000	137,087,000	11,508,000	4,543,000	3,378,000
1947	105,390	111,356,000	11,884,000	16,138,000	27,634,000	17,774,000	35,380,000	14,750,000	9,906,000	32,577,000	44,097,000	178,173,000	16,477,000	6,241,000	4,143,000
1948	110,078	121,708,000	11,778,000	17,090,000	30,355,000	18,685,000	41,227,000	15,253,000	11,757,000	33,577,000	50,506,000	198,260,000	17,985,000	6,760,000	4,617,000
1949	110,269	123,755,000	12,610,000	16,067,000	27,780,000	20,789,000	44,118,000	13,286,000	12,262,000	34,780,000	54,105,000	185,285,000	14,158,000	5,446,000	4,838,000
1950	109,537	141,600,000	13,370,000	21,753,000	33,008,000	24,528,000	46,377,000	17,559,000	12,269,000	35,502,000	61,539,000	218,272,000	23,608,000	10,575,000	6,037,000
1951	114,142	160,876,000	14,542,000	24,011,000	40,774,000	26,014,000	52,643,000	20,823,000	15,797,000	37,676,000	67,049,000	258,956,000	24,697,000	14,060,000	5,715,000
1952	113,711	170,282,000	14,748,000	26,907,000	41,801,000	25,922,000	57,723,000	22,783,000	19,372,000	38,730,000	70,767,000	258,969,000	20,228,000	11,348,000	5,665,000
1953	115,254	176,805,000	14,847,000	26,368,000	42,992,000	27,267,000	61,657,000	22,258,000	20,392,000	39,265,000	74,549,000	278,495,000	21,290,000	12,054,000	5,848,000
1954	115,820	181,891,000	15,745,000	27,767,000	39,872,000	28,730,000	65,364,000	22,257,000	21,547,000	40,519,000	79,384,000	264,966,000	18,194,000	9,385,000	5,818,000
1955	124,199	201,360,000	15,999,000	32,380,000	44,422,000	34,095,000	69,892,000	25,853,000	22,426,000	42,986,000	88,007,000	303,211,000	25,816,000	12,891,000	6,770,000
1956	128,457	216,363,000	15,514,000	36,276,000	49,788,000	32,274,000	77,330,000	29,338,000	26,121,000	44,923,000	94,065,000	316,679,000	24,504,000	12,209,000	7,121,000
1957	133,558	224,910,000	15,165,000	36,083,000	50,358,000	33,574,000	83,801,000	28,434,000	29,032,000	46,194,000	100,081,000	330,749,000	22,677,000	11,481,000	7,366,000
1958	145,531	235,836,000	16,231,000	39,609,000	49,643,000	36,414,000	87,733,000	30,226,000	31,274,000	47,778,000	107,072,000	326,940,000	18,424,000	9,877,000	7,239,000
1959	156,297	252,134,000	15,289,000	42,245,000	54,799,000	42,559,000	89,997,000	33,444,000	32,132,000	49,498,000	112,392,000	363,157,000	25,026,000	12,435,000	7,666,000
1960	165,862	262,308,000	15,373,000	43,378,000	55,763,000	44,190,000	94,201,000	34,870,000	33,177,000	51,047,000	118,022,000	371,093,000	22,200,000	11,362,000	8,028,000
1961	173,558	275,964,000	16,064,000	48,810,000	57,523,000	45,900,000	96,917,000	37,893,000	35,133,000	52,429,000	124,087,000	377,580,000	22,538,000	11,403,000	8,409,000
1962	183,149	292,640,000	—	—	60,941,000	—	—	—	—	—	—	407,865,000	25,386,000	12,643,000	9,508,000
1963	181,800	310,207,000	17,463,000	55,906,000	64,664,000	53,781,000	104,782,000	43,692,000	38,673,000	54,029,000	139,432,000	429,507,000	28,825,000	14,323,000	10,330,000
1964	184,961	335,190,000	17,817,000	67,449,000	68,108,000	53,486,000	113,693,000	48,849,000	43,969,000	55,230,000	150,132,000	464,820,000	32,552,000	15,488,000	11,509,000

Year	Corporate tax returns [1] Ch570 Number	Total assets or liabilities Ch571	Cash Ch572	Notes and accounts receivable less allowance for bad debts [2] Ch573	Inventories Ch574	Investments Ch575	Capital assets less reserves [3] Ch576	Accounts payable and short-term debt Ch577	Long-term debt Ch578	Capital Ch579	Surplus and retained earnings Ch580	Receipts Total Ch581	Receipts Total less total deductions Ch582	Income tax (not adjusted for credits) Ch583	Dividends paid other than own stock Ch584
		Thousand dollars	Thousand dollars	Thousand dollars	Thousand dollars	Thousand dollars	Thousand dollars	Thousand dollars	Thousand dollars	Thousand dollars	Thousand dollars	Thousand dollars	Thousand dollars	Thousand dollars	Thousand dollars
1965	185,924	311,524,000	18,673,000	76,544,000	75,994,000	57,902,000	125,493,000	56,159,000	50,997,000	56,096,000	165,482,000	514,719,000	39,509,000	18,415,000	12,205,000
1966	187,642	405,967,000	18,993,000	84,669,000	85,829,000	56,624,000	140,711,000	65,561,000	59,844,000	56,996,000	180,233,000	571,009,000	43,490,000	20,143,000	12,879,000
1967	197,023	448,026,000	20,432,000	92,521,000	91,955,000	63,185,000	155,823,000	73,556,000	69,703,000	59,848,000	198,661,000	590,822,000	39,486,000	18,589,000	13,215,000
1968	191,915	500,564,000	21,271,000	105,122,000	98,231,000	75,725,000	170,505,000	85,609,000	81,132,000	60,177,000	216,589,000	648,965,000	43,560,000	22,427,000	14,461,000
1969	202,102	572,127,000	21,026,000	125,403,000	108,635,000	89,330,000	191,253,000	106,172,000	95,725,000	64,673,000	239,523,000	710,084,000	40,386,000	21,621,000	16,029,000
1970	197,807	612,912,516	21,172,895	132,068,461	112,824,459	94,853,833	204,009,256	115,428,627	110,030,468	65,112,101	248,572,088	722,911,319	30,497,428	16,981,466	14,616,282
1971	200,973	646,645,886	22,806,365	137,601,803	112,740,929	110,028,891	210,730,527	115,196,071	119,564,836	66,006,207	264,763,581	748,478,571	37,155,368	19,615,770	14,675,256
1972	230,238	698,659,684	23,959,555	153,932,070	123,125,391	117,893,833	219,250,643	125,620,533	127,075,557	66,808,731	287,418,607	870,463,407	46,642,648	22,842,078	15,626,374
1973	209,259	786,163,347	26,403,147	177,391,772	143,267,915	132,925,619	238,770,165	153,340,859	138,742,681	67,970,349	318,647,255	1,038,045,522	60,876,741	28,536,338	17,245,232
1974	211,563	885,822,652	27,436,871	194,963,858	173,702,196	144,389,082	269,906,921	187,955,036	153,677,009	70,570,964	348,429,596	1,297,265,793	69,564,173	32,288,865	18,706,198
1975	217,354	944,581,970	31,054,917	203,845,270	172,948,362	163,454,651	293,844,902	186,866,591	175,162,951	72,261,787	378,361,289	1,296,359,650	65,670,154	32,475,947	19,973,061
1976	212,333	1,034,602,790	36,699,412	225,309,352	187,915,521	180,421,939	321,341,514	198,498,682	193,442,808	77,488,665	409,977,722	1,462,652,852	84,954,334	41,452,853	22,884,452
1977	231,149	1,182,263,458	39,726,110	263,833,820	207,458,384	213,831,496	361,247,151	227,399,912	210,589,393	79,846,023	477,475,576	1,653,531,899	93,988,965	47,434,803	26,913,367
1978	223,471	1,308,673,807	44,695,714	306,964,685	223,353,223	229,153,058	402,693,309	260,412,041	237,682,006	82,590,174	523,294,484	1,836,552,260	106,542,635	53,092,051	31,173,451
1979	236,564	1,528,575,203	47,667,575	357,594,626	256,278,072	280,318,672	464,512,922	323,453,473	267,817,415	89,506,305	598,209,941	2,152,660,164	120,529,086	58,976,752	38,121,235
1980	242,550	1,709,471,700	50,387,699	385,069,638	268,446,932	300,600,412	532,618,549	333,337,261	305,689,825	97,030,393	666,677,559	2,404,323,844	113,730,036	60,184,725	37,306,509
1981	251,294	1,933,710,383	55,886,455	419,235,308	285,204,131	394,733,442	605,318,125	374,158,173	337,893,659	104,294,746	764,009,109	2,613,512,581	104,378,012	59,554,935	41,434,134
1982	259,106	2,060,710,683	54,468,342	439,300,826	274,567,278	429,217,913	669,524,667	412,720,542	371,551,511	111,859,814	806,135,983	2,488,331,915	65,076,979	45,760,800	43,912,134
1983	261,927	2,232,987,922	68,812,454	483,908,291	270,385,611	471,389,357	693,120,061	416,397,967	378,514,253	119,082,436	857,809,388	2,552,830,718	83,572,992	50,950,876	43,295,901
1984	272,050	2,417,631,605	65,145,271	501,359,041	298,374,824	558,105,530	733,201,858	454,327,878	423,898,964	128,155,097	935,708,135	2,768,247,655	107,093,801	58,542,710	45,630,537
1985	276,545	2,644,393,424	78,384,536	585,442,919	299,379,832	627,719,666	770,021,474	535,325,463	457,693,586	127,862,443	1,023,322,103	2,831,062,496	97,957,150	56,687,476	—
1986	285,119	2,931,610,462	82,651,314	655,687,933	309,880,755	693,046,503	836,435,939	556,852,522	581,898,174	138,351,988	1,047,111,692	2,810,713,781	87,014,878	50,222,612	—
1987	294,211	3,111,708,665	88,739,062	688,748,762	331,733,231	737,186,010	879,664,471	590,193,026	635,648,257	139,335,934	1,132,473,595	3,141,406,444	129,295,213	57,286,912	—
1988	299,538	3,390,433,557	93,799,272	750,676,283	354,494,099	810,312,865	958,250,392	668,559,039	727,540,706	149,174,956	1,196,881,509	3,348,965,911	178,991,266	68,661,707	—
1989	301,346	3,721,219,914	90,661,255	785,857,093	373,518,748	945,608,887	1,072,354,134	760,527,517	747,966,622	164,807,753	1,304,867,902	3,531,219,028	154,073,758	63,780,169	—
1990	301,669	3,921,323,756	93,352,597	822,329,911	379,419,902	955,838,096	1,156,133,727	847,809,780	821,829,592	179,575,026	1,323,890,016	3,688,693,895	143,572,053	64,385,522	—
1991	300,122	4,028,360,038	107,165,214	790,086,253	373,792,878	1,048,592,045	1,177,420,557	784,392,611	825,893,110	181,011,196	1,411,976,708	3,658,501,307	109,754,514	53,891,094	—
1992	300,071	4,113,123,804	109,289,289	872,779,884	371,341,238	1,053,833,119	1,189,091,211	818,190,145	871,762,206	183,082,955	1,347,010,702	3,760,265,837	126,421,265	53,369,555	—
1993	307,419	4,225,134,395	117,284,200	900,216,922	377,241,078	1,042,535,665	1,216,722,053	844,506,576	864,109,659	189,495,231	1,378,900,564	3,890,747,271	149,154,611	61,912,971	—
1994	312,383	4,525,455,926	121,737,999	897,459,541	402,664,510	1,185,426,520	1,282,881,851	934,663,483	907,436,537	199,816,746	1,528,537,337	4,218,791,583	194,490,801	74,398,479	—
1995	319,699	4,941,082,530	137,694,522	992,269,530	432,291,778	1,220,126,262	1,380,691,087	1,051,033,313	982,394,009	216,871,453	1,695,641,793	4,585,549,761	230,985,684	83,817,532	—
1996	325,689	5,425,184,573	162,579,575	1,035,023,065	442,240,560	1,393,733,604	1,490,482,173	1,148,834,841	1,067,137,841	238,585,048	1,922,325,270	4,902,669,122	249,708,599	95,502,448	—
1997	325,045	5,966,306,398	175,165,261	1,150,855,449	465,751,279	1,519,592,048	1,595,405,825	1,317,597,308	1,132,773,540	249,993,302	2,082,069,833	5,177,663,770	266,959,713	101,849,787	—

[1] Through 1956, number of returns filing balance sheets.

[2] Through 1958, includes loans to stockholders.

[3] Through 1938, excludes intangible assets.

[4] Includes inactive corporations.

Sources

U.S. Internal Revenue Service (and its predecessor, U.S. Bureau of Internal Revenue), *Statistics of Income* and *Statistics of Income: Corporation Income Tax Returns*, various issues.

Documentation

See the text for Table Ch510–524.

TABLE Ch585–599   Corporate assets, liabilities, receipts, dividends, and income tax: 1926–1997   [Transportation, communications, and utilities]

Contributed by Naomi R. Lamoreaux

Year	Corporate tax returns Ch585 [1] Number	Total assets or liabilities Ch586 Thousand dollars	Selected assets					Selected liabilities				Receipts		Income tax (not adjusted for credits) Ch598 Thousand dollars	Dividends paid other than own stock Ch599 Thousand dollars
			Cash Ch587 Thousand dollars	Notes and accounts receivable less allowance for bad debts Ch588 [2] Thousand dollars	Inventories Ch589 Thousand dollars	Investments Ch590 Thousand dollars	Capital assets less reserves Ch591 [3] Thousand dollars	Accounts payable and short-term debt Ch592 Thousand dollars	Long-term debt Ch593 Thousand dollars	Capital Ch594 Thousand dollars	Surplus and retained earnings Ch595 Thousand dollars	Total Ch596 Thousand dollars	Total less total deductions Ch597 Thousand dollars		
1926	18,297 [4]	57,245,000	1,358,000	1,528,000	942,000	—	40,699,000	2,337,000	19,932,000	20,466,000	6,045,000	—	—	—	—
1927	16,858	66,559,000	1,549,000	2,115,000	1,024,000	—	46,487,000	2,604,000	23,542,000	25,296,000	7,594,000	—	—	—	—
1928	16,770	71,380,000	1,571,000	3,628,000	1,000,000	—	48,887,000	3,585,000	25,696,000	25,741,000	9,837,000	—	—	—	—
1929	17,258	77,792,000	1,634,000	3,974,000	1,119,000	9,614,000	52,205,000	4,449,000	26,619,000	28,131,000	10,955,000	—	—	—	—
1930	17,248	80,479,000	1,693,000	3,670,000	973,000	14,505,000	55,060,000	4,146,000	28,739,000	28,345,000	12,431,000	—	—	—	—
1931	16,457	72,337,000	1,333,000	2,826,000	889,000	11,616,000	52,214,000	3,494,000	27,024,000	26,642,000	10,332,000	13,297,000	958,000	104,000	1,789,000
1932	17,547	72,149,000	1,299,000	2,539,000	713,000	12,956,000	50,058,000	3,382,000	27,006,000	27,793,000	8,036,000	10,735,000	341,000	97,000	1,300,000
1933	17,706	69,049,000	1,290,000	2,210,000	741,000	11,323,000	50,141,000	2,798,000	26,959,000	26,191,000	8,000,000	10,110,000	249,000	92,000	994,000
1934	21,265	68,461,000	1,306,000	2,660,000	629,000	10,535,000	50,472,000	3,908,000	25,654,000	27,131,000	6,785,000	10,997,000	631,000	126,000	1,213,000
1935	21,149	66,478,000	1,233,000	1,869,000	617,000	10,050,000	49,581,000	3,189,000	26,391,000	26,119,000	6,243,000	11,353,000	638,000	126,000	1,281,000
1936	20,667	62,715,000	1,499,000	1,602,000	651,000	8,377,000	47,673,000	2,987,000	24,619,000	24,786,000	5,263,000	11,938,000	980,000	166,000	1,285,000
1937	20,775	64,648,000	1,181,000	1,592,000	818,000	8,825,000	49,629,000	2,925,000	25,803,000	25,420,000	7,172,000	13,235,000	1,084,000	192,000	1,334,000
1938	18,595	60,843,000	1,444,000	1,422,000	692,000	8,159,000	47,064,000	2,830,000	24,418,000	23,815,000	6,468,000	12,037,000	687,000	166,000	1,114,000
1939	18,744	60,230,000	1,582,000	1,394,000	715,000	8,031,000	46,694,000	2,801,000	23,994,000	23,602,000	6,250,000	12,945,000	1,179,000	215,000	1,196,000
1940	18,680	56,748,000	1,851,000	1,440,000	745,000	5,243,000	45,977,000	2,118,000	23,331,000	21,661,000	5,955,000	13,574,000	1,320,000	359,000	1,067,000
1941	18,405	58,472,000	2,024,000	1,628,000	1,013,000	6,179,000	45,966,000	2,059,000	23,709,000	21,926,000	6,183,000	15,739,000	1,918,000	695,000	1,068,000
1942	16,873	63,581,000	2,476,000	2,059,000	1,027,000	11,336,000	44,647,000	2,090,000	23,652,000	23,765,000	8,267,000	18,450,000	3,624,000	1,567,000	1,118,000
1943	16,227	64,910,000	3,130,000	2,391,000	991,000	12,171,000	44,117,000	2,233,000	22,863,000	23,593,000	9,149,000	21,186,000	4,500,000	2,402,000	1,171,000
1944	16,183	64,958,000	2,703,000	2,275,000	1,096,000	12,945,000	43,635,000	2,221,000	21,854,000	23,804,000	9,967,000	22,328,000	4,188,000	2,382,000	1,221,000
1945	16,656	63,217,000	2,754,000	2,203,000	1,115,000	12,962,000	41,955,000	2,287,000	20,902,000	23,619,000	10,701,000	22,485,000	2,928,000	1,538,000	1,238,000
1946	18,561	63,812,000	2,858,000	2,276,000	1,427,000	12,256,000	42,756,000	2,669,000	21,463,000	23,964,000	10,685,000	22,738,000	2,336,000	891,000	1,338,000
1947	20,376	68,037,000	2,921,000	2,476,000	1,811,000	12,512,000	46,092,000	3,349,000	23,425,000	24,182,000	11,947,000	25,957,000	2,662,000	979,000	1,292,000
1948	21,749	73,705,000	2,876,000	2,565,000	2,059,000	13,993,000	50,001,000	3,573,000	26,125,000	25,828,000	13,033,000	29,272,000	3,413,000	1,189,000	1,432,000
1949	22,496	71,620,000	2,853,000	2,621,000	1,756,000	8,295,000	53,986,000	3,411,000	25,534,000	24,349,000	13,624,000	28,410,000	2,835,000	1,041,000	1,303,000
1950	22,973	79,209,000	3,178,000	3,296,000	1,909,000	10,259,000	57,444,000	3,633,000	28,912,000	25,034,000	15,714,000	31,857,000	4,312,000	1,752,000	1,640,000
1951	23,641	84,707,000	3,170,000	3,553,000	2,360,000	10,258,000	62,955,000	3,902,000	31,275,000	26,084,000	16,747,000	36,007,000	4,676,000	2,299,000	1,782,000
1952	25,139	90,041,000	3,503,000	3,703,000	2,352,000	10,537,000	67,517,000	4,111,000	33,062,000	27,159,000	18,824,000	38,348,000	4,900,000	2,472,000	1,909,000
1953	26,314	95,220,000	3,281,000	3,732,000	2,381,000	10,429,000	72,862,000	4,213,000	35,053,000	28,517,000	20,303,000	40,570,000	5,018,000	2,537,000	2,012,000
1954	26,067	98,637,000	3,658,000	3,495,000	2,468,000	8,567,000	77,608,000	4,260,000	36,556,000	28,810,000	21,641,000	42,038,000	4,424,000	2,296,000	2,057,000
1955	29,704	106,378,000	3,634,000	3,904,000	2,623,000	9,436,000	83,444,000	5,164,000	38,727,000	30,183,000	24,157,000	47,983,000	5,763,000	2,895,000	2,380,000
1956	32,895	113,838,000	3,641,000	4,603,000	3,050,000	9,155,000	89,978,000	6,123,000	41,317,000	32,150,000	25,726,000	52,070,000	5,953,000	3,017,000	2,535,000
1957	34,492	121,316,000	3,666,000	4,834,000	3,004,000	9,200,000	97,083,000	6,315,000	45,905,000	32,350,000	28,623,000	55,834,000	5,753,000	2,953,000	2,682,000
1958	35,161	128,678,000	3,672,000	5,019,000	2,710,000	9,736,000	103,747,000	6,379,000	49,166,000	34,151,000	30,637,000	55,788,000	5,719,000	2,994,000	2,803,000
1959	43,195	137,319,000	3,559,000	5,439,000	3,007,000	10,437,000	110,216,000	6,961,000	52,321,000	35,414,000	32,421,000	62,309,000	6,798,000	3,528,000	3,040,000
1960	43,852	144,774,000	3,632,000	5,747,000	3,093,000	10,296,000	117,081,000	7,606,000	55,791,000	36,287,000	33,877,000	65,922,000	6,602,000	3,695,000	3,199,000
1961	49,048	155,535,000	3,893,000	6,140,000	3,126,000	12,322,000	124,624,000	7,241,000	60,955,000	38,779,000	35,941,000	68,154,000	7,496,000	3,916,000	3,440,000
1962	52,701	161,025,000	—	—	3,112,000	—	—	—	—	—	—	73,156,000	8,026,000	4,180,000	3,579,000
1963	56,291	167,379,000	4,120,000	6,951,000	3,310,000	12,499,000	133,984,000	8,340,000	62,211,000	39,650,000	41,133,000	77,870,000	8,947,000	4,570,000	3,801,000
1964	56,338	174,913,000	4,023,000	7,384,000	3,471,000	12,962,000	140,084,000	8,258,000	65,027,000	40,496,000	44,458,000	81,726,000	9,760,000	4,741,000	4,214,000

Year	Corporate tax returns [1] Ch585 Number	Total assets or liabilities Ch586 Thousand dollars	Selected assets Cash Ch587 Thousand dollars	Notes and accounts receivable less allowance for bad debts [2] Ch588 Thousand dollars	Inventories Ch589 Thousand dollars	Investments Ch590 Thousand dollars	Capital assets less reserves Ch591 [3] Thousand dollars	Selected liabilities Accounts payable and short-term debt Ch592 Thousand dollars	Long-term debt Ch593 Thousand dollars	Capital Ch594 Thousand dollars	Surplus and retained earnings Ch595 Thousand dollars	Receipts Total Ch596 Thousand dollars	Total less total deductions Ch597 Thousand dollars	Income tax (not adjusted for credits) Ch598 Thousand dollars	Dividends paid other than own stock Ch599 Thousand dollars
1965	59,676	186,854,000	4,257,000	8,357,000	3,812,000	13,150,000	150,025,000	9,832,000	69,454,000	40,746,000	49,092,000	88,957,000	10,711,000	4,951,000	4,590,000
1966	59,925	204,061,000	4,674,000	9,999,000	4,243,000	14,848,000	161,985,000	11,561,000	77,090,000	42,742,000	53,444,000	97,098,000	11,628,000	5,383,000	4,953,000
1967	66,045	221,144,000	4,647,000	10,892,000	4,947,000	15,889,000	175,641,000	13,123,000	85,760,000	44,594,000	57,458,000	102,398,000	10,617,000	5,029,000	5,146,000
1968	65,554	238,568,000	4,986,000	12,012,000	5,189,000	17,173,000	188,705,000	16,205,000	93,636,000	45,890,000	60,673,000	112,587,000	10,526,000	5,639,000	5,439,000
1969	66,945	262,357,000	4,917,000	14,543,000	6,035,000	21,142,000	203,320,000	19,905,000	101,598,000	47,672,000	66,184,000	125,262,000	10,068,000	5,573,000	5,678,000
1970	67,398	287,740,207	5,335,334	15,038,685	6,998,837	26,392,188	219,811,933	21,641,591	114,437,722	51,166,337	70,504,366	135,492,476	7,564,140	4,372,068	5,837,565
1971	71,104	309,902,216	5,941,496	16,762,857	7,756,378	26,910,887	237,259,930	23,431,492	126,059,402	54,154,132	74,720,335	149,722,193	7,878,257	4,192,767	6,228,480
1972	72,550	337,715,312	5,914,071	17,408,256	8,149,156	28,930,455	259,320,782	24,585,760	135,085,055	58,366,927	84,914,492	167,212,641	8,604,565	4,363,110	6,911,309
1973	76,952	371,435,400	6,523,007	21,855,724	9,392,932	31,177,591	283,690,650	30,065,153	145,224,141	61,697,444	92,705,099	186,995,128	8,899,202	4,604,338	7,869,533
1974	80,232	414,691,198	6,969,496	24,837,639	12,953,067	35,586,279	312,283,037	40,022,954	159,446,213	66,221,677	97,799,270	222,074,759	8,662,536	4,719,299	8,323,023
1975	80,701	443,326,797	7,470,870	25,977,578	14,177,279	38,011,188	333,149,412	35,522,556	171,680,499	71,002,497	106,401,143	243,480,637	10,071,471	5,146,272	8,900,353
1976	81,373	486,241,965	8,188,887	32,368,370	15,265,600	42,458,879	358,832,631	40,557,176	179,360,163	76,997,187	119,923,064	282,758,334	14,446,185	7,143,518	10,797,172
1977	85,215	538,778,308	8,660,721	37,644,971	18,692,638	50,480,269	392,554,311	45,462,262	191,793,390	83,821,529	135,660,502	330,112,349	18,326,909	8,870,780	11,836,726
1978	92,686	597,721,008	8,633,367	45,208,079	20,185,622	56,415,270	434,739,189	52,578,972	204,786,763	91,119,066	151,367,284	372,898,491	20,871,346	10,394,378	13,666,472
1979	103,770	674,479,897	9,487,437	55,335,217	25,594,576	61,442,905	485,079,644	68,043,215	223,921,235	98,895,875	166,779,278	445,978,021	18,184,361	9,252,511	15,264,900
1980	111,324	758,364,400	10,324,282	66,060,643	29,070,462	70,222,150	539,265,732	77,636,989	249,839,439	103,436,042	189,027,986	523,807,396	19,853,111	10,733,055	17,329,807
1981	109,127	837,300,816	11,191,169	74,086,799	31,851,445	79,037,188	585,131,766	90,069,538	226,827,497	113,453,430	209,560,529	598,507,994	19,335,925	10,727,390	19,622,705
1982	115,470	919,861,069	14,175,410	82,641,078	30,487,943	93,979,531	641,350,717	98,101,573	296,998,401	123,501,628	232,463,347	632,294,442	17,897,123	11,638,542	21,438,500
1983	122,567	998,870,785	16,992,530	91,492,082	30,052,453	115,005,070	681,082,225	105,098,674	306,356,849	156,415,831	241,484,834	657,421,487	19,227,115	11,621,625	24,540,824
1984	128,184	1,084,873,718	21,703,981	106,426,352	32,703,620	137,731,923	703,983,869	118,636,103	325,998,783	135,428,953	292,077,532	725,631,232	28,391,143	15,579,597	27,505,378
1985	138,337	1,246,426,899	27,377,081	120,053,622	33,925,331	187,524,909	783,391,609	135,104,786	366,167,141	159,157,248	335,339,055	772,358,188	24,522,030	15,214,129	—
1986	138,428	1,310,227,440	26,611,886	113,944,572	30,517,206	203,162,384	818,475,581	128,192,387	400,851,705	161,637,748	347,000,194	762,231,202	21,513,071	16,156,499	—
1987	147,893	1,352,512,937	29,505,063	117,518,525	31,236,728	206,780,038	840,060,339	134,621,532	423,390,784	163,777,175	354,340,745	786,179,466	37,154,661	17,696,185	—
1988	149,248	1,411,201,395	28,873,302	132,796,944	29,452,644	234,679,965	844,226,340	153,203,024	428,201,824	159,878,446	371,338,529	838,753,393	46,213,082	17,762,410	—
1989	156,037	1,474,412,864	27,342,868	141,516,336	29,300,311	226,283,939	889,568,974	159,102,517	459,614,272	163,044,605	366,276,059	906,501,335	38,944,918	17,176,596	—
1990	160,353	1,522,045,738	26,815,809	157,196,511	29,292,799	219,216,094	917,509,780	176,796,172	489,173,429	161,697,630	365,108,173	936,277,062	35,316,230	17,114,547	—
1991	164,980	1,573,824,265	27,653,046	156,619,778	29,847,667	244,040,302	938,516,330	171,211,719	507,392,874	174,397,515	375,427,647	954,944,592	37,106,989	17,143,124	—
1992	178,284	1,641,997,827	28,839,727	165,781,043	29,240,373	253,281,257	1,021,588,612	198,684,916	506,309,738	171,664,973	384,079,758	997,640,581	41,171,441	17,942,081	—
1993	175,980	1,770,691,651	34,137,234	191,376,050	28,035,020	293,680,841	997,905,639	227,757,188	510,987,466	172,692,164	425,681,086	1,037,156,438	52,255,424	20,717,373	—
1994	186,474	1,826,272,914	38,195,442	183,876,127	29,690,927	295,713,097	1,048,574,842	195,877,461	525,332,216	180,032,821	456,388,377	1,103,212,254	67,137,141	25,104,099	—
1995	194,456	1,903,213,778	40,960,551	172,072,859	30,298,489	308,554,330	1,077,319,960	215,230,530	547,618,913	183,872,004	465,689,865	1,156,709,979	72,033,574	27,186,351	—
1996	205,277	2,069,453,023	45,238,614	199,572,910	32,328,824	372,542,984	1,160,196,387	219,176,222	599,894,964	184,959,194	547,045,070	1,257,010,639	74,641,349	28,376,759	—
1997	209,412	2,219,019,293	57,414,098	226,132,493	26,997,729	441,040,171	1,198,744,828	259,689,566	662,338,281	188,435,929	595,927,021	1,330,726,431	69,814,587	28,506,843	—

[1] Through 1956, number of returns filing balance sheets.

[2] Through 1958, includes loans to stockholders.

[3] Through 1938, excludes intangible assets.

[4] Includes inactive corporations.

Sources

U.S. Internal Revenue Service (and its predecessor, U.S. Bureau of Internal Revenue), *Statistics of Income* and *Statistics of Income: Corporation Income Tax Returns*, various issues.

Documentation

See the text for Table Ch510–524.

TABLE Ch600–614   Corporate assets, liabilities, receipts, dividends, and income tax: 1926–1997   [Wholesale and retail trade]

Contributed by Naomi R. Lamoreaux

			Selected assets					Selected liabilities				Receipts			
Year	Corporate tax returns Number Ch600 [1][4]	Total assets or liabilities Ch601	Cash Ch602	Notes and accounts receivable less allowance for bad debts Ch603 [2]	Inventories Ch604	Investments Ch605	Capital assets less reserves Ch606 [3]	Accounts payable and short-term debt Ch607	Long-term debt Ch608	Capital Ch609	Surplus and retained earnings Ch610	Total Ch611	Total less total deductions Ch612	Income tax (not adjusted for credits) Ch613	Dividends paid other than own stock Ch614
	Number	Thousand dollars	Thousand dollars	Thousand dollars	Thousand dollars	Thousand dollars	Thousand dollars	Thousand dollars	Thousand dollars	Thousand dollars	Thousand dollars	Thousand dollars	Thousand dollars	Thousand dollars	Thousand dollars
1926	100,395 [4]	19,140,000	1,164,000	5,632,000	5,569,000	—	4,079,000	4,997,000	584,000	8,558,000	3,502,000	—	—	—	—
1927	110,280	20,083,000	1,198,000	5,614,000	5,631,000	—	4,309,000	5,046,000	846,000	8,858,000	3,832,000	—	—	—	—
1928	114,068	21,481,000	1,293,000	6,297,000	5,908,000	—	4,910,000	5,646,000	1,044,000	9,252,000	4,359,000	—	—	—	—
1929	117,583	21,842,000	1,283,000	6,305,000	5,862,000	1,764,000	4,967,000	5,730,000	1,252,000	9,317,000	4,204,000	—	—	—	—
1930	119,792	20,115,000	1,269,000	5,652,000	5,046,000	2,032,000	4,889,000	5,029,000	1,331,000	9,174,000	3,619,000	—	—	—	—
1931	113,886	17,900,000	1,033,000	4,688,000	3,986,000	2,120,000	4,729,000	4,074,000	1,315,000	8,520,000	2,925,000	29,540,000	−453,000	45,000	430,000
1932	119,346	15,759,000	1,041,000	4,006,000	3,368,000	2,068,000	4,158,000	3,443,000	1,204,000	8,237,000	1,936,000	22,609,000	−705,000	30,000	249,000
1933	120,064	15,654,000	990,000	3,944,000	3,809,000	2,032,000	3,810,000	3,625,000	1,126,000	7,732,000	2,155,000	23,653,000	36,000	62,000	213,000
1934	127,457	17,434,000	1,251,000	4,787,000	4,374,000	2,267,000	3,698,000	4,951,000	892,000	8,054,000	2,445,000	32,170,000	415,000	93,000	392,000
1935	130,317	17,486,000	1,270,000	4,832,000	4,568,000	2,168,000	3,662,000	5,030,000	1,029,000	7,725,000	2,560,000	36,669,000	558,000	107,000	505,000
1936	130,073	18,224,000	1,314,000	5,224,000	5,054,000	2,160,000	3,615,000	5,381,000	998,000	7,648,000	2,788,000	40,532,000	915,000	167,000	736,000
1937	128,200	18,853,000	1,287,000	5,180,000	5,328,000	2,561,000	3,671,000	5,382,000	1,279,000	7,902,000	3,348,000	44,199,000	845,000	166,000	702,000
1938	124,765	18,346,000	1,452,000	4,990,000	4,808,000	2,660,000	3,655,000	4,781,000	1,461,000	7,900,000	3,456,000	37,974,000	435,000	113,000	432,000
1939	124,627	19,030,000	1,501,000	5,224,000	5,157,000	2,714,000	3,961,000	5,071,000	1,544,000	7,822,000	3,824,000	41,849,000	830,000	165,000	497,000
1940	125,474	19,514,000	1,684,000	5,626,000	5,522,000	2,203,000	4,003,000	5,366,000	1,537,000	7,494,000	4,172,000	46,060,000	1,089,000	292,000	504,000
1941	123,439	22,134,000	1,920,000	6,454,000	6,841,000	2,325,000	4,068,000	6,356,000	1,718,000	7,500,000	5,099,000	56,512,000	2,071,000	853,000	576,000
1942	114,165	21,063,000	2,687,000	5,021,000	6,313,000	2,564,000	3,870,000	4,977,000	1,467,000	7,063,000	5,795,000	54,642,000	2,548,000	1,385,000	487,000
1943	107,667	21,489,000	3,152,000	4,494,000	6,032,000	3,495,000	3,661,000	4,426,000	1,311,000	7,026,000	6,615,000	57,193,000	3,057,000	1,760,000	530,000
1944	106,193	22,674,000	3,505,000	4,678,000	5,941,000	4,289,000	3,543,000	4,673,000	1,305,000	6,999,000	7,320,000	60,660,000	3,228,000	1,895,000	543,000
1945	110,587	24,041,000	3,946,000	4,636,000	6,582,000	4,675,000	3,532,000	5,034,000	1,366,000	7,182,000	8,045,000	65,654,000	3,337,000	1,886,000	547,000
1946	139,816	31,958,000	4,300,000	7,130,000	10,746,000	4,213,000	4,732,000	7,803,000	2,017,000	8,434,000	10,459,000	94,936,000	5,487,000	1,992,000	915,000
1947	163,300	38,122,000	5,049,000	9,169,000	12,758,000	4,044,000	6,158,000	9,229,000	2,621,000	9,516,000	12,876,000	120,960,000	5,969,000	2,174,000	980,000
1948	181,353	42,270,000	5,322,000	10,354,000	14,016,000	4,120,000	7,417,000	9,770,000	3,088,000	10,505,000	15,025,000	135,092,000	5,681,000	2,094,000	1,063,000
1949	187,520	42,985,000	5,348,000	10,778,000	13,446,000	4,257,000	8,081,000	9,528,000	3,286,000	10,946,000	15,853,000	129,965,000	3,810,000	1,469,000	965,000
1950	193,496	51,759,000	5,547,000	14,068,000	17,394,000	4,558,000	9,028,000	13,115,000	3,951,000	11,518,000	18,585,000	152,895,000	6,273,000	2,593,000	1,135,000
1951	201,594	55,102,000	5,992,000	14,682,000	18,089,000	5,272,000	9,831,000	13,536,000	4,401,000	12,282,000	19,856,000	166,422,000	5,473,000	2,754,000	1,076,000
1952	205,848	55,792,000	6,023,000	15,365,000	17,802,000	5,169,000	10,145,000	14,043,000	4,572,000	12,468,000	20,058,000	166,063,000	4,388,000	2,226,000	989,000
1953	212,931	56,370,000	6,185,000	15,193,000	17,828,000	5,445,000	10,263,000	13,902,000	4,968,000	12,608,000	20,197,000	167,705,000	3,922,000	2,050,000	926,000
1954	222,801	59,132,000	6,317,000	16,594,000	18,138,000	5,651,000	10,695,000	15,402,000	4,973,000	12,856,000	21,066,000	170,589,000	3,629,000	1,867,000	909,000
1955	248,071	69,113,000	6,808,000	20,287,000	21,578,000	6,533,000	12,037,000	19,460,000	5,795,000	14,366,000	23,500,000	204,924,000	5,099,000	2,435,000	993,000
1956	270,951	73,468,000	6,917,000	21,134,000	23,124,000	6,856,000	13,280,000	21,134,000	6,478,000	15,017,000	24,496,000	215,914,000	5,239,000	2,532,000	1,060,000
1957	305,117	76,830,000	7,046,000	21,767,000	24,021,000	7,582,000	13,843,000	21,888,000	7,335,000	15,534,000	25,568,000	229,816,000	4,725,000	2,392,000	1,036,000
1958	311,477	79,346,000	7,484,000	23,654,000	24,230,000	7,635,000	14,001,000	22,559,000	8,350,000	15,656,000	26,355,000	225,939,000	4,411,000	2,228,000	982,000
1959	334,717	87,557,000	7,651,000	26,113,000	26,704,000	9,122,000	14,998,000	25,252,000	9,624,000	16,508,000	28,253,000	256,648,000	5,573,000	2,640,000	1,131,000
1960	355,623	92,219,000	8,423,000	26,386,000	28,434,000	9,296,000	15,891,000	27,247,000	9,894,000	17,401,000	29,057,000	269,581,000	4,535,000	2,359,000	1,232,000
1961	364,947	94,591,000	8,262,000	27,566,000	28,783,000	9,429,000	16,257,000	27,947,000	10,390,000	17,479,000	29,278,000	270,847,000	4,573,000	2,272,000	1,239,000
1962	388,852	101,563,000	—	—	30,715,000	—	—	—	—	—	—	298,336,000	5,179,000	2,508,000	1,314,000
1963	403,435	105,722,000	8,723,000	30,665,000	32,523,000	9,812,000	18,761,000	31,531,000	11,949,000	18,447,000	51,543,000	309,590,000	5,366,000	2,593,000	1,250,000
1964	421,553	113,939,000	9,343,000	34,055,000	34,892,000	9,828,000	20,434,000	35,361,000	12,475,000	18,769,000	33,803,000	335,319,000	6,641,000	2,843,000	1,462,000

Year	Corporate tax returns¹ Ch600 Number	Total assets or liabilities Ch601	Cash Ch602	Notes and accounts receivable less allowance for bad debts² Ch603	Inventories Ch604	Investments Ch605	Capital assets less reserves³ Ch606	Accounts payable and short-term debt Ch607	Long-term debt Ch608	Capital Ch609	Surplus and retained earnings Ch610	Total Ch611	Total less total deductions Ch612	Income tax (not adjusted for credits) Ch613	Dividends paid other than own stock Ch614
1965	440,304	125,487,000	9,708,000	37,696,000	39,410,000	10,353,000	22,693,000	41,329,000	13,563,000	19,049,000	36,744,000	365,166,000	7,623,000	3,193,000	1,653,000
1966	453,174	135,943,000	10,011,000	39,834,000	43,300,000	11,009,000	25,307,000	45,994,000	14,979,000	19,969,000	40,226,000	389,155,000	8,215,000	3,361,000	1,780,000
1967	465,841	144,129,000	11,163,000	41,023,000	45,794,000	11,597,000	27,212,000	47,802,000	15,950,000	20,638,000	43,739,000	410,370,000	8,834,000	3,641,000	1,885,000
1968	471,987	162,115,000	11,878,000	46,232,000	51,054,000	13,501,000	30,538,000	54,626,000	19,110,000	21,232,000	48,774,000	451,898,000	10,317,000	4,570,000	2,138,000
1969	524,586	184,644,000	12,666,000	51,349,000	58,695,000	15,034,000	35,488,000	63,934,000	22,115,000	23,464,000	53,376,000	508,265,000	10,728,000	4,889,000	2,470,000
1970	518,062	192,181,800	13,533,294	51,997,705	58,746,728	16,747,892	39,086,314	66,172,928	24,835,057	23,304,189	55,708,024	522,546,369	9,637,730	4,485,128	2,068,501
1971	538,664	210,883,481	14,303,363	56,600,735	65,376,550	18,088,710	43,319,586	73,234,889	28,038,555	24,082,087	61,127,594	575,729,510	11,313,926	5,026,658	2,310,294
1972	568,228	241,756,673	16,176,130	64,822,214	75,939,528	20,232,546	48,637,664	86,302,566	32,179,884	25,345,783	69,358,750	674,507,820	14,317,898	5,700,493	2,431,237
1973	581,867	279,894,989	18,789,946	74,647,842	88,827,573	23,970,269	53,580,190	101,457,825	36,247,383	26,012,964	82,199,330	789,892,441	19,552,044	7,249,137	3,206,761
1974	602,423	313,305,334	20,928,097	84,777,597	100,043,924	27,225,233	59,766,668	113,082,604	40,919,566	27,527,948	93,390,605	923,364,748	22,482,310	8,315,540	4,378,033
1975	614,632	323,496,726	22,918,920	84,688,034	104,245,065	25,246,296	64,924,011	114,783,555	42,295,119	28,972,678	97,522,673	969,938,872	22,427,092	8,131,078	5,029,897
1976	635,540	368,793,060	24,291,434	96,482,129	118,766,741	33,020,019	73,416,140	130,380,795	49,267,489	30,806,178	112,839,319	1,113,913,736	25,064,271	9,144,428	5,402,867
1977	672,394	414,650,094	26,081,480	108,887,906	135,571,381	36,759,789	82,562,249	150,446,797	54,851,783	32,134,576	125,215,622	1,239,882,173	29,485,464	10,547,774	6,845,280
1978	721,443	486,146,204	29,467,519	127,457,934	158,135,586	41,739,047	98,992,342	177,767,157	71,427,941	33,971,813	143,757,682	1,461,404,863	35,166,504	12,479,414	7,272,502
1979	772,598	573,306,508	33,605,354	150,081,836	177,252,484	52,650,079	116,660,162	206,940,862	88,195,310	36,116,859	166,684,408	1,752,708,933	39,002,174	13,419,871	8,828,705
1980	799,628	646,901,005	36,682,163	166,871,894	188,789,045	74,028,158	131,881,486	245,927,452	97,627,525	39,790,578	189,308,726	1,955,523,778	36,069,560	13,655,104	10,343,087
1981	816,836	708,060,408	39,958,553	174,442,396	211,130,734	84,647,165	146,753,553	245,176,098	106,765,438	41,824,467	201,986,861	2,039,628,384	32,736,913	12,515,795	10,034,841
1982	839,547	753,351,132	43,455,917	175,241,736	214,824,922	91,221,072	156,767,137	247,343,998	114,283,891	44,451,055	216,164,978	2,017,701,364	27,962,078	11,584,691	12,069,015
1983	851,785	804,242,963	48,460,707	195,313,239	237,519,820	101,421,896	161,413,896	279,119,966	119,681,889	45,457,731	229,741,512	2,119,444,862	34,961,910	12,910,870	12,722,120
1984	896,524	899,032,645	52,263,643	214,653,799	264,789,285	117,983,838	178,114,721	316,115,765	137,593,385	48,125,890	253,924,334	2,307,612,139	41,769,011	15,082,817	13,057,047
1985	917,301	1,009,965,739	57,376,921	220,216,752	296,465,709	133,793,509	202,187,355	353,548,769	159,615,461	51,458,492	248,410,682	2,473,865,453	33,462,080	16,392,896	—
1986	939,159	1,073,523,697	63,781,982	235,969,601	303,014,310	132,557,816	222,201,972	368,205,275	184,334,941	53,740,426	261,417,343	2,547,440,986	35,359,047	17,097,449	—
1987	971,758	1,177,668,920	62,569,896	260,675,766	336,380,034	132,742,946	251,395,409	408,614,727	220,577,820	56,760,360	277,814,829	2,766,717,240	38,225,913	14,956,044	—
1988	984,553	1,295,819,375	68,702,177	280,679,479	359,148,953	154,414,419	278,697,467	451,993,285	248,668,211	64,025,600	288,262,121	2,977,982,750	42,449,652	14,116,720	—
1989	1,102,980	1,390,555,774	70,479,143	302,702,318	371,700,159	164,399,634	306,966,923	487,561,290	268,522,067	66,866,511	298,916,711	3,184,946,370	36,130,112	13,595,625	—
1990	1,023,057	1,447,296,828	76,088,721	315,564,118	380,666,945	166,676,393	327,886,814	498,604,395	277,196,982	75,120,030	302,307,185	3,308,988,336	29,921,649	13,839,310	—
1991	1,043,534	1,483,427,907	79,808,073	320,687,700	384,005,805	184,827,246	340,947,593	497,527,404	283,642,854	83,925,073	315,649,408	3,380,598,972	29,690,115	13,227,114	—
1992	1,052,713	1,581,910,771	82,665,205	333,154,648	421,263,752	215,218,778	356,796,574	543,400,811	283,339,263	87,203,145	341,159,668	3,503,944,396	40,565,241	14,844,365	—
1993	1,072,905	1,702,833,504	89,324,197	340,778,306	499,801,204	209,175,987	382,351,853	578,110,738	298,140,122	89,326,258	384,579,301	3,709,494,745	49,730,227	16,373,907	—
1994	1,106,363	1,795,187,540	90,086,374	371,543,869	486,013,026	214,662,945	411,899,034	610,133,706	316,405,299	92,324,187	428,363,915	4,052,225,816	68,251,804	19,885,265	—
1995	1,132,409	1,919,717,823	95,540,441	379,278,386	482,138,131	270,321,080	441,100,758	607,341,352	337,176,522	97,133,335	466,893,478	4,310,346,947	62,786,174	20,301,551	—
1996	1,142,491	2,016,232,163	106,795,194	399,640,222	499,824,641	243,334,164	482,129,882	664,231,069	348,294,751	101,762,023	500,052,301	4,490,073,608	71,752,497	22,694,239	—
1997	1,149,132	1,947,931,949	110,892,077	405,577,145	512,060,591	222,889,974	527,445,792	648,927,983	361,518,312	108,081,282	543,333,137	4,703,816,853	79,620,667	23,871,953	—

¹ Through 1956, number of returns filing balance sheets.
² Through 1958, includes loans to stockholders.
³ Through 1938, excludes intangible assets.
⁴ Includes inactive corporations.

Sources

U.S. Internal Revenue Service (and its predecessor, U.S. Bureau of Internal Revenue), *Statistics of Income* and *Statistics of Income: Corporation Income Tax Returns*, various issues.

Documentation

See the text for Table Ch510–524.

TABLE Ch615–629 Corporate assets, liabilities, receipts, dividends, and income tax: 1926–1997   [Finance, insurance, and real estate]

Contributed by Naomi R. Lamoreaux

All figures in Thousand dollars except Ch615 (Number).

Year	Corporate tax returns, Number Ch615 [1]	Total assets or liabilities Ch616	Cash Ch617	Notes and accounts receivable less allowance for bad debts Ch618 [2]	Inventories Ch619	Investments Ch620	Capital assets less reserves Ch621 [3]	Accounts payable and short-term debt Ch622	Long-term debt Ch623	Capital Ch624	Surplus and retained earnings Ch625	Receipts Total Ch626	Receipts Total less total deductions Ch627	Income tax (not adjusted for credits) Ch628	Dividends paid other than own stock Ch629
1926	98,417 [4]	99,452,000	9,778,000	5,790,000	923,000	—	13,429,000	6,682,000	4,740,000	13,733,000	7,436,000	—	—	—	—
1927	106,016	112,917,000	9,721,000	32,131,000	1,068,000	—	15,251,000	6,179,000	6,047,000	15,725,000	9,394,000	—	—	—	—
1928	108,123	125,692,000	14,278,000	41,029,000	675,000	—	16,969,000	7,724,000	8,103,000	18,056,000	11,995,000	—	—	—	—
1929	113,463	140,724,000	14,471,000	44,129,000	921,000	41,401,000	17,819,000	8,654,000	10,135,000	23,682,000	15,108,000	—	—	—	—
1930	114,275	140,035,000	13,207,000	39,158,000	462,000	62,136,000	18,792,000	7,640,000	11,079,000	24,356,000	16,177,000	—	—	—	—
1931	107,892	121,043,000	9,385,000	31,202,000	249,000	57,611,000	17,638,000	6,962,000	11,000,000	21,583,000	12,167,000	10,565,000	-328,000	53,000	1,222,000
1932	104,141	110,753,000	9,581,000	24,647,000	151,000	57,397,000	14,638,000	5,625,000	9,395,000	19,635,000	10,619,000	8,155,000	-954,000	35,000	753,000
1933	100,989	105,475,000	9,252,000	21,235,000	141,000	56,518,000	13,712,000	2,825,000	8,652,000	18,482,000	9,965,000	7,422,000	-936,000	34,000	560,000
1934	105,535	140,840,000	13,702,000	23,640,000	134,000	83,626,000	14,689,000	8,031,000	13,611,000	32,739,000	14,074,000	8,022,000	721,000	59,000	1,226,000
1935	104,146	144,747,000	16,986,000	22,886,000	109,000	86,809,000	13,320,000	7,147,000	13,037,000	33,100,000	14,143,000	8,662,000	1,817,000	81,000	1,535,000
1936	96,869	144,109,000	18,872,000	24,028,000	65,000	87,108,000	10,238,000	6,814,000	10,707,000	29,046,000	13,606,000	8,692,000	1,834,000	136,000	1,738,000
1937	98,438	140,402,000	17,685,000	24,611,000	47,000	84,835,000	9,785,000	6,349,000	10,674,000	27,156,000	16,966,000	8,927,000	1,757,000	134,000	1,736,000
1938	118,631	150,926,000	20,314,000	23,040,000	53,000	85,377,000	18,439,000	5,504,000	16,451,000	28,582,000	16,688,000	8,548,000	1,273,000	127,000	1,326,000
1939	120,945	155,975,000	25,518,000	23,777,000	42,000	85,668,000	18,099,000	5,410,000	15,944,000	27,136,000	16,711,000	8,768,000	1,386,000	127,000	1,421,000
1940	120,725	168,414,000	31,103,000	25,616,000	61,000	90,565,000	18,131,000	5,609,000	16,159,000	28,264,000	17,394,000	9,455,000	1,369,000	192,000	1,622,000
1941	120,647	174,403,000	30,434,000	28,333,000	107,000	94,928,000	17,740,000	5,684,000	15,734,000	26,732,000	17,515,000	10,199,000	1,499,000	315,000	1,631,000
1942	114,866	175,483,000	30,837,000	23,185,000	68,000	101,264,000	17,255,000	3,937,000	11,507,000	17,631,000	13,079,000	8,749,000	2,385,000	387,000	1,004,000
1943	112,892	194,564,000	30,714,000	22,026,000	51,000	122,082,000	16,384,000	3,241,000	10,916,000	16,514,000	13,654,000	9,001,000	2,686,000	455,000	965,000
1944	113,221	221,043,000	33,152,000	24,624,000	35,000	143,870,000	15,836,000	3,675,000	10,937,000	16,000,000	14,818,000	9,614,000	3,123,000	544,000	1,004,000
1945	116,186	249,119,000	38,105,000	29,407,000	46,000	162,424,000	15,221,000	4,352,000	10,286,000	15,562,000	16,457,000	10,612,000	3,680,000	654,000	1,076,000
1946	124,564	246,364,000	38,404,000	35,984,000	69,000	151,177,000	16,363,000	5,294,000	11,232,000	15,822,000	17,878,000	12,097,000	4,146,000	713,000	1,261,000
1947	131,825	257,833,000	42,318,000	44,933,000	46,000	149,696,000	16,281,000	6,353,000	11,448,000	15,828,000	18,167,000	13,581,000	3,982,000	628,000	1,265,000
1948	140,872	265,124,000	43,254,000	50,699,000	11,000	148,524,000	17,380,000	6,628,000	13,143,000	15,928,000	19,550,000	15,132,000	4,612,000	792,000	1,428,000
1949	146,120	281,983,000	40,447,000	52,065,000	6,000	165,077,000	19,053,000	7,061,000	17,397,000	18,236,000	22,504,000	16,768,000	5,411,000	992,000	1,656,000
1950	151,540	298,624,000	46,104,000	64,529,000	20,000	162,872,000	20,111,000	8,406,000	16,508,000	15,750,000	24,318,000	18,233,000	5,849,000	1,228,000	1,748,000
1951	158,335	317,026,000	50,129,000	70,912,000	23,000	167,642,000	21,309,000	9,331,000	16,850,000	15,769,000	26,788,000	20,017,000	6,088,000	1,515,000	1,700,000
1952	166,749	374,891,000	52,174,000	88,544,000	27,000	206,476,000	20,970,000	10,818,000	18,779,000	16,424,000	32,351,000	23,343,000	6,662,000	1,745,000	1,712,000
1953	175,653	401,976,000	52,637,000	96,456,000	31,000	222,418,000	22,609,000	11,364,000	21,378,000	16,911,000	35,153,000	25,829,000	7,167,000	1,879,000	1,817,000
1954	187,172	432,477,000	52,413,000	103,697,000	48,000	243,959,000	24,129,000	13,502,000	22,724,000	17,484,000	39,979,000	29,406,000	8,308,000	2,068,000	2,027,000
1955	213,680	474,858,000	57,210,000	126,800,000	47,000	255,680,000	25,581,000	18,176,000	25,697,000	17,825,000	45,124,000	32,320,000	8,543,000	2,030,000	2,238,000
1956	244,755	504,571,000	59,773,000	138,584,000	59,000	266,632,000	28,590,000	19,911,000	28,824,000	19,881,000	50,639,000	35,718,000	8,676,000	2,015,000	2,491,000
1957	255,976	528,509,000	59,159,000	124,872,000	94,000	301,072,000	31,201,000	24,754,000	32,763,000	21,920,000	51,746,000	39,019,000	9,154,000	2,214,000	2,688,000
1958	272,305	572,513,000	61,134,000	130,276,000	81,000	332,652,000	34,542,000	26,868,000	34,985,000	22,139,000	61,800,000	59,335,000	8,085,000	2,724,000	2,780,000
1959	318,592	606,825,000	60,780,000	142,887,000	96,000	348,808,000	38,583,000	28,406,000	38,912,000	24,285,000	65,408,000	65,912,000	7,949,000	2,559,000	3,283,000
1960	334,388	650,591,000	64,935,000	154,916,000	141,000	371,608,000	42,512,000	29,633,000	44,017,000	25,678,000	71,525,000	70,842,000	9,161,000	3,101,000	3,466,000
1961	340,210	699,888,000	68,380,000	163,801,000	176,000	401,151,000	46,495,000	33,339,000	46,795,000	26,885,000	81,099,000	75,584,000	10,051,000	3,138,000	3,618,000
1962	359,229	764,797,000	—	—	231,000	—	—	—	—	—	—	81,859,000	9,847,000	3,092,000	3,778,000
1963	375,375	825,415,000	72,434,000	222,048,000	216,000	448,210,000	54,814,000	63,195,000	53,556,000	30,848,000	91,753,000	93,343,000	9,739,000	3,119,000	4,080,000
1964	383,727	883,959,000	76,053,000	220,127,000	355,000	497,949,000	59,643,000	43,745,000	55,546,000	31,942,000	97,983,000	101,297,000	10,640,000	3,059,000	4,627,000

		Selected assets						Selected liabilities				Receipts			
	Corporate tax returns [1]	Total assets or liabilities	Cash	Notes and accounts receivable less allowance for bad debts [2]	Inventories	Investments	Capital assets less reserves [3]	Accounts payable and short-term debt	Long-term debt	Capital	Surplus and retained earnings	Total	Total less deductions	Income tax (not adjusted for credits)	Dividends paid other than own stock
	Ch615 [1]	Ch616	Ch617	Ch618 [2]	Ch619	Ch620	Ch621 [3]	Ch622	Ch623	Ch624	Ch625	Ch626	Ch627	Ch628	Ch629
Year	Number	Thousand dollars	Thousand dollars	Thousand dollars	Thousand dollars	Thousand dollars	Thousand dollars	Thousand dollars	Thousand dollars	Thousand dollars	Thousand dollars	Thousand dollars	Thousand dollars	Thousand dollars	Thousand dollars
1965	388,428	955,902,000	77,347,000	251,348,000	357,000	528,586,000	63,158,000	45,370,000	59,770,000	33,673,000	103,027,000	110,466,000	12,429,000	5,115,000	5,924,000
1966	402,740	1,007,717,000	84,934,000	259,895,000	293,000	562,048,000	66,665,000	50,818,000	61,848,000	35,621,000	109,579,000	119,815,000	12,731,000	3,202,000	5,612,000
1967	399,115	1,097,348,000	95,224,000	283,550,000	622,000	610,292,000	67,978,000	55,977,000	60,422,000	38,506,000	119,461,000	131,983,000	15,146,000	3,640,000	6,062,000
1968	407,199	1,202,918,000	102,771,000	312,700,000	873,000	671,818,000	70,462,000	66,007,000	68,355,000	40,507,000	139,396,000	146,905,000	17,477,000	4,226,000	7,395,000
1969	428,972	1,298,161,000	114,512,000	343,461,000	1,237,000	706,846,000	79,405,000	79,632,000	78,835,000	45,386,000	151,108,000	164,291,000	15,832,000	4,292,000	9,068,000
1970	406,235	1,401,153,520	126,317,340	366,857,535	1,288,792	769,283,976	80,363,927	82,205,086	82,871,518	45,608,659	153,328,052	177,320,048	15,691,113	4,442,733	7,387,211
1971	417,736	1,572,631,205	141,570,114	408,628,153	1,467,686	869,632,379	83,291,872	85,011,170	96,535,988	48,221,574	176,065,180	198,468,720	19,864,955	5,358,133	7,053,702
1972	425,088	1,810,200,797	169,007,109	491,881,483	2,286,648	976,686,474	91,843,526	107,320,413	113,311,031	52,494,769	196,783,878	225,581,228	20,787,410	5,933,209	8,045,468
1973	426,650	2,011,951,079	192,358,173	575,755,228	3,092,223	1,047,684,507	98,570,934	124,981,717	128,570,934	54,552,239	204,387,850	260,092,291	20,787,410	6,050,310	9,082,485
1974	425,249	2,176,652,153	209,607,023	646,189,745	3,761,428	1,099,094,328	102,354,024	142,189,809	137,093,071	56,891,586	200,792,999	303,198,775	16,798,876	5,570,370	8,661,214
1975	411,846	2,321,965,956	210,336,337	654,734,081	3,525,486	1,228,844,692	103,173,121	139,772,665	141,707,857	59,049,099	215,461,912	315,795,981	17,832,164	5,644,729	8,729,977
1976	411,984	2,549,799,105	224,101,900	727,308,401	4,076,011	1,360,329,494	105,964,562	144,543,213	155,206,984	61,195,557	241,233,447	353,774,035	24,392,753	7,203,750	9,590,282
1977	432,919	2,861,478,449	261,972,218	827,447,193	5,496,153	1,516,947,025	111,785,790	166,432,136	164,180,619	66,158,696	263,253,605	405,131,593	34,921,510	9,302,917	11,604,616
1978	454,301	3,249,397,057	302,242,597	996,610,016	6,195,753	1,659,870,328	116,448,101	206,817,805	183,378,965	76,252,103	299,197,235	474,690,489	42,395,629	11,920,213	13,599,824
1979	471,222	3,626,872,420	338,472,797	1,120,635,991	5,665,968	1,837,191,706	121,184,425	234,187,015	208,303,187	100,643,138	359,210,145	561,106,822	46,826,112	11,749,927	18,294,307
1980	493,426	4,022,206,073	393,811,864	1,222,825,342	7,833,456	2,036,105,742	133,186,681	295,037,140	223,214,607	147,124,623	428,128,815	697,460,846	44,823,059	9,804,884	24,692,146
1981	469,795	4,486,191,441	384,213,439	1,418,751,746	12,829,156	2,183,958,363	148,930,696	365,610,305	249,604,965	238,686,511	508,727,765	877,808,946	39,044,142	8,159,015	41,998,295
1982	461,630	4,987,466,401	382,408,496	1,568,156,224	12,118,589	2,425,252,388	171,683,945	441,205,075	286,709,958	339,927,110	583,605,918	949,867,877	34,703,115	7,809,420	46,504,963
1983	479,656	5,487,225,439	410,284,773	1,746,471,794	12,064,445	2,648,567,827	184,568,113	485,529,690	343,429,407	424,784,739	634,220,589	902,822,472	46,143,784	8,540,701	41,592,101
1984	497,366	5,938,984,929	397,539,172	1,894,997,902	14,634,205	2,863,661,284	208,307,708	551,545,264	412,524,245	481,569,057	682,311,487	1,033,146,416	47,459,109	9,619,055	51,315,346
1985	518,432	7,029,452,681	456,840,952	2,188,433,899	25,172,871	3,461,438,207	231,140,465	685,064,024	503,061,319	532,896,560	950,492,646	1,182,034,309	77,462,107	13,598,201	—
1986	537,384	7,985,641,912	521,578,576	2,366,805,251	27,914,055	4,078,557,694	261,001,755	760,751,320	570,555,962	786,664,412	1,231,042,332	1,365,095,368	119,622,259	18,097,479	—
1987	521,136	8,732,320,235	497,778,506	2,442,473,105	64,581,790	4,501,979,632	271,783,419	924,823,625	620,941,700	880,321,412	1,380,630,960	1,589,218,435	112,481,040	19,264,979	—
1988	572,418	9,411,547,140	515,298,105	2,651,210,250	34,886,177	4,894,675,911	322,042,665	957,864,576	678,904,915	1,001,057,996	1,505,473,727	1,714,352,381	118,307,815	20,899,804	—
1989	592,832	9,957,481,118	555,177,191	2,674,433,070	33,865,422	4,935,696,577	336,204,120	1,060,928,886	725,346,436	1,022,289,379	1,843,047,886	1,868,003,359	137,466,388	22,693,200	—
1990	609,138	10,193,295,357	489,499,753	2,601,210,250	36,588,933	5,031,105,163	361,479,474	1,145,008,959	788,556,220	1,104,404,319	1,931,864,904	1,954,709,651	144,842,076	22,556,387	—
1991	617,557	10,780,681,276	483,045,301	2,617,751,348	31,454,985	5,614,390,102	366,569,751	1,503,865,772	792,003,552	1,232,826,606	2,264,068,851	1,924,317,623	153,148,605	27,281,531	—
1992	635,268	11,480,469,997	493,868,099	2,483,804,042	29,140,429	6,004,621,893	370,480,188	1,385,410,556	801,769,579	1,365,100,286	2,666,866,069	1,900,428,224	176,120,894	35,433,128	—
1993	641,397	12,831,680,335	471,203,424	2,767,096,931	20,966,238	6,787,677,946	389,732,064	1,151,729,477	897,765,772	1,510,478,867	3,300,182,647	1,940,315,739	216,980,212	44,409,373	—
1994	681,671	13,895,294,545	490,265,358	2,959,447,845	133,355,286	7,234,176,574	419,648,406	1,434,278,387	1,018,266,842	1,575,675,146	3,642,193,169	1,976,491,348	203,439,111	39,014,557	—
1995	683,211	15,677,286,629	558,503,767	3,352,671,280	22,311,856	8,372,710,170	451,637,281	1,610,380,143	1,112,529,728	1,595,736,200	4,521,050,445	2,278,103,923	292,308,309	51,874,358	—
1996	723,754	17,360,053,164	633,506,830	3,725,106,683	21,916,687	9,430,326,181	502,408,385	1,886,873,524	1,230,842,321	1,649,370,957	5,401,360,205	2,406,855,250	330,241,653	58,301,659	—
1997	744,545	20,905,619,903	785,248,373	4,372,702,580	20,503,418	11,536,401,817	579,816,808	2,123,467,714	1,439,125,751	2,289,727,277	6,505,474,253	2,711,269,836	406,930,001	63,604,700	—

[1] Through 1956, number of returns filing balance sheets.
[2] Through 1958, includes loans to stockholders.
[3] Through 1938, excludes intangible assets.
[4] Includes inactive corporations.

Sources
U.S. Internal Revenue Service (and its predecessor, U.S. Bureau of Internal Revenue), *Statistics of Income* and *Statistics of Income: Corporation Income Tax Returns*, various issues.

Documentation
See the text for Table Ch510–524.

TABLE Ch630–644 Corporate assets, liabilities, receipts, dividends, and income tax: 1926–1997   [Services]

Contributed by Naomi R. Lamoreaux

	Corporate tax returns		Selected assets						Selected liabilities				Receipts			
	Number	Total assets or liabilities	Cash	Notes and accounts receivable less allowance for bad debts	Inventories	Investments	Capital assets less reserves	Accounts payable and short-term debt	Long-term debt	Capital	Surplus and retained earnings	Total	Total less total deductions	Income tax (not adjusted for credits)	Dividends paid other than own stock
Year	Ch630 [1]	Ch631	Ch632	Ch633 [2]	Ch634	Ch635	Ch636 [3]	Ch637	Ch638	Ch639	Ch640	Ch641	Ch642	Ch643	Ch644
	Number	Thousand dollars	Thousand dollars	Thousand dollars	Thousand dollars	Thousand dollars	Thousand dollars	Thousand dollars	Thousand dollars	Thousand dollars	Thousand dollars	Thousand dollars	Thousand dollars	Thousand dollars	Thousand dollars
1926	23,264 [4]	4,873,000	300,000	384,000	184,000	—	2,783,000	821,000	842,000	1,963,000	596,000	—	—	—	—
1927	25,388	5,618,000	240,000	459,000	177,000	—	3,340,000	869,000	1,163,000	2,189,000	736,000	—	—	—	—
1928	26,505	5,857,000	249,000	548,000	178,000	—	3,521,000	928,000	1,291,000	2,386,000	697,000	—	—	—	—
1929	28,710	7,820,000	440,000	833,000	191,000	1,876,000	3,814,000	954,000	1,563,000	2,519,000	1,982,000	—	—	—	—
1930	30,312	7,518,000	292,000	686,000	241,000	1,705,000	3,880,000	963,000	1,719,000	2,573,000	1,716,000	—	—	—	—
1931	28,515	6,555,000	211,000	636,000	198,000	1,189,000	3,719,000	878,000	1,636,000	2,427,000	1,045,000	1,486,000	−67,000	11,000	115,000
1932	34,552	8,480,000	231,000	637,000	145,000	1,228,000	5,611,000	983,000	3,008,000	3,078,000	712,000	2,953,000	−371,000	9,000	71,000
1933	34,546	7,429,000	204,000	625,000	139,000	744,000	5,070,000	954,000	2,724,000	2,761,000	179,000	2,662,000	−255,000	9,000	42,000
1934	37,171	7,771,000	246,000	597,000	166,000	677,000	5,447,000	1,166,000	3,004,000	2,705,000	54,000	3,231,000	−144,000	15,000	63,000
1935	40,093	8,427,000	285,000	526,000	157,000	826,000	6,033,000	1,231,000	3,560,000	2,734,000	−18,000	3,528,000	−97,000	18,000	71,000
1936	48,590	10,853,000	365,000	602,000	167,000	1,077,000	8,085,000	1,408,000	5,002,000	3,185,000	175,000	4,345,000	13,000	31,000	156,000
1937	49,751	10,835,000	356,000	558,000	175,000	970,000	8,271,000	1,384,000	5,128,000	3,101,000	529,000	4,605,000	36,000	33,000	148,000
1938	33,816	4,294,000	241,000	406,000	205,000	625,000	2,496,000	714,000	1,311,000	1,564,000	400,000	3,409,000	59,000	23,000	83,000
1939	34,177	4,255,000	261,000	388,000	218,000	626,000	2,610,000	686,000	1,289,000	1,579,000	422,000	1,512,000	85,000	26,000	85,000
1940	34,094	4,273,000	303,000	386,000	213,000	640,000	2,586,000	675,000	1,269,000	1,485,000	573,000	3,702,000	117,000	38,000	90,000
1941	33,296	4,366,000	313,000	420,000	264,000	611,000	2,605,000	656,000	1,307,000	1,465,000	614,000	4,029,000	189,000	74,000	97,000
1942	31,692	4,475,000	411,000	423,000	301,000	672,000	2,458,000	610,000	1,197,000	1,417,000	813,000	4,457,000	157,000	179,000	86,000
1943	29,799	4,584,000	530,000	427,000	351,000	756,000	2,331,000	573,000	1,122,000	1,370,000	1,000,000	4,964,000	537,000	303,000	104,000
1944	29,389	4,739,000	556,000	481,000	391,000	901,000	2,198,000	567,000	1,147,000	1,344,000	1,143,000	5,481,000	575,000	317,000	114,000
1945	30,043	5,017,000	660,000	502,000	419,000	994,000	2,240,000	640,000	1,193,000	1,354,000	1,283,000	5,801,000	596,000	312,000	130,000
1946	34,229	5,869,000	755,000	631,000	537,000	991,000	2,692,000	816,000	1,273,000	1,517,000	1,631,000	7,143,000	785,000	284,000	203,000
1947	39,896	6,517,000	814,000	724,000	618,000	919,000	3,135,000	1,003,000	1,389,000	1,595,000	1,867,000	8,285,000	720,000	260,000	184,000
1948	43,882	6,950,000	827,000	779,000	546,000	990,000	3,516,000	1,035,000	1,493,000	1,689,000	2,061,000	8,766,000	623,000	241,000	172,000
1949	46,588	7,063,000	854,000	810,000	467,000	911,000	3,726,000	1,059,000	1,531,000	1,750,000	2,059,000	8,850,000	534,000	212,000	154,000
1950	47,834	8,053,000	913,000	996,000	570,000	1,271,000	4,004,000	1,252,000	1,717,000	1,834,000	2,461,000	9,350,000	568,000	236,000	170,000
1951	51,357	8,667,000	973,000	1,144,000	633,000	1,328,000	4,284,000	1,321,000	1,903,000	1,855,000	2,711,000	10,432,000	637,000	325,000	179,000
1952	54,690	8,916,000	1,043,000	1,260,000	602,000	1,304,000	4,398,000	1,410,000	1,925,000	1,858,000	2,807,000	11,168,000	620,000	324,000	174,000
1953	56,473	9,471,000	1,110,000	1,309,000	551,000	1,469,000	4,652,000	1,543,000	2,133,000	1,962,000	2,897,000	11,815,000	607,000	318,000	157,000
1954	58,117	10,017,000	1,228,000	1,420,000	574,000	1,588,000	4,756,000	1,813,000	2,241,000	1,902,000	3,028,000	12,267,000	585,000	319,000	159,000
1955	66,011	11,264,000	1,296,000	1,808,000	630,000	1,666,000	5,334,000	2,244,000	2,413,000	2,169,000	3,283,000	14,103,000	699,000	361,000	173,000
1956	74,372	13,090,000	1,430,000	2,220,000	718,000	1,881,000	6,190,000	2,823,000	2,904,000	2,317,000	3,661,000	16,273,000	840,000	409,000	189,000
1957	82,429	14,858,000	1,506,000	2,481,000	772,000	2,159,000	7,111,000	3,244,000	3,734,000	2,593,000	3,705,000	17,779,000	784,000	423,000	187,000
1958	89,494	15,870,000	1,613,000	2,902,000	837,000	2,129,000	7,558,000	3,605,000	3,963,000	2,581,000	3,173,000	18,295,000	749,000	412,000	181,000
1959	110,005	18,355,000	1,736,000	3,160,000	807,000	2,720,000	8,737,000	4,003,000	4,790,000	3,056,000	4,448,000	22,227,000	970,000	491,000	215,000
1960	121,024	19,853,000	1,787,000	3,449,000	856,000	2,799,000	9,538,000	4,418,000	5,444,000	3,272,000	4,401,000	23,347,000	853,000	486,000	277,000
1961	137,955	22,829,000	2,072,000	4,001,000	1,095,000	3,249,000	10,762,000	5,040,000	6,353,000	3,723,000	4,811,000	25,920,000	893,000	525,000	233,000
1962	150,082	25,219,000	—	—	1,113,000	—	—	—	—	—	—	28,095,000	837,000	524,000	221,000
1963	163,766	27,526,000	2,345,000	4,661,000	1,319,000	3,466,000	13,624,000	6,025,000	7,851,000	4,327,000	5,181,000	31,615,000	908,000	558,000	285,000
1964	176,902	29,951,000	2,545,000	5,017,000	1,546,000	3,751,000	14,840,000	6,713,000	8,806,000	4,489,000	5,438,000	34,101,000	1,154,000	587,000	297,000

	Corporate tax returns[1]	Total assets or liabilities	Selected assets					Selected liabilities				Receipts			
			Cash	Notes and accounts receivable less allowance for bad debts	Inventories	Investments	Capital assets less reserves[3]	Accounts payable and short-term debt	Long-term debt	Capital	Surplus and retained earnings	Total	Total less total deductions	Income tax (not adjusted for credits)	Dividends paid other than own stock
	Ch630	Ch631	Ch632	Ch633[2]	Ch634	Ch635	Ch636[3]	Ch637	Ch638	Ch639	Ch640	Ch641	Ch642	Ch643	Ch644
Year	Number	Thousand dollars	Thousand dollars	Thousand dollars	Thousand dollars	Thousand dollars	Thousand dollars	Thousand dollars	Thousand dollars	Thousand dollars	Thousand dollars	Thousand dollars	Thousand dollars	Thousand dollars	Thousand dollars
1965	188,177	33,481,000	2,773,000	5,864,000	1,585,000	4,329,000	16,507,000	7,684,000	9,536,000	4,628,000	6,378,000	38,377,000	1,582,000	699,000	177,000
1966	202,065	36,858,000	3,092,000	6,481,000	1,800,000	4,349,000	19,171,000	8,530,000	10,832,000	4,991,000	7,271,000	43,083,000	1,820,000	797,000	423,000
1967	220,561	39,984,000	3,584,000	6,737,000	1,883,000	4,742,000	19,558,000	9,034,000	11,865,000	5,186,000	8,255,000	47,441,000	1,976,000	864,000	521,000
1968	228,904	47,234,000	4,052,000	7,921,000	2,345,000	6,756,000	22,160,000	10,370,000	13,420,000	5,735,000	10,567,000	51,046,000	2,016,000	1,032,000	565,000
1969	261,640	55,398,000	4,204,000	9,296,000	2,414,000	7,702,000	26,328,000	12,248,000	16,286,000	6,549,000	11,928,000	60,037,000	1,654,000	1,115,000	656,000
1970	281,218	61,875,140	4,654,863	9,899,922	2,557,436	8,893,496	28,999,630	13,373,966	17,988,570	7,136,082	13,153,813	69,571,428	1,188,174	1,062,678	558,452
1971	287,780	62,225,735	4,966,907	9,770,752	2,542,263	8,851,506	29,438,949	13,371,425	18,182,820	7,207,395	13,077,515	73,595,971	1,474,107	1,025,791	552,111
1972	314,795	68,259,469	5,657,083	10,856,029	2,888,018	9,318,803	31,780,755	14,432,299	20,737,926	7,352,882	14,914,798	83,987,745	2,304,490	1,173,965	631,299
1973	368,099	79,780,844	6,261,005	12,866,781	3,619,794	10,986,886	36,705,949	17,058,381	24,074,948	8,415,421	17,218,152	101,840,902	2,681,987	1,324,566	772,167
1974	388,832	84,979,681	6,399,667	13,617,176	4,229,163	11,847,814	39,208,361	18,928,248	25,835,661	7,992,473	18,414,599	115,589,142	2,494,750	1,431,617	826,292
1975	435,672	90,534,067	7,613,280	14,481,901	4,452,947	12,882,696	41,312,793	19,559,762	27,083,346	9,080,364	19,216,538	131,377,364	3,380,921	1,640,778	855,402
1976	466,317	99,489,782	8,926,925	16,437,826	4,651,469	13,019,629	45,138,766	21,852,657	4,614,793	9,422,721	21,644,027	150,157,645	4,292,358	1,918,952	1,148,065
1977	516,387	119,286,766	11,252,556	20,841,219	5,613,150	15,492,820	52,481,034	26,253,850	34,089,293	10,522,473	26,001,383	183,007,786	6,547,349	2,584,017	1,441,254
1978	560,016	134,379,134	13,102,050	22,591,412	6,468,683	16,311,817	60,243,185	28,143,976	38,078,766	11,213,167	29,828,006	210,606,073	7,620,863	3,190,125	1,490,937
1979	603,445	154,038,119	14,820,487	24,931,245	7,575,358	19,804,531	66,928,609	32,267,134	43,496,104	11,106,389	36,846,998	245,107,695	8,237,020	3,323,418	1,822,529
1980	671,338	178,163,737	16,963,540	29,006,681	8,502,383	26,257,441	74,177,721	35,327,403	50,637,921	12,186,041	43,735,479	279,883,187	8,090,213	3,554,144	1,841,845
1981	752,813	213,724,531	19,723,171	35,586,617	11,030,812	31,386,318	87,040,142	42,380,782	60,919,966	13,475,705	51,457,741	346,846,723	8,056,674	4,100,151	2,491,324
1982	819,706	237,876,895	22,287,575	35,628,825	12,179,103	35,141,789	95,626,155	49,018,015	66,153,599	14,166,815	57,874,990	380,767,394	7,049,553	3,982,538	3,269,285
1983	848,394	269,797,251	26,954,231	41,751,071	13,401,687	38,821,403	108,225,420	58,696,728	78,072,728	15,994,263	63,802,377	416,462,427	5,975,865	3,779,735	2,407,362
1984	899,370	307,895,160	30,312,297	49,905,586	13,839,981	44,707,365	122,803,504	65,218,663	89,196,573	18,474,532	72,493,176	490,332,811	5,342,650	4,458,267	3,126,700
1985	939,390	330,982,941	33,150,421	55,571,720	14,896,218	46,980,605	130,853,398	64,247,047	103,250,383	20,362,516	75,710,930	534,587,609	5,901,996	4,742,347	—
1986	1,072,178	381,609,099	35,924,305	65,048,707	16,327,613	53,296,245	150,150,486	69,863,336	120,911,882	22,287,286	85,742,775	591,849,715	7,553,785	4,942,317	—
1987	1,119,604	435,561,919	40,435,500	74,618,503	18,485,400	66,063,384	164,568,317	78,249,932	134,920,822	24,834,272	97,198,314	663,133,101	9,179,501	5,033,943	—
1988	995,425	530,326,395	41,065,098	95,327,925	20,942,836	89,384,265	183,902,645	108,456,235	160,617,186	28,781,409	109,207,384	695,265,170	8,997,242	5,049,797	—
1989	989,850	552,132,138	40,985,161	94,029,449	23,060,757	92,864,019	212,053,217	108,000,546	173,460,868	32,967,230	108,982,551	735,497,193	10,574,489	5,785,655	—
1990	1,029,447	572,842,266	44,479,929	95,104,277	21,060,115	102,463,459	223,016,889	107,964,836	177,224,463	36,259,780	117,891,560	779,329,609	10,293,701	5,368,531	—
1991	1,061,657	636,751,574	49,421,040	100,305,198	21,487,205	130,267,839	236,901,660	109,912,882	178,117,978	40,916,430	148,232,758	809,724,469	9,560,529	5,230,030	—
1992	1,100,449	661,597,099	51,974,981	105,501,541	21,825,238	137,627,342	244,331,197	111,753,806	177,398,197	44,846,738	163,984,141	869,533,422	18,410,778	5,920,338	—
1993	1,157,724	744,758,261	58,293,812	119,147,681	25,066,204	161,139,586	263,826,628	118,215,132	200,427,097	50,037,646	201,082,568	941,642,864	25,189,394	7,401,280	—
1994	1,424,394	833,929,557	69,963,386	133,130,365	25,067,980	186,827,383	294,249,156	140,608,019	227,305,762	52,653,438	229,534,298	1,198,029,951	35,530,623	9,990,309	—
1995	1,504,230	950,737,457	82,154,665	159,315,569	28,167,527	203,929,342	335,098,007	160,526,922	245,734,087	65,448,936	264,046,360	1,335,694,559	38,219,196	10,358,678	—
1996	1,557,401	1,092,310,137	96,394,037	168,343,324	30,160,220	232,784,455	397,539,909	171,524,237	288,045,826	65,796,662	324,512,794	1,496,215,552	43,011,056	12,588,705	—
1997	1,592,854	1,259,381,543	112,107,735	202,857,608	32,572,535	255,149,274	448,930,152	192,329,401	338,562,482	75,248,267	368,836,157	1,638,587,903	49,577,216	14,804,587	—

[1] Through 1956, number of returns filing balance sheets.
[2] Through 1958, includes loans to stockholders.
[3] Through 1938, excludes intangible assets.
[4] Includes inactive corporations.

Sources

U.S. Internal Revenue Service (and its predecessor, U.S. Bureau of Internal Revenue), *Statistics of Income* and *Statistics of Income: Corporation Income Tax Returns*, various issues.

Documentation

See the text for Table Ch510–524.

TABLE Ch645–658   Corporate assets, liabilities, receipts, and dividends: 1965–1997   [S-corporations]

Contributed by Naomi R. Lamoreaux

	Corporate tax returns		Selected assets					Selected liabilities				Receipts		
	Number	Total assets or liabilities	Cash	Notes and accounts receivable less allowance for bad debts	Inventories	Investments	Capital assets less reserves	Accounts payable and short-term debt	Long-term debt	Capital	Surplus and retained earnings	Total	Total less total deductions	Dividends paid other than own stock
Year	Ch645	Ch646	Ch647	Ch648	Ch649	Ch650	Ch651	Ch652	Ch653	Ch654	Ch655	Ch656	Ch657	Ch658
		Thousand dollars	Thousand dollars	Thousand dollars	Thousand dollars	Thousand dollars	Thousand dollars	Thousand dollars	Thousand dollars	Thousand dollars	Thousand dollars	Thousand dollars	Thousand dollars	Thousand dollars
1965	173,410	19,239,447	1,889,866	4,711,061	4,059,438	863,316	6,086,426	5,722,065	2,870,865	4,276,195	3,604,069	46,442,511	1,448,277	1,139,694
1966	181,851	21,351,389	—	—	—	—	—	—	—	—	—	50,909,933	—	1,366,843
1967	200,784	24,234,096	—	5,346,717	4,800,989	—	7,963,309	7,001,399	3,715,068	—	—	56,752,764	—	1,467,535
1968	217,134	26,450,189	—	5,661,036	5,288,925	—	8,560,762	7,881,203	3,954,840	—	—	61,765,015	2,252,455	1,621,024
1969	233,807	31,976,473	3,143,755	7,096,931	6,470,721	1,847,197	10,121,561	9,842,416	4,997,186	5,898,834	8,594,303	73,260,632	—	—
1970	257,475	33,397,424	—	7,006,280	6,534,014	—	11,066,614	10,098,155	5,350,268	—	—	77,631,396	—	1,135,180
1971	262,066	34,745,158	—	7,261,483	6,936,399	—	11,455,285	10,609,469	6,060,129	—	—	79,788,892	—	1,294,221
1972	287,906	40,543,020	—	8,309,391	7,824,436	—	13,401,276	12,542,010	7,533,807	—	—	90,999,639	2,878,649	1,517,807
1973	313,080	48,934,906	5,047,080	9,536,496	9,652,989	2,486,085	16,554,351	15,417,558	9,765,416	6,697,023	8,214,077	110,890,533	3,675,279	1,835,241
1974	333,099	53,919,325	—	10,166,189	10,917,010	—	18,714,522	17,267,469	10,923,165	—	—	123,143,669	—	2,108,297
1975	358,413	55,529,316	5,510,920	10,211,698	11,460,274	3,064,089	19,516,146	17,367,672	11,401,107	7,381,093	8,528,550	128,016,555	3,250,876	2,200,720
1976	391,685	62,197,040	—	11,193,732	13,040,445	—	21,735,782	19,830,686	12,756,801	—	—	148,438,448	—	2,440,099
1977	428,204	71,570,536	7,149,043	12,928,127	14,720,223	3,672,211	25,240,957	23,056,680	15,069,322	8,666,085	11,601,171	164,317,459	4,763,920	2,767,894
1978	478,679	79,448,133	7,551,598	14,266,556	16,632,652	4,233,648	27,844,060	25,255,871	17,752,924	9,239,747	9,791,341	194,224,117	5,355,802	2,944,466
1979	514,907	85,777,842	7,798,782	14,312,898	17,465,476	4,650,036	31,587,691	27,665,023	20,430,300	10,161,402	8,420,825	212,706,226	3,801,883	3,180,183
1980	545,389	87,412,922	8,020,977	14,719,355	16,328,626	5,817,526	32,557,172	27,555,514	21,898,027	9,636,760	6,361,364	210,322,424	2,526,608	2,932,620
1981	541,489	91,171,986	7,876,585	14,582,675	16,159,941	6,472,696	34,694,885	27,664,865	23,970,683	9,473,357	4,909,684	212,514,030	1,885,773	3,264,671
1982	564,219	110,512,890	10,721,652	17,795,793	19,358,751	9,388,005	38,685,456	32,322,315	26,216,431	10,402,125	9,864,236	243,056,569	3,066,957	4,484,018
1983	648,267	142,211,607	14,064,692	23,777,567	23,783,466	14,340,919	47,881,592	40,192,109	33,579,619	12,371,229	16,026,276	300,248,422	5,082,069	909,186
1984	701,339	180,173,410	17,804,462	31,727,463	28,925,232	17,911,858	62,685,218	51,493,064	45,653,407	13,791,118	22,655,103	385,026,843	6,906,667	1,736,227
1985	724,749	207,935,175	19,811,793	36,149,279	35,792,468	20,057,969	70,005,276	58,598,720	54,392,612	14,107,758	29,205,182	430,641,781	7,752,553	—
1986	826,214	250,975,543	24,405,166	41,081,179	44,173,919	24,532,825	85,633,171	68,082,967	65,243,714	16,662,036	37,166,245	483,986,301	8,669,204	—
1987	1,127,905 [1]	443,723,257	44,333,827	83,064,919	94,372,378	38,981,502	132,010,289	127,334,595	94,253,472	23,106,941	104,373,004	972,246,266	24,207,077	—
1988	1,257,191	584,533,143	55,565,702	109,255,556	122,007,283	49,019,402	182,093,065	165,432,730	132,543,936	28,192,817	140,868,538	1,263,988,377	33,537,144	—
1989	1,422,967	687,394,399	62,981,398	126,361,315	138,706,407	58,059,022	221,633,038	198,293,852	161,662,030	31,536,301	159,833,608	1,463,966,315	32,548,424	—
1990	1,575,092	744,307,752	68,969,946	138,628,048	146,150,954	66,003,700	244,392,990	210,380,303	178,387,605	35,094,732	171,274,973	1,620,702,664	32,928,086	—
1991	1,698,271	769,648,961	73,244,012	138,424,024	146,298,190	71,484,958	257,769,714	213,692,970	181,550,423	37,973,247	177,117,293	1,682,984,576	29,440,136	—
1992	1,785,371	808,090,676	77,366,319	147,783,192	153,561,103	73,287,786	269,768,091	219,074,632	180,851,262	42,268,498	197,656,966	1,821,882,961	46,664,314	—
1993	1,901,505	870,298,964	83,607,463	163,510,961	166,773,466	79,450,852	286,639,303	234,868,809	189,787,445	44,235,721	218,799,944	1,997,596,803	54,531,671	—
1994	2,023,754	943,679,740	90,239,607	179,885,773	183,409,745	86,114,352	307,469,260	256,965,058	202,528,875	47,060,882	239,829,062	2,210,945,344	74,422,618	—
1995	2,153,119	1,019,592,855	96,692,242	194,091,372	194,348,354	95,145,586	335,321,036	277,610,937	220,462,442	49,111,227	259,516,422	2,405,073,461	77,511,418	—
1996	2,304,416	1,100,360,936	110,477,442	206,252,429	203,470,594	106,435,493	361,721,577	297,041,883	237,076,624	51,418,421	291,138,974	2,618,094,172	93,858,493	—
1997	2,452,254	1,307,473,289	130,898,379	267,797,259	221,503,423	152,920,085	404,996,673	338,651,190	272,619,511	52,589,889	344,497,877	2,895,237,519	112,665,933	—

1 Firms that shifted from fiscal to calendar years are counted twice.

Sources

U.S. Internal Revenue Service, *Statistics of Income* and *Statistics of Income: Corporation Income Tax Returns*, various issues.

Documentation

See the text for Tables Ch1–18 and Ch510–524.

The figures for S-corporations are also included in Table Ch510-524. The series "surplus and retained earnings" includes "shareholders' undistributed taxable income previously taxed," "accumulated adjustments account," and "other adjustments account" for years where these categories were reported separately.

TABLE Ch659–679   Corporate assets, liabilities, capital, net income, and dividends: 1914–1943
[Two samples of large manufacturing corporations]
Contributed by Naomi R. Lamoreaux

	Total assets or liabilities	Assets								Liabilities	
		Current assets					Investments and advances	Fixed assets (net)	Other assets	Current liabilities	
		Total	Cash	Marketable securities	Receivables	Inventory				Total	Notes payable
	Ch659	Ch660 [1]	Ch661	Ch662	Ch663	Ch664	Ch665	Ch666	Ch667	Ch668 [1]	Ch669
Year	Million dollars	Million dollars	Million dollars	Million dollars	Million dollars	Million dollars	Million dollars	Million dollars	Million dollars	Million dollars	Million dollars
1914	5,254.1	1,532.4	236.8	42.0	465.6	780.5	253.6	3,116.6	351.5	385.0	181.1
1915	5,919.1	1,920.5	316.4	99.8	581.8	886.4	306.1	3,277.1	415.4	527.8	177.4
1916	6,754.0	2,579.3	448.3	190.6	674.8	1,216.4	310.4	3,434.7	429.6	658.9	204.4
1917	8,197.0	3,662.7	552.9	461.2	863.0	1,717.6	407.8	3,667.6	458.9	1,331.3	345.4
1918	9,340.7	4,512.5	581.6	621.0	1,071.2	2,158.0	455.8	3,866.3	506.1	1,737.1	447.2
1919	9,693.5	4,500.6	573.8	534.7	1,065.5	2,242.2	563.2	4,136.1	493.6	1,459.9	511.3
1920	10,463.5	4,646.3	520.0	369.6	1,209.8	2,464.5	651.2	4,652.4	513.6	1,556.1	670.8
1921	9,915.1	3,786.5	526.6	432.2	985.4	1,837.1	775.4	4,874.8	478.4	948.2	436.9
1922 [2]	12,701.1	5,102.3	650.7	583.9	1,379.6	2,488.1	1,032.6	6,005.8	560.4	1,111.0	273.0
1922 [2]	9,911.5	3,753.2	547.7	430.8	943.7	1,826.7	785.3	4,882.3	490.7	799.1	220.0
1923	13,761.3	5,555.9	735.9	620.0	1,437.3	2,762.7	1,104.7	6,571.7	529.0	1,297.5	319.2
1924	14,030.7	5,728.9	818.6	665.0	1,472.8	2,772.5	1,025.7	6,752.3	523.8	1,225.9	232.7
1925	15,029.9	6,218.9	911.9	694.4	1,595.0	3,017.6	1,029.5	7,302.9	478.6	1,344.2	162.4
1926	16,048.3	6,651.5	937.1	877.9	1,658.2	3,178.3	1,035.9	7,847.6	513.3	1,385.0	166.6
1927	16,360.7	6,467.1	1,026.7	928.5	1,403.3	3,108.6	1,089.7	8,255.1	548.8	1,178.1	152.5
1928	17,292.3	6,999.5	1,187.2	1,079.6	1,529.9	3,202.8	1,221.7	8,459.8	611.3	1,344.7	171.7
1929	18,684.2	7,394.1	1,124.3	1,059.1	1,675.7	3,535.0	1,643.8	8,972.7	673.6	1,364.5	161.8
1930	18,689.2	6,855.1	1,219.1	910.0	1,453.9	3,272.1	1,434.7	9,735.3	664.1	1,059.6	72.4
1931	18,035.6	6,031.3	1,080.4	1,030.3	1,180.8	2,739.8	1,362.1	10,021.3	620.9	757.3	44.7
1932	16,799.4	5,360.4	1,219.5	782.2	987.3	2,371.4	1,466.2	9,391.6	581.2	649.1	34.8
1933	16,588.0	5,448.2	1,041.3	899.2	962.5	2,545.2	1,673.7	8,757.5	708.6	787.2	65.0
1934	16,257.0	5,553.1	1,109.1	705.8	947.8	2,790.4	1,604.7	8,600.2	499.0	957.1	129.5
1935	16,338.9	5,933.0	1,299.1	613.8	1,093.2	2,926.9	1,547.6	8,356.4	501.9	1,201.0	193.6
1936	16,985.4	6,280.8	1,270.1	522.6	1,266.7	3,221.4	1,594.0	8,592.7	517.9	1,480.0	197.5
1937	18,034.0	6,663.3	1,105.4	493.9	1,282.2	3,781.8	1,637.9	9,156.9	575.9	1,597.1	289.2
1938	17,769.2	6,641.1	1,593.9	451.9	1,223.8	3,371.5	1,650.2	8,937.8	540.1	1,279.9	145.4
1939	18,212.5	7,033.9	1,772.1	576.0	1,297.9	3,387.9	1,850.8	8,807.4	520.4	1,440.4	88.2
1940	19,048.2	7,858.0	2,184.0	602.5	1,511.0	3,560.5	1,985.9	8,715.6	488.7	2,081.6	120.4
1941	21,071.8	9,643.3	2,059.2	1,280.6	2,097.8	4,205.7	1,902.8	8,911.1	614.6	3,547.7	263.9
1942	23,074.1	11,664.6	2,120.6	1,751.2	3,168.2	4,624.6	1,833.5	8,853.4	722.6	4,928.9	321.7
1943	24,632.3	13,259.6	2,610.4	2,666.1	3,241.6	4,741.5	1,775.5	8,727.0	870.2	5,870.8	202.7

	Liabilities				Capital					
	Current liabilities		Long-term debt	Other liabilities	Preferred stock	Common stock	Capital reserves	Surplus	Net income	Dividends
	Accounts payable	Other								
	Ch670	Ch671	Ch672	Ch673	Ch674	Ch675	Ch676	Ch677	Ch678	Ch679
Year	Million dollars	Million dollars	Million dollars	Million dollars	Million dollars	Million dollars	Million dollars	Million dollars	Million dollars	Million dollars
1914	111.3	53.4	1,027.9	22.4	1,064.7	1,865.6	77.0	811.5	190.5	154.1
1915	220.0	67.5	1,030.0	122.5	1,149.6	1,955.9	126.8	1,006.5	381.5	172.1
1916	227.0	122.7	1,067.3	68.3	1,173.3	2,108.0	150.0	1,528.2	914.0	305.6
1917	332.8	471.1	1,114.2	82.4	1,236.4	2,337.9	237.7	1,857.1	875.1	357.4
1918	435.4	700.0	1,221.0	79.8	1,298.4	2,472.9	370.6	2,160.9	627.4	331.9
1919	385.0	323.7	1,204.0	88.4	1,404.1	2,610.7	440.7	2,485.7	610.7	297.1
1920	370.1	285.1	1,286.2	47.2	1,453.5	2,959.6	474.2	2,686.7	587.8	311.3
1921	230.9	198.8	1,470.6	60.0	1,450.1	3,028.0	552.5	2,405.7	139.2	297.2
1922 [2]	604.1	233.9	1,648.6	59.7	1,877.2	4,864.2	435.4	2,705.0	645.2	410.5
1922 [2]	289.9	204.5	1,460.3	40.4	1,547.3	3,592.9	505.4	1,966.1	511.1	535.9
1923	685.1	293.2	1,780.4	59.5	1,913.8	5,251.0	405.7	3,053.4	868.1	499.1
1924	689.5	303.7	1,745.2	55.4	1,935.2	5,384.8	423.8	3,260.4	889.7	527.2

Notes appear at end of table

(continued)

TABLE Ch659–679 Corporate assets, liabilities, capital, net income, and dividends: 1914–1943
[Two samples of large manufacturing corporations] *Continued*

	Liabilities					Capital					
	Current liabilities										
	Accounts payable	Other	Long-term debt	Other liabilities		Preferred stock	Common stock	Capital reserves	Surplus	Net income	Dividends
	Ch670	Ch671	Ch672	Ch673		Ch674	Ch675	Ch676	Ch677	Ch678	Ch679
Year	Million dollars	Million dollars	Million dollars	Million dollars		Million dollars	Million dollars	Million dollars	Million dollars	Million dollars	Million dollars
1925	790.0	391.8	1,756.8	66.4		1,983.5	5,551.1	447.5	3,880.4	1,214.7	613.9
1926	760.2	458.2	1,887.0	67.4		2,041.1	5,974.0	429.1	4,264.7	1,311.0	764.8
1927	575.8	449.8	2,114.3	242.1		1,907.0	6,283.2	460.0	4,176.0	1,098.7	839.5
1928	685.5	487.5	2,162.2	279.9		1,918.9	6,582.8	456.4	4,547.4	1,485.3	905.3
1929	708.2	494.5	1,850.7	329.4		1,964.0	7,421.7	544.8	5,209.1	1,721.1	1,011.6
1930	588.9	398.3	2,001.2	299.4		1,995.1	7,521.9	544.9	5,267.1	964.1	971.7
1931	425.4	287.2	1,972.1	459.6		1,979.6	7,684.6	550.2	4,632.2	289.7	809.8
1932	385.2	229.1	1,933.4	406.2		1,955.0	7,307.3	459.3	4,089.1	0.5	497.1
1933	465.7	256.5	1,768.9	413.0		1,945.2	7,243.3	461.2	3,969.2	314.3	384.0
1934	448.1	379.5	1,662.3	476.0		1,938.4	6,782.2	492.2	3,948.8	467.2	440.1
1935	504.0	503.4	1,592.0	440.8		1,882.4	6,805.0	519.9	3,897.8	791.7	514.6
1936	613.0	669.5	1,551.4	374.6		1,871.2	7,015.2	567.3	4,125.7	1,269.3	922.5
1937	557.0	750.9	1,717.0	469.5		1,956.0	7,110.4	634.0	4,550.0	1,427.4	1,019.2
1938	532.2	602.3	2,048.4	454.1		1,956.5	6,840.8	596.3	4,593.2	651.6	562.2
1939	626.2	726.0	2,089.9	423.2		1,963.1	6,856.5	639.2	4,800.2	1,048.4	750.7
1940	729.0	1,232.2	2,013.5	421.1		1,946.6	6,805.5	813.3	4,966.6	1,317.6	868.8
1941	925.1	2,358.7	2,014.3	444.5		1,907.4	6,821.4	960.5	5,376.0	1,501.6	949.8
1942	1,159.6	3,447.6	1,993.5	461.4		1,898.2	6,830.2	1,208.8	5,753.1	1,154.6	750.2
1943	1,466.3	4,201.8	1,984.3	495.7		1,831.1	6,843.0	1,408.8	6,198.6	1,247.7	770.7

[1] For 1914–1922, exceeds sum of components by amount of unsegregable items.

[2] Two sets of values are shown for 1922, the first comparable with earlier years, the second with later years.

Source

Historical Statistics of the United States (1975), series V285–305, based on unpublished data provided by the National Bureau of Economic Research.

Documentation

These series represent financial data for two samples of large corporations (companies with total assets over $10 million each). The data for 1914–1922 are based on a sample of 81 corporations, and the data for 1922–1943 are based on a sample of 84 corporations. For both samples, companies were selected from among the largest and most important concerns in eleven major manufacturing industries. Some very large corporations (for example, the Ford Motor Company) had to be omitted because of lack of published financial statements, but the number of such omissions was small. Consequently, both samples, though small in terms of the number of firms included, represent substantial portions of the entire manufacturing universe in terms of total assets and total volume of operations. For example, in 1933 firms in the sample represented 29 percent of the total assets of all manufacturing corporations and as much as 45 percent of the total assets of all manufacturing corporations with total assets over $10 million (A. R. Koch, *The Financing of Large Corporations* (National Bureau of Economic Research, 1943), p. 13).

In the sample for 1914–1922, data were not available for eight companies in 1914, three in 1915, one in 1916, and one in 1917. In the sample for 1922–1943, three companies had to be omitted in 1922, one in 1923, one in 1924, and one in 1925. Because the excluded firms were among the smallest in the samples, however, their omission had a relatively minor effect on the composite balance sheets and income statements.

The amounts of total assets, income, and dividends for the sample for 1922–1943 are considerably greater than those for the sample for earlier years, mainly because, in the 1922–1943 sample, a number of larger companies were substituted for smaller concerns included in the sample for 1914–1922. These differences should be borne in mind when trends over the entire period are examined.

For a more detailed description of these samples, see the unpublished manuscript *Corporate Financial Data for Studies in Business Finance* (May 1945) available at the National Bureau of Economic Research.

The accounting terms used in these series are defined as follows: "total assets" is the sum of all asset items less reserves for depreciation and revaluation; "cash" is cash on hand and bank deposits; "marketable securities" are government securities and call and time loans; "receivables" are notes and accounts receivable less a reserve for bad debts; "inventory" is raw materials, goods and work in process, finished goods, and supplies, all less reserves for inventory; "investments and advances" are investments in, or advances to, subsidiaries or affiliated concerns, and other stocks and bonds; "fixed assets (net)" are land, plant, machinery, equipment, and nonoperating property, all less reserves for depreciation, depletion, and obsolescence; "other assets" are prepaid expenses, deferred charges, intangibles, amounts due from officers, directors, and stockholders, and cash set aside for specific purposes or not available for immediate use; "notes payable" are all notes or bills to banks, trade, and others; "accounts payable" are accounts payable to trade; "other current liabilities" are accruals and current reserves; "long-term debt" is all funded debt or mortgages, whether current or not, less sinking funds listed on asset side, and purchase obligations; "other liabilities" are minority interest, deferred liabilities, amounts appropriated from surplus for specific purposes, and amounts due to officers, employees, and affiliates; "preferred stock" is preferred and debenture stock less treasury preferred stock when listed on asset side; "common stock" is common stock (A and B) or capital stock less common treasury stock when listed on asset side; "capital reserves" are special appropriations from income or surplus for contingencies; "surplus" is capital and earned surplus less profit and undivided surplus when carried on asset side; "net income" is net amount after all expenses, interest, and taxes; "dividends" are cash dividends on preferred and common shares. Stock dividends are not included.

CHAPTER Cj
Financial Markets and Institutions

Editor: Michael D. Bordo

Associate Editors: Richard G. Anderson, Howard Bodenhorn, John A. James, Hugh Rockoff,
Peter L. Rousseau, Richard Sylla, David C. Wheelock, and Eugene N. White

Michael D. Bordo

This chapter assembles historical statistics on the monetary and financial systems of the United States since colonial times. The tables cover various monetary aggregates, indicators of monetary policy, statistics on banking, insurance, and other financial institutions, financial markets, debt and the flow of funds, and interest rates. This essay provides an overview of the roles of money and the financial system in the historical functioning and growth of the American economy, with individual essays setting the background for each of the major topics: monetary aggregates; monetary statistics before the national banking era; monetary policy; financial institutions and their regulation; securities markets; debt and the flow of funds; and interest rates and yields.

Money and the Economy

Money has a central role in the creation of a modern economy based on exchange, production, and an effective division of labor. Money facilitates exchange across space and over time; indeed, it is at the base of the credit system, which allocates resources over time. Historically, three basic functions of money have been identified: unit of account, store of value, and medium of exchange (Friedman and Meltzer 2003). The *unit of account* function refers to announcing prices and recording transactions in units of the asset. The *store of value* function refers to an asset retaining its value over time, allowing money to serve as a standard of deferred payments. Most fundamentally, money is a means of payment, a way of discharging debts that arise from exchanging goods and services. A financial instrument is said to be a *medium of exchange* if it is widely accepted to discharge debts, including debts arising from the purchase and sale of goods and services. The stock of money, in turn, is defined to include those financial instruments that either are media of exchange or may be converted, quickly and at low cost, into media of exchange. Examples of such instruments include metal coins, paper currency, and certain deposits at banks and other financial institutions (see the essay on monetary aggregates in this chapter).

Acknowledgments
Michael D. Bordo thanks Antu Panini Murshid for his help on the project. David C. Wheelock thanks Heidi Beyer for valuable research assistance.

Money began as full-bodied coins whose face value equaled their value as a commodity. Precious metals – gold, silver, and copper – were used in the United States as commodity money from 1790 to 1933 because they possessed the valuable properties of divisibility, storability, portability, and high value relative to weight. Fiduciary money, whose face value exceeds its value as a commodity, evolved to economize on the resource cost of using gold and silver coin. In order to circulate, fiduciary money requires basic trust by the public in the issuer's intent not to overissue to capture the social saving inherent in fiduciary money. Indeed, fiduciary money is a social contrivance. People accept it because in their experience other people also do so. Commodity money, certified by the government in the form of coin, was eventually replaced by fiduciary money, which evolved from bank-issued notes convertible into coin to the present-day government-issued pure fiat money backed by a credible commitment by the monetary authorities to maintain stable prices.

Commercial banks play an integral part in the monetary system. They evolved from the goldsmiths of medieval Europe who would take in gold for safekeeping in return for warehouse receipts, which began circulating as money. Their modern-day descendants borrow short-term and lend long-term to firms and households. Their liabilities (including notes before 1934) and deposits are the largest part of the money supply (as discussed in the following sections; also see the essay on financial institutions and their regulation in this chapter).

Government has played a crucial role in the monetary system from the beginning, but active pursuit of "monetary policy" is a relatively recent phenomenon. In the U.S. Constitution, Congress certified the value of the dollar as a coin with a fixed weight in gold or silver. Under this system, the monetary authority (the U.S. Treasury until 1914, the Federal Reserve since then) was charged with preserving the convertibility of paper currency into gold. In the twentieth century, the Federal Reserve has accepted a much broader responsibility for general macroeconomic stability. The monetary authority is also charged with maintaining the stability of the financial system. This involves both maintaining the smooth functioning of the payments system and serving as a lender of last resort in the event of a banking panic.

In the United States, monetary policy since the 1920s has largely achieved its aims by using open market operations (buying and selling of government securities from and to the banking system and the public) to produce changes in the monetary base. The monetary base is the sum of currency outstanding and prudential bank reserves at Federal Reserve banks. The monetary base changes in response to changes in the federal funds rate, which is the overnight rate banks charge for the sale of surplus bank reserves at Federal Reserve banks. The change in short-term interest rates in turn affects the cost of borrowing funds and hence both business investment and household consumption expenditures.

Over the past two centuries, financial innovation – the development of new types of financial instruments – has changed the structure of the financial system by creating new types of financial institutions and markets (see the essays on monetary statistics before the national banking era and on financial institutions and their regulation, both in this chapter). This evolution has changed the channels by which monetary policy can affect the economy (for example, through the substitution between different financial assets and by affecting bank lending directly). Financial innovation has vastly increased the size of the financial system relative to the monetary base, which the Federal Reserve can control using open market operations. Despite these developments, the basic role of the Federal Reserve remains unchanged. It is to provide a nominal anchor for the price level by its control over the monetary base.

The Financial System

The function of the financial system is to allocate resources by matching the surplus funds of savers (lenders) with the demands for funds by investors (borrowers). The financial system provides three key services: risk sharing, liquidity, and information. The financial system enables risk sharing by diversifying portfolios, through the provision of financial instruments to lenders who in turn pool the risks across borrowers. Providing such a service encourages higher levels of lending than would be the case if savers could place their funds in only one industry or sector of the economy.

An asset is said to be "liquid" if it can be quickly sold for very near the price for which it can be purchased. By definition, the most liquid asset is money. The financial system provides facilities to ease the exchange of financial assets, which may be risky and may be long-lived, for money.

Finally, the financial system provides information to savers about potential investors. It reduces the costs of asymmetric information in which investors (borrowers) have better information about the likely success of the projects to be funded than do savers. After delivering credit, the system continues to produce information by monitoring the performance of borrowers in utilizing the funds and servicing and repaying the loans. The three services the financial system provides are defined by two types of entities: financial institutions (see the essay on financial institutions and their regulation in this chapter) and financial markets (see the essays on securities markets and on debt and the flow of funds, both in this chapter).

A financial institution is an intermediary that collects funds from savers and transfers them to borrowers. The primary financial institutions in the United States have been commercial banks. A commercial bank receives deposits and makes loans. The loans earn interest, generated by the productive activity financed. The depositors are paid interest or are provided other services (for example, transaction facilities) to compensate them for the use of their funds. The bank earns profits from the spread between the interest paid on deposits and the interest earned on loans, and from fees charged for other financial services. The bank reduces risk by lending to diverse entities facing diverse risks. It also provides liquidity by ensuring that savers can always convert their deposits into cash.

Banks are the most important financial intermediaries in the U.S. economy. Until the middle of the twentieth century, the banking sector had the largest share of financial assets. Other types of financial intermediaries, such as savings and loan associations, trust companies, investment banks, and insurance companies, perform many of the same functions as banks, but they are specialized in terms of the activities they finance and the liquidity of their liabilities. Traditionally, the liabilities of the banking system have been the most liquid and, as previously noted, comprise the largest component of the money supply.

Commercial banks and related financial institutions in the United States are regulated by various authorities, such as the Federal Reserve, the Comptroller of the Currency, the Federal Deposit Insurance Corporation, and state agencies. Regulation serves to ensure the soundness of these institutions, to prevent fraud, and to reduce the costs of asymmetric information (see the essay on financial institutions and their regulation in this chapter).

Financial markets are arenas in which savers and investors are directly matched. Investors (borrowers) issue claims, which are purchased by savers (lenders). Primary markets are those in which newly issued claims are sold to buyers. Secondary markets trade in already-issued claims. Funds are raised in financial markets either as debt (bonds), whose principal a borrower must repay with interest, or as equity (stocks), which involves an ownership claim to the profits or assets of the firm.

Financial markets also provide the services of risk sharing, liquidity, and information. As in the case of financial institutions, financial markets in the United States are regulated by agencies such as the Securities and Exchange Commission to ensure the free flow of information (see the essays on securities markets and on debt and the flow of funds, both in this chapter).

Interest rates are relative prices, which equilibrate demand and supply for various financial assets in financial markets (see the essay on interest rates and yields in this chapter). Nominal or market interest rates encompass both the "real" rate of interest representing the return on capital and the marginal rate of time preference, and expectations of inflation. The term structure of interest rates from short-term to long-term reflects the longevity and liquidity of the asset as well as expectations of future monetary and fiscal policy and the business cycle.

Finally, the financial system, by matching savers and investors and facilitating diversification of portfolios, has contributed in important ways to the growth of the U.S. economy. The financial system assists growth by fostering an environment that raises the savings rate and thereby accelerates capital accumulation. It also provides the funds to finance new technology (Levine 1997). The existence of robust and flexible financial markets has been frequently identified as an important contributor to the reemergence of the United States as the world technological leader at the end of the twentieth century (Gompers and Lerner 2001).

References

Friedman, Milton, and Allan Meltzer. 2003. "Money." In *Encyclopedia Britannica*. Merriam-Webster.

Gompers, Paul, and Josh Lerner. 2001. *The Money of Invention*. Harvard Business School Press.

Hubbard, R. Glenn. 2000. *Money, the Financial System and the Economy*. 3rd edition. Addison-Wesley.

Levine, Ross. 1997. "Development and Economic Growth: Views and Agenda." *Journal of Economic Literature* 35 (June): 688–726.

MONETARY AGGREGATES

Richard G. Anderson

Monetary aggregates are measures of the total stock of money held by the public. Empirical measures of U.S. monetary aggregates have changed and adapted through time in response to changes in the range of available instruments and the transaction cost of exchanging one asset for another. Friedman and Schwartz (1970, p. 198) note that "the purpose of a definition is to facilitate organizing the data in a useful way, not to prejudge conclusions." As a result, monetary aggregates "cannot be defined by any single set of hard and fast rules. It is a question of judgment on the basis of criteria that are inevitably incomplete and often unformulated."

Historically, alternative monetary aggregates have been constructed simultaneously at various levels of aggregation because of uncertainty regarding the correspondence among financial instruments, the functions of money, and the cost of converting less-liquid assets into a medium of exchange. Over time, financial innovation has both introduced new assets and changed the feasibility and cost of conversion among existing assets. As a result, definitions of U.S. monetary aggregates have changed. Prior to the imposition of federal statutory reserve requirements in 1914, for example, banks often did not distinguish sharply among demand, savings, and time deposits. Demand deposits sometimes paid interest, and time deposits sometimes were transferable via checks. During the 1980s, thrift institutions began offering checkable deposits, commercial banks began paying explicit interest on certain checkable deposits, and the popularity of money market mutual funds soared.

The U.S. economy comprises a wide variety of financial assets, and there is no simple rule for determining which assets should be included in a monetary aggregate. The tables in this chapter focus on four aggregates: currency, M1, M2, and M3. Two currency aggregates are included. The *currency stock* refers to the total amount of currency in the economy, including currency issued by U.S. firms and by the monetary authorities (the U.S. Treasury and, after 1914, the Federal Reserve), whether held in the United States or abroad. *Currency in circulation* refers to the currency stock minus currency held by the monetary authorities. Table Cj54–69 shows currency in circulation, by kind, and Table Cj70–74 compares the currency stock and currency in circulation. The Treasury has compiled figures on currency in circulation since 1800, and the tables are based on these data. Depending on date, the currency aggregates may include specie coin (gold and silver), nominal coin (nonprecious metals), paper currency legally convertible into specie coin or bullion, and paper currency not convertible into specie. Historically, many types of firms have issued currency. Prior to the Civil War, currency was issued, with the approval of state governments, by railroad and canal development companies as well as by banks. Following the Civil War, a federal excise tax on notes issued by state-chartered banks made their issue unprofitable; as a result, most currency came to be issued by national banks. Today, Federal Reserve notes are dominant (see Tables Cj54–74 for details).

The M1, M2, and M3 monetary aggregates in Table Cj84–99 are the measures currently published by the Board of Governors of the Federal Reserve System. Unfortunately, owing to limited source data, these figures begin only in 1959 (Anderson and Kavajecz 1994; Kavajecz 1994). Tables Cj42–53 display monetary aggregate measures for earlier years. Data in Table Cj42–48 are annual aver-

ages for years through 1947, calculated from the mixed-frequency figures compiled by Friedman and Schwartz; data in Table Cj49–53 are annual averages for 1947–1958 of the monthly figures compiled by Rasche (Friedman and Schwartz 1970; Rasche 1987, 1990).

The M1 aggregate includes currency in circulation outside the vaults of depository financial institutions; travelers' checks issued by nonbank financial institutions; and certain deposits, transferable by check, that are held by the nonbank public. The nonbank public is defined to consist of households, firms other than depository institutions, state and local governments, and federal government agencies other than the Treasury. The financial assets included in M1 function as a medium of exchange, that is, they are commonly used to settle debts resulting from the exchange of goods and services. Checks have been used in the United States to transfer ownership of deposits since at least 1800. Prior to the Banking Act of 1933, little distinction was drawn between demand deposits (which the bank was required to pay out immediately, on demand) and other types of savings deposits. Although only demand deposits could be transferred to third parties via negotiable instruments (checks), banks often allowed customers to shift funds among different types of accounts without penalty, and interest could be paid to customers. The Banking Act of 1933, however, prohibited banks from paying explicit interest on demand deposits, and it required banks to impose penalties on customers who withdrew time deposits prior to the contractual maturity. Since 1994, the Federal Reserve's published measure of M1 has been distorted by the operation of automated retail-deposit sweep programs. As of December 1999, such programs were estimated to have reduced the amount of checkable deposits included in M1 by approximately $369 billion, relative to the level of checkable deposits that the nonbank public perceives itself to be holding at depository institutions (for details, see Anderson and Rasche 2001).

The M2 aggregate equals the sum of M1 plus the nonbank public's holdings of certain savings and time deposits at depository institutions and of shares in retail-oriented money market mutual funds. These deposits, although not commonly used as a medium of exchange, are highly liquid (that is, they may be converted quickly and at very low cost into a medium of exchange). Deposits and mutual fund shares linked to retirement accounts, such as IRAs and Keoghs, are excluded because high penalties are imposed for their early conversion (prior to legal specifications) into a medium of exchange.

The M3 aggregate equals the sum of M2 plus the nonbank public's holdings of large-denomination time deposits at depository financial institutions, plus institutionally oriented money market mutual funds. The aggregate also includes certain repurchase agreements and Eurodollar deposits issued by depository institutions (see Table Cj84–99).

Traditionally, monetary aggregates have been constructed by summing, for each time period, the aggregate dollar values of the included assets. This practice ignores economic aggregation theory, which suggests that liquid financial instruments should be aggregated in a manner similar to durable goods. Barnett established that a superlative statistical index number, as defined by Diewert, provides an approximation to the appropriate economic aggregator function (Barnett 1980; Diewert 1976). Table Cj100–107 displays a set of such *monetary index numbers* and their (economically) dual user costs as produced by the Research Division of the Federal Reserve Bank of St. Louis (for details, see Anderson, Jones, and Nesmith 1997; or Barnett and Serletis 2000).

References

Anderson, Richard G., Barry E. Jones, and Travis D. Nesmith. 1997. "Special Report: The Monetary Services Index Project of the Federal Reserve Bank of St. Louis." *Federal Reserve Bank of St. Louis Review* 79 (January/February): 25–82.

Anderson, Richard G., and Kenneth A. Kavajecz. 1994. "A Historical Perspective on the Federal Reserve's Monetary Aggregates: Definition, Construction and Targeting." *Federal Reserve Bank of St. Louis Review* 76 (March/April): 1–31.

Anderson, Richard G., and Robert H. Rasche. 2001. "Retail Sweep Programs and Bank Reserves, 1994–1999." *Federal Reserve Bank of St. Louis Review* 83 (January/February): 51–72.

Barnett, William A. 1980. "Economic Monetary Aggregates: An Application of Index Number and Aggregation Theory." *Journal of Econometrics* 13 (Summer): 11–48.

Barnett, William A., and Apostolos Serletis, editors. 2000. *The Theory of Monetary Aggregation.* Elsevier Science.

Diewert, W. E. 1976. "Exact and Superlative Index Numbers." *Journal of Econometrics* 4 (2): 115–45.

Friedman, Milton, and Anna Jacobson Schwartz. 1970. *Monetary Statistics of the United States: Estimates, Sources, Methods.* Columbia University Press.

Kavajecz, Kenneth A. 1994. "The Evolution of the Federal Reserve's Monetary Aggregates: A Timeline." *Federal Reserve Bank of St. Louis Review* 76 (March/April): 32–66.

Rasche, Robert H. 1987. "M1-Velocity and Money Demand Functions: Do Stable Relationships Exist?" *Carnegie–Rochester Conference Series on Public Policy* 27 (Autumn): 9–88.

Rasche, Robert H. 1990. "Demand Functions for U.S. Money and Credit Measures." In P. Hooper, Karen H. Johnson, et al., editors. *Financial Sectors in Open Economies: Empirical Analysis and Policy Issues.* Board of Governors of the Federal Reserve System.

MONETARY STATISTICS BEFORE THE NATIONAL BANKING ERA

Hugh Rockoff

From the establishment of the federal government through the Civil War, money in the United States consisted mainly of specie (gold and silver coins), bank notes (paper money issued by banks), bank deposits, and at times currency issued by the federal government. The U.S. Mint, established in 1792, produced coins of gold, silver, and copper. Foreign coins also circulated, especially Mexican, Latin American, and Spanish silver pesos. These and other designated foreign coins were legal tender for most of the period. The Mint assayed specimens of these coins and determined their legal tender values. Legal tender status for foreign coins was discontinued in 1857.

During this period, the United States was on a bimetallic standard. Both gold and silver coins were legal tenders, and when specific amounts of gold and silver were brought to the Mint, it was required by law to convert the metals into coin. The content of the silver dollar was set at 371.25 grains of silver, and the content of the gold dollar was set at 24.75 grains of gold, thus establishing a "bimetallic ratio" or "mint ratio" of 15 : 1. One rationale for bimetallism was that gold coins would provide a convenient medium for large transactions, while silver coins would be convenient for small transactions. A second rationale, one that became more important after the Civil War, was that bimetallism would reduce the threat of deflation and produce greater price stability. If the stock of one

metal, say gold, grew too slowly to produce stable prices, the other metal, silver, might be used in its place.

In practice, the ability of the United States to maintain both metals in circulation, and thus to satisfy the first rationale, was limited by the tendency of the coins made from the metal worth relatively more in world markets to be withdrawn from circulation and exported. In the early decades of the nineteenth century, the rising price of gold on world markets produced a situation in which most of the coin in circulation was silver. Partly to remedy this situation, the amount of gold in the gold dollar was reduced from 24.75 grains to 23.22 grains in 1834, thus establishing a mint ratio of 16 : 1, which was more in line with world markets. Although this change encouraged the circulation of gold, the main reason gold began to replace silver was the discovery of gold in California in 1848 and the related discoveries in other areas. Although silver did not entirely disappear, the circulation shifted rapidly toward gold in the 1850s. The idea that the cheaper money would replace the dearer (provided the two monies circulate at a fixed exchange rate owing to law, custom, or convenience) is known as Gresham's law, often summarized as "bad money drives out good," although "cheap money drives out dear" is more accurate.

Bank notes were payable in specie on demand except during financial crises or wars, when convertibility was suspended. Bank notes were issued by local private banks and by the First and Second Banks of the United States. The local banks were chartered by the states; the First and Second Banks were chartered by the federal government. The legal procedures for chartering local banks and the rules regulating banks varied greatly from state to state. In some states, banks were chartered individually by the state legislature but, under the so-called free banking laws, anyone could start a bank provided that the bank complied with certain rules and regulations. One of those regulations was that notes issued by free banks had to be backed by government bonds, typically bonds of the state where the bank was located. Perhaps the most important common feature of the early banking laws was that banks with charters from one state were not permitted to set up branches in other states. Restrictions on branching, particularly the ban on interstate branching, produced a system of geographically isolated banks that persisted well into the twentieth century and distinguished the U.S. banking system from the systems prevailing in other industrialized countries. In those countries, bank offices typically were branches of a few large banks with headquarters in the nation's financial center.

The large number of distinct bank notes in existence (because each bank issued its own notes) gave rise to an unusual currency system. Bank notes generally circulated in the vicinity of the bank that issued them. Notes taken into another region had to be converted into local money. Generally, a discount would be charged on nonlocal notes, analogous to the charges sometimes levied for withdrawing cash from an automated teller machine (ATM). The appropriate discounts on bank notes issued by solvent banks – and lists of notes of bankrupt banks, and counterfeits – were published in reference books known as bank note reporters. Although considerable research has been conducted on the determinants of the discounts and other aspects of the system, it is still not known whether the volume of discounted or counterfeit notes was sufficient to affect the accuracy of the monetary statistics from the era.

The First Bank of the United States was chartered in 1791 for a term of twenty years; the Second Bank was chartered in 1816, again for a term of twenty years. The notes issued by the First and Second Banks of the United States enjoyed a higher status than those issued by state-chartered banks. The high status of their notes flowed from the decision to make them a legal tender for the payment of taxes, from the fact that the First and Second Banks alone had a nationwide system of branches, and from the patronage of the federal government enjoyed by the First and Second Banks. As might be expected, the competition between the state-chartered banks and the federally chartered banks was intense, and it was a major factor in the decisions not to renew the charters of the First and Second Banks.

Deposit banking in those days was similar in many respects to our modern system of deposit banking, but it was restricted, especially in the early years of the nineteenth century, to a relatively small class of people who were literate, numerate, and possessed of sufficient means to make deposit banking worthwhile. The share of deposits in the total supply of money, however, grew dramatically between 1800 and 1865. By 1860, deposits were a larger component of the stock of money than bank notes were (see Table Cj7–21).

The federal government did not issue paper money in peacetime, but during the War of 1812 and especially during the Civil War, large amounts of fiat paper money (money not redeemable in specie) were issued. The motive was simply the need for revenues to finance the wars. Taxes and borrowing were also used to finance the wars, but the printing press was an attractive alternative. In effect, printing new money was a low-cost (in terms of administrative expenses) way of taxing a widely held asset: money held by the public. The result of relying on money creation was substantial inflation. During the Civil War, both the North and the South experienced major inflation, but the inflation in the South was far more severe, in part because the South relied far more on printing money than did the North.

Data on the stock of money and its components before 1867 are often incomplete and available at irregular intervals. Data on the notes and deposits issued by private banks after the mid-1830s are available in reports the banks made to state government regulatory agencies, which in turn reported them to the Secretary of the Treasury. Considerable data for earlier decades were uncovered by Joseph Van Fenstermaker (1965), who combed government records, newspapers, and other sources for the balance sheets of the banks. Data on the issue of fiat paper money are also available in the Reports of the Secretary of the Treasury. The figures on the amount of coin in circulation are more problematic. Although the amount minted is known, the amount of coin (of domestic or foreign origin) entering or leaving the United States can only be approximated from imprecise and incomplete statistics on foreign trade.

Since the nineteenth century, scholars have attempted to combine estimates of coin, bank notes, and deposits into estimates of the stock of money. The work of Milton Friedman and Anna J. Schwartz (1963, 1970) clarified the conceptual framework for estimating the stock of money. The first effort to apply their framework to the antebellum period was made by George Macesich (1960), who prepared estimates of the stock of specie and the stock of money for the years 1834–1845, and used them to reinterpret the monetary disturbances of the Jacksonian Era. Peter Temin (1969), building on the work of Macesich, prepared estimates covering the years 1820–1858 for his study of the Jacksonian Era. Temin's data are shown in Table Cj22–25. Comprehensive estimates from 1790

of the stock of money and its components were first assembled by Milton Friedman and Anna J. Schwartz (1970). Table Cj7–21 is a version of Friedman and Schwartz's Table 13. It has been simplified for the general reader in several ways: (1) when Friedman and Schwartz give alternative estimates, we present only what appears to us to be the best estimate; (2) when Friedman and Schwartz present data for different months toward the end of the year, we have combined them into a single end-of-year estimate; and (3) we have omitted certain minor monetary variables. Readers engaged in detailed research should consult the original source.

The monetary aggregates presented here are, with the exception of certain figures for the North in the Civil War, simple arithmetic sums of the amount of coins, paper money, and deposits. This is probably the best that can be done for now, but it is unlikely that this method is ideal. If acceptable procedures existed for weighting assets on the basis of their "moneyness," then the weight on coins in the monetary aggregates would be higher than the weight on notes and deposits, and the weight on notes and deposits issued by the First and Second Banks of the United States would be higher than the weight on notes and deposits issued by the state-chartered banks. However, practical systems for assigning the weights are lacking.

During some of the banking panics – there were banking panics in 1819, 1837, 1839, and 1857 – and during the War of 1812 and the Civil War, convertibility of bank notes and deposits into coin was suspended. The price of coin in terms of notes and deposits then became a market price that varied over time. Valuing coin at market prices would produce a larger estimate of the stock of money, and valuing paper at coin prices would produce a smaller estimate, than the arithmetic sum that included coins and notes and deposits all at face value. Economic theory, however, does not provide a clear basis for choosing among these approaches.

The Civil War also created additional problems for interpreting the monetary statistics. The nation was split into several distinct currency areas. In the North and Midwest, the famous greenback dollar, a fiat paper currency, dominated. Gold and silver could be purchased at a premium in the bullion market, but typically gold and silver were not used in domestic transactions. Similarly, in the Confederacy, the Confederate dollar reigned. On the Pacific Coast of the United States, however, gold remained the dominant form of money, and the greenback dollar was treated as a "foreign" currency that circulated at a discount. In part, this odd state of affairs was achieved through social pressure that stigmatized individuals who insisted on paying debts with or otherwise using greenbacks. The South also was split into two currency areas after the North gained control of the Mississippi River. In both the North and the South, moreover, the governments issued interest-bearing notes designed to circulate as money. The extent to which they circulated from hand to hand and whether they should be included in estimates of the stock of money, however, remain controversial topics. Estimates for the South in the Civil War are presented in Tables Eh111–127 and for the North in Table Cj26–41.

Despite all the problems noted in the preceding paragraphs, the monetary statistics from the antebellum and Civil War eras compare favorably in terms of breadth of coverage and accuracy with other sorts of quantitative data from this period. Modern monetary data, it is true, are available more frequently and are based on more comprehensive underlying sources. However, the simpler structure of the financial system during the antebellum and Civil War eras may make the interpretation of the monetary statistics, and the choice among candidate estimates of the money stock, easier than they are today. In any case, the antebellum and Civil War monetary statistics clearly provide a valuable tool for understanding the early history of the United States and a rich field in which to test the principles of monetary economics.

References

Fenstermaker, Joseph Van. 1965. *The Development of American Commercial Banking: 1782–1837.* Kent State University Press.

Friedman, Milton, and Anna Jacobson Schwartz. 1963. *A Monetary History of the United States, 1867–1960.* Princeton University Press.

Friedman, Milton, and Anna Jacobson Schwartz. 1970. *Monetary Statistics of the United States: Estimates, Sources, Methods.* Columbia University Press.

Macesich, George. 1960. "Sources of Monetary Disturbances in the United States, 1834–1845." *Journal of Economic History* 20 (3): 407–34.

Rockoff, Hugh. 2000. "Banking and Finance, 1789–1914." In Stanley L. Engerman and Robert E. Gallman, editors. *The Cambridge Economic History of the United States,* Volume 2, *The Long Nineteenth Century.* Cambridge University Press.

Temin, Peter. 1969. *The Jacksonian Economy.* Norton.

MONETARY POLICY

Michael D. Bordo and David C. Wheelock

"Monetary policy" is commonly interpreted as either the intent or outcome of actions taken by a government authority affecting either the stock of money or the level of interest rates. Under the Employment Act of 1946 and the Full Employment and Balanced Growth Act of 1978, the federal government accepted responsibility for pursuing macroeconomic policies that promote high employment and price level stability. Actions by the Federal Reserve System that affect money or interest rates comprise one form of policy focused on achieving those employment and price level goals.

Monetary policy in this sense is a comparatively recent phenomenon. Traditionally, governments defined their currencies in terms of gold or silver, either minting coin with intrinsic value or offering to convert paper currency or minor coin into bullion at a set price. Currency and deposits issued by commercial banks were similarly backed by the commodity. Changes in the commodity stock, over which governments typically had little control, were thus the principal source of changes in the nation's money stock. Historically, monetary policy consisted of changes in the price at which the government would convert its currency into a commodity, the occasional issuance of unconvertible fiat currency to finance wars, and the manipulation of a central bank discount rate to protect convertibility in a financial crisis. For most countries, however, such actions were rare and not made for the purposes of stabilizing national output or prices.

Government manipulation of money or interest rates to achieve general macroeconomic stability became widely accepted after the Great Depression of the 1930s. To gain such control, governments sought to lessen the constraint that commodity (gold) convertibility imposed on their ability to manipulate monetary conditions. Eventually, commodity backing was completely eliminated, and today no currency of a developed country is convertible into a commodity.

The evolution of monetary policy in the United States was similar to that of other countries. The major turning points in the history of metallic standards may be seen in Table Cj108–112. The Coinage Act of 1792 defined the dollar as the unit of account in terms of coins of a fixed weight in gold or silver. The official bimetallic ratio (silver to gold) was set at 15 : 1. The ratio was changed in 1834 to 16 : 1. That ratio prevailed until silver was officially demonetized in 1900 under the Gold Standard Act. The United States was on the gold standard de facto from 1834 to 1971, save for a period of suspension from 1862 to 1879 during and after the Civil War. The Civil War was partly financed by the issuance of inconvertible greenbacks. At war's end, the government deliberately sought to contract the money supply to restore the original parity of $20.67 per ounce. This official gold price prevailed from 1834 to 1933. After a transition of several months, the official price of gold was fixed at $35 per ounce in 1934. On August 15, 1971, President Richard Nixon closed the gold window, thus ending official convertibility of the dollar into gold. In 1973, the government's gold stock was revalued at $42.22 per ounce, where it has since remained.

The United States had no formal central bank until the establishment of the Federal Reserve System in 1914. Two federal banks, the First and Second Banks of the United States (1791–1811; 1816–1836), however, at times pursued the monetary policy objectives of stabilizing the exchange rate and acting as lender of last resort. Following the Second Bank's demise, the Independent U.S. Treasury (founded in 1847) occasionally engaged in monetary policy by switching deposits from the Treasury to commercial banks, usually to ease financial crises. In the late nineteenth and early twentieth centuries, the Treasury increased its monetary policy activities and in a rudimentary way performed many of the functions of a modern central bank.

Periodic financial crises and general dissatisfaction with the functioning of the payments system led to the establishment of the Federal Reserve System (the "Fed") in 1914. The Fed was created as a quasi-public institution consisting of twelve privately owned reserve banks with an overseeing government board. The reserve banks were designed to serve as bankers' banks, providing check clearing and other payments services, and holding commercial bank reserve accounts. By rediscounting commercial bank loans and issuing currency, the Fed also was intended to be a mechanism by which the nation's stocks of currency and bank reserves could expand and contract to meet changes in demand.

In providing reserves and currency, the Fed's founders intended that the system's operations be consistent with the Real Bills Doctrine and preservation of the gold standard. By basing the extension of Federal Reserve credit (currency and reserves) on the rediscount of short-term, commercial loans (that is, "real bills"), the Fed's founders sought to accommodate the credit and currency needs of a growing economy without supplying excessive funds that might cause financial speculation or inflation. A gold reserve requirement placed on the reserve banks served as a further check on the overextension of Federal Reserve credit. The banks were expected to defend their reserve positions, if they were threatened, by making discount rate adjustments.

The Federal Reserve Act also permitted the reserve banks to purchase Treasury securities, presumably as a source of revenue, and bankers' acceptances, so as to support the growth of an acceptance market. Although the Federal Reserve Act seemed to leave little scope for policy discretion, by the 1920s the Fed had begun to use open market operations in government securities to affect money market conditions with the aim of achieving macroeconomic policy objectives. Confidence in the Fed's expertise at monetary management was one of the factors that underlay the optimistic faith in the "New Era" of that decade.

During its first major test, however – the downward economic slide of 1929–1933 – the Fed proved unequal to the task. In August 1929, amidst signs that the economy was already slowing down, the Fed raised the discount rate (the rate charged for borrowing by member banks) to 6 percent (see Table Cj113–117). Intended to discourage stock market speculation, the action may have precipitated the Crash of October 1929. From that point the Fed quickly reversed course. But its major critics have charged the Fed with neglecting its obligation to serve as lender of last resort, doing little or nothing to prevent several waves of bank failures, while allowing the money supply to fall by one third (Friedman and Schwartz 1963). Subsequent writers have questioned the primacy of the Fed's role in the crisis, pointing out that the stock of high-powered money (currency plus bank reserves) actually rose between 1929 and 1933, while interest rates fell (see Tables Cj113–117 and Cj141), suggesting that deflationary pressures were emanating from elsewhere in the economy (Temin 1976). Nonetheless, interpretations of the Fed's thought and action during this episode continue to be debated (Wicker 1966; Epstein and Ferguson 1984; Wheelock 1991).

Legislation of the 1930s reorganized the Fed's Open Market Committee, giving greater authority to the Board of Governors. The Banking Act of 1935 extended the Fed's authority to change commercial bank reserve requirements. Concerned about expanding levels of excess reserves, the Fed raised reserve requirements in two steps, in 1936 and 1937 (see Table Cj131–134). The economy subsequently slipped into recession in 1937 and 1938, and although analysts are not agreed on the causal connection, the Fed was highly criticized for these actions and has largely avoided the use of reserve requirements as a policy instrument since then.

During World War II and in the postwar period to 1951, the Fed conducted its operations in coordination with the U.S. Treasury to maintain ceiling yields on government securities. In March 1951, the Fed and the Treasury agreed to an accord, which permitted the Fed to pursue other objectives, such as the control of inflation. The Fed then returned to a strategy of targeting net borrowed or "free" reserves (excess less borrowed reserves) with the aim of influencing market interest rates and, ultimately, achieving the system's goals for inflation, employment, and the international balance of payments. Over time, this strategy focused increasingly on influencing the federal funds rate – the interest rate at which commercial banks borrow reserves from one another (series Cj117). Since the early 1970s, the Fed has specified target rates or ranges for the federal funds rate and carried out its open market operations to achieve those targets.

The Fed's free reserves and money market operating strategies have been criticized by proponents of monetary aggregate targeting. These critics point out that the Fed's focus on interest rates led to substantial contraction of the money stock during the Great Depression and to rapid growth of the money stock and inflation from the mid-1960s to 1980. Proponents of monetary aggregate targeting argue that while money market interest rates and free reserves may reflect the intent of policymakers, the growth of monetary aggregates better reflects the true stance of monetary policy. The

monetary base, which consists of bank reserves and currency held by the public, is one such aggregate. Because the reserve requirements that depository institutions are required to meet have varied over time, two measures of the monetary base adjusted for such charges have been created – one by the Board of Governors of the Federal Reserve System and one by the Federal Reserve Bank of St. Louis (see Table Cj135–140).

The Fed has never targeted the monetary base, though at times the Fed has sought to influence the growth of monetary aggregates. In particular, from 1979 to 1982, the Fed acted to reduce inflation by enhancing its control over money supply growth, which entailed a substantial expansion of its federal funds rate target range. Since 1982, the Fed has again rejected monetary aggregate targeting in favor of tight control of the federal funds rate. The evolution of monetary policy since the 1930s is traced in Calomiris and Wheelock (1998).

References

Calomiris, Charles, and David Wheelock. 1998. "The Great Depression as a Watershed for American Monetary Policy?" In Michael D. Bordo, Claudia Goldin, and Eugene N. White, editors. *The Defining Moment: The Great Depression and the American Economy in the Twentieth Century.* University of Chicago Press.

Epstein, Gerald, and Thomas Ferguson. 1984. "Monetary Policy, Loan Liquidation, and Industrial Conflict: The Federal Reserve and the Open Market Operations of 1932." *Journal of Economic History* 44 (December): 957–83.

Friedman, Milton, and Anna Jacobson Schwartz. 1963. *A Monetary History of the United States, 1867–1960.* Princeton University Press.

Temin, Peter. 1976. *Did Monetary Forces Cause the Great Depression?* Norton.

Wheelock, David. 1991. *The Strategy and Consistency of Federal Reserve Monetary Policy, 1924–1933.* Cambridge University Press.

Wicker, Elmus. 1966. *Federal Reserve Monetary Policy 1917–1933.* Random House.

FINANCIAL INSTITUTIONS AND THEIR REGULATION

Howard Bodenhorn and Eugene N. White

Encouraged by Alexander Hamilton, in 1781 Robert Morris persuaded the Continental Congress to charter the Bank of North America, the first commercial bank in the New World. The bank made loans to the cash-strapped Revolutionary government as well as to private citizens, mostly Philadelphia merchants. In addition to supplying a medium of exchange and intermediary services, early American financial institutions were expected to support private enterprise and public infrastructure projects, including bridges, roads, and canals. In many respects, contemporaries viewed banks as one of many government-sponsored infrastructure investments.

Early National and Antebellum Banking

By 1800, each major U.S. port city had at least one commercial bank serving the local business community. As Americans grew more familiar and comfortable with the corporate form, banking spread to smaller communities and expanded its clientele. Thus, in 1818, there were 338 banks that specialized in short-term credit to merchants, artisans, and farmers (Table Cj142–148). In addition to commercial banks, mutual savings banks were organized, initially as charitable organizations (modeled after British "friendly" societies) to promote thrift among the working poor. The first mutual savings banks were founded in Boston and Philadelphia in 1816, and they soon spread throughout the Northeast. In the West and the South, building and loan societies later fulfilled the same role.

Gradually, explicit public interest justifications for banks were no longer necessary and banks were seen as profit-making enterprises that served the public interest only indirectly. Yet, the growth of banks was not unrestricted. Politicians often limited the number of charters, concerned about excessive expansion and competition, and the need to protect the monopolies of political allies. Worries about overexpansion seemed justified when America first experienced widespread bank failures during the depression of the early 1820s. Not until 1827 did the United States have as many banks as it had in 1818.

Federal involvement in banking and bank regulation began with the charter of the First Bank of the United States in 1791 (Table Cj177–188). Congress granted it a twenty-year charter in 1791, with provisions that it be both a commercial bank and the government's fiscal agent. Proposed by Alexander Hamilton and modeled after the Bank of England, the bank was based in Philadelphia with branches in eight other cities. It was a well-managed institution but was widely criticized for its Federalist affiliations, its restraining influence on state bank operations, and ownership of its stock by English and Dutch investors. For these and other reasons, Jeffersonian Democrats opposed the bank. When the bank's charter came up for renewal in 1811, they refused to support it even though the Treasury Secretary, Albert Gallatin, argued that its closure represented a greater danger than its continuance. The rechartering bill failed by a single vote.

Difficulties in financing the War of 1812 and in regulating state banks discredited the antibank position, and in 1816 the Second Bank of the United States was granted a twenty-year charter (Tables Cj189–202). Modeled after its predecessor, the Second Bank acted as the federal government's fiscal agent, engaged in commercial bank lending, and practiced some very limited central bank functions. The Second Bank's first two administrations provided ineffectual leadership. Nicholas Biddle assumed leadership of the bank in 1823 and reconstructed a more centralized national institution out of one whose twenty-five branches had previously acted semiautonomously.

Like the First Bank of the United States, the Second Bank had powerful enemies. By 1832 there were 464 state banks that chafed at the Second Bank's ability to control their note issues, which limited their lending. In 1832, Henry Clay, an ardent bank supporter, opposed Andrew Jackson, a bank detractor, in the presidential election. The Second Bank's recharter, due in 1836, became a political flashpoint. Congress approved the recharter, but Jackson vetoed it and interpreted his reelection as broad support for his antibank stance. He removed federal deposits from the bank, and its charter expired in 1836.

The Second Bank's closing left a void in U.S. financial markets. Many states responded by chartering new banks. Eighteen others responded by enacting so-called free banking acts. Such acts allowed prospective bankers to establish banks without the formality of legislative charters. After meeting a number of regulatory demands – notably minimum capital restrictions and depositing government bonds with a regulatory agency's guaranty

fund – these banking associations were granted most corporate powers. Between 1836 and 1860, the number of state banks grew from 713 to 1,562, and total industry assets increased from about $622 million to nearly $1 billion (Table Cj149–157).[1]

Banking after the Civil War

The free banking era effectively came to an end with the passage of the National Banking Acts of 1863 and 1864. Proposed by Salmon Chase, the acts invited state banks to take out federal charters. Designed to assist war finance and establish a more uniform currency, the system was modeled after New York's 1838 Free Banking Act in that it required national banks to buy federal bonds as a guarantee for note issues. Banks turned these bonds over to the U.S. Treasury, which issued bank notes equal to 90 percent of the value of the deposited bonds, thus protecting noteholders from losses.

The banking acts vested oversight of national banks in the Office of the Comptroller of the Currency (OCC), a bureau of the U.S. Department of the Treasury. The subsequent National Bank Act authorized the Comptroller of the Currency to employ a staff of bank examiners to oversee bank activities, including their lending and investments. In addition to examinations, the OCC approved applications for new national bank charters or changes to the capital or branches of existing banks. As the regulator of national banks, the OCC remains one of the most important institutions of bank regulation.

In the post–Civil War era, most state banks gave up their state charters for national ones that imposed higher operating costs. National banks were forced to buy U.S. government bonds, which sold above par and increased the costs of note issue, and were subject to aggregate note issue limits. They also faced minimum capital and reserve requirements and were denied the right to make real estate loans. Hindered by these regulations, the national banking system grew slowly until Congress imposed a 10 percent tax on state bank notes in 1865. Although this action initially brought a drastic reduction in the number of state-chartered banks, the post-1870 growth of deposit banking spurred the recovery of the state banking systems. Regulated by state banking authorities and the OCC, the United States developed a dual banking system. The banking system was further shaped by the Comptroller's 1866 ruling that banned branch banking for national banks, a regulation adopted by many states. Consequently, the rapid growth in the demand for banking services resulted in a vast increase in the number of banks rather than in the number of branches. Although the more lightly regulated state banks outnumbered them by the end of the nineteenth century, the national banks were generally the larger and more prominent institutions (Tables Cj203–250).

Trust companies first developed before the Civil War, but at the end of the nineteenth century they emerged as competitors for commercial banks. Combining deposit taking and lending with their trust business, they became the fastest growing intermediaries at the turn of the century. Similarly, insurance companies were transformed into important intermediaries late in the century. Initially, the industry was dominated by marine and fire insurance companies, but the innovating life insurance companies – first stock and later mutual firms – became major forces in the financial markets by

---

[1] The evolution of banks and financial markets in this era is surveyed in Bodenhorn (2000).

investing the steady inflow of funds provided by premiums (Tables Cj713–796).

The regulations derived from the National Bank Act had important consequences for the stability of the banking system. Economic fluctuations were amplified because of an "inelastic currency," the inability to increase national bank note issues in a timely manner in response to transitory or seasonal increases in the demand for currency. Bank reserves were subject to rapid withdrawals from financial centers in times of crisis, partly because of the "pyramiding" of reserves, which encouraged country banks to place their reserves in designated reserve cities and central reserve cities. Furthermore, the prohibition on branch banking created thousands of small, undiversified country banks, less able to withstand economic shocks. Thus, autumn pressure in the money markets had a tendency to produce financial panics, bank runs, and the suspension of specie payments.

The Reforms of the Federal Reserve Act and the New Deal

Following the panic of 1907, Congress commissioned the National Monetary Commission to study contemporary and historical banking systems, providing the intellectual background and information needed for extensive banking reforms. The vehicle for reform was the Federal Reserve Act of 1913. Designed to prevent crises, the Act left the structure of the banking system unchanged but created a central bank to correct its perceived weaknesses. Supervised by the Federal Reserve Board, the Federal Reserve System divided the United States into twelve districts, each with a reserve bank. Reserve banks were organized as federally chartered corporations owned by member banks in their districts. They were to hold the legal reserves of member banks, provide check clearing and settlement services, and act as fiscal agents and depositories for the U.S. Treasury and other federal government agencies. Even though the Federal Reserve Act conferred central banking powers on the Federal Reserve to maintain the gold standard and provide liquidity to the banking system in times of crisis, it also made the Fed the regulator of member banks. Members include all national banks and those eligible state banks seeking membership. As membership for state banks was voluntary, the dual banking system was left intact and a tripartite division emerged, comprising national banks, state member banks, and nonmember banks (Table Cj289–297).

Unlike banking, the insurance industry had always been regulated primarily by the states. The increasingly close ties among investment banks, commercial banks, and insurance companies prompted New York State's 1905 Armstrong investigation. The findings of this investigation produced punitive laws that broke interlocking relationships and forced insurance companies to sell their stocks and eliminate semitontine policies. Most other states copied New York's law, creating a more narrowly defined insurance industry that invested almost exclusively in bonds, real estate mortgages, and policy loans. The progressives who attacked the practices of the insurance companies also sought to offer small savers a safe repository for their funds, and they persuaded Congress to create the Postal Savings System in 1911. Administered by the Post Office, it enjoyed considerable growth during the Great Depression and World War II but declined afterward, when banks and savings associations sought smaller accounts and paid higher rates. The system was closed in 1967 (Table Cj432–436).

In the stable economic environment of the 1920s, the financial system boomed with the economy. However, constrained by limits on branching and lending, commercial banks and mutual savings banks saw their share of financial intermediation shrink, as the securities industry, insurance companies, and savings and loans became more important. The larger banks adapted to the new environment and offered new financial services, but many smaller banks failed in stagnating rural areas. The Great Depression of 1929–1933 brought the financial system to the brink of total collapse. The decline in national income and rise in unemployment led the public to withdraw funds from financial intermediaries, who in turn reduced lending. Already beset by defaults on loans and securities, insolvency threatened many institutions. Three banking crises in 1930, 1931, and 1933 winnowed the banking system before President Roosevelt declared a bank holiday on March 6, 1933.

Deteriorating economic conditions and the rush for liquidity forced huge contractions of the savings and loan and insurance industries. States declared holidays for insurance companies to protect them from withdrawals of funds by policyholders, and Congress attempted to bolster the thrift industry by passing the Federal Home Loan Bank Act of 1932. Modeled on the Federal Reserve System, the law provided for twelve regional home loan banks, owned by member thrifts, operating under the supervision of the Federal Home Loan Bank Board (FHLBB). These home loan banks borrowed at favorable rates and re-lent to member thrifts (Tables Cj448–463).

Dramatic Congressional hearings, the Democrats' electoral landslide, and intense political lobbying produced the New Deal legislation that reshaped the banking industry. The Banking Act of 1933, often known as the Glass-Steagall Act, and the Banking Act of 1935 determined the basic structure of commercial banking for the next half century. The Federal Deposit Insurance Corporation (FDIC) was created by the first Act (Tables Cj486–550). All Federal Reserve member banks were required to join, but fearful of exposure to banking runs, most nonmember banks quickly signed up. Insured banks paid a premium to create a mutual guarantee fund to compensate depositors of failed banks.[2]

The Glass-Steagall Act also required an almost complete divorce of commercial and investment banking, narrowly defining each industry. The Banking Acts of 1933 and 1935 placed new legal restrictions on competition. Interest rate ceilings for deposits were imposed, and charters became increasingly difficult to obtain. National banks were limited to the branching rights enjoyed by the state-chartered banks where they were domiciled, whereas bank holding companies were brought under the regulation and supervision of the Federal Reserve.

In this wave of legislation, dual regulatory systems were created for the thrift industry and credit unions. States had been solely responsible for chartering savings and loan associations. The Home Owners Loan Act of 1933 gave the FHLBB new authority to charter federal mutual savings and loan associations. Similarly, Congress made federal charters available in the Federal Credit Union Act of 1934, competing with the issuance of credit union charters by the states. Concerned that the FDIC would give commercial banks an advantage over the savings and loan associations, Congress

---

[2] For the historical background to federal deposit insurance, see Calomiris and White (1994).

established the Federal Savings and Loan Insurance Corporation (FSLIC) in 1934 to provide insurance for the thrift industry.

The New Deal in banking appeared to be a great success. Bank failures almost disappeared. Even though the public was less inclined to run on the banks, thrifts, and insurance companies, there was little need for concern as the surviving institutions had become extraordinarily liquid and conservative in the wake of the collapse of the early 1930s. The long period of prosperity from the end of World War II to the early 1970s was marked by growing incomes and price stability. Although the New Deal legislation may have contributed to stability in the financial sector, the tight regulations left commercial banks, mutual savings banks, and life insurance companies with a shrinking share of intermediation. The more lightly and favorably regulated savings and loan associations, finance companies, pension funds, and mutual funds benefited and captured a greater share of the flow of funds. Chafing under New Deal regulations, commercial banks tried to grow in size by mergers, acquisitions, and bank holding companies when state laws limiting branching could not be changed. However, the courts limited mergers, and Congress ensured that one-bank and multibank holding companies remained under the supervision of the Federal Reserve in the Bank Holding Company Acts of 1956 and 1970.

Crisis, Competition, and the Emergence of Financial Services Conglomerates

Higher inflation, hard recessions, and crises between 1970 and 1990 gradually undermined the regulation governing the financial sector. Burdened by New Deal restrictions, commercial banks, mutual savings banks, and life insurance companies lost further ground not only to more lightly regulated intermediaries but also to financial markets. Commercial bank failures began to reappear in the 1970s and then burgeoned in the 1980s, as interest rates soared and real estate and oil booms and busts ravaged the industry. The wave of bank failures helped to ease opposition to mergers and branching, while automated teller machines (ATMs) crept around the restrictions on branching (Table Cj354–361). Merger policy relaxed, holding companies were allowed to buy out-of-state banks, and the Riegle-Neal Interstate Banking and Branching Efficient Act of 1994 cleared the final obstacles to nationwide branch banking.

Like banks, insurance companies faced a weak demand for their traditional products. Inflation and high interest rates of the early 1980s increased policy surrenders and policy loans, reducing companies' liquidity and producing a number of failures. To survive, insurance companies moved aggressively into new activities, including the pension and annuity business. Credit crunches in the 1960s led Congress to create the National Credit Union Administration in 1970 to provide short-term lending for troubled credit unions and the National Credit Union Share Insurance Fund (NCUSIF) to set up an insurance fund for them.

Although the savings and loan industry first enjoyed a rapid expansion, its profits and net worth disappeared when inflation rose unexpectedly. Congress tried to revive the industry with the Depository Institutions Deregulation and Monetary Control Act of 1980 and the Garn–St. Germain Act of 1982, which lifted interest rate ceilings and allowed thrifts to invest in riskier loans. These efforts did not make savings and loans solvent; instead, their losses made the FSLIC insolvent. The FSLIC and the FHLBB were closed, and

insurance of the remaining thrifts was transferred to the FDIC's new Savings Association Insurance Fund, while the Office of Thrift Supervision became their regulator. Insolvent thrifts were liquidated by the Resolution Trust Corporation.

Since the early nineteenth century, the segmentation of the financial industry into distinct types of intermediaries had been a steady feature of the American system. This narrow definition of intermediaries, bolstered by the New Deal banking laws, gradually began to erode in the 1980s. Many of the remaining barriers among commercial banks, securities firms, and insurance companies were dissolved by the Gramm-Leach-Bliley Act of 1999. The formation of financial conglomerates with highly diverse financial activities may be the hallmark and challenge of the twenty-first century.

References

Bodenhorn, Howard. 2000. *A History of Banking in Antebellum America.* Cambridge University Press.

Calomiris, Charles, and Eugene N. White. 1994. "The Origins of Federal Deposit Insurance." In Claudia Goldin and Gary Libecap, editors. *The Regulated Economy.* University of Chicago Press.

SECURITIES MARKETS

Peter L. Rousseau

Despite their central role in today's economy, the development of securities markets in the early United States has received relatively little attention from researchers, perhaps because the historical record of the banking sector, owing to reporting requirements, is far more accessible and complete. Nevertheless, securities markets, starting with informal groups of brokers in Boston, New York, Philadelphia, and Baltimore that traded securities in coffee houses and in the street shortly after the framing of the federal Constitution, have been a fundamental part of the U.S. financial landscape. By early 1792, trading in New York had become adequately voluminous and competition for brokering services so intense that a group of street brokers met beneath a buttonwood tree on Wall Street on May 17 to form an alliance for setting commissions and providing preferential treatment to trades among themselves as opposed to trades with nonmembers. And so with the "Buttonwood Agreement," the precursor of the New York Stock Exchange (NYSE) was born. By 1830, all of the nation's major cities had developed a network for the trading of debt and equity securities. As communications technologies improved in the late nineteenth century, however, trading became increasingly concentrated in New York, and that city's dominant position in the securities industry persists to this day. The data presented in this chapter offer an overview of the securities markets across the nineteenth and twentieth centuries and reflect the considerable progress that has been made to date in building the historical record of securities market activity from primary sources such as contemporary newspapers.

Common stock represents the residual claim to a firm's assets after all other obligations, including those to employees, suppliers, the government, and creditors, have been paid. This makes common stock the most risky of corporate securities; however, it has provided by far the largest cumulative return over the long term. As the value of a firm's common stock, which includes the potential of the firm's current or future assets to generate future residual claims, depends on investor perceptions of fundamental characteristics of the firm and the overall economic conditions, common stocks tend to fluctuate more widely in price than other direct corporate claims. Preferred stocks operate much like debt in that they promise periodic fixed payments to shareholders. They differ importantly from debt, however, in that failure to keep these promises does not offer grounds for legal action by investors against the firm. Both types of equities are represented in the tables in this chapter.

The tables include a set of stock market price indexes and dividend yield records that track equity performance on an annual basis in New York from 1802 (series Cj797), with separate categories for industrial, railroad, and utilities stocks after 1870 (series Cj800–803). Because Boston was the premier market for trading industrial securities from early in the nineteenth century until New York surpassed it around 1900, the chapter also presents prices and dividend yields for those industrial and bank stocks traded in Boston both at auction and over the formal stock exchange from 1835 to 1897 (series Cj809–810). A wide range of indexes of market performance have become available in recent years, and the most widely used are represented here from their inception dates, including the Dow Jones Industrial Average, the Standard and Poor's 500 Index, the NYSE Composite, the NASDAQ Composite, and the Wilshire 5000 (series Cj804–807). The yields of high-grade preferred stocks also appear in series Cj815–816.

Although stocks often trade frequently in the secondary market after their issue, it is in the primary market, or the market for new securities, that corporations raise external funds for investments and new ventures. In this respect, the aggregate value of new issues reflects the business climate at a point in time because firms are more likely to raise funds when they can do so at low cost, or when interest rates are low. Although bonds are the securities whose prices are most directly linked to interest rates, these rates also figure prominently in determining the returns that investors will require to hold common stocks in a given risk class, and thus affect offering prices. The role of primary markets in the distribution of both initial public offerings (IPOs) and the new issues of firms that have sold stock to the public before ("seasoned" offerings) is one of mobilizing and directing an economy's resources to projects that offer the highest returns. The size of this market in each year since 1933 is included here to document the ebbs and flows of new corporate capital, along with that of new issues of state and local government securities (Table Cj817–830).

For financial markets to function well, investors must be able to sell their assets quickly at prices that reflect their intrinsic or "true" value. Though a high volume of transactions may simply reflect the disruptive phenomenon of "churning," it is also closely related to market liquidity. Where there is a liquid financial market, there will be firms hoping to raise funds and list there because listing provides a mechanism through which the venture capitalist can "cash in" on successful projects. Because firms hope to maximize their stock price and because a share in a liquid market will trade at a higher price than an identical share in an illiquid market, the existence of a liquid stock exchange will tend to concentrate transactions within an institutional structure where informational asymmetries are smallest, promoting efficiency in the asset allocation process.

A number of series for transactions quantities are reported in this chapter as a means of observing growth in the securities markets generally. They include the annual volume and value of shares traded on the NYSE from 1879, and those of bonds from 1910

(Table Cj857–858). Also included are the annual values of trades on all registered stock exchanges, and on the New York Curb/American Stock Exchange (AMEX) specifically from 1935 (series Cj853–854). Overall, activity on the AMEX and the regional stock exchanges has been small compared to that on the NYSE, but the emergence of the NASDAQ system (operated by the National Association of Securities Dealers, or NASD) has contributed very significantly to trading volume over the past decade, often exceeding that on the NYSE in terms of the number of shares changing hands. The chapter thus includes annual NASDAQ trades since its start in 1971 (series Cj855–856).

As participation in securities markets by institutions and individuals becomes more widespread, the role of mutual funds in channeling funds to the capital markets has become increasingly important. Mutual funds are popular because they save many investors, for a fee, the time and expense of maintaining portfolios with small holdings of any individual security. Such portfolios would be costly to adjust, yet mutual funds, by spreading management and maintenance costs across a number of investor accounts, can offer a diversified portfolio to investors at low cost. The table that presents the number, value, and net redemptions of mutual fund shares since the passage of the Investment Company Act in 1940 reflects the recent and rapid rise in ownership of these shares (Table Cj859–862).

To buy stocks, investors often tender cash to their brokers, yet brokers will also lend to their customers to finance security purchases. If many such loans are made during a bull market that later experiences an unanticipated correction, the brokerage industry and the economy in general could be adversely affected by defaults. To avoid the excessive use of credit in the purchase of stocks, the Federal Reserve limits the degree to which this can be done by imposing a "margin" requirement. As can be seen in Table Cj863–865, the margin requirement changed fairly frequently from 1934 on, but it has remained at 50 percent since January 1974.

DEBT AND THE FLOW OF FUNDS

John A. James and Richard Sylla

Production and consumption in a modern economy, as well as savings and investment, are financed by a wide variety of fund flows among economic sectors. These flows result at any given point in time in a complex structure of assets, liabilities or debts, and net worth.

For the U.S. economy, the most comprehensive source for data on financial flows and outstanding stocks of debt, as well as total financial assets (including equities in corporate and noncorporate business) and liabilities, are the flow-of-funds accounts maintained by the Board of Governors of the Federal Reserve System. These data begin with the year 1945 and extend to the present. They are updated quarterly and annually, and they can be accessed at the Federal Reserve Internet site. The flow-of-funds accounts are voluminous and can serve a multitude of purposes. To facilitate their use, the Federal Reserve publishes a *Guide to the Flow of Funds Accounts*. This chapter presents a sampling of the flow-of-funds data and the stocks of assets and liabilities resulting from the flows. These data illustrate the nature of the Federal Reserve accounts and include additional tables on net debt outstanding and savings flows for years before 1945, as well as a more detailed rendering than appears in the flow-of-funds accounts of mortgage debt outstanding, by type of property and type of holder, since 1970.

The flow-of-funds accounts measure the acquisition of physical and financial assets throughout the U.S. economy and the sources of funds used to acquire the assets. In doing this, the accounts record the net volume of transactions in financial instruments. They provide a means of analyzing, for example, the development of financial instruments and the behavior of sectors over time, and they record the role of financial intermediaries, such as banks, mutual funds, and pension funds, in transferring funds from sectors that have positive savings to those that borrow funds.

In showing the relationship among various financial activities and their relation with nonfinancial activities that generate income and production, the flow-of-funds accounts provide a broad measure of investment activities. In theory, the accounts encompass all net changes in financial claims or liabilities resulting from (1) current transactions in the economy, (2) the allocation of saving between investment in physical capital and investment in financial capital, and (3) decisions to change the composition of financial assets and liabilities. The flow-of-funds accounts are consistent with, but broader than, the national income and product accounts, which focus on activity related to current production and income. Unlike the national income and product accounts, the flow-of-funds accounts include financial flows among various sectors of the economy that arise from transfers of existing physical assets, as well as shifts in the composition of financial portfolios that may be unrelated to, or only indirectly related to, current production.

The flow-of-funds accounts are a component of a system of accounts that describes the U.S. economy. Other components of the system are the national income and product accounts and the balance-of-payments accounts. The latter two components measure production and income activity and international capital flows during a particular time period. The flow-of-funds accounts and related national balance sheets detail how current investment in tangible and financial assets contributes to a buildup of the stock of assets in each sector of the economy and to the creation of national wealth. One can view the flow-of-funds accounts as combining data on the flows of savings and investment in the national income and product accounts with further details on the borrowing and lending of specific economic sectors.

The flow-of-funds accounts embody the principle that all movements of funds in the economy must be accounted for because total sources of funds equal total uses of funds. Savings equals investment in the economy, and all funds supplied by economic sectors become uses of funds by other sectors.

Sources of funds for a sector are its savings from current income and the amount it raises from sources outside the sector. Saving is equal to receipts of current income less outlays for consumption, operating expenses, interest, and other current expenses. The value of capital consumption allowances – that is, depreciation on tangible assets – is added to net saving to obtain gross saving. Funds raised from outside sources constitute the sectors' net increase in liabilities or debts to other sectors.

Uses of funds for a sector are its investment in physical assets and net increases in financial assets, such as deposits, loans made, and securities purchased.

The requirement that sources of funds must equal uses of funds applies not only to sectors but also to individual types of transactions. That is, total funds borrowed by means of each type of financial instrument must equal total funds lent through that instrument. For the economy as a whole, funds borrowed by all sectors must equal funds lent by all sectors, and funds borrowed through all types of financial instruments must equal funds lent through all types of instruments.

The flow-of-funds accounts are published in both flow and levels versions. Most flow tables have a corresponding levels table. A flow variable is one that shows an amount of change over a period of time. Examples of flows are Tables Ce1–68, covering 1897–1949 and showing national savings by major saver groups as well as personal savings and nonagricultural individuals' saving by major components or instruments. Here one can see, for example, how much of personal savings was channeled into the stock market in the 1920s. Other examples of flow variables are personal income, the net acquisition of government securities, and the amount of borrowing from banks, all during a particular period of time such as a year.

A level, also referred to as a stock, a position, or an outstanding, shows a value at a particular point in time. An example is the balance in an individual's checking account at the end of a month or a year. Other examples are holdings of equities by households and nonprofit organizations, and the credit market debt outstanding of (owed by) households at the end of a particular year.

In the flow-of-funds accounts, many flow series are determined by calculating changes in levels between two periods. In some cases, however, the change in a level does not equal the flow. One reason is that some series are shown at market rather than book value (that is, historical cost). For series shown at book value, the flow ordinarily equals the change in the level. However, for series shown at market value, the change in the level between two periods is not equal to the flow. Corporate equities held as assets, for example, are valued in the accounts at market values. Hence, the level for corporate equities shown in the tables for any period differs from that of the previous period by the flow, or net issuance, plus the change in market value (that is, the capital gain or loss).

The flow-of-funds tables presented here for the period beginning 1945 are in levels (Tables Cj1021–1178). They show the outstanding levels of assets and liabilities by sector or by instrument at the end of each year. In most cases, the flow-of-funds tables published by the Federal Reserve (and also available at its Internet site) would have a corresponding flows table.

INTEREST RATES AND YIELDS

John A. James and Richard Sylla

Interest rates and yields of securities indicate the cost of credit to borrowers and the income received by those who lend and invest. Borrowers traditionally were business concerns and governments, but in the modern economy they also include consumers and homeowners. Lenders include individuals, banks, trusts, endowments, and a variety of other financial institutions, both private and public. This chapter presents a variety of money market rates of interest, bond yield data, rates paid to depositors and charged to consumers by financial institutions, and rates of interest paid by homeowners on mortgage loans.

Borrowers, depending on their needs and the availability to them of various forms of credit, have a choice of borrowing for either short or long periods of time, and in either open markets (for example, the money market or the bond market) or institution-based markets (for example, banks). In open markets, large numbers of borrowers and lenders meet and trade at market rates determined by the demand for and supply of available funds. In institution-based markets, interest rates on loans are determined more by negotiations between the institution and individual borrowers with characteristics that vary widely from one borrower to another.

The open markets, with rates determined by supply and demand, and the institution-based markets, with rates determined by characteristics of individual borrowers are, of course, related and interact with one another. In the early nineteenth century, only governments and large, well-established corporations had access to either open market credit or bank loans, while small businesses and individuals were restricted to borrowing from local banks and other lenders who knew them. In the latter case, negotiated-rate markets, banks collected loanable funds from local depositors and then lent out funds to local borrowers. The interest rate on a loan was negotiated individually with each customer. That rate could differ greatly from borrower to borrower, and even the average of such rates could differ substantially from one geographical area to another, as Table Cj1198–1222 on bank rates on short-term business loans indicates. The average loan rate in local markets could also differ substantially from open market rates in the national money market.

In recent decades, however, banks no longer lend out merely what local depositors bring in to them. If a bank has a loan it wants to make but cannot fund from its deposit base, it can borrow from another bank or itself issue a money market instrument such as a certificate of deposit (CD) or commercial paper to fund its desired lending. Such links between open markets and negotiated loan markets have tended to narrow the spreads of interest rates across geographical regions and over time (see Table Cj1198–1222). The narrowing of spreads indicates a more efficient market, one that allocates funds over the whole economy based on return and risk characteristics. Another way of saying this is that markets tend increasingly to be integrated rather than segmented, so that interest rates and yields are determined more by the overall supply of and demand for funds in the economy, rather than widely varying supplies and demands in separate markets that have few links with one another.

Another aspect of financial market integration is the increasing variety of choices available to participants. In earlier times, a nonfinancial corporation would deposit its surplus funds in a bank or banks. When it needed to borrow, it would borrow from the same bank or banks. Or, if the corporation were sufficiently large and well known, it might be able to borrow by issuing a money market instrument. In more recent times, nonfinancial corporations have not had to rely on banks as the main outlets for temporary surpluses of funds. Instead of lodging such funds with banks as deposits, the corporations can purchase money market instruments

such as commercial paper. The development of the open money markets has thus tended to erode the share of banks in the overall financial system. Again, the widening variety of options both for placing funds and for borrowing has tended to make allocation across the financial system more efficient.

The tables in this chapter illustrate many of the general points made in the preceding paragraphs. The interest rate data on money market instruments such as stock exchange call loans and commercial paper extend well back into the nineteenth century (Table Cj1223–1237). The twentieth century expanded the scope of the money market with the innovation of open markets for newer instruments such as Treasury bills, finance company paper, and CDs (Tables Cj1179–1191, Cj1223–1237, and Cj1250–1256). The advent of the Federal Reserve System early in the century was based in part on the desire of market participants and policymakers to widen the scope and utility of open money markets. The Federal Reserve itself is a constant participant in the money market, where it takes actions designed to implement monetary policies. To do so, it can vary the discount rate at which it lends to member banks and the so-called federal funds rate at which banks with excess reserves trade them with banks that have deficient reserves for very short terms, often overnight. An indication of how much the money market grew over the twentieth century is provided by data on the outstanding volumes of commercial and finance paper and bankers' acceptances (Table Cj1179–1191).

Several tables here present data on long-term bond yields over two centuries. The longest series is for U.S. government bonds (series Cj1192). This market began with Treasury Secretary Alexander Hamilton's restructuring of Revolutionary War debts in 1790. Other series show yields of bonds issued by state and local governments (municipals), railroads, and other corporations, as well as – for the twentieth century – what financial economists call the "term structure" of yields or the yields to maturity at a given point in time of similar bonds with varying terms to maturity (Tables Cj1192–1197 and Cj1238–1242). A normal yield curve is often said to be one that shows higher yields the longer the term to maturity of a bond, presumably because the bond investor has to wait longer for the return of principal. However, yield curves sometimes invert, showing higher yields for shorter maturities than longer ones.

The tables also show what may be called consumer interest rates, including the rates consumers earned when they deposited their funds in financial institutions and the rates they paid when borrowing from banks for auto, personal, and credit card loans. Finally, the tables present interest rates on home mortgage loans in recent decades. Before the 1930s, there was no nationwide market for home mortgage credit. However, that changed in the later decades of the twentieth century with the advent of federal programs to make mortgage credit more widely available and of mortgage securitization that packaged mortgages and used the packages to back mortgage securities. This once again represented the inroads the open markets made on activity once confined to the negotiated, institution-based markets.

MONETARY AGGREGATES

Richard G. Anderson and Hugh Rockoff

TABLE Cj1–6   U.S. monetary gold stock: 1879–1971[1]

Contributed by Michael D. Bordo

Year	Monetary gold stock, end of year Cj1 [2] Million dollars	Increase in monetary gold stock Cj2 Million dollars	Gold production Cj3 Million dollars	Excess of gold imports over exports Cj4 Million dollars	Increase in gold under earmark Cj5 Million dollars	Gold under earmark, end of year Cj6 Million dollars
1879	336.5	102.9 [5]	38.9	74.7	—	—
1880	436.1	99.2	30.4	70.6	—	—
1881	521.9	84.7	34.7	57.8	—	—
1882	524.6	2.1	32.5	−25.3	—	—
1883	566.2	41.3	30.0	16.0	—	—
1884	576.1	10.3	30.8	−13.0	—	—
1885	613.1	37.2	31.8	12.2	—	—
1886	640.4	26.9	34.9	(Z)	—	—
1887	704.6	64.1	33.1	35.7	—	—
1888	704.6	— [6]	33.2	−23.6	—	—
1889	689.6	−16.5	33.0	−38.9	—	—
1890	704.0	16.5	33.0	−3.8	—	—
1891	686.9	−16.5	33.2	−34.1	—	—
1892	651.3	−35.1	33.0	−59.1	—	—
1893	666.8	16.5	35.9	−7.0	—	—
1894	625.1	−41.3	39.5	−80.6	—	—
1895	598.0	−26.9	46.6	−70.6	—	—
1896	692.9	95.1	53.1	46.5	—	—
1897	744.9	51.7	57.4	−0.3	—	—
1898	949.6	204.6	64.4	142.0	—	—
1899	1,015.9	66.1	71.0	6.0	—	—
1900	1,108.5	93.0	79.2	12.6	—	—
1901	1,176.1	68.2	78.7	−3.0	—	—
1902	1,246.8	70.3	80.0	8.2	—	—
1903	1,314.6	68.2	73.6	20.9	—	—
1904	1,346.0	31.0	80.4	−36.4	—	—
1905	1,420.0	74.4	88.2	3.5	—	—
1906	1,587.0	167.4	94.4	108.9	—	—
1907	1,604.6	16.5	90.4	88.2	—	—
1908	1,653.8	49.6	94.3	−30.9	—	—
1909	1,638.1	−16.5	99.4	−88.8	—	—
1910	1,708.8	70.3	96.1	0.4	—	—
1911	1,797.0	88.9	96.7	20.3	—	—
1912	1,878.5	80.6	93.0	19.1	—	—
1913	1,917.6	39.3	88.2	−28.1	—	—
1914	1,526.0 [3]	−100.2	93.4	−165.2	—	—
1915	2,025.0	499.1	99.7	420.5	—	—
1916	2,556.0	530.7	91.1	530.2	6.1	6.1
1917	2,868.0	312.2	82.3	180.6	−51.7 [9]	6.9
1918	2,873.0	4.9	67.3	21.0	46.7 [9]	6.9
1919	2,707.0	−165.8	59.5	−291.7	−127.4 [9]	5.0
1920	2,639.0	−68.4	49.9	95.0	145.0 [9]	22.0
1921	3,373.0	734.6	48.8	667.4	−18.7 [9]	—
1922	3,642.0	268.5	47.3	238.3	3.7	3.7
1923	3,957.0	315.1	50.1	294.1	−0.7	3.0
1924	4,212.0	255.6	50.6	258.1	42.2	45.2
1925	4,112.0	−100.1	48.0	−134.4	−32.2	13.0
1926	4,205.0	92.6	46.3	97.3	26.3	39.3
1927	4,092.0	−112.8	43.8	6.1	160.2	199.4
1928	3,854.0	−237.9	44.3	−391.9	−119.5	79.9
1929	3,997.0	142.5	42.5	175.0	55.4	135.3
1930	4,306.0	309.6	43.4	280.0	2.4	137.7
1931	4,173.0	−133.4	45.8	145.3	320.3	453.5
1932	4,226.0	52.9	45.9	−446.2	−457.5 [9]	73.7
1933	4,036.0	−190.4	47.1	−173.5	58.0 [9]	59.1
1934	8,258.0	4,222.5	92.9	1,133.9	−82.6	9.0

Notes appear at end of table

TABLE Cj1–6   U.S. monetary gold stock: 1879–1971   *Continued*

Year	Monetary gold stock, end of year Cj1 [2] Million dollars	Increase in monetary gold stock Cj2 Million dollars	Gold production Cj3 Million dollars	Excess of gold imports over exports Cj4 Million dollars	Increase in gold under earmark Cj5 Million dollars	Gold under earmark, end of year Cj6 Million dollars
1935	10,125.0	1,867.2	110.7	1,739.0	−0.2	8.8
1936	11,423.0	1,296.5	131.6	1,116.6	85.9	94.7
1937	12,790.0	1,367.5	143.9	1,585.5	200.4	295.1
1938	14,592.0	1,801.5	148.6	1,973.6	333.5	628.6
1939	17,800.0	3,208.0	161.7	3,574.2	534.4	1,163.0
1940	22,042.0	4,242.2	170.2	4,744.5	644.7	1,807.7
1941	22,762.0	719.8	169.1	982.4	407.7	2,215.4
1942	22,739.0	−23.0	125.4	315.7	453.4	2,673.8
1943	21,981.0	−757.9	48.3	68.9	303.6	3,477.4
1944	20,631.0	−1,349.8	35.3	−845.4	459.3	3,937.2
1945	20,083.0	−547.8	32.0	−106.3	356.7	4,293.3
1946	20,706.0	623.1	51.2	311.5	−465.4	3,328.4
1947	22,868.0	2,162.1 [7]	75.3	1,866.3	−210.0	3,613.4
1948	24,399.0	1,530.4	70.9	1,680.4	159.2	3,777.7
1949	24,563.0	164.6	67.3	686.5	495.7	4,273.3
1950	22,820.0	−1,743.3	30.1	−371.3	1,352.4	5,625.7
1951	22,873.0	52.7	66.3	−549.0	−617.6	5,003.2
1952	23,252.0	379.8	67.4	684.3	304.3	5,313.0
1953	22,091.0	−1,161.9	69.0	2.0	1,170.3	6,483.3
1954	21,793.0	−297.2	65.1	16.6	325.2	6,308.9
1955	21,753.0	−40.9	65.7	97.6	132.4	6,941.3
1956	22,058.0	305.9	65.3	106.1	−318.5	6,622.3
1957	22,857.0	798.8	63.6	104.3	−600.1	6,022.7
1958	20,582.0	−2,275.1	61.6	259.6	2,515.0	3,537.6
1959	19,507.0	−1,075.2 [8]	57.2	302.4	1,323.6	9,361.2
1960	17,804.0	−1,702.3	53.3	333.4	1,981.4	11,842.6
1961	16,947.0	−857.2	54.3	−718.8	62.6	11,905.2
1962	16,057.0	−889.9	54.5	−230.0	795.3	12,700.4
1963	15,596.0	−461.0	51.4	−159.4	254.0	12,954.0
1964	15,471.0	−125.0	51.4	−381.9	−256.0	12,693.0
1965	13,806.0 [4]	−1,665.0 [8]	58.6	−1,183.4	198.0	12,896.0
1966	13,235.0	−571.0	63.1	−415.3	50.0	12,946.0
1967	12,065.0	−1,170.0	53.4	−972.7	307.0	13,253.0
1968	10,892.0	−1,173.0	53.9	−612.9	−187.0	13,066.0
1969	11,859.0	967.0	60.1	224.6	−755.0	12,311.0
1970	11,072.0	−787.0 [8]	63.5	196.7	615.0	12,926.0
1971	10,206.0	−866.0 [5]	52.3	175.0	889.0 [10]	13,815.0

(Z) Less than $0.05 million.

[1] Gold valued at $20.67 per fine ounce through January 1934, and at $35 thereafter.

[2] From 1934, when the Exchange Stabilization Fund was established, figures include gold in the Exchange Stabilization Fund; prior to that time, figures represent changes in Treasury gold stock only.

[3] *Report to the Congress of the Commission on the Role of Gold*, p. 203, Table SC-9, reports a figure of 87.86 million fine ounces, with gold valued at $20.67; this is equivalent to $1,816 million. The major reason for this discrepancy is that $287 million was deducted by the Federal Reserve in each year from 1914 to 1933 because this amount was not returned to the Treasury in 1934, when gold holdings outside the Treasury were prohibited. For more details, see the notes accompanying this table; also see Board of Governors of the Federal Reserve System, *Banking and Monetary Statistics* (Board of Governors of the Federal Reserve System, 1943), p. 522.

[4] Excludes $259 million gold subscription to the International Monetary Fund in June 1965 for a U.S. quota increase that became effective on February 23, 1966.

[5] The increase in U.S. monetary gold stock for 1879 and 1971 was calculated by taking the first difference of the figures for U.S. monetary gold stock. In 1878, U.S. monetary gold stock was 11.21 million ounces and gold was valued at $20.84 per fine ounce.

[6] Less than 50,000 ounces.

[7] Net after payment of $687.5 million in gold as U.S. gold subscription to the International Monetary Fund (IMF).

[8] Includes payment of increases in U.S. gold subscription to the IMF as follows: 1959, $344 million; 1965, $259 million; and 1970, $385 million.

[9] Adjusted for changes in gold held under earmark abroad by the Federal Reserve banks.

[10] The increase in gold under earmark for 1971 was calculated by taking the first difference of the figures for gold under earmark held at the Federal Reserve banks.

Sources

Series Cj1–3, for 1879–1913, from the *Report to the Congress of the Commission on the Role of Gold in the Domestic and International Monetary Systems,* Volume 1 (1982), Table SC-5, pp. 193-4, Table SC-9, pp. 203-4, Table SC-14, pp. 212-15, except for series Cj2 for 1879, which was calculated using the first difference of series Cj1 (see footnote for details). Series Cj4, for 1879–1913, was constructed from monthly series posted on the National Bureau of Economic Research Web site, series number 14112.

All series, 1914–1941, are from Board of Governors of the Federal Reserve System, *Banking and Monetary Statistics* (Board of Governors of the Federal Reserve System, 1943), Table 156, p. 536.

Series Cj1–5, for 1942–1957 (except series Cj1 beginning in 1953, and series Cj4 beginning in 1956), are reported in the *Federal Reserve Bulletin* (June 1949): 745, and (April 1958): 503. Series Cj2 and Cj5, 1958–1970, were constructed from unpublished data. Series Cj1, 1953–1970, series Cj3, 1958–1971, and series Cj6, 1942–1971, are reported in the *Federal Reserve Bulletin*, January issues. Series Cj4 for the years 1956–1970, *U.S. Bureau of the Census, Report FT 2402,* annual issues. The source for series Cj1 and Cj4 for 1971 was the *Report to the Congress of the Commission on the Role of Gold in the Domestic and International Monetary Systems,* Volume 1 (1982), Tables 2-1, p. 84, SC-5, p. 194, and SC-14, p. 214. The 1971 figures for series Cj2 and Cj5 were calculated by taking the first difference of series Cj1 and Cj6, respectively.

TABLE Cj7–21 Stock of money and its components: 1790–1859 [Friedman and Schwartz]
Contributed by Hugh Rockoff

All values in millions of dollars.

End of year	Total stock of money held by public (Cj7)	Specie: Total stock in United States (Cj8)	Specie: Held by the Treasury (Cj9)	Specie: Held by state banks (Cj10)	Specie: Held by the First or Second Bank of the United States (Cj11)	Specie: Held by the public (Cj12)	Paper, outstanding from banks: Total (Cj13)	Paper, outstanding: From state banks (Cj14)	Paper, outstanding: From First or Second Bank of the United States (Cj15)	Government currency issues (Cj16)	Paper: Held by the public (Cj17)	Deposits, total in banking sector: Total (Cj18)	Deposits: Held at state banks (Cj19)	Deposits: Held at the First or Second Bank of United States (Cj20)	Adjusted deposits (held by the public) (Cj21)
1790	—	9.0 [2]	—	3.0 [5]	—	7.0 [2]	2.5 [9]	2.5	—	—	3.0 [9]	—	—	—	—
1791	—	16.0	—	—	—	—	9.0	—	—	—	—	—	—	—	—
1792	—	18.0	—	5.0	1.0	12.0	11.5	9.8	1.7	—	7.0	—	—	1.7	—
1793	—	20.0	—	—	1.2	—	11.0	9.0	2.0	—	—	—	—	1.9	—
1794	—	21.5	—	—	0.7	—	11.6	7.9	3.7	—	—	—	—	2.6	—
1795	—	19.0	—	—	1.4	—	11.0	7.3	3.7	—	—	—	—	2.5	—
1796	—	16.5	—	—	1.6	—	10.5	7.1	3.4	—	—	—	—	2.3	—
1797	—	16.0	—	—	2.7	—	10.0	6.9	3.1	—	—	—	—	3.7	—
1798	—	14.0	—	—	3.1	—	9.0	4.9	4.1	—	—	—	—	4.2	—
1799	—	17.0	—	—	4.0	—	10.0	5.7	4.3	—	—	13.0 [4]	8.6 [4]	4.4	—
1800	—	17.5	1.5	—	5.7 [6]	—	10.5	5.0	5.5	—	—	—	—	—	—
1801	—	17.0	—	—	5.2 [7]	—	11.0	6.0	5.0 [7]	—	—	—	—	—	—
1802	—	16.5	—	—	—	—	10.0	—	—	—	—	—	—	—	—
1803	—	16.0	—	—	—	—	11.0	—	—	—	—	—	—	—	—
1804	—	17.5 [3]	—	—	12.0	17.5	14.0	—	—	—	13.0	—	—	—	—
1805	—	18.0	—	—	—	—	15.0	—	—	—	—	—	—	—	—
1806	—	18.5	—	—	—	—	17.0	—	—	—	—	—	—	—	—
1807	—	20.0	—	—	—	—	18.0	—	—	—	—	—	—	—	—
1808	—	38.0	—	—	—	14.0	—	—	4.5	—	22.8	27.0 [4]	—	—	—
1809	—	—	—	—	—	—	—	—	—	—	—	—	—	—	—
1810	—	33.4 [4]	3.0	9.6	5.8	15.0	28.1	22.7	5.4	—	15.0	—	—	7.8	—
1812	—	—	—	—	—	—	—	—	—	2.8	—	—	—	—	—
1813	—	—	—	28.0 [6]	—	8.0	62.0 [10]	62.0 [10]	—	4.9	52.0	18.0	18.0	—	—
1814	—	24.0 [4]	—	17.0 [4]	—	7.0	45.5	45.5	—	10.6	40.0	—	—	—	—
1815	—	26.5	—	19.0	—	7.5	68.0 [11]	68.0 [11]	—	17.6	— [12]	—	—	—	—
1816	—	—	—	—	1.7	—	—	—	1.9	3.4	—	—	—	11.2	—
1817	—	—	—	—	2.5	—	—	—	8.3	—	—	—	—	12.3	—
1818	—	—	—	—	2.7	—	—	—	6.6	—	—	—	—	5.8	—
1819	—	25.0	—	16.7	3.1 [2]	5.2 [4]	44.8	40.6	4.2 [4]	—	—	37.8 [2]	31.2	6.6 [4]	—
1820	—	41.0 [4]	2.0	13.4	7.6	18.0 [4]	—	—	4.6	—	—	—	—	7.9	—
1821	—	39.0	—	19.2	4.8	15.0	—	—	5.6	—	—	—	—	8.1	—
1822	—	32.0	—	8.6	4.4	19.0	—	—	4.4	—	—	—	—	7.6	—
1823	—	31.0	—	12.2	5.8	13.0	—	—	4.6	—	—	—	—	13.7	—
1824	—	32.0	—	14.3	6.7	11.0	—	—	6.1	—	—	—	—	12.0	—
1825	—	29.0	—	14.0	4.0	11.0	—	—	9.5	—	—	—	—	11.2	—
1826	—	32.0	—	12.5	6.5	13.0	—	—	8.5	—	—	—	—	14.3	—
1827	—	32.0	—	11.8	6.2	14.0	—	—	9.9	—	—	—	—	14.5	—
1828	—	31.0	—	11.9	6.1	13.0	—	—	11.9	—	—	—	—	17.1	—
1829	—	33.0 [4]	—	14.9	7.6 [4]	10.5 [8]	61.3	48.3	13.0 [4]	—	53.5	55.6 [13]	40.8	14.8 [2]	—

End of year	Specie (coin) Total stock of money held by public Cj7 Million dollars	Total stock in the United States Cj8 Million dollars	Held by the Treasury Cj9 Million dollars	Held by state banks Cj10 Million dollars	Held by the First or Second Bank of the United States Cj11 Million dollars	Held by the public Cj12 Million dollars	Paper money Outstanding, from banks Total Cj13 Million dollars	From state banks Cj14 Million dollars	From First or Second Bank of the United States Cj15 Million dollars	Government currency issues Cj16 Million dollars	Held by the public Cj17 Million dollars	Deposits (excluding interbank deposits) Total in the banking sector Total Cj18 Million dollars	Held at state banks Cj19 Million dollars	Held at the First or Second Bank of United States Cj20 Million dollars	Adjusted deposits (held by the public) Cj21 Million dollars
1830	—	32.0	—	13.2	10.8	8.0	77.0	60.7	16.3	—	67.0	—	—	17.3	—
1831	—	30.4	—	15.0	7.0	8.4	91.5	70.1	21.4	—	—	—	—	22.8	—
1832	—	30.6	—	14.0	9.0	7.6	91.5	74.0	17.5	—	76.3 [2]	50.3	30.0	20.3	—
1833	152.0	42.7 [4]	—	15.0	10.0	15.8 [4]	94.8	75.6	19.2	—	72.7	75.7	64.9	10.8	63.5
1834	174.8 [1]	55.0 [4]	—	19.3	15.7	20.0 [4]	103.7	86.4	17.3	—	82.6	83.1	71.3	11.8	72.2
1835	217.8	65.0 [2]	—	31.6	8.4	25.0	140.3	117.2	23.1	—	108.2	115.1	110.0	5.1	84.6
1836	224.7	73.0	0.7	35.3	2.6	35.0	149.2	137.8	11.4	—	112.7 [4]	127.4	125.1	2.3	77.0
1837	221.2	87.5	1.0	31.4	3.8	52.0	116.1	109.3	6.8	3.0	91.2 [4]	84.7	82.1	2.6	78.0
1838	231.1	87.0	1.3	40.9	4.2	42.0	135.2	129.2	6.0	7.8	107.8 [4]	90.2 [2]	83.4	6.8	81.3 [2]
1839	204.3	83.0	0.7	31.6	1.5	50.0	107.0	100.3	6.7	1.0	86.2 [4]	75.7 [2]	72.4 [2]	3.3	68.1 [2]
1840	188.0	80.0 [4]	1.4	34.8	—	45.0 [4]	107.3	107.3	—	2.6	81.6 [4]	64.9	64.9	—	61.4
1841	175.4	80.0	0.2	28.4	—	52.0	83.7	83.7	—	7.4	64.3 [4]	62.4	62.4	—	59.1
1842	149.2	90.0	0.4	33.5	—	56.0	58.6	58.6	—	10.1	45.3 [4]	56.2	56.2	—	47.9
1843	181.9	100.0	0.6	49.9	—	50.0	75.2	75.2	—	2.3	63.5 [4]	84.6	84.6	—	68.4
1844	203.0	96.0	0.6	44.2	—	52.0	89.6	89.6	—	0.8	77.6 [4]	88.0	88.0	—	73.4
1845	227.2	97.0	0.7	42.0	—	54.2	105.6	105.6	—	0.6	92.6 [4]	96.9	96.9	—	80.4
1846	252.5	120.0	2.8	35.1	—	82.1	105.5	105.5	—	15.5	92.4	91.8	91.8	—	78.0
1847	267.3	112.0	3.1	46.4	—	62.5	128.5	128.5	—	14.7	112.1	103.2	103.2	—	92.7
1848	258.9	120.0	2.0	43.6	—	74.4	114.7	114.7	—	3.6	102.0	91.2 [2]	91.2 [2]	—	82.5
1849	316.4	154.0	5.3	45.4	—	103.3	131.4	131.4	—	0.7	115.1	109.6 [2]	109.6 [2]	—	98.0
1850	360.4 [1]	186.0	9.6	48.7	—	127.7	155.2	155.2	—	—	138.0	110.0	110.0	—	94.7
1851	408.5	204.0	13.5	48.4	—	142.1	171.7	171.7	—	—	147.9	137.3	137.3	—	118.5
1852	451.4	236.0	18.7	47.1	—	170.2	188.2	188.2	—	—	157.8	145.6	145.6	—	123.4
1853	504.9	241.0	21.3	59.4	—	160.3	204.7	204.7	—	—	182.0	188.2	188.2	—	162.6
1854	508.7	250.0	19.5	53.9	—	176.6	187.0	187.0	—	—	163.6	190.4	190.4	—	168.5
1855	534.5	250.0	19.9	59.3	—	170.8	195.7	195.7	—	—	170.9	212.7	212.7	—	192.8
1856	574.5	260.0	19.1	58.3	—	182.5	214.8	214.8	—	—	186.7	230.4	230.4	—	205.3
1857	477.2	260.0	11.8	74.4	—	173.8	155.2	155.2	—	19.8	132.8	185.9	185.9	—	170.6
1858	546.8	250.0	5.8	104.5	—	139.6	193.3	193.3	—	14.7	174.4	259.6 [2]	259.6 [2]	—	232.8
1859	565.2	237.0	4.3	83.6	—	149.1	207.1	207.1	—	—	181.6	253.8 [2]	253.8 [2]	—	234.5

[1] Table 14 from the source shows Macesich's estimates for 1834 and 1850 to be 162 and 379, respectively.

[2] Lower bound of the range reported in the source.

[3] Lower bound; from a different primary source than that used for series Cj11–12.

[4] Upper bound of the range reported in the source.

[5] Estimate from a different primary source than that used for the other estimates of specie.

[6] September.

[7] November. From James O. Wettereau, *Statistical Records of the First Bank of the United States* (Garland, 1985).

[8] Derived as a residual. Table 13 shows estimates ranging from 8.5 to 13.0.

[9] Estimates for series Cj13 and Cj17 are inconsistent and derive from different primary sources.

[10] September; lower bound.

[11] Estimates for September range from 99 to 110.

[12] There is an estimate for September of 110.

[13] Sum of series Cj19–20. Table 13 in the source shows estimates from other sources ranging from 61 to 65.

Source

Milton Friedman and Anna J. Schwartz, *Monetary Statistics of the United States* (Columbia University Press, 1970), Table 13, pp. 216–30, and Table 14, pp. 231–3.

(continued)

TABLE Cj7–21 Stock of money and its components: 1790–1859 [Friedman and Schwartz] *Continued*

Documentation

Data for the pre–Civil War era are often incomplete, and the estimates that do exist often do not agree. Friedman and Schwartz compile the estimates available in secondary sources and government documents. They adopt the practice of reporting upper and lower bounds when more than one estimate is available. Here, however, in order to make the data more accessible to the general reader, we report what appears to be the best estimate based on the quality of the primary source and the consistency of the estimate in question with other data. For additional estimates, consult Friedman and Schwartz (1970) and the sources cited there.

The estimates refer to the end of the calendar year.

Series Cj7. This estimate of the total stock of money is the sum of series Cj12, Cj17, and Cj21. The Treasury notes shown occasionally in series Cj16 after 1837 are excluded.

Series Cj8–12. These series are estimates of the amount of specie (money in the form of coin) in the United States. The amount of specie varied from year to year based on imports and exports of specie, the mining of monetary metals, and the minting of coins. Until 1857, some foreign coins were legal tender. The estimates for 1831–1858 exclude Treasury holdings, except for 1836–1844, when they may be included. Series Cj12 is the amount in the hands of the public, calculated as the difference between series Cj8 and the sum of series Cj9–11, except as described in the footnotes.

Series Cj13–15 and Cj17. Estimates of notes issued by banks. These notes were redeemable in specie on demand, except when a bank had suspended payments owing to individual difficulties or during financial crises. Series Cj14 shows notes issued by state banks (generally private banks chartered by state governments, although some state-owned banks are included). Series Cj15 shows notes issued by the First (1791–1811) and Second (1816–1836) Banks of the United States. Series Cj13 is the sum of series Cj14–15. Series Cj17 is the amount of bank notes in the hands of the public. It was estimated by deducting estimates of the amount of notes held by banks from series Cj13.

Series Cj16. Currency issued by the federal government. The series includes one-year Treasury notes, some bearing interest and some not, that served as bank reserves, and may have circulated as currency, that were issued occasionally between 1837 and 1858. See Friedman and Schwartz 1970, p. 257.

Series Cj18–21. Deposits were generally subject to check and often bore interest. Series Cj18 is the sum of series Cj19–20. Series Cj21 was calculated by deducting estimates of float (checks in the process of collection) and Treasury balances at banks from series Cj18.

TABLE Cj22–25   Stock of money and its components: 1820–1858   [Temin]

Contributed by Hugh Rockoff

End of year	Total stock of money	Components			End of year	Total stock of money	Components		
		Stock of specie	Reserve ratio of the banking system	Proportion of money held as specie			Stock of specie	Reserve ratio of the banking system	Proportion of money held as specie
	Cj22	Cj23	Cj24	Cj25		Cj22	Cj23	Cj24	Cj25
	Million dollars	Million dollars	Ratio	Ratio		Million dollars	Million dollars	Ratio	Ratio
1820	85	41	0.32	0.24	1840	186	80	0.25	0.24
1821	96	39	0.30	0.16	1841	174	80	0.23	0.30
1822	81	32	0.21	0.23	1842	158	90	0.33	0.35
1823	88	31	0.25	0.15	1843	194	100	0.35	0.26
1824	88	32	0.27	0.13	1844	214	96	0.27	0.24
1825	106	29	0.19	0.10	1845	241	97	0.23	0.23
1826	108	32	0.20	0.12	1846	267	120	0.19	0.32
1827	101	32	0.20	0.14	1847	281	112	0.21	0.23
1828	114	31	0.18	0.11	1848	267	120	0.23	0.28
1829	105	33	0.22	0.12	1849	329	154	0.20	0.33
1830	114	32	0.23	0.06	1850	399	186	0.19	0.34
1831	155	30	0.15	0.05	1851	—	204	—	—
1832	150	31	0.16	0.05	1852	451	236	0.18	0.42
1833	168	41	0.18	0.08	1853	546	241	0.16	0.33
1834	172	51	0.27	0.04	1854	539	250	0.16	0.36
1835	246	65	0.18	0.10	1855	565	250	0.16	0.34
1836	276	73	0.16	0.13	1856	611	260	0.14	0.33
1837	232	88	0.20	0.23	1857	498	260	0.24	0.37
1838	240	87	0.23	0.18	1858	569	250	0.25	0.25
1839	215	83	0.20	0.23					

Source

Peter Temin, *The Jacksonian Economy* (Norton, 1969), Table 3.3, p. 71, and Table 5.2, p. 159.

Documentation

The estimates shown in this table are similar to those reported by Milton Friedman and Anna J. Schwartz, *Monetary Statistics of the United States* (Columbia University Press, 1970), Table 13, pp. 216–30, in years when both are available, but were created by methods that differ in a number of details. The margin of error surrounding the estimates expands as one goes back in time.

Series Cj22. Includes specie, bank notes, and deposits held by the nonbank public. Federal and state governments are considered part of the public. Series Cj23–25 are known as the "determinants" of series Cj22, which is equal to series Cj23 divided by the following: series Cj24 plus series Cj25 minus the product of series Cj24–25. In some cases, the result of this formula, when applied to the figures in the table, differs from series Cj22 because of rounding. Additional estimates for this period, for selected dates, were made by Clark

Warburton, "The Secular Trend in Monetary Velocity," *Quarterly Journal of Economics* 63 (February 1949): 76–7, and John G. Gurley and E. S. Shaw, "The Growth of Debt and Money in the United States, 1800–1950: A Suggested Interpretation," *Review of Economics and Statistics* 39 (August 1957): 258.

Series Cj23–25. Series Cj23 estimates the amount of money in the form of coin in the United States whether in banks or held by the public. From 1829 on, Temin relied on estimates of the stock of specie reported by the Comptroller of the Currency. Temin extended these estimates back to 1820 by using data on mining and foreign trade. In calculating the amount of bank notes and deposits issued by state banks and their specie holdings, Temin relied on data reported by the U.S. Treasury for 1834 onward. He extended these estimates back to 1820 by relying on the bank balance sheets compiled by J. Van Fenstermaker, *The Development of American Commercial Banking, 1782–1837* (Kent State University Press, 1965). Totals derived from Van Fenstermaker's balance sheets were adjusted upward to allow for non-reporting banks. Combined with data on the Second Bank of the United States, these procedures produced sufficient information to calculate series Cj23–25.

TABLE Cj26–41 Stock of money and its components: 1859–1866[1]   [Friedman, Schwartz, and Mitchell]

Contributed by Hugh Rockoff

		Stock of money			Specie (money in the form of coin)					Paper money					Deposits (excluding interbank deposits)		
		Excluding specie		Including specie and interest-bearing currency[2]						Government currency issues		Bank notes					
Year	Month	Excluding interest-bearing currency[2]	Including interest-bearing currency[2]		Total stock	Held by the Treasury	Held by state banks	Held by national banks	Held by the public	Non-interest-bearing	Interest-bearing	From state banks	From national banks	Held by the public	At state banks	At national banks	Adjusted deposits held by the public
		Cj26[2]	Cj27[2]	Cj28[2]	Cj29	Cj30	Cj31	Cj32	Cj33	Cj34	Cj35	Cj36	Cj37	Cj38	Cj39	Cj40	Cj41
		Million dollars	Million dollars	Million dollars	Million dollars	Million dollars	Million dollars	Million dollars	Million dollars	Million dollars	Million dollars	Million dollars	Million dollars	Million dollars	Million dollars	Million dollars	Million dollars
1859	Dec	562.1	562.1	562.1	237.0	4.3	83.6	—	149.1	—	—	207.1	—	181.6	253.8[4]	—	231.4
1860	June	554.2	554.2	554.2	235.0	3.9[4]	85.0[5]	—	145.1	—	—	204.5[3]	—	180.9	253.9[3]	—	227.2
1860	Dec	570.6	570.6	570.6	259.2[3]	2.8[3]	87.7	—	168.8[5]	—	—	202.0	—	180.1	254.0	—	221.7
1861	June	557.9	557.9	557.9	286.0	2.0[4]	101.0[5]	—	183.0	—	—	192.7[3]	—	169.1	274.3[3]	—	242.7
1861	Dec	564.6	564.6	564.6	291.0[3]	6.0[3]	102.1	—	182.8[5]	—	—	183.8	—	158.5	296.3	—	260.3
1862	June	602.6	602.6	729.4	296.0	18.3[4]	101.0[5]	—	175.7	149.6	—	209.5[3]	—	296.9	341.5[3]	—	283.8
1862	Dec	727.6	727.6	881.0	283.2[3]	12.4[3]	101.2	—	169.6[5]	248.0[3]	—	238.7	—	385.0	393.7	—	320.6
1863	June	741.9	741.9	972.5	271.0	8.4[4]	50.8	—	211.8	411.2	—	163.4	—	405.5	393.6[3]	—	314.4
1863	Dec	778.2	778.2	999.1	240.3[3]	12.7[3]	29.7[3]	—	197.8[5]	440.1[3]	—	171.1[3]	—	445.1	393.6[3]	—	311.1
1864	June	956.9	1,125.4	1,396.7	213.0	19.3	17.4[3]	—	176.3[5]	471.0	168.5	179.2	31.2	681.7	393.5[3]	119.4	421.7
1864	Nov	1,025.2	1,219.1	1,506.2	206.8[3]	26.5[3]	11.1[3]	—	169.3[5]	464.9[3]	193.9[3]	163.1[3]	59.4[3]	685.6	393.5	208.9[3]	511.6
1865	June	1,032.5	1,268.6	1,445.4	198.5	41.2	5.9[6]	9.4	142.0[5]	456.6	236.1	142.9	146.1	646.4	237.0[3]	456.4	600.2
1865	Nov	957.9	1,159.9	1,330.5	188.8[3]	43.7[3]	3.5[6]	10.6[3]	131.0[5]	444.5[3]	202.0[3]	62.9[3]	192.1[3]	578.9	165.0	501.6[3]	559.0
1866	June	1,013.3	1,175.8	1,314.9	176.0	47.5	3.3[6]	12.6	112.6[5]	428.1	162.5	20.0	281.5	539.7	200.5[3]	572.4	614.2

[1] The data beginning in June 1861 and ending in November 1864 are for the Northern states.

[2] Northern states only, 1861–1864.

[3] Calculated by linear interpolation of natural logarithms of prior and subsequent observations.

[4] Lower bound.

[5] Calculated as the difference between the appropriate subtotal and the other components of that subtotal.

[6] Estimated by applying the ratio of specie to the sum of notes and deposits at national banks to the sum of notes and deposits at state banks.

Sources

Series Cj34–35. Wesley Clair Mitchell, *A History of the Greenbacks: With Special Reference to the Economic Consequence of Their Issue, 1862–65* (University of Chicago Press, 1903), Table V, p. 179.

All other series. Milton Friedman and Anna J. Schwartz, *Monetary Statistics of the United States: Estimates, Sources, Methods* (University of Chicago Press, 1970), Table 13, pp. 224–5.

Documentation

The existing data for the Civil War (April 1861 to April 1865) are often incomplete or difficult to interpret because of the disturbed monetary conditions that prevailed. Friedman and Schwartz adopt the practice of frequently reporting upper and lower bounds because of the unreliability of the underlying data. Here, however, in order to make the data more accessible to the general reader, we report what appears to be the best estimate based on the quality of the primary source and the consistency of the estimate in question with other data. All of the figures were rounded.

Series Cj26–28. Any attempt to measure the total stock of money in the North must be considered somewhat speculative. For the interested reader, however, three totals are shown. Series Cj26 includes only items known to have circulated from hand to hand as money. Series Cj27–28 add items that may have enjoyed limited use for transaction purposes, and were extremely close substitutes for the items included in series Cj26. Series Cj26 includes non-interest-bearing government currency issues held by the public, bank notes held by the public, and bank deposits held by the public for all dates. Specie in the hands of the public, series Cj33, is included for the period prior to the suspension of specie payments on December 30, 1861. A deduction for specie in the hands of the public in the South, Godfrey's lower bound estimate of $37 million, is made in June and December 1861, the observations that occur between the outbreak of the war and the suspension of specie payments. An estimate of the amount of gold circulating on the Pacific Coast, $22 million (Mitchell 1903, p. 179), is included throughout. Series Cj27 adds interest-bearing government currency issues, series Cj35, to series Cj26. Series Cj28 adds an estimate of specie in the North, after the suspension of specie payments, valued at market prices to series Cj27. For this purpose, all specie in the North, including specie on the Pacific Coast, held by the public was valued at the greenback price of gold. This adjustment overstates the value of that part of the stock of specie that was silver. On the eve of the war, about 18 percent of the stock of specie consisted of silver and subsidiary coins.

TABLE Cj26–41   Stock of money and its components: 1859–1866   [Friedman, Schwartz, and Mitchell]   *Continued*

Series Cj29–33. Series Cj29 is an estimate of the stock of specie in the nation as a whole at face value. John Munro Godfrey, "Monetary Expansion in the Confederacy," Ph.D. dissertation, University of Georgia, 1976, p. 113, estimates Confederate specie holdings at the outbreak of the war as $26 million held by the banks and between $37 million and $55 million held by the public. The estimates of series Cj30–32 often had to be interpolated or derived from limited additional evidence, so series Cj33, an estimate of the total stock of specie in the hands of the public, is estimated with a substantial margin of error.

Series Cj34–35. Series Cj34 consists mostly of the famous greenbacks, a fiat paper money, although it also includes small amounts of postage and fractional currencies, and demand notes issued prior to the greenbacks. Series Cj35 includes several kinds of short-term, legal-tender, interest-bearing Treasury notes that were intended to circulate as money, although the extent to which they actually did so is controversial.

Series Cj36–38. Series Cj36–37 are probably reliable estimates of the amount of bank notes outstanding of state and national banks, although a number of estimates had to be interpolated. In principle, all currency held by banks and the Treasury should be deducted to reach currency in the hands of the public. But the total shown in series Cj38 may be inaccurate because only scattered figures are available on the currency holdings of the Treasury and state and national banks. Estimates of currency held by the Treasury may not include state bank notes. Currency held by state banks after December 1862 was estimated by multiplying the December 1862 ratio of specie and bank notes held by banks to bank notes and deposits issued by banks by the current amount of bank notes and deposits and deducting current specie holdings. The estimate of notes held by national banks may exclude state bank notes.

Series Cj39–41. Series Cj39–40 are probably reliable estimates of deposits held at state and national banks, although a number of estimates had to be interpolated. Series Cj41 is an estimate of deposits adjusted by deducting float and Treasury deposits at banks. Estimates of state bank float are not available after December 1862 and were estimated by multiplying the ratio of state bank float to deposits outstanding in December 1862 by the current amount of deposits outstanding. Treasury balances at depository banks are not available for the early years of the war and were estimated by multiplying current government spending by the ratio of Treasury deposits to spending in June 1864. The corresponding figure in Table Cj7–21 omits this adjustment.

TABLE Cj42–48   Stock of money and its components: 1867–1947
[Friedman and Schwartz]

Contributed by Richard G. Anderson

	M1			M2			
	Total	Currency	Demand deposits	Total	Deposits at commercial banks	M3	M4
	Cj42	Cj43	Cj44	Cj45	Cj46	Cj47	Cj48
Year	Billion dollars	Billion dollars	Billion dollars	Billion dollars	Billion dollars	Billion dollars	Billion dollars
1867	—	0.58	—	1.28	0.70	1.58	—
1868	—	0.54	—	1.27	0.73	1.60	—
1869	—	0.55	—	1.28	0.73	1.68	—
1870	—	0.54	—	1.35	0.81	1.81	—
1871	—	0.54	—	1.50	0.96	2.04	—
1872	—	0.55	—	1.61	1.06	2.24	—
1873	—	0.56	—	1.62	1.06	2.31	—
1874	—	0.54	—	1.65	1.11	2.39	—
1875	—	0.54	—	1.72	1.18	2.52	—
1876	—	0.53	—	1.68	1.15	2.52	—
1877	—	0.54	—	1.65	1.11	2.47	—
1878	—	0.54	—	1.58	1.04	2.34	—
1879	—	0.58	—	1.66	1.08	2.46	—
1880	—	0.67	—	2.03	1.36	2.85	—
1881	—	0.78	—	2.44	1.66	3.35	—
1882	—	0.84	—	2.63	1.79	3.59	—
1883	—	0.87	—	2.80	1.93	3.79	—
1884	—	0.84	—	2.80	1.96	3.81	—
1885	—	0.80	—	2.87	2.07	3.94	—
1886	—	0.78	—	3.10	2.32	4.22	—
1887	—	0.83	—	3.31	2.48	4.46	—
1888	—	0.85	—	3.40	2.55	4.62	—
1889	—	0.87	—	3.60	2.73	4.87	—
1890	—	0.93	—	3.92	2.99	5.25	—
1891	—	0.96	—	4.08	3.12	5.52	—
1892	—	0.96	—	4.43	3.47	5.89	—
1893	—	1.00	—	4.26	3.26	5.76	—
1894	—	0.93	—	4.28	3.35	5.83	—
1895	—	0.91	—	4.43	3.52	6.07	—
1896	—	0.89	—	4.35	3.46	6.02	—
1897	—	0.92	—	4.64	3.72	6.34	—
1898	—	1.00	—	5.26	4.26	7.08	7.47
1899	—	1.10	—	6.09	4.99	7.99	8.37
1900	—	1.21	—	6.60	5.39	8.62	8.99
1901	—	1.27	—	7.48	6.21	9.60	9.97
1902	—	1.34	—	8.17	6.83	10.42	10.79
1903	—	1.42	—	8.68	7.26	11.05	11.44
1904	—	1.44	—	9.24	7.80	11.71	12.11
1905	—	1.50	—	10.24	8.74	12.82	13.23
1906	—	1.63	—	11.08	9.45	13.81	14.13
1907	—	1.72	—	11.60	9.88	14.45	14.44
1908	—	1.76	—	11.44	9.68	14.38	15.06
1909	—	1.71	—	12.68	10.97	15.71	16.17
1910	—	1.74	—	13.34	11.60	16.50	17.13
1911	—	1.76	—	14.12	12.36	17.43	18.05
1912	—	1.82	—	15.13	13.31	18.59	19.20
1913	—	1.89	—	15.73	13.84	19.31	20.13
1914	—	1.91	—	16.39	14.48	20.07	20.82
1915	12.48	1.93	10.55	17.59	15.66	21.41	22.59
1916	14.70	2.17	12.53	20.85	18.68	24.91	25.98
1917	17.08	2.17	14.91	24.37	22.20	28.62	29.67
1918	18.96	2.76	16.20	26.73	23.97	31.07	33.14
1919	21.79	4.02	17.77	31.01	26.99	35.74	37.44
1920	23.73	4.48	19.25	34.80	30.32	39.83	40.86
1921	21.51	4.04	17.47	32.85	28.81	38.11	40.61
1922	21.67	3.69	17.98	33.72	30.03	39.49	41.70
1923	22.93	3.96	18.97	36.60	32.64	42.70	45.01
1924	23.67	3.96	19.71	38.58	34.62	45.11	48.05

**TABLE Cj42–48   Stock of money and its components: 1867–1947
[Friedman and Schwartz]   Continued**

	M1			M2			
	Total	Currency	Demand deposits	Total	Deposits at commercial banks	M3	M4
	Cj42	Cj43	Cj44	Cj45	Cj46	Cj47	Cj48
Year	Billion dollars	Billion dollars	Billion dollars	Billion dollars	Billion dollars	Billion dollars	Billion dollars
1925	25.66	3.96	21.70	42.05	38.09	49.01	52.03
1926	26.18	4.00	22.18	43.68	39.68	50.93	54.59
1927	26.10	3.98	22.12	44.73	40.75	52.60	56.68
1928	26.38	3.89	22.49	46.42	42.53	54.84	59.67
1929	26.64	3.90	22.74	46.60	42.70	55.20	60.99
1930	25.76	3.73	22.03	45.73	42.00	54.49	60.36
1931	24.14	4.16	19.98	42.69	38.53	51.94	56.73
1932	21.11	4.92	16.19	36.05	31.13	45.49	51.83
1933	19.91	5.09	14.82	32.22	27.13	41.52	48.09
1934	21.86	4.63	17.23	34.36	29.73	44.18	48.20
1935	25.88	4.80	21.08	39.07	34.27	49.35	52.84
1936	29.55	5.23	24.32	43.48	38.25	54.09	57.84
1937	30.91	5.59	25.32	45.68	40.09	56.34	59.73
1938	30.52	5.55	24.97	45.51	39.96	56.37	60.58
1939	34.15	6.04	28.11	49.27	43.23	60.35	64.39
1940	39.65	6.76	32.89	55.20	48.44	66.38	70.23
1941	46.52	8.40	38.12	62.51	54.11	73.70	76.92
1942	55.36	11.54	43.82	71.16	59.62	82.73	87.84
1943	72.24	16.35	55.89	89.91	73.56	102.80	106.49
1944	85.34	21.22	64.12	106.82	85.60	121.58	127.00
1945	99.23	25.33	73.90	126.63	101.30	143.89	147.13
1946	106.46	26.48	79.98	138.73	112.25	157.69	163.71
1947	111.79	26.58	85.22	146.00	119.42	166.76	174.22

Source

Constructed from figures in Milton Friedman and Anna Jacobson Schwartz, *Monetary Statistics of the United States* (Columbia University Press, 1970).

Documentation

Figures are annual averages constructed from the Friedman and Schwartz data. Where figures were available for all months or quarters in a year, annual figures are an arithmetic average of these figures; otherwise, annual figures are constructed by linear interpolation of monthly or quarterly figures.

These figures are extensively documented in the source. The figures begin in 1867 because, after a careful review, Friedman and Schwartz (1970, Chapter 8) conclude that the quality of the data prior to 1867 is too uncertain to include them in a monetary aggregate. All monetary aggregates reflect, to some extent, the institutional characteristics of their eras. During the period examined by Friedman and Schwartz, thrift institutions, such as mutual savings banks and saving and loan associations, did not issue deposits transferable by check. (The cashiers' checks that they often gave to customers typically were drawn on a demand deposit at a commercial bank.) Hence, only demand deposits at commercial banks are included in Friedman and Schwartz's M1. Some analysts have argued that the inability of thrifts to issue transaction deposits sharply separated, in the behavior of households and firms, deposits at thrifts from deposits at commercial banks. Hence, Friedman and Schwartz's M2 includes only such deposits at commercial banks. Their M3 and M4 aggregates, however, include deposits at both commercial banks and thrifts.

A frequently asked question is how closely Friedman and Schwartz's figures resemble today's Federal Reserve monetary aggregates (shown in Table Cj84–99). For M1, the resemblance is close. Both consist of currency held by the public and checkable (transaction) deposits. Friedman and Schwartz's M1 includes only demand deposits at banks, whereas the current Federal Reserve aggregate also includes checkable deposits at thrift institutions; however, there were no such thrift deposits during the era examined by Friedman and Schwartz. Because Friedman and Schwartz's M2 includes only deposits at commercial banks, it does not resemble any currently published monetary aggregate. Prior to redefinition in 1980, the Federal Reserve's

M1 and M2 also included only commercial bank deposits. See Richard G. Anderson and Kenneth A. Kavajecz, "A Historical Perspective on the Federal Reserve's Monetary Aggregates," *Federal Reserve Bank of St. Louis Review* 76 (March/April 1994). Friedman and Schwartz's M4 in many respects resembles the Federal Reserve's current M2, which includes all deposits at commercial banks and thrifts except large-denomination (more than $100,000) time deposits. The resemblance between the two aggregates is not exact. By excluding large-denomination time deposits (such as negotiable certificates of deposit), the Federal Reserve's current M2 excludes a significant amount of the funds bought wholesale by larger banks. Yet, it seems likely that Friedman and Schwartz's total bank-deposit figures include some wholesale funds. Further, the Federal Reserve's current M2 includes retail-type money market mutual fund shares, a financial instrument that did not exist during the era examined by Friedman and Schwartz. In these aspects, currently published aggregates differ from those of Friedman and Schwartz. However, during the era examined by Friedman and Schwartz, it seems likely that a good deal of the *type* of funds that now reside in money market mutual funds instead resided in bank and thrift-institution deposits. Hence, from an economic viewpoint, Friedman and Schwartz's M4 and the currently published Federal Reserve M2 aggregates are more similar than first appearances may suggest.

See Table Cj49–53 for data covering the period 1947–1958.

Series Cj42. Friedman and Schwartz's M1 money stock is the sum of "currency held by the nonbank public" plus "demand deposits adjusted" at commercial banks. The currency and demand deposit figures are of their own construction through, respectively, 1942 and 1945. Thereafter, they use data from the *Federal Reserve Bulletin* (Board of Governors of the Federal Reserve System). This aggregate begins in 1915 because for earlier periods it generally is not feasible to separate demand and time deposits at banks.

Series Cj43. These figures equal currency in circulation (outside the Treasury and, beginning November 1914, the Federal Reserve banks), series Cj73, minus the vault cash held by those depository institutions whose deposit liabilities are included in the monetary aggregate. This measure of currency is referred to as "currency held by the nonbank public." For details of its measurement, see Friedman and Schwartz (1970), Chapters 6, 8–12.

(continued)

TABLE Cj42–48   Stock of money and its components: 1867–1947   [Friedman and Schwartz]   *Continued*

Series Cj44. Demand deposits are deposits at commercial banks that (legally) may be immediately transferred to a third party or withdrawn in currency. "Demand deposits adjusted" excludes demand deposits due to the U.S. Treasury and demand deposits due to other banks (interbank deposits). It also excludes "float," that is, the deposit amounts for which checks are in the process of collection. Because sorting, transporting, and collecting checks takes some time, the aggregate amount of demand deposits reported by all banks exceeds, by the value of checks in collection, the dollar amount of deposits available to households and firms for spending.

Series Cj45–46. Friedman and Schwartz's M2 money stock equals the sum of currency held by the nonbank public, series Cj43, plus total deposits at commercial banks. They note that the characteristics of time deposits at banks have changed through time. During some periods, there was little or no penalty for withdrawing time deposits before the end of their contract period. During other periods, the penalties were quite high. Also, the available data, especially for earlier years and some states, do not permit drawing

clear distinctions between demand and time deposits. These figures also include what later came to be known as *saving deposits*, that is, interest-bearing deposits with no contractual maturity date.

Series Cj47–48. Friedman and Schwartz's M3 money stock equals the sum of M2 plus deposits at mutual savings banks and deposits in the postal saving system. Their M4 monetary aggregate equals the sum of M3 plus shares (deposits) in savings and loan associations. These aggregates are constructed by consolidation, not summation. During consolidation, liabilities (deposits) issued by one included institution and held by another included institution – such as demand deposits at commercial banks held by mutual savings banks – are netted out. (Note that demand deposits held by one commercial bank at another commercial bank similarly are netted out during the construction of the "demand deposit adjusted" figures.) M4 is measured less precisely than M3 because for all years only December figures are available for savings and loan shares; beginning May 1907, M3 is calculated from monthly figures.

TABLE Cj49–53   Stock of money and its components: 1947–1958   [Rasche]

Contributed by Richard G. Anderson

	M1				
	Total	Currency	Demand deposits	M2	M3
Year	Cj49	Cj50	Cj51	Cj52	Cj53
	Billion dollars	Billion dollars	Billion dollars	Billion dollars	Billion dollars
1947	108.47	26.74	81.73	—	172.62
1948	109.01	26.27	82.74	171.18	174.19
1949	107.82	25.66	82.16	172.75	179.96
1950	110.80	25.24	85.56	178.47	179.96
1951	115.89	25.73	90.17	186.39	187.95
1952	121.89	26.86	95.03	199.19	200.85
1953	125.03	27.88	97.15	210.82	212.58
1954	126.96	27.73	99.23	222.76	224.63
1955	131.13	27.83	103.30	236.84	238.82
1956	132.75	28.20	104.55	246.21	248.28
1957	133.43	28.46	104.97	258.00	260.16
1958	135.06	28.57	106.49	274.69	276.99

Sources

Constructed from figures from Robert H. Rasche, "M1-Velocity and Money Demand Functions: Do Stable Relationships Exist?" *Carnegie-Rochester Conference Series on Public Policy* 27 (Autumn 1987), Appendix A, pp. 70–1, and Robert H. Rasche, "Demand Functions for U.S. Money and Credit Measures," in P. Hooper, Karen H. Johnson, et al., editors, *Financial Sectors in Open Economies: Empirical Analysis and Policy Issues* (Board of Governors of the Federal Reserve System, 1990), Appendix, p. 159. As of January 2002, these data were available at Rasche's Michigan State University Internet site.

Documentation

These figures represent an effort by Robert H. Rasche to construct monetary aggregates for 1947–1958 using the Federal Reserve Board's currently published definitions. Monetary aggregates published by the Board of Governors begin in 1959; Board staff members have not constructed comparable figures for earlier periods. Rasche constructs his figures by making adjustments to previously published figures on demand deposits and time deposits. Rasche makes no adjustments to currency. Figures presented here are annual averages of monthly data from Rasche. The methods used to construct these series can be found in the source.

See Table Cj42–48 for data covering the period 1867–1947.

Series Cj49–51. For M1, Rasche makes an adjustment for traveler's checks. Figures on M1 currently published by the Federal Reserve Board, for dates beginning January 1959, include the amount of traveler's checks issued by institutions other than commercial banks (such as American Express and certain subsidiaries of bank holding companies). Published figures for earlier periods do not, and exact figures for earlier periods do not exist. To adjust for the change, Rasche multiplies M1 figures for 1947–1958 by 1.0138, the 1959 ratio of the sum of currency plus nonbank traveler's checks to currency. (Note that traveler's checks issued by commercial banks are not a part of this calculation. Banks include these checks in demand deposit figures reported to the Federal Reserve.)

Series Cj51. For demand deposits, Rasche notes that figures currently published by the Federal Reserve Board for years beginning 1959 exclude demand deposits held by foreign commercial banks and foreign official institutions.

Previously published figures for 1947–1958, however, include such foreign deposits. No exact figures exist regarding the amount of such deposits. From published descriptions, Rasche estimates that the level of such deposits had a mean of approximately $2.7 billion and a very small variance from January 1947 through December 1958. He subtracts this amount from previously published, not seasonally adjusted, monthly demand deposit figures, and then uses the Board staff's published seasonal adjustment factors to create seasonally adjusted demand deposit figures.

Series Cj52–53. An adjustment is necessary because the Federal Reserve Board's currently published monetary aggregates include a special consolidation adjustment that removes deposits held by some depository institutions at other depository institutions. In the course of business, depositories often hold deposits at other depository institutions. Thrift institutions, for example, often hold deposits at commercial banks. Such deposits are excluded from monetary aggregates because monetary aggregates seek to measure assets held by the nonbank public. Figures currently published by the Federal Reserve Board, beginning with January 1959, include such adjustments. Previously published figures for 1948–1958 covered commercial banks and thrift institutions separately, and hence there is no available consolidation adjustment for their combination. Rasche approximates such an adjustment for M2 for 1948–1958 by adding to M1 previously published separate figures on the amounts of time deposits at commercial banks and at thrifts. At the beginning of 1959, this combined figure, which includes no consolidation adjustment, is approximately 1.6 percent larger than the M2 figure currently published by the Federal Reserve Board, which does include such a consolidation adjustment. He chains the earlier data to the later data by multiplying the figures for 1948–1958 by 0.984. Rasche uses the same method to approximate a consolidation adjustment for M3. He chains the 1948–1958 figures to the Federal Reserve Board's currently published figures by multiplying the older data by 0.991935. This method is feasible because the financial assets that are included in the Board's currently published M3 but are not included in the M2 monetary aggregate (large-denomination time deposits, repurchase agreements, Eurodollar deposits, and institutional money market mutual funds) generally were unimportant or did not exist prior to 1959.

TABLE Cj54–69 Currency in circulation, by kind: 1800–1999
Contributed by Richard G. Anderson

	Coin			Fractional		Paper notes			Currency no longer issued					Nineteenth-century notes		
	Gold	Dollars	Total	Subsidiary silver coin	Minor coin	Federal Reserve notes	U.S. notes	Total	Gold certificates	Silver certificates	Treasury notes of 1890	National bank notes	Federal Reserve Bank notes	Fractional currency	Other U.S. currency	State bank notes
	Cj54	Cj55	Cj56	Cj57	Cj58	Cj59	Cj60	Cj61	Cj62	Cj63	Cj64	Cj65	Cj66	Cj67	Cj68	Cj69
Fiscal year	Thousand dollars	Thousand dollars	Thousand dollars	Thousand dollars	Thousand dollars	Thousand dollars	Thousand dollars	Thousand dollars	Thousand dollars	Thousand dollars	Thousand dollars	Thousand dollars	Thousand dollars	Thousand dollars	Thousand dollars	Thousand dollars
1800	—	—	—	—	—	—	—	—	—	—	—	—	—	—	—	10,500
1810	—	—	—	—	—	—	—	—	—	—	—	—	—	—	—	28,000
1820	—	—	—	—	—	—	—	—	—	—	—	—	—	—	—	44,800
1830	—	—	—	—	—	—	—	—	—	—	—	—	—	—	—	61,000
1831	—	—	—	—	—	—	—	—	—	—	—	—	—	—	—	77,000
1832	—	—	—	—	—	—	—	—	—	—	—	—	—	—	—	91,500
1833	—	—	—	—	—	—	—	—	—	—	—	—	—	—	—	91,500
1834	—	—	—	—	—	—	—	—	—	—	—	—	—	—	—	94,840
1835	—	—	—	—	—	—	—	—	—	—	—	—	—	—	—	103,692
1836	—	—	—	—	—	—	—	—	—	—	—	—	—	—	—	140,301
1837	—	—	—	—	—	—	—	—	—	—	—	—	—	—	—	149,186
1838	—	—	—	—	—	—	—	—	—	—	—	—	—	—	—	116,139
1839	—	—	—	—	—	—	—	—	—	—	—	—	—	—	—	135,171
1840	—	—	—	—	—	—	—	—	—	—	—	—	—	—	—	106,969
1841	—	—	—	—	—	—	—	—	—	—	—	—	—	—	—	107,290
1842	—	—	—	—	—	—	—	—	—	—	—	—	—	—	—	83,734
1843	—	—	—	—	—	—	—	—	—	—	—	—	—	—	—	58,564
1844	—	—	—	—	—	—	—	—	—	—	—	—	—	—	—	75,168
1845	—	—	—	—	—	—	—	—	—	—	—	—	—	—	—	89,609
1846	—	—	—	—	—	—	—	—	—	—	—	—	—	—	—	105,552
1847	—	—	—	—	—	—	—	—	—	—	—	—	—	—	—	105,520
1848	—	—	—	—	—	—	—	—	—	—	—	—	—	—	—	128,506
1849	—	—	—	—	—	—	—	—	—	—	—	—	—	—	—	114,743
1850	—	—	—	—	—	—	—	—	—	—	—	—	—	—	—	131,367
1851	—	—	—	—	—	—	—	—	—	—	—	—	—	—	—	155,165
1852	—	—	—	—	—	—	—	—	—	—	—	—	—	—	—	171,673
1853	—	—	—	—	—	—	—	—	—	—	—	—	—	—	—	188,181
1854	—	—	—	—	—	—	—	—	—	—	—	—	—	—	—	204,689
1855	—	—	—	—	—	—	—	—	—	—	—	—	—	—	—	186,952
1856	—	—	—	—	—	—	—	—	—	—	—	—	—	—	—	195,748
1857	—	—	—	—	—	—	—	—	—	—	—	—	—	—	—	214,779
1858	—	—	—	—	—	—	—	—	—	—	—	—	—	—	—	155,208
1859	—	—	—	—	—	—	—	—	—	—	—	—	—	—	—	193,307
1860	207,305	—	—	21,000 [1]	—	—	—	—	—	—	—	—	—	—	—	207,102
1861	266,400	—	—	16,000 [1]	—	—	—	—	—	—	—	—	—	—	—	202,006
1862	283,000 [1]	—	—	13,000 [1]	—	—	72,866	—	—	—	—	—	—	—	53,040	183,792
1863	260,000 [1]	—	—	11,000 [1]	—	—	312,481	—	—	—	—	—	—	15,884	93,230	238,677
1864	184,346	—	—	9,375	—	—	415,116	—	—	—	—	31,235	—	19,133	169,252	179,158

	Coin			Fractional		Paper notes								Nineteenth-century notes		
								Currency no longer issued								
Fiscal year	Gold	Dollars	Total	Subsidiary silver coin	Minor coin	Federal Reserve notes	U.S. notes	Total	Gold certificates	Silver certificates	Treasury notes of 1890	National bank notes	Federal Reserve Bank notes	Fractional currency	Other U.S. currency	State bank notes
	Cj54	Cj55	Cj56	Cj57	Cj58	Cj59	Cj60	Cj61	Cj62	Cj63	Cj64	Cj65	Cj66	Cj67	Cj68	Cj69
	Thousand dollars	Thousand dollars	Thousand dollars	Thousand dollars	Thousand dollars	Thousand dollars	Thousand dollars	Thousand dollars	Thousand dollars	Thousand dollars	Thousand dollars	Thousand dollars	Thousand dollars	Thousand dollars	Thousand dollars	Thousand dollars
1865	148,557	—	—	8,713	—	—	378,917	—	—	—	—	146,138	—	21,729	236,567	142,920
1866	109,705	—	—	8,241	—	—	327,792	—	10,505	—	—	276,013	—	24,687	162,739	19,996
1867	72,882	—	—	7,082	—	—	319,438	—	18,678	—	—	286,764	—	26,306	123,727	4,484
1868	63,758	—	—	6,520	—	—	328,572	—	17,643	—	—	294,369	—	28,999	28,859	3,164
1869	62,129	—	—	5,695	—	—	314,767	—	29,956	—	—	291,750	—	30,442	3,343	2,559
1870	81,183	—	—	8,978	—	—	324,963	—	32,085	—	—	288,648	—	34,379	2,507	2,223
1871	72,391	—	—	12,022	—	—	343,069	—	17,790	—	—	311,406	—	34,446	1,064	1,968
1872	76,575	—	—	12,064	—	—	346,169	—	26,412	—	—	329,037	—	36,403	849	1,701
1873	62,718	—	—	13,679	—	—	348,464	—	34,251	—	—	338,962	—	38,076	701	1,399
1874	78,948	—	—	14,940	—	—	371,421	—	18,015	—	—	340,266	—	38,234	620	1,162
1875	64,446	—	—	22,141	—	—	349,686	—	17,549	—	—	340,547	—	37,905	551	964
1876	74,839	—	—	26,055	—	—	331,447	—	24,175	—	—	316,121	—	32,939	500	1,047
1877	78,111	—	—	42,885	—	—	337,899	—	32,298	—	—	301,289	—	20,242	456	909
1878	84,740	1,209	—	58,918	—	—	320,906	—	24,898	7	—	311,724	—	16,368	428	806
1879	110,505	8,036	—	61,347	—	—	301,644	—	15,280	414	—	321,405	—	—	—	—
1880	225,696	20,111	—	48,512	—	—	327,895	—	7,964	5,790	—	337,415	—	—	—	—
1881	315,313	29,342	—	46,839	—	—	328,127	—	5,760	39,111	—	349,746	—	—	—	—
1882	358,251	32,404	—	46,380	—	—	325,255	—	5,029	54,506	—	352,465	—	—	—	—
1883	344,653	35,651	—	46,474	—	—	323,242	—	59,807	72,621	—	347,856	—	—	—	—
1884	340,624	40,690	—	45,661	—	—	318,687	—	71,147	96,427	—	330,690	—	—	—	—
1885	341,668	39,087	—	43,703	—	—	331,219	—	126,730	101,531	—	308,631	—	—	—	—
1886	358,220	52,669	—	46,174	—	—	323,813	—	76,044	88,116	—	307,665	—	—	—	—
1887	376,541	55,549	—	48,584	—	—	326,667	—	91,225	142,118	—	276,855	—	—	—	—
1888	391,114	55,527	—	50,362	—	—	308,000	—	121,095	200,760	—	245,313	—	—	—	—
1889	376,482	54,457	—	51,477	—	—	316,439	—	117,130	257,156	—	207,221	—	—	—	—
1890	374,259	56,279	—	54,033	—	—	334,689	—	130,831	297,556	—	181,605	—	—	—	—
1891	407,319	58,826	—	58,219	—	—	343,207	—	120,063	307,236	40,349	162,221	—	—	—	—
1892	408,569	56,817	—	63,294	—	—	339,400	—	141,094	326,693	98,259	167,222	—	—	—	—
1893	408,536	56,930	—	65,470	—	—	330,774	—	92,642	326,824	140,856	174,670	—	—	—	—
1894	495,977	52,565	—	58,511	—	—	325,525	—	66,340	326,991	134,681	200,220	—	—	—	—
1895	479,638	51,986	—	60,350	—	—	319,094	—	48,381	319,623	115,943	206,953	—	—	—	—
1896	454,905	52,117	—	60,204	—	—	256,140	—	42,198	330,657	95,045	215,168	—	—	—	—
1897	517,590	51,940	—	59,616	—	—	306,915	—	37,285	357,849	83,470	226,318	—	—	—	—
1898	657,950	58,483	—	64,057	—	—	310,134	—	35,812	390,127	98,306	222,991	—	—	—	—
1899	679,738	61,481	—	69,066	—	—	328,627	—	32,656	402,137	92,562	237,805	—	—	—	—
1900	610,806	65,889	—	76,161	26,080	—	317,677	—	200,733	408,466	75,304	300,115	—	—	—	—
1901	632,394	66,921	—	79,235	27,890	—	330,045	—	247,036	429,644	47,525	345,111	—	—	—	—
1902	617,261	68,747	—	85,721	29,724	—	334,292	—	306,399	446,558	29,803	345,477	—	—	—	—
1903	645,818	72,391	—	92,727	32,040	—	334,249	—	377,259	454,733	19,077	399,997	—	—	—	—
1904	—	71,314	—	95,528	33,763	—	333,759	—	465,655	461,139	12,902	433,028	—	—	—	—

Notes appear at end of table

(continued)

TABLE Cj54–69 Currency in circulation, by kind: 1800–1999 Continued

Fiscal year	Coin — Gold Cj54 (Thousand dollars)	Coin — Dollars Cj55 (Thousand dollars)	Coin — Total Cj56 (Thousand dollars)	Fractional — Subsidiary silver coin Cj57 (Thousand dollars)	Fractional — Minor coin Cj58 (Thousand dollars)	Federal Reserve notes Cj59 (Thousand dollars)	U.S. notes Cj60 (Thousand dollars)	Total Cj61 (Thousand dollars)	Gold certificates Cj62 (Thousand dollars)	Paper notes, Currency no longer issued — Silver certificates Cj63 (Thousand dollars)	Treasury notes of 1890 Cj64 (Thousand dollars)	National bank notes Cj65 (Thousand dollars)	Federal Reserve Bank notes Cj66 (Thousand dollars)	Nineteenth-century notes — Fractional currency Cj67 (Thousand dollars)	Other U.S. currency Cj68 (Thousand dollars)	State bank notes Cj69 (Thousand dollars)
1905	651,064	73,584	—	101,438	35,458	—	332,421	—	485,211	454,865	9,272	480,029	—	—	—	—
1906	668,655	77,001	—	111,630	38,043	—	335,940	—	516,562	471,520	7,337	548,001	—	—	—	—
1907	561,697	81,710	—	121,777	40,907	—	342,270	—	600,072	470,211	5,976	589,242	—	—	—	—
1908	613,245	76,329	—	124,178	41,139	—	339,396	—	782,977	465,279	4,964	631,649	—	—	—	—
1909	599,338	71,988	—	132,332	42,585	—	340,118	—	815,005	477,717	4,203	665,539	—	—	—	—
1910	590,878	72,433	—	135,584	46,328	—	334,788	—	802,754	478,597	3,663	683,660	—	—	—	—
1911	589,296	72,446	—	138,422	49,049	—	338,989	—	930,368	453,544	3,237	687,701	—	—	—	—
1912	610,724	70,340	—	145,034	50,707	—	337,697	—	943,436	469,224	2,916	705,142	—	—	—	—
1913	608,401	72,127	—	154,458	54,954	—	337,215	—	1,003,998	469,129	2,657	715,754	—	—	—	—
1914	611,545	70,300	—	159,966	57,419	—	337,846	—	1,026,149	478,602	2,428	715,180	—	—	—	—
1915	587,537	64,499	—	159,043	58,516	70,810	309,796	—	821,869	463,147	2,245	782,120	—	—	—	—
1916	624,939	66,234	—	171,178	62,998	149,152	328,227	—	1,050,266	476,279	2,098	716,204	1,683	—	—	—
1917	666,545	71,754	—	193,745	68,411	506,756	311,595	—	1,082,926	468,365	1,970	690,635	3,702	—	—	—
1918	537,230	77,201	—	216,492	74,958	1,698,190	291,859	—	511,190	370,349	1,851	691,407	10,970	—	—	—
1919	474,875	79,041	—	229,316	81,780	2,450,278	274,119	—	327,552	163,445	1,745	639,472	155,014	—	—	—
1920	474,822	76,749	—	248,863	90,958	3,064,742	278,144	—	259,007	97,606	1,656	689,608	185,431	—	—	—
1921	447,272	65,883	—	235,295	91,409	2,599,598	259,170	—	200,582	158,843	1,576	721,421	129,942	—	—	—
1922	415,937	57,973	—	229,310	89,157	2,138,715	292,343	—	173,342	265,335	1,510	727,681	71,868	—	—	—
1923	404,181	57,262	—	247,307	93,897	2,234,660	302,749	—	386,456	364,258	1,460	711,076	19,969	—	—	—
1924	393,330	54,015	—	252,995	96,952	1,843,106	297,790	—	801,381	364,414	1,423	733,835	10,066	—	—	—
1925	402,297	54,289	—	262,009	100,307	1,636,108	282,578	—	1,004,823	382,780	1,387	681,709	6,921	—	—	—
1926	391,703	51,577	—	270,072	104,194	1,679,407	294,916	—	1,057,371	377,741	1,356	651,477	5,453	—	—	—
1927	384,957	48,717	—	275,605	108,132	1,702,843	292,205	—	1,007,075	375,798	1,327	650,057	4,606	—	—	—
1928	377,028	46,222	—	278,175	111,061	1,626,433	298,438	—	1,019,149	384,577	1,304	650,212	4,029	—	—	—
1929	368,488	43,684	—	284,226	115,210	1,692,721	262,188	—	934,994	387,073	1,283	652,812	3,616	—	—	—
1930	357,236	38,629	—	281,231	117,436	1,402,066	288,389	—	994,841	386,915	1,260	650,779	3,206	—	—	—
1931	363,020	34,326	—	273,147	117,393	1,708,429	299,427	—	996,510	377,149	1,240	648,363	2,929	—	—	—
1932	452,763	30,115	—	256,220	113,619	2,780,229	289,076	—	715,683	352,605	1,222	700,894	2,746	—	—	—
1933	320,939	27,995	—	256,865	112,532	3,060,793	268,809	—	265,487	360,699	1,186	919,614	125,845	—	—	—
1934	—	30,013	—	280,400	119,142	3,068,404	279,608	—	149,740	401,456	1,189	901,872	141,645	—	—	—
1935	—	32,308	—	295,773	125,125	3,222,913	285,417	—	117,167	701,474	1,182	704,263	81,470	—	—	—
1936	—	35,029	—	316,476	134,691	4,002,216	278,190	—	100,771	954,592	1,177	366,105	51,954	—	—	—
1937	—	38,046	—	340,827	144,107	4,168,780	281,459	—	88,116	1,078,071	1,172	268,862	37,616	—	—	—
1938	—	39,446	—	341,942	145,625	4,114,338	262,155	—	78,500	1,230,156	1,169	217,441	30,118	—	—	—
1939	—	42,407	—	361,209	154,869	4,483,552	265,962	—	71,930	1,453,573	1,166	186,480	25,593	—	—	—
1940	—	46,020	—	384,187	168,977	5,163,284	247,887	—	66,793	1,581,662	1,163	165,155	22,373	—	—	—
1941	—	52,992	—	433,485	193,963	6,684,209	299,514	—	62,872	1,713,508	1,161	150,460	20,268	—	—	—
1942	—	66,093	—	503,947	213,144	9,310,135	316,886	—	59,399	1,754,255	1,158	139,131	18,717	—	—	—
1943	—	83,701	—	610,005	235,672	13,746,612	322,343	—	56,909	1,648,571	1,155	132,130	584,162	—	—	—
1944	—	103,325	—	700,022	262,775	18,750,201	322,293	—	53,964	1,587,691	1,154	125,887	597,030	—	—	—

		Coin		Fractional		Paper notes			Currency no longer issued					Nineteenth-century notes		
	Gold	Dollars	Total	Subsidiary silver coin	Minor coin	Federal Reserve notes	U.S. notes	Total	Gold certificates	Silver certificates	Treasury notes of 1890	National bank notes	Federal Reserve Bank notes	Fractional currency	Other U.S. currency	State bank notes
Fiscal year	Cj54	Cj55	Cj56	Cj57	Cj58	Cj59	Cj60	Cj61	Cj62	Cj63	Cj64	Cj65	Cj66	Cj67	Cj68	Cj69
	Thousand dollars	Thousand dollars	Thousand dollars	Thousand dollars	Thousand dollars	Thousand dollars	Thousand dollars	Thousand dollars	Thousand dollars	Thousand dollars	Thousand dollars	Thousand dollars	Thousand dollars	Thousand dollars	Thousand dollars	Thousand dollars
1945	—	125,178	—	788,283	291,996	22,867,459	322,587	—	52,084	1,650,689	1,150	120,012	527,001	—	—	—
1946	—	140,319	—	843,122	316,994	23,973,006	316,743	—	50,223	2,025,178	1,149	113,948	464,315	—	—	—
1947	—	148,452	—	875,971	331,039	23,999,004	320,403	—	47,794	2,060,728	1,147	106,429	406,260	—	—	—
1948	—	156,340	—	918,691	346,112	23,600,323	321,485	—	45,158	2,060,869	1,146	99,235	353,499	—	—	—
1949	—	163,894	—	939,568	355,316	23,209,437	318,688	—	42,665	2,060,852	1,145	92,524	308,821	—	—	—
1950	—	170,185	—	964,709	360,886	22,760,285	320,781	—	40,772	2,177,251	1,145	86,488	273,788	—	—	—
1951	—	180,013	—	1,019,824	378,350	23,456,018	318,173	—	39,070	2,092,174	1,145	81,202	243,261	—	—	—
1952	—	191,306	—	1,092,891	393,482	24,605,158	318,330	—	37,855	2,087,811	1,145	77,364	220,584	—	—	—
1953	—	202,424	—	1,150,499	412,952	25,608,669	317,702	—	36,596	2,121,511	1,143	73,403	200,054	—	—	—
1954	—	211,533	—	1,164,912	418,754	25,384,606	320,224	—	35,481	2,135,016	1,142	70,005	180,277	—	—	—
1955	—	223,047	—	1,202,209	432,512	25,617,775	319,064	—	34,466	2,169,726	1,142	66,810	162,573	—	—	—
1956	—	236,837	—	1,258,555	453,044	26,055,247	317,643	—	33,483	2,148,369	1,142	64,239	146,629	—	—	—
1957	—	252,607	—	1,315,325	473,904	26,329,345	321,148	—	32,541	2,161,589	1,142	61,745	132,566	—	—	—
1958	—	267,927	—	1,346,429	486,571	26,341,854	316,851	—	31,797	2,199,532	1,142	59,411	120,225	—	—	—
1959	—	285,491	—	1,415,483	513,876	27,028,617	316,166	—	31,046	2,154,916	1,142	57,385	110,051	—	—	—
1960	—	305,083	—	1,484,033	549,367	27,093,693	318,436	—	30,394	2,126,833	1,142	55,652	99,987	—	—	—
1961	—	328,680	—	1,548,135	585,234	27,352,908	318,338	—	29,803	2,094,379	1,142	54,262	91,811	—	—	—
1962	—	359,590	—	1,663,485	629,423	28,622,224	318,420	—	29,270	2,009,073	142	53,066	84,835	—	—	—
1963	—	411,489	—	1,789,924	676,291	30,291,625	318,537	—	19,858	1,846,537	142	37,148	78,247	—	—	—
1964	—	481,721	—	1,987,138	736,049	32,355,954	320,721	—	19,379	1,722,995	142	36,320	73,276	—	—	—
1965	—	481,698	—	2,355,380	824,585	34,823,233	301,978	—	13,209	829,177	42	22,167	68,333	—	—	—
1966	—	481,694	—	2,907,355	874,769	37,315,989	302,781	—	4,107	581,715	11	21,300	64,301	—	—	—
1967	—	481,691	—	3,238,822	920,815	39,290,336	300,178	—	3,973	394,656	11	20,906	61,057	—	—	—
1968	—	481,689	—	3,877,813	949,604	41,723,506	299,188	—	3,868	225,266	11	20,664	58,854	—	—	—
1969	—	481,688	—	4,260,860	1,047,364	44,547,642	294,478	—	3,804	222,828	11	20,467	56,885	—	—	—
1970	—	481,675	—	4,519,799	1,126,617	47,626,751	296,784	—	3,731	220,061	11	20,271	55,272	—	—	—
1971	—	481,675	—	4,790,952	1,198,961	51,304,990	321,401	—	3,676	217,516	11	20,116	53,894	—	—	—
1972	—	632,899	—	5,100,151	1,283,291	54,572,723	320,276	—	3,609	215,255	11	19,971	52,561	—	—	—
1973	—	704,881	—	5,413,938	1,379,210	59,665,019	319,792	—	3,546	213,456	11	19,843	51,532	—	—	—
1974	—	764,956	—	5,770,589	1,504,082	65,186,131	321,309	—	3,493	211,953	11	19,762	50,830	—	—	—
1975	—	815,566	—	6,069,276	1,611,568	72,093,807	322,200	—	3,464	210,655	11	19,692	50,119	—	—	—
1976	—	940,799	—	6,602,212	1,701,536	79,029,427	321,705	—	3,425	209,491	11	19,645	49,417	—	—	—
(TQ)	—	951,389	—	6,669,300	1,727,364	79,598,211	321,002	—	3,415	209,227	11	19,635	49,357	—	—	—
1977	—	998,932	—	7,017,118	1,859,692	87,350,004	317,338	—	3,390	208,135	11	19,581	48,860	—	—	—
1978	—	1,063,180	—	7,427,862	2,012,735	96,566,832	313,485	—	3,338	207,126	8	19,542	48,455	—	—	—
1979	—	1,434,980	—	7,833,581	2,177,387	106,681,190	311,571	—	3,318	206,508	8	19,511	48,153	—	—	—
1980	—	1,482,744	—	8,342,258	2,352,944	117,152,826	309,542	—	3,300	205,877	8	19,508	47,881	—	—	—
1981	—	1,491,561	11,385,546	—	—	125,047,751	306,779	276,190	—	—	—	—	—	—	—	—
1982	—	1,504,164	11,948,767	—	—	135,173,614	303,346	275,150	—	—	—	—	—	—	—	—
1983	—	1,523,841	12,549,767	—	—	148,167,037	298,840	274,076	—	—	—	—	—	—	—	—
1984	—	1,530,775	13,189,973	—	—	160,043,377	293,641	272,870	—	—	—	—	—	—	—	—

Notes appear at end of table

(continued)

TABLE Cj54–69 Currency in circulation, by kind: 1800–1999 *Continued*

	Coin			Fractional		Paper notes			Currency no longer issued					Nineteenth-century notes		
	Gold	Dollars	Total	Subsidiary silver coin	Minor coin	Federal Reserve notes	U.S. notes	Total	Gold certificates	Silver certificates	Treasury notes of 1890	National bank notes	Federal Reserve Bank notes	Fractional currency	Other U.S. currency	State bank notes
Fiscal year	Cj54	Cj55	Cj56	Cj57	Cj58	Cj59	Cj60	Cj61	Cj62	Cj63	Cj64	Cj65	Cj66	Cj67	Cj68	Cj69
	Thousand dollars	Thousand dollars	Thousand dollars	Thousand dollars	Thousand dollars	Thousand dollars	Thousand dollars	Thousand dollars	Thousand dollars	Thousand dollars	Thousand dollars	Thousand dollars	Thousand dollars	Thousand dollars	Thousand dollars	Thousand dollars
1985	—	1,510,366	13,781,121	—	—	171,481,319	293,003	271,581	—	—	—	—	—	—	—	—
1986	—	1,535,226	14,350,565	—	—	184,175,870	292,335	270,302	—	—	—	—	—	—	—	—
1987	—	1,552,720	14,979,342	—	—	199,672,479	291,754	269,192	—	—	—	—	—	—	—	—
1988	—	1,564,477	15,699,692	—	—	217,671,916	291,138	268,029	—	—	—	—	—	—	—	—
1989	—	1,572,343	16,378,796	—	—	229,070,581	290,385	266,763	—	—	—	—	—	—	—	—
1990	—	1,602,449	17,008,614	—	—	252,731,683	289,633	265,514	—	—	—	—	—	—	—	—
1991	—	1,619,843	17,478,627	—	—	273,778,955	288,461	264,438	—	—	—	—	—	—	—	—
1992	—	1,612,276	18,111,592	—	—	297,617,547	288,116	263,132	—	—	—	—	—	—	—	—
1993	—	1,622,662	18,939,450	—	—	330,414,467	284,811	261,904	—	—	—	—	—	—	—	—
1994	—	1,697,707	19,820,157	—	—	363,501,640	283,464	260,455	—	—	—	—	—	—	—	—
1995	—	1,764,875	20,710,069	—	—	386,257,165	281,118	258,954	—	—	—	—	—	—	—	—
1996	—	1,832,801	21,603,383	—	—	406,514,866	318,626	257,544	—	—	—	—	—	—	—	—
1997	—	1,892,053	22,271,691	—	—	433,566,154	271,783	256,207	—	—	—	—	—	—	—	—
1998	—	1,946,455	22,982,620	—	—	468,747,233	269,662	255,026	—	—	—	—	—	—	—	—
1999	2,012,891	24,537,438		—	—	517,010,907	267,783	253,988	—	—	—	—	—	—	—	—

(TQ) Transition quarter.

1 Total stock; figures for amount held outside the Treasury not available.

Sources

1800–1969: U.S. Department of the Treasury, *Annual Report of the Secretary of the Treasury* (1947), p. 543; (1961), p. 636; (1964), p. 598; (1967), p. 656; and (1970), p. 240. Series Cj69, 1800–1859: *Annual Report of the Comptroller of the Currency* (1916), Volume 2, p. 45.

1970–1980: *Annual Report of the Secretary of the Treasury, Statistical Appendix* (1970), Tables 54, 55, 56; 1971, 1976–1980, Tables 56, 57, 58; 1972–1975, Tables 57, 58, 59.

1981–1982: *Statement of United States Currency and Coin,* as of September 30, 1981, and September 30, 1982 (Department of the Treasury – Fiscal Service, Bureau of Government Financial Operations).

1983–1999: "U.S. Currency and Coin Outstanding and in Circulation," *Treasury Bulletin* (1983–1999).

1994–1999: Some unpublished data regarding currency in circulation by kind were furnished by the Treasury Department's Financial Management Service. Data are not available for other years. Most of these figures also are available, for dates through 1965, in *Circulation Statement of United States Money* and, for dates thereafter, in *[Monthly] Statement of United States Currency and Coin,* both published by the Treasury Department.

Documentation

Figures shown in this table include coin and paper notes issued by the U.S. government and by banks. The term "currency in circulation" refers to currency, regardless of issuer, held outside the Treasury and Federal Reserve banks. The Treasury Department has compiled figures on currency in circulation since 1800. The figures include paper notes held within the United States, paper notes and coin exported or carried abroad, coin (except gold coin since January 30, 1934), paper notes and coins in the vaults of banks, currency lost or destroyed, and gold and silver not appearing in the official gold and silver export figures. The figures exclude gold and silver coin known to have been exported and, beginning January 31, 1934, all gold coin. For further discussion, see *Banking and Monetary Statistics* (1943), section 11; *Banking and Monetary Statistics: 1941–1970* (1976), section 11; and Milton Friedman and Anna J. Schwartz,

Monetary Statistics of the United States: Estimates, Sources, Methods (Columbia University Press, 1970), Chapter 12.

In some historical discussions, currency in circulation has been separated into three components: Treasury currency, Federal Reserve notes, and the monetary gold stock (gold coins and certificates). Although such a schema is not shown here, Treasury currency usually is taken to include standard silver dollars; silver certificates; Treasury notes of 1890; subsidiary silver; minor coin; U.S. notes; and those (older) national bank notes and Federal Reserve Bank notes for which lawful money has been deposited with the Treasury for their redemption (all outstanding Federal Reserve Bank notes and national bank notes have been Treasury currency since March 1935 and August 1935, respectively). (The reader is cautioned not to confuse Federal Reserve Bank notes with Federal Reserve notes; see the text in the following paragraphs for the individual series). For further discussion, see *Banking and Monetary Statistics* (1943), section 11.

The right to redeem currency in specie (gold and silver) is a long and contentious thread in U.S. monetary history. The brief discussion here can do no more than scratch the surface. Major events since the Civil War include the 1875 Resumption Act and the return in 1879 to specie payments at the pre-War parity; the 1933 Congressional abrogation of contractual gold clauses; the 1934 Gold Reserve Act and the prohibition of private gold holdings; and the 1961 Old Series Currency Adjustment Act, which removed specie backing from some older currency. On the early controversies, see Friedman and Schwartz (1970), pp. 79–85 and 462–70. On the Old Series Currency Adjustment Act of 1961 (U.S. Code, Title 31, Section 913), see *Annual Report of the Secretary of the Treasury* (1961). This Act was repealed and replaced in 1982 by Public Law 97-258, the first section of which became the current Title 31 of the U.S. Code.

Annual figures regarding currency in circulation in dollars (rather than thousands of dollars), by kind, are shown in the various annual reports of the Secretary of the Treasury and the Comptroller of the Currency that were cited earlier. The security and reserve provisions applicable to the issuers of various types of currency are described in *The Annual Report of the Secretary of the Treasury, 1972,* p. 245.

TABLE Cj54–69   Currency in circulation, by kind: 1800–1999   *Continued*

Series Cj54. Careful estimates of the amount of gold coin in circulation, 1837–1907, were published in Bureau of the Mint, *Annual Report of the Director of the Mint, 1907*, pp. 66–95. These are the figures reported here. Alternative figures for 1914–1933, which excluded $287 million of gold, were published by the Board of Governors of the Federal Reserve System in *Banking and Monetary Statistics* (1943), p. 409. The Board staff's rationale for excluding $287 million was that when all privately held gold was recalled to the Treasury in January 1934, the amount received was less than the amount believed to be in circulation by approximately $287 million. Board staff asserted that this amount had been largely lost, melted down, or otherwise disappeared from circulation prior to 1934. In *A Monetary History of the United States, 1867–1960* (Princeton University Press, 1963), pp. 463–4, Milton Friedman and Anna Jacobson Schwartz argue that the evidence for the Board's adjustment is not persuasive, and we omit it here.

Series Cj55. Through 1971, the figures shown are for standard silver dollars only. Beginning in 1972, the figures include $481,781,898 in standard silver dollars, in addition to other one-dollar coins in circulation.

Series Cj56–58. Beginning in 1981, individual figures are no longer reported by the Treasury for minor coin and subsidiary silver coin. Rather, the sum is reported as fractional coin.

Series Cj59. Federal Reserve notes are issued by Federal Reserve banks against collateral specified by law. In each Federal Reserve Bank, the *Federal Reserve agent* monitors the issuance of notes and related collateral. Under the Federal Reserve Act, the Federal Reserve agent is a Class C director appointed by the Board of Governors of the Federal Reserve System and the chair of the Bank's board of directors. Acceptable collateral includes gold certificates issued by the Treasury; certain discounted or purchased commercial paper; securities issued by the Treasury; special drawing rights certificates; and certain discounts and advances (loans) made by Federal Reserve banks to depository institutions. Federal Reserve notes issued before the series of 1928 are a part of Treasury currency rather than a liability of the Federal Reserve banks; funds have been deposited by the Federal Reserve banks with the Treasurer of the United States for the redemption of these notes.

Series Cj60. U.S. notes – also referred to as U.S. currency notes and known as the "greenbacks" of the Civil War era – were issued under various acts during 1862 and 1863. These are the only kind of paper money now being issued by the Treasury. Early on, until the requirement was repealed, these notes were secured by a gold reserve. The most common denominations historically have been $2 and $5 notes, but issuance of both denominations had ended by 1968, when the Treasury began issue of a $100 denomination. Although the Act of May 31, 1879, required a permanent issue of $346.7 million, the amount in circulation (outside the Treasury) tended to vary greatly (see, for example, Friedman and Schwartz 1970, Table 8, pp. 179–80). Cur-

rently, Title 31, Section 5115 of the U.S. Code specifies that the amount outstanding and in circulation shall be less than $300 million and that the Secretary of the Treasury is not required to reissue notes after redemption.

Series Cj61–66. Beginning in 1981, the Treasury stopped reporting individual data for gold certificates, silver certificates, Treasury notes of 1890, Federal Reserve Bank notes, and national bank notes. Rather, a combined series, "currency no longer issued," is reported. However, for dates where the series overlap, the reported series Cj61 does not add up exactly to the sum of those items – a discrepancy that was not resolved.

Series Cj62. Prior to 1961, gold certificates were fully secured by gold in the U.S. Treasury. Since 1961, gold certificates that were issued prior to January 30, 1934, are redeemed from the general fund of the Treasury and are retired on redemption – that is, no new certificates are issued (U.S. Code, Title 31, Section 5119). Currently, the Treasury issues gold certificates only to the Federal Reserve. These (special) certificates are not a part of currency in circulation.

Series Cj63. Silver certificates were secured when issued by standard silver dollars and silver bullion held by the Treasury at the monetary value of $1.29+ per fine troy ounce. The Treasury ceased issuing silver certificates in mid-1966. Silver certificates issued on or after July 1, 1929, were redeemable in silver prior to June 24, 1968; after that date, certificates were not redeemable at the Treasury for silver. Today, they are redeemed from the general fund of the Treasury and are retired on redemption (U.S. Code, Title 31, Section 5119).

Series Cj64. Treasury notes of 1890 were issued to purchase silver under provisions of the Act of July 14, 1890 (the Sherman Silver Purchase Act). Within only a few years after issue, the Treasury began to redeem the notes through the issue of silver certificates (Friedman and Schwartz 1970, pp. 179–81). Redeemable in silver and gold until 1961, these notes today are redeemed from the general fund of the Treasury and are retired on redemption (U.S. Code, Title 31, Section 5119).

Series Cj65. National bank notes were issued by national banks against U.S. government securities. These notes have been in the process of retirement since December 23, 1915, when issue of such notes ceased. Lawful money has been deposited with the Treasurer of the United States for their redemption. These notes are retired on redemption.

Series Cj66. Federal Reserve Bank notes, not to be confused with Federal Reserve notes, were issued in 1916–1917, 1918–1920, 1933, and 1942–1943 against U.S. government bonds. Authority to issue such notes was ended by the Act of June 12, 1945, and they have since been in redemption. The Reserve Banks have eliminated their liability for these notes by depositing lawful money with the Treasurer of the United States. See *Banking and Monetary Statistics: 1941–1970*, p. 615, and Friedman and Schwartz (1970), p. 353.

TABLE Cj70–74   Currency stock and currency in circulation, by holder: 1800–1999[1]

Contributed by Richard G. Anderson

Fiscal year	Total Cj70 Thousand dollars	U.S. Treasury Cj71 Thousand dollars	Federal Reserve Banks Cj72 Thousand dollars	In circulation Total Cj73 Thousand dollars	In circulation Outside the United States Cj74 Thousand dollars	Fiscal year	Total Cj70 Thousand dollars	U.S. Treasury Cj71 Thousand dollars	Federal Reserve Banks Cj72 Thousand dollars	In circulation Total Cj73 Thousand dollars	In circulation Outside the United States Cj74 Thousand dollars
1800	28,000	1,500 [3]	—	26,500	—	1880	1,185,550	212,169	—	973,382	—
1810	58,000	3,000 [3]	—	55,000	—	1881	1,349,592	235,355	—	1,114,238	—
1820	69,100	2,000 [3]	—	67,100	—	1882	1,409,398	235,108	—	1,174,290	—
1830	93,100	5,756	—	87,344	—	1883	1,472,494	242,189	—	1,230,306	—
1831 [2]	109,100	6,015	—	93,085	—	1884	1,487,250	243,324	—	1,243,926	—
1832	121,900	4,503	—	117,397	—	1885	1,537,434	244,865	—	1,292,569	—
1833	122,150	2,012	—	120,138	—	1886	1,561,408	308,707	—	1,252,701	—
1834	135,840	11,703	—	124,137	—	1887	1,633,413	315,874	—	1,317,539	—
1835	154,692	8,893	—	145,800	—	1888	1,691,441	319,270	—	1,372,171	—
1836	205,301	5,000 [3]	—	200,301	—	1889	1,658,672	278,311	—	1,380,362	—
1837	222,186	5,000 [3]	—	217,186	—	1890	1,685,123	255,872	—	1,429,251	—
1838	203,639	5,000 [3]	—	198,639	—	1891	1,677,794	180,353	—	1,497,441	—
1839	222,171	2,467	—	219,704	—	1892	1,752,219	150,872	—	1,601,347	—
1840	189,969	3,663	—	186,305	—	1893	1,738,808	142,107	—	1,596,701	—
1841	187,290	987	—	186,303	—	1894	1,805,079	144,270	—	1,660,809	—
1842	163,734	230	—	163,504	—	1895	1,819,360	217,392	—	1,601,968	—
1843	148,564	1,449	—	147,114	—	1896	1,799,975	293,540	—	1,506,435	—
1844	175,168	7,857	—	167,310	—	1897	1,906,770	265,787	—	1,640,983	—
1845	185,609	7,658	—	177,950	—	1898	2,073,574	235,714	—	1,837,860	—
1846	202,552	9,126	—	193,426	—	1899	2,190,094	286,022	—	1,904,072	—
1847	225,520	1,701	—	223,819	—	1900	2,366,220	284,989	—	2,081,231	—
1848	240,506	8,101	—	232,405	—	1901	2,511,472	308,275	—	2,203,198	—
1849	234,743	2,185	—	232,558	—	1902	2,593,910	314,796	—	2,279,114	—
1850	285,367	6,605	—	278,762	—	1903	2,717,646	317,914	—	2,399,732	—
1851	341,165	10,912	—	330,254	—	1904	2,838,023	285,117	—	2,552,906	—
1852	375,673	14,632	—	361,041	—	1905	2,919,494	296,154	—	2,623,340	—
1853	424,181	21,943	—	402,238	—	1906	3,109,380	334,690	—	2,774,690	—
1854	445,689	20,138	—	425,551	—	1907	3,158,111	344,248	—	2,813,863	—
1855	436,952	18,932	—	418,020	—	1908	3,423,068	343,913	—	3,079,155	—
1856	445,748	19,901	—	425,847	—	1909	3,451,521	302,695	—	3,148,826	—
1857	474,779	17,710	—	457,069	—	1910	3,466,856	318,172	—	3,148,684	—
1858	415,208	6,398	—	408,810	—	1911	3,606,989	343,935	—	3,263,053	—
1859	443,307	4,339	—	438,968	—	1912	3,701,965	366,744	—	3,335,220	—
1860	442,102	6,695	—	435,407 [4]	—	1913	3,777,021	358,329	—	3,418,692	—
1861	488,006	3,600	—	484,406 [4]	—	1914	3,797,825	338,391	—	3,459,434	—
1862	629,452	23,754	—	605,698 [4]	—	1915	4,050,783	348,236	382,965	3,319,582	—
1863	1,010,747	79,473	—	931,274 [4]	—	1916	4,541,730	299,127	593,345	3,649,258	—
1864	1,062,841	55,226	—	1,007,615	—	1917	5,678,774	796,005	816,365	4,066,404	—
1865	1,180,197	96,657	—	1,083,541	—	1918	6,906,237	1,568,557	855,984	4,481,697	—
1866	1,068,066	128,388	—	939,678	—	1919	7,688,413	2,001,139	810,636	4,876,638	—
1867	1,020,927	161,567	—	859,360	—	1920	8,158,496	1,675,026	1,015,881	5,467,589	—
1868	888,413	116,529	—	771,884	—	1921	8,174,528	2,001,446	1,262,089	4,910,992	—
1869	873,759	133,118	—	740,641	—	1922	8,276,070	2,515,005	1,297,893	4,463,172	—
1870	899,876	124,909	—	774,966	—	1923	8,702,788	2,671,678	1,207,836	4,823,275	—
1871	894,376	100,220	—	794,156	—	1924	8,846,542	2,620,299	1,376,935	4,849,307	—
1872	900,571	71,361	—	829,209	—	1925	8,299,382	2,116,582	1,367,591	4,815,208	—
1873	903,316	65,065	—	838,252	—	1926	8,428,971	2,070,588	1,473,118	4,885,266	—
1874	950,116	86,510	—	863,606	—	1927	8,667,282	2,062,851	1,753,110	4,851,321	—
1875	925,702	91,912	—	833,789	—	1928	8,118,091	1,738,889	1,582,576	4,796,626	—
1876	905,238	98,114	—	807,124	—	1929	8,538,796	1,935,513	1,856,986	4,746,297	—
1877	916,548	102,458	—	814,090	—						
1878	984,225	164,221	—	820,004	—						
1879	1,033,641	215,009	—	818,632	—						

Notes appear at end of table

TABLE Cj70–74   Currency stock and currency in circulation, by holder: 1800–1999   *Continued*

				In circulation	
		U.S. Treasury	Federal Reserve Banks	Total	Outside the United States
	Total				
	Cj70	Cj71	Cj72	Cj73	Cj74
Fiscal year	Thousand dollars	Thousand dollars	Thousand dollars	Thousand dollars	Thousand dollars
1930	8,306,564	2,043,489	1,741,087	4,521,988	—
1931	9,079,624	2,031,632	2,226,059	4,821,933	—
1932	9,004,505	1,513,985	1,795,349	5,695,171	—
1933	10,078,417	2,085,971	2,271,682	5,720,764	—
1934 [2]	13,634,381	6,953,734	1,305,985	5,373,470	—
1935	15,113,035	8,398,521	1,147,422	5,567,093	—
1936	17,402,493	7,800,438	3,360,854	6,241,200	—
1937	19,376,690	9,475,429	3,454,205	6,447,056	—
1938	20,096,865	10,132,397	3,503,576	6,460,891	—
1939	23,754,736	13,271,527	3,436,467	7,046,743	—
1940	28,457,960	17,124,764	3,485,695	7,847,501	—
1941	32,774,611	19,781,266	3,380,914	9,612,432	—
1942	35,840,908	19,937,577	3,520,465	12,382,866	—
1943	40,868,266	19,676,674	3,770,331	17,421,260	—
1944	44,805,301	18,489,163	3,811,797	22,504,342	—
1945	48,009,400	17,517,449	3,745,512	26,746,438	—
1946	49,648,011	17,539,072	3,863,941	28,244,997	—
1947	50,599,352	18,538,131	3,763,994	28,297,227	—
1948	52,601,129	20,769,375	3,928,896	27,902,859	—
1949	53,103,980	21,736,254	3,874,816	27,492,910	—
1950	52,440,353	21,464,308	3,819,755	27,156,290	—
1951	50,985,939	18,979,646	4,197,063	27,809,230	—
1952	53,853,745	20,610,303	4,217,518	29,025,925	—
1953	54,015,346	19,729,629	4,160,765	30,124,952	—
1954	53,429,405	19,234,197	4,273,259	29,921,949	—
1955	53,308,618	18,989,892	4,089,403	30,229,323	—
1956	54,008,743	19,060,827	4,232,727	30,715,189	—
1957	55,363,063	19,887,518	4,393,632	31,081,913	—
1958	54,058,080	18,642,860	4,243,480	31,171,739	—
1959	53,260,402	16,994,973	4,351,256	31,914,173	—
1960	53,070,922	16,608,562	4,397,741	32,064,619	—
1961	51,947,136	14,818,780	4,723,662	32,404,694	—
1962	52,194,980	13,720,548	4,704,904	33,769,527	—
1963	53,334,680	13,010,106	4,854,775	35,469,798	—
1964	55,450,634	12,760,173	4,956,767	37,733,694	—
1965 [2]	56,689,683	14,411,477	2,554,020	39,719,801	3,736,000
1966	46,641,417	320,797	3,766,598	42,554,022	4,064,000
1967	48,126,693	799,071	2,615,178	44,712,443	4,338,000
1968	51,138,815	496,863	3,001,489	47,640,463	4,555,000
1969	54,019,573	292,960	2,790,588	50,936,024	4,929,000
1970	57,416,085	117,164	2,947,949	54,350,972	5,445,000
1971	61,914,778	197,123	3,324,464	58,393,190	5,983,000
1972	66,351,352	244,633	3,905,971	62,200,747	6,438,000
1973	72,184,607	261,887	4,151,493	67,771,228	7,102,000
1974	78,413,597	167,772	4,412,710	73,833,116	7,957,000
1975	86,689,445	364,281	5,128,806	81,196,358	9,156,000
1976	94,551,377	480,064	5,193,645	88,877,667	10,835,000
(TQ)	96,268,025	495,921	6,223,193	89,548,910	—
1977	104,966,499	434,246	6,709,172	97,823,061	12,759,000
1978	121,272,546	299,299	13,310,683	107,662,564	15,242,000
1979	135,281,270	336,700	16,228,363	118,716,207	18,397,000
1980	150,938,443	465,634	20,555,922	129,916,887	22,341,000
1981	164,107,796	457,114	25,142,854	138,507,828	26,002,000
1982	171,324,130	437,089	21,681,999	149,205,042	29,857,000
1983	188,661,044	479,491	25,367,992	162,813,560	34,711,000
1984	206,119,414	477,929	30,310,848	175,330,637	39,494,000
1985	222,372,875	544,257	34,491,228	187,337,391	44,497,000
1986	241,365,914	495,010	40,246,605	200,624,298	48,074,000
1987	270,944,811	477,550	53,701,774	216,765,487	53,106,000
1988	284,295,559	408,537	48,391,771	235,495,251	59,365,000
1989	297,100,581	441,412	49,080,302	247,578,867	64,895,000
1990	317,134,369	527,367	44,709,109	271,897,893	80,411,000
1991	387,004,877	661,019	92,913,535	293,430,323	96,832,000
1992	378,833,511	568,202	60,374,646	317,890,663	109,634,000
1993	417,285,130	385,389	65,376,447	351,523,294	129,853,000
1994	471,785,273	364,123	85,857,728	385,563,422	150,006,000
1995	496,634,759	315,915	87,046,663	409,272,181	167,128,000
1996	558,179,845	185,408	127,467,217	430,527,220	178,769,000
1997	575,145,363	196,990	116,690,485	458,257,889	201,480,000
1998	606,504,679	69,397	112,234,287	494,200,995	221,751,000
1999	854,531,574	110,940	310,337,624	544,083,009	238,195,000

(TQ) Transition quarter.

[1] Prior to 1860, figures refer to an estimated annual amount, without reference to a specific day or period within the year; for 1860–1976, as of June 30; thereafter, as of September 30.

[2] Figures agree with source; however, they do not add to total shown.

[3] Estimated.

[4] Includes stock of silver dollars and subsidiary silver, 1860–1863, and gold coin and bullion, 1862–1863. It is not practical to present the amounts in circulation separately for these years.

Sources

Series Cj70–73, 1800–1859. U.S. Department of the Treasury, *Annual Report of the Comptroller of the Currency to the Second Session of the Fifty-Fourth Congress of the United States* (December 7, 1896), Volume 1, Table 35, p. 544. These data were repeated, without revision, in some later volumes. The 1916 *Annual Report*, for example, shows the same data in Volume 2, Table 26, p. 44.

Series Cj70–73, 1860–1980. U.S. Department of the Treasury, *Statistical Appendix to Annual Report of the Secretary of the Treasury for the Year Ending June 30, 1980*, Table 57, p. 365. This table contains figures for 1978–1980 and certain earlier years. Figures for years not included in the table are available in the *Statistical Appendix* and *Annual Report of the Secretary of the Treasury* as follows: 1976–1977, *Statistical Appendix* (1977), p. 302; 1972–1974, *Statistical Appendix* (1974), p. 250; 1969–1971, *Statistical Appendix* (1971), p. 234; 1966–1968, *Statistical Appendix* (1968), p. 224; 1962–1964, *Annual Report* (1964), p. 596; 1951–1961, *Annual Report* (1961), p. 634; 1948–1949, *Annual Report* (1956), p. 542; 1860–1947, *Annual Report* (1947), p. 482. Because confusion sometimes arises

regarding sources, it is worth noting previous publication. The figures for 1860–1928 in the 1947 *Annual Report* are the same as those published in the 1928 *Annual Report*, Table 60, pp. 550–1. The figures for 1860–1916 previously appeared in, and often are cited from, the 1916 *Annual Report of the Comptroller of the Currency*, Volume 2, Table 27, pp. 44–5. For 1860–1884, these figures are the same as those in the Treasury's 1928 *Annual Report* but, for dates beginning with 1885, they are not. For details, see the Treasury's 1928 *Annual Report*, pp. 70–1.

Series Cj70–73, 1981–1982. *Statement of United States Currency and Coin, as of September 30, 1981, and September 30, 1982* (Department of the Treasury, Fiscal Service, Bureau of Government Financial Operations).

Series Cj70–73, 1983–1999. "U.S. Currency and Coin Outstanding and in Circulation," *Treasury Bulletin* (1983–1999).

Series Cj70–73. Most of these figures also are available, for dates through 1965, in *Circulation Statement of United States Money* and, for dates thereafter, in *[Monthly] Statement of United States Currency and Coin*, both published by the Treasury.

Series Cj74. Board of Governors of the Federal Reserve System, *Flow of Funds Accounts of the United States: Annual Flows and Outstandings* (March 9, 2001), Table L.204, p. 76, line 22.

Documentation

The term "currency stock" refers to coin, paper currency, and certain amounts of specie (gold and silver) issued in the United States and denominated in U.S. dollars plus, for some periods, gold held outside the United States by

(continued)

TABLE Cj70–74   Currency stock and currency in circulation, by holder: 1800–1999   *Continued*

the Federal Reserve. It includes all currency held by the public outside banks, both in the United States and abroad; all currency held by depository institutions, including currency in automated teller machines; and all issued currency held by the Treasury and the Federal Reserve banks.

Currency in circulation equals the currency stock minus coin, paper currency, and certain specie held by the Treasury and the Federal Reserve. It includes all currency held outside the Treasury and Federal Reserve banks, both in the United States and abroad.

Construction of the figures shown in this table varies somewhat by year.

For 1800–1859, series Cj70 is the sum of all outstanding bank notes and specie (gold and silver) held in the United States. These figures, compiled by the Treasury Department and first published in the 1896 annual report of the Comptroller of the Currency, are recognized as the best available but necessarily are subject to substantial uncertainty.

The Treasury has compiled and published data on the currency stock since 1800. Significant revisions to the published figures and procedures occurred in 1922 and 1927, after which each issue of the Treasury's *Annual Report* or its *Statistical Appendix* included a footnote similar to the following: "The figures from 1860–1889 are the best data available in annual reports of the Secretary of the Treasury. The records are not complete and the figures for gold and silver in those years are only estimates. The figures beginning 1890 were compiled based on revised figures for June 30 of each year and therefore differ slightly from the [previously published] monthly circulation statements." Because Treasury staff carried their efforts backward to figures for earlier dates, the specific revisions are unimportant unless one wishes to compare the revised figures to the previously published monthly currency statements. For details, see *Annual Report of the Secretary of the Treasury* (1922), p. 433, and (1928), pp. 70–1.

For 1915–1933 (when all gold was transferred to the Treasury by the Gold Reserve Act), the currency stock includes the Federal Reserve's holdings of gold bullion and foreign gold coin. Because Federal Reserve money holdings are subtracted from the currency stock to obtain currency in circulation, these items are not included in currency in circulation whether held as a reserve (collateral) against Federal Reserve notes or otherwise. For the same years, the currency stock also includes gold coin and bullion held abroad for the account of the Federal Reserve banks.

For all years, the currency stock and currency in circulation exclude earmarked gold coin (or bullion) held by the Treasury as backing for certain paper note issues (gold and silver certificates and Treasury notes of 1890) that are included in the currency stock. To illustrate the calculation, consider data for June 30, 1930. On this date, the Treasury's total currency stock was $4.022 billion (not shown in this volume) of which $1.978 billion (of gold and silver), earmarked as security against gold and silver certificates and Treasury notes of 1890, is not included in the currency stock. The Federal Reserve's stock was $1.741 billion, and the public's stock was $4.522 billion. The currency stock of the United States equaled $8.307 billion, including $2.044 billion (equals $4.022 billion minus $1.978 billion) held by the Treasury, $1.741 billion held by the Federal Reserve, and $4.522 held by the public. By definition, currency in circulation was $4.522 billion, equal to the currency stock minus the Treasury's currency stock, $2.044 billion, and the Federal Reserve System's currency stock, $1.741 billion. Calculations for later years are similar but are affected by the end of the earmarking of gold and silver in 1961 (the Old Currency Adjustment Act) and the end of the convertibility of silver certificates in 1968. For a detailed discussion

of the specie backing of various paper currencies, see, for example, *Statistical Appendix to Annual Report of the Secretary of the Treasury* (1972), p. 245.

For some years, the currency stock involves a duplication because some included paper currencies (U.S. notes, Federal Reserve notes, Federal Reserve Bank notes, and national bank notes) are, at least in part, secured by gold, which also is included in full. A potential additional duplication is avoided by the omission of earmarked gold held by the Treasury. Otherwise, the currency stock would include both paper notes – gold certificates, silver certificates, and Treasury notes of 1890 – plus the equal amounts of gold or silver held by the Treasury as security for these issues.

For years beginning 1900, the currency stock includes minor coin (the bronze one-cent piece and nickel five-cent piece). Minor coin is not included for earlier years because satisfactory figures are not available.

The Bureau of Printing and Engraving, a part of the U.S. Treasury Department, prints all U.S. currency. Almost all such currency is Federal Reserve notes. Neither the Bureau of Printing and Engraving nor the Treasury, however, issues currency to the public. Federal Reserve notes are issued into circulation only by Federal Reserve banks, acting as agents for the Treasury. At the time of issue, the Bank must pledge certain collateral against the notes. Until such collateral is posted and the newly printed notes are issued to the public, printed paper notes are not part of the U.S. currency stock and are not included in this table. For details, see the footnotes to the money stock tables in the 1980 *Statistical Appendix to Annual Report of the Secretary of the Treasury*.

Series Cj70. This series is as calculated and published by the Treasury. As discussed earlier, it excludes gold and silver held by the Treasury as security against gold certificates, silver certificates, and Treasury notes of 1890.

Series Cj71. Prior to 1860, the figures consist of specie only; the Treasury held little, if any, paper currency and figures are not available. Beginning in 1860, the figures include coin, bullion, and paper currency. The figures exclude gold and silver held by the Treasury as security against gold and silver certificates and Treasury notes of 1890 because an equal amount of these paper currencies is also included. For 1860–1933, prior to the Gold Reserve Act, these paper currencies are referred to by the Treasury as currency outside the Treasury. Beginning in 1934, they are referred to either as currency outside the Treasury or as currency amounts held in the Treasury for Federal Reserve banks and agents, payable in gold certificate.

Series Cj74. In recent years, a great deal of U.S. currency has been exported. In countries with political turmoil and uncertainty regarding future inflation, U.S. currency is an attractive liquid asset and, often, a popular medium of exchange. See, for example, Richard D. Porter and Ruth A. Judson, "The Location of U.S. Currency: How Much Is Abroad?" *Federal Reserve Bulletin* 82 (October 1996): 883–903. In 1997, quarterly estimates of the amount of U.S. currency held abroad were introduced into the Federal Reserve's flow-of-funds accounts and the Bureau of Economic Analysis's estimates of the net international investment position of the United States. At that time, the latter reduced the estimated net foreign asset position of the United States by more than $300 billion. See Russell B. Scholl, "The International Investment Position of the United States in 1996," *Survey of Current Business* (July 1997): 24–33. The figures shown here for 1964–1999 are from the Federal Reserve Board's flow-of-funds accounts, as of March 2001. The estimates suggest that about 11 percent of currency outside banks was held abroad in 1964 and about 45 percent in 1999.

TABLE Cj75–83 Monetary aggregates, by type of financial institution: 1959–1999

Contributed by Richard G. Anderson

	At commercial banks					At thrift institutions			
				Time deposits				Time deposits	
	Demand deposits adjusted	Other checkable deposits	Savings deposits	Small denomination	Large denomination	Other checkable deposits	Savings deposits	Small denomination	Large denomination
	Cj75	Cj76	Cj77	Cj78	Cj79	Cj80	Cj81	Cj82	Cj83
Year	Billion dollars	Billion dollars	Billion dollars	Billion dollars	Billion dollars	Billion dollars	Billion dollars	Billion dollars	Billion dollars
1959	111.3	(Z)	52.9	9.6	1.4	(Z)	88.0	2.4	0.0
1960	111.2	0.0	55.5	9.5	1.5	(Z)	96.2	2.7	0.0
1961	113.8	0.0	61.2	11.0	3.2	(Z)	106.3	3.3	0.0
1962	116.2	0.0	67.6	14.4	5.5	(Z)	117.5	4.2	0.0
1963	119.2	0.0	74.2	18.0	8.8	0.1	131.3	5.2	0.0
1964	123.1	0.0	79.5	21.4	13.1	0.1	145.5	6.2	0.0
1965	127.9	0.0	87.6	25.3	18.4	0.1	159.0	7.2	0.0
1966	133.2	0.0	90.5	33.7	23.3	0.1	164.3	11.8	0.0
1967	138.0	0.0	91.7	45.5	28.9	0.1	166.8	22.0	0.0
1968	147.8	(Z)	95.0	57.4	32.7	0.1	170.4	32.5	0.0
1969	156.2	0.0	94.7	68.3	28.3	0.1	171.5	42.8	0.0
1970	160.9	0.0	94.5	74.3	30.1	0.2	160.7	62.7	0.4
1971	171.4	0.0	107.0	88.2	50.7	0.2	171.9	84.2	1.2
1972	183.7	0.0	119.4	101.4	63.2	0.2	188.1	110.2	2.0
1973	196.1	0.0	125.9	113.5	93.7	0.3	199.2	136.9	3.0
1974	203.2	(Z)	132.0	121.0	129.0	0.4	199.6	158.3	4.4
1975	208.7	0.2	149.5	133.8	128.9	0.5	216.2	180.3	6.2
1976	216.4	0.8	183.2	146.9	115.7	1.0	240.4	216.8	7.0
1977	230.1	1.6	213.4	163.8	118.3	1.9	263.3	259.2	9.0
1978	246.0	2.5	220.6	175.0	159.7	2.8	273.9	303.4	13.9
1979	253.9	10.7	205.7	209.3	183.2	3.7	247.2	372.7	23.5
1980	259.7	16.6	187.0	265.3	197.1	5.4	217.8	421.4	39.3
1981	235.5	53.5	166.4	321.8	237.9	12.9	193.7	465.6	49.9
1982	230.2	71.6	162.7	375.8	262.4	19.3	188.8	482.5	58.9
1983	237.0	90.8	342.5	336.3	220.0	30.9	316.5	415.5	75.7
1984	241.7	101.5	374.6	371.4	239.6	38.7	319.3	469.5	125.6
1985	254.8	115.5	432.1	386.7	259.7	48.9	341.1	498.8	150.2
1986	280.9	140.8	493.5	382.2	273.1	64.4	379.2	499.7	155.8
1987	294.1	174.6	542.8	371.7	289.8	79.7	416.5	497.8	151.6
1988	288.7	188.2	545.8	419.7	321.0	86.0	395.3	566.5	169.8
1989	279.9	192.1	526.6	504.0	369.6	86.1	355.8	610.2	172.6
1990	277.0	203.9	564.3	571.3	372.0	87.2	351.0	590.9	138.7
1991	279.7	224.8	622.5	616.6	355.8	88.0	362.1	514.4	99.5
1992	318.7	261.9	719.5	546.3	309.3	98.4	416.5	401.6	72.9
1993	362.6	292.5	769.9	485.4	275.7	107.5	433.1	331.9	64.2
1994	386.1	299.6	778.0	473.5	281.3	110.6	423.9	306.7	62.4
1995	385.9	276.0	740.0	555.9	323.1	105.5	369.3	345.9	71.1
1996	403.7	205.0	845.9	583.3	377.5	106.5	364.3	353.3	76.0
1997	397.3	155.6	963.1	611.3	457.1	98.5	373.5	349.3	82.3
1998	383.3	145.8	1,104.8	627.2	526.6	101.2	397.0	336.4	86.8
1999	362.3	140.9	1,253.6	621.3	549.6	104.6	442.9	318.3	89.7

(Z) Less than $0.05 billion.

Sources
Division of Monetary Affairs, Board of Governors of the Federal Reserve System, Washington, D.C. These data are as of May 2000. Revised data are available on the Internet from the Federal Reserve Board Internet site and the Federal Reserve Bank of St. Louis Internet site. For current definitions and data, see the Board's weekly H.6 release, "Monetary Aggregates and the Monetary Base," and the *Federal Reserve Bulletin*.

Documentation
Data are annual averages of monthly, not seasonally, adjusted figures.

Series Cj75. Demand deposits are deposits at commercial banks and some foreign-related institutions in the United States that, under law, may be immediately transferred to a third party or withdrawn in currency. *Demand deposits adjusted* excludes demand deposits due to the U.S. Treasury, due to other banks (interbank deposits), and due to foreign banks and official institutions. It also excludes *float*, that is, the deposit amounts for which checks

are in the process of collection. Because sorting, transporting, and collecting checks take some time, the aggregate amount of demand deposits reported by all banks exceeds, by the value of checks in collection, the dollar amount of deposits available to households and firms for spending. Subtracting float removes these excess deposits.

Series Cj76 and Cj80. *Other checkable deposits* at commercial banks (including branches and agencies of foreign banks located in the United States and Edge Act corporations) consist of negotiable order of withdrawal (NOW) and automatic transfer service (ATS) accounts. (Edge Act corporations are subsidiaries of U.S. commercial banks, located in the United States, that are restricted to conducting international banking business only.) *Other checkable deposits* at thrift institutions include NOW and ATS accounts at mutual savings banks, share draft accounts at credit unions, and certain demand deposits at thrift institutions. In most cases, these deposits are savings deposits for which a depository institution has a right to require prior notice of withdrawal. In practice, such notice is never requested, and depositors regard the accounts as immediately available funds. Regulations limit the

(continued)

TABLE Cj75–83 Monetary aggregates, by type of financial institution: 1959–1999 *Continued*

use of such checkable deposits by businesses, and hence most are held by households, nonprofit organizations, and state and local governments. These series also are referred to as *other deposits transferable by check*.

Series Cj77 and Cj81. *Savings deposits* include passbook and statement savings accounts, and money market deposit accounts (MMDA). Savings deposits exclude deposits transferable by check except for MMDA, an unusual hybrid of transaction and savings deposits that was created by Congress in 1982. By statute, MMDA customers are permitted no more than six third-party withdrawals each month, by check or transfer. The Federal Reserve ceased collecting separate data on MMDA accounts in 1992; since that time, depositories have reported to the Federal Reserve only their combined total of MMDA and other savings deposits.

Series Cj75–77 and Cj80–81. Beginning January 1994, the amounts reported to the Federal Reserve have been increased (savings deposits series) or decreased (other series) by the spread of retail-deposit sweep programs. See the text for series Cj99.

Series Cj78–79 and Cj82–83. Time deposits are deposits with initial maturity of seven days or more. (For some older dates, this category consists of deposits with initial maturity of fourteen days or more.) *Small-denomination time deposits* are those of less than $100,000; *large-denomination time deposits* are those of $100,000 or more. Deposits at commercial banks with less than the minimum maturity are classified as demand deposits; deposits at thrifts with less than the minimum maturity are classified as savings deposits. Often, these deposits are referred to as "certificates of deposit" even when no certificate is issued. For some older dates, these figures include so-called retail repurchase agreements issued in amounts of less than $100,000. The figures exclude all deposits held as part of an individual retirement account or, for self-employed workers, as a Keogh account. The figures also exclude all time deposits held by other financial firms whose liabilities are included in the monetary aggregates – for example, time deposits issued by banks to money market mutual funds are excluded from these figures.

TABLE Cj84–99 Federal Reserve Board monetary aggregates and major components: 1959–1999
Contributed by Richard G. Anderson

	M1 money stock				M2 money stock				M3 money stock				L money stock		Nonfinancial-sector debt	Retail sweep program deposits
	Total	Currency held by the nonbank public	Demand deposits adjusted	Other deposits transferable by check	Total	Savings deposits	Small-denomination time deposits	Retail-type money market mutual fund shares	Total	Large-denomination time deposits	Institutional-type money market mutual fund shares	Repurchase agreements and Eurodollars	Total	Treasury bills, bankers' acceptances, and commercial paper held by the nonbank public		
	Cj84	Cj85	Cj86	Cj87	Cj88	Cj89	Cj90	Cj91	Cj92	Cj93	Cj94	Cj95	Cj96	Cj97	Cj98	Cj99
Year	Billion dollars	Billion dollars	Billion dollars	Billion dollars	Billion dollars	Billion dollars	Billion dollars	Billion dollars	Billion dollars	Billion dollars	Billion dollars	Billion dollars	Billion dollars	Billion dollars	Billion dollars	Billion dollars
1959	140.4	28.7	111.3	0.0	293.3	140.9	12.0	0.0	295.4	1.4	0.0	0.7	382.8	87.4	662.5	—
1960	140.3	28.8	111.2	0.0	304.3	151.8	12.2	0.0	306.6	1.5	0.0	0.8	396.2	89.6	703.7	—
1961	143.1	28.9	113.8	0.0	324.8	167.5	14.3	0.0	329.3	3.2	0.0	1.3	417.8	88.5	740.1	—
1962	146.5	29.8	116.2	0.0	350.1	185.1	18.5	0.0	357.1	5.5	0.0	1.5	449.4	92.3	789.5	—
1963	150.9	31.3	119.2	0.1	379.6	205.5	23.2	0.0	390.2	8.8	0.0	1.8	486.3	96.1	843.6	—
1964	156.8	33.2	123.1	0.1	409.4	225.0	27.6	0.0	424.6	13.1	0.0	2.2	522.6	98.0	902.0	—
1965	163.5	34.9	128.0	0.1	442.5	246.6	32.5	0.0	462.9	18.4	0.0	2.0	563.3	100.4	968.4	—
1966	171.0	37.1	133.2	0.1	471.4	254.9	45.5	0.0	496.6	23.3	0.0	1.9	602.0	105.4	1,037.6	—
1967	177.7	39.0	138.0	0.1	503.6	258.5	67.5	0.0	534.6	28.9	0.0	2.1	642.1	107.5	1,101.1	—
1968	190.1	41.6	147.8	0.1	545.3	265.3	89.8	0.0	580.9	32.7	0.0	2.9	699.2	118.3	1,188.4	—
1969	201.4	44.4	156.2	0.1	578.7	266.2	111.1	0.0	610.6	28.3	0.0	3.6	747.2	136.6	1,279.0	—
1970	209.1	47.2	160.9	0.2	601.4	255.2	137.1	0.0	638.3	30.5	0.0	6.4	787.1	148.8	1,366.0	—
1971	223.2	50.6	171.4	0.2	674.4	278.9	172.4	0.0	732.8	51.8	0.0	6.6	863.5	130.7	1,479.8	—
1972	239.0	54.0	183.7	0.2	758.1	307.5	211.6	0.0	832.7	65.2	0.0	9.3	963.7	131.0	1,623.4	—
1973	256.4	58.6	196.1	0.3	831.8	325.1	250.3	(Z)	943.7	96.7	0.0	15.2	1,091.1	147.4	1,806.2	—
1974	269.2	64.1	203.2	0.4	880.8	331.6	279.3	0.6	1,036.3	133.3	0.1	22.1	1,206.4	170.1	1,980.2	—
1975	281.4	70.1	208.7	0.7	964.0	365.7	314.1	2.8	1,122.7	135.0	0.3	23.2	1,305.8	183.1	2,152.1	—
1976	297.2	76.6	216.4	1.8	1,087.1	423.7	363.7	2.5	1,243.8	122.7	0.5	33.6	1,445.7	201.9	2,375.8	—
1977	320.0	83.6	230.1	3.5	1,222.1	476.8	423.0	2.4	1,396.1	127.3	0.8	45.9	1,615.0	218.9	2,652.1	—
1978	340.3	91.9	246.0	5.3	1,323.3	494.5	478.4	4.2	1,564.3	173.6	2.3	65.1	1,809.2	244.9	3,012.1	—
1979	372.7	100.9	253.9	14.5	1,426.8	452.8	582.0	19.3	1,737.9	206.7	6.9	97.5	2,032.6	294.7	3,402.3	—
1980	395.7	110.4	259.7	22.0	1,541.6	404.7	686.7	54.4	1,902.0	236.4	15.3	108.6	2,226.3	324.4	3,763.3	—
1981	424.9	119.0	235.5	66.4	1,681.0	360.2	787.4	108.5	2,133.5	287.8	26.0	138.7	2,482.3	348.8	4,143.2	—
1982	453.0	127.8	230.2	90.9	1,835.0	351.5	858.3	172.2	2,371.1	321.3	42.8	172.0	2,756.0	384.9	4,561.4	—
1983	503.2	140.1	237.0	121.7	2,059.6	659.0	751.8	145.7	2,593.6	295.7	43.0	195.3	3,027.1	433.5	5,062.9	—
1984	538.7	152.0	241.7	140.2	2,224.3	694.0	841.0	150.8	2,856.8	365.2	48.2	219.1	3,375.1	518.3	5,758.9	—
1985	587.0	162.3	254.8	164.5	2,422.1	773.2	885.6	176.3	3,111.2	409.9	64.5	214.7	3,690.1	578.9	6,591.5	—
1986	666.5	174.4	280.9	205.3	2,619.1	872.6	881.8	198.2	3,368.9	428.9	78.9	241.9	3,994.6	625.7	7,514.0	—
1987	743.6	188.8	294.1	254.3	2,789.2	959.4	869.6	216.6	3,606.4	441.4	86.9	288.9	4,252.2	645.8	8,305.0	—
1988	775.0	205.3	288.7	274.2	2,939.7	941.1	986.2	237.5	3,838.2	490.8	93.2	314.5	4,540.4	702.2	9,070.8	—
1989	782.5	217.6	279.9	278.2	3,063.4	882.4	1,114.2	284.3	4,016.6	542.3	101.3	309.6	4,802.4	785.8	9,815.8	—
1990	811.1	235.5	277.0	291.1	3,231.7	915.2	1,162.1	343.2	4,129.1	510.7	120.7	266.1	4,963.6	834.5	10,512.9	—
1991	859.5	259.5	279.7	312.8	3,351.9	984.6	1,131.0	376.7	4,202.5	455.3	163.2	232.1	5,029.8	827.3	11,060.7	—
1992	966.3	279.5	318.7	360.3	3,416.2	1,136.0	947.9	365.9	4,226.1	382.2	209.4	218.4	5,073.7	847.6	11,561.9	—
1993	1,079.0	308.3	362.6	400.0	3,455.3	1,203.1	817.3	356.0	4,236.1	340.0	207.1	233.7	5,131.9	895.8	12,097.9	—
1994	1,145.5	340.9	386.1	410.2	3,503.3	1,201.9	780.2	375.7	4,303.8	343.7	196.4	260.4	5,257.4	953.6	12,694.8	8.0
1995	1,143.1	366.7	385.9	381.5	3,575.2	1,109.3	901.7	421.1	4,499.9	394.2	232.3	298.2	5,563.6	1,063.7	13,357.9	25.1
1996	1,106.3	382.2	403.7	311.5	3,747.0	1,210.2	936.5	493.9	4,796.4	453.5	285.4	310.5	5,944.7	1,148.3	14,071.2	115.9
1997	1,069.9	409.9	397.3	254.1	3,931.6	1,336.6	960.6	564.5	5,179.1	539.3	347.1	361.0	6,404.3	1,225.2	14,802.0	220.6
1998	1,080.7	442.0	383.3	247.0	4,221.0	1,501.7	963.6	675.0	5,710.1	613.4	446.9	428.8	6,944.3	1,234.2	15,759.8	293.1
1999	1,102.4	486.2	362.3	245.5	4,538.2	1,696.5	939.6	799.7	6,208.5	639.3	558.5	472.5		—	16,831.6	348.9

TABLE Cj84–99   Federal Reserve Board monetary aggregates and major components: 1959–1999   *Continued*

(Z) Less than $0.05 billion.

Sources

Division of Monetary Affairs, Board of Governors of the Federal Reserve System, Washington, D.C. These data are as of May 2000. Revised data are available on the Internet from the Federal Reserve Board Internet site and the Federal Reserve Bank of St. Louis Internet site. For current definitions and data, see the Board's weekly H.6 release, "Monetary Aggregates and the Monetary Base," and the *Federal Reserve Bulletin*.

Documentation

Data are annual averages of monthly, not seasonally, adjusted data.

In what follows, the term *depository institution* includes commercial banks and those thrift institutions (mutual saving banks, credit unions, and savings and loan associations) that issue deposits transferable by check and are subject to the Federal Reserve System's statutory reserve requirements.

Series Cj84. Equals the sum of series Cj85–87.

Series Cj85. *Currency held by the nonbank public* consists of U.S. currency held outside the Treasury, Federal Reserve banks, and the vaults of depository institutions plus the outstanding amount of U.S. dollar-denominated traveler's checks issued by nonbank financial institutions (including subsidiaries of bank holding companies). Traveler's checks issued by commercial banks are included in demand deposits.

Series Cj86–87 and Cj89. Beginning January 1994, the amounts reported to the Federal Reserve have been increased (savings deposit series) or reduced (other series) by the spread of retail-deposit sweep programs; see the text for series Cj99.

Series Cj86. Demand deposits are deposits at commercial banks and some foreign-related institutions that, under law, may be immediately transferred to a third party or withdrawn in currency. *Demand deposits adjusted* exclude demand deposits due to the U.S. Treasury, due to other banks (interbank deposits), and due to foreign banks and official institutions. They also exclude *float*, that is, the deposit amounts for which checks are in the process of collection. Because sorting, transporting, and collecting checks take some time, the aggregate amount of demand deposits reported by all banks exceeds, by the value of checks in collection, the dollar amount of deposits available to households and firms for spending. Subtracting float removes these excess deposits.

Series Cj87. *Other deposits transferable by check* include negotiable order of withdrawal and automatic transfer service accounts at depository institutions; share draft accounts at credit unions; and certain demand deposits at thrift institutions. Regulations concerning these deposits vary by type of financial institution. In most cases, these deposits, in fact, are savings deposits for which a depository institution has a right to require prior notice of withdrawal. In practice, such notice is never requested, and depositors regard the accounts as immediately available funds. Regulations limit the use of such checkable deposits by businesses, and hence most are held by households, nonprofit organizations, and state and local governments.

Series Cj88. Equals the sum of series Cj84 and Cj89–91.

Series Cj89. *Savings deposits* include passbook and statement savings accounts, and money market deposit accounts (MMDA). Savings deposits exclude deposits transferable by check except for MMDA, an unusual hybrid of transaction and savings deposits that was created by Congress in 1982. At the time, its proponents argued that the MMDA would enable banks and thrifts to better compete for deposits against retail-type money market mutual funds. By statute, MMDA customers are permitted no more than six third-party withdrawals each month, by check or transfer. The Federal Reserve ceased collecting separate data on MMDA accounts in 1992; since that time, depositories have reported to the Federal Reserve only their combined total of MMDA and savings deposits.

Series Cj90. *Small-denomination time deposits* consist of deposits at commercial banks and thrift institutions in amounts of less than $100,000 with a fixed maturity of seven days or more. For some older dates, this category consists of deposits with a maturity of fourteen days or more. Deposits at commercial banks with less than the minimum maturity are classified as

demand deposits; deposits at thrifts with less than the minimum maturity are classified as savings deposits. Often, these deposits are referred to as "certificates of deposit" even when no certificate is issued. For some older dates, these figures include so-called retail repurchase agreements issued in amounts of less than $100,000. The figures exclude all deposits held as part of an individual retirement account (IRA) or, for self-employed workers, as a Keogh account.

Series Cj91. *Retail-type money market mutual funds* are mutual funds that satisfy Securities and Exchange Commission (SEC) rules for marketing to smaller, less sophisticated investors. Such funds usually require an initial investment of less than $50,000 and, by SEC rules, hold as assets highly liquid, short-maturity, low default-risk money market instruments such as prime commercial paper, Treasury bills, and certificates of deposit issued by large banks. These figures exclude mutual fund shares held as part of an IRA or, for self-employed workers, as a Keogh account.

Series Cj92. Equals the sum of series Cj88 and Cj93–95.

Series Cj93. *Large-denomination time deposits* consist of deposits in amounts of $100,000 or more with initial maturity of seven days or more. *Negotiable certificates of deposit*, usually issued in amounts of $1 million or more, are a special type of time deposit. Ownership of such deposits may be bought and sold freely prior to maturity, but the depository may not pay out the deposited funds prior to maturity.

Series Cj94. *Institutional-type money market mutual funds* are funds that agree to abide by SEC rules intended to discourage sale of the funds to smaller, less sophisticated investors. Such funds often require initial investments of $50,000 or more. Estimates by the mutual fund industry suggest that individuals hold approximately one fourth of institutional-type money market mutual shares; the balance is held by corporations, pension funds, and similar investors.

Series Cj95. *Repurchase agreements* (RPs) are contracts in which a depository institution sells a security (perhaps a Treasury bill) to a customer while agreeing to the date and price at which it will repurchase the security. The economics of entering into a repurchase agreement are similar to those of issuing a large-denomination time deposit: simultaneously, the customer obtains an interest-bearing investment and the depository acquires new liquid funds. *Eurodollar deposits* are U.S. dollar-denominated deposits in banks outside the United States held by owners with U.S. addresses. Deposits due to depository institutions in the United States are excluded. The figures include such deposits at all foreign offices of U.S. banks and at offices of all banks in Canada and the United Kingdom.

Series Cj96. The L monetary aggregate, intended to measure the total stock of liquid assets held by the nonbank public, equals the sum of series Cj92 and Cj97. Publication of the L monetary aggregate was discontinued in 1998.

Series Cj97. In addition to the deposit-type assets previously discussed, households and firms hold several types of highly liquid, low default-risk liquid assets. *Treasury bills* are short-term debt instruments of the U.S. government issued in three-, six-, and twelve-month maturities. *Bankers' acceptances* are debt instruments issued by business firms and payable at a specified future date. For a fee, a bank has "accepted" the debt and guarantees payment at maturity. *Commercial paper* is a short-term debt instrument issued by large banks and well-known corporations.

Series Cj98. *Nonfinancial-sector debt* includes all credit-market debt issued by households, firms, and state and federal governments. It excludes debt issued by government-sponsored enterprises and related mortgage securities, but includes home mortgages, corporate bonds, consumer credit, bank loans, and commercial paper. Although constructed from the same underlying sources, these figures are adjusted for discontinuities in available data and hence differ from those reported in the Federal Reserve Board's flow-of-funds accounts. In addition, these figures are estimates of month-average debt levels, while the flow-of-funds figures are last-day-of-the-quarter estimates.

Series Cj99. *Retail sweep program deposits* are estimates of the amounts of transaction deposits being reclassified as MMDA deposits in retail deposit sweep programs. A retail deposit sweep program consists of computer software that reclassifies transaction deposits (demand deposits and/or other checkable deposits) as MMDA for the purpose of reducing a depository

TABLE Cj84–99 Federal Reserve Board monetary aggregates and major components: 1959–1999 *Continued*

institution's statutory reserve requirements. Introduced in January 1994, retail deposit sweep programs had expanded by December 1999 to include almost $370 billion of transaction deposits. Because retail deposit sweep programs are invisible to depository institutions' customers, it seems unlikely that the programs have affected the demand for M1. If so, then the M1 monetary aggregate, series Cj84, which seeks to measure the amount of currency and transaction deposits that households and firms perceive them-

selves to hold, is understated by the amount of reclassified deposits. For further discussion, see Richard Anderson and Robert Rasche, "Retail Deposit Sweep Programs and Bank Reserves 1994-1999," *Federal Reserve Bank of St. Louis Review* 83 (January/February 2001). This article and these data are available from the Internet site of the Federal Reserve Bank of St. Louis. Separate data on the amounts swept from demand deposits and from other checkable deposits are not available.

TABLE Cj100–107 Divisia monetary aggregates – monetary services and real dual user cost indexes: 1960–1999

Contributed by Richard G. Anderson

	Monetary services indexes				Real dual user cost indexes			
	MSI-M1	MSI-M2	MSI-M3	MSI-L	MSI-M1	MSI-M2	MSI-M3	MSI-L
	Cj100	Cj101	Cj102	Cj103	Cj104	Cj105	Cj106	Cj107
Year	Billion dollars	Billion dollars	Billion dollars	Billion dollars	Billion dollars	Billion dollars	Billion dollars	Billion dollars
1960	102.04	318.71	341.32	414.65	56.44	31.22	29.33	28.58
1961	103.86	336.50	362.50	434.67	56.79	30.62	28.77	28.50
1962	106.46	357.80	387.56	463.50	56.25	26.78	25.09	24.85
1963	109.90	381.35	415.35	494.99	52.98	24.53	22.90	22.24
1964	114.47	406.15	444.76	526.67	51.55	23.70	22.04	21.11
1965	119.51	432.30	475.53	560.05	52.28	21.33	19.73	18.93
1966	125.19	454.54	501.45	589.56	66.21	33.88	31.24	29.91
1967	130.44	479.20	530.67	620.13	65.92	34.45	32.10	31.19
1968	139.52	514.35	570.52	667.73	73.06	41.28	38.12	36.58
1969	147.91	543.54	600.59	707.21	105.41	70.76	65.30	63.02
1970	154.09	565.54	627.48	738.53	96.11	60.50	55.94	53.82
1971	164.54	630.48	712.17	812.72	95.01	55.47	52.74	52.60
1972	176.21	704.03	803.09	902.81	89.10	51.94	49.66	49.64
1973	189.15	770.18	895.67	1,007.32	107.93	65.23	58.25	56.54
1974	199.50	814.77	956.67	1,078.53	123.16	78.36	68.79	66.44
1975	209.86	891.05	1,040.37	1,171.85	113.07	74.14	71.34	71.24
1976	222.60	999.52	1,149.04	1,294.92	104.31	64.49	63.45	63.80
1977	239.89	1,118.71	1,282.53	1,440.25	94.55	55.76	54.06	53.82
1978	260.10	1,211.90	1,416.38	1,591.52	99.31	63.46	57.78	56.00
1979	281.28	1,296.27	1,527.41	1,723.35	122.42	78.21	68.43	65.24
1980	300.38	1,375.23	1,626.68	1,832.38	154.50	112.27	101.27	98.20
1981	329.84	1,468.80	1,753.15	1,969.58	168.45	124.14	109.50	104.99
1982	354.29	1,566.31	1,880.13	2,114.45	153.46	131.54	122.60	119.33
1983	387.38	1,647.30	1,965.22	2,225.83	130.55	107.84	104.28	101.92
1984	414.71	1,772.25	2,143.37	2,451.25	133.50	102.52	98.48	96.50
1985	449.28	1,907.88	2,314.97	2,658.13	122.73	101.38	99.97	98.62
1986	503.50	2,044.40	2,486.24	2,855.70	102.00	80.86	80.17	79.80
1987	555.05	2,160.56	2,639.51	3,018.00	104.69	92.12	90.15	89.80
1988	581.40	2,300.18	2,825.22	3,234.87	106.58	87.67	84.05	82.81
1989	591.84	2,390.50	2,946.33	3,399.27	97.51	59.14	52.55	50.13
1990	618.24	2,513.24	3,065.67	3,544.02	100.69	69.77	65.19	63.46
1991	659.56	2,603.53	3,138.01	3,613.39	97.81	83.22	81.84	81.50
1992	736.45	2,599.80	3,108.43	3,592.16	100.00	100.00	100.00	100.00
1993	820.57	2,593.39	3,082.26	3,590.15	92.31	93.13	92.91	92.69
1994	873.66	2,619.29	3,117.68	3,654.10	99.44	102.32	99.27	97.43
1995	876.50	2,680.85	3,237.99	3,825.02	94.40	79.20	73.72	70.02
1996	845.92	2,777.50	3,393.70	4,020.60	93.50	82.41	77.74	74.80
1997	822.66	2,893.19	3,598.56	4,257.37	91.11	78.65	73.30	69.98
1998	839.06	3,083.51	3,896.79	—	85.96	70.23	64.39	—
1999	866.51	3,292.04	4,191.70	—	94.61	85.91	80.39	—

Source

Internet site of the Federal Reserve Bank of St. Louis – Monetary Services Index Project. Data are as of September 2000.

Documentation

Monetary Services Indexes (MSI) measure the flow of monetary services received each period by households and firms from their holdings of monetary assets. Levels of these indexes are sometimes referred to as Divisia monetary aggregates. Unlike conventional monetary aggregates, such as the figures

published by the Federal Reserve Board (see Table Cj84–99), the MSI and their dual user cost indexes are statistical index numbers based on economic aggregation theory. Perhaps the definitive reference is William A. Barnett and Apostolos Serletis, *The Theory of Monetary Aggregation* (Elsevier, 2000). The indexes presented here are discussed in Richard Anderson, Barry Jones, and Travis Nesmith, "The Monetary Services Index Project of the Federal Reserve Bank of St. Louis," *Federal Reserve Bank of St. Louis Review* 79 (January/February 1997): 25-82. The variables shown in this table are defined in Richard

TABLE Cj100–107   Divisia monetary aggregates – monetary services and real dual user cost indexes: 1960–1999
Continued

Anderson, Barry Jones, and Travis Nesmith, "Building New Monetary Services Indexes: Concepts, Data and Methods," *Federal Reserve Bank of St. Louis Review* 79 (January/February 1997), p. 57, Table 1, section A. These publications are available at the Federal Reserve Bank of St. Louis Internet site.

The annual index-number figures shown here are constructed directly from annual data. The underlying data, including figures such as the amounts of various assets held by households and firms, are annual averages of monthly, not seasonally, adjusted figures.

Series Cj100–103. These MSI are nominal Törnqvist-Theil index numbers, as defined in Anderson, Jones, and Nesmith (1997). The index numbers are constructed for four levels of aggregation – M1, M2, M3, and L – corresponding to the aggregation levels of the Federal Reserve Board's currently published monetary aggregates.

Series Cj100. MSI-M1 is constructed from figures on currency, nonbank traveler's checks, demand deposits, other checkable deposits at commercial banks and thrift institutions, and Super negotiable order of withdrawal (NOW) accounts at commercial banks and thrift institutions.

Series Cj101. MSI-M2 is constructed from the figures used in MSI-M1 plus money market deposit accounts at commercial banks and thrift institutions, savings deposits at commercial banks and thrift institutions,

small-denomination time deposits at commercial banks and thrift institutions, and retail money market mutual funds.

Series Cj102. MSI-M3 is constructed from the figures used in MSI-M2 plus total repurchase agreements, total Eurodollar deposits, total large-denomination time deposits at commercial banks and thrift institutions, and institutional money market mutual funds.

Series Cj103. MSI-L is constructed from the figures used in MSI-M3 plus U.S. savings bonds, short-term Treasury securities, bankers' acceptances, and commercial paper.

Series Cj103 and Cj107. Discontinued after September 1998 owing to unavailability of data.

Series Cj104–107. Figures are real dual user cost indexes, as defined in Anderson, Jones, and Nesmith (1997). These indexes are dual to the MSI quantity indexes in the sense that, for each of the levels of aggregation, the corresponding quantity and user cost indexes satisfy the Fisher weak factor-reversal test. The user cost indexes are constructed from the same figures on the quantities of assets held by households and firms as are the corresponding MSI quantity indexes, plus figures on households' and firms' real (inflation-adjusted) total expenditures (or, alternatively, opportunity costs) incurred due to holding these assets.

MONETARY POLICY

David C. Wheelock

TABLE Cj108–112   U.S. monetary standards – official value of the dollar: 1792–1973

Contributed by Michael D. Bordo

Year	Official value of U.S. dollar in fine grains		U.S. Mint ratio	Official U.S. dollar price of fine troy ounce	
	Gold	Silver		Gold	Silver
	Cj108	Cj109 [1]	Cj110	Cj111	Cj112 [1]
	Fine grains	Fine grains	Ratio	Dollars	Dollars
1792	24.75	371.25	15.00	19.39	1.29
1834	23.20	371.25	16.00	20.69	1.29
1837	23.22	371.25	15.98	20.67	1.29
1879 [2]	23.22	—	—	20.67	—
1913	23.22	—	—	20.67	—
1934	13.71	— [3]	—	35.00	— [3]
1972	12.63	—	—	38.00	—
1973	11.37	—	—	42.22	—

[1] The Coinage Act of 1792 fixed the value of the dollar at 371.25 fine grains of silver, or $1.29 per fine ounce of silver. Thereafter, the official price of the dollar in terms of silver remained unchanged, even after silver was demonetized in 1879.

[2] Silver is demonetized; however, the official book price of silver remains $1.29 per fine ounce.

[3] Under the Thomas Amendment, coinage of domestically produced silver began at the official price of $1.2929 per fine ounce, although seignorage fees of 50 percent were charged, making the effective official price of silver $0.6464 per fine ounce.

Source

Report to the Congress of the Commission on the Role of Gold in the Domestic and International Monetary Systems (1982), Volume 1, Chapter 2, pp. 51–110.

Documentation

The Coinage Act of 1792 established a bimetallic standard in the United States. The value of the dollar was defined to be 371.25 grains of pure silver or 24.75 grains of pure gold (that is, the official mint ratio was 15 : 1). However, the United States operated on a de facto silver standard until 1834 as the market price of gold rose above the official 15 : 1 ratio. By 1834, the market ratio had risen to 15.625 : 1. Largely for political reasons, the official mint ratio was set higher than this market ratio at 16 : 1; thus, the official price of gold was set at $20.67 per fine troy ounce (see Milton Friedman,

Money Mischief (Harcourt, Brace, 1986), p. 56). Given this discrepancy between official and market prices of gold, the United States remained on a de facto gold standard until the beginning of the Civil War. During the war, convertibility of the Union currency was suspended, resulting in a temporary fiduciary standard – the greenback standard. Resumption of a specie standard on the basis of gold came into effect on January 1, 1879. The value of the dollar was set at the pre–Civil War level, with a fine troy ounce of gold continuing to be valued at $20.67. After a brief embargo on gold exports from September 1917 to June 1919 during World War I, full convertibility was resumed, and the legal price of gold remained at $20.67 per fine troy ounce until the United States abandoned the gold standard in April 1933. The currency was then devalued in stages before finally being pegged at $35 per fine troy ounce on January 31, 1934. (See Milton Friedman and Anna Schwartz, *A Monetary History of the United States, 1860–1960* (Princeton University Press, 1963), p. 465.) During the Bretton Woods period, from 1944 to 1971, gold continued to be valued at $35 per fine troy ounce; however, the United States was the only country maintaining a peg with gold. On August 15, 1971, Richard Nixon closed the gold window and broke the final link with gold. In 1973, the official price of gold was raised to $42.22, where it has since remained.

TABLE Cj113–117   Federal Reserve monetary policy – interest rates: 1914–1999

Contributed by David C. Wheelock

	Discount rate							Discount rate				
	Lowest during year	Highest during year	Annual average	Buying rate on 1- to 90-day acceptances	Average federal funds trading rate			Lowest during year	Highest during year	Annual average	Buying rate on 1- to 90-day acceptances	Average federal funds trading rate
	Cj113	Cj114	Cj115	Cj116 [1]	Cj117			Cj113	Cj114	Cj115	Cj116 [1]	Cj117
Year	Percent	Percent	Percent	Percent	Percent		Year	Percent	Percent	Percent	Percent	Percent
1914	5.00	6.00	5.50	—	—		1960	3.00	4.00	3.50	—	3.22
1915	4.00	5.00	4.08	—	—		1961	3.00	3.00	3.00	—	1.96
1916	3.00	4.00	3.67	—	—		1962	3.00	3.00	3.00	—	2.71
1917	3.00	3.50	3.04	—	—		1963	3.00	3.50	3.25	—	3.18
1918	3.50	4.00	3.88	—	—		1964	3.50	4.00	3.58	—	3.50
1919	4.00	4.75	4.13	4.750 [2]	—		1965	4.00	4.50	4.04	—	4.07
1920	4.75	7.00	6.58	5.750 [2]	—		1966	4.50	4.50	4.50	—	5.11
1921	4.50	7.00	5.88	4.125 [2]	—		1967	4.00	4.50	4.21	—	4.22
1922	4.00	4.50	4.21	3.875 [2]	—		1968	4.50	5.50	5.21	—	5.66
1923	4.00	4.50	4.46	4.000 [2]	—		1969	5.50	6.00	5.88	—	8.20
1924	3.00	4.50	3.67	2.750 [2]	—		1970	5.50	6.00	5.94	—	7.18
1925	3.00	3.50	3.46	3.250 [2]	—		1971	4.50	5.50	4.83	—	4.66
1926	3.50	4.00	3.83	3.500 [2]	—		1972	4.50	4.50	4.50	—	4.43
1927	3.50	4.00	3.79	3.000 [2]	—		1973	4.50	7.50	6.54	—	8.73
1928	3.50	5.00	4.54	4.500	—		1974	7.50	8.00	7.85	—	10.50
1929	4.50	6.00	5.17	4.000	—		1975	6.00	7.75	6.21	—	5.82
1930	2.00	4.50	2.96	1.750	—		1976	5.25	6.00	5.46	—	5.05
1931	1.50	3.50	2.17	3.000 [2]	—		1977	5.25	6.00	5.52	—	5.54
1932	2.50	3.50	2.75	1.000	—		1978	6.00	9.50	7.54	—	7.93
1933	2.00	3.50	2.50	0.500	—		1979	9.50	12.00	10.38	—	11.19
1934	1.50	2.00	1.54	0.500	—		1980	10.00	13.00	11.75	—	13.36
1935	1.50	1.50	1.50	0.500	—		1981	12.00	14.00	13.42	—	16.38
1936	1.50	1.50	1.50	0.500	—		1982	8.50	12.00	10.88	—	12.26
1937	1.00	1.50	1.29	0.500	—		1983	8.50	8.50	8.50	—	9.09
1938	1.00	1.00	1.00	0.500	—		1984	8.00	9.00	8.75	—	10.23
1939	1.00	1.00	1.00	0.500	—		1985	7.50	8.00	7.67	—	8.10
1940	1.00	1.00	1.00	0.500	—		1986	5.50	7.50	6.25	—	6.81
1941	1.00	1.00	1.00	0.500	—		1987	5.50	6.00	5.67	—	6.66
1942	0.50	1.00	0.88	0.500	—		1988	6.00	6.50	6.21	—	7.57
1943	0.50	0.50	0.50	0.500	—		1989	6.50	7.00	6.96	—	9.22
1944	0.50	0.50	0.50	0.500	—		1990	6.50	7.00	6.96	—	8.10
1945	0.50	0.50	0.50	0.500	—		1991	3.50	6.50	5.33	—	5.69
1946	0.50	1.00	0.88	1.000	—		1992	3.00	3.50	3.25	—	3.52
1947	1.00	1.00	1.00	1.125	—		1993	3.00	3.00	3.00	—	3.02
1948	1.00	1.50	1.35	1.500	—		1994	3.00	4.75	3.67	—	4.20
1949	1.50	1.50	1.50	1.500	—		1995	4.75	5.25	5.21	—	5.84
1950	1.50	1.75	1.60	1.750	—		1996	5.00	5.25	5.00	—	5.30
1951	1.75	1.75	1.75	1.875	—		1997	5.00	5.00	5.00	—	5.46
1952	1.75	1.75	1.75	1.875	—		1998	4.50	5.00	4.90	—	5.35
1953	1.75	2.00	2.00	2.125	—		1999	4.50	5.00	4.65	—	4.97
1954	1.50	2.00	1.58	1.500	1.07							
1955	1.50	2.50	1.92	—	1.78							
1956	2.50	3.00	2.79	—	2.73							
1957	3.00	3.50	3.13	—	3.11							
1958	1.75	3.00	2.13	—	1.57							
1959	2.50	4.00	3.42	—	3.30							

[1] Rates at the lower end of a range were applied to shorter maturities.

[2] Minimum rate is given, but source provides a range. The maximum rates in this range are as follows: 1919, 5.00; 1920, 6.00; 1921, 4.25; 1922, 4.00; 1923, 4.125; 1924, 3.00; 1925, 3.375; 1926, 3.75; 1927, 3.25; 1931, 3.125.

Sources

Board of Governors of the Federal Reserve System. 1914–1941, *Banking and Monetary Statistics, 1914–1941*, pp. 439–45; 1942–1970, *Banking and Monetary Statistics, 1941–1970*, pp. 667–70, 689; 1971–1999, *Annual Statistical Digest* (annual issues).

These data are updated monthly in the *Federal Reserve Bulletin* and are available from the Federal Reserve Board Internet site.

Documentation

Series Cj113–115. The Federal Reserve Bank of New York discount rates shown are the lowest and highest rates during the year, and an annual average of month-end rates, on discounts for and advances to depository institutions under Sections 13 and 13a of the Federal Reserve Act. For the period before 1921, when a multiplicity of rates prevailed, discount rates on paper of a single class and maturity – usually the type of paper and maturity for which the rate was lowest – are shown. Specifically, from November 16, 1914, the day the Reserve Banks opened, through August 1916, the rate applies to discounts of commercial, agricultural, and livestock paper with maturities of from 31 to 60 days; and from September 1916 to December 1920, to

TABLE Cj113–117   Federal Reserve monetary policy – interest rates: 1914–1999   *Continued*

discounts of, and advances secured by, commercial, agricultural, and live-stock paper with maturities of 15 days or less. For 1942–1945, the low rate shown is the preferential rate for advances secured by U.S. government securities maturing or callable in one year or less. In this period, the rate of 1 percent was continued for discounts of eligible paper and advances secured by such paper or by U.S. government obligations with maturities beyond one year.

Series Cj116. The Federal Reserve Bank of New York acceptance buying rate shown is the minimum rate prevailing at the end of the calendar year on prime bankers' acceptances maturing in 90 days or less. Comparable data prior to

1919 are unavailable. On March 2, 1955, the Federal Reserve discontinued setting official buying rates and authorized open-market purchases and sales of acceptances at market rates of discount. In 1977, the Federal Reserve suspended transactions in bankers' acceptances on an outright basis, and in 1984, the Federal Reserve discontinued the use of repurchase agreements involving bankers' acceptances. In 1998, the Federal Reserve formally terminated its authority to conduct any transactions in bankers' acceptances.

Series Cj117. The federal funds trading rate shown is a weighted average of rates on trades through New York brokers (annual average of daily trading rates). These data are available only since 1954.

TABLE Cj118–130   Depository institution reserve funds – sources, uses, and reserves: 1917–1999

Contributed by David C. Wheelock

	Sources					Uses			Reserves				
	Federal Reserve												
Year	Security holdings	Loans to depository institutions	Total credit outstanding	Gold and special drawing rights	U.S. Treasury currency outstanding	Currency in circulation	U.S. Treasury cash holdings and deposits at Federal Reserve banks	Other Federal Reserve accounts	Reserve balances with Federal Reserve banks	Vault cash available to meet reserve requirements	Required	Excess	Free
	Cj118	Cj119	Cj120	Cj121	Cj122	Cj123	Cj124	Cj125	Cj126	Cj127	Cj128	Cj129	Cj130
	Million dollars	Million dollars	Million dollars	Million dollars	Million dollars	Million dollars	Million dollars	Million dollars	Million dollars	Million dollars	Million dollars	Million dollars	Million dollars
1917	288	376	778	2,871	1,911	3,865	314	109	1,272	—	—	—	—
1918	421	1,134	1,723	2,871	1,867	4,371	391	203	1,497	—	—	—	—
1919	578	1,906	2,625	2,842	1,716	4,729	464	270	1,719	—	—	—	—
1920	709	2,523	3,390	2,582	1,695	5,191	293	347	1,835	—	—	—	—
1921	345	1,797	2,198	3,004	1,758	4,663	263	364	1,671	—	—	—	—
1922	614	571	1,226	3,515	1,871	4,248	268	316	1,781	—	—	—	—
1923	413	736	1,205	3,774	1,991	4,535	255	307	1,873	—	—	—	—
1924	574	373	996	4,152	2,017	4,592	260	290	2,023	—	—	—	—
1925	646	490	1,195	4,094	2,000	4,582	244	295	2,167	—	—	—	—
1926	631	572	1,258	4,165	1,985	4,645	242	312	2,209	—	—	—	—
1927	680	442	1,175	4,277	2,000	4,605	226	331	2,290	—	—	—	—
1928	625	840	1,505	3,919	2,008	4,496	225	356	2,355	—	—	—	—
1929	449	952	1,459	3,996	2,015	4,476	229	406	2,358	—	2,315	43	−909
1930	777	272	1,087	4,173	2,025	4,245	239	421	2,379	—	2,324	55	−217
1931	914	327	1,274	4,417	2,025	4,672	251	470	2,323	—	2,234	89	−238
1932	1,532	521	2,077	3,952	2,096	5,328	275	407	2,114	—	1,858	256	−265
1933	2,135	283	2,429	4,059	2,271	5,576	343	497	2,343	—	1,788 [1]	528 [1]	245
1934	2,457	36	2,502	7,512	2,381	5,403	2,879	438	3,676	—	2,104 [1]	1,564 [1]	1,528
1935	2,436	7	2,475	9,059	2,478	5,585	2,919	507	5,001	—	2,532	2,469	2,462
1936	2,435	6	2,481	10,578	2,503	6,101	2,920	551	5,989	—	3,477	2,512	2,506
1937	2,507	14	2,554	12,162	2,567	6,475	3,384	595	6,830	—	5,610	1,220	1,206
1938	2,566	9	2,600	13,250	2,711	6,510	3,457	658	7,935	—	5,413	2,522	2,513
1939	2,584	5	2,628	16,085	2,879	7,058	3,307	877	10,352	—	5,960	4,392	4,387
1940	2,417	4	2,487	19,865	3,018	7,879	2,796	1,446	13,249	—	6,923	6,326	6,322
1941	2,187	5	2,293	22,546	3,156	9,594	2,917	2,082	13,404	—	8,080	5,324	5,319
1942	3,191	7	3,408	22,729	3,324	12,687	2,498	1,628	12,648	—	9,980	2,668	2,661
1943	7,724	25	8,182	22,371	4,025	17,617	2,596	1,739	12,626	—	11,116	1,510	1,485
1944	14,772	135	15,358	21,204	4,105	22,557	2,733	2,156	13,222	—	12,176	1,046	911
1945	21,363	376	22,211	20,255	4,186	26,855	2,799	1,942	15,055	—	13,934	1,121	745
1946	23,258	310	24,029	20,283	4,510	28,292	2,870	1,691	15,969	—	14,993	976	666
1947	22,330	219	22,989	21,383	4,555	28,421	2,419	1,627	16,461	—	15,608	853	634
1948	21,511	331	22,283	23,516	4,566	28,064	2,759	1,542	18,001	—	17,164	837	506
1949	19,560	231	20,161	24,432	4,592	27,519	2,080	1,811	17,774	—	16,952	822	591
1950	18,410	129	19,062	23,903	4,608	27,175	1,894	2,104	16,400	—	15,617	783	654
1951	22,756	293	24,070	22,027	4,659	27,824	1,784	1,855	19,293	—	18,536	757	464
1952	23,066	801	24,801	23,253	4,756	29,065	1,701	1,687	20,356	—	19,642	714	−87
1953	24,661	777	26,262	22,422	4,850	30,137	1,664	1,738	19,996	—	19,319	677	−100
1954	24,646	217	25,602	21,885	4,949	30,030	1,315	1,815	19,276	—	18,501	775	558

Note appears at end of table

(continued)

TABLE Cj118–130   Depository institution reserve funds – sources, uses, and reserves: 1917–1999   *Continued*

	Sources					Uses			Reserves				
	Federal Reserve												
	Security holdings	Loans to depository institutions	Total credit outstanding	Gold and special drawing rights	U.S. Treasury currency outstanding	Currency in circulation	U.S. Treasury cash holdings and deposits at Federal Reserve banks	Other Federal Reserve accounts	Reserve balances with Federal Reserve banks	Vault cash available to meet reserve requirements	Required	Excess	Free
	Cj118	Cj119	Cj120	Cj121	Cj122	Cj123	Cj124	Cj125	Cj126	Cj127	Cj128	Cj129	Cj130
Year	Million dollars	Million dollars	Million dollars	Million dollars	Million dollars	Million dollars	Million dollars	Million dollars	Million dollars	Million dollars	Million dollars	Million dollars	Million dollars
1955	23,904	666	25,472	21,690	5,000	30,252	1,289	1,779	18,843	—	18,257	586	−80
1956	23,732	833	25,702	21,810	5,033	30,689	1,271	1,619	18,965	—	18,403	562	−271
1957	23,372	850	25,373	22,494	5,106	31,006	1,236	1,710	19,021	—	18,504	517	−333
1958	24,694	295	25,982	21,563	5,199	31,181	1,180	1,738	18,647	—	18,057	590	295
1959	26,229	812	28,089	19,949	5,273	31,799	1,045	1,856	18,611	25	18,191	447	−353
1960	26,412	436	28,008	19,010	5,357	32,059	922	1,529	17,865	664	17,980	547	119
1961	27,439	83	28,839	17,384	5,482	32,510	895	1,573	16,725	2,538	18,662	601	522
1962	29,571	137	31,299	16,359	5,580	33,778	910	1,457	17,095	2,785	19,356	520	418
1963	31,824	269	33,837	15,734	5,581	35,511	1,283	1,489	16,869	3,020	19,441	447	196
1964	24,700	295	36,879	15,460	5,551	37,718	1,338	1,434	17,399	3,271	20,276	395	105
1965	39,749	492	41,071	14,260	5,443	39,901	1,651	1,073	18,149	3,572	21,341	377	−91
1966	41,980	650	44,720	13,458	5,933	42,524	1,726	911	18,950	3,893	22,481	358	−277
1967	46,253	178	48,067	13,020	6,609	44,774	2,232	872	19,817	4,173	23,621	371	196
1968	51,376	569	53,858	10,707	6,771	47,730	1,864	148	21,594	4,457	25,692	346	−215
1969	54,112	1,103	59,838	10,367	6,777	50,891	1,486	1,907	22,698	4,685	27,145	238	−867
1970	58,260	835	63,623	11,641	6,989	54,186	1,608	3,146	23,314	4,997	28,116	193	−610
1971	65,431	412	69,922	10,796	7,400	58,072	1,780	3,144	25,121	5,325	30,234	202	−210
1972	71,063	322	75,744	10,588	8,039	62,174	2,244	3,119	26,834	5,667	32,364	207	−114
1973	76,159	1,678	81,617	11,048	8,510	67,617	2,873	3,768	26,917	6,218	33,062	226	−1,442
1974	83,450	2,054	89,470	11,972	8,911	73,960	2,472	4,251	29,670	6,784	36,287	178	−1,266
1975	89,247	195	94,805	12,075	9,618	80,674	3,762	4,272	27,790	7,237	34,848	199	31
1976	97,439	84	103,910	12,319	10,593	88,433	7,742	4,440	26,207	7,981	34,119	221	139
1977	104,239	461	111,301	12,828	11,123	96,554	7,856	4,335	26,506	8,694	34,977	213	−248
1978	114,415	871	123,386	12,960	11,598	106,208	8,342	5,011	28,383	9,525	37,781	202	−668
1979	117,813	1,339	131,201	12,946	12,371	116,587	3,574	5,547	30,810	10,455	41,195	225	−1,114
1980	128,336	1,416	139,965	14,197	13,258	127,305	3,516	5,698	30,903	11,550	42,372	276	−950
1981	130,858	1,361	145,255	14,102	13,595	136,911	3,632	5,810	26,570	14,150	40,410	313	−943
1982	139,918	1,052	152,761	15,048	13,774	146,452	4,265	6,002	24,627	15,885	40,149	362	−520
1983	151,466	1,039	162,969	15,750	13,786	159,015	4,573	6,017	22,016	16,796	38,323	489	−177
1984	161,292	3,730	175,361	15,723	16,083	173,923	4,904	8,263	20,078	17,820	37,237	675	−389
1985	175,048	1,321	190,064	15,732	16,759	185,535	4,623	8,703	23,695	19,399	42,251	815	191
1986	192,514	836	209,990	15,936	17,322	198,875	5,151	9,012	30,214	21,080	50,356	887	542
1987	216,635	756	234,685	16,092	17,869	214,822	7,627	9,676	36,515	22,905	58,297	1,007	557
1988	231,442	2,357	251,152	16,082	18,490	233,219	5,442	10,056	36,987	24,880	60,801	1,027	499
1989	232,302	1,140	263,423	18,336	19,334	248,622	7,715	10,549	34,096	26,559	59,677	977	460
1990	236,441	926	278,138	19,850	20,039	267,054	6,045	11,854	32,890	28,221	60,142	969	509
1991	256,496	373	292,708	21,078	20,730	291,991	7,493	12,023	23,104	27,757	49,690	1,170	877
1992	282,855	172	315,172	20,949	21,237	312,903	6,883	14,020	23,576	29,091	51,641	1,025	854
1993	320,260	180	352,753	19,073	21,726	343,850	7,033	16,154	26,494	31,237	56,653	1,079	899
1994	353,656	259	387,493	19,071	22,540	379,420	6,217	17,174	26,293	33,892	59,118	1,067	808
1995	375,807	203	410,130	20,234	23,486	408,050	6,502	17,958	21,316	36,220	56,525	1,011	808
1996	390,014	202	422,440	21,026	24,516	426,008	5,974	20,294	15,730	37,136	51,775	1,091	889
1997	417,446	276	449,300	20,298	25,283	454,049	7,107	22,920	10,772	36,381	45,858	1,296	1,020
1998	446,851	162	480,271	20,246	25,843	486,049	6,495	24,187	9,637	35,527	43,642	1,521	1,360
1999	485,550	221	529,819	19,038	27,062	536,750	5,918	25,268	8,015	34,851	41,625	1,242	1,021

[1] Includes average balances of unlicensed banks; see text.

Sources

Board of Governors of the Federal Reserve System. 1914–1941, *Banking and Monetary Statistics, 1914–1941*, p. 368; 1942–1970, *Banking and Monetary Statistics, 1942–1970*, pp. 524–5; 1971–1999, *Annual Statistical Digest* (annual issues).

These data are updated monthly in the *Federal Reserve Bulletin* and are available from the Federal Reserve Board Internet site.

Documentation

Values are annual averages of daily figures. For additional detail about the data shown in this table, see *Banking and Monetary Statistics, 1942–1970*, pp. 509–21.

Series Cj118–120. Series Cj120 consists of Federal Reserve holdings of U.S. government and agency securities and bankers' acceptances (series Cj118), Federal Reserve loans to depository institutions (series Cj119), and miscellaneous items, including Federal Reserve Bank float, Federal Reserve deposits in foreign banks, and other items. Beginning in 1969, Federal Reserve credit is the sum of all Federal Reserve assets.

Series Cj121. Beginning in 1934, includes only gold and special drawing rights held by the U.S. Treasury. For prior years, this series includes gold coin in circulation and gold held by Federal Reserve banks.

Series Cj122. Beginning in 1966, includes standard silver dollars, fractional coin, and U.S. notes. For prior years, this series also includes silver bullion against the pledge of which silver certificates and Treasury notes of 1890

TABLE Cj118–130   Depository institution reserve funds – sources, uses, and reserves: 1917–1999   *Continued*

were outstanding, subsidiary silver, and those notes issued by national banks and Federal Reserve banks for the retirement of which funds have been deposited with the Treasurer of the United States.

Series Cj123. Includes all U.S. money outside of the Federal Reserve banks and U.S. Treasury, except gold and silver coin known to have been exported and, beginning in 1934, all gold coin outstanding. The principal components of currency in circulation are Federal Reserve notes and Treasury currency outstanding.

Series Cj124. Includes Treasury holdings of currency and coin, and the general account of the U.S. Treasurer with the Federal Reserve.

Series Cj125. For 1917–1968, includes deposits with Federal Reserve banks other than those of the U.S. Treasury and depository institution reserve accounts, Federal Reserve Bank capital accounts, and other liabilities, less Reserve Bank premises and other assets. For 1969–1999, the series excludes Reserve Bank premises and other assets, which are included in total Federal Reserve credit.

Series Cj126. Consists of depository institution deposits with Federal Reserve banks that may be used to satisfy statutory reserve requirements. They do not include other depository institution deposits, such as contracted clearing balances, that are not used to satisfy reserve requirements.

Series Cj127. Includes currency and coin held by depository institutions that may be used to satisfy statutory reserve requirements. Until June 21, 1917, and since December 1, 1959, commercial banks were authorized to count part of their vault cash as legal reserves. Since November 23, 1960, this privilege was extended to include all vault cash.

Series Cj128–130. Depository institutions are required to hold reserve balances with Federal Reserve banks or vault cash equal to a fixed fraction of their outstanding deposit liabilities. This sum is termed required reserves and is shown in series Cj128. Federal Reserve requirements were applicable only to Federal Reserve member banks until 1980, but to all depository institutions since then. Excess reserves equal depository institution holdings of reserve deposits with Federal Reserve banks and vault cash in excess of what is required. Free reserves equal the excess reserves of depository institutions less Federal Reserve loans to depository institutions, series Cj119. Series Cj128–129 include average balances of unlicensed banks as follows: $27 million in 1933 and $8 million in 1934. Required and excess reserves for March 1933 were estimated by the Federal Reserve; from then through April 1934, they cover licensed banks only. After April 1934, the Federal Reserve made no distinction between reports from licensed and unlicensed banks.

TABLE Cj131–134   Depository institution reserve requirements: 1913–1992

Contributed by David C. Wheelock

	Effective date		Central reserve city banks	Reserve city banks	Country banks	Time deposits
	Central reserve city or reserve city banks	Country banks	Cj131	Cj132	Cj133	Cj134
Year			Percent	Percent	Percent	Percent
1913	Dec 23	—	18.00	15.0	12.00	5.00
1917	Jun 21	—	13.00	10.0	7.00	3.00
1936	Aug 16	—	19.50	15.0	10.50	4.50
1937	Mar 01	—	22.75	17.5	12.25	5.25
1937	May 01	—	26.00	20.0	14.00	6.00
1938	Apr 16	—	22.75	17.5	12.00	5.00
1941	Nov 01	—	26.00	20.0	14.00	6.00
1942	Aug 20	—	24.00	20.0	14.00	6.00
1942	Sep 14	—	22.00	20.0	14.00	6.00
1942	Oct 03	—	20.00	20.0	14.00	6.00
1948	Feb 27	—	22.00	20.0	14.00	6.00
1948	Jun 11	—	24.00	20.0	14.00	6.00
1949	Sep 16	Sep 24	26.00	22.0	16.00	7.50
1949	May 01	May 05	24.00	21.0	15.00	7.00
1949	Jun 30	Jul 01	24.00	20.0	14.00	6.00
1949	Aug 01	—	24.00	20.0	13.00	6.00
1949	Aug 11	Aug 16	23.50	19.5	12.00	5.00
1949	Aug 18	—	23.00	19.0	12.00	5.00
1949	Aug 25	—	22.50	18.5	12.00	5.00
1949	Sep 01	—	22.00	18.0	12.00	5.00
1951	Jan 11	Jan 16	23.00	19.0	13.00	6.00
1951	Jan 25	Feb 01	24.00	20.0	14.00	6.00
1953	Jul 01	Jul 09	22.00	19.0	13.00	6.00
1954	Jun 16	Jun 24	21.00	19.0	13.00	5.00
1954	Jul 29	Aug 01	20.00	18.0	12.00	5.00
1958	Feb 27	Mar 01	19.50	17.5	11.50	5.00
1958	Mar 20	Apr 01	19.00	17.0	11.00	5.00
1958	Apr 17	—	18.50	17.0	11.00	5.00
1958	Apr 24	—	18.00	16.5	11.00	5.00
1960	Sep 01	—	17.50	16.5	11.00	5.00

(continued)

TABLE Cj131–134   Depository institution reserve requirements: 1913–1992   *Continued*

	Effective date		Central reserve city banks	Reserve city banks	Country banks	Time deposits
	Central reserve city or reserve city banks	Country banks	Cj131	Cj132	Cj133	Cj134
Year			Percent	Percent	Percent	Percent
1960	Nov 24	—	17.50	16.5	12.00	5.00
1960	Dec 01	—	16.50	16.5	12.00	5.00
1962	Oct 25	Nov 01	—	16.5	12.00	4.00
1966	Jul 14	Jul 21	—	16.5	12.00	5.00
1966	Sep 08	Sep 11	—	16.5	12.00	6.00
1968	Jan 11	Jan 18	—	17.0	12.50	6.00
1969	Apr 17	—	—	17.5	13.00	6.00
1970	Oct 01	—	—	17.5	13.00	5.00
1972	Nov 09	—	—	—	17.50	5.00
1973	Jul 19	—	—	—	18.00	5.00
1974	Dec 12	—	—	—	17.50	6.00
1975	Feb 13	—	—	—	16.50	6.00
1976	Dec 30	—	—	—	16.25	6.00
1980	Nov 13	—	—	—	12.00	3.00
1990	Dec 26	—	—	—	12.00	0.00
1992	Apr 02	—	—	—	10.00	0.00

Sources

Joshua N. Feinman, "Reserve Requirements: History, Current Practice, and Potential Reform," *Federal Reserve Bulletin* 79 (June 1993): 569–89.

More recent data are available from the Board of Governors of the Federal Reserve System.

Documentation

Values shown are maximum rates applicable on various deposit classes. Values are expressed as a percentage of net demand deposits for series Cj131–133 and as a percentage of time deposits for series Cj134.

The reserve requirements listed here prior to 1980 were applicable to Federal Reserve member banks only. Beginning in 1980 (after a phase-in period), uniform reserve requirements on transactions accounts (series Cj131–133) and nontransactions accounts (series Cj134) were applied to all depository institutions.

Since 1966, different reserve requirements have applied to different levels of deposits within each deposit class. Only the rate applied to the largest level of deposits is shown. Between 1972 and 1976, reserve requirements on time deposits also varied by maturity, with lower requirements on deposits of longer maturity. Only the requirements applicable to time deposits of the shortest maturity are shown here.

On July 28, 1962, Federal Reserve's authority to classify cities as central reserve cities was terminated. Thereafter, reserve city reserve requirements applied to banks located in cities previously designated as central reserve cities (New York City and Chicago). The reserve city and country designations were discontinued in 1972, and reserve requirements were applied uniformly across all Federal Reserve member banks. Beginning in 1972, reserve requirements listed in series Cj133 applied to all Federal Reserve member banks, and, since 1980, to all depository institutions.

The Federal Reserve Act of 1913 provided for temporary reserve requirements for member banks to be effective for a period of approximately three years. A 1917 amendment to the Act established percentages below which reserve requirements could not be set, but fixed no upper limits. Maximum limits at twice the legal minimums were provided by the Banking Act of 1935. Beginning August 16, 1948, maximum limits were again increased, but on June 30, 1949, returned to their former levels. A 1959 Act changed the maximum reserve requirement on demand deposits of banks in central reserve cities and in reserve cities from twice the legal minimum to 22 percent. That Act also discontinued the central reserve city designation effective July 28, 1962. Since 1966, reserve requirements have been graduated, based on the level of deposits at each bank. Only the rate applied to the largest level of deposits is shown. The designation between reserve city and country member banks was eliminated in 1972. Between 1972 and 1976, reserve requirements on time deposits varied by deposit maturity, with lower requirements applied to deposits of longer maturity. Only the requirements applied

to time deposits of the shortest maturity are shown. Beginning in 1969, reserve requirements were extended to net balances due from domestic bank offices to their foreign branches. Beginning November 16, 1978, domestic deposits of Edge corporations were subject to the same reserve requirements as member banks. Effective October 25, 1979, reserve requirements were applied to managed liabilities of banks in excess of a base amount. These liabilities included large time deposits, Eurodollar borrowings, repurchase agreements against U.S. government and agency securities, and federal funds borrowings from nonmember institutions. This requirement was eliminated on July 24, 1980. The Monetary Control Act of 1980 subjected all depository institutions, after a phase-in period, to uniform reserve requirements, applying to both transaction accounts and nontransaction accounts (although since 1990 the required reserve ratio on nontransaction accounts has been zero). Transaction accounts include all deposits on which the account holder is permitted to make withdrawals by negotiable or transferable instruments, payment orders of withdrawal, and telephone and preauthorized transfers (in excess of three per month) for the purpose of making payments.

The temporary reserve requirements in effect until 1917 authorized member banks to hold a part of their reserves as cash in their own vaults and a part on deposit with other banks. For a fuller discussion of these requirements and the 1917 amendment of the Federal Reserve Act, see *Federal Reserve Bulletin,* November 1938. Only balances with Federal Reserve banks could be counted as legal reserves from June 21, 1917, until 1959. Since that time, member banks have also been allowed to count some portion of their vault cash as reserves. Effective December 1, 1959, vault cash in excess of 4 percent of net demand deposits could be counted by country banks. The percentage was decreased to 2.5 percent on August 25, 1960. Central reserve city and reserve city banks were allowed to count vault cash in excess of 2 percent of net demand deposits effective December 3, 1959, and amounts greater than 1 percent beginning September 1, 1960. All member banks were allowed to count all vault cash as reserves effective November 24, 1960.

Net demand deposits are demand deposits subject to reserve requirements. In general, prior to 1917, net demand deposits were made up of (1) the gross amount of all demand deposits except those due to other banks, and (2) the net excess (if any) of demand deposits due to other banks over demand balances due from other banks and cash items in process of collection. From 1917 to August 23, 1935, the definition was substantially the same, except that U.S. government deposits were exempt by law from all reserve requirements and were therefore excluded from net demand deposits. Beginning August 23, 1935, net demand deposits have been defined as total demand deposits minus cash items in the process of collection and demand balances due from domestic banks (also minus war loan and Series E bond accounts during the period April 13, 1943, to June 30, 1947).

TABLE Cj135–140   Commercial bank reserves and the monetary base: 1918–1999

Contributed by David C. Wheelock

Year	Board of Governors measure			Federal Reserve Bank of St. Louis measure		
	Monetary base	Adjusted monetary base	Adjusted reserves	Monetary base	Adjusted monetary base	Adjusted reserves
	Cj135	Cj136	Cj137	Cj138	Cj139	Cj140
	Million dollars	Million dollars	Million dollars	Million dollars	Million dollars	Million dollars
1918	—	—	—	5,869	5,177	—
1919	—	—	—	6,446	5,687	—
1920	—	—	—	7,025	6,197	—
1921	—	—	—	6,336	5,590	—
1922	—	—	—	6,027	5,315	—
1923	—	—	—	6,402	5,642	—
1924	—	—	—	6,614	5,829	—
1925	—	—	—	6,747	5,947	—
1926	—	—	—	6,853	6,040	—
1927	—	—	—	6,895	6,077	—
1928	—	—	—	6,851	6,038	—
1929	—	—	—	6,833	6,022	—
1930	—	—	—	6,637	5,850	—
1931	—	—	—	6,994	6,164	—
1932	—	—	—	7,441	6,558	—
1933	—	—	—	7,918	6,978	—
1934	—	—	—	9,073	7,996	—
1935	—	—	—	10,583	9,341	—
1936	—	—	—	12,089	10,110	—
1937	—	—	—	13,304	9,371	—
1938	—	—	—	14,440	10,709	—
1939	—	—	—	17,400	13,200	—
1940	—	—	—	21,124	16,119	—
1941	—	—	—	22,995	17,146	—
1942	—	—	—	25,328	18,299	—
1943	—	—	—	30,235	22,475	—
1944	—	—	—	35,771	26,894	—
1945	—	—	—	41,897	31,617	—
1946	—	—	—	44,256	33,243	—
1947	—	—	—	44,878	33,538	6,643
1948	—	—	—	46,060	33,117	6,643
1949	—	—	—	45,303	33,095	6,983
1950	—	—	—	43,571	32,740	6,993
1951	—	—	—	47,111	33,738	7,371
1952	—	—	—	49,416	35,342	7,755
1953	—	—	—	50,133	36,458	7,922
1954	—	—	—	49,305	36,746	8,202
1955	—	—	—	49,091	36,945	8,271
1956	—	—	—	49,651	37,381	8,350
1957	—	—	—	50,022	37,692	8,399
1958	—	—	—	49,824	38,379	8,792
1959	50,483	40,789	11,089	50,405	38,930	8,964
1960	49,996	40,832	11,021	49,918	39,132	9,057
1961	49,306	41,176	11,248	49,228	39,928	9,526
1962	50,938	42,333	11,397	50,859	41,482	9,988
1963	52,444	43,913	11,494	52,365	43,319	10,372
1964	55,186	46,081	11,714	55,108	45,728	10,859
1965	58,109	48,273	12,044	58,031	48,300	11,532
1966	61,533	50,765	12,248	61,454	51,083	12,086
1967	64,656	53,137	12,661	64,577	53,820	12,809
1968	69,389	56,492	13,342	69,312	57,336	13,637
1969	73,657	59,881	13,816	73,578	60,584	14,109
1970	77,565	63,324	14,228	77,486	63,894	14,639
1971	83,260	67,633	14,968	83,184	68,934	16,020
1972	89,065	72,230	15,942	89,082	74,129	17,440
1973	94,643	78,303	16,866	94,676	80,912	19,246
1974	103,622	84,939	17,341	103,652	87,647	20,529

(continued)

TABLE Cj135–140   Commercial bank reserves and the monetary base: 1918–1999
Continued

	Board of Governors measure			Federal Reserve Bank of St. Louis measure		
	Monetary base	Adjusted monetary base	Adjusted reserves	Monetary base	Adjusted monetary base	Adjusted reserves
	Cj135	Cj136	Cj137	Cj138	Cj139	Cj140
Year	Million dollars	Million dollars	Million dollars	Million dollars	Million dollars	Million dollars
1975	108,542	90,810	17,586	108,573	93,692	21,076
1976	114,698	98,004	17,976	114,728	99,900	21,458
1977	122,930	106,061	18,688	122,967	107,543	22,507
1978	134,551	115,907	19,737	134,599	117,363	24,211
1979	147,559	125,712	19,926	147,608	126,433	25,039
1980	158,589	136,838	21,008	158,641	136,769	26,385
1981	163,916	145,330	22,233	164,087	145,809	26,855
1982	172,069	154,425	22,658	172,317	156,355	28,578
1983	183,362	169,273	24,905	183,559	172,858	32,764
1984	195,244	182,318	26,144	195,564	187,999	35,986
1985	210,637	195,576	29,094	210,960	201,846	39,502
1986	230,796	212,944	34,446	231,002	220,448	46,017
1987	253,086	232,222	39,359	253,340	241,163	52,357
1988	271,881	249,584	40,125	272,211	258,970	53,703
1989	283,232	261,954	39,847	283,732	271,385	54,002
1990	301,658	280,886	40,879	302,428	290,731	55,664
1991	318,119	307,229	43,117	318,285	318,324	59,324
1992	341,539	333,910	50,235	341,758	347,878	68,753
1993	376,353	369,778	57,403	376,670	386,185	78,335
1994	411,133	405,231	60,035	411,498	421,571	81,104
1995	433,695	429,191	57,630	433,940	443,486	77,261
1996	447,789	441,583	53,016	448,033	455,562	73,920
1997	471,451	464,430	47,204	471,934	478,714	69,514
1998	502,109	495,221	45,216	502,599	508,958	67,816
1999	550,529	543,529	42,992	551,895	557,926	72,426

Sources

Series Cj135–137. 1959–1970, *Banking and Monetary Statistics, 1941–1970*; 1971–1999, *Annual Statistical Digest* (annual issues).

Series Cj138–140. Federal Reserve Bank of St. Louis Internet site.

More recent data are available from the *Federal Reserve Bulletin* and the Federal Reserve Bank of St. Louis Internet site.

Documentation

All figures in this table are annual averages of daily data.

Adjusted series are those for which an adjustment has been made to account for the impact of reserve requirement changes on bank reserves, so as to make the data more comparable from year to year as a measure of the trend of monetary policy.

For additional explanation of the Federal Reserve Bank of St. Louis measures, see Richard G. Anderson and Robert H. Rasche, "Eighty Years of Observations on the Adjusted Monetary Base: 1918–1997," *Federal Reserve Bank of St. Louis Review* 81 (January/February 1999): 3–22.

Series Cj135. Consists of total depository institution reserve balances with Federal Reserve banks plus vault cash used to satisfy reserve requirements, required clearing balances, and adjustments to compensate for float at Federal Reserve banks plus the currency component of the money stock plus the difference between current vault cash and the amount applied to satisfy current reserve requirements.

Series Cj136. Consists of total reserves (Board of Governors measure) adjusted for the effects of changes in reserve requirements plus the currency component of the money stock plus the difference between current vault cash and the amount applied to satisfy current reserve requirements (adjusted for changes in reserve requirements).

Series Cj137. Consists of required reserves adjusted for changes in reserve requirements plus excess reserves.

Series Cj138. Consists of total depository institution reserve balances with Federal Reserve banks plus total vault cash, required clearing balances, and adjustments to compensate for float at Federal Reserve banks plus the currency component of the money stock.

Series Cj139. Consists of total reserves (Federal Reserve Bank of St. Louis measure) adjusted for changes in reserve requirements plus the currency component of the money stock.

Series Cj140. Consists of total depository institution reserve balances with Federal Reserve banks, required clearing balances, and adjustments to compensate for float at Federal Reserve banks plus vault cash, adjusted to account for changes in reserve requirements.

TABLE Cj141   High-powered money: 1867–1960

Contributed by David C. Wheelock

Year	High-powered money Cj141 Billion dollars	Year	High-powered money Cj141 Billion dollars	Year	High-powered money Cj141 Billion dollars	Year	High-powered money Cj141 Billion dollars	Year	High-powered money Cj141 Billion dollars	Year	High-powered money Cj141 Billion dollars
1867	0.852	1885	1.233	1900	1.954	1915	3.686	1930	6.937	1945	41.750
1868	0.775	1886	1.195	1901	2.070	1916	4.204	1931	7.319	1946	43.925
1869	0.761	1887	1.257	1902	2.143	1917	5.059	1932	7.786	1947	44.658
1870	0.758	1888	1.309	1903	2.257	1918	6.078	1933	8.163	1948	45.817
1871	0.776	1889	1.318	1904	2.406	1919	6.620	1934	9.132	1949	45.092
1872	0.782	1890	1.366	1905	2.470	1920	7.187	1935	10.735	1950	43.208
1873	0.783	1891	1.433	1906	2.628	1921	6.539	1936	12.244	1951	46.258
1874	0.801	1892	1.529	1907	2.869	1922	6.283	1937	13.443	1952	48.592
1875	0.783	1893	1.514	1908	3.094	1923	6.676	1938	14.618	1953	49.400
1876	0.758	1894	1.569	1909	3.123	1924	6.874	1939	17.646	1954	48.650
1877	0.757	1895	1.502	1910	3.177	1925	7.026	1940	21.480	1955	48.258
1878	0.763	1896	1.399	1911	3.279	1926	7.123	1941	23.314	1956	48.633
1879	0.752	1897	1.524	1912	3.346	1927	7.172	1942	25.466	1957	48.975
1880	0.897	1898	1.721	1913	3.421	1928	7.123	1943	30.042	1958	48.933
1881	1.005	1899	1.806	1914	3.532	1929	7.120	1944	35.692	1959	49.450
1882	1.124									1960	48.850
1883	1.184										
1884	1.189										

Source

Milton Friedman and Anna J. Schwartz, *A Monetary History of the United States, 1867–1960* (Princeton University Press, 1963), pp. 799–808.

Documentation

There are three principal determinants of changes in the stock of money: changes in the public's holdings of currency relative to bank deposits; changes in the banking system's holdings of reserves relative to its deposit liabilities; and changes in high-powered money, which is commonly referred to as the monetary base.

Friedman and Schwartz estimated the stock of high-powered money for the period 1867–1960 as the sum of hand-to-hand currency held by the public plus vault cash in banks plus, after 1914, deposit liabilities of the Federal Reserve System to commercial banks. "The total is called high-powered money because one dollar of such money held as bank reserves may give rise to the creation of several dollars of deposits" (Friedman and Schwartz 1963, p. 50).

The Friedman–Schwartz high-powered money series differs from Federal Reserve System measures of the monetary base presented in series Cj135 in several respects. The Friedman–Schwartz series is based on end-of-month figures through 1946, whereas the data reported in series Cj135 for this period are derived from monthly averages of daily data. In addition, the Friedman–Schwartz series is based on seasonally adjusted data that include an adjustment for float, whereas the monetary base figures in series Cj135 covering the same period make no allowance for float and are based on seasonally unadjusted data. See Richard G. Anderson and Robert H. Rasche, "Eighty Years of Observations on the Adjusted Monetary Base: 1918–1997," *Federal Reserve Bank of St. Louis Review* 81 (January/February 1999): 3–22, for an additional explanation of differences between Federal Reserve and Friedman–Schwartz estimates of the monetary base.

Data for 1867–1872 are January figures; data for 1873–1881 are February figures; data for 1882–1907 are June figures; and data for 1907–1960 are annual averages of monthly figures.

BANKS

Howard Bodenhorn and Eugene N. White

TABLE Cj142–148   State banks – number, assets, and liabilities: 1782–1837
Contributed by Howard Bodenhorn and Eugene N. White

	State-chartered banks	Authorized capital stock	Reporting banks				
			Number	Notes in circulation	Consolidated deposits	Specie	Loans and discounts
	Cj142	Cj143	Cj144	Cj145	Cj146	Cj147	Cj148
Year	Number	Dollars	Number	Dollars	Dollars	Dollars	Dollars
1782	1	400,000	—	—	—	—	—
1783	1	400,000	—	—	—	—	—
1784	2	1,200,000	—	—	—	—	—
1785	2	1,200,000	—	—	—	—	—
1786	1	800,000	—	—	—	—	—
1787	2	2,800,000	—	—	—	—	—
1788	2	2,800,000	—	—	—	—	—
1789	2	2,800,000	—	—	—	—	—
1790	3	3,100,000	—	—	—	—	—
1791	5	4,600,000	—	—	—	—	—
1792	12	6,310,000	—	—	—	—	—
1793	15	10,470,000	—	—	—	—	—
1794	15	10,470,000	—	—	—	—	—
1795	20	13,470,000	—	—	—	—	—
1796	22	14,170,000	—	—	—	—	—
1797	22	14,170,000	—	—	—	—	—
1798	22	14,170,000	—	—	—	—	—
1799	25	16,870,000	—	—	—	—	—
1800	28	17,420,000	—	—	—	—	—
1801	32	19,170,000	—	—	—	—	—
1802	35	20,030,000	—	—	—	—	—
1803	53	24,900,000	—	—	—	—	—
1804	64	31,165,000	—	—	—	—	—
1805	71	38,865,000	—	—	—	—	—
1806	78	41,340,000	—	—	—	—	—
1807	83	43,429,000	—	—	—	—	—
1808	86	41,490,000	—	—	—	—	—
1809	92	45,190,000	—	—	—	—	—
1810	102	56,190,000	—	—	—	—	—
1811	117	66,290,000	—	—	—	—	—
1812	143	84,485,000	—	—	—	—	—
1813	147	87,000,000	—	—	—	—	—
1814	202	110,024,233	—	—	—	—	—
1815	212	115,232,353	—	—	—	—	—
1816	232	123,976,890	—	—	—	—	—
1817	262	137,843,926	—	—	—	—	—
1818	338	160,308,873	—	—	—	—	—
1819	341	160,980,443	185	21,552,539	12,394,590	6,498,968	67,579,755
1820	327	159,602,121	145	15,379,583	11,505,592	5,735,453	55,092,834
1821	273	146,232,121	153	27,260,864	17,246,077	10,986,461	71,927,534
1822	267	142,532,121	135	18,290,614	11,154,129	4,446,394	56,027,523
1823	274	138,673,787	169	25,383,864	15,617,482	7,752,996	75,979,765
1824	300	150,748,787	181	27,956,905	17,600,532	8,282,824	73,790,775
1825	330	156,078,787	198	31,794,185	21,148,973	8,502,212	88,665,337
1826	331	155,978,787	211	32,255,919	22,272,117	7,845,406	104,807,877
1827	333	157,513,787	223	28,652,055	20,252,004	7,816,466	90,543,197
1828	355	162,413,884	228	29,927,277	22,659,423	7,809,535	100,325,906
1829	369	166,063,884	245	28,144,192	21,480,472	8,420,217	102,976,130
1830	381	170,403,884	273	38,403,155	27,796,122	9,563,540	115,344,320
1831	424	185,579,484	296	48,204,627	36,362,462	10,486,662	149,025,534
1832	464	207,953,484	321	46,341,758	39,877,788	9,410,713	152,470,522
1833	517	150,117,884	414	65,020,891	54,059,311	13,736,134	222,885,468
1834	558	275,778,618	472	68,911,172	70,310,295	23,683,201	249,033,558
1835	584	308,383,619	529	106,902,095	102,646,292	29,999,207	332,821,968
1836	703	435,614,059	619	146,500,041	133,188,491	38,878,770	511,072,319
1837	729	471,526,482	667	118,608,455	100,413,101	35,440,216	486,388,025

TABLE Cj142–148 State banks – number, assets, and liabilities: 1782–1837 *Continued*

Sources

J. Van Fenstermaker, *The Development of American Commercial Banking: 1782–1837* (Kent State University Press, 1965), pp. 66B65, 111, 186–236. Albert Gallatin, *Considerations on the Currency and the Banking System of the United Sates* (1831), pp. 101–2, contains data for the series Cj142–143, for the years 1811, 1815, 1816, 1820, and 1830; for the series Cj144–147, it contains data for the years 1820 and 1830. The data shown there are somewhat different from those reported in Fenstermaker.

Documentation

These represent the most consistent series for state-chartered banks operating in the first third of the nineteenth century. Inferences based on these data should be drawn with caution. Not every operating bank reported in every year, and reporting was not consistent from year to year. Fenstermaker constructed many of these series by extrapolation. Despite their shortcomings, these data are broadly indicative of trends in banking in the late eighteenth and early nineteenth centuries. Those interested in early American banking are encouraged to return to the source as Fenstermaker includes detailed appendixes that provide state-level aggregates. Because of reporting differences between states, these data are often better used for drawing inferences.

For the years 1782–1837 inclusive, would-be bankers needed to obtain a legislative charter before they could legally open a commercial bank. In the early Federal period, a combined wariness of corporate privilege and limited demand for banking services led to slow growth in the financial sector. By the early 1790s, a major American city such as New York, Philadelphia, Boston, and Charleston typically had one chartered bank. Industry growth increased markedly in the early 1810s with the closing of the First Bank of the United States and increased familiarity with the corporate form. A second rapid expansion in the sector occurred in response to increased commercial activity and the threat of the closing of the Second Bank of the United States in the mid-1830s.

TABLE Cj149–157 State banks – number, assets, and liabilities: 1834–1896[1]

Contributed by Howard Bodenhorn

			Assets				Liabilities		
	Banks	Assets or liabilities	Loans and discounts	Investments in government and other securities	Cash and cash items	Due from other banks	Deposits	Notes in circulation	Capital account
	Cj149	Cj150	Cj151	Cj152	Cj153	Cj154	Cj155	Cj156	Cj157
Year	Number	Thousand dollars	Thousand dollars	Thousand dollars	Thousand dollars	Thousand dollars	Thousand dollars	Thousand dollars	Thousand dollars
1834	506	418,933	324,119	6,113	48,797	27,330	102,269	94,840	200,006
1835	704	498,326	365,164	9,211	68,085	40,084	122,054	103,692	231,250
1836	713	622,197	457,506	11,709	76,935	51,877	165,507	140,301	251,875
1837	788	706,490	525,116	12,407	79,815	59,664	189,818	149,186	290,772
1838	829	682,058	485,632	33,909	61,052	58,195	145,707	116,139	317,637
1839	840	702,382	492,278	36,128	76,118	52,898	143,376	135,171	327,133
1840	901	657,750	462,897	42,412	57,527	41,140	119,856	106,969	358,443
1841	784	608,143	386,488	64,811	63,626	47,877	107,752	107,290	313,609
1842	692	471,812	323,958	24,586	50,988	30,752	88,273	83,734	260,172
1843	691	393,162	254,545	28,380	53,401	20,666	77,625	58,564	228,862
1844	696	426,602	264,906	22,859	68,301	35,861	116,549	75,168	210,872
1845	707	433,910	288,617	20,356	63,068	29,619	114,358	89,609	206,046
1846	707	455,617	312,114	21,487	63,313	31,690	125,132	105,552	196,894
1847	715	457,691	310,283	20,158	62,035	31,789	120,332	105,520	203,071
1848	751	511,928	344,477	26,498	73,287	38,905	142,641	128,506	204,838
1849	782	478,588	332,323	23,572	65,008	32,228	121,274	114,743	207,309
1850	824	532,261	364,204	20,607	73,286	41,632	146,304	131,367	217,317
1851	879	597,227	413,757	22,388	81,208	50,718	175,375	155,165	227,808
1852 [2]	913	620,328	429,761	23,254	84,350	52,680	182,158	161,167	236,620
1853 [3]	750	577,185	408,944	22,285	77,570	48,920	195,179	146,073	207,909
1854	1,208	794,870	557,398	44,350	107,649	55,516	238,511	204,689	301,376
1855	1,307	816,729	576,145	52,727	99,310	55,739	235,557	186,952	332,177
1856	1,398	880,087	634,183	49,485	104,031	62,640	265,426	195,748	343,874
1857	1,416	953,178	684,457	59,272	111,555	65,849	288,026	214,779	370,835
1858	1,422	848,596	583,165	60,305	112,241	58,053	237,102	155,208	394,623
1859	1,476	983,436	657,184	63,502	150,205	78,245	327,784	193,307	401,976
1860	1,562	999,859	691,946	70,344	128,429	67,235	309,735	207,102	421,880
1861	1,601	1,015,859	696,778	74,005	138,876	58,794	318,505	202,006	429,593
1862	1,492	1,012,149	646,678	99,011	155,228	65,257	357,466	183,792	418,140
1863	1,466	1,191,750	648,602	180,508	205,563	96,934	494,213	238,677	405,046
1864 [4]	1,089	720,661	483,906	57,183	99,633	50,409	233,155	150,431	311,554
1865 [4]	349	230,956	155,081	18,326	31,930	16,155	74,721	48,210	71,182
1866 [4]	297	196,544	131,974	15,595	27,173	13,748	63,588	41,026	66,479
1867 [4]	272	180,000	120,866	14,282	24,885	12,591	58,235	37,573	65,204
1868 [4]	247	163,456	109,757	12,970	22,598	11,433	52,883	34,120	66,364
1869 [4]	259	171,397	115,089	13,600	23,696	11,989	55,452	35,777	66,969

Notes appear at end of table

(continued)

TABLE Cj149–157   State banks – number, assets, and liabilities: 1834–1896   *Continued*

				Assets				Liabilities		
	Banks	Assets or liabilities	Loans and discounts	Investments in government and other securities	Cash and cash items	Due from other banks	Deposits	Notes in circulation	Capital account
	Cj149	Cj150	Cj151	Cj152	Cj153	Cj154	Cj155	Cj156	Cj157
Year	Number	Thousand dollars	Thousand dollars	Thousand dollars	Thousand dollars	Thousand dollars	Thousand dollars	Thousand dollars	Thousand dollars
1870 [4]	325	215,073	144,416	17,066	29,734	15,044	69,582	44,894	86,513
1871 [4]	452	299,117	200,850	23,734	41,354	20,923	96,773	62,438	111,444
1872 [4]	566	374,558	251,507	29,720	51,783	26,200	121,180	78,185	122,129
1873	1,330 [5]	880,111	514,319	276,436	19,704	28,071	788,956	175	86,191
1874	1,569 [5]	1,038,634	638,187	280,797	42,822	37,482	912,121	153	113,826
1875	1,260	1,291,427	775,083	359,164	49,588	45,068	1,111,233	178	159,861
1876	1,357	1,357,256	793,491	390,797	50,951	51,781	1,151,314	388	185,088
1877	1,306	1,429,665	819,307	420,569	55,634	56,753	1,187,839	388	218,687
1878	1,173	1,330,203	726,141	414,265	51,810	53,195	1,107,004	388	196,431
1879	1,287	1,292,796	671,479	423,906	55,787	51,061	1,059,082	389	211,270
1880	1,279	1,363,452	667,543	452,699	75,479	62,403	1,136,966	283	201,070
1881	1,312	1,543,291	757,048	500,995	59,075	95,266	1,284,676	275	222,822
1882	1,333	1,686,802	841,520	583,771	60,158	96,951	1,412,461	286	240,216
1883	1,418	1,843,271	947,947	563,062	59,513	111,455	1,546,615	188	266,408
1884	1,488	1,938,690	990,841	592,409	72,668	117,713	1,615,793	177	297,273
1885	1,661	2,004,978	1,014,580	609,786	84,231	128,646	1,658,559	98	314,889
1886	1,529	2,067,851	1,035,232	644,154	70,352	109,597	1,726,939	103	315,964
1887	3,156	2,556,047	1,382,937	682,129	161,337	160,906	2,068,490	231	452,756
1888	3,527	2,739,010	1,533,091	774,776	161,496	156,574	2,174,881	169	505,779
1889	4,005	3,006,931	1,698,541	806,225	201,264	185,883	2,390,937	120	552,374
1890	4,717	3,295,855	1,920,024	862,505	185,861	207,185	2,597,662	120	623,584
1891	4,989	3,448,785	2,067,319	869,994	165,634	212,521	2,708,609	111	661,373
1892	5,577	3,751,649	2,209,132	936,327	197,789	261,279	2,970,209	137	710,110
1893	5,685	3,979,009	2,348,193	1,009,605	205,645	250,701	3,126,187	10	752,213
1894	5,738	3,868,475	2,140,628	1,010,248	229,373	309,015	3,039,359	5	751,160
1895	6,103	4,138,991	2,252,283	1,118,159	227,743	320,721	3,259,742	0	792,450
1896	5,780	4,200,125	2,279,515	1,210,827	169,199	295,862	3,345,229	0	763,434

[1] Reports on or about June 30 each year.

[2] Number of banks estimated based on previous five years; all other amounts estimated using ten years, 1854–1863 inclusive.

[3] Incomplete owing to nonreporting banks.

[4] All figures, except number of banks and capital, estimated.

[5] Estimated.

Source

Comptroller of the Currency, *Annual Report* (1931), Table 94, pp. 1018–19.

Documentation

The historical tables appearing in the 1931 *Annual Report* of the Comptroller of the Currency provide summary statistics by single years beginning in 1834 for all reporting state-chartered commercial banks and private banks. The original sources from which the Comptroller's estimates are derived are: U.S. Congress, House Executive Document number 111, 26th Congress, 2nd Session (for years 1834–1840 inclusive); House Executive Document number 68, 31st Congress, 2nd Session (for years 1841–1850 inclusive); reports of condition made in 1863 (for years 1851–1863 inclusive, except 1852 and 1853). The 1853 figures are based on reports included in House Executive Document number 66, 32nd Congress, 2nd Session, but these reports are incomplete. For 1852, the reported number of banks is estimated from number of banks reporting between 1847 and 1851; the reported assets and liabilities are estimated on assets and liabilities reported in the ten years

1854–1863, inclusive. The Comptroller did not report the source of the post–Civil War reports, but they were presumably collected from reports made to state banking authorities. The statistics are further contaminated because they may include mutual savings banks in addition to loan and trust companies chartered by the various states as well as unchartered private banks.

Thus, data for all years should be used with caution. The original sources on which the Comptroller relied are notoriously incomplete. Prior to the establishment of the Comptroller of the Currency and the formation of national banks, state banks (both chartered and free banks) reported to a state legislative committee or regulatory agency. Although reports were typically required by law or charter terms, banks sometimes failed to report. It should also be kept in mind that the banks' reports of condition were not audited and, hence, were subject to both uncorrected mistakes and purposive misreporting. Errors and omissions were also highly likely as the U.S. House documents on which the Comptroller relied were compilations of various state reports forwarded to the Secretary of the Treasury. Some state reports were not forwarded and were not included in the House documents. Despite their known shortcomings, series Cj149–157 represent the best extant estimates of state bank accounts for the period.

Series Cj154. Includes balances held with clearinghouses and correspondent banks.

Series Cj157. Includes paid-in capital and retained earnings.

TABLE Cj158–168   State banks – number and assets: 1896–1955[1]

Contributed by Howard Bodenhorn

		Loans		Securities			Cash			
					U.S. government	States and political subdivisions		Items in process of collection	Currency and coin	Bankers' balances (including reserves)
	Banks	Total assets	Total	Real estate	Total			Total			
	Cj158	Cj159	Cj160 [2]	Cj161 [2]	Cj162	Cj163	Cj164	Cj165	Cj166	Cj167	Cj168
Year	Number	Million dollars	Million dollars	Million dollars	Million dollars	Million dollars	Million dollars	Million dollars	Million dollars	Million dollars	Million dollars
1896	7,785	2,813	1,770	418	355	75	80	528	46	187	295
1897	7,828	2,912	1,723	399	402	79	89	622	52	203	367
1898	7,949	3,193	1,897	401	447	81	100	671	40	208	423
1899	8,253	3,780	2,210	421	555	88	120	836	111	220	505
1900	8,696	4,115	2,421	457	635	88	128	874	96	227	551
1901	9,261	4,897	2,854	513	791	75	139	1,059	195	264	600
1902	9,956	5,420	3,275	581	877	57	143	1,046	108	264	674
1903	10,897	5,905	3,611	661	991	56	160	1,073	96	283	694
1904	11,707	6,382	3,674	718	1,135	48	192	1,326	119	325	882
1905	12,488	7,217	4,292	829	1,319	44	210	1,339	149	321	869
1906	13,739	7,820	4,778	979	1,322	35	200	1,431	175	354	902
1907	14,939	8,390	5,148	1,060	1,383	29	223	1,549	181	399	969
1908	15,714	7,954	4,604	1,052	1,394	27	230	1,621	159	463	999
1909	16,212	8,780	5,029	1,141	1,559	28	256	1,843	226	527	1,090
1910	17,376	9,432	5,618	1,327	1,591	24	260	1,838	274	556	1,008
1911	17,913	9,941	5,822	1,448	1,708	26	302	1,980	201	561	1,218
1912	18,478	10,638	6,267	1,602	1,854	29	351	2,045	200	564	1,281
1913	19,197	11,024	6,661	1,733	1,851	19	360	2,022	195	580	1,247
1914	19,718	11,679	6,973	1,698	1,991	18	389	2,160	230	593	1,337
1915	19,793	12,316	7,171	1,809	2,131	17	419	2,397	183	596	1,618
1916	20,168	14,297	8,300	1,961	2,551	37	508	2,796	254	644	1,898
1917	20,699	16,571	9,645	2,210	2,876	257	548	3,271	238	712	2,321
1918	21,157	18,090	10,494	2,299	3,643	1,018	605	3,043	271	483	2,289
1919	21,368	21,357	11,912	2,425	4,711	1,922	625	3,666	553	517	2,596
1920	22,267	24,242	15,063	2,995	4,350	1,501	607	3,771	601	562	2,608
1921	22,306	23,194	14,410	3,074	4,441	1,345	650	3,236	560	482	2,194
1922	21,876	23,473	13,849	3,300	4,846	1,607	732	3,633	737	451	2,445
1923	21,593	25,878	15,620	3,780	5,297	1,948	780	3,717	654	453	2,610
1924	20,908	27,612	16,323	4,175	5,576	1,813	878	4,332	1,036	510	2,786
1925	20,376	30,150	17,630	4,636	6,055	1,942	933	4,874	1,149	534	3,191
1926	19,770	31,579	18,762	5,056	6,387	1,948	1,076	4,780	1,115	552	3,113
1927	18,860	32,518	19,083	4,930	6,777	1,900	1,170	4,924	1,255	530	3,139
1928	18,113	33,298	19,567	4,908	7,324	2,044	1,160	4,478	997	455	3,026
1929	17,440	35,181	21,308	4,901	7,032	2,071	1,117	4,725	1,165	444	3,116
1930	16,432	35,297	20,169	4,678	7,517	2,126	1,218	5,502	1,851	459	3,192
1931	14,854	31,587	16,145	4,177	8,024	2,760	1,327	5,029	1,264	449	3,316
1932	12,598	23,985	11,735	3,342	7,094	2,903	1,185	3,490	680	379	2,431
1933	9,310	19,698	8,355	2,880	6,719	3,469	1,109	3,259	742	296	2,221
1934	9,931	21,124	8,039	2,335	7,741	4,477	1,135	3,959	463	292	3,204
1935	10,063	22,896	7,597	2,200	9,037	5,614	1,293	4,941	536	327	4,078
1936	9,961	25,929	7,852	2,164	10,618	6,909	1,338	6,129	968	417	4,744
1937	9,801	26,635	8,674	2,224	10,042	6,377	1,338	6,627	973	434	5,220
1938	9,625	25,868	7,811	2,241	9,491	6,108	1,355	7,361	846	412	6,103
1939	9,464	28,303	7,858	2,278	10,476	6,986	1,595	8,792	993	423	7,376
1940	9,370	30,988	8,237	2,399	10,911	7,503	1,685	10,769	618	461	9,690
1941	9,304	34,128	9,427	2,570	12,398	9,028	1,655	11,322	1,004	587	9,731
1942	9,252	35,691	9,369	2,638	14,848	11,562	1,608	10,569	1,020	618	8,931
1943	9,137	45,539	8,500	2,505	25,389	22,393	1,496	10,921	1,292	692	8,837
1944	9,102	54,889	9,816	2,414	32,655	29,841	1,443	11,664	1,617	700	9,347
1945	9,111	64,754	11,329	2,424	40,108	37,085	1,582	12,613	1,218	709	10,686
1946	9,140	67,810	12,690	3,105	40,609	37,278	1,631	13,811	2,249	723	10,839
1947	9,170	63,825	14,915	4,094	34,858	31,262	2,067	13,363	2,273	884	10,206
1948	9,191	64,718	17,622	4,983	32,595	28,707	2,384	13,753	2,209	998	10,546
1949	9,164	64,852	18,522	5,346	31,738	27,734	2,523	13,844	2,410	995	10,439

Notes appear at end of table

(continued)

TABLE Cj158–168   State banks – number and assets: 1896–1955   *Continued*

			Loans		Securities			Cash			
	Banks	Total assets	Total	Real estate	Total	U.S. government	States and political subdivisions	Total	Items in process of collection	Currency and coin	Bankers' balances (including reserves)
	Cj158	Cj159	Cj160 [2]	Cj161 [2]	Cj162	Cj163	Cj164	Cj165	Cj166	Cj167	Cj168
Year	Number	Million dollars	Million dollars	Million dollars	Million dollars	Million dollars	Million dollars	Million dollars	Million dollars	Million dollars	Million dollars
1950	9,175	67,223	20,208	6,076	32,841	28,205	3,104	13,355	2,478	883	9,994
1951	9,161	71,109	24,341	6,920	30,690	25,556	3,555	15,187	2,793	905	11,489
1952	9,144	76,164	26,180	7,234	32,222	26,574	4,044	16,775	3,348	1,156	12,271
1953	9,131	78,009	28,606	7,787	31,503	25,687	4,324	16,878	3,279	1,254	12,345
1954	9,102	81,974	29,664	8,117	34,238	27,750	4,990	16,933	3,391	1,290	12,252
1955	9,037	91,508	35,759	9,410	36,189	28,599	5,774	18,134	4,357	1,317	12,460

[1] Reports dated on or about June 30 each year.

[2] Beginning June 30, 1948, figures for real estate loans are shown gross (that is, before deduction of valuation reserves). They are not entirely compatible with earlier figures. Total loans continue to be shown net.

Source

Board of Governors of the Federal Reserve System, *All-Bank Statistics, United States, 1896–1955* (April 1959), Table A-3, pp. 42–5.

Documentation

The Board of Governors of the Federal Reserve System compiled these series from annual reports of state banking authorities. Most state banking authorities provide condensed balance sheets of individual banks collected at one or more call dates each year. In some instances, these reports did not include all the information needed, and the Board of Governors requested additional unpublished data from the state authorities.

The Board of Governors reported that sources of this information varied between states, and the form in which the data were organized and reported changed yearly for a given state. The Board did not provide detailed bibliographic sources for this information but wrote that the sources should be understood to include: (1) annual or regular reports published by state banking authorities; (2) abstracts or summaries of condition published by those authorities, sometimes for their own internal use; (3) summaries prepared by the state authorities at the request of the Comptroller of the Currency, the Federal Reserve banks, or the Federal Deposit Insurance Corporation; and (4) summaries prepared by Federal Reserve banks from reports forwarded by state banking authorities. Given the unique and scattered sources of the data underlying this table, it was deemed too demanding a task to bring these series up to date. Nevertheless, the statistics reported in this table provide valuable insights into U.S. banking structure, especially when used in conjunction with statistics on national banks, insured commercial banks, savings and loans, and mutual savings banks. Those interested in detailed reports at the state level should consult the original source.

This series ends in 1955 because no regulatory agency continued the series. Detailed information on state banks is available from reports issued by fifty state banking authorities, but this information is not collected and combined to form a national series comparable to these data.

TABLE Cj169–176   State banks – liabilities: 1896–1955[1]

Contributed by Howard Bodenhorn

		Deposits						
	Total liabilities	Total	Interbank	U.S. government	Other demand deposits	Other time deposits	Capital accounts	Other liabilities
	Cj169	Cj170	Cj171	Cj172	Cj173	Cj174	Cj175	Cj176
Year	Million dollars	Million dollars	Million dollars	Million dollars	Million dollars	Million dollars	Million dollars	Million dollars
1896	2,813	2,001	116	—	1,241	644	483	66
1897	2,912	2,101	129	—	1,299	673	471	68
1898	3,193	2,376	152	—	1,488	736	469	70
1899	3,780	2,934	194	—	1,852	888	475	74
1900	4,115	3,171	198	—	1,984	989	516	79
1901	4,897	3,864	230	—	2,467	1,167	546	99
1902	5,420	4,246	256	—	2,595	1,395	626	92
1903	5,905	4,546	267	—	2,745	1,532	697	89
1904	6,382	4,905	344	—	2,944	1,617	762	98
1905	7,217	5,622	362	—	3,360	1,900	782	157
1906	7,820	6,101	362	—	3,637	2,102	848	149
1907	8,390	6,539	409	—	3,818	2,312	887	180
1908	7,954	6,096	390	—	3,530	2,176	910	161
1909	8,780	6,857	455	—	4,033	2,369	949	149
1910	9,432	7,390	404	—	4,280	2,706	1,000	198
1911	9,941	7,780	486	—	4,232	3,062	1,008	250
1912	10,638	8,394	458	—	4,605	3,331	1,036	273
1913	11,024	8,667	464	—	4,646	3,557	1,099	285
1914	11,679	9,246	534	—	5,198	3,514	1,126	312
1915	12,316	9,794	603	—	5,468	3,723	1,149	340
1916	14,297	11,742	797	—	6,526	4,419	1,192	290
1917	16,571	13,733	989	13	7,655	5,076	1,272	423
1918	18,090	14,693	922	506	7,907	5,358	1,329	903
1919	21,357	17,319	975	349	9,669	6,326	1,386	1,386
1920	24,242	19,523	904	88	10,895	7,636	1,553	1,741
1921	23,194	18,289	771	158	9,858	7,502	1,673	1,764
1922	23,473	19,210	871	56	10,479	7,804	1,677	1,067
1923	25,878	21,276	1,032	115	11,259	8,870	1,752	1,256
1924	27,612	22,994	1,453	64	11,894	9,583	1,792	1,112
1925	30,150	25,318	1,476	76	13,296	10,470	1,844	1,164
1926	31,579	26,307	1,425	92	13,668	11,122	1,926	1,338
1927	32,518	26,926	1,708	95	13,749	11,374	1,967	1,437
1928	33,298	26,937	1,581	90	13,392	11,874	2,017	1,962
1929	35,181	27,799	1,755	149	14,252	11,643	2,257	2,276
1930	35,297	28,032	2,279	128	13,966	11,659	2,256	1,917
1931	31,587	25,113	2,288	213	11,916	10,696	2,064	1,477
1932	23,985	18,229	1,509	221	8,914	7,585	1,793	1,545
1933	19,698	15,337	1,467	410	7,879	5,581	1,431	1,021
1934	21,124	16,914	1,814	848	8,327	5,925	1,776	580
1935	22,896	18,985	2,234	386	10,214	6,151	1,735	390
1936	25,929	21,965	2,735	454	12,311	6,465	1,703	420
1937	26,635	22,629	2,547	292	12,793	6,997	1,645	426
1938	25,868	22,051	2,628	204	12,177	7,042	1,614	314
1939	28,303	24,478	3,338	289	13,692	7,159	1,560	311
1940	30,988	27,233	4,085	287	15,458	7,403	1,516	264
1941	34,128	30,315	4,339	232	18,103	7,641	1,491	272
1942	35,691	31,860	3,781	690	19,874	7,515	1,482	248
1943	45,539	41,586	3,732	3,484	25,947	8,423	1,472	248
1944	54,889	50,650	3,798	8,766	28,039	10,047	1,469	328
1945	64,754	60,193	4,335	11,246	31,888	12,724	1,482	371
1946	67,810	62,830	4,493	5,765	37,468	15,104	1,516	450
1947	63,825	58,786	4,249	523	38,097	15,917	1,526	457
1948	64,718	59,408	4,131	850	38,074	16,353	1,549	558
1949	64,852	59,319	3,993	885	37,870	16,571	1,576	566
1950	67,223	61,416	4,073	1,436	39,134	16,773	1,607	599
1951	71,109	64,886	4,321	2,459	41,385	16,721	1,664	777
1952	76,164	69,645	4,927	2,489	44,540	17,689	1,729	798
1953	78,009	71,073	5,004	1,506	45,548	19,015	1,800	881
1954	81,974	74,706	5,747	2,315	46,169	20,475	1,864	915
1955	91,508	82,881	6,928	2,315	52,064	21,574	2,129	1,435

Note appears at end of table

(continued)

TABLE Cj169–176   State banks – liabilities: 1896–1955   *Continued*

[1] Reports dated on or about June 30 each year.

Source

Board of Governors of the Federal Reserve System, *All Bank Statistics, United States, 1896–1955* (April 1959), Table A-3, pp. 42–5.

Documentation

For a discussion of the data, its reliability, and its compilation, see the text for Table Cj158–168.

TABLE Cj177–188   First Bank of the United States – assets and liabilities: 1792–1800[1]

Contributed by Howard Bodenhorn and Eugene N. White

	Assets							Liabilities				
	Loans, discounts, and bills of exchange	Stocks and bonds	Real estate and banking houses	Due from state banks and intrabank debits	Notes of state banks and state paper	Specie	Other assets	Capital	Notes in circulation	Deposits	Due to state banks and intrabank credits	Other liabilities
	Cj177	Cj178	Cj179	Cj180	Cj181	Cj182	Cj183	Cj184	Cj185	Cj186	Cj187	Cj188
Year	Dollars	Dollars	Dollars	Dollars	Dollars	Dollars	Dollars	Dollars	Dollars	Dollars	Dollars	Dollars
1792	7,997,359	50,000 [4]	—	346,555	112,828	976,910	22,525	3,915,345 [5]	1,689,486	2,657,359	433,902	164,304
1793	8,380,942 [3]	5,999,700	—	320,566	180,173	1,201,884	1,171,862	9,993,497	2,022,501	3,301,586	1,082,221 [4]	154,429
1794	10,482,516	6,000,000	23,333	477,948	281,321	745,735	61,464	10,000,000	3,677,805	3,172,286	365,035	46,103
1795	13,142,369	3,595,957	53,761	168,925	384,216	1,436,780	95,551	10,000,000	3,653,715	2,981,687	350,007	254,545
1796	13,909,089	3,524,332	91,021	682,558	484,894	1,579,407	33,531	10,000,000	3,383,136	3,795,831	688,336	261,641
1797	13,029,001	3,448,409	210,151	1,068,990	404,592	2,707,596	50,392	10,000,000	3,126,149	5,659,154	1,145,120	272,212
1798	13,541,674	3,281,880	282,913	1,443,954	399,852	3,075,303	44,365	10,000,000	4,079,391	5,201,030	664,626	291,131
1799	15,271,074	3,280,109	317,461	895,242	434,892	4,001,358	34,092	10,000,000	4,276,685	7,412,941	942,212	357,574
1800 [2]	16,899,257	3,187,707	359,835	881,542	978,656	5,671,949	19,534	10,000,000	5,469,063	9,869,732	1,005,535	325,510

[1] Figures are nearest year-end.

[2] Data for August 23 to November 26, 1800.

[3] Plus 199,000 guilders.

[4] Funded debt purchased by order of the Secretary of the Treasury.

[5] Capital stock not including certificates of U.S.-funded debt.

Source

James O. Wettereau, *Statistical Records of the First Bank of the U.S.* (Garland Publishing, 1985), pp. 232–3, 238–9, 244–5, 250–1, 256–7, 265–6, 273–4, 279–80.

Documentation

Although the First Bank of the United States operated between 1791 and 1811, the only known data on its assets and liabilities are restricted to the years 1792–1800.

The reporting dates of the branches of the First Bank of the United States were spread over several days. Typically, the branches compiled reports at some time during December of each year, though some branches reported as late as early January of the following year. In some instances, the reporting dates closest to the end of the year were taken from the January reports of the following year.

The First Bank of the United States was the first bank chartered by Congress after adoption of the Constitution. The original impetus behind the bank was a proposal by Alexander Hamilton for a national bank that would have resembled the Bank of England. Hamilton's proposal aroused fervent opposition from the emerging Republican Party as expressed by James Madison and Thomas Jefferson. They feared that Hamilton's programs, which included the creation of a national bank, would consolidate federal power. However, Hamilton's arguments carried the day, and President George Washington signed the Bank Act into law in January 1791.

The bank's charter ran for twenty years and included a promise that Congress would charter no competing bank during that period. The bank's authorized capital was $10 million, one fifth of which was owned by the federal government. In addition to acting as the federal government's fiscal agent, the First Bank loaned to individuals and businesses, issued bank notes, and accepted private deposits.

With a main office in Philadelphia, the bank established branches in Boston, New York, Baltimore, Washington, Norfolk, Charleston, Savannah, and New Orleans. The bank appears to have been conservatively managed and returned its shareholders about 8–10 percent dividends. The Secretary of the Treasury was authorized to request financial reports from the bank as often as once each week, but the Treasury Department never shared any of the reports it requested with Congress. With such secrecy surrounding the bank as well as substantial foreign ownership, Jeffersonian Republicans opposed it. Secretary of the Treasury Albert Gallatin convinced them that revoking its charter represented a greater danger than allowing it to continue.

When the bank's charter came up for renewal in 1811, however, the Republicans refused to support the rechartering bill despite overwhelming support from state banks. Even with the support of the Madison administration and the Federalists, the rechartering bill failed by a single vote. Treasury Secretary Gallatin presided over the bank's liquidation, selling many of the bank's assets, including its branch office buildings, to newly chartered state banks.

TABLE Cj189–200   Second Bank of the United States – assets and liabilities: 1817–1840[1]

Contributed by Howard Bodenhorn and Eugene N. White

	Assets							Liabilities				
	Loans and discounts	Stocks	Real estate	Banking houses	Due from state and foreign banks	Notes of state banks	Specie	Capital	Circulation	Deposits	Due to state and foreign banks	Other liabilities
	Cj189	Cj190	Cj191	Cj192	Cj193	Cj194	Cj195	Cj196	Cj197	Cj198	Cj199	Cj200
Year	Thousand dollars	Thousand dollars	Thousand dollars	Thousand dollars	Thousand dollars	Thousand dollars	Thousand dollars	Thousand dollars	Thousand dollars	Thousand dollars	Thousand dollars	Thousand dollars
1817	13,485 [2]	4,829	—	—	8,848	587	1,724	35,000	1,911	11,233	—	—
1818	41,182	9,476	—	175	2,238	1,837	2,516	35,000	8,339	12,279	1,358	400
1819	35,786	7,392	—	434	3,246	1,878	2,667	35,000	6,564	5,793	1,434	2,600
1820	31,401	7,193	—	1,297	2,989	1,443	3,393	35,000	3,589	6,569	2,054	500
1821	30,905	9,156	—	1,887	1,262	677	7,643	35,000	4,567	7,895	2,053	2,000
1822	28,061	13,319	563	1,856	2,825	918	4,761	35,000	5,579	8,075	2,040	1,700
1823	30,736	11,019	627	1,957	1,432	766	4,425	35,000	4,361	7,622	1,293	2,600
1824	33,432	10,874	1,303	1,872	2,722	705	5,814	35,000	4,647	13,702	1,020	2,400
1825	31,813	18,422	1,495	1,853	2,154	1,056	6,747	35,000	6,068	12,033	2,407	8,000
1826	33,425	18,304	1,848	1,793	1,169	1,115	3,960	35,000	9,475	11,215	251	5,500
1827	30,938	17,764	2,039	1,678	2,144	1,068	6,457	35,000	8,549	14,320	280	4,100
1828	33,683	17,625	2,295	1,634	357	1,447	6,170	35,000	9,856	14,497	3,165	600
1829	39,220	16,099	2,346	1,557	2,206	1,294	6,098	35,000	11,902	17,062	1,448	3,400
1830	40,664	11,610	2,886	1,445	2,730	1,465	7,608	35,000	12,924	16,046	—	4,500
1831	44,032	8,675	2,629	1,345	2,383	1,495	10,808	35,000	16,251	17,297	735	2,000
1832	66,294	—	2,137	1,160	4,037	2,172	7,038	35,000	21,356	22,761	1,951	1,600
1833	61,696	—	1,855	1,181	6,795	2,293	8,952	35,000	17,518	20,348	2,092	8,000
1834	54,911	—	1,741	1,189	4,861	1,983	10,039	35,000	19,208	10,839	1,522	8,200
1835	51,809	—	1,761	1,219	6,532	1,506	15,708	35,000	17,340	11,757	3,119	11,300
1836	59,232	—	1,487	967	4,161	1,736	8,418	35,000	23,075	5,061	2,661	10,100
1837	57,394	—	817	420	2,285	1,207	2,638	35,000	11,448	2,332	9,211	6,800
1838	45,257	14,862	1,062	443	3,657	867	3,771	35,000	6,768	2,617	17,449	7,987
1839	41,619	17,957	1,055	424	5,833	1,792	4,154	35,000	5,983	6,779	15,832	9,260
1840	36,840	16,316	1,229	611	7,469	1,384	1,470	35,000	6,696	3,339	9,127	8,119

[1] Reports dated January 1 of each year.

[2] Carried to contingent fund.

Sources

U.S. Comptroller of the Currency, *Annual Report* (1876), Appendix, p. lxxxiii; except series Cj199 for 1818–1837, U.S. Comptroller of the Currency, *Annual Report* (1916), p. 912.

Documentation

The Second Bank of the United States was chartered by Congress in 1816, five years after Congress's refusal to recharter the First Bank of the United States. Fiscal difficulties that arose during the War of 1812 and the lack of an effective fiscal agent convinced the Madison administration and Congress that a national bank would prove useful. Treasury Secretary Alexander Dallas was also an ardent supporter of a national bank. Congress's first chartering act, passed in 1815, failed to meet the Madison administration's demands, however, and it was vetoed. It was not until April 1816, after the war was over, that Congress passed a charter acceptable to Madison and Dallas.

The Second Bank's charter differed from the First Bank's mostly in details. It was given a twenty-year charter; it was authorized to have $35 million in capital, of which the government owned one fifth; the president with Senate approval appointed five of its twenty-five directors; and the bank acted as the federal government's fiscal agent, transferring government funds without charge. The bank's main office was located in Philadelphia, and it eventually opened twenty-five branches throughout the United States.

The Second Bank was not as warmly received by investors as the First Bank, and the Philadelphia capitalist Stephen Girard finally bought the final $3 million in stock so the bank could open for business. William Jones, a loyal Republican with an undistinguished record as Navy Secretary and Acting Treasury Secretary, was appointed its first president. Under his leadership, many branch officers engaged in several barely legal activities that nearly bankrupted the institution. A congressional investigation in 1819 focused on Jones's alleged mismanagement, and he resigned in 1819.

Langdon Cheves, an attorney from South Carolina and former Speaker of the House, was appointed as Jones's replacement. To save the bank, he ordered nearly every branch to contract its lending and note issues. Some commentators argue that the bank's contraction initiated a financial panic that spread to state banks.

Cheves's contractionary policy reduced the bank's profitability, and in 1823 the stockholders replaced him with Nicolas Biddle. Biddle's more informed policies increased the bank's profitability. Although Biddle's expansionary policies quieted the bank's critics, they did not allay fears of the bank's size or questions concerning its constitutionality. President Andrew Jackson believed that the bank was unconstitutional and vetoed a rechartering act passed by Congress in 1832. The veto became the defining issue of the 1832 presidential election, which ultimately degenerated into what historians now label the "Bank War." Jackson withdrew government deposits, placing them with state banks whose leaders supported Jackson's reelection campaign. Biddle responded by forcing a larger contraction than was called for by the loss of government deposits. But Biddle's actions only convinced critics that they had been correct when they claimed that the bank was too large and too powerful.

The bank retained sufficient congressional support following the election that the Senate censured Jackson for his removal of government deposits and rejected his nomination of Roger B. Taney as Secretary of the Treasury. It did not have enough support, however, to override Jackson's veto. Between 1834 and 1836, the bank wound down, selling its branch assets to state banks. It received a charter from the Pennsylvania Assembly, and the Philadelphia office continued as the Bank of the United States of Pennsylvania. Cotton speculations and a new economic downturn in 1839 finally drove the bank into liquidation in 1840.

TABLE Cj201–202   Second Bank of the United States – dividend rate and profits: 1817–1834

Contributed by Eugene N. White

Year	Month	Profits Cj201 Dollars	Dividend rate Cj202 Percent	Year	Month	Profits Cj201 Dollars	Dividend rate Cj202 Percent
1817	July	1,021,873	2.60	1826	Jan	1,162,486	2.75
1818	Jan	1,382,217	4.00	1826	July	1,218,141	3.00
1818	July	1,266,187	3.50	1827	Jan	1,147,562	3.00
1819	Jan	899,011	2.50	1827	July	1,273,501	3.00
1819	July	983,479	— [1]	1828	Jan	1,202,595	3.00
1820	Jan	784,843	— [1]	1828	July	1,349,352	3.50
1820	July	718,591	— [1]	1829	Jan	1,325,275	3.50
1821	Jan	733,868	— [1]	1829	July	1,381,200	3.50
1821	July	750,439	1.50	1830	Jan	1,392,442	3.50
1822	Jan	719,007	2.00	1830	July	1,414,352	3.50
1822	July	1,009,728	2.25	1831	Jan	1,344,780	3.50
1823	Jan	884,106	2.50	1831	July	1,590,242	3.50
1823	July	932,488	2.50	1832	Jan	1,716,292	3.50
1824	Jan	929,083	2.50	1832	July	1,861,219	3.50
1824	July	976,932	2.50	1833	Jan	1,594,116	3.50
1825	Jan	1,031,256	2.50	1833	July	1,601,951	3.50
1825	July	1,154,940	2.75	1834	Jan	1,430,320	3.50
				1834	July	1,498,435	3.50

[1] Carried to contingent fund.

Source

Ralph C. H. Catterall, *The Second Bank of the United States* (University of Chicago Press, 1902), Appendix V, p. 504.

TABLE Cj203–211   National banks – number, assets, and liabilities: 1863–1896[1]

Contributed by Howard Bodenhorn

Year	Banks	Assets or liabilities	Loans and discounts	Investments in government and other securities	Cash and cash items	Due from banks	Deposits	Notes in circulation	Capital account
	Cj203	Cj204	Cj205	Cj206 [2]	Cj207	Cj208 [3]	Cj209	Cj210	Cj211 [4]
	Number	Thousand dollars	Thousand dollars	Thousand dollars	Thousand dollars	Thousand dollars	Thousand dollars	Thousand dollars	Thousand dollars
1863	66	16,798	5,466	5,665 [5]	2,212	3,118	9,479	—	7,317
1864	467	252,274	70,747	92,531 [5]	47,628	38,330	146,796	25,826 [6]	79,438
1865	1,294	1,126,455	362,443	393,988 [5]	199,515	144,370	614,242	131,452 [6]	380,298
1866	1,634	1,476,395	550,353	467,601	231,921	206,756	694,892	267,799	493,708
1867	1,636	1,494,085	588,450	521,967	130,334	230,284	685,384	291,770	512,447
1868	1,640	1,572,167	655,730	507,307	136,338	247,153	744,607	294,908	529,488
1869	1,619	1,564,174	686,348	466,204	112,718	269,225	716,044	292,753	548,691
1870	1,612	1,565,757	719,341	452,668	144,201	216,629	705,518	291,184	561,788
1871	1,723	1,703,415	789,417	455,689	163,325	259,051	791,066	307,794	594,188
1872	1,853	1,770,837	871,531	449,790	165,574	246,098	805,397	327,093	625,959
1873	1,968	1,851,235	925,558	444,912	179,290	259,500	836,227	338,789	662,264
1874	1,983	1,851,841	926,196	451,203	199,026	230,504	827,928	338,539	675,576
1875	2,076	1,913,239	972,926	442,780	180,646	251,285	897,387	318,148	686,898
1876	2,091	1,825,761	933,687	427,417	166,396	233,450	841,716	294,445	678,900
1877	2,078	1,774,353	901,731	431,044	165,008	205,907	818,360	290,002	656,267
1878	2,056	1,750,465	835,078	460,213	155,474	232,028	813,894	299,621	629,055
1879	2,048	2,019,885	835,875	714,717	151,704	246,258	1,090,110	307,329	615,369
1880	2,076	2,035,493	994,713	451,494	198,783	318,746	1,085,140	318,088	624,455
1881	2,115	2,325,833	1,144,989	484,303	218,912	408,307	1,364,386	312,223	641,592
1882	2,239	2,344,343	1,208,933	471,138	208,539	389,448	1,364,960	308,922	660,393
1883	2,417	2,364,833	1,285,592	464,729	226,607	314,166	1,337,362	311,963	706,984
1884	2,625	2,282,599	1,269,863	448,726	230,644	257,327	1,232,761	295,175	738,877
1885	2,689	2,421,852	1,257,656	432,238	305,568	357,508	1,419,594	269,148	725,028
1886	2,809	2,474,544	1,398,552	407,405	276,467	316,701	1,459,240	244,893	760,415
1887	3,014	2,637,276	1,560,372	328,970	270,982	405,836	1,650,149	166,626	806,292
1888	3,120	2,731,448	1,628,125	356,331	297,579	373,623	1,716,215	155,313	841,787
1889	3,239	2,937,976	1,779,055	322,983	313,731	443,449	1,919,579	128,867	875,297
1890	3,484	3,061,771	1,933,509	310,698	302,887	427,454	1,978,771	126,324	934,543
1891	3,652	3,113,415	1,963,705	309,399	332,297	414,185	1,974,086	123,916	987,551
1892	3,759	3,493,795	2,127,757	347,616	388,616	530,309	2,327,251	141,062	1,011,145
1893	3,807	3,213,262	2,020,484	310,343	310,343	422,994	1,939,235	155,071	1,028,870
1894	3,770	3,422,096	1,944,441	459,624	459,624	475,307	2,228,310	171,715	1,001,388
1895	3,715	3,470,553	2,016,640	447,171	403,368	490,195	2,278,892	178,816	987,228
1896	3,689	3,535,797	1,971,642	463,820	362,657	438,627	2,140,953	199,214	982,997

[1] Data are for all reporting banks. Reports dated on or about June 30 each year.

[2] Prior to 1903 includes borrowed securities.

[3] Includes lawful reserves and, prior to 1915, checks and other cash items not reported separately.

[4] Includes paid-in capital and retained earnings.

[5] Includes only U.S. securities.

[6] Includes state bank circulation outstanding.

Source

U.S. Comptroller of the Currency, *Annual Report* (1931), Table 95, pp. 1021–2.

Documentation

The National Banking Act was passed and signed into law by Abraham Lincoln in February 1863. All banks in the national system were chartered by the federal government, through the Office of the Comptroller of the Currency overseen by the Treasury department. The national bank was a war measure instituted, in part, to create a demand for the burgeoning volume of federal bonds issued to finance the war. Banks were not required to join and, in fact, some banks were refused membership. Members were subject to common regulations, such as minimum capital requirements, reserve ratios, and collateral security for note issues, designed to promote consistency and confidence in banking operations.

Membership promised certain advantages, including the possibility of becoming a Treasury depository. After 1865, membership became more attractive with passage of the 10 percent tax on bank notes issued by state-chartered banks. The 1865 law had two effects. First, the number of national banks increased sharply. Second, banks unwilling to adopt a national charter promoted the use of demand deposits, which grew rapidly after 1870. Not every bank preferred a national charter because there were offsetting costs of membership. Most important was the initial aggregate cap on national bank note issues. Moreover, the apportionment scheme favored existing state banks that switched charters over newly formed national banks. A second problem was the seasonal inelasticity of the bank note currency. It was simply too expensive for national banks to buy additional collateral bonds in the late summer to increase their note issues in anticipation of the annual autumn increase in money demand and then to redeem the notes and sell the bonds in the winter and spring.

Passage of the Federal Reserve Act in 1913 reduced the importance of national banking and the Office of the Comptroller of the Currency because all national banks were required to join the Federal Reserve System and became subject to Federal Reserve regulations. Federal Reserve notes also supplanted national bank notes as hand-to-hand currency. Despite the Federal Reserve's overriding presence, national banks and the Office of Comptroller of the Currency remain a feature of the banking system. The prominence of

TABLE Cj203–211   National banks – number, assets, and liabilities: 1863–1896   *Continued*

national banking is seen in many bank names, which include the abbreviation "N.A." for National Association.

Reports used in compiling the series are those dated closest to June 30 each year, as specific reporting dates varied. The series for 1863–1896 reflect consistent continuous reporting requirements.

Reporting requirements for national banks have changed since the inception of the Office of the Comptroller of the Currency in 1863. An Act of February 25, 1863, provided for banks to compile reports of condition on the first day of each quarter. An Act of June 3, 1864, required reports dated on the first Monday of January, April, July, and October on a form distributed by the Comptroller. On March 3, 1869, the reporting requirements were changed to not less than five reports each year, to be compiled on a day specified by the Comptroller. On December 22, 1922, the minimum number of call reports was reduced to three, with dates specified by the Comptroller. It was not until February 25, 1927, that an Act of Congress

required a semi-independent audit of the reports, conducted by an officer of the bank other than the president and cashier, who were responsible for compiling the report. An Act of June 16, 1933, required national banks to compile and publish at least three reports of condition each year for affiliated nonnational banks (that is, private or investment banking affiliates of national banks). This provision was repealed in 1935. The Federal Deposit Insurance Act of July 14, 1960, required insured national banks to provide the Comptroller of the Currency with at least four reports annually on dates selected by the Comptroller, the Chairman of the Board of Directors of the Federal Reserve System, and the Chairman of the Board of Directors of the Federal Deposit Insurance Corporation, or a majority thereof. Two of these reports must be called for in the period January to June, and two in the period July to December. In addition, the Comptroller retained the right to call for additional reports of condition whenever the Comptroller deemed them necessary to effectively supervise the national banking system.

TABLE Cj212–224   National banks – number and assets: 1896–1998[1]

Contributed by Howard Bodenhorn and Eugene N. White

				Assets									
				Loans		Securities			Cash				
Year	Banks	Total domestic assets	Total consolidated domestic and foreign assets	Total	Real estate	Total	U.S. government	States and political subdivisions	Total	Items in process of collection	Currency and coin	Bankers' balances (including reserves)	Other
	Cj212	Cj213	Cj214	Cj215 [2]	Cj216 [2]	Cj217 [3]	Cj218	Cj219	Cj220	Cj221	Cj222	Cj223	Cj224
	Number	Million dollars	Million dollars	Million dollars	Million dollars	Million dollars	Million dollars	Million dollars	Million dollars	Million dollars	Million dollars	Million dollars	Million dollars
1896	3,689	3,354	—	1,972	18	464	274	22	801	89	363	349	117
1897	3,610	3,563	—	1,978	18	484	279	24	982	101	435	446	119
1898	3,581	3,978	—	2,164	20	555	304	29	1,129	112	493	524	130
1899	3,582	4,709	—	2,508	24	652	346	36	1,428	229	512	687	121
1900	3,731	4,944	—	2,644	26	775	418	41	1,400	180	529	691	125
1901	4,163	5,674	—	2,980	31	885	450	51	1,681	326	567	788	128
1902	4,532	6,007	—	3,246	35	945	460	57	1,685	269	597	819	131
1903	4,935	6,285	—	3,441	37	1,025	486	63	1,633	250	581	802	186
1904	5,330	6,653	—	3,625	38	1,091	514	67	1,740	172	689	879	197
1905	5,664	7,325	—	3,928	41	1,204	527	76	1,982	296	679	1,007	211
1906	6,047	7,781	—	4,236	47	1,240	562	78	2,071	345	681	1,045	234
1907	6,422	8,472	—	4,662	52	1,361	587	93	2,157	306	721	1,130	292
1908	6,817	8,710	—	4,639	52	1,518	679	105	2,264	271	889	1,104	289
1909	6,886	9,365	—	4,986	57	1,594	705	157	2,496	338	926	1,232	289
1910	7,138	9,892	—	5,454	65	1,575	712	149	2,549	483	865	1,201	314
1911	7,270	10,378	—	5,632	65	1,724	717	164	2,691	317	998	1,376	331
1912	7,366	10,857	—	5,972	75	1,822	745	179	2,714	295	996	1,423	349
1913	7,467	11,032	—	6,160	77	1,845	752	175	2,659	295	968	1,396	368
1914	7,518	11,477	—	6,443	114	1,870	764	176	2,770	358	1,022	1,390	394
1915	7,597	11,790	—	6,663	151	2,025	749	245	2,695	250	857	1,588	407
1916	7,571	13,920	—	7,767	161	2,319	703	278	3,352	522	818	2,012	482
1917	7,599	16,231	—	8,936	185	2,961	1,043	315	3,739	530	752	2,457	595
1918	7,699	18,262	—	10,077	185	3,836	2,025	320	3,570	598	382	2,590	779
1919	7,779	21,105	—	10,903	184	4,809	2,941	322	4,395	1,183	424	2,788	998
1920	8,024	23,267	—	13,499	230	4,048	2,137	338	4,493	1,406	449	2,638	1,227
1921	8,150	20,475	—	11,976	280	3,919	1,917	393	3,535	1,106	373	2,056	1,045
1922	8,244	20,633	—	11,191	371	4,514	2,240	414	3,969	1,251	325	2,393	959
1923	8,236	21,454	—	11,778	463	5,027	2,655	401	3,660	1,023	290	2,347	989
1924	8,080	22,525	—	11,955	535	5,103	2,446	505	4,455	1,468	345	2,642	1,012
1925	8,066	24,252	—	12,592	636	5,701	2,512	594	4,789	1,605	359	2,825	1,170
1926	7,972	25,202	—	13,322	725	5,837	2,466	647	4,788	1,568	359	2,861	1,255
1927	7,790	26,455	—	13,849	1,062	6,388	2,593	743	4,978	1,635	363	2,980	1,240
1928	7,685	28,265	—	14,921	1,285	7,141	2,888	839	4,738	1,412	314	3,012	1,465
1929	7,530	27,260	—	14,805	1,412	6,651	2,801	838	4,279	1,228	297	2,754	1,525
1930	7,247	28,828	—	14,874	1,468	6,875	2,748	893	5,408	1,808	340	3,260	1,671
1931	6,800	27,430	—	13,162	1,580	7,662	3,251	1,107	4,988	1,262	367	3,359	1,618
1932	6,145	22,318	—	10,265	1,612	7,183	3,347	1,114	3,480	692	336	2,452	1,390
1933	4,897	20,813	—	8,102	1,322	7,358	4,026	1,158	4,110	764	286	3,060	1,243
1934	5,417	23,854	—	7,681	1,326	9,331	5,847	1,225	5,688	633	350	4,705	1,154
1935	5,425	26,009	—	7,353	1,293	10,698	7,164	1,396	6,857	639	402	5,766	1,101
1936	5,368	29,643	—	7,749	1,367	12,459	8,435	1,535	8,368	1,236	528	6,604	1,067
1937	5,293	30,272	—	8,797	1,503	12,097	8,206	1,462	8,365	1,284	441	6,640	1,013
1938	5,242	30,317	—	8,316	1,621	11,618	7,973	1,424	9,438	1,107	525	7,806	945
1939	5,203	33,119	—	8,553	1,821	12,528	8,753	1,691	11,061	1,257	527	8,277	977
1940	5,164	36,816	—	9,156	1,993	12,882	9,094	1,926	13,857	980	575	12,302	921
1941	5,130	41,228	—	10,897	2,712	14,922	11,111	2,016	14,496	1,512	703	12,281	913
1942	5,101	44,584	—	10,880	2,237	18,584	14,878	1,956	14,274	1,671	715	11,888	846
1943	5,060	58,783	—	9,173	2,129	33,632	30,102	2,022	15,154	2,258	793	12,103	824
1944	5,036	70,143	—	11,213	2,032	42,130	38,640	2,029	15,998	2,509	803	12,686	802
1945	5,015	81,491	—	12,369	2,077	50,808	47,051	2,196	17,544	2,184	801	14,559	770
1946	5,012	85,698	—	14,469	2,740	51,809	47,271	2,451	18,607	3,004	788	14,815	813
1947	5,012	83,149	—	18,764	4,215	44,218	39,271	2,898	19,341	3,558	966	14,817	826
1948	4,998	85,081	—	22,243	5,250	41,395	36,092	3,204	20,415	3,829	1,105	15,481	1,028
1949	4,987	84,853	—	22,505	5,677	41,012	35,487	3,406	20,324	3,692	1,077	15,555	1,012

Notes appear at end of table

(continued)

TABLE Cj212–224   National banks – number and assets: 1896–1998   *Continued*

				Assets									
				Loans		Securities			Cash				
	Banks	Total domestic assets	Total consolidated domestic and foreign assets	Total	Real estate	Total	U.S. government	States and political subdivisions	Total	Items in process of collection	Currency and coin	Bankers' balances (including reserves)	Other
	Cj212	Cj213	Cj214	Cj215 [2]	Cj216 [2]	Cj217 [3]	Cj218	Cj219	Cj220	Cj221	Cj222	Cj223	Cj224
Year	Number	Million dollars	Million dollars	Million dollars	Million dollars	Million dollars	Million dollars	Million dollars	Million dollars	Million dollars	Million dollars	Million dollars	Million dollars
1950	4,971	89,691	—	24,591	6,335	44,132	37,548	4,288	19,914	4,334	946	14,634	1,054
1951	4,946	94,394	—	30,479	7,224	40,535	32,965	4,959	22,198	4,616	968	16,614	1,182
1952	4,925	101,253	—	33,054	7,785	42,982	34,604	5,800	23,927	5,271	1,239	17,417	1,290
1953	4,874	103,418	—	36,420	8,443	41,429	32,958	6,209	24,279	5,547	1,336	17,396	1,290
1954	4,867	108,607	—	37,671	9,109	44,808	35,757	6,941	24,635	5,489	1,369	17,777	1,493
1955	4,743	107,736	—	39,422	10,366	43,890	34,671	7,011	22,890	5,405	1,364	16,121	1,534
1956	4,667	110,703	—	45,860	11,552	39,595	30,555	7,079	23,545	6,175	1,162	16,208	1,703
1957	4,647	112,460	—	48,415	12,022	39,495	30,345	7,243	22,525	5,187	1,388	15,950	2,025
1958	4,599	122,100	—	50,744	12,685	45,154	34,498	8,247	23,964	5,918	1,545	16,504	2,238
1959	4,559	126,255	—	55,816	14,505	44,166	33,152	9,072	23,835	6,331	1,603	15,901	2,438
1960	4,542	131,433	—	62,398	15,278	39,912	29,298	8,984	26,380	8,267	1,670	16,443	2,743
1961	4,524	137,299	—	63,440	15,838	45,403	33,522	10,124	25,274	8,063	1,491	15,720	3,182
1962	4,500	149,559	—	69,771	17,542	49,470	34,508	12,809	26,860	8,902	1,687	16,271	3,458
1963	4,537	162,748	—	78,383	20,064	51,763	34,011	15,174	28,641	10,206	1,867	16,568	3,961
1964	4,702	175,250	—	89,469	22,806	51,729	31,560	17,527	29,511	10,354	2,466	16,691	4,541
1965	4,803	193,748	—	103,377	25,407	53,612	30,230	20,403	31,595	11,565	2,732	17,307	5,164
1966	4,811	226,050	—	125,212	29,407	57,212	28,891	23,975	36,794	13,967	2,986	19,841	6,832
1967	4,780	242,685	—	133,161	31,343	62,614	29,544	27,660	39,490	16,450	2,766	20,275	7,420
1968	4,742	266,259	—	144,272	34,565	68,558	31,627	30,646	44,830	20,055	2,967	21,807	8,599
1969	4,701	307,019	—	171,505	39,930	71,441	29,489	35,651	52,344	25,741	3,638	22,966	11,729
1970	4,638	314,334	—	177,211	40,846	71,526	28,212	37,064	52,001	22,872	4,151	24,978	13,596
1971	4,599	352,964	—	182,867	—	89,532	41,207	46,254	57,255	—	—	—	23,310
1972	4,607	392,163	—	207,414	—	96,810	42,892	51,033	60,197	—	—	—	27,742
1973	4,631	449,924	—	254,211	—	99,700	43,428	53,277	61,356	—	—	—	34,657
1974	4,695	516,770	—	293,362	—	104,676	43,843	57,396	73,719	—	—	—	45,013
1975	4,732	536,987	—	288,396	—	114,351	54,838	55,796	75,715	—	—	—	58,525
1976	4,749	548,726	—	287,151	—	121,731	63,913	56,894	75,491	—	—	—	64,353
1977	4,703	599,798	—	316,262	—	131,625	67,931	60,667	74,666	—	—	—	77,245
1978	4,616	671,166	892,272	367,083	—	132,481	67,130	62,841	90,729	—	—	—	80,873
1979	4,493	745,114	996,286	416,466	—	144,851	66,058	68,427	98,175	—	—	—	85,622
1980	4,426	1,035,011	1,095,123	567,927	—	161,416	72,360	74,189	195,697	—	—	—	109,971
1981	4,453	1,131,133	1,200,901	620,513	—	175,128	80,918	78,295	210,315	—	—	—	125,177
1982	4,507	—	1,225,253	694,243	—	180,414	83,139	80,736	202,225	—	—	—	148,371
1983	4,713	—	1,324,958	752,445	—	214,520	—	—	210,601	—	—	—	147,392
1984	4,823	—	1,433,096	875,477	—	206,352	—	—	99,429	—	—	—	251,838
1985	4,962	—	1,528,168	948,031	—	221,648	—	—	106,917	—	—	—	251,572
1986	4,913	—	1,649,531	1,023,840	—	252,508	—	—	122,035	—	—	—	251,148
1987	4,744	—	1,717,393	1,077,064	—	279,401	—	—	119,083	—	—	—	241,845
1988	4,458	—	1,796,976	1,149,143	—	271,063	—	—	116,620	—	—	—	260,150
1989	4,263	—	1,893,674	1,218,936	—	284,044	—	—	124,915	—	—	—	265,779
1990	4,063	—	1,973,231	1,266,939	—	307,027	—	—	123,595	—	—	—	275,670
1991	3,908	—	1,960,790	1,246,020	—	328,855	—	—	113,837	—	—	—	272,078
1992	3,702	—	1,971,586	1,204,859	—	381,312	—	—	114,588	—	—	—	270,827
1993	3,444	—	2,013,865	1,207,473	—	420,881	—	—	159,779	—	—	—	225,732
1994	3,187	—	2,184,623	1,299,604	—	440,157	—	—	161,059	—	—	—	283,803
1995	2,946	—	2,299,720	1,409,785	—	391,654	—	—	171,555	—	—	—	326,726
1996	2,763	—	2,538,682	1,629,136	—	399,979	—	—	181,470	—	—	—	328,097
1997	2,656	—	2,688,044	1,746,593	—	408,303	—	—	198,539	—	—	—	334,609
1998	2,546	—	2,978,601	1,923,469	—	474,122	—	—	204,510	—	—	—	376,500

[1] Reports dated on or about June 30 each year.

[2] Beginning in June 1948, figures for real estate loans are gross (that is, before deduction of valuation reserves) and are not completely comparable to earlier figures. Total loans are reported net.

[3] Before 1903, includes securities borrowed.

Sources

1896–1955: Board of Governors of the Federal Reserve System, *All-Bank Statistics, United States, 1896–1955* (April 1959), Table A-2, pp. 38–41. 1956–1979: Comptroller of the Currency, *Annual Report* (various issues). 1971–1982:

Federal Deposit Insurance Corporation, *Assets and Liabilities, Commercial and Mutual Savings Banks* (various issues). 1981–1998: Comptroller of the Currency, *Quarterly Journal* (various issues); see the Internet site for the Comptroller of the Currency for updates.

Documentation

For a discussion of national banks, see the text for Table Cj203–211.

Series Cj215–224. Beginning in 1991, series report consolidated figures for domestic and foreign assets of national banks.

TABLE Cj225–237   National banks – liabilities: 1896–1998[1]

Contributed by Howard Bodenhorn and Eugene N. White

	Total domestic liabilities	Total consolidated domestic and foreign liabilities	Total domestic	Total consolidated domestic and foreign	Interbank	U.S. government	Other demand	All domestic and foreign non-interest-bearing deposits	Other time	All domestic and foreign interest-bearing deposits	Notes in circulation	Capital accounts	Other liabilities
	Cj225	Cj226	Cj227	Cj228	Cj229 [2]	Cj230 [3]	Cj231 [4]	Cj232 [5]	Cj233 [6]	Cj234 [5]	Cj235	Cj236	Cj237
Year	Million dollars	Million dollars	Million dollars	Million dollars	Million dollars	Million dollars	Million dollars	Million dollars	Million dollars	Million dollars	Million dollars	Million dollars	Million dollars
1896	2,141	—	2,141	—	454	16	1,603	—	68	—	199	983	31
1897	2,386	—	2,386	—	597	16	1,700	—	73	—	196	962	19
1898	2,799	—	2,799	—	720	53	1,943	—	83	—	190	955	34
1899	3,539	—	3,539	—	933	76	2,443	—	87	—	199	947	24
1900	3,621	—	3,621	—	1,063	99	2,361	—	98	—	265	1,014	44
1901	4,249	—	4,249	—	1,207	99	2,811	—	132	—	319	1,062	44
1902	4,467	—	4,467	—	1,243	124	2,945	—	155	—	309	1,184	47
1903	4,561	—	4,561	—	1,212	147	3,026	—	176	—	359	1,285	80
1904	4,834	—	4,834	—	1,412	110	3,113	—	199	—	399	1,349	71
1905	5,406	—	5,406	—	1,547	75	3,538	—	246	—	445	1,406	68
1906	5,691	—	5,691	—	1,545	90	3,766	—	290	—	511	1,490	89
1907	6,188	—	6,188	—	1,686	180	3,890	—	432	—	547	1,603	134
1908	6,328	—	6,328	—	1,823	130	3,850	—	525	—	613	1,667	102
1909	6,932	—	6,932	—	2,037	70	4,082	—	743	—	636	1,728	69
1910	7,254	—	7,257	—	1,900	54	4,286	—	1,017	—	675	1,850	113
1911	7,673	—	7,683	—	2,147	48	4,394	—	1,094	—	681	1,932	92
1912	8,061	—	8,061	—	2,178	58	4,611	—	1,214	—	708	1,983	105
1913	8,140	—	8,140	—	2,120	49	4,603	—	1,368	—	722	2,045	125
1914	8,560	—	8,560	—	2,186	66	5,107	—	1,201	—	722	2,049	146
1915	8,817	—	8,817	—	2,208	48	5,235	—	1,326	—	722	2,105	146
1916	10,872	—	10,872	—	2,713	39	6,391	—	1,729	—	675	2,102	271
1917	12,767	—	12,767	—	3,025	133	7,430	—	2,179	—	660	2,197	607
1918	14,015	—	14,015	—	2,796	1,036	7,840	—	2,343	—	681	2,249	1,317
1919	15,935	—	15,935	—	2,974	565	9,612	—	2,784	—	677	2,362	2,131
1920	17,159	—	17,159	—	2,824	174	10,676	—	3,485	—	688	2,621	2,799
1921	15,142	—	15,142	—	2,132	247	9,068	—	3,695	—	704	2,795	1,834
1922	16,323	—	16,323	—	2,482	102	9,628	—	4,111	—	725	2,847	738
1923	16,899	—	16,899	—	2,384	191	9,570	—	4,754	—	719	2,874	962
1924	18,349	—	18,349	—	2,794	121	10,175	—	5,259	—	729	2,915	532
1925	19,912	—	19,912	—	2,855	106	11,028	—	5,923	—	648	2,969	723
1926	20,644	—	20,644	—	2,864	143	11,325	—	6,312	—	651	3,088	819
1927	21,778	—	21,778	—	2,820	138	11,507	—	7,313	—	650	3,237	790
1928	22,645	—	22,645	—	2,701	184	11,466	—	8,294	—	649	3,569	1,402
1929	21,586	—	21,586	—	2,219	226	10,908	—	8,233	—	649	3,672	1,353
1930	23,235	—	13,235	—	2,850	170	1,682	—	8,533	—	649	3,969	975
1931	22,164	—	22,164	—	2,862	234	10,653	—	8,415	—	636	3,749	881
1932	17,428	—	17,428	—	1,814	212	8,196	—	7,206	—	649	3,274	967
1933	16,742	—	16,742	—	2,000	448	8,141	—	6,153	—	727	2,850	494
1934	19,896	—	19,896	—	2,767	887	9,469	—	6,773	—	695	2,995	268
1935	22,477	—	22,477	—	3,410	435	11,517	—	7,115	—	222	3,080	230
1936	26,153	—	26,153	—	4,167	690	13,786	—	7,510	—	—	3,160	330
1937	26,716	—	26,716	—	3,790	377	14,785	—	7,764	—	—	3,205	351
1938	26,763	—	26,763	—	4,210	392	14,210	—	7,951	—	—	3,266	288
1939	29,416	—	29,416	—	4,881	500	15,999	—	8,036	—	—	3,382	321
1940	33,014	—	33,014	—	6,083	537	18,189	—	8,205	—	—	3,468	334
1941	37,273	—	37,273	—	6,589	516	21,812	—	8,356	—	—	3,590	365
1942	40,533	—	40,533	—	6,497	1,146	24,737	—	8,153	—	—	3,671	380
1943	54,590	—	54,590	—	7,156	4,542	33,715	—	9,177	—	—	3,816	377
1944	65,585	—	65,585	—	7,402	10,746	36,214	—	11,223	—	—	4,101	457
1945	76,534	—	76,534	—	8,251	13,138	40,638	—	14,507	—	—	4,461	496
1946	80,212	—	80,212	—	7,816	7,648	47,356	—	17,392	—	—	4,862	624
1947	77,146	—	77,146	—	7,432	843	49,932	—	18,939	—	—	5,296	707
1948	78,753	—	78,753	—	7,305	1,327	50,680	—	19,441	—	—	5,533	795
1949	78,219	—	78,219	—	6,945	1,417	50,130	—	19,727	—	—	5,815	819
1950	82,430	—	82,430	—	7,362	2,363	52,748	—	19,957	—	—	6,180	1,081
1951	86,589	—	86,589	—	7,625	3,870	55,014	—	20,080	—	—	6,504	1,301
1952	92,719	—	92,719	—	8,584	3,629	58,862	—	21,644	—	—	6,879	1,655
1953	94,475	—	94,475	—	8,594	2,434	60,186	—	23,261	—	—	7,220	1,723
1954	99,358	—	99,358	—	9,750	3,576	60,826	—	25,206	—	—	4,668	1,563

Notes appear at end of table   (continued)

TABLE Cj225–237   National banks – liabilities: 1896–1998   *Continued*

	Total domestic liabilities	Total consolidated domestic and foreign liabilities	Deposits					All domestic and foreign non-interest-bearing deposits		All domestic and foreign interest-bearing deposits	Notes in circulation	Capital accounts	Other liabilities
			Total domestic	Total consolidated domestic and foreign	Interbank	U.S. government	Other demand		Other time				
	Cj225	Cj226	Cj227	Cj228	Cj229 [2]	Cj230 [3]	Cj231 [4]	Cj232 [5]	Cj233 [6]	Cj234 [5]	Cj235	Cj236	Cj237
Year	Million dollars	Million dollars	Million dollars	Million dollars	Million dollars	Million dollars	Million dollars	Million dollars	Million dollars	Million dollars	Million dollars	Million dollars	Million dollars
1955	98,631	—	98,631	—	8,314	3,099	60,917	—	26,301	—	—	7,714	1,391
1956	100,826	—	100,826	—	7,364	3,167	62,655	—	27,640	—	—	8,232	1,645
1957	100,989	—	100,988	—	6,854	2,014	62,305	—	29,815	—	—	8,722	2,750
1958	110,065	—	110,065	—	7,383	4,941	63,417	—	34,324	—	—	9,451	2,584
1959	112,659	—	112,658	—	7,344	1,755	66,975	—	36,584	—	—	10,041	3,555
1960	116,178	—	116,179	—	7,490	3,770	67,765	—	37,154	—	—	10,686	4,569
1961	122,485	—	122,486	—	7,463	3,749	67,952	—	43,322	—	—	11,439	3,375
1962	133,728	—	133,727	—	7,823	5,630	69,661	—	50,613	—	—	12,243	3,588
1963	145,513	—	145,513	—	8,183	6,203	72,800	—	58,327	—	—	13,008	4,226
1964	155,978	—	155,979	—	8,154	5,989	75,823	—	66,013	—	—	14,262	5,010
1965	171,528	—	171,528	—	8,838	6,903	79,494	—	76,293	—	—	15,853	6,367
1966	198,314	—	198,315	—	10,246	6,954	89,559	—	91,556	—	—	18,021	9,715
1967	211,731	—	211,732	—	11,143	3,381	94,091	—	103,117	—	—	19,098	11,856
1968	229,772	—	229,772	—	11,831	3,021	103,335	—	111,585	—	—	20,503	15,984
1969	252,680	—	252,680	—	13,595	3,734	114,540	—	120,811	—	—	22,635	31,704
1970	255,819	—	255,820	—	14,106	5,207	114,841	—	121,666	—	—	24,113	34,402
1971	323,005	—	294,025	—	16,774	5,489	142,788	—	151,236	—	—	25,999	28,980
1972	359,367	—	322,288	—	15,980	6,023	149,864	—	172,423	—	—	27,712	37,079
1973	413,606	—	364,129	—	17,502	6,679	159,937	—	204,191	—	—	31,867	49,477
1974	476,840	—	407,915	—	21,933	5,294	171,077	—	236,837	—	—	34,966	68,925
1975	494,073	—	431,646	—	24,222	2,042	175,395	—	256,251	—	—	37,483	62,427
1976	506,584	—	444,251	—	22,527	2,886	175,570	—	268,679	—	—	39,504	62,333
1977	553,787	—	476,382	—	23,697	2,189	185,867	—	290,514	—	—	43,143	77,405
1978	621,050	—	526,932	—	27,493	5,231	202,925	—	324,007	—	—	47,020	94,118
1979	697,546	—	553,914	—	—	1,627	207,401	—	346,511	—	—	51,873	143,632
1980	806,466	—	597,090	—	—	—	177,614	—	335,102	—	—	57,180	193,504
1981	877,735	—	656,645	—	—	—	162,849	—	406,515	—	—	62,999	202,920 [7]
1982	939,878	1,153,125	713,772	939,878	—	—	153,075	—	472,105	—	—	68,619	199,356
1983	—	1,249,915	—	1,016,607	—	—	—	210,375	—	594,893	—	75,043	233,308
1984	—	1,350,299	—	1,099,911	—	—	—	220,747	—	651,927	—	82,716	250,388
1985	—	1,435,985	—	1,167,963	—	—	—	235,320	—	721,127	—	92,119	479,538
1986	—	1,550,440	—	1,256,222	—	—	—	273,900	—	777,614	—	99,021	294,218
1987	—	1,619,985	—	1,312,264	—	—	—	272,896	—	830,688	—	97,331	307,721
1988	—	1,688,721	—	1,356,085	—	—	—	263,224	—	894,052	—	102,690	332,636
1989	—	1,780,065	—	1,430,213	—	—	—	264,736	—	970,472	—	113,769	349,852
1990	—	1,854,263	—	1,512,293	—	—	—	263,663	—	1,044,428	—	119,325	341,970
1991	—	1,837,458	—	1,531,699	—	—	—	264,051	—	1,078,420	—	123,746	305,759
1992	—	1,834,914	—	1,539,639	—	—	—	285,680	—	1,060,580	—	136,649	295,275
1993	—	1,855,842	—	1,527,145	—	—	—	303,022	—	1,024,098	—	155,654	328,697
1994	—	2,017,026	—	1,564,275	—	—	—	309,159	—	1,014,903	—	168,225	452,751
1995	—	2,119,608	—	1,617,100	—	—	—	310,831	—	1,022,174	—	181,814	502,508
1996	—	2,332,955	—	1,794,667	—	—	—	363,163	—	1,125,591	—	207,994	538,288
1997	—	2,455,705	—	1,879,289	—	—	—	405,587	—	1,473,702	—	232,656	576,416
1998	—	2,714,914	—	2,035,448	—	—	—	422,097	—	1,613,351	—	263,687	679,466

[1] Reports dated on or about June 30 each year.

[2] Beginning in 1966, includes domestic interbank deposits only; 1961–1965 includes domestic interbank and postal savings deposits. Prior to 1966, includes deposits of foreign banks.

[3] Beginning in 1971, includes deposits of states and political subdivisions.

[4] Beginning in 1971, all demand deposits are reported instead of other demand deposits.

[5] 1982–1996, these are domestic deposits; beginning in 1997, the figures are for consolidated domestic and foreign deposits.

[6] Beginning in 1971, all time deposits are reported instead of other time deposits. In 1976, all savings deposits are included in all time deposits.

[7] Other liabilities for the consolidated domestic and foreign balance sheet were $213,247 million.

Sources

1896–1955: Board of Governors of the Federal Reserve System, *All-Bank Statistics, United States, 1896–1955* (April 1959), Table A-2, pp. 38–41. 1956–1979: Comptroller of the Currency, *Annual Report* (various issues). 1971–1982: Federal Deposit Insurance Corporation, *Assets and Liabilities, Commercial and Mutual Savings Banks* (various issues). 1981–1998: Comptroller of the Currency, *Quarterly Journal* (various issues); see the Internet site for the Comptroller of the Currency for updates.

Documentation

Series Cj231 and Cj233. Excludes interbank and U.S. government deposits.

TABLE Cj238–250   National banks – number, earnings, and expenses: 1869–1998[1]

Contributed by Howard Bodenhorn and Eugene N. White

Year	Banks	Earnings		Expenses		Net earnings		Net losses		Profits or income			
		Gross domestic earnings	Consolidated domestic and foreign operating income	Domestic expenses	Consolidated domestic and foreign operating expenses	Net current earnings	Income before income taxes and extraordinary items	Including depreciation or net recoveries	Loan	Net profits	Net income	Cash dividends declared	Net profits as percentage of total capital accounts
	Cj238	Cj239	Cj240	Cj241 [2]	Cj242 [3]	Cj243 [2]	Cj244	Cj245 [4]	Cj246 [5]	Cj247	Cj248	Cj249	Cj250
	Number	Million dollars	Million dollars	Million dollars	Million dollars	Million dollars	Million dollars	Million dollars	Million dollars	Million dollars	Million dollars	Million dollars	Percent
1869	1,619	—	—	—	—	—	—	—	—	29	—	22	10.7
1870	1,612	—	—	—	—	—	—	—	—	56	—	43	9.9
1871	1,723	—	—	—	—	—	—	—	—	55	—	44	9.2
1872	1,853	—	—	—	—	—	—	—	—	58	—	47	9.3
1873	1,968	—	—	—	—	—	—	—	—	65	—	50	9.8
1874	1,983	—	—	—	—	—	—	—	—	60	—	48	8.8
1875	2,076	—	—	—	—	—	—	—	—	58	—	49	8.4
1876	2,091	—	—	—	—	—	—	—	—	44	—	47	6.4
1877	2,078	—	—	—	—	—	—	—	—	35	—	44	5.3
1878	2,056	—	—	—	—	—	—	—	—	31	—	37	4.9
1879	2,048	—	—	—	—	—	—	—	—	32	—	35	5.1
1880	2,076	—	—	—	—	—	—	—	—	45	—	36	7.2
1881	2,115	—	—	—	—	—	—	—	—	54	—	38	8.4
1882	2,239	—	—	—	—	—	—	—	—	53	—	41	8.1
1883	2,417	—	—	—	—	—	—	—	—	54	—	41	7.6
1884	2,625	—	—	—	—	—	—	—	—	52	—	41	7.1
1885	2,689	—	—	—	—	—	—	—	—	44	—	41	6.0
1886	2,809	—	—	—	—	—	—	—	—	55	—	42	7.3
1887	3,014	—	—	—	—	—	—	—	—	65	—	44	8.0
1888	3,120	129	—	45	—	84	—	−19	—	65	—	47	7.8
1889	3,239	135	—	50	—	86	—	−16	—	70	—	47	8.0
1890	3,484	145	—	51	—	93	—	−21	—	72	—	51	7.7
1891	3,652	151	—	55	—	96	—	−20	—	76	—	51	7.7
1892	3,759	149	—	59	—	90	—	−23	—	67	—	50	6.6
1893	3,807	152	—	61	—	91	—	−22	—	69	—	50	6.7
1894	3,770	140	—	60	—	80	—	−38	—	42	—	45	4.2
1895	3,715	135	—	60	—	75	—	−28	—	47	—	46	4.8
1896	3,689	142	—	61	—	81	—	−31	—	50	—	46	5.1
1897	3,610	138	—	61	—	77	—	−33	—	44	—	42	4.6
1898	3,582	143	—	62	—	81	—	−31	—	50	—	44	5.2
1899	3,583	157	—	68	—	88	—	−34	—	54	—	47	5.7
1900	3,732	194	—	73	—	121	—	−34	—	87	—	48	8.6
1901	4,165	188	—	78	—	111	—	−29	—	82	—	52	7.7
1902	4,535	221	—	85	—	136	—	−29	—	107	—	68	9.0
1903	4,939	235	—	93	—	141	—	−31	—	110	—	64	8.6
1904	5,331	249	—	103	—	146	—	−33	—	113	—	76	8.4
1905	5,668	249	—	112	—	136	—	−30	—	106	—	73	7.5
1906	6,053	279	—	120	—	159	—	−31	—	128	—	89	8.6
1907 [6]	6,429	315	—	132	—	183	—	−31	—	152	—	100	11.4
1908	6,824	332	—	151	—	182	—	−51	—	131	—	97	7.9
1909	6,926	349	—	177	—	172	—	−41	—	131	—	93	7.5
1910	7,145	403	—	210	—	193	—	−39	—	154	—	103	8.3
1911	7,277	429	—	232	—	197	—	−40	—	157	—	115	8.1
1912	7,372	450	—	259	—	191	—	−42	—	149	—	120	7.5
1913	7,473	499	—	285	—	215	—	−54	—	161	—	120	7.9
1914	7,525	516	—	301	—	214	—	−65	—	149	—	131	7.3
1915	7,605	528	—	322	—	206	—	−79	—	127	—	114	6.0
1916	7,579	591	—	371	—	220	—	−63	—	157	—	115	7.5
1917	7,604	667	—	411	—	257	—	−63	—	194	—	126	8.8
1918	7,705	814	—	510	—	304	—	−92	—	212	—	130	9.4
1919	7,890	993	—	671	—	322	—	−73	—	249	—	135	10.2
1920	8,130	1,211	—	817	—	393	—	−132	—	261	—	162	9.9
1921	8,169	1,121	—	775	—	347	—	−166	—	181	—	153	6.5
1922	8,225	1,043	—	717	—	326	—	−115	—	211	—	161	7.4
1923	8,184	1,065	—	758	—	307	—	−112	—	195	—	152	6.7
1924	8,049	1,094	—	776	—	318	—	−104	—	214	—	155	7.4

Notes appear at end of table

(continued)

TABLE Cj238–250　National banks – number, earnings, and expenses: 1869–1998　*Continued*

		Earnings		Expenses		Net earnings		Net losses		Profits or income			
		Gross domestic earnings	Consolidated domestic and foreign operating income	Domestic expenses	Consolidated domestic and foreign operating expenses	Net current earnings	Income before income taxes and extraordinary items	Including depreciation or net recoveries	Loan	Net profits	Net income	Cash dividends declared	Net profits as percentage of total capital accounts
	Banks												
	Cj238	Cj239	Cj240	Cj241 [2]	Cj242 [3]	Cj243 [2]	Cj244	Cj245 [4]	Cj246 [5]	Cj247	Cj248	Cj249	Cj250
Year	Number	Million dollars	Million dollars	Million dollars	Million dollars	Million dollars	Million dollars	Million dollars	Million dollars	Million dollars	Million dollars	Million dollars	Percent
1925	8,054	1,160	—	823	—	338	—	−94	—	244	—	163	8.2
1926	7,912	1,212	—	857	—	354	—	−109	—	245	—	169	8.0
1927	7,765	1,227	—	919	—	308	—	−50	—	258	—	184	7.9
1928	7,635	1,351	—	988	—	363	—	−72	—	291	—	195	8.2
1929	7,408	1,407	—	988	—	418	—	−126	—	292	—	227	7.8
1930	7,038	1,325	—	990	—	336	—	−178	—	158	—	211	4.0
1931	6,373	1,153	—	850	—	303	—	−358	—	−55	—	193	−1.5
1932	6,016	1,000	—	750	—	250	—	−415	—	−165	—	135	−5.0
1933 [7]	5,159	802	—	565	—	236	—	−522	—	−286	—	72	−9.6
1934 [7]	5,467	809	—	558	—	251	—	−404	—	−153	—	91	−5.2
1935	5,392	794	—	549	—	245	—	−87	—	158	—	113	5.1
1936	5,331	825	—	565	—	260	—	54	—	314	—	120	10.0
1937	5,266	859	—	586	—	273	—	−45	—	228	—	122	7.1
1938	5,230	838	—	577	—	261	—	−62	—	199	—	123	6.1
1939	5,193	848	—	581	—	267	—	−15	—	252	—	131	7.4
1940	5,150	865	—	599	—	265	—	−24	—	241	—	133	7.0
1941	5,123	926	—	642	—	284	—	−15	—	269	—	133	7.5
1942	5,087	963	—	695	—	268	—	−25	—	243	—	128	6.6
1943	5,046	1,062	—	746	—	315	—	35	—	350	—	132	9.1
1944	5,031	1,206	—	846	—	360	—	52	—	412	—	144	10.0
1945	5,023	1,349	—	987	—	362	—	128	—	490	—	156	11.0
1946	4,013	1,574	—	1,138	—	436	—	59	—	495	—	170	10.1
1947	5,011	1,725	—	1,263	—	461	—	−8	—	453	—	184	8.6
1948	4,997	1,900	—	1,361	—	540	—	−116	—	424	—	194	7.6
1949	4,981	2,005	—	1,442	—	563	—	−88	—	475	—	205	8.2
1950	4,965	2,193	—	1,593	—	600	—	−62	—	538	—	230	8.7
1951	4,946	2,454	—	1,812	—	642	—	−135	—	507	—	248	7.8
1952	4,916	2,751	—	2,067	—	684	—	−123	—	561	—	259	8.2
1953	4,864	3,068	—	2,310	—	758	—	−185	—	573	—	275	7.9
1954	4,796	3,226	—	2,528	—	699	—	42	—	741	—	300	9.6
1955	4,700	3,437	—	2,551	—	885	—	−242	—	643	—	310	8.1
1956	4,659	3,833	—	2,768	—	1,065	—	−418	—	647	—	330	7.9
1957	4,627	4,284	—	3,252	—	1,031	—	−301	—	730	—	364	8.3
1958	4,585	4,539	—	3,660	—	878	—	11	—	889	—	393	9.4
1959	4,542	5,183	—	3,845	—	1,338	—	−538	—	800	—	423	8.0
1960	4,530	5,756	—	4,450	—	1,305	—	−259	—	1,046	—	451	9.8
1961	4,513	5,955	—	4,751	—	1,203	—	−161	—	1,042	—	486	9.1
1962	4,503	6,596	—	5,304	—	1,292	—	−223	—	1,069	—	518	8.7
1963	4,615	7,302	—	5,917	—	1,386	—	−180	—	1,206	—	548	9.2
1964	4,773	9,148	—	6,536	—	1,612	—	−399	—	1,213	—	593	8.5
1965	4,815	9,705	—	7,836	—	1,870	—	−483	—	1,387	—	683	8.6
1966	4,799	11,305	—	9,099	—	2,207	—	−624	—	1,583	—	738	8.8
1967	4,758	12,651	—	10,375	—	2,276	—	−519	—	1,757	—	796	9.2
1968	4,716	14,998	—	12,218	—	2,779	—	−847	—	1,932	—	897	9.4
1969	4,669	18,221	—	15,565	—	2,656	—	−634	—	2,022	—	1,068	9.0
1970	4,621	20,434	—	17,542	—	2,892	—	−593	—	2,299	—	1,278	9.5
1971	4,600	21,310	—	17,430	—	3,879	—	−838	—	3,041	—	1,390	11.7
1972	4,614	23,543	—	19,315	—	4,228	—	−920	—	3,308	—	1,310	10.8
1973	4,661	31,214	—	26,247	—	4,967	—	−1,199	—	3,768	—	1,449	11.4
1974	4,708	40,448	—	35,241	—	5,207	—	−1,162	—	4,045	—	1,671	11.3
1975	4,744	38,907	—	33,616	—	5,290	—	−1,031	—	4,259	—	1,821	10.9
1976	4,737	48,021	—	42,103	—	5,918	—	−1,327	—	4,591	—	1,821	11.6
1977	4,655	53,789	—	46,956	—	6,833	—	−1,694	—	5,139	—	1,994	11.4
1978	4,564	67,842	—	58,975	—	6,276	—	−103	—	6,173	—	2,196	12.5
1979	4,493	89,886	—	79,726	—	7,407	—	−158	—	7,247	—	2,650	13.3

Notes appear at end of table

TABLE Cj238–250   National banks – number, earnings, and expenses: 1869–1998 *Continued*

		Earnings		Expenses		Net earnings		Net losses		Profits or income			
	Banks	Gross domestic earnings	Consolidated domestic and foreign operating income	Domestic expenses	Consolidated domestic and foreign operating expenses	Net current earnings	Income before income taxes and extraordinary items	Including depreciation or net recoveries	Loan	Net profits	Net income	Cash dividends declared	Net profits as percentage of total capital accounts
	Cj238	Cj239	Cj240	Cj241 [2]	Cj242 [3]	Cj243 [2]	Cj244	Cj245 [4]	Cj246 [5]	Cj247	Cj248	Cj249	Cj250
Year	Number	Million dollars	Million dollars	Million dollars	Million dollars	Million dollars	Million dollars	Million dollars	Million dollars	Million dollars	Million dollars	Million dollars	Percent
1980	4,426	57,231	—	51,792	—	5,439	—	−1,657	—	7,666	—	2,951	12.8
1981	4,453	—	148,942	—	137,664	—	8,678	—	2,272	—	8,201	3,378	12.5
1982	4,507	—	153,865	—	143,349	—	10,516	—	4,137	—	8,236	3,808	11.8
1983	4,713	—	143,585	—	133,245	—	10,340	—	5,404	—	8,095	4,184	10.2
1984	4,823	—	167,464	—	147,150	—	11,116	—	6,669	—	8,424	4,248	12.5
1985	4,962	—	169,024	—	145,520	—	12,973	—	8,537	—	9,991	4,877	10.4
1986	4,913	—	164,766	—	140,352	—	12,751	—	10,341	—	9,742	5,315	4.4
1987	4,744	—	173,273	—	146,731	—	2,995	—	10,684	—	442	6,323	0.4
1988	4,392	—	193,284	—	163,247	—	19,035	—	12,362	—	13,825	8,434	12.5
1989	4,263	—	226,255	—	192,690	—	16,995	—	14,865	—	10,769	7,955	7.3
1990	3,981	—	226,635	—	194,810	—	11,333	—	18,798	—	7,398	7,623	6.7
1991	3,789	—	206,623	—	174,261	—	12,337	—	21,140	—	9,514	8,772	7.5
1992	3,591	—	188,102	—	149,912	—	25,086	—	15,676	—	17,287	7,553	11.9
1993	3,304	—	190,099	—	158,502	—	35,773	—	10,073	—	25,688	13,278	16.4
1994	3,075	—	195,597	—	149,592	—	40,152	—	6,015	—	26,837	17,669	15.5
1995	2,858	—	221,195	—	186,376	—	44,439	—	6,499	—	28,641	20,516	15.8
1996	2,726	—	233,423	—	193,911	—	47,859	—	9,968	—	30,097	25,279	15.3
1997	2,597	—	265,703	—	218,069	—	55,570	—	12,649	—	35,027	28,587	15.0
1998	2,458	—	295,404	—	245,321	—	56,852	—	14,482	—	35,582	25,415	14.3

[1] Data on earnings and expenses are for the calendar year, except for the years ending June 30, 1907–1918; and years ending August 31, 1869–1906. The number of banks is for dates closest to the end of the accounting year.

[2] Income taxes have been treated as an expense before 1981. Beginning in 1943, these figures differ from those shown in the source volume because income taxes in the source volume are shown separately from other expenses and as a deduction from net current earnings.

[3] Income taxes are not treated as an expense after 1981.

[4] Losses here are traditionally entered as negative numbers.

[5] Losses here are recorded as positive numbers.

[6] Ten months only.

[7] Licensed banks, that is, those operating on an unrestricted basis.

Sources
1869–1941: Board of Governors of the Federal Reserve System, *Banking and Monetary Statistics* (1943), pp. 2601. 1942–1980: U.S. Comptroller of the Currency, *Annual Report* (various issues). 1981–1998: U.S. Comptroller of the Currency, *Quarterly Journal* (various issues), and the Internet site for the Comptroller of the Currency.

Documentation
For those interested in the details of sources of national bank income and expenses, the reader is referred to the original sources, especially the Comptroller's reports before 1941. Those sources report much more detailed earning reports categorized by type of asset, recoveries and profits from bad debts, and transfers to and from valuation reserve accounts. Data are also available for state, region, and Federal Reserve district, as well as bank class and size. Some issues also report various earnings and operating ratios.

The figures for gross and net current earnings before 1927 include profits on securities sold. The figures for gross and net earnings up to and including the fiscal year ending June 1919 also include recoveries on charged-off assets. Beginning in 1927 and 1919, respectively, these items are included in series Cj242.

Data after 1968 are not comparable with data for 1968 and before. Beginning in 1969, net current earnings are reduced by a provision for loan losses; expenses reported in series Cj240 include only those income taxes applicable to current earnings; the effect of taxes on other earnings is reflected in series Cj242; and series Cj242 is computed by summing securities gains or losses, extraordinary charges or credits, and the excess of transfers from reserves over transfers to reserves, all adjusted for tax effects.

Beginning in 1981, the Comptroller began to report income and expenses for the consolidated domestic and foreign operations of national banks.

TABLE Cj251–264   Commercial banks – number and assets: 1834–1980[1]

Contributed by Howard Bodenhorn

			Assets											
			Loans			Investments				Cash				
Year	Banks	Total assets or liabilities and capital	Total	Real estate	Other	Total	U.S. government obligations	Obligations of state and political subdivisions	Other	Total	Cash items in process of collection	Currency and coin	Bankers' balances	Other
	Cj251	Cj252	Cj253 [2,3]	Cj254	Cj255	Cj256 [3]	Cj257	Cj258	Cj259	Cj260	Cj261	Cj262	Cj263 [4]	Cj264 [5]
	Number	Million dollars	Million dollars	Million dollars	Million dollars	Million dollars	Million dollars	Million dollars	Million dollars	Million dollars	Million dollars	Million dollars	Million dollars	Million dollars
1834	506	419	324	—	—	6	—	—	—	76	—	49	27	13
1835	704	498	365	—	—	9	—	—	—	108	—	68	40	16
1836	713	622	458	—	—	12	—	—	—	129	—	77	52	24
1837	788	706	525	—	—	12	—	—	—	140	—	80	60	29
1838	829	682	485	—	—	34	—	—	—	119	—	61	58	43
1839	840	702	492	—	—	36	—	—	—	129	—	76	53	45
1840	901	658	463	—	—	42	—	—	—	99	—	58	41	54
1841	784	608	386	—	—	65	—	—	—	112	—	64	48	45
1842	692	472	324	—	—	25	—	—	—	82	—	51	31	42
1843	691	393	255	—	—	28	—	—	—	74	—	53	21	36
1844	696	427	265	—	—	23	—	—	—	104	—	68	36	35
1845	707	434	289	—	—	20	—	—	—	93	—	63	30	32
1846	707	456	312	—	—	21	—	—	—	95	—	63	32	27
1847	715	458	310	—	—	20	—	—	—	94	—	62	32	33
1848	751	512	344	—	—	26	—	—	—	112	—	73	39	29
1849	782	479	332	—	—	24	—	—	—	97	—	65	32	25
1850	824	532	364	—	—	21	—	—	—	115	—	73	42	33
1851	879	597	414	—	—	22	—	—	—	132	—	81	51	29
1852	913	620	430	—	—	23	—	—	—	137	—	84	53	30
1853	750	577	409	—	—	22	—	—	—	127	—	78	49	19
1854	1,208	795	557	—	—	44	—	—	—	164	—	108	56	30
1855	1,307	817	576	—	—	53	—	—	—	155	—	99	56	33
1856	1,398	880	634	—	—	49	—	—	—	167	—	104	63	30
1857	1,416	953	684	—	—	59	—	—	—	178	—	112	66	32
1858	1,422	849	583	—	—	60	—	—	—	170	—	112	58	35
1859	1,476	983	657	—	—	64	—	—	—	228	—	150	78	34
1860	1,562	1,000	692	—	—	70	—	—	—	195	—	128	67	42
1861	1,601	1,016	697	—	—	74	—	—	—	198	—	139	59	47
1862	1,492	1,012	647	—	—	99	—	—	—	220	—	155	65	46
1863	1,532	1,209	654	—	—	186	—	—	—	308	—	208	100	60
1864	1,556	973	555	—	—	150	—	—	—	236	—	147	89	33
1865	1,643	1,357	518	—	—	412	—	—	—	392	—	231	161	36
1866	1,931	1,672	682	—	—	483	—	—	—	480	—	259	221	28
1867	1,908	1,674	709	—	—	536	—	—	—	398	—	155	243	30
1868	1,887	1,736	765	—	—	521	—	—	—	418	—	159	259	32
1869	1,878	1,736	801	—	—	480	—	—	—	417	—	136	281	37
1870	1,937	1,781	864	—	—	470	—	—	—	406	—	174	232	42
1871	2,175	2,003	990	—	—	479	—	—	—	485	—	205	280	48
1872	2,419	2,145	1,123	—	—	480	—	—	—	489	—	217	272	53
1873	3,298	2,731	1,440	—	—	721	—	—	—	487	—	199	288	84
1874	3,552	2,890	1,564	—	—	732	—	—	—	510	—	242	268	84
1875	3,336	3,205	1,748	—	—	802	—	—	—	526	—	230	296	128
1876	3,448	3,183	1,727	—	—	818	—	—	—	502	—	217	285	135
1877	3,384	3,204	1,721	—	—	852	—	—	—	484	—	221	263	148
1878	3,229	3,081	1,561	—	—	874	—	—	—	492	—	207	285	152
1879	3,335	3,313	1,507	—	—	1,139	—	—	—	504	—	207	297	162
1880	3,355	3,399	1,662	—	—	904	—	—	—	655	—	274	381	177
1881	3,427	3,869	1,902	—	—	985	—	—	—	782	—	278	504	200
1882	3,572	4,031	2,050	—	—	1,055	—	—	—	755	—	269	486	171
1883	3,835	4,208	2,234	—	—	1,028	—	—	—	712	—	286	426	235
1884	4,113	4,221	2,261	—	—	1,041	—	—	—	678	—	303	375	241
1885	4,350	4,427	2,272	—	—	1,042	—	—	—	876	—	390	486	237
1886	4,338	4,542	2,434	—	—	1,051	—	—	—	773	—	347	426	284
1887	6,170	5,193	2,943	—	—	1,011	—	—	—	999	—	432	567	240
1888	6,647	5,470	3,161	—	—	1,131	—	—	—	989	—	459	530	189
1889	7,244	5,945	3,478	—	—	1,129	—	—	—	1,144	—	515	629	194

Notes appear at end of table

TABLE Cj251–264 Commercial banks – number and assets: 1834–1980 *Continued*

			Loans			Investments				Cash				
	Banks	Total assets or liabilities and capital	Total	Real estate	Other	Total	U.S. government obligations	Obligations of state and political subdivisions	Other	Total	Cash items in process of collection	Currency and coin	Bankers' balances	Other
	Cj251	Cj252	Cj253 [2,3]	Cj254	Cj255	Cj256 [3]	Cj257	Cj258	Cj259	Cj260	Cj261	Cj262	Cj263 [4]	Cj264 [5]
Year	Number	Million dollars	Million dollars	Million dollars	Million dollars	Million dollars	Million dollars	Million dollars	Million dollars	Million dollars	Million dollars	Million dollars	Million dollars	Million dollars
1890	8,201	6,358	3,854	—	—	1,173	—	—	—	1,124	—	489	635	208
1891	8,641	6,562	4,031	—	—	1,179	—	—	—	1,125	—	498	627	227
1892	9,336	7,245	4,337	—	—	1,283	—	—	—	1,378	—	586	792	247
1893	9,492	7,192	4,369	—	—	1,366	—	—	—	1,190	—	516	674	268
1894	9,508	7,291	4,085	—	—	1,445	—	—	—	1,473	—	689	784	287
1895	9,818	7,610	4,269	—	—	1,565	—	—	—	1,442	—	631	811	333
1896	11,474	6,167	3,741	436	3,305	818	348	102	368	1,330	136	550	644	278
1897	11,438	6,475	3,701	417	3,284	886	358	113	415	1,604	153	638	813	284
1898	11,530	7,170	4,060	420	3,640	1,002	386	128	488	1,800	151	701	948	308
1899	11,835	8,489	4,718	446	4,272	1,207	435	157	615	2,264	339	732	1,193	300
1900	12,427	9,059	5,065	484	4,581	1,410	506	169	735	2,274	276	756	1,242	310
1901	13,424	10,572	5,835	545	5,290	1,676	525	190	961	2,740	521	831	1,388	321
1902	14,488	11,427	6,521	617	5,904	1,821	517	199	1,105	2,731	377	862	1,492	354
1903	15,814	12,190	7,052	698	6,354	2,016	542	223	1,251	2,706	345	865	1,496	416
1904	17,037	13,035	7,299	756	6,543	2,226	562	259	1,405	3,066	291	1,014	1,761	444
1905	18,152	14,542	8,220	870	7,350	2,523	571	286	1,666	3,321	445	1,001	1,875	478
1906	19,786	15,601	9,013	1,026	7,987	2,563	598	279	1,686	3,502	519	1,036	1,947	523
1907	21,361	16,862	9,810	1,111	8,699	2,744	616	316	1,812	3,706	487	1,120	2,099	602
1908	22,531	16,664	9,243	1,104	8,139	2,912	706	335	1,871	3,885	431	1,351	2,103	624
1909	23,098	18,145	10,015	1,199	8,816	3,153	733	412	2,008	4,340	565	1,453	2,322	637
1910	24,514	19,324	11,072	1,392	9,680	3,156	737	408	2,011	4,387	757	1,421	2,209	709
1911	25,183	20,320	11,455	1,513	9,942	3,431	742	466	2,223	4,672	519	1,559	2,594	762
1912	25,844	21,495	12,239	1,677	10,562	3,676	774	530	2,372	4,758	495	1,559	2,704	822
1913	26,664	22,056	12,820	1,809	11,011	3,697	770	536	2,391	4,681	490	1,548	2,643	858
1914	27,236	23,155	13,416	1,812	11,604	3,861	782	565	2,514	4,930	587	1,615	2,728	948
1915	27,390	24,106	13,834	1,960	11,874	4,156	767	663	2,726	5,092	434	1,452	3,206	1,024
1916	27,739	28,217	16,067	2,122	13,945	4,870	740	786	3,344	6,148	775	1,463	3,910	1,132
1917	28,298	32,802	18,581	2,395	16,186	5,837	1,300	863	3,674	7,010	768	1,464	4,778	1,374
1918	28,856	36,352	20,571	2,484	18,087	7,478	3,043	824	3,511	6,613	869	865	4,879	1,690
1919	29,147	42,462	22,814	2,609	20,205	9,521	4,864	947	3,710	8,061	1,737	941	5,383	2,066
1920	30,291	47,509	28,562	3,225	25,337	8,393	3,638	944	3,816	8,264	2,007	1,012	5,245	2,285
1921	30,456	43,669	26,386	3,354	23,032	8,360	3,262	1,043	4,055	6,771	1,665	856	4,250	2,152
1922	30,120	44,106	25,040	3,671	21,369	9,359	3,846	1,146	4,367	7,602	1,988	776	4,838	2,105
1923	29,829	47,332	27,397	4,243	23,154	10,325	4,604	1,182	4,539	7,377	1,677	746	4,957	2,233
1924	28,988	50,136	28,278	4,710	23,568	10,679	4,260	1,382	5,037	8,787	2,504	855	5,428	2,392
1925	28,442	54,401	30,222	5,273	24,949	11,755	4,454	1,527	5,774	9,663	2,755	892	6,016	2,761
1926	27,742	56,781	32,084	5,781	26,303	12,224	4,414	1,723	6,087	9,568	2,683	911	5,974	2,905
1927	26,650	58,973	32,932	5,992	26,940	13,165	4,494	1,912	6,759	9,901	2,890	893	6,118	2,975
1928	25,798	61,563	34,488	6,193	28,295	14,466	4,933	1,999	7,534	9,215	2,409	768	6,038	3,394
1929	24,970	62,442	36,114	6,313	29,801	13,683	4,872	1,955	6,856	9,004	2,394	740	5,870	3,641
1930	23,679	64,125	35,043	6,146	28,897	14,392	4,874	2,111	7,407	10,910	3,659	799	6,452	3,780
1931	21,654	59,017	29,307	5,757	23,550	15,686	6,011	2,434	7,241	10,017	2,526	816	6,675	4,007
1932	18,734	46,304	22,001	4,955	17,046	14,277	6,250	2,299	5,728	6,970	1,372	715	4,883	3,056
1933	14,207	40,511	16,457	4,202	12,255	14,078	7,496	2,267	4,315	7,368	1,506	582	5,280	2,608
1934	15,348	44,978	15,719	3,661	12,058	17,072	10,324	2,360	4,388	9,648	1,097	642	7,909	2,539
1935	15,438	48,905	14,950	3,494	11,456	19,735	12,778	2,689	4,268	11,799	1,226	729	9,844	2,421
1936	15,329	55,572	15,600	3,530	12,070	23,077	15,344	2,873	4,860	14,497	2,204	945	11,348	2,398
1937	15,094	56,907	17,471	3,727	13,744	22,138	14,583	2,799	4,756	14,993	2,257	875	11,861	2,305
1938	14,867	56,185	16,128	3,863	12,265	21,109	14,081	2,779	4,249	16,798	1,953	936	13,909	2,150
1939	14,667	61,422	16,411	4,099	12,312	23,004	15,740	3,286	3,978	19,852	2,249	950	16,653	2,155
1940	14,534	67,804	17,393	4,392	13,001	23,793	16,597	3,610	3,586	24,626	1,598	1,037	21,991	1,992
1941	14,434	75,356	20,324	4,742	15,582	27,319	20,139	3,670	3,510	25,819	2,517	1,290	22,012	1,894
1942	14,353	80,276	20,249	4,875	15,374	33,431	26,439	3,564	3,428	24,844	2,691	1,334	20,819	1,752
1943	14,197	104,322	17,673	4,633	13,040	59,020	52,495	3,517	3,008	25,976	3,550	1,485	20,941	1,653
1944	14,138	125,031	21,029	4,447	16,582	74,784	68,480	3,472	2,832	27,662	4,126	1,503	22,033	1,556

Notes appear at end of table

(continued)

TABLE Cj251–264   Commercial banks – number and assets: 1834–1980 *Continued*

			Loans			Investments				Cash				
	Banks	Total assets or liabilities and capital	Total	Real estate	Other	Total	U.S. government obligations	Obligations of state and political subdivisions	Other	Total	Cash items in process of collection	Currency and coin	Bankers' balances	Other
	Cj251	Cj252	Cj253 [2,3]	Cj254	Cj255	Cj256 [3]	Cj257	Cj258	Cj259	Cj260	Cj261	Cj262	Cj263 [4]	Cj264 [5]
Year	Number	Million dollars	Million dollars	Million dollars	Million dollars	Million dollars	Million dollars	Million dollars	Million dollars	Million dollars	Million dollars	Million dollars	Million dollars	Million dollars
1945	14,126	146,245	23,697	4,501	19,196	90,917	84,136	3,778	3,003	30,157	3,402	1,509	25,246	1,474
1946	14,152	153,507	27,159	5,845	21,314	92,417	84,549	4,082	3,786	32,418	5,253	1,510	25,655	1,513
1947	14,182	146,974	33,679	8,310	25,369	79,076	70,533	4,965	3,578	32,705	5,831	1,851	25,023	1,514
1948	14,189	149,799	39,866	10,233	29,963	73,990	64,798	5,588	3,604	34,168	6,038	2,103	26,027	1,775
1949	14,151	149,705	41,028	11,023	30,459	72,750	63,221	5,929	3,600	34,167	6,102	2,072	25,993	1,760
1950	14,146	159,914	44,798	12,411	32,978	76,973	65,753	7,392	3,828	33,270	6,813	1,829	24,628	1,873
1951	14,107	165,503	54,821	14,144	41,392	71,224	58,521	8,514	4,189	37,385	7,409	1,873	28,103	2,073
1952	14,069	177,417	59,233	15,019	45,067	75,204	61,178	9,844	4,182	40,703	8,619	2,396	29,688	2,277
1953	14,005	181,427	65,025	16,230	49,734	72,932	58,645	10,533	3,754	41,157	8,826	2,590	29,741	2,313
1954	13,936	190,581	67,335	17,226	51,099	79,046	63,508	11,930	3,608	41,568	8,880	2,659	30,029	2,632
1955	13,780 [6]	199,244	75,181	19,779	56,527	80,080	63,270	12,785	4,025	41,024	9,762	2,681	28,581	2,959
1956	13,719 [6]	206,846	87,447	21,990	66,810	73,461	56,869	12,988	3,603	42,623	11,105	2,321	29,196	3,315
1957	13,658 [6]	209,601	91,635	22,736	70,543	73,851	56,895	13,388	3,568	40,175	8,957	2,791	28,427	3,941
1958	13,574	229,182	96,244	23,927	74,159	84,722	64,463	15,789	4,471	43,711	10,952	3,076	29,684	4,505
1959	13,492	234,782	103,994	26,857	79,151	83,005	62,208	17,043	3,754	43,035	11,258	3,156	28,622	4,747
1960	13,503	243,274	115,767	28,439	89,554	74,961	54,987	16,827	3,147	47,192	14,875	3,277	29,039	5,354
1961	13,474	254,627	118,462	29,383	91,503	84,050	61,921	18,766	3,362	45,679	14,912	2,922	27,846	6,436
1962	13,434	277,211	129,779	32,194	100,254	91,643	64,550	23,206	3,887	48,844	16,782	3,204	28,858	6,945
1963	13,494	301,063	145,733	36,939	111,813	96,160	63,676	27,863	4,621	51,309	18,380	3,506	29,423	7,861
1964	13,682	323,349	165,336	41,648	126,946	95,928	59,456	31,477	4,995	53,342	18,867	4,571	29,903	8,742
1965	13,805	356,110	189,688	46,548	146,776	99,315	56,986	36,614	5,715	57,221	20,968	5,012	31,241	9,887
1966	13,821	388,373	214,386	52,306	166,165	102,500	53,619	40,702	8,180	60,187	22,949	5,267	31,970	11,300
1967	13,762	415,437	226,516	55,731	175,198	111,214	54,387	46,994	9,833	65,244	26,470	4,879	33,896	12,462
1968	13,743	460,575	247,283	61,967	190,156	123,408	58,805	52,794	11,809	75,562	33,627	5,220	36,705	14,322
1969	13,694	521,242	289,911	69,079	217,833	126,910	54,242	60,261	12,407	88,530	44,384	6,302	37,845	18,892
1970	13,690	534,932	288,153	71,291	216,862	127,701	51,860	63,153	12,687	85,910	38,516	7,142	40,252	21,966
1971	13,749	605,151	310,656	76,639	234,017	154,194	58,651	76,765	18,778	96,584	42,528	7,695	46,361	43,717
1972	13,896	673,016	353,942	90,121	263,821	169,167	59,050	85,605	24,512	100,095	39,206	6,845	54,044	49,812
1973	14,069	776,709	433,369	109,114	324,255	175,111	56,400	89,464	33,244	104,303	40,290	7,718	56,293	63,926
1974	14,360	891,956	498,559	127,320	371,239	184,421	51,828	91,848	40,745	127,217	52,449	8,431	66,338	81,759
1975	14,597	939,420	501,968	133,011	368,957	213,416	68,619	102,255	42,542	129,525	49,640	10,170	69,715	94,511
1976	14,668	972,770	509,387	143,699	365,688	238,733	88,231	102,842	47,660	129,304	45,767	12,062	71,506	95,346
1977	14,746	1,084,674	569,707	163,007	406,700	257,551	98,383	109,340	49,828	140,148	53,495	12,812	73,841	117,273
1978	14,729	1,226,598	663,502	194,467	469,035	265,171	94,510	116,813	53,848	168,152	69,514	12,019	86,619	129,773
1979	14,730	1,354,574	770,734	228,813	541,921	276,229	87,109	127,032	62,087	183,323	78,167	13,335	91,772	124,288
1980	14,729	1,446,638	792,395	252,728	539,667	299,794	91,103	138,116	79,575	199,399	80,100	16,117	103,110	155,050

[1] Reports dated on or about June 30 each year.

[2] Beginning in 1948, figures for all loan categories are gross (that is, before deduction of valuation reserves). They do not add to the totals in 1948–1968 and are not entirely comparable with earlier figures. Total loans are shown net beginning in 1969.

[3] Beginning in 1969, all loan and security categories are gross.

[4] For 1834–1895, includes lawful reserves. Beginning in 1966, includes domestic interbank deposits only. For 1961–1965, includes domestic interbank and postal savings deposits. Prior to 1966, includes deposits of foreign banks.

[5] Beginning in 1966, excludes corporate stock other than Federal Reserve Bank stock held by national banks, which is reported with other assets.

[6] Figures for member commercial banks exclude, and figures for uninsured nonmember commercial banks include, one member nondeposit trust company that is not insured by the Federal Deposit Insurance Corporation.

Sources

1834–1895: Comptroller of the Currency, *Annual Report* (1931), pp. 1023–4.
1896–1955: Board of Governors of the Federal Reserve System, *All-Bank Statistics, United States, 1896–1955* (1959). 1956–1980: Federal Deposit Insurance Corporation, *Annual Report* and *Assets and Liabilities* (various issues).

Documentation

For a description of the data and cautions concerning its use, see the text for Tables Cj149–168 and Cj203–211.

The Federal Reserve System ceased collection and reporting of combined statistical series on all state, national, and savings banks after 1955. Although the Federal Deposit Insurance Corporation (FDIC) did not report the series separately, it continued to collect and report aggregate series for all commercial banks up to 1980. After 1980, the FDIC reported statistics only for all FDIC-insured commercial banks, thus leaving out the few small, uninsured banks.

Data include Alaska and Hawai'i beginning in 1956.

TABLE Cj265–272   Commercial banks – liabilities: 1834–1980[1]

Contributed by Howard Bodenhorn

Year	Total	Interbank	U.S. government	Other demand	Other time	Bank notes in circulation	Capital accounts	Other liabilities
	Cj265	Cj266 [2]	Cj267	Cj268	Cj269	Cj270	Cj271	Cj272
	Million dollars	Million dollars	Million dollars	Million dollars	Million dollars	Million dollars	Million dollars	Million dollars
1834	102	—	—	—	—	95	200	22
1835	122	—	—	—	—	104	231	41
1836	166	—	—	—	—	140	252	65
1837	190	—	—	—	—	149	291	77
1838	146	—	—	—	—	116	318	103
1839	143	—	—	—	—	135	327	97
1840	120	—	—	—	—	107	358	72
1841	108	—	—	—	—	107	314	79
1842	88	—	—	—	—	84	260	40
1843	78	—	—	—	—	59	229	28
1844	117	—	—	—	—	75	211	24
1845	114	—	—	—	—	90	206	24
1846	125	—	—	—	—	106	197	28
1847	120	—	—	—	—	106	203	29
1848	143	—	—	—	—	129	205	36
1849	121	—	—	—	—	115	207	35
1850	146	—	—	—	—	131	217	37
1851	175	—	—	—	—	155	228	39
1852	182	—	—	—	—	161	237	40
1853	195	—	—	—	—	146	208	28
1854	239	—	—	—	—	205	301	50
1855	236	—	—	—	—	187	332	62
1856	265	—	—	—	—	196	344	75
1857	288	—	—	—	—	215	371	80
1858	237	—	—	—	—	155	395	62
1859	328	—	—	—	—	193	402	60
1860	310	—	—	—	—	207	422	61
1861	319	—	—	—	—	202	430	66
1862	357	—	—	—	—	184	418	53
1863	504	—	—	—	—	239	412	54
1864	380	—	—	—	—	176	391	26
1865	689	—	—	—	—	180	451	37
1866	758	—	—	—	—	309	560	45
1867	744	—	—	—	—	329	578	23
1868	797	—	—	—	—	329	595	13
1869	771	—	—	—	—	329	616	20
1870	775	—	—	—	—	336	649	21
1871	888	—	—	—	—	370	706	38
1872	927	—	—	—	—	405	748	66
1873	1,625	—	—	—	—	339	749	19
1874	1,740	—	—	—	—	339	789	23
1875	2,009	—	—	—	—	318	847	31
1876	1,993	—	—	—	—	295	864	31
1877	2,006	—	—	—	—	290	875	32
1878	1,921	—	—	—	—	300	826	34
1879	2,149	—	—	—	—	308	826	29
1880	2,222	—	—	—	—	318	826	33
1881	2,649	—	—	—	—	312	864	43
1882	2,777	—	—	—	—	309	901	44
1883	2,884	—	—	—	—	312	974	38
1884	2,849	—	—	—	—	295	1,036	42
1885	3,078	—	—	—	—	269	1,040	40
1886	3,186	—	—	—	—	245	1,076	35
1887	3,719	—	—	—	—	167	1,259	49
1888	3,891	—	—	—	—	155	1,348	76
1889	4,311	—	—	—	—	129	1,428	78

Notes appear at end of table   (continued)

TABLE Cj265–272   Commercial banks – liabilities: 1834–1980   *Continued*

		Deposits						
	Total	Interbank	U.S. government	Other demand	Other time	Bank notes in circulation	Capital accounts	Other liabilities
	Cj265	Cj266 [2]	Cj267	Cj268	Cj269	Cj270	Cj271	Cj272
Year	Million dollars	Million dollars	Million dollars	Million dollars	Million dollars	Million dollars	Million dollars	Million dollars
1890	4,576	—	—	—	—	126	1,559	97
1891	4,683	—	—	—	—	124	1,649	107
1892	5,297	—	—	—	—	141	1,721	86
1893	5,065	—	—	—	—	155	1,781	190
1894	5,268	—	—	—	—	172	1,753	98
1895	5,539	—	—	—	—	179	1,779	112
1896	4,142	571	15	2,844	712	199	1,730	96
1897	4,486	726	16	2,999	745	197	1,705	87
1898	5,175	872	53	3,431	819	190	1,701	104
1899	6,472	1,126	76	4,295	975	199	1,720	98
1900	6,792	1,261	99	4,345	1,087	265	1,878	124
1901	8,114	1,437	99	5,279	1,299	319	1,996	143
1902	8,713	1,498	124	5,541	1,550	309	2,266	139
1903	9,107	1,479	147	5,771	1,710	359	2,555	169
1904	9,739	1,756	110	6,057	1,816	399	2,727	170
1905	11,028	1,909	75	6,898	2,146	445	2,844	225
1906	11,791	1,908	89	7,403	2,391	511	3,060	239
1907	12,727	2,094	180	7,708	2,745	547	3,274	314
1908	12,425	2,213	130	7,381	2,701	613	3,364	262
1909	13,789	2,492	70	8,115	3,112	636	3,501	219
1910	14,644	2,304	54	8,566	3,720	675	3,694	311
1911	15,452	2,633	48	8,625	4,146	681	3,843	344
1912	16,455	2,636	58	9,217	4,544	709	3,955	376
1913	16,808	2,585	49	9,249	4,925	722	4,116	410
1914	17,806	2,720	66	10,306	4,714	722	4,169	458
1915	18,612	2,811	48	10,703	5,050	722	4,286	486
1916	22,613	3,510	39	12,917	6,147	676	4,367	561
1917	26,501	4,015	146	15,085	7,255	660	4,612	1,029
1918	28,708	3,718	1,541	15,747	7,702	681	4,742	2,221
1919	33,254	3,948	914	19,282	9,110	677	5,014	3,517
1920	36,682	3,729	261	21,571	11,121	688	5,599	4,540
1921	33,432	2,904	405	18,926	11,197	703	5,936	3,598
1922	35,532	3,353	158	20,106	11,915	725	6,044	1,805
1923	38,175	3,417	305	20,829	13,624	719	6,220	2,218
1924	41,343	4,247	185	22,069	14,842	729	6,420	1,644
1925	45,230	4,330	182	24,325	16,393	648	6,636	1,887
1926	46,952	4,289	235	24,993	17,435	651	7,021	2,157
1927	48,704	4,527	232	25,257	18,688	650	7,392	2,227
1928	49,582	4,282	274	24,857	20,169	649	7,968	3,364
1929	49,385	3,975	375	25,160	19,875	649	8,780	3,628
1930	51,267	5,129	298	25,648	20,192	649	9,318	2,891
1931	47,277	5,150	447	22,569	1,911	636	8,749	2,358
1932	35,658	3,323	433	17,111	14,791	649	7,484	2,513
1933	32,078	3,467	858	16,019	11,734	727	6,190	1,516
1934	36,810	4,581	1,735	17,796	12,698	695	6,625	848
1935	41,462	5,644	820	21,731	13,267	222	6,601	620
1936	48,118	6,903	1,144	26,096	13,975	—	6,703	751
1937	49,345	6,336	669	27,578	14,762	—	6,786	776
1938	48,814	6,838	596	26,387	14,993	—	6,770	60
1939	53,894	8,220	788	29,691	15,195	—	3,896	632
1940	60,246	10,168	824	33,646	15,608	—	6,960	598
1941	67,588	10,929	748	39,915	15,996	—	7,131	637
1942	72,394	10,278	1,837	44,611	15,668	—	7,254	628
1943	96,175	10,888	8,026	59,661	17,600	—	7,521	626
1944	116,235	11,201	19,511	64,254	21,269	—	8,011	785
1945	136,727	12,586	24,384	72,526	27,231	—	8,652	866
1946	143,042	12,309	13,413	84,824	32,496	—	9,392	1,073
1947	135,933	11,681	1,365	88,030	34,857	—	9,877	1,164
1948	138,162	11,435	2,178	88,754	35,795	—	10,284	1,353
1949	137,538	10,938	2,302	87,999	36,299	—	10,781	1,386

Notes appear at end of table

TABLE Cj265-272   Commercial banks – liabilities: 1834–1980   *Continued*

		Deposits				Bank notes in circulation	Capital accounts	Other liabilities
	Total	Interbank	U.S. government	Other demand	Other time			
	Cj265	Cj266 [2]	Cj267	Cj268	Cj269	Cj270	Cj271	Cj272
Year	Million dollars	Million dollars	Million dollars	Million dollars	Million dollars	Million dollars	Million dollars	Million dollars
1950	143,845	11,435	3,799	91,882	36,729	—	11,389	1,630
1951	151,475	11,946	6,329	96,399	36,801	—	11,950	2,078
1952	162,365	13,512	6,118	103,402	39,333	—	12,599	2,453
1953	165,548	13,598	3,940	105,735	42,275	—	13,276	2,603
1954	174,065	15,497	5,862	106,995	45,681	—	14,038	2,478
1955	181,512	15,242	5,414	112,981	47,875	—	14,906	2,826
1956	187,299	12,368	5,632	117,854	51,446	—	16,027	3,520
1957	187,348	11,494	3,713	116,766	55,375	—	16,941	5,313
1958	205,500	12,514	9,561	119,296	64,129	—	18,293	5,390
1959	208,513	12,204	3,117	125,560	67,631	—	19,192	7,078
1960	214,425	12,719	6,684	126,615	68,408	—	20,392	8,456
1961	225,765	12,929	6,667	126,591	79,577	—	21,812	7,050
1962	246,149	13,583	9,870	130,379	92,317	—	23,254	7,808
1963	267,207	14,214	11,336	135,362	106,295	—	24,660	9,195
1964	286,133	14,468	10,544	140,968	120,153	—	26,861	10,355
1965	312,912	15,477	12,100	147,248	138,086	—	29,588	13,610
1966	340,598	16,337	11,275	155,947	157,044	—	31,435	16,339
1967	362,486	17,603	5,467	163,325	176,090	—	33,419	19,532
1968	397,275	19,521	5,324	180,541	191,889	—	35,923	27,377
1969	429,277	23,647	6,021	196,840	202,769	—	39,002	52,963
1970	436,650	24,515	8,309	196,477	207,349	—	41,905	56,377
1971	507,459	30,843	9,032	193,135	230,548	—	45,538	52,154
1972	557,205	28,674	9,601	205,597	262,088	—	50,382	65,429
1973	634,419	32,505	11,212	223,970	307,279	—	56,029	86,261
1974	715,515	44,095	8,844	240,500	354,449	—	61,952	114,489
1975	760,423	44,898	3,665	272,503	439,358	—	66,907	112,090
1976	794,986	41,011	5,394	276,071	287,282	—	69,888	107,896
1977	869,235	46,144	3,671	297,169	305,182	—	76,673	138,771
1978	973,776	49,034	9,278	328,149	359,911	—	84,342	168,480
1979	1,027,393	57,343	3,063	386,764	416,928	—	93,014	106,404
1980	1,111,863	48,000	2,972	415,216	140,000	—	103,031	231,744

[1] Reports dated on or about June 30 each year.

[2] Beginning in 1966, includes domestic interbank deposits only. For 1961–1965, includes domestic interbank and postal savings deposits. Prior to 1966, includes deposits of foreign banks.

Sources
1834–1895: Comptroller of the Currency, *Annual Report* (1931), pp. 1023–4. 1896–1955: Board of Governors of the Federal Reserve System, *All-Bank Statistics, United States, 1896–1955* (1959). 1956–1980: Federal Deposit Insurance Corporation, *Annual Report* and *Assets and Liabilities* (various issues).

Documentation
See the text for Table Cj251–264.

TABLE Cj273–282   Federal Reserve banks – assets and liabilities: 1914–1998

Contributed by Howard Bodenhorn and Eugene N. White

		Reserve bank credit outstanding					Deposits			
	Total reserves	Total loans and securities	Discounts and advances	Bills bought	U.S. government securities	Total assets or liabilities and capital	Total	Member bank reserve account	Federal Reserve notes in circulation	Capital accounts
	Cj273	Cj274 [1]	Cj275	Cj276	Cj277	Cj278	Cj279	Cj280	Cj281 [2]	Cj282
Year	Million dollars	Million dollars	Million dollars	Million dollars	Million dollars	Million dollars	Million dollars	Million dollars	Million dollars	Million dollars
1914	268	11	10	0	0	330	31	265 [4]	11	18
1915	555	84	32	24	16	697	452	401 [4]	189	55
1916	757	222	29	129	55	1,211	879	722 [4]	275	56
1917	1,672	1,060	660	273	122	3,164	1,583	1,447	1,247	71
1918	2,146	2,291	1,766	287	239	5,250	1,808	1,636	2,659	104
1919	1,990	3,090	2,215	574	300	6,324	2,022	1,890	3,009	208
1920	2,250	3,235	2,687	260	287	6,254	1,861	1,781	3,336	302
1921	3,010	1,524	1,144	145	234	5,151	1,876	1,753	2,409	319
1922	3,166	1,326	618	272	436	5,252	1,974	1,934	2,396	326
1923	3,169	1,211	723	355	134	5,066	1,960	1,898	2,247	331
1924	3,047	1,249	320	387	540	5,096	2,311	2,220	1,862	330
1925	2,824	1,395	643	374	375	5,109	2,257	2,212	1,838	338
1926	2,948	1,335	637	381	315	5,150	2,276	2,194	1,851	354
1927	2,867	1,591	582	392	617	5,346	2,531	2,487	1,790	366
1928	2,709	1,783	1,056	489	228	5,352	2,440	2,389	1,838	401
1929	3,011	1,548	632	392	511	5,458	2,414	2,355	1,910	448
1930	3,082	1,352	251	364	729	5,201	2,517	2,471	1,664	444
1931	3,158	1,825	638	339	817	5,672	2,125	1,961	2,624	420
1932	3,331	2,128	235	33	1,855	6,115	2,561	2,509	2,739	430
1933	3,794	2,670	98	133	2,437	7,041	2,865	2,729	3,080	445
1934	5,401	2,457	7	6	2,430	8,442	4,405	4,096	3,221	331
1935	7,835	2,473	5	5	2,431	11,026	6,386	5,587	3,709	335
1936	9,121	2,461	3	3	2,430	12,525	7,190	6,606	4,284	341
1937	9,481	2,592	10	1	2,564	12,880	7,577	7,027	4,284	341
1938	12,166	2,584	4	1	2,564	15,581	10,088	8,724	4,452	344
1939	15,524	2,502	7	0	2,484 [3]	19,027	12,941	11,653	4,959	349
1940	20,036	2,195	3	0	2,184 [3]	23,262	16,127	14,026	5,931	369
1941	20,764	2,267	3	0	2,254 [3]	24,353	14,678	12,450	8,192	373
1942	20,908	6,208	6	0	6,189 [3]	29,019	15,194	13,117	12,193	381
1943	20,096	11,558	5	0	11,543 [3]	33,955	15,181	12,886	16,906	429
1944	18,687	18,930	80	0	18,846 [3]	40,269	16,411	14,373	21,731	486
1945	17,863	24,513	249	0	24,262 [3]	45,063	18,200	15,915	24,649	587
1946	18,381	23,513	163	0	23,350	45,006	17,353	16,139	24,945	678
1947	21,497	22,646	85	0	22,559	47,712	19,731	17,899	24,820	696
1948	22,966	23,556	223	0	23,333	50,043	22,791	20,479	24,161	761
1949	23,176	18,965	78	0	18,885	45,643	18,906	16,568	23,483	832
1950	21,458	20,848	67	0	20,778	47,172	19,810	17,681	23,587	869
1951	21,468	23,825	19	0	23,801	49,900	21,192	20,056	25,064	909
1952	21,986	24,857	156	0	24,697	52,852	21,344	19,950	26,250	972
1953	21,354	25,945	28	0	25,916	52,315	21,422	20,160	26,558	1,025
1954	21,033	25,076	143	0	24,932	50,872	20,371	18,876	26,253	1,084
1955	21,009	24,921	108	28	24,785	52,340	20,355	19,005	26,921	1,132
1956	21,269	25,034	50	69	24,915	52,910	20,249	19,059	27,476	1,209
1957	22,085	24,360	55	66	24,238	53,028	20,117	19,034	27,535	1,291
1958	19,951	26,460	64	49	26,347	53,095	19,526	18,504	27,872	1,341
1959	19,164	27,181	458	75	26,648	54,028	19,716	18,174	28,262	1,174
1960	17,479	27,491	33	74	27,384	50,859	18,316	17,081	27,924	1,226
1961	16,615	29,062	130	51	28,881	52,470	18,451	17,387	28,802	1,333
1962	15,696	30,968	38	110	30,820	53,931	18,722	17,454	30,151	1,401
1963	15,237	33,818	63	162	33,593	56,176	18,391	17,049	32,381	1,487
1964	15,075	37,324	186	94	37,044	60,389	19,456	18,086	34,659	1,048
1965	13,436	41,092	137	187	40,768	62,652	19,620	18,447	37,074	1,102
1966	12,674	44,682	173	193	44,316	67,043	20,957	19,779	39,339	1,140
1967	11,481	49,455	141	164	49,150	72,026	22,920	20,999	41,642	1,196
1968	10,026	53,183	188	58	52,937	75,885	23,484	21,818	44,726	1,260
1969	10,036	57,401	183	64	57,154	80,854	24,338	22,083	47,473	1,338

Notes appear at end of table

TABLE Cj273–282 Federal Reserve banks – assets and liabilities: 1914–1998 *Continued*

		Reserve bank credit outstanding					Deposits			
Year	Total reserves	Total loans and securities	Discounts and advances	Bills bought	U.S. government securities	Total assets or liabilities and capital	Total	Member bank reserve account	Federal Reserve notes in circulation	Capital accounts
	Cj273	Cj274 [1]	Cj275	Cj276	Cj277	Cj278	Cj279	Cj280	Cj281 [2]	Cj282
	Million dollars	Million dollars	Million dollars	Million dollars	Million dollars	Million dollars	Million dollars	Million dollars	Million dollars	Million dollars
1970	10,457	62,534	335	57	62,142	85,913	26,687	24,150	50,323	1,404
1971	9,875	71,104	39	261	70,218	94,595	31,101	27,788	53,819	1,484
1972	10,303	73,317	1,981	106	69,906	94,765	28,667	25,647	58,757	1,586
1973	11,460	81,821	1,258	68	78,516	103,272	31,486	27,060	64,262	1,688
1974	11,652	87,012	299	999	80,501	110,828	30,649	25,843	70,916	1,794
1975	11,599	95,461	211	1,126	87,934	120,402	34,780	26,052	77,159	1,858
1976	11,598	105,109	25	991	97,021	129,284	37,260	25,158	83,727	1,966
1977	11,718	112,493	265	954	102,819	137,802	35,550	26,870	93,153	2,058
1978	11,671	120,352	1,174	587	110,562	151,066	36,972	31,152	103,325	2,156
1979	11,112	128,325	1,454	704	117,458	160,824	35,708	29,520	113,355	2,290
1980	11,161	121,328	1,809	776	133,177	168,545	31,546	27,456	124,241	2,406
1981	11,151	128,230	1,601	195	142,144	174,777	30,815	25,228	131,906	2,556
1982	11,148	151,034	717	1,480	139,312	186,935	32,883	26,489	141,990	2,718
1983	11,121	162,131	918	418	151,942	196,759	26,123	21,446	157,097	2,930
1984	11,096	173,204	3,577	0	160,850	207,184	28,252	21,818	168,327	3,252
1985	11,090	194,308	3,060	0	181,327	236,052	39,503	28,631	181,450	3,562
1986	11,084	223,024	1,565	0	211,316	266,030	56,905	48,107	195,360	3,746
1987	11,078	235,235	3,815	0	222,551	275,566	48,368	41,784	212,890	4,094
1988	11,060	249,659	2,170	0	238,422	293,674	48,898	39,347	229,640	4,226
1989	11,059	235,898	481	0	228,367	304,424	46,430	38,327	241,739	4,486
1990	11,058	259,975	190	0	244,985	327,573	48,228	38,658	267,657	4,846
1991	11,059	288,647	218	0	281,831	353,061	49,783	49,783	287,906	5,304
1992	11,056	309,192	675	0	302,474	367,368	40,148	32,079	314,208	6,108
1993	11,053	349,960	94	0	344,202	409,251	50,543	34,951	343,925	6,802
1994	11,051	378,969	223	0	374,084	436,487	39,075	30,789	381,505	7,366
1995	11,050	394,829	135	0	390,959	454,723	36,908	29,611	400,935	7,932
1996	11,048	414,800	85	0	410,878	481,140	33,325	24,524	426,522	9,098
1997	11,047	457,295	2,035	0	451,924	517,847	37,639	30,838	457,469	10,653
1998	11,046	482,872	17	0	471,815	548,101	34,165	26,306	491,657	11,904

[1] Statistics for 1914–1959 include industrial advances not shown separately.

[2] Includes Federal Reserve notes held by the U.S. Treasury or by a Federal Reserve bank other than the issuing bank. Effective January 1, 1977, Federal Reserve notes of other Federal Reserve banks were merged into liability accounts for Federal Reserve notes.

[3] Includes guaranteed obligations not issued until late 1933. Reserve banks were first authorized to purchase them in 1934. The only holdings of such securities prior to 1939 were $181,000 at the end of 1935, which were included in other securities.

[4] Figures not comparable with later years because prior to June 21, 1917, member banks were not required to keep all their legal reserves with Reserve banks; also for 1914–1916, deferred availability accounts, subsequently shown separately in the original sources, are included in total deposits.

Sources
1914–1941: Board of Governors of the Federal Reserve System, *Banking and Monetary Statistics* (1943), pp. 330–2. 1942–1998: Board of Governors of the Federal Reserve System, *Federal Reserve Bulletin* (various issues).

Documentation
Complete and detailed accounts and notes for the combined Federal Reserve banks as well as individual banks can be found in the original sources.

The Federal Reserve System was founded by an Act signed into law by Woodrow Wilson in December 1913. For purposes of administering the Federal Reserve System, the country is divided into twelve districts. There is a Federal Reserve Bank, and generally one or more branches, located in each district. Federal Reserve banks are organized as federally chartered corporations with capital stock owned by member banks in the respective districts. Member banks include all national banks and those state-chartered banks that seek membership and meet the requirements for joining the system.

The Federal Reserve banks are the principal medium through which the credit, monetary, and exchange policies, as well as the general regulatory and supervisory powers of the Federal Reserve authorities, are carried out. Federal Reserve banks hold the legal reserves of member banks and perform several services for members, including collection and clearing of checks and discount facilities. The Reserve banks also act as fiscal agents, depositories, and custodians for the U.S. Treasury and other federal government units. The actions of the twelve Federal Reserve banks and their branches are coordinated and administered by the Board of Governors of the Federal Reserve System, housed in Washington, D.C. For more details on the history and structure of the Federal Reserve System, see Federal Reserve Board of Governors, *Federal Reserve System: Purposes and Functions*, sixth edition (1974).

Since 1934, the reserves of the Federal Reserve banks have consisted primarily of the gold certificate account, which is backed dollar-for-dollar by gold in the Treasury. The supply of these reserves is dependent primarily on the size of the monetary gold stock, specifically that part of the gold stock against which the Treasury has issued gold certificates or gold certificate credits. For a discussion of changes in the items affecting the reserves of Federal Reserve banks, 1914–1934, see *Banking and Monetary Statistics*, p. 325.

Deposits of Federal Reserve banks consist mainly of reserves of member banks, shown in series Cj280. They also include the checking account of the U.S. Treasurer, deposits of foreign banks and governments, and other accounts of certain nonmember banks maintained for use in collecting and clearing checks and checking accounts of U.S. government agencies. For further descriptions, see sources.

TABLE Cj283–288   Federal Reserve banks – earnings and expenses: 1915–1998

Contributed by Howard Bodenhorn and Eugene N. White

Year	Current earnings	Current expenses	Net earnings before payments to U.S. Treasury	Disposition of net earnings		
				Dividends paid	Paid to U.S. Treasury	Transferred to surplus
	Cj283	Cj284	Cj285	Cj286	Cj287 [1]	Cj288
	Thousand dollars	Thousand dollars	Thousand dollars	Thousand dollars	Thousand dollars	Thousand dollars
1915	2,173	2,321	−141	217	—	—
1916	5,218	2,274	2,751	1,743	—	—
1917	16,128	5,160	9,582	6,804	1,134	1,134
1918	67,584	10,960	52,716	5,541	—	48,334
1919	102,381	19,340	78,368	5,012	2,704	70,652
1920	181,297	28,258	149,295	5,654	60,725	82,916
1921	122,866	34,464	82,087	6,120	59,974	15,993
1922	50,499	29,559	16,498	6,307	10,851	−660
1923	50,709	29,764	12,711	6,553	3,613	2,546
1924	38,340	28,431	3,718	6,682	114	−3,078
1925	41,801	27,528	9,449	6,916	59	2,474
1926	47,600	27,350	16,612	7,329	818	8,464
1927	43,024	27,518	13,048	7,755	250	5,044
1928	64,053	26,905	32,122	8,458	2,585	21,079
1929	70,955	29,691	36,403	9,584	4,283	22,536
1930	36,424	28,343	7,988	10,269	17	−2,298
1931	29,701	27,041	2,972	10,030	—	−7,058
1932	50,019	26,291	22,314	9,282	2,011	11,021
1933	49,487	29,223	7,957	8,874	—	−917
1934	48,903	29,241	15,231	8,782	—	6,450
1935	42,752	31,577	9,438	8,505	—	635
1936	37,901	29,874	8,512	7,830	227	455
1937	41,233	28,801	10,801	7,941	117	2,684
1938	36,261	28,912	9,582	8,019	120	1,443
1939	38,501	28,647	12,243	8,110	25	4,108
1940	43,538	29,165	25,860	8,215	82	17,563
1941	41,380	32,963	9,138	8,430	141	566
1942	52,663	38,624	12,470	8,669	198	3,604
1943	69,306	43,546	49,528	8,911	245	40,372
1944	104,392	49,176	58,438	9,500	327	48,611
1945	142,210	48,717	92,662	10,183	248	82,232
1946	150,385	57,235	92,524	10,962	67	81,495
1947	158,656	65,393	95,236	11,523	75,260	8,453
1948	304,161	72,710	197,133	11,920	166,690	18,523
1949	316,537	77,478	226,937	12,329	193,146	21,462
1950	275,839	80,572	231,561	13,083	196,629	21,849
1951	394,656	95,469	297,059	13,865	254,874	28,321
1952	456,060	104,694	352,950	14,682	291,935	46,334
1953	513,037	113,515	398,463	15,558	342,568	40,337
1954	438,486	109,733	328,619	16,442	276,289	35,888
1955	412,488	110,060	302,162	17,712	251,741	32,710
1956	595,649	121,182	474,443	18,905	401,556	53,983
1957	763,348	131,814	624,393	20,081	542,708	61,603
1958	742,068	137,722	604,471	21,197	524,059	59,215
1959	886,226	144,703	839,771	22,722	910,650	−93,601
1960	1,103,385	153,882	963,378	23,948	896,816	42,613
1961	941,648	161,275	783,855	25,570	687,393	70,892
1962	1,048,508	176,136	872,316	27,412	799,366	45,588
1963	1,151,120	187,273	964,462	28,912	879,685	55,864
1964	1,343,747	197,396	1,147,077	30,782	1,582,119	−465,823
1965	1,559,484	204,290	1,356,215	32,352	1,296,810	27,054
1966	1,908,500	207,401	1,702,095	33,696	1,649,455	18,944
1967	2,190,404	220,121	1,972,377	35,027	1,907,498	29,851
1968	2,764,446	242,350	2,530,616	36,959	2,463,629	30,027
1969	3,373,361	274,973	3,097,830	39,237	3,019,161	39,432
1970	3,877,218	321,373	3,567,287	41,137	3,493,571	32,580
1971	3,723,370	377,185	3,440,451	43,488	3,356,560	40,403
1972	3,792,334	414,606	3,328,112	46,183	3,231,268	50,661
1973	5,016,769	495,117	4,440,998	49,140	4,340,680	51,178
1974	6,280,091	547,541	5,654,063	52,580	5,549,999	51,484

Note appears at end of table

TABLE Cj283–288   Federal Reserve banks – earnings and expenses: 1915–1998
Continued

Year	Current earnings	Current expenses	Net earnings before payments to U.S. Treasury	Disposition of net earnings		
				Dividends paid	Paid to U.S. Treasury	Transferred to surplus
	Cj283	Cj284	Cj285	Cj286	Cj287 [1]	Cj288
	Thousand dollars	Thousand dollars	Thousand dollars	Thousand dollars	Thousand dollars	Thousand dollars
1975	6,257,937	585,066	5,470,501	54,609	5,382,064	33,828
1976	6,623,000	649,000	5,981,000	57,000	5,870,000	54,000
1977	6,890,000	624,000	6,043,000	60,000	5,937,000	46,000
1978	8,455,000	653,000	7,116,000	63,000	7,006,000	47,000
1979	10,312,000	694,000	9,415,000	67,000	9,279,000	69,000
1980	12,802,000	791,000	11,834,000	70,000	11,707,000	57,000
1981	15,509,000	897,000	14,177,000	75,000	14,025,000	77,000
1982	16,520,000	998,000	15,365,000	79,000	15,208,000	78,000
1983	16,070,000	1,022,000	14,424,000	85,000	14,232,000	107,000
1984	18,068,000	1,101,000	16,309,000	93,000	16,054,000	162,000
1985	18,132,000	1,127,000	18,056,000	103,000	17,798,000	155,000
1986	17,465,000	1,156,000	18,009,000	110,000	17,807,000	92,000
1987	17,633,000	1,147,000	18,032,000	117,000	17,740,000	174,000
1988	19,524,000	1,208,000	17,548,000	126,000	17,356,000	65,000
1989	22,230,000	1,331,000	21,888,000	130,000	21,627,000	131,000
1990	23,475,000	1,211,000	23,954,000	141,000	23,633,000	180,000
1991	22,551,000	1,208,000	21,158,000	153,000	20,778,000	222,000
1992	20,234,000	1,440,000	17,348,000	172,000	16,774,000	402,000
1993	18,913,000	1,609,000	16,528,000	195,000	15,985,000	348,000
1994	20,911,000	1,796,000	20,964,000	212,000	20,470,000	282,000
1995	25,395,000	1,695,000	23,896,000	230,500	23,382,000	283,500
1996	25,163,000	1,781,000	20,974,000	255,900	20,083,000	635,100
1997	26,916,000	1,813,000	21,793,000	299,700	20,662,000	831,300
1998	28,147,000	1,785,000	27,623,000	343,000	26,549,000	731,000

[1] Several policy changes affect series. See text.

Sources
1915–1962, Board of Governors of the Federal Reserve System, *Annual Report* (various issues); 1963–1998, *Federal Reserve Bulletin* (various issues).

Documentation
Federal Reserve banks are not operated for a profit, but they are self-supporting. The nature and amount of Reserve bank earnings depend largely on the demand for Reserve bank credit on the part of member banks and on Federal Reserve policy as to open market operations. Income of the Federal Reserve System is derived primarily from interest accrued on U.S. Treasury securities acquired through open market operations. The remainder arises from the provision of various financial services, such as check clearing, offered to members. The bulk of the Reserve banks' expenses are incurred in collecting checks, supplying currency, and performing other services from which no revenues are earned.

Until 1933, the law required that the net earnings of the Federal Reserve banks, after deduction of the annual 6 percent cumulative dividend on paid-in capital, be allocated to surplus and to a franchise tax paid to the U.S. Treasury. In 1933, Congress abolished the franchise tax at a time when Reserve bank earnings were small and after Congress had directed the Reserve

banks to contribute one half of their surplus to the capital of the Federal Deposit Insurance Corporation. Between 1947 and 1958, the Reserve banks paid the U.S. Treasury nine tenths of their net earnings after dividends and adjustments to maintain their surplus at the level of subscribed capital. In 1959, they began paying all such earnings to the Treasury. Since 1964, surplus has been maintained at the level of paid-in capital (which is one half subscribed capital). Since the end of 1964, the Reserve System has distributed all of its net earnings, after payment of the statutory dividend and additions to surplus, to the U.S. Treasury as interest on Federal Reserve notes.

Series Cj285 and Cj287. Current earnings less current expenses plus other additions and other deductions.

Series Cj287. The Banking Act of 1933 eliminated the provision in the original 1913 Federal Reserve Act requiring payment of franchise tax, payable to the U.S. Treasury. Payments after 1934 were made pursuant to Section 13b of the Federal Reserve Act relating to loans and discounts for industrial purposes, provided for by the Act of June 19, 1934. Beginning in 1947, payments also represent interest on Federal Reserve notes. Under policy adopted by the Board of Governors of the Federal Reserve System at the end of 1964, all net earnings after the statutory dividend to member banks and additions to surplus were paid to the U.S. Treasury as interest on Federal Reserve notes.

TABLE Cj289–297   Commercial banks – number and assets, by Federal Reserve membership and type of bank: 1896–1998[1]

Contributed by Howard Bodenhorn and Eugene N. White

	Member banks of the Federal Reserve System						Nonmember banks		
	National banks			State banks					
Year	Number	Domestic assets	Domestic and foreign assets	Number	Domestic assets	Domestic and foreign assets	Number	Domestic assets	Domestic and foreign assets
	Cj289	Cj290 [2]	Cj291	Cj292 [3]	Cj293 [2,3]	Cj294	Cj295	Cj296 [2]	Cj297
	Number	Million dollars	Million dollars	Number	Million dollars	Million dollars	Number	Million dollars	Million dollars
1896	3,689	3,354	—	—	—	—	7,785	2,813	—
1897	3,610	3,563	—	—	—	—	7,828	2,912	—
1898	3,581	3,978	—	—	—	—	7,949	3,193	—
1899	3,582	4,709	—	—	—	—	8,253	3,780	—
1900	3,731	4,944	—	—	—	—	8,696	4,115	—
1901	4,163	5,674	—	—	—	—	9,261	4,897	—
1902	4,532	6,007	—	—	—	—	9,956	5,420	—
1903	4,935	6,285	—	—	—	—	10,879	5,905	—
1904	5,330	6,653	—	—	—	—	11,707	6,382	—
1905	5,664	7,325	—	—	—	—	12,488	7,217	—
1906	6,047	7,781	—	—	—	—	13,739	7,820	—
1907	6,422	8,472	—	—	—	—	14,939	8,390	—
1908	6,817	8,710	—	—	—	—	15,714	7,954	—
1909	6,886	9,365	—	—	—	—	16,212	8,780	—
1910	7,138	9,892	—	—	—	—	17,376	9,432	—
1911	7,270	10,378	—	—	—	—	17,913	9,941	—
1912	7,366	10,857	—	—	—	—	18,478	10,638	—
1913	7,467	11,032	—	—	—	—	19,197	11,024	—
1914	7,518	11,477	—	—	—	—	19,718	11,679	—
1915	7,597	11,790	—	17	97	—	19,776	12,219	—
1916	7,571	13,920	—	34	307	—	20,134	13,990	—
1917	7,599	16,231	—	53	756	—	20,646	15,815	—
1918	7,699	18,262	—	513	6,104	—	20,644	11,987	—
1919	7,779	21,105	—	1,042	8,629	—	20,326	12,727	—
1920	8,024	23,267	—	1,374	10,351	—	20,893	13,891	—
1921	8,150	20,475	—	1,595	10,375	—	20,711	12,820	—
1922	8,244	20,633	—	1,648	10,960	—	20,228	12,513	—
1923	8,236	21,454	—	1,620	12,212	—	19,973	13,666	—
1924	8,080	22,525	—	1,570	13,192	—	19,338	14,419	—
1925	8,066	24,252	—	1,472	14,694	—	18,904	15,455	—
1926	7,972	25,202	—	1,403	15,436	—	18,367	16,143	—
1927	7,790	26,455	—	1,309	16,144	—	17,551	16,374	—
1928	7,685	28,265	—	1,244	16,390	—	16,869	16,908	—
1929	7,530	27,260	—	1,177	18,194	—	16,263	16,988	—
1930	7,247	28,828	—	1,068	18,521	—	15,364	16,776	—
1931	6,800	27,430	—	982	17,406	—	13,872	14,181	—
1932	6,145	22,318	—	835	13,538	—	11,754	10,448	—
1933	4,897	20,813	—	709	12,226	—	8,601	7,472	—
1934	5,417	23,854	—	958	13,529	—	8,973	7,595	—
1935	5,425	26,009	—	985	14,710	—	9,078	8,186	—
1936	5,368	29,643	—	1,032	16,881	—	8,929	9,048	—
1937	5,293	30,272	—	1,064	17,181	—	8,737	9,454	—
1938	5,242	30,317	—	1,096	16,826	—	8,529	9,042	—
1939	5,203	33,119	—	1,127	18,789	—	8,337	9,514	—
1940	5,164	36,816	—	1,234	21,030	—	8,136	9,958	—
1941	5,130	41,228	—	1,423	23,620	—	7,881	10,508	—
1942	5,101	44,584	—	1,543	25,353	—	7,709	10,340	—
1943	5,060	58,783	—	1,640	32,028	—	7,497	13,511	—
1944	5,036	70,143	—	1,734	38,528	—	7,368	16,360	—
1945	5,015	81,491	—	1,822	44,930	—	7,289	19,824	—
1946	5,012	85,698	—	1,872	45,686	—	7,268	22,123	—
1947	5,012	83,149	—	1,913	41,630	—	7,257	22,195	—
1948	4,998	85,081	—	1,924	42,199	—	7,267	22,519	—
1949	4,987	84,853	—	1,913	42,388	—	7,251	22,464	—

Notes appear at end of table

TABLE Cj289–297   Commercial banks – number and assets, by Federal Reserve membership and type of bank: 1896–1998   *Continued*

	Member banks of the Federal Reserve System						Nonmember banks		
	National banks			State banks					
Year	Number	Domestic assets	Domestic and foreign assets	Number	Domestic assets	Domestic and foreign assets	Number	Domestic assets	Domestic and foreign assets
	Cj289	Cj290 [2]	Cj291	Cj292 [3]	Cj293 [2,3]	Cj294	Cj295	Cj296 [2]	Cj297
	Number	Million dollars	Million dollars	Number	Million dollars	Million dollars	Number	Million dollars	Million dollars
1950	4,971	89,691	—	1,911	44,033	—	7,264	23,190	—
1951	4,946	94,394	—	1,910	47,199	—	7,251	23,910	—
1952	4,925	101,253	—	1,887	50,266	—	7,257	25,898	—
1953	4,874	103,418	—	1,888	50,817	—	7,243	27,192	—
1954	4,834	108,607	—	1,883	53,568	—	7,219	28,406	—
1955	4,743	107,736	—	1,864	61,919	—	7,173	29,589	—
1956	4,667	110,703	—	1,828	64,090	—	6,734	29,460	—
1957	4,647	112,460	—	1,794	64,019	—	6,770	30,703	—
1958	4,599	122,100	—	1,754	70,874	—	6,791	32,650	—
1959	4,559	126,255	—	1,717	70,980	—	6,821	35,252	—
1960	4,542	131,433	—	1,672	72,713	—	6,933	37,183	—
1961	4,524	137,299	—	1,615	76,405	—	6,997	38,928	—
1962	4,500	149,559	—	1,568	82,784	—	7,043	42,787	—
1963	4,537	162,749	—	1,519	88,453	—	7,140	47,607	—
1964	4,702	175,250	—	1,477	94,174	—	7,222	51,659	—
1965	4,803	193,748	—	1,431	102,289	—	7,301	56,758	—
1966	4,811	226,050	—	1,382	95,767	—	7,366	63,091	—
1967	4,780	242,685	—	1,327	100,220	—	7,426	69,011	—
1968	4,742	266,259	—	1,296	112,340	—	7,481	77,705	—
1969	4,701	307,019	—	1,236	119,358	—	7,536	90,202	—
1970	4,638	314,334	—	1,166	117,209	—	7,683	98,368	—
1971	4,598	352,807	—	1,138	107,484	—	7,811	113,058	—
1972	4,606	392,043	—	1,108	138,021	—	7,955	131,774	—
1973	4,629	449,772	—	1,076	155,017	—	8,137	157,461	—
1974	4,693	516,632	—	1,072	182,837	—	8,347	179,457	—
1975	4,730	536,836	—	1,064	179,789	—	8,526	198,157	—
1976	4,747	548,698	—	1,029	179,644	—	8,597	214,167	—
1977	4,701	599,743	—	1,019	195,455	—	9,705	245,753	—
1978	4,616	671,166	—	1,005	217,384	—	8,760	284,221	—
1979	4,493	749,419	928,205	988	240,793	316,572	8,886	327,689	316,573
1980	4,426	820,919	1,034,905	981	250,907	339,019	9,001	368,551	371,253
1981	4,453	—	1,123,947	1,019	—	379,676	8,971	—	414,747
1982	4,507	—	1,224,644	1,031	—	391,545	8,875	—	451,909
1983	4,683	—	1,321,912	1,041	—	417,895	8,741	—	492,596
1984	4,774	—	1,434,041	1,051	—	446,311	8,548	—	531,051
1985	4,910	—	1,528,173	1,069	—	468,739	8,388	—	574,424
1986	4,870	—	1,649,179	1,086	—	503,415	8,219	—	621,494
1987	4,696	—	1,716,910	1,098	—	526,093	8,011	—	669,620
1988	4,459	—	1,801,877	1,071	—	540,579	7,744	—	713,407
1989	4,269	—	1,898,045	1,036	—	550,153	7,571	—	758,689
1990	4,049	—	1,983,910	1,016	—	566,562	7,371	—	810,968
1991	3,907	—	1,964,402	986	—	573,401	7,197	—	839,511
1992	3,702	—	1,974,289	950	—	612,150	7,037	—	851,822
1993	3,342	—	2,012,397	972	—	699,402	6,785	—	857,569
1994	3,187	—	2,184,623	968	—	820,953	6,560	—	886,947
1995	2,942	—	2,299,720	996	—	943,912	6,231	—	927,074
1996	2,763	—	2,538,682	1,024	—	950,586	5,903	—	907,578
1997	2,656	—	2,688,044	993	—	1,203,470	5,659	—	879,649
1998	2,546	—	2,978,601	989	—	1,295,268	5,449	—	908,889

[1] Reports dated on or about June 30 each year.

[2] Beginning in 1969, loans and securities are included on a gross basis in total assets.

[3] For 1941–1962, member banks include mutual savings banks as follows: three through 1959, two in 1960, and one in 1961–1962. For 1955–1970, data include one nondeposit trust company that was not insured by the Federal Deposit Insurance Corporation.

Sources

1896–1970: U.S. Bureau of the Census, *Historical Statistics of the United States, Bicentennial Edition* (1975), series X610–X615 (original sources cited in the Bicentennial Edition were incorrect, but the series were not reconstructed from correct originals); for the period before 1956, series Cj293–294 were constructed by deducting the total assets for all member banks reported in series Cj290 and Cj292 from the total assets of all commercial banks reported in series Cj252.

For series Cj289–290, Cj292–293, and Cj295–296, for 1971–1980, data were obtained from the Federal Deposit Insurance Corporation (FDIC), *Assets and Liabilities* (various issues). The consolidated assets reported in series Cj291, Cj294, and Cj297 for 1979–1980 and all series for 1981–1993 were

(continued)

TABLE Cj289–297   Commercial banks – number and assets, by Federal Reserve membership and type of bank: 1896–1998   *Continued*

obtained directly from unpublished FDIC sources. The data for 1994–1998 are found on the FDIC Internet site, *Statistics on Banking.*

Documentation

The Federal Reserve System was established in 1913 with the passage of the Federal Reserve Act. Statistics on Federal Reserve member banks refer to banks that either were members or eventually would become members.

State member commercial banks are those banks chartered by the various state banking authorities that voluntarily seek membership in the Federal Reserve System and meet all necessary requirements. Nonmember commercial banks are all other state-chartered banks, excluding mutual savings banks. National banks are required to be members of the Federal Reserve System.

TABLE Cj298–307   Bank debits and deposit turnover: 1919–1942[1]

Contributed by Howard Bodenhorn

	Bank debits to deposit accounts at reporting centers				Bank debits and deposit turnover, all commercial banks					
					Total demand and time deposits			Demand deposits		
Year	All reporting centers	New York City	140 other centers	Other reporting centers	Debits	Deposits	Annual turnover rate	Debits	Deposits	Annual turnover rate
	Cj298 [2]	Cj299	Cj300	Cj301 [2]	Cj302	Cj303	Cj304	Cj305	Cj306	Cj307
	Million dollars	Million dollars	Million dollars	Million dollars	Million dollars	Million dollars	Rate	Million dollars	Million dollars	Rate
1919	460,249	244,119	211,175	4,955	663,000	27,060	24.5	646,000	18,480	35.0
1920	490,468	241,431	241,595	7,442	721,000	30,350	23.8	700,000	19,800	35.4
1921	409,338	207,096	191,946	10,300	591,000	28,400	20.8	569,000	17,470	32.6
1922	451,513	239,855	199,510	12,148	643,000	29,750	21.6	620,000	18,150	34.2
1923	494,412	238,396	225,331	30,685	685,000	32,920	20.8	658,000	19,280	34.1
1924	522,627	263,530	228,161	30,936	716,000	34,590	20.7	687,000	19,990	34.4
1925	605,843	313,373	256,689	35,781	820,000	37,720	21.7	788,000	21,720	36.3
1926	646,587	339,055	268,902	38,630	872,000	39,340	22.2	838,000	22,210	37.7
1927	714,328	391,558	282,303	40,467	852,000	40,670	23.4	915,000	22,340	41.0
1928	850,521	500,211	306,194	44,116	1,114,000	42,570	26.2	1,075,000	22,950	46.8
1929	982,531	603,088	331,942	47,501	1,276,000	42,720	29.9	1,237,000	23,080	53.6
1930	702,959	384,639	277,317	41,003	931,000	41,550	22.4	892,000	22,090	40.4
1931	515,294	263,834	217,523	33,937	685,000	37,830	18.1	658,000	19,810	33.2
1932	347,264	167,964	154,401	24,899	471,000	31,720	14.8	456,000	16,720	27.3
1933	303,216	148,449 [4]	134,259 [4]	20,508 [4]	437,000	28,500	15.3	424,000	15,850	26.8
1934	356,613	165,948	165,555	25,110	491,000	30,640	16.0	479,000	18,220	26.3
1935	402,718	184,006	190,167	28,545	547,000	34,610	15.8	534,000	21,480	24.9
1936	461,889	208,936	219,669	33,284	628,000	38,660	16.2	614,000	24,810	24.7
1937	469,462	197,836	235,207	36,419	650,000	40,290	16.1	635,000	25,710	24.7
1938	405,930	168,778	204,744	32,408	566,000	40,410	14.0	551,000	25,520	21.6
1939	423,933	171,382	218,295	34,256	592,000	43,670	13.6	577,000	28,550	20.2
1940	445,863	171,582	236,952	37,329	627,000	48,610	12.9	611,000	33,040	18.5
1941	537,343	197,724	293,925	45,694	756,000	54,110	14.0	740,000	38,220	19.4
1942 [3]	641,778	226,865	347,837	67,074	—	—	—	—	—	—

[1] Excludes interbank deposits and collection items.

[2] The exact number of centers in this group varied considerably.

[3] Partly estimated for first four months.

[4] Eleven months only; data for March 1933 not available because of federal bank holiday.

Sources

1919–1941: Board of Governors of the Federal Reserve System, *Banking and Monetary Statistics* (1943), pp. 234–7. 1942: Board of Governors of the Federal Reserve System, *Federal Reserve Bulletin* (June 1946), p. 630.

Documentation

Deposits in commercial banks form a major component of the current means of payment. The extent to which such deposits are used is measured by the statistics of bank debits. In conjunction with deposit figures, debits are a means of determining the rate of turnover of deposits in commercial banks. Although these two measurements illuminate current economic developments, the data must be used with care to measure changes in business conditions. Because factors unrelated to business activity may affect debits

and deposits, these data reflect changes in general business conditions only in a broad way.

Figures represent debits or charges on books of reporting member and nonmember commercial banks in deposit accounts of individuals, partnerships, and corporations; the U.S. government; and state, county, and municipal governments, including debits to time and savings accounts, payments from funds on deposit in the banking department, and payments of certificates of deposit. Debits to accounts of other banks or in settlement of clearinghouse balances, payment of certified and officers' checks, charges to expense and miscellaneous accounts, corrections, and similar charges are not included. For a more detailed description of the data, see *Banking and Monetary Statistics*, pp. 230–3, and George Garvey, *Development of Bank Debits and Clearings and Their Use in Economic Analysis* (Board of Governors of the Federal Reserve System, 1952), especially pp. 27–48.

Satisfactory figures are available for New York City and 140 other reporting centers, but the number of other reporting centers, and consequently the total number of all reporting counties, increased substantially over the relevant period.

TABLE Cj308–315   Bank debits and deposit turnover: 1943–1976

Contributed by Howard Bodenhorn

	Debits to demand deposit accounts				Annual rate of turnover			
	All reporting centers	Leading centers		Other centers	All reporting centers	Leading centers		Other centers
		New York	6 other leading centers			New York	6 other leading centers	
	Cj308	Cj309	Cj310	Cj311	Cj312	Cj313	Cj314	Cj315
Year	Billion dollars	Billion dollars	Billion dollars	Billion dollars	Rate	Rate	Rate	Rate
1943	757	281	175	301	17.5	20.4	18.0	15.3
1944	849	327	195	326	17.8	22.3	18.3	14.6
1945	924	383	200	342	17.6	24.1	17.5	13.5
1946	1,017	407	218	392	19.2	25.1	18.3	14.1
1947	1,104	398	247	459	18.7	23.8	19.7	15.5
1948	1,227	443	271	513	20.4	26.9	21.6	16.6
1949	1,206	446	261	499	20.2	27.9	20.9	15.9
1950	1,380	509	299	572	21.9	31.1	22.6	17.2
1951	1,543	544	337	661	23.0	31.9	24.0	18.4
1952	1,643	598	350	695	23.5	34.4	24.1	18.4
1953	1,759	633	386	740	24.6	36.7	25.6	18.9
1954	1,887	739	390	758	26.2	42.3	25.8	19.2
1955	2,044	767	432	845	27.1	42.7	27.3	20.4
1956	2,201	816	463	922	28.9	45.8	28.8	21.8
1957	2,357	888	489	979	30.8	49.5	30.4	23.0
1958	2,440	959	487	994	31.5	53.6	30.0	22.9
1959	2,679	1,024	545	1,110	33.4	56.4	32.5	24.5
1960	2,839	1,103	578	1,158	35.5	60.0	34.8	25.7
1961	3,111	1,279	623	1,210	38.2	70.0	36.9	26.2
1962	3,436	1,416	702	1,319	41.5	77.8	41.2	27.7
1963	3,755	1,556	776	1,423	44.3	84.8	44.6	29.0
1964 [1]	4,141	1,736	842	1,563	47.7	93.8	47.8	30.8
1964 [2]	4,631	1,925	1,031	1,675	44.8	90.2	41.6	29.2
1965	5,162	2,138	1,141	1,883	48.1	98.8	44.7	31.2
1966	5,923	2,502	1,328	2,093	52.8	109.4	50.1	33.3
1967	6,662	2,921	1,472	2,269	56.7	120.8	53.4	34.5
1968	8,010	3,635	1,756	2,619	62.0	135.5	59.2	36.0
1969	9,223	4,069	2,124	3,031	68.0	143.6	68.1	39.8
1970	10,237	4,518	2,404	3,315	72.9	154.4	77.6	41.9
1971	11,847	5,411	2,682	3,754	81.2	188.1	81.0	44.8
1972	13,584	6,524	3,125	4,405	86.4	209.4	88.0	47.7
1973	18,641	8,098	4,463	6,081	110.2	269.8	115.0	60.6
1974	22,192	9,932	5,153	7,108	128.0	312.8	131.8	69.3
1975	23,565	10,971	4,938	7,662	131.0	351.8	118.4	71.6
1976	26,698	12,835	5,515	8,346	144.1	358.7	129.7	75.6

[1] Comparable with earlier years.

[2] Comparable with later years.

Sources

1943–1963, Board of Governors of the Federal Reserve System, *Supplement to Banking and Monetary Statistics* (various issues), Section 5, "Bank Debits"; 1964–1977, *Federal Reserve Bulletin* (various issues).

Documentation

Deposits in commercial banks form a major component of the current means of payment. The extent to which such deposits are used is measured by the statistics of bank debits. In conjunction with deposit figures, debits are a means of determining the rate of turnover of deposits in commercial banks. Although these two measurements illuminate current economic developments, the data must be used with care to measure changes in business conditions. Because factors unrelated to business activity may affect debits and deposits, these data reflect changes in general business conditions only in a broad way.

Beginning in May 1942, sixty new reporting centers and a number of banks in previously included reporting centers were added to those centers and banks included in the years prior to 1942. The figures for the pre-1943 period are therefore not directly comparable with those reported here.

Beginning in March 1953, the Board of Governors of the Federal Reserve System began publishing revised monthly bank debit series comprising only debits to demand deposit accounts of individuals, partnerships, corporations, and states and political subdivisions. Series Cj308–311, which classify reporting centers into three groups (New York City, six other leading centers, and 338 other reporting centers), provide a better measure of the activity of checking accounts than the pre-1942 series, which covered fewer centers and included demand deposit activity of the U.S. government and debits to time deposits.

The turnover of demand deposits, series Cj312–315, which is computed by dividing debits during a period (converted to an annual rate) by average deposits against which the debits are made, indicates the number of times a deposit dollar is used during the period.

In 1964, the Federal Reserve System again revised its debit and deposit turnover series. The 1964 changes involved three significant revisions designed to make the series more useful indicators of economic and financial developments. The changes included expanded geographic coverage for reporting centers from the city proper to the SMSA (Standard Metropolitan Statistical Area); figures in the revised series represent estimates of SMSA totals instead of reported figures only; and monthly debits and deposit turnover for the national aggregate series are published on an annual rate basis adjusted for seasonal variations.

Expanding the reporting basis to the SMSA increased deposit coverage by about 19 percent and debit coverage by about 12 percent. The number of reporting areas was reduced from 344 to 225, which reflects the consolidation of some city reporting centers into a single SMSA and the elimination of several smaller reporting centers that are not part of an SMSA. Seventeen cities

(continued)

TABLE Cj308–315   Bank debits and deposit turnover: 1943–1976   *Continued*

or counties that are not SMSAs were retained, however, to maintain broad regional coverage. No attempt was made to revise the series in Table Cj298–307 because of the difficulties of the newly included suburban banks whose characteristics are substantially different from those of city banks. Changes in the reporting basis, combined with the new seasonal adjustments, resulted in a new series that is about 11.6 percent higher than the old series. The changes pushed the New York City series 10.9 percent higher; the six other centers series 22.5 percent higher; and the all other centers series 6.5 percent

higher. A more detailed discussion of the changes and their effects on the series can be found in Board of Governors of the Federal Reserve System, *Federal Reserve Bulletin* 51 (March 1965): 390–3. Beginning in March 1967, the Federal Reserve issues a special report (available on request) on debits and deposit turnover for each of the SMSA included in the national series.

Series Cj310 and Cj314. Includes Boston, Philadelphia, Chicago, Detroit, San Francisco–Oakland, and Los Angeles–Long Beach.

TABLE Cj316–323   Bank debits and deposit turnover: 1977–1996

Contributed by Howard Bodenhorn

	Debits to demand deposits				Annual rates of turnover			
	Commercial banks				Commercial banks			
Year	Total	Major New York City banks	Other banks	Other checkable deposits	Total	Major New York City banks	Other banks	Other checkable deposits
	Cj316 [1]	Cj317	Cj318	Cj319 [2]	Cj320	Cj321	Cj322	Cj323 [2]
	Billion dollars	Billion dollars	Billion dollars	Billion dollars	Rate	Rate	Rate	Rate
1977	34,322.8	13,860.6	20,462.2	5.5	129.2	506.0	85.9	6.5
1978	40,297.8	15,008.7	25,289.1	17.1	139.4	541.9	96.8	7.0
1979	49,775.0	18,512.7	31,262.3	83.3	163.5	646.2	113.3	7.8
1980	63,013.4	25,192.5	37,820.9	158.4	201.6	813.7	134.3	9.7
1981	80,858.7	33,891.9	46,966.9	761.0	285.8	1,105.1	186.2	14.4
1982	90,914.4	37,932.9	52,981.6	1,036.2	324.2	1,287.6	211.1	14.5
1983	109,642.5	47,769.4	61,873.1	1,405.5	380.5	1,528.0	240.9	15.6
1984	128,440.8	57,392.7	71,048.1	1,588.7	434.4	1,843.0	268.6	15.8
1985	154,556.0	70,445.1	84,110.9	1,920.8	496.5	2,168.9	301.8	16.7
1986	188,345.8	91,397.3	96,948.8	2,182.5	556.5	2,498.2	321.2	15.6
1987	217,116.2	104,496.3	112,619.8	2,402.7	612.1	2,670.6	357.0	13.8
1988	226,888.4	107,547.3	119,341.2	2,757.7	641.2	2,903.5	376.8	14.7
1989	256,150.4	129,319.9	126,830.5	2,910.5	735.1	3,421.5	408.3	15.2
1990	277,916.3	131,784.0	146,132.3	3,349.6	800.6	3,804.1	467.7	16.5
1991	281,050.1	140,905.5	140,144.6	3,624.6	817.6	4,391.9	449.6	16.1
1992	313,179.6	165,484.6	147,695.1	3,780.7	825.8	4,794.5	428.7	14.4
1993	334,375.0	171,310.7	163,064.2	3,468.9	785.4	4,200.5	423.7	11.8
1994	369,029.1	191,168.8	177,860.3	3,798.6	817.4	4,481.5	435.1	12.6
1995	397,649.3	201,161.4	196,487.9	4,207.4	874.1	4,867.3	475.2	15.4
1996	452,481.0	238,194.5	214,281.8	6,750.1	940.6	5,841.9	486.7	34.3

[1] All debit and deposit data are seasonally adjusted annual averages of monthly figures.

[2] For 1977–1992, other checkable deposits include accounts authorized for automatic transfer to demand deposits (ATS accounts) and accounts authorized for negotiable order of withdrawal (NOW accounts). For 1993–1996, other checkable deposits include ATS and NOW accounts, plus telephone and preauthorized transfer accounts.

Source

Board of Governors of the Federal Reserve System, *Federal Reserve Bulletin* (various issues).

Documentation

Deposits in commercial banks form a major component of the current means of payment. The extent to which such deposits are used is measured by the statistics of bank debits. In conjunction with deposit figures, debits are a means of determining the rate of turnover of deposits in commercial banks. Although these two measurements illuminate current economic developments, the data must be used with care to measure changes in business conditions. Because factors unrelated to business activity may affect debits

and deposits, these data reflect changes in general business conditions only in a broad way.

Data for bank debits and deposit turnover were revised again in 1977 to take account of geographic changes in bank density, changes in industry concentration, and innovations in financial intermediation. The amended series, which begins in 1977, is based on reports from a national sample of about 300 Federal Reserve member banks, replacing the series in Table Cj308–315 based on 233 SMSAs. The Federal Reserve's new series is based on monthly estimates of debits, deposits, and deposit turnover in all commercial banks for demand deposits, total savings deposits, business savings deposits, and savings deposits of other customers. As in series in related tables, demand deposits are defined as deposits of individuals, partnerships, corporations and of states and political subdivisions of the United States. All debits and turnover estimates are expressed in annual rates.

In September 1996, the Federal Reserve System discontinued its survey of debits and deposit turnover and its reports were discontinued.

TABLE Cj324–335 Branch banking – number of branches, by type of bank: 1900–1998[1]

Contributed by Howard Bodenhorn and Eugene N. White

		Commercial banks					Mutual savings banks			Number of banking facilities	All insured commercial banks	All insured savings institutions
			Member banks		Nonmember banks							
	Total	Total	National	State	Insured	Noninsured	Total	Insured	Noninsured			
	Cj324	Cj325 [2]	Cj326	Cj327 [3]	Cj328 [3]	Cj329 [3]	Cj330	Cj331	Cj332	Cj333 [4]	Cj334	Cj335
Year	Number	Number	Number	Number	Number	Number	Number	Number	Number	Number	Number	Number
1900	—	119	5	—	114	—	—	—	—	—	—	—
1905	—	350	5	—	345	—	—	—	—	—	—	—
1910	—	548	12	—	536	—	—	—	—	—	—	—
1915	—	785	26	—	759	—	—	—	—	—	—	—
1920	—	1,281	63	—	1,218	—	—	—	—	—	—	—
1921	—	1,455	72	—	1,383	—	—	—	—	—	—	—
1922	—	1,801	140	—	1,661	—	—	—	—	—	—	—
1923	—	2,054	204	—	1,850	—	—	—	—	—	—	—
1924	—	2,297	256	—	2,041	—	—	—	—	—	—	—
1925	—	2,525	318	—	2,207	—	—	—	—	—	—	—
1926	—	2,703	421	—	2,282	—	—	—	—	—	—	—
1927	—	2,914	723	—	2,191	—	—	—	—	—	—	—
1928	—	3,138	934	—	2,204	—	—	—	—	—	—	—
1929	—	3,353	995	—	2,358	—	—	—	—	—	—	—
1930	—	3,522	1,042	—	2,480	—	—	—	—	—	—	—
1931	—	3,467	1,110	—	2,357	—	—	—	—	—	—	—
1932	—	3,195	1,220	—	1,975	—	—	—	—	—	—	—
1933	2,911	2,786	1,121	960	705	—	125	—	—	—	—	—
1934	3,133	3,007	1,243	981	783	—	126	—	—	—	0	—
1935	3,284	3,156	1,329	952	828	47	128	11	117	—	3,112	—
1936	3,399	3,271	1,398	981	848	44	128	11	117	—	3,261	—
1937	3,540	3,412	1,485	994	891	42	128	11	117	—	3,381	—
1938	3,580	3,445	1,499	992	908	46	135	16	119	—	3,412	—
1939	3,629	3,497	1,518	1,002	927	50	132	24	108	—	3,456	—
1940	3,666	3,531	1,539	1,002	940	50	135	31	104	—	3,489	—
1941	3,699	3,564	1,565	1,015	932	52	135	32	103	—	3,517	—
1942	3,712	3,575	1,571	1,020	932	52	137	35	102	27	3,555	—
1943	3,716	3,580	1,573	1,020	935	52	136	95	41	217	3,744	—
1944	3,772	3,632	1,589	1,035	954	54	140	99	41	292	3,875	—
1945	3,866	3,723	1,641	1,061	964	57	143	101	42	224	3,896	—
1946	4,059	3,902	1,721	1,118	1,001	62	157	115	42	79	3,928	—
1947	4,261	4,090	1,817	1,168	1,038	67	171	124	47	71	4,096	—
1948	4,461	4,279	1,913	1,219	1,079	68	182	132	50	70	4,283	—
1949	4,684	4,485	2,012	1,288	1,132	53	199	141	58	94	4,530	—
1950	4,934	4,721	2,136	1,343	1,190	52	213	152	61	122	4,832	—
1951	5,224	4,994	2,244	1,449	1,260	41	230	165	65	159	5,157	—
1952	5,520	5,274	2,403	1,530	1,300	41	246	177	69	191	5,486	—
1953	5,897	5,627	2,590	1,631	1,365	41	270	192	78	199	5,855	—
1954	6,416	6,108	2,900	1,710	1,462	36	308	221	87	198	6,346	—
1955	7,040	6,710	3,196	1,916	1,563	35	330	234	96	213	6,965	—
1956	7,728	7,362	3,629	2,053	1,643	37	366	257	109	227	7,639	—
1957	8,373	7,968	3,993	2,173	1,765	37	405	296	109	236	8,367	—
1958	9,038	9,613	4,341	2,360	1,873	39	425	305	120	248	8,955	—
1959	9,835	9,388	4,769	2,490	2,087	42	447	318	129	264	9,743	—
1960	10,702	10,216	5,298	2,597	2,274	47	486	381	105	267	10,556	—
1961	11,620	11,077	5,827	2,826	2,380	44	543	427	116	276	11,436	—
1962	12,655	12,068	6,423	2,981	2,614	50	587	466	121	277	12,421	—
1963	13,844	13,220	7,204	3,166 [5]	2,800	50	624	502	122	278	13,581	—
1964	14,995	14,321	7,940	3,056	3,275	50	674	549	125	280	14,699	—
1965	16,201	15,486	8,754	3,309	3,369	54	715	583	132	270	15,872	—
1966	17,405	16,648	9,407	3,493	3,686	62	757	614	143	260	17,029	—
1967	18,519	17,690	9,991	3,658	3,995	46	829	669	160	238	18,079	—
1968	19,675	18,777	10,797	3,555	4,379	46	898	729	169	236	19,183	—
1969	20,973	19,985	11,550	3,465	4,923	47	988	810	178	223	20,379	—
1970	22,508	21,424	12,363	3,642	5,371	48	1,084	891	193	219	21,839	—
1971	22,967	21,880	12,570	3,651	5,589	62	1,087	894	193	—	23,336	—
1972	26,226	24,872	14,012	3,983	6,803	66	1,354	1,112	242	—	24,829	—
1973	28,210	26,718	14,966	4,053	7,624	66	1,492	1,241	251	—	26,673	—
1974	30,347	28,705	15,788	4,209	8,632	67	1,642	1,387	255	—	28,651	—

Notes appear at end of table

(continued)

TABLE Cj324–335 Branch banking – number of branches, by type of bank: 1900–1998 *Continued*

		Commercial banks					Mutual savings banks			Number of banking facilities	All insured commercial banks	All insured savings institutions
	Total	Total	Member banks		Nonmember banks		Total	Insured	Noninsured			
			National	State	Insured	Noninsured						
	Cj324	Cj325 [2]	Cj326	Cj327 [3]	Cj328 [3]	Cj329 [3]	Cj330	Cj331	Cj332	Cj333 [4]	Cj334	Cj335
Year	Number	Number	Number	Number	Number	Number	Number	Number	Number	Number	Number	Number
1975	32,108	30,262	16,330	4,406	9,447	69	1,846	1,568	278	—	30,205	—
1976	33,484	31,404	16,723	4,672	9,927	71	2,080	1,796	284	—	31,344	—
1977	35,485	33,171	17,630	4,595	10,863	71	2,314	1,979	335	—	33,108	—
1978	37,398	34,857	18,167	4,721	11,903	54	2,541	2,192	349	—	34,791	—
1979	39,728	36,853	18,860	4,879	13,054	48	2,875	2,516	359	—	37,971	—
1980	41,902	38,779	19,792	4,771	14,173	31	3,123	2,743	380	—	38,738	—
1981	43,995	40,838	20,766	5,173	14,848	33	3,157	2,886	271	—	40,786	—
1982	42,501	39,835	20,289	5,014	14,481	32	2,666	2,418	248	—	39,783	—
1983	43,610	40,913	21,329	4,814	14,714	37	2,697	2,466	231	—	40,853	—
1984	44,344	41,907	22,178	4,718	15,011	—	—	2,437	—	—	41,799	20,470
1985	46,051	43,347	22,860	4,935	15,552	—	—	2,734	—	—	43,293	21,083
1986	47,216	44,356	23,343	5,226	15,785	—	—	2,860	—	—	44,392	21,455
1987	48,742	45,701	24,117	5,356	15,228	—	—	3,041	—	—	45,357	21,886
1988	50,331	47,083	24,912	5,434	15,717	—	—	3,268	—	—	46,381	22,038
1989	51,735	48,450	25,844	5,702	16,904	—	—	3,285	—	—	48,005	20,584
1990	54,126	50,815	27,300	5,913	17,602	—	—	3,311	—	—	50,406	18,809
1991	55,804	52,484	28,282	6,522	17,680	—	—	3,320	—	—	51,969	17,028
1992	55,780	52,438	27,470	7,250	17,718	—	—	3,342	—	—	51,935	15,413
1993	—	53,121	27,575	7,789	17,757	—	—	—	—	—	52,868	14,669
1994	—	55,144	28,558	8,380	18,196	—	—	—	—	—	55,145	13,926
1995	—	56,513	28,786	9,735	17,992	—	—	—	—	—	56,512	13,445
1996	—	57,788	30,833	8,981	17,974	—	—	—	—	—	57,788	13,833
1997	—	60,320	34,092	9,448	16,780	—	—	—	—	—	60,325	12,951
1998	—	61,957	34,955	10,256	16,746	—	—	—	—	—	61,957	12,451

[1] For years prior to 1924, figures are not for any uniform month. For 1925, 1926, and 1932–1983, figures are as of December; for 1924 and 1927–1931, as of June. Otherwise, reports dated December 31.

[2] Includes one national bank in the Virgin Islands with two branches, which became a member of the Federal Reserve System in 1957.

[3] Figures for 1900–1932 comprise state-chartered commercial banks operating branches and their branches in addition to those unincorporated private banks operating branches and their branches reporting to state banking authorities. Beginning in 1934, the proportion of private banks reporting was larger than in prior years.

[4] Banking facilities are provided at military installations and other government establishments through arrangements made with banks by the Treasury Department. Some of these facilities are operated by banks that have no other type of branch or additional office.

[5] State member bank figure includes one noninsured trust company without deposits.

Sources

Series Cj324–333. 1900–1941: Board of Governors of the Federal Reserve System, *Banking and Monetary Statistics* (1943), pp. 297, 311. For number of private and mutual savings banks, see tables in *Federal Reserve Bulletin* (various issues). For number of branches, 1900–1951: Joint Committee on the Economy Report, *Monetary Policy and the Management of the Public Debt*, 82nd Congress, 2nd Session (1952), Part 1, p. 555. 1952–1970 and earlier years as indicated: *Federal Reserve Bulletin* (various issues). 1971–1983: Federal Deposit Insurance Corporation (FDIC), *Changes among Operating Banks and Branches*, various issues; 1984–1990: FDIC, *Data Book Operating Banks and Branches*; 1991–1998: the FDIC Internet site.

Series Cj334–335. Available at the FDIC Internet site, Historical Statistics on Banking.

Documentation

The figures for number of branches represent some revisions of data previously published in *Banking and Monetary Statistics*. Detailed statistics on branch banking by states, by class of bank, and by location of branches relative to the head office, for selected years since 1900, are available in the sources indicated.

Branch banking is defined as a type of multiple-office banking under which a bank, as a single legal entity, operates more than one banking office. If a bank operates a single branch office, irrespective of size or function, other than a banking facility, as defined in the following, it is included here.

The statistics on branches include all branches or additional offices in the coterminous United States prior to 1959, and include Alaska and Hawai'i thereafter, within the meaning of Section 5155, United States Revised Statutes, which defines a branch as "any branch bank, branch office, branch agency, additional office, or any branch place of business . . . at which deposits are received, or checks paid, or money lent." Branch figures, however, do not include banking facilities at military installations or other government establishments, which began in 1942 through arrangements made by the Treasury Department with banks designated as depositories and financial agents of the government. The number of such facilities is shown separately in series Cj345.

Branch banking should not be confused with group and chain banking. Group and chain banking refers to types of multiple-office banking that differ from branch banking principally in legal form and type of control. For data on group and chain banking, see sources cited previously.

For mutual savings banks, data are not available for banks operating branches until 1933. Branches of unincorporated private banks not reporting to state banking authorities are not included prior to 1934.

Beginning in 1983, reporting practices began to change. First, data on noninsured institutions were no longer reported, ending series Cj329 and Cj332 and eliminating them in the totals for series Cj324. Reporting of insured mutual savings banks, series Cj331, ceased in 1992. Information on these institutions was recorded with all savings institutions, series Cj335, which includes all savings institutions insured by the FDIC's Bank Insurance Fund and Savings Association Insurance Fund. See the text for Table Cj621–628 concerning the development of the insurance funds. Series Cj334 is an alternative to series Cj325.

Series Cj326. Federal deposit insurance is mandatory for national banks and member banks of the Federal Reserve System.

TABLE Cj336–346   Branch banking – number of banks operating branches, by type of bank: 1900–1998[1]

Contributed by Howard Bodenhorn and Eugene N. White

		Commercial banks					Mutual savings banks			All insured commercial banks	All insured savings institutions
	Total	Total	Member banks		Nonmember banks		Total	Insured	Noninsured		
			National	State	Insured	Noninsured					
	Cj336	Cj337 [2]	Cj338	Cj339 [3]	Cj340 [3]	Cj341 [3]	Cj342	Cj343	Cj344	Cj345	Cj346
Year	Number	Number	Number	Number	Number	Number	Number	Number	Number	Number	Number
1900	—	87	5	—	82	—	—	—	—	—	—
1905	—	196	5	—	191	—	—	—	—	—	—
1910	—	292	9	—	283	—	—	—	—	—	—
1915	—	397	12	—	385	—	—	—	—	—	—
1920	—	530	21	—	509	—	—	—	—	—	—
1921	—	547	23	—	524	—	—	—	—	—	—
1922	—	610	55	—	555	—	—	—	—	—	—
1923	—	671	91	—	580	—	—	—	—	—	—
1924	—	706	112	—	594	—	—	—	—	—	—
1925	—	720	130	—	590	—	—	—	—	—	—
1926	—	744	148	—	596	—	—	—	—	—	—
1927	—	740	153	—	587	—	—	—	—	—	—
1928	—	775	171	—	604	—	—	—	—	—	—
1929	—	764	167	—	597	—	—	—	—	—	—
1930	—	751	166	—	585	—	—	—	—	—	—
1931	—	723	164	—	559	—	—	—	—	—	—
1932	—	681	157	—	524	—	—	—	—	—	—
1933	660	584	146	—	438	—	76	—	—	—	—
1934	807	729	176	—	553	—	78	—	—	0	—
1935	901	822	181	—	641	—	79	—	—	796	—
1936	938	859	188	—	671	—	79	—	—	854	—
1937	981	903	194	159	527	23	78	—	—	885	—
1938	1,001	921	194	161	566	—	80	—	—	899	—
1939	1,019	939	195	165	649	30	80	—	—	913	—
1940	1,040	959	200	170	560	29	81	—	—	933	—
1941	1,054	973	205	174	563	31	81	—	—	945	—
1942	1,065	985	212	177	565	31	80	—	—	974	—
1943	1,069	989	214	181	563	31	80	49	31	1,066	—
1944	1,082	999	216	188	563	32	83	51	32	1,113	—
1945	1,101	1,016	222	190	570	34	85	52	33	1,092	—
1946	1,143	1,053	235	193	591	34	90	56	34	1,058	—
1947	1,188	1,089	253	194	604	38	99	60	39	1,083	—
1948	1,242	1,140	276	202	626	36	102	62	40	1,132	—
1949	1,301	1,191	298	214	648	31	110	65	45	1,198	—
1950	1,354	1,241	324	218	669	30	113	67	46	1,267	—
1951	1,422	1,299	352	226	692	29	123	75	48	1,339	—
1952	1,483	1,359	385	237	708	29	124	78	46	1,413	—
1953	1,609	1,474	444	258	745	27	135	85	50	1,534	—
1954	1,720	1,571	502	276	769	24	149	92	57	1,631	—
1955	1,814	1,659	543	304	790	22	155	94	61	1,728	—
1956	1,962	1,790	627	327	815	21	172	100	72	1,862	—
1957	2,066	1,893	677	340	856	20	173	106	67	1,969	—
1958	2,187	2,010	739	352	899	20	177	107	70	2,087	—
1959	2,351	2,164	805	383	956	20	187	113	74	2,228	—
1960	2,523	2,329	905	404	1,001	19	194	131	63	2,386	—
1961	2,696	2,484	986	418	1,062	18	212	146	66	2,539	—
1962	2,840	2,619	1,036	425	1,139	19	221	154	67	2,669	—
1963	3,016	2,791	1,133	439 [4]	1,200	19	225	160	65	2,843	—
1964	3,204	2,966	1,233	445	1,269	19	237	172	66	3,020	—
1965	3,386	3,140	1,331	452	1,336	21	246	176	70	3,192	—
1966	3,573	3,313	1,406	454	1,435	18	260	183	77	3,369	—
1967	3,756	3,487	1,477	459	1,530	21	269	190	79	3,535	—
1968	3,946	3,665	1,550	462	1,633	20	281	199	83	3,714	—
1969	4,084	3,794	1,591	446	1,738	19	290	206	84	3,846	—
1970	4,294	3,994	1,684	450	1,840	20	300	213	87	3,993	—
1971	4,316	4,016	1,687	453	1,853	19	300	213	87	4,196	—
1972	4,789	4,459	1,798	470	2,168	19	330	238	92	4,437	—
1973	5,140	4,799	1,879	480	2,416	19	341	246	95	4,775	—
1974	5,540	5,186	1,990	488	2,684	19	354	258	96	5,163	—

Notes appear at end of table   (continued)

TABLE Cj336–346   Branch banking – number of banks operating branches, by type of bank: 1900–1998   *Continued*

		Commercial banks					Mutual savings banks			All insured commercial banks	All insured savings institutions
	Total	Total	Member banks		Nonmember banks		Total	Insured	Noninsured		
			National	State	Insured	Noninsured					
	Cj336	Cj337 [2]	Cj338	Cj339 [3]	Cj340 [3]	Cj341 [3]	Cj342	Cj343	Cj344	Cj345	Cj346
Year	Number	Number	Number	Number	Number	Number	Number	Number	Number	Number	Number
1975	5,919	5,540	2,095	502	2,919	18	379	271	108	5,516	—
1976	6,131	5,739	2,134	497	3,082	19	392	283	109	5,712	—
1977	6,460	6,061	2,228	506	3,300	19	399	285	114	6,033	—
1978	6,796	6,393	2,288	500	3,578	19	403	290	113	6,366	—
1979	6,995	6,590	2,282	487	3,795	18	405	293	112	6,564	—
1980	7,266	6,858	2,328	502	4,012	8	407	296	112	6,842	—
1981	7,450	7,052	2,377	524	4,131	8	398	306	92	7,033	—
1982	7,411	7,037	2,334	529	4,155	7	374	290	84	7,019	—
1983	7,406	7,054	2,344	528	4,162	8	352	273	79	7,035	—
1984	7,337	7,068	2,354	534	4,180	—	—	267	—	7,069	2,478
1985	7,371	7,024	2,341	535	4,148	—	—	347	—	7,024	2,569
1986	7,389	7,004	2,359	550	4,096	—	—	385	—	7,003	2,635
1987	7,377	6,988	2,362	557	4,089	—	—	389	—	6,987	2,608
1988	7,314	6,917	2,344	548	4,025	—	—	397	—	6,916	2,472
1989	7,246	6,850	2,324	550	3,976	—	—	396	—	6,850	2,242
1990	7,246	6,861	2,317	547	3,997	—	—	385	—	6,861	2,051
1991	7,212	6,835	2,310	515	3,974	—	—	377	—	6,835	1,863
1992	7,237	6,819	2,261	575	3,983	—	—	418	—	6,819	1,739
1993	—	6,718	2,167	601	3,850	—	—	—	—	6,720	1,637
1994	—	6,549	2,051	626	3,872	—	—	—	—	6,550	1,561
1995	—	6,446	1,983	713	3,750	—	—	—	—	6,443	1,467
1996	—	6,248	1,905	708	3,635	—	—	—	—	6,249	1,403
1997	—	6,024	1,837	699	3,474	—	—	—	—	6,026	1,293
1998	—	5,881	1,763	724	3,394	—	—	—	—	5,882	1,210

[1] For years prior to 1924, figures are not for any uniform month. For 1925, 1926, and 1932–1983, figures are as of December; for 1924 and 1927–1931, as of June. Otherwise, reports dated December 31.

[2] Includes one national bank in the Virgin Islands, with two branches, which became a member of the Federal Reserve System in 1957.

[3] Figures for 1900–1932 comprise state-chartered commercial banks operating branches and their branches in addition to those unincorporated private banks operating branches and their branches reporting to state banking authorities. Beginning in 1934, the proportion of private banks reporting was larger than in prior years.

[4] State member bank figure includes one noninsured trust company without deposits.

Sources

Series Cj336–344. 1900–1941, Board of Governors of the Federal Reserve System, *Banking and Monetary Statistics* (1943), pp. 297, 311. For number of private and mutual savings banks, see tables in *Federal Reserve Bulletin* (various issues). For number of branches, 1900–1951: Joint Committee on the Economy Report, *Monetary Policy and the Management of the Public Debt*, 82nd Congress, 2nd Session (1952), Part 1, p. 555. 1952–1970 and earlier years as indicated: *Federal Reserve Bulletin* (various issues). 1971–1983: Federal Deposit Insurance Corporation (FDIC), *Changes among Operating Banks and Branches* (various issues); 1984–1990: FDIC, *Data Book Operating Banks and Branches*; 1991–1998: the FDIC Internet site.

Series Cj345–346. Available at the FDIC Internet site, Historical Statistics on Banking.

Documentation

See the text for Table Cj324–335.

TABLE Cj347–353   National banks issuing credit cards – number and outstanding credit balances: 1970–1992[1]

Contributed by Howard Bodenhorn

			Banks offering credit card and related revolving credit plans				
				Banks offering credit card plans		Banks offering related revolving credit plans	
	National banks	Number	Outstanding balances	Number	Outstanding balances	Number	Outstanding balances
	Cj347	Cj348 [2]	Cj349	Cj350	Cj351	Cj352	Cj353
Year	Number	Number	Thousand dollars	Number	Thousand dollars	Number	Thousand dollars
1970	4,638	—	3,508,000	688	2,755,000	660	753,000
1971	4,599	—	4,064,500	740	3,246,962	701	817,538
1972	4,607	—	4,888,722	801	3,930,645	789	958,077
1973	4,631	—	6,147,762	839	4,999,338	900	1,148,424
1974	4,695	—	7,450,556	861	6,052,634	1,040	1,397,922
1975	4,732	—	8,434,699	927	6,952,298	1,130	1,482,401
1976	4,749	—	9,861,793	958	8,215,846	1,216	1,645,947
1977	4,703	—	12,875,882	1,020	10,679,513	1,305	2,196,369
1978	4,616	1,850	17,542,357	—	—	—	—
1979	4,493	1,830	21,528,485	—	—	—	—
1980	4,426	1,839	22,066,505	—	—	—	—
1981	4,453	1,832	23,780,888	—	—	—	—
1982 [3]	4,507	1,866	23,753,011	—	—	—	—
1983 [3]	4,713	1,927	26,537,637	—	—	—	—
1984 [3]	4,823	2,063	37,376,064	—	—	—	—
1985 [3]	4,962	2,295	52,216,992	—	—	—	—
1986 [3]	4,913	2,404	64,298,968	—	—	—	—
1987 [3]	4,744	2,385	57,073,363	—	—	—	—
1988 [4]	4,458	2,207	61,972,203	—	—	—	—
1989	4,263	2,350	89,496,754	—	—	—	—
1990	3,967	2,320	74,427,762	—	—	—	—
1991	3,908	2,324	74,466,790	—	—	—	—
1992	3,691	2,247	75,101,621	—	—	—	—

[1] Number does not sum to figures reported in series Cj350 and Cj352 because some national banks offered both types of plans.

[2] As of June 30.

[3] As of March 31.

[4] As of December 31, except where noted.

Sources

1970–1980: Comptroller of the Currency, *Annual Report* (various issues); 1981–1992: Comptroller of the Currency, *Quarterly Journal* (various issues).

Documentation

Despite the growing popularity of bank-issued debit cards and point-of-sale transactions (see series Cj356), credit cards account for the largest proportion of electronic payments. In 1997, there were about 17 billion credit card transactions, representing about 18 percent of all transactions.

Credit card transactions take place over electronic networks that link card holders, merchants, card-issuing banks, merchants' banks, and the credit card companies themselves. In 1997, approximately 500 million general-purpose credit cards were in use. MasterCard and Visa cards account for 85 percent of those cards. Nonbank general-purpose cards, such as American Express, Discover, and Diners Club cards, account for about 25 percent of all general-purpose credit card use. So-called private label cards, such as those issued by retailers, department stores, and oil companies, account for nearly one fifth of all credit card dollar volume. Interested readers are referred to the original Comptroller's Reports, as well as to the *Nilson Report*, which provides regular updates on credit card usage.

TABLE Cj354–361   Automated teller machines and point of sale terminals – number and transactions: 1980–1998

Contributed by Howard Bodenhorn and Eugene N. White

	Transactions			ATM terminals				
	All	ATM	POS	Number			Monthly transactions per terminal	POS terminals
				Total	Shared	Proprietary		
	Cj354	Cj355	Cj356	Cj357 [1]	Cj358	Cj359	Cj360	Cj361 [2]
Year	Million	Million	Million	Thousand	Thousand	Thousand	Number	Thousand
1980	—	—	—	18.5	—	—	5,405	—
1985	3,579	3,565	14	60.0	35.5	24.5	4,951	—
1986	3,661	3,625	36	64.0	48.6	15.4	4,720	—
1987	4,108	4,048	60	68.0	55.0	13.0	4,962	—
1988	4,581	4,480	92	72.5	65.1	7.4	5,151	—
1989	5,274	5,116	157	75.6	70.1	5.5	5,638	—
1990	5,942	5,751	191	80.2	75.3	4.9	5,980	53.1
1991	6,642	6,418	223	83.5	79.6	4.0	6,403	78.1
1992	7,537	7,206	289	87.3	84.7	2.6	6,876	95.2
1993	8,135	7,705	430	94.8	92.6	2.3	6,772	155.0
1994	8,958	8,334	624	109.1	108.1	1.0	6,459	340.5
1995	10,464	9,689	775	122.7	122.6	0.1	6,580	528.6
1996	11,830	10,684	1,146	139.1	139.0	0.1	6,399	875.4
1997	12,362	10,920	1,442	165.0	165.0	—	5,515	1,300.0
1998	12,960	11,160	1,800	187.0	187.0	—	4,977	1,700.0

[1] As of September each year.

[2] As of June each year.

Source

U.S. Bureau of the Census, *Statistical Abstract of the United States* (various issues).

Documentation

Cash and checks remain the dominant forms of payment in the United States. Although the use of cash is difficult to measure, some estimates place its share at 50 percent of the total number of transactions. Ironically, the popularity of cash has been bolstered in recent years by an electronic device, namely the automated teller machine (ATM). ATMs offer more convenient access to cash than the traditional method of cashing a check at a banking office.

An ATM allows a customer to withdraw cash from his or her account by entering a personal identification number (PIN) and the withdrawal is immediately debited to the customer's account. ATM transactions were made possible through the development of a communications network that includes all four parties to the transaction: the customer, the card-issuing bank, the ATM owner, and the network or networks to which the card issuer and ATM owner belong. Point of sale (POS) or debit cards operate in a similar fashion. A customer presents a retailer with a debit card at the point of purchase. Unlike a credit card, a debit card transaction immediately debits the customer's bank account. Most debit card or POS transactions operate through the same networks as ATM transactions.

Between 1985 and 1997, the number of ATM transactions increased threefold, while the number of POS transactions increased tenfold. The rapid growth in the use of both types of electronic fund transfers resulted from an increasing availability of ATMs, with more than 50 percent located at non-bank premises, such as convenience stores, gas stations, and shopping malls. Similarly, the use of debit cards has increased markedly, so POS transactions accounted for about 4 percent of total transactions in 1997. More than 250 million debit cards have been issued; a 1997 Federal Reserve Bank of Kansas City survey revealed that 77 percent of all banks issue debit cards, and an additional 14 percent plan to do so. A number of factors account for the increased use of POS transactions: growing familiarity among bank customers, increased merchant acceptance, aggressive marketing by banks, and the coupling of ATM and POS capabilities with a single card. Interested readers are referred to Stuart E. Weiner, "Electronic Payments in the U.S. Economy: An Overview," *Federal Reserve Bank of Kansas City Economic Review* 84 (1999): 1–12, and sources therein.

Howard Bodenhorn

TABLE Cj362–374 Mutual savings banks – assets and liabilities: 1896–1977[1]

Contributed by Howard Bodenhorn

		Assets									Liabilities		
	Total assets or liabilities and reserve accounts	Loans			Securities								
		Total	Mortgage	Other	Total	U.S. government	State and local government	Corporate and other	Cash	Other	Deposits	Other	General reserve accounts
	Cj362	Cj363	Cj364	Cj365	Cj366	Cj367	Cj368	Cj369	Cj370	Cj371	Cj372	Cj373	Cj374
Year	Million dollars	Million dollars	Million dollars	Million dollars	Million dollars	Million dollars	Million dollars	Million dollars	Million dollars	Million dollars	Million dollars	Million dollars	Million dollars
1896	1,881	874	728	146	870	158	482	230	91	46	1,717	1	163
1897	1,957	895	752	143	916	156	508	252	99	47	1,785	1	171
1898	2,048	915	777	138	968	147	544	277	115	50	1,870	1	177
1899	2,190	971	815	156	1,047	139	561	347	117	55	2,000	2	188
1900	2,328	1,027	858	169	1,134	105	567	462	121	46	2,129	2	197
1901	2,466	1,080	901	179	1,215	78	595	542	125	46	2,261	2	203
1902	2,599	1,143	948	195	1,277	62	624	591	124	55	2,390	2	207
1903	2,711	1,205	999	206	1,325	46	652	627	122	59	2,505	1	205
1904	2,814	1,246	1,049	197	1,370	38	657	675	135	63	2,602	3	209
1905	2,969	1,320	1,121	199	1,452	30	673	749	134	63	2,744	3	222
1906	3,139	1,429	1,202	227	1,517	22	694	801	133	60	2,911	3	225
1907	3,252	1,509	1,282	227	1,540	20	684	836	142	61	3,032	2	218
1908	3,281	1,519	1,326	193	1,544	16	682	846	158	60	3,016	2	263
1909	3,344	1,533	1,349	184	1,593	14	719	860	159	59	3,094	1	249
1910	3,598	1,694	1,500	194	1,684	13	765	906	156	64	3,306	2	290
1911	3,706	1,773	1,570	203	1,705	12	759	934	170	58	3,407	8	291
1912	3,877	1,885	1,677	208	1,764	13	750	1,001	167	61	3,558	4	315
1913	4,047	2,001	1,780	221	1,803	12	804	987	172	71	3,715	5	327
1914	4,194	2,085	1,866	219	1,840	12	842	986	196	73	3,859	2	333
1915	4,257	2,143	1,916	227	1,825	11	813	1,001	208	81	3,893	8	356
1916	4,480	2,196	1,986	210	1,963	14	851	1,098	237	84	4,124	5	351
1917	4,739	2,321	2,109	212	2,089	50	864	1,175	240	89	4,355	8	376
1918	4,745	2,292	2,094	198	2,131	200	783	1,148	224	98	4,353	21	371
1919	5,141	2,318	2,100	218	2,503	561	748	1,194	225	95	4,728	18	395
1920	5,586	2,627	2,291	336	2,646	783	650	1,213	225	88	5,157	9	420
1921	5,964	2,850	2,502	348	2,809	939	680	1,190	209	96	5,503	12	449
1922	6,262	2,961	2,715	246	2,968	971	697	1,300	228	105	5,695	12	555
1923	6,812	3,337	3,086	251	3,150	1,112	670	1,368	218	107	6,202	12	598
1924	7,284	3,753	3,529	224	3,164	1,122	644	1,398	247	120	6,618	13	653
1925	7,831	4,155	3,923	232	3,302	1,076	709	1,517	240	134	7,071	12	748
1926	8,298	4,574	4,325	249	3,337	970	758	1,609	238	149	7,465	13	820
1927	9,820	5,017	4,760	257	3,484	852	827	1,805	255	164	7,996	15	909
1928	9,557	5,458	5,171	287	3,681	738	900	2,043	238	180	8,555	16	986
1929	9,873	5,830	5,483	347	3,621	604	905	2,112	219	203	8,884	18	971

Notes appear at end of table

(continued)

TABLE Cj362–374 Mutual savings banks – assets and liabilities: 1896–1977 Continued

		Assets									Liabilities		
	Total assets or liabilities and reserve accounts	Loans			Securities				Cash	Other	Deposits	Other	General reserve accounts
		Total	Mortgage	Other	Total	U.S. government	State and local government	Corporate and other					
Year	Cj362	Cj363	Cj364	Cj365	Cj366	Cj367	Cj368	Cj369	Cj370	Cj371	Cj372	Cj373	Cj374
	Million dollars	Million dollars	Million dollars	Million dollars	Million dollars	Million dollars	Million dollars	Million dollars	Million dollars	Million dollars	Million dollars	Million dollars	Million dollars
1930	10,164	5,947	5,635	312	3,697	499	920	2,278	291	229	9,099	12	1,053
1931	11,052	6,108	5,869	239	4,287	590	1,038	2,659	388	269	9,910	17	1,125
1932	10,991	6,071	5,903	168	4,129	687	957	2,485	437	354	9,911	39	1,041
1933	10,848	5,880	5,752	128	4,047	733	911	2,403	425	496	9,606	44	1,198
1934	10,938	5,590	5,480	110	4,190	984	896	2,310	511	647	9,670	27	1,241
1935	11,046	5,289	5,196	93	4,441	1,538	866	2,037	520	796	9,809	24	1,213
1936	11,283	5,040	4,956	84	4,780	2,049	773	1,958	541	922	9,950	20	1,313
1937	11,496	4,965	4,884	81	5,074	3,250	793	1,031	527	930	10,141	18	1,337
1938	11,545	4,905	4,826	79	5,158	2,680	704	1,774	575	907	10,186	22	1,337
1939	11,771	4,889	4,812	77	5,336	3,040	647	1,649	697	849	10,409	22	1,340
1940	11,925	4,917	4,835	82	5,247	3,108	551	1,588	977	784	10,608	25	1,292
1941	11,969	4,949	4,858	91	5,348	3,420	536	1,392	966	706	10,624	35	1,310
1942	11,655	4,815	4,743	72	5,522	3,880	388	1,254	751	567	10,372	37	1,246
1943	12,407	4,575	4,522	53	6,654	5,279	234	1,141	720	458	11,122	41	1,244
1944	13,810	4,405	4,351	54	8,545	7,294	156	1,095	533	327	12,449	39	1,322
1945	16,962	4,264	4,202	62	11,849	10,650	— [2]	1,199 [2]	606	243	15,332	48	1,582
1946	18,662	4,526	4,451	75	13,118	11,745	— [2]	1,372 [2]	815	203	16,813	61	1,788
1947	19,724	4,950	4,856	94	13,680	11,984	— [2]	1,696 [2]	881	213	17,759	71	1,894
1948	20,482	5,689	5,583	106	13,692	11,509	— [2]	2,183 [2]	877	224	18,400	80	2,002
1949	21,503	6,585	6,479	106	13,812	11,444	— [2]	2,368 [2]	872	234	19,287	95	2,121
1950	22,446	8,166	8,039	127	13,233	10,877	— [2]	2,356 [2]	792	255	20,025	138	2,283
1951	23,504	9,876	9,747	129	12,457	9,827	140	2,490	883	288	20,900	154	2,450
1952	25,301	11,375	11,231	144	12,703	9,443	335	2,925	917	306	22,610	164	2,527
1953	27,199	12,957	12,792	165	12,930	9,191	428	3,311	983	329	24,388	203	2,608
1954	29,350	15,033	14,845	188	12,911	8,755	608	3,548	1,026	380	26,351	261	2,738
1955	31,346	17,490	17,297	193	12,473	8,463	646	3,364	966	417	28,182	310	2,854
1956	33,381	19,807	19,559	248	12,206	7,982	676	3,548	920	448	30,026	369	2,986
1957	35,215	21,224	20,971	253	12,612	7,583	685	4,344	889	490	31,684	426	3,105
1958	37,784	23,358	23,038	320	12,970	7,270	729	4,971	921	535	34,031	526	3,227
1959	38,945	25,127	24,769	358	12,437	6,871	721	4,845	829	552	34,977	606	3,362
1960	40,571	27,118	26,702	416	11,991	6,243	672	5,076	874	588	36,343	678	3,550
1961	42,829	29,377	28,902	475	11,877	6,160	677	5,040	937	638	38,277	781	3,771
1962	46,121	32,658	32,056	602	11,811	6,107	527	5,177	956	696	41,336	828	3,957
1963	49,702	36,614	36,007	607	11,377	5,863	440	5,074	912	799	44,606	943	4,153
1964	54,238	41,067	40,328	739	11,281	5,791	391	5,099	1,004	886	48,849	989	4,400
1965	58,232	45,295	44,433	862	10,975	5,485	320	5,170	1,017	945	52,443	1,124	4,665
1966	60,982	48,271	47,193	1,078	10,734	4,764	251	5,719	953	1,024	55,006	1,113	4,863
1967	66,365	51,514	50,311	1,203	12,721	4,319	219	8,183	993	1,137	60,121	1,260	4,984
1968	71,152	54,693	53,286	1,407	14,208	3,834	194	10,180	996	1,255	64,507	1,372	5,273
1969	74,144	57,605	55,781	1,824	14,320	3,296	200	10,824	912	1,307	67,026	1,588	5,530

	Total assets or liabilities and reserve accounts	Loans			Assets — Securities				Cash	Other	Liabilities — Deposits	Other	General reserve accounts
		Total	Mortgage	Other	Total	U.S. government	State and local government	Corporate and other					
Year	Cj362	Cj363	Cj364	Cj365	Cj366	Cj367	Cj368	Cj369	Cj370	Cj371	Cj372	Cj373	Cj374
	Million dollars	Million dollars	Million dollars	Million dollars	Million dollars	Million dollars	Million dollars	Million dollars	Million dollars	Million dollars	Million dollars	Million dollars	Million dollars
1970	78,995	60,030	57,775	2,255	16,224	3,151	197	12,876	1,270	1,471	71,580	1,689	5,726
1971	89,573	64,186	61,978	2,208	21,684	6,267	392	15,025	1,396	2,307	87,817	1,756	6,328
1972	100,600	69,801	67,556	2,245	26,254	7,588	1,241	17,425	1,645	2,900	92,225	1,414	6,961
1973	106,660	75,587	73,230	2,357	25,232	6,994	936	17,302	1,976	3,865	97,166	1,902	7,592
1974	109,544	77,499	74,920	2,579	25,967	6,844	937	18,186	2,193	3,885	99,379	2,208	7,957
1975	121,071	80,154	77,249	2,905	34,222	10,799	1,550	21,873	2,347	4,348	110,583	2,067	8,421
1976	134,820	85,295	81,640	3,655	41,977	14,765	2,407	24,805	2,370	5,178	123,654	2,112	9,054
1977	147,329	92,349	88,227	4,122	46,578	17,444	2,842	26,292	2,421	5,981	134,917	2,433	9,979

[1] 1896–1944, reports dated nearest June 30; 1945–1977, reports dated December 31.

[2] State and local government securities included in corporate and other.

Sources

1896–1944: Board of Governors of the Federal Reserve System, *All-Bank Statistics* (1959), Table A-4. 1945–1962: Board of Governors of the Federal Reserve System, *Supplement to Banking and Monetary Statistics* (various issues), Section 12, Table 26. 1963–1970: *Federal Reserve Bulletin* 59 (March 1973): A39. 1971–1972: Federal Deposit Insurance Corporation (FDIC), *Assets and Liabilities – Commercial and Mutual Savings Banks* (1974). 1973–1977: FDIC, *Assets and Liabilities – Commercial and Mutual Savings Banks* (1978).

Documentation

Mutual savings banks are organized without explicit capital stock and operated for the benefit of their depositors. Mutuals are similar to cooperatives in that all of the institution's net assets are the property of depositors. They differ from cooperatives, however, in that depositors manage neither the bank nor its assets; that responsibility is vested with a board of trustees, which selects the bank's operating officers.

Historically, mutual savings banks were promoted and organized to encourage saving and thrift among the working classes. Many were initially formed as self-help or benevolent institutions that provided a social service for depositors with savings too modest to justify the expense of opening demand or savings deposit accounts with commercial banks. Thus, mutuals attracted funds that may have otherwise been hoarded and allowed savers to earn moderate yields on their savings. To maintain the mutuals' place as a repository for small savers, most states set limits on the maximum deposit maintained by an individual.

Mutual savings banks do not contract for an interest rate on deposits in advance. Rather, most mutuals are required to invest in investment-grade government and corporate securities and high-grade mortgages. Dividends on these investments are distributed, pro rata, to depositors after the bank's expenses are paid and any contributions to the firm's reserve fund are made. Because mutuals are required to return to depositors dividends only as large as the trustees deem advisable, the amounts that are periodically credited to the depositors' accounts are better thought of as dividends than as interest.

Data for 1930 and earlier are from the Board of Governors of the Federal Reserve System. For 1931–1945, figures were obtained by the National Association of Mutual Savings Banks from state banking departments and directly from some individual savings banks. Reporting procedures for state banking departments were not completely uniform in this period and differed in some respects from those prescribed by the FDIC. Beginning in 1946, the data were collected by the National Association of Mutual Savings Banks directly from individual savings banks and generally conform to FDIC reporting procedures.

These series end in 1977 when the FDIC ceased to report them.

TABLE Cj375–381   Savings and loan associations – number, by organizational form and regulatory membership: 1900–1989

Contributed by Howard Bodenhorn

Year	All operating savings and loan associations and insured savings banks	Federal Home Loan Bank members					Federal Home Loan Bank nonmember, uninsured state savings and loan associations
		Total	FSLIC-insured			Uninsured state savings and loan associations	
			Savings banks	Savings and loan associations			
				Federal	State		
	Cj375	Cj376	Cj377 [1]	Cj378 [1]	Cj379 [1]	Cj380	Cj381
	Number	Number	Number	Number	Number	Number	Number
1900	5,356	—	—	—	—	—	5,356
1902	5,299	—	—	—	—	—	5,299
1904	5,265	—	—	—	—	—	5,265
1906	5,316	—	—	—	—	—	5,316
1908	5,599	—	—	—	—	—	5,599
1910	5,869	—	—	—	—	—	5,869
1912	6,273	—	—	—	—	—	6,273
1914	6,612	—	—	—	—	—	6,612
1916	7,072	—	—	—	—	—	7,072
1918	7,484	—	—	—	—	—	7,484
1920	8,633	—	—	—	—	—	8,633
1922	10,009	—	—	—	—	—	10,009
1923	10,744	—	—	—	—	—	10,744
1924	11,844	—	—	—	—	—	11,844
1925	12,403	—	—	—	—	—	12,403
1926	12,626	—	—	—	—	—	12,626
1927	12,804	—	—	—	—	—	12,804
1928	12,666	—	—	—	—	—	12,666
1929	12,342	—	—	—	—	—	12,342
1930	11,777	—	—	—	—	—	11,777
1931	11,442	—	—	—	—	—	11,442
1932	10,915	101	—	—	—	101	10,814
1933	10,596	2,073	—	6	—	2,067	8,523
1934	10,744	3,054	—	539	2	2,513	7,690
1935	10,266	3,455	—	987	130	2,338	6,811
1936	10,042	3,750	—	1,200	375	2,175	6,292
1937	9,225	3,895	—	1,318	566	2,011	5,330
1938	8,762	3,903	—	1,357	741	1,805	4,859
1939	8,006	3,870	—	1,398	801	1,671	4,136
1940	7,521	3,824	—	1,437	840	1,547	3,697
1941	7,211	3,783	—	1,460	883	1,440	3,428
1942	6,941	3,744	—	1,467	931	1,346	3,197
1943	6,498	3,705	—	1,466	981	1,258	2,793
1944	6,279	3,659	—	1,464	1,002	1,193	2,620
1945	6,149	3,658	—	1,467	1,008	1,183	2,491
1946	6,093	3,661	—	1,471	1,025	1,165	2,432
1947	6,045	3,670	—	1,478	1,058	1,134	2,375
1948	6,011	3,733	—	1,485	1,131	1,117	2,278
1949	5,983	3,822	—	1,508	1,248	1,066	2,161
1950	5,992	3,894	—	1,526	1,334	1,036	2,098
1951	5,995	3,950	—	1,549	1,471	931	2,045
1952	6,004	4,028	—	1,581	1,591	856	1,976
1953	6,012	4,108	—	1,604	1,700	804	1,904
1954	6,037	4,209	—	1,640	1,793	776	1,828
1955	6,071	4,307	—	1,683	1,861	763	1,764
1956	6,136	4,398	—	1,739	1,927	732	1,738
1957	6,169	4,475	—	1,772	2,000	703	1,694
1958	6,207	4,543	—	1,804	2,077	662	1,664
1959	6,223	4,599	—	1,841	2,138	620	1,624
1960	6,320	4,694	—	1,873	2,225	596	1,626
1961	6,246	4,795	—	1,906	2,315	574	1,451
1962	6,289	4,888	—	1,941	2,391	556	1,401
1963	6,248	4,960	—	1,968	2,451	541	1,288
1964	6,222	4,985	—	1,981	2,482	516	1,237

Note appears at end of table

TABLE Cj375–381   Savings and loan associations – number, by organizational form and regulatory membership: 1900–1989   *Continued*

	All operating savings and loan associations and insured savings banks	Federal Home Loan Bank members					Federal Home Loan Bank nonmember, uninsured state savings and loan associations
		Total	FSLIC-insured			Uninsured state savings and loan associations	
			Savings banks	Savings and loan associations			
				Federal	State		
	Cj375	Cj376	Cj377 [1]	Cj378 [1]	Cj379 [1]	Cj380	Cj381
Year	Number	Number	Number	Number	Number	Number	Number
1965	6,185	5,006	—	2,011	2,497	498	1,179
1966	6,112	4,982	—	2,051	2,459	472	1,130
1967	6,036	4,919	—	2,056	2,431	432	1,117
1968	5,947	4,849	—	2,063	2,407	379	1,098
1969	5,835	4,747	—	2,071	2,367	309	1,088
1970	5,669	4,601	—	2,067	2,298	236	1,068
1971	5,474	4,471	—	2,049	2,222	200	1,003
1972	5,298	4,362	—	2,044	2,147	171	936
1973	5,170	4,311	—	2,040	2,123	148	859
1974	5,086	4,281	—	2,070	2,071	140	805
1975	4,931	4,202	—	2,048	2,030	124	729
1976	4,821	4,159	—	2,019	2,025	115	661
1977	4,761	4,173	—	2,012	2,053	108	588
1978	4,725	4,154	—	2,000	2,053	101	571
1979	4,684	4,139	—	1,990	2,049	99	546
1980	4,594	4,101	3	1,985	2,017	96	493
1981	4,298	3,878	6	1,907	1,872	93	420
1982	3,831	3,428	6	1,727	1,616	79	403
1983	3,645	3,260	143	1,553	1,487	77	385
1984	3,591	3,209	229	1,460	1,447	73	382
1985	3,535	3,307	302	1,419	1,525	61	228
1986	3,487	3,279	403	1,344	1,473	59	208
1987	3,385	3,206	499	1,288	1,360	59	179
1988	3,175	3,011	621	1,123	1,205	62	164
1989	3,011	2,891	770	1,075	1,033	13	120

[1] Beginning in 1989, the Savings Association Insurance Fund replaced the Federal Savings and Loan Insurance Corporation as the guarantor of deposits.

Source
Office of Thrift Supervision, *Savings and Home Financing Source Book* (1989), Table A-1.

Documentation
The information in this table is for savings banks and savings and loan associations, commonly classed together as thrifts. Industry numbers roughly doubled in the first three decades of the twentieth century, increasing from 5,356 to 12,804 institutions between 1900 and 1927. During the Great Depression of the 1930s, the industry witnessed widespread failures and closures. The federal government organized two institutions to stabilize the industry and promote home ownership. The Federal Home Loan Bank Board (FHLBB) was established in 1932. The FHLBB raises funds for the thrift industry by securitizing mortgages and selling them to investors. The Federal Savings and Loan Insurance Corporation (FSLIC) was established in 1933. The FSLIC insured depositors in insured savings and loans from loss due to thrift failure. The Savings Association Insurance Fund (SAIF) is the successor to the FSLIC.

The series show that thrifts were quick to join the FHLBB, largely because membership provided access to relatively low-cost funds. FSLIC membership lagged as one quarter to one third of the industry operated without federal insurance guarantees up to the early 1970s. The thrift crisis of the 1980s is also evident in the series. The total number of operating thrifts declined by one third between 1980 and 1989. By the end of the decade, the proportion of uninsured state-chartered thrifts also declined markedly.

TABLE Cj382–388   Savings and loan associations – assets, by organizational form and regulatory membership: 1900–1989

Contributed by Howard Bodenhorn

	All operating savings and loan associations and insured savings banks	Federal Home Loan Bank members					Federal Home Loan Bank nonmember, uninsured state savings and loan associations
		Total	FSLIC-insured			Uninsured state savings and loan associations	
			Savings banks	Savings and loan associations			
				Federal	State		
	Cj382	Cj383	Cj384 [1]	Cj385 [1]	Cj386 [1]	Cj387	Cj388
Year	Million dollars	Million dollars	Million dollars	Million dollars	Million dollars	Million dollars	Million dollars
1900	571	—	—	—	—	—	571
1902	577	—	—	—	—	—	577
1904	600	—	—	—	—	—	600
1906	673	—	—	—	—	—	673
1908	784	—	—	—	—	—	784
1910	932	—	—	—	—	—	932
1912	1,138	—	—	—	—	—	1,138
1914	1,358	—	—	—	—	—	1,358
1916	1,599	—	—	—	—	—	1,599
1918	1,898	—	—	—	—	—	1,898
1920	2,520	—	—	—	—	—	2,520
1922	3,343	—	—	—	—	—	3,343
1923	3,943	—	—	—	—	—	3,943
1924	4,766	—	—	—	—	—	4,766
1925	5,509	—	—	—	—	—	5,509
1926	6,334	—	—	—	—	—	6,334
1927	7,179	—	—	—	—	—	7,179
1928	8,016	—	—	—	—	—	8,016
1929	8,695	—	—	—	—	—	8,695
1930	8,829	—	—	—	—	—	8,829
1931	8,417	—	—	—	—	—	8,417
1932	7,737	203	—	—	—	203	7,737
1933	7,018	2,576	—	2	—	2,574	7,018
1934	6,406	2,740	—	138	12	2,590	6,256
1935	5,875	2,891	—	495	216	2,180	5,164
1936	5,772	3,187	—	783	498	1,906	4,491
1937	5,682	3,548	—	1,099	659	1,790	3,924
1938	5,632	3,753	—	1,311	816	1,626	3,505
1939	5,597	4,048	—	1,576	933	1,539	3,088
1940	5,733	4,411	—	1,867	1,059	1,485	2,807
1941	6,049	4,798	—	2,164	1,189	1,445	2,696
1942	6,150	5,025	—	2,296	1,347	1,382	2,507
1943	6,604	5,539	—	2,616	1,557	1,366	2,431
1944	7,458	6,423	—	3,168	1,827	1,428	2,463
1945	8,747	7,681	—	3,921	2,202	1,558	2,624
1946	10,202	9,017	—	4,671	2,623	1,723	2,908
1947	11,687	10,427	—	5,458	3,070	1,899	3,159
1948	13,028	11,733	—	6,164	3,551	2,018	3,313
1949	14,622	13,278	—	7,104	4,174	2,000	3,344
1950	16,893	15,516	—	8,457	5,234	1,825	3,202
1951	19,222	17,916	—	9,792	6,412	1,712	3,018
1952	22,660	21,332	—	11,762	7,894	1,676	3,004
1953	26,733	25,312	—	14,045	9,548	1,719	3,140
1954	31,633	30,155	—	16,775	11,592	1,788	3,266
1955	37,656	36,147	—	20,035	14,163	1,949	3,458
1956	42,875	41,274	—	22,973	16,365	1,936	3,537
1957	48,138	46,454	—	25,733	18,726	1,995	3,679
1958	56,139	53,368	—	29,652	21,659	2,057	4,828
1959	63,530	61,636	—	34,362	25,188	2,086	3,980
1960	71,476	69,492	—	38,511	28,919	2,062	4,046
1961	82,135	80,135	—	43,805	34,179	2,151	4,151
1962	93,605	91,880	—	49,633	39,912	2,335	4,060
1963	107,559	105,627	—	56,368	46,786	2,473	4,405
1964	119,355	117,382	—	61,643	53,009	2,730	4,703

Note appears at end of table

TABLE Cj382–388   Savings and loan associations – assets, by organizational form and regulatory membership: 1900–1989   *Continued*

	All operating savings and loan associations and insured savings banks	Federal Home Loan Bank members					Federal Home Loan Bank nonmember, uninsured state savings and loan associations
		Total		FSLIC-insured		Uninsured state savings and loan associations	
			Savings banks	Savings and loan associations			
				Federal	State		
	Cj382	Cj383	Cj384 [1]	Cj385 [1]	Cj386 [1]	Cj387	Cj388
Year	Million dollars	Million dollars	Million dollars	Million dollars	Million dollars	Million dollars	Million dollars
1965	129,580	127,594	—	66,715	57,861	3,018	5,004
1966	133,933	132,014	—	69,581	59,464	2,969	4,888
1967	143,535	141,360	—	75,279	63,210	2,871	5,045
1968	152,890	150,505	—	81,077	66,659	2,769	5,154
1969	162,148	158,723	—	87,302	69,486	1,935	5,361
1970	176,183	172,093	—	96,259	74,386	1,448	5,538
1971	206,024	201,373	—	114,229	85,755	1,389	6,039
1972	243,127	237,816	—	136,925	99,424	1,467	6,778
1973	271,905	266,287	—	152,240	112,557	1,490	7,108
1974	295,545	290,082	—	167,671	120,552	1,359	6,822
1975	338,233	332,445	—	195,410	134,849	2,186	7,974
1976	391,908	385,640	—	225,763	157,409	2,468	8,735
1977	459,241	452,727	—	261,920	188,078	2,729	9,243
1978	523,542	516,103	—	298,195	215,115	2,793	10,232
1979	578,962	571,126	—	323,058	245,049	3,019	10,855
1980	632,872	624,046	2,160	348,462	270,005	3,419	8,827
1981	671,627	662,180	7,460	407,351	243,717	3,652	9,447
1982	714,577	702,896	6,859	483,898	208,765	3,374	11,681
1983	838,385	822,851	64,968	499,255	254,945	3,683	15,534
1984	1,000,489	981,287	98,439	527,888	351,124	3,836	19,202
1985	1,080,096	1,073,751	131,887	552,624	385,501	3,739	6,345
1986	1,172,076	1,167,906	210,281	536,891	416,679	4,055	4,170
1987	1,258,554	1,255,178	284,270	541,937	424,648	4,323	3,376
1988	1,359,354	1,356,018	425,966	550,166	374,368	5,517	3,336
1989	1,253,619	1,249,791	497,885	474,189	276,951	765	3,828

[1] Beginning in 1989, the Savings Association Insurance Fund replaced the Federal Savings and Loan Insurance Corporation as the guarantor of deposits.

Source

Office of Thrift Supervision, *Savings and Home Financing Source Book* (1989), pp. A3–A4.

Documentation

The table reports total assets for savings banks and savings and loan associations, commonly classed together as thrifts, by insurance status and type of regulatory oversight. The table demonstrates the rapid growth in the industry in the first thirty years of the twentieth century. Between 1900 and 1930, total thrift assets grew fifteenfold. Diminishing confidence in banks and thrifts during the Great Depression resulted in a brief period of sharp disintermediation. By 1937, total industry assets declined to about 64 percent of the 1930 peak.

The New Deal establishment of the Federal Home Loan Bank Board, giving thrifts access to low-cost funds to finance and encourage home ownership, and the Federal Savings and Loan Insurance Corporation (FSLIC), which insured savings and loan depositors from loss, led to a limited industry-wide recovery in the 1940s. The late 1950s and early 1960s witnessed a marked recovery. Industry assets continued to grow through the 1980s despite the failure of more than 500 insured savings and loans and the bankruptcy of the FSLIC.

See the text for Table Cj375–381 for more information.

TABLE Cj389–397 Savings and loan associations – number, assets, and liabilities: 1922–1989
[All operating associations]

Contributed by Howard Bodenhorn

			Assets				Liabilities and capital		
	Savings and loans	Total assets or total liabilities and capital	Mortgage loans	Mortgage-backed securities	Nonmortgage loans	Cash and investments	Total deposits	All other borrowed money	Capital accounts
	Cj389	Cj390 [1]	Cj391	Cj392	Cj393	Cj394 [2]	Cj395	Cj396 [3]	Cj397
Year	Number	Million dollars	Million dollars	Million dollars	Million dollars	Million dollars	Million dollars	Million dollars	Million dollars
1922	10,009	3,343	3,009	—	—	—	2,210	—	—
1923	10,744	3,943	3,549	—	—	—	2,626	—	—
1924	11,844	4,766	4,289	—	—	—	3,153	—	—
1925	12,403	5,509	5,085	—	—	—	3,811	—	—
1926	12,626	6,334	5,842	—	—	—	4,378	—	—
1927	12,804	7,179	6,586	—	—	—	5,027	—	—
1928	12,666	8,016	7,267	—	—	—	5,762	—	—
1929	12,342	8,695	7,791	—	—	—	6,237	—	—
1930	11,777	8,829	7,760	—	—	238	6,296	—	—
1931	11,442	9,417	7,214	—	—	370	5,916	—	—
1932	10,915	7,737	6,407	—	—	642	5,326	—	—
1933	10,596	7,018	5,559	—	—	828	4,750	—	—
1934	10,744	6,406	4,593	—	—	1,012	4,458	—	—
1935	10,266	5,875	3,947	—	—	1,163	4,254	—	—
1936	10,042	5,772	3,810	—	—	1,477	4,194	194	490
1937	9,225	5,682	3,886	—	—	1,313	4,080	247	485
1938	8,762	5,632	3,967	—	—	1,199	4,077	244	496
1939	8,006	5,597	4,126	—	—	1,036	4,118	227	478
1940	7,521	5,733	4,415	—	—	877	4,322	233	464
1941	7,211	6,049	4,823	—	—	783	4,682	256	475
1942	6,941	6,150	4,810	—	—	934	4,941	153	502
1943	6,498	6,604	4,793	—	—	1,435	5,494	135	533
1944	6,279	7,458	4,983	—	—	2,144	6,305	199	572
1945	6,149	8,747	5,521	—	—	2,903	7,365	336	644
1946	6,093	10,202	7,276	—	—	2,571	8,548	402	751
1947	6,045	11,687	8,971	—	—	2,313	9,753	542	855
1948	6,011	13,028	10,409	—	—	2,130	10,964	590	969
1949	5,983	14,622	11,714	—	—	2,357	12,471	499	1,106
1950	5,992	16,846	13,714	—	—	2,461	13,978	880	1,279
1951	5,995	19,164	15,610	—	—	2,701	16,073	884	1,453
1952	6,004	22,585	18,416	—	—	3,118	19,143	934	1,656
1953	6,012	26,638	21,957	—	—	3,443	22,778	1,014	1,895
1954	6,037	31,508	26,088	—	—	3,991	27,164	932	2,180
1955	6,071	37,533	31,354	—	—	4,437	32,058	1,522	2,534
1956	6,136	42,781	35,716	—	—	4,901	37,073	1,343	2,912
1957	6,169	48,053	39,969	—	—	5,368	41,856	1,373	3,321
1958	6,208	54,978	45,478	—	—	6,430	47,894	1,427	3,796
1959	6,223	63,530	53,141	—	—	7,323	54,583	2,387	4,393
1960	6,320	71,476	60,070	—	—	7,888	62,142	2,197	4,983
1961	6,246	82,135	68,834	—	—	9,189	70,885	2,856	5,708
1962	6,289	93,605	78,770	—	—	10,175	80,236	3,629	6,520
1963	6,248	107,559	90,944	—	270	11,224	91,307	5,027	7,386
1964	6,216	119,355	101,333	—	320	11,825	101,887	5,615	8,098
1965	6,185	129,580	110,304	—	347	12,200	110,385	6,457	8,986
1966	6,112	133,933	114,427	—	338	12,128	113,969	7,470	9,385
1967	6,036	143,535	121,804	—	375	13,955	124,493	4,779	9,838
1968	5,947	152,890	130,801	—	398	14,117	131,618	5,679	10,613
1969	5,835	162,148	140,230	—	441	13,898	135,539	9,728	11,543
1970	5,669	176,183	150,331	—	450	16,526	146,404	10,911	12,311
1971	5,474	206,024	174,250	—	433	21,042	174,198	8,992	13,481
1972	5,298	243,127	206,182	—	477	24,356	206,764	9,778	15,060
1973	5,170	271,905	231,733	—	572	21,055	226,968	17,166	17,056
1974	5,086	295,545	249,302	—	520	23,251	242,975	24,744	18,442
1975	4,931	338,233	278,590	—	526	30,853	285,743	20,634	19,778
1976	4,821	391,908	323,005	10,681	590	35,724	335,913	19,083	21,998
1977	4,761	459,241	381,163	13,052	651	39,150	386,799	27,839	25,184
1978	4,725	523,542	432,808	16,654	8,465	44,883	430,953	42,906	29,056
1979	4,684	578,962	475,688	20,581	10,460	46,341	470,004	55,226	32,637

Notes appear at end of table

TABLE Cj389–397   Savings and loan associations – number, assets, and liabilities: 1922–1989
[All operating associations]   *Continued*

			Assets				Liabilities and capital		
	Savings and loans	Total assets or total liabilities and capital	Mortgage loans	Mortgage-backed securities	Nonmortgage loans	Cash and investments	Total deposits	All other borrowed money	Capital accounts
	Cj389	Cj390 [1]	Cj391	Cj392	Cj393	Cj394 [2]	Cj395	Cj396 [3]	Cj397
Year	Number	Million dollars	Million dollars	Million dollars	Million dollars	Million dollars	Million dollars	Million dollars	Million dollars
1980	4,594	632,872	503,927	27,905	12,387	58,598	513,564	64,734	33,473
1981	4,298	971,627	522,284	34,495	13,981	65,437	531,242	89,605	28,652
1982	3,831	714,577	486,967	63,684	16,842	87,567	573,837	98,543	26,414
1983	3,645	838,385	533,486	91,647	23,903	114,710	687,683	99,564	33,975
1984	3,591	1,000,489	606,733	112,934	46,629	141,906	804,362	139,290	38,361
1985	3,535	1,080,096	652,433	115,695	61,498	145,255	852,679	158,283	47,169
1986	3,487	1,172,076	661,470	158,225	72,422	166,639	897,761	197,188	53,012
1987	3,385	1,258,554	684,595	201,964	77,991	171,177	939,178	250,138	47,136
1988	3,175	1,359,354	733,072	214,736	93,227	188,260	979,311	299,725	56,004
1989	3,011	1,253,619	712,059	170,532	87,697	167,383	949,718	256,026	24,034

[1] Beginning in 1982, balances reflect regulatory change adopted in July 1982, which provided that certain balances previously reported as liabilities be reported as contra-asset items (deductions from assets accounts, namely for mortgage loans). This change reduced total assets by about $26.2 billion in 1982.

[2] For 1922–1958, includes cash, U.S. government and agency securities, and real estate owned, the last of which represents a small proportion of the total. For 1959–1989, includes cash and all investment securities, which include U.S. government and agency securities as well as corporate and other securities.

[3] Includes Federal Home Loan Bank advances as well as all other borrowed money, which includes reverse repurchase agreements, mortgage-backed bonds issued, commercial bank loans, commercial paper issued, overdrafts in transaction accounts, and all other borrowed funds.

Sources

1922–1958: Federal Home Loan Bank Board, *Trends in the Savings and Loan Field, 1958* (November 1959), Table 1. 1959–1962: Federal Home Loan Bank Board, *Annual Report* (1970), Table A-11. 1963–1989: Office of Thrift Supervision, *Savings and Home Financing Source Book* (1989), Table A-3.

Documentation

Unlike commercial banks, most savings and loan associations did not immediately join the Federal Savings and Loan Insurance Corporation (FSLIC) when it was established in 1933. The difference in the total number and assets of operating thrifts reported in this table and the insured thrifts reported in Table Cj398–406 remained significant for many years. Most of the data were obtained from publications of the FSLIC. These savings and loan associations formerly insured by the FSLIC are currently insured by the Savings Association Insurance Fund. Subgroups of the banks classified as all FSLIC-insured institutions include FSLIC-insured savings and loan associations, FSLIC-insured savings banks, FSLIC-insured federally chartered thrift institutions, and FSLIC-insured stock thrift institutions.

All FSLIC-insured thrift institutions are Federal Home Loan Bank (FHLB) members. Non-FSLIC-insured savings institutions may also be members if they meet certain regulatory requirements. Selected assets and liabilities for only FHLB members are reported in Table Cj407–415. Selected assets and liabilities for FSLIC-insured savings institutions are reported in Table Cj398–406.

The primary sources of information were the FHLB's monthly or quarterly supervisory reports, supervisory reports for FSLIC-insured institutions, and annual state supervisory reports for non-FSLIC-insured savings associations. When data were available, they were presented as reported. Otherwise, they were estimated. Estimated data include all figures for non-FSLIC-insured associations, as well as selected balance sheet items for FSLIC-insured savings banks, non-FHLB members, and non-FSLIC-insured state-chartered savings associations. This remains the best available series.

TABLE Cj398–406   Savings and loan associations – number, assets, and liabilities: 1963–1989[1]
[Insured associations]

Contributed by Howard Bodenhorn

		Assets				Liabilities and capital		
Insured savings and loans	Total assets or total liabilities and capital	Mortgage loans	Mortgage-backed securities	Nonmortgage loans	Cash and investments	Total deposits	All other borrowed money	Capital accounts
Cj398	Cj399 [2]	Cj400	Cj401	Cj402	Cj403 [3]	Cj404	Cj405 [4]	Cj406
Number	Million dollars	Million dollars	Million dollars	Million dollars	Million dollars	Million dollars	Million dollars	Million dollars
Year								
1963	4,419	103,154	87,453	—	—	10,694	87,526	4,971	6,986
1964	4,463	114,652	97,612	—	—	11,285	97,861	5,547	7,685
1965	4,508	124,576	106,333	—	—	11,647	106,103	6,376	9,553
1966	4,510	129,045	110,511	—	—	11,609	109,772	7,396	8,957
1967	4,487	138,489	117,832	—	—	13,395	120,184	4,675	9,411
1968	4,470	147,736	126,756	—	—	13,529	127,244	5,576	10,173
1969	4,438	156,788	136,031	—	—	13,295	130,995	9,622	11,072
1970	4,365	170,645	146,043	—	—	15,846	141,703	10,817	11,820
1971	4,271	199,984	169,568	—	—	20,245	169,045	8,898	12,985
1972	4,191	236,349	200,876	—	—	23,552	200,970	9,689	14,526
1973	4,163	264,797	226,155	—	—	20,304	220,893	16,978	16,509
1974	4,141	288,223	243,554	—	—	22,444	236,689	24,585	17,868
1975	4,078	330,259	272,456	—	—	29,900	287,774	20,542	19,175
1976	4,044	383,172	316,332	10,377	—	34,606	328,214	18,983	21,372
1977	4,065	449,998	374,089	12,698	—	38,038	378,782	27,621	24,525
1978	4,053	513,310	424,969	16,243	7,760	43,623	422,194	42,563	28,281
1979	4,039	568,107	467,262	20,115	9,784	45,201	460,694	54,890	31,769
1980	4,005	620,626	494,914	27,275	11,708	56,953	503,156	64,222	32,579
1981	3,785	658,528	512,870	33,849	13,281	63,324	519,937	89,097	27,829
1982	3,349	699,522	477,009	62,793	16,070	84,430	560,461	98,152	25,567
1983	3,183	819,168	521,308	90,902	22,949	109,923	671,058	98,511	32,980
1984	3,136	977,451	593,034	112,686	44,983	136,745	784,468	137,945	37,162
1985	3,246	1,070,012	645,498	115,525	60,712	143,538	843,932	157,666	46,657
1986	3,220	1,163,851	655,652	158,193	72,264	164,844	890,664	196,930	52,282
1987	3,147	1,250,855	679,249	201,828	77,598	169,717	932,616	249,916	46,382
1988	2,949	1,350,500	726,562	214,587	92,755	186,986	671,700	299,400	55,185
1989	2,878	1,249,025	708,929	170,535	87,243	166,023	945,656	255,981	23,583

[1] As of December 31 each year.

[2] Beginning in 1982, balances reflect regulatory change adopted in July 1982, which provided that certain balances previously reported as liabilities be reported as contra-asset items (deductions from assets accounts, namely for mortgage loans). This change reduced total assets by about $26.2 billion in 1982.

[3] Includes cash and all investment securities, which include U.S. government and agency securities as well as corporate and other securities.

[4] Includes Federal Home Loan Bank advances as well as all other borrowed money, which includes reverse repurchase agreements, mortgage-backed bonds issued, com-mercial bank loans, commercial paper issued, overdrafts in transaction accounts, and all other borrowed funds.

Sources
Office of Thrift Supervision, *Savings and Home Financing Source Book* (1989), Table A-4.

Documentation
For a description of the data, see the text for Table Cj389–397.

TABLE Cj407–415 Savings and loan associations – number, assets, and liabilities: 1963–1989[1]
[Federal Home Loan Bank member stock institutions]
Contributed by Howard Bodenhorn

	Federal Home Loan Bank member stock institutions	Total assets or total liabilities and capital	Assets				Liabilities and capital		
			Mortgage loans	Mortgage-backed securities	Nonmortgage loans	Cash and investments	Total deposits	All other borrowed money	Capital accounts
	Cj407	Cj408 [2]	Cj409	Cj410	Cj411	Cj412 [3]	Cj413	Cj414 [4]	Cj415
Year	Number	Million dollars	Million dollars	Million dollars	Million dollars	Million dollars	Million dollars	Million dollars	Million dollars
1963	678	21,063	17,923	—	172	2,070	17,073	1,368	1,381
1964	690	24,748	21,174	—	181	2,133	20,253	1,920	1,678
1965	705	27,204	23,157	—	180	2,238	22,405	2,142	1,860
1966	699	28,199	23,821	—	180	2,253	23,059	2,646	1,934
1967	697	30,140	25,227	—	197	2,649	25,390	1,913	1,973
1968	691	31,897	27,098	—	231	2,675	26,367	2,403	2,126
1969	676	33,524	28,992	—	271	2,409	26,229	3,778	2,357
1970	649	36,028	30,944	—	352	2,821	27,699	4,416	2,453
1971	628	41,455	35,378	—	542	3,538	33,613	3,181	2,706
1972	600	49,566	42,568	310	853	4,079	41,035	3,148	3,128
1973	604	55,438	47,669	418	1,130	3,778	44,682	5,059	3,547
1974	615	60,119	51,214	616	1,239	4,200	47,121	7,166	3,819
1975	626	68,194	57,221	846	1,449	5,569	56,020	5,344	4,092
1976	649	83,789	70,176	1,288	1,959	6,974	69,895	5,407	4,763
1977	720	105,356	88,886	1,480	2,683	8,479	85,420	8,965	5,779
1978	729	122,280	102,607	2,112	3,013	10,054	96,835	13,178	6,792
1979	749	143,579	119,552	2,907	4,600	11,201	111,903	17,699	7,926
1980	797	168,343	135,255	5,457	5,882	15,006	129,168	24,039	8,722
1981	799	188,767	146,039	9,204	5,673	18,069	136,714	36,502	7,671
1982	759	207,236	151,624	10,663	6,002	23,003	154,813	39,952	7,927
1983	742	298,546	190,706	32,186	10,389	37,149	231,599	46,806	12,779
1984	936	511,238	305,065	61,773	23,870	68,254	392,717	88,161	20,160
1985	1,088	602,185	359,535	67,120	35,286	74,952	451,536	109,302	27,889
1986	1,200	721,700	401,565	108,452	46,953	88,622	520,161	150,538	34,724
1987	1,275	872,747	457,831	157,219	55,584	110,143	612,793	207,467	36,535
1988	1,292	994,785	519,763	171,180	71,938	129,971	679,459	255,276	41,309
1989	1,203	880,682	486,847	127,163	65,424	111,694	629,775	205,438	27,743

[1] As of December 31 each year.

[2] Beginning in 1982, balances reflect regulatory change adopted in July 1982, which provided that certain balances previously reported as liabilities be reported as contra-asset items (deductions from assets accounts, namely for mortgage loans). This change reduced total assets by about $26.2 billion in 1982.

[3] Includes cash and all investment securities, which include U.S. government and agency securities as well as corporate and other securities.

[4] Includes Federal Home Loan Bank advances as well as all other borrowed money, which includes reverse repurchase agreements, mortgage-backed bonds issued, com-mercial bank loans, commercial paper issued, overdrafts in transaction accounts, and all other borrowed funds.

Source
Office of Thrift Supervision, *Savings and Home Financing Source Book* (1989), Table A-8.

Documentation
For a description of the data, see the text for Table Cj389–397.

TABLE Cj416–422 Savings and loan associations – income and expenses: 1957–1988 [Insured associations]

Contributed by Howard Bodenhorn

Year	Operating income			Operating expenses			Net operating income
	Total gross	Mortgages and loans	Investments and bank deposits	Total	Employee compensation	Marketing expenses	
	Cj416 [1]	Cj417	Cj418	Cj419	Cj420	Cj421	Cj422 [2]
	Million dollars	Million dollars	Million dollars	Million dollars	Million dollars	Million dollars	Million dollars
1957	2,130	1,789	101	506	233	59	1,583
1958	2,475	2,069	120	576	261	63	1,865
1959	2,971	2,457	151	675	302	77	2,236
1960	3,503	2,917	178	766	338	90	2,658
1961	4,602	3,414	198	873	384	102	3,122
1962	4,822	4,035	240	979	429	111	3,753
1963	5,482	4,629	262	1,174	496	131	4,178
1964	6,230	5,346	338	1,243	575	121	4,796
1965	6,821	5,922	371	1,317	613	127	5,262
1966	7,299	6,381	423	1,368	631	135	5,559
1967	7,792	6,707	502	1,421	655	126	6,087
1968	8,610	7,329	597	1,546	710	139	6,780
1969	9,609	8,157	677	1,713	781	167	7,443
1970	10,675	9,002	822	1,902	863	193	8,010
1971	12,668	10,463	1,116	2,113	994	195	9,951
1972	15,209	12,615	1,196	2,485	1,157	237	12,244
1973	18,280	15,180	1,513	2,975	1,371	308	14,388
1974	20,981	17,197	1,892	3,443	1,584	348	15,867
1975	23,719	19,267	2,038	3,949	1,817	352	19,170
1976	28,217	22,711	2,153	4,582	2,137	345	22,243
1977	33,890	27,380	2,310	5,328	2,512	381	27,057
1978	40,589	32,677	3,042	6,177	2,936	481	31,745
1979	48,639	38,325	4,443	7,107	3,412	575	37,232
1980	56,149	43,350	5,596	7,936	3,804	619	42,417
1981	65,170	48,838	7,548	8,883	4,278	739	47,074
1982	71,170	50,522	8,109	9,936	4,562	726	49,640
1983	81,947	53,129	9,303	12,534	5,479	731	59,751
1984	100,669	62,658	11,984	15,437	6,912	816	72,473
1985	110,637	69,165	11,733	19,576	8,124	833	76,937
1986	110,775	67,018	11,003	22,939	9,477	870	72,377
1987	107,515	63,889	11,662	24,176	10,428	948	65,219
1988	113,634	67,244	13,074	23,957	10,452	919	68,481

[1] Includes items not shown separately.

[2] Gross operating income plus net nonoperating income less operating expenses, non-operating expenses, interest on savings accounts, borrowed funds, and income taxes.

Sources

Federal Home Loan Bank System, *Member Savings and Loan Associations of the Federal Home Loan Bank System: Combined Financial Statements* (1968); Federal Home Loan Bank Board, *Annual Report* (1988).

Documentation

These income and expense series may be combined with those reported in Table Cj398–406 to construct commonly used operating ratios, such as gross income to assets or capital, or net income to assets or capital. Analysts typically use such ratios as comparative measures of performance and industry efficiency. Comparisons to other financial institutions can be made by constructing similar ratios for national banks using Tables Cj212–224 and Cj238–250 or Federal Deposit Insurance Corporation–insured commercial banks using Tables Cj551–562 and Cj572–580.

Data pertain to calendar years.

OTHER FINANCIAL INSTITUTIONS

Howard Bodenhorn and Eugene N. White

TABLE Cj423–431 Employees of finance, insurance, and real estate firms, by industry division: 1947–2000

Contributed by Richard Sutch

		Finance					Insurance		
	Total	Total	Depository institutions	Nondepository institutions	Securities and commodities	Holding and other investment offices	Carriers	Agents, brokers, and service	Real estate
	Cj423	Cj424	Cj425	Cj426	Cj427	Cj428	Cj429	Cj430	Cj431
Year	Thousand	Thousand	Thousand	Thousand	Thousand	Thousand	Thousand	Thousand	Thousand
1947	1,728	—	—	—	63	—	—	—	—
1948	1,800	—	—	—	61	—	—	—	—
1949	1,828	—	—	—	58	—	—	—	—
1950	1,888	—	—	—	62	—	—	—	—
1951	1,956	—	—	—	67	—	—	—	—
1952	2,035	—	—	—	68	—	—	—	—
1953	2,111	—	—	—	69	—	—	—	—
1954	2,200	—	—	—	71	—	—	—	—
1955	2,298	—	—	—	81	—	—	—	—
1956	2,389	—	—	—	87	—	—	—	—
1957	2,438	—	—	—	90	—	—	—	—
1958	2,481	—	—	—	94	—	814	—	—
1959	2,549	—	—	—	107	—	817	—	—
1960	2,628	—	—	—	114	—	832	—	—
1961	2,688	—	—	—	129	—	844	—	—
1962	2,754	—	—	—	132	—	852	—	—
1963	2,830	—	—	—	124	—	872	—	—
1964	2,911	—	—	—	126	—	890	—	—
1965	2,977	—	—	—	129	—	893	—	—
1966	3,058	—	—	—	141	—	908	—	—
1967	3,185	—	—	—	156	—	947	—	—
1968	3,337	—	—	—	192	—	981	—	—
1969	3,512	—	—	—	226	—	999	—	—
1970	3,645	—	—	—	205	—	1,030	—	—
1971	3,772	—	—	—	198	—	1,047	—	—
1972	3,908	1,778	—	—	203	73	1,054	319	756
1973	4,046	1,866	—	—	192	77	1,071	330	778
1974	4,148	1,936	—	—	174	82	1,087	346	778
1975	4,165	1,964	—	—	170	87	1,085	357	760
1976	4,271	2,026	—	—	176	91	1,101	367	776
1977	4,467	2,113	—	—	182	95	1,141	388	826
1978	4,724	2,233	—	—	189	103	1,174	418	900
1979	4,975	2,369	—	—	204	111	1,200	443	963
1980	5,160	2,483	—	—	227	115	1,224	464	989
1981	5,298	2,593	—	—	259	123	1,237	476	992
1982	5,340	2,647	—	—	274	134	1,237	486	970
1983	5,466	2,741	—	—	308	136	1,229	499	997
1984	5,684	2,852	—	—	339	144	1,240	525	1,067
1985	5,948	2,974	—	—	355	166	1,292	548	1,135
1986	6,273	3,145	—	—	393	190	1,365	579	1,184
1987	6,533	3,264	—	—	442	201	1,415	612	1,242
1988	6,630	3,274	2,255	363	447	209	1,435	640	1,280
1989	6,668	3,283	2,273	361	430	218	1,438	652	1,296
1990	6,709	3,268	2,251	373	424	221	1,462	663	1,315
1991	6,646	3,187	2,164	379	420	224	1,495	666	1,299
1992	6,602	3,160	2,096	406	440	219	1,496	657	1,290
1993	6,757	3,238	2,089	455	472	223	1,529	668	1,322
1994	6,896	3,299	2,066	491	516	227	1,552	684	1,361

(continued)

TABLE Cj423–431   Employees of finance, insurance, and real estate firms, by industry division: 1947–2000
Continued

		Finance				Insurance		
	Total	Total	Depository institutions	Nondepository institutions	Securities and commodities	Holding and other investment offices	Carriers	Agents, brokers, and service	Real estate
	Cj423	Cj424	Cj425	Cj426	Cj427	Cj428	Cj429	Cj430	Cj431
Year	Thousand	Thousand	Thousand	Thousand	Thousand	Thousand	Thousand	Thousand	Thousand
1995	6,806	3,231	2,025	463	525	217	1,529	696	1,351
1996	6,911	3,303	2,019	522	553	210	1,517	709	1,382
1997	7,109	3,424	2,027	577	596	223	1,539	725	1,421
1998	7,389	3,588	2,046	658	647	238	1,591	744	1,465
1999	7,555	3,688	2,056	709	689	234	1,610	758	1,500
2000	7,560	3,710	2,029	681	748	251	1,589	757	1,504

Sources

U.S. Bureau of Labor Statistics (BLS), "Employment, Hours, and Earnings: United States, 1909–94," *Bulletin* number 2445, 2 volumes (1994). BLS, "Employment, Hours, and Earnings: United States, 1990–95," *Bulletin* number 2465 (1995). BLS, *National Employment, Hours, and Earnings*, BLS Internet site. Also see the periodical *Employment and Earnings*, published monthly by the BLS. For series Cj429–430, 1919–1938: BLS, "Employment, Hours, and Earnings: United States, 1909–90," *Bulletin* number 2370 (1990). These data are also available at the BLS Internet site.

Documentation

See the text for Table Ba840–848.

Series Cj423. Equals series Ba846.

Series Cj424–428. Series 425–428 are Standard Industrial Classification (SIC) codes 60–62 and 67, respectively. See the Introduction to Part D for a discussion of SIC codes. Series Cj424 equals the sum of series Cj425–428.

Series Cj429–431. SIC codes 63–65, respectively.

TABLE Cj432–436   Postal Savings System – offices, depositors, and deposits: 1911–1967[1]

Contributed by Howard Bodenhorn

Year	Offices in operation Cj432 Number	Depositors Cj433 [2] Number	Deposits Cj434 Thousand dollars	Withdrawals Cj435 Thousand dollars	Balance to credit of depositors Cj436 [3] Thousand dollars
1911	400	11,918	778	101	677
1912	10,170	243,801	30,732	11,172	20,237
1913	12,820	331,006	41,701	28,120	33,819
1914	10,347	388,511	47,815	38,190	43,444
1915	9,546	525,414	70,315	48,074	65,685
1916	9,421	602,937	76,776	56,441	86,020
1917	7,161	674,728	132,112	86,177	131,955
1918	6,656	612,188	116,893	100,376	148,471
1919	6,439	565,509	136,690	117,838	167,323
1920	6,314	508,508	139,209	149,256	157,276
1921	6,300	466,109	133,575	138,461	152,390
1922	6,774	420,242	96,508	111,161	137,736
1923	6,802	417,902	88,008	94,073	131,671
1924	6,758	412,584	94,933	93,790	132,814
1925	6,655	402,325	89,708	90,349	132,173
1926	6,623	399,305	90,751	88,746	134,179
1927	6,672	411,394	103,607	90,426	147,359
1928	6,683	412,250	96,386	91,602	152,143
1929	6,770	416,584	112,446	110,945	153,645
1930	6,795	466,401	159,959	138,332	175,272
1931	7,459	770,859	366,901	194,756	347,417
1932	7,549	1,545,190	860,196	422,792	784,821
1933	7,888	2,342,133	1,166,327	763,961	1,187,186
1934	8,059	2,562,082	966,651	955,917	1,197,920
1935	8,111	2,598,391	944,960	938,017	1,204,863
1936	8,103	2,705,152	933,071	906,261	1,231,673
1937	8,068	2,791,371	972,743	936,743	1,267,674
1938	8,050	2,741,569	929,480	945,355	1,251,799
1939	7,964	2,767,417	897,339	886,846	1,262,292
1940	7,980	2,816,408	923,266	892,149	1,293,409
1941	8,038	2,882,886	923,660	912,916	1,304,153
1942	8,063	2,812,806	895,080	883,710	1,315,523
1943	8,060	3,064,054	1,033,550	771,548	1,577,526
1944	8,057	3,493,079	1,363,028	906,417	2,034,137
1945	8,050	3,921,937	1,739,341	1,113,902	2,659,575
1946	8,089	4,135,565	2,127,038	1,666,956	3,119,656
1947	8,141	4,196,517	2,163,619	1,890,502	3,392,773
1948	8,183	4,111,373	2,055,651	2,069,295	3,379,130
1949	8,195	3,964,509	1,947,238	2,048,965	3,277,402
1950	8,235	3,779,784	1,827,913	2,007,999	3,097,316
1951	8,247	3,529,527	1,603,327	1,912,444	2,788,199
1952	8,261	3,339,378	1,460,415	1,631,050	2,617,564
1953	8,247	3,162,176	1,342,675	1,502,691	2,457,548
1954	7,872	2,934,795	1,197,325	1,403,454	2,251,419
1955	7,750	2,711,110	1,140,503	1,383,926	2,007,996
1956	7,622	2,482,026	606,100	848,627	1,765,470
1957	7,369	2,200,508	353,628	656,830	1,462,268
1958	6,871	1,925,852	241,239	489,900	1,213,608
1959	6,324	1,740,052	192,887	363,042	1,043,453
1960	5,923	1,550,930	145,082	350,475	838,060
1961	5,484	1,397,538	114,884	251,248	701,696
1962	5,205	1,271,858	193,675	212,303	583,067
1963	4,250	1,164,634	76,442	174,752	484,756
1964	3,644	1,076,225	63,155	131,945	415,965
1965	3,130	997,029	50,428	122,159	344,234
1966	2,791	803,130	32,750	176,688	200,296
1967	2,658	607,304	0	0	52,950

Notes appear at end of table   (continued)

TABLE Cj432–436 Postal Savings System – offices, depositors, and deposits: 1911–1967 Continued

[1] Beginning in 1957, data reported on basis of postal fiscal year, which ends in June.

[2] Includes depositors whose accounts are reported on balance sheet as unclaimed.

[3] Includes items shown on balance sheet as unclaimed.

Sources

U.S. Post Office Department, *Annual Report of the Postmaster General* (1957, 1969), and unpublished data.

Documentation

An Act of Congress in June 1910 established the Postal Savings System effective January 1911. The legislation aimed to pull money from hoards, attract the savings of people who had lost confidence in commercial and savings banks following the panic of 1907, attract the savings of immigrants accustomed to postal savings systems in their home countries, and provide a convenient depository for working people. Because post offices were open from 8 A.M. to 6 P.M., Monday through Saturday, accounts could be accessed with relative ease.

The system paid 2 percent per annum on deposits. The minimum deposit was $1; the maximum deposit was $2,500. Deposits grew slowly in the 1910s and 1920s, but increased rapidly in the 1930s with the widespread failure of commercial banks during the Great Depression. Deposits peaked in 1947 at nearly $3.4 billion. But after the war, restored confidence in the commercial banking sector, as well as rising interest rates paid by commercial and savings banks for small accounts, produced declining use of postal savings accounts. In 1964, deposit balances fell to $416 million.

Beginning on April 27, 1966, the post office no longer accepted new deposits in existing accounts, no longer opened new accounts, and stopped interest payments. When the system officially ended on July 1, 1967, the system retained about $60 million in unclaimed accounts. These funds were turned over to the Treasury Department to be held in trust. A law of August 13, 1971, authorized the Treasury to distribute the funds to various states and jurisdictions. A small fund was retained to meet future claims, but the Postal Savings System Statute of Limitations Act of 1984 provided that no new claims would be considered or honored after July 1985.

For additional information, see the U.S. Postal Service Internet site.

TABLE Cj437–447   Federal and state-chartered credit unions – number, members, savings, loans, and assets: 1931–1998[1]

Contributed by Howard Bodenhorn and Eugene N. White

	Operating credit unions			Members		Members' savings		Outstanding loans		Total assets	
	Total	Federal	State	Federal	State	Federal	State	Federal	State	Federal	State
	Cj437	Cj438	Cj439 [2]	Cj440	Cj441	Cj442 [3]	Cj443 [4]	Cj444 [3]	Cj445 [5]	Cj446 [3]	Cj447 [5]
Year	Number	Number	Number	Thousand	Number	Million dollars	Million dollars	Million dollars	Million dollars	Million dollars	Million dollars
1931	1,244	—	1,244	—	286	—	—	—	—	—	34
1932	1,472	—	1,472	—	301	—	22	—	25	—	31
1933	1,772	—	1,772	—	360	—	23	—	26	—	35
1934	2,067	39	2,028	3	427	(Z)	28	(Z)	28	(Z)	40
1935	2,894	772	2,122	119	523	2	36	2	34	2	48
1936	4,485	1,751	2,734	310	854	9	59	7	52	9	74
1937	5,441	2,313	3,128	484	1,056	18	80	16	62	19	97
1938	6,737	2,760	3,977	632	1,237	27	100	24	84	30	118
1939	7,859	3,182	4,677	851	1,459	43	126	38	111	48	146
1940	8,931	3,756	5,175	1,128	1,700	66	157	56	135	73	181
1941	9,734	4,228	5,506	1,409	1,908	97	190	69	151	106	217
1942	9,545	4,145	5,400	1,357	1,797	110	193	43	106	120	221
1943	9,062	3,938	5,124	1,312	1,721	117	206	35	87	127	228
1944	8,722	3,815	4,907	1,306	1,630	134	221	34	87	144	254
1945	8,615	3,757	4,858	1,217	1,626	141	243	35	91	153	282
1946	8,715	3,761	4,954	1,302	1,718	160	291	57	131	173	322
1947	8,942	3,845	5,097	1,446	1,894	192	341	91	189	210	381
1948	9,329	4,058	5,271	1,628	2,121	235	395	138	261	258	443
1949	9,897	4,495	5,402	1,820	2,271	285	445	186	329	316	511
1950	10,571	4,984	5,587	2,127	2,483	362	552	264	416	406	600
1951	11,284	5,398	5,886	2,464	2,732	457	622	300	447	505	694
1952	12,249	5,925	6,324	2,853	3,035	597	758	415	570	662	854
1953	13,564	6,578	6,986	3,255	3,380	768	923	574	734	854	1,041
1954	14,940	7,227	7,713	3,599	3,757	931	1,109	682	870	1,033	1,237
1955	16,064	7,806	8,258	4,032	4,121	1,135	1,312	863	1,071	1,267	1,476
1956	17,113	8,350	8,763	4,502	4,549	1,366	1,548	1,049	1,277	1,529	1,742
1957	18,049	8,735	9,314	4,898	4,964	1,589	1,792	1,257	1,521	1,789	2,021
1958	18,770	9,030	9,740	5,210	5,329	1,812	2,057	1,380	1,698	2,035	2,312
1959	19,408	9,447	9,961	5,643	5,677	2,075	2,366	1,667	2,051	2,353	2,676
1960	20,056	9,905	10,151	6,087	5,971	2,344	2,637	2,021	2,381	2,670	2,989
1961	20,567	10,271	10,296	5,643	6,336	2,673	2,966	2,245	2,607	3,028	3,354
1962	20,969	10,632	10,337	7,008	6,745	3,020	3,311	2,561	2,917	3,430	3,758
1963	21,301	10,955	10,346	7,500	7,080	3,453	3,711	2,911	3,260	3,917	4,213
1964	21,730	11,278	10,452	8,092	7,530	4,017	4,208	3,349	3,699	4,559	4,800
1965	22,064	11,543	10,521	8,641	8,115	4,538	4,682	3,865	4,233	5,166	5,385
1966	22,585	11,941	10,644	9,272	8,651	4,944	5,127	4,324	4,769	5,669	5,938
1967	22,997	12,210	10,787	9,874	9,189	5,421	5,682	4,677	5,204	6,208	6,568
1968	23,378	12,584	10,794	10,509	9,720	5,986	6,326	5,398	5,895	6,902	7,310
1969	23,759	12,921	10,838	11,302	10,326	6,713	7,027	6,329	6,630	7,794	8,124
1970	23,656	12,977	10,679	11,966	10,853	7,629	7,894	6,969	7,137	8,861	9,089
1971	23,253	12,717	10,536	12,702	11,391	9,191	9,167	8,071	8,081	10,553	10,568
1972	23,062	12,708	10,354	13,572	12,118	10,956	10,622	9,424	9,239	12,514	12,275
1973	22,950	12,733	10,217	14,666	12,886	12,598	11,914	11,109	10,650	14,569	13,806
1974	22,853	12,748	10,105	15,906	13,575	14,456	13,218	12,607	11,636	16,689	15,246
1975	22,871	12,858	10,013	17,090	14,198	17,624	15,608	14,750	12,855	20,437	17,812
1976	22,540	12,757	9,783	18,624	15,246	21,295	18,152	18,095	15,993	24,413	20,892
1977	22,330	12,750	9,580	20,427	16,375	25,576	19,107	23,007	19,389	29,688	24,500
1978	22,106	12,759	9,347	23,259	17,461	29,803	21,086	27,687	22,582	34,760	27,588
1979	17,507	12,738	4,769	24,790	12,219	31,831	15,871	28,547	15,204	36,468	18,460
1980	17,350	12,440	4,910	24,519	12,337	36,263	18,469	26,350	14,582	37,515	20,870
1981	16,963	11,969	4,994	25,459	12,954	37,789	20,007	27,204	15,341	39,181	22,584
1982	16,654	11,631	5,023	26,115	13,113	41,352	21,636	28,192	15,282	45,494	24,089
1983	15,891	10,976	4,915	26,799	14,278	49,891	24,297	33,201	17,215	54,482	27,479
1984	15,193	10,548	4,645	28,192	15,205	57,929	26,327	42,133	19,951	63,656	29,188
1985	15,045	10,125	4,920	29,579	15,689	71,616	37,917	48,241	26,168	78,188	41,525
1986	14,693	9,758	4,935	31,041	17,363	87,954	48,097	55,305	30,834	95,484	52,244
1987	14,335	9,401	4,934	32,067	17,999	96,346	52,083	64,104	35,436	105,190	56,972
1988	13,878	9,118	4,760	34,438	18,519	104,431	55,217	73,766	39,977	114,564	60,740
1989	13,371	8,821	4,550	35,612	18,859	109,653	57,517	80,272	42,336	120,666	63,022

Notes appear at end of table

(continued)

TABLE Cj437–447   Federal and state-chartered credit unions – number, members, savings, loans, and assets: 1931–1998 *Continued*

	Operating credit unions			Members		Members' savings		Outstanding loans		Total assets	
	Total	Federal	State	Federal	State	Federal	State	Federal	State	Federal	State
	Cj437	Cj438	Cj439 [2]	Cj440	Cj441	Cj442 [3]	Cj443 [4]	Cj444 [3]	Cj445 [5]	Cj446 [3]	Cj447 [5]
Year	Number	Number	Number	Thousand	Number	Million dollars	Million dollars	Million dollars	Million dollars	Million dollars	Million dollars
1990	12,860	8,511	4,349	36,242	19,454	117,892	62,082	83,029	44,102	130,073	68,133
1991	12,960	8,229	4,731	37,081	21,619	130,164	75,626	84,150	49,268	143,940	83,133
1992	12,653	7,916	4,737	38,205	23,859	146,078	89,648	87,633	53,727	162,544	98,767
1993	12,317	7,696	4,621	39,756	23,997	153,506	93,482	94,640	57,695	172,854	104,316
1994	11,991	7,498	4,493	40,837	24,295	160,226	94,797	110,090	65,769	182,529	106,937
1995	11,687	7,329	4,358	42,163	24,927	170,300	99,838	120,514	71,606	193,781	112,861
1996	11,392	7,152	4,240	43,545	25,666	180,964	105,728	134,120	79,651	206,692	120,176
1997	11,238	6,981	4,257	43,501	27,922	187,817	119,359	140,100	92,117	215,097	136,107
1998	10,995	6,815	4,180	43,864	29,674	202,651	137,347	144,849	100,890	231,904	156,787

(Z) Less than $500,000.

[1] As of December 31 each year.

[2] Reports not received from all operating credit unions. For 1979–1998, state figures include only federally insured, state-chartered credit unions.

[3] Data for 1935–1944 partly estimated. For 1979–1998, state figures include only federally insured, state-chartered credit unions.

[4] Includes members' deposits. For 1979–1998, state figures include only federally insured, state-chartered credit unions.

[5] For 1979–1989, state figures include only federally insured, state-chartered credit unions.

Sources

1931–1970: U.S. National Credit Union Administration, *1970 Annual Report of the National Credit Union Administration* and *1970 State-Chartered Credit Union Annual Report;* 1971–1977: National Credit Union Administration, *Quarterly Report* (various issues); 1978–1989: National Credit Union Administration, *Annual Report* (1990–1998).

Documentation

A credit union is a nonprofit, cooperative financial institution owned and run by its members. Credit unions provide their members with a safe place to save and opportunities to save and borrow at low rates. Members pool their funds and make loans to one another. The volunteer board that manages each credit union is elected by its members. Eligibility for membership is usually based on residence in a particular community, employment at one or more employers, or membership in another organization or association. It is common for employees at a large corporation, for example, to establish and operate a credit union. Community development credit unions principally serve low-income individuals who reside in areas or communities unserved by traditional financial intermediaries. To promote the establishment and success of such credit union, the National Credit Union Administration has in recent years provided technical assistance and grants to designated low-income credit unions. Another form of credit union is the corporate credit union. These institutions do not serve people; rather, they act as credit unions for credit unions. Currently, there are thirty-five federally insured corporate credit unions that provide investment, liquidity, and payment services for member credit unions.

The earliest financial cooperatives date back to early nineteenth-century Britain, but the legitimate forerunner of the modern credit union originated in Germany in the mid-nineteenth century. These early credit unions were organized by Herman Schulze-Delitzsch and Friedrich Raiffeisen, who during the crop failure and famine of 1846 opened a cooperative mill and bakery, which sold bread at below-market prices, adapting the cooperative organizational form to provide credit to low-income individuals. Early German credit unions assisted farmers, providing them with credit to purchase livestock, equipment, and so forth.

The first credit union organized in North America was founded by Alphonse Desjardins in Levis, Quebec, Canada. Desjardins reportedly organized his credit union to provide relief to the working poor who paid high rates to loan sharks, if they could borrow at all. In 1909, Desjardins assisted a group to open a credit union in Manchester, New Hampshire. The St. Mary's Cooperative Credit Association quickly came to the attention of Edward Filene, merchant and philanthropist, and Pierre Jay, the Massachusetts Banking Commissioner, who pushed through the Massachusetts Credit Union Act of 1909, which served as the basis for other state credit union acts, as well as the Federal Credit Union Act of 1934.

Between the 1910s and 1930s, credit unions became increasingly popular. In 1931, there were 1,244 credit unions in thirty-two states. Credit unions, like other financial institutions, experienced sharp deposit outflows during the early 1930s. In 1934, the Federal Credit Union Act, which authorized the establishment of federally chartered credit unions, was signed into law. In the congressional debate surrounding the Act, it became clear that neither the Comptroller of the Currency nor the Federal Reserve wanted to take regulatory responsibility for credit unions, so it was placed in the hands of the Farm Credit Administration. Over the years, responsibility shifted to the Federal Deposit Insurance Corporation, the Federal Security Agency, and the Department of Health, Education, and Welfare. Finally, in 1970 the National Credit Union Administration was established and given the power to charter, supervise, and regulate credit unions. The Act also established the National Credit Union Insurance Fund, which insures deposits held by credit unions.

Turbulent economic conditions in the 1970s and 1980s adversely affected credit unions. In 1977, legislation allowed credit unions to offer expanded services, including mortgage lending. Even while the number of credit unions declined, the number of members, savings, loans, and assets all increased. As of 1999, there were about 12,000 credit unions, with about seventy million members and $316 billion in assets.

Data on the early operations of credit unions are available in U.S. Bureau of Labor Statistics (BLS), *Monthly Labor Review* (1936–1953), and in the BLS *Bulletin*, numbers 797, 850, 894, and 922.

Data for federal credit unions, which were authorized by the 1934 legislation, represent all operating credit unions. Data on state-chartered credit unions were furnished by state officials charged with supervision of such credit unions to the National Credit Union Administration (formerly Bureau of Federal Credit Unions) since 1951, and to the BLS prior to 1951. Figures for state credit unions represent reporting unions that, in recent years, have included more than 99 percent of all active credit unions; prior to 1939, about 80 percent reported.

TABLE Cj448–453   Federal Home Loan Banks – lending: 1935–1989

Contributed by Howard Bodenhorn

Year	Advances to members	Repayments by members	Borrowings outstanding			Borrowing members
			Total	Secured	Unsecured	
	Cj448 [1]	Cj449 [1]	Cj450 [2]	Cj451 [2]	Cj452 [2]	Cj453 [2]
	Million dollars	Million dollars	Million dollars	Million dollars	Million dollars	Number
1935	59	43	103	77	26	2,192
1940	134	114	201	143	59	2,262
1945	278	213	195	159	36	916
1950	675	292	816	568	248	2,279
1955	1,252	702	1,417	943	474	2,408
1960	1,943	2,097	1,981	1,306	674	2,371
1961	2,882	220	2,662	1,787	875	2,455
1962	4,111	3,294	2,479	2,250	1,229	2,722
1963	5,601	4,296	4,784	3,288	1,496	2,856
1964	5,563	5,023	5,325	4,090	1,234	2,795
1965	5,007	4,335	5,997	4,864	1,133	2,857
1966	3,804	2,866	6,935	6,457	478	2,580
1967	1,537	4,076	4,386	4,176	208	1,956
1968	2,734	1,861	5,259	4,946	313	2,193
1969	5,531	1,501	9,289	8,682	607	2,782
1970	3,255	1,930	10,615	10,419	195	2,391
1971	2,714	5,392	7,936	7,169	767	2,023
1972	4,792	4,750	7,979	7,271	707	2,104
1973	10,013	2,845	15,147	14,550	597	2,515
1974	12,763	6,106	21,804	21,508	297	2,607
1975	5,468	9,125	17,845	17,449	296	2,542
1976	8,115	10,097	15,862	15,228	635	2,547
1977	13,757	9,446	20,173	18,411	1,762	2,820
1978	25,300	12,802	32,670	30,193	2,477	3,139
1979	29,184	20,016	41,838	39,013	2,825	2,983
1980	36,585	29,460	48,963	46,466	2,497	2,819
1981	53,941	37,709	65,194	63,781	1,413	2,637
1982	53,744	52,928	66,011	65,596	414	2,202
1983	44,724	51,758	58,977	58,665	312	1,904
1984	91,239	75,598	74,618	74,446	171	1,902
1985	133,651	119,417	88,852	88,846	6	1,804
1986	181,648	161,832	108,668	108,668	0	1,908
1987	194,381	170,000	133,054	133,054	0	2,204
1988	187,536	167,809	152,777	152,777	0	2,172
1989	218,876	229,874	141,795	141,795	0	1,866

[1] Calendar year.

[2] As of year-end.

Source

Office of Thrift Supervision, *Savings and Home Financing Source Book* (1989), Table D-2.

Documentation

For a discussion of the operations of the Federal Home Loan Bank system, see the text for Table Cj454–463.

TABLE Cj454–463   Federal Home Loan Banks – assets and liabilities: 1949–1988

Contributed by Howard Bodenhorn

	Assets					Liabilities			Capital accounts	
Year	Total assets or liabilities and capital	Cash and deposits	U.S. government securities	Advances	Other	Deposits and borrowings	Consolidated obligations	Other liabilities	Paid-in capital	Retained earnings
	Cj454	Cj455	Cj456	Cj457	Cj458	Cj459	Cj460	Cj461	Cj462	Cj463
	Million dollars	Million dollars	Million dollars	Million dollars	Million dollars	Million dollars	Million dollars	Million dollars	Million dollars	Million dollars
1949	734	23	275	433	3	267	204	4	232 [1]	27
1950	1,058	40	199	816	3	224	560	6	238 [2]	30
1951	1,095	36	249	806	4	262	525	6	270	32
1952	1,222	43	311	864	4	420	445	7	316	34
1953	1,388	45	387	952	4	559	414	9	369	37
1954	1,561	47	641	868	5	803	272	7	438	41
1955	2,249	62	765	1,417	5	699	975	13	516	46
1956	2,325	62	1,026	1,228	9	683	962	21	607	52
1957	2,245	63	908	1,265	9	653	825	24	685	58
1958	2,383	75	999	1,298	11	819	714	17	769	64
1959	3,343	103	1,093	2,135	12	590	1,774	42	866	71
1960	3,316	90	1,234	1,981	11	939	1,266	39	989	83
1961	3,988	159	1,153	2,662	14	1,181	1,571	35	1,107	94
1962	5,204	173	1,531	3,479	21	1,214	2,707	49	1,127	107
1963	6,875	159	1,906	4,784	26	1,151	4,363	68	1,171	122
1964	7,019	141	1,523	5,325	30	1,199	4,369	86	1,227	138
1965	7,806	129	1,640	5,997	40	1,045	5,221	105	1,277	158
1966	9,649	113	2,523	6,935	78	1,037	6,859	197	1,369	187
1967	7,186	127	2,598	4,386	75	1,432	4,060	100	1,395	199
1968	7,808	126	2,375	5,259	48	1,383	4,701	102	1,403	219
1969	11,373	124	1,862	9,289	98	1,041	8,422	192	1,478	240
1970	14,723	105	3,864	10,615	139	2,332	10,183	341	1,607	260
1971	10,701	142	2,420	7,936	203	1,789	6,840	173	1,617	282
1972	10,431	129	2,125	7,979	198	1,548	6,671	157	1,756	299
1973	19,007	157	3,437	15,147	266	1,745	14,449	317	2,122	374
1974	25,498	144	3,097	21,804	453	2,484	19,445	406	2,624	539
1975	22,712	108	4,376	17,845	383	2,700	16,383	334	2,705	590
1976	22,481	164	6,079	15,862	376	4,024	14,620	313	2,889	635
1977	24,566	134	3,749	20,173	510	4,286	16,009	296	3,295	680
1978	36,767	201	3,414	32,670	482	6,243	25,109	459	4,120	836
1979	46,428	251	3,693	41,838	646	9,368	30,372	596	5,149	943
1980	54,347	304	4,328	48,963	752	10,147	37,268	903	5,160	869
1981	74,680	395	8,157	65,194	934	12,185	54,131	1,563	5,827	974
1982	80,262	358	12,575	66,001	1,328	15,155	55,967	1,727	6,269	1,144
1983	72,490	556	9,841	58,978	3,115	14,153	48,930	1,672	6,395	1,340
1984	96,992	1,128	17,584	74,616	3,664	21,024	65,085	2,179	7,200	1,504
1985	112,152	799	19,243	88,835	3,275	25,215	74,447	2,383	8,313	1,794
1986	131,427	2,607	17,388	108,645	2,787	28,030	88,752	2,900	9,485	2,260
1987	154,104	1,587	16,538	133,058	2,921	21,624	115,725	2,897	11,281	2,577
1988	174,564	1,549	16,981	152,781	3,253	19,843	135,834	2,900	13,177	2,817

[1] Includes $96 million in temporary operating capital supplied by the U.S. Treasury. The Treasury's original contribution in 1933 amounted to $100 million.

[2] Includes $56 million in temporary operating capital supplied by the U.S. Treasury. By year-end 1951, capital subscriptions by member institutions were sufficient to repay the Treasury. Thereafter, paid-in capital represents subscriptions by member institutions.

Sources

Federal Home Loan Bank Board, *Annual Report* (1969), Table A-2, pp. 94–5; Federal Home Loan Bank Board, *Journal* (April 1972), Table S.2.1, p. 82; *Journal* (August 1976), Table S.3.1, p. 36; *Journal* (May 1989), Table 8.

Documentation

Designed to restore confidence in the nation's financial institutions and promote home ownership, the Federal Home Loan Bank System was created by the 1932 Federal Home Loan Bank Act. The Federal Home Loan Bank Board (FHLBB) comprises twelve district banks located in Atlanta, Boston, Chicago, Cincinnati, Dallas, Des Moines, Indianapolis, New York, Pittsburgh, San Francisco, Seattle, and Topeka. The district banks are federally chartered corporations wholly owned by member financial institutions. The Federal Housing Finance Board regulates and supervises the twelve district banks.

Each bank is governed by at least fourteen directors. Six directors are appointed by the Federal Housing Finance Board to promote the public interest. At least eight directors are elected by each district bank's member institutions. The Finance Board annually appoints a board chair from the appointed directors and a vice-chair from the elected members.

FHLBB members include federal and state-chartered thrift institutions, commercial banks, credit unions, and insurance companies. Financial institutions can become members upon meeting several criteria, the most important being that they have at least 10 percent of their assets invested in long-term mortgage loans. They must also be subject to inspection and supervision and maintain safe financial ratios.

The FHLBB's principal function is to raise funds by selling consolidated obligations to institutional investors. In 1999, the FHLBB was, in fact, the third largest issuer of debt in the world, and the system's debt receives both Standard & Poor's and Moody's highest (AAA) ratings. Through the FHLBB, small institutions gain access to national capital markets at rates and maturities typically available only to very large banks.

TABLE Cj454–463   Federal Home Loan Banks – assets and liabilities: 1949–1988   *Continued*

In addition to credit, the FHLBB banks provide their members with correspondent services and check-processing services. The system acts as a lender of last resort; it provides long-term advances on mortgage collateral; it provides low-cost advances to members to support the federal government's Affordable Housing and Community Investment programs; and it makes advances to member institutions at interest rates lower than those in commercial markets. Member institutions earn dividends on their capital stock

investment from the bank's earnings. Dividends may be paid in cash or capital stock.

With the dissolution of the FHLBB in 1989, consistent reporting of these series ceased. Limited information on the operations of the individual Federal Home Loan Banks can be obtained from their individual annual reports and from their various Web sites.

TABLE Cj464–475   National Credit Union Administration – income, expenses, liquidations, and assistance transactions: 1971–1998[1]

Contributed by Howard Bodenhorn and Eugene N. White

	Income			Expenses		Net income	Involuntary liquidations			Assistance to avoid liquidation		
								Share payouts				
Year	Total	Insurance premiums	Interest on investments and other income	Share insurance losses and expenses	Operating and administrative expenses	added to share insurance fund	Number of cases	Total	As a percentage of total insured shares	Number of cases	Capital notes and cash advances	Noncash guaranty accounts
	Cj464	Cj465 [2]	Cj466	Cj467	Cj468	Cj469	Cj470	Cj471	Cj472	Cj473	Cj474	Cj475
	Thousand dollars	Thousand dollars	Thousand dollars	Thousand dollars	Thousand dollars	Thousand dollars	Number	Thousand dollars	Percent	Number	Thousand dollars	Thousand dollars
1971	3,268	3,168	100	0	515	2,753	—	—	—	—	—	—
1972	8,534	8,037	497	1	596	7,937	—	—	—	—	—	—
1973	11,812	10,723	1,089	864	1,358	9,590	—	—	—	—	—	—
1974	15,148	12,871	2,277	1,589	1,871	11,688	—	—	—	—	—	—
1975	19,293	15,678	3,615	290	3,775	15,228	—	—	—	—	—	—
1976	22,799	18,432	4,367	1,222	5,535	16,042	—	—	—	—	—	—
1977 [3]	30,394	24,625	5,730	3,024	5,455	21,914	—	—	—	—	—	—
1978 [3]	37,396	29,631	7,674	2,557	5,788	29,051	—	—	—	—	—	—
1980 [4]	53,532	38,495	15,037	29,801	11,062	12,669	239	59,957	0.110	59	15,447	29,247
1981 [4]	62,422	41,734	20,688	43,746	9,433	9,243	251	78,639	0.136	114	8,388	42,922
1982 [4]	95,041	74,800 [5]	20,241	77,458	14,440	3,143	160	39,892	0.058	124	16,839	48,786
1983 [4]	125,036	103,538 [6]	21,498	55,060	12,688	57,288	50	9,954	0.012	113	31,838	52,736
1984 [4]	91,151	60,185	30,966	28,068	12,752	50,331	38	34,840	0.039	72	36,413	54,213
1985 [4]	100,213	15,716	84,497	25,472	10,927	63,814	31	15,499	0.014	45	33,266	36,946
1986	121,426	0	121,426	37,864	16,822	66,740	36	22,168	0.020	30	22,396	39,903
1987	112,746	0	112,746	55,732	21,466	35,548	33	3,213	0.002	16	5,031	39,564
1988	127,605	0	127,605	60,122	26,588	40,894	35	36,110	0.023	25	5,117	41,127
1989	148,800	0	148,800	93,608	30,817	24,375	54	21,687	0.013	43	39,360	53,959
1990	160,264	0	160,264	89,982	35,153	35,130	83	70,875	0.040	42	67,891	98,576
1991	207,409	41,235	166,174	163,000	40,353	4,056	89	117,710	0.067	51	35,101	179,595
1992	278,045	123,874	154,171	112,000	46,161	119,884	81	124,857	0.057	27	101,228	88,286
1993	146,250	0	146,250	60,000	43,574	42,676	54	57,303	0.024	15	6,634	16,587
1994	149,822	0	149,822	26,000	44,132	79,690	29	27,279	0.011	7	2,673	2,849
1995	175,073	0	175,073	0	48,384	126,690	15	11,737	0.004	9	0	1,134
1996	186,863	0	186,863	0	47,220	139,643	13	1,028	0.000	12	265	1,197
1997	204,089	0	204,089	0	49,767	154,322	8	17,888	0.006	7	1,211	1,343
1998	219,998	0	219,998	0	51,071	168,927	13	6,298	0.002	12	1,466	1,557

[1] Fiscal year ended June 30, except as indicated.

[2] Assessments are charged at rate of one twelfth of 1 percent of total shares as of December 31 and are net rebates paid to liquidating credit unions.

[3] Fiscal year ended September 30.

[4] Fiscal year ended December 31.

[5] Includes special premium assessment totaling $29,945,000.

[6] Includes special premium assessment totaling $52,286,000.

Sources
1971–1978: National Credit Union Administration (NCUA), *Annual Report* (1978), p. 50; 1980–1984: NCUA, *Annual Report* (1989), pp. 24–6; 1985–1998: NCUA, *Annual Report* (1992), pp. 30–1, and (1999), pp. 56–7.

Documentation
The National Credit Union Administration was created by Title II of the Federal Credit Union Act in October 1970. It was funded without taxpayer

money, but it is guaranteed with the full faith and credit of the U.S. government. The insurance fund is a revolving fund in the U.S. Treasury under the management of the NCUA Board. The Act requires the Board to insure member accounts in all federal credit unions and in qualifying state credit unions that seek membership. The maximum insurance per member account was initially $20,000; it was raised to $40,000 in 1974 and to $100,000 in 1980, placing credit union accounts on the same footing as deposits held in commercial banks, savings banks, and savings association accounts.

The National Credit Union Share Insurance Fund maintains approximately 1.3 percent of insured credit union deposits. Money in the Fund can be used by the Board for insurance payments, for assistance transactions to troubled credit unions, and for expenses incurred in connection with routine business. By law, federally insured credit unions maintain 1 percent of their deposits in the insurance fund, and the NCUA Board can levy special premiums if deemed necessary. Credit unions capitalized the Fund in 1985

(continued)

TABLE Cj464–475 National Credit Union Administration – income, expenses, liquidations, and assistance transactions: 1971–1998 *Continued*

by depositing 1 percent of their deposits with the Fund. Since then, the Board has charged only one premium, when three large New England credit unions failed in 1992.

The NCUA's central office is located in Washington, D.C., and the agency maintains regional offices in Albany, New York; Washington, D.C.; Atlanta, Georgia; Itasca, Illinois; Austin, Texas; and Concord, California. The regional offices are responsible for examining and supervising all insured credit unions. In addition, the regional offices engage in initial reviews of insurance applications and requests for financial assistance. They are also responsible for continuing insurability reviews and assisting receivers in liquidating failed credit unions.

Credit unions experiencing financial difficulties may be assisted by the Fund if their difficulties are considered correctable. Such special assistance may be a waiver of statutory reserve requirements, whereby the credit union

is allowed to cease augmenting its reserves or to charge operating losses against its regular reserve. If its reserves are depleted, the Fund may provide a special guarantee equal to the reserve shortfall. In addition, the Fund may provide cash assistance in share deposits or capital notes, or may even purchase assets from the credit union.

In many cases, the Fund seeks to orchestrate the merger of troubled credit unions with stronger ones. Such transactions often require assistance in the form of cash payments to the acquiring credit union, the purchase of certain assets, or guarantees of some assets, usually loans.

When a credit union is no longer viable and the Fund cannot locate a merger partner, the Fund will liquidate the credit union, sell its assets, and pay members' shares up to the insurance limit. In some instances, the Fund will provide guarantees to third-party purchasers of the failed credit union's assets (primarily loans).

TABLE Cj476–485 Domestic finance companies – assets and liabilities: 1972–1998[1]

Contributed by Howard Bodenhorn and Eugene N. White

		Assets					Liabilities			
	Total assets or liabilities	Accounts receivable			Less reserve for losses and unearned income	Other	Bank loans	Commercial paper	Other debt and liabilities	Capital, surplus, and undivided profits
		Consumer	Business	Real estate						
	Cj476	Cj477	Cj478	Cj479	Cj480	Cj481	Cj482	Cj483	Cj484	Cj485
Year	Billion dollars	Billion dollars	Billion dollars	Billion dollars	Billion dollars	Billion dollars	Billion dollars	Billion dollars	Billion dollars	Billion dollars
1972	65.6	31.9	27.4	—	7.4	13.7	5.6	17.3	31.8	10.9
1973	73.2	35.4	32.3	—	8.4	14.0	7.2	19.7	34.8	11.5
1974	79.6	36.1	37.2	—	9.0	15.4	9.7	20.7	36.9	12.4
1975	81.6	36.0	39.3	—	9.4	15.7	8.0	22.2	38.9	12.5
1976	89.2	38.6	44.7	—	10.5	16.3	6.3	23.7	45.8	13.4
1977	104.3	44.0	55.2	—	12.7	17.8	5.9	29.6	53.7	15.1
1978	122.4	52.6	63.3	—	15.6	22.1	6.5	34.5	64.3	17.2
1979	140.9	65.7	70.3	—	20.0	24.9	8.5	43.3	69.1	19.9
1980	150.1	73.6	72.3	—	23.3	27.5	13.2	43.4	74.2	19.4
1981	171.4	85.5	80.6	—	28.9	34.2	15.4	51.2	82.2	22.8
1982	179.5	89.5	81.0	—	30.5	39.7	18.6	45.8	90.9	24.2
1983	217.6	83.3	113.4	20.5	34.0	34.4	18.3	60.5	110.0	28.9
1984	249.2	89.9	137.8	23.8	38.0	35.7	20.0	73.1	124.6	31.5
1985	298.6	111.9	157.5	28.0	44.1	45.3	18.0	99.2	148.6	32.8
1986	351.9	134.7	173.4	32.6	47.3	58.6	18.6	117.8	179.1	36.4
1987	394.3	141.1	207.6	39.5	52.1	58.2	16.4	128.4	217.9	31.5
1988	441.3	146.2	236.5	43.5	57.3	72.4	15.4	142.0	248.3	35.6
1989	477.6	140.8	256.0	48.9	59.7	91.6	14.5	149.5	274.2	39.4
1990	520.6	136.0	290.8	59.9	65.8	99.6	19.4	152.7	305.7	42.8
1991	561.6	121.9	292.9	65.8	68.0	149.0	42.3	159.5	294.8	64.8
1992	566.1	117.1	296.5	68.4	66.6	150.6	37.6	156.4	304.3	67.8
1993	593.4	117.5	290.1	68.6	60.0	177.3	25.3	159.2	337.1	71.7
1994	666.9	134.8	337.6	78.5	67.4	183.4	21.2	184.6	385.5	75.7
1995	748.0	152.0	375.9	86.6	77.3	210.7	23.1	184.5	453.2	87.2
1996	826.9	154.5	398.1	105.7	73.9	242.5	27.8	192.9	508.3	97.9
1997	910.0	256.8	318.5	87.9	65.7	312.4	24.1	201.5	583.1	101.3
1998	979.5	261.8	347.5	102.3	70.1	337.9	26.3	231.5	604.7	117.0

[1] As of December 31 each year.

Source

Board of Governors of the Federal Reserve System, *Federal Reserve Bulletin* (various issues).

Documentation

Consumer finance companies make small, secured, personal loans, usually limited to a few thousand dollars. These companies typically charge higher interest rates and loan fees than commercial banks or credit unions because finance companies tend to make riskier loans to less creditworthy individuals. Because of the higher costs, consumer finance companies are not the lender of choice for most small businesses.

Commercial finance companies also take on greater risks than a typical commercial bank. These companies finance automobile sales and handle larger commercial loans (often as much as $500,000) than those made by consumer finance companies. Firms that rely on commercial finance companies tend to be young, potentially high-growth companies with spotty credit histories, or companies with high debt-to-net-worth ratios but reasonably strong cash flows. The cost of relying on finance companies can be significant. Commercial finance companies' rates and fees often exceed commercial bank rates and fees by 2–5 percentage points, sometimes even more.

DEPOSIT INSURANCE

Howard Bodenhorn and Eugene N. White

TABLE Cj486–494   Federal Deposit Insurance Corporation – assets, liabilities, insured deposits, and insurance fund: 1934–1998

Contributed by Howard Bodenhorn and Eugene N. White

	Assets								
	Total	Cash and cash equivalents	U.S. government securities	Net assets acquired through bank resolutions	Miscellaneous	Total liabilities	Bank insurance fund	Insured deposits	Bank insurance fund as a percentage of insured deposits
	Cj486	Cj487	Cj488 [1]	Cj489 [2]	Cj490 [3]	Cj491	Cj492 [4]	Cj493	Cj494
Year	Thousand dollars	Thousand dollars	Thousand dollars	Thousand dollars	Thousand dollars	Thousand dollars	Thousand dollars	Million dollars	Percent
1934	333,283	15,984	316,679	474	146	41,631	291,653	18,075	1.61
1935	337,210	33,478	298,258	5,418	56	31,152	306,057	20,158	1.52
1936	353,172	9,089	332,642	11,391	49	9,767	343,405	22,330	1.54
1937	385,340	20,635	348,486	16,154	66	2,191	383,149	22,557	1.70
1938	421,622	22,230	372,758	26,550	84	1,078	420,545	23,121	1.82
1939	456,114	28,276	363,542	64,231	64	3,403	452,711	24,650	1.84
1940	497,209	20,461	384,514	92,172	62	1,224	495,985	26,638	1.86
1941	555,662	19,964	453,892	81,741	65	2,163	553,500	28,249	1.96
1942	618,744	19,360	536,827	62,056	501	1,801	616,943	32,837	1.88
1943	705,464	19,961	638,776	46,250	476	2,409	703,055	48,440	1.45
1944	806,246	17,804	762,064	26,069	309	1,905	804,341	56,398	1.43
1945	931,090	15,723	899,944	15,122	301	1,939	929,151	67,021	1.39
1946	1,060,739	7,337	1,047,721	5,552	130	2,254	1,058,485	73,759	1.44
1947	1,030,742	4,589	1,022,457	3,579	116	24,652	1,006,090	76,254	1.32
1948	1,072,027	2,286	1,066,056	3,597	89	6,176	1,065,851	75,320	1.42
1949	1,211,724	1,402	1,207,289	2,861	171	7,781	1,203,943	76,589	1.57
1950	1,314,345	2,454	1,309,459	2,315	117	70,398	1,243,947	91,359	1.36
1951	1,360,345	750	1,356,255	3,040	300	78,157	1,282,188	96,713	1.33
1952	1,444,022	386	1,441,392	2,025	219	80,530	1,363,492	101,841	1.34
1953	1,536,749	3,981	1,530,547	2,104	118	86,066	1,450,684	105,610	1.37
1954	1,632,781	2,614	1,628,897	1,105	165	90,084	1,542,697	110,973	1.39
1955	1,734,097	4,131	1,725,477	4,352	141	94,508	1,639,589	116,380	1.41
1956	1,840,009	4,222	1,831,238	4,425	124	97,932	1,742,077	121,008	1.44
1957	1,950,912	2,289	1,944,947	3,531	146	100,452	1,850,459	127,055	1.46
1958	2,067,593	3,159	2,060,695	3,617	122	102,147	1,965,446	137,698	1.43
1959	2,197,484	2,907	2,189,528	3,310	1,739	107,693	2,089,790	142,131	1.47
1960	2,336,685	3,492	2,324,773	6,376	2,044	114,507	2,222,178	149,684	1.48
1961	2,481,511	2,855	2,470,460	3,815	4,381	127,717	2,353,794	160,309	1.47
1962	2,645,532	1,669	2,634,812	1,304	7,747	143,519	2,502,013	170,210	1.47
1963	2,823,147	1,955	2,798,130	14,618	8,444	155,238	2,667,910	177,381	1.50
1964	3,008,873	4,885	2,981,511	14,156	8,321	164,208	2,844,665	191,787	1.48
1965	3,211,733	3,754	3,190,208	9,579	8,192	175,407	3,036,326	209,690	1.45
1966	3,443,285	4,441	3,413,988	16,668	8,188	191,322	3,251,963	234,150	1.39
1967	3,691,724	4,159	3,661,441	17,996	8,128	206,238	3,485,486	261,149	1.33
1968	3,970,753	6,242	3,942,980	13,519	8,012	221,532	3,749,221	296,701	1.26
1969	4,297,472	6,347	4,261,152	22,232	7,741	246,363	4,051,108	313,085	1.29
1970	4,631,367	8,927	4,575,104	39,580	7,755	251,797	4,379,570	349,581	1.25
1971	4,993,246	10,293	4,831,006	144,253	7,693	253,386	4,739,859	374,568	1.27
1972	5,455,652	5,405	5,332,980	71,923	45,344	296,937	5,158,715	419,756	1.23
1973	5,923,333	8,645	5,639,516	179,910	95,262	307,997	5,615,336	465,600	1.21
1974	8,177,751	18,857	5,996,242	2,148,236	44,416	2,053,561	6,124,190	520,309	1.18
1975	8,349,861	17,359	6,472,294	1,814,911	45,297	1,633,822	6,716,039	569,101	1.18
1976	8,555,903	22,860	6,760,229	1,727,422	45,392	1,287,278	7,268,625	628,263	1.16
1977	8,462,534	8,663	7,267,012	1,178,071	8,788	469,746	7,992,788	692,533	1.15
1978	9,282,683	4,343	8,373,161	896,137	9,042	486,690	8,795,993	760,706	1.16
1979	10,359,380	1,523	9,636,106	712,838	8,913	566,648	9,792,732	808,555	1.21

Notes appear at end of table   (continued)

TABLE Cj486–494   Federal Deposit Insurance Corporation – assets, liabilities, insured deposits, and insurance fund: 1934–1998   *Continued*

	Assets								Bank insurance fund as a percentage of insured deposits
	Total	Cash and cash equivalents	U.S. government securities	Net assets acquired through bank resolutions	Miscellaneous	Total liabilities	Bank insurance fund	Insured deposits	
	Cj486	Cj487	Cj488 [1]	Cj489 [2]	Cj490 [3]	Cj491	Cj492 [4]	Cj493	Cj494
Year	Thousand dollars	Thousand dollars	Thousand dollars	Thousand dollars	Thousand dollars	Thousand dollars	Thousand dollars	Million dollars	Percent
1980	11,635,620	1,986	10,720,901	884,366	28,367	616,079	11,019,541	948,717	1.16
1981	13,241,785	382	12,236,398	977,531	27,474	995,645	12,246,140	988,898	1.24
1982	15,233,525	1,335	13,559,481	1,628,763	43,946	1,462,581	13,770,944	1,134,221	1.21
1983	16,945,486	88,785	14,362,701	2,010,952	483,048	1,516,306	15,429,180	1,268,332	1.22
1984	22,037,941	4,158	14,830,230	6,600,969	602,584	4,876,009	17,161,932	1,389,874	1.19
1985	22,073,098	23,186	16,341,098	5,071,396	590,254	4,116,108	17,956,990	1,503,393	1.19
1986	22,407,626	42,477	17,106,516	4,545,533	713,100	4,154,309	18,253,317	1,634,302	1.12
1987	22,426,524	18,499	16,563,166	5,213,783	631,076	4,124,682	18,301,842	1,658,802	1.10
1988	22,654,758	12,644	16,877,253	5,687,327	77,534	8,593,628	14,061,130	1,750,259	0.80
1989	19,614,407	4,813,914	9,204,693	5,498,127	97,673	6,404,884	13,209,523 [6]	1,873,837	0.70
1990	19,986,240	1,216,185	5,846,017	12,778,820	145,218	15,941,754	4,044,486	1,929,612	0.21
1991	26,415,163	1,770,016	5,806,921 [5]	18,674,760	163,466	33,443,105	−7,027,942	1,957,722	−0.36
1992	34,837,525	3,592,629	3,259,175 [5]	27,823,964	161,757	34,938,100	−100,575	1,945,623	−0.01
1993	20,381,795	483,239	6,115,836 [5]	13,624,302	158,418	7,260,135	13,121,660	1,906,885	0.69
1994	23,504,238	1,621,456	13,400,186 [5]	8,327,517	155,079	1,656,456	21,847,782	1,896,060	1.15
1995	26,175,231	531,308	21,349,143 [5]	4,143,040	151,740	721,533	25,453,698	1,952,543	1.30
1996	27,279,410	258,132	22,531,724 [5]	4,341,154	148,400	425,031	26,854,379	2,007,447	1.34
1997	28,605,670	219,207	27,071,643	1,169,759	145,061	313,122	28,292,548	2,055,874	1.38
1998	29,918,861	2,117,644	26,816,281	775,321	209,615	306,551	29,612,310	2,141,268	1.38

[1] Valued at cost less reserve for amortization of premium and includes accrued interest receivable.

[2] Includes claims of depositors against closed insured banks, net balances of depositors in closed banks pending settlement or not claimed, loans to merging banks to avert deposit insurance losses, assistance to insured banks to avert deposit insurance losses, and reserves for losses.

[3] Beginning in 1959, includes cost of land and buildings.

[4] Equal to capital and surplus from 1934 through 1948. Capital stock was returned by payments to U.S. Treasury in 1947 and 1948.

[5] Includes investments in corporate-owned assets.

[6] Passage of the Financial Institutions Reform, Recovery, and Enforcement Act of 1989 forced the Federal Deposit Insurance Corporation to assume responsibility for ninety-eight insolvent savings and loans formerly insured by the Federal Savings and Loan Insurance Corporation.

Sources

Series Cj486–492, Federal Deposit Insurance Corporation, *Annual Report* (1934–1998). Series Cj493–494, Federal Deposit Insurance Corporation, *Annual Report* (1996, 1998).

Documentation

The Federal Deposit Insurance Corporation (FDIC) was established in June 1933 to reimburse depositors in failed banks. All national banks and member banks of the Federal Reserve System are required by law to be members of the FDIC. Nonnational and non–Federal Reserve System banks may be admitted to FDIC membership on meeting prescribed conditions. At the end of 1996, the FDIC was the principal federal regulator of 5,785 state-chartered banks that were not members of the Federal Reserve System, and 590 state-chartered savings banks. The FDIC also retained secondary supervisory responsibility for 5,077 federally insured banks and savings associations. The FDIC's supervisory efforts consist of bank examinations, as well as development and enforcement of regulations. These efforts are designed to identify poor management and avoid excessive risk taking by FDIC members.

Historically, the FDIC's principal assets have been U.S. Treasury securities and cash or cash equivalents. In the 1980s, however, it acquired increasingly large amounts of assets (mostly loans and securities) of failed or failing banks. By the mid-1990s, in fact, the FDIC's assets acquired through resolutions reached more than $27 billion, an amount that represented the bulk of the insurer's assets. The Omnibus Budget Reconciliation Act of 1990 and the Federal Deposit Insurance Corporation Improvement Act of 1991 changed the insurer's assessment authority, and the latter Act required the Bank Insurance Fund to maintain funds equal to at least 1.25 percent of insured deposits. Sales and other divestitures of assets acquired through resolutions in combination with higher assessments brought the insurance fund into compliance with the 1.25 percent requirement.

Details on the assets, liabilities, and earnings of the FDIC itself, as well as the assets, liabilities, earnings, and dividends of insured banks, can be found in the FDIC's *Annual Report*s or on the FDIC's Internet site.

TABLE Cj495–503   Federal Deposit Insurance Corporation – income, expenses, and effective assessment rate: 1934–1998

Contributed by Howard Bodenhorn and Eugene N. White

	Income					Expenses			
	Total	Assessment income	Assessment credits	Investment and other income	Effective assessment rate	Total	Deposit insurance losses and expenses	Administrative and operating	Net income/loss
	Cj495	Cj496	Cj497	Cj498	Cj499	Cj500	Cj501	Cj502	Cj503
Year	Million dollars	Million dollars	Million dollars	Million dollars	Percent	Million dollars	Million dollars	Million dollars	Million dollars
1934	7	0	0	7	—	10	0.2	10	−3
1935	21	12	0	9	0.0833	11	2.8	9	10
1936	44	36	0	8	0.0833	11	2.6	8	33
1937	48	39	0	9	0.0833	12	3.7	9	36
1938	48	38	0	9	0.0833	11	2.5	9	36
1939	51	41	0	11	0.0833	16	7.2	9	35
1940	56	46	0	10	0.0833	13	3.5	9	43
1941	62	51	0	11	0.0833	10	0.6	10	52
1942	69	57	0	13	0.0833	10	0.5	10	59
1943	87	70	0	17	0.0833	10	0.2	10	77
1944	99	81	0	18	0.0833	9	0.1	9	90
1945	121	94	0	27	0.0833	9	0.1	9	112
1946	131	107	0	24	0.0833	10	0.1	10	121
1947	158	114	0	43	0.0833	10	0.1	10	148
1948	146	119	0	26	0.0833	7	0.7	6	139
1949	151	123	0	28	0.0833	6	0.3	6	145
1950	85	123	69	31	0.0370	8	1.4	6	77
1951	84	124	70	29	0.0370	7	0.0	7	77
1952	89	131	74	31	0.0370	8	0.8	7	81
1953	94	139	79	34	0.0357	7	0.1	7	87
1954	100	144	82	37	0.0357	8	0.1	8	92
1955	106	152	85	40	0.0370	9	0.3	9	97
1956	112	156	87	44	0.0370	9	0.3	9	103
1957	117	159	90	48	0.0357	10	0.1	10	108
1958	127	167	93	53	0.0370	12	0.0	12	115
1959	137	178	100	58	0.0370	12	0.2	12	124
1960	145	180	101	65	0.0370	13	0.1	12	132
1961	147	189	116	74	0.0323	15	1.6	13	133
1962	161	203	127	85	0.0313	14	0.1	14	147
1963	182	221	136	98	0.0313	15	0.7	14	167
1964	197	238	145	104	0.0323	18	2.9	16	179
1965	215	261	158	112	0.0323	23	5.2	18	192
1966	241	284	173	129	0.0323	20	0.1	20	221
1967	263	303	182	142	0.0333	27	2.9	24	236
1968	295	335	202	163	0.0333	29	0.1	29	266
1969	336	364	220	192	0.0333	35	1.0	34	301
1970	383	369	210	223	0.0357	46	3.8	42	337
1971	415	417	241	240	0.0345	60	13.4	47	355
1972	467	469	280	279	0.0333	60	10.1	50	407
1973	561	529	283	315	0.0385	108	53.8	54	453
1974	668	587	285	366	0.0435	159	100.0	59	509
1975	689	641	362	410	0.0357	98	29.8	68	592
1976	765	676	380	468	0.0370	212	31.9	180	553
1977	838	731	412	518	0.0370	114	24.3	89	724
1978	952	810	443	585	0.0385	149	45.6	103	803
1979	1,090	881	525	734	0.0333	94	−13.1	107	997
1980	1,310	952	521	880	0.0370	84	−34.6	118	1,227
1981	2,075	1,039	117	1,153	0.0714	848	720.9	127	1,227
1982	2,525	1,109	96	1,512	0.0769	1,000	869.9	130	1,525
1983	2,628	1,215	164	1,577	0.0714	970	834.2	136	1,658
1984	3,100	1,322	0	1,778	0.0800	1,999	1,848.0	151	1,100
1985	3,385	1,433	0	1,952	0.0833	1,958	1,778.7	179	1,428
1986	3,260	1,517	0	1,743	0.0833	2,964	2,783.4	180	296
1987	3,319	1,696	0	1,623	0.0833	3,271	3,066.0	205	49
1988	3,348	1,773	0	1,575	0.0833	7,588	7,364.5	224	−4,241
1989	3,495	1,885	0	1,610	0.0833	4,346	4,132.3	214	−852

(continued)

TABLE Cj495–503   Federal Deposit Insurance Corporation – income, expenses, and effective assessment rate: 1934–1998 *Continued*

	Income					Expenses			
	Total	Assessment income	Assessment credits	Investment and other income	Effective assessment rate	Total	Deposit insurance losses and expenses	Administrative and operating	Net income/loss
	Cj495	Cj496	Cj497	Cj498	Cj499	Cj500	Cj501	Cj502	Cj503
Year	Million dollars	Million dollars	Million dollars	Million dollars	Percent	Million dollars	Million dollars	Million dollars	Million dollars
1990	3,838	2,855	0	983	0.1200	13,003	12,783.7	220	−9,165
1991	5,790	5,161	0	629	0.2125	16,862	16,578.2	284	−11,072
1992	6,302	5,588	0	714	0.2300	−626	−1,196.6	571	6,927
1993	6,431	5,784	0	647	0.2440	−6,791	−7,179.9	389	13,222
1994	6,467	5,591	0	876	0.2360	−2,259	−2,682.3	423	8,726
1995	4,089	2,907	0	1,182	0.1240	483	12.6	471	3,606
1996	1,655	73	0	1,583	0.0024	255	−250.7	505	1,401
1997	1,616	25	0	1,591	0.0008	177	−427.9	605	1,438
1998	2,000	22	0	1,979	0.0008	692	−6.1	698	1,309

Source

Federal Deposit Insurance Corporation, *Annual Report* (various years).

Documentation

The primary purpose of the Federal Deposit Insurance Corporation's Bank Insurance Fund is to insure deposits, protect depositors of insured banks, and liquidate failed banks. The Bank Insurance Fund is funded through interest on investments in U.S. Treasury securities; Bank Insurance Fund premiums; income earned on and funds received from the management and liquidation of failed banks; and borrowings from the U.S. Treasury and the Federal Financing Bank, if necessary. The Federal Deposit Insurance Corporation Improvement Act of 1991 (FDICIA) sets limits on maximum obligations that can be incurred by the Bank Insurance Fund. At year-end 1996, the limit was $49 billion.

The Omnibus Budget Reconciliation Act of 1990 removed caps on assessment rate increases and authorized the Federal Deposit Insurance Corporation (FDIC) to establish new rates semiannually. The FDICIA also required the FDIC to implement risk-based insurance assessments; authorized the FDIC to increase assessment rates on member banks to ensure sufficient funds to meet the Bank Insurance Fund's obligations; and authorized the FDIC to increase assessment rates more often than semiannually and impose emergency special assessments to ensure the FDIC's ability to repay U.S. Treasury borrowings.

The FDICIA mandated that the Bank Insurance Fund equal 1.25 percent of insured deposits. The Bank Insurance Fund reached that level in May 1995. In 1996, the Deposit Insurance Fund Act of 1996 provided for the elimination of minimum assessments.

Effective assessment rates from 1950 through 1984 vary from the statutory rate of 0.0833 percent due to assessment credits provided in those years. The statutory rate increased to 0.12 percent in 1990 and to a minimum of 0.15 percent in 1991. Effective rates in 1991 and 1992 vary because the FDIC exercised its authority to increase assessments above the statutory rate when necessary. Beginning in 1993, the effective rate is determined by a risk premium system through which institutions pay assessments in the range of 0.23 percent to 0.31 percent, depending on perceived risk exposure. In May 1995, the Bank Insurance Fund reached the mandated level of 1.25 percent of insured deposits. As a result, the assessment rate was reduced to 4.4 cents per $100 of insured deposits, and assessment premiums totaling $1.5 billion were returned to insured banks in September 1995. In November 1996, the FDIC Board of Directors voted to maintain an assessment schedule of 0–27 cents per $100 of insured deposits, depending on a bank's risk exposure.

TABLE Cj504–510   Federal Deposit Insurance Corporation – deposit insurance coverage, banks closed, and deposits of banks closed: 1934–1998

Contributed by Howard Bodenhorn and Eugene N. White

		Insured banks closed					
		Number			Total deposits		
Year	Deposit insurance limit	Total	Not requiring insurance fund disbursements	Requiring insurance fund disbursements	Total	Not requiring insurance fund disbursements	Requiring insurance fund disbursements
	Cj504	Cj505	Cj506	Cj507	Cj508	Cj509	Cj510
	Thousand dollars	Number	Number	Number	Thousand dollars	Thousand dollars	Thousand dollars
1934	5	9	0	9	1,968	0	1,968
1935	5	26	1	25	13,405	85	13,320
1936	5	69	0	69	27,508	0	27,508
1937	5	77	2	75	33,677	328	33,349
1938	5	74	0	74	59,684	0	59,684
1939	5	60	0	60	157,772	0	157,772
1940	5	43	0	43	142,430	0	142,430
1941	5	15	0	15	29,717	0	29,717
1942	5	20	0	20	19,185	0	19,185
1943	5	5	0	5	12,525	0	12,525
1944	5	2	0	2	1,915	0	1,915
1945	5	1	0	1	5,695	0	5,695
1946	5	1	0	1	347	0	347
1947	5	5	0	5	7,040	0	7,040
1948	5	3	0	3	10,674	0	10,674
1949	5	5	1	4	6,665	1,190	5,475
1950	10	4	0	4	5,513	0	5,513
1951	10	2	0	2	3,408	0	3,408
1952	10	3	0	3	3,170	0	3,170
1953	10	4	2	2	44,711	26,449	18,262
1954	10	2	0	2	998	0	998
1955	10	5	0	5	11,953	0	11,953
1956	10	2	0	2	11,330	0	11,330
1957	10	2	1	1	11,247	10,084	1,163
1958	10	4	0	4	8,240	0	8,240
1959	10	3	0	3	2,593	0	2,593
1960	10	1	0	1	6,930	0	6,930
1961	10	5	0	5	8,936	0	8,936
1962	10	1	1	0	3,011	3,011	0
1963	10	2	0	2	23,444	0	23,444
1964	10	7	0	7	23,438	0	23,438
1965	10	5	0	5	43,861	0	43,861
1966	15	7	0	7	103,523	0	103,523
1967	15	4	0	4	10,878	0	10,878
1968	15	3	0	3	22,524	0	22,524
1969	20	9	0	9	40,134	0	40,134
1970	20	7	0	7	54,806	0	54,806
1971	20	6	0	6	132,058	0	132,058
1972	20	1	0	1	20,480	0	20,480
1973	20	6	0	6	971,296	0	971,296
1974	40	4	0	4	1,575,832	0	1,575,832
1975	40	13	0	13	339,574	0	339,574
1976	40	16	0	16	864,859	0	864,859
1977	40	6	0	6	205,208	0	205,208
1978	40	7	0	7	854,154	0	854,154
1979	40	10	0	10	110,696	0	110,696
1980	100	10	0	10	216,300	0	216,300
1981	100	10	0	10	3,826,022	0	3,826,022
1982	100	42	0	42	9,908,379	0	9,908,379
1983	100	48	0	48	5,441,608	0	5,441,608
1984	100	79	0	79	2,883,162	0	2,883,162
1985	100	120	0	120	8,059,441	0	8,059,441
1986	100	138	0	138	6,471,100	0	6,471,100
1987	100	184	0	184	6,281,500	0	6,281,500
1988	100	200	0	200	24,931,302	0	24,931,302
1989	100	206	0	206	24,090,551	0	24,090,551

(continued)

TABLE Cj504–510 Federal Deposit Insurance Corporation – deposit insurance coverage, banks closed, and deposits of banks closed: 1934–1998 *Continued*

		Insured banks closed					
		Number			Total deposits		
	Deposit insurance limit	Total	Not requiring insurance fund disbursements	Requiring insurance fund disbursements	Total	Not requiring insurance fund disbursements	Requiring insurance fund disbursements
	Cj504	Cj505	Cj506	Cj507	Cj508	Cj509	Cj510
Year	Thousand dollars	Number	Number	Number	Thousand dollars	Thousand dollars	Thousand dollars
1990	100	168	0	168	14,473,300	0	14,473,300
1991	100	124	0	124	53,751,763	0	53,751,763
1992	100	120	10	110	41,150,898	4,257,667	36,893,231
1993	100	41	0	41	3,132,177	0	3,132,177
1994	100	13	1	12	1,236,488	0	1,236,488
1995	100	6	0	6	632,700	0	632,700
1996	100	5	0	5	168,228	0	168,228
1997	100	1	0	1	26,800	0	26,800
1998	100	3	0	3	335,076	0	335,076

Source

Federal Deposit Insurance Corporation, *Annual Report* (1998), pp. 119, 122.

Documentation

The Federal Deposit Insurance Corporation (FDIC) was established in June 1933 to reimburse depositors in failed member banks. FDIC disbursements are made when insured depositors in closed banks are paid off, or when the deposits of closed institutions are assumed by a continuing bank with the financial assistance of the FDIC. Additional details on closings of insured banks by type of resolution are shown in Tables Cj298–307 and Cj523–550.

TABLE Cj511–522   Federal Deposit Insurance Corporation – disbursements and losses on disbursements for closed banks: 1934–1998

Contributed by Howard Bodenhorn and Eugene N. White

	All bank closings			Deposit payoff closings			Deposit assumption closings			Assistance transactions		
	Banks	Disbursements	Losses on disbursements	Banks	Disbursements	Losses on disbursements	Banks	Disbursements	Losses on disbursements	Banks	Disbursements	Losses on disbursements
	Cj511	Cj512	Cj513 [1]	Cj514	Cj515	Cj516	Cj517	Cj518	Cj519	Cj520	Cj521	Cj522
Year	Number	Thousand dollars	Thousand dollars	Number	Thousand dollars	Thousand dollars	Number	Thousand dollars	Thousand dollars	Number	Thousand dollars	Thousand dollars
1934	9	941	207	9	941	207	—	—	—	—	—	—
1935	25	9,108	2,685	24	6,026	1,752	1	3,082	933	—	—	—
1936	69	15,206	2,333	42	7,735	1,338	27	7,471	995	—	—	—
1937	75	20,204	3,672	50	12,365	2,647	25	7,839	1,025	—	—	—
1938	74	34,394	2,425	50	9,092	1,184	24	25,302	1,241	—	—	—
1939	60	81,828	7,152	32	26,196	5,797	28	55,632	1,355	—	—	—
1940	43	87,899	3,796	19	4,895	582	24	83,004	3,214	—	—	—
1941	15	25,061	591	8	12,278	213	7	12,783	378	—	—	—
1942	20	11,684	688	6	1,320	292	14	10,072	396	—	—	—
1943	5	7,230	123	4	5,500	123	1	1,730	0	—	—	—
1944	2	1,532	40	1	404	40	1	1,128	0	—	—	—
1945	1	1,845	0	0	0	0	1	1,845	0	—	—	—
1946	1	274	0	0	0	0	1	274	0	—	—	—
1947	5	2,038	59	0	0	0	5	2,038	59	—	—	—
1948	3	3,150	641	0	0	0	3	3,150	641	—	—	—
1949	4	2,685	369	0	0	0	4	2,685	369	—	—	—
1950	4	4,404	1,385	0	0	0	4	4,404	1,385	—	—	—
1951	2	1,986	0	0	0	0	2	1,986	0	—	—	—
1952	3	1,525	792	0	0	0	3	1,525	792	—	—	—
1953	2	5,359	0	0	0	0	2	5,359	0	—	—	—
1954	2	1,029	258	0	0	0	2	1,029	258	—	—	—
1955	5	7,315	230	4	4,438	230	1	2,877	0	—	—	—
1956	2	3,499	213	1	2,795	213	1	704	0	—	—	—
1957	1	1,031	0	1	1,031	0	0	0	0	—	—	—
1958	4	3,051	28	3	2,796	28	1	255	0	—	—	—
1959	3	1,835	97	3	1,835	97	0	0	0	—	—	—
1960	1	4,765	0	1	4,765	0	0	0	0	—	—	—
1961	5	6,201	1,502	5	6,201	1,502	0	0	0	—	—	—
1962	0	0	0	0	0	0	0	0	0	—	—	—
1963	2	19,172	286	2	19,172	286	0	0	0	—	—	—
1964	7	13,712	1,541	7	13,712	1,541	0	0	0	—	—	—
1965	5	11,479	663	3	10,908	517	2	571	146	—	—	—
1966	7	10,020	245	1	735	0	6	9,285	245	—	—	—
1967	4	8,097	1,010	4	8,097	1,010	0	0	0	—	—	—
1968	3	6,476	12	0	0	0	3	6,476	12	—	—	—
1969	9	42,072	82	4	7,596	82	5	34,476	0	—	—	—
1970	7	51,566	272	4	29,265	272	3	22,301	0	—	—	—
1971	6	171,646	193	5	53,767	193	1	117,846	0	—	—	—
1972	1	16,189	1,696	1	16,189	1,704	0	0	0	—	—	—
1973	6	435,238	66,386	3	16,771	0	3	418,425	64,723	—	—	—
1974	4	2,403,277	40	0	0	0	4	2,403,277	39	—	—	—
1975	13	332,046	16,312	3	25,918	68	10	306,128	16,244	—	—	—
1976	16	599,388	247	3	11,416	73	13	587,921	174	—	—	—
1977	6	26,650	2,093	0	0	0	6	26,650	2,093	—	—	—
1978	7	547,369	9,015	1	817	204	6	544,921	8,850	—	—	—
1979	10	90,351	10,872	3	9,936	927	7	80,415	9,934	—	—	—
1980	11	152,355	30,680	3	13,732	2,305	7	138,623	28,375	1	—	—
1981	10	888,999	781,778	2	35,736	1,138	5	79,208	7,850	3	774,055	772,790
1982	42	2,275,150	1,168,571	7	277,240	70,993	25	268,372	54,794	10	1,729,538	1,042,784
1983	48	3,807,082	1,376,609	9	148,423	25,939	35	2,893,969	1,043,086	4	764,690	307,584
1984	80	7,696,215	1,640,155	16	791,838	92,355	62	1,373,198	431,525	2	5,531,179	1,116,275
1985	120	2,920,687	1,007,152	29	523,789	112,576	87	1,631,166	535,520	4	765,732	359,056
1986	145	4,790,969	1,781,742	40	1,155,981	416,324	98	3,476,140	1,272,059	7	158,848	93,359
1987	203	5,037,871	2,022,996	51	2,103,792	702,587	133	2,773,202	1,160,245	19	160,877	160,164
1988	280	12,163,006	6,949,197	36	1,252,160	429,597	164	9,180,495	4,956,868	80	1,730,351	1,562,732
1989	207	11,445,829	6,209,686	32	2,116,556	855,182	174	9,326,725	5,352,016	1	2,548	2,488

Note appears at end of table

(continued)

TABLE Cj511–522   Federal Deposit Insurance Corporation – disbursements and losses on disbursements for closed banks: 1934–1998   *Continued*

	All bank closings			Deposit payoff closings			Deposit assumption closings			Assistance transactions		
	Banks	Disbursements	Losses on disbursements	Banks	Disbursements	Losses on disbursements	Banks	Disbursements	Losses on disbursements	Banks	Disbursements	Losses on disbursements
	Cj511	Cj512	Cj513 [1]	Cj514	Cj515	Cj516	Cj517	Cj518	Cj519	Cj520	Cj521	Cj522
Year	Number	Thousand dollars	Thousand dollars	Number	Thousand dollars	Thousand dollars	Number	Thousand dollars	Thousand dollars	Number	Thousand dollars	Thousand dollars
1990	169	10,816,602	2,787,145	20	2,182,583	736,879	148	8,629,084	2,045,470	1	4,935	4,796
1991	127	21,412,647	6,249,485	21	1,468,407	473,455	103	19,938,123	5,770,125	3	6,117	5,905
1992	122	14,084,663	3,756,786	25	1,802,655	494,132	95	12,280,522	3,261,464	2	1,486	1,190
1993	41	1,797,297	649,810	5	261,069	101,295	36	1,536,094	548,515	0	0	0
1994	13	1,224,797	181,617	0	0	0	13	1,224,797	181,617	0	0	0
1995	6	717,799	93,234	0	0	0	6	717,799	93,234	0	0	0
1996	5	169,397	43,696	0	0	0	5	169,397	43,696	0	0	0
1997	1	25,546	3,500	0	0	0	1	25,546	3,500	0	0	0
1998	3	286,086	178,976	0	0	0	3	286,086	178,976	0	0	0

[1] Includes estimated losses in active cases. Amounts are not adjusted for interest received, which was collected in some cases in which the disbursement was fully recovered. Because they are estimated, loss amounts are subject to change, especially those after 1990.

Sources

Federal Deposit Insurance Corporation, *Annual Report* (1988), p. 72; *Annual Report* (1998), p. 120.

Documentation

Disbursements by the Federal Deposit Insurance Corporation (FDIC) are made when depositors of closed, insured banks are paid off, or when the deposits of a closed bank are assumed by a continuing bank with the financial assistance of the FDIC. In cases where depositors are paid off, disbursements equal the amount paid by the FDIC on insured deposits. In deposit assumption cases, the FDIC transfers the closed bank's insured deposits to another bank, while uninsured depositors share with other creditors, including the FDIC, the proceeds realized from the liquidation of the closed bank's assets.

Although the principal disbursement in deposit assumption cases is to facilitate the transfer of deposits to a continuing bank, additional disbursements are sometimes made to protect assets during liquidation and for liquidation expenses. The FDIC may also assume contingent liability by providing guarantees to the bank assuming the deposits and assets of a closed bank.

The FDIC also provides assistance to troubled banks to avoid claims on the Bank Insurance Fund. This assistance usually takes the form of mergers concluded with the financial assistance of the FDIC. From 1980 to 1997, the FDIC provided more than $11.6 billion in assistance to 141 banks. Its realized and expected losses on those assistance transactions amounted to nearly $5.5 billion.

For additional information and updated loss estimates, refer to a recent FDIC *Annual Report.*

TABLE Cj523–531 Federal Deposit Insurance Corporation – number of banks closed, by type of assistance transaction: 1934–1998

Contributed by Howard Bodenhorn and Eugene N. White

Year	Purchase and assumption	Payoff	Reopen	Assistance transaction	Insured deposit transfer	Insured deposit assumption	Bridge bank	Pass-through receivership	Purchase and assumption, insured deposits
	Cj523	Cj524	Cj525	Cj526	Cj527	Cj528	Cj529	Cj530	Cj531
	Number	Number	Number	Number	Number	Number	Number	Number	Number
1934	0	9	0	—	—	—	—	—	—
1935	1	24	1	—	—	—	—	—	—
1936	27	42	0	—	—	—	—	—	—
1937	25	50	2	—	—	—	—	—	—
1938	24	50	0	—	—	—	—	—	—
1939	28	32	0	—	—	—	—	—	—
1940	24	19	0	—	—	—	—	—	—
1941	7	8	0	—	—	—	—	—	—
1942	14	6	0	—	—	—	—	—	—
1943	1	4	0	—	—	—	—	—	—
1944	1	1	0	—	—	—	—	—	—
1945	1	0	0	—	—	—	—	—	—
1946	1	0	0	—	—	—	—	—	—
1947	5	0	0	—	—	—	—	—	—
1948	3	0	0	—	—	—	—	—	—
1949	4	0	1	—	—	—	—	—	—
1950	4	0	0	—	—	—	—	—	—
1951	2	0	0	—	—	—	—	—	—
1952	3	0	0	—	—	—	—	—	—
1953	2	0	2	—	—	—	—	—	—
1954	2	0	0	—	—	—	—	—	—
1955	1	4	0	—	—	—	—	—	—
1956	1	1	0	—	—	—	—	—	—
1957	0	1	1	—	—	—	—	—	—
1958	1	3	0	—	—	—	—	—	—
1959	0	3	0	—	—	—	—	—	—
1960	0	1	0	—	—	—	—	—	—
1961	0	5	0	—	—	—	—	—	—
1962	1	0	0	—	—	—	—	—	—
1963	0	2	0	—	—	—	—	—	—
1964	0	7	0	—	—	—	—	—	—
1965	2	3	0	—	—	—	—	—	—
1966	5	1	0	—	—	—	—	—	—
1967	0	4	0	—	—	—	—	—	—
1968	3	0	0	—	—	—	—	—	—
1969	5	4	0	—	—	—	—	—	—
1970	3	4	0	—	—	—	—	—	—
1971	1	5	0	1	—	—	—	—	—
1972	0	1	0	1	—	—	—	—	—
1973	3	3	0	0	—	—	—	—	—
1974	3	0	0	1	—	—	—	—	—
1975	10	3	0	0	—	—	—	—	—
1976	13	3	0	1	—	—	—	—	—
1977	6	0	0	0	—	—	—	—	—
1978	6	1	0	0	—	—	—	—	—
1979	7	3	0	0	—	—	—	—	—
1980	7	3	0	1	—	—	—	—	—
1981	5	2	0	3	—	—	—	—	—
1982	25	7	0	10	—	—	—	—	—
1983	35	9	0	4	—	—	—	—	—
1984	62	4	0	2	12	—	—	—	—
1985	88	21	0	4	7	—	—	—	—
1986	98	21	0	7	19	—	—	—	—
1987	133	11	0	19	40	—	—	—	—
1988	163	6	0	22	30	—	—	—	—
1989	175	8	0	1	23	—	—	—	—
1990	148	8	0	1	12	—	—	—	—
1991	104	4	0	2	17	—	—	—	—
1992	72	11	0	2	14	1	21	1	0
1993	4	5	0	0	2	0	1	0	29
1994	3	0	0	0	0	0	1	0	8

(continued)

TABLE Cj523–531 Federal Deposit Insurance Corporation – number of banks closed, by type of assistance transaction: 1934–1998 *Continued*

	Purchase and assumption	Payoff	Reopen	Assistance transaction	Insured deposit transfer	Insured deposit assumption	Bridge bank	Pass-through receivership	Purchase and assumption, insured deposits
	Cj523	Cj524	Cj525	Cj526	Cj527	Cj528	Cj529	Cj530	Cj531
Year	Number	Number	Number	Number	Number	Number	Number	Number	Number
1995	0	0	0	0	0	0	0	0	6
1996	1	0	0	0	0	0	0	0	4
1997	0	0	0	0	0	0	0	0	1
1998	0	0	0	0	0	0	0	0	3

Sources

Federal Deposit Insurance Corporation, *Statistics on Banking: Historical, 1934–1994,* Volume 1, *A Statistical History of the United States Banking Industry* (1995), pp. C1–C110; *Statistics on Banking* (1997); and the FDIC Internet site, Historical Statistics on Banking.

Documentation

Section 11(f) of the Federal Deposit Insurance Corporation Act provided that upon failure of a Federal Deposit Insurance Corporation (FDIC)-insured bank, depositors shall be reimbursed as quickly as possible. Typically, reimbursement has taken one of two forms: (1) direct payment by the insurer in cash or (2) transfer of the insured deposit to a continuing bank. Although there is little empirical evidence concerning the timing of these payments, it is believed that the FDIC begins issuing deposit insurance checks or transferring deposits between three and five working days after a bank closing. This is the period in which payouts begin. Completion of payments depends on a multitude of factors including bank size, the condition and accuracy of the bank's records, and the cooperation of depositors, among others. All depositors must provide evidence of deposit ownership and file appropriate claim forms before payout commences.

Resolution of failed banks and reimbursement of depositors may take several forms. A *deposit payoff* occurs when the FDIC issues checks directly to depositors for the amounts of insured deposits.

A *purchase and assumption* transaction occurs when both the insured and uninsured deposits of a failed or failing bank are assumed by another insured bank. Generally, the FDIC subsidizes some part of the transfer by providing financial assistance to the assuming bank. All of the deposit liabilities of the failed bank become liabilities of the assuming bank on the same terms and conditions (namely, interest rates and maturities) as those offered by the failing bank. A *purchase and assumption of insured deposits* is similar to a simple purchase and assumption except that the assuming bank assumes only the insured deposit of a failed bank.

An *insured deposit transfer* occurs when the FDIC transfers the insured deposits of a failed bank to an agent bank, which makes these funds available to the depositors of the failed bank. The agent bank usually makes these funds available on the first business day after the failed bank closes.

Open bank *assistance transactions,* unlike FDIC resolutions that take place subsequent to a bank failure, are completed in anticipation of bank failure. In assistance transactions, the FDIC provides financial assistance to prevent a troubled bank from failing. The bank continues, and the deposits remain available to customers on the same terms as before FDIC intervention.

A *bridge bank* is formed when one or more insured banks have defaulted, or are about to default, and the FDIC organizes and the Office of the Comptroller of the Currency charters a new national bank that assumes the deposits of the defaulting bank(s). The newly organized institution is referred to as a bridge bank. Such bridge banks are chartered if the FDIC determines, in consultation with the Office of the Comptroller of the Currency (OCC), that the amount required to operate such a bank will not exceed the costs of liquidating the defaulting bank, or if it is in the best interests of the depositors and the community to have a bank in operation. It is Congress's intent that bridge banks will be established to prevent undue hardships on or losses to customers of insured banks, especially creditworthy farmers, small businesses, and households. Bridge banks are given all the powers and privileges granted to national banks, but they are not required to purchase Federal Reserve Bank stock, and the OCC may waive its indemnity bond requirement. Bridge banks operate without explicit capital, and the FDIC provides necessary operating funds. Once the bridge bank has established itself and can convince the FDIC and the OCC that it is a viable institution, it is authorized to issue and sell stock, or it may be sold outright with the buyer providing the capitalization.

A *pass-through receivership* occurs when all deposits, most assets, and certain nondeposit liabilities of the defaulting bank instantly pass through the receiver to a newly chartered institution or bridge bank.

A *reopen* occurs when the defaulting bank is reorganized and allowed by the FDIC to start its operation.

Series Cj523–524 show that, historically, the most common forms of FDIC resolution of defaulting institutions have been deposit payoff or purchase and assumption. Only a handful of defaulting banks were allowed to or were capable of reorganization and reopening. Beginning in the early 1970s, however, the FDIC embarked on a policy of preemptive assistance transactions to ward off default (series Cj526), and the number of assistance transactions increased in the 1980s, though the number remained small relative to the number of payoff and assumption cases. The 1980s witnessed an increasing number of insured deposit-only transfers, perhaps reflecting the deteriorating condition of some failing banks' balance sheets during the banking and savings and loan crises of the mid-1980s. In the early 1990s, the bridge bank appeared and was a relatively common resolution method in 1992. In the mid-1990s, there was an increasing use of the purchase and assumption of insured deposits only. Series Cj523–531, seen in conjunction with series Cj532–540, reflect changing resolution methods and changing attitudes within the FDIC itself on the best way of resolving failed banks.

TABLE Cj532–540   Federal Deposit Insurance Corporation–insured deposits of banks closed, by type of assistance transaction: 1934–1998

Contributed by Howard Bodenhorn and Eugene N. White

Year	Purchase and assumption	Payoff	Reopen	Assistance transaction	Insured deposit transfer	Insured deposit assumption	Bridge bank	Pass-through receivership	Purchase and assumption, insured deposits
	Cj532	Cj533	Cj534	Cj535	Cj536	Cj537	Cj538	Cj539	Cj540
	Thousand dollars	Thousand dollars	Thousand dollars	Thousand dollars	Thousand dollars	Thousand dollars	Thousand dollars	Thousand dollars	Thousand dollars
1934	0	1,966	0	—	—	—	—	—	—
1935	4,357	9,020	85	—	—	—	—	—	—
1936	16,696	10,847	0	—	—	—	—	—	—
1937	18,296	14,508	328	—	—	—	—	—	—
1938	51,943	10,121	0	—	—	—	—	—	—
1939	128,219	32,558	0	—	—	—	—	—	—
1940	138,172	5,600	0	—	—	—	—	—	—
1941	14,991	14,626	0	—	—	—	—	—	—
1942	16,072	1,379	0	—	—	—	—	—	—
1943	5,898	6,274	0	—	—	—	—	—	—
1944	1,459	405	0	—	—	—	—	—	—
1945	5,695	0	0	—	—	—	—	—	—
1946	316	0	0	—	—	—	—	—	—
1947	6,966	0	0	—	—	—	—	—	—
1948	40,455	0	0	—	—	—	—	—	—
1949	4,978	0	1,190	—	—	—	—	—	—
1950	5,765	0	0	—	—	—	—	—	—
1951	3,408	0	0	—	—	—	—	—	—
1952	3,157	0	0	—	—	—	—	—	—
1953	36,370	0	8,341	—	—	—	—	—	—
1954	990	0	0	—	—	—	—	—	—
1955	5,465	6,498	0	—	—	—	—	—	—
1956	6,578	4,703	0	—	—	—	—	—	—
1957	0	1,163	10,084	—	—	—	—	—	—
1958	4,084	4,155	0	—	—	—	—	—	—
1959	0	2,539	0	—	—	—	—	—	—
1960	0	6,955	0	—	—	—	—	—	—
1961	0	8,819	—	—	—	—	—	—	—
1962	3,011	0	—	—	—	—	—	—	—
1963	0	23,441	—	—	—	—	—	—	—
1964	0	23,323	—	—	—	—	—	—	—
1965	1,012	42,865	—	—	—	—	—	—	—
1966	102,748	774	—	—	—	—	—	—	—
1967	0	10,878	—	—	—	—	—	—	—
1968	22,524	0	—	—	—	—	—	—	—
1969	31,123	9,005	—	—	—	—	—	—	—
1970	21,332	31,008	—	—	—	—	—	—	—
1971	57,547	74,135	—	9,300	—	—	—	—	—
1972	0	20,385	—	—	—	—	—	—	—
1973	945,500	25,791	—	0	—	—	—	—	—
1974	1,459,858	0	—	112,703	—	—	—	—	—
1975	299,672	39,925	—	0	—	—	—	—	—
1976	846,000	19,108	—	370,000	—	—	—	—	—
1977	204,576	0	—	0	—	—	—	—	—
1978	852,868	1,282	—	0	—	—	—	—	—
1979	98,066	12,687	—	0	—	—	—	—	—
1980	199,847	16,265	—	5,300,000	—	—	—	—	—
1981	49,507	47,421	—	3,729,016	—	—	—	—	—
1982	552,365	534,928	—	8,817,025	—	—	—	—	—
1983	2,275,312	160,998	—	3,005,297	—	—	—	—	—
1984	1,603,923	319,302	—	17,945,028	465,295	—	—	—	—
1985	2,000,044	255,647	—	5,510,411	293,339	—	—	—	—
1986	5,311,700	445,800	—	585,600	713,600	—	—	—	—
1987	4,050,310	331,400	—	2,118,000	1,899,790	—	—	—	—
1988	23,633,031	131,200	—	11,520,952	1,147,200	—	—	—	—
1989	20,597,800	109,300	—	6,400	1,566,100	—	—	—	—

(continued)

TABLE Cj532–540   Federal Deposit Insurance Corporation–insured deposits of banks closed, by type of assistance transaction: 1934–1998   *Continued*

Year	Purchase and assumption	Payoff	Reopen	Assistance transaction	Insured deposit transfer	Insured deposit assumption	Bridge bank	Pass-through receivership	Purchase and assumption, insured deposits
	Cj532	Cj533	Cj534	Cj535	Cj536	Cj537	Cj538	Cj539	Cj540
	Thousand dollars	Thousand dollars	Thousand dollars	Thousand dollars	Thousand dollars	Thousand dollars	Thousand dollars	Thousand dollars	Thousand dollars
1990	12,215,700	777,200	—	15,600	1,480,500	—	—	—	—
1991	52,303,320	61,448	—	51,573	1,415,800	—	—	—	—
1992	22,408,350	1,120,315	—	33,491	1,069,691	19,480	9,772,506	6,535,247	—
1993	147,125	271,172	—	0	125,994	0	196,655	0	2,391,232
1994	313,273	0	0	0	0	0	0	0	923,215
1995	0	0	—	0	0	0	0	0	774,690
1996	22,288	0	—	0	0	0	0	0	175,357
1997	0	0	0	0	0	0	0	0	27,511
1998	0	0	0	0	0	0	0	0	260,675

Sources

Federal Deposit Insurance Corporation (FDIC), *Statistics on Banking: Historical, 1934–1994*, Volume 1, *A Statistical History of the United States Banking Industry* (1995), pp. C1–C110; *Statistics on Banking* (1997); and the FDIC Internet site, Historical Statistics on Banking.

Documentation

For discussion and description of the series, see the text for Table Cj523–531.

TABLE Cj541–550   Federal Deposit Insurance Corporation – number and insured deposits of closed banks, by charter type: 1934–1998

Contributed by Howard Bodenhorn and Eugene N. White

	Number of banks					Insured deposits				
	National	State member	Nonmember	Federal savings	State savings	National banks	State member banks	Nonmember banks	Federal savings banks	State savings banks
	Cj541	Cj542	Cj543	Cj544	Cj545	Cj546	Cj547	Cj548	Cj549	Cj550
Year	Number	Number	Number	Number	Number	Thousand dollars	Thousand dollars	Thousand dollars	Thousand dollars	Thousand dollars
1934	1	0	8	—	0	42	0	1,924	—	0
1935	4	0	22	—	0	5,461	0	8,001	—	0
1936	2	1	66	—	0	2,166	3,734	21,643	—	0
1937	13	2	62	—	0	15,947	1,709	15,476	—	0
1938	5	2	66	—	1	6,556	22,775	30,254	—	2,479
1939	10	4	46	—	0	18,997	25,816	115,964	—	0
1940	8	6	29	—	0	11,074	115,306	17,392	—	0
1941	6	2	7	—	0	10,768	2,907	15,942	—	0
1942	10	2	8	—	0	11,337	2,858	3,256	—	0
1943	3	0	2	—	0	10,931	0	1,241	—	0
1944	1	0	1	—	0	1,459	0	405	—	0
1945	0	0	1	—	0	0	0	5,695	—	0
1946	0	0	1	—	0	0	0	316	—	0
1947	3	0	2	—	0	5,449	0	1,517	—	0
1948	1	2	0	—	0	1,925	8,530	0	—	0
1949	1	0	4	—	0	3,090	0	3,078	—	0
1950	2	0	2	—	0	3,648	0	24,117	—	0
1951	1	0	1	—	0	3,260	0	148	—	0
1952	0	0	3	—	0	0	0	3,157	—	0
1953	0	0	4	—	0	0	0	44,711	—	0
1954	0	0	2	—	0	0	0	990	—	0
1955	2	0	3	—	0	4,606	0	7,357	—	0
1956	1	0	1	—	0	6,578	0	4,703	—	0
1957	1	1	0	—	0	10,084	1,163	0	—	0
1958	1	0	3	—	0	1,368	0	6,871	—	0
1959	0	0	3	—	0	0	0	2,539	—	0
1960	0	0	1	—	0	0	0	6,955	—	0
1961	2	1	2	—	0	5,393	1,652	1,774	—	0
1962	1	0	0	—	0	3,011	0	0	—	0
1963	0	0	2	—	0	0	0	23,441	—	0
1964	1	0	6	—	0	3,459	0	19,864	—	0
1965	2	0	3	—	0	42,430	0	1,447	—	0
1966	2	0	5	—	0	3,692	0	99,830	—	0
1967	1	1	2	—	0	3,818	3,885	3,175	—	0
1968	1	0	2	—	0	11,757	0	10,767	—	0
1969	3	2	4	—	0	11,592	3,252	25,284	—	0
1970	1	0	6	—	0	15,912	0	36,428	—	0
1971	1	0	6	—	0	1,201	0	139,781	—	0
1972	0	1	1	—	0	0	—	20,385	—	0
1973	3	0	3	—	0	945,500	0	25,791	—	0
1974	1	1	2	—	0	1,444,982	14,876	115,974	—	0
1975	2	1	10	—	0	105,766	60,603	173,228	—	0
1976	2	1	14	—	0	338,902	165,079	731,127	—	0
1977	1	0	5	—	0	4,912	0	199,664	—	0
1978	1	0	5	—	1	197,166	0	645,153	—	11,831
1979	3	0	7	—	0	43,615	0	67,138	—	0
1980	2	0	9	—	0	5,310,428	0	205,684	—	0
1981	1	2	4	—	3	9,627	30,194	57,107	—	3,914,268
1982	10	2	22	—	7	1,056,800	184,405	289,779	—	7,988,258
1983	9	2	34	—	2	909,683	127,944	3,330,361	—	2,169,207
1984	18	6	55	—	1	17,916,126	112,385	1,810,395	—	498,033
1985	29	11	78	—	2	1,053,921	167,177	1,497,602	—	5,406,945
1986	48	11	85	1	0	3,408,850	130,200	3,647,850	28,200	0
1987	70	10	121	1	1	2,482,800	315,000	4,026,900	474,800	1,099,485
1988	89	21	111	0	0	19,881,000	662,716	15,888,667	0	0
1989	110	17	79	0	1	30,649,343	661,516	973,859	0	683,356

(continued)

TABLE Cj541–550   Federal Deposit Insurance Corporation – number and insured deposits of closed banks,
by charter type: 1934–1998   *Continued*

	Number of banks					Insured deposits				
	National	State member	Nonmember	Federal savings	State savings	National banks	State member banks	Nonmember banks	Federal savings banks	State savings banks
	Cj541	Cj542	Cj543	Cj544	Cj545	Cj546	Cj547	Cj548	Cj549	Cj550
Year	Number	Number	Number	Number	Number	Thousand dollars	Thousand dollars	Thousand dollars	Thousand dollars	Thousand dollars
1990	98	10	52	1	8	8,988,300	178,700	2,686,400	493,700	2,243,533
1991	44	7	64	2	17	31,232,286	155,511	6,463,696	1,330,951	14,806,988
1992	32	16	54	1	21	6,520,598	3,801,774	5,426,316	6,535,247	19,648,447
1993	23	1	16	0	1	1,505,420	111,994	1,020,191	0	720,512
1994	3	1	6	0	2	160,246	93,008	488,661	0	505,146
1995	1	1	4	0	0	8,677	297,948	468,065	0	0
1996	2	0	3	0	0	107,145	0	90,500	0	0
1997	0	0	1	0	0	0	0	27,511	0	0
1998	0	2	1	0	0	0	54,350	206,325	0	0

Sources

Federal Deposit Insurance Corporation (FDIC), *Statistics on Banking: Historical, 1934–1994*, Volume 1, *A Statistical History of the United States Banking Industry* (1995), pp. C1–C110; FDIC, *Statistics on Banking* (1997); and the FDIC Internet site, Historical Statistics on Banking.

Documentation

See the text for Tables Cj523–531 and Cj551–562.

TABLE Cj551–562   Insured commercial banks and trust companies – number and assets: 1934–1998[1, 2, 3]

Contributed by Howard Bodenhorn and Eugene N. White

	Insured commercial banks and trust companies	Assets										
		Total	Cash and amounts due from other banks	Investment securities	Loans and leases			Other earning assets	Bank premises and equipment	Other real estate	Intangible assets	All other assets
					Total	Allowance for losses	Net loans and leases					
	Cj551	Cj552 [4]	Cj553	Cj554	Cj555 [5]	Cj556 [6]	Cj557	Cj558 [7]	Cj559 [8]	Cj560	Cj561	Cj562
Year	Number	Million dollars	Million dollars	Million dollars	Million dollars	Million dollars	Million dollars	Million dollars	Million dollars	Million dollars	Million dollars	Million dollars
1934	14,137	46,448	11,202	18,172	14,614	—	14,614	—	1,212	465	—	783
1935	14,123	50,926	13,851	20,116	14,719	—	14,719	—	1,196	551	—	493
1936	13,969	56,210	15,730	22,307	15,965	—	15,965	—	1,178	560	—	470
1937	13,795	54,212	14,931	20,476	16,750	—	16,750	—	1,161	520	—	375
1938	13,657	56,800	17,176	21,451	16,024	—	16,024	—	1,123	646	—	380
1939	13,534	63,147	21,876	22,428	16,866	—	16,866	—	1,091	566	—	320
1940	13,438	70,720	26,291	24,163	18,398	—	18,398	—	1,071	463	—	334
1941	13,427	76,827	25,793	28,032	21,262	—	21,262	—	1,060	370	—	310
1942	13,347	95,459	27,593	47,344	18,907	—	18,907	—	1,048	301	—	266
1943	13,274	112,246	27,191	64,678	18,844	—	18,844	—	994	207	—	332
1944	13,268	134,613	29,746	82,053	21,355	—	21,355	—	940	139	—	380
1945	13,302	157,582	34,303	96,066	25,769	—	25,769	—	903	100	—	441
1946	13,359	147,365	33,704	81,469	30,740	—	30,740	—	902	85	—	465
1947	13,403	152,773	36,936	76,712	37,592	—	37,592	—	936	80	—	516
1948	13,419	152,163	38,097	70,339	42,388	409	41,979	—	999	80	—	669
1949	13,436	155,319	35,222	75,824	43,047	548	42,499	—	1,046	93	—	635
1950	13,446	166,792	39,865	73,198	52,482	673	51,809	—	1,109	110	—	702
1951	13,455	177,449	44,242	73,673	58,184	814	57,371	—	1,193	123	—	848
1952	13,439	186,682	44,299	76,280	64,728	904	63,824	—	1,291	123	—	864
1953	13,432	191,062	44,478	76,851	68,227	961	67,266	—	1,392	128	—	946
1954	13,323	200,589	43,235	84,142	71,412	1,071	70,341	—	1,523	124	—	1,224
1955	13,237	209,145	46,560	77,240	83,628	1,268	82,360	—	1,700	154	—	1,130
1956	13,218	216,146	48,444	73,947	91,705	1,562	90,143	—	1,894	176	—	1,542
1957	13,165	221,534	48,219	75,330	95,577	1,776	93,801	—	2,096	219	—	1,869
1958	13,124	237,474	48,792	86,056	100,087	1,955	98,132	—	2,322	249	—	1,922
1959	13,114	243,422	49,211	78,582	112,867	2,172	110,695	—	2,624	276	—	2,033
1960	13,126	256,322	51,902	81,020	119,878	2,356	117,522	—	2,829	375	—	2,674
1961	13,115	277,374	56,181	89,662	127,414	2,606	124,807	—	3,102	442	—	3,180
1962	13,124	295,983	53,799	94,912	142,718	2,694	140,023	—	3,403	481	—	3,364
1963	13,291	311,790	50,445	97,472	158,928	2,995	155,933	—	3,945	449	—	3,545
1964	13,493	345,130	60,033	100,960	178,649	3,553	175,096	—	4,754	—	—	4,288
1965	13,544	375,394	30,437	103,651	203,061	4,011	199,050	2,064	5,144	—	—	5,048
1966	13,538	402,899	68,649	104,271	220,306	4,337	215,969	2,461	5,619	—	—	5,930
1967	13,514	450,647	77,529	123,241	237,489	4,732	232,757	3,924	6,007	283	—	6,906
1968	13,487	500,160	83,266	135,202	264,640	5,215	259,425	6,527	6,657	323	—	8,760
1969	13,473	524,645	89,335	122,019	286,752	5,886	280,866	12,894	8,070	361	—	11,100
1970	13,511	570,158	93,048	141,370	298,186	5,999	292,187	21,616	9,143	407	—	12,387
1971	13,612	633,573	98,691	163,681	328,226	6,151	322,075	24,951	10,285	391	—	13,500
1972	13,733	730,902	111,844	178,459	388,902	6,624	382,278	30,763	11,525	369	—	15,664
1973	13,976	820,400	116,939	179,401	459,756	7,527	452,229	43,035	12,789	434	—	20,134
1974	14,230	1,037,197	178,307	188,892	584,055	8,611	575,444	46,921	14,683	829	—	32,121
1975	14,384	1,086,674	189,408	226,024	590,218	9,004	581,214	42,677	16,054	1,935	—	29,362
1976	14,410	1,182,412	203,783	246,513	633,015	6,340	626,675	53,757	17,235	2,975	—	31,474
1977	14,411	1,339,376	242,953	258,125	729,705	6,891	722,814	56,279	19,009	3,130	—	37,066
1978	14,391	1,507,936	274,029	269,120	840,935	7,956	832,979	56,015	21,326	2,507	—	51,961
1979	14,364	1,691,789	306,566	284,092	944,703	9,182	935,521	71,049	23,539	2,131	—	68,891
1980	14,434	1,855,687	331,909	325,058	1,016,461	10,053	1,006,408	79,737	26,652	2,209	—	83,714
1981	14,414	2,028,982	327,410	339,337	1,131,536	11,415	1,120,121	103,948	30,378	2,608	—	105,180
1982	14,451	2,193,339	334,216	366,676	1,224,284	13,203	1,211,081	122,927	33,970	4,411	—	120,058
1983	14,469	2,342,101	341,850	424,295	1,316,780	15,472	1,301,308	110,538	36,605	5,175	1,655	120,675
1984	14,496	2,508,870	323,727	385,549	1,508,601	18,705	1,489,896	139,328	38,444	5,860	2,315	123,752
1985	14,417	2,730,672	340,689	439,407	1,630,790	23,262	1,607,527	173,716	40,662	7,209	2,863	118,597
1986	14,210	2,940,699	379,331	484,865	1,756,438	28,900	1,727,538	182,104	42,663	9,178	4,374	110,646
1987	13,723	2,999,949	358,339	520,713	1,829,174	49,890	1,779,284	163,134	44,950	10,991	4,843	117,694
1988	13,137	3,130,796	355,563	535,995	1,932,376	46,666	1,885,710	163,216	45,733	11,354	5,178	128,047
1989	12,715	3,299,362	350,234	558,639	2,058,195	53,743	2,004,452	189,241	48,212	13,828	6,038	128,718

Notes appear at end of table   (continued)

TABLE Cj551-562 Insured commercial banks and trust companies – number and assets: 1934-1998 *Continued*

	Insured commercial banks and trust companies	Assets										
					Loans and leases							
		Total	Cash and amounts due from other banks	Investment securities	Total	Allowance for losses	Net loans and leases	Other earning assets	Bank premises and equipment	Other real estate	Intangible assets	All other assets
	Cj551	Cj552 [4]	Cj553	Cj554	Cj555 [5]	Cj556 [6]	Cj557	Cj558 [7]	Cj559 [8]	Cj560	Cj561	Cj562
Year	Number	Million dollars	Million dollars	Million dollars	Million dollars	Million dollars	Million dollars	Million dollars	Million dollars	Million dollars	Million dollars	Million dollars
1990	12,347	3,389,470	317,997	604,622	2,110,170	55,532	2,054,638	194,601	51,437	21,607	10,645	133,923
1991	11,927	3,430,640	304,820	691,385	2,052,754	55,146	1,997,608	215,858	52,249	27,553	12,246	128,921
1992	11,466	3,505,674	298,088	772,939	2,031,977	54,477	1,977,500	238,970	53,102	26,378	15,551	123,146
1993	10,960	3,706,189	272,988	836,598	2,149,733	52,756	2,096,977	273,097	55,528	16,784	18,027	136,200
1994	10,451	4,010,664	303,554	822,949	2,358,177	52,101	2,306,076	343,033	58,922	10,189	23,985	141,956
1995	9,941	4,312,679	306,545	811,107	2,602,745	52,817	2,549,928	—	61,425	6,650	30,167	148,825
1996	9,528	4,579,343	335,998	800,827	2,811,016	53,621	2,757,395	—	64,605	5,439	44,681	164,344
1997	9,143	5,014,884	355,120	871,870	2,970,667	54,718	2,915,949	—	67,178	4,454	61,673	180,015
1998	8,774	5,440,943	356,611	979,654	3,238,559	57,279	3,181,281	—	71,302	3,654	80,159	205,014

[1] Reports dated December 31 each year.

[2] Beginning in 1942, demand deposits due from and due to other banks exclude reciprocal interbank deposits.

[3] Beginning in 1984, obligations, other than securities, of states, counties, and municipalities are reported as loans.

[4] For 1934-1969, assets and liabilities are reported on a cash or cash accrual basis. For 1934-1973, assets and liabilities were reported on a domestic basis only. See text.

[5] For 1934-1963, includes federal funds sold. For 1934-1975, unearned income is not reflected in total loans but is included in other assets. For 1976-1997, represents total of all loans and leases net of unearned income.

[6] For 1948-1975, represents the reserve for bad debt losses on loans. See text.

[7] Items included in the series change in 1968, 1970, and 1984. See text.

[8] For 1934-1997, figure represents bank premises, furniture and equipment, net of depreciation. For 1934-1968, the value is reported net of mortgage indebtedness. Beginning in 1969, value is reported gross of mortgage indebtedness, which is included in other borrowed money (series Cj564).

Sources

Federal Deposit Insurance Corporation (FDIC), *Statistics on Banking: Historical, 1934–1994* (1995); FDIC, *Quarterly Reports* (various issues). These data and subsequent updates can be accessed through the FDIC's Internet site.

Documentation

The Federal Deposit Insurance Corporation was established in June 1933 to provide deposit insurance to depositors of member banks. All national banks and member banks of the Federal Reserve System are required by law to be members of the FDIC. Nonnational and non–Federal Reserve System banks may be admitted to FDIC membership upon meeting prescribed conditions. The FDIC is the principal federal regulator of those state-chartered banks that are not members of the Federal Reserve System and of state-chartered savings banks. The FDIC also retains secondary supervisory responsibility for the federally insured banks and savings associations. The FDIC's supervisory efforts consist of bank examinations as well as development and enforcement of regulations. These efforts are designed to identify poor management and avoid excessive risk taking by FDIC members.

The Financial Institutions Reform, Recovery, and Enforcement Act of 1989 (FIRREA) provided for the reform, recapitalization, and consolidation of the Federal Deposit Insurance System. The act created the Bank Insurance Fund (BIF), the Savings Association Insurance Fund (SAIF), and the Federal Savings and Loan Insurance Corporation Resolution Fund (FRF). The FDIC was made the administrator of these three funds, though each is administered separately. BIF members are predominantly commercial and savings banks supervised by the FDIC, the Comptroller of the Currency, and the Federal Reserve System. SAIF members are predominantly thrifts supervised by the Office of Thrift Supervision. FRF is responsible for winding up the affairs of the former Federal Savings and Loan Insurance Corporation and liquidating the assets and liabilities transferred from the former Resolution Trust Corporation.

Series Cj552. For 1934–1969, assets and liabilities are reported on a cash or cash accrual basis, depending on each bank's bookkeeping methods. For 1934–1973, assets and liabilities were reported on a domestic basis only. Net amounts due from foreign branches or branches located outside the fifty states (that is, Guam, Puerto Rico, Virgin Islands, and other U.S. territories and possessions) are included in all other assets (series Cj562). Net amounts due to foreign branches and other branches are included in all other liabilities (series Cj566).

Series Cj556. For 1948–1975, represents the reserve for bad debt losses on loans as permitted by Internal Revenue Service (IRS) ruling of December 8, 1947. Beginning 1976, the IRS reserve for bad debt losses on loans is divided into three categories as follows: (1) a "valuation" portion as an offset against gross loans, (2) a "deferred income tax portion" that is included in other liabilities (reported in series Cj566), and (3) a "contingency" portion included in undivided profits or reserve for contingencies (reported in series Cj570).

Series Cj558. For 1965–1967, includes only federal funds sold, which were previously included in loans. For 1968–1969, includes federal funds sold and securities sold under repurchase agreements; the latter were previously included in loans (series Cj555). For 1970–1983, includes federal funds sold, securities sold under repurchase agreements, and trading account securities; the latter were previously included in securities (series Cj554). For 1984–1997, includes federal funds sold, securities sold under repurchase agreements, trading accounts securities, and all other trading accounts assets, the last of which were reported in various asset categories.

TABLE Cj563–571   Insured commercial banks and trust companies – liabilities: 1934–1998[1]

Contributed by Howard Bodenhorn and Eugene N. White

	Liabilities				Equity capital				
						Stock			
	Total deposits	Borrowed funds	Subordinated notes	Other liabilities	Total	Preferred	Common	Surplus	Undivided profits
	Cj563	Cj564 [2]	Cj565 [3]	Cj566 [4]	Cj567	Cj568	Cj569	Cj570	Cj571 [5]
Year	Million dollars	Million dollars	Million dollars	Million dollars	Million dollars	Million dollars	Million dollars	Million dollars	Million dollars
1934	39,015	93	—	40,297	6,152	—	3,349	1,915	470
1935	44,147	66	—	44,716	6,209	—	3,300	1,946	547
1936	49,283	56	—	49,882	6,329	—	3,081	2,185	662
1937	47,224	49	—	47,808	6,404	—	3,030	2,268	704
1938	49,779	31	—	50,365	6,435	—	2,982	2,347	742
1939	56,076	14	—	56,622	6,524	—	2,914	2,443	789
1940	63,470	11	—	64,047	6,673	—	2,872	2,563	838
1941	69,421	10	—	69,985	6,842	—	2,849	2,686	895
1942	87,820	10	—	88,403	7,056	—	2,849	2,801	972
1943	104,116	45	—	104,792	7,454	—	2,875	3,090	1,006
1944	125,752	121	50	126,669	7,944	202	2,663	3,402	1,169
1945	174,811	215	43	148,953	8,629	153	2,839	3,785	1,291
1946	137,030	39	35	138,112	9,253	112	2,996	4,060	1,494
1947	141,889	61	30	143,067	9,706	87	3,079	4,316	1,649
1948	140,683	54	22	142,025	10,138	78	3,164	4,504	1,872
1949	143,194	14	22	144,692	10,627	69	3,305	4,803	1,953
1950	153,498	87	20	155,531	11,261	62	3,437	5,200	2,093
1951	163,172	38	18	165,544	11,904	51	3,631	5,504	2,258
1952	171,357	189	25	174,122	12,560	33	3,818	5,938	2,307
1953	175,083	59	22	177,820	13,242	30	3,979	6,284	2,498
1954	183,309	23	24	186,334	14,255	24	4,239	6,857	2,653
1955	190,989	150	30	194,166	14,980	20	4,518	7,209	2,777
1956	196,507	63	29	200,154	15,992	18	4,825	7,760	2,941
1957	200,485	68	28	204,476	17,059	18	5,124	8,242	3,232
1958	215,169	70	28	219,310	18,165	19	5,371	8,789	3,458
1959	219,012	609	26	224,217	19,205	17	5,818	9,276	3,631
1960	228,993	152	23	235,688	20,634	15	6,170	9,916	4,020
1961	247,905	462	22	255,273	22,101	15	6,585	10,798	4,157
1962	261,444	3,584	20	272,251	23,732	35	6,882	11,458	4,790
1963	274,647	3,577	130	286,598	25,192	38	7,283	12,163	5,112
1964	306,230	2,591	811	318,503	26,627	42	7,886	12,893	5,113
1965	331,513	4,337	1,653	347,142	28,252	40	8,508	13,465	5,438
1966	352,840	4,729	1,730	372,935	29,964	62	8,857	13,999	6,167
1967	395,796	5,549	1,984	418,629	32,018	87	9,254	14,983	6,607
1968	434,652	8,683	2,110	465,641	34,519	91	9,773	16,174	7,421
1969	436,990	18,654	1,998	486,958	37,688	103	10,529	17,461	8,428
1970	482,506	19,850	2,092	529,569	40,589	107	11,138	18,073	10,145
1971	539,184	26,312	2,956	589,511	44,062	92	11,811	19,896	11,135
1972	616,908	38,811	4,093	682,515	48,387	69	12,854	21,528	13,012
1973	681,619	58,432	4,117	771,130	53,829	66	13,846	23,593	15,362
1974	871,225	60,073	4,261	977,976	59,221	43	14,789	25,313	18,033
1975	915,856	61,317	4,422	1,022,820	63,854	48	15,565	26,706	20,565
1976	991,913	80,771	5,221	1,110,143	72,270	67	16,221	28,894	27,088
1977	1,116,618	97,510	5,831	1,260,112	79,264	99	17,265	31,085	30,815
1978	1,233,403	126,447	6,159	1,420,495	87,441	114	18,182	33,203	35,942
1979	1,362,805	154,023	6,253	1,594,548	97,241	126	20,274	35,329	41,512
1980	1,481,162	177,705	6,554	1,748,093	107,594	135	21,672	37,776	48,011
1981	1,588,782	211,798	6,460	1,910,679	118,303	171	23,557	40,301	54,274
1982	1,705,689	237,593	7,330	2,064,506	128,833	316	24,729	43,229	60,559
1983	1,842,503	236,380	7,093	2,201,564	140,537	664	25,723	47,894	66,256
1984	1,962,935	261,260	10,204	2,354,767	154,103	818	28,082	53,004	72,199
1985	2,118,088	320,432	14,659	2,561,554	169,117	994	29,142	58,737	80,245
1986	2,283,527	358,970	16,941	2,758,556	182,143	1,394	29,574	63,991	87,183
1987	2,335,441	361,767	17,614	2,819,298	180,651	1,682	30,165	70,594	78,210
1988	2,431,735	381,411	16,862	2,934,250	196,546	1,771	30,160	75,326	89,289
1989	2,548,505	419,092	19,774	3,094,540	204,822	1,557	30,537	82,150	90,578

Notes appear at end of table

(continued)

TABLE Cj563–571   Insured commercial banks and trust companies – liabilities: 1934–1998 *Continued*

	Liabilities				Equity capital				
			Subordinated notes	Other liabilities	Total	Stock		Surplus	Undivided profits
	Total deposits	Borrowed funds				Preferred	Common		
	Cj563	Cj564 [2]	Cj565 [3]	Cj566 [4]	Cj567	Cj568	Cj569	Cj570	Cj571 [5]
Year	Million dollars	Million dollars	Million dollars	Million dollars	Million dollars	Million dollars	Million dollars	Million dollars	Million dollars
1990	2,650,131	385,292	23,920	3,170,854	218,616	1,673	30,858	92,382	93,703
1991	2,687,622	379,726	24,962	3,198,942	231,698	1,524	31,260	101,522	97,392
1992	2,698,691	406,671	33,731	3,242,271	263,403	1,610	32,130	117,352	112,311
1993	2,754,332	497,888	37,372	3,409,666	296,523	1,523	32,869	126,508	135,623
1994	2,874,351	681,015	40,747	3,698,477	312,187	1,505	34,634	136,024	140,024
1995	3,027,553	770,098	43,536	3,963,018	349,661	1,836	35,857	146,809	166,153
1996	3,197,234	828,585	51,177	4,203,047	375,295	2,011	35,099	167,664	171,633
1997	3,421,696	977,319	61,989	4,596,989	417,896	2,384	34,423	190,658	191,792
1998	3,681,523	1,135,262	72,787	4,978,718	462,225	2,699	34,969	217,446	208,481

[1] Reports dated December 31 each year.

[2] For 1934–1968, does not include mortgage indebtedness, which is charged against bank premises. Beginning 1969, this represents federal funds purchased, securities sold under repurchase agreements, demand notes issued to the U.S. Treasury, mortgage indebtedness, liabilities under capitalized leases, and all other liabilities for borrowed money.

[3] For 1934–1943, does not include capital notes and debentures, which are included in common stock. Beginning in 1944, represents all notes and debentures subordinated to deposits, and all capital notes and debentures.

[4] In 1934, includes bank notes outstanding; 1980–1984, includes limited life preferred stock.

[5] For 1984–1990, includes foreign currency translation adjustment account.

Sources

Federal Deposit Insurance Corporation (FDIC), *Statistics on Banking: Historical, 1934–1994*; FDIC, *Quarterly Reports* (various issues). These data and subsequent updates can be accessed through the FDIC's Internet site.

Documentation

For a description of the FDIC, see text for Table Cj551–562.

TABLE Cj572–580   Insured commercial banks and trust companies – number and income: 1934–1998

Contributed by Howard Bodenhorn and Eugene N. White

			Interest income				Noninterest income			
	Banks	Total	Loans and leases		Investment securities	Total	Services charges on deposit accounts	Capital gains (losses) on securities	Net income
			Domestic offices	Foreign offices					
	Cj572	Cj573	Cj574	Cj575	Cj576	Cj577	Cj578	Cj579	Cj580
Year	Number	Million dollars	Million dollars	Million dollars	Million dollars	Million dollars	Million dollars	Million dollars	Million dollars
1934	14,146	1,241	691	—	550	470	—	−377	−357
1935	14,125	1,191	643	—	548	583	—	−211	174
1936	13,973	1,237	663	—	574	505	—	113	490
1937	13,797	1,282	710	—	572	410	—	−59	357
1938	13,661	1,237	705	—	532	409	—	−49	281
1939	13,538	1,249	727	—	522	423	—	0	370
1940	13,442	1,268	769	—	500	436	—	−15	383
1941	13,430	1,357	848	—	509	446	—	−16	436
1942	13,347	1,427	817	—	610	420	84	−54	426
1943	13,274	1,567	706	—	861	484	95	−13	623
1944	13,268	1,788	698	—	1,090	519	107	19	736
1945	13,302	2,027	727	—	1,300	578	110	134	894
1946	13,359	2,346	951	—	1,395	576	125	76	894
1947	13,403	2,541	1,282	—	1,259	602	148	−18	775
1948	13,419	2,798	1,600	—	1,198	642	174	−19	941
1949	13,436	2,975	1,760	—	1,215	651	194	35	968
1950	13,446	3,249	2,008	—	1,241	700	212	52	1,072
1951	13,455	3,658	2,425	—	1,233	755	231	−27	1,047
1952	13,439	4,160	2,784	—	1,376	787	245	−64	1,067
1953	13,432	4,660	3,156	—	1,505	837	271	−117	1,070
1954	13,323	4,861	3,263	—	1,598	931	312	350	1,473
1955	13,237	5,381	3,697	—	1,685	1,020	340	−164	1,320
1956	13,218	6,126	4,413	—	1,713	1,122	385	−286	1,476
1957	13,165	6,818	4,963	—	1,855	1,244	441	−173	1,578
1958	13,124	7,187	5,141	—	2,046	1,334	487	588	2,082
1959	13,114	8,247	5,969	—	2,278	1,456	532	−698	1,553
1960	13,126	9,176	6,807	—	2,369	1,578	590	110	2,251
1961	13,115	9,540	7,009	—	2,531	1,550	630	409	2,374
1962	13,124	10,570	7,718	—	2,852	1,660	681	198	2,348
1963	13,291	11,770	8,672	—	3,098	1,750	729	118	2,393
1964	13,493	13,111	9,785	—	3,326	1,925	781	−14	2,602
1965	13,547	14,715	11,205	—	3,510	2,114	843	0	2,861
1966	13,538	17,136	13,286	—	3,849	2,373	915	−392	3,040
1967	13,514	19,152	14,647	—	4,505	2,626	986	−21	3,509
1968	13,487	22,501	17,121	—	5,308	2,975	1,055	−457	3,786
1969	13,473	27,285	20,728	—	5,745	3,520	1,120	−237	4,334
1970	13,511	30,513	22,969	—	6,538	4,202	1,178	−104	4,837
1971	13,612	31,628	23,079	—	7,678	4,747	1,231	213	5,236
1972	13,733	35,030	25,645	—	8,358	5,220	1,262	92	5,656
1973	13,976	47,034	35,373	—	9,174	6,000	1,327	−27	6,582
1974	14,230	61,218	47,126	—	10,380	6,926	1,460	−87	7,079
1975	14,384	57,915	43,380	—	12,242	8,643	1,555	37	7,255
1976	14,410	73,033	51,645	—	14,382	7,631	1,635	312	7,843
1977	14,411	82,252	58,991	—	15,198	8,106	1,807	142	8,879
1978	14,391	103,957	76,182	—	16,518	9,625	2,049	−447	10,759
1979	14,364	138,901	102,192	—	18,839	11,381	2,529	−650	12,838
1980	14,434	176,420	126,954	—	23,075	14,348	3,187	−854	14,010
1981	14,414	231,271	128,658	34,846	29,452	17,525	3,921	−1,583	14,803
1982	14,451	238,315	136,147	31,049	33,514	20,176	4,594	−1,280	14,996
1983	14,469	217,226	128,245	23,724	36,992	23,269	5,429	−21	14,931
1984	14,496	250,350	147,517	33,623	37,136	26,515	6,554	−140	15,502
1985	14,417	248,220	151,364	29,884	37,739	31,054	7,374	1,565	17,977
1986	14,210	237,765	148,998	24,161	38,363	35,877	7,962	3,951	17,418
1987	13,723	244,839	154,680	22,736	39,416	41,481	8,719	1,427	2,803
1988	11,137	272,277	170,972	26,906	42,038	44,953	9,434	279	24,812
1989	12,715	317,371	201,832	32,142	46,784	50,916	10,267	801	15,575

(continued)

TABLE Cj572–580   Insured commercial banks and trust companies – number and income: 1934–1998 *Continued*

Year	Banks	Interest income Total	Loans and leases Domestic offices	Loans and leases Foreign offices	Investment securities	Noninterest income Total	Services charges on deposit accounts	Capital gains (losses) on securities	Net income
	Cj572	Cj573	Cj574	Cj575	Cj576	Cj577	Cj578	Cj579	Cj580
	Number	Million dollars	Million dollars	Million dollars	Million dollars	Million dollars	Million dollars	Million dollars	Million dollars
1990	11,927	320,476	203,658	30,749	51,126	54,899	11,439	481	15,991
1991	11,433	289,214	185,539	24,206	52,535	59,739	12,814	2,972	17,935
1992	10,433	255,224	157,538	23,388	51,936	65,620	13,978	4,006	31,987
1993	10,960	245,058	150,221	24,942	48,883	74,961	14,919	3,061	43,069
1994	10,451	257,843	163,970	23,148	48,585	76,222	15,337	−570	44,680
1995	9,941	302,663	200,106	23,349	51,213	82,440	16,046	545	48,836
1996	11,452	385,078	208,691	25,522	50,694	101,081	16,937	2,016	59,398
1997	9,143	339,554	226,447	23,314	52,844	104,500	18,546	1,843	59,236
1998	8,774	362,073	237,922	26,943	57,040	123,745	19,803	3,127	61,921

Sources

Federal Deposit Insurance Corporation (FDIC), *Statistics on Banking: Historical, 1934–1994;* FDIC, *Quarterly Reports* (various issues). More detailed income accounts are reported in the original sources, and updates can be accessed through the FDIC's Internet site.

Documentation

All data apply to calendar years.

Interest income on loans and leases in domestic and foreign offices of FDIC-insured commercial banks includes all interest charges, commitment fees, and service charges associated with assets generally classified as loans. Interest and fees on loans in foreign offices are not available prior to 1984. Similarly, interest income on investment securities represents interest and dividends, net of premium amortization and discount accretion, on all assets considered investment securities.

Noninterest income on deposits represents service charges – such as maintenance fees, activity charges, administrative charges, overdraft charges, and check certification charges – on deposit accounts in domestic offices. All other noninterest income includes income from fiduciary activities, gains and losses and fees related to foreign currency and foreign exchange transactions, net gains from the sale of loans or premises and other real estate, fees charges on bank-issued credit cards, net gains on forward and futures contracts, and other miscellaneous income. Unfortunately, the FDIC sources do not report these amounts in finer categories. It should be noted, however, that total noninterest income represented about 25 percent of total bank income in 1934, fell through the 1970s to about 15 percent of total bank income, and began increasing thereafter. By 1997, noninterest income once again represented about 25 percent of bank income.

TABLE Cj581–590 Insured commercial banks and trust companies – expenses: 1934–1998

Contributed by Howard Bodenhorn and Eugene N. White

		Interest expenses					Noninterest expenses			
		Interest on deposits		Federal funds purchased and securities sold	Borrowed money	Subordinated notes and debentures		Employee salaries and benefits	Provision for loan and lease losses	Income taxes
	Total	Domestic offices	Foreign offices				Total			
	Cj581	Cj582	Cj583	Cj584	Cj585	Cj586	Cj587	Cj588	Cj589	Cj590
Year	Million dollars	Million dollars	Million dollars	Million dollars	Million dollars	Million dollars	Million dollars	Million dollars	Million dollars	Million dollars
1934	328	303	—	—	7	18	836	402	500	—
1935	298	262	—	—	3	33	854	411	237	—
1936	273	237	—	—	2	35	950	427	140	2
1937	261	235	—	—	1	24	958	452	52	5
1938	250	230	—	—	1	19	968	462	94	4
1939	234	215	—	—	1	18	992	471	71	5
1940	219	201	—	—	0	17	1,033	485	48	6
1941	208	190	—	—	0	18	1,102	514	32	8
1942	190	175	—	—	0	15	1,085	553	12	80
1943	179	164	—	—	1	14	1,118	582	−10	128
1944	202	187	—	—	1	14	1,199	627	−14	203
1945	248	233	—	—	2	12	1,309	691	−11	299
1946	279	269	—	—	2	8	1,505	831	−3	323
1947	307	298	—	—	3	6	1,687	947	53	302
1948	325	317	—	—	3	5	1,852	1,044	28	275
1949	337	328	—	—	4	5	1,971	1,111	59	325
1950	352	343	—	—	4	4	2,120	1,202	29	428
1951	399	385	—	—	10	4	2,345	1,351	35	559
1952	483	458	—	—	21	4	2,603	1,495	35	695
1953	562	534	—	—	24	3	2,902	1,652	59	786
1954	630	618	—	—	9	3	3,087	1,762	44	908
1955	704	678	—	—	23	3	3,370	1,896	49	794
1956	854	806	—	—	45	2	3,725	2,093	92	815
1957	1,193	1,142	—	—	50	2	4,047	2,268	72	998
1958	1,407	1,381	—	—	24	2	4,286	2,400	61	1,271
1959	1,662	1,580	—	—	79	2	4,853	2,577	53	884
1960	1,874	1,785	—	—	87	2	5,142	2,798	206	1,384
1961	2,146	2,107	—	—	38	2	5,383	3,276	190	1,406
1962	2,911	2,845	—	—	64	2	5,746	3,493	167	1,256
1963	3,574	3,464	—	—	107	3	6,206	3,741	238	1,227
1964	4,241	4,088	—	—	127	26	6,780	4,010	251	1,148
1965	5,316	5,071	—	—	190	56	7,298	4,288	324	1,029
1966	6,628	6,259	—	—	301	67	8,001	4,694	417	1,030
1967	7,734	7,383	—	—	267	84	8,903	5,204	434	1,177
1968	9,315	8,685	—	—	529	101	10,140	5,856	512	1,266
1969	11,533	9,793	—	1,206	433	101	12,024	6,782	521	2,164
1970	12,456	10,486	—	1,401	464	105	14,428	7,716	703	2,173
1971	13,603	12,225	—	1,096	140	142	15,191	8,397	868	1,689
1972	15,603	13,845	—	1,429	114	214	16,423	9,086	972	1,708
1973	24,489	19,833	—	3,899	503	254	18,571	10,127	1,264	2,122
1974	35,071	27,886	—	5,986	916	283	21,545	11,585	2,290	2,084
1975	30,240	26,246	—	3,323	377	294	23,729	12,687	3,612	1,793
1976	39,328	26,254	8,750	3,312	667	345	27,731	14,751	3,691	2,409
1977	44,565	28,596	10,216	4,543	818	392	30,925	16,346	3,303	2,875
1978	59,383	35,655	14,558	7,264	1,458	448	35,573	18,744	3,526	3,940
1979	87,912	47,364	24,524	12,356	3,167	501	40,692	21,562	3,785	4,442
1980	120,122	63,478	34,941	16,770	4,387	546	46,662	24,673	4,478	4,658
1981	169,840	92,706	46,735	23,878	5,904	617	53,658	28,044	5,066	3,904
1982	169,343	99,994	41,746	20,747	6,218	661	61,531	31,424	8,342	3,037
1983	143,887	91,386	29,022	16,497	6,293	689	66,909	33,877	10,802	4,017
1984	169,084	104,670	35,782	19,479	8,353	801	73,817	36,887	13,816	4,721
1985	157,323	100,683	30,129	16,623	8,785	1,103	82,365	40,003	17,774	5,629
1986	142,829	93,078	24,484	15,923	8,034	1,310	90,250	42,920	22,106	5,266
1987	144,953	89,701	25,998	15,841	11,996	1,417	97,244	45,183	37,544	5,404
1988	165,028	101,048	28,448	18,657	15,404	1,471	101,330	46,560	17,163	9,988
1989	205,142	123,945	33,610	24,900	20,963	1,724	108,121	49,166	31,020	9,540

(continued)

TABLE Cj581–590   Insured commercial banks and trust companies – expenses: 1934–1998 *Continued*

	Interest expenses						Noninterest expenses			
		Interest on deposits		Federal funds purchased and securities sold	Borrowed money	Subordinated notes and debentures		Employee salaries and benefits	Provision for loan and lease losses	Income taxes
	Total	Domestic offices	Foreign offices				Total			
	Cj581	Cj582	Cj583	Cj584	Cj585	Cj586	Cj587	Cj588	Cj589	Cj590
Year	Million dollars	Million dollars	Million dollars	Million dollars	Million dollars	Million dollars	Million dollars	Million dollars	Million dollars	Million dollars
1990	204,952	127,439	34,085	22,744	18,919	1,765	115,768	51,765	32,088	7,704
1991	167,302	113,287	25,168	14,325	12,462	2,060	124,794	53,111	34,314	8,265
1992	121,805	76,885	21,326	9,268	12,464	1,862	130,965	54,802	26,048	14,481
1993	105,742	59,171	20,423	8,486	15,498	2,164	139,689	58,189	16,812	19,838
1994	111,266	59,272	20,135	12,590	16,806	2,463	144,196	60,600	10,912	22,426
1995	148,441	79,404	25,977	18,548	21,050	3,193	149,670	63,440	12,550	26,176
1996	192,188	82,935	24,457	16,761	22,309	3,540	160,697	67,046	18,746	31,297
1997	165,039	90,760	26,538	20,633	23,073	4,035	169,958	71,768	19,785	31,898
1998	179,291	95,304	29,986	22,433	26,780	3,249	194,047	79,098	22,209	31,986

Sources

Federal Deposit Insurance Corporation (FDIC), *Statistics on Banking: Historical, 1934–1994*; FDIC, *Quarterly Reports* (various issues). These data and subsequent updates can be accessed through the FDIC's Internet site.

Documentation

All data apply to calendar years.

The FDIC adjusted historical amounts to reflect current definitions and reporting requirements. Interest on deposits in domestic and foreign offices (series Cj582–583) represents all payments on liabilities reportable as deposits, which may include finders' and brokers' fees that represent an added expense on deposits acquired through brokers. Early withdrawal penalties that represent forfeiture of interest are deducted from gross interest paid. Before 1976, interest expenses at foreign offices are not available, as banks were required to report on domestic operations only. Interest expenses on borrowed money, series Cj585, represent expenses related to demand notes issued to the U.S. Treasury, mortgage indebtedness, obligations on capitalized leases, and other borrowed money.

Employee salaries and benefits, series Cj588, include salaries, benefits, and taxes paid on behalf of all officers and employees of the banks and their subsidiaries, including guards, temporary office help, and building and maintenance employees. In 1934 and 1935, the series includes fees paid to directors and committee members, as well as professional fees, which were subsequently included in noninterest expenses other than salaries and benefits. Before 1968, the difference between total noninterest expenses (series Cj587) and salaries and benefits (series Cj588) includes net losses and charge-offs on assets other than loans and securities and additions to valuation allowances (other than those related to loans and securities). Beginning in 1969, the difference is made up of fees paid to directors, trustees, and advisory boards; deposit insurance premiums; retainer and other legal fees; net losses from the sale or disposition of loans, premises, and fixed assets; management fees assessed by parent bank holding companies; advertising and promotional expenses; amortization of intangible assets; charitable contributions; net losses on forward and futures contracts; office supplies; telephone expenses; examination and audit fees; and other miscellaneous expenses.

TABLE Cj591–611 Banks – number and assets, by deposit insurance status and type of bank: 1934–1998[1]
Contributed by Howard Bodenhorn and Eugene N. White

	All banks					Commercial banks				
	Insured		Noninsured			Insured				
									Member banks	
	Number	Assets	Number	Assets	Number	Domestic assets	Domestic and foreign assets	Number	Domestic assets	Domestic and foreign assets
	Cj591 [2]	Cj592	Cj593	Cj594	Cj595	Cj596	Cj597	Cj598	Cj599	Cj600
Year	Number	Million dollars	Number	Million dollars	Number	Million dollars	Million dollars	Number	Million dollars	Million dollars
1934	14,150	50,946	1,807	5,149	13,915	43,449	—	6,375	37,383	—
1935	14,242	48,468	1,849	11,672	14,179	47,273	—	6,410	40,719	—
1936	14,121	54,718	1,807	12,343	14,065	53,596	—	6,400	46,524	—
1937	13,943	56,047	1,744	12,585	13,887	54,908	—	6,357	47,452	—
1938	13,783	55,520	1,676	12,449	13,727	54,383	—	6,338	47,144	—
1939	13,621	60,832	1,630	12,604	13,572	59,439	—	6,330	51,908	—
1940	13,534	67,187	1,585	12,825	13,483	65,602	—	6,398	57,846	—
1941	13,479	74,976	1,540	12,679	13,426	72,997	—	6,553	64,848	—
1942	13,456	80,765	1,474	11,582	13,403	78,709	—	6,644	69,937	—
1943	13,363	105,414	1,411	11,927	13,302	102,405	—	6,700	90,811	—
1944	13,461	131,766	1,254	7,894	13,269	122,646	—	6,770	108,670	—
1945	13,474	154,115	1,228	9,010	13,282	143,457	—	6,837	126,421	—
1946	13,526	162,881	1,203	9,646	13,335	150,743	—	6,884	131,384	—
1947	13,582	157,542	1,179	9,747	13,091	144,373	—	6,925	124,779	—
1948	13,613	161,177	1,154	9,805	13,420	147,244	—	6,922	127,280	—
1949	13,614	161,888	1,109	9,788	13,423	147,216	—	6,900	127,241	—
1950	13,641	170,364	1,077	9,679	13,449	154,701	—	6,882	133,724	—
1951	13,652	179,946	1,026	9,309	13,451	163,351	—	6,856	141,592	—
1952	13,655	193,222	983	9,547	13,450	175,339	—	6,812	151,519	—
1953	13,648	199,176	926	9,579	13,440	179,586	—	6,762	154,235	—
1954	13,619	209,880	888	10,038	13,400	188,643	—	6,718	162,179	—
1955	13,505	220,327	845	10,359	13,287	197,566	—	6,607 [4]	169,660	—
1956	13,449	228,524	798	10,743	13,229	177,253	—	6,495 [4]	147,793	—
1957	13,445	233,423	739	10,432	13,211	207,182	—	6,441 [4]	176,479	—
1958	13,383	255,645	712	10,216	13,144	226,624	—	6,353	193,974	—
1959	13,348	263,714	663	9,594	13,097	232,486	—	6,276	197,234	—
1960	13,415	273,540	604	9,331	13,147	241,329	—	6,214	204,146	—
1961	13,461	288,706	528	7,740	13,136	252,632	—	6,139	213,704	—
1962	13,442	313,496	505	8,134	13,111	275,130	—	6,068	232,343	—
1963	13,527	340,389	479	8,694	13,196	298,808	—	6,056	251,201	—
1964	13,728	366,106	461	9,243	13,401	321,084	—	6,179	269,425	—
1965	13,862	401,601	448	10,891	13,535	352,795	—	6,234	296,037	—
1966	13,891	436,359	437	11,429	13,559	384,908	—	6,193	321,817	—
1967	13,867	467,727	400	11,863	13,533	411,916	—	6,107	342,905	—
1968	13,851	516,434	394	13,172	13,519	456,304	—	6,038	378,599	—
1969	13,806	580,323	388	14,219	13,473	516,579	—	5,937	426,377	—
1970	13,818	596,027	369	15,278	13,487	529,911	—	5,804	431,543	—
1971	13,874	670,171	346	15,774	13,547	595,818	—	5,736	482,761	—
1972	14,201	745,281	369	18,505	13,875	661,837	—	5,714	530,064	—
1973	14,163	853,966	364	21,977	13,839	762,077	—	5,705	604,789	—
1974	14,428	966,663	389	26,666	14,108	871,985	—	5,761	692,528	—
1975	14,655	1,017,056	420	30,857	14,332	914,783	—	5,796	716,624	—
1976	14,721	1,056,526	416	35,715	14,393	942,512	—	5,776	728,344	—
1977	14,750	1,168,143	437	48,000	14,441	1,048,911	—	5,720	795,199	—
1978	14,719	1,319,303	389	60,674	14,395	1,181,635	—	5,621	893,037	—
1979	14,689	1,168,424	503	48,393	14,367	1,317,902	1,574,174	5,477	990,213	1,244,777
1980	14,733	1,590,754	395	18,709	14,408	1,440,377	1,745,179	5,403	1,071,826	1,373,925
1981	—	—	—	—	14,458	—	1,927,371	5,467	—	1,512,624
1982	—	—	—	—	14,435	—	2,068,100	5,515	—	1,616,190
1983	—	—	—	—	14,455	—	2,232,405	5,712	—	1,739,809
1984	—	—	—	—	14,456	—	2,411,000	5,878	—	1,880,353
1985	—	—	—	—	14,472	—	2,571,000	6,032	—	1,996,912
1986	—	—	—	—	14,312	—	2,774,000	5,999	—	2,152,595
1987	—	—	—	—	13,947	—	2,913,000	5,839	—	2,243,004
1988	—	—	—	—	13,412	—	3,056,000	5,552	—	2,342,457
1989	—	—	—	—	12,945	—	3,207,000	5,323	—	2,448,199

Notes appear at end of table

(continued)

TABLE Cj591–611   Banks – number and assets, by deposit insurance status and type of bank: 1934–1998 *Continued*

	All banks				Commercial banks					
	Insured		Noninsured		Insured					
									Member banks	
	Number	Assets	Number	Assets	Number	Domestic assets	Domestic and foreign assets	Number	Domestic assets	Domestic and foreign assets
	Cj591 [2]	Cj592	Cj593	Cj594	Cj595	Cj596	Cj597	Cj598	Cj599	Cj600
Year	Number	Million dollars	Number	Million dollars	Number	Million dollars	Million dollars	Number	Million dollars	Million dollars
1990	—	—	—	—	12,505	—	3,361,000	5,080	—	2,550,473
1991	—	—	—	—	12,154	—	3,377,000	4,904	—	2,537,803
1992	—	—	—	—	11,686	—	3,438,000	4,650	—	2,586,440
1993	—	—	—	—	11,199	—	3,569,000	4,414	—	2,711,800
1994	—	—	—	—	10,717	—	3,893,000	4,155	—	3,005,576
1995	—	—	—	—	10,169	—	4,171,000	3,940	—	3,243,632
1996	—	—	—	—	9,690	—	4,397,000	3,787	—	3,489,268
1997	—	—	—	—	9,308	—	4,771,000	3,648	—	3,891,513
1998	—	—	—	—	8,983	—	5,181,000	3,535	—	4,273,870

	Commercial banks					Mutual savings banks				All savings institutions – insured	
	Insured		Noninsured nonmember			Insured		Noninsured			
	Nonmember banks										
	Number	Domestic assets	Domestic and foreign assets	Number	Assets	Number	Assets	Number	Assets	Number	Domestic and foreign assets
	Cj601	Cj602	Cj603	Cj604	Cj605	Cj606 [3]	Cj607	Cj608 [3]	Cj609	Cj610	Cj611
Year	Number	Million dollars	Million dollars	Number	Million dollars	Number	Million dollars	Number	Million dollars	Number	Million dollars
1934	7,540	6,066	—	1,476	1,708	235	7,497	331	3,441	—	—
1935	7,769	6,554	—	1,352	1,821	63	1,195	497	9,851	—	—
1936	7,665	7,072	—	1,307	2,182	56	1,122	500	10,161	—	—
1937	7,530	7,456	—	1,247	2,228	56	1,139	498	10,357	—	—
1938	7,389	7,239	—	1,179	2,041	56	1,137	497	10,408	—	—
1939	7,242	7,531	—	1,135	2,226	49	1,393	495	10,378	—	—
1940	7,085	7,756	—	1,093	2,485	51	1,585	492	10,340	—	—
1941	6,873	8,149	—	1,051	2,689	53	1,979	489	9,990	—	—
1942	6,759	8,772	—	988	1,983	53	2,056	486	9,599	—	—
1943	6,602	11,594	—	934	2,529	61	3,009	477	9,398	—	—
1944	6,499	13,976	—	909	3,203	192	9,119	345	4,691	—	—
1945	6,445	17,036	—	885	3,744	192	10,658	343	5,266	—	—
1946	6,451	19,359	—	860	3,763	191	12,138	343	5,883	—	—
1947	6,466	19,594	—	836	3,554	191	13,169	343	6,193	—	—
1948	6,498	19,964	—	814	3,485	193	13,933	340	6,320	—	—
1949	6,523	19,975	—	769	3,355	191	14,672	340	6,433	—	—
1950	6,567	20,977	—	738	3,090	192	15,663	339	6,589	—	—
1951	6,595	21,759	—	697	3,069	201	16,595	329	6,240	—	—
1952	6,638	23,820	—	658	3,052	205	17,883	325	6,495	—	—
1953	6,678	25,351	—	610	2,836	213	19,590	316	6,743	—	—
1954	6,682	26,464	—	578	2,960	219	21,237	310	7,078	—	—
1955	6,680	27,906	—	534	2,738	218	22,761	311	7,621	—	—
1956	6,734	29,460	—	490	2,593	220	24,271	308	8,150	—	—
1957	6,770	30,703	—	447	2,419	234	26,241	292	8,013	—	—
1958	6,791	32,650	—	430	2,558	239	29,021	282	7,657	—	—
1959	6,821	35,252	—	395	2,295	251	31,228	268	7,299	—	—
1960	6,933	37,183	—	356	1,944	268	32,211	248	7,387	—	—
1961	6,997	38,928	—	338	1,995	325	36,074	190	5,744	—	—
1962	7,043	42,787	—	323	2,081	331	38,366	182	6,052	—	—
1963	7,140	47,607	—	298	2,254	331	41,580	181	6,441	—	—
1964	7,222	51,659	—	281	2,266	327	45,022	180	6,978	—	—
1965	7,301	56,758	—	270	3,315	327	48,806	178	7,577	—	—
1966	7,366	63,091	—	262	3,465	332	51,452	175	7,965	—	—
1967	7,426	69,011	—	229	3,520	334	55,810	171	8,343	—	—
1968	7,481	77,705	—	224	4,271	332	60,130	170	8,901	—	—
1969	7,536	90,202	—	221	4,664	333	63,745	167	9,555	—	—

Notes appear at end of table

TABLE Cj591–611   Banks – number and assets, by deposit insurance status and type of bank: 1934–1998   *Continued*

	Commercial banks						Mutual savings banks				All savings institutions – insured	
	Insured			Noninsured nonmember			Insured		Noninsured			
	Nonmember banks											
	Number	Domestic assets	Domestic and foreign assets	Number	Assets		Number	Assets	Number	Assets	Number	Domestic and foreign assets
	Cj601	Cj602	Cj603	Cj604	Cj605		Cj606 [3]	Cj607	Cj608 [3]	Cj609	Cj610	Cj611
Year	Number	Million dollars	Million dollars	Number	Million dollars		Number	Million dollars	Number	Million dollars	Number	Million dollars
1970	7,683	98,368	—	203	5,021		331	66,116	166	10,257	—	—
1971	7,811	113,057	—	182	4,356		327	74,353	164	11,418	—	—
1972	8,161	131,773	—	206	5,884		326	83,444	163	12,621	—	—
1973	8,134	157,288	—	204	8,196		324	91,889	160	13,781	—	—
1974	8,347	179,457	—	229	12,769		320	94,678	160	13,897	—	—
1975	8,536	198,159	—	265	16,356		323	102,273	155	14,501	—	—
1976	8,617	214,168	—	270	21,272		328	114,014	146	14,443	—	—
1977	8,705	245,753	—	293	33,390		325	127,191	144	14,610	—	—
1978	8,774	288,598	—	246	45,176		324	137,668	143	15,498	—	—
1979	8,881	327,689	329,397	363	36,672		322	145,522	140	11,721	—	—
1980	8,995	368,551	371,254	256	6,260		325	150,377	139	12,449	—	—
1981	8,978	—	414,747	—	—		336	—	118	—	—	—
1982	8,881	—	451,910	—	—		325	—	105	—	—	—
1983	8,743	—	492,596	—	—		297	—	—	—	—	—
1984	8,578	—	531,051	—	—		294	—	—	—	3,435	1,068,294
1985	8,440	—	574,424	—	—		290	—	96	—	3,464	1,187,000
1986	8,313	—	621,494	—	—		468	—	3	—	3,704	1,332,000
1987	8,108	—	669,620	—	—		480	—	—	—	3,658	1,441,000
1988	7,860	—	713,407	—	—		492	—	—	—	3,581	1,556,000
1989	7,622	—	758,690	—	—		491	—	—	—	3,197	1,511,000
1990	7,425	—	810,968	—	—		479	—	—	—	2,930	1,317,000
1991	7,250	—	839,511	—	—		468	—	—	—	2,684	1,161,000
1992	7,036	—	851,822	—	—		477	—	—	—	2,489	1,078,000
1993	6,785	—	857,569	—	—		576	—	—	—	2,314	1,004,000
1994	6,560	—	886,947	—	—		623	—	—	—	2,216	999,000
1995	6,228	—	927,074	—	—		625	—	—	—	2,082	1,017,000
1996	5,902	—	907,578	—	—		—	—	—	—	1,980	1,023,000
1997	5,660	—	879,649	—	—		—	—	—	—	1,852	1,029,000
1998	5,449	—	908,889	—	—		—	—	—	—	1,729	1,126,000

[1] Reports dated on or about June 30 each year.

[2] For 1969–1980, loans and securities are stated on a gross basis in total assets of commercial banks. Total loans were calculated net prior to 1969.

[3] Beginning in 1986, mutual savings banks include all Bank Insurance Fund–insured savings banks as well as the state-chartered Savings Association Insured Fund–insured savings banks that were regulated by the Federal Deposit Insurance Corporation.

[4] Figures for member commercial banks exclude, and figures for noninsured nonmember commercial banks include, one member nondeposit trust company that is not insured by the Federal Deposit Insurance Corporation.

Sources

1934–1970: U.S. Bureau of the Census, *Historical Statistics of the United States,* Bicentennial Edition (1975), pp. 1023–4; 1970–1980: Federal Deposit Insurance Corporation (FDIC), *Annual Report* (various issues). The sources reported for the 1934–1970 data were as follows: 1934–1955: Board of Governors of the Federal Reserve System, unpublished data (compiled in connection with *All-Bank Statistics, United States, 1896–1955*); 1956–1970: FDIC, *Annual Reports* and *Report of Call: Assets, Liabilities, and Capital Accounts – Commercial and Mutual Savings Banks* (June issues), and unpublished data.

For all series for the years 1971–1980 and for series Cj606 and Cj608 for 1971–1995, data were obtained from the FDIC, *Assets and Liabilities* and *Statistics on Banking* (various issues). The consolidated assets reported in series Cj597, Cj600, Cj603, and Cj611 for 1979–1980 and all series for 1981–1993 were obtained directly from unpublished FDIC sources. The data for 1994–1998 are from the FDIC Internet site, Statistics on Banking.

Documentation

Savings institutions include all mutual savings banks and the savings and loans associations now insured by the FDIC.

Series Cj595–609. Comparability of figures for classes of banks is affected somewhat by changes in Federal Reserve System membership, deposit insurance status, and reserve classifications of cities and individual banks and by mergers and so forth.

Series Cj595–596, Cj598–599, Cj601–602, and Cj604–609. Member commercial banks exclude, and mutual savings banks include, mutual savings banks that are members of the Federal Reserve System, as follows: three for 1941–1959; two in 1960; and one for 1961–1970.

TABLE Cj612–620   Insured commercial banks – number, branches, and offices: 1934–1998[1]

Contributed by Howard Bodenhorn and Eugene N. White

				Additions		Deletions			
							Failures		
	Banks	Offices	Branches	New charters	Conversions	Unassisted mergers	Mergers	Paid off	Other
	Cj612	Cj613	Cj614	Cj615	Cj616	Cj617	Cj618	Cj619	Cj620
Year	Number	Number	Number	Number	Number	Number	Number	Number	Number
1934	14,146	14,146	—	1,220	740	335	0	9	23
1935	14,125	17,237	3,112	45	197	153	0	26	84
1936	13,973	17,234	3,261	32	52	139	22	40	35
1937	13,797	17,178	3,381	46	36	150	20	50	38
1938	13,661	17,073	3,412	22	26	72	22	48	42
1939	13,538	16,994	3,456	26	18	90	20	32	25
1940	13,442	16,931	3,489	28	20	72	20	19	33
1941	13,430	16,947	3,517	37	33	45	6	6	25
1942	13,347	16,902	3,555	15	21	63	13	6	37
1943	13,274	17,017	3,744	36	16	76	1	4	44
1944	13,268	17,142	3,875	56	35	66	1	1	29
1945	13,302	17,198	3,896	101	21	72	0	0	16
1946	13,359	17,287	3,928	130	31	88	1	0	15
1947	13,402	17,499	4,096	99	29	74	3	0	7
1948	13,419	17,702	4,283	61	34	69	2	0	8
1949	13,436	17,966	4,530	58	41	73	4	0	5
1950	13,446	18,278	4,832	58	47	84	4	0	7
1951	13,455	18,612	5,157	51	34	70	2	0	4
1952	13,439	18,925	5,486	61	26	93	2	0	8
1953	13,432	19,287	5,855	59	46	108	1	0	3
1954	13,323	19,669	6,346	66	32	201	2	0	4
1955	13,237	20,202	6,965	103	41	221	1	4	4
1956	13,218	20,857	7,639	107	64	183	0	1	6
1957	13,165	21,432	8,267	73	22	147	0	1	0
1958	13,124	22,079	8,955	83	29	146	1	3	3
1959	13,114	22,846	9,732	102	54	163	0	2	1
1960	13,126	23,682	10,556	111	27	126	0	0	0
1961	13,115	24,551	11,436	98	31	135	0	5	0
1962	13,124	25,545	12,421	167	20	176	0	1	1
1963	13,291	26,872	13,581	281	39	150	0	2	1
1964	13,793	28,192	14,699	323	20	133	0	7	1
1965	13,544	29,416	15,872	182	17	140	0	5	3
1966	13,538	30,567	17,029	99	24	121	6	1	1
1967	13,514	31,593	18,079	94	21	131	0	4	4
1968	13,487	32,670	19,183	82	19	125	3	0	0
1969	13,473	33,852	20,379	115	18	138	5	4	0
1970	13,511	33,350	21,839	178	13	146	2	4	1
1971	13,612	36,948	23,336	197	5	95	1	5	0
1972	13,733	38,562	24,829	236	4	118	0	1	0
1973	13,976	40,649	26,673	332	11	94	3	3	0
1974	14,230	42,881	28,651	364	6	113	3	0	0
1975	14,384	44,589	30,205	246	5	84	10	3	0
1976	14,410	45,754	31,344	161	6	125	13	3	0
1977	14,411	47,519	33,108	157	3	152	6	0	1
1978	14,391	49,182	34,791	149	2	165	5	1	0
1979	14,364	51,155	36,791	204	3	224	7	3	0
1980	14,434	53,172	38,738	205	1	126	7	3	0
1981	14,414	55,200	40,786	198	0	210	5	2	1
1982	14,451	54,232	39,783	317	8	256	25	7	0
1983	14,469	55,322	40,853	361	22	314	36	9	6
1984	14,496	56,295	41,799	391	49	332	72	4	5
1985	14,417	57,710	43,293	331	45	336	94	22	3
1986	14,210	58,602	44,392	257	31	341	120	21	13
1987	13,723	59,080	45,357	219	37	543	175	11	14
1988	13,137	59,518	46,381	229	3	598	203	6	11
1989	12,715	60,720	48,005	192	9	411	197	9	6

Note appears at end of table

TABLE Cj612–620   Insured commercial banks – number, branches, and offices: 1934–1998 *Continued*

				Additions		Deletions			
							Failures		
	Banks	Offices	Branches	New charters	Conversions	Unassisted mergers	Mergers	Paid off	Other
	Cj612	Cj613	Cj614	Cj615	Cj616	Cj617	Cj618	Cj619	Cj620
Year	Number	Number	Number	Number	Number	Number	Number	Number	Number
1990	12,347	62,753	50,406	165	24	393	150	8	6
1991	11,927	63,896	51,969	106	35	447	101	4	9
1992	11,466	63,402	51,935	72	11	428	87	11	18
1993	10,960	63,828	52,868	59	12	481	55	5	36
1994	10,452	65,597	55,145	50	17	549	11	0	16
1995	9,942	66,454	56,612	102	37	609	6	0	34
1996	9,530	67,319	57,789	148	49	554	5	0	47
1997	9,143	69,465	60,325	188	55	601	1	0	28
1998	8,774	70,731	61,957	194	24	564	3	0	20

[1] As of December 31 each year.

Sources

Federal Deposit Insurance Corporation (FDIC), *Statistics on Banking: Historical, 1934–1994;* FDIC, *Quarterly Reports* (various issues). Updates are available through the FDIC's Internet site.

Documentation

On January 1, 1934, there were 15,034 banks – 12,551 insured commercial banks, 1,904 noninsured commercial banks, 214 insured mutual savings banks, and 365 noninsured mutual savings banks. When the Temporary Federal Deposit Insurance plan went into effect on January 1, 1934, 12,551 commercial banks were admitted to the temporary plan and 214 mutual savings banks were admitted to a separate temporary fund for mutuals. The two funds were combined on July 1, 1935.

In 1936, the FDIC's definition of a commercial bank included all national banks, all incorporated state banks, trust companies, and bank and trust companies regularly engaged in the business of receiving deposits (except mutual savings banks and guaranty savings banks chartered in New Hampshire); all stock savings banks, banks in conservatorship provided they were authorized to accept deposits; industrial banks or Morris Plan banks operating under general banking codes; branches of foreign banks that engaged in a regular deposit business; private banks under state banking authority supervision; insured trust companies even if they were not engaged in a regular deposit business; and the chief office of banks operating in the U.S. possessions engaged in a general deposit business.

This definition was substantially revised in 1947, reflecting new forms of commercial, deposit-taking banks and depositories chartered in South Carolina, Arkansas, Georgia, New Hampshire, New York, and Texas, as well as government-operated banks in American Samoa, Guam, and North Dakota. Similar, more inclusive revisions in the definition were adopted in 1970, 1982, 1984, and 1992. The most recent revision defines FDIC-insured commercial banks and trust companies as national banks; state-chartered banks and trust companies, excluding savings banks; commercial banks, either national or state-chartered insured by the Bank Insurance Fund (BIF) or Savings Association Insurance Fund (SAIF); and other financial institutions operating under general banking codes that are specifically authorized to, and do, accept deposits or obligations classified as insurable deposits by the FDIC.

Offices include all offices of banks operating more than one office, other than head offices, at which deposits are received and checks cashed, and all offices of insured trust companies not engaged in deposit banking. The term "branch" includes any branch bank, branch office, agency, or additional office or place of business located in any state of the United States plus Puerto Rico and the Virgin Islands at which deposits are received, checks are cashed, and money is lent.

Series Cj612–614 reflect only net changes in the number of branches, offices, and banks (that is, additions less deletions, or entry less exit). While these data are sufficient for some types of analysis, it is often informative to observe gross entry and exit as well as the causes of exit. Series Cj615–620 provide detailed statistics on entry through new bank formation and through conversions of noninsured to insured status, as well as exit and the causes thereof, whether by voluntary merger, FDIC-facilitated merger, failure, or voluntary liquidation. Banking difficulties in the 1930s are evident, as are the problems of the 1980s as seen in the sharp rise in FDIC-assisted mergers and failures beginning in 1982 and continuing through 1994. The intervening period was one of relative calm in the financial industry, with few failures and few insurer-assisted mergers.

Series Cj613. Offices include all offices where deposits are received and checks are paid. In many instances, offices are operated on or near military installations at the request of the Secretary of the Treasury or of the commanding officer of the installation.

Series Cj614. In 1934, the FDIC did not draw a distinction between a branch and an office, which is why it reports zero branches in that year. Beginning in 1936, branches include all offices, other than the head office, where deposits are received, checks are paid, and money is lent.

Series Cj615. Represents institutions newly licensed by the Office of the Comptroller of the Currency in the case of national banks, or state banking authorities in the case of state banks. These include de novo charters as well as charters issued to take control of a failing institution.

Series Cj616. Represents conversions of existing commercial banks that applied for and received FDIC insurance.

Series Cj618. Represents mergers, consolidations, and absorptions entered into in response to supervisory actions. These transactions may or may not have required FDIC assistance.

Series Cj619. Represents institutions declared insolvent whose deposits the FDIC paid off.

Series Cj620. Represents withdrawals from FDIC insurance, voluntary liquidations, and conversions to institutions not considered commercial banks.

TABLE Cj621–628   Savings institutions insured by the FDIC – number, by regulatory agent and insurance fund: 1984–1998[1]

Contributed by Howard Bodenhorn and Eugene N. White

		FDIC supervised			Office of Thrift Supervision supervised			
	Savings institutions insured by the FDIC	Total	Savings Association Insurance Fund member	Bank Insurance Fund member	Total	Savings Association Insurance Fund member	Bank Insurance Fund member	Resolution Trust Corporation conservatorships
	Cj621	Cj622	Cj623	Cj624	Cj625	Cj626	Cj627	Cj628 [2]
Year	Number	Number	Number	Number	Number	Number	Number	Number
1984	3,418	268	—	268	3,150	3,126	24	—
1985	3,626	364	—	364	3,262	3,234	28	—
1986	3,677	445	—	445	3,232	3,206	26	—
1987	3,622	463	—	463	3,159	3,137	22	—
1988	3,438	471	—	471	2,967	2,946	21	—
1989	3,087	469	—	469	2,618	2,598	20	281
1990	2,815	456	5	451	2,359	2,341	18	179
1991	2,561	449	23	426	2,112	2,097	15	91
1992	2,390	518	120	398	1,872	1,856	16	81
1993	2,262	593	205	388	1,669	1,653	16	63
1994	2,152	609	238	371	1,543	1,526	17	1
1995	2,030	593	234	359	1,437	1,411	26	0
1996	1,925	590	234	356	1,335	1,308	27	0
1997	1,780	565	233	322	1,215	1,180	35	0
1998	1,687	544	222	322	1,143	1,105	38	0

[1] Data represent the number of reporting institutions; see text.

[2] The Resolution Trust Company was created in 1989; see text.

Sources

Federal Deposit Insurance Corporation (FDIC), *Statistics on Banking: Historical, 1934–1984*, Volume 1, *A Statistical History of the United States Banking Industry* (1995), Table SI-1; FDIC, *Statistics on Banking* (1997 update); and the FDIC Internet site, Historical Statistics on Banking.

Documentation

FDIC-insured savings institutions include all institutions insured by either the Bank Insurance Fund (BIF) or the Savings Association Insurance Fund (SAIF) that operate under state or federal banking codes applicable to thrift institutions. Savings institutions that were transferred to Resolution Trust Corporation conservatorship are excluded from these tables while they were in conservatorship. The institutions reported here are regulated and submit financial reports to either the FDIC or the Office of Thrift Supervision (OTS). Data for FDIC-insured institutions were taken from FDIC call reports. Data for savings institutions regulated by the OTS are taken from Thrift Financial Reports.

In 1984, deposit insurance was made available for mutual savings banks (banks with no capital stock and whose earnings are distributed as dividends among depositors). Mutual savings banks include all those operating under special state banking codes applicable to mutual savings banks and all guaranty savings banks in New Hampshire and all insured savings banks in Massachusetts.

The 1989 Financial Institutions Reform, Recovery, and Enforcement Act (FIRREA) made the FDIC the sole insurer of all financial institutions and required that all such institutions acquire deposit insurance through either the BIF or the SAIF, depending on their charter type. The SAIF replaced the closed Federal Savings and Loan Insurance Corporation insurance fund. Regulatory supervision continued to be provided by the FDIC or the OTS, depending on the institution's charter.

Data in Tables Cj621–658 are as of December 31. The data represent the number of reporting institutions, which may differ from the actual number of institutions because some institutions may not have supplied a call report. This typically occurs when an institution merges or closes on or near December 31. The count does not include institutions transferred to the Resolution Trust Corporation (RTC).

Additional information can be found in the FDIC's annual reports or the FDIC's Internet site.

Series Cj628. In 1989, FIRREA created and funded the RTC to manage and dispose of any failed savings institution transferred from the OTS through September 30, 1993. The RTC Completion Act extended the RTC's responsibility to manage and dispose of failed savings institutions transferred from the OTS through July 1, 1995, and terminated the RTC effective December 31, 1995. Resolution of all failed savings institutions after 1995 is handled by either the BIF or the SAIF.

TABLE Cj629-638   Savings institutions insured by the FDIC – assets: 1984-1998[1]

Contributed by Howard Bodenhorn and Eugene N. White

Year	Total	Cash	Securities	Total loans and leases	Reserve for loan and lease losses	Other earning assets	Bank premises and equipment	Other real estate	Intangible assets	All other assets
	Cj629	Cj630 [2]	Cj631 [3]	Cj632	Cj633	Cj634	Cj635	Cj636	Cj637	Cj638 [4]
	Thousand dollars	Thousand dollars	Thousand dollars	Thousand dollars	Thousand dollars	Thousand dollars	Thousand dollars	Thousand dollars	Thousand dollars	Thousand dollars
1984	1,144,246,523	17,076,864	288,204,890	737,657,960	3,193,876	3,098,192	12,642,734	10,508,179	25,803,117	52,448,442
1985	1,262,654,097	19,660,442	298,590,995	825,907,461	5,145,828	4,124,273	13,820,962	15,469,354	27,764,613	62,461,757
1986	1,386,866,491	25,326,266	367,275,702	869,049,328	9,092,199	4,568,663	14,945,935	21,808,572	27,050,903	65,933,187
1987	1,502,110,585	23,317,341	421,685,353	924,205,231	12,556,242	3,526,507	16,294,746	28,803,094	29,638,963	67,195,536
1988	1,606,488,808	25,888,270	431,026,664	1,006,093,682	10,547,564	3,758,146	17,449,212	33,155,428	27,473,651	72,191,307
1989	1,427,511,565	22,301,128	358,113,919	923,923,016	8,113,421	5,885,304	16,006,141	27,293,545	18,642,295	63,459,656
1990	1,259,177,997	39,978,145	285,420,184	821,936,839	9,655,145	16,199,471	13,971,150	27,822,061	13,304,302	49,200,961
1991	1,113,001,663	36,453,310	252,941,875	733,602,663	9,536,543	14,733,455	12,400,188	22,209,005	10,870,198	39,327,485
1992	1,030,214,478	34,764,042	267,585,268	656,828,172	8,911,403	13,750,577	11,468,923	15,870,155	7,260,786	31,597,955
1993	1,000,891,303	31,259,265	275,773,438	635,042,105	8,661,954	12,365,007	11,118,770	8,420,109	5,975,810	29,598,759
1994	1,008,568,282	25,188,667	290,276,346	642,787,265	7,726,056	6,739,666	11,001,964	4,830,945	5,745,963	29,723,527
1995	1,025,742,103	26,783,665	288,582,397	655,215,683	7,307,706	11,871,289	10,783,716	3,472,771	6,864,499	29,475,790
1996	1,028,294,428	23,641,580	262,355,763	688,814,691	7,483,834	11,106,806	11,148,837	3,004,491	8,225,856	27,480,244
1997	1,026,185,798	24,251,457	248,680,981	698,752,719	6,979,903	10,251,772	10,820,243	2,679,773	10,984,159	26,744,597
1998	1,087,684,108	30,115,013	269,245,737	720,907,859	6,922,051	16,753,618	11,097,525	2,166,629	14,212,950	30,106,827

[1] Data represent the number of reporting institutions; see the text for Table Cj621-628.

[2] Represents currency and coin, balances due from institutions, and cash items. For 1990-1998, it includes interest earning accounts held at a Federal Home Loan Bank (FHLB) by FHLB members.

[3] Represents securities of the U.S. government and agencies, states, counties, municipalities, corporate bonds, notes and debentures, and equity securities. The amount is net of valuation allowances. For FHLB members, in 1984-1989, it also includes interest-earning accounts held at a FHLB, as well as federal funds sold and assets held in trading accounts.

[4] For 1990-1998, represents all assets not previously mentioned, which includes all non-real estate repossessed property, investment in service corporations and subsidiaries, property leased to others, income earned but not yet collected, assets held in trading accounts, and miscellaneous assets. For 1984-1989, same as for 1990-1998 except assets held in trading accounts are included in securities accounts (series Cj631).

Source
Federal Deposit Insurance Corporation's (FDIC) Internet site.

Documentation
For a discussion of FDIC-insured savings institutions, see the text for Table Cj621-628. For the number of such institutions, see series Cj621.

Series Cj634. Represents federal funds sold and securities purchased under agreements to resell.

Series Cj637. Represents goodwill, mortgage servicing rights, and other identifiable intangible assets.

TABLE Cj639-647   Savings institutions insured by the FDIC – liabilities and capital: 1984-1998[1]

Contributed by Howard Bodenhorn and Eugene N. White

Year	Liabilities					Capital			
	Total	Total deposits	Borrowed funds	Subordinated notes	Other	Total	Shareholder equity	Surplus	Undivided profits
	Cj639	Cj640	Cj641 [2]	Cj642	Cj643 [3]	Cj644	Cj645	Cj646	Cj647
	Thousand dollars	Thousand dollars	Thousand dollars	Thousand dollars	Thousand dollars	Thousand dollars	Thousand dollars	Thousand dollars	Thousand dollars
1984	1,109,180,710	944,732,761	146,713,629	2,122,828	15,611,462	35,065,815	1,514,625	10,943,568	22,139,376
1985	1,217,865,484	1,022,739,280	171,822,146	3,302,787	20,001,171	44,781,047	2,601,173	15,744,661	26,435,213
1986	1,331,088,491	1,083,166,920	219,080,752	4,580,158	24,260,646	55,772,662	3,022,359	25,636,877	26,601,902
1987	1,448,352,860	1,137,819,400	283,931,841	4,947,961	21,653,576	53,754,308	3,779,484	29,523,934	20,100,781
1988	1,540,490,476	1,193,133,708	317,230,322	5,504,131	24,622,300	65,997,301	4,921,259	33,374,049	27,370,799
1989	1,358,140,508	1,081,416,562	249,158,792	4,675,428	22,889,717	69,371,055	3,973,925	31,480,395	33,680,473
1990	1,191,643,186	987,142,157	183,580,333	4,331,165	16,589,504	67,534,817	3,536,623	30,915,532	32,916,616
1991	1,044,373,553	906,681,075	120,910,415	3,523,797	13,258,269	68,628,117	3,458,481	30,093,980	35,023,910
1992	955,864,578	828,352,685	113,430,881	3,055,945	11,025,065	74,349,889	3,079,284	30,145,542	41,124,984
1993	922,470,205	774,157,010	134,007,374	2,533,460	11,772,355	78,421,102	3,197,186	32,034,232	43,189,574
1994	928,633,375	737,180,175	178,358,727	2,395,207	10,699,266	79,934,907	3,279,946	33,987,393	42,667,568
1995	939,688,331	741,906,813	182,508,312	2,581,403	12,691,803	96,053,762	2,931,048	36,909,715	46,213,000
1996	942,499,872	727,922,862	200,909,478	2,400,551	11,266,980	85,794,559	2,701,630	38,559,564	44,533,365
1997	936,853,493	704,136,219	216,257,598	2,935,121	13,524,555	89,332,312	2,628,512	40,848,069	45,855,732
1998	993,256,809	704,531,040	267,574,926	2,812,330	18,338,511	94,427,281	2,254,636	45,690,750	46,481,895

Notes appear at end of table

(continued)

TABLE Cj639–647   Savings institutions insured by the FDIC – liabilities and capital: 1984–1998   *Continued*

[1] Data represent the number of reporting institutions; see the text for Table Cj621–628.

[2] For institutions reporting to the Federal Deposit Insurance Corporation, includes federal funds purchased, securities sold under repurchase agreements, demand notes issued to the U.S. Treasury, mortgage indebtedness, liabilities under capitalized leases, and all other borrowed money. For institutions reporting to the Office of Thrift Supervision, includes only reverse repurchase agreements and Federal Savings and Loan Insurance Corporation net worth certificates.

[3] Includes all liabilities not otherwise categorized as well as limited life preferred stock.

Source

Federal Deposit Insurance Corporation's (FDIC) Internet site.

Documentation

For a discussion of FDIC-insured savings institutions, see the text for Table Cj621–628. For the number of such institutions, see series Cj621.

TABLE Cj648–658   Savings institutions insured by the FDIC – income and expenses: 1984–1998[1]

Contributed by Howard Bodenhorn and Eugene N. White

Year	Total interest income	Total interest expenses	Net interest income	Total noninterest income	Total noninterest expense	Provision for loan losses	Pre-tax operating income	Securities gains or losses	Income taxes	Net extraordinary items	Net income
	Cj648	Cj649	Cj650	Cj651	Cj652	Cj653 [2]	Cj654	Cj655 [3]	Cj656 [4]	Cj657	Cj658
	Thousand dollars	Thousand dollars	Thousand dollars	Thousand dollars	Thousand dollars	Thousand dollars	Thousand dollars	Thousand dollars	Thousand dollars	Thousand dollars	Thousand dollars
1984	108,169,907	99,124,183	9,045,724	11,441,908	20,918,653	68,019	−499,040	2,549,584	914,864	18,678	1,154,358
1985	118,683,609	101,469,922	17,213,687	12,141,894	26,885,788	180,450	2,289,343	5,814,461	2,668,071	96,180	5,531,913
1986	119,846,495	97,015,483	22,761,530	13,095,065	36,563,328	272,003	−978,736	7,930,278	4,307,709	155,924	2,799,757
1987	119,899,465	94,213,291	25,775,173	11,522,830	31,907,338	9,626,544	−4,235,879	2,719,515	3,890,511	78,318	−5,328,557
1988	126,899,257	101,170,376	25,728,879	9,768,370	29,769,467	9,674,391	−3,946,609	2,087,028	2,959,445	47,128	−4,771,898
1989	134,192,315	109,583,904	24,608,411	9,580,792	30,804,093	9,661,654	−6,276,545	1,843,983	1,184,188	34,379	−5,582,440
1990	117,215,480	90,948,750	26,266,730	7,320,174	28,474,434	9,266,704	−4,163,203	701,957	1,359,944	96,906	−4,722,723
1991	97,635,716	69,491,519	28,144,197	6,645,524	26,462,300	6,998,598	1,328,824	2,175,523	2,810,099	144,118	838,362
1992	77,651,599	45,852,061	31,799,534	6,311,292	25,232,038	5,176,489	7,702,303	2,439,151	3,755,185	305,745	6,692,022
1993	66,138,020	34,518,273	31,619,753	6,415,920	24,897,501	4,311,745	8,826,432	1,878,899	3,859,788	−3,892	6,843,650
1994	63,469,619	33,410,608	30,059,007	6,123,215	23,231,414	2,480,735	10,470,086	94,020	3,779,546	−422,917	6,361,630
1995	70,994,651	42,528,781	28,465,870	7,121,274	21,834,723	2,117,816	11,634,610	463,222	4,158,690	−320,512	7,618,630
1996	72,270,593	42,170,713	30,099,871	7,493,100	25,700,618	2,535,140	6,357,204	940,815	3,035,696	−246,176	7,016,150
1997	69,175,314	40,559,366	28,315,945	7,029,141	21,072,548	2,186,424	12,386,114	1,259,837	4,852,161	−4,688	8,789,098
1998	71,058,800	41,888,492	29,170,308	9,200,255	23,545,201	1,773,113	13,052,243	2,456,069	5,269,087	−82,547	10,156,678

[1] Data represent the number of reporting institutions; see the text for Table Cj621–628.

[2] For 1984–1986, this number was not reported by those filing reports with the Office of Thrift Supervision (OTS). For 1987–1998, number represents the amount needed to make the allowance for loan losses adequate to absorb expected loan losses based on management's evaluation of its current loan portfolio. The amount reported here may differ from the bad debt expense deduction taken for income tax purposes.

[3] For 1984–1986, institutions reporting to the OTS reported only gains; losses were included in noninterest expense. For 1987–1989, includes gains and losses on loans held by institutions reporting to the OTS. For 1990–1998, represents the net value of profits on securities sold or redeemed less losses on securities held. Actual recoveries on securities are included in noninterest income; actual charge-offs are included in noninterest expense.

[4] Represents federal, state, and local taxes on income. It does not include taxes on securities transactions or extraordinary items.

Source

Federal Deposit Insurance Corporation's (FDIC) Internet site.

Documentation

For a discussion of FDIC-insured savings institutions, see the text for Table Cj621–628. For the number of such institutions, see series Cj621.

Detailed information on interest and noninterest income by source, as well as interest and noninterest expense on each type of liability, can be found in the source. Updates are also available.

Data pertain to calendar years.

TABLE Cj659–662   Insured savings institutions – failures and deposits in failed institutions: 1934–1998

Contributed by Howard Bodenhorn and Eugene N. White

	Failed savings associations		Failed savings banks			Failed savings associations		Failed savings banks	
	Number	Deposits	Number	Deposits		Number	Deposits	Number	Deposits
	Cj659 [1]	Cj660	Cj661 [2]	Cj662		Cj659 [1]	Cj660	Cj661 [2]	Cj662
Year(s)	Number	Thousand dollars	Number	Thousand dollars	Year(s)	Number	Thousand dollars	Number	Thousand dollars
1934–1979	1 [3]	1,584	2 [4]	14,310	1990	215	101,594,680	8	2,243,533
1980	11	955,879	0	0	1991	146	66,513,349	17	14,806,988
1981	30	10,363,515	3	3,914,268	1992	60	40,288,211	21	19,648,447
1982	77	20,862,380	7	7,988,258	1993	7	4,735,267	1	720,512
1983	51	8,687,003	2	2,169,207	1994	2	127,508	2	505,146
1984	26	4,409,981	1	498,033	1995	2	414,692	0	0
1985	60	20,600,041	2	5,406,945	1996	1	32,745	0	0
1986	60	16,020,957	0	0	1997	0	0	0	0
1987	60	14,489,457	1	1,099,485	1998	0	0	0	0
1988	190	80,241,912	0	0					
1989	327	113,924,969	1	683,356					

[1] Includes state or federally chartered savings associations supervised by the Office of Thrift Supervision. Deposit insurance was supplied by the Federal Savings and Loan Insurance Corporation between 1934 and 1988, and by the Federal Deposit Insurance Corporation through the Savings Association Insurance Fund thereafter. Numbers have been revised several times. These figures may vary from previously published figures due to changes in charter status and to the continuing resolution of failed and troubled thrifts.

[2] Includes state-chartered savings banks supervised by the Federal Deposit Insurance Corporation.

[3] One savings association failed in 1939 with deposits of $1,584 (thousands).

[4] Includes one failed savings bank in 1938 with deposits of $2,479 (thousands) and one in 1978 with deposits of $11,831 (thousands).

Source

Federal Deposit Insurance Corporation's (FDIC) Internet site, Historical Statistics on Banking.

Documentation

Before 1989, two federal deposit insurance systems operated side by side. The FDIC insured deposits in commercial banks and state-chartered savings banks. The Federal Savings and Loan Insurance Corporation (FSLIC) was an agency placed within the Federal Home Loan Bank Board (FHLBB) and insured deposits in state and federally chartered savings associations. The savings and loan crisis bankrupted the FSLIC, which brought about the closure of the FHLBB and the transfer of savings association deposit insurance to the FDIC. The Financial Institutions Reform, Recovery, and Enforcement Act (FIRREA) in 1989 made the FDIC the sole federal deposit insurer for commercial banks, savings banks, and savings associations. The former FDIC and FSLIC funds remain effectively separated; the former is now called the Bank Insurance Fund (BIF), the latter the Savings Association Insurance Fund (SAIF).

Failing savings institutions have been resolved in several different ways. The FDIC categorizes failures using three broad categories. Category 1 failures occur when a failed institution's charter survives. In such cases, the insurer offers temporary assistance to the failing bank, so that it emerges from bankruptcy without closing. In other instances, the institution is closed and later reopened under the original charter. Category 2 failures occur when the failed institution's charter is terminated, and the insured deposits as well as some assets and other liabilities are transferred to a successor institution operating under a new charter. In some instances, known as "purchase and assumption," the successor institution purchases the assets and assumes the liabilities of the failed institution. In other instances, the transfer of assets and liabilities to a successor institution required FSLIC or FDIC assistance. In yet other instances of Category 2 failures, failed institutions were placed under government control through the FSLIC's Management Consignment Program or through the Resolution Trust Corporation's (RTC) conservatorship program after the RTC was established. In 1984, there were five such cases. Finally, Category 3 failures occur when insured depositors are paid by the insurer, the failed institution's charter is terminated, and there is no successor institution. Most failures fall into the first category.

For details and updated series, see the source.

TABLE Cj663–673   Insured mutual savings banks – number, assets, and liabilities: 1934–1982[1]
Contributed by Howard Bodenhorn

			Assets						Liabilities		
		Total assets or liabilities and reserve accounts	Loans		Securities						
	Banks		Real estate	Other	U.S. government	Other	Cash	Other assets	Deposits	Other liabilities	Reserve accounts
	Cj663	Cj664	Cj665	Cj666	Cj667	Cj668	Cj669	Cj670	Cj671	Cj672	Cj673
Year	Number	Million dollars	Million dollars	Million dollars	Million dollars	Million dollars	Million dollars	Million dollars	Million dollars	Million dollars	Million dollars
1934	68	1,174	545	9	160	316	60	12	1,045	1	1,124
1935	56	1,108	489	—	179	284	68	88	978	4	1,257
1936	56	1,132	469	—	237	262	70	94	988	3	1,318
1937	56	1,141	472	—	250	246	72	101	1,004	3	1,344
1938	56	1,137	461	—	280	232	71	93	1,012	3	1,311
1939	51	1,566	605	—	421	303	133	104	1,409	4	1,299
1940	53	1,984	637	—	548	470	202	127	1,818	5	1,263
1941	52	1,958	642	—	629	421	151	115	1,788	6	1,257
1942	56	2,089	662	30	726	416	141	115	1,900	6	182
1943	184	7,946	3,105	28	3,322	663	494	333	7,135	22	789
1944	192	9,165	3,086	30	4,723	629	450	247	8,281	24	860
1945	192	10,636	3,056	37	6,345	605	417	175	9,648	27	961
1946	191	12,066	3,113	42	7,589	654	530	139	10,923	33	1,110
1947	194	13,129	3,352	48	8,127	814	650	137	11,870	42	1,217
1948	193	13,861	3,756	57	8,043	1,190	668	147	12,520	45	1,296
1949	192	14,627	4,382	58	7,856	1,504	665	162	13,201	48	1,378
1950	194	15,543	5,328	68	7,755	1,561	653	178	14,013	64	1,466
1951	202	16,695	6,765	79	7,293	1,663	662	230	15,001	80	1,613
1952	206	17,906	8,012	85	6,755	2,065	729	255	16,103	94	1,710
1953	219	19,625	9,288	103	6,621	2,591	744	276	17,719	119	1,787
1954	218	21,873	10,802	120	6,755	3,016	874	302	19,739	160	1,974
1955	220	22,741	12,467	130	5,993	3,009	809	330	20,577	199	1,964
1956	223	24,534	14,494	155	5,730	3,035	757	359	22,202	250	2,082
1957	239	26,904	16,446	185	5,592	3,559	724	394	24,322	318	2,264
1958	241	29,161	18,046	227	5,339	4,378	742	424	26,305	431	2,425
1959	268	31,249	19,938	244	5,237	4,677	690	456	28,136	512	2,600
1960	325	31,249	22,628	355	5,093	5,036	721	495	30,823	598	2,918
1961	330	34,340	24,255	353	4,792	5,228	758	511	32,320	507	3,089
1962	331	35,917	26,435	442	4,749	5,152	794	561	34,351	538	3,264
1963	330	38,152	29,539	543	4,563	5,116	786	612	37,175	589	3,417
1964	327	41,181	33,122	588	4,352	5,058	769	692	40,334	660	3,615
1965	329	48,467	36,992	672	4,031	5,069	892	783	43,986	653	3,827
1966	332	51,400	40,095	843	3,595	5,153	839	845	46,591	764	4,045
1967	333	55,173	42,795	1,003	3,156	6,312	954	925	50,248	731	4,194
1968	334	59,674	45,445	1,176	3,050	8,136	826	1,005	54,535	794	4,346
1969	331	63,315	47,971	1,463	2,703	9,334	716	1,090	57,835	888	4,592
1970	329	65,788	49,629	1,903	2,387	9,898	778	1,135	59,863	1,163	4,762
1971	327	73,662	52,365	2,309	4,438	11,932	1,156	1,386	67,443	983	5,236
1972	326	82,996	56,554	2,566	5,740	15,033	1,330	1,656	76,226	1,075	5,695
1973	322	90,851	61,600	2,968	6,299	16,239	1,676	1,898	83,212	1,381	6,257
1974	320	94,427	64,696	3,251	5,950	16,411	1,825	2,087	85,994	1,764	6,668
1975	329	101,714	66,698	3,389	7,824	19,036	2,067	2,380	92,850	1,803	7,060
1976	329	114,218	70,258	2,804	11,584	23,091	1,767	4,249	104,711	1,856	7,448
1977	323	126,894	75,389	3,337	14,611	25,907	1,962	5,202	116,565	1,940	8,126
1978	325	137,597	81,915	3,897	15,927	27,162	2,343	5,942	125,820	2,725	8,901
1979	324	145,331	86,683	4,673	16,840	26,943	3,084	6,768	131,842	3,555	9,559
1980	323	150,259	88,883	5,958	18,446	25,931	3,266	7,488	134,909	5,216	9,756
1981	331	155,577	89,636	8,140	19,974	24,529	4,359	8,615	138,977	7,176	9,069
1982	315	156,272	86,591	9,722	20,493	22,815	5,540	10,757	139,322	8,633	7,867

[1] Reports dated December 31 each year.

Source
Federal Deposit Insurance Corporation (FDIC), *Annual Report* (1934–1983).

Documentation
For a discussion of the FDIC, see the text for Table Cj551–562. For a discussion of mutual savings banks, see the text for Table Cj362–374.

These series end in 1982, when the FDIC stopped reporting them.

TABLE Cj674–680   Insured mutual savings banks – number, earnings, and expenses: 1934–1982

Contributed by Howard Bodenhorn

Year	Banks	Total operating income	Total operating expenses	Income before income taxes and net realized gains or losses	Net realized gains or losses	Net income	Capital or reserve account
	Cj674	Cj675	Cj676	Cj677	Cj678	Cj679	Cj680
	Number	Thousand dollars	Thousand dollars	Thousand dollars	Thousand dollars	Thousand dollars	Thousand dollars
1934	68	47,819	11,943	41,357	11,097	30,260	—
1935	56	42,732	12,889	36,810	8,475	28,335	—
1936	56	41,381	14,349	38,693	11,631	27,062	131,707
1937	56	42,084	15,813	36,657	15,237	21,420	133,371
1938	48	44,471	16,303	36,520	28,354	8,166	122,145
1939	51	56,956	19,706	51,182	26,090	25,092	152,529
1940	53	70,965	22,542	60,665	47,771	12,894	160,600
1941	52	69,547	23,344	46,203	11,931	34,272	1,958
1942	56	76,287	24,520	51,767	47,954	3,813	182,243
1943	184	273,479	87,847	185,632	158,355	27,277	788,696
1944	192	295,709	86,575	209,134	145,252	63,882	859,901
1945	192	322,795	77,705	245,090	99,456	145,634	961,007
1946	191	350,951	85,523	265,428	121,936	143,492	1,109,800
1947	194	375,592	93,613	281,979	199,915	82,064	1,217,056
1948	193	403,156	100,768	302,388	217,726	84,662	1,296,175
1949	192	436,869	104,187	332,682	250,717	81,965	1,378,290
1950	194	478,695	115,470	363,225	272,050	91,175	1,466,351
1951	202	513,817	106,654	407,163	284,030	123,133	1,613,414
1952	206	568,498	116,763	451,735	400,776	50,959	1,709,615
1953	219	647,067	127,336	519,731	457,065	62,666	1,787,113
1954	218	721,323	139,931	581,392	482,584	98,808	1,974,410
1955	220	801,682	147,678	656,004	569,258	86,746	1,964,152
1956	223	898,440	158,317	740,123	641,678	98,445	2,081,904
1957	239	1,026,327	174,758	851,569	761,165	90,404	2,263,550
1958	241	1,149,643	187,758	961,885	836,288	125,597	2,424,941
1959	268	1,280,347	201,402	1,078,945	944,789	134,156	2,600,089
1960	325	1,461,763	224,789	1,236,974	1,068,834	168,140	2,918,714
1961	330	1,595,183	241,685	1,353,498	1,166,158	187,340	3,089,358
1962	331	1,755,582	252,963	1,502,619	1,355,256	147,363	2,363,771
1963	330	1,946,776	274,544	1,672,323	1,493,073	179,250	3,416,709
1964	327	2,164,115	290,471	1,973,644	1,779,790	193,854	3,615,099
1965	329	2,391,753	331,755	2,079,996	1,838,835	241,161	3,827,293
1966	322	2,606,012	334,451	2,271,561	2,124,552	147,009	4,044,734
1967	333	2,884,789	353,947	2,530,842	2,433,470	97,372	4,194,283
1968	334	3,238,735	389,780	2,848,955	2,660,348	188,607	4,345,524
1969	331	3,581,559	442,151	3,139,408	2,870,014	269,394	4,591,909
1970	329	3,874,870	519,499	3,355,371	3,065,621	289,750	4,762,424
1971	327	4,529,014	581,693	3,947,321	3,603,732	343,589	5,235,706
1972	326	5,295,449	671,818	4,623,631	4,144,466	479,165	5,695,035
1973	322	6,064,895	811,689	5,253,206	4,775,050	478,156	6,257,277
1974	320	6,483,654	938,705	5,544,949	5,227,438	317,511	6,668,439
1975	329	7,188,000	6,625,000	563,000	197,609	365,391	6,894,000
1976	329	8,331,000	7,646,000	685,000	178,000	507,000	7,448,000
1977	323	9,434,000	8,520,000	914,000	232,000	682,000	8,126,000
1978	325	10,668,000	9,503,000	1,165,000	356,000	809,000	8,901,000
1979	324	11,967,000	11,060,000	907,000	258,000	649,000	9,559,000
1980	323	13,029,000	13,268,000	−238,000	11,000	−249,000	9,756,000
1981	331	14,640,000	16,289,000	−1,515,000	−67,000	−1,448,000	9,069,000
1982	315	15,140,000	16,585,000	−1,421,000	−192,000	−1,229,000	7,867,000

Sources

Federal Deposit Insurance Corporation (FDIC), *Annual Report* (various years); FDIC, *Statistics on Banking* (1982).

Documentation

The sources, especially the annual reports, provide considerably more detailed statistics on income and expenses. Because the series and the defi-

nitions are not reported consistently over the entire period and change frequently, only broad aggregates are provided here. Those interested in the details on loan and security interest earnings as well as realized loan losses are referred to the original sources.

These series end in 1982, when the FDIC stopped reporting them.

Data pertain to calendar years.

TABLE Cj681–692   Federal Savings and Loan Insurance Corporation – assets and liabilities: 1938–1985

Contributed by Howard Bodenhorn

	Assets					Liabilities or capital accounts						
						Liabilities		Capital or surplus				
Year	Total assets or liabilities and capital accounts	Cash	Accounts receivable (insurance premiums due)	Investments (U.S. Treasury securities)	Accrued interest	Accounts payable for purchases and services and funds held in escrow	Deferred income – unearned and prepaid insurance premiums	Total	Capital outstanding	Reserve fund less contributions to insured institutions	Secondary reserve	Contingency fund
	Cj681	Cj682	Cj683	Cj684	Cj685	Cj686	Cj687	Cj688	Cj689	Cj690	Cj691	Cj692
	Thousand dollars	Thousand dollars	Thousand dollars	Thousand dollars	Thousand dollars	Thousand dollars	Thousand dollars	Thousand dollars	Thousand dollars	Thousand dollars	Thousand dollars	Thousand dollars
1938	114,078	118	527	112,850	583	5	948	113,125	100,000	4,125	—	9,000
1939	119,400	320	619	117,863	597	5	1,112	118,283	100,000	3,843	—	14,440
1940	124,914	615	729 [1]	122,777	604	7	1,289	123,621	100,000	5,752	—	17,869
1941	130,920	925	821	128,062	604	39	1,492	129,681	100,000	29,389	—	292
1942	134,371	4,369	963	122,716	566	6	1,699	132,666	100,000	11,666	—	21,000
1943	143,240	961	1,052	137,288	110	8	1,834	141,407	100,000	17,407	—	24,000
1944	151,632	950	1,179	146,802	182	11	2,240	149,280	100,000	22,280	—	27,000
1945	160,263	1,644	1,419	155,483	163	11	2,662	157,493	100,000	27,493	—	30,000
1946	170,729	1,288	1,757	1,659,983	623	17	3,236	167,350	100,000	34,350	—	33,000
1947	182,400	1,270	2,113	178,331	695	87	3,855	178,458	100,000	42,458	—	36,000
1948	—	—	—	—	—	—	—	—	100,000	—	—	—
1949	—	—	—	—	—	—	—	—	100,000	—	—	—
1950	199,593	536	2,237	192,628	928	1,079	4,923	188,590	100,000	83,205	—	5,385
1951	208,212	3,204	3,112	199,782	994	3,400	5,409	199,403	93,284	99,762	—	6,357
1952	213,691	1,208	3,748	208,297	291	943	6,508	207,694	85,755	112,944	—	8,995
1953	223,443	1,073	4,508	216,831	867	842	7,867	213,279	76,987	128,751	—	7,541
1954	235,517	1,497	5,483	227,694	678	745	9,512	225,260	66,779	147,620	—	10,861
1955	250,318	1,400	6,491	240,657	1,579	630	11,408	238,280	54,847	170,726	—	12,707
1956	267,082	2,058	7,600	256,224	758	586	13,317	253,179	40,971	197,157	—	15,051
1957	286,202	1,994	8,635	274,059	1,102	432	15,101	270,669	24,801	228,403	—	17,465
1958	301,541	1,487	9,788	287,883	1,924	77	17,247	284,216	0	264,441	—	19,775
1959	348,650	2,314	11,663	331,921	2,311	51	20,177	328,340	—	305,419	—	22,921
1960	404,048	3,529	13,604	331,397	2,568	64	22,964	380,936	—	353,590	—	27,346
1961	467,465	3,431	18,767	394,153	—	165	26,414	440,887	—	440,887	—	0
1962	708,537	4,616	23,681	236,810	—	262	30,295	677,980	—	506,858	171,122	—
1963	981,053	4,171	19,313	854,595	7,879	1,322	34,923	944,709	—	579,740	364,969	—
1964	1,289,889	7,139	23,240	1,143,668	8,353	1,200	39,716	1,248,928	—	658,517	590,411	—
1965	1,584,028	6,051	26,401	1,341,333	0	3,141	43,684	1,537,141	—	725,039	812,102	—
1966	1,867,760	8,053	28,343	1,548,025	1,613	16,205	47,535	1,803,957	—	805,170	998,787	—
1967	2,120,092	2,441	29,181	1,792,877	4,048	17,560	53,342	2,049,121	—	921,669	1,127,452	—
1968	2,493,064	4,527	3,597	2,058,510	21,436	6,950	61,178	2,409,440	—	1,037,057	1,372,383	—
1969	2,829,013	5,977	5,463	2,387,898	27,913	7,473	9,651	2,801,328	—	1,243,107	1,558,221	—
1970	2,942,869	2,012	1,348	2,491,385	27,022	5,065	20,930	2,888,881	—	1,361,444	1,527,437	—
1971	3,011,640	1,023	1,282	2,677,702	25,668	12,343	18,141	2,952,260	—	1,467,936	1,484,324	—
1972	3,151,050	994	1,312	2,836,105	31,113	6,465	14,738	3,101,368	—	1,682,847	1,418,521	—
1973	3,367,394	122	5,321	3,098,281	41,833	4,317	812	3,340,655	—	1,958,376	1,382,279	—
1974	3,717,953	353	5,960	3,497,654	45,565	4,950	817	3,685,524	—	2,281,530	1,403,994	—
1975	4,059,511	409	4,293	3,842,880	61,061	8,421	454	4,025,741	—	2,646,924	1,378,817	—
1976	4,405,416	203	3,605	4,235,644	60,840	9,126	1,334	4,363,178	—	3,046,563	1,316,615	—
1977	4,793,557	231	4,100	4,655,930	73,160	8,878	3,561	4,743,550	—	3,518,852	1,224,698	—
1978	5,206,702	30	4,705	5,070,532	78,915	5,702	4,019	5,164,405	—	4,051,306	1,113,099	—
1979	5,717,769	56	6,173	5,542,713	96,657	5,856	5,193	5,649,796	—	4,681,066	968,730	—
1980	6,315,369	459	9,053	4,996,251	89,017	27,461	6,351	6,148,668	—	5,333,255	815,413	—
1981	6,891,954	2,436	22,709	5,803,556	86,934	39,370	—	6,167,326	—	5,568,065	599,261	—
1982	7,512,253	203	22,941	6,354,939	82,422	43,073	—	6,307,320	—	5,693,670	613,650	—
1983	8,347,292	1,160	—	—	—	33,359	—	6,425,421	—	5,764,261	661,160	—
1984	8,937,588	2,764	—	—	—	55,680	—	5,605,767	—	4,885,037	720,730	—
1985	10,499,000	9,442	—	—	—	30,544	—	4,557,402	—	3,783,169	774,233	—

[1] Does not include accounts receivable due from insured institutions in receivership.

Source

Federal Home Loan Bank Board, *Annual Reports* (1938–1986).

Documentation

Savings and loan associations, often called building and loan societies, first appeared in the 1830s and were designed to fill an explicit niche, namely, lenders who specialized in financing home ownership. Thus, savings institutions or thrifts and commercial banks held very different portfolios. A second difference between commercial banking and thrifts is their very different failure histories. The thrift industry experienced a significant number of failures only in the 1890s, the 1930s, and the 1980s.

TABLE Cj681–692   Federal Savings and Loan Insurance Corporation – assets and liabilities: 1938–1985   *Continued*

During the 1930s, thrifts did not issue demand liabilities so they, unlike the commercial banking industry, did not experience widespread and systemic runs. They did experience disintermediation as members drew down their accounts as the Depression deepened. Thrifts were squeezed by these withdrawals because they held long-term assets, mostly mortgages, making their portfolios relatively illiquid. Moreover, few thrifts had accumulated significant reserves, which meant that declining housing values quickly reduced the market value of their portfolios. The negative and declining net worth of numerous thrifts drove many into bankruptcy. Shareholders and owners suffered large losses and the flow of funds into housing was sharply curtailed.

The federal government responded by subsidizing and regulating the thrift industry. President Herbert Hoover signed the Federal Home Loan Bank Act on July 22, 1932. The Act established the Federal Home Loan Bank (FHLB) system, whose main purpose was to give members access to a steady flow of reasonably priced funds to promote home ownership. The FHLBs issued consolidated obligations in national capital markets and then advanced these funds to member institutions at low rates.

Initially, FHLB members included only state-chartered institutions that chose to join. Passage of the Home Owners' Loan Act in 1933 established a federal charter for thrifts and gave the chartering and regulatory authority to the FHLB. This created a dual chartering system equivalent to that of commercial banks. Members of the FHLB system included all federally chartered savings institutions and any state-chartered institutions that opted to join and met certain requirements.

Demands for deposit insurance resulted in the creation of the Federal Deposit Insurance Corporation (FDIC) in 1933 and the Federal Savings and Loan Insurance Corporation (FSLIC) in 1934. Title IV of the National Housing Act created the FSLIC to provide federally sponsored deposit insurance for savings institutions. Unlike the FDIC, the FSLIC was not established as a separate agency, but was housed in and administered by the Federal Home Loan Bank Board (FHLBB). All federally chartered thrifts were made members of the FSLIC; state-chartered institutions could voluntarily seek coverage. Insured institutions accepted regulatory supervision by the FHLBB and accepted regulations on the geographic area in which each thrift could loan, on advertising, and on capital requirements. The FSLIC gave thrifts an equal footing with insured commercial banks.

The policy intent of this layered regulatory and insurance program was clear: Thrifts were to be the principal providers of home mortgage financing. FSLIC insurance assured depositors, which provided thrifts with a reliable source of low-cost funds. Similarly, the FHLB system provided thrifts with indirect access to low-cost funds in national capital markets. Moreover, the FHLB was designed to serve as a lender of last resort in the event that one or more thrifts experienced short-run liquidity problems. The FSLIC and the FHLB system served the same purposes for thrifts that the FDIC and the Federal Reserve served for commercial banks. Although thrift and bank regulatory structures were parallel, thrifts focused on mortgage lending. The explicit and implicit guarantees involved in the FSLIC/FHLB structure and the indirect subsidies they provided made fifteen-, twenty-, even thirty-year mortgages economical because part of the risk was transferred from the lender to the insurer and the regulator.

The system worked well until the late 1970s and early 1980s, when thrifts experienced continued disintermediation in a high-interest-rate and high-inflation environment. Thrift portfolios were heavily laden with assets returning 5 or 6 percent per annum while short-term market interest rates rose into double digits in the early 1980s. Thus, thrifts could not profitably meet the competition, which was growing ever more intense with the financial innovation. Depositors, even small depositors, grew more sophisticated and sought out alternative repositories of funds paying higher rates, principally money market mutual funds offered by commercial banks. Regulation Q (which limited interest rates payable by financial institutions) no longer protected thrifts from external interest rate (or price) competition. In addition, most states prohibited thrifts from issuing mortgages with variable interest rates tied to other interest rates (loans now known as adjustable rate mortgages or ARMs).

In the early 1980s, several reforms were made. On the asset side, thrifts were allowed to offer ARMs and to invest in a much broader array of assets. They could offer credit cards, consumer loans, commercial real estate loans, and commercial loans and take direct ownership positions in certain ventures. These changes were not designed to encourage thrifts to turn from residential mortgage lending; rather, they were designed to allow a degree of previously unavailable portfolio diversification. On the liability side, thrifts were allowed to raise interest rates on time deposits to reflect market rates, they were allowed to offer de facto checking accounts, and the maximum insured deposit limit was raised to $100,000.

For many thrifts, however, these changes were either too little or too late, and the number of insolvent and failing thrifts increased markedly (see series Cj659 and Cj661). By the mid-1980s, the FSLIC's contingent liability grew so large that it was effectively bankrupted. The federal government responded by closing the FSLIC, turning the resolution of already-failed thrifts over to the newly formed Resolution Trust Corporation, and placing insured thrifts under the regulatory control of the FDIC.

Those interested in the details of the history of the FSLIC and the thrift crisis of the 1980s are referred to Edward J. Kane, *The S&L Insurance Mess: How Did It Happen?* (Washington University, 1989); Lawrence J. White, *The S&L Debacle* (Oxford University Press, 1991); and James R. Barth, *The Great Savings and Loan Debacle* (AEI Press, 1991).

TABLE Cj693–699   Federal Savings and Loan Insurance Corporation – income and expenses: 1938–1985

Contributed by Howard Bodenhorn

Year	Insurance premiums	Interest on investments	Interest on loans to insured institutions	Administrative expenses	Total operating income	Total operating expenses	Net income
	Cj693	Cj694	Cj695	Cj696	Cj697	Cj698	Cj699
	Thousand dollars	Thousand dollars	Thousand dollars	Thousand dollars	Thousand dollars	Thousand dollars	Thousand dollars
1938	1,881	3,263	—	192	1,947	193	4,992
1939	2,292	3,367	—	213	2,337	223	5,440
1940	261	3,389	—	240	6,038	256	5,869
1941	3,063	3,481	—	256	6,568	265	6,320
1942	3,535	3,481	—	324	7,043	358	6,802
1943	4,000	3,557	—	293	7,594	332	9,324
1944	4,245	3,277	—	426	7,535	453	8,218
1945	5,087	3,549	—	430	8,679	553	8,213
1946	6,119	3,764	—	491	10,030	499	9,857
1947	7,423	4,004	—	527	11,578	544	11,107
1950	8,451	4,624	—	580	13,209	595	10,483
1951	10,125	4,515	—	489	14,801	644	12,528
1952	12,027	4,813	—	430	16,938	720	14,366
1953	14,450	5,083	—	431	19,618	725	17,262
1954	17,438	5,282	—	443	22,720	756	20,734
1955	20,901	5,536	—	481	26,437	847	24,952
1956	25,180	5,921	—	549	31,100	987	28,774
1957	29,043	6,615	—	611	35,658	1,065	33,660
1958	32,949	7,068	—	740	40,017	1,362	38,349
1959	37,819	7,861	0	760	45,680	1,484	44,197
1960	43,817	9,431	891	783	54,139	1,610	52,596
1961	49,992	10,547	1,273	868	61,811	1,876	59,951
1962	57,363	16,934	376	1,075	74,745	2,306	65,971
1963	65,882	27,522	0	1,137	93,182	2,451	72,882
1964	75,612	34,905	0	717	116,148	4,584	78,777
1965	84,691	44,985	165	216	132,361	4,853	66,523
1966	92,024	56,816	696	231	155,131	7,104	80,131
1967	96,779	71,638	1,524	248	175,007	10,384	116,499
1968	102,643	89,956	1,877	292	200,952	12,116	115,388
1969	161,771	114,330	2,832	322	286,783	13,329	206,050
1970	111,170	138,766	3,764	381	264,535	17,356	151,003
1971	122,593	142,876	7,477	442	275,632	20,403	106,492
1972	144,290	154,121	8,829	500	315,841	17,886	214,910
1973	169,968	180,133	12,991	521	369,690	17,314	275,529
1974	185,785	217,637	4,235	634	412,315	17,790	323,154
1975	203,960	251,240	3,551	728	489,562	18,898	365,394
1976	239,750	281,642	2,601	740	529,920	19,476	399,639
1977	279,455	313,520	1,097	816	604,165	25,092	472,290
1978	318,882	344,930	1,110	794	668,488	23,910	532,453
1979	356,536	407,362	1,627	745	784,696	46,357	629,760
1980	385,323	444,242	8,190	837	931,817	47,255	652,189
1981	425,070	539,615	33,417	990	1,045,690	1,031,040	146,500
1982	426,988	603,592	33,982	1,014	1,090,096	953,233	136,864
1983	508,491	604,656	20,200	1,076	1,162,472	1,067,648	47,067
1984	596,941	655,266	42,397	1,234	1,324,978	2,143,053	−879,223
1985	703,913	489,773	82,460	—	2,388,161	3,490,030	−1,101,868

Source

Federal Home Loan Bank Board, *Annual Reports* (1938–1986).

Documentation

For a discussion of the origins and end of the Federal Savings and Loan Insurance Corporation (FSLIC), see the text for Table Cj681–692.

Complete figures on income and expenses are not available. The FSLIC's income and expense series demonstrate the extent of the thrift crisis of the 1980s by the agency's unprecedented and large negative net income in 1984 and 1985. In 1989, insurance coverage for savings institutions was transferred to the Federal Deposit Insurance Corporation through the Savings Association Insurance Fund (SAIF). See Table Cj700–708 for assets, liabilities, income, and expenses of the SAIF.

TABLE Cj700–708 Savings Association Insurance Fund – income, expenses, and effective assessment rate: 1989–1998

Contributed by Howard Bodenhorn and Eugene N. White

	Income			Expenses					Effective assessment rate
	Total	Assessment	Investment and other	Total	Interest and other	Administrative and operating	Provision for losses	Net income	
	Cj700	Cj701	Cj702	Cj703	Cj704	Cj705	Cj706	Cj707	Cj708
Year	Thousand dollars	Thousand dollars	Thousand dollars	Thousand dollars	Thousand dollars	Thousand dollars	Thousand dollars	Thousand dollars	Percent
1989	2	0	2	5,602	0	5,602	0	2	0.208
1990	18,195	18,195	0	56,088	0	56,088	0	18,195	0.208
1991	96,446	93,530	2,916	63,085	609	42,362	20,114	75,723	0.230
1992	178,643	172,079	6,564	28,982	−5	43,932	−14,945	185,107	0.230
1993	923,516	897,692	25,824	46,814	0	30,283	16,531	876,702	0.250
1994	1,215,289	1,132,102	83,187	434,303	0	20,303	414,000	780,986	0.244
1995	1,139,916	970,027	169,889	−281,216	0	39,784	−321,000	1,421,132	0.234
1996	5,501,684	5,221,560	280,124	−28,890	128	62,618	−91,636	5,530,574	0.204
1997	549,912	13,914	535,998	69,986	0	71,865	−1,879	479,926	0.004
1998	583,859	15,352	568,507	116,629	9	84,628	31,992	467,230	0.002

Source
Federal Deposit Insurance Corporation, *Annual Report* (1996), p. 111.

Documentation
The Financial Institutions Reform, Recovery, and Enforcement Act of 1989 (FIRREA) was enacted to reform and recapitalize the two principal federal deposit insurance programs, namely, the Federal Deposit Insurance Corporation (FDIC) and the Federal Savings and Loan Insurance Corporation. FIRREA created the Savings Association Insurance Fund (SAIF), the Bank Insurance Fund, and the Resolution Funding Corporation. All three funds were to be administered by the FDIC, though each is maintained separately.

The Omnibus Budget Reconciliation Act of 1990 (OBR) removed caps on assessment rate increases and authorized the FDIC to set assessment rates for the SAIF semiannually, based on a member's average assessment base. In 1991, the Federal Deposit Insurance Corporation Improvement Act (FDICIA) further required the FDIC to implement risk-based assessments of SAIF members; authorized the FDIC to increase assessment rates of SAIF members to ensure that sufficient funds are available to meet the SAIF's obligations; required the FDIC to accumulate insurance fund reserves equal to 1.25 percent

of insured deposits; and authorized the FDIC to increase assessments more often than semiannually and to impose special assessments to ensure that the SAIF can repay U.S. Treasury borrowings.

Because the SAIF was slow in accumulating the required 1.25 percent of insured member deposits, the Deposit Insurance Funds Act of 1996 provided for the full capitalization of the SAIF by a one-time special assessment. On October 1, 1996, the SAIF reached the mandated 1.25 percent level following a $4.5 billion special assessment.

The FDIC employs a risk-based assessment system and charges higher rates to those institutions believed to pose greater risks to the SAIF. The FDIC places each institution in one of nine categories, using a two-step process based first on capitalization ratios and then on other considerations. Between 1993 and 1995, thrifts were assessed between 23 and 31 cents per $100 of domestic deposits, depending on risk category. In December 1996, assessments were decreased to 0–27 cents per $100 in domestic insured deposits, depending on risk category. The assessments rates established in December 1996 were identical to rates paid by Bank Insurance Fund members.

TABLE Cj709–712   Savings Association Insurance Fund – insurance coverage, insured deposits, and insurance fund: 1989–1998

Contributed by Howard Bodenhorn and Eugene N. White

	Insurance coverage	Insured deposits	Deposit insurance fund	
			Amount	As a percentage of insured deposits
	Cj709	Cj710	Cj711	Cj712
Year	Thousand dollars	Million dollars	Million dollars	Percent
1989	100	882,920	0.0	0.00
1990	100	830,028	18.2	0.00
1991	100	776,351	93.9	0.01
1992	100	729,458	279.0	0.04
1993	100	695,158	1,155.7	0.17
1994	100	692,626	1,936.7	0.28
1995	100	711,017	3,357.8	0.47
1996	100	683,090	8,888.4	1.30
1997	100	690,132	9,368.3	1.36
1998	100	708,959	9,839.8	1.39

Source

Federal Deposit Insurance Corporation, *Annual Report* (1998), p. 123.

Documentation

The Financial Institutions Reform, Recovery, and Enforcement Act of 1989 created the Savings Association Insurance Fund (SAIF) as part of the consolidation and recapitalization of federal deposit insurance following the thrift crisis of the 1980s. The SAIF's principal purposes are to protect depositors in insured thrifts from loss due to failure of the institution, and to liquidate and settle the accounts of failed thrifts. Although the SAIF's members are predominantly savings and loan associations supervised by the Office of Thrift Supervision, the SAIF insurance fund is maintained by the Federal Deposit Insurance Corporation (FDIC).

Subsequent laws that affect the SAIF's operations are the Omnibus Budget Reconciliation Act of 1990 and the Federal Deposit Insurance Corporation Improvement Act of 1991 (FDICIA). These acts changed the FDIC's assessment and borrowing authority. The laws allowed the FDIC to change its assessment rates semiannually and to charge different rates to different institutions depending on perceived risk of a thrift's asset portfolio. In addition, the FDICIA required the FDIC to resolve thrift failures in such a way as to minimize the costs to the insurance fund and to maintain the insurance fund at no less than 1.25 percent of insured deposits.

Because of the SAIF's inability to attain its 1.25 percent requirement in a timely manner, the Deposit Insurance Fund Act of 1996 provided for the full capitalization of the SAIF by means of a one-time special assessment on SAIF-insured institutions. Other than the special assessment in 1996, the SAIF is primarily funded through assessments on insured members and interest earned on U.S. Treasury obligations. It can also borrow from the Federal Home Loan Bank Board, the U.S. Treasury, and the Federal Financing Bank.

LIFE AND PROPERTY INSURANCE

Eugene N. White

TABLE Cj713–722 Life insurance – number of companies and life insurance in force, by type: 1759–1998

Contributed by Eugene N. White

			Life insurance in force					Average size policy		
			Value							
	Companies	Policies	Total	Ordinary	Group	Industrial	Credit	Ordinary	Group	Industrial
	Cj713	Cj714	Cj715	Cj716	Cj717 [1]	Cj718 [2]	Cj719 [3]	Cj720	Cj721	Cj722
Year	Number	Million	Million dollars	Million dollars	Million dollars	Million dollars	Million dollars	Dollars	Dollars	Dollars
1759	1	—	—	—	—	—	—	—	—	—
1760	1	—	—	—	—	—	—	—	—	—
1761	1	—	—	—	—	—	—	—	—	—
1762	1	—	—	—	—	—	—	—	—	—
1763	1	—	—	—	—	—	—	—	—	—
1764	1	—	—	—	—	—	—	—	—	—
1765	1	—	—	—	—	—	—	—	—	—
1766	1	—	—	—	—	—	—	—	—	—
1767	1	—	—	—	—	—	—	—	—	—
1768	1	—	—	—	—	—	—	—	—	—
1769	2	—	—	—	—	—	—	—	—	—
1770	2	—	—	—	—	—	—	—	—	—
1771	2	—	—	—	—	—	—	—	—	—
1772	2	—	—	—	—	—	—	—	—	—
1773	2	—	—	—	—	—	—	—	—	—
1774	2	—	—	—	—	—	—	—	—	—
1775	2	—	—	—	—	—	—	—	—	—
1776	2	—	—	—	—	—	—	—	—	—
1777	2	—	—	—	—	—	—	—	—	—
1778	2	—	—	—	—	—	—	—	—	—
1779	2	—	—	—	—	—	—	—	—	—
1780	2	—	—	—	—	—	—	—	—	—
1781	2	—	—	—	—	—	—	—	—	—
1782	2	—	—	—	—	—	—	—	—	—
1783	2	—	—	—	—	—	—	—	—	—
1784	2	—	—	—	—	—	—	—	—	—
1785	2	—	—	—	—	—	—	—	—	—
1786	2	—	—	—	—	—	—	—	—	—
1787	3	—	—	—	—	—	—	—	—	—
1788	3	—	—	—	—	—	—	—	—	—
1789	3	—	—	—	—	—	—	—	—	—
1790	3	—	—	—	—	—	—	—	—	—
1791	2	—	—	—	—	—	—	—	—	—
1792	2	—	—	—	—	—	—	—	—	—
1793	2	—	—	—	—	—	—	—	—	—
1794	4	—	—	—	—	—	—	—	—	—
1795	4	—	—	—	—	—	—	—	—	—
1796	4	—	—	—	—	—	—	—	—	—
1797	4	—	—	—	—	—	—	—	—	—
1798	4	—	—	—	—	—	—	—	—	—
1799	4	—	—	—	—	—	—	—	—	—
1800	4	—	—	—	—	—	—	—	—	—
1801	4	—	—	—	—	—	—	—	—	—
1802	2	—	—	—	—	—	—	—	—	—
1803	2	—	—	—	—	—	—	—	—	—
1804	2	—	—	—	—	—	—	—	—	—
1805	2	—	—	—	—	—	—	—	—	—
1806	2	—	—	—	—	—	—	—	—	—
1807	2	—	—	—	—	—	—	—	—	—
1808	2	—	—	—	—	—	—	—	—	—
1809	2	—	—	—	—	—	—	—	—	—

Notes appear at end of table   (continued)

TABLE Cj713-722   Life insurance – number of companies and life insurance in force, by type: 1759-1998   *Continued*

			Life insurance in force							
			Value					Average size policy		
	Companies	Policies	Total	Ordinary	Group	Industrial	Credit	Ordinary	Group	Industrial
	Cj713	Cj714	Cj715	Cj716	Cj717 [1]	Cj718 [2]	Cj719 [3]	Cj720	Cj721	Cj722
Year	Number	Million	Million dollars	Million dollars	Million dollars	Million dollars	Million dollars	Dollars	Dollars	Dollars
1810	2	—	—	—	—	—	—	—	—	—
1811	2	—	—	—	—	—	—	—	—	—
1812	4	—	—	—	—	—	—	—	—	—
1813	3	—	—	—	—	—	—	—	—	—
1814	4	—	—	—	—	—	—	—	—	—
1815	4	—	(Z)	(Z)	—	—	—	—	—	—
1816	4	—	—	—	—	—	—	—	—	—
1817	4	—	—	—	—	—	—	—	—	—
1818	5	—	—	—	—	—	—	—	—	—
1819	5	—	—	—	—	—	—	—	—	—
1820	6	—	0.1	0.1	—	—	—	—	—	—
1821	6	—	—	—	—	—	—	—	—	—
1822	7	—	—	—	—	—	—	—	—	—
1823	7	—	—	—	—	—	—	—	—	—
1824	7	—	—	—	—	—	—	—	—	—
1825	7	—	0.2	0.2	—	—	—	—	—	—
1826	7	—	—	—	—	—	—	—	—	—
1827	7	—	—	—	—	—	—	—	—	—
1828	7	—	—	—	—	—	—	—	—	—
1829	7	—	—	—	—	—	—	—	—	—
1830	9	—	0.6	0.6	—	—	—	—	—	—
1831	9	—	—	—	—	—	—	—	—	—
1832	10	—	—	—	—	—	—	—	—	—
1833	12	—	—	—	—	—	—	—	—	—
1834	13	—	—	—	—	—	—	—	—	—
1835	15	—	2.8	2.8	—	—	—	—	—	—
1836	17	—	—	—	—	—	—	—	—	—
1837	18	—	—	—	—	—	—	—	—	—
1838	18	—	—	—	—	—	—	—	—	—
1839	17	—	—	—	—	—	—	—	—	—
1840	15	—	4.7	4.7	—	—	—	—	—	—
1841	14	—	—	—	—	—	—	—	—	—
1842	15	—	—	—	—	—	—	—	—	—
1843	15	—	—	—	—	—	—	—	—	—
1844	16	—	—	—	—	—	—	—	—	—
1845	18	—	14.5	14.5	—	—	—	—	—	—
1846	20	—	—	—	—	—	—	—	—	—
1847	25	—	—	—	—	—	—	—	—	—
1848	30	—	—	—	—	—	—	—	—	—
1849	38	—	—	—	—	—	—	—	—	—
1850	48	—	97.1	97.1	—	—	—	—	—	—
1851	50	—	—	—	—	—	—	—	—	—
1852	45	—	—	—	—	—	—	—	—	—
1853	41	—	—	—	—	—	—	—	—	—
1854	43	—	94.0	94.0	—	—	—	—	—	—
1855	42	—	106.0	106.0	—	—	—	—	—	—
1856	38	—	106.5	106.5	—	—	—	—	—	—
1857	37	—	120.6	120.6	—	—	—	—	—	—
1858	36	—	130.5	130.5	—	—	—	—	—	—
1859	38	—	151.7	151.7	—	—	—	—	—	—
1860	43	—	173.3	173.3	—	—	—	—	—	—
1861	44	—	173.3	173.3	—	—	—	—	—	—
1862	48	—	191.8	191.8	—	—	—	—	—	—
1863	50	—	276.1	276.1	—	—	—	—	—	—
1864	53	—	404.3	404.3	—	—	—	—	—	—
1865	61	—	589.9	589.9	—	—	—	—	—	—
1866	79	—	874.2	874.2	—	—	—	—	—	—
1867	100	—	1,168.0	1,168.0	—	—	—	—	—	—
1868	113	—	1,534.6	1,534.6	—	—	—	—	—	—
1869	127	—	1,824.8	1,824.8	—	—	—	—	—	—

Notes appear at end of table

TABLE Cj713–722   Life insurance – number of companies and life insurance in force, by type: 1759–1998 *Continued*

			Life insurance in force							
			Value					Average size policy		
	Companies	Policies	Total	Ordinary	Group	Industrial	Credit	Ordinary	Group	Industrial
	Cj713	Cj714	Cj715	Cj716	Cj717 [1]	Cj718 [2]	Cj719 [3]	Cj720	Cj721	Cj722
Year	Number	Million	Million dollars	Million dollars	Million dollars	Million dollars	Million dollars	Dollars	Dollars	Dollars
1870	129	—	2,006.1	2,006.1	—	—	—	—	—	—
1871	123	—	2,083.0	2,083.0	—	—	—	—	—	—
1872	108	—	2,079.2	2,079.2	—	—	—	—	—	—
1873	96	—	2,040.8	2,040.8	—	—	—	—	—	—
1874	96	—	1,947.6	1,947.6	—	—	—	—	—	—
1875	86	—	1,873.9	1,873.9	—	—	—	—	—	—
1876	76	—	1,690.6	1,690.2	—	(Z)	—	—	—	—
1877	69	—	1,512.1	1,511.1	—	1	—	—	—	—
1878	65	—	1,519.7	1,517.7	—	2	—	—	—	—
1879	61	—	1,474.9	1,469.5	—	5	—	—	—	—
1880	59	—	1,522.7	1,502.2	—	21	—	—	—	—
1881	58	—	1,606.5	1,573.0	—	34	—	—	—	—
1882	55	—	1,720.8	1,664.6	—	56	—	—	—	—
1883	56	—	1,872.1	1,784.9	—	87	—	—	—	—
1884	56	—	1,995.9	1,884.8	—	111	—	—	—	—
1885	56	—	2,007.1	1,861.3	—	146	—	—	—	—
1886	59	—	2,096.9	1,899.1	—	198	—	—	—	—
1887	60	—	2,456.3	2,201.8	—	255	—	—	—	—
1888	60	—	2,742.0	2,437.8	—	304	—	—	—	—
1889	60	—	3,122.6	2,758.1	—	365	—	—	—	—
1890	60	—	3,522.2	3,094.7	—	428	—	—	—	—
1891	63	—	3,868.0	3,388.0	—	481	—	—	—	—
1892	66	—	4,267.0	3,685.0	—	582	—	—	—	—
1893	66	—	4,609.0	3,948.0	—	661	—	—	—	—
1894	66	—	4,847.0	4,048.0	—	799	—	—	—	—
1895	67	9	4,988.0	4,170.0	—	818	—	2,440	—	120
1896	67	9	5,207.0	4,323.0	—	884	—	2,420	—	120
1897	69	10	5,555.0	4,563.0	—	992	—	2,340	—	120
1898	73	11	6,053.0	4,952.0	—	1,101	—	2,310	—	130
1899	82	12	6,822.0	5,547.0	—	1,275	—	2,210	—	130
1900	84	14	7,573.0	6,124.0	—	1,449	—	2,160	—	130
1901	86	16	8,369.0	6,766.0	—	1,603	—	2,040	—	130
1902	95	17	9,369.0	7,594.0	—	1,775	—	2,020	—	130
1903	101	19	10,217.0	8,264.0	—	1,953	—	1,970	—	140
1904	106	20	11,165.0	9,059.0	—	2,106	—	1,930	—	140
1905	126	22	11,863.0	9,585.0	—	2,278	—	1,880	—	140
1906	163	23	12,285.0	9,871.0	—	2,414	—	1,870	—	140
1907	190	24	12,639.0	10,103.0	—	2,536	—	1,860	—	140
1908	211	25	13,085.0	10,450.0	—	2,635	—	1,850	—	140
1909	254	27	13,878.0	10,960.0	—	2,918	—	1,830	—	140
1910	284	29	14,908.0	11,783.0	—	3,125	—	1,830	—	140
1911	304	31	16,125.0	12,772.0	(Z)	3,353	—	1,790	—	140
1912	305	34	17,301.0	13,709.0	13	3,579	—	1,800	1,080	140
1913	302	37	18,683.0	14,827.0	31	3,825	—	1,810	910	130
1914	307	39	19,737.0	15,661.0	65	4,011	—	1,810	970	130
1915	295	41	21,029.0	16,650.0	100	4,279	—	1,800	830	130
1916	293	45	22,853.0	18,081.0	155	4,617	—	1,800	780	130
1917	295	49	25,243.0	19,868.0	349	5,026	—	1,830	780	130
1918	295	53	27,924.0	21,818.0	630	5,474	2	1,840	840	140
1919	314	60	32,971.0	25,783.0	1,092	6,092	4	1,860	920	130
1920	335	65	40,540.0	32,018.0	1,570	6,948	4	1,990	960	150
1921	339	70	43,944.0	34,777.0	1,527	7,633	7	2,040	1,070	150
1922	347	76	48,342.0	38,053.0	1,795	8,486	8	2,090	1,150	150
1923	358	83	55,097.0	43,077.0	2,393	9,618	9	2,160	1,180	160
1924	369	90	61,327.0	47,283.0	3,127	10,905	12	2,200	1,280	170
1925	379	97	69,475.0	52,892.0	4,247	12,318	18	2,270	1,340	170
1926	396	104	77,642.0	58,453.0	5,362	13,803	24	2,350	1,400	180
1927	407	110	84,775.0	63,334.0	6,333	15,078	30	2,400	1,450	190
1928	433	116	92,590.0	68,430.0	7,889	16,231	40	2,410	1,580	200
1929	438	123	102,086.0	75,686.0	8,994	17,349	57	2,470	1,590	190

Notes appear at end of table

(continued)

TABLE Cj713–722   Life insurance – number of companies and life insurance in force, by type: 1759–1998 *Continued*

			Life insurance in force							
			Value					Average size policy		
Year	Companies	Policies	Total	Ordinary	Group	Industrial	Credit	Ordinary	Group	Industrial
	Cj713	Cj714	Cj715	Cj716	Cj717 [1]	Cj718 [2]	Cj719 [3]	Cj720	Cj721	Cj722
	Number	Million	Million dollars	Million dollars	Million dollars	Million dollars	Million dollars	Dollars	Dollars	Dollars
1930	438	124	106,413.0	78,576.0	9,801	17,963	73	2,460	1,700	210
1931	413	124	106,970.0	79,514.0	9,736	17,635	85	2,420	1,730	210
1932	392	116	101,559.0	75,898.0	8,923	16,669	69	2,380	1,860	210
1933	375	115	96,246.0	70,872.0	8,681	16,630	63	2,260	1,780	210
1934	371	117	96,677.0	70,094.0	9,472	17,036	75	2,210	1,710	220
1935	373	121	98,464.0	70,684.0	10,208	17,471	101	2,160	1,590	220
1936	372	124	102,653.0	72,361.0	11,291	18,863	138	2,160	1,670	230
1937	436	128	107,794.0	74,836.0	12,638	20,104	216	2,180	1,710	240
1938	435	129	108,927.0	75,772.0	12,503	20,396	256	2,150	1,890	240
1939	446	131	111,569.0	77,121.0	13,641	20,500	307	2,130	1,790	240
1940	444	134	115,530.0	79,346.0	14,938	20,866	380	2,130	1,700	240
1941	438	140	122,178.0	82,525.0	17,359	21,825	469	2,100	1,710	250
1942	435	144	127,721.0	85,139.0	19,316	22,911	355	2,090	1,740	250
1943	437	151	137,158.0	89,596.0	22,413	24,874	275	2,080	1,760	270
1944	451	159	145,771.0	95,085.0	23,922	26,474	290	2,080	1,860	270
1945	473	163	151,762.0	101,550.0	22,172	27,675	365	2,100	1,930	270
1946	514	173	170,066.0	112,818.0	27,206	29,313	729	2,150	2,060	280
1947	539	182	186,035.0	122,393.0	32,026	30,406	1,210	2,200	2,050	290
1948	584	187	201,208.0	131,158.0	37,068	31,253	1,729	2,240	2,280	290
1949	612	194	213,672.0	138,862.0	40,207	32,087	2,516	2,264	2,330	300
1950	649	202	234,168.0	149,116.0	47,793	33,415	3,844	2,319	2,478	310
1951	679	210	253,140.0	159,109.0	54,398	34,870	4,763	2,378	2,535	320
1952	730	219	276,591.0	170,875.0	62,913	36,448	6,355	2,452	2,667	330
1953	832	229	304,259.0	185,007.0	72,913	37,781	8,558	2,530	2,755	340
1954	917	237	333,719.0	198,599.0	86,410	38,664	10,046	2,619	3,018	350
1955	1,107	251	372,332.0	216,812.0	101,345	39,682	14,493	2,721	3,202	350
1956	1,191	261	412,630.0	238,348.0	117,399	40,109	16,774	2,853	3,361	360
1957	1,273	266	458,359.0	264,949.0	133,905	40,139	19,366	3,041	3,580	370
1958	1,365	267	493,561.0	288,607.0	144,772	39,646	20,536	3,227	3,736	380
1959	1,425	275	542,128.0	317,158.0	160,163	39,809	24,998	3,424	3,875	390
1960	1,441	282	586,448.0	341,881.0	175,903	39,563	29,101	3,597	4,034	390
1961	1,448	286	629,493.0	366,141.0	192,794	39,451	31,107	3,766	4,167	400
1962	1,469	290	675,977.0	391,048.0	209,950	39,638	35,341	3,932	4,323	420
1963	1,488	299	730,623.0	420,808.0	229,477	39,672	40,666	4,136	4,494	420
1964	1,547	308	797,808.0	457,868.0	253,620	39,833	46,487	4,382	4,637	430
1965	1,629	320	900,554.0	499,638.0	308,078	39,818	53,020	4,662	5,056	450
1966	1,704	331	984,689.0	541,022.0	345,945	39,663	58,059	4,938	5,356	450
1967	1,715	336	1,079,821.0	584,570.0	394,501	39,215	61,535	5,150	5,733	470
1968	1,763	346	1,183,354.0	633,392.0	442,778	38,827	68,357	5,453	6,074	480
1969	1,773	351	1,284,529.0	682,453.0	488,864	38,614	74,598	5,773	6,473	490
1970	1,780	355	1,402,123.0	734,730.0	551,357	38,644	77,392	6,105	6,905	500
1971	1,765	357	1,503,334.0	792,318.0	589,883	39,202	81,931	6,442	7,194	516
1972	1,753	365	1,627,985.0	853,911.0	640,689	39,975	93,410	6,777	7,538	526
1973	1,766	369	1,778,300.0	928,192.0	708,322	40,632	101,154	7,252	8,049	542
1974	1,757	380	1,985,120.0	1,009,038.0	827,018	39,441	109,623	7,703	8,798	556
1975	1,746	380	2,139,571.0	1,083,421.0	904,695	39,423	112,032	8,085	9,424	563
1976	1,742	382	2,343,063.0	1,177,672.0	1,002,647	39,175	123,569	8,596	10,026	585
1977	1,789	390	2,582,815.0	1,289,321.0	1,115,047	39,045	139,402	9,276	10,519	592
1978	1,840	401	2,870,250.0	1,425,095.0	1,243,994	38,080	163,081	10,036	11,207	595
1979	1,895	407	3,222,340.0	1,585,878.0	1,419,418	37,794	179,250	10,862	12,343	610
1980	1,958	402	3,541,038.0	1,760,474.0	1,579,355	35,994	165,215	11,895	13,384	621
1981	1,991	400	4,063,595.0	1,978,080.0	1,888,612	34,547	162,356	13,276	15,355	628
1982	2,060	389	4,476,659.0	2,216,388.0	2,066,361	32,766	161,144	15,181	16,664	630
1983	2,117	387	4,965,861.0	2,544,275.0	2,219,573	31,354	170,659	17,427	17,477	627
1984	2,193	385	5,499,987.0	2,887,574.0	2,392,358	30,104	189,951	19,914	18,837	641
1985	2,261	386	6,053,107.0	3,247,289.0	2,561,595	28,250	215,973	22,868	19,705	642
1986	2,254	391	6,750,279.0	3,658,203.0	2,801,049	27,168	233,859	25,582	20,749	647
1987	2,337	395	7,452,498.0	4,139,071.0	3,043,782	26,668	242,977	28,545	22,381	650
1988	2,343	391	8,020,159.0	4,511,608.0	3,232,080	25,456	251,015	31,331	23,421	653
1989	2,270	394	8,694,015.0	4,939,964.0	3,469,498	24,446	260,107	34,305	24,606	661

Notes appear at end of table

TABLE Cj713–722 **Life insurance – number of companies and life insurance in force, by type: 1759–1998** *Continued*

			Life insurance in force							
			Value					Average size policy		
Year	Companies	Policies	Total	Ordinary	Group	Industrial	Credit	Ordinary	Group	Industrial
	Cj713	Cj714	Cj715	Cj716	Cj717 [1]	Cj718 [2]	Cj719 [3]	Cj720	Cj721	Cj722
	Number	Million	Million dollars	Million dollars	Million dollars	Million dollars	Million dollars	Dollars	Dollars	Dollars
1990	2,195	389	9,392,597.0	5,366,982.0	3,753,506	24,071	248,038	38,064	26,621	669
1991	2,064	375	9,968,336.0	5,677,777.0	4,057,606	22,475	228,478	41,444	28,777	681
1992	1,944	366	10,405,792.0	5,941,810.0	4,240,919	20,973	202,090	43,057	29,866	699
1993	1,844	363	11,104,741.0	6,428,434.0	4,456,338	20,451	199,518	45,917	31,383	705
1994	2,136	366	11,081,335.0	6,429,811.0	4,443,179	18,947	189,398	45,927	30,643	653
1995	2,079	370	11,696,325.0	6,872,252.0	4,604,856	18,134	201,083	49,441	31,326	672
1996	1,679	355	12,704,296.0	7,407,682.0	5,067,804	18,064	210,746	52,912	36,459	695
1997	1,620	351	13,363,858.0	7,854,570.0	5,279,042	17,991	212,255	57,333	37,176	720
1998	1,563	358	14,471,449.0	8,505,894.0	5,735,273	17,365	212,917	62,543	37,732	724

(Z) Series Cj715–716, less than $50,000. Series Cj717–718, less than $500,000.

[1] Initial year 1911.

[2] First weekly premium policy issued 1873; industrial agency system introduced 1875.

[3] Initial year 1917.

Sources

Series Cj713. 1759–1936: J. Owen Stalson, *Marketing Life Insurance: Its History in America* (Harvard University Press, 1942), pp. 748–53. 1937–1939: Institute of Life Insurance estimates. 1940–1998: Institute of Life Insurance, *Life Insurance Fact Book* (various years).

Series Cj714–716. 1815–1850: Stalson (1942). 1854–1894: Spectator Company, *Spectator Insurance Year Book* (various issues); Institute of Life Insurance, unpublished data. 1895–1998: Frederick L. Hoffman, "Fifty Years of American Life Insurance," *Quarterly Publications of the American Statistical Association*, New Series, 95 (12) (1911), 667–760; *Life Insurance Fact Book* (various issues).

Series Cj717–722. *Life Insurance Fact Book* (various issues).

Documentation

The figures comprise the total number of companies in operation and domiciled in the United States and the life insurance in force in the United States at the end of the year. The number of companies is larger than the number of companies for which life insurance in force data are available. Alaska and Hawai'i are first included in the data in 1960.

Ordinary life insurance refers to life insurance usually issued in amounts of $1,000 or more, with premiums payable on an annual, semiannual, quarterly, or monthly basis. Group life insurance is life insurance issued, usually without medical examination, on a group of persons under a master policy. It is usually issued to an employer for the benefit of employees. The individual members of the group hold certificates as evidence of their insurance. Industrial life insurance is life insurance issued in small amounts, usually not more than $500. Premiums are payable on a weekly or monthly basis and are generally collected at the home by an agent of the company. Credit life insurance is term life insurance sold through a lender or lending agency to cover payment of a loan, installment purchase, or other obligation, in case of death. Lending agencies are defined to include agencies that sell merchandise on time and mortgage departments of life insurance companies, as well as banks, finance companies, and other institutions or agencies to or through which financial obligations are incurred. The data refer to insurance on loans of duration of ten years or less.

Life insurance in force is the sum total of the face amounts (plus additions purchased with dividends) of the life insurance outstanding at a given time. The additional amount of life insurance payable under accidental death provisions (providing for payment of an additional death benefit in case of death as a result of accidental means, often called double indemnity) is not included. Data represent all life insurance in force with U.S. life companies, including both direct business and reinsurance acquired. Data include group certificates and credit life insurance. For the policies in force for 1854–1894,

the series were derived by deducting from the insurance in force figures of U.S. life insurance companies the amount of their Canadian and other foreign business, and adding thereto the U.S. business of Canadian and other foreign companies. Data for 1895–1948 were derived from the totals of individual state estimates given in the "Life Insurance in Force by States" section of each *Spectator Insurance Year Book*. For ordinary life insurance, the figures for 1815–1850 are for all available companies; for 1854–1877, the figures are for life insurance companies reporting to the New York Insurance Department. Beginning with 1878, the data are for all available companies. All the data for group, industrial, and credit life insurance are for all available companies.

Ordinary insurance in force of U.S. companies was compiled from the following sources: 1854–1858, Spectator Company, *Spectator Insurance Year Book* (1878), p. 71; 1859–1877, Stalson (1942), p. 820; 1878–1894, *Spectator Insurance Year Book* (various issues: for certain years, adjustments were made). Ordinary business of U.S. companies in Canada: 1869–1894, Stalson (1942), pp. 833–4 (1873 figure adjusted; 1885–1894, industrial business in Canada of U.S. companies subtracted to get ordinary business in Canada). Ordinary business of U.S. companies in foreign countries other than Canada: 1868–1885, Stalson (1942), p. 824; 1886–1888, Hoffman (1911), p. 86; 1889–1894, *Spectator Insurance Year Book* (1899), p. 466. Ordinary business of Canadian companies in the United States: 1889–1894, Stalson (1942), p. 839. Ordinary business of other foreign companies in the United States: 1854–1870, series for U.S. branches of British companies estimated by the Institute of Life Insurance; 1871–1881, 1885–1886, State of New York Insurance Department, *New York Insurance Report* (various issues); 1882–1884, data not available, but probably insignificant.

Industrial insurance in force of U.S. companies was compiled from the following sources: 1876–1894, Spectator Company, *Spectator Insurance Year Book* (various issues; for certain years, adjustments were made); industrial business of U.S. companies in Canada: 1885–1894, *Spectator Insurance Year Book* (various issues). Canadian and other foreign companies have never written industrial life insurance in the United States, according to available information.

Life insurance in force figures have been adjusted to represent insurance in force on the lives of residents of the United States, whether issued by U.S. or by foreign companies. For statistics of life insurance in force with U.S. life insurance companies, whether the policyholders are residents of the United States or of some other country, and for the number of policies outstanding, see the *Life Insurance Fact Book*. Estimates by states are available from the "Life Insurance in Force by States" section of the annual *Spectator Insurance Year Book* and the *Life Insurance Fact Book*.

For an alternative series on life insurance in force in the United States for selected years, 1815–1937, see Stalson (1942), pp. 816–17. The alternative series includes fraternal, assessment, and other types of life insurance and is derived from aggregate figures of U.S., Canadian, and foreign companies, rather than as totals of state figures.

TABLE Cj723–726 Life insurance – sales, by type of insurance: 1854–1998

Contributed by Eugene N. White

Year	Total Cj723 [1] Million dollars	Ordinary Cj724 Million dollars	Group Cj725 Million dollars	Industrial Cj726 Million dollars	Year	Total Cj723 [1] Million dollars	Ordinary Cj724 Million dollars	Group Cj725 Million dollars	Industrial Cj726 Million dollars
1854	15	15	—	—	1915	3,285	2,437	48	800
1855	17	17	—	—	1916	3,893	2,986	90	817
1856	20	20	—	—	1917	4,553	3,500	184	869
1857	21	21	—	—	1918	4,731	3,520	268	943
1858	23	23	—	—	1919	7,882	6,369	433	1,080
1859	30	30	—	—	1920	9,415	7,634	441	1,340
1860	36	36	—	—	1921	7,957	6,248	128	1,581
1861	25	25	—	—	1922	8,885	6,720	298	1,867
1862	44	44	—	—	1923	11,061	8,273	549	2,239
1863	90	90	—	—	1924	12,039	8,764	649	2,626
1864	156	156	—	—	1925	14,278	10,060	1,075	3,143
1865	245	245	—	—	1926	15,217	10,508	1,174	3,535
1866	405	405	—	—	1927	15,582	10,777	1,008	3,797
1867	472	472	—	—	1928	16,942	11,654	1,508	3,780
1868	580	580	—	—	1929	17,755	12,305	1,379	4,071
1869	615	615	—	—	1930	17,265	11,905	1,381	3,979
1870	588	588	—	—	1931	15,066	10,161	927	3,978
1871	489	489	—	—	1932	12,305	7,896	720	3,689
1872	490	490	—	—	1933	10,846	6,786	427	3,633
1873	466	466	—	—	1934	11,928	7,363	534	4,031
1874	352	352	—	—	1935	12,298	7,550	715	4,033
1875	299	299	—	—	1936	12,165	7,314	626	4,225
1876	233	233	—	1	1937	12,572	7,593	800	4,179
1877	179	178	—	1	1938	11,045	6,745	507	3,793
1878	168	166	—	2	1939	10,935	6,886	844	3,205
1879	178	173	—	5	1940	11,087	7,022	747	3,318
1880	228	193	—	35	1941	12,564	7,935	1,197	3,432
1881	268	231	—	37	1942	11,888	7,041	1,657	3,190
1882	321	269	—	52	1943	13,281	8,022	1,924	3,335
1883	394	317	—	77	1944	14,124	9,184	1,621	3,319
1884	418	329	—	89	1945	15,391	10,577	1,302	3,512
1885	432	339	—	94	1946	22,805	16,244	2,152	4,409
1886	609	477	—	133	1947	23,637	16,131	2,768	4,738
1887	697	538	—	159	1948	23,380	15,787	2,998	4,595
1888	723	545	—	178	1949	24,215	15,848	2,911	5,456
1889	871	669	—	202	1950	29,989	18,260	6,237	5,492
1890	984	742	—	242	1951	28,857	19,000	4,261	5,596
1891	1,006	779	—	227	1952	32,954	21,579	5,285	6,090
1892	1,096	819	—	277	1953	38,134	24,908	6,609	6,617
1893	1,131	797	—	334	1954	47,453 [2]	26,824	13,669 [2]	6,960
1894	1,274	712	—	562	1955	50,243 [2]	32,207	11,637 [2]	6,399
1895	1,113	744	—	369	1956	60,037	38,941	14,518	6,578
1896	1,034	687	—	347	1957	71,748	48,937	16,016	6,795
1897	1,196	803	—	393	1958	72,918	50,839	15,061	7,018
1898	1,286	883	—	403	1959	75,107	55,138	13,077	6,892
1899	1,609	1,118	—	491	1960	78,417	56,183	15,328	6,906
1900	1,755	1,221	—	534	1961	85,317	58,888	19,181	7,248
1901	1,895	1,326	—	569	1962	84,624	61,259	16,260	7,105
1902	2,064	1,488	—	576	1963	95,882	68,862	19,854	7,166
1903	2,217	1,660	—	557	1964	111,899	79,430	25,149	7,320
1904	2,316	1,729	—	587	1965	142,166 [3]	83,485	51,385 [3]	7,296
1905	2,283	1,666	—	617	1966	121,990	88,693	26,219	7,078
1906	1,963	1,377	—	586	1967	140,868 [2]	94,694	39,118 [2]	7,056
1907	1,782	1,272	—	510	1968	150,495 [2]	103,944	39,877 [2]	6,674
1908	1,884	1,379	—	505	1969	159,283	113,500	39,329	6,454
1909	2,232	1,574	—	658	1970	193,122 [3]	122,820	63,690 [3]	6,612
1910	2,371	1,742	—	629	1971	188,811	132,130	49,407	7,274
1911	2,688	2,008	(Z)	680	1972	208,730	145,479	55,857	7,394
1912	2,886	2,125	13	748	1973	234,191	162,506	64,461	7,224
1913	3,175	2,414	22	739	1974	301,057 [3]	182,755	111,622 [3]	6,680
1914	3,098	2,305	41	752					

Notes appear at end of table

TABLE Cj723–726   Life insurance – sales, by type of insurance: 1854–1998   *Continued*

Year	Total Cj723 [1] Million dollars	Ordinary Cj724 Million dollars	Group Cj725 Million dollars	Industrial Cj726 Million dollars	Year	Total Cj723 [1] Million dollars	Ordinary Cj724 Million dollars	Group Cj725 Million dollars	Industrial Cj726 Million dollars
1975	289,922 [3]	188,003	95,190 [3]	6,729	1990	1,529,151	1,069,880	459,271	—
1976	324,849	213,784	104,683	6,382	1991	1,615,659 [3]	1,041,706	573,953 [3]	—
1977	369,796	247,453	115,839	6,504	1992	1,488,500	1,048,357	440,143	—
1978	414,211	283,067	125,129	6,015	1993	1,678,299	1,101,476	576,823	—
1979	492,812	329,571	157,906	5,335	1994	1,617,465	1,057,233	560,232	—
1980	572,602	385,575	183,418	3,609	1995	1,577,086	1,039,258	537,828	—
1981	831,114 [2,3]	481,895	346,702 [2,3]	2,517	1996	1,703,833	1,089,268	614,565	—
1982	837,874	585,444	250,532	1,898	1997	1,892,270	1,203,681	688,589	—
1983	1,026,441	753,444	271,609	1,388	1998	2,064,179	1,324,671	739,508	—
1984	1,114,779	820,315	293,521	943					
1985	1,231,169	910,944	319,503	722					
1986	1,308,751 [2,3]	933,592	374,741 [2,3]	418					
1987	1,352,513	986,660	365,529	324					
1988	1,406,854	995,686	410,848	320					
1989	1,441,678	1,020,719	420,707	252					

(Z) Less than $500,000.

[1] First weekly premium policy issued in 1873; industrial agency system introduced in 1875. Yearly sales for 1873–1875 were probably less than $500,000. Includes industrial life insurance sales for 1990–1998. Industrial life insurance sales amounted to $106 million in 1998.

[2] Includes federal employees' group life insurance of $6,756 million in 1954, $1,928 million in 1955, $8.2 billion in 1967, $3.4 billion in 1968, $84.4 billion in 1981, and $10.8 billion in 1985.

[3] Includes servicemen's group life insurance of $27.4 billion in 1965, $17.1 billion in 1970, $29.2 billion in 1974, $1.7 billion in 1975, $45.6 billion in 1981, $51.0 billion in 1986, and $166.7 billion in 1991.

Sources

Series Cj723. 1854–1920: a summation of series Cj724–726; 1921–1998: Institute of Life Insurance, *Life Insurance Fact Book* (1958), p. 23; (1974), p. 16; (1983), p. 10; (1990), p. 10; (1999), pp. 20–1.

Series Cj724. 1854–1910: Spectator Company, *Spectator Insurance Year Book* (various issues; for certain years, adjustments were made by the Institute of Life Insurance); 1911–1920: Institute of Life Insurance, unpublished data (based on data from summary table of Spectator Company, *Spectator Compendium of Official Life Insurance Reports* for each year); 1921–1998: Institute of Life Insurance, *Life Insurance Fact Book* (1958), p. 23; (1974), p. 16; (1983), p. 10; (1990), p. 10; (1999), pp. 20–1.

Series Cj725. 1911–1920, Institute of Life Insurance, unpublished data (1911–1918, estimated from a survey of companies writing group life insurance at that time; 1919–1920, compiled from Group Life Exhibit in Spectator Company, *Spectator Compendium of Official Life Insurance Reports* (various issues)); 1921–1998, Institute of Life Insurance, *Life Insurance Fact Book* (1958), p. 23; (1972), p. 21; (1983), p. 10; (1990), p. 10; (1999), pp. 20–1.

Series Cj726. 1873–1910: Spectator Company, *Spectator Insurance Year Book* (various issues); 1911–1920: *Spectator Compendium of Official Life Insurance Reports* (various issues); 1921–1989: Institute of Life Insurance, *Life Insurance Fact Book* (1958), p. 23; (1972), p. 21; (1983), p. 10; (1990), p. 10; (1999), pp. 20–1.

Documentation

Figures represent U.S. life insurance companies' sales in the United States and in other countries. Alaska and Hawai'i are first included in the 1959 figures. Credit life insurance is excluded. The data also exclude revivals, increases, and dividend additions. The figures include reinsurance until 1964 and exclude reinsurance thereafter.

Life insurance sales represent the sum total of the face amount of life insurance sold in a given period (in this case, one year). The additional amount of life insurance payable under accidental death provisions is not included. Total life insurance sales in the United States, representing all sales to residents of the United States, whether issued by U.S. or foreign companies, are available beginning with 1940.

Sales of ordinary life insurance estimates for 1854–1877 are for life insurance companies reporting to the New York Insurance Department. Thereafter, the data are for all available companies. Beginning in 1888, the data are on a paid-for basis; beginning in 1893, they exclude revivals, increases, and dividend additions. The group life insurance figures are on a paid-for basis. Figures for 1912–1918 may reflect increases in existing contracts to some extent. Beginning in 1919, figures exclude revivals, increases, and dividend additions. Figures for industrial life insurance exclude revivals, increases, and dividend additions starting in 1893.

TABLE Cj727–732   Life insurance – company income, by type: 1854–1998

Contributed by Eugene N. White

Year	Total	Premiums		Health insurance	Investment income	Other
		Life insurance	Annuity			
	Cj727	Cj728 [1]	Cj729 [1]	Cj730	Cj731 [2]	Cj732 [2]
	Million dollars	Million dollars	Million dollars	Million dollars	Million dollars	Million dollars
1854	3.2	2.6	—	—	—	0.6
1855	3.5	3.0	—	—	—	0.5
1856	3.8	3.0	—	—	—	0.8
1857	4.0	3.2	—	—	—	0.8
1858	4.5	3.6	—	—	—	0.9
1859	5.2	4.0	—	—	—	1.2
1860	6.0	4.8	—	—	—	1.2
1861	6.3	4.9	—	—	—	1.4
1862	7.4	5.7	—	—	—	1.7
1863	10.6	8.5	—	—	—	2.1
1864	16.1	13.1	—	—	—	3.0
1865	24.9	21.6	—	—	—	3.3
1866	40.4	35.8	(Z)	—	—	4.6
1867	56.5	50.4	(Z)	—	—	6.1
1868	77.4	67.8	0.1	—	—	9.5
1869	98.5	86.0	0.1	—	—	12.4
1870	105.0	90.2	0.1	—	—	14.7
1871	113.5	96.6	0.1	—	—	16.8
1872	117.3	96.5	0.1	—	—	20.7
1873	118.4	95.8	0.2	—	—	22.4
1874	115.7	89.2	0.2	—	—	26.3
1875	108.6	83.4	0.4	—	—	24.8
1876	96.4	71.8	0.3	—	—	24.3
1877	86.2	62.7	0.3	—	—	23.2
1878	80.5	56.8	0.5	—	—	23.2
1879	77.8	53.1	0.7	—	—	24.0
1880	77.7	53.0	1.2	—	—	23.5
1881	80.2	54.9	1.9	—	—	23.4
1882	85.7	59.4	1.7	—	—	24.6
1883	93.4	66.0	2.2	—	—	25.2
1884	98.1	71.8	1.3	—	—	25.0
1885	107.0	78.8	1.2	—	—	27.0
1886	119.1	89.1	1.7	—	—	28.3
1887	133.7	101.6	1.9	—	—	30.2
1888	153.9	117.9	2.4	—	—	33.6
1889	176.2	137.2	2.9	—	—	36.1
1890	195.6	153.6	3.2	—	—	38.8
1891	213.4	170.0	2.9	—	—	40.5
1892	227.6	181.9	2.6	—	—	43.1
1893	241.7	195.0	2.0	—	—	44.7
1894	262.0	207.1	2.6	—	—	52.3
1895	271.9	216.1	3.6	—	—	52.2
1896	283.7	222.9	5.0	—	—	55.8
1897	304.9	237.3	6.0	—	—	61.6
1898	325.5	252.6	5.1	—	—	67.8
1899	365.4	285.6	6.2	—	—	73.6
1900	400.6	318.4	6.3	—	—	75.9
1901	458.0	357.6	8.7	—	—	91.7
1902	504.5	396.5	10.4	—	—	97.6
1903	553.6	438.7	8.8	—	—	106.1
1904	599.1	477.2	11.1	—	—	110.8
1905	642.1	507.7	8.3	—	—	126.1
1906	667.2	521.5	5.1	—	—	140.6
1907	678.7	528.4	4.7	—	—	145.6
1908	703.9	542.0	3.9	—	—	158.0
1909	748.0	560.2	5.0	—	—	182.8

Notes appear at end of table

TABLE Cj727–732   Life insurance – company income, by type: 1854–1998 *Continued*

Year	Total	Premiums		Health insurance	Investment income	Other
		Life insurance	Annuity			
	Cj727	Cj728 [1]	Cj729 [1]	Cj730	Cj731 [2]	Cj732 [2]
	Million dollars	Million dollars	Million dollars	Million dollars	Million dollars	Million dollars
1910	781.0	587.7	5.7	—	—	187.6
1911	836.1	625.9	4.2	—	—	206.0
1912	893.4	666.3	4.9	—	—	222.2
1913	945.6	708.5	4.6	—	—	232.5
1914	985.0	738.8	5.4	—	—	240.8
1915	1,043.1	776.4	5.7	—	—	261.0
1916	1,118	835	10	—	—	273
1917	1,249	916	10	—	—	323
1918	1,325	980	11	—	—	334
1919	1,560	1,187	17	—	—	356
1920	1,764	1,374	7	—	—	383
1921	1,951	1,523	11	—	—	417
1922	2,149	1,671	11	—	—	467
1923	2,427	1,881	13	—	—	533
1924	2,703	2,096	20	—	—	587
1925	3,018	2,340	38	—	—	640
1926	3,330	2,577	39	—	—	714
1927	3,673	2,814	52	—	—	807
1928	4,088	3,037	98	—	—	953
1929	4,337	3,251	92	—	—	994
1930	4,594	3,416	101	—	—	1,077
1931	4,850	3,477	176	—	—	1,197
1932	4,653	3,314	181	—	—	1,158
1933	4,622	3,057	254	—	—	1,311
1934	4,786	3,107	400	—	—	1,279
1935	5,072	3,182	491	—	—	1,399
1936	5,180	3,216	440	—	—	1,524
1937	5,257	3,354	376	—	—	1,527
1938	5,357	3,368	393	—	—	1,596
1939	5,453	3,431	345	—	—	1,677
1940	5,658	3,501	386	—	—	1,771
1941	5,855	3,607	413	—	—	1,835
1942	6,029	3,753	368	—	—	1,908
1943	6,442	3,942	415	—	—	2,085
1944	7,011	4,265	528	—	—	2,218
1945	7,674	4,589	570	—	—	2,515
1946	8,068	4,982	644	—	—	2,442
1947	9,114	5,370	718	1,567	565	894
1948	9,751	5,679	799	1,707	679	887
1949	10,376	5,926	768	1,899	817	966
1950	11,337	6,249	939	2,075	1,001	1,073
1951	12,012	6,785	961	1,948	1,294	1,024
1952	13,076	7,228	1,094	2,160	1,561	1,033
1953	14,271	7,778	1,190	2,353	1,879	1,071
1954	15,280	8,239	1,209	2,590	2,115	1,127
1955	16,544	8,903	1,288	2,801	2,355	1,197
1956	17,865	9,592	1,293	3,063	2,699	1,218
1957	19,333	10,241	1,408	3,331	3,126	1,227
1958	20,249	10,753	1,424	3,492	3,294	1,286
1959	21,790	11,487	1,494	3,879	3,641	1,289
1960	23,007	11,998	1,341	4,304	4,026	1,338
1961	24,397	12,546	1,385	4,668	4,327	1,471
1962	26,000	13,215	1,484	5,044	4,674	1,583
1963	28,584	14,266	1,742	5,821	5,105	1,650
1964	30,674	15,128	1,912	6,276	5,613	1,745
1965	33,167	16,083	2,260	6,778	6,261	1,785
1966	36,134	17,160	2,416	7,353	7,244	1,961
1967	38,635	18,094	2,671	7,929	7,887	2,054
1968	41,863	19,364	2,993	8,613	8,730	2,163
1969	45,628	20,491	3,762	9,354	9,743	2,278

Notes appear at end of table

(continued)

TABLE Cj727–732 Life insurance – company income, by type: 1854–1998 *Continued*

	Total	Premiums			Investment income	Other
		Life insurance	Annuity	Health insurance		
	Cj727	Cj728 [1]	Cj729 [1]	Cj730	Cj731 [2]	Cj732 [2]
Year	Million dollars	Million dollars	Million dollars	Million dollars	Million dollars	Million dollars
1970	49,054	21,679	3,721	10,144	11,367	2,143
1971	54,202	22,935	4,910	11,031	12,897	2,429
1972	58,848	24,678	5,503	12,127	14,318	2,222
1973	64,753	26,373	6,771	13,670	15,524	2,415
1974	70,010	27,750	7,737	15,144	17,123	2,256
1975	78,022	29,336	10,165	16,488	19,074	2,959
1976	88,558	31,358	13,962	18,758	21,059	3,421
1977	97,985	33,765	14,974	21,713	23,580	3,953
1978	108,206	36,592	16,339	25,294	25,829	4,152
1979	119,139	39,083	17,939	29,562	27,894	4,661
1980	130,888	40,829	22,429	33,928	29,366	4,336
1981	151,866	46,246	27,579	39,774	31,803	6,464
1982	170,044	50,800	34,644	45,532	34,960	4,108
1983	176,026	50,265	30,544	50,862	38,201	6,154
1984	206,109	51,274	42,859	59,213	40,671	12,092
1985	234,027	60,127	53,899	67,952	41,837	10,212
1986	282,257	66,213	83,712	75,435	44,153	12,744
1987	314,298	76,737	88,677	82,875	47,549	18,460
1988	338,140	73,531	103,278	92,042	52,306	16,983
1989	367,318	73,290	114,997	103,965	56,079	18,987
1990	402,200	76,692	129,064	111,853	58,254	26,337
1991	411,022	79,301	123,590	118,984	60,900	28,247
1992	426,916	83,868	132,645	121,389	65,545	23,469
1993	466,350	94,448	156,445	124,205	68,658	22,594
1994	492,628	98,948	153,019	125,999	86,184	28,478
1995	528,054	102,766	158,389	143,967	90,038	32,894
1996	561,087	107,598	178,416	152,700	92,183	30,190
1997	610,646	115,039	197,529	170,713	92,737	34,628
1998	663,383	119,897	229,493	176,801	94,881	42,311

(Z) Less than $50,000.

[1] Annuity premiums included with life insurance 1854–1865.

[2] Investment income and health insurance premiums are included in other income for 1854–1946.

Sources

1854–1910: Spectator Company, *Spectator Insurance Year Book* (various issues); 1911–1998: Institute of Life Insurance, *Life Insurance Fact Book* (1958), p. 53; (1970), p. 57; (1999), pp. 93–4.

Documentation

The data for 1854–1887 are for life insurance companies reporting to the New York Insurance Department. Thereafter, the data are for all available U.S. companies. Alaska and Hawai'i are first included in the data in 1959.

In general, before 1951, income and disbursement items were reported on a cash basis (in the accounting use of the term). Beginning in 1951, income and disbursement items are reported on an accrual basis (reflecting earned income and incurred claims and expenses).

Before 1951, gross investment income (without deduction of investment expenses) was reported as income, and investment expenses were reported as disbursements (included with "commissions, expenses, taxes, and other disbursements"). Beginning in 1951, investment expenses are deducted from gross investment income and the resulting net figure is reported as income.

Life insurance premiums for 1911–1998 were obtained by subtracting from premium income, as reported in the source, the annuity premium series. Since 1947, accident and health premiums have also been subtracted from premium income. This series includes premiums for ordinary, group, and industrial life insurance, including disability and accidental death provi-

sions. A premium is defined as the payment, or one of the regular periodical payments, a policyholder is required to make for an insurance policy.

An annuity is defined as a contract that provides an income for a specified period of time, such as a number of years or for life. A supplementary contract is an agreement by the company to retain the lump sum payable under an insurance policy and to make payments in accordance with the settlement option chosen. Annuity premiums include considerations for group and individual annuities. Annuity premiums are included with life insurance payments for the years 1854–1865. Before 1911, figures include considerations for supplementary contracts with life contingencies. Annuity premiums data for 1911–1931 were obtained by subtracting, from the "consideration for annuities" figures given in the aggregates of the *Spectator Compendium* each year, the amount of supplementary contracts involving life contingencies. The series on supplementary contracts involving life contingencies was compiled by the Institute of Life Insurance from data in the *New York Insurance Reports* and the annual editions of Alfred M. Best Company, *Best's Life Insurance Reports*. For 1932–1951, data were obtained directly by summing annuity income items from *Spectator Insurance Year Book* aggregates each year. For 1952–1955, data were obtained by summing group and individual annuity data given in Institute of Life Insurance, *The Tally of Life Insurance Statistics* (August 1956), p. 1; for 1956, Institute of Life Insurance, unpublished data; for 1957, *Life Insurance Fact Book* (1958), p. 54; for 1958–1998, *Life Insurance Fact Book* (various issues).

Beginning in 1951, investment income is net of investment expenses. For 1911–1970, figures include considerations for supplementary contracts both with and without life contingencies. Before 1911, figures include considerations for supplementary contracts without life contingencies.

TABLE Cj733–740   Life insurance – benefit payments: 1854–1998

Contributed by Eugene N. White

Year	Total	Death benefits	Matured endowments	Annuity payments	Policy dividends	Surrender values under Life	Surrender values under Annuity	Disability payments and accidental death benefits
	Cj733 [1]	Cj734	Cj735	Cj736 [2]	Cj737 [2,3]	Cj738	Cj739 [4]	Cj740 [5]
	Million dollars	Million dollars	Million dollars	Million dollars	Million dollars	Million dollars	Million dollars	Million dollars
1854	—	1.0	—	—	—	—	—	—
1855	—	1.2	—	—	—	—	—	—
1856	—	1.0	—	—	—	—	—	—
1857	—	1.2	—	—	—	—	—	—
1858	—	1.2	—	—	—	—	—	—
1859	1.9	1.3 [6]	— [6]	— [6]	0.4	0.1	—	—
1860	2.1	1.4 [6]	— [6]	— [6]	0.5	0.2	—	—
1861	2.8	1.5 [6]	— [6]	— [6]	0.6	0.7	—	—
1862	2.8	1.7 [6]	— [6]	— [6]	0.6	0.5	—	—
1863	3.7	2.3 [6]	— [6]	— [6]	1.0	0.4	—	—
1864	4.6	3.1 [6]	— [6]	— [6]	1.0	0.4	—	—
1865	6.3	4.1 [6]	— [6]	— [6]	1.5	0.7	—	—
1866	10.2	6.1	0.3	(Z)	2.5	1.2	—	—
1867	16.5	7.6	0.6	(Z)	6.2	2.1	—	—
1868	26.5	10.1	0.9	0.1	11.7	3.8	—	—
1869	36.6	15.6 [7]	— [7]	0.1	15.7	5.1	—	—
1870	44.9	19.5 [7]	— [7]	0.1	15.8	9.6	—	—
1871	56.7	28.7 [7]	— [7]	0.1	14.6	13.3	—	—
1872	59.7	25.6 [7]	— [7]	0.1	20.1	13.9	—	—
1873	66.8	27.1 [7]	— [7]	0.1	22.9	16.7	—	—
1874	64.9	25.7 [7]	— [7]	0.1	16.6	22.5	—	—
1875	65.5	25.0	2.0	0.2	17.9	20.4	—	—
1876	63.1	22.3	3.0	0.2	16.2	21.4	—	—
1877	60.7	21.0	4.9	0.2	15.4	19.2	—	—
1878	60.9	19.7	9.2	0.3	14.6	17.1	—	—
1879	57.4	22.6	8.8	0.3	13.5	12.2	—	—
1880	53.2	21.9	7.9	0.3	13.2	9.9	—	—
1881	52.7	22.8	7.9	0.5	12.6	8.9	—	—
1882	52.8	23.0	6.4	0.6	13.6	9.3	—	—
1883	56.4	25.4	7.9	0.8	13.4	8.8	—	—
1884	59.5	27.1	8.8	1.0	13.0	9.5	—	—
1885	61.6	30.3	7.6	1.1	13.0	9.6	—	—
1886	61.5	30.8	6.9	1.1	13.2	9.4	—	—
1887	68.9	35.9	6.5	1.2	14.9	10.4	—	—
1888	76.5	41.1	8.1	1.4	14.5	11.5	—	—
1889	82.1	44.9	9.1	1.5	14.1	12.4	—	—
1890	90.0	50.9	8.9	1.8	14.5	14.0	—	—
1891	97.0	55.8	8.5	2.0	14.2	16.5	—	—
1892	104.5	63.9	8.0	2.1	14.7	15.9	—	—
1893	112.7	66.6	8.5	2.3	15.1	20.2	—	—
1894	118.4	69.3	8.3	2.3	14.8	23.6	—	—
1895	125.1	73.1	10.9	2.4	15.4	23.4	—	—
1896	136.2	77.3	12.3	2.6	17.2	26.7	—	—
1897	139.4	78.6	12.4	3.0	18.5	27.0	—	—
1898	146.8	82.7	14.0	3.4	20.0	26.8	—	—
1899	160.0	96.2	15.4	3.7	21.4	23.4	—	—
1900	168.7	100.7	18.3	4.1	22.9	22.7	—	—
1901	192.4	117.9	21.3	4.4	24.3	24.6	—	—
1902	199.9	118.4	22.4	4.9	26.9	27.3	—	—
1903	225.8	131.7	24.6	5.6	31.4	32.6	—	—
1904	247.1	144.5	25.3	6.3	33.6	37.4	—	—
1905	265.0	149.7	28.0	6.8	36.1	44.4	—	—
1906	287.3	153.0	29.3	7.1	40.3	57.7	—	—
1907	309.7	164.2	33.0	7.3	46.3	58.9	—	—
1908	335.8	164.7	34.9	7.2	54.5	74.5	—	—
1909	360.7	172.3	41.2	7.4	63.0	76.8	—	—
1910	387.3	180.7	46.4	7.4	75.4	77.5	—	—
1911	414.3	194.1	48.5	7.4	83.1	81.2	—	—
1912	448.8	205.2	55.7	7.8	92.8	87.4	—	—
1913	469.6	209.6	56.0	8.4	101.2	94.4	—	—
1914	509.5	222.1	60.7	8.1	107.9	110.6	—	—

Notes appear at end of table

(continued)

TABLE Cj733–740   Life insurance – benefit payments: 1854–1998   *Continued*

Year	Total	Death benefits	Matured endowments	Annuity payments	Policy dividends	Surrender values under Life	Surrender values under Annuity	Disability payments and accidental death benefits
	Cj733 [1]	Cj734	Cj735	Cj736 [2]	Cj737 [2,3]	Cj738	Cj739 [4]	Cj740 [5]
	Million dollars	Million dollars	Million dollars	Million dollars	Million dollars	Million dollars	Million dollars	Million dollars
1915	544.7	237.4	63.4	8.9	111.3	123.8	—	—
1916	566.4	256.4	63.5	9.1	125.3	112.0	—	—
1917	590.2	264.6	74.6	10.0	136.7	104.3	—	—
1918	710.2	372.9	80.0	11.1	145.2	101.0	—	—
1919	739.9	354.1	103.7	10.9	159.5	111.7	—	—
1920	744.6	350.0	101.2	9.4	157.5	119.0	—	7.5
1921	840.0	338.9	121.9	10.7	192.0	167.2	—	9.3
1922	1,005.7	370.1	138.3	9.5	259.8	218.4	—	9.6
1923	1,089.1	420.8	142.9	10.0	274.7	225.3	—	15.4
1924	1,205.1	449.7	138.6	10.1	351.1	235.7	—	19.9
1925	1,246.2	493.4	114.5	10.0	351.1	248.6	—	28.6
1926	1,373.2	569.1	98.7	11.3	376.9	282.9	—	34.3
1927	1,499.9	613.5	89.2	13.0	417.9	324.5	—	41.8
1928	1,698.7	705.9	89.9	16.8	465.8	369.2	—	51.1
1929	1,961.5	807.8	108.8	21.2	513.2	448.0	—	62.5
1930	2,246.8	855.8	112.0	23.3	553.7	614.2	—	87.8
1931	2,606.6	915.2	117.0	29.0	584.6	861.0	—	99.8
1932	3,087.0	905.3	122.6	36.5	562.7	1,346.1	—	113.8
1933	3,016.4	877.1	121.0	42.2	499.4	1,356.6	—	120.1
1934	2,704.9	875.4	129.4	58.2	437.7	1,077.8	—	126.4
1935	2,535.1	877.4	145.0	76.1	424.2	882.5	—	129.9
1936	2,429.2	919.2	154.2	94.8	418.3	712.7	—	130.0
1937	2,437.0	937.3	154.7	109.9	435.4	669.3	—	130.4
1938	2,578.1	934.0	175.9	123.2	446.9	771.2	—	126.9
1939	2,641.5	943.2	241.6	133.6	456.5	731.6	—	135.0
1940	2,664.3	995.0	269.2	176.5	468.1	652.0	—	103.5
1941	2,525.2	1,009.6	260.3	187.2	432.2	534.2	—	101.7
1942	2,402.5	1,003.0	261.5	195.4	434.7	412.6	—	95.3
1943	2,365.2	1,098.5	318.1	193.4	404.0	262.4	—	88.8
1944	2,481.3	1,204.7	354.7	200.0	431.1	204.8	—	86.0
1945	2,667.3	1,279.6	406.7	216.4	466.1	210.9	—	87.6
1946	2,792.7	1,280.4	398.3	236.1	501.6	284.5	—	91.8
1947	2,971.2	1,339.4	408.5	256.2	536.6	338.6	—	91.9
1948	3,236.9	1,446.6	431.1	280.3	567.7	416.4	—	94.8
1949	3,478.4	1,489.8	467.3	297.3	600.2	527.9	—	95.9
1950	3,730.7	1,589.7	495.1	319.4	634.6	592.3	—	99.6
1951	3,984.8	1,709.4	503.2	355.1	719.1	596.9	—	101.1
1952	4,147.0	1,833.5	449.7	367.7	765.9	626.3	—	103.9
1953	4,515.2	1,989.9	472.6	423.9	828.4	693.5	—	106.9
1954	4,947.1	2,072.2	540.8	456.8	933.2	833.9	—	110.2
1955	5,382.7	2,240.7	613.9	462.3	1,059.9	895.9	—	110.0
1956	5,878.2	2,419.0	653.1	510.8	1,180.5	1,003.0	—	111.8
1957	6,660.7	2,710.7	726.9	549.4	1,292.6	1,267.0	—	114.1
1958	7,231.5	2,909.1	743.5	610.1	1,413.5	1,436.3	—	119.0
1959	7,531.4	3,109.7	632.1	656.0	1,521.2	1,493.4	—	119.0
1960	8,118.5	3,346.1	673.1	722.0	1,620.1	1,633.4	—	123.8
1961	8,811.0	3,581.4	714.9	769.9	1,819.0	1,793.1	—	132.7
1962	9,324.8	3,878.1	713.9	838.1	1,980.2	1,772.8	—	141.7
1963	10,028.2	4,208.6	809.0	901.1	2,165.1	1,789.3	—	154.5
1964	10,757.8	4,533.5	898.7	961.0	2,370.3	1,833.7	—	160.6
1965	11,417	4,832	931	1,300	2,259	1,932	—	163
1966	12,342	5,218	982	1,437	2,416	2,120	—	169
1967	13,294	5,665	1,017	1,598	2,596	2,243	—	175
1968	14,385	6,209	967	1,754	2,803	2,456	—	196
1969	15,525	6,758	953	1,920	2,967	2,722	—	205
1970	16,449	7,017	978	2,120	3,214	2,887	—	233
1971	17,177	7,423	990	2,325	3,300	2,882	—	257
1972	18,574	8,007	1,001	2,628	3,640	3,027	—	271
1973	20,313	8,572	1,025	3,033	3,948	3,418	—	317
1974	21,452	8,885	991	3,351	4,208	3,642	—	375

Notes appear at end of table

TABLE Cj733–740   Life insurance – benefit payments: 1854–1998   *Continued*

	Total	Death benefits	Matured endowments	Annuity payments	Policy dividends	Surrender values under Life	Surrender values under Annuity	Disability payments and accidental death benefits
	Cj733 [1]	Cj734	Cj735	Cj736 [2]	Cj737 [2,3]	Cj738	Cj739 [4]	Cj740 [5]
Year	Million dollars	Million dollars	Million dollars	Million dollars	Million dollars	Million dollars	Million dollars	Million dollars
1975	22,536	9,192	946	3,665	4,544	3,763	—	426
1976	24,611	9,593	976	4,419	5,017	4,148	—	458
1977	26,462	10,196	932	5,267	5,263	4,309	—	495
1978	28,614	11,108	916	5,863	5,674	4,520	—	533
1979	32,385	11,766	913	7,548	6,131	5,473	—	554
1980	38,042	12,884	908	10,195	6,785	6,678	—	592
1981	43,484	14,154	883	12,021	7,838	7,961	—	627
1982	47,994	15,066	839	12,814	7,922	10,779	—	574
1983	51,860	15,660	824	13,564	8,641	12,605	—	566
1984	60,432	16,752	771	17,912	9,700	14,731	—	566
1985	66,510	18,226	779	21,259	10,121	15,589	—	536
1986	68,305	19,479	766	22,657	10,122	14,741	—	540
1987	71,432	20,530	752	24,316	10,466	14,864	—	504
1988	74,091	21,660	751	25,665	11,046	14,456	—	513
1989	80,201	23,261	727	29,383	11,417	14,859	—	554
1990	88,385	24,567	700	32,575	11,953	18,022	—	568
1991	91,585	25,407	668	36,615	12,066	16,282	—	547
1992	95,043	27,235	649	37,550	12,203	16,814	—	592
1993	99,975	28,819	598	40,325	12,714	16,904	—	615
1994	200,809	32,583	647	40,412	15,915	18,014	92,779	459
1995	227,635	34,545	1,007	48,457	17,816	19,501	105,449	860
1996	246,946	36,257	741	51,069	18,064	24,454	115,747	614
1997	276,578	37,488	563	55,080	17,981	24,016	140,842	608
1998	301,834	40,101	572	60,410	18,865	26,816	154,463	607

(Z) Less than $50,000.

[1] Beginning in 1947, includes data on operations of accident and health departments of U.S. life insurance companies, not shown separately.

[2] Beginning in 1965, annuity payments include some dividend payments formerly classified as policy dividends.

[3] Beginning in 1947, includes policy dividends paid by accident and health departments of U.S. life insurance companies.

[4] Beginning in 1994, "surrender values" include annuity withdrawals of funds. An amount comparable to that of prior years is not available.

[5] Beginning in 1951, accidental death benefits included with death benefits. Accidental death benefits were approximately $30 million in 1951.

[6] Matured endowments and annuity payments included with death benefits.

[7] Matured endowments included with death benefits.

Sources

1854–1918: Spectator Company, *Spectator Insurance Year Book* (various issues; for certain years, adjustments were made by the Institute of Life Insurance); 1919–1939: Spectator Company, *Spectator Compendium of Official Life Insurance Reports* for each year; 1940–1998: Institute of Life Insurance, *Life Insurance Fact Book* (1965), p. 38; (1983), p. 37; (1999), pp. 107–8.

Documentation

These data cover life insurance benefit payments in the United States.

Matured endowment payments are defined as the proceeds paid under a policy which provides that a definite sum of money be paid to the policyholder after a specified number of years if he or she is then living. If the policyholder dies during the endowment period, payment is made to a beneficiary (such proceeds are included as death benefits).

A policy dividend is defined as a refund of part of the premium on a participating life insurance policy. It is a share of the surplus earnings apportioned for distribution and reflects the difference between the premium charged and actual experience.

A surrender value payment is the amount paid to policyholders upon surrender, for cash, of a policy before it becomes payable by death or maturity.

Disability benefits are payments under a feature added to a life insurance policy, providing for waiver of premium and sometimes payment of monthly income if the insured becomes totally and permanently disabled. Disability provisions became general around 1910, and benefits under these were usually included with annuity payments until 1920. Accidental death benefit provisions became general around 1917, and benefits under these were usually included with death benefits until 1920.

TABLE Cj741–747   Life insurance – company assets and earning rate: 1854–1998

Contributed by Eugene N. White

	Assets						Net rate of interest earned on assets
	Total	Bonds	Stocks	Mortgages	Real estate	Policy loans and other assets	
	Cj741	Cj742 [1]	Cj743 [1]	Cj744	Cj745	Cj746	Cj747
Year	Million dollars	Million dollars	Million dollars	Million dollars	Million dollars	Million dollars	Million dollars
1854	11.4	—	—	—	—	—	—
1855	12.7	—	—	—	—	—	—
1856	15.0	—	—	—	—	—	—
1857	14.0	—	—	—	—	—	—
1858	15.9	—	—	—	—	—	—
1859	20.5	—	—	—	—	—	—
1860	24.1	—	—	—	—	—	—
1861	26.7	—	—	—	—	—	—
1862	30.1	—	—	—	—	—	—
1863	37.8	—	—	—	—	—	—
1864	49.0	—	—	—	—	—	—
1865	64.2	22.4	—	16.5	1.7	23.6	—
1866	91.6	28.3	—	23.7	2.3	37.3	—
1867	125.6	33.2	—	37.0	3.6	51.8	—
1868	176.8	40.9	—	58.0	4.8	73.1	—
1869	229.1	45.1	—	83.6	7.0	93.4	—
1870	269.5	48.1	—	108.0	9.0	104.4	—
1871	302.6	52.4	—	134.9	10.8	104.5	—
1872	335.2	54.7	—	164.3	12.5	103.7	6.90
1873	360.1	56.6	—	189.8	15.0	98.7	6.93
1874	387.3	65.3	—	210.1	18.3	93.6	6.89
1875	403.1	73.9	—	219.7	22.6	86.9	6.79
1876	407.4	85.7	—	217.9	29.2	74.6	6.55
1877	396.4	100.8	—	201.1	31.6	62.9	6.37
1878	404.1	112.8	—	189.1	42.8	59.4	5.94
1879	401.7	116.2	—	173.8	49.2	62.5	5.83
1880	418.1	124.8	—	164.8	51.6	76.9	5.48
1881	429.6	129.2	—	160.2	51.1	89.1	5.51
1882	450.0	124.0	—	172.7	51.4	101.9	5.55
1883	472.4	137.6	—	187.6	51.7	95.5	5.54
1884	492.2	152.1	—	205.7	54.6	79.8	5.48
1885	524.7	182.6	—	212.9	58.0	71.2	5.42
1886	561.6	197.7	—	227.5	59.9	76.5	5.39
1887	597.6	207.8	—	244.9	63.4	81.5	5.47
1888	657.1	231.6	—	262.5	68.6	94.4	5.43
1889	714.5	251.7	—	283.3	75.7	103.8	5.27
1890	771.0	241.0	30	310.0	81.0	109.0	5.10
1891	841.0	270.0	31	334.0	86.0	120.0	5.36
1892	919.0	306.0	39	351.0	97.0	126.0	5.08
1893	988.0	323.0	47	374.0	105.0	139.0	4.95
1894	1,073.0	369.0	50	394.0	117.0	143.0	4.93
1895	1,160.0	423.0	53	412.0	125.0	147.0	5.00
1896	1,244.0	445.0	54	442.0	135.0	168.0	4.91
1897	1,345.0	503.0	56	452.0	138.0	196.0	4.86
1898	1,463.0	581.0	72	455.0	145.0	210.0	4.87
1899	1,595.0	654.0	83	468.0	154.0	236.0	4.81
1900	1,742.0	707.0	95	501.0	158.0	281.0	4.67
1901	1,911.0	792.0	103	532.0	166.0	318.0	4.61
1902	2,092.0	872.0	132	573.0	170.0	345.0	4.58
1903	2,265.0	897.0	165	624.0	178.0	401.0	4.61
1904	2,499.0	1,066.0	173	672.0	181.0	407.0	4.63
1905	2,706.0	1,211.0	173	724.0	171.0	427.0	4.68
1906	2,924.0	1,299.0	160	826.0	170.0	469.0	4.68
1907	3,053.0	1,281.0	133	921.0	170.0	548.0	4.80
1908	3,380.0	1,473.0	147	987.0	167.0	606.0	4.77
1909	3,644.0	1,616.0	146	1,084.0	167.0	631.0	4.79
1910	3,876.0	1,660.0	130	1,227.0	173.0	686.0	4.55
1911	4,164.0	1,787.0	100	1,358.0	171.0	748.0	4.59
1912	4,409.0	1,859.0	96	1,485.0	176.0	793.0	4.59
1913	4,659.0	1,909.0	86	1,618.0	166.0	880.0	4.67
1914	4,935.0	1,982.0	83	1,706.0	171.0	993.0	4.69

Note appears at end of table

TABLE Cj741–747   Life insurance – company assets and earning rate: 1854–1998   *Continued*

	Assets						Net rate of interest earned on assets
	Total	Bonds	Stocks	Mortgages	Real estate	Policy loans and other assets	
	Cj741	Cj742 [1]	Cj743 [1]	Cj744	Cj745	Cj746	Cj747
Year	Million dollars	Million dollars	Million dollars	Million dollars	Million dollars	Million dollars	Million dollars
1915	5,190.0	2,095.0	81	1,779.0	173.0	1,062.0	4.77
1916	5,537.0	2,309.0	83	1,893.0	174.0	1,078.0	4.80
1917	5,941.0	2,537.0	83	2,021.0	179.0	1,121.0	4.81
1918	6,475.0	3,012.0	82	2,075.0	179.0	1,127.0	4.72
1919	6,791.0	3,241.0	76	2,094.0	168.0	1,212.0	4.66
1920	7,320.0	3,298.0	75	2,442.0	172.0	1,333.0	4.83
1921	7,936.0	3,390.0	69	2,792.0	186.0	1,499.0	5.02
1922	8,652.0	3,656.0	56	3,122.0	197.0	1,621.0	5.12
1923	9,455.0	3,783.0	57	3,662.0	243.0	1,710.0	5.18
1924	10,394.0	4,034.0	64	4,175.0	239.0	1,882.0	5.17
1925	11,538.0	4,333.0	81	4,808.0	266.0	2,050.0	5.11
1926	12,940.0	4,653.0	125	5,580.0	303.0	2,279.0	5.09
1927	14,392.0	5,146.0	145	6,200.0	351.0	2,550.0	5.05
1928	15,961.0	5,655.0	285	6,778.0	403.0	2,840.0	5.05
1929	17,482.0	6,001.0	416	7,316.0	464.0	3,285.0	5.05
1930	18,880.0	6,431.0	519	7,598.0	548.0	3,784.0	5.05
1931	20,160.0	6,806.0	567	7,673.0	684.0	4,430.0	4.93
1932	20,754.0	6,843.0	574	7,336.0	935.0	5,066.0	4.65
1933	20,896.0	7,189.0	487	6,701.0	1,267.0	5,252.0	4.25
1934	21,844.0	8,533.0	482	5,875.0	1,693.0	5,261.0	3.92
1935	23,216.0	10,041.0	583	5,357.0	1,990.0	5,245.0	3.70
1936	24,874.0	11,869.0	615	5,128.0	2,149.0	5,113.0	3.71
1937	26,249.0	13,272.0	558	5,230.0	2,192.0	4,997.0	3.69
1938	27,755.0	14,473.0	586	5,445.0	2,179.0	5,072.0	3.59
1939	29,243.0	15,734.0	587	5,683.0	2,139.0	5,100.0	3.54
1940	30,802.0	17,092.0	605	5,972.0	2,065.0	5,068.0	3.45
1941	32,731.0	19,051.0	601	6,442.0	1,878.0	4,759.0	3.42
1942	34,931.0	21,558.0	608	6,726.0	1,663.0	4,376.0	3.44
1943	37,766.0	24,836.0	652	6,714.0	1,352.0	4,212.0	3.33
1944	41,054.0	28,711.0	756	6,686.0	1,063.0	3,838.0	3.23
1945	44,797.0	32,605.0	999	6,636.0	857.0	3,700.0	3.11
1946	48,191.0	35,350.0	1,249	7,155.0	735.0	3,702.0	2.93
1947	51,743.0	36,757.0	1,390	8,675.0	860.0	4,061.0	2.88
1948	55,512.0	37,979.0	1,428	10,833.0	1,055.0	4,217.0	2.96
1949	59,630.0	39,274.0	1,718	12,906.0	1,247.0	4,485.0	3.06
1950	64,020.0	39,366.0	2,103	16,102.0	1,445.0	5,004.0	3.13
1951	68,278.0	39,650.0	2,221	19,314.0	1,631.0	5,462.0	3.18
1952	73,375.0	41,974.0	2,446	21,251.0	1,903.0	5,801.0	3.28
1953	78,533.0	44,402.0	2,573	23,322.0	2,020.0	6,216.0	3.36
1954	84,486.0	46,294.0	3,268	25,976.0	2,298.0	6,650.0	3.46
1955	90,432.0	47,741.0	3,633	29,445.0	2,581.0	7,032.0	3.51
1956	96,011.0	49,107.0	3,503	32,989.0	2,817.0	7,595.0	3.63
1957	101,309.0	51,356.0	3,391	35,236.0	3,119.0	8,207.0	3.75
1958	107,580.0	54,233.0	4,109	37,062.0	3,364.0	8,812.0	3.85
1959	113,650.0	56,686.0	4,561	39,197.0	3,651.0	9,555.0	3.96
1960	119,576.0	58,555.0	4,981	41,771.0	3,765.0	10,504.0	4.11
1961	126,816.0	60,932.0	6,258	44,203.0	4,007.0	11,416.0	4.22
1962	133,291.0	63,722.0	6,302	46,902.0	4,107.0	12,258.0	4.34
1963	141,121.0	66,083.0	7,135	50,544.0	4,319.0	13,040.0	4.45
1964	149,470.0	67,963.0	7,938	55,152.0	4,528.0	13,889.0	4.53
1965	158,884.0	70,152.0	9,126	60,013.0	4,681.0	14,912.0	4.61
1966	167,455.0	72,215.0	8,832	64,609.0	4,885.0	16,914.0	4.73
1967	177,832.0	75,766.0	10,877	67,516.0	5,187.0	18,486.0	4.82
1968	188,636.0	79,406.0	13,230	69,973.0	5,571.0	20,456.0	4.95
1969	197,208.0	81,773.0	13,707	72,027.0	5,912.0	23,789.0	5.12
1970	207,254.0	84,166.0	15,420	74,375.0	6,320.0	26,973.0	5.30
1971	222,102.0	90,198.0	20,607	75,496.0	6,904.0	28,897.0	5.44
1972	239,730.0	97,512.0	26,845	76,948.0	7,295.0	31,130.0	5.56
1973	252,436.0	103,199.0	25,919	81,369.0	7,693.0	34,256.0	5.88
1974	263,349.0	108,617.0	21,920	86,234.0	8,331.0	38,247.0	6.25

Note appears at end of table

(continued)

TABLE Cj741–747   Life insurance – company assets and earning rate: 1854–1998   *Continued*

	Assets						Net rate of interest earned on assets
	Total	Bonds	Stocks	Mortgages	Real estate	Policy loans and other assets	
	Cj741	Cj742 [1]	Cj743 [1]	Cj744	Cj745	Cj746	Cj747
Year	Million dollars	Million dollars	Million dollars	Million dollars	Million dollars	Million dollars	Million dollars
1975	289,304.0	121,014.0	28,061	89,167.0	9,621.0	41,441.0	6.36
1976	321,552.0	140,926.0	34,262	91,552.0	10,476.0	44,336.0	6.55
1977	351,722.0	161,444.0	33,763	96,848.0	11,060.0	48,607.0	6.89
1978	389,924.0	182,596.0	35,518	106,167.0	11,764.0	53,879.0	7.31
1979	432,282.0	198,709.0	39,757	118,421.0	13,007.0	62,388.0	7.73
1980	479,210.0	212,618.0	47,366	131,080.0	15,033.0	73,113.0	8.02
1981	525,803.0	233,308.0	47,670	137,747.0	18,278.0	88,800.0	8.57
1982	588,163.0	268,288.0	55,730	141,989.0	20,624.0	101,532.0	8.91
1983	654,948.0	308,738.0	64,868	150,999.0	22,234.0	108,109.0	8.96
1984	722,979.0	358,897.0	63,335	156,699.0	25,767.0	118,281.0	9.45
1985	825,901.0	421,446.0	77,496	171,797.0	28,822.0	126,340.0	9.63
1986	937,551.0	486,583.0	90,864	193,842.0	31,615.0	134,647.0	9.35
1987	1,044,459.0	557,110.0	96,515	213,450.0	34,172.0	143,212.0	9.10
1988	1,166,870.0	640,094.0	104,373	232,863.0	37,371.0	152,169.0	9.03
1989	1,299,756.0	716,204.0	125,614	254,215.0	39,908.0	163,815.0	9.10
1990	1,408,208.0	793,443.0	128,484	270,109.0	43,367.0	172,805.0	8.89
1991	1,551,201.0	893,005.0	164,515	265,258.0	46,711.0	181,712.0	8.63
1992	1,664,531.0	990,315.0	192,403	246,702.0	50,595.0	184,516.0	8.08
1993	1,839,127.0	1,113,853.0	251,885	229,061.0	54,249.0	190,079.0	7.52
1994	1,942,273.0	1,186,139.0	281,816	215,332.0	53,813.0	205,173.0	7.14
1995	2,143,544.0	1,278,416.0	371,867	211,815.0	52,437.0	229,009.0	7.41
1996	2,327,924.0	1,372,637.0	453,919	211,743.0	50,444.0	239,182.0	7.25
1997	2,579,078.0	1,451,289.0	598,358	209,898.0	46,076.0	273,457.0	7.35
1998	2,826,520.0	1,518,998.0	757,958	216,336.0	41,313.0	291,917.0	6.95

[1]   Through 1889, stocks are included in the bond series.

Sources

Series Cj741–746. 1854–1889: Spectator Company, *Spectator Insurance Year Book* (various issues); 1890–1998: Institute of Life Insurance, *Life Insurance Fact Book* (various issues).

Series Cj747. 1872–1909: Spectator Company, *Spectator Insurance Year Book* (various issues); 1910–1914: Institute of Life Insurance, unpublished data; 1915–1998: Institute of Life Insurance, *Life Insurance Fact Book* (1958), pp. 64–91; (1971), p. 68; (1999), pp. 131–2.

Documentation

Data for life insurance companies assets for 1854–1887 are for companies reporting to the New York Insurance Department. Thereafter, the data are for all available U.S. companies. Figures for Hawai'i and Alaska are first included in 1959.

Assets are on an admitted asset value basis, which is the aggregate value of all the assets used for determination of a company's balance sheet in accord with principles adopted by the insurance departments of the various states. Until about 1909, stocks and bonds were reported at market value. Until 1906, this value was determined by each individual company and, since 1907, by the insurance commissioners. In 1909, New York State required amortization of amply secured bonds, and this soon became the general practice. Stocks and nonamortizable bonds are generally reported at market value. Assets include the assets, distributed by type, of the accident and health departments of life insurance companies.

Shares of federal savings and loan associations are included in stocks. Real estate includes real estate sold on contract but does not include real estate owned subject to redemption. Foreclosed liens subject to redemption are included in "mortgages" and not transferred to "real estate" until the redemption period is past.

The net rate of interest earned is the ratio of the investment income for the year to the mean assets decreased by one half the investment income. For 1872–1909, the investment income is gross investment income, that is, there was no deduction of investment expenses. For 1910–1939, the investment income is net of investment expenses (including direct investment taxes) and the federal income taxes are treated as investment expenses. Beginning in 1940, the investment income is net of investment expenses (including direct investment taxes) and all federal income taxes. For 1872–1950, the assets used in the formula are ledger assets; beginning in 1951, the assets are invested assets (including cash) and interest due and accrued.

For a discussion of the level of interest earnings before 1872, see Lester W. Zartman, *The Investments of Life Insurance Companies* (Henry Holt, 1906).

TABLE Cj748–750   Life insurance – company liabilities, policy reserves, capital, and surplus: 1859–1998

Contributed by Eugene N. White

Year	Total liabilities Cj748 Million dollars	Policy reserves Cj749 Million dollars	Capital and surplus Cj750 Million dollars	Year	Total liabilities Cj748 Million dollars	Policy reserves Cj749 Million dollars	Capital and surplus Cj750 Million dollars
1859	15.4	—	5.1	1920	6,752.0	6,338.0	568.0
1860	17.1	14.4	7.0	1921	7,332.0	6,903.0	604.0
1861	18.3	15.3	8.4	1922	7,943.0	7,449.0	709.0
1862	23.8	17.5	6.3	1923	8,657.0	8,130.0	798.0
1863	28.6	24.0	9.2	1924	9,551.0	8,939.0	843.0
1864	34.7	31.0	14.3	1925	10,623.0	9,927.0	915.0
1865	49.3	42.8	14.9	1926	11,919.0	11,061.0	1,021.0
1866	65.6	59.8	26.0	1927	13,238.0	12,279.0	1,154.0
1867	88.6	81.2	37.0	1928	14,711.0	13,596.0	1,250.0
1868	135.8	126.0	41.0	1929	16,159.0	14,948.0	1,323.0
1869	180.3	170.9	.48.8	1930	17,524.0	16,231.0	1,356.0
1870	221.0	209.3	48.5	1931	18,750.0	17,384.0	1,410.0
1871	254.6	243.3	48.0	1932	19,308.0	17,839.0	1,446.0
1872	288.3	277.4	46.9	1933	19,475.0	18,077.0	1,421.0
1873	311.5	300.2	48.6	1934	20,417.0	19,030.0	1,427.0
1874	328.4	320.3	58.9	1935	21,826.0	20,404.0	1,390.0
1875	342.3	334.1	60.8	1936	23,274.0	21,800.0	1,600.0
1876	346.3	337.5	61.1	1937	24,706.0	23,202.0	1,543.0
1877	334.8	326.3	61.6	1938	26,122.0	24,495.0	1,633.0
1878	339.6	329.5	64.5	1939	27,512.0	25,827.0	1,731.0
1879	336.3	328.3	65.4	1940	28,964.0	27,238.0	1,838.0
1880	346.5	338.8	71.6	1941	30,769.0	28,945.0	1,962.0
1881	357.1	349.9	72.5	1942	32,775.0	30,797.0	2,156.0
1882	373.1	366.4	76.9	1943	35,343.0	33,049.0	2,423.0
1883	391.9	385.2	80.5	1944	38,318.0	35,577.0	2,736.0
1884	410.1	403.3	82.1	1945	41,556.0	38,667.0	3,241.0
1885	431.5	425.0	93.2	1946	44,885.0	41,702.0	3,306.0
1886	459.8	452.8	101.8	1947	48,307.0	44,882.0	3,436.0
1887	524.7	518.4	72.9	1948	51,803.0	48,158.0	3,709.0
1888	574.6	566.8	82.5	1949	55,472.0	51,498.0	4,158.0
1889	624.3	616.3	90.2	1950	59,381.0	54,946.0	4,639.0
1890	679.0	670.0	92.0	1951	63,428.0	58,547.0	4,850.0
1891	740.0	727.0	101.0	1952	68,119.0	62,579.0	5,256.0
1892	802.0	789.0	117.0	1953	72,819.0	66,683.0	5,714.0
1893	869.0	853.0	119.0	1954	78,103.0	70,903.0	6,383.0
1894	931.0	915.0	142.0	1955	83,424.0	75,359.0	7,008.0
1895	998.0	980.0	162.0	1956	88,321.0	79,738.0	7,690.0
1896	1,067.0	1,048.0	177.0	1957	93,085.0	84,075.0	8,224.0
1897	1,141.0	1,119.0	204.0	1958	98,773.0	88,604.0	8,807.0
1898	1,246.0	1,203.0	217.0	1959	104,533.0	93,975.0	9,117.0
1899	1,366.0	1,322.0	229.0	1960	109,902.0	98,473.0	9,674.0
1900	1,493.0	1,443.0	249.0	1961	116,240.0	103,285.0	10,576.0
1901	1,640.0	1,584.0	271.0	1962	122,035.0	108,384.0	11,256.0
1902	1,798.0	1,738.0	294.0	1963	129,088.0	114,301.0	12,033.0
1903	1,979.0	1,916.0	286.0	1964	136,589.0	120,698.0	12,881.0
1904	2,168.0	2,101.0	331.0	1965	145,048.0	127,620.0	13,836.0
1905	2,372.0	2,295.0	334.0	1966	152,539.0	134,711.0	14,916.0
1906	2,557.0	2,473.0	367.0	1967	162,084.0	142,418.0	15,748.0
1907	2,736.0	2,651.0	317.0	1968	171,804.0	150,308.0	16,832.0
1908	2,939.0	2,829.0	441.0	1969	180,154.0	158,550.0	17,054.0
1909	3,171.0	3,029.0	473.0	1970	189,931.0	167,556.0	17,323.0
1910	3,386.0	3,226.0	490.0	1971	204,263.0	179,250.0	17,839.0
1911	3,646.0	3,473.0	518.0	1972	220,775.0	192,146.0	18,955.0
1912	3,880.0	3,695.0	529.0	1973	232,542.0	203,668.0	19,894.0
1913	4,137.0	3,934.0	522.0	1974	244,708.0	215,447.0	18,641.0
1914	4,364.0	4,166.0	571.0	1975	268,741.0	237,116.0	20,563.0
1915	4,648.0	4,399.0	542.0	1976	299,541.0	262,775.0	22,011.0
1916	4,967.0	4,696.0	570.0	1977	328,105.0	287,932.0	23,617.0
1917	5,336.0	5,033.0	605.0	1978	363,677.0	318,483.0	26,247.0
1918	5,903.0	5,407.0	572.0	1979	402,279.0	351,637.0	30,003.0
1919	6,209.0	5,830.0	582.0				

(continued)

TABLE Cj748–750   Life insurance – company liabilities, policy reserves, capital, and surplus: 1859–1998   *Continued*

Year	Total liabilities Cj748 Million dollars	Policy reserves Cj749 Million dollars	Capital and surplus Cj750 Million dollars	Year	Total liabilities Cj748 Million dollars	Policy reserves Cj749 Million dollars	Capital and surplus Cj750 Million dollars
1980	444,852.0	390,339.0	34,358.0	1990	1,316,835.0	1,196,967.0	91,373.0
1981	488,381.0	428,031.0	37,422.0	1991	1,445,163.0	1,304,778.0	106,038.0
1982	546,712.0	479,360.0	41,451.0	1992	1,549,294.0	1,407,091.0	115,237.0
1983	608,564.0	532,441.0	46,384.0	1993	1,711,107.0	1,549,803.0	128,020.0
1984	672,632.0	584,193.0	50,347.0	1994	1,805,532.0	1,644,043.0	136,741.0
1985	769,121.0	665,302.0	56,780.0	1995	1,992,600.0	1,812,325.0	150,944.0
1986	873,402.0	761,924.0	64,149.0	1996	2,180,684.0	1,965,790.0	147,240.0
1987	977,089.0	862,133.0	67,370.0	1997	2,418,992.0	2,164,559.0	160,086.0
1988	1,091,920.0	968,963.0	74,950.0	1998	2,653,825.0	2,377,449.0	172,695.0
1989	1,216,073.0	1,083,678.0	83,683.0				

Sources

Series Cj748. 1859–1917: Spectator Company, *Spectator Insurance Year Book* (various issues); 1918–1920: *Spectator Compendium of Official Life Insurance Reports* (various issues); 1921–1998: Institute of Life Insurance, *Life Insurance Fact Book* (1953–1958, 1971, 1999).

Series Cj749. 1860–1864: State of New York Insurance Department, New York Insurance Report (1865), pp. clxxv–clxxix; 1865–1889: Spectator Company, *Spectator Insurance Year Book* (various issues; for certain years, adjustments were made by Institute of Life Insurance); 1890–1998: Institute of Life Insurance, *Life Insurance Fact Book* (1958), p. 61; (1970), p. 57; (1971), p. 65; (1971), p. 64; (1999), p. 144.

Series Cj750. 1859–1917 (except 1868, 1869, 1870, 1879, and 1881, which are from various New York Insurance Reports): Spectator Company, *Spectator Insurance Year Book* (various issues); 1918–1951: *Spectator Compendium of Official Life Insurance Reports* (various issues); 1952–1998: Institute of Life Insurance, *Life Insurance Fact Book* (1953–1958, 1971, 1999).

Documentation

Figures pertain to U.S. companies.

Total liabilities include operations of accident and health departments of life insurance companies. The 1918–1931 figures were compiled by subtracting, from total liabilities as given, the amount shown as "amounts set apart." The 1932–1942 figures were compiled by subtracting, from total liabilities as given, the amounts shown as "special, voluntary contingency, etc., reserves." The 1943–1951 figures are those shown as total liabilities. The 1952–1998 figures were compiled by adding, all the reserve and obligation items shown, excluding only special surplus funds, unassigned surplus, and capital. Alaska and Hawai'i are first included in 1959.

Policy reserves are defined as the funds that an insurance company holds specifically for the fulfillment of its policy obligations. Reserves are so calculated that, together with future premiums and interest earnings, they will enable the company to pay all future claims. The policy reserves series includes life, annuity, supplementary contract, disability, and accidental death reserves and, beginning in 1947, business of accident and health departments of life insurance companies.

The capital and surplus figures for 1919–1931 figures were compiled by adding, to the "unassigned funds and capital" as given, the amounts shown as "amounts set apart." The 1932–1950 figures were compiled by adding, to the "unassigned funds and capital" as given, the amounts shown as "special, voluntary, contingency, etc., reserves" (for 1932–1942, "special, voluntary, contingency, etc., reserves" are shown as "liabilities"; for 1943–1950, this item is shown separately). The 1951–1998 figures were compiled by adding the items "special surplus funds," "unassigned surplus," and "capital." This series includes operations of accident and health departments of life insurance companies.

TABLE Cj751–765 Property liability insurance – business assets, policyholders' surplus, and premiums written: 1931–1998

Contributed by Eugene N. White

	Assets					Policyholders' surplus					Premiums written				
	Total	Stock companies	Mutual companies	Reciprocals	Lloyds	Total	Stock companies	Mutual companies	Reciprocals	Lloyds	Total	Stock companies	Mutual companies	Reciprocals	Lloyds
	Cj751	Cj752	Cj753	Cj754	Cj755	Cj756	Cj757	Cj758	Cj759	Cj760	Cj761	Cj762	Cj763	Cj764	Cj765
Year	Million dollars	Million dollars	Million dollars	Million dollars	Million dollars	Million dollars	Million dollars	Million dollars	Million dollars	Million dollars	Million dollars	Million dollars	Million dollars	Million dollars	Million dollars
1931	4,440	3,830	537	64	8	1,728	1,466	219	37	6	1,833	1,532	261	38	2
1932	4,142	3,571	507	58	6	1,478	1,243	197	34	4	1,547	1,288	226	31	2
1933	3,627	3,111	456	54	6	1,528	1,288	205	32	3	1,437	1,182	226	27	2
1934	3,689	3,128	499	58	4	1,749	1,472	241	33	3	1,580	1,282	264	32	2
1935	4,160	3,528	564	62	6	2,095	1,784	272	36	3	1,668	1,332	295	37	3
1936	4,690	3,987	629	66	9	2,416	2,079	296	36	6	1,827	1,445	332	43	7
1937	4,549	3,800	669	72	9	2,184	1,828	319	33	3	2,029	1,579	394	49	8
1938	4,781	3,976	720	75	9	2,354	1,972	342	37	3	1,929	1,508	370	46	5
1939	4,921	4,063	768	79	10	2,563	2,179	342	38	4	2,022	1,571	397	49	5
1940	5,145	4,229	822	82	12	2,633	2,209	378	41	5	2,230	1,730	444	51	6
1941	5,435	4,432	903	88	12	2,606	2,164	397	41	5	2,583	1,989	529	59	6
1942	5,798	4,661	1,023	100	14	2,721	2,222	448	45	6	2,841	2,165	602	67	7
1943	6,408	5,141	1,144	109	14	3,050	2,494	501	49	5	2,774	2,091	610	66	7
1944	7,010	5,617	1,259	119	15	3,335	2,729	547	53	6	2,985	2,258	650	70	8
1945	7,851	6,309	1,398	128	16	3,806	3,151	595	53	7	3,230	2,425	720	78	7
1946	8,315	6,630	1,525	142	18	3,546	2,879	607	54	6	4,052	3,063	879	100	9
1947	9,408	7,465	1,745	176	21	3,636	2,905	658	65	7	5,113	3,862	1,104	133	13
1948	10,530	8,288	2,003	212	27	3,897	3,066	743	80	8	5,877	4,403	1,299	159	17
1949	12,100	9,520	2,295	252	34	4,720	3,708	902	101	10	6,356	4,760	1,393	180	23
1950	13,476	10,603	2,552	287	35	5,331	4,217	990	114	9	6,866	5,138	1,506	199	23
1951	14,756	11,535	2,861	320	40	5,739	4,543	1,062	125	10	7,775	5,759	1,761	229	25
1952	16,397	12,779	3,211	368	39	6,246	4,964	1,136	138	8	8,770	6,411	2,058	277	24
1953	17,872	13,772	3,641	420	40	6,573	5,192	1,211	162	9	9,673	7,000	2,325	321	26
1954	20,416	15,789	4,115	475	37	8,392	6,697	1,494	191	10	9,908	7,144	2,412	331	22
1955	22,305	17,275	4,481	513	35	9,461	7,694	1,553	208	7	10,539	7,662	2,510	347	20
1956	23,106	17,811	4,727	529	39	9,607	7,800	1,587	212	8	11,130	7,991	2,759	358	22
1957	23,449	17,889	4,981	535	43	8,859	7,073	1,575	202	9	12,096	8,640	3,035	399	22
1958	26,309	20,115	5,539	608	46	10,679	8,619	1,825	224	10	12,828	9,077	3,282	445	24
1959	28,602	21,801	6,080	669	52	11,633	9,381	1,993	247	12	14,084	9,931	3,646	481	27
1960	30,132	22,777	6,581	727	48	11,930	9,495	2,163	263	9	14,973	10,527	3,900	523	23
1961	33,690	25,585	7,270	787	48	14,594	11,719	2,565	299	11	15,474	10,783	4,134	531	25
1962	34,217	25,780	7,588	802	47	14,144	11,146	2,697	288	12	16,034	11,207	4,239	566	22
1963	37,076	27,909	8,164	876	46	15,747	12,642	2,788	306	11	17,175	11,881	4,656	616	22
1964	39,865	30,077	8,788	950	50	16,990	13,691	2,970	315	15	18,317	12,648	4,973	673	24
1965	41,843	31,299	9,437	1,051	56	17,112	13,660	3,106	326	20	20,063	13,855	5,413	769	26
1966	42,288	31,035	10,046	1,150	57	15,556	12,007	3,189	338	22	22,090	15,197	6,017	849	27
1967	46,562	34,183	11,020	1,296	62	17,501	13,580	3,512	382	26	23,829	16,343	6,509	948	28
1968	51,226	37,691	12,032	1,442	60	19,107	14,887	3,775	423	22	26,026	17,833	7,111	1,054	29
1969	52,369	37,992	12,746	1,574	56	16,719	12,699	3,606	395	19	29,225	19,970	8,023	1,206	25

(continued)

TABLE Cj751–765 Property liability insurance – business assets, policyholders' surplus, and premiums written: 1931–1998 Continued

	Assets					Policyholders' surplus					Premiums written				
	Total	Stock companies	Mutual companies	Reciprocals	Lloyds	Total	Stock companies	Mutual companies	Reciprocals	Lloyds	Total	Stock companies	Mutual companies	Reciprocals	Lloyds
	Cj751	Cj752	Cj753	Cj754	Cj755	Cj756	Cj757	Cj758	Cj759	Cj760	Cj761	Cj762	Cj763	Cj764	Cj765
Year	Million dollars	Million dollars	Million dollars	Million dollars	Million dollars	Million dollars	Million dollars	Million dollars	Million dollars	Million dollars	Million dollars	Million dollars	Million dollars	Million dollars	Million dollars
1970	58,594	42,568	14,140	1,831	55	18,521	14,014	4,046	443	18	32,867	22,430	8,980	1,433	25
1971	67,284	49,333	15,681	2,213	57	22,749	17,308	4,846	578	17	35,715	24,824	9,179	1,686	26
1972	78,885	58,461	17,734	2,628	62	28,211	21,398	6,039	755	19	39,318	27,595	9,829	1,869	25
1973	83,862	62,214	18,667	2,918	64	27,091	20,056	6,181	835	19	42,480	30,051	10,390	2,015	23
1974	82,115	60,294	18,635	3,110	76	20,898	14,831	5,204	832	31	45,152	32,110	10,915	2,101	25
1975	94,118	69,716	20,811	3,508	83	26,303	18,451	5,961	858	33	49,967	35,644	11,892	2,398	33
1976	112,975	83,573	24,940	4,370	92	31,394	23,021	7,311	1,027	35	60,959	43,138	14,666	3,117	38
1977	135,513	99,648	30,084	5,678	103	37,372	27,062	8,861	1,415	33	73,030	51,165	17,843	3,978	45
1978	160,060	117,545	35,460	6,923	132	45,004	32,510	10,596	1,856	42	82,341	57,433	20,302	4,548	58
1979	187,406	137,289	41,817	8,143	158	54,418	39,170	12,940	2,257	51	91,359	63,058	23,162	5,077	61
1980	212,807	156,223	47,070	9,335	179	65,697	47,499	15,422	2,722	55	96,556	66,957	24,058	5,476	65
1981	228,229	166,693	50,934	10,392	211	67,720	47,524	17,095	3,027	74	100,294	69,269	25,090	5,869	65
1982	248,362	182,403	54,091	11,622	246	75,670	53,333	18,907	3,366	94	104,038	71,884	25,654	6,438	63
1983	266,641	193,639	59,922	12,764	315	81,756	56,422	21,560	3,666	109	109,247	74,822	27,468	6,891	65
1984	279,865	202,970	62,672	13,845	378	78,913	53,284	21,525	3,987	117	118,591	81,428	29,558	7,544	61
1985	329,005	241,483	71,376	15,702	444	93,107	64,375	24,102	4,509	121	144,860	100,722	35,333	8,711	94
1986	395,953	291,697	84,836	18,844	574	116,105	81,845	28,647	5,479	134	176,993	125,446	41,016	10,421	109
1987	451,289	332,708	96,545	21,433	603	128,530	89,859	32,578	5,950	143	193,689	135,618	46,424	11,535	111
1988	504,536	373,810	105,776	24,363	587	145,738	102,307	36,373	6,897	162	202,285	140,737	49,073	12,377	99
1989	589,983	441,930	119,716	27,642	695	166,449	117,742	40,487	8,028	191	208,834	143,191	52,236	13,250	158
1990	621,491	464,458	126,325	29,994	714	172,536	122,948	40,966	8,407	215	218,100	148,574	55,209	14,164	152
1991	673,740	501,474	138,670	32,825	770	197,188	140,841	46,512	9,611	224	223,243	150,652	57,279	15,120	192
1992	707,401	525,871	146,259	33,941	1,330	200,543	142,604	47,127	10,191	620	227,751	152,323	60,073	15,003	352
1993	745,017	552,195	155,991	35,264	1,567	224,817	159,867	52,746	11,580	625	241,691	162,769	63,325	14,893	704
1994	778,458	577,148	164,816	34,874	1,620	237,780	167,449	58,134	11,579	619	250,709	169,733	65,349	14,891	737
1995	848,047	631,305	178,559	36,589	1,595	284,694	202,416	67,962	13,778	539	259,803	177,281	66,489	15,305	727
1996	887,040	658,014	188,620	38,630	1,776	311,900	217,576	77,535	15,921	867	268,730	185,076	66,366	16,502	787
1997	977,661	726,521	208,626	40,395	2,119	384,136	268,755	96,356	18,006	1,020	276,568	190,468	67,882	17,284	934
1998	1,031,680	767,990	217,818	43,420	2,452	419,868	292,354	106,216	20,097	1,200	281,621	194,754	68,362	17,427	1,078

Source

A. M. Best Company, *Best's Aggregates and Averages* (1959, 1971, 1999).

Documentation

The aggregates in these series represent the totals of the property-liability insurance business except that the mutual company aggregates do not include a very large number of small companies operated on the township or county plans or on the assessment basis. Life insurance companies writing accident and health policies are excluded unless they maintained completely segregated departments and statistics so separate department figures could be developed.

Aggregates through 1944 are based on the reported statutory underwriting results, with some companies including federal income taxes as an expense of operation and others excluding them. For 1942 and 1943, the statutory profit before federal income was estimated at $115 million for each year and at about $70 million and $65 million, respectively, after federal income taxes. For 1944, the corresponding figures were $100 million and $60 million. Beginning in 1945, underwriting experience is recorded before federal income taxes and underwriting results are on a cash basis for reserves.

Prior to 1951, figures included only business written by casualty companies. Figures for all years include credit, livestock, and miscellaneous unsegregated and reinsurance unsegregated lines.

Series Cj756–760. Policyholders' surplus represents the sum of paid-in capital, if any, and net reported surplus.

Series Cj761–765. Net premiums written represent retained premium income, direct or through reinsurance, less payments made for reinsurance ceded.

TABLE Cj766–786   Life insurance – finances of stock companies, mutual companies, and reciprocals: 1925–1998

Contributed by Eugene N. White

	Stock companies								Mutual companies		
	Net premiums			Losses incurred as a percentage of premiums earned	Expenses incurred as a percentage of premiums written	Underwriting profit or loss			Net premiums		
						Total	As a percentage of premiums earned				
	Written	Earned	Unearned						Written	Earned	Unearned
	Cj766	Cj767	Cj768	Cj769	Cj770	Cj771	Cj772		Cj773	Cj774	Cj775
Year	Million dollars	Million dollars	Million dollars	Percent	Percent	Million dollars	Percent		Million dollars	Million dollars	Million dollars
1925	633	599	270	57.7	39.3	−11	−1.8		70	67	19
1926	710	682	296	59.5	39.4	−8	−1.2		88	84	24
1927	763	740	316	58.7	39.2	−8	−1.1		105	100	27
1928	805	779	345	58.0	39.5	4	0.5		121	116	33
1929	866	841	366	60.0	39.7	−22	−2.5		135	130	36
1930	838	840	359	63.4	40.9	−39	−4.7		132	131	36
1931	769	777	332	65.7	41.2	−51	−6.6		122	123	36
1932	636	673	281	66.3	41.9	−31	−4.6		108	110	33
1933	591	598	260	62.7	40.3	−17	−2.8		110	108	34
1934	645	636	269	61.2	38.7	−5	−0.7		141	135	40
1935	673	659	281	58.5	38.3	11	1.6		168	162	46
1936	746	726	313	55.1	38.1	34	4.7		200	192	53
1937	824	800	336	52.9	39.2	52	6.6		235	228	60
1938	812	800	349	51.6	40.5	55	6.9		231	226	64
1939	821	813	354	50.8	41.0	62	7.7		257	253	70
1940	870	849	374	51.9	40.6	54	6.3		294	287	78
1941	997	951	421	52.7	39.1	58	6.0		364	350	94
1942	1,110	1,084	446	51.1	40.1	81	7.4		427	416	105
1943	1,130	1,126	449	53.3	39.0	83	7.4		440	435	111
1944	1,223	1,183	497	53.8	37.0	94	8.0		485	474	123
1945	1,325	1,251	568	58.0	36.1	47	3.8		540	517	146
1946	1,614	1,482	701	61.2	37.7	−33	−2.2		688	648	192
1947	2,075	1,913	863	58.1	36.3	48	2.5		887	844	230
1948	2,442	2,284	1,019	56.6	35.6	121	5.3		1,059	1,017	273
1949	2,664	2,562	1,130	55.7	36.1	173	6.7		1,171	1,139	306
1950	2,933	2,821	1,239	60.0	35.7	84	3.0		1,327	1,289	346
1951	5,759	5,377	4,007	60.2	36.9	13	0.2		1,659	1,551	777
1952	6,411	5,994	4,422	58.4	36.0	186	3.1		1,884	1,770	886
1953	7,000	6,658	4,756	57.2	35.9	336	5.0		2,186	2,080	1,005
1954	7,144	6,992	4,921	56.9	36.7	387	5.5		2,278	2,223	1,055
1955	7,662	7,342	5,232	58.2	36.7	259	3.5		2,385	2,331	1,112
1956	7,991	7,744	5,455	63.4	37.1	−134	−1.7		2,609	2,527	1,206
1957	8,640	8,325	5,771	66.2	36.7	−359	−4.3		2,890	2,791	1,306
1958	9,077	8,841	6,003	63.7	36.3	−87	−1.0		3,120	3,022	1,403
1959	9,931	9,526	6,407	62.5	35.3	74	0.8		3,475	3,357	1,518
1960	10,527	10,264	6,672	63.6	34.8	70	0.7		3,723	3,650	1,594
1961	10,783	10,707	6,744	64.4	35.0	36	0.3		3,945	3,883	1,657
1962	11,599	11,285	7,061	64.5	34.5	9	0.1		4,038	4,047	1,649
1963	11,881	11,595	7,285	66.3	34.7	−210	−1.8		4,447	4,240	1,855
1964	12,648	12,347	7,578	68.0	33.9	−341	−2.8		4,767	4,651	1,970
1965	13,855	13,379	8,025	69.2	32.7	−419	−3.1		5,196	5,036	2,126
1966	15,197	14,655	8,522	66.1	31.9	110	0.8		5,788	5,617	2,290
1967	16,343	15,853	8,994	67.2	31.7	28	0.2		6,278	6,121	2,447
1968	17,833	17,236	9,589	68.8	31.2	−187	−1.1		6,887	6,659	2,664
1969	19,970	19,108	10,426	70.3	30.3	−384	−2.0		7,773	7,463	2,969
1970	22,430	21,448	11,386	69.7	29.6	−146	−0.7		8,713	8,383	3,304
1971	24,824	23,789	12,325	66.7	29.1	695	2.9		8,795	8,494	3,389
1972	27,596	26,556	13,370	66.0	29.4	920	3.5		9,424	9,189	3,618
1973	30,051	29,066	14,350	68.6	29.6	219	0.8		9,953	9,814	3,763
1974	32,071	31,382	15,051	75.3	29.7	−1,764	−5.6		10,459	10,216	3,953
1975	35,618	34,505	16,133	78.8	28.7	−2,899	−8.4		11,533	11,061	4,430
1976	43,116	40,933	18,351	74.6	27.4	−1,400	−3.4		14,148	13,289	5,288
1977	51,149	48,720	20,764	70.1	26.9	793	1.6		17,226	16,368	6,150
1978	57,418	55,441	22,753	69.0	27.6	1,324	2.4		19,666	18,879	6,959
1979	63,038	60,731	25,026	71.6	27.9	−386	−0.6		21,946	21,230	7,696

(continued)

TABLE Cj766–786 Life insurance – finances of stock companies, mutual companies, and reciprocals: 1925–1998
Continued

Year	Stock companies Net premiums Written	Earned	Unearned	Losses incurred as a percentage of premiums earned	Expenses incurred as a percentage of premiums written	Underwriting profit or loss Total	As a percentage of premiums earned	Mutual companies Net premiums Written	Earned	Unearned
	Cj766	Cj767	Cj768	Cj769	Cj770	Cj771	Cj772	Cj773	Cj774	Cj775
	Million dollars	Million dollars	Million dollars	Percent	Percent	Million dollars	Percent	Million dollars	Million dollars	Million dollars
1980	66,875	65,522	26,379	73.9	28.5	−1,949	−3.0	23,168	22,765	8,078
1981	69,215	67,964	27,626	75.5	29.4	−3,692	−5.4	24,132	23,761	8,451
1982	71,834	70,596	28,892	78.6	30.1	−6,507	−9.2	25,638	25,197	8,894
1983	74,577	73,050	30,511	81.0	30.8	−9,079	−12.4	27,456	27,161	9,247
1984	81,063	78,671	32,800	88.8	30.1	−15,838	−19.9	29,508	28,545	10,055
1985	100,081	91,482	40,883	88.8	27.7	−17,473	−19.1	35,300	32,724	12,562
1986	125,005	116,296	49,595	80.3	26.6	−10,351	−8.9	41,016	39,637	13,884
1987	135,491	131,232	54,083	76.2	27.1	−5,508	−4.2	46,141	45,966	14,114
1988	140,483	138,964	55,790	76.2	27.8	−5,877	−4.2	49,057	48,512	14,557
1989	142,835	141,850	—	67.6	28.2	—	—	52,148	51,292	—
1990	148,390	147,288	—	67.5	28.2	—	—	55,136	54,418	—
1991	150,464	150,464	—	67.5	28.6	—	—	57,225	56,491	—
1992	152,123	151,601	—	76.3	28.7	—	—	60,022	58,961	—
1993	162,710	158,457	—	66.0	28.2	—	—	63,260	61,954	—
1994	169,700	165,061	—	67.1	27.8	—	—	65,307	63,792	—
1995	177,216	172,837	—	64.8	27.8	—	—	66,434	65,619	—
1996	184,951	180,727	—	64.9	27.8	—	—	66,311	65,604	—
1997	190,373	186,406	—	60.0	28.3	—	—	67,821	67,015	—
1998	194,679	191,319	—	62.3	29.0	—	—	68,326	68,055	—

Year	Mutual companies Losses incurred as a percentage of premiums earned	Expenses incurred as a percentage of premiums written	Underwriting profit or loss Total	As a percentage of premiums earned	Reciprocals Net premiums Written	Earned	Unearned	Losses incurred as a percentage of premiums earned	Expenses incurred as a percentage of premiums written	Underwriting profit or loss Total	As a percentage of premiums earned
	Cj776	Cj777	Cj778	Cj779	Cj780	Cj781	Cj782	Cj783	Cj784	Cj785	Cj786
	Percent	Percent	Million dollars	Percent	Million dollars	Million dollars	Million dollars	Percent	Percent	Million dollars	Percent
1925	63.0	19.0	11	15.9	—	—	—	—	—	—	—
1926	58.3	20.7	14	16.2	—	—	—	—	—	—	—
1927	61.3	20.6	16	15.9	—	—	—	—	—	—	—
1928	61.8	20.1	18	15.9	—	—	—	—	—	—	—
1929	65.1	21.6	15	11.9	—	—	—	—	—	—	—
1930	62.9	22.6	18	14.0	—	—	—	—	—	—	—
1931	62.1	23.4	17	14.0	—	—	—	—	—	—	—
1932	60.4	24.5	17	15.2	—	—	—	—	—	—	—
1933	61.4	23.7	15	14.1	—	—	—	—	—	—	—
1934	63.7	21.4	18	13.2	—	—	—	—	—	—	—
1935	61.1	21.4	26	15.8	—	—	—	—	—	—	—
1936	61.4	21.2	30	15.7	—	—	—	—	—	—	—
1937	60.2	21.1	41	18.2	—	—	—	—	—	—	—
1938	58.8	22.0	42	18.7	—	—	—	—	—	—	—
1939	57.7	23.5	46	18.2	—	—	—	—	—	—	—
1940	59.9	23.9	45	15.6	—	—	—	—	—	—	—
1941	60.3	23.7	52	14.9	—	—	—	—	—	—	—
1942	57.0	23.2	79	19.0	—	—	—	—	—	—	—
1943	59.4	23.8	72	16.5	—	—	—	—	—	—	—
1944	61.4	23.9	67	14.2	—	—	—	—	—	—	—

TABLE Cj766–786   Life insurance – finances of stock companies, mutual companies, and reciprocals: 1925–1998
Continued

	Mutual companies				Reciprocals						
	Losses incurred as a percentage of premiums earned	Expenses incurred as a percentage of premiums written	Underwriting profit or loss		Net premiums			Losses incurred as a percentage of premiums earned	Expenses incurred as a percentage of premiums written	Underwriting profit or loss	
			Total	As a percentage of premiums earned	Written	Earned	Unearned			Total	As a percentage of premiums earned
	Cj776	Cj777	Cj778	Cj779	Cj780	Cj781	Cj782	Cj783	Cj784	Cj785	Cj786
Year	Percent	Percent	Million dollars	Percent	Million dollars	Million dollars	Million dollars	Percent	Percent	Million dollars	Percent
1945	64.0	23.9	57	11.0	—	—	—	—	—	—	—
1946	64.6	24.3	62	9.6	—	—	—	—	—	—	—
1947	61.5	23.8	114	13.4	—	—	—	—	—	—	—
1948	58.7	23.7	169	16.6	—	—	—	—	—	—	—
1949	61.0	23.1	174	15.3	—	—	—	—	—	—	—
1950	65.6	22.2	150	11.6	—	—	—	—	—	—	—
1951	60.3	24.8	204	13.1	—	—	—	—	—	—	—
1952	60.5	24.7	233	13.2	—	—	—	—	—	—	—
1953	60.3	24.4	292	14.1	—	—	—	—	—	—	—
1954	59.3	25.3	329	14.8	—	—	—	—	—	—	—
1955	61.3	26.0	285	12.2	—	—	—	—	—	—	—
1956	65.0	26.3	201	7.9	—	—	—	—	—	—	—
1957	65.5	25.8	215	7.7	—	—	—	—	—	—	—
1958	64.9	25.6	263	8.7	—	—	—	—	—	—	—
1959	64.7	25.3	306	9.1	—	—	—	—	—	—	—
1960	64.2	25.6	352	9.6	—	—	—	—	—	—	—
1961	63.6	25.6	404	10.4	—	—	—	—	—	—	—
1962	66.7	25.7	307	7.6	—	—	—	—	—	—	—
1963	71.4	26.5	35	0.8	—	—	—	—	—	—	—
1964	73.4	25.9	3	0.1	—	—	—	—	—	—	—
1965	73.1	25.0	56	1.1	—	—	—	—	—	—	—
1966	70.9	24.2	234	4.2	—	—	—	—	—	—	—
1967	72.7	24.5	129	2.1	—	—	—	—	—	—	—
1968	74.4	24.6	13	0.2	—	—	—	—	—	—	—
1969	76.5	24.1	−123	−1.6	1,200	1,135	499	75.7	23.1	−2	−0.2
1970	73.3	23.4	202	2.4	1,427	1,333	593	73.9	21.8	37	2.8
1971	69.1	23.1	592	7.0	1,684	1,584	691	69.9	21.0	123	7.8
1972	68.1	23.8	688	7.5	1,870	1,815	747	67.4	21.7	186	10.2
1973	71.2	24.3	416	4.2	2,015	1,958	804	70.3	21.9	142	7.2
1974	76.4	24.8	−184	−1.8	2,101	2,066	838	74.6	22.4	55	2.7
1975	80.2	24.2	−599	−5.4	2,398	2,264	973	81.9	22.3	−125	−5.5
1976	77.1	22.5	−142	−1.1	3,116	2,897	1,192	78.5	20.9	−30	−1.0
1977	72.4	21.5	813	5.0	3,978	3,735	1,443	71.1	20.2	277	7.4
1978	72.9	21.7	848	4.5	4,548	4,366	1,629	71.5	20.0	337	7.7
1979	76.3	21.7	251	1.2	5,077	4,895	1,813	76.7	20.3	110	2.2
1980	77.0	22.1	116	0.5	5,472	5,378	1,907	78.4	20.5	38	0.7
1981	79.8	23.1	−773	−3.3	5,684	5,673	2,094	79.6	20.8	−67	−1.2
1982	82.1	23.5	−1,504	−6.0	6,433	6,148	2,380	84.0	21.5	−402	−6.5
1983	81.9	23.4	−1,522	−5.6	6,886	6,692	2,571	85.2	22.0	−526	−7.9
1984	87.3	23.3	−3,239	−11.3	7,534	7,358	2,745	84.5	22.0	−515	−7.0
1985	88.6	21.9	−3,983	−12.2	8,711	8,348	3,109	87.9	21.5	−860	−10.3
1986	84.3	21.8	−2,713	−6.8	10,421	9,908	3,616	84.6	20.7	−633	−6.4
1987	82.2	21.4	−1,666	−3.6	11,515	11,225	3,887	80.7	20.2	−158	−1.4
1988	83.5	21.1	−2,366	−4.9	12,377	12,065	4,200	82.7	20.2	−415	−3.4
1989	73.7	21.2	—	—	13,246	12,944	—	69.2	20.4	—	—
1990	74.4	21.5	—	—	14,149	13,833	—	70.4	21.1	—	—
1991	70.6	22.0	—	—	15,114	14,798	—	70.4	21.6	—	—
1992	71.4	22.3	—	—	15,003	15,017	—	71.0	22.4	—	—
1993	68.7	21.9	—	—	14,890	14,553	—	65.8	22.0	—	—
1994	69.5	22.4	—	—	14,891	14,663	—	73.0	22.1	—	—
1995	67.5	23.1	—	—	15,304	14,883	—	66.3	22.2	—	—
1996	67.1	23.1	—	—	16,505	16,113	—	64.5	23.0	—	—
1997	61.9	24.3	—	—	17,284	17,061	—	58.4	24.1	—	—
1998	65.9	24.9	—	—	17,426	17,196	—	61.9	23.6	—	—

(continued)

TABLE Cj766–786   Life insurance – finances of stock companies, mutual companies, and reciprocals: 1925–1998 Continued

Sources

A. M. Best Company, *Best's Aggregates and Averages* (1955), pp. 122–5, 182–5; (1963), pp. 141–4, 209–12; (1971), pp. 139–42, 208–11; (1999), pp. 273, 277, 280.

Documentation

Premiums earned are the net premiums written with the increase or decrease during the year in the liability for unearned premiums. Unearned premiums represent the estimated aggregate net amount, after deduction of reinsurance credits, that an insurance company would be obliged to tender to its policyholders as return premiums for the unexpired terms, should it wish to cancel every policy in force. For losses, the ratio of losses and claim expenses incurred to premiums earned is used, but expenses incurred are ratioed to premiums written. When premium volume is increasing or decreasing, the combined loss and expense ratio thus calculated is a more accurate gauge of underwriting than the statutory figure. The underwriting profit or loss is the statutory figure taken from the annual statements of insurance companies and represents a comparison of losses and expenses incurred with premiums earned, adjusted with minor profit and loss items. This statutory figure does not include any adjustment for the estimated gain or loss in the equity in unearned premium liability.

TABLE Cj787–796   Life insurance – stock company resources and operating results: 1910–1998

Contributed by Eugene N. White

	Resources					Operating results				
						Investment income			Underwriting profit or loss	
	Assets	Liabilities	Capital	Surplus	Policyholders' surplus	Total	Ratio of to mean assets	Investment profit or loss	Total	As a percentage of premiums earned
	Cj787	Cj788	Cj789	Cj790	Cj791 [1]	Cj792	Cj793	Cj794 [2]	Cj795 [3]	Cj796
Year	Million dollars	Million dollars	Million dollars	Million dollars	Million dollars	Million dollars	Million dollars	Million dollars	Million dollars	Percent
1910	799	432	122	246	367	38	4.78	20	23	5.70
1911	860	460	128	271	399	41	4.90	31	6	1.49
1912	917	495	138	284	422	49	5.48	28	9	2.02
1913	935	515	150	269	419	45	4.84	9	5	1.01
1914	984	561	152	271	423	54	5.61	11	−17	−3.26
1915	1,039	582	158	300	457	56	5.58	41	15	2.71
1916	1,142	652	169	321	491	64	5.89	49	3	0.56
1917	1,271	776	173	323	496	61	5.05	15	5	0.77
1918	1,447	917	184	346	529	63	4.64	37	20	2.34
1919	1,739	1,106	205	428	633	86	5.38	42	51	5.18
1920	2,004	1,336	236	432	668	105	5.61	53	−29	−2.47
1921	2,080	1,335	246	498	745	109	5.32	114	−23	−1.90
1922	2,225	1,365	296	563	859	113	5.25	151	7	0.58
1923	2,348	1,479	323	546	869	115	5.02	71	−12	−0.94
1924	2,557	1,584	341	631	973	113	4.59	190	−48	−3.57
1925	2,809	1,742	372	695	1,067	116	4.31	163	−57	−4.01
1926	3,058	1,897	397	764	1,161	112	3.83	158	−49	−3.17
1927	3,463	2,039	443	981	1,424	124	3.80	285	26	1.59
1928	4,009	2,186	552	1,270	1,822	140	3.76	242	62	3.65
1929	4,322	2,285	639	1,398	2,037	152	3.65	84	31	1.74
1930	4,021	2,197	650	1,174	1,824	164	3.92	−148	−23	−1.30
1931	3,830	2,364	604	862	1,466	154	3.92	60	−11	−0.69
1932	3,571	2,328	449	794	1,243	125	3.38	−9	−3	−0.24
1933	3,111	1,824	418	869	1,288	106	3.17	107	64	5.10
1934	3,128	1,655	419	1,053	1,472	112	3.58	25	59	4.62
1935	3,528	1,744	429	1,355	1,784	108	3.23	332	83	6.35
1936	3,987	1,908	444	1,635	2,079	120	3.21	359	69	4.98
1937	3,800	1,972	448	1,389	1,828	126	3.24	−286	85	5.64
1938	3,976	2,004	461	1,511	1,972	115	2.97	233	97	6.40
1939	4,063	1,884	473	1,561	2,179	116	2.88	138	89	5.78
1940	4,229	2,020	484	1,573	2,209	122	2.93	58	70	4.28
1941	4,432	2,268	491	1,520	2,164	128	2.95	39	55	2.96
1942	4,661	2,440	493	1,575	2,222	123	2.71	84	74	3.43
1943	5,141	2,646	513	1,781	2,494	133	2.72	332	153	7.42
1944	5,617	2,888	530	1,946	2,729	141	2.62	331	72	3.37
1945	6,309	3,158	579	2,199	3,151	147	2.47	517	33	1.47
1946	6,630	3,751	594	1,960	2,879	154	2.38	−12	−152	−5.78
1947	7,465	4,560	615	2,050	2,905	172	2.44	109	−49	−1.44
1948	8,288	5,222	620	2,187	3,066	188	2.39	152	200	4.99
1949	9,520	5,812	671	2,656	3,708	215	2.42	528	421	9.51

Notes appear at end of table

TABLE Cj787–796 Life insurance – stock company resources and operating results: 1910–1998 *Continued*

	Resources					Operating results				
						Investment income			Underwriting profit or loss	
	Assets	Liabilities	Capital	Surplus	Policyholders' surplus	Total	Ratio of to mean assets	Investment profit or loss	Total	As a percentage of premiums earned
	Cj787	Cj788	Cj789	Cj790	Cj791 [1]	Cj792	Cj793	Cj794 [2]	Cj795 [3]	Cj796
Year	Million dollars	Million dollars	Million dollars	Million dollars	Million dollars	Million dollars	Million dollars	Million dollars	Million dollars	Percent
1950	10,603	6,386	736	3,034	4,217	253	2.52	600	191	4.00
1951	11,535	6,992	739	3,264	4,543	273	2.47	545	13	0.24
1952	12,779	7,815	759	3,598	4,964	294	2.30	549	185	3.08
1953	13,772	8,580	797	3,793	5,192	326	2.37	267	333	5.00
1954	15,789	9,091	832	4,858	6,697	363	2.46	1,583	385	5.50
1955	17,275	9,581	911	5,532	7,694	394	2.38	1,147	255	3.49
1956	17,811	10,011	934	5,536	7,800	430	2.45	580	−136	−1.75
1957	17,889	10,816	957	5,009	7,073	461	2.58	−166	−361	−4.33
1958	20,115	11,496	951	5,995	8,619	489	2.57	2,074	−93	−1.05
1959	21,801	12,419	1,030	6,502	9,381	534	2.55	1,021	71	0.74
1960	22,777	13,282	1,112	6,745	9,495	592	2.66	655	66	0.64
1961	25,585	13,865	1,175	8,126	11,719	621	2.57	2,516	30	0.28
1962	25,780	14,633	1,251	7,843	11,146	673	2.62	−230	3	0.02
1963	27,989	15,347	1,290	8,868	12,642	721	2.69	2,017	−219	−1.89
1964	30,077	16,386	1,350	9,576	13,691	782	2.69	1,821	−348	−2.81
1965	31,297	17,639	1,316	9,391	13,660	852	2.78	1,466	−425	−3.19
1966	31,035	19,028	1,320	8,388	12,007	896	2.87	−552	103	0.70
1967	34,183	20,603	1,367	9,324	13,580	987	3.03	2,302	10	0.07
1968	37,691	22,804	1,500	10,136	14,887	1,101	3.06	2,279	−201	−1.17
1969	37,992	24,293	1,578	8,690	12,699	1,238	3.27	−492	−396	−2.07
1970	42,568	28,553	1,878	9,326	14,014	1,439	3.57	1,250	−154	−0.72
1971	49,333	32,025	—	—	17,308	1,785	3.88	3,417	679	2.85
1972	58,461	37,063	—	—	21,398	2,068	3.84	4,724	915	3.44
1973	62,214	42,158	—	—	20,056	2,491	4.13	−1,441	226	0.78
1974	60,294	45,463	—	—	14,831	2,891	4.72	−3,251	−1,761	−5.60
1975	69,716	51,265	—	—	18,451	3,143	4.83	6,569	−2,880	−8.34
1976	83,573	60,552	—	—	23,021	3,629	4.73	6,871	−1,406	−3.43
1977	99,648	72,586	—	—	27,062	4,648	5.07	4,720	804	1.65
1978	117,545	85,035	—	—	32,510	5,724	5.27	7,062	1,335	2.41
1979	137,289	98,119	—	—	39,170	7,601	5.97	10,805	−365	−0.60
1980	156,223	108,724	—	—	47,499	8,836	6.02	13,780	−1,956	−2.98
1981	166,693	119,169	—	—	47,524	10,291	6.37	8,643	−3,681	−5.41
1982	182,403	129,070	—	—	53,333	11,846	6.79	14,460	−6,475	−9.17
1983	193,639	137,217	—	—	56,422	12,381	6.58	14,797	−9,090	−12.41
1984	202,970	149,686	—	—	53,284	13,695	6.91	12,871	−15,670	−19.84
1985	241,483	177,108	—	—	64,375	14,957	6.73	22,408	−17,879	−19.40
1986	291,697	209,852	—	—	81,845	16,872	6.35	24,186	−10,446	−8.95
1987	332,708	242,849	—	—	89,859	18,824	6.03	19,845	−5,450	−4.14
1988	373,810	271,503	—	—	102,307	22,380	6.32	27,853	−5,838	−4.19
1989	441,930	324,188	—	—	117,742	25,027	5.90	35,281	−12,289	−8.64
1990	464,458	341,510	—	—	122,948	25,193	5.56	24,149	−12,622	−8.56
1991	501,474	360,633	—	—	140,841	27,071	5.60	40,994	−12,843	−8.53
1992	525,871	383,267	—	—	142,604	26,472	5.16	33,278	−27,761	−18.29
1993	552,195	392,328	—	—	159,867	24,978	4.64	34,358	−12,270	−7.74
1994	577,148	409,699	—	—	167,449	25,717	4.55	25,458	−14,180	−8.59
1995	631,305	428,889	—	—	202,416	28,507	4.72	49,828	−11,091	−6.41
1996	658,014	440,438	—	—	217,576	30,191	4.68	46,757	−11,233	−6.21
1997	726,521	457,766	—	—	268,755	34,477	4.98	71,191	−2,184	−1.17
1998	767,990	475,636	—	—	292,354	33,318	4.46	54,599	−8,317	−4.35

[1] Includes voluntary reserves.

[2] Includes investment income.

[3] Beginning in 1942, before federal income taxes.

Sources

A. M. Best Company, *Best's Aggregates and Averages* (1959), pp. 20, 22; (1971), pp. 30, 32; (1999), pp. 260–1.

Documentation

Investment profit or loss is the statutory figure taken from the annual statements of insurance companies. From 1931 to 1934, arbitrary average values were used in valuing stocks owned by insurance companies; since 1934, market prices have been used for stocks, but all bonds not in default have been listed at amortized values. This item, therefore, does not reflect actual market prices for all securities since December 31, 1931, although in most recent years the market prices of high-grade bonds have usually exceeded the amortized values at which they are carried in the statements.

EQUITY AND BOND MARKETS

Peter L. Rousseau

TABLE Cj797–807   Common stock prices: 1802–1999
Contributed by Peter L. Rousseau

| Year | Schwert's index of common stocks Cj797 Index 1802 = 10 | Boston | | Cowles Commission/Standard and Poor | | | | Dow Jones Industrial Average Cj804 Index | NYSE composite Cj805 Index 1965 = 50 | NASDAQ composite Cj806 Index | Wilshire 5000 total market Cj807 Index |
		Banks Cj798 Index 1835 = 10	Industrials Cj799 Index 1835 = 10	Composite Cj800 Index 1941– 1943 = 10	Industrials Cj801 Index 1941– 1943 = 10	Railroads Cj802 Index 1941– 1943 = 10	Utilities Cj803 Index 1941– 1943 = 10				
1802	10.00	—	—	—	—	—	—	—	—	—	—
1803	9.04	—	—	—	—	—	—	—	—	—	—
1804	8.66	—	—	—	—	—	—	—	—	—	—
1805	8.28	—	—	—	—	—	—	—	—	—	—
1806	8.66	—	—	—	—	—	—	—	—	—	—
1807	9.04	—	—	—	—	—	—	—	—	—	—
1808	9.03	—	—	—	—	—	—	—	—	—	—
1809	9.13	—	—	—	—	—	—	—	—	—	—
1810	8.94	—	—	—	—	—	—	—	—	—	—
1811	8.25	—	—	—	—	—	—	—	—	—	—
1812	8.54	—	—	—	—	—	—	—	—	—	—
1813	8.64	—	—	—	—	—	—	—	—	—	—
1814	7.19	—	—	—	—	—	—	—	—	—	—
1815	7.39	—	—	—	—	—	—	—	—	—	—
1816	7.11	—	—	—	—	—	—	—	—	—	—
1817	7.97	—	—	—	—	—	—	—	—	—	—
1818	7.72	—	—	—	—	—	—	—	—	—	—
1819	7.14	—	—	—	—	—	—	—	—	—	—
1820	7.51	—	—	—	—	—	—	—	—	—	—
1821	7.96	—	—	—	—	—	—	—	—	—	—
1822	7.57	—	—	—	—	—	—	—	—	—	—
1823	7.56	—	—	—	—	—	—	—	—	—	—
1824	7.93	—	—	—	—	—	—	—	—	—	—
1825	7.48	—	—	—	—	—	—	—	—	—	—
1826	7.47	—	—	—	—	—	—	—	—	—	—
1827	7.25	—	—	—	—	—	—	—	—	—	—
1828	7.25	—	—	—	—	—	—	—	—	—	—
1829	7.18	—	—	—	—	—	—	—	—	—	—
1830	7.71	—	—	—	—	—	—	—	—	—	—
1831	7.94	—	—	—	—	—	—	—	—	—	—
1832	8.33	—	—	—	—	—	—	—	—	—	—
1833	8.25	—	—	—	—	—	—	—	—	—	—
1834	9.38	—	—	—	—	—	—	—	—	—	—
1835	9.70	10.00	10.00	—	—	—	—	—	—	—	—
1836	8.53	9.25	9.98	—	—	—	—	—	—	—	—
1837	7.86	8.72	8.36	—	—	—	—	—	—	—	—
1838	7.67	8.60	8.48	—	—	—	—	—	—	—	—
1839	6.75	8.15	8.18	—	—	—	—	—	—	—	—
1840	7.13	8.65	8.13	—	—	—	—	—	—	—	—
1841	6.20	8.84	8.52	—	—	—	—	—	—	—	—
1842	5.02	8.32	7.75	—	—	—	—	—	—	—	—
1843	7.41	8.62	8.15	—	—	—	—	—	—	—	—
1844	8.64	9.27	8.84	—	—	—	—	—	—	—	—
1845	9.37	9.40	9.43	—	—	—	—	—	—	—	—
1846	8.00	9.26	8.92	—	—	—	—	—	—	—	—
1847	8.10	9.02	8.31	—	—	—	—	—	—	—	—
1848	7.81	8.90	7.18	—	—	—	—	—	—	—	—
1849	7.82	9.17	6.91	—	—	—	—	—	—	—	—
1850	9.27	9.60	6.98	—	—	—	—	—	—	—	—
1851	8.97	9.83	6.77	—	—	—	—	—	—	—	—
1852	10.72	9.97	6.40	—	—	—	—	—	—	—	—
1853	9.37	10.07	7.64	—	—	—	—	—	—	—	—
1854	6.55	9.78	6.75	—	—	—	—	—	—	—	—

TABLE Cj797-807   Common stock prices: 1802-1999 *Continued*

	Schwert's index of common stocks	Boston		Cowles Commission/Standard and Poor				Dow Jones Industrial Average	NYSE composite	NASDAQ composite	Wilshire 5000 total market
		Banks	Industrials	Composite	Industrials	Railroads	Utilities				
	Cj797	Cj798	Cj799	Cj800	Cj801	Cj802	Cj803	Cj804	Cj805	Cj806	Cj807
Year	Index 1802 = 10	Index 1835 = 10	Index 1835 = 10	Index 1941– 1943 = 10	Index 1941– 1943 = 10	Index 1941– 1943 = 10	Index 1941– 1943 = 10	Index	Index 1965 = 50	Index	Index
1855	6.65	9.31	5.77	—	—	—	—	—	—	—	—
1856	6.94	9.58	5.65	—	—	—	—	—	—	—	—
1857	4.79	9.78	5.30	—	—	—	—	—	—	—	—
1858	5.47	9.17	4.22	—	—	—	—	—	—	—	—
1859	4.89	9.99	5.46	—	—	—	—	—	—	—	—
1860	5.57	9.92	5.90	—	—	—	—	—	—	—	—
1861	5.46	9.65	5.98	—	—	—	—	—	—	—	—
1862	8.48	8.89	5.99	—	—	—	—	—	—	—	—
1863	11.34	9.60	8.29	—	—	—	—	—	—	—	—
1864	11.90	9.90	7.76	—	—	—	—	—	—	—	—
1865	10.94	11.11	8.96	—	—	—	—	—	—	—	—
1866	11.34	10.51	9.18	—	—	—	—	—	—	—	—
1867	11.61	11.35	8.97	—	—	—	—	—	—	—	—
1868	12.85	11.21	7.45	—	—	—	—	—	—	—	—
1869	12.86	11.52	8.53	—	—	—	—	—	—	—	—
1870	13.55	11.54	7.31	—	—	—	—	—	—	—	—
1871	—	12.15	6.73	5.44	2.40	15.76	17.29	—	—	—	—
1872	—	12.19	8.05	5.81	2.79	16.70	18.74	—	—	—	—
1873	—	11.85	8.11	5.07	2.54	14.60	15.01	—	—	—	—
1874	—	12.03	7.52	5.21	2.70	14.89	16.33	—	—	—	—
1875	—	12.74	7.12	5.00	2.55	14.24	16.21	—	—	—	—
1876	—	11.81	6.42	4.10	2.42	11.64	12.16	—	—	—	—
1877	—	11.87	6.34	3.72	1.97	10.63	11.49	—	—	—	—
1878	—	11.30	6.61	3.94	2.01	11.31	12.24	—	—	—	—
1879	—	10.15	5.95	5.64	2.42	16.56	17.32	—	—	—	—
1880	—	11.51	7.99	6.69	2.41	20.46	16.26	—	—	—	—
1881	—	12.07	8.69	6.89	2.80	20.60	19.44	—	—	—	—
1882	—	11.91	9.05	6.69	2.61	20.03	19.51	—	—	—	—
1883	—	11.39	7.71	6.12	2.43	18.36	17.53	—	—	—	—
1884	—	11.35	7.03	4.97	2.28	14.86	13.44	—	—	—	—
1885	—	11.12	6.37	6.02	2.74	17.88	17.49	—	—	—	—
1886	—	11.65	6.55	6.45	2.92	19.30	17.03	—	—	—	—
1887	—	11.37	6.66	6.06	2.88	18.04	16.22	—	—	—	—
1888	—	11.44	6.41	6.00	3.39	17.29	17.60	—	—	—	—
1889	—	11.92	6.53	6.13	3.38	17.81	18.15	—	—	—	—
1890	—	12.06	6.78	5.40	3.03	15.80	14.87	—	—	—	—
1891	—	12.32	6.68	6.30	3.43	18.60	17.14	—	—	—	—
1892	—	11.70	6.57	6.32	3.84	17.88	19.64	—	—	—	—
1893	—	11.62	6.93	4.83	2.51	13.91	16.80	—	—	—	—
1894	—	10.64	6.11	4.84	2.54	13.80	17.83	—	—	—	—
1895	—	10.92	6.15	4.88	2.49	13.96	18.52	—	—	—	—
1896	—	10.76	6.39	4.78	2.47	13.63	18.30	40.53	—	—	—
1897	—	10.36	5.96	5.49	2.79	15.66	21.76	49.41	—	—	—
1898	—	—	—	6.60	3.73	18.44	26.01	60.52	—	—	—
1899	—	—	—	6.86	3.84	19.73	24.23	66.08	—	—	—
1900	—	—	—	8.17	4.43	24.14	26.73	70.71	—	—	—
1901	—	—	—	9.28	4.33	29.78	27.75	64.56	—	—	—
1902	—	—	—	9.47	4.19	31.29	27.20	64.29	—	—	—
1903	—	—	—	7.73	3.12	25.87	23.28	49.11	—	—	—
1904	—	—	—	9.49	4.19	32.07	25.52	69.61	—	—	—
1905	—	—	—	11.15	5.49	37.35	25.46	96.20	—	—	—
1906	—	—	—	11.16	5.63	37.91	21.51	94.35	—	—	—
1907	—	—	—	7.49	3.24	27.12	13.07	58.75	—	—	—
1908	—	—	—	10.46	5.03	36.57	18.80	86.15	—	—	—
1909	—	—	—	11.94	6.57	40.44	20.36	99.05	—	—	—
1910	—	—	—	10.43	5.48	35.34	18.96	81.36	—	—	—
1911	—	—	—	10.49	5.34	35.68	19.65	81.68	—	—	—
1912	—	—	—	10.70	5.80	35.48	20.04	87.87	—	—	—
1913	—	—	—	9.31	5.00	30.93	17.62	78.78	—	—	—
1914	—	—	—	8.35	4.58	27.16	16.78	54.58	—	—	—

(continued)

TABLE Cj797–807   Common stock prices: 1802–1999   *Continued*

Year	Schwert's index of common stocks Cj797 Index 1802 = 10	Boston Banks Cj798 Index 1835 = 10	Boston Industrials Cj799 Index 1835 = 10	Composite Cj800 Index 1941–1943 = 10	Industrials Cj801 Index 1941–1943 = 10	Railroads Cj802 Index 1941–1943 = 10	Utilities Cj803 Index 1941–1943 = 10	Dow Jones Industrial Average Cj804 Index	NYSE composite Cj805 Index 1965 = 50	NASDAQ composite Cj806 Index	Wilshire 5000 total market Cj807 Index
1915	—	—	—	11.03	7.47	32.48	20.01	99.15	—	—	—
1916	—	—	—	11.01	7.72	31.33	20.33	95.00	—	—	—
1917	—	—	—	8.19	5.80	24.19	14.63	74.38	—	—	—
1918	—	—	—	9.07	6.74	25.83	14.38	82.20	—	—	—
1919	—	—	—	10.34	8.83	23.45	13.22	107.23	—	—	—
1920	—	—	—	7.98	5.77	22.36	12.68	71.95	—	—	—
1921	—	—	—	8.35	6.20	22.79	14.98	81.10	—	—	—
1922	—	—	—	10.30	7.75	26.87	17.76	98.73	—	—	—
1923	—	—	—	9.99	7.69	25.31	17.86	95.52	—	—	—
1924	—	—	—	11.97	9.04	31.52	20.78	120.51	—	—	—
1925	—	—	—	14.59	11.46	36.35	24.35	156.66	—	—	—
1926	—	—	—	15.03	11.73	38.67	24.99	157.20	—	—	—
1927	—	—	—	19.15	15.28	45.59	30.84	202.40	—	—	—
1928	—	—	—	25.61	20.93	50.32	44.16	300.00	—	—	—
1929	—	—	—	22.05	16.41	48.73	50.42	248.48	—	—	—
1930	—	—	—	15.31	11.07	33.27	38.04	164.58	—	—	—
1931	—	—	—	7.89	5.81	11.40	21.96	77.90	—	—	—
1932	—	—	—	6.80	4.99	9.03	19.10	59.93	—	—	—
1933	—	—	—	10.19	8.92	14.76	16.49	99.90	—	—	—
1934	—	—	—	10.10	9.21	12.89	13.98	104.04	—	—	—
1935	—	—	—	13.91	12.47	15.01	22.51	144.13	—	—	—
1936	—	—	—	17.60	15.93	19.79	26.78	179.90	—	—	—
1937	—	—	—	11.14	10.11	10.26	18.11	120.85	—	—	—
1938	—	—	—	13.60	12.63	11.17	19.66	154.76	—	—	—
1939	—	—	—	13.19	12.12	10.78	20.82	150.24	—	—	—
1940	—	—	—	11.51	10.49	9.74	18.76	131.13	—	—	—
1941	—	—	—	9.59	8.98	8.36	13.43	110.96	—	—	—
1942	—	—	—	10.45	9.87	9.65	13.72	119.40	—	—	—
1943	—	—	—	12.59	11.71	11.92	17.46	135.89	—	—	—
1944	—	—	—	14.33	13.30	16.21	19.21	152.32	—	—	—
1945	—	—	—	18.87	17.53	21.31	24.80	192.91	—	—	—
1946	—	—	—	17.08	16.00	15.97	23.01	177.20	—	—	—
1947	—	—	—	16.74	16.13	14.79	19.42	181.16	—	—	—
1948	—	—	—	16.11	15.48	14.24	19.09	177.30	—	—	—
1949	—	—	—	18.11	17.47	14.20	21.57	200.13	—	—	—
1950	—	—	—	21.94	21.64	19.80	21.80	235.41	—	—	—
1951	—	—	—	24.98	24.91	20.56	23.90	269.23	—	—	—
1952	—	—	—	26.94	26.70	25.50	25.50	291.90	—	—	—
1953	—	—	—	25.85	25.55	20.59	25.78	280.90	13.60	—	—
1954	—	—	—	36.73	37.67	31.12	29.96	404.39	19.40	—	—
1955	—	—	—	43.89	46.88	34.98	31.55	488.40	23.71	—	—
1956	—	—	—	46.30	49.42	32.12	31.47	499.47	24.35	—	—
1957	—	—	—	39.99	42.86	20.95	32.14	435.69	21.11	—	—
1958	—	—	—	55.21	58.97	34.39	43.28	583.65	28.85	—	—
1959	—	—	—	59.89	64.50	33.82	44.74	679.36	32.15	—	—
1960	—	—	—	58.11	61.49	29.55	51.76	615.89	30.94	—	—
1961	—	—	—	71.55	75.72	33.25	64.83	731.14	38.93	—	—
1962	—	—	—	63.10	66.00	32.73	61.09	652.10	33.81	—	—
1963	—	—	—	75.02	79.25	40.65	66.42	762.95	39.92	—	—
1964	—	—	—	84.75	89.62	45.82	74.52	874.13	45.65	—	—
1965	—	—	—	92.43	98.47	51.28	75.51	969.26	50.00	—	—
1966	—	—	—	80.33	85.24	41.04	69.35	785.69	43.72	—	—
1967	—	—	—	96.47	105.11	43.71	66.08	905.11	53.83	—	—
1968	—	—	—	103.86	113.02	54.15	69.69	943.75	58.90	—	—
1969	—	—	—	92.06	101.49	37.16	56.09	800.36	51.53	—	—
1970	—	—	—	92.15	100.90	26.25	61.71	838.92	50.23	—	—
1971	—	—	—	102.09	112.72	51.31	59.83	890.20	56.43	114.12	—
1972	—	—	—	118.05	131.87	49.84	61.05	1,020.02	64.48	133.73	—
1973	—	—	—	97.55	109.14	43.29	46.91	850.86	51.82	92.19	—
1974	—	—	—	68.56	76.47	32.13	33.54	616.24	36.13	59.82	—

TABLE Cj797–807   Common stock prices: 1802–1999   *Continued*

	Schwert's index of common stocks	Boston		Cowles Commission/Standard and Poor				Dow Jones Industrial Average	NYSE composite	NASDAQ composite	Wilshire 5000 total market
		Banks	Industrials	Composite	Industrials	Railroads	Utilities				
	Cj797	Cj798	Cj799	Cj800	Cj801	Cj802	Cj803	Cj804	Cj805	Cj806	Cj807
Year	Index 1802 = 10	Index 1835 = 10	Index 1835 = 10	Index 1941– 1943 = 10	Index 1941– 1943 = 10	Index 1941– 1943 = 10	Index 1941– 1943 = 10	Index	Index 1965 = 50	Index	Index
1975	—	—	—	90.19	100.88	39.23	44.45	852.41	47.64	77.62	—
1976	—	—	—	107.46	119.46	49.78	54.24	1,004.65	57.88	97.88	—
1977	—	—	—	95.10	104.71	44.29	54.73	831.17	52.50	105.05	—
1978	—	—	—	96.11	107.21	41.50	48.47	805.01	53.62	117.98	—
1979	—	—	—	107.94	121.02	48.90	50.24	838.74	61.95	151.14	1,100.71
1980	—	—	—	135.76	154.45	80.44	52.45	963.99	77.86	202.34	1,404.60
1981	—	—	—	122.55	137.12	70.38	52.98	875.00	71.11	195.84	1,286.24
1982	—	—	—	140.64	157.62	78.45	60.45	1,046.54	81.03	232.41	1,451.59
1983	—	—	—	164.93	186.24	101.20	66.17	1,258.64	95.18	278.60	1,723.62
1984	—	—	—	167.24	186.36	91.71	75.89	1,211.57	96.38	247.35	1,702.01
1985	—	—	—	211.28	234.56	120.27	93.17	1,546.67	121.58	324.93	2,164.69
1986	—	—	—	242.17	269.93	125.72	112.29	1,895.95	138.58	348.83	2,434.95
1987	—	—	—	247.08	285.86	121.19	102.12	1,938.83	138.23	330.47	2,417.12
1988	—	—	—	277.72	321.26	145.41	112.64	2,168.57	156.26	381.38	2,738.42
1989	—	—	—	353.40	403.49	177.47	156.34	2,753.20	195.04	454.82	3,419.88
1990	—	—	—	330.22	387.42	149.55	143.59	2,633.66	180.49	373.84	3,101.36
1991	—	—	—	417.09	492.72	217.61	155.16	3,168.83	229.44	586.34	4,014.10
1992	—	—	—	435.71	507.46	231.81	158.46	3,301.11	240.21	676.95	4,289.74
1993	—	—	—	466.45	540.19	271.23	172.58	3,754.09	259.08	776.80	4,657.83
1994	—	—	—	459.27	547.51	223.12	150.12	3,843.44	250.94	751.96	4,540.62
1995	—	—	—	615.93	721.19	305.27	202.58	5,177.12	329.51	1,052.13	6,057.21
1996	—	—	—	740.74	869.97	343.66	198.81	6,448.27	392.30	1,291.03	7,189.29
1997	—	—	—	970.43	1,121.38	439.22	235.81	7,908.25	511.19	1,570.35	9,296.19
1998	—	—	—	1,229.23	1,479.16	425.93	259.62	9,181.43	595.81	2,192.69	11,317.59
1999	—	—	—	1,469.25	1,841.92	380.40	227.22	11,497.12	650.30	4,069.31	13,812.67

Sources

Series Cj797. G. William Schwert, "Indexes of U.S. Stock Prices from 1802 to 1987," *Journal of Business* 63 (3) (1990): 399–426; Walter B. Smith and Arthur H. Cole, *Fluctuations in American Business, 1790–1860* (Harvard University Press, 1935); Frederick R. Macaulay, *The Movements of Interest Rates, Bond Yields and Stock Prices in the United States since 1856* (National Bureau of Economic Research, 1938).

Series Cj798–799. Peter L. Rousseau, "The Boston Market for Banking and Industrial Equities, 1835–1897," *Historical Methods* 11 (3) (2000): 163–9; Joseph G. Martin, *Twenty-One Years in the Boston Stock Market* (Redding, 1856), and *A Century of Finance: The Boston Stock and Money Markets, 1798 to 1898* (published by the author, 1898), and underlying worksheets.

Series Cj800–803. Jack W. Wilson and Charles P. Jones, "An Analysis of the S&P 500 Index and Cowles' Extensions: Price Indexes and Stock Returns, 1870–1999," *Journal of Business* 75 (3) (2002): 505–33; Arthur Cowles and Associates, *Common Stock Indexes for 1940* (mimeographed, University of Chicago Graduate School of Business, 1942); Standard Statistics Company, *Standard Statistical Bulletin* (various issues); Standard and Poor's Statistical Service, *Security Price Index Record* (various issues).

Series Cj804. 1896–1990: Dow Jones and Company, *The Dow Jones Averages, 1885–1990*, edited by Phyllis S. Pierce (Business One Irwin, 1991); 1991–1999: Dow Jones and Company Internet site.

Series Cj805. New York Stock Exchange, *Fact Book, 1999*.

Series Cj806. Nasdaq-Amex Market Group, *NASDAQ–Amex Fact Book and Company Directory* (1999), and *NASDAQ Stock Market Fact Book and Company Directory* (various issues).

Series Cj807. Wilshire Associates Internet site.

Documentation

All indexes reflect values at the end of the calendar year.

Series Cj797. This index of common stock prices for the early United States includes selected bank stocks for 1802–1814, bank and insurance stocks for 1815–1833, and banks, insurance, and railroad stocks for 1834–1845, all from Smith and Cole. The index includes only railroad stock prices for 1846–1869, with 1846–1862 from Smith and Cole and 1863–1869 from Macaulay's average monthly prices. Schwert describes the construction of a continuous series from the original sources and the methodology used to adjust the 1863–1869 values to reflect year-end timing.

Series Cj798–799. These indexes include all banking and industrial common stocks, respectively, traded in the Boston stock market both over the formal stock exchange and by auction. For 1835–1853, these series are based on annual low prices of individual stocks from contemporary broker Joseph G. Martin and are imprecisely timed. Price observations closest to the end of each year are used for 1854–1897 based on worksheets that underlie Martin's volumes. These "chained" indexes weight individual securities by their market valuations. See Rousseau (2000) for additional details.

Series Cj800–803. These internally consistent price indexes, which cover 130 years, were obtained by reconstructing the broadly defined Standard and Poor's (S&P) weekly index from 1918 to join with the modern S&P indexes from 1957 to the present. The S&P weekly index included 198 common stocks in 1918, included 223 stocks by 1923, and rose sharply to more than 400 stocks in 1930 before joining in 1957 with the S&P "500." Thus, coverage of the index in series Cj800 is broader than the ninety common stocks used in the index published by S&P for 1927–1956. The Cowles Commission's price indexes are used to extend the series back from 1918 to 1871 and have been adjusted to reflect month-end estimates after 1885. The entries from 1871 to 1884 are averages of high and low prices in December of each year. The formula used for this index is a "base-weighted aggregative" expressed in relatives with the average value for the base period (1941–1943) equal to 10, and with adjustments for arbitrary price changes caused by the issuance of rights, stock dividends, and split-ups.

Series Cj804. The Dow Jones Industrial Average (DJIA) was first published in its present form in 1896, though other price performance indexes that mix railroad and industrial stocks are available from 1885 on. The DJIA is a summation of the prices of thirty selected industrial common stocks, to

(continued)

TABLE Cj797–807   Common stock prices: 1802–1999   *Continued*

which a divisor is applied to account for stock splits and changes in the firms that comprise the index. The value of the DJIA at its inception on May 26, 1896, was 40.94. As an index that includes a representative sample of large industrial stocks, the DJIA aims to capture broad price trends in the U.S. equity market.

Series Cj805. The New York Stock Exchange (NYSE) Composite measures changes in the aggregate market value of all common stocks listed on the NYSE, with adjustments to eliminate the effects of capitalization changes, new listings, and delistings. The aggregate market value is then expressed as a relative of the base period market value of 50.00 on December 31, 1965. The NYSE publishes the Composite index going back to 1953 by linking it with the U.S. Security and Exchange Commission's index for 1953–1964.

Series Cj806. The National Association of Securities Dealers Automated Quotation System (NASDAQ) is the automated version of what was once the over-the-counter market. The NASDAQ Composite is a capitalization-weighted price index of all issues trading over the system, with a starting value of 100 in February 1971.

Series Cj807. The Wilshire 5000 index measures the performance of all U.S. headquartered equity securities with readily available price data. In 1999, more than 7,000 capitalization-weighted security returns were used to adjust the index. The index base is its December 31, 1980, capitalization of $1,404.6 billion. Thus, the Wilshire 5000 index aims to approximate dollar changes in the U.S. equity market. It has been computed on a daily basis since 1979.

TABLE Cj808–816   Stock dividend yields: 1802–1999

Contributed by Peter L. Rousseau

		Common stocks						Preferred stocks	
	Schwert's index	Boston		Cowles Commission/Standard and Poor					High-grade industrials
		Banks	Industrials	Composite	Industrials	Railroads	Utilities	High-grade	
	Cj808	Cj809	Cj810	Cj811	Cj812	Cj813	Cj814	Cj815	Cj816
Year	Index 1941–1943 = 10	Percent annually	Percent annually	Percent annually	Percent annually	Percent annually	Percent annually	Percent annually	Percent annually
1802	4.52	—	—	—	—	—	—	—	—
1803	5.18	—	—	—	—	—	—	—	—
1804	5.12	—	—	—	—	—	—	—	—
1805	5.14	—	—	—	—	—	—	—	—
1806	5.02	—	—	—	—	—	—	—	—
1807	5.05	—	—	—	—	—	—	—	—
1808	5.07	—	—	—	—	—	—	—	—
1809	5.06	—	—	—	—	—	—	—	—
1810	5.08	—	—	—	—	—	—	—	—
1811	5.16	—	—	—	—	—	—	—	—
1812	5.08	—	—	—	—	—	—	—	—
1813	5.05	—	—	—	—	—	—	—	—
1814	5.21	—	—	—	—	—	—	—	—
1815	5.08	—	—	—	—	—	—	—	—
1816	5.17	—	—	—	—	—	—	—	—
1817	4.93	—	—	—	—	—	—	—	—
1818	5.08	—	—	—	—	—	—	—	—
1819	5.22	—	—	—	—	—	—	—	—
1820	5.00	—	—	—	—	—	—	—	—
1821	5.00	—	—	—	—	—	—	—	—
1822	5.15	—	—	—	—	—	—	—	—
1823	5.07	—	—	—	—	—	—	—	—
1824	5.02	—	—	—	—	—	—	—	—
1825	5.12	—	—	—	—	—	—	—	—
1826	5.12	—	—	—	—	—	—	—	—
1827	5.06	—	—	—	—	—	—	—	—
1828	5.12	—	—	—	—	—	—	—	—
1829	5.09	—	—	—	—	—	—	—	—
1830	4.98	—	—	—	—	—	—	—	—
1831	5.04	—	—	—	—	—	—	—	—
1832	5.04	—	—	—	—	—	—	—	—
1833	5.07	—	—	—	—	—	—	—	—
1834	4.94	—	—	—	—	—	—	—	—
1835	4.91	5.90	11.38	—	—	—	—	—	—
1836	5.30	7.14	10.60	—	—	—	—	—	—
1837	5.18	6.74	5.47	—	—	—	—	—	—
1838	5.04	6.12	6.72	—	—	—	—	—	—
1839	5.24	7.10	9.15	—	—	—	—	—	—

TABLE Cj808–816   Stock dividend yields: 1802–1999   *Continued*

		Common stocks						Preferred stocks	
	Schwert's index	Boston		Cowles Commission/Standard and Poor				High-grade	High-grade industrials
		Banks	Industrials	Composite	Industrials	Railroads	Utilities		
	Cj808	Cj809	Cj810	Cj811	Cj812	Cj813	Cj814	Cj815	Cj816
Year	Index 1941–1943 = 10	Percent annually	Percent annually	Percent annually	Percent annually	Percent annually	Percent annually	Percent annually	Percent annually
1840	5.07	6.16	4.08	—	—	—	—	—	—
1841	5.20	5.97	9.12	—	—	—	—	—	—
1842	5.28	6.21	3.81	—	—	—	—	—	—
1843	4.75	5.87	6.23	—	—	—	—	—	—
1844	4.74	5.54	14.35	—	—	—	—	—	—
1845	5.07	6.50	14.57	—	—	—	—	—	—
1846	5.16	6.80	16.37	—	—	—	—	—	—
1847	4.99	7.44	11.19	—	—	—	—	—	—
1848	5.23	8.11	8.74	—	—	—	—	—	—
1849	5.05	8.41	8.10	—	—	—	—	—	—
1850	4.96	7.87	9.23	—	—	—	—	—	—
1851	5.05	7.65	6.07	—	—	—	—	—	—
1852	4.91	7.52	8.20	—	—	—	—	—	—
1853	5.16	7.56	8.36	—	—	—	—	—	—
1854	5.38	7.89	8.00	—	—	—	—	—	—
1855	5.05	7.79	6.34	—	—	—	—	—	—
1856	5.16	7.54	7.59	—	—	—	—	—	—
1857	5.40	7.23	5.51	—	—	—	—	—	—
1858	4.92	7.41	5.82	—	—	—	—	—	—
1859	5.20	6.61	9.24	—	—	—	—	—	—
1860	4.70	6.65	10.90	—	—	—	—	—	—
1861	5.28	6.50	8.26	—	—	—	—	—	—
1862	4.58	6.69	19.18	—	—	—	—	—	—
1863	4.58	6.76	15.31	—	—	—	—	—	—
1864	5.08	11.07	13.88	—	—	—	—	—	—
1865	5.12	18.95	11.64	—	—	—	—	—	—
1866	5.02	9.17	12.78	—	—	—	—	—	—
1867	5.06	8.26	8.08	—	—	—	—	—	—
1868	4.95	8.83	11.20	—	—	—	—	—	—
1869	5.04	8.50	8.36	—	—	—	—	—	—
1870	5.01	8.20	6.69	—	—	—	—	—	—
1871	—	7.62	11.42	5.96	5.62	6.30	2.60	—	—
1872	—	7.54	9.80	5.58	6.71	6.48	2.36	—	—
1873	—	7.56	7.53	5.76	6.43	6.52	2.47	—	—
1874	—	7.25	7.24	7.38	6.72	7.14	8.07	—	—
1875	—	6.05	6.03	6.28	6.49	6.26	7.71	—	—
1876	—	5.14	5.04	6.47	7.26	6.54	6.08	—	—
1877	—	4.75	6.47	5.33	4.08	5.02	4.68	—	—
1878	—	3.92	5.42	5.40	5.16	5.53	5.04	—	—
1879	—	4.31	8.00	5.95	4.94	5.62	5.66	—	—
1880	—	4.91	7.37	5.24	6.54	5.04	4.24	—	—
1881	—	4.50	6.88	4.98	5.95	5.00	5.01	—	—
1882	—	5.11	5.00	5.12	5.08	4.95	6.30	—	—
1883	—	4.66	5.04	5.54	5.68	5.26	7.06	—	—
1884	—	4.70	4.16	5.97	6.09	5.46	6.79	—	—
1885	—	4.55	3.93	5.34	6.50	4.92	9.26	—	—
1886	—	4.39	4.29	3.74	5.36	3.88	4.03	—	—
1887	—	4.63	7.65	4.15	5.83	4.00	4.42	—	—
1888	—	4.82	6.31	4.15	4.43	3.74	6.55	—	—
1889	—	4.34	6.23	4.21	4.57	3.41	6.27	—	—
1890	—	4.39	5.70	3.83	4.94	3.39	5.68	—	—
1891	—	4.21	5.80	4.61	6.26	4.14	5.79	—	—
1892	—	4.39	7.60	4.36	6.40	3.75	5.68	—	—
1893	—	4.26	5.62	4.11	5.71	3.73	4.99	—	—
1894	—	4.40	4.41	4.60	6.76	4.33	6.34	—	—
1895	—	4.19	5.55	4.61	6.21	3.73	5.63	—	—
1896	—	4.33	4.54	4.24	6.80	3.72	4.40	—	—
1897	—	4.50	3.84	4.44	5.64	3.78	4.80	—	—
1898	—	—	—	3.79	5.71	3.39	5.14	—	—
1899	—	—	—	4.02	7.14	3.46	3.68	—	—

(continued)

TABLE Cj808–816   Stock dividend yields: 1802–1999   *Continued*

	Common stocks							Preferred stocks	
	Schwert's index	Boston		Cowles Commission/Standard and Poor					High-grade industrials
		Banks	Industrials	Composite	Industrials	Railroads	Utilities	High-grade	
	Cj808	Cj809	Cj810	Cj811	Cj812	Cj813	Cj814	Cj815	Cj816
Year	Index 1941–1943 = 10	Percent annually	Percent annually	Percent annually	Percent annually	Percent annually	Percent annually	Percent annually	Percent annually
1900	—	—	—	4.38	4.90	4.10	4.01	—	—
1901	—	—	—	4.29	5.13	3.76	4.14	—	—
1902	—	—	—	3.95	5.02	3.35	3.86	—	—
1903	—	—	—	4.00	5.12	3.42	3.93	—	—
1904	—	—	—	4.42	5.33	4.07	4.67	—	—
1905	—	—	—	4.18	4.50	3.54	4.96	—	—
1906	—	—	—	3.88	4.13	3.64	3.98	—	—
1907	—	—	—	4.02	4.80	4.27	3.97	—	—
1908	—	—	—	6.10	6.94	5.73	6.06	—	—
1909	—	—	—	5.28	6.10	4.65	4.61	—	—
1910	—	—	—	4.11	4.43	4.14	4.51	6.30	—
1911	—	—	—	5.05	5.23	4.80	5.41	6.28	—
1912	—	—	—	5.19	10.20	4.88	5.25	6.27	—
1913	—	—	—	5.28	6.41	4.76	5.00	6.57	—
1914	—	—	—	4.96	5.17	4.71	6.13	6.49	—
1915	—	—	—	5.66	5.80	5.62	6.53	6.48	—
1916	—	—	—	6.29	5.95	4.94	6.24	6.19	—
1917	—	—	—	7.63	8.82	5.45	6.02	6.42	—
1918	—	—	—	8.16	9.48	6.62	7.07	6.70	—
1919	—	—	—	6.35	6.20	6.09	7.49	6.31	—
1920	—	—	—	5.45	4.54	6.78	7.87	6.79	—
1921	—	—	—	6.36	5.88	7.11	9.23	6.80	—
1922	—	—	—	6.69	6.23	6.86	8.62	6.14	—
1923	—	—	—	5.63	5.08	6.07	7.54	6.12	—
1924	—	—	—	6.13	5.36	7.09	7.88	6.08	—
1925	—	—	—	5.57	5.13	5.78	6.69	5.90	—
1926	—	—	—	5.15	5.09	5.51	5.56	5.78	—
1927	—	—	—	5.38	5.28	5.45	5.51	5.51	—
1928	—	—	—	4.38	4.27	4.82	4.88	5.12	—
1929	—	—	—	3.71	3.72	4.56	3.08	5.12	—
1930	—	—	—	4.07	4.22	4.88	3.26	4.95	—
1931	—	—	—	4.97	5.10	5.37	4.11	5.04	—
1932	—	—	—	5.86	5.79	4.51	6.35	6.13	—
1933	—	—	—	5.37	5.34	3.81	6.16	5.75	—
1934	—	—	—	3.92	3.49	2.82	6.59	5.29	—
1935	—	—	—	4.04	3.86	2.81	7.35	4.63	—
1936	—	—	—	4.91	4.83	6.59	4.81	4.33	—
1937	—	—	—	4.41	4.51	3.39	4.34	4.45	—
1938	—	—	—	4.63	4.23	3.23	5.84	4.34	—
1939	—	—	—	4.32	4.17	4.46	5.31	4.19	—
1940	—	—	—	5.06	4.96	5.27	5.21	4.14	—
1941	—	—	—	6.51	6.18	7.04	5.41	4.08	—
1942	—	—	—	6.69	5.73	9.93	6.58	4.31	—
1943	—	—	—	6.13	5.35	9.74	6.61	4.06	—
1944	—	—	—	5.41	4.94	8.22	5.30	3.99	—
1945	—	—	—	4.71	4.64	6.79	4.76	3.70	—
1946	—	—	—	4.06	3.82	4.88	4.07	3.53	—
1947	—	—	—	5.41	5.34	6.08	4.77	3.79	3.51
1948	—	—	—	6.26	6.51	7.44	5.79	4.15	3.81
1949	—	—	—	7.07	7.43	7.80	6.13	3.97	3.63
1950	—	—	—	7.72	8.49	8.03	5.75	3.85	3.52
1951	—	—	—	6.17	6.38	6.41	6.06	4.11	3.69
1952	—	—	—	5.49	5.58	6.42	5.63	4.13	3.75
1953	—	—	—	5.22	5.34	5.80	5.55	4.27	3.88
1954	—	—	—	5.77	6.20	7.29	5.80	4.02	3.69
1955	—	—	—	4.56	4.36	5.62	5.20	4.01	3.69
1956	—	—	—	4.14	4.21	5.40	5.18	4.25	3.90
1957	—	—	—	4.04	3.64	5.17	5.31	4.63	4.36
1958	—	—	—	4.38	4.41	7.64	5.16	4.45	4.24
1959	—	—	—	3.31	3.52	4.83	4.09	4.69	4.45

TABLE Cj808–816   Stock dividend yields: 1802–1999   *Continued*

		Common stocks						Preferred stocks	
	Schwert's index	Boston		Cowles Commission/Standard and Poor				High-grade	High-grade industrials
		Banks	Industrials	Composite	Industrials	Railroads	Utilities		
	Cj808	Cj809	Cj810	Cj811	Cj812	Cj813	Cj814	Cj815	Cj816
Year	Index 1941–1943 = 10	Percent annually	Percent annually	Percent annually	Percent annually	Percent annually	Percent annually	Percent annually	Percent annually
1960	—	—	—	3.26	3.10	5.03	4.16	4.75	4.48
1961	—	—	—	3.48	3.38	5.48	3.79	4.66	4.36
1962	—	—	—	2.98	2.91	4.93	3.16	4.50	4.21
1963	—	—	—	3.61	3.61	5.26	3.54	4.30	4.04
1964	—	—	—	3.33	3.28	4.80	3.49	4.32	4.05
1965	—	—	—	3.21	3.18	4.58	3.34	4.33	4.07
1966	—	—	—	3.11	3.03	4.37	3.56	4.97	4.67
1967	—	—	—	3.64	3.53	5.46	4.17	5.34	5.13
1968	—	—	—	3.18	3.03	5.10	4.52	5.78	5.62
1969	—	—	—	3.04	2.89	4.16	4.42	6.41	6.15
1970	—	—	—	3.41	3.19	5.44	5.65	7.22	7.03
1971	—	—	—	3.33	3.15	7.16	5.27	6.75	6.55
1972	—	—	—	3.09	2.86	3.71	5.53	6.88	6.56
1973	—	—	—	2.86	2.64	2.76	5.57	7.23	6.65
1974	—	—	—	3.69	3.41	3.92	7.38	8.24	7.48
1975	—	—	—	5.37	4.94	5.62	10.70	8.36	7.83
1976	—	—	—	4.49	4.21	4.17	8.46	7.98	7.37
1977	—	—	—	4.35	4.15	3.58	7.47	7.61	7.12
1978	—	—	—	5.33	5.11	4.62	7.91	8.25	7.76
1979	—	—	—	5.88	5.58	5.39	9.61	9.11	8.54
1980	—	—	—	5.71	5.41	4.93	9.87	10.60	10.11
1981	—	—	—	4.88	4.53	3.15	10.18	12.36	11.64
1982	—	—	—	5.61	5.24	3.83	10.80	12.53	11.68
1983	—	—	—	5.04	4.68	3.36	10.01	11.02	10.05
1984	—	—	—	4.57	3.99	2.76	9.78	11.59	10.21
1985	—	—	—	4.72	4.15	3.29	8.87	10.44	9.41
1986	—	—	—	3.92	3.47	2.59	7.55	8.76	8.13
1987	—	—	—	3.64	3.22	2.53	6.57	8.37	7.94
1988	—	—	—	3.94	3.41	2.80	7.46	9.23	8.17
1989	—	—	—	3.98	3.49	2.63	7.00	9.04	7.82
1990	—	—	—	3.42	3.07	2.19	5.30	8.96	8.28
1991	—	—	—	3.69	3.25	2.77	5.93	8.17	7.87
1992	—	—	—	2.97	2.59	1.99	5.51	7.46	7.05
1993	—	—	—	2.89	2.47	1.87	5.47	6.90	6.32
1994	—	—	—	2.83	2.41	1.72	5.13	—	6.96
1995	—	—	—	3.00	2.55	2.26	5.92	—	6.87
1996	—	—	—	2.42	2.16	1.75	4.76	—	6.74
1997	—	—	—	2.09	1.92	1.64	5.07	—	6.60
1998	—	—	—	1.67	1.54	1.07	4.30	—	7.01
1999	—	—	—	1.36	1.18	1.11	3.81	—	—

Sources

Series Cj808. William G. Schwert, "Indexes of U.S. Stock Prices from 1802 to 1987," *Journal of Business* 63 (3) (1990): 399–426; Walter B. Smith and Arthur H. Cole, *Fluctuations in American Business, 1790–1860* (Harvard University Press, 1935); Frederick R. Macaulay, *The Movements of Interest Rates, Bond Yields and Stock Prices in the United States since 1856* (National Bureau of Economic Research, 1938).

Series Cj809–810. Peter L. Rousseau, "The Boston Market for Banking and Industrial Equities, 1835-1897." *Historical Methods* 11 (3) (2000): 163–9; Joseph G. Martin, *Twenty-One Years in the Boston Stock Market* (Redding, 1856), and *A Century of Finance: The Boston Stock and Money Markets, 1798 to 1898* (published by the author, 1898), and underlying worksheets.

Series Cj811–814. Jack W. Wilson and Charles P. Jones, "An Analysis of the S&P 500 Index and Cowles' Extensions: Price Indexes and Stock Returns, 1870-1999," *Journal of Business*, 75 (3) (2002): 505–33; Arthur Cowles and Associates, *Common Stock Indexes for 1940* (mimeographed, University of Chicago Graduate School of Business, 1942); Standard Statistics Company,

Standard Statistical Bulletin (various issues); Standard and Poor's Statistical Service, *Security Price Index Record* (various issues).

Series Cj815. Standard and Poor's Statistical Service, *Security Price Index Record* (various issues).

Series Cj816. Mergent Technologies, *Moody's Industrial Manual, 1999*, p. a79.

Documentation

For a discussion of coverage, see the text for Table Cj797–807.

Series Cj808. An index of dividend yields.

Series Cj809–814. These series reflect actual dividend yields that would have obtained with a "buy and hold" investment strategy in the securities comprising the corresponding price index over a given calendar year.

Series Cj815. Based on one price weekly (as of Wednesday's close), averaged across four or five weeks per month and then across twelve months per year to produce annual yields. This series is based on high-grade, noncallable preferred issues.

Series Cj816. Formed from high-grade industrial issues.

TABLE Cj817–830   Security issues and net change in outstanding corporate securities: 1934–1999
Contributed by Peter L. Rousseau

		Security issues								Net change in outstanding securities			Net issuance of corporate securities		
		Use of proceeds		Corporate											
				Bonds and notes		Stocks								
Year	Noncorporate	Total gross proceeds	Retirement of securities	Other	Publicly offered	Privately placed	Preferred	Common	Total	Bonds and notes	Stocks	Total	Corporate and foreign bonds	Stocks
	Cj817	Cj818	Cj819	Cj820	Cj821	Cj822	Cj823	Cj824	Cj825	Cj826	Cj827	Cj828	Cj829	Cj830
	Million dollars	Million dollars	Million shares	Million dollars	Million dollars	Million dollars	Million dollars	Million dollars	Million dollars	Million shares	Million dollars	Billion dollars	Billion dollars	Billion dollars
1934 [1]	4,512	397	231	152	280	92	6	19	−260	−250	−10	—	—	—
1935	4,352	2,332	1,865	401	1,840	385	86	22	−343	−200	−143	—	—	—
1936	5,411	4,572	3,368	1,062	3,660	369	271	272	626	575	51	—	—	—
1937	3,018	2,310	1,100	1,138	1,291	327	406	285	−48	−452	404	—	—	—
1938	3,771	2,155	1,206	904	1,353	691	86	25	549	578	−29	—	—	—
1939	3,523	2,164	1,695	420	1,276	703	98	87	−559	−621	62	—	—	—
1940	3,887	2,677	1,854	761	1,628	758	183	108	−273	−342	69	—	—	—
1941	12,490	2,667	1,583	1,041	1,578	811	167	110	−24	−125	101	—	—	—
1942	34,376	1,062	396	646	506	411	112	34	−336	−389	53	—	—	—
1943	43,348	1,170	739	408	621	369	124	56	−800	−767	−33	—	—	—
1944	53,108	3,202	2,389	753	1,892	778	369	163	−516	−653	136	—	—	—
1945	48,701	6,011	4,555	1,347	3,851	1,004	758	397	−573	−1,038	464	—	—	—
1946	11,786	6,900	2,868	3,889	3,019	1,863	1,127	891	2,226	1,114	1,111	2.1	0.9	1.2
1947	13,364	6,577	1,352	5,114	2,889	2,147	762	779	4,191	3,005	1,186	4.4	2.9	1.5
1948	13,172	7,078	307	6,652	2,965	3,008	492	614	5,818	4,725	1,093	6.0	4.8	1.2
1949	15,059	6,052	401	5,558	2,437	2,453	425	736	4,592	3,285	1,307	4.7	3.2	1.5
1950	13,532	6,361	1,271	4,990	2,360	2,560	631	811	3,469	2,004	1,465	3.8	2.1	1.7
1951	13,523	7,741	486	7,120	2,364	3,326	838	1,212	5,886	3,583	2,303	6.6	4.0	2.6
1952	17,675	9,534	664	8,716	3,645	3,957	564	1,369	7,383	4,942	2,441	7.4	4.7	2.7
1953	19,926	8,898	260	8,495	3,856	3,228	489	1,326	6,688	4,757	1,932	7.2	4.8	2.4
1954	20,249	9,516	1,875	7,490	4,003	3,484	816	1,213	5,602	3,799	1,802	4.8	3.2	1.6
1955	16,532	10,240	1,227	8,821	4,119	3,301	635	2,185	6,081	4,188	1,893	4.9	3.2	1.7
1956	11,467	10,939	364	10,384	4,225	3,777	636	2,301	7,158	4,611	2,548	8.1	5.1	3.0
1957	17,687	12,884	214	12,447	6,118	3,839	411	2,516	9,739	7,026	2,713	11.5	7.7	3.8
1958	22,885	11,558	549	10,823	6,332	3,320	571	1,334	7,977	5,850	2,127	8.3	6.4	1.9
1959	21,326	9,748	135	9,392	3,557	3,632	531	2,027	6,448	4,073	2,376	7.3	4.5	2.8
1960	17,387	10,154	271	9,653	4,806	3,275	409	1,664	6,690	4,994	1,696	10.3	7.2	3.1
1961	22,363	13,165	868	12,017	4,700	4,720	450	3,294	7,819	5,170	2,650	7.6	5.6	2.0
1962	19,251	10,705	754	9,747	4,440	4,529	422	1,314	5,552	4,864	688	7.1	5.4	1.7
1963	22,989	12,211	1,528	10,553	4,713	6,143	343	1,011	5,328	5,577	−249	8.1	6.3	1.8
1964	23,165	13,957	—	—	3,623	7,243	412	2,679	8,068	6,637	1,431	9.4	7.6	1.8
1965	24,116	15,992	—	—	5,570	8,150	725	1,547	8,061	8,098	−37	6.5	6.5	0.0
1966	26,941	18,074	—	—	8,018	7,542	574	1,939	12,258	11,088	1,169	14.9	12.5	2.4
1967	43,716	24,798	—	—	14,990	6,964	885	1,959	18,229	15,960	2,267	19.7	16.8	2.9
1968	43,596	21,966	—	—	10,731	6,651	637	3,946	13,062	13,962	−900	17.1	14.6	2.5
1969	26,003	26,744	—	—	12,735	5,613	682	7,714	18,027	13,755	4,272	20.5	14.0	6.5

	Security issues								Net change in outstanding securities			Net issuance of corporate securities		
	Use of proceeds				Corporate / Class of securities									
					Bonds and notes		Stocks							
Year	Noncorporate	Total gross proceeds	Retirement of securities	Other	Publicly offered	Privately placed	Preferred	Common	Total	Bonds and notes	Stocks	Total	Corporate and foreign bonds	Stocks
	Cj817	Cj818	Cj819	Cj820	Cj821	Cj822	Cj823	Cj824	Cj825	Cj826	Cj827	Cj828	Cj829	Cj830
	Million dollars	Million dollars	Million shares	Million dollars	Million dollars	Million dollars	Million dollars	Million dollars	Million dollars	Million shares	Million dollars	Billion dollars	Billion dollars	Billion dollars
1970	49,721	38,944	—	—	25,385	4,913	1,390	7,240	29,628	22,825	6,801	29.5	23.2	6.3
1971	—	44,914	—	—	24,790	7,209	3,679	9,236	—	—	—	40.2	24.5	15.7
1972	—	40,787	—	—	18,347	9,378	3,373	9,689	—	—	—	34.8	20.6	14.2
1973	—	33,391	—	—	13,649	8,620	3,372	7,750	—	—	—	29.2	15.5	13.7
1974	—	38,313	—	—	25,903	6,160	2,253	3,994	—	—	—	34.2	29.0	5.2
1975	—	53,619	—	—	32,583	10,172	3,458	7,405	—	—	—	50.3	42.5	7.8
1976	—	53,488	—	—	26,453	15,927	2,803	8,305	—	—	—	50.9	38.3	12.6
1977	—	53,792	—	—	24,072	17,943	3,916	7,861	—	—	—	45.2	40.2	5.0
1978	—	47,230	—	—	19,815	17,057	2,832	7,526	—	—	—	34.7	31.7	3.0
1979	—	51,533	—	—	25,814	14,394	3,574	7,751	—	—	—	20.2	24.6	-4.4
1980	—	73,694	—	—	41,587	11,619	3,631	16,858	—	—	—	50.9	36.4	14.5
1981	—	70,441	—	—	38,103	6,989	1,797	23,552	—	—	—	26.5	36.9	-10.4
1982	—	84,638	—	—	44,278	9,798	5,113	25,449	—	—	—	59.7	52.1	7.6
1983	—	120,149	—	—	47,444	21,126	7,213	44,366	—	—	—	73.2	46.5	26.7
1984	—	132,531	—	—	73,579	36,324	4,118	18,510	—	—	—	15.6	88.2	-72.6
1985	—	201,269	—	—	119,559	46,195	6,505	29,010	—	—	—	72.0	143.4	-71.4
1986	—	423,726	—	—	274,532	80,760	11,514	50,316	—	—	—	152.7	222.5	-69.8
1987	—	392,339	—	—	209,455	92,070	10,123	43,225	—	—	—	100.7	164.7	-64.0
1988	—	410,849	—	—	202,170	127,700	6,544	35,911	—	—	—	55.6	162.2	-106.6
1989	—	377,836	—	—	179,694	117,420	6,194	26,030	—	—	—	16.9	119.5	-102.6
1990	—	340,049	—	—	188,848	86,982	3,998	19,443	—	—	—	79.5	125.2	-45.7
1991	—	465,483	—	—	287,125	74,930	17,408	47,860	—	—	—	253.0	180.7	72.3
1992	—	559,827	—	—	378,058	65,853	21,339	57,118	—	—	—	272.5	172.9	99.6
1993	—	769,088	—	—	487,029	121,226	18,897	82,657	—	—	—	414.2	281.2	133.0
1994	—	583,240	—	—	365,222	76,065	12,570	48,828	—	—	—	170.1	157.3	12.8
1995	—	673,779	—	—	408,707	87,942	10,917	57,556	—	—	—	320.7	336.7	-16.0
1996	—	668,687	—	—	465,489	83,433	33,208	83,052	—	—	—	320.4	348.9	-28.5
1997	—	929,256	—	—	811,376	54,990	—	—	—	—	—	307.1	406.7	-99.6
1998	—	1,128,491	—	—	1,001,736	37,845	—	—	—	—	—	337.5	535.6	-198.1
1999	—	1,072,866	—	—	941,298	28,506	—	—	—	—	—	384.7	452.5	-67.8

[1] Estimated gross proceeds, which represent the amount paid for the securities by investors.

Sources

Series Cj817–824. 1934–1969: U.S. Securities and Exchange Commission, *Annual Report* (1952), pp. 210–21, and (1958), pp. 208–16; and *Statistical Bulletin* (May 1958), pp. 9–11, and subsequent issues. 1970–1999: *Federal Reserve Bulletin* (January issues).

Series Cj825–827. SEC sources list above for 1960–1970, and unpublished data prior to 1960.

Series Cj828–830. Board of Governors of the Federal Reserve System's *Flow of Funds Accounts*.

Documentation

Series Cj817–824. These series cover substantially all new issues of securities offered for cash sale in the United States in amounts greater than $100,000 and with terms to maturity of more than one year. Figures include issues privately placed and publicly offered, whether unregistered or registered with the Securities and Exchange Commission.

Series Cj821–822. The figures for privately placed issues include securities actually issued but exclude securities that institutions had contracted to purchase but had not actually taken during the period covered by the statistics. Also excluded are intercorporate transactions; U.S. government "Special Series" issues and other sales directly to federal agencies and trust accounts; notes issued exclusively to commercial banks; and corporate issues sold through continuous offering, such as issues of open-end investment companies. Issues sold directly to ultimate investors by competitive bidding are classified as publicly offered issues.

Series Cj825–830. Derived by deducting from estimated gross proceeds received by corporations through the sale of securities the amount of estimated gross payments by corporations to investors for securities retired. Included in the latter figures are payments for issues retired with internal funds as well as with proceeds from new issues sold for refunding purposes. These series are based primarily on cash transactions but include conversions and exchanges of one type of security for another, such as bonds for stocks.

TABLE Cj831–837   Corporate security issues: 1910–1934

Contributed by Peter L. Rousseau

				Class of security			
	Total	New capital	Retirement of securities	Bonds and notes	Preferred	Common	Preferred and common
	Cj831	Cj832	Cj833	Cj834	Cj835	Cj836	Cj837
Year	Million dollars	Million dollars	Million dollars	Million dollars	Million dollars	Million dollars	Million dollars
1910	—	—	—	1,113	—	—	405
1911	—	—	—	1,387	—	—	352
1912	—	—	—	1,350	—	—	904
1913	—	—	—	1,194	—	—	452
1914	—	—	—	1,175	—	—	262
1915	—	—	—	1,111	—	—	325
1916	—	—	—	1,405	—	—	782
1917	—	—	—	1,076	—	—	455
1918	—	—	—	1,047	—	—	298
1919	2,668	2,246	422	1,122	793	753	1,546
1920	2,788	2,563	225	1,750	483	555	1,038
1921	2,270	1,702	568	1,994	75	200	275
1922	2,949	2,215	734	2,329	333	288	621
1923	3,165	2,635	530	2,430	407	329	736
1924	3,521	3,029	492	2,655	346	519	865
1925	4,223	3,605	618	2,975	637	610	1,247
1926	4,574	3,754	820	3,354	543	677	1,220
1927	6,507	4,657	1,850	4,769	1,054	684	1,738
1928	6,930	5,346	1,584	3,439	1,397	2,094	3,491
1929	9,376	8,002	1,374	2,620	1,695	5,062	6,757
1930	4,957	4,483	474	3,431	421	1,105	1,526
1931	2,372	1,551	821	2,028	148	195	343
1932	644	325	319	620	10	13	23
1933	380	161	219	227	15	137	152
1934	490	178	312	456	3	31	34

Sources

1910–1918: U.S. Bureau of Foreign and Domestic Commerce, *Statistical Abstract of the United States* (1932), p. 292. 1919–1934: Board of Governors of the Federal Reserve System, *Banking and Monetary Statistics, 1914–1943* (1943), p. 487.

Documentation

The *Commercial and Financial Chronicle* data used for these series, for 1919–1934, include all security issues publicly offered for sale by companies incorporated in the United States. Securities sold privately were included when the compilers were aware of the sale. Issues of foreign companies sold in the United States are excluded. Data are based on the offering price for preferred stock of no par value and for common stock, and on par amounts for bonds, notes,

and preferred stock with stated par value. The data prior to 1919 include offerings of foreign corporations.

The series differ from those compiled by the Securities and Exchange Commission (SEC) and the Federal Reserve (Table Cj817–830) in a number of respects. The latter include issues on the basis of gross and/or net proceeds, whereas the *Chronicle* series include issues on the basis noted earlier. The *Chronicle* series include issues for exchange purposes, whereas the SEC figures include only that portion of such an offering that is sold for cash. The SEC series also include foreign corporate security issues sold in the United States, whereas the *Chronicle* series exclude them except for the period noted. The bases for inclusion of privately sold securities in the two sets of series also differ.

TABLE Cj838   New state and local government security issues: 1919–1999
Contributed by Peter L. Rousseau

Year	Security issues Cj838 Million dollars	Year	Security issues Cj838 Million dollars	Year	Security issues Cj838 Million dollars	Year	Security issues Cj838 Million dollars
1919	691	1940	1,238	1960	7,292	1980	48,367
1920	683	1941	956	1961	8,566	1981	47,732
1921	1,207	1942	524	1962	8,845	1982	79,138
1922	1,101	1943	435	1963	10,538	1983	86,421
1923	1,063	1944	661	1964	10,847	1984	106,641
1924	1,399	1945	795	1965	11,329	1985	214,189
1925	1,400	1946	1,204	1966	11,405	1986	147,011
1926	1,366	1947	2,354	1967	14,766	1987	102,407
1927	1,510	1948	3,004	1968	16,600	1988	114,522
1928	1,415	1949	2,996	1969	11,897	1989	113,646
1929	1,431	1950	3,694	1970	18,164	1990	120,339
1930	1,487	1951	3,278	1971	24,962	1991	154,402
1931	1,256	1952	4,401	1972	23,652	1992	226,818
1932	849	1953	5,558	1973	23,970	1993	279,945
1933	520	1954	6,969	1974	24,315	1994	153,950
1934	939	1955	5,977	1975	30,607	1995	145,657
1935	1,232	1956	5,446	1976	35,313	1996	171,222
1936	1,121	1957	6,926	1977	46,769	1997	214,694
1937	908	1958	7,526	1978	48,607	1998	262,342
1938	1,108	1959	7,697	1979	43,365	1999	215,427
1939	1,126						

Sources

1919–1933: Board of Governors of the Federal Reserve System, *Banking and Monetary Statistics, 1914–1943* (1943), p. 487. 1934–1945: U.S. Securities and Exchange Commission, *Annual Report* (1952), Part 3, p. 211. 1946–1963: Board of Governors of the Federal Reserve System, *Supplement to Banking and Monetary Statistics* (1966), section 12, "Money Rates and Securities Markets," p. 166. 1964–1999: *Federal Reserve Bulletin* (January issues).

Documentation

These data represent principal amounts of securities offered publicly for sale in the United States by all political subdivisions either for new money or for refunding, retiring, or otherwise acquiring existing securities. They include loans from the U.S. government.

For 1919–1933, figures are as compiled and published by the *Commercial and Financial Chronicle;* for 1934–1956, they are from totals published by the *Chronicle* and the *Bond Buyer;* beginning in 1957, the figures are compilations of the Investment Bankers Association of America.

TABLE Cj839–856   Sales of stocks and bonds on registered securities exchanges – market value and volume: 1935–1998
Contributed by Peter L. Rousseau

	All exchanges							New York Stock Exchange							New York Curb/AMEX, stocks		NASDAQ, stocks	
	Market value, all sales	Stocks		Bonds		Rights and warrants		Market value, all sales	Stocks		Bonds		Rights and warrants					
		Market value	Shares	Market value	Par value	Market value	Number of units		Market value	Shares	Market value	Par value	Market value	Number of units	Market value	Shares	Market value	Shares
Year	Cj839	Cj840	Cj841	Cj842	Cj843	Cj844	Cj845	Cj846	Cj847	Cj848	Cj849	Cj850	Cj851	Cj852	Cj853	Cj854	Cj855	Cj856
	Million dollars	Million dollars	Million	Million dollars	Million dollars	Million dollars	Million	Million dollars	Million dollars	Million	Million dollars	Million dollars	Million dollars	Million	Million dollars	Million	Million dollars	Million
1935	19,115	15,376	662	3,739	4,723	—	—	16,138	13,338	499	2,800	3,505	—	—	1,205	85	—	—
1936	27,283	23,621	956	3,661	4,652	25	23	23,323	20,387	702	2,937	3,791	—	—	2,055	158	—	—
1937	23,709	21,010	837	2,699	3,429	42	35	20,769	18,468	614	2,301	2,967	—	—	1,589	124	—	—
1938	13,927	12,338	542	1,589	2,310	8	11	12,306	11,016	424	1,290	1,932	3	6	687	57	—	—
1939	13,347	11,426	467	1,921	2,590	5	5	11,488	9,970	366	1,518	2,121	2	3	749	52	—	—
1940	9,726	8,404	372	1,314	2,081	8	5	8,223	7,166	283	1,053	1,760	4	2	643	48	—	—
1941	7,603	6,240	310	1,363	2,530	6	7	6,408	5,257	230	1,151	2,269	4	4	394	28	—	—
1942	5,570	4,309	220	1,261	2,666	(Z)	2	4,796	3,674	169	1,122	2,478	(Z)	1	285	25	—	—
1943	10,986	9,024	485	1,962	3,839	5	6	9,457	7,672	362	1,785	3,593	1	2	800	77	—	—
1944	11,780	9,799	464	1,981	3,122	10	6	10,089	8,255	342	1,834	2,925	3	3	904	76	—	—
1945	18,112	16,226	744	1,842	2,691	45	22	15,190	13,462	496	1,716	2,509	12	11	1,728	152	—	—
1946	20,001	18,814	802	1,187	1,572	97	46	16,675	15,562	531	1,113	1,489	42	29	1,972	141	—	—
1947	12,541	11,587	512	954	1,274	59	39	10,617	9,742	358	875	1,176	36	22	1,000	74	—	—
1948	13,749	12,904	570	846	1,172	21	30	11,731	10,932	413	798	1,110	10	21	1,032	80	—	—
1949	11,443	10,740	516	703	933	25	38	9,674	9,012	380	662	880	14	26	898	68	—	—
1950	22,840	21,777	857	1,038	1,278	25	35	19,735	18,725	655	1,000	1,228	10	27	1,481	115	—	—
1951	22,127	21,302	863	825	955	45	77	19,013	18,215	643	797	915	27	63	1,597	120	—	—
1952	18,179	17,388	732	791	899	59	105	15,531	14,761	522	769	868	42	90	1,274	112	—	—
1953	17,488	16,708	716	781	909	47	82	15,010	14,250	520	760	875	32	71	1,126	110	—	—
1954	29,156	28,130	1,053	1,026	1,121	55	59	25,267	24,264	749	1,003	1,089	15	46	1,873	170	—	—
1955	39,261	37,868	1,212	1,231	1,261	161	108	34,038	32,745	820	1,207	1,226	85	89	2,594	244	—	—
1956	36,360	35,133	1,182	1,227	1,253	114	98	31,064	29,855	784	1,209	1,229	68	85	2,696	242	—	—
1957	33,360	32,206	1,292	1,154	1,253	147	222	28,686	27,547	914	1,140	1,235	96	200	2,315	225	—	—
1958	39,962	38,408	1,400	1,554	1,583	144	93	34,351	32,818	999	1,533	1,561	64	77	2,793	257	—	—
1959	53,877	51,864	1,605	1,892	1,816	122	94	45,368	43,476	1,039	1,864	1,783	28	76	4,863	403	—	—
1960	46,901	45,219	1,389	1,607	1,614	75	51	39,552	37,960	958	1,580	1,587	13	29	4,175	301	—	—
1961	66,068	63,802	2,010	2,023	1,954	243	131	54,785	52,699	1,292	1,964	1,909	122	100	6,752	525	—	—
1962	56,564	54,732	1,664	1,730	1,786	102	47	49,019	47,341	1,187	1,666	1,719	13	34	3,648	333	—	—
1963	66,157	64,314	1,838	1,740	1,654	103	41	56,564	54,887	1,351	1,667	1,586	11	21	4,755	336	—	—
1964	75,328	72,147	2,045	2,882	2,641	298	81	63,284	60,424	1,482	2,783	2,542	77	60	5,921	397	—	—
1965	93,325	89,225	2,587	3,794	3,289	305	82	76,878	73,200	1,809	3,643	3,150	34	58	8,612	582	—	—
1966	127,914	123,034	3,188	4,261	3,740	619	123	102,754	98,565	2,205	4,101	3,590	88	93	14,130	731	—	—
1967	168,258	161,746	4,504	6,087	5,394	424	141	130,791	125,329	2,886	5,428	4,862	34	107	23,111	1,290	—	—
1968	202,772	196,358	5,312	5,670	5,459	744	96	149,395	144,978	3,299	4,402	4,448	14	54	34,775	1,571	—	—
1969	180,877	175,297	4,963	4,501	5,124	1,079	171	133,173	129,603	3,174	3,550	4,123	19	70	30,074	1,341	—	—
1970	136,465	131,126	4,539	4,763	6,300	576	294	107,649	103,063	3,213	4,328	5,555	257	233	14,366	879	—	—
1971	195,173	185,027	5,916	8,803	10,158	1,342	256	155,382	147,098	4,265	8,010	9,081	274	139	17,664	1,049	—	—
1972	215,063	204,026	6,299	9,515	10,077	1,500	145	168,895	159,700	4,496	8,717	9,169	467	47	20,453	1,103	—	—
1973	187,157	177,878	5,723	8,295	9,420	984	176	154,664	146,451	4,337	7,865	8,737	348	84	10,270	735	—	—
1974	125,102	118,252	4,839	6,457	8,120	394	104	105,566	99,181	3,822	6,194	7,741	192	63	5,048	475	—	—

	All exchanges							New York Stock Exchange							New York Curb/ AMEX, stocks		NASDAQ, stocks	
	Market value, all sales	Stocks		Bonds		Rights and warrants		Market value, all sales	Stocks		Bonds		Rights and warrants					
		Market value	Shares	Market value	Par value	Market value	Number of units		Market value	Shares	Market value	Par value	Market value	Number of units	Market value	Shares	Market value	Shares
	Cj839	Cj840	Cj841	Cj842	Cj843	Cj844	Cj845	Cj846	Cj847	Cj848	Cj849	Cj850	Cj851	Cj852	Cj853	Cj854	Cj855	Cj856
Year	Million dollars	Million dollars	Million	Million dollars	Million dollars	Million dollars	Million	Million dollars	Million dollars	Million	Million dollars	Million dollars	Million dollars	Million	Million dollars	Million	Million dollars	Million
1975	166,900	157,260	6,231	9,346	10,707	295	150	143,066	133,819	5,056	9,079	10,314	169	108	5,678	541	21,213	1,390
1976	206,959	194,969	7,036	—	—	256	89	164,679	164,545	5,649	—	—	133	53	7,468	637	24,831	1,684
1977	198,292	187,203	7,023	—	—	190	112	157,339	157,250	5,613	—	—	89	62	8,532	652	24,666	1,932
1978	268,509	249,257	9,602	—	—	346	82	210,550	210,426	7,618	—	—	124	42	15,205	922	36,141	2,762
1979	323,900	299,973	10,863	—	—	755	115	251,583	251,098	8,675	—	—	484	84	20,596	1,161	44,300	3,651
1980	522,206	475,850	15,486	—	—	567	99	398,009	397,670	12,390	—	—	338	71	34,697	1,659	68,669	6,692
1981	532,713	490,688	15,910	—	—	329	59	416,079	415,913	12,843	—	—	165	41	26,385	1,472	71,057	7,823
1982	657,021	602,937	22,423	—	—	424	78	514,553	514,263	18,211	—	—	290	58	19,621	1,550	84,189	8,432
1983	1,017,798	957,139	30,146	—	—	1,165	170	815,897	815,113	24,253	—	—	785	112	31,492	2,209	188,285	15,909
1984	993,469	959,207	30,456	—	—	440	91	823,024	822,714	25,150	—	—	309	65	21,349	1,584	153,454	15,159
1985	1,307,945	1,199,420	37,046	—	—	770	142	1,023,863	1,022,827	30,222	—	—	332	93	26,332	2,115	233,454	20,699
1986	1,867,887	1,705,124	48,338	—	—	2,023	243	1,452,543	1,450,150	39,258	—	—	1,303	151	43,433	2,999	378,216	28,737
1987	2,491,721	2,284,166	83,771	—	—	2,737	312	1,986,549	1,983,311	53,038	—	—	1,518	206	52,548	2,496	499,855	37,890
1988	1,702,047	1,587,012	52,533	—	—	939	132	1,380,303	1,377,717	44,018	—	—	714	83	31,111	2,576	347,089	31,070
1989	2,004,034	1,884,768	54,239	—	—	3,029	178	1,581,460	1,576,899	44,140	—	—	2,690	118	43,351	3,248	431,381	33,530
1990	1,746,869	1,611,667	53,338	—	—	5,131	408	1,394,424	1,390,090	43,829	—	—	2,837	165	35,639	3,125	452,430	33,380
1991	1,903,509	1,776,275	58,031	—	—	2,123	265	1,534,334	1,531,813	47,674	—	—	1,193	129	40,200	3,103	693,852	41,311
1992	2,149,906	2,033,200	65,501	—	—	742	242	1,759,117	1,757,494	53,344	—	—	251	99	41,559	3,631	890,785	48,455
1993	2,726,667	2,609,854	82,807	—	—	650	247	2,277,919	2,276,281	66,732	—	—	232	118	53,895	4,470	1,350,100	66,541
1994	2,956,599	2,816,810	90,482	—	—	861	305	2,482,967	2,481,586	76,665	—	—	241	95	55,952	4,300	1,449,301	74,353
1995	3,678,327	3,506,785	106,392	—	—	1,206	677	3,078,473	3,076,377	90,062	—	—	513	399	72,942	4,843	2,398,214	101,158
1996	4,719,336	4,510,875	125,747	—	—	905	176	4,012,961	4,010,627	108,151	—	—	618	77	86,044	5,306	3,301,777	138,112
1997	—	—	—	—	—	—	—	—	—	—	—	—	—	—	—	—	4,481,691	163,882
1998	—	—	—	—	—	—	—	—	—	—	—	—	—	—	—	—	5,758,558	202,040

(Z) Less than $500,000.

Sources

U.S. Securities and Exchange Commission, *Statistical Bulletin* and *Annual Report* (various issues), annual data.

Documentation

The data presented in these series are of two types, depending on the method of aggregation used by each exchange. Reports of some exchanges cover transactions cleared during the calendar month; clearances appear for the most part within five days of the execution of a trade. Reports for other exchanges cover transactions effected on trade dates falling within the report month. The variance introduced by these two different methods of aggregating the data is not considered significant, and, accordingly, all registered exchanges are aggregated and reported in annual summaries.

Stock data include voting trust certificates, certificates of deposit for stocks, and American Depository Receipts for stocks. Bond data have excluded transactions covering U.S. government issues since March 1944. Warrants data include trading in rights for all periods.

Stock and bond sales for the New York Stock Exchange and the New York Curb Exchange, January to March, exclude stopped sales; stock sales for these exchanges also exclude odd-lot sales.

Series Cj853–854. The New York Curb Exchange changed its name to the American Stock Exchange in 1952.

TABLE Cj857–858   Sales of stocks and bonds on the New York Stock Exchange: 1879–1999
Contributed by Peter L. Rousseau

Year	Stocks – shares Cj857 Million	Bonds – par value Cj858 Million dollars	Year	Stocks – shares Cj857 Million	Bonds – par value Cj858 Million dollars	Year	Stocks – shares Cj857 Million	Bonds – par value Cj858 Million dollars
1879	73	—	1920	227	3,977	1960	767	1,346
1880	96	—	1921	173	3,324	1961	1,021	1,636
1881	117	—	1922	259	4,370	1962	962	1,455
1882	117	—	1923	236	2,790	1963	1,146	1,483
1883	98	—	1924	282	3,804	1964	1,237	2,524
1884	96	—	1925	454	3,384	1965	1,556	2,975
1885	93	—	1926	451	2,987	1966	1,899	3,093
1886	104	—	1927	577	3,269	1967	2,530	3,956
1887	86	—	1928	920	2,903	1968	2,932	3,814
1888	66	—	1929	1,125	2,982	1969	2,851	3,646
1889	72	—	1930	810	2,764	1970	2,937	4,495
1890	71	—	1931	577	3,051	1971	3,891	6,564
1891	73	—	1932	425	2,967	1972	4,138	5,444
1892	87	—	1933	655	3,369	1973	4,053	4,425
1893	78	—	1934	324	3,726	1974	3,518	4,052
1894	49	—	1935	382	3,339	1975	4,693	5,178
1895	66	—	1936	496	3,576	1976	5,360	5,262
1896	54	—	1937	409	2,793	1977	5,274	4,646
1897	78	—	1938	297	1,860	1978	7,205	4,554
1898	113	—	1939	262	2,046	1979	8,156	4,088
1899	173	—	1940	208	1,669	1980	11,352	5,190
1900	139	—	1941	171	2,112	1981	11,854	5,733
1901	265	—	1942	126	2,311	1982	16,458	7,155
1902	187	—	1943	279	3,255	1983	21,590	7,572
1903	159	—	1944	263	2,695	1984	23,071	6,982
1904	187	—	1945	378	2,262	1985	27,511	9,047
1905	261	—	1946	364	1,364	1986	35,680	10,464
1906	282	—	1947	254	1,076	1987	47,801	9,727
1907	195	—	1948	295	1,014	1988	40,850	7,702
1908	195	—	1949	271	818	1989	41,699	8,836
1909	212	—	1950	525	1,112	1990	39,665	10,893
1910	164	635	1951	444	824	1991	45,266	12,698
1911	127	890	1952	338	773	1992	51,376	11,629
1912	131	675	1953	355	776	1993	66,923	9,743
1913	83	502	1954	573	980	1994	73,420	7,197
1914	48	462	1955	650	1,046	1995	87,218	6,979
1915	173	961	1956	556	1,069	1996	104,636	5,529
1916	233	1,150	1957	560	1,082	1997	133,312	5,046
1917	186	1,057	1958	747	1,382	1998	169,745	3,838
1918	144	2,063	1959	820	1,586	1999	203,914	3,221
1919	317	3,809						

Sources

1879–1899, Edmund C. Stedman, *The New York Stock Exchange* (Greenwood Press, 1969; originally published 1905), pp. 473–4. 1900–1909, Board of Governors of the Federal Reserve System, *Banking and Monetary Statistics* (1943), p. 485. 1910–1970, *Commercial and Financial Chronicle* (various issues). 1971–1999, *New York Stock Exchange Fact Book, 1999*.

Documentation

Series Cj857. Data on stocks from 1900 to 1999 show the volume of share trading in round lots on the New York Stock Exchange as reported by the exchange ticker. This series excludes odd lots, stopped sales, private sales, split openings, covered transactions, and errors of omission. This segment of series Cj857 matches up precisely with that of Stedman for the 1879–1899 period.

Series Cj858. Data on bonds are exclusive of stopped sales and, beginning in July 1947, include bonds of the International Bank for Reconstruction and Development.

TABLE Cj859–862   Mutual funds – number, net assets, sales, and redemptions: 1940–1999

Contributed by Peter L. Rousseau

Year	Number of funds Cj859 Number	Net assets Cj860 Million dollars	Sales Cj861 [1] Million dollars	Redemptions Cj862 [1] Million dollars	Year	Number of funds Cj859 Number	Net assets Cj860 Million dollars	Sales Cj861 [1] Million dollars	Redemptions Cj862 [1] Million dollars
1940	—	448.0	—	—	1970	361	47,618.1	4,625.8	2,987.6
1941	68	401.6	53.3	45.0	1971	392	55,045.3	5,147.2	4,750.2
1942	68	486.9	73.1	25.4	1972	410	59,830.6	4,892.5	6,562.9
1943	68	653.7	116.1	51.2	1973	421	46,519.0	4,359.3	5,651.1
1944	68	882.2	169.2	70.8	1974	431	35,777.1	5,323.5	3,936.9
1945	73	1,284.2	292.4	110.0	1975	426	45,874.7	10,055.9	9,570.2
1946	74	1,311.1	370.4	143.6	1976	452	51,267.8	13,721.4	16,410.4
1947	80	1,409.2	266.9	88.7	1977	477	48,936.7	17,072.6	16,688.7
1948	87	1,505.8	273.8	127.2	1978	505	55,838.0	37,157.5	31,526.9
1949	91	1,973.5	385.5	107.6	1979	524	94,194.2	118,681.2	86,368.4
1950	98	2,530.6	518.8	280.7	1980	564	134,761.3	247,421.4	216,077.7
1951	103	3,129.6	674.6	321.6	1981	665	241,365.2	472,133.0	362,442.5
1952	110	3,931.4	782.9	196.0	1982	857	296,678.5	626,941.2	588,350.2
1953	110	4,146.1	672.0	238.8	1983	1,026	292,985.5	547,772.1	565,828.9
1954	115	6,109.4	862.8	399.7	1984	1,241	370,679.8	680,083.7	607,022.8
1955	125	7,837.5	1,207.5	442.6	1985	1,527	495,385.4	953,731.8	864,883.1
1956	135	9,046.4	1,346.7	432.8	1986	1,835	715,669.6	1,205,104.2	1,015,611.3
1957	143	8,714.1	1,390.6	405.7	1987	2,312	769,177.1	1,251,156.4	1,178,580.3
1958	151	13,242.4	1,619.8	511.3	1988	2,708	809,379.5	1,176,817.7	1,166,700.4
1959	155	15,818.0	2,280.0	785.6	1989	2,900	980,678.2	1,444,831.6	1,327,169.5
1960	161	17,025.7	2,097.2	841.8	1990	3,086	1,065,474.9	1,564,803.9	1,470,779.5
1961	170	22,788.8	2,950.9	1,160.4	1991	3,408	1,393,199.7	2,036,724.0	1,879,236.7
1962	169	21,270.7	2,699.0	1,122.7	1992	3,830	1,642,571.5	2,749,341.1	2,548,098.8
1963	165	25,214.4	2,459.1	1,505.3	1993	4,537	2,070,069.1	3,187,460.1	2,904,368.7
1964	160	29,116.3	3,403.0	1,874.1	1994	5,329	2,155,434.5	3,075,771.1	2,928,062.2
1965	170	35,220.2	4,358.1	1,962.4	1995	5,729	2,811,536.8	3,600,538.8	3,314,785.8
1966	182	34,829.4	4,671.8	2,005.1	1996	6,254	3,526,270.0	4,671,579.0	4,266,320.9
1967	204	44,701.3	4,669.6	2,744.2	1997	6,684	4,468,200.7	5,799,591.9	5,324,083.2
1968	240	52,677.2	6,819.8	3,838.7	1998	7,314	5,525,209.3	7,230,380.5	6,649,271.6
1969	269	48,290.7	6,718.3	3,661.6	1999	7,791	6,846,339.2	9,043,614.3	8,562,100.4

[1] Data from U.S. Bureau of the Census, *Historical Statistics of the United States* (1975), have been corrected to reflect annual sales and redemptions rather than those for the fourth quarter only.

Source

Investment Company Institute, *Mutual Fund Fact Book* (1966–2000), various issues.

Documentation

A mutual fund may be defined as a company that combines the funds of many investors whose investment goals are similar, and invests those funds in a wide variety of securities. The selection, purchase, and sale of individual securities by the mutual fund are conducted under the supervision of professional managers. Different mutual funds have a variety of investment objectives, management policies, and degrees of risk. Some funds place strong emphasis on capital growth; others stress current income or a balance between growth and income; some are highly speculative.

Most mutual funds are technically known as open-end investment companies because they stand ready at any time to redeem outstanding shares upon request by the investor. As open-end companies, the number of their shares is not fixed, with the outstanding total varying as new shares are sold to investors and shares are redeemed by investors upon presentation to the company. Shares are generally available from investment dealers or fund sales representatives. In most cases, the offering price includes a sales charge of up to 8.5 percent, with a lower percentage applying for some funds or on larger purchases. The redemption price is generally the net asset value prevailing at the time the shares to be redeemed are received by the company. The net asset value per share is determined by most companies at least once a day and is computed by dividing the current market value of the company's total net assets by the number of its shares outstanding.

The origin of investment companies and the concept of diversification date well back into the nineteenth century. However, most of the growth in mutual funds in the United States, in both the number of companies and total assets, has occurred since World War II, and particularly in the 1980s and 1990s. Growth in net assets over the years has been due not only to excess of share purchases over redemptions but also to the long-term upward trend in the market value of securities in which the mutual funds have typically invested.

Mutual funds are regulated by both federal and state governments. The major federal statutes regulating investment companies are the Securities Act of 1933, the Securities Exchange Act of 1934, and the Investment Company Act of 1940. The latter regulates the creation and structure and many of the operations of investment companies. The federal acts are administered by the Securities and Exchange Commission.

TABLE Cj863–865   Federal Reserve Board margin requirements: 1934–1974

Contributed by Peter L. Rousseau

		Regulation T		Regulation U, for loans by banks on stocks
		For extensions of credit by brokers and dealers on listed securities	For short sales	
		Cj863	Cj864	Cj865
Year	Date	Percent	Percent	Percent
1934	Oct 1	25 [3]	— [5]	—
1936	Feb 1	25 [3]	— [5]	—
1936	Apr 1	55 [4]	— [5]	55
1937	Nov 1	40	50	40
1945	Feb 5	50	50	50
1945	Jul 5	75	75	75
1946	Jan 20	100	100	100
1947	Feb 1	75	75	75
1949	Mar 1	50	50	50
1951	Jan 17	75	75	75
1953	Feb 21	50	50	50
1955	Jan 5 [1]	60	60	60
1955	Apr 23 [1]	70	70	70
1958	Jan 16	50	50	50
1958	Aug 5	70	70	70
1958	Oct 16	90	90	90
1960	Jul 28	70	70	70
1962	Jul 10	50	50	50
1963	Nov 6	70	70	70
1968	Mar 11	70	70	70
1968	Jun 8	80	80	80
1970	May 6	65	65	65
1971	Dec 6	55	55	55
1972	Nov 23	65	65	65
1974	Jan 3 [2]	50	50	50

[1] Effective after close of business.

[2] In effect.

[3] Figures are minimum margin requirement. Exact requirements ranged from 25 to 45 percent based on the relation of the security's current price to its lowest price since July 1, 1933.

[4] Effective May 1, 1936.

[5] Requirement prior to November 1, 1937, was margin "customarily required" by broker.

Sources

1931–1963: Board of Governors of the Federal Reserve System, *Supplement to Banking and Monetary Statistics* (1966), section 12, "Money Rates and Securities Markets," p. 141; 1964–1999: Board of Governors of the Federal Reserve System, *Federal Reserve Bulletin* (January issues).

Documentation

Regulations T and U, administered by the Federal Reserve Board in accordance with the Securities Exchange Act of 1934, limit the amount of credit that may be extended on a security by prescribing a maximum loan value, which is a specified percentage of its market value at the time of extension. The "margin requirements" shown are the difference between the market value (100 percent) and the maximum loan value. The current limits have been in effect since January 3, 1974. Data are expressed as percentage of market value, effective the date shown.

TABLE Cj866–869   Brokers' loans: 1918–1938

Contributed by Peter L. Rousseau

		Loans by		
	Total	New York City banks	Outside banks	Others
	Cj866	Cj867	Cj868	Cj869
Year	Million dollars	Million dollars	Million dollars	Million dollars
1918	1,000	575	145	280
1919	1,610	715	420	475
1920	1,080	390	285	405
1921	1,190	545	265	380
1922	1,860	945	410	505
1923	1,580	720	410	450
1924	2,230	1,150	530	550
1925	3,550	1,450	1,050	1,050
1926	3,290	1,160	830	1,300
1927	4,430	1,550	1,050	1,830
1928	6,440	1,640	915	3,885
1929	4,110	1,200	460	2,450
1930	2,105	1,280	215	610
1931	715	540	35	140
1932	430	335	20	75
1933	915	705	135	75
1934	905	660	180	65
1935	1,080	1,020	30	30
1936	1,185	1,095	50	40
1937	770	705	35	30
1938	770	715	15	40

Source

Board of Governors of the Federal Reserve System, *Banking and Monetary Statistics* (1943), p. 494.

Documentation

These data were assembled from various sources, and where gaps occurred, estimates were made. The figures represent loans to brokers by principal groups of lenders – New York City banks, outside banks, and others. Other lenders comprise foreign banking agencies, corporations, other brokers, and individuals. The figures cover primarily loans to brokers and dealers in New York City, most of whom are members of the New York Stock Exchange, but they also include loans to certain investment banking houses that do not have stock exchange seats and to brokers and dealers belonging to other stock exchanges. Comparable data are not available after 1938. For a more detailed description of the series, see the source, pp. 434–5.

DEBT AND FLOW OF FUNDS

John A. James and Richard Sylla

TABLE Cj870–889   Net public and private debt, by major sector: 1916–1976

Contributed by John A. James and Richard Sylla

	Public					Private			
	Total	Total	Federal	Federal financial agencies	State and local	Total	Corporate		
							Total	Long term	Short term
	Cj870	Cj871	Cj872	Cj873	Cj874	Cj875	Cj876	Cj877	Cj878
Year	Billion dollars	Billion dollars	Billion dollars	Billion dollars	Billion dollars	Billion dollars	Billion dollars	Billion dollars	Billion dollars
1916	82.2	5.7	1.2	—	4.5	76.5	40.2	—	—
1917	94.5	12.1	7.3	—	4.8	82.4	43.7	—	—
1918	117.5	26.0	20.9	—	5.1	91.5	47.0	—	—
1919	128.3	31.1	25.6	—	5.5	97.2	53.3	—	—
1920	135.7	29.9	23.7	—	6.2	105.8	57.7	—	—
1921	136.3	30.1	23.1	—	7.0	106.2	57.0	—	—
1922	140.2	30.7	22.8	—	7.9	109.5	58.6	—	—
1923	146.7	30.4	21.8	—	8.6	116.3	62.6	—	—
1924	153.4	30.4	21.0	—	9.4	123.0	67.2	—	—
1925	162.9	30.6	20.3	—	10.3	132.3	72.7	—	—
1926	169.2	30.3	19.2	—	11.1	138.9	76.2	—	—
1927	177.9	30.3	18.2	—	12.1	147.6	81.2	—	—
1928	186.3	30.2	17.5	—	12.7	156.1	86.1	—	—
1929	191.9	30.1	16.5	—	13.6	161.8	88.9	47.3	41.6
1930	192.3	31.2	16.5	—	14.7	161.1	89.3	51.1	38.2
1931	182.9	34.5	18.5	—	16.0	148.4	83.5	50.3	33.2
1932	175.0	37.9	21.3	—	16.6	137.1	80.0	49.2	30.8
1933	168.5	40.6	24.3	—	16.3	127.9	76.9	47.9	29.0
1934	171.6	46.3	30.4	—	15.9	125.3	75.5	44.6	30.9
1935	175.0	50.5	34.4	—	16.1	124.5	74.8	43.6	31.2
1936	180.6	53.9	37.7	—	16.2	126.7	76.1	42.5	33.5
1937	182.2	55.3	39.2	—	16.1	126.9	75.8	43.5	32.3
1938	179.9	56.6	40.5	—	16.1	123.3	73.3	44.8	28.5
1939	183.3	59.0	42.6	—	16.4	124.3	73.5	44.4	29.2
1940	189.8	61.2	44.8	—	16.4	128.6	75.6	43.7	31.9
1941	211.4	72.4	56.3	—	16.1	139.0	83.4	43.6	39.8
1942	258.6	117.1	101.7	—	15.4	141.5	91.6	42.7	49.0
1943	313.2	168.9	154.4	—	14.5	144.3	95.5	41.0	54.5
1944	370.6	225.8	211.9	—	13.9	144.8	94.1	39.8	54.3
1945	405.9	265.9	252.5	—	13.4	140.0	85.3	38.3	47.0
1946	396.6	243.2	229.5	—	13.7	153.4	93.5	41.3	52.2
1947	415.7	237.4	221.7	0.7	15.0	178.3	108.9	46.1	62.8
1948	431.3	232.9	215.3	0.6	17.0	198.4	117.8	52.5	65.3
1949	445.8	237.4	217.6	0.7	19.1	208.4	118.0	56.5	61.4
1950	486.2	239.8	217.4	0.7	21.7	246.4	142.1	60.1	81.9
1951	519.2	242.4	216.9	1.3	24.2	276.8	162.5	66.6	95.9
1952	550.2	249.8	221.5	1.3	27.0	300.4	171.0	73.3	97.7
1953	581.6	258.9	226.8	1.4	30.7	322.7	179.5	78.3	101.2
1954	605.9	265.9	229.1	1.3	35.5	340.0	182.8	82.9	100.0
1955	665.8	273.6	229.6	2.9	41.1	392.2	212.1	90.0	122.2
1956	698.4	271.2	224.3	2.4	44.5	427.2	231.7	100.1	131.7
1957	728.3	274.0	223.0	2.4	48.6	454.3	246.7	112.1	134.6
1958	769.6	287.2	231.0	2.5	53.7	482.4	259.5	121.2	138.4
1959	833.0	304.7	241.4	3.7	59.6	528.3	283.3	129.3	154.0
1960	874.2	308.1	239.8	3.5	64.9	566.1	302.8	139.1	163.7
1961	930.3	321.2	246.7	4.0	70.5	609.1	324.3	149.3	174.9
1962	996.0	335.9	253.6	5.3	77.0	660.1	348.2	161.2	187.0
1963	1,070.9	348.6	257.5	7.2	83.9	722.3	376.4	174.8	201.7
1964	1,151.6	361.9	264.0	7.5	90.4	789.7	409.6	192.5	217.1

TABLE Cj870–889   Net public and private debt, by major sector: 1916–1976   *Continued*

	Public					Private			
							Corporate		
	Total	Total	Federal	Federal financial agencies	State and local	Total	Total	Long term	Short term
	Cj870	Cj871	Cj872	Cj873	Cj874	Cj875	Cj876	Cj877	Cj878
Year	Billion dollars	Billion dollars	Billion dollars	Billion dollars	Billion dollars	Billion dollars	Billion dollars	Billion dollars	Billion dollars
1965	1,252.5	373.6	266.4	8.9	98.3	878.9	454.3	209.4	244.9
1966	1,349.1	387.8	271.8	11.2	104.7	961.3	506.6	231.3	275.3
1967	1,450.8	408.1	286.5	9.0	112.8	1,042.7	553.6	255.6	298.1
1968	1,596.8	436.0	291.9	21.5	122.7	1,160.9	631.5	283.6	347.9
1969	1,753.4	453.2	289.3	30.6	133.3	1,300.2	734.1	323.5	410.6
1970	1,881.9	484.7	301.1	38.8	144.8	1,397.2	797.3	360.2	437.1
1971	2,067.3	528.5	325.9	39.9	162.7	1,538.8	871.3	400.0	471.3
1972	2,299.8	560.6	341.2	41.4	178.0	1,739.2	975.3	443.6	531.7
1973	2,562.3	601.2	349.1	59.8	192.3	1,961.1	1,106.7	491.8	615.0
1974	2,793.5	648.4	360.8	76.4	211.2	2,145.1	1,223.0	540.9	682.1
1975	3,028.8	747.8	446.3	78.8	222.7	2,281.0	1,286.6	585.3	701.8
1976	3,354.9	833.4	515.8	81.4	236.3	2,521.5	1,414.7	626.1	788.5

	Private									
	Individual and noncorporate									
	Farm			Nonfarm						
				Mortgage			Other			
	Total	Production	Mortgage	Total	1–4 family	Multifamily, residential and commercial	Total	Commercial	Financial	Commercial and financial	Consumer
	Cj879	Cj880	Cj881	Cj882	Cj883	Cj884	Cj885	Cj886	Cj887	Cj888	Cj889
Year	Billion dollars	Billion dollars	Billion dollars	Billion dollars	Billion dollars	Billion dollars	Billion dollars	Billion dollars	Billion dollars	Billion dollars	Billion dollars
1916	36.3	2.0	5.8	8.4	—	—	20.1	—	—	—	—
1917	38.7	2.5	6.5	9.3	—	—	20.4	—	—	—	—
1918	44.5	2.7	7.1	9.6	—	—	25.4	—	—	—	—
1919	43.9	3.5	8.4	10.1	—	—	—	—	—	19.3	2.6
1920	48.1	3.9	10.2	11.7	—	—	—	—	—	19.3	3.0
1921	49.2	3.3	10.7	12.8	—	—	—	—	—	19.4	3.0
1922	50.9	3.1	10.8	14.1	—	—	—	—	—	19.7	3.2
1923	53.7	3.0	10.7	16.3	—	—	—	—	—	20.0	3.7
1924	55.8	2.7	9.9	18.6	—	—	—	—	—	20.6	4.0
1925	59.6	2.8	9.7	21.3	—	—	—	—	—	21.1	4.7
1926	62.7	2.6	9.7	24.0	—	—	—	—	—	21.2	5.2
1927	66.4	2.6	9.8	26.9	—	—	—	—	—	21.8	5.3
1928	70.0	2.7	9.8	29.6	—	—	—	—	—	21.6	6.3
1929	72.9	2.6	9.6	—	18.0	13.2	—	—	—	22.4	7.1
1930	71.8	2.4	9.4	—	17.9	14.1	—	—	—	21.6	6.4
1931	64.9	2.0	9.1	—	17.2	13.7	—	—	—	17.6	5.3
1932	57.1	1.6	8.5	—	15.8	13.2	—	—	—	14.0	4.0
1933	51.0	1.4	7.7	—	14.6	11.7	—	—	—	11.7	3.9
1934	49.8	1.3	7.6	—	14.8	10.7	—	—	—	11.2	4.2
1935	49.7	1.5	7.4	—	14.7	10.1	—	—	—	10.8	5.2
1936	50.6	1.4	7.2	—	14.6	9.8	—	—	—	11.2	6.4
1937	51.1	1.6	7.0	—	14.7	9.6	—	—	—	11.3	6.9
1938	50.0	2.2	6.8	—	15.0	9.5	—	—	—	10.1	6.4
1939	50.8	2.2	6.6	—	15.5	9.5	—	3.8	6.0	—	7.2
1940	53.0	2.6	6.5	—	16.5	9.6	—	4.3	5.2	—	8.3
1941	55.6	2.9	6.4	—	17.4	9.7	—	5.0	5.0	—	9.2
1942	49.9	3.0	6.0	—	17.3	9.5	—	4.1	4.0	—	6.0
1943	48.8	2.8	5.4	—	16.9	9.2	—	3.8	5.7	—	4.9
1944	50.7	2.8	4.9	—	17.0	9.0	—	3.7	8.1	—	5.1
1945	54.7	2.5	4.8	—	17.7	9.3	—	4.4	10.3	—	5.7
1946	59.9	2.7	4.9	—	22.1	9.7	—	6.2	5.9	—	8.4
1947	69.4	3.5	5.1	—	27.1	10.1	—	7.1	4.8	—	11.6
1948	80.6	5.5	5.3	—	32.0	10.4	—	7.8	5.1	—	14.4
1949	90.4	6.4	5.6	—	36.4	10.7	—	7.9	6.0	—	17.4

(continued)

TABLE Cj870–889 Net public and private debt, by major sector: 1916–1976 *Continued*

					Private						
					Individual and noncorporate						
	Farm					Nonfarm					
				Mortgage			Other				
	Total	Production	Mortgage	Total	1–4 family	Multifamily, residential and commercial	Total	Commercial	Financial	Commercial and financial	Consumer
	Cj879	Cj880	Cj881	Cj882	Cj883	Cj884	Cj885	Cj886	Cj887	Cj888	Cj889
Year	Billion dollars	Billion dollars	Billion dollars	Billion dollars	Billion dollars	Billion dollars	Billion dollars	Billion dollars	Billion dollars	Billion dollars	Billion dollars
1950	104.3	6.2	6.1	—	43.9	10.9	—	8.9	6.9	—	21.5
1951	114.3	7.0	6.7	—	50.4	11.3	—	9.5	6.7	—	22.7
1952	129.4	8.0	7.2	—	57.1	11.8	—	10.3	7.5	—	27.5
1953	143.2	9.1	7.7	—	64.7	12.0	—	9.9	8.5	—	31.4
1954	157.2	9.3	8.2	—	74.1	12.3	—	10.4	10.4	—	32.5
1955	180.1	9.7	9.0	—	86.3	12.4	—	12.4	11.6	—	38.8
1956	195.5	9.6	9.8	—	96.8	12.6	—	13.3	11.1	—	42.3
1957	207.6	9.8	10.4	—	105.2	12.9	—	13.2	11.1	—	45.0
1958	222.9	12.1	11.1	—	114.5	13.6	—	13.7	12.8	—	45.1
1959	245.0	11.7	12.1	—	127.3	13.7	—	15.3	13.4	—	51.5
1960	263.3	12.3	12.8	—	137.4	13.9	—	16.6	14.2	—	56.1
1961	284.8	13.6	13.9	—	148.9	15.6	—	17.9	16.9	—	58.0
1962	311.9	15.0	15.2	—	161.9	18.4	—	19.3	18.3	—	63.8
1963	345.8	16.4	16.8	—	177.1	21.5	—	21.5	20.8	—	71.7
1964	380.1	17.1	18.9	—	193.3	25.6	—	23.5	21.5	—	80.3
1965	424.6	18.1	21.2	—	216.2	28.1	—	27.0	24.1	—	89.9
1966	454.7	19.1	23.1	—	228.8	32.0	—	29.4	26.0	—	96.2
1967	489.1	22.8	25.1	—	243.2	34.9	—	31.2	31.0	—	100.8
1968	529.3	24.3	27.4	—	260.0	38.4	—	33.3	35.2	—	110.8
1969	566.2	26.0	29.2	—	277.4	42.4	—	35.8	34.2	—	121.1
1970	600.0	27.5	30.3	—	291.1	53.2	—	34.9	35.3	—	127.0
1971	667.5	30.3	32.2	—	321.1	68.2	—	36.8	40.2	—	138.6
1972	763.9	32.4	35.8	—	363.5	85.2	—	39.8	50.0	—	157.2
1973	854.4	37.7	41.3	—	406.9	103.5	—	42.0	44.1	—	179.0
1974	922.1	42.9	46.3	—	444.8	116.2	—	40.7	42.4	—	188.7
1975	994.4	47.1	51.1	—	486.1	126.7	—	39.3	46.9	—	197.3
1976	1,106.8	52.4	56.1	—	546.8	137.3	—	40.4	56.0	—	217.8

Sources

U.S. Bureau of Economic Analysis (formerly Office of Business Economics), *Survey of Current Business* (May 1969): 11; (May 1970): 14; (May 1973): 13.

Documentation

Data are as of end of year.

After 1976, the source no longer reported these data. The Federal Reserve's flow-of-funds data – some of which are reported elsewhere in this edition of *Historical Statistics of the United States* – continually update and report similar information. They are accessible at the Federal Reserve's Internet site. The source publications include details for the sectors shown here as well as data on gross debt.

All sectors of both gross and net debt exclude (1) deposit liability of banks and bank notes in circulation, (2) value of outstanding policies and annuities of life insurance carriers, (3) short-term debt of individuals and unincorporated nonfinancial business concerns held by other individuals and unincorporated businesses, and (4) nominal corporate debt, such as bonds authorized but not reacquired.

Series Cj871–874. Net debt for the public sectors of the economy represents total outstanding indebtedness minus intrasector holdings of such debt, for example, total federal debt minus such portions of that debt as are held by the Treasury and by federal agencies. The debt of federal agencies not included in the budget is shown in series Cj874. State and local debt includes state loans to local units.

Series Cj873. Comprises the debt of federally sponsored agencies, in which there is no longer any federal proprietary interest. Includes obligations of the Federal Land Banks beginning in 1947; debt of the Federal Home Loan Banks beginning in 1951; and debts of the Federal National Mortgage Association, Federal Intermediate Credit Banks, and Banks for Cooperatives beginning in 1968.

Series Cj876–878. Net corporate debt represents total corporate debt minus intercompany debts of affiliated companies.

Series Cj877–878. Long-term debt has a maturity of one year or more; short-term debt, less than one year.

Series Cj879–889. Figures for the noncorporate private debt are gross, with no adjustment for intrasector holdings.

Series Cj880. Represents agricultural loans to farmers and farmers' cooperatives by institutional lenders.

Series Cj887–888. Financial debt is owed to banks for purchasing or carrying securities, customers' debt to brokers, and debt owed to life insurance companies by policyholders.

Series Cj887 and Cj889. Includes debt owed by farmers for financial and consumer purposes.

TABLE Cj890–898 Mortgage debt outstanding, by type of holder and property: 1970–1997

Contributed by John A. James and Richard Sylla

		Type of property				Type of holder			
	Total	1–4 family	Multifamily	Commercial	Farm	Major financial institutions	Federal and related agencies	Mortgage pools or trusts	Individuals and others
	Cj890	Cj891	Cj892	Cj893	Cj894	Cj895	Cj896	Cj897	Cj898
Year	Million dollars	Million dollars	Million dollars	Million dollars	Million dollars	Million dollars	Million dollars	Million dollars	Million dollars
1970	474,188	298,102	60,111	85,629	30,346	355,929	33,579	4,755	79,925
1971	526,467	328,330	70,062	95,868	32,207	394,239	36,825	9,526	85,877
1972	603,417	372,154	82,840	112,665	35,758	450,000	40,157	14,404	98,856
1973	682,321	416,211	93,132	131,725	41,253	606,500	46,721	18,040	112,160
1974	742,512	449,371	99,976	146,877	46,288	542,560	58,320	23,799	117,833
1975	801,537	490,761	100,601	159,298	50,877	581,193	66,891	34,138	119,315
1976	889,202	556,456	104,505	171,210	57,031	647,525	66,753	49,801	125,123
1977	1,023,505	656,566	111,841	189,274	65,824	745,011	70,006	70,289	138,199
1978	1,172,754	761,843	121,972	212,746	76,193	848,095	81,853	88,633	154,173
1979	1,334,373	872,191	130,758	239,093	92,331	940,268	97,293	119,278	177,534
1980	1,460,375	965,051	142,343	255,494	97,487	996,799	114,556	145,921	203,099
1981	1,566,682	1,039,786	142,145	277,522	107,229	1,040,507	126,410	167,957	231,808
1982	1,637,947	1,080,044	145,699	300,893	111,311	1,021,327	138,741	224,422	253,457
1983	1,825,380	1,198,479	160,739	352,441	113,721	1,108,249	148,328	297,422	271,381
1984	2,051,437	1,334,329	185,435	419,251	112,422	1,245,915	158,993	350,669	295,860
1985	2,303,252	1,501,418	214,470	481,514	105,850	1,361,492	166,928	439,058	335,774
1986	2,618,324	1,719,673	247,831	555,039	95,781	1,474,343	203,800	565,428	374,753
1987	2,977,293	1,959,607	273,954	654,863	88,869	1,664,211	192,721	718,297	402,064
1988	3,242,267	2,168,803	287,056	699,620	86,788	1,805,428	200,570	810,887	425,382
1989	3,519,833	2,388,857	302,216	758,819	86,459	1,891,568	211,524	948,714	468,026
1990	3,803,696	2,676,175	289,799	748,313	78,903	1,914,315	239,003	1,080,684	569,694
1991	3,961,810	2,849,780	284,412	700,604	79,305	1,846,726	266,146	1,258,155	590,783
1992	4,092,984	3,037,408	274,234	689,296	80,738	1,769,187	286,263	1,434,264	603,270
1993	4,268,420	3,227,134	270,796	684,803	81,194	1,767,835	327,014	1,564,571	609,000
1994	4,473,100	3,430,023	275,303	708,467	82,971	1,815,810	319,401	1,718,297	619,592
1995	4,715,884	3,634,698	288,090	768,027	84,629	1,890,539	320,828	1,853,613	650,904
1996	4,929,439	3,761,711	312,588	768,027	87,134	1,979,114	300,935	2,070,436	578,945
1997	5,277,185	4,019,228	338,135	829,476	90,346	2,084,728	292,522	2,282,566	617,369

Sources

Board of Governors of the Federal Reserve System, *Annual Statistical Digest, 1970–1979* (1981), Table 40, p. 281; *Annual Statistical Digest, 1980–1989* (1991), Table 37, pp. 237–41; *Federal Reserve Bulletin* (July 1999), Table 1.54, p. A35.

Documentation

Total mortgage debt of all holders, series Cj890, is broken down by type of property in series Cj891–894 and by type of holder in series Cj895–898. The series by type of holder are broad categories; the sources provide more detail on each type of holder and the types of property on which it holds mortgage debt.

Figures are as of end of year.

Series Cj898. Other holders include mortgage companies, real estate investment trusts, state and local credit agencies, state and local retirement funds, noninsured pension funds, credit unions, and finance companies.

TABLE Cj899–957   Credit market debt outstanding: 1945–1997[1]

Contributed by John A. James and Richard Sylla

				Credit market debt owed						
				Domestic nonfinancial sectors						
						Nonfederal sectors				
	Total	Total	Federal government	Total	Household sector	Nonfinancial corporate business	Nonfarm noncorporate business	Farm business	State and local governments	Rest of world
	Cj899	Cj900	Cj901	Cj902	Cj903	Cj904	Cj905	Cj906	Cj907	Cj908
Year	Billion dollars	Billion dollars	Billion dollars	Billion dollars	Billion dollars	Billion dollars	Billion dollars	Billion dollars	Billion dollars	Billion dollars
1945	354.9	348.1	251.5	96.6	27.4	45.1	4.8	6.6	12.6	5.0
1946	350.8	339.8	228.0	111.8	34.1	50.8	7.2	7.0	12.7	8.0
1947	367.7	351.6	220.8	130.8	42.5	58.0	8.5	7.4	14.3	12.3
1948	382.2	363.2	215.1	148.1	50.5	64.5	9.2	8.1	15.7	13.7
1949	397.5	377.5	217.7	159.8	58.1	66.3	10.2	8.5	16.6	13.9
1950	425.2	402.7	216.5	186.2	69.8	73.4	12.3	9.5	21.2	14.0
1951	449.3	425.0	216.1	209.0	78.2	82.1	14.3	10.8	23.6	14.7
1952	484.6	458.4	221.4	237.0	89.7	88.8	16.1	11.6	30.8	15.1
1953	516.6	487.7	228.4	259.3	101.7	93.2	17.1	11.5	35.8	16.3
1954	541.7	512.9	230.8	282.1	112.3	97.4	18.9	12.3	41.1	16.6
1955	581.9	550.1	230.0	320.1	132.3	106.4	21.5	13.7	46.1	16.6
1956	611.4	576.0	224.1	351.9	147.2	116.0	23.7	14.6	50.4	17.4
1957	642.6	603.1	221.9	381.2	159.4	125.9	25.2	15.6	55.0	18.8
1958	681.5	639.8	231.1	408.7	169.7	133.7	27.7	17.0	60.7	20.8
1959	738.6	689.5	238.0	451.5	191.2	142.7	31.9	18.9	66.7	21.4
1960	780.0	724.2	236.0	488.3	208.2	152.1	35.8	20.0	72.2	23.2
1961	828.1	767.7	243.2	524.6	224.0	160.2	41.0	21.6	77.8	25.5
1962	887.5	820.6	250.0	570.5	245.1	171.4	46.4	23.9	83.8	27.5
1963	953.4	876.0	253.8	622.1	270.9	183.0	52.6	26.4	89.2	30.8
1964	1,027.8	939.9	259.9	680.0	299.1	197.8	58.5	29.0	95.6	35.0
1965	1,106.4	1,007.1	261.5	745.6	326.6	218.7	64.7	32.3	103.2	37.5
1966	1,186.9	1,074.6	265.1	809.5	348.4	244.1	71.5	35.5	110.0	39.5
1967	1,267.5	1,150.6	278.1	872.6	366.9	270.8	78.7	38.8	117.4	43.3
1968	1,372.7	1,242.7	290.6	952.1	397.4	299.9	87.1	41.6	126.1	46.1
1969	1,492.8	1,332.0	287.4	1,044.6	426.8	335.3	99.6	44.6	138.3	49.2
1970	1,602.1	1,422.3	299.5	1,122.8	445.3	367.4	112.2	47.6	150.3	52.1
1971	1,752.9	1,557.5	324.4	1,233.1	487.1	395.6	132.1	51.6	166.7	56.6
1972	1,937.4	1,713.5	339.4	1,374.1	544.5	433.0	159.2	56.8	180.7	61.1
1973	2,175.2	1,898.0	346.3	1,551.7	614.1	497.0	180.4	65.4	194.8	67.4
1974	2,411.8	2,072.3	358.2	1,714.1	663.5	554.6	214.4	73.3	208.2	81.2
1975	2,621.7	2,264.7	443.9	1,820.8	715.3	575.2	228.9	82.1	219.4	95.6
1976	2,909.3	2,508.3	513.1	1,995.3	802.3	614.2	248.7	92.2	237.8	116.0
1977	3,297.8	2,829.6	569.4	2,260.2	934.6	687.6	275.9	105.9	256.2	129.4
1978	3,785.6	3,214.5	621.9	2,592.6	1,094.2	761.6	319.1	122.2	295.6	157.6
1979	4,285.4	3,606.5	657.7	2,948.9	1,259.1	844.8	377.0	145.7	322.2	172.9
1980	4,734.0	3,957.9	735.0	3,222.9	1,375.6	910.2	431.2	161.5	344.4	197.2
1981	5,269.4	4,366.4	820.5	3,545.9	1,483.5	1,026.0	486.6	177.8	372.1	220.7
1982	5,776.8	4,788.3	981.8	3,806.5	1,551.0	1,114.6	542.6	184.5	413.8	210.4
1983	6,475.4	5,364.9	1,167.0	4,197.9	1,709.6	1,225.5	613.3	188.4	461.1	227.7
1984	7,439.2	6,151.2	1,364.2	4,787.0	1,921.9	1,431.3	732.2	187.9	513.6	235.5
1985	8,627.7	7,132.7	1,589.9	5,542.8	2,239.4	1,608.9	843.1	173.4	677.9	236.7
1986	9,804.9	7,973.1	1,805.9	6,167.2	2,494.1	1,827.8	937.2	156.0	752.1	238.3
1987	10,816.4	8,675.0	1,949.8	6,725.3	2,751.5	1,996.3	992.1	144.4	841.0	244.8
1988	11,855.8	9,457.6	2,104.9	7,352.8	3,024.3	2,201.2	1,098.5	133.7	895.0	252.4
1989	12,822.5	10,161.0	2,251.2	7,909.8	3,298.9	2,378.9	1,152.5	134.4	945.2	262.2
1990	13,745.1	10,843.4	2,498.1	8,345.3	3,582.0	2,487.7	1,147.9	135.4	992.3	285.9
1991	14,395.3	11,307.6	2,776.4	8,531.2	3,758.6	2,430.0	1,130.1	134.8	1,077.7	301.1
1992	15,195.3	11,833.2	3,080.3	8,752.9	3,923.1	2,470.5	1,115.3	135.3	1,108.7	315.8
1993	16,167.9	12,436.0	3,336.5	9,099.6	4,134.3	2,525.5	1,118.5	137.9	1,183.4	385.8
1994	17,210.9	13,016.8	3,492.3	9,524.5	4,446.2	2,663.1	1,121.8	142.2	1,151.1	371.8
1995	18,443.7	13,719.6	3,636.7	10,082.8	4,800.4	2,876.5	1,145.8	145.1	1,115.1	442.9
1996	19,798.2	14,447.4	3,781.8	10,665.6	5,143.9	3,052.1	1,190.2	149.9	1,129.4	513.4
1997	21,222.4	15,210.1	3,804.9	11,405.2	5,497.0	3,289.3	1,253.7	156.3	1,209.0	558.8

Note appears at end of table

TABLE Cj899–957   Credit market debt outstanding: 1945–1997   *Continued*

			Credit market debt owed									
			Financial sectors									
		Commercial banking										
Year	Total	Total	U.S.-chartered commercial banks	Foreign banking offices in the United States	Bank holding companies	Savings institutions	Credit unions	Life insurance companies	Government-sponsored enterprises	Federally related mortgage pools	Asset-backed securities (ABS) issuers	Finance companies
	Cj909	Cj910	Cj911	Cj912	Cj913	Cj914	Cj915	Cj916	Cj917	Cj918	Cj919	Cj920
	Billion dollars	Billion dollars	Billion dollars	Billion dollars	Billion dollars	Billion dollars	Billion dollars	Billion dollars	Billion dollars	Billion dollars	Billion dollars	Billion dollars
1945	1.9	0.2	0.1	0.0	—	0.4	—	—	0.9	—	—	0.4
1946	3.0	0.2	0.2	0.0	—	0.4	—	—	1.2	—	—	1.0
1947	3.8	0.3	0.2	0.1	—	0.5	—	—	1.3	—	—	1.5
1948	5.3	0.3	0.2	0.1	—	0.6	—	—	1.6	—	—	2.7
1949	6.1	0.3	0.2	0.1	—	0.5	—	—	1.4	—	—	3.6
1950	8.5	0.4	0.3	0.1	—	0.9	—	—	1.8	—	—	4.9
1951	9.6	0.5	0.4	0.1	—	1.0	—	—	2.1	—	—	5.6
1952	11.1	0.5	0.4	0.1	—	1.0	—	—	2.1	0.1	—	6.9
1953	12.7	0.6	0.5	0.1	—	1.0	—	—	2.1	0.1	—	8.3
1954	12.3	0.9	0.7	0.2	—	1.0	—	—	2.1	0.1	—	7.5
1955	15.3	0.6	0.5	0.1	—	1.6	—	—	3.1	0.1	—	8.5
1956	17.9	1.0	0.8	0.2	—	1.4	—	—	3.8	0.1	—	10.3
1957	20.8	1.3	1.1	0.3	—	1.4	—	—	4.9	0.2	—	12.0
1958	21.0	1.2	1.0	0.2	—	1.4	—	—	5.0	0.2	—	11.7
1959	27.7	1.2	0.9	0.2	—	2.4	—	—	7.3	0.2	—	15.0
1960	32.5	2.0	1.6	0.4	—	2.2	—	—	7.9	0.2	—	18.6
1961	34.9	2.7	2.2	0.5	—	2.9	—	—	8.6	0.3	—	18.2
1962	39.4	2.7	2.1	0.5	—	3.6	—	—	10.1	0.4	—	19.9
1963	46.6	3.2	2.6	0.6	—	5.0	—	—	11.5	0.5	—	22.9
1964	53.0	4.2	3.5	0.7	—	5.6	—	—	12.1	0.6	—	26.5
1965	61.9	5.0	4.3	0.7	—	6.5	—	—	14.2	0.9	—	30.9
1966	72.9	5.3	4.6	0.7	—	7.5	—	—	19.0	1.3	—	35.8
1967	73.6	6.3	5.5	0.9	—	4.8	—	—	18.4	2.0	—	37.8
1968	84.0	6.7	5.8	0.9	—	5.7	—	—	21.9	2.5	—	41.5
1969	111.5	11.8	6.4	1.1	4.3	9.8	—	—	30.6	3.2	—	48.8
1970	127.8	12.7	7.8	1.4	3.4	11.0	—	—	38.9	4.8	—	51.3
1971	138.9	15.2	9.4	1.6	4.2	9.0	—	—	40.0	9.5	—	52.1
1972	162.8	17.9	9.7	1.4	6.8	9.5	—	—	43.5	14.4	—	58.1
1973	209.8	23.1	11.3	1.8	10.0	17.1	—	—	59.8	18.0	—	65.6
1974	258.3	37.4	19.2	3.7	14.4	23.3	—	—	77.1	21.5	—	74.5
1975	261.4	42.0	19.6	3.8	18.7	19.1	—	—	80.3	28.5	—	75.0
1976	284.9	48.6	23.4	4.6	20.7	16.8	—	—	82.4	40.7	—	82.1
1977	338.8	56.1	26.4	5.2	24.5	22.7	—	—	88.7	56.8	—	101.0
1978	413.5	63.2	26.2	4.9	32.0	37.8	—	—	112.2	70.4	—	115.1
1979	505.9	76.4	33.5	6.8	36.1	47.9	—	—	137.0	94.8	—	132.6
1980	578.9	91.4	39.9	8.6	42.8	55.4	—	—	162.6	114.0	—	126.9
1981	682.4	113.0	48.3	11.9	52.8	71.4	—	—	195.0	129.0	—	141.6
1982	778.1	131.9	58.4	13.4	60.1	72.5	—	—	210.4	178.5	—	144.9
1983	882.8	152.1	63.0	15.7	73.5	66.8	—	—	211.8	244.9	3.7	159.7
1984	1,052.4	175.9	63.5	22.9	89.5	90.3	—	—	242.2	289.0	23.4	183.6
1985	1,258.3	188.3	57.8	24.4	106.2	111.4	—	—	263.9	368.9	39.4	224.3
1986	1,593.6	195.9	51.9	27.2	116.8	135.7	—	—	278.7	531.6	81.4	275.9
1987	1,896.5	217.4	52.5	33.8	131.1	164.4	—	—	308.2	670.4	131.3	299.1
1988	2,145.8	219.4	48.8	34.4	136.2	186.0	—	—	353.1	745.3	169.0	323.0
1989	2,399.3	224.6	46.7	35.4	142.5	171.0	—	—	378.3	869.5	225.1	350.4
1990	2,615.8	197.7	48.5	34.5	114.8	140.1	—	—	398.5	1,019.9	286.6	373.5
1991	2,786.7	184.6	47.4	24.9	112.3	95.4	—	—	407.7	1,156.5	355.0	389.6
1992	3,046.3	194.6	58.8	21.2	114.6	88.4	—	—	447.9	1,272.0	422.5	386.4
1993	3,346.1	208.0	68.6	16.0	123.4	99.6	0.2	0.2	528.5	1,356.8	506.1	385.1
1994	3,822.2	228.1	81.0	13.4	133.6	112.4	0.5	0.6	700.6	1,472.1	579.0	433.7
1995	4,281.2	250.6	92.2	10.4	148.0	115.0	0.4	0.5	806.5	1,570.3	720.1	483.9
1996	4,837.3	263.6	103.9	9.6	150.0	140.5	0.4	1.6	896.9	1,711.4	873.8	529.8
1997	5,453.5	309.2	133.4	7.2	168.6	160.3	0.6	1.8	995.3	1,825.8	1,088.1	554.5

(continued)

TABLE Cj899–957   Credit market debt outstanding: 1945–1997   *Continued*

	Credit market debt owed				Credit market assets held							
	Financial sectors				Domestic nonfederal nonfinancial sectors							
Year	Mortgage companies	Real estate investment trusts (REITs)	Brokers and dealers	Funding corporations	Total	Total	Household sector	Nonfinancial corporate business	Nonfarm noncorporate business	State and local governments	Federal government	Rest of world
	Cj921	Cj922	Cj923	Cj924	Cj925	Cj926	Cj927	Cj928	Cj929	Cj930	Cj931	Cj932
	Billion dollars	Billion dollars	Billion dollars	Billion dollars	Billion dollars	Billion dollars	Billion dollars	Billion dollars	Billion dollars	Billion dollars	Billion dollars	Billion dollars
1945	0.1	—	—	—	354.9	120.6	90.8	21.6	0.6	7.7	5.2	3.1
1946	0.2	—	—	—	350.8	114.2	90.0	16.4	0.7	7.1	8.3	2.4
1947	0.2	—	—	—	367.7	116.6	91.1	16.9	0.8	7.9	12.6	3.0
1948	0.2	—	—	—	382.2	121.1	93.4	18.4	0.9	8.5	13.9	3.1
1949	0.3	—	—	—	397.5	125.1	94.3	20.9	1.0	8.9	15.3	3.4
1950	0.5	—	—	—	425.2	131.9	95.7	25.3	1.1	9.8	16.0	4.8
1951	0.4	—	—	—	449.3	135.1	96.6	26.8	1.3	10.4	17.3	4.9
1952	0.6	—	—	—	484.6	144.7	104.6	25.7	2.7	11.7	18.8	5.1
1953	0.6	—	—	—	516.6	152.8	109.6	27.8	2.8	12.6	20.8	5.8
1954	0.8	—	—	—	541.7	152.2	109.5	26.4	2.8	13.5	20.5	6.4
1955	1.4	—	—	—	581.9	166.6	117.6	31.4	2.9	14.7	21.1	6.7
1956	1.3	—	—	—	611.4	171.3	124.9	27.4	3.1	15.9	21.8	7.3
1957	0.9	—	—	—	642.6	177.9	131.9	27.0	3.1	15.9	22.4	7.5
1958	1.4	—	—	—	681.5	179.5	132.7	27.7	3.1	16.1	23.9	7.5
1959	1.6	—	—	—	738.6	199.2	142.8	35.5	3.4	17.5	25.7	11.7
1960	1.6	—	—	—	780.0	202.9	150.9	29.7	3.2	19.1	26.7	12.6
1961	2.2	—	—	—	828.1	206.6	154.9	28.4	3.1	20.1	28.4	13.1
1962	2.7	—	—	—	887.5	211.2	158.2	28.0	3.3	21.7	30.4	14.8
1963	3.5	—	—	—	953.4	219.5	159.8	32.8	3.6	23.3	31.9	15.9
1964	3.9	—	—	—	1,027.8	228.1	166.2	33.1	3.8	25.0	34.7	16.9
1965	4.5	—	—	—	1,106.4	234.7	170.2	33.0	4.0	27.5	37.6	17.2
1966	3.9	—	—	—	1,186.9	254.3	190.9	32.0	4.0	27.5	42.7	16.5
1967	4.3	—	—	—	1,267.5	258.5	196.3	30.6	4.0	27.6	47.3	18.9
1968	4.9	0.8	—	—	1,372.7	275.4	206.7	33.1	4.2	31.4	52.3	19.3
1969	5.7	1.5	—	—	1,492.8	289.6	217.0	31.7	4.5	36.4	55.4	18.8
1970	6.9	2.2	—	—	1,602.1	290.3	216.3	33.7	5.2	35.1	58.2	29.8
1971	8.9	4.1	—	—	1,752.9	285.6	204.0	41.7	6.5	33.4	60.3	56.5
1972	10.6	8.8	—	—	1,937.4	291.6	199.5	44.3	7.7	40.1	62.2	65.1
1973	12.5	13.7	—	—	2,175.2	320.9	220.6	42.6	7.9	49.8	64.9	66.0
1974	10.6	14.0	—	—	2,411.8	373.4	262.3	47.0	7.7	56.4	72.2	71.9
1975	6.7	9.7	—	—	2,621.7	405.6	272.9	61.7	7.2	63.8	85.8	80.7
1976	6.5	7.9	—	—	2,909.3	439.6	276.4	73.0	8.1	82.0	93.7	94.4
1977	7.4	6.0	—	—	3,297.8	479.1	287.6	70.9	9.9	110.6	103.6	142.1
1978	9.5	5.4	—	—	3,785.6	562.6	328.3	74.0	12.8	147.5	120.6	170.5
1979	12.1	5.1	—	—	4,285.4	666.0	399.7	76.4	14.7	175.2	140.0	161.0
1980	11.6	4.6	—	12.5	4,734.0	724.2	424.7	91.2	14.9	193.4	163.8	186.5
1981	11.8	3.7	—	16.8	5,269.4	802.4	443.7	109.5	23.7	225.6	187.8	216.7
1982	13.4	3.7	—	22.8	5,776.8	898.1	506.3	113.5	28.2	250.1	203.6	255.1
1983	14.0	3.5	0.4	25.9	6,475.4	1,047.2	589.3	140.2	35.3	282.4	213.2	281.2
1984	15.5	4.2	1.1	27.1	7,439.2	1,221.8	694.2	163.8	44.8	319.0	230.1	357.9
1985	16.7	5.5	1.3	38.7	8,627.7	1,534.8	848.8	180.7	49.7	455.6	248.6	431.9
1986	25.7	6.7	3.4	58.7	9,804.9	1,619.0	862.7	175.1	55.4	525.8	255.2	543.7
1987	14.5	8.3	3.2	79.7	10,816.4	1,835.8	1,030.1	174.3	47.7	583.6	240.2	595.5
1988	14.5	10.3	7.5	117.8	11,855.8	2,102.4	1,232.3	193.3	58.2	618.6	215.0	698.3
1989	24.6	11.6	13.8	130.3	12,822.5	2,233.2	1,296.6	225.5	47.1	664.1	206.6	816.2
1990	24.6	12.4	15.3	147.1	13,745.1	2,446.1	1,499.8	199.4	43.6	703.4	240.1	902.4
1991	22.2	13.6	19.0	143.1	14,395.3	2,611.4	1,592.5	230.0	38.3	750.6	248.0	928.8
1992	30.2	13.9	21.7	168.6	15,195.3	2,694.1	1,645.8	257.8	38.1	752.3	236.0	1,023.0
1993	30.2	17.4	33.7	180.3	16,167.9	2,728.5	1,635.1	271.5	37.0	784.9	231.9	1,147.8
1994	18.7	31.1	34.3	211.0	17,210.9	3,002.4	1,945.7	289.2	37.6	729.9	204.4	1,254.8
1995	19.1	36.8	29.3	248.6	18,443.7	2,874.6	1,913.3	280.4	42.3	638.6	204.2	1,563.1
1996	31.5	47.8	27.3	312.7	19,798.2	2,926.9	1,979.3	286.0	46.7	614.8	196.5	1,953.6
1997	36.4	72.6	35.3	373.8	21,222.4	2,793.6	1,833.8	295.9	49.4	614.5	201.4	2,274.0

TABLE Cj899–957   Credit market debt outstanding: 1945–1997   *Continued*

				Credit market assets held								
				Financial sectors								
			Commercial banking									
	Total	Monetary authority	Total	U.S.-chartered commercial banks	Foreign banking offices in the United States	Bank holding companies	Banks in U.S.-affiliated areas	Savings institutions	Credit unions	Bank personal trusts and estates	Life insurance companies	Other insurance companies
	Cj933	Cj934	Cj935	Cj936	Cj937	Cj938	Cj939	Cj940	Cj941	Cj942	Cj943	Cj944
Year	Billion dollars	Billion dollars	Billion dollars	Billion dollars	Billion dollars	Billion dollars	Billion dollars	Billion dollars	Billion dollars	Billion dollars	Billion dollars	Billion dollars
1945	226.0	24.3	117.7	116.7	0.4	—	0.6	23.9	0.2	—	41.2	3.5
1946	226.0	23.5	111.6	110.6	0.5	—	0.6	26.7	0.2	—	44.4	4.1
1947	235.4	22.6	114.9	113.9	0.5	—	0.5	29.1	0.3	—	47.4	4.8
1948	244.0	23.5	113.2	112.1	0.6	—	0.5	31.2	0.5	—	50.9	5.7
1949	253.8	19.0	119.0	117.7	0.8	—	0.5	33.6	0.6	—	54.4	6.4
1950	272.5	20.7	125.6	124.1	1.0	—	0.5	36.7	0.7	—	57.9	7.2
1951	292.0	23.6	132.8	131.1	1.3	—	0.5	39.5	0.8	—	61.6	7.8
1952	316.0	24.1	141.4	139.5	1.5	—	0.5	44.1	1.1	—	65.9	8.7
1953	337.2	25.3	145.2	143.3	1.5	—	0.5	49.5	1.4	—	70.6	9.9
1954	362.6	25.0	154.9	152.8	1.6	—	0.5	55.5	1.6	—	75.4	10.8
1955	387.5	24.4	159.2	157.1	1.6	—	0.5	63.2	2.0	—	80.5	11.5
1956	411.0	24.7	164.8	162.6	1.6	—	0.6	70.2	2.4	—	85.6	11.9
1957	434.8	23.8	170.1	168.0	1.5	—	0.6	77.0	2.9	—	90.5	12.6
1958	470.6	26.3	185.0	182.8	1.5	—	0.7	85.5	3.1	—	95.5	13.4
1959	502.0	26.7	189.7	187.9	1.6	—	0.2	95.1	3.8	—	100.5	14.6
1960	537.7	27.0	199.7	197.6	1.9	—	0.2	104.2	4.5	—	105.6	15.5
1961	580.0	28.8	215.9	213.2	2.4	—	0.3	115.3	4.9	—	110.9	16.5
1962	631.2	30.5	235.2	232.3	2.6	—	0.4	128.3	5.6	—	116.9	18.0
1963	686.1	33.7	252.8	249.9	2.4	—	0.5	144.5	6.3	—	123.3	18.7
1964	748.1	36.6	276.1	273.0	2.6	—	0.5	160.2	7.2	—	130.3	19.5
1965	816.9	40.6	305.1	301.6	2.8	—	0.6	173.5	8.2	—	137.8	20.6
1966	873.4	43.7	323.1	319.1	3.3	—	0.7	181.7	9.4	—	145.9	22.0
1967	942.9	49.1	359.8	355.0	4.0	—	0.9	195.0	10.2	—	153.3	23.5
1968	1,025.7	53.0	398.7	393.4	4.4	—	1.0	208.9	11.7	—	160.7	25.4
1969	1,129.0	57.2	418.3	407.2	6.0	3.9	1.2	221.5	13.8	30.9	167.6	27.0
1970	1,223.8	62.2	455.3	441.6	9.5	3.0	1.3	236.8	15.2	33.6	174.6	30.9
1971	1,350.5	69.6	506.5	492.5	9.5	2.8	1.6	271.7	17.2	38.0	182.8	34.6
1972	1,518.6	71.2	575.7	558.6	12.6	2.6	1.9	314.5	20.1	41.1	192.5	38.3
1973	1,723.4	80.5	662.4	638.6	17.5	4.3	2.0	348.0	23.7	45.5	204.8	41.8
1974	1,894.4	85.3	737.5	703.5	26.6	4.9	2.5	369.7	26.4	48.3	217.7	46.4
1975	2,049.6	93.5	768.8	733.2	27.8	4.9	2.9	415.2	31.7	53.2	234.6	53.7
1976	2,281.6	100.3	833.2	791.0	32.9	5.8	3.5	477.5	38.4	59.5	258.3	66.2
1977	2,573.1	108.9	924.6	875.2	38.4	7.2	3.8	548.1	45.6	65.4	285.8	83.7
1978	2,932.0	117.4	1,052.6	984.1	57.7	6.7	4.0	614.4	52.0	72.6	318.9	100.2
1979	3,318.5	124.5	1,181.8	1,095.6	74.3	8.0	4.0	671.9	53.8	83.6	352.0	113.7
1980	3,659.5	128.0	1,289.9	1,183.2	94.1	7.6	5.0	722.7	53.0	88.8	385.1	123.5
1981	4,062.6	136.9	1,398.2	1,278.1	106.6	8.0	5.5	748.7	55.0	96.7	419.8	132.0
1982	4,419.9	144.5	1,482.9	1,386.1	83.1	5.8	7.9	756.7	57.3	100.3	463.2	137.0
1983	4,933.7	159.2	1,626.1	1,522.7	86.8	7.2	9.5	879.5	69.4	109.4	513.8	138.6
1984	5,629.3	167.6	1,800.1	1,681.4	99.6	8.1	11.0	1,018.6	85.0	123.1	570.1	150.3
1985	6,412.3	186.0	1,989.5	1,846.9	117.1	11.8	13.7	1,097.6	98.4	132.8	646.6	176.5
1986	7,387.0	205.5	2,187.6	2,009.4	152.0	11.5	14.6	1,191.0	113.9	151.4	734.5	219.2
1987	8,144.8	230.1	2,323.0	2,108.6	186.2	13.5	14.7	1,310.3	131.3	163.9	823.1	258.6
1988	8,840.1	240.6	2,479.5	2,235.0	215.6	13.4	15.5	1,409.3	148.8	177.8	927.2	287.9
1989	9,566.5	233.3	2,647.4	2,371.9	242.3	16.2	17.1	1,316.0	156.0	197.5	1,028.3	317.5
1990	10,156.6	241.4	2,772.5	2,466.7	270.8	13.4	21.6	1,176.5	166.6	213.4	1,134.5	344.0
1991	10,607.1	272.5	2,853.3	2,502.5	319.2	11.9	19.7	1,013.2	179.4	223.5	1,218.9	376.6
1992	11,242.2	300.4	2,948.6	2,571.9	335.8	17.5	23.4	937.4	197.1	231.5	1,304.4	389.4
1993	12,059.6	336.7	3,090.8	2,721.5	326.0	17.5	25.8	914.1	218.7	240.9	1,416.0	422.7
1994	12,749.2	368.2	3,254.3	2,869.6	337.1	18.4	29.2	920.8	246.8	248.0	1,482.6	446.4
1995	13,801.8	380.8	3,520.1	3,056.1	412.6	18.0	33.4	913.3	263.0	239.7	1,581.8	468.7
1996	14,721.2	393.1	3,707.7	3,175.8	475.8	22.0	34.1	933.2	288.5	232.0	1,654.3	491.2
1997	15,953.4	431.4	4,032.5	3,450.7	516.1	27.4	38.3	928.5	305.3	239.5	1,767.4	514.4

(continued)

TABLE Cj899–957   Credit market debt outstanding: 1945–1997   *Continued*

Credit market assets held

Financial sectors

Year	Private pension funds	State and local govt. retirement funds	Money market mutual funds	Mutual funds	Closed-end funds	Government-sponsored enterprises	Federally related mortgage pools	Asset-backed securities (ABS) issuers	Finance companies	Mortgage companies	Real estate investment trusts (REITs)	Brokers and dealers	Funding corporations
	Cj945	Cj946	Cj947	Cj948	Cj949	Cj950	Cj951	Cj952	Cj953	Cj954	Cj955	Cj956	Cj957
	Billion dollars	Billion dollars	Billion dollars	Billion dollars	Billion dollars	Billion dollars	Billion dollars	Billion dollars	Billion dollars	Billion dollars	Billion dollars	Billion dollars	Billion dollars
1945	3.9	2.5	—	0.2	0.2	2.0	—	—	3.6	0.1	—	2.7	—
1946	4.1	2.8	—	0.3	0.2	2.1	—	—	4.1	0.2	—	1.6	—
1947	4.4	3.1	—	0.3	0.3	2.3	—	—	4.7	0.2	—	0.9	—
1948	4.7	3.5	—	0.3	0.3	2.7	—	—	5.7	0.2	—	1.5	—
1949	5.0	4.1	—	0.4	0.3	2.6	—	—	6.6	0.3	—	1.5	—
1950	5.3	4.7	—	0.4	0.4	3.1	—	—	7.8	0.5	—	1.4	—
1951	6.0	5.4	—	0.5	0.4	3.5	—	—	8.3	0.4	—	1.2	—
1952	7.2	6.4	—	0.5	0.5	3.6	0.1	—	10.2	0.6	—	1.5	0.1
1953	8.5	7.7	—	0.5	0.6	3.7	0.1	—	11.9	0.6	—	1.6	0.1
1954	9.8	9.2	—	0.7	0.6	4.0	0.1	—	12.3	0.8	—	1.6	0.1
1955	11.2	10.5	—	0.8	0.7	5.0	0.1	—	15.6	1.4	—	1.4	0.1
1956	12.7	11.7	—	1.1	0.8	6.0	0.1	—	16.7	1.3	—	1.0	0.1
1957	14.5	13.3	—	1.2	0.9	7.3	0.2	—	18.3	0.9	—	1.4	0.1
1958	16.2	15.0	—	1.5	1.0	7.7	0.2	—	17.6	1.4	—	1.2	0.1
1959	17.9	16.8	—	1.8	1.2	9.9	0.2	—	20.8	1.6	—	1.2	0.2
1960	19.7	18.9	—	2.0	1.4	11.1	0.2	—	24.3	1.6	—	1.9	0.2
1961	21.2	21.1	—	2.4	1.4	12.1	0.3	—	24.7	2.2	—	2.0	0.2
1962	22.9	23.2	—	2.6	1.4	13.7	0.4	—	26.5	2.7	—	3.0	0.3
1963	24.8	25.6	—	2.8	1.8	15.3	0.5	—	30.1	3.5	—	1.9	0.3
1964	27.2	28.3	—	3.2	2.1	16.0	0.6	—	34.0	3.9	—	2.7	0.3
1965	29.1	31.3	—	3.9	2.1	18.3	0.9	—	38.2	4.5	—	2.4	0.5
1966	31.9	34.9	—	5.1	2.0	23.3	1.3	—	41.0	3.9	—	3.2	0.8
1967	32.8	38.3	—	4.3	2.2	23.3	2.0	—	41.2	4.3	—	2.9	0.8
1968	33.8	41.6	—	4.1	2.6	26.5	2.5	—	45.7	4.9	0.8	3.5	1.0
1969	34.6	45.5	—	5.1	2.6	35.1	3.2	—	53.4	5.7	2.0	3.7	1.6
1970	36.6	49.6	—	5.7	1.8	43.9	4.8	—	54.6	6.9	3.9	6.0	1.4
1971	35.0	52.9	—	5.5	2.4	45.0	9.5	—	58.7	8.9	6.2	4.6	1.3
1972	40.5	57.4	—	6.0	2.7	49.0	14.4	—	66.9	10.6	10.4	6.0	1.2
1973	46.8	63.1	—	6.6	3.3	64.5	18.0	—	77.0	12.5	16.0	7.5	1.7
1974	55.6	69.4	0.8	7.4	3.0	85.3	21.5	—	84.2	10.6	16.1	7.8	1.4
1975	71.2	78.3	1.5	8.0	3.1	89.8	28.5	—	85.7	9.3	13.2	8.8	1.3
1976	77.8	87.7	2.1	8.4	3.4	94.5	40.7	—	97.6	9.0	9.4	16.6	1.1
1977	88.2	99.2	1.9	12.3	2.7	101.4	56.8	—	118.4	10.2	7.0	11.3	1.6
1978	98.7	116.0	5.1	12.5	3.0	128.1	70.4	—	141.0	13.2	5.8	7.6	2.4
1979	120.8	126.6	24.9	14.5	3.0	158.1	94.8	—	166.6	16.8	4.9	3.9	2.4
1980	151.4	147.2	42.0	17.1	3.0	184.5	114.0	—	179.7	16.1	4.2	6.6	2.9
1981	178.6	169.0	107.5	20.2	2.9	217.7	129.0	—	202.2	16.4	2.6	20.9	8.3
1982	225.9	190.7	137.6	25.4	3.4	233.7	178.5	—	210.2	18.6	2.6	36.2	15.2
1983	268.1	198.8	119.7	34.9	3.1	236.4	244.9	3.0	234.5	19.5	2.7	25.5	46.4
1984	306.7	233.2	164.1	53.9	2.7	265.9	289.0	21.9	267.4	21.6	3.5	54.1	30.5
1985	330.5	252.4	178.2	129.9	4.1	291.0	368.9	36.9	311.2	24.7	5.9	58.2	93.0
1986	335.5	297.1	213.1	259.9	7.0	307.6	531.6	78.1	351.0	36.6	5.9	66.3	94.5
1987	348.4	324.1	215.0	291.1	11.0	330.9	670.4	126.2	396.4	23.9	7.0	39.8	120.4
1988	373.3	342.8	225.5	304.5	28.8	364.1	745.3	162.2	431.3	29.0	8.7	23.5	130.1
1989	434.5	389.3	293.7	327.2	35.4	359.9	869.5	216.4	449.2	49.2	8.4	103.7	134.1
1990	487.4	424.0	371.3	360.1	36.7	373.9	1,019.9	267.7	471.2	49.2	7.7	106.5	132.2
1991	524.4	396.4	403.9	440.2	49.5	388.8	1,156.5	331.6	453.0	60.3	7.0	124.0	134.2
1992	561.9	410.8	408.6	566.4	69.7	457.6	1,272.0	394.8	453.3	60.5	8.1	122.7	147.0
1993	611.4	433.5	429.0	725.9	89.7	545.5	1,356.8	475.9	427.9	60.4	8.6	137.5	117.8
1994	656.9	455.8	459.0	718.8	86.0	663.3	1,472.1	541.7	476.2	36.5	13.3	93.3	109.3
1995	718.2	483.3	545.5	771.3	96.4	748.0	1,570.3	661.0	526.2	33.0	15.5	183.4	82.2
1996	766.5	529.2	634.3	820.2	98.7	813.6	1,711.4	784.4	544.5	41.2	17.5	167.7	92.0
1997	834.2	565.8	718.8	899.5	99.8	908.6	1,825.8	949.2	566.4	57.6	15.5	181.4	111.7

TABLE Cj899–957   Credit market debt outstanding: 1945–1997   *Continued*

[1] Data are not seasonally adjusted. Excludes corporate equities and mutual fund shares.

Sources

Flow-of-funds data are available at the Federal Reserve Board's Internet site. The data for 1945–1996 are also available in a series of six hard copy releases by the Board of Governors of the Federal Reserve System, *Flow of Funds Accounts of the United States, Annual Flows and Outstandings, 1945–1953, 1954–1962, 1963–1972, 1973–1981, 1982–1990,* and *1991–1996,* all dated December 11, 1997. Updates are available in Federal Reserve Statistical Release Z.1, *Flow of Funds Accounts of the United States, Flows and Outstandings*, published quarterly.

Documentation

The data are year-end estimates of the levels of credit market debt outstanding.

Series Cj899 gives the total credit market debt owed by each of the individual sectors described in series Cj900–924. Debt owed must be debt held by other sectors; the total of credit market assets held is given in series Cj925, which matches series Cj899. Series Cj926–957 show the amounts of credit market debt held by various sectors, most but not all of which are the same sectors that owe.

TABLE Cj958–985   Credit market debt owed – nonfinancial sectors: 1945–1997[1]

Contributed by John A. James and Richard Sylla

		Domestic debt												
			Federal government			Nonfederal								
											By instrument		Mortgages	
Year	Domestic and foreign debt	Total	Total	Treasury securities	Budget agency securities and mortgages	Total	Commercial paper	Municipal securities and loans	Corporate bonds	Bank loans not elsewhere classified	Other loans and advances	Mortgages	Home	Multifamily residential
	Cj958	Cj959	Cj960	Cj961	Cj962	Cj963	Cj964	Cj965	Cj966	Cj967	Cj968	Cj969	Cj970	Cj971
	Billion dollars	Billion dollars	Billion dollars	Billion dollars	Billion dollars	Billion dollars	Billion dollars	Billion dollars	Billion dollars	Billion dollars	Billion dollars	Billion dollars	Billion dollars	Billion dollars
1945	353.1	348.1	251.5	251.2	0.3	96.6	0.1	12.1	23.9	10.5	7.5	35.7	18.6	4.9
1946	347.8	339.8	228.0	227.9	0.1	111.8	0.1	12.2	24.9	14.8	8.2	41.9	22.9	5.3
1947	363.9	351.6	220.8	220.7	0.1	130.8	0.2	13.8	27.7	18.5	8.4	49.0	28.0	5.8
1948	376.9	363.2	215.1	214.2	0.9	148.1	0.2	15.1	32.0	19.2	9.0	56.2	33.1	6.7
1949	391.4	377.5	217.7	216.7	1.0	159.8	0.2	16.1	34.9	17.2	9.3	62.7	37.4	7.8
1950	416.8	402.7	216.5	216.1	0.4	186.2	0.2	20.7	36.5	21.9	10.2	72.8	44.9	9.3
1951	439.7	425.0	216.1	215.8	0.2	209.0	0.3	22.8	39.8	27.2	11.4	82.3	51.5	10.6
1952	473.5	458.4	221.4	220.8	0.6	237.0	0.3	29.7	44.5	28.2	12.5	91.2	58.1	11.5
1953	504.0	487.7	228.4	226.2	2.3	259.3	0.4	35.0	48.0	27.2	13.0	101.1	65.7	12.1
1954	529.5	512.9	230.8	228.5	2.3	282.1	0.5	40.7	51.5	26.9	13.3	113.2	75.0	12.7
1955	566.7	550.1	230.0	228.4	1.6	320.1	0.4	45.7	54.6	33.1	14.1	129.4	87.5	13.5
1956	593.5	576.0	224.1	222.8	1.4	351.9	0.4	49.9	58.0	38.1	15.0	144.0	98.3	14.1
1957	621.9	603.1	221.9	220.1	1.8	381.2	0.4	54.4	64.1	40.1	16.9	156.1	106.9	14.5
1958	660.6	639.8	231.1	229.0	2.1	408.7	0.7	59.8	69.7	39.9	18.0	171.1	116.7	16.0
1959	710.9	689.5	238.0	236.2	1.8	451.5	0.3	65.7	72.8	45.0	20.7	189.8	129.6	17.9
1960	747.5	724.2	236.0	234.0	1.9	488.3	0.8	71.0	76.2	48.4	24.1	206.6	140.8	19.5
1961	793.2	767.7	243.2	240.7	2.5	524.6	1.1	76.3	80.6	50.6	25.7	226.7	153.3	22.1
1962	848.1	820.6	250.0	246.8	3.3	570.5	1.2	81.8	84.6	55.8	27.9	249.8	167.4	25.0
1963	906.8	876.0	253.8	250.7	3.2	622.1	1.0	87.0	88.4	60.8	30.7	276.4	184.0	28.2
1964	974.9	939.9	259.9	255.9	4.0	680.0	1.1	93.2	92.4	67.5	34.3	304.2	201.3	32.8
1965	1,044.5	1,007.1	261.5	257.0	4.5	745.6	0.8	100.4	97.3	79.5	38.4	331.7	218.6	36.4
1966	1,114.0	1,074.6	265.1	259.3	5.8	809.5	1.6	106.6	107.5	90.9	43.6	355.8	232.0	39.5
1967	1,194.0	1,150.6	278.1	268.2	9.9	872.6	3.0	113.8	122.1	99.2	46.4	379.4	245.3	43.1
1968	1,288.7	1,242.7	290.6	277.6	13.0	952.1	4.2	122.1	135.0	111.2	51.4	408.7	262.5	46.5
1969	1,381.3	1,332.0	287.4	276.8	10.6	1,044.6	5.4	133.5	147.0	128.0	62.1	439.5	280.7	51.5
1970	1,474.4	1,422.3	299.5	289.9	9.6	1,122.8	7.1	145.5	166.8	132.6	67.9	469.3	294.9	58.4
1971	1,614.1	1,557.5	324.4	315.9	8.5	1,233.1	6.2	161.7	185.6	140.1	72.3	518.0	321.5	68.4
1972	1,774.7	1,713.5	339.4	330.1	9.3	1,374.1	7.0	175.8	197.8	156.0	79.2	589.6	361.0	81.1
1973	1,965.4	1,898.0	346.3	336.7	9.6	1,551.7	8.4	192.7	206.9	194.1	90.3	666.2	404.0	91.4
1974	2,153.6	2,072.3	358.2	348.8	9.4	1,714.1	12.5	208.0	226.6	230.5	106.6	728.0	438.2	98.3
1975	2,360.2	2,264.7	443.9	434.9	8.9	1,820.8	9.6	223.0	253.8	224.4	117.2	785.8	477.7	99.0
1976	2,624.3	2,508.3	513.1	503.7	9.3	1,995.3	11.0	243.9	276.6	227.0	137.2	870.5	540.4	104.0
1977	2,959.0	2,829.6	569.4	560.9	8.4	2,260.2	12.8	273.6	299.5	250.5	159.9	999.5	633.6	112.5
1978	3,372.1	3,214.5	621.9	614.9	7.0	2,592.6	15.5	324.9	320.6	286.1	184.0	1,151.2	743.8	123.5
1979	3,779.5	3,606.5	657.7	652.1	5.6	2,948.9	24.5	364.2	337.9	330.5	220.7	1,318.0	862.0	133.6
1980	4,155.1	3,957.9	735.0	730.0	5.0	3,222.9	28.0	399.4	365.6	365.0	249.8	1,459.7	966.2	141.2
1981	4,587.0	4,366.4	820.5	815.9	4.5	3,545.9	42.7	443.7	390.3	413.5	300.8	1,581.8	1,041.0	141.1
1982	4,998.7	4,788.3	981.8	978.1	3.7	3,806.5	37.6	508.0	421.0	465.7	320.1	1,663.7	1,082.8	144.8
1983	5,592.6	5,364.9	1,167.0	1,163.4	3.6	4,197.9	36.8	575.1	447.0	490.9	354.0	1,853.8	1,200.4	160.0
1984	6,386.7	6,151.2	1,364.2	1,360.8	3.4	4,787.0	58.5	650.6	495.1	545.4	422.5	2,093.9	1,336.3	184.7

Domestic debt — Federal government and Nonfederal (1985–1997)

Year	Domestic and foreign debt Cj958	Total Cj959	Federal government Total Cj960	Treasury securities Cj961	Budget agency securities and mortgages Cj962	Total Cj963	Commercial paper Cj964	Municipal securities and loans Cj965	Corporate bonds Cj966	Bank loans not elsewhere classified Cj967	Other loans and advances Cj968	Mortgages Cj969	Home Cj970	Multifamily residential Cj971
	Billion dollars	Billion dollars	Billion dollars	Billion dollars	Billion dollars	Billion dollars	Billion dollars	Billion dollars	Billion dollars	Billion dollars	Billion dollars	Billion dollars	Billion dollars	Billion dollars
1985	7,369.4	7,132.7	1,589.9	1,586.6	3.3	5,542.8	72.2	859.5	578.2	589.1	465.1	2,374.8	1,537.0	204.3
1986	8,211.4	7,973.1	1,805.9	1,802.2	3.6	6,167.2	62.9	920.4	705.4	646.4	515.1	2,658.9	1,743.0	237.5
1987	8,919.8	8,675.0	1,949.8	1,944.6	5.2	6,725.3	73.8	1,010.4	784.1	659.8	549.2	2,959.3	1,948.6	256.9
1988	9,710.0	9,457.6	2,104.9	2,082.3	22.6	7,352.6	85.7	1,082.3	887.2	700.1	590.8	3,274.6	2,188.8	272.6
1989	10,423.2	10,161.0	2,251.2	2,227.0	24.2	7,909.8	107.1	1,135.2	961.1	728.3	641.2	3,543.7	2,422.6	285.2
1990	11,129.3	10,843.4	2,498.1	2,465.8	32.4	8,345.3	116.9	1,184.4	1,008.2	732.6	701.7	3,796.4	2,674.2	285.5
1991	11,608.6	11,307.6	2,776.4	2,757.8	18.6	8,531.2	98.5	1,272.2	1,086.9	690.3	639.3	3,949.4	2,850.2	282.5
1992	12,149.0	11,833.2	3,080.3	3,061.6	18.8	8,752.9	107.1	1,302.8	1,154.5	678.4	648.3	4,063.5	3,018.7	272.2
1993	12,821.8	12,436.0	3,336.5	3,309.9	26.6	9,099.6	117.8	1,377.5	1,229.7	684.8	629.3	4,201.4	3,177.3	266.9
1994	13,388.7	13,016.8	3,492.3	3,465.6	26.7	9,524.5	139.2	1,341.7	1,253.0	759.9	669.6	4,377.2	3,355.9	268.8
1995	14,162.5	13,719.6	3,636.7	3,608.5	28.2	10,082.8	157.4	1,293.5	1,326.3	862.1	736.9	4,583.9	3,530.4	279.5
1996	14,960.8	14,447.4	3,781.8	3,755.1	26.6	10,665.6	156.4	1,296.0	1,398.8	928.3	770.6	4,903.8	3,761.6	301.7
1997	15,768.9	15,210.1	3,804.9	3,778.3	26.5	11,405.2	168.6	1,367.5	1,489.5	1,029.8	837.4	5,248.3	4,030.3	319.0

Domestic debt — Nonfederal, By instrument and By sector (1945–1964)

Year	Commercial Cj972	Farm Cj973	Consumer credit Cj974	Household sector Cj975	Nonfinancial business Cj976	Corporate Cj977	Nonfarm noncorporate Cj978	Farm Cj979	State and local governments Cj980
	Billion dollars	Billion dollars	Billion dollars	Billion dollars	Billion dollars	Billion dollars	Billion dollars	Billion dollars	Billion dollars
1945	7.5	4.8	6.8	27.4	56.6	45.1	4.8	6.6	12.6
1946	8.8	4.9	9.7	34.1	64.9	50.8	7.2	7.0	12.7
1947	10.1	5.1	13.2	42.5	74.0	58.0	8.5	7.4	14.3
1948	11.2	5.3	16.3	50.5	81.8	64.5	9.2	8.1	15.7
1949	11.9	5.6	19.4	58.1	85.0	66.3	10.2	8.5	16.6
1950	12.5	6.1	23.9	69.8	95.2	73.4	12.3	9.5	21.2
1951	13.5	6.7	25.4	78.2	107.2	82.1	14.3	10.8	23.6
1952	14.4	7.2	30.5	89.7	116.4	88.8	16.1	11.6	30.8
1953	15.6	7.7	34.6	101.7	121.8	93.2	17.1	11.5	35.8
1954	17.3	8.2	36.0	112.3	128.6	97.4	18.9	12.3	41.1
1955	19.4	9.0	42.9	132.3	141.6	106.4	21.5	13.7	46.1
1956	21.8	9.8	46.6	147.2	154.4	116.0	23.7	14.6	50.4
1957	24.3	10.4	49.2	159.4	166.7	125.9	25.2	15.6	55.0
1958	27.2	11.1	49.5	169.7	178.4	133.7	27.7	17.0	60.7
1959	30.2	12.1	57.2	191.2	193.6	142.7	31.9	18.9	66.7
1960	33.4	12.8	61.2	208.2	207.9	152.1	35.8	20.0	72.2
1961	37.4	13.9	63.4	224.0	222.7	160.2	41.0	21.6	77.8
1962	42.2	15.2	69.3	245.1	241.6	171.4	46.4	23.9	83.8
1963	47.3	16.8	77.9	270.9	262.0	183.0	52.6	26.4	89.2
1964	51.1	18.9	87.4	299.1	285.3	197.8	58.5	29.0	95.6

Foreign credit market debt held in United States (1945–1964)

Year	Total Cj981	Commercial paper Cj982	Bonds Cj983	Bank loans not elsewhere classified Cj984	Other loans and advances Cj985
	Billion dollars	Billion dollars	Billion dollars	Billion dollars	Billion dollars
1945	5.0	—	2.9	0.5	1.6
1946	8.0	—	2.8	0.8	4.4
1947	12.3	—	2.8	1.0	8.5
1948	13.7	—	2.9	1.2	9.6
1949	13.9	—	2.9	0.9	10.1
1950	14.0	—	3.1	0.7	10.3
1951	14.7	—	3.4	0.8	10.5
1952	15.1	—	3.4	0.9	10.9
1953	16.3	—	3.3	0.7	12.2
1954	16.6	—	3.3	1.2	12.1
1955	16.6	—	3.1	1.4	12.1
1956	17.4	—	3.4	1.8	12.3
1957	18.8	—	3.8	2.1	12.8
1958	20.8	—	4.7	2.6	13.4
1959	21.4	—	5.2	2.9	13.4
1960	23.2	—	5.8	3.0	14.4
1961	25.5	—	6.2	3.7	15.5
1962	27.5	—	7.2	4.2	16.2
1963	30.8	—	8.2	4.8	17.8
1964	35.0	—	8.7	6.5	19.8

Note appears at end of table

(continued)

TABLE Cj958–985   Credit market debt owed – nonfinancial sectors: 1945–1997   Continued

	Domestic debt									Foreign credit market debt held in United States				
	Nonfederal													
	By instrument					By sector							Bank loans not elsewhere	Other loans
	Commercial	Farm	Consumer credit	Household sector	Nonfinancial business	Corporate	Nonfarm noncorporate	Farm	State and local governments	Total	Commercial paper	Bonds	classified	and advances
Year	Cj972	Cj973	Cj974	Cj975	Cj976	Cj977	Cj978	Cj979	Cj980	Cj981	Cj982	Cj983	Cj984	Cj985
	Billion dollars	Billion dollars	Billion dollars	Billion dollars	Billion dollars	Billion dollars	Billion dollars	Billion dollars	Billion dollars	Billion dollars	Billion dollars	Billion dollars	Billion dollars	Billion dollars
1965	55.6	21.2	97.5	326.6	315.7	218.7	64.7	32.3	103.2	37.5	—	9.1	7.1	21.2
1966	61.3	23.1	103.4	348.4	351.1	244.1	71.5	35.5	110.0	39.5	—	9.9	7.1	22.5
1967	65.9	25.0	108.6	366.9	388.3	270.8	78.7	38.8	117.4	43.3	—	11.1	6.7	25.6
1968	72.5	27.2	119.3	397.4	428.6	299.9	87.1	41.6	126.1	46.1	—	12.2	6.3	27.6
1969	78.3	29.0	129.2	426.8	479.5	335.3	99.6	44.6	138.3	49.2	—	13.2	6.0	30.0
1970	85.5	30.5	133.7	445.3	527.2	367.4	112.2	47.6	150.3	52.1	—	14.1	5.8	32.2
1971	95.7	32.4	149.2	487.1	579.2	395.6	132.1	51.6	166.7	56.6	—	15.0	7.3	34.3
1972	112.1	35.4	168.8	544.5	649.0	433.0	159.2	56.8	180.7	61.1	—	16.0	10.4	34.7
1973	131.1	39.8	193.0	614.1	742.8	497.0	180.4	65.4	194.8	67.4	—	17.0	13.1	37.3
1974	146.6	44.9	201.9	663.5	842.4	554.6	214.4	73.3	208.2	81.2	0.2	19.4	17.8	43.9
1975	159.2	49.9	207.0	715.3	886.2	575.2	228.9	82.1	219.4	95.6	0.6	26.5	21.6	46.8
1976	170.7	55.4	229.0	802.3	955.1	614.2	248.7	92.2	237.8	116.0	1.3	35.1	28.4	51.3
1977	189.4	63.9	264.4	934.6	1,069.4	687.6	275.9	105.9	256.2	129.4	1.8	40.1	31.4	56.0
1978	211.1	72.8	310.4	1,094.2	1,202.9	761.6	319.1	122.2	295.6	157.6	2.9	44.1	49.9	60.7
1979	235.6	86.8	353.1	1,259.1	1,367.6	844.8	377.0	145.7	322.2	172.9	4.6	47.8	53.0	67.6
1980	254.8	97.5	355.4	1,375.6	1,502.9	910.0	431.2	161.5	344.4	197.2	7.0	49.0	64.8	76.5
1981	292.5	107.2	373.1	1,483.5	1,690.4	1,026.0	486.6	177.8	372.1	220.7	10.8	54.5	67.8	87.5
1982	324.8	111.3	390.3	1,551.0	1,841.7	1,114.6	542.6	184.5	413.8	210.4	15.1	61.1	33.8	100.5
1983	379.7	113.7	440.3	1,709.6	2,027.2	1,225.5	613.3	188.4	461.1	227.7	21.5	64.2	37.4	104.6
1984	460.5	112.4	521.0	1,921.9	2,351.5	1,431.3	732.2	187.9	513.6	235.5	27.7	68.0	30.8	109.0
1985	527.7	105.9	603.8	2,239.4	2,625.5	1,608.9	843.1	173.4	677.9	236.7	33.9	71.8	27.9	103.0
1986	583.2	95.2	658.2	2,494.1	2,921.0	1,827.8	937.2	156.0	752.1	238.3	37.4	74.9	26.9	99.1
1987	666.1	87.7	688.6	2,751.5	3,132.8	1,996.5	992.1	144.4	841.0	244.8	41.2	82.3	23.3	98.0
1988	730.2	83.0	732.0	3,024.3	3,433.4	2,201.2	1,098.5	133.7	895.0	252.4	49.9	89.2	21.5	91.8
1989	755.4	80.5	793.3	3,298.9	3,665.8	2,378.9	1,152.5	134.4	945.2	262.2	63.0	94.0	21.4	83.8
1990	757.8	78.9	805.1	3,582.0	3,771.0	2,487.7	1,147.9	135.4	992.3	285.9	75.3	115.4	18.5	76.6
1991	737.6	79.2	794.5	3,758.6	3,695.0	2,430.0	1,130.1	134.8	1,077.7	301.1	82.1	130.4	21.6	67.0
1992	692.8	79.7	798.3	3,923.1	3,721.1	2,470.5	1,115.3	135.3	1,108.7	315.8	78.4	147.2	23.9	66.3
1993	676.4	80.7	859.0	4,134.3	3,781.9	2,525.5	1,118.5	137.9	1,183.4	385.8	68.8	230.1	24.6	62.3
1994	669.5	83.0	983.9	4,446.2	3,927.1	2,663.1	1,121.8	142.2	1,151.1	371.8	42.7	242.3	26.1	60.8
1995	689.4	84.6	1,122.8	4,800.4	4,167.3	2,876.5	1,145.8	145.1	1,115.1	442.9	56.2	291.9	34.6	60.2
1996	753.4	87.1	1,211.6	5,143.9	4,392.3	3,052.1	1,190.2	149.9	1,129.4	513.4	67.5	341.3	43.7	61.0
1997	808.6	90.4	1,264.1	5,497.0	4,699.3	3,289.3	1,253.7	156.3	1,209.0	558.8	65.1	382.6	52.1	59.0

1 Data are not seasonally adjusted.

Sources

Flow-of-funds data are available at the Federal Reserve Board's Internet site. The data for 1945–1996 are also available in a series of six hard copy releases by the Board of Governors of the Federal Reserve System, *Flow of Funds Accounts of the United States, Annual Flows and Outstandings, 1945–1953, 1954–1962, 1963–1972, 1973–1981, 1982–1990,* and *1991–1996,* all dated December 11, 1997. Updates are available in Federal Reserve Statistical Release Z.1, *Flow of Funds Accounts of the United States, Flows and Outstandings,* published quarterly.

Documentation

The data are levels outstanding at year-end. Whereas Table Cj899–957 gives breakdowns of total credit market debt outstanding for all sectors, financial and nonfinancial, this table provides more detail on credit market debt owed by nonfinancial sectors, including several domestic sectors and the foreign sector. In this table, credit market debt is also broken down by type of debt instrument. For similar detail on financial-sector components and the types of credit instruments used by them in raising funds, see Table Cj986–1009.

TABLE Cj986-1009   Credit market debt owed – financial sectors: 1945–1997[1]

Contributed by John A. James and Richard Sylla

						By instrument					
	Total	Federal government– related	Government- sponsored enterprise securities	Mortgage pool securities	U.S. government loans	Private financial sectors	Open market paper	Corporate bonds	Bank loans not elsewhere classified	Other loans and advances	Mortgages
	Cj986	Cj987	Cj988	Cj989	Cj990	Cj991	Cj992	Cj993	Cj994	Cj995	Cj996
Year	Billion dollars	Billion dollars	Billion dollars	Billion dollars	Billion dollars	Billion dollars	Billion dollars	Billion dollars	Billion dollars	Billion dollars	Billion dollars
1945	1.9	0.9	0.9	—	—	1.0	0.2	0.1	0.4	0.2	—
1946	3.0	1.2	1.2	—	—	1.8	0.4	0.2	0.9	0.3	—
1947	3.8	1.3	1.3	—	—	2.5	0.6	0.3	1.2	0.4	—
1948	5.3	1.6	1.6	—	—	3.8	0.8	0.8	1.7	0.5	—
1949	6.1	1.5	1.4	—	—	4.7	1.0	1.1	2.2	0.4	—
1950	8.5	1.9	1.8	—	—	6.6	1.1	1.3	3.4	0.8	—
1951	9.6	2.1	2.1	—	—	7.5	1.6	1.7	3.3	0.9	—
1952	11.1	2.2	2.1	0.1	—	8.9	1.9	1.7	4.4	0.9	—
1953	12.7	2.2	2.1	0.1	—	10.5	2.2	3.1	4.3	1.0	—
1954	12.3	2.1	2.1	0.1	—	10.1	2.4	2.8	4.1	0.9	—
1955	15.3	3.2	3.0	0.1	0.1	12.1	2.4	3.2	5.1	1.4	—
1956	17.9	4.0	3.4	0.1	0.4	13.9	2.8	4.5	5.4	1.2	—
1957	20.8	5.1	4.8	0.2	0.1	15.7	3.6	5.7	5.1	1.3	—
1958	21.0	5.2	4.9	0.2	0.1	15.8	3.4	5.6	5.5	1.3	—
1959	27.7	7.5	7.1	0.2	0.1	20.2	4.1	6.5	7.5	2.1	—
1960	32.5	8.1	7.9	0.2	0.0	24.4	5.8	9.8	6.9	2.0	—
1961	34.9	8.9	8.5	0.3	0.1	26.0	6.3	10.5	6.5	2.7	—
1962	39.4	10.5	10.0	0.4	0.1	28.9	7.5	10.8	7.2	3.5	—
1963	46.6	12.0	11.5	0.5	0.0	34.6	8.7	12.4	8.7	4.8	—
1964	53.0	12.7	11.9	0.6	0.1	40.3	10.7	15.5	8.7	5.3	—
1965	61.9	15.1	13.8	0.9	0.3	46.8	11.9	16.7	12.2	6.0	—
1966	72.9	20.3	18.9	1.3	0.1	52.5	15.7	18.3	11.6	6.9	—
1967	73.6	20.4	18.4	2.0	0.0	53.2	18.4	19.3	11.1	4.4	—
1968	84.0	24.4	21.6	2.5	0.3	59.6	21.4	19.9	12.8	5.3	0.2
1969	111.5	33.8	30.6	3.2	0.0	77.7	32.8	20.9	14.3	9.3	0.4
1970	127.8	43.6	38.9	4.8	0.0	84.1	33.1	23.5	16.4	10.6	0.5
1971	138.9	49.5	40.0	9.5	0.0	89.3	33.8	28.2	18.6	7.9	0.7
1972	162.8	57.9	43.5	14.4	0.0	104.8	34.7	35.6	25.4	8.0	1.2
1973	209.8	77.9	59.8	18.0	0.0	131.9	41.7	41.0	32.6	15.1	1.5
1974	258.3	98.6	76.4	21.5	0.7	159.7	55.1	47.9	33.3	21.8	1.6
1975	261.4	108.9	78.8	28.5	1.6	152.6	56.4	57.1	19.7	17.8	1.5
1976	284.9	123.1	81.2	40.7	1.2	161.8	62.5	64.0	17.5	15.9	2.0
1977	338.8	145.5	88.2	56.8	0.5	193.3	75.1	76.3	19.9	20.2	1.8
1978	413.5	182.6	111.3	70.4	0.9	230.9	89.1	82.9	24.4	32.7	2.0
1979	505.9	231.8	135.5	94.8	1.5	274.1	115.9	86.4	28.0	41.8	2.0
1980	578.9	276.6	159.9	114.0	2.7	302.3	128.8	93.8	28.7	49.0	1.9
1981	682.4	324.0	190.4	129.0	4.6	358.3	161.5	98.9	30.8	65.2	1.9
1982	778.1	388.9	205.4	178.5	5.0	389.2	174.2	113.7	33.3	66.0	2.0
1983	882.8	456.7	206.8	244.9	5.0	426.1	195.5	131.3	35.8	61.4	2.1
1984	1,052.4	531.2	237.2	289.0	5.0	521.2	219.5	176.6	44.8	77.8	2.5
1985	1,258.3	632.7	257.8	368.9	6.1	625.6	252.4	233.1	44.6	92.9	2.5
1986	1,593.6	810.3	273.0	531.6	5.7	783.3	284.6	325.4	56.9	113.5	2.8
1987	1,896.5	978.6	303.2	670.4	5.0	917.9	322.9	404.0	48.6	139.3	3.1
1988	2,145.8	1,098.4	348.1	745.3	5.0	1,047.4	377.7	456.1	51.4	158.8	3.4
1989	2,399.3	1,247.8	373.3	869.5	5.0	1,151.4	409.1	525.5	64.9	148.3	3.7
1990	2,615.8	1,418.4	393.7	1,019.9	4.9	1,197.4	417.7	582.1	68.9	124.4	4.3
1991	2,786.7	1,564.2	402.9	1,156.5	4.8	1,222.5	385.3	669.0	76.2	87.1	4.8
1992	3,046.3	1,720.0	443.1	1,272.0	4.8	1,326.3	393.5	763.9	77.0	86.6	5.4
1993	3,346.1	1,885.2	523.7	1,356.8	4.8	1,460.8	393.4	887.0	62.6	108.9	8.9
1994	3,822.2	2,172.7	700.6	1,472.1	0.0	1,649.5	441.6	1,008.8	48.9	131.6	18.7
1995	4,281.2	2,376.8	806.5	1,570.3	0.0	1,904.4	486.9	1,205.4	52.8	135.0	24.3
1996	4,837.3	2,608.3	896.9	1,711.4	0.0	2,229.1	579.1	1,385.1	69.7	162.9	32.2
1997	5,453.5	2,821.0	995.3	1,825.8	0.0	2,632.5	745.7	1,558.9	89.4	198.5	40.0

Note appears at end of table

(continued)

TABLE Cj986-1009   Credit market debt owed – financial sectors: 1945–1997   *Continued*

					By sector								
Year	Commercial banks	Bank holding companies	Savings institutions	Credit unions	Life insurance companies	Government-sponsored enterprises	Federally related mortgage pools	Asset-backed securities (ABS) issuers	Brokers and dealers	Finance companies	Mortgage companies	Real estate investment trusts (REITS)	Funding corporations
	Cj997	Cj998	Cj999	Cj1000	Cj1001	Cj1002	Cj1003	Cj1004	Cj1005	Cj1006	Cj1007	Cj1008	Cj1009
	Billion dollars	Billion dollars	Billion dollars	Billion dollars	Billion dollars	Billion dollars	Billion dollars	Billion dollars	Billion dollars	Billion dollars	Billion dollars	Billion dollars	Billion dollars
1945	0.2	—	0.4	—	—	0.9	—	—	—	0.4	0.1	—	—
1946	0.2	—	0.4	—	—	1.2	—	—	—	1.0	0.2	—	—
1947	0.3	—	0.5	—	—	1.3	—	—	—	1.5	0.2	—	—
1948	0.3	—	0.6	—	—	1.6	—	—	—	2.7	0.2	—	—
1949	0.3	—	0.5	—	—	1.4	—	—	—	3.6	0.3	—	—
1950	0.4	—	0.9	—	—	1.8	—	—	—	4.9	0.5	—	—
1951	0.5	—	1.0	—	—	2.1	—	—	—	5.6	0.4	—	—
1952	0.5	—	1.0	—	—	2.1	0.1	—	—	6.9	0.6	—	—
1953	0.6	—	1.0	—	—	2.1	0.1	—	—	8.3	0.6	—	—
1954	0.9	—	1.0	—	—	2.1	0.1	—	—	7.5	0.8	—	—
1955	0.6	—	1.6	—	—	3.1	0.1	—	—	8.5	1.4	—	—
1956	1.0	—	1.4	—	—	3.8	0.1	—	—	10.3	1.3	—	—
1957	1.3	—	1.4	—	—	4.9	0.2	—	—	12.0	0.9	—	—
1958	1.2	—	1.4	—	—	5.0	0.2	—	—	11.7	1.4	—	—
1959	1.2	—	2.4	—	—	7.3	0.2	—	—	15.0	1.6	—	—
1960	2.0	—	2.2	—	—	7.9	0.2	—	—	18.6	1.6	—	—
1961	2.7	—	2.9	—	—	8.6	0.3	—	—	18.2	2.2	—	—
1962	2.7	—	3.6	—	—	10.1	0.4	—	—	19.9	2.7	—	—
1963	3.2	—	5.0	—	—	11.5	0.5	—	—	22.9	3.5	—	—
1964	4.2	—	5.6	—	—	12.1	0.6	—	—	26.5	3.9	—	—
1965	5.0	—	6.5	—	—	14.2	0.9	—	—	30.9	4.5	—	—
1966	5.3	—	7.5	—	—	19.0	1.3	—	—	35.8	3.9	—	—
1967	6.3	—	4.8	—	—	18.4	2.0	—	—	37.8	4.3	—	—
1968	6.7	—	5.7	—	—	21.9	2.5	—	—	41.5	4.9	0.8	—
1969	7.5	4.3	9.8	—	—	30.6	3.2	—	—	48.8	5.7	1.5	—
1970	9.3	3.4	11.0	—	—	38.9	4.8	—	—	51.3	6.9	2.2	—
1971	11.0	4.2	9.0	—	—	40.0	9.5	—	—	52.1	8.9	4.1	—
1972	11.1	6.8	9.5	—	—	43.5	14.4	—	—	58.1	10.6	8.8	—
1973	13.1	10.0	17.1	—	—	59.8	18.0	—	—	65.6	12.5	13.7	—
1974	23.0	14.4	23.3	—	—	77.1	21.5	—	—	74.5	10.6	14.0	—
1975	23.4	18.7	19.1	—	—	80.3	28.5	—	—	75.0	6.7	9.7	—
1976	27.9	20.7	16.8	—	—	82.4	40.7	—	—	82.1	6.5	7.9	—
1977	31.6	24.5	22.7	—	—	88.7	56.8	—	—	101.0	7.4	6.0	—
1978	31.1	32.0	37.8	—	—	112.2	70.4	—	—	115.1	9.5	5.4	—
1979	40.2	36.1	47.9	—	—	137.0	94.8	—	—	132.6	12.1	5.1	—
1980	48.5	42.8	55.4	—	—	162.6	114.0	—	—	126.9	11.6	4.6	12.5
1981	60.1	52.8	71.4	—	—	195.0	129.0	—	—	141.6	11.8	3.7	16.8
1982	71.8	60.1	72.5	—	—	210.4	178.5	—	—	144.9	13.4	3.7	22.8
1983	78.6	73.5	66.8	—	—	211.8	244.9	3.7	0.4	159.7	14.0	3.5	25.9
1984	86.4	89.5	90.3	—	—	242.2	289.0	23.4	1.1	183.6	15.5	4.2	27.1
1985	82.2	106.2	111.4	—	—	263.9	368.9	39.4	1.3	224.3	16.7	5.5	38.7
1986	79.1	116.8	135.7	—	—	278.7	531.6	81.4	3.4	275.9	25.7	6.7	58.7
1987	86.3	131.1	164.4	—	—	308.2	670.4	131.3	3.2	299.1	14.5	8.3	79.7
1988	83.1	136.2	186.0	—	—	353.1	745.3	169.0	7.5	323.0	14.5	10.3	117.8
1989	82.1	142.5	171.0	—	—	378.3	869.5	225.1	13.8	350.4	24.6	11.6	130.3
1990	83.0	114.8	140.1	—	—	398.5	1,019.9	286.6	15.3	373.5	24.6	12.4	147.1
1991	72.3	112.3	95.4	—	—	407.7	1,156.5	355.0	19.0	389.6	22.2	13.6	143.1
1992	80.0	114.6	88.4	—	—	447.9	1,272.0	422.5	21.7	386.4	30.2	13.9	168.6
1993	84.6	123.4	99.6	0.2	0.2	528.5	1,356.8	506.1	33.7	385.1	30.2	17.4	180.3
1994	94.5	133.6	112.4	0.5	0.6	700.6	1,472.1	579.0	34.3	433.7	18.7	31.1	211.0
1995	102.6	148.0	115.0	0.4	0.5	806.5	1,570.3	720.1	29.3	483.9	19.1	36.8	248.6
1996	113.6	150.0	140.5	0.4	1.6	896.9	1,711.4	873.8	27.3	529.8	31.5	47.8	312.7
1997	140.6	168.6	160.3	0.6	1.8	995.3	1,825.8	1,088.1	35.3	554.5	36.4	72.6	373.8

[1] Data are not seasonally adjusted.

Sources

Flow-of-funds data are available at the Federal Reserve Board's Internet site. The data for 1945–1996 are also available in a series of six hard copy releases by the Board of Governors of the Federal Reserve System, *Flow of Funds Accounts of the United States, Annual Flows and Outstandings, 1945–1953, 1954–1962, 1963–1972, 1973–1981, 1982–1990,* and *1991–1996,* all dated December 11, 1997. Updates are available in Federal Reserve Statistical Release Z.1, *Flow of Funds Accounts of the United States, Flows and Outstandings,* published quarterly.

Documentation

The data are year-end levels. A variety of financial institutions fund themselves in credit markets by issuing a variety of financial instruments. This table gives totals and detailed breakdowns of credit market debt owed by several types of financial institutions, series Cj997–1009, and by the types of instruments used to borrow, series Cj987–996.

TABLE Cj1010–1020   Credit market debt and equity securities – all sectors: 1945–1997[1]

Contributed by John A. James and Richard Sylla

			Credit market debt									
Year	Total	Open market paper	U.S. government securities	Municipal securities	Corporate and foreign bonds	Bank loans not elsewhere classified	Other loans and advances	Mortgages	Consumer credit	Corporate equities	Mutual fund shares
	Cj1010	Cj1011	Cj1012	Cj1013	Cj1014	Cj1015	Cj1016	Cj1017	Cj1018	Cj1019 [2]	Cj1020 [2]
	Billion dollars	Billion dollars	Billion dollars	Billion dollars	Billion dollars	Billion dollars	Billion dollars	Billion dollars	Billion dollars	Billion dollars	Billion dollars
1945	354.9	0.3	252.4	12.1	26.9	11.4	9.3	35.7	6.8	117.7	1.3
1946	350.8	0.6	229.2	12.2	27.9	16.5	12.8	41.9	9.7	109.7	1.3
1947	367.7	0.8	222.1	13.8	30.8	20.7	17.3	49.0	13.2	107.6	1.4
1948	382.2	0.9	216.7	15.1	35.6	22.2	19.1	56.2	16.3	106.5	1.5
1949	397.5	1.1	219.1	16.1	38.8	20.4	19.9	62.7	19.4	116.9	3.1
1950	425.2	1.3	218.4	20.7	40.9	26.0	21.3	72.8	23.9	142.7	3.3
1951	449.3	1.8	218.2	22.8	44.9	31.3	22.7	82.3	25.4	166.5	3.5
1952	484.6	2.2	223.6	29.7	49.6	33.5	24.3	91.2	30.5	168.6	3.9
1953	516.6	2.6	230.6	35.0	54.4	32.2	26.1	101.1	34.6	164.6	4.1
1954	541.7	2.9	233.0	40.7	57.6	32.2	26.2	113.2	36.0	224.3	6.1
1955	581.9	2.7	233.2	45.7	60.8	39.6	27.6	129.4	42.9	281.8	7.8
1956	611.4	3.2	227.7	49.9	65.9	45.2	28.9	144.0	46.6	307.0	9.0
1957	642.6	4.1	226.8	54.4	73.6	47.3	31.1	156.2	49.2	279.6	8.7
1958	681.5	4.1	235.7	59.8	80.0	48.1	32.8	171.6	49.5	370.9	13.2
1959	738.6	4.4	244.5	65.7	84.5	55.4	36.3	190.7	57.2	413.7	15.8
1960	780.0	6.5	242.8	71.0	91.8	58.3	40.5	207.9	61.2	420.3	17.0
1961	828.1	7.4	250.5	76.3	97.3	60.9	44.0	228.2	63.4	521.1	22.9
1962	887.5	8.7	258.7	81.8	102.7	67.1	47.7	251.6	69.3	503.8	21.3
1963	953.4	9.7	264.1	87.0	109.0	74.3	53.2	278.2	77.9	558.5	25.2
1964	1,027.8	11.9	270.6	93.2	116.6	82.7	59.6	306.0	87.4	647.2	29.1
1965	1,106.4	12.7	274.4	100.4	123.1	98.8	66.0	333.5	97.5	734.9	35.2
1966	1,186.9	17.3	283.6	106.6	135.7	109.6	73.2	357.6	103.4	660.4	34.8
1967	1,267.5	21.4	296.7	113.8	152.5	117.0	76.4	381.1	108.6	835.1	44.3
1968	1,372.7	25.6	313.0	122.1	167.1	130.4	84.5	410.6	119.3	996.1	51.2
1969	1,492.8	38.1	319.7	133.5	181.1	148.3	101.4	441.5	129.2	849.9	47.6
1970	1,602.1	40.2	341.6	145.5	204.3	154.8	110.7	471.4	133.7	841.4	46.8
1971	1,752.9	40.1	372.5	161.7	228.8	166.0	114.6	520.1	149.2	987.5	55.4
1972	1,937.4	41.7	396.0	175.8	249.4	191.8	121.9	592.1	168.8	1,219.5	58.9
1973	2,175.2	50.1	422.9	192.7	264.9	239.8	142.8	669.0	193.0	948.8	46.6
1974	2,411.8	67.8	455.0	208.0	293.9	281.5	173.0	730.7	201.9	636.8	35.2
1975	2,621.7	66.6	550.1	223.0	337.4	265.8	183.5	788.4	207.0	845.7	43.0
1976	2,909.3	74.8	634.0	243.9	375.7	272.9	205.6	873.5	229.0	1,041.6	46.5
1977	3,297.8	89.8	713.5	273.6	415.9	301.8	236.6	1,002.2	264.4	928.7	45.5
1978	3,785.6	107.5	802.8	324.9	447.6	360.4	278.3	1,153.9	310.4	977.5	46.1
1979	4,285.4	145.0	887.3	364.2	472.1	411.5	331.6	1,320.6	353.1	1,160.2	51.8
1980	4,734.0	163.8	1,008.3	399.4	508.4	458.5	377.9	1,462.2	355.4	1,513.8	61.8
1981	5,269.4	215.1	1,139.5	443.7	543.7	512.2	458.1	1,584.1	373.1	1,402.6	59.8
1982	5,776.8	226.8	1,365.4	508.0	595.8	532.8	491.6	1,666.1	390.2	1,588.3	76.9
1983	6,475.4	253.8	1,618.4	575.1	642.5	564.2	525.0	1,856.1	440.3	1,889.0	112.1
1984	7,439.2	305.7	1,890.3	650.6	739.7	621.0	614.3	2,096.6	521.0	1,824.7	135.6
1985	8,627.7	358.5	2,216.5	859.5	883.1	661.7	667.2	2,377.5	603.8	2,319.0	245.9
1986	9,804.9	384.9	2,610.4	920.4	1,105.6	730.2	733.5	2,661.7	658.2	2,745.9	426.5
1987	10,816.4	437.9	2,923.4	1,010.4	1,270.4	731.8	791.5	2,962.4	688.6	2,762.7	480.2
1988	11,855.8	513.4	3,198.3	1,082.3	1,432.5	773.0	846.3	3,278.0	732.0	3,115.4	500.5
1989	12,822.5	579.2	3,494.1	1,135.2	1,580.6	814.5	878.3	3,547.4	793.3	3,831.6	589.6
1990	13,745.1	609.9	3,911.7	1,184.4	1,705.7	820.0	907.5	3,800.8	805.1	3,536.7	608.4
1991	14,395.3	565.9	4,335.7	1,272.2	1,886.4	788.2	798.2	3,954.2	794.5	4,866.0	769.5
1992	15,195.3	579.0	4,795.5	1,302.8	2,065.6	779.2	805.9	4,068.9	798.3	5,458.3	992.5
1993	16,167.9	580.0	5,216.9	1,377.5	2,346.8	772.0	805.3	4,210.3	859.0	6,257.6	1,375.4
1994	17,210.9	623.5	5,665.0	1,341.7	2,504.0	834.9	862.0	4,395.9	983.9	6,237.9	1,477.3
1995	18,443.7	700.4	6,013.6	1,293.5	2,823.6	949.6	932.1	4,608.2	1,122.8	8,331.3	1,852.8
1996	19,798.2	803.0	6,390.0	1,296.0	3,125.3	1,041.7	994.5	4,936.0	1,211.6	10,061.1	2,342.4
1997	21,222.4	979.4	6,625.9	1,367.5	3,431.0	1,171.3	1,094.9	5,288.3	1,264.1	12,958.6	2,994.7

[1] Data are not seasonally adjusted.

[2] Not included in series Cj1010.

Sources

Flow-of-funds data are available at the Federal Reserve Board's Internet site. The data for 1945–1996 are also available in a series of six hard copy releases by the Board of Governors of the Federal Reserve System, *Flow of Funds Accounts of the United States, Annual Flows and Outstandings, 1945–1953, 1954–1962, 1963–1972, 1973–1981, 1982–1990,* and *1991–1996,* all dated December 11, 1997. Updates are available in Federal Reserve Statistical Release Z.1, *Flow of Funds Accounts of the United States, Flows and Outstandings,* published quarterly.

(continued)

TABLE Cj1010–1020   Credit market debt and equity securities – all sectors: 1945–1997   *Continued*

Documentation

The data are year-end levels.

This table provides a comprehensive view, by type of financial instrument, of the amounts of debt and equity securities outstanding. The issuance of corporate equities is an alternative to credit market borrowing for corporations. Mutual fund shares are liabilities of the mutual funds, issued to provide them with resources for their role as financial intermediaries serving businesses, governments, and other financial institutions through purchases of equities and other securities. Mutual fund shares and corporate equities, valued here at market prices, are not considered credit instruments in the flow-of-funds accounts, but the information on funds raised in equity markets is presented for completeness and to allow users to compare the sizes of equity and credit markets. Corporate firms shift their financing between the two markets depending on the relative costs of funds.

TABLE Cj1021–1053　Flow-of-funds balance sheet – national: 1945–1997[1]

Contributed by John A. James and Richard Sylla

							Liabilities					
	Total	Credit market debt	Official foreign exchange	Special drawing right certificates	Treasury currency	Foreign deposits	Net interbank liabilities	Checkable deposits and currency	Small time and savings deposits	Large time deposits	Money market fund shares	Security repurchase agreements
	Cj1021	Cj1022	Cj1023	Cj1024	Cj1025	Cj1026	Cj1027	Cj1028	Cj1029	Cj1030	Cj1031	Cj1032
Year	Billion dollars	Billion dollars	Billion dollars	Billion dollars	Billion dollars	Billion dollars	Billion dollars	Billion dollars	Billion dollars	Billion dollars	Billion dollars	Billion dollars
1945	681.0	354.9	0.0	—	2.3	0.0	19.9	133.7	50.3	3.2	—	-3.6
1946	676.4	350.8	-0.2	—	2.4	0.1	19.7	119.1	56.6	3.4	—	-1.6
1947	714.8	367.7	0.9	—	2.4	0.1	21.8	120.2	60.0	3.6	—	-1.3
1948	746.3	382.2	1.3	—	2.4	0.0	24.2	119.6	62.2	3.9	—	-1.1
1949	769.5	397.5	1.5	—	2.4	0.0	20.7	119.6	64.9	4.3	—	-1.0
1950	838.2	425.2	1.4	—	2.4	0.1	23.1	124.9	67.3	4.6	—	-1.1
1951	890.8	449.3	1.4	—	2.4	0.1	26.1	132.1	72.3	4.5	—	-1.0
1952	954.0	484.6	1.5	—	2.4	0.1	26.1	138.7	80.2	4.9	—	-1.1
1953	1,008.6	516.6	1.4	—	2.5	0.1	25.9	138.7	88.5	5.8	—	-1.2
1954	1,064.0	541.7	1.2	—	2.5	0.2	24.5	143.3	97.8	7.0	—	-1.5
1955	1,151.4	581.9	1.0	—	2.5	0.1	26.0	145.7	106.6	6.7	—	-2.0
1956	1,213.8	611.4	1.6	—	2.5	0.1	27.0	147.6	116.2	6.5	—	-1.9
1957	1,271.1	642.6	2.0	—	2.6	0.1	26.5	147.1	128.3	6.7	—	-1.9
1958	1,360.1	681.5	2.0	—	2.6	0.1	26.0	153.0	142.6	9.3	—	-2.1
1959	1,458.8	738.6	2.0	—	2.6	0.1	26.3	154.4	154.1	7.5	—	-1.9
1960	1,536.7	780.0	1.6	—	2.7	0.1	26.2	156.3	165.8	11.1	—	-2.1
1961	1,650.1	828.1	1.8	—	2.7	0.2	28.1	162.4	184.1	13.5	—	-2.1
1962	1,765.0	887.5	1.2	—	2.8	0.8	28.8	167.7	209.9	16.4	—	-2.1
1963	1,906.3	953.4	1.2	—	2.8	0.7	28.2	172.9	235.5	20.3	—	-2.6
1964	2,065.8	1,027.8	1.2	—	2.8	1.1	29.2	181.8	261.2	25.1	—	-2.3
1965	2,240.8	1,106.4	1.6	—	3.1	0.8	30.1	189.1	288.5	31.0	—	-1.5
1966	2,383.2	1,186.9	1.6	—	4.0	0.9	35.8	193.6	306.5	33.3	—	-1.5
1967	2,580.5	1,267.5	2.8	—	4.6	1.1	38.0	208.9	341.2	39.2	—	-2.2
1968	2,819.0	1,372.7	4.8	—	5.1	1.6	44.0	224.0	367.8	45.9	—	-1.5
1969	3,143.9	1,492.8	5.1	—	5.3	1.2	51.6	232.1	382.3	30.9	—	4.7
1970	3,367.0	1,602.1	2.6	0.4	5.6	0.8	48.5	244.8	412.9	55.1	—	1.1
1971	3,751.9	1,752.9	0.9	0.4	6.0	1.2	47.3	262.9	481.3	68.6	—	5.0
1972	4,219.3	1,937.4	0.7	0.4	6.6	2.2	45.0	287.0	551.0	87.4	—	6.7
1973	4,653.6	2,175.2	0.6	0.4	7.0	3.3	42.6	304.7	590.4	126.4	—	23.1
1974	4,930.7	2,411.8	1.9	0.4	7.3	4.9	42.1	311.7	628.1	167.4	2.4	25.4
1975	5,737.3	2,621.7	2.3	0.5	8.2	5.8	30.4	331.1	726.5	158.3	3.7	29.1
1976	6,497.3	2,909.3	4.8	1.2	8.7	7.4	21.3	356.2	848.0	144.4	3.7	45.1
1977	7,280.0	3,297.8	5.0	1.3	8.9	8.8	21.6	386.3	943.2	173.0	3.9	52.3
1978	8,360.9	3,785.6	5.4	1.3	9.4	17.1	38.4	419.0	1,009.6	228.1	10.8	76.1
1979	9,520.0	4,285.4	5.1	1.8	10.5	26.9	57.7	455.8	1,070.2	257.4	45.2	92.7
1980	10,681.3	4,734.0	13.0	2.5	11.1	31.4	24.7	477.5	1,154.1	316.9	76.4	116.2
1981	11,856.6	5,269.4	14.8	3.3	11.5	41.8	-25.9	505.6	1,204.0	378.6	186.3	144.6
1982	13,074.6	5,776.8	17.6	4.6	11.9	49.5	-31.1	543.3	1,342.9	395.8	219.9	176.7
1983	14,588.3	6,475.4	17.6	4.6	12.3	141.6	-32.8	582.8	1,559.6	384.6	179.5	188.6
1984	16,344.6	7,439.2	18.2	4.6	12.9	140.0	-19.9	629.7	1,710.8	471.4	232.2	224.1

Note appears at end of table　　　(continued)

TABLE Cj1021–1053   Flow-of-funds balance sheet – national: 1945–1997   *Continued*

Liabilities (1985–1997)

Year	Total Cj1021 (Billion dollars)	Credit market debt Cj1022 (Billion dollars)	Official foreign exchange Cj1023 (Billion dollars)	Special drawing right certificates Cj1024 (Billion dollars)	Treasury currency Cj1025 (Billion dollars)	Foreign deposits Cj1026 (Billion dollars)	Net interbank liabilities Cj1027 (Billion dollars)	Checkable deposits and currency Cj1028 (Billion dollars)	Small time and savings deposits Cj1029 (Billion dollars)	Large time deposits Cj1030 (Billion dollars)	Money market fund shares Cj1031 (Billion dollars)	Security repurchase agreements Cj1032 (Billion dollars)
1985	18,999.0	8,627.7	24.8	4.7	13.3	148.5	9.0	713.5	1,853.4	488.5	242.4	250.6
1986	21,198.8	9,804.9	29.1	5.0	13.8	179.9	36.9	837.9	1,978.7	492.1	290.6	298.7
1987	23,006.9	10,816.4	24.4	5.0	14.2	213.3	72.5	841.9	2,048.5	541.9	313.8	292.7
1988	25,097.1	11,855.8	27.1	5.0	14.7	228.7	77.1	884.6	2,187.8	595.1	335.0	318.7
1989	27,492.3	12,822.5	53.6	8.5	15.3	266.8	62.5	891.0	2,285.5	613.0	424.7	396.5
1990	29,077.3	13,745.1	61.3	10.0	16.3	297.9	94.9	934.6	2,349.0	546.9	493.3	372.3
1991	30,902.8	14,395.3	55.4	10.0	16.3	273.5	96.4	1,020.9	2,350.7	488.4	535.0	355.9
1992	32,815.3	15,195.3	51.8	8.0	16.5	267.7	138.5	1,134.4	2,293.4	415.2	539.5	400.0
1993	35,368.3	16,167.9	53.4	8.0	17.0	271.8	189.3	1,251.7	2,223.1	391.7	559.6	471.3
1994	37,364.7	17,210.9	53.2	8.0	17.6	324.6	280.1	1,242.0	2,183.2	411.2	602.9	549.5
1995	40,805.7	18,443.7	63.7	10.2	18.2	359.2	290.7	1,229.3	2,279.7	476.9	745.3	659.9
1996	44,377.7	19,798.2	53.7	9.7	18.2	438.1	240.8	1,245.1	2,377.0	590.9	891.1	699.9
1997	49,040.3	21,222.4	48.9	9.2	18.2	527.0	192.8	1,286.6	2,474.1	713.4	1,048.7	815.1

Liabilities / Assets (1945–1959)

				Liabilities						Assets		
												Assets not included in liabilities
Year	Mutual fund shares Cj1033 (Billion dollars)	Security credit Cj1034 (Billion dollars)	Life insurance reserves Cj1035 (Billion dollars)	Pension fund reserves Cj1036 (Billion dollars)	Trade payables Cj1037 (Billion dollars)	Taxes payable Cj1038 (Billion dollars)	Investment in bank personal trusts Cj1039 (Billion dollars)	Miscellaneous Cj1040 (Billion dollars)	Totals identified to sectors Cj1041 (Billion dollars)	Gold and special drawing rights Cj1042 (Billion dollars)	Corporate equities Cj1043 (Billion dollars)	Household equity in noncorporate business Cj1044 (Billion dollars)
1945	1.3	8.9	39.6	12.3	21.5	10.5	—	26.2	1,014.7	20.1	117.7	194.8
1946	1.3	4.6	43.4	13.5	27.6	8.6	—	27.2	1,027.9	20.7	109.7	225.1
1947	1.4	3.4	46.5	15.8	31.7	10.7	—	30.0	1,102.0	22.9	107.6	260.0
1948	1.5	3.6	49.4	18.3	34.6	11.6	—	32.5	1,144.9	24.4	106.5	271.6
1949	3.1	4.4	52.1	21.1	34.7	9.5	—	34.7	1,180.8	24.6	116.9	275.5
1950	3.3	5.5	55.0	24.3	45.2	16.9	—	39.8	1,290.8	22.8	142.7	294.4
1951	3.5	5.1	57.8	27.9	46.9	21.6	—	40.7	1,397.6	22.9	166.5	319.4
1952	3.9	5.7	60.7	33.5	48.6	18.8	—	45.5	1,457.6	23.3	168.6	319.6
1953	4.1	6.5	63.6	38.5	48.8	19.9	—	48.8	1,503.6	22.1	164.6	319.9
1954	6.1	8.6	66.3	43.9	52.6	16.4	—	53.3	1,622.2	21.8	224.3	324.2
1955	7.8	9.6	69.3	52.0	63.3	19.7	—	61.2	1,769.4	21.8	281.8	331.7
1956	9.0	9.0	72.7	58.2	69.1	18.2	—	66.5	1,878.1	22.1	307.0	348.6
1957	8.7	8.7	75.5	64.6	71.6	16.3	—	71.8	1,922.6	22.9	279.6	360.9
1958	13.2	10.4	78.5	74.9	77.4	13.7	—	76.8	2,117.6	20.6	370.9	375.9
1959	15.8	10.5	82.0	85.0	83.0	15.5	—	83.1	2,256.4	19.5	413.7	376.5

	Liabilities								Assets			
										Assets not included in liabilities		
	Mutual fund shares	Security credit	Life insurance reserves	Pension fund reserves	Trade payables	Taxes payable	Investment in bank personal trusts	Miscellaneous	Totals identified to sectors	Gold and special drawing rights	Corporate equities	Household equity in noncorporate business
Year	Cj1033	Cj1034	Cj1035	Cj1036	Cj1037	Cj1038	Cj1039	Cj1040	Cj1041	Cj1042	Cj1043	Cj1044
	Billion dollars	Billion dollars	Billion dollars	Billion dollars	Billion dollars	Billion dollars	Billion dollars	Billion dollars	Billion dollars	Billion dollars	Billion dollars	Billion dollars
1960	17.0	10.9	85.2	93.9	87.8	14.9	—	85.2	2,354.4	17.8	420.3	388.0
1961	22.9	13.1	88.6	107.2	91.9	14.7	—	92.9	2,584.5	16.9	521.1	404.8
1962	21.3	13.8	92.4	113.7	95.9	16.3	—	98.5	2,700.2	16.1	503.8	422.4
1963	25.2	16.4	96.6	128.0	102.5	17.3	—	107.8	2,897.6	15.6	558.5	426.0
1964	29.1	16.8	101.1	144.8	110.3	18.0	—	117.7	3,163.1	15.5	647.2	443.7
1965	35.2	18.0	105.9	162.0	123.0	20.1	—	127.6	3,455.3	14.1	734.9	470.6
1966	34.8	18.7	110.6	172.5	133.0	19.2	—	133.4	3,560.0	13.2	660.4	503.9
1967	44.3	25.8	115.5	195.6	141.2	14.8	—	142.2	3,969.0	12.1	835.1	528.2
1968	51.2	32.3	120.3	218.7	157.2	16.0	—	158.7	4,408.2	10.9	996.1	572.0
1969	47.6	25.7	125.4	230.9	179.2	14.5	135.2	179.4	4,627.8	11.9	849.9	606.1
1970	46.8	24.9	130.7	253.8	187.6	12.5	137.9	199.0	4,876.4	11.9	841.1	636.5
1971	55.4	28.7	137.1	293.5	202.6	16.6	163.0	228.4	5,479.9	11.4	987.5	702.3
1972	58.9	37.4	143.9	349.5	229.1	20.5	187.1	268.6	6,291.8	12.4	1,219.5	788.0
1973	46.6	29.5	151.3	358.5	285.1	25.9	175.0	308.0	6,568.2	13.8	948.8	926.6
1974	35.2	25.9	158.4	367.8	232.2	32.8	147.3	327.9	6,750.5	14.0	636.8	1,030.5
1975	43.0	28.5	166.5	467.5	253.4	31.3	169.3	660.4	7,679.2	13.9	845.7	1,133.1
1976	46.5	39.9	175.3	535.4	281.5	38.5	195.9	834.3	8,684.7	14.0	1,041.6	1,265.3
1977	45.5	44.2	184.8	591.0	322.0	41.9	194.0	954.7	9,483.4	14.3	928.7	1,423.8
1978	46.1	46.7	196.0	692.7	382.5	48.8	206.6	1,140.6	10,795.3	13.2	977.5	1,653.7
1979	51.8	48.0	206.7	802.6	453.5	58.8	230.6	1,359.4	12,338.9	13.9	1,160.2	1,916.3
1980	61.8	61.9	216.4	962.5	499.6	64.4	265.3	1,591.6	14,067.2	13.8	1,513.8	2,156.2
1981	59.8	64.0	225.6	1,056.2	536.4	58.1	271.6	1,850.9	15,324.4	15.2	1,402.6	2,337.7
1982	76.9	69.8	232.8	1,280.9	551.6	55.7	288.5	2,010.4	16,812.4	16.4	1,588.3	2,400.1
1983	112.1	83.4	240.8	1,530.3	569.0	60.4	318.1	2,160.6	18,764.8	16.1	1,889.0	2,481.9
1984	135.6	87.9	246.0	1,699.2	618.4	65.0	331.1	2,298.2	20,748.6	16.7	1,824.7	2,518.1
1985	245.9	131.2	257.0	2,047.0	681.4	66.3	384.3	2,809.5	24,026.0	18.4	2,319.0	2,607.7
1986	426.5	141.1	274.9	2,274.3	682.8	72.9	429.1	2,929.6	26,916.0	19.5	2,745.9	2,704.6
1987	480.2	115.3	301.0	2,432.4	747.3	79.1	442.1	3,225.0	28,982.3	21.4	2,762.7	2,839.8
1988	500.5	118.3	326.6	2,668.7	834.0	80.2	470.3	3,568.9	31,808.8	20.7	3,115.4	3,020.1
1989	589.6	133.9	355.3	3,137.5	891.4	80.9	541.4	3,922.4	35,140.6	21.0	3,831.6	3,161.4
1990	608.4	137.4	380.9	3,388.2	927.2	82.8	551.7	4,079.1	36,611.2	22.0	3,536.7	3,247.6
1991	769.5	188.9	406.8	3,876.9	948.3	76.8	639.3	4,398.4	39,783.8	22.3	4,866.0	3,197.5
1992	992.5	217.7	434.8	4,217.9	995.1	87.4	660.6	4,749.0	42,158.8	19.6	5,458.3	3,156.7
1993	1,375.4	279.0	470.8	4,662.0	1,047.8	98.8	691.3	5,138.5	45,677.5	20.1	6,257.6	3,222.6
1994	1,477.3	279.0	505.3	4,880.1	1,141.5	101.4	699.4	5,397.3	47,852.8	21.1	6,237.9	3,422.6
1995	1,852.8	305.7	550.2	5,599.6	1,243.4	106.5	803.0	5,767.7	53,850.5	22.1	8,331.3	3,647.5
1996	2,342.4	358.1	593.8	6,329.5	1,315.5	121.5	871.7	6,082.7	59,735.7	21.4	10,061.1	3,863.3
1997	2,994.7	468.2	649.7	7,452.2	1,411.8	135.4	1,082.8	6,489.0	67,780.8	21.1	12,958.6	4,156.7

(continued)

TABLE Cj1021–1053   Flow-of-funds balance sheet – national: 1945–1997   *Continued*

	Assets						Floats not included in assets		
	Liabilities not included in assets								
Year	Treasury currency	Foreign deposits	Net interbank transactions	Security repurchase agreements	Taxes payable	Miscellaneous	Checkable deposits: federal government	Other	Trade credit
	Cj1045	Cj1046	Cj1047	Cj1048	Cj1049	Cj1050	Cj1051	Cj1052	Cj1053
	Billion dollars	Billion dollars	Billion dollars	Billion dollars	Billion dollars	Billion dollars	Billion dollars	Billion dollars	Billion dollars
1945	-1.9	—	0.9	-3.6	0.4	1.4	0.8	5.4	-4.6
1946	-2.0	—	0.7	-1.6	-0.1	1.4	1.4	5.7	-1.5
1947	-2.0	—	0.7	-1.3	-0.5	2.8	-0.1	6.4	-2.7
1948	-2.0	—	0.7	-1.1	-0.5	2.8	-0.1	6.0	-1.9
1949	-2.1	—	0.7	-1.0	-0.3	2.8	0.0	6.3	-1.0
1950	-2.1	—	0.8	-1.2	-0.4	5.3	-0.2	6.9	-1.9
1951	-2.2	—	0.5	-1.2	-0.9	3.4	-0.2	7.1	-4.5
1952	-2.2	—	0.6	-2.2	8.6	3.8	-0.8	8.8	-8.7
1953	-2.3	—	0.6	-2.1	11.7	3.3	-0.7	9.0	-8.1
1954	-2.3	—	0.6	-1.9	11.1	4.1	0.0	8.5	-7.8
1955	-2.3	—	0.8	-3.4	12.8	7.2	-0.4	9.0	-6.4
1956	-2.4	—	0.8	-3.8	11.7	5.5	-0.1	9.5	-7.9
1957	-2.4	—	0.7	-4.6	10.5	5.1	0.0	9.2	-6.5
1958	-2.5	—	0.8	-3.9	9.2	4.7	-0.2	9.6	-7.7
1959	-2.5	—	1.0	-2.9	8.9	5.6	-0.2	9.0	-6.8
1960	-2.6	—	0.9	-2.8	8.8	2.2	-0.3	9.6	-7.5
1961	-2.7	—	1.5	-2.7	8.5	3.0	-0.2	11.2	-10.1
1962	-2.7	—	0.9	-3.6	9.6	1.7	0.0	11.6	-10.6
1963	-2.6	—	1.0	-2.6	9.4	1.9	0.1	12.5	-10.9
1964	-2.4	—	0.4	-2.3	9.9	3.2	-0.1	12.8	-12.5
1965	-2.4	—	0.6	-2.9	12.1	-3.2	0.2	14.3	-13.7
1966	-2.2	—	1.2	-5.6	13.3	-4.1	0.2	16.6	-18.7
1967	-2.0	—	1.1	-5.1	8.5	-10.3	0.2	16.2	-21.8
1968	-1.7	—	1.9	-3.5	8.8	-11.3	1.3	19.7	-25.3
1969	-1.5	—	1.8	-4.4	9.8	-13.3	0.1	20.6	-29.0
1970	-1.6	—	2.2	-1.7	10.1	-21.5	-0.3	22.0	-28.8
1971	-1.6	—	1.7	-0.9	9.6	-32.0	-0.6	22.9	-26.1
1972	-1.7	—	-2.0	-0.9	11.3	-58.5	-0.2	27.6	-28.0
1973	-1.7	—	-1.1	-0.2	14.0	-47.4	0.1	27.2	-16.3
1974	-1.9	—	1.9	6.6	18.3	-139.7	-0.2	27.7	-51.3
1975	-2.0	3.6	-2.4	15.3	17.1	51.8	-0.3	29.3	-61.6
1976	-2.2	4.5	-3.1	27.2	18.2	131.7	-1.1	29.9	-71.5
1977	-2.4	3.6	-6.9	31.1	20.6	167.1	0.2	31.7	-81.5
1978	-2.4	9.1	-6.0	45.3	22.3	207.0	-0.1	31.2	-96.2
1979	-2.6	12.6	-8.3	43.1	27.2	274.8	-0.1	31.2	-106.4
1980	-2.8	15.9	-11.7	52.2	32.6	300.5	-0.8	33.5	-121.6
1981	-3.0	11.8	-17.3	67.3	38.6	293.6	-1.8	37.6	-139.0
1982	-3.2	14.4	-18.1	76.5	36.4	260.5	-2.2	35.7	-133.1
1983	-3.4	99.8	-27.4	63.4	36.2	192.3	-0.8	38.3	-188.0
1984	-3.5	100.3	-22.9	51.4	34.0	16.6	-0.5	36.5	-223.2

Assets

		Liabilities not included in assets					Floats not included in assets		
Year	Treasury currency	Foreign deposits	Net interbank transactions	Security repurchase agreements	Taxes payable	Miscellaneous	Checkable deposits: federal government	Other	Trade credit
	Cj1045	Cj1046	Cj1047	Cj1048	Cj1049	Cj1050	Cj1051	Cj1052	Cj1053
	Billion dollars	Billion dollars	Billion dollars	Billion dollars	Billion dollars	Billion dollars	Billion dollars	Billion dollars	Billion dollars
1985	-3.8	107.5	-18.3	28.1	27.9	-45.2	1.7	37.3	-217.2
1986	-3.8	131.9	-24.5	40.2	24.7	-213.4	2.7	28.3	-233.4
1987	-4.0	167.7	-28.1	29.8	29.6	-332.7	6.0	28.8	-248.6
1988	-4.1	168.4	-28.5	33.3	21.8	-507.6	5.9	29.6	-274.4
1989	-4.3	215.6	-31.0	40.5	19.7	-632.3	6.1	27.5	-276.1
1990	-4.1	244.6	-32.0	-19.4	23.2	-703.4	15.0	35.9	-287.3
1991	-4.7	222.6	-4.2	-53.3	23.4	-763.2	3.8	40.4	-260.2
1992	-4.9	217.6	-9.3	-48.0	33.0	-698.1	6.8	42.0	-248.0
1993	-5.1	233.2	-4.7	-1.5	40.8	-872.6	5.6	40.7	-245.3
1994	-5.4	276.2	-6.5	67.8	48.8	-983.1	3.4	38.0	-245.8
1995	-5.8	300.6	-9.0	90.7	61.3	-1,260.8	3.1	34.2	-258.1
1996	-6.8	353.1	-10.6	90.0	74.7	-1,650.8	-1.6	30.1	-290.3
1997	-7.4	424.6	-32.1	162.0	88.5	-1,960.4	-8.1	26.2	-297.5

1 Data are not seasonally adjusted.

Sources

Flow-of-funds data are available at the Federal Reserve Board's Internet site. The data for 1945–1996 are also available in a series of six hard copy releases by the Board of Governors of the Federal Reserve System, *Flow of Funds Accounts of the United States, Annual Flows and Outstandings, 1945–1953, 1954–1962, 1963–1972, 1973–1981, 1982–1990,* and *1991–1996,* all dated December 11, 1997. Updates are available in Federal Reserve Statistical Release Z.1, *Flow of Funds Accounts of the United States, Flows and Outstandings,* published quarterly.

Documentation

Figures are year-end levels. A financial asset of one entity is often a financial liability of another entity. A bank deposit, for example, is an asset to its owner, but a liability of the bank that holds it. This table identifies the components of financial liabilities and financial assets. Most of the difference between total liabilities, series Cj1021, and total financial assets, series Cj1041, is accounted for by corporate equities, series Cj1043, and household equity in noncorporate business, series Cj1044.

TABLE Cj1054–1080   Flow-of-funds balance sheet – personal sector: 1945–1997[1]

Contributed by John A. James and Richard Sylla

						Assets				Securities					
Year	Total	Foreign deposits	Checkable deposits and currency	Time and savings deposits	Money market fund shares	Total	Open market paper	U.S. savings bonds	Other Treasury securities	Agency securities	Municipal securities	Corporate and foreign bonds	Corporate equities[2]	Mutual fund shares
	Cj1054	Cj1055	Cj1056	Cj1057	Cj1058	Cj1059	Cj1060	Cj1061	Cj1062	Cj1063	Cj1064	Cj1065	Cj1066	Cj1067
	Billion dollars	Billion dollars	Billion dollars	Billion dollars	Billion dollars	Billion dollars	Billion dollars	Billion dollars	Billion dollars	Billion dollars	Billion dollars	Billion dollars	Billion dollars	Billion dollars
1945	388.9	—	71.1	50.3	—	189.4	0.0	42.9	23.6	-0.1	3.9	8.4	109.5	1.3
1946	398.4	—	76.7	56.6	—	178.9	0.1	44.2	21.0	-0.2	3.8	7.5	101.3	1.3
1947	406.3	—	76.7	60.1	—	176.2	0.1	46.2	18.8	-0.3	4.5	6.6	98.8	1.4
1948	412.7	—	73.7	62.3	—	176.2	0.2	47.8	18.0	-0.2	4.6	6.7	97.5	1.5
1949	430.3	—	71.7	65.0	—	185.4	0.3	49.3	18.0	-0.2	3.7	6.3	105.0	3.1
1950	469.0	—	74.4	67.4	—	210.1	0.4	49.6	16.9	-0.4	5.5	6.0	128.7	3.3
1951	508.7	—	79.1	72.2	—	232.6	0.8	49.1	16.3	-0.2	5.7	6.3	151.1	3.5
1952	537.8	—	80.7	79.6	—	240.3	1.0	49.2	18.2	0.0	11.0	6.0	151.0	3.9
1953	556.3	—	81.6	87.8	—	239.2	1.3	49.4	18.7	0.2	13.9	6.0	145.8	4.1
1954	631.5	—	83.8	96.9	—	293.1	1.1	50.0	16.1	0.1	16.0	4.9	198.8	6.1
1955	712.0	—	85.1	105.4	—	351.0	1.4	50.2	18.6	0.6	19.2	5.0	248.2	7.8
1956	765.9	—	87.0	114.7	—	380.7	1.4	50.1	20.1	1.0	21.9	6.1	271.0	9.0
1957	766.7	—	86.7	126.5	—	358.9	1.7	48.2	23.3	1.5	23.9	7.2	244.5	8.7
1958	882.6	—	90.7	140.3	—	439.4	1.8	47.7	20.9	0.8	24.6	7.9	322.3	13.2
1959	955.5	—	91.3	151.5	—	485.1	1.6	45.9	25.7	2.3	28.4	8.2	357.3	15.8
1960	993.3	—	92.4	163.4	—	494.2	2.6	45.6	26.6	1.0	31.0	10.6	359.8	17.0
1961	1,121.5	—	91.3	181.6	—	584.2	2.2	46.4	25.5	0.6	32.5	10.8	443.2	22.9
1962	1,147.0	—	90.9	207.4	—	571.4	3.0	47.0	26.8	0.2	32.1	10.2	431.2	20.9
1963	1,240.8	—	95.5	233.3	—	614.0	4.2	48.1	24.7	0.0	32.1	10.1	469.9	24.8
1964	1,380.9	—	102.1	259.3	—	696.7	5.2	49.1	24.5	0.2	34.9	10.3	544.1	28.4
1965	1,521.9	—	108.9	286.8	—	778.2	6.0	49.7	25.1	1.1	36.5	9.2	616.1	34.4
1966	1,513.3	—	111.6	305.5	—	728.3	8.3	50.2	28.8	5.9	41.2	11.9	548.3	33.9
1967	1,740.7	—	122.4	340.4	—	875.0	10.1	51.2	27.8	6.3	38.2	16.3	682.1	43.0
1968	1,962.5	—	132.3	370.8	—	1,022.9	12.2	51.9	30.1	6.1	36.5	21.4	815.3	49.5
1969	1,896.2	—	129.5	378.3	—	797.2	14.8	51.8	36.9	7.2	36.4	21.3	587.4	41.5
1970	1,962.9	—	137.3	420.8	—	779.9	12.5	52.1	26.1	11.5	35.4	29.5	572.5	40.4
1971	2,198.1	—	151.2	486.3	—	856.6	8.6	54.4	15.7	10.6	31.9	36.5	650.9	48.1
1972	2,541.2	—	163.5	558.7	—	1,016.6	3.4	57.7	15.6	4.9	32.4	38.4	813.7	50.6
1973	2,395.5	—	146.2	621.7	—	810.9	7.5	60.4	22.7	3.7	39.0	41.3	597.5	38.7
1974	2,260.0	—	151.0	677.8	2.4	614.6	15.6	63.3	25.7	8.3	47.1	52.9	373.4	28.2
1975	2,618.5	—	165.3	741.7	3.7	763.3	12.1	67.4	35.3	1.1	50.0	63.9	499.0	34.4
1976	2,991.8	—	181.8	838.8	3.4	903.6	8.2	72.0	20.5	4.6	52.5	72.1	637.4	36.2
1977	3,109.1	—	206.8	934.1	3.0	816.4	22.6	76.8	20.6	0.3	56.3	61.8	542.5	35.6
1978	3,433.7	—	230.6	1,029.8	8.5	858.3	36.4	80.7	22.6	0.6	80.1	51.5	550.3	36.2
1979	3,925.1	—	253.7	1,102.0	38.3	1,047.2	43.5	79.9	67.5	0.3	96.2	45.6	674.9	39.4
1980	4,573.1	—	266.6	1,227.5	62.2	1,290.0	38.3	72.5	90.1	5.3	104.5	30.8	902.9	45.6
1981	4,874.7	—	286.4	1,318.2	148.1	1,201.9	26.6	68.2	87.8	1.2	131.3	30.5	809.7	46.6
1982	5,461.7	2.4	302.1	1,435.6	180.3	1,325.5	30.3	68.3	104.3	1.2	170.0	24.4	869.7	57.3
1983	6,231.0	6.9	334.0	1,622.6	149.1	1,555.7	25.0	71.5	147.7	2.0	211.2	26.7	983.8	87.7
1984	6,827.2	6.9	347.9	1,856.6	191.0	1,616.0	42.0	74.5	184.3	18.1	250.7	27.5	914.3	104.6

Assets

Year	Total	Foreign deposits	Checkable deposits and currency	Time and savings deposits	Money market fund shares	Total	Securities: Open market paper	U.S. savings bonds	Other Treasury securities	Agency securities	Municipal securities	Corporate and foreign bonds	Corporate equities [2]	Mutual fund shares
	Cj1054	Cj1055	Cj1056	Cj1057	Cj1058	Cj1059	Cj1060	Cj1061	Cj1062	Cj1063	Cj1064	Cj1065	Cj1066	Cj1067
	Billion dollars	Billion dollars	Billion dollars	Billion dollars	Billion dollars	Billion dollars	Billion dollars	Billion dollars	Billion dollars	Billion dollars	Billion dollars	Billion dollars	Billion dollars	Billion dollars
1985	7,966.0	7.8	389.5	1,981.5	193.3	2,060.4	35.0	79.8	167.5	28.8	346.4	77.5	1,127.5	197.9
1986	8,978.6	8.8	510.0	2,067.2	228.8	2,509.4	30.6	93.3	146.1	27.9	352.6	107.3	1,418.3	333.2
1987	9,506.2	9.8	510.6	2,187.8	250.0	2,681.6	32.9	101.1	168.2	35.0	452.6	125.9	1,384.2	381.7
1988	10,533.7	10.7	496.3	2,386.9	265.3	3,158.0	67.3	109.6	242.9	52.0	523.8	121.2	1,639.9	401.3
1989	11,762.1	11.9	489.6	2,480.2	341.7	3,606.7	56.9	117.7	216.7	80.1	547.2	155.3	1,963.6	469.1
1990	12,159.8	13.4	470.2	2,528.6	368.6	3,631.4	63.2	126.2	279.9	123.6	574.5	200.8	1,795.4	467.8
1991	13,783.6	14.6	513.0	2,474.6	383.1	4,621.7	33.3	138.1	255.1	111.9	614.1	304.7	2,577.9	586.6
1992	14,715.9	15.6	616.8	2,397.6	342.2	5,169.6	29.9	157.3	314.2	137.8	585.5	297.3	2,919.7	727.9
1993	15,774.8	15.8	673.3	2,291.1	341.8	5,731.1	45.5	171.9	316.4	99.4	552.6	333.7	3,220.7	990.9
1994	16,264.8	18.8	649.1	2,287.3	355.3	5,942.2	46.7	179.9	496.3	242.4	502.2	373.7	3,048.9	1,052.1
1995	18,603.8	23.4	596.0	2,466.0	454.1	7,115.7	59.9	185.0	411.2	260.5	459.1	440.3	4,042.5	1,257.2
1996	20,671.1	35.5	534.7	2,640.7	534.6	8,061.8	82.6	187.0	395.1	336.9	441.1	445.4	4,602.3	1,571.3
1997	23,776.9	49.3	527.1	2,821.5	645.7	9,375.5	122.6	186.5	162.0	368.6	463.3	445.8	5,624.6	2,002.1

Assets

Year	Private life insurance reserves	Private insured pension reserves	Private noninsured pension reserves	Government insurance and pension reserves	Investment in bank personal trusts	Miscellaneous assets
	Cj1068	Cj1069	Cj1070	Cj1071	Cj1072	Cj1073
	Billion dollars	Billion dollars	Billion dollars	Billion dollars	Billion dollars	Billion dollars
1945	36.0	2.7	4.1	9.1	—	26.3
1946	38.6	3.1	4.3	10.9	—	29.4
1947	41.1	3.6	4.9	12.7	—	31.1
1948	43.8	4.2	5.5	14.1	—	32.9
1949	46.4	4.8	6.1	15.8	—	35.0
1950	49.1	5.6	7.1	17.6	—	37.7
1951	51.6	6.6	8.2	19.2	—	39.2
1952	54.5	7.7	10.7	21.2	—	43.0
1953	57.4	8.8	12.8	23.2	—	45.4
1954	60.4	10.0	15.0	24.8	—	47.5
1955	63.5	11.3	19.8	26.7	—	49.2
1956	66.6	12.5	22.8	29.1	—	52.6
1957	69.3	14.1	25.4	31.3	—	54.5
1958	72.3	15.6	31.5	34.1	—	58.8
1959	75.6	17.6	36.7	37.1	—	60.5
1960	78.8	18.9	41.2	40.2	—	64.2
1961	82.1	20.3	49.7	43.8	—	68.6
1962	85.8	21.6	51.6	47.2	—	71.2
1963	89.9	23.3	60.1	51.3	—	73.3
1964	94.2	25.3	70.5	55.9	—	77.0

Liabilities

Year	Total	Mortgage debt on nonfarm homes	Other mortgage debt [3]	Consumer credit	Policy loans	Security credit	Other liabilities [3]
	Cj1074	Cj1075	Cj1076	Cj1077	Cj1078	Cj1079	Cj1080
	Billion dollars	Billion dollars	Billion dollars	Billion dollars	Billion dollars	Billion dollars	Billion dollars
1945	44.8	18.3	8.4	6.8	2.1	1.2	8.1
1946	55.4	22.4	9.2	9.7	2.0	0.6	11.5
1947	66.8	27.3	9.8	13.2	2.1	0.6	13.7
1948	77.4	32.2	10.8	16.3	2.2	0.6	15.4
1949	87.2	36.4	12.2	19.4	2.4	0.9	15.9
1950	103.9	43.4	13.7	23.9	2.6	1.5	18.8
1951	116.0	49.8	15.9	25.4	2.8	1.4	20.8
1952	130.9	56.2	17.8	30.5	2.9	1.5	22.0
1953	144.7	63.6	19.3	34.6	3.1	1.8	22.2
1954	160.7	72.6	21.3	36.0	3.4	2.6	24.8
1955	186.8	84.9	23.0	42.9	3.6	3.0	29.3
1956	206.0	95.6	26.0	46.6	3.8	3.1	30.9
1957	221.1	104.2	28.0	49.2	4.2	2.7	32.7
1958	237.5	113.7	31.3	49.5	4.5	3.7	34.8
1959	265.4	126.4	36.1	57.2	5.0	3.7	37.0
1960	288.1	137.4	40.5	61.2	5.7	3.6	39.6
1961	311.6	149.6	46.3	63.4	6.2	4.6	41.4
1962	340.5	163.5	52.5	69.3	6.8	4.5	44.0
1963	375.7	179.7	59.2	77.9	7.2	6.0	45.7
1964	411.8	196.6	65.8	87.4	7.8	5.5	48.8

Notes appear at end of table

(continued)

TABLE Cj1054–1080 Flow-of-funds balance sheet – personal sector: 1945–1997 Continued

Year	Assets						Liabilities						
	Private life insurance reserves	Private insured pension reserves	Private noninsured pension reserves	Government insurance and pension reserves	Investment in bank personal trusts	Miscellaneous assets	Total	Mortgage debt on nonfarm homes	Other mortgage debt	Consumer credit	Policy loans	Security credit	Other liabilities [3]
	Cj1068	Cj1069	Cj1070	Cj1071	Cj1072	Cj1073	Cj1074	Cj1075	Cj1076 [3]	Cj1077	Cj1078	Cj1079	Cj1080 [3]
	Billion dollars	Billion dollars	Billion dollars	Billion dollars	Billion dollars	Billion dollars	Billion dollars	Billion dollars	Billion dollars	Billion dollars	Billion dollars	Billion dollars	Billion dollars
1965	98.9	27.3	80.9	60.8	—	80.2	449.7	213.4	73.1	97.5	8.3	5.9	51.4
1966	103.5	29.4	84.0	66.2	—	84.8	480.8	226.4	79.8	103.4	9.8	5.8	55.5
1967	108.3	31.9	98.8	72.1	—	91.6	513.8	239.5	86.4	108.6	10.8	8.9	59.7
1968	113.1	34.7	112.4	78.9	—	97.5	556.9	256.1	95.6	119.3	12.1	11.5	62.2
1969	118.1	37.6	115.0	85.6	135.2	99.7	600.3	273.5	105.3	129.2	14.7	8.2	69.3
1970	123.3	41.0	125.0	95.2	137.9	102.5	633.5	287.1	117.4	133.7	17.0	6.9	71.4
1971	129.6	46.1	148.0	106.8	163.0	110.5	706.1	312.9	135.4	149.2	18.0	9.5	81.1
1972	136.3	52.1	183.3	121.5	187.1	122.1	805.5	352.2	160.6	168.8	19.0	13.1	91.8
1973	143.5	56.1	182.2	127.9	175.0	132.0	918.5	395.0	165.3	193.0	21.2	8.9	135.1
1974	150.5	60.4	181.2	134.1	147.3	140.7	1,016.4	429.1	191.7	201.9	23.9	7.4	162.4
1975	158.5	72.3	248.4	154.8	169.3	141.2	1,096.9	468.4	204.7	207.0	25.5	8.3	183.0
1976	167.1	88.7	279.7	175.2	195.9	157.8	1,225.1	530.9	222.0	229.0	26.9	12.5	203.8
1977	176.4	103.2	302.2	194.0	194.0	179.0	1,409.3	624.0	245.8	264.4	28.6	14.5	232.0
1978	187.3	121.6	357.0	222.8	206.6	211.2	1,641.4	733.9	276.1	310.4	31.2	17.1	272.7
1979	197.7	143.5	420.9	247.2	230.6	243.8	1,903.7	851.7	324.0	353.1	35.9	17.5	321.5
1980	207.4	172.0	515.1	284.5	265.3	282.6	2,112.0	955.5	373.4	355.4	42.6	24.7	360.3
1981	216.3	199.8	544.9	320.8	271.6	366.6	2,292.2	1,030.0	416.1	373.1	50.0	23.0	400.1
1982	223.3	242.9	676.4	371.1	288.5	413.6	2,458.8	1,071.3	472.3	390.3	54.2	25.8	444.8
1983	231.1	281.7	824.0	434.3	318.1	473.4	2,718.6	1,188.5	517.5	440.3	55.2	34.2	482.9
1984	236.1	328.3	882.5	498.3	331.1	532.5	3,064.9	1,323.7	607.8	521.0	55.6	31.8	524.9
1985	246.5	260.4	1,231.1	566.0	384.3	645.3	3,525.4	1,523.7	692.2	603.8	55.5	50.7	599.5
1986	263.7	327.9	1,292.4	665.2	429.1	676.2	3,854.4	1,729.0	758.1	658.2	55.4	57.4	596.3
1987	289.5	348.6	1,359.6	735.8	442.1	690.9	4,137.1	1,934.0	810.8	688.6	55.3	41.8	606.6
1988	314.4	438.4	1,400.3	842.1	470.3	751.0	4,520.3	2,173.5	880.0	732.0	55.3	43.5	636.0
1989	342.8	510.1	1,615.5	1,024.4	541.4	797.8	4,901.5	2,406.6	903.6	793.3	58.4	42.5	697.1
1990	368.1	596.0	1,601.1	1,203.9	551.7	826.8	5,181.1	2,657.6	909.9	805.1	62.5	38.8	707.1
1991	393.8	659.1	1,889.0	1,341.8	639.3	853.7	5,377.4	2,833.2	903.6	794.5	67.3	55.1	723.8
1992	421.5	743.0	1,983.1	1,505.1	660.6	860.8	5,546.5	3,001.2	868.4	798.3	73.0	53.5	752.0
1993	457.2	836.4	2,216.3	1,622.9	691.3	897.7	5,797.5	3,159.2	844.1	859.0	78.6	76.1	780.5
1994	491.5	884.5	2,317.2	1,692.2	699.4	927.3	6,132.3	3,337.2	820.3	983.9	86.4	75.1	829.5
1995	536.3	997.3	2,681.4	1,934.8	803.0	995.8	6,547.6	3,511.1	817.6	1,122.8	96.9	78.6	920.5
1996	580.1	1,088.9	3,072.6	2,181.6	871.7	1,068.9	6,978.9	3,741.6	850.0	1,211.6	101.4	94.4	979.9
1997	635.7	1,266.4	3,604.2	2,595.7	1,082.8	1,173.1	7,460.9	4,009.6	891.3	1,264.1	104.6	131.2	1,060.1

[1] Data are year-end levels; not seasonally adjusted.

[2] Only directly held and those in closed-end funds. Other equities are included in series Cj1067–1072.

[3] Includes corporate farms.

Sources

Flow-of-funds data are available at the Federal Reserve Board's Internet site. The data for 1945–1996 are also available in a series of six hard copy releases by the Board of Governors of the Federal Reserve System, Flow of Funds Accounts of the United States, Annual Flows and Outstandings, 1945–1953, 1954–1962, 1963–1972, 1973–1981, 1982–1990, and 1991–1996, all dated December 11, 1997. Updates are available in Federal Reserve Statistical Release Z.1, Flow of Funds Accounts of the United States, Flows and Outstandings, published quarterly.

Documentation

This table represents the combined statement for the household sector, nonfarm noncorporate business, and farm business. The personal sector excludes corporate business and government.

The table is useful in separating securities directly held by the personal sector from those it held indirectly through mutual funds, life insurance and pension reserves, and bank personal trusts (see footnote to series Cj1066).

TABLE Cj1081–1132   Flow-of-funds balance sheet – households and nonprofit organizations: 1945–1997[1, 2]

Contributed by John A. James and Richard Sylla

					Assets					
		Tangible assets						**Financial assets**		
		Real estate							**Deposits**	
					Equipment owned by nonprofit organizations					Checkable deposits and currency
	Total	Total	Households	Nonprofit organizations		Consumer durable goods	Total	Total	Foreign	
	Cj1081	Cj1082	Cj1083	Cj1084	Cj1085	Cj1086	Cj1087	Cj1088	Cj1089	Cj1090	Cj1091
Year	Billion dollars	Billion dollars	Billion dollars	Billion dollars	Billion dollars	Billion dollars	Billion dollars	Billion dollars	Billion dollars	Billion dollars	Billion dollars
1945	757.4	198.0	150.6	131.2	19.4	0.4	47.0	559.3	104.2	—	54.0
1946	828.0	230.3	175.5	150.8	24.6	0.5	54.3	597.8	115.5	—	58.9
1947	914.3	273.7	207.8	178.6	29.2	0.6	65.3	640.6	118.8	—	58.7
1948	966.0	307.1	231.6	200.7	30.9	0.7	74.8	658.8	118.6	—	56.3
1949	1,013.7	334.2	249.8	218.0	31.8	0.8	83.6	679.5	119.4	—	54.4
1950	1,114.9	379.4	279.6	244.3	35.3	1.1	98.7	735.5	124.3	—	56.9
1951	1,222.3	422.8	310.8	271.9	38.9	1.3	110.7	799.6	133.3	—	61.0
1952	1,282.5	455.7	336.8	295.8	41.0	1.4	117.6	826.7	142.7	—	63.1
1953	1,330.1	485.2	358.2	316.1	42.0	1.6	125.5	844.9	152.0	—	64.3
1954	1,436.4	512.6	381.9	338.5	43.4	1.8	128.9	923.8	162.9	—	66.0
1955	1,567.4	556.1	416.0	368.1	47.9	2.0	138.1	1,011.3	172.4	—	67.0
1956	1,679.1	598.6	447.6	395.1	52.5	2.3	148.7	1,080.5	183.4	—	68.7
1957	1,727.0	633.6	473.3	418.0	55.3	2.5	157.8	1,093.4	194.3	—	67.8
1958	1,881.9	660.4	496.0	439.3	56.7	2.8	161.6	1,221.5	210.4	—	70.1
1959	1,989.9	692.9	522.9	464.4	58.5	3.1	166.9	1,297.0	223.9	—	72.4
1960	2,071.1	724.3	549.4	487.6	61.7	3.3	171.7	1,346.8	237.6	—	74.1
1961	2,246.7	755.6	577.8	511.7	66.1	3.4	174.3	1,491.1	254.5	—	72.9
1962	2,323.1	788.8	605.0	533.8	71.2	3.6	180.1	1,534.3	279.9	—	72.5
1963	2,455.9	824.1	630.2	553.9	76.4	3.8	190.0	1,631.8	310.6	—	77.3
1964	2,656.6	867.9	663.6	580.4	83.1	4.1	200.3	1,788.6	343.0	—	83.7
1965	2,870.2	914.3	697.8	606.2	91.5	4.4	212.1	1,955.9	377.2	—	90.5
1966	2,966.4	986.9	750.1	649.6	100.5	4.8	232.0	1,979.6	398.7	—	93.1
1967	3,284.1	1,054.4	795.6	686.3	109.4	5.1	253.6	2,229.8	444.2	—	103.8
1968	3,674.5	1,178.9	891.3	768.8	122.5	5.5	282.1	2,495.6	484.2	—	113.5
1969	3,745.8	1,284.4	971.4	833.1	138.3	6.0	307.1	2,461.4	488.9	—	110.6
1970	3,922.3	1,365.8	1,028.5	875.0	153.5	6.4	331.0	2,556.5	537.7	—	118.2
1971	4,337.7	1,490.0	1,130.8	957.8	173.0	6.8	352.4	2,847.7	615.3	—	132.0
1972	4,952.4	1,685.8	1,296.1	1,099.3	196.8	8.0	381.8	3,266.6	698.1	—	144.0
1973	5,157.2	1,912.4	1,480.1	1,252.2	227.9	9.6	422.8	3,244.8	737.6	—	122.2
1974	5,228.1	2,020.3	1,520.3	1,261.8	258.5	12.6	487.4	3,207.9	799.2	—	126.9
1975	5,908.9	2,243.2	1,691.6	1,414.2	277.4	14.7	536.9	3,665.7	877.9	—	140.6
1976	6,655.9	2,494.6	1,888.1	1,590.6	297.4	16.9	589.7	4,161.3	987.7	—	155.1
1977	7,312.0	2,891.6	2,219.1	1,887.5	331.6	18.5	654.1	4,420.4	1,102.3	—	177.4
1978	8,300.3	3,347.8	2,587.5	2,212.0	375.5	20.8	739.5	4,952.4	1,220.6	—	197.9
1979	9,573.7	3,889.2	3,034.8	2,604.8	430.0	23.0	831.3	5,684.5	1,337.2	—	218.1
1980	10,923.1	4,366.1	3,421.8	2,944.6	477.2	26.1	918.2	6,557.0	1,493.6	—	228.1
1981	11,802.5	4,830.0	3,813.8	3,294.9	518.9	28.3	987.9	6,972.5	1,686.2	—	245.6
1982	12,645.0	5,056.4	3,999.4	3,449.8	549.6	30.2	1,026.8	7,588.6	1,847.7	2.4	257.5
1983	13,683.8	5,300.5	4,181.0	3,605.2	575.8	32.0	1,087.6	8,383.3	2,027.9	6.9	281.0
1984	14,776.4	5,833.9	4,629.8	4,018.3	611.5	33.9	1,170.2	8,942.4	2,309.2	6.9	289.8
1985	16,634.5	6,535.5	5,235.3	4,592.2	643.1	35.2	1,265.0	10,099.0	2,461.2	7.8	319.3
1986	18,333.0	7,146.6	5,719.3	5,040.7	678.6	37.6	1,389.6	11,186.4	2,695.6	8.8	436.4
1987	19,590.4	7,724.4	6,176.7	5,465.2	711.5	40.8	1,506.9	11,866.0	2,840.6	9.8	436.5
1988	21,419.3	8,398.6	6,712.6	5,954.4	758.2	44.6	1,641.4	13,020.7	3,029.2	10.7	414.6
1989	23,475.1	9,107.9	7,296.0	6,494.9	801.1	48.5	1,763.4	14,367.1	3,182.8	11.9	404.1
1990	24,184.5	9,324.7	7,405.8	6,608.5	797.3	52.6	1,866.3	14,859.9	3,241.5	13.4	385.6
1991	25,912.9	9,470.0	7,478.4	6,716.0	762.3	56.6	1,935.1	16,442.9	3,244.3	14.6	426.6
1992	27,050.3	9,732.9	7,665.8	6,948.8	717.0	62.0	2,005.0	17,317.4	3,226.7	15.6	523.6
1993	28,401.9	9,981.8	7,807.0	7,105.0	702.0	67.0	2,107.9	18,420.0	3,160.3	15.8	570.8
1994	29,386.8	10,319.2	8,020.6	7,281.9	738.8	72.2	2,226.3	19,067.6	3,135.1	18.8	541.0
1995	32,381.7	10,805.6	8,404.5	7,631.0	773.5	77.7	2,323.4	21,576.1	3,349.7	23.4	483.2
1996	35,208.2	11,396.9	8,897.3	8,088.0	809.3	84.4	2,415.2	23,811.3	3,542.9	35.5	416.9
1997	39,333.9	12,170.8	9,588.2	8,688.3	899.9	89.1	2,493.5	27,163.1	3,828.7	49.3	404.0

Notes appear at end of table

(continued)

TABLE Cj1081–1132   Flow-of-funds balance sheet – households and nonprofit organizations: 1945–1997 *Continued*

							Assets					
							Financial assets					
	Deposits						Credit market instruments					
							U.S. government securities					
							Treasury					
	Time and savings	Money market mutual fund shares	Total	Open market paper	Total	Total	Savings bonds	Other Treasury	Agency	Municipal securities	Corporate and foreign bonds	Mortgages
	Cj1092	Cj1093	Cj1094	Cj1095	Cj1096	Cj1097	Cj1098	Cj1099	Cj1100	Cj1101	Cj1102	Cj1103
Year	Billion dollars	Billion dollars	Billion dollars	Billion dollars	Billion dollars	Billion dollars	Billion dollars	Billion dollars	Billion dollars	Billion dollars	Billion dollars	Billion dollars
1945	50.3	—	90.8	0.0	66.4	66.5	42.9	23.6	−0.1	3.9	8.4	12.2
1946	56.6	—	90.0	0.1	64.9	65.1	44.2	21.0	−0.2	3.8	7.5	13.7
1947	60.1	—	91.1	0.1	64.8	65.1	46.2	18.8	−0.3	4.5	6.6	15.0
1948	62.3	—	93.4	0.2	65.6	65.8	47.8	18.0	−0.2	4.6	6.7	16.2
1949	65.0	—	94.3	0.3	67.0	67.3	49.3	18.0	−0.2	3.7	6.3	17.0
1950	67.4	—	95.7	0.4	66.1	66.5	49.6	16.9	−0.4	5.5	6.0	17.6
1951	72.2	—	96.6	0.8	65.2	65.4	49.1	16.3	−0.2	5.7	6.3	18.6
1952	79.6	—	104.6	1.0	67.4	67.4	49.2	18.2	0.0	11.0	6.0	19.2
1953	87.8	—	109.6	1.3	68.2	68.0	49.4	18.7	0.2	13.9	6.0	20.2
1954	96.9	—	109.5	1.1	66.2	66.1	50.0	16.1	0.1	16.0	4.9	21.4
1955	105.4	—	117.6	1.4	69.4	68.8	50.2	18.6	0.6	19.2	5.0	22.7
1956	114.7	—	124.9	1.4	71.2	70.2	50.1	20.1	1.0	21.9	6.1	24.3
1957	126.5	—	131.9	1.7	73.0	71.5	48.2	23.3	1.5	23.9	7.2	26.2
1958	140.3	—	132.7	1.8	69.5	68.6	47.7	20.9	0.8	24.6	7.9	28.8
1959	151.5	—	142.8	1.6	73.9	71.6	45.9	25.7	2.3	28.4	8.2	30.7
1960	163.4	—	150.9	2.6	73.2	72.2	45.6	26.6	1.0	31.0	10.6	33.5
1961	181.6	—	154.9	2.2	72.5	71.9	46.4	25.5	0.6	32.5	10.8	36.8
1962	207.4	—	158.2	3.0	74.0	73.7	47.0	26.8	0.2	32.1	10.2	39.0
1963	233.3	—	159.8	4.2	72.9	72.9	48.1	24.7	0.0	32.1	10.1	40.5
1964	259.3	—	166.2	5.2	73.8	73.6	49.1	24.5	0.2	34.9	10.3	42.0
1965	286.8	—	170.2	6.0	75.9	74.8	49.7	25.1	1.1	36.5	9.2	42.6
1966	305.5	—	190.9	8.3	84.9	79.1	50.2	28.8	5.9	41.2	11.9	44.6
1967	340.4	—	196.3	10.1	85.2	78.9	51.2	27.7	6.3	38.2	16.3	46.5
1968	370.8	—	206.7	12.2	87.8	81.6	51.9	29.8	6.1	36.5	21.4	49.0
1969	378.3	—	217.0	14.8	95.4	88.2	51.8	36.4	7.2	36.4	21.3	49.1
1970	419.4	—	216.3	12.5	89.0	77.5	52.1	25.4	11.5	35.4	29.5	50.0
1971	483.3	—	204.0	8.6	79.8	69.2	54.4	14.8	10.6	31.9	36.5	47.3
1972	554.1	—	199.5	3.4	77.1	72.2	57.7	14.5	4.9	32.4	38.4	48.2
1973	615.5	—	220.6	7.5	85.6	81.9	60.4	21.5	3.7	39.0	41.3	47.2
1974	670.0	2.4	262.3	15.6	96.1	87.8	63.3	24.5	8.3	47.1	52.9	50.5
1975	733.7	3.7	272.9	12.1	102.5	101.4	67.4	34.0	1.1	50.0	63.9	44.4
1976	829.3	3.4	276.4	8.2	95.6	91.0	72.0	19.0	4.6	52.5	72.1	48.0
1977	921.9	3.0	287.6	22.6	95.2	94.9	76.8	18.2	0.3	56.3	61.8	51.7
1978	1,014.3	8.5	328.3	36.4	100.7	100.1	80.7	19.4	0.6	80.1	51.5	59.6
1979	1,080.8	38.3	399.7	43.5	144.8	144.5	79.9	64.7	0.3	96.2	45.6	69.6
1980	1,203.3	62.2	424.7	38.3	165.4	160.0	72.5	87.5	5.3	104.5	30.8	85.8
1981	1,292.5	148.1	443.7	26.6	153.9	152.7	68.2	84.5	1.2	131.3	30.5	101.4
1982	1,407.5	180.3	506.3	30.3	170.6	169.4	68.3	101.0	1.2	170.0	24.4	111.1
1983	1,590.9	149.1	589.3	25.0	215.2	213.2	71.5	141.7	2.0	211.2	26.7	111.2
1984	1,821.5	191.0	694.2	42.0	271.5	253.4	74.5	178.9	18.1	250.7	27.5	102.5
1985	1,940.9	193.3	848.8	35.0	270.3	241.5	79.8	161.7	28.8	346.4	77.5	119.7
1986	2,024.9	225.6	862.7	30.6	256.6	228.7	93.3	135.4	27.9	352.6	107.3	115.5
1987	2,147.4	246.9	1,030.1	32.9	294.5	259.5	101.1	158.4	35.0	452.6	125.9	124.2
1988	2,342.1	261.8	1,232.3	67.3	394.1	342.2	109.6	232.6	52.0	523.8	121.2	129.9
1989	2,428.8	338.0	1,296.6	56.9	402.6	322.5	117.7	204.8	80.1	547.2	155.3	134.5
1990	2,477.5	364.9	1,499.8	63.2	517.2	393.6	126.2	267.4	123.6	574.5	200.8	144.2
1991	2,423.7	379.5	1,592.5	33.3	492.9	381.0	138.1	242.8	111.9	614.1	304.7	147.6
1992	2,349.0	338.6	1,645.8	29.9	596.3	458.5	157.3	301.2	137.8	585.5	297.3	136.8
1993	2,235.9	337.9	1,635.1	45.5	574.5	475.0	171.9	303.1	99.4	552.6	333.7	128.9
1994	2,223.9	351.3	1,945.7	46.7	904.7	662.2	179.9	482.3	242.4	502.2	373.7	118.5
1995	2,393.9	449.2	1,913.3	59.9	841.0	580.6	185.0	395.6	260.5	459.1	440.3	112.9
1996	2,561.9	528.7	1,979.3	82.6	901.4	564.4	187.0	377.4	336.9	441.1	445.4	108.8
1997	2,736.3	639.0	1,833.8	122.6	697.8	329.2	186.5	142.7	368.6	463.3	445.8	104.2

TABLE Cj1081–1132   Flow-of-funds balance sheet – households and nonprofit organizations: 1945–1997 *Continued*

	Assets								Liabilities		
	Financial assets								Credit market instruments		
	Corporate equities	Mutual fund shares	Security credit	Life insurance reserves	Pension fund reserves	Investment in bank personal trusts	Equity in noncorporate business	Miscellaneous assets	Total	Total	Home mortgages
	Cj1104	Cj1105	Cj1106	Cj1107	Cj1108	Cj1109	Cj1110	Cj1111	Cj1112	Cj1113	Cj1114
Year	Billion dollars	Billion dollars	Billion dollars	Billion dollars	Billion dollars	Billion dollars	Billion dollars	Billion dollars	Billion dollars	Billion dollars	Billion dollars
1945	109.5	1.3	0.7	39.6	12.3	—	194.8	6.3	29.7	27.4	18.0
1946	101.3	1.3	0.7	43.4	13.5	—	225.1	7.1	36.1	34.1	21.9
1947	98.8	1.4	0.7	46.5	15.8	—	260.0	7.6	44.7	42.5	26.6
1948	97.5	1.5	0.7	49.4	18.3	—	271.6	8.0	52.8	50.5	31.3
1949	105.0	3.1	0.7	52.1	21.1	—	275.5	8.4	60.9	58.1	35.4
1950	128.7	3.3	1.0	55.0	24.3	—	294.4	8.7	73.2	69.8	41.8
1951	151.1	3.5	0.9	57.8	27.9	—	319.4	9.3	81.7	78.2	48.1
1952	151.0	3.9	0.7	60.7	33.5	—	319.6	10.0	93.5	89.7	54.3
1953	145.8	4.1	0.7	63.6	38.5	—	319.9	10.6	106.0	101.7	61.6
1954	198.8	6.1	1.0	66.3	43.9	—	324.2	10.9	117.6	112.3	70.2
1955	248.2	7.8	0.9	69.3	52.0	—	331.7	11.4	138.2	132.3	82.3
1956	271.0	9.0	0.9	72.7	58.2	—	348.6	11.7	153.5	147.2	93.0
1957	244.5	8.7	0.9	75.5	64.6	—	360.9	12.0	165.7	159.4	101.5
1958	322.3	13.2	1.2	78.5	74.9	—	375.9	12.3	177.1	169.7	110.7
1959	357.3	15.8	1.0	82.0	85.0	—	376.5	12.8	199.2	191.2	123.1
1960	359.8	17.0	1.1	85.2	93.9	—	388.0	13.3	216.4	208.2	133.9
1961	443.2	22.9	1.2	88.6	107.2	—	404.8	13.8	233.6	224.0	145.7
1962	431.2	20.9	1.2	92.4	113.7	—	422.4	14.3	254.9	245.1	159.1
1963	469.9	24.8	1.2	96.6	128.0	—	426.0	14.8	282.6	270.9	174.8
1964	544.1	28.4	1.7	101.1	144.8	—	443.7	15.7	310.8	299.1	191.1
1965	616.1	34.4	2.5	105.9	162.0	—	470.6	17.0	339.4	326.6	207.3
1966	548.3	33.9	2.7	110.6	172.5	—	503.9	18.2	361.8	348.4	219.8
1967	682.1	43.0	4.9	115.5	195.6	—	528.2	19.8	384.3	366.9	232.3
1968	815.3	49.5	7.0	120.3	218.7	—	572.0	21.6	418.4	397.4	247.4
1969	587.4	41.5	5.2	125.4	230.9	135.2	606.1	23.8	445.5	426.8	262.7
1970	572.5	40.4	4.4	130.7	253.8	137.9	636.5	26.3	463.8	445.3	274.2
1971	650.9	48.1	4.9	137.1	293.5	163.0	702.3	28.7	509.4	487.1	297.2
1972	813.7	50.6	5.0	143.9	349.3	187.1	788.0	31.3	571.7	544.5	332.5
1973	597.5	38.7	4.9	151.3	358.5	175.0	926.6	34.1	638.3	614.1	371.4
1974	373.4	28.2	3.9	158.4	367.8	147.3	1,030.5	36.8	688.1	663.5	402.5
1975	499.0	34.4	4.5	166.5	467.5	169.3	1,133.1	40.6	741.8	715.3	439.9
1976	637.4	36.2	5.7	175.3	535.4	195.9	1,265.3	46.0	833.9	802.3	500.4
1977	542.5	35.6	5.7	184.8	591.0	194.0	1,423.8	52.9	969.5	934.6	590.9
1978	550.3	36.2	8.5	196.0	692.7	206.6	1,653.7	59.5	1,133.5	1,094.2	697.4
1979	674.9	39.4	10.4	206.7	802.6	230.6	1,916.3	66.7	1,300.9	1,259.1	809.7
1980	902.9	45.6	16.2	216.4	962.5	265.3	2,156.2	73.5	1,427.1	1,375.6	906.1
1981	809.7	46.6	14.7	225.6	1,056.2	271.6	2,337.7	80.4	1,536.0	1,483.5	974.5
1982	869.7	57.3	17.8	232.8	1,280.9	288.5	2,400.1	87.4	1,607.9	1,551.0	1,005.7
1983	983.8	87.7	20.6	240.8	1,530.3	318.1	2,481.9	102.9	1,777.9	1,709.6	1,093.8
1984	914.3	104.6	21.6	246.0	1,699.2	331.1	2,518.1	104.2	1,990.1	1,921.9	1,221.5
1985	1,127.5	197.9	35.1	257.0	2,047.0	384.3	2,607.7	132.5	2,329.6	2,239.4	1,411.2
1986	1,418.3	333.2	44.0	274.9	2,274.3	429.1	2,704.6	149.8	2,592.0	2,494.1	1,605.1
1987	1,384.2	381.7	39.1	301.0	2,432.4	442.1	2,839.8	174.9	2,839.8	2,751.5	1,824.2
1988	1,639.9	401.3	40.9	326.6	2,668.7	470.3	3,020.1	191.3	3,124.9	3,024.3	2,034.6
1989	1,963.6	469.1	53.2	355.3	3,137.5	541.4	3,161.4	206.2	3,415.4	3,298.9	2,238.7
1990	1,795.4	467.8	62.4	380.9	3,388.2	551.7	3,247.6	224.4	3,706.1	3,582.0	2,488.9
1991	2,577.9	586.6	87.0	406.8	3,876.9	639.3	3,197.5	234.1	3,907.1	3,758.6	2,654.8
1992	2,919.7	727.9	76.2	434.8	4,217.9	660.6	3,156.7	251.0	4,074.8	3,923.1	2,796.9
1993	3,220.7	990.9	102.3	470.8	4,662.0	691.3	3,222.6	264.1	4,316.5	4,134.3	2,923.3
1994	3,048.9	1,052.1	109.0	505.3	4,880.1	699.4	3,422.6	269.5	4,632.1	4,446.2	3,096.1
1995	4,042.5	1,257.2	127.6	550.2	5,599.6	803.0	3,647.5	285.4	4,999.0	4,800.4	3,272.1
1996	4,602.3	1,571.3	162.9	593.8	6,329.5	871.7	3,863.3	294.3	5,360.0	5,143.9	3,503.9
1997	5,624.6	2,002.1	214.5	649.7	7,452.2	1,082.8	4,156.7	318.0	5,755.1	5,497.0	3,768.6

(continued)

TABLE Cj1081–1132   Flow-of-funds balance sheet – households and nonprofit organizations: 1945–1997 *Continued*

	Liabilities								
	Credit market instruments							Deferred and unpaid life insurance premiums	Net worth
	Consumer credit	Municipal securities	Bank loans not elsewhere classified	Other loans and advances	Commercial mortgages	Security credit	Trade payables		
	Cj1115	Cj1116 [3]	Cj1117	Cj1118	Cj1119 [3]	Cj1120	Cj1121 [3]	Cj1122	Cj1123
Year	Billion dollars	Billion dollars	Billion dollars	Billion dollars	Billion dollars	Billion dollars	Billion dollars	Billion dollars	Billion dollars
1945	6.8	—	0.2	2.1	0.3	1.2	0.5	0.6	727.6
1946	9.7	—	0.1	2.0	0.4	0.6	0.7	0.7	791.9
1947	13.2	—	0.1	2.1	0.5	0.6	0.8	0.8	869.7
1948	16.3	—	0.1	2.2	0.7	0.6	0.9	0.8	913.2
1949	19.4	—	0.1	2.4	0.9	0.9	0.9	0.9	952.8
1950	23.9	—	0.2	2.6	1.2	1.5	1.0	1.0	1,041.7
1951	25.4	—	0.4	2.8	1.5	1.4	1.0	1.1	1,140.7
1952	30.5	—	0.2	2.9	1.8	1.5	1.1	1.2	1,189.0
1953	34.6	—	0.3	3.1	2.1	1.8	1.2	1.3	1,224.1
1954	36.0	—	0.4	3.4	2.3	2.6	1.3	1.3	1,318.8
1955	42.9	—	1.7	3.6	1.9	3.0	1.4	1.5	1,429.2
1956	46.6	—	1.0	3.9	2.7	3.1	1.5	1.7	1,525.7
1957	49.2	—	1.4	4.4	3.0	2.7	1.7	1.8	1,561.3
1958	49.5	—	1.0	4.8	3.7	3.7	1.8	2.0	1,704.8
1959	57.2	—	1.2	5.4	4.2	3.7	2.2	2.2	1,790.7
1960	61.2	—	1.9	6.3	4.9	3.6	2.3	2.4	1,854.7
1961	63.4	—	2.6	7.0	5.3	4.6	2.5	2.5	2,013.0
1962	69.3	—	3.1	7.7	5.8	4.5	2.6	2.7	2,068.2
1963	77.9	—	3.5	8.4	6.3	6.0	2.9	2.9	2,173.3
1964	87.4	—	4.8	9.2	6.7	5.5	3.2	3.0	2,345.7
1965	97.5	—	4.4	10.0	7.5	5.9	3.6	3.3	2,530.8
1966	103.4	—	5.1	11.9	8.1	5.8	4.0	3.7	2,604.6
1967	108.6	—	5.5	13.3	7.2	8.9	4.6	3.9	2,899.9
1968	119.3	—	6.2	15.3	9.2	11.5	5.2	4.3	3,256.1
1969	129.2	—	6.8	18.3	9.8	8.2	5.8	4.7	3,300.3
1970	133.7	—	6.1	20.9	10.6	6.9	6.5	5.1	3,458.5
1971	149.2	—	7.3	22.3	11.2	9.5	7.3	5.4	3,828.3
1972	168.8	—	7.6	23.6	11.9	13.1	8.2	6.0	4,380.7
1973	193.0	0.4	11.2	26.2	11.9	8.9	8.9	6.4	4,518.9
1974	201.9	1.3	16.8	29.4	11.6	7.4	10.1	7.1	4,540.1
1975	207.0	2.7	23.0	31.5	11.1	8.3	10.6	7.7	5,167.1
1976	229.0	4.7	23.4	33.4	11.5	12.5	10.7	8.4	5,822.0
1977	264.4	8.1	23.4	35.7	12.1	14.5	11.1	9.3	6,342.5
1978	310.4	10.7	23.1	39.5	13.0	17.1	11.9	10.3	7,166.8
1979	353.1	13.6	22.4	45.9	14.4	17.5	12.6	11.7	8,272.8
1980	355.4	16.7	27.8	54.7	14.8	24.7	13.8	12.9	9,496.0
1981	373.1	21.1	33.5	65.8	15.5	23.0	14.8	14.7	10,266.5
1982	390.3	29.6	35.1	73.2	17.1	25.8	15.6	15.5	11,037.1
1983	440.3	41.0	35.6	73.4	25.5	34.2	18.0	16.1	11,905.9
1984	521.0	51.2	22.0	75.4	30.9	31.8	21.2	15.1	12,786.3
1985	603.8	81.3	31.0	79.0	33.1	50.7	24.3	15.2	14,304.8
1986	658.2	78.4	31.0	83.2	38.3	57.4	26.6	13.9	15,741.0
1987	688.6	78.1	31.9	84.4	44.4	41.8	31.4	15.1	16,750.7
1988	732.0	79.9	30.0	88.9	59.0	43.5	41.5	15.5	18,294.5
1989	793.3	83.3	20.4	90.3	72.8	42.5	57.6	16.4	20,059.7
1990	805.1	86.6	17.9	100.9	82.5	38.8	68.9	16.5	20,478.4
1991	794.5	90.6	13.1	110.2	95.5	55.1	77.7	15.7	22,005.8
1992	798.3	90.0	17.6	119.5	100.9	53.5	82.5	15.8	22,975.5
1993	859.0	89.5	27.4	126.6	108.5	76.1	89.8	16.3	24,085.4
1994	983.9	91.0	40.0	133.7	101.5	75.1	94.0	16.8	24,754.7
1995	1,122.8	91.9	56.0	160.3	97.3	78.6	102.4	17.5	27,382.7
1996	1,211.6	97.9	52.3	172.7	105.5	94.4	103.9	17.9	29,848.2
1997	1,264.1	108.8	55.5	190.7	109.2	131.2	106.8	20.1	33,578.7

Notes appear at end of table

TABLE Cj1081–1132   Flow-of-funds balance sheet – households and nonprofit organizations: 1945–1997   *Continued*

	Replacement cost value of structures								
	Residential								
							Household net worth as a percentage of disposable personal income	Owners' equity in household real estate	Owners' equity as a percentage of household real estate
	Total	Households	Farm households	Nonprofit organizations	Nonresidential (nonprofits)	Disposable personal income			
	Cj1124	Cj1125	Cj1126	Cj1127	Cj1128	Cj1129	Cj1130	Cj1131	Cj1132
Year	Billion dollars	Billion dollars	Billion dollars	Billion dollars	Billion dollars	Billion dollars	Percent	Billion dollars	Percent
1945	117.6	96.4	16.2	5.0	10.7	150.7	482.8	113.2	86.3
1946	140.6	115.7	19.0	5.9	13.5	160.6	493.1	128.9	85.5
1947	169.0	140.2	21.9	6.9	16.5	170.8	509.2	152.0	85.1
1948	187.8	157.2	23.3	7.3	17.6	190.1	480.4	169.5	84.4
1949	201.1	169.4	24.1	7.5	17.9	189.8	502.0	182.6	83.8
1950	225.8	192.3	25.5	8.0	19.9	209.6	497.0	202.5	82.9
1951	249.3	213.9	26.9	8.5	22.4	230.2	495.5	223.8	82.3
1952	265.9	229.7	27.5	8.7	23.6	242.5	490.3	241.5	81.6
1953	280.1	243.5	27.8	8.8	24.2	258.0	474.4	254.6	80.5
1954	297.9	260.6	28.3	9.0	25.2	263.9	499.8	268.3	79.2
1955	323.1	284.7	29.0	9.3	27.8	282.7	505.6	285.9	77.7
1956	344.0	304.7	29.6	9.6	31.0	301.8	505.5	302.1	76.5
1957	358.7	319.2	29.7	9.8	32.8	318.4	490.4	316.6	75.7
1958	372.5	332.6	29.8	10.1	34.0	329.5	517.5	328.6	74.8
1959	391.8	351.4	30.0	10.4	35.0	349.9	511.8	341.3	73.5
1960	400.6	359.3	30.2	11.1	36.9	363.8	509.8	353.7	72.5
1961	408.0	365.7	30.5	11.8	39.2	379.7	530.2	366.0	71.5
1962	416.1	372.6	30.7	12.8	42.3	402.2	514.2	374.7	70.2
1963	429.8	386.2	30.5	13.1	45.5	422.0	514.9	379.1	68.4
1964	465.7	419.6	31.7	14.4	49.3	458.5	511.7	389.4	67.1
1965	496.7	448.6	32.6	15.5	54.3	494.9	511.4	398.9	65.8
1966	534.9	483.4	34.4	17.1	59.4	534.7	487.1	429.8	66.2
1967	572.9	518.7	36.0	18.2	64.6	572.9	506.2	454.0	66.1
1968	635.2	576.0	38.9	20.3	72.3	622.5	523.1	521.4	67.8
1969	678.9	616.3	40.7	21.9	81.6	669.4	493.0	570.3	68.5
1970	717.0	651.6	42.2	23.2	91.5	728.1	475.0	600.9	68.7
1971	803.9	732.0	45.7	26.1	103.8	791.5	483.7	660.6	69.0
1972	895.7	817.0	49.2	29.5	118.2	856.8	511.3	766.7	69.7
1973	1,028.0	940.0	54.3	33.6	134.4	967.0	467.3	880.8	70.3
1974	1,161.1	1,061.8	61.0	38.3	151.4	1,056.8	429.6	859.3	68.1
1975	1,258.2	1,152.2	65.0	41.1	163.3	1,162.6	444.4	974.3	68.9
1976	1,412.1	1,296.8	70.7	44.6	173.6	1,277.1	455.9	1,090.2	68.5
1977	1,657.0	1,526.2	80.0	50.8	190.8	1,406.1	451.1	1,296.6	68.7
1978	1,936.0	1,789.1	90.1	56.8	213.5	1,585.8	451.9	1,514.6	68.5
1979	2,259.0	2,093.0	101.5	64.5	240.6	1,775.7	465.9	1,795.1	68.9
1980	2,544.4	2,360.2	112.3	71.9	268.2	1,980.6	479.5	2,038.5	69.2
1981	2,740.0	2,544.4	118.7	77.0	292.1	2,208.3	464.9	2,320.4	70.4
1982	2,861.4	2,659.0	121.9	80.6	310.3	2,355.8	468.5	2,444.1	70.8
1983	2,983.7	2,777.4	123.3	83.0	324.3	2,531.5	470.3	2,511.3	69.7
1984	3,166.3	2,953.5	126.2	86.6	342.1	2,819.9	453.4	2,796.8	69.6
1985	3,344.5	3,125.3	128.6	90.5	357.2	3,012.2	474.9	3,181.0	69.3
1986	3,616.6	3,386.4	133.6	96.6	377.0	3,198.5	492.1	3,435.6	68.2
1987	3,876.6	3,636.3	138.4	102.0	398.1	3,374.5	496.4	3,641.0	66.6
1988	4,150.4	3,901.4	142.5	106.5	420.7	3,652.7	500.9	3,919.9	65.8
1989	4,408.5	4,151.4	146.9	110.2	444.3	3,906.1	513.5	4,256.2	65.5
1990	4,607.3	4,343.1	151.2	113.0	465.0	4,179.4	490.0	4,119.6	62.3
1991	4,710.0	4,445.9	152.0	112.1	474.9	4,356.8	505.1	4,061.3	60.5
1992	4,985.5	4,713.9	156.8	114.8	493.3	4,626.7	496.6	4,151.9	59.8
1993	5,328.8	5,049.6	162.2	117.0	521.6	4,829.2	498.7	4,181.6	58.9
1994	5,749.9	5,459.0	170.7	120.2	551.5	5,052.7	489.9	4,185.8	57.5
1995	6,020.5	5,724.0	175.0	121.5	575.1	5,355.7	511.3	4,358.9	57.1
1996	6,348.5	6,044.6	179.6	124.4	597.3	5,608.4	532.2	4,584.1	56.7
1997	6,712.8	6,402.8	183.0	127.0	630.9	5,885.2	570.6	4,919.6	56.6

[1] Includes farm households.

[2] Data are levels; not seasonally adjusted.

[3] Liabilities of nonprofit organizations.

Sources

Flow-of-funds data are available at the Federal Reserve Board's Internet site. The data for 1945–1996 are also available in a series of six hard copy

(continued)

TABLE Cj1081–1132   Flow-of-funds balance sheet – households and nonprofit organizations: 1945–1997 *Continued*

releases by the Board of Governors of the Federal Reserve System, *Flow of Funds Accounts of the United States, Annual Flows and Outstandings, 1945–1953, 1954–1962, 1963–1972, 1973–1981, 1982–1990,* and *1991–1996,* all dated December 11, 1997. Updates are available in Federal Reserve Statistical Release Z.1, *Flow of Funds Accounts of the United States, Flows and Outstandings,* published quarterly.

Documentation

For households and nonprofit organizations, the table shows total assets broken down into tangible assets and real assets, and components of each of these asset categories. It also shows total liabilities, again broken down into components, and net worth. Finally, the table gives the value of various classes of structures, the amount of owners' equity in household real estate, owners' equity as a percentage of the value of household real estate, and household net worth as a percentage of disposable personal income.

Series Cj1084. At market value. Includes vacant land and vacant homes for sale.

Series Cj1086–1087. At replacement (current) cost.

Series Cj1104. At market value.

Series Cj1105. Value based on market values of equities held and the book value of other assets held by mutual funds.

Series Cj1110. Owners' equity in noncorporate business, farm business, and unincorporated security brokers and dealers.

Series Cj1131. Equals series Cj1084 less series Cj1114.

Series Cj1132. Equals series Cj1131 divided by series Cj1084.

TABLE Cj1133–1178   Flow-of-funds balance sheet – nonfarm, nonfinancial corporate businesses: 1945–1997[1]

Contributed by John A. James and Richard Sylla

						With tangible assets stated at market value or replacement cost						
						Assets						
			Tangible					Financial assets				
	Assets	Total	Real estate	Equipment	Inventories	Total	Foreign deposits	Checkable deposits and currency	Time and savings deposits	Money market fund shares	Security repurchase agreements	Commercial paper
	Cj1133	Cj1134	Cj1135 [2]	Cj1136 [3]	Cj1137 [3]	Cj1138	Cj1139	Cj1140	Cj1141	Cj1142	Cj1143	Cj1144
Year	Billion dollars	Billion dollars	Billion dollars	Billion dollars	Billion dollars	Billion dollars	Billion dollars	Billion dollars	Billion dollars	Billion dollars	Billion dollars	Billion dollars
1945	266.1	197.3	131.7	32.1	33.4	68.8	0.0	19.0	0.9	—	—	—
1946	302.4	235.3	159.4	39.4	36.5	67.2	0.1	19.5	0.9	—	—	—
1947	354.6	278.8	188.0	48.3	42.5	75.9	0.1	21.4	0.9	—	—	0.1
1948	384.6	303.2	199.6	56.1	47.5	81.4	0.0	21.9	0.9	—	—	0.2
1949	393.9	308.6	203.8	61.4	43.4	85.3	0.0	22.9	0.9	—	—	0.3
1950	444.9	342.8	220.5	69.2	53.1	102.1	0.1	24.2	0.9	—	—	0.1
1951	488.6	378.6	240.5	77.1	61.0	110.1	0.1	25.9	0.9	—	—	0.1
1952	511.2	395.7	251.3	82.7	61.7	115.5	0.1	26.6	0.9	—	—	0.2
1953	529.8	411.3	258.9	89.0	63.4	118.5	0.1	26.6	0.9	—	—	0.2
1954	544.5	420.5	264.4	94.2	61.9	124.0	0.2	28.3	1.1	—	—	0.3
1955	597.9	456.5	284.2	103.6	68.6	141.4	0.1	29.3	1.0	—	—	0.2
1956	652.0	505.5	312.4	117.2	75.8	146.4	0.1	29.0	1.0	—	—	0.3
1957	686.2	535.2	328.6	129.1	77.5	151.0	0.1	29.0	1.0	—	—	0.4
1958	707.0	544.4	336.4	134.1	73.9	162.5	0.1	30.1	1.9	—	—	0.2
1959	744.8	567.2	342.7	140.8	83.7	177.6	0.1	29.2	1.5	—	—	0.7
1960	763.1	582.5	350.1	145.7	86.7	180.5	0.1	28.2	3.0	—	—	0.8
1961	790.4	597.2	358.7	149.4	89.2	193.2	0.2	31.7	4.1	—	—	1.1
1962	823.5	618.2	368.1	155.6	94.5	205.3	0.8	34.6	5.0	—	—	1.3
1963	862.1	641.3	378.5	162.4	100.4	220.8	0.7	33.4	5.7	—	—	1.0
1964	910.3	674.9	394.7	172.7	107.4	235.5	1.1	32.7	6.7	—	0.3	1.7
1965	985.6	722.6	419.1	186.3	117.1	263.0	0.8	33.1	9.0	—	0.6	1.4
1966	1,066.5	788.9	447.4	208.2	133.2	277.7	0.9	32.4	8.6	—	0.9	2.9
1967	1,149.2	853.6	478.8	229.6	145.1	295.7	1.1	34.8	9.7	—	0.7	4.0
1968	1,260.3	931.3	519.7	254.6	157.0	328.9	1.6	37.5	9.1	—	1.1	5.1
1969	1,392.3	1,028.8	574.7	281.5	172.5	363.5	1.2	43.1	3.7	—	3.3	7.6
1970	1,510.1	1,124.7	633.6	309.7	181.4	385.4	0.8	44.1	5.3	—	0.2	9.4
1971	1,651.6	1,224.4	702.3	331.2	190.9	427.2	1.2	42.6	9.5	—	1.1	11.3
1972	1,835.5	1,339.4	779.4	354.0	206.0	496.1	2.2	44.9	11.9	—	2.7	14.2
1973	2,105.7	1,531.1	895.3	393.4	242.3	574.6	3.3	46.3	16.6	—	11.3	14.9
1974	2,457.0	1,837.3	1,047.2	486.8	303.2	619.7	4.9	47.8	20.5	—	5.5	16.5
1975	2,818.8	2,040.4	1,170.8	556.5	313.1	778.4	2.2	45.2	38.3	—	1.2	8.4
1976	3,118.7	2,250.0	1,284.9	616.0	349.1	868.6	2.9	45.7	47.5	—	1.5	10.5
1977	3,477.3	2,507.0	1,419.9	693.8	393.2	970.3	5.1	41.1	63.6	0.2	2.1	9.4
1978	3,948.1	2,842.2	1,600.2	788.7	453.2	1,105.9	7.6	40.2	74.8	0.6	2.5	9.5
1979	4,551.7	3,265.5	1,824.1	912.5	528.9	1,286.2	9.2	43.5	80.4	3.0	3.1	9.6
1980	5,186.1	3,731.0	2,079.9	1,060.7	590.5	1,455.1	8.7	46.9	80.8	7.0	3.9	9.1
1981	5,817.7	4,166.6	2,342.9	1,177.6	646.1	1,651.2	11.1	50.5	69.8	18.4	1.8	8.2
1982	6,145.3	4,381.2	2,514.4	1,240.2	626.5	1,764.1	8.9	63.8	70.2	19.0	2.4	7.9
1983	6,462.7	4,518.7	2,587.7	1,282.3	648.8	1,944.0	12.9	69.4	93.2	11.2	3.2	12.2
1984	7,012.7	4,790.7	2,731.9	1,342.5	716.3	2,222.0	11.7	85.1	87.9	16.1	3.9	9.7
1985	7,502.3	5,006.3	2,853.9	1,421.0	731.4	2,496.1	14.3	96.2	99.8	14.5	3.4	10.5
1986	7,837.8	5,169.6	2,936.3	1,502.1	731.2	2,668.2	17.2	93.0	119.7	18.1	5.1	10.2
1987	8,342.9	5,440.1	3,083.4	1,567.7	789.0	2,902.7	14.4	104.8	116.6	18.9	3.4	15.0
1988	9,074.0	5,788.3	3,288.5	1,652.5	847.4	3,285.7	20.2	134.9	98.8	15.6	5.0	13.6
1989	9,620.8	6,101.7	3,471.9	1,735.8	894.0	3,519.1	13.3	151.1	89.7	16.2	2.8	14.3
1990	9,828.1	6,193.7	3,440.1	1,828.1	925.4	3,634.4	13.2	166.8	73.4	26.3	2.1	13.8
1991	9,806.9	6,042.7	3,253.9	1,875.8	913.0	3,764.2	15.0	182.5	66.8	31.5	1.6	14.7
1992	9,791.7	5,860.0	3,010.5	1,925.1	924.4	3,931.7	14.3	189.4	51.8	47.3	5.1	17.0
1993	10,146.0	5,857.0	2,900.1	1,994.1	962.7	4,289.0	12.9	203.1	74.1	44.8	2.5	19.4
1994	10,775.2	6,207.9	3,073.9	2,092.3	1,041.7	4,567.3	14.0	221.6	67.5	52.2	2.2	18.8
1995	11,589.3	6,530.5	3,205.3	2,222.2	1,103.0	5,058.8	15.6	252.9	42.9	77.0	2.4	20.1
1996	12,403.9	6,844.3	3,351.4	2,360.6	1,132.3	5,559.6	26.4	302.7	44.7	84.2	3.8	31.0
1997	13,457.7	7,368.5	3,771.0	2,424.8	1,172.7	6,089.2	30.0	313.2	46.1	98.3	4.3	33.9

Notes appear at end of table

(continued)

TABLE Cj1133–1178 Flow-of-funds balance sheet – nonfarm, nonfinancial corporate businesses: 1945–1997
Continued

	With tangible assets stated at market value or replacement cost												
	Assets								Liabilities				
	Financial assets									Credit market instruments			
	U.S. government securities	Municipal securities	Mortgages	Consumer credit	Trade receivables	Mutual fund shares	Miscellaneous assets	Total	Total	Commercial paper	Municipal securities	Corporate bonds
	Cj1145	Cj1146	Cj1147	Cj1148	Cj1149	Cj1150 [2]	Cj1151	Cj1152	Cj1153	Cj1154	Cj1155	Cj1156 [4]
Year	Billion dollars	Billion dollars	Billion dollars	Billion dollars	Billion dollars	Billion dollars	Billion dollars	Billion dollars	Billion dollars	Billion dollars	Billion dollars	Billion dollars
1945	18.5	0.3	—	2.8	19.8	—	7.5	70.2	45.1	0.1	—	23.9
1946	12.8	0.3	—	3.3	22.6	—	7.7	80.2	50.8	0.1	—	24.9
1947	12.3	0.4	—	4.1	27.6	—	9.1	93.0	58.0	0.2	—	27.7
1948	12.9	0.5	—	4.9	29.6	—	10.6	101.8	64.5	0.2	—	32.0
1949	14.7	0.5	—	5.5	28.6	—	11.9	101.1	66.3	0.2	—	34.9
1950	17.9	0.7	—	6.6	38.6	—	13.0	123.6	73.4	0.2	—	36.5
1951	18.7	0.8	—	7.2	42.0	—	14.5	136.4	82.1	0.3	—	39.8
1952	17.6	0.8	—	7.1	45.9	—	16.3	141.2	88.8	0.3	—	44.5
1953	19.2	1.0	—	7.3	45.0	—	18.2	146.1	93.2	0.4	—	48.0
1954	17.5	1.0	—	7.7	48.4	—	19.6	149.3	97.4	0.5	—	51.5
1955	21.6	1.2	—	8.3	58.0	—	21.6	171.3	106.4	0.4	—	54.6
1956	17.1	1.3	—	8.6	63.8	—	25.1	183.5	116.0	0.4	—	58.0
1957	16.4	1.5	—	8.7	65.4	—	28.4	192.9	125.9	0.4	—	64.1
1958	16.7	2.0	—	8.8	71.8	—	30.9	202.4	133.7	0.7	—	69.7
1959	22.8	1.8	—	10.1	77.4	—	34.0	219.2	142.7	0.3	—	72.8
1960	16.9	2.4	—	9.6	82.3	—	37.2	229.6	152.1	0.8	—	76.2
1961	15.3	2.4	—	9.6	88.3	—	40.5	242.1	160.2	1.1	—	80.6
1962	13.6	2.7	—	10.4	92.8	0.2	44.0	257.4	171.4	1.2	—	84.6
1963	16.7	3.8	—	11.3	99.1	0.2	48.8	277.9	183.0	1.0	—	88.4
1964	15.5	3.7	—	12.3	107.6	0.3	53.6	300.0	197.8	1.1	—	92.4
1965	13.8	4.6	—	13.2	120.9	0.3	65.4	335.2	218.7	0.8	—	97.3
1966	12.1	3.6	—	13.4	133.3	0.4	69.2	369.2	244.1	1.6	—	107.5
1967	9.6	3.3	—	13.7	141.6	0.6	76.7	397.0	270.8	3.0	—	122.1
1968	10.4	3.8	—	13.8	160.1	0.8	85.6	446.0	299.9	4.2	—	135.0
1969	7.3	2.8	—	13.9	183.0	0.7	96.8	500.4	335.3	5.4	—	147.0
1970	7.5	2.2	—	14.7	191.4	0.6	109.2	539.6	367.4	7.1	—	166.8
1971	10.0	3.2	—	17.3	203.8	0.7	126.6	585.3	395.6	6.2	0.1	185.6
1972	7.9	4.2	—	18.0	230.2	0.7	159.2	649.5	433.0	7.0	0.6	197.8
1973	4.5	4.0	—	19.2	269.3	0.8	184.4	760.8	497.0	8.4	2.4	206.9
1974	5.6	4.7	—	20.3	245.5	0.8	247.7	764.6	554.6	12.5	4.1	226.6
1975	17.5	4.8	9.7	21.2	271.4	0.9	357.5	1,086.9	575.2	9.6	6.7	253.8
1976	24.4	4.2	10.4	23.5	302.4	1.0	394.7	1,189.3	614.2	11.0	9.2	276.6
1977	19.2	4.4	13.6	24.4	346.4	0.8	440.0	1,335.3	687.6	12.8	17.4	299.5
1978	17.8	4.6	15.5	26.5	407.3	0.6	498.3	1,532.3	761.6	15.5	25.0	320.6
1979	15.3	4.5	18.8	28.3	479.7	1.1	589.9	1,789.3	844.8	24.5	35.0	337.9
1980	15.9	9.4	27.4	29.4	529.4	1.5	685.8	2,011.2	910.2	28.0	45.9	365.6
1981	24.4	10.6	35.9	30.3	574.1	1.6	814.3	2,293.5	1,026.0	42.7	59.3	390.3
1982	24.3	12.2	38.2	30.8	569.1	3.1	914.0	2,453.7	1,114.6	37.6	74.5	421.0
1983	34.3	18.3	40.0	35.4	626.5	4.5	982.9	2,609.6	1,225.5	36.8	83.9	447.0
1984	41.8	22.5	51.4	38.4	694.1	7.2	1,152.2	2,928.5	1,431.3	58.5	104.4	495.1
1985	45.1	25.6	57.0	42.5	739.3	10.8	1,337.0	3,308.2	1,608.9	72.2	127.0	578.2
1986	42.7	25.1	50.2	47.0	741.5	15.7	1,482.8	3,498.2	1,827.8	62.9	117.1	705.4
1987	34.4	19.4	51.5	54.0	805.3	12.8	1,652.1	3,774.0	1,996.3	73.8	116.2	784.1
1988	34.0	16.8	68.1	60.8	895.9	10.6	1,911.2	4,191.7	2,201.2	85.7	116.4	887.2
1989	60.6	32.4	54.4	63.8	938.0	11.7	2,070.9	4,532.7	2,378.9	107.1	115.5	961.1
1990	40.9	24.7	52.8	67.1	967.2	9.7	2,176.3	4,729.4	2,487.7	116.9	115.2	1,008.2
1991	48.5	44.8	59.0	63.0	961.4	14.8	2,260.5	4,829.8	2,430.4	98.5	114.0	1,086.9
1992	69.2	45.8	60.0	65.7	988.9	21.1	2,355.8	5,109.7	2,470.5	107.1	114.0	1,154.5
1993	67.9	54.7	52.3	77.2	1,035.0	29.8	2,615.3	5,388.6	2,525.5	117.8	113.9	1,229.7
1994	70.7	56.7	56.4	86.6	1,107.0	31.1	2,782.6	5,627.4	2,663.1	139.2	108.8	1,253.0
1995	80.5	36.8	57.9	85.1	1,184.9	45.7	3,156.9	6,009.5	2,876.5	157.4	96.3	1,326.3
1996	81.5	26.7	69.0	77.7	1,247.4	58.6	3,505.7	6,324.1	3,052.1	156.4	78.8	1,398.8
1997	75.7	30.4	77.0	78.9	1,284.6	81.8	3,935.1	6,651.3	3,289.3	168.6	58.6	1,489.5

Notes appear at end of table

TABLE Cj1133-1178   Flow-of-funds balance sheet – nonfarm, nonfinancial corporate businesses: 1945-1997
Continued

							With tangible assets stated at market value or replacement cost				
	Liabilities							Replacement cost value of structures		Market value of equities outstanding (includes corporate farm equities)	Debt as a percentage of net worth
	Credit market instruments										
Year	Bank loans not elsewhere classified	Other loans and advances	Mortgages	Trade payables	Taxes payable	Miscellaneous liabilities	Net worth (market value)	Residential	Nonresidential		
	Cj1157	Cj1158	Cj1159	Cj1160	Cj1161	Cj1162	Cj1163	Cj1164	Cj1165	Cj1166	Cj1167
	Billion dollars	Billion dollars	Billion dollars	Billion dollars	Billion dollars	Billion dollars	Billion dollars	Billion dollars	Billion dollars	Billion dollars	Percent
1945	8.9	3.2	9.1	13.7	10.1	1.2	195.9	2.4	108.1	103.7	23.0
1946	12.5	3.0	10.3	20.0	8.1	1.2	222.3	2.8	127.4	97.3	22.8
1947	15.5	2.9	11.8	23.4	10.3	1.2	261.7	3.2	148.2	95.1	22.2
1948	16.1	2.9	13.3	25.0	11.1	1.3	282.7	3.4	158.9	94.1	22.8
1949	14.2	2.9	14.2	24.7	8.8	1.3	292.8	3.5	162.2	103.8	22.6
1950	17.9	3.1	15.7	32.7	16.1	1.5	321.2	3.8	174.3	126.7	22.9
1951	22.1	3.4	16.5	32.3	20.5	1.5	352.2	4.0	189.9	147.6	23.3
1952	22.9	3.8	17.2	33.1	17.4	2.0	369.9	4.1	199.3	146.6	24.0
1953	22.4	4.3	18.1	32.8	18.0	2.1	383.7	4.1	204.9	144.1	24.3
1954	21.7	4.3	19.3	34.8	14.8	2.3	395.3	4.2	210.2	194.8	24.6
1955	25.6	4.4	21.5	43.9	18.4	2.6	426.6	4.4	225.1	244.2	24.9
1956	30.7	4.6	22.3	48.0	16.8	2.7	468.5	4.5	246.1	268.4	24.8
1957	31.9	5.7	23.9	49.6	14.6	2.8	493.3	4.6	258.3	245.7	25.5
1958	31.5	5.7	26.1	53.8	12.0	2.9	504.6	4.7	264.0	324.7	26.5
1959	35.3	7.0	27.3	59.1	14.2	3.2	525.6	5.0	269.4	362.2	27.2
1960	37.4	9.1	28.6	61.9	12.6	2.9	533.5	5.6	274.3	365.2	28.5
1961	38.3	9.4	30.8	65.7	13.3	3.0	548.3	6.1	278.8	437.7	29.2
1962	41.9	9.8	33.9	68.6	14.4	3.0	566.1	6.7	284.7	424.3	30.3
1963	45.3	10.8	37.5	76.0	15.7	3.1	584.2	7.1	291.6	465.8	31.3
1964	49.9	12.6	41.8	82.9	16.2	3.1	610.3	8.0	302.3	546.0	32.4
1965	60.7	14.8	45.1	94.6	18.3	3.6	650.4	8.6	319.7	623.8	33.6
1966	69.1	16.3	49.5	103.8	17.4	3.8	697.4	9.8	340.4	547.9	35.0
1967	75.6	16.5	53.5	109.7	13.2	3.2	752.2	10.8	364.0	712.2	36.0
1968	85.4	18.2	57.0	126.2	14.3	5.6	814.3	11.9	393.8	843.2	36.8
1969	98.8	23.5	60.6	145.7	12.6	6.8	891.9	12.7	432.0	694.6	37.6
1970	103.6	25.0	64.9	153.6	10.0	8.6	970.5	13.4	475.4	677.0	37.9
1971	107.7	26.4	69.6	167.2	13.1	9.4	1,066.3	15.2	525.9	792.9	37.1
1972	120.5	30.4	76.8	190.4	15.5	10.7	1,186.0	17.2	581.7	994.3	36.5
1973	137.1	36.2	106.0	228.4	19.3	16.1	1,344.9	19.8	665.3	759.2	37.0
1974	159.4	44.9	107.2	165.2	24.5	20.3	1,692.3	22.6	778.5	510.7	32.8
1975	143.5	48.9	112.7	176.4	22.3	313.1	1,731.8	24.3	871.0	699.1	33.2
1976	140.1	59.7	117.6	195.2	27.8	352.2	1,929.4	26.4	953.4	848.3	31.8
1977	154.9	73.3	129.7	227.0	29.1	391.6	2,141.9	30.2	1,048.2	740.4	32.1
1978	175.1	84.1	141.2	271.8	34.1	464.8	2,415.8	33.7	1,178.3	777.3	31.5
1979	204.3	100.8	142.3	327.4	41.0	576.1	2,762.3	38.3	1,339.7	922.5	30.6
1980	230.3	109.6	130.8	356.5	43.9	700.6	3,174.9	42.8	1,529.2	1,214.6	28.7
1981	261.7	136.2	135.7	383.4	39.9	844.3	3,524.2	46.2	1,725.6	1,110.7	29.1
1982	318.5	143.0	120.1	394.2	35.6	909.4	3,691.5	49.0	1,845.0	1,264.4	30.2
1983	340.9	169.1	147.8	402.0	38.6	943.5	3,853.1	50.7	1,877.6	1,486.1	31.8
1984	391.1	219.8	162.4	436.7	42.2	1,018.4	4,084.2	52.9	1,977.0	1,370.7	35.0
1985	424.1	248.4	159.0	479.7	39.0	1,180.6	4,194.1	55.6	2,057.5	1,674.7	38.4
1986	481.1	289.6	171.8	478.0	42.8	1,149.6	4,339.6	59.3	2,102.5	1,978.1	42.1
1987	485.1	322.6	214.5	522.4	47.9	1,207.4	4,568.9	62.6	2,207.1	2,014.6	43.7
1988	517.9	372.9	221.1	576.1	44.4	1,370.0	4,882.3	65.3	2,348.2	2,216.7	45.1
1989	542.8	418.9	233.5	597.9	38.3	1,517.6	5,088.1	67.1	2,464.2	2,673.1	46.8
1990	545.5	473.1	228.9	626.3	38.3	1,577.1	5,098.6	68.6	2,563.5	2,529.7	48.8
1991	507.7	410.2	212.7	649.4	28.9	1,721.5	4,977.1	69.4	2,592.8	3,497.0	48.8
1992	488.4	412.6	193.9	682.8	35.3	1,921.1	4,682.0	72.3	2,666.1	3,827.9	52.8
1993	477.6	388.4	198.1	719.3	40.7	2,103.1	4,757.4	74.0	2,805.0	4,126.0	53.1
1994	521.0	421.4	219.7	796.5	40.3	2,127.4	5,147.8	76.1	2,955.8	4,141.8	51.7
1995	587.7	453.7	255.1	877.5	40.3	2,215.3	5,579.8	78.4	3,086.8	5,481.1	51.6
1996	633.5	472.4	312.2	932.5	49.9	2,289.6	6,079.8	81.9	3,217.2	6,367.4	50.2
1997	706.5	518.6	347.4	997.3	58.1	2,306.6	6,806.4	85.0	3,402.8	7,898.5	48.3

(continued)

TABLE Cj1133–1178   Flow-of-funds balance sheet – nonfarm, nonfinancial corporate businesses: 1945–1997
Continued

	With tangible assets stated at market value or replacement cost		With tangible assets stated at historical cost								
	Debt as a percentage of equities	Equities as a percentage of net worth	Assets	Tangible assets				Net worth (historical cost)	Historical-cost value of structures		Debt as percentage of net worth
				Total	Real estate	Equipment	Inventories		Residential	Nonresidential	
	Cj1168	Cj1169	Cj1170	Cj1171	Cj1172	Cj1173	Cj1174	Cj1175	Cj1176	Cj1177	Cj1178
Year	Percent	Percent	Billion dollars	Billion dollars	Billion dollars	Billion dollars	Billion dollars	Billion dollars	Billion dollars	Billion dollars	Percent
1945	43.5	52.9	196.5	127.8	70.0	31.5	26.3	126.4	1.2	61.4	35.7
1946	52.2	43.8	213.5	146.4	73.6	35.2	37.5	133.4	1.2	64.1	38.1
1947	61.0	36.4	239.3	163.4	77.7	41.1	44.6	146.3	1.3	67.7	39.7
1948	68.5	33.3	259.9	178.5	82.5	47.1	48.9	158.0	1.3	72.2	40.8
1949	63.9	35.5	268.7	183.4	86.7	51.4	45.3	167.6	1.4	76.3	39.6
1950	57.9	39.4	304.7	202.6	91.5	56.1	55.1	181.0	1.5	80.7	40.5
1951	55.6	41.9	334.7	224.6	97.9	61.9	64.8	198.2	1.6	86.7	41.4
1952	60.5	39.6	353.3	237.8	104.0	67.8	66.0	212.0	1.6	93.0	41.9
1953	64.7	37.6	371.6	253.1	111.5	74.1	67.4	225.5	1.7	99.9	41.3
1954	50.0	49.3	387.0	263.0	118.2	79.3	65.5	237.7	1.8	106.4	41.0
1955	43.6	57.2	425.5	284.1	126.0	85.1	73.0	254.2	1.9	113.2	41.9
1956	43.2	57.3	456.5	310.0	136.6	92.8	80.6	273.0	1.9	122.5	42.5
1957	51.2	49.8	482.1	331.1	146.8	101.9	82.3	289.2	2.0	131.9	43.5
1958	41.2	64.3	507.0	344.4	156.0	106.6	81.9	304.6	2.1	139.4	43.9
1959	39.4	68.9	544.5	366.8	165.1	113.2	88.4	325.3	2.5	146.7	43.9
1960	41.7	68.4	568.3	387.8	175.4	120.7	91.6	338.8	3.1	154.9	44.9
1961	36.6	79.8	601.3	408.1	186.0	127.1	95.0	359.2	3.7	162.8	44.6
1962	40.4	75.0	637.0	431.8	196.3	134.9	100.6	379.7	4.3	170.6	45.1
1963	39.3	79.7	677.9	457.1	206.9	143.5	106.8	400.0	4.7	178.5	45.8
1964	36.2	89.5	720.9	485.4	218.3	153.9	113.1	420.8	5.3	187.7	47.0
1965	35.1	95.9	791.2	528.2	233.2	168.4	126.6	456.0	5.7	199.3	48.0
1966	44.6	78.6	856.7	579.1	250.1	186.2	142.8	487.5	6.5	212.9	50.1
1967	38.0	94.7	917.9	622.2	266.7	202.5	153.1	520.9	7.1	226.4	52.0
1968	35.6	103.5	999.6	670.7	283.9	220.8	166.0	553.6	7.5	241.2	54.2
1969	48.3	77.9	1,097.5	733.9	305.8	241.7	186.4	597.0	8.0	258.2	56.2
1970	54.3	69.8	1,165.3	779.9	326.7	259.9	193.3	625.7	8.5	276.3	58.7
1971	49.9	74.4	1,252.8	825.6	348.0	277.2	200.4	667.5	9.1	294.8	59.3
1972	43.5	83.8	1,392.9	896.8	373.2	297.9	225.7	743.3	10.1	315.6	58.2
1973	65.5	56.4	1,569.8	995.2	404.4	326.9	263.9	809.0	10.9	340.8	61.4
1974	108.6	30.2	1,737.7	1,118.0	438.3	360.2	319.5	973.1	11.9	370.7	57.0
1975	82.3	40.4	1,955.3	1,177.0	469.8	390.7	316.5	868.4	12.3	401.0	66.2
1976	72.4	44.0	2,147.5	1,278.9	504.3	427.6	346.9	958.2	12.7	433.0	64.1
1977	92.9	34.6	2,379.0	1,408.7	543.7	480.0	385.0	1,043.6	13.2	468.6	65.9
1978	98.0	32.2	2,684.1	1,578.2	594.0	545.7	438.4	1,151.8	14.0	514.3	66.1
1979	91.6	33.4	3,064.8	1,778.6	657.4	621.5	499.6	1,275.4	15.1	572.2	66.2
1980	74.9	38.3	3,416.7	1,961.6	733.2	695.1	533.3	1,405.5	16.0	641.1	64.8
1981	92.4	31.5	3,847.6	2,196.4	824.9	775.0	596.5	1,554.1	17.0	723.0	66.0
1982	88.2	34.3	4,108.3	2,344.2	914.8	841.5	587.9	1,654.6	17.6	806.2	67.4
1983	82.5	38.6	4,451.5	2,507.5	989.8	904.9	612.8	1,841.9	18.5	873.7	66.5
1984	104.4	33.6	4,968.6	2,746.6	1,077.5	989.2	679.9	2,040.1	19.7	952.2	70.2
1985	96.1	39.9	5,467.2	2,971.1	1,175.1	1,071.3	724.8	2,159.0	20.9	1,036.5	74.5
1986	92.4	45.6	5,782.1	3,114.0	1,249.5	1,143.0	721.5	2,283.9	22.5	1,103.1	80.0
1987	99.1	44.1	6,210.6	3,308.2	1,321.0	1,204.7	782.6	2,437.0	23.8	1,164.8	81.9
1988	99.3	45.4	6,790.4	3,504.7	1,400.3	1,269.4	834.9	2,598.7	25.0	1,225.5	84.7
1989	89.0	52.5	7,199.3	3,680.1	1,474.5	1,341.8	863.9	2,666.5	26.1	1,286.2	89.2
1990	98.3	49.6	7,483.9	3,849.5	1,561.7	1,412.4	875.4	2,754.5	27.2	1,356.9	90.3
1991	69.5	70.3	7,732.4	3,968.2	1,629.8	1,471.7	866.8	2,902.6	28.2	1,420.1	83.7
1992	64.5	81.8	8,059.4	4,128.2	1,688.8	1,536.9	902.5	2,950.2	29.3	1,474.6	83.7
1993	61.2	86.7	8,610.4	4,321.4	1,759.2	1,621.5	940.6	3,221.7	29.8	1,538.6	78.4
1994	64.3	80.5	9,124.1	4,556.7	1,833.1	1,727.7	996.0	3,496.7	30.6	1,605.4	76.2
1995	52.5	98.2	9,868.9	4,810.1	1,914.8	1,863.8	1,031.5	3,859.4	32.1	1,687.7	74.5
1996	47.9	104.7	10,637.3	5,077.7	2,010.1	2,009.7	1,057.9	4,313.2	33.6	1,781.7	70.8
1997	41.6	116.0	11,488.5	5,399.3	2,116.2	2,179.2	1,103.9	4,837.1	35.1	1,883.4	68.0

TABLE Cj1133–1178   Flow-of-funds balance sheet – nonfarm, nonfinancial corporate businesses: 1945–1997
Continued

[1] Data are year-end levels; not seasonally adjusted.

[2] At market value.

[3] At replacement (current) cost.

[4] Through 1992, corporate bonds include net issues by Netherlands Antillean financial subsidiaries, and U.S. direct investment abroad excludes net inflows from those bond issues.

Source

Flow-of-funds data are available at the Federal Reserve Board's Internet site. The data for 1945–1996 are also available in a series of six hard copy releases by the Board of Governors of the Federal Reserve System, *Flow of Funds Accounts of the United States, Annual Flows and Outstandings, 1945–1953, 1954–1962, 1963–1972, 1973–1981, 1982–1990,* and *1991–1996,* all dated December 11, 1997. Updates are available in Federal Reserve Statistical Release Z.1, *Flow of Funds Accounts of the United States, Flows and Outstandings,* published quarterly.

Documentation

Analogous to Table Cj1081–1132, this table shows for the nonfinancial corporate business sector its assets, liabilities, and net worth, at both replacement and historical costs. Assets are broken down into various categories (major ones are tangible and financial assets), as are liabilities. Also shown are various ratios, such as debt to net worth.

Series Cj1155. Industrial revenue bonds are issued by state and local governments to finance private investment and are secured in interest and principal by the industrial user of the funds.

Series Cj1167. Equals series Cj1153 expressed as a percentage of series Cj1163.

Series Cj1168. Equals series Cj1153 expressed as a percentage of series Cj1166.

Series Cj1169. Equals series Cj1166 expressed as a percentage of series Cj1171.

Series Cj1170. Equals the sum of series Cj1138 and Cj1171.

Series Cj1175. Equals series Cj1170 less series Cj1152.

Series Cj1178. Equals series Cj1153 expressed as a percentage of series Cj1175.

TABLE Cj1179–1191   Commercial and finance company paper and bankers' acceptances outstanding: 1918–1997

Contributed by John A. James and Richard Sylla

	Commercial paper and finance company paper			Commercial paper			Bankers' acceptances						
				Financial companies				Held by			Based on		
Year	Total	Placed through dealers	Placed directly	Placed through dealers	Placed directly	Nonfinancial companies	Total	Accepting banks	Federal Reserve banks	Others	Imports into United States	Exports from United States	Other
	Cj1179 [1]	Cj1180 [1]	Cj1181 [1]	Cj1182	Cj1183	Cj1184	Cj1185	Cj1186	Cj1187	Cj1188	Cj1189	Cj1190	Cj1191
	Million dollars	Million dollars	Million dollars	Million dollars	Million dollars	Million dollars	Million dollars	Million dollars	Million dollars	Million dollars	Million dollars	Million dollars	Million dollars
1918	881	—	—	—	—	—	—	—	—	—	—	—	—
1919	1,186	—	—	—	—	—	—	—	—	—	—	—	—
1920	948	—	—	—	—	—	—	—	—	—	—	—	—
1921	663	—	—	—	—	—	—	—	—	—	—	—	—
1922	722	—	—	—	—	—	—	—	—	—	—	—	—
1923	763	—	—	—	—	—	—	—	—	—	—	—	—
1924	798	—	—	—	—	—	821	—	430	—	292	305	223
1925	621	—	—	—	—	—	774	93	442	239	311	297	165
1926	526	—	—	—	—	—	755	77	437	242	284	261	211
1927	555	—	—	—	—	—	1,081	105	619	357	313	391	377
1928	383	—	—	—	—	—	1,284	76	813	395	316	497	472
1929	334	—	—	—	—	—	1,732	191	939	602	383	524	825
1930	358	—	—	—	—	—	1,556	371	767	417	221	415	919
1931	120	—	—	—	—	—	974	262	556	156	159	222	594
1932	81	—	—	—	—	—	710	604	44	62	79	164	468
1933	109	—	—	—	—	—	764	442	131	190	94	207	463
1934	166	—	—	—	—	—	543	497	1	46	89	140	314
1935	171	—	—	—	—	—	397	368	0	29	107	94	196
1936	215	—	—	—	—	—	373	315	0	57	126	86	161
1937	279	—	—	—	—	—	343	278	2	63	117	87	139
1938	187	—	—	—	—	—	270	212	0	58	95	60	116
1939	210	—	—	—	—	—	233	175	0	57	103	39	92
1940	218	—	—	—	—	—	209	167	0	42	109	18	81
1941	375	—	—	—	—	—	194	146	0	49	116	15	63
1942	230	—	—	—	—	—	118	93	0	25	57	9	52
1943	202	—	—	—	—	—	117	90	0	37	66	11	39
1944	166	—	—	—	—	—	129	93	0	35	86	14	28
1945	159	—	—	—	—	—	154	112	0	42	103	18	33
1946	228	—	—	—	—	—	227	169	7	52	162	29	36
1947	287	—	—	—	—	—	261	197	2	62	159	63	39
1948	674	277	397	—	—	—	259	146	3	109	164	57	38
1949	838	270	568	—	—	—	272	128	11	133	184	49	39
1950	921	345	576	—	—	—	394	192	21	180	245	87	62
1951	1,333	449	884	—	—	—	490	197	21	272	235	133	122
1952	1,749	552	1,197	—	—	—	492	183	20	289	232	125	135
1953	1,973	564	1,409	—	—	—	574	172	24	378	274	154	147
1954	1,933	733	1,200	—	—	—	873	289	19	565	285	182	406
1955	2,035	510	1,525	—	—	—	642	175	61	405	252	210	180
1956	2,183	506	1,677	—	—	—	967	227	119	621	261	329	377
1957	2,672	551	2,121	—	—	—	1,307	287	142	878	278	456	574
1958	2,751	840	1,911	—	—	—	1,194	302	117	775	254	349	590
1959	3,202	677	2,525	—	—	—	1,151	319	157	675	357	309	485
1960	4,497	1,358	3,139	—	—	—	2,027	662	304	1,060	403	669	954
1961	4,686	1,711	2,975	—	—	—	2,683	1,272	177	1,234	485	969	1,229
1962	6,000	2,088	3,912	—	—	—	2,650	1,153	196	1,301	541	778	1,331
1963	6,790	1,928	4,862	—	—	—	2,890	1,291	254	1,345	567	908	1,414
1964	8,442	2,223	6,219	—	—	—	3,385	1,671	216	1,498	667	999	1,719
1965	9,300	1,903	7,397	—	—	—	3,392	1,223	331	1,837	792	974	1,626
1966	13,645	3,089	10,556	—	—	—	3,604	1,198	384	2,022	997	829	1,778
1967	17,085	4,901	12,184	—	—	—	4,317	1,906	320	2,090	1,086	989	2,241
1968	21,173	7,201	13,972	—	—	—	4,428	1,544	167	2,717	1,423	952	2,053
1969	32,600	11,817	20,783	—	—	—	5,451	1,567	210	3,674	1,889	1,153	2,408
1970	33,071	12,671	20,400	—	—	—	7,058	2,694	307	4,057	2,601	1,561	2,895
1971	32,552	—	—	5,270	20,684	6,598	7,889	3,480	515	3,894	2,834	1,546	3,509
1972	35,207	—	—	5,630	22,219	7,358	6,898	2,706	385	3,907	2,531	1,909	2,458
1973	41,690	—	—	5,467	27,346	8,877	8,892	2,837	649	5,406	2,273	3,499	3,120
1974	50,020	—	—	4,594	31,959	13,470	18,484	4,226	2,108	12,150	4,023	4,067	10,394

Note appears at end of table

TABLE Cj1179–1191 Commercial and finance company paper and bankers' acceptances outstanding: 1918–1997
Continued

	Commercial paper and finance company paper			Commercial paper			Bankers' acceptances						
				Financial companies				Held by			Based on		
Year	Total	Placed through dealers	Placed directly	Placed through dealers	Placed directly	Nonfinancial companies	Total	Accepting banks	Federal Reserve banks	Others	Imports into United States	Exports from United States	Other
	Cj1179 [1]	Cj1180 [1]	Cj1181 [1]	Cj1182	Cj1183	Cj1184	Cj1185	Cj1186	Cj1187	Cj1188	Cj1189	Cj1190	Cj1191
	Million dollars	Million dollars	Million dollars	Million dollars	Million dollars	Million dollars	Million dollars	Million dollars	Million dollars	Million dollars	Million dollars	Million dollars	Million dollars
1975	48,471	—	—	6,212	31,404	10,835	18,727	7,333	1,419	9,975	3,726	4,001	11,000
1976	52,971	—	—	7,261	32,511	13,125	22,523	10,422	1,366	10,715	4,992	4,818	12,713
1977	65,101	—	—	8,884	40,484	15,536	25,450	10,434	1,316	13,904	6,378	5,863	13,209
1978	83,665	—	—	12,296	51,630	19,365	33,700	8,579	1,251	24,456	8,574	7,586	17,540
1979	112,803	—	—	17,579	45,321	30,293	45,321	9,865	2,086	33,370	10,270	9,640	25,411
1980	124,374	—	—	19,599	67,854	36,921	54,744	10,564	2,567	41,614	11,776	12,712	30,257
1981	165,829	—	—	30,333	81,660	53,836	69,226	10,857	1,637	56,731	14,765	15,400	39,060
1982	166,436	—	—	34,605	84,393	47,437	79,543	10,910	2,429	66,204	17,683	16,328	45,531
1983	187,658	—	—	44,455	97,042	46,161	73,309	9,355	1,147	67,807	15,649	16,880	45,781
1984	237,586	—	—	56,485	110,543	70,558	78,364	9,811	671	67,881	17,845	16,305	44,214
1985	298,779	—	—	78,443	135,320	85,016	68,413	11,197	937	56,279	15,147	13,204	40,062
1986	329,991	—	—	101,072	151,820	77,099	64,974	13,423	1,317	50,234	14,670	12,960	37,344
1987	358,056	—	—	102,844	173,980	81,232	70,565	10,943	965	58,658	16,483	15,227	38,855
1988	457,297	—	—	160,094	194,537	102,666	66,631	9,086	1,493	56,052	14,984	14,410	37,237
1989	529,055	—	—	187,084	212,210	129,761	62,972	9,433	1,066	52,473	15,651	13,683	33,638
1990	562,656	—	—	214,706	200,036	147,914	54,771	9,017	918	44,836	13,095	12,703	28,973
1991	528,832	—	—	212,999	182,463	133,370	43,770	11,017	1,739	31,014	12,843	10,351	20,577
1992	545,619	—	—	226,456	171,605	147,558	38,194	10,555	1,276	26,364	12,209	8,096	17,890
1993	555,075	—	—	218,947	180,389	155,739	32,348	12,421	725	19,202	10,217	7,293	14,838
1994	595,382	—	—	223,038	207,701	164,643	29,835	11,783	410	17,642	10,062	6,355	13,417
1995	674,903	—	—	275,815	210,828	188,260	29,242	—	—	—	—	—	—
1996	775,371	—	—	361,147	229,662	184,563	25,754	—	—	—	—	—	—
1997	966,699	—	—	513,307	252,536	200,857	—	—	—	—	—	—	—

[1] Prior to 1948, total for commercial paper represents only paper maturing within seven months as reported by principal paper dealers; thereafter, figures for commercial paper and finance combined by method of placement represent paper with an original maturity of nine months or less as reported by varying number of dealers.

Sources
Board of Governors of the Federal Reserve System. 1918–1941: *Banking and Monetary Statistics* (1943), pp. 465–7; 1942–1952: *Federal Reserve Bulletin* (February 1944), p. 170; (January 1946), p. 59; (February 1953), p. 146; 1953–1997: *Federal Reserve Bulletin* (various issues).

Documentation
Data given are as of the end of the year.

Series Cj1179–1184. Prior to 1948, figures for commercial paper represent the amount of paper outstanding as reported by the principal commercial paper dealers in the country. Some finance company paper sold in the open market is included. Beginning in 1948, figures are for commercial paper and finance company paper combined, shown by method of placement. These data represent paper with an original maturity of nine months or less (including some finance company paper sold in open markets) as reported by a varying number of dealers. Finance company paper represents the amount reported by a varying number of institutions engaged primarily in commercial, savings, and mortgage banking; sales, personal, and mortgage financing; factoring, finance leasing, and other business lending; insurance underwriting; and other investment activities. Prior to 1958, a small amount of finance company paper with original maturity of more than 270 days was included; thereafter, all paper in this maturing group is included.

Series Cj1182. Includes all financial company paper sold by dealers in the open market.

Series Cj1183. Data are as reported by financial companies that place their paper directly with investors.

Series Cj1184. Includes public utilities and firms engaged primarily in activities such as communications, construction, manufacturing, mining, wholesale and retail trade, transportation, and services.

Series Cj1185–1191. Figures for bankers' acceptances are amounts outstanding as reported by makers of bankers' acceptances, including banks and bankers in the United States and agencies of foreign banks in this country.

INTEREST RATES AND YIELDS

John A. James and Richard Sylla

TABLE Cj1192–1197   Long-term bond yields: 1798–1997

Contributed by John A. James and Richard Sylla

		Municipal		Corporate		
	U.S. government	High-grade	New England	Unadjusted index of American railroad	High-grade	Medium-grade
	Cj1192	Cj1193	Cj1194	Cj1195	Cj1196	Cj1197
Year	Percent per annum	Percent per annum	Percent per annum	Percent per annum	Percent per annum	Percent per annum
1798	7.56	—	6.30	—	—	—
1799	7.42	—	6.16	—	—	—
1800	6.94	—	6.13	—	—	—
1801	6.44	—	5.63	—	—	—
1802	6.02	—	5.25	—	—	—
1803	6.16	—	5.06	—	—	—
1804	6.29	—	5.14	—	—	—
1805	6.38	—	5.36	—	—	—
1806	6.14	—	5.32	—	—	—
1807	6.08	—	5.29	—	—	—
1808	5.96	—	5.19	—	—	—
1809	5.85	—	5.02	—	—	—
1810	5.82	—	5.02	—	—	—
1811	5.95	—	5.09	—	—	—
1812	6.12	—	5.13	—	—	—
1813	6.30	—	5.03	—	—	—
1814	7.64	—	5.26	—	—	—
1815	7.30	—	5.29	—	—	—
1816	7.25	—	5.72	—	—	—
1817	5.86	—	5.27	—	—	—
1818	5.78	—	5.08	—	—	—
1819	5.90	—	5.17	—	—	—
1820	5.16	—	5.00	—	—	—
1821	4.57	—	4.93	—	—	—
1822	4.65	—	—	—	—	—
1823	4.72	—	5.00	—	—	—
1824	4.25	—	4.52	—	—	—
1825	4.32	—	4.52	—	—	—
1826	4.50	—	—	—	—	—
1827	4.37	—	4.61	—	—	—
1828	4.48	—	—	—	—	—
1829	4.50	—	4.77	—	—	—
1830	4.37	—	4.90	—	—	—
1831	4.41	—	—	—	—	—
1832	4.45	—	5.00	—	—	—
1833	—	—	4.87	—	—	—
1834	—	—	4.87	—	—	—
1835	—	—	4.83	—	—	—
1836	—	—	4.96	—	—	—
1837	—	—	4.95	—	—	—
1838	—	—	5.01	—	—	—
1839	—	—	5.21	—	—	—
1840	—	—	5.07	—	—	—
1841	—	—	4.99	—	—	—
1842	6.07	—	4.95	—	—	—
1843	5.03	—	4.88	—	—	—
1844	4.85	—	4.84	—	—	—
1845	5.16	—	4.86	—	—	—
1846	5.50	—	4.92	—	—	—
1847	5.77	—	5.14	—	—	—
1848	5.71	—	5.31	—	—	—
1849	5.16	—	5.31	—	—	—

TABLE Cj1192–1197   Long-term bond yields: 1798–1997   *Continued*

Year	U.S. government	Municipal		Corporate		
		High-grade	New England	Unadjusted index of American railroad	High-grade	Medium-grade
	Cj1192	Cj1193	Cj1194	Cj1195	Cj1196	Cj1197
	Percent per annum	Percent per annum	Percent per annum	Percent per annum	Percent per annum	Percent per annum
1850	4.58	—	5.13	—	—	—
1851	4.47	—	5.08	—	—	—
1852	4.39	—	4.98	—	—	—
1853	4.02	—	4.99	—	—	—
1854	4.14	—	5.13	—	—	—
1855	4.18	—	5.16	—	—	—
1856	4.11	—	5.10	—	—	—
1857	4.30	—	5.19	10.25	—	—
1858	4.32	—	5.03	9.34	—	—
1859	4.72	—	4.81	8.91	—	—
1860	5.57	—	4.79	8.59	—	—
1861	6.45	—	5.04	8.88	—	—
1862	6.25	—	4.91	7.56	—	—
1863	6.00	—	4.37	6.34	—	—
1864	5.10	—	4.80	6.27	—	—
1865	5.19	—	5.51	7.62	—	—
1866	5.17	—	5.50	7.95	—	—
1867	4.97	—	5.34	7.87	—	—
1868	4.62	—	5.28	7.80	—	—
1869	4.07	—	5.37	8.13	—	—
1870	4.24	—	5.44	7.92	—	—
1871	4.18	—	5.32	7.78	—	—
1872	3.70	—	5.36	7.60	—	—
1873	3.51	—	5.58	7.76	—	—
1874	3.42	—	5.47	7.53	—	—
1875	3.30	—	5.07	7.06	—	—
1876	3.66	—	4.59	6.68	—	—
1877	3.81	—	4.45	6.62	—	—
1878	3.97	—	4.34	6.45	—	—
1879	3.96	—	4.22	5.98	—	—
1880	3.63	—	4.02	5.60	—	—
1881	3.13	—	3.70	5.19	—	—
1882	2.91	—	3.62	5.24	—	—
1883	2.88	—	3.63	5.23	—	—
1884	2.76	—	3.62	5.15	—	—
1885	2.68	—	3.52	4.89	—	—
1886	2.43	—	3.37	4.55	—	—
1887	2.32	—	3.52	4.65	—	—
1888	2.27	—	3.67	4.59	—	—
1889	2.13	—	3.45	4.43	—	—
1890	2.37	—	3.42	4.55	—	—
1891	2.58	—	3.62	4.71	—	—
1892	2.73	—	3.60	4.53	—	—
1893	2.96	—	3.75	4.65	—	—
1894	2.72	—	3.70	4.41	—	—
1895	2.82	—	3.46	4.27	—	—
1896	3.06	—	3.60	4.34	—	—
1897	2.57	—	3.40	4.11	—	—
1898	2.50	—	3.35	4.03	—	—
1899	2.22	—	3.10	3.85	—	—
1900	—	3.12	3.15	3.89	—	—
1901	—	3.13	—	3.83	—	—
1902	—	3.20	—	3.84	—	—
1903	—	3.38	—	4.03	—	—
1904	—	3.45	—	3.98	—	—
1905	—	3.40	—	3.89	—	—
1906	—	3.57	—	4.00	—	—
1907	—	3.86	—	4.27	—	—
1908	—	3.93	—	4.22	—	—
1909	—	3.78	—	4.07	—	—

(continued)

TABLE Cj1192–1197   Long-term bond yields: 1798–1997   *Continued*

Year	U.S. government	Municipal		Corporate		
		High-grade	New England	Unadjusted index of American railroad	High-grade	Medium-grade
	Cj1192	Cj1193	Cj1194	Cj1195	Cj1196	Cj1197
	Percent per annum	Percent per annum	Percent per annum	Percent per annum	Percent per annum	Percent per annum
1910	—	3.97	—	4.18	—	—
1911	—	3.98	—	4.19	—	—
1912	—	4.02	—	4.23	—	—
1913	—	4.22	—	4.44	—	—
1914	—	4.12	—	4.44	—	—
1915	—	4.16	—	4.62	—	—
1916	—	3.94	—	4.49	—	—
1917	—	4.20	—	4.79	—	—
1918	—	4.50	—	5.23	—	—
1919	4.73	4.46	—	5.29	5.49	—
1920	5.32	4.98	—	5.81	6.12	—
1921	5.09	5.09	—	5.57	5.97	—
1922	4.30	4.23	—	4.85	5.10	—
1923	4.36	4.25	—	4.98	5.12	—
1924	4.06	4.20	—	4.84	5.00	—
1925	3.86	4.09	—	4.73	4.88	—
1926	3.68	4.08	—	4.47	4.73	—
1927	3.34	3.98	—	4.34	4.57	—
1928	3.33	4.05	—	4.35	4.55	—
1929	3.60	4.27	—	4.60	4.73	—
1930	3.29	4.07	—	4.41	4.55	—
1931	3.34	4.01	—	4.66	4.58	—
1932	3.68	4.65	—	5.73	5.01	—
1933	3.31	4.71	—	5.35	4.49	—
1934	3.12	4.03	—	4.53	4.00	—
1935	2.79	3.40	—	4.24	3.60	—
1936	2.69	3.07	—	3.88	3.24	—
1937	2.74	3.10	—	—	3.26	—
1938	2.61	2.91	—	—	3.19	—
1939	2.41	2.76	—	—	3.01	—
1940	2.26	2.50	—	—	2.84	—
1941	2.05	2.10	—	—	2.77	—
1942	2.46	2.36	—	—	2.83	—
1943	2.47	2.06	—	—	2.73	—
1944	2.48	1.86	—	—	2.72	—
1945	2.37	1.67	—	—	2.62	—
1946	2.19	1.10	—	—	2.53	3.05
1947	2.25	1.45	—	—	2.61	3.24
1948	2.44	1.87	—	—	2.82	3.47
1949	2.31	1.66	—	—	2.66	3.42
1950	2.32	1.57	—	—	2.62	3.24
1951	2.57	1.60	—	—	2.86	3.41
1952	2.68	1.79	—	—	2.96	3.52
1953	2.94	2.31	—	—	3.20	3.74
1954	2.55	2.03	—	—	2.90	3.51
1955	2.84	2.17	—	—	3.06	3.53
1956	3.08	2.50	—	—	3.36	3.88
1957	3.47	3.10	—	—	3.89	4.71
1958	3.43	2.92	—	—	3.79	4.73
1959	4.07	3.35	—	—	4.38	5.05
1960	4.01	3.26	—	—	4.41	5.19
1961	3.90	3.27	—	—	4.35	5.08
1962	3.95	3.03	—	—	4.33	5.02
1963	4.00	3.06	—	—	4.26	4.86
1964	4.15	3.09	—	—	4.40	4.83
1965	4.21	3.16	—	—	4.49	4.87
1966	4.66	3.67	—	—	5.13	5.67
1967	4.85	3.74	—	—	5.51	6.23
1968	5.25	4.20	—	—	6.18	6.94
1969	6.10	5.45	—	—	7.03	7.81

TABLE Cj1192–1197   Long-term bond yields: 1798–1997   *Continued*

Year	U.S. government	Municipal High-grade	Municipal New England	Corporate Unadjusted index of American railroad	Corporate High-grade	Corporate Medium-grade
	Cj1192	Cj1193	Cj1194	Cj1195	Cj1196	Cj1197
	Percent per annum	Percent per annum	Percent per annum	Percent per annum	Percent per annum	Percent per annum
1970	6.59	6.12	—	—	8.04	9.11
1971	5.74	5.22	—	—	7.39	8.56
1972	5.63	5.04	—	—	7.21	8.16
1973	6.30	4.99	—	—	7.44	8.24
1974	6.99	5.89	—	—	8.57	9.50
1975	6.98	6.42	—	—	8.83	10.61
1976	6.78	5.66	—	—	8.43	9.75
1977	7.06	5.20	—	—	8.02	8.97
1978	7.89	5.52	—	—	8.73	9.49
1979	8.74	5.92	—	—	9.63	10.69
1980	10.81	7.85	—	—	11.94	13.67
1981	13.43	10.43	—	—	14.17	16.04
1982	12.23	10.88	—	—	13.79	16.11
1983	10.84	8.80	—	—	12.04	13.55
1984	12.00	9.61	—	—	12.71	14.19
1985	10.75	8.60	—	—	11.37	12.72
1986	8.14	6.95	—	—	9.02	10.39
1987	8.64	7.14	—	—	9.38	10.58
1988	8.98	7.36	—	—	9.71	10.83
1989	8.58	7.00	—	—	9.26	10.18
1990	8.74	6.96	—	—	9.32	10.36
1991	8.16	6.56	—	—	8.77	9.80
1992	7.52	6.09	—	—	8.14	8.98
1993	6.45	5.38	—	—	7.22	7.93
1994	7.41	5.77	—	—	7.97	8.63
1995	6.93	5.80	—	—	7.59	8.20
1996	6.80	5.52	—	—	7.37	8.05
1997	6.67	5.32	—	—	7.26	7.87

Sources

Series 1192. 1798–1900: Sidney Homer and Richard Sylla, *A History of Interest Rates*, 3rd edition (Rutgers University Press, 1996), pp. 286–8; 1919–1940: Board of Governors of the Federal Reserve System, *Federal Reserve Bulletin* (May 1945), p. 483; 1941–1963: *Supplement to Banking and Monetary Statistics* (1966), section 12, "Money Rates and Securities Markets," p. 68; 1964–1997: *Federal Reserve Bulletin* (various issues).

Series Cj1193. 1900–1970: Standard and Poor's Corporation, *Trade and Securities Statistics, Security Price Index Record* (1971); 1971–1997: Moody's Aaa series from *Federal Reserve Bulletin*, variously numbered tables titled "Interest Rates – Money and Capital Markets."

Series Cj1194. 1798–1856: Homer and Sylla (1996), pp. 286–8; 1857–1900: Frederick R. Macaulay, *Some Theoretical Problems Suggested by the Movements of Interest Rate, Bond Yields and Stock Prices in the United States since 1856* (National Bureau of Economic Research, 1938), pp. A169–76.

Series Cj1195. Macaulay (1938), pp. A121–61.

Series Cj1196. 1919–1970: Moody's Investors Service, *Moody's Industrial Manual* (1971). 1971–1997: *Federal Reserve Bulletin* (various issues), variously numbered tables titled "Interest Rates – Money and Capital Markets," continuing the Moody's series.

Series Cj1197. Moody's Investors Service, *Moody's Industrial Manual* (1971), thereafter reported in *Federal Reserve Bulletin* (various issues), variously numbered tables titled "Interest Rates – Money and Capital Markets."

Documentation

Series Cj1192. Figures are unweighted averages of yields. For 1798–1900, they are derived from average annual prices of those longer-term issues with the least discount or premium. Yields were selected to reflect what appeared to be a realistic going average rate for the year. For 1919–1925, yields cover all outstanding partially tax-exempt government bonds due or callable after

eight years; for 1926–1934, all such bonds due or callable after twelve years; for 1935–1941, all such bonds due or callable after fifteen years. For further description of the series, see *Banking and Monetary Statistics*, p. 429, and *Federal Reserve Bulletin* (May 1945), pp. 483, 490. Beginning in 1942, the series is for fully taxable bonds. For 1942 to March 31, 1952, yields cover the bonds due or callable after fifteen years; for April 1, 1952 to March 31, 1953, due or callable after twelve years; and for April 1, 1953 to 1997, due or callable in ten years or more.

Series Cj1193. Prior to 1929, this series is an arithmetic average of the yield to maturity of fifteen high-grade municipal bonds, based on the mean of monthly high-low prices. Beginning 1929, the series is an average of the four or five weekly indexes for the month. Annual figures are averages of monthly data. Monthly and weekly data are available in the sources.

Series Cj1194. Before 1857, the yields are annual averages of those on Massachusetts or Boston 5s; after 1857 they are taken from Frederick Macaulay's Average of New England Municipals.

Series Cj1195. The railroad industry was selected as the basis for a long-term study of bond yields because no other industry had securities of comparable importance as early as 1857, and for many years no other industry had as high a credit rating. The series is available before and after adjustment to eliminate economic drift owing to secular changes in the quality of the bonds included. The unadjusted series is more comparable with currently available series. The series is a chain index number based on the arithmetic average of yields on long-term high-grade railroad bonds. Yields for individual bonds are based on arithmetic averages of monthly high and low sale prices. With a few exceptions, the index includes no bonds with maturities under ten years, and since 1909, the minimum has been fourteen years. The number of bonds on which the index is based was 13 in 1857 and increased gradually to 37 in 1900; it varied between 36 and 45 until 1930 and declined to about 28 in 1933. Annual figures are averages of monthly data.

TABLE Cj1192–1197   Long-term bond yields: 1798–1997   *Continued*

Series Cj1196. This series is an unweighted arithmetic average of the yields for individual Aaa-rated bonds, based on closing prices. Prior to 1928, yields are based on the average of the month's high and low sale price for each bond; for 1928 and 1929, on biweekly closing quotations; for 1930 through October 1931, on weekly quotations; beginning November 1931, on daily closing quotations. Annual figures are averages of monthly data.

Series Cj1197. This series represents the average yield to maturity on selected Baa long-term bonds. Annual figures are averages of monthly averages.

TABLE Cj1198–1222   Bank rates on short-term business loans: 1815–1997

Contributed by John A. James and Richard Sylla

	Business loan rates				Customer loan rates					Regional interest rates			
	Total 19 cities	New York City	7 northern and eastern cities	11 southern and western cities	Total leading cities	New York City	Northern and eastern cities	Southern and western cities	Prime rate for commercial loans	Northeast	South	Plains	West
	Cj1198 [1]	Cj1199 [1]	Cj1200 [1]	Cj1201 [1]	Cj1202 [1]	Cj1203 [1]	Cj1204 [1]	Cj1205 [1]	Cj1206 [1]	Cj1207 [1]	Cj1208 [1]	Cj1209 [1]	Cj1210 [1]
Year	Percent per annum	Percent per annum	Percent per annum	Percent per annum	Percent per annum	Percent per annum	Percent per annum	Percent per annum	Percent per annum	Percent per annum	Percent per annum	Percent per annum	Percent per annum
1880	—	—	—	—	—	—	—	—	—	6.90	9.37	10.89	10.30
1881	—	—	—	—	—	—	—	—	—	7.25	10.00	11.45	20.02
1882	—	—	—	—	—	—	—	—	—	6.74	9.05	10.07	12.84
1883	—	—	—	—	—	—	—	—	—	6.57	8.30	10.41	10.88
1884	—	—	—	—	—	—	—	—	—	6.51	8.99	11.44	14.59
1885	—	—	—	—	—	—	—	—	—	6.26	8.06	8.65	9.98
1886	—	—	—	—	—	—	—	—	—	6.23	8.32	8.55	8.35
1887	—	—	—	—	—	—	—	—	—	6.81	8.30	8.36	7.81
1888	—	—	—	—	—	—	—	—	—	6.75	8.58	8.54	12.30
1889	—	—	—	—	—	—	—	—	—	6.58	8.36	8.26	11.28
1890	—	—	—	—	—	—	—	—	—	6.92	8.03	8.20	10.54
1891	—	—	—	—	—	—	—	—	—	6.54	8.82	9.68	11.85
1892	—	—	—	—	—	—	—	—	—	5.89	8.33	9.02	9.85
1893	—	—	—	—	—	—	—	—	—	7.08	9.90	12.32	13.11
1894	—	—	—	—	—	—	—	—	—	5.87	8.26	9.37	10.60
1895	—	—	—	—	—	—	—	—	—	5.82	8.74	9.17	10.74
1896	—	—	—	—	—	—	—	—	—	6.32	8.74	10.96	15.66
1897	—	—	—	—	—	—	—	—	—	5.93	8.60	9.08	10.11
1898	—	—	—	—	—	—	—	—	—	5.83	8.45	9.31	10.40
1899	—	—	—	—	—	—	—	—	—	5.44	8.12	8.71	10.90
1900	—	—	—	—	—	—	—	—	—	6.59	8.07	8.24	9.60
1901	—	—	—	—	—	—	—	—	—	5.38	6.91	7.06	7.76
1902	—	—	—	—	—	—	—	—	—	5.24	6.78	7.70	8.01
1903	—	—	—	—	—	—	—	—	—	5.32	6.40	7.79	7.35
1904	—	—	—	—	—	—	—	—	—	5.28	6.59	7.75	7.90
1905	—	—	—	—	—	—	—	—	—	5.11	6.63	7.22	7.58
1906	—	—	—	—	—	—	—	—	—	4.91	6.35	6.86	6.48
1907	—	—	—	—	—	—	—	—	—	6.71	7.70	9.02	7.95
1908	—	—	—	—	—	—	—	—	—	5.49	6.89	7.68	8.16
1909	—	—	—	—	—	—	—	—	—	5.01	6.84	7.38	7.86
1910	—	—	—	—	—	—	—	—	—	5.38	6.90	8.04	7.61
1911	—	—	—	—	—	—	—	—	—	5.62	7.41	8.45	8.97
1912	—	—	—	—	—	—	—	—	—	5.49	7.20	8.65	8.28
1913	—	—	—	—	—	—	—	—	—	5.99	7.41	9.16	8.25
1914	—	—	—	—	—	—	—	—	—	6.10	7.68	8.84	8.85
1915	—	—	—	—	—	—	—	—	—	6.18	7.74	8.84	8.32
1916	—	—	—	—	—	—	—	—	—	6.65	7.48	8.29	8.10
1917	—	—	—	—	—	—	—	—	—	5.85	7.34	7.54	7.17
1918	—	—	—	—	—	—	—	—	—	6.20	7.08	8.22	7.76
1919	—	—	—	—	5.7	5.5	5.7	6.0	—	6.52	7.24	8.18	8.04
1920	—	—	—	—	6.6	6.3	6.7	6.8	—	6.38	7.57	7.72	7.34
1921	—	—	—	—	6.7	6.3	6.8	7.0	—	6.93	8.35	9.81	9.27
1922	—	—	—	—	5.5	5.1	5.5	6.1	—	6.45	7.39	8.16	8.05
1923	—	—	—	—	5.5	5.2	5.5	5.9	—	5.79	6.56	7.40	7.20
1924	—	—	—	—	5.1	4.6	5.1	5.7	—	6.07	6.76	7.96	7.59

Notes appear at end of table

TABLE Cg1198–1222   Bank rates on short-term business loans: 1815–1997   *Continued*

	Business loan rates				Customer loan rates					Regional interest rates			
	Total 19 cities	New York City	7 northern and eastern cities	11 southern and western cities	Total leading cities	New York City	Northern and eastern cities	Southern and western cities	Prime rate for commercial loans	Northeast	South	Plains	West
	Cj1198 [1]	Cj1199 [1]	Cj1200 [1]	Cj1201 [1]	Cj1202 [1]	Cj1203 [1]	Cj1204 [1]	Cj1205 [1]	Cj1206 [1]	Cj1207 [1]	Cj1208 [1]	Cj1209 [1]	Cj1210 [1]
Year	Percent per annum	Percent per annum	Percent per annum	Percent per annum	Percent per annum	Percent per annum	Percent per annum	Percent per annum	Percent per annum	Percent per annum	Percent per annum	Percent per annum	Percent per annum
1925	—	—	—	—	5.0	4.5	5.0	5.6	—	5.46	5.98	7.25	6.73
1926	—	—	—	—	5.1	4.7	5.1	5.6	—	5.94	6.74	7.38	7.23
1927	—	—	—	—	5.0	4.5	4.9	5.6	—	5.55	6.47	7.13	6.62
1928	5.2	5.0	5.2	5.4	5.4	5.2	5.3	5.7	—	5.39	6.43	6.46	6.80
1929	5.8	5.8	5.8	5.9	6.0	5.9	6.0	6.1	—	5.90	6.74	7.25	6.65
1930	4.9	4.4	4.8	5.4	—	—	—	—	—	6.13	7.10	7.85	7.43
1931	4.3	3.8	4.3	4.9	—	—	—	—	—	5.87	6.85	7.53	7.45
1932	4.7	4.2	4.8	5.2	—	—	—	—	—	6.04	6.81	7.82	7.43
1933	4.3	3.4	4.5	5.0	—	—	—	—	—	6.78	6.96	8.32	8.69
1934	3.5	2.5	3.7	4.3	—	—	—	—	—	5.33	6.25	7.08	7.02
1935	2.9	1.8	3.4	3.8	—	—	—	—	—	5.13	5.34	5.88	5.53
1936	2.7	1.7	3.0	3.4	—	—	—	—	—	4.65	5.40	5.81	5.36
1937	2.6	1.7	2.9	3.3	—	—	—	—	—	4.28	4.98	5.40	5.18
1938	2.5	1.7	2.8	3.3	—	—	—	—	—	4.59	4.97	5.81	5.55
1939	2.1	1.8	2.0	2.5	—	—	—	—	—	4.45	4.89	5.45	5.66
1940	2.1	1.8	2.0	2.5	—	—	—	—	—	4.23	4.94	5.15	5.23
1941	2.0	1.8	1.9	2.5	—	—	—	—	—	4.03	4.81	4.77	5.16
1942	2.2	2.0	2.3	2.6	—	—	—	—	—	1.61	2.61	3.03	4.17
1943	2.6	2.2	2.9	2.8	—	—	—	—	—	1.41	2.16	2.79	3.43
1944	2.4	2.1	2.7	2.8	—	—	—	—	—	3.72	3.71	4.09	4.33
1945	2.2	2.0	2.5	2.5	—	—	—	—	—	3.21	3.06	3.95	3.62
1946	2.1	1.8	2.1	2.5	—	—	—	—	1.50	3.12	3.39	3.79	3.55
1947	2.1	1.8	2.2	2.6	—	—	—	—	1.51	3.45	3.81	4.17	4.15
1948	2.5	2.2	2.6	2.9	—	—	—	—	1.83	3.92	4.24	4.22	4.54
1949	2.7	2.4	2.7	3.1	—	—	—	—	2.00	4.24	4.55	4.60	4.99
1950	2.7	2.4	2.7	3.2	—	—	—	—	2.05	3.93	4.42	4.32	4.65
1951	3.1	2.8	3.1	3.5	—	—	—	—	2.75	4.49	4.85	4.84	5.02
1952	3.5	3.3	3.5	3.8	—	—	—	—	3.00	4.41	4.90	5.02	5.15
1953	3.7	3.5	3.7	4.0	—	—	—	—	3.17	4.67	5.05	5.11	5.49
1954	3.6	3.4	3.6	4.0	—	—	—	—	3.06	4.65	5.02	5.05	5.28
1955	3.7	3.5	3.7	4.0	—	—	—	—	3.41	4.65	5.02	4.96	5.35
1956	4.2	4.0	4.2	4.4	—	—	—	—	3.77	4.92	5.34	5.41	5.35
1957	4.6	4.5	4.6	4.8	—	—	—	—	4.17	5.33	5.72	5.57	5.78
1958	4.3	4.1	4.3	4.7	—	—	—	—	3.85	5.26	5.58	5.47	5.75
1959	5.0	4.8	5.0	5.2	—	—	—	—	4.48	5.54	5.79	5.82	5.84
1960	5.2	5.0	5.2	5.5	—	—	—	—	4.83	5.64	6.00	6.01	6.42
1961	5.0	4.8	5.0	5.3	—	—	—	—	4.50	—	—	—	—
1962	5.0	4.8	5.0	5.3	—	—	—	—	4.50	—	—	—	—
1963	5.0	4.8	5.0	5.3	—	—	—	—	4.50	—	—	—	—
1964	5.0	4.8	5.0	5.3	—	—	—	—	4.50	—	—	—	—
1965	5.1	5.0	5.1	5.3	—	—	—	—	4.54	—	—	—	—
1966	6.0	5.8	6.1	6.2	—	—	—	—	5.62	—	—	—	—
1967	—	—	—	—	—	—	—	—	5.62	—	—	—	—
1968	—	—	—	—	—	—	—	—	6.31	—	—	—	—
1969	—	—	—	—	—	—	—	—	7.90	—	—	—	—
1970	—	—	—	—	—	—	—	—	7.87	—	—	—	—
1971	—	—	—	—	—	—	—	—	5.75	—	—	—	—
1972	—	—	—	—	—	—	—	—	5.30	—	—	—	—
1973	—	—	—	—	—	—	—	—	8.02	—	—	—	—
1974	—	—	—	—	—	—	—	—	10.69	—	—	—	—
1975	—	—	—	—	—	—	—	—	7.88	—	—	—	—
1976	—	—	—	—	—	—	—	—	6.84	—	—	—	—
1977	—	—	—	—	—	—	—	—	6.82	—	—	—	—
1978	—	—	—	—	—	—	—	—	9.06	—	—	—	—
1979	—	—	—	—	—	—	—	—	12.67	—	—	—	—
1980	—	—	—	—	—	—	—	—	15.27	—	—	—	—
1981	—	—	—	—	—	—	—	—	18.87	—	—	—	—
1982	—	—	—	—	—	—	—	—	14.86	—	—	—	—
1983	—	—	—	—	—	—	—	—	10.79	—	—	—	—
1984	—	—	—	—	—	—	—	—	12.04	—	—	—	—

Notes appear at end of table

(continued)

TABLE Cg1198-1222   Bank rates on short-term business loans: 1815–1997   *Continued*

	Business loan rates				Customer loan rates					Regional interest rates			
Year	Total 19 cities	New York City	7 northern and eastern cities	11 southern and western cities	Total leading cities	New York City	Northern and eastern cities	Southern and western cities	Prime rate for commercial loans	Northeast	South	Plains	West
	Cj1198 [1]	Cj1199 [1]	Cj1200 [1]	Cj1201 [1]	Cj1202 [1]	Cj1203 [1]	Cj1204 [1]	Cj1205 [1]	Cj1206 [1]	Cj1207 [1]	Cj1208 [1]	Cj1209 [1]	Cj1210 [1]
	Percent per annum	Percent per annum	Percent per annum	Percent per annum	Percent per annum	Percent per annum	Percent per annum	Percent per annum	Percent per annum	Percent per annum	Percent per annum	Percent per annum	Percent per annum
1985	—	—	—	—	—	—	—	—	9.93	—	—	—	—
1986	—	—	—	—	—	—	—	—	8.33	—	—	—	—
1987	—	—	—	—	—	—	—	—	8.21	—	—	—	—
1988	—	—	—	—	—	—	—	—	9.32	—	—	—	—
1989	—	—	—	—	—	—	—	—	10.87	—	—	—	—
1990	—	—	—	—	—	—	—	—	10.01	—	—	—	—
1991	—	—	—	—	—	—	—	—	8.46	—	—	—	—
1992	—	—	—	—	—	—	—	—	6.25	—	—	—	—
1993	—	—	—	—	—	—	—	—	6.00	—	—	—	—
1994	—	—	—	—	—	—	—	—	7.15	—	—	—	—
1995	—	—	—	—	—	—	—	—	8.83	—	—	—	—
1996	—	—	—	—	—	—	—	—	8.27	—	—	—	—
1997	—	—	—	—	—	—	—	—	8.44	—	—	—	—

	Net rates of return on earning assets											
Year	Boston	Massachusetts	Rhode Island	New York City	Philadelphia	Pennsylvania	Virginia	South Carolina	New Orleans	Kentucky	Tennessee	Indiana
	Cj1211 [2]	Cj1212 [2]	Cj1213 [2]	Cj1214 [2]	Cj1215 [2]	Cj1216 [2]	Cj1217 [2]	Cj1218 [2]	Cj1219 [2]	Cj1220 [2]	Cj1221 [2]	Cj1222 [2]
	Percent per annum	Percent per annum	Percent per annum	Percent per annum	Percent per annum	Percent per annum	Percent per annum	Percent per annum	Percent per annum	Percent per annum	Percent per annum	Percent per annum
1815	—	—	—	—	4.62	—	—	8.55	—	—	—	—
1816	—	—	—	—	5.70	—	—	5.55	—	—	—	—
1817	—	—	—	—	3.69	—	—	5.45	—	—	—	—
1818	—	—	—	—	5.55	—	—	8.35	—	—	—	—
1819	5.48	4.99	—	—	3.84	—	—	4.23	—	—	—	—
1820	6.12	5.34	—	—	5.60	4.24	—	4.36	—	—	—	—
1821	5.61	4.76	—	—	4.78	4.16	—	4.34	—	—	—	—
1822	4.28	4.61	—	—	5.65	4.52	4.08	5.77	—	6.33	—	—
1823	4.70	4.65	—	—	3.42	4.35	3.81	4.86	—	4.42	—	—
1824	—	—	—	—	5.21	3.92	4.14	4.62	—	4.01	—	—
1825	—	—	—	—	4.24	4.48	4.61	4.15	—	3.93	—	—
1826	—	—	—	—	5.86	4.32	3.97	2.53	—	3.00	—	—
1827	4.05	5.50	—	—	4.95	4.28	4.97	7.81	—	3.12	—	—
1828	4.64	5.08	—	—	5.82	4.62	3.97	4.50	—	3.83	—	—
1829	4.93	5.07	—	—	4.58	4.37	4.23	4.09	—	3.51	—	—
1830	4.88	—	—	—	4.97	5.89	4.45	4.14	—	5.02	—	—
1831	5.42	—	—	—	5.15	5.19	4.84	4.49	—	3.48	—	—
1832	4.05	—	—	—	4.48	5.61	6.28	4.24	—	3.35	—	—
1833	4.94	5.21	—	5.03	6.54	5.95	8.02	4.37	—	2.85	—	—
1834	4.31	5.07	—	5.69	3.41	4.04	3.75	3.54	6.82	—	—	—
1835	4.52	5.19	6.24	5.11	6.12	5.69	4.43	4.12	7.54	5.89	—	7.97
1836	4.56	5.28	5.78	6.82	5.74	6.35	7.22	4.37	7.16	7.97	—	7.60
1837	5.09	5.53	4.88	5.91	4.75	4.96	5.70	6.11	11.28	6.03	—	8.50
1838	5.21	5.30	5.27	5.33	5.47	4.05	4.41	6.00	7.68	5.93	—	8.35
1839	6.09	4.94	5.46	4.24	3.44	4.78	6.78	5.11	10.15	4.38	—	—
1840	5.45	4.83	4.39	5.57	5.73	4.34	5.43	3.10	9.01	3.30	6.85	—
1841	5.46	—	5.80	5.27	4.41	4.81	4.21	5.75	8.86	4.91	5.48	7.65
1842	5.51	—	5.34	3.95	2.50	—	4.20	5.97	8.85	6.88	7.41	5.05
1843	4.89	—	4.86	5.37	3.72	3.40	4.12	6.20	—	6.02	4.85	2.85
1844	4.28	—	3.94	5.80	5.18	5.13	4.15	6.03	—	6.41	6.99	5.74
1845	4.31	4.34	5.40	5.21	4.20	4.82	5.10	5.76	—	6.29	4.24	7.86
1846	5.25	5.00	6.03	4.69	6.39	4.13	3.95	5.42	—	5.72	5.66	—
1847	4.51	4.92	5.57	5.04	5.21	4.08	4.99	7.11	—	5.44	4.92	6.32
1848	5.87	5.10	4.58	5.32	4.83	4.97	4.43	5.07	7.73	7.57	5.62	8.36
1849	6.02	5.49	6.18	7.17	6.35	4.48	4.19	6.03	4.84	5.02	5.50	7.77

Notes appear at end of table

TABLE Cg1198–1222   Bank rates on short-term business loans: 1815–1997   *Continued*

Net rates of return on earning assets

Year	Boston Cj1211 [2] Percent per annum	Massachusetts Cj1212 [2] Percent per annum	Rhode Island Cj1213 [2] Percent per annum	New York City Cj1214 [2] Percent per annum	Philadelphia Cj1215 [2] Percent per annum	Pennsylvania Cj1216 [2] Percent per annum	Virginia Cj1217 [2] Percent per annum	South Carolina Cj1218 [2] Percent per annum	New Orleans Cj1219 [2] Percent per annum	Kentucky Cj1220 [2] Percent per annum	Tennessee Cj1221 [2] Percent per annum	Indiana Cj1222 [2] Percent per annum
1850	5.15	5.16	5.31	5.62	6.47	4.79	4.53	9.28	7.42	6.22	4.01	9.45
1851	5.14	5.23	5.58	6.32	4.69	5.07	4.72	7.67	7.79	7.00	6.08	5.95
1852	5.13	5.42	5.24	7.23	5.56	4.07	5.53	6.38	7.91	7.01	4.77	6.81
1853	5.73	5.92	5.94	4.99	5.10	5.50	4.46	6.71	7.38	5.80	4.38	6.37
1854	5.57	5.47	5.82	4.98	5.31	5.84	5.04	5.57	8.50	5.00	5.19	7.70
1855	5.87	5.75	5.20	5.87	5.70	5.96	5.18	6.03	12.81	8.42	4.65	10.89
1856	6.11	5.90	5.18	6.09	4.45	6.19	4.29	6.30	—	4.80	7.35	9.25
1857	6.01	5.59	5.81	5.45	3.16	5.28	3.88	5.93	—	4.96	7.46	—
1858	4.75	5.58	5.53	4.95	6.46	5.32	2.92	5.98	—	5.78	6.79	—
1859	4.67	5.18	5.49	4.62	4.32	6.04	5.96	6.76	—	6.25	4.48	—

[1] No data before 1880.

[2] No data after 1859.

Sources

Series Cj1198–1205. Board of Governors of the Federal Reserve System. 1919–1938: *Banking and Monetary Statistics*, pp. 463–4. 1939–1963, *Supplement to Banking and Monetary Statistics* (1966), section 12, "Money Rates and Securities Markets," p. 61. 1964–1966: *Federal Reserve Bulletin* (various issues).

Series Cj1206. Board of Governors of the Federal Reserve System. 1946–1963: *Supplement to Banking and Monetary Statistics* (1941–1970), section 12, "Money Rates and Securities Markets." 1964–1997: *Annual Statistical Digest* and *Federal Reserve Bulletin* (various issues).

Series Cj1207–1210. Howard Bodenhorn, "A More Perfect Union: Regional Interest Rates in the United States, 1880–1960," in M. Bordo and R. Sylla, editors, *Anglo-American Financial Systems* (Irwin, 1995), pp. 447–51.

Series Cj1211-1222. Howard Bodenhorn and Hugh Rockoff, "Regional Interest Rates in Antebellum America," in C. Goldin and H. Rockoff, editors, *Strategic Factors in Nineteenth-Century American Economic History* (University of Chicago Press, 1992), pp. 167–8.

Documentation

Series Cj1198–1205

Data by months through 1938 and by quarters thereafter are available in the source publications. These data are compiled by the Board of Governors of the Federal Reserve System from reports submitted by member banks in leading cities throughout the country.

The reporting cities are representative financial centers that have large loan markets. Interest rates charged by banks in these cities are more responsive to changes in general monetary conditions than are rates in other places. Because of the financial importance of the cities, their influence would predominate in any compilation designed to show movements of interest rates in large cities.

Figures for series Cj1202–1205 represent averages of prevailing rates reported monthly by banks in a varying number of leading cities on commercial loans and time and demand security loans. These figures are not strictly comparable with those in series Cj1198–1201, but they are believed to represent bank rates on business loans. For series Cj1198-1201, the figures for 1928–1938 are averages of prevailing rates reported monthly by banks in nineteen principal cities on business loans only; beginning in 1939, the figures are averages of interest rates charged by banks in the nineteen cities on short-term business loans made during the first half of March, June, September, and December. For a description of the figures prior to 1939, see *Banking and Monetary Statistics* (1943), pp. 426–7; beginning in 1939, see *Supplement to Banking and Monetary Statistics* (1966), pp. 9–11. Beginning in 1948, the source publication includes data on average interest rates by size of loan.

In 1967, these series were revised for expanded coverage. The new series cover new loans and loan renewals made during the first half of the middle month of each calendar quarter. The number of financial centers covered by the survey has been raised from 19 to 35 and the number of respondent banks from 66 to 1126. For further details, see *Federal Reserve Bulletin* (May 1967), pp. 721–7. The weighted average interest rate on short-term commercial and industrial loans from these quarterly surveys, as well as rates on several classes of longer-term loans, are reported in the Federal Reserve's *Annual Statistical Digest*, 1970–1979 and 1980–1989, but do not appear in the 1990–1995 edition of the *Annual Statistical Digest*.

Series Cj1206. This rate is that posted by a majority of the top twenty-five (by assets in domestic offices) insured U.S.-chartered commercial banks. The prime is one of the several base rates banks use to price short-term business loans.

Series Cj1207–1210. These figures are average loan rates charged by national banks by region constructed from earnings and balance sheet data reported to the U.S. Comptroller of the Currency. Returns from other earning assets besides loans and discounts – that is, holdings of U.S. securities, bonds of other governmental units, corporate bonds, and interest-bearing balances held with correspondent banks – are subtracted from gross earnings to calculate the revenue generated by the banks' loan portfolios. The rates of return to loans and discounts are then constructed by dividing by loans and discounts plus overdrafts less loan losses. For 1880–1887, the Comptroller reported only net earnings rather than gross earnings, and so expenses had to be estimated in order to calculate the gross figure from the net. For 1927–1960, reported "Interest and Discounts on Loans" and "Service Charge on Loans" are used in the numerator of the rate of return calculation.

Series Cj1211–1222. These figures are calculated average rates of returns on discounts and bills of exchange similar to those in series Cj1207–1210 based primarily on state legislative reports and documents. Net earnings are computed as dividends plus changes in surplus plus taxes less securities earnings.

TABLE Cj1223–1237   Money market rates: 1831–1997
Contributed by John A. James and Richard Sylla

	Commercial paper		Finance company paper, placed directly, 3–6 months	Stock exchange time loans, 90 days	Stock exchange call loans			Prime bankers' acceptances, 90 days	U.S. government securities				Federal Reserve Bank of New York discount rate		Federal funds rate
									3-month bills		Certificates and selected note and bond issues, 9–12 months	Selected note and bond issues, 3–5 years			
		Prime, 4–6 months			All	New	Renewals		Rate on new issues	Market yield			Low	High	
	60–90 day														
	Cj1223	Cj1224 [1,2]	Cj1225 [2,3]	Cj1226 [1]	Cj1227 [4]	Cj1228 [4]	Cj1229 [4]	Cj1230 [1,2]	Cj1231 [2,5,6]	Cj1232 [2,5,6]	Cj1233 [5]	Cj1234 [5]	Cj1235	Cj1236	Cj1237 [2]
Year	Percent per annum	Percent per annum	Percent per annum	Percent per annum	Percent per annum	Percent per annum	Percent per annum	Percent per annum	Percent per annum	Percent per annum	Percent per annum	Percent per annum	Percent per annum	Percent per annum	Percent per annum
1831	6.12	—	—	—	—	—	—	—	—	—	—	—	—	—	—
1832	6.25	—	—	—	—	—	—	—	—	—	—	—	—	—	—
1833	7.83	—	—	—	—	—	—	—	—	—	—	—	—	—	—
1834	14.70	—	—	—	—	—	—	—	—	—	—	—	—	—	—
1835	7.00	—	—	—	—	—	—	—	—	—	—	—	—	—	—
1836	18.00	—	—	—	—	—	—	—	—	—	—	—	—	—	—
1837	14.25	—	—	—	—	—	—	—	—	—	—	—	—	—	—
1838	9.04	—	—	—	—	—	—	—	—	—	—	—	—	—	—
1839	12.58	—	—	—	—	—	—	—	—	—	—	—	—	—	—
1840	7.75	—	—	—	—	—	—	—	—	—	—	—	—	—	—
1841	6.80	—	—	—	—	—	—	—	—	—	—	—	—	—	—
1842	8.08	—	—	—	—	—	—	—	—	—	—	—	—	—	—
1843	4.41	—	—	—	—	—	—	—	—	—	—	—	—	—	—
1844	4.87	—	—	—	—	—	—	—	—	—	—	—	—	—	—
1845	4.71	—	—	—	—	—	—	—	—	—	—	—	—	—	—
1846	8.33	—	—	—	—	—	—	—	—	—	—	—	—	—	—
1847	9.59	—	—	—	—	—	—	—	—	—	—	—	—	—	—
1848	15.10	—	—	—	—	—	—	—	—	—	—	—	—	—	—
1849	10.25	—	—	—	—	—	—	—	—	—	—	—	—	—	—
1850	8.04	—	—	—	—	—	—	—	—	—	—	—	—	—	—
1851	9.66	—	—	—	—	—	—	—	—	—	—	—	—	—	—
1852	6.33	—	—	—	—	—	—	—	—	—	—	—	—	—	—
1853	10.25	—	—	—	—	—	—	—	—	—	—	—	—	—	—
1854	10.37	—	—	—	—	—	—	—	—	—	—	—	—	—	—
1855	8.92	—	—	—	—	—	—	—	—	—	—	—	—	—	—
1856	8.83	—	—	—	—	—	—	—	—	—	—	—	—	—	—
1857	11.56	—	—	—	—	—	9.34	—	—	—	—	—	—	—	—
1858	4.81	—	—	—	—	—	4.15	—	—	—	—	—	—	—	—
1859	6.14	—	—	—	—	—	5.43	—	—	—	—	—	—	—	—
1860	7.31	—	—	—	—	—	5.99	—	—	—	—	—	—	—	—
1861	6.70	—	—	—	—	—	5.51	—	—	—	—	—	—	—	—
1862	5.32	—	—	—	—	—	5.23	—	—	—	—	—	—	—	—
1863	5.65	—	—	—	—	—	6.19	—	—	—	—	—	—	—	—
1864	7.36	—	—	—	—	—	6.59	—	—	—	—	—	—	—	—

	Commercial paper		Finance company paper, placed directly, 3–6 months	Stock exchange time loans, 90 days	Stock exchange call loans			Prime bankers' acceptances, 90 days	U.S. government securities				Federal Reserve Bank of New York discount rate		Federal funds rate
	60–90 day	Prime, 4–6 months			All	New	Renewals		3-month bills		Certificates and selected note and bond issues, 9–12 months	Selected note and bond issues, 3–5 years	Low	High	
									Rate on new issues	Market yield					
Year	Cj1223	Cj1224 [1,2]	Cj1225 [2,3]	Cj1226 [1]	Cj1227 [4]	Cj1228 [4]	Cj1229 [4]	Cj1230 [1,2]	Cj1231 [2,5,6]	Cj1232 [2,5,6]	Cj1233 [5]	Cj1234 [5]	Cj1235	Cj1236	Cj1237 [2]
	Percent per annum	Percent per annum	Percent per annum	Percent per annum	Percent per annum	Percent per annum	Percent per annum	Percent per annum	Percent per annum	Percent per annum	Percent per annum	Percent per annum	Percent per annum	Percent per annum	Percent per annum
1865	7.77	—	—	—	—	—	6.17	—	—	—	—	—	—	—	—
1866	6.33	—	—	—	—	—	5.23	—	—	—	—	—	—	—	—
1867	7.32	—	—	—	—	—	6.26	—	—	—	—	—	—	—	—
1868	7.28	—	—	—	—	—	7.54	—	—	—	—	—	—	—	—
1869	9.66	—	—	—	—	—	10.29	—	—	—	—	—	—	—	—
1870	7.23	—	—	—	—	—	5.72	—	—	—	—	—	—	—	—
1871	6.98	—	—	—	—	—	5.55	—	—	—	—	—	—	—	—
1872	8.63	—	—	—	—	—	8.38	—	—	—	—	—	—	—	—
1873	10.27	—	—	—	—	—	14.24	—	—	—	—	—	—	—	—
1874	5.98	—	—	—	—	—	3.42	—	—	—	—	—	—	—	—
1875	5.44	—	—	—	—	—	3.11	—	—	—	—	—	—	—	—
1876	5.13	—	—	—	—	—	3.35	—	—	—	—	—	—	—	—
1877	5.01	—	—	—	—	—	3.87	—	—	—	—	—	—	—	—
1878	4.82	—	—	—	—	—	4.22	—	—	—	—	—	—	—	—
1879	5.14	—	—	—	—	—	5.44	—	—	—	—	—	—	—	—
1880	5.23	—	—	—	—	—	4.86	—	—	—	—	—	—	—	—
1881	5.36	—	—	—	—	—	5.76	—	—	—	—	—	—	—	—
1882	5.64	—	—	—	—	—	4.53	—	—	—	—	—	—	—	—
1883	5.62	—	—	—	—	—	3.71	—	—	—	—	—	—	—	—
1884	5.21	—	—	—	—	—	3.03	—	—	—	—	—	—	—	—
1885	4.05	—	—	—	—	—	1.66	—	—	—	—	—	—	—	—
1886	4.77	—	—	—	—	—	4.03	—	—	—	—	—	—	—	—
1887	5.73	—	—	—	—	—	5.01	—	—	—	—	—	—	—	—
1888	4.91	—	—	—	—	—	2.51	—	—	—	—	—	—	—	—
1889	4.85	—	—	—	—	—	4.18	—	—	—	—	—	—	—	—
1890	5.62	6.91	—	5.31	—	—	5.84	—	—	—	—	—	—	—	—
1891	5.46	6.48	—	4.83	—	—	3.42	—	—	—	—	—	—	—	—
1892	4.10	5.40	—	3.80	—	—	3.08	—	—	—	—	—	—	—	—
1893	6.78	7.64	—	5.08	—	—	4.57	—	—	—	—	—	—	—	—
1894	3.04	5.22	—	2.30	—	—	1.07	—	—	—	—	—	—	—	—
1895	2.83	5.80	—	2.82	—	—	1.88	—	—	—	—	—	—	—	—
1896	5.82	7.02	—	4.83	—	—	4.28	—	—	—	—	—	—	—	—
1897	3.50	4.72	—	2.68	—	—	1.75	—	—	—	—	—	—	—	—
1898	3.83	5.34	—	3.31	—	—	2.18	—	—	—	—	—	—	—	—
1899	4.15	5.50	—	4.19	—	—	5.08	—	—	—	—	—	—	—	—
1900	4.38	5.71	—	3.94	—	—	2.94	—	—	—	—	—	—	—	—
1901	—	5.40	—	4.24	—	—	4.00	—	—	—	—	—	—	—	—
1902	—	5.81	—	5.05	—	—	5.15	—	—	—	—	—	—	—	—
1903	—	6.16	—	4.84	—	—	3.71	—	—	—	—	—	—	—	—
1904	—	5.14	—	3.10	—	—	1.78	—	—	—	—	—	—	—	—

Notes appear at end of table

(continued)

TABLE Cj1223–1237 Money market rates: 1831–1997 Continued

	Commercial paper		Finance company paper, placed directly, 3–6 months	Stock exchange time loans, 90 days	Stock exchange call loans			Prime bankers' acceptances, 90 days	U.S. government securities				Federal Reserve Bank of New York discount rate		Federal funds rate
	60–90 day	Prime, 4–6 months			All	New	Renewals		3-month bills		Certificates and selected note and bond issues, 9–12 months	Selected note and bond issues, 3–5 years			
									Rate on new issues	Market yield			Low	High	
Year	Cj1223	Cj1224 [1,2]	Cj1225 [2,3]	Cj1226 [1]	Cj1227 [4]	Cj1228 [4]	Cj1229 [4]	Cj1230 [1,2]	Cj1231 [2,5,6]	Cj1232 [2,5,6]	Cj1233 [5]	Cj1234 [5]	Cj1235	Cj1236	Cj1237 [2]
	Percent per annum	Percent per annum	Percent per annum	Percent per annum	Percent per annum	Percent per annum	Percent per annum	Percent per annum	Percent per annum	Percent per annum	Percent per annum	Percent per annum	Percent per annum	Percent per annum	Percent per annum
1905	—	5.18	—	3.82	—	—	4.44	—	—	—	—	—	—	—	—
1906	—	6.25	—	5.71	—	—	6.54	—	—	—	—	—	—	—	—
1907	—	6.66	—	6.49	—	—	7.01	—	—	—	—	—	—	—	—
1908	—	5.00	—	3.24	—	—	1.92	—	—	—	—	—	—	—	—
1909	—	4.67	—	3.26	—	—	2.71	—	—	—	—	—	—	—	—
1910	—	5.72	—	4.03	—	—	2.98	—	—	—	—	—	—	—	—
1911	—	4.75	—	3.22	—	—	2.57	—	—	—	—	—	—	—	—
1912	—	5.41	—	4.16	—	—	3.52	—	—	—	—	—	—	—	—
1913	—	6.20	—	4.64	—	—	3.22	—	—	—	—	—	—	—	—
1914	—	5.47	—	4.37	—	—	3.43	—	—	—	—	—	5.00	6.00	—
1915	—	4.01	—	2.85	—	—	1.92	—	—	—	—	—	4.00	5.00	—
1916	—	3.84	—	3.25	—	—	2.62	—	—	—	—	—	3.00	4.00	—
1917	—	5.07	—	4.62	—	—	3.43	—	—	—	—	—	3.00	3.50	—
1918	—	6.02	—	5.90	—	—	5.28	4.19	—	—	—	—	3.50	4.00	—
1919	—	5.37	—	5.83	—	6.70	6.32	4.37	—	—	—	—	4.00	4.75	—
1920	—	7.50	—	8.06	—	8.07	7.74	6.06	—	—	—	—	4.75	7.00	—
1921	—	6.62	—	6.15	—	5.97	5.97	5.28	—	—	—	—	4.50	7.00	—
1922	—	4.52	—	4.53	—	4.36	4.29	3.51	—	—	—	—	4.00	4.50	—
1923	—	5.07	—	5.14	—	4.87	4.86	4.09	—	—	—	—	4.00	4.50	—
1924	—	3.98	—	3.64	—	3.10	3.08	2.98	—	—	—	—	3.00	4.50	—
1925	—	4.02	—	4.23	—	4.20	4.18	3.29	—	—	—	—	3.00	3.50	—
1926	—	4.34	—	4.60	—	4.52	4.50	3.59	—	—	—	—	3.50	4.00	—
1927	—	4.11	—	4.35	—	4.05	4.06	3.45	—	—	—	—	3.50	4.00	—
1928	—	4.85	—	5.86	—	6.10	6.04	4.09	—	—	—	—	3.50	5.00	—
1929	—	5.85	—	7.75	—	7.74	7.61	5.03	—	—	—	—	4.50	6.00	—
1930	—	3.59	—	3.26	—	2.87	2.94	2.48	—	—	—	—	2.00	4.50	—
1931	—	2.64	—	2.15	—	1.74	1.74	1.57	1.402	1.40	—	—	1.50	3.50	—
1932	—	2.73	—	1.87	—	2.05	2.05	1.28	0.879	0.88	—	—	2.50	3.50	—
1933	—	1.73	—	1.11	—	1.14	1.16	0.63	0.515	0.52	—	—	2.00	3.50	—
1934	—	1.02	—	0.90	—	1.00	1.00	0.25	0.256	0.26	—	—	1.50	2.00	—
1935	—	0.75	—	0.55	—	0.56	0.55	0.13	0.137	0.14	—	—	1.50	1.50	—
1936	—	0.75	—	1.16	—	0.91	0.91	0.15	0.143	0.14	—	—	1.50	1.50	—
1937	—	0.94	—	1.25	—	1.00	1.00	0.43	0.447	0.45	—	—	1.00	1.50	—
1938	—	0.81	—	1.25	—	1.00	1.00	0.44	0.053	0.05	—	—	1.00	1.00	—
1939	—	0.59	—	1.25	—	1.00	1.00	0.44	0.023	0.02	—	—	1.00	1.00	—
1940	—	0.56	—	1.25	—	1.00	1.00	0.44	0.014	0.01	—	—	1.00	1.00	—
1941	—	0.53	—	1.25	—	1.00	1.00	0.44	0.103	0.13	—	—	1.00	1.00	—
1942	—	0.66	—	1.25	—	1.00	1.00	0.44	0.326	0.34	—	0.73	0.50	1.00	—
1943	—	0.69	—	1.25	—	1.00	1.00	0.44	0.373	0.38	0.75	1.46	0.50	1.00	—
1944	—	0.73	—	1.25	—	1.00	1.00	0.44	0.375	0.38	0.79	1.33	0.50	1.00	—

	Commercial paper		Finance company paper, placed directly, 3-6 months	Stock exchange time loans, 90 days	Stock exchange call loans			Prime bankers' acceptances, 90 days	U.S. government securities				Federal Reserve Bank of New York discount rate		Federal funds rate
	60-90 day	Prime, 4-6 months				All	New	Renewals		3-month bills		Certificates and selected note and bond issues, 9-12 months	Selected note and bond issues, 3-5 years			
										Rate on new issues	Market yield			Low	High	
Year	Cj1223	Cj1224 [1,2]	Cj1225 [2,3]	Cj1226 [1]	Cj1227 [4]	Cj1228 [4]	Cj1229 [4]	Cj1230 [1,2]	Cj1231 [2,5,6]	Cj1232 [2,5,6]	Cj1233 [5]	Cj1234 [5]	Cj1235	Cj1236	Cj1237 [2]
	Percent per annum	Percent per annum	Percent per annum	Percent per annum	Percent per annum	Percent per annum	Percent per annum	Percent per annum	Percent per annum	Percent per annum	Percent per annum	Percent per annum	Percent per annum	Percent per annum	Percent per annum
1945	—	0.75	—	1.25	—	1.00	1.00	0.44	0.375	0.38	0.81	1.18	0.50	1.00	—
1946	—	0.81	—	1.35	—	1.16	1.16	0.61	0.375	0.38	0.82	1.16	0.50	1.00	—
1947	—	1.03	0.94	1.50	—	1.38	1.38	0.87	0.594	0.61	0.88	1.32	1.00	1.00	—
1948	—	1.44	1.34	1.50	—	1.55	1.55	1.11	1.040	1.05	1.14	1.62	1.00	1.50	—
1949	—	1.49	1.46	1.50	—	1.63	1.63	1.13	1.102	1.11	1.14	1.43	1.50	1.50	—
1950	—	1.45	1.41	1.59	—	1.63	1.63	1.15	1.218	1.20	1.26	1.50	1.50	1.75	—
1951	—	2.16	1.87	2.15	—	2.17	2.17	1.60	1.552	1.52	1.73	1.93	1.75	1.75	—
1952	—	2.33	2.16	2.42	—	2.48	2.48	1.75	1.766	1.72	1.81	2.13	1.75	1.75	—
1953	—	2.52	2.33	2.85	—	3.06	3.06	1.87	1.931	1.90	2.07	2.56	1.75	2.00	—
1954	—	1.58	1.27	2.80	—	3.05	3.05	1.35	0.953	0.94	0.92	1.82	1.50	2.00	—
1955	—	2.18	1.98	3.01	—	3.20	3.20	1.71	1.753	1.73	1.89	2.50	1.50	2.50	1.79
1956	—	3.31	3.08	3.89	—	4.08	4.03	2.64	2.658	2.62	2.83	3.12	2.50	3.00	2.73
1957	—	3.81	3.56	4.35	4.50	—	—	3.45	3.267	3.23	3.53	3.62	3.00	3.50	3.11
1958	—	2.46	2.12	3.62	3.72	—	—	2.04	1.839	1.78	2.09	2.90	1.75	3.00	1.57
1959	—	3.97	3.84	4.22	4.22	—	—	3.49	3.405	3.37	4.11	4.33	2.50	4.00	3.31
1960	—	3.85	3.60	4.99	4.99	—	—	3.51	2.928	2.87	3.55	3.99	3.00	4.00	3.21
1961	—	2.97	2.73	4.50	4.50	—	—	2.81	2.378	2.36	2.91	3.60	3.00	3.00	1.95
1962	—	3.26	3.08	4.50	4.50	—	—	3.01	2.778	2.77	3.02	3.57	3.00	3.00	2.71
1963	—	3.55	3.41	—	4.50	—	—	3.36	3.157	3.16	3.28	3.72	3.00	3.50	3.18
1964	—	3.97	3.84	—	4.50	—	—	3.77	3.560	3.54	3.76	4.06	3.50	4.00	3.50
1965	—	4.38	4.27	—	4.69	—	—	4.34	3.954	3.95	4.09	4.22	4.00	4.50	4.07
1966	—	5.55	5.42	—	5.78	—	—	5.42	4.881	4.86	1.17	1.16	4.50	4.50	5.11
1967	—	5.10	4.89	—	5.67	—	—	4.82	4.321	4.29	4.84	5.07	4.00	4.50	4.22
1968	—	5.90	5.68	—	6.31	—	—	5.79	5.339	5.34	5.62	5.59	4.50	5.50	5.66
1969	—	7.83	7.09	—	7.96	—	—	7.75	6.677	6.67	7.06	6.85	5.50	6.00	8.21
1970	—	7.72	7.20	—	7.92	—	—	7.23	6.430	6.39	6.90	7.37	5.00	5.75	7.17
1971	—	5.11	4.89	—	—	—	—	4.67	4.350	4.33	—	—	4.50	5.25	4.67
1972	—	4.72	4.55	—	—	—	—	4.33	4.070	4.06	—	—	4.50	4.50	4.44
1973	—	8.15	7.38	—	—	—	—	8.27	7.040	7.04	—	—	5.00	7.50	8.74
1974	—	9.88	8.62	—	—	—	—	9.74	7.890	7.85	—	—	7.50	8.00	10.51
1975	—	6.33	6.17	—	—	—	—	6.33	5.840	5.79	—	—	6.00	7.25	5.82
1976	—	5.35	5.23	—	—	—	—	5.08	4.990	4.98	—	—	5.50	6.00	5.05
1977	—	5.61	5.50	—	—	—	—	5.53	5.270	5.26	—	—	5.25	6.50	5.54
1978	—	7.99	7.77	—	—	—	—	8.05	7.220	7.18	—	—	6.50	9.50	7.93
1979	—	10.90	10.24	—	—	—	—	10.97	10.050	10.05	—	—	9.50	12.00	11.20
1980	—	12.24	11.25	—	—	—	—	12.67	11.510	11.39	—	—	10.00	13.00	13.35
1981	—	14.77	13.74	—	—	—	—	15.34	14.030	14.04	—	—	12.00	14.00	16.39
1982	—	11.89	11.20	—	—	—	—	11.89	10.690	10.60	—	—	8.50	12.00	12.24
1983	—	8.90	8.70	—	—	—	—	8.91	8.630	8.62	—	—	8.50	8.50	9.09
1984	—	10.18	9.67	—	—	—	—	10.17	9.350	9.54	—	—	8.00	9.00	10.23

Notes appear at end of table   (continued)

TABLE Cj1223–1237   Money market rates: 1831–1997   Continued

Year	Commercial paper 60–90 day Cj1223 Percent per annum	Commercial paper Prime, 4–6 months Cj1224 [1,2] Percent per annum	Finance company paper, placed directly, 3–6 months Cj1225 [2,3] Percent per annum	Stock exchange time loans, 90 days Cj1226 [1] Percent per annum	Stock exchange call loans All Cj1227 [4] Percent per annum	Stock exchange call loans New Cj1228 [4] Percent per annum	Stock exchange call loans Renewals Cj1229 [4] Percent per annum	Prime bankers' acceptances, 90 days Cj1230 [1,2] Percent per annum	U.S. government securities 3-month bills Rate on new issues Cj1231 [2,5,6] Percent per annum	U.S. government securities 3-month bills Market yield Cj1232 [2,5,6] Percent per annum	Certificates and selected note and bond issues, 9–12 months Cj1233 [5] Percent per annum	Selected note and bond issues, 3–5 years Cj1234 [5] Percent per annum	Federal Reserve Bank of New York discount rate Low Cj1235 Percent per annum	Federal Reserve Bank of New York discount rate High Cj1236 Percent per annum	Federal funds rate Cj1237 [2] Percent per annum
1985	—	8.00	7.74	—	—	—	—	7.91	7.470	7.47	—	—	7.50	8.00	8.10
1986	—	6.39	6.31	—	—	—	—	6.38	5.980	5.97	—	—	5.50	7.50	6.80
1987	—	6.85	6.37	—	—	—	—	6.75	5.820	5.78	—	—	5.50	6.00	6.66
1988	—	7.68	7.14	—	—	—	—	7.56	6.690	6.67	—	—	6.00	6.50	7.57
1989	—	8.80	8.16	—	—	—	—	8.87	8.120	8.11	—	—	6.50	7.00	9.21
1990	—	7.95	7.53	—	—	—	—	7.93	7.510	7.50	—	—	6.50	7.00	8.10
1991	—	5.85	5.60	—	—	—	—	5.70	5.420	5.38	—	—	3.50	6.50	5.69
1992	—	3.80	3.63	—	—	—	—	3.62	3.450	3.43	—	—	3.00	3.50	3.52
1993	—	3.30	3.15	—	—	—	—	3.13	3.020	3.00	—	—	3.00	3.00	3.02
1994	—	4.93	4.56	—	—	—	—	4.56	4.290	4.25	—	—	3.00	4.75	4.21
1995	—	5.93	5.68	—	—	—	—	5.81	5.510	5.49	—	—	4.75	5.25	5.83
1996	—	5.42	5.21	—	—	—	—	5.31	5.020	5.01	—	—	5.00	5.25	5.30
1997	—	5.62	5.48	—	—	—	—	5.54	5.070	5.06	—	—	5.00	5.00	5.46

[1] Averages of weekly prevailing rates through 1934; averages of the most representative daily offering rates quoted by dealers thereafter.

[2] Annualized using a 360-day year for bank interest.

[3] Averages of the most representative daily offering rates published by finance companies, for varying maturities in the 90- to 179-day range.

[4] Seven-day average for week ending Wednesday.

[5] Yields are averages computed from daily closing bid prices.

[6] Bills quoted on bank discount rate basis.

Sources

Series Cj1223. Frederick R. Macaulay, *Some Theoretical Problems Suggested by the Movements of Interest Rate, Bond Yields and Stock Prices in the United States since 1856* (National Bureau of Economic Research, 1938), pp. A237–50, 340–51.

Series Cj1224–1237. Board of Governors of the Federal Reserve System. 1890–1941: *Banking and Monetary Statistics* (1943), pp. 439–42, 448, 460; 1941–1963: *Supplement to Banking and Monetary Statistics* (1966), section 12, "Money Rates and Securities Markets," pp. 37, 48, 50; 1964–1997: *Annual Statistical Digest* and *Federal Reserve Bulletin* (various issues).

Documentation

Available statistics on interest rates and security prices indicate the cost of credit to borrowers (mainly business concerns and the federal government) and the income received by those who lend and invest (primarily individuals, trusts, endowments, banks, and other financial institutions). Tables Cj1179–1260 present a variety of money rate and security market statistics, including principal short-term open market rates in New York City, the discount rate of the Federal Reserve Bank of New York, the federal funds rate, commercial paper and bankers' acceptances outstanding, bank rates on short-term loans to business, bond yields and prices, and interest rates charged and paid by financial institutions.

Series Cj1223. The 1831–1857 figures are taken from Erastus B. Bigelow, *The Tariff Question, Considered in Regard to the Policy of England and the Interests of the United States; with Statistical and Comparative Tables* (Little, Brown, 1863), Appendix Table 112, and refer to "street rates on first class paper in Boston." Those from 1857 are for 60–90 prime double name paper in New York, although Macaulay notes that in the 1857–1865 period it is "not clear what grade of paper is being [actually] quoted." Sources of the original data from which Macaulay constructed monthly averages are January 1857 to December 1859, *Journal of Commerce*; January 1860 to December 1861, *Hunt's Merchants' Magazine* and *Bankers' Magazine*; January 1862 to June 1862, *Hunt's Merchants' Magazine, Bankers' Magazine*, and New York newspapers; July 1862 to December 1865, New York newspapers; January 1866 to December 1900, *Financial Review* and *Commercial and Financial Chronicle*.

Series Cj1224–1237. The rates shown here cover the most important short-term open market instruments in New York City, which is the chief money market of the country. The New York money market is composed of a number of specialized markets for certain types of borrowing, and there are usually differences in rates corresponding to differences in the supply of funds relative to the demand for particular types of short-term funds in which the market deals. These markets are called "open" markets because transactions in them are usually made on an impersonal basis with the borrower and lender dealing through agents, as distinct from a "customer" market, where the borrower and lender deal directly with each other and where transactions are often made on a personal basis. As a result, lenders may sell paper held, call loans, or refrain from renewing credits upon maturity more freely in the case of open market paper than in the case of customer loans. Monthly and weekly figures for most of the series shown here are given in the source.

Series Cj1226–1229. Rates on stock exchange loans are no longer published by the Board of Governors of the Federal Reserve System, but data for these series for 1942–1962 were supplied by that agency.

TABLE Cj1223–1237   Money market rates: 1831–1997   *Continued*

Series Cj1231–1233. Beginning in 1929, a new measure of short-term rates became available with the issuance by the Treasury of a new type of security, the Treasury bill, which differs from other types of Treasury marketable securities in that it is sold on a discount basis instead of being offered in the market with a fixed coupon rate. Maturities of Treasury bills have varied up to nine months, but usually have been three months. Series for two short-term maturities are available, series Cj1231–1232, beginning in 1931, and series Cj1233, beginning 1943.

Series Cj1235–1236. The Federal Reserve Bank of New York discount rates shown are the lowest and highest rates during the year on discounts for and advances to member banks under sections 13 and 13a of the Federal Reserve Act. For the period prior to 1921, when a multiplicity of rates prevailed, discount rates on paper of a single class and maturity – usually the type of paper and maturity for which the rate was lowest – are shown. Specifically, from November 16, 1914, the day the Reserve Banks opened, through August 1916, the rate applies to discounts of commercial, agricultural, and livestock paper with maturities of from thirty-one to sixty days; and from September 1916 to December 1920, to discounts of, and advances secured by, commercial, agricultural, and livestock paper with maturities of fifteen days or less. Rates also apply to advances secured by obligations of federal intermediate credit banks maturing in six months. For 1942–1945, the low rate shown is the preferential rate for advances secured by government securities maturing or callable in one year or less. In this period, the rate of 1 percent was continued for discounts of eligible paper and advances secured by such paper or by U.S. government obligations with maturities beyond one year. The discount rates at all Federal Reserve banks and a description of the series through 1941 are contained in *Banking and Monetary Statistics* (1943), pp. 422–4, 439–42, and thereafter in the *Federal Reserve Bulletin*.

Series Cj1237. The federal funds rate is the cost of borrowing immediately available funds, primarily for one day. The daily effective rate is a weighted average of rates on trades through New York brokers.

TABLE Cj1238-1242   Basic yields of corporate bonds, by term to maturity: 1900-1975

Contributed by John A. James and Richard Sylla

Year	1 year Cj1238 Percent per annum	5 years Cj1239 Percent per annum	10 years Cj1240 Percent per annum	20 years Cj1241 Percent per annum	30 years Cj1242 Percent per annum	Year	1 year Cj1238 Percent per annum	5 years Cj1239 Percent per annum	10 years Cj1240 Percent per annum	20 years Cj1241 Percent per annum	30 years Cj1242 Percent per annum
1900	3.97 [1]	3.36 [1]	3.30	3.30	3.30	1940	0.41	1.28	1.95	2.55	2.70
1901	3.25	3.25	3.25	3.25	3.25	1941	0.41	1.21	1.88	2.50	2.65
1902	3.30 [2]	3.30 [2]	3.30 [2]	3.30 [2]	3.30 [2]	1942	0.81	1.50	2.16	2.61	2.65
1903	3.45	3.45	3.45	3.45	3.45	1943	1.17	1.71	2.16	2.61	2.65
1904	3.60	3.60	3.60	3.60	3.60	1944	1.08 [1]	1.58	2.20	2.60	2.60
1905	3.50	3.50	3.50	3.50	3.50	1945	1.02	1.53	2.14	2.55	2.55
1906	4.75 [1]	3.67 [1]	3.55	3.55	3.55	1946	0.86 [2]	1.32	1.88 [2]	2.35	2.43
1907	4.87 [1]	3.87 [1]	3.80	3.80	3.80	1947	1.05 [2]	1.65	2.08 [2]	2.40	2.50
1908	5.10 [1]	4.30 [1]	4.02 [1]	3.95	3.95	1948	1.60	2.03	2.53	2.73	2.80
1909	4.03	3.97	3.91	3.82	3.77	1949	1.60	1.92	2.32	2.62	2.74
1910	4.25	4.10	3.99	3.87	3.80	1950	1.42 [2]	1.90 [2]	2.30	2.48	2.58
1911	4.09	4.05	4.01	3.94	3.90	1951	2.05 [2]	2.22 [2]	2.39	2.59	2.67
1912	4.04	4.00	3.96	3.91	3.90	1952	2.73 [2]	2.73 [2]	2.73	2.88	3.00
1913	4.74	4.31	4.12	4.02	4.00	1953	2.62 [2]	2.75 [2]	2.88	3.05	3.15
1914	4.64	4.45	4.32	4.16	4.10	1954	2.40	2.52	2.66	2.88	3.00
1915	4.47	4.39	4.31	4.20	4.15	1955	—	2.70 [2]	2.80	2.95	3.04
1916	3.48	4.03	4.05	4.05	4.05	1956	2.70	2.78	2.86	2.99	3.09
1917	4.05	4.05	4.05	4.05	4.05	1957	3.50 [2]	3.50 [2]	3.50	3.50 [2]	3.68
1918	5.48	5.25	5.05	4.82	4.75	1958	3.21 [2]	3.25 [2]	3.33	3.47	3.61
1919	5.58	5.16	4.97	4.81	4.75	1959	3.67	3.80	4.03	4.10	4.10
1920	6.11	5.72	5.43	5.17	5.10	1960	4.95	4.73	4.60	4.55	4.55
1921	6.94 [2]	6.21	5.73	5.31	5.17	1961	3.10	3.75	4.00	4.12	4.22
1922	5.31	5.19	5.06	4.85	4.71	1962	3.50	3.97	4.28	4.40	4.42
1923	5.01	4.90	4.80	4.68	4.61	1963	3.25	3.77	3.98	4.10	4.16
1924	5.02	4.90	4.80	4.69	4.66	1964	4.00	4.15	4.25	4.33	4.33
1925	3.85	4.46	4.50	4.50	4.50	1965	4.15	4.29	4.33	4.35	4.35
1926	4.40	4.40	4.40	4.40	4.40	1966	5.00	4.97	4.91	4.80	4.75
1927	4.30	4.30	4.30	4.30	4.30	1967	5.29	5.28	5.23	5.00	4.95
1928	4.05	4.05	4.05	4.05	4.05	1968	6.24	6.24	6.20	6.00	5.93
1929	5.27	4.72	4.57	4.45	4.42	1969	7.05	7.05	7.05	6.77	6.54
1930	4.40	4.40	4.40	4.40	4.40	1970	8.15	8.10	8.00	7.60	7.60
1931	3.05	3.90	4.03	4.10	4.10	1971	4.60	5.88	7.05	7.12	7.12
1932	3.99 [1]	4.58 [1]	4.70	4.70	4.70	1972	4.25	6.50	7.05	7.05	7.01
1933	2.60 [2]	3.68	4.00	4.11	4.15	1973	6.25	6.85	7.05	7.20	7.20
1934	2.62 [2]	3.48	3.70	3.91	3.99	1974	7.26	7.47	7.67	7.80	7.80
1935	1.05	2.37	3.00	3.37	3.50	1975	7.55	7.70	8.00	8.35	8.35
1936	0.61	1.86	2.64	3.04	3.20						
1937	0.69	1.68	2.38	2.90	3.08						
1938	0.85	1.97	2.60	2.91	3.00						
1939	0.57	1.55	2.18	2.65	2.75						

[1] One alternative value; the other is equal to the longest-term yield shown.

[2] More than usually liable to error.

Sources

1900-1942: David Durand, *Basic Yields of Corporate Bonds, 1900-1942* (National Bureau of Economic Research, 1942).

1943-1955: National Bureau of Economic Research, unpublished data.

1956-1970: Unpublished data provided by the investment firm of Scudder, Stevens, and Clark (now Scudder Kemper Investments).

1971-1975: Sidney Homer and Richard Sylla, *A History of Interest Rates,* 3rd edition, revised (Rutgers University Press, 1996), Table 52A, pp. 397, 432-35.

Estimates were prepared by Sidney Homer using methods similar to Durand's.

Documentation

Yield by years to maturity appears in greater detail in Durand's volume than here. Through 1950, the basic yield series represent the yields estimated as prevailing in the first quarter of each year on the highest grade corporate issues, classified by term to maturity; thereafter, the yields estimated in February only. These series are based on monthly high and low quotations of practically all the actively traded high-grade corporate issues outstanding since 1900.

TABLE Cj1243–1249   Yields of government bonds, by term to maturity: 1950–1998

Contributed by John A. James and Richard Sylla

Year	1 year	2 years	3 years	5 years	10 years	20 years	30 years
	Cj1243	Cj1244	Cj1245	Cj1246	Cj1247	Cj1248	Cj1249
	Percent per annum	Percent per annum	Percent per annum	Percent per annum	Percent per annum	Percent per annum	Percent per annum
1950	1.17	1.23	1.29	1.45	1.98	2.29	—
1951	1.52	1.60	1.63	1.75	2.32	2.45	—
1952	1.77	1.99	2.12	2.22	2.50	2.73	—
1953	2.12	2.21	2.28	2.42	2.65	2.79	—
1954	1.13	1.32	1.53	1.99	2.49	2.64	2.91
1955	1.28	1.87	2.12	2.33	2.55	2.74	2.98
1956	2.48	2.55	2.60	2.63	2.78	2.80	2.87
1957	3.28	3.36	3.39	3.35	3.28	3.19	3.25
1958	1.98	2.37	2.64	2.76	2.97	3.28	3.32
1959	3.40	3.68	3.82	3.88	3.89	3.95	3.97
1960	4.44	4.58	4.69	4.82	4.51	4.39	4.34
1961	2.77	3.18	3.42	3.69	3.85	3.91	3.95
1962	3.22	3.57	3.75	3.95	4.12	4.15	4.16
1963	3.04	3.20	3.37	3.68	3.86	3.97	4.01
1964	3.77	3.92	3.98	4.05	4.15	4.16	4.19
1965	3.94	3.97	4.02	4.08	4.19	4.18	4.18
1966	4.81	4.87	4.92	4.93	4.67	4.58	4.54
1967	4.62	4.61	4.61	4.60	4.50	4.44	4.42
1968	5.30	5.37	5.41	5.47	5.47	5.37	5.29
1969	6.30	6.23	6.17	6.07	6.00	6.00	6.00
1970	8.11	8.12	8.16	8.16	7.50	6.84	6.82
1971	4.31	4.59	5.23	5.73	5.99	5.97	5.95
1972	4.20	4.85	5.24	5.67	6.19	5.90	5.89
1973	6.08	6.23	6.32	6.41	6.49	6.85	6.89
1974	7.10	6.79	6.79	6.82	6.93	7.38	7.39
1975	6.14	6.92	6.90	7.20	7.00	7.64	7.95
1976	5.48	6.35	6.88	7.40	7.38	7.85	8.01
1977	5.50	6.13	6.49	6.91	7.40	7.68	7.74
1978	7.22	7.40	7.51	7.68	7.89	8.09	8.12
1979	10.12	9.60	9.19	8.94	8.92	8.84	8.80
1980	12.32	11.73	11.10	11.09	11.11	11.11	11.08
1981	13.93	13.26	12.91	12.73	12.64	12.40	12.23
1982	14.05	14.17	14.23	14.09	14.19	14.17	13.88
1983	8.92	9.59	9.98	10.44	10.75	11.08	11.18
1984	9.76	10.54	10.78	11.31	11.59	11.77	11.73
1985	9.15	9.99	10.29	10.80	11.07	11.30	11.19
1986	7.55	7.94	8.14	8.59	9.04	9.41	9.33
1987	5.92	6.33	6.42	6.73	7.17	7.74	7.51
1988	6.68	7.27	7.49	7.82	8.31	8.53	8.50
1989	9.02	9.10	9.11	9.04	8.98	8.92	8.83
1990	8.11	8.37	8.39	8.42	8.47	—	8.50
1991	6.27	6.87	7.08	7.47	7.85	—	8.03
1992	4.29	5.21	5.72	6.58	7.34	—	7.85
1993	3.39	4.10	4.58	5.43	6.26	—	7.09
1994	3.87	4.47	4.83	5.40	5.97	6.57	6.49
1995	6.70	7.11	7.25	7.37	7.47	7.73	7.61
1996	4.94	5.03	5.14	5.38	5.81	6.30	6.24
1997	5.53	5.90	5.43	6.20	6.42	6.77	6.69
1998	5.31	5.42	5.43	5.49	5.57	5.96	5.89

Sources

1950–1989: Sidney Homer and Richard Sylla, *A History of Interest Rates,* 3rd edition, revised (Rutgers University Press, 1996), Table 53B, pp. 398–9. 1990–1995: Board of Governors of the Federal Reserve System, *Annual Statistical Digest, 1990–1995* (1996), Table 18, pp. 92–7. 1996–1998: *Federal Reserve Bulletin* (July 1999), Table 1.35, p. A23.

Documentation

Figures are yields of actively traded issues adjusted to constant maturities. Figures are based on February data.

TABLE Cj1250–1256   Interest rates on household savings and consumer credit: 1835–1997

Contributed by John A. James and Richard Sylla

Year	Regular deposits of mutual savings banks	Demand deposits	Insured savings and loan dividend rate	Certificates of deposit	Consumer credit commercial bank rates New autos	Personal loans	Credit card plans
	Cj1250	Cj1251	Cj1252	Cj1253	Cj1254	Cj1255	Cj1256
	Percent per annum	Percent per annum	Percent per annum	Percent per annum	Percent per annum	Percent per annum	Percent per annum
1835	5.0	—	—	—	—	—	—
1836	5.0	—	—	—	—	—	—
1837	5.0	—	—	—	—	—	—
1838	5.0	—	—	—	—	—	—
1839	5.0	—	—	—	—	—	—
1840	5.0	—	—	—	—	—	—
1841	5.0	—	—	—	—	—	—
1842	5.0	—	—	—	—	—	—
1843	5.0	—	—	—	—	—	—
1844	5.0	—	—	—	—	—	—
1845	5.0	—	—	—	—	—	—
1846	5.0	—	—	—	—	—	—
1847	5.0	—	—	—	—	—	—
1848	5.0	—	—	—	—	—	—
1849	6.0	—	—	—	—	—	—
1850	6.0	—	—	—	—	—	—
1851	6.0	—	—	—	—	—	—
1852	5.0	—	—	—	—	—	—
1853	5.0	—	—	—	—	—	—
1854	5.0	—	—	—	—	—	—
1855	5.0	—	—	—	—	—	—
1856	5.0	—	—	—	—	—	—
1857	5.0	—	—	—	—	—	—
1858	5.0	—	—	—	—	—	—
1859	5.0	—	—	—	—	—	—
1860	5.0	—	—	—	—	—	—
1861	5.0	—	—	—	—	—	—
1862	5.0	—	—	—	—	—	—
1863	5.0	—	—	—	—	—	—
1864	5.0	—	—	—	—	—	—
1865	5.0	—	—	—	—	—	—
1866	5.0	—	—	—	—	—	—
1867	6.0	—	—	—	—	—	—
1868	6.0	—	—	—	—	—	—
1869	6.0	—	—	—	—	—	—
1870	6.0	—	—	—	—	—	—
1871	6.0	—	—	—	—	—	—
1872	6.0	—	—	—	—	—	—
1873	6.0	—	—	—	—	—	—
1874	6.0	—	—	—	—	—	—
1875	6.0	—	—	—	—	—	—
1876	6.0	—	—	—	—	—	—
1877	6.0	—	—	—	—	—	—
1878	5.0	—	—	—	—	—	—
1879	5.0	—	—	—	—	—	—
1880	5.0	—	—	—	—	—	—
1881	4.0	—	—	—	—	—	—
1882	4.0	—	—	—	—	—	—
1883	4.0	—	—	—	—	—	—
1884	4.0	—	—	—	—	—	—
1885	4.0	—	—	—	—	—	—
1886	4.0	—	—	—	—	—	—
1887	4.0	—	—	—	—	—	—
1888	4.0	—	—	—	—	—	—
1889	4.0	—	—	—	—	—	—
1890	4.0	—	—	—	—	—	—
1891	4.0	—	—	—	—	—	—
1892	4.0	—	—	—	—	—	—
1893	4.0	—	—	—	—	—	—
1894	4.0	—	—	—	—	—	—

TABLE Cj1250–1256   Interest rates on household savings and consumer credit: 1835–1997   *Continued*

Year	Regular deposits of mutual savings banks	Demand deposits	Insured savings and loan dividend rate	Certificates of deposit	Consumer credit commercial bank rates		
					New autos	Personal loans	Credit card plans
	Cj1250	Cj1251	Cj1252	Cj1253	Cj1254	Cj1255	Cj1256
	Percent per annum	Percent per annum	Percent per annum	Percent per annum	Percent per annum	Percent per annum	Percent per annum
1895	4.0	—	—	—	—	—	—
1896	4.0	—	—	—	—	—	—
1897	4.0	—	—	—	—	—	—
1898	4.0	—	—	—	—	—	—
1899	3.5	—	—	—	—	—	—
1900	3.5	—	—	—	—	—	—
1901	4.0	—	—	—	—	—	—
1902	4.0	—	—	—	—	—	—
1903	3.5	—	—	—	—	—	—
1904	3.5	—	—	—	—	—	—
1905	4.0	—	—	—	—	—	—
1906	3.5	—	—	—	—	—	—
1907	4.0	—	—	—	—	—	—
1908	4.0	—	—	—	—	—	—
1909	4.0	—	—	—	—	—	—
1910	3.5	—	—	—	—	—	—
1911	3.5	—	—	—	—	—	—
1912	3.5	—	—	—	—	—	—
1913	3.5	—	—	—	—	—	—
1914	3.5	—	—	—	—	—	—
1915	3.5	—	—	—	—	—	—
1916	3.5	—	—	—	—	—	—
1917	4.0	—	—	—	—	—	—
1918	4.0	—	—	—	—	—	—
1919	4.0	2.00	—	—	—	—	—
1920	4.0	2.25	—	—	—	—	—
1921	4.0	2.25	—	—	—	—	—
1922	4.0	2.00	—	—	—	—	—
1923	4.0	2.00	—	—	—	—	—
1924	4.0	2.00	—	—	—	—	—
1925	4.0	2.00	—	—	—	—	—
1926	4.0	2.00	—	—	—	—	—
1927	4.0	2.00	—	—	—	—	—
1928	4.0	2.00	—	—	—	—	—
1929	4.5	2.00	—	—	—	—	—
1930	4.5	1.50	—	—	—	—	—
1931	4.0	1.00	—	—	—	—	—
1932	3.5	0.50	—	—	—	—	—
1933	3.0	0.00	—	—	—	—	—
1934	3.0	—	—	—	—	—	—
1935	2.5	—	—	—	—	—	—
1936	2.0	—	—	—	—	—	—
1937	2.0	—	—	—	—	—	—
1938	2.0	—	—	—	—	—	—
1939	2.0	—	—	—	—	—	—
1940	2.0	—	—	—	—	—	—
1941	2.0	—	—	—	—	—	—
1942	2.0	—	—	—	—	—	—
1943	2.0	—	—	—	—	—	—
1944	1.5	—	—	—	—	—	—
1945	1.5	—	—	—	—	—	—
1946	—	—	2.31	—	—	—	—
1947	—	—	2.34	—	—	—	—
1948	—	—	2.43	—	—	—	—
1949	—	—	2.52	—	—	—	—
1950	—	—	2.55	—	—	—	—
1951	—	—	2.62	—	—	—	—
1952	—	—	2.75	—	—	—	—
1953	—	—	2.87	—	—	—	—
1954	—	—	2.95	—	—	—	—

(continued)

TABLE Cj1250–1256   **Interest rates on household savings and consumer credit: 1835–1997**   *Continued*

Year	Regular deposits of mutual savings banks	Demand deposits	Insured savings and loan dividend rate	Certificates of deposit	Consumer credit commercial bank rates		
					New autos	Personal loans	Credit card plans
	Cj1250	Cj1251	Cj1252	Cj1253	Cj1254	Cj1255	Cj1256
	Percent per annum	Percent per annum	Percent per annum	Percent per annum	Percent per annum	Percent per annum	Percent per annum
1955	—	—	3.01	—	—	—	—
1956	—	—	3.13	—	—	—	—
1957	—	—	3.37	—	—	—	—
1958	—	—	3.49	—	—	—	—
1959	—	—	3.66	—	—	—	—
1960	—	—	3.86	—	—	—	—
1961	—	—	3.90	—	—	—	—
1962	—	—	4.08	—	—	—	—
1963	—	—	4.17	—	—	—	—
1964	—	—	4.19	3.91	—	—	—
1965	—	—	4.23	4.35	—	—	—
1966	—	—	4.48	5.47	—	—	—
1967	—	—	4.68	5.02	—	—	—
1968	—	—	4.71	5.86	—	—	—
1969	—	—	4.81	7.77	—	—	—
1970	—	—	5.14	7.56	—	—	—
1971	—	—	5.30	4.99	—	—	—
1972	—	—	5.37	4.67	10.05	12.46	17.21
1973	—	—	5.51	8.41	10.21	12.60	17.21
1974	—	—	5.96	10.24	10.97	12.99	17.21
1975	—	—	6.21	6.44	11.36	13.08	17.16
1976	—	—	6.31	5.27	11.07	12.77	17.05
1977	—	—	6.39	5.64	10.92	12.97	16.89
1978	—	—	6.56	8.22	11.02	13.19	17.03
1979	—	—	7.29	11.22	12.02	13.85	17.03
1980	—	—	8.78	14.00	14.30	15.47	17.31
1981	—	—	10.71	16.79	16.54	18.09	17.78
1982	—	—	11.19	13.12	16.83	18.65	18.51
1983	—	—	9.71	9.07	13.92	16.88	18.78
1984	—	—	9.93	10.37	13.71	16.47	18.77
1985	—	—	9.03	8.05	12.91	15.94	18.69
1986	—	—	7.84	6.51	11.33	14.82	18.26
1987	—	—	6.92	6.87	10.46	14.23	17.93
1988	—	—	7.20	7.73	10.85	14.68	17.78
1989	—	—	7.70	9.09	12.07	15.44	18.02
1990	—	—	7.68	8.15	11.78	15.46	18.14
1991	—	—	6.89	5.83	11.14	15.18	18.23
1992	—	—	5.19	3.68	9.29	14.04	17.78
1993	—	—	4.12	3.17	8.09	13.47	16.83
1994	—	—	3.95	4.63	8.12	13.19	16.20
1995	—	—	4.85	5.92	9.57	13.84	16.02
1996	—	—	4.87	5.39	9.05	13.54	15.63
1997	—	—	4.92	5.62	9.02	13.90	15.77

Sources

Series Cj1250–1251. Sidney Homer and Richard Sylla, *A History of Interest Rates*, 3rd edition, revised (Rutgers University Press, 1996), pp. 318–20, 362–3.

Series Cj1252. 1946–1989: See source for series Cj1250, pp. 391–3. 1990–1997: Office of Thrift Supervision's Internet site, *Cost of Funds Report – Historical Data*.

Series Cj1253. Board of Governors of the Federal Reserve System, *Federal Reserve Bulletin* and *Annual Statistical Digest*, 1970–1979, 1980–1989, and 1990–1995.

Series Cj1254–1256. Board of Governors of the Federal Reserve System, *Federal Reserve Bulletin* and *Annual Statistical Digest*, variously numbered tables titled "Terms of Consumer Credit."

Documentation

Series Cj1250. Compiled from records of the Bowery Savings Bank of New York City, as of January 1.

Series Cj1251. Represents the maximum rate on demand deposits paid by New York Clearinghouse banks. The series was privately compiled.

Series Cj1252. Compiled from reports of Federal Housing Administration, Federal Home Loan Bank Board, and Office of Thrift Supervision.

Series Cj1254. Annual averages based on Federal Reserve quarterly surveys.

TABLE Cj1257–1260   Mortgage interest rates: 1970–1997

Contributed by John A. James and Richard Sylla

Year	Contract rate		FHA mortgages	GNMA securities
	FHFB	HUD		
	Cj1257	Cj1258	Cj1259	Cj1260
	Percent per annum	Percent per annum	Percent per annum	Percent per annum
1970	8.27	8.52	9.03	—
1971	7.59	7.75	7.70	7.07
1972	7.45	7.64	7.53	6.97
1973	7.78	8.30	8.19	7.65
1974	8.71	9.22	9.55	8.70
1975	8.75	9.10	9.20	8.52
1976	8.76	8.99	8.82	8.17
1977	8.80	8.95	8.68	8.04
1978	9.30	9.68	9.70	8.98
1979	10.48	11.15	10.87	10.22
1980	12.25	13.94	13.43	12.62
1981	14.16	16.52	16.31	15.30
1982	14.46	15.79	15.30	14.70
1983	12.19	13.43	13.11	12.28
1984	11.86	13.79	13.81	13.13

Year	Contract rate		FHA mortgages	GNMA securities
	FHFB	HUD		
	Cj1257	Cj1258	Cj1259	Cj1260
	Percent per annum	Percent per annum	Percent per annum	Percent per annum
1985	11.11	12.28	12.23	11.61
1986	9.82	10.07	9.91	9.28
1987	8.93	10.16	10.15	9.43
1988	8.81	10.29	10.49	9.82
1989	9.75	10.21	10.24	9.71
1990	9.68	10.08	10.17	9.51
1991	9.02	9.20	9.25	8.59
1992	7.98	8.43	8.46	7.71
1993	7.03	7.37	7.46	6.65
1994	7.26	8.58	8.68	7.96
1995	7.65	8.05	8.18	7.57
1996	7.56	8.03	8.19	7.48
1997	7.57	7.76	7.89	7.26

Sources

Board of Governors of the Federal Reserve System. 1970–1979: *Annual Statistical Digest* (1981), Table 39, p. 270; 1980–1989: *Annual Statistical Digest* (1991), Table 36, p. 236; 1990–1995: *Annual Statistical Digest,* Table 31, p. 148; 1996–1997: *Federal Reserve Bulletin* (July 1999), Table 1.53, p. A34.

Documentation

Series Cj1257. Values are weighted averages based on sample surveys of mortgages originated by major institutional lender groups for purchase of newly built homes. This series is compiled by the Federal Housing Finance Board (FHFB), formerly the Federal Home Loan Bank Board, in cooperation with the Federal Deposit Insurance Corporation.

Series Cj1258. Values are average contract rates on new commitments for conventional first mortgages. The data are from U.S. Department of Housing and Urban Development (HUD).

Series Cj1259. Values are average gross yields on thirty-year, minimum-down-payment first mortgages insured by the Federal Housing Administration (FHA) for immediate delivery in the private secondary market.

Series Cj1260. Values are average net yields to investors on fully modified pass-through securities backed by mortgages and guaranteed by the Government National Mortgage Association (GNMA), assuming prepayment in twelve years on pools of thirty-year mortgages insured by the FHA or guaranteed by the Department of Veterans Affairs.

INDEX

Note: The number before the colon is the volume; the number after the colon is the page. A number range indicates inclusive pages in the same volume. Numbers in italics refer to pages in essays; numbers not in italics refer to pages in statistical tables.

Numbers in italics refer to pages in essays; numbers not in italics refer to pages in statistical tables.

Numbers in italics refer to pages in essays; numbers not in italics refer to pages in statistical tables.

Corn (*continued*)
　price support, *4:35*
　sweet, acreage, price, and production, 4:155–60
Corn oil, 4:138–9
Corporate income tax, 3:561–9
Corporations, *3:482–6. See also* S-corporations
　in agriculture, forestry, and fishing industries,
　　3:499–502, 3:563–5
　assets, 3:561–79, 3:581–2
　balance sheets, 3:561–82
　capital, 3:581–2
　charitable giving, 2:931–3
　in construction industries, 3:505–7, 3:568–9
　in distribution industries, 3:574–5
　dividends, 3:561–79, 3:581–2
　in finance, insurance, and real estate industries,
　　3:514–15, 3:576–7
　during the Great Depression, 3:129
　income, 3:581–2
　income tax, corporate, 3:561–79
　incorporations, 3:531–52
　　in New England, *3:483,* 3:548
　　in New Jersey, *3:483*
　　number and liabilities, 3:550–1
　　by type of incorporation law, *3:483,* 3:531–6,
　　　3:548
　liabilities, 3:561–79, 3:581–2
　in manufacturing industries, 3:508–9, 3:570–1,
　　4:702–4
　in mining industries, 3:503–5, 3:566–7
　profits, national income originating in,
　　3:29–30
　receipts of, 3:561–79
　saving of, 3:298–9
　securities of, 3:764–6
　in service industries, 3:578–9
　in trade, wholesale, and retail industries,
　　3:512–13
　in transportation, communications, and utilities
　　industries, 3:572–3
Correctional institutions, *5:222,* 5:820–1
　See also Prisoners
　population, *1:13,* 1:669–70
　state and federal, 5:256–61
Corruption, public, federal prosecution of, 5:331
Costa Rica, U.S. population born in, 1:611
Cotton and cottonseed
　acreage, 4:110–15
　Commodity Credit Corporation, owned by,
　　4:253–5
　Confederate States of America, *5:778*
　　cotton, 5:778–9, 5:802
　consumption, 4:694–5
　cottonseed oil, price and production, 4:138–9
　exports, 5:546–53
　freight rates, 4:884
　inventory, 4:110–14
　prices, 3:71, 3:207–11, 4:110–14, *5:778*
　production, 4:110–15
Courier services, 4:857
Courts, *5:220–2,* 5:311–31
　juvenile courts, 5:326–9
　state courts, 5:326
　U.S. District Courts, 5:321–5
　U.S. Supreme Court, 5:315–20
Crab. *See* Shellfish
Craftsmen, foremen, and kindred workers,
　2:146–8
　American Indian, 1:768–70
　economically active, 2:238–41
　immigrants, prior occupation of, 1:590–6,
　　1:618–20
　by nativity, 2:216–18, 2:226–8
　by race, 2:176–8, 2:186–8, 2:196–8, 2:206–8
　by sex, 1:618–20, 1:768–70, 2:156–8, 2:166–8,
　　2:176–8, 2:186–8, 2:196–8, 2:206–8

Credit cards, 3:669
Credit market debt, 3:789–90
　outstanding, 3:777, 3:784–8
　by sector, 3:784–8
Credit unions, 3:687–8. *See also* National Credit
　Union Administration
Crime, 5:209–22, 5:223–36
　criminal behavior, definition, *5:210–11*
　estimated, 5:236
　justice, criminal, *5:211*
　known to police, by type of offense,
　　5:223–4
　measurement, 5:209–10
　property
　　high school seniors involved in, 5:278–9,
　　　5:286–91
　　known to police, *5:215,* 5:223–5
　　by race and sex, 5:286–91
　　victimization, 5:234–5, 5:274–5
　public corruption, 5:331
　rates, by type of offense, 5:224–5
　recorded, 5:236
　statistics, reliability of, *5:211–17*
　urban, by type of offense, 5:225
　victims, *5:209–19,* 5:236
　　high school seniors as, 5:267–96
　　of personal crimes, 5:232–3
　　of property crimes, 5:232–5, 5:269,
　　　5:274–5
　　by type of offense, 5:232–5
　　of violent crimes, 5:234–5, 5:267–8,
　　　5:270–3
Crippled Children's Program, 2:805–6
Cropland, 3:360–1. *See also* Crops;
　　specific crops
　acreage harvested, 4:89–91
　acreage reduction programs, *4:35,*
　　4:267–8
　harvested, *4:11, 4:15*
　use, *4:15,* 4:89–91
　utilization, *4:15–17*
　yield, per acre, 4:89–91
Crops, *4:15–18,* 4:89–192. *See also* Cropland
　acreage, *4:16 (see also specific crops)*
　greenhouse, 4:143
　insurance programs for, 4:268–9
　inventory, 4:101–4
　nursery, 4:143
　in outlying areas, 5:608–9
　output, 4:193–6, 5:785
　yields, *4:21,* 4:199–201
Crude oil reserves, 4:344–5
Cuba
　aliens naturalized from, 1:644–7
　immigration from, 1:571–4, 1:576
　U.S. population born in, 1:604, 1:608,
　　1:611
Cucumbers, acreage, price, and production,
　4:155–60
Currency
　in circulation, 3:588–92, 3:608–16
　coin, 3:588, 3:608–13
　paper notes, 3:588, 3:592–3, 3:608–13,
　　3:623
　stock of, 3:589–92, 3:614–16
　U.S. Treasury, 3:589–92, 3:614–16
　value of, 3:592–3, 3:623
Cyprus, U.S. population born in, 1:610
Czechoslovakia, U.S. population born in, 1:602,
　1:606, 1:609

Dairy products
　consumption, 2:574
　livestock kept for milk, 4:178–86
　prices and price indexes, 3:161–2, 4:178–86
　production, 4:178–86

Dams, *4:1070*
　federal government owned, 4:1101–2
Deaf and hard-of-hearing population
　benevolent institutions for, 2:865–7
　special education programs for, 2:410
Deaf-blind children, special education programs
　for, 2:410
Death registration areas, 1:397–8
Deaths and death rates, 1:391–6, 1:458–85, 1:487,
　　1:745. *See also* Accidents and fatalities;
　　Casualties; Death registration areas;
　　Mortality rates
　causes of, *1:387,* 1:463–6, 1:483–5,
　　1:745
　motor vehicle, *4:765,* 4:840–6
　trends in, *1:387*
Debt, *3:593–4, 3:624–5,* 3:774–811
　credit market, 3:784–8
　　outstanding, 3:778–90
　government, *5:6*
　　federal, 5:80–1, 5:96–9, 5:100–2
　　by level, 5:25–6
　mortgage, 3:777
　private, 3:774–6
　public, 3:774–6
Defense. *See also* Armed forces
　government expenditures for, 5:19–25
　　federal, 5:32–7, 5:91–4, 5:105–8, 5:369
　national, *5:333–9,* 5:350–439
　　veterans' benefits, 5:367–8
　research and development, 3:453–5
Deformities, 2:618–19
Degrees conferred, 2:444–9
　bachelor's, 2:457–61
　doctorate, 2:450–7
　by field of study, 2:450–61
　by sex, 2:454–7, 2:459–61
Delaware. *See* State data
Delinquency
　by high school seniors, 5:267–96
　violent crimes, by race and sex, 5:281–6
Democratic Party
　congressional affiliations with, 5:200–3
　House candidates, votes cast, 5:193
　party identification, 5:204
　presidential affiliations with, 5:200–3
　presidential candidates, 5:172–9
　presidential elections
　　electoral votes, 5:180–3
　　popular votes, 5:184–92
　Senate candidates, votes cast, 5:194
Democratic-Republican Party, 5:172–9,
　　5:200–3
Denmark, U.S. population born in, 1:601, 1:606,
　　1:609. *See also* Scandinavia
Dental care. *See also* Dentists
　consumer expenditures on, 3:230–66
　price indexes, 3:165–6
Dentists, 2:541–5, 2:549
Department stores, sales and inventories,
　　4:737
Deportation, 1:648–9
Deposit insurance, 3:693–730. *See also* Federal
　　Deposit Insurance Corporation
　Savings Association Insurance Fund, 3:730
Depository institution reserve funds
　requirements, 3:627–8
　sources, uses, and reserves, 3:594–5, 3:625–7
Depressions, *3:71–7. See also* Business cycles;
　　Great Depression
　definition, *3:71, 3:207–11*
Dermatitis, 2:616–17
Diabetes, 2:617–18
Diet, *2:506–7. See also* Nutrition
Digestive conditions, 2:611–13, 2:620
Diphtheria, 2:564–6

Numbers in italics refer to pages in essays; numbers not in italics refer to pages in statistical tables.

Numbers in italics refer to pages in essays; numbers not in italics refer to pages in statistical tables.

Numbers in italics refer to pages in essays; numbers not in italics refer to pages in statistical tables.

Numbers in italics refer to pages in essays; numbers not in italics refer to pages in statistical tables.

Numbers in italics refer to pages in essays; numbers not in italics refer to pages in statistical tables.

Numbers in italics refer to pages in essays; numbers not in italics refer to pages in statistical tables.

Numbers in italics refer to pages in essays; numbers not in italics refer to pages in statistical tables.

Numbers in italics refer to pages in essays; numbers not in italics refer to pages in statistical tables.

Numbers in italics refer to pages in essays; numbers not in italics refer to pages in statistical tables.

Numbers in italics refer to pages in essays; numbers not in italics refer to pages in statistical tables.

Numbers in italics refer to pages in essays; numbers not in italics refer to pages in statistical tables.

Numbers in italics refer to pages in essays; numbers not in italics refer to pages in statistical tables.

Numbers in italics refer to pages in essays; numbers not in italics refer to pages in statistical tables.

Numbers in italics refer to pages in essays; numbers not in italics refer to pages in statistical tables.

Numbers in italics refer to pages in essays; numbers not in italics refer to pages in statistical tables.

Numbers in italics refer to pages in essays; numbers not in italics refer to pages in statistical tables.

Numbers in italics refer to pages in essays; numbers not in italics refer to pages in statistical tables.